BICENTENNIAL EDITION

HISTORICAL STATISTICS
of the United States

COLONIAL TIMES TO 1970

PART 1

U.S. Department of Commerce
Rogers C. B. Morton, Secretary

James L. Pate, Assistant Secretary
for Economic Affairs

BUREAU OF THE CENSUS
Vincent P. Barabba, Director

BUREAU OF THE CENSUS

Vincent P. Barabba, Director
Robert L. Hagan, Deputy Director
James W. Turbitt, Associate Director for Field
Operations and User Services

DATA USER SERVICES DIVISION
Michael G. Garland, Chief

ACKNOWLEDGMENTS

Preparation of this edition was
under the direction of
William Lerner
Chief, Statistical Compendia Staff

The bicentennial edition of *Historical Statistics of the United States* is the third in the series of volumes inaugurated in 1949. In both form and content, the bicentennial edition has drawn heavily from, and built upon, the two prior editions. Both the first volume, *Historical Statistics of the United States, 1789 to 1945,* issued in 1949, and the second volume, *Historical Statistics of the United States, Colonial Times to 1957,* issued in 1960, were prepared by the Bureau of the Census with the cooperation of the Social Science Research Council (SSRC). Although the SSRC did not participate in the preparation of the bicentennial edition, its cooperation in the first two volumes was invaluable in establishing those volumes as the basis for continuing work in the field of historical statistics. Similarly, the many individuals and agencies who made important and distinctive contributions to the first two volumes were instrumental in the preparation of the present one. Immediately following the table of contents, therefore, are reprinted the "official roster and credits" pages from the first two volumes. Also, incorporated within the "Acknowledgments for Chapter Contributions," under the title of each edition, are the credits to contributors as they appeared in the first two volumes.

Analytical review and editing of text tables was primarily the responsibility of **Helen E. Teir,** Assistant Chief, Statistical Compendia Staff, Data User Services Division. During the period January 1972 to June 1973, **Elma D. Beynon** was primarily responsible for obtaining the cooperation and assistance of the many subject consultants and for immediate supervision of compilation operations. **Suzanne L. Worth** assisted Mrs. Beynon and, from July 1973 to November 1974, was responsible for working with consultants and for supervision of the technical and clerical staff. **Alma L. Butler,** assisted by **Kay Swenson,** was responsible for final editing and preparation

of manuscript for the printer. The Census Library, **Dorothy W. Kaufman,** Chief, also lent valuable assistance.

The cooperation of the many contributors to this volume and to the prior editions is gratefully acknowledged. Following the practice established by the prior editions, every data series shown in this volume is, to the extent possible, specifically identified by source as to issuing agency and/or individual author, publication title, publisher, and date of issue. Frequently all five items are shown; frequently additional information is given.

September 1975

For Library of Congress Cataloging in Publication Data, see p. A-32.

Suggested Citation

U.S. Bureau of the Census

Historical Statistics of the United States, Colonial Times to 1970, Bicentennial Edition, Part 2

Washington, D.C., 1975

For sale by the Superintendent of Documents
U.S. Government Printing Office, Washington, D.C. 20402
Price $26 per 2 part set (Sold only in sets)
Stock Number 003-024-00120-9

Contents of Parts 1 and 2

Part 1

Part 2

Part 1—Detailed Contents

DETECTED CONTENTS

Replica of
"Official Roster and
Credits Page" from
**Historical Statistics
of the United States,
Colonial Times to 1957**

Bureau of the Census

ROBERT W. BURGESS, *Director*
A. Ross Eckler, *Deputy Director*
Howard C. Grieves, *Assistant Director*
Conrad Taeuber, *Assistant Director*
Morris H. Hansen, *Assistant Director for Statistical Standards*
Lowell T. Galt, *Assistant Director for Operations*
Walter L. Kehres, *Assistant Director for Administration*
Calvert L. Dedrick, *Chief, International Statistical Programs Office*
A. W. von Struve, *Acting Public Information Officer*

HERMAN P. MILLER, *Historical Statistics Project Director*

This volume stems from a joint interest by the Bureau of the Census and the Social Science Research Council. It was planned, assembled, edited, and published by the Bureau, with the advice and assistance of the Committee on Historical Statistics appointed by the Council. Many other individuals and agencies cooperated and made significant contributions to this project. General acknowledgments for each chapter are presented on p. VII; other acknowledgments frequently appear in the text discussions of the various chapters.

The volume was prepared in the Bureau of the Census under the general direction of Edwin D. Goldfield, Chief, Statistical Reports Division. Herman P. Miller served as the Project Director and was primarily responsible for the planning, organizing, and supervising of all aspects of the compilation of the data. Dr. Miller also served

as executive secretary of the Committee on Historical Statistics, handled liaison matters for the Committee, and participated in its selection of experts to serve as consultants. O. Halbert Goolsby acted as staff assistant.

Morris B. Ullman, who supervised the preparation of the previous volume, *Historical Statistics of the United States, 1789–1945*, was responsible for planning during the early stages of the project.

William Lerner, Assistant Chief, Statistical Reports Division, was primarily responsible for the planning and supervising of the publication aspects of the volume and for the review and editing of the text and tables. Dorothy M. Belzer was responsible for the tabular presentation of the data and preparation of the material for the printer. The Census Library Branch, Louise H. Clickner, Chief, also lent valuable assistance.

Social Science Research Council

The Committee on Historical Statistics appointed by the Social Science Research Council participated actively in the preparation of this volume, in the extension of the subjects to be added, and in planning the general procedures for securing expert assistance on each subject. As the project was developed the Committee, especially the Chairman, was primarily responsible for consideration of prob-

lems of data selection and format, for general appraisal of the quality of the series suggested for inclusion, and for the selection of consultant-specialists for the various subjects. The Committee as a whole, or through specially qualified members, reviewed the plans for inclusion of specific series and discussed areas of study which presented unusual problems.

Committee on Historical Statistics of the Social Science Research Council
(Advisory to the Bureau of the Census)

G. Heberton Evans, Jr., *Chairman*
Chairman of Department of Political Economy
The Johns Hopkins University

Herman P. Miller, *Executive Secretary*
Bureau of the Census

Otis Dudley Duncan
Associate Director of Population
Research and Training Center
The University of Chicago

Maurice I. Gershenson
Department of Industrial Relations
State of California

Willard L. Thorp
Director of Merrill Center for
Economics
Amherst College

Solomon Fabricant
Director of Research
National Bureau of Economic
Research, Inc.

Richard M. Scammon
Director of Elections Research
Governmental Affairs Institute

Harold F. Williamson
Professor of Economics
Northwestern University

Paul Webbink, Vice President, Social Science Research Council, attended Committee meetings and acted as the Council's representative. Stanley Lebergott, Office of Statistical Standards, Bureau of the Budget, also participated in the meetings.

BUREAU OF THE CENSUS

J. C. CAPT, *Director*

PHILIP M. HAUSER, *Deputy Director*

A. ROSS ECKLER, *Assistant Director*

HOWARD C. GRIEVES, *Assistant Director*

MORRIS H. HANSEN, *Statistical Assistant to the Director*

ROBERT Y. PHILLIPS, *Executive Assistant to the Director*

CALVERT L. DEDRICK, *Coordinator, International Statistics*

FRANK R. WILSON, *Information Assistant to the Director*

While this volume has been planned, assembled, and edited in the Bureau of the Census, with the advice and assistance of the Social Science Research Council, many other individuals and agencies contributed to its preparation, directly and indirectly. In some instances, individuals devoted themselves full-time for the period necessary to complete their phase of the project. In other instances, contributions were prepared by individuals while they maintained heavy responsibilities in their own offices. A number of private publishers, authors, and research organizations generously granted permission to use their materials. In some cases, they also made additional contributions in time and energy. General acknowledgments for each chapter are given on p. IV; other specific acknowledgments appear within the text in the various sections of the volume.

This volume was prepared in the office of Morris H. Hansen, Statistical Assistant to the Director of the Bureau of the Census, under the supervision of Morris B. Ullman, Chief, Statistical Reports Section, by Bruce L. Jenkinson, A. Benjamin Handler, and William Lerner. Mr. Jenkinson, Chief, Statistical Abstract Unit, was primarily responsible for the planning and preparation of the report; Mr. Handler, Executive Secretary of the Social Science Research Council Committee on the Source Book of Historical Statistics, was primarily responsible for procurement of data and relationships with the agencies and individuals who contributed to the publication; and Mr. Lerner, Statistician, Statistical Abstract Unit, was primarily responsible for the review and editing of the materials as to content, adequacy, and coverage.

Dorothy M. Belzer acted as staff assistant, particularly with respect to tabular presentation, and was responsible for preparation of the materials for the printer. Claire F. Cahill checked all citations by reference to the original published sources and offered many constructive suggestions as to the content of the book.

Social Science Research Council

The Social Science Research Council Committee on the Source Book of Historical Statistics, Advisory to the Bureau of the Census, played an important role in the preparation of this volume. The Chairman of the Committee and its members gave considerable time and thought to the review of plans, to advising on proper courses of action, and contributed in other ways. In particular, J. Frederic Dewhurst, Chairman, was in a large measure responsible for the initiation of the project. The completed volume owes much to his original outline of purpose, coverage, and arrangement. For a detailed statement of the origins of this historical volume, see introductory text.

Through a grant by the Committee on Research in Economic History (Arthur H. Cole, Chairman) of the Social Science Research Council, the full-time services of the Executive Secretary of the Advisory Committee were made available to the Bureau of the Census.

The Social Science Research Council Committee on the Source Book of Historical Statistics
(Advisory to the Bureau of the Census)

J. Frederic Dewhurst (Chairman), The Twentieth Century Fund

Shepard Clough
    Columbia University
Arthur H. Cole
    Harvard University
Morris A. Copeland
    National Bureau of Economic Research
Ernest S. Griffith
    The Library of Congress
Edward P. Hutchinson
    University of Pennsylvania

Stacy May
    International Basic Economy Corp.
Walter Mitchell, Jr.
    Controllers Institute of America
Amos E. Taylor
    Bureau of Foreign and Domestic Commerce
Harold Williamson
    Northwestern University
A. Benjamin Handler (Executive Secretary)
    Social Science Research Council

R. H. Coats, University of Toronto, attended meetings of the Committee as a representative of the Social Science Research Council of Canada

Acknowledgments for Chapter Contributions *

Chapter A.   Population

Historical Statistics . . . Colonial Times to 1970
Consultant—Philip M. Hauser, University of Chicago
Major contributor—Campbell J. Gibson, Population Division, Bureau of the Census

Historical Statistics . . . Colonial Times to 1957
Principal consultant—Population Division, Bureau of the Census
Review consultant—Irene B. Taeuber, Princeton University
Other contributor—Donald S. Akers, Bureau of the Census

Historical Statistics . . . 1789–1945
Material on population prepared by Bureau of the Census staff.

Chapter B.   Vital Statistics and Health and Medical Care

Historical Statistics . . . Colonial Times to 1970

VITAL STATISTICS

Consultant—Irene B. Taeuber, Princeton University
Major contributors—Wilson H. Grabill, Bureau of the Census; Michael J. Zugzda, National Center for Health Statistics

HEALTH AND MEDICAL CARE

Consultant—Herbert E. Klarman, New York University

Historical Statistics . . . Colonial Times to 1957

VITAL STATISTICS

Principal consultant—Robert D. Grove, National Office of Vital Statistics
Review consultant—Irene B. Taeuber, Princeton University
Other contributors—Joseph Schachter and Mildred L. McKinnon, National Office of Vital Statistics; Wilson H. Grabill, Bureau of the Census

HEALTH AND MEDICAL CARE

Principal consultant—Maryland Y. Pennell, Public Health Service
Review consultant—Antonio Ciocco, University of Pittsburgh

Historical Statistics . . . 1789–1945
Basic text and series on vital statistics supplied by National Office of Vital Statistics, Public Health Service, Federal Security Agency.
Basic text and series on health supplied by Division of Public Health Methods, Office of the Surgeon General, Public Health Service, Federal Security Agency.
Basic text and series on nutrition supplied by Bureau of Human Nutrition and Home Economics and Bureau of Agricultural Economics, Department of Agriculture.

Chapter C.   Migration

Historical Statistics . . . Colonial Times to 1970
Consultant—Henry S. Shryock, Jr., Georgetown University

---

* See also Appendix, p. A–1.

Historical Statistics . . . Colonial Times to 1957

INTERNAL MIGRATION

Principal consultants—Everett S. Lee and Dorothy S. Thomas, University of Pennsylvania
Review consultant—Irene B. Taeuber, Princeton University
Other contributor—Anne S. Lee, University of Pennsylvania

INTERNATIONAL MIGRATION AND NATURALIZATION

Principal consultant—Edward P. Hutchinson, University of Pennsylvania
Review consultant—Niles Carpenter, The University of Buffalo
Other contributors—Helen F. Eckerson and Gertrude D. Krichefsky, Immigration and Naturalization Service

Historical Statistics . . . 1789–1945
Material on internal migration, citizenship, and country of birth prepared by Bureau of the Census staff.
Basic text and series for immigration, emigration, and naturalization supplied by Mrs. Helen F. Eckerson, Supervisor of the Statistics Section, Division of Research and Education, Immigration and Naturalization Service, Department of Justice.

Chapter D.   Labor

Historical Statistics . . . Colonial Times to 1970
Consultant—Stanley Lebergott, Wesleyan University

Historical Statistics . . . Colonial Times to 1957

LABOR FORCE

Principal consultant—Seymour L. Wolfbein, Bureau of Labor Statistics
Review consultant—Clarence D. Long, The Johns Hopkins University

HOURS, WAGES, AND WORKING CONDITIONS

Principal consultants—H. Gregg Lewis and Albert Rees, The University of Chicago
Review consultant—Harry M. Douty, Bureau of Labor Statistics

Historical Statistics . . . 1789–1945
Material on labor force prepared by Bureau of the Census staff.
Basic text and series on wages and working conditions largely supplied by Bureau of Labor Statistics, Department of Labor, Margaret H. Schoenfeld, Economic Editor, coordinating.

Chapter E.   Prices and Price Indexes

Historical Statistics . . . Colonial Times to 1970
Consultant—Irving B. Kravis, University of Pennsylvania

Historical Statistics . . . Colonial Times to 1957
Principal consultant—Ethel D. Hoover, Bureau of Labor Statistics
Review consultants—Arthur H. Cole, Harvard University; Geoffrey H. Moore, National Bureau of Economic Research, Inc.

Historical Statistics . . . 1789–1945
Basic text and series supplied by Prices and Cost of Living Branch, Bureau of Labor Statistics, Department of Labor.

Chapter F.   National Income and Wealth

Historical Statistics ... Colonial Times to 1970

NATIONAL PRODUCT AND INCOME; NATIONAL WEALTH AND SAVING

Consultant—Edward F. Denison, The Brookings Institution

Major contributors—Nora E. Dollymore, Robert E. Graham, and Allan H. Young, Bureau of Economic Analysis; Raymond W. Goldsmith, Yale University; Stephen P. Taylor, Board of Governors of the Federal Reserve System

INPUT-OUTPUT STRUCTURE OF THE U.S. ECONOMY

Consultant—Albert J. Walderhaug, Bureau of Economic Analysis

Historical Statistics ... Colonial Times to 1957

Principal consultant—Richard A. Easterlin, University of Pennsylvania

Review consultant—Simon Kuznets, The Johns Hopkins University

Other contributor—Raymond W. Goldsmith, National Bureau of Economic Research, Inc.

Historical Statistics ... 1789–1945

Chapter prepared by Harlow D. Osborne, Economic Analyst, National Income Division, Bureau of Foreign and Domestic Commerce, Department of Commerce.

Chapter G.   Consumer Income and Expenditure

Historical Statistics ... Colonial Times to 1970

Consultant—Herman P. Miller, Temple University

Major contributors—Henry Aaron, The Brookings Institution; Roger A. Herriot, Bureau of the Census

Historical Statistics ... Colonial Times to 1957

FAMILY AND INDIVIDUAL INCOME

Principal consultant—Selma F. Goldsmith, Office of Business Economics

Review consultant—Dorothy S. Brady, University of Pennsylvania

CONSUMER EXPENDITURE PATTERNS

Principal consultant—Faith M. Williams, Bureau of Labor Statistics

Review consultant—Rose D. Friedman, Chicago, Illinois

Other contributors—Joseph A. Clorety, Anna-Stina L. Ericson, Helen H. Lamale, Bureau of Labor Statistics; Marguerite C. Burk, Agricultural Marketing Service, and Jean L. Pennock, Agricultural Research Service

Chapter H.   Social Statistics

Historical Statistics ... Colonial Times to 1970

SOCIAL SECURITY AND WELFARE

Consultant—Ida C. Merriam, Social Security Administration

Major contributor—Alfred M. Skolnik, Social Security Administration

EDUCATION

Consultant—Abbott L. Ferriss, Emory University

Major contributors—J. Fred Beamer and C. George Lind, Office of Education

RELIGIOUS AFFILIATION

Consultant—Constant H. Jacquet, Jr., National Council of the Churches of Christ

RECREATION

Consultant—Marion Clawson, Resources for the Future, Inc.

CRIME AND CORRECTION

Consultants—Thorsten Sellin and Marvin E. Wolfgang, University of Pennsylvania

Major contributors—James A. McCafferty, Administrative Office of the United States Courts; Paul White, Law Enforcement Assistance Administration

Historical Statistics ... Colonial Times to 1957

SOCIAL SECURITY AND WELFARE

Principal consultant—Ida C. Merriam, Social Security Administration

Review consultant—Eveline M. Burns, Columbia University

Other contributor—George Rohrlich, Bureau of Employment Security

EDUCATION

Principal consultant—Emery M. Foster, Office of Education

Review consultants—Helen M. Walker, Columbia University; John Walton, The Johns Hopkins University

Other contributors—Henry G. Badger, W. Vance Grant, and Rose Marie Smith, Office of Education; Charles B. Nam, Bureau of the Census

RELIGIOUS AFFILIATION

Principal consultant—Benson Y. Landis, National Council of the Churches of Christ in the United States of America

Review consultant—Edmund deS. Brunner, Columbia University

RECREATION

Principal consultant—Marion Clawson, Resources for the Future, Inc.

Review consultant—Thomas C. Fichandler, The Twentieth Century Fund

Other contributor—George D. Butler, National Recreation Association

CRIME AND CORRECTION

Principal consultant—Ronald H. Beattie, California Department of Justice, State of California

Review consultant—Thorsten Sellin, University of Pennsylvania

Other contributors—Benjamin Frank, Henry C. Lanpher, James A. McCafferty, Bureau of Prisons

Chapter J.   Land, Water, and Climate

Historical Statistics ... Colonial Times to 1970

LAND AND WATER UTILIZATION

Consultant—Marion Clawson, Resources for the Future, Inc.

CLIMATE

Consultant—George S. Benton, The Johns Hopkins University

Major contributor—Harry Torbitt, National Climatic Center

Historical Statistics ... Colonial Times to 1957

LAND AND WATER UTILIZATION

Principal consultants—Ernst H. Wiecking and Hugh H. Wooten, Agricultural Research Service; Walter L. Picton, Business and Defense Services Administration

Review consultant—Marion Clawson, Resources for the Future, Inc.

CLIMATE

Principal consultants—Helmut E. Landsberg and J. Murray Mitchell, Jr., Weather Bureau

Review consultant—George S. Benton, The Johns Hopkins University

Other contributor—Milton L. Blanc, Weather Bureau

Historical Statistics ... 1789–1945

Basic text and series on public lands supplied largely by Branch of Research, Bureau of Land Management, Department of the Interior.

Basic text and series on land utilization supplied by Bureau of Agricultural Economics, Department of Agriculture.

ACKNOWLEDGMENTS FOR CHAPTER CONTRIBUTIONS

Chapter K. Agriculture

Historical Statistics . . . Colonial Times to 1970

Consultant—Earl E. Houseman, Department of Agriculture

Major contributors—J. Richard Grant, Department of Agriculture; Arnold L. Bollenbacher and Orvin L. Wilhite, Bureau of the Census

Historical Statistics . . . Colonial Times to 1957

Principal consultant—Department of Agriculture (Earl E. Houseman, Coordinator)

Review consultant—Theodore W. Schultz, The University of Chicago

Historical Statistics . . . 1789–1945

Basic text and series supplied by Bureau of Agricultural Economics and Farm Credit Administration, Department of Agriculture, Robert M. Walsh, Special Assistant to the Chief of the Bureau of Agricultural Economics, coordinating.

Chapter L. Forestry and Fisheries

Historical Statistics . . . Colonial Times to 1970

FORESTS AND FOREST PRODUCTS

Consultant—Robert S. Manthy, Michigan State University

Major contributor—Dwight Hair, Forest Service

FISHERIES

Consultant—Howard Horton, Oregon State University

Major contributor—William Robinson, National Marine Fisheries Service

Historical Statistics . . . Colonial Times to 1957

FORESTS AND FOREST PRODUCTS

Principal consultant—Dwight Hair, Forest Service

Review consultant—William A. Duerr, Syracuse University

FISHERIES

Principal consultant—Harvey L. Moore, Fish and Wildlife Service

Review consultant—F. Heward Bell, International Pacific Halibut Commission

Other contributor—Edward A. Power, Fish and Wildlife Service

Historical Statistics . . . 1789–1945

Series on forestry supplied by Division of Forest Economics, Forest Service, Department of Agriculture.

Series of fisheries supplied by Statistical Section, Division of Commercial Fisheries, Fish and Wildlife Service, Department of the Interior.

Chapter M. Minerals

Historical Statistics . . . Colonial Times to 1970

Consultant—Vivian E. Spencer, University of Connecticut

Historical Statistics . . . Colonial Times to 1957

Principal consultants—Sam H. Schurr and Elizabeth K. Vogely, Resources for the Future, Inc.

Review consultant—Vivian E. Spencer, Bureau of the Census

Other contributor—Robert E. Herman, Bureau of Mines

Historical Statistics . . . 1789–1945

Basic text and series on minerals supplied by Economics and Statistics Branch, Bureau of Mines, Department of the Interior, Hubert D. Keiser and Allan F. Matthews, former and present editors of the *Minerals Yearbook*, coordinating.

Introduction

This volume is the third in the *Historical Statistics* series issued by the Bureau of the Census as a supplement to the annual *Statistical Abstract of the United States.*

Statistics are a valuable adjunct to historical analysis. They often clarify and enrich qualitative history and on occasion become important parts of a historical record on their own. However, users of historical data are faced with the paradox of over-abundance and scarcity. A burdensome multiplicity of sources has frequently to be consulted in order to reconstruct one quantitative aspect of a particular subject. Just as often, users are confronted by a discouraging barrenness of data, discoverable only after much costly work and delay.

The objective of the *Historical Statistics* volumes is to provide a convenient reference source which has two functions, *collecting* and *referring*. The *collecting* function consists of assembling, selecting, and arranging data from hundreds of sources and making them available within a single source. The *referring* function consists of text annotations to the data which act as a guide to sources of greater detail. The annotations also define terms used in the tables and include essential qualifying statements.

The first volume in this series, *Historical Statistics of the United States, 1789–1945*, was published in 1949. It provided a wide range of series quantifying various aspects of the development of the Nation. An interim *Continuation to 1952* was issued in 1954 to provide data for 1946 to 1952 for the still-active series shown in the first volume. Limited resources confined the scope of the first volume to data most readily available, usually from governmental agency sources. Nevertheless, some 3,000 statistical time series were presented.

Historical Statistics of the United States, Colonial Times to 1957, issued in 1960, represented a substantial expansion of the data shown in the original volume. It presented more than 8,000 time series, mostly annual, on a greater variety of subjects and for longer time periods. The statistics were also more fully annotated and more precise references to original sources were provided. For a greater number of series, in addition, there were more detailed descriptions of the development and reliability of the data. A *Continuation to 1962 and Revisions* was issued in 1965, presenting revisions of data in the basic volume and extensions to 1962 of the more than 6,000 series still current at that time.

Each of the first two volumes was prepared with the cooperation of the Social Science Research Council, the guidance of a distinguished Advisory Committee, and the assistance of numerous scholars, research analysts, and particular subject specialists. A description tracing the development of the first two editions appears below under "Origin of Historical Statistics of the United States."

During the latter 1960's, the supply of copies of *Historical Statistics ... to 1957* available for sale from the U.S. Superintendent of Documents was exhausted. The edition had already been through a cycle of five printings and a question was raised concerning the advisability of further printings in the light of a possible new edition. The question was timely. Experience with the first two editions and their *Continuation* supplements had shown that a new edition was desirable at 10 to 12 year intervals. The *Continuation* supplements were at best handy stopgaps for researchers, a serviceable minimum seriously lacking in documentation. As each year lengthened the interval between editions, the "convenience" value of both the *Continuation to 1962* and its parent *Historical Statistics ... to 1957* diminished. More and more time series were revised in part or entirely replaced. Further, the task for the user of updating the still active, unrevised, series became more burdensome despite the special efforts of the an-

nual *Statistical Abstract* to maintain a direct linkage to as many historical series as possible in its current tables. As a result, a decision was made in 1969 to begin preparation of a new edition.

The plans for the new edition immediately encountered the problem of funding and resources. It was clearly impractical at that time, given the available resources, to consider undertaking a full-fledged new edition of *Historical Statistics*. The determination to make a start, however, was very strong and more modest objectives were adopted. In effect, the early plans for the present edition proposed that it comprise little more than: (1) An extension to 1970 of those series for which current data were available; (2) revisions of data which had occurred since issuance of the *Continuation to 1962*; and (3) a reprinting of those series in *Historical Statistics ... to 1957* which had not been affected by either updating or revisions. No time span was specifically set down to complete the work because there was a clear understanding that it was a part-time staff project.

Two other aspects of this plan differed considerably from the procedures followed for the last edition. For that edition, a large number of consultants were enlisted for their expertise in assembling and developing new time series, reviewing and adjusting old time series, and providing explanatory and bibliographic notes for both. Although most of these consultants, especially those in Federal agencies, contributed their own and their agencies services without compensation, many were compensated from funds provided by the Ford Foundation (by arrangement through the Social Science Research Council). For the new edition, given the limited resources, consultants' contributions were recruited on a public service basis entirely. Partly for the same reason, it was decided not to revive the collaboration of the Census Bureau with the Social Science Research Council which had proved so highly effective for the first two *Historical Statistics* editions. Even more convincing for the Bureau decision to undertake the project alone was the solidity of the base which those editions now provided for the next edition. Seeking such collaboration again seemed unwarranted in the light of the modest objectives outlined above.

As the work slowly progressed and as the many consultants and contributors gave generously of their knowledge and talent, it became clear that our objectives were too restrictive; that our contemplated mere updating would, if adhered to, have to ignore a large accumulation of new time series which were either ineligible for the last edition (at that time they covered a period of less than 20 years) or had not been discovered or properly developed prior to that edition. The gradual accretion of new material plus the additions to old material substantially changed the planned scope of the present edition. What follows are some measures of the changes in content introduced in the present edition.

All of the broad subject fields shown as separate chapters in the last edition are included in this edition and follow the same sequence. Within some of the chapters, however, chapter segments have been regrouped into new subchapters (as in chapters K and X) and in others, the sequence of the subchapters has been changed (as in chapters H, Q, and U) to achieve minor improvements in the juxta-position of subjects.

In two chapters, two entirely new subchapters have been added: "Input-Output Structure of the U.S. Economy" to chapter F and "Flow of Funds" to chapter X.

The present edition presents more than 12,500 time series, a 50-percent increase over the last edition. Every chapter has undergone some expansion with respect to new time series. Chapter F, national income and wealth, and chapter H, social statistics, doubled in number of series; the former from 345 to 723 and the latter from 543 to 1,170. The increase in chapter F was largely due to newly-added data for economic growth rates, greater detail than was previously shown for national and personal income, and data showing valuation of capital stocks. Unsurprisingly, the largest increase in series occurred in chapter H where the data for social insurance and welfare, education, and crime and correction reflect the great public attention given to these subjects in recent decades. Almost equally large increases took place for chapter K, agriculture, and chapter X, financial markets and institutions (formerly banking and finance); chapter K from 328 series to 623; chapter X from 480 to 962. Partly to accommodate the increase in series, chapter K has been subdivided into 4 parts. Most of the new series in chapter K relate to farm population and farm-operator characteristics, farm marketings, government payments and price supports, and a number of new measures of farm productivity. For chapter X, the bulk of the increase in series is in the new flow-of-funds subchapter.

Several chapters now include for the first time a number of data series below the national level. In all, there are 13 new tables (comprising 484 series) in this category, 9 of which present data for the individual States and 4 for either regions (e.g. the South or the West) or the smaller geographic divisions (e.g. New England, South Atlantic). Perhaps of special interest among these tables are the series on population characteristics and land area for each State (A 195–263), those on selected items for farms and farm population by State (K 17–81), those on voter participation in presidential elections by State (Y 27–78), and those on population censuses taken in the colonies and States during the colonial and pre-Federal period (Z 24–132).

In addition, each of 4 chapters (D, G, Q, and Z) includes at least 200 or more new series and each of 10 chapters (A, B, L, N, P, S, T, U, V, and Y) includes 100 or more. A summary of selected new series included in each chapter is shown on p. XV.

One other important change is the reinstatement of a time period index (see p. A–4) which first appeared in *Historical Statistics . . . , 1789 to 1945*. The index enables users to identify quickly which time series (or statistics for particular subjects) begin in the specified 10- or 20-year time segment (e.g. 1800–1819, 1820–1839).

As a result of the complete review and updating of the contents of the last edition of *Historical Statistics*, many changes, apart from the entirely new series, have occurred in both the tables, the descriptive text, and the bibliographic notes. Most of the changes are due to revisions and corrections made during the interval between the last and present editions by the sources of the data affected. Where users of both editions become aware of discrepancies in what purport to be identical sets of data, it is safe to assume that the figures, descriptive text, and notes in the present edition supersede those in the last edition.

With rare exception, all of the series shown in the last edition are also included here. 76 series were omitted. They were primarily discontinued series replaced on recommendations of consultants by other series of a similar kind or were considered of marginal importance or relatively weak in other respects. In one or two instances, space was also a factor.

Origin of *Historical Statistics of the United States*

The first edition, *Historical Statistics of the United States, 1789–1945*, was formally initiated by a recommendation in 1945 by the Social Science Research Council that the Secretary of Commerce consider compilation and publication by the Bureau of the Census of a source book of economic statistics.

Earlier the same year, J. Frederic Dewhurst urged the development of an historical source book in a proposal to the American Statistical Association and the American Economic Association. A joint committee was named by these associations, joined by the Economic History Association, to explore the practical problems of preparing such a volume. Dr. Dewhurst's proposal coincided closely with

Bureau of the Census plans to prepare an historical supplement to the *Statistical Abstract of the United States*. The formal decision in 1945 by the Bureau of the Census to compile and publish such a volume led to the reconstitution of the joint committee, which then became the Social Science Research Council Committee on the Source Book of Historical Statistics, Advisory to the Bureau of the Census.

After the first edition was issued in June 1949, the Economic History Association, in response to a request from the Bureau of the Census, appointed an advisory committee in September 1950 to evaluate the volume and to make specific recommendations affecting the question of its revision. This committee, formally designated as the Committee of the Economic History Association on the Revision of *Historical Statistics of the United States, 1789–1945*, was under the chairmanship of G. Heberton Evans, Jr., The Johns Hopkins University, and included the following as members: Arthur H. Cole, Harvard University; Shepard Clough, Columbia University; T. C. Cochran, University of Pennsylvania, and Solomon Fabricant, National Bureau of Economic Research, Inc. In April 1952 the committee submitted a report to the Bureau of the Census entitled "On the Revision of *Historical Statistics of the United States, 1789–1945*." The conclusions and comments presented in this report were subsequently influential in getting underway the project for a revised volume.

For the second edition, *Historical Statistics of the United States, Colonial Times to 1957*, the Bureau designated a project director who also acted as secretary of the Committee on Historical Statistics appointed by the Social Science Research Council to serve as an advisory group similar to the committee which participated in the preparation of the first edition. The Census Bureau again assumed the responsibility for publishing the volume as a part of its *Statistical Abstract* program. The Social Science Research Council, in turn, obtained a grant from the Ford Foundation which provided funds for the procurement of services of experts in each field. More than 125 such specialists were engaged to serve as consultants. The Council also made arrangements with some of the consultants for the preparation of bibliographic essays on statistics in selected fields, five of which were subsequently published in the *Journal of the American Statistical Association*.

The Problem of Historical Statistics

The scattered sources of historical statistics of the United States include the annual reports of the executive heads of the agencies of the Federal Government, reports of special Federal commissions, the U.S. census volumes, printed debates of the Congress, published reports of committees of the Congress and transcripts of hearings on important legislative measures, published reports and documents of the State governments, statistical publications of private research organizations and of the universities and colleges of the Nation, together with the great mass of statistical volumes printed by other private organizations and individuals.

It has been noted that on occasion compilers, desiring to save the time and effort required to obtain data directly from the original sources, make use of successive issues of the annual *Statistical Abstract of the United States* to construct long-term time series. The results of such a procedure are not always sound, since the space available in the *Statistical Abstract* for describing major revisions in time series may not permit adequate clarification. Of the many revised figures appearing in each issue, most revisions apply to the immediate preceding years, but revisions of much earlier years are not uncommon. Moreover, the revisions shown have followed no systematic pattern and may be scattered irregularly over many issues.

Impediments to the use of historical statistics, then, include the initial difficulty of determining whether the data in fact exist, of identifying the document in which the data may be found, of constructing time series where the data may not be arranged in suitable form, and of identifying and interpreting changes in concept and coverage. Definitions employed in published historical tables, moreover, may have to be sought in separate publications if, indeed, they have been published at all.

Technical Notes and Explanations

Arrangement of the data. Data are arranged for broad subjects in lettered chapters and for more specific and detailed subjects in numbered series within each chapter. To facilitate reference, subject groups are organized in summary form under chapter and subchapter titles in the table of contents (p. IV). In addition, there is a detailed alphabetical subject index (p. A–10). The data are presented in conventional tabular form, each table comprising a group of subject-related series. Each series or tabular column is assigned a unique letter and number. The letter prefix identifies the chapter and the number represents the order of the series in the chapter. Thus the 44th series in the chapter on agriculture is designated K 44 to distinguish it from the 44th series in the chapter on transportation, Q 44. Because of possible confusion with numerals, the capital letters I and O have been omitted in identifying chapters. Source citations and descriptive text material (see below) are linked to the data series by use of the assigned series numbers.

All series begin with the most recent year for which data have been obtained and run backward in time. This arrangement was selected because it lent itself to more compact, less space-consuming presentation than the alternative of beginning with the earliest year. Insofar as possible, there are uniformly placed spaces above every year ending in 0 or 5. No data are shown for years subsequent to 1970. Figures for later years for most of the current series are presented in the *Statistical Abstract of the United States* beginning with the 1973 edition.

Basic guidelines. The guidelines adopted for this edition to aid Census Bureau staff members, subject matter consultants, and other participants with respect to selection and presentation of the data are quite similar to those of the last edition. As was the case then, however, the guidelines were not followed with complete rigidity. At times, the scope, variety, and complexity of the data involved made it necessary to modify the rules for the sake of clarity or internal consistency. The guidelines applied and the elements subject to application are discussed below.

Area coverage. Except as otherwise specified, data generally represent conterminous United States or the 48 States (including the District of Columbia) prior to the admission of Alaska and Hawaii to statehood and the 50 States thereafter. Asterisks on individual tables or series indicate the first year for which the figures include Alaska and Hawaii to the extent that their inclusion could be ascertained. For some series, especially in chapter K, the notes specifying inclusion or exclusion of Alaska and Hawaii appear in the text. In some instances, the sources used for data failed to specify the area covered. Where practicable, the data were examined and the appropriate qualifications were added.

Because of limitations of space, data are not generally shown for regions, States, or localities. Some exceptions were permitted, however, as noted above with respect to data for regions and States. Other exceptions were of a more specialized nature as in the following instances: Where regional statistics are helpful for correct interpretation of data, such as presentation of merchant marine statistics separately for each coast and for inland waters; where data in the subject field cannot (by definition) be summarized effectively for the United States, such as internal migration data; where summary data for a given subarea or market are indicative of general trend or level, such as prices on the New York Stock Exchange or in specified cities; where data for a given area effectively represent the national picture because of concentration of production, etc., as Pennsylvania anthracite; where data are available for only a given area as in the case of many series concerned with early American history and limited to the Atlantic seaboard.

Time coverage. In general, only annual or census-period data which cover at least 20 years are presented. A major exception was made for series covering the colonial or pre-Federal period. Other exceptions were permitted where newly developed series of recent origin were the only data available to represent an important subject field or where a short series was an important extension of other longer series.

The general requirements as to time coverage were specifically designed to permit inclusion of "lapsed" series, particularly those falling within the nineteenth century or extending into the early twentieth century. The lapsed series, which begin and terminate in the past, represent major fields of interest during various phases of American historical development; frequently they must be sought in out-of-print documents which are available in few libraries.

The identification of time-periods was complicated by failure of some sources to state whether the data were prepared on a calendar-year or on a fiscal-year basis; by shifts in time coverage from calendar to fiscal year during the period of the series, and, in some instances, by the lack of identification of the beginning or ending date of the fiscal year. In all such cases, particularly where time shifts seemed likely to have occurred, an effort was made to identify the correct basis.

Frequency of data. Annual data are given preference but certain series are presented only for years in which a national census was conducted, and, in some instances (for example, telephone and telegraph rates), only for the scattered dates for which the data are available. Where both annual figures and decennial or quinquennial benchmark or census data exist, both series are frequently shown.

Series linkage. No formal attempt was made to extend a single series back through time by linking it to another series which terminated at or near the date on which the first began. In a number of instances, however, such series are presented in adjoining columns, with an overlap for a period of years, when available.

Selection of data. The criteria of selection varied broadly, depending on a number of factors applicable to the subject matter involved. Generally, summary measures or one-dimensional aggregates at gross levels and immediately below were given highest priority for inclusion. Below such levels, selection was governed by the interplay of: The amount of space already devoted to a particular subject; the attempt to achieve a relatively balanced presentation among subject fields; the "uniqueness" (in the sense that other data did or did not fairly cover a particular subject) of the data; the quantity of data available; the quality of the data available; and the extent to which data might be related to and enhance the value of other data.

Among less discretionary factors, both area detail (see above under area coverage) and subject detail, such as cross-classifications or data for specific commodities, were held to a minimum because of space limitations. Inevitably, there were exceptions where synthesis or summarization did serious damage to the value of a series or where it was clearly more meaningful to show series for specific commodities than a group aggregate.

Presentation of absolute rather than derived data. Primary emphasis was placed on the presentation of absolute figures rather than on derived data since the absolute figures offer somewhat greater flexibility to the user. The major exception was the presentation of index numbers. In general, percentage distributions of absolute data already shown are not presented. Other percentage data, and averages, medians, ratios, and rates were used only where they resulted in a significant economy in space or where they significantly facilitated interpretation. No attempt was made to convert various series of index numbers to a base year or period other than that shown in the source. Large numbers (8 digits or more, for example) shown in the source documents have been rounded to thousands, millions, or billions for ease of use and reference only as staff resources allowed.

Omissions of data, "blank" cells. The significance of dashes in tabular cells varies from series to series. In general, the presence of cell "leaders" or "dashes" indicates merely that no information was provided. Dash entries may mean that no information exists for the given year; the entry, if shown, would be zero; the information was not available; or the information is believed to exist in published form but it was not practicable to do the research necessary to locate the appropriate source. The user will have to judge from the context which meaning is appropriate in each particular instance.

The practices of the various sources of information differ as to the meaning of dashes in cells, the extent to which they label data as "not available," the meaning of the term "not available," the use of the zero entry, etc. In general, the policy adopted in preparing this volume was to retain "not available" notations where they appeared for intermediate years in the series; to change them to dashes where they appeared at the beginning or end of the series. Where cells were left blank in the sources, they were filled with dashes unless there was evidence that "not available" was a more appropriate entry.

Since series of varying length taken from different sources are frequently found in adjoining columns in a table, the stub listings for years necessarily encompass the earliest and latest date for which any of the series in the table are shown. In itself, this tends to create many additional blank cells since missing entries have been replaced by dashes in order to make it easier for the user's eye to trace the entries for a given year across the entire table.

Source citations and text. For every series shown, the text notes present the source or sources of the data. In most cases, precise publication dates and page or table numbers are given. However, where numerous issues of a certain publication were used, the source citations are usually limited to "annual issues," "various monthly issues," or similar notations. The term "unpublished data" means that the data were not in published form at the time they were obtained for use in this edition. In many cases, such data were scheduled for inclusion in forthcoming publications.

Where possible the descriptive text includes definitions of concepts and terms used, and sufficient methodological and historical information to permit intelligent use of the data. For many series the text also includes reference to where more detail can be found. Unusual values in a series are explained and major changes which affect comparability are noted. Methods used for adjusted or derived figures are described, often with reference to a more complete description.

Copyright material. Copyright restrictions, where applicable, are noted in source citations. Permission to quote or reprint copyright material should be obtained directly from the copyright owner.

Statistical Reliability and Responsibility

The contents of this volume were obtained from a large number of sources. All data from either censuses and surveys or based on estimates or administrative records are subject to error arising from a number of sources: Sampling variability (for statistics based on samples), reporting errors in the data for individual units, incomplete coverage, nonresponse, imputation, and processing error. The Bureau of the Census cannot accept responsibility for the accuracy or the limitations of data presented here, other than for those which it collects. Every attempt has been made, within the limits of time and available personnel, to verify and correctly identify the material. Final responsibility for selection of the material, and for its accurate and proper presentation, rests with the Bureau of the Census, even though carried out with the cooperation of many individuals and agencies who devoted much time and energy in providing data and descriptions of series for this publication.

The information presented in this volume supersedes all similar information presented in *Historical Statistics of the United States, Colonial Times to 1957*, and in *Historical Statistics of the United States, Colonial Times to 1957: Continuation to 1962 and Revisions.*

FOR ADDITIONAL INFORMATION ON DATA PRESENTED

please consult the source publications available in local libraries or write to the agency indicated in the source note in the descriptive text for the given statistical series. Write to the Bureau of the Census only if it is indicated as the source.

SUGGESTIONS AND COMMENTS

should be sent to:

**The Director
Bureau of the Census
Washington, D.C. 20233**

Summary of Selected New Series in This Edition

Chapter and title	Number of new series	Summary of selected new series	Chapter and title	Number of new series	Summary of selected new series
A. Population	198	Urban population characteristics (A 82–90); foreign born, by sex and race (A 105–118); population characteristics and land area, by States (A 195–263); households, by number of persons (A 335–349); inmates of institutions (A 359–371)	**L. Forestry and Fisheries**	153	Forest products production, imports, exports, and consumption (L 56–71, L 87–97, L 138–165, L 178–198); fishery imports and exports (L 224–235); value of landed fish catches (L 244–253); prices received by fishermen (L 321–337)
B. Vital Statistics and Health and Medical Care	180	Fertility and birth rates, by age of mother (B 11–19); illegitimate births and rates (B 28–35); health expenditures (B 221–261); hospital use rates, expenses, personnel, and insurance coverage (B 381–422)	**M. Minerals**	26	Employment and man-hours in mineral industries (M 287–306)
C. Migration	36	Aliens naturalized (C 162–167); passenger arrivals and departures (C 296–331)	**N. Construction and Housing**	120	Wholesale price indexes for construction materials (N 140–155); new publicly-owned housing starts (N 171–179); value and mean age of stocks of residential structures (N 200–231); housing vacancy rates (N 246–258)
D. Labor	227	Working women (D 49–74); unemployment rates (D 87–115); employee output (D 683–704); employee earnings (D 705–786); union membership and work stoppages (D 927–939, D 986–1021)	**P. Manufactures**	132	General statistics (P 58–67); horsepower of power equipment (P 68–73); shipments, inventories, and orders (P 74–92); corporation sales, profits, and equity (P 93–106); shares of largest companies (P 177–204); consumption of selected commodities (P 216–230)
E. Prices	22	GNP implicit price deflators (E 1–22)	**Q. Transportation**	240	Intercity passenger traffic (Q 1–11); revenues and employment, by type of transport (Q 23–46); intercity motor carriers (Q 69–81); long-term public highway debt (Q 136–147); motor vehicle insurance, ownership, and financing (Q 163–186); motor vehicle speed, miles of travel, and accidents (Q 187–232); merchant vessels built, repaired, launched, and active (Q 438–480, Q 487–502)
F. National Income and Wealth	362	GNP growth rates and per capita (F 10–31); GNP summary and by type of industry (F 32–46), F 130–162); national and personal income (F 163–209, F 250–348); national tangible assets (F 349–376); value and age of capital stocks (F 470–534)			
G. Consumer Income and Expenditures	292	Distribution of families and persons, by money income levels (G 1–268); nutritive value of city diets (G 857–865); food used at home (G 866–880)	**R. Communications**	53	Cable TV (R 98–101); radio and TV finances (R 113–120, R 130–137); new books published (R 195–217); newsprint consumption (R 218–223)
H. Social Statistics	675	Employee benefit plans (H 70–114); OASDHI (social security) coverage, benefits, and trust fund (H 186–259); Civil Service retirement (H 260–270); private philanthropy (H 398–411); schools and school enrollment (H 418–432, H 442–522); school retention rates (H 587–597); income, by years of school completed (H 648–663); illiteracy (H 669–688); doctorates, by field (H 766–787); foreign travel, passports issued, and foreign visitors to U.S. (H 894–951); crimes and crime rates (H 952–961); homicides and suicides (H 971–986); criminal justice expenditures (H 1012–1027); lawyers (H 1028–1062); courts (H 1063–1124)	**S. Energy**	124	Consumption of raw materials and fuel resources (S 15–31); privately-owned electric utility generating plants and balance sheet and income items (S 58–73, S 133–146); REA summary of operations (S 147–159); waterpower (S 160–175); natural gas consumption and gas utility industry (S 178–218)
			T. Distribution and Services	100	Annual earnings of full-time employees (T 29–42); legal form of organization of industries (T 43–57); merchant wholesalers sales and stocks (T 375–383); index of national advertising expenditures (T 472–484)
J. Land, Water, and Climate	15	Indian lands (J 16–19); tornadoes, floods, and cyclones (J 268–278)	**U. International Transactions and Foreign Commerce**	155	Value of direct foreign investment in U.S. (U 47–74); U.S. Government foreign grants and credits (U 75–186); exports and imports, by broad end-use class (U 249–263)
K. Agriculture	315	Farm population, land in farms, farm property, farm products sold (K 1–81); farm operator characteristics (K 82–108); balance sheet of farming and value of gross farm product (K 204–239); farm income and farm marketings (K 256–343); farm productivity (K 407–495)	**V. Business Enterprise**	115	Number of firms, by type of ownership (V 1–12); income of unincorporated firms (V 66–77); manufacturing and trade sales and inventories (V 78–107); gross product and unit costs of nonfinancial corporations

Summary of Selected New Series in This Edition—Con.

Chapter and title	Number of new series	Summary of selected new series	Chapter and title	Number of new series	Summary of selected new series
		(V 141–166); business expenditures for new plant and equipment (V 306–332)	Y. Government	158	Voter participation in presidential elections (Y 28–78); costs of presidential elections (Y 187–188); congressional bills vetoed (Y 199–203); Federal Government full-time civilian employment (Y 318–331); Federal grants to State and local governments (Y 638–651); selective service registrants (Y 917–926); defendants charged with violation of selective service acts (Y 927–942)
W. Productivity and Technological Development	60	Indexes of output per man-hour and per employed person (W 22–29); funds for research and development (W 109–125, W 161–167); employment of natural scientists and engineers (W 168–180)			
X. Financial Markets and Institutions	517	Flow of funds (X 1–392); sales of stocks and bonds on registered exchanges (X 517–530); savings and other time deposits, by institution (X 687–697); assets and liabilities of mutual savings banks and savings and loan associations (X 821–844); selected items of property-liability insurance (X 918–932); stock and mutual insurance companies (X 933–956)	Z. Colonial and Pre-Federal Statistics	200	Population censuses taken in the colonies and States (Z 24–132); components of private wealth for the thirteen colonies (Z 169–191); exports to and imports from Scotland, by colonies and States (Z 227–244); commodity imports and exports, shipping earnings, and value of slaves imported (Z 286–290); vessels built in colonies and West Florida (Z 510–529)

Chapter A

Population

A 1–371. General note.

The principal source of population data is the Decennial Census of Population, a house-by-house enumeration made by the Bureau of the Census. In accordance with a Constitutional provision for a decennial canvass of the population, the first census enumeration was made in 1790. The primary reason for the Census of Population, as set forth in the Constitution, is to provide a basis for the apportionment of Members of the House of Representatives among the several States. Until 1902, the census organization was temporary. It was assembled before each decennial census and disbanded after the work was finished. In 1902, the Bureau of the Census was established as a permanent agency of the Government, charged with responsibility for the decennial census and for compiling statistics on other subjects as needed. Currently (1973), this Bureau provides population data based on surveys and estimates in addition to making the comprehensive decennial census enumeration.

In accordance with census practice dating back to 1790, each person is counted as an inhabitant of his usual place of residence or usual place of abode, that is, the place where he lives and sleeps most of the time. This place is not necessarily the same as his legal residence, voting residence, or domicile, although, in the vast majority of cases, the use of these different bases of classification would produce identical results. Indians living in Indian Territory or on reservations were not included in the population count until 1890, and in earlier censuses large tracts of unorganized and sparsely settled territory were not covered by enumerators. Alaska and Hawaii were territories through 1950 and were first included in the United States in the 1960 census. Many tables in this chapter show two sets of 1960 data, one for the conterminous United States and one for the United States including Alaska and Hawaii.

Through 1930, the data presented are based on complete counts. Many of the data shown from subsequent censuses are based on sample tabulations (ranging from 3⅓ percent to 25 percent), as indicated in footnotes to the tables.

Several tables present data from the Current Population Survey, conducted monthly by the Bureau of the Census since 1947. Originally, the Survey covered a representative sample of approximately 21,000 interviewed households in areas throughout the United States. This sample was increased to approximately 35,000 in May 1956, and to approximately 50,000 in January 1967.

Exact agreement is not to be expected among the various samples, nor between them and the complete census count, but the sample data may be used with confidence where large numbers are involved, and may be assumed to indicate patterns and relationships where small numbers are involved. Detailed statements regarding the sampling errors are given in the original sources.

Many errors appear in the census publications of 1790–1840. The data for these censuses were adjusted by county and race, and the revised figures were published in the 1870 census. Revised figures by sex for the United States population by race for 1790–1840 were published in the 1910 census. Official revisions by age have not been made, and thus the 1790–1840 age data in this chapter for most race-sex groups add to totals which differ slightly from the revised figures for race-sex groups.

The Bureau of the Census has always been concerned about the degree of completeness of enumeration in the decennial censuses, although public interest in census coverage and statistical techniques for estimating coverage were quite limited prior to 1950. Discussions of coverage in earlier censuses were limited mostly to qualitative statements.

The quantitative evaluation of census coverage can be done at the individual and aggregate levels. At the individual level, the approaches include reinterview (e.g., postenumeration surveys) and record checks (e.g., matching of census records and birth records). At the aggregate level, the approaches include demographic analysis (i.e., the use of data on births, deaths, and migration, and of life tables, expected sex ratios, etc.) and the use of aggregated data from administrative records (e.g., comparing the enrollment in "Medicare" with the census count of the aged population).

In 1950, the postenumeration survey was thought to be a satisfactory method of determining net census underenumeration. The number missed in the 1950 census was estimated at about 2.1 million, or 1.4 percent with corresponding estimates of 1.6 percent for 1940 and 0.7 percent for 1930. However, demographers now generally believe that postenumeration surveys tend to understate census omissions because persons missed in a census have an above-average probability of being missed in a postenumeration survey. Evaluations of census coverage now rely heavily on demographic analysis. An analysis of coverage conducted in conjunction with the 1970 census shows the following estimates and revisions of net census underenumeration: for 1970, 5.3 million, or 2.5 percent; for 1960, 5.1 million, or 2.7 percent; for 1950, 5.1 million, or 3.3 percent. Analyses of census coverage are subject to revision on the basis of additional information and research.

While the earlier censuses no doubt were characterized by underenumeration, the amounts generally are difficult to determine. One technique is the comparison of rates of change with respect to consistency and reasonableness. On this basis, it is believed that figures for the South show unreasonably low rates of increase for the decade 1860–1870 and abnormally high rates of increase for 1870–1880. The differences are so great that it appears evident that the enumeration of 1870 in this area was seriously incomplete, undoubtedly as a result of the unsettled conditions of the Reconstruction period. For the portion of the United States outside the South, the rate of increase for 1860–1870 was about the same as for 1870–1880. Therefore, the number initially enumerated in 1870 for the South was revised upward. For a detailed discussion of the adjustment, see *U.S. Census of Population: 1890*, vol. I, pp. xi–xii.

For analyses of the completeness of census enumerations from 1880 to 1970, see the following sources. Ansley J. Coale and Melvin Zelnik, *New Estimates of Fertility and Population in the United States* (Princeton University Press, Princeton, New Jersey), 1963. Jacob S. Siegel, "Estimates of Coverage of the Population by Sex, Race, and Age in the 1970 Census," *Demography*, vol. 11, No. 1 (February 1974), pp. 1–23. Ansley J. Coale and Norfleet W. Rives, Jr., "A Statistical Reconstruction of the Black Population of the United States, 1880–1970: Estimates of True Numbers by Age and Sex, Birth Rates, and Total Fertility," *Population Index*, vol. 39, No. 1 (January 1973), pp. 3–36.

A 1–5. Area and population of the United States, 1790–1970.

Source: U.S. Bureau of the Census. 1790–1950, land area, *U.S. Census of Population: 1960*, vol. I, part A, p. 1–4; gross area, *Historical Statistics of the United States, Colonial Times to 1957*, p. 8. 1960, land area and gross area, *Area Measurement Reports*, GE-20, No. 1, 1970, p. 5. 1970, land area and gross area, *U.S. Census of Population: 1970*, vol. I, part A, section 1, pp. 1–41, 1–42. 1790–1960, population, *U.S. Census of Population: 1960*, vol. I, part A, p. 1–4. 1970, population, *U.S. Census of Population: 1970*, vol. I, part A, section 1, pp. 1–37, 1–42.

Area figures for each census year represent the conterminous area under the jurisdiction of the United States, with the addition in 1960 and 1970 of Alaska and Hawaii. In some cases, large areas are included that were not yet settled or covered by the census. Area figures prior to 1940 have been adjusted to bring them into agreement with remeasurements made in 1940. For area measurements prior to 1940, see text for series A 210–266. For a further discussion of areas covered by the censuses, see *U.S. Census of Population: 1940, Areas of the United States: 1940*, and *U.S. Census of Population: 1950*, vol. I, p. XI. For a discussion of the revision of the 1870 census of population, see *U.S. Census of Population: 1890*, vol. I, pp. xi–xii.

A 6–8. Annual population estimates for the United States, 1790–1970.

Source: U.S. Bureau of the Census. 1790–1899, *Historical Statistics of the United States, Colonial Times to 1957*, p. 7; 1900–1970, *Current Population Reports*, series P–25, No. 499, pp. 11–12.

The estimates are as of July 1, and thus figures for the resident population for census years differ from decennial census populations. Estimates prior to 1900 are based on linear interpolation between decennial censuses. Estimates for the 1900–1919 period are based on interpolation techniques applied to census age data. Estimates for subsequent years are based on census data and information on births, deaths, and international migration. For a discussion of the methodology, see Bureau of the Census, *Current Population Reports*, series P–25, No. 311, pp. 1–3.

Estimates subsequent to the 1960 census are preliminary and are subject to revision on the basis of final estimates of births, deaths, and international migration for the 1960–1970 decade. These population estimates are controlled to 1970 census results, which are final, and thus subsequent revisions in the preliminary estimates will be small.

A 9–22. Population of the United States and outlying areas, 1880–1970.

Source: U.S. Bureau of the Census. For the United States, see source for series A 1–5. For population abroad and other: *U.S. Census of Population: 1910*, vol. I, p. 23; *1920*, vol. I, p. 13; *1950*, vol. I, part A, p. 1–3; *1960*, vol. I, part A, p. 1–3; *1970*, vol. I, part A, section 1, p. 1–41. For the Philippines, *Historical Statistics of the United States, 1789–1945*, p. 25. For Puerto Rico and outlying areas, *U.S. Census of Population: 1970*, vol. I, part A, sections 1 and 2, pp. 3–7, 13–7, 53–9, 54–5, 56–5, 57–5, 55–5, and 58–9.

A 23–28. Annual estimates of the population, by sex and race, 1900–1970.

Source: U.S. Bureau of the Census. 1900–1949, *Current Population Reports*, series P–25, No. 311, pp. 24–123; 1950–1959, *Current Population Reports*, series P–25, No. 310, pp. 14–15, 30–31. 1960–1970, *Current Population Reports*, series P–25, No. 519, pp. 15–25.

Estimates by race for the 1960–1970 period are consistent with the 20-percent sample data on race in the 1970 census. For a discussion of the 1970 data and the definition of race, see text for series A 91–104. For a discussion of methodology, see text for series A 6–8.

A 29–42. Annual estimates of the population, by age, 1900–1970.

Source: U.S. Bureau of the Census. 1900–1949, *Current Population Reports*, series P–25, No. 311, pp. 24–123; 1950–1959, *Current Population Reports*, series P–25, No. 310, pp. 11, 14, 27, 30, and unpublished estimates; 1960–1970, *Current Population Reports*, series P–25, No. 519, pp. 15–25.

For a discussion of methodology, see text for series A 6–8.

A 43–72. Number of places and population in urban and rural territory, by size of place, 1790–1970.

Source: U.S. Bureau of the Census. 1790–1960, *U.S. Census of Population: 1960*, vol. I, part A, pp. 1–13 to 1–15; 1970, *U.S. Census of Population: 1970*, vol. I, part A, section 1, p. 1–46.

The Bureau of the Census has employed several definitions of urban population. According to the definition adopted for use in the 1970 census, the urban population comprises all persons living in urbanized areas (see text for series A 82–90) and in places of 2,500 inhabitants or more outside urbanized areas. More specifically, the urban population consists of all persons living in (a) places of 2,500 inhabitants or more incorporated as cities, villages, boroughs (except Alaska), and towns (except in the New England States, New York, and Wisconsin), but excluding those persons living in the rural portions of extended cities; (b) unincorporated places of 2,500 inhabitants or more; and (c) other territory, incorporated or unincorporated, included in urbanized areas.

In censuses prior to 1950, the urban population comprised all persons living in incorporated places of 2,500 or more and areas (usually minor civil divisions) classified as urban under special rules relating to population size and density. The most important component of the urban territory in any definition is the group of incorporated places having 2,500 inhabitants or more. A definition of urban territory restricted to such places, however, would exclude a number of large and densely settled areas merely because they are not considered "incorporated places." Prior to 1950, an effort was made to avoid some of the more obvious omissions by inclusion of selected areas which were classified as urban under special rules. Even with these rules, however, many large and closely built-up areas were excluded from the urban territory.

To improve its measure of the urban population, the Bureau of the Census adopted, in 1950, the concept of the urbanized area and delineated, in advance of enumeration, boundaries for unincorporated places. With the adoption of the urbanized area and unincorporated place concepts for the 1950 census, the urban population was defined as all persons residing in urbanized areas and, outside these areas, in all places incorporated or unincorporated, which had 2,500 inhabitants or more. With the following two exceptions, the 1950 definition of urban was continued substantially unchanged to 1960 and 1970. In 1960 (but not in 1970), certain towns in the New England States, townships in New Jersey and Pennsylvania, and counties elsewhere were designated as urban. However, most of the population of these "special rule" areas would have been classified as urban in any event because they were residents of an urbanized area or an unincorporated place of 2,500 or more.

In all urban and rural definitions, the population not classified as urban constitutes the rural population.

The first official publication of figures formally presenting the urban population was made following the Census of 1870 in the *Statistical Atlas of the United States*. The population of cities and towns of 8,000 inhabitants or more was presented as the "urban population." In the reports of the 1880, 1890, and 1900 censuses, the urban population was variously defined as the population living in places of 4,000 inhabitants or more, or 8,000 inhabitants or more. The first publication in which the population of places having 2,500 inhabitants or more was officially designated as urban was the *Supplementary Analysis of the Twelfth Census (1900)*, published in 1906. This definition, with minor modifications, was used in later censuses up to and including 1940. For purposes of comparison, the data for 1950 were also tabulated in accordance with this urban definition.

A time series on the urban population since 1790 according to the 1940 definition of urban was published in the 1940 census. These data are shown in series A 43–56 and A 57–72. Data on the urban population by selected characteristics are not always available on this basis, and thus the total urban populations shown in other tables may differ slightly.

For detailed discussions of the urban definitions used up to 1940 and of the major changes implemented in 1950, see Bureau of the

Census, *Current Population Reports*, series P–23, No. 1, "The Development of the Urban–Rural Classification in the United States: 1874 to 1949," and *U.S. Census of Population: 1950*, vol. I, pp. XV–XVIII.

A 73–81.   Population, by type of residence, sex, and race, 1880–1970.

Source: U.S. Bureau of the Census. 1880–1900, *Supplementary Analysis of the Twelfth Census (1900)*, pp. 597–607, 632–642. 1910–1940, *U.S. Census of Population: 1940*, vol. II, part 1, pp. 19–20. 1950, *U.S. Census of Population: 1950*, vol. II, part 1, pp. 88, 91. 1960, *U.S. Census of Population: 1960*, vol. I, part 1, pp. 144, 359; part 3, pp. 17, 117–118; part 13, pp. 17, 113–114. 1970, *U.S. Census of Population: 1970*, vol. I, part 1, section 1, pp. 262, 380–381.

The rural population is subdivided into rural farm and rural nonfarm components. In 1960 and 1970, the farm population was defined as persons living on places of 10 or more acres from which sales of farm products amounted to $50 or more in the preceding calendar year or on places of fewer than 10 acres from which sales of farm products amounted to $250 or more in the preceding year. In 1950, the farm population was defined as all persons living on farms and depended on the respondent's conception of farm (or ranch) with the exception that persons living on what might have been considered farmland were classified as nonfarm if they paid cash rent for their homes and yards only. In 1930 and 1940, the farm population comprised all persons living on farms and depended primarily upon the interviewer's conception of what was meant by the word farm. In 1920, the farm population comprised all persons living on farms and those farm laborers (and their families) who, while not living on a farm, lived in rural, unincorporated territory. Farms were defined in 1920 (as in the census of agriculture) to include all tracts of 3 acres or more used for agricultural purposes and smaller tracts which produced as much as $250 worth of farm products in 1919 or required for their agricultural operations the continuous services of at least one person.

For further discussion, see *U.S. Census of Population: 1930*, vol. II, p. 8; *U.S. Census of Population: 1950*, vol. II, part 1, pp. 33–35; *U.S. Census of Population: 1960*, vol. I, part 1, pp. XXXVII–XXXVIII. See text for series A 43–56 for the definition of urban and rural. See text for series A 91–104 for the definition of race.

A 82–90.   Urban population, by type of residence, sex, and race, 1950–1970.

Source: U.S. Bureau of the Census. 1950, all races and white, *U.S. Census of the Population: 1960*, vol. I, part 1, p. 143; 1950, Negro and other races, *U.S. Census of Population: 1950*, vol. IV, part 5, chapter A, pp. 16–18. 1960, *U.S. Census of Population: 1960*, vol. I, part 1, p. 144; parts 3 and 13, p. 17. 1970, *U.S. Census of Population: 1970*, vol. I, part 1, section 1, p. 262.

The first systematic attempt to define the metropolitan population of the United States was presented in the 1910 census in which Metropolitan Districts were defined for cities of 200,000 or more. Each Metropolitan District included contiguous minor civil divisions which met certain rules of proximity and population density. The Metropolitan District concept was used with changes in definition up through the 1940 census, when Metropolitan Districts were defined for cities of 50,000 or more. Metropolitan Districts were seldom cross-tabulated with census data on social and economic characteristics and thus were of limited usefulness.

In 1950, Metropolitan Districts were replaced in census reports by Standard Metropolitan Areas (see text for series A 267–278) and Urbanized Areas. Urbanized Areas, with minor changes in definition, were delineated in the 1950, 1960, and 1970 censuses. In general, an Urbanized Area is defined as a city of 50,000 or more (or twin cities meeting this criterion) and surrounding closely settled areas, including incorporated places and unincorporated territory. The urban population can be divided into the Urbanized Area population

and the Other Urban population. The Urbanized Area population can be further divided into Central City and Urban Fringe components.

For a further discussion, see the following sources: *U.S. Census of Population: 1910*, vol. I, pp. 73–77; *U.S. Census of Population: 1930, Metropolitan Districts*; *U.S. Census of Population: 1940, The Growth of Metropolitan Districts in the United States: 1900–1940*; *U.S. Census of Population: 1950*, vol. I, pp. XXVII–XXVIII; *U.S. Census of Population: 1970*, vol. I, part A, section 1, p. XIII.

See text for series A 43–56 for definition of urban and rural. See text for series A 91–104 for definition of race.

A 91–104.   Population, by sex and race, 1790–1970.

Source: U.S. Bureau of the Census. 1790–1920, *U.S. Census of Population: 1920*, vol. II, p. 107; slave population, *U.S. Census of Population: 1870*, vol. I, p. 7. 1930–1960, *U.S. Census of Population: 1960*, vol. I, part 1, pp. 144–145. 1970, *U.S. Census of Population: 1970*, vol. I, part 1, section 1, p. 262.

The classification of the population by race reflects common usage rather than an attempt to define biological stock. As a result, the white and Negro populations usually have not been divided into racial subgroups (although the white population has been classified by ethnic origin), but American Indians and some Asian groups (e.g., Japanese, Chinese, Filipino, Korean, etc.) have typically been identified with country of origin.

Through 1950, the classification of the population by race was usually obtained by the enumerator's observation. Persons of mixed white and other parentage were usually classified with the other race. A person of mixed parentage other than white was usually classified by the race of his father, except that mixtures of Negro and Indian were classified as Negro unless the Indian stock was clearly predominant or unless the individual was accepted in the community in which he resided as an Indian.

The category Indian included unmixed American Indians together with persons who were of mixed white and Indian ancestry if they were enrolled on an Indian reservation or agency roll. Persons who were part Indian were included as Indian if they were one-fourth or more Indian, or if they were regarded as Indians in the community in which they resided.

In the 1960 census, data on race were collected by a combination of self-classification, direct interview, and observation by the enumerator; the classification rules were essentially the same as in 1950.

In the 1970 census, data on race were obtained primarily through self-classification. In a change from earlier censuses, a person of mixed white and other parentage who was in doubt as to his classification was classified according to the race of his father. It is believed that self-identification of race may lead to a somewhat higher proportion of the population being classed in the "Other races" category than does observation by the enumerator.

In the 1930 census, persons of Mexican origin were included with "Other races"; however, the tables in this volume have been revised to include Mexicans in the white population.

In the 1970 census, the edit and review of questionnaires were not completed when the complete-count data were processed. As a result, some information which pertained to nationality or ethnicity was accepted as identifying race. For example, some persons who classified themselves in the race item as Mexican or Spanish American were thus included in the "Other races" population, but should have been included in the white population. In the tabulation of sample data, this error was corrected. The result in the case of 20-percent sample data was that the population of "Other races" was reduced from 2,882,662 to 2,555,872 (1,270,625 males and 1,285,247 females), or by 326,790, which is roughly the amount added to the white population in the sample tabulations.

The Census of 1860 was the first in which Indians were distinguished from other classes in the population. Prior to 1890, enumeration of

Indians was limited to Indians living in the general population of the various States; Indians in Indian Territory and on Indian reservations were excluded. In 1910, a special effort was made to secure a complete enumeration of persons with any perceptible amount of Indian ancestry. This probably resulted in the enumeration as Indian of a considerable number of persons who would have been reported as white in earlier censuses. There were no special efforts in 1920, and the returns showed a much smaller number of Indians than in 1910. Again in 1930, emphasis was placed on securing a complete count of Indians, with the result that the returns probably overstated the decennial increase in the number of Indians.

For further discussion of race in census statistics, see *U.S. Census of Population: 1950*, vol. II, part 1, pp. 35–36; *1960*, vol. I, part 1, pp. XLI–XLIII; *1970*, vol. I, part 1, section 2, pp. App. 15–16.

A 105–118. Foreign born population, by sex and race, 1850–1970.

Source: U.S. Bureau of the Census. 1850 and 1870, *U.S. Census of Population: 1870*, vol. I, pp. 606–609, 614–615. 1860, white, *U.S. Census of Population: 1930*, vol. II, p. 97. 1860, all races and Negro, *U.S. Census of Population: 1870*, vol. I, pp. 610–613. 1880, *U.S. Census of Population: 1880*, vol. I, pp. 542–545. 1890, all races and white, *U.S. Census of Population: 1890*, vol. I, part 1, pp. 486–487. 1890, other races, *U.S. Census of Population: 1900*, vol. II, part II, p. xvii. 1900–1940, *U.S. Census of Population: 1940*, vol. II, p. 19. 1950, *U.S. Census of Population: 1950*, vol. II, part 1, p. 171. 1960, *U.S. Census of Population: 1960*, vol. I, part 1, p. 354; part 3, p. 118; part 13, p. 115. 1970, *U.S. Census of Population: 1970*, vol. I, part 1, section 2, pp. 593–596.

The native born population is comprised of persons born in the United States, or in outlying areas of the United States (see series A 9–22) and persons born elsewhere to United States citizens. The remainder of the population is foreign born. Through 1950, persons for whom place of birth was not reported were included in the native population. In 1960 and 1970, such persons were classified as native unless their census report contained contradictory information, such as an entry of a language spoken prior to coming to the United States.

The outlying areas are as defined at each census. Thus, persons born in the Philippines (which was granted independence in 1946) were classified as native born in 1940 and foreign born in 1950.

A 119–134. Population, by age, sex, race, and nativity, 1790–1970.

Source: U.S. Bureau of the Census. (1) For all races, white, Negro, other races, free Negro, and slave: 1790–1840, *U.S. Census of Population: 1840*, Compendium (Blair and Rives edition), pp. 96–98, 366–371. 1850–1870, *U.S. Census of Population: 1870*, vol. II, pp. 552–558. 1880–1950, all races and white, *U.S. Census of Population: 1950*, vol. II, part 1, pp. 93–94. 1890–1930, Negro, *U.S. Census of Population: 1930*, vol. II, p. 580. 1890–1930, other races—by subtraction of Negro (as cited) from Negro and other races (*U.S. Census of Population: 1950*, vol. II, part 1, pp. 93–94). 1940, Negro and other races, *U.S. Census of Population: 1940*, vol. II, part 1, p. 22. 1950, Negro and other races, *U.S. Census of Population: 1950*, vol. II, part 1, p. 172. 1960, all races and white, *U.S. Census of Population: 1960*, vol. I, part 1, pp. 153–154; parts 3 and 13, pp. 23–24. 1960, Negro and other races, *U.S. Census of Population: 1960*, vol. I, part 1, p. 359; part 3, p. 117; part 13, p. 113. 1970, *U.S. Census of Population: 1970*, vol. I, part 1, section 1, pp. 269–296. (2) For foreign-born white: 1870, *U.S. Census of Population: 1870*, vol. II, p. 553. 1880, *U.S. Census of Population: 1880*, vol. I, pp. 549, 551. 1890–1950, *U.S. Census of Population: 1950*, vol. IV, part 3, chapter A, p. 16. 1960, *U.S. Census of Population: 1960*, vol. I, part 1, pp. 354, 359. 1970, *U.S. Census of Population: 1970*, vol. I, part 1, section 2, p. 591.

The censuses of 1790–1840 contain numerous inconsistencies and other errors. Total population by race (including a division of the Negro population into free and slave) for each State and county were corrected in *U.S. Census of Population: 1870*, vol. I, pp. xliv–xlix, 3–8. Adjusted totals by sex appear in *U.S. Census of Population: 1920*, vol. II, p. 107; however, the age data were not adjusted, and thus the totals in series A 119–134, which are consistent with the age data shown, differ slightly in some cases from the totals in series A 91–104.

See text for series A 91–104 and A 105–118 for definitions of race and nativity.

A 135–142. Native born white population, by sex and parentage, 1850–1970.

Source: U.S. Bureau of the Census. 1850–1880, *U.S. Census of Population: 1930*, vol. II, pp. 33, 97. 1890–1930, *U.S. Census of Population: 1950*, vol. IV, part 3, chapter A, p. 11. 1940, parentage, *U.S. Census of Population: 1940*, Nativity and Parentage of the White Population, p. 7; total native population, *U.S. Census of Population: 1940*, vol. II, part 1, p. 19. 1950, *U.S. Census of Population: 1950*, vol. IV, part 3, chapter A, p. 11. 1960, parentage, *U.S. Census of Population: 1960*, PC(2)-1A, p. 2; total native population, *U.S. Census of Population: 1960*, vol. I, part 1, pp. 354, 359. 1970, *U.S. Census of Population: 1970*, Final Report PC(2)-1A, *National Origin and Language*, p. 1.

The procedures for determining the nativity of parents are generally the same as those for determining the nativity of the individual himself. The native-born population can be subdivided into native born of native (American) parents, native born of mixed parentage (one American parent and one foreign-born parent), and native born of foreign parentage (both parents foreign born).

The figures for total native-born population in series A 135–142 and the figures for foreign-born population in series A 105–118 for each year are from the same census count or sample. For 1850–1940, these are complete-count data which add to the totals in series A 91–104. For 1950–1970, these are sample data which do not agree with the totals in A 91–104.

Similarly, the figures by parentage in A 135–142 for each year are from the same census count or sample. For 1870–1930, these are complete-count data which add to the totals in A 135–142. For 1940–1970, these are sample data which add to the totals in A 135–142 only when all figures are from the same tabulation of the same sample.

A 143–157. Median age of the population, by race, sex, and nativity, 1790–1970.

Source: Derived from series A 119–134.

The median age is that age which divides the population into two equal groups, one half being older and one half being younger. Medians have been computed on the basis of the population for which age is available and on the assumption that population is evenly distributed within the age groups shown in series A 119–134. In most cases, the median falls in a 5-year age group, and the assumption of linearity introduces little error. In cases where the median falls near the center of a large age span (e.g., Negro in 1830 and 1840), this assumption may introduce considerable error. The fluctuations in median ages for the "Other races" population are due in part to changing race composition (e.g., the majority of the Indian population was not included in tabulations by age until 1900).

A 158–159. Median age at first marriage, by sex, 1890–1970.

Source: U.S. Bureau of the Census, *Current Population Reports*, series P-20, No. 242, "Marital Status and Living Arrangements: March 1972," p. 2.

The median age at first marriage, as shown here, is an approximation derived indirectly from tabulations of marital status and age. (See source for detailed explanation of computation procedures.) These estimates differ from those based on annual marriage records or census questions on age at first marriage. The median age at first marriage shown here can be interpreted as applying to the cohort born "n" years earlier, where "n" is the median age at first marriage. Estimates from 1947 to 1970 are subject to sampling variability.

A 160–171. Marital status of the population, by age and sex, 1890–1970.

Source: U.S. Bureau of the Census. 1890–1950, *U.S. Census of Population: 1950*, vol. II, part 1, pp. 179–181; 1960, *U.S. Census of Population: 1960*, vol. I, part 1, pp. 424–425; 1970, *U.S. Census of Population: 1970*, vol. I, part 1, section 2, pp. 640–641.

Marital status (single, married, widowed, and divorced) represents the status of persons at the time of the enumeration. Persons classified as "married" include those who have been married only once, remarried after having been widowed or divorced, separated, and living in common-law marriages. Persons reported as never married or with annulled marriages are classified as single. Since it is probable that some divorced persons are reported as single, married, or widowed, the census figures may understate somewhat the actual number of divorced persons who have not remarried.

A 172–194. Population of regions, by sex, race, residence, age, and nativity, 1790–1970.

Source: U.S. Bureau of the Census. **Series A 172** and **A 178–179**, *U.S. Census of Population: 1970*, vol. I, part A, tables 8 and 18. **Series A 173–177** and **A 184–189**, 1790–1830, *Fifth Census of the United States: 1830*; 1840, *Sixth Census of the United States: 1840*; 1850, *Seventh Census of the United States: 1850*, table 1; 1860, *Eighth Census of the United States: 1860*, table 1; 1870–1890, *Sixteenth Census of the United States: 1940*, *Population*, vol. II, parts 1–7, table 4; 1900–1970, *U.S. Census of Population: 1970*, vol. I, parts 1–52. **Series A 180–183**, 1900–1920, *Fourteenth Census of the United States: 1920*, vol. III, table 1; 1930, *Fifteenth Census of the United States: 1930*, vol. III, part 1, table 40; 1940, *Sixteenth Census of the United States: 1940*, vol. II, part 2; 1950, *U.S. Census of Population: 1950*, vol. II, part 1, table 60; 1960–1970, *U.S. Census of Population: 1970*, vol. I, part 1, section 1, table 55. **Series A 190–194**, 1850–1870, *Ninth Census of the United States: 1870*, vol. I, table VI; 1880, *Tenth Census of the United States: 1880*, tables XII and XIX; 1960, *U.S. Census of Population: 1960*, vol. I, part 1, table 108; 1970, *U.S. Census of Population: 1970*, vol. I, part 1, section 1, table 141. **Series A 190–192**, 1890–1950, *U.S. Census of Population: 1950*, vol. IV, Special Reports, part 3, table 2. **Series A 193–194**, 1890, *Twelfth Census of the United States: 1900*, vol. I, part 1, tables 11 and 15; 1900–1940, *Sixteenth Census of the United States: 1940*, vol. II, parts 1–7, table 4; 1950, *U.S. Census of Population: 1950*, vol. II, table 54.

The divisional and State composition of census regions is as follows:

Northeast Region:
  New England Division:
    Maine
    New Hampshire
    Vermont
    Massachusetts
    Rhode Island
    Connecticut
  Middle Atlantic Division:
    New York
    New Jersey
    Pennsylvania
North Central Region:
  East North Central Division:
    Ohio
    Indiana
    Illinois
    Michigan
    Wisconsin
  West North Central Division:
    Minnesota
    Iowa
    Missouri
    North Dakota
    South Dakota
    Nebraska
    Kansas
South Region:
  South Atlantic Division:
    Delaware
    Maryland
    District of Columbia
    Virginia

South Region—Con.
  South Atlantic Division—Con.
    West Virginia
    North Carolina
    South Carolina
    Georgia
    Florida
  East South Central Division:
    Kentucky
    Tennessee
    Alabama
    Mississippi
  West South Central Division:
    Arkansas
    Louisiana
    Oklahoma
    Texas
West Region:
  Mountain Division:
    Montana
    Idaho
    Wyoming
    Colorado
    New Mexico
    Arizona
    Utah
    Nevada
  Pacific Division:
    Washington
    Oregon
    California
    Alaska
    Hawaii

For definition of residence, see text for series A 43–56; for definition of race, see text for series A 91–104; for definition of nativity, see text for series A 105–118. See also general note for series A 1–371 and text for series A 195–209.

A 195–209. Population of States by sex, race, urban-rural residence, and age, 1790–1970.

Source: U.S. Bureau of the Census. **Series A 195** and **A 202–203**, *U.S. Census of Population: 1970*, vol. I, part 1, section 1, tables 8 and 18. **Series A 196**, 1790–1890, *Fourteenth Census of the United States: 1920*, *Population*, table 18; 1900–1910, *Census of Population: 1950*, vol. II, part 1, table 9; 1920–1970, *U.S. Census of Population: 1970*, vol. I, part 1, section 1, table 11. **Series A 197–201** and **A 204–209**, 1790–1830, *Fifth Census of the United States: 1830*; 1840, *Sixth Census of the United States: 1840*; 1850, *Seventh Census of the United States: 1850*, table 1; 1860, *Eighth Census of the United States: 1860*, table 1; 1870–1890, *Sixteenth Census of the United States: 1940*, *Population*, vol. II, parts 1–7, table 4; 1900–1970, *U.S. Census of Population: 1970*, vol. I, parts 1–52.

For a discussion of changes in State boundaries, see *U.S. Census of Population: 1960*, vol. I, part 1, pp. XVI–XVIII.

For definition of residence, see text for series A 43–56; for definition of race, see text for series A 91–104. See also general note for series A 1–371.

A 210–263. Land area of the United States, by States and territories, 1790–1970.

Source: U.S. Bureau of the Census. 1790–1920, *Fourteenth Census of the United States: 1920*, vol. I, *Population*, table 14; 1930, *Fifteenth Census of the United States, 1930*, vol. I, *Population*, table 7; 1940, *Sixteenth Census of the United States: 1940*, *Areas of the United States, 1940*, table 1; 1950, *Census of Population: 1950*, vol. II, *Characteristics of the Population*, part 1, U.S. Summary, table 9; 1960, *Area Measurement Reports, 1960*, series GE-20; 1970, *U.S. Census of Population: 1970*, vol. I, part 1, section 1, table 11.

Area measurements of the States and former territories rest on three periods of measurement. The first period is for the 1880 Census of Population when, under Henry Gannett, Census Geographer, "the foundation for accurate and detailed area measurement in the United States" was laid (Proudfoot, *Measurement of Geographic Area*, 1946, p. 27). The second period is for the 1940 census when, under Batschelet and Proudfoot, a basic remeasurement of all the areas was accomplished, which still remains the basis for subsequent remeasurements. The third period was during the 1960's when remeasurements of land and water areas based on the 1940 total or gross areas were undertaken with the use of recent maps and greatly improved measurement techniques.

Remeasurements of land and water areas between and since those three periods occurred but they were largely in terms of adjusting the earlier figures because of relatively minor boundary changes or because of land and water changes resulting mainly from the construction of known dams and reservoirs.

According to the 1940 definitions of land and water areas (used also in the 1960's), ponds, lakes, or similar areas were counted as inland water if their areas were 40 acres or more; streams and canals had to be ⅛-mile or more in width to be counted. All other areas were tabulated as land with the exception of "water other than inland water" such as the Great Lakes, coastal waters, bays, etc. The definitions were based on maps, not on inspection of the surface of the earth. Accordingly, features such as new reservoirs which were not shown in the maps used in the measurement work were reported as land rather than water.

The land areas shown for the United States, which are consistent with data available for States and territories, differ slightly from the figures shown in series A 1–5. The latter figures reflect adjustments made only at the national level in conjunction with remeasurements made in 1940.

A 264–275. Number and population of standard metropolitan statistical areas, as defined in 1950, 1960, and 1970, by region and size, 1950–1970.

Source: U.S. Bureau of the Census. 1950 delineations, *U.S. Census of Population: 1950*, vol. I, pp. 1–66 to 1–73; 1960 delineations, *U.S. Census of Population: 1960*, vol. I, part A, pp. 1–100 to 1–111; 1970 delineations, *U.S. Census of Population: 1970*, vol. I, part A, section 1, pp. 1–171 to 1–186.

Standard Metropolitan Areas (SMA's) were first defined in conjunction with the 1950 census. The concept was continued with some changes in definition in the 1960 and 1970 censuses, although the title was changed to Standard Metropolitan Statistical Areas (SMSA's). (For a discussion of other definitions of the metropolitan population, see text for series A 82–90).

Except in the New England States, a standard metropolitan statistical area is a county or group of contiguous counties which contains at least one city of 50,000 inhabitants or more, or "twin cities" with a combined population of at least 50,000. In addition to the county, or counties, containing such a city or cities, contiguous counties are included in an SMSA if, according to certain criteria, they are socially and economically integrated with the central county. In the New England States, SMSA's consist of towns and cities instead of counties. Each SMSA must include at least one central city, and the complete title of an SMSA identifies the central city or cities. The population of SMSA's can be divided into the portions living Inside Central Cities and Outside Central Cities. For a detailed description of the official criteria for defining SMSA's in the 1970 census, see Bureau of the Budget (now U.S. Office of Management and Budget), *Standard Metropolitan Statistical Areas: 1967*.

Urbanized Areas, as discussed in the text for series A 82–90, and SMSA's differ considerably. An Urbanized Area represents the physical or continuously built-up urban area without regard to political boundaries. SMSA's conform to political boundaries. It is thus possible to assemble historical series for SMSA's as defined at a specified time; however, SMSA's include substantial rural population, especially when the current definition is used to present information for an earlier date. In 1970, 12 percent of the SMSA population was rural, and 30 percent of the rural population of the United States was included in SMSA's. See *U.S. Census of Population: 1970*, vol. I, part 1, section 1, pp. 1–206 to 1–212. For a discussion of the criteria for defining SMSA's and the inconsistencies in the application of these criteria, see Ira Rosenwaike, "A Critical Examination of the Designation of Standard Metropolitan Statistical Areas," *Social Forces*, vol. 48, No. 3 (March 1970), pp. 322–333.

A 276–287. Population of standard metropolitan statistical areas, by region, size, and race, 1950–1970.

Source: U.S. Bureau of the Census. 1950, *U.S. Census of Population: 1950*, vol. II, parts 2–50 (State reports), table 34; 1960, *U.S. Census of Population: 1960*, vol. I, parts 2–52 (State reports), table 21; 1970, *U.S. Census of Population: 1970*, vol. I, parts 2–50 (State reports), table 23.

A 288–319. Households, families, subfamilies, married couples, and unrelated individuals, 1790–1970.

Source: U.S. Bureau of the Census. 1790–1880, Twelfth Census Special Reports, *A Century of Population Growth, 1790–1900*; 1890–1930, *U.S. Census of Population: 1950*, vol. IV, Special Reports, *General Characteristics of Families*; 1940–1970, *Current Population Reports*, series P–20, Nos. 176 and 251.

According to the 1970 Census Bureau definition, a household consists of all the persons who occupy a housing unit. A house, an apartment or other group of rooms, or a single room is regarded as a housing unit when it is occupied or intended for occupancy as separate living quarters; that is, when the occupants do not live and eat with any other persons in the structure and there is either (1) direct access from the outside or through a common hall or (2) a kitchen or cooking equipment for the exclusive use of the occupants. A household includes the related family members and all the unrelated persons, if any, such as lodgers, foster children, wards, or employees who share the housing unit. A person living alone in a housing unit, or a group of unrelated persons sharing a housing unit as partners, is also counted as a household.

Households classified as having a male head include those where the head of the household is a married man whose wife lives with him and all other households with a male designated as head. Female household heads include women who are not married or not living with their husbands and who are designated as household heads.

The count of households excludes group quarters (referred to as "quasi-households" in the previous edition of *Historical Statistics*), which are living arrangements for institutional inmates, regardless of the number of inmates, or for other groups containing 5 or more persons unrelated to the person in charge.

The figures for number of households are not strictly comparable from year to year. In general, the definitions of household for 1790, 1900, 1930, 1940, 1950, 1960, and 1970 are similar. Very minor differences result from the fact that in 1950, 1960, and 1970, housing units with 5 or more lodgers were excluded from the count of households, whereas in 1930 and 1940, housing units with 11 lodgers or more were excluded, and in 1790 and 1900, no precise definition of the maximum allowable number of lodgers was made. The definition of household for 1850–1890, 1910, and 1920 differs slightly from that given above. For these years, no distinction was made between households and group quarters (quasi-households), and thus the numbers include both households and group quarters.

In 1950–1970, the number of households was equal, by definition, to the number of occupied housing units enumerated for housing statistics. In 1940, the definition of household was not completely the same as that of occupied housing units. In that year there were 95,000 more households than occupied housing units.

Average size figures were computed by dividing the total population (the total free population for 1790, 1850, and 1860) by the number of household heads. The number of household heads for 1850–1890, 1910, and 1920 also includes the heads of group quarters (quasi-households). Since these are such a small fraction of the total number of household heads, the population per household is only slightly affected by a change in definition for these years.

Data for families are shown only for 1940 and later years. Prior to 1940 the concept of "family" was basically synonymous with the present concept of "household" wherein a family comprised the head of a household and all other members of the household related to the head. Under this definition, a head of a household living alone was counted as a family but a mutually related group of lodgers or resident employees was not counted as a family.

The term "family," as shown here, refers to a group of two or more persons related by blood, marriage, or adoption and residing together in a household. A primary family consists of the head of a household and all other persons in the household related to the head. A secondary family comprises two or more persons such as guests, lodgers, or resident employees and their relatives, living in a household and related to each other.

A subfamily is a married couple with or without children, or one parent with one or more unmarried children under 18 years old, living in a household and related to, but not including, the head of the household or his wife. Members of a subfamily are also members of the primary family with whom they live. The number of subfamilies, therefore, is not included in the number of families.

A married couple is defined as a husband and his wife living together in the same household, with or without children and other relatives.

Unrelated individuals refers to persons (other than inmates of institutions) who are not living with any relatives. A primary individual is a household head living alone or with nonrelatives only. A secondary individual in a household is a person such as a guest, lodger, or resident employee who is not related to any other person in the household. Persons in group quarters, except inmates of institutions, are classified as secondary individuals.

Selected data for 1940–1970, which are from the *Current Population Reports*, have been revised on the basis of new population controls from the 1960 and 1970 censuses. The revisions have been made only for series A 288–319 and A 353–358 and, therefore, the data, especially for 1961–1970, are not comparable with those in series A 320–334, A 335–349, and A 350–352.

A 320–334. Households, by race, sex, and age of head, 1890–1970.

Source: U.S. Bureau of the Census. 1890, Eleventh Census Reports, *Farms and Homes: Proprietorship and Indebtedness;* 1900, Twelfth Census Reports, *Population,* vol. II, part 2; 1910–1940, Fifteenth Census Reports, *Population,* vol. VI, and Sixteenth Census Reports, *Population, Families—Size of Family and Age of Head* and *Population—Characteristics of the Nonwhite Population by Race;* 1950, *U.S. Census of Population: 1950,* vol. IV, Special Reports, *General Characteristics of Families;* 1960, *U.S. Census of Population: 1960,* vol. I, *Characteristics of the Population,* part 1, U.S. Summary; 1965–1970, *Current Population Reports,* series P-20.

See text for series A 91–104 and A 288–319.

A 335–349. Households, by number of persons, 1790–1970.

Source: U.S. Bureau of the Census. 1790–1940, unpublished, computed from household data compiled from the decennial censuses; 1950–1970, *Current Population Reports,* series P-20.

See text for series A 288–319.

A 350–352. Households, by residence, 1900–1970.

Source: U.S. Bureau of the Census, *Current Population Reports.* 1900–1946, series P-20, No. 92; 1947–1949, series P-20, No. 59; 1950–1970, series P-20, Nos. 176, 200, and 218.

See text for series A 288–319 for definition of household, and A 43–56 for definition of residence.

Data for 1900–1946 represent estimates of the number of married women with their spouses in their own households, and the number of household heads in the remaining population. These estimates were based on available census and survey data and on additional information on construction activity, vacancy rates, marriage rates, divorce rates, economic indexes, etc. Although the figures are shown as of a given date, they should be regarded as an approximation of the annual average number of households.

The estimates by residence were made by subdividing the total into farm and nonfarm components, using estimates of the average size of farm households in conjunction with annual estimates of the farm population (see joint report of Bureau of the Census and Bureau of Agricultural Economics, *Estimates of the Farm Population: 1910 to 1950,* series Census-BAE, No. 16A). Since the annual changes in the number of households which are implied in these series may be subject to substantial sampling variability, caution should be used in the interpretation of small changes.

The farm household series for 1910–1946 relates to the total farm population, whereas that for 1947–1970 relates to the rural-farm population. There were 88,000 urban-farm households in 1940 and 96,000 in 1950.

A 353–358. Families and percent distribution of own children under 18 years old, 1950–1970.

Source: U.S. Bureau of the Census, *Current Population Reports,* series P-20.

See text for series A 288–319.

Data for 1955–1970 have been revised on the basis of new population controls from the 1960 and 1970 censuses.

A 359–371. Inmates of institutions, by sex, race, age, and type of institution, 1940–1970.

Source: U.S. Bureau of the Census. 1940, *U.S. Census of Population: 1940, Institutional Population,* p. 10; 1950, *U.S. Census of Population: 1950,* vol. IV, part 2, chapter C, Institutional Population, pp. 15–17; 1960, *U.S. Census of Population: 1960,* Final Report PC(2)-8A, *Inmates of Institutions,* pp. 3–5, 7, and 12; 1970, *U.S. Census of Population: 1970,* Final Report PC(2)-4E, *Persons in Institutions and Other Group Quarters,* pp. 2–3, 5, 7, 11, and 21.

In the 1970 census, "inmates of institutions" were defined as persons under care or custody in institutions at the time of enumeration, regardless of their length of stay in that place and regardless of the number of people in that place. Statistics shown in this table for 1960 are based on similar criteria with the exception of "length of stay" as a criterion for defining inmates in 1960. Differences in the classification and definition of inmates between the 1950 and 1960 censuses are minimal and, thus, the estimates for both dates are comparable. However, several major differences exist between the estimates of inmates for 1940 and those for later years: In 1940 the coverage of inmates was for the population 14 years old and over rather than for all ages; inmates in tuberculosis hospitals were excluded from the 1940 inmate count; and a more detailed classification of inmates in homes for the aged and dependent was designed following the 1940 census which enabled enumerators in subsequent censuses to increase the field coverage in this area, particularly with respect to such places as commercial boarding homes for the aged, and rest, convalescent, and nursing homes.

Although data on types of institutions are generally comparable for each year shown, it should be noted that the use of progressively refined techniques to identify types of institutions in each census since 1940 has resulted in more inclusive and definitive classification of these types.

★ ★ ★ ★ ★ ★ ★ ★ ★ **More Recent Data for *Historical Statistics* Series** ★ ★ ★ ★ ★ ★ ★ ★ ★

★   ★

★   **Statistics for more recent years in continuation of many of the still-active series shown here appear**   ★

★   **in annual issues of the *Statistical Abstract of the United States,* beginning with the 1975 edition. For**   ★

★   **direct linkage of the historical series to the tables in the *Abstract,* see Appendix I in the *Abstract.***   ★

★   ★

★ ★

Series A 1–5. Area and Population of the United States: 1790 to 1970

Year	Land area [1] (square miles) 1	Population Number 2	Increase from preceding census Number 3	Increase from preceding census Percent [2] 4	Per square mile of land area 5	Year	Land area [1] (square miles) 1	Population Number 2	Increase from preceding census Number 3	Increase from preceding census Percent [2] 4	Per square mile of land area 5
1970 (Apr. 1) [3]	3,536,855	[3]203,235,298	23,912,123	13.3	57.5	1880 (June 1)	2,969,640	50,155,783	10,337,334	26.0	16.9
1960 (Apr. 1) *	3,540,911	179,323,175	28,625,814	19.0	50.6	1870 (June 1)	2,969,640	[5]39,818,449	8,375,128	26.6	13.4
1960 (Apr. 1) [4]	2,968,054	178,464,236	27,766,875	18.4	60.1	1860 (June 1)	2,969,640	31,443,321	8,251,445	35.6	10.6
1950 (Apr. 1)	2,974,726	150,697,361	19,028,086	14.5	50.7	1850 (June 1)	2,940,042	23,191,876	6,122,423	35.9	7.9
1940 (Apr. 1)	2,977,128	131,669,275	8,894,229	7.2	44.2	1840 (June 1)	1,749,462	17,069,453	4,203,433	32.7	9.8
1930 (Apr. 1)	2,977,128	122,775,046	17,064,426	16.1	41.2	1830 (June 1)	1,749,462	12,866,020	3,227,567	33.5	7.4
1920 (Jan. 1)	2,969,451	105,710,620	13,738,354	14.9	35.6	1820 (Aug. 7)	1,749,462	9,638,453	2,398,572	33.1	5.5
1910 (Apr. 15)	2,969,565	91,972,266	15,977,691	21.0	31.0	1810 (Aug. 6)	1,681,828	7,239,881	1,931,398	36.4	4.3
1900 (June 1)	2,969,834	75,994,575	13,046,861	20.7	25.6	1800 (Aug. 4)	864,746	5,308,483	1,379,269	35.1	6.1
1890 (June 1)	2,969,640	62,947,714	12,791,931	25.5	21.2	1790 (Aug. 2)	864,746	3,929,214	(X)	(X)	4.5

* Denotes first year for which figures include Alaska and Hawaii.
X   Not applicable.
[1] Gross area (including inland water) in square miles: 1790–1800—888,811; 1810—1,716,003; 1820–1840—1,788,006; 1850—2,992,747; 1860–1950—3,022,387; 1960 conterminous—3,022,261; 1960 including Alaska and Hawaii—3,615,123; 1970—3,615,122.

[2] Based on interval since preceding census which is not always exactly 10 years.
[3] Official resident population. 1970 census tables show a population of 203,211,926. The net difference of 23,372 reflects errors found after the tabulations were completed.
[4] Conterminous United States (excludes Alaska and Hawaii).
[5] Revised to include adjustment of 1,260,078 for underenumeration in the Southern States.   Unrevised census count is 38,558,371. See text.

Series A 6–8. Annual Population Estimates for the United States: 1790 to 1970

[In thousands.   As of July 1.   1960–1970, preliminary; for description of estimates, see text]

Year	Total, including Armed Forces overseas 6	Total resident population 7	Civilian resident population 8
1970	204,879	203,810	201,722
1969	202,677	201,385	199,145
1968	200,706	199,399	197,113
1967	198,712	197,457	195,264
1966	196,560	195,576	193,420
1965	194,303	193,526	191,605
1964	191,889	191,141	189,141
1963	189,242	188,483	186,493
1962	186,538	185,771	183,677
1961	183,691	182,992	181,143
1960	180,671	179,979	178,140
1959 *	177,830	177,135	175,277
1959	177,073	176,289	174,521
1958	174,141	173,320	171,485
1957	171,274	170,371	168,400
1956	168,221	167,306	165,373
1955	165,275	164,308	162,311
1954	162,391	161,164	159,059
1953	159,565	158,242	155,975
1952	156,954	155,687	153,292
1951	154,287	153,310	151,009
1950	151,684	151,235	150,203
1949	149,188	148,665	147,578
1948	146,631	146,093	145,168
1947	144,126	143,446	142,566
1946	141,389	140,054	138,385
1945	139,928	132,481	127,573
1944	138,397	132,885	126,708
1943	136,739	134,245	127,499
1942	134,860	133,920	130,942
1941	133,402	133,121	131,595
1940	132,122	131,954	131,658
1939	131,028	130,880	130,683
1938	129,969	129,825	129,635
1937	128,961	128,825	128,639
1936	128,181	128,053	127,879
1935	127,362	127,250	127,099
1934	126,485	126,374	126,228
1933	125,690	125,579	125,436
1932	124,949	124,840	124,694
1931	124,149	124,040	123,886
1930	123,188	123,077	122,923

Year	Total resident population 7	Year	Total resident population 7	Year	Total resident population 7	Year	Total resident population 7
1929	121,767	1894	68,275	1859	30,687	1824	10,924
1928	120,509	1893	66,970	1858	29,862	1823	10,596
1927	119,035	1892	65,666	1857	29,037	1822	10,268
1926	117,397	1891	64,361	1856	28,212	1821	9,939
1925	115,829	1890	63,056	1855	27,386	1820	9,618
1924	114,109	1889	61,775	1854	26,561	1819	9,379
1923	111,947	1888	60,496	1853	25,736	1818	9,139
1922	110,049	1887	59,217	1852	24,911	1817	8,899
1921	108,538	1886	57,938	1851	24,086	1816	8,659
1920	106,461	1885	56,658	1850	23,261	1815	8,419
1919	[1]104,514	1884	55,379	1849	22,631	1814	8,179
1918	[1]103,208	1883	54,100	1848	22,018	1813	7,939
1917	[1]103,268	1882	52,821	1847	21,406	1812	7,700
1916	101,961	1881	51,542	1846	20,794	1811	7,460
1915	100,546	1880	50,262	1845	20,182	1810	7,224
1914	99,111	1879	49,208	1844	19,569	1809	7,031
1913	97,225	1878	48,174	1843	18,957	1808	6,838
1912	95,335	1877	47,141	1842	18,345	1807	6,644
1911	93,863	1876	46,107	1841	17,733	1806	6,451
1910	92,407	1875	45,073	1840	17,120	1805	6,258
1909	90,490	1874	44,040	1839	16,684	1804	6,065
1908	88,710	1873	43,006	1838	16,264	1803	5,872
1907	87,008	1872	41,972	1837	15,843	1802	5,679
1906	85,450	1871	40,938	1836	15,423	1801	5,486
1905	83,822	1870	39,905	1835	15,003	1800	5,297
1904	82,166	1869	39,051	1834	14,582	1799	5,159
1903	80,632	1868	38,213	1833	14,162	1798	5,021
1902	79,163	1867	37,376	1832	13,742	1797	4,883
1901	77,584	1866	36,538	1831	13,321	1796	4,745
1900	76,094	1865	35,701	1830	12,901	1795	4,607
1899	74,799	1864	34,863	1829	12,565	1794	4,469
1898	73,494	1863	34,026	1828	12,237	1793	4,332
1897	72,189	1862	33,188	1827	11,909	1792	4,194
1896	70,885	1861	32,351	1826	11,580	1791	4,056
1895	69,580	1860	31,513	1825	11,252	1790	3,929

* Denotes first year for which figures include Alaska and Hawaii.

[1] Total population, including Armed Forces overseas (in thousands): 1917—103,414; 1918—104,550; 1919—105,063. Civilian population (in thousands): 1917—102,796; 1918—101,488; 1919—104,153.

Series A 9–22. Population of the United States and Outlying Areas: 1880 to 1970

Year	Total	United States [1]	Population abroad [2]	Outlying areas										
				Total	Alaska [1]	Hawaii [1]	Philippines [3]	Puerto Rico	Guam	American Samoa	Canal Zone	Virgin Islands	Trust Territory of the Pacific Islands	Other
	9	10	11	12	13	14	15	16	17	18	19	20	21	22
1970	207,999,824	[4]203,235,298	1,737,836	3,026,690	---------	---------	---------	2,712,033	84,996	27,159	44,198	62,468	90,940	[5]4,896
1960	183,285,009	179,323,175	1,374,421	2,587,413	---------	---------	---------	2,349,544	67,044	20,051	42,122	32,099	[6]70,724	[7]5,829
1950	154,233,234	150,697,361	[8]481,545	3,054,328	128,643	499,794	---------	2,210,703	59,498	18,937	52,822	26,665	[9]54,843	[10]2,423
1940	150,622,754	131,669,275	118,933	18,834,546	[11]72,524	422,770	16,356,000	1,869,255	22,290	12,908	51,827	24,889	---------	[12]2,083
1930	138,439,069	122,775,046	89,453	15,574,570	[11]59,278	368,300	13,513,000	1,543,913	18,509	10,055	39,467	22,012	---------	[13]36
1920	118,107,855	105,710,620	117,238	12,279,997	55,036	255,881	10,599,000	1,299,809	13,275	8,056	22,858	[14]26,051	---------	[13]31
1910	102,370,018	91,972,266	55,608	10,342,144	64,356	191,874	8,886,000	1,118,012	[15]7,251		[15]62,810	---------	---------	[13]35
1900	84,371,985	75,994,575	91,219	8,286,191	63,592	154,001	7,100,000	[16]953,243	[17]9,676	5,679	---------	---------	---------	
1890	62,979,766	62,947,714	---------	32,052	32,052	---------	---------	---------	---------	---------	---------	---------	---------	
1880	50,189,209	50,155,783	---------	33,426	33,426	---------	---------	---------	---------	---------	---------	---------	---------	

[1] Alaska and Hawaii included with outlying areas through 1950 and with United States thereafter. Alaska's population not enumerated in 1870 census.
[2] Excludes U.S. citizens temporarily abroad on private business, travel, etc.
[3] Estimates derived by extrapolation and interpolation of censuses of 1903, 1918, and 1939. The Philippines became independent in 1946.
[4] Official 1970 resident population. See series A 1–5, footnote 3.
[5] Includes Midway (2,220), Wake (1,647), Johnston (1,007), and Swan (22) Islands.
[6] Population as of 1958 census.
[7] Includes Midway (2,356), Corn (1,872), Wake (1,097), Canton (320), Johnston (156), and Swan (28) Islands.
[8] Estimate based on 20-percent sample of reports received.

[9] Estimated civilian population as of June 30, 1950.
[10] Includes Corn (1,304), Midway (416), Wake (349), Canton (272), Johnston (46), and Swan (36) Islands.
[11] Census taken as of October 1 of preceding year.
[12] Includes Corn (1,523), Midway (437), Johnston (69), Canton and Enderbury (44), and Baker, Howland, and Jarvis (10) Islands.
[13] Population for Midway Islands.
[14] Population as of 1917 census.
[15] Population as of 1912 census.
[16] Population as of 1899 census.
[17] Population as of 1901 census.

Series A 23–28. Annual Estimates of the Population, by Sex and Race: 1900 to 1970

[In thousands. As of July 1. 1900–1939, resident population; 1940–1970, total population, including Armed Forces overseas. 1960–1970, preliminary; for description of estimates, see text for series A 6–8]

Year	Total	Sex		Race			Year	Total	Sex		Race	
		Male	Female	White	Negro	Other			Male	Female	White	Negro and other
	23	24	25	26	27	28		23	24	25	26	27–28
1970	204,879	100,266	104,613	179,491	22,787	2,600	1934	126,374	63,726	62,648	113,527	12,847
1969	202,677	99,287	103,390	177,782	22,431	2,464	1933	125,579	63,384	62,195	112,815	12,764
1968	200,706	98,426	102,280	176,246	22,117	2,343	1932	124,840	63,070	61,770	112,154	12,686
1967	198,712	97,564	101,148	174,695	21,780	2,237	1931	124,040	62,726	61,314	111,433	12,606
1966	196,560	96,620	99,941	172,998	21,434	2,129	1930	123,077	62,297	60,780	110,559	12,518
1965	194,303	95,609	98,694	171,205	21,064	2,034	1929	121,767	61,680	60,087	109,383	12,384
1964	191,889	94,518	97,371	169,257	20,672	1,960	1928	120,509	61,101	59,408	108,244	12,265
1963	189,242	93,303	95,939	167,104	20,255	1,882	1927	119,035	60,397	58,638	106,941	12,094
1962	186,538	92,066	94,472	164,885	19,852	1,801	1926	117,397	59,588	57,809	105,468	11,929
1961	183,691	90,740	92,952	162,533	19,437	1,721	1925	115,829	58,813	57,016	104,061	11,768
1960	180,671	89,320	91,352	160,023	19,006	1,642	1924	114,109	57,985	56,124	102,512	11,597
1959 *	177,830	87,995	89,834	157,655	20,175		1923	111,947	56,861	55,086	100,510	11,437
1959	177,073	87,621	89,453	157,368	19,706		1922	110,049	55,886	54,163	98,768	11,281
1958	174,141	86,236	87,905	154,922	19,220		1921	108,538	55,292	53,246	97,416	11,122
1957	171,274	84,892	86,382	152,512	18,762		1920	106,461	54,291	52,170	95,510	10,951
1956	168,221	83,434	84,786	149,923	18,298		1919	[1]104,514	[2]53,103	51,411	93,684	10,830
1955	165,275	82,030	83,246	147,428	17,847		1918	[1]103,208	[2]51,974	51,234	92,352	10,856
1954	162,391	80,647	81,744	144,981	17,409		1917	[1]103,268	[2]52,788	50,480	92,435	10,833
1953	159,565	79,295	80,270	142,573	16,991		1916	101,961	52,234	49,727	91,196	10,765
1952	156,954	78,061	78,893	140,344	16,609		1915	100,546	51,573	48,973	89,848	10,698
1951	154,287	76,792	77,496	138,049	16,238		1914	99,111	50,883	48,228	88,480	10,631
1950	151,684	75,539	76,146	135,814	15,870		1913	97,225	49,957	47,268	86,705	10,520
1949	149,188	74,335	74,853	133,598	15,590		1912	95,335	49,025	46,310	84,928	10,407
1948	146,631	73,130	73,502	131,308	15,323		1911	93,863	48,290	45,573	83,524	10,339
1947	144,126	71,946	72,180	129,059	15,067		1910	92,407	47,554	44,853	82,137	10,270
1946	141,389	70,631	70,757	126,565	14,824		1909	90,490	46,545	43,945	80,339	10,151
1945	139,928	70,035	69,893	125,266	14,662		1908	88,710	45,594	43,116	78,658	10,052
1944	138,397	69,378	69,020	124,009	14,388		1907	87,008	44,682	42,326	77,055	9,953
1943	136,739	68,546	68,194	122,605	14,134		1906	85,450	43,841	41,609	75,583	9,867
1942	134,860	67,597	67,263	120,992	13,868		1905	83,822	42,965	40,857	74,059	9,763
1941	133,402	66,920	66,482	119,731	13,671		1904	82,166	42,089	40,077	72,520	9,646
1940	132,122	66,352	65,770	118,629	13,494		1903	80,632	41,262	39,370	71,084	9,548
1939	130,880	65,713	65,166	117,524	13,355		1902	79,163	40,483	38,680	69,722	9,441
1938	129,825	65,235	64,590	116,592	13,233		1901	77,584	39,649	37,935	68,267	9,317
1937	128,825	64,790	64,035	115,706	13,118		1900	76,094	38,867	37,227	66,900	9,194
1936	128,053	64,460	63,594	115,022	13,031							
1935	127,250	64,110	63,140	114,309	12,941							

* Denotes first year for which figures include Alaska and Hawaii.
[1] Estimates including Armed Forces overseas, in thousands: 1917—103,414; 1918—104,550; 1919—105,063.
[2] Estimates including Armed Forces overseas, in thousands: 1917—52,934; 1918—53,316; 1919—53,658.

Series A 29–42. Annual Estimates of the Population, by Age: 1900 to 1970

[In thousands. As of July 1. 1900–1939, resident population; 1940–1970, total population, including Armed Forces overseas. 1960–1970, preliminary; for description of estimates, see text for series A 6–8]

Year	Total	Age group (in years)								Selected cumulative age groups (in years)				
		Under 5	5–14	15–24	25–34	35–44	45–54	55–64	65 and over	14 and over	16 and over	18 and over	21 and over	62 and over
	29	30	31	32	33	34	35	36	37	38	39	40	41	42
1970	204,879	17,156	40,733	36,496	25,293	23,142	23,310	18,664	20,085	151,087	142,949	135,177	124,024	25,050
1969	202,677	17,376	40,884	35,236	24,681	23,383	23,047	18,390	19,680	148,465	140,462	132,905	122,019	24,552
1968	200,706	17,913	40,772	34,090	23,990	23,731	22,758	18,088	19,365	145,988	138,171	130,815	120,098	24,073
1967	198,712	18,563	40,496	33,196	23,156	24,038	22,440	17,752	19,071	143,520	135,905	128,785	117,823	23,625
1966	196,560	19,208	40,051	32,012	22,725	24,276	22,125	17,408	18,755	141,069	133,651	126,665	116,523	23,184
1965	194,303	19,824	39,426	30,773	22,465	24,447	21,839	17,077	18,451	138,726	131,542	124,572	115,198	22,800
1964	191,889	20,165	38,783	29,519	22,396	24,562	21,580	16,758	18,127	136,480	129,427	122,206	113,844	22,426
1963	189,242	20,342	38,124	28,223	22,410	24,584	21,346	16,436	17,778	134,322	127,275	120,822	112,274	22,039
1962	186,538	20,469	37,435	26,909	22,494	24,519	21,124	16,131	17,457	132,172	124,864	119,412	111,063	21,682
1961	183,691	20,522	37,031	25,242	22,692	24,392	20,875	15,847	17,089	129,952	123,404	117,900	109,926	21,277
1960	180,671	20,341	35,735	24,576	22,919	24,221	20,578	15,625	16,675	127,365	121,835	116,146	108,856	20,836
1959*	177,830	20,175	34,564	23,988	23,169	24,023	20,262	15,401	16,248	125,888	120,287	114,780	107,824	20,402
1959	177,073	20,055	34,390	23,890	23,062	23,917	20,189	15,357	16,213	125,411	119,837	114,356	107,425	20,356
1958	174,141	19,768	33,322	23,162	23,430	23,693	19,857	15,139	15,771	123,875	118,108	113,139	106,394	19,895
1957	171,274	19,379	32,515	22,311	23,737	23,496	19,513	14,973	15,353	122,365	116,790	112,108	105,517	19,459
1956	168,221	18,895	31,423	21,869	24,015	23,160	19,143	14,815	14,902	120,531	115,489	110,956	104,500	18,962
1955	165,275	18,467	30,248	21,667	24,175	22,818	18,824	14,586	14,489	119,011	114,276	109,803	103,436	18,455
1954	162,391	17,962	29,092	21,641	24,233	22,571	18,501	14,350	14,040	117,662	113,088	108,739	102,459	17,899
1953	159,565	17,548	27,880	21,658	24,233	22,359	18,171	14,135	13,582	116,430	111,922	107,673	101,445	17,354
1952	156,954	17,228	26,656	21,796	24,197	22,109	17,881	13,918	13,169	115,333	110,957	106,683	100,446	16,874
1951	154,287	17,252	25,055	22,018	24,085	21,833	17,623	13,654	12,768	114,141	109,878	105,678	99,250	16,384
1950	151,684	16,331	24,477	22,260	23,932	21,557	17,400	13,364	12,362	113,031	108,753	104,624	97,998	15,886
1949	149,188	15,607	23,770	22,570	23,729	21,187	17,260	13,145	11,921	111,947	107,729	103,445	96,684	15,386
1948	146,631	14,919	23,089	22,866	23,494	20,794	17,107	12,824	11,538	110,722	106,503	102,066	95,265	14,925
1947	144,126	14,406	22,257	23,122	23,236	20,421	16,970	12,528	11,185	109,602	105,252	100,724	93,871	14,498
1946	141,389	13,244	21,844	23,282	22,954	20,073	16,820	12,244	10,828	108,520	104,042	99,501	92,595	14,068
1945	139,928	12,979	21,599	23,705	22,734	19,787	16,642	11,988	10,494	107,623	103,042	98,372	91,326	13,662
1944	138,397	12,524	21,573	23,999	22,511	19,505	16,419	11,719	10,147	106,627	101,924	97,153	89,976	13,233
1943	136,739	12,016	21,699	24,065	22,194	19,226	16,199	11,472	9,867	105,404	100,630	95,836	88,592	12,871
1942	134,860	11,301	21,823	24,093	21,911	18,950	15,976	11,220	9,584	104,132	99,328	94,489	87,151	12,499
1941	133,402	10,850	22,089	24,074	21,691	18,692	15,759	10,959	9,288	102,878	98,036	93,136	85,766	12,115
1940	132,122	10,579	22,363	24,033	21,446	18,422	15,555	10,694	9,031	101,607	96,732	91,763	84,429	11,781
1939	130,880	10,418	22,701	23,819	21,176	18,178	15,336	10,487	8,764	100,209	95,283	90,311	83,104	11,467
1938	129,825	10,176	23,146	23,655	20,953	18,001	15,077	10,310	8,508	98,981	94,018	89,073	81,978	11,163
1937	128,825	10,009	23,564	23,487	20,723	17,866	14,785	10,132	8,258	97,734	92,754	87,876	80,867	10,854
1936	128,053	10,044	23,942	23,309	20,505	17,783	14,495	9,949	8,027	96,575	91,594	86,791	79,825	10,553
1935	127,250	10,170	24,213	23,130	20,275	17,712	14,208	9,739	7,804	95,350	90,435	85,698	78,751	10,256
1934	126,374	10,331	24,402	22,963	20,022	17,640	13,933	9,502	7,582	94,079	89,247	84,553	77,619	9,961
1933	125,579	10,612	24,531	22,820	19,750	17,569	13,684	9,249	7,363	92,838	88,070	83,393	76,482	9,680
1932	124,840	10,903	24,614	22,716	19,484	17,504	13,481	8,992	7,147	91,699	86,968	82,295	75,411	9,411
1931	124,040	11,179	24,629	22,617	19,242	17,412	13,296	8,735	6,928	90,598	85,877	81,209	74,358	9,144
1930	123,077	11,372	24,631	22,487	19,039	17,270	13,096	8,477	6,705	89,439	84,722	80,069	73,256	8,867
1929	121,767	11,734	24,470	22,151	18,941	16,921	12,761	8,315	6,474	87,902	83,233	78,619	71,897	8,576
1928	120,509	11,978	24,320	21,811	18,953	16,540	12,430	8,178	6,299	86,536	81,898	77,325	70,701	8,328
1927	119,035	12,111	24,152	21,430	18,948	16,172	12,092	8,003	6,127	85,071	80,489	75,978	69,472	8,076
1926	117,397	12,189	23,906	21,037	18,867	15,847	11,786	7,805	5,960	83,575	79,050	74,619	68,244	7,840
1925	115,829	12,316	23,614	20,691	18,720	15,576	11,521	7,605	5,786	82,149	77,677	73,324	67,068	7,615
1924	114,109	12,269	23,358	20,314	18,557	15,337	11,278	7,387	5,609	80,704	76,297	72,035	65,914	7,399
1923	111,947	12,119	23,089	19,798	18,231	15,066	11,068	7,165	5,411	78,915	74,606	70,461	64,518	7,184
1922	110,049	12,031	22,788	19,402	17,924	14,823	10,899	6,951	5,231	77,362	73,144	69,102	63,297	6,998
1921	108,538	11,879	22,515	19,140	17,747	14,665	10,721	6,791	5,080	76,233	72,102	68,154	62,446	6,847
1920	106,461	11,631	22,158	18,821	17,416	14,382	10,505	6,619	4,929	74,708	70,683	66,839	61,235	6,663
1919	104,514	11,536	21,849	18,465	16,912	14,008	10,402	6,456	4,886	73,144	69,170	65,407	59,911	6,577
1918	103,208	11,606	21,732	18,071	16,445	13,879	10,293	6,356	4,826	71,886	67,899	64,092	58,670	6,490
1917	103,268	11,527	21,369	18,836	16,913	13,647	10,068	6,194	4,714	72,361	68,425	64,646	59,030	6,332
1916	101,961	11,442	21,008	18,872	16,776	13,388	9,846	6,026	4,603	71,476	67,579	63,811	58,176	6,176
1915	100,546	11,347	20,660	18,844	16,580	13,130	9,618	5,866	4,501	70,482	66,623	62,863	57,244	6,029
1914	99,111	11,244	20,816	18,796	16,370	12,875	9,398	5,711	4,401	69,470	65,652	61,907	56,272	5,887
1913	97,225	11,082	19,904	18,649	16,070	12,562	9,135	5,542	4,281	68,127	64,364	60,650	55,048	5,719
1912	95,335	10,915	19,503	18,477	15,772	12,252	8,875	5,372	4,169	66,775	63,068	59,387	53,828	5,562
1911	93,863	10,796	19,214	18,355	15,530	12,003	8,657	5,234	4,074	65,688	62,022	58,369	52,839	5,427
1910	92,407	10,671	18,950	18,212	15,274	11,759	8,454	5,101	3,986	64,598	60,974	57,346	51,852	5,301
1909	90,490	10,509	18,670	17,871	14,923	11,471	8,204	4,964	3,878	63,093	59,531	55,970	50,579	5,155
1908	88,710	10,364	18,440	17,526	14,585	11,202	7,974	4,840	3,779	61,659	58,157	54,660	49,375	5,021
1907	87,008	10,220	18,240	17,184	14,257	10,945	7,755	4,724	3,684	60,275	56,828	53,397	48,216	4,894
1906	85,450	10,092	18,067	16,864	13,952	10,705	7,554	4,621	3,595	58,993	55,595	52,224	47,142	4,778
1905	83,822	9,944	17,888	16,526	13,631	10,461	7,350	4,517	3,505	57,668	54,322	51,014	46,036	4,658
1904	82,166	9,791	17,697	16,178	13,315	10,211	7,150	4,410	3,414	56,331	53,035	49,792	44,919	4,541
1903	80,632	9,645	17,524	15,858	13,019	9,974	6,964	4,313	3,335	55,094	51,848	48,661	43,886	4,436
1902	79,163	9,502	17,360	15,555	12,737	9,745	6,788	4,220	3,256	53,911	50,710	47,578	42,896	4,333
1901	77,584	9,336	17,158	15,242	12,442	9,504	6,606	4,122	3,174	52,676	49,523	46,448	41,862	4,229
1900	76,094	9,181	16,966	14,951	12,161	9,273	6,437	4,026	3,099	51,511	48,403	45,379	40,879	4,130

* Denotes first year for which figures include Alaska and Hawaii.

Series A 43–56. Number of Places in Urban and Rural Territory, by Size of Place: 1790 to 1970

[For definition of urban, see text]

Series No.	Class and population size	1970[1]	1960 Including Alaska and Hawaii	1960 Conterminous United States	1950 1950 urban definition	1950 1940 urban definition	1940	1930[2]	1920	1910	1900	1890
43	**Urban territory**	7,062	6,041	6,015	4,741	4,023	3,464	3,165	2,722	2,262	1,737	1,348
44	Places of 1,000,000 or more	6	5	5	5	5	5	5	3	3	3	3
45	Places of 500,000–999,999	20	16	16	13	13	9	8	9	5	3	1
46	Places of 250,000–499,999	30	30	29	23	23	23	24	13	11	9	7
47	Places of 100,000–249,999	100	81	81	65	66	55	56	43	31	23	17
48	Places of 50,000–99,999	240	201	201	126	128	107	98	76	59	40	30
49	Places of 25,000–49,999	520	432	429	252	271	213	185	143	119	82	66
50	Places of 10,000–24,999	1,385	1,134	1,130	778	814	665	606	465	369	280	230
51	Places of 5,000–9,999	1,839	1,394	1,388	1,176	1,133	965	851	715	605	465	340
52	Places of 2,500–4,999	2,295	2,152	2,140	1,846	1,570	1,422	1,332	1,255	1,060	832	654
53	Places under 2,500	627	596	596	457	---	---	---	---	---	---	---
54	**Rural territory**	13,706	13,749	13,693	13,807	13,235	13,288	13,433	12,855	11,830	8,931	6,490
55	Places of 1,000–2,499	4,191	4,151	4,113	4,158	3,408	3,205	3,087	3,030	2,717	2,128	1,603
56	Places under 1,000	9,515	9,598	9,580	9,649	9,827	10,083	10,346	9,825	9,113	6,803	4,887

Series No.	Class and population size	1880	1870	1860	1850[3]	1840[3]	1830	1820	1810	1800	1790
43	**Urban territory**	939	663	392	236	131	90	61	46	33	24
44	Places of 1,000,000 or more	1	---	---	---	---	---	---	---	---	---
45	Places of 500,000–999,999	3	2	2	1	---	---	---	---	---	---
46	Places of 250,000–499,999	4	5	1	–	1	---	---	---	---	---
47	Places of 100,000–249,999	12	7	6	5	2	1	1	---	---	---
48	Places of 50,000–99,999	15	11	7	4	2	3	2	2	1	---
49	Places of 25,000–49,999	42	27	19	16	7	3	2	2	2	2
50	Places of 10,000–24,999	146	116	58	36	25	16	8	7	3	3
51	Places of 5,000–9,999	249	186	136	85	48	33	22	17	15	7
52	Places of 2,500–4,999	467	309	163	89	46	34	26	18	12	12

– Represents zero.

[1] In 1970, relatively sparsely settled portions of certain incorporated places were classified as rural. The size class to which these places were assigned, however, was based on the population of the places within their legal boundaries.

[2] In 1930 each pair of the following was counted as a single place: Bluefield, Va., and Bluefield, W. Va.; Bristol, Tenn., and Bristol, Va.; Delmar, Del., and Delmar, Md.; Harrison, Ohio, and West Harrison, Ind.; Junction City, Ark., and Junction City, La.; Texarkana, Ark., and Texarkana, Tex.; Texhoma, Okla., and Texhoma, Tex.; and Union City, Ind., and Union City, Ohio. In all other years they were counted as separate incorporated places.

[3] Erroneously excludes Williamsburgh Village, New York, from the count of urban places. See series A 57–72, footnote 3.

Series A 57–72. Population in Urban and Rural Territory, by Size of Place: 1790 to 1970

[**In thousands.** For U.S. total population, see series A 2. For definition of urban, see text for series A 43–56]

Series No.	Class and population size	1970[1]	1960 Including Alaska and Hawaii	1960 Conterminous United States	1950 1950 urban definition	1950 1940 urban definition	1940	1930	1920	1910	1900
57	**Urban territory**	149,325	125,269	124,699	96,468	88,927	74,424	68,955	54,158	41,999	30,160
58	Places of 1,000,000 or more	18,769	17,484	17,484	17,404	17,404	15,911	15,065	10,146	8,501	6,429
59	Places of 500,000–999,999	12,967	11,111	11,111	9,187	9,187	6,457	5,764	6,224	3,011	1,645
60	Places of 250,000–499,999	10,442	10,766	10,472	8,242	8,242	7,828	7,956	4,541	3,950	2,861
61	Places of 100,000–249,999	14,286	11,652	11,652	9,479	9,614	7,793	7,541	6,519	4,840	3,272
62	Places of 50,000–99,999	16,724	13,836	13,836	8,931	9,073	7,344	6,491	5,265	4,179	2,709
63	Places of 25,000–49,999	17,848	14,951	14,855	8,808	9,496	7,417	6,426	5,075	4,023	2,801
64	Places of 10,000–24,999	21,415	17,568	17,513	11,867	12,467	9,967	9,097	7,035	5,549	4,338
65	Places of 5,000–9,999	12,924	9,780	9,739	8,139	7,879	6,682	5,897	4,968	4,217	3,204
66	Places of 2,500–4,999	8,038	7,580	7,542	6,490	5,565	5,026	4,718	4,386	3,728	2,899
67	Places under 2,500	727	690	690	578	---	---	---	---	---	---
68	Other urban territory	15,186	9,851	9,806	7,344	---	---	---	---	---	---
69	**Rural territory**	53,887	54,054	53,765	54,230	61,770	57,246	53,820	51,553	49,973	45,835
70	Places of 1,000–2,499	6,656	6,497	6,440	6,473	5,383	5,027	4,821	4,712	4,234	3,298
71	Places under 1,000	3,852	3,894	3,888	4,031	4,129	4,316	4,363	4,255	3,930	3,003
72	Other rural territory	43,379	43,664	43,437	43,725	52,258	47,903	44,637	42,586	41,809	39,533

See footnotes at end of table.

Series A 57–72.   Population in Urban and Rural Territory, by Size of Place: 1790 to 1970—Con.

[In thousands]

Series No.	Class and population size	1890	1880	1870[2]	1860	1850[3]	1840[3]	1830	1820	1810	1800	1790
57	**Urban territory**	22,106	14,130	9,902	6,217	3,544	1,845	1,127	693	525	322	202
58	Places of 1,000,000 or more	3,662	1,206									
59	Places of 500,000–999,999	806	1,917	1,616	1,379	516						
60	Places of 250,000–499,999	2,448	1,301	1,524	267	-	313					
61	Places of 100,000–249,999	2,782	1,787	990	993	659	205	203	124			
62	Places of 50,000–99,999	2,028	948	768	452	284	187	222	127	150	61	
63	Places of 25,000–49,999	2,269	1,446	930	670	611	235	105	70	80	68	62
64	Places of 10,000–24,999	3,451	2,189	1,710	884	561	405	240	122	109	54	48
65	Places of 5,000–9,999	2,384	1,717	1,278	976	596	329	231	155	116	94	48
66	Places of 2,500–4,999	2,277	1,618	1,086	595	316	172	126	96	70	45	44
69	**Rural territory**	40,841	36,026	28,656	25,227	19,648	15,224	11,739	8,945	6,714	4,986	3,728
70	Places of 1,000–2,499	2,509										
71	Places under 1,000	2,249										
72	Other rural territory	36,083										

- Represents zero.

[1] In 1970, relatively sparsely settled portions of certain incorporated places were classified as rural. The population of these portions was excluded from the items under "Urban" and included in "Other rural." The size class to which these places were assigned however, was based on the population of the places within their legal boundaries. Excludes 23,377 persons for whom urban-rural residence is not available. See series A 1–5, footnote 3.

[2] Excludes 1,260,078 persons for whom urban-rural residence is not available. See series A 1–5, footnote 5, and text for series A 1–5.

[3] Erroneously excludes population (30,780 in 1850 and 5,094 in 1840) of Williamsburgh Village, New York.

Series A 73–81.   Population, by Type of Residence, Sex, and Race: 1880 to 1970

[For definition of urban, see text for series A 43–56; for definition of rural farm, see text for series A 73–81]

Year	All races			White		Negro		Other races	
	Total	Male	Female	Male	Female	Male	Female	Male	Female
	73	74	75	76	77	78	79	80	81
TOTAL									
1970[1]	203,211,926	98,912,192	104,299,734	86,720,987	91,027,988	10,748,316	11,831,973	1,442,889	1,439,773
1960[2] *	179,323,175	88,331,494	90,991,681	78,367,149	80,464,583	9,113,408	9,758,423	850,937	768,675
1960[2]	178,464,236	87,864,510	90,599,726	78,153,040	80,301,916	9,105,702	9,754,415	605,768	543,395
1950	150,697,361	74,833,239	75,864,122	67,129,192	67,812,836	7,298,722	7,743,564	405,325	307,722
1940	131,669,275	66,061,592	65,607,683	59,448,548	58,766,322	6,269,038	6,596,480	344,006	244,881
1930	122,775,046	62,137,080	60,637,966	55,922,528	54,364,212	5,855,669	6,035,474	358,883	238,280
1920	105,710,620	53,900,431	51,810,189	48,430,655	46,390,260	5,209,436	5,253,695	260,340	166,234
1910	91,972,266	47,332,277	44,639,989	42,178,245	39,553,712	4,885,881	4,941,882	268,151	144,395
1900[3]	75,994,575	38,816,448	37,178,127	34,201,735	32,607,461	4,386,547	4,447,447	228,166	123,219
1890[3]	62,947,714	32,237,101	30,710,613	28,270,379	26,830,879	7,488,676		357,780	
1880[3]	50,155,783	50,155,783		43,402,970		6,580,793		172,020	
URBAN									
1970 (1970 urban def.)[1]	149,324,930	71,958,564	77,366,366	62,210,243	66,562,997	8,657,231	9,710,087	1,091,090	1,093,282
1960 (1960 urban def.)[2] *	125,268,750	60,733,005	64,535,745	53,631,145	56,797,187	6,557,123	7,250,517	544,737	488,041
1960 (1960 urban def.)[2]	124,699,022	60,436,481	64,262,541	53,510,814	56,691,185	6,553,529	7,247,735	372,138	323,621
1950 (1950 urban def.)	96,467,686	46,891,782	49,575,904	42,249,894	44,506,541	4,449,766	4,942,842	192,122	126,521
1950 (1940 urban def.)	88,927,464	43,117,270	45,810,194	38,697,282	40,970,582	(NA)	(NA)	(NA)	(NA)
1940 (1940 urban def.)	74,423,702	36,363,706	38,059,996	33,304,701	34,668,122	2,929,423	3,324,165	129,582	67,709
1930 (1930 urban def.)	68,954,823	34,154,760	34,800,063	31,538,288	32,021,745	2,479,158	2,714,755	137,314	63,563
1920 (1920 urban def.)	54,304,603	27,203,312	27,101,291	25,373,627	25,246,457	1,737,820	1,821,653	91,865	33,181
1910 (1910 urban def.)	42,623,383	21,496,181	21,127,202	20,129,679	19,702,234	1,279,484	1,409,745	87,018	15,223
1900 (1906 urban def.)	30,583,411	15,190,726	15,392,685	14,187,311	14,318,835	936,731	1,067,390	66,684	6,460
1900 (1906 urban def.)[3]	28,372,392	14,083,330	14,289,062	13,176,238	13,317,892	844,797	965,453	62,295	5,717
1890 (1906 urban def.)	22,559,367	11,283,148	11,276,219	10,525,811	10,485,556	1,482,651		65,349	
1890 (1906 urban def.)[3]	20,693,924	10,349,963	10,343,961	9,676,685	9,640,865	1,317,062		59,312	
1880 (1906 urban def.)[3]	13,184,902	13,184,902		12,297,612		849,721		37,569	
RURAL									
1970 (1970 urban def.)[1]	53,886,996	26,953,628	26,933,368	24,510,744	24,464,991	2,091,085	2,121,886	351,799	346,491
1960 (1960 urban def.)[2] *	54,054,425	27,598,489	26,455,936	24,736,004	23,667,396	2,556,285	2,507,906	306,200	280,634
1960 (1960 urban def.)[2]	53,765,214	27,428,029	26,337,185	24,642,226	23,610,731	2,552,173	2,506,680	233,630	219,774
1950 (1950 urban def.)	54,229,675	27,941,457	26,288,218	24,879,298	23,306,295	2,848,956	2,800,722	213,203	181,201
1950 (1940 urban def.)	61,769,897	31,715,969	30,053,928	28,431,910	26,842,254	(NA)	(NA)	(NA)	(NA)
1940 (1940 urban def.)	57,245,573	29,697,886	27,547,687	26,143,847	24,098,200	3,339,615	3,272,315	214,424	177,172
1930 (1930 urban def.)	53,820,223	27,982,320	25,837,903	24,384,240	22,342,467	3,376,511	3,320,719	221,569	174,717
1920 (1920 urban def.)	51,406,017	26,697,119	24,708,898	23,057,028	21,143,803	3,471,616	3,432,042	168,475	133,053
1910 (1910 urban def.)	49,348,883	25,836,096	23,512,787	22,048,566	19,851,478	3,606,397	3,532,137	181,133	129,172
1900 (1906 urban def.)	45,411,164	23,625,722	21,785,442	20,014,424	18,288,626	3,449,816	3,380,057	161,482	116,759
1900 (1906 urban def.)[3]	47,622,183	24,733,118	22,889,065	21,025,497	19,289,569	3,541,750	3,481,994	165,871	117,502
1890 (1906 urban def.)	40,388,347	20,953,953	19,434,394	17,744,568	16,345,323	6,006,025		292,431	
1890 (1906 urban def.)[3]	42,253,790	21,887,138	20,366,652	18,593,694	17,190,014	6,171,614		298,468	
1880 (1906 urban def.)[3]	36,970,881	36,970,881		31,105,358		5,731,072		134,451	

See footnotes at end of table.

Series A 73–81. Population, by Type of Residence, Sex, and Race: 1880 to 1970—Con.

Year	All races			White		Negro		Other races	
	Total	Male	Female	Male	Female	Male	Female	Male	Female
	73	74	75	76	77	78	79	80	81
RURAL NONFARM									
1970 (1970 urban def.) 1	45,586,707	22,683,834	22,902,873	20,537,870	20,722,994	1,865,126	1,899,159	280,838	280,720
1960 (1960 urban def.) 2 *	40,567,121	20,598,091	19,969,030	18,547,804	17,970,872	1,804,715	1,769,962	245,572	228,196
1960 (1960 urban def.) 2	40,291,215	20,435,131	19,856,084	18,455,737	17,915,558	1,800,610	1,768,704	178,784	171,822
1950 (1950 urban def.)	31,181,325	15,862,847	15,318,478	14,489,275	13,981,064	1,256,115	1,235,262	117,457	102,152
1950 (1940 urban def.)	38,693,358	19,622,272	19,071,086	18,028,680	17,505,535	(NA)	(NA)	(NA)	(NA)
1940 (1940 urban def.)	27,029,385	13,757,516	13,271,869	12,627,240	12,151,345	1,053,699	1,055,931	76,577	64,593
1930 (1930 urban def.)	23,662,710	12,117,945	11,544,765	11,012,799	10,487,663	1,022,066	994,641	83,080	62,461
1920 (1920 urban def.)	20,047,377	10,337,060	9,710,317	9,352,304	8,775,727	918,382	885,313	66,374	49,277
RURAL FARM									
1970 (1970 urban def.) 1	8,292,150	4,260,965	4,031,185	4,002,398	3,774,179	223,241	223,868	35,326	33,138
1960 (1960 urban def.) 2 *	13,474,771	6,986,175	6,488,596	6,177,614	5,698,719	747,075	734,910	61,486	54,967
1960 (1960 urban def.) 2	13,461,466	6,978,998	6,482,468	6,175,864	5,697,223	747,070	734,901	56,064	50,344
1950 (1950 urban def.)	23,048,350	12,078,610	10,969,740	10,390,023	9,325,231	1,592,841	1,565,460	95,746	79,049
1950 (1940 urban def.)	23,076,539	12,093,697	10,982,842	10,403,230	9,336,719	(NA)	(NA)	(NA)	(NA)
1940 (1940 urban def.)	30,216,188	15,940,370	14,275,818	13,516,607	11,946,855	2,285,916	2,216,384	137,847	112,579
1930 (1930 urban def.)	30,157,513	15,864,375	14,293,138	13,371,441	11,854,804	2,354,445	2,326,078	138,489	112,256
1920 (1920 urban def.)	31,358,640	16,360,059	14,998,581	13,704,724	12,368,076	2,553,234	2,546,729	102,101	83,776

* Denotes first year for which figures include Alaska and Hawaii.
NA Not available.
1 Complete-count data for total, urban, and rural; 20-percent sample data for rural nonfarm and rural farm. See text for series A 91–104 for discussion of 1970 data by race. Complete-count figures exclude 23,372 persons for whom data are not available. See series A 1–5, footnote 3.

2 Complete-count data for total, urban, and rural; 25-percent sample data for rural nonfarm and rural farm.
3 Definition modified to exclude population in incorporated places and New England towns in the 2,500–3,999 size range.

Series A 82–90. Urban Population, by Type of Residence, Sex, and Race: 1950 to 1970

[For definition of urbanized areas, see text]

Year	All races			White		Negro		Other races	
	Total	Male	Female	Male	Female	Male	Female	Male	Female
	82	83	84	85	86	87	88	89	90
URBANIZED AREAS—TOTAL									
1970 1	118,446,566	57,035,148	61,411,418	48,751,475	52,200,027	7,384,180	8,308,505	899,493	902,886
1960 *	95,848,487	46,494,210	49,354,277	40,706,094	43,063,841	5,352,291	5,905,276	435,825	385,160
1960	95,497,151	46,310,655	49,186,496	40,646,972	43,014,130	5,350,802	5,904,446	312,881	267,920
1950 2	69,249,148	33,670,714	35,578,434	30,160,082	31,764,954	3,338,340	3,715,560	154,320	103,680
URBANIZED AREAS—CENTRAL CITIES									
1970 1	63,921,684	30,409,942	33,511,742	23,642,104	25,904,467	6,151,899	6,992,899	615,939	614,376
1960 *	57,975,132	27,927,624	30,047,508	22,976,282	24,650,950	4,606,147	5,095,965	345,195	300,593
1960	57,680,938	27,777,916	29,903,022	22,935,746	24,611,212	4,605,401	5,095,392	236,769	196,418
1950 2	48,377,240	23,432,038	24,945,202	20,402,408	21,639,560	2,886,420	3,221,310	129,690	85,500
URBANIZED AREAS—URBAN FRINGE									
1970 1	54,524,882	26,625,206	27,899,676	25,109,371	26,295,560	1,232,281	1,315,606	283,554	288,510
1960 *	37,873,355	18,566,586	19,306,769	17,729,812	18,412,891	746,144	809,311	90,630	84,567
1960	37,816,213	18,532,739	19,283,474	17,711,226	18,402,918	745,401	809,054	76,112	71,502
1950 2	20,871,908	10,238,676	10,633,232	9,757,674	10,125,394	451,920	494,250	24,630	18,180
OTHER URBAN									
1970 1	30,878,364	14,923,416	15,954,948	13,458,768	14,362,970	1,273,051	1,401,582	191,597	190,396
1960 *	29,420,263	14,238,795	15,181,468	12,925,051	13,733,346	1,204,832	1,345,241	108,912	102,881
1960	29,201,871	14,125,826	15,076,045	12,863,842	13,677,055	1,202,727	1,343,289	59,257	55,701
1950 2	27,218,538	13,221,068	13,997,470	12,089,812	12,741,587	1,090,110	1,226,880	34,950	27,060

* Denotes first year for which figures include Alaska and Hawaii.
1 See text for series A 91–104 for discussion of 1970 data by race. Excludes 23,372 persons for whom data are not available. See series A 1–5, footnote 3.

2 Complete-count data for all races and for white; 3⅓-percent sample for Negro and for other races.

Series A 91–104. Population, by Sex and Race: 1790 to 1970

	Male			Other races				Female			Other races			
Year	All races	White	Negro[1]	Total[2]	Indian	Japanese	Chinese	All races	White	Negro[1]	Total[2]	Indian	Japanese	Chinese
	91	92	93	94	95	96	97	98	99	100	101	102	103	104
1970[3]	98,912,192	86,720,987	10,748,316	1,442,889	388,691	271,300	228,565	104,299,734	91,027,988	11,831,973	1,439,773	404,039	319,990	206,497
1960*	88,331,494	78,367,149	9,113,408	850,937	263,369	224,828	135,549	90,991,681	80,464,583	9,758,423	768,675	260,222	239,504	101,743
1960	87,864,510	78,153,040	9,105,702	605,768	255,677	124,323	115,849	90,599,726	80,301,916	9,754,415	543,395	252,998	135,736	83,109
1950	74,833,239	67,129,192	7,298,722	405,325	178,824	76,649	77,008	75,864,122	67,812,836	7,743,564	307,722	164,586	65,119	40,621
1940	66,061,592	59,448,548	6,269,038	344,006	171,427	71,967	57,389	65,607,683	58,766,322	6,596,480	244,881	162,542	54,980	20,115
1930	62,137,080	55,922,528	5,855,669	358,883	170,350	81,771	59,802	60,637,966	54,364,212	6,035,474	238,280	162,047	57,063	15,152
1920	53,900,431	48,430,655	5,209,436	260,340	125,068	72,707	53,891	51,810,189	46,390,260	5,253,695	166,234	119,369	38,303	7,748
1910	47,332,277	42,178,245	4,885,881	268,151	135,133	63,070	66,856	44,639,989	39,553,712	4,941,882	144,395	130,550	9,087	4,675
1900	38,816,448	34,201,735	4,386,547	228,166	119,484	23,341	85,341	37,178,127	32,607,461	4,447,447	123,219	117,712	985	4,522
1890	32,237,101	28,270,379	3,735,603	231,119	125,719	1,780	103,620	30,710,613	26,830,879	3,753,073	126,661	122,534	259	3,868
1880	25,518,820	22,130,900	3,253,115	134,805	33,985	134	100,686	24,636,963	21,272,070	3,327,678	37,215	32,422	14	4,779
1870[4]	19,493,565	17,029,088	2,393,263	71,214	12,534	47	58,633	19,064,806	16,560,289	2,486,746	17,771	13,197	8	4,566
1860	16,085,204	13,811,387	2,216,744	57,073	23,924		33,149	15,358,117	13,111,150	2,225,086	21,881	20,097		1,784
1850	11,837,660	10,026,402	1,811,258					11,354,216	9,526,666	1,827,550				
1840	8,688,532	7,255,544	1,432,988					8,380,921	6,940,261	1,440,660				
1830	6,532,489	5,366,213	1,166,276					6,333,531	5,171,165	1,162,366				
1820	4,896,605	3,995,809	900,796					4,741,848	3,870,988	870,860				
1810	(5)	2,988,130	(1)					(5)	2,873,943	(1)				
1800	(5)	2,195,305	(1)					(5)	2,111,141	(1)				
1790	(5)	1,615,434	(1)					(5)	1,556,572	(1)				

* Denotes first year for which figures include Alaska and Hawaii.
[1] Sex not reported before 1820. Total for both sexes: 1790—757,208; 1800—1,002,037; 1810—1,377,808. Total slave population: 1790—697,681; 1800—893,602; 1810—1,191,362; 1820—1,538,022; 1830—2,009,043; 1840—2,487,355; 1850—3,204,313; 1860—3,953,760. For slave population by sex, 1820–1860, see series A 119–134.
[2] Includes races not shown separately, of which Filipinos are most numerous. Filipino males: 1910—144; 1920—5,232; 1930—42,268; 1950—46,101; 1960 (conterminous U.S.)—67,351; 1960 (including Alaska and Hawaii)—112,286; 1970—189,498. Filipino females: 1910—16; 1920—371; 1930—2,940; 1940—5,840; 1950—15,535; 1960 (conterminous U.S.)—39,075; 1960 (including Alaska and Hawaii)—64,024; 1970—153,562.
[3] The population of other races (i.e., neither white nor Negro) was overstated by about 327,000 in the 1970 census. See text for series A 91–104. Excludes 23,372 persons for whom sex and race are not available. See series A 1–5, footnote 3.
[4] Revisions to include adjustments for underenumeration in the Southern States show a total (both sexes) of 34,337,292 for white and 5,392,172 for Negro.
[5] Data by sex not available. See series A 1–5 for total population.

Series A 105–118. Foreign Born Population, by Sex and Race: 1850 to 1970

	Male			Other races				Female			Other races			
Year	All races	White	Negro	Total[1]	Indian	Japanese	Chinese	All races	White	Negro	Total[1]	Indian	Japanese	Chinese
	105	106	107	108	109	110	111	112	113	114	115	116	117	118
1970[2]	4,403,687	3,982,797	115,406	305,484	7,153	39,375	105,907	5,215,615	4,750,973	138,052	326,590	7,335	83,125	98,325
1960[3]*	4,760,432	4,507,502	65,952	186,978	(NA)	40,709	59,083	4,977,659	4,786,490	59,370	131,799	(NA)	60,947	34,205
1960[3]	4,714,545	4,500,434	214,111		(NA)	(NA)	(NA)	4,946,422	4,778,835	167,587		(NA)	(NA)	(NA)
1950[4]	5,258,255	[5] 5,098,370	[6] 159,885		(6)	(6)	(6)	5,089,140	[5] 4,997,045	[6] 92,095		(6)	(6)	(6)
1940	6,121,647	6,011,015	44,488	66,144	2,463	29,651	31,687	5,473,249	5,408,123	39,453	25,673	2,028	17,654	5,555
1930	7,647,090	7,502,491	54,081	90,518	1,888	45,897	39,109	6,557,059	6,480,914	44,539	31,606	1,664	24,580	4,977
1920	7,675,435	7,528,322	42,641	104,472	3,539	57,213	40,573	6,245,257	6,184,432	31,162	29,663	2,760	24,125	2,534
1910	7,667,748	7,523,788	23,888	120,072	1,464	60,730	54,935	5,848,138	5,821,757	16,451	9,930	1,289	6,925	1,661
1900	5,630,190	5,515,285	11,829	103,076	1,207	23,185	78,684	4,711,086	4,698,532	8,507	4,047	1,006	872	2,169
1890[7]	5,067,130	4,951,858	(8)	(8)	(8)	(8)	(8)	4,182,417	4,170,009	(8)	(8)	(8)	(8)	(8)
1880	3,630,566	3,521,635	7,758	101,173	1,002	133	100,038	3,049,377	3,038,044	6,259	5,074	818	12	4,244
1870[9]	3,006,943	2,942,579	5,346	59,018	647	46	58,325	2,560,286	2,551,133	4,299	4,854	489	8	4,357
1860		2,192,230	[10] 3,512	33,149					1,904,523	[10] 3,499	1,784			
1850		1,239,434	[10] 2,015						1,001,101	[10] 2,052				

* Denotes first year for which figures include Alaska and Hawaii.
NA Not available.
[1] Includes races not shown separately, of which Filipinos are most numerous. Filipino males: 1960 (including Alaska and Hawaii,)—66,226; 1970—101,051; Filipino females: 1960 (including Alaska and Hawaii)—22,579; 1970—77,919.
[2] 15-percent sample data. These data vary in degree of comparability with data on total population by race. See text for series A 91–104.
[3] 25-percent sample data.
[4] 20-percent sample data. Complete-count data available only for the white population.
[5] Complete-count data: Males—5,176,390; females—4,984,778.
[6] Data for specific races in the Negro and Other races grouping are based on various samples and are extremely unreliable. See Census of Population: 1950, vol. IV, part 3, chapter B.
[7] Excludes population enumerated in the Indian Territory and on Indian reservations (totaling 325,464) which was not classified by nativity. Totals by race and sex: Males—169,221; females—156,243; white males—64,047; white females—53,321; Negro males—10,042; Negro females—8,594; Indian males—95,119; Indian females—94,328; Chinese males—13.
[8] Data by sex not available. Totals for both sexes: Negro—19,979; Indian—1,235; Japanese—1,921; Chinese—104,545.
[9] Excludes 1,260,078 persons for whom data on nativity are not available. See series A 1–5, footnote 3.
[10] Free Negroes only. Data on nativity were not collected for slaves.

Series A 119–134. Population, by Age, Sex, Race, and Nativity: 1790 to 1970

[Age at last birthday, except for 1890, which is age at nearest birthday. For 1940–1970, age not reported was allocated on the basis of other characteristics]

Year	Total	Under 5 years	5-9 years	10-14 years	15-19 years	20-24 years	25-29 years	30-34 years	35-39 years	40-44 years	45-49 years	50-54 years	55-59 years	60-64 years	65 years and over	Age not stated
	119	120	121	122	123	124	125	126	127	128	129	130	131	132	133	134
TOTAL																
1970 [1]	203,211,926	17,154,337	19,956,247	20,789,468	19,070,348	16,371,021	13,476,993	11,430,436	11,106,851	11,980,954	12,115,939	11,104,018	9,973,028	8,616,784	20,065,502	—
1960 *	179,323,175	20,320,901	18,691,780	16,773,492	13,219,243	10,800,761	10,869,186	11,949,186	10,869,124	11,600,243	10,879,485	9,605,954	8,429,865	7,142,452	16,559,580	—
1960	178,464,236	20,205,746	18,592,413	16,689,953	13,147,223	10,726,632	10,803,977	11,881,172	12,414,091	11,545,677	10,834,998	9,571,934	8,402,132	7,123,256	16,525,082	—
1950	150,697,361	16,163,571	13,199,685	11,119,268	10,616,598	11,481,828	12,242,260	11,517,007	11,246,386	10,203,973	9,070,465	8,272,188	7,235,120	6,059,475	12,269,537	—
1940	131,669,275	10,541,524	10,684,622	11,745,935	12,333,523	11,587,835	11,096,638	10,242,388	9,545,377	8,787,843	8,255,225	7,256,846	5,843,865	4,728,340	9,019,314	—
1930	122,775,046	11,444,390	12,607,609	12,004,877	11,552,115	10,870,378	9,833,608	9,120,421	9,208,645	7,990,195	7,042,279	5,975,804	4,645,677	3,751,221	6,633,805	94,022
1920	105,710,620	11,573,230	11,398,075	10,641,137	9,430,556	9,277,021	9,086,491	8,071,193	7,775,281	6,345,557	5,763,620	4,734,873	3,549,124	2,982,548	4,933,215	148,699
1910	91,972,266	10,631,364	9,760,632	9,107,140	9,063,603	9,056,984	8,180,003	6,972,185	6,396,100	5,261,587	4,469,197	3,900,791	2,786,951	2,267,150	3,949,524	169,055
1900	75,994,575	9,170,628	8,874,123	8,080,234	7,556,089	7,335,016	6,529,441	5,556,039	4,964,761	4,247,166	3,454,612	2,942,829	2,211,172	1,791,363	3,080,498	200,584
1890 [2]	62,622,250	7,634,693	7,573,998	7,033,509	6,557,563	6,196,676	5,227,777	4,578,630	3,866,761	3,185,518	2,731,640	2,326,262	1,672,336	1,458,034	2,417,288	162,165
1880	50,155,783	6,914,516	6,479,660	5,715,186	5,011,415	5,087,772	4,080,621	3,368,943	3,000,419	2,468,811	2,089,445	1,839,883	1,271,434	1,104,219	1,723,459	5,161
1870 [3]	38,558,371	5,514,713	4,814,713	4,786,189	4,040,588	3,748,299	3,075,118	2,562,829	2,314,976	1,939,712	1,578,932	1,367,969	876,552	778,971	1,153,649	51,511
1860	31,443,321	4,842,496	4,171,200	3,720,780	3,361,495	5,726,400		4,021,248		2,614,330		1,585,603		1,347,982		14,285
1850	23,191,876	3,497,773	3,241,268	2,890,629	2,529,792	4,277,318		2,825,819		1,846,660		1,109,540		958,792		
MALE																
1970 [1]	98,912,192	8,745,499	10,168,496	10,590,737	9,633,847	7,917,269	6,621,567	5,595,790	5,412,423	5,818,813	5,851,334	5,347,916	4,765,821	4,026,972	8,415,708	—
1960 *	88,331,494	10,329,729	9,504,368	8,524,289	6,633,661	5,272,340	5,333,075	5,846,224	6,079,512	5,675,881	5,357,925	4,734,829	4,127,245	3,409,319	7,503,097	—
1960	87,864,510	10,270,966	9,453,586	8,481,598	6,592,215	5,225,940	5,298,813	5,811,157	6,044,485	5,646,279	5,331,969	4,714,262	4,110,628	3,398,572	7,484,040	—
1950	74,833,239	8,236,164	6,714,555	5,660,399	5,311,342	5,606,293	5,972,078	5,624,723	5,517,544	5,070,269	4,526,366	4,128,648	3,630,046	3,037,888	5,796,974	—
1940	66,061,592	5,354,808	5,418,823	5,952,329	6,180,153	5,692,392	5,450,662	5,070,312	4,745,659	4,419,135	4,209,269	3,752,750	3,011,364	2,397,816	4,406,120	—
1930	62,137,080	5,806,174	6,381,108	6,068,777	5,757,825	5,336,815	4,860,180	4,561,786	4,679,860	4,136,459	3,671,924	3,181,645	2,425,992	1,941,508	3,325,211	51,816
1920	53,900,431	5,857,461	5,753,001	5,369,306	4,673,792	4,527,045	4,538,233	4,130,783	4,074,361	3,285,543	3,117,550	2,535,545	1,880,065	1,585,866	2,483,071	92,875
1910	47,332,277	5,380,596	4,924,123	4,601,753	4,527,282	4,580,290	4,244,348	3,656,768	3,367,016	2,786,016	2,378,916	2,110,013	1,488,437	1,185,966	1,985,976	114,443
1900	38,816,448	4,633,612	4,479,396	4,083,041	3,750,451	3,624,580	3,323,643	2,901,321	2,616,865	2,255,916	1,837,836	1,564,622	1,145,257	917,167	1,555,418	127,423
1890 [2]	32,067,880	3,884,869	3,830,352	3,574,787	3,248,711	3,104,893	2,698,311	2,425,664	2,051,044	1,654,604	1,418,102	1,208,922	871,663	758,710	1,233,719	103,529
1880	25,518,820	3,507,709	3,275,131	2,907,481	2,476,088	2,554,684	2,109,741	1,744,308	1,527,159	1,243,773	1,078,695	966,702	674,927	584,858	867,564	3,795
1870 [3]	19,493,565	2,797,257	2,437,442	2,435,585	1,989,695	1,835,946	1,515,671	1,273,633	1,179,366	990,021	839,578	740,360	469,495	407,491	578,230	27,890
1860	16,085,204	2,449,547	2,109,545	1,900,868	1,650,012	2,911,558		2,129,017		1,392,223		835,074		679,194		9,173
1850	11,837,660	1,769,460	1,640,407	1,473,116	1,237,680	2,194,469		1,490,135		967,573		575,685		479,962		
FEMALE																
1970 [1]	104,299,734	8,408,838	9,787,751	10,198,731	9,436,501	8,453,752	6,855,426	5,834,646	5,694,428	6,162,141	6,264,605	5,756,102	5,207,207	4,589,812	11,649,794	—
1960 *	90,991,681	9,991,172	9,187,412	8,249,203	6,585,582	5,528,421	5,536,164	6,102,962	6,401,597	5,924,362	5,521,560	4,871,125	4,302,620	3,733,133	9,056,483	—
1960	90,599,726	9,934,780	9,138,827	8,208,355	6,555,008	5,500,692	5,505,164	6,070,015	6,369,606	5,899,398	5,503,029	4,857,672	4,291,504	3,724,684	9,040,992	—
1950	75,864,122	7,927,407	6,485,130	5,458,869	5,305,256	5,875,535	6,270,182	5,892,284	5,728,842	5,133,704	4,544,099	4,143,540	3,605,074	3,021,637	6,472,563	—
1940	65,607,683	5,186,716	5,265,799	5,793,606	6,153,370	5,895,443	5,645,976	5,172,076	4,799,718	4,368,708	4,045,956	3,504,096	2,832,501	2,330,524	4,613,194	—
1930	60,637,966	5,638,216	6,226,501	5,936,100	5,794,290	5,533,563	4,973,428	4,558,635	4,528,785	3,853,736	3,370,355	2,844,159	2,219,685	1,809,713	3,308,594	42,206
1920	51,810,189	5,715,769	5,645,074	5,271,831	4,756,764	4,749,976	4,548,258	3,940,410	3,700,920	3,060,014	2,646,070	2,199,328	1,669,059	1,400,748	2,450,144	55,824
1910	44,639,989	5,250,768	4,836,509	4,505,387	4,536,321	4,476,694	3,935,655	3,315,417	3,029,084	2,475,237	2,090,281	1,790,778	1,298,514	1,081,184	1,963,548	54,612
1900	37,178,127	4,537,016	4,394,727	3,997,193	3,805,638	3,710,436	3,205,898	2,654,718	2,347,916	1,991,250	1,616,776	1,378,207	1,065,915	874,196	1,525,080	73,161
1890 [2]	30,554,370	3,749,824	3,743,646	3,458,722	3,308,852	3,091,783	2,529,466	2,152,966	1,815,117	1,530,914	1,313,538	1,117,340	800,673	699,324	1,183,569	58,636
1880	24,636,963	3,406,807	3,204,529	2,807,705	2,535,327	2,533,088	1,970,880	1,624,635	1,473,260	1,225,088	1,010,750	873,181	596,507	519,361	855,895	1,366
1870 [3]	19,064,806	2,717,456	2,377,271	2,350,604	2,050,893	1,912,353	1,559,447	1,289,196	1,135,610	949,691	739,354	627,609	407,057	371,480	575,419	23,621
1860	15,358,117	2,392,949	2,061,655	1,819,912	1,711,483	2,814,842		1,892,231		1,222,107		750,529		668,788		5,112
1850	11,354,216	1,728,313	1,600,861	1,417,513	1,292,112	2,082,849		1,335,684		879,087		533,855		478,830		

See footnotes at end of table.

Series A 119–134. Population, by Age, Sex, Race, and Nativity: 1790 to 1970—Con.

Year	Total	Under 5 years	5-9 years	10-14 years	15-19 years	20-24 years	25-29 years	30-34 years	35-39 years	40-44 years	45-49 years	50-54 years	55-59 years	60-64 years	65 years and over	Age not stated
	119	120	121	122	123	124	125	126	127	128	129	130	131	132	133	134
WHITE, MALE																
1970 [1]	86,720,987	7,874,333	8,633,093	9,033,725	8,291,270	6,940,820	5,849,792	4,925,069	4,784,375	5,194,497	5,257,619	4,832,555	4,310,921	3,647,243	7,645,675	—
1960 *	78,367,149	8,849,181	8,202,157	7,456,573	5,837,093	4,645,822	4,721,783	5,218,188	5,446,833	5,117,038	4,828,179	4,286,023	3,728,599	3,121,664	6,908,016	—
1960	78,153,040	8,823,480	8,182,144	7,440,898	5,817,598	4,614,204	4,702,477	5,200,541	5,429,784	5,102,661	4,817,693	4,278,441	3,722,948	3,117,954	6,902,217	—
1950	67,129,192	7,244,211	5,915,130	4,944,535	4,685,825	5,002,782	5,349,707	5,080,610	4,955,941	4,573,529	4,080,174	3,756,125	3,350,888	2,829,399	5,360,336	—
1940	59,448,548	4,701,470	4,744,537	5,259,007	5,515,920	5,113,642	4,892,013	4,573,316	4,254,368	3,995,190	3,842,613	3,451,717	2,790,046	2,232,453	4,082,256	—
1930	55,922,528	5,158,439	5,662,102	5,415,256	5,132,461	4,746,792	4,324,314	4,116,726	4,225,332	3,772,619	3,327,142	2,835,808	2,239,604	1,799,730	3,122,827	43,376
1920	48,430,655	5,260,714	5,099,205	4,735,150	4,141,331	4,018,576	4,094,301	3,776,266	3,665,341	2,987,412	2,779,175	2,293,604	1,740,661	1,461,619	2,298,475	78,325
1910	42,178,245	4,728,650	4,285,366	4,006,104	3,999,143	4,070,955	3,792,224	3,297,169	3,024,002	2,537,219	2,161,848	1,915,860	1,363,821	1,076,753	1,825,019	94,112
1900	34,201,735	4,011,455	3,862,349	3,519,303	3,258,090	3,145,481	2,942,882	2,619,446	2,360,348	2,055,176	1,651,972	1,396,035	1,040,235	825,213	1,415,924	97,826
1890 [2]	28,206,332	3,351,104	3,276,983	3,044,068	2,818,914	2,740,864	2,407,153	2,200,903	1,831,443	1,495,923	1,271,113	1,083,091	793,301	686,462	1,124,304	80,646
1880 [3]	22,130,900	2,949,449	2,756,201	2,482,572	2,150,068	2,219,317	1,838,054	1,548,077	1,353,221	1,111,763	962,027	856,178	610,080	516,416	777,477	2,199
1870 [3]	17,029,088	2,398,615	2,103,986	2,103,425	1,731,015	1,591,909	1,328,232	1,131,799	1,048,443	881,637	751,745	654,500	424,553	358,940	518,090	14,073
1860	13,811,387	2,091,460	1,788,711	1,590,420	1,400,536	2,497,210		[7]766,283	1,288,682	1,224,086		740,429	495,065	411,411	597,032	7,153
1850	10,026,402	1,472,053	1,372,438	1,225,575	1,041,116	1,869,092		[7]571,997	866,462	840,222		498,660	364,836	278,966	411,411	6,100
1840 [4]	7,255,534	1,270,743	1,024,050	879,530	756,106	1,322,453		[7]431,589		536,606		314,528	262,487	211,002		—
1830 [4]	5,360,451	972,980	782,075	669,734	573,196	956,487		592,535		367,840		229,284			211,002	5,318
1820 [4]	3,995,133	1,345,220		[5]612,535	[6]776,283											
1810 [4]	2,987,571	1,035,058		[5]468,083	[6]547,597											
1800 [4]	2,204,421	764,118		[5]353,071	[6]393,156											
1790 [4]	1,615,625		[8]802,327													
WHITE, FEMALE																
1970 [1]	91,027,988	7,048,807	8,264,333	8,647,392	8,079,090	7,341,007	5,962,122	5,042,368	4,936,494	5,412,335	5,587,023	5,169,302	4,695,581	4,157,467	10,684,667	—
1960 *	80,464,583	8,509,371	7,885,385	7,182,319	5,771,136	4,824,957	4,833,802	5,370,642	5,694,008	5,305,312	4,956,983	4,407,505	3,897,612	3,429,009	8,395,872	—
1960	80,301,916	8,484,716	7,866,039	7,167,491	5,761,253	4,811,363	4,819,304	5,356,568	5,679,699	5,295,312	4,948,180	4,401,423	3,893,296	3,426,023	8,390,528	—
1950	67,812,836	6,940,293	5,681,442	4,749,994	4,644,695	5,176,405	5,575,097	5,275,721	5,102,532	4,616,761	4,089,180	3,779,314	3,344,844	2,823,207	6,013,351	—
1940	58,766,322	4,528,035	4,584,414	5,093,688	5,448,127	5,226,507	5,012,257	4,633,162	4,262,292	3,940,893	3,690,143	3,228,590	2,636,799	2,184,240	4,297,175	—
1930	54,364,212	4,983,730	5,499,561	5,279,168	5,116,318	4,865,877	4,384,684	4,094,186	4,052,936	3,494,273	3,054,428	2,609,935	2,079,591	1,697,047	3,117,146	35,226
1920	46,390,260	5,113,207	4,988,040	4,634,172	4,172,324	4,166,765	4,047,389	3,562,524	3,300,464	2,768,133	2,408,865	2,023,662	1,565,010	1,309,814	2,284,551	45,338
1910	39,553,712	4,594,264	4,189,807	3,912,304	3,969,248	3,915,456	3,464,912	2,970,107	2,707,843	2,243,053	1,899,214	1,639,453	1,200,385	992,570	1,814,984	40,112
1900	32,637,558	3,908,497	3,775,977	3,439,193	3,285,099	3,189,563	2,820,098	2,384,998	2,100,227	1,796,967	1,453,706	1,237,946	980,982	795,945	1,390,795	47,226
1890 [2]	26,777,558	3,228,544	3,196,185	2,947,914	2,856,433	2,707,603	2,239,534	1,943,859	1,608,487	1,369,725	1,178,107	1,007,858	738,358	636,648	1,077,808	40,495
1880 [3]	21,272,070	2,850,702	2,686,218	2,397,959	2,201,582	2,183,155	1,703,647	1,431,177	1,295,271	1,078,972	899,865	771,714	544,835	460,892	766,081	864
1870 [3]	16,560,289	2,321,177	2,047,729	2,033,036	1,780,021	1,643,119	1,353,320	1,133,266	998,877	833,618	654,870	549,743	370,218	327,739	512,692	11,085
1860	13,111,150	2,025,985	1,739,387	1,523,281	1,452,045	2,420,139		[7]736,600	1,128,257	1,128,246		659,246	585,523	408,460	523,246	3,154
1850	9,526,666	1,424,405	1,331,690	1,176,554	1,087,600	1,758,469		[7]544,256	779,120	748,566		459,511		281,404		—
1840 [4]	6,940,161	1,203,319	986,940	836,630	792,223	1,253,490		[7]411,694		502,183		304,852				—
1830 [4]	5,171,115	921,934	750,741	638,856	596,254	918,411		555,531		356,046		223,504		209,838		—
1820 [4]	3,866,804	981,421		[5]605,375	[6]781,030											
1810 [4]	2,874,433	715,197		[5]448,322	[6]561,956											
1800 [4]	2,100,068 [10]			[5]323,648	[6]401,499											
1790 [4]	1,556,839															
FOREIGN-BORN WHITE, MALE																
1970 [11]	3,982,797	41,809	94,967	122,194	149,214	184,966	212,082	236,906	232,179	247,359	272,021	219,606	282,728	351,105	1,335,661	—
1960 [12] *	4,507,502	46,307	76,961	112,140	92,606	121,207	149,510	184,949	243,569	204,179	293,870	396,801	514,193	521,795	1,549,415	—
1960 [12]	4,500,434	46,120	76,684	111,895	92,399	120,582	149,090	184,663	243,122	203,839	293,465	396,254	513,546	521,186	1,547,589	—
1950 [13]	5,098,370	31,735	31,430	32,930	47,640	86,140	154,555	147,275	244,470	383,225	534,395	627,215	703,470	715,185	1,358,705	—
1940	6,011,015	4,219	10,937	27,114	82,391	98,917	193,647	342,991	530,164	656,782	816,955	883,342	735,848	573,300	1,054,408	—
1930	7,502,491	17,232	71,872	90,104	183,215	368,631	571,039	693,851	933,999	992,135	907,537	737,822	565,334	491,843	871,210	6,667
1920	7,528,322	22,857	85,774	167,152	259,270	456,988	792,088	946,818	1,008,677	803,195	744,423	651,546	503,789	392,629	679,384	13,732
1910	7,523,788	51,940	150,652	181,303	351,754	823,920	990,576	888,668	812,007	751,519	656,455	526,256	380,110	331,914	607,008	19,706
1900	5,515,285	26,567	73,727	157,632	271,381	456,186	589,521	660,702	672,804	557,300	468,466	440,079	345,241	285,783	493,760	16,136
1890 [2]	4,951,858	44,040	126,070	201,159	257,658	476,224	602,545	549,099	493,471	475,106	433,466	382,987	278,485	254,401	360,817	16,630
1880 [3]	3,521,635	31,256	61,803	120,740	184,320	274,038	365,094	419,769	432,957	384,931	340,863	318,045	206,820	170,841	210,158	—
1870 [3]	2,942,579	42,322	88,322	104,726	157,050	306,735	379,577	368,420	359,484	328,020	260,805	215,717	115,553	98,703	115,857	1,288

See footnotes at end of table.

Series A 119–134. Population, by Age, Sex, Race, and Nativity: 1790 to 1970—Con.

Year	Total	Under 5 years	5–9 years	10–14 years	15–19 years	20–24 years	25–29 years	30–34 years	35–39 years	40–44 years	45–49 years	50–54 years	55–59 years	60–64 years	65 years and over	Age not stated
	119	120	121	122	123	124	125	126	127	128	129	130	131	132	133	134
FOREIGN-BORN WHITE, FEMALE																
1970 [11]	4,750,973	40,097	89,354	120,721	149,534	229,069	277,961	299,307	282,098	317,950	333,321	250,963	323,164	398,068	1,639,366	---
1960 [12]*	4,786,490	45,022	75,273	110,061	98,620	155,965	189,889	248,375	293,022	226,832	318,702	413,841	507,576	538,949	1,564,363	---
1960 [12]	4,778,835	44,826	74,965	109,863	98,413	155,336	189,107	247,287	292,123	226,353	318,373	413,346	507,045	538,581	1,563,217	---
1950 [13]	4,997,045	31,815	30,605	30,330	44,605	121,415	198,090	174,980	282,565	403,795	523,085	598,190	621,545	599,620	1,336,405	---
1940	5,408,123	4,102	10,647	26,637	82,394	110,592	230,629	366,100	518,231	606,288	686,950	682,226	582,902	495,575	1,004,850	---
1930	6,480,914	16,777	70,501	88,430	193,891	378,557	543,893	626,959	768,432	753,765	702,515	607,308	483,142	434,050	808,645	4,049
1920	6,184,432	22,127	84,110	164,210	268,672	469,856	662,275	704,657	729,128	624,904	555,252	515,831	404,933	323,102	648,843	6,532
1910	5,821,757	50,567	147,585	177,027	322,007	606,461	672,120	617,047	596,086	551,956	489,905	398,799	313,410	295,669	576,341	6,505
1900	4,698,532	25,802	73,465	153,933	290,365	463,296	507,708	512,981	504,762	408,812	371,754	363,313	297,762	259,248	456,587	8,744
1890 [2]	4,170,009	42,589	122,281	195,220	263,637	441,150	469,694	393,221	377,121	384,848	354,349	326,233	246,646	223,546	321,487	7,987
1880 [3]	3,038,044	31,115	60,894	117,699	194,492	254,217	306,022	342,862	356,308	327,959	290,078	259,042	166,294	139,622	191,440	305
1870 [3]	2,551,133	41,590	85,911	100,812	168,376	302,333	328,949	321,175	308,508	272,729	192,021	154,061	87,963	82,228	104,172	
NEGRO, MALE																
1970 [1]	10,748,316	1,219,567	1,377,355	1,406,715	1,201,605	839,848	657,544	568,086	540,539	543,737	520,095	458,526	404,704	334,425	675,570	---
1960 [12]*	9,097,704	1,362,831	1,195,123	989,360	740,971	569,398	547,941	563,502	569,082	508,082	479,437	406,991	365,302	258,918	540,522	---
1960 [12]	9,090,095	1,362,000	1,194,593	989,150	740,196	567,483	546,779	562,859	568,530	507,715	479,437	406,796	365,205	258,875	540,477	---
1950 [13]	7,269,170	947,740	761,430	674,480	591,550	563,730	579,880	510,970	530,210	468,595	418,690	350,255	264,085	195,155	412,400	7,064
1940	6,269,038	621,689	643,781	661,351	630,079	550,193	529,613	467,887	462,559	400,249	348,251	283,120	207,220	154,245	308,801	13,510
1930	5,855,669	611,231	679,748	623,228	595,646	553,622	500,520	416,869	430,472	339,329	323,162	277,532	174,367	133,349	189,530	17,076
1920	5,209,436	568,633	631,341	616,251	513,416	487,169	424,305	331,579	383,587	275,926	320,506	227,995	129,153	112,137	173,881	25,157
1910	4,885,881	629,320	619,175	578,074	473,750	482,157	421,805	332,130	320,450	229,680	199,993	179,387	115,090	101,149	152,482	18,435
1900	4,386,547	604,487	600,410	548,642	422,258	458,921	360,597	262,130	233,371	179,090	168,495	155,188	97,323	85,961	133,025	
1890 [2]	3,725,561	529,985	[14]549,405	[14]526,450		350,392	272,044	203,361	343,371	179,858	257,301		144,761		107,311	
1880 [3]	[15]3,253,115	[14]517,589														
1870 [3]	2,393,263	396,812	331,795	329,339	251,822	232,490	175,068	130,517	123,129	101,580	85,010	83,941	44,237	47,811	59,701	11
1860	2,216,744	354,999	317,999	307,374	245,104	394,185	[17]270,707	247,853	247,378	162,220		93,106		80,615		13,764
1850	1,811,268	297,407	267,969	247,541	196,564	325,377	[17]213,235	201,453	201,453	127,351		77,025		68,551		2,020
1840 [4]	1,432,998	478,868	[19]391,511		[16]444,011			[7]187,173		[18]173,534						
1830	1,166,276	402,173								[18]141,151						
1820 [4]	900,762	394,994			[20]227,100											
NEGRO, FEMALE																
1970 [1]	11,831,973	1,213,071	1,370,073	1,403,154	1,221,440	974,372	770,713	684,849	655,188	654,128	602,684	530,941	468,824	399,352	883,184	---
1960 [12]*	9,750,915	1,359,569	1,195,515	983,572	756,020	642,315	630,858	663,092	652,195	578,429	533,714	444,591	393,439	290,249	627,357	---
1960 [12]	9,746,972	1,358,732	1,195,013	983,302	755,837	641,897	630,322	662,699	651,926	578,212	533,621	444,494	393,392	290,201	627,324	---
1950 [13]	7,757,505	942,880	768,400	677,965	634,585	667,815	669,295	592,570	608,650	503,960	444,215	351,960	264,650	189,685	454,225	13,964
1940	6,596,480	627,391	650,765	669,309	674,527	645,034	615,671	524,992	523,274	414,847	344,556	267,315	189,999	141,669	307,141	17,378
1930	6,035,474	618,975	688,633	628,314	654,882	649,569	571,267	447,645	460,428	348,094	306,903	227,058	135,030	108,820	183,189	6,667
1920	5,253,695	575,066	634,866	620,663	562,799	567,678	485,387	366,286	390,344	283,775	231,083	171,115	100,827	87,981	158,832	9,993
1910	4,941,882	629,968	627,378	577,192	552,471	548,638	459,422	335,926	312,999	225,733	185,981	146,683	94,532	85,353	141,642	13,964
1900	4,447,447	611,168	602,348	543,348	508,272	510,251	376,882	262,477	241,316	188,126	157,889	135,799	81,853	75,726	128,338	23,654
1890 [2]	3,744,479	[14]517,589	[14]544,089	[14]507,251	448,860	381,156	287,507	206,616	363,723		242,378	123,559			104,373	17,378
1880 [3]	[15]3,327,678															
1870 [3]	2,486,746	394,609	328,036	315,972	268,728	266,364	203,980	154,232	135,709	115,240	83,958	77,421	36,620	43,503	62,357	17
1860	2,225,086	364,085	319,807	294,273	256,489	389,418	[17]281,507	253,202	135,220	162,299		90,587		82,414		12,494
1850	1,827,550	303,908	269,171	240,959	204,512	324,380	[17]218,327	207,427	207,427	130,521		74,344		70,370		1,958
1840 [4]	1,440,760	476,527	[19]370,242		[16]446,709			[7]179,874		[18]169,575				66,442		
1830	1,162,366	394,994								[18]136,214				55,923		
1820 [4]	870,800				[20]231,186											
OTHER, MALE																
1970 [1]	1,442,889	151,599	158,048	150,297	140,972	136,601	114,231	102,635	87,509	80,579	73,620	56,835	50,196	45,304	94,463	---
1960 [12]*	857,707	118,812	102,276	84,592	63,920	56,364	59,861	60,361	59,119	46,016	44,820	42,769	44,732	25,533	48,040	---
1960 [12]	612,962	86,651	71,504	57,800	42,478	43,656	46,016	43,721	41,866	31,642	30,061	30,064	33,617	18,628	35,258	---
1950 [13]	401,525	48,045	36,145	36,690	30,440	35,930	34,690	25,985	26,985	23,696	25,300	20,370	14,655	14,310	24,510	---
1940	344,006	31,649	30,505	31,971	34,154	28,557	29,036	29,109	28,732		18,405	17,913	14,098	11,118	15,063	---
1930	358,883	36,504	39,258	30,293	29,718	36,401	35,346	28,191	24,056	24,511	21,620	18,305	12,021	8,429	12,854	1,376
1920	260,340	28,114	22,455	17,905	20,545	21,300	19,580	22,938	25,433	22,205	17,869	13,946	10,251	8,044	10,715	1,040
1910	268,151	22,626	19,582	17,575	20,194	27,178	30,319	27,436	22,564	19,451	17,140	14,766	9,526	8,064	6,469	3,255
1900	228,166	17,670	16,637	15,096	18,611	20,178	20,064	19,745	23,146	21,650	17,369	13,399	7,699	8,475	2,104	3,440
1890 [2]	135,987	[3]3,780	[3]3,964	[14]4,279	7,539	13,637	19,114	21,330	34,424		15,519		5,849	5,993		4,448
1880	134,805 [15]	1,830	1,661	2,821	6,858	11,547	12,371	11,317	7,794	6,804	2,823	1,919	705	740	439	1,585
1870	71,214												89,498			
1860	57,073	3,088	2,835	3,022	4,372	20,163		14,261		5,917		1,815		1,547		53

See footnotes at end of table.

Series A 119–134. Population, by Age, Sex, Race, and Nativity: 1790 to 1970—Con.

Year	Total	Under 5 years	5-9 years	10-14 years	15-19 years	20-24 years	25-29 years	30-34 years	35-39 years	40-44 years	45-49 years	50-54 years	55-59 years	60-64 years	65 years and over	Age not stated
	119	120	121	122	123	124	125	126	127	128	129	130	131	132	133	134
OTHER, FEMALE																
1970[1]	1,439,773	146,960	153,345	148,185	135,971	138,373	122,591	107,429	102,746	95,678	74,898	55,859	42,802	32,993	81,943	—
1960[12]*	781,670	115,094	98,834	81,118	60,161	55,245	66,264	68,690	57,439	41,736	31,736	31,021	25,027	17,568	32,370	—
1960[13]	556,008	84,393	70,204	55,792	39,552	41,500	50,547	50,124	40,072	27,252	21,234	17,278	23,851	12,031	22,178	—
1950	309,545	47,195	35,875	31,480	28,725	31,950	29,140	21,820	17,480	13,665	12,615	11,460	8,855	6,460	12,825	—
1940	244,881	31,290	30,620	30,609	30,716	23,902	18,048	13,902	14,152	12,968	11,257	8,191	5,703	4,625	8,878	—
1930	238,280	35,511	38,307	28,618	23,090	18,117	17,477	16,804	15,421	11,369	9,024	7,166	4,958	3,846	8,259	313
1920	166,234	27,496	22,168	16,996	14,641	15,533	15,482	11,600	10,112	8,104	6,122	4,551	3,222	2,953	6,761	493
1910	144,445	22,536	19,374	15,891	14,602	12,600	11,321	9,384	8,242	6,451	5,086	4,642	3,597	3,261	6,922	536
1900	123,219	17,351	16,402	13,910	12,267	10,622	8,918	7,243	6,373	6,157	5,181	4,462	3,080	3,025	5,947	2,281
1890[2]	82,333	[14]3,691	[14]3,372	[14]3,557	3,559	3,024	—	2,491	4,096	—	2,535	—	1,432	—	1,388	763
1880	[15]37,215	—	—	—	—	—	—	—	—	—	—	—	—	—	—	485
1870	17,771	1,670	1,506	1,596	2,144	2,870	2,147	1,698	1,024	833	526	445	219	238	370	485
1860	21,881	2,879	2,461	2,358	2,949	5,285	—	2,798	—	1,562	—	—	696	851	—	42
FREE NEGRO, MALE																
1860	234,119	32,843	30,700	30,446	24,739	39,167	—	29,032	—	21,429	—	13,330	—	12,348	—	85
1850	208,724	30,319	28,806	26,061	20,395	35,782	—	26,153	—	18,199	—	11,771	—	11,088	—	150
1840[4]	186,481	56,284	—	—	[16]52,805	—	[17]35,321	—	—	[18]28,274	—	—	—	13,797	—	—
1830	153,453	48,675	—	—	[16]43,079	—	[17]27,650	—	—	[18]22,271	—	—	—	11,778	—	—
1820[4]	112,734	[19]47,659	—	—	[20]24,012	—	—	[7]23,450	—	—	—	—	17,613	—	—	—
FREE NEGRO, FEMALE																
1860	253,951	33,075	31,157	29,953	28,008	46,395	—	32,700	—	23,297	—	14,661	—	14,618	—	87
1850	225,771	30,502	29,246	26,247	23,399	41,765	—	29,072	—	19,741	—	12,582	—	13,081	—	136
1840[4]	199,322	55,062	—	—	[16]56,592	—	[17]41,682	—	—	[18]30,371	—	—	—	15,615	—	—
1830	166,146	47,329	—	—	[16]48,138	—	[17]32,541	—	—	[18]24,327	—	—	—	13,811	—	—
1820[4]	120,790	[19]45,898	—	—	[20]28,850	—	—	[7]27,181	—	—	—	—	18,861	—	—	—
SLAVE, MALE																
1860	1,982,625	322,156	287,299	276,928	220,365	355,018	—	218,346	—	140,791	—	79,776	—	16,115	68,267	13,679
1850	1,602,534	267,088	239,163	221,480	176,169	289,595	—	175,300	—	109,152	—	65,254	—	13,811	57,463	1,870
1840[4]	1,246,517	422,584	—	—	[16]391,206	—	[17]235,386	—	—	[18]145,260	—	—	—	52,081	—	—
1830	1,012,823	353,498	—	—	[16]312,567	—	[17]185,585	—	—	[18]118,880	—	—	—	42,293	—	—
1820[4]	788,028	[19]343,852	—	—	[20]203,088	—	—	[7]163,723	—	—	—	—	77,365	—	—	—
SLAVE, FEMALE																
1860	1,971,135	331,010	288,650	264,320	228,481	343,023	—	220,520	—	139,002	—	75,926	—	—	67,796	12,407
1850	1,601,779	273,406	239,925	214,712	181,113	282,615	—	178,355	—	110,780	—	61,762	—	—	57,289	1,822
1840[4]	1,240,938	421,465	—	—	[16]390,117	—	[17]239,825	—	—	[18]139,204	—	—	—	50,327	—	—
1830	996,220	347,665	—	—	[16]308,770	—	[17]185,786	—	—	[18]111,887	—	—	—	42,112	—	—
1820[4]	750,010	[19]324,344	—	—	[20]202,336	—	—	[7]152,693	—	—	—	—	70,637	—	—	—

* Denotes first year for which figures include Alaska and Hawaii.

— Represents zero.

[1] Excludes 23,372 persons for whom age is not available. See series A 1–5, footnote 3.

[2] Exclusive of 325,464 persons enumerated in the Indian Territory and on Indian reservations. See series A 105–118, footnote 7, for composition by race and sex.

[3] Excludes 1,260,078 persons (747,915 white and 512,163 Negro) for whom age is not available. See series A 1–5, footnote 5, and series A 91–104, footnote 4.

[4] Totals differ slightly from corrected totals shown in series A 91–104. Corrections by age are not available. See U.S. Census of Population: 1870, vol. I, pp. xliv–xlix, and 3–8.

[5] 10–15 years old.

[6] 16–25 years old.

[7] 26–44 years old.

[8] Under 16 years old.

[9] 16 years old and over

[10] Age for 1790 available only for white males.

[11] 15-percent sample data.

[12] 25-percent sample data.

[13] 20-percent sample data.

[14] Estimates based on population under 15 and age distribution of Negro and other races.

[15] Age for 1880 available only for all races, white, and for Negro and other races combined.

[16] 10–23 years old.

[17] 24–35 years old.

[18] 36–54 years old.

[19] Under 14 years old.

[20] 14–25 years old.

Series A 135–142. Native Born White Population, by Sex and Parentage: 1850 to 1970

Year	Male				Female			
	Total	Native parentage	Foreign or mixed parentage		Total	Native parentage	Foreign or mixed parentage	
			Foreign	Mixed			Foreign	Mixed
	135	136	137	138	139	140	141	142
1970 [1]	82,910,031	71,823,652	11,086,379		86,475,420	74,407,634	12,067,786	
1960 [2] *	73,840,267	62,271,351	6,674,831	4,894,053	75,703,420	63,487,912	7,115,615	5,099,872
1960 [2]	73,633,549	62,090,878	6,662,816	4,879,826	75,547,881	63,353,734	7,106,238	5,087,888
1950 [3]	61,431,020	50,004,910	7,195,325	4,230,785	62,951,930	50,799,665	7,620,435	4,531,830
1940 [4]	53,437,533	42,126,520	7,613,220	3,945,060	53,358,199	41,998,320	7,570,520	4,028,780
1930	48,420,037	35,595,286	8,645,951	4,178,800	47,883,298	34,805,666	8,761,576	4,316,056
1920	40,902,333	29,636,781	7,810,531	3,455,021	40,205,828	28,785,176	7,884,008	3,536,644
1910	34,654,457	25,229,218	6,456,793	2,968,446	33,731,955	24,259,357	6,459,518	3,013,080
1900	28,686,450	20,849,847	5,341,350	2,495,253	27,908,929	20,099,515	5,290,930	2,518,484
1890 [5]	23,318,521	17,536,950	[6] 5,781,571		22,660,870	16,938,766	[6] 5,722,104	
1880	18,609,265	(7)	(7)	(7)	18,234,026	(7)	(7)	(7)
1870 [8]	14,086,509	(9)	(9)	(9)	14,009,156	(9)	(9)	(9)
1860	11,619,157				11,206,627			
1850	8,786,968				8,525,565			

* Denotes first year for which figures include Alaska and Hawaii.
[1] 15-percent sample data. These data are not entirely comparable with data on total white population, by sex. See text for series A 91–104.
[2] 25-percent sample data. Total native, and data by parentage, are from different tabulations.
[3] 20-percent sample data.
[4] Complete-count data for totals by sex; 5-percent sample data for parentage.
[5] Excludes population enumerated in the Indian Territory and on Indian reservations (including 64,047 white males and 53,321 white females) not classified by nativity.

[6] Totals for both sexes: Foreign parentage—8,085,019; mixed parentage—3,418,656.
[7] Data not available by sex. Totals for both sexes: Native parentage—28,568,424; foreign parentage—6,363,769; mixed parentage—1,911,098.
[8] Excludes 747,915 white persons for whom data on nativity are not available. See series A 1–5, footnote 5, and series A 91–104, footnote 4.
[9] Data not available by sex. Totals for both sexes: Native parentage—22,771,397; foreign parentage—4,167,098; mixed parentage—1,157,170.

Series A 143–157. Median Age of the Population, by Race, Sex, and Nativity: 1790 to 1970

Year	All races			White			Negro			Other races			Foreign-born white		
	Total	Male	Female	Total	Male	Female	Total	Male	Female	Total	Male	Female	Total	Male	Female
	143	144	145	146	147	148	149	150	151	152	153	154	155	156	157
1970	28.1	26.8	29.3	28.9	27.6	30.2	22.4	21.0	23.6	24.7	24.4	24.9	54.6	54.5	54.7
1960 *	29.5	28.7	30.3	30.3	29.4	31.1	23.5	22.3	24.5	24.3	25.2	23.2	57.7	58.4	57.1
1960	29.6	28.7	30.4	30.3	29.5	31.2	23.5	22.3	24.5	24.5	25.5	23.4	57.7	58.2	57.2
1950	30.2	29.9	30.5	30.8	30.4	31.1	26.1	25.8	26.4	24.5	26.9	21.8	56.1	59.0	55.5
1940	29.0	29.1	29.0	29.5	29.5	29.5	25.3	25.3	25.3	24.1	27.6	19.9	51.0	51.4	50.5
1930	26.5	26.7	26.2	26.9	27.1	26.6	23.5	23.7	23.3	23.3	25.9	18.6	43.9	44.1	43.7
1920	25.3	25.8	24.7	25.6	26.1	25.1	22.3	22.8	22.0	26.1	30.4	20.5	40.0	40.1	39.9
1910	24.1	24.6	23.5	24.5	24.9	23.9	21.0	21.0	20.7	26.5	29.2	19.8	37.2	36.9	37.6
1900	22.9	23.3	22.4	23.4	23.8	22.9	19.5	19.5	19.5	27.3	30.9	20.3	38.5	38.8	38.1
1890	22.0	22.3	21.6	22.5	22.9	22.1	18.1	17.9	18.3	28.9	33.2	27.2	37.1	37.1	37.0
1880	20.9	21.2	20.7	21.4	21.6	21.1	(NA)	(NA)	(NA)	(NA)	(NA)	(NA)	38.3	38.5	38.0
1870	20.2	20.2	20.1	20.4	20.6	20.3	18.3	17.8	18.8	28.1	29.1	23.0	34.6	35.3	33.9
1860	19.4	19.8	19.1	19.7	20.1	19.3	17.5	17.5	17.5	26.1	27.5	20.5			
1850	18.9	19.2	18.6	19.2	19.5	18.8	17.4	17.3	17.4						
1840	17.8	17.9	17.8	17.9	18.0	17.8	17.6	17.5	17.6						
1830	17.2	17.2	17.3	17.3	17.2	17.3	17.2	17.1	17.3						
1820	16.7	16.6	16.8	16.6	16.5	16.6	17.2	17.1	17.4						
1810				16.0	15.9	16.1									
1800				16.0	15.7	16.3									
1790					(1)										

* Denotes first year for which figures include Alaska and Hawaii.
NA Not available.

[1] Median falls in the open-ended age group, 16 years and over, which includes 50.3 percent of the white male population.

Series A 158–159. Median Age at First Marriage, by Sex: 1890 to 1970

[In years. 1947 to 1970 based on sample data from Current Population Survey. See text for method of computation]

Year	Male 158	Female 159	Year	Male 158	Female 159	Year	Male 158	Female 159	Year	Male 158	Female 159
1970	23.2	20.8	1962	22.7	20.3	1954	23.0	20.3	1947	23.7	20.5
1969	23.2	20.8	1961	22.8	20.3	1953	22.8	20.2	1940	24.3	21.5
1968	23.1	20.8	1960	22.8	20.3	1952	23.0	20.2	1930	24.3	21.3
1967	23.1	20.6	1959	22.5	20.2	1951	22.9	20.4	1920	24.6	21.2
1966	22.8	20.5	1958	22.6	20.2				1910	25.1	21.6
1965	22.8	20.6	1957	22.6	20.3	1950	22.8	20.3	1900	25.9	21.9
1964	23.1	20.5	1956	22.5	20.1	1949	22.7	20.3	1890	26.1	22.0
1963	22.8	20.5	1955	22.6	20.2	1948	23.3	20.4			

Series A 160–171. Marital Status of the Population, by Age and Sex: 1890 to 1970

[For 1940–1970, marital status not reported was allocated on the basis of other characteristics]

Year and age	Males, 14 years old and over						Females, 14 years old and over					
	Total	Single	Married	Widowed	Divorced	Status not reported	Total	Single	Married	Widowed	Divorced	Status not reported
	160	161	162	163	164	165	166	167	168	169	170	171
1970 [1]												
Total, 14 years and over	71,485,878	20,426,937	47,001,412	2,130,932	1,926,597	–	77,910,094	17,624,105	47,666,431	9,615,280	3,004,278	–
14 years	2,136,818	2,111,778	20,768	2,451	1,821	–	2,049,056	2,019,680	22,010	5,421	1,945	–
15–19 years	9,718,189	9,315,441	381,500	8,529	12,719	–	9,485,229	8,358,248	1,073,147	23,038	30,796	–
15–17 years	6,071,485	5,986,895	74,740	5,057	4,793	–	5,825,133	5,553,582	250,529	12,382	8,640	–
18 and 19 years	3,646,704	3,328,546	306,760	3,472	7,926	–	3,660,096	2,804,666	822,618	10,656	22,156	–
20–24 years	7,761,209	4,307,592	3,329,772	12,878	110,967	–	8,354,509	3,030,876	5,054,321	56,508	212,804	–
25–29 years	6,569,934	1,288,594	5,066,314	19,196	195,830	–	6,810,076	827,906	5,616,300	71,530	294,340	–
30–34 years	5,607,593	601,868	4,803,203	19,574	182,948	–	5,868,858	435,897	5,055,678	86,494	290,789	–
35–44 years	11,261,731	884,372	9,895,931	75,546	405,882	–	11,860,315	672,255	10,187,753	353,760	646,547	–
45–54 years	11,138,181	711,099	9,813,513	186,144	427,425	–	11,996,408	662,506	9,728,095	942,796	663,011	–
55–64 years	8,858,893	574,425	7,587,085	364,665	332,718	–	9,827,142	669,051	6,677,855	1,988,096	492,146	–
65 years and over	8,433,330	631,768	6,103,326	1,441,949	256,287	–	11,658,495	947,686	4,251,272	6,087,637	371,900	–
1960 [2] *												
Total, 14 years and over	61,315,358	15,313,822	42,630,422	2,071,910	1,299,204	–	64,961,189	12,320,199	42,905,285	7,880,607	1,855,098	–
14 years	1,402,724	1,394,426	7,756	163	379	–	1,345,136	1,330,089	14,250	391	406	–
15–19 years	6,698,837	6,437,186	254,377	1,784	5,490	–	6,588,597	5,528,745	1,033,804	4,751	21,297	–
15–17 years	4,341,635	4,290,310	48,850	897	1,578	–	4,171,262	3,886,610	277,151	1,874	5,627	–
18 and 19 years	2,357,202	2,146,876	205,527	887	3,912	–	2,417,335	1,642,135	756,653	2,877	15,670	–
20–24 years	5,283,228	2,807,784	2,417,552	4,780	53,112	–	5,519,937	1,567,622	3,833,956	17,252	101,107	–
25–29 years	5,333,282	1,111,768	4,117,072	9,548	94,894	–	5,537,104	582,114	4,772,006	37,047	145,937	–
30–34 years	5,840,287	694,924	5,000,763	17,246	127,354	–	6,111,422	422,915	5,423,228	74,109	191,170	–
35–44 years	11,739,191	948,784	10,410,091	76,436	303,880	–	12,336,341	748,766	10,741,606	374,216	471,753	–
45–54 years	10,139,671	749,390	8,896,768	182,260	311,253	–	10,485,709	738,266	8,379,825	921,258	446,360	–
55–64 years	7,569,153	605,187	6,351,408	380,508	232,050	–	8,138,691	648,264	5,375,362	1,819,043	296,022	–
65 years and over	7,308,985	564,373	5,174,635	1,399,185	170,792	–	8,898,252	753,418	3,331,248	4,632,540	181,046	–
1950 [3]												
Total, 14 years and over	54,601,105	14,399,840	36,866,055	2,263,850	1,071,360	–	57,102,295	11,418,335	37,576,800	6,734,275	1,372,885	–
14 years	1,090,020	1,080,370	6,660	1,670	1,320	–	1,047,370	1,039,610	6,980	565	215	–
15–19 years	5,323,470	5,146,610	166,955	4,995	4,910	–	5,321,755	4,412,565	887,615	5,260	16,315	–
15–17 years	3,187,510	3,151,360	30,410	3,460	2,280	–	3,116,230	2,893,350	217,325	2,055	3,500	–
18 and 19 years	2,135,960	1,995,250	136,545	1,535	2,630	–	2,205,525	1,519,215	670,290	3,205	12,815	–
20–24 years	5,559,265	3,281,540	2,217,810	9,060	50,855	–	5,878,040	1,898,910	3,856,760	25,280	97,090	–
25–29 years	5,904,975	1,404,860	4,381,375	15,485	103,255	–	6,277,480	833,040	5,227,960	57,490	158,990	–
30–34 years	5,562,315	734,195	4,690,995	20,945	116,180	–	5,896,625	546,245	5,082,260	91,945	176,175	–
35–44 years	10,402,195	996,570	9,046,675	94,865	264,085	–	10,837,650	900,480	9,140,055	409,250	387,865	–
45–54 years	8,484,515	725,355	7,267,615	240,755	250,790	–	8,687,605	680,150	6,737,675	967,595	302,185	–
55–64 years	6,540,100	551,185	5,320,670	495,140	173,105	–	6,633,170	525,405	4,310,160	1,636,660	160,945	–
65 years and over	5,734,250	479,155	3,767,300	1,380,935	106,860	–	6,522,600	581,930	2,327,335	3,540,230	73,105	–
1940												
Total, 14 years and over	50,553,748	17,593,379	30,192,334	2,143,612	624,423	–	50,549,176	13,935,866	30,090,488	5,700,202	822,620	–
14 years	1,218,116	1,216,784	1,247	60	25	–	1,187,614	1,184,094	3,353	110	57	–
15–19 years	6,180,153	6,073,165	104,935	1,031	1,022	–	6,153,370	5,424,023	713,940	6,423	8,984	–
15–17 years	3,684,780	3,670,287	14,002	311	180	–	3,629,909	3,461,246	165,131	1,729	1,803	–
18 and 19 years	2,495,373	2,402,878	90,933	720	842	–	2,523,461	1,962,777	548,809	4,694	7,181	–
20–24 years	5,692,392	4,109,304	1,557,104	8,394	17,590	–	5,895,443	2,781,001	3,025,923	32,751	55,768	–
25–29 years	5,450,662	1,964,118	3,417,046	20,973	48,525	–	5,645,976	1,288,092	4,185,325	71,878	100,681	–
30–34 years	5,070,312	1,050,199	3,912,820	36,714	70,579	–	5,172,076	761,698	4,155,872	128,256	126,250	–
35–44 years	9,164,794	1,283,994	7,551,974	155,405	173,421	–	9,168,426	950,876	7,430,791	537,584	249,175	–
45–54 years	7,962,019	885,004	6,590,954	328,130	157,931	–	7,550,052	654,312	5,736,614	991,448	167,678	–
55–64 years	5,409,180	577,170	4,245,427	488,620	97,963	–	5,163,025	462,407	3,254,768	1,365,044	80,806	–
65 years and over	4,406,120	433,641	2,810,827	1,104,285	57,367	–	4,613,194	429,363	1,583,902	2,566,708	33,221	–
1930												
Total, 14 years and over	45,035,691	16,143,512	26,311,682	2,022,588	488,688	69,221	43,970,842	12,465,795	26,159,771	4,728,565	572,574	44,137
14 years	1,206,486	1,205,662	761	42	21	–	1,175,899	1,171,393	4,241	167	98	–
15–19 years	5,757,825	5,645,359	100,362	1,513	1,348	9,243	5,794,290	5,032,174	731,967	12,337	12,371	5,441
15–17 years	3,493,718	3,482,706	10,553	281	178	–	3,465,118	3,279,560	179,404	3,284	2,870	–
18 and 19 years	2,264,107	2,162,653	89,809	1,232	1,170	9,243	2,329,172	1,752,614	552,563	9,053	9,501	5,441
20–24 years	5,336,815	3,779,443	1,500,493	17,657	21,900	17,322	5,533,563	2,547,057	2,857,665	56,375	62,464	10,002
25–29 years	4,860,180	1,785,413	2,977,004	39,013	50,229	8,521	4,973,428	1,079,923	3,697,645	102,041	89,124	4,695
30–34 years	4,561,786	965,945	3,468,176	59,493	62,669	5,503	4,558,635	603,048	3,715,648	148,571	88,219	3,149
35–44 years	8,816,319	1,261,705	7,189,452	218,881	137,180	9,101	8,382,521	839,130	6,832,581	547,562	157,650	5,598
45–54 years	6,803,569	776,863	5,551,146	357,047	111,471	7,042	6,214,514	564,466	4,673,539	872,676	98,874	4,959
55–64 years	4,367,500	442,505	3,407,751	445,262	66,499	5,483	4,029,398	360,188	2,499,285	1,119,802	45,881	4,242
65 years and over	3,325,211	280,617	2,116,537	883,680	37,371	7,006	3,308,594	268,416	1,147,200	1,869,034	17,893	6,051

See footnotes at end of table.

Series A 160–171. Marital Status of the Population, by Age and Sex: 1890 to 1970—Con.

Year and age	Males, 14 years old and over						Females, 14 years old and over					
	Total	Single	Married	Widowed	Divorced	Status not reported	Total	Single	Married	Widowed	Divorced	Status not reported
	160	161	162	163	164	165	166	167	168	169	170	171
1920												
Total, 14 years and over	37,861,085	13,969,763	21,823,326	1,754,302	234,519	79,175	36,134,659	10,608,384	21,301,014	3,909,736	272,736	42,789
14 years	1,033,297	1,029,971	3,173	118	35	–	1,012,968	1,007,088	5,554	269	57	–
15–19 years	4,673,792	4,567,770	96,374	1,830	759	7,059	4,756,764	4,137,650	596,542	12,239	6,017	4,316
15–17 years	2,828,546	2,815,533	12,521	384	108	–	2,861,030	2,711,081	145,390	3,091	1,468	–
18 and 19 years	1,845,246	1,752,237	83,853	1,446	651	7,059	1,895,734	1,426,569	451,152	9,148	4,549	4,316
20–24 years	4,527,045	3,200,623	1,280,318	20,511	10,280	15,313	4,749,976	2,164,051	2,483,697	65,414	28,582	8,232
25–29 years	4,538,233	1,789,721	2,662,124	51,470	22,856	12,062	4,548,258	1,048,285	3,336,501	117,387	41,243	4,842
30–34 years	4,130,783	995,869	3,023,357	74,454	28,080	9,023	3,940,410	588,119	3,155,854	152,893	40,188	3,356
35–44 years	7,359,904	1,188,586	5,873,308	220,700	63,592	13,718	6,760,934	767,882	5,426,434	485,493	75,027	6,098
45–54 years	5,653,095	677,420	4,580,056	329,976	56,162	9,481	4,845,398	464,838	3,587,794	739,058	48,562	5,146
55–64 years	3,461,865	337,592	2,697,429	386,587	34,249	6,008	3,069,807	257,029	1,878,478	906,362	23,451	4,487
65 years and over	2,483,071	182,211	1,607,187	668,656	18,506	6,511	2,450,144	173,442	830,160	1,430,621	9,609	6,312
1910												
Total, 14 years and over	33,247,336	13,455,690	18,066,188	1,466,839	155,604	103,015	30,904,861	9,826,911	17,667,119	3,167,432	184,621	58,778
14 years	935,974	934,980	898	82	14	–	912,148	908,435	3,482	198	33	–
15–19 years	4,527,282	4,448,067	51,877	1,110	347	25,881	4,536,321	3,985,764	513,239	10,261	3,650	23,407
15–17 years	2,688,370	2,667,874	4,990	252	70	15,184	2,683,806	2,543,264	121,803	2,697	867	15,175
18 and 19 years	1,838,912	1,780,193	46,887	858	277	10,697	1,852,515	1,442,500	391,436	7,564	2,783	8,232
20–24 years	4,580,290	3,432,161	1,100,093	18,815	6,732	22,489	4,476,694	2,163,683	2,225,362	55,354	20,370	11,925
25–29 years	4,244,348	1,816,137	2,353,525	45,092	15,503	14,091	3,935,655	981,556	2,823,935	95,385	29,153	5,626
30–34 years	3,656,768	951,820	2,611,244	65,339	19,068	9,297	3,315,417	535,170	2,619,959	128,942	28,109	3,237
35–44 years	6,153,366	1,026,502	4,873,153	198,701	42,688	12,322	5,504,321	628,516	4,410,310	411,896	49,269	4,330
45–54 years	4,488,929	499,751	3,658,931	286,222	36,502	7,523	3,881,059	331,573	2,904,043	610,386	31,934	3,123
55–64 years	2,674,403	222,950	2,112,699	312,420	21,675	4,659	2,379,698	167,991	1,479,454	714,452	15,200	2,601
65 years and over	1,985,976	123,322	1,303,768	539,058	13,075	6,753	1,963,548	124,223	687,335	1,140,558	6,903	4,529
1900												
Total, 14 years and over	26,286,316	11,053,813	13,920,057	1,173,509	83,828	55,109	24,951,254	8,319,285	13,784,538	2,706,332	114,176	26,923
14 years	793,340	792,267	667	33	7	366	775,224	770,742	3,783	126	30	543
15–19 years	3,750,451	3,706,382	37,781	871	194	5,223	3,805,638	3,374,814	415,682	9,336	2,418	3,388
20–24 years	3,624,580	2,812,113	782,907	14,332	3,322	11,906	3,710,436	1,913,552	1,726,296	52,545	13,124	4,919
25–29 years	3,323,543	1,520,782	1,746,620	38,781	9,142	8,218	3,205,898	882,875	2,209,357	91,847	18,461	3,358
30–34 years	2,901,321	800,664	2,025,729	58,312	10,307	6,309	2,654,718	441,409	2,071,698	121,944	17,384	2,283
35–44 years	4,872,781	826,201	3,840,575	174,535	22,630	8,840	4,339,166	481,668	3,451,375	372,677	29,953	3,493
45–54 years	3,402,458	349,429	2,797,354	230,656	19,498	5,521	2,994,983	234,413	2,212,223	526,456	19,111	2,780
55–64 years	2,062,424	156,823	1,644,373	245,424	12,297	3,507	1,940,111	128,954	1,172,904	626,271	9,566	2,416
65 years and over	1,555,418	89,152	1,044,051	410,565	7,355	4,295	1,525,080	90,858	521,220	905,130	4,129	3,743
1890												
Total, 14 years and over	21,397,501	9,331,617	11,176,124	811,110	48,708	29,942	20,239,343	6,906,714	11,101,645	2,144,496	71,584	14,904
14 years	723,158	723,015	23	–	1	119	695,801	694,281	1,411	17	12	80
15–19 years	3,248,711	3,230,835	16,746	137	28	965	3,308,852	2,987,949	313,983	4,845	1,101	974
20–24 years	3,104,893	2,505,460	585,748	7,610	1,468	4,607	3,091,783	1,601,266	1,444,712	36,456	6,931	2,418
25–29 years	2,698,311	1,240,797	1,421,407	26,601	4,340	5,166	2,529,466	641,988	1,805,064	69,965	10,588	1,861
30–34 years	2,425,664	642,827	1,728,930	43,777	5,832	4,298	2,152,966	326,306	1,717,204	96,797	11,161	1,498
35–44 years	3,705,648	568,511	2,997,030	120,796	12,837	6,474	3,346,031	330,139	2,698,266	296,302	18,899	2,425
45–54 years	2,627,024	239,928	2,213,901	157,920	11,393	3,882	2,430,878	171,454	1,796,979	447,370	13,080	1,995
55–64 years	1,630,373	111,144	1,342,414	166,686	7,835	2,294	1,499,997	86,573	905,627	499,420	6,721	1,656
65 years and over	1,233,719	69,100	869,925	287,583	4,974	2,137	1,183,569	66,758	418,399	693,324	3,091	1,997

* Denotes first year for which figures include Alaska and Hawaii.
– Represents zero.
[1] 5-percent sample.
[2] 25-percent sample.
[3] 20-percent sample.

Series A 172–194.　Population of Regions, by Sex, Race, Residence, Age, and Nativity: 1790 to 1970

[In thousands.　For definition of residence, see text for series A 43–72; for definition of race, see text for series A 91–104; for definition of nativity, see text for series A 105–118]

Region and year	Total popula-tion	Sex [1]		Race			Residence [2]		Urban		Rural	
		Male	Female	White	Negro	Other races	Urban	Rural	White	Negro and other	White	Negro and other
	172	173	174	175	176	177	178	179	180	181	182	183
NORTHEAST												
1970	49,041	23,563	25,478	44,311	4,344	386	39,450	9,591	34,883	4,567	9,427	163
1960	44,678	21,726	22,952	41,522	3,028	127	35,840	8,838	32,836	3,004	8,686	151
1950	39,478	19,347	20,131	37,399	2,018	61	31,373	8,105	29,427	1,946	7,972	133
1940	35,977	17,865	18,111	34,567	1,370	40	27,568	8,409	26,303	1,265	8,264	145
1930	34,427	17,213	17,214	33,237	1,147	43	26,707	7,720	25,652	1,055	7,585	135
1920	29,662	14,879	14,783	28,958	679	25	22,404	7,258	21,931	607	7,027	97
1910	25,869	13,078	12,790	25,361	484	23	18,563	7,305	18,311	410	7,050	97
1900	21,047	10,525	10,522	20,638	385	24	13,911	7,136	13,817	312	6,821	96
1890	17,407	8,681	8,726	17,122	270	15	10,266	7,141	--------	--------	--------	--------
1880	14,507	7,161	7,347	14,274	229	4	7,370	7,137	--------	--------	--------	--------
1870	12,299	6,080	6,219	12,117	180	2	5,448	6,851	--------	--------	--------	--------
1860	10,594	5,266	5,329	10,438	156	(Z)	3,787	6,807	--------	--------	--------	--------
1850	8,627	4,339	4,287	8,477	150	–	2,289	6,338	--------	--------	--------	--------
1840	6,761	3,397	3,364	6,619	142	–	1,253	5,508	--------	--------	--------	--------
1830 [3]	5,542	2,784	2,751	5,417	125	–	785	4,758	--------	--------	--------	--------
1820	4,360	2,187	2,169	4,246	114	–	480	3,880	--------	--------	--------	--------
1810	3,487	1,714	1,670	3,384	102	–	380	3,107	--------	--------	--------	--------
1800	2,636	1,303	1,248	2,553	83	–	245	2,391	--------	--------	--------	--------
1790	1,968	961	940	1,901	67	–	160	1,809	--------	--------	--------	--------
NORTH CENTRAL												
1970	56,572	27,563	29,009	51,641	4,572	359	40,481	16,091	35,773	4,708	15,868	223
1960	51,619	25,472	26,147	48,003	3,446	170	35,481	16,138	32,085	3,396	15,917	220
1950	44,461	22,179	22,282	42,119	2,228	114	28,491	15,970	26,354	2,137	15,765	205
1940	40,143	20,268	19,876	38,640	1,420	83	23,437	16,706	22,159	1,278	16,481	225
1930	38,594	19,690	18,904	37,151	1,262	181	22,351	16,243	21,149	1,203	16,003	240
1920	34,020	17,494	16,526	33,164	793	62	17,776	16,244	17,103	674	16,061	182
1910	29,889	15,486	14,403	29,279	543	66	13,487	16,401	13,088	403	16,191	206
1900	26,333	13,589	12,744	25,776	496	61	10,165	16,168	9,843	324	15,933	233
1890	22,410	11,619	10,792	21,914	431	65	7,418	14,992	--------	--------	--------	--------
1880	17,364	9,016	8,348	16,961	386	17	4,198	13,166	--------	--------	--------	--------
1870 [4]	12,981	6,705	6,262	12,699	273	10	2,702	10,279	--------	--------	--------	--------
1860	9,097	4,743	4,354	8,900	184	13	1,263	7,833	--------	--------	--------	--------
1850	5,404	2,814	2,589	5,268	136	–	499	4,904	--------	--------	--------	--------
1840	3,352	1,758	1,594	3,262	89	–	129	3,222	--------	--------	--------	--------
1830	1,610	838	772	1,569	42	–	42	1,569	--------	--------	--------	--------
1820	859	453	406	841	18	–	10	850	--------	--------	--------	--------
1810	292	151	135	286	7	–	3	290	--------	--------	--------	--------
1800	51	27	23	50	1	–	–	51	--------	--------	--------	--------
SOUTH												
1970	62,795	30,588	32,208	50,420	11,970	405	40,540	22,255	32,212	8,328	18,208	4,048
1960	54,973	27,065	27,908	43,477	11,312	185	32,160	22,813	25,472	6,688	18,004	4,809
1950	47,197	23,424	23,774	36,850	10,225	122	22,956	24,241	18,034	4,922	18,816	5,426
1940	41,666	20,795	20,871	31,659	9,905	103	15,290	26,375	11,659	3,631	19,999	6,376
1930	37,858	19,015	18,843	27,674	9,362	822	12,904	24,953	9,594	3,310	18,080	6,874
1920	33,126	16,773	16,352	24,132	8,912	81	9,300	23,826	7,043	2,261	17,089	6,733
1910	29,389	14,924	14,465	20,547	8,749	92	6,623	22,767	4,761	1,862	15,786	6,980
1900	24,524	12,405	12,119	16,522	7,923	79	4,421	20,103	3,052	1,369	13,470	6,633
1890 [5]	20,028	10,118	9,910	13,193	6,761	74	3,261	16,767	--------	--------	--------	--------
1880	16,517	8,272	8,244	10,555	5,954	7	2,017	14,500	--------	--------	--------	--------
1870	12,288	6,091	6,197	7,863	4,421	4	1,497	10,791	--------	--------	--------	--------
1860	11,133	5,655	5,478	7,034	4,097	2	1,067	10,067	--------	--------	--------	--------
1850	8,983	4,552	4,430	5,630	3,352	–	744	8,239	--------	--------	--------	--------
1840	6,951	3,528	3,423	4,309	2,642	–	463	6,488	--------	--------	--------	--------
1830	5,708	2,900	2,808	3,546	2,162	–	301	5,407	--------	--------	--------	--------
1820	4,419	2,255	2,163	2,776	1,644	–	204	4,216	--------	--------	--------	--------
1810	3,461	1,123	1,069	2,191	1,268	–	143	3,318	--------	--------	--------	--------
1800	2,622	874	830	1,704	918	–	78	2,544	--------	--------	--------	--------
1790	1,961	655	616	1,271	690	–	42	1,919	--------	--------	--------	--------
WEST [6]												
1970	34,804	17,199	17,606	31,377	1,695	1,732	28,854	5,950	25,905	2,949	5,472	478
1960	28,053	14,067	13,986	25,830	1,086	1,137	21,787	6,266	20,035	1,752	5,795	471
1950	20,190	9,884	9,677	18,574	571	416	14,027	6,163	12,941	707	5,633	280
1940	14,379	7,134	6,750	13,350	171	363	8,409	5,969	7,851	276	5,498	257
1930	12,324	6,218	5,678	10,802	120	974	7,199	5,125	6,442	551	4,360	543
1920	9,214	4,754	4,149	8,567	79	258	4,773	4,440	4,543	143	4,023	193
1910	7,082	3,844	2,982	6,544	51	231	3,391	3,691	3,219	111	3,325	170
1900	4,309	2,298	1,794	3,873	30	188	1,718	2,591	1,594	70	2,279	148
1890	3,134	1,820	1,283	2,872	27	203	1,161	1,974	--------	--------	--------	--------
1880	1,801	1,070	698	1,612	12	144	544	1,257	--------	--------	--------	--------
1870	991	609	381	910	6	74	256	735	--------	--------	--------	--------
1860	619	422	197	551	4	64	99	520	--------	--------	--------	--------
1850	179	132	47	178	1	–	11	167	--------	--------	--------	--------

See footnotes at end of table.

Series A 172–194. Population of Regions, by Sex, Race, Residence, Age, and Nativity: 1790 to 1970—Con.

[In thousands]

Region and year	Under 5 years	5–14 years	15–24 years	25–44 years	45–64 years	65 years and over	White — Native born: Native stock	White — Native born: Foreign stock	White — Foreign born	Negro and other races — Native born	Negro and other races — Foreign born
	184	185	186	187	188	189	190	191	192	193	194
NORTHEAST											
1970	3,991	9,359	8,015	11,570	10,905	5,199	31,051	9,573	3,778	4,300	342
1960	4,656	8,093	5,506	12,029	9,895	4,498	26,822	10,274	4,432	3,011	143
1950	3,766	5,603	5,481	12,269	8,912	3,446	21,468	10,611	5,184	1,976	103
1940	2,391	5,546	6,381	11,280	7,784	2,594	18,131	10,560	6,021	1,328	82
1930	2,905	6,448	6,031	10,679	6,416	1,949	14,617	11,518	7,109	1,090	93
1920	3,107	5,638	4,950	9,284	5,200	1,453	12,434	9,741	6,783	641	63
1910	2,691	4,686	4,940	8,183	4,101	1,235	11,076	7,644	6,641	472	36
1900	2,244	4,018	3,913	6,584	3,227	1,018	9,918	5,981	4,739	385	24
1890	1,781	3,399	3,513	5,126	2,662	881	8,891	4,356	3,875	272	13
1880	1,646	3,080	2,861	4,035	2,187	700	11,465		2,808	227	6
1870	1,506	2,735	2,409	3,393	1,741	512	9,600		2,517	178	3
1860	1,448	2,387	3,042	3,103	561	52	8,419		2,019	151	5
1850	1,136	2,037	2,596	2,396	411	48	7,143		1,324	146	2
1840	1,017	1,626	1,965	1,685	293	33	------	------	------	------	------
1830 [3]	866	1,410	1,598	1,277	234	25					
1820	1,335	655	847	843		567					
1810	1,121	528	641	655	439						
1800	846	402	461	513	329						
1790		466			495						
NORTH CENTRAL											
1970	4,837	11,662	9,786	13,067	11,493	5,727	43,620	6,299	1,780	4,773	93
1960	6,009	10,212	6,682	13,222	10,415	5,078	38,532	7,237	2,237	3,578	40
1950	4,677	6,940	6,280	13,083	9,508	3,973	31,458	7,807	2,683	2,309	24
1940	3,087	6,457	7,043	11,974	8,501	3,081	27,155	8,284	3,349	1,493	10
1930	3,414	7,363	6,771	11,596	7,035	2,415	23,051	9,852	4,347	1,332	13
1920	3,561	6,652	5,889	10,309	5,781	1,787	19,266	9,303	4,595	843	13
1910	3,219	5,881	5,877	8,740	4,654	1,462	16,276	8,323	4,680	600	10
1900	3,039	5,818	5,092	7,507	3,680	1,143	14,149	7,476	4,151	550	7
1890	2,744	5,168	4,551	6,072	2,928	855	12,252	5,608	4,053	490	7
1880	2,370	4,273	3,616	4,448	2,133	525	14,049		2,912	398	5
1870 [4]	1,958	3,381	2,587	3,285	1,444	313	10,368		2,331	280	2
1860	1,523	2,345	2,620	2,297	289	18	7,370		1,543	69	1
1850	883	1,451	1,553	1,277	154	11	4,699		650	48	(Z)
1840	631	911	945	690	80	6	------	------	------	------	------
1830	331	453	435	308	38	3					
1820	318	130	163	152	78						
1810	113	44	51	53	26						
1800	20	8	9	9	4						
SOUTH											
1970	5,389	12,736	11,346	14,783	12,498	6,043	46,564	2,718	1,220	12,195	96
1960	6,416	11,527	8,020	14,038	10,389	4,582	40,298	2,258	913	11,445	50
1950	5,573	8,739	7,623	13,763	8,246	3,253	34,209	1,794	739	10,316	28
1940	4,007	8,336	8,131	12,113	6,778	2,300	29,647	1,484	626	9,993	14
1930	4,152	8,682	7,615	10,150	5,628	1,630	25,888	1,683	801	9,468	18
1920	4,034	8,111	6,442	8,770	4,447	1,271	21,832	1,453	847	8,972	21
1910	4,053	7,132	6,015	7,560	3,591	983	18,561	1,260	726	8,828	14
1900	3,464	6,306	5,152	5,870	2,889	765	14,862	1,097	563	7,990	11
1890 [5]	2,791	5,455	4,105	4,633	2,004	603	11,843	830	521	6,825	9
1880	2,690	4,486	3,283	3,937	1,748	467	10,113		442	5,955	6
1870	1,920	3,275	2,621	2,844	1,315	317	7,468		396	4,421	4
1860	1,793	3,066	3,206	2,605	377	38	6,644		392	258	1
1850	1,464	2,546	2,578	2,055	299	35	5,383		240	234	2
1840	826	1,191	1,215	929	135	13	------	------	------	------	------
1830	695	979	1,011	740	110	11					
1820	973	433	548	508		314					
1810	783	344	418	408	238						
1800	613	267	324	322	178						
1790		336			319						
WEST [6]											
1970	2,937	6,989	6,295	8,574	6,914	3,096	24,997	4,564	1,955	2,937	354
1960	3,239	5,634	3,812	7,609	5,357	2,401	20,108	4,015	1,711	2,010	212
1950	2,148	3,036	2,715	6,095	3,970	1,598	13,670	3,366	1,489	886	96
1940	1,057	2,091	2,365	4,305	3,022	1,043	9,191	2,830	1,424	464	70
1930	973	2,119	2,006	3,728	2,336	715	6,844	2,850	1,727	378	97
1920	870	1,638	1,427	2,916	1,602	422	4,890	2,190	1,487	225	111
1910	668	1,168	1,289	2,327	1,078	269	3,575	1,671	1,298	171	111
1900	424	812	734	1,337	604	154	2,021	1,092	761	132	85
1890	318	586	586	1,028	414	78	1,490	710	673	230	98
1880	208	357	340	593	237	32	1,215		397	52	103
1870	128	208	168	370	101	12	661		250	17	63
1860	79	95	217	216	10	1	436		179	4	(Z)
1850	15	26	80	52	3	(Z)	150		27	1	(Z)

- Represents zero. Z Less than 500.

[1] For 1790–1810, white persons only. [2] Series A 178 and A 179, 1950–1970, based on current definition of urban and rural; 1790–1940, based on 1940 definition. Series A 180–183, 1950–1970, based on current definition; 1930–1940, based on 1940 definition and 1900–1920 based on 1920 definition. See text for series A 43–56. [3] Includes 5,602 persons for whom sex, race, and age detail are not available. [4] Sex and age detail for the Dakota Territory not available. [5] Age detail excludes all persons residing in Indian Territory or on Indian reservations. [6] Total population, series A 172, and urban and rural population, series A 178 and A 179, include Alaska beginning 1890, and Hawaii beginning 1900. Sex, race, age, and nativity detail, series A 173–177 and A 180–194, include Alaska and Hawaii beginning 1960. [7] Ages not reported and ages unknown are not included. Prior to 1850 age detail for white only. Age detail columns have changed for early censuses as follows: 1790: Under 16 years and over 16 years, for males only; 1800–1820: Under 10 years, 10–15 years, 16–25 years, 26–44 years, and 45 and over; 1830–1860: Under 5 years, 5–14 years, 15–29 years, 30–59 years, 60–79 years, 80 and over. See also footnote 5. [8] Nativity data for 1850–1930 are based on complete-count data; data for 1940–1970 are sample data. For the 1850 and 1860 censuses, nativity detail for slaves was not compiled; nativity unknown or not reported is not included.

Series A 195–209. Population of States, by Sex, Race, Urban-Rural Residence, and Age: 1790 to 1970

[In thousands, except series A 196. For definition of residence, see text for series A 43–72; for definition of race, see text for series A 91–104]

State and year	Resident population Total	Per square mile of land area	Sex Male	Female	Race White	Negro	Other races	Residence Urban	Rural	Age Under 5 years	5–14 years	15–24 years	25–44 years	45–64 years	65 years and over
	195	196	197	198	199	200	201	202	203	204	205	206	207	208	209
ALABAMA															
1970	3,444	67.9	1,662	1,782	2,534	903	7	2,012	1,432	301	719	616	791	691	326
1960	3,267	64.2	1,592	1,675	2,284	980	3	1,792	1,475	390	718	487	803	607	261
1950³	3,062	59.9	1,503	1,559	2,080	980	3	1,341	1,721	380	620	508	857	497	199
1950⁴								1,228	1,834	---					
1940	2,833	55.5	1,400	1,433	1,849	983	1	856	1,977	297	619	562	793	426	136
1930	2,646	51.8	1,315	1,331	1,701	945	1	744	1,902	314	635	554	669	374	99
1920	2,348	45.8	1,173	1,175	1,447	901	(Z)	509	1,839	300	618	456	587	302	83
1910	2,138	41.7	1,074	1,064	1,229	908	1	370	1,768	312	538	441	524	254	65
1900	1,829	35.7	917	912	1,001	827	(Z)	217	1,612	267	485	394	406	214	54
1890	1,513	29.5	758	756	834	678	1	152	1,361	219	433	315	336	164	42
1880	1,263	24.6	623	640	662	600	(Z)	69	1,194	214	351	254	276	134	34
1870	997	19.4	489	508	521	476	(Z)	63	934	156	273	218	223	103	23
1860	964	18.8	489	475	526	438	(Z)	49	915	159	276	284	214	29	3
1850	772	15.0	392	379	427	345	---	35	736	131	224	224	169	21	2
1840	591	11.5	305	286	335	256	---	13	578	71	100	91	66	7	1
1830	310	6.0	161	149	190	119		3	306	44	54	51	37	4	(Z)
1820	128	2.5	68	60	85	42		–	128	33	13	17	16	7	
1810⁵	9								9						
1800⁵	1								1						
ALASKA															
1970	300	.5	163	137	237	9	55	146	155	32	71	62	87	41	7
1960	226	.4	129	97	175	7	45	86	140	34	46	41	72	28	5
1950	129	.2	79	49	93	–	36	34	94	16	19	28	45	17	5
1940⁶	73	.1	43	30	39	(Z)	33	17	55	8	13	12	22	14	4
1930⁷	59	.1	36	24	29	(Z)	31	8	51	6	11	9	17	13	3
1920	55	.1	35	20	28	(Z)	27	3	52	6	10	7	19	11	2
1910	64	.1	46	18	36	(Z)	28	6	58	5	7	10	30	11	1
1900	64	.1	46	18	30	(Z)	33	16	48	4	7	8	21	7	1
1890	32	.1	19	13	4		28	–	32						
1880	33				(Z)		33	–	33						
ARIZONA															
1970	1,771	15.6	871	900	1,605	53	113	1,409	362	159	379	318	412	342	161
1960	1,302	11.5	655	647	1,170	43	89	971	332	167	286	187	343	229	90
1950³	750	6.6	379	371	655	26	69	416	334	93	146	114	222	130	44
1950⁴								274	476	---					
1940	499	4.4	258	241	427	15	57	174	325	53	101	92	146	83	24
1930	436	3.8	231	204	379	11	46	150	286	50	93	80	131	64	16
1920	334	2.9	184	151	291	8	35	121	213	41	71	60	107	44	10
1910	204	1.8	119	86	171	2	31	63	141	25	40	38	69	26	6
1900	123	1.1	72	51	93	2	28	19	103	15	26	22	39	16	3
1890	88	.8	51	38	56	1	31	8	80	7	12	11	21	8	1
1880	40	.4	28	12	35	(Z)	5	7	33	4	6	8	18	4	(Z)
1870	10	.1	7	3	10	(Z)	(Z)	3	6	1	1	2	5	1	(Z)
ARKANSAS															
1970	1,923	37.0	932	991	1,566	352	5	961	962	158	383	325	412	407	238
1960	1,786	34.2	879	907	1,396	389	2	765	1,021	194	375	251	398	373	194
1950³	1,910	36.3	952	958	1,482	427	1	631	1,279	228	382	295	506	349	150
1950⁴								617	1,292	---					
1940	1,949	37.0	983	966	1,466	483	1	432	1,517	198	407	377	537	324	107
1930	1,854	35.2	940	915	1,375	478	1	383	1,472	209	437	378	475	279	76
1920	1,752	33.4	895	857	1,280	472	(Z)	290	1,462	221	450	336	450	231	62
1910	1,574	30.0	810	764	1,131	443	1	203	1,372	231	390	326	395	186	45
1900	1,312	25.0	675	636	945	367	(Z)	112	1,200	190	354	279	302	151	31
1890	1,128	21.5	586	542	819	309	(Z)	73	1,055	173	322	236	257	115	23
1880	803	15.3	416	386	592	211	(Z)	32	771	142	226	156	191	74	13
1870	484	9.2	248	236	362	122	(Z)	12	472	82	129	114	112	41	7
1860	435	8.3	228	208	324	111	(Z)	4	432	75	129	131	91	8	1
1850	210	4.0	110	100	162	48	---	–	210	38	63	62	43	4	(Z)
1840	98	1.9	53	45	77	20	---	–	98	17	22	22	15	1	(Z)
1830	30	.6	17	14	26	5	---	–	30	6	7	7	5	(Z)	(Z)
1820	14	.1	8	6	13	2	---	–	14	5	2	3	2	1	
1810	1							–	1						

See footnotes at end of table.

Series A 195–209.   Population of States, by Sex, Race, Urban-Rural Residence, and Age: 1790 to 1970—Con.

[In thousands, except series A 196]

State and year	Resident population Total	Resident population Per square mile of land area	Sex[1] Male	Sex[1] Female	Race White	Race Negro	Race Other races	Residence Urban	Residence Rural	Age[2] Under 5 years	Age[2] 5–14 years	Age[2] 15–24 years	Age[2] 25–44 years	Age[2] 45–64 years	Age[2] 65 years and over
	195	196	197	198	199	200	201	202	203	204	205	206	207	208	209
CALIFORNIA															
1970	19,953	127.6	9,817	10,136	17,761	1,400	792	18,136	1,817	1,643	3,882	3,558	5,036	4,034	1,801
1960	15,717	100.4	7,837	7,880	14,455	884	378	13,573	2,144	1,746	3,018	2,080	4,408	3,089	1,376
1950[3]	10,586	67.5	5,296	5,291	9,915	462	209	8,539	2,047	1,099	1,500	1,403	3,439	2,250	895
1950[4]								7,209	3,377						
1940	6,907	44.1	3,516	3,392	6,597	124	186	4,902	2,005	453	914	1,120	2,271	1,595	555
1930	5,677	36.2	2,943	2,735	5,408	81	188	4,161	1,517	405	890	904	1,911	1,188	366
1920	3,427	22.0	1,814	1,613	3,265	39	123	2,327	1,100	276	540	518	1,186	697	200
1910	2,378	15.3	1,323	1,055	2,260	22	96	1,468	909	194	350	430	847	423	125
1900	1,485	9.5	821	665	1,403	11	71	777	708	126	264	265	491	253	77
1890	1,213	7.8	703	511	1,112	11	90	589	624	107	223	235	398	198	40
1880	865	5.5	518	347	767	6	91	371	494	93	171	165	285	133	17
1870	560	3.6	349	211	499	4	57	208	352	68	113	90	221	61	6
1860	380	2.4	273	107	323	4	53	79	301	43	45	137	149	5	(Z)
1850	93	.6	86	7	92	1	—	7	86	2	4	52	33	1	(Z)
COLORADO															
1970	2,207	21.3	1,089	1,118	2,112	66	28	1,733	474	186	458	422	547	406	188
1960	1,754	16.9	870	883	1,701	40	13	1,293	461	209	360	243	464	320	158
1950[3]	1,325	12.8	665	660	1,297	20	8	831	494	148	216	199	389	257	116
1950[4]								760	565						
1940	1,123	10.8	569	555	1,107	12	5	591	533	97	191	197	324	227	86
1930	1,036	10.0	531	505	1,019	12	5	520	516	96	204	182	298	194	62
1920	940	9.1	493	447	924	11	4	453	486	97	184	157	288	164	41
1910	799	7.7	431	368	783	11	4	402	397	83	145	150	265	127	27
1900	540	5.2	295	244	529	9	2	261	279	57	106	95	187	77	14
1890	413	4.0	246	167	405	6	3	186	227	44	73	80	158	47	6
1880	194	1.9	129	65	191	2	1	61	133	19	30	41	83	19	2
1870	40	.4	25	15	39	(Z)	(Z)	5	35	5	7	8	16	3	(Z)
1860	34	.3	33	2	34	(Z)	(Z)	5	30	(Z)	1	19	13	(Z)	(Z)
CONNECTICUT															
1970	3,032	623.6	1,470	1,561	2,835	181	15	2,345	687	253	600	494	731	665	289
1960	2,535	520.6	1,244	1,291	2,424	107	4	1,986	550	278	469	306	705	535	243
1950[3]	2,007	409.7	988	1,019	1,952	53	1	1,559	449	195	282	266	642	445	177
1950[4]								1,391	617						
1940	1,709	348.9	850	859	1,675	33	1	1,158	551	109	254	315	526	377	129
1930	1,607	328.0	801	806	1,577	29	1	1,132	475	133	313	280	486	301	93
1920	1,381	286.4	695	685	1,359	21	1	936	444	154	261	223	435	238	69
1910	1,115	231.3	564	551	1,099	15	1	732	383	112	197	209	353	182	60
1900	908	188.5	454	454	892	15	1	544	365	92	163	165	290	147	51
1890	746	154.8	370	377	733	12	1	380	366	69	133	150	222	124	45
1880	623	129.2	306	317	611	12	(Z)	261	362	63	122	120	176	105	37
1870	537	111.5	265	272	528	10	(Z)	177	360	59	108	102	154	85	29
1860	460	95.5	226	234	452	9	(Z)	122	338	55	91	133	145	33	3
1850	371	76.9	184	187	363	8	—	59	311	40	78	111	113	25	3
1840	310	64.3	152	158	302	8	—	39	271	37	68	86	87	21	3
1830	298	61.8	147	151	290	8	—	28	270	37	69	85	76	19	2
1820	275	57.1	135	141	267	8	—	21	254	72	41	53	55	47	
1810	262	54.3	126	129	255	7	—	16	246	74	39	49	50	43	
1800	251	52.1	121	124	245	6	—	13	238	74	38	45	48	40	
1790	238	49.4	115	118	233	6	—	7	231		54			61	
DELAWARE															
1970	548	276.5	267	281	466	78	3	396	153	48	117	95	136	108	44
1960	446	225.2	221	225	384	61	1	293	154	55	88	57	127	83	36
1950[3]	318	160.8	157	161	274	44	1	199	119	33	49	44	100	65	26
1950[4]								148	170						
1940	267	134.7	134	132	231	36	(Z)	139	127	19	41	48	83	55	21
1930	238	120.5	121	117	206	33	(Z)	123	115	19	45	41	70	46	17
1920	223	113.5	114	109	193	30	(Z)	121	102	23	41	39	67	40	12
1910	202	103.0	103	99	171	31	(Z)	97	105	20	39	39	59	35	10
1900	185	94.0	94	91	154	31	(Z)	86	99	20	38	35	54	29	8
1890	168	85.7	86	83	140	28	(Z)	71	97	18	37	34	47	24	8
1880	147	74.6	74	73	120	26	(Z)	49	98	18	34	31	38	20	6
1870	125	63.6	63	62	102	23	—	31	94	17	32	26	31	16	4
1860	112	57.1	57	56	91	22	—	21	91	17	29	33	29	4	(Z)
1850	92	46.6	46	46	71	20	—	14	78	13	25	26	23	4	(Z)
1840	78	39.7	39	39	59	20	—	8	70	10	15	18	14	2	(Z)
1830	77	39.1	39	38	58	19	—	—	77	9	16	18	13	2	(Z)
1820	73	37.0	37	36	55	17	—	—	73	18	9	11	11	7	
1810	73	37.0	28	27	55	17	—	—	73	19	9	11	11	6	
1800	64	32.7	25	25	50	14	—	—	64	16	9	11	10	5	
1790	59	30.1	24	22	46	13	—	—	59		12			12	

See footnotes at end of table.

Series A 195–209. Population of States, by Sex, Race, Urban-Rural Residence, and Age: 1790 to 1970—Con.

[In thousands, except series A 196]

State and year	Resident population		Sex [1]		Race			Residence		Age [2]					
	Total	Per square mile of land area	Male	Female	White	Negro	Other races	Urban	Rural	Under 5 years	5–14 years	15–24 years	25–44 years	45–64 years	65 years and over
	195	196	197	198	199	200	201	202	203	204	205	206	207	208	209
DIST. OF COLUMBIA															
1970	757	12,401.8	351	405	209	538	10	757	–	60	129	145	197	155	71
1960	764	12,523.9	358	406	345	412	7	764	–	78	116	109	216	176	69
1950	802	13,150.5	378	424	518	281	4	802	–	71	90	117	294	174	57
1940	663	10,870.3	318	346	474	187	1	663	–	40	78	114	252	137	41
1930	487	7,981.5	232	255	354	132	1	487	–	32	68	84	173	100	27
1920	438	7,292.9	204	234	327	110	1	438	–	30	60	85	161	79	21
1910	331	5,517.8	158	173	236	94	(Z)	331	–	27	50	63	119	54	17
1900	279	4,645.3	132	147	192	87	(Z)	279	–	23	46	56	94	46	12
1890	230	3,972.3	110	121	155	76	(Z)	230	–	20	44	50	69	37	9
1880	178	3,062.5	84	94	118	60	(Z)	160	18	21	38	34	54	25	6
1870	132	2,270.7	62	70	88	43	(Z)	121	11	18	28	26	40	16	4
1860	75	1,294.5	35	40	61	14	(Z)	70	5	10	17	22	22	3	(Z)
1850	52	891.2	24	28	38	14	–	48	3	7	13	16	14	2	(Z)
1840	34	485.7	16	18	24	10	–	31	3	4	6	8	6	1	(Z)
1830	30	442.6	15	15	21	9	–	27	3	3	5	7	5	1	(Z)
1820	23	367.1	11	12	16	7	–	21	3	5	2	3	4	2	
1810	15	266.9	5	5	10	5	–	13	2	3	1	2	2	1	1
1800	8	156.6	3	3	6	2	–	6	2	2	1	1	1		1
FLORIDA															
1970	6,789	125.5	3,276	3,514	5,719	1,042	28	5,468	1,321	501	1,249	1,073	1,509	1,468	989
1960	4,952	91.5	2,437	2,515	4,064	880	7	3,661	1,290	541	926	634	1,279	1,019	553
1950[3]	2,771	51.1	1,367	1,404	2,166	603	2	1,814	957	291	435	395	853	560	237
1950[4]								1,567	1,205						
1940	1,897	35.0	943	954	1,382	514	1	1,046	852	151	324	339	602	349	131
1930	1,468	27.1	738	731	1,035	432	1	760	708	142	295	276	441	242	71
1920	968	17.7	495	473	638	329	1	354	615	105	218	178	277	147	41
1910	753	13.7	394	358	444	309	(Z)	219	534	97	171	155	215	90	22
1900	529	9.6	275	253	297	231	(Z)	107	422	73	131	111	136	60	14
1890	391	7.1	202	189	225	166	(Z)	77	314	54	104	81	98	43	10
1880	269	4.9	136	133	143	127	(Z)	27	243	44	74	54	65	27	6
1870	188	3.4	95	93	96	92	(Z)	15	172	30	52	41	44	18	4
1860	140	2.6	73	67	78	63	(Z)	6	135	23	39	40	32	4	(Z)
1850	87	1.6	46	42	47	40	–	–	87	15	24	25	21	2	(Z)
1840	54	1.0	30	25	28	27	–	–	54	5	7	9	7	(Z)	(Z)
1830	35	.6	19	16	18	16	–	–	35	4	5	5	4	(Z)	(Z)
GEORGIA															
1970	4,590	79.0	2,231	2,359	3,391	1,187	11	2,768	1,822	422	951	860	1,122	868	367
1960	3,943	67.8	1,926	2,017	2,817	1,123	3	2,180	1,763	472	852	603	1,013	713	291
1950[3]	3,445	58.9	1,689	1,756	2,381	1,063	1	1,559	1,885	422	667	568	1,006	562	220
1950[4]								1,426	2,018						
1940	3,124	53.4	1,535	1,589	2,038	1,085	1	1,074	2,050	313	644	633	897	477	159
1930	2,909	49.7	1,435	1,474	1,837	1,071	(Z)	895	2,013	316	693	623	744	417	113
1920	2,896	49.3	1,445	1,451	1,689	1,206	(Z)	728	2,168	363	748	580	737	362	102
1910	2,609	44.4	1,305	1,304	1,432	1,177	(Z)	539	2,070	377	663	541	645	299	81
1900	2,216	37.7	1,103	1,113	1,181	1,035	(Z)	346	1,870	325	591	471	510	246	66
1890	1,837	31.3	920	917	978	859	(Z)	257	1,580	267	523	381	424	186	52
1880	1,542	26.3	763	779	817	725	(Z)	145	1,397	262	427	307	352	150	44
1870	1,184	20.2	579	605	639	545	(Z)	100	1,084	189	325	258	265	116	30
1860	1,057	18.0	532	525	592	466	(Z)	75	982	177	303	307	232	35	4
1850	906	15.4	456	450	522	385	–	39	867	155	269	261	189	29	3
1840	691	11.8	351	340	408	284	–	25	667	84	119	110	82	11	1
1830	517	8.8	263	253	297	220	–	14	503	64	83	82	59	8	1
1820	341	5.8	175	166	190	151	–	8	333	69	30	38	33	20	
1810	252	4.3	76	70	145	107	–	5	247	54	23	28	27	14	9
1800	163	1.5	54	48	102	60	–	5	158	38	16	19	20		
1790	83	.6	27	26	53	30	–	–	83		14			13	
HAWAII															
1970	769	119.6	399	369	298	8	463	639	130	71	160	153	203	138	44
1960	633	98.5	338	295	202	5	426	484	149	81	137	105	183	97	29
1950	500	78.0	274	226	115	3	382	345	155	64	92	94	159	70	20
1940	423	66.0	245	178	104	(Z)	319	264	159	40	91	99	127	53	13
1930	368	57.5	223	146	80	1	287	198	170	48	85	76	105	46	8
1920	256	39.9	151	105	55	(Z)	201	92	164	39	52	45	79	36	5
1910	192	30.0	123	69	44	1	147	59	133	24	33	34	76	23	3
1900	154	24.0	106	48	29	(Z)	125	39	115	15	20	32	70	14	3

See footnotes at end of table.

Series A 195-209. Population of States, by Sex, Race, Urban-Rural Residence, and Age: 1790 to 1970—Con.

[In thousands, except series A 196]

State and year	Resident population		Sex [1]		Race			Residence		Age [2]					
	Total	Per square mile of land area	Male	Female	White	Negro	Other races	Urban	Rural	Under 5 years	5–14 years	15–24 years	25–44 years	45–64 years	65 years and over
	195	196	197	198	199	200	201	202	203	204	205	206	207	208	209
IDAHO															
1970	713	8.6	356	357	699	2	12	385	327	64	152	127	158	143	68
1960	667	8.1	338	329	657	2	8	317	350	82	149	94	161	123	58
1950 [3]	589	7.1	303	285	581	1	6	253	336	73	114	86	167	105	44
1950 [4]								234	354						
1940	525	6.3	277	248	519	1	5	177	348	52	98	100	146	97	32
1930	445	5.4	237	208	439	1	6	130	316	46	100	82	119	76	22
1920	432	5.2	234	198	426	1	5	119	313	55	98	74	126	64	15
1910	326	3.9	186	140	319	1	6	70	256	40	68	62	101	44	9
1900	162	1.9	93	68	154	(Z)	7	10	152	22	37	29	49	20	4
1890	89	1.1	53	35	82	(Z)	6	–	89	11	19	15	27	11	2
1880	33	.4	22	11	29	(Z)	4	–	33	4	6	5	12	5	(Z)
1870	15	.2	12	3	11	(Z)	4	–	15	1	1	2	9	1	(Z)
ILLINOIS															
1970	11,114	199.4	5,392	5,722	9,600	1,426	88	9,230	1,884	937	2,233	1,855	2,653	2,343	1,094
1960	10,081	180.4	4,953	5,128	9,010	1,037	33	8,140	1,941	1,130	1,871	1,268	2,674	2,163	975
1950 [3]	8,712	155.8	4,319	4,393	8,046	646	20	6,759	1,953	843	1,250	1,182	2,705	1,979	754
1950 [4]								6,487	2,226						
1940	7,897	141.2	3,957	3,940	7,504	387	6	5,810	2,088	547	1,161	1,361	2,519	1,741	568
1930	7,631	136.4	3,873	3,757	7,295	329	6	5,636	1,995	616	1,365	1,351	2,472	1,399	421
1920	6,485	115.7	3,305	3,180	6,299	182	4	4,404	2,082	655	1,241	1,102	2,078	1,103	298
1910	5,639	100.6	2,912	2,727	5,527	109	3	3,480	2,159	598	1,068	1,122	1,749	843	243
1900	4,822	86.1	2,473	2,349	4,735	85	2	2,616	2,205	550	1,039	915	1,475	641	191
1890	3,826	68.3	1,972	1,854	3,768	57	1	1,719	2,107	471	848	793	1,076	494	138
1880	3,078	55.0	1,587	1,491	3,031	46	(Z)	941	2,137	416	755	650	792	378	87
1870	2,540	45.4	1,317	1,223	2,511	29	(Z)	596	1,944	391	662	503	663	269	52
1860	1,712	30.6	903	809	1,704	8	(Z)	246	1,466	293	432	507	431	46	3
1850	851	15.2	448	403	846	5	–	64	787	142	244	244	200	19	1
1840	476	8.5	257	219	472	4	–	10	467	93	132	140	98	9	1
1830	157	2.8	83	74	155	2	–	–	157	36	44	43	29	3	(Z)
1820	55	1.0	30	25	54	1	–	–	55	20	8	11	10	4	
1810	12	.1	6	5	12	1	–	–	12	4	2	2	2	1	
INDIANA															
1970	5,194	143.9	2,531	2,662	4,820	357	16	3,372	1,822	456	1,075	917	1,222	1,030	494
1960	4,662	128.8	2,299	2,364	4,389	269	5	2,910	1,752	543	939	629	1,204	903	446
1950 [3]	3,934	108.7	1,959	1,976	3,759	174	2	2,357	1,577	422	631	569	1,148	803	361
1950 [4]								2,217	1,717						
1940	3,428	94.7	1,725	1,703	3,305	122	1	1,888	1,540	269	554	601	995	721	288
1930	3,239	89.4	1,640	1,598	3,126	112	1	1,796	1,443	285	612	551	927	629	233
1920	2,930	81.3	1,489	1,441	2,849	81	1	1,483	1,448	289	559	497	854	543	184
1910	2,701	74.9	1,383	1,318	2,640	60	1	1,144	1,557	276	521	510	782	459	149
1900	2,516	70.1	1,285	1,231	2,459	58	(Z)	863	1,654	275	538	489	712	379	118
1890	2,192	61.1	1,118	1,074	2,147	45	(Z)	590	1,602	254	507	452	584	299	91
1880	1,978	55.1	1,010	968	1,939	39	(Z)	386	1,592	258	495	429	497	239	61
1870	1,681	46.8	858	823	1,656	25	(Z)	248	1,433	253	453	347	402	184	42
1860	1,350	37.6	699	651	1,339	11	(Z)	116	1,235	227	365	393	320	43	3
1850	988	27.5	512	477	977	11	–	45	944	168	292	281	219	26	2
1840	686	19.1	357	329	679	7	–	11	675	137	200	189	136	15	1
1830	343	9.6	178	163	338	4	–	–	343	77	100	90	63	8	1
1820	147	4.1	77	70	146	1	–	–	147	57	22	28	26	12	2
1810	25	.6	13	11	24	1	–	–	25	9	4	5	4	2	
1800	6	(8)	3	2	5	(Z)	–	–	6	2	1	1	1	(Z)	
IOWA															
1970	2,824	50.5	1,373	1,452	2,783	33	9	1,616	1,208	233	574	477	612	579	350
1960	2,758	49.2	1,359	1,398	2,729	25	3	1,463	1,295	307	551	358	652	562	328
1950 [3]	2,621	46.8	1,310	1,311	2,600	20	2	1,251	1,370	280	426	374	710	558	273
1950 [4]								1,229	1,392						
1940	2,538	45.3	1,280	1,258	2,521	17	1	1,084	1,454	207	417	443	706	537	228
1930	2,471	44.1	1,255	1,216	2,453	17	1	979	1,492	220	479	425	691	471	184
1920	2,404	43.2	1,229	1,175	2,384	19	1	875	1,529	251	468	426	694	418	144
1910	2,225	40.0	1,148	1,077	2,209	15	1	680	1,545	236	451	436	620	352	125
1900	2,232	40.2	1,157	1,075	2,219	13	(Z)	572	1,659	263	496	439	614	308	106
1890	1,912	34.4	995	918	1,901	11	1	406	1,507	234	455	397	490	257	78
1880	1,625	29.2	848	776	1,615	10	(Z)	247	1,377	230	409	341	396	202	47
1870	1,194	21.5	626	568	1,188	6	(Z)	156	1,038	191	320	234	296	128	24
1860	675	12.1	354	320	674	1	(Z)	60	615	125	177	186	168	17	1
1850	192	3.5	101	91	192	(Z)	–	10	182	34	56	53	45	4	(Z)
1840	43	.2	24	19	43	(Z)	–	–	43	8	11	14	9	1	(Z)

See footnotes at end of table.

Series A 195–209. Population of States, by Sex, Race, Urban-Rural Residence, and Age: 1790 to 1970—Con.

[In thousands, except series A 196]

State and year	Resident population — Total	Per square mile of land area	Sex — Male	Female	Race — White	Negro	Other races	Residence — Urban	Rural	Age — Under 5 years	5–14 years	15–24 years	25–44 years	45–64 years	65 years and over
	195	196	197	198	199	200	201	202	203	204	205	206	207	208	209
KANSAS															
1970	2,247	27.5	1,102	1,145	2,122	107	18	1,485	762	175	440	406	501	459	266
1960	2,179	26.6	1,081	1,097	2,079	91	9	1,329	850	246	426	290	545	432	240
1950³	1,905	23.2	954	952	1,829	73	3	993	912	200	299	278	535	399	194
1950⁴								903	1,002						
1940	1,801	21.9	906	895	1,734	65	1	754	1,047	138	301	314	509	382	157
1930	1,881	22.9	961	920	1,812	66	3	730	1,151	171	371	337	525	346	129
1920	1,769	21.6	909	860	1,709	58	2	616	1,153	187	365	316	502	292	105
1910	1,691	20.7	886	805	1,634	54	3	492	1,199	192	346	338	468	255	88
1900	1,470	18.0	769	702	1,416	52	2	330	1,141	172	341	298	383	214	60
1890	1,428	17.5	753	675	1,377	50	2	270	1,159	186	357	289	365	189	40
1880	996	12.2	537	459	952	43	1	105	891	152	261	195	265	107	17
1870	364	4.5	202	162	346	17	1	52	313	59	89	75	106	31	4
1860	107	1.3	59	48	106	1	(Z)	10	97	18	27	35	26	1	(Z)
KENTUCKY															
1970	3,219	81.2	1,579	1,640	2,982	231	6	1,684	1,535	271	651	584	731	644	337
1960	3,038	76.2	1,508	1,530	2,820	216	2	1,353	1,685	342	637	447	737	582	292
1950³	2,945	73.9	1,475	1,470	2,742	202	1	1,084	1,861	346	562	474	798	529	235
1950⁴								986	1,959						
1940	2,846	70.9	1,436	1,410	2,631	214	(Z)	849	1,996	285	579	541	769	483	189
1930	2,615	65.2	1,323	1,292	2,388	226	(Z)	799	1,816	293	596	480	677	425	142
1920	2,417	60.2	1,227	1,189	2,181	236	(Z)	634	1,783	292	559	446	637	368	114
1910	2,290	57.0	1,162	1,128	2,028	262	(Z)	555	1,734	295	526	457	603	313	94
1900	2,147	53.4	1,090	1,057	1,862	285	(Z)	468	1,680	284	525	439	550	265	77
1890	1,859	46.3	943	916	1,590	268	(Z)	357	1,502	249	481	391	452	215	64
1880	1,649	41.0	833	816	1,377	271	(Z)	250	1,399	248	444	344	386	178	47
1870	1,321	32.9	666	655	1,099	222	(Z)	196	1,125	207	363	277	303	137	34
1860	1,156	28.8	592	563	919	236	(Z)	121	1,035	193	322	330	267	40	4
1850	982	24.4	503	480	761	221	————	74	909	164	285	283	215	32	4
1840	780	19.4	400	380	590	190	————	31	749	115	167	167	122	18	2
1830	688	17.1	353	336	519	170	————	16	672	105	148	146	102	16	2
1820	564	14.0	289	275	435	129	————	9	555	161	71	83	74	46	
1810	407	10.1	169	155	324	82	————	4	402	126	53	59	55	31	
1800	221	5.5	94	86	180	41	————	–	221	72	27	31	33	16	
1790	74	1.8	32	29	61	13	————	–	74		17			15	
LOUISIANA															
1970	3,641	81.0	1,771	1,870	2,541	1,087	13	2,406	1,235	348	808	675	826	677	307
1960	3,257	72.2	1,592	1,665	2,212	1,039	6	2,061	1,196	423	725	467	808	592	242
1950³	2,684	59.4	1,319	1,364	1,797	882	4	1,472	1,212	334	510	423	773	466	177
1950⁴								1,380	1,304						
1940	2,364	52.3	1,172	1,191	1,512	849	3	980	1,383	231	472	457	712	374	119
1930	2,102	46.5	1,048	1,054	1,323	776	3	834	1,268	231	476	424	593	302	76
1920	1,799	39.6	903	895	1,097	700	2	628	1,170	209	442	360	493	230	59
1910	1,656	36.5	835	821	941	714	1	497	1,160	224	413	340	440	185	50
1900	1,382	30.4	695	687	730	651	1	366	1,015	199	361	285	340	152	40
1890	1,119	24.6	559	559	558	559	1	284	835	163	306	231	260	124	32
1880	940	20.7	469	471	455	484	1	239	701	151	252	177	228	108	25
1870	727	16.0	362	365	362	364	1	203	524	111	181	145	187	87	17
1860	708	15.6	370	338	357	350	(Z)	185	523	102	168	207	199	19	2
1850	518	11.4	275	243	255	262	————	134	383	73	123	156	151	13	1
1840	352	7.8	188	165	158	194	————	105	247	28	37	50	42	3	(Z)
1830	216	4.8	115	101	89	126	————	46	170	16	23	26	22	2	(Z)
1820	153	3.4	82	71	74	80	————	27	126	23	10	15	17	8	
1810	77	2.2	19	15	34	42	————	17	59	11	5	6	8	4	
MAINE															
1970	992	32.1	483	509	985	3	4	504	488	85	201	168	219	204	115
1960	969	31.3	479	490	963	3	3	497	472	109	192	133	235	194	107
1950³	914	29.4	454	460	911	1	2	472	442	100	154	137	246	184	94
1950⁴								375	539						
1940	847	27.3	426	421	845	1	1	343	504	70	151	145	227	173	80
1930	797	25.7	401	396	795	1	1	322	476	75	154	129	207	163	69
1920	768	25.7	389	379	766	1	1	300	468	75	142	125	210	154	62
1910	742	24.8	377	365	740	1	1	262	480	72	131	127	209	141	61
1900	694	23.2	351	343	692	1	1	233	462	66	124	124	195	129	55
1890	661	22.1	333	328	659	1	1	186	475	58	124	126	179	120	52

See footnotes at end of table.

Series A 195–209. Population of States, by Sex, Race, Urban-Rural Residence, and Age: 1790 to 1970—Con.

[In thousands, except series A 196]

State and year	Resident population Total	Per square mile of land area	Male	Female	White	Negro	Other races	Urban	Rural	Under 5 years	5–14 years	15–24 years	25–44 years	45–64 years	65 years and over
	195	196	197	198	199	200	201	202	203	204	205	206	207	208	209
MAINE—Con.															
1880	649	21.7	324	325	647	1	1	147	502	64	130	126	171	109	49
1870	627	21.0	313	314	625	2	1	132	495	68	135	125	160	100	39
1860	628	21.0	317	311	627	1	(Z)	104	524	78	144	181	178	42	4
1850	583	19.5	297	286	582	1	- - -	79	504	76	146	167	158	31	4
1840	502	16.8	254	248	500	1	- - -	39	462	79	132	140	124	23	3
1830	399	13.4	201	198	398	1	- - -	13	387	67	106	115	91	17	
1820	298	10.0	150	149	297	1	- - -	9	290	96	49	59	56	38	2
1810	229	7.7	116	112	228	1	- - -	7	222	80	36	42	44	26	
1800	152	5.1	77	74	151	1	- - -	4	148	55	24	26	30	16	
1790	97	3.2	49	47	96	1	- - -	—	97		25			24	
MARYLAND															
1970	3,922	396.6	1,916	2,006	3,195	699	28	3,004	918	344	814	682	996	786	300
1960	3,101	313.5	1,533	1,567	2,574	518	8	2,254	847	367	626	414	880	587	227
1950 [3]	2,343	237.1	1,167	1,176	1,955	386	2	1,616	727	258	368	343	761	450	164
1950 [4]								1,426	917						
1940	1,821	184.2	915	906	1,518	302	1	1,080	741	137	297	333	573	358	124
1930	1,632	165.0	821	811	1,354	276	1	975	657	145	315	292	488	295	93
1920	1,450	145.8	729	720	1,205	244	(Z)	869	580	147	284	264	431	250	72
1910	1,295	130.3	644	651	1,063	232	(Z)	658	637	138	263	251	376	205	61
1900	1,188	119.5	589	599	952	235	1	591	597	135	259	235	334	171	50
1890	1,042	104.9	516	527	826	216	(Z)	496	547	121	239	212	278	145	44
1880	935	94.0	462	473	725	210	(Z)	376	559	123	223	190	241	123	34
1870	781	78.6	385	396	605	175	(Z)	295	485	108	193	157	197	101	24
1860	687	69.1	341	346	516	171	- - -	233	454	101	172	196	186	29	3
1850	583	58.6	292	291	418	165	- - -	188	395	86	151	168	153	23	3
1840	470	47.3	234	235	318	152	- - -	114	356	53	76	96	80	12	1
1830	447	45.0	226	221	291	156	- - -	91	356	46	73	90	70	10	1
1820	407	41.0	207	200	260	147	- - -	66	341	81	39	54	54	33	
1810	381	38.3	120	115	235	145	- - -	47	334	75	36	47	48	29	
1800	342	34.4	111	106	216	125	- - -	27	315	70	34	44	44	25	
1790	320	32.0	107	101	209	111	- - -	14	306		51			56	
MASSACHUSETTS															
1970	5,689	727.0	2,719	2,970	5,478	176	36	4,810	879	470	1,098	979	1,295	1,212	636
1960	5,149	657.3	2,486	2,662	5,023	112	14	4,303	846	548	932	656	1,330	1,110	572
1950 [3]	4,691	596.2	2,270	2,420	4,612	73	6	3,959	731	449	660	660	1,392	1,061	468
1950 [4]								4,066	625						
1940	4,317	545.9	2,102	2,214	4,258	55	4	3,859	457	282	659	755	1,286	966	369
1930	4,250	537.4	2,072	2,178	4,193	52	4	3,831	418	350	778	712	1,277	856	274
1920	3,852	479.2	1,890	1,962	3,804	45	3	3,469	383	386	693	630	1,211	723	206
1910	3,366	418.8	1,655	1,711	3,325	38	3	2,996	371	329	580	622	1,094	563	175
1900	2,805	349.0	1,367	1,438	2,770	32	4	2,412	393	282	485	517	922	446	143
1890	2,239	278.5	1,088	1,151	2,215	22	1	1,835	404	204	388	459	698	362	122
1880	1,783	221.8	858	925	1,764	19	1	1,332	452	179	333	352	534	289	96
1870	1,457	181.3	704	754	1,443	14	(Z)	972	485	157	288	287	433	223	69
1860	1,231	153.1	597	634	1,221	10	(Z)	733	498	151	243	365	391	73	8
1850	995	123.7	489	506	985	9	- - -	504	491	114	201	317	300	55	6
1840	738	91.7	365	372	729	9	- - -	279	458	93	155	228	207	41	5
1830	610	75.9	298	312	603	7	- - -	190	421	80	139	186	157	36	5
1820	523	65.1	255	268	516	7	- - -	119	404	140	77	102	112	85	
1810	472	58.7	230	236	465	7	- - -	101	371	136	68	91	95	75	
1800	423	52.6	205	211	417	6	- - -	65	358	125	63	79	84	67	
1790	379	47.1	183	191	373	5	- - -	51	328		87			95	
MICHIGAN															
1970	8,875	156.2	4,349	4,526	7,833	991	51	6,554	2,321	804	1,903	1,575	2,085	1,755	753
1960	7,823	137.7	3,883	3,940	7,086	718	20	5,739	2,084	969	1,623	1,011	2,077	1,505	638
1950 [3]	6,372	111.7	3,212	3,160	5,918	442	12	4,503	1,869	704	1,041	922	1,941	1,303	462
1950 [4]								4,166	2,206						
1940	5,256	92.2	2,695	2,561	5,040	208	8	3,455	1,801	431	883	935	1,612	1,063	331
1930	4,842	84.9	2,519	2,323	4,664	169	9	3,302	1,540	463	942	835	1,538	805	255
1920	3,668	63.8	1,928	1,740	3,602	60	7	2,242	1,427	405	695	612	1,158	604	191
1910	2,810	48.9	1,455	1,356	2,785	17	8	1,327	1,483	299	534	532	812	474	157
1900	2,421	42.1	1,249	1,172	2,399	16	7	952	1,469	261	512	456	689	379	121
1890	2,094	36.4	1,092	1,002	2,073	15	6	730	1,364	237	458	408	592	302	92
1880	1,637	28.5	862	775	1,615	15	7	405	1,232	208	371	333	451	217	57
1870	1,184	20.6	618	566	1,167	12	5	238	946	164	287	235	321	145	33
1860	749	13.0	395	354	736	7	6	100	649	113	181	222	205	26	2
1850	398	6.9	210	188	395	3	- - -	29	369	60	109	112	104	11	1
1840	212	3.7	114	98	212	1	- - -	9	203	38	56	63	50	4	(Z)
1830	32	.2	18	13	31	(Z)	- - -	—	32	6	8	10	6	1	(Z)
1820	9	(8)	5	3	9	(Z)	- - -	—	9	2	1	2	2	1	
1810	5	.1	3	2	5	(Z)	- - -	—	5	1	1	1	1	(Z)	

See footnotes at end of table.

Series A 195–209. Population of States, by Sex, Race, Urban-Rural Residence, and Age: 1790 to 1970—Con.

[In thousands, except series A 196]

State and year	Resident population		Sex [1]		Race			Residence		Age [2]					
	Total	Per square mile of land area	Male	Female	White	Negro	Other races	Urban	Rural	Under 5 years	5–14 years	15–24 years	25–44 years	45–64 years	65 years and over
	195	196	197	198	199	200	201	202	203	204	205	206	207	208	209
MINNESOTA															
1970	3,805	48.0	1,864	1,941	3,736	35	34	2,527	1,278	332	818	665	852	729	409
1960	3,414	43.1	1,693	1,721	3,372	22	20	2,123	1,291	416	705	446	816	676	354
1950 [3]	2,982	37.3	1,501	1,481	2,954	14	15	1,625	1,358	332	491	421	829	640	269
1950 [4]								1,607	1,375						
1940	2,792	34.9	1,428	1,365	2,769	10	13	1,390	1,402	230	459	503	809	579	213
1930	2,564	32.0	1,317	1,247	2,543	9	12	1,258	1,306	231	511	454	749	454	163
1920	2,387	29.5	1,246	1,142	2,369	9	9	1,052	1,336	261	483	438	707	385	111
1910	2,076	25.7	1,109	967	2,059	7	9	850	1,225	227	435	432	594	298	86
1900	1,751	21.7	932	819	1,737	5	9	598	1,153	228	410	331	502	210	67
1890	1,310	16.2	699	611	1,296	4	10	443	867	177	301	258	366	154	42
1880	781	9.7	419	362	777	2	2	149	632	117	191	161	197	95	19
1870	440	5.4	235	204	438	1	1	71	369	71	118	77	118	47	8
1860	172	2.1	93	79	169	(Z)	2	16	156	34	39	47	48	4	(Z)
1850	6	(8)	4	2	6	(Z)			6	1	1	2	2	(Z)	(Z)
MISSISSIPPI															
1970	2,217	46.9	1,074	1,143	1,393	816	8	987	1,230	210	490	406	466	422	222
1960	2,178	46.0	1,068	1,110	1,258	916	5	821	1,357	278	502	331	475	401	190
1950 [3]	2,179	46.1	1,077	1,102	1,189	986	4	607	1,572	283	457	363	568	355	153
1950 [4]								602	1,577						
1940	2,184	46.1	1,084	1,099	1,106	1,075	3	433	1,751	235	477	428	607	321	115
1930	2,010	42.4	1,005	1,005	998	1,010	2	339	1,671	234	478	422	514	283	77
1920	1,791	38.6	897	893	854	935	1	240	1,550	216	472	355	452	226	67
1910	1,797	38.8	906	891	786	1,009	2	207	1,590	260	464	373	449	193	54
1900	1,551	33.5	781	770	641	908	2	120	1,431	229	421	337	353	163	45
1890	1,290	27.8	650	640	545	743	2	70	1,220	192	378	272	285	124	35
1880	1,132	24.4	567	564	479	650	2	35	1,097	196	324	223	255	106	28
1870	828	17.9	413	415	383	444	1	33	795	137	222	182	188	81	18
1860	791	17.1	406	385	354	437	(Z)	21	771	126	216	233	171	20	2
1850	607	13.1	312	295	296	311		11	596	105	176	177	132	15	1
1840	376	8.1	196	180	179	197		4	372	38	50	52	36	3	(Z)
1830	137	2.9	72	65	70	66		3	134	15	20	20	14	1	(Z)
1820	75	1.6	40	35	42	33			75	15	6	8	8	4	
1810 [5]	31	.4	13	10	23	17			31	8	3	5	5	2	
1800 [5]	8	.3	3	2	5	4			8	2	1	1	1	(Z)	
MISSOURI															
1970	4,677	67.8	2,256	2,421	4,177	480	19	3,278	1,399	371	919	784	1,060	981	561
1960	4,320	62.6	2,108	2,212	3,923	391	6	2,877	1,443	466	799	561	1,055	936	503
1950 [3]	3,955	57.1	1,941	2,014	3,656	297	2	2,433	1,522	384	602	553	1,132	876	407
1950 [4]								2,290	1,665						
1940	3,785	54.6	1,881	1,903	3,539	244	1	1,961	1,824	279	606	639	1,127	807	326
1930	3,629	52.4	1,823	1,807	3,404	224	2	1,859	1,770	306	664	640	1,068	704	245
1920	3,404	49.5	1,723	1,681	3,225	178	1	1,587	1,817	328	673	599	1,011	603	186
1910	3,293	47.9	1,688	1,606	3,135	157	1	1,394	1,900	361	662	654	960	498	150
1900	3,107	45.2	1,596	1,511	2,945	161	1	1,128	1,979	364	718	624	867	413	113
1890	2,679	39.0	1,385	1,294	2,528	150	1	857	1,822	343	656	568	698	325	81
1880	2,168	31.6	1,127	1,041	2,023	145	(Z)	546	1,622	311	569	458	547	235	49
1870	1,721	25.0	896	825	1,603	118	(Z)	430	1,292	276	467	348	437	164	28
1860	1,182	17.2	622	560	1,063	119	(Z)	203	979	204	318	351	279	28	2
1850	682	9.9	358	324	592	90		81	601	116	198	201	152	14	1
1840	384	5.6	203	181	324	60		16	367	67	91	94	65	6	(Z)
1830	140	2.1	74	66	115	26		5	135	26	33	31	22	2	(Z)
1820	67	1.0	37	30	56	11			67	20	8	12	11	5	
1810	20	(NA)	9	8	17	4			20	7	3	3	3	2	
MONTANA															
1970	694	4.8	347	347	663	2	29	371	324	57	151	122	155	141	69
1960	675	4.6	344	331	651	1	23	338	336	83	144	90	167	125	65
1950 [3]	591	4.1	309	282	572	1	18	258	333	68	102	82	170	118	51
1950 [4]								253	338						
1940	559	3.8	299	260	540	1	18	212	348	49	93	102	157	122	36
1930	538	3.7	293	244	520	1	16	181	357	49	110	94	156	101	27
1920	549	3.8	300	249	534	2	13	172	377	67	111	83	185	84	17
1910	376	2.6	227	149	361	2	14	133	243	38	64	73	137	52	9
1900	243	1.7	150	93	226	2	16	85	159	27	44	41	95	30	5
1890	143	1.0	93	50	128	1	14	39	104	13	19	25	57	15	2
1880	39	.3	28	11	35	(Z)	3	7	32	4	6	7	17	5	(Z)
1870	21	.1	17	4	18	(Z)	2	3	17	1	2	3	11	2	(Z)

See footnotes at end of table.

Series A 195–209.   Population of States, by Sex, Race, Urban-Rural Residence, and Age: 1790 to 1970—Con.

[In thousands, except series A 196]

State and year	Resident population		Sex [1]		Race			Residence		Age [2]					
	Total	Per square mile of land area	Male	Female	White	Negro	Other races	Urban	Rural	Under 5 years	5–14 years	15–24 years	25–44 years	45–64 years	65 years and over
	195	196	197	198	199	200	201	202	203	204	205	206	207	208	209
NEBRASKA															
1970	1,483	19.4	724	759	1,433	40	11	913	571	120	300	258	326	296	184
1960	1,411	18.4	700	711	1,375	29	7	766	645	160	276	183	340	288	164
1950 [3]	1,326	17.3	667	658	1,301	19	5	622	704	140	209	196	365	286	130
1950 [4]								607	719						
1940	1,316	17.2	666	650	1,298	14	4	514	802	105	227	232	370	276	106
1930	1,378	18.0	706	672	1,360	14	4	486	892	130	278	253	394	236	86
1920	1,296	16.9	673	624	1,279	13	4	405	891	143	273	236	377	200	64
1910	1,192	15.5	628	564	1,180	8	4	311	881	140	250	248	330	172	51
1900	1,066	13.9	565	502	1,057	6	4	253	814	134	255	213	291	138	35
1890	1,063	13.8	575	488	1,047	9	7	292	771	148	256	214	303	113	23
1880	452	5.9	249	203	450	2	(Z)	61	391	72	112	88	129	44	7
1870	123	1.6	70	53	122	1	(Z)	22	101	20	28	25	38	10	1
1860	29	.2	17	12	29	(Z)	(Z)	–	29	5	6	10	8	(Z)	(Z)
NEVADA															
1970	489	4.4	248	241	448	28	13	395	93	44	100	79	134	100	31
1960	285	2.6	148	138	263	13	8	201	85	33	54	38	84	58	18
1950 [3]	160	1.5	85	75	150	4	6	92	68	17	24	20	54	34	11
1950 [4]								84	76						
1940	110	1.0	61	49	104	1	6	43	67	9	16	18	36	24	7
1930	91	.8	53	38	85	1	6	34	57	7	15	14	30	20	5
1920	77	.7	46	31	71	(Z)	6	15	62	7	12	11	29	15	3
1910	82	.7	53	29	74	1	7	13	69	6	11	13	34	14	3
1900	42	.4	26	17	35	(Z)	7	7	35	4	7	8	13	8	2
1890	47	.4	30	17	39	(Z)	8	16	31	4	8	8	16	9	1
1880	62	.6	42	20	54	(Z)	8	19	43	6	9	10	28	8	1
1870	42	.4	32	10	39	(Z)	3	7	35	3	4	6	25	4	(Z)
1860	7	.1	6	1	7	(Z)		–	7	(Z)	(Z)	4	3	(Z)	–
NEW HAMPSHIRE															
1970	738	81.7	361	377	733	3	2	416	322	65	149	126	171	149	78
1960	607	67.2	298	309	604	2	1	354	253	66	116	79	151	127	68
1950 [3]	533	59.1	262	271	532	1	(Z)	307	226	55	81	75	148	116	58
1950 [4]								312	221						
1940	492	54.5	245	247	491	(Z)	(Z)	283	208	36	79	83	138	107	49
1930	465	51.6	232	234	464	1	(Z)	273	192	39	86	74	125	99	42
1920	443	49.1	222	221	442	1	(Z)	250	193	41	79	71	125	91	35
1910	431	47.7	216	214	430	1	(Z)	223	207	40	73	75	126	83	34
1900	412	45.6	205	206	411	1	(Z)	192	219	38	68	73	123	76	32
1890	377	41.7	187	190	376	1	(Z)	148	229	30	63	74	107	70	32
1880	347	38.4	171	176	346	1	(Z)	104	243	31	61	67	95	64	29
1870	318	35.2	156	163	318	1	(Z)	83	235	30	60	61	85	57	25
1860	326	36.1	160	166	326	(Z)		72	254	35	65	92	102	29	3
1850	318	35.2	156	162	317	1		54	264	33	69	93	96	24	3
1840	285	31.5	139	145	284	1		29	256	36	67	78	81	20	3
1830	269	29.8	131	138	269	1		13	256	38	67	75	70	17	2
1820	244	27.0	120	124	243	1		7	237	70	39	48	49	38	
1810	214	23.7	106	108	214	1		7	208	67	35	40	42	30	
1800	184	20.4	91	92	184	1		5	179	61	29	34	36	24	
1790	142	15.7	71	70	142	1		5	137		35			36	
NEW JERSEY															
1970	7,168	953.1	3,467	3,701	6,350	770	48	6,373	795	589	1,403	1,121	1,746	1,612	697
1960	6,067	805.5	2,972	3,095	5,539	515	13	5,374	692	642	1,107	717	1,716	1,324	560
1950 [3]	4,835	642.8	2,383	2,453	4,512	319	5	4,186	649	459	662	646	1,571	1,103	394
1950 [4]								3,918	917						
1940	4,160	553.1	2,069	2,091	3,931	227	2	3,395	765	256	618	752	1,341	914	279
1930	4,041	537.3	2,031	2,011	3,830	209	3	3,339	702	330	765	715	1,294	734	201
1920	3,156	420.0	1,590	1,566	3,037	117	2	2,522	633	339	614	526	1,009	532	133
1910	2,537	337.7	1,286	1,251	2,446	90	2	1,939	599	267	471	487	816	387	107
1900	1,884	250.7	942	942	1,812	70	2	1,329	555	206	371	345	597	281	80
1890	1,445	192.3	721	724	1,397	48	1	905	540	153	291	292	426	217	62
1880	1,131	150.5	560	571	1,092	39	(Z)	615	516	135	251	220	316	164	45
1870	906	120.6	450	456	875	31	(Z)	396	510	120	210	173	254	120	30
1860	672	89.4	335	337	647	25		220	452	98	154	192	193	32	3
1850	490	65.2	245	244	466	24		86	403	68	122	142	132	23	3
1840	373	49.7	188	185	352	22		40	334	56	89	102	87	15	2
1830	321	42.7	163	158	300	21		18	302	49	80	87	70	13	1
1820	278	36.9	140	137	258	20		7	270	82	39	50	49	37	
1810	246	32.7	115	112	227	19		6	240	74	37	42	43	31	
1800	211	28.1	99	96	194	17		–	211	67	31	33	39	24	
1790	184	24.5	87	83	170	14		–	184		41			45	

See footnotes at end of table.

Series A 195–209. Population of States, by Sex, Race, Urban-Rural Residence, and Age: 1790 to 1970—Con.

[In thousands, except series A 196]

State and year	Resident population		Sex[1]		Race			Residence		Age[2]					
	Total	Per square mile of land area	Male	Female	White	Negro	Other races	Urban	Rural	Under 5 years	5–14 years	15–24 years	25–44 years	45–64 years	65 years and over
	195	196	197	198	199	200	201	202	203	204	205	206	207	208	209
NEW MEXICO															
1970	1,016	8.4	501	515	916	20	81	709	307	97	242	188	241	178	71
1960	951	7.8	480	471	876	17	58	626	325	136	225	144	251	144	51
1950[3]	681	5.6	348	334	630	8	43	342	339	95	142	115	194	102	33
1950[4]								315	367						
1940	532	4.4	272	260	492	5	35	176	355	64	120	101	147	77	23
1930	423	3.5	219	204	391	3	29	107	317	54	101	81	112	58	17
1920	360	2.9	190	170	335	6	20	65	295	46	87	67	97	49	12
1910	327	2.7	175	152	305	2	21	47	281	45	75	63	90	43	10
1900	195	1.6	104	91	180	2	13	27	168	27	49	34	54	25	6
1890	160	1.3	86	74	143	2	15	10	150	22	34	30	44	19	4
1880	120	1.0	64	55	109	1	10	7	113	16	29	24	34	14	3
1870	92	.7	47	45	90	(Z)	1	5	87	13	24	19	25	9	2
1860[9]	94	.4	49	44	83	(Z)	11	5	89	14	24	28	23	3	1
1850[10]	62	.3	32	30	62	(Z)	--------	5	57	9	16	20	15	2	(Z)
NEW YORK															
1970	18,237	381.3	8,715	9,522	15,834	2,169	234	15,602	2,634	1,487	3,391	2,946	4,417	4,036	1,961
1960	16,782	350.6	8,123	8,659	15,287	1,418	78	14,332	2,450	1,691	2,936	2,028	4,548	3,892	1,688
1950[3]	14,830	309.3	7,240	7,590	13,872	918	40	12,682	2,148	1,365	1,987	1,989	4,702	3,529	1,258
1950[4]								11,907	2,923						
1940	13,479	281.2	6,690	6,789	12,880	571	28	11,166	2,313	836	1,942	2,271	4,510	2,999	922
1930	12,588	262.6	6,313	6,276	12,153	413	22	10,522	2,066	989	2,163	2,210	4,201	2,346	667
1920	10,385	217.9	5,187	5,198	10,172	198	15	8,589	1,797	1,010	1,875	1,743	3,402	1,850	493
1910	9,114	191.2	4,585	4,529	8,967	134	13	7,188	1,925	899	1,590	1,781	2,960	1,454	418
1900	7,269	152.5	3,615	3,654	7,157	99	13	5,298	1,971	753	1,358	1,343	2,336	1,120	348
1890	6,003	126.0	2,980	3,023	5,924	70	9	3,910	2,093	601	1,130	1,204	1,822	931	298
1880	5,083	106.7	2,505	2,578	5,016	65	2	2,869	2,214	559	1,053	1,004	1,449	785	233
1870	4,383	92.0	2,163	2,220	4,330	52	(Z)	2,189	2,193	521	967	849	1,257	619	167
1860	3,881	81.4	1,934	1,947	3,832	49	(Z)	1,524	2,356	530	861	1,122	1,163	188	16
1850	3,097	65.0	1,568	1,529	3,048	49	--------	873	2,224	403	720	960	867	131	13
1840	2,429	51.0	1,231	1,198	2,379	50	--------	471	1,958	368	587	726	598	90	9
1830[11]	1,919	40.3	974	940	1,868	45	--------	287	1,632	310	504	552	430	66	6
1820	1,373	28.8	698	674	1,333	39	--------	161	1,212	439	206	265	269	154	
1810	959	20.1	474	444	919	40	--------	121	838	324	143	171	181	101	
1800	589	12.4	297	259	556	31	--------	75	514	186	94	97	118	61	
1790	340	7.1	162	152	314	26	--------	39	301		78		84		
NORTH CAROLINA															
1970	5,082	104.1	2,488	2,594	3,902	1,126	54	2,285	2,797	437	1,016	984	1,233	999	414
1960	4,556	93.2	2,247	2,309	3,399	1,116	41	1,802	2,754	526	995	726	1,192	805	312
1950[3]	4,062	82.7	2,017	2,045	2,983	1,047	31	1,368	2,694	502	810	722	1,178	625	225
1950[4]								1,238	2,824						
1940	3,572	72.7	1,773	1,799	2,568	981	23	974	2,597	376	785	761	993	501	157
1930	3,170	64.5	1,575	1,595	2,235	919	17	810	2,360	391	809	665	779	408	116
1920	2,559	52.5	1,279	1,280	1,784	763	12	490	2,069	359	674	500	613	311	99
1910	2,206	45.3	1,098	1,108	1,501	698	8	318	1,888	333	561	452	510	269	78
1900	1,894	38.9	939	955	1,264	624	6	187	1,707	284	499	400	412	229	66
1890	1,618	33.2	799	819	1,055	561	2	116	1,502	233	459	326	357	182	57
1880	1,400	28.7	688	712	867	531	1	55	1,345	233	375	280	310	155	47
1870	1,071	22.0	519	553	678	392	1	36	1,035	163	285	233	232	123	34
1860	993	20.4	496	497	630	362	1	25	968	158	280	278	230	40	5
1850	869	17.8	431	438	553	316	--------	21	848	142	249	244	194	34	5
1840	753	15.5	375	379	485	269	--------	13	740	90	133	134	107	19	2
1830	738	15.1	371	367	473	265	--------	10	728	89	130	134	101	17	2
1820	639	13.1	322	317	419	220	--------	13	626	146	66	82	74	51	
1810	556	11.4	189	188	376	179	--------	–	556	133	60	73	68	42	
1800	478	9.8	172	166	338	140	--------	–	478	122	53	65	62	36	
1790	394	8.1	147	141	288	106	--------	–	394		78		70		
NORTH DAKOTA															
1970	618	8.9	312	306	599	2	16	273	344	51	135	114	130	122	66
1960	632	9.1	323	309	620	1	12	223	410	80	138	90	146	120	59
1950	620	8.8	323	297	608	(Z)	11	165	455	75	117	99	167	113	48
1940	642	9.2	335	307	631	(Z)	10	132	510	62	129	124	172	117	39
1930	681	9.7	360	321	672	(Z)	9	113	568	76	158	137	175	104	30
1920	647	9.2	342	305	640	(Z)	6	88	559	91	161	116	176	83	19
1910	577	8.2	318	260	570	1	7	63	514	82	129	118	167	65	13
1900	319	4.5	177	142	312	(Z)	7	23	296	48	78	60	93	33	7
1890	191	2.7	106	85	182	(Z)	8	11	180	30	41	33	58	17	4
1880[12]	37	.9	82	53	133	(Z)	1	3	34	20	27	27	46	13	2
1870[12]	2	.1	(NA)	(NA)	13	(Z)	1	–	2	(NA)	(NA)	(NA)	(NA)	1	(NA)
1860[12]	5	([8])	3	2	3	–	2	–	5	1	1	1	1	(Z)	(Z)

See footnotes at end of table.

Series A 195–209. Population of States, by Sex, Race, Urban-Rural Residence, and Age: 1790 to 1970—Con.

[In thousands, except series A 196]

State and year	Resident population Total	Per square mile of land area	Sex[1] Male	Female	Race White	Negro	Other races	Residence Urban	Rural	Age[2] Under 5 years	5–14 years	15–24 years	25–44 years	45–64 years	65 years and over
	195	196	197	198	199	200	201	202	203	204	205	206	207	208	209
OHIO															
1970	10,652	260.0	5,163	5,489	9,647	970	35	8,026	2,626	921	2,187	1,846	2,515	2,186	998
1960	9,706	236.6	4,764	4,942	8,910	786	11	7,123	2,583	1,139	1,939	1,247	2,588	1,896	897
1950[3]	7,947	193.8	3,929	4,018	7,428	513	5	5,578	2,368	847	1,207	1,101	2,403	1,680	709
1950[4]								5,346	2,600						
1940	6,908	168.0	3,461	3,447	6,567	339	2	4,613	2,295	507	1,072	1,225	2,068	1,496	540
1930	6,647	161.6	3,361	3,286	6,335	309	2	4,507	2,139	573	1,252	1,142	2,011	1,250	415
1920	5,759	141.4	2,956	2,803	5,572	186	1	3,677	2,082	586	1,057	965	1,809	1,018	319
1910	4,767	117.0	2,435	2,332	4,655	111	1	2,665	2,102	479	865	900	1,455	799	262
1900	4,158	102.1	2,103	2,055	4,060	97	(Z)	1,998	2,159	432	851	801	1,216	641	210
1890	3,672	90.1	1,856	1,817	3,585	87	(Z)	1,510	2,162	400	811	751	1,006	521	177
1880	3,198	78.5	1,614	1,584	3,118	80	(Z)	1,031	2,167	405	761	660	823	419	129
1870	2,665	65.4	1,338	1,328	2,602	63	(Z)	683	1,982	375	671	544	657	328	90
1860	2,340	57.4	1,190	1,149	2,303	37	(Z)	400	1,939	364	600	673	596	98	8
1850	1,980	48.6	1,017	964	1,955	25		242	1,738	310	546	573	473	72	6
1840	1,519	37.3	784	735	1,502	17		83	1,436	282	415	433	324	45	3
1830	938	23.3	485	453	928	10		37	901	186	268	260	186	26	2
1820	581	14.5	303	278	577	5		10	572	218	90	110	103	55	
1810	231	5.7	120	109	229	2		3	228	91	35	40	42	21	
1800	45	1.1	24	21	45	(Z)		–	45	18	7	8	8	3	
OKLAHOMA															
1970	2,559	37.2	1,246	1,313	2,280	172	107	1,740	819	197	491	449	586	536	300
1960	2,328	33.8	1,148	1,180	2,108	153	67	1,465	863	243	455	329	567	485	249
1950[3]	2,233	32.4	1,116	1,118	2,033	146	55	1,139	1,094	240	399	345	624	431	194
1950[4]								1,107	1,126						
1940	2,336	33.7	1,182	1,155	2,104	169	63	880	1,457	219	464	440	669	399	145
1930	2,396	34.6	1,233	1,163	2,131	172	93	822	1,574	265	544	484	660	346	97
1920	2,028	29.2	1,058	970	1,821	149	58	538	1,490	253	509	392	543	263	65
1910	1,657	23.9	882	776	1,445	138	75	319	1,338	242	404	333	441	193	41
1900	790	11.4	423	367	670	56	65	58	732	119	208	157	201	87	15
1890[13]	259	3.7	140	119	173	22	64	9	249	9	15	11	18	7	1
OREGON															
1970	2,091	21.7	1,024	1,067	2,032	26	33	1,403	689	164	406	366	480	449	227
1960	1,769	18.4	880	889	1,732	18	19	1,100	669	185	360	227	439	374	184
1950[3]	1,521	15.8	773	749	1,497	12	13	819	702	164	240	202	457	325	133
1950[4]								732	789						
1940	1,090	11.3	563	527	1,076	3	11	532	558	76	155	183	328	254	93
1930	954	9.9	500	454	939	2	13	490	464	69	164	161	290	201	67
1920	783	8.2	416	367	769	2	12	390	393	71	142	126	252	149	43
1910	673	7.0	384	289	655	1	16	307	366	60	113	131	226	112	28
1900	414	4.3	233	181	395	1	18	133	280	41	85	78	129	63	16
1890	318	3.3	184	134	302	1	15	88	229	34	68	62	98	41	9
1880	175	1.8	103	71	163	(Z)	11	26	149	23	40	35	51	22	4
1870	91	1.0	53	38	87	(Z)	4	8	83	14	24	16	27	9	1
1860	52	.5	32	21	52	(Z)	(Z)	3	50	10	13	15	14	1	(Z)
1850[14]	12	(8)	8	5	13	(Z)		–	12	2	3	4	3	(Z)	(Z)
PENNSYLVANIA															
1970	11,794	262.3	5,665	6,128	10,738	1,017	40	8,430	3,363	926	2,251	1,928	2,683	2,733	1,272
1960	11,319	251.4	5,510	5,810	10,454	853	13	8,102	3,217	1,188	2,107	1,415	3,029	2,452	1,129
1950[3]	10,498	233.1	5,170	5,328	9,854	638	6	7,403	3,095	1,026	1,603	1,531	3,225	2,227	887
1950[4]								6,985	3,513						
1940	9,900	219.8	4,951	4,949	9,427	470	3	6,587	3,313	726	1,670	1,867	2,941	2,019	677
1930	9,631	213.8	4,846	4,786	9,196	431	4	6,534	3,098	896	1,989	1,732	2,793	1,708	508
1920	8,720	194.5	4,429	4,291	8,433	285	3	5,672	3,048	1,005	1,797	1,473	2,612	1,431	394
1910	7,665	171.0	3,942	3,723	7,468	194	3	4,631	3,034	884	1,485	1,473	2,350	1,136	326
1900	6,302	140.6	3,205	3,098	6,142	157	4	3,449	2,854	730	1,311	1,203	1,888	896	262
1890	5,258	117.3	2,666	2,592	5,148	108	2	2,557	2,701	604	1,143	1,075	1,479	722	224
1880	4,283	95.5	2,137	2,146	4,197	86	(Z)	1,783	2,500	552	1,008	855	1,126	571	170
1870	3,522	78.6	1,758	1,763	3,457	65	(Z)	1,313	2,209	492	854	706	901	448	119
1860	2,906	64.8	1,454	1,452	2,849	57	(Z)	895	2,012	442	724	820	780	129	11
1850	2,312	51.6	1,168	1,144	2,258	54		545	1,767	345	596	673	594	93	9
1840	1,724	38.5	868	856	1,676	48		308	1,416	291	432	493	393	60	6
1830	1,348	30.1	684	664	1,310	38		206	1,142	229	351	387	291	46	4
1820	1,049	23.4	532	516	1,017	30		136	913	342	155	204	191	124	
1810	810	18.1	402	385	787	23		104	706	270	124	150	145	98	
1800	602	13.4	301	285	586	16		68	534	203	90	108	113	72	
1790	434	9.7	218	206	424	10		44	390	111		107			

See footnotes at end of table.

Series A 195–209. Population of States, by Sex, Race, Urban-Rural Residence, and Age: 1790 to 1970—Con.

[In thousands, except series A 196]

State and year	Resident population Total	Per square mile of land area	Sex Male	Female	Race White	Negro	Other races	Residence Urban	Rural	Age Under 5 years	5–14 years	15–24 years	25–44 years	45–64 years	65 years and over
	195	196	197	198	199	200	201	202	203	204	205	206	207	208	209
RHODE ISLAND															
1970	947	902.5	464	482	915	25	7	825	122	76	174	174	210	209	104
1960	859	819.3	422	438	839	18	2	743	117	90	154	117	225	184	90
1950 ³	792	748.5	391	401	777	14	1	667	125	77	109	121	243	172	70
1950 ⁴								689	103						
1940	713	674.2	349	364	702	11	1	653	60	47	111	132	216	154	54
1930	687	649.8	335	352	677	10	1	635	52	60	132	119	202	135	40
1920	604	566.4	298	307	594	10	(Z)	555	49	62	112	104	185	111	30
1910	543	508.5	270	272	532	10	1	494	49	54	95	106	173	88	25
1900	429	401.6	211	218	419	9	(Z)	378	50	43	77	82	137	68	20
1890	346	323.8	168	177	338	7	(Z)	295	51	32	64	72	105	55	17
1880	277	259.2	133	144	270	6	(Z)	227	50	29	54	54	82	44	14
1870	217	203.7	105	113	212	5	(Z)	162	55	23	43	44	63	34	10
1860	175	163.7	84	90	171	4	(Z)	111	64	21	35	52	55	11	1
1850	148	138.3	72	75	144	4	---	82	65	18	31	46	44	8	1
1840	109	102.0	53	56	106	3	---	48	61	14	23	32	30	6	1
1830	97	91.1	47	50	94	4	---	30	67	13	22	29	24	5	1
1820	83	77.8	40	43	79	4	---	19	64	22	12	16	16	13	
1810	77	72.1	36	37	73	4	---	18	59	21	11	15	14	12	
1800	69	64.8	32	34	65	4	---	14	55	19	10	12	13	11	
1790	69	64.5	32	33	65	4	---	13	56			16		16	
SOUTH CAROLINA															
1970	2,591	85.7	1,272	1,318	1,794	789	7	1,232	1,358	236	552	519	606	487	191
1960	2,383	78.7	1,176	1,207	1,551	829	2	981	1,401	295	555	396	597	389	151
1950 ³	2,117	69.9	1,041	1,076	1,293	822	2	778	1,339	280	456	371	589	306	115
1950 ⁴								653	1,464						
1940	1,900	62.1	935	965	1,084	814	1	466	1,434	211	430	418	500	260	81
1930	1,739	56.8	853	886	944	794	1	371	1,368	205	464	378	411	224	57
1920	1,684	55.2	838	845	819	865	(Z)	294	1,390	229	459	343	409	189	53
1910	1,515	49.7	752	764	679	836	(Z)	225	1,291	228	401	324	355	160	44
1900	1,340	44.0	665	675	558	782	(Z)	171	1,169	204	369	296	288	142	40
1890	1,151	37.7	572	579	462	689	(Z)	116	1,035	170	345	236	250	114	34
1880	996	32.6	490	505	391	604	(Z)	75	921	174	277	192	221	101	32
1870	706	23.1	344	362	290	416	(Z)	61	645	109	187	149	161	78	21
1860	704	23.1	347	356	291	412	(Z)	49	655	111	195	198	169	28	3
1850	669	21.9	330	339	275	394	---	49	619	107	185	187	157	26	3
1840	594	19.5	293	301	259	335	---	34	561	48	71	73	57	9	1
1830	581	19.1	290	292	258	323	---	34	548	49	71	73	55	8	1
1820	503	16.5	255	248	237	265	---	25	478	83	37	48	43	27	
1810	415	13.6	110	105	214	201	---	25	390	77	34	42	39	22	
1800	346	11.3	101	95	196	149	---	19	327	72	32	36	37	20	
1790	249	8.2	73	67	140	109	---	16	233			38		36	
SOUTH DAKOTA															
1970	666	8.8	330	335	630	2	34	297	369	54	143	119	136	133	80
1960	681	9.0	344	336	653	1	26	267	413	83	145	91	159	131	72
1950 ³	653	8.5	337	315	629	1	24	217	436	77	114	101	175	131	55
1950 ⁴								216	437						
1940	643	8.4	333	310	619	(Z)	23	158	485	58	121	120	173	127	44
1930	693	9.1	364	329	670	1	22	131	562	71	153	129	191	110	37
1920	637	8.3	337	299	619	1	17	102	535	80	141	116	183	89	26
1910	584	7.6	317	267	564	1	19	76	507	73	127	122	164	77	19
1900	402	5.2	216	185	381	(Z)	20	41	361	55	99	76	106	51	13
1890	349	4.5	190	159	328	1	20	29	320	49	78	60	96	37	8
1880 ¹²	98	.			97	(Z)	1	7	91						
1870 ¹²	12	.			11	(Z)	(Z)	–	12						
1860 ¹²															
TENNESSEE															
1970	3,924	94.9	1,898	2,026	3,294	621	8	2,305	1,618	325	772	699	938	806	384
1960	3,567	86.2	1,741	1,826	2,978	587	2	1,865	1,702	394	734	526	908	696	309
1950 ³	3,292	78.8	1,623	1,669	2,760	531	1	1,453	1,839	380	610	536	958	574	235
1950 ⁴								1,264	2,028						
1940	2,916	69.5	1,446	1,470	2,407	509	(Z)	1,027	1,889	278	578	562	844	482	172
1930	2,617	62.4	1,305	1,312	2,139	478	(Z)	897	1,720	282	587	525	689	411	119
1920	2,338	56.1	1,174	1,164	1,886	452	(Z)	611	1,727	281	563	445	611	334	101
1910	2,185	52.4	1,103	1,081	1,711	473	(Z)	441	1,744	295	512	449	558	284	83
1900	2,021	48.5	1,021	999	1,540	480	(Z)	327	1,694	275	509	431	483	248	66
1890	1,768	42.4	892	876	1,337	431	(Z)	238	1,529	245	479	376	405	201	55

See footnotes at end of table.

Series A 195–209.   Population of States, by Sex, Race, Urban-Rural Residence, and Age: 1790 to 1970—Con.

[In thousands, except series A 196]

State and year	Resident population Total	Per square mile of land area	Male	Female	White	Negro	Other races	Urban	Rural	Under 5 years	5–14 years	15–24 years	25–44 years	45–64 years	65 years and over
	195	196	197	198	199	200	201	202	203	204	205	206	207	208	209
TENNESSEE—Con.															
1880	1,542	37.0	769	773	1,139	403	(Z)	116	1,426	250	425	313	349	162	43
1870	1,259	30.2	623	635	936	322	(Z)	94	1,164	201	341	274	287	126	31
1860	1,110	26.6	563	547	827	283	(Z)	47	1,063	184	316	324	245	36	4
1850	1,003	24.1	504	499	757	246	--------	22	981	170	300	291	207	31	4
1840	829	19.9	420	410	641	189	--------	7	822	130	192	173	125	19	2
1830	682	16.4	348	334	536	146	--------	6	676	115	158	148	99	14	1
1820	423	10.1	215	208	340	83	--------	–	423	131	56	63	55	34	
1810	262	6.3	112	104	216	46	--------	–	262	86	33	39	38	19	
1800	106	2.5	47	45	92	14	--------	–	106	38	14	17	15	8	
1790	36	.8	17	15	32	4	--------	–	36		10			6	
TEXAS															
1970	11,197	42.7	5,481	5,716	9,717	1,399	81	8,921	2,276	1,001	2,328	2,051	2,685	2,140	992
1960	9,580	36.4	4,745	4,835	8,375	1,187	18	7,187	2,392	1,162	2,010	1,372	2,499	1,791	745
1950 ³	7,711	29.3	3,863	3,848	6,727	977	7	4,838	2,873	901	1,346	1,235	2,318	1,398	513
1950 ⁴								4,613	3,099						
1940	6,415	24.3	3,221	3,194	5,488	924	3	2,911	3,503	576	1,221	1,205	1,987	1,080	347
1930	5,825	22.1	2,966	2,859	4,967	855	3	2,389	3,435	611	1,265	1,187	1,684	841	232
1920	4,663	17.8	2,409	2,254	3,918	742	3	1,513	3,151	534	1,118	945	1,300	593	163
1910	3,897	14.8	2,018	1,879	3,205	690	2	938	2,958	539	965	813	1,008	452	111
1900	3,049	11.6	1,579	1,470	2,427	621	1	521	2,528	452	816	639	722	333	74
1890	2,236	8.5	1,173	1,063	1,746	488	1	350	1,886	336	634	452	535	221	47
1880	1,592	6.1	838	754	1,197	393	1	147	1,445	280	438	311	388	147	28
1870	819	3.1	424	395	565	253	(Z)	55	764	135	229	177	190	76	12
1860	604	2.3	320	284	421	183	(Z)	27	578	106	168	177	133	12	1
1850	213	.8	114	99	154	59	--------	8	205	37	61	63	48	4	(Z)
UTAH															
1970	1,059	12.9	523	536	1,032	7	21	851	208	112	241	214	238	177	78
1960	891	10.8	445	446	874	4	13	667	223	126	208	137	217	142	60
1950 ³	689	8.4	348	341	677	3	9	450	239	93	138	113	191	112	42
1950 ⁴								433	256						
1940	550	6.7	279	272	543	1	6	305	245	59	114	109	148	90	30
1930	508	6.2	260	248	500	1	7	266	242	59	122	99	132	73	23
1920	449	5.5	232	217	442	1	6	216	234	61	108	82	122	59	16
1910	373	4.5	197	176	367	1	6	173	200	53	86	74	103	44	12
1900	277	3.4	142	135	272	1	4	105	171	42	71	54	68	30	10
1890	211	2.6	112	99	206	1	4	75	136	31	54	41	52	22	7
1880	144	1.8	75	69	142	(Z)	1	34	110	26	39	28	31	16	4
1870	87	1.1	44	43	86	(Z)	1	16	71	17	25	15	19	9	2
1860	40	.3	20	20	40	(Z)	(Z)	8	32	10	10	10	10	1	(Z)
1850	11	(8)	6	5	11	(Z)	--------	–	11	2	3	3	3	(Z)	(Z)
VERMONT															
1970	444	47.9	217	227	443	1	1	143	301	40	92	80	99	86	47
1960	390	42.0	192	198	389	1	(Z)	150	240	44	79	54	91	78	44
1950	378	40.7	188	190	377	(Z)	(Z)	138	240	42	64	56	101	76	40
1940	359	38.7	182	177	359	(Z)	1	123	236	30	63	62	97	74	34
1930	360	38.8	183	176	359		(Z)	119	241	33	68	59	94	74	31
1920	352	38.6	179	174	352	1	(Z)	110	242	35	66	56	95	71	30
1910	356	39.0	183	173	354	2	(Z)	99	257	34	64	60	101	67	29
1900	344	37.7	175	169	343	1	(Z)	76	268	33	62	60	96	64	28
1890	332	36.4	169	163	331	1	(Z)	51	282	30	63	62	89	60	28
1880	332	36.4	167	165	331	1	(Z)	33	299	34	68	62	86	56	26
1870	331	36.2	166	165	330	1	(Z)	23	308	37	69	63	84	54	22
1860	315	34.5	159	156	314	1	(Z)	6	309	37	69	86	95	25	3
1850	314	34.4	160	154	313	1	--------	6	308	38	74	88	91	20	3
1840	292	32.0	147	145	291	1	--------	–	292	42	72	80	78	17	2
1830	281	30.8	140	140	280	1	--------	–	281	43	73	81	68	14	1
1820	236	25.9	118	118	235	1	--------	–	236	71	38	49	46	31	
1810	218	23.9	110	107	217	1	--------	–	218	75	36	41	41	25	
1800	154	16.9	79	75	154	1	--------	–	154	58	23	26	32	15	
1790	85	9.4	45	40	85	(Z)	--------	–	85		22			22	

See footnotes at end of table.

Series A 195–209. Population of States, by Sex, Race, Urban-Rural Residence, and Age: 1790 to 1970—Con.

[In thousands, except series A 196]

State and year	Resident population Total	Per square mile of land area	Male	Female	White	Negro	Other races	Urban	Rural	Under 5 years	5–14 years	15–24 years	25–44 years	45–64 years	65 years and over
	195	196	197	198	199	200	201	202	203	204	205	206	207	208	209
VIRGINIA															
1970	4,648	116.9	2,297	2,351	3,762	861	26	2,935	1,714	392	931	881	1,165	913	366
1960	3,967	99.6	1,979	1,988	3,142	816	8	2,205	1,762	458	810	609	1,083	717	289
1950 [3]	3,319	83.2	1,675	1,643	2,582	734	3	1,560	1,759	381	584	558	1,020	560	215
1950 [4]								1,375	1,944						
1940	2,678	67.1	1,349	1,329	2,016	661	1	945	1,733	244	523	535	770	450	155
1930	2,422	60.7	1,216	1,206	1,770	650	1	786	1,636	257	562	473	628	384	117
1920	2,309	57.4	1,168	1,141	1,618	690	1	674	1,635	277	549	447	606	327	100
1910	2,062	51.2	1,035	1,026	1,390	671	1	477	1,585	269	494	413	526	272	85
1900	1,854	46.1	926	928	1,193	661	1	340	1,514	249	461	386	444	238	73
1890	1,656	41.1	824	832	1,020	635	(Z)	283	1,373	215	450	341	383	198	65
1880	1,513	37.6	746	767	881	632	(Z)	189	1,323	235	406	293	348	175	56
1870	1,225	30.4	597	628	712	513	(Z)	146	1,080	183	314	252	283	149	43
1860 [15]	1,220	24.8	806	790	1,047	549	(Z)	116	1,104	252	436	444	387	70	7
1850 [15]	1,119	22.1	718	704	895	527	----	89	1,030	220	399	395	339	60	8
1840 [15]	1,025	19.3	628	621	748	502	----	71	954	136	197	212	171	29	3
1830 [15]	1,044	18.9	614	607	701	520	----	50	994	129	189	202	153	25	3
1820 [15]	938	16.6	545	529	610	465	----	35	903	204	92	123	115	75	
1810 [15]	878	15.2	283	274	557	426	----	32	846	190	86	107	105	68	
1800 [15]	808	13.7	264	254	518	367	----	21	786	181	80	100	99	58	
1790 [15]	692	11.6	227	215	442	306	----	12	679		111	100		116	
WASHINGTON															
1970	3,409	51.2	1,694	1,715	3,251	71	87	2,476	933	280	677	626	806	698	322
1960	2,853	42.8			2,752	49	53	1,943	910	316	577	382	734	566	279
1950 [3]	2,379	35.6	1,224	1,155	2,316	31	32	1,503	876	263	363	333	724	484	211
1950 [4]								1,274	1,105						
1940	1,736	25.9	906	830	1,698	7	31	922	814	122	245	296	525	405	144
1930	1,563	23.3	826	737	1,522	7	35	885	679	115	274	268	477	325	102
1920	1,357	20.3	735	622	1,320	7	30	743	614	126	246	217	453	249	60
1910	1,142	17.1	659	483	1,109	6	27	606	536	109	192	222	400	175	37
1900	518	7.8	304	214	496	3	19	211	307	53	105	91	177	71	15
1890	357	5.3	222	136	341	2	15	127	230	38	65	67	132	39	6
1880	75	1.1	46	29	67	(Z)	8	7	68	10	17	14	24	9	1
1870	24	.4	15	9	22	(Z)	2	–	24	4	5	4	9	2	(Z)
1860 [16]	12	.1	8	3	11	(Z)	(Z)	–	12	2	2	4	4	(Z)	(Z)
1850 [14]	1							–	1						
WEST VIRGINIA															
1970	1,744	72.5	845	900	1,673	67	3	679	1,065	138	336	301	383	392	194
1960	1,860	77.2	915	945	1,770	89	1	711	1,149	196	402	262	455	372	173
1950 [3]	2,006	83.3	1,006	999	1,890	115	(Z)	694	1,311	240	396	326	561	344	139
1950 [4]								641	1,365						
1940	1,902	79.0	969	933	1,784	118	(Z)	534	1,368	197	398	379	525	302	101
1930	1,729	71.8	890	839	1,614	115	(Z)	492	1,238	207	414	329	454	251	73
1920	1,464	60.9	763	701	1,377	86	(Z)	369	1,095	196	349	271	396	194	56
1910	1,221	50.8	644	577	1,157	64	(Z)	228	993	169	279	247	335	147	42
1900	959	39.9	499	460	915	43	(Z)	125	833	135	232	201	243	112	32
1890	763	31.8	390	373	730	33	(Z)	81	681	106	205	161	178	84	26
1880	618	25.7	314	304	593	26	(Z)	54	564	99	170	124	140	65	19
1870	442	18.4	223	219	424	18	(Z)	36	406	73	121	91	97	47	13
1860 [15]	377							20	357						
1850 [15]	302							11	291						
1840 [15]	225							8	217						
1830 [15]	177							–	177						
1820 [15]	137							–	137						
1810 [15]	105							–	105						
1800 [15]	79							–	79						
1790 [15]	56							–	56						

See footnotes at end of table.

Series A 195–209. Population of States, by Sex, Race, Urban-Rural Residence, and Age: 1790 to 1970—Con.

[In thousands, except series A 196]

State and year	Resident population		Sex [1]		Race			Residence		Age [2]					
	Total	Per square mile of land area	Male	Female	White	Negro	Other races	Urban	Rural	Under 5 years	5–14 years	15–24 years	25–44 years	45–64 years	65 years and over
	195	196	197	198	199	200	201	202	203	204	205	206	207	208	209
WISCONSIN															
1970	4,418	81.1	2,167	2,250	4,259	128	31	2,910	1,507	382	935	770	977	880	473
1960	3,952	72.6	1,965	1,987	3,859	75	18	2,522	1,430	470	800	507	968	806	403
1950 [3]	3,435	62.8	1,727	1,708	3,393	28	14	1,988	1,447	372	555	484	974	740	310
1950 [4]								1,949	1,485						
1940	3,138	57.3	1,600	1,537	3,113	12	13	1,679	1,458	254	528	547	912	654	242
1930	2,939	53.7	1,511	1,428	2,916	11	12	1,554	1,385	271	578	516	855	525	192
1920	2,632	47.6	1,357	1,275	2,617	5	10	1,245	1,387	285	537	467	759	441	140
1910	2,334	42.2	1,209	1,125	2,321	3	10	1,004	1,330	256	494	465	638	360	119
1900	2,069	37.4	1,068	1,001	2,058	3	9	790	1,279	257	483	391	558	274	103
1890	1,693	30.6	878	815	1,681	3	10	562	1,131	216	400	327	438	220	82
1880	1,315	23.8	680	635	1,310	3	3	317	998	181	322	273	305	184	50
1870	1,055	19.1	545	510	1,051	2	1	207	848	157	286	198	247	137	29
1860	776	14.0	407	368	774	1	1	112	664	138	198	197	217	25	1
1850	305	5.5	165	141	305	1	---	29	277	51	76	87	83	7	(Z)
1840	31	.4	19	12	31	(Z)	---	--	31	5	6	12	7	(Z)	(Z)
WYOMING															
1970	332	3.4	167	166	323	3	7	201	131	28	70	58	78	67	30
1960	330	3.4	169	161	323	2	5	188	143	41	71	44	87	61	26
1950	291	3.0	155	136	284	3	4	145	146	34	50	47	87	54	18
1940	251	2.6	135	116	247	1	3	94	157	23	44	47	76	48	13
1930	226	2.3	125	101	221	1	3	70	155	22	46	41	72	36	9
1920	194	2.0	110	84	190	1	3	57	137	23	38	32	69	26	6
1910	146	1.5	92	54	140	2	3	43	103	15	24	31	55	18	3
1900	93	.9	58	34	89	1	3	27	66	11	18	18	34	10	2
1890	63	.6	40	22	59	1	2	21	41	7	11	12	24	6	1
1880	21	.2	14	7	19	(Z)	1	6	15	2	3	4	9	2	(Z)
1870	9	.1	7	2	9	(Z)	(Z)	--	9	1	1	3	5	(Z)	(Z)

– Represents zero.
NA Not available.
Z Less than 500.

[1] For 1790–1810, white persons only.
[2] Ages not reported and ages unknown are not included. Prior to 1850, age detail for white only. Age detail columns have changed for early censuses as follows: 1790: Under 16 years and over 16 years, for males only; 1800–1820: Under 10 years, 10–15 years, 16–25 years, 26–44 years, and 45 and over; 1830–1860: Under 5 years, 5–14 years, 15–29 years, 30–59 years, 60–79 years, 80 and over. See also footnote 13.
[3] Urban definition comparable with later data.
[4] Urban definition comparable with earlier data.
[5] Population of those parts of Mississippi Territory now in present State. Population per square mile, sex, race, and age detail for Alabama included with Mississippi.
[6] Census taken October 1, 1939.
[7] Census taken October 1, 1929.

[8] Less than 1/10 of a person.
[9] Includes population of area taken to form part of Arizona Territory in 1863.
[10] Data for Territory of New Mexico which included parts of present States of Arizona and New Mexico, and smaller parts of Colorado and Nevada.
[11] Includes 5,602 persons for whom sex, race, and age detail are not available.
[12] North and South Dakota comprised Dakota Territory. Population per square mile, sex, and age detail for South Dakota included with North Dakota.
[13] Age detail excludes all persons residing in Indian Territory or on Indian reservations.
[14] Population total of those parts of Oregon Territory taken to form part of Washington Territory in 1853 and 1859 excluded from Oregon included under Washington. Population per square mile, sex, race, and age detail for Washington included with Oregon.
[15] Sex, race, and age detail for West Virginia, 1790–1860, included with Virginia.
[16] Includes population of Idaho and parts of Montana and Wyoming.

Series A 210–263.　Land Area of the United States, by States and Territories: 1790 to 1970

[In square miles]

Series No.	State or territory	Year of admission to statehood	1970	1960	1950	1940	1930	1920	1910	1900	1890
210	**United States**	(X)	**3,536,855**	**3,540,911**	**2,974,726**	**2,977,128**	**2,973,776**	**2,973,774**	**2,973,890**	**2,974,159**	**2,973,965**
211	Alabama	1819	50,708	50,851	51,078	51,078	51,279	51,279	51,279	51,279	51,279
212	Alaska	1959	566,432	566,432							
213	Arizona	1912	113,417	113,563	113,575	113,580	113,810	113,810	113,810	113,840	113,840
214	Arkansas	1836	51,945	52,175	52,675	52,725	52,525	52,525	52,525	52,525	52,525
215	California	1850	156,361	156,537	156,740	156,803	155,652	155,652	155,652	156,092	155,900
216	Colorado	1876	103,766	103,794	103,922	103,967	103,658	103,658	103,658	103,658	103,658
217	Connecticut	[1] 1788	4,862	4,870	4,899	4,899	4,820	4,820	4,820	4,820	4,820
218	Delaware	[1] 1787	1,982	1,982	1,978	1,978	1,965	1,965	1,965	1,965	1,965
219	District of Columbia	(X)	61	61	61	61	62	60	60	60	58
220	Florida	1845	54,090	54,136	54,262	54,262	54,861	54,861	54,861	54,861	54,861
221	Georgia	[1] 1788	58,073	58,197	58,483	58,518	58,725	58,725	58,725	58,725	58,725
222	Hawaii	1959	6,425	6,425							
223	Idaho	1890	82,677	82,677	82,769	82,808	83,354	83,354	83,354	83,354	83,354
224	Illinois	1818	55,748	55,875	55,935	55,947	56,043	56,043	56,043	56,002	56,002
225	Indiana	1816	36,097	36,189	36,205	36,205	36,045	36,045	36,045	35,885	35,885
226	Iowa	1846	55,941	56,043	56,045	55,986	55,586	55,586	55,586	55,586	55,586
227	Kansas	1861	81,787	82,056	82,108	82,113	81,774	81,774	81,774	81,774	81,774
228	Kentucky	1792	39,650	39,851	39,864	40,109	40,181	40,181	40,181	40,181	40,181
229	Louisiana	1812	44,930	45,131	45,162	45,177	45,409	45,409	45,409	45,409	45,409
230	Maine	1820	30,920	30,933	31,040	31,040	29,895	29,895	29,895	29,895	29,895
231	Maryland	[1] 1788	9,891	9,891	9,881	9,887	9,941	9,941	9,941	9,941	9,941
232	Massachusetts	[1] 1788	7,826	7,833	7,867	7,907	8,039	8,039	8,039	8,039	8,039
233	Michigan	1837	56,817	56,817	57,022	57,022	57,480	57,480	57,480	57,480	57,480
234	Minnesota	1858	79,289	79,289	80,009	80,009	80,858	80,858	80,858	80,858	80,858
235	Mississippi	1817	47,296	47,358	47,248	47,420	46,362	46,362	46,362	46,362	46,362
236	Missouri	1821	68,995	69,046	69,226	69,270	68,727	68,727	68,727	68,727	68,727
237	Montana	1889	145,587	145,603	145,878	146,316	146,131	146,131	146,201	146,201	146,201
238	Nebraska	1867	76,483	76,522	76,663	76,653	76,808	76,808	76,808	76,808	76,808
239	Nevada	1864	109,889	109,889	109,789	109,802	109,821	109,821	109,821	109,821	109,821
240	New Hampshire	[1] 1788	9,027	9,033	9,017	9,024	9,031	9,031	9,031	9,031	9,031
241	New Jersey	[1] 1787	7,521	7,532	7,522	7,522	7,514	7,514	7,514	7,514	7,514
242	New Mexico	1912	121,412	121,445	121,511	121,511	122,503	122,503	122,503	122,503	122,503
243	New York	[1] 1788	47,831	47,869	47,944	47,929	47,654	47,654	47,654	47,654	47,654
244	North Carolina	[1] 1789	48,798	48,880	49,097	49,142	48,740	48,740	48,740	48,740	48,740
245	North Dakota	1889	69,273	69,280	70,057	70,054	70,183	70,183	70,183	70,183	70,183
246	Ohio	1803	40,975	41,018	41,000	41,122	40,740	40,740	40,740	40,740	40,740
247	Oklahoma	1907	68,782	68,983	69,031	69,283	69,414	69,414	69,414	38,624	38,624
248	Oregon	1859	96,184	96,209	96,315	96,350	95,607	95,607	95,607	95,607	95,607
249	Pennsylvania	[1] 1787	44,966	45,025	45,045	45,045	44,832	44,832	44,832	44,832	44,832
250	Rhode Island	[1] 1790	1,049	1,049	1,058	1,058	1,067	1,067	1,067	1,067	1,067
251	South Carolina	[1] 1788	30,225	30,280	30,305	30,594	30,495	30,495	30,495	30,495	30,495
252	South Dakota	1889	75,955	75,956	76,536	76,536	76,868	76,868	76,868	76,868	76,868
253	Tennessee	1796	41,328	41,366	41,797	41,961	41,687	41,687	41,687	41,687	41,687
254	Texas	1845	262,134	262,970	263,513	263,644	262,398	262,398	262,398	262,398	262,398
255	Utah	1896	82,096	82,381	82,346	82,346	82,184	82,184	82,184	82,184	82,184
256	Vermont	1791	9,267	9,274	9,278	9,278	9,124	9,124	9,124	9,124	9,124
257	Virginia	[1] 1788	39,780	39,841	39,893	39,899	40,262	40,262	40,262	40,262	40,262
258	Washington	1889	66,570	66,663	66,786	66,977	66,836	66,836	66,836	66,836	66,836
259	West Virginia	1863	24,070	24,084	24,080	24,090	24,022	24,022	24,022	24,022	24,022
260	Wisconsin	1848	54,464	54,466	54,705	54,715	55,256	55,256	55,256	55,256	55,256
261	Wyoming	1890	97,203	97,281	97,506	97,506	97,548	97,548	97,594	97,594	97,594
262	Indian Territory and unorganized territory	(X)	--------	--------	--------	--------	--------	--------	--------	30,790	30,790

X　Not applicable.
[1] Year of ratification of Constitution; one of the original 13 States.

Series A 210–263.   Land Area of the United States, by States and Territories: 1790 to 1970—Con.

[In square miles]

Series No.	State or territory	1880	1870	1860	1850	1840	1830	1820	1810	1800	1790
210	United States	2,973,965	2,973,965	2,973,965	2,944,337	1,753,588	1,753,588	1,753,588	1,685,865	867,980	867,980
211	Alabama	51,279	51,279	51,279	51,279	51,279	51,279	51,279			
213	Arizona	113,840	113,840								
214	Arkansas	52,525	52,525	52,525	52,525	52,525	52,525	105,275			
215	California	155,900	155,900	155,900	155,900						
216	Colorado	103,658	103,658	103,658							
217	Connecticut	4,820	4,820	4,820	4,820	4,820	4,820	4,820	4,820	4,820	4,820
218	Delaware	1,965	1,965	1,965	1,965	1,965	1,965	1,965	1,965	1,965	1,965
219	District of Columbia	58	58	58	58	90	90	90	90	90	
220	Florida	54,861	54,861	54,861	54,861	54,861	54,861	54,861			
221	Georgia	58,725	58,725	58,725	58,725	58,725	58,725	58,725	58,725	111,877	145,196
223	Idaho	83,354	83,360								
224	Illinois	56,002	56,002	56,002	56,002	56,002	56,002	56,002	192,381		
225	Indiana	35,885	35,885	35,885	35,885	35,885	35,885	35,885	42,933	252,084	
226	Iowa	55,586	55,586	55,586	55,586	191,656					
227	Kansas	81,774	81,774	81,774							
228	Kentucky	40,181	40,181	40,181	40,181	40,181	40,181	40,181	40,181	40,181	40,181
229	Louisiana	45,409	45,409	45,409	45,409	45,409	45,409	45,409	34,065		
230	Maine	29,895	29,895	29,895	29,895	29,895	29,895	29,895	29,895	29,895	29,895
231	Maryland	9,941	9,941	9,941	9,941	9,941	9,941	9,941	9,941	9,941	9,999
232	Massachusetts	8,039	8,039	8,039	8,041	8,041	8,041	8,041	8,041	8,041	8,041
233	Michigan	57,480	57,480	57,480	57,480	57,480	186,052	186,052	42,625		
234	Minnesota	80,858	80,858	80,858	163,457						
235	Mississippi	46,362	46,362	46,362	46,362	46,362	46,362	46,362	97,641	33,319	
236	Missouri	68,727	68,727	68,727	68,727	68,727	65,618	65,618			
237	Montana	146,201	146,195								
238	Nebraska	76,172	76,172	118,915							
239	Nevada	109,821	109,821	61,260							
240	New Hampshire	9,031	9,031	9,031	9,031	9,031	9,031	9,031	9,031	9,031	9,031
241	New Jersey	7,514	7,514	7,514	7,514	7,514	7,514	7,514	7,514	7,514	7,514
242	New Mexico	122,503	122,503	247,782	236,548						
243	New York	47,654	47,654	47,654	47,652	47,652	47,652	47,652	47,652	47,652	47,652
244	North Carolina	48,740	48,740	48,740	48,740	48,740	48,740	48,740	48,740	48,740	48,740
246	Ohio	40,740	40,740	40,740	40,740	40,740	40,228	40,228	40,228	40,228	
248	Oregon	95,607	95,607	95,607	282,257						
249	Pennsylvania	44,832	44,832	44,832	44,832	44,832	44,832	44,832	44,832	44,832	44,832
250	Rhode Island	1,067	1,067	1,067	1,067	1,067	1,067	1,067	1,067	1,067	1,067
251	South Carolina	30,495	30,495	30,495	30,495	30,495	30,495	30,495	30,495	30,495	30,495
253	Tennessee	41,687	41,687	41,687	41,687	41,687	41,687	41,687	41,687	41,687	46,977
254	Texas	262,398	262,398	262,398	262,398						
255	Utah	82,184	82,184	122,887	230,610						
256	Vermont	9,124	9,124	9,124	9,124	9,124	9,124	9,124	9,124	9,124	9,124
257	Virginia	40,262	40,262	64,284	64,284	64,252	64,252	64,252	64,252	64,252	64,284
258	Washington	66,836	66,836	183,254							
259	West Virginia	24,022	24,022								
260	Wisconsin	55,256	55,256	55,256	55,256	82,643					
261	Wyoming	97,594	97,594								
262	Indian Territory and unorganized territory	69,414	69,414	69,414	535,003	511,967	52,750				
263	Other Territory:										
	Territory Northwest of Ohio River									25,855	318,167
	Territory South of Tennessee									5,290	
	Missouri Territory						608,565	608,565	777,940		
	Dakota Territory	147,687	147,687	312,094							

Series A 264–275.   Number and Population of Standard Metropolitan Statistical Areas, as Defined in 1950, 1960, and 1970, by Region and Size: 1950 to 1970

[For definition of Standard Metropolitan Statistical Areas (SMSA's), see text]

Series No.	Region and size	Number of SMSA's			SMSA population as defined in terms of—						Central city population as defined at each census		
					1970 area			1960 area		1950 area			
		1970 [1]	1960*	1950	1970 [1]	1960	1950*	1960	1950*	1950	1970	1960*	1950
264	United States	243	212	168	139,418,811	119,594,754	94,579,008	112,885,178	89,316,903	84,500,680	63,796,943	58,004,334	49,412,792
	REGION [2]												
265	Northeast	51	47	39	39,188,328	36,043,708	31,825,560	35,346,505	31,267,169	31,053,322	17,256,146	17,321,731	17,249,033
266	North Central	67	59	52	37,658,273	33,350,785	26,944,997	30,959,961	25,074,674	24,170,135	17,068,167	16,510,746	15,230,330
267	South	88	77	59	35,199,352	28,872,540	21,417,235	26,447,395	19,417,751	17,360,208	17,917,474	15,061,777	10,941,370
268	West	37	29	18	27,372,858	21,327,721	14,391,216	20,131,317	13,557,309	11,917,015	11,555,156	9,110,080	5,992,059
	POPULATION SIZE												
269	5,000,000 and over	3	3	2	25,582,921	22,954,317	18,885,498	23,658,242	19,101,722	18,407,358	14,436,513	14,155,571	12,250,712
270	3,000,000–4,999,999	3	2	3	12,127,364	10,754,019	8,823,179	8,105,257	6,687,245	11,055,156	4,537,326	3,672,656	5,891,531
271	2,000,000–2,999,999	6	5	3	14,513,949	12,895,423	10,880,541	11,840,095	10,047,952	6,823,989	4,196,596	3,923,375	2,638,182
272	1,000,000–1,999,999	21	14	6	28,432,512	22,466,699	15,934,977	17,978,476	13,810,161	8,153,993	11,653,630	8,784,128	4,936,689
273	500,000–999,999	32	29	19	21,936,284	18,588,623	14,424,019	19,214,817	14,125,628	12,398,635	10,758,973	10,126,684	7,805,511
274	250,000–499,999	60	48	44	19,760,861	16,991,831	13,363,939	15,829,067	12,603,137	14,594,878	8,745,284	7,750,597	7,744,565
275	Under 250,000	118	111	91	17,064,920	14,943,842	12,266,855	16,259,224	12,941,058	13,066,671	9,468,621	9,591,323	8,145,602

* Denotes first year for which figures include Alaska and Hawaii.
[1] Excludes 23,372 persons for whom type of residence is not available. See series A 1–5, footnote 3.

[2] In the data on number of SMSA's those located in two regions are included in the region containing most of the SMSA's population; in the data on population, they are divided into their component regions.

Series A 276–287. Population of Standard Metropolitan Statistical Areas, by Region, Size, and Race: 1950 to 1970

[For definition of Standard Metropolitan Statistical Areas (SMSA's), see text for series A 267–278]

Series No.	Region, size, and race	1970 [1] Total	1970 [1] Inside central city	1970 [1] Outside central city	1960 * Total	1960 * Inside central city	1960 * Outside central city	1950 Total	1950 Inside central city	1950 Outside central city
276	**United States**	**139,418,811**	**63,796,943**	**75,621,868**	**112,885,178**	**58,004,334**	**54,880,844**	**84,500,680**	**49,412,792**	**35,087,888**
	White	120,578,729	49,430,443	71,148,286	99,687,658	47,653,833	52,033,825	76,250,470	43,001,634	33,248,836
	Negro	16,770,610	13,140,331	3,630,279	12,207,231	9,703,584	2,503,647	7,931,469	6,194,948	1,736,521
	Other races	2,069,472	1,226,169	843,303	990,289	646,917	343,372	318,741	216,210	102,531
	REGION									
277	**Northeast**	**39,188,328**	**17,256,146**	**21,932,182**	**35,346,505**	**17,321,731**	**18,024,774**	**31,053,322**	**17,249,033**	**13,804,289**
	White	34,695,275	13,632,546	21,062,729	32,382,629	14,922,738	17,459,891	29,090,116	15,687,312	13,402,804
	Negro	4,146,869	3,369,526	777,343	2,855,137	2,320,019	535,118	1,912,303	1,522,382	389,921
	Other races	346,184	254,074	92,110	108,739	78,974	29,765	50,903	39,339	11,564
278	**North Central**	**37,658,273**	**17,068,167**	**20,590,106**	**30,959,961**	**16,510,746**	**14,449,215**	**24,170,135**	**15,230,330**	**8,939,805**
	White	33,136,332	13,211,120	19,925,212	27,714,230	13,666,826	14,047,404	22,156,571	13,548,014	8,608,557
	Negro	4,292,753	3,708,004	584,749	3,163,076	2,781,924	381,152	1,974,223	1,649,926	324,297
	Other races	229,188	149,043	80,145	82,655	61,996	20,659	39,341	32,390	6,951
279	**South**	**35,199,352**	**17,917,474**	**17,281,878**	**26,447,395**	**15,061,777**	**11,385,618**	**17,360,208**	**10,941,370**	**6,418,838**
	White	28,256,870	12,848,348	15,408,522	21,191,838	11,142,949	10,048,889	13,784,680	8,251,383	5,533,297
	Negro	6,714,199	4,945,456	1,768,743	5,186,706	3,876,934	1,309,772	3,555,654	2,675,386	880,268
	Other races	228,283	123,670	104,613	68,851	41,894	26,957	19,874	14,601	5,273
280	**West**	**27,372,858**	**11,555,156**	**15,817,702**	**20,131,317**	**9,110,080**	**11,021,237**	**11,917,015**	**5,992,059**	**5,924,956**
	White	24,490,252	9,738,429	14,751,823	18,398,961	7,921,320	10,477,641	11,219,103	5,514,925	5,704,178
	Negro	1,616,789	1,117,345	499,444	1,002,312	724,707	277,605	489,289	347,254	142,035
	Other races	1,265,817	699,382	566,435	730,044	464,053	265,991	208,623	129,880	78,743
	POPULATION SIZE									
281	**5,000,000 and over**	**25,582,921**	**14,436,513**	**11,146,408**	**23,658,242**	**14,155,571**	**9,502,671**	**18,407,358**	**12,250,712**	**6,156,646**
	White	21,168,440	10,759,292	10,409,148	20,855,887	11,744,617	9,111,270	16,756,075	10,869,166	5,886,909
	Negro	3,879,066	3,293,332	585,734	2,582,496	2,245,015	337,481	1,600,022	1,335,596	264,426
	Other races	535,415	383,889	151,526	219,859	165,939	53,920	51,261	45,950	5,311
282	**3,000,000–4,999,999**	**12,127,364**	**4,537,326**	**7,590,038**	**8,105,257**	**3,672,656**	**4,432,601**	**11,055,156**	**5,891,531**	**5,163,625**
	White	9,939,406	2,842,292	7,097,114	6,856,959	2,650,449	4,206,510	9,932,972	4,997,257	4,935,715
	Negro	1,931,490	1,535,007	396,483	1,230,174	1,011,463	218,711	1,056,645	847,756	208,889
	Other races	256,468	160,027	96,441	18,124	10,744	7,380	65,539	46,518	19,021
283	**2,000,000–2,999,999**	**14,513,949**	**4,196,596**	**10,317,353**	**11,840,095**	**3,923,375**	**7,916,720**	**6,823,989**	**2,638,182**	**4,185,807**
	White	12,218,729	2,449,174	9,769,555	10,445,438	2,885,490	7,559,948	6,420,456	2,375,210	4,045,246
	Negro	2,202,106	1,709,565	492,541	1,260,090	947,972	312,118	335,076	213,574	121,502
	Other races	93,114	37,857	55,257	134,567	89,913	44,654	68,457	49,398	19,059
284	**1,000,000–1,999,999**	**28,432,512**	**11,653,630**	**16,778,882**	**17,978,476**	**8,784,128**	**9,194,348**	**8,153,993**	**4,936,689**	**3,217,304**
	White	25,170,467	9,211,308	15,959,159	15,882,015	7,052,090	8,829,925	7,111,522	4,069,944	3,041,578
	Negro	2,930,563	2,269,554	661,009	2,015,484	1,677,733	337,751	1,027,784	856,632	171,152
	Other races	331,482	172,768	158,714	80,977	54,305	26,672	14,687	10,113	4,574
285	**500,000–999,999**	**21,936,284**	**10,758,973**	**11,177,311**	**19,214,817**	**10,126,684**	**9,088,133**	**12,398,635**	**7,744,565**	**4,654,070**
	White	19,011,773	8,469,582	10,542,191	16,783,125	8,237,981	8,545,144	11,019,272	6,655,905	4,363,367
	Negro	2,396,877	1,979,136	417,741	2,015,290	1,623,526	391,764	1,341,107	1,060,425	280,682
	Other races	527,634	310,255	217,379	416,402	265,177	151,225	38,256	28,235	10,021
286	**250,000–499,999**	**19,760,861**	**8,745,284**	**11,015,577**	**15,829,067**	**7,750,597**	**8,078,470**	**14,594,878**	**7,805,511**	**6,789,367**
	White	17,634,982	7,359,641	10,275,341	14,380,530	6,709,971	7,670,559	13,414,218	6,911,778	6,502,440
	Negro	1,919,299	1,289,357	629,942	1,382,055	1,010,675	371,380	1,127,126	870,996	256,130
	Other races	206,580	96,286	110,294	66,482	29,951	36,531	53,534	22,737	30,797
287	**Under 250,000**	**17,064,920**	**9,468,621**	**7,596,299**	**16,259,224**	**9,591,323**	**6,667,901**	**13,066,671**	**8,145,602**	**4,921,069**
	White	15,434,932	8,339,154	7,095,778	14,483,704	8,373,235	6,110,469	11,595,955	7,122,374	4,473,581
	Negro	1,511,209	1,064,380	446,829	1,721,642	1,187,200	534,442	1,443,709	1,009,969	433,740
	Other races	118,779	65,087	53,692	53,878	30,888	22,990	27,007	13,259	13,748

* Denotes first year for which figures include Alaska and Hawaii.

[1] Excludes 23,372 persons for whom type of residence is not available. See series A 1–5, footnote 3. See text for series A 91–104 for discussion of 1970 data by race.

Series A 288–319. Households, Families, Subfamilies, Married Couples, and Unrelated Individuals: 1790 to 1970

[In thousands, except average size. As of March, except as noted]

Year	Households Total	Households Primary families	Households Primary individuals	Households Average size	Families Total	Families Husband-wife	Families Other male head	Families Female head	Primary families Total	Primary families Husband-wife	Primary families Other male head	Primary families Female head	Secondary families Total	Secondary families Husband-wife	Secondary families Other male head	Secondary families Female head	Average size
	288	289	290	291	292	293	294	295	296	297	298	299	300	301	302	303	304
1970	63,401	51,456	11,945	3.14	51,586	44,755	1,239	5,591	51,456	44,728	1,228	5,500	130	27	11	91	3.58
1969	62,214	50,729	11,485	3.16	50,823	44,110	1,232	5,481	50,729	44,086	1,221	5,422	94	24	11	59	3.60
1968	60,813	50,012	10,801	3.20	50,111	43,530	1,211	5,370	50,012	43,507	1,195	5,310	99	23	16	60	3.63
1967	59,236	49,086	10,150	3.26	49,214	42,805	1,203	5,206	49,086	42,743	1,190	5,153	128	62	13	53	3.67
1966	58,406	48,399	10,007	3.27	48,509	42,312	1,178	5,019	48,399	42,263	1,163	4,973	110	49	15	46	3.69
1965	57,436	47,838	9,598	3.29	47,956	41,749	1,181	5,026	47,838	41,689	1,167	4,982	118	60	14	44	3.70
1964	56,149	47,381	8,768	3.33	47,540	41,395	1,245	4,900	47,381	41,341	1,204	4,836	159	54	41	64	3.70
1963	55,270	46,872	8,398	3.33	47,059	40,975	1,333	4,751	46,872	40,888	1,295	4,689	187	87	38	62	3.68
1962	54,764	46,262	8,502	3.31	46,418	40,470	1,296	4,652	46,262	40,404	1,268	4,590	156	66	28	62	3.67
1961	53,557	45,383	8,174	3.34	45,539	39,678	1,222	4,639	45,383	39,620	1,199	4,564	156	58	23	75	3.70
1960*	52,799	44,905	7,895	3.33	45,111	39,329	1,275	4,507	44,905	39,254	1,228	4,422	207	75	47	85	3.67
1959	51,435	43,971	7,464	3.34	44,232	38,574	1,319	4,339	43,971	38,410	1,285	4,276	261	164	33	63	3.65
1958	50,474	43,426	7,047	3.34	43,696	38,056	1,324	4,315	43,426	37,911	1,278	4,237	269	145	46	78	3.64
1957	49,673	43,262	6,411	3.33	43,497	37,856	1,263	4,378	43,262	37,718	1,241	4,304	235	138	22	75	3.60
1956	48,902	42,593	6,309	3.32	42,889	37,204	1,440	4,245	42,593	37,047	1,408	4,138	296	157	32	107	3.58
1955[1]	47,874	41,732	6,142	3.33	41,951	36,378	1,339	4,234	41,732	36,251	1,328	4,153	219	127	11	81	3.59
1950	43,554	38,838	4,716	3.37	39,303	34,440	1,184	3,679	38,838	34,075	1,169	3,594	465	365	15	85	3.54
1947[1]	39,107	34,964	4,143	(NA)	35,794	31,211	1,186	3,397	34,964	30,612	1,129	3,223	830	599	57	174	(NA)
1940[1]	34,949	31,491	3,458	3.67	32,166	26,971	1,579	3,616	31,491	26,571	1,510	3,410	675	400	69	206	3.76

Year	Households Total	Average size	Year	Households Total	Average size	Year	Households Total	Average size	Year	Households Total	Average size	Year	Households Total	Average size
	288	291		288	291		288	291		288	291		288	291
1930[1]	29,905	4.11	1910[2]	20,256	4.54	1890[2]	12,690	4.93	1870[1]	7,579	5.09	1850[1]	3,598	5.55
1920[2]	24,352	4.34	1900	15,964	4.76	1880[1]	9,946	5.04	1860[1]	5,211	5.28	1790[1]	558	5.79

Year	Subfamilies Total	Subfamilies Husband-wife	Subfamilies Other male head	Subfamilies Female head	Married couples Total	Married couples With own household	Without own household Total	Without own household Percent	Unrelated individuals Total	Primary individuals Total	Primary individuals Male	Primary individuals Female	Secondary individuals Total	Secondary individuals Male	Secondary individuals Female
	305	306	307	308	309	310	311	312	313	314	315	316	317	318	319
1970	1,150	617	48	484	45,373	44,728	645	1.4	14,988	11,945	4,063	7,882	3,043	1,631	1,412
1969	1,168	603	66	499	44,713	44,086	627	1.4	14,154	11,485	3,890	7,595	2,669	1,415	1,254
1968	1,225	661	80	484	44,191	43,507	684	1.5	13,425	10,801	3,658	7,143	2,624	1,294	1,330
1967	1,292	679	91	522	43,484	42,743	741	1.7	12,725	10,150	3,419	6,731	2,575	1,286	1,289
1966	1,383	721	92	570	43,033	42,263	770	1.8	12,558	10,007	3,299	6,708	2,551	1,350	1,201
1965	1,293	729	72	492	42,478	41,689	789	1.9	12,333	9,598	3,277	6,321	2,735	1,432	1,303
1964	1,343	742	83	518	42,137	41,341	796	1.9	11,433	8,768	2,965	5,803	2,665	1,428	1,237
1963	1,375	786	87	502	41,761	40,888	873	2.1	11,330	8,398	2,838	5,560	2,932	1,561	1,371
1962	1,407	815	82	510	41,285	40,404	881	2.1	11,563	8,502	2,932	5,570	3,061	1,654	1,407
1961	1,532	903	78	551	40,581	39,620	961	2.4	11,231	8,174	2,779	5,395	3,057	1,548	1,509
1960*	1,514	871	115	528	40,200	39,254	946	2.4	11,092	7,895	2,716	5,179	3,198	1,746	1,451
1959	1,630	943	103	584	39,518	38,410	1,108	2.8	11,062	7,464	2,449	5,015	3,598	2,077	1,520
1958	1,730	1,068	75	587	39,124	37,911	1,213	3.1	10,568	7,047	2,329	4,718	3,520	1,987	1,534
1957	1,804	1,091	97	615	38,947	37,718	1,229	3.2	9,901	6,411	2,038	4,374	3,489	2,057	1,432
1956	1,825	1,106	120	600	38,310	37,047	1,263	3.3	10,019	6,309	2,058	4,250	3,710	2,187	1,523
1955[1]	1,973	1,178	69	726	37,556	36,251	1,305	3.5	9,891	6,142	2,059	4,083	3,749	2,128	1,621
1950	2,402	1,651	113	638	36,091	34,075	2,016	5.6	9,136	4,716	1,668	3,048	4,420	2,541	1,879
1947[1]	3,123	2,332	83	708	33,543	30,612	2,931	8.7	8,491	4,143	1,388	2,755	4,348	2,464	1,884
1946[2]	(NA)	(NA)	(NA)	(NA)	31,550	28,850	2,700	8.6	(NA)	(NA)	(NA)	(NA)	(NA)	(NA)	(NA)
1945[3]	(NA)	(NA)	(NA)	(NA)	28,200	26,835	1,365	4.8	(NA)	(NA)	(NA)	(NA)	(NA)	(NA)	(NA)
1940[1]	2,062	1,546	52	464	28,517	26,571	1,946	6.8	9,277	3,458	1,599	1,859	5,819	3,343	2,476
1930[1]	---	---	---	---	25,174	23,649	1,525	6.1	---	---	---	---	---	---	---
1910[2]	---	---	---	---	17,175	16,250	925	5.4	---	---	---	---	---	---	---

* Denotes first year for which figures include Alaska and Hawaii.
NA Not available.
[1] As of April.
[2] As of June.
[3] As of September.

POPULATION

Series A 320–334. Households, by Race, Sex, and Age of Head: 1890 to 1970

[In thousands. 1965–1970 based on sample figures from Current Population Survey]

Year	Race of head			Male head						Female head					
	White	Negro	Other	Total	Under 25 years	25–34 years	35–44 years	45–54 years	55 years and over	Total	Under 25 years	25–34 years	35–44 years	45–54 years	55 years and over
	320	321	322	323	324	325	326	327	328	329	330	331	332	333	334
1970	56,248	6,053	573	49,588	3,485	10,328	10,286	10,278	15,211	13,287	820	1,324	1,401	1,959	7,782
1969	55,394	5,870	541	48,927	3,360	9,990	10,250	10,177	15,149	12,877	706	1,291	1,489	1,973	7,417
1968	54,188	5,728	530	48,121	3,150	9,457	10,452	10,096	14,968	12,323	679	1,141	1,480	1,869	7,157
1967	52,826	6,018		47,082	3,023	9,234	10,486	9,969	14,372	11,763	540	1,084	1,433	1,845	6,861
1966	52,135	5,954		46,517	3,046	8,952	10,467	9,904	14,146	11,575	506	1,071	1,413	1,839	6,748
1965	51,441	5,808		46,027	2,918	8,912	10,449	9,726	14,022	11,224	484	984	1,521	1,760	6,475
1960 [1] *	47,868	5,153		43,873	2,369	8,964	10,480	9,194	12,866	9,151	330	803	1,227	1,607	5,184
1950 [1]	38,429	3,822		35,863	1,850	8,139	8,676	7,274	9,925	6,389	164	541	935	1,264	3,486
1940	31,680	3,142	127	29,680	1,260	6,539	7,286	6,716	7,879	5,269	113	470	879	1,144	2,663
1930	[2] 26,983	2,804	118	[3] 26,112	1,266	5,879	7,082	5,743	6,123	[3] 3,793	[4] 120	[4] 371	[4] 685	[4] 862	[4] 1,749
1920	21,826	2,431	95	(NA)	(NA)	(NA)	(NA)	(NA)	(NA)	(NA)	(NA)	(NA)	(NA)	(NA)	(NA)
1910	(NA)	2,173	(NA)	(NA)	(NA)	(NA)	(NA)	(NA)	(NA)	(NA)	(NA)	(NA)	(NA)	(NA)	(NA)
1900	14,064	1,834	66	14,023	(NA)	(NA)	(NA)	(NA)	(NA)	(NA)	(NA)	(NA)	(NA)	(NA)	(NA)
1890	11,255	1,411	24	10,857	572	2,962	2,883	2,184	2,256	1,833	59	230	387	466	691

* Denotes first year for which figures include Alaska and Hawaii.
NA Not available.
[1] Based on 20-percent sample of census returns.
[2] Figures for race of head revised to include Mexicans as white. Mexicans were classified as other races in the 1930 reports.

[3] Total for males includes 18,345 persons of unknown age and total for females, 6,567 of unknown age.
[4] Number of female heads in each age group estimated from data on white and Negro heads with marital status and age reported.

Series A 335–349. Households, by Number of Persons: 1790 to 1970

[Number in thousands. As of March, except as noted]

Year	Number of households	Size of household							Percent distribution of number of households						
		1 person	2 persons	3 persons	4 persons	5 persons	6 persons	7 or more persons	1 person	2 persons	3 persons	4 persons	5 persons	6 persons	7 or more persons
	335	336	337	338	339	340	341	342	343	344	345	346	347	348	349
1970	62,874	10,692	18,129	10,903	9,935	6,532	3,505	3,178	17.0	28.8	17.3	15.8	10.4	5.6	5.1
1969	61,806	10,333	17,916	10,698	9,714	6,345	3,534	3,266	16.7	29.0	17.3	15.7	10.3	5.7	5.3
1968	60,446	9,743	17,272	10,513	9,565	6,281	3,605	3,467	16.1	28.6	17.4	15.8	10.4	6.0	5.7
1967	58,845	9,139	16,659	10,334	9,496	6,235	3,468	3,527	15.5	28.3	17.6	16.1	10.6	5.9	6.0
1966	58,092	9,044	16,589	9,939	9,414	6,223	3,446	3,446	15.6	28.6	17.1	16.2	10.7	5.9	5.9
1965	57,251	8,603	16,067	10,230	9,239	6,293	3,316	3,503	15.0	28.1	17.9	16.1	11.0	5.8	6.1
1964	55,996	7,800	15,579	10,007	9,539	6,311	3,364	3,396	13.9	27.8	17.9	17.0	11.3	6.0	6.1
1963	55,189	7,490	15,257	9,974	9,431	6,231	3,468	3,337	13.6	27.6	18.1	17.1	11.3	6.3	6.0
1962	54,652	7,458	15,429	10,056	9,328	6,004	3,361	3,016	13.6	28.2	18.4	17.1	11.0	6.1	5.5
1961	53,291	7,077	15,110	9,731	9,343	6,022	3,070	2,938	13.3	28.4	18.3	17.5	11.3	5.8	5.5
1960*	52,610	6,871	14,616	9,941	9,277	6,064	2,976	2,865	13.1	27.8	18.9	17.6	11.5	5.7	5.4
1959	51,302	6,317	14,538	9,788	9,123	5,793	2,948	2,795	12.3	28.4	19.1	17.8	11.3	5.7	5.4
1958	50,402	6,078	14,303	9,715	8,933	5,609	3,002	2,762	12.1	28.4	19.3	17.7	11.1	6.0	5.5
1957	49,543	5,451	14,274	9,743	9,096	5,487	2,848	2,644	11.0	28.8	19.7	18.4	11.1	5.7	5.3
1956	48,785	5,396	13,827	9,936	9,152	5,287	2,624	2,563	11.1	28.3	20.4	18.8	10.8	5.4	5.3
1955	47,788	5,212	13,612	9,725	9,052	5,291	2,568	2,328	10.9	28.5	20.4	18.9	11.1	5.4	4.9
1954	46,893	5,032	13,249	9,776	8,820	5,170	2,521	2,325	10.7	28.3	20.8	18.8	11.0	5.4	5.0
1953 [1]	46,828	6,148	13,530	9,868	8,300	4,658	2,332	1,992	13.1	28.9	21.1	17.7	9.9	5.0	4.3
1952 [2]	45,464	5,388	13,460	9,908	8,106	4,378	2,142	2,082	11.9	29.6	21.8	17.8	9.6	4.7	4.6
1951 [2]	44,564	(NA)	(NA)	(NA)	(NA)	(NA)	(NA)	(NA)	(NA)	(NA)	(NA)	(NA)	(NA)	(NA)	(NA)
1950 [1]	43,468	4,737	12,529	9,808	7,729	4,357	2,196	2,113	10.9	28.8	22.6	17.8	10.0	5.1	4.9
1940 [2]	34,949	2,481	8,667	7,829	6,326	4,019	2,377	3,250	7.1	24.8	22.4	18.1	11.5	6.8	9.3
1930 [2]	29,905	2,357	6,983	6,227	5,235	3,574	2,273	3,255	7.9	23.4	20.8	17.5	12.0	7.6	10.9
1900	15,964	814	2,395	2,810	2,698	2,267	1,740	3,257	5.1	15.0	17.6	16.9	14.2	10.9	20.4
1890 [3]	12,690	457	1,675	2,119	2,132	1,916	1,472	2,919	3.6	13.2	16.7	16.8	15.1	11.6	23.0
1790	558	21	44	65	77	78	74	200	3.7	7.8	11.7	13.8	13.9	13.2	35.8

* Denotes first year for which figures include Alaska and Hawaii.
NA Not available.
[1] Covers related persons only; therefore, not strictly comparable with other years.

[2] As of April.
[3] As of June; includes a small number of quasi-households.

Series A 350–352. Households, by Residence: 1900 to 1970

[In thousands. 1900–1946 as of July; 1947–1949 and 1951–1955 as of April; and 1950 and 1956–1970 as of March]

Year	Total 350	Nonfarm 351	Farm 352	Year	Total 350	Nonfarm 351	Farm 352	Year	Total 350	Nonfarm 351	Farm 352	Year	Total 350	Nonfarm 351	Farm 352
1970	62,874	60,150	2,724	1952	45,538	39,584	5,954	1934	31,306	24,118	7,188	1916	22,926	16,291	6,635
1969	61,805	58,935	2,870	1951	44,673	38,602	6,071	1933	30,802	23,653	7,149	1915	22,501	15,949	6,552
1968	60,444	57,501	2,944	1950	43,554	37,279	6,275	1932	30,439	23,541	6,898	1914	22,110	15,630	6,480
1967	58,845	55,910	2,934	1949	42,182	35,687	6,495	1931	30,272	23,476	6,796	1913	21,606	15,187	6,419
1966	58,092	54,875	3,214	1948	40,532	34,116	6,416	1930	29,997	23,268	6,729	1912	21,075	14,727	6,348
1965	57,251	53,899	3,350	1947	39,107	32,673	6,434	1929	29,582	22,851	6,731	1911	20,620	14,358	6,262
1964	55,996	52,651	3,345	1946	38,370	31,944	6,426	1928	29,124	22,416	6,708	1910	20,183	13,989	6,194
1963	55,189	51,725	3,464	1945	37,503	31,158	6,345	1927	28,632	21,941	6,691	1909	19,734		
1962	54,652	50,890	3,762	1944	37,115	30,722	6,393	1926	28,101	21,325	6,776	1908	19,294		
1961	53,464	49,715	3,749	1943	36,833	30,206	6,627	1925	27,540	20,745	6,795	1907	18,863		
1960*	52,799	48,708	4,091	1942	36,445	29,433	7,012	1924	26,941	20,182	6,759	1906	18,394		
1959	51,435	46,028	5,407	1941	35,929	28,786	7,143	1923	26,298	19,492	6,806	1905	17,939		
1958	50,474	45,289	5,185	1940	35,153	28,001	7,152	1922	25,687	18,780	6,907	1904	17,521		
1957	49,673	44,441	5,232	1939	34,409	27,249	7,160	1921	25,119	18,255	6,864	1903	17,108		
1956	48,902	43,239	5,663	1938	33,683	26,518	7,165	1920	24,467	17,668	6,799	1902	16,716		
1955	47,874	42,319	5,555	1937	33,088	25,917	7,171	1919	23,873	17,307	6,566	1901	16,345		
1954	46,962	41,460	5,502	1936	32,454	25,253	7,201	1918	23,519	16,846	6,673	1900	15,992		
1953	46,385	40,548	5,837	1935	31,892	24,665	7,227	1917	23,323	16,643	6,680				

* Denotes first year for which figures include Alaska and Hawaii.

Series A 353–358. Families and Percent Distribution of Own Children Under 18 Years Old: 1950 to 1970

[As of March, except as noted]

Year	Families (1,000) 353	Percent distribution of own children					Year	Families (1,000) 353	Percent distribution of own children				
		No children 354	1 child 355	2 children 356	3 children 357	4 or more children 358			No children 354	1 child 355	2 children 356	3 children 357	4 or more children 358
1970	51,586	44.1	18.2	17.4	10.6	9.8	1959	44,232	43.3	18.4	18.3	10.5	9.5
1969	50,823	44.2	18.1	16.9	10.5	10.3	1958	43,696	43.8	18.6	18.0	10.4	9.1
1968	50,111	44.2	17.5	17.0	10.5	10.7	1957	43,497	44.2	18.5	18.2	10.4	8.7
1967	49,214	44.0	17.8	16.8	10.6	10.8	1956 [1]	42,889	44.6	18.8	18.5	9.8	8.3
1966	48,509	44.3	17.2	16.8	10.7	11.0	1955 [1]	41,951	44.7	19.1	18.7	9.9	7.6
1965	47,956	43.4	17.7	16.8	11.0	11.1	1954 [1]	41,202	45.4	19.9	17.9	9.4	7.4
1964	47,540	43.1	17.3	17.4	11.3	11.0	1953 [1]	40,832	46.9	20.2	17.0	9.1	6.8
1963	47,059	42.8	17.6	17.4	11.2	11.0	1952 [1]	40,578	47.4	20.2	17.0	8.5	6.9
1962	46,418	43.4	18.0	17.3	10.9	10.5	1951 [1]	39,929	46.7	21.5	17.0	8.3	6.5
1961	45,539	43.1	18.4	17.7	11.0	9.8	1950	39,303	48.3	21.1	16.5	7.8	6.3
1960 *	45,111	43.0	18.5	18.0	11.1	9.4							

* Denotes first year for which figures include Alaska and Hawaii.   [1] As of April.

Series A 359–371. Inmates of Institutions by Sex, Race, Age, and Type of Institution: 1940 to 1970

[For definition of institutions, see text]

Year	Total 359	Sex		Race			Age			Type of institution			
		Male 360	Female 361	White 362	Negro 363	Other 364	Under 18 365	18–64 366	65 and over 367	Correctional 368	Mental 369	Homes for aged and dependent 370	Other 371
ALL INMATES													
1970 [1]	2,126,719	1,126,327	1,000,392	1,785,085	318,991	22,643	238,090	921,014	967,615	328,020	433,890	927,514	437,295
1960 [2] *	1,886,967	1,116,825	770,142	1,581,611	305,356		237,588	1,034,323	615,056	346,015	630,046	469,717	441,189
1950	1,566,846		949,628	617,218	1,351,152	215,694	204,644	976,783	385,419	264,557	613,628	296,783	391,878
INMATES, 15 YEARS AND OVER													
1970 [1]	1,990,644	1,040,381	950,263	1,678,055	292,191	20,398	102,015	921,014	967,615	326,720	419,768	925,847	318,309
1960 [2] *	1,736,830	1,026,305	710,525	1,455,204	281,626		87,451	1,034,323	615,056	345,280	622,559	468,410	300,581
1950	1,424,434	867,455	556,979	1,221,060	203,374		62,232	976,783	385,419	263,896	609,805	294,085	256,648
1940	1,156,298	755,290	401,008	989,839	166,459		69,788	864,545	221,965	312,423	587,328	234,054	22,493

* Denotes first year for which figures include Alaska and Hawaii.   [2] 25-percent sample.
[1] 20-percent sample.

Vital Statistics and Health and Medical Care

Vital Statistics (Series B 1-220)

B 1–220. General note.

Vital statistics, including statistics of births, deaths, marriages, and divorces, are compiled for the country as a whole by the National Center for Health Statistics, successor in recent years to the former National Office of Vital Statistics. Beginning 1900, the collection of these data was the responsibility of the Bureau of the Census. In July 1946, this function was transferred to the Federal Security Agency, which, in 1953, was reconstituted as the Department of Health, Education, and Welfare. The National Center for Health Statistics is a part of the Public Health Service in that Department.

The live-birth, death, and fetal-death statistics prepared by the National Center for Health Statistics are based on copies of vital records received from registration offices of all States, of certain cities, and of the District of Columbia. Marriage and divorce statistics are based on information from two sources: (1) Complete counts of events obtained from all States and the District of Columbia and (2) samples of marriage and divorce certificates obtained from States meeting certain reporting criteria. In the statistical tabulations, *United States* refers only to the aggregate of the 50 States and the District of Columbia. Alaska has been included in the United States totals since 1959 and Hawaii since 1960.

The annual report, *Vital Statistics of the United States*, presents final figures and an annual life table. A series of national summaries *Vital Statistics—Special Reports* containing data on particular subjects was issued each year from 1934 to 1959. This series was superseded by *Vital and Health Statistics*, Series 20, 21, and 22.

Although every State has adopted a law requiring the registration of births, deaths, and fetal deaths, these laws are not uniformly observed. One condition for admission to the national registration areas was a demonstration of registration completeness of at least 90 percent. On the basis of this criterion, all of the States were admitted to both the birth- and death-registration areas by 1933. It is recognized, however, that the methods then used in testing completeness were subject to considerable error.

The annual collection of mortality statistics for the national death-registration area began in 1900 with 10 registration States and the District of Columbia; the collection of birth statistics for the national birth-registration area began in 1915, also with 10 States and the District of Columbia. The changing composition of the two registration areas makes it impossible to obtain geographically comparable birth and death data for the entire United States before 1933. Although the national birth-registration area was not started until 1915, annual estimates of births have been prepared for the period 1909–34. These estimates include adjustments for underregistration and for States not in the birth-registration area before 1933. Beginning 1933, the birth- and death-registration areas have comprised the entire United States, including Alaska beginning 1959 and Hawaii beginning 1960. National statistics on fetal deaths were compiled for 1918 and annually since 1922.

Prior to 1951, birth statistics were the result of a complete count of the records received in the Public Health Service. Since 1951, they have been based on a 50-percent sample of all registered births (except for 1955 when they reverted to a complete count and for 1967 when they were based on a 20–50 percent sample).

Mortality statistics are compiled in accordance with World Health Organization regulations, which specify that member nations classify causes of death according to the *International Statistical Classification*

Growth of Birth- and Death-Registration Area: 1900 to 1933

Year	Conterminous United States, midyear population	Birth-registration area [1]			Death-registration area [1]		
		Midyear population		Number of States	Midyear population		Number of States
		Number	Percent of total		Number	Percent of total	
	1,000	*1,000*			*1,000*		
1933	125,579	125,579	100.0	48	125,579	100.0	48
1932	124,840	118,904	95.2	47	118,904	95.2	47
1931	124,040	117,455	94.7	46	118,149	95.3	47
1930	123,077	116,545	94.7	46	117,238	95.3	47
1929	121,770	115,317	94.7	46	115,317	94.7	46
1928	120,501	113,636	94.3	44	113,636	94.3	44
1927	119,038	104,321	87.6	40	107,085	90.0	42
1926	117,399	90,401	77.0	35	103,823	88.4	41
1925	115,832	88,295	76.2	33	102,032	88.1	40
1924	114,113	87,000	76.2	33	99,318	87.0	39
1923	111,950	81,072	72.4	30	96,788	86.5	38
1922	110,055	79,561	72.3	30	92,703	84.2	37
1921	108,541	70,807	65.2	27	87,814	80.9	34
1920	106,466	63,597	59.7	23	86,079	80.9	34
1919	104,512	61,212	58.6	22	83,158	79.6	33
1918	103,203	55,154	53.4	20	79,008	76.6	30
1917	103,266	55,198	53.5	20	70,235	68.0	27
1916	101,966	32,944	32.3	11	66,971	65.7	26
1915	100,549	31,097	30.9	10	61,895	61.6	24
1914	99,118	---------	---------	---------	60,963	61.5	24
1913	97,227				58,157	59.8	23
1912	95,331				54,848	57.5	22
1911	93,868				53,930	57.5	22
1910	92,407.				47,470	51.4	20
1909	90,492				44,224	48.9	18
1908	88,709				38,635	43.6	17
1907	87,000				34,553	39.7	15
1906	85,437				33,782	39.5	15
1905	83,820				21,768	26.0	10
1904	82,165				21,332	26.0	10
1903	80,632				20,943	26.0	10
1902	79,160				20,583	26.0	10
1901	77,585				20,237	26.1	10
1900	76,094				19,965	26.2	10

[1] District of Columbia excluded from count of number of States but included in the population figures.

of Diseases, Injuries, and Causes of Death. The current (1973) classification, "Eighth Revision International Classification of Diseases, Adapted for Use in the United States," has been used since 1968.

Accurate measures of birth-registration completeness on a nationwide basis were obtained for the first time in 1940, when studies were made in connection with the population census of that year. They showed that, for the United States as a whole, birth registration was 92.5 percent complete. A corresponding study 10 years later indicated that registration had improved considerably, with 97.9 percent of the births in 1950 being recorded. Only in a few States was underregistration shown to be still a problem. The results of this study have been published in considerable detail (Bureau of the Census, *Infant Enumeration Study*, 1950) and provide a basis for adjusting registered birth data for underreporting and for making estimates of registration completeness in post-censal years. Birth registration has continued to improve since 1930 and, in 1968, 99.1 percent of the live births were registered. (See National Office of Vital Statistics, "Birth-Registration Completeness in the United States and Geographic Areas, 1950," parts I, II, and III, *Vital Statistics—Special Reports*, vol. 39, Nos. 2 and 4, and vol. 45, No. 9.)

Death registration is believed to be at least as complete as birth registration. However, quantitative information on the completeness with which deaths are reported is limited to that obtained years ago in applying the "90-percent" standard for entry into the death-registration area and to information obtained from occasional local area studies. While underregistration for the country as a whole is negligible, local studies furnish evidence that in certain isolated places underreporting of deaths may still be a problem. Registration of fetal deaths is probably significantly incomplete in all areas.

National collections of statistics on marriages and divorces in the United States were made for various years from 1867 to 1940 and for each year since 1944. Estimates have been made for intervening years and for years in which collections were not complete. A marriage-registration area was established by the Public Health Service in 1957, and a divorce-registration area in 1958. At the beginning of 1971, the marriage-registration area covered 40 States and 3 independent registration areas; the divorce-registration area, 29 States and 1 independent area.

Population statistics published or made available by the Bureau of the Census have been used in computing the vital rates shown here. Rates for 1940, 1950, 1960, and 1970 are based on the population enumerated in the censuses of those years which were taken as of April 1. Rates for all other years are based on midyear (July 1) estimates of population made by the Bureau of the Census.

Except for 1941–1946, vital rates are based on the population residing in conterminous United States. In those years, the transfer overseas of several million men precluded the computation of birth and divorce rates strictly comparable with such rates for prewar years. For 1941–1946, the birth and divorce rates are based on the population including the Armed Forces overseas. (For a discussion of the interpretation of rates during wartime, see "Summary of Natality and Mortality Statistics, United States, 1943," *Vital Statistics—Special Reports*, vol. 21, No. 1, and "Marriage and Divorce in the United States, 1937 to 1945," *Vital Statistics—Special Reports*, vol. 23, No. 9.)

Vital statistics showing color and race are compiled from entries which appear on certificates filed with vital registration offices. The classification "white" includes persons reported as Mexican, Cuban, and Puerto Rican. The Negro group includes persons of mixed Negro and other ancestry. For births, the newborn child is ordinarily assigned to the race of the parents. If parents are of different races, the following applies: (1) When only one parent is white, the child is assigned the other parent's race; (2) when neither is white, the child is assigned the father's race. For additional details, see source.

B 1. Live births, 1909–1970.

Source: U.S. Public Health Service, 1909–1968, *Vital Statistics of the United States, 1968*, vol. I, p. 1–4; 1969–1970, same report, annual issues.

See general note for series B 1–220.

B 2. Deaths, 1933–1970.

Source: U.S. Public Health Service, 1933–1967, *Vital Statistics of the United States, 1967*, vol. II, part A, p. 1–2; 1968–1970, same report, annual issues.

See general note for series B 1–220.

B 3–4. Marriages and divorces, 1920–1970.

Source: U.S. Public Health Service, 1920–1965, *Vital Statistics of the United States, 1965*, vol. III, pp. 1–5 and 2–5; 1966–1970, same report, annual issues.

See general note for series B 1–220.

B 5–10. Birth rate—total and for women 15–44 years old, by race, 1800–1970.

Source: **Series B 5**, 1820–1900, Henry D. Sheldon, *The Older Population of the United States*, John Wiley and Sons, New York, 1958, p. 145 (copyright). **Series B 6** and **B 9**, 1800–1900, Warren S. Thompson and P. K. Whelpton, *Population Trends in the United States*, McGraw-Hill, New York, 1933, p. 263 (copyright). **Series B 5–10**, 1909–1968, U.S. Public Health Service, *Vital Statistics of the United States, 1968*, vol. I. p. 1–4; 1969–1970, same report, annual issues.

Estimates for 1909–1934 were prepared by Pascal K. Whelpton. For 1915–1932, the figures include adjustments for States not in the registration area; for years prior to 1915, figures are estimates based on the number of registered births in the 10 original registration States for the same period.

See also general note for series B 1–220.

B 11–19. Fertility rate and birth rate, by age of mother, by race, 1940–1970.

Source: U.S. Public Health Service, 1940–1968, *Vital Statistics of the United States, 1968*, vol. I, p. 1–7; 1969, *Monthly Vital Statistics Report, 1969*, vol. 22, No. 7, p. 5; 1970, *Vital Statistics of the United States, 1970*, vol. I.

Series B 11–19 is an age-adjusted rate because it is based on the assumption that there are the same number of women in each age group. The rate of 2,480 in 1970, for example, means that if a hypothetical group of 1,000 women were to have the same birth rate in each age group observed in the actual childbearing population in 1970, the women would have a total of 2,480 children by the time they reached the end of the reproductive period (taken here as age 50), assuming that all of the women survive to that age.

See also general note for series B 1–220.

B 20–27. Birth rate, by race, by live-birth order, 1940–1970.

Source: U.S. Public Health Service, 1940–1968, see source note for series B 11–19, p. 1–9; 1969, see same source note, p. 6–7; 1970, see same source note.

B 28–35. Illegitimate live births and birth rates, by age and race of mother, 1940–1970.

Source: U.S. Public Health Service, *Vital Statistics of the United States, 1970*, vol. I.

These are estimated data based on certificates of live birth filed for each child born in the United States. During the 1930's almost all States had a query concerning legitimacy or illegitimacy on their certificates. During the 1940's, concern for confidentiality prompted a number of States to remove it. These data are based on reports of 34 States and the District of Columbia for 1940–1965 and on reports of 40 States and the District of Columbia for 1966–1970.

In making estimates of the number of illegitimate births occurring in the country as a whole, the States were grouped into nine geographic divisions. The combined ratio of illegitimate births per 1,000 total live births for all reporting States in a single geographic division was then applied to all live births to residents of that division. This estimating procedure was separately applied for white persons and for Negro and other persons. The sum of these estimates for the nine geographic divisions represents the estimate for the United States. No adjustments were made for misstatements of legitimacy status on the birth record or for failure to register illegitimate births because the extent of such reporting problems is unknown. A birth with legitimacy status not recorded was considered to be legitimate.

The rates shown for the years 1951–65 differ from those published in earlier issues of *Vital Statistics of the United States*. The rates shown here are based on a smoothed series of population estimates for unmarried women by race and age which were not available when the rates previously published were computed. For details concerning these estimates and other data for illegitimate births, see U.S. Public Health Service, National Center for Health Statistics, "Trends in Illegitimacy, United States, 1940-1965," *Vital and Health Statistics*, PHS Pub. No. 1000-Series 21-No. 15, February 1968.

B 36-41. Gross and net reproduction rates, by race, 1905-10 to 1970.

Source: U.S. Bureau of the Census, 1905-10 to 1935-40, Sixteenth Census Reports, *Differential Fertility, 1940 and 1910—Standardized Fertility Rates and Reproduction Rates;* U.S. Public Health Service, 1935, *Vital Statistics of the United States, 1950*, vol. I, p. 87; 1940-1956, *Vital Statistics of the United States, 1956*, vol. I, p. lxxix; 1957-70, same report, annual issues.

The gross reproduction rate represents the number of daughters a hypothetical cohort of 1,000 women entering the child-bearing period would have during their lives, if they were subject to the age-specific birth rates observed in a given time period, and if none of the cohort were to die before the child-bearing period was completed. Age-specific birth rate is the ratio of births by age of mother to women in each age interval for a specified year. The gross reproduction rate is the sum of the age-specific birth rates of female infants per 1,000 women. It shows the maximum possible replacement of women that might be expected from the given set of age-specific birth rates. If no migration took place and if the gross rate remained below 1,000, no improvement in mortality alone could prevent the population from declining when a stable age distribution had been reached.

The net reproduction rate is based on the specific fertility and mortality conditions existing in a given time period. If the age-specific birth and death rates of a certain year (or years) were to continue until the population became stable, a net reproduction rate of 1,000 would mean that a cohort of 1,000 newly born girls would bear just enough daughters to replace themselves.

Reproduction rates are useful in the analyses of fertility and mortality conditions of a given period, but they are not indicators of future population growth. They do not take into account such factors as nuptiality, marital duration, and size of family, and they assume the continuation of the age-specific rates in a given year throughout the lifetime of a cohort of women. Since the United States has experienced major changes in marriage and fertility rates over short periods of time, variations in reproduction rates should not be taken as indications of long-run movements in family formation and rates of fertility and mortality.

B 42-48. Percent distribution of ever-married women (survivors of birth cohorts of 1835-39 to 1920-24), by race and by number of children ever born, as reported in censuses of 1910, 1940, 1950, 1960, and 1970.

Source: 1910-1950, all races, Conrad and Irene Taeuber, *The Changing Population of the United States, 1790-1955*, John Wiley and Sons, New York, 1957, pp. 255-256 (copyright). By race, U.S. Bureau of the Census, 1910 and 1940, Sixteenth Census Reports, *Population, Differential Fertility, 1940 and 1910*, part 2; 1950, *U.S. Census of Population: 1950*, Special Reports, P-E, No. 5C, *Fertility*. 1960 and 1970, *U.S. Census of Population: 1960* and *1970*, PC(2)3A, *Women by Number of Children Ever Born*.

These data are based on an analysis of the decennial censuses. In each of these censuses women who had ever married were asked about the number of children they had ever borne. When these women are classified according to age, it is possible to suggest the trend in fertility among women who had completed their childbearing at each census.

Caution should be used in comparing the data from the 1910 census with those from later censuses. The 1910 census may have inadvertently obtained some stillbirths in the counts of children ever born, resulting in overstatements of fertility. Comparisons of the

average number of children ever born to women age 40-44 in 1910 with the average for those surviving to age 70-74 in 1940 show about ten percent more children at the earlier date. In contrast, there is little difference when the average numbers of children ever born are compared for women of recently completed fertility in 1940 with the average for survivors at much older ages in the censuses of 1950 to 1970, suggesting that the memory factor does not cause much undercount of children by women long past the childbearing ages.

Illegitimate births are represented in the data insofar as the women ever married included births before marriage (as they were supposed to do) in their reported total number of children ever born. Comparisons of cumulations of birth data from annual vital statistics (that include all illegitimate births) with recent census data on children ever born suggest that the census data may be short by about 5 percent for all races and about 3 percent for whites.

B 49-66. Children ever born to women ever married, by race and age of women, 1910-1970.

Source: U.S. Bureau of the Census. 1910 and 1940, Sixteenth Census of Population, Special Reports, *Differential Fertility, 1940 and 1910—Fertility for States and Large Cities*, tables 3 and 4; *Differential Fertility, 1940 and 1910—Women by Number of Children Ever Born*, tables 9 and 12; and unpublished data. 1950, *U.S. Census of Population: 1950*, Special Report P-E No. 5C, *Fertility*, tables 1, 2, and 12; and unpublished data. 1960, *U.S. Census of Population: 1960*, vol. I, *Characteristics of the Population*, part 1, *U.S. Summary*, table 190, and Final Report PC(2)-3A, *Women by Number of Children Ever Born*, tables 2 and 8. 1970, *U.S. Census of Population: 1970*, part 1, *U.S. Summary*, table 213.

These data are based on an 8.9 percent sample for 1910, 3.3 percent for 1940, 2.4 percent for 1950, 25 percent for 1960 (except that the separate data for Negroes are from a 5 percent sample), and 20 percent for 1970. The data shown for 1940 in series B 42-48 and series B 49-66 include special adjustments to allow for the fertility of women with no original report on number of children ever born and therefore differ slightly from the data published in the reports on *Differential Fertility, 1940 and 1910*.

See the text for series B 42-48 for cautions regarding the comparability of data from the 1910 census with data from later censuses, and possible minor shortages in counts of children ever born due to underreporting of illegitimate births.

B 67-98. Number of children under 5 years old per 1,000 women 20 to 44 years old, by race and residence, by geographic divisions, 1800-1970.

Source: **Series B 67-68**, 1800-1940, and **series B 69-98**, 1800-1840 and 1910-1950, Wilson H. Grabill, Clyde V. Kiser, and Pascal K. Whelpton, *The Fertility of American Women*, John Wiley and Sons, New York, 1958 (copyright). **Series B 67-68**, 1950-1970 and **series B 69-98**, 1850-1900 and 1960-1970, U.S. Bureau of the Census, special computations from decennial census reports.

Figures for series B 67-68 were adjusted for underreporting of children in 1800-1940 on the basis of factors obtained for 1925-1930 and for underreporting of both women and children in 1950-1970 on the basis of estimates derived by analytical methods. The ratios have been standardized for age of women (except for white women for 1800-1820) using the 1930 age distribution of women to offset the effect of changes in the age distribution of the female population. Therefore, the figures represent the fertility ratios of women having the same age distribution as those in 1930. Rates for 1800-1860 are partly estimated.

For composition of geographic divisions, see text for series A 172-194. The urban-rural classification shown for 1800-1950 is based on the rules used in 1940. That shown for 1960-1970 is based on rules used for those censuses. For definition of residence by old and new rules of classification, see text for series A 43-56. The change in rules is known to have relatively little effect on the fertility ratios for 1950 and probably has little effect on the comparability of the fertility ratios for 1960–1970 with those of earlier years.

B 99–106. Median interval between births, by race, 1930–1969.

Source: U.S. Bureau of the Census, *Current Population Reports*, series P-20, Nos. 180 and 186, and unpublished data.

The median interval between two sets of events is an estimate of the length of time after the first set of events in which half of the second set takes place. If the first set of events is births of a first child and the second set is births of a second child and the estimate of the median interval is 32.2 months, the interpretation is that half of the second births occur within 32.2 months of the first births.

Data on median intervals between births and first marriage and between births of successive orders are useful for comparing child-spacing and family building patterns between subgroups within a population at a given point in time and between different cohorts either of women or (as in series B 67–98) of their children.

B 107–115. Expectation of life at birth, by race and sex, 1900–1970.

Source: U.S. Public Health Service, 1900–1967, *Vital Statistics of the United States, 1967*, vol. II, part A, p. 5–8; 1968–1970, same report, annual issues.

Derivation of estimates is described in "Estimated Average Length of Life in the Death-Registration States," *Vital Statistics—Special Reports*, vol. 33, No. 9.

The expectation of life at birth is the average number of years that members of a hypothetical cohort would live if they were subject throughout their lives to the age-specific mortality rates observed at the time of their birth. This is the most usual measure of the comparative longevity of different populations. There is some objection to the use of the average duration of life as a standard of comparison because the method of calculating it gives great weight to the relatively large number of deaths occurring in the first year of life. This influence may be entirely eliminated by considering instead the average lifetime remaining to those members of the cohort surviving to age 1, or, in other words, the expectation of life at age 1. However, this objection is growing less valid as infant mortality decreases.

B 116–125. Expectation of life at specified ages, by sex and race, 1900–1970.

Source: 1901–1910, white population, U.S. Bureau of the Census, *United States Life Tables, 1900–1931*, pp. 40–47. 1900–1902 and 1909–11 to 1956, U.S. Public Health Service, *Vital Statistics of the United States, 1956*, vol. I, p. xciii; 1957–1970, same report, annual issues, vol. I, 1957–1959, and vol. II, thereafter.

The expectation of life at a specified age is the average number of years that members of a hypothetical cohort would continue to live if they were subject throughout the remainder of their lives to the mortality rates for specified age groups observed in a given time period.

B 126–135. Expectation of life at specified ages, by sex, for Massachusetts, 1850 to 1949–51.

Source: 1850, Metropolitan Life Insurance Company, *Statistical Bulletin*, vol. 9, No. 3, March 1928, pp. 7–8; 1855, Edgar Sydenstricker, *Health and Environment*, McGraw-Hill, New York, 1933, p. 164 (copyright); 1878–82 to 1939–41, Louis I. Dublin, Alfred J. Lotka, and Mortimer Spiegelman, *Length of Life*, Ronald Press, New York, 1949 pp. 326 and 334 (copyright); 1949–51, U.S. Bureau of the Census and U.S. Public Health Service, *Vital Statistics—Special Reports*, vol. 41, Supplement 20, March 21, 1956, pp. 193 and 195.

See text for series B 116–125.

B 136–138. Fetal death ratio, by race, 1922–1970.

Source: U.S. Public Health Service, 1922–1944, *Vital Statistics of the United States, 1956*, vol. I, p. lxxxviii; 1945–1967, same report, *1967*, vol. II, part A, p. 3–4; 1968–1970, same report, annual issues.

Lack of uniformity in requirements for registration and variation in completeness of registration influence the comparability of the data over the years, especially in the series based on all reported fetal deaths. Considering the probable total effect of these factors, as well as that of incompleteness of the registration area until 1933, it appears likely that the ratios understate any decline in fetal mortality. Changes in the regulations have more often been in the direction of broadening the base of fetal death reporting, than in the other direction. With respect to completeness of reporting, the situation has probably improved because of the increases in the number of women receiving hospital and medical care at childbirth and also because of the general strengthening of the vital registration system.

B 139–141. Neonatal mortality rate, by race, 1915–1970.

Source: U.S. Public Health Service, 1915–1929, *Vital Statistics of the United States, 1950*, vol. I, pp. 258–259; 1930–1939, *Vital Statistics—Special Reports*, vol. 45, No. 1, pp. 8–10; 1940–1967, *Vital Statistics of the United States, 1967*, vol. II, part A, p. 2–3; 1968–1970, same report, annual issues.

The neonatal mortality rate represents the number of deaths of infants under 28 days (exclusive of fetal deaths) per 1,000 live births.

B 142–144. Infant mortality rate, by race, 1915–1970.

Source: U.S. Public Health Service, 1915–1939, *Vital Statistics—Special Reports*, vol. 45, No. 1, p. 7; 1940–1970, see source for series B 139–141.

The infant mortality rate represents the number of deaths under 1 year (exclusive of fetal deaths) per 1,000 live births. The rates have been computed by the conventional method in which the infant deaths occurring in a specified period are related to the number of live births occurring during the same period. Rates computed in this way are influenced by changes in the number of births and will not be comparable if the birth rate is fluctuating widely. Deaths under 1 year of age occurring during any calendar year are deaths not only of infants born during that year but also of infants born during parts of the previous year. An approximate correction of this error can be made by relating infant deaths during a specified year to the year in which those infants were born. See Bureau of the Census, "Effect of Changing Birth Rates Upon Infant Mortality Rates," *Vital Statistics—Special Reports*, vol. 19, No. 21.

B 145–147. Maternal mortality rate, by race, 1915–1970.

Source: U.S. Public Health Service, 1915–1939, *Vital Statistics—Special Reports*, vol. 46, No. 17, p. 438; 1940–1967, *Vital Statistics of the United States, 1967*, vol. II, part A, p. 1–41; 1968–1970, same report, annual issues.

The maternal mortality rate represents the number of deaths from deliveries and complications of pregnancy, childbirth, and the puerperium per 10,000 live births.

B 148. Infant mortality rate, for Massachusetts, 1851–1970.

Source: 1851–1899, *77th Annual Report of Vital Statistics of Massachusetts*, p. 132; 1900–1956, U.S. Bureau of the Census and U.S. Public Health Service, *Vital Statistics of the United States*, vol. I, annual issues; 1957–1970, U.S. Public Health Service, *Vital Statistics of the United States*, vol. II, part A, annual issues.

B 149–166. Death rate, for selected causes, 1900–1970.

Source: U.S. Public Health Service. **Series B 149–150, B 152–163**, and **B 166**, 1900–1970, *Vital Statistics of the United States* (vol. I to 1954 and vol. II, part A, thereafter), various annual issues.   **Series B 151**, 1900–1920, *Vital Statistics of the United States, 1950*, vol. I, p. 218; 1921–1940, *Vital Statistics Rates in the United States, 1900–1940*, p. 266; 1941–1970, unpublished data.   **Series B 164–165**, U.S. Bureau of the Census, 1900–1933, *Mortality Statistics*, various annual issues; 1934–1938, *Vital Statistics of the United States, Special Reports, Deaths From Each Cause, United States: 1934–1938*; 1939–1949, *Vital Statistics of the United States*, part I; 1950–1970, *Vital Statistics of the United States*, vol. II, part A, various annual issues.

Mortality data are classified according to the numbers and titles of the detailed International List of Causes of Death.   A large proportion of the death certificates filed annually in the United States report two or more diseases or conditions as joint causes of death. General statistical practice requires that cases involving more than one cause of death be changed to a single cause.

In the French edition of the International List (1900), certain principles for determining the single cause to be selected from the joint causes given were incorporated as a part of the general classification scheme.   As an outgrowth of practices in this country after 1902, definite relationships among the various conditions represented by items in the International List were put in concrete form in the *Manual of Joint Causes of Death*, first published in 1914, and revised to conform with successive revisions of the International List.   This manual, which was developed for use in the United States, was followed until 1949, when an international procedure for joint-cause selection was adopted.   The new international rules place the responsibility on the medical practitioner to indicate the underlying cause of death.   This change, in conjunction with the Sixth Revision of the International List in 1949, the Seventh Revision in 1958, and the Eighth Revision in 1968, has introduced rather serious breaks in statistical continuity.

Time-trend studies of causes of death would be facilitated if the International List were maintained without change over a long period of years.   However, if the list were rigidly fixed it would be inconsistent with current medical knowledge and terminology.   To obtain the advantages of frequent revision, and yet to retain a fixed list for a number of years, revisions are made at an international conference every 10 years.   In the process of revision, discontinuities are introduced into the time trends of death rates for certain specific causes of death (see National Office of Vital Statistics, "The Effect of the Sixth Revision of the International List of Diseases and Causes of Death Upon Comparability of Mortality Trends," *Vital Statistics—Special Reports*, vol. 36, No. 10).

Improvement in diagnostic procedures and development of medical knowledge and facilities are other important factors in the study of changes in death rates for certain causes.

B 167–173.   Death rate, by race and sex, 1900–1970.

Source: 1900–1968, U.S. Public Health Service, *Vital Statistics of the United States, 1968*, vol. II, part A; 1969–1970, unpublished data.

B 174–180.   Age-adjusted death rate, by race and sex, 1900–1970.

Source: See source for series B 167–173.

The age-adjusted death rate is a convenient summary index that "corrects" for differences in age composition.   These rates were computed by taking the age-distribution of the population in 1940 as the "standard" without regard to sex, color, or other characteristics. The age-specific death rates actually observed in a given year were applied to the age distribution of this standard population and a total death rate was computed.   The age-specific death rate is the

rate of deaths per 1,000 population in each age interval for a specified year.   For a detailed description of the direct method by which these rates were computed, see *Vital Statistics Rates in the United States, 1900–1940*, pp. 66–69.

B 181–192.   Death rate, by age and sex, 1900–1970.

Source: 1900–1939, U.S. Public Health Service, *Vital Statistics—Special Reports*, vol. 43, No. 1, pp. 10–12; 1940–1954, U.S. Bureau of the Census, *Vital Statistics of the United States, 1954*, vol. I, p. xlix; 1955–1957, *Vital Statistics of the United States, 1956*, vol. I, p. xcviii; 1958–1970, *Vital Statistics of the United States, 1968*, vol. II, part A; and unpublished data.

B 193–200.   Death rate, by sex and by selected cause, for Massachusetts, 1860–1970.

Source: 1860–1899, computed from *48th Annual Registration Report for Massachusetts* and *77th Annual Report on the Vital Statistics of Massachusetts;* 1900–1956, U.S. Bureau of the Census and U.S. Public Health Service, *Vital Statistics of the United States*, vol. I, annual issues; 1957–1970, U.S. Public Health Service, *Vital Statistics of the United States*, vol. II, part A, annual issues.

B 201–213.   Death rate, by age, for Massachusetts, 1865–1900.

Source: *48th Annual Registration Report for Massachusetts*, p. 321, and *77th Annual Report on the Vital Statistics of Massachusetts*, p. 126.

B 214–220.   Marriage rate and divorce, 1920–1970.

Source: **Series B 214–218**, U.S. Public Health Service, *Vital Statistics of the United States*, vol. III, annual issues; **series B 219–220**, U.S. Bureau of the Census, *Current Population Reports*, series P-20.

See also: U.S. Commissioner of Labor, *A Report on Marriage and Divorce in the United States, 1867 to 1886;* U.S. Bureau of the Census, *Marriage and Divorce, 1867–1906; Vital Statistics—Special Reports*, vol. 9, No. 60, "A Review of Marriage and Divorce Statistics: United States: 1887–1937"; *Marriage and Divorce, 1916* and annual issues for 1922–1932; S. A. Stauffer and L. M. Spencer, "Recent Increases in Marriage and Divorce," *American Journal of Sociology*, vol. 44, No. 4 (for 1933–1936); U.S. Bureau of the Census, *Vital Statistics—Special Reports*, vol. 15, Nos. 13 and 18, "Estimated Number of Marriages by State: United States, 1937–1940" and "Estimated Number of Divorces by State: United States, 1937–1940," respectively.   For exact population base figures, see *Vital Statistics—Special Reports*, vol. 46, No. 12, p. 330.

Marriage and divorce records are filed only at the county level in some States, but gradually the various States are requiring by law that such events be recorded at the State level.   The completeness of reporting to the State offices varies, but there has been no nationwide test.   A marriage-registration area covering 30 States and 5 independent areas was established by the National Office of Vital Statistics in 1957.   A major criterion for admission of a State to the registration areas was agreement with the National Office of Vital Statistics to conduct a test of marriage registration completeness. By 1971, the marriage-registration area covered 40 States and 3 independent areas.   A divorce-registration area with 14 States and 3 independent areas was inaugurated in 1958.   By 1971, it covered 29 States and 1 independent area.

The marriage and divorce rates shown in series B 215 and B 217 are based on those segments of the female population that may be considered as subject to possible marriage and divorce.

Series B 1–4. Live Births, Deaths, Marriages, and Divorces: 1909 to 1970

[In thousands. Birth, marriage, and divorce figures represent estimates of all such events; death figures, the number of registered events]

Year	Live births [1][2] (1)	Deaths [3] (2)	Marriages (3)	Divorces [4] (4)	Year	Live births [1] (1)	Deaths [3] (2)	Marriages (3)	Divorces [4] (4)	Year	Live births [1] (1)	Marriages (3)	Divorces [4] (4)
1970	3,731	1,921	2,163	708	1950	3,632	1,452	1,667	385	1930	2,618	1,127	196
1969	3,600	1,922	2,145	639	1949	3,649	1,444	1,580	397	1929	2,582	1,233	206
1968	3,502	1,930	2,069	584	1948	3,637	1,444	1,811	408	1928	2,674	1,182	200
1967	[5] 3,521	1,851	1,927	523	1947	3,817	1,445	1,992	483	1927	2,802	1,201	196
1966	3,606	1,863	1,857	499	1946	3,411	1,396	2,291	610	1926	2,839	1,203	185
1965	3,760	1,828	1,800	479	1945	2,858	1,402	1,613	485	1925	2,909	1,188	175
1964	4,027	1,798	1,725	450	1944	2,939	1,411	1,452	400	1924	2,979	1,185	171
1963	4,098	1,814	1,654	428	1943	3,104	1,460	1,577	359	1923	2,910	1,230	165
1962	4,167	1,757	1,577	413	1942	2,989	1,385	1,772	321	1922	2,882	1,134	149
1961	4,268	1,702	1,548	414	1941	2,703	1,398	1,696	293	1921	3,055	1,164	160
1960 *	4,258	1,712	1,523	393	1940	2,559	1,417	1,596	264	1920	2,950	1,274	171
1959 [6]	4,245	1,657	1,494	395	1939	2,466	1,388	1,404	251	1919	2,740	--------	--------
1958	4,255	1,648	1,451	368	1938	2,496	1,381	1,331	244	1918	2,948	--------	--------
1957	4,308	1,633	1,518	381	1937	2,413	1,450	1,451	249	1917	2,944	--------	--------
1956	4,218	1,564	1,585	382	1936	2,355	1,479	1,369	236	1916	2,964	--------	--------
1955	4,104	1,529	1,531	377	1935	2,377	1,393	1,327	218	1915	2,965	--------	--------
1954	4,078	1,481	1,490	379	1934	2,396	1,397	1,302	204	1914	2,966	--------	--------
1953	3,965	1,518	1,546	390	1933	2,307	1,342	1,098	165	1913	2,869	--------	--------
1952	3,913	1,497	1,539	392	1932	2,440	--------	982	164	1912	2,840	--------	--------
1951	3,823	1,482	1,595	381	1931	2,506	--------	1,061	188	1911	2,809	--------	--------
										1910	2,777	--------	--------
										1909	2,718	--------	--------

* Denotes first year for which figures include Alaska and Hawaii.
[1] 1959–1970, registered live births; 1909–1958, adjusted for underregistration.
[2] Based on 50-percent sample for 1951–1954, 1956–1966, and 1968–1970.
[3] Excludes fetal deaths.
[4] Includes reported annulments.
[5] Based on 20- to 50-percent sample.
[6] Includes Alaska.

Series B 5–10. Birth Rate—Total and for Women 15–44 Years Old, by Race: 1800 to 1970

[Based on estimated total live births per 1,000 population for specified group. Based on a 50-percent sample of births for 1951–1954, 1956–1966, and 1968–1970; on 20- to 50-percent sample for 1967. Prior to 1959, births adjusted for underregistration; thereafter, registered live births]

Year	Rate, total population — Total (5)	White (6)	Negro and other (7)	Rate, women 15–44 years [1] — Total (8)	White (9)	Negro and other (10)	Year	Rate, total population — Total (5)	White (6)	Negro and other (7)	Rate, women 15–44 years [1] — Total (8)	White (9)	Negro and other (10)
1970	18.4	17.4	25.1	87.9	84.1	113.0	1932	19.5	18.7	26.9	81.7	79.0	103.0
1969	17.8	16.9	24.4	86.5	82.4	114.8	1931	20.2	19.5	26.6	84.6	82.4	102.1
1968	17.5	16.6	24.2	85.7	81.5	114.9							
1967 [2]	17.8	16.8	25.0	87.6	83.1	119.8	1930	21.3	20.6	27.5	89.2	87.1	105.9
1966	18.4	17.4	26.1	91.3	86.4	125.9	1929	21.2	20.5	27.3	89.3	87.3	106.1
							1928	22.2	21.5	28.5	93.8	91.7	111.0
1965	19.4	18.3	27.6	96.6	91.4	133.9	1927	23.5	22.7	31.1	99.8	97.1	121.7
1964	21.0	20.0	29.1	105.0	99.9	141.7	1926	24.2	23.1	33.4	102.6	99.2	130.3
1963 [3]	21.7	20.7	29.7	108.5	103.7	144.9							
1962 [3]	22.4	21.4	30.5	112.2	107.5	148.8	1925	25.1	24.1	34.2	106.6	103.3	134.0
1961	23.3	22.2	31.6	117.2	112.2	153.5	1924	26.1	25.1	34.6	110.9	107.8	135.6
							1923	26.0	25.2	33.2	110.5	108.0	130.5
1960 *	23.7	22.7	32.1	118.0	113.2	153.6	1922	26.2	25.4	33.2	111.2	108.8	130.8
1959 [4]	24.0	22.9	32.9	118.8	113.9	156.0	1921	28.1	27.3	35.8	119.8	117.2	140.8
1958	24.5	23.3	34.3	120.2	114.9	160.5							
1957	25.3	24.0	35.3	122.9	117.7	163.0	1920	27.7	26.9	35.0	117.9	115.4	137.5
1956	25.2	24.0	35.4	121.2	116.0	160.9	1919	26.1	25.3	32.4	111.2	(NA)	---------
							1918	28.2	27.6	33.0	119.8	(NA)	---------
1955	25.0	23.8	34.7	118.5	113.8	155.3	1917	28.5	27.9	32.9	121.0	(NA)	---------
1954	25.3	24.2	34.9	118.1	113.6	153.2	1916	29.1	28.5	---------	123.4	121.8	---------
1953	25.0	24.0	34.1	115.2	111.0	147.3							
1952	25.1	24.1	33.6	113.9	110.1	143.3	1915	29.5	28.9	---------	125.0	123.2	---------
1951	24.9	23.9	33.8	111.5	107.7	142.1	1914	29.9	29.3	---------	126.6	124.6	---------
							1913	29.5	28.8	---------	124.7	122.4	---------
1950	24.1	23.0	33.3	106.2	102.3	137.3	1912	29.8	29.0	---------	125.8	123.3	---------
1949	24.5	23.6	33.0	107.1	103.6	135.1	1911	29.9	29.1	---------	126.3	123.6	---------
1948	24.9	24.0	32.4	107.3	104.3	131.6							
1947	26.6	26.1	31.2	113.3	111.8	125.9	1910	30.1	29.2	---------	126.8	123.8	---------
1946	24.1	23.6	38.4	101.9	100.4	113.9	1909	30.0	29.2	---------	126.8	123.6	---------
							1900	32.3	30.1	---------	---------	130	---------
1945	20.4	19.7	26.5	85.9	83.4	106.0	1890	(NA)	31.5	---------	---------	137	---------
1944	21.2	20.5	27.4	88.8	86.3	108.5	1880	39.8	35.2	---------	---------	155	---------
1943	22.7	22.1	28.3	94.3	92.3	111.0							
1942	22.2	21.5	27.7	91.5	89.5	107.6	1870	(NA)	38.3	---------	---------	167	---------
1941	20.3	19.5	27.3	83.4	80.7	105.4	1860	44.3	41.4	---------	---------	184	---------
							1850	(NA)	43.3	---------	---------	194	---------
1940	19.4	18.6	26.7	79.9	77.1	102.4	1840	51.8	48.3	---------	---------	222	---------
1939	18.8	18.0	26.1	77.6	74.8	100.1							
1938	19.2	18.4	26.3	79.1	76.5	100.5	1830	(NA)	51.4	---------	---------	240	---------
1937	18.7	17.9	26.0	77.1	74.4	99.4	1820	55.2	52.8	---------	---------	260	---------
1936	18.4	17.6	25.1	75.8	73.3	95.9	1810		54.3	---------	---------	274	---------
							1800		55.0	---------	---------	278	---------
1935	18.7	17.9	25.8	77.2	74.5	98.4							
1934	19.0	18.1	26.3	78.5	75.8	100.4							
1933	18.4	17.6	25.5	76.3	73.7	97.3							

* Denotes first year for which figures include Alaska and Hawaii.
NA Not available.
[1] Computed by relating total births, regardless of age of mother, to women aged 15–44 years.
[2] Based on 20- to 50-percent sample of births.
[3] Figures by race exclude New Jersey; State did not require reporting of race.
[4] Includes Alaska.

Series B 11–19. Fertility Rate and Birth Rate, by Age of Mother, by Race: 1940 to 1970

[Total fertility rates are the sums of birth rates, by age of mother, multiplied by 5.   Birth rates are live births per 1,000 women in specified group.   Prior to 1959, births adjusted for underregistration; thereafter, registered live births.   Based on 50-percent sample of births for 1951–1954, 1956–1966, and 1968–1970; on 20- to 50-percent sample for 1967]

Year and race	Total fertility rate	Birth rate, by age of mother							
		10–14 years	15–19 years	20–24 years	25–29 years	30–34 years	35–39 years	40–44 years	45–49 years
	11	12	13	14	15	16	17	18	19
TOTAL									
1970	2,480	1.2	68.3	167.8	145.1	73.3	31.7	8.1	0.5
1969	2,465	1.0	66.1	166.0	143.0	74.1	33.4	8.8	.5
1968	2,477	1.0	66.1	167.4	140.3	74.9	35.6	9.6	.6
1967	2,573	.9	67.9	174.0	142.6	79.3	38.5	10.6	.7
1966	2,736	.9	70.6	185.9	149.4	85.9	42.2	11.7	.7
1965	2,928	.8	70.4	196.8	162.5	95.0	46.4	12.8	.8
1964	3,208	.9	72.8	219.9	179.4	103.9	50.0	13.8	.8
1963	3,333	.9	76.4	231.2	185.8	106.2	51.3	14.2	.9
1962	3,474	.8	81.2	243.7	191.7	108.9	52.7	14.8	.9
1961	3,629	.9	88.0	253.7	197.9	113.3	55.6	15.6	.9
1960	3,654	.8	89.1	258.1	197.4	112.7	56.2	15.5	.9
1959	3,670	.9	89.1	257.5	198.6	114.4	57.3	15.3	.9
1958	3,701	.9	91.4	258.2	198.3	116.2	58.3	15.7	.9
1957	3,767	1.0	96.3	260.6	199.4	118.9	59.9	16.3	1.1
1956	3,689	1.0	94.6	253.7	194.7	117.3	59.3	16.3	1.0
1955	3,580	.9	90.5	242.0	190.5	116.2	58.7	16.1	1.0
1954	3,543	.9	90.6	236.2	188.4	116.9	57.9	16.2	1.0
1953	3,424	1.0	88.2	224.6	184.1	113.4	56.6	15.8	1.0
1952	3,358	.9	86.1	217.6	182.0	112.6	55.8	15.5	1.3
1951	3,269	.9	87.6	211.6	175.3	107.9	54.1	15.4	1.1
1950	3,091	1.0	81.6	196.6	166.1	103.7	52.9	15.1	1.2
1949	3,110	1.0	83.4	200.1	165.4	102.1	53.5	15.3	1.3
1948	3,109	1.0	81.8	200.3	163.4	103.7	54.5	15.7	1.3
1947	3,274	.9	79.3	209.7	176.0	111.9	58.9	16.6	1.4
1946	2,943	.7	59.3	181.8	161.2	108.9	58.7	16.5	1.5
1945	2,491	.8	51.1	138.9	132.2	100.2	56.9	16.6	1.6
1944	2,568	.8	54.3	151.8	136.5	98.1	54.6	16.1	1.4
1943	2,718	.8	61.7	164.0	147.8	99.5	52.8	15.7	1.5
1942	2,628	.7	61.1	165.1	142.7	91.8	47.9	14.7	1.6
1941	2,399	.7	56.9	145.4	128.7	85.3	46.1	15.0	1.7
1940	2,301	.7	54.1	135.6	122.8	83.4	46.3	15.6	1.9
WHITE									
1970	2,385	.5	57.4	163.4	145.9	71.9	30.0	7.5	.4
1969	2,360	.4	55.2	161.4	142.8	72.0	31.6	8.1	.5
1968	2,368	.4	55.3	162.6	139.7	72.5	33.8	8.9	.5
1967	2,453	.3	57.3	168.8	140.7	76.5	36.6	9.8	.6
1966	2,609	.3	60.8	179.9	146.6	82.7	40.0	10.8	.7
1965	2,790	.3	60.7	189.8	158.8	91.7	44.1	12.0	.7
1964	3,074	.3	63.2	213.1	176.2	100.5	47.7	13.0	.7
1963 [1]	3,201	.3	68.1	224.7	181.5	102.6	48.9	13.4	.8
1962 [1]	3,348	.4	73.1	238.0	187.7	105.2	50.2	14.1	.8
1961	3,502	.4	78.8	247.9	194.4	110.1	53.2	14.8	.9
1960	3,533	.4	79.4	252.8	194.9	109.6	54.0	14.7	.8
1959	3,544	.4	79.2	251.7	195.5	111.3	55.1	14.7	.9
1958	3,560	.5	81.0	251.4	194.8	113.0	55.8	14.8	.8
1957	3,625	.5	85.2	253.8	195.8	115.9	57.4	15.4	.8
1956	3,546	.3	83.2	247.1	190.6	114.4	57.0	15.4	.8
1955	3,446	.3	79.2	236.0	186.8	114.1	56.7	15.4	.9
1954	3,415	.4	79.0	230.7	185.0	115.1	56.2	15.4	.9
1953	3,306	.4	77.2	219.6	181.5	111.9	55.1	15.0	.9
1952	3,250	.4	75.0	212.5	180.5	111.4	54.4	14.8	.9
1951	3,157	.4	75.9	206.0	174.2	106.5	52.6	14.6	1.0
1950	2,977	.4	70.0	190.4	165.1	102.6	51.4	14.5	1.0
1949	3,009	.4	72.1	194.6	165.2	101.5	52.2	14.6	1.1
1948	3,022	.4	71.1	195.5	163.9	103.6	53.5	15.2	1.1
1947	3,230	.4	69.8	207.9	179.1	113.0	58.4	16.1	1.2
1946	2,901	.3	50.6	179.8	164.0	110.0	58.4	15.9	1.3
1945	2,421	.3	42.1	134.7	133.1	100.5	56.3	16.0	1.4
1944	2,501	.3	45.3	147.9	137.7	98.2	54.1	15.5	1.2
1943	2,664	.3	52.1	161.1	150.7	100.2	52.2	15.0	1.3
1942	2,577	.3	51.8	162.9	145.6	92.3	47.2	14.1	1.3
1941	2,328	.2	47.6	141.6	130.1	85.2	45.1	14.3	1.4
1940	2,229	.2	45.3	131.4	123.6	83.4	45.3	15.0	1.6
NEGRO AND OTHER									
1970	3,067	4.8	133.4	196.8	140.1	82.5	42.2	12.6	.9
1969	3,148	4.6	133.3	197.8	144.2	88.9	45.9	13.9	1.0
1968	3,197	4.4	133.3	200.8	144.8	91.2	48.6	15.0	1.2
1967	3,385	4.1	135.2	212.1	155.9	99.1	52.4	16.8	1.2
1966	3,615	4.0	135.5	228.9	169.3	107.9	57.7	18.4	1.4
1965	3,891	4.0	136.1	247.3	188.1	118.3	63.8	19.2	1.5
1964	4,153	4.0	138.7	268.6	202.0	127.5	67.5	20.9	1.5
1963 [1]	4,269	4.0	139.9	277.3	211.8	129.3	68.9	21.0	1.5
1962 [1]	4,396	3.9	144.6	285.7	217.4	132.4	72.0	21.7	1.5
1961	4,533	4.0	152.8	292.9	221.9	136.2	74.9	22.3	1.5

[1] Excludes New Jersey; State did not require reporting of race.

Series **B 11–19.** Fertility Rate and Birth Rate, by Age of Mother, by Race: 1940 to 1970—Con.

Year and race	Total fertility rate	Birth rate, by age of mother							
		10–14 years	15–19 years	20–24 years	25–29 years	30–34 years	35–39 years	40–44 years	45–49 years
	11	**12**	**13**	**14**	**15**	**16**	**17**	**18**	**19**
NEGRO AND OTHER—Con.									
1960	4,522	4.0	158.2	294.2	214.6	135.6	74.2	22.0	1.7
1959	4,595	4.2	160.5	297.9	220.2	138.1	75.0	21.2	1.8
1958	4,727	4.3	167.3	305.2	224.2	142.3	78.4	21.8	1.9
1957	4,798	5.6	172.8	307.0	228.1	143.5	78.7	23.5	2.0
1956	4,730	4.7	172.5	299.1	225.9	139.4	78.8	23.6	2.0
1955	4,550	4.8	168.3	283.4	219.6	133.5	75.4	22.1	2.1
1954	4,474	4.9	170.3	274.7	215.7	131.3	72.9	22.5	2.1
1953	4,283	5.1	165.4	261.4	206.4	125.7	70.0	23.0	2.2
1952	4,147	5.2	162.9	254.0	194.2	122.0	66.6	21.9	2.2
1951	4,091	5.4	166.7	252.5	184.2	117.9	66.5	22.6	2.2
1950	3,928	5.1	163.5	242.6	173.8	112.6	64.3	21.2	2.6
1949	3,855	5.1	162.8	241.3	167.0	107.3	63.9	21.1	2.5
1948	3,742	4.9	157.3	237.0	159.6	104.1	62.5	20.4	2.8
1947	3,575	4.6	146.6	223.7	150.6	102.4	62.7	21.4	3.1
1946	3,238	3.7	121.9	197.3	139.2	99.3	61.0	21.8	3.5
1945	3,017	3.9	117.5	172.1	125.4	97.1	61.3	22.3	3.7
1944	3,075	3.9	121.5	182.4	126.8	97.3	58.4	21.5	3.2
1943	3,128	4.0	133.4	187.2	125.1	93.9	56.9	21.5	3.7
1942	3,022	3.9	131.8	182.3	119.6	88.1	54.0	20.8	4.0
1941	2,956	4.0	128.3	175.0	118.1	86.2	54.1	21.5	4.1
1940	2,870	3.7	121.7	168.5	116.3	83.5	53.7	21.5	5.2

Series **B 20–27.**   Birth Rate, by Race, by Live-Birth Order: 1940 to 1970

[Rates are live births per 1,000 women aged 15–44 years in specified race group. Live-birth order refers to number of children born alive to mother. Prior to 1959, births adjusted for underregistration; thereafter, registered live births. Figures for not stated birth order have been distributed. Based on 50-percent sample of births for 1951–1954, 1956–1966, and 1968–1970; on 20- to 50-percent sample for 1967]

Year and race	Total	Birth rate, by live-birth order							Year and race	Total	Birth rate, by live-birth order						
		1st	2d	3d	4th	5th	6th and 7th	8th and over			1st	2d	3d	4th	5th	6th and 7th	8th and over
	20	**21**	**22**	**23**	**24**	**25**	**26**	**27**		**20**	**21**	**22**	**23**	**24**	**25**	**26**	**27**
TOTAL									WHITE								
1970	87.9	34.1	24.2	13.7	7.2	3.8	3.2	1.8	1970	84.1	32.8	23.7	13.3	6.8	3.4	2.7	1.2
1969	86.5	32.8	23.4	13.4	7.4	4.0	3.5	2.0	1969	82.4	31.5	22.9	13.1	7.0	3.6	2.9	1.4
1968	85.7	32.1	22.5	13.2	7.5	4.2	3.9	2.3	1968	81.5	30.9	22.1	12.8	7.1	3.8	3.2	1.6
1967	87.6	30.8	22.6	13.9	8.3	4.8	4.5	2.7	1967	83.1	29.7	22.1	13.5	7.9	4.3	3.7	1.8
1966	91.3	31.0	22.5	14.8	9.2	5.4	5.2	3.2	1966	86.4	30.1	22.0	14.4	8.7	4.9	4.3	2.1
1965	96.6	29.8	23.4	16.6	10.7	6.4	6.0	3.7	1965	91.4	28.9	23.0	16.2	10.2	5.8	5.0	2.4
1964	105.0	30.4	25.1	18.8	12.3	7.3	6.9	4.1	1964	99.9	29.8	24.8	18.5	11.7	6.7	5.7	2.7
1963	108.5	29.9	26.1	19.9	13.1	7.8	7.3	4.3	1963 [1]	103.7	29.4	25.9	19.6	12.6	7.1	6.1	2.9
1962	112.2	30.1	27.0	21.1	13.8	8.2	7.5	4.4	1962 [1]	107.5	29.8	26.9	20.9	13.3	7.5	6.2	2.9
1961	117.2	31.1	28.4	22.4	14.6	8.5	7.8	4.5	1961	112.2	30.7	28.3	22.2	14.0	7.7	6.4	2.9
1960 *	118.0	31.1	29.2	22.8	14.6	8.3	7.6	4.3	1960 *	113.2	30.8	29.2	22.7	14.1	7.5	6.1	2.8
1959	118.8	31.5	29.9	23.0	14.5	8.2	7.4	4.2	1959	113.9	31.2	29.9	22.9	13.9	7.3	5.9	2.8
1958	120.2	32.2	30.6	23.3	14.4	8.1	7.3	4.2	1958	114.9	31.9	30.6	23.1	13.8	7.2	5.7	2.7
1957	122.9	33.7	31.7	23.9	14.4	7.9	7.1	4.2	1957	117.7	33.4	31.7	23.7	13.7	7.0	5.6	2.7
1956	121.2	33.5	31.9	23.6	13.9	7.6	6.8	4.0	1956	116.0	33.2	31.9	23.4	13.1	6.6	5.2	2.6
1955	118.5	32.9	31.9	23.1	13.3	7.2	6.4	3.8	1955	113.8	32.6	32.0	22.9	12.6	6.2	4.9	2.5
1954	118.1	33.6	32.4	22.7	12.8	6.8	6.0	3.8	1954	113.6	33.3	32.8	22.6	12.0	5.9	4.6	2.5
1953	115.2	33.4	32.5	21.9	12.0	6.3	5.5	3.6	1953	111.0	33.3	32.9	21.6	11.1	5.4	4.3	2.5
1952	113.9	34.0	32.7	21.3	11.3	5.8	5.2	3.6	1952	110.0	34.1	33.1	21.0	10.4	5.0	4.0	2.5
1951	111.5	34.9	32.6	20.0	10.2	5.3	5.0	3.6	1951	107.7	35.0	32.9	19.5	9.4	4.5	3.9	2.5
1950	106.2	33.3	32.1	18.4	9.2	4.8	4.7	3.6	1950	102.3	33.3	32.3	17.9	8.4	4.1	3.7	2.5
1949	107.1	36.2	32.1	17.1	8.6	4.7	4.7	3.7	1949	103.6	36.3	32.2	16.6	7.9	4.0	3.8	2.7
1948	107.3	39.6	30.9	16.1	8.0	4.5	4.6	3.6	1948	104.3	39.9	31.1	15.7	7.4	3.9	3.7	2.6
1947	113.3	46.7	30.3	15.6	7.9	4.5	4.6	3.7	1947	111.8	47.8	30.8	15.3	7.4	4.0	3.8	2.7
1946	101.9	38.5	27.9	14.5	7.8	4.5	4.7	3.8	1946	100.4	39.5	28.5	14.4	7.3	4.0	3.9	2.8
1945	85.9	28.9	22.9	13.4	7.5	4.5	4.8	4.0	1945	83.4	29.0	23.3	13.2	7.0	3.9	4.0	3.0
1944	88.8	30.2	23.8	13.8	7.6	4.5	4.9	4.0	1944	86.3	30.4	24.2	13.6	7.1	4.0	4.1	3.1
1943	94.3	34.7	25.5	13.5	7.4	4.4	4.8	4.0	1943	92.3	35.2	25.9	13.2	6.9	3.9	4.0	3.1
1942	91.5	37.5	22.9	11.9	6.6	4.1	4.6	3.9	1942	89.5	38.3	23.1	11.5	6.1	3.6	3.8	3.1
1941	83.4	32.2	20.7	11.2	6.4	4.1	4.7	4.1	1941	80.7	32.5	20.7	10.7	5.9	3.6	3.9	3.2
1940	79.9	29.3	20.0	10.9	6.4	4.1	4.8	4.3	1940	77.1	29.4	20.0	10.5	5.9	3.6	4.1	3.5

See footnotes at end of table.

Series **B 20–27**. Birth Rate, by Race, by Live-Birth Order: 1940 to 1970—Con.

Year and race	Total	1st	2d	3d	4th	5th	6th and 7th	8th and over	Year and race	Total	1st	2d	3d	4th	5th	6th and 7th	8th and over
	20	21	22	23	24	25	26	27		20	21	22	23	24	25	26	27
NEGRO AND OTHER									**NEGRO AND OTHER—Con.**								
1970	113.0	42.4	26.9	15.9	9.7	6.2	6.7	5.3	1955	155.3	35.0	30.7	24.4	19.1	14.6	17.4	14.1
1969	114.8	42.2	26.4	15.9	10.1	6.6	7.4	6.3	1954	153.2	35.6	29.7	24.4	19.1	14.2	16.5	13.5
1968	114.9	40.6	25.3	15.7	10.4	7.0	8.5	7.4	1953	147.2	34.1	29.5	23.8	18.4	13.3	15.4	12.8
1967	119.8	38.4	25.9	16.8	11.5	8.1	10.1	9.0	1952	143.3	33.1	29.2	24.0	18.1	12.4	14.2	12.4
1966	125.9	37.4	26.0	18.0	12.8	9.4	11.6	10.7	1951	142.1	34.1	29.9	23.9	16.9	11.2	13.5	12.2
1965	133.9	35.8	26.6	19.6	14.6	10.8	13.8	12.6	1950	137.3	33.8	30.3	22.9	15.3	10.4	12.6	12.0
1964	141.7	34.8	27.4	21.1	16.0	12.1	15.8	14.4	1949	135.1	35.4	30.8	21.2	14.0	9.8	12.2	11.8
1963[1]	144.9	33.8	27.6	21.8	16.9	13.1	16.6	15.1	1948	131.6	37.3	29.5	19.4	12.9	9.2	11.7	11.6
1962[1]	148.8	33.1	28.0	22.8	17.8	13.7	17.6	15.7	1947	125.9	38.4	26.2	17.3	12.1	8.8	11.4	11.6
1961	153.5	33.6	28.8	23.7	18.8	14.1	18.4	16.0	1946	113.9	31.1	23.4	16.0	11.8	8.7	11.3	11.7
1960*	153.6	33.6	29.3	24.0	18.6	14.1	18.4	15.6	1945	106.0	27.9	20.1	14.7	11.3	8.7	11.3	11.9
1959	156.0	33.9	29.8	24.4	19.1	14.5	18.7	15.6	1944	108.5	28.7	21.1	15.6	11.7	8.6	11.3	11.6
1958	160.5	34.7	31.0	25.4	19.5	14.9	19.1	15.9	1943	111.0	31.0	22.2	15.5	11.4	8.4	11.0	11.6
1957	163.0	36.1	31.6	25.7	19.8	15.3	19.0	15.6	1942	107.6	31.0	21.1	14.9	10.8	8.1	10.5	11.1
1956	160.9	35.9	31.7	25.2	19.7	15.0	18.7	15.0	1941	105.4	29.8	20.6	14.5	10.6	8.0	10.6	11.3
									1940	102.4	28.6	19.6	14.1	10.5	7.8	10.4	11.3

* Denotes first year for which figures includes Alaska and Hawaii.   [1] Excludes New Jersey; State did not require reporting of race.

Series **B 28–35**.   Illegitimate Live Births and Birth Rates, by Age and Race of Mother: 1940 to 1970

[Refers only to illegitimate births occurring within the United States.   Rates are illegitimate live births per 1,000 unmarried females in specified group.   Figures for age of mother not stated are distributed.   Based on 50-percent sample of births for 1951–1954, 1956–1966, and 1968–1970; on 20- to 50-percent sample for 1967]

Year and race	Births (1,000)	Rate, all ages[1]	15–19 years	20–24 years	25–29 years	30–34 years	35–39 years	40–44 years	Year and race	Births (1,000)	Rate, all ages[1]	15–19 years	20–24 years	25–29 years	30–34 years	35–44 years
	28	29	30	31	32	33	34	35		28	29	30	31	32	33	34–35
TOTAL									**WHITE—Con.**							
1970	399	26.4	22.4	38.4	37.1	27.0	13.3	3.6	1967	142	12.5	9.0	23.1	22.7	14.0	4.7
1969	361	25.0	20.6	37.4	38.1	27.4	13.6	3.6	1966	133	12.0	8.5	22.5	23.5	15.7	4.9
1968	339	24.4	19.8	37.3	38.6	28.2	14.9	3.8	1965	124	11.6	7.9	22.1	24.3	16.6	4.9
1967	318	23.9	18.6	38.3	41.4	29.2	15.4	4.0	1964	114	11.0	7.3	21.2	24.1	15.9	4.8
1966	302	23.4	17.5	39.1	45.6	33.0	16.4	4.1	1963[4]	102	10.5	7.0	20.8	22.0	14.2	4.6
1965	291	23.5	16.7	39.9	49.3	37.5	17.4	4.5	1962[4]	93	9.8	6.5	20.0	19.8	12.6	4.3
1964	276	23.0	15.8	39.9	50.2	37.2	16.3	4.4	1961	91	10.0	7.0	19.7	19.4	11.3	4.2
1963	259	22.5	15.2	40.3	49.0	33.2	16.1	4.3	1960*	83	9.2	6.6	18.2	18.2	10.8	3.9
1962	245	21.9	14.8	40.9	46.7	29.7	15.6	4.0	1959[3]	80	9.2	6.5	18.3	17.6	10.7	3.6
1961	240	22.7	15.9	41.7	46.5	28.3	15.4	3.9	1958	75	8.8	6.3	17.3	15.8	10.8	3.4
1960*	224	21.6	15.3	39.7	45.1	27.8	14.1	3.6	1957	71	8.6	6.4	16.6	14.6	10.5	3.0
1959[3]	221	21.9	15.5	40.2	44.1	28.1	14.1	3.3	1956	68	8.3	6.2	16.3	14.0	9.2	3.0
1958	209	21.2	15.3	38.2	40.5	27.5	13.3	3.2	1955	64	7.9	6.0	15.0	13.3	8.6	2.8
1957	202	21.0	15.8	37.3	36.8	26.8	12.1	3.1	1950	54	6.1	5.1	10.0	8.7	5.9	2.0
1956	194	20.4	15.6	36.4	35.6	24.6	11.1	2.8	1940	40	3.6	3.3	5.7	4.0	2.5	1.2
1955	183	19.3	15.1	33.5	33.5	22.0	10.5	2.7	**NEGRO AND OTHER**							
1954	177	18.7	14.9	31.4	31.0	20.4	10.3	2.5	1970	224	89.9	90.8	120.9	93.7	69.9	21.6
1953	161	16.9	13.9	28.0	27.6	17.3	9.0	2.4	1969	197	86.6	85.6	116.6	98.0	73.5	22.3
1952	150	15.8	13.5	25.4	24.8	15.7	8.2	1.9	1968	184	86.6	82.8	118.3	104.4	80.6	25.2
1951	147	15.1	13.2	23.2	22.8	14.6	7.6	2.2	1967	176	89.5	80.2	128.2	118.4	97.2	28.9
1950	142	14.1	12.6	21.3	19.9	13.3	7.2	2.0	1966	170	92.8	76.9	139.4	143.8	119.4	33.8
1949	133	13.3	12.0	21.0	18.0	11.4	6.8	1.9	1965	168	97.6	75.8	152.6	164.7	137.8	39.0
1948	130	12.5	11.4	19.8	16.4	10.0	5.8	1.6	1964	161	97.2	74.0	164.2	168.7	132.3	34.5
1947	132	12.1	11.0	18.9	15.7	9.2	5.6	1.8	1963[4]	151	97.1	73.8	161.8	171.5	124.3	34.4
1946	125	10.9	9.5	17.3	15.6	7.3	4.4	1.8	1962[4]	147	97.5	74.1	163.6	172.7	115.2	35.5
1945	117	101.1	9.5	15.3	12.1	7.1	4.1	1.6	1961	149	100.8	77.6	169.6	172.7	112.0	37.4
1944	105	9.0	8.8	13.1	10.1	7.0	4.0	1.3	1960*	142	98.3	76.5	166.5	171.8	104.0	35.6
1943	98	8.3	8.4	11.4	8.8	6.7	3.8	1.3	1959[3]	141	100.8	80.8	167.8	168.0	106.5	34.9
1942	97	8.0	8.2	11.0	8.4	6.3	3.8	1.2	1958	134	97.8	80.4	153.2	161.2	110.5	32.5
1941	96	7.8	8.0	10.5	7.8	6.0	3.7	1.4	1957	131	95.3	81.4	147.7	142.6	115.1	30.3
1940	90	7.1	7.4	9.5	7.2	5.1	3.4	1.2	1956	126	92.1	79.6	143.5	132.7	113.7	27.0
WHITE									1955	119	87.2	77.6	133.0	125.2	100.9	25.3
1970	175	13.8	10.9	22.5	21.1	14.2		4.4	1950	88	71.2	68.5	105.4	94.2	63.5	20.0
1969	164	13.5	10.0	23.0	22.4	15.1		4.4	1940	49	35.6	42.5	46.1	32.5	23.4	9.3
1968	155	13.2	9.8	23.1	22.1	15.1		4.7								

* Denotes first year for which figures include Alaska and Hawaii.   [3] Includes Alaska.
[1] Rates computed by relating total illegitimate births regardless of age of mother to women aged 15–44 years.   [4] Excludes New Jersey; State did not require reporting of race.
[2] Rates for total computed by relating illegitimate births to mothers aged 40 and over to unmarried women aged 40–44 years.   Rates for race detail computed by relating births to mothers aged 35 and over to women aged 35–44 years.

Series B 36–41. Gross and Net Reproduction Rates, by Race: 1905–10 to 1970

[Based on 50-percent sample of estimated total live births for 1951–1954, 1956–1966, and 1968–1970; on 20- to 50-percent sample for 1967]

Year	Gross reproduction rate			Net reproduction rate			Year or period	Gross reproduction rate			Net reproduction rate		
	Total	White	Negro and other	Total	White	Negro and other		Total	White	Negro and other	Total	White	Negro and other
	36	37	38	39	40	41		36	37	38	39	40	41
1970	1,207	1,158	1,509	1,168	1,125	1,433	1952	1,637	1,579	2,062	1,563	1,516	1,897
1969	1,201	1,147	1,554	1,161	1,113	1,473	1951	1,593	1,534	2,027	1,521	1,472	1,865
1968	1,206	1,151	1,577	1,166	1,116	1,495							
1967	1,255	1,193	1,676	1,213	1,158	1,582	1950	1,505	1,446	1,940	1,435	1,387	1,780
1966	1,336	1,271	1,785	1,288	1,231	1,678	1949	1,515	1,462	1,906	1,439	1,397	1,743
							1948	1,514	1,469	1,845	1,430	1,400	1,679
1965	1,428	1,357	1,919	1,376	1,314	1,802	1947	1,593	1,568	1,766	1,505	1,492	1,594
1964	1,564	1,495	2,051	1,507	1,447	1,923	1946	1,430	1,406	1,600	1,344	1,331	1,435
1963 ¹	1,623	1,556	2,102	1,564	1,506	1,973							
1962 ¹	1,695	1,630	2,170	1,633	1,577	2,033	1945	1,212	1,175	1,493	1,132	1,106	1,323
1961	1,770	1,704	2,240	1,704	1,648	2,100	1944	1,249	1,214	1,520	1,163	1,139	1,334
							1943	1,323	1,294	1,543	1,228	1,211	1,348
1960 *	1,783	1,720	2,241	1,715	1,662	2,093	1942	1,277	1,250	1,487	1,185	1,171	1,293
1959 ²	1,791	1,725	2,271	1,722	1,667	2,118	1941	1,168	1,131	1,458	1,075	1,052	1,242
1958	1,807	1,735	2,339	1,736	1,675	2,178							
1957	1,837	1,764	2,371	1,765	1,701	2,206	1940	1,121	1,082	1,422	1,027	1,002	1,209
1956	1,798	1,724	2,339	1,729	1,665	2,184	1935	1,091	1,059	1,350	975	958	1,108
							1935–40	1,101	1,063	1,413	978	957	1,137
1955	1,745	1,675	2,255	1,676	1,617	2,101	1930–35	1,108	1,080	1,336	984	972	1,074
1954	1,727	1,660	2,216	1,657	1,601	2,062	1905–10	1,793	1,740	2,240	1,336	1,339	1,329
1953	1,668	1,607	2,118	1,597	1,546	1,959							

* Denotes first year for which figures include Alaska and Hawaii.   ² Includes Alaska.
¹ Excludes New Jersey; State did not require reporting of race.

Series B 42–48. Percent Distribution of Ever-Married Women (Survivors of Birth Cohorts of 1835–39 to 1920–24) by Race and by Number of Children Ever Born, as Reported in Censuses of 1910, 1940, 1950, 1960, and 1970

Year of birth of women	Census year	Age of women reporting (years)	Percent of women, by number of births						Children per 1,000 women	Year of birth of women	Census year	Age of women reporting (years)	Percent of women, by number of births						Children per 1,000 women
			None	1 and 2	3 and 4	5 and 6	7 to 9	10 or more					None	1 and 2	3 and 4	5 and 6	7 to 9	10 or more	
			42	43	44	45	46	47	48				42	43	44	45	46	47	48
TOTAL										**WHITE—Con.**									
1920–24	1970	45–49	10.6	39.9	32.8	10.7	4.5	1.5	2,701	1870–74	1940	65–69	15.7	28.3	25.0	14.6	11.2	5.2	3,558
1915–19	1970	50–54	13.8	43.1	28.9	8.8	3.9	1.4	2,854	1865–69	1940	70–74	14.3	26.6	25.7	15.7	11.8	5.8	3,741
1910–14	1960*	45–49	18.1	44.2	24.7	7.8	3.8	1.5	2,402	1860–64	1910	45–49	9.6	22.9	22.7	17.7	17.4	9.8	4,594
1905–09	1960*	50–54	20.8	43.2	22.3	7.8	4.2	1.7	2,355	1855–59	1910	50–54	9.0	20.9	22.0	18.3	19.0	10.8	4,817
1900–04	1950	45–49	20.4	41.5	22.4	8.4	5.0	2.2	2,492	1850–54	1910	55–59	8.4	19.1	21.3	18.2	20.5	12.5	5,082
1895–99	1950	50–54	18.6	39.0	23.9	10.0	5.8	2.6	2,706	1845–49	1910	60–64	8.3	18.8	20.8	18.7	20.9	12.6	5,123
1890–94	1940	45–49	16.8	35.3	25.0	12.2	7.7	3.1	2,998	1840–44	1910	65–69	8.0	18.2	20.6	18.5	21.7	13.0	5,237
1885–89	1940	50–54	16.6	33.1	25.1	13.1	8.6	3.6	3,146	1835–39	1910	70–74	7.9	17.5	20.3	19.1	21.8	13.4	5,278
1880–84	1940	55–59	16.7	30.7	24.7	14.1	9.6	4.2	3,301	**NEGRO**									
1875–79	1940	60–64	15.0	30.5	25.2	14.4	10.3	4.7	3,462	1920–24	1970	45–49	17.9	31.3	21.4	13.1	10.5	5.8	3,394
1870–74	1940	65–69	13.9	28.4	25.1	15.2	11.6	5.8	3,700	1915–19	1970	50–54	23.0	33.0	18.9	10.9	8.8	5.4	3,030
1865–69	1940	70–74	12.3	26.6	26.1	16.0	12.5	6.4	3,901	1910–14	1960*	45–49	27.9	33.2	16.9	8.9	7.8	5.2	2,761
1860–64	1910	45–49	9.5	22.4	22.0	17.3	17.6	11.2	4,744	1905–09	1960*	50–54	28.5	34.0	16.0	8.9	7.6	5.0	2,696
1855–59	1910	50–54	8.9	20.6	21.3	17.9	19.0	12.3	4,972	1900–04	1950	45–49	28.4	31.9	17.6	9.2	8.0	4.9	2,767
1850–54	1910	55–59	8.3	18.8	20.8	17.8	20.4	13.9	5,218	1895–99	1950	50–54	25.5	30.9	17.4	10.9	8.8	6.5	3,085
1845–49	1910	60–64	8.2	18.5	20.3	18.3	20.8	14.0	5,266	1890–94	1940	45–49	23.8	28.1	19.5	12.6	9.9	6.1	3,255
1840–44	1910	65–69	7.9	17.9	20.1	18.1	21.6	14.3	5,364	1885–89	1940	50–54	20.1	25.6	22.1	14.2	10.7	7.3	3,594
1835–39	1910	70–74	7.7	17.3	20.0	18.7	21.6	14.7	5,395	1880–84	1940	55–59	19.3	25.5	21.4	14.1	10.9	8.8	3,751
WHITE										1875–79	1940	60–64	17.0	23.0	21.3	16.5	13.0	9.2	4,046
1920–24	1970	45–49	9.9	40.9	33.9	10.5	3.8	1.0	2,791	1870–74	1940	65–69	14.5	22.1	20.9	17.5	14.1	11.0	4,347
1915–19	1970	50–54	12.9	44.3	29.9	8.6	3.3	1.0	2,553	1865–69	1940	70–74	12.8	18.1	22.6	15.1	17.6	13.8	4,892
1910–14	1960*	45–49	17.1	45.4	25.6	7.6	3.3	1.1	2,354	1860–64	1910	45–49	8.6	17.9	15.5	13.8	18.7	25.5	6,162
1905–09	1960*	50–54	20.0	44.3	23.0	7.6	3.8	1.4	2,313	1855–59	1910	50–54	7.8	16.4	14.0	13.6	19.5	28.7	6,580
1900–04	1950	45–49	19.5	42.7	23.0	8.3	4.6	1.9	2,456	1850–54	1910	55–59	7.2	16.1	14.5	12.7	18.7	30.8	6,910
1895–99	1950	50–54	18.0	39.9	24.5	10.0	5.4	2.3	2,665	1845–49	1910	60–64	5.9	13.9	13.8	14.2	21.3	30.9	6,883
1890–94	1940	45–49	16.3	36.0	25.5	12.1	7.4	2.7	2,968	1840–44	1910	65–69	6.9	16.3	14.1	14.0	18.4	30.3	7,035
1885–89	1940	50–54	16.4	33.6	25.3	13.0	8.4	3.2	3,106	1835–39	1910	70–74	5.4	12.4	14.1	11.3	21.4	35.4	6,947
1880–84	1940	55–59	16.7	31.4	24.7	13.7	9.2	4.2	3,270										
1875–79	1940	60–64	16.6	30.3	24.9	13.9	9.9	4.3	3,349										

* Denotes first year for which figures include Alaska and Hawaii.

Series B 49–66.　Children Ever Born to Women Ever Married, by Race and Age of Women: 1910 to 1970

Year and race	Percent childless among women ever married, by age of women									Children ever born per 1,000 women ever married, by age of women								
	15–44 years	15–19 years	20–24 years	25–29 years	30–34 years	35–39 years	40–44 years	45–49 years	50–59 years	15–44 years	15–19 years	20–24 years	25–29 years	30–34 years	35–39 years	40–44 years	45–49 years	50–59 years
	49	50	51	52	53	54	55	56	57	58	59	60	61	62	63	64	65	66
TOTAL																		
1970	16.4	50.9	35.7	15.8	8.3	7.3	8.6	10.6	15.6	2,360	636	1,071	1,984	2,806	3,170	3,097	2,854	2,520
1960	15.0	43.6	24.2	12.6	10.4	11.1	14.1	18.1	20.7	2,314	792	1,441	2,241	2,627	2,686	2,564	2,402	2,420
1950	22.8	52.8	33.3	21.1	17.3	19.1	20.0	20.4	18.1	1,859	604	1,082	1,654	2,059	2,247	2,492	2,492	2,822
1940	26.5	54.6	39.9	30.1	23.3	19.9	17.4	16.8	16.6	1,904	572	987	1,463	1,964	2,414	2,754	2,998	3,215
1910	16.2	42.7	24.2	17.2	13.7	11.6	10.4	9.5	8.7	2,866	725	1,407	2,180	2,956	3,781	4,383	4,744	5,076
WHITE																		
1970	16.7	53.7	37.5	16.1	8.1	6.9	8.1	9.9	14.7	2,285	579	1,006	1,922	2,734	3,086	3,012	2,791	2,470
1960	14.6	46.0	25.0	12.3	9.7	10.2	13.0	17.1	20.0	2,253	729	1,370	2,171	2,559	2,629	2,516	2,354	2,378
1950	21.8	55.4	34.0	20.1	15.8	17.5	18.9	19.5	17.5	1,828	548	1,028	1,620	2,034	2,218	2,329	2,456	2,786
1940	25.9	56.4	40.3	29.7	22.3	18.9	16.7	16.3	16.5	1,870	539	941	1,413	1,922	2,369	2,717	2,968	3,180
1910	15.9	43.5	24.2	16.8	13.4	11.5	10.4	9.6	8.8	2,806	699	1,344	2,099	2,880	3,683	4,263	4,594	4,929
NEGRO																		
1970	13.8	32.2	20.7	12.6	9.4	9.8	13.0	17.9	24.4	2,976	1,026	1,631	2,541	3,395	3,839	3,795	3,394	2,938
1960	18.7	25.3	17.0	12.4	15.8	20.0	24.7	28.1	28.1	2,808	1,258	2,030	2,835	3,190	3,139	2,949	2,761	2,756
1950	30.8	38.0	28.9	30.0	30.8	32.3	30.1	28.4	25.1	2,089	921	1,474	1,931	2,250	2,450	2,619	2,767	3,175
1940	32.8	46.6	38.7	35.1	31.0	28.8	25.8	23.8	19.8	2,096	723	1,234	1,761	2,243	2,666	3,012	3,255	3,660
1910	18.7	39.7	24.2	19.6	16.5	13.3	10.5	8.6	7.4	3,237	834	1,696	2,645	3,532	4,515	5,484	6,162	6,709

Series B 67–98.　Number of Children Under 5 Years Old Per 1,000 Women 20 to 44 Years Old, by Race and Residence, by Geographic Divisions: 1800 to 1970

[Adjusted data standardized for age of women, and allowance made for undercount in censuses; see text.　For composition of geographic divisions, see text for series A 172–194]

Series No.	Area	1970	1960*	1950	1940	1930	1920	1910	1900	1890	1880	1870	1860	1850	1840	1830	1820	1810	1800
	Adjusted number of children per 1,000 women:																		
67	White	507	717	580	419	506	604	631	666	685	780	814	905	892	1,085	1,145	1,295	1,358	1,342
68	Negro	689	895	663	513	554	608	736	845	930	1,090	997	1,072	1,087	-----	-----	-----	-----	-----
	Unadjusted number of children per 1,000 white women:																		
69	United States	503	667	551	400	485	581	609	644	667	754	792	886	877	1,070	1,134	1,236	1,290	1,281
70	Urban	483	636	479	311	388	471	469	----	----	----	----	----	----	701	708	831	900	845
71	Rural	558	747	673	551	658	744	782	----	----	----	----	----	----	1,134	1,189	1,276	1,329	1,319
72	New England	521	664	516	347	441	518	482	478	440	498	544	622	621	752	812	930	1,052	1,098
73	Urban	504	636	486	321	417	500	468	----	----	----	----	----	----	592	614	764	845	827
74	Rural	574	755	612	443	541	602	566	----	----	----	----	----	----	800	851	952	1,079	1,126
75	Middle Atlantic	486	602	471	320	424	539	533	549	547	624	679	767	763	940	1,036	1,183	1,289	1,279
76	Urban	466	574	432	286	386	501	495	----	----	----	----	----	----	711	722	842	924	852
77	Rural	568	720	596	457	590	680	650	----	----	----	----	----	----	1,006	1,100	1,235	1,344	1,339
78	East North Central	530	704	552	388	458	548	555	599	653	757	869	999	1,022	1,270	1,467	1,608	1,702	1,840
79	Urban	510	674	491	326	400	485	470	----	----	----	----	----	----	841	910	1,059	1,256	-----
80	Rural	585	783	679	533	605	668	672	----	----	----	----	----	----	1,291	1,484	1,616	1,706	1,840
81	West North Central	530	743	600	431	495	584	630	710	781	905	990	1,105	1,114	1,445	1,678	1,685	1,810	-----
82	Urban	497	699	514	324	365	416	426	----	----	----	----	----	----	705	1,181	-----	-----	-----
83	Rural	597	816	702	538	614	711	760	----	----	----	----	----	----	1,481	1,703	1,685	1,810	-----
84	South Atlantic	469	625	572	464	593	694	760	779	777	851	811	918	937	1,140	1,174	1,280	1,325	1,345
85	Urban	443	588	450	305	401	458	485	----	----	----	----	----	----	770	767	881	936	861
86	Rural	514	681	677	596	744	851	894	----	----	----	----	----	----	1,185	1,209	1,310	1,347	1,365
87	East South Central	490	656	631	539	655	734	817	834	850	926	903	1,039	1,099	1,408	1,519	1,631	1,700	1,799
88	Urban	453	609	494	333	414	441	469	----	----	----	----	----	----	859	863	1,089	1,348	-----
89	Rural	537	707	720	648	781	846	922	----	----	----	----	----	----	1,424	1,529	1,635	1,701	1,799
90	West South Central	512	695	607	474	584	686	845	925	968	1,043	935	1,084	1,046	1,297	1,359	1,418	1,383	-----
91	Urban	500	680	542	342	410	445	504	----	----	----	----	----	----	846	877	866	727	-----
92	Rural	547	736	703	591	723	823	977	----	----	----	----	----	----	1,495	1,463	1,522	1,557	-----
93	Mountain	542	775	663	526	582	664	661	720	757	872	967	1,051	886	-----	-----	-----	-----	-----
94	Urban	525	742	584	404	428	470	466	----	----	----	----	----	----	-----	-----	-----	-----	-----
95	Rural	596	859	754	643	712	807	810	----	----	----	----	----	----	-----	-----	-----	-----	-----
96	Pacific	482	653	539	339	360	425	460	512	587	775	888	1,026	901	-----	-----	-----	-----	-----
97	Urban	474	633	478	283	306	344	360	----	----	----	----	----	----	-----	-----	-----	-----	-----
98	Rural	537	751	652	466	507	603	640	----	----	----	----	----	----	-----	-----	-----	-----	-----

* Denotes first year for which figures include Alaska and Hawaii.

Series B 99–106. Median Interval Between Births, by Race: 1930 to 1969

[In months. Excludes Alaska and Hawaii. Excludes institutional population. Based on sample]

Series No.	Race and interval	Year of birth of child							
		1965–1969	1960–1964	1955–1959	1950–1954	1945–1949	1940–1944	1935–1939	1930–1934
	WHITE								
	Median interval in months from—								
99	First marriage of mother to birth of first child____	15.5	14.5	16.2	17.7	18.4	20.2	20.1	20.3
100	Birth of first child to birth of second child_____	29.3	25.9	28.2	30.7	32.9	32.8	32.0	32.2
101	Birth of second child to birth of third child_____	33.1	31.6	33.0	31.3	33.1	34.0	34.2	31.8
102	Birth of third child to birth of fourth child_____	35.0	31.2	30.4	30.0	32.5	34.4	32.8	33.1
	NEGRO AND OTHER								
	Median interval in months from—								
103	First marriage of mother to birth of first child____	----------	9.0	11.9	12.7	11.1	10.7	12.9	11.9
104	Birth of first child to birth of second child_____	----------	23.3	23.4	23.3	24.9	27.3	22.8	27.6
105	Birth of second child to birth of third child_____	----------	23.8	23.3	23.4	24.6	24.1	22.6	(B)
106	Birth of third child to birth of fourth child_____	----------	22.1	22.9	22.4	23.8	24.0	(B)	(B)

B Not shown; base for estimate is too small (number of children reported by women surviving to 1969 is less than 150,000).

Series B 107–115. Expectation of Life (in Years) at Birth, by Race and Sex: 1900 to 1970

[Prior to 1929, for death-registration area only. See general note for series B 1–220]

Year	Total			White			Negro and other			Year	Total			White			Negro and other		
	Both sexes	Male	Female	Both sexes	Male	Female	Both sexes	Male	Female		Both sexes	Male	Female	Both sexes	Male	Female	Both sexes	Male	Female
	107	108	109	110	111	112	113	114	115		107	108	109	110	111	112	113	114	115
1970	70.9	67.1	74.8	71.7	68.0	75.6	65.3	61.3	69.4	1935	61.7	59.9	63.9	62.9	61.0	65.0	53.1	51.3	55.2
1969	70.5	66.8	74.3	71.3	67.8	75.1	64.3	60.5	68.4	1934	61.1	59.3	63.3	62.4	50.6	64 6	51.8	50.2	53.7
1968	70.2	66.6	74.0	71.1	67.5	74.9	63.7	60.1	67.5	1933	63.3	61.7	65.1	64.3	62.7	66.3	54.7	53.5	56.0
1967	70.5	67.0	74.2	71.3	67.8	75.1	64.6	61.1	68.2	1932	62.1	61.0	63.5	63.2	62.0	64.5	53.7	52.8	54.6
1966	70.1	66.7	73.8	71.0	67.6	74.7	64.0	60.7	67.4	1931	61.1	59.4	63.1	62.6	60.8	64.7	50.4	49.5	51.5
1965	70.2	66.8	73.7	71.0	67.6	74.7	64.1	61.1	67.4	1930	59.7	58.1	61.6	61.4	59.7	63.5	48.1	47.3	49.2
1964	70.2	66.9	73.7	71.0	67.7	74.6	64.1	61.1	67.2	1929	57.1	55.8	58.7	58.6	57.2	60.3	46.7	45.7	47.8
1963 [1]	69.9	66.6	73.4	70.8	67.5	74.4	63.6	60.9	66.5	1928	56.8	55.6	58.3	58.4	57.0	60.0	46.3	45.6	47.0
1962 [1]	70.0	66.9	73.4	70.9	67.7	74.4	64.1	61.5	66.8	1927	60.4	59.0	62.1	62.0	60.5	63.9	48.2	47.6	48.9
1961	70.2	67.0	73.6	71.0	67.8	74.5	64.4	61.9	67.0	1926	56.7	55.5	58.0	58.2	57.0	59.6	44.6	43.7	45.6
1960 *	69.7	66.6	73.1	70.6	67.4	74.1	63.6	61.1	66.3	1925	59.0	57.6	60.6	60.7	59.3	62.4	45.7	44.9	46.7
1959 [2]	69.9	66.8	73.2	70.7	67.5	74.2	63.9	61.3	66.5	1924	59.7	58.1	61.5	61.4	59.8	63.4	46.6	45.5	47.8
1958	69.6	66.6	72.9	70.5	67.4	73.9	63.4	61.0	65.8	1923	57.2	56.1	58.5	58.3	57.1	59.6	48.3	47.7	48.9
1957	69.5	66.4	72.7	70.3	67.7	73.7	63.0	60.7	65.5	1922	59.6	58.4	61.0	60.4	59.1	61.9	52.4	51.5	53.0
1956	69.7	66.7	72.9	70.5	67.5	73.9	63.6	61.3	66.1	1921	60.8	60.0	61.8	61.8	60.8	62.9	51.5	51.6	51.3
1955	69.6	66.7	72.8	70.5	67.4	73.7	63.7	61.4	66.1	1920	54.1	53.6	54.6	54.9	54.4	55.6	45.3	45.5	45.2
1954	69.6	66.7	72.8	70.5	67.5	73.7	63.4	61.1	65.9	1919	54.7	53.5	56.0	55.8	54.5	57.4	44.5	44.5	44.4
1953	68.8	66.0	72.0	69.7	66.8	73.0	62.0	59.7	64.5	1918	39.1	36.6	42.2	39.8	37.1	43.2	29.9	29.9	32.5
1952	68.6	65.8	71.6	69.5	66.6	72.6	61.4	59.1	63.8	1917	50.9	48.4	54.0	52.0	49.3	55.3	38.8	37.0	40.8
1951	68.4	65.6	71.4	69.3	66.5	72.4	61.2	59.2	63.4	1916	51.7	49.6	54.3	52.5	50.2	55.2	41.3	39.6	43.1
1950	68.2	65.6	71.1	69.1	66.5	72.2	60.8	59.1	62.9	1915	54.5	52.5	56.8	55.1	53.1	57.5	38.9	37.5	40.5
1949	68.0	65.2	70.7	68.8	66.2	71.9	60.6	58.9	62.7	1914	54.2	52.0	56.8	54.9	52.7	57.5	38.9	37.1	40.8
1948	67.2	64.6	69.9	68.0	65.5	71.0	60.0	58.1	62.5	1913	52.5	50.3	55.0	53.0	50.8	55.7	38.4	36.7	40.3
1947	66.8	64.4	69.7	67.6	65.2	70.5	59.7	57.9	61.9	1912	53.5	51.5	55.9	53.9	51.9	56.2	37.9	35.9	40.0
1946	66.7	64.4	69.4	67.5	65.1	70.3	59.1	57.5	61.0	1911	52.6	50.9	54.4	53.0	51.3	54.9	36.4	34.6	38.2
1945	65.9	63.6	67.9	66.8	64.4	69.5	57.7	56.1	59.6	1910	50.0	48.4	51.8	50.3	48.6	52.0	35.6	33.8	37.5
1944	65.2	63.6	66.8	66.2	64.5	68.4	56.6	55.8	57.7	1909	52.1	50.5	53.8	52.5	50.9	54.2	35.7	34.2	37.3
1943	63.3	62.4	64.4	64.2	63.2	65.7	55.6	55.4	56.1	1908	51.1	49.5	52.8	51.5	49.9	53.3	34.9	33.8	36.0
1942	66.2	64.7	67.9	67.3	65.9	69.4	56.6	55.4	58.2	1907	47.6	45.6	49.9	48.1	46.0	50.4	32.5	31.1	34.0
1941	64.8	63.1	66.8	66.2	64.4	68.5	53.8	52.5	55.3	1906	48.7	46.9	50.8	49.3	47.3	51.4	32.9	31.8	33.9
1940	62.9	60.8	65.2	64.2	62.1	66.6	53.1	51.5	54.9	1905	48.7	47.3	50.2	49.1	47.6	50.6	31.3	29.6	33.1
1939	63.7	62.1	65.4	64.9	63.3	66.6	54.5	53.2	56.0	1904	47.6	46.2	49.1	48.0	46.6	49.5	30.8	29.1	32.7
1938	63.5	61.9	65.3	65.0	63.2	66.8	52.9	51.7	54.3	1903	50.5	49.1	52.0	50.9	49.5	52.5	33.1	31.7	34.6
1937	60.0	58.0	62.4	61.4	59.3	63.8	50.3	48.3	52.5	1902	51.5	49.8	53.4	51.9	50.2	53.8	34.6	32.9	36.4
1936	58.5	56.6	60.6	59.8	58.0	61.9	49.0	47.0	51.4	1901	49.1	47.6	50.6	49.4	48.0	51.0	33.7	32.2	35.3
										1900	47.3	46.3	48.3	47.6	46.6	48.7	33.0	32.5	33.5

* Denotes first year for which figures include Alaska and Hawaii.
[1] Excludes New Jersey; State did not require reporting of race.
[2] Includes Alaska.

Series B 116–125.　Expectation of Life at Specified Ages, by Sex and Race: 1900 to 1970

[In years]

Year or period [1]	At birth Male 116	At birth Female 117	Age 20 Male 118	Age 20 Female 119	Age 40 Male 120	Age 40 Female 121	Age 60 Male 122	Age 60 Female 123	Age 70 Male 124	Age 70 Female 125
WHITE										
1970	68.0	75.6	50.3	57.4	31.9	38.3	16.2	21.0	10.5	13.6
1969	67.8	75.1	50.1	56.9	31.8	37.8	16.0	20.5	10.4	13.0
1968	67.5	74.9	49.9	56.7	31.6	37.6	15.8	20.2	10.2	12.9
1967	67.8	75.1	50.2	56.9	31.8	37.8	16.1	20.4	10.4	13.0
1966	67.6	74.7	50.1	56.7	31.6	37.5	15.9	20.2	10.3	12.8
1965	67.6	74.7	50.2	56.6	31.7	37.5	16.0	20.1	10.3	12.8
1964	67.7	74.6	50.2	56.6	31.8	37.5	16.0	20.1	10.4	12.8
1963 [2]	67.5	74.4	50.1	56.4	31.6	37.3	15.8	19.9	10.2	12.5
1962 [2]	67.6	74.4	50.2	56.4	31.7	37.3	16.0	19.9	10.3	12.5
1961	67.8	74.5	50.4	56.6	31.9	37.4	16.1	20.0	10.4	12.6
1960 *	67.4	74.1	50.1	56.2	31.6	37.1	15.9	19.7	10.2	12.4
1959 [3]	67.6	74.2	50.3	56.3	31.8	37.2	16.1	19.7	10.4	12.5
1958	67.2	73.7	50.0	55.9	31.5	36.7	15.7	19.2	10.1	12.0
1957	67.1	73.5	49.9	55.7	31.4	36.6	15.7	19.2	10.1	12.1
1956	67.3	73.7	50.1	55.9	31.6	36.7	15.9	19.3	10.3	12.2
1955	67.3	73.6	50.1	55.8	31.7	36.7	16.0	19.3	10.3	12.2
1949–51	66.3	72.0	49.5	54.6	31.2	35.6	15.8	18.6	10.1	11.7
1939–41	62.8	67.3	47.8	51.4	30.0	33.3	15.1	17.0	9.4	10.5
1929–31	59.1	62.7	46.0	48.5	29.2	31.5	14.7	16.1	9.2	10.0
1919–21	56.3	58.5	45.6	46.5	29.9	30.9	15.3	15.9	9.5	9.9
1909–11	50.2	53.6	42.7	44.9	27.4	29.3	14.0	14.9	8.8	9.4
1901–10	49.3	52.5	42.4	44.4	27.6	29.3	14.2	15.1	(NA)	(NA)
1900–02	48.2	51.1	42.2	43.8	27.7	29.2	14.4	15.2	9.0	9.6
NEGRO AND OTHER										
1970	61.3	69.4	44.7	52.2	28.6	34.2	15.7	19.4	11.2	13.7
1969	60.5	68.4	43.9	51.2	27.8	33.3	14.9	18.5	10.9	13.7
1968	60.1	67.5	43.6	50.5	27.4	32.7	14.5	17.9	10.5	13.2
1967	61.1	68.2	44.8	51.3	28.3	33.4	15.3	18.7	11.2	13.9
1966	60.7	67.4	44.6	50.7	28.0	32.8	14.9	18.1	11.0	13.4
1965	61.1	67.4	45.1	50.8	28.3	32.8	15.1	18.2	11.2	13.5
1964	61.1	67.2	45.3	50.6	28.5	32.7	15.2	18.1	11.4	13.4
1963 [2]	60.9	66.5	45.1	50.0	28.1	32.1	14.6	17.5	10.7	12.8
1962 [2]	61.5	66.8	45.6	50.2	28.6	32.4	15.0	17.7	10.9	12.9
1961	61.9	67.0	46.0	50.5	29.0	32.6	15.3	18.0	11.2	13.0
1960 *	61.1	66.3	45.5	49.9	28.4	32.1	14.9	17.7	10.7	12.7
1959 [3]	61.4	66.5	45.8	50.2	28.8	32.4	15.5	18.2	11.2	13.0
1958	60.6	65.5	45.0	49.3	28.0	31.5	14.5	17.4	10.9	13.1
1957	60.3	65.2	44.7	48.9	27.8	31.3	14.5	17.4	11.1	13.2
1956	61.1	65.9	45.4	49.4	28.5	31.8	15.2	17.9	11.5	13.6
1955	61.2	65.9	45.5	49.6	28.6	32.0	15.4	18.1	11.7	13.8
1949–51	58.9	62.7	43.7	46.8	27.3	29.8	14.9	17.0	10.7	12.3
1939–41 [4]	52.3	55.5	39.7	42.1	25.2	27.3	14.4	16.1	10.1	11.8
1929–31 [4]	47.6	49.5	36.0	37.2	23.4	24.3	13.2	14.2	8.8	10.4
1919–21 [4]	47.1	46.9	38.4	37.2	26.5	25.6	14.7	14.7	9.6	10.3
1909–11 [4]	34.1	37.7	33.5	36.1	21.6	23.3	11.7	12.8	8.0	9.2
1900–02 [4]	32.5	35.0	35.1	36.9	23.1	24.4	12.6	13.6	8.3	9.6

* Denotes first year for which figures include Alaska and Hawaii.
NA Not available.
[1] Data for 1929–31 to 1958 are for conterminous United States; those for 1919–21, for death-registration States of 1920 (34 States and the District of Columbia); those for earlier years, for death-registration States of 1900 (20 States and the District of Columbia).
[2] Excludes New Jersey; State did not require reporting of race.
[3] Includes Alaska.
[4] Negroes only.

Series B 126–135.　Expectation of Life at Specified Ages, by Sex, for Massachusetts: 1850 to 1949–51

[In years]

Year or period	At birth Male 126	At birth Female 127	Age 20 Male 128	Age 20 Female 129	Age 40 Male 130	Age 40 Female 131	Age 60 Male 132	Age 60 Female 133	Age 70 Male 134	Age 70 Female 135	Year or period	At birth Male 126	At birth Female 127	Age 20 Male 128	Age 20 Female 129	Age 40 Male 130	Age 40 Female 131	Age 60 Male 132	Age 60 Female 133	Age 70 Male 134	Age 70 Female 135
1949–51	66.7	72.1	49.3	54.2	30.7	35.2	15.4	18.3	9.9	11.6	1893–97	44.1	46.6	41.2	42.8	27.4	29.0	14.4	15.7	9.3	10.4
1939–41 [1]	63.3	67.6	47.4	51.0	29.3	32.6	14.5	16.4	9.1	10.2	1890	42.5	44.5	40.7	42.0	27.4	28.8	14.7	15.7	9.4	10.2
1929–31 [1]	59.3	62.6	46.1	48.5	29.0	31.2	14.3	15.8	8.9	9.9	1878–82	41.7	43.5	42.2	42.8	28.9	30.3	15.6	16.9	10.3	11.3
1919–20 [1]	54.1	56.6	44.6	45.5	28.8	30.0	14.4	15.4	8.9	9.6	1855	38.7	40.9	39.8	39.9	27.0	28.8	14.4	15.6	(NA)	(NA)
1909–11	49.3	53.1	42.5	44.9	27.0	29.0	13.4	14.8	8.6	9.5	1850	38.3	40.5	40.1	40.2	27.9	29.8	15.6	17.0	10.2	11.3
1900–02	46.1	49.4	41.8	43.7	27.2	28.8	13.9	15.1	8.9	9.6											

NA Not available.
[1] For white population only.

Series B 136–147. Fetal Death Ratio; Neonatal, Infant, and Maternal Mortality Rates, by Race: 1915 to 1970

[Prior to 1933, for registration area only.   See general note for series B 1–220]

Year	Fetal death ratio per 1,000 live births [1]			Neonatal mortality rate per 1,000 live births			Infant mortality rate per 1,000 live births			Maternal mortality rate per 10,000 live births		
	Total	White	Negro and other	Total	White	Negro and other	Total	White	Negro and other	Total	White	Negro and other
	136	137	138	139	140	141	142	143	144	145	146	147
1970	14.2	12.4	22.6	15.1	13.8	21.4	20.0	17.8	30.9	2.2	1.4	5.6
1969	14.1	12.4	22.5	15.6	14.2	22.5	20.9	18.4	32.9	2.2	1.5	5.6
1968	15.8	13.8	25.6	16.1	14.7	23.0	21.8	19.2	34.5	2.5	1.7	6.4
1967	15.6	13.5	25.8	16.5	15.0	23.8	22.4	19.7	35.9	2.8	2.0	7.0
1966	15.7	13.6	26.1	17.2	15.6	24.8	23.7	20.6	38.8	2.9	2.0	7.2
1965	16.2	13.9	27.2	17.7	16.1	25.4	24.7	21.5	40.3	3.2	2.1	8.4
1964	16.4	14.1	28.2	17.9	16.2	26.5	24.8	21.6	41.1	3.3	2.2	9.0
1963 [2]	15.8	13.7	26.7	18.2	16.7	26.1	25.2	22.2	41.5	3.6	2.4	9.7
1962 [2]	15.9	13.9	26.7	18.3	16.9	26.1	25.3	22.3	41.4	3.5	2.4	9.6
1961	16.1	14.1	27.0	18.4	16.9	26.2	25.3	22.4	40.7	3.7	2.5	10.1
1960 *	16.1	14.1	26.8	18.7	17.2	26.9	26.0	22.9	43.2	3.7	2.6	9.8
1959 [3]	16.2	14.2	27.3	19.0	17.5	27.7	26.4	23.2	44.0	3.7	2.6	10.2
1958	16.5	14.5	27.5	19.5	17.8	29.0	27.1	23.8	45.7	3.8	2.6	10.2
1957	16.3	14.5	26.8	19.1	17.5	27.8	26.3	23.3	43.7	4.1	2.8	11.8
1956	16.5	14.6	27.2	18.9	17.5	27.0	26.0	23.2	42.1	4.1	2.9	11.1
1955	17.1	15.2	28.4	19.1	17.7	27.2	26.4	23.6	42.8	4.7	3.3	13.0
1954	17.5	15.5	28.9	19.1	17.8	27.0	26.6	23.9	42.9	5.2	3.7	14.4
1953	17.8	15.9	29.6	19.6	18.3	27.4	27.8	25.0	44.7	6.1	4.4	16.6
1952	18.3	16.1	32.2	19.8	18.5	28.0	28.4	25.5	47.0	6.8	4.9	18.8
1951	18.8	16.7	32.1	20.0	18.9	27.3	28.4	25.8	44.8	7.5	5.5	20.1
1950	19.2	17.1	32.5	20.5	19.4	27.5	29.2	26.8	44.5	8.3	6.1	22.2
1949	19.8	17.5	34.6	21.4	20.3	28.6	31.3	28.9	47.3	9.0	6.8	23.5
1948	20.6	18.3	36.5	22.2	21.2	29.1	32.0	29.9	46.5	11.7	8.9	30.1
1947	21.1	18.7	39.6	22.8	21.7	31.0	32.2	30.1	48.5	13.5	10.9	33.5
1946	22.8	20.4	40.9	24.0	23.1	31.5	33.8	31.8	49.5	15.7	13.1	35.9
1945	23.9	21.4	42.0	24.3	23.3	32.0	38.3	35.6	57.0	20.7	17.2	45.5
1944	27.0	24.5	45.4	24.7	23.6	32.5	39.8	36.9	60.3	22.8	18.9	50.6
1943	26.7	24.2	46.2	24.7	23.7	32.9	40.4	37.5	62.5	24.5	21.1	51.0
1942	28.2	25.5	49.3	25.7	24.5	34.6	40.4	37.3	64.6	25.9	22.2	54.4
1941	29.9	26.5	54.0	27.7	26.1	39.0	45.3	41.2	74.8	31.7	26.6	67.8
1940	31.3	27.7	56.7	28.8	27.2	39.7	47.0	43.2	73.8	37.6	32.0	77.4
1939	32.0	28.2	59.0	29.3	27.8	39.6	48.0	44.3	74.2	40.4	35.3	76.2
1938	32.1	28.1	61.1	29.6	28.3	39.1	51.0	47.1	79.1	43.5	37.7	84.9
1937	33.4	29.2	63.2	31.3	29.7	42.1	54.4	50.3	83.2	48.9	43.6	85.8
1936	34.4	29.8	66.9	32.6	31.0	43.9	57.1	52.9	87.6	56.8	51.2	97.2
1935	35.8	31.1	68.7	32.4	31.0	42.7	55.7	51.9	83.2	58.2	53.1	94.6
1934	36.2	31.4	70.1	34.1	[4] 32.3	[4] 45.3	60.1	[4] 54.5	[4] 94.4	59.3	[4] 54.4	[4] 89.7
1933	37.0	32.2	71.1	34.0	[4] 32.1	[4] 45.8	58.1	[4] 52.8	[4] 91.3	61.9	[4] 56.4	[4] 96.7
1932	37.8	32.7	74.4	33.5	[4] 32.0	[4] 43.7	57.6	[4] 53.3	[4] 86.2	63.3	[4] 58.1	[4] 97.6
1931	38.2	33.4	74.1	34.6	33.2	45.2	61.6	57.4	93.1	66.1	60.1	111.4
1930	39.2	34.0	79.9	35.7	34.2	47.4	64.6	60.1	99.9	67.3	60.9	117.4
1929	39.5	34.4	79.7	36.9	35.6	47.3	67.6	63.2	102.2	69.5	63.1	119.9
1928	40.2	35.0	81.5	37.2	35.7	48.8	68.7	64.0	106.2	69.2	62.7	121.0
1927	38.8	34.8	74.8	36.1	35.0	46.1	64.6	60.6	100.1	64.7	59.4	113.3
1926	38.1	35.1	73.0	37.9	37.1	48.0	73.3	70.0	111.8	65.6	61.9	107.1
1925	38.1	35.1	73.1	37.8	36.8	49.5	71.7	68.3	110.8	64.7	60.3	116.2
1924	39.3	35.8	76.2	38.6	37.4	51.2	70.8	66.8	112.9	65.6	60.7	117.9
1923	38.9	35.9	71.8	39.5	38.6	49.9	77.1	73.5	117.4	66.5	62.6	109.5
1922	39.4	36.4	73.4	39.7	38.8	49.9	76.2	73.2	110.0	66.4	62.8	106.8
1921				39.7	38.7	50.3	75.6	72.5	108.5	68.2	64.4	107.7
1920				41.5	40.4	55.0	85.8	82.1	131.7	79.9	76.0	128.1
1919				41.5	40.3	55.2	86.6	83.0	130.5	73.7	69.6	124.4
1918				44.2	43.3	60.5	100.9	97.4	161.2	91.6	88.9	139.3
1917				43.4	42.6	58.0	93.8	90.5	150.7	66.2	63.2	117.7
1916				44.1	43.5	68.9	101.0	99.0	184.9	62.2	60.8	117.9
1915				44.4			99.9	98.6	181.2	60.8	60.1	105.6

* Denotes first year for which figures include Alaska and Hawaii.

[1] For 1945–1970, includes only deaths for which the period of gestation was given as 20 weeks or more or not stated.   For earlier years, includes all fetal deaths, regardless of gestation.   In 1945 ratios based on all fetal deaths, regardless of gestation, were: Total, 26.6; white, 24.1; Negro and other, 44.6.

[2] Figures by race exclude New Jersey; State did not require reporting of race.
[3] Includes Alaska.
[4] Mexicans included with Negro and other.

Series B 148.   Infant Mortality Rate, for Massachusetts: 1851 to 1970

[Deaths under 1 year per 1,000 live births.   Excludes fetal deaths.   Data for 1940 to 1968 are by place of residence; for other years, by place of occurrence]

Year	Rate 148	Year or period	Rate 148	Period	Rate 148	Period	Rate 148
1970	16.8	1961	21.6	1940–44	34.3	1895–99	153.2
1969	18.3	1960	21.6	1935–39	43.2	1890–94	163.2
1968	19.9	1959	22.3	1930–34	53.9	1885–89	158.5
1967	20.0	1958	22.8	1925–29	67.6	1880–84	161.3
1966	21.2	1957	22.7	1920–24	78.7	1875–79	156.3
1965	22.2	1956	22.4	1915–19	100.2	1870–74	170.3
1964 [1]	19.8	1955	21.9	1910–14	116.7	1865–69	146.3
1963	20.6	1950–54	22.8	1905–09	134.3	1860–64	142.5
1962	21.8	1945–49	28.4	1900–04	141.4	1855–59	122.9
						1851–54	131.1

[1] Excludes approximately 6,000 deaths registered in Massachusetts, primarily to residents of the State, covering all ages.

Series B 149–166. Death Rate, for Selected Causes: 1900 to 1970

[Number of deaths, excluding fetal deaths, per 100,000 population. Prior to 1933, for death-registration area only; see general note for series B 1–220]

Year	Tuberculosis, all forms	Syphilis and its sequelae [1]	Typhoid and paratyphoid fever	Scarlet fever and streptococcal sore throat	Hepatitis	Diphtheria	Whooping cough	Measles	Malignant neoplasms [2]	Diabetes mellitus	Major cardiovascular-renal diseases	Influenza and pneumonia [3]	Gastritis, duodenitis, enteritis, and colitis [4]	Cirrhosis of liver	Motor vehicle accidents [5]	Accidental falls	All other accidents [6]	Suicide
	149	150	151	152	153	154	155	156	157	158	159	160	161	162	163	164	165	166
1970	2.6	0.2	(Z)	(Z)	0.5	(Z)	(Z)	(Z)	162.8	18.9	496.0	30.9	0.6	15.5	26.9	8.3	21.2	11.6
1969	2.8	.3	(Z)	(Z)	.5	(Z)	(Z)	(Z)	160.0	19.1	501.7	33.9	.9	14.8	27.6	8.8	21.2	11.1
1968	3.1	.3	(Z)	(Z)	.4	(Z)	(Z)	(Z)	159.4	19.2	512.1	36.8	.3	14.6	27.5	9.3	20.7	10.7
1967	3.5	1.2	(Z)	(Z)	.4	(Z)	(Z)	(Z)	157.2	17.7	511.5	28.8	3.8	14.1	26.7	10.2	20.2	10.8
1966	3.9	1.1	(Z)	(Z)	.4	(Z)	(Z)	.1	155.1	17.7	521.4	32.5	3.9	13.6	27.1	10.2	20.7	10.9
1965	4.1	1.3	(Z)	(Z)	.4	(Z)	(Z)	.1	153.5	17.1	516.4	31.9	4.1	12.8	25.4	10.3	20.1	11.1
1964	4.3	1.4	(Z)	(Z)	.4	(Z)	(Z)	.2	151.3	16.9	514.3	31.1	4.3	12.1	24.5	9.9	19.8	10.8
1963	4.9	1.4	(Z)	(Z)	.5	(Z)	(Z)	.2	151.3	17.2	527.3	37.5	4.4	11.9	23.1	10.2	20.1	11.0
1962	5.1	1.5	(Z)	(Z)	.5	(Z)	(Z)	.2	149.9	16.8	521.2	32.3	4.4	11.7	22.0	10.5	19.8	10.9
1961	5.4	1.6	(Z)	.1	.5	(Z)	(Z)	.2	149.4	16.4	511.4	30.1	4.3	11.3	20.8	10.2	19.4	10.4
1960 *	6.1	1.6	(Z)	.1	.5	(Z)	.1	.2	149.2	16.7	521.8	37.3	4.4	11.3	21.3	10.6	20.4	10.6
1959 [7]	6.5	1.7	(Z)	.1	.5	(Z)	.2	.2	147.3	15.9	515.9	31.2	4.4	10.9	21.5	10.6	20.1	10.6
1958	7.1	2.0	(Z)	.1	.5	(Z)	.1	.3	146.8	15.9	523.5	33.1	4.5	10.8	21.3	10.5	20.4	10.7
1957	7.8	2.2	(Z)	.1	.5	(Z)	.1	.2	148.6	16.0	523.4	35.8	4.7	11.3	22.7	12.1	21.1	9.8
1956	8.4	2.3	(Z)	.1	.5	.1	.1	.2	147.8	15.7	510.5	28.2	4.5	10.7	23.7	12.1	20.9	10.0
1955	9.1	2.3	(Z)	.1	.5	.1	.3	.2	146.5	15.5	506.0	27.1	4.7	10.2	23.4	12.3	21.2	10.2
1954	10.2	3.0	(Z)	.1	.5	.1	.2	.3	145.6	15.6	495.1	25.4	4.9	10.1	22.1	12.3	21.5	10.1
1953	12.3	3.3	.1	.1	.5	.1	.2	.3	144.7	16.3	514.8	33.0	5.4	10.4	24.0	13.0	23.1	10.1
1952	15.8	3.7	.1	.2	.5	.1	.3	.4	143.3	16.4	511.9	29.7	5.6	10.2	24.3	13.5	24.0	10.0
1951	20.1	4.1	.1	.2	.4	.2	.6	.4	140.5	16.3	513.2	31.4	5.2	9.8	24.1	13.9	24.5	10.4
1950	22.5	5.0	.1	.2	.4	.3	.7	.3	139.8	16.2	510.8	31.3	5.1	9.2	23.1	13.8	23.7	11.4
1949	26.3	5.8	.1	.3	.4	.4	.5	.6	138.8	16.9	502.1	30.0	6.7	9.2	21.3	15.0	24.3	11.4
1948	30.0	8.0	.2	(Z)	------	.4	.8	.6	134.9	26.4	488.0	38.7	6.0	11.3	22.1	16.6	28.2	11.2
1947	33.5	8.8	.2	.1	------	.6	1.4	.3	132.3	26.2	491.0	43.1	5.6	10.4	22.8	16.7	29.7	11.5
1946	36.4	9.3	.3	.1	------	.9	.9	.9	130.0	24.8	476.8	44.5	5.8	9.6	23.9	16.1	29.8	11.5
1945	39.9	10.6	.4	.2	------	1.2	1.3	.2	134.0	26.5	508.2	51.6	8.7	9.5	21.2	17.7	33.2	11.2
1944	41.2	11.2	.4	.3	------	.9	1.4	1.4	128.8	26.3	500.5	61.6	9.9	8.6	18.3	17.0	36.0	10.0
1943	42.5	12.1	.5	.3	------	.9	2.5	1.0	124.3	27.1	510.8	67.1	9.6	9.3	17.7	18.0	37.7	10.2
1942	43.1	12.2	.6	.3	------	1.0	1.9	1.0	122.0	25.4	479.5	55.7	8.8	9.4	21.1	16.6	33.5	12.0
1941	44.5	13.3	.8	.3	------	1.0	2.8	1.7	120.1	25.4	475.3	63.8	10.5	8.9	30.0	16.7	29.2	12.8
1940	45.9	14.4	1.1	.5	------	1.1	2.2	.5	120.3	26.6	485.7	70.3	10.3	8.6	26.2	17.2	29.8	14.4
1939	47.1	15.0	1.5	.7	------	1.5	2.3	.9	117.5	25.5	466.3	75.7	11.6	8.3	24.7	17.5	28.1	14.1
1938	49.1	15.9	1.9	.9	------	2.0	3.7	2.5	114.9	23.9	456.8	80.4	14.3	8.3	25.1	19.5	27.2	15.3
1937	53.8	16.1	2.1	1.4	------	2.0	3.9	1.2	112.4	23.7	454.6	114.9	14.7	8.5	30.8	20.4	30.0	15.0
1936	55.9	16.2	2.5	1.9	------	2.4	2.1	1.0	111.4	23.7	461.1	119.6	16.4	8.8	29.7	20.8	34.9	14.3
1935	55.1	15.4	2.8	2.1	------	3.1	3.7	3.1	108.2	22.3	431.2	104.2	14.1	7.9	28.6	19.2	30.1	14.3
1934	56.7	15.9	3.4	2.0	------	3.3	5.9	5.5	106.4	22.2	430.0	96.9	18.4	7.7	28.6	18.8	32.0	14.9
1933	59.6	15.1	3.6	2.0	------	3.9	3.6	2.2	102.3	21.4	413.6	95.7	17.3	7.4	25.0	15.1	31.8	15.9
1932	62.5	15.4	3.7	2.2	------	4.4	4.5	1.6	102.3	22.0	418.2	107.3	16.1	7.2	23.6	14.8	32.4	17.4
1931	67.8	15.4	4.5	2.2	------	4.8	3.9	3.0	99.0	20.4	407.1	107.5	20.5	7.4	27.1	14.6	36.1	16.8
1930	71.1	15.7	4.8	1.9	------	4.9	4.8	3.2	97.4	19.1	414.4	102.5	26.0	7.2	26.7	14.7	38.4	15.6
1929	75.3	15.6	4.2	2.1	------	6.5	6.2	2.5	95.8	18.8	418.9	146.5	23.3	7.2	25.5	14.5	39.7	13.9
1928	78.3	16.4	4.9	1.9	------	7.2	5.4	5.2	95.7	19.0	419.1	142.5	26.4	7.5	23.2	14.1	40.8	13.5
1927	79.6	16.4	5.3	2.3	------	7.7	6.8	4.1	95.2	17.4	398.3	102.2	27.1	7.4	21.6	14.0	41.5	13.2
1926	85.5	17.1	6.4	2.5	------	7.4	8.8	8.3	94.6	17.9	410.6	141.7	32.9	7.2	19.9	14.0	43.3	12.6
1925	84.8	17.3	7.8	2.7	------	7.8	6.7	2.3	92.0	16.8	391.5	121.7	38.6	7.2	16.8	13.4	46.3	12.0
1924	87.9	17.4	6.6	3.1	------	9.3	8.1	8.2	90.4	16.4	383.4	115.2	33.7	7.3	15.3	13.1	45.4	11.9
1923	91.7	17.9	6.7	3.5	------	12.0	9.6	10.7	88.4	17.7	380.8	151.7	39.1	7.1	14.6	12.8	46.9	11.5
1922	95.3	18.0	7.4	3.5	------	14.6	5.5	4.3	86.2	18.3	366.6	132.3	38.9	7.4	12.4	12.1	43.8	11.7
1921	97.6	17.5	8.8	5.3	------	17.7	9.1	4.2	85.5	16.7	351.2	98.7	50.7	7.3	11.3	11.4	44.1	12.4
1920	113.1	16.5	7.6	4.6	------	15.3	12.5	8.8	83.4	16.1	364.9	207.3	53.7	7.1	10.3	11.8	47.9	10.2
1919	125.6	16.2	9.2	2.8	------	14.9	5.6	3.9	81.0	15.0	348.6	223.0	55.2	7.9	9.3	11.3	50.5	11.5
1918	149.8	18.7	12.3	3.1	------	14.0	17.0	10.8	80.8	16.1	387.0	588.5	72.2	9.6	9.3	12.7	59.5	12.3
1917	143.5	19.1	13.3	3.5	------	15.6	10.5	14.1	80.8	16.9	396.4	164.5	75.2	10.9	8.6	14.8	62.6	13.0
1916	138.4	18.6	13.2	3.1	------	13.9	10.5	11.4	81.0	16.9	389.4	163.8	75.5	11.8	7.1	15.1	59.4	13.7
1915	140.1	17.7	11.8	3.6	------	15.2	8.2	5.2	80.7	17.6	383.5	145.9	67.5	12.1	5.8	14.8	52.9	16.2
1914	141.7	16.7	14.7	6.6	------	17.2	10.2	6.8	78.7	16.2	374.5	132.4	75.1	12.5	4.2	15.0	57.5	16.1
1913	143.5	16.2	17.5	7.7	------	18.1	10.1	12.8	78.5	15.4	370.6	140.8	86.7	12.9	3.8	15.4	64.5	15.4
1912	145.4	15.1	16.1	6.0	------	17.6	9.2	7.2	77.0	15.1	375.7	138.4	79.6	13.1	2.8	15.4	62.6	15.6
1911	155.1	15.3	20.1	8.6	------	18.4	11.0	9.9	74.2	15.1	366.5	145.4	86.8	13.6	2.1	15.0	66.5	16.0
1910	153.8	13.5	22.5	11.4	------	21.1	11.6	12.4	76.2	15.3	371.9	155.9	115.4	13.3	1.8	15.4	67.0	15.3
1909	156.3	12.9	20.2	11.1	------	19.9	10.0	12.4	74.0	14.1	362.0	148.1	101.8	13.4	1.2	------	77.5	16.0
1908	162.1	12.4	23.4	12.4	------	21.9	10.7	10.6	71.5	13.8	356.7	150.9	112.5	13.5	.8	------	82.1	16.8
1907	174.2	12.4	28.2	9.3	------	24.2	11.3	9.6	71.4	14.2	389.8	180.0	115.0	14.8	.7	------	94.1	14.5
1906	175.8	14.1	30.9	7.3	------	26.3	16.1	12.9	69.3	13.4	364.3	156.3	123.6	14.1	.4	------	94.0	12.8
1905	179.9	13.8	22.4	6.8	------	23.5	8.9	7.4	73.4	14.1	384.0	169.3	118.4	14.0	------	------	81.3	13.5
1904	188.1	13.9	23.9	11.6	------	29.3	5.8	11.3	71.5	14.2	388.8	192.1	111.5	13.9	------	------	85.4	12.2
1903	177.2	13.2	24.6	12.3	------	31.1	14.3	8.8	70.0	12.7	364.4	169.3	100.3	13.5	------	------	81.4	11.3
1902	174.2	12.9	26.4	11.9	------	29.8	12.4	9.3	66.3	11.7	349.8	161.3	104.9	13.0	------	------	72.5	10.3
1901	189.9	12.5	27.6	13.6	------	33.5	8.7	7.4	66.4	11.6	347.7	197.2	118.5	13.1	------	------	83.8	10.4
1900	194.4	12.0	31.3	9.6	------	40.3	12.2	13.3	64.0	11.0	345.2	202.2	142.7	12.5	------	------	72.3	10.2

* Denotes first year for which figures include Alaska and Hawaii.

Z   Less than 0.05.

[1] 1900–1920, excludes aneurysm of the aorta.

[2] Includes neoplasms of lymphatic and hematopoietic tissues.

[3] All years, excludes pneumonia of newborn; 1900–1920, excludes capillary bronchitis.

[4] All years, excludes diarrhea of newborn; 1900–1920, includes ulcer of duodenum.

[5] 1906–1925, excludes automobile collisions with trains and streetcars, and motorcycle accidents.

[6] 1900–1921, includes legal executions; 1900–1908, food poisoning; and 1900–1905, motor vehicle accidents.

[7] Includes Alaska.

Series B 167–180. Death Rate, by Race and Sex: 1900 to 1970

[Number of deaths, excluding fetal deaths, per 1,000 population. Prior to 1933 for death-registration area only; see general note for series B 1–220]

Year	Death rate							Age-adjusted death rate						
	Total	White			Negro and other			Total	White			Negro and other		
		Both sexes	Male	Female	Both sexes	Male	Female		Both sexes	Male	Female	Both sexes	Male	Female
	167	168	169	170	171	172	173	174	175	176	177	178	179	180
1970	9.5	9.5	10.9	8.1	9.4	11.2	7.8	7.1	6.8	8.9	5.0	9.8	12.3	7.7
1969	9.5	9.5	10.9	8.2	9.6	11.3	8.0	7.3	6.9	9.0	5.2	10.5	13.0	8.3
1968	9.7	9.6	11.1	8.2	9.9	11.6	8.3	7.5	7.1	9.2	5.3	10.8	13.3	8.6
1967	9.4	9.4	10.8	8.0	9.4	10.9	7.9	7.3	6.9	9.0	5.2	10.2	12.4	8.2
1966	9.5	9.5	10.9	8.1	9.7	11.3	8.3	7.5	7.1	9.2	5.3	10.5	12.7	8.6
1965	9.4	9.4	10.8	8.0	9.6	11.1	8.2	7.4	7.1	9.1	5.3	10.3	12.4	8.5
1964	9.4	9.4	10.8	8.0	9.7	11.1	8.3	7.4	7.1	9.0	5.3	10.3	12.2	8.6
1963 ¹	9.6	9.5	11.0	8.1	10.1	11.5	8.7	7.6	7.2	9.2	5.5	10.6	12.5	8.9
1962 ¹	9.5	9.4	10.8	8.0	9.8	11.2	8.5	7.5	7.1	9.0	5.4	10.3	12.0	8.7
1961	9.3	9.3	10.7	7.8	9.6	10.9	8.4	7.4	7.0	8.9	5.4	10.0	11.6	8.6
1960 *	9.5	9.5	11.0	8.0	10.1	11.5	8.7	7.6	7.3	9.2	5.6	10.5	12.1	8.9
1959 ²	9.4	9.3	10.8	7.9	9.9	11.3	8.6	7.5	7.2	9.0	5.5	10.3	11.9	8.8
1958	9.5	9.4	10.9	8.0	10.3	11.6	9.0	7.7	7.3	9.1	5.7	10.6	12.2	9.2
1957	9.6	9.5	11.0	8.0	10.5	11.9	9.1	7.8	7.4	9.2	5.8	10.8	12.4	9.4
1956	9.4	9.3	10.8	7.8	10.1	11.4	8.8	7.6	7.3	9.1	5.7	10.5	11.9	9.1
1955	9.3	9.2	10.7	7.8	10.0	11.3	8.8	7.7	7.4	9.1	5.7	10.4	11.9	9.1
1954	9.2	9.1	10.6	7.6	10.1	11.4	8.8	7.6	7.3	9.0	5.8	10.6	12.0	9.2
1953	9.6	9.4	11.0	8.0	10.8	12.3	9.4	8.0	7.7	9.4	6.1	11.4	13.0	9.9
1952	9.6	9.4	11.0	8.0	11.0	12.5	9.6	8.1	7.8	9.5	6.2	11.7	13.2	10.2
1951	9.7	9.5	11.0	8.0	11.1	12.5	9.8	8.3	7.9	9.6	6.3	11.9	13.3	10.5
1950	9.6	9.5	10.9	8.0	11.2	12.5	9.9	8.4	8.0	9.6	6.5	12.3	13.6	10.9
1949	9.7	9.5	11.0	8.1	11.2	12.5	10.0	8.5	8.1	9.7	6.6	12.3	13.5	11.1
1948	9.9	9.7	11.2	8.3	11.4	12.7	10.1	8.8	8.3	10.0	6.8	12.5	13.8	11.2
1947	10.1	9.9	11.4	8.5	11.4	12.5	10.3	9.0	8.6	10.1	7.1	12.5	13.6	11.4
1946	10.0	9.8	11.2	8.5	11.1	12.2	10.0	9.1	8.8	10.2	7.3	12.4	13.5	11.3
1945	10.6	10.4	12.5	8.6	11.9	13.5	10.5	9.5	9.1	10.7	7.5	13.1	14.5	11.9
1944	10.6	10.4	12.2	8.8	12.4	13.8	11.1	9.7	9.3	10.8	7.8	13.8	14.9	12.6
1943	10.9	10.7	12.2	9.2	12.8	14.0	11.6	10.2	9.7	11.2	8.2	14.5	15.7	13.4
1942	10.3	10.1	11.4	8.7	12.7	14.0	11.4	9.9	9.4	10.9	8.0	14.5	15.8	13.3
1941	10.5	10.2	11.4	8.9	13.5	14.8	12.2	10.3	9.7	11.2	8.3	15.6	16.9	14.3
1940	10.8	10.4	11.6	9.2	13.8	15.1	12.6	10.8	10.2	11.6	8.8	16.3	17.6	15.0
1939	10.6	10.3	11.3	9.2	13.5	14.7	12.4	10.7	10.2	11.4	8.9	16.0	17.1	14.9
1938	10.6	10.3	11.3	9.2	14.0	15.2	12.9	10.9	10.3	11.5	9.1	16.6	17.7	15.5
1937	11.3	10.8	12.0	9.6	14.9	16.4	13.4	11.7	11.1	12.4	9.7	17.8	19.2	16.3
1936	11.6	11.1	12.3	9.9	15.4	16.9	13.9	12.2	11.5	12.8	10.1	18.5	20.1	17.0
1935	10.9	10.6	11.6	9.5	14.3	15.6	13.0	11.6	11.1	12.3	9.8	17.3	18.5	16.1
1934	11.1	10.6	11.7	9.6	14.8	16.0	13.5	11.9	11.3	12.5	10.0	17.9	19.0	16.7
1933	10.7	10.3	11.2	9.3	14.1	15.1	13.1	11.6	11.0	12.2	9.9	17.2	18.1	16.4
1932	10.9	10.5	11.3	9.6	14.5	15.4	13.5	11.9	11.3	12.3	10.2	17.8	18.6	17.0
1931	11.1	10.6	11.5	9.6	15.5	16.5	14.5	12.1	11.4	12.5	10.3	19.0	19.9	18.1
1930	11.3	10.8	11.7	9.8	16.3	17.4	15.3	12.5	11.7	12.8	10.6	20.1	21.0	19.2
1929	11.9	11.3	12.2	10.4	16.9	18.0	15.8	13.2	12.4	13.5	11.4	21.0	21.9	20.0
1928	12.0	11.4	12.3	10.5	17.1	18.0	16.2	13.4	12.6	13.6	11.5	20.9	21.7	20.2
1927	11.3	10.8	11.6	10.0	16.4	17.2	15.6	12.6	11.9	12.8	10.9	19.8	20.4	19.3
1926	12.1	11.6	12.3	10.8	17.8	18.7	16.9	13.5	12.7	13.6	11.8	21.4	22.1	20.8
1925	11.7	11.1	11.8	10.4	17.4	18.2	16.6	13.0	12.3	13.2	11.4	20.9	21.4	20.4
1924	11.6	11.0	11.8	10.3	17.1	17.9	16.3	12.9	12.2	13.1	11.3	20.5	21.1	20.0
1923	12.1	11.7	12.3	11.0	16.5	17.0	16.0	13.5	12.9	13.7	12.1	19.8	20.0	19.7
1922	11.7	11.3	11.9	10.7	15.2	15.7	14.8	13.0	12.6	13.3	11.8	18.3	18.4	18.4
1921	11.5	11.1	11.6	10.6	15.5	15.7	15.4	12.7	12.2	12.7	11.6	18.2	18.0	18.6
1920	13.0	12.6	13.0	12.1	17.7	17.8	17.5	14.2	13.7	14.2	13.1	20.6	20.4	21.0
1919	12.9	12.4	13.0	11.8	17.9	18.1	17.8	14.0	13.4	14.1	12.8	20.5	20.3	20.8
1918	18.1	17.5	19.3	15.8	25.6	26.7	24.4	19.0	18.4	20.2	16.6	28.0	28.9	27.1
1917	14.0	13.5	14.6	12.4	20.4	21.4	19.4	15.3	14.7	16.0	13.4	23.4	24.1	22.7
1916	13.8	13.4	14.4	12.4	19.1	19.9	18.4	15.1	14.7	15.8	13.4	22.2	22.6	21.6
1915	13.2	12.9	13.7	12.0	20.2	20.8	19.5	14.4	14.1	15.1	13.0	23.1	23.5	22.6
1914	13.3	13.0	13.9	12.1	20.2	20.9	19.4	14.5	14.1	15.2	13.0	22.6	23.3	21.9
1913	13.8	13.5	14.5	12.5	20.3	21.0	19.6	15.0	14.6	15.8	13.4	22.7	23.3	22.0
1912	13.6	13.4	14.3	12.4	20.6	21.3	19.7	14.8	14.6	15.7	13.4	23.1	24.0	22.2
1911	13.9	13.7	14.5	12.8	21.3	21.9	20.6	15.2	14.9	15.9	13.8	23.7	24.4	22.9
1910	14.7	14.5	15.4	13.6	21.7	22.3	21.0	15.8	15.6	16.7	14.4	24.1	24.8	23.2
1909	14.2	14.0	14.9	13.2	21.8	22.3	21.2	15.3	15.0	16.1	14.0	24.1	24.8	23.3
1908	14.7	14.5	15.3	13.6	22.4	22.8	22.0	15.8	15.5	16.6	14.4	24.7	25.3	24.1
1907	15.9	15.7	16.8	14.5	24.3	25.0	23.5	17.1	16.8	18.2	15.4	26.6	27.5	25.7
1906	15.7	15.5	16.5	14.4	24.2	24.7	23.6	16.7	16.4	17.6	15.1	26.2	27.0	25.5
1905	15.9	15.7	16.5	14.8	25.5	26.8	24.3	16.7	16.5	17.6	15.4	28.3	29.7	26.9
1904	16.4	16.2	17.1	15.3	26.1	27.6	24.7	17.3	17.1	18.1	16.0	29.1	30.7	27.4
1903	15.6	15.4	16.2	14.6	24.5	25.5	23.4	16.5	16.2	17.2	15.3	27.2	28.5	25.9
1902	15.5	15.3	16.2	14.4	23.6	24.8	22.3	16.2	16.0	17.0	14.9	25.9	27.5	24.5
1901	16.4	16.2	17.1	15.4	24.3	25.6	23.1	17.2	17.0	18.0	16.0	26.9	28.4	25.5
1900	17.2	17.0	17.7	16.3	25.0	25.7	24.4	17.8	17.6	18.4	16.8	27.8	28.7	27.1

* Denotes first year for which figures include Alaska and Hawaii.
¹ Excludes New Jersey; State did not require reporting of race.
² Includes Alaska.

Series B 181–192. Death Rate, by Age and Sex: 1900 to 1970

[Number of deaths, excluding fetal deaths, per 1,000 population for specified group. Prior to 1933, for death-registration area only; see general note for series B 1–220]

Year	Total [1]	Under 1 year	1–4 years	5–14 years	15–24 years	25–34 years	35–44 years	45–54 years	55–64 years	65–74 years	75–84 years	85 years and over
	181	182	183	184	185	186	187	188	189	190	191	192
BOTH SEXES												
1970	9.5	21.4	0.8	0.4	1.3	1.6	3.1	7.3	16.6	35.8	80.0	163.4
1969	9.5	21.5	.9	.4	1.3	1.6	3.2	7.3	16.8	37.4	79.0	190.8
1968	9.7	22.3	.9	.4	1.2	1.6	3.2	7.5	17.2	38.5	80.8	196.1
1967	9.4	22.3	.9	.4	1.2	1.5	3.1	7.3	16.7	37.5	79.0	194.2
1966	9.5	23.3	.9	.4	1.2	1.5	3.1	7.4	17.0	38.4	81.7	200.5
1965	9.4	24.1	.9	.4	1.1	1.5	3.1	7.4	16.9	37.9	81.9	202.0
1964	9.4	24.6	1.0	.4	1.1	1.5	3.1	7.4	17.0	37.8	81.8	200.2
1963	9.6	25.3	1.0	.4	1.1	1.5	3.0	7.5	17.3	38.9	85.2	210.1
1962	9.5	25.3	1.0	.4	1.0	1.5	3.0	7.4	16.9	38.0	84.3	204.7
1961	9.3	25.4	1.0	.4	1.0	1.4	2.9	7.3	16.7	37.2	83.6	195.9
1960 *	9.5	27.0	1.1	.5	1.1	1.5	3.0	7.6	17.4	38.2	87.5	198.6
1959	9.4	27.5	1.1	.5	1.1	1.5	2.9	7.4	17.1	37.6	85.8	194.2
1958	9.5	28.1	1.1	.5	1.1	1.5	3.0	7.5	17.4	38.4	87.9	198.0
1957	9.6	28.0	1.1	.5	1.2	1.5	3.1	7.7	17.8	38.9	88.4	188.4
1956	9.4	28.3	1.1	.5	1.1	1.5	3.0	7.5	17.5	37.8	88.5	181.8
1955	9.3	28.5	1.1	.5	1.1	1.5	3.1	7.5	17.3	37.9	89.0	179.3
1954	9.2	29.2	1.2	.5	1.1	1.5	3.1	7.7	17.4	37.6	87.6	172.6
1953	9.6	30.7	1.3	.5	1.2	1.6	3.3	8.1	18.4	39.1	92.5	183.4
1952	9.6	32.1	1.4	.6	1.3	1.7	3.4	8.3	18.6	39.2	91.9	183.0
1951	9.7	32.3	1.4	.6	1.3	1.8	3.5	8.4	18.8	40.0	93.3	192.3
1950	9.6	33.0	1.4	.6	1.3	1.8	3.6	8.5	[2] 19.0	[2] 41.0	93.3	202.0
1949	9.7	35.2	1.5	.7	1.3	1.8	3.7	8.7	19.3	40.8	93.0	203.2
1948	9.9	35.7	1.6	.7	1.4	2.0	3.9	9.0	19.7	41.4	95.1	213.2
1947	10.1	34.5	1.6	.7	1.5	2.1	4.1	9.2	20.1	42.1	97.0	216.9
1946	10.0	46.3	1.8	.8	1.7	2.3	4.2	9.2	19.8	41.2	95.1	210.6
1945	10.6	42.5	2.0	.9	1.9	2.7	4.6	9.6	20.5	42.6	98.4	209.6
1944	10.6	44.2	2.3	.9	2.0	2.7	4.6	9.7	20.8	43.9	101.7	215.3
1943	10.9	44.0	2.6	1.0	2.1	2.7	4.8	10.2	21.5	46.2	107.5	230.3
1942	10.3	48.8	2.4	.9	1.9	2.8	4.8	10.1	21.0	44.9	101.6	211.1
1941	10.5	52.6	2.8	1.0	2.0	2.9	5.0	10.3	21.3	46.2	105.8	218.7
1940	10.8	54.9	2.9	1.0	2.0	3.1	5.2	10.3	[2] 22.2	[2] 48.4	112.0	235.7
1939	10.6	53.7	3.2	1.1	2.1	3.2	5.3	10.7	22.1	47.2	112.5	223.3
1938	10.6	58.0	3.8	1.2	2.3	3.4	5.6	10.9	22.1	47.1	110.9	212.6
1937	11.3	61.3	4.2	1.4	2.6	3.9	6.2	11.8	23.5	49.0	117.0	227.2
1936	11.6	62.9	4.4	1.5	2.8	4.1	6.5	12.1	24.1	50.8	121.7	242.7
1935	10.9	60.9	4.4	1.5	2.7	4.0	6.2	11.6	23.2	48.7	113.1	224.6
1934	11.1	66.8	5.1	1.5	2.8	4.1	6.2	11.8	23.5	49.4	114.1	224.8
1933	10.7	61.3	4.7	1.5	2.7	4.1	6.2	11.4	23.2	49.0	111.3	222.3
1932	10.9	61.3	4.6	1.5	2.9	4.2	6.3	11.6	23.4	50.0	114.3	233.3
1931	11.1	64.4	5.3	1.7	3.2	4.5	6.7	12.0	23.6	49.9	110.5	222.8
1930	11.3	69.0	5.6	1.7	3.3	4.7	6.8	12.2	24.0	51.4	112.7	228.0
1929	11.9	71.6	6.3	1.9	3.6	5.0	7.3	12.7	24.5	54.0	122.2	254.3
1928	12.0	73.1	6.5	1.9	3.7	5.0	7.5	12.8	24.2	54.3	125.2	268.3
1927	11.3	68.8	5.9	1.9	3.5	4.7	7.1	12.0	22.9	51.2	115.9	250.1
1926	12.1	77.9	7.2	1.9	3.7	4.9	7.4	12.7	24.1	53.8	125.4	279.7
1925	11.7	75.4	6.4	2.0	3.8	4.8	7.2	12.2	23.3	51.7	119.3	272.3
1924	11.6	76.8	6.8	2.0	3.8	4.8	7.1	12.1	23.0	51.0	117.2	261.8
1923	12.1	81.1	8.1	2.1	3.9	5.0	7.3	12.2	23.9	53.3	123.5	279.7
1922	11.7	77.6	7.4	2.1	3.8	5.0	7.1	11.8	23.2	52.2	117.5	258.1
1921	11.5	80.6	8.0	2.5	3.9	4.9	6.8	11.2	22.1	49.0	111.2	239.1
1920	13.0	92.3	9.9	2.6	4.9	6.8	8.1	12.2	23.6	52.5	118.9	248.3
1919	12.9	91.0	9.3	2.7	5.3	7.5	8.6	12.3	23.1	50.0	107.8	222.2
1918	18.1	111.7	15.7	4.1	10.7	16.4	13.4	15.2	26.5	55.1	113.0	222.1
1917	14.0	104.6	10.7	2.6	4.7	6.5	9.0	13.9	26.8	57.3	123.9	245.9
1916	13.8	105.7	11.1	2.5	4.4	6.2	8.8	13.6	26.5	57.2	123.9	250.4
1915	13.2	102.4	9.2	2.3	4.1	5.8	8.3	13.1	25.5	55.6	120.1	240.3
1914	13.3	107.2	10.2	2.5	4.2	6.0	8.5	13.1	25.1	54.1	115.6	231.5
1913	13.8	114.8	11.9	2.7	4.4	6.2	8.7	13.5	25.5	54.1	117.9	235.9
1912	13.6	111.1	10.9	2.5	4.3	6.1	8.6	13.4	25.8	54.5	120.2	242.2
1911	13.9	114.0	11.8	2.7	4.5	6.4	8.9	13.5	25.8	55.0	120.1	246.4
1910	14.7	131.8	14.0	2.9	4.5	6.5	9.0	13.7	26.2	55.6	122.2	250.3
1909	14.2	126.7	13.5	2.8	4.4	6.3	8.7	13.3	25.6	53.9	118.4	244.9
1908	14.7	133.2	14.0	3.0	4.8	6.7	9.0	13.8	26.2	53.8	119.5	248.6
1907	15.9	138.6	14.7	3.2	5.3	7.5	10.2	15.1	28.6	58.8	128.7	269.1
1906	15.7	144.8	15.8	3.3	5.3	7.5	9.8	14.5	27.1	55.0	120.4	255.1
1905	15.9	141.2	15.0	3.4	5.2	7.4	9.8	14.7	27.7	56.2	122.4	261.5
1904	16.4	139.2	15.9	3.7	5.5	7.8	10.2	15.1	28.5	58.2	126.1	270.0
1903	15.6	132.6	15.4	3.4	5.2	7.5	9.8	14.3	27.2	55.0	120.8	253.7
1902	15.5	138.9	16.6	3.3	5.1	7.5	9.6	14.0	25.9	52.9	114.1	235.6
1901	16.4	141.4	17.0	3.5	5.5	8.0	10.3	15.0	27.8	56.2	124.6	260.8
1900	17.2	162.4	19.8	3.9	5.9	8.2	10.2	15.0	27.2	56.4	123.3	260.9

See footnotes at end of table.

Series B 181–192. Death Rate, by Age and Sex: 1900 to 1970—Con.

Year	Total [1]	Under 1 year	1–4 years	5–14 years	15–24 years	25–34 years	35–44 years	45–54 years	55–64 years	65–74 years	75–84 years	85 years and over
	181	182	183	184	185	186	187	188	189	190	191	192
MALE												
1970	10.9	24.1	0.9	0.5	1.9	2.2	4.0	9.6	22.8	48.7	100.1	178.2
1969	11.0	24.2	.9	.5	1.9	2.2	4.1	9.6	23.1	50.3	97.6	195.5
1968	11.1	25.2	.9	.5	1.8	2.1	4.1	9.8	23.7	51.9	98.8	203.9
1967	10.8	25.2	1.0	.5	1.7	2.0	3.9	9.6	23.0	50.2	96.2	203.8
1966	11.0	26.3	1.0	.5	1.7	2.0	3.9	9.8	23.3	51.2	98.5	209.3
1965	10.9	27.1	1.0	.5	1.6	2.0	3.9	9.7	23.1	50.5	98.2	212.8
1964	10.8	27.7	1.0	.5	1.5	2.0	3.8	9.7	23.0	49.9	97.1	210.4
1963	11.1	28.6	1.1	.5	1.5	1.9	3.8	9.8	23.2	51.1	100.7	224.6
1962	10.9	28.7	1.0	.5	1.5	1.9	3.7	9.7	22.6	49.4	98.7	219.0
1961	10.7	28.6	1.1	.5	1.5	1.8	3.7	9.6	22.4	48.1	97.8	209.1
1960 *	11.0	30.6	1.2	.6	1.5	1.9	3.7	9.9	23.1	49.1	101.8	211.9
1959	10.8	31.1	1.2	.6	1.5	1.9	3.7	9.7	22.8	47.9	99.1	205.4
1958	11.0	31.6	1.2	.6	1.5	1.9	3.7	9.8	23.0	48.5	101.4	208.3
1957	11.1	31.6	1.2	.6	1.6	1.9	3.8	9.9	23.5	48.8	100.7	201.9
1956	10.8	32.1	1.2	.6	1.7	1.9	3.7	9.6	23.0	47.2	100.6	195.1
1955	10.8	32.1	1.2	.6	1.6	1.9	3.8	9.7	22.7	46.9	101.5	191.7
1954	10.7	33.0	1.3	.6	1.6	2.0	3.8	9.9	22.7	46.3	98.5	185.0
1953	11.1	34.7	1.4	.7	1.7	2.1	4.1	10.4	23.9	47.6	103.4	197.8
1952	11.1	36.2	1.5	.7	1.8	2.2	4.2	10.5	24.0	47.5	102.6	194.6
1951	11.1	36.6	1.5	.7	1.7	2.2	4.3	10.6	23.9	48.6	103.9	207.4
1950	11.1	37.3	1.5	.7	1.7	2.2	4.3	10.7	²24.0	²49.3	104.3	216.4
1949	11.1	39.6	1.6	.8	1.7	2.2	4.4	10.8	24.2	48.4	103.8	215.0
1948	11.3	40.2	1.7	.8	1.8	2.3	4.7	11.2	24.6	48.8	105.1	226.4
1947	11.5	38.8	1.8	.8	1.9	2.4	4.8	11.3	25.0	49.2	106.6	229.3
1946	11.3	52.1	2.0	1.0	2.1	2.6	4.9	11.2	24.3	47.5	104.1	221.1
1945	12.6	47.6	2.2	1.1	2.7	3.5	5.5	11.6	25.0	49.1	107.7	220.7
1944	12.4	49.1	2.5	1.1	2.8	3.2	5.4	11.7	25.0	50.2	110.7	225.5
1943	12.4	49.3	2.8	1.1	2.6	3.2	5.5	12.2	25.7	52.6	117.2	242.6
1942	11.7	54.4	2.6	1.1	2.3	3.2	5.6	12.1	25.1	51.3	111.0	222.1
1941	11.8	58.6	3.0	1.1	2.3	3.3	5.7	12.2	25.3	52.6	115.2	231.9
1940	12.0	61.9	3.1	1.2	2.3	3.4	5.9	12.5	²26.1	²54.6	121.3	246.4
1939	11.7	60.3	3.4	1.3	2.4	3.4	6.0	12.5	25.5	52.7	120.7	232.6
1938	11.7	65.2	4.1	1.4	2.5	3.6	6.2	12.6	25.3	52.5	118.8	222.2
1937	12.5	68.7	4.5	1.5	2.9	4.2	7.0	13.8	27.2	54.5	126.4	238.0
1936	12.7	70.7	4.7	1.7	3.0	4.4	7.4	14.1	27.7	56.1	130.6	252.7
1935	12.0	68.9	4.7	1.7	2.9	4.3	7.0	13.3	26.3	53.7	121.7	234.7
1934	12.1	74.8	5.4	1.7	3.0	4.3	7.0	13.5	26.6	54.3	122.2	235.1
1933	11.6	68.3	5.0	1.7	2.9	4.3	6.8	12.9	26.0	53.6	118.3	232.7
1932	11.7	68.5	4.9	1.7	3.0	4.3	6.9	12.9	26.1	54.1	121.1	242.3
1931	12.0	72.2	5.6	1.8	3.4	4.7	7.4	13.4	26.2	54.4	117.5	234.1
1930	12.3	77.0	6.0	1.9	3.5	4.9	7.5	13.6	26.6	55.8	119.1	236.7
1929	12.8	80.0	6.6	2.1	3.7	5.2	8.0	14.1	26.9	58.4	128.9	259.8
1928	12.8	82.3	6.8	2.1	3.8	5.1	8.0	14.1	26.5	58.5	132.3	271.5
1927	12.1	77.5	6.2	2.1	3.5	4.8	7.6	13.2	25.0	55.2	122.6	254.2
1926	12.9	87.1	7.6	2.1	3.7	5.0	7.9	13.9	26.0	57.6	131.8	281.3
1925	12.4	84.6	6.7	2.2	3.8	4.9	7.6	13.3	25.1	55.4	125.3	273.5
1924	12.3	86.2	7.2	2.2	3.8	4.8	7.6	13.1	24.9	54.7	122.8	263.8
1923	12.7	90.2	8.5	2.3	3.9	5.1	7.7	13.1	25.6	56.2	127.4	279.4
1922	12.3	87.0	7.9	2.3	3.8	5.0	7.4	12.5	24.7	55.1	121.8	257.8
1921	11.9	90.1	8.4	2.7	3.8	4.8	6.9	11.6	23.3	51.1	114.4	241.2
1920	13.4	103.6	10.3	2.8	4.8	6.4	8.2	12.6	24.6	54.5	122.1	253.0
1919	13.5	101.9	9.7	2.8	5.3	7.4	9.1	12.9	24.4	51.9	111.0	229.6
1918	19.8	124.5	16.0	4.2	12.2	19.0	15.3	16.7	28.7	58.5	118.1	227.6
1917	15.0	117.4	11.2	2.7	5.0	7.1	10.1	15.5	29.3	61.1	129.0	251.1
1916	14.8	118.2	11.7	2.6	4.5	6.6	9.7	15.1	29.0	60.6	128.7	255.5
1915	14.0	114.5	9.7	2.4	4.2	6.2	9.1	14.4	27.7	58.8	124.6	246.7
1914	14.2	118.9	10.7	2.6	4.4	6.4	9.4	14.5	27.4	57.8	120.5	236.9
1913	14.8	127.6	12.5	2.8	4.7	6.7	9.7	15.0	27.9	57.7	122.8	241.4
1912	14.5	123.3	11.5	2.6	4.5	6.5	9.5	14.9	28.2	57.9	125.2	248.6
1911	14.7	125.9	12.2	2.8	4.7	6.7	9.8	14.9	28.0	58.1	125.1	249.3
1910	15.6	145.5	14.6	3.0	4.8	6.9	10.0	15.2	28.7	58.7	127.4	255.8
1909	15.1	139.7	14.1	2.9	4.6	6.6	9.5	14.8	27.7	57.0	123.9	251.4
1908	15.5	147.0	14.6	3.1	5.0	7.0	9.8	15.2	28.4	56.4	125.9	251.5
1907	17.0	152.9	15.3	3.3	5.8	8.1	11.4	16.8	31.1	62.7	134.0	275.0
1906	16.7	160.2	16.4	3.4	5.7	7.9	10.9	16.0	29.4	58.2	126.5	261.6
1905	16.7	156.6	15.8	3.4	5.3	7.6	10.6	16.0	29.8	59.0	128.8	270.5
1904	17.3	153.9	16.6	3.7	5.5	8.0	11.1	16.4	31.1	61.7	132.6	280.7
1903	16.4	146.6	15.9	3.5	5.3	7.7	10.4	15.5	29.0	58.5	126.8	262.7
1902	16.4	153.4	17.1	3.4	5.2	7.7	10.3	15.1	28.0	56.5	120.5	248.6
1901	17.3	156.4	17.7	3.7	5.7	8.3	11.0	16.1	29.5	59.2	129.7	268.1
1900	17.9	179.1	20.5	3.8	5.9	8.2	10.7	15.7	28.7	59.3	128.3	268.8

See footnotes at end of table.

Series B 181–192.　Death Rate, by Age and Sex: 1900 to 1970—Con.

Year	Total [1]	Under 1 year	1–4 years	5–14 years	15–24 years	25–34 years	35–44 years	45–54 years	55–64 years	65–74 years	75–84 years	85 years and over
	181	182	183	184	185	186	187	188	189	190	191	192
FEMALE												
1970	8.1	18.6	0.8	0.3	0.7	1.0	2.3	5.2	11.0	25.8	66.8	155.2
1969	8.1	18.6	.8	.3	.7	1.0	2.4	5.1	11.1	27.1	66.3	188.0
1968	8.2	19.2	.8	.3	.7	1.0	2.4	5.3	11.4	27.8	68.3	191.7
1967	8.0	19.4	.8	.3	.6	1.0	2.3	5.1	11.2	27.3	66.9	188.6
1966	8.1	20.3	.8	.3	.6	1.1	2.3	5.2	11.2	28.1	69.6	195.1
1965	8.0	20.9	.8	.3	.6	1.1	2.3	5.2	11.3	27.7	70.0	195.3
1964	8.0	21.4	.9	.3	.6	1.1	2.3	5.2	11.4	27.8	70.4	193.8
1963	8.2	21.8	.9	.4	.6	1.1	2.3	5.2	11.8	28.6	73.5	201.4
1962	8.1	21.9	.9	.4	.6	1.1	2.3	5.2	11.6	28.3	73.3	196.0
1961	7.9	22.0	.9	.3	.6	1.0	2.2	5.1	11.5	27.9	72.8	187.8
1960 *	8.1	23.2	1.0	.4	.6	1.1	2.3	5.3	12.0	28.7	76.3	190.1
1959	8.0	23.8	1.0	.4	.6	1.1	2.2	5.2	11.8	28.6	75.5	186.8
1958	8.1	24.5	1.0	.4	.6	1.1	2.3	5.4	12.1	29.4	77.4	191.0
1957	8.1	24.3	1.0	.4	.7	1.1	2.4	5.5	12.4	30.0	78.5	179.5
1956	7.9	24.3	1.0	.4	.7	1.1	2.3	5.4	12.3	29.4	78.7	173.0
1955	7.9	24.7	1.0	.4	.7	1.1	2.4	5.4	12.2	29.7	79.5	171.1
1954	7.8	25.3	1.1	.4	.7	1.1	2.4	5.7	12.3	29.6	78.4	164.3
1953	8.1	26.5	1.2	.4	.7	1.2	2.6	6.0	13.1	31.2	83.1	173.7
1952	8.1	27.9	1.3	.5	.8	1.3	2.7	6.1	13.4	31.5	82.8	175.1
1951	8.2	27.8	1.3	.5	.9	1.4	2.8	6.3	13.8	32.2	84.1	182.0
1950	8.2	28.5	1.3	.5	.9	1.4	2.9	6.4	[2] 14.0	[2] 33.3	84.0	191.9
1949	8.3	30.6	1.4	.5	.9	1.5	3.0	6.6	14.3	33.6	83.8	194.4
1948	8.5	31.0	1.5	.6	1.1	1.6	3.2	6.8	14.8	34.3	86.4	203.1
1947	8.7	30.0	1.5	.6	1.2	1.8	3.3	7.1	15.2	35.3	88.5	207.2
1946	8.6	40.1	1.7	.7	1.3	1.9	3.5	7.1	15.3	35.1	87.3	203.0
1945	8.8	37.2	1.9	.7	1.4	2.1	3.8	7.5	15.9	36.3	90.2	201.3
1944	9.0	39.0	2.2	.8	1.4	2.2	3.9	7.6	16.4	37.8	93.7	207.8
1943	9.4	38.5	2.4	.8	1.5	2.4	4.1	8.1	17.2	39.9	99.0	221.2
1942	9.0	42.9	2.3	.7	1.6	2.4	4.1	8.0	16.7	38.7	93.4	202.9
1941	9.2	46.3	2.6	.8	1.7	2.6	4.3	8.3	17.1	39.8	97.3	208.8
1940	9.5	47.7	2.7	.9	1.8	2.7	4.5	8.6	[2] 18.0	[2] 42.2	103.7	227.6
1939	9.5	46.8	2.9	.9	1.9	2.9	4.6	8.9	18.6	41.7	105.1	216.3
1938	9.6	50.7	3.6	1.1	2.1	3.1	4.9	9.1	18.6	41.8	103.7	205.4
1937	10.0	53.6	3.9	1.2	2.3	3.5	5.4	9.7	19.6	43.4	108.4	219.0
1936	10.4	54.9	4.1	1.3	2.5	3.8	5.6	10.0	20.3	45.4	113.5	235.3
1935	9.9	52.8	4.1	1.4	2.5	3.8	5.4	9.8	19.8	43.7	105.1	217.0
1934	10.0	58.5	4.7	1.4	2.5	3.8	5.5	9.9	20.2	44.4	106.5	217.1
1933	9.7	54.0	4.4	1.3	2.6	3.9	5.5	9.8	20.1	44.3	104.7	214.4
1932	10.0	53.9	4.4	1.4	2.7	4.0	5.7	10.1	20.6	45.8	108.0	226.6
1931	10.1	56.5	4.9	1.5	3.0	4.3	6.0	10.4	20.7	45.4	104.0	214.3
1930	10.4	60.7	5.2	1.5	3.2	4.4	6.1	10.6	21.2	46.8	106.6	221.4
1929	11.0	62.9	5.9	1.7	3.5	4.8	6.6	11.1	21.8	49.4	116.0	250.2
1928	11.1	63.6	6.1	1.7	3.6	4.8	6.9	11.3	21.8	49.9	118.6	265.9
1927	10.5	60.0	5.6	1.7	3.4	4.6	6.5	10.8	20.6	47.0	109.6	247.0
1926	11.3	68.4	6.8	1.7	3.7	4.8	6.8	11.4	22.0	49.9	119.5	278.4
1925	10.9	66.0	6.1	1.8	3.8	4.8	6.7	11.0	21.2	47.9	113.8	271.3
1924	10.9	67.0	6.4	1.8	3.8	4.7	6.6	11.1	21.0	47.1	112.0	260.3
1923	11.5	71.6	7.7	2.0	3.9	5.0	6.9	11.2	22.0	50.4	119.8	279.9
1922	11.1	67.9	7.0	2.0	3.8	5.1	6.8	11.0	21.5	49.2	113.7	258.4
1921	11.0	70.8	7.6	2.3	3.9	5.0	6.8	10.7	20.8	46.8	108.3	237.6
1920	12.6	80.7	9.5	2.5	5.0	7.1	8.0	11.7	22.4	50.5	115.9	244.7
1919	12.3	79.7	8.8	2.6	5.3	7.6	8.1	11.5	21.6	48.0	105.0	216.8
1918	16.4	98.5	15.5	4.1	9.4	14.0	11.3	13.6	24.0	51.5	108.3	218.1
1917	12.9	91.5	10.1	2.4	4.4	5.9	7.9	12.0	24.0	53.4	119.2	242.1
1916	12.8	92.8	10.5	2.3	4.2	5.7	7.7	11.9	23.9	53.6	119.5	246.6
1915	12.3	90.0	8.8	2.2	3.9	5.4	7.4	11.6	23.2	52.5	116.0	235.3
1914	12.4	95.1	9.7	2.4	4.0	5.6	7.5	11.6	22.7	50.4	111.0	227.3
1913	12.8	101.7	11.4	2.5	4.1	5.7	7.7	11.8	22.9	50.5	113.4	231.7
1912	12.7	98.5	10.4	2.3	4.0	5.7	7.6	11.6	23.3	51.1	115.5	237.1
1911	13.0	101.8	11.3	2.6	4.3	6.0	7.9	11.9	23.4	51.9	115.5	244.2
1910	13.7	117.6	13.4	2.9	4.2	6.1	7.9	12.1	23.7	52.4	117.4	246.0
1909	13.4	113.2	12.9	2.7	4.2	6.0	7.8	11.7	23.4	50.8	113.3	239.9
1908	13.8	119.1	13.4	2.9	4.5	6.3	8.0	12.2	23.9	51.1	113.7	246.4
1907	14.8	123.9	14.1	3.0	4.8	6.9	8.8	13.1	25.9	54.9	124.0	264.7
1906	14.7	129.2	15.2	3.2	4.9	7.0	8.5	12.9	24.6	51.8	114.8	250.3
1905	15.0	125.5	14.2	3.3	5.1	7.2	8.9	13.3	25.6	53.5	116.7	254.9
1904	15.5	124.2	15.2	3.6	5.5	7.6	9.2	13.7	26.0	54.9	120.3	262.1
1903	14.8	118.3	14.9	3.4	5.0	7.3	9.0	13.0	25.4	51.8	115.4	247.1
1902	14.6	124.1	16.0	3.2	5.1	7.3	8.8	12.8	23.9	49.5	108.3	226.1
1901	15.6	126.1	16.2	3.4	5.4	7.8	9.6	13.9	26.0	53.4	120.0	255.6
1900	16.5	145.4	19.1	3.9	5.8	8.2	9.8	14.2	25.8	53.6	118.8	255.2

* Denotes first year for which figures include Alaska and Hawaii.
[1] Age not reported included in "Total," but not distributed among specified age groups.

[2] Based on enumerated population adjusted for age bias in the population for Negro and other races, 55 to 69 years old.

Series B 193–200.　Death Rate, by Sex and by Selected Cause, for Massachusetts: 1860 to 1970

[Includes only deaths, excluding fetal deaths, occurring within Massachusetts, except for 1940–1970; for these years, data are for deaths occurring to residents of Massachusetts]

| Year | By sex per 1,000 population | | | By cause per 100,000 population | | | | | Year | By sex per 1,000 population | | | By cause per 100,000 population | | | | |
| | Total | Male | Female | Tuberculosis of respiratory system | Diphtheria | Typhoid and paratyphoid fever [1] | Measles | Smallpox | | Total | Male | Female | Tuberculosis of respiratory system | Diphtheria | Typhoid and paratyphoid fever | Measles | Smallpox |
	193	194	195	196	197	198	199	200		193	194	195	196	197	198	199	200
1970	10.1			2.4	–	(Z)	(Z)	-------	1892	20.9	(NA)	(NA)	244.8	62.2	35.3	3.8	0.1
1969	10.6			2.4	–	–	(Z)	-------	1891	19.7	(NA)	(NA)	239.6	53.2	35.9	10.3	.1
1968	10.9			2.9	–	(Z)	(Z)	-------									
1967	10.7			3.5	–	(Z)	–	-------	1890	19.4	20.0	18.9	258.6	72.6	37.3	5.1	(Z)
1966	10.7			3.3	–	(Z)	–	-------	1889	19.2	(NA)	(NA)	256.5	101.7	40.9	7.9	.3
									1888	19.9	(NA)	(NA)	270.8	86.6	44.6	10.4	.4
1965	11.0			4.0	–	(Z)	0.1	-------	1887	19.8	(NA)	(NA)	285.6	79.2	44.8	22.1	.1
1964	[2] 9.6			3.3	–	(Z)	(Z)	-------	1886	18.6	(NA)	(NA)	295.1	78.0	40.0	6.5	(Z)
1963	10.5			4.4	(Z)	(Z)	–	-------									
1962	10.8			4.8	–	(Z)	.1	-------	1885	19.6	20.2	19.0	306.6	78.4	39.5	16.1	1.0
1961	10.8			5.7	–	0.1	(Z)	-------	1884	19.0	(NA)	(NA)	303.6	86.2	45.8	3.9	.2
									1883	20.1	(NA)	(NA)	316.0	86.4	45.8	17.1	.3
1960	11.0			6.0	–	(Z)	.1	-------	1882	19.9	(NA)	(NA)	317.9	96.0	58.5	3.7	2.4
1959	10.7			6.6	–	(Z)	–	-------	1881	20.1	(NA)	(NA)	324.5	131.4	59.1	12.7	2.6
1958	11.3			6.5	–	(Z)	.1	-------									
1957	11.1			8.2	(Z)	–	.1	-------	1880	19.8	20.3	19.3	308.1	134.3	49.5	13.2	2.1
1956	10.9			8.6	0.1	(Z)	(Z)	(Z)	1879	18.1	(NA)	(NA)	297.4	130.6	36.3	1.1	.4
									1878	18.1	(NA)	(NA)	308.4	145.5	39.3	17.6	.1
1955	10.9			9.3	(Z)	(Z)	.4	(Z)	1877	18.4	(NA)	(NA)	320.4	166.6	47.8	7.9	1.4
1950	10.5	11.6	9.5	20.2	.2	(Z)	(Z)	(Z)	1876	19.8	(NA)	(NA)	317.6	196.4	52.5	2.8	1.8
1945	12.2	(NA)	(NA)	36.9	.3	.1	.2	(Z)									
1940	11.9	12.6	11.1	34.6	.2	.2	.3	(Z)	1875	21.7	21.8	20.5	347.4	113.8	64.1	14.1	2.1
1935	11.5	12.2	10.8	42.9	.7	.3	.8	(Z)	1874	18.6	(NA)	(NA)	328.0	56.7	71.2	10.0	1.6
									1873	21.6	(NA)	(NA)	353.6	47.4	89.5	11.5	42.5
1930	11.6	12.2	11.1	57.2	4.3	.9	3.3	(Z)	1872	22.9	(NA)	(NA)	362.6	49.1	111.1	27.9	67.2
1925	12.5	13.0	11.9	70.1	8.0	1.8	8.4	(Z)	1871	18.7	(NA)	(NA)	339.3	50.0	74.7	8.8	19.7
1920	13.8	13.9	13.6	96.8	15.1	2.4	9.1	.1									
1915	14.3	15.0	13.7	116.8	19.8	6.7	7.3	.3	1870	18.8	19.5	18.6	343.3	46.4	91.5	18.5	9.0
1910	16.1	17.0	15.3	138.3	21.0	12.5	11.6	(Z)	1869	18.4	(NA)	(NA)	328.8	54.3	85.0	15.7	4.2
									1868	18.6	(NA)	(NA)	322.0	56.7	65.0	20.8	1.5
1905	16.7	17.6	15.8	163.5	22.1	17.9	8.4	.1	1867	17.0	(NA)	(NA)	325.5	45.3	72.0	14.5	14.6
1900	18.4	19.2	17.6	190.3	52.8	22.1	11.7	.1	1866	18.2	(NA)	(NA)	353.0	63.7	83.7	8.4	10.8
1899	17.4	(NA)	(NA)	190.4	38.2	22.3	8.8	.5									
1898	17.5	(NA)	(NA)	197.4	26.4	24.7	3.1	(Z)	1865	20.6	21.7	19.6	367.9	92.8	133.7	10.7	17.4
1897	18.1	(NA)	(NA)	207.4	54.5	23.2	6.0	.2	1864	22.8	(NA)	(NA)	375.7	106.7	107.6	25.4	19.2
									1863	22.2	(NA)	(NA)	372.6	182.4	115.1	11.3	3.4
1896	19.3	(NA)	(NA)	216.4	65.5	28.3	5.4	(Z)	1862	18.5	(NA)	(NA)	342.8	92.1	91.1	29.6	3.2
1895	19.0	19.9	18.2	223.4	71.4	27.2	4.7	(Z)	1861	19.5	(NA)	(NA)	365.2	89.2	79.9	16.9	2.7
1894	19.1	(NA)	(NA)	223.4	73.6	30.6	4.0	1.3	1860	18.7	19.3	18.4	--------	68.0	76.1	18.2	27.1
1893	20.5	(NA)	(NA)	231.0	58.3	31.4	11.5	.4									

– Represents zero.　NA Not available.　Z Less than 0.05.
[1] Beginning 1958, includes "other salmonella infections."

[2] Excludes approximately 6,000 deaths registered in Massachusetts, primarily to residents of the State.

Series B 201–213.　Death Rate, by Age, for Massachusetts: 1865 to 1900

[Includes only deaths, excluding fetal deaths, occurring within Massachusetts.　Rate per 1,000 population for specified group]

| Year | Total | Under 1 year | 1–4 years | 5–9 years | 10–14 years | 15–19 years | 20–29 years | 30–39 years | 40–49 years | 50–59 years | 60–69 years | 70–79 years | 80 years and over |
	201	202	203	204	205	206	207	208	209	210	211	212	213
1900	18.2	190.1	57.8	5.3	2.9	4.8	7.0	8.8	12.0	21.3	41.0	85.8	197.8
1895	19.0	215.9	64.5	6.2	3.2	5.3	7.1	9.7	12.7	20.5	39.4	82.4	184.7
1890	19.4	223.6	68.1	6.6	3.6	6.3	8.4	10.4	13.4	20.4	37.5	76.0	174.2
1885	19.6	212.5	67.0	7.5	3.8	6.4	9.1	10.6	13.0	19.7	36.2	76.2	182.3
1880	19.8	191.3	68.1	8.5	3.8	6.6	9.5	10.3	11.7	17.9	33.9	73.1	184.0
1875	21.2	226.6	74.0	9.8	4.7	7.7	10.5	11.3	13.0	18.3	34.8	71.1	176.4
1870	18.8	188.1	62.9	5.9	3.7	7.2	10.5	10.6	12.0	17.0	30.1	68.9	170.0
1865	20.6	205.3	68.6	9.6	5.1	9.6	12.6	11.7	11.9	17.5	32.9	70.5	168.2

Series B 214–215.　Marriage Rate: 1920 to 1970

Year	Per 1,000 population	Per 1,000 unmarried females [1]	Year	Per 1,000 population	Per 1,000 unmarried females [1]	Year	Per 1,000 population	Per 1,000 unmarried females [1]	Year	Per 1,000 population	Per 1,000 unmarried females [1]
	214	215		214	215		214	215		214	215
1970	10.6	76.7	1957	8.9	78.0	1944	10.9	76.5	1931	8.6	61.9
1969	10.6	80.0	1956	9.5	82.4	1943	11.7	83.0	1930	9.2	67.6
1968	10.4	79.1	1955	9.3	80.9	1942	13.2	93.0			
1967	9.7	76.4	1954	9.2	79.8	1941	12.7	88.5	1929	10.1	75.5
1966	9.5	75.6	1953	9.8	83.7	1940	12.1	82.8	1928	9.8	74.1
									1927	10.1	77.0
1965	9.3	75.0	1952	9.9	83.2	1939	10.7	73.0	1926	10.2	78.7
1964	9.0	74.6	1951	10.4	86.6	1938	10.3	69.9	1925	10.3	79.2
1963	8.8	73.4	1950	11.1	90.2	1937	11.3	78.0			
1962	8.5	71.2	1949	10.6	86.7	1936	10.7	74.0	1924	10.4	80.3
1961	8.5	72.2	1948	12.4	98.5	1935	10.4	72.5	1923	11.0	85.2
									1922	10.3	79.7
1960 *	8.5	73.5	1947	13.9	106.2	1934	10.3	71.8	1921	10.7	83.0
1959 [2]	8.5	73.6	1946	16.4	118.1	1933	8.7	61.3	1920	12.0	92.0
1958	8.4	72.0	1945	12.2	83.6	1932	7.9	56.0			

* Denotes first year for which figures include Alaska and Hawaii.　　　　[2] Includes Alaska.
[1] 15 years old and over.

Series B 216–220.　Divorce: 1920 to 1970

[Includes reported annulments]

Year	Divorce rate Per 1,000 population	Divorce rate Per 1,000 married females [1]	Median duration of marriage (years)	Percent of spouses separated	Divorced persons per 1,000 married, spouse present [2]	Year	Divorce rate Per 1,000 population	Divorce rate Per 1,000 married females [1]
	216	217	218	219	220		216	217
1970	3.5	14.9	6.7	1.8	47	1944	2.9	12.0
1969	3.2	13.4	6.9	1.9	46	1943	2.6	11.0
1968	2.9	12.4	7.0	1.8	45	1942	2.4	10.1
1967	2.6	11.2	7.1	1.8	43	1941	2.2	9.4
1966	2.5	10.9	7.1	1.9	43			
						1940	2.0	8.8
1965	2.5	10.6	7.2	2.0	41	1939	1.9	8.5
1964	2.4	10.0	7.4	1.9	41	1938	1.9	8.4
1963	2.3	9.6	7.5	1.8	39	1937	1.9	8.7
1962	2.2	9.4	7.3	1.9	37	1936	1.8	8.3
1961	2.3	9.6	7.1	1.9	37			
						1935	1.7	7.8
1960 *	2.2	9.2	7.2	1.8	35	1934	1.6	7.5
1959 [3]	2.2	9.3	7.0	1.9	33	1933	1.3	6.1
1958	2.1	8.9	6.4	1.8	32	1932	1.3	6.1
1957	2.2	9.2	6.7	1.6	31	1931	1.5	7.1
1956	2.3	9.4	6.5	1.8	32			
						1930	1.6	7.5
1955	2.3	9.3	6.4	1.8	31	1929	1.7	8.0
1954	2.4	9.5	6.4	1.7	33	1928	1.7	7.8
1953	2.5	9.9	6.1	1.5	31	1927	1.6	7.8
1952	2.5	10.1	6.1	1.4	29	1926	1.6	7.5
1951	2.5	9.9	6.0	1.5	29			
						1925	1.5	7.2
1950	2.6	10.3	5.8	1.8	29	1924	1.5	7.2
1949	2.7	10.6	-----	-----	29	1923	1.5	7.1
1948	2.8	11.2	-----	-----	33	1922	1.4	6.6
1947	3.4	13.6	-----	-----	-----	1921	1.5	7.2
1946	4.3	17.9	-----	-----	-----	1920	1.6	8.0
1945	3.5	14.4	-----	-----	-----			

* Denotes first year for which figures include Alaska and Hawaii.
[1] 15 years old and over. Population enumerated as of April 1 for 1940, 1950, and 1960, and estimated as of July 1 for all other years; includes Armed Forces abroad for 1941–1946.
[2] Persons 14 years old and over.　　[3] Includes Alaska.

Chapter B

Health and Medical Care (Series B 221-459)

B 221-235. Total and per capita national health expenditures, by type of service, 1929-1970.

Source: U.S. Social Security Administration. 1929-1968, *Compendium of National Health Expenditures Data*, DHEW Pub. No.(SSA)73-11903, table 6; 1969-1970, *National Health Expenditures, Calendar Years 1929-71*, Research and Statistics Note, No. 3, 1973, DHEW Pub. No. (SSA)73-11701, tables 2 and 8.

The general method of estimating national health expenditures is to estimate the total outlays for each type of medical service or expenditure and to deduct the amounts paid to public and private hospitals, physicians in private practice, etc., under each public program. The figures for each public program are allocated by type of expenditure on the basis of published and unpublished reports for each program.

B 223, hospital care. The estimates of expenditures for hospital care are based on the data on hospital finances published by the American Hospital Association, and increased slightly to allow for nonreporting and for osteopathic hospitals. Salaries of physicians and dentists on the staffs of hospitals and hospital outpatient facilities are considered a component of hospital care and are, therefore, included. Expenditures for the education and training of physicians and other health personnel are included only where they are not separable from the cost of hospital operations.

B 224-226, physicians' services, dentists' services, and other professional services. The estimates of expenditures for the services of physicians, dentists, and other health professions in private practice are based on the gross incomes from self-employment practice reported to the Internal Revenue Service on Schedule C of the income-tax return (as shown in *Statistics of Income*, published by the Internal Revenue Service). Data are totaled for practitioners in sole proprietorships and partnerships. The total also includes the estimated gross income of offices that are organized as corporations, the gross receipts of medical and dental laboratories estimated to represent patient payments to medical laboratories, and the estimated expenses of group-practice prepayment plans in providing physicians' services (to the extent that these are not included in physicians' income from self-employment). Estimated receipts of physicians for making life insurance examinations are deducted.

Salaries of physicians and dentists on the staffs of hospitals and hospital outpatient facilities are considered a component of hospital care (series B 223).

Salaries of visiting nurse associations, estimated from surveys conducted by the National League for Nursing, are added to the private income of other health professionals. Deductions and exclusions are made in the same manner as for expenditures for physicians' and dentists' services.

B 227-228, drugs and drug sundries, and eyeglasses and appliances. The basic source of the estimates for these items is the report of personal consumption expenditures in the Department of Commerce national income accounts in the monthly *Survey of Current Business*. Total expenditures for drugs and appliances are the sum of the Department of Commerce estimates and the expenditures under all public programs for these products.

B 229, nursing-home care. Expenditures for nursing-home care are derived by applying an estimated cost per patient day to the total days of care. Total days of care are estimated by applying an average occupancy rate, as reported by the Federal Housing Administration, to the number of nursing-home beds, as reported by the Division of Hospital and Medical Facilities of the Public Health Service in their annual report, *Hill-Burton State Plan Data*.

The cost per patient day was based on unpublished data from a survey of nursing homes financed by the Social Security Administration.

B 230, expenses for prepayment and administration. Prepayment expenses represent the difference between the earned premiums or subscription charges of health insurance organizations and their claim or benefit expenditures (expenditures in providing such services in the case of organizations that directly provide services). In other words, it is the amount retained by health insurance organizations for operating expenses, additions to reserves, and profits, and is considered a consumer expenditure. The data on the financial experience of health insurance organizations are reported annually in a *Social Security Bulletin* article on private health insurance.

The administration component represents the administrative expenses (where they are reported) of federally financed health programs.

B 231, government public health activities. The Federal portion consists of outlays for the organization and delivery of health services and prevention and control of health problems by the Health Services and Mental Health Administration, the National Institutes of Health, and the Environmental Health Service of the Public Health Service. Also included are outlays by other Federal agencies for similar health activities. The data for these programs are taken from Office of Management and Budget, *Special Analyses, Budget of the United States*.

The State and local portion represents expenditures of all State and local health departments and intergovernmental payments to the States and localities for public health activities. It excludes expenditures by other State and local government departments for air-pollution and water-pollution control, sanitation, water supplies, and sewage treatment. The source of these data is *Government Finances*, published annually by the Bureau of the Census.

B 232, other health services. This series covers items of expenditures not elsewhere classified. It includes, for each public program, the residual amount of expenditures not classified as a specific type of medical service. In addition, it includes the following programs: (1) Industrial in-plant services and activities of private voluntary health agencies in the private sector and (2) school health services and nonhospital Federal medical activities in the public sector.

B 233-235, research and medical-facilities construction. Expenditures for medical research, series B 234, include all such spending by agencies whose primary object is the advancement of human health. Also included are those research expenditures directly related to health that are made by other agencies, such as those of the Department of Defense or the National Aeronautics and Space Administration. Research expenditures of drug and medical supply companies are excluded since they are included in the cost of the product. The Federal amounts represent those reported as medical research in the Office of Management and Budget, *Special Analyses, Budget of the United States*. The amounts shown for State and local governments and private expenditures are based on published estimates that have been prepared by the Resources Analysis Branch of the National Institutes of Health, primarily in the periodic publication, *Basic Data Relating to the National Institutes of Health*.

Expenditures for construction, series B 235, represent "value put in place" for hospitals, nursing homes, medical clinics, and medical-research facilities but not for private office buildings providing office space for private practitioners. Excluded are amounts spent for construction of water-treatment or sewage-treatment plants and Federal grants for these purposes.

The data for value put in place for construction of publicly and privately owned medical facilities in each year are taken from the Department of Commerce monthly report, *Construction Review*.

B 236–247.   National and personal health care expenditures, by source of funds, 1929–1970.

Source: See sources for series B 221–235 (tables 3, 4, and 6 in first source; tables 2 and 5 in second).

For the general method of estimating national health expenditures, see text for series B 221–235.   For the dollar amounts of gross national product used as the bases for series B 237, see series F 1.

For the most part, private expenditures represent direct payments made by private consumers and insurance benefits paid in their behalf by private insurers.   In addition, they include private philanthropy; amounts spent by industry for maintenance of in-plant health services; expenditures made from capital funds for expansion, renovation, or new construction of medical facilities; and outlays for research by private foundations.

Public funds come from Federal, State, and local governments.

Personal health care expenditures include all such expenditures except research, construction, expenses for prepayment and administration, government public health activities, and expenses of private voluntary agencies for fund-raising and general-health activities.

B 248–261.   National health expenditures, by type of expenditure, 1929–1970.

Source: See sources for series B 221–235 (tables 6 and 10 in first source; tables 2 and 3 in second).

For the general method of estimating national health expenditures, see text for series B 221–235.   For the dollar amounts of gross national product used as the bases for series B 249, see series F 1.

See also text for series B 236–247.

B 253, veterans' hospital and medical care.   All veterans with service-connected disabilities are eligible for a wide range of hospital and medical services, as are veterans with nonservice-connected disabilities who are unable to pay for care.   The medical care program includes inpatient and outpatient hospital and clinic care, nursing bed care (and a community nursing-home program where nursing bed facilities are not available), day-care centers for psychiatric patients, outpatient dental care, and the provision of prosthetic appliances.

There were 165 Veterans Administration hospitals which collectively in 1970 had a capacity of about 100,000 beds.   Medical care is also given to veterans in other Federal hospitals, in hospitals attached to VA domiciliaries, and in State and local government and private hospitals at the expense of the Veterans Administration.

All veterans' health and medical benefit data are provided by the Veterans Administration together with administrative costs. See also series Y 993–994 and Y 1010–1027.

B 254, general hospital and medical care.   The Federal Government has directly provided hospital and medical care for specified groups of beneficiaries since 1798 when President John Adams signed into law "An Act for the relief of sick and disabled seamen." Since that time, federally sponsored and financed medical care for specified beneficiaries has been expanded to include Indians, Alaskan natives, lepers, narcotic addicts, commissioned officers of the Public Health Service and their dependents, personnel of the Coast Guard and the former Coast and Geodetic Survey (now part of the National Oceanic and Atmospheric Administration) and their dependents, and owners of commercial fishing boats. The Federal Government also provides medical care in Federal prisons, in-plant health services for Federal employees, medical care for certain Foreign Service employees overseas, medical care in the Ryukyu Islands (returned to Japan in 1972), the Trust Territories, American Samoa, and the Canal Zone, and support for certain medical institutions in the District of Columbia.

Federal outlays include operation of hospitals and medical care

units other than military and veterans' facilities and reimbursements to public and private hospitals for the care of Federal civilian beneficiaries.   Excluded where separately identifiable are training grants and fellowships and expenditures for research and the construction of medical facilities.

The main source of these Federal civilian expenditures data is the Office of Management and Budget, *The Budget of the United States Government* and its *Appendix* and *Special Analyses*.

State, local, and county governments also provide hospital and medical care for their residents.   They own and operate long- and short-term general, psychiatric, and tuberculosis hospitals and also pay to or for the support of a few nongovernment facilities.   Expenditures for psychiatric and tuberculosis care, traditionally considered a government responsibility, represent the largest portion of all State and local expenditures for hospital and medical care.

Data shown for series B 254 represent net expenditures for services. State and local vendor payments for specific programs covered in other series, as well as capital outlays and patient revenues, have been excluded. State and local gross totals, as well as figures on capital outlays and patient revenues are shown annually in Bureau of the Census, *Governmental Finances*.

B 255, public assistance.   Public assistance programs existed prior to most of the social insurance programs.   They comprise old-age assistance, medical assistance for the aged, aid to the blind, aid to families with dependent children, aid to the permanently and totally disabled, medical assistance, and State and locally financed general assistance programs.   See also text for series H 346–367.

Health expenditures for public assistance include money payments to needy recipients, assistance in kind, and vendor payments on behalf of recipients for medical care and for other goods and services (payments directly to the suppliers of service) made from Federal, State, and local funds for the categorical assistance programs and from State and local funds for the general assistance programs. Administrative expenditures under the public assistance programs are included, along with grants for demonstration projects under section 1115 of the Social Security Act.

Beginning in 1966 the Medicaid program, enacted as Title XIX of the Social Security Act in 1965, enabled the States to provide a single health program for the indigent and medically indigent, with Federal financial participation. Benefit standards required that a participating State must provide a minimum of five basic services to all Medicaid recipients (inpatient hospital care, out-patient hospital services, other laboratory and X-ray services, skilled nursing-home services for individuals aged 21 or older, and physicians' services).   In addition, States may offer other services—such as drugs and dental care—for which they receive Federal matching funds. Wide variation exists among the individual State programs in terms of eligibility, and scope and duration of benefits.

Many States, with and without Medicaid programs, contribute additional vendor medical payments out of State and local funds under the category of general assistance.

Vendor payments for medical care under public assistance programs are published annually by the National Center for Social Statistics in *Source of Funds Expended for Public Assistance Payments* (report F–1).

B 256, workmen's compensation. Workmen's compensation legislation, designed to provide cash benefits and medical care when a worker is injured on the job and an income to his survivors if he is killed, was the first form of social insurance to develop widely in the United States.   The Federal Government led the way covering its civilian employees with an act in 1908, reenacted in 1916.   Similar laws were enacted by 10 States in 1911; by the beginning of 1929, all but five States had such laws and, by 1948, all States had them. See also text for series H 332–345.

Each of the States operates its own workmen's compensation program, independent of any Federal legislative or administrative responsibility.   As a result, there are wide differences among States in the scope of employments covered, the amount and duration of benefits paid, and the methods used to insure that compensation will be paid when due.

Workmen's compensation expenditures include: (1) Periodic cash payments to the worker during periods of disability and (in some States) to his dependents; (2) death and funeral benefits to the worker's survivors; (3) lump-sum settlements; (4) medical and rehabilitative services; and (5) the administrative costs incurred by government bodies in operating or supervising the programs.

Workmen's compensation medical benefits include those for medical and rehabilitative services. Specific medical benefits are included in the law of each State; they are provided without limit as to time and amount in about four-fifths of the States.

Medical benefit payments include the estimated amounts paid out by private insurance carriers, by State insurance funds, and by employers as self-insurers. Also included are the amounts paid under the Federal workmen's compensation programs such as the Federal Employees' Compensation Act, Longshoremen's and Harbor Workers' Compensation Act, War Hazards Compensation Act, and the Defense Bases Compensation Act. Data for periods prior to 1959 exclude expenditures under the laws in Alaska and Hawaii.

Workmen's compensation medical benefit data are estimated annually by the Social Security Administration, using data primarily compiled by the National Council on Compensation Insurance. The data are published regularly in the *Social Security Bulletin* (for recent years, in January issues).

See also text for series H 332–345.

B 257, Defense Department hospital and medical care. Hospital and medical care for military personnel have been a Federal responsibility since the 18th century. Active-duty personnel have been provided with complete medical care incident to other necessities of life—food, shelter, and clothing. The armed services provide preventive treatment, curative and rehabilitative services in military hospitals, outpatient clinics, dispensaries, and field and shipboard stations. In 1965 there were 187 hospitals owned and operated by the armed services—51 Army hospitals, 37 Navy hospitals and 99 Air Force hospitals—with a total complement of 36,066 beds.

Figures for series B 257 include the expenses of operating military hospitals, clinics and other medical facilities, the salaries of military medical personnel, payments for medical care in nonmilitary facilities and expenditures for the dependents' medical care program.

B 258, school, maternal, and child health services. School health programs of educational agencies are programs financed and administered by State and local departments of education. These programs include medical and dental screening, first aid, the salaries of school nurses and/or doctors employed by local school districts and the expenses of health supplies. Data are from the Office of Education.

Programs for maternal and child health at the Federal level were established under Title V of the Social Security Act. They are designed to encourage, extend, and improve health services for mothers and children, especially in rural and low-income areas.

Under the maternal and child health program, Federal grants are matched and used by State health agencies to provide maternity clinics, well-child and pediatric clinics, inpatient hospital services, health services for school children, dental care, and immunization.

Under the crippled children's program, Federal grants are used by State health and crippled children's agencies to locate crippled children; to provide medical, surgical, corrective and other services and care for crippled children; and to provide facilities for diagnosis, hospitalization, and after-care for these children.

B 259, other. The category "other" includes the following: (1) temporary disability insurance, (2) other public health activities, (3) medical vocational rehabilitation, (4) special Office of Economic Opportunity (OEO) programs, and (5) beginning 1966, health insurance for the aged (Medicare).

The temporary disability programs, as enacted by four States (Rhode Island, California, New Jersey, and New York) in the 1940's, are designed to replace one-half or more of the weekly wage loss attributable to illness or off-the-job injury.

For a description of other public health activities, see text above for series B 231.

Medical vocational rehabilitation refers to assistance given the physically and mentally handicapped so that they may be prepared for and placed in gainful occupations. Included among vocational rehabilitation basic services are such medical services as study and diagnosis to assess the extent of disability and the individual's work capacities; medical, surgical, and hospital treatment and related therapy to remove or reduce the disability; and provision of prosthetic devices. Data on Federal, State, and local expenditures for this program are provided by the Rehabilitation Services Administration.

The OEO programs are aimed at developing and demonstrating more effective ways of delivering quality health care to poor families. OEO health funds include grants and contracts to aid local health services and resources and are reported in the *Special Analysis* of the *Budget* (see above for series B 254).

Federal health insurance for the aged (Medicare) became effective July 1, 1966, providing hospital and medical protection to an enrolled population aged 65 and over. Benefits under the hospital program (Part A) cover specified inpatient hospital services, post-hospital services in a "participating" extended-care facility, and home health visits. Under the supplementary medical program (Part B), payment is provided for physicians' services (including home and office visits), home health visits, outpatient hospital services, outpatient physical therapy services, diagnostic X-ray and laboratory tests, radiation therapy, prosthetic devices, ambulance services, and certain other medical supplies. Payments for deductibles, coinsurance, and noncovered services are not included here.

Financing of the hospital insurance program is on a self-supporting basis through a Federal tax applied to a portion of current earnings and paid by employees, employers, and self-employed persons. The tax proceeds are placed in the hospital insurance trust fund, from which benefits and administrative expenses are paid. The supplementary medical insurance program is financed through monthly premium payments paid by enrollees and matched by the Federal Government. These amounts are paid into the supplementary medical insurance trust fund from which benefits and administrative expenses are paid. Premium payments are thus included in the expenditures of the Medicare program.

For additional detail for public program expenditures, see U.S. Social Security Administration, *Personal Health Care Expenditures, by State*, vol. I, Public Funds, 1966 and 1969.

B 262–274. Indexes of medical care prices, 1935–1970.

Source: U.S. Bureau of Labor Statistics, *Consumer Price Index*, various monthly issues.

For description and historical development of the consumer price index, see text for series E 135–166.

See the source for more detail for various component indexes of medical care prices.

B 275–276. Physicians, 1850–1970.

Source: Superintendent of the U.S. Census, 1850, *Statistical View of the United States . . . a Compendium of the Seventh Census;* 1860, *Population of the United States in 1860.* U.S. Bureau of the Census, 1870–1930 (decennial years), Sixteenth Census Reports, *Comparative Occupation Statistics for the United States, 1870 to 1940*, p. 111; 1940 and 1950, *U.S. Census of Population, 1950*, vol. II, part 1, pp. 1–266 to 1–269. American Medical Association, 1870–1934, R. G. Leland, *Distribution of Physicians in the United States*, Chicago, 1936, pp. 7 and 79 (copyright); 1936–1957, the *American Medical Directory,* vols. 14–20 (copyright). 1958 edition includes summary for 1906–1957. U.S. Public Health Service, 1958–1970, *Health Resources Statistics*, 1971, p. 147, and unpublished data; compiled from data provided by American Medical Association and American Osteopathic Association.

The census data for 1940 and 1950 are for employed civilian physicians; figures for prior census years are largely for gainful workers and may include physicians not in active medical practice. See text for series D 75–84 for explanation of difference between employed persons and gainful workers. The 1910 census figure includes osteopaths; earlier census figures include osteopaths, chiropractors, and healers (not elsewhere classified).

The *American Medical Directory* figures pertain to the total number of physicians, including those retired or not in practice for other reasons and those in the Federal service. They exclude graduates of the years concerned.

Population figures used to compute physician-population rate for census years, 1850–1930, include Armed Forces overseas; only the civilian population is used for 1940 and 1950. Rates for years prior to 1963, excluding 1960, are based on the Census Bureau population estimates as of July 1, including Armed Forces overseas. Rates for years 1960 and 1963–1970 are based on Census Bureau estimates of civilian population in the 50 States, District of Columbia, outlying areas, U.S. citizens in foreign countries, and the Armed Forces in the United States and abroad as of December 31.

B 277. Physicians admitted to U.S. as immigrants, 1901–1970.

Source: U.S. Public Health Service, *Foreign Trained Physicians and American Medicine*, DHEW Publication No.(NIH)73–325, table A1. Compiled from the U.S. Immigration and Naturalization Service data.

B 278–280. Medical schools, students, and graduates, 1810–1970.

Source: 1810–1840, American Medical Association, *1956 American Medical Directory* (copyright); later years, annual reports of the Council on Medical Education and Hospitals of the American Medical Association as follows: 1850–1919, *Journal of the American Medical Association*, vol. 79, No. 8, pp. 629–633, Aug. 1922; 1920–1930, *Journal of the American Medical Association*, vol. 105, No. 9, p. 686, Aug. 1935; 1931–1957, Edward L. Turner, *et al.*, *Journal of the American Medical Association*, vol. 165, No. 11, p. 1420, November 1957. (Copyright.) 1958–1970, U.S. Public Health Service, *Health Resources Statistics*, 1971, p. 88, and unpublished data.

Data on the number of medical schools, students, and graduates prior to 1900 are fragmentary and of dubious accuracy. The first medical school in the United States was founded in 1765. In 1800 three schools graduated students, with the number of schools increasing steadily from 52 in 1850 to a maximum of 162 in 1906. From 1906 to 1929, the number of schools declined sharply, largely because of the inspection and classification system begun in 1904 by the American Medical Association Council on Medical Education. By 1929, only one unapproved school remained.

B 281–282. Dentists, 1810–1970.

Source: 1810 and 1840, John T. O'Rourke and Leroy M. S. Miner, *Dental Education in the United States*, W. B. Saunders Co., Philadelphia, 1941, p. 298 (copyright). 1820 and 1830, Harris' *Principles and Practice of Dental Surgery*, Lindsay and Blakiston, Philadelphia, 1848, pp. 36–37. 1850–1950 (decennial years), same sources as series B 275–276. 1893–1928, *Polk's Dental Register and Directory of the United States and Dominion of Canada*, R. L. Polk and Co., Chicago, 1928, and prior editions (copyright). 1947–1957, *Distribution of Dentists in the United States by State, Region, District, and County*, American Dental Association, Chicago, 1958, and prior editions. (Copyright by the American Dental Association. Reprinted by permission.) 1958–1970, U.S. Public Health Service, *Health Resources Statistics*, annual issues, and unpublished data; compiled from American Dental Association data.

The census data for 1940 and 1950 are for employed civilian dentists; figures for prior census years are largely for gainful workers and may include dental students and dentists not in active dental practice. See text for series D 75–84 for explanation of difference between employed persons and gainful workers.

The 14 editions of *Polk's Dental Register and Directory of the United States and Dominion of Canada* list by State all dentists for 1893–1928. The *American Dental Directory*, first published in 1947, lists by State all dentists, including those retired or not in practice for other reasons and those in the Federal dental service. The figures for all dates include graduates of the years concerned.

Prior to 1963, the population figures used to compute the dentist-population rate are the same as those used for the physician-population rate. See text for series B 275–276. Population figures used to compute the dentist-population rate for 1963–1970 include all persons in the United States and in the Armed Forces overseas as of July 1.

B 283. Dental schools, 1840–1970.

Source: 1840–1945, Harlan Hoyt Horner, *Dental Education Today*, p. 30 (copyright 1947 by University of Chicago); 1946–1957, American Dental Association Council on Dental Education, *Dental Students' Register*, Chicago, annual publications (copyright). 1958–1970, U.S. Public Health Service, *Health Resources Statistics*, 1971, p. 77, and unpublished data.

Horner's data are compiled from Dorothy Fahs Beck, *The Development of the Dental Profession in the United States*, dissertation of the University of Chicago, 1932, and from records of the Council on Dental Education of the American Dental Association. Additional data may be obtained from the following sources cited by Beck: W. J. Gies, *Dental Education in the United States and Canada*, Carnegie Foundation for the Advancement of Teaching, Bulletin No. 19, 1926, p. 42; *Polk's Dental Register and Directory of the United States and Canada*, R. L. Polk and Co., Chicago, 1925, p. 35; W. J. Gies, "Additional Remarks on a Reference to the Carnegie Foundation's Study of Dental Education," *Journal of Dental Research*, vol. 10, p. 32, February 1930; W. J. Greenleaf, *Dentistry*, Career Series, Leaflet No. 7, Office of Education, pp. 7–10. The Beck tabulation also appears in Frederick B. Noyes, "Dental Education, 1911–36," *Oral Hygiene*, vol. 26, p. 24, January 1936.

The first dental school in the United States was organized in 1840. Before that, all physicians practiced some dentistry, a few limiting their practice to this specialty. The dental practitioners who were not physicians learned their trade as apprentices or were self-taught. From 1840 to 1880 apprentice training was the chief source of supply, but by 1880 most States had enacted laws requiring graduation from a dental school.

B 284. Dental students, 1921–1970.

Source: 1921–1934, Frederick B. Noyes, "Dental Education, 1911–36," *Oral Hygiene*, vol. 26, January 1936, p. 28 (copyright); 1935–1957, American Dental Association Council on Dental Education, *Dental Students' Register*, annual publications (copyright); 1958–1970, see source for series B 283.

Sources cited by Noyes are: W. J. Gies, *Journal of the American Dental Association*, vol. 18, p. 593, April 1931, and Dental Educational Council of America, statistical reports.

B 285. Dental graduates, 1850–1970.

Source: See source for series B 283.

Annual figures for graduates for 1841–1924, are also presented in *Polk's Dental Register*, 1925, p. 34; but the figures for the early years far exceed those shown elsewhere in histories of dentistry as well as those shown here.

B 286–287. Graduate nurses, 1910–1970.

Source: 1910–1950, U.S. Public Health Service, *Health Manpower Source Book 2, Nursing Personnel*, pp. 14–15. 1953 and 1955, American Nurses Association, *Facts About Nursing*, New York, 1956–57 edition, p. 8 (copyright). 1956–1970, U.S. Public Health Service, *Health Resources Statistics*, 1971, p. 177, and unpublished data; compiled from data provided by American Nurses Association.

The estimates for 1910–1950 were obtained by subtracting student nurses from the number of nurses reported in the decennial censuses.

Census data for 1910–1930 are for gainful workers; for 1940 they include employed nurses and those seeking work; and for 1950 they include employed civilian nurses. See text for series D 75–84 for explanation of difference between employed persons and gainful workers.

The estimates for 1953 and 1955 were prepared jointly by the American Nurses Association, the National League for Nursing, and the Public Health Service. They are based partly on information supplied by hospitals, schools of nursing, public health agencies, boards of education, and nursing homes. Estimates of nurses in private duty, doctors' offices, industry, and other nursing fields were based on the American Nurses Association Inventory of 1951 adjusted according to trends observed in more recent State surveys of nursing needs and resources.

Population figures used to compute nurse-population rates for 1910–1940 include Armed Forces overseas. The 1950 rate is based on the civilian population. Rates for 1953–1955 and 1958–1962 are based on the Census Bureau population estimates, including Armed Forces overseas, as of January 1 of the following year. Rates for 1964–1970 are based on Census Bureau population estimates for civilians and the Armed Forces in the United States as of December 31.

B 288–290. Nursing schools, students, and graduates, 1880–1970.

Source: 1880–1927 and 1931, U.S. Office of Education, *Biennial Survey of Education in the United States: 1934–36*, vol. II, chap. IV, p. 294. 1929 and 1932, The Committee on the Grading of Nursing Schools, *The Second Grading of Nursing Schools*, New York, 1932, p. 9. 1935–1939, American Nurses Association, *Facts About Nursing, 1946*, New York, 1946, pp. 32 and 34; 1940–1955, *Facts About Nursing, 1957*, pp. 67 and 71 (copyright). 1956–1970, U.S. Public Health Service, *Health Resources Statistics*, 1971, p. 181; compiled from data provided by American Nurses Association.

Nursing education began in this country in 1873 with the opening of three schools. These schools offered students an opportunity to learn by doing, under the tutorship for 1 year of a superintendent who had been trained in one of the European schools.... By 1893 about 70 schools were in operation.... As State licensing bodies came into existence, counts of State approved schools and of their students began to be available. Since only graduates of State approved schools could stand for licensure examinations, nonapproved schools tended to close as the effect of licensure became felt. Not until 1923 was machinery for approving schools in operation in every State. (U.S. Public Health Service, *Health Manpower Source Book 2, Nursing Personnel*, p. 33.)

B 291–304. Rates per 100,000 population for specified reportable diseases, 1912–1970.

Source: 1912–1919, U.S. Public Health Service, *Public Health Reports*, various issues; 1920–1950, U.S. National Office of Vital Statistics, *Vital Statistics—Special Reports*, vol. 37, No. 9; 1951–1970, U.S. Center for Disease Control, *Morbidity and Mortality, Weekly Report*, Annual Supplement, Summary, 1960 and 1970.

The rates refer to the number of notifiable diseases occurring within the United States per 100,000 population. For 1920–1970, rates are based on the total resident population. Each State makes its own laws and regulations prescribing the diseases to be reported, the agencies and persons required to report, and penalities for failure to report. All States have entered voluntarily into a cooperative agreement to report to the Federal Government.

The notification of disease in the United States began in the colonial period on a local basis, particularly in port cities. It was usually limited to periods when epidemics of pestilential disease threatened or were in progress. Statewide notification was not required until 1883, when Michigan passed a law requiring physicians and householders to report certain diseases to health officers or boards of health. During the next three decades all States made similar requirements.

In response to the need for nationwide statistical information on epidemic diseases, a law was passed in 1878 providing for the collection of such statistics. By 1912, data were supplied regularly by 19 States and the District of Columbia on diphtheria, measles, poliomyelitis, scarlet fever, tuberculosis, typhoid fever, and smallpox. State health authorities now report weekly on 25 diseases and annually on about 40. Most States require the reporting of additional diseases.

The Public Health Service has changed its form of reporting several times and some of the rates shown here do not appear in the published reports. Since the data were originally shown only for the individual States, a rate for the country was obtained for each disease by combining the information only for those States reporting it, the denominators being the population of the reporting States.

For trends of sickness and accident among groups of male and female industrial workers (1917–1950, for cases disabling for 1 day or longer, and 1921–1952, for cases disabling for 8 days or longer), see W. M. Gafafer, "Industrial Sickness Absenteeism Among Males and Females During 1950," *Public Health Reports*, vol. 66, No. 47, pp. 1550–1552, November 1951. See also "Rates for Specific Causes in 1952 for the Year and Last Two Quarters—Industrial Sickness Absenteeism," *Public Health Report*, vol. 68, No. 11, pp. 1052–1055, November 1953; and S. D. Collins, "Long-Time Trends in Illness and Medical Care," *Public Health Monograph*, No. 48, p. 32.

Civilian illness rates for the United States are not available for a long period. However, records of illness (admission to sick report) among the active-duty personnel of the Army are available back to 1819, and those for the Navy back to 1865. See U.S. Army, *Annual Reports of the Surgeon General on Medical Statistics*, and U.S. Navy, *Annual Reports of the Surgeon General on Medical Statistics*. For annual days sick per person, computed from Army and Navy data, see S. D. Collings, "Long-Time Trends in Illness and Medical Care," *Public Health Monograph*, No. 48, p. 37.

B 305–400 and B 413–422. General note.

Until 1953, when it discontinued registration of hospitals, the American Medical Association (AMA) collected data annually from all hospitals registered by it, and published them in the Hospital Number of the *Journal of the American Medical Association*. Registration was a basic recognition extended to hospitals and related institutions in accordance with requirements officially adopted by its House of Delegates.

Figures from the AMA presented in series B 319–330, B 345–358, and B 371–380 are not entirely comparable with similar data provided by the American Hospital Association (AHA) because the standards required for "listing" or "recognition" of hospitals by the AHA differ from those required by the AMA. Statistics of hospitals obtained from the AHA's annual survey of hospitals are published annually in *Hospitals*, Guide Issue, and cover all hospitals accepted for registration by the AHA. To be accepted for registration, a hospital must meet certain requirements, as follows: It must have at least 6 beds for the care of nonrelated patients for an average stay of over 24 hours per admission; be constructed and equipped to insure safety of patients and to provide sanitary facilities for their treatment; have an organized medical staff, registered nurse supervision, and nursing care for round-the-clock patient care; maintain clinical records on all patients and submit evidence of patient care by doctors; provide minimal surgical and obstetrical facilities or relatively complete diagnostic and treatment facilities; have diagnostic X-ray and clinical laboratory services readily available; and offer services more intensive than those required merely for room, board, personal services, and general nursing care.

Short-term hospitals are those in which over 50 percent of all patients admitted have a stay of less than 30 days; long-term, those in which over 50 percent of all patients admitted have a stay of 30 days or more. General hospitals accept patients for a variety of acute medical and surgical conditions, and, for the most part, do not admit cases of contagious disease, tuberculosis, and nervous and mental disease. Special hospitals are those devoted to the treatment of some particular disease or group of diseases or some particular group in the population. Among the former are orthopedic, contagious disease, chronic and convalescent, and eye, ear, nose, and throat hospitals; the latter include maternity, children's, and industrial hospitals. Psychiatric hospitals include those providing temporary or prolonged care for the mentally ill, the mentally retarded, epileptic, and persons with alcoholic or other addictive diseases. Tuberculosis hospitals include sanatoria or hospitals specifically for the care of tubercular patients.

Governmental hospitals include those operated by Federal, State, and local governments, the latter including county, city, city-county, and hospital district. Nonprofit hospitals are those operated not for profit by churches and by associations of citizens or fraternal organizations. Proprietary hospitals are operated for profit by individuals, partnerships, or corporations.

Number of beds includes beds, cribs, and pediatric bassinets normally available for inpatients. It excludes newborn infant bassinets.

Data from the AHA relate generally to the year ending September 30 or to the fiscal year closest to that date.

B 305–318. Hospitals and beds, by type of service and ownership (AHA), 1946–1970.

Source: American Hospital Association, Chicago, *Hospitals*, Guide Issue, part II, annual issues (copyright; reprinted with permission).

See general note for series B 305–400 and B 413–422.

B 319–330. Hospitals and beds, by type of service (AMA), 1909–1953.

Source: American Medical Association, Chicago, 1909, 1914, 1918, and 1921, *American Medical Directory*, 1921 and prior editions; 1920 and 1923–1953, *Journal of the American Medical Association*, Hospital Number: 1920, April 1921 issue, pp. 1083–1103; 1923 and 1927–1933, March 1934 issue, pp. 1008–1009; 1924, March 1925 issue, pp. 961–970; 1925, April 1926 issue, pp. 1009–1055; 1926, March 1927 issue, pp. 789–839; 1934–1953, May 1954 issue, pp. 9–10. (Copyright.)

Although the AMA's annual census was begun in 1920, complete data on the number of hospital beds classified by type of service are available only from 1925. In addition to information on number of hospitals and beds, the Hospital Number of the AMA Journal presented statistics on admissions, average daily census, and births.

See also general note for series B 305–400 and B 413–422.

B 331–344. Hospitals and beds, by ownership or control (AHA), 1946–1970.

Source: See source for series B 305–318.

See general note for series B 305–400 and B 413–422.

B 345–358. Hospitals and beds, by ownership or control (AMA), 1909–1953.

Source: American Medical Association, Chicago, *Journal of the American Medical Association*, Hospital Number: 1909, 1914, 1918, and 1934–1953, May 1954 issue, pp. 4, 7–8; 1923 and 1927–1933, March 1934 issue, pp. 1006–1007; 1924, March 1925 issue, pp. 961–970; 1925, April 1926 issue, pp. 1009–1055; 1926, March 1927 issue, pp. 789–839. (Copyright.)

See general note for series B 305–400 and B 413–422.

B 359–370. Average daily census and admissions to hospitals, by type of service and ownership (AHA), 1946–1970.

Source: See source for series B 305–318.

Average daily census is defined as the average number of inpatients receiving care each day during the 12-month period, excluding the newborn.

Admissions refer to the number of patients accepted for inpatient service during the 12-month period, either as first admissions or readmissions. Births are excluded.

See also general note for series B 305–400 and B 413–422.

B 371–380. Average daily census and admissions to hospitals, by type of service (AMA), 1923–1953.

Source: American Medical Association, Chicago, *Journal of the American Medical Association*, Hospital Number: 1925, April 1926 issue, p. 1009; 1923, 1927, and 1929–1933, March 1934 issue, pp. 1008–1009; 1934–1953, May 1954 issue, pp. 9–10. (Copyright.)

See text for series B 359–370 and general note for series B 305–400 and B 413–422.

B 381–388. Hospital use rates, 1931–1970.

Source: 1931–1966, U.S. Public Health Service, *Health, Education, and Welfare Trends*, part 1, various annual issues (based on data prepared by American Medical Association and American Hospital Association); 1967–1970, American Hospital Association, Chicago, unpublished data.

See text for series B 359–370 and general note for series B 305–400 and B 413–422.

B 389–400. Hospital expense per patient day, 1946–1970.

Source: American Hospital Association, Chicago, 1946–1964, *Hospitals*, Guide Issue, part 2, Aug. 1, 1965, pp. 448–449; 1965–1970, *Hospitals*, Guide Issue, part 2, Aug. 1, 1972, pp. 460–462. (Copyright.)

Payroll expenses include all salaries and wages except, beginning 1951, those paid to interns, residents, student nurses, and other trainees. All professional fees and the salary expenditures excluded from payroll are defined as nonpayroll expenses and are included in total expenses.

See also general note for series B 305–400 and B 413–422.

B 401–412. Persons covered by private health insurance for hospital and surgical benefits, 1939–1970.

Source: U.S. Social Security Administration, *Social Security Bulletin*, February 1973 and earlier issues.

The data for insurance companies are from the Health Insurance Institute, *Source Book of Health Insurance Data*, and were developed from surveys and reports of insurance companies and other health insurance plans, government agencies, and hospital and medical associations. The data for Blue Cross–Blue Shield are from annual reports of the Blue Cross–Blue Shield Associations. The data for independent plans—plans other than Blue Cross–Blue Shield and insurance companies—are from annual surveys of these plans by the Social Security Administration.

In 1970, there were many different health insurance organizations in the United States—75 Blue Cross plans, 72 Blue Shield plans, about 1,000 commercial insurance companies, and more than 500 independent plans. They insured in varying degree against the costs of hospital and surgical care, other physicians' services, nursing care, dental and vision care, and prescribed drugs.

Health insurance policies, both group and individual, are written by health insurance companies, as well as by life and health, casualty, and multiple line companies.

Because one plan may provide only one type of benefit and because the benefits may be limited, families frequently carry several forms of health insurance; for example, Blue Cross for hospital insurance, Blue Shield for surgical insurance, in-hospital medical expense insurance, and an insurance policy applicable to all three types of expense. Multiple coverage may also occur when husband and wife are both employed and both cover self, spouse, and dependents under the insurance plan at the work place.

Hospitalization insurance provides benefits for hospital charges incurred by an insured person because of an illness or injury. Surgical insurance pays benefits toward physicians' surgical fees. The Social Security Administration publishes its own estimates of the net number (of different persons) and the percentage of the civilian population covered by hospital and surgical insurance. These estimates, which usually run 5–10 percentage points lower than those published by the Health Insurance Institute, are based on household interviews conducted by the National Center for Health Statistics (NCHS) during 1967 and 1968, and on findings of various household surveys by the Health Information Foundation and the Public Health Service in 1953–1963.

B 413–422. Hospitals—assets, expenses, and personnel, by type of control and service, 1946–1970.

Source: See source for series B 389–400.

Assets comprise plant assets (land, buildings, equipment, and reserves for construction, improvement, and replacement—less deductions for depreciation) plus all other assets, including endowment fund principal and general and temporary fund balances.

Expenses include all expenses covering the 12-month period, both total and payroll. Payroll expenses include all salaries and wages except those paid to interns, residents, student nurses, and other trainees. All professional fees and those salary expenditures excluded from payroll are defined as nonpayroll expenses and are included in total expenses.

Data on personnel refer to the number of persons on the payroll at the close of the 12-month reporting period. Except as noted, they include full-time equivalents of part-time personnel but exclude trainees (student nurses, interns, residents, and other trainees), private duty nurses, and volunteers. Full-time equivalents are calculated on the basis that two part-time persons are equal to one full-time person.

See also general note for series B 305–400 and B 413–422.

B 423–427. Patients in mental hospitals, by type of hospital, 1904–1970.

Source: U.S. Census Office, 1904, *Insane and Feeble-Minded in Hospitals and Institutions, 1904* (special report). U.S. Bureau of the Census, 1910, *Insane and Feeble-Minded in Institutions, 1910*; 1923–1946, *Patients in Mental Institutions* (annual reports, varying titles). U.S. National Institute of Mental Health, 1947–1966, *Patients in Mental Institutions*, annual issues; 1967–1970, *Mental Health Statistics*, Series A, Reference Tables, and unpublished data.

For 1923–1932, the annual enumerations of patients in mental institutions, conducted by the Bureau of the Census, were confined to State hospitals for mental disease and State institutions for mental defectives and epileptics. Since 1933, the annual censuses conducted by the Bureau of the Census until 1946 and subsequently by the National Institute of Mental Health (NIMH) have covered all types of hospitals and institutions caring for the mentally ill, mental defectives, and epileptics. For a discussion of these developments, see the 1947 issue of NIMH, *Patients in Mental Institutions*, pp. 1–4. Additional information on admissions, patients, personnel, and expenditures of institutions for mental defectives and epileptics, as well as for hospitals for mental diseases, appear in various issues of that report.

The figures represent patients who are resident in hospitals which provide care solely for the mentally ill, as distinguished from the physically ill and from the mentally deficient and epileptic. These hospitals may provide care over an unlimited period of time or temporary care, as in psychopathic hospitals. Hospitals included are those under control of State and local governments, nonprofit and proprietary organizations, the Veterans Administration, and the Federal Government in the District of Columbia (included here under State hospitals).

These facilities contain 93 percent of the psychiatric beds. (The other 7 percent are in general hospitals and residential treatment centers for emotionally disturbed children.) The number of resident patients in these hospitals peaked in 1955 (the year during which the use of tranquilizers became widespread in these hospitals) and has decreased since. Coupled with this decrease in residents is an increase in admissions offset by the practice of returning many hospitalized patients to the community for treatment.

There are also programs for preventing hospitalization in the many outpatient psychiatric clinics and community mental health centers. These, along with the general hospital psychiatric services, provide about three-fourths of the care to the mentally ill in the existing psychiatric facilities.

B 428–443. Public institutions for the mentally retarded, 1936–1970.

Source: 1936–1945, U.S. Bureau of the Census, *Patients in Mental Institutions, 1945*, pp. 31 and 35–37; 1946–1970, U.S. Social and Rehabilitation Service, *Residents in Public Institutions for the Mentally Retarded*, annual issues.

From 1946 to 1968 the National Institute of Mental Health was responsible for collecting and publishing data on the institutionalized mentally retarded in the United States. Since 1969, the annual census of the public institutions of the mentally retarded has been the responsibility of the Social and Rehabilitation Service.

B 432–433, admissions. Includes first and readmissions. First admissions are all patients admitted to a public institution for the mentally retarded without a record of previous care, i.e., a record of an admission and a formal discharge, in either a public or private institution anywhere. Thus, a patient coming into a public institution for the mentally retarded from a hospital for mental disease would be considered a first admission. Readmissions are all patients admitted with a record of previous care in a public or private institution. Admissions per 100,000 civilian population, series B 433, measures the proportion of people coming under care during the year.

B 435, deaths in institutions. This category includes only deaths occurring to patients resident in the institution and does not include deaths among patients on leave, even though these patients are still on the institution books.

B 436, net live releases. This concept takes into account movement of patients into and out of the institution since this quantity is the number of placements on extramural care plus direct discharge from the institution less the number of returns from extramural care, all occurring during any one year. National data on placements and returns from extramural care are not available but net releases may be computed from less detailed movement data as:

Net live releases	=	Resident patients beginning of year	+	All admissions excluding transfers	−	Deaths in institution	−	Resident patients end of year

Interpretation of net live releases should be made with caution. This quantity is the net number of releases alive from the public institutions in the State system and includes not only direct discharges to the community and placement on leave but also direct discharges to other inpatient facilities outside the State system such as public mental hospitals, boarding care homes, and public institutions in other States. The number of net releases is used as a measure of movement out of the institution rather than the total number of discharges because many discharges occur while patients are already outside the institution on extramural care. The number of net releases may be considered an estimate of the number of effective releases from the institution under the assumption that subtracting returns from leave during the year removes only the short term visits, leaves, and escapes, and retains the effective releases; i.e., those from which the patients did not return to the institution within the time period covered.

B 442–443, expenditures per average daily resident patient. The most commonly used ratio for comparing institution expenditures. Its major limitation is that it does not adequately take into account the number of admissions for which a large share of the expenditure is required. If the patient base were enlarged to include admissions during the year, the resulting sum would be the best available estimate of patients under treatment during the year.

B 444–447. Four indexes of per capita food consumption, 1909–1970.

Source: U.S. Department of Agriculture, Economic Research Service, *Food Consumption, Prices, and Expenditures*, Agricultural Economics Report No. 138 and its *Supplement for 1971*, tables 1, 5, 6, and 38.

Three methods are commonly used to measure the total amount of food consumed, or otherwise "disappearing" through the marketing system. Total food consumed is measured in terms of its monetary value, physical weight, or nutritive value.

Civilian disappearance, the residual from all other known uses, normally is the estimate of annual U.S. civilian food consumption. This estimate is usually derived from supply and utilization "balance sheets," which summarize production, imports, and beginning stocks; and deduct exports, all known nonfood uses, military procurement, and end-of-year inventories of each commodity. The residual, after adjustment for marketing losses up to the retail level, is assumed to have been consumed for food.

B 444, food consumption. This index measures per capita consumption (civilian, beginning 1941) of quantities of individual foods measured in pounds equivalent to the form sold at retail food stores. The quantities used for this series have been combined into indexes on the basis of average 1947–49 retail prices through 1954 and 1957–59 prices thereafter; the indexes are linked at 1955. Component indexes for individual groups of animal and crop products are presented in the source (table 1). For comparison with the food use index, see below.

B 445, food use. In concept, this index parallels the food consumption index, except that it combines farm products ultimately used for food (farm weight or an equivalent) weighted by constant prices received by farmers, or an equivalent. It is a component of the system of index numbers that integrates the entire supply and utilization of farm commodities at the farm level (see tables 91–93 in the source). It is not available in as much detail as the food consumption index, but serves as a check on it.

The food consumption and food use indexes are based on roughly the same kind of data. But development of the food consumption index at the retail rather than the farm level introduces variations among products in farm-retail marketing margins into its weighting scheme. Consequently, crop products are more heavily weighted in the food consumption index than in the food use index (see tables 4 and 93 in source).

Shifts in consumption are reflected in these indexes. A 1-pound increase in consumption of a relatively high-priced food (meat, for example) and a simultaneous 1-pound decrease in consumption of a relatively low-priced food (potatoes, for example) would result in an increase in both indexes. Major differences in the forms in which food is sold affect the food consumption index. For example, fruits and vegetables sold fresh and those sold in processed form are weighted separately. Accordingly, the index reflects, to a limited extent, the trend toward consumption of more highly processed foods.

The food use index tends to reflect changes in the form of agricultural commodities sold by farmers. Instead of weighting individual food items on the basis of price, as is done in the food consumption index, the food use index weights food groups, such as dairy products, fruits, and vegetables. This difference makes the food consumption index more sensitive to smaller shifts in food consumption patterns than the food use index.

B 446, food consumed, pounds. This index was based on data

presented in pounds in the source (table 6). Pounds of the various foods consumed are totaled on the basis of retail weight, or an equivalent, to achieve consistency in aggregating grossly different foods. Nevertheless, the different forms in which food is marketed and the problems of summing pounds of liquids, solids, and concentrated products make it difficult to interpret changes in these data. Quantities of food consumed are roughly equivalent to the weight of food sold (or at least saleable) by retail food stores. No aggregation of pounds at the farm level has been made, partly because of the problem of allocating joint raw farm products among various ultimate food and nonfood uses.

B 447, calories per day. This index was computed from data presented in calories of food energy available for consumption per capita per day in the source (table 38). These data were in turn based on estimates of per capita food consumption (retail weight), including estimates of produce of home gardens. No deduction was made for loss or waste of food in the home nor use for pet food.

B 448–452. Index of per capita consumption of selected nutrients, 1909–1970.

Source: U.S. Department of Agriculture, Economic Research Service, *Food Consumption, Prices, and Expenditures*, Agricultural Economics Report No. 138 and its *Supplement for 1971*, table 38; and *National Food Situation*, NFS-142, table 10.

These indexes were computed from data presented in the source in terms of grams and milligrams. The nutritive value of food is measured by the amount of food energy (see calories per day, series B 447), protein, fat, carbohydrate, and several vitamins and minerals it contains.

The data on nutrients are derived by applying composition values to food consumption data reported in terms of retail weight equivalents. Allowances are made for bones, rinds, and peelings, but not for bruises and rot. No deduction is made for nutrient losses that occur in household storage and meal preparation. Quantities of food discarded as plate waste or fed to pets are not deducted. As a result, these data overstate nutrients actually ingested.

For additional data on other nutrients, see source.

B 453–459. Controlled fluoridation of water systems, 1945–1970.

Source: **Series B 453–455** and **B 457–459**, 1945–1969, U.S. Public Health Service, *Fluoridation Census 1969*, table 3; 1970, unpublished data. **Series B 456**, computed on basis of U.S. resident population in series A 7.

Controlled fluoridation is defined as the conscious maintenance of the optimal fluoride concentration in the water supply. This may be accomplished by adding fluoride chemicals to fluoride-deficient water; by blending two or more sources of water naturally containing fluoride to the optimal concentration; or by defluoridation, that is, removing fluorides in excess of the recommended level. Water supply systems are considered to have natural fluoridation if they contain 0.7 parts per million or more naturally occurring fluoride. (See *Natural Fluoride Content of Community Water Supplies, 1969*, Division of Dental Health, U.S. National Institutes of Health.)

The current population on controlled fluoridation was estimated by applying the Bureau of the Census population projection factors to the population on fluoridated water expressed in terms of the 1960 census population.

The data on operative and discontinued systems are based upon the year in which institution, discontinuation, or reinstitution of fluoridation (shown separately in the source) were reported to the U.S. Public Health Service and not necessarily the year in which the event occurred.

Series B 221–235. Total and Per Capita National Health Expenditures, by Type of Service: 1929 to 1970

[Calendar year data]

Year	Total	Health services and supplies											Research and medical-facilities construction		
		Total	Hospital care	Physicians' services	Dentists' services	Other professional services [1]	Drugs and drug sundries [2]	Eyeglasses and appliances [3]	Nursing home care	Expenses for prepayment and administration [4]	Government public health activities	Other health services	Total	Research [2]	Construction
	221	222	223	224	225	226	227	228	229	230	231	232	233	234	235
TOTAL (mil. dol.)															
1970	71,573	66,365	27,597	14,294	4,419	1,466	7,297	1,866	3,070	2,098	1,568	2,690	5,208	1,842	3,366
1969	64,142	59,351	24,093	12,654	4,047	1,313	6,812	1,765	2,650	2,109	1,316	2,592	4,791	1,818	2,973
1968	56,587	52,532	20,926	11,099	3,623	1,271	6,165	1,731	2,280	2,007	1,098	2,332	4,055	1,795	2,260
1967	50,696	46,987	18,145	10,287	3,360	1,158	5,652	1,609	1,858	1,877	942	2,099	3,709	1,703	2,006
1966	44,974	41,440	15,583	9,156	2,964	1,123	5,309	1,413	1,526	1,681	885	1,800	3,534	1,574	1,960
1965	40,468	37,087	13,605	8,745	2,808	1,038	4,850	1,230	1,328	1,293	698	1,492	3,381	1,469	1,912
1964	37,461	34,375	12,697	8,065	2,648	940	4,446	1,072	1,214	1,172	610	1,511	3,086	1,324	1,762
1963	33,530	30,890	11,709	6,891	2,277	921	4,235	952	891	1,094	540	1,380	2,640	1,184	1,456
1962	31,295	28,857	10,658	6,498	2,234	902	4,095	908	695	1,085	505	1,277	2,438	1,032	1,406
1961	28,783	26,766	9,921	5,895	2,067	882	3,824	804	606	995	452	1,320	2,018	844	1,174
1960	26,895	25,185	9,092	5,684	1,977	862	3,657	776	526	861	414	1,336	1,710	662	1,048
1959	24,878	23,354	8,177	5,481	1,894	801	3,525	722	434	754	428	1,138	1,524	526	998
1958	22,848	21,442	7,548	4,910	1,850	729	3,242	678	383	633	424	1,045	1,406	416	990
1957	21,108	19,885	6,892	4,419	1,737	673	3,010	678	368	682	415	1,011	1,223	344	879
1956	19,246	18,348	6,347	4,067	1,625	610	2,686	668	358	620	402	965	898	270	628
1955	17,745	16,884	5,900	3,689	1,508	562	2,384	604	312	624	377	924	861	210	651
1954	16,799	15,946	5,502	3,574	1,406	541	2,181	606	270	587	374	904	853	183	670
1953	15,745	14,895	5,085	3,278	1,234	499	2,152	612	248	498	378	911	850	164	686
1952	14,988	13,949	4,685	3,042	1,098	459	2,071	586	228	401	427	952	1,039	150	889
1951	13,992	12,912	4,254	2,868	997	426	1,989	551	207	321	416	883	1,080	134	946
1950	12,662	11,702	3,851	2,747	961	396	1,726	491	187	316	361	666	960	117	843
1949	11,576	10,811	3,557	2,633	920	371	1,557	458	168	271	338	539	765	105	660
1948	10,612	10,184	3,203	2,611	900	354	1,466	436	150	287	306	470	428	89	339
1940	3,987	3,868	1,011	973	419	174	637	189	33	167	153	112	119	3	116
1935	2,936	2,875	763	773	302	153	475	133	---------	95	117	64	61	---------	61
1929	3,649	3,436	663	1,004	482	252	606	133	---------	110	96	91	213	---------	213
PER CAPITA (dollars) [5]															
1970	343.44	318.45	132.42	68.59	21.20	7.03	35.01	8.95	14.73	10.07	7.52	12.91	24.99	8.83	16.15
1969	311.06	287.83	116.84	61.37	19.63	6.37	33.04	8.56	12.85	10.23	6.38	12.57	23.23	8.81	14.41
1968	277.14	257.28	102.49	54.36	17.74	6.22	30.19	8.48	11.17	9.83	5.38	11.42	19.86	8.79	11.07
1967	250.77	232.42	89.76	50.89	16.62	5.73	27.96	7.96	9.19	9.28	4.66	10.38	18.35	8.42	9.92
1966	224.89	207.22	77.92	45.78	14.82	5.62	26.55	7.07	7.63	8.41	4.43	9.00	17.67	7.87	9.80
1965	204.68	187.58	68.81	44.23	14.20	5.25	24.53	6.22	6.72	6.54	3.53	7.55	17.10	7.43	9.67
1964	191.88	176.07	65.04	41.31	13.56	4.81	22.77	5.49	6.22	6.00	3.12	7.74	15.81	6.78	9.03
1963	174.15	160.44	60.81	35.79	11.83	4.78	22.00	4.94	4.63	5.68	2.80	7.17	13.71	6.15	7.56
1962	164.89	152.05	56.16	34.24	11.77	4.75	21.58	4.78	3.66	5.72	2.66	6.73	12.85	5.44	7.41
1961	154.02	143.23	53.09	31.55	11.06	4.72	20.46	4.30	3.24	5.32	2.42	7.06	10.80	4.52	6.28
1960	146.30	137.00	49.46	30.92	10.75	4.69	19.89	4.22	2.86	4.68	2.25	7.27	9.30	3.60	5.70
1959	137.94	129.49	45.34	30.39	10.50	4.44	19.54	4.00	2.41	4.18	2.37	6.31	8.45	2.92	5.53
1958	128.81	120.88	42.55	27.68	10.43	4.11	18.28	3.82	2.16	3.57	2.39	5.89	7.93	2.35	5.58
1957	121.00	113.99	39.51	25.33	9.96	3.86	17.25	3.89	2.11	3.91	2.38	5.80	7.01	1.97	5.04
1956	112.32	107.07	37.04	23.73	9.48	3.56	15.67	3.90	2.09	3.62	2.35	5.63	5.24	1.58	3.66
1955	105.38	100.27	35.04	21.91	8.96	3.34	14.16	3.59	1.85	3.71	2.24	5.49	5.11	1.25	3.87
1954	101.54	96.37	33.26	21.60	8.50	3.27	13.18	3.66	1.63	3.55	2.26	5.46	5.16	1.11	4.05
1953	96.84	91.61	31.27	20.16	7.59	3.07	13.24	3.76	1.53	3.06	2.32	5.60	5.23	1.01	4.22
1952	93.69	87.19	29.29	19.02	6.86	2.87	12.95	3.66	1.43	2.51	2.67	5.95	6.49	.94	5.56
1951	88.95	82.08	27.04	18.23	6.34	2.71	12.64	3.50	1.32	2.04	2.64	5.61	6.87	.85	6.01
1950	81.86	75.66	24.90	17.76	6.21	2.56	11.16	3.17	1.21	2.04	2.33	4.31	6.21	.76	5.45
1949	76.11	71.08	23.39	17.31	6.05	2.44	10.24	3.01	1.10	1.78	2.22	3.54	5.03	.69	4.34
1948	70.97	68.11	21.42	17.46	6.02	2.37	9.80	2.92	1.00	1.92	2.05	3.14	2.86	.60	2.27
1940	29.62	28.74	7.51	7.23	3.11	1.29	4.73	1.40	.25	1.24	1.14	.83	.88	.02	.86
1935	22.65	22.18	5.89	5.96	2.33	1.18	3.67	1.03	---------	.73	.90	.49	.47	---------	.47
1929	29.49	27.77	5.36	8.11	3.90	2.04	4.90	1.07	---------	.89	.78	.74	1.72	---------	1.72

[1] Services of registered and practical nurses in private duty, visits of nurses, podiatrists, physical therapists, clinical psychologists, chiropractors, naturopaths, and Christian Science practitioners.
[2] Research expenditures of drug companies included in expenditures for drugs and drug sundries and excluded from research expenditures.
[3] Includes fees of optometrists and expenditures for hearing aids, orthopedic appliances, artificial limbs, crutches, wheelchairs, etc.
[4] Includes the net cost of insurance and administrative expenses of federally financed health programs.
[5] Based on July 1 data from the Bureau of the Census for total U.S. population, including Armed Forces and Federal civilian employees overseas and the civilian population of outlying areas.

Series B 236–247. National and Personal Health Care Expenditures, by Source of Funds: 1929 to 1970

[In millions of dollars, except percent. Calendar year data]

Year	National health expenditures						Personal health care expenditures					
	Total		Private			Public	Total	Private				Public
	Amount	Percent of gross national product	Total	Consumers	Philanthropy and other			Total	Direct payments	Insurance benefits	Other	
	236	237	238	239	240	241	242	243	244	245	246	247
1970	71,573	7.3	44,685	40,943	3,742	26,887	62,282	40,430	23,758	15,744	928	21,851
1969	64,142	6.9	40,047	36,615	3,432	24,095	55,541	35,881	21,958	13,068	855	19,660
1968	56,587	6.5	34,999	32,282	2,717	21,588	49,060	31,522	19,383	11,344	795	17,537
1967	50,696	6.4	32,555	30,070	2,485	18,141	43,853	29,275	18,965	9,545	765	14,578
1966	44,974	6.0	32,153	29,729	2,422	12,821	38,594	29,051	19,166	9,142	744	9,543
1965	40,468	5.9	30,398	28,050	2,348	10,066	34,821	27,475	18,049	8,729	697	7,346
1964	37,461	5.9	28,193	25,898	2,295	9,266	32,322	25,415	16,915	7,832	668	6,905
1963	33,530	5.7	24,970	23,001	1,969	8,558	28,990	22,568	14,947	6,980	641	6,420
1962	31,295	5.6	23,373	21,515	1,858	7,924	27,023	21,056	14,104	6,344	608	5,968
1961	28,783	5.5	21,507	19,905	1,602	7,278	25,082	19,504	13,232	5,695	577	5,579
1960	26,895	5.3	20,259	18,831	1,428	6,637	23,680	18,523	12,990	4,996	537	5,157
1959	24,878	5.1	18,596	17,329	1,267	6,280	21,953	17,141	12,190	4,399	552	4,810
1958	22,848	5.1	16,932	15,763	1,169	5,918	20,177	15,645	11,266	3,877	502	4,534
1957	21,108	4.8	15,648	14,547	1,101	5,461	18,591	14,357	10,403	3,474	480	4,235
1956	19,246	4.6	14,278	13,374	904	4,968	17,140	13,221	9,750	3,015	456	3,919
1955	17,745	4.4	13,190	12,282	908	4,555	15,708	12,100	9,132	2,536	432	3,608
1954	16,799	4.6	12,421	11,572	849	4,378	14,818	11,408	8,816	2,179	413	3,410
1953	15,745	4.3	11,388	10,629	759	4,357	13,860	10,525	8,224	1,919	382	3,335
1952	14,988	4.3	10,558	9,690	868	4,431	12,968	9,662	7,697	1,604	361	3,307
1951	13,992	4.3	9,846	8,962	884	4,148	12,031	8,997	7,302	1,353	342	3,035
1950	12,662	4.5	9,222	8,425	797	3,440	10,885	8,445	7,133	992	320	2,440
1949	11,576	4.5	8,716	8,042	674	2,860	10,073	8,078	7,026	767	285	1,995
1948	10,612	4.1	8,208	7,691	517	2,404	9,473	7,694	6,829	606	259	1,779
1940	3,987	4.0	3,178	3,051	127	811	3,548	2,980	2,886		94	570
1935	2,936	4.0	2,372	2,288	84	563	2,663	2,269	2,195		74	392
1929	3,649	3.5	3,154	2,937	217	495	3,202	2,913	2,829		84	289

Series B 248–261. National Health Expenditures, by Type of Expenditure: 1929 to 1970

[In millions of dollars, except percent. Calendar year data]

Year	Total		Private expenditures			Public expenditures								
						Health and medical services								
	Amount	Percent of gross national product	Health and medical services	Medical research	Medical-facilities construction	Veterans' hospital and medical care	General hospital and medical care	Public assistance	Workmen's compensation	Defense Department hospital and medical care [1]	School, maternal, and child health services	Other	Medical research	Medical-facilities construction
	248	249	250	251	252	253	254	255	256	257	258	259	260	261
1970	71,573	7.3	42,288	194	2,203	1,763	3,560	5,745	1,043	1,858	676	[2]9,432	[2]1,648	1,163
1969	64,142	6.9	37,855	192	2,000	1,541	3,196	4,871	930	1,755	657	[2]8,547	[2]1,626	973
1968	56,587	6.5	33,444	188	1,367	1,387	2,969	4,254	833	1,699	589	[2]7,358	[2]1,608	893
1967	50,696	6.4	31,150	181	1,224	1,297	2,868	2,944	752	1,540	514	[2]5,921	[2]1,522	782
1966	44,974	6.0	30,753	172	1,228	1,206	2,772	2,040	678	1,269	451	[2]2,272	[2]1,402	732
1965	40,468	5.9	29,023	166	1,210	1,138	2,618	1,479	610	1,022	377	818	1,303	703
1964	37,461	5.9	26,837	158	1,198	1,092	2,481	1,258	562	1,104	346	693	1,166	564
1963	33,530	5.7	23,908	151	911	1,038	2,360	1,068	527	1,042	327	618	1,033	545
1962	31,295	5.6	22,367	141	865	988	2,204	919	492	1,003	310	575	892	541
1961	28,783	5.5	20,719	132	656	955	2,179	686	463	961	284	520	712	518
1960	26,895	5.3	19,598	125	536	913	2,100	514	435	896	254	474	538	512
1959	24,878	5.1	18,100	106	390	862	1,909	451	405	907	234	484	420	608
1958	22,848	5.1	16,473	86	373	822	1,803	365	380	911	216	473	330	617
1957	21,108	4.8	15,224	78	346	769	1,718	304	362	851	200	458	266	533
1956	19,246	4.6	14,016	70	192	732	1,573	270	345	788	184	439	200	436
1955	17,745	4.4	12,889	60	241	723	1,384	232	325	754	168	408	150	410
1954	16,799	4.6	12,152	54	215	701	1,263	194	305	777	153	402	129	455
1953	15,745	4.3	11,170	51	167	661	1,206	165	282	890	117	403	113	519
1952	14,988	4.3	10,204	45	309	643	1,137	137	257	1,046	76	450	105	580
1951	13,992	4.3	9,449	40	357	613	1,034	110	230	976	66	435	94	589
1950	12,662	4.5	8,885	38	299	582	933	76	204	584	63	376	79	544
1949	11,576	4.5	8,456	36	224	579	834	26	186	325	60	345	69	436
1948	10,612	4.1	8,068	32	108	554	739	--------	174	280	57	312	57	231
1940	3,987	4.0	3,145	--------	33	63	306	--------	94	75	32	153	3	83
1935	2,936	4.0	2,362	--------	10	50	231	--------	69	29	15	117	--------	51
1929	3,649	3.5	3,049	--------	105	49	125	--------	75	29	13	96	--------	108

[1] Includes military dependents.
[2] Beginning 1966 includes the following amounts for "Medicare," health insurance payments for the aged (in millions): 1966, $1,199; 1967, $4,736; 1968, $5,979; 1969, $6,918; and 1970, $7,494.

Series B 262–274. Indexes of Medical Care Prices: 1935 to 1970

[1967 = 100. U.S. city average, consumer price index for urban wage earners and clerical workers]

Year	Total medical care	Medical care services	Drugs and prescriptions		Professional services							Hospital services	
			Total	Prescriptions	Physicians' fees			Obstetrical cases	Tonsillectomy and adenoidectomy	Dentists' fees	Optometric examination and eyeglasses	Daily service charges	Private rooms
					Total	Office visits	House visits						
	262	263	264	265	266	267	268	269	270	271	272	273	274
1970	120.6	124.2	103.6	101.2	121.4	122.6	122.4	121.8	117.1	119.4	113.5	143.9	141.7
1969	113.4	116.0	101.3	99.6	112.9	113.3	114.5	113.5	110.3	112.9	107.6	127.9	126.7
1968	106.1	107.3	100.2	98.3	105.6	105.8	106.5	105.2	104.9	105.5	103.2	113.2	112.7
1967	100.0	100.0	100.0	100.0	100.0	100.0	100.0	100.0	100.0	100.0	100.0	100.0	100.0
1966	93.4	92.0	100.5	101.8	93.4	92.7	93.5	93.0	94.9	95.2	95.3	84.0	84.7
1965	89.5	87.3	100.2	102.0	88.3	87.3	87.6	89.0	91.0	92.2	92.8	76.6	77.7
1964	87.3	84.6	100.5	103.1	85.2	84.1	84.1	87.1	88.4	89.4	90.9	72.4	73.4
1963	85.6	82.6	100.8	104.5	83.1	82.1	81.6	85.0	85.9	87.1	89.7	69.0	70.1
1962	83.5	80.2	101.7	107.1	81.3	80.0	79.7	83.7	83.8	84.7	89.2	64.9	66.6
1961	81.4	77.7	103.3	111.5	79.0	77.7	77.2	81.1	81.9	82.5	87.8	60.6	62.4
1960	79.1	74.9	104.5	115.3	77.0	75.9	75.0	79.4	80.3	82.1	85.1	56.3	57.8
1959	76.4	72.0	104.4	115.7	75.1	74.5	72.8	77.7	77.1	80.5	83.0	52.7	53.8
1958	73.2	68.7	102.8	113.1	72.7	72.1	70.1	75.5	74.3	78.6	82.1	49.9	51.0
1957	69.9	65.5	99.3	108.2	70.3	69.5	67.5	73.5	71.9	76.2	81.3	47.2	48.7
1956	67.2	62.8	96.7	104.7	67.4	67.2	63.5	70.9	69.5	74.4	78.2	43.7	46.0
1955	64.8	60.4	94.7	101.6	65.4	65.4	61.2	68.6	69.0	73.0	77.0	41.5	44.1
1954	63.4	58.7	93.7	100.2	63.2	63.7	58.8	64.4	67.4	72.3	75.9	39.6	42.2
1953	61.4	57.0	92.6	98.3	61.4	61.2	57.6	61.5	66.0	70.0	76.9	37.4	39.7
1952	59.3	55.0	91.8	98.3	59.8	59.2	56.3	60.2	64.3	67.8	77.8	35.2	37.5
1951	56.3	51.7	91.0	97.1	57.3	56.8	54.6	54.4	62.0	66.4	76.8	32.0	34.2
1950	53.7	49.2	88.5	92.6	55.2	54.9	52.9	51.2	60.7	63.9	73.5	28.9	31.3
1949	52.7	48.1	87.4	90.2	54.4	54.2	51.9	50.6	60.2	62.4	72.8	27.8	30.5
1948	51.1	46.4	86.1	88.1	53.4	53.3	50.8	49.9	58.5	60.0	70.5	25.7	28.6
1947	48.1	43.5	81.8	81.3	51.4	51.2	49.5	46.7	55.1	56.9	67.7	22.0	24.9
1946	44.4	40.1	76.2	74.0	48.3	48.1	46.6	43.5	51.5	52.5	65.1	18.5	21.3
1945	42.1	37.9	74.8	71.5	46.0	45.7	44.7	41.0	48.8	49.6	63.9	16.2	18.9
1944	41.1	36.9	74.3	70.6	44.9	44.3	44.0	40.2	47.5	47.6	63.1	15.7	18.3
1943	39.9	35.4	73.5	69.4	43.2	42.2	42.5	38.5	45.4	45.1	61.6	15.1	17.6
1942	38.0	33.7	73.0	68.8	40.6	39.9	40.4	35.1	43.0	43.1	59.0	14.0	16.4
1941	37.0	32.7	71.4	67.0	39.8	39.1	39.6	33.6	41.8	42.0	58.3	12.9	15.4
1940	36.8	32.5	70.8	66.2	39.6	39.1	39.6	33.0	41.5	42.0	58.1	12.7	15.1
1939	36.7	32.5	71.1	66.2	39.6	39.0	39.6	33.0	42.6	42.0	57.6	12.6	15.1
1938	36.7	32.4	71.3	66.2	39.5	38.9	39.6	32.8	42.4	41.9	57.2	12.6	15.0
1937	36.6	32.3	70.9	65.7	39.6	39.0	39.7	32.5	42.1	41.8	57.1	12.3	14.7
1936	36.3	31.9	70.5	65.4	39.4	38.9	39.6	32.3	41.9	40.9	56.8	12.0	14.3
1935	36.1	31.8	70.7	65.4	39.2	38.8	39.1	32.1	41.8	40.8	56.7	11.9	14.2

Series B 275–290. Physicians, Dentists, and Nurses; and Medical, Dental, and Nursing Schools: 1810 to 1970

[Census figures in italics. Figures for schools and students are for academic session ending in the specified year]

Year	Physicians [1]			Medical schools [2]			Dentists [4]		Dental schools			Active professional graduate nurses		Professional nursing schools [6]		
	Number	Rate per 100,000 population	Physicians admitted to U.S. as immigrants	Number [3]	Students	Graduates	Number	Rate per 100,000 population	Number [5]	Students	Graduates	Number	Rate per 100,000 population	Number	Students	Graduates
	275	276	277	278	279	280	281	282	283	284	285	286	287	288	289	290
1970	348,328	166	3,158	107	39,666	8,799	118,175	58	53	16,008	3,700	700,000	345	1,328	150,795	43,639
1969	338,942	163	2,756	104	37,712	8,486	115,610	57	52	15,408	3,433	680,000	338	1,287	145,588	42,196
1968	330,732	161	3,128	100	36,368	8,400	113,636	57	50	14,955	3,457	659,000	331	2,262	141,948	41,555
1967	322,045	158	3,326	95	35,212	8,148	112,152	56	49	14,421	3,360	640,000	325	1,219	139,070	38,237
1966	313,559	156	2,552	93	34,516	7,934	111,130	56	49	14,020	3,198	621,000	319	1,191	135,702	35,125
1965	305,115	153	2,012	93	34,089	7,803	109,301	56	49	13,876	3,181	613,188	319	1,153	129,629	34,686
1964	297,089	159	2,249	92	33,595	7,691	107,820	56	48	13,691	3,213	582,000	306	1,142	124,744	35,259
1963	289,188	149	2,093	92	33,072	7,631	106,230	56	48	13,576	3,233			1,128	123,861	32,398
1962	270,136	145	1,797	92	32,633	7,530	105,252	56	47	13,513	3,207	550,000	297	1,118	123,012	31,186
1961				92	32,232	7,500	103,596	56	47	13,580	3,290			1,123	118,849	30,267
1960	274,833	148	1,574	*91	*31,999	*7,508	101,947	56	*47	*13,581	*3,253	*504,000	*282	*1,119	*115,057	*30,113
1959	*236,818	*133	1,630	85	29,614	6,860	*100,615	*57	47	13,509	3,156			1,126	113,518	30,312
1958			1,934	85	29,473	6,861	98,540	57	47	13,279	3,083	460,000	268	1,118	112,989	30,410
1957	226,625	132	1,990	85	29,130	6,796	100,534	59	45	13,004	3,050			1,115	114,674	29,933
1956			1,388	82	28,639	6,845	99,227	59	43	12,730	3,038	430,000	262	1,125	114,423	30,236
1955	218,061	132	1,046	81	28,583	6,977	97,529	59	43	12,601	3,081	7 430,000	259	1,139	107,572	28,729
1954	214,200	132	1,040	80	28,227	6,861	95,883	59	43	12,516	3,084	7 389,600	244	1,141	103,019	28,539
1953	210,900	132	845	79	27,688	6,668	93,726	59	42	12,370	2,945			1,148	102,019	29,308
1952	207,900	132	1,210	79	27,076	6,080	91,638	58	42	12,169	2,975			1,167	102,550	29,016
1951	205,500	133	1,388	79	26,186	6,135			42	11,891	2,830			1,183	103,433	28,794

See footnotes at end of table.

Series B 275–290. Physicians, Dentists, and Nurses; and Medical, Dental, and Nursing Schools: 1810 to 1970—Con.

Year	Physicians [1]			Medical schools [2]			Dentists [4]		Dental schools			Active professional graduate nurses		Professional nursing schools [6]		
	Number	Rate per 100,000 population	Physicians admitted to U.S. as immigrants	Number [3]	Students	Graduates	Number	Rate per 100,000 population	Number [5]	Students	Graduates	Number	Rate per 100,000 population	Number	Students	Graduates
	275	276	277	278	279	280	281	282	283	284	285	286	287	288	289	290
1950	203,400	134	1,878	79	25,103	5,553	89,441	59	41	11,460	2,565	[7]375,000	249	1,203	98,712	25,790
1950	*191,947*	*128*					*74,855*	*50*								
1949	201,277	135	1,141	78	23,670	5,094			41	10,132	1,574			1,215	88,817	21,379
1948				77	22,739	5,543			40	8,996	1,755			1,245	91,643	34,268
1947				77	23,900	6,389	82,990	58	40	8,287	2,225			1,253	106,900	40,744
1946				77	23,216	5,826			39	7,274	2,666			1,271	128,828	36,195
1945			202	77	24,028	5,136			39	[8]8,590	3,212			1,295	126,576	31,721
1944			156	77	[8]48,195	[8]10,303			39	[8]9,014	2,470			1,307	112,249	28,276
1943			218	76	22,631	5,223			39	[8]8,847	1,926			1,297	100,486	26,816
1942	180,496	134	290	77	22,031	5,163			39	[8]8,355	1,784			1,299	91,457	25,613
1941			706	77	21,379	5,275			39	7,720	1,568			1,303	87,588	24,899
1940	175,163	133	1,095	77	21,271	5,097			39	7,407	1,757	[7]284,200	216	1,311	85,156	23,600
1940	*165,989*	*126*					*69,921*	*53*								
1939			1,384	77	21,302	5,089			39	7,331	1,794			1,328	82,095	22,485
1938	169,628	131	738	77	21,587	5,194			39	7,184	1,704			1,349	74,305	20,655
1937			533	77	22,095	5,377			39	7,397	1,739			1,389	73,286	20,400
1936	165,163	129	462	77	22,564	5,183			39	7,306	1,736			1,417	69,589	18,600
1935			304	77	22,888	5,101			39	7,175	1,840			1,472	67,533	19,600
1934	161,359	128	353	77	22,799	5,035			39	7,160	1,864					
1933			187	77	22,466	4,895			39	7,508	1,986					
1932			259	76	22,135	4,936			38	8,031	1,840			1,781	84,290	25,312
1931	156,406	126	329	76	21,982	4,735			38	8,129	1,842			1,844	100,419	25,971
1930			390	76	21,597	4,565			38	7,813	1,561	[7]214,300	174			
1930	*153,803*	*125*					*71,055*	*58*								
1929	152,503	125	398	76	20,878	4,446			40	8,200	2,442			1,885	78,771	23,810
1928			454	80	20,545	4,262	67,334	56	40		2,563					
1927	149,521	126	486	80	19,662	4,035			40	10,333	2,642			1,797	77,768	18,623
1926			487	79	18,840	3,962			44		2,610					
1925	147,010	127	540	80	18,200	3,974	64,481	56	43	11,863	2,590					
1924			1,391	79	17,728	3,562			43		3,422					
1923	145,966	130	704	80	16,960	3,120			45	13,099	3,271					
1922			458	81	15,635	2,520			45		1,765					
1921	145,404	134	597	83	14,466	3,186			45	11,745	1,795					
1920			459	85	13,798	3,047			46		906	[7]103,900	98	1,755	54,953	14,980
1920	*144,977*	*137*					*56,152*	*53*								
1919			236	85	13,052	2,656			46		3,587					
1918	147,812	141	182	90	13,630	2,670			46		3,345					
1917			326	96	13,764	3,379	45,988	44	46		3,010					
1916	145,241	142	326	95	14,012	3,518			49		2,835					
1915			476	96	14,891	3,536			49		2,388			1,509	46,141	11,118
1914	142,332	144	504	102	16,502	3,594	42,606	43	48		2,254					
1913			508	107	17,015	3,981			51		2,022					
1912	137,199	144	459	118	18,412	4,483	38,866	41	52		1,940					
1911			429	122	19,786	4,273			54		1,742					
1910	135,000	146	365	131	21,526	4,440	37,684	41	54		1,646	[7]50,500	55	1,129	32,636	8,140
1910	*151,132*	*164*					*39,997*	*43*								
1909	134,402	149	332	140	22,145	4,515			56		1,761					
1908			504	151	22,602	4,741	36,670	41	55		2,005					
1907			480	159	24,276	4,980			55		1,724					
1906	134,688	158	725	162	25,204	5,364	35,238	41	55		1,519					
1905			1,043	158	26,147	5,600			55		2,621			862	19,824	5,795
1904	128,950	157	907	160	28,142	5,747	32,204	39	56		2,168					
1903			343	160	27,615	5,698			55		2,198					
1902	123,196	156	116	160	27,501	5,009	28,109	36	56		2,294					
1901			100	160	26,417	5,444			57		2,304					
1900	119,749	157		160	25,171	5,214	25,189	33	57		2,091			432	11,164	3,456
1900	*132,002*	*173*					*29,665*	*39*								
1898	115,524	157					23,911	33	54		1,894					
1896	104,554	147					20,063	28	48		1,432					
1893	103,090	154							37							
1890	100,180	159		133	15,404	4,454			31		960			35	1,552	471
1890	*104,805*	*166*					*17,498*	*28*								
1886	87,521	151							23		473					
1880	82,000	163		100	11,826	3,241			14		315			15	323	157
1880	*85,671*	*171*					*12,314*	*25*								
1870	60,000	150		75					10		147					
1870	*64,414*	*162*					*7,988*	*20*								
1860	55,055	175		65			5,606	18	3		64					
1850	*40,755*	*176*		52			*2,923*	*13*	2		17					
1840				35			1,000	6	1							
1830				20			300	2								
1820				10			100	1								
1810				5			50	1								

* Denotes first year for which figures include Alaska and Hawaii.
NA Not available.
[1] Beginning 1960, includes osteopaths.
[2] Beginning 1954, includes Puerto Rico; beginning 1960, includes osteopaths and their schools.
[3] Approved medical and basic science schools.
[4] Beginning 1958, excludes graduates of year stated.

[5] For 1840 and 1926–1931, schools offering courses in dentistry; for 1850–1925, schools conferring degrees; for other years, schools in operation. Includes Puerto Rico.
[6] Includes Hawaii and Puerto Rico beginning 1950 for number and students and 1952 for graduates.
[7] Census estimate adjusted to exclude student nurses enumerated as graduates.
[8] Reflects enrollment of more than 1 class in some schools under accelerated program in operation during World War II.

Series B 291–304. Rates Per 100,000 Population for Specified Reportable Diseases: 1912 to 1970

[Rate per 100,000 population enumerated as of April 1 for 1940, 1950, 1960, and 1970, and estimated as of July 1 for all other years]

Year	Tuberculosis, all forms [1]	Syphillis and its sequelae	Gonorrhea	Malaria	Typhoid and paratyphoid fever [2]	Scarlet fever and streptococcal sore throat [3]	Hepatitis [4]	Brucellosis	Diphtheria	Whooping cough	Measles	Meningococcal infections	Acute poliomyelitis	Smallpox
	291	292	293	294	295	296	297	298	299	300	301	302	303	304
1970	18.3	43.8	285.2	1.5	0.2	239.2	32.0	0.1	0.2	2.1	23.2	1.2	(Z)	
1969	19.4	48.1	245.9	1.5	.2	238.2	27.3	.1	.1	1.6	12.8	1.5	(Z)	
1968	21.3	49.9	219.2	1.2	.2	226.3	25.7	.1	.1	2.4	11.1	1.3	(Z)	
1967	23.1	53.2	193.0	1.0	.2	238.1	21.2	.1	.1	4.9	31.7	1.1	(Z)	
1966	24.4	57.1	173.6	.3	.2	226.8	17.8	.1	.1	3.9	104.2	1.7	.1	
1965	25.3	59.7	163.8	.1	.2	204.3	17.7	.1	.1	3.5	135.1	1.6	(Z)	
1964	26.6	62.9	154.5	(Z)	.3	210.6	20.0	.2	.2	6.8	239.4	1.5	.1	
1963	28.7	69.3	145.7	.1	.3	181.6	23.1	.2	.2	9.1	204.2	1.3	.2	
1962	28.7	68.1	142.8	.1	.3	170.0	28.9	.2	.2	9.6	259.0	1.2	.5	
1961	29.4	69.7	147.8	(Z)	.4	185.0	40.1	.3	.3	6.3	231.6	1.2	.7	
1960*	30.8	68.0	139.6	(Z)	.5	175.8	23.4	.4	.5	8.3	245.4	1.3	1.8	
1959 [5]	32.5	69.3	137.1	(Z)	.5	189.6	13.4	.5	.5	22.7	230.1	1.2	4.8	
1958	36.5	68.5	129.3	(Z)	.6	152.4	9.4	.5	.5	18.6	440.5	1.5	3.3	
1957	39.2	78.3	129.8	.1	.7	113.3	8.8	.6	.7	16.6	285.9	1.6	3.2	
1956	41.6	77.1	142.4	.1	1.0	105.5	11.5	.8	.9	19.0	365.9	1.6	9.1	
1955	46.9	76.0	149.2	.3	1.0	89.8	19.5	.9	1.2	38.2	337.9	2.1	17.6	
1954	49.3	87.5	152.0	.4	1.3	91.7	31.1	1.1	1.3	37.8	423.5	2.8	23.9	
1953	53.0	100.8	157.4	.8	1.4	84.0	21.7	1.3	1.5	23.5	283.7	3.2	22.5	
1952	70.5	110.8	161.3	4.5	1.5	73.0	11.8	1.6	1.9	28.9	438.5	3.1	37.2	
1951	77.3	131.8	179.5	3.7	1.4	54.9	5.5	2.0	2.6	44.8	345.6	2.7	18.5	
1950	80.4	154.2	204.0	1.4	1.6	42.8	2.5	2.3	3.8	80.1	210.1	2.5	22.1	
1949	90.7	197.3	226.7	2.8	2.7	58.7		2.8	5.4	46.7	420.6	2.4	28.3	(Z)
1948	93.8	234.7	252.0	6.6	2.5	62.5		3.4	6.5	51.1	421.0	2.3	19.0	(Z)
1947	94.1	264.6	284.2	10.5	2.8	65.2		4.4	8.5	109.1	155.0	2.4	7.5	.1
1946	85.2	271.7	275.0	34.7	2.8	89.6		4.2	11.7	78.4	496.8	4.1	18.3	.2
1945	86.8	282.3	225.8	47.4	3.7	140.1		3.8	14.1	101.0	110.2	6.2	10.3	.3
1944	95.0	367.9	236.5	43.4	4.0	150.9		3.3	10.6	82.7	474.3	12.3	14.3	.3
1943	89.6	447.0	213.6	40.6	4.1	112.0		2.8	11.0	142.9	472.0	13.6	9.3	.6
1942	87.5	363.4	160.9	44.9	4.6	101.4		2.4	12.1	142.9	408.8	2.9	3.1	.6
1941	79.3	368.2	146.7	51.1	6.5	104.7		2.6	13.5	166.9	671.7	1.5	6.8	1.0
1940	78.0	359.7	133.8	59.2	7.4	125.9		2.5	11.8	139.6	220.7	1.3	7.4	2.1
1939	79.4	367.1	139.8	63.2	10.0	132.3		2.7	18.4	140.0	308.2	1.5	5.6	7.5
1938	82.4	372.0	153.8	64.9	11.5	152.8		3.4	23.5	175.1	633.8	2.2	1.3	11.5
1937	87.2	264.3	143.4	84.2	12.4	183.5		2.1	22.2	166.6	249.6	4.3	7.4	9.1
1936	83.6	212.6	129.8	104.6	12.4	195.6		1.6	23.4	115.0	234.0	5.7	3.5	6.1
1935	87.9	205.6	130.8	108.1	14.4	211.0		1.6	30.8	141.9	584.6	4.6	8.5	6.3
1934	89.4	186.7	124.1	105.4	17.6	180.0		1.6	34.1	209.9	632.6	2.0	5.9	4.3
1933	91.1	193.4	121.4	100.0	18.6	174.4		1.4	40.2	142.6	319.2	2.3	4.0	5.2
1932	97.7	208.2	132.5	55.0	21.4	172.7			48.0	172.5	323.2	2.5	3.1	9.0
1931	100.7	197.4	137.0	56.7	21.4	166.3			57.1	139.1	382.8	4.4	12.8	24.4
1930	101.5	185.4	135.5	80.0	22.1	144.5			54.1	135.6	340.8	6.8	7.5	39.7
1929		169.2	135.4	134.7	19.1	152.9			70.1	162.1	300.6	8.7	2.4	34.7
1928		174.2	138.3	138.2	22.6	148.9			75.9	134.3	466.3	4.8	4.3	32.7
1927		171.9	140.7	118.2	29.2	179.8			89.8	152.4	387.6	2.6	8.8	31.6
1926		196.1	157.2	98.9	35.5	166.7			80.7	172.2	587.1	1.8	2.3	28.7
1925		181.2	149.3	86.8	40.0	161.9			82.1	131.2	194.3	1.5	5.3	34.2
1924		174.2	144.5	98.4	31.0	164.2			105.6	145.0	463.7	1.4	4.6	49.6
1923		156.2	142.2	124.2	31.0	158.8			131.4	146.7	680.0	1.9	3.1	27.6
1922		157.7	140.4	142.9	33.0	148.1			156.9	97.7	241.8	1.9	2.0	30.3
1921		172.3	177.7	174.7	43.5	178.7			190.7		274.5	2.2	5.8	94.7
1920		145.3	175.4	173.0	33.8	151.6			139.0		480.5	2.6	2.2	95.9
1919		113.2	147.8		42.9	118.3			144.7		203.2	3.1	2.3	63.8
1918					50.0	94.5			101.5		474.9	7.2	2.8	83.1
1917					63.0	139.2			133.0		611.6	6.2	4.9	52.7
1916					82.3	114.5			129.2		621.8	2.7	41.1	23.4
1915					74.0	108.6			132.7		254.1	2.9	3.1	50.2
1914					82.4	133.0			152.5		295.8	3.4	2.4	66.4
1913					84.2	143.1			142.1		368.5	3.4	4.0	55.7
1912					81.8	138.2			139.0		310.0		5.5	30.8

* Denotes first year for which figures include Alaska and Hawaii.
Z Less than 0.05.
[1] Includes Alaska and Hawaii for all years. Prior to 1953, active and inactive cases; thereafter, new active cases only.

[2] Beginning 1950, excludes paratyphoid fever.
[3] 1912–1919, excludes streptococcal sore throat.
[4] 1950–1952, infectious only; thereafter, infectious and serum. Reporting incomplete.
[5] Includes Alaska.

Series B 305–318. Hospitals and Beds, by Type of Service and Ownership (AHA): 1946 to 1970

Year	Total		Non-Federal								Federal, all types		Beds per 1,000 population	
			Short-term general and special		Long-term general and special		Psychiatric		Tuberculosis					
	Hospitals	Beds	Hospitals	Beds	Hospitals	Beds	Hospitals	Beds	Hospitals	Beds	Hospitals	Beds	Total	Short-term [1]
	305	306	307	308	309	310	311	312	313	314	315	316	317	318
1970___	7,123	1,615,771	5,859	848,232	236	59,961	519	526,889	101	19,720	408	160,969	8.0	4.2
1969___	7,144	1,649,662	5,853	825,795	260	63,075	509	570,550	107	20,562	415	169,681	8.3	4.1
1968___	7,137	1,663,203	5,820	805,912	280	66,517	505	593,916	116	22,213	416	174,645	8.4	4.1
1967___	7,172	1,671,125	5,850	788,446	331	80,311	470	609,075	105	18,228	416	175,065	8.5	4.0
1966___	7,160	1,678,658	5,812	768,479	291	67,337	476	639,041	156	30,796	425	173,005	8.7	4.0
1965___	7,123	1,703,522	5,736	741,292	283	65,897	483	685,175	178	37,196	443	173,962	8.9	3.9
1964___	7,127	1,696,039	5,712	720,810	300	68,783	487	691,367	187	39,589	441	175,490	9.0	3.8
1963___	7,138	1,701,839	5,684	698,191	323	73,525	499	714,661	186	39,144	446	176,318	9.1	3.7
1962___	7,028	1,689,414	5,564	676,795	323	73,474	491	716,781	203	44,687	447	177,677	9.2	3.7
1961___	6,923	1,669,789	5,460	658,521	321	70,536	483	714,622	222	48,556	437	177,554	9.2	3.6
1960___	6,876	1,657,970	5,407	639,057	308	67,214	488	722,493	238	52,101	435	177,105	9.3	3.6
1959*_	6,845	1,612,822	5,364	619,877	330	68,323	459	688,410	254	57,392	438	178,820	9.2	3.5
1958___	6,786	1,572,036	5,290	609,732	321	78,383	475	646,270	261	57,077	439	180,574	9.1	3.5
1957___	6,818	1,588,691	5,309	594,529	340	77,608	452	641,455	280	62,097	437	183,002	9.2	3.5
1956___	6,966	1,607,692	5,299	586,498	395	75,646	525	695,331	315	66,096	432	184,121	9.6	3.5
1955___	6,956	1,604,408	5,237	567,612	402	76,278	542	707,162	347	70,194	428	183,162	9.8	3.5
1954___	6,970	1,577,961	5,212	553,068	406	70,926	554	691,176	368	73,558	430	189,233	9.8	3.4
1953___	6,978	1,580,654	5,212	545,903	406	68,039	541	691,855	384	72,253	435	202,604	10.0	3.5
1952___	6,903	1,561,809	5,122	530,669	405	69,731	546	675,749	391	72,642	439	213,018	10.0	3.4
1951___	6,832	1,521,959	5,066	516,020	394	62,768	551	655,932	399	72,642	422	214,597	9.9	3.4
1950___	6,788	1,455,825	5,031	504,504	412	70,136	533	619,530	398	72,178	414	189,477	9.6	3.3
1949___	6,277	1,435,288	4,585	476,584	395	79,145	507	614,465	414	78,330	376	186,764	9.7	3.2
1948___	6,160	1,411,450	4,499	471,555	362	77,040	504	601,103	409	75,906	386	185,846	9.7	3.2
1947___	6,173	1,400,318	4,475	465,209	385	84,758	499	580,273	411	70,307	403	199,771	9.8	3.2
1946___	6,125	1,435,778	4,444	473,059	389	83,415	476	568,473	412	74,867	404	235,964	10.3	3.4

* Denotes first year for which figures include Alaska and Hawaii.   [1] Non-Federal short-term general and special hospitals.

Series B 319–330. Hospitals and Beds, by Type of Service (AMA): 1909 to 1953

Year	Total		General		Mental		Tuberculosis		All other		Beds per 1,000 population	
	Hospitals	Beds	Hospitals	Beds	Hospitals	Beds	Hospitals	Beds	Hospitals	Beds	Total	General
	319	320	321	322	323	324	325	326	327	328	329	330
1953_____	6,840	1,573,014	5,087	653,752	593	749,393	420	88,406	740	81,463	9.9	4.1
1952_____	6,665	1,541,615	4,924	640,923	585	732,929	428	89,571	728	78,192	9.9	4.1
1951_____	6,637	1,529,988	4,890	640,207	596	728,187	430	88,379	721	73,215	10.0	4.2
1950_____	6,430	1,456,912	4,713	587,917	579	711,921	431	85,746	707	71,328	9.6	3.9
1949_____	6,572	1,439,030	4,761	574,683	606	705,423	444	83,470	761	75,454	9.7	3.9
1948_____	6,335	1,423,520	4,589	576,459	586	691,499	438	81,993	722	73,569	9.7	3.9
1947_____	6,276	1,425,222	4,539	592,453	585	680,913	441	81,328	711	70,528	9.9	4.1
1946_____	6,280	1,468,714	4,523	641,331	575	674,930	450	83,187	732	69,266	10.5	4.6
1945_____	6,511	1,738,944	4,744	922,549	563	657,393	449	78,774	755	80,228	13.1	7.0
1944_____	6,611	1,729,945	4,833	925,818	566	648,745	453	79,848	759	75,534	13.0	7.0
1943_____	6,655	1,649,254	4,885	850,576	575	650,993	455	79,860	740	67,825	12.3	6.3
1942_____	6,345	1,383,827	4,557	594,260	586	646,118	468	82,372	734	61,077	10.3	4.4
1941_____	6,358	1,324,381	4,518	533,498	596	638,144	477	82,365	767	70,374	9.9	4.0
1940_____	6,291	1,226,245	4,432	462,360	602	621,284	479	78,246	778	64,355	9.3	3.5
1939_____	6,226	1,195,026	4,356	444,947	600	606,284	480	75,972	790	67,823	9.1	3.4
1938_____	6,166	1,161,380	4,286	425,324	592	591,822	493	76,022	795	68,212	8.9	3.3
1937_____	6,128	1,124,548	4,245	412,091	579	570,616	508	76,751	796	65,090	8.7	3.2
1936_____	6,189	1,096,721	4,207	402,605	584	548,952	506	73,692	892	71,472	8.6	3.1
1935_____	6,246	1,075,139	4,257	406,174	592	529,311	496	70,373	901	69,281	8.4	3.2
1934_____	6,334	1,048,101	4,198	393,425	614	513,845	495	70,063	1,027	70,768	8.3	3.1
1933_____	6,437	1,027,046	4,237	386,713	621	498,955	497	70,682	1,082	70,696	8.2	3.1
1932_____	6,562	1,014,354	4,305	395,543	624	479,548	512	69,676	1,121	69,587	8.1	3.2
1931_____	6,613	974,115	4,309	384,333	587	451,245	509	65,923	1,208	72,614	7.9	3.1
1930_____	6,719	955,869	4,302	371,609	561	437,919	515	65,940	1,341	80,401	7.8	3.0
1929_____	6,665	907,133	4,268	357,034	572	414,386	502	61,310	1,323	74,403	7.4	2.9
1928_____	6,852	892,934	4,361	363,337	553	394,268	508	62,113	1,430	73,216	7.4	3.0
1927_____	6,807	853,318	4,322	345,364	563	373,364	508	63,170	1,414	71,420	7.2	2.9
1926_____	6,946	859,445									7.3	
1925_____	6,896	802,065	4,041	293,301	589	341,480	466	49,131	1,800	118,153	6.9	2.5
1924_____	7,370	813,926									7.1	
1923_____	6,830	755,722	3,793		593		476		1,968		6.8	
1921_____	[1] 6,236											
1920_____	6,152	817,020	4,013	311,159	521	295,382	52	10,150	1,566	200,329	7.7	2.9
1918_____	5,323	612,251									5.9	
1914_____	5,047	532,481									5.4	
1909_____	4,359	421,065									4.7	

[1] Excludes hospitals with less than 10 beds.

Series B 331–344. Hospitals and Beds, by Ownership or Control (AHA): 1946 to 1970

Year	Total		Governmental						Nonprofit				Proprietary	
			Federal		State		Local		Church		Other			
	Hospitals	Beds	Hospitals	Beds	Hospitals	Beds	Hospitals	Beds	Hospitals	Beds	Hospitals	Beds	Hospitals	Beds
	331	332	333	334	335	336	337	338	339	340	341	342	343	344
1970___	7,123	1,615,771	408	160,969	577	557,571	1,680	219,353	(1)	(1)	[1] 3,600	[1] 618,548	858	59,330
1969___	7,144	1,649,663	415	169,681	565	598,064	1,665	220,447	(1)	(1)	[1] 3,643	[1] 606,186	856	55,285
1968___	7,137	1,663,203	416	174,645	559	620,455	1,631	218,623	(1)	(1)	[1] 3,660	[1] 594,845	871	54,635
1967___	7,172	1,671,125	416	175,065	552	646,929	1,589	216,338	(1)	(1)	[1] 3,692	[1] 578,560	923	54,233
1966___	7,160	1,678,658	425	173,005	550	669,118	1,554	218,630	(1)	(1)	[1] 3,675	[1] 563,320	956	54,585
1965___	7,123	1,703,522	443	173,962	546	707,974	1,495	215,554	1,266	215,723	2,404	336,201	969	54,108
1964___	7,127	1,696,039	441	175,490	555	719,343	1,500	215,891	1,227	210,837	2,424	320,798	980	53,680
1963___	7,138	1,701,839	446	176,318	561	738,839	1,446	210,527	1,271	205,774	2,392	317,261	1,022	53,120
1962___	7,028	1,689,414	447	177,677	558	746,490	1,410	208,200	1,259	201,919	2,364	305,189	990	49,939
1961___	6,923	1,669,789	437	177,554	551	745,392	1,374	205,732	1,260	199,284	2,328	294,840	973	46,987
1960___	6,876	1,657,970	435	177,105	556	752,148	1,324	201,322	1,241	192,743	2,338	288,843	982	45,809
1959*__	6,845	1,612,822	438	178,820	555	725,455	1,280	195,328	1,232	186,912	2,328	281,424	1,012	44,883
1958___	6,786	1,572,036	439	180,574	548	691,226	1,257	195,778	1,220	183,437	2,288	275,365	1,034	45,656
1957___	6,818	1,558,691	437	183,002	543	686,255	1,238	194,740	1,220	180,291	2,291	267,555	1,089	46,848
1956___	6,966	1,607,692	432	184,121	553	728,151	1,263	202,368	1,206	176,972	2,304	265,633	1,208	50,447
1955___	6,956	1,604,408	428	183,162	552	739,153	1,253	203,179	1,101	162,283	2,339	264,761	1,283	51,870
1954___	6,970	1,577,961	430	189,233	552	717,558	1,248	202,312	1,196	169,685	2,225	247,658	1,319	51,515
1953___	6,978	1,580,654	435	202,604	556	710,802	1,239	203,836	1,110	157,597	2,259	251,712	1,379	54,103
1952___	6,903	1,561,809	439	213,018	(2)	(2)	[2] 1,747	[2] 896,596	(1)	(1)	[1] 3,348	[1] 398,530	1,369	53,665
1951___	6,832	1,521,959	422	214,597	(2)	(2)	[2] 1,701	[2] 870,517	(1)	(1)	[1] 3,297	[1] 383,102	1,412	53,743
1950___	6,788	1,455,825	414	189,477	(2)	(2)	[2] 1,654	[2] 843,672	(1)	(1)	[1] 3,250	[1] 368,137	1,470	54,539
1949___	6,277	1,435,288	376	186,764	(2)	(2)	[2] 1,511	[2] 842,089	(1)	(1)	[1] 3,044	[1] 355,331	1,346	51,104
1948___	6,160	1,411,450	386	185,846	(2)	(2)	[2] 1,474	[2] 826,377	(1)	(1)	[1] 3,022	[1] 349,310	1,278	49,917
1947___	6,173	1,400,318	403	199,771	(2)	(2)	[2] 1,490	[2] 807,602	(1)	(1)	[1] 2,981	[1] 342,120	1,299	50,825
1946___	6,125	1,435,778	404	235,964	(2)	(2)	[2] 1,504	[2] 811,702	(1)	(1)	[1] 2,921	[1] 334,867	1,296	53,245

* Denotes first year for which figures include Alaska and Hawaii.
[1] Church-operated and affiliated hospitals included with "Other."
[2] State hospitals included with "Local."

Series B 345–358. Hospitals and Beds, by Ownership or Control (AMA): 1909 to 1953

Year	Total		Governmental						Nonprofit				Proprietary	
			Federal		State		Local		Church		Other			
	Hospitals	Beds	Hospitals	Beds	Hospitals	Beds	Hospitals	Beds	Hospitals	Beds	Hospitals	Beds	Hospitals	Beds
	345	346	347	348	349	350	351	352	353	354	355	356	357	358
1953___	6,840	1,573,014	392	200,535	550	711,824	1,194	200,645	1,169	164,053	2,206	243,653	1,329	52,304
1952___	6,665	1,541,615	386	211,510	549	691,408	1,143	196,705	1,136	158,389	2,146	232,598	1,305	51,005
1951___	6,637	1,529,988	388	216,939	554	683,376	1,090	197,405	1,116	154,053	2,121	225,903	1,368	52,312
1950___	6,430	1,456,912	355	186,793	552	665,019	1,005	185,229	1,097	150,078	2,072	218,788	1,349	51,005
1949___	6,572	1,439,030	361	182,254	573	656,611	1,003	186,290	1,090	146,315	2,067	213,576	1,478	53,984
1948___	6,335	1,423,520	372	185,098	567	648,386	961	186,283	1,068	144,036	2,016	208,936	1,351	50,781
1947___	6,276	1,425,222	401	213,204	563	626,648	953	190,353	1,051	141,920	1,965	202,661	1,343	50,436
1946___	6,280	1,468,714	464	264,486	557	628,363	941	189,885	1,050	138,096	1,942	198,885	1,326	48,999
1945___	6,511	1,738,944	705	546,384	549	619,642	929	190,692	1,036	135,481	1,954	195,805	1,338	50,940
1944___	6,611	1,729,945	798	551,135	539	609,025	925	192,118	1,020	133,090	1,961	195,624	1,368	48,953
1943___	6,655	1,649,254	827	476,673	531	610,115	926	189,351	1,004	130,488	1,952	192,219	1,415	50,408
1942___	6,345	1,383,827	474	220,938	530	606,437	920	188,406	977	126,141	1,949	190,150	1,495	51,755
1941___	6,358	1,324,381	428	179,202	530	600,320	906	185,989	993	123,331	1,917	182,140	1,584	53,399
1940___	6,291	1,226,245	336	108,928	521	572,079	910	192,682	998	120,809	1,903	177,681	1,623	54,066
1939___	6,226	1,195,026	329	96,338	523	560,575	888	188,233	1,001	120,740	1,839	172,765	1,646	56,375
1938___	6,166	1,161,380	330	92,248	523	541,279	875	181,609	981	119,521	1,776	169,980	1,681	56,743
1937___	6,128	1,124,548	329	97,951	522	508,913	871	181,885	975	115,283	1,718	162,474	1,713	58,042
1936___	6,189	1,096,721	323	84,234	524	503,306	877	176,300	969	113,288	1,742	162,586	1,754	57,007
1935___	6,246	1,075,139	316	83,353	526	483,994	882	174,365	970	113,268	1,670	155,300	1,882	64,859
1934___	6,334	1,048,101	313	77,865	544	473,035	892	166,988	970	113,263	1,676	154,449	1,939	62,501
1933___	6,437	1,027,046	295	75,635	557	459,646	924	159,192	984	115,840	[1] 3,677	[1] 216,733	(1)	(1)
1932___	6,562	1,014,354	301	74,151	568	442,601	935	162,615	1,001	117,555	[1] 3,757	[1] 217,432	(1)	(1)
1931___	6,613	974,115	291	69,170	576	419,282	949	153,072	1,011	116,935	[1] 3,786	[1] 215,656	(1)	(1)
1930___	6,719	955,869	288	63,581	581	405,309	943	150,836	1,017	116,846	[1] 3,890	[1] 219,297	(1)	(1)
1929___	6,665	907,133	292	59,901	578	385,706	925	136,930	1,024	113,555	[1] 3,846	[1] 211,041	(1)	(1)
1928___	6,852	892,934	294	61,765	595	369,759	924	135,910	1,056	114,613	[1] 3,983	[1] 210,887	(1)	(1)
1927___	6,807	853,318	301	60,444	592	354,786	916	129,939	1,060	108,582	[1] 3,938	[1] 199,567	(1)	(1)
1926___	6,946	859,445	(NA)	63,553	(NA)	334,984	(NA)	(NA)	(NA)	(NA)	(NA)	(NA)	(NA)	(NA)
1925___	6,896	802,065	299	57,091	351	317,264	(NA)	(NA)	(NA)	(NA)	(NA)	(NA)	(NA)	(NA)
1924___	7,370	813,926	310	62,352	632	321,399	1,050	125,302	1,233	110,760	1,748	131,439	2,397	62,674
1923___	6,830	755,722	220	53,869	601	302,208	915	115,871	893	77,941	2,439	160,114	1,762	45,719
1918___	5,323	612,251	110	18,815	303	262,064								
1914___	5,047	532,481	93	12,602	294	232,834								
1909___	4,359	421,056	71	8,827	232	189,049								

NA   Not available.   [1] Proprietary hospitals and beds included with "Other nonprofit."

Series B 359–370.   Average Daily Census and Admissions to Hospitals, by Type of Service and Ownership (AHA): 1946 to 1970

[In thousands]

Year	Total		Non-Federal								Federal, all types	
			Short-term general and special		Long-term general and special		Psychiatric		Tuberculosis			
	Average daily census	Admissions during year	Average daily census	Admissions during year	Average daily census	Admissions during year	Average daily census	Admissions during year	Average daily census	Admissions during year	Average daily census	Admissions during year
	359	360	361	362	363	364	365	366	367	368	369	370
1970	1,298	31,759	662	29,252	49	132	447	598	12	36	128	1,741
1969	1,346	30,729	651	28,254	52	105	490	565	13	36	140	1,769
1968	1,378	29,766	630	27,276	55	149	532	538	14	36	146	1,766
1967	1,380	29,361	612	26,988	68	155	540	492	12	26	149	1,700
1966	1,398	29,151	588	26,897	57	144	582	451	21	45	151	1,615
1965	1,403	28,812	563	26,463	56	166	607	491	26	52	150	1,640
1964	1,421	28,266	550	25,987	59	157	632	442	28	62	152	1,619
1963	1,430	27,502	530	25,267	62	148	657	435	29	55	152	1,598
1962	1,407	26,531	509	24,307	62	159	649	413	33	60	154	1,592
1961	1,393	25,474	489	23,375	60	155	654	376	36	65	153	1,503
1960	1,402	25,027	477	22,970	58	151	672	362	39	68	154	1,476
1959 *	1,363	23,605	462	21,605	59	149	642	349	45	79	156	1,424
1958	1,323	23,697	451	21,684	67	160	604	359	44	69	157	1,425
1957	1,320	22,993	438	21,002	67	198	609	303	49	71	157	1,419
1956	1,356	22,090	425	20,107	63	175	659	343	53	76	156	1,388
1955	1,363	21,073	407	19,100	65	158	677	312	56	87	157	1,415
1954	1,343	20,345	393	18,392	61	155	668	289	61	89	160	1,421
1953	1,342	20,184	394	18,098	56	160	663	291	62	77	168	1,558
1952	1,336	19,624	385	17,413	58	156	651	392	62	76	180	1,586
1951	1,298	18,783	378	16,677	51	163	636	275	62	83	171	1,586
1950	1,253	18,483	372	16,663	60	164	607	293	62	79	152	1,284
1949	1,240	17,224	352	15,428	68	132	597	269	66	128	157	1,268
1948	1,241	16,821	361	15,072	70	128	595	267	66	112	149	1,241
1947	1,190	17,689	354	15,908	73	149	558	266	55	94	150	1,271
1946	1,142	15,675	341	13,655	63	139	517	202	55	85	166	1,593

* Denotes first year for which figures include Alaska and Hawaii.

Series B 371–380.   Average Daily Census and Admissions to Hospitals, by Type of Service (AMA): 1923 to 1953

[In thousands]

Year	Total		General		Mental		Tuberculosis		All other	
	Average daily census	Admissions during year	Average daily census	Admissions during year	Average daily census	Admissions during year	Average daily census	Admissions during year	Average daily census	Admissions during year
	371	372	373	374	375	376	377	378	379	380
1953	1,333	19,869	477	18,693	719	328	75	108	61	739
1952	1,309	18,915	475	17,760	704	312	75	110	55	733
1951	1,294	18,237	471	17,066	698	307	74	107	52	757
1950	1,243	17,024	433	15,830	688	307	72	113	49	773
1949	1,225	16,660	429	15,450	675	308	69	113	51	789
1948	1,217	16,423	438	15,160	664	305	66	106	49	852
1947	1,217	15,830	457	14,665	652	292	63	99	46	773
1946	1,239	15,153	496	14,052	636	271	62	100	45	731
1945	1,405	16,257	665	15,228	624	249	60	86	56	694
1944	1,299	16,037	570	15,060	619	226	63	88	47	662
1943	1,257	15,375	529	14,455	619	209	65	92	43	620
1942	1,126	12,546	405	11,634	610	214	70	102	41	596
1941	1,087	11,596	364	10,647	603	209	71	101	50	639
1940	1,026	10,088	325	9,219	591	190	67	91	43	587
1939	996	9,879	308	9,018	577	190	65	91	46	580
1938	966	9,421	293	8,546	562	199	66	101	44	576
1937	944	9,222	288	8,350	547	196	65	102	44	574
1936	909	8,647	272	7,756	525	185	63	99	49	607
1935	876	7,717	261	6,875	507	173	61	86	46	583
1934	830	7,147	237	6,292	488	172	60	82	45	601
1933	810	7,038	232	6,072	475	171	60	84	43	711
1932	808	7,228	250	6,304	455	170	60	93	43	662
1931	775	7,156	248	6,322	427	------------	56	81	45	------------
1930	763	------------	240	------------	415	------------	56	------------	52	------------
1929	727	------------	234	------------	395	------------	51	------------	47	------------
1927	672	------------	228	------------	350	------------	51	------------	43	------------
1925	629	------------	194	------------	322	------------	40	------------	74	------------
1923	553	------------	------------	------------	------------	------------	------------	------------	------------	------------

Series **B 381–388.** Hospital Use Rates: 1931 to 1970

[Data are annual rates per 1,000 population, except as noted, based on Bureau of the Census estimated resident population as of July 1]

Year	General and special hospitals			Mental hospitals		Tuberculosis hospitals			Year	General and special hospitals			Mental hospitals		Tuberculosis hospitals		
	Admissions	Total days in hospital	Average length of stay (days)	Admissions	Total days in hospital	Admissions	Total days in hospital	Average length of stay (days)		Admissions	Total days in hospital	Average length of stay (days)	Admissions	Total days in hospital	Admissions	Total days in hospital	Average length of stay (days)
	381	382	383	384	385	386	387	388		381	382	383	384	385	386	387	388
1970	152	1,440	9.5	3.3	862	0.2	22	122	1953	123	1,241	10.1	2.1	1,659	0.7	173	252
1969	149	1,452	9.8	3.1	958	.2	24	136	1952	119	1,242	10.5	2.0	1,650	.7	176	250
1968	146	1,438	9.9	3.0	1,060	.2	27	145	1951	116	1,244	10.7	2.0	1,660	.7	175	251
1967	146	1,440	9.9	2.7	1,084	.1	23	167									
1966	146	1,387	9.5	2.6	1,179	.2	40	168	1950	110	1,165	10.6	2.0	1,659	.7	175	233
									1949	109	1,179	10.8	2.1	1,658	.8	171	224
1965	146	1,329	9.1	2.9	1,261	.3	52	183	1948	110	1,215	11.1	2.1	1,660	.7	166	230
1964	145	1,327	9.2	2.7	1,326	.3	57	168	1947	108	1,280	11.9	2.0	1,658	.7	159	231
1963	143	1,314	9.2	2.6	1,393	.3	60	172	1946	106	1,412	13.4	1.9	1,657	.7	161	227
1962	140	1,295	9.3	2.6	1,399	.4	70	186									
1961	136	1,269	9.3	2.4	1,431	.4	78	190	1945	120	1,987	16.5	1.9	1,720	.7	165	253
									1944	118	1,696	14.3	1.7	1,700	.7	173	261
1960 *	136	1,265	9.3	2.3	1,491	.4	86	200	1943	112	1,556	13.9	1.6	1,684	.7	178	260
1959	131	1,252	9.6	2.3	1,453	.6	104	188	1942	91	1,216	13.3	1.6	1,662	.8	191	252
1958	134	1,274	9.5	2.3	1,406	.5	108	211									
1957	132	1,265	9.6	2.1	1,443	.6	123	223	1940	74	1,019	13.7	1.4	1,634	.7	185	269
1956	129	1,248	9.7	2.3	1,576	.6	135	231	1935	59	882	15.0	1.4	1,455	.7	174	257
									1931	56	860	15.3	0.8	1,257	.6	165	254
1955	125	1,238	9.9	2.2	1,645	.7	146	219									
1954	124	1,232	10.0	2.1	1,650	.7	157	232									

* Denotes first year for which figures include Alaska and Hawaii.

Series **B 389–400.** Hospital Expense Per Patient Day: 1946 to 1970

[**In dollars.** Covers hospitals accepted for registration by the American Hospital Association]

Year	Total expenses						Payroll expenses [1]					
	Amount	Federal	Non-Federal				Total	Federal	Non-Federal			
			Short-term, general and special	Long-term, general and special	Psychiatric (including short-term)	Tuberculosis			Short-term, general and special	Long-term, general and special	Psychiatric (including short-term)	Tuberculosis
	389	390	391	392	393	394	395	396	397	398	399	400
1970	53.95	53.10	81.01	36.17	16.63	34.20	33.16	37.44	47.30	24.00	12.24	23.94
1969	45.01	45.89	70.03	29.77	13.61	29.47	29.47	33.41	41.36	20.60	10.00	20.40
1968	37.78	37.97	61.38	27.00	11.25	25.13	23.78	27.48	36.61	18.58	8.29	17.38
1967	32.54	33.04	54.08	21.45	9.62	21.36	20.76	25.35	32.44	15.10	7.10	14.66
1966	27.94	29.69	48.15	20.59	8.11	19.16	18.27	23.96	29.41	14.39	6.11	13.36
1965	25.29	28.67	44.48	19.79	7.50	17.39	16.70	23.12	27.44	13.96	5.60	12.20
1964	23.20	27.17	41.58	18.91	6.97	15.72	15.38	22.38	25.26	13.21	5.16	10.78
1963	21.00	26.28	38.91	16.57	5.98	15.13	13.93	21.58	24.01	11.61	4.40	10.31
1962	19.73	24.97	36.83	15.10	5.72	15.22	13.12	20.42	22.79	10.62	4.16	10.38
1961	18.46	23.34	34.98	14.49	5.53	14.72	12.25	19.15	21.54	10.12	4.00	9.89
1960	16.46	20.11	32.23	12.82	4.91	13.37	10.92	16.34	20.08	9.01	3.45	8.92
1959 *	15.65	19.62	30.19	12.50	4.71	12.80	10.37	15.98	18.76	8.39	3.26	8.54
1958 [2]	14.74	18.38	28.27	10.32	4.40	12.08	9.63	14.80	17.19	6.91	3.08	7.91
1957	13.48	17.68	26.02	10.33	3.91	11.16	8.76	14.27	15.74	6.79	2.66	7.14
1956	12.16	16.97	24.15	10.20	3.63	10.19	7.98	13.74	14.85	6.84	2.41	6.51
1955	11.24	14.60	23.12	8.06	3.73	10.13	7.20	11.63	14.26	5.36	2.17	6.48
1954	10.67	15.92	21.76	8.53	3.22	9.32	6.83	12.06	13.21	5.63	2.03	5.77
1953	9.73	13.93	19.95	8.26	2.83	8.54	6.10	10.44	11.86	5.28	1.74	5.11
1952	9.14	14.10	18.35	6.63	2.68	7.85	5.63	10.35	10.66	4.05	1.58	4.61
1951	8.26	11.91	16.77	6.30	2.46	7.37	5.01	8.68	9.65	3.89	1.43	4.25
1950	7.98	12.77	15.62	5.39	2.43	7.22	4.79	9.35	8.86	3.32	1.38	4.06
1949	7.70	13.30	14.33	4.07	2.84	6.68	4.53	9.53	7.96	2.35	1.53	3.70
1948	6.35	8.81	13.09	3.81	1.95	6.25	3.60	6.19	7.17	1.99	1.03	3.17
1947	5.42	7.39	11.09	3.03	1.60	5.44	3.07	5.23	5.99	1.64	.84	2.82
1946	5.21	6.14	9.39	2.97	1.39	4.57	2.93	4.06	4.98	1.64	.80	2.38

* Denotes first year for which figures include Alaska and Hawaii.   [2] Includes Alaska.
[1] Includes full-time equivalents of part-time personnel; beginning 1951, excludes residents, interns, and students.

Series B 401–412. Persons Covered by Private Health Insurance for Hospital and Surgical Benefits: 1939 to 1970

[In thousands. As of end of year]

Year	Hospitalization insurance						Surgical insurance					
	Persons covered [1]		Blue Cross-Blue Shield	Insurance companies		Independent plans [3]	Persons covered [1]		Blue Cross-Blue Shield	Insurance companies		Independent plans [3]
	Number	Percent of population [2]		Group policies	Individual policies		Number	Percent of population [2]		Group policies	Individual policies	
	401	402	403	404	405	406	407	408	409	410	411	412
1970	175,382	86.4	75,464	82,712	43,480	8,131	162,655	80.1	69,110	84,133	30,128	10,532
1969	170,855	85.0	73,211	80,093	41,469	7,702	158,584	78.9	66,595	81,363	29,097	9,950
1968	167,209	84.1	70,510	76,059	39,709	7,277	153,977	77.5	63,279	77,415	28,201	8,752
1967	160,649	81.6	67,513	73,351	37,908	7,050	148,729	75.6	60,433	74,318	28,719	8,580
1966	155,864	80.1	65,638	69,570	38,641	6,633	143,284	73.6	57,916	70,268	29,301	8,325
1965	151,483	78.5	63,662	67,104	37,372	6,984	139,437	72.3	56,330	67,557	29,239	8,684
1964	148,338	77.8	62,429	64,506	35,857	6,840	135,433	71.0	54,473	64,939	27,506	8,297
1963	144,575	76.8	60,698	62,817	34,462	7,165	131,954	70.1	52,371	63,288	26,973	8,608
1962	139,176	75.1	59,618	59,153	32,921	6,937	126,900	68.4	50,876	59,787	25,491	8,287
1961	134,417	73.7	57,960	57,013	30,951	7,102	122,951	67.4	49,374	57,373	24,862	8,494
1960	130,007	72.3	57,464	55,218	30,187	5,994	117,304	65.2	48,266	55,504	23,012	7,336
1959	125,753	71.1	55,054	51,255	28,971	6,380	112,842	63.8	46,386	51,756	22,198	6,188
1958	121,018	69.6	53,623	49,508	26,784	6,389	107,527	61.9	44,331	49,917	20,808	6,080
1957	119,493	69.9	53,282	48,439	26,337	6,411	105,229	61.6	43,305	48,955	20,349	5,990
1956	114,342	68.2	51,455	45,211	25,570	6,430	98,015	58.4	40,542	45,906	18,831	5,899
1955	105,452	64.1	48,924	39,029	24,131	6,545	88,856	54.0	37,395	39,725	18,769	5,930
1954	101,493	62.9	45,355	35,090	22,172	6,680	85,890	53.3	33,081	35,723	16,825	5,970
1953	97,303	61.5	43,684	33,575	21,860	6,973	80,982	51.2	29,527	34,039	17,039	6,007
1952	90,965	58.5	41,353	29,455	21,412	6,120	72,459	46.6	25,775	29,621	18,354	5,258
1951	85,348	55.9	39,412	26,663	20,802	5,290	64,892	42.5	22,052	29,376	15,623	4,510
1950	76,639	50.7	37,645	22,305	17,296	4,445	54,156	35.8	17,253	21,219	13,718	3,760
1949	66,044	44.2	33,576	17,697	14,729	3,623	41,143	27.5	12,842	15,590	9,315	3,026
1948	60,995	41.5	30,619	16,741	11,286	3,280	34,060	23.2	10,516	14,199	6,944	2,670
1947	52,584	36.4	27,646	14,190	7,584	3,040	26,247	18.2	6,187	11,103	4,875	2,550
1946	42,112	29.9	24,342	11,315	3,000	2,820	18,609	13.2	4,236	8,661	2,000	2,460
1945	32,068	24.0	18,961	7,804	2,700	2,670	12,890	9.7	2,335	5,537	1,800	2,420
1944	29,232	22.9	15,828	8,400	2,400	2,495	11,713	9.2	1,583	5,625	1,600	2,375
1943	24,160	18.9	12,696	6,800	2,100	2,319	10,069	7.9	1,065	4,700	1,400	2,323
1942	19,695	15.2	10,295	5,080	1,800	2,290	8,140	6.3	815	3,275	1,200	2,290
1941	16,349	12.4	8,469	3,850	1,500	2,270	6,775	5.1	645	2,300	1,000	2,270
1940	12,312	9.3	6,072	2,500	1,200	2,250	5,350	4.0	260	1,430	850	2,250
1939	7,976	6.1	---	---	---	---	3,103	2.4	---	---	---	---

[1] Net number of different persons covered as estimated by Health Insurance Association of America (HIAA), an association of insurance companies. Estimate of net number enrolled exceeds summary of individual categories for early years because HIAA data include estimated enrollment of college and university health services.

[2] For 1939, based on total population; all other years based on Bureau of the Census estimates of the civilian population as of end of year.

[3] Plans—community group and individual practice plans, employer-employee-union group and individual practice plans, private group clinics, and dental service corporations— not affiliated with Blue Cross-Blue Shield or insurance companies.

Series B 413–422. Hospitals—Assets, Expenses, and Personnel, by Type of Control and Service: 1946 to 1970

[Covers hospitals accepted for registration by the American Hospital Association]

Year	Total	Federal	Non-Federal							
			Total	Psychiatric	Tuberculosis	Long-term [1]	Short-term [1]			
							Total	Voluntary nonprofit	For profit	State and local government
	413	414	415	416	417	418	419	420	421	422
	ASSETS (mil. dol.)									
1970	36,159	3,183	32,976	4,816	311	1,176	26,674	20,502	871	5,301
1969	33,547	3,036	30,511	4,922	307	1,128	24,153	18,567	647	4,938
1968	31,019	3,180	27,839	4,659	317	1,085	21,778	16,954	539	4,286
1967	27,922	2,817	25,105	4,189	225	1,179	19,512	15,075	484	3,953
1966	26,336	3,057	23,280	4,084	356	1,057	17,783	13,734	412	3,637
1965	24,502	2,552	21,950	4,167	421	998	16,364	12,476	414	3,474
1964	23,275	2,505	20,770	4,297	442	1,143	14,888	11,423	413	3,052
1963	21,309	2,450	18,859	3,716	420	1,073	13,651	10,507	343	2,801
1962	19,980	2,342	17,638	3,558	470	1,008	12,602	9,656	288	2,658
1961	19,079	2,285	16,795	3,515	505	992	11,783	8,949	266	2,568
1960	17,714	2,124	15,590	3,437	508	787	10,858	8,422	243	2,193
1959 *	16,682	2,115	14,566	3,107	528	777	10,154	7,807	226	2,121
1958 [2]	15,470	2,018	13,451	2,773	517	742	9,419	7,221	219	1,980
1957	14,538	1,940	12,598	2,422	553	818	8,805	6,505	300	1,999
1956	13,035	1,903	11,133	2,318	514	766	7,535	5,741	173	1,621
1955	11,986	1,664	10,322	2,232	530	575	6,985	5,223	148	1,614
1954	10,820	1,805	9,016	1,931	484	422	6,177	4,709	145	1,323
1953	10,159	1,529	8,630	1,842	486	562	5,739	4,348	145	1,246
1952	9,418	1,532	7,886	1,802	437	509	5,138	3,901	147	1,090
1951	8,206	1,439	6,766	1,476	421	351	4,518	3,460	141	918
1950	7,791	1,131	6,660	1,441	421	449	4,349	3,350	138	861
1949	6,946	874	6,072	1,261	442	435	3,934	3,101	131	702
1948	6,490	905	5,586	1,143	395	349	3,699	2,889	136	675
1947	5,881	812	5,070	966	322	343	3,439	2,697	129	612

See footnotes at end of table.

Series B 413–422.   Hospitals—Assets, Expenses, and Personnel, by Type of Control and Service: 1946 to 1970—Con.

Year	Total	Federal	Non-Federal							
			Total	Psychiatric	Tuberculosis	Long-term [1]	Short-term [1]			
							Total	Voluntary nonprofit	For profit	State and local government
	413	414	415	416	417	418	419	420	421	422

EXPENSES [3] (mil. dol.)

Year	413	414	415	416	417	418	419	420	421	422
1970	25,556	2,483	23,073	2,712	152	649	19,560	14,163	1,068	4,328
1969	22,103	2,350	19,753	2,433	143	565	16,613	12,137	852	3,624
1968	19,061	2,032	17,030	2,192	133	543	14,162	10,317	720	3,125
1967	16,395	1,795	14,600	1,896	94	529	12,081	8,806	653	2,622
1966	14,198	1,633	12,565	1,716	147	427	10,276	7,435	553	2,288
1965	12,948	1,568	11,380	1,662	165	406	9,147	6,643	510	1,994
1964	12,031	1,503	10,528	1,608	163	407	8,349	6,039	493	1,817
1963	10,956	1,458	9,498	1,433	158	376	7,532	5,491	417	1,624
1962	10,129	1,408	8,721	1,355	182	343	6,841	4,999	346	1,496
1961	9,387	1,308	8,080	1,322	192	316	6,250	4,584	304	1,362
1960	8,421	1,134	7,287	1,205	192	273	5,617	4,139	275	1,203
1959 *	7,789	1,119	6,670	1,102	208	269	5,091	3,760	242	1,089
1958 [2]	7,133	1,051	6,084	972	195	262	4,655	3,427	225	1,003
1957	6,496	1,013	5,483	870	200	252	4,161	3,050	200	911
1956	6,017	968	5,049	873	197	236	3,743	2,739	188	816
1955	5,594	837	4,757	923	208	192	3,434	2,508	174	752
1954	5,229	927	4,303	786	206	190	3,121	2,276	162	683
1953	4,765	853	3,912	685	192	167	2,868	2,080	169	619
1952	4,456	925	3,531	636	177	141	2,577	1,879	151	547
1951	3,913	743	3,169	571	167	117	2,314	1,688	139	486
1950	3,651	712	2,938	539	162	117	2,120	1,523	143	454
1949	3,486	764	2,722	619	160	101	1,842	1,333	125	383
1948	2,875	480	2,396	424	150	98	1,724	1,264	119	341
1947	2,354	405	1,949	325	109	81	1,434	1,048	109	276
1946	1,963	373	1,590	262	91	68	1,169	848	94	227

PERSONNEL [4] (1,000)

Year	413	414	415	416	417	418	419	420	421	422
1970	2,537	216	2,321	305	18	69	1,929	1,387	97	444
1969	2,426	213	2,213	303	18	68	1,824	1,330	88	407
1968	2,309	210	2,100	292	19	72	1,717	1,251	84	382
1967	2,203	214	1,988	277	15	78	1,619	1,175	81	363
1966	2,106	206	1,900	274	24	69	1,532	1,104	77	352
1965	1,952	199	1,754	274	29	65	1,386	1,011	70	306
1964	1,887	193	1,693	264	30	67	1,333	962	67	304
1963	1,840	206	1,634	261	29	67	1,277	921	64	291
1962	1,763	207	1,556	251	34	64	1,207	875	57	276
1961	1,696	202	1,494	248	37	60	1,149	835	51	263
1960	1,598	186	1,412	238	39	55	1,080	792	48	241
1959 *	1,520	179	1,341	215	41	54	1,031	758	46	227
1958 [2]	1,465	181	1,284	203	41	56	984	720	45	219
1957	1,401	186	1,215	191	43	55	926	680	43	203
1956	1,375	198	1,177	201	45	53	878	639	41	198
1955	1,301	192	1,109	188	48	47	826	597	41	188
1954	1,246	195	1,051	178	49	46	777	568	40	169
1953	1,169	198	971	165	47	40	719	520	40	159
1952	1,119	206	913	155	47	37	674	486	39	149
1951	1,075	197	878	151	47	32	648	464	38	146
1950	1,058	169	888	147	45	34	662	473	41	148
1949	963	161	803	132	45	30	596	435	35	126
1948	939	154	785	126	43	30	586	427	34	124
1947	883	161	722	117	36	30	539	392	35	111
1946	830	162	668	99	36	28	505	362	35	108

See footnotes at end of table.

Series B 413–422. Hospitals—Assets, Expenses, and Personnel, by Type of Control and Service: 1946 to 1970—Con.

Year	Total	Federal	Non-Federal				Short-term [1]			
			Total	Psychiatric	Tuberculosis	Long-term [1]	Total	Voluntary nonprofit	For profit	State and local government
	413	414	415	416	417	418	419	420	421	422

PERSONNEL PER 100 PATIENTS [4]

Year	413	414	415	416	417	418	419	420	421	422
1970	196	169	198	68	146	140	292	292	256	298
1969	180	152	183	62	138	131	280	284	244	279
1968	168	144	171	55	128	131	272	276	237	270
1967	160	144	161	51	122	115	265	268	233	262
1966	151	137	152	47	117	120	261	264	234	257
1965	139	133	140	45	111	115	246	252	218	234
1964	133	128	133	42	105	113	242	247	212	236
1963	129	135	128	40	102	108	241	244	214	237
1962	125	134	124	39	104	102	237	241	208	232
1961	122	132	121	38	103	100	235	240	205	227
1960	114	120	113	35	99	95	226	232	196	215
1959 *	112	114	111	34	93	91	223	229	195	210
1958 [2]	111	116	110	34	93	84	218	224	189	206
1957	107	118	104	32	88	82	211	218	185	197
1956	101	127	98	31	85	83	207	213	179	195
1955	95	122	92	28	85	71	203	210	182	188
1954	93	122	89	27	81	76	198	207	178	175
1953	87	118	83	25	76	72	183	193	161	161
1952	84	115	-------	24	76	63	175	184	162	153
1951	83	116	-------	24	75	63	171	181	155	151
1950	84	111	81	24	74	57	178	191	161	149
1949	78	102	-------	22	68	43	169	180	152	144
1948	76	103	-------	21	65	43	162	173	145	136
1947	79	97	-------	21	65	41	151	161	139	126
1946	73	97	-------	19	66	45	148	156	137	129

* Denotes first year for which figures include Alaska and Hawaii.
[1] Composed of both general and other special.
[2] Includes Alaska.

[3] Excludes cost of new construction.
[4] Beginning 1951, excludes residents, interns, and students; beginning 1954, includes full-time equivalents of part-time personnel.

Series B 423–427. Patients in Mental Hospitals, by Type of Hospital: 1904 to 1970

[In thousands, except rate. As of end of year. Completeness of reporting varies from year to year]

Year	Total		Federal [2]	State and county [3]	Private hospitals	Year	Total		Federal [2]	State and county [3]	Private hospitals	Year	Total		Federal [2]	State and county [3]	Private hospitals
	Number	Rate [1]					Number	Rate [1]					Number	Rate [1]			
	423	424	425	426	427		423	424	425	426	427		423	424	425	426	427
1970	391	194	43	338	11	1955	634	390	60	559	15	1940	479	364	34	434	11
1969	424	212	43	370	11	1954	625	393	57	554	14	1939	476	364	32	433	11
1968	457	231	48	399	10	1953	612	392	53	545	14	1938	462	356	30	421	11
1967	493	252	53	426	14	1952	599	390	53	532	13	1937	448	348	27	409	12
1966	523	270	57	452	14	1951	587	389	53	520	14	1936	435	340	24	400	11
1965	550	287	62	475	13	1950	580	386	54	513	14	1935	422	331	23	389	11
1964	566	299	62	490	13	1949	567	384	54	499	14	1934	407	322	21	376	10
1963	579	311	62	505	13	1948	558	384	55	490	13	1933	395	315	19	366	10
1962	591	322	62	516	14	1947	544	381	54	477	12	1931	353	284	12	332	8
1961 *	603	333	63	527	13	1946	531	384	49	470	12						
1960 [4]	611	343	[5] 62	536	14	1945	522	409	45	463	13	1923	268	239	[6] 29	[7] 230	9
1959	618	354	[5] 63	542	14	1944	510	402	41	456	12	1910	188	203	-------	-------	-------
1958	621	363	62	545	14	1943	503	394	38	453	12	1904	150	183	-------	-------	-------
1957	622	369	61	549	14	1942	502	383	36	454	12						
1956	628	380	62	551	14	1941	496	377	35	450	11						

* Denotes first year for which figures include Alaska and Hawaii.
[1] Patients per 100,000 population estimated as of July 1. Total population used prior to 1936; civilian, thereafter.
[2] Includes veterans with mental disorders resident in VA hospitals and, through 1965, all patients in public health service hospitals at Fort Worth, Tex., and Lexington, Ky.

[3] Includes patients in State-operated psychopathic hospitals and, through 1950, in city hospitals.
[4] Includes Alaska.
[5] Beginning 1959, includes Alaska; 1960, Hawaii.
[6] Includes county hospitals.
[7] State mental hospitals only.

Series B 428–443. Public Institutions for the Mentally Retarded: 1936 to 1970

Year	Number of facilities	Resident patients, beginning of year	Patients per 100,000 population [1]	Patients in public institutions [2] (1,000)	Admissions, excluding transfers		Patients under treatment	Deaths in institutions	Net live releases [4]	Resident patients, end of year	Average daily resident patient population	Personnel, full-time [5]		Maintenance expenditures [5][6]		
					Number	Rate per 100,000 civilian population [3]						Total	Rate per 100 average daily resident patient population	Total (mil. dol.)	Per average daily resident patient	
															Per year (dol.)	Per day (dol.)
	428	429	430	431	432	433	434	435	436	437	438	439	440	441	442	443
1970	190	189,956	--------	187	14,985	7.5	204,941	3,496	14,702	186,743	187,897	117,327	62.4	871	4,635	12.70
1969	180	192,848	--------	189	14,868	7.4	207,716	3,621	14,701	189,394	191,363	107,737	56.3	765	3,996	10.95
1968	170	193,121	98	193	14,688	7.4	207,809	3,614	11,675	192,520	193,690	100,804	52.0	673	3,472	9.51
1967	165	192,774	99	193	15,714	8.1	208,488	3,635	11,665	193,188	194,650	94,900	48.8	577	2,965	8.12
1966	154	189,858	102	192	14,998	7.8	204,856	3,601	9,268	191,987	192,384	88,974	46.3	505	2,615	7.16
1965	143	181,549	101	187	17,300	9.1	198,849	3,583	7,993	187,273	189,172	79,056	41.8	442	2,335	6.40
1964	134	177,207	99	180	15,018	7.9	190,636	3,384	9,292	179,599	181,779	74,128	40.8	397	2,189	6.00
1963	129	174,187	99	177	15,151	8.1	187,536	3,498	8,156	176,516	179,022	69,494	38.8	354	1,984	5.44
1962	124	170,575	99	174	14,132	7.7	184,707	3,244	7,764	173,699	175,445	63,810	36.4	326	1,859	5.09
1961	113	163,913	96	167	14,515	8.0	178,428	3,158	7,979	167,291	166,169	57,666	34.7	288	1,727	4.73
1960	108	158,682	96	164	14,701	8.3	173,383	3,202	6,451	163,730	163,282	54,277	33.2	266	1,650	4.52
1959	106	156,633	95	158	13,949	8.0	170,582	3,122	6,262	161,198	158,119	49,892	31.6	235	1,503	4.12
1958	102	152,876	94	154	13,463	7.9	166,339	3,499	6,050	156,790	153,453	46,218	30.1	215	1,409	3.86
1957	99	147,857	94	151	13,970	8.3	161,827	2,818	5,616	153,393	149,705	41,235	27.5	190	1,280	3.51
1956	100	145,997	93	146	12,972	7.8	158,969	2,730	9,998	146,241	145,700	39,470	27.1	169	1,166	3.19
1955	99	141,053	93	144	13,096	8.1	154,149	2,698	5,581	145,870	142,265	36,333	25.5	153	1,008	2.76
1954	97	136,926	93	140	13,511	8.5	150,437	2,703	5,517	142,217	138,595	34,336	24.8	141	1,017	2.79
1953	98	133,431	91	135	12,627	8.1	146,058	2,780	6,148	137,130	134,053	31,025	23.1	130	970	2.66
1952	96	130,743	91	132	12,262	8.0	143,005	2,721	6,902	133,382	130,076	29,416	22.6	120	923	2.53
1951	95	130,294	91	130	11,957	7.9	142,251	2,552	8,216	131,483	127,415	26,902	21.1	103	808	2.21
1950	96	125,375	90	128	12,233	6.9	137,608	2,678	5,531	129,399	125,704	25,744	20.1	92	732	2.01
1949	99	123,557	90	126	12,384	8.4	135,941	2,833	6,133	126,975	123,717	24,162	19.5	87	703	1.93
1948	95	119,214	88	122	12,294	8.5	131,508	2,742	6,315	122,451	119,653	21,554	18.0	75	627	1.72
1947	--------	113,475	88	119	11,770	8.3	125,245	2,873	3,669	118,703	113,633	18,810	16.6	61	537	1.47
1946	--------	114,199	86	113	11,216	8.1	125,415	3,063	8,877	113,475	111,648	17,490	15.7	49	439	1.20
1945	--------	112,758	94	113	11,128	8.7	123,886	2,720	6,967	114,199	111,648	15,926	14.0	43	379	1.04
1944	--------	112,792	94	112	10,822	8.5	123,614	2,999	7,489	113,126	112,641	15,467	13.7	40	355	.97
1943	--------	107,285	89	107	10,726	8.4	118,011	2,673	7,675	107,663	107,948	--------	--------	36	333	.91
1942	--------	109,385	88	109	11,543	8.8	120,928	2,531	7,831	110,566	--------	--------	--------	--------	--------	--------
1941	--------	99,720	80	102	11,980	9.1	111,700	2,310	7,263	102,127	--------	--------	--------	--------	--------	--------
1940	--------	99,222	80	101	10,714	8.1	109,936	2,262	6,091	101,583	--------	--------	--------	--------	--------	--------
1939	--------	96,757	79	99	10,447	8.0	107,204	2,382	5,241	99,581	--------	--------	--------	--------	--------	--------
1938	--------	97,516	82	101	11,226	8.7	108,742	2,555	4,170	102,017	--------	--------	--------	--------	--------	--------
1937	--------	95,112	79	98	12,230	9.5	107,342	2,907	5,726	98,709	--------	--------	--------	--------	--------	--------
1936	--------	92,572	78	95	10,710	8.4	103,282	2,686	5,792	94,804	--------	--------	--------	--------	--------	--------

[1] Population estimated as of July 1. Total population used prior to 1936; civilian, thereafter.
[2] Includes city institutions through 1945.
[3] Based on Bureau of the Census estimated resident population as of July 1.
[4] Excess of patients released alive from hospital over those returning to hospital.
[5] Reporting facilities only.
[6] Includes salaries and wages, purchased provisions, fuel, light, water, etc.

Series B 444–447. Four Indexes of Per Capita Food Consumption: 1909 to 1970

[1967 = 100. Beginning 1941, civilian consumption only]

Year	Food consumption	Food use	Food consumed, pounds	Calories per day	Year	Food consumption	Food use	Food consumed, pounds	Calories per day	Year	Food consumption	Food use	Food consumed, pounds	Calories per day
	444	445	446	447		444	445	446	447		444	445	446	447
1970	103	102	101	103	1950	95	96	105	102	1930	86	89	108	107
1969	102	102	101	102	1949	94	95	106	100	1929	87	90	110	108
1968	101	102	101	102	1948	94	96	107	100	1928	87	89	109	109
1967	100	100	100	100	1947	97	100	112	102	1927	87	90	108	108
1966	98	98	99	99	1946	99	103	115	103	1926	88	92	110	108
1965	97	97	99	98	1945	97	101	115	103	1925	86	91	109	107
1964	98	98	99	99	1944	96	100	114	104	1924	87	92	110	108
1963	97	98	99	98	1943	93	97	111	105	1923	87	--------	109	107
1962	96	96	99	97	1942	92	94	110	103	1922	85	--------	109	107
1961	96	97	100	97	1941	93	95	110	106	1921	80	--------	105	100
1960 *	96	96	101	98	1940	91	93	108	104	1920	83	--------	108	102
1959	97	98	101	99	1939	89	91	108	104	1919	84	--------	107	107
1958	95	96	101	97	1938	86	88	106	102	1918	83	--------	109	105
1957	96	98	102	97	1937	86	89	106	102	1917	81	--------	106	104
1956	98	100	103	99	1936	86	88	106	102	1916	81	--------	105	105
1955	97	99	103	99	1935	83	85	105	100	1915	82	--------	110	107
1954	96	97	103	98	1934	85	88	104	102	1914	83	--------	109	107
1953	96	97	104	99	1933	84	88	104	102	1913	83	--------	110	108
1952	95	96	104	99	1932	84	87	105	103	1912	85	--------	113	108
1951	94	95	105	98	1931	86	89	108	106	1911	84	--------	109	108
										1910	83	--------	111	109
										1909	85	--------	113	110

* Denotes first year for which figures include Alaska and Hawaii.

Series B 448–452. Index of Per Capita Consumption of Selected Nutrients: 1909 to 1970

[1967=100. Beginning 1941, civilian only]

Year	Protein 448	Fat 449	Carbo-hydrate 450	Iron 451	Ascorbic acid 452	Year	Protein 448	Fat 449	Carbo-hydrate 450	Iron 451	Ascorbic acid 452	Year	Protein 448	Fat 449	Carbo-hydrate 450	Iron 451	Ascorbic acid 452
1970	102	105	102	103	105	1950	96	97	108	96	97	1930	95	89	127	83	95
1969	102	103	102	100	100	1949	96	93	107	95	101	1929	96	91	126	83	103
1968	101	103	101	99	98	1948	96	93	106	95	104	1928	96	90	129	84	97
1967	100	100	100	100	100	1947	99	95	110	100	110	1927	97	89	128	84	97
1966	99	98	99	96	94	1946	104	95	110	106	114	1926	96	89	128	84	96
1965	98	97	99	95	94	1945	104	92	112	104	116	1925	97	89	127	83	98
1964	99	99	100	97	93	1944	101	95	114	102	116	1924	98	90	127	85	100
1963	98	97	99	96	94	1943	102	95	115	94	106	1923	98	90	125	86	101
1962	96	95	100	95	99	1942	99	93	114	90	108	1922	96	86	129	84	96
1961	97	95	100	95	99	1941	96	96	119	84	106	1921	93	81	118	82	96
1960	97	95	101	95	100	1940	95	95	115	83	106	1920	95	82	123	85	96
1959	97	98	101	94	98	1939	94	93	118	81	107	1919	99	87	128	88	93
1958	96	95	101	94	94	1938	92	89	116	80	106	1918	99	86	124	89	94
1957	97	94	100	94	99	1937	92	89	116	79	102	1917	98	81	126	85	91
1956	98	97	101	95	97	1936	93	89	117	81	101	1916	98	84	126	83	89
1955	97	97	101	94	98	1935	90	85	117	78	104	1915	99	84	129	85	97
1954	96	95	102	93	97	1934	93	89	115	81	100	1914	100	85	129	84	93
1953	97	95	103	95	98	1933	92	89	117	79	97	1913	102	83	131	86	95
1952	96	95	104	94	97	1932	93	89	120	80	99	1912	104	83	131	88	96
1951	95	93	105	94	99	1931	94	89	123	82	101	1911	103	84	131	88	92
												1910	104	83	133	89	99
												1909	106	85	133	90	97

Series B 453–459. Controlled Fluoridation of Water Systems: 1945 to 1970

[As of December 31]

Year	Operative systems				Discontinued systems			Year	Operative systems				Discontinued systems		
	Number		Population served	Percent of total U.S. population	Number		Population served		Number		Population served	Percent of total U.S. population	Number		Population served
	Water supply systems	Com-munities			Water supply systems	Com-munities			Water supply systems	Com-munities			Water supply systems	Com-munities	
	453	454	455	456	457	458	459		453	454	455	456	457	458	459
1970			83,725,771	41.1				1957	879	1,717	36,215,208	21.3	59	84	1,909,455
1969	2,653	4,834	80,096,860	39.8	109	146	4,296,868	1956	772	1,583	33,905,474	20.3	56	73	1,767,320
1968	2,372	4,229	74,579,666	37.4	98	122	4,628,507								
1967	2,091	3,827	71,916,682	36.4	97	122	3,983,707	1955	672	1,347	26,278,820	16.0	47	60	1,604,914
1966	1,785	3,145	62,427,290	31.9	87	112	4,018,710	1954	572	1,194	22,336,884	13.9	30	32	1,191,370
								1953	482	1,007	17,666,339	11.2	12	12	84,868
1965	1,692	3,030	59,855,024	30.9	89	111	4,018,195	1952	353	751	13,875,005	8.9	7	7	204,125
1964	1,573	2,758	48,363,066	25.3	86	111	2,815,953	1951	171	368	5,079,321	3.3	2	2	29,450
1963	1,482	2,612	46,678,380	24.8	85	111	2,324,486								
1962	1,350	2,321	44,045,392	23.7	83	108	2,243,764	1950	62	100	1,578,578	1.0	1	1	16,550
1961	1,249	2,197	42,201,115	23.1	79	104	2,217,635	1949	29	49	1,062,779	.7			
								1948	13	26	581,683	.4			
1960	1,172	2,111	41,179,694	22.9	79	110	2,211,230	1947	11	16	458,748	.3			
1959	1,081	1,990	39,628,377	22.4	72	103	2,173,363	1946	8	12	332,467	.2			
1958	995	1,890	38,461,589	22.2	65	96	2,001,877	1945	3	6	231,920	.2			

Chapter C

Migration

Internal Migration (Series C 1-88)

C 1–75. General note.

Data in these series are based on comparison of State of birth and State of residence of the native population enumerated at successive decennial censuses of population. The migration measured is the net movement from the time of birth to the census date. Migrants defined in this way include only those persons who have moved from one State to another and are, *on the census date*, living in States other than those in which they were born.

These statistics for migrants do not represent the total number of persons who have moved from the State or geographic division in which they were born to other States or divisions during any given period of time. Some of those who moved from one State to another died before the following census date. Some moved from and returned, between censuses, to their State of birth. Others moved to places outside the conterminous United States.

A native is defined as a person born in the United States, Puerto Rico, or an outlying area of the United States or persons born in a foreign country who have at least one parent born in the United States. Persons for whom place of birth was not reported are included under native. See also text for series A 105–118, A 119–134, and A 135–142 and general note, A 1–371.

Through 1950, the figures showing classification by race were not ordinarily based on replies to census questions asked by enumerators, but were rather obtained by observation. The figures do not, therefore, reflect a clear-cut definition of biological stock. The population of Negro and other races consists of Negroes, American Indians, Japanese, Chinese, Filipinos, and some other groups. Persons of mixed white and other parentage were placed in the classification of the parent who was not white. Persons of Mexican birth or ancestry who are not definitely Indian or of stock other than white have been classified as white in all censuses except that of 1930. The lack of comparability introduced by this factor is substantial in the West South Central, Mountain, and Pacific Divisions. For revised 1930 figures for regions showing Mexicans classified as white, see series B 215–230 in *Historical Statistics of the United States, 1789–1945*.

For a discussion of 1960 and 1970 data on race and a more complete statement concerning earlier years, see text for series A 91–104.

C 1–14. Native population, by residence within or outside State, division, and region of birth, by race, 1850–1970.

Source: Special compilations made by the University of Pennsylvania Studies of Population Redistribution and Economic Growth from the following U.S. Bureau of the Census reports: 1850, *The Seventh Census of the United States: 1850*, pp. xxxvi–xxxviii; 1860, *Eighth Census of the United States: 1860*, table 5 for each State, pp. 10–589 (various pages) and pp. 616–619; 1870, Ninth Census Reports, vol. I, pp. 327–335; 1880, Tenth Census Reports, *Population*; pp. 484–491; 1890, Eleventh Census Reports, *Population*, part 1, pp. 564–567 and 576–579; 1900, Twelfth Census Reports, *Population*, vol. I, part 1, pp. 686–693 and 702–705; 1910, Thirteenth Census Reports, *Population*, vol. I, pp. 730–744; 1920, Fourteenth Census Reports, *Population*, vol. II, pp. 626–640; 1930, Fifteenth Census

Reports, *Population*, vol. II, pp. 153–167; 1940, Sixteenth Census Reports, *State of Birth of the Native Population*, pp. 20–39; 1950, *U.S. Census of Population: 1950*, vol. IV, Special Reports, *State of Birth*; pp. 4A–24 to 4A–43; 1960, *U.S. Census of Population: 1960*, vol. II, Subject Reports, *State of Birth*; 1970, *U.S. Census of Population: 1970*, vol. II, Subject Reports, *State of Birth*.

In 1860, persons who were born in territories and who were then residing in territories were assumed to be residing in the territory of their birth.

See general note for series C 1–75 for definition of race and nativity; see also text for series A 172–194 for definition of division and region.

C 15–24. Native population born in each division, by division of residence, by race, 1850–1970.

Source: See source for series C 1–14.

See also general note for series C 1–75 for definition of race and nativity.

C 25–75. Estimated net intercensal migration of total, native white, foreign-born white, and Negro population, by States, 1870–1970.

Source: Components of change method, U.S. Bureau of the Census, Current Population Reports, *Population Estimates and Projections*, series p. 25, No. 72, p. 5; No. 304, p. 12; and No. 406, pp. 10 and 14. Survival rate method, 1870–1950, Everett S. Lee, Ann Ratner Miller, Carol P. Brainerd, and Richard A. Easterlin, *Population Redistribution and Economic Growth: United States, 1870–1950*, vol. I, the American Philosophical Society, Philadelphia, 1957, pp. 107–231 (copyright). 1950–1960, Hope T. Eldridge, *Net Intercensal Migration for States and Geographic Divisions of the United States, 1950–1960* (Analytical and Technical Reports, No. 5) Population Studies Center, University of Pennsylvania, Philadelphia, table A-1 (copyright).

The estimate of the net migration data shown for the component of change method was obtained by subtracting the national increase for the intercensal period (births minus deaths) from the difference between the census counts at the beginning and the end of the period.

The estimates of net migration by the survival rate method were obtained by a residual method, using survival ratios derived from census data. The loss through mortality during an intercensal period was estimated on the basis of the ratios of appropriate age groups as enumerated in successive decennial censuses. The difference between the enumerated population at the end of the decennial period and the estimated survivors from the beginning to the end of the period was assumed to be net migration. Computations were by age groups for each sex, the figures presented in series C 25–75 being summations for ages 10 years and over at the end of each intercensal period. For the native population, the figures show the estimated amount of net internal migration. For the foreign born, the figures represent the estimated net change attributable to direct movement into the State from abroad and the net gain or loss in the exchange of foreign-born residents with other States.

See general note for series C 1–75 for definition of race and nativity.

C 76–80.   Estimated annual movement of the farm population, 1920–1970.

Source: U.S. Department of Agriculture, Economic Research Service, 1920–1962, *Farm Population Estimates for 1910–1962*, ERS-130, 1963; 1963–1970, *Farm Population Estimates*, annual issues.

Estimates of the total farm population and of the annual changes in its components have utilized data from the censuses of population and agriculture and the Current Population Survey, conducted by the Bureau of the Census, and surveys of the Department of Agriculture. For a history of the procedures used and the successive revisions of the series, see Department of Agriculture, *Major Statistical Series of the U.S. Department of Agriculture*, vol. 7, Agricultural Handbook No. 365, 1969.

Farm population figures relate to the rural civilian population living on farms, regardless of occupation or source of income. From 1850 to 1960 the definition of a farm has varied. See general note for series K 1–203 and text for series K 1–3 for discussion of the changes in definition. Since 1960 a farm is defined as a place of 10 acres or more from which at least $50 worth of farm products were sold in the preceding year, or a place of less than 10 acres from which at least $250 worth of products were sold. Persons living on or what might be considered farmland are classed as nonfarm if they rent for cash a house and yard only. Likewise, persons in institutions, summer camps, motels, and tourist camps located in the open country are also classed as nonfarm.

C 81–88.   Mobility status and type of mobility of the population one year old and over, 1947–1970.

Source: U.S. Bureau of the Census, *Current Population Reports*, series P-20, No. 235.

The population was classified by mobility status on the basis of a comparison between the place of residence of each individual on the survey date and the place of residence one year earlier. Persons classified as movers include all those whose place of residence in the United States was different at the end of the period and at the beginning of the period.

For similar information for earlier years, see Donald J. Bogue, Henry S. Shryock, Jr., and Siegfried A. Hoermann, "Subregional Migration in the United States, 1935–40," vol. 1, *Streams of Migration Between Subregions*, Scripps Foundation Studies in Population Distribution, No. 5, Miami, Ohio, 1957.

★ ★ ★ ★ ★ ★ ★ ★ ★ ★   **More Recent Data for *Historical Statistics* Series**   ★ ★ ★ ★ ★ ★ ★ ★ ★ ★

★   ★
★   Statistics for more recent years in continuation of many of the still-active series shown here appear   ★
★   in annual issues of the *Statistical Abstract of the United States*, beginning with the 1975 edition. For   ★
★   direct linkage of the historical series to the tables in the *Abstract*, see Appendix I in the *Abstract*.   ★
★   ★

★ ★

Series C 1–14. Native Population, by Residence Within or Outside State, Division, and Region of Birth, by Race: 1850 to 1970

Race and year	Native population	Born in State of residence [1]		Born in other States [1]				Born in outlying areas [1]	Born abroad or at sea	State of birth not reported	Born in division of residence		Born in region of residence	
				Contiguous to State of residence		Noncontiguous to State of residence								
		Number	Percent	Number	Percent	Number	Percent				Number	Percent	Number	Percent
1	2	3	4	5	6	7	8	9	10	11	12	13	14

TOTAL														
1970 [2]	193,454,051	131,296,419	67.9	18,081,446	9.3	33,577,139	17.4	873,241	744,155	8,881,651	145,349,492	75.1	153,603,453	79.4
1960 [3]	169,587,580	119,293,462	70.3	16,640,284	9.8	28,050,769	16.5	660,425	401,510	4,541,130	131,889,464	77.8	139,065,350	82.0
1950 [4]	139,868,715	102,788,395	73.5	14,589,035	10.4	20,695,175	14.8	329,970	96,355	1,369,785	113,477,925	81.1	119,490,525	85.4
1940	120,074,379	92,609,754	77.1	12,583,482	10.5	14,322,504	11.9	156,956	122,169	279,514	101,694,396	84.7	106,734,907	88.9
1930	108,570,897	82,677,619	76.2	12,200,290	11.2	13,187,810	12.1	136,032	130,677	238,469	91,382,402	84.2	96,447,180	88.8
1920	91,789,928	71,071,013	77.4	9,741,781	10.6	10,532,669	11.5	38,020	92,863	313,582	77,906,515	84.9	82,308,490	89.7
1910	78,456,380	61,185,305	78.0	7,959,860	10.1	8,950,254	11.4	7,365	67,911	285,685	66,746,379	85.1	70,864,304	90.3
1900	65,653,299	51,901,722	79.0	6,308,975	9.6	7,192,070	11.0	2,923	67,151	180,458	56,248,496	85.7	60,025,002	91.4
1890 [5]	53,372,703	41,872,656	78.5	4,628,768	8.7	6,464,295	12.1	322	10,010	396,652	45,022,600	84.4	48,398,175	90.7
1880	43,475,840	33,882,734	77.9	4,083,004	9.4	5,509,760	12.7	51	291	–	36,582,390	84.1	39,530,266	90.9
1870	32,991,142	25,321,340	76.8	3,182,563	9.6	4,474,757	13.6	51	169	12,262	27,363,803	82.9	29,634,393	89.8

WHITE														
1970 [2]	169,273,531	115,156,268	68.0	16,633,079	9.8	29,039,976	17.2	790,751	680,042	6,973,415	127,824,055	75.5	135,541,644	80.1
1960 [3]	149,543,683	105,655,834	70.7	15,174,128	10.1	24,070,953	16.1	621,762	377,398	3,643,608	116,915,448	78.2	123,605,716	82.7
1950 [4]	124,382,950	91,984,045	74.0	13,195,215	10.6	17,629,435	14.2	289,435	88,065	1,196,755	101,491,060	81.6	107,061,715	86.1
1940	106,795,732	82,533,805	77.3	11,298,723	10.6	12,492,817	11.7	99,170	117,933	253,284	90,586,586	84.8	95,225,370	89.2
1930 [6]	95,497,800	72,821,481	76.2	10,824,966	11.3	11,452,788	12.0	71,582	125,060	201,923	80,492,581	84.3	85,075,201	89.1
1920	81,108,161	62,524,789	77.1	8,675,416	10.7	9,521,420	11.7	26,476	88,838	271,222	68,601,740	84.6	72,563,235	89.5
1910	68,386,412	52,806,091	77.2	7,018,331	10.3	8,245,872	12.0	6,413	64,356	245,349	57,703,559	84.4	61,361,087	89.7
1900	56,595,379	44,278,021	78.2	5,534,957	9.8	6,562,833	11.6	2,563	63,366	153,639	48,102,508	85.0	51,407,811	90.8
1890 [5]	45,862,023	35,524,287	77.5	4,064,121	8.9	5,926,722	12.9	279	9,543	337,071	38,315,138	83.5	41,227,682	89.9
1880	36,843,291	28,310,081	76.8	3,576,340	9.7	4,956,596	13.5	50	224	30,681,197		83.3	33,126,949	89.9
1870	28,095,665	21,355,242	76.0	2,779,526	9.9	3,951,487	14.1	38	160	9,212	23,130,521	82.3	24,914,093	88.7
1860 [7]	23,353,385	17,527,069	75.1	2,529,494	10.8	3,242,190	13.9	_____	2,618	52,014	18,969,880	81.2	20,481,089	87.7
1850 [7]	17,772,270	13,624,902	76.7	2,105,724	11.9	2,006,033	11.3	_____	_____	35,611	14,707,719	82.8	15,765,010	88.7

NEGRO AND OTHER RACES														
1970 [2]	24,180,520	16,140,151	66.7	1,448,367	6.0	4,537,163	18.8	82,490	64,113	1,908,236	17,525,437	72.5	18,061,809	74.7
1970 [8]	22,260,196	14,775,004	66.4	1,353,981	6.1	4,259,605	19.1	53,968	37,106	1,780,532	16,020,511	72.0	16,498,493	74.1
1960 [3]	20,043,897	13,637,628	68.0	1,466,156	7.3	3,979,816	19.9	38,663	24,112	897,522	14,974,016	74.7	15,459,634	77.1
1950 [4]	15,485,765	10,804,350	69.8	1,393,820	9.0	3,065,740	19.8	40,535	8,290	173,030	11,986,865	77.4	12,428,810	80.3
1940	13,278,647	10,075,949	75.9	1,284,759	9.7	1,829,687	13.8	57,786	4,236	26,230	11,107,810	83.7	11,509,537	86.7
1930 [9]	13,073,097	9,856,138	75.4	1,375,324	10.5	1,735,022	13.3	64,450	5,617	36,546	10,889,821	83.3	11,371,979	87.0
1920	10,681,767	8,546,224	80.0	1,066,365	10.0	1,011,249	9.5	11,544	4,025	42,360	9,304,775	87.1	9,745,255	91.2
1910	10,069,968	8,379,214	83.2	941,529	9.3	704,382	7.0	952	3,555	40,336	9,042,820	89.8	9,503,217	94.4
1900	9,057,920	7,623,701	84.2	774,018	8.5	629,237	6.9	360	3,785	26,819	8,145,988	89.9	8,617,191	95.1
1890 [5]	7,510,680	6,348,369	84.5	564,647	7.5	537,573	7.2	43	467	59,581	6,707,462	89.3	7,170,493	95.5
1880	6,632,549	5,572,653	84.0	506,664	7.6	553,164	8.3	1	67		5,901,193	89.0	6,403,317	96.5
1870	4,895,477	3,966,098	81.0	403,037	8.2	523,270	10.7	13	9	3,050	4,233,282	86.5	4,720,300	96.4

– Represents zero. [1] Prior to 1960, Alaska and Hawaii included in outlying areas. [2] Based on 5-percent sample of persons enumerated. [3] Based on 25-percent sample of persons enumerated. [4] Based on 20-percent sample of persons enumerated. [5] Excludes population of Indian Territory and Indian reservations, specially enumerated in 1890, with a native population of 117,368 white, and 208,083 Negro and other races, not distributed by State of birth. [6] Excludes Mexicans; classified under "other races." [7] 434,495 free Negroes included with white in 1850, 487,970 in 1860. [8] Negro only. [9] Includes Mexicans.

Series C 15–24. Native Population Born in Each Division, by Division of Residence, by Race: 1850 to 1970

[Excludes persons born outside United States and persons for whom State of birth was not reported]

Division of birth, race, and census year	Total	Division of residence								
		New England	Middle Atlantic	East North Central	West North Central	South Atlantic	East South Central	West South Central	Mountain	Pacific
	15	16	17	18	19	20	21	22	23	24

WHITE										
1970 [1]	160,829,323	10,491,117	31,485,397	34,048,261	18,187,380	19,609,673	11,892,067	15,776,495	6,235,092	13,103,841
New England	9,988,571	8,639,976	727,930	196,779	71,586	163,267	37,328	49,641	27,654	74,410
Middle Atlantic	28,254,639	518,674	25,946,240	587,629	182,941	594,163	109,618	116,093	60,032	139,249
East North Central	33,326,277	198,334	1,097,309	28,014,272	1,055,465	889,657	1,297,743	397,803	143,989	231,705
West North Central	14,654,554	57,232	166,661	783,411	12,598,459	136,850	135,052	409,795	180,791	186,303
South Atlantic	22,102,985	474,328	1,813,354	1,256,454	399,709	16,389,562	1,025,285	367,518	119,593	257,182
East South Central	9,719,571	34,980	118,221	360,325	107,802	454,197	8,305,511	243,510	30,607	64,418
West South Central	14,938,789	77,014	237,659	437,381	602,993	306,955	517,380	12,291,853	215,004	252,550
Mountain	7,158,450	79,605	256,491	560,130	897,031	152,724	111,158	492,089	4,174,510	434,352
Pacific	20,685,487	410,974	1,121,532	1,851,880	2,271,394	522,298	352,632	1,408,193	1,282,912	11,463,672
1960 [2] *	144,900,915	8,860,751	26,514,136	30,582,096	14,065,699	18,980,114	9,132,225	13,395,232	6,126,688	17,243,974
New England	9,379,371	7,867,550	501,445	161,376	41,355	339,937	27,450	54,718	53,109	332,431
Middle Atlantic	28,792,297	563,705	24,484,595	996,389	131,702	1,292,957	90,898	172,495	180,074	879,482
East North Central	30,831,621	130,905	503,605	25,809,611	771,484	876,755	269,049	356,533	451,384	1,662,295
West North Central	17,598,319	56,135	163,403	1,017,835	12,224,504	286,651	87,599	555,159	849,164	2,357,869
South Atlantic	17,490,468	114,501	526,613	736,366	100,832	14,879,459	377,346	242,667	112,871	399,813
East South Central	11,416,161	30,940	104,069	1,288,476	138,456	859,016	8,028,843	533,910	104,099	328,352
West South Central	14,333,384	35,774	95,707	330,036	393,228	245,390	197,496	11,188,447	483,802	1,363,504
Mountain	5,241,623	19,514	46,859	104,479	138,863	68,215	20,095	145,481	3,605,164	1,092,953
Pacific	9,817,671	41,727	87,840	137,528	125,275	131,734	33,449	145,822	287,021	8,827,275

See footnotes at end of table.

Series C 15–24. Native Population Born in Each Division, by Division of Residence, by Race: 1850 to 1970—Con.

Division of birth, race, and census year	Total	Division of residence								
		New England	Middle Atlantic	East North Central	West North Central	South Atlantic	East South Central	West South Central	Mountain	Pacific
	15	16	17	18	19	20	21	22	23	24
WHITE—Con.										
1950³	122,808,695	7,765,220	23,667,205	26,038,680	12,848,660	15,490,860	8,652,720	11,564,885	4,543,490	12,236,975
New England	8,123,805	7,040,420	445,570	130,600	31,000	185,885	16,245	35,245	30,575	208,265
Middle Atlantic	25,133,805	456,510	21,967,895	883,575	119,430	800,840	61,425	124,225	113,220	606,685
East North Central	26,253,590	90,555	434,780	22,344,070	801,785	498,185	208,910	292,995	314,300	1,268,010
West North Central	15,804,720	40,080	142,145	925,255	11,186,855	180,270	66,485	532,565	697,650	2,033,415
South Atlantic	14,808,625	66,925	434,560	461,355	70,370	12,976,725	326,755	174,420	63,965	233,550
East South Central	10,389,290	19,555	82,350	908,915	132,160	613,630	7,795,585	523,035	75,205	238,855
West South Central	12,022,265	18,830	69,435	223,550	314,375	141,435	150,350	9,699,470	357,420	1,047,400
Mountain	3,945,625	11,210	34,890	79,265	109,840	36,690	10,845	98,400	2,721,865	842,620
Pacific	6,326,970	21,135	55,580	82,095	82,845	57,200	16,120	84,530	169,290	5,758,175
1940	106,325,345	6,788,754	21,562,277	22,892,971	12,296,354	12,766,703	7,936,741	10,255,758	3,698,071	8,127,716
New England	7,091,608	6,292,313	410,907	101,637	25,600	91,015	6,952	12,776	16,803	133,605
Middle Atlantic	22,321,593	340,901	20,113,804	765,363	123,075	440,461	30,373	64,963	66,229	376,424
East North Central	23,255,752	62,294	393,318	20,031,073	896,605	301,011	155,711	238,290	242,314	935,136
West North Central	14,401,132	25,609	120,901	818,929	10,705,594	102,722	45,398	516,685	633,440	1,431,854
South Atlantic	12,601,815	35,011	360,021	314,513	54,368	11,290,451	246,371	135,018	39,439	126,623
East South Central	9,333,222	9,258	59,151	616,381	133,904	432,330	7,336,524	531,150	59,299	155,225
West South Central	10,085,283	7,189	43,268	142,119	237,853	69,671	105,050	8,669,708	270,484	539,941
Mountain	3,089,040	6,431	26,562	59,659	85,530	18,445	5,519	61,359	2,271,873	553,662
Pacific	4,145,900	9,748	34,345	43,297	33,825	20,597	4,843	25,809	98,190	3,875,246
1930⁴	95,099,235	6,204,011	19,780,421	20,990,462	11,778,688	11,025,521	7,158,480	8,906,478	2,999,731	6,255,443
New England	6,535,693	5,752,888	392,102	114,311	36,849	65,025	6,084	12,825	19,829	135,780
Middle Atlantic	20,610,693	321,693	18,427,461	834,310	179,234	314,394	27,532	69,246	78,751	358,072
East North Central	21,523,034	53,302	362,359	18,167,867	1,102,154	229,645	151,942	278,633	275,415	901,717
West North Central	13,113,754	21,386	106,542	760,889	9,918,618	68,103	39,461	558,788	562,360	1,077,607
South Atlantic	11,319,720	29,326	353,731	322,548	72,008	9,955,907	271,607	166,797	42,096	105,700
East South Central	8,531,783	7,315	52,209	596,959	153,991	326,357	6,563,867	635,683	61,895	133,507
West South Central	8,039,544	5,401	34,716	101,431	202,164	44,638	90,120	7,117,591	179,510	263,973
Mountain	2,317,079	5,090	22,734	53,880	82,608	10,884	4,219	47,331	1,699,814	390,519
Pacific	3,107,935	7,610	28,567	38,267	31,062	10,568	3,648	19,584	80,061	2,888,568
1920	80,721,625	5,420,554	16,651,261	17,641,695	10,798,750	9,311,926	6,286,445	7,615,242	2,730,830	4,264,922
New England	5,613,387	5,003,487	251,361	103,025	53,349	49,436	5,803	13,680	25,804	107,442
Middle Atlantic	17,754,221	305,384	15,714,467	746,504	252,354	264,186	27,434	74,672	99,028	270,192
East North Central	18,836,603	48,079	273,633	15,606,106	1,292,533	179,169	136,431	306,576	319,171	674,905
West North Central	11,077,968	17,259	72,434	462,835	8,699,489	50,549	32,428	534,721	529,090	679,163
South Atlantic	9,605,593	24,111	246,672	232,580	90,706	8,487,281	222,844	180,365	45,179	75,855
East South Central	7,445,580	5,815	36,076	377,338	179,126	234,259	5,791,383	663,654	63,268	94,661
West South Central	6,358,200	4,562	21,272	53,305	141,216	30,900	64,080	5,791,839	133,956	117,070
Mountain	1,785,103	4,997	15,165	32,948	62,656	7,714	3,300	34,621	1,442,878	180,824
Pacific	2,244,970	6,860	20,181	27,054	27,321	8,432	2,742	15,114	72,456	2,064,810
1910	68,070,294	4,641,157	14,003,037	14,791,593	9,682,750	7,765,765	5,657,676	6,344,580	2,063,208	3,120,528
New England	4,867,376	4,305,759	215,838	97,016	73,131	28,394	5,221	11,024	30,999	99,994
Middle Atlantic	15,123,715	247,999	13,264,960	652,982	337,132	191,251	26,602	60,485	110,309	231,995
East North Central	16,287,667	37,814	211,088	13,239,961	1,411,304	111,408	129,227	309,955	291,913	544,997
West North Central	9,210,184	13,453	48,916	323,844	7,410,156	22,494	26,257	484,944	378,359	501,761
South Atlantic	8,273,219	19,347	201,618	167,764	109,371	7,244,553	220,304	204,527	42,174	63,561
East South Central	6,631,841	4,461	24,205	250,933	196,661	145,352	5,198,232	686,321	52,956	72,720
West South Central	4,909,800	3,879	13,329	27,218	91,459	15,183	48,275	4,563,489	84,119	62,849
Mountain	1,206,525	3,876	11,416	17,638	36,206	3,417	2,055	15,963	1,024,876	91,078
Pacific	1,559,967	4,569	11,667	14,237	17,330	3,713	1,503	7,872	47,503	1,451,573
1900	56,375,811	4,063,335	11,764,269	13,037,883	8,501,171	6,487,097	4,947,654	4,494,019	1,281,152	1,799,231
New England	4,304,088	3,782,347	175,529	117,475	95,473	21,464	4,972	7,981	27,658	71,189
Middle Atlantic	12,994,778	213,818	11,203,366	725,710	410,130	152,668	24,477	39,005	88,623	136,981
East North Central	13,990,407	31,065	162,945	11,539,208	1,424,563	83,300	119,432	192,025	180,312	257,557
West North Central	7,211,362	11,316	33,376	267,723	6,142,945	15,230	22,391	305,129	190,402	222,850
South Atlantic	7,028,299	14,206	152,680	154,152	125,802	6,105,309	221,912	197,884	24,638	31,716
East South Central	5,696,181	3,111	16,105	195,986	209,595	95,892	4,515,686	597,479	26,407	35,920
West South Central	3,330,565	1,888	7,950	18,745	58,754	9,877	36,961	3,143,786	28,208	24,396
Mountain	765,078	1,716	4,543	9,280	21,396	1,446	823	6,401	685,356	34,117
Pacific	1,055,053	3,868	7,775	9,604	12,513	1,911	1,000	4,329	29,548	984,505
1890⁵	45,515,130	3,498,667	9,620,523	10,679,859	7,053,073	5,376,140	4,186,475	2,937,889	856,949	1,305,555
New England	3,869,022	3,308,754	157,962	141,909	126,561	21,469	5,802	7,058	28,966	70,541
Middle Atlantic	11,026,901	149,620	9,222,526	769,746	507,162	115,883	24,664	29,588	84,419	123,293
East North Central	11,459,737	18,588	95,477	9,280,356	1,464,505	57,959	94,521	112,084	138,062	198,195
West North Central	5,083,535	5,555	16,549	137,664	4,511,678	8,284	14,461	121,395	113,722	154,227
South Atlantic	5,988,960	9,927	107,554	159,824	151,969	5,101,959	232,107	177,366	20,095	28,159
East South Central	4,794,666	2,026	9,597	171,757	238,208	62,460	3,790,050	466,533	20,572	33,463
West South Central	2,138,369	1,275	5,167	11,125	36,260	6,446	23,931	2,019,570	15,988	18,607
Mountain	452,657	756	1,664	3,155	10,025	523	341	2,074	417,647	16,472
Pacific	701,283	2,166	4,027	4,323	6,705	1,167	598	2,221	17,478	662,598
1880	36,843,017	3,177,460	8,287,904	9,098,915	4,950,250	4,483,127	3,563,017	2,067,174	468,678	746,492
New England	3,614,346	3,031,308	176,366	178,124	123,105	17,545	4,886	6,645	21,169	55,198
Middle Atlantic	9,693,744	116,499	7,921,093	899,051	479,473	103,764	21,758	23,520	51,848	76,738
East North Central	9,062,808	12,806	73,777	7,521,118	1,126,361	42,533	67,865	69,347	62,709	86,292
West North Central	3,117,714	3,176	11,055	101,161	2,801,794	4,361	11,515	78,285	43,790	62,577
South Atlantic	5,169,015	8,618	90,530	192,311	149,700	4,256,663	52,704	272,498	12,170	18,422
East South Central	4,077,215	1,725	7,269	192,398	232,785	52,704	3,164,256	390,416	12,557	23,105
West South Central	1,410,432	1,016	4,219	9,494	28,023	4,633	19,693	1,328,521	5,920	8,913
Mountain	265,689	711	1,096	1,941	4,925	339	177	1,083	248,307	7,110
Pacific	432,054	1,601	2,499	3,317	4,084	585	369	1,254	10,208	408,137

See footnotes at end of table.

Series C 15–24.   Native Population Born in Each Division, by Division of Residence, by Race: 1850 to 1970—Con.

Division of birth, race, and census year	Total	Division of residence								
		New England	Middle Atlantic	East North Central	West North Central	South Atlantic	East South Central	West South Central	Mountain	Pacific
	15	16	17	18	19	20	21	22	23	24
WHITE—Con.										
1870	28,086,255	2,807,945	6,788,821	7,325,414	3,038,215	3,469,244	2,835,457	1,161,542	224,834	434,783
New England	3,270,626	2,704,882	180,779	212,928	97,087	14,708	5,552	4,418	9,181	41,091
Middle Atlantic	8,065,869	83,537	6,479,733	967,899	339,388	84,225	23,259	13,223	20,533	54,072
East North Central	6,550,805	8,463	48,589	5,625,542	704,106	19,407	48,469	24,893	20,631	50,705
West North Central	1,684,544	1,621	5,031	62,386	1,524,350	2,051	8,851	33,449	11,644	35,161
South Atlantic	4,206,178	6,497	65,515	230,689	138,450	3,308,462	313,905	123,369	5,032	14,259
East South Central	3,165,831	1,206	4,920	214,814	210,645	37,442	2,420,279	253,883	4,766	17,876
West South Central	765,053	730	2,651	7,885	20,005	2,591	14,865	707,821	1,487	7,018
Mountain	153,772	66	138	432	2,169	52	65	159	147,771	2,920
Pacific	223,577	943	1,465	2,839	2,015	306	212	327	3,789	211,681
1860 [6]	23,298,753	2,663,062	5,898,979	5,715,955	1,702,245	3,358,465	2,538,909	984,856	150,116	286,166
New England	3,144,598	2,584,262	212,218	224,230	57,324	12,213	7,269	5,930	6,006	35,146
Middle Atlantic	6,944,042	64,518	5,582,854	946,080	184,972	68,452	24,020	15,661	10,348	47,137
East North Central	4,562,911	5,057	29,662	4,044,329	358,725	10,445	32,248	24,038	17,053	41,354
West North Central	848,692	652	1,965	27,496	756,018	915	5,842	23,459	7,188	25,157
South Atlantic	4,264,749	6,777	66,971	265,569	125,982	3,236,171	411,919	133,672	3,046	14,642
East South Central	2,781,432	797	3,061	202,798	210,990	28,932	2,048,662	263,132	4,306	18,754
West South Central	550,043	522	1,648	4,322	7,759	1,230	8,887	518,799	950	5,926
Mountain	100,739	(NA)	(NA)	(NA)	(NA)	(NA)	(NA)	(NA)	100,739	(NA)
Pacific	101,547	477	600	1,131	475	107	62	165	480	98,050
1850 [6]	17,736,659	2,423,178	4,884,300	3,965,269	695,231	2,907,947	2,207,677	503,295	68,484	81,278
New England	2,821,823	2,367,932	237,367	171,172	9,404	11,074	5,922	5,522	1,131	12,299
Middle Atlantic	5,483,951	46,635	4,566,495	725,056	39,123	55,210	19,778	12,656	2,286	16,712
East North Central	2,757,356	2,410	16,349	2,582,600	96,708	7,048	21,821	14,616	2,511	13,293
West North Central	373,500	181	568	12,794	334,662	495	2,951	11,619	1,341	8,889
South Atlantic	3,764,808	5,100	60,734	286,195	80,838	2,811,305	446,391	65,489	482	8,274
East South Central	2,179,505	507	1,840	184,634	131,053	21,951	1,705,017	123,282	823	10,398
West South Central	286,016	378	934	2,812	3,435	858	5,796	270,104	88	1,611
Mountain	59,802	(NA)	(NA)	(NA)	(NA)	(NA)	(NA)	(NA)	59,802	(NA)
Pacific	9,898	35	13	6	8	6	1	7	20	9,802
NEGRO AND OTHER RACES										
1970 [1]	22,152,681	258,577	2,454,261	2,346,566	629,565	7,133,334	3,808,822	3,653,069	349,703	1,518,784
New England	341,142	193,028	18,139	5,437	2,298	91,102	20,359	6,025	1,079	3,675
Middle Atlantic	3,410,327	14,410	2,257,280	32,370	7,982	901,078	143,726	38,188	2,785	12,508
East North Central	3,633,676	31,759	37,755	2,150,800	56,701	282,870	824,905	222,589	5,869	20,428
West North Central	714,238	920	4,592	19,068	476,071	15,460	92,914	92,607	4,748	7,858
South Atlantic	6,000,302	8,522	86,691	29,594	7,748	5,670,277	140,497	35,030	3,745	18,198
East South Central	2,440,828	1,283	6,727	22,995	4,905	43,959	2,327,288	27,718	1,480	4,473
West South Central	2,928,778	1,333	7,468	13,898	12,533	26,021	93,127	2,752,576	6,496	15,326
Mountain	396,456	583	3,670	7,439	11,698	12,944	13,709	51,926	278,143	16,344
Pacific	2,286,934	6,739	31,939	64,965	49,629	89,623	152,297	426,410	45,358	1,419,974
1960 [2] *	19,083,600	224,801	2,527,559	2,715,123	595,583	5,692,481	2,660,976	2,763,662	318,112	1,585,303
New England	144,829	119,877	11,807	2,731	508	5,096	564	675	334	3,237
Middle Atlantic	1,515,818	11,258	1,388,304	26,523	2,665	59,936	4,516	4,495	2,012	16,109
East North Central	1,442,437	3,132	24,857	1,317,877	14,858	18,671	16,622	9,088	3,735	33,597
West North Central	485,700	1,236	7,075	50,981	367,449	4,989	3,453	8,567	8,989	32,961
South Atlantic	6,896,680	70,680	930,590	301,498	12,028	5,448,369	53,412	21,303	6,289	52,511
East South Central	3,911,070	11,970	123,760	789,358	96,597	125,386	2,547,807	106,306	10,550	99,336
West South Central	3,405,655	4,623	30,858	208,938	93,669	21,587	32,197	2,600,442	50,239	363,102
Mountain	267,216	308	1,741	3,166	3,131	1,386	483	3,650	226,396	26,955
Pacific	1,014,195	1,717	8,567	14,051	4,678	7,061	1,922	9,136	9,568	957,495
1950 [3]	15,263,910	136,825	1,771,205	1,799,890	469,245	5,068,460	2,687,045	2,473,610	214,980	642,650
New England	95,105	74,260	11,345	2,245	350	3,780	410	515	270	1,930
Middle Atlantic	884,085	6,990	798,465	20,225	1,675	41,660	3,180	3,280	1,175	7,435
East North Central	754,760	1,605	19,745	675,230	11,170	13,040	11,310	5,920	1,915	14,825
West North Central	362,865	790	6,165	45,560	268,130	3,660	3,420	7,830	5,980	21,330
South Atlantic	6,125,045	43,895	810,945	269,290	8,740	4,882,210	60,780	18,125	2,960	28,100
East South Central	3,634,040	5,730	91,980	604,445	89,670	104,760	2,569,950	108,770	6,020	52,715
West South Central	2,954,750	2,575	25,165	169,690	85,170	15,965	36,775	2,323,380	32,520	263,510
Mountain	183,685	145	1,425	2,520	2,150	1,015	355	1,800	158,355	15,920
Pacific	269,575	835	5,970	10,685	2,190	2,370	865	3,990	5,785	236,885
1940	13,190,395	95,035	1,208,567	1,084,123	401,916	4,706,493	2,779,679	2,489,075	163,606	261,901
New England	72,448	58,883	9,094	1,190	142	2,143	228	150	58	560
Middle Atlantic	571,445	4,352	526,569	12,397	945	22,910	1,084	779	324	2,085
East North Central	469,788	762	13,421	420,714	9,676	8,114	7,444	3,391	1,111	5,155
West North Central	304,282	275	3,971	31,247	240,766	1,918	2,635	8,471	4,933	10,066
South Atlantic	5,484,716	27,275	585,734	188,711	8,733	4,579,081	62,448	19,370	1,753	11,611
East South Central	3,359,873	2,016	50,942	340,816	74,444	82,512	2,664,877	125,376	4,036	14,854
West South Central	2,615,711	735	13,731	85,882	64,924	8,126	40,421	2,329,478	17,136	55,278
Mountain	144,576	69	793	1,357	1,610	596	240	1,151	131,955	6,805
Pacific	167,556	668	4,312	1,809	676	1,093	302	909	2,300	155,487
1930 [7]	12,966,484	85,473	980,056	957,610	394,534	4,421,188	2,655,398	2,797,906	298,651	375,668
New England	60,784	47,909	8,543	1,308	191	1,964	152	166	83	468
Middle Atlantic	405,404	4,380	365,212	12,886	1,046	17,792	1,109	917	405	1,657
East North Central	355,312	617	11,840	307,789	10,799	6,950	7,522	4,144	1,366	4,285
West North Central	295,827	243	3,229	33,085	229,087	1,531	2,675	11,592	5,841	8,544
South Atlantic	5,215,766	29,024	531,014	197,586	11,337	4,316,289	85,900	31,498	2,444	10,674
East South Central	3,197,521	1,779	45,220	321,450	74,933	68,994	2,515,818	153,257	4,486	11,584
West South Central	2,855,954	574	11,050	79,125	62,438	6,528	41,697	2,588,627	20,299	45,616
Mountain	303,676	73	783	2,162	3,782	368	219	5,937	258,301	32,051
Pacific	276,240	874	3,165	2,219	921	772	306	1,768	5,426	260,789

See footnotes at end of table.

Series C 15–24. Native Population Born in Each Division, by Division of Residence, by Race: 1850 to 1970—Con.

Division of birth, race, and census year	Total	Division of residence								
		New England	Middle Atlantic	East North Central	West North Central	South Atlantic	East South Central	West South Central	Mountain	Pacific
	15	16	17	18	19	20	21	22	23	24
NEGRO AND OTHER RACES—Con.										
1920	10,623,838	68,704	562,963	522,270	311,204	4,315,975	2,516,980	2,110,266	105,563	109,913
New England	46,726	36,756	5,356	1,023	292	2,051	343	453	152	300
Middle Atlantic	265,307	4,315	235,108	8,594	1,178	13,020	733	705	689	965
East North Central	225,537	501	6,458	190,121	10,630	4,709	5,336	3,390	1,686	2,706
West North Central	242,757	220	2,089	20,419	194,448	2,093	2,721	10,710	5,407	4,650
South Atlantic	4,771,502	24,251	280,607	86,850	12,137	4,231,573	76,086	47,528	5,097	7,373
East South Central	2,923,262	1,423	25,506	190,571	58,241	56,648	2,399,065	178,676	6,134	6,998
West South Central	1,981,385	371	5,096	22,118	31,599	4,588	32,076	1,867,040	6,868	11,629
Mountain	85,376	85	593	840	2,020	472	331	951	77,728	2,356
Pacific	81,986	782	2,150	1,734	659	821	289	813	1,802	72,936
1910	10,025,125	60,931	407,348	311,737	278,717	4,103,893	2,646,426	2,048,401	95,408	72,264
New England	39,839	32,693	3,944	598	265	1,414	185	344	133	263
Middle Atlantic	219,137	4,018	196,486	5,117	1,178	9,186	966	989	415	782
East North Central	192,088	405	4,471	162,724	9,180	3,160	5,131	3,718	1,397	1,902
West North Central	238,996	211	1,294	13,386	198,839	1,138	3,076	12,660	5,225	3,167
South Atlantic	4,497,605	21,394	191,612	35,299	12,656	4,048,161	108,763	71,118	2,700	5,902
East South Central	2,849,182	967	5,787	88,363	40,006	37,547	2,494,110	173,531	4,361	4,510
West South Central	1,848,608	285	1,448	5,011	14,034	2,203	33,650	1,783,963	3,363	4,651
Mountain	82,771	64	581	281	2,145	462	320	1,415	76,130	1,373
Pacific	56,899	894	1,725	958	414	622	225	663	1,684	49,714
1900	9,026,956	56,174	325,698	267,124	276,104	3,723,920	2,496,880	1,750,800	80,317	49,939
New England	34,186	28,948	2,803	625	206	1,002	136	186	120	160
Middle Atlantic	183,339	3,999	166,691	4,070	947	5,640	520	676	332	464
East North Central	170,049	346	3,494	148,199	7,232	2,002	4,267	2,805	978	726
West North Central	237,297	122	752	10,828	203,858	507	3,032	12,603	4,182	1,413
South Atlantic	4,133,276	21,417	145,557	30,787	14,038	3,684,080	134,831	96,632	2,772	3,162
East South Central	2,628,985	633	4,066	68,777	38,282	28,514	2,327,272	156,214	3,327	1,900
West South Central	1,524,820	241	1,052	3,405	8,624	1,790	26,633	1,480,511	1,317	1,247
Mountain	70,780	27	335	152	2,741	77	70	868	66,036	474
Pacific	44,224	441	948	281	176	308	119	305	1,253	40,393
1890 [5]	7,450,589	42,248	219,834	210,343	225,426	3,249,541	2,105,538	1,342,049	26,286	29,324
New England	28,981	24,677	2,201	468	216	736	142	242	102	197
Middle Atlantic	150,505	3,438	136,516	3,555	1,051	3,738	605	665	389	548
East North Central	136,704	142	1,483	121,167	6,422	1,292	2,752	2,027	915	504
West North Central	178,589	56	569	6,448	157,506	372	2,765	7,100	2,741	1,032
South Atlantic	3,627,912	13,252	76,277	27,938	15,723	3,223,865	148,595	116,874	2,700	2,688
East South Central	2,183,937	322	1,639	48,570	37,128	18,188	1,932,764	141,602	2,365	1,359
West South Central	1,103,866	274	663	2,059	7,086	1,100	17,493	1,073,379	790	1,022
Mountain	17,177	11	284	47	225	29	364	85	15,873	259
Pacific	22,918	76	202	91	69	221	58	75	411	21,715
1880	6,632,481	39,430	188,000	191,082	206,963	2,939,779	1,926,935	1,087,916	23,548	28,828
New England	29,078	25,077	1,843	466	210	648	235	399	41	159
Middle Atlantic	149,988	3,309	136,808	3,445	900	3,061	995	895	155	420
East North Central	116,353	150	739	105,676	3,728	1,236	2,753	1,641	233	197
West North Central	159,284	29	147	6,194	141,665	180	2,981	6,742	1,005	341
South Atlantic	3,340,699	10,369	46,950	30,110	16,439	2,917,316	197,100	120,570	729	1,116
East South Central	1,942,781	288	963	43,205	35,325	16,183	1,708,900	136,846	657	414
West South Central	847,230	167	419	1,902	8,583	1,073	13,918	820,685	220	263
Mountain	19,932	24	80	52	78	37	19	100	19,345	197
Pacific	27,136	17	51	32	35	45	34	38	1,163	25,721
1870	4,892,405	30,847	146,581	134,896	145,086	2,216,892	1,463,794	738,385	3,456	12,468
New England	22,477	19,514	1,426	405	135	345	155	236	43	218
Middle Atlantic	120,810	2,904	110,845	2,941	664	1,786	444	611	113	502
East North Central	67,523	100	430	62,667	2,220	375	857	718	69	87
West North Central	117,168	31	78	4,817	101,335	159	3,096	7,011	296	345
South Atlantic	2,622,615	7,873	32,620	27,869	15,027	2,201,827	210,996	124,766	384	1,253
East South Central	1,426,109	244	828	34,648	21,324	11,437	1,238,885	118,026	295	422
West South Central	504,139	167	328	1,512	4,306	940	9,345	486,997	352	192
Mountain	1,952	2	3	9	59	4	3	9	1,813	50
Pacific	9,612	12	23	28	16	19	13	11	91	9,399

* Denotes first year for which figures include Alaska and Hawaii.
NA   Not available.
[1] Based on 5-percent sample.
[2] Based on 25-percent sample.
[3] Based on 20-percent sample.
[4] Excludes Mexicans; classified under "other races."

[5] Excludes population of Indian Territory and Indian reservations, specially enumerated in 1890, with a native population of 117,368 white and 208,083 Negro and other races, not distributed by State of birth.
[6] Includes free Negroes.
[7] Includes Mexicans.

Series C 25–75. Estimated Net Intercensal Migration of Total, Native White, Foreign-Born White, and Negro Population, by States: 1870 to 1970

[In thousands]

Series No.	State	Components of change method (Bureau of the Census)			Survival-rate method (see text for sources)								
		1960–1970	1950–1960	1940–1950	1950–1960	1940–1950	1930–1940	1920–1930	1910–1920	1900–1910	1890–1900	1880–1890	1870–1880
	TOTAL WHITE AND NEGRO POPULATION [1]												
	New England:												
25	Maine	−69	−67	−27	−70.5	−35.8	−1.2	−39.3	−8.3	10.6	4.1	−15.9	−33.3
26	New Hampshire	69	12	(²)	−2.1	−9.1	9.1	−10.2	−3.6	3.2	20.4	20.7	10.1
27	Vermont	15	−38	−19	−38.4	−23.8	−18.7	−20.6	−17.6	−3.7	−2.4	−13.3	−26.2
28	Massachusetts	74	−96	23	−154.0	−29.5	−69.5	22.1	192.2	307.3	334.9	295.7	140.2
29	Rhode Island	13	−26	11	−36.5	2.7	−2.3	11.4	12.8	66.1	45.9	42.5	27.9
30	Connecticut	214	234	113	−172.7	89.5	39.2	64.1	122.1	112.7	90.8	72.9	22.4
	Middle Atlantic:												
31	New York	−101	210	270	1.2	83.8	396.3	1,062.1	467.4	1,061.0	604.8	395.4	61.7
32	New Jersey	488	578	294	409.9	200.7	−28.2	442.3	278.2	376.1	218.3	151.3	48.4
33	Pennsylvania	−378	−475	−355	−594.0	−447.2	−301.0	−252.9	51.9	444.6	262.0	285.1	19.1
	East North Central:												
34	Ohio	−126	407	245	265.9	151.6	−56.6	214.7	499.4	207.7	77.7	41.9	−12.9
35	Indiana	−16	61	97	21.0	56.7	10.6	−.9	−54.4	33.4	340.0	−86.7	−70.2
36	Illinois	−43	124	75	−10.1	−22.1	−60.8	414.0	255.6	223.0	340.0	170.3	−59.0
37	Michigan	27	155	336	88.0	251.4	17.1	549.6	465.2	117.2	62.0	172.3	161.4
38	Wisconsin	4	−53	−84	85.2	−95.1	−10.9	−17.9	37.6	9.2	84.3	100.8	9.0
	West North Central:												
39	Minnesota	−25	−98	−173	−109.2	−160.9	36.0	−106.2	59.1	72.6	148.4	264.1	156.2
40	Iowa	−183	−234	−196	−220.7	−178.5	−73.4	−167.2	−18.3	−207.5	21.7	−5.6	85.1
41	Missouri	2	−134	−190	−150.0	−168.6	−20.8	−98.7	−134.7	−163.8	−17.2	56.4	−30.4
42	North Dakota	−94	−105	−121	−91.0	−109.4	−105.8	−76.3	−46.0	137.3	63.8	}243.4	86.8
43	South Dakota	−94	−95	−79	−76.1	−71.2	−101.4	−45.0	−31.2	86.9	.3		
44	Nebraska	−73	−117	−135	−102.4	−123.0	−139.5	−78.1	−34.5	−28.8	−153.9	362.5	204.4
45	Kansas	−130	−44	−91	−29.6	−86.8	−163.8	−83.1	−74.5	20.0	−149.8	159.7	366.8
	South Atlantic:												
46	Delaware	38	63	21	51.1	14.5	16.0	−3.5	5.1	2.7	−1.2	4.3	−2.3
47	Maryland	385	321	270	231.1	213.3	87.0	10.2	43.1	−8.3	8.2	−10.7	−11.2
48	District of Columbia	−100	−160	49	−115.1	78.5	157.8	27.3	97.0	41.0	34.3	36.1	18.1
49	Virginia	141	15	169	−2.0	152.0	.2	−231.6	−27.7	−73.7	−91.5	−80.9	−51.1
50	West Virginia	−265	−446	−235	−401.6	−210.8	−73.6	−53.8	−1.7	46.1	17.2	−4.8	24.0
51	North Carolina	−94	−328	−258	−277.6	−202.8	−85.4	−7.9	−74.3	−80.4	−88.8	−57.7	−14.4
52	South Carolina	−149	−222	−230	−179.1	−172.4	−102.5	−256.9	−80.9	−80.6	−75.5	−35.9	25.7
53	Georgia	51	−212	−290	−169.7	−224.3	−134.1	−414.9	−98.1	−41.7	−56.1	−19.5	−40.0
54	Florida	1,326	1,616	578	1,385.6	510.9	280.3	297.6	101.6	103.5	36.9	51.1	12.1
	East South Central:												
55	Kentucky	−153	−390	−366	−350.2	−319.2	−93.5	−206.1	−167.1	−177.8	−65.1	−96.8	−47.2
56	Tennessee	−45	−274	−143	−252.6	−102.8	−14.9	−113.8	−131.2	−156.9	−95.4	−77.7	−91.8
57	Alabama	−233	−369	−342	−332.3	−271.0	−165.3	−149.2	−113.9	−47.8	−40.4	−11.5	−60.7
58	Mississippi	−267	−433	−433	−369.6	−349.9	−90.3	−101.6	−199.3	−46.4	−44.5	−60.6	−5.6
	West South Central:												
59	Arkansas	−71	−433	−415	−353.0	−320.4	−128.8	−191.3	−74.7	−27.2	−82.8	75.1	84.0
60	Louisiana	−130	−49	−147	−39.0	−112.1	5.7	−23.2	−64.7	10.6	1.4	−3.0	−12.0
61	Oklahoma	13	−219	−434	−196.0	−356.1	−269.4	−51.8	62.4	491.5	501.3	44.5	(NA)
62	Texas	146	121	73	174.5	132.9	−72.8	243.5	114.3	131.1	147.7	151.2	308.5
	Mountain:												
63	Montana	−58	−25	−40	−25.3	−42.2	−19.3	−72.9	90.1	86.5	63.5	70.6	12.1
64	Idaho	−42	−40	−27	−39.3	−29.6	−20.5	−50.6	37.3	104.1	39.8	34.2	11.7
65	Wyoming	−39	−20	−1	−18.7	−4.6	−.1	−1.2	20.7	33.3	15.6	28.7	7.2
66	Colorado	215	164	41	132.4	32.4	1.0	−16.6	39.8	159.8	51.9	146.8	119.1
67	New Mexico	−130	52	16	51.7	9.8	18.6	−22.9	−20.2	63.1	1.2	6.4	−3.3
68	Arizona	228	329	137	289.3	117.4	−3.5	23.5	75.4	50.7	21.4	10.9	19.8
69	Utah	−11	9	9	4.9	6.4	−30.5	−30.8	−.2	24.9	8.9	17.9	16.7
70	Nevada	144	86	34	74.9	28.8	12.5	6.9	−6.4	32.9	−5.1	−15.6	6.6
	Pacific:												
71	Washington	249	87	392	49.5	351.3	109.2	81.6	97.5	464.7	80.4	205.4	28.7
72	Oregon	159	16	286	1.2	244.0	94.1	56.0	189.9	43.0	85.9	39.0	
73	California	2,113	3,142	2,658	2,573.1	2,339.1	974.6	1,695.2	804.1	694.1	172.7	214.2	129.6
74	Alaska	16	41	--------	48.0								
75	Hawaii	11	3	--------	47.9								
	NATIVE WHITE POPULATION [3]												
	New England:												
25	Maine	−69	−69	−27	−71.4	−41.6	−2.2	−46.6	−22.7	−18.4	−20.6	−40.8	−46.5
26	New Hampshire	68	11	−1	−2.7	−12.6	8.3	−14.4	−12.8	−15.7	−2.5	−7.1	−7.1
27	Vermont	14	−38	−20	−38.1	−25.8	−14.6	−25.2	−19.7	−17.2	−10.9	−21.9	−24.7
28	Massachusetts	23	−122	8	−185.0	−73.8	−45.6	−101.7	−6.0	−23.3	46.9	31.9	13.5
29	Rhode Island	4	−28	9	−34.2	−.2	.8	−8.7	−10.5	5.1	3.3	2.4	4.1
30	Connecticut	166	195	98	106.6	49.0	30.2	6.4	18.7	−10.9	5.4	2.8	−6.5
	Middle Atlantic:												
31	New York	−638	−72	−6	−392.6	−270.8	140.3	138.1	−76.5	−74.9	−18.6	−146.4	−167.4
32	New Jersey	336	466	231	214.5	88.6	−18.8	179.3	72.0	71.4	46.3	9.4	−8.9
33	Pennsylvania	−423	−552	−467	−657.9	−531.3	−260.9	−380.2	−199.4	−178.1	−60.2	−70.0	−105.2
	East North Central:												
34	Ohio	−191	274	110	116.8	28.5	−58.6	58.2	233.4	−40.4	−29.6	−96.7	−92.8
35	Indiana	−58	17	57	−24.6	15.0	7.1	−43.3	−33.1	−111.9	−7.6	−120.4	−101.2
36	Illinois	−215	−64	−142	−229.6	−202.9	−58.7	80.3	−36.2	−198.9	44.0	−170.7	−192.5
37	Michigan	−124	28	146	−57.7	51.7	18.1	239.9	181.5	−35.9	−26.8	−19.7	25.8
38	Wisconsin	−29	−82	−96	−120.8	−110.3	−10.0	−53.2	−37.3	−103.3	−25.7	−75.6	−78.8

See footnotes at end of table.

Series C 25–75. Estimated Net Intercensal Migration of Total, Native White, Foreign-Born White, and Negro Population, by States: 1870 to 1970—Con.

[In thousands]

Series No.	State	Components of change method (Bureau of the Census)			Survival-rate method (see text for sources)									
		1960–1970	1950–1960	1940–1950	1950–1960	1940–1950	1930–1940	1920–1930	1910–1920	1900–1910	1890–1900	1880–1890	1870–1880
	NATIVE WHITE POPULATION [3]—Con.												
	West North Central:												
39	Minnesota	−39	−102	−175	−111.1	−163.1	27.1	−113.6	−1.2	−61.4	25.9	37.2	38.2
40	Iowa	−189	−236	−198	−218.3	−180.9	−70.5	−164.0	−45.9	−249.1	−29.9	−108.2	2.7
41	Missouri	−25	−161	−222	−173.7	−197.4	−36.8	−141.4	−173.7	−228.1	−50.0	2.4	−43.2
42	North Dakota	−94	−103	−119	−87.5	−103.6	−99.1	−72.8	−46.3	81.8	20.4	} 126.0	43.5
43	South Dakota	−92	−90	−74	−74.0	−71.3	−96.8	−46.1	−33.7	59.6	−26.5	}	43.5
44	Nebraska	−76	−121	−139	−106.0	−125.9	−135.5	−81.1	−53.2	−62.4	−159.2	244.3	139.2
45	Kansas	−139	−49	−96	−33.6	−90.1	−156.2	−84.6	−86.9	−18.2	−156.6	106.3	290.1
	South Atlantic:												
46	Delaware	32	57	17	43.6	11.2	12.8	−3.8	.3	−3.0	−3.7	−11.	−2.6
47	Maryland	290	284	231	187.6	167.6	72.2	−4.5	16.8	−26.9	−5.8	−29.4	−16.1
48	District of Columbia	−137	−213	−14	−165.4	6.7	101.2	5.5	69.3	22.2	20.1	18.1	8.6
49	Virginia	206	85	194	58.4	169.1	33.7	−111.7	−9.5	−35.6	−25.8	−33.6	−16.5
50	West Virginia	−247	−406	−219	−361.3	−193.0	−66.7	−62.7	−29.3	−6.2	3.5	−12.3	18.1
51	North Carolina	81	−121	−95	−109.9	−81.6	−27.1	5.2	−47.7	−54.4	−41.7	−19.8	−7.6
52	South Carolina	44	−4	−24	−.7	−15.7	−8.7	−52.4	−8.0	−10.5	−10.8	−17.5	9.1
53	Georgia	198	−8	−49	−10.8	−38.2	−44.2	−155.1	−27.4	−30.8	−31.4	−35.1	−20.8
54	Florida	1,340	1,516	564	1,152.8	438.7	208.4	221.1	84.5	46.6	10.1	24.8	7.3
	East South Central:												
55	Kentucky	−158	−375	−349	−334.8	−299.1	−83.8	−188.4	−153.1	−159.9	−58.9	−85.6	−39.6
56	Tennessee	1	−217	−97	−201.6	−68.6	−24.4	−100.6	−103.2	−127.3	−76.7	−64.9	−67.0
57	Alabama	−5	−145	−140	−142.5	−108.6	−101.0	−69.7	−45.3	−32.8	−41.1	−12.1	−25.9
58	Mississippi	10	−110	−108	−104.8	−94.3	−32.0	−33.8	−70.3	−19.0	−35.8	−47.7	−22.7
	West South Central:												
59	Arkansas	38	−283	−259	−243.8	−207.1	−95.5	−144.4	−74.4	−55.2	−77.6	25.3	53.0
60	Louisiana	26	43	−2	23.0	−4.7	15.3	2.9	−17.8	15.8	9.2	−12.2	−11.8
61	Oklahoma	−4	−193	−361	−179.5	−319.5	−253.4	−51.2	54.5	414.2	404.3	39.6	(NA)
62	Texas	92	147	173	155.3	134.4	−1.7	197.5	−28.4	60.5	95.5	90.9	233.9
	Mountain:												
63	Montana	−57	−23	−36	−23.5	−41.9	−14.8	−66.9	75.4	51.0	37.1	39.8	8.2
64	Idaho	−44	−41	−28	−39.5	−30.7	20.8	−49.5	31.5	81.9	31.0	24.6	8.5
65	Wyoming	−39	−19	−2	−17.0	−5.6	2.2	−1.8	19.9	19.8	11.7	19.1	5.5
66	Colorado	187	149	32	110.1	21.1	7.4	−17.6	29.2	108.8	33.1	101.1	86.7
67	New Mexico	−120	53	17	43.3	3.8	22.5	−17.2	−32.0	52.7	−2.3	2.7	−5.9
68	Arizona	248	339	135	255.5	97.6	12.4	31.8	39.9	25.7	15.1	7.2	11.7
69	Utah	−16	8	6	−2.0	1.0	−27.5	−31.5	−7.6	2.8	−2.5	2.7	.6
70	Navada	136	80	31	66.0	24.2	13.8	5.1	−6.1	21.5	−3.9	−10.0	.8
	Pacific:												
71	Washington	220	69	375	27.8	303.9	100.3	49.2	51.9	311.4	54.0	133.2	20.8
72	Oregon	145	10	278	−4.5	222.9	90.4	74.3	38.2	132.0	29.2	57.4	25.7
73	California	1,528	2,788	2,373	1,964.6	1,874.7	899.5	1,244.5	537.7	425.2	96.3	109.6	56.0
74	Alaska	22	42	---------	41.1	---------	---------	---------	---------	---------	---------	---------	---------
75	Hawaii	58	55	---------	44.5	---------	---------	---------	---------	---------	---------	---------	---------
	FOREIGN-BORN WHITE POPULATION [3]												
	New England:												
25	Maine				−.4	5.9	.8	7.5	14.3	28.9	24.4	25.0	13.4
26	New Hampshire				(Z)	3.3	1.0	4.0	9.2	18.9	22.7	27.9	17.1
27	Vermont				−.3	2.0	−4.0	4.7	3.0	12.7	8.6	8.6	−1.4
28	Massachusetts				14.2	33.6	−26.6	120.9	191.3	324.8	278.0	259.3	123.7
29	Rhode Island				−2.6	1.7	−3.6	21.0	22.7	60.3	41.1	38.9	22.9
30	Connecticut				37.6	27.5	6.8	52.5	98.1	123.2	82.9	69.0	28.1
	Middle Atlantic:												
31	New York				150.0	111.0	120.1	751.3	480.9	1,100.2	589.7	532.0	221.5
32	New Jersey				103.2	58.5	−18.9	196.0	181.6	286.2	154.2	133.5	54.4
33	Pennsylvania				3.4	−5.5	−60.4	25.6	168.7	589.8	282.9	334.3	115.6
	East North Central:												
34	Ohio				41.7	16.5	−18.8	65.8	196.5	232.5	102.1	133.4	77.3
35	Indiana				10.3	9.5	−5.0	19.3	28.8	53.4	32.9	29.9	24.3
36	Illinois				60.2	1.0	−51.5	214.4	222.0	398.3	273.4	332.6	124.8
37	Michigan				35.7	36.4	−29.0	223.6	245.1	151.1	88.3	193.2	134.0
38	Wisconsin				12.1	3.4	−1.9	30.9	72.7	112.0	107.0	176.3	86.5
	West North Central:												
39	Minnesota				−1.7	−.5	7.8	6.9	58.1	131.7	116.5	225.4	116.5
40	Iowa				−3.4	1.1	−2.6	−1.3	23.7	39.4	50.1	102.1	80.2
41	Missouri				4.5	3.0	−3.3	6.7	11.8	63.3	32.8	58.1	17.2
42	North Dakota				−3.9	−5.8	−6.6	−3.4	.3	55.2	38.6	} 117.4	43.0
43	South Dakota				−2.2	−.2	−4.4	1.2	2.5	27.0	12.7	}	43.0
44	Nebraska				(Z)	−.2	−4.6	3.0	13.4	32.0	7.7	110.9	64.1
45	Kansas				1.6	1.1	−7.5	−4.4	7.0	35.6	7.4	50.7	62.0
	South Atlantic:												
46	Delaware				2.9	.8	.8	−.3	5.3	6.0	3.1	5.1	1.7
47	Maryland				18.6	15.7	4.1	9.7	19.4	30.0	20.6	26.2	12.4
48	District of Columbia				−.9	10.7	9.1	5.8	9.3	9.1	5.5	4.7	3.3
49	Virginia				10.7	13.4	3.4	−2.7	9.0	11.3	5.1	6.2	2.9
50	West Virginia				−3.5	−1.1	−2.8	−3.9	12.1	37.0	8.0	4.0	3.8
51	North Carolina				3.6	6.1	1.6	2.7	2.2	2.3	1.5	.6	1.1
52	South Carolina				2.5	2.3	.6	−.2	1.6	2.0	.7	.3	1.1
53	Georgia				6.2	5.1	.5	.2	4.0	5.4	2.5	3.3	.9
54	Florida				152.9	65.0	22.0	22.4	13.9	16.2	3.4	10.5	1.1
	East South Central:												
55	Kentucky				1.2	2.7	−.7	−1.0	2.7	4.4	6.0	11.2	5.5
56	Tennessee				1.0	4.0	1.0	.7	1.3	4.7	.4	5.9	−.2
57	Alabama				1.8	3.0	−.5	1.1	2.2	7.0	2.4	6.3	1.3
58	Mississippi				−.6	2.5	−.2	1.1	.7	3.4	1.7	.3	−.6

See footnotes at end of table.

Series C 25–75. Estimated Net Intercensal Migration of Total, Native White, Foreign-Born White, and Negro Population, by States: 1870 to 1970—Con.

[In thousands]

Series No.	State	Components of change method (Bureau of the Census)			Survival-rate method (see text for sources)								
		1960–1970	1950–1960	1940–1950	1950–1960	1940–1950	1930–1940	1920–1930	1910–1920	1900–1910	1890–1900	1880–1890	1870–1880
	FOREIGN-BORN WHITE POPULATION [3]—Con.												
	West South Central:												
59	Arkansas				−0.6	2.8	(Z)	−.6	0.8	5.5	2.6	5.1	5.6
60	Louisiana				4.3	6.4	−1.1	−.6	4.3	10.9	13.8	5.8	1.2
61	Oklahoma				2.2	2.3	−2.9	−2.4	7.1	22.6	17.8	2.7	(NA)
62	Texas				38.7	65.8	−76.1	36.4	137.5	80.8	45.0	47.6	53.6
	Mountain:												
63	Montana				−1.8	−.5	−4.4	−5.9	14.8	35.2	26.4	30.9	4.0
64	Idaho				(Z)	.7	−.3	−.9	5.6	21.9	8.9	9.5	3.3
65	Wyoming				−.8	−.3	−2.1	.6	1.4	12.3	4.0	9.6	1.7
66	Colorado				11.3	5.1	−7.3	.3	9.9	47.9	18.7	45.6	32.4
67	New Mexico				4.3	3.7	−5.4	−2.7	7.8	10.4	3.5	3.6	2.6
68	Arizona				26.8	13.0	−19.4	−10.2	29.8	24.8	6.4	3.8	8.2
69	Utah				6.4	4.2	−3.2	1.0	7.1	21.6	11.4	15.2	16.1
70	Nevada				3.6	1.7	−1.5	1.6	−.2	11.1	−1.1	−5.7	5.8
	Pacific:												
71	Washington				15.0	29.6	7.7	32.3	44.4	149.8	26.4	72.2	8.0
72	Oregon				3.3	14.3	3.3	22.1	17.2	57.5	13.8	28.5	13.4
73	California				388.2	265.4	33.8	414.2	250.3	259.1	76.4	104.7	73.6
74	Alaska				1.7								
75	Hawaii				2.2								
	NEGRO POPULATION												
	New England:												
25	Maine	−2	2	(4)	1.4	−.1	.2	−.2	.1	.2	.3	−.1	−.2
26	New Hampshire	(4)	1	(4)	.7	.2	−.3	.2	(Z)	(Z)	.1	(Z)	.1
27	Vermont	(4)	(4)	(4)	(Z)	.1	−.2	(Z)	−.9	.8	−.1	(Z)	(Z)
28	Massachusetts	33	20	12	16.8	10.6	2.7	2.9	6.9	5.9	9.9	4.4	3.0
29	Rhode Island	2	1	1	.3	1.2	.6	−.7	.6	.6	1.5	1.2	.8
30	Connecticut	38	37	15	28.5	12.9	2.2	5.2	5.3	.5	2.5	1.1	.8
	Middle Atlantic:												
31	New York	396	255	266	243.8	243.6	135.9	172.8	63.1	35.8	33.8	9.9	7.6
32	New Jersey	120	107	61	92.2	53.6	9.5	67.0	24.5	18.5	17.7	8.4	2.9
33	Pennsylvania	25	75	107	60.4	89.6	20.3	101.7	82.5	32.9	39.2	20.8	8.7
	East North Central:												
34	Ohio	45	129	131	107.4	106.7	20.7	90.7	69.4	15.6	5.2	5.2	2.6
35	Indiana	32	42	39	35.3	32.1	8.6	23.2	20.3	4.1	8.1	3.9	6.6
36	Illinois	127	182	203	159.2	179.8	49.4	119.3	69.8	23.5	22.7	8.4	8.7
37	Michigan	124	122	186	109.9	163.3	28.0	86.1	38.7	1.9	.4	−1.2	1.6
38	Wisconsin	27	29	14	23.5	11.9	1.0	4.4	2.2	.5	3.0	.1	1.3
	West North Central:												
39	Minnesota	7	5	4	3.6	2.7	1.0	.6	2.1	2.3	5.9	1.5	1.5
40	Iowa	2	2	2	.9	1.0	−.4	−1.9	3.9	2.1	1.6	.4	2.3
41	Missouri	14	24	31	19.2	25.7	19.2	35.9	27.2	1.0	(Z)	−4.0	−4.3
42	North Dakota	1	1	(4)	.3	.1	−.1	−.1	−.1	.3	4.9	}	
43	South Dakota	(4)	(4)	(4)	.2	.2	−.1	−.2	(Z)	.3	14.0	} (Z)	.3
44	Nebraska	2	4	4	3.6	3.0	.6	(Z)	5.2	1.6	−2.3	7.3	1.2
45	Kansas	−1	2	4	2.4	2.3	−.1	6.0	5.4	2.6	−.6	2.7	14.7
	South Atlantic:												
46	Delaware	4	6	4	4.6	2.4	2.4	.5	−.6	−.4	−.7	.3	−1.4
47	Maryland	79	31	37	24.9	29.9	10.7	5.0	7.0	−11.4	−6.5	−7.5	−7.5
48	District of Columbia	36	51	61	51.3	61.2	47.5	16.0	18.3	9.8	8.7	13.4	6.2
49	Virginia	−79	−74	−29	−71.1	−30.6	−36.9	−117.2	−27.2	−49.3	−70.8	−53.4	−37.6
50	West Virginia	−20	−41	−17	−36.8	−16.7	−4.1	12.8	15.5	15.3	5.8	3.6	2.1
51	North Carolina	−175	−204	−164	−171.3	−127.3	−60.0	−15.7	−28.9	−28.4	−48.7	−38.4	−7.9
52	South Carolina	−197	−218	−208	−180.8	−159.0	−94.4	−204.3	−74.5	−72.0	−65.5	−18.6	15.7
53	Georgia	−154	−205	−243	−165.1	−191.2	−90.3	−260.0	−74.7	−16.2	−27.3	12.3	−20.3
54	Florida	−32	96	12	79.8	7.2	49.9	54.2	3.2	40.7	23.4	15.8	1.4
	East South Central:												
55	Kentucky	1	−16	−18	−16.6	−22.8	−9.1	−16.6	−16.6	−22.3	−12.2	−22.4	−13.1
56	Tennessee	−51	−59	−48	−52.2	−38.2	8.6	−14.0	−29.3	−34.3	−19.0	−18.7	−24.6
57	Alabama	−231	−224	−204	−191.6	−165.4	−63.8	−80.7	−70.8	−22.1	−1.7	−5.8	−36.1
58	Mississippi	−279	−323	−326	−264.2	−258.2	−58.2	−68.8	−129.6	−30.9	−10.4	−13.2	17.6
	West South Central:												
59	Arkansas	−112	−150	−158	−108.6	−116.1	−33.3	−46.3	−1.0	22.5	−7.9	44.7	25.4
60	Louisiana	−163	−93	−147	−66.2	−113.8	−8.4	−25.5	−51.2	−16.1	−21.6	3.3	−1.3
61	Oklahoma	−3	−21	−47	−18.8	−38.9	−13.0	1.9	.8	54.8	79.3	2.3	(NA)
62	Texas	−4	−33	−107	−19.6	−67.2	4.9	9.7	5.2	−10.2	7.1	12.6	21.0
	Mountain:												
63	Montana	(4)	(4)	(4)	(Z)	.1	(Z)	−.2	−.1	.3	——	——	——
64	Idaho	(4)	(4)	(4)	.3	.1	(Z)	−.1	.3	.3	——	——	——
65	Wyoming	(4)	−1	2	−.8	1.3	−.2	−.1	−.6	1.2	——	——	——
66	Colorado	16	13	7	11.0	6.1	.9	.8	.7	3.1	——	——	——
67	New Mexico	−4	4	2	4.1	2.3	1.5	−2.9	4.1	(NA)	——	——	——
68	Arizona	−4	4	6	7.0	6.7	3.5	1.9	5.8	.2	——	——	——
69	Utah	1	1	1	.5	1.1	.2	−.3	.4	.5	——	——	——
70	Nevada	6	6	3	5.3	2.8	.2	.2	−.1	.4	——	——	——
	Pacific:												
71	Washington	10	8	21	6.7	17.8	1.2	.2	1.1	3.4	——	——	——
72	Oregon	4	3	8	2.4	6.9	.5	.2	.7	.5	——	——	——
73	California	272	255	289	220.4	258.9	41.2	36.4	16.1	9.8	——	——	——
74	Alaska	(4)	(4)	——	5.2	——	——	——	——	——	——	——	——
75	Hawaii	1	(4)	——	1.2	——	——	——	——	——	——	——	——

NA Not available.   Z Less than 50.
[1] For 1870–1890, only white population in Mountain and Pacific States; no estimates made for Negroes.   [2] Less than 1,000.
[3] For component of change method, 1950–1970, total white population; no estimates separately for native white and foreign-born white.
[4] Less than 500.

Series C 76–80. Estimated Annual Movement of the Farm Population: 1920 to 1970

[In thousands]

Year	Farm population, April 1	Net change: Births and deaths	Change through migration and reclassification of residence [1]			Year	Farm population, April 1	Net change: Births and deaths	Change through migration and reclassification of residence [1]		
			Net	To farms	From farms				Net	To farms	From farms
	76	77	78	79	80		76	77	78	79	80
1970	9,712	47	−642			1945	24,420	353	−748	(NA)	(NA)
1969	10,307	51	−198	284	−481	1944	24,815	370	−1,740	(NA)	(NA)
1968	10,454	60	−481	268	−749	1943	26,186	418	−3,145	(NA)	(NA)
1967	10,875	73	−793	299	−1,092	1942	28,914	383	−1,587	(NA)	(NA)
1966	11,595	90	−858	250	−1,108	1941	30,118	359	−788	(NA)	(NA)
1965	12,363	112	−703	275	−978	1940	30,547	410	−703	819	(NA)
1964	12,954	121	−533	283	−816	1939	30,840	405	−545	823	−1,368
1963	13,367	140	−1,086	352	−1,438	1938	30,980	375	−661	872	−1,533
1962	14,313	156	−646	287	−933	1937	31,266	363	−834	719	−1,553
1961	14,803	168	−1,000	309	−1,309	1936	31,737	375	−799	825	−1,624
1960 *	15,635	184	−1,142	356	−1,498	1935	32,161	383	−527	783	−1,310
1959 ²	16,592	203	−740	(NA)	(NA)	1934	32,305	375	−463	970	−1,433
1958	17,128	220	−748	(NA)	(NA)	1933	32,393	398	607	1,826	−1,219
1957	17,656	239	−1,295	(NA)	(NA)	1932	31,388	387	156	1,918	−1,762
1956	18,712	261	−627	(NA)	(NA)	1931	30,845	377	−61	1,985	−2,046
1955	19,078	268	−210	(NA)	(NA)	1930	30,529	426	−477	1,604	−2,081
1954	19,019	296	−1,151	(NA)	(NA)	1929	30,580	454	−422	1,698	−2,120
1953	19,874	328	−2,201	(NA)	(NA)	1928	30,548	475	−457	1,705	−2,162
1952	21,748	341	−483	(NA)	(NA)	1927	30,530	458	−907	1,427	−2,334
1951	21,890	373	−1,531	(NA)	(NA)	1926	30,979	491	−702	1,336	−2,038
1950	23,048	392	−1,537	(NA)	(NA)	1925	31,190	500	−487	1,581	−2,068
1949	24,194	397	−586	(NA)	(NA)	1924	31,177	494	−807	1,355	−2,162
1948	24,383	443	−1,889	(NA)	(NA)	1923	31,490	518	−1,137	1,115	−2,252
1947	25,829	470	−44	(NA)	(NA)	1922	32,109	550	−564	759	−1,323
1946	25,403	312	671	(NA)	(NA)	1921	32,123	485	−336	560	−896
						1920	31,974				

* Denotes first year for which figures include Alaska and Hawaii.
NA Not available.

[1] Includes persons who did not move but who were in or out of the farm population because agricultural operations on the places where they were living either ceased or were begun.
² Includes Alaska.

Series C 81–88. Mobility Status and Type of Mobility of the Population One Year Old and Over: 1947 to 1970

[In thousands. Includes members of the Armed Forces living off post or with their families on post but excludes all other members of the Armed Forces]

Period	Total [1]	Same house (nonmovers)	Different house in the United States (movers)					Abroad at beginning of period
			Total	Same county	Different county (migrants)			
					Total	Within a State	Between States	
	81	82	83	84	85	86	87	88
March 1969 to March 1970	198,955	160,860	36,541	23,225	13,316	6,250	7,066	1,554
March 1968 to March 1969	196,642	159,310	35,933	22,993	12,940	6,316	6,625	1,399
March 1967 to March 1968	194,621	156,735	36,603	22,960	13,643	6,607	7,035	1,283
March 1966 to March 1967	192,233	155,710	35,200	22,339	12,861	6,308	6,553	1,323
March 1965 to March 1966	190,242	152,656	36,703	24,165	12,538	6,275	6,263	883
March 1964 to March 1965	187,974	149,128	37,866	25,122	12,744	6,597	6,147	978
March 1963 to March 1964	185,312	148,125	36,327	24,089	12,238	6,191	6,047	859
March 1962 to March 1963	182,541	146,109	35,411	23,059	12,352	5,712	6,640	1,021
April 1961 to April 1962	179,663	144,445	34,364	23,341	11,023	5,461	5,562	854
March 1960 to March 1961	177,354	140,821	35,535	24,289	11,246	5,493	5,753	998
March 1959 to March 1960 *	174,451	139,766	33,811	22,564	11,247	5,724	5,523	874
April 1958 to April 1959	170,658	137,018	32,804	22,315	10,489	5,419	5,070	836
March 1957 to March 1958	167,604	133,501	33,263	22,023	11,240	5,656	5,584	840
April 1956 to April 1957	164,371	131,648	31,834	21,566	10,268	5,192	5,076	889
March 1955 to March 1956	161,497	127,457	33,098	22,186	10,912	5,859	5,053	942
April 1954 to April 1955	158,609	126,190	31,492	21,086	10,406	5,511	4,895	927
April 1953 to April 1954	155,679	125,654	29,027	19,046	9,981	4,947	5,034	998
April 1952 to April 1953	153,038	121,512	30,786	20,638	10,148	4,626	5,522	740
April 1951 to April 1952	150,494	120,016	29,840	19,874	9,966	4,854	5,112	638
April 1950 to April 1951	148,400	116,936	31,158	20,694	10,464	5,276	5,188	306
March 1949 to March 1950	146,864	118,849	27,526	19,276	8,250	4,360	3,889	491
April 1948 to April 1949	144,101	116,498	27,127	18,792	8,335	3,992	4,344	476
April 1947 to April 1948	141,698	113,026	28,210	19,202	9,008	4,638	4,370	462

* Denotes first year for which figures include Alaska and Hawaii.   [1] Population 1 year old and over at end of survey interval.

Chapter C

International Migration and Naturalization (Series C 89-331)

C 89-157. General note.

The continuous record of immigration to the United States began in 1819, under the Act of 1819, which required the captain or master of a vessel arriving from abroad to deliver to the local collector of customs a list or manifest of all passengers taken on board. This list was to designate the age, sex, and occupation of each passenger, "the country to which they severally belonged," and the number that had died on the voyage. Copies of these manifests were to be transmitted to the Secretary of State, who reported the information periodically to Congress. Subsequently, the Act of 1855 prescribed quarterly reports to the Secretary of State and annual reports to Congress. Later acts have continued to require the collection of such information.

Although the reporting of alien arrivals was required by the Act of 1798, which expired two years later, the number arriving before 1819 is not known. William J. Bromwell, in his *History of Immigration to the United States*, 1856 (pp. 18–19), estimated the number of passengers of foreign birth arriving here from the close of the Revolutionary War to 1819, at 250,000. This estimate was used by the Bureau of Statistics which later compiled the official statistics of immigration.

Immigration statistics were compiled by the Department of State for 1820–1870; by the Treasury Department, Bureau of Statistics, for 1867–1895; and since 1892, by a separate Office or Bureau of Immigration, now a part of the Immigration and Naturalization Service. For 1892–1932, the Bureau of Immigration issued annual reports. For 1933–1940, the data were summarized in the *Annual Report of the Secretary of Labor*; for 1941, they were issued in the *Annual Report of the Attorney General*; for 1942, no report was published; and for subsequent years, the statistics appeared in the *Annual Report of the Immigration and Naturalization Service*.

Since 1820 the official immigration data have undergone many changes in the reporting area covered. During the first decades only arrivals by vessel at Atlantic and Gulf ports were reported. Arrivals at Pacific ports were first included in 1850. During the Civil War the only Southern ports that reported were those controlled by the Federal Government. Later the reporting area was expanded to include arrivals at outlying possessions. Arrivals in Alaska were first reported in 1871, but only irregularly thereafter until 1904, after which Alaska was regularly included among the places of entry. Arrivals in Hawaii were first included in 1901, Puerto Rico in 1902, and the Virgin Islands in 1942.

Counting arrivals at the land borders was not required by the early immigration acts, and the counting of such arrivals did not approach completeness until after 1904. For 1820–1823, a few arrivals by land borders were included. Complete reporting was attempted in 1855 with only partial success, was interrupted for several years by the Civil War, and was discontinued in 1885. Beginning in 1894, European immigrants who arrived at Canadian ports with the declared intention of proceeding to the United States were included in the immigration statistics. Some immigration was reported at land border stations established in 1904. More stations were opened in the following years, but reporting of land border arrivals was not fully established until 1908.

The statistical treatment of Canadian and Mexican immigrants at times has differed from that of other immigrants. When reporting of arrivals by land borders was discontinued in 1885, regular reporting of Canadian and Mexican arrivals by vessel was also discontinued; however, a few Canadian and Mexican immigrants were reported in most of the following years. Arrivals of Canadians and Mexicans by land borders began to be reported in 1906, and reporting was fully established in 1908 under authority of the Act of 1907, which provided for the inspection of Canadians and Mexicans at the land borders.

Not all aliens entering via the Canadian and Mexican borders are counted for inclusion in the immigration statistics. Before 1930, no count was made of residents of a year or longer of Canada, Newfoundland, or Mexico who planned to remain in the United States less than 6 months. For 1930–1945 the following classes of aliens entering via the land borders were counted and included in the statistics of immigration:

(1) Those who have not been in the United States within 6 months, who come to stay more than 6 months; (2) those for whom straight head tax is a prerequisite to admission, or for whom head tax is specially deposited and subsequently converted to straight head tax account; (3) those required by law or regulation to present an immigration visa or re-entry permit, and those who surrender either, regardless of whether they are required by law or regulation to do so; (4) those announcing an intention to depart via a seaport of the United States for Hawaii or insular possessions of the United States, or for foreign countries, except arrivals from Canada intending to return thereto by water; and (5) those announcing an intention to depart across the other land boundary.

These classes were revised in 1945 so that the statistics of arriving aliens at land border ports of entry for 1945–1952 included (1) arriving aliens who came into the United States for 30 days or more; and (2) returning alien residents who had been out of the United States more than 6 months. Arriving aliens who came into the United States for 29 days or less were not counted except those certified by public health officials, aliens held for a board of special inquiry, aliens excluded and deported, and aliens in transit who announced an intention to depart across another land boundary, or by sea.

Since 1953, all arriving aliens at land border ports of entry are counted and included except Canadian citizens and British subjects resident in Canada who were admitted for 6 months or less, and Mexican citizens who were admitted for 72 hours or less in the United States.

Persons who cross the land borders for brief periods (border crossers) are not included in the immigration and emigration statistics. The Immigration and Naturalization Service publishes statistics on alien and citizen border crossers in the *Annual Report*, however.

Arrivals in and departures from the Philippines were recorded in the port tables for 1910–1924, but were not included in the total immigration data. For 1925–1931, such arrivals and departures were obtained annually from the Bureau of Insular Affairs, War Department, and published in separate tables. The Immigration Service has no records since 1932 of arrivals in, or departures from, the Philippines to foreign countries.

Data on aliens admitted to conterminous United States from insular possessions were compiled from 1908 through 1964. Aliens admitted from the Virgin Islands were first recorded in 1917. The departure of aliens from the mainland to Puerto Rico was first recorded in 1918. Data on aliens from Guam began in 1929; Samoa, in 1932.

Definition of terms. For 1820–1867, immigration totals (compiled by the Department of State) were shown as alien passenger arrivals, but may have included alien passengers who died before arrival, and did include, for 1856–1867, temporary visitors among arriving alien passengers. For the 12-year period, the temporary visitors constituted about 1½ percent of the alien passenger arrivals.

For 1868–1891, the Bureau of Statistics immigrant arrival figures (excluding temporary visitors), were reported. Since 1892, official immigration data have been compiled by the Office of Immigration (and its successors) and for 1892–1895 its totals were 7 to 8 percent lower than those for the Bureau of Statistics for that period. The difference is largely attributable to the limitation of the Office of Immigration figures to alien steerage passengers; cabin class passengers were not again included as immigrants until 1904. A further difference was that the Bureau of Statistics figures were for arrivals and those of the Office of Immigration were for admissions.

For 1895–1897, the Office of Immigration readopted arrivals and the figures include the 2,419 aliens debarred in 1895, the 2,799 in 1896, and 1,880 in 1897. In later years, the immigration data were further refined to exclude aliens in transit through the United States (1904), and resident aliens returning from a visit abroad (1906).

In 1906 arriving aliens were divided into two classes: Immigrants, or those who intended to settle in the United States, and nonimmigrants, or admitted aliens who declared an intention not to settle in the United States, and all aliens returning to resume domiciles formerly acquired in the United States.

The official record of emigration began in 1907 and ended in 1957. It was made possible by the Immigration Act of 1907, which required all steamship companies carrying departing aliens to furnish manifests similar to those required for arriving aliens.

For 1908–1932, aliens arriving in or departing from the United States were classified as follows: Arriving aliens with permanent domicile outside the United States who intended to reside permanently in the United States were classed as immigrants; departing aliens with permanent residence in the United States who intended to reside permanently abroad were classed as emigrants; all alien residents making a temporary trip abroad and all aliens residing abroad making a temporary trip to the United States were classed as nonimmigrants on the inward journey and nonemigrants on the outward. Permanent residence was defined as residence of 1 year or longer. (*Annual Report of the Commissioner General of Immigration, 1908*, p. 6.)

Since 1933, aliens arriving in the United States have been classified as immigrants or nonimmigrants. Immigrants are nonresident aliens admitted to the United States for permanent residence. Until July 1, 1968, they were further classified as quota and nonquota immigrants. Quota immigrants were those subject to the established quotas of Eastern Hemisphere countries and their dependencies. Nonquota immigrants included natives of the Western Hemisphere and their spouses and children, immediate relatives of U.S. citizens, and certain groups of special immigrants. Beginning July 1, 1968, immigrants have been classified as those subject to the numerical limitations of the Eastern Hemisphere, those subject to the numerical limitations of the Western Hemisphere, and those exempt from numerical limitations. Those that are exempt include immediate relatives (parents, spouses, and children) of U.S. citizens and various classes of special immigrants.

Nonimmigrants are nonresident aliens admitted to the United States for a temporary period. Included in this group are visitors for business and pleasure, students and their spouses and children, temporary workers and trainees and their spouses and children, foreign government officials, exchange visitors and their spouses and children, international representatives, treaty traders and investors, representatives of foreign information media, fiances(ees) of U.S. citizens and their children, intracompany transferees and their spouses and children, NATO officials, aliens in transit, and, for statistical purposes, permanent resident aliens returning after short trips abroad. Excluded are border crossers, crewmen, and insular travelers.

Data on emigrants have not been kept since 1957. Emigrants were aliens who resided in the United States for a year or longer and who left for a permanent residence abroad. Nonemigrants were resident aliens of the United States who left the United States for a temporary period abroad, or nonresident aliens of the United States who were in the United States for less than a year who were returning to their permanent residence abroad. Since 1957 data have been

kept only on aliens departing. They include all aliens departing by sea or air except for direct departures to Canada.

The old definitions of immigrant, emigrant, nonimmigrant, and nonemigrant somewhat impaired the reliability of net immigration figures. While immigrants were admitted for permanent residence, they could depart prior to residence of 1 year, in which case they were counted as immigrants on arrival and nonemigrants on departure. Persons coming in temporarily, however, as nonimmigrants who failed to leave within a year would have been counted as emigrants on departure.

C 89–119. Immigrants, by country, 1820–1970.

Source: 1820–1932, U.S. Immigration and Naturalization Service, unpublished data, and U.S. Bureau of Immigration, *Annual Report of the Commissioner General of Immigration*, as follows: 1820–1926 *Report for 1926*, pp. 170–178; 1927–1931, *Report for 1931*, pp. 222–223; 1932, *Report for 1932*, pp. 120–125; 1933–1957, U.S. Immigration and Naturalization Service, unpublished data; 1958–1970, *Annual Report of the Immigration and Naturalization Service*, annual issues.

Prior to 1906, data cover countries from which the aliens came; thereafter, countries of last permanent residence. Owing to changes in the list of countries separately reported and to changes in boundaries, data for certain countries are not comparable throughout. Under the provisions of the Immigration and Nationality Act, subquotas of 100 each were established for colonies or dependencies, to be charged against the quota of the mother country. Because of these provisions, statistics were compiled, between January 1953 and July 1968, for each colony or dependency having a subquota. Under the Act of October 3, 1965, colonies and dependencies of foreign states are alloted 200 visa numbers each, chargeable to the mother country.

The principal changes in reporting immigrants by country since 1820 are shown in the detailed listing below.

See also general note for series C 89–157.

C 90–101. Immigration from Europe, 1820–1970.

Source: See source for series C 89–119.

Since 1820, territorial transfers in Europe have, to a certain extent, impaired the comparability of immigration statistics from that continent. Data for Austria–Hungary were not reported until 1861. Austria and Hungary have been reported separately since 1905. For 1938–1945, Austria is included with Germany. Bulgaria, Serbia, and Montenegro were first reported in 1899. In 1920, Bulgaria was reported separately, as was the Kingdom of Serbs, Croats, and Slovenes (identified as Yugoslavia since 1922). Prior to 1925, Northern Ireland was included with Ireland (Eire). The figures for Norway and Sweden were combined from 1820–1868; since 1869, each country has been reported separately. Poland was recorded as a separate country for 1820–1898 and since 1920. During 1899–1919, Poland was included with Austria-Hungary, Germany, and Russia. There is no record of immigration from Romania prior to 1880.

International transfers in territory following World War I resulted in the establishment of several countries. In 1920, Czechoslovakia, Finland, Poland, and the Kingdom of Serbs, Croats, and Slovenes (designated as Yugoslavia in 1922) were added to the immigration lists; in 1924, Albania, Estonia, Latvia, and Lithuania were added; in 1925, the Free City of Danzig and Luxembourg were added.

The Immigration Act of 1924, which established quotas for all independent countries in Europe, Asia, Africa, and the Pacific, effected a further change in the immigration lists of countries. This change, however, was not fully felt until 1931. In that year, Andorra, Iceland, Liechtenstein, Monaco, and San Marino were added to the European countries, and the Russian Empire was classified into European Russia (designated as U.S.S.R. in Europe from 1947 through 1963) and Siberia, or Asiatic Russia. Since 1964, all the U.S.S.R. has been included in Europe. The principal effect of the 1924 Act, however, was in the extension of the lists of Asian, African, and Western Hemisphere countries.

In 1950, Bessarabia and the northern portion of Bukovina were included in the U.S.S.R. instead of in Romania. The Dodecanese Islands were included in Greece instead of Italy. The Free Territory of Trieste, formerly a part of Italy and Yugoslavia, was established as an independent country until 1959, when it again became part of Italy and Yugoslavia in immigration statistics.

C 102–109. Immigration from Asia, 1820–1970.

Source: See source for series C 89–119.

China and India are the only countries in Asia for which the records of immigration to the United States date back to 1820. A few immigrants from Japan were recorded in 1861, 1866, and 1867, but complete records for Japan begin with 1869. Figures for Turkey in Asia are available since 1869. Data on some immigration from Arabia are recorded for 1876–1895; from Armenia for 1874–1895; and from Persia for 1871–1895. For 1896–1923, immigration from Asia included only China, India, Japan, Turkey in Asia, and "other Asia." In 1924, Syria was added, and in 1925, Armenia, Palestine, and Persia (Iran) were added to the lists of Asian countries. Since 1934, Armenia has been included in Russia. In 1931, Siberia, or Asiatic Russia, was separated from European Russia, and Iraq and Siam (Thailand) were added to the lists. Since 1964, all the U.S.S.R. has been included in Europe.

In 1945, the classification of country in the country-of-birth statistics (on which the Quota Law was based) was adopted for the immigration statistics. This change resulted in the addition to the immigration lists of Afghanistan, Arabian Peninsula, Bhutan, Muscat, Nepal, Saudi Arabia, and Asiatic colonies, dependencies, and protectorates of European countries. Since 1948, the following countries have been added to the immigration lists: (1948) Burma, Ceylon, Jordan, Korea, and Pakistan; (1949) Israel (formerly included with Palestine), Lebanon (formerly included with Syria), and Yemen; (1950) Indonesia; (1952) Bonin Volcano Islands, Ryukyu Islands, Cambodia, Laos, and Vietnam; (1957) Formosa; (1961) Cyprus; (1963) Kuwait; (1964) Malaysia; (1967) Singapore.

C 110–114. Immigration from America, 1820–1970.

Source: See source for series C 89–119.

Prior to 1920, Canada and Newfoundland were recorded under country of last permanent residence as British North America. For 1920–1924, combined figures are available for Canada and Newfoundland; for 1925–1948, each was reported separately. Since 1950, Newfoundland has been included in Canada. Inspection of Canadians and Mexicans was first authorized by the Act of 1907. The first complete year for which all immigration via the land borders was recorded is, therefore, 1908.

Immigration from Mexico has been recorded for 1820–1885 and for 1894 to the present. Immigration statistics for the West Indies have been available since 1820. For 1820–1860, there was no classification of the West Indies, by country. For 1861–1898, some immigration was recorded from Antigua (1873–1895), Bahamas (1871–1895), Barbados (1869–1895), Bermuda (1861–1895), Cuba (1869–1898), Curacao (1873–1895), Haiti (1869–1895), Jamaica (1869–1895), Puerto Rico (1869–1895), Saint Croix (1871–1895), Saint Thomas (1872–1895), and Trinidad (1874–1895). For 1899–1924, there again was no classification by country of immigration from the West Indies. Immigration from Cuba has been separately recorded since 1925; from the British West Indies, Dominican Republic, Dutch West Indies, French West Indies, and Haiti since 1931; and from Bermuda since 1945. For detailed data, see *Annual Report of Commissioner General of Immigration* for each year, 1892–1932. Since January 1953, all countries in the West Indies have been reported.

Immigration from Central America has been recorded since 1820, but not by country during most of that period. Separate statistics are available for 1895–1898 for Guatemala, Honduras, Nicaragua, and

El Salvador; and for 1895–1897 for Costa Rica. British Honduras was also enumerated separately for 1874–1910. With the above exceptions, only figures for total immigration were available for Central America until 1925. Immigration has been reported separately from British Honduras since 1925, and from the Canal Zone, Costa Rica, Guatemala, Honduras, Nicaragua, Panama, and El Savador since 1931.

Immigration from South America has also been reported in total since 1820 but, with the following exceptions, not by country until 1925. For 1869–1895, separate enumerations were made for Brazil, Chile, Colombia, Ecuador, Guiana, Peru, and Venezuela; and for 1871–1895 for the Argentine Republic. Separate figures for Brazil have been again available since 1925; and since 1931 for Argentina, Bolivia, British Guiana (since 1967, Guyana), Dutch Guiana (Surinam), French Guiana, Chile, Colombia, Ecuador, Paraguay, Peru, Uruguay, and Venezuela.

C 115. Immigration from Africa, 1820–1970.

Source: See source for series C 89–119.

Immigration from Africa has been recorded since 1820, but, with few exceptions, was not classified by country until 1931. There is record of some immigration from Liberia in 1829, 1839, 1844, and 1857–1893; Algeria, 1872–1894; Egypt, 1869–1895; and South Africa, 1869–1895. For 1890–1924, only immigration for continental Africa was reported. Immigration from Ethiopia (Abyssinia), Liberia, Morocco, and Union of South Africa has been recorded since 1931. In 1945, "other Africa" was classified into Cameroons (British Mandate), Cameroons (French Mandate), Ruanda and Urundi (trust territory, Belgium), South-West Africa (Mandate of the Union of South Africa), Tanganyika (trust territory, United Kingdom), Togoland (British Mandate), Togoland (trust territory, France), and colonies, dependencies, or protectorates of Belgium, France, Great Britain, Italy, Portugal, and Spain. Many of these countries have since gained their independence.

Since 1945, the following countries have been added: 1953: Libya and Somaliland (Italian administration), and Southern Rhodesia. Eritrea, which was federated with Ethiopia, was included with Ethiopia. 1957: Ghana (composed of British territories, Gold Coast and British Togoland), Sudan, and Tunisia. 1961: Congo, Republic of the Congo, Dahomey, Gabon, Ivory Coast, Malagasy Republic, Republic of Mali, Niger, Nigeria, Republic of Senegal, Somali Republic, and Upper Volta. 1963: Burundi and Rwanda, formerly Ruanda-Urundi. 1967: Botswana and Lesotho.

C 116–118. Immigration from Australasia, 1870–1970.

Source: See source for series C 89–119.

Immigration from Australia was recorded separately in 1822, 1839–1840, and for most of the years 1854–1898. For 1899–1924, a combined total was recorded for Australia, Tasmania, and New Zealand, and, since 1925, Australia has again been reported separately. Separate figures for New Zealand are available for 1870–1890. For 1891–1893, New Zealand was included in "all other countries"; for 1894–1898, in "Pacific Islands, not specified," and for 1899–1924, with Australia and Tasmania. Separate figures for New Zealand have again been available since 1925.

The following countries were added to the immigration lists of the Pacific in 1945: Nauru (British Mandate); Territory of New Guinea including appertaining islands (Australian Mandate); Western Samoa (New Zealand Mandate); Yap and other Pacific Islands under Japanese Mandate; and colonies, dependencies, or protectorates of France, Great Britain, Japan, Netherlands, and Portugal. In 1952, the Pacific Islands (trust territory, U.S. administration) were added. In 1962, Western Samoa gained its independence and, since 1968, Nauru has also been an independent nation. Yap and several of the other islands once under the mandate of Japan are now included in Japan.

C 120-137. Immigrants, by major occupation group, 1820-1970.

Source: U.S. Department of the Treasury, Bureau of Statistics, 1820-1890, *Arrivals of Alien Passengers and Immigrants in the United States, 1820-1890*, pp. 42-49; 1891, *Immigration into the United States Showing Number, Nationality, Sex, Age, Occupation, Destination, ... from 1820-1903.* U.S. Bureau of Immigration 1892-1898, *Annual Report of Commissioner General of Immigration*, annual issues. U.S. Immigration and Naturalization Service, 1899-1944, unpublished data; 1945-1970, *Annual Report of the Immigration and Naturalization Service*, annual issues, and unpublished data.

The major occupation groups for 1820-1898 include the following categories: Professional—occupations which involve a liberal education or its equivalent and mental rather than manual skills; commercial—agents, bankers, hotelkeepers, manufacturers, and merchants and dealers; skilled—occupations requiring special training of a manual rather than mental nature. A "farmer" is one who operates a farm, either for himself or for others; a "farm laborer" is one who works on a farm for the man who operates it. The "no occupation" group includes dependent women and children, other aliens without occupation, and aliens whose occupations were not stated.

Although the data are shown in broad occupation groups, the instructions for compiling statistics specified that the occupation should be described as precisely as possible. For example, civil engineer, stationary engineer, mining engineer, brass polisher, steel polisher, iron molder, wood turner, etc., should be so described, and not entered simply as engineer, polisher, molder, turner, or other indefinite designation.

From 1945 to 1951, the Immigration and Naturalization Service applied the major occupation groups as shown in the *Sixteenth Census of the United States, Alphabetical Index of Occupations and Industries.* It also grouped occupations of immigrants for 1899-1944 (compiled in unpublished records) as closely as possible into the new groups. From 1952 to 1961, occupations were coded and grouped in accordance with the definitions in *U.S. Census of Population: 1950, Alphabetical Index of Occupations and Industries;* beginning with 1962, occupations have been grouped according to the 1960 index.

The occupation figures include all immigrants, those with and without work experience. The "no occupation" group includes housewives, unemployed, retired persons, students, children under 14 years of age, aliens with no occupation, and occupation unknown or not reported.

See also general note for series C 89-157.

C 138, 140-142. Immigrants, by age, 1820-1970.

Source: U.S. Department of the Treasury, Bureau of Statistics, 1820-1897, *Monthly Summary of Commerce and Finance of the U.S.*, No. 12, series 1902-1903, pp. 4358 and 4362; U.S. Bureau of Immigration, 1898-1932, *Annual Report of the Commissioner General of Immigration*, annual issues; U.S. Immigration and Naturalization Service, 1933-1957, unpublished data; 1958-1970, *Annual Report of the Immigration and Naturalization Service*, annual issues, and unpublished data.

Some of the published estimates have been revised because of apparent printing errors in the source.

The age groups used to classify immigrants have changed a number of times since 1820, thereby impairing to a certain extent their comparability. For 1820-1898, the classification was: Under 15 years, 15 to 40, and over 40. In addition, the age of nearly 250,000 immigrants, or 4 percent of the total, for 1820-1866 was not reported.

For 1899-1917, the age classification was: Under 14 years, 14 to 44, and 45 years and over; for 1918-1924: Under 16 years, 16 to 44, and 45 years and over.

Although only three age groups were generally used before 1925, a more detailed classification was used for 1910-1924 for single females: 15 to 19 years, 20 to 24, 25 to 29, and 30 to 34 in 1910; 14 to 21 years, 22 to 29, 30 to 37, and 38 to 44 for 1911-1917; 16 to 21 years, 22 to 29, 30 to 37, and 38 to 44 for 1918-1924.

In 1925 the age classification was enlarged from 3 to 6 groups: Under 16 years, 16 to 21, 22 to 29, 30 to 37, 38 to 44, and 45 years and over. In 1940, it was enlarged to 12 groups, with a lower limit of under 11 years, 5-year age groups until 60, and an upper limit of over 60 years. In 1945, it was further enlarged into 5-year groups, with a lower age limit of under 5 years and an upper open-end limit of 100 years and over. The upper limit has since been changed to 95 and over.

See also general note for series C 89-157.

C 139. Male immigrants, 1820-1970.

Source: Senate Doc. No. 756, 61st Congress, 1820-1910, *Reports of the Immigration Commission*, vol. 3. U.S. Bureau of Immigration, 1911-1931, *Annual Report of the Commissioner General of Immigration*, 1931; 1932, *Annual Report of the Commissioner General of Immigration*, 1932. U.S. Immigration and Naturalization Service, 1933-1939, unpublished data; 1940-1970, *Annual Report of the Immigration and Naturalization Service*, annual issues.

Although the Act of 1819 required that arriving immigrants be recorded by sex, these data were not satisfactorily compiled before 1869. (See Senate Doc. No. 756 cited above.) The earlier reports of the Secretary of State to Congress contain partial data on this subject, and in 1911 the Immigration Commission compiled percentage data to show the approximate sex distribution for 1820-1867. The data are not complete, as in most years sex was not reported for a considerable number of immigrants, but on the whole the percentages may be accepted as fairly representative of the sex distribution in the years considered. For continuity of data throughout the 1820-1970 period, the above mentioned percentages have been applied to the total immigration figures for the years 1820 through 1867 to arrive at an estimate of the number of male immigrants. Data for 1869 through 1970 reflect actual data of immigration by sex.

C 143-157. Annual quota and aliens admitted, by classes, 1925-1970.

Source: U.S. Immigration and Naturalization Service, *Annual Report of Immigration and Naturalization Service*, annual issues, Presidential Proclamations on quotas, and unpublished data.

For 1925-1929, the annual quota (series C 143) of 164,667 was based on 2 percent of the foreign-born residents in the United States as determined by the 1890 census. The "national origin" formula which determined quotas from 1929 until the Act of October 3, 1965, went into effect, provided that the annual quota equal one-sixth of one percent of the number of white inhabitants in the continental United States in 1920, less Western Hemisphere immigrants and their descendants. The annual quota for each nationality was then determined by the same ratio to 150,000 as the number of inhabitants of each nationality living in the continental United States in 1920 to the total inhabitants, although a minimum quota for any nationality was 100. As territorial boundaries changed and new countries were established, slight changes in quotas occurred.

The Act of October 3, 1965, abolished the quota system and in its place set up an annual numerical limitation of 170,000 immigrants from the Eastern Hemisphere, with no more than 20,000 immigrants to come from any one country. From December 1, 1965, through June 30, 1968, countries retained their old quotas, but unused visa numbers from each year went into a general pool of numbers available on a first-come, first-served basis during the next year. On July 1, 1968, the new law and the system of numerical limitations went fully into effect. Also at that time a numerical limitation of 120,000 per year was imposed on Western Hemisphere immigration, which had previously been unrestricted. The Act of October 3, 1965, thereby abolished the "national origins" system and gave persons from every country within each hemisphere an equal chance to immigrate to the United States.

The classes presented in these series are legal classes of admission defined in the Act of 1924 and the Immigration and Nationality Act of 1952 as amended by the Act of October 3, 1965. Returning resident aliens, who have been counted before as immigrants, are included with nonimmigrants.

In general, statistics on aliens admitted have been derived from manifests or entry documents. Changes in regulations extending documentary waivers for nonimmigrants entering via the Canadian or Mexican border, or from adjacent islands, have impaired comparability of the nonimmigrant statistics.

See also general note for series C 89–157.

C 158–161. Aliens deported, required to depart, and excluded, 1892–1970.

Source: U.S. Immigration and Naturalization Service, *Annual Report of Immigration and Naturalization Service*, 1957, pp. 46, 50, and 1970, p. 85.

C 159, aliens deported. Undesirable aliens who have violated certain immigration laws may be expelled or deported under formal deportation proceedings. Deportation of alien contract laborers within one year after entry was authorized by the Act of 1888. Deportation statistics, however, have been compiled only since 1892, shortly after enactment of the Act of 1891, which provided for the deportation of all aliens who entered unlawfully. The classes of deportable aliens were extended by subsequent acts and are now defined in the Immigration and Nationality Act of 1952 as amended by the Act of October 3, 1965. The principal deportable classes are criminals (including violators of narcotic laws), immoral classes, mental or physical defectives, public charges, subversives, and those who entered illegally or failed to maintain or comply with the conditions of admission.

C 160, aliens required to depart. Aliens who would be deportable under certain sections of the law may forego formal deportation hearings and depart voluntarily either at their own expense, or if deemed desirable, at the expense of the Government. Statistics on aliens required to depart have been recorded since 1927.

C 161, aliens excluded. Prior to 1882, various State laws were enacted excluding from admission to the United States undesirable aliens such as paupers, felons, and diseased aliens. The first Chinese exclusion law was passed in 1882. Lunatics, idiots, and persons likely to become public charges were first excluded by the Act of 1882.

Statistics on aliens excluded were first compiled in 1892, shortly after passage of the Act of 1891, which extended the classes of excludable aliens. Subsequent acts, principally the Immigration Act of 1917, and the Immigration and Nationality Act of 1952, extended these classes further. At present, the principal classes excluded are attempted illegal entries, criminals (including violators of narcotic laws), immoral persons, subversive or anarchistic persons, attempted entry without proper documents, mental or physical defectives, stowaways, and those likely to become a public charge.

C 162–167. Aliens naturalized, by type of provision, 1907–1970.

Source: 1907–1930, U.S. Bureau of Naturalization, *Annual Report of the Commissioner of Naturalization;* 1931–1970, U.S. Immigration and Naturalization Service, *Annual Report of the Immigration and Naturalization Service*, annual issues.

See also general note for series C 168–180.

General naturalization provisions. Since the first naturalization statute of 1790, residence in the United States, good moral character, and an oath to support the Constitution have been required of persons seeking U.S. citizenship. The Act of April 14, 1802, incorporated the requisites of 5 years' residence in the United States, favorable disposition to the happiness of the nation, good moral character, and attachment to the principles of the Constitution. These prerequisites for naturalization are still in basically the same form today.

Married to U.S. citizens. Prior to 1922, married women were ineligible for judicial naturalization during coverture. The Act of September 22, 1922, however, eliminated sex and marital status as factors for eligibility and established a one year residence require-

ment for a woman who married a U.S. citizen. On May 24, 1934, another act provided similar benefits but extended them to the spouse of a U.S. citizen, woman or man, and set a 3-year residence requirement which has continued into the current statute.

Children of U.S. citizens. Statutes prior to the Act of October 14, 1940, made no provisions for the naturalization of a minor child except under special circumstances. Beginning with the 1940 Act, a child born outside the United States, one or both of whose parents is a U.S. citizen at the time of petitioning, may be naturalized if under the age of 18, if not otherwise disqualified, and if residing permanently in the United States with the citizen parent. No particular period of residence is required and if the child is of "tender years" he may be presumed to be of good moral character and attached to the principles of the Constitution. Children adopted by U.S. citizens before attaining 16 years of age were also first provided for in the 1940 Act and similar legislation was reenacted in the Act of October 3, 1965. The current law requires a specified period of residence, generally 2 years, but adoption does not have to be in the United States as specified in the earlier law.

Military. Prior to 1918, special provisions were not made for persons who had served in the U.S. Armed Forces. The Act of May 9, 1918, and subsequent amendments expiring December 8, 1943, provided for the simplified naturalization of veterans of World War I and prior conflicts. The Act of March 27, 1942, for which the termination date for filing petitions was set on December 31, 1946, gave special benefits to World War II servicemen. The Act of June 1, 1948, made permanent the provisions for the expeditious naturalization of persons serving honorably in the U.S. Armed Forces during World Wars I and II. On September 26, 1961, another act amended the above to include those serving in the Korean Conflict occurring between June 25, 1950, and July 1, 1955. The Act of October 24, 1968, added the Vietnam Conflict for a period beginning February 28, 1961, and ending on a date to be fixed by the President.

C 168–180. General note.

Prior to 1906, individual courts kept records of naturalizations, but no national data were compiled. The Act of 1906 required all courts conducting naturalization proceedings to file with a central Federal agency a copy of each declaration of intention and petition of naturalization filed and of each certificate of naturalization issued.

For 1907–1912, naturalization statistics were compiled by the Bureau of Immigration and Naturalization. For 1913–1932, they were compiled by the Bureau of Naturalization. For 1933–1940, they were given in the *Annual Report of the Secretary of Labor* and, for 1941, in the *Annual Report of the Attorney General*. No report was published in 1942. For subsequent years, the statistics appeared in the *Annual Report of the Immigration and Naturalization Service*.

C 168. Declarations filed, 1907–1970.

Source: 1907–1910, U.S. Department of Labor, *Annual Report of the Secretary of Labor*, 1940, p. 115; 1911–1970, U.S. Immigration and Naturalization Service, *Annual Report of Immigration and Naturalization Service*, annual issues.

See also general note for series C 168–180.

Section 331 of the Nationality Act of 1940 provided that an applicant for naturalization after reaching the age of 18 years must make, under oath, not less than 2 nor more than 7 years prior to his petition for naturalization, a signed declaration of intention to become a citizen. This section contained substantially the requirements of the Basic Naturalization Act of 1906 concerning the declaration of intention. The Immigration and Nationality Act of 1952, which repealed the Nationality Act of 1940, provides that a declaration of intention may be filed, but it is not a prerequisite to naturalization. In a number of States, in order to obtain employment, a license, etc., an alien applicant must prove that he intends to become a citizen. The law permits the filing of a declaration to show such intent.

Prior to 1930, the number of declarations of intention was far in excess of the number of aliens naturalized. This was due mainly to the failure of many aliens to file a petition for naturalization within the prescribed time limit, as well as the denial of a number of petitions for naturalization. In most of the years since 1930 the number of aliens naturalized has exceeded the declarations filed, because of the increasing number of persons who were exempted from the general requirements for a declaration of intention.

Since 1907, a number of laws were passed exempting special classes of persons from the general requirement of a declaration of intention. Most of these laws were codified into the Nationality Act of 1940. Included among such exempted classes were noncitizen spouses of United States citizens; certain former citizens; noncitizens who, because of misinformation, erroneously exercised the rights of citizenship; noncitizens who, at the time of entering the United States, were under 16 years of age; certain noncitizens who served honorably in the United States Armed Forces or on certain vessels; and certain noncitizen children.

C 169. Aliens naturalized, 1907–1970.

Source: See source for series C 168.

"Aliens naturalized" are aliens upon whom naturalization was conferred in the United States by a naturalization court or outside of the United States by a representative of the Immigration and Naturalization Service. The total number of aliens naturalized includes both civilian and military naturalizations. Statistics on naturalizations do not include repatriations.

Separate statistics on repatriations are compiled by the Immigration and Naturalization Service which also compiles statistics on certificates of derivative citizenship granted and denied, expatriations and certificates of naturalization revoked, and petitions for naturalization denied.

C 170–171. Aliens naturalized, by sex, 1923–1970.

Source: 1923–1932, U.S. Bureau of Naturalization, *Annual Report of the Commissioner of Naturalization*, annual issues; 1933–1940, U.S. Department of Labor, *Annual Report of the Secretary of Labor*, annual issues; 1941–1970, U.S. Immigration and Naturalization Service, *Annual Report of the Immigration and Naturalization Service*, annual issues.

See also general note for series C 168–180 and text for series C 169.

C 172–179. Aliens naturalized, by area of former allegiance, 1923–1970.

Source: U.S. Bureau of Naturalization, 1923–1932, *Annual Report of the Commissioner of Naturalization*, annual issues; U.S. Immigration and Naturalization Service, 1933–1935, unpublished data; 1936–1970, *Annual Report of the Immigration and Naturalization Service*, annual issues.

See also general note for series C 168–180.

"Country of former allegiance or nationality" is the country of which the alien at the time was a citizen or subject. Data on the number of aliens naturalized, by country or region of former allegiance, have been compiled only from 1922. Owing to changes in the list of countries separately reported and to changes in boundaries, data for certain countries are not comparable throughout. The principal changes in reporting since 1923 are shown for individual series below.

C 172, Northwestern Europe. Includes the British Empire, Norway, Sweden, Denmark, Netherlands, Belgium, Luxembourg, Switzerland, France, and, beginning 1948, Iceland. Beginning 1948, Ireland has been reported separately. Australia has been reported separately from 1951, and included in "All other" (series C 179). For earlier years, Ireland and Australia are included under the British Empire. See text for series C 176, C 177, and C 179 for former British territories.

C 173, Central Europe. Includes Germany, Poland, Czechoslovakia, Austria, Hungary, and Yugoslavia. For 1938–1947, Austria was included with Germany.

C 174, Eastern Europe. Includes the Union of Soviet Socialist Republics, Latvia, Estonia, Lithuania, Finland, Romania, Bulgaria, and Turkey. For 1923–1927, Lithuania comprised portions of Russia and Germany. European and Asiatic Turkey are included in Eastern Europe.

C 175, Southern Europe. Includes Greece, Italy, Spain, Portugal, and for 1929–1970, "Other Europe," which comprises Albania, the Free City of Danzig, Liechtenstein, San Marino, Monaco, Andorra, and for the years 1950–1959, Trieste. For 1923–1928, "Other Europe" was recorded under the "miscellaneous" group of countries and is included with "All other" (C 179).

C 176, Asia. The Asian countries reported separately and the beginning dates are shown below:

Afghanistan (1929); Arabian Peninsula (1943); Bhutan (1945); Burma (1949); Cambodia (1959); Ceylon (1948); China (1932); Cyprus (1961); India (1948, British Empire formerly); Indonesia (1950); Iran (1929); Iraq (1929); Israel (1950, Palestine formerly); Japan (1932); Jordan (1948, formerly called Trans-Jordan and included with Palestine prior to 1948); Korea (1948, Japan formerly); Kuwait (1962); Laos (1960); Lebanon (1950, included in Syria formerly); Malaysia (1963); Maldive Republic (1970); Muscat and Oman (1945); Nepal (1945); Pakistan (1948, included in British Empire formerly); Palestine (reported separately 1929–1944 and since 1948; included in British Empire 1945–1947); Philippines (1929); Saudi Arabia (1945); Singapore (1967); Southern Yemen (1969); Syria (reported separately 1928–1944, 1948–1958, and 1962–1970; included in France, 1944–1947 and in United Arab Republic, 1959–1961; Thailand (Siam, 1944); Vietnam (1952); Yemen (1950); and Tiawan (Formosa, 1957).

Until 1953, racial restrictions upon naturalization limited the naturalization of aliens who were citizens or subjects of countries located in Asia. (See text for series C 180.)

C 178, other America. Includes Mexico, the West Indies, Central and South America. Figures for Mexico date from 1924; for the West Indies (Cuba, Dominican Republic, and Haiti separately) from 1929. For 1924–1928, the figures for Central and South America were combined. Separate figures have been compiled for independent countries in Central and South America beginning with 1929, except in 1933.

C 179, all other. Includes "miscellaneous" countries 1923–1928; repatriated Americans, 1924–1934; "stateless" nationals from 1945; Ethiopia from 1929; Liberia from 1929; and countries which were former territories. Former territories and the beginning dates of separate report are shown below:

Formerly French territories: Libya (1953); Tunisia (1957); Sudan (1957); Morocco (1958); Guinea (1960); Central African Republic, Chad, Congo, Dahomey, Gabon, Ivory Coast, Malagasy Republic, Republic of Mali, Mauritania, Niger, Republic of Senegal, Togo, and Upper Volta (1961); Algeria and Cameroon (1963). Formerly British Territories: Egypt, included in British Empire, 1945–1947, reported separately 1929–1944 and since 1948; South West Africa (1952); Southern Rhodesia (1953); Union of South Africa (1948); Australia (1951); Nauru (1952); New Guinea (1952); New Zealand (1952); and Western Samoa (1952). Ghana (1959), Nigeria and Sierra Leone (1961); Tanganyika (1962); Kenya (1964), Malawi, Uganda, and Zanzibar (1965); Zambia (1966); Gambia (1967); Tanzania (1968), Botswana and Lesotho (1969), Mauritius and Swaziland (1970). Formerly Belgian territories: Republic of the Congo (1961), Burundi and Rwanda (1964). Formerly Italian Administration: Somaliland (1953; Somali Republic as of

1961). Formerly international administration: Tangier (1953). Separate figures are available for the following United States possessions: American Samoa, Canal Zone, Puerto Rico, Virgin Islands, and Wake and Midway Islands (1945–1951 and since 1955); Hawaii (1955–1959); Guam (1944–1951, and since 1955); Bonin Islands (1962–1968); Christmas Islands (since 1964); the Ryukyu Islands (since 1960); and Swains Island (since 1962).

C 180. Petitions denied, 1907–1970.

Source: 1907–1921, U.S. Bureau of Naturalization, *Report of Commissioner of Naturalization*, as follows: 1907–1917, *Report* for 1917, p. 5; 1918–1919, *Report* for 1919, p. 4; 1920, *Report* for 1920, pp. 5–6; 1921–1957, U.S. Immigration and Naturalization Service, *Annual Report of Immigration and Naturalization Service*, annual issues.

See also general note for series C 168–180.

Statistics on petitions denied have been compiled since 1907. The Basic Naturalization Act of 1906 and subsequent naturalization laws specified the eligibility requirements for naturalization. Petitions for naturalization of aliens who fail to meet the prerequisites for naturalization may be denied by the courts at the final naturalization hearing. Included among the reasons for denial are lack of knowledge and understanding of history, principles, and form of government of the United States, failure to establish good moral character, lack of attachment to the Constitution of the United States, inability to speak (read, write) the English language, failure to establish lawful admission to the United States or to meet residence requirements, etc.

In the early laws the right to become naturalized was limited to white persons, and petitions of persons of ineligible races were denied. Gradually such restrictions were removed with respect to Negroes, Filipinos, races indigenous to North and South America and adjacent islands, Chinese, and Guamanians. In 1952, the Immigration and Nationality Act removed all racial restrictions to naturalization.

C 181–194. Citizenship status of the population, 1890–1970.

Source: U.S. Bureau of the Census. 1890–1940, total, native, and total foreign-born population, and 1930–1940, citizenship status of foreign born and persons 21 years old and over, Sixteenth Census Reports, *Population*, vol. II, part 1; 1890–1920, data on persons 21 years old and over, and 1920, citizenship status of foreign born, Fifteenth Census Reports, *Population*, vol. II; 1950, *U.S. Census of Population: 1950*, vol. II, part 1; 1960, *U.S. Census of Population: 1960*, vol. I, part 1; 1970, *U.S. Census of Population: 1970*, vol. II, *Subject Reports*.

Citizenship. Information on citizenship was used to classify the population into two major categories, citizens and aliens. Citizens are further classified as native or naturalized. "Native" includes all persons born in the United States, Puerto Rico, the Canal Zone, Guam, American Samoa, or the Virgin Islands and persons born abroad of American parents or at sea. It was assumed that all natives were citizens. See also text for series A 105–118.

In 1970, when information on citizenship was missing, it was assigned on the basis of related information.

These statistics relate to the citizenship status of the population at the date of the specified decennial census.

C 195–227. Native population of foreign or mixed parentage, by country of origin of parents, 1900–1970.

Source: U.S. Bureau of the Census. 1900–1940, Sixteenth Census Reports, *Population, Country of Origin of Foreign Stock*; 1950, *U.S. Census of Population: 1950*, vol. IV, Special Reports, *Nativity and Parentage*; 1960, *U.S. Census of Population: 1960*, vol. I, part 1; 1970, *U.S. Census of Population: 1970*, vol. II, *Subject Reports*.

The category "native" comprises persons born in the United States, in the Commonwealth of Puerto Rico, in an outlying area of the

United States, or at sea. Also included in this category is the small number of persons who, although they were born in a foreign country, have at least one native American parent. When information on place of birth was missing, nativity was assigned on the basis of related information. In previous censuses, persons for whom nativity was not reported were generally classified as native. The rules for determining the nativity of parents are generally the same as those for determining the nativity of the person himself.

Parentage. Information on birthplace of parents is used to classify the native population into two categories: native of native parentage and native of foreign or mixed parentage. The category "native of native parentage" comprises native persons with both parents born in the United States. The category "native of foreign or mixed parentage" includes native persons with one or both parents foreign born.

The definition of country of birth of parents is similar to that used in series C 228–295, below, with one important exception. The classification by country of birth of parents for 1930 and later years is made on the basis of boundaries existing at the date of the specified decennial census. This is the same procedure used for all of the years in series C 228–295. However, the 1920 data on country of birth of parents shown in this series are based on pre-World War I boundaries because of the difficulty of obtaining correct replies on the basis of postwar boundaries for parents of persons enumerated.

See also text for series A 91–104, A 105–118, A 119–134, and A 135–142.

C 228–295. Foreign-born population, by country of birth, 1850–1970.

Source: U.S. Bureau of the Census. 1850–1930, total foreign born, Fifteenth Census Reports, *Population*, vol. II, p. 233; 1910–1940, foreign-born white, Sixteenth Census Reports, *Population*, vol. II, part 1, p. 43; 1950, *U.S. Census of Population: 1950*, vol. IV, *Special Reports, Nativity and Parentage*, p. 3A-71 and vol. IV, *Special Reports, Nonwhite Population by Race*, p. 3B-82, and unpublished data; 1960, *U.S. Census of Population: 1960*, vol. I, part 1; 1970, *U.S. Census of Population: 1970*, vol. II, *Subject Reports*.

The foreign born population comprises all persons born outside the United States, Puerto Rico, or an outlying area of the United States, except those persons with at least one American parent. Persons born in any of the outlying areas, and American citizens born abroad or at sea, are regarded as native.

The statistics on country of birth are generally based on the political boundaries of foreign nations existing at the date of the specified decennial census. Because of boundary changes following World War I and World War II, accurate comparisons over the entire period, 1850–1950, can be made for relatively few countries. These countries include England, Scotland, Wales, Norway, Sweden, Netherlands, Switzerland, Spain, Portugal, Canada (total of Canada-French, Canada-other, and Newfoundland), and Mexico. For several other countries, as for example, Italy, France, and Belgium, the figures are slightly affected by boundary changes; but these changes have not been so great as to destroy entirely the value of comparative figures. The boundaries of other countries, as for example, U.S.S.R., Austria, Hungary, Romania, and Greece, have been so changed that comparisons over time are subject to a large margin of error.

Statistics on country of birth of the foreign born have generally been restricted to those countries which had at the time of the census a separate political entity. For 1860–1900, however, an exception was made in the case of Poland. Although Poland was not restored to its original status as an independent country until the end of World War I, its historical position was such that Polish immigrants generally regarded Poland as their country of birth regardless of the political sovereignty over their birthplace. For 1860–1890, persons reported as born in Poland were so tabulated without qualification. In the census of 1900, an attempt was made to distinguish Austrian, German, and Russian Poland, and separate statistics for each were presented. In the census of 1910, persons reported as born in Poland were assigned either to Russia, Germany, or Austria. The figures for 1910, however, have been adjusted on the basis of mother tongue data, to conform as nearly as possible to the conditions in 1930.

Since World War I, the greatest difficulties encountered in the country-of-birth statistics have been the classification of persons born in the former Austro-Hungarian Empire. Many persons born within the prewar boundaries of this Empire could not or did not give the census enumerator the information needed for the determination of their country of birth on the basis of postwar geography. It is therefore quite possible that some persons were assigned to Austria who were really born within the present areas of either Czechoslovakia or Yugoslavia, and that persons were assigned to Hungary who were born within the present areas of Romania or Yugoslavia. Similarly, it is possible that some persons born in Latvia, Estonia, or Lithuania were assigned to Russia. Persons for whom Austria-Hungary was reported in the 1950 census were allocated on the basis of surname to the various countries created out of the territory of the old empire after World War I. Even with this procedure, however, there appears to be some indication that Austria and Hungary are overreported at the expense of Yugoslavia and Czechoslovakia. In 1950 the situation was further complicated by the fact that, although there were extensive de facto boundary changes as a result of World War II, only a small number of these changes were officially recognized by the United States at that time.

Since 1950, persons have been allocated to a specific country based on mother tongue data.

See also text for series A 91–104 and A 105–118.

C 296–301. Passenger arrivals and departures, 1908–1970.

Source: U.S. Bureau of Immigration, 1908–1930, *Annual Report of the Commissioner General of Immigration.* U.S. Immigration and Naturalization Service, 1931–1949, *Report of Passenger Travel Between the United States and Foreign Countries,* annual issues; 1950–1970, *Annual Report of the Immigration and Naturalization Service,* annual issues.

Statistics on passenger travel are obtained from passenger manifests or lists required by law to be prepared by carriers for vessels and aircraft traveling between the United States and foreign countries. Arrival manifests were first required under the Act of 1819, while similar manifests of departing passengers were first required under the Act of 1907.

Prior to 1908, statistical information on passenger travel is incomplete. From 1820 through 1856, reports showed the total number of alien passengers arrived. During the years 1857 through 1867, data reflected the arrivals of immigrants as well as all alien passenger arrivals. Beginning in 1868, the data related to immigrant arrivals only, a practice that continued until 1906, when alien arrivals were classified into two groups: immigrants and nonimmigrants. No record of the movement of U.S. citizen passengers was made before 1908.

Data relating to the inward and outward movement of passengers became complete in 1908, when, as the result of the Act of 1907, departure records were first compiled. U.S. citizen passengers were also reported for the first time during that year.

C 302–331. Passengers arriving and departing by area of embarkation or debarkation, flag of carrier, and mode of travel, 1931–1970.

Source: U.S. Immigration and Naturalization Service, 1931–1949, *Report of Passenger Travel Between the United States and Foreign Countries,* annual issues; 1950–1970, *Annual Report of the Immigration and Naturalization Service,* annual issues.

Detailed statistics relating to the inward and outward movement of passengers were first reported in 1931. These data have, since their inception, been derived from passenger manifests or lists required by law of international carriers arriving in and departing from the United States.

Country of embarkation is the foreign country where the passenger boards the vessel or aircraft which brings him to the United States; country of debarkation is the foreign country where the passenger disembarks from the vessel or aircraft which he boarded in a U.S. port. The origin or final destination of the passenger is not reported. For example, a passenger proceeding from Frankfurt to Paris, where he boards a plane for New York, is counted as arrived in New York from France. Flag of carrier means the nationality of the carrier; cruise travel denotes movement of passengers who embark on a carrier at a U.S. port for a round trip cruise to foreign territory and return on the same carrier. Cruise travel is counted for both inbound and outbound passengers.

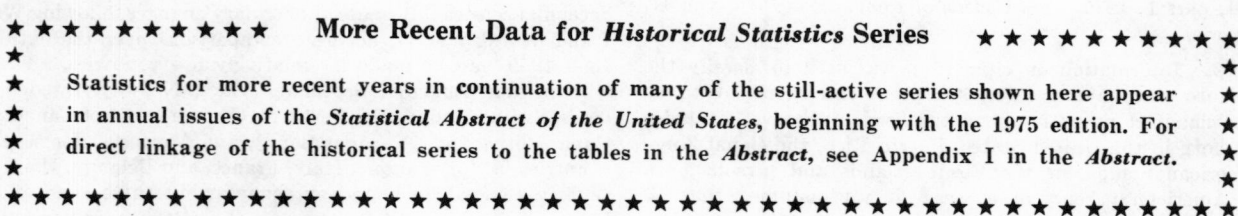

★ ★ ★ ★ ★ ★ ★ ★ ★ ★ **More Recent Data for *Historical Statistics* Series** ★ ★ ★ ★ ★ ★ ★ ★ ★ ★

★ Statistics for more recent years in continuation of many of the still-active series shown here appear in annual issues of the *Statistical Abstract of the United States,* beginning with the 1975 edition. For direct linkage of the historical series to the tables in the *Abstract,* see Appendix I in the *Abstract.*

Series C 89–119. Immigrants, by Country: 1820 to 1970

[For years ending June 30, except: 1820–1831 and 1844–1849, years ending Sept. 30; 1833–1842 and 1851–1867, years ending Dec. 31; 1832 covers 15 months ending Dec. 31; 1843, 9 months ending Sept. 30; 1850, 15 months ending Dec. 31; 1868, 6 months ending June 30]

Year	All countries [1]	Total	Northwestern Europe — Great Britain	Ireland [2]	Scandinavia [3]	Other Northwestern [4]	Central Europe — Germany [5]	Poland	Other Central [6]	U.S.S.R. and Baltic States [7]	Other Eastern [8]	Italy	Other Southern [9]
	89	90	91	92	93	94	95	96	97	98	99	100	101
1970	373,326	110,653	14,089	1,583	2,110	6,961	10,632	2,013	10,411	836	1,357	27,369	33,292
1969	358,579	114,052	15,072	1,981	2,149	5,944	10,380	2,115	8,889	574	1,158	27,033	38,757
1968	454,448	129,022	26,025	2,995	4,203	9,873	16,590	3,676	5,659	974	883	25,882	32,262
1967	361,972	128,775	23,004	2,765	4,230	9,881	16,595	4,356	5,116	876	899	28,487	32,566
1966	323,040	115,898	18,777	3,267	4,549	9,049	17,654	8,490	3,972	768	878	26,447	22,047
1965	296,697	101,468	24,135	5,187	5,853	11,526	22,432	7,093	3,693	632	859	10,874	9,184
1964	292,248	108,215	25,758	6,055	5,497	11,120	24,494	7,097	3,248	763	1,054	12,769	10,360
1963	306,260	109,066	22,708	5,746	5,208	11,938	24,727	6,785	3,244	591	996	16,175	10,948
1962	283,763	103,989	18,066	5,118	4,716	13,117	21,477	5,660	2,533	753	753	20,119	11,677
1961	271,344	108,532	18,719	5,738	4,943	14,635	25,815	6,254	2,911	996	620	18,956	8,945
1960	265,398	120,178	19,967	6,918	6,185	17,234	29,452	4,216	9,073	856	761	13,369	12,147
1959	260,686	138,191	18,325	6,595	6,100	14,217	32,039	2,800	30,738	775	726	16,804	9,072
1958	253,265	115,198	24,147	9,134	5,873	11,364	29,498	1,470	3,508	641	673	23,115	5,775
1957	326,867	169,625	24,020	8,227	6,189	25,109	60,353	571	15,498	663	558	19,624	8,813
1956	321,625	156,866	19,008	5,607	5,681	15,254	44,409	263	10,284	643	394	40,430	14,893
1955	237,790	110,591	15,761	5,222	5,159	10,707	29,596	129	4,133	523	134	30,272	8,955
1954	208,177	92,121	16,672	4,655	5,459	11,853	33,098	67	2,873	475	104	13,145	3,720
1953	170,434	82,352	16,639	4,304	5,537	11,145	27,329	136	2,885	609	86	8,432	5,250
1952	265,520	193,626	22,177	3,526	5,416	12,476	104,236	235	23,529	548	137	11,342	10,004
1951	205,717	149,545	14,898	3,144	5,502	10,973	87,755	98	10,365	555	223	8,958	7,074
1950	249,187	199,115	12,755	5,842	5,661	10,857	128,592	696	17,792	526	277	12,454	3,663
1949	188,317	129,592	21,149	8,678	6,665	12,288	55,284	1,673	7,411	694	246	11,695	3,809
1948	170,570	103,544	26,403	7,534	6,127	13,721	19,368	2,447	6,006	897	485	16,075	4,481
1947	147,292	83,535	23,788	2,574	4,918	14,562	13,900	745	4,622	761	249	13,866	3,550
1946	108,721	52,852	33,552	1,816	1,278	8,651	2,598	335	511	153	98	2,636	1,224
1945	38,119	5,943	3,029	427	224	365	172	195	206	98	97	213	917
1944	28,551	4,509	1,321	112	281	619	238	292	316	157	109	120	944
1943	23,725	4,920	974	165	239	1,531	248	394	206	159	54	49	901
1942	28,781	11,153	907	83	371	5,622	2,150	343	396	197	117	103	864
1941	51,776	26,541	7,714	272	1,137	9,009	4,028	451	786	665	299	450	1,730
1940	70,756	50,454	6,158	839	1,260	7,743	21,520	702	3,628	898	491	5,302	1,913
1939	82,998	63,138	3,058	1,189	1,178	5,214	33,515	3,072	5,334	1,021	620	6,570	2,367
1938	67,895	44,495	2,262	1,085	1,393	3,352	17,199	2,403	5,195	960	542	7,712	2,392
1937	50,244	31,863	1,726	531	971	2,512	10,895	1,212	3,763	629	533	7,192	1,899
1936	36,329	23,480	1,310	444	646	1,745	6,346	869	2,723	378	424	6,774	1,821
1935	34,956	22,778	1,413	454	688	1,808	5,201	1,504	2,357	418	453	6,566	1,916
1934	29,470	17,210	1,305	443	557	1,270	4,392	1,032	1,422	607	347	4,374	1,461
1933	23,068	12,383	979	338	511	1,045	1,919	1,332	981	458	352	3,477	991
1932	35,576	20,579	2,057	539	938	1,558	2,670	1,296	1,749	636	592	6,662	1,882
1931	97,139	61,909	9,110	7,305	3,144	4,420	10,401	3,664	4,500	1,396	1,192	13,399	3,438
1930	241,700	147,438	31,015	23,445	6,919	9,170	26,569	9,231	9,184	2,772	2,159	22,327	4,647
1929	279,678	158,598	21,327	19,921	17,379	9,091	46,751	9,002	8,081	2,450	2,153	18,008	4,435
1928	307,255	158,513	19,958	25,268	16,184	9,079	45,778	8,755	7,091	2,652	1,776	17,728	4,244
1927	335,175	168,368	23,669	28,545	16,860	9,134	48,513	9,211	6,559	2,933	1,708	17,297	3,939
1926	304,488	155,562	25,528	24,897	16,818	8,773	50,421	7,126	6,020	3,323	1,596	8,253	2,807
1925	294,314	148,366	27,172	26,650	16,810	8,548	46,068	5,341	4,701	3,121	1,566	6,203	2,186
1924	706,896	364,339	59,490	17,111	35,577	16,077	75,091	28,806	32,700	20,918	13,173	56,246	9,150
1923	522,919	307,920	45,759	15,740	34,184	12,469	48,277	26,538	34,038	21,151	16,082	46,674	7,008
1922	309,556	216,385	25,153	10,579	14,625	11,149	17,931	28,635	29,363	19,910	12,244	40,319	6,477
1921	805,228	652,364	51,142	28,435	22,854	29,317	6,803	95,089	77,069	10,193	32,793	222,260	76,409
1920	430,001	246,295	38,471	9,591	13,444	24,491	1,001	4,813	5,666	1,751	3,913	95,145	48,009
1919	141,132	24,627	6,797	474	5,590	5,126	52	(10)	53	1,403	51	1,884	3,197
1918	110,618	31,063	2,516	331	6,506	3,146	447	(10)	61	4,242	93	5,250	8,471
1917	295,403	133,083	10,735	5,406	13,771	6,731	1,857	(10)	1,258	12,716	369	34,596	45,644
1916	298,826	145,699	16,063	8,639	14,761	8,715	2,877	(10)	5,191	7,842	1,167	33,665	46,779
1915	326,700	197,919	27,237	14,185	17,883	12,096	7,799	(10)	18,511	26,187	2,892	49,688	21,441
1914	1,218,480	1,058,391	48,729	24,688	29,391	25,591	35,734	(10)	278,152	255,660	21,420	283,738	55,288
1913	1,197,892	1,055,855	60,328	27,876	32,267	28,086	34,329	(10)	254,825	291,040	18,036	265,542	43,526
1912	838,172	718,875	57,148	25,879	27,554	22,921	27,788	(10)	178,882	162,395	20,925	157,134	38,249
1911	878,587	764,757	73,384	29,112	42,285	25,549	32,061	(10)	159,057	158,721	21,655	182,882	40,051
1910	1,041,570	926,291	68,941	29,855	48,267	23,852	31,283	(10)	258,737	186,792	25,287	215,537	37,740
1909	751,786	654,875	46,793	25,033	32,496	17,756	25,540	(10)	170,191	120,460	11,659	183,218	21,729
1908	782,870	691,901	62,824	30,556	30,175	22,177	32,309	(10)	168,509	156,711	27,345	128,503	32,792
1907	1,285,349	1,199,566	79,037	34,530	49,965	26,512	37,807	(10)	338,452	258,943	36,510	285,731	52,079
1906	1,100,735	1,018,365	67,198	34,995	52,781	23,277	37,564	(10)	265,138	215,665	18,652	273,120	29,975
1905	1,026,499	974,273	84,189	52,945	60,625	24,693	40,574	(10)	275,693	184,897	11,022	221,479	18,156
1904	812,870	767,933	51,448	36,142	60,096	23,321	46,380	(10)	177,156	145,141	12,756	193,296	22,197
1903	857,046	814,507	33,637	35,310	77,647	17,009	40,086	(10)	206,011	136,093	12,600	230,622	25,492
1902	648,743	619,068	16,898	29,138	54,038	10,322	28,304	(10)	171,989	107,347	8,234	178,375	14,423
1901	487,918	469,237	14,985	30,561	39,234	9,279	21,651	(10)	113,390	85,257	8,199	135,996	10,685
1900	448,572	424,700	12,509	35,730	31,151	5,822	18,507	(10)	114,847	90,787	6,852	100,135	8,360
1899	311,715	297,349	13,456	31,673	22,192	5,150	17,476	(10)	62,491	60,982	1,738	77,419	4,772
1898	229,299	217,786	12,894	25,128	19,282	4,698	17,111	4,726	39,797	29,828	1,076	58,613	4,633
1897	230,832	216,397	12,752	28,421	21,089	5,323	22,533	4,165	33,031	25,816	943	59,431	2,893
1896	343,267	329,067	24,565	40,262	33,199	7,611	31,885	691	65,103	51,445	954	68,060	5,292
1895	258,536	250,342	28,833	46,304	26,852	7,313	32,173	790	33,401	35,907	768	35,427	2,574
1894	285,631	277,052	22,520	30,231	32,400	9,514	53,989	1,941	38,638	39,278	1,027	42,977	4,537
1893	439,730	429,324	35,189	43,578	58,945	17,888	78,756	16,374	57,420	42,310	625	72,145	6,094
1892	579,663	570,876	42,215	51,383	66,295	21,731	119,168	40,536	76,937	81,511	1,331	61,631	8,138
1891	560,319	546,085	66,605	55,706	60,107	21,824	113,554	27,497	71,042	47,426	1,222	76,055	5,047

See footnotes at end of p. 106.

Series C 89–119. Immigrants, by Country: 1820 to 1970—Con.

[For years ending June 30, except: 1820–1831 and 1844–1849, years ending Sept. 30; 1833–1842 and 1851–1867, years ending Dec. 31; 1832 covers 15 months ending Dec. 31; 1843, 9 months ending Sept. 30; 1850, 15 months ending Dec. 31; 1868, 6 months ending June 30]

			Europe										
			Northwestern Europe				Central Europe			Eastern Europe		Southern Europe	
Year	All countries [1]	Total	Great Britain	Ireland [2]	Scandinavia [3]	Other North-western [4]	Germany [5]	Poland	Other Central [6]	U.S.S.R. and Baltic States [7]	Other Eastern [8]	Italy	Other Southern [9]
	89	90	91	92	93	94	95	96	97	98	99	100	101
1890	455,302	445,680	69,730	53,024	50,368	20,575	92,427	11,073	56,199	35,598	723	52,003	3,960
1889	444,427	434,790	87,992	65,557	57,504	22,010	99,538	4,922	34,174	33,916	1,145	25,307	2,725
1888	546,889	538,131	108,692	73,513	81,924	23,251	109,717	5,826	45,811	33,487	1,393	51,558	2,959
1887	490,109	482,829	93,378	68,370	67,629	17,307	106,865	6,128	40,265	30,766	2,251	47,622	2,248
1886	334,203	329,529	62,929	49,619	46,735	11,737	84,403	3,939	28,680	17,800	670	21,315	1,702
1885	395,346	353,083	57,713	51,795	40,704	13,732	124,443	3,085	27,309	17,158	941	13,642	2,561
1884	518,592	453,686	65,950	63,344	52,728	18,768	179,676	4,536	36,571	12,689	388	16,510	2,526
1883	603,322	522,587	76,606	81,486	71,994	24,271	194,786	2,011	27,625	9,909	163	31,792	1,944
1882	788,992	648,186	102,991	76,432	105,326	27,796	250,630	4,672	29,150	16,918	134	32,159	1,978
1881	669,431	528,545	81,376	72,342	81,582	26,883	210,485	5,614	27,935	5,041	102	15,401	1,784
1880	457,257	348,691	73,273	71,603	65,657	15,042	84,638	2,177	17,267	5,014	35	12,354	1,631
1879	177,826	134,259	29,955	20,013	21,820	9,081	34,602	489	5,963	4,453	29	5,791	2,063
1878	138,469	101,612	22,150	15,932	12,254	6,929	29,313	547	5,150	3,048	29	4,344	1,916
1877	141,857	106,195	23,581	14,569	11,274	8,621	29,298	533	5,396	6,599	32	3,195	3,097
1876	169,986	120,920	29,291	19,575	12,323	10,923	31,937	925	6,276	4,775	38	3,015	1,842
1875	227,498	182,961	47,905	37,957	14,322	11,987	47,769	984	7,658	7,997	27	3,631	2,724
1874	313,339	262,783	62,021	53,707	19,178	15,998	87,291	1,795	8,850	4,073	62	7,666	2,142
1873	459,803	397,541	89,500	77,344	35,481	22,892	149,671	3,338	7,112	1,634	53	8,757	1,759
1872	404,806	352,155	84,912	68,732	28,575	15,614	141,109	1,647	4,410	1,018	20	4,190	1,928
1871	321,350	265,145	85,455	57,439	22,132	7,174	82,554	535	4,887	673	23	2,816	1,457
1870	387,203	328,626	103,677	56,996	30,742	9,152	118,225	223	4,425	907	6	2,891	1,382
1869	352,768	315,963	84,438	40,786	43,941	10,585	131,042	184	1,499	343	18	1,489	1,638
1868	138,840	130,090	24,127	32,068	11,985	4,293	55,831	-	192	141	4	891	558
1867	315,722	283,751	52,641	72,879	8,491	12,417	133,426	310	692	205	26	1,624	1,040
1866	318,568	278,916	94,924	36,690	14,495	13,648	115,892	412	93	287	18	1,382	1,075
1865	248,120	214,048	82,465	29,772	7,258	7,992	83,424	528	422	183	14	924	1,066
1864	193,418	185,233	53,428	63,523	2,961	5,621	57,276	165	230	256	11	600	1,162
1863	176,282	163,733	66,882	55,916	3,119	3,245	33,162	94	85	77	16	547	590
1862	91,985	83,710	24,639	23,351	2,550	4,386	27,529	63	111	79	11	566	425
1861	91,918	81,200	19,675	23,797	850	3,769	31,661	48	51	34	5	811	499
1860	153,640	141,209	29,737	48,637	840	5,278	54,491	82	----------	65	4	1,019	1,056
1859	121,282	110,949	26,163	35,216	1,590	3,727	41,784	106	----------	91	10	932	1,330
1858	123,126	111,354	28,956	26,873	2,662	4,580	45,310	9	----------	246	17	1,240	1,461
1857	251,306	224,224	58,479	54,361	2,747	6,879	91,781	124	----------	25	11	1,007	810
1856	200,436	186,083	44,658	54,349	1,330	12,403	71,028	20	----------	9	5	1,365	916
1855	200,877	187,729	47,572	49,627	1,349	14,571	71,918	462	----------	13	9	1,052	1,156
1854	427,833	405,542	58,647	101,606	4,222	23,070	215,009	208	----------	2	7	1,263	1,508
1853	368,645	361,576	37,576	162,649	3,396	14,205	141,946	33	----------	3	15	555	1,198
1852	371,603	362,484	40,699	159,548	4,106	11,278	145,918	110	----------	2	3	351	469
1851	379,466	369,510	51,487	221,253	2,438	20,905	72,482	10	----------	1	2	447	485
1850	369,980	308,323	51,085	164,004	1,589	11,470	78,896	5	----------	31	15	431	797
1849	297,024	286,501	55,132	159,398	3,481	7,634	60,235	4	----------	44	9	209	355
1848	226,527	218,025	35,159	112,934	1,113	9,877	58,465	-	----------	1	3	241	232
1847	234,968	229,117	23,302	105,536	1,320	24,336	74,281	8	----------	5	2	164	163
1846	154,416	146,315	22,180	51,752	2,030	12,303	57,561	4	----------	248	4	151	82
1845	114,371	109,301	19,210	44,821	982	9,466	34,355	6	----------	1	3	137	320
1844	78,615	74,745	14,353	33,490	1,336	4,343	20,731	36	----------	13	10	141	292
1843	52,496	49,013	8,430	19,670	1,777	4,364	14,441	17	----------	6	5	117	186
1842	104,565	99,945	22,005	51,342	588	5,361	20,370	10	----------	28	2	100	139
1841	80,289	76,216	16,188	37,772	226	6,077	15,291	15	----------	174	6	179	288
1840	84,066	80,126	2,613	39,430	207	7,978	29,704	5	----------	-	1	37	151
1839	68,069	64,148	10,271	23,963	380	7,891	21,028	46	----------	7	1	84	477
1838	38,914	34,070	5,420	12,645	112	3,839	11,683	41	----------	13	-	86	231
1837	79,340	71,039	12,218	28,508	399	5,769	23,740	81	----------	19	-	36	269
1836	76,242	70,465	13,106	30,578	473	5,189	20,707	53	----------	2	3	115	239
1835	45,374	41,987	8,970	20,927	68	3,369	8,311	54	----------	9	-	60	219
1834	65,365	57,510	10,490	24,474	66	4,468	17,686	54	----------	15	1	105	151
1833	58,640	29,111	4,916	8,648	189	5,355	6,988	1	----------	159	1	1,699	1,155
1832	60,482	34,193	5,331	12,436	334	5,695	10,194	34	----------	52	-	3	114
1831	22,633	13,039	2,475	5,772	36	2,277	2,413	-	----------	1	-	28	37
1830	23,322	7,217	1,153	2,721	19	1,305	1,976	2	----------	3	2	9	27
1829	22,520	12,523	3,179	7,415	30	1,065	597	1	----------	1	1	23	212
1828	27,382	24,729	5,352	12,488	60	4,700	1,851	1	----------	7	6	34	230
1827	18,875	16,719	4,186	9,766	28	1,829	432	1	----------	19	1	35	422
1826	10,837	9,751	2,319	5,408	26	968	511	-	----------	4	2	57	456
1825	10,199	8,543	2,095	4,888	18	719	450	1	----------	10	-	75	287
1824	7,912	4,965	1,264	2,345	20	671	230	4	----------	7	2	45	377
1823	6,354	4,016	1,100	1,908	7	528	183	3	----------	7	2	33	245
1822	6,911	4,418	1,221	2,267	28	522	148	3	----------	10	4	35	180
1821	9,127	5,936	3,210	1,518	24	521	383	1	----------	7	-	35	209
1820	8,385	7,691	2,410	3,614	23	452	968	5	----------	14	1	30	174

- Represents zero.

[1] For 1820–1867 excludes returning citizens; therefore, for those years, does not agree with series C 120 and C 138.
[2] Comprises Eire and Northern Ireland.
[3] Comprises Norway, Sweden, Denmark, and Iceland.
[4] Comprises Netherlands, Belgium, Luxembourg, Switzerland, and France.
[5] Includes Austria, 1938 to 1945.
[6] Comprises Czechoslovakia (since 1920), Yugoslavia (since 1920), Hungary (since 1861), and Austria (since 1861, except for the years 1938–1945, when Austria was included with Germany).
[7] Comprises U.S.S.R. (excluding Asian U.S.S.R. between 1931 and 1963, Latvia, Estonia, Lithuania, and Finland).
[8] Comprises Romania, Bulgaria, and Turkey in Europe.
[9] Comprises Spain, Portugal, Greece, and other Europe, not elsewhere classified.
[10] Between 1899 and 1919, included with Austria-Hungary, Germany, and Russia.

Series C 89–119. Immigrants, by Country: 1820 to 1970—Con.

For years ending June 30, except: 1820–1831 and 1844–1849, years ending Sept. 30; 1833–1842 and 1851–1867, years ending Dec. 31; 1832 covers 15 months ending Dec. 31; 1843, 9 months ending Sept. 30; 1850, 15 months ending Dec. 31; 1868, 6 months ending June 30]

Year	Asia								America				
	Total	Turkey in Asia [11]	China [12]	India	Japan [13]	Korea [14]	Philippines	Other Asia	Total	Canada and Newfoundland [15]	Mexico	West Indies	Other America
	102	103	104	105	106	107	108	109	110	111	112	113	114
1970	90,215	495	6,427	8,795	4,731	8,888	30,507	30,372	161,727	26,850	44,821	56,614	33,442
1969	72,959	556	5,264	5,205	4,095	5,854	20,263	31,722	164,045	29,303	45,748	53,190	35,804
1968	56,298	325	4,851	4,165	3,810	3,592	16,086	23,469	262,736	41,716	44,716	140,827	35,477
1967	57,574	491	7,118	4,129	4,125	3,845	10,336	27,530	170,235	34,768	43,034	61,987	30,446
1966	40,113	365	2,948	2,293	3,468	2,414	5,894	22,731	162,551	37,273	47,217	37,999	40,062
1965	20,040	365	1,611	467	3,294	2,139	2,963	9,201	171,019	50,035	40,686	31,141	49,157
1964	21,279	331	2,684	488	3,774	2,329	2,862	8,811	158,644	51,114	34,448	24,067	49,015
1963	23,242	307	1,605	965	4,147	2,560	3,483	10,175	169,966	50,509	55,986	22,951	40,520
1962	20,249	304	1,356	390	4,054	1,463	3,354	9,328	155,871	44,272	55,805	20,917	34,877
1961	19,495	296	900	292	4,490	1,442	2,628	9,447	139,580	47,470	41,476	20,520	30,114
1960	21,604	200	1,380	244	5,699	1,410	2,791	9,880	119,525	46,668	32,708	13,636	26,513
1959	25,259	229	1,702	351	6,248	1,614	2,503	12,612	93,061	34,599	22,909	12,109	23,444
1958	20,870	197	1,143	323	6,847	1,470	2,034	8,856	113,132	45,143	26,791	16,983	24,215
1957	20,008	77	2,098	196	6,829	577	1,874	8,357	134,160	46,354	49,321	18,362	20,123
1956	17,327	48	1,386	185	5,967	579	1,792	7,370	144,713	42,363	61,320	19,512	21,518
1955	10,935	54	568	194	4,150	263	1,598	4,108	110,436	32,435	43,702	12,876	21,423
1954	9,970	33	254	144	3,846	175	1,234	4,284	95,587	34,873	30,645	8,411	21,658
1953	8,231	13	528	104	2,579	75	1,074	3,858	77,650	36,283	17,183	8,628	15,556
1952	9,328	12	263	123	3,814	47	1,179	3,890	61,049	33,354	9,079	6,672	11,944
1951	7,149	3	335	109	271	21	3,228	3,182	47,631	25,880	6,153	5,902	9,696
1950	4,508	13	1,280	121	100	24	729	2,241	44,191	21,885	6,744	6,206	9,356
1949	7,595	40	3,415	175	529	39	1,157	2,240	49,334	25,156	8,083	6,733	9,362
1948	11,907	16	7,203	263	423	44	1,168	2,790	52,746	25,485	8,384	6,932	11,945
1947	6,733	22	3,191	432	131	----------	910	2,047	52,753	24,342	7,558	6,728	14,125
1946	2,108	16	252	425	14	----------	475	926	46,066	21,344	7,146	5,878	11,698
1945	461	13	71	103	1	----------	19	254	29,646	11,530	6,702	5,452	5,962
1944	231	15	50	41	4	----------	4	117	23,084	10,143	6,598	3,198	3,145
1943	342	36	65	71	20	----------	8	142	18,162	9,761	4,172	2,312	1,917
1942	615	31	179	36	44	----------	51	274	16,377	10,599	2,378	1,599	1,801
1941	1,971	16	1,003	94	289	----------	170	399	22,445	11,473	2,824	4,687	3,461
1940	2,050	7	643	52	102	----------	137	1,109	17,822	11,078	2,313	2,675	1,756
1939	2,281	15	642	36	102	----------	119	1,367	17,139	10,813	2,640	2,231	1,455
1938	2,492	11	613	34	93	----------	116	1,625	20,486	14,404	2,502	2,110	1,470
1937	1,149	13	293	47	132	----------	84	580	16,903	12,011	2,347	1,322	1,223
1936	793	20	273	13	91	----------	72	324	11,786	8,121	1,716	985	964
1935	682	31	229	32	88	----------	(16)	302	11,174	7,782	1,560	931	901
1934	597	22	187	28	86	----------	----------	274	11,409	7,945	1,801	861	802
1933	552	27	148	44	75	----------	----------	258	9,925	6,187	1,936	862	940
1932	1,931	43	750	87	526	----------	----------	525	12,577	8,003	2,171	1,029	1,374
1931	3,345	139	1,150	123	653	----------	----------	1,280	30,816	22,183	3,333	2,496	2,804
1930	4,535	118	1,589	110	837	----------	----------	1,881	88,104	65,254	12,703	5,225	4,922
1929	3,758	70	1,446	103	771	----------	----------	1,368	116,177	66,451	40,154	4,306	5,266
1928	3,380	80	1,320	102	550	----------	----------	1,328	144,281	75,281	59,016	4,058	5,926
1927	3,669	73	1,471	102	723	----------	----------	1,300	161,872	84,580	67,721	4,019	5,552
1926	3,413	37	1,751	93	654	----------	----------	878	144,393	93,368	43,316	3,222	4,487
1925	3,578	51	1,937	65	723	----------	----------	802	141,496	102,753	32,964	2,106	3,673
1924	22,065	2,820	6,992	183	8,801	----------	----------	3,269	318,855	200,690	89,336	17,559	11,270
1923	13,705	2,183	4,986	257	5,809	----------	----------	470	199,972	117,011	63,768	13,181	6,012
1922	14,263	1,998	4,406	360	6,716	----------	----------	783	77,448	46,810	19,551	7,449	3,638
1921	25,034	11,735	4,009	511	7,878	----------	----------	901	124,118	72,317	30,758	13,774	7,269
1920	17,505	5,033	2,330	300	9,432	----------	----------	410	162,666	90,025	52,361	13,808	6,472
1919	12,674	19	1,964	171	10,064	----------	----------	456	102,286	57,782	29,818	8,826	5,860
1918	12,701	43	1,795	130	10,213	----------	----------	520	65,418	32,452	18,524	8,879	5,563
1917	12,756	393	2,237	109	8,991	----------	----------	1,026	147,779	105,399	17,869	15,507	9,004
1916	13,204	1,670	2,460	112	8,680	----------	----------	282	137,424	101,551	18,425	12,007	5,421
1915	15,211	3,543	2,660	161	8,613	----------	----------	234	111,206	82,215	12,340	11,598	5,053
1914	34,273	21,716	2,502	221	8,929	----------	----------	905	122,695	86,139	14,614	14,451	7,491
1913	35,358	23,955	2,105	179	8,281	----------	----------	838	103,907	73,802	11,926	12,458	5,721
1912	21,449	12,788	1,765	175	6,114	----------	----------	607	95,926	55,990	23,238	12,467	4,231
1911	17,428	10,229	1,460	524	4,520	----------	----------	695	94,364	56,830	19,889	13,403	4,242
1910	23,533	15,212	1,968	1,696	2,720	----------	----------	1,937	89,534	56,555	18,691	11,244	3,044
1909	12,904	7,506	1,943	203	3,111	----------	----------	141	82,208	51,941	16,251	11,180	2,836
1908	28,365	9,753	1,397	1,040	15,803	----------	----------	372	59,997	38,510	6,067	11,888	3,532
1907	40,524	8,053	961	898	30,226	----------	----------	386	41,762	19,918	1,406	16,689	3,749
1906	22,300	6,354	1,544	216	13,835	----------	----------	351	24,613	5,063	1,997	13,656	3,897
1905	23,925	6,157	2,166	190	10,331	----------	----------	5,081	25,217	2,168	2,637	16,641	3,771
1904	26,186	5,235	4,309	261	14,264	----------	----------	2,117	16,420	2,837	1,009	10,193	2,381
1903	29,966	7,118	2,209	94	19,968	----------	----------	577	11,023	1,058	528	8,170	1,267
1902	22,271	6,223	1,649	93	14,270	----------	----------	36	6,698	636	709	4,711	642
1901	13,593	5,782	2,459	22	5,269	----------	----------	61	4,416	540	347	3,176	353
1900	17,946	3,962	1,247	9	12,635	----------	----------	93	5,455	396	237	4,656	166
1899	8,972	4,436	1,660	17	2,844	----------	----------	15	4,316	1,322	161	2,585	248
1898	8,637	4,275	2,071	–	2,230	----------	----------	61	2,627	352	107	2,124	44
1897	9,662	4,732	3,363	–	1,526	----------	----------	41	4,537	291	91	4,101	54
1896	6,764	4,139	1,441	–	1,110	----------	----------	74	7,303	278	150	6,828	47
1895	4,495	2,767	539	–	1,150	----------	----------	39	3,508	244	116	3,096	52
1894	4,690	–	1,170	–	1,931	----------	----------	1,589	3,551	194	109	3,177	71
1893	2,392	–	472	–	1,380	----------	----------	540	2,593	(17)	(18)	2,593	–
1892	(17)					----------	----------		(17)	(17)	(18)	(17)	(17)
1891	7,678	2,488	2,836	42	1,136	----------	----------	1,176	5,082	234	(18)	3,906	942

See footnotes at end of p. 109.

Series C 89–119. Immigrants, by Country: 1820 to 1970—Con.

[For years ending June 30, except: 1820–1831 and 1844–1849, years ending Sept. 30; 1833–1842 and 1851–1867, years ending Dec. 31; 1832 covers 15 months ending Dec. 31; 1843, 9 months ending Sept. 30; 1850, 15 months ending Dec. 31; 1868, 6 months ending June 30]

Year	Asia						America				
	Total	Turkey in Asia [11]	China [12]	India	Japan [13]	Other Asia	Total	Canada and Newfoundland	Mexico	West Indies	Other America
	102	103	104	105	106	109	110	111	112	113	114
1890	4,448	1,126	1,716	43	691	872	3,833	183	(18)	3,070	580
1889	1,725	593	118	59	640	315	5,459	28	(18)	4,923	508
1888	843	273	26	20	404	120	5,402	15	(18)	4,880	507
1887	615	208	10	32	229	136	5,270	9	(18)	4,876	385
1886	317	15	40	17	194	51	3,026	17	(18)	2,734	275
1885	198	---------	22	34	49	93	41,203	38,336	323	2,477	67
1884	510	---------	279	12	20	199	63,339	60,626	430	2,208	75
1883	8,113	---------	8,031	9	27	46	71,729	70,274	469	903	83
1882	39,629	---------	39,579	10	5	35	100,129	98,366	366	1,291	106
1881	11,982	5	11,890	33	11	43	127,577	125,450	325	1,680	122
1880	5,839	4	5,802	21	4	8	101,692	99,744	492	1,351	105
1879	9,660	31	9,604	15	4	6	33,043	31,286	556	1,123	78
1878	9,014	7	8,992	8	2	5	27,204	25,592	465	1,019	128
1877	10,640	3	10,594	17	7	19	24,065	22,137	445	1,390	93
1876	22,943	8	22,781	25	4	125	24,686	22,505	631	1,382	168
1875	16,499	1	16,437	19	3	39	26,640	24,097	610	1,790	143
1874	13,838	6	13,776	17	21	18	35,339	33,020	386	1,777	156
1873	20,325	3	20,292	15	9	6	40,335	37,891	606	1,634	204
1872	7,825	–	7,788	12	17	5	42,205	40,204	569	1,322	110
1871	7,240	4	7,135	14	78	9	48,835	47,164	402	1,169	100
1870	15,825	–	15,740	24	48	13	42,658	40,414	463	1,679	102
1869	12,949	2	12,874	3	63	7	23,767	21,120	320	2,233	94
1868	5,171	---------	5,157	–	–	14	3,415	2,785	129	419	82
1867	3,961	---------	3,863	2	67	29	24,715	23,379	292	817	227
1866	2,411	---------	2,385	17	7	2	33,582	32,150	239	895	298
1865	2,947	---------	2,942	5	–	–	22,778	21,586	193	851	148
1864	2,982	---------	2,975	6	–	1	4,607	3,636	99	718	154
1863	7,216	---------	7,214	1	–	1	4,147	3,464	96	491	96
1862	3,640	---------	3,633	5	–	2	4,175	3,275	142	585	173
1861	7,528	---------	7,518	6	1	3	2,763	2,069	218	358	118
1860	5,476	---------	5,467	5	---------	4	6,343	4,514	229	1,384	216
1859	3,461	---------	3,457	2	---------	2	5,466	4,163	265	879	159
1858	5,133	---------	5,128	5	---------	–	5,821	4,603	429	647	142
1857	5,945	---------	5,944	1	---------	–	6,811	5,670	133	923	85
1856	4,747	---------	4,733	13	---------	1	9,058	6,493	741	1,337	487
1855	3,540	---------	3,526	6	---------	8	9,260	7,761	420	887	192
1854	13,100	---------	13,100	–	---------	–	8,533	6,891	446	1,036	160
1853	47	---------	42	5	---------	–	6,030	5,424	162	406	38
1852	4	---------	–	4	---------	–	7,695	6,352	72	1,232	39
1851	2	---------	–	2	---------	–	9,703	7,438	181	1,929	155
1850	7	---------	3	4	---------	–	15,768	9,376	597	3,171	2,624
1849	11	---------	3	8	---------	–	8,904	6,890	518	1,073	423
1848	8	---------	–	6	---------	2	7,989	6,473	24	1,338	154
1847	12	---------	4	8	---------	–	5,231	3,827	62	1,251	91
1846	11	---------	7	4	---------	–	5,525	3,855	222	1,351	97
1845	6	---------	6	–	---------	–	5,035	3,195	498	1,241	101
1844	6	---------	3	1	---------	2	3,740	2,711	197	771	61
1843	11	---------	3	2	---------	6	2,854	1,502	398	880	74
1842	7	---------	4	2	---------	1	3,994	2,078	403	1,410	103
1841	3	---------	2	1	---------	–	3,429	1,816	352	1,042	219
1840	1	---------	–	1	---------	–	3,815	1,938	395	1,446	36
1839	---------	---------	–	–	---------	–	3,617	1,926	353	1,289	49
1838	1	---------	–	1	---------	–	2,990	1,476	211	1,231	72
1837	11	---------	–	11	---------	–	3,628	1,279	627	1,627	95
1836	4	---------	–	4	---------	–	4,936	2,814	798	1,178	146
1835	17	---------	8	8	---------	1	3,312	1,193	1,032	938	149
1834	6	---------	–	6	---------	–	2,779	1,020	885	791	83
1833	3	---------	–	3	---------	–	3,282	1,194	779	1,264	45
1832	4	---------	–	4	---------	–	2,871	608	827	1,256	180
1831	1	---------	–	1	---------	–	2,194	176	692	1,281	45
1830	---------	---------	–	–	---------	–	2,296	189	983	937	187
1829	2	---------	1	1	---------	–	3,299	409	2,290	517	83
1828	3	---------	–	–	---------	–	2,090	267	1,089	652	82
1827	1	---------	–	1	---------	–	580	165	127	227	61
1826	1	---------	–	1	---------	–	831	223	106	427	75
1825	1	---------	1	–	---------	–	846	314	68	389	75
1824	1	---------	–	1	---------	–	559	155	110	259	35
1823	---------	---------	–	–	---------	–	382	167	35	160	20
1822	1	---------	–	1	---------	–	378	204	5	159	10
1821	---------	---------	–	–	---------	–	303	184	4	107	8
1820	5		1	1	---------	3	387	209	1	164	13

See footnotes at end of p. 109.

Series C 89–119. Immigrants, by Country: 1820 to 1970—Con.

[For years ending June 30, except: 1820–1831 and 1844–1849, years ending Sept. 30; 1833–1842 and 1851–1867, years ending Dec. 31; 1832 covers 15 months ending Dec. 31; 1843, 9 months ending Sept. 30; 1850, 15 months ending Dec. 31; 1868, 6 months ending June 30]

Year	Africa, total	Australasia Total	Australia and New Zealand	Other Pacific Islands	All other countries
	115	116	117	118	119
1970	7,099	3,632	2,693	939	---
1969	4,460	3,061	2,278	783	2
1968	3,220	3,172	2,374	798	---
1967	2,577	2,811	2,128	683	---
1966	1,967	2,500	1,894	606	11
1965	1,949	2,199	1,803	396	22
1964	2,015	2,070	1,767	303	25
1963	1,982	1,977	1,642	335	27
1962	1,834	1,819	1,427	392	1
1961	1,851	1,881	1,556	325	5
1960	1,925	2,140	1,892	248	26
1959	1,992	2,162	1,878	284	21
1958	2,008	2,045	1,783	262	12
1957	1,600	1,458	1,228	230	16
1956	1,351	1,346	1,171	175	22
1955	1,203	1,028	932	96	3,597
1954	1,248	910	845	65	8,341
1953	989	782	742	40	430
1952	931	578	545	33	8
1951	845	527	490	37	20
1950	849	517	460	57	7
1949	995	776	661	115	25
1948	1,027	1,336	1,218	118	10
1947	1,284	2,960	2,821	139	27
1946	1,516	6,106	6,009	97	73
1945	406	1,663	1,625	38	---
1944	112	615	577	38	---
1943	141	160	120	40	---
1942	473	163	120	43	---
1941	564	255	194	61	---
1940	202	228	207	21	---
1939	218	222	213	9	---
1938	174	248	228	20	---
1937	155	174	145	29	---
1936	105	165	147	18	---
1935	118	141	132	9	63
1934	104	147	130	17	3
1933	71	137	122	15	---
1932	186	303	291	12	---
1931	417	652	616	36	---
1930	572	1,051	1,026	25	---
1929	509	636	619	17	---
1928	475	606	578	28	---
1927	520	746	712	34	---
1926	529	591	556	35	---
1925	412	462	416	46	---
1924	900	679	635	44	58
1923	548	759	711	48	15
1922	520	915	855	60	25
1921	1,301	2,281	2,191	90	130
1920	648	2,185	2,066	119	702
1919	189	1,310	1,234	76	46
1918	299	1,090	925	165	47
1917	566	1,142	1,014	128	77
1916	894	1,574	1,484	90	31
1915	934	1,399	1,282	117	31
1914	1,539	1,446	1,336	110	136
1913	1,409	1,340	1,229	111	23
1912	1,009	898	794	104	15
1911	956	1,043	984	59	39
1910	1,072	1,097	998	99	43
1909	858	892	839	53	49
1908	1,411	1,179	1,098	81	17
1907	1,486	1,989	1,947	42	22
1906	712	1,733	1,682	51	[19] 33,012
1905	757	2,166	2,091	75	161
1904	686	1,555	1,461	94	90
1903	176	1,349	1,150	199	25
1902	37	566	384	182	103
1901	173	498	325	173	1
1900	30	428	214	214	13
1899	51	810	456	354	217
1898	48	201	153	48	---
1897	37	199	139	60	---
1896	21	112	87	25	---

Year	Africa, total	Australasia Total	Australia and New Zealand	Other Pacific Islands	All other countries
	115	116	117	118	119
1895	36	155	155		70
1894	24	244	244	---	
1893	[17]	248	248	[17]	5,173
1892	[17]	267	267	[17]	8,520
1891	103	1,301	777	524	70
1890	112	1,167	699	468	62
1889	187	2,196	1,000	1,196	70
1888	65	2,387	697	1,690	61
1887	40	1,282	528	754	73
1886	122	1,136	522	614	73
1885	112	679	449	230	71
1884	59	900	502	398	98
1883	67	747	554	193	79
1882	60	889	878	11	99
1881	33	1,191	1,188	3	103
1880	18	954	953	1	63
1879	12	816	813	3	36
1878	18	606	606	-	15
1877	16	914	912	2	27
1876	89	1,312	1,205	107	36
1875	54	1,268	1,104	164	76
1874	58	1,193	960	233	128
1873	28	1,414	1,135	279	160
1872	41	2,416	2,180	236	164
1871	24	21	18	3	85
1870	31	36	36	---	27
1869	72	---	---	---	17
1868	3	---	---	---	161
1867	25	---	---	---	3,270
1866	33	---	---	---	3,626
1865	49	---	---	---	8,298
1864	37	---	---	---	559
1863	3	---	---	---	1,183
1862	12	---	---	---	448
1861	47	---	---	---	380
1860	126				486
1859	11				1,395
1858	17				801
1857	25				22,301
1856	6				542
1855	14				334
1854					658
1853	8				984
1852					1,420
1851	3				248
1850					45,882
1849	3				1,605
1848	10				495
1847					608
1846	1				2,564
1845	4				25
1844	14				110
1843	6				612
1842	3				616
1841	14				627
1840	6				118
1839	10				294
1838	10				1,843
1837	2				4,660
1836	6				831
1835	14				44
1834	1				5,069
1833	1				26,243
1832	2				23,412
1831	2				7,397
1830	2				13,807
1829	1				6,695
1828	6				554
1827	4				1,571
1826					254
1825	1				808
1824	1				2,387
1823					1,956
1822					2,114
1821	2				2,886
1820	1				301

- Represents zero.
[11] No record of immigration from Turkey in Asia until 1869.
[12] Beginning 1957, includes Taiwan.
[13] No record of immigration from Japan until 1861.
[14] No record of immigration from Korea prior to 1948.
[15] Prior to 1920, Canada and Newfoundland were recorded as British North America.
[16] Philippines included in "All other countries" prior to 1936.
[17] Included in "All other countries."
[18] No record of immigration from Mexico for 1886 to 1893.
[19] Includes 32,897 persons returning to their homes in the United States.

Series C 120–137. Immigrants, by Major Occupation Group: 1820 to 1970

[For years ending June 30, except: 1820–1831 and 1844–1850, years ending Sept. 30; 1833–1842 and 1850–1865, years ending Dec. 31; 1832 covers 15 months ending Dec. 31; 1843, 9 months ending Sept. 30; 1851, 15 months ending Dec. 31]

Year	Total	Professional, technical, and kindred workers	Farmers and farm managers	Managers, officials, and proprietors, exc. farm	Clerical, sales, and kindred workers	Craftsmen, foremen, operatives, and kindred workers	Private household workers	Service workers, exc. private household	Farm laborers and foremen	Laborers, exc. farm and mine	No occupation
	120	121	122	123	124	125	126	127	128	129	130
1970	373,326	46,151	3,839	5,829	16,517	46,622	10,479	9,272	4,332	14,148	216,137
1969	358,579	40,427	3,687	5,356	17,448	43,266	16,822	10,461	5,224	13,062	202,826
1968	454,448	48,753	2,727	9,436	29,090	56,819	25,419	16,411	6,002	14,374	245,417
1967	361,972	41,652	3,276	7,974	19,783	34,596	17,406	12,832	5,277	10,129	209,047
1966	323,040	30,039	2,964	6,773	22,676	30,725	10,558	10,541	4,227	9,830	194,707
1965	296,697	28,790	1,833	7,090	29,779	31,676	9,706	10,743	2,638	8,556	165,886
1964	292,248	28,756	1,732	6,822	30,015	31,811	8,451	10,396	3,988	9,127	161,150
1963	306,260	27,930	1,776	5,986	28,094	32,444	9,522	9,392	9,463	16,062	165,591
1962	283,763	23,710	1,589	5,554	26,304	30,148	9,690	9,414	10,801	17,614	148,939
1961	271,344	21,455	3,002	5,363	25,198	30,967	8,811	8,399	4,799	15,694	147,656
1960	265,398	21,940	3,050	5,309	24,386	34,135	8,173	8,812	3,914	12,838	142,841
1959	260,686	23,287	2,187	4,688	21,475	36,552	7,465	9,641	2,729	11,937	140,725
1958	253,265	22,482	2,221	4,646	22,140	31,518	7,521	7,362	2,511	11,100	141,764
1957	326,867	24,489	3,506	6,127	25,897	46,338	11,457	8,761	4,585	21,826	173,881
1956	321,625	18,995	5,727	5,814	23,413	44,950	15,347	7,922	9,050	27,807	162,600
1955	237,790	14,109	4,446	5,114	18,060	34,218	11,824	6,512	5,486	17,518	120,503
1954	208,177	13,817	3,846	5,296	16,018	32,151	8,096	5,203	1,622	10,061	112,067
1953	170,434	12,783	3,393	5,025	15,171	26,975	6,852	4,390	1,538	5,369	88,938
1952	265,520	16,496	10,566	5,968	16,724	42,315	9,653	6,418	6,289	8,969	142,122
1951	205,717	15,269	10,214	5,493	14,098	34,041	7,243	5,292	4,972	5,481	103,614
1950	249,187	20,502	17,642	6,396	16,796	41,450	8,900	4,970	3,976	5,693	122,862
1949	188,317	13,884	8,937	6,014	14,797	27,964	6,990	3,937	933	6,192	98,669
1948	170,570	12,619	4,884	6,207	15,298	23,816	6,389	4,350	946	4,826	91,235
1947	147,292	10,891	3,462	5,886	13,961	19,306	4,922	3,882	442	2,831	81,709
1946	108,721	6,198	947	3,616	8,378	8,826	2,464	2,153	189	1,473	74,477
1945	38,119	2,852	497	1,457	3,715	4,511	1,495	1,047	225	886	21,434
1944	28,551	2,616	349	894	2,368	3,533	1,125	811	203	1,030	15,622
1943	23,725	2,695	235	988	1,840	2,587	770	707	164	681	13,058
1942	28,781	3,518	254	2,305	1,638	2,061	872	740	92	493	16,808
1941	51,776	6,232	356	5,640	2,837	3,513	1,503	829	129	732	30,005
1940	70,756	6,802	847	7,415	4,361	5,710	2,891	949	252	2,120	39,409
1939	82,998	7,199	1,186	8,929	4,794	6,532	5,420	1,979	415	2,070	44,474
1938	67,895	5,418	1,508	5,408	3,119	5,697	5,919	1,794	609	2,411	36,012
1937	50,244	4,130	852	3,422	2,126	3,996	3,213	1,426	378	1,904	28,797
1936	36,329	2,564	535	1,782	1,449	2,490	1,944	1,056	324	1,195	22,990
1935	34,956	2,244	593	1,347	1,024	2,689	1,418	1,390	408	1,355	22,488
1934	29,470	2,101	425	1,207	933	2,267	805	1,216	233	1,154	19,129
1933	23,068	1,615	292	690	600	1,821	550	933	134	887	15,546
1932	35,576	2,100	403	1,331	919	2,053	1,232	1,063	254	1,157	25,064
1931	97,139	4,120	2,743	2,384	4,229	9,555	9,740	3,128	3,422	4,806	53,012
1930	241,700	8,585	8,375	4,620	14,414	32,474	29,073	6,749	13,736	18,080	105,594
1929	279,678	8,792	8,309	4,709	15,354	36,437	31,841	6,820	19,849	27,873	119,694
1928	307,255	9,332	9,332	5,287	16,344	42,765	28,751	8,846	24,161	37,904	125,092
1927	335,175	9,883	10,324	5,772	20,140	42,394	31,344	10,070	23,698	55,989	125,561
1926	304,488	9,203	9,720	5,374	19,086	38,682	30,587	14,340	17,390	45,199	114,907
1925	294,314	8,942	13,875	5,508	15,363	36,927	26,924	15,399	16,022	36,610	118,744
1924	706,896	20,926	20,320	15,668	27,373	123,923	51,680	29,621	27,492	112,344	277,909
1923	522,919	13,926	12,503	12,086	17,931	87,899	52,223	22,244	25,905	86,617	191,585
1922	309,556	9,696	7,676	9,573	10,055	40,309	44,531	12,340	10,529	33,797	131,050
1921	805,228	12,852	22,282	18,286	18,922	109,710	102,478	24,298	32,400	162,859	301,141
1920	430,001	10,540	12,192	9,654	14,054	55,991	37,197	18,487	15,257	83,496	173,133
1919	141,132	5,261	3,933	4,247	6,524	21,671	6,277	11,571	4,412	18,922	58,314
1918	110,618	3,529	2,583	3,940	4,239	17,501	7,816	6,367	4,538	15,142	44,963
1917	295,403	7,499	7,764	8,329	10,554	38,660	31,885	11,784	22,328	52,182	104,418
1916	298,826	9,024	6,840	8,725	9,907	36,086	29,258	10,989	26,250	56,981	104,766
1915	326,700	11,453	6,518	10,728	9,377	45,591	39,774	11,976	24,723	49,620	116,940
1914	1,218,480	13,454	14,442	21,903	17,933	149,515	144,409	19,621	288,053	228,935	320,215
1913	1,197,892	12,552	13,180	19,094	15,173	139,091	140,218	17,609	320,105	223,682	297,188
1912	838,172	10,913	7,664	14,715	13,782	107,893	116,529	13,580	184,154	137,872	231,070
1911	878,587	11,275	9,709	15,416	14,723	128,717	107,153	11,051	176,003	158,518	246,022
1910	1,041,570	9,689	11,793	14,731	12,219	121,847	96,658	8,977	288,745	216,909	260,002
1909	751,786	7,603	8,914	11,562	8,467	75,730	64,568	5,849	171,310	176,490	221,293
1908	782,870	10,504	7,720	16,410	11,523	106,943	89,942	10,367	138,844	147,940	242,677
1907	1,285,349	12,016	13,476	20,132	12,735	169,394	121,587	13,578	323,854	293,868	304,709
1906	1,100,735	13,015	15,288	23,515	12,226	156,902	115,984	10,439	239,125	228,781	285,460
1905	1,026,499	12,582	18,474	27,706	12,759	159,442	125,473	5,849	142,187	290,009	232,018
1904	812,870	12,195	4,507	26,914	11,055	133,748	104,937	6,400	85,850	212,572	214,692
1903	857,046	6,999	13,363	15,603	7,226	110,644	92,686	11,482	77,518	321,824	199,701
1902	648,743	2,937	8,168	9,340	3,836	71,131	69,913	6,298	80,562	243,399	153,159
1901	487,918	2,665	3,035	8,294	3,197	57,346	42,027	5,352	54,753	162,563	148,686
1900	448,572	2,392	5,433	7,216	2,870	54,793	40,311	4,406	31,949	164,261	134,941
1899	311,715	1,972	3,973	6,815	2,473	38,608	34,120	4,580	17,343	92,452	109,379

Series C 120–137.   Immigrants, by Major Occupation Group: 1820 to 1970—Con.

[For years ending June 30, except: 1820–1831 and 1844–1850, years ending Sept. 30; 1833–1842 and 1850–1865, years ending Dec. 31; 1832 covers 15 months ending Dec. 31; 1843, 9 months ending Sept. 30; 1851, 15 months ending Dec. 31]

Year	Total [1]	No occupation	Professional	Commercial	Skilled	Farmers	Servants	Laborers	Miscellaneous
	120	130	131	132	133	134	135	136	137
1898	229,299	90,569	1,347	5,959	33,145	16,243	23,656	52,531	5,849
1897	230,832	91,624	1,732	7,159	33,161	22,560	23,739	46,198	4,659
1896	343,267	123,196	2,324	6,174	46,807	29,251	38,926	91,262	5,327
1895	258,536	92,193	2,029	5,314	43,844	13,055	35,960	61,430	4,711
1894	285,631	113,247	1,791	6,033	49,736	21,762	29,653	56,732	6,677
1893	439,730	209,767	2,362	837	51,145	34,070	(2)	114,295	[2] 27,254
1892	579,663	255,832	2,932	2,683	63,128	51,630	(2)	171,483	[2] 31,975
1891	560,319	248,635	3,431	11,340	54,951	36,398	32,596	167,290	5,678
1890	455,302	195,770	3,236	7,802	44,540	29,296	28,625	139,365	6,668
1889	444,427	208,761	2,815	7,359	50,457	28,962	30,220	111,809	4,044
1888	546,889	243,900	3,360	7,597	59,985	29,335	27,310	170,273	5,129
1887	490,109	224,073	2,882	8,032	52,403	30,932	27,510	140,938	3,339
1886	334,203	157,952	2,078	6,237	36,522	20,600	20,198	86,853	3,763
1885	395,346	211,730	2,097	6,707	39,817	27,585	20,213	83,068	4,129
1884	518,592	277,052	2,284	7,691	55,061	42,050	24,249	106,478	3,727
1883	603,322	322,318	2,450	8,280	62,505	39,048	27,988	136,071	4,662
1882	788,992	402,835	2,992	10,102	72,664	61,888	23,010	209,605	5,896
1881	669,431	355,670	2,812	9,371	66,457	58,028	19,342	147,816	9,935
1880	457,257	217,446	1,773	7,916	49,929	47,204	18,580	105,012	9,397
1879	177,826	81,772	1,639	5,202	21,362	19,907	6,804	36,897	4,243
1878	138,469	62,622	1,510	4,475	16,531	14,843	6,157	26,656	5,675
1877	141,857	63,316	1,885	4,667	21,006	13,188	5,158	25,482	7,155
1876	169,986	71,111	2,400	4,963	24,200	14,536	6,493	38,847	7,436
1875	227,498	106,723	2,426	5,029	33,803	16,447	10,579	46,877	5,614
1874	313,339	155,122	2,476	5,641	38,700	28,775	12,427	65,895	4,303
1873	459,803	239,307	2,980	7,593	48,792	36,983	16,259	104,423	3,466
1872	404,806	213,959	1,905	7,156	44,967	38,159	11,108	85,934	1,618
1871	321,350	172,215	2,247	5,553	33,577	27,042	13,814	65,936	966
1870	387,203	207,174	1,831	7,139	35,698	35,656	14,261	84,577	867
1869	352,768	181,453	1,700	8,837	33,345	28,102	10,265	88,649	417
1868	282,189	150,983	1,398	8,556	32,197	23,046	6,561	59,151	297
1867	342,162	182,794	2,288	14,706	44,097	32,626	7,715	57,419	517
1866	359,957	202,456	2,242	15,827	41,091	30,302	8,883	58,629	527
1865	287,399	161,580	1,743	12,700	36,522	20,012	9,231	45,247	364
1864	221,535	106,656	1,120	9,473	26,542	13,837	15,623	48,041	243
1863	199,811	99,039	1,173	7,590	24,155	12,348	9,103	46,198	205
1862	114,463	62,860	788	7,774	11,986	9,265	3,683	17,752	355
1861	112,702	60,760	668	7,683	11,601	11,668	739	19,413	170
1860	179,691	93,925	792	11,207	19,342	21,742	1,415	31,268	----------
1859	155,509	78,228	858	12,495	24,628	16,323	1,281	21,696	----------
1858	144,906	71,320	662	10,217	18,742	20,506	1,142	22,317	----------
1857	271,982	153,963	570	12,114	26,062	34,702	1,322	43,249	----------
1856	224,496	130,647	462	11,101	18,797	24,722	1,748	37,019	----------
1855	230,476	117,603	780	14,759	17,463	34,693	2,598	42,580	----------
1854	460,474	235,216	699	15,173	36,468	87,188	3,357	82,373	----------
1853	400,982	223,390	722	12,782	20,806	56,322	3,938	83,022	----------
1852	397,343	223,861	572	11,502	27,176	58,023	942	75,267	----------
1851	474,398	257,376	938	14,983	36,297	59,095	3,733	101,976	----------
1850	315,334	188,931	918	6,400	26,369	42,873	3,203	46,640	----------
1849	299,683	157,657	972	3,508	32,021	39,675	3,671	62,179	----------
1848	229,483	118,528	517	3,407	24,705	31,670	4,433	46,223	----------
1847	239,482	126,005	703	4,218	25,895	43,594	3,198	35,869	----------
1846	158,649	91,132	592	4,189	13,250	27,944	3,349	18,193	----------
1845	119,896	65,055	542	5,049	10,857	19,349	2,492	16,552	----------
1844	84,764	49,843	755	3,960	9,476	9,831	1,174	9,725	----------
1843	56,529	32,842	578	3,226	6,093	8,031	413	5,346	----------
1842	110,980	60,526	744	4,976	14,553	12,966	1,264	15,951	----------
1841	87,805	46,197	541	5,267	11,111	12,343	923	11,423	----------
1840	92,207	47,305	481	5,311	10,811	18,476	183	9,640	----------
1839	74,666	37,985	584	5,692	10,026	12,410	99	7,870	----------
1838	45,159	24,627	459	4,005	5,675	6,667	42	3,684	----------
1837	84,959	52,011	522	3,893	8,483	10,835	120	9,095	----------
1836	80,972	50,684	472	3,379	8,879	8,770	39	8,749	----------
1835	48,716	28,736	487	3,875	6,005	6,117	599	2,897	----------
1834	67,948	45,906	561	3,021	7,190	7,160	1,236	2,874	----------
1833	59,925	30,944	459	4,913	12,800	6,618	82	4,109	----------
1832	61,654	33,840	176	5,424	10,333	8,502	56	3,323	----------
1831	23,880	15,218	183	2,368	2,383	2,685	115	928	----------
1830	24,837	19,363	136	1,427	1,745	1,424	22	720	----------
1829	24,513	15,535	252	2,661	2,579	1,264	337	1,885	----------
1828	30,184	18,066	331	2,328	3,868	2,542	421	2,628	----------
1827	21,777	12,415	262	2,076	3,056	2,071	136	1,761	----------
1826	13,908	7,478	190	1,943	2,129	1,382	70	716	----------
1825	12,858	7,031	204	1,841	1,416	1,647	69	650	----------
1824	9,627	4,965	187	1,926	1,237	918	13	381	----------
1823	8,265	4,247	179	1,427	1,268	800	6	338	----------
1822	8,549	4,302	151	1,431	1,397	834	20	414	----------
1821	11,644	6,670	204	1,441	1,533	1,249	94	453	----------
1820	10,311	6,836	105	933	1,090	874	139	334	----------

[1] For 1820–1867, includes returning citizens.   [2] Servants included with "Miscellaneous" (series C 137).

Series C 138–142. Immigrants, by Age: 1820 to 1970

[For years ending as follows (except as noted): 1820–1832, ending Sept. 30; 1833–1842, ending Dec. 31; 1843–1850, ending Sept. 30; 1851–1865, ending Dec. 31; 1866–1970, ending June 30. Note variability for series C 140–142 in composition of age groups for different periods; see text]

Year	Total Both sexes [1] (138)	Total Males (139)	Age group Under 16 years (140)	Age group 16–44 years (141)	Age group 45 years and over (142)
1970	373,326	176,990	104,880	221,534	46,912
1969	358,579	165,472	98,167	210,681	49,731
1968	454,448	199,732	111,794	262,598	80,056
1967	361,972	158,324	97,598	207,434	56,940
1966	323,040	141,456	89,715	189,526	43,799
1965	296,697	127,171	72,431	188,652	35,614
1964	292,248	126,214	70,444	186,821	34,983
1963	306,260	139,297	72,510	197,506	36,244
1962	283,763	131,575	64,531	182,464	36,768
1961	271,344	121,380	64,544	170,881	35,919
1960	265,398	116,687	59,895	170,084	35,419
1959	260,686	114,367	58,826	165,366	36,494
1958	253,265	109,121	60,124	162,240	30,901
1957	326,867	155,201	80,140	207,664	39,063
1956	321,625	156,410	74,429	206,770	40,426
1955	237,790	112,032	51,829	156,001	29,960
1954	208,177	95,594	45,105	135,731	27,341
1953	170,434	73,073	37,016	110,860	22,558
1952	265,520	123,609	64,513	159,788	41,219
1951	205,717	99,327	44,023	121,823	39,871
1950	249,187	119,130	50,468	152,358	46,361
1949	188,317	80,340	32,728	123,340	32,249
1948	170,570	67,322	24,095	112,453	34,022
1947	147,292	53,769	18,831	101,459	27,002
1946	108,721	27,275	11,092	85,797	11,832
1945	38,119	13,389	5,645	25,482	6,992
1944	28,551	11,410	4,092	[2]18,511	[2]5,948
1943	23,725	9,825	3,179	[2]15,282	[2]5,264
1942	28,781	12,008	3,710	[2]17,529	[2]7,542
1941	51,776	23,519	7,982	[2]30,747	[2]13,047
1940	70,756	33,460	9,602	[2]45,026	[2]16,128
1939	82,998	39,423	12,204	54,235	16,559
1938	67,895	29,959	10,181	47,068	10,646
1937	50,244	21,664	8,326	33,907	8,011
1936	36,329	14,776	6,925	23,391	6,013
1935	34,956	14,010	6,893	22,557	5,506
1934	29,470	12,101	5,389	18,987	5,094
1933	23,068	9,219	4,131	15,033	3,904
1932	35,576	13,917	6,781	22,905	5,890
1931	97,139	40,621	17,320	67,100	12,719
1930	241,700	117,026	40,777	177,059	23,864
1929	279,678	142,132	47,935	207,990	23,753
1928	307,255	165,977	49,680	230,832	26,743
1927	335,175	194,163	51,689	254,574	28,912
1926	304,488	170,567	47,347	228,527	28,614
1925	294,314	163,252	50,722	213,980	29,612
1924	706,896	423,186	132,264	513,788	60,844
1923	522,919	307,522	91,816	383,960	47,143
1922	309,556	149,741	63,710	210,164	35,682
1921	805,228	449,422	146,613	587,965	70,650
1920	430,001	247,625	81,890	307,589	40,522
1919	141,132	83,272	26,373	97,341	17,418
1918	110,618	61,880	21,349	76,098	13,171

Year	Both sexes [1] (138)	Males (139)	Under 14 years (140)	14–44 years (141)	45 years and over (142)
1917	295,403	174,479	47,467	214,616	33,320
1916	298,826	182,229	47,070	220,821	30,935
1915	326,700	187,021	52,982	244,472	29,246
1914	1,218,480	798,747	158,621	981,692	78,167
1913	1,197,892	808,144	147,158	986,355	64,379
1912	838,172	529,931	113,700	678,480	45,992
1911	878,587	570,057	117,837	714,709	46,041
1910	1,041,570	736,038	120,509	868,310	52,751
1909	751,786	519,969	88,393	624,876	38,517
1908	782,870	506,912	112,148	630,671	40,051
1907	1,285,349	929,976	138,344	1,100,771	46,234
1906	1,100,735	764,463	136,273	913,955	50,507
1905	1,026,499	724,914	114,668	855,419	56,412
1904	812,870	549,100	109,150	657,155	46,565
1903	857,046	613,146	102,431	714,053	40,562
1902	648,743	466,369	74,063	539,254	35,426
1901	487,918	331,055	62,562	396,516	28,840
1900	448,572	304,148	54,624	370,382	23,566
1899	311,715	195,277	43,983	248,187	19,545

Year	Total Both sexes [1] (138)	Total Males [3] (139)	Age group Under 15 years (140)	Age group 15–40 years (141)	Age group 40 years and over (142)
1898	229,299	135,775	38,267	164,905	26,127
1897	230,832	135,107	38,627	165,181	27,024
1896	343,267	212,466	52,741	254,519	36,007
1895	279,948	149,016	33,289	233,543	13,116
1894	314,467	169,274	41,755	258,162	14,550
1893	502,917	280,344	57,392	419,701	25,824
1892	623,084	361,864	89,167	491,839	42,078
1891	560,319	354,059	95,879	405,843	58,597
1890	455,302	281,853	86,404	315,054	53,844
1889	444,427	263,024	92,534	303,835	48,058
1888	546,889	345,375	97,287	396,990	52,612
1887	490,109	306,658	94,278	345,575	50,256
1886	334,203	200,704	66,188	232,118	35,897
1885	395,346	226,382	92,880	257,551	44,915
1884	518,592	308,509	123,562	335,572	59,458
1883	603,322	363,863	143,865	390,406	69,051
1882	788,992	498,814	171,021	540,677	77,294
1881	669,431	410,729	153,480	454,495	61,456
1880	457,257	287,623	87,154	327,662	42,441
1879	177,826	111,882	34,554	122,731	20,541
1878	138,469	86,259	24,285	95,938	18,246
1877	141,857	92,033	23,754	100,366	17,737
1876	169,986	111,786	27,875	121,734	20,377
1875	227,498	139,950	44,254	154,621	28,623
1874	313,339	189,225	63,578	199,840	49,921
1873	459,803	275,792	104,672	288,272	66,859
1872	404,806	240,170	90,510	263,213	51,083
1871	321,350	190,428	71,148	210,366	39,836
1870	387,203	235,612	89,129	250,965	47,109
1869	352,768	214,865	79,803	232,397	40,568
1868	282,189	(⁴)	57,637	188,359	36,193
1867	342,162	212,140	65,335	236,017	40,810
1866 [5]	185,892	116,554	27,011	112,692	18,034
1865	287,399	172,152	46,524	175,501	32,190
1864	221,535	131,592	41,912	151,711	27,778
1863	199,811	120,086	37,433	142,009	20,108
1862	114,463	66,846	20,641	80,725	12,888
1861	112,702	64,353	18,878	81,515	11,221
1860	179,691	105,299	28,620	133,919	16,795
1859	155,509	90,506	24,670	114,110	16,115
1858	144,906	83,756	25,914	102,921	15,545
1857	271,982	146,598	50,548	177,093	22,808
1856	224,496	129,759	42,732	141,986	19,905
1855	230,476	135,520	53,045	151,440	25,155
1854	460,474	265,233	100,013	312,301	47,377
1853	400,982	227,357	87,331	267,876	44,558
1852	397,343	233,638	90,274	246,076	43,394
1851	408,828	235,894	89,241	274,359	44,072
1850 [6]	65,570	40,785	13,825	43,699	7,621
1850	315,334	196,138	62,543	181,468	26,085
1849	299,683	179,810	67,331	200,899	30,679
1848	229,483	135,165	53,213	151,148	23,066
1847	239,482	138,660	57,161	156,627	20,800
1846	158,649	91,223	36,878	103,263	17,160
1845	119,896	69,180	26,182	79,448	12,059
1844	84,764	47,468	19,913	54,745	8,655
1843 [7]	56,529	32,448	14,930	34,606	5,197
1842	110,980	67,698	25,516	74,499	9,709
1841	87,805	54,000	19,732	58,864	8,590
1840	92,207	59,197	21,727	62,461	7,556
1839	74,666	47,786	15,167	51,063	7,201
1838	45,159	28,586	8,822	28,713	5,748
1837	84,959	53,864	16,014	54,312	8,421
1836	80,972	51,660	16,665	54,738	8,141
1835	48,716	30,204	10,635	32,412	5,431
1834	67,948	46,069	15,383	42,811	6,818
1833	59,925	40,449	17,425	35,002	4,855
1832 [6]	7,303	4,791	1,946	3,774	425
1832	54,351	35,654	16,485	31,069	4,273
1831	23,880	15,379	7,040	13,598	1,863
1830	24,837	18,007	2,878	6,347	1,173
1829	24,513	15,982	3,686	11,603	1,764
1828	30,184	19,740	8,117	18,397	3,036
1827	21,777	15,614	3,905	14,089	2,148
1826	13,908	9,861	2,261	10,025	1,281
1825	12,858	9,541	1,825	9,392	1,151
1824	9,627	7,711	94	6,550	1,106
1823	8,265	6,529	17	5,314	984
1822	8,549	6,625	51	5,430	956
1821	11,644	8,640	170	7,047	1,396
1820	10,311	7,197	1,313	6,064	1,518

[1] For 1820–1867, figures include returning citizens; for 1820–1866, figures include immigrants not shown separately, whose age was not reported.
[2] For 1940–1944, figures in series C 141 include, and those in series C 142 exclude, immigrants 45 years old.   [3] For 1820–1867, data by sex are available only by percentages. These percentages have been applied to the total number of immigrants to estimate the number of males during those years.
[4] Not reported.   [5] 6 months ending June 30.
[6] 3 months ending December 31.   [7] 9 months ending September 30.

Series C 143–157. Annual Quota and Aliens Admitted, by Classes: 1925 to 1970

[For years ending June 30]

Year	Annual quota	Immigrants					Nonimmigrants								
		Total	Natives of Eastern Hemisphere countries [1]	Immediate relatives of U.S. citizens [2]	Natives of Western Hemisphere countries [3]	Other	Total	Temporary visitors	Transit aliens	Students	Foreign government and international officials	Returning resident aliens [4]	Exchange visitors	Temporary workers and industrial trainees	Other
	143	144	145	146	147	148	149	150	151	152	153	154	155	156	157
1970	[5]	373,326	172,546	79,337	114,737	6,706	4,431,880	3,345,169	231,891	98,179	74,241	493,522	50,817	85,688	52,373
1969	[5]	358,579	157,306	60,016	133,689	7,568	3,645,328	2,682,008	210,543	90,486	64,896	441,082	47,175	62,952	46,186
1968	158,261	454,448	156,212	43,677	245,449	9,110	3,200,336	2,300,466	232,731	73,303	65,146	373,252	45,320	68,969	41,149
1967	158,261	361,972	153,079	46,903	151,034	10,956	2,608,193	1,848,999	204,936	63,370	61,302	284,330	38,630	70,010	36,616
1966	158,561	323,040	126,310	39,231	147,906	9,593	2,341,923	1,674,188	177,827	55,716	55,696	238,013	35,253	75,848	29,382
1965	158,561	296,697	99,381	32,714	153,199	11,403	2,075,967	1,498,979	142,686	50,435	52,570	203,235	33,768	67,869	26,425
1964	158,161	292,248	102,844	33,669	139,284	16,451	1,744,808	1,249,948	119,360	44,952	47,519	165,429	33,371	60,470	23,759
1963	156,987	306,260	103,036	30,606	147,744	24,874	1,507,091	1,067,444	105,815	38,991	45,961	135,701	30,002	63,477	19,700
1962	156,687	283,763	90,319	30,316	133,505	29,623	1,331,383	928,021	110,276	41,202	43,120	112,261	26,977	57,608	11,918
1961	156,487	271,344	96,104	32,551	112,836	29,853	1,220,315	858,472	106,888	35,072	40,087	103,931	24,346	44,263	7,256
1960	154,887	265,398	101,373	34,215	91,701	38,109	1,140,736	779,205	118,291	35,415	39,967	97,895	25,233	38,479	6,251
1959	154,857	260,686	97,657	36,402	68,196	58,431	1,024,945	689,416	116,814	35,583	38,308	85,915	24,293	29,339	5,277
1958	154,957	253,265	102,153	35,320	88,575	27,217	847,764	596,004	99,190	34,848	36,046	32,747	20,349	24,402	4,178
1957	154,857	326,867	97,178	32,359	113,488	83,842	758,858	537,760	107,399	30,760	34,904	10,617	17,849	16,856	2,713
1956	154,657	321,625	89,310	31,742	124,032	76,541	686,259	471,969	65,214	28,013	32,299	52,136	17,204	17,077	2,347
1955	154,657	237,790	82,232	30,882	94,274	30,402	620,946	401,090	71,301	27,192	32,291	61,442	16,077	9,750	1,803
1954	154,657	208,177	94,098	30,689	80,526	2,864	566,613	353,754	78,526	25,425	28,696	55,887	15,260	7,479	1,586
1953	154,657	170,434	84,175	22,543	61,099	2,617	485,714	306,715	67,684	13,533	30,614	50,397	12,584	3,021	1,166
1952	154,277	265,520	194,247	19,315	48,408	3,550	516,082	356,351	77,899	8,613	27,404	44,980	_____	_____	835
1951	154,277	205,717	156,547	11,462	35,274	2,434	465,106	314,205	72,027	7,355	26,407	44,212	_____	_____	900
1950	154,206	249,187	197,460	16,275	33,238	2,214	426,837	287,794	68,640	9,744	18,985	40,903	_____	_____	771
1949	153,929	188,317	113,046	35,854	36,394	3,023	447,272	299,083	81,615	10,481	18,445	36,984	_____	_____	664
1948	153,929	170,570	92,526	36,830	37,968	3,246	476,006	284,983	124,780	11,914	20,881	32,464	_____	_____	984
1947	153,929	147,292	70,701	38,739	35,640	2,212	366,305	214,558	96,825	11,003	20,320	22,818	_____	_____	781
1946	153,879	108,721	29,095	49,267	29,502	857	203,469	134,826	31,124	5,855	17,689	13,306	_____	_____	669
1945	153,879	38,119	11,623	3,078	22,828	590	164,247	107,729	28,174	2,866	18,054	6,896	_____	_____	528
1944	153,774	28,551	9,394	1,302	17,614	241	113,641	48,689	34,856	1,643	23,630	4,745	_____	_____	78
1943	153,774	23,725	9,045	875	13,522	283	81,117	27,700	31,906	1,021	16,328	4,102	_____	_____	60
1942	153,774	28,781	14,597	1,262	12,596	326	82,457	25,135	28,305	1,368	12,038	15,462	_____	_____	149
1941	153,774	51,776	36,220	2,122	12,586	848	100,008	34,660	18,749	1,766	9,269	35,246	_____	_____	318
1940	153,774	70,756	51,997	5,474	11,985	1,300	138,032	65,325	36,304	2,044	7,448	26,105	_____	_____	806
1939	153,774	82,998	62,402	7,043	12,223	1,330	185,333	88,309	44,115	2,182	7,777	42,196	_____	_____	754
1938	153,774	67,895	42,494	10,262	14,379	760	184,802	79,840	45,146	2,451	6,221	50,266	_____	_____	878
1937	153,774	50,244	27,762	9,536	12,152	794	181,640	89,455	31,822	1,828	6,493	51,223	_____	_____	819
1936	153,774	36,329	18,675	8,824	8,066	764	154,570	73,313	26,571	1,515	5,312	47,166	_____	_____	693
1935	153,774	34,956	17,207	9,228	7,747	774	144,765	61,633	24,931	1,377	5,194	50,885	_____	_____	745
1934	153,774	29,470	12,483	7,891	8,237	859	134,434	49,833	23,687	1,048	4,363	54,928	_____	_____	575
1933	153,831	23,068	8,220	6,658	7,549	641	127,660	36,899	22,693	877	4,053	62,460	_____	_____	678
1932	153,831	35,576	12,983	9,490	9,461	3,642	139,295	40,465	28,678	147	2,966	66,879	_____	_____	160
1931	153,714	97,139	54,118	17,264	21,287	4,470	183,540	55,636	32,169	272	3,951	91,201	_____	_____	311
1930	153,714	241,700	141,497	32,105	63,147	4,951	204,514	70,823	27,991	552	5,326	99,056	_____	_____	766
1929	164,667	279,678	146,918	30,245	97,548	[6]4,967	199,649	64,310	27,776	561	5,273	100,879	_____	_____	850
1928	164,667	307,255	153,231	25,678	123,534	[6]4,812	193,376	64,581	27,257	517	5,340	94,368	_____	_____	1,313
1927	164,667	335,175	158,070	18,361	147,399	[6]11,345	202,826	60,508	28,312	524	4,769	95,502	_____	_____	13,211
1926	164,667	304,488	157,432	11,061	134,305	1,690	191,618	56,614	25,574	1,878	5,638	83,744	_____	_____	18,170
1925	164,667	294,314	145,971	7,159	139,389	1,795	164,121	35,326	22,697	1,397	1,930	64,617	_____	_____	38,154

[1] Represents quota immigrants through June 30, 1968; see text for series C 143–157. Effective July 1, 1968, natives of the Eastern Hemisphere became subject to an annual numerical limitation of 170,000.

[2] Spouses and children of U.S. citizens; beginning 1966, data also include parents of adult U.S. citizens.

[3] Data include Cuban refugees adjusting their status and the spouses and children of natives of Western Hemisphere countries. Beginning July 1, 1968, natives of Western Hemisphere countries and their spouses and children became subject to an annual numerical limitation of 120,000.

[4] Figures are not comparable because of changes in documentary requirements. Returning resident aliens who have once been counted as immigrants are included with nonimmigrants.

[5] The Act of October 3, 1965, abolished the quota system as of July 1, 1968, and in its place set up an annual limitation of 170,000 on immigration from the Eastern Hemisphere and 120,000 from the Western Hemisphere.

[6] Does not agree with source; adjusted to conform to definitions used in later years.

Series C 158–161.   Aliens Deported, Required to Depart, and Excluded: 1892 to 1970

[For years ending June 30]

Year	Aliens expelled			Aliens excluded	Year	Aliens expelled			Aliens excluded	Year	Aliens deported	Aliens excluded
	Total	Deported	Required to depart			Total	Deported	Required to depart				
	158	159	160	161		158	159	160	161		159	161
1970	320,241	16,893	303,348	576	1944	39,449	7,179	32,270	1,642	1917	1,853	16,028
1969	251,463	10,505	240,958	525	1943	16,154	4,207	11,947	1,495	1916	2,781	18,867
1968	189,082	9,130	179,952	460	1942	10,613	3,709	6,904	1,833	1915	2,564	24,111
1967	151,603	9,260	142,343	468	1941	10,938	4,407	6,531	2,929	1914	4,610	33,041
1966	132,851	9,168	123,683	512	1940	15,548	6,954	8,594	5,300	1913	3,461	19,938
1965	105,406	10,143	95,263	429	1939	17,792	8,202	9,590	6,498	1912	2,456	16,057
1964	81,788	8,746	73,042	421	1938	18,553	9,275	9,278	8,066	1911	2,788	22,349
1963	76,846	7,454	69,392	309	1937	17,617	8,829	8,788	8,076	1910	2,695	24,270
1962	61,801	7,637	54,164	388	1936	17,446	9,195	8,251	7,000	1909	2,124	10,411
1961	59,821	7,438	52,383	743	1935	16,297	8,319	7,978	5,558	1908	2,069	10,902
1960	59,625	6,829	52,796	411	1934	16,889	8,879	8,010	5,384	1907	995	13,064
1959	64,598	7,988	56,610	480	1933	30,212	19,865	10,347	5,527	1906	676	12,432
1958	67,742	7,142	60,600	733	1932	30,201	19,426	10,775	7,064	1905	845	11,879
1957	68,461	5,082	63,379	907	1931	29,861	18,142	11,719	9,744	1904	779	7,994
1956	88,188	7,297	80,891	1,709	1930	28,018	16,631	11,387	8,233	1903	547	8,769
1955	247,797	15,028	232,769	2,667	1929	38,796	12,908	25,888	18,127	1902	465	4,974
1954	1,101,228	26,951	1,074,277	3,313	1928	31,571	11,625	19,946	18,839	1901	363	3,516
1953	905,236	19,845	885,391	2,637	1927	26,674	11,662	15,012	19,755	1900	356	4,246
1952	723,959	20,181	703,778	2,944	1926	10,904	10,904	----------	20,550	1899	263	3,798
1951	686,713	13,544	673,169	3,784	1925	9,495	9,495	----------	25,390	1898	199	3,030
1950	579,105	6,628	572,477	3,571	1924	6,409	6,409	----------	30,284	1897	263	1,617
1949	296,337	20,040	276,297	3,834	1923	3,661	3,661	----------	20,619	1896	238	2,799
1948	217,555	20,371	197,184	4,905	1922	4,345	4,345	----------	13,731	1895	177	2,419
1947	214,543	18,663	195,880	4,771	1921	4,517	4,517	----------	13,779			
1946	116,320	14,375	101,945	2,942	1920	2,762	2,762	----------	11,795	1894	417	1,389
1945	80,760	11,270	69,490	2,341	1919	3,068	3,068	----------	8,626	1893	577	1,053
					1918	1,569	1,569	----------	7,297	1892	637	2,164

Series C 162–167.   Aliens Naturalized, by Type of Provision: 1907 to 1970

[For years ending June 30]

Year	Total naturalized	Under general naturalization provisions	Married to U.S. citizens	Children of U.S. citizens [1]	Military	Other	Year	Total naturalized	Military	Other	Year	Total naturalized
	162	163	164	165	166	167		162	166	167		162
1970	110,399	79,761	14,899	5,023	10,616	100	1944	441,979	49,213	392,766	1917	88,104
1969	98,709	73,489	14,346	5,271	5,458	145	1943	318,933	37,474	281,459	1916	87,831
1968	102,726	76,377	17,156	6,579	2,438	176	1942	270,364	1,602	268,762	1915	91,848
1967	104,902	78,544	16,778	6,740	2,691	149	1941	277,294	1,547	275,747	1914	104,145
1966	103,059	76,214	16,448	7,695	2,561	141	1940	235,260	2,760	232,500	1913	83,561
1965	104,299	76,630	16,602	7,914	3,085	68	1939	188,813	3,638	185,175	1912	70,310
1964	112,234	82,621	17,867	9,056	2,605	85	1938	162,078	3,936	158,142	1911	56,683
1963	124,178	93,325	19,048	9,136	2,560	109	1937	164,976	2,053	162,923	1910	39,448
1962	127,307	98,739	17,379	8,723	2,335	131	1936	141,265	481	140,784	1909	38,374
1961	132,450	104,341	18,674	7,416	1,719	300	1935	118,945	–	118,945	1908	25,975
1960	119,442	91,548	19,799	6,149	1,594	352	1934	113,669	2,802	110,867	1907	7,941
1959	103,931	77,230	19,512	5,632	1,308	249	1933	113,363	995	112,368		
1958	119,866	94,380	19,353	4,966	916	251	1932	136,600	2	136,598		
1957	138,043	114,827	18,212	3,779	845	380	1931	143,495	3,224	140,271		
1956	145,885	117,161	18,224	2,865	7,204	431	1930	169,377	1,740	167,637		
1955	2 209,526	173,954	20,460	2,600	2 11,958	554	1929	224,728	531	224,197		
1954	117,831	86,166	15,977	1,208	13,745	735	1928	233,155	5,149	228,006		
1953	92,051	46,793	42,088	698	1,575	897	1927	199,804	4,311	195,493		
1952	88,655	26,920	58,027	760	1,585	1,363	1926	146,331	92	146,239		
1951	54,716	14,864	36,433	487	975	1,957	1925	152,457	–	152,457		
1950	66,346	19,403	40,684	499	2,067	3,693	1924	150,510	10,170	140,340		
1949	66,594	24,566	35,131	448	2,456	3,993	1923	145,084	7,109	137,975		
1948	70,150	34,347	28,898	419	1,070	5,416	1922	170,447	9,468	160,979		
1947	93,904	46,339	27,066	245	16,462	3,792	1921	181,292	17,636	163,656		
1946	150,062	93,346	40,190	118	15,213	1,195	1920	177,683	51,972	125,711		
1945	231,402	137,729	69,526	182	22,695	1,270	1919	217,358	128,335	89,023		
							1918	151,449	63,993	87,456		

–   Represents zero.
[1] Includes adopted children.
[2] Includes aliens in U.S. Armed Forces who were naturalized abroad.

Series C 168–180. Aliens Naturalized, by Sex and Area of Former Allegiance: 1907 to 1970

[For years ending June 30, except as noted]

Year	Declarations filed	Total naturalized	Sex		Area of former allegiance [1]								Petitions denied
			Male	Female	North-western Europe	Central Europe	Eastern Europe	Southern Europe	Asia	Canada	Other America	All other	
	168	169	170	171	172	173	174	175	176	177	178	179	180
1970	18,799	110,399	52,679	57,720	14,976	18,002	2,678	13,122	16,466	6,340	36,032	2,783	1,980
1969	14,102	98,709	45,177	53,532	16,065	18,822	2,725	14,235	15,362	6,387	22,202	2,911	2,043
1968	13,594	102,726	45,102	57,624	17,734	22,054	3,258	15,221	14,980	6,984	19,264	3,231	1,962
1967	12,465	104,902	46,014	58,888	18,487	23,059	2,832	17,156	14,259	8,120	17,542	3,447	2,008
1966	12,957	103,059	46,536	56,523	18,391	23,837	2,736	17,446	14,369	8,579	14,858	2,843	2,029
1965	13,082	104,299	48,495	55,804	19,205	26,734	3,461	16,620	14,680	8,489	12,273	2,837	2,059
1964	14,374	112,234	51,408	60,826	20,807	29,180	3,878	17,771	15,724	9,479	12,442	2,953	2,309
1963	14,478	124,178	58,303	65,875	23,861	37,789	4,952	18,338	15,253	9,944	11,602	2,439	2,436
1962	15,120	127,307	60,988	66,319	21,586	34,841	6,155	25,720	14,573	9,272	12,533	2,627	3,557
1961	15,921	132,450	58,795	73,655	22,168	34,858	8,908	27,188	12,308	10,033	14,178	2,809	3,175
1960	16,255	119,442	50,896	68,546	22,978	33,796	8,094	20,248	11,071	10,215	10,606	2,434	2,277
1959	16,115	103,931	43,719	60,212	21,842	32,594	7,975	12,202	8,313	10,324	8,804	1,877	2,208
1958	16,196	119,866	51,350	68,516	23,992	42,358	11,520	13,725	7,496	10,211	8,463	2,101	2,688
1957	15,911	138,043	60,289	77,754	25,878	47,656	18,062	15,762	7,548	10,891	8,977	3,269	2,948
1956	12,870	[2] 145,885	64,962	80,923	28,183	47,186	21,017	14,200	10,412	11,539	10,795	2,553	3,935
1955	10,855	[2] 209,526	95,850	113,676	46,253	62,557	22,795	23,955	16,000	18,151	15,321	4,494	4,571
1954	9,100	[2] 117,831	54,477	63,354	31,085	28,341	7,848	16,024	12,170	13,062	7,210	2,091	2,084
1953	23,558	92,051	34,657	57,394	23,238	26,676	5,440	13,507	4,966	10,303	5,181	2,740	1,122
1952	111,461	88,655	28,597	60,058	23,688	25,933	5,392	13,360	3,749	10,004	4,548	1,981	2,163
1951	91,497	54,716	18,711	36,005	17,069	11,864	3,485	8,503	2,886	5,872	3,827	1,210	2,395
1950	93,527	66,346	25,745	40,601	20,260	13,946	4,300	12,200	4,802	5,882	4,133	823	2,276
1949	64,866	66,594	27,865	38,729	20,782	14,471	5,244	11,716	4,993	5,347	3,607	434	2,271
1948	60,187	70,150	33,147	37,003	18,834	17,495	6,150	13,059	7,201	3,860	3,183	368	2,887
1947	37,771	[2] 93,904	52,998	40,906	27,017	24,220	7,281	15,661	11,741	[3]	4,676	3,308	3,953
1946	28,787	[2] 150,062	76,296	73,766	41,772	46,802	14,481	30,336	3,450	[3]	7,144	6,077	6,575
1945	31,195	[2] 231,402	[4] 116,691	[4] 114,711	57,997	82,195	23,948	51,629	2,545	[3]	8,590	4,498	9,782
1944	42,368	[2] 441,979	[4] 202,698	[4] 239,281	114,801	139,304	48,382	122,638	5,592	[3]	11,099	163	7,297
1943	115,664	[2] 318,933	[4] 157,663	[4] 161,270	122,708	86,365	42,012	51,758	6,133	[3]	9,866	91	13,656
1942	221,796	270,364	112,040	158,324	117,607	71,762	41,586	31,047	2,075	[3]	6,247	40	8,348
1941	224,123	277,294	136,348	140,946	96,375	86,122	35,844	51,819	1,844	[3]	5,249	41	7,769
1940	203,536	235,260	132,406	102,854	78,357	75,024	29,146	47,236	1,523	[3]	3,930	44	6,549
1939	155,691	188,813	113,934	74,879	62,430	59,636	22,209	40,452	1,331	[3]	2,709	46	5,630
1938	150,673	162,078	92,041	70,037	55,359	51,359	19,809	32,235	1,311	[3]	1,976	29	4,854
1937	176,195	164,976	97,696	67,280	58,002	55,789	18,970	29,169	1,290	[3]	1,710	46	4,042
1936	148,118	141,265	86,777	54,488	54,852	47,289	14,781	22,194	901	[3]	1,220	28	3,124
1935	136,524	118,945	82,182	36,763	44,605	39,554	11,825	21,171	760	[3]	987	43	2,765
1934	108,079	113,669	82,465	31,204	39,481	38,859	11,476	20,349	703	[3]	896	1,905	1,133
1933	83,046	113,363	78,293	35,070	40,795	37,068	12,544	19,498	706	[3]	780	1,972	4,703
1932	101,345	136,600	95,901	40,699	39,123	43,334	14,884	24,851	676	10,144	721	2,867	5,478
1931	106,272	143,495	106,715	36,780	38,465	48,041	17,428	27,793	822	7,173	989	2,784	7,514
1930	62,138	169,377	120,572	48,805	38,915	56,540	24,046	37,481	993	7,566	651	3,185	9,068
1929	280,645	224,728	167,665	57,063	50,554	72,267	33,652	53,234	1,445	8,223	664	4,689	11,848
1928	254,588	233,155	181,875	51,280	46,059	72,111	34,962	63,989	1,334	7,712	506	6,482	12,479
1927	258,295	199,804	165,833	33,971	37,293	65,592	27,399	55,924	[5]	5,237	455	7,904	11,946
1926	277,539	146,331	121,561	24,770	28,317	49,696	23 158	33,750	[5]	5,078	283	6,049	13,274
1925	277,218	152,457	133,881	18,576	29,006	55,262	23,154	31,671	[5]	7,013	290	6,061	15,613
1924	424,540	150,510	135,739	14,771	28,780	55,915	23,348	32,232	[5]	5,765	270	4,200	18,324
1923	296,636	145,084	[6] 139,073	6,011	29,107	56,112	22,897	28,392	[5]	6,546	[5]	2,030	24,884
1922	273,511	170,447											29,076
1921	303,904	181,292											18,981
1920	299,076	177,683											15,586
1919	391,156	217,358											13,119
1918	342,283	151,449											12,182
1917	440,651	88,104											9,544
1916	209,204	87,831											11,927
1915	247,958	91,848											13,691
1914	214,104	104,145											13,133
1913	182,095	83,561											10,891
1912	171,133	70,310											9,635
1911	189,249	56,683											9,017
1910	169,348	39,448											7,781
1909	145,745	38,374											6,341
1908	137,571	25,975											3,330
1907 [7]	73,658	7,941											250

[1] See text for list of countries.
[2] Data for 1943–1947 and 1954–1956 include naturalizations in various theaters of war or areas occupied by U.S. Forces.
[3] Included in Northwestern Europe as part of British Empire.
[4] Data are from unpublished data of the Immigration and Naturalization Service and do not agree with source quoted. Source excludes Armed Forces overseas whereas the data shown here include them.

[5] Included in "All other."
[6] Includes data for both male and female for the first quarter of the year when sexes were not reported separately.
[7] September 27, 1906, to June 30, 1907.

Series C 181–194. Citizenship Status of the Population: 1890 to 1970

[Prior to 1920, the citizenship inquiry of the Population Census was restricted to males 21 years old and over.   1970 figures based on 5-percent sample, 1960 on 25-percent, and 1950 on 20-percent; therefore differ from series for 1890–1940 based on complete count]

Year	All ages							21 years old and over						
	Total population	Native population	Foreign-born population					Total population	Native population	Foreign-born population				
			Total	Natural-ized	Having first papers	No papers	Unknown citizen-ship			Total	Natural-ized	Having first papers	No papers	Unknown citizen-ship
	181	182	183	184	185	186	187	188	189	190	191	192	193	194
BOTH SEXES														
1970	203,193,774	193,454,051	9,739,723	6,198,173	3,541,550			122,597,202	114,076,804	8,520,398	5,795,027	2,725,371		
1960 *	179,325,657	169,587,566	9,738,091	(NA)	(NA)	(NA)	731,785	108,051,172	99,071,648	8,979,524	(NA)	(NA)	(NA)	674,105
1950	150,216,110	139,868,715	10,347,395	7,562,970	2,052,640		731,785	96,732,900	86,712,450	10,020,450	7,466,445	1,879,900		674,105
1940	131,669,275	120,074,379	11,594,896	7,280,265	924,524	2,555,128	834,979	83,996,629	72,703,808	11,292,821	7,159,643	910,416	2,424,976	797,786
1930	122,775,046	108,570,897	14,204,149	7,919,536	1,266,419	4,518,341	499,853	72,943,624	59,607,271	13,336,353	7,681,681	1,237,255	3,946,176	471,241
1920	105,710,620	91,789,928	13,920,692	6,489,883	1,222,553	5,406,780	801,476	60,886,520	48,200,127	12,686,393	6,218,801	1,197,698	4,529,756	740,138
MALE														
1970	98,896,402	94,424,109	4,472,293	2,918,753	1,553,540			57,992,895	54,128,061	3,864,834	2,719,383	1,145,451		
1960 *	88,303,167	83,542,735	4,760,432	(NA)	(NA)	(NA)	349,465	52,147,983	47,765,139	4,382,844	(NA)	(NA)	(NA)	320,035
1950	74,200,085	68,941,830	5,258,255	4,033,070	875,720		349,465	47,137,460	42,045,230	5,092,230	3,981,895	790,300		320,035
1940	66,061,592	59,939,945	6,121,647	4,137,027	581,713	1,008,071	394,836	42,004,816	36,035,228	5,969,588	4,076,207	574,296	942,855	376,230
1930	62,137,080	54,489,990	7,647,090	4,365,403	955,942	2,081,710	244,035	37,056,757	29,837,780	7,218,977	4,247,704	939,875	1,800,295	231,103
1920	53,900,431	46,224,996	7,675,435	3,449,547	1,137,021	2,695,042	393,825	31,403,370	24,339,776	7,063,594	3,320,226	1,119,982	2,259,310	364,076
1910	47,332,277	39,664,529	7,667,748					26,999,151	20,218,937	6,780,214	3,038,303	571,521	2,390,426	779,964
1900	38,816,448	33,186,258	5,630,190					21,134,299	16,124,013	5,010,286	2,848,807	412,271	1,014,219	734,989
1890	32,237,101							16,940,311	12,591,852	4,348,459	2,545,753	236,061	1,189,452	377,193
FEMALE														
1970	104,297,372	99,029,942	5,267,430	3,279,420	1,988,010			64,604,307	59,948,743	4,655,564	3,075,644	1,579,920		
1960 *	91,022,490	86,044,831	4,977,659	(NA)	(NA)	(NA)	382,320	55,903,189	51,306,509	4,596,680	(NA)	(NA)	(NA)	354,070
1950	76,016,025	70,926,885	5,089,140	3,529,900	1,176,920		382,320	49,595,440	44,667,220	4,928,220	3,484,550	1,089,600		354,070
1940	65,607,683	60,134,434	5,473,249	3,143,238	342,811	1,547,057	440,143	41,991,813	36,668,580	5,323,233	3,083,436	336,120	1,482,121	421,556
1930	60,637,966	54,080,907	6,557,059	3,554,133	310,477	2,436,631	255,818	35,886,867	29,769,491	6,117,376	3,433,977	297,380	2,145,881	240,138
1920	51,810,189	45,564,932	6,245,257	3,040,336	85,532	2,711,738	407,651	29,483,150	23,860,351	5,622,799	2,898,575	77,716	2,270,446	376,062

* Denotes first year for which figures include Alaska and Hawaii.   NA   Not available.

Series C 195–227. Native Population of Foreign or Mixed Parentage, by Country of Origin of Parents: 1900 to 1970

[1940 figures based on 5-percent sample; 1950 on 20-percent; 1960 on 25-percent; and 1970 on 15-percent]

Series No.	Country of origin of parents	Total		White					
		1970	1960 *	1950	1940	1930	1920	1910	1900
195	**Total**	**23,955,930**	**24,312,263**	**23,589,485**	**23,157,580**	**25,902,383**	**22,686,204**	**18,897,837**	**15,646,017**
196	England and Wales	1,268,643	1,409,159	1,443,230	1,466,900	1,890,051	1,864,345	1,822,264	1,695,558
197	Scotland	411,121	455,453	463,325	446,540	545,268	514,436	484,699	447,524
198	Northern Ireland	99,187	186,984	29,890	270,820	517,167	} 3,122,013	} 3,304,015	} 3,375,546
199	Ireland (Eire)	1,198,845	1,434,590	1,891,495	1,838,920	2,341,712			
200	Norway	517,406	622,056	652,380	662,600	752,246	701,096	609,068	478,531
201	Sweden	679,068	832,451	864,695	856,320	967,453	888,497	752,695	542,032
202	Denmark [1]	264,151	314,290	318,710	305,640	349,668	320,410	256,175	187,844
203	Netherlands	273,139	280,243	272,535	261,320	280,833	249,339	188,015	(2)
204	Belgium	89,238	89,972	85,500	76,400	82,897	68,961	46,222	(2)
205	Switzerland	168,976	201,486	215,660	205,680	260,993	257,341	217,459	178,691
206	France	237,982	240,099	253,665	246,120	336,373	288,350	226,059	214,592
207	Germany	2,789,070	3,330,849	3,742,615	3,998,840	5,264,289	5,346,004	5,670,611	5,340,147
208	Poland	1,826,137	2,032,276	1,925,015	1,912,380	2,073,615	1,303,351	725,924	326,764
209	Czechoslovakia	598,682	690,212	705,890	664,620	890,441	(3)	(3)	(3)
210	Austria	761,311	794,123	816,465	781,340	583,734	[4] 1,235,097	716,753	391,636
211	Hungary	420,432	456,385	437,080	371,840	316,318	[4] 538,518	215,295	81,897
212	Yugoslavia	293,526	282,705	239,920	222,300	257,979	(3)	(3)	(3)
213	U.S.S.R.	1,479,733	1,599,669	1,647,420	1,569,360	1,516,214	1,508,604	775,654	} 288,098
214	Lithuania	254,976	281,371	249,825	229,040	245,589			
215	Finland	158,327	173,203	172,370	167,080	178,058	152,161	85,672	
216	Romania	146,116	149,230	130,100	131,760	147,060	64,776	26,934	(2)
217	Greece	257,296	219,419	195,235	163,420	129,225	52,083	9,985	(2)
218	Italy	3,232,246	3,286,936	3,143,405	2,971,200	2,756,453	1,751,091	771,645	254,550
219	Spain	97,668	81,164	69,490	61,700	52,305	} 137,284	} 74,548	{ (2)
220	Portugal	149,532	148,602	117,675	114,060	97,917			(2)
221	Other Europe	168,082	121,984	128,000	75,660	101,652			(2)
222	Asia	920,475	642,520	239,525	183,260	152,347	(2)	(2)	(2)
223	Canada-French	} 2,222,135	2,228,551	{ 519,495	635,020	735,307	562,360	562,709	456,030
224	Canada-Other			{ 1,468,325	1,231,020	1,323,617	1,279,245	1,088,112	933,440
225	Mexico	1,579,440	1,160,090	891,980	699,220	583,422	253,176	162,959	(2)
226	Other America	479,439	248,272	101,240	91,980	75,220	51,259	30,169	(2)
227	All other and not reported	913,605	317,919	157,300	245,220	96,960	176,407	74,196	453,137

* Denotes first year for which figures include Alaska and Hawaii.
[1] Includes Iceland prior to 1930.
[2] Included with "All other and not reported."
[3] Included with Austria and Hungary.
[4] Areas as defined in 1910.

Series C 228–295.   Foreign-Born Population, by Country of Birth: 1850 to 1970

[Data are given for each country for all census years since 1850 for which figures are available]

Series No.	Country of birth	Total foreign born									
		1970[1]	1960[2]	1950[3]	1930	1920	1910	1900	1890	1880	1870
228	All countries	9,619,302	9,738,091	10,420,908	14,204,149	13,920,692	13,515,886	10,341,276	9,249,560	6,679,943	5,567,229
229	Northwestern Europe	1,536,722	1,973,025	(NA)	3,728,050	3,830,094	4,239,067	4,202,683	4,380,752	3,494,484	3,124,638
230	England	458,114	528,205	}	809,563	813,853	877,719	840,513	909,092	664,160	555,046
231	Scotland	170,134	213,219	846,570	354,323	254,570	261,076	233,524	242,231	170,136	140,835
232	Wales	17,014	23,469		60,205	67,066	82,488	93,586	100,079	83,302	74,533
233	Northern Ireland	40,837	68,162	}	178,832	1,037,234	1,352,251	1,615,459	1,871,509	1,854,571	1,855,827
234	Ireland (Eire)	251,375	338,722	505,285	744,810						
235	Norway	97,243	152,698	202,448	347,852	363,863	403,877	336,388	322,665	181,729	114,246
236	Sweden	127,070	214,491	325,118	595,250	625,585	665,207	582,014	478,041	194,337	97,332
237	Denmark	61,410	85,060	107,982	179,474	189,154	181,649	153,690	132,543	64,196	30,107
238	Iceland	2,895	2,780	(NA)	2,764						
239	Netherlands[4]	110,570	118,415	102,224	133,133	131,766	120,063	94,931	81,828	58,090	46,802
240	Belgium	41,412	50,294	(NA)	64,194	62,687	49,400	29,757	22,639	15,535	12,553
241	Luxembourg	3,531	4,360	(NA)	9,048	12,585	3,071	3,031	2,882	12,836	5,802
242	Switzerland	49,732	61,568	71,636	113,010	118,659	124,848	115,593	104,069	88,621	75,153
243	France	105,385	111,582	108,547	135,592	153,072	117,418	104,197	113,174	106,971	116,402
244	Central and Eastern Europe	2,811,094	3,717,907	(NA)	5,897,799	6,134,845	6,014,028	4,136,646	3,420,629	2,187,776	1,784,449
245	Germany	832,965	989,815	991,321	1,608,814	1,686,108	[5]2,311,237	2,663,418	2,784,894	1,966,742	1,690,533
246	Poland	548,107	747,750	861,655	1,268,583	1,139,979	[5]937,884	383,407	147,440	48,557	14,436
247	Czechoslovakia	160,899	227,618	278,438	491,638	362,438					
248	Austria	214,014	304,507	409,043	370,914	575,627	[5]845,555	432,798	241,377	124,024	70,797
249	Hungary	183,236	245,252	268,183	274,450	397,283	495,609	145,714	62,435	11,526	3,737
250	Yugoslavia	153,745	165,798	144,070	211,416	169,439					
251	U.S.S.R.	[6]463,462	[6]690,598	896,000	1,153,628						
252	Latvia	41,707	50,681	(NA)	20,673	1,400,495	[5]1,184,412	423,726	182,644	35,722	4,644
253	Estonia	12,163	13,991	(NA)	3,550						
254	Lithuania	76,001	121,475	147,872	193,606	135,068					
255	Finland	45,499	67,624	95,686	142,478	149,824	129,680	62,641			
256	Romania	70,687	84,575	85,230	146,393	102,823	65,923	15,032			
257	Bulgaria	8,609	8,223	(NA)	9,399	10,477	11,498				
258	Turkey in Europe	(7)	(7)	(7)	2,257	5,284	[8]32,230	[7]9,910	[7]1,839	[7]1,205	[7]302
259	Southern Europe	1,343,510	1,528,473	(NA)	2,106,295	1,911,213	1,525,875	530,200	206,648	58,265	25,853
260	Greece	177,275	159,167	169,335	174,526	175,976	101,282	8,515	1,887	776	390
261	Albania	9,180	9,618	(NA)	8,814	5,608	(8)				
262	Italy	1,008,533	1,256,999	1,427,952	1,790,429	1,610,113	1,343,125	484,027	182,580	44,230	17,157
263	Spain	57,488	44,999	(NA)	59,362	49,535	22,108	7,050	6,185	5,121	3,764
264	Portugal	91,034	57,690	56,591	73,164	69,981	59,360	30,608	15,996	8,138	4,542
265	Other Europe	20,700	14,320	[9]185,685	16,255	5,901	12,871	2,251	12,579	3,786	1,678
266	Danzig	---	---	---	1,483	2,049					
267	Europe, not specified	---	---	---	14,772	3,852	[10]12,871	2,251	12,579	3,786	1,678
268	Asia	[7]824,887	[7]499,312	[7]275,990	275,665	237,950	191,484	120,248	113,396	107,630	64,565
269	Armenia	(6)	(6)	(NA)	32,166	36,628					
270	Palestine	(11)	(11)	(NA)	6,137	3,203	59,729				
271	Syria	14,962	16,717	(NA)	57,227	51,901					
272	Turkey in Asia	[7]48,085	[7]52,228	(NA)	46,654	11,019		(7)	(7)	(7)	(7)
273	China	172,132	99,735	(NA)	46,129	43,560	56,756	81,534	106,701	104,468	63,042
274	Japan	120,235	109,175	(NA)	70,993	81,502	67,744	24,788	2,292	401	73
275	India	51,000	12,296	(NA)	5,850	4,901	4,664	2,031	2,143	1,707	586
276	Korea	38,711	11,171								
277	Philippines	184,842	104,843	---							
278	Other Asia	[11]194,920	[11]93,147	(NA)	10,509	5,236	2,591	11,895	2,260	1,054	864
279	America	2,616,391	1,860,809	[9]1,655,324	2,102,209	1,727,017	1,489,231	1,317,380	1,088,245	807,230	551,335
280	Canada-French				370,852	307,786	385,083	[12]395,126	[12]302,496		
281	Canada-Other	812,421	952,500	1,003,038	915,537	817,139	819,554	[12]784,796	[12]678,442	717,157	493,464
282	Newfoundland				23,980	13,249	5,080	(12)	(12)		
283	Cuba	439,048	79,150	(NA)	18,493	14,872	15,133	11,081	23,256	6,917	5,319
284	Other West Indies	[13]34,513	[13]114,772	(NA)	87,748	64,090	32,502	14,354		9,484	6,251
285	Mexico	759,711	575,902	454,417	641,462	486,418	221,915	103,393	77,853	68,399	42,435
286	Central America	315,460	48,949	(NA)	10,514	4,912	1,736	3,897	1,192	707	301
287	South America	255,238	89,536	(NA)	33,623	18,551	8,228	4,733	5,006	4,566	3,565
288	All other	465,998	144,245	[9]202,723	77,876	73,672	43,330	31,868	27,311	20,772	14,711
289	Africa	61,463	18,737	(NA)	8,859	5,781	3,992	2,538	2,207	2,204	2,657
290	Australia	24,271	22,209	(NA)	12,816	10,914	9,035	6,807	5,984	4,906	3,118
291	Azores	28,865	22,586	(NA)	35,611	33,995	18,274	9,768	9,739	7,641	4,434
292	Other Atlantic Islands	18,680	8,302	(NA)	9,467	10,345					
293	Pacific Islands	[14]8,870	[14]12,521	(NA)	4,527	3,712	2,415	2,013	3,369	1,953	910
294	Country not specified	323,849	59,890	89,691	1,588	3,589	2,687	2,546	479	---	954
295	Born at sea	---	---	---	5,008	5,336	6,927	8,196	5,533	4,068	2,638

See footnotes at end of table.

Series C 228–295. Foreign-Born Population, by Country of Birth: 1850 to 1970—Con.

[Data are given for each country for all census years since 1850 for which figures are available]

Series No.	Country of birth	Total foreign born—Con.		Foreign-born, white						
		1860	1850	1970[1]	1960[2]	1950[3]	1940[15]	1930	1920	1910
228	All countries	4,138,697	2,244,602	8,733,770	9,293,992	10,158,854	11,419,138	13,983,405	13,712,754	13,345,545
229	Northwestern Europe	2,472,211	1,437,475	1,528,092	1,968,797	2,326,887	2,825,671	3,726,844	3,828,876	4,237,373
230	England	433,494	278,675	453,867	526,157	554,625	621,975	808,684	812,828	876,455
231	Scotland	108,518	70,550	169,636	213,026	244,200	279,321	354,323	254,567	261,034
232	Wales	45,763	29,868	16,904	23,407	30,060	35,360	60,205	67,066	82,479
233	Northern Ireland			40,733	68,083	15,398	106,416	178,832		
234	Ireland (Eire)	1,611,304	961,719	250,492	338,350	504,961	572,031	744,810	1,037,233	1,352,155
235	Norway	43,995	12,678	96,938	152,644	202,294	262,088	347,852	363,862	403,858
236	Sweden	18,625	3,559	126,843	214,313	324,944	445,070	595,250	625,580	665,183
237	Denmark	9,962	1,838	61,307	84,989	107,897	138,175	179,474	189,154	181,621
238	Iceland			2,868	2,769	2,455	2,104	2,764		
239	Netherlands[4]	28,281	9,848	109,709	118,160	102,133	111,064	133,133	131,766	120,053
240	Belgium	9,072	1,313	41,259	50,210	52,891	53,958	64,194	62,686	49,397
241	Luxembourg			3,498	4,335	5,590	6,886	9,048	12,585	3,068
242	Switzerland	53,327	13,358	49,547	61,490	71,515	88,293	113,010	118,659	124,834
243	France	109,870	54,069	104,491	110,864	107,924	102,930	135,265	152,890	117,236
244	Central and Eastern Europe	1,311,722	586,240	2,802,546	3,711,725	4,218,903	4,958,368	5,897,795	6,134,825	6,013,720
245	Germany	1,276,075	583,774	830,498	986,564	984,331	1,237,772	1,608,814	1,686,102	[5]2,311,085
246	Poland	7,298		547,010	747,250	861,184	993,479	1,268,583	1,139,978	[5]937,884
247	Czechoslovakia			160,672	227,467	278,268	319,971	491,638	362,436	
248	Austria	25,061	946	213,501	304,192	408,785	479,906	370,914	575,625	[5]845,506
249	Hungary			182,681	244,945	268,022	290,228	274,450	397,282	495,600
250	Yugoslavia			153,020	165,658	143,956	161,093	211,416	169,437	
251	U.S.S.R.			[6]461,444	[6]689,462	894,844	1,040,884	1,153,624		
252	Latvia			41,558	50,658	31,590	18,636	20,673	1,400,489	
253	Estonia	3,160	1,414	12,130	13,974	10,085	4,178	3,550		
254	Lithuania			75,806	121,349	147,765	165,771	193,606	135,068	[5]1,184,382
255	Finland			45,372	67,540	95,506	117,210	142,478	149,824	129,669
256	Romania			70,364	84,471	84,952	115,940	146,393	102,823	65,920
257	Bulgaria			8,490	8,195	9,615	8,888	9,399	10,477	11,453
258	Turkey in Europe	[7]128	[7]106	(7)	(7)	(7)	4,412	2,257	5,284	[8]32,221
259	Southern Europe	20,365	8,152	1,337,283	1,525,251	1,706,640	1,896,886	2,093,976	1,902,781	1,523,934
260	Greece	328	86	176,025	158,894	169,083	163,252	174,526	175,972	101,264
261	Albania			8,895	9,572	10,510	(8)	(8)		(8)
262	Italy	11,677	3,679	1,005,687	1,255,812	1,427,145	1,623,580	1,790,424	1,610,109	1,343,070
263	Spain	4,244	3,113	56,866	44,815	45,565	47,707	59,033	49,247	21,977
264	Portugal	4,116	1,274	89,810	56,158	54,357	62,347	69,993	67,453	57,623
265	Other Europe	1,403		20,232	14,166	15,670	[8]19,819	[8]25,065	11,509	[10]12,851
268	Asia	36,796	1,135	273,598	201,330	[7]179,900	149,909	157,580	110,450	64,314
269	Armenia			(6)	(6)	(6)	(6)	(6)	(6)	
270	Palestine			(11)	(11)	(11)	7,047	6,135	3,202	
271	Syria			14,840	16,566	35,325	50,859	57,227	51,900	59,702
272	Turkey in Asia	(7)	(7)	47,705	[7]51,887	[7]71,730	52,479	46,651	11,014	
273	China	35,565	758	11,839	12,858	11,985		2,279	716	333
274	Japan			6,085	11,686	4,650		632	278	198
275	India			41,412	6,414	5,370		3,300	2,532	2,078
276	Korea			2,094	2,681					
277	Philippines			11,187	15,624					
278	Other Asia	1,231	377	[11]138,436	[11]83,614	[6][11]50,840	[6]39,524	[6]41,356	[6]40,808	2,003
279	America	288,285	168,484	2,360,490	1,743,058	1,564,139	1,509,855	2,011,224	1,656,801	1,453,186
280	Canada-French					[12]238,409	273,366	370,852	307,786	385,083
281	Canada-Other	249,970	147,711	798,782	941,906	[12]756,153	770,753	907,660	810,092	810,987
282	Newfoundland					(12)	21,361	23,971	13,242	5,076
283	Cuba			425,974	74,921	29,295	15,277	16,089	12,843	12,869
284	Other West Indies	7,353	5,772	[13]5,388	[13]30,876	[13]22,735	15,257	15,511	13,526	10,300
285	Mexico	27,466	13,317	746,327	572,564	450,562	377,433	639,017	478,383	219,802
286	Central America	233	141	145,251	38,773	23,475	7,638	7,791	4,074	1,507
287	South America	3,263	1,543	238,768	84,018	43,510	28,770	30,333	16,855	7,562
288	All other	7,915	43,116	411,529	129,665	146,715	58,630	70,921	67,512	40,167
289	Africa	526	551	48,021	16,545	13,260		7,868	5,222	3,518
290	Australia	1,419		23,699	22,060	19,900	10,998	12,720	10,801	8,938
291	Azores	1,361		28,397	22,467	26,025	25,751	35,432	33,788	
292	Other Atlantic Islands			9,140	4,949	4,595	3,232	4,053	5,196	15,795
293	Pacific Islands	721	588	[14]2,570	[14]7,665	[14]5,760		4,367	3,643	2,344
294	Country not specified	1,366	41,977	299,702	55,979	77,175	17,638	1,518	3,560	2,687
295	Born at sea	2,522					1,011	4,963	5,302	6,885

NA Not available.
[1] Based on 15-percent sample.
[2] Based on 25-percent sample.
[3] Foreign-born white based on 20-percent sample; total foreign born, on complete count.
[4] Listed as Holland prior to 1910.
[5] Persons reported in 1910 as of Polish mother tongue born in Austria, Germany, and U.S.S.R. have been deducted from their respective countries and combined as Poland.
[6] White foreign born for 1920–1950, Armenia included with "Other Asia"; beginning 1960, total and white foreign born with U.S.S.R.
[7] 1850–1900, Turkey in Asia included with Turkey in Europe; beginning 1950, Turkey in Europe included with Turkey in Asia.

[8] 1910, Albania included with Turkey in Europe; 1930 and 1940, with "Other Europe."
[9] Includes countries for which figures are not shown separately.
[10] Includes persons born in Serbia and Montenegro, which became part of Yugoslavia in 1918.
[11] Palestine included with "Other Asia."
[12] Newfoundland included with Canada prior to 1910.
[13] Excludes U.S. outlying areas.
[14] Includes New Zealand and Trust Territories of the Pacific Islands, but excludes outlying areas of the U.S.
[15] There were 11,656,641 total foreign born persons in 1940; data by country of birth are not available.

Series C 296–301. Passenger Arrivals and Departures: 1908 to 1970

[For years ending June 30. Excludes travel over international land borders, crewmen, military personnel, and travelers between the United States and its outlying areas]

Year	Arrivals Total	Arrivals U.S. citizens	Arrivals Aliens	Departures Total	Departures U.S. citizens	Departures Aliens	Year	Arrivals Total	Arrivals U.S. citizens	Arrivals Aliens	Departures Total	Departures U.S. citizens	Departures Aliens
	296	297	298	299	300	301		296	297	298	299	300	301
1970	10,039,426	6,208,226	3,831,200	9,353,738	6,107,257	3,246,481	1939	567,773	343,096	224,677	501,500	327,814	173,686
1969	8,800,147	5,457,266	3,342,881	8,029,192	5,221,574	2,807,618	1938	602,263	392,796	209,467	589,091	393,186	195,905
1968	7,549,492	4,645,045	2,904,447	7,061,131	4,587,389	2,473,742	1937	567,043	373,132	193,911	584,990	386,059	198,931
1967	6,627,010	4,073,538	2,553,472	6,177,410	4,033,283	2,144,127	1936	470,682	307,981	162,701	476,172	306,060	170,112
1966	5,867,001	3,613,855	2,253,146	5,462,702	3,542,751	1,919,951	1935	429,543	275,199	154,344	430,744	265,095	165,649
1965	5,059,458	3,099,951	1,959,507	4,819,860	3,084,921	1,734,939	1934	405,877	264,143	141,734	412,376	255,071	157,305
1964	4,475,324	2,786,907	1,688,417	4,139,932	2,709,196	1,430,736	1933	424,324	295,760	128,564	534,728	322,553	212,175
1963	3,948,226	2,433,463	1,514,763	3,688,191	2,421,348	1,266,843[9]	1932	471,590	326,720	144,870	585,561	350,788	234,773
1962	3,612,678	2,199,326	1,413,352	3,318,817	2,159,857	1,158,960	1931	650,548	420,200	230,348	683,586	429,219	254,367
1961	3,360,606	2,043,416	1,317,190	3,063,056	1,969,119	1,093,937	1930	813,481	467,298	346,183	683,759	445,485	238,274
1960	3,111,530	1,920,582	1,190,948	2,939,330	1,934,953	1,004,377	1929	803,621	441,758	361,863	632,602	414,379	218,223
1959	2,865,567	1,804,435	1,061,132	2,624,959	1,739,046	885,913	1928	777,838	422,449	355,389	644,869	414,265	230,604
1958	2,427,540	1,469,262	958,278	2,194,343	1,483,915	710,428	1927	728,950	367,908	361,042	575,854	358,278	217,576
1957	2,338,768	1,365,075	973,693	1,976,715	1,402,107	574,608	1926	688,252	359,321	328,931	569,425	360,342	209,083
1956	2,071,130	1,281,110	790,020	1,813,498	1,272,516	540,982	1925	601,942	304,277	297,665	524,843	314,341	210,502
1955	1,839,156	1,167,593	671,563	1,584,188	1,096,146	488,042	1924	849,845	285,516	564,329	457,607	267,056	190,551
1954	1,612,767	1,009,503	603,264	1,413,767	971,025	442,742	1923	758,792	287,321	471,471	439,415	260,765	178,650
1953	1,486,440	921,384	565,056	1,340,295	923,560	416,735	1922	571,442	228,082	343,360	617,494	293,317	324,177
1952	1,433,010	797,108	635,902	1,198,503	812,644	385,859	1921	1,041,470	203,715	837,755	645,041	247,503	397,538
1951	1,282,165	749,702	532,463	999,574	663,773	335,801	1920	575,533	135,520	440,013	556,956	167,602	389,354
1950	1,182,152	651,943	530,209	981,124	651,595	329,529	1919	194,099	73,487	120,612	363,501	194,252	169,249
1949	1,104,473	606,992	497,481	863,951	548,352	315,599	1918	157,605	44,757	112,848	362,920	232,371	130,549
1948	1,023,742	533,531	490,211	786,319	474,048	312,271	1917	312,392	82,738	229,654	195,093	81,156	113,937
1947	829,540	428,009	401,531	695,441	446,320	249,121	1916	326,220	88,789	237,431	297,885	87,500	210,385
1946	485,007	263,322	221,685	389,584	226,308	163,276	1915	522,032	192,653	329,379	483,342	142,291	341,051
1945	310,113	168,726	141,387	186,301	100,490	85,811	1914	1,532,533	240,867	1,291,666	836,689	299,470	537,219
1944	205,775	101,108	104,667	118,109	60,598	57,511	1913	1,557,307	230,623	1,326,684	736,388	256,367	480,021
1943	169,870	99,233	70,637	87,233	59,083	28,150	1912	1,164,233	240,369	923,864	799,226	274,101	525,125
1942	180,631	112,055	68,576	108,504	67,179	41,325	1911	1,173,241	236,660	936,581	694,876	258,452	436,424
1941	261,189	169,064	92,125	230,130	163,270	66,860	1910	1,327,958	220,254	1,107,704	589,185	271,331	317,854
1940	422,273	250,887	171,386	360,908	218,485	142,423	1909	1,074,388	217,173	857,215	586,452	215,768	370,684
							1908	1,114,668	200,447	914,221	874,686	159,858	714,828

Series C 302–316. Passengers Arriving, by Area of Embarkation, Flag of Carrier, and Mode of Travel: 1931 to 1970

[In thousands. For years ending June 30. Excludes travel over international land borders, crewmen, military personnel, and travelers between the United States and its outlying areas]

Year	Passengers arriving	Europe	Asia[1]	Africa	Oceania[1]	Canada and Greenland[2]	Mexico[3]	West Indies	Central America	South America	Cruise[4]	United States	Foreign	By sea	By air
	302	303	304	305	306	307	308	309	310	311	312	313	314	315	316
1970	10,039	4,087	893	30	225	79	880	2,481	264	531	569	5,106	4,933	867	9,172
1969	8,800	3,466	686	21	186	84	827	2,333	243	495	460	4,581	4,219	764	8,036
1968	7,549	3,044	565	15	161	77	710	1,931	219	429	397	3,883	3,666	713	6,836
1967	6,627	2,758	482	19	133	77	621	1,618	199	358	362	3,208	3,419	754	5,873
1966	5,867	2,497	406	18	115	64	538	1,373	175	324	356	2,744	3,123	816	5,051
1965	5,059	2,212	351	15	96	54	441	1,118	148	277	347	2,246	2,813	840	4,220
1964	4,475	1,952	326	16	81	43	388	927	130	252	360	1,981	2,494	877	3,598
1963	3,948	1,704	284	17	85	45	332	827	118	218	319	1,753	2,195	834	3,114
1962	3,613	1,514	248	15	78	41	296	819	120	209	272	1,620	1,992	796	2,816
1961	3,361	1,444	223	14	63	29	268	801	99	207	214	1,469	1,891	751	2,609
1960	3,112	1,256	197	14	55	23	257	847	93	194	175	1,472	1,640	754	2,358
1959	2,866	1,172	175	12	51	32	226	807	92	156	142	1,431	1,435	747	2,119
1958	2,428	1,065	161	13	57	25	76	794	89	148	--------	1,291	1,137	635	1,793
1957	2,339	1,049	148	11	51	39	32	802	81	127	--------	1,256	1,083	683	1,656
1956	2,071	950	130	11	37	40	30	688	73	112	--------	1,164	907	664	1,407
1955	1,839	811	135	11	34	72	29	577	65	104	--------	1,047	792	662	1,178
1954	1,613	722	108	7	22	74	16	511	58	94	--------	907	706	607	1,006
1953	1,486	648	89	10	9	63	21	491	58	97	--------	837	649	576	910
1952	1,433	653	83	8	9	50	25	460	53	91	--------	842	591	623	810
1951	1,282	582	66	4	26	36	15	430	45	77	--------	763	519	548	734
1950	1,182	588	50	5	19	35	4	363	51	67	--------	750	432	602	581
1949	1,104	480	49	7	16	97	4	337	47	67	--------	697	407	503	602
1948	1,024	441	51	8	20	78	4	313	46	63	--------	648	375	491	532
1947	830	325	33	8	23	51	3	323	36	28	--------	586	244	356	473
1946	485	159	18	15	24	34	7	196	23	9	--------	377	108	200	285

See footnotes at end of table.

Series C 302–316. Passengers Arriving, by Area of Embarkation, Flag of Carrier, and Mode of Travel: 1931 to 1970—Con.

[In thousands]

Year	Passengers arriving	Europe	Asia [1]	Africa	Oceania [1]	Canada and Greenland [2]	Mexico [3]	West Indies	Central America	South America	United States	Foreign	By sea	By air
	302	303	304	305	306	307	308	309	310	311	313	314	315	316
1945	310	73	10	28	20	31	3	121	19	5	252	58	107	203
1944	206	41	6	16	9	14	2	89	16	13	139	67	84	121
1943	170	27	4	6	8	10	(NA)	75	17	23	133	37	76	94
1942	181	22	7	5	9	10	2	85	23	17	145	36	118	62
1941	261	38	27	2	9	6	6	129	24	21	202	59	211	51
1940	422	200	19	1	7	10	6	141	20	18	211	211	379	43
1939	568	321	18	1	9	13	5	166	19	16	179	389	536	32
1938	602	350	24	1	9	13	9	164	20	13	184	418	577	25
1937	567	317	24	1	6	16	10	159	21	14	173	394	544	23
1936	471	255	23	1	7	15	7	132	19	11	155	316	454	17
1935	430	248	21	1	6	16	8	102	19	9	136	293	414	16
1934	406	244	18	1	3	14	10	91	18	8	119	287	394	11
1933	424	267	16	1	2	11	10	96	15	7	122	303	414	11
1932	472	287	21	1	1	14	11	111	17	8	135	337	463	8
1931	651	422	25	1	2	16	11	143	19	12	176	475	641	9

[1] Philippines included with Oceania prior to 1950, with Asia thereafter; prior to 1935, the Philippines was a U.S. possession and, therefore, was not included in the total for Oceania.   [2] Includes Newfoundland; Greenland not included prior to 1943.   [3] Mexico is not reported separately prior to 1942; figures prior to 1942 are for "Other North America."   [4] Data on cruise travel not available prior to 1959.

Series C 317–331. Passengers Departing, by Area of Debarkation, Flag of Carrier and Mode of Travel: 1931 to 1970

[In thousands. For years ending June 30. Excludes travel over international land borders, crewmen, military personnel, and travelers between the United States and its outlying areas]

Year	Passengers departing	Europe	Asia [1]	Africa	Oceania [1]	Canada and Greenland [2]	Mexico [3]	West Indies	Central America	South America	Cruise [4]	United States	Foreign	By sea	By air
	317	318	319	320	321	322	323	324	325	326	327	328	329	330	331
1970	9,354	3,907	808	33	222	55	846	2,157	243	490	594	4,612	4,742	859	8,494
1969	8,029	3,223	611	28	191	66	777	1,997	216	444	477	4,044	3,985	764	7,266
1968	7,061	2,880	533	21	169	95	687	1,674	201	398	403	3,587	3,474	691	6,370
1967	6,177	2,565	466	22	137	74	609	1,430	192	319	364	2,919	3,258	713	6,370
1966	5,463	2,312	449	22	119	46	516	1,239	180	264	316	2,532	2,931	734	4,729
1965	4,820	2,111	357	19	105	32	427	1,030	145	252	343	2,089	2,731	813	4,007
1964	4,140	1,833	307	17	90	25	364	831	116	214	343	1,785	2,355	833	3,307
1963	3,688	1,648	271	16	71	21	316	738	110	196	302	1,593	2,095	805	2,883
1962	3,319	1,461	236	16	72	27	283	663	104	190	266	1,388	1,930	772	2,547
1961	3,063	1,360	195	12	57	23	253	677	90	192	204	1,303	1,760	718	2,345
1960	2,939	1,231	169	13	47	23	246	805	84	175	146	1,378	1,561	720	2,219
1959	2,625	1,059	141	13	44	30	204	758	81	151	144	1,278	1,347	680	1,945
1958	2,194	959	126	13	52	20	78	734	74	138	--------	1,117	1,078	585	1,609
1957	1,977	812	126	12	42	20	41	728	72	124	--------	1,053	924	580	1,397
1956	1,813	785	107	12	35	18	37	645	63	112	--------	1,013	801	578	1,236
1955	1,582	703	86	14	25	20	34	546	54	102	--------	900	683	554	1,028
1954	1,412	642	78	12	19	26	17	482	47	90	--------	795	617	565	847
1953	1,340	600	73	12	9	28	21	459	49	90	--------	781	560	536	805
1952	1,199	486	65	12	10	31	21	441	44	89	--------	690	508	479	719
1951	1,000	400	29	7	18	7	14	406	38	80	--------	568	431	399	601
1950	981	433	46	6	19	13	5	352	38	68	--------	577	404	467	514
1949	864	364	40	6	17	7	4	316	42	69	--------	528	336	408	456
1948	786	292	55	7	25	6	4	288	41	68	--------	503	283	375	411
1947	695	228	49	7	25	12	8	281	39	45	--------	508	188	295	400
1946	390	96	9	12	11	23	17	170	23	28	--------	296	94	137	253
1945	186	46	2	15	3	17	11	61	14	16	--------	137	49	47	139
1944	118	20	1	4	1	10	1	52	13	16	--------	84	34	27	91
1943	87	11	1	3	1	5	1	34	11	21	--------	67	20	15	72
1942	150	6	4	3	2	9	3	88	18	16	--------	123	27	91	59
1941	230	9	20	1	8	4	5	136	25	21	--------	191	39	181	49
1940	361	133	21	1	14	12	6	133	21	20	--------	185	176	322	39
1939	502	250	19	1	14	15	8	161	19	15	--------	165	336	472	29
1938	589	333	19	1	13	14	10	164	20	15	--------	182	407	565	24
1937	585	325	29	1	12	15	10	162	18	13	--------	167	418	562	23
1936	476	255	27	1	11	12	8	130	20	13	--------	153	323	461	15
1935	431	246	28	1	11	10	7	99	18	10	--------	132	299	416	15
1934	412	247	30	1	3	10	9	87	17	9	--------	109	303	402	11
1933	535	360	35	1	2	10	10	95	13	9	--------	125	409	526	9
1932	586	392	32	1	2	12	11	108	16	10	--------	137	449	579	7
1931	684	451	32	1	4	13	11	142	18	12	--------	167	516	677	7

[1] Philippines included with Oceania prior to 1950, with Asia thereafter; prior to 1935, the Philippines was a U.S. possession and, therefore, was not included in the total for Oceania.   [2] Includes Newfoundland; Greenland not included prior to 1943.   [3] Mexico is not reported separately prior to 1942; figures prior to 1942 are for "Other North America."   [4] Data on cruise travel not available prior to 1959.

Labor

Labor Force (Series D 1-682)

D 1-74. General note.

The conceptual structure and techniques for measurement of current labor force data were developed during the late 1930's by the Work Projects Administration (see John N. Webb, "Concepts Used in Unemployment Surveys," *Journal of the American Statistical Association*, March 1939). However, prior to 1940, especially during the 1930's, the economically active sector was differentiated on the basis of its ability and willingness to work. Thus, most surveys during the 1930's counted as unemployed those persons not working but "willing and able to work." Willingness and ability, however, turned out to be extremely subjective in practice, and since these concepts were dependent on the attitudes of the persons involved, it was difficult to compile data on a comparable basis from place to place and from time to time.

The estimates shown here, prior to 1940, were prepared on as comparable a basis as possible with the concepts used since 1940. For the techniques used in preparing these data, see their source. In contrast, the decennial census data shown here are not directly comparable with annual data because of differences in collection techniques, time reference, and other factors.

For another set of labor force estimates, 1890–1950, see Clarence D. Long, *The Labor Force Under Changing Income and Employment*, National Bureau of Economic Research, New York, 1958, appendix tables A-4, A-6, and A-20.

The concepts and procedures used since 1940 are based principally upon an individual's actual activity, that is, whether he was working, looking for work, or doing something else during the time reference of the survey. Instead of questions about a person's attitudes with respect to his labor market status (e.g., "Are you able to work?" or "Are you willing to work?" or "Do you want work?"), the present concept makes labor market participation depend on the more overt test of working or actively seeking work.

Current labor force data are collected for the week containing the 12th of each month for the Bureau of Labor Statistics by the Bureau of the Census as a part of the latter's Current Population Survey. The Survey is based on a scientifically designed sample of households in 461 areas (1966–1970), with coverage in every State and the District of Columbia. From May 1956 through December 1966, the sample covered 330 areas, all of which were continued in the new and expanded sample. From January 1954 through April 1956, the sample covered 230 areas and, prior to 1954, the interviewed households were concentrated in 68 sample areas. The number of households interviewed totaled about 35,000 from May 1956 until January 1967, when it was raised to about 47,000. Before May 1956, a total of about 21,000 household interviews were conducted monthly.

The household interview method (population approach) involves direct enumeration and interrogation of individuals to obtain information on employment activity from workers or members of workers' households. This approach encompasses direct enumeration of all employed and unemployed persons including the self-employed, unpaid family workers, domestic servants, and others who do not ordinarily appear on the payrolls of any establishment. For a more detailed description of the concepts, techniques, estimation procedures, and adequacy and reliability of these data, see Bureau of the Census, *Current Population Reports*, series P-23, No. 22.

Labor force data have also been collected in the decennial censuses

of population. The sample size for labor force data has varied from census to census (e.g., 20-percent sample in 1970, 25-percent sample in 1960). Also, the concepts have changed over time in a manner corresponding to the Current Population Survey. (See the Decennial Census reports cited for series D 11–25.)

In the surveys and censuses conducted by the Bureau of the Census, persons are currently classified with regard to employment status by the following criteria.

Employed persons comprise: (a) All those who, during the survey week, worked at all as paid employees, in their own business or profession or on their own farm, or who worked 15 hours or more as unpaid workers in an enterprise operated by a family member; and (b) all those who were not working but who had jobs or businesses from which they were temporarily absent because of illness, bad weather, vacation, labor-management dispute, or personal reasons, whether or not they were paid by their employers for the time off, and whether or not they were seeking other jobs.

Each employed person is counted only once. Those who hold more than one job are counted in the job at which they worked the greatest number of hours during the survey week. Included are employed citizens of foreign countries, temporarily in the United States, but not living on the premises of an Embassy. Excluded are persons whose only activity consisted of work around the house (such as own home housework and painting or repairing own home) or volunteer work for religious, charitable, and similar organizations.

Unemployed persons comprise all persons who did not work during the survey week, who made specific efforts to find a job within the past 4 weeks, and who were available for work during the survey week except for temporary illness. Also included as unemployed are those who did not work at all, were available for work, and (a) were waiting to be called back to a job from which they had been laid off; (b) were waiting to report to a new wage or salary job within 30 days.

The *civilian labor force* (persons 14 years old and over through 1966 and to persons 16 years old and over thereafter) is the sum of the employed and the unemployed. Data on the size of the Armed Forces (except for decennial data) is obtained from the Defense Department and added to the civilian labor force to provide the total labor force figures.

Persons not in the labor force include all persons 14 years old and over (or 16 years old and over) not classified as employed, unemployed, or in the Armed Forces.

The foregoing criteria or concepts of measuring employment and unemployment include several revisions made in January 1967 by the President's Committee to Appraise Employment and Unemployment Statistics. The principal revisions are as follows:

a. A specific jobseeking activity within the past 4 weeks must be reported in order to have a person counted as unemployed. Previously, the household interview questionnaire was ambiguous as to the time period for jobseeking, and there was no specific question concerning methods of seeking work.

b. A person must be currently available for work in order to be counted as unemployed. This revision in concept primarily affects the classification of students, who, for example, begin to look for work in the spring when they may not be available until June. They were previously counted as unemployed but are now classified as not in the labor force.

c. Persons with a job are classified as employed, even though they were absent from their jobs in the survey week and were looking for other jobs. Previously, persons absent from their jobs because of strikes, bad weather, etc., who were looking for other jobs were classified as unemployed.

d. The new definition of unemployment excludes those who would have been looking for work except for the belief that no work was available (theoretically counted in the past, but without explicit questions).

Historical data have not been revised to take account of these changes because the differences between the old and the new series are relatively small. For most analytical purposes, the data may be regarded as reasonably comparable. The table below presents comparisons for employment status in 1966, by sex and age. Additional tables comparing the published figures for 1966 on an annual average basis with the estimates derived from the new definitions and procedures appear in Bureau of Labor Statistics *Employment and Earnings and Monthly Report on the Labor Force*, Feb. 1967.

Item	New definitions	Old definitions
TOTAL, 16 YEARS AND OVER		
Civilian labor force	75,715	75,770
Employed	72,939	72,895
Agriculture	3,904	3,979
Nonagricultural industries	69,035	68,916
Unemployed	2,776	2,875
Not in labor force	52,343	52,288
MEN, 20 YEARS AND OVER		
Civilian labor force	44,637	44,786
Employed	43,650	43,667
Agriculture	2,901	2,894
Nonagricultural industries	40,750	40,773
Unemployed	987	1,119
Not in labor force	8,967	8,818
WOMEN, 20 YEARS AND OVER		
Civilian labor force	24,512	24,427
Employed	23,493	23,507
Agriculture	626	675
Nonagricultural industries	22,867	22,832
Unemployed	1,019	919
Not in labor force	36,348	36,434
BOTH SEXES, 16 TO 19 YEARS		
Civilian labor force	6,565	6,557
Employed	5,795	5,721
Agriculture	377	410
Nonagricultural industries	5,418	5,310
Unemployed	770	836
Not in labor force	7,029	7,036

D 1–10. Labor force and its components, 1900–1947.

Source: Stanley Lebergott, *Manpower in Economic Growth: The American Record Since 1800*, table A-3. (Copyright 1964; used with permission of McGraw-Hill Book Co., New York.)

Lebergott's estimates are designed to be comparable with those of the Current Population Survey. That survey, conducted by the Census Bureau, with its labor-force data presented by the Bureau of Labor Statistics (BLS) provides the continuing official source of reliable data on these subjects. Hence, Lebergott seeks to link to the levels it provides for the years since 1940, when it began. However, the Survey estimates are not wholly consistent with the decennial census levels for 1940. Lebergott's estimates, in consequence, will be at variance with studies tied to decennial census figures. Because the Survey estimates are not consistent with the farm-employment series of the Department of Agriculture, nor with the employees in nonagricultural establishment series of the Department of Labor, Lebergott's series will also not be consistent with them.

See source pp. 355–420. Lebergott's methods may be briefly described as follows: Preliminary annual labor force and employment estimates were derived by interpolating between detailed worker rates in the census years, and applying the resultant series to un-

published census estimates of population annually from 1900 to 1930. Special adjustments were made for labor force variation in World War I, and for immigration effects between 1900 and 1914. Tests of nonlinearity in the 1930's were made.

For 1900, 1910, 1920, and 1930, Lebergott computed worker rates separately for males and females in each of three nativity groups—native white, foreign-born white, and Negro—and within each group for the separate age intervals (10–13, 14–19, 20–24, 25–44, 45–64, 65 and over). For 1920 and 1930, he used the census data without adjustment. For 1900, minor adjustment was required in the reported data to develop estimates for the 10–13, 14–19, and 20–24 groups. For 1910, he used a preliminary set of rates roughly consistent with the adjusted U.S. estimate. The worker rates used for 1900, 1920, and 1930 necessarily differ from Durand's estimates (John Durand, *The Labor Force in the United States, 1890–1960*), as the latter are all adjusted to be comparable with the 1940 census totals, whereas the present series is comparable with the Current Population Survey estimates beginning 1940.

The worker rates for each age-sex-nativity group were interpolated to give annual estimates for 1900 to 1930, then applied to unpublished census data on population. Two adjustments were made in the data thus derived. Armed Forces overseas, excluded from the census series, were added to the preliminary labor-force series for 1917 to 1919. Secondly, the census estimates were based largely on school-attendance figures and other series not particularly sensitive to the inmigration of adult workers. Lebergott, therefore, computed a direct estimate for 1900 to 1914 of immigrant worker arrivals, and used that series as a measure of 1900 to 1914 labor-force trends among the foreign born.

The preliminary 1900 to 1930 employment trend series thus derived for persons aged 14 and over was used to interpolate between gainful-worker figures for 1900, 1910, 1920, and 1930. The decennial rates of gain were used to adjust from reported census date figures to annual averages. In addition, the reported 1910 figure was adjusted to allow for the overcount of that year. Lebergott estimated the adjustment for males 14 and over as for females, on the assumption that the overcounted group included only home-farm workers having the same age distribution as reported home-farm workers.

Interpolation between 1930 and 1940 benchmark totals was by means of the BLS total labor force series. The BLS series was derived by applying annual worker rates for age-sex groups to census population data for the corresponding groups. The worker rates were interpolations between estimated 1930 labor-force rates and those shown for 1940 by the Current Population Survey. The resultant series reflects changing proportions among the various age-sex groups, and these changes are reflected in the Lebergott series.

The unemployment series for 1900 to 1930 was derived by making direct benchmark estimates of unemployment in 1900, 1910, and 1930, using the population census data on unemployment in those years. Intercensal estimates were then obtained by estimating civilian labor force and employment and deducting one series from the other.

The estimate of unemployment in 1900 was based on data collected in two enumerations. One was the 1900 Census of Population, which secured information on unemployment during the year preceding the taking of the census. The second was a Cost of Living Survey made by the Commissioner of Labor of family income and expenditures that secured detailed information for about 25,000 families on cause and duration of unemployment during 1900–1901.

Although the census of 1910 secured data on unemployment of wage earners in the previous year, these data were not tabulated until 1948. The 1910 data on unemployment are in the form of distributions for unemployed wage earners 16 years and over by duration of unemployment. By applying the distribution to the total for wage earners 16 years and over, and deducting estimates made similarly for teachers and home-farm laborers (wage earners), Lebergott secured a preliminary estimate for the number of unemployed wage earners by duration group. The resultant distribution was reduced to exclude unemployment that would not be counted by current definitions. He used the same proportions within each group as indicated in the 1901 Cost of Living Survey—multiplying by the same average duration figures, within each group, as used for 1900, and computing man-years of unemployment.

An annual average unemployment benchmark for 1930 was estimated as follows. Prior estimates (John Durand and Edwin Goldfield, *Estimates of Labor Force, Employment and Unemployment in the United States, 1940 and 1930*) indicated that 5.17 percent of the gainfully occupied total for April were unemployed. This ratio, applied to the census gainful-worker total for April, gives an April unemployment figure and, by subtraction, an employment figure. The annual average employment was estimated at 97.02 percent of the April level, using ratios for its agricultural, manufacturing, and other components. Adding Armed Forces overseas to this figure and subtracting from the annual average gainful-worker total gives an unemployment figure for 1930.

Following the procedure used for the original BLS estimates, but adopting a variety of revisions in the labor force and the component employment series, gives unemployment estimates for 1929–1939 that differ in trivial amount from those in the published BLS series except for 1929, which is approximately 20 percent different. Because of the widespread use of the BLS figures and because the differences are well within the error involved in the computation of the duplicating item, Lebergott adopted the BLS figures beginning 1930 as his unemployment totals, then subtracted these from the labor-force totals to give the employment series.

Beginning 1940, Lebergott adopted the Census Bureau's Current Population Survey reports, supplementing them for certain omissions. These data appear in *Current Population Reports*, series P-50.

See general note for series D 1–74 and also table and text for series D 11–25.

D 11–25. Labor force status of the population, 1870–1970.

Source: Annual data: 1947–1970, U.S. Bureau of Labor Statistics, **series D 11–19**, *Employment and Earnings*, monthly issues, tables A-1 and A-2; **series D 20–23**, unpublished data. Decennial data: U.S. Bureau of the Census, 1870–1930, *Twelfth Census of the United States: 1900*, Special Reports, *Occupations*, table IV, and *Fifteenth Census of the United States: 1930*, vol. IV, *Occupations by States*, tables 1.2 and 11; 1940–1950, *U.S. Census of Population: 1950*, vol. II, part 1, tables 52 and 118; 1960, *U.S. Census of Population: 1960*, vol. I, part 1, table 82; 1970, *U.S. Census of Population: 1970*, vol. I, part 1, table 90.

In 1953, population data from the 1950 census were introduced into the estimating procedure, affecting the comparability of the labor force figures with earlier years. Population levels were raised by 600,000; labor force, total employment, and agricultural employment levels were raised by 350,000, primarily in the figures for all persons and for males. Similarly, population data from the 1960 census were introduced in 1962, reducing the population totals by 50,000 and the labor force and employment totals by 200,000.

The inclusion of Alaska and Hawaii in 1960 resulted in an increase of about 600,000 in population and 300,000 in the labor force, four-fifths of which was in nonagricultural employment.

See general note for series D 1–74.

D 26–28. Gainful workers, by sex, by State, 1870–1950.

Source: Everett S. Lee, Ann Ratner Miller, Carol P. Brainerd, and Richard A. Easterlin, *Population Redistribution and Economic Growth, United States, 1870–1950*, vol. I, *Methodological Considerations and Reference Tables*, The American Philosophical Society, Philadelphia, 1957, table L-4. (Copyright.)

These series cover persons engaged in agricultural and nonagricultural occupations, shown separately in the source. The basic data are from the decennial censuses. To facilitate tabulation, the agriculture series was compiled directly and nonagricultural totals were obtained by subtraction from totals for all occupations.

Census tabulations of gainful workers during the period 1870–1930 included all persons 10 years of age and over. Beginning in 1940, however, tabulations of the labor force included only persons 14 years of age and over. The authors therefore constructed estimates of 10–13 year-old workers by sex for each State on the basis of the occupational distributions of 14–15 year-olds.

For 1870 through 1930 all gainful workers are included in the series. All experienced persons in the labor force are included for 1950, that is, all persons except those looking for their first jobs. The 1940 data refer to employed persons and to experienced workers seeking work but exclude persons on public emergency work.

For definition of "gainful workers," see text for series D 75–84.

D 29–41. Labor force, by age and sex, 1890–1970.

Source: Annual data, 1940–1946, U.S. Bureau of the Census, *Current Population Reports*, series P-50 and P-25; 1947–1970, U.S. Department of Labor, *Manpower Report of the President, March 1972*, pp. 158–159. Decennial census data, 1890–1930, John D. Durand, *The Labor Force in the United States, 1890–1960*, Social Science Research Council, New York, 1948; 1940 and 1960, U.S. Bureau of the Census, *U.S. Census of Population: 1960*, vol. I, part 1, tables 82–84; 1950, *U.S. Census of Population: 1950*, vol. IV, Special Reports, *Employment and Personal Characteristics*, p. 1A-62; and 1970, *U.S. Census of Population: 1970*, vol. I, part 1, table 215, and unpublished data.

The civilian labor force data are annual averages. However, the data on the Armed Forces and on the total population (the base for labor force participation rates) are estimates as of July 1 of the specified year.

See general note for series D 1–74 and also text for series D 11–25.

D 42–48. Civilian labor force as percent of civilian noninstitutional population, by race and sex, 1940–1970.

Source: See source for series D 29–41.
See general note for series D 1–74 and text for series D 11–25.

D 49–62. Marital status of women in the civilian labor force, 1890–1970.

Source: Annual data, 1940–1958, U.S. Bureau of the Census, *Current Population Reports*, series P-50; 1959–1970, U.S. Bureau of Labor Statistics, *Special Labor Force Reports*, various issues. Decennial data, U.S. Bureau of the Census, 1890–1930, *U.S. Census of Population: 1930*, vol. IV, table 25; 1940–1970, *U.S. Census of Population: 1970*, vol. I, tables 2, 3, and 5.

In the annual series, data for 1940 are based on complete count census data revised for comparability with the Current Population Survey; data for 1944–1970 are based on the Current Population Survey.

See general note for series D 1–74 and text for series D 11–25.

D 63–74. Married women (husband present) in the labor force, by age and presence of children, 1948–1970.

Source: U.S. Bureau of Labor Statistics, *Handbook of Labor Statistics, 1972*, table 14.

Children refer to "own" children of the family head and include stepchildren and adopted children.
See general note for series D 1–74.

D 75–84. Gainful workers, by age, sex, and farm-nonfarm occupations, 1820–1930.

Source: U.S. Bureau of the Census, Sixteenth Census Reports, *Comparative Occupation Statistics for the United States, 1870–1940*, pp. 93, 100, and 142.

The gainful worker concept differs radically from current labor force concepts as described in the general note for series D 1–74. The primary purpose of the gainful worker statistics was a count of occupations. The data were based on a question relating to occupational status and not to employment status as currently defined. Census enumerators were instructed to find and enter the occupation of each person 10 years of age and over who followed an occupation in which he earned money or its equivalent, or in which he assisted in the production of marketable goods. Thus, the term "gainful workers" includes all persons who usually followed a gainful occupation although they may not have been employed when the census was taken. It does not include women doing housework in their own homes, without wages, and having no other employment, nor children working at home, merely on general household work, or chores, or at odd times on other work.

The question as posed by the enumerator made no reference to time. The response thus varied substantially with the individual. Many persons who were retired or permanently disabled and who had not worked for some time reported their former line of work and were counted as gainful workers. On the other hand, many employed persons did not enter themselves as gainful workers, because they considered themselves as students or housewives and their current employment as only temporary.

These and other factors made for incomparabilities among different age and occupational groups from one decennial census to the next. The gainful worker statistics, however, are considered as a generally reliable measure of long-term trends during the time period covered.

For a more detailed discussion of the gainful worker concept and the data themselves, see John D. Durand, *The Labor Force in the United States, 1890–1960*, Social Science Research Council, New York, 1948, p. 191 *et seq.*; John D. Durand, "Development of the Labor Force Concept, 1930–40," *Labor Force Definition and Measurement*, appendix A, Social Science Research Council, Bulletin 56, 1947; and U.S. Bureau of the Census, Sixteenth Census Reports, *Population*, "Estimates of Labor Force, Employment, and Unemployment in the U.S.: 1940 and 1930."

D 85–86. Unemployment, 1890–1970.

Source: 1890–1928, see source for series D 1–10, tables A–3 and A–15; 1929–1970, U.S. Bureau of Labor Statistics, *Employment and Earnings*, May 1972.

For data prior to 1900, an 1890 benchmark was derived from the unemployment data reported in the 1890 and 1900 censuses. Data for the primary male groups in the labor force showed unemployment in 1890 at 79.31 percent of that in 1900. Applying this ratio to the 1900 unemployment rate gives an 1890 rate of 3.96 percent. This rate applied to an estimated 1890 total for the labor force aged 14 and over gives the 1890 unemployment figure.

Intercensal unemployment figures for 1891–1899 were derived by deducting an employment series from a labor-force series. The employment series is the adjusted sum of a number of detailed series, whose derivation is described in *Manpower in Economic Growth*, pp. 421–478.

The figures for 1900–1939 represent estimates of unemployment on as comparable a basis as possible to current labor force concepts. There have been many estimates of unemployment for these years prepared by such agencies as the National Industrial Conference Board and by authors such as Paul Douglas in *Real Wages in the United States, 1890–1926* (these are discussed and compared in Lebergott, cited above). In all of these, including the series presented here, unemployment was calculated as a residual. That is, estimates were first made of the civilian labor force, then of employment; the difference between the two provides the estimates of unemployment. The figures for decennial census years were used as benchmarks, with interpolations made for intercensal years from a variety of available sources.

Beginning with 1940, figures were obtained from the U.S. Bureau of the Census Current Population Survey. These data appear in the Census Bureau's series P–50 reports and, beginning 1958, in the Bureau of Labor Statistics monthly *Employment and Earnings*.

See general note for series D 1–74 and text for series D 87–101.

D 87–101. Unemployment rates for selected groups, 1947–1970.

Source: U.S. Bureau of Labor Statistics, *Handbook of Labor Statistics, 1972*, pp. 128–129, and 144.

The unemployment rate represents the percent of the civilian labor force reported as unemployed by the Current Population Survey during the survey week (the week containing the 12th of each month). Annual figures shown here are averages of monthly figures.

Duration of unemployment represents the length of time (through the end of the current survey week) during which persons classified as unemployed had been continuously looking for work. For persons on layoff, duration of unemployment represents the number of full weeks since the termination of their most recent employment. A period of two weeks or more during which a person was employed or ceased looking for work breaks the continuity of the present period of seeking work. Series D 99 represents the unemployment rate calculated as a percent of the civilian labor force. Average duration, series D 100, is an arithmetic mean computed from a distribution by single weeks of unemployment.

State insured unemployment refers to persons seeking benefits under State unemployment insurance programs. Series D 101 represents the unemployment rate for the survey week calculated as a percent of average covered employment.

See general note for series D 1–74.

D 102–115. Unemployment rates, by industry, 1948–1970.

Source: U.S. Bureau of Labor Statistics, *Handbook of Labor Statistics, 1972*, p. 151.

See general note for series D 1–74 and text for series D 87–101.

D 116–126. Persons with a job but not at work and civilians employed, by hours worked, 1950–1970.

Source: U.S. Bureau of Labor Statistics, *Employment and Earnings*, May issues.

Hours of work statistics relate to the actual number of hours worked during the survey week. (See general note for series D 1–74.) For example, a person who normally works 40 hours a week but who was off on the Veterans Day holiday would be reported as working 32 hours even though he was paid for the holiday.

For persons working in more than one job, the figures relate to the number of hours worked in all jobs during the week, and all the hours are credited to the longest job.

Persons who worked 35 hours or more in the survey week are designated as working "full time"; persons who worked between 1 and 34 hours are designated as working "part time."

D 127–141. Employees on nonagricultural payrolls, by major industry divisions, 1900–1970.

Source: 1900–1928, see source for series D 1–10, table A–5; 1929–1970, U.S. Bureau of Labor Statistics, *Handbook of Labor Statistics, 1972*, p. 89.

Data from payroll records, submitted voluntarily by over 160,000 employers, provide (1) current information on wage and salary employment, hours, and earnings in nonagricultural establishments, and (2) job vacancies and labor turnover in manufacturing, by industry and geographic location. These statistical programs are conducted by the Bureau of Labor Statistics (BLS) in cooperation with State agencies.

The two types of data collection documents used are of the "shuttle" type, with spaces for each month of the calendar year. The cooperating State agencies mail the reporting forms to the participating establishments each month, use the information to prepare State and area estimates, and then send the basic data to BLS in Washington for use in preparing national series.

Employment data refer to persons on establishment payrolls who receive pay for any part of the reference pay period, and include workers on paid sick leave (when pay is received directly from the firm), on paid holiday or paid vacation, and those who work during a part of the pay period and are unemployed or on strike during the rest of the period. Proprietors, the self-employed, unpaid family workers, farmworkers, and domestic workers in households are excluded. Government employment covers civilian employees only.

Periodically, the industry employment series are adjusted to recent benchmarks to improve their accuracy. These adjustments may also affect the hours, earnings, and labor turnover series since employment levels are used as weights. Industry data for these series have been adjusted to March 1970 benchmarks.

Total employment in nonagricultural establishments from the "payroll" survey is not directly comparable with the estimates of nonagricultural employment obtained from the monthly "household" survey (Current Population Survey). The household survey includes the self-employed, unpaid family workers, and private household workers and is basically a count of persons. The payroll series, in contrast, excludes these workers and is basically a count of jobs. Thus, the multiple jobholder, counted only once in the household survey, would be counted once for each job by the payroll survey. Employment estimates developed by quinquennial censuses may differ from payroll estimates due, primarily, to the reporting practices of multiproduct establishments, and administrative handling of central offices and auxiliary units.

For a more detailed description of these programs see Chapter 2, "Employment, Hours, and Earnings," of the *Handbook of Methods for Surveys and Studies*, BLS Bulletin 1711.

The data summarized in these series are available in considerable detail (estimates are provided for about 400 different industries each month). For a discussion of available historical data, see Bureau of Labor Statistics, *Employment and Earnings, United States, 1909–1971*, Bulletin No. 1312–8; for an analysis of historical trends, see Seymour L. Wolfbein, "Changing Patterns of Industrial Employment," *Monthly Labor Review*, March 1956.

D 142–151. Production or nonsupervisory workers on private nonagricultural payrolls, by industry division, 1909–1970.

Source: U.S. Bureau of Labor Statistics, *Handbook of Labor Statistics, 1972*, p. 92.

See text for series D 127–141.

D 152–166. Industrial distribution of gainful workers, 1820–1940.

Source: Solomon Fabricant, "The Changing Industrial Distribution of Gainful Workers: Some Comments on the American Decennial Statistics for 1820–1940," *Studies in Income and Wealth*, vol. 11, National Bureau of Economic Research, New York, 1949, p. 42. (Copyright.)

For definition of "gainful workers," see text for series D 75–84. The data are based almost entirely on estimates in the following monographs which were prepared mainly from data collected in the

decennial censuses of population: P. K. Whelpton, "Occupational Groups in the United States, 1820–1920," *Journal of the American Statistical Association*, September 1926; U.S. Bureau of the Census, Sixteenth Census Reports, *Comparative Occupation Statistics for the United States, 1870 to 1940*; and Daniel Carson, "Industrial Composition of Manpower in the United States, 1870–1940," *Studies in Income and Wealth*, vol. 11.

D 167–181. Labor force and employment, by industry, 1800–1960.

Source: See source for series D 1–10, table A–1.

The individual series on labor force and employment for 1800 to 1960 were derived in extensive detail. A full description of the procedures used appears in a Conference on Research in Income and Wealth, *Studies in Income and Wealth*, vol. 30, pp. 132 ff. The data represent revisions of some of the materials used for series D 152–166 and are intended to be comparable with current official series.

D 182–232. Major occupation group of the experienced civilian labor force, by sex, 1900–1970.

Source: U.S. Bureau of the Census. 1900–1950 (1950 classification), David L. Kaplan and M. Claire Casey, *Occupational Trends in the United States, 1900–1950*, Working Paper No. 5, 1958; 1950–1960 (1960 classification), *U.S. Census of Population: 1960*, vol. I, part 1, table 201; 1960 (1970 classification)–1970, *U.S. Census of Population: 1970*, vol. I, part 1, table 221.

The data for 1900–1950 (1950 classification) constitute primarily an updating by Kaplan and Casey of the material in Sixteenth Census Reports, *Comparative Occupation Statistics in the United States, 1870–1940*. Separate series developed by Alba M. Edwards in that report were brought together and a number of new estimates were prepared to fill gaps. The appropriate figures were then adjusted to conform to the definitions used in the 1950 occupational classification system. Except where there was firm evidence to support a change, Edwards' basic assumptions and estimates were utilized throughout.

The source cautions that the data, particularly those for 1900, are approximations only. The estimates for 1900 "were included mainly for the purpose of rounding out a half-century of information, despite some obvious deficiencies. Particularly prior to 1910, there is little information available on the exact definitions used for the several occupational categories. And, even for fairly recent years, there is often only meager statistical intelligence on which to base adjustments for comparability with the 1950 definitions."

The universe covered in the Kaplan and Casey series is described as the "economically active population." Prior to 1940, this refers to civilian gainful workers 10 years old and over; for 1940 and 1950, it refers to persons 14 years old and over in the experienced civilian labor force (all employed and unemployed workers with previous work experience). Two incomparabilities should be noted. First, there are important differences between the gainful worker and labor force concepts (see general note for series D 1–74, and text for series D 75–84). Second, there is the difference in age limitation. The inclusion of the 10-to-13 group prior to 1940, and their exclusion in 1940 and 1950, follows the census practice in those years.

The occupation classification system used in the 1970 census is similar to that used in each decennial census since 1940. However, the changes made for each of the censuses affect the comparability of data from one census to another. For example, many of the larger 1960 occupation categories were divided into several smaller categories which increased the number of categories in the 1970 system to 441, compared with 297 in 1960.

A new major group, "transport equipment operatives," added to the occupation classification in 1970, includes occupations formerly part of the "operatives" major group. The arrangement of some major groups was changed to form more "families" of occupations. This applies especially to the "professional" and "service" major groups. Although there was an effort to limit changes between major groups, there were many cases where such changes were necessary. One such change is the treatment of apprentices. They were moved from "operatives" to "craftsmen" and are classified as a subcategory of their craft.

Two other changes in the census have an important effect on comparability: (1) The allocation of "not reported" cases to the major groups in 1970 increased the size of those totals relative to the totals for 1950 and 1960 when there was no allocation of these characteristics; and (2) the age coverage for statistics on these subjects to accord with past and current definitions of the labor force, as indicated in the table for series D 182–232.

The population census occupational classification system is generally comparable with the system used in U.S. Bureau of Employment Security, *Dictionary of Occupational Titles* (DOT), 3d edition, with the exception of the blue collar workers (i.e. manual and service workers). The DOT structure for these occupations is quite differ-

ent from that used by the Bureau of the Census. An important reason for this is that the two systems are designed to meet different needs and to be used under different circumstances. The DOT system is designed primarily for employment service needs, such as placement and counseling, and is ordinarily used to classify very detailed occupational information obtained in an interview with the worker himself. The census system, on the other hand, is designed for statistical purposes and is ordinarily used in the classification of limited occupational descriptions obtained in a self-enumeration questionnaire or in an interview with a member of the worker's family.

D 233–682. Detailed occupation of the economically active population, 1900–1970.

Source: See source for series D 182–232.

Dashes (------) are used in the columns of this table to denote that comparable data are not available because of changes in definitions and occupations.

See also text for series D 182–232.

Series D 1–10. Labor Force and Its Components: 1900 to 1947

[In thousands of persons 14 years old and over. Annual averages]

Year	Total labor force — Number	Total labor force — Percent of noninstitutional population	Armed Forces	Civilian labor force	Employed — Total	Employed — Farm	Employed — Nonfarm	Unemployed — Total	Unemployed — Percent of — Civilian labor force	Unemployed — Percent of — Nonfarm employees
	1	2	3	4	5	6	7	8	9	10
1947	61,758	57.4	1,590	60,168	57,812	8,256	49,557	2,356	3.9	5.4
1946	60,970	57.2	3,450	57,520	55,250	8,320	46,930	2,270	3.9	5.5
1945	65,290	61.9	11,430	53,860	52,820	8,580	44,240	1,040	1.9	2.7
1944	66,040	63.1	11,410	54,630	53,960	8,950	45,010	670	1.2	1.7
1943	64,560	62.3	9,020	55,540	54,470	9,080	45,390	1,070	1.9	2.7
1942	60,380	58.8	3,970	56,410	53,750	9,250	44,500	2,660	4.7	6.8
1941	57,530	56.7	1,620	55,910	50,350	9,100	41,250	5,560	9.9	14.4
1940	56,180	56.0	540	55,640	47,520	9,540	37,980	8,120	14.6	21.3
1939	55,588	56.0	370	55,218	45,738	9,710	36,028	9,480	17.2	25.2
1938	54,872	56.0	340	54,532	44,142	9,840	34,302	10,390	19.1	27.9
1937	54,088	55.9	320	53,768	46,068	10,000	36,068	7,700	14.3	21.3
1936	53,319	55.7	300	53,019	43,989	10,090	33,899	9,030	17.0	25.4
1935	52,553	55.6	270	52,283	41,673	10,110	31,563	10,610	20.3	30.2
1934	51,910	55.7	260	51,650	40,310	9,990	30,320	11,340	22.0	32.6
1933	51,132	55.6	250	50,882	38,052	10,090	27,962	12,830	25.2	37.6
1932	50,348	55.4	250	50,098	38,038	10,120	27,918	12,060	24.1	36.3
1931	49,585	55.2	260	49,325	41,305	10,240	31,065	8,020	16.3	25.2
1930	48,783	55.0	260	48,523	44,183	10,340	33,843	4,340	8.9	14.2
1929	48,017	55.1	260	47,757	46,207	10,541	35,666	1,550	3.2	5.3
1928	47,367	55.2	262	47,105	45,123	10,497	34,626	1,982	4.2	6.9
1927	46,634	55.2	259	46,375	44,856	10,529	34,327	1,519	3.3	5.4
1926	45,885	55.3	256	45,629	44,828	10,690	34,138	801	1.8	2.9
1925	45,431	55.4	262	45,169	43,716	10,662	33,054	1,453	3.2	5.4
1924	44,502	55.5	267	44,235	42,045	10,599	31,446	2,190	5.0	8.3
1923	43,699	55.8	255	43,444	42,395	10,621	31,774	1,049	2.4	4.1
1922	42,772	55.7	276	42,496	39,637	10,561	29,076	2,859	6.7	11.4
1921	42,341	55.9	362	41,979	37,061	10,443	26,618	4,918	11.7	19.5
1920	41,720	55.6	380	41,340	39,208	10,440	28,768	2,132	5.2	8.6
1919	41,239	56.4	1,543	39,696	39,150	10,498	28,652	546	1.4	2.4
1918	41,980	57.7	2,904	39,076	38,540	10,674	27,866	536	1.4	2.4
1917	40,742	56.6	719	40,023	38,175	10,788	27,387	1,848	4.6	8.2
1916	40,238	56.6	181	40,057	38,014	10,802	27,212	2,043	5.1	9.1
1915	39,774	56.8	174	39,600	36,223	10,953	25,270	3,377	8.5	15.6
1914	39,564	57.3	163	39,401	36,281	10,945	25,336	3,120	7.9	14.7
1913	38,832	57.3	157	38,675	37,004	10,974	26,030	1,671	4.3	8.2
1912	38,081	57.4	149	37,932	36,173	11,136	25,037	1,759	4.6	9.0
1911	37,623	57.6	145	37,478	34,960	11,107	23,853	2,518	6.7	13.0
1910	36,850	57.4	141	36,709	34,559	11,260	23,299	2,150	5.9	11.6
1909	35,855	57.2	134	35,721	33,897	11,163	22,734	1,824	5.1	10.3
1908	35,039	57.2	123	34,916	32,136	11,238	20,898	2,780	8.0	16.4
1907	34,295	57.2	112	34,183	33,238	11,493	21,745	945	2.8	6.0
1906	33,321	56.8	109	33,212	32,638	11,479	21,159	574	1.7	3.9
1905	32,408	56.5	109	32,299	30,918	11,187	19,731	1,381	4.3	9.5
1904	31,548	56.3	107	31,441	29,750	11,076	18,674	1,691	5.4	12.0
1903	30,804	56.2	106	30,698	29,494	10,869	18,625	1,204	3.9	9.0
1902	30,012	56.0	108	29,904	28,807	10,753	18,054	1,097	3.7	8.6
1901	29,268	55.8	115	29,153	27,948	10,916	17,032	1,205	4.0	10.1
1900	28,500	55.5	124	28,376	26,956	11,050	15,906	1,420	5.0	12.6

Series D 11–25. Labor Force Status of the Population: 1870 to 1970

[In thousands of persons 16 years old and over, except as noted. Annual estimates are averages of monthly figures. The introduction of data from the decennial censuses into the estimation procedure in 1953 and 1962 and the inclusion of Alaska and Hawaii beginning 1960 have resulted in 3 periods of noncomparability; see text]

Year	Total noninstitutional population [1]	Total labor force		Civilian labor force					Not in labor force				
		Number [2]	Percent of population	Total	Employed			Unemployed	Total	Keeping house	In school	Unable to work	Other
					Total	Agriculture	Nonagricultural						
	11	12	13	14	15	16	17	18	19	20	21	22	23
TOTAL													
1970	140,182	85,903	61.3	82,715	78,627	3,462	75,165	4,088	54,280	35,118	7,033	2,409	9,719
1969	137,841	84,240	61.1	80,734	77,902	3,606	74,296	2,832	53,602	34,888	7,013	2,328	9,373
1968	135,562	82,272	60.7	78,737	75,920	3,817	72,103	2,817	53,291	35,204	6,900	2,264	8,923
1967	133,319	80,793	60.6	77,347	74,372	3,844	70,527	2,975	52,527	34,993	6,657	2,341	8,536
1966	131,180	78,893	60.1	75,770	72,895	3,979	68,915	2,875	52,288	35,230	6,423	1,909	8,728
1965	129,236	77,178	59.7	74,455	71,088	4,361	66,726	3,366	52,058	35,463	6,399	1,727	8,468
1964	127,224	75,830	59.6	73,091	69,305	4,523	64,782	3,786	51,394	35,346	5,948	1,690	8,410
1963	125,154	74,571	59.6	71,833	67,762	4,687	63,076	4,070	50,583	35,209	5,476	1,813	8,085
1962	122,981	73,442	59.7	70,614	66,702	4,944	61,759	3,911	49,539	35,241	4,921	1,768	7,608
1961	121,343	73,031	60.2	70,459	65,746	5,200	60,546	4,714	48,312	34,802	4,739	1,747	7,024
1960*	119,759	72,142	60.2	69,628	65,778	5,458	60,318	3,852	47,617	34,464	4,489	1,772	6,893
1959	117,881	70,921	60.2	68,369	64,630	5,565	59,065	3,740	46,960	34,374	4,239	1,765	6,583
1958	116,363	70,275	60.4	67,639	63,036	5,586	57,450	4,602	46,088	34,135	3,929	1,777	6,246
1957	115,065	69,729	60.6	66,929	64,071	5,947	58,123	2,859	45,336	33,780	3,627	1,827	6,103
1956	113,811	69,409	61.0	66,552	63,802	6,283	57,517	2,750	44,402	33,291	3,468	1,932	5,711
1955	112,732	68,072	60.4	65,023	62,171	6,449	55,724	2,852	44,660	33,613	3,518	2,173	5,357
1954	111,671	66,993	60.0	63,643	60,110	6,206	53,903	3,532	44,678	33,752	3,378	2,288	5,260
1953	110,601	66,560	60.2	63,015	61,181	6,261	54,922	1,834	44,041	(3)	(3)	(3)	(3)
1952	108,823	65,730	60.4	62,138	60,254	6,501	53,753	1,883	43,093	33,197	3,177	2,272	4,446
1951	107,721	65,117	60.4	62,017	59,962	6,726	53,239	2,055	42,604	32,960	3,120	2,321	4,204
1950	106,645	63,858	59.9	62,208	58,920	7,160	51,760	3,288	42,787	32,912	3,542	2,363	3,970
1949	105,611	62,903	59.6	61,286	57,649	7,656	49,990	3,637	42,708	32,925	3,493	6,289	
1948	104,527	62,080	59.4	60,621	58,344	7,629	50,713	2,276	42,447	32,703	3,610	6,135	
1947	103,418	60,941	58.9	59,350	57,039	7,891	49,148	2,311	42,477	---	---	---	---
Decennial census:													
1970 (April)	139,130	82,049	59.0	80,051	76,554	2,750	73,804	3,497	57,082	(3)	9,666	(3)	47,415
1960 (April)*[4]	124,517	69,877	56.1	68,144	64,639	4,257	60,383	3,505	54,639	(3)	10,327	(3)	44,312
1950 (April)[4]	110,267	59,643	54.1	58,646	55,788	[5] 6,876	[5] 48,912	2,858	50,624	32,338	(3)	4,620	13,666
1940 (April)[4]	[5] 100,147	53,011	52.9	52,705	45,070	8,449	36,621	7,635	[5] 47,136	28,932	9,013	5,269	3,922
1930 (April)[6]	98,723	48,830	49.5	---	---	10,472	38,358	---	49,893				
1920 (Jan.)[6]	82,739	41,614	50.3	---	---	10,666	30,948	---	41,125				
1910 (April)[6]	71,580	38,167	53.3	---	---	12,388	25,779	---	33,413				
1900 (June)[6]	57,950	29,073	50.2	---	---	10,382	18,691	---	28,877				
1890 (June)[6][7]	47,414	23,318	49.2	---	---	9,148	14,170	---	24,095				
1880 (June)[6]	36,762	17,392	47.3	---	---	7,714	9,678	---	19,370				
1870 (June)[6]	28,229	12,506	44.3	---	---	5,949	6,557	---	15,723				
MALE													
1970	67,409	54,343	80.6	51,195	48,960	2,861	46,099	2,235	13,066	---	---	---	---
1969	66,365	53,688	80.9	50,221	48,818	2,963	45,855	1,403	12,677	---	---	---	---
1968	65,345	53,030	81.2	49,533	48,114	3,157	44,957	1,419	12,315	---	---	---	---
1967	64,316	52,398	81.5	48,987	47,479	3,164	44,315	1,508	11,919	---	---	---	---
1966	63,351	51,560	81.4	48,471	46,919	3,243	43,675	1,551	11,792	---	---	---	---
1965	62,473	50,946	81.5	48,255	46,340	3,547	42,792	1,914	11,527	---	---	---	---
1964	61,556	50,387	81.9	47,679	45,474	3,691	41,782	2,205	11,169	---	---	---	---
1963	60,627	49,835	82.2	47,129	44,657	3,809	40,849	2,472	10,792	---	---	---	---
1962	59,626	49,395	82.8	46,600	44,177	4,069	40,108	2,423	10,231	---	---	---	---
1961	58,826	49,193	83.6	46,653	43,656	4,298	39,359	2,997	9,633	---	---	---	---
1960*	58,144	48,870	84.0	46,388	43,904	4,472	39,431	2,486	9,274	---	---	---	---
1959	57,312	48,405	84.5	45,886	43,466	4,532	38,934	2,420	8,907	---	---	---	---
1958	56,640	48,126	85.0	45,521	42,423	4,596	37,827	3,098	8,514	---	---	---	---
1957	56,082	47,964	85.5	45,197	43,357	4,824	38,532	1,841	8,118	---	---	---	---
1956	55,547	47,914	86.3	45,091	43,380	5,039	38,340	1,711	7,633	---	---	---	---
1955	55,122	47,488	86.2	44,475	42,621	5,265	37,357	1,854	7,634	---	---	---	---
1954	54,706	47,275	86.4	43,965	41,620	5,200	36,418	2,344	7,431	---	---	---	---
1953	54,248	47,131	86.9	43,633	42,431	5,253	37,178	1,202	7,117	---	---	---	---
1952	53,248	46,416	87.2	42,869	41,684	5,389	36,294	1,185	6,832	---	---	---	---
1951	52,788	46,063	87.3	43,001	41,780	5,533	36,248	1,221	6,725	---	---	---	---
1950	52,352	45,446	86.8	43,819	41,580	6,001	35,578	2,239	6,906	---	---	---	---
1949	51,922	45,097	86.9	43,498	40,926	6,342	34,584	2,572	6,825	---	---	---	---
1948	51,439	44,729	87.0	43,286	41,726	6,358	35,368	1,559	6,710	---	---	---	---
1947	50,968	44,258	86.8	42,686	40,994	6,643	34,351	1,692	6,710	---	---	---	---
Decennial census:													
1970 (April)	66,218	51,502	77.8	49,549	47,624	2,521	45,103	1,925	14,716	---	---	---	---
1960 (April)*[4]	60,274	47,468	78.8	45,763	43,467	3,846	39,621	2,296	12,807	---	---	---	---
1950 (April)[4]	53,728	43,091	80.2	42,126	40,037	6,406	33,631	2,089	10,637	---	---	---	---
1940 (April)[4]	50,770	40,123	79.0	39,818	33,892	7,887	26,005	5,926	10,647	---	---	---	---
1930 (April)[6]	49,950	38,078	76.2	---	---	9,562	28,516	---	11,872	---	---	---	---
1920 (Jan.)[6]	42,290	33,065	78.2	---	---	9,583	23,482	---	9,225	---	---	---	---
1910 (April)[6]	37,028	30,092	81.3	---	---	10,582	19,510	---	6,936	---	---	---	---
1900 (June)[6]	29,703	23,754	80.0	---	---	9,404	14,350	---	5,950	---	---	---	---
1890 (June)[6][7]	24,353	19,313	79.3	---	---	8,379	10,934	---	5,040	---	---	---	---
1880 (June)[6]	18,736	14,745	78.7	---	---	7,119	7,626	---	3,991	---	---	---	---
1870 (June)[6]	14,259	10,670	74.8	---	---	5,552	5,118	---	3,589	---	---	---	---

See footnotes at end of table.

Series D 11–25. Labor Force Status of the Population: 1870 to 1970—Con.

[In thousands of persons 16 years old and over, except as noted.   Annual estimates are averages of monthly figures]

Year	Total noninsti-tutional population [1]	Total labor force		Civilian labor force					Not in labor force
		Number [2]	Percent of population	Total	Employed			Unemployed	
					Total	Agriculture	Nonagri-cultural		
	11	12	13	14	15	16	17	18	19

FEMALE

1970	72,774	31,560	43.4	31,520	29,667	601	29,066	1,853	41,214
1969	71,476	30,551	42.7	30,513	29,084	643	28,441	1,429	40,924
1968	70,217	29,242	41.6	29,204	27,807	660	27,147	1,397	40,976
1967	69,003	28,395	41.2	28,360	26,893	680	26,212	1,468	40,608
1966	67,829	27,333	40.3	27,299	25,976	736	25,240	1,324	40,496
1965	66,763	26,232	39.3	26,200	24,748	814	23,934	1,452	40,531
1964	65,668	25,443	38.7	25,412	23,831	832	23,000	1,581	40,225
1963	64,527	24,736	38.3	24,704	23,105	878	22,227	1,598	39,791
1962	63,355	24,047	38.0	24,014	22,525	875	21,651	1,488	39,308
1961	62,517	23,838	38.1	23,806	22,090	902	21,187	1,717	38,679
1960*	61,615	23,272	37.8	23,240	21,874	986	20,887	1,366	38,343
1959	60,569	22,516	37.2	22,483	21,164	1,033	20,131	1,320	38,053
1958	59,723	22,149	37.1	22,118	20,613	990	19,623	1,504	37,574
1957	58,983	21,765	36.9	21,732	20,714	1,123	19,591	1,018	37,218
1956	58,264	21,495	36.9	21,461	20,422	1,244	19,177	1,039	36,769
1955	57,610	20,584	35.7	20,548	19,550	1,184	18,367	998	37,026
1954	56,965	19,718	34.6	19,678	18,490	1,006	17,486	1,188	37,247
1953	56,353	19,429	34.5	19,382	18,750	1,008	17,744	632	36,924
1952	55,575	19,314	34.8	19,269	18,570	1,112	17,459	698	36,261
1951	54,933	19,054	34.7	19,016	18,182	1,193	16,990	834	35,879
1950	54,293	18,412	33.9	18,389	17,340	1,159	16,182	1,049	35,881
1949	53,689	17,806	33.2	17,788	16,723	1,314	15,409	1,065	35,883
1948	53,088	17,351	32.7	17,335	16,618	1,271	15,347	717	35,737
1947	52,450	16,683	31.8	16,664	16,045	1,248	14,797	619	35,767

Decennial census:

1970 (April)	72,913	30,547	41.9	30,502	28,930	319	28,611	1,572	42,366
1960 (April)* [4]	64,242	22,410	34.9	22,381	21,172	410	20,762	1,209	41,832
1950 (April) [4]	56,539	16,552	30.9	16,520	15,751	590	15,161	769	39,987
1940 (April) [4]	50,688	12,887	25.4	12,887	11,178	485	10,693	1,709	37,800
1930 (April) [6]	48,773	10,752	22.0	--------	--------	910	9,842	--------	38,021
1920 (Jan.) [6]	40,449	8,550	21.0	--------	--------	1,083	7,467	--------	31,900
1910 (April) [6]	34,553	8,076	23.4	--------	--------	1,807	6,269	--------	26,477
1900 (June) [6]	28,246	5,319	18.8	--------	--------	977	4,342	--------	22,927
1890 (June) [6 7]	23,061	4,006	17.4	--------	--------	770	3,236	--------	19,055
1880 (June) [6]	18,026	2,647	14.7	--------	--------	595	2,053	--------	15,378
1870 (June) [6]	13,970	1,836	13.1	--------	--------	397	1,439	--------	12,134

Year	Civilian noninsti-tutional population [1]	Civilian labor force				Not in labor force	Civilian noninsti-tutional population [1]	Civilian labor force				Not in labor force
		Number	Percent of population	Employed	Unemployed			Number	Percent of population	Employed	Unemployed	
	24	14	25	15	18	19	24	14	25	15	18	19

	WHITE						NEGRO AND OTHER RACES					
1970	122,112	73,518	60.2	70,182	3,337	48,594	14,883	9,197	61.8	8,445	752	5,686
1969	119,913	71,779	59.9	69,518	2,261	48,133	14,422	8,954	62.1	8,384	570	5,468
1968	117,948	69,977	59.3	67,751	2,226	47,971	14,080	8,760	62.2	8,169	590	5,320
1967	116,099	68,699	59.2	66,361	2,338	47,401	13,775	8,648	62.8	8,011	638	5,127
1966	114,564	67,274	58.7	65,019	2,253	47,292	13,492	8,496	63.0	7,875	621	4,995
1965	113,284	66,136	58.4	63,445	2,691	47,148	13,230	8,319	62.9	7,643	676	4,912
1964	111,534	64,921	58.2	61,922	2,999	46,613	12,951	8,169	63.1	7,383	786	4,781
1963	109,705	63,830	58.2	60,622	3,208	45,875	12,710	8,004	63.0	7,140	864	4,707
1962	107,715	62,750	58.3	59,698	3,052	44,965	12,439	7,863	63.2	7,004	859	4,577
1961	106,603	62,654	58.8	58,912	3,742	43,950	12,168	7,802	64.1	6,832	970	4,364
1960*	105,282	61,913	58.8	58,850	3,063	43,369	11,965	7,714	64.5	6,927	787	4,250
1959	103,802	60,953	58.7	58,005	2,947	42,850	11,527	7,418	64.4	6,624	794	4,110
1958	102,391	60,293	58.9	56,614	3,679	42,099	11,334	7,347	64.8	6,422	925	3,987
1957	101,117	59,741	59.1	57,452	2,289	41,378	11,144	7,188	64.5	6,619	569	3,958
1956	99,976	59,427	59.4	57,265	2,162	40,549	10,978	7,127	64.9	6,535	592	3,850
1955	98,881	58,082	58.7	55,834	2,248	40,798	10,806	6,942	64.2	6,341	601	3,864
1954	97,705	56,817	58.2	53,957	2,860	40,888	10,615	6,824	64.3	6,150	674	3,791

Decennial census:

1970 (April)	123,590	71,177	58.4	68,283	2,895	52,413	15,500	8,874	57.3	8,271	603	6,626
1960 (April)* [4]	111,530	60,885	54.6	58,010	2,875	50,645	13,013	7,259	55.8	6,629	630	5,754
1950 (April) [4]	100,732	53,178	52.8	50,804	2,374	47,553	11,044	6,125	55.5	5,645	480	4,918
1940 (April) [4]	91,407	47,052	51.5	40,369	6,683	44,355	9,772	5,680	58.1	4,728	952	4,092
1930 (April) [6]	87,981	42,584	48.4	39,776	2,808	45,396	10,742	6,245	58.1	5,866	379	4,497
1920 (Jan.) [6]	74,360	36,616	49.2	--------	--------	37,744	8,380	4,998	59.6	--------	--------	3,381
1910 (April) [6]	63,934	32,774	51.3	--------	--------	31,160	7,646	5,393	70.5	--------	--------	2,253
1900 (June) [6]	51,251	24,913	48.6	--------	--------	26,338	6,699	4,160	62.1	--------	--------	2,539
1890 (June) [6 7]	41,931	19,542	46.6	--------	--------	22,389	5,482	3,193	58.2	--------	--------	2,289

* Denotes first year for which figures include Alaska and Hawaii.
[1] 1870–1930, total population includes institutional.
[2] 1940–1970, includes Armed Forces.
[3] Not available on basis consistent with "total not in labor force."
[4] Data for persons 14 years old and over.
[5] Estimated from data based on different sample.
[6] Data for persons 10 years old and over reporting a gainful occupation.
[7] Revised figures for total and male and female; uncorrected figures for white and Negro and other races.

Series D 26–28. Gainful Workers, by Sex, by State: 1870 to 1950

[In thousands of workers 10 years old and over]

State and year	Total (26)	Male (27)	Female (28)
UNITED STATES			
1950	60,200.8	43,678.3	16,522.6
1940	49,625.4	37,511.9	12,113.4
1930	48,829.9	38,077.8	10,752.1
1920	41,614.2	33,064.7	8,549.5
1910	38,167.3	30,091.6	8,075.8
1900	29,073.2	23,753.8	5,319.4
1890	22,735.7	18,821.1	3,914.6
1880	17,392.1	14,744.9	2,647.2
1870	12,505.9	10,669.6	1,836.3
ALABAMA			
1950	1,099.2	807.8	291.5
1940	965.6	735.6	230.1
1930	1,026.3	772.3	254.0
1920	908.2	684.3	223.9
1910	997.5	683.2	314.3
1900	763.2	563.2	200.0
1890	541.6	411.6	130.0
1880	492.8	368.7	124.1
1870	365.3	275.6	89.6
ARIZONA			
1950	266.5	198.1	68.5
1940	168.8	133.2	35.6
1930	165.3	135.3	30.0
1920	130.6	112.2	18.4
1910	87.8	77.2	10.6
1900	53.4	46.6	6.8
1890	26.4	24.8	1.6
1880	22.3	21.8	.5
1870	6.0	5.7	.3
ARKANSAS			
1950	655.3	511.0	144.3
1940	634.3	525.6	108.7
1930	667.8	548.7	119.2
1920	634.6	518.8	115.8
1910	672.4	510.4	162.0
1900	485.8	407.9	77.9
1890	347.2	299.0	48.2
1880	260.7	230.1	30.6
1870	135.9	120.2	15.8
CALIFORNIA			
1950	4,417.5	3,163.5	1,253.9
1940	2,815.3	2,119.3	695.9
1930	2,500.6	1,943.3	557.4
1920	1,512.8	1,226.1	286.6
1910	1,107.7	932.8	174.9
1900	644.3	556.3	87.9
1890	544.2	483.6	60.5
1880	376.5	348.3	28.2
1870	238.6	224.9	13.8
COLORADO			
1950	514.7	377.8	136.9
1940	386.5	301.7	84.8
1930	402.9	321.9	81.0
1920	366.5	303.9	62.6
1910	338.7	285.1	53.6
1900	218.3	190.3	28.0
1890	191.9	172.8	19.1
1880	101.3	96.5	4.8
1870	17.6	17.1	.4
CONNECTICUT			
1950	880.6	603.6	277.0
1940	736.7	519.7	217.0
1930	677.2	499.2	178.0
1920	589.9	443.7	146.3
1910	490.5	370.5	120.0
1900	385.6	297.0	88.6
1890	317.0	245.6	71.4
1880	241.3	192.7	48.7
1870	193.4	159.5	34.0
DELAWARE			
1950	131.2	93.9	37.3
1940	110.3	82.0	28.3
1930	98.1	77.2	20.9
1920	91.2	73.1	18.1
1910	85.9	68.3	17.5
1900	73.0	60.0	13.0
1890	64.3	53.9	10.3
1880	54.6	46.7	7.9
1870	40.3	34.3	6.0

State and year	Total (26)	Male (27)	Female (28)
DISTRICT OF COLUMBIA			
1950	404.0	236.6	167.4
1940	300.0	202.8	127.1
1930	243.9	155.0	88.8
1920	236.0	143.4	92.6
1910	158.0	105.0	52.9
1900	126.9	85.8	41.2
1890	101.1	69.0	32.1
1880	66.6	47.0	19.7
1870	49.0	35.2	13.8
FLORIDA			
1950	1,102.9	769.2	333.7
1940	741.9	526.2	215.7
1930	598.9	449.0	150.0
1920	385.3	300.0	85.3
1910	322.1	248.9	73.2
1900	201.6	164.0	37.6
1890	136.8	110.4	26.4
1880	91.5	73.8	17.8
1870	60.8	50.9	9.8
GEORGIA			
1950	1,350.1	951.1	399.0
1940	1,176.7	853.7	323.0
1930	1,162.2	850.2	311.9
1920	1,129.2	840.4	288.7
1910	1,160.1	807.2	352.9
1900	864.5	645.9	218.5
1890	668.7	508.8	159.9
1880	597.9	445.5	152.3
1870	444.7	329.2	115.5
IDAHO			
1950	219.1	171.5	47.6
1940	177.2	149.2	28.0
1930	162.2	139.9	22.3
1920	153.5	136.0	17.5
1910	131.1	118.0	13.0
1900	62.7	58.2	4.5
1890	35.2	33.3	1.9
1880	15.6	15.3	.3
1870	10.9	10.8	.1
ILLINOIS			
1950	3,729.6	2,659.6	1,070.1
1940	3,132.0	2,328.8	803.2
1930	3,184.7	2,469.2	715.5
1920	2,627.7	2,086.8	540.9
1910	2,296.8	1,865.4	431.4
1900	1,804.0	1,509.4	294.6
1890	1,353.6	1,153.2	200.3
1880	999.8	893.7	106.1
1870	742.0	678.7	63.3
INDIANA			
1950	1,573.0	1,162.1	410.8
1940	1,242.9	977.3	265.6
1930	1,251.1	1,015.8	235.3
1920	1,117.0	931.6	185.4
1910	1,036.7	881.0	155.7
1900	899.0	782.2	116.7
1890	724.1	639.2	84.9
1880	635.1	583.7	51.4
1870	459.4	428.3	31.1
IOWA			
1950	1,024.8	775.0	249.9
1940	919.6	740.6	179.0
1930	912.8	749.3	163.5
1920	858.7	717.4	141.3
1910	826.3	694.8	131.5
1900	789.4	682.5	106.9
1890	631.8	551.4	80.4
1880	528.3	483.5	44.8
1870	344.3	321.2	23.1
KANSAS			
1950	740.8	562.8	178.0
1940	626.8	502.0	124.8
1930	694.3	575.1	119.2
1920	624.4	531.9	92.5
1910	621.3	540.6	80.7
1900	507.7	452.2	55.6
1890	452.3	406.8	45.5
1880	322.3	302.9	19.4
1870	123.9	117.3	6.5

State and year	Total (26)	Male (27)	Female (28)
KENTUCKY			
1950	1,018.9	804.0	214.8
1940	933.3	768.9	164.4
1930	907.1	760.4	146.7
1920	851.1	719.6	131.5
1910	867.0	719.4	147.6
1900	752.5	646.9	105.6
1890	590.3	506.9	83.4
1880	519.9	465.4	54.4
1870	414.6	364.3	50.3
LOUISIANA			
1950	934.3	694.1	240.2
1940	839.7	640.1	199.5
1930	815.6	624.2	191.4
1920	681.2	528.5	152.7
1910	679.2	501.6	177.6
1900	536.1	405.2	130.9
1890	423.1	314.3	108.8
1880	363.2	268.2	95.1
1870	256.5	198.2	58.3
MAINE			
1950	345.1	250.3	94.8
1940	314.7	233.4	81.4
1930	308.6	240.1	68.5
1920	309.9	245.0	64.8
1910	305.5	242.2	63.3
1900	276.8	224.8	51.9
1890	257.1	212.0	45.1
1880	232.0	198.5	33.5
1870	208.2	179.8	28.4
MARYLAND			
1950	972.0	698.1	274.0
1940	738.6	545.4	193.2
1930	672.9	515.2	157.7
1920	603.5	466.3	137.2
1910	541.2	410.9	130.3
1900	458.7	359.8	99.0
1890	393.3	308.5	84.8
1880	324.4	265.6	58.8
1870	258.5	213.7	44.9
MASSACHUSETTS			
1950	1,959.9	1,329.6	630.3
1940	1,703.1	1,174.5	528.6
1930	1,814.3	1,285.3	529.0
1920	1,728.3	1,225.2	503.2
1910	1,531.1	1,086.8	444.3
1900	1,208.4	879.4	329.0
1890	982.4	719.2	263.3
1880	720.8	546.6	174.2
1870	579.8	451.5	128.3
MICHIGAN			
1950	2,542.6	1,900.7	641.9
1940	1,989.8	1,561.4	428.4
1930	1,927.3	1,567.5	359.8
1920	1,474.0	1,228.6	245.4
1910	1,113.0	926.8	186.2
1900	906.0	772.3	133.7
1890	759.6	663.6	95.9
1880	569.2	514.2	55.0
1870	404.2	346.7	57.4
MINNESOTA			
1950	1,191.0	876.5	314.4
1940	1,028.3	802.2	226.0
1930	992.8	791.8	201.0
1920	907.0	742.9	164.1
1910	835.5	689.8	145.6
1900	645.9	548.9	96.9
1890	469.1	403.5	65.6
1880	255.1	230.0	25.1
1870	132.7	121.8	10.9
MISSISSIPPI			
1950	775.2	583.7	191.5
1940	780.1	590.1	190.0
1930	844.9	613.2	231.7
1920	721.4	526.4	195.0
1910	879.6	574.3	305.4
1900	645.1	466.8	178.4
1890	462.7	337.9	124.8
1880	415.5	305.1	110.4
1870	318.8	232.3	86.5

Series D 26–28. Gainful Workers, by Sex, by State: 1870 to 1950—Con.

[In thousands of workers 10 years old and over]

State and year	Total	Male	Female	State and year	Total	Male	Female	State and year	Total	Male	Female
	26	27	28		26	27	28		26	27	28
MISSOURI				**NORTH CAROLINA**				**SOUTH DAKOTA**			
1950	1,579.6	1,143.1	436.5	1950	1,564.9	1,122.3	442.6	1950	253.0	198.9	54.0
1940	1,410.0	1,077.0	333.0	1940	1,279.4	945.3	334.1	1940	218.8	179.2	39.5
1930	1,458.0	1,158.7	299.2	1930	1,141.0	868.0	273.0	1930	247.7	210.3	37.3
1920	1,317.2	1,072.5	244.6	1920	895.9	693.2	202.7	1920	216.6	186.9	29.7
1910	1,288.3	1,076.8	211.6	1910	947.8	674.8	273.0	1910	219.1	190.4	28.7
1900	1,121.4	966.9	154.5	1900	716.7	556.6	160.2	1900	137.2	121.5	15.6
1890	884.4	771.6	112.8	1890	537.4	422.2	115.2	1890	114.1	102.6	11.5
1880	693.0	630.0	62.9	1880	480.2	393.2	87.0	1880	(1)	(1)	(1)
1870	505.6	466.8	38.7	1870	351.3	292.4	58.9	1870	(1)	(1)	(1)
MONTANA				**NORTH DAKOTA**				**TENNESSEE**			
1950	232.9	181.8	51.1	1950	233.7	186.4	47.3	1950	1,206.7	894.8	311.9
1940	207.2	172.2	35.0	1940	216.5	180.3	36.2	1940	1,015.7	784.9	230.9
1930	216.5	184.2	32.3	1930	240.3	204.1	36.2	1930	958.4	763.1	195.3
1920	214.2	185.9	28.3	1920	207.1	178.8	28.3	1920	830.1	678.0	152.1
1910	178.7	159.9	18.9	1910	217.4	188.4	29.0	1910	855.5	682.2	173.3
1900	114.8	105.0	9.8	1900	117.6	103.5	14.1	1900	727.6	611.4	116.2
1890	72.2	67.6	4.6	1890	67.8	60.0	7.8	1890	553.8	473.2	80.6
1880	22.3	21.7	.5	1880	1 57.8	1 55.0	1 2.9	1880	448.0	391.6	56.4
1870	14.0	13.9	.2	1870	1 5.9	1 5.7	1 .2	1870	368.0	322.6	45.4
NEBRASKA				**OHIO**				**TEXAS**			
1950	528.2	398.7	129.5	1950	3,216.2	2,352.5	863.7	1950	2,991.0	2,235.1	755.9
1940	463.4	369.8	93.6	1940	2,560.6	1,967.8	592.8	1940	2,327.3	1,821.7	505.6
1930	507.0	417.3	89.7	1930	2,615.8	2,076.2	539.6	1930	2,206.8	1,785.1	421.7
1920	457.1	385.3	71.8	1920	2,301.5	1,891.5	410.0	1920	1,719.0	1,415.2	303.8
1910	441.1	377.8	63.3	1910	1,919.1	1,572.3	346.7	1910	1,556.9	1,228.4	328.4
1900	374.0	327.4	46.6	1900	1,546.0	1,299.9	246.1	1900	1,033.0	892.6	140.4
1890	368.1	325.4	42.6	1890	1,272.8	1,088.6	184.2	1890	696.2	610.2	86.0
1880	152.6	142.2	10.5	1880	994.5	881.8	112.6	1880	522.1	463.2	58.9
1870	43.8	41.9	1.9	1870	840.9	757.4	83.5	1870	237.1	208.5	28.6
NEVADA				**OKLAHOMA**				**UTAH**			
1950	71.1	53.3	17.8	1950	800.5	603.8	196.6	1950	243.9	186.6	57.4
1940	45.6	38.3	7.3	1940	734.6	592.9	141.7	1940	165.0	134.1	31.0
1930	42.9	37.0	5.9	1930	828.0	698.7	129.3	1930	170.0	141.0	29.0
1920	37.5	33.2	4.3	1920	681.4	586.8	94.6	1920	149.2	127.4	21.8
1910	44.9	40.5	4.4	1910	598.6	520.4	78.3	1910	131.5	113.1	18.4
1900	19.8	17.8	2.0	1900	266.4	243.9	22.5	1900	84.6	73.8	10.8
1890	23.4	21.6	1.8	1890	20.9	19.8	1.1	1890	66.9	59.8	7.1
1880	32.2	30.7	1.5	1880				1880	40.1	37.2	2.9
1870	26.9	26.5	.4	1870				1870	21.5	20.4	1.1
NEW HAMPSHIRE				**OREGON**				**VERMONT**			
1950	217.3	149.5	67.8	1950	621.3	458.9	162.4	1950	145.6	105.7	39.9
1940	195.3	139.6	55.8	1940	431.0	337.8	93.2	1940	134.5	103.9	30.6
1930	192.7	142.7	50.0	1930	409.6	328.5	81.1	1930	141.2	112.8	28.4
1920	192.8	143.5	49.3	1920	322.3	267.8	54.5	1920	138.5	111.6	26.9
1910	191.7	143.4	48.3	1910	305.2	264.7	40.5	1910	144.1	115.8	28.3
1900	178.7	137.0	41.8	1900	169.6	151.2	18.4	1900	134.9	112.2	22.8
1890	164.7	127.8	36.9	1890	126.8	116.0	10.8	1890	128.8	108.8	20.0
1880	142.5	112.3	30.1	1880	67.3	64.6	2.8	1880	118.6	102.4	16.2
1870	120.2	96.0	24.1	1870	30.7	30.0	.7	1870	108.8	95.3	13.5
NEW JERSEY				**PENNSYLVANIA**				**VIRGINIA**			
1950	2,100.1	1,483.4	616.7	1950	4,168.3	3,022.8	1,145.5	1950	1,307.6	976.2	331.4
1940	1,745.2	1,252.1	493.1	1940	3,676.1	2,778.1	898.0	1940	989.8	764.0	225.8
1930	1,712.1	1,295.6	416.5	1930	3,722.1	2,918.2	803.9	1930	880.2	697.9	182.3
1920	1,310.7	1,014.7	296.0	1920	3,426.4	2,740.1	686.2	1920	833.6	677.4	156.2
1910	1,074.4	834.8	239.6	1910	3,130.7	2,525.2	605.4	1910	795.6	626.9	168.7
1900	757.8	603.2	154.5	1900	2,448.6	2,017.1	431.5	1900	662.4	536.9	125.5
1890	570.7	459.5	111.3	1890	1,959.1	1,635.1	323.9	1890	551.8	445.5	106.4
1880	396.9	330.1	66.8	1880	1,456.1	1,239.1	217.0	1880	494.2	411.0	83.2
1870	296.0	251.6	44.4	1870	1,020.5	886.2	134.3	1870	412.7	337.5	75.2
NEW MEXICO				**RHODE ISLAND**				**WASHINGTON**			
1950	231.0	179.6	51.4	1950	343.9	233.9	110.0	1950	959.7	720.8	238.9
1940	160.2	129.9	30.3	1940	296.8	201.8	94.9	1940	672.4	532.0	140.4
1930	142.6	120.5	22.1	1930	297.2	209.3	87.8	1930	664.7	538.1	126.7
1920	122.0	107.1	14.9	1920	275.0	194.4	80.6	1920	578.7	485.8	92.9
1910	121.5	106.4	15.1	1910	251.9	181.0	70.9	1910	521.5	455.4	66.1
1900	66.0	59.7	6.3	1900	191.9	139.8	52.1	1900	225.4	204.6	20.8
1890	54.2	50.2	3.9	1890	155.9	113.2	42.7	1890	164.7	153.6	11.1
1880	40.8	38.6	2.3	1880	117.0	87.1	29.9	1880	30.1	29.1	1.1
1870	29.4	26.3	3.1	1870	88.6	66.9	21.7	1870	9.8	9.5	.2
NEW YORK				**SOUTH CAROLINA**				**WEST VIRGINIA**			
1950	6,347.3	4,402.2	1,945.1	1950	808.7	560.5	248.2	1950	659.5	521.7	137.8
1940	5,676.8	4,051.5	1,625.3	1940	693.8	489.2	204.6	1940	574.4	472.4	101.9
1930	5,523.3	4,108.2	1,415.1	1930	687.7	481.0	206.8	1930	570.5	488.3	82.2
1920	4,503.2	3,367.9	1,135.3	1920	674.3	468.6	205.7	1920	491.1	433.7	57.4
1910	4,003.8	3,020.2	983.7	1910	728.6	460.8	267.8	1910	448.5	394.4	54.1
1900	2,996.5	2,324.4	672.0	1900	571.0	389.6	181.4	1900	325.7	294.5	31.2
1890	2,435.7	1,921.8	513.9	1890	440.9	311.4	129.4	1890	223.8	202.1	21.7
1880	1,884.6	1,524.3	360.4	1880	392.1	272.0	120.1	1880	176.2	164.7	11.5
1870	1,491.0	1,234.0	257.0	1870	263.3	182.4	80.9	1870	115.2	107.1	8.2

1 South Dakota included with North Dakota.

Series D 26–28. Gainful Workers, by Sex, by State: 1870 to 1950—Con.

[In thousands of workers 10 years old and over]

State and year	Total	Male	Female	State and year	Total	Male	Female
	26	27	28		26	27	28
WISCONSIN				**WYOMING**			
1950	1,400.1	1,030.7	369.4	1950	120.4	94.6	25.8
1940	1,147.5	902.2	245.3	1940	94.9	80.0	14.9
1930	1,129.5	914.2	215.2	1930	92.4	79.7	12.7
1920	995.5	813.2	182.4	1920	81.5	72.1	9.4
1910	892.4	729.8	162.6	1910	73.6	67.6	6.0
1900	732.5	616.4	116.1	1900	44.3	41.3	3.0
1890	576.3	495.2	81.1	1890	30.6	28.7	1.9
1880	417.5	371.1	46.4	1880	8.9	8.4	.5
1870	292.8	267.3	25.5	1870	6.6	6.3	.3

Series D 29–41. Labor Force, by Age and Sex: 1890 to 1970

[Labor force in thousands of persons 16 years old and over except, prior to 1947, 14 years old and over. Annual estimates are averages of monthly figures. Includes Armed Forces overseas, except for decennial data. The introduction of data from the decennial censuses into the estimation procedure in 1953 and 1962 and the inclusion of Alaska and Hawaii beginning 1960 have resulted in 3 periods of noncomparability; see text for series D 11–25]

Year	Total labor force	Male						Female					
		Total	16 to 19 years [1]	20 to 24 years	25 to 44 years	45 to 64 years	65 and over	Total	16 to 19 years [1]	20 to 24 years	25 to 44 years	45 to 64 years	65 and over
	29	30	31	32	33	34	35	36	37	38	39	40	41
LABOR FORCE													
1970	85,903	54,343	4,395	7,378	22,792	17,614	2,164	31,560	3,250	4,893	11,675	10,686	1,056
1969	84,239	53,688	4,282	7,088	22,652	17,494	2,170	30,551	3,109	4,615	11,306	10,465	1,056
1968	82,272	53,030	4,195	6,788	22,498	17,394	2,154	29,242	2,948	4,251	10,973	10,070	999
1967	80,793	52,398	4,214	6,546	22,283	17,239	2,118	28,395	2,897	3,981	10,700	9,841	978
1966	78,893	51,560	4,123	6,139	22,156	17,054	2,089	27,333	2,880	3,601	10,277	9,612	963
1965	77,178	50,946	3,831	5,926	22,157	16,899	2,131	26,232	2,519	3,375	10,060	9,301	976
1964	75,830	50,387	3,575	5,704	22,195	16,788	2,123	25,443	2,321	3,220	9,805	9,129	966
1963	74,571	49,835	3,406	5,471	22,224	16,602	2,135	24,736	2,238	2,970	9,785	8,837	905
1962	73,442	49,395	3,252	5,272	22,262	16,368	2,241	24,047	2,152	2,814	9,590	8,581	911
1961	73,031	49,193	3,229	5,187	22,283	16,276	2,220	23,838	2,148	2,708	9,545	8,510	926
1960*	72,142	48,870	3,184	5,089	22,270	16,039	2,287	23,272	2,062	2,590	9,448	8,266	907
1959	70,921	48,405	3,042	4,987	22,216	15,838	2,321	22,516	1,902	2,484	9,328	7,966	836
1958	70,275	48,126	2,951	4,849	22,269	15,677	2,379	22,149	1,838	2,510	9,391	7,589	822
1957	69,729	47,964	2,985	4,781	22,293	15,428	2,477	21,765	1,866	2,453	9,384	7,249	813
1956	69,409	47,914	2,947	4,814	22,285	15,268	2,604	21,495	1,868	2,467	9,321	7,017	821
1955	68,072	47,488	2,812	4,851	22,297	15,002	2,526	20,584	1,729	2,458	9,069	6,546	780
1954	66,993	47,275	2,726	4,959	22,215	14,853	2,525	19,718	1,688	2,441	8,939	5,988	666
1953	66,560	47,131	2,777	5,084	22,138	14,591	2,544	19,429	1,713	2,447	8,843	5,730	693
1952	65,730	46,416	2,812	5,223	21,635	14,331	2,415	19,314	1,758	2,519	8,779	5,669	590
1951	65,117	46,063	2,865	5,267	21,325	14,136	2,469	19,054	1,763	2,670	8,612	5,458	551
1950	63,858	45,446	2,821	5,224	20,996	13,952	2,453	18,412	1,714	2,681	8,267	5,167	584
1949	62,903	45,097	2,899	5,198	20,746	13,798	2,454	17,806	1,813	2,662	7,999	4,778	556
1948	62,080	44,729	3,002	5,117	20,481	13,745	2,385	17,351	1,835	2,721	7,744	4,538	514
1947	60,941	44,258	3,053	5,094	20,201	13,532	2,376	16,683	1,835	2,725	7,426	4,252	445
1946	60,520	43,690	3,700	4,800	19,450	13,400	2,340	16,840	2,170	2,800	7,400	4,020	450
1945	66,210	46,910	4,610	5,850	20,620	13,370	2,460	19,304	2,720	3,310	8,370	4,410	490
1944	66,320	46,930	5,170	5,840	20,210	13,290	2,420	19,390	2,900	3,340	8,330	4,320	500
1943	64,780	45,950	4,950	5,740	19,770	13,170	2,320	18,830	2,930	3,180	8,260	3,970	490
1942	60,330	44,200	4,260	5,500	19,470	12,780	2,190	16,120	2,370	2,910	7,030	3,420	400
1941	57,720	43,070	9,380		[2] 26,820		[3] 6,880	14,650	4,840		[2] 8,390		[3] 1,410
1940	56,100	41,940	8,770		[2] 26,560		[3] 6,610	14,160	4,600		[2] 8,270		[3] 1,290
Decennial census:													
1970 (April)	82,049	51,502	3,593	6,271	22,111	17,434	2,092	30,547	2,609	4,683	11,652	10,432	1,171
1960 (April)*	69,234	47,013	2,634	4,554	21,829	15,765	2,231	22,222	1,703	2,475	9,382	7,742	919
1950 (April)	59,223	42,779	2,204	4,537	20,389	13,275	2,373	16,443	1,331	2,521	7,666	4,416	509
1940 (April)	52,966	39,959	2,565	4,993	18,705	11,859	1,838	13,007	1,396	2,698	6,081	2,554	279
1930 (April)	47,404	37,008	2,795	4,747	17,498	10,173	1,795	10,396	1,591	2,316	4,404	1,842	243
1920 (Jan.)	40,282	32,053	2,947	4,080	15,353	8,290	1,383	8,229	1,640	1,785	3,314	1,310	180
1900 (June)	27,640	22,641	2,834	3,302	10,560	4,958	987	4,999	1,230	1,179	1,791	672	127
1890 (June)	21,833	18,129	1,997	2,836	8,513	3,937	846	3,704	984	938	1,216	476	90
LABOR FORCE PARTICIPATION RATE (Percent)													
1970	61.3	80.6	58.4	86.6	96.8	89.3	26.8	43.4	44.0	57.8	47.9	49.3	9.7
1969	61.1	80.9	58.3	86.6	97.0	89.7	27.2	42.7	43.3	56.8	46.8	49.0	9.9
1968	60.7	81.2	58.3	86.5	97.2	90.3	27.3	41.6	42.0	54.6	45.8	47.7	9.6
1967	60.6	81.5	59.2	87.5	97.4	90.6	27.7	41.1	41.7	53.4	45.1	47.4	9.6
1966	60.1	81.4	58.1	87.9	97.4	90.7	27.0	40.3	41.5	51.5	43.5	47.4	9.6
1965	59.7	81.5	56.7	88.0	97.4	90.9	27.9	39.3	38.1	50.0	42.5	46.6	10.0
1964	59.6	81.9	56.1	88.2	97.4	91.4	28.0	38.7	37.1	49.5	41.4	46.5	10.1
1963	59.6	82.2	56.8	88.3	97.5	91.7	28.4	38.3	38.0	47.6	41.3	45.9	9.6
1962	59.7	82.8	57.7	89.1	97.5	91.6	30.3	38.0	39.1	47.4	40.4	45.1	9.9
1961	60.2	83.6	58.2	89.8	97.6	92.1	31.7	38.1	39.7	47.1	40.3	44.8	10.7

See footnotes at end of table.

Series D 29–41. Labor Force, by Age and Sex: 1890 to 1970—Con.

[In thousands of persons 16 years old and over except, prior to 1947, 14 years old and over. Annual estimates are averages of monthly figures.]

Year	Total labor force	Male						Female					
		Total	16 to 19 years	20 to 24 years	25 to 44 years	45 to 64 years	65 and over	Total	16 to 19 years	20 to 24 years	25 to 44 years	45 to 64 years	65 and over
	29	30	31	32	33	34	35	36	37	38	39	40	41
LABOR FORCE PARTICIPATION RATE (Percent) —Con.													
1960*	60.2	84.0	59.4	90.2	97.7	92.0	33.1	37.8	39.4	46.2	39.9	44.3	10.8
1959	60.2	84.5	59.7	90.1	97.7	92.4	34.2	37.2	40.7	45.2	39.4	43.6	10.2
1958	60.4	85.0	61.3	89.5	97.6	92.7	35.6	37.1	39.1	46.4	39.6	42.4	10.3
1957	60.6	85.5	64.2	89.8	97.6	92.6	37.5	36.9	41.1	46.0	39.4	41.3	10.5
1956	61.0	86.3	65.0	90.8	97.7	93.1	40.0	36.9	42.3	46.4	39.2	40.9	10.9
1955	60.4	86.2	63.0	90.8	97.9	92.8	39.6	35.7	39.8	46.0	38.2	38.9	10.6
1954	60.0	86.4	62.2	91.5	97.8	93.1	40.5	34.6	39.5	45.3	37.8	36.3	9.3
1953	60.2	86.9	64.9	92.2	97.9	92.8	41.6	34.5	40.8	44.5	37.5	35.5	10.0
1952	60.4	87.2	66.2	92.1	98.1	92.5	42.6	34.8	42.2	44.8	37.9	35.1	9.1
1951	60.4	87.3	67.9	91.1	97.6	92.2	44.9	34.7	42.5	46.6	37.5	34.4	8.9
1950	59.9	86.8	66.3	89.1	97.1	92.0	45.8	33.9	41.0	46.1	36.4	33.2	9.7
1949	59.6	86.9	66.7	87.8	97.2	92.1	46.9	33.2	42.3	45.0	35.6	33.2	9.6
1948	59.4	87.0	67.3	85.7	97.2	93.1	46.8	32.7	42.0	45.3	35.0	31.3	9.1
1947	58.9	86.8	67.0	84.9	97.1	93.0	47.8	31.8	41.1	44.9	34.0	30.4	9.1
1946	55.8	81.1	54.8	79.9	91.4	91.5	45.0	30.8	31.8	46.6	34.0	27.9	8.0
1945	61.6	87.6	66.4	96.8	97.9	92.4	48.7	35.8	39.2	55.3	39.0	31.2	9.0
1944	62.2	88.2	72.2	96.4	97.0	93.2	49.4	36.3	41.1	55.6	39.3	31.1	9.5
1943	61.5	87.4	68.9	94.5	96.4	93.8	48.6	35.7	41.0	53.1	39.5	29.2	9.6
1942	58.0	85.1	58.6	91.9	96.4	92.3	47.1	30.9	32.8	48.7	34.0	25.6	8.1
1941	56.1	83.8	70.8		[2]95.5		[3]68.0	28.5	36.6		[2]29.9	[3]13.9	
1940	55.2	82.5	66.4		[2]95.6		[3]66.9	27.9	34.7		[2]29.9	[3]13.1	
Decennial census:													
1970 (April)	58.2	76.6	47.2	80.9	94.3	87.2	24.8	41.4	34.9	56.1	47.5	47.8	10.0
1960 (April)*	57.3	80.4	50.0	86.2	95.3	89.0	30.5	35.7	32.6	44.8	39.1	41.6	10.3
1950 (April)	55.1	81.6	51.7	81.9	93.3	88.2	41.4	29.9	31.1	42.9	33.3	28.8	7.8
1940 (April)	52.4	79.1	34.7	88.1	94.9	88.7	41.8	25.8	18.9	45.6	30.5	20.2	6.1
1930 (April)	53.2	82.1	40.1	88.8	95.8	91.0	54.0	23.6	22.8	41.8	24.6	18.0	7.3
1920 (Jan.)	54.3	84.6	51.5	89.9	95.6	90.7	55.6	22.7	28.4	37.5	21.7	16.5	7.3
1900 (June)	53.7	85.7	62.0	90.6	94.7	90.3	63.1	20.0	26.8	31.7	17.5	13.6	8.3
1890 (June)	52.2	84.3	50.0	90.9	96.0	92.0	68.3	18.2	24.5	30.2	15.1	12.1	7.6
PERCENT DISTRIBUTION													
1970	100.0	63.3	5.1	8.6	26.5	20.5	2.5	36.7	3.8	5.7	13.6	12.4	1.2
1969	100.0	63.7	5.1	8.4	26.9	20.8	2.6	36.3	3.7	5.5	13.4	12.4	1.3
1968	100.0	64.5	5.1	8.3	27.3	21.1	2.6	35.5	3.6	5.2	13.3	12.2	1.3
1967	100.0	64.9	5.2	8.1	27.6	21.3	2.6	35.1	3.6	4.9	13.2	12.2	1.2
1966	100.0	65.4	5.2	7.8	28.1	21.6	2.6	34.6	3.7	4.6	13.0	12.2	1.2
1965	100.0	66.0	5.0	7.7	28.7	21.9	2.8	34.0	3.3	4.4	13.0	12.1	1.3
1964	100.0	66.4	4.7	7.5	29.3	22.1	2.8	33.6	3.1	4.2	12.9	12.0	1.3
1963	100.0	66.8	4.6	7.3	29.8	22.3	2.9	33.2	3.0	4.0	13.1	11.9	1.2
1962	100.0	67.3	4.4	7.2	30.3	22.3	3.1	32.7	2.9	3.8	13.1	11.7	1.2
1961	100.0	67.4	4.4	7.1	30.5	22.3	3.0	32.6	2.9	3.7	13.1	11.7	1.3
1960*	100.0	67.7	4.4	7.1	30.9	22.2	3.2	32.3	2.9	3.6	13.1	11.5	1.3
1959	100.0	68.3	4.3	7.0	31.3	22.3	3.3	31.7	2.7	3.5	13.2	11.2	1.2
1958	100.0	68.5	4.2	6.9	31.7	22.3	3.4	31.5	2.6	3.6	13.4	10.8	1.2
1957	100.0	68.8	4.3	6.9	32.0	22.1	3.6	31.2	2.7	3.5	13.5	10.4	1.2
1956	100.0	69.0	4.2	6.9	32.1	22.0	3.8	31.0	2.7	3.5	13.4	10.1	1.2
1955	100.0	69.8	4.1	7.1	32.8	22.0	3.7	30.2	2.5	3.6	13.3	9.6	1.1
1954	100.0	70.6	4.1	7.4	33.2	22.2	3.8	29.4	2.5	3.6	13.3	8.9	1.0
1953	100.0	70.8	4.2	7.6	33.3	21.9	3.8	29.2	2.6	3.7	13.3	8.6	1.0
1952	100.0	70.6	4.3	7.9	32.9	21.8	3.7	29.4	2.7	3.8	13.4	8.6	.9
1951	100.0	70.7	4.4	8.1	32.7	21.7	3.8	29.3	2.7	4.1	13.2	8.4	.8
1950	100.0	71.2	4.4	8.2	32.9	21.8	3.8	28.8	2.7	4.2	12.9	8.1	.9
1949	100.0	71.7	4.6	8.3	33.0	21.9	3.9	28.3	2.9	4.2	12.7	7.6	.9
1948	100.0	72.0	4.8	8.2	33.0	22.1	3.8	28.0	3.0	4.4	12.5	7.3	.8
1947	100.0	72.6	5.0	8.4	33.1	22.2	3.9	27.4	3.0	4.5	12.2	7.0	.7
1946	100.0	72.2	6.1	7.9	32.1	22.1	3.9	27.8	3.6	4.6	12.2	6.6	.7
1945	100.0	70.8	7.0	8.8	31.1	20.2	3.7	29.2	4.1	5.0	12.6	6.7	.7
1944	100.0	70.8	7.8	8.8	30.5	20.0	3.7	29.2	4.4	5.0	12.6	6.5	.8
1943	100.0	70.9	7.6	8.9	30.5	20.3	3.6	29.1	4.5	4.9	12.7	6.1	.8
1942	100.0	73.3	7.1	9.1	32.3	21.2	3.6	26.7	3.9	4.8	11.6	5.7	.7
1941	100.0	74.6	16.2		[2]46.5		[3]11.9	25.4	8.4		[2]14.5	[3]2.4	
1940	100.0	74.8	15.6		[2]47.3		[3]11.8	25.2	8.2		[2]14.7	[3]2.3	
Decennial census:													
1970 (April)	100.0	62.8	4.4	7.6	26.9	21.2	2.5	37.2	3.2	5.7	14.2	12.7	1.4
1960 (April)*	100.0	67.9	3.8	6.6	31.5	22.8	3.2	32.1	2.5	3.6	13.6	11.2	1.3
1950 (April)	100.0	72.2	3.7	7.7	34.4	22.4	4.0	27.8	2.2	4.3	12.9	7.5	.9
1940 (April)	100.0	75.4	4.8	9.4	35.3	22.4	3.5	24.6	2.6	5.1	11.5	4.8	.5
1930 (April)	100.0	78.1	5.9	10.0	36.9	21.5	3.8	21.9	3.4	4.9	9.3	3.9	.5
1920 (Jan.)	100.0	79.6	7.3	10.1	38.1	20.6	3.4	20.4	4.1	4.4	8.2	3.3	.4
1900 (June)	100.0	81.9	10.3	11.9	38.2	17.9	3.6	18.1	4.5	4.3	6.5	2.4	.5
1890 (June)	100.0	83.0	9.1	13.0	39.0	18.0	3.9	17.0	4.5	4.3	5.6	2.2	.4

* Denotes first year for which figures include Alaska and Hawaii.
[1] 14 to 19 years for 1940 through 1946.
[2] 25 to 54 years.
[3] 55 and over.

Series D 42–48. Civilian Labor Force as Percent of Civilian Noninstitutional Population, by Race and Sex: 1940 to 1970

[Based on persons 16 years old and over except, prior to 1947, 14 years old and over. See headnote for series D 11–25]

Year	Both sexes			Male		Female		Year	Total, both sexes
	Total	White	Negro and other races	White	Negro and other races	White	Negro and other races		
	42	43	44	45	46	47	48		42
1970	60.4	60.2	61.8	80.0	76.5	42.6	49.5	1953	58.9
1969	60.1	59.9	62.1	80.2	76.9	41.8	49.8	1952	59.0
1968	59.6	59.3	62.2	80.4	77.6	40.7	49.3	1951	59.3
1967	59.6	59.2	62.8	80.7	78.5	40.1	49.5		
1966	59.2	58.7	63.0	80.6	79.0	39.2	49.3	1950	59.2
								1949	58.9
1965	58.9	58.4	62.9	80.8	79.6	38.1	48.6	1948	58.8
1964	58.7	58.2	63.1	81.1	80.0	37.5	48.5	1947	58.3
1963	58.7	58.2	63.0	81.5	80.2	37.2	48.1	1946	55.2
1962	58.8	58.3	63.2	82.1	80.8	36.7	48.0		
1961	59.3	58.8	64.1	83.0	82.2	36.9	48.3	1945	56.5
								1944	57.9
1960	59.4	58.8	64.5	83.4	83.0	36.5	48.2	1943	58.0
1959	59.3	58.7	64.3	83.8	83.4	36.0	47.7	1942	56.5
1958	59.5	58.9	64.8	84.3	84.0	35.8	48.0	1941	55.3
1957	59.6	59.1	64.4	84.8	84.3	35.7	47.2		
1956	61.6	59.4	64.9	85.6	85.1	35.7	47.3	1940	55.1
1955	59.3	58.7	64.2	85.4	85.0	34.5	46.1		
1954	58.8	58.2	64.3	85.6	85.2	33.3	46.1		

Series D 49–62. Marital Status of Women in the Civilian Labor Force: 1890 to 1970

[Persons 15 years old and over, 1890–1930; 14 years old and over, 1940–1966; 16 years old and over, thereafter. As of March, except as indicated]

Year	Female labor force (1,000)					Percent distribution of female labor force				Female labor force as percent of female population				
	Total	Single	Married		Widowed or divorced	Single	Married		Widowed or divorced	Total	Single	Married		Widowed or divorced
			Total	Husband present			Total	Husband present				Total	Husband present	
	49	50	51	52	53	54	55	56	57	58	59	60	61	62
1970	31,233	6,965	19,799	18,377	4,469	22.3	63.4	58.8	14.3	42.6	53.0	41.4	40.8	36.2
1969	29,898	6,501	19,100	17,595	4,297	21.7	63.9	58.9	14.4	41.6	51.2	40.4	39.6	35.8
1968	28,778	6,357	18,234	16,821	4,187	22.1	63.4	58.5	14.6	40.7	51.3	39.1	38.3	35.8
1967	27,545	5,915	17,486	15,908	4,144	21.5	63.5	57.8	15.0	39.7	50.7	37.8	36.8	35.9
1966	26,820	6,106	16,676	15,178	4,038	22.7	62.2	56.6	15.1	37.3	40.8	36.5	35.4	36.4
1965	25,952	5,912	16,154	14,708	3,886	22.8	62.2	56.7	15.0	36.7	40.5	35.7	34.7	35.7
1964	25,399	5,781	15,790	14,461	3,828	22.8	62.2	56.9	15.1	36.5	40.9	35.3	34.4	36.1
1963	24,675	5,614	15,362	14,061	3,699	22.8	62.3	57.0	15.0	36.1	41.0	34.6	33.7	35.8
1962	23,978	5,481	14,770	13,485	3,727	22.9	61.6	56.2	15.5	35.7	41.7	33.7	32.7	36.6
1961	24,199	5,663	14,612	13,266	3,924	23.4	60.4	54.8	16.2	36.8	44.4	34.0	32.7	39.0
1960*	22,516	5,401	13,485	12,253	3,629	24.0	59.9	54.4	16.1	34.8	44.1	31.7	30.5	37.1
1959	22,376	5,162	13,586	12,205	3,628	23.1	60.7	54.5	16.2	35.2	43.4	32.3	30.9	38.0
1958	22,000	5,365	13,032	11,826	3,604	24.4	59.2	53.8	16.4	35.0	45.4	31.4	30.2	37.9
1957	21,524	5,378	12,696	11,529	3,450	25.0	59.0	53.6	16.0	34.8	46.8	30.8	29.6	37.6
1956	20,842	5,167	12,278	11,126	3,397	24.8	58.9	53.4	16.3	34.2	46.4	30.2	29.0	36.9
1955 [1]	20,154	5,087	11,839	10,423	3,227	25.2	58.7	51.7	16.0	33.5	46.4	29.4	27.7	36.0
1954 [1]	19,726	5,412	11,209	9,923	3,105	27.4	56.8	50.3	15.7	33.1	49.0	28.1	26.6	36.0
1953 [1]	19,304	5,223	10,908	9,763	3,174	27.1	56.5	50.6	16.4	32.8	48.5	27.7	26.3	36.3
1952 [1]	18,812	5,532	10,350	9,222	2,930	29.4	55.0	49.0	15.6	32.4	50.0	26.8	25.3	35.3
1951 [1]	18,602	5,430	10,182	9,086	2,990	29.2	54.7	48.8	16.1	32.4	49.6	26.7	25.2	36.1
1950	17,795	5,621	9,273	8,550	2,901	31.6	52.1	48.0	16.3	31.4	50.5	24.8	23.8	36.0
1949 [1]	17,167	5,682	8,739	7,959	2,746	33.1	50.9	46.4	16.0	30.7	50.9	23.6	22.5	35.1
1948 [1]	17,155	5,943	8,281	7,553	2,931	34.6	48.3	44.0	17.1	31.0	51.1	23.1	22.0	36.8
1947 [1]	16,323	6,181	7,545	6,676	2,597	37.9	46.2	40.9	15.9	29.8	51.2	21.4	20.0	34.6
1944 [1]	18,449	7,542	8,433	6,226	2,474	40.9	45.7	33.7	13.4	35.0	58.6	25.6	21.7	35.7
1940	13,840	6,710	5,040	[1] 4,200	2,090	48.5	36.4	[1] 30.3	15.1	27.4	48.1	16.7	[1] 14.7	32.0
Decennial census:														
1970 (April)	30,756	6,936	19,178	17,583	4,642	22.5	62.3	57.1	15.0	41.6	50.9	40.2	39.6	36.8
1960 (April)*	22,410	5,282	13,610	12,365	3,518	23.6	60.7	55.2	15.7	34.5	42.9	31.7	30.6	36.1
1950 (April)	16,553	5,274	8,635	7,697	2,644	31.9	52.2	46.5	16.0	29.0	46.3	23.0	21.6	32.7
1940 (April)	13,007	6,377	4,675	3,918	1,955	49.0	35.9	30.1	15.0	25.8	45.5	15.6	13.8	30.2
1930 (April)	10,632	5,735	3,071	--------	1,826	53.9	28.9	--------	17.2	24.8	50.5	11.7	--------	34.4
1920 (Jan.)	8,347	[2] 6,427	1,920	--------	(2)	[2] 77.0	23.0	--------	(2)	23.7	[2] 46.4	9.0	--------	(2)
1910 (April) [3]	7,640	4,602	1,891	--------	1,147	60.2	24.7	--------	15.0	25.4	51.1	10.7	--------	34.1
1900 (June)	4,997	3,307	769	--------	920	66.2	15.4	--------	18.4	20.6	43.5	5.6	--------	32.5
1890 (June)	3,712	2,531	515	--------	665	68.2	13.9	--------	17.9	18.9	40.5	4.6	--------	29.9

* Denotes first year for which figures include Alaska and Hawaii.
[1] As of April.   [2] Single includes widowed or divorced.
[3] Data not comparable with earlier or later censuses due to difference in basis of enumeration. The importance of returning "the occupation, if any, followed by a child of any age or by a woman," was emphasized in the printed instructions to census enumerators in 1910, but not in instructions in other censuses, and it is believed that enumerators in 1910 enumerated as gainful workers many women who would not have been enumerated in other censuses—particularly as agricultural laborers.

Series D 63–74. Married Women (Husband Present) in the Labor Force, by Age and Presence of Children: 1948 to 1970

[As of March, except as noted]

Year	Number in labor force (1,000)			With children under 6 years			Labor force participation rate [1]			With children under 6 years		
	Total	With no children under 18 years	With children 6 to 17 years only	Total	No children 6 to 17 years	Also children 6 to 17 years	Total	With no children under 18 years	With children 6 to 17 years only	Total	No children 6 to 17 years	Also children 6 to 17 years
	63	64	65	66	67	68	69	70	71	72	73	74
1970	18,377	8,174	6,289	3,914	1,874	2,040	40.8	42.2	49.2	30.3	30.2	30.5
1969	17,595	7,853	6,146	3,596	1,756	1,840	39.6	41.0	48.6	28.5	29.3	27.8
1968	16,821	7,564	5,693	3,564	1,641	1,923	38.3	40.1	46.9	27.6	27.8	27.4
1967	15,908	7,158	5,269	3,480	1,629	1,851	36.8	38.9	45.0	26.5	26.9	26.2
1966	15,178	7,043	4,949	3,186	1,431	1,755	35.4	38.4	43.7	24.2	24.0	24.3
1965	14,708	6,755	4,836	3,117	1,408	1,709	34.7	38.3	42.7	23.3	23.8	22.8
1964	14,461	6,545	4,866	3,050	1,408	1,642	34.4	37.8	43.0	22.7	23.6	21.9
1963	14,061	6,366	4,689	3,006	1,346	1,660	33.7	37.4	41.5	22.5	22.4	22.5
1962	13,485	6,156	4,445	2,884	1,282	1,602	32.7	36.1	41.8	21.3	21.1	21.5
1961	13,266	6,186	4,419	2,661	1,178	1,483	32.7	37.3	41.7	20.0	19.6	20.3
1960*	12,253	5,692	4,087	2,474	1,123	1,351	30.5	34.7	39.0	18.6	18.2	18.9
1959	12,205	5,679	4,055	2,471	1,118	1,353	30.9	35.2	39.8	18.7	18.3	19.0
1958	11,826	5,713	3,714	2,399	1,122	1,277	30.2	35.4	37.6	18.2	18.4	18.1
1957	11,529	5,805	3,517	2,208	961	1,247	29.6	35.6	36.6	17.0	15.9	17.9
1956	11,126	5,694	3,384	2,048	971	1,077	29.0	35.3	36.4	15.9	15.6	16.1
1955 [2]	10,423	5,227	3,183	2,012	927	1,086	27.7	32.7	34.7	16.2	15.1	17.3
1954 [2]	9,923	5,096	3,019	1,808	883	925	26.6	31.6	33.2	14.9	14.3	15.5
1953 [2]	9,763	5,130	2,749	1,884	1,047	837	26.3	31.2	32.2	15.5	15.8	15.2
1952 [2]	9,222	5,042	2,492	1,688	916	772	25.3	30.9	31.1	13.9	13.7	14.1
1951 [2]	9,086	5,016	2,400	1,670	886	784	25.2	31.0	30.3	14.0	13.6	14.6
1950	8,550	4,946	2,205	1,399	748	651	23.8	30.3	28.3	11.9	11.2	12.6
1949 [2]	7,959	4,544	2,130	1,285	654	631	22.5	28.7	27.3	11.0	10.0	12.2
1948 [2]	7,553	4,400	1,927	1,226	594	632	22.0	28.4	26.0	10.8	9.2	12.7

* Denotes first year for which figures include Alaska and Hawaii.   [2] As of April.
[1] Married women in the labor force as percent of married women in the population.

Series D 75–84. Gainful Workers, by Age, Sex, and Farm-Nonfarm Occupations: 1820 to 1930

[In thousands of persons 10 years old and over]

Year	Total workers	Occupation		Sex		Age (in years)					Year	Total workers	Occupation	
		Farm	Non-farm	Male	Female	10 to 15	16 to 44	45 to 64	65 and over	Un-known			Farm	Non-farm
	75	76	77	78	79	80	81	82	83	84		75	76	77
1930	48,830	10,472	38,358	38,078	10,752	667	33,492	12,422	2,205	44	1860	10,533	6,208	4,325
1920	42,434	11,449	30,985	33,797	8,637	1,417	29,339	9,914	1,691	73	1850	7,697	4,902	2,795
1910	37,371	11,592	25,779	29,926	7,445	1,622	26,620	7,606	1,440	83	1840	5,420	3,720	1,700
1900	29,073	10,912	18,161	23,754	5,319	1,750	20,223	5,804	1,202	94	1830	3,932	2,772	1,160
1890	23,318	9,938	13,380	19,313	4,006	1,504	16,162	4,547	1,009	97	1820	2,881	2,069	812
1880	17,392	8,585	8,807	14,745	2,647	1,118	16,274							
1870	12,925	6,850	6,075	11,008	1,917	765	12,160							

Series D 85–86. Unemployment: 1890 to 1970

[In thousands of persons 16 years old and over except, prior to 1947, 14 years old and over. Annual averages]

Year	Unemployed 85	Percent of civilian labor force 86	Year	Unemployed 85	Percent of civilian labor force 86	Year	Unemployed 85	Percent of civilian labor force 86	Year	Unemployed 85	Percent of civilian labor force 86	Year	Unemployed 85	Percent of civilian labor force 86
1970	4,088	4.9	1954	3,532	5.5	1938	10,390	19.0	1922	2,859	6.7	1906	574	1.7
1969	2,832	3.5	1953¹	1,834	2.9	1937	7,700	14.3	1921	4,918	11.7	1905	1,381	4.3
1968	2,817	3.6	1952	1,883	3.0	1936	9,030	16.9				1904	1,691	5.4
1967	2,975	3.8	1951	2,055	3.3				1920	2,132	5.2	1903	1,204	3.9
1966	2,875	3.8				1935	10,610	20.1	1919	546	1.4	1902	1,097	3.7
			1950	3,288	5.3	1934	11,340	21.7	1918	536	1.4	1901	1,205	4.0
1965	3,366	4.5	1949	3,637	5.9	1933	12,830	24.9	1917	1,848	4.6			
1964	3,786	5.2	1948	2,276	3.8	1932	12,060	23.6	1916	2,043	5.1	1900	1,420	5.0
1963	4,070	5.7	1947	2,311	3.9	1931	8,020	15.9				1899	1,819	6.5
1962¹	3,911	5.5	1946	2,270	3.9				1915	3,377	8.5	1898	3,351	12.4
1961	4,714	6.7				1930	4,340	8.7	1914	3,120	7.9	1897	3,890	14.5
			1945	1,040	1.9	1929	1,550	3.2	1913	1,671	4.3	1896	3,782	14.4
1960¹*	3,852	5.5	1944	670	1.2	1928	1,982	4.2	1912	1,759	4.6	1895	3,510	13.7
1959	3,740	5.5	1943	1,070	1.9	1927	1,519	3.3	1911	2,518	6.7			
1958	4,602	6.8	1942	2,660	4.7	1926	801	1.8				1894	4,612	18.4
1957	2,859	4.3	1941	5,560	9.9				1910	2,150	5.9	1893	2,860	11.7
1956	2,750	4.1				1925	1,453	3.2	1909	1,824	5.1	1892	728	3.0
			1940	8,120	14.6	1924	2,190	5.0	1908	2,780	8.0	1891	1,265	5.4
1955	2,852	4.4	1939	9,480	17.2	1923	1,049	2.4	1907	945	2.8	1890	904	4.0

* Denotes first year for which figures include Alaska and Hawaii.

¹ See headnote for series D 11–25.

Series D 87–101. Unemployment Rates for Selected Groups in the Labor Force: 1947 to 1970

[Percent of each group specified of persons 16 years old and over in the civilian labor force]

Year	All civilian workers Total 87	Male 88	Female 89	White Total 90	Male 91	Female 92	Negro and other races Total 93	Male 94	Female 95	Both sexes, 16–19 years old 96	Men, 20 years and over 97	Women, 20 years and over 98	Unemployed 15 weeks and over, total 99	Average duration of unemployment, weeks 100	State insured unemployment 101
1970	4.9	4.4	5.9	4.5	4.0	5.4	8.2	7.3	9.3	15.2	3.5	4.8	0.8	8.8	3.4
1969	3.5	2.8	4.7	3.1	2.5	4.2	6.4	5.3	7.8	12.2	2.1	3.7	.5	8.0	2.2
1968	3.6	2.9	4.8	3.2	2.6	4.3	6.7	5.6	8.3	12.7	2.2	3.8	.5	8.5	2.2
1967	3.8	3.1	5.2	3.4	2.7	4.6	7.4	6.0	9.1	12.9	2.3	4.2	.6	8.8	2.5
1966	3.8	3.2	4.8	3.3	2.8	4.3	7.3	6.3	8.6	12.8	2.5	3.8	.7	10.4	2.4
1965	4.5	4.0	5.5	4.1	3.6	5.0	8.1	7.4	9.2	14.8	3.2	4.5	1.0	11.8	3.0
1964	5.2	4.6	6.2	4.6	4.1	5.5	9.6	8.9	10.6	16.2	3.9	5.2	1.3	13.3	3.7
1963	5.7	5.2	6.5	5.0	4.7	5.8	10.8	10.5	11.2	17.2	4.5	5.4	1.5	14.0	4.3
1962	5.5	5.2	6.2	4.9	4.6	5.5	10.9	10.9	11.0	14.7	4.6	5.4	1.6	14.7	4.4
1961	6.7	6.4	7.2	6.0	5.7	6.5	12.4	12.8	11.8	16.8	5.7	6.3	2.2	15.6	5.7
1960	5.5	5.4	5.9	4.9	4.8	5.3	10.2	10.7	9.4	14.7	4.7	5.1	1.4	12.8	4.8
1959	5.5	5.3	5.9	4.8	4.6	5.3	10.7	11.5	9.4	14.6	4.7	5.2	1.5	14.4	4.4
1958	6.8	6.8	6.8	6.1	6.1	6.2	12.6	13.8	10.8	15.9	6.2	6.1	2.1	13.9	6.3
1957	4.3	4.1	4.7	3.8	3.6	4.3	7.9	8.3	7.3	11.6	3.6	4.1	.8	10.5	3.7
1956	4.1	3.8	4.8	3.6	3.4	4.2	8.3	7.9	8.9	11.1	3.4	4.2	.8	11.3	3.4
1955	4.4	4.2	4.9	3.9	3.7	4.3	8.7	8.8	8.4	11.0	3.8	4.4	1.1	13.0	3.5
1954	5.5	5.3	6.0	5.0	4.8	5.6	9.9	10.3	9.3	12.6	4.9	5.5	1.3	11.8	5.1
1953	2.9	2.8	3.3	2.7	2.5	3.1	4.5	4.8	4.1	7.6	2.5	2.9	.3	8.0	2.8
1952	3.0	2.8	3.6	2.8	2.5	3.3	5.4	5.2	5.7	8.5	2.4	3.2	.4	8.4	3.0
1951	3.3	2.8	4.4	3.1	2.6	4.2	5.3	4.9	6.1	8.2	2.5	4.0	.5	9.7	3.0
1950	5.3	5.1	5.7	4.9	4.7	5.3	9.0	9.4	8.4	12.2	4.7	5.1	1.3	12.1	4.8
1949	5.9	5.9	6.0	5.6	5.6	5.7	8.9	9.6	7.9	13.4	5.4	5.3	1.1	10.0	6.0
1948	3.8	3.6	4.1	3.5	3.4	3.8	5.9	5.8	6.1	9.2	3.2	3.6	.5	8.6	3.1
1947	3.9	4.0	3.7	--------	--------	--------	--------	--------	--------	--------	--------	--------	--------	--------	--------

Series D 102–115. Unemployment Rates, by Industry: 1948 to 1970

[Percent of each industry specified of persons 16 years old and over in the civilian labor force]

				Experienced wage and salary workers										
					Wage and salary workers in private nonagricultural industries									
Year	Total unemployed [1]	Total	Agriculture	Total	Mining	Construction	Manufacturing			Transportation and public utilities	Wholesale and retail trade	Finance, insurance, real estate	Service industries	Government
							Total	Durable	Non-durable					
	102	103	104	105	106	107	108	109	110	111	112	113	114	115
1970	4.9	4.8	7.5	5.2	3.1	9.7	5.6	5.7	5.4	3.2	5.3	2.8	4.7	2.2
1969	3.5	3.3	6.0	3.0	2.8	5.4	3.3	3.0	3.7	2.1	4.1	2.1	3.5	1.9
1968	3.6	3.4	6.3	3.0	3.1	6.2	3.3	3.0	3.7	1.9	4.0	2.2	3.6	1.8
1967	3.8	3.6	6.9	3.9	3.4	6.6	3.6	3.4	4.1	2.3	4.2	2.5	3.9	1.8
1966	3.8	3.5	6.6	3.8	3.5	7.1	3.2	2.7	3.8	2.0	4.4	2.1	3.9	1.8
1965	4.5	4.3	7.5	4.6	5.3	10.1	4.0	3.5	4.7	2.9	5.0	2.3	4.6	1.9
1964	5.2	5.0	9.7	5.4	6.7	11.2	5.0	4.7	5.4	3.5	5.7	2.6	5.3	2.1
1963	5.7	5.6	9.2	6.1	7.3	13.3	5.7	5.5	6.0	4.2	6.2	2.7	5.7	2.2
1962	5.5	5.6	7.5	6.1	7.7	13.5	5.8	5.7	6.0	4.1	6.3	3.0	5.5	2.1
1961	6.7	6.8	9.6	7.5	11.1	15.7	7.8	8.5	6.8	5.3	7.3	3.3	6.2	2.5
1960	5.5	5.7	8.3	6.2	9.5	13.5	6.2	6.4	6.1	4.6	5.9	2.4	5.1	2.4
1959	5.5	5.7	6.1	6.1	9.7	13.4	6.1	6.2	6.0	4.4	5.8	2.5	5.3	2.2
1958	6.8	7.3	10.3	7.9	10.9	15.3	9.3	10.6	7.7	6.1	6.8	2.8	5.7	2.5
1957	4.3	4.6	6.9	4.9	5.8	10.9	5.1	4.9	5.3	3.3	4.5	1.8	4.2	1.9
1956	4.1	4.4	7.3	4.7	6.8	10.0	4.7	4.4	5.2	3.0	4.5	1.7	4.6	1.7
1955	4.4	4.8	7.2	5.1	9.0	10.9	4.7	4.4	5.2	4.0	4.7	2.3	5.2	2.0
1954	5.5	7.0	8.9	6.7	14.4	12.9	7.1	7.3	6.9	5.6	5.7	2.3	5.5	2.2
1953	2.9	3.2	5.6	3.4	4.6	7.2	3.1	2.6	3.8	2.2	3.4	1.7	3.4	1.5
1952	3.0	3.3	4.8	3.6	3.8	6.7	3.5	3.0	4.1	2.3	3.5	1.7	3.6	1.6
1951	3.3	3.7	4.3	3.9	4.0	7.2	3.8	3.1	4.7	2.3	3.9	1.5	4.2	1.8
1950	5.3	6.0	9.0	3.9	6.7	12.2	6.2	5.7	6.8	4.7	6.0	2.2	6.4	3.0
1949	5.9	6.8	7.1	7.3	8.9	13.9	8.0	8.1	7.8	4.7	6.2	2.1	6.7	3.1
1948	3.8	4.3	5.5	4.5	3.0	8.7	4.2	4.0	4.4	3.5	4.7	1.8	4.8	2.2

[1] Also includes the self-employed, unpaid family workers, and those with no previous work experience, not shown separately.

Series D 116–126. Persons With a Job but Not at Work and Civilians Employed, by Hours Worked: 1950 to 1970

[In thousands of persons 14 years old and over through 1965; 16 years old and over, thereafter. Data are for the survey week in May of each year]

	Persons with a job but not at work			Civilians employed							
				In nonagricultural industries [1]					In agriculture [1]		
Year	All industries, total	Reasons for not working		Total	Worked 1–14 hours	Worked 15–34 hours	Worked 35 or more hours		Total	Worked 35 or more hours	
		Vacation	Illness				Total	Percent of total		Total	Percent of total
	116	117	118	119	120	121	122	123	124	125	126
1970	3,140	974	1,321	74,632	4,354	11,383	55,827	74.8	3,725	2,533	68.0
1969	2,801	933	1,120	73,370	3,845	10,775	56,019	76.4	3,894	2,661	68.3
1968	2,694	917	1,021	71,935	3,984	10,198	55,176	76.7	3,996	2,663	66.6
1967	2,485	758	1,033	69,812	3,827	9,646	53,950	77.3	3,824	2,578	67.4
1966	2,415	808	947	69,472	4,363	8,407	54,392	78.2	4,293	2,806	65.4
1965	2,402	759	1,063	67,278	4,403	7,563	53,008	78.8	5,128	3,475	67.7
1964	2,396	833	911	66,094	4,466	7,817	51,507	77.9	5,007	3,450	68.9
1963	2,172	643	921	63,883	4,147	7,261	50,382	78.9	5,178	3,490	67.4
1962	2,032	663	870	62,775	3,912	7,209	49,711	79.2	5,428	3,801	70.0
1961	2,026	641	902	61,234	3,858	7,533	47,926	78.3	5,544	3,701	66.8
1960*	2,086	645	873	61,371	3,578	7,203	48,594	79.2	5,837	4,128	70.7
1959	2,007	661	918	59,608	3,349	6,431	47,936	80.4	6,408	4,488	70.0
1958	1,902	584	836	57,789	3,224	7,147	45,619	78.9	6,272	4,452	71.0
1957	2,056	707	810	58,519	2,942	6,576	47,115	80.5	6,659	4,615	69.3
1956	1,803	535	859	58,092	2,980	6,557	46,587	80.2	7,146	5,185	72.6
1955	1,783	575	736	55,740	2,440	5,617	45,831	82.2	6,963	5,176	74.3
1954	1,752	470	809	54,297	2,133	6,214	43,959	81.0	6,822	4,955	72.6
1953	1,715	364	738	55,557	1,926	5,608	45,988	82.8	6,422	4,346	67.7
1952	1,930	398	750	54,216	1,934	4,946	45,284	83.5	6,960	5,416	77.8
1951	1,585	462	659	53,753	2,071	4,930	45,055	83.8	7,440	5,797	77.9
1950	1,475	353	629	51,669	1,949	5,149	43,034	83.3	8,062	5,970	74.1

* Denotes first year for which figures include Alaska and Hawaii.

[1] Includes persons who had a job or business, but did not work at all during entire survey week because of illness, bad weather, vacation, industrial dispute, or various personal reasons.

Series D 127–141. Employees on Nonagricultural Payrolls, by Major Industry Divisions: 1900 to 1970

[In thousands. Annual averages of monthly figures]

Year	Total	Goods-producing					Service-producing						Government		
		Mining	Contract construc-tion	Manufacturing			Trans-portation and public utilities	Wholesale and retail trade			Finance, insurance, and real estate	Services			
				Total	Durable	Non-durable		Total	Whole-sale trade	Retail trade			Total	Federal	State and local
	127	128	129	130	131	132	133	134	135	136	137	138	139	140	141
1970	70,616	622	3,345	19,369	11,198	8,171	4,504	14,922	3,824	11,098	3,690	11,630	12,535	2,705	9,830
1969	70,284	619	3,435	20,167	11,895	8,272	4,429	14,639	3,733	10,906	3,564	11,229	12,202	2,758	9,444
1968	67,915	606	3,285	19,781	11,626	8,155	4,310	14,084	3,611	10,473	3,382	10,623	11,845	2,737	9,109
1967	65,857	613	3,208	19,447	11,459	8,008	4,261	13,606	3,525	10,081	3,225	10,099	11,398	2,719	8,679
1966	63,955	627	3,275	19,214	11,284	7,930	4,151	13,245	3,437	9,808	3,100	9,551	10,792	2,564	8,227
1965	60,815	632	3,186	18,062	10,406	7,656	4,036	12,716	3,312	9,404	3,023	9,087	10,074	2,378	7,696
1964	58,331	634	3,050	17,274	9,816	7,458	3,951	12,160	3,189	8,709	2,957	8,709	9,596	2,348	7,248
1963	56,702	635	2,963	16,995	9,616	7,380	3,903	11,778	3,104	8,675	2,877	8,325	9,225	2,358	6,868
1962	55,596	650	2,902	16,853	9,480	7,373	3,906	11,566	3,056	8,511	2,800	8,028	8,890	2,340	6,550
1961	54,042	672	2,816	16,326	9,070	7,256	3,903	11,337	2,993	8,344	2,731	7,664	8,594	2,279	6,315
1960	54,234	712	2,885	16,796	9,459	7,336	4,004	11,391	3,004	8,388	2,669	7,423	8,353	2,270	6,083
1959	53,313	732	2,960	16,675	9,373	7,303	4,011	11,127	2,946	8,182	2,594	7,130	8,083	2,233	5,850
1958	51,363	751	2,778	15,945	8,830	7,116	3,976	10,750	2,848	7,902	2,519	6,806	7,839	2,191	5,648
1957	52,894	828	2,923	17,174	9,856	7,319	4,241	10,886	2,893	7,992	2,477	6,749	7,616	2,217	5,399
1956	52,408	822	2,999	17,243	9,834	7,409	4,244	10,858	2,884	7,974	2,429	6,536	7,277	2,209	5,069
1955	50,675	792	2,802	16,882	9,541	7,340	4,141	10,535	2,796	7,740	2,335	6,274	6,914	2,187	4,723
1954	49,022	791	2,612	16,314	9,129	7,185	4,084	10,235	2,739	7,496	2,234	6,002	6,751	2,188	4,567
1953	50,232	866	2,623	17,549	10,110	7,438	4,290	10,247	2,727	7,520	2,146	5,867	6,645	2,305	4,340
1952	48,825	898	2,634	16,632	9,349	7,284	4,248	10,004	2,687	7,317	2,069	5,730	6,609	2,420	4,188
1951	47,849	929	2,603	16,393	9,089	7,304	4,226	9,742	2,606	7,136	1,991	5,576	6,389	2,302	4,087
1950	45,222	901	2,333	15,241	8,094	7,147	4,034	9,386	2,518	6,868	1,919	5,382	6,026	1,928	4,098
1949	43,778	930	2,165	14,441	7,489	6,953	4,001	9,264	2,487	6,778	1,857	5,264	5,856	1,908	3,948
1948	44,891	994	2,169	15,582	8,326	7,256	4,189	9,272	2,489	6,783	1,829	5,206	5,650	1,863	3,787
1947	43,881	955	1,982	15,545	8,385	7,159	4,166	8,955	2,361	6,595	1,754	5,050	5,474	1,892	3,582
1946	41,674	862	1,661	14,703	7,742	6,962	4,061	8,376	2,190	6,186	1,697	4,719	5,595	2,254	3,341
1945	40,394	836	1,132	15,524	9,074	6,450	3,906	7,314	1,862	5,452	1,497	4,241	5,944	2,808	3,137
1944	41,883	892	1,094	17,328	10,856	6,472	3,829	7,058	1,762	5,296	1,476	4,163	6,043	2,928	3,116
1943	42,452	925	1,567	17,602	11,084	6,518	3,647	6,982	1,741	5,241	1,502	4,148	6,080	2,905	3,174
1942	40,125	992	2,170	15,280	8,823	6,458	3,460	7,118	1,821	5,297	1,538	4,084	5,483	2,213	3,270
1941	36,554	957	1,790	13,192	6,968	6,225	3,274	7,210	1,873	5,338	1,549	3,921	4,660	1,340	3,320
1940	32,376	925	1,294	10,985	5,363	5,622	3,038	6,750	1,754	4,996	1,502	3,681	4,202	996	3,206
1939	30,618	854	1,150	10,278	4,715	5,564	2,936	6,426	1,684	4,742	1,462	3,517	3,995	905	3,090
1938	29,209	891	1,055	9,440	----------	----------	2,863	6,179	----------	----------	1,425	3,473	3,883	829	3,054
1937	31,026	1,015	1,112	10,794	----------	----------	3,134	6,265	----------	----------	1,432	3,518	3,756	833	2,923
1936	29,082	946	1,145	9,827	----------	----------	2,973	5,809	----------	----------	1,388	3,326	3,668	826	2,842
1935	27,053	897	912	9,069	----------	----------	2,786	5,431	----------	----------	1,335	3,142	3,481	753	2,728
1934	25,953	883	862	8,501	----------	----------	2,750	5,281	----------	----------	1,319	3,058	3,299	652	2,647
1933	23,711	744	809	7,397	----------	----------	2,672	4,755	----------	----------	1,295	2,873	3,166	565	2,601
1932	23,628	731	970	6,931	----------	----------	2,816	4,683	----------	----------	1,341	2,931	3,225	559	2,666
1931	26,649	873	1,214	8,170	----------	----------	3,254	5,284	----------	----------	1,407	3,183	3,264	560	2,704
1930	29,424	1,009	1,372	9,562	----------	----------	3,685	5,797	----------	----------	1,475	3,376	3,148	526	2,622
1929	31,339	1,087	1,497	10,702	----------	----------	3,916	6,123	----------	----------	1,509	3,440	3,065	533	2,532
1928	30,539	1,038	1,704	9,942	----------	----------	3,886	6,047	----------	----------	1,484	3,399	3,039	----------	----------
1927	30,481	1,100	1,761	9,996	----------	----------	3,997	5,942	----------	----------	1,380	3,360	2,945	----------	----------
1926	30,599	1,168	1,756	10,156	----------	----------	4,077	5,864	----------	----------	1,328	3,397	2,853	----------	----------
1925	29,751	1,065	1,680	9,942	----------	----------	4,018	5,717	----------	----------	1,264	3,300	2,765	----------	----------
1924	28,577	1,091	1,556	9,675	----------	----------	4,063	5,047	----------	----------	1,211	3,298	2,636	----------	----------
1923	29,231	1,181	1,408	10,317	----------	----------	4,185	5,194	----------	----------	1,175	3,247	2,524	----------	----------
1922	26,616	880	1,315	9,129	----------	----------	3,897	4,708	----------	----------	1,081	3,151	2,455	----------	----------
1921	24,542	906	1,035	8,262	----------	----------	3,929	3,960	----------	----------	968	3,085	2,397	----------	----------
1920	27,434	1,180	850	10,702	----------	----------	4,317	4,012	----------	----------	902	3,100	2,371	----------	----------
1919	27,270	1,067	1,011	10,702	----------	----------	4,055	4,213	----------	----------	868	2,905	2,449	----------	----------
1918	26,432	1,311	928	10,167	----------	----------	3,877	4,110	----------	----------	809	2,769	2,461	----------	----------
1917	25,762	1,267	1,027	9,872	----------	----------	3,722	4,320	----------	----------	771	2,783	2,000	----------	----------
1916	25,510	1,168	1,208	9,629	----------	----------	3,579	4,476	----------	----------	738	2,796	1,916	----------	----------
1915	23,149	1,022	1,195	8,210	----------	----------	3,439	4,091	----------	----------	694	2,637	1,861	----------	----------
1914	23,190	1,027	1,267	8,210	----------	----------	3,445	4,128	----------	----------	657	2,647	1,809	----------	----------
1913	24,143	1,182	1,412	8,751	----------	----------	3,570	4,232	----------	----------	613	2,626	1,757	----------	----------
1912	23,191	1,083	1,337	8,322	----------	----------	3,552	4,073	----------	----------	568	2,539	1,717	----------	----------
1911	22,093	1,052	1,249	7,870	----------	----------	3,426	3,813	----------	----------	520	2,491	1,672	----------	----------
1910	21,697	1,068	1,342	7,828	----------	----------	3,366	3,570	----------	----------	483	2,410	1,630	----------	----------
1909	21,203	998	1,376	7,661	----------	----------	3,229	3,585	----------	----------	464	2,326	1,564	----------	----------
1908	19,259	900	1,308	6,570	----------	----------	3,069	3,299	----------	----------	442	2,164	1,507	----------	----------
1907	20,523	1,051	1,436	7,322	----------	----------	3,114	3,486	----------	----------	423	2,243	1,448	----------	----------
1906	20,069	894	1,391	7,226	----------	----------	3,110	3,442	----------	----------	405	2,215	1,386	----------	----------
1905	18,707	889	1,208	6,739	----------	----------	2,905	3,170	----------	----------	385	2,076	1,335	----------	----------
1904	17,640	801	1,257	6,199	----------	----------	2,743	2,992	----------	----------	369	2,002	1,277	----------	----------
1903	17,858	834	1,290	6,527	----------	----------	2,666	2,979	----------	----------	351	1,982	1,229	----------	----------
1902	17,395	685	1,393	6,305	----------	----------	2,754	2,827	----------	----------	337	1,903	1,191	----------	----------
1901	16,294	703	1,274	5,817	----------	----------	2,404	2,765	----------	----------	322	1,880	1,129	----------	----------
1900	15,178	637	1,147	5,468	----------	----------	2,282	2,502	----------	----------	308	1,740	1,094	----------	----------

Series D 142–151. Production or Nonsupervisory Workers on Private Nonagricultural Payrolls, by Industry Division: 1909 to 1970

[In thousands. Relates to production workers in mining and manufacturing, to construction workers in contract construction, and to nonsupervisory workers in other industries]

Year	Total private [1]	Mining	Contract construction	Manufacturing Total	Durable goods	Nondurable goods	Wholesale and retail trade Total	Wholesale	Retail trade	Finance, insurance, and real estate [2]	Year	Manufacturing, total
	142	143	144	145	146	147	148	149	150	151		145
1970	47,950	472	2,790	14,033	8,043	5,990	13,269	3,212	10,057	2,919	1938	7,478
1969	48,105	472	2,896	14,767	8,651	6,116	13,034	3,139	9,895	2,835	1937	8,791
1968	46,475	461	2,768	14,514	8,457	6,056	12,528	3,036	9,492	2,687	1936	8,014
1967	45,169	469	2,708	14,308	8,364	5,944	12,121	2,971	9,151	2,566		
1966	44,281	487	2,784	14,297	8,370	5,926	11,820	2,911	8,909	2,476	1935	7,374
											1934	6,909
1965	42,309	494	2,710	13,434	7,715	5,719	11,358	2,814	8,544	2,426	1933	5,924
1964	40,589	497	2,597	12,781	7,213	5,569	10,869	2,719	8,151	2,386	1932	5,351
1963	39,553	498	2,523	12,555	7,027	5,527	10,560	2,656	7,904	2,329	1931	6,301
1962	38,979	512	2,462	12,488	6,935	5,553	10,400	2,625	7,775	2,274		
1961	37,989	532	2,390	12,083	6,618	5,465	10,234	2,584	7,650	2,225	1930	7,464
											1929	8,567
1960	38,516	570	2,459	12,586	7,028	5,559	10,315	2,605	7,710	2,181	1928	8,051
1959*	38,080	590	2,538	12,603	7,033	5,570	10,087	2,562	7,525	2,121	1927	8,037
1958	36,608	611	2,384	11,997	6,579	5,419	9,736	2,477	7,259	2,063	1926	8,214
1957	38,384	695	2,537	13,189	7,550	5,638	9,923	2,541	7,382	2,031		
1956	38,495	701	2,613	13,436	7,669	5,767	9,933	2,547	7,386	1,994	1925	8,061
											1924	7,789
1955	37,500	680	2,440	13,288	7,548	5,740	9,675	2,479	7,196	1,920	1923	8,388
1954	36,276	686	2,281	12,817	7,194	5,623	9,456	2,442	7,014	1,837	1922	7,327
1953	37,694	765	2,305	14,055	8,154	5,901	9,510	2,459	7,051	1,771	1921	6,622
1952	36,643	801	2,324	13,359	7,550	5,810	9,333	2,439	6,894	1,711		
1951	36,225	840	2,308	13,368	7,480	5,888	9,091	2,365	6,726	1,649	1920	8,652
											1919	8,617
1950	34,349	816	2,069	12,523	6,705	5,817	8,742	2,294	6,448	1,591	1914	6,624
1949	33,159	839	1,919	11,790	6,122	5,669	8,595	2,267	6,328	1,542	1909	6,272
1948	34,489	906	1,924	12,910	6,925	5,986	8,629	2,274	6,355	1,521		
1947	33,747	871	1,759	12,990	7,028	5,962	8,241	2,165	6,076	1,460		
1946				12,274	6,412	5,862						
1945				13,009	7,541	5,468						
1944				14,740	9,197	5,543						
1943				15,147	9,548	5,599						
1942				12,996	7,589	5,407						
1941				11,016	5,947	5,070						
1940				8,940	4,477	4,463						
1939				8,318	3,895	4,423						

* Denotes first year for which figures include Alaska and Hawaii.
[1] Beginning 1964, includes "transportation and public utilities" and "service industries," not shown separately.
[2] Excludes nonoffice salesmen.

Series D 152–166. Industrial Distribution of Gainful Workers: 1820 to 1940

[In thousands]

Year	Total	Agriculture	Forestry and fisheries	Mining	Manufacturing and hand trades	Construction	Transportation and other public utilities	Trade	Finance and real estate	Educational service	Other professional service	Domestic service	Personal service	Government not elsewhere classified	Not allocated
	152	153	154	155	156	157	158	159	160	161	162	163	164	165	166
1940	53,300	9,000	140	1,110	11,940	3,510	4,150	7,180	1,550	1,680	2,320	2,610	3,100	1,690	3,330
1930 [1]	47,400	10,180	120	1,160	10,770	3,030	4,810	6,190	1,470	1,630	1,720	2,550	2,500	1,130	[2]145
1930 [3]	48,830	10,480	270	1,150	10,990	3,030	4,850	6,030	1,420	1,650	1,760	2,330	2,490	1,050	1,340
1920	41,610	11,120	280	1,230	10,880	2,170	4,190	4,060	800	1,170	1,080	1,700	1,630	920	380
1910	36,730	11,340	250	1,050	8,230	2,300	3,190	3,370	520	900	770	2,150	1,520	540	600
1900	29,070	10,710	210	760	6,340	1,660	2,100	2,760		650	500	1,740	970	300	370
1890	23,740	9,990	180	480	4,750	1,440	1,530	1,990		510	350	1,520	640	190	170
1880	17,390	8,610	95	310	3,170	830	860	1,220		330	190	1,080	360	140	195
1870 [4]	12,920	6,430	60	200	2,250	750	640	830		190	140	940	250	100	140
1870 [3]	12,920	6,850	60	180	2,750		1,350			[5]1,700					30
1860	10,530	6,210	50	170	1,930		780			1,310					80
1850	7,700	4,900	25	90	1,260		420			940					65
1840	5,420	3,720		15	790										895
1830	3,930	2,770													1,160
1820	2,880	2,070			350										460

[1] Comparable with 1940.
[2] Difference between number of persons not reporting industrial affiliation (1,335,000) and excess of the "gainful worker" total over the "labor force" total (1,190,000).
[3] Comparable with data for earlier years.
[4] Comparable with data for later years.
[5] Figure corrected for apparent error in source; components now add to total, series D 152.

Series D 167–181. Labor Force and Employment, by Industry: 1800 to 1960

[In thousands of persons 10 years old and over]

Year	Labor force — Total	Free	Slave	Agriculture	Fishing	Mining	Construction	Manufacturing — Total persons engaged	Cotton textile wage earners	Primary iron and steel wage earners	Trade	Transport — Ocean vessels	Railway	Service — Teachers	Domestics
	167	168	169	170	171	172	173	174	175	176	177	178	179	180	181
1960	74,060			5,970	45	709	3,640	17,145	300	530	14,051	135	883	1,850	2,489
1950	65,470			7,870	77	901	3,029	15,648	350	550	12,152	130	1,373	1,270	1,995
1940	56,290			9,575	60	925	1,876	11,309	400	485	9,328	150	1,160	1,086	2,300
1930	48,830			10,560	73	1,009	1,988	9,884	372	375	8,122	160	1,659	1,044	2,270
1920	41,610			10,790	53	1,180	1,233	11,190	450	460	5,845	205	2,236	752	1,660
1910	37,480			11,770	68	1,068	1,949	8,332	370	306	5,320	150	1,855	595	2,090
1900	29,070			11,680	69	637	1,665	5,895	303	222	3,970	105	1,040	436	1,800
1890	23,320			9,960	60	440	1,510	4,390	222	149	2,960	120	750	350	1,580
1880	17,390			8,920	41	280	900	3,290	175	130	1,930	125	416	230	1,130
1870	12,930			6,790	28	180	780	2,470	135	78	1,310	135	160	170	1,000
1860	11,110	8,770	2,340	5,880	31	176	520	1,530	122	43	890	145	80	115	600
1850	8,250	6,280	1,970	4,520	30	102	410	1,200	92	35	530	135	20	80	350
1840	5,660	4,180	1,480	3,570	24	32	290	500	72	24	350	95	7	45	240
1830	4,200	3,020	1,180	2,965	15	22		(NA)	55	20		70		30	160
1820	3,135	2,185	950	2,470	14	13		(NA)	12	5		50		20	110
1810	2,330	1,590	740	1,950	6	11		75	10	5		60		12	70
1800	1,900	1,370	530	1,400	5	10			1	1		40		5	40

NA Not available.

Series D 182–232. Major Occupation Group of the Experienced Civilian Labor Force, by Sex: 1900 to 1970

[In thousands of persons 14 years old and over, except as indicated.   Census data for 1900, June 1; 1910, April 15; 1920, Jan. 1; 1930–1970, April 1]

Series No.	Major occupation group and sex	1970 — 16 years old and over	1970 — 14 years old and over	1960 — 1970 classification	1960 — 1960 classification	1950 — 1960 classification	1950 — 1950 classification	1940	1930	1920	1910	1900
	BOTH SEXES											
182	Total	79,802[1]	80,603[2]	67,990[3]	67,990[3]	59,230[4]	58,999	51,742	48,686	42,206	37,291	29,030
183	White-collar workers	37,857	36,131	27,028	27,244	21,253	21,601	16,082	14,320	10,529	7,962	5,115
184	Professional, technical, and kindred workers	11,561	11,018	7,090	7,336	5,000	5,081	3,879	3,311	2,283	1,758	1,234
185	Managers, officials, and proprietors[5]	6,463	6,224	5,708	5,489	5,096	5,155	3,770	3,614	2,803	2,462	1,697
186	Clerical and kindred workers	14,208	13,457	9,431	9,617	7,132	7,232	4,982	4,336	3,385	1,987	877
187	Salesworkers	5,625	5,433	4,799	4,801	4,025	4,133	3,450	3,059	2,058	1,755	1,307
188	Manual and service workers	39,420	36,947	33,377	33,207	29,749	30,445	26,666	24,044	20,287	17,797	13,027
189	Manual workers	29,169	27,356	25,475	25,617	23,733	24,266	20,597	19,272	16,974	14,234	10,401
190	Craftsmen, foremen, and kindred workers	11,082	10,435	9,465	9,241	8,205	8,350	6,203	6,246	5,482	4,315	3,062
191	Operative and kindred workers	14,335	13,406	12,254	12,846	11,754	12,030	9,518	7,691	6,587	5,441	3,720
192	Laborers, except farm and mine	3,751	3,515	3,755	3,530	3,774	3,885	4,875	5,335	4,905	4,478	3,620
193	Service workers	10,251	9,591	7,902	7,590	6,015	6,180	6,069	4,772	3,313	3,562	2,626
194	Private household workers	1,204	1,143	1,817	1,825	1,492	1,539	2,412	1,998	1,411	1,851	1,579
195	Service workers, exc. private household	9,047	8,449	6,086	5,765	4,524	4,641	3,657	2,774	1,901	1,711	1,047
196	Farmworkers	2,448	2,345	4,132	4,085	6,858	6,953	8,995	10,321	11,390	11,533	10,888
197	Farmers and farm managers	1,428	1,350	2,528	2,526	4,325	4,375	5,362	6,032	6,442	6,163	5,763
198	Farm laborers and foremen	1,022	995	1,604	1,560	2,533	2,578	3,632	4,290	4,948	5,370	5,125
	MALE											
199	Total	49,455[1]	50,002[2]	45,686[3]	45,686[3]	42,722[4]	42,554	39,168	37,933	33,569	29,847	23,711
200	White-collar workers	19,428	18,693	15,316	15,413	12,798	12,974	10,434	9,564	7,176	6,019	4,166
201	Professional, technical, and kindred workers	6,917	6,621	4,366	4,543	3,025	3,074	2,271	1,829	1,275	1,032	800
202	Managers, officials, and proprietors[5]	5,386	5,189	4,864	4,695	4,408	4,456	3,356	3,321	2,612	2,312	1,623
203	Clerical and kindred workers	3,748	3,547	3,024	3,120	2,723	2,730	2,282	2,090	1,771	1,300	665
204	Salesworkers	3,378	3,336	3,063	3,055	2,642	2,715	2,525	2,323	1,518	1,376	1,079
205	Manual and service workers	27,807	26,154	24,477	24,422	22,746	23,228	20,247	18,956	16,172	13,469	9,664
206	Manual workers	23,760	22,315	21,465	21,612	20,159	20,581	17,877	17,138	14,923	12,320	8,924
207	Craftsmen, foremen, and kindred workers	10,530	9,911	9,170	8,973	7,959	8,098	6,069	6,140	5,377	4,209	2,985
208	Operative and kindred workers	9,789	9,183	8,733	9,234	8,566	8,743	7,067	5,822	4,839	3,739	2,457
209	Laborers, except farm and mine	3,440	3,221	3,562	3,405	3,634	3,740	4,742	5,177	4,707	4,372	3,482
210	Service workers	4,048	3,839	3,012	2,810	2,587	2,647	2,370	1,818	1,250	1,149	740
211	Private household workers	38	40	65	65	78	80	135	89	51	67	53
212	Service workers, exc. private household	4,010	3,800	2,947	2,745	2,509	2,568	2,235	1,729	1,199	1,082	687
213	Farmworkers	2,205	2,123	3,737	3,696	6,271	6,352	8,487	9,414	10,221	10,359	9,880
214	Farmers and farm managers	1,357	1,288	2,408	2,406	4,207	4,255	5,205	5,769	6,165	5,884	5,451
215	Farm laborers and foremen	848	835	1,329	1,290	2,064	2,097	3,282	3,645	4,056	4,475	4,429

See footnotes at end of table.

Series D 182–232. Major Occupation Group of the Experienced Civilian Labor Force, by Sex: 1900 to 1970—Con.
[In thousands of persons 14 years old and over, except as indicated]

Series No.	Major occupation group and sex	1970 16 years old and over	1970 14 years old and over	1960 1970 classification	1960 1960 classification	1950 1960 classification	1950 1950 classification	1940	1930	1920	1910	1900
	FEMALE											
216	Total	[1] 30,347	[2] 30,601	[3] 22,304	[3] 22,304	[4] 16,507	16,445	12,574	10,752	8,637	7,445	5,319
217	White-collar workers	18,430	17,438	11,711	11,831	8,456	8,627	5,648	4,756	3,353	1,943	949
218	Professional, technical, and kindred workers	4,644	4,398	2,724	2,793	1,976	2,007	1,608	1,482	1,008	726	434
219	Managers, officials, and proprietors [5]	1,077	1,034	844	794	688	700	414	292	191	150	74
220	Clerical and kindred workers	10,461	9,910	6,407	6,497	4,408	4,502	2,700	2,246	1,614	688	212
221	Salesworkers	2,247	2,097	1,736	1,746	1,383	1,418	925	736	541	379	228
222	Manual and service workers	11,612	10,793	8,900	8,786	7,003	7,217	6,419	5,088	4,115	4,327	3,363
223	Manual workers	5,409	5,041	4,010	4,006	3,574	3,685	2,720	2,134	2,052	1,914	1,477
224	Craftsmen, foremen, and kindred workers	552	524	295	268	246	253	135	106	105	106	76
225	Operative and kindred workers	4,546	4,223	3,521	3,612	3,188	3,287	2,452	1,870	1,748	1,702	1,264
226	Laborers, except farm and mine	311	295	193	125	140	145	133	158	199	106	137
227	Service workers	6,203	5,752	4,890	4,780	3,429	3,532	3,699	2,954	2,063	2,413	1,886
228	Private household workers	1,166	1,103	1,752	1,760	1,414	1,459	2,277	1,909	1,360	1,784	1,526
229	Service workers, exc. private household	5,037	4,649	3,139	3,020	2,015	2,073	1,422	1,045	703	629	359
230	Farmworkers	245	222	395	390	587	601	508	908	1,169	1,175	1,008
231	Farmers and farm managers	72	63	120	120	118	120	157	263	277	279	311
232	Farm laborers and foremen	173	160	275	270	469	481	351	645	892	895	697

[1] Includes 74,911 unemployed persons whose occupations were not reported; 14,781 males and 60,130 females.
[2] Includes 5,179,626 unemployed persons whose occupations were not reported; 3,032,524 males and 2,147,102 females.
[3] Includes 3,453,279 unemployed persons whose occupations were not reported; 2,155,586 males and 1,297,693 females.
[4] Includes 1,369,621 unemployed persons whose occupations were not reported; 907,615 males and 462,006 females. [5] Except farm.

Series D 233–682. Detailed Occupation of the Economically Active Population: 1900 to 1970
[In thousands of persons 14 years old and over, except as indicated. "N.e.c." means not elsewhere classified. Census data for 1900 as of June 1; 1910, April 15; 1920, Jan. 1; 1930–1970, April 1]

Series No.	Occupation	1970 16 years old and over	1970 14 years old and over	1960 1970 classification	1960 1960 classification	1950 1960 classification	1950 1950 classification	1940	1930	1920	1910	1900
233	Total	[1] 79,802	[1] 80,603	[1] 67,990	[1] 67,990	[1] 59,230	58,999	51,742	48,686	42,206	37,291	29,030
234	Professional, technical, and kindred workers	[2] 11,561	[2] 11,018	[2] 7,090	7,336	5,000	5,081	3,879	3,311	2,283	1,758	1,234
235	Accountants and auditors	712	713	496	477	385	390	238	192	118	39	23
236	Actors and actresses	15	15	12	13	18	20	21				
237	Athletes				5	12	13	9				
238	Dancers and dancing teachers				22	17	18	14				
239	Entertainers (n.e.c.)				12	16	17	12	76	48	48	31
240	Sports instructors and officials				78	46	47	25				
241	Airplane pilots and navigators	52	52	28	28	15	14	5	6	1		
242	Architects	57	57	38	31	24	25	22	23	17	16	11
243	Artists and art teachers				105	81	83	66	57	35	34	25
244	Authors	26	26	29	29	16	17	14	12	7	4	3
245	Chemists	110	110	96	84	76	77	57	45	28	16	9
246	Clergymen	219	219	202	202	169	171	141	149	127	118	
247	Religious workers	36	36	61	57	42	42	42				
248	Recreation and group workers	53	54	29	38	17			71	46	19	114
249	Social and welfare workers, except group	221	221	95	98	77	95	77				
250	College presidents, professors, and instructors (n.e.c.)				179	126	127	77	62	33	16	7
251	Dentists	91	91	83	83	76	76	71	71	56	40	30
252	Designers	112	112	69	68	29	41	32				
253	Draftsmen	294	295	219	219	136	127	82	98	67	45	18
254	Editors and reporters	151	151	106	103	73	93	66	61	39	36	32
255	Engineers, technical	1,230	1,231	871	872	535	543	297	217	134	77	38
256	Engineers, civil	175	175	158	158	126	128	128	97	88	56	40
257	Engineers, chemical	53	53	42	41	33	34	13				20
258	Engineers, metallurgical, and metallurgists	16	16	9	19	12						
259	Engineers, mining	5	5	7	12		23	12	14	11	7	3
260	Engineers, electrical	286	286	188	185	108	110	65	58	27	15	
261	Engineers, industrial	188	188	115	98	41	42	13				
262	Engineers, aeronautical	69	69	53	53	18						14
263	Engineers, mechanical	181	181	162	160	115	207	97	58	39	15	
264	Engineers (n.e.c.)	259	259	137	145	67						
265	Farm and home management advisors	13	13	14	14	12	13	12	4	3	1	
266	Funeral directors and embalmers	41	41	39	37	40	41	40	34	24	21	16
267	Lawyers and judges	273	274	218	213	182	184	182	161	123	115	108
268	Librarians	124	124	76	85	56	57	39	30	15	7	3
269	Musicians and music teachers				198	162	166	167	165	130	139	92
270	Nurses, professional	841	842	630	592	406	491	377	294	149	82	12
271	Nurses, student professional					58	77					
272	Optometrists	17	17	16	16	15	15	10	8	7	1	
273	Pharmacists	110	110	96	93	89	90	83	84	64	54	46
274	Photographers	67	67	53	53	55	56	38	33	29	30	25
275	Physicians and surgeons	282	282	233	230	193	195	168	157	146	152	131
276	Osteopaths				4	5	5	6	6	5		
277	Chiropractors	14	14	14	14	13	13	11	12			
278	Therapists and healers (n.e.c.)				37	25	25	18	14	12	5	

See footnotes at end of table.

Series D 233–682. Detailed Occupation of the Economically Active Population: 1900 to 1970—Con.

[In thousands of persons 14 years old and over, except as indicated]

Series No.	Occupation	1970 16 years old and over	1970 14 years old and over	1960 1970 classi-fication	1960 1960 classi-fication	1950 1960 classi-fication	1950 1950 classi-fication	1940	1930	1920	1910	1900
	Professional, technical, and kindred workers—Con.											
279	Radio operators	29	29	18	29	17	17	7	5	5	4	
280	Surveyors	62	62	47	46	27	27	17	15	9	8	6
281	Teachers (n.e.c.)			1,684	1,133	1,149	1,086	1,044	752	595	436	
282	Technicians, medical and dental	264	264	129	141	78	158	73	20	4		
283	Technicians, testing	471	471	346	281	104	28	11	20	4		
284	Technicians (n.e.c.)	74	74	73	67	19	28	11				
285	Veterinarians	20	20	15	15	14	14	11	12	13	12	8
286	Dietitians and nutritionists	41	41	27	27	23						
287	Foresters and conservationists	42	42	34	34	27						
288	Natural scientists (n.e.c.)	95	95	62	67	43	302	153	73	32	20	12
289	Personnel and labor relations workers	296	296	103	99	53						
290	Social scientists	110	110	42	57	36						
291	Professional, technical, and kindred workers (n.e.c.)				345	108						
292	**Farmers and farm managers**	[1]1,428	1,350	2,528	2,526	4,325	4,375	5,362	6,032	6,412	6,163	5,763
293	Farmers (owners and tenants)	1,286	1,289	2,503	2,501	4,290	4,339	5,324	5,992	6,384	6,132	5,752
294	Farm managers	61	61	25	25	35	36	38	40	58	31	10
295	**Managers, officials, and proprietors, exc. farm**	[2]6,463	[2]6,224	[2]5,708	5,489	5,096	5,155	3,770	3,614	2,803	2,462	1,697
296	Buyers and department heads, store	387	387	210	238	145	147	74	35	20	15	
297	Buyers and shippers, farm products	20	20	31	18	29	29	43	42	48	51	12
298	Conductors, railroad	40	40	45	45	56	57	48	73	75	66	43
299	Credit men	60	60	48	48	33	34	30	22	14	2	2
300	Floormen and floor managers, store				11	11	11	7	6	4	4	2
301	Inspectors (n.e.c.), public administration	[3]81	[3]82	[3]62	[3]77	[3]58	[3]58	[3]43	124	100	72	58
302	Officials (n.e.c.), public administration	[4]248	[4]248	[4]195	[4]201	[4]156	[4]158	[4]122				
303	Inspectors (n.e.c.), Federal public administration and postal service	51	51	43	41	29	28	20	40	42	20	18
304	Officials and administrators (n.e.c.), Federal public administration and postal service	120	120	79	69	51	51	40				
305	Inspectors (n.e.c.), State public administration	20	20	10	14	10	10	11	15	9	7	4
306	Officials & admins. (n.e.c.), State public admin	49	49	37	37	23	24	21				
307	Inspectors (n.e.c.), local public administration	10	10	9	22	20	20	12	70	49	44	35
308	Officials and admins. (n.e.c.), local public admin	79	79	79	96	82	83	61				
309	Managers and superintendents, building	85	85	46	54	67	68	72	71	43	32	
310	Officers, pilots, pursers, and engineers, ship	26	26	31	37	42	43	35	49	49	45	43
311	Officials, lodge, society, union, etc	51	51	43	34	27	28	26	15	12	8	
312	Postmasters	35	36	38	37	39	39	40	34	29	25	19
313	Purchasing agents and buyers (n.e.c.)	164	164	111	105	64	65	34	29	18	8	7
314	Managers, officials, and proprietors (n.e.c.)	3,753	3,756	4,268	4,586	4,368	4,419	3,197	3,113	2,390	2,135	1,511
315	Construction	399	397	378	378	293	296	175	199	107	183	58
316	Manufacturing	760	752	801	826	669	665	432	447	406	350	174
317	Transportation	164	164	167	159	150	151	90	98	83	82	66
318	Telecommunications, utilities, & sanitary services	117	115	108	108	86	68	54	39	25	19	6
319	Wholesale trade	312	310	340	338	338	343	225	152	143	104	78
320	Retail trade	1,122	1,119	1,341	1,628	1,943	1,977	1,620	1,592	1,220	1,119	930
321	Eating and drinking places				287	365	370	270	165	106	129	110
322	Food & dairy products stores, & milk retailing	255	255	327	327	495	512	469	540	444	395	
323	General merchandise and five and ten cent stores	128	128	136	135	139	128	111	184	162	167	
324	Apparel and accessories stores	82	82	108	108	128	130	99	96	97	85	
325	Motor vehicles and accessories retailing	130	130	143	143	117	119	65	62	29	5	820
326	Gasoline service stations	169	170	197	197	184	186	183	89	15	2	
327	Furniture, home furnishings, and equipment stores	71	71	81	81	97	98	57				
328	Hardware, farm implement, & bldg. material, retail	81	81	122	122	129	131	95	456	368	336	
329	Other retail trade	206	202	228	229	288	305	271				
330	Banking and other finance	214	212	397	227	142	143	126	174	122	75	76
331	Insurance and real estate				191	116	117	65	66	38	29	14
332	Automobile repair services and garages	[5]196	[5]195	[5]191	60	85	86	66	93	56	5	
333	Miscellaneous repair services				28	34	35	14	9	8	7	
334	Personal services	225	223	212	211	213	216	129	105	76	88	72
335	Business services	(5)	(5)	(5)	103	59	63	33	140	107	74	36
336	All other industries (incl. not reported)	245	270	332	330	241	259	169				
337	**Clerical and kindred workers**	14,208	13,457	9,431	9,617	7,132	7,232	4,982	4,336	3,385	1,987	877
338	Agents (n.e.c.)				163	126	128	73	102	64	28	59
339	Collectors, bill and account	53	53	34	32	24	24	45	43	31	36	
340	Attendants and assistants, library	126	129	37	33	13	13	24	2	2	3	1
341	Attendants, physician's and dentist's office				73	42	43	35	28	14	6	
342	Baggagemen, transportation				6	8	8	6	9	12	12	19
343	Bookkeepers	1,572	1,574	951	936	739	994	721	738	616	447	232
344	Cashiers	869	878	510	492	239	19	23	26	25	22	
345	Express messengers and railway mail clerks				7	19	19					
346	Mail carriers	256	256	199	202	168	171	124	121	91	81	28
347	Stenographers, typists, and secretaries	3,914	3,920	2,316	2,313	1,629	1,661	1,223	1,097	786	387	134
348	Messengers and office boys	59	61	63	63	59	60	64	80	110	103	66
349	Telegraph messengers				5	8	8	17	16	9	9	
350	Telegraph operators	13	13	21	21	35	36	42	68	75	66	56
351	Telephone operators	420	421	372	372	367	375	214	249	190	98	19
352	Ticket, station, and express agents	100	100	75	73	68	61	47	38	37	35	27
353	Office machine operators	571	572	322	318	146	150	66	38			
354	Shipping and receiving clerks	427	427	325	295	297	304	233				
355	Bank tellers	253	254	135	131	65				1,681	1,323	654	235
356	Dispatchers and starters, vehicle	61	61	48	59	32	3,178	2,026				
357	Clerical and kindred workers (n.e.c.)	5,514	4,737	4,025	4,026	3,047						

See footnotes at end of table.

Series D 233–682. Detailed Occupation of the Economically Active Population: 1900 to 1970—Con.

[In thousands of persons 14 years old and over, except as indicated]

Series No.	Occupation	1970 16 years old and over	1970 14 years old and over	1960 1970 classification	1960 1960 classification	1950 1960 classification	1950 1950 classification	1940	1930	1920	1910	1900
358	**Salesworkers**	[1] 5,625	5,433	4,799	4,801	4,025	4,133	3,450	3,059	2,058	1,755	1,307
359	Advertising agents and salesmen	64	65	35	35	34	35	41	40	25	11	12
360	Auctioneers	5	5	4	4	5	6	4	4	5	4	3
361	Demonstrators	40	40	29	26	14	14	10	8	5	4	3
362	Hucksters and peddlers	122	122	62	57	24	24	55	57	50	80	77
363	Insurance agents and brokers	460	461	371	369	276	312	253	257	120	88	78
364	Newsboys	65	188	197	197	100	101	58	39	28	30	7
365	Real estate agents and brokers	266	266	196	196	143	145	119	150	89	78	34
366	Stock and bond salesmen	99	99	35	29	11	11	18	22	11	6	4
	Salesmen and sales clerks (n.e.c.):											
367	Manufacturing	419	420	475	474	334						
368	Wholesale trade	650	651	508	504	413						
369	Retail trade	2,845	2,868	2,669	2,724	2,536	3,485	2,893	2,482	1,724	1,454	1,089
370	Other industries (incl. not reported)	244	247	217	186	136						
371	**Craftsmen, foremen, and kindred workers**	[2] 11,082	[2] 10,435	[2] 9,465	9,241	8,205	8,350	6,203	6,246	5,482	4,315	3,062
372	Bakers	112	113	117	113	125	128	139	141	98	90	70
373	Boilermakers	31	31	28	27	39	40	33	50	74	45	31
374	Bookbinders	36	36	30	28	32	33	19	19	19	17	26
375	Brickmasons, stonemasons, and tile setters	213	213	222	208	177	181	141	171	135	160	149
376	Cabinetmakers	70	70	71	69	77	78	60	63	50	43	36
377	Carpenters	922	923	936	924	993	1,016	776	917	885	815	596
378	Cement and concrete finishers	75	75	48	48	33	34	32	15	8	9	------
379	Electrotypers and stereotypers	7	7	9	9	12	12	8	8	5	4	3
380	Engravers, except photoengravers	9	9	12	12	10	10	9	28	23	22	136
381	Photoengravers and lithographers	33	33	28	25	29	29	23				
382	Compositors and typesetters	163	163	193	183	179	182	181	184	140	128	
383	Pressmen and plate printers, printing	160	160	85	75	50	51	36	31	19	20	
384	Decorators and window dressers	72	73	53	53	45	46	30	20	9	5	3
385	Electricians	483	483	365	356	326	332	221	253	192	108	51
386	Cranemen, derrickmen, and hoistmen	159	159	133	132	108	223	123	294	258	219	134
387	Excavating, grading, and road machinery operators	345	346	284	226	111						
388	Stationary engineers	173	173	293	276	219	222	201				
389	Blacksmiths	10	10	20	21	45	60	99	136	209	238	220
390	Forgemen and hammermen	16	16	13	12	14						
391	Foremen (n.e.c.)	1,617	1,618	1,186	1,199	856	867	585	551	485	318	162
392	Construction	159	158	103	103	61	62	79	43	14	15	------
393	Manufacturing	938	934	662	756	520	525	310	293	296	164	90
394	Metal industries	------	------	------	131	84						
395	Machinery, including electrical	------	------	------	134	81	218	112				
396	Transportation equipment	------	------	------	82	51						
397	Textiles, textile products, and apparel	------	------	------	76	70	72	53	293	296	164	90
398	Other durable goods	------	------	------	102	77						
399	Other nondurable goods (incl. not specified mfg.)	------	------	------	230	157	235	144				
400	Railroads and railway express service				36	54	55	51	83	81	69	38
401	Transportation, except railroad	157	156	202	28	20	20	15	44	31	24	10
402	Telecommunications, utilities, & sanitary services				58	41	41	27				
403	Other industries (incl. not reported)	363	369	218	218	161	164	104	88	63	45	24
404	Furriers	3	3	5	4	13	14	16	12	9	8	7
405	Painters, construction and maintenance	359	361	384	416	433	447	451	446	265	288	221
406	Glaziers	26	26	18	16	11	11	8				
407	Heat treaters, annealers, and temperers	21	21	22	20	18	19	11	6	3	2	------
408	Inspectors, scalers, and graders, log and lumber	18	18	22	21	20	18	17	7	7	7	2
409	Inspectors (n.e.c.)	121	121	101	102	98	99	82	78	77	53	22
410	Construction	23	23	15	15	8	8	9	7	3	4	1
411	Railroads and railway express service	25	25	30	30	37	37	30	39	43	28	20
412	Transp. exc. railroad, commun., & other pub. util.	72	73	56	15	13	13	14	14	10	8	1
413	Other industries (incl. not reported)				42	40	40	30	17	21	14	------
414	Jewelers, watchmakers, goldsmiths, and silversmiths	38	38	38	38	48	49	36	39	40	33	23
415	Linemen & servicemen, telegraph, telephone, & power	397	397	273	278	217	219	116	106	51	35	18
416	Locomotive engineers	50	50	60	58	73	74	67	104	113	99	107
417	Locomotive firemen	14	14	39	39	56	57	50	67	91	76	
418	Loom fixers	21	21	24	24	31	32	25	19	16	13	9
419	Job setters, metal	------	------	------	41	25						
420	Machinists	390	390	521	516	535	571	535				
421	Mechanics and repairmen, airplane	146	146	116	119	74	75	28				
422	Mechanics and repairmen, automobile	936	938	684	703	682	693	448				
423	Mechanics and repairmen, railroad and car shop	56	57	62	41	48	49	46	1,387	1,168	520	304
424	Mechanics and repairmen, office machine	40	40	30	30	31						
425	Mechanics and repairmen, radio and television	140	141	105	106	79	987	436				
426	Mechanics and repairmen (n.e.c.)	1,135	1,165	1,185	1,302	875						
427	Toolmakers, and die makers and setters	207	207	188	187	157	160	100				
428	Millers, grain, flour, feed, etc.	7	7	9	9	10	10	16	16	23	23	25
429	Millwrights	81	81	69	68	60	61	44	42	38	17	8
430	Molders, metal	57	57	53	52	64	65	86	105	124	121	97
431	Motion picture projectionists	16	16	18	18	27	27	24	20	10	4	------
432	Opticians, and lens grinders and polishers	28	28	21	21	20	20	12	13	11	9	6
433	Paperhangers	11	11	27	11	23	23	31	28	19	26	22
434	Pattern and model makers, except paper	40	40	42	40	37	38	30	30	28	24	15
435	Piano and organ tuners and repairmen	7	7	6	6	8	8	5	7	7	7	4
436	Plasterers	31	31	54	53	64	66	53	70	38	48	35
437	Plumbers and pipefitters	398	398	340	331	298	304	211	238	207	148	92
438	Rollers and roll hands, metal	20	20	20	31	31	32	33	31	25	18	6
439	Roofers and slaters	65	65	57	55	49	50	33	24	12	14	9
440	Shoemakers and repairers, except factory	32	32	43	37	59	60	68	76	79	70	102
441	Stone cutters and stone carvers	7	7	7	7	9	9	15	23	23	36	37

See footnotes at end of table.

Series D 233–682. Detailed Occupation of the Economically Active Population: 1900 to 1970—Con.

[In thousands of persons 14 years old and over, except as indicated]

Series No.	Occupation	1970 — 16 years old and over	1970 — 14 years old and over	1960 — 1970 classification	1960 — 1960 classification	1950 — 1960 classification	1950 — 1950 classification	1940	1930	1920	1910	1900
	Craftsmen, foremen, and kindred workers—Con.											
442	Structural metalworkers	79	79	66	66	55	57	47	33	31	18	4
443	Tailors and tailoresses	71	71	87	43	86	88	120	169	192	205	134
444	Tinsmiths, coppersmiths, and sheet metal workers	162	162	150	145	130	133	91	83	75	60	49
445	Upholsterers	65	65	63	62	64	65	43	42	24	20	26
446	Craftsmen and kindred workers (n.e.c.)	996	335	281	112	74	76	47	43	66	73	60
447	Members of the Armed Forces [2]	36	36	18	18	30	38	3	----	----	----	----
448	**Operatives and kindred workers**	[2]14,335	[2]13,406	[2]12,254	[2]12,846	[2]11,754	12,030	9,518	7,691	6,587	5,441	3,720
449	Apprentice carpenters				6	11	11	8	4	5	6	2
450	Apprentice electricians				10	9	9	3	5	10	3	----
451	Apprentice plumbers and pipefitters				8	12	13	5	6	7	10	3
452	Apprentices, printing trades				12	16	16	10	11	12	12	4
453	Apprentice machinists and toolmakers				16	16	16	20	14	39		
454	Apprentice auto mechanics				2	4						
455	Apprentice bricklayers and masons				3	6						
456	Apprentice mechanics, except auto				4	7	42	33	49	66	86	57
457	Apprentices, building trade (n.e.c.)				3	4						
458	Apprentices, metalworking trades (n.e.c.)				6	7						
459	Apprentices, other specified trades				9	13						
460	Apprentices, trade not specified				10	15	15	12				
461	Asbestos and insulation workers	26	26	20	20	15	17	6	3	1	2	----
462	Attendants, auto service and parking				378	248	253	245	144	18	----	----
463	Blasters and powdermen	8	8	6	7	12	12	7	7	7	2	1
464	Boatmen, canalmen, and lock keepers				7	8	9	6	6	6	5	13
465	Brakemen, railroad	49	49	65	65	81	82	77	173	208	160	107
466	Switchmen, railroad	53	53	60	60	62	63	50				
467	Chainmen, rodmen, and axmen, surveying	12	12	11	11	8	8	11	4	3	4	----
468	Conductors, bus and street railway	10	10	12	4	11	12	18	37	64	57	24
469	Deliverymen and routemen	643	649	462	438	249	253	294	187	170	230	167
470	Dressmakers and seamstresses, except factory	102	102	126	124	147	147	172	198	259	467	413
471	Dyers	25	25	19	19	25	26	28	18	15	14	5
472	Filers, grinders, and polishers, metal	123	123	152	159	156	160	117	79	60	50	17
473	Fruit, nut, & veget. graders & packers, exc. factory				28	34	37	25	10	8	5	----
474	Furnacemen, smeltermen, and pourers	67	68	56	57	58	59	33	20	24	26	13
475	Heaters, metal	7	7	8	8	10	10	10	15	16	10	5
476	Laundry and dry cleaning operatives				412	451	462	314	265	142	132	91
477	Meatcutters, except slaughter and packing house	205	206	189	186	177	180	160	120	61	41	33
478	Milliners	2	2	4	4	13	13	15	25	50	100	75
	Mine operatives and laborers (n.e.c.):											
479	Coal mining	164	164	247	140	381	620	845	892	995	907	660
480	Crude petroleum and natural gas extraction				102	108						
481	Mining and quarrying, except fuel				89	116						
482	Motormen, mine, factory, logging camp, etc.	10	10	15	15	24	25	20	17	12	3	----
483	Motormen, street, subway, and elevated railway				8	27	27	39	58	63	56	37
484	Oilers and greasers, except auto	49	49	57	57	62	63	40	31	25	14	55
485	Painters, except construction and maintenance				148	123	126	104	83	61	49	2
486	Photographic process workers	67	67	47	44	29	30	15	8	3	2	----
487	Power station operators	18	18	27	27	22	22	22	29	21	12	----
488	Sailors and deckhands	29	29	41	41	52	55	47	65	55	47	40
489	Sawyers	108	108	104	95	99	100	50	36	34	43	18
490	Spinners, textile				52	85	88	113	81	83	74	56
491	Stationary firemen	97	97	106	93	128	130	128	127	144	111	73
492	Bus drivers	239	239	185	185	158	1,808	1,515	972	285	46	----
493	Taxicab drivers and chauffeurs	158	158	171	171	214						
494	Truck and tractor drivers	[6]1,453	[6]1,455	[6]1,550	1,663	1,397						
495	Weavers, textile	52	52	69	66	103	105	109	225	219	202	155
496	Welders and flame-cutters	566	566	388	387	277	283	137	37	54	3	----
497	Operatives and kindred workers (n.e.c.)				4,993	4,752	6,627	4,654	3,634	3,284	2,451	1,592
498	Manufacturing				4,305	4,079	5,847	4,225	3,189	3,076	2,318	1,443
499	Sawmills, planing mills, and millwork				104	144	151	63	91	92	105	75
500	Miscellaneous wood products				38	39	46	36				19
501	Furniture and fixtures				107	112	132	82	72	52	44	25
502	Glass and glass products				55	56	76	54	41	45	42	5
503	Cement & concrete, gypsum, & plaster products				35	28	30	13	11	8	9	7
504	Structural clay products				21	21	23	16	13	10	13	10
505	Pottery and related products				21	32	35	25	23	17	16	9
506	Miscellaneous nonmetallic mineral & stone prod				38	24	28	18	8	6	9	
507	Motor vehicles and motor vehicle equipment				174	216	371	208	170	125	21	
508	Ship and boat building and repairing				20	15	15	19	11	53	6	
509	Blast furnaces, steelworks, and rolling mills				100	120	133	105				
510	Other primary iron and steel industries				65	65	324	209				
511	Fabricated steel products				288	216						121
512	Office and store machines and devices				26	28	40	24	397	370	286	
513	Miscellaneous machinery				231	165	273	123				
514	Not specified metal industries				2	4	4	12				
515	Agricultural machinery and tractors				24	36	52	21				
516	Aircraft and parts				78	31	67	27				
517	Railroad & miscellaneous transportation equipment				18	17	19	11				
518	Primary nonferrous industries				85	66	98	48	34	32	27	11
519	Fabricated nonferrous metal products				313	218	356	150	117	65	25	18
520	Electrical machinery, equipment, and supplies				44	30	60	29				
521	Professional equipment and supplies				11	10	60	29	172	192	133	102
522	Photographic equipment and supplies				10	16	258	172				
523	Watches, clocks, and clockwork-operated devices				10	16						
524	Miscellaneous manufacturing industries				140	141	258	172				

See footnotes at end of table.

Series D 233–682. Detailed Occupation of the Economically Active Population: 1900 to 1970—Con.

[In thousands of persons 14 years old and over, except as indicated]

Series No.	Occupation	1970 16 yrs+	1970 14 yrs+	1970 class.	1960 class.	1960 class. (1950)	1950 class.	1940	1930	1920	1910	1900
	Operatives and kindred workers—Con.											
	Operatives and kindred workers (n.e.c.)—Con.											
	Manufacturing—Con.											
525	Meat products				134	93	132	91	53	50	26	} 11
526	Canning & preserving fruits, veget., & seafood				92	65	95	52	26	18	8	
527	Dairy products				57	58	62	36	26	19	12	13
528	Grain-mill products				30	29	33	17	7	8	4	4
529	Bakery products				44	33	68	45	28	20	9	5
530	Confectionery and related products				26	27	51	49	44	52	31	27
531	Beverage industries				48	51	57	36	7	10	20	13
532	Miscellaneous food preparations & kindred products				35	32	} 51	29	30	21	16	2
533	Not specified food industries				5	5						
534	Tobacco manufacturers				41	54	70	86	104	145	152	116
535	Knitting mills				62	26	154	192	129	104	85	41
536	Dyeing and finishing textiles, except knit goods				24	25	26	24	20	18	16	13
537	Carpets, rugs, and other floor covering				12	20	26	21	17	14	15	10
538	Yarn, thread, and fabric mills				251	373	477	426	324	323	269	202
539	Miscellaneous textile mill products				21	28	32	35	35	46	48	31
540	Apparel and accessories				395	384	824	734	422	365	336	225
541	Miscellaneous fabricated textile products				42	37	58	53	15	21	18	21
542	Pulp, paper, and paperboard mills				110	99	106	87	64	55	36	} 21
543	Miscellaneous paper and pulp products				48	50	61	28	17	14	10	
544	Paperboard containers and boxes				69	58	64	41	14	20	18	} 19
545	Printing, publishing, and allied industries				97	71	80	59	51	48	42	
546	Synthetic fibers				23	26	27	31	21	----	----	16
547	Paints, varnishes, and related products				17	16	18	12	8	6	4	3
548	Drugs and medicines				17	13	} 149	72	53	51	33	9
549	Miscellaneous chemicals and allied products				136	113						
550	Petroleum refining				44	43	48	30	27	14	4	1
551	Miscellaneous petroleum and coal products				6	7	7	5	2	2	2	2
552	Rubber products				162	136	127	85	81	86	32	15
553	Leather: tanned, curried, and finished				18	30	32	35	29	32	34	26
554	Footwear, except rubber				148	169	226	228	210	206	181	98
555	Leather products, except footwear				31	39	50	44	26	33	29	31
556	Not specified manufacturing industries				10	19	43	74	139	207	93	67
557	Nonmanufacturing industries (incl. not reported)				688	673	780	429	445	208	132	149
558	Construction				102	72	71	40	15	4	8	7
559	Railroads and railway express service				56	94	96	73	98	111	61	}
560	Transportation, except railroad				36	31	37	24	} 57	30	19	} 137
561	Telecommunications, utilities, and sanitary serv				50	52	52	24				
562	Wholesale and retail trade				220	224	311	145	74	40	27	
563	Business and repair services				72	50	54	38	30	8	6	
564	Public administration				46	51	54	11	6	4	3	
565	Personal services				15	20	} 105	75	165	12	9	5
566	All other industries (incl. not reported)				90	80						
567	**Private household workers**	1,204	1,143	1,817	[7]1,825	[7]1,492	1,539	2,412	1,998	1,411	1,851	1,579
568	Laundresses, private household—living in	12	13	41	(Z)	1	76	203	344	375	513	280
569	Laundresses, private household—living out				41	73						
570	Housekeepers, private household—living in	105	105	156	56	53	150	410				
571	Housekeepers, private household—living out				96	93						
572	Private household workers (n.e.c.)—living in	1,087	1,025	1,619	104	163	1,313	1,799	1,654	1,036	1,338	1,299
573	Private household workers (n.e.c.)—living out				1,178	1,034						
574	**Service workers, except private household**	9,047	8,449	6,086	5,765	4,524	4,641	3,657	2,774	1,901	1,711	1,047
575	Attendants, hospital and other institution	746	749	420	409	212	216	102				
576	Midwives	1	1	1	1	2						
577	Practical nurses	242	242	175	217	145	151	115	198	157	133	109
578	Attendants, professional & personal service (n.e.c.)	64	65	84	75	43	52	42	4	3	2	----
579	Attendants, recreation and amusement	76	83	74	63	65	66	64	29	13	9	6
580	Ushers, recreation and amusement	15	16	16	16	25	26	22				
581	Barbers, beauticians, and manicurists	650	651	489	487	391	396	449	371	214	193	133
582	Bartenders	199	199	184	184	209	214	131	----	26	101	89
583	Boarding and lodging housekeepers	7	8	30	30	29	30	74	144	133	165	71
584	Bootblacks	4	5	10	10	15	15	16	19	15	14	8
585	Charwomen and cleaners	461	470	402	192	124	128	72	52	31	29	29
586	Cooks, except private household	873	886	603	597	466	478	349	292	200	174	117
587	Elevator operators	37	37	77	77	94	97	87	68	41	25	13
588	Firemen, fire protection	178	178	139	139	112	112	82	73	51	36	15
589	Guards, watchmen, and doorkeepers	329	329	259	258	250	255	216	148	116	78	
590	Policemen and detectives, government	378	378	262	238	175	176	135	145	94	68	116
591	Policemen and detectives, private				17	21	21	21				
592	Marshals and constables	5	5	6	6	7	7	9	9	7	9	
593	Housekeepers and stewards, except private household				152	110	112	90	61	52	45	34
594	Janitors and sextons	1,274	1,301	785	621	475	482	377	310	179	113	57
595	Porters				155	174	179	182	151	102	96	42
596	Sheriffs and bailiffs	35	35	24	24	19	19	16	15	11	7	5
597	Counter and fountain workers	161	168	168	167	93	} 836	636	415	242	200	107
598	Waiters and waitresses	1,100	1,127	899	896	717						
599	Watchmen (crossing) and bridge tenders	42	42	29	26	9	12	10	13	13	10	4
600	Service workers, except private household (n.e.c.)	2,168	1,472	950	709	544	561	360	259	203	203	93
601	**Farm laborers and foremen**	[1]1,022	995	1,604	1,560	2,533	2,578	3,632	4,290	4,948	5,370	5,125
602	Farm foremen	33	34	25	25	18	17	17	28	35	19	7
603	Farm laborers, wageworkers	808	848	1,288	1,244	1,584	1,617	2,405	2,597	2,271	2,832	} 5,115
604	Farm laborers, unpaid family workers	94	109	286	284	921	934	1,208	1,660	2,633	2,514	
605	Farm service laborers, self-employed	4	4	5	5	10	10	3	5	10	6	4

See footnotes at end of table.

Series D 233–682. Detailed Occupation of the Economically Active Population: 1900 to 1970—Con.

[In thousands of persons 14 years old and over, except as indicated]

Series No.	Occupation	1970		1960		1950		1940	1930	1920	1910	1900
		16 years old and over	14 years old and over	1970 classification	1960 classification	1960 classification	1950 classification					
606	**Laborers, except farm and mine**	[8]3,751	[8]3,515	[8]3,755	[8]3,530	[8]3,774	3,885	4,875	5,335	4,905	4,478	3,620
607	Fishermen and oystermen	31	31	41	41	78	75	64	73	53	68	69
608	Garage laborers, and car washers and greasers	—	—	—	93	70	72	63	77	33	4	—
609	Gardeners, except farm, and groundskeepers	—	—	—	216	156	159	163	168	71	65	24
610	Longshoremen and stevedores	47	47	61	61	73	73	74	74	86	63	29
611	Lumbermen, raftsmen, and woodchoppers	89	90	132	136	189	196	169	147	180	139	117
612	Teamsters	8	8	22	22	22	23	31	120	412	441	374
613	Laborers (n.e.c.)	675	688	1,165	2,763	2,997	3,288	4,312	4,675	4,070	3,696	3,007
614	Manufacturing	349	347	662	961	1,154	1,209	1,598	1,960	2,169	1,487	723
615	Sawmills, planing mills, and millwork	26	26	47	97	147	152	230	292	280	289	139
616	Miscellaneous wood products				13	18	18	27				
617	Furniture and fixtures	7	7	13	18	20	21	35	40	35	24	7
618	Glass and glass products				14	14	16	21	28	29	25	15
619	Cement & concrete, gypsum, & plaster products	24	24	53	28	24	24	26	39	30	36	13
620	Structural clay products				26	28	29	39	60	49	78	42
621	Pottery and related products				5	7	7	7	11	12	9	6
622	Miscellaneous nonmetallic mineral & stone products				10	9	9	14	8	5	7	7
623	Motor vehicles and motor vehicle equipment	13	13	20	36	50	51	71	124	83	16	
624	Ship and boat building and repairing	—	—	—	14	16	16	23	17	69	12	
625	Blast furnaces, steelworks, and rolling mills	43	43	109	119	141	145	201				
626	Other primary iron and steel industries				42	52	111	128				
627	Fabricated steel products				62	60						
628	Office and store machines and devices				2	2	2	2				145
629	Miscellaneous machinery				37	39	43	46	492	544	419	
630	Not specified metal industries				(Z)	1	1	6				
631	Agricultural machinery and tractors				7	13	14	11				
632	Aircraft and parts				6	4	4	4				
633	Railroad & miscellaneous transportation equipment				6	6	6	8				
634	Primary nonferrous industries				25	27	33	43	39	43	33	15
635	Fabricated nonferrous metal products				—	—						
636	Electrical machinery, equipment, and supplies	13	13	23	33	34	33	30	37	27	11	8
637	Professional equipment and supplies				3	3	4	4				
638	Photographic equipment and supplies	2	2	3	1	1						
639	Watches, clocks, and clockwork-operated devices				(Z)	1			74	101	43	30
640	Miscellaneous manufacturing industries	11	11	13	12	15	18	27				
641	Meat products				30	36	37	47	43	60	34	12
642	Canning & preserving fruits, veget., & seafood				24	23	27	34	26	19	10	
643	Dairy products				18	23	15	17	17	15	5	5
644	Grain-mill products				17	18	20	21	16	18	9	10
645	Bakery products	44	44	90	9	5	10	8	12	8	5	3
646	Confectionery and related products				3	4	4	8	6	7	3	3
647	Beverage industries				17	21	25	22	9	11	19	12
648	Miscellaneous food preparations & kindred prod				17	29	24	29	26	32	17	3
649	Not specified food industries				2	2						
650	Tobacco manufacturers	2	2	4	7	7	10	17	21	35	16	14
651	Knitting mills				—	—	3	5	9	12	8	4
652	Dyeing and finishing textiles, except knit goods				—	—	3	5	8	11	10	9
653	Carpets, rugs, and other floor coverings	12	12	14	—	—	6	7	5	4	4	2
654	Yarn, thread, and fabric mills				30	45	50	71	94	120	59	44
655	Miscellaneous textile mill products				10	14	4	7	5	8	8	5
656	Apparel and accessories	4	4	4	11	11	9	10	14	12	8	5
657	Miscellaneous fabricated textile products				3	3	1	1	1	1	1	
658	Pulp, paper, and paperboard mills	15	15	29	25	28	29	44	52	52	31	14
659	Miscellaneous paper and pulp products				5	8	9	6	4	3	2	
660	Paperboard containers and boxes				9	10	10	10	3	3	1	1
661	Printing, publishing, and allied industries	5	5	7	13	12	12	10	11	8	5	4
662	Synthetic fibers				3	3	3	5	5	—	—	—
663	Paints, varnishes, and related products				3	5	5	6	6	5	3	2
664	Drugs and medicines				2	2	61	77	80	79	45	15
665	Miscellaneous chemical and allied products				41	45						
666	Petroleum, refining				14	24	25	28	41	32	11	5
667	Miscellaneous petroleum and coal products				3	3	6	8	5	9	11	11
668	Rubber products				18	21	17	20	29	51	14	6
669	Leather: tanned, curried, and finished	4	4	8	11	15	8	11	17	27	21	16
670	Footwear, except rubber				6		6	12	18	19	10	5
671	Leather products, except footware				2		2	3	3	8	4	3
672	Not specified manufacturing industries	3	3	2	2	11	11	44	114	191	109	79
673	Nonmanufacturing industries (incl. not reported)	—	—	—	1,802	1,843	2,079	2,714	2,715	1,901	2,210	2,284
674	Construction	645	649	802	751	699	788	1,340	710	391	531	20
675	Railroads and railway express service				136	284	293	278	490	543	599	284
676	Transportation, except railroad	105	105	191	91	87	119	98	249	199	195	86
677	Telecommunications, utilities, & sanitary serv				123	132	135	103				
678	Wholesale and retail trade	96	98	130	372	270	345	250	253	182	152	68
679	Business and repair services	22	23	15	24	16	15	7	15	2	2	1
680	Public administration	95	95	74	77	98	107	52	134	93	56	—
681	Personal services	—	—	—	77	79	83	64	864	490	675	1,825
682	All other industries (incl. not reported)	83	95	128	151	179	194	520				

Z Less than 500.
[1] Includes persons for whom occupations were not reported.
[2] Includes occupations not shown separately.
[3] Includes data in series D 303, D 305, and D 307.
[4] Includes data in series D 304, D 306, and D 308.
[5] Business services included with automobile and miscellaneous repair services and garages.
[6] Excludes tractor drivers.
[7] Includes babysitters, not shown separately.
[8] Includes carpenters' helpers, truck drivers, helpers, and warehousemen, not shown separately.

Chapter D

Earnings, Hours, and Working Conditions (Series D 683-1036)

D 683–688. Indexes of employee output (NBER), 1869–1969.

Source: U.S. Bureau of Economic Analysis, *Long Term Economic Growth, 1860–1970*, pp. 210–211.

The productivity indexes in the source publication are from John W. Kendrick, *Productivity Trends in the United States*, 1961, and *Postwar Productivity Trends in the United States, 1948–1969*, National Bureau of Economic Research, New York (copyright).

D 683 and **D 684–686**, indexes of output per man-hour. Kendrick derived these series by dividing the appropriate output series (gross private domestic product, gross nonfarm product, manufacturing output, and gross farm product) by the corresponding man-hours series.

D 689–704. Indexes of output, man-hours, compensation per man-hour, and unit labor cost (BLS), 1947–1970.

Source: U.S. Council of Economic Advisors, *Economic Report of the President*, January 1972, p. 234. Data are from the U.S. Bureau of Labor Statistics (BLS).

These series are based primarily on BLS surveys of establishments. The output measure, gross national product (GNP), represents the market value, in 1958 dollars, of final goods and services produced in the economy. It includes the purchases of goods and services by consumers, business establishments, foreign investors, and various government agencies. The GNP data (see series F 3) were prepared by the U.S. Bureau of Economic Analysis. In developing the man-hour series, data from labor force reports and national income series were used to supplement BLS payrolls series data.

The indexes of compensation per man-hour and unit labor cost were developed from man-hour estimates based on data from establishments. Compensation includes wages and salaries, plus supplemental payments such as contributions of employers to social security and private health and pension funds. The compensation data include an estimate for proprietors' salaries and contributions for supplementary benefits. Real compensation per man-hour can be derived by adjusting the compensation data by the consumer price index to reflect changes in purchasing power. The indexes of unit labor costs were developed by dividing compensation per man-hour by output per man-hour (see series W 22–25).

See also general note for series D 1–74 and data and text for series W 22–29.

D 705–714. Farm laborers—average monthly earnings with board, by geographic divisions, 1818–1948.

Source: Stanley Lebergott, *Manpower in Economic Growth: The American Record Since 1800*, tables A-23 and A-24, pp. 257ff. (Copyright 1964; used with permission of McGraw-Hill Book Co., New York.)

For most of the nineteenth century and well into the twentieth, the common method of wage payment in agriculture was monthly, with board included. Reasonably satisfactory data for individual States are available at something like decennial intervals for the entire period beginning with 1818. These figures have been supplemented with partial information to provide national estimates for the years for which this is not so. State data for 1818–1919 were combined into division and U.S. averages using weights from the population census. For 1909 and 1919, they therefore differ from U.S. Department of Agriculture (USDA) division totals.

For 1818, 1826, and 1830, estimates were made in 1832 by Senator John Holmes of Maine, and reported by him in the Congressional *Register of Debates*. For certain States there are, in addition, the results of a survey in 1832–1834 on 1832 farm wages made by Secretary of State Edward Livingstone, drawing on returns from many individual towns in these States—i.e., 59 of 134 towns in Connecticut, 101 of 444 in Maine, 109 of 230 in New Hampshire, etc. Given the broader basis of the Secretary's survey, his figures were used to represent the 1830 average (other data indicating virtually no 1830–1832 change) with the Holmes series used to extrapolate these values to 1818 and 1826. For 1818, 1826, and 1830, the total number of persons reported by the 1820 census as having agricultural occupations was used for weighting.

For 1850 and 1860, special wage-rate inquiries made in connection with census reports on social statistics gave monthly rates paid to farmhands (with board) and were used here.

For 1850, the number of free white male farmers aged 15 and over was used for weighting, and for 1860, the number of farm laborers. Examination of the ratios of farmers to farm laborers in 1860 indicated a marked degree of intrastate uniformity so that the shift from one type of weights to the other would not make a marked difference.

The source used for 1870 was a study made by Edward Young, Chief of the Bureau of Statistics of the Treasury Department, in which figures on wage rates in a host of occupations were collected. Because of the timing, it is possible that these data were collected in connection with the 1870 census. The data were more probably developed as the other materials in the volume were, from information secured by the assistant assessors of internal revenue in the various States. Their issuance, however, under the sponsorship of a competent statistician, who was experienced in data evaluation and presentation and who had worked under David A. Wells, entitles them to serious consideration.

For 1880 and 1890, the crop-reporter surveys of the USDA were used to provide State estimates.

For 1899, the USDA survey reported not rates for men hired "by the year"—as do the reports used for earlier periods—but "by the year or season." In examining the extent of noncomparability, Lebergott was limited to a comparison between the two types of rates for 1909, that being the only year for which the USDA reported both types of rates.

Day rates (other than harvest) were charted against monthly rates by the year and season for the years 1891 to 1909. The scatter showed a close and simple correlation for all years except 1909. Given the scatter and the day rate for 1909, Lebergott deduced a 1909 rate for the year and season that is virtually the same as the enumerated "year" rate for that date. On this basis he took the year-season rate for 1899 as roughly identical with the desired year rate for that date. He secured the same result by charting the year rates for 1866 to 1890 and 1909 against the daily rate (other than harvest) and interpolating for 1899 by the daily rate. It was therefore concluded that the "year–season" State rates for 1899 as actually reported could be used as satisfactory approximations of the year rates for that date.

For 1870 and 1880, the population census counts of agricultural laborers aged 16 to 59 were used as weights. For 1890 and 1899, the census count of male agricultural laborers aged 16 and over in

1900 was used. For 1909 and 1919, the division estimates of the USDA were not used because they were weighted by the number of farms employing hired labor at any time during the year. Such weights will distort the relative importance of States that characteristically hired above (or below) average proportions of migrant labor, or short-term labor. Thus, while New Jersey reported roughly as many farms with hired labor in the agricultural census as it did hired laborers in the population census, North Dakota reported almost twice as many. The population census count of farm laborers (working off-farm) was therefore used to compute regional and U.S. averages.

For 1929 and 1940, the USDA division figures were used, these having been weighted by the count of hired farm workers derived from the surveys themselves. For 1948, the 1950 Census of Agriculture count of hired farm workers was used.

D 715–717. Average daily wage rates of artisans, laborers, and agricultural workers, in the Philadelphia area, 1785–1830.

Source: Donald R. Adams, Jr., "Wage Rates in the Early National Period: Philadelphia, 1785–1830," *The Journal of Economic History*, Economic History Association, New York, September 1968. (Copyright.)

The ranges of wage rates shown for certain years are the result of multiple observations within those years. Single rates for a given year indicate that all observations for that date were identical.

The principal manuscript sources utilized in constructing these series are as follows: Pennsylvania Historical Society, *Joshua Humphreys Shipyard Accounts*, and *Moses Lancaster Account Book*; American Philosophical Society, *Treasurer's Account Book*; Records of the Ship *North Carolina*, *American State Papers*, I, Class VI (Washington: Gales and Seaton, 1834), p. 836; Stephen Girard Collection: *Ship Disbursements and Repair Records* (Ship *Good Friends*, Ship *Liberty*, Brig *Polly*, Brig *Kitty*, Ship *Two Brothers*, Ship *North America*, Ship *Helvetius*, and Ship *Superb*); *Bills and Receipts*; *Bills and Receipts Alphabetically*; *Place Accounts*; *New Houses and Stores in Water Street No. 2*; and *Real Estate Accounts*. Wage rates were obtained from the actual receipts, bills, day books, and account books.

Wage contracts in agriculture were often stated on a monthly or annual basis. The problem of determining average monthly wage rates was enhanced by the wide range of rates observable within any given year. Since the manuscript sources do not indicate any discernible seasonal trend, the differences encountered most likely lie in the differences in payment in kind or "found." In practice, the averages are simple arithmetic means of the observations for a given year.

A few examples of the variety in the content of such nonmonetary payments from the *Peale Day Book* and the *Peale-Sellers Belfield Farm Book* indicate the difficulty of making total wage estimates:

Date	Wage Rate ($)	Content of Found
June 1810	100/yr.	Mending, washing, and lodging
Oct. 1810	120/yr.	Meat, drink, washing, and lodging
Apr. 1811	10/mo.	Board and washing
July 1818	11/mo.	Finding his own wash

Special daily rates often applied at harvest time or for particular tasks:

Date	Wage Rate ($)	Sex	Function
1812	0.50/day	Female	Mowing hay
1814	1.25/day	Male	Mower
1814	0.625/day	Male	Making hay
1815	1.25/day	Male	Reaper

Examples of piece rates can also be found. During harvest periods in 1817 and 1818, according to the Girard *Place Accounts*, mowers were paid at the rate of $2.00 per acre.

As indicated in the manuscripts, $8.00 to $12.00 per month was perhaps the most common range for agricultural laborers—falling below $8.00 in only three years and rising above $12.00 in only four years—while the average monthly wage fell into the narrower range of $9.00 to $11.00 per month.

D 718–721. Daily wage rates on the Erie Canal, 1828–1881.

Source: Walter B. Smith, "Wage Rates on the Erie Canal, 1828–1881," *The Journal of Economic History*, Economic History Association, New York, September 1963, p. 298. (Copyright.)

The original sources of Smith's data are the check-rolls and workmen's receipts for payment for repair and maintenance work on the canal, as given in the Erie Canal Papers on deposit in the New York State Library in Albany. The tasks of the work gangs were such enterprises as: Leveling the tow path, cleaning the canal each spring, raising sunken boats, making emergency repairs of breaches caused by floods, breaking the ice in late autumn and keeping the locks and "feeders" in good working order. The data come largely from work of repair rather than of enlargement and new construction. On the check-rolls are the names of the workmen, their classification, the number of days worked, the daily wage rates, and the total wages paid. Most reports contain brief descriptions of the kinds of projects undertaken by the gangs. The reports in 1828 and later years are much clearer than those of earlier dates. The attempt accurately to determine the wage rates before 1828 was frustrated by the earlier practice of recording a man's name and the amount paid to him without specifying clearly the kind of work done. In 1819, it seems probable that the common labor rate was $1.00 a day and in 1823 and 1826, 75 cents. But there is a certain amount of conjecture in these statements, and not until 1828 were wage payments accompanied by a clear indication of occupational status.

For operation and maintenance purposes the 350-odd miles of the Erie Canal (the main line) were administered in three main divisions: The first extended from Albany to Utica (later to a point a little farther west), the second from Utica to Montezuma, and the third from Montezuma to Buffalo. The divisions were subdivided into sections of about 25 miles each, for which a Superintendent of Repairs was responsible. Under their control were the gang foremen, who not merely hired the men and supervised the work but who usually prepared the check-rolls. The gangs were by no means all alike; some were specialized, for example, carpenters; others were general purpose groups; some worked regularly month after month for full months, others worked only occasionally and only for a few days; and some included several hundred men (usually for emergency employment), others consisted of only five or six. The check-rolls, an integral part of the accounting and payments process on the canal, were forwarded bimonthly by the superintendents of repairs to the canal auditor as vouchers attached to his Abstract of Returns. From these records were collected about 30,000 cases of wage rates, a number sufficiently large to give a stable and dependable average rate, by months, for each of the three main divisions of the canal. The continuity of the record is, unfortunately, broken between 1867 and 1870 owing to the adoption of the "contracting-out system" for repairs in those years.

The Erie Canal was important not only as a carrier, but also as an institution of great interest to the politicians concerned with patronage. The outcome of numerous legislative inquiries was a statute specifying that repair work be let to contractors; the statistical consequence was an almost complete absence of reports of wages for the interesting years of post-Civil War price adjustment, January 1867 to April 1870. The contracting-out system did not work very well, and the former system of making repairs was soon restored. Beginning with April 1870, wage statistics once more became abundant and continuous, and continued to be so until 1879 when the responsibility for repairs was taken over by the New York State Superintendent of Public Works.

Eight hours became the legal workday in April 1870. In the midst of the confusion attendant on a return to the older method of making repairs, it became necessary to adjust the reporting system to this eight-hour day regulation. Actually, the effect of the law regarding the length of the working day was nominal rather than substantive. Men continued to work for ten hours a day on the canal as they had for many years and the only immediately observable change was the quotation of daily wage rates at four-fifths of the previous amount and a recording of all workmen as working at time-and-a-quarter a day. In series D 718–721, the check-roll quotations beginning with May 1870 were multiplied by five-fourths in order that the rates shown be for a ten-hour day.

About nine-tenths of the wage quotations in the vouchers were for male common labor, and almost all of the remainder were for carpenters, masons, foremen, and that combination of a team of horses and their driver consistently recorded as "teamwork." The large number of reported wage payments to common labor made it easily possible to determine a modal wage rate by months for each of the three divisions of the canal. The annual wage rate figures for series D 718–721 were derived from the monthly rates. Carpenters and teamworkers were sufficiently numerous to warrant confidence in the annual wage rate series for the canal as a whole. The reports about masons were less satisfactory: the number was small and there are gaps in the reports extending for months at a time. The data for masons suggest that masons' wages were about the same as those of carpenters. The only wages for women on the rolls were for cooks. They were invariably employed on the State scow and generally they received wages half those of common labor.

The mode was used to represent the central tendency in the wage returns. In over 60 percent of the months *all* common laborers received identical wages and in the remaining months the deviations from the mode were small both in number and amount. Wage records on the canal were specified in New York shillings (eight to the dollar) and pence, and when deviations from the mode occurred or when wages changed generally the amount of change was sometimes a sixpence but more often a shilling. Owing to the size of the unit in which wage changes took place, the mode seems to be unstable in periods of transition. A computed mean would have been more continuous but would not necessarily have been more representative of the general wage rate than the mode.

The difference between the mode and the arithmetic mean was not great. The average deviation of the means from the corresponding modes for common labor in the eastern division for the month of June (1828–81) was eight-tenths of a cent. In 31 out of 48 years for which data existed, the means and the modes were identical. The record for 1857, a good year for testing the differences between the mean and the mode, disclosed that out of 778 cases of wage rates for common labor in the eastern division, 759 men received $1.00 a day and only 19 received $1.125. The mean exceeded the mode by three-tenths of a cent.

The sampling procedure used in this study was dominated by the condition of the surviving records and by the practical difficulty of finding the reports of the superintendents of repairs among the thousands of bundles of manuscripts. The surviving data are ample for some times and places of employment and very scarce or non-existent for others. The author made a complete tabulation of all the data on rolls when only a few were found; when abundant, the data on five or six rolls were transcribed in entirety. Rolls containing several hundreds of cases were not used. Further search for data after the total number of wage rates approached a thousand in a given year hardly seemed worthwhile.

Lack of elegance in sampling technique was less significant for the validity of the results than were the occasional gaps in the continuity of the records. For example, no statistics could be found for the period between October 1849 and 1851 for the eastern division of the canal. This and other similar gaps in the records affected the geographical composition of the sample.

To test the reliability of the findings, the modal wage rates, by months, were subjected to an internal check. The rates for the eastern and western divisions were compared and found to be in agreement in 45 percent of the cases. Where differences existed they were small and temporary—rarely by more than a New York shilling or for more than a month or two. Wages tended to be lower in the western division than in the eastern part of the canal, but this was far from being consistently the case. The agreement between wages in the eastern and the middle divisions was close. This internal agreement suggests that the quotation of an annual wage for the canal as a whole is not seriously misleading.

D 722–727. Average annual earnings of employees, 1900–1970.

Source: **Series D 722**, U.S. Office of Business Economics (OBE), 1929–1963, *The National Income and Product Accounts of the United States, 1929–65, Statistical Tables;* 1964–1967, *U.S. National Income and Product Accounts, 1964–67;* 1968–1970, U.S. Bureau of Economic Analysis, *Survey of Current Business,* July 1971, table 6.5. **Series D 723–727,** see source for series D 705–714, table A-16.

See also text for series D 739–764.

Full-time earnings, series D 722, were computed as weighted averages of the series for individual industries as described in text for series D 739–764. The weights were the numbers employed by industry. The income loss from unemployment was estimated by applying to the full-time earnings figure the relevant unemployment percentage—for civilian labor force or nonfarm employees. This income loss, when subtracted from the full-time earnings (i.e., "when employed"), gave the earnings after deduction for unemployment. Both series D 723 and D 724 were deflated by the consumer price index to yield real earnings when employed and after deduction for unemployment, series D 725 and D 726. The price index was the Bureau of Labor Statistics index 1913–1960 extrapolated by Albert Rees to 1900. (Albert Rees, *Real Wages in Manufacturing, 1890 to 1914*, National Bureau of Economic Research, New York, 1961.)

D 728–734. Daily wages of five skilled occupations and of laborers, in manufacturing establishments, 1860–1880.

Source: Clarence D. Long, *Wages and Earnings in the United States, 1860–1890*, National Bureau of Economic Research, New York, 1960, p. 144 (copyright).

These series were compiled from Tenth Census Reports, *Report on the Statistics of Wages in the Manufacturing Industries With Supplementary Reports on the Average Retail Prices of Necessaries of Life and on Trade Societies, and Strikes and Lockouts,* vol. XX, 1886, by Joseph D. Weeks.

Weeks gathered his data from payroll records to give a continuous wage history of the same occupations in the same firms for some one date each year over a considerable period. In each of the more prominent manufacturing, mechanical, and mining industries in various sections of the country, "typical" establishments were selected, based on their age, standing, productive capacity, and general reputation. The mailing list of firms was said to be prepared after much correspondence with experts in each industry and recourse to trade directories and publications. No important branch of manufacturing was overlooked, but information on some was not returned or was unsatisfactory. Of the more than 50 industries with satisfactory returns, less than 20 could be used in Weeks' investigation, for only that many had wage data covering the entire period 1860–1880. The data do not usually cover overtime, holiday and Sunday work, and other extra earnings, and any payments to helpers and underhands have been deducted, so that the worker's wage covers what he received only for his own work. Weeks attempted to convert piece rates into daily wages wherever the firms could furnish information on time put in by piece workers.

For these series, Long used 85 establishments to compute the average daily wage: 26 for blacksmiths' wage; 10 for carpenters'; 25 for engineers'; 15 for machinists'; 9 for painters'; and 78 for laborers'.

D 735–738. Average annual and daily earnings of nonfarm employees, 1860–1900.

Source: See source for series D 705–714, table A-19 and pp. 289ff.

See also text for series D 722–727, D 728–734, and D 739–764.

There are two sets of data collected in the 1880–1890 period relative to the course of wage rates during and after the Civil War. One, "Report on Wholesale Prices, on Wages and on Transportation" (52d Cong., 2d Sess., 1893), termed the "Aldrich reports," was based on reports collected by the Commissioner of Labor in the early nineties; the other, "Report on the Statistics of Wages in Manufacturing Industries" (1886), collected as part of the 1880 census, is termed the "Weeks reports."

Lebergott rejected the Aldrich reports with their geographic, industrial, and occupational biases and relied on the Weeks reports, which have an enormously broader scope because they come from many more establishments, in more States, without the occupational biases in some of the key Aldrich reports. He used the Weeks reports primarily for interpolating between benchmarks derived from the population census and other reports and checked the movement of the series thus derived against an extensive set of contemporary investigations made by David A. Wells as Special Commissioner of the Revenue.

The wider scope of the Weeks reports has made them attractive to previous investigators. Their lack of use reflects the fact that, although many wage series are reported, no occupational weights are attached to them. To develop reasonable weights for the Weeks materials from the population census data on gainful workers by occupation, Lebergott utilized the occupational wage series to measure the trend of wages within a given occupation. Thus, he used a report for the trend of earnings by common labor in Pennsylvania and combined it with other Weeks reports on common-labor rate trends in Pennsylvania machine shops, blast furnaces, rolling mills, hardware, paper, tanneries, furniture, etc. He treated each of these as random observations of the trend for wages of that group and combined these series to interpolate between benchmark estimates for common labor in Pennsylvania. Similar combinations and interpolations were made for common labor in the other States. The State benchmarks for 1850 and 1860 are from the population census reports for those years; for 1870 from the Treasury *Report on Immigration*; and for 1880 from the census data on rates paid in iron and steel, coke, stone, and other industries.

Employees in other nonfarm occupations were allocated to 1860 wage intervals and the trend in the Weeks data for these wage intervals was used as the trend series for these groups. This amounts to saying that the trend of earnings for machinists, wheelwrights, carpenters, painters, and others reported by Weeks, who were classifiable in the $1.50 to $1.99 wage interval in 1860, should be similar to the trend for all other workmen in that interval.

The parallelism of wage movement for individual occupations within a wage-rate interval can be verified by study of the trend for individual occupations, such trends being apparent in the raw data.

The key figures involved are summarized below:

1860 Census

(In thousands)

Total nonfarm employees	2,983
Laborers	972
Miners, boatmen, and others earning $1.00 to $1.49	453
Carpenters, blacksmiths, and others earning $1.50 to $1.99	744
Domestic servants	566
All others	248

Given the above distribution of employees and their derived average daily earnings in 1860, Lebergott utilized the Weeks data (as summarized in Wesley Mitchell, *Gold Prices and Wages Under the Greenback Standard*, 1908) as follows. Mitchell had combined the hundreds of quotations into wage-interval groups and computed indices of

medians for each interval—e.g., 25–99 cents, $1–$1.49, etc.—for 1860 to 1880. Lebergott weighted these indices by the 1860 employment distribution shown above and computed an index for all nonfarm employees. Then, for each year, he computed the ratio of the resultant median to that shown by Mitchell as the median for the $1–$1.49 interval.

This ratio was then applied to the series for laborers previously derived to give an overall average. Because the trend in medians would not be satisfactory as a measure of the trend in averages, the median data were used only to derive adjustment ratios with which to step down the laborers trend to an all-employees trend.

D 739–764. Average annual earnings per full-time employee, by industry, 1900–1970.

Source: 1900–1928, see source for series D 705–714, table A-18 and pp. 480ff. 1929–1967, U.S. Office of Business Economics, 1929–1963, *The National Income and Product Accounts of the United States, 1929–1965, Statistical Tables*; 1964–1967, *U.S. National Income and Product Accounts, 1964–67*; 1968–1970, U.S. Bureau of Economic Analysis, *Survey of Current Business*, July 1971, table 6.5.

These estimates are ratios of aggregate wage and salary payments, by industry, to the aggregate number of full-time equivalent employees, by industry. Wages and salaries include executives' compensation, bonuses, tips, and payments in kind, and exclude those sources of labor income appearing in series D 893–912 as "supplements to wages and salaries."

Full-time equivalent employment measures man-years of full-time employment of wage and salary earners and its equivalent in work performed by part-time workers. For a discussion of the concept of full-time equivalent employment and the methods of estimation involved in converting part-time work to its full-time equivalent, see the *Survey of Current Business*, June 1945, pp. 17–18.

Since 1939, private industry employment and payrolls have been based principally upon records of the Social Security programs. For 1929–1938, the employment and payrolls figures are extrapolations backward from 1939, based on sources and methods similar to those used by Lebergott. The mainstay of the private industry estimates has been data of the State Unemployment Insurance (UI) programs as compiled by the U.S. Department of Labor. Additions were made for employment covered by Old-Age, Survivors, Disability, and Health Insurance (OASDHI) but not by UI—e.g. employment in small firms omitted from UI coverage under some State laws. Railroad Retirement Act coverage came from the Interstate Commerce Commission's *Transport Statistics* except that certain employment covered by the Railroad Retirement Act but not reported to the Interstate Commerce Commission was estimated from Railroad Retirement Board data.

This general method was followed except for categories for which more reliable data were available from other sources or where the proportion of firms not covered by Social Security programs was large: Agriculture, forestry, and fisheries; hospitals; private higher education; religious organizations; and private households. Data for these were obtained from the U.S. Department of Agriculture (USDA), the American Hospital Association, the Office of Education, and various governmental censuses and surveys.

Employment and payroll figures used as a basis for earnings in government and in private households were: (1) For the Federal Government, reports of the Civil Service Commission, records of the Armed Services, and (for 1933–1943) records of the Federal work relief projects; (2) for State and local governments, reports of the Bureau of the Census, the Office of Education, etc.; and (3) for private households, the Census of Population and the Current Population Survey of the Bureau of the Census. For further details, see U.S. Office of Business Economics, *National Income: 1954 Edition*.

The earnings figures for 1900–1928 were computed to link to those of the U.S. Department of Commerce national income accounts beginning 1929. Substantial use was made of a wide variety of sources, including special census reports, Simon Kuznets, *National Income and Its Composition, 1919 to 1938*; and Paul Douglas, *Real Wages in the United States, 1890–1926*.

The following summaries from Lebergott's book cover the derivation of estimates for individual industries for the 1900–1928 period:

D 739, agriculture, forestry, and fisheries. For 1910 to 1928, average earnings were computed from estimates of wages of hired labor (including the value of perquisites) and the average employment of such labor. For 1899, the total cost of hired labor as reported in the agriculture census and total employment of hired labor as reported in the population census were used for computing an earnings figure. For 1902, 1906, and 1909, figures were interpolated between 1899 and 1910 averages by the average monthly farm wage rates as derived from the surveys of the USDA.

Analysis by Louis Ducoff indicates the close relationship over the 1910–1943 period between farm wage-rate changes and prices received by farmers. Lebergott therefore used the U.S. Bureau of Labor Statistics wholesale price index component for farm prices for interpolating between the above estimates.

D 740, manufacturing. For manufacturing employees, Lebergott relied on the census of manufactures series for census years, interpolating for the pre-1919 years by the State data as combined by Paul Douglas, and for the post-1919 years by similar data as combined by Simon Kuznets.

D 741, mining, total. The estimates for all mining were computed as the weighted sum of series for anthracite, bituminous, metal, and oil mining for 1902, 1909, and the years 1914 to 1928. For the remaining years in the 1900–1913 period, total mining was estimated from the trend in coal mining, the ratio of one average to the other being much the same in 1902, 1909, and 1914. All mining earnings were 108.5 percent of coal mining in 1914 and 107.8 percent in 1909. For 1902 they were 11.3 percent, a difference explained by the anthracite strike of that year. The 1909 ratio was therefore used for 1900 to 1913.

D 742 and **D 743,** anthracite and bituminous coal. Separate estimates were computed for each industry for the years 1900 to 1928. For 1919 to 1928, the averages can be readily derived from Kuznets' estimates. For earlier years, the census data were interpolated by Paul Douglas on the basis of the relevant State series; his figures were used for extrapolation after some adjustments. For both the anthracite coal strike of 1902 and the bituminous coal strike of 1919, Lebergott followed Douglas in showing a decline in earnings, relating total payrolls to the average number customarily employed in the nonstrike months. Since this decline is also reflected in employment data, the two may not be multiplied together for these years to give total payrolls.

D 744, metal mining. For metal mining, Lebergott interpolated between census benchmark data by the weighted trend of earnings in copper and iron mining. Because the precious metals, lead, and zinc, were mined primarily in the West during this period, the employment weight for these industries was given to the series for copper, which is primarily one for the Mountain States.

D 745, construction. The 1929 Department of Commerce average was extrapolated to 1919 by the implicit full-time earnings figures in the Kuznets' estimates. Lebergott then extrapolated to 1900 by an adjusted index of weekly earnings, using Douglas' series for building tradesmen and for unskilled laborers, and weighting these together by population census weights. To adjust this series for the varying volume of employment from year to year, Lebergott multiplied by an adjustment ratio—computed as the ratio of an index of weekly to one of annual earnings in manufacturing.

D 746–752, transport and utilities. The group average, as those for utilities and for communications, is a weighted average of earnings in individual industry sectors. The weights used were the employment estimates derived above. The average earnings were in general the Department of Commerce 1929 figure extrapolated to 1919 by Kuznets' series, and to 1900 by Douglas' series. There were three partial exceptions to this primary procedure: (1) For gas and electricity, alternative estimates of the 1900 to 1904 trend were made because Douglas' figures, based on Wisconsin reports, show an unreasonable trend; (2) for telephone and telegraph, the 1902 estimate was extrapolated to 1900 by the trend for street-railway earnings, the two showing similar trends in immediately subsequent years; and (3) for water transport, the 1900 to 1918 trend of average weekly earnings of seamen was adjusted to the trend for annual earnings by the ratios of weekly to annual series for earnings on steam railroads.

D 753, wholesale and retail trade. Direct estimates for trade were made, using as basic sources a variety of direct studies of earnings made in the period 1900 to 1919. Benchmark estimates were made for 1900 using the 1901 Cost of Living Survey (of 24,000 families), an 1895–1896 study by the Commissioner of Labor on earnings in the various industries of 30 States, and the 1899 Census of Manufactures. Benchmark estimates for 1909 and 1919 were developed from censuses of manufactures, laundries, and the telephone industry, from a massive 1909 Bureau of Labor study of women's earnings, and from a 1921 study by the National Bureau of Economic Research and the Census Bureau. Interpolations were then made between these benchmark averages.

D 754, finance, insurance, and real estate. Earnings were computed as the weighted sum of earnings in the two major occupational categories, agents and clerical personnel. Estimates of the number of agents who were employees were made from population census data. Average earnings of agents in 1900, 1905, 1910, and 1920 were available for Metropolitan Life Insurance Company agents, the largest company in the field. Interpolation for 1901 to 1904 and 1910 to 1920 was by the movement of earnings in trade. For 1906 to 1909, a linear trend was used to reflect the readjustment of agents' earnings after the Armstrong investigation, leading to a much greater 1905 to 1910 growth than appears in trade earnings.

Unpublished figures on earnings of salaried clerical employees in one of the five largest insurance companies were used for the years 1909 and 1914 to 1919. These were extrapolated to 1900 and interpolated for 1910 to 1913 by the trend in earnings of salaried clerical personnel in manufacturing. The two series thus estimated were combined with employment weights derived from the 1910 census, giving a trend series for 1900 to 1919. This series was used to extrapolate the 1919 to 1929 figures derived from Kuznets' estimates.

D 756, personal services. The first step in developing this series was to make a benchmark earnings estimate for 1900, by estimating averages for key occupations and industries, then weighting them together by the number of employees in each. (Consistent weights were available from the special class-of-worker tabulations from the 1910 census.)

For 1920 and 1921, the results of a Census-National Bureau of Economic Research nationwide survey for the President's Conference on Unemployment were used.

The personal-service earnings figures thus derived for 1900 and 1920, as well as that for 1929 shown in Department of Commerce estimates, are virtually identical with the average earnings in laundries for those years. Therefore, the census of manufactures data on laundry earnings in 1909, 1914, 1919, 1925, and 1927 were used to extrapolate the 1919 service earnings figure to these additional years.

Ratios of personal service earnings to those for trade, a segment for which yearly estimates had already been made and which is similar in certain key respects to that of service, were computed. The ratios were as follows: 1900, 65; 1909, 69; 1914, 67; 1921, 73; 1925, 69; 1927, 70. The relationship appears to be quite reasonable and steady, even to the extent of indicating a relatively greater rise for the lower-paid industry than the higher during World War I and after—a phenomenon apparent in other series based on very solid annual or biennial reports.   These ratios were, therefore, interpolated and applied to the trade series to give the estimates of earnings in personal service.

D 762, State and local government.   An initial benchmark for earnings in 1905 was established as follows:

(1) For policemen and firemen, the largest single group, averages of earnings data available for cities of 30,000 and over in population in 1905 were adjusted to apply to all cities on the basis of the ratio of teachers' earnings in larger and smaller cities.   (2) For the next largest occupation group, city labor, the 1905 census data for employees of street-cleaning departments were used, after an adjustment similar to that noted for policemen and firemen to make the figures apply to the United States as a whole.   (3) For city officials and other city employees, the average for policemen and firemen was used.   (4) For State and county officials, the Office of Education data on average earnings of teachers were used since the two were very similar in level during stable periods in the 1920's.   (5) In addition, an estimate of the number employed in State mental hospitals and institutions for the feebleminded was prepared as part of the employment estimates. The average salary for this group was assumed the same as that for all hospitals, computed as part of the estimates for service.   These five earnings averages were then weighted together by the occupation data for local government in 1910 as shown by the Census of Population.

For 1919 to 1928, Kuznets' estimates based on a review of available reports for individual cities and States were used.   The 1905–1919–1928 data show a close similarity of trend to that for the earnings of urban teachers, suggesting that the latter could be used for interpolation.   In the critical overlap period of 1919 to 1921, however, the rate of change in teachers' salaries was not proportionate to that for other State employees, salaries of the former lagging behind increases previously granted to other local employees and, in addition, reflecting the impact of heavy postwar enrollments.   The procedure used, therefore, was to extrapolate the 1919 estimate to 1916 by the movement of earnings for policemen and firemen in selected cities as estimated by W. I. King, *The National Income and Its Purchasing Power* (1930).   The resultant estimate of local government earnings in 1916 was 91 percent of the average salary of urban teachers, a ratio almost identical with the 88 percent implicit in the 1905 figures estimated earlier.   By extrapolating and interpolating these percentages and those for 1905 and 1919 and applying them to the urban teachers' salary estimates, the final series for local government was derived.

D 763, public education.   For this series, the biennial surveys of the Office of Education provide the basic raw materials.   These were developed into consistent estimates by Douglas and Kuznets; their series were used to extrapolate the 1929 Department of Commerce benchmark.

D 764, Federal civilian government.   Separate earnings series were derived for postal and for nonpostal civilian employees of the Federal government, the two series being weighted together and then used to interpolate between benchmark estimates for 1899 and 1929. The 1899 benchmark was derived by sampling the complete list of Federal employees and their salaries as recorded in the U.S. *Official Register* for 1899.   For 1929, Department of Commerce data were used.

A benchmark estimate for 1899 earnings in postal service was computed by sampling from the *Official Register* for that year, with interpolation between that figure and the implicit Department of Commerce 1929 average by a series for all postal employees.   Benchmark averages for all Federal employees outside the postal service were computed for 1899 and 1919 by sampling from the complete list of employees shown in the *Official Register* for those years.   The procedure was identical with that used for postal employees.   Interpolation from 1899 to 1919 was by the trend of salaries of government employees in the District of Columbia.   For 1920 to 1928, Lebergott interpolated between the 1919 figure and Kuznets' 1929 figure.

D 765–778. Average hours and average earnings in manufacturing, in selected nonmanufacturing industries, and for "lower-skilled" labor, 1890–1926.

Source: Paul H. Douglas, *Real Wages in the United States, 1890–1926*, Houghton Mifflin Company, New York, 1930 (copyright).

D765–766 are weighted averages of series D 767 and D 769, and series D 768 and D 770, respectively.   The union scales of wages are substantially higher and less flexible than the wages of all workers in the "union" industries.   Since the weight of the "union" industries in the all-manufacturing average is based on the total number of skilled and semiskilled workers in the industries, the total manufacturing average is too high (see Leo Wolman, "American Wages," *Quarterly Journal of Economics*, XLVI, 1932, pp. 398–406).

D 767–768, beginning in 1907, are weighted averages of trade union scales for occupations.   The weights are union membership by crafts.   The series are extrapolated back to 1890 by use of payroll data from the sources of series D 769 and D 770.

D 769–770, average hours and earnings for "payroll" manufacturing industries, are averages weighted by employment data from employer payrolls (see text for series D 794–801), given in various U.S. Bureau of Labor Statistics (BLS) bulletins and in the *Nineteenth Annual Report of the Commissioner of Labor*.   Until 1913, the original data are for selected occupations only, and exclude most laborers and some other unskilled workers.   Therefore, for 1890–1913, the series are extrapolations backward from the 1914 level.

Differences between series D 767–768 and D 769–770 are not necessarily reliable indicators of differences in wages and hours between workers in union and nonunion industries.   Because the biases in series D 767–768 are probably much greater than those in series D 769–770, it may sometimes be desirable to use only the latter to represent all manufacturing.

D 771, average hours (standard) in bituminous coal mining, is estimated from union contracts and their coverage for 1890–1903; after 1903, it is based on data from the U.S. Geological Survey.

D 772, average hourly earnings, was obtained by dividing series D 788, average annual earnings, by average days worked, as reported by the U. S. Geological Survey; the resulting series was divided by daily hours worked.

D 773, average full-time earnings on railroads, is based on average daily wages by occupations, 1895–1914; for 1914–1926, it is based on average hourly wages as reported by the U.S. Interstate Commerce Commission and estimated daily hours.

D 774–775, average hours and earnings in the building trades, were obtained in the same way as series D 767–768.

D 776, average hours for postal employees, is based on nominal hours as set by law, adjusted (after 1920) for sick leave.

D 777, average hourly earnings, is estimated by dividing series D 791 by 52 to obtain weekly earnings and then by dividing again by series D 776 to obtain hourly earnings.

D 778, average full-time weekly earnings for "lower-skilled" labor, is reproduced in the source from Whitney Coombs, *The Wages of Unskilled Labor in Manufacturing Industries in the United States, 1890–1924*, Columbia University Press, New York, 1926, p. 99.   It is based on the wages of the least skilled or lowest paid occupations reported for each industry in BLS bulletins and in the *Nineteenth Annual Report of the Commissioner of Labor*, except that the figure for 1920 is based on the data of the National Industrial Conference Board.   Since these sources exclude most laborers before 1914, the series is labeled here as "lower skilled," though it is called "unskilled" by Coombs and by Douglas.

D 779–793. Average annual earnings in all and selected industries and in occupations, 1890–1926.

Source: See source for series D 765–778.

D 779–780, all industries averages, are weighted averages of series D 781–793 and an additional series beginning in 1902 for anthracite coal.   The weights change annually and are based on decennial census employment estimates. Interpolations of weights for intercensal years are based on State employment data when available; elsewhere they are linear.

The weights for decennial census years and 1926 are shown in the source, p. 390.

D 781, wage earners in manufacturing, is based on data from the census of manufactures for census years (total wages paid and wage earners). Figures for intercensal years are interpolated using similar data from the labor bureaus of a number of States. Census data for 1890 are adjusted to eliminate the hand trades.

D 782, wage earners in steam railroads, is based on Interstate Commerce Commission data since 1905, and extrapolated back to 1890 using data from several State railroad commissions.

D 783, street railways, is based on the Eleventh Census (1890) and the censuses of electrical industries. Figures for intercensal years are interpolations based on data from several State railroad and public utility commissions and State labor bureaus.

D 784–785, telephone and telegraph industries, are based on censuses of electrical industries. Figures for intercensal years are interpolations based on data published by the Pennsylvania Department of Internal Affairs.

D 786, gas and electricity, is based on the censuses of electrical industries (electricity) and on the censuses of manufactures (gas). Figures for intercensal years are interpolations based on data for New York City, Wisconsin, Illinois, and Pennsylvania, from State sources.

D 787, clerical workers in manufacturing and steam railroads, is based on: Average earnings of salaried workers in manufacturing computed from the censuses of manufactures for census years, with data from three States used to interpolate for other years; and, beginning in 1895, earnings of salaried workers in railroads from the Interstate Commerce Commission, with data from two State railway commissions and one railroad used to extrapolate back to 1890.

D 788, bituminous coal mining, is based on aggregate wage payments from the censuses of mines and quarries of 1889, 1902, 1909, and 1919 as revised in the Fourteenth Census (1920), divided by employment figures reported by the U. S. Geological Survey. Figures for intercensal years are interpolations based on data from the State labor bureaus or departments of mines of five major coal-producing States.

D 789, farm labor, is based on the U.S. Department of Agriculture series of daily wages of farm labor without board and of monthly wages of farm labor without board. Data for 1900–1909 are linear interpolations covering from one to three years each.

D 790, Federal employees, covers employees of Federal executive departments in Washington, D.C., only. The data are from the *Official Register*, adjusted to include bonuses paid during 1917–1924.

D 791, postal employees, covers letter carriers and, beginning in 1906, postal clerks in first and second class post offices. The data are from the *Annual Reports of the Postmaster General*, adjusted to calendar years.

D 792, public school teachers, covers teachers, principals, and supervisors in public elementary and secondary schools. The data are from the *Annual Reports of the U.S. Commissioner of Education*, adjusted to a calendar-year basis. Data for some years after 1915 are interpolations based on studies of the National Education Association.

D 793, ministers, covers salaries of Methodist and Congregational ministers as reported in the *Methodist Year Book* and the *Annual Congregational Gray Book*.

D 794–801. Indexes of wages, hours, and earnings in manufacturing and in the building trades, 1890–1907.

Source: **Series D 794–796**, U.S. Department of Commerce and Labor, *Bulletin of the Bureau of Labor, No. 77*, 1908, p. 7. **Series D 797**, Leo Wolman, "Hours of Work in American Industry," *Bulletin 71*, National Bureau of Economic Research, New York, 1938, p. 2 (copyright).

Beginning in 1900, the Bureau of Labor of the Department of Commerce and Labor undertook, in somewhat modified form, a continuation of the Aldrich reports (see text for series D 735–738). The *Nineteenth Annual Report of the Commissioner of Labor*, 1904, contains the results of the studies for 1890–1903. Somewhat similar surveys were made for 1904–1907 and the information for the entire period was summarized in *Bulletin No. 77*, cited above. The *Nineteenth Annual Report* and the subsequent *Bulletins* (Nos. 59, 65, 71, and 77) show the basic wage, hour, and employment averages for each of the individual occupations and industries and for selected occupations by States and for large cities.

The Bureau of Labor figures, series D 794–796, include the building and other hand and neighborhood trades. Wolman's figures, series D 797, exclude the building and hand trades.

The data in the *Nineteenth Annual Report* are based on information obtained from 3,475 establishments in 67 industries, covering 519 occupations. Agents of the Bureau of Labor collected wages, hours, and employment data separately by occupation and sex from the records of each establishment. Such data were taken only for what were judged principal occupations in each industry and only for the period within each year that was judged "normal" for the establishment. By and large, the basic data for each occupation (separately by sex) were for establishments whose records were complete enough to supply the data for each year 1890–1903.

For 1890–1903, average hourly wages and average full-time weekly hours, weighted by employment, were computed for each occupation, separately by sex. Each of the occupational series was converted to an index number with the average for 1890–1899 as the base. Within each industry, simple arithmetic means of the individual occupational indexes were then computed. Series D 798 and D 800 are unweighted means of the occupational indexes in the building trades. The "all manufacturing" index numbers (series D 794 and D 796), however, are weighted means of the indexes of the 67 separate industries included, each industry weighted by the payroll of that industry as estimated from the 1900 census. Series D 795 is the product of series D 794 and D 796; series D 799 is the product of series D 798 and D 800.

For 1904–1907, the procedures used by the Bureau of Labor were similar to those used for 1890–1903, with the following exceptions: (1) Some small industries covered in 1890–1903 were dropped although the number of establishments covered was increased; and (2) the indexes were chain-linked to those for 1890–1903.

Series D 797 and D 801, for average full-time weekly hours, are based on Wolman's reworking of the basic data for series D 796 and D 800. Series D 797 shows the index numbers computed from the weighted average of the hours figures in the *Nineteenth Annual Report* for 456 occupations in 48 manufacturing industries and excludes the building trades and other hand and neighborhood trades covered in the report. The weight for each occupation in each year is the number of employees covered in the survey of that occupation in the year. Series D 801 is the index number calculated from the similarly weighted average computed by Wolman for the 19 building trades occupations. For the building trades, Wolman expressed the opinion that the hours data in the *Nineteenth Annual Report* were those established by unions.

Wolman's report is a basic source of information of hours of work in American industry. It contains 15 summary tables of historical data on hours of work in manufacturing, building construction, steam railroads, and coal mining for various dates, 1890–1937.

D 802–810. Earnings and hours of production workers in manufacturing, 1909–1970.

Source: U.S. Bureau of Labor Statistics, *Employment and Earnings, United States, 1909–71*, Bulletin No. 1312–8.

The figures for 1909–1931 represent estimates based largely on periodic wage and hour surveys conducted by the Bureau of Labor Statistics (BLS) during that period for a narrow list of manufacturing industries. These figures are an extension of, and are adjusted for comparability with, the figures for 1932–1957. For a discussion of the methods and data used to derive the figures for 1909–1931, see BLS, *Monthly Labor Review*, July 1955, pp. 801–806.

The estimates of average weekly earnings for 1909–1931, based primarily on census data, tend to be more accurate than those for average hourly earnings and average weekly hours. It is likely that the hourly earnings figures are overstated and the weekly hours understated because the BLS surveys of wages tended to sample large firms more heavily than small firms.

For 1932–1970, the underlying employment, payroll, and man-hour figures were obtained by means of a mail questionnaire sent monthly to cooperating establishments. Each establishment reported the following information: (1) The number of production workers or nonsupervisory employees who worked or received pay for any part of the payroll period which includes the 12th of the month; (2) the total gross payrolls for these employees before such deductions as Social Security taxes, withholding taxes, union dues, etc. (the payroll figures include pay for overtime, shift premiums, sick leave, holidays, vacations, and production bonuses, but exclude payments in kind, retroactive pay, nonproduction bonuses, employer contributions to private welfare funds, insurance and pension plans, and similar fringe payments); and (3) total man-hours paid for these employees including hours paid for vacations, holidays, sick leave, travel time, lunch time, etc.

Within each detailed industry the payroll, employment, and man-hours figures for reporting establishments are aggregated, and average hourly earnings, average weekly hours, and average weekly earnings are computed. The average hourly earnings and average weekly hours for a group of industries are weighted arithmetic means of the corresponding averages for the industries within the group. The weights used for earnings are estimates of aggregate production-worker man-hours and those used for hours are estimates of aggregate production-worker employment. Average weekly earnings for the group is the product of the average hourly earnings and the average weekly hours for the group.

Average weekly hours worked or paid for differ from average full-time or standard hours (before payment at overtime premium rates) and from average hours worked per week. During periods of substantial unemployment, average weekly hours paid for often may be considerably below the full-time level of hours or the level at which premium payments for overtime begin. On the other hand, during periods of relatively full employment, overtime hours tend to raise the average weekly hours above the full-time level.

Until the 1940's, the distinction in most industries between hours paid for and hours actually worked was relatively unimportant. The widespread adoption of paid vacations of increasing length and of an increasing number of paid holidays (and in some industries paid travel time, lunch time, etc.), however, has raised average weekly hours (which are hours paid for) above average hours worked by increasing amounts.

Average hourly earnings figures exclude such fringe payments as employer contributions to private health, welfare, and insurance funds and include premium payments for overtime and for night work.

D 811–813. Earnings and hours for bituminous coal-lignite mining (BLS), 1909–1970.

Source: See source for series D 802–810.

For 1909–1931, estimates are based on a variety of sources including special studies by the BLS and data collected by the Bureau of the Census, the Bureau of Mines, and reports of State coal commissions. For 1932–1970, figures are strictly comparable in concept and method of estimation with those for manufacturing in series D 802–810. See text for same series regarding hours paid for in contrast to hours worked and the exclusion from average hourly earnings of fringe payments which are particularly applicable to coal mining.

Before 1945, lunch time was not paid for in the mines. Beginning April 1945, mine operators paid for 15 minutes of lunch time per day; in July 1947, the lunch time paid for was increased to one-half hour. Similarly, before November 1943, working time was computed on a "face-to-face" basis. From November 1943 to April 1945, inside mine workers were paid for 45 minutes of travel time per day at two-thirds of the regular rate. Since April 1945, inside workers have been paid for all travel time at the applicable hourly rate.

Data published by the Bureau of Mines (*Minerals Yearbook*, 1946, p. 81) show that in 1944 travel time amounted, on the average, to 10–15 percent of total time paid for. Therefore, average weekly hours figures since 1945 may have a serious upward bias if used to measure hours actually worked, and the average hourly earnings figures may have a correspondingly serious downward bias if used to measure average earnings per hour actually worked.

Average hourly earnings figures exclude contributions of coal mine employers to the miners' welfare and retirement fund, established in 1946. This fund was financed by mine operators through contributions of 5 cents for each ton of coal produced. In 1947, the contribution was raised to 10 cents. The medical and hospital fund, previously financed by miners, was combined with the welfare and retirement fund, and the rate of contribution was raised several more times until, in 1952, it reached the current (1970) rate of 40 cents a ton. In 1969, wage supplements in bituminous coal mining, chiefly employer contributions to the welfare and retirement fund, amounted to 20 percent of total compensation.

D 814. Earnings for bituminous coal mining (Lewis), 1890–1957.

Source: H. G. Lewis, *Unionism and Relative Wages in the United States*, pp. 75–76 (© 1963, by The University of Chicago).

In constructing this series, Lewis used the following sources: 1890–1928, Rush V. Greenslade, "The Economic Effects of Collective Bargaining in Bituminous Coal Mining," unpublished Ph. D. dissertation, University of Chicago, 1952, table 8; 1929–1957, Ethel B. Jones, "Hours of Work in the United States, 1900–1957," unpublished Ph. D. dissertation, University of Chicago, 1961, table 2.

Average hourly compensation includes wage supplements.

D 815–817. Earnings and hours for Class I railroads, 1939–1970.

Source: See source for series D 802–810.

Figures for Class I railroads are based on their monthly reports to the Interstate Commerce Commission. Until 1951, the figures covered all hourly rated employees of Class I railroads excluding Class I switching and terminal companies. Since 1951, the figures cover all employees (excluding switching and terminal companies) except executives, officials, and staff assistants. Although the figures since 1951 are not strictly comparable with those for earlier years, the difference is not large.

Average hourly earnings are computed by dividing the total compensation of covered employees by total man-hours paid for. Average weekly earnings are derived by multiplying average weekly hours by average hourly earnings. Average weekly hours equal total man-hours paid for (during a month) reduced to a weekly basis, divided by the full-month count of employees on the payroll. The full-month count generally tends to be somewhat larger than a count for the payroll period which includes the 12th of the month and is used for other industries. For this reason both the weekly earnings and the weekly hours figures tend to be slightly lower than they would be if computed on the latter basis.

D 818–829. Indexes of union hourly wage rates and weekly hours, building and printing trades, 1907–1970.

Source: U.S. Bureau of Labor Statistics, *Union Wages and Hours: Building Trades, 1970*, BLS Bulletin No. 1709, pp. 3 and 6; and

Union Wages and Hours: Printing Industry, 1970, BLS Bulletin No. 1707, pp. 3 and 6.

Studies by the Bureau of Labor Statistics of union wage rates and hours prior to 1936 included at various times building and printing trades, barbers, linemen, longshoremen, and workers employed in breweries, laundries, metal trades, millwork, restaurants, soft drink production, theaters, baking, trucking, and local transit. Since 1936, the studies have been confined to the printing and building trades, trucking, local transit, and baking. The baking study was discontinued in 1953.

For each trade, the local union is asked to submit data on the minimum union wage rate, the weekly hours (before overtime becomes effective), and the number of active union members working or available for work on a single specified date (recently July 1) each year.

The earliest studies covered 13 journeymen and 7 helper and labor classifications in building construction, and 7 book and job and 4 newspaper classifications in the printing trades in 39 cities. Since 1964, the studies have covered 24 journeymen and 9 helper and labor classifications in the building trades in 68 cities of over 100,000 population; and 12 book and job and 8 newspaper classifications, and, since 1968, 6 lithographic crafts in the printing trades in 69 such cities.

Indexes for all years were computed by the chain-link relative method, except 1921–1929, which were based on weighted arithmetic means for each year. The figures reflect minimum union contract rates and exclude premium pay for overtime. During periods of unemployment, the contract rates may be higher than the actual wage rates paid. Wage rates above contract rates may be paid during periods of high employment or rapid inflation. Thus, the union figures tend to have smaller cyclical fluctuations than actual wage rates paid to union employees. Furthermore, since overtime pay is excluded, union wage rates fluctuate less cyclically than average hourly earnings.

The hours figures also reflect union contract straight-time hours. They do not measure hours actually worked, which for the building trades vary with climatic conditions and the amount of construction work available.

D 830–844. Earnings and hours of production workers in 25 manufacturing industries, by sex and degree of skill, 1914–1948.

Source: The Conference Board, Inc., *The Economic Almanac for 1950*, New York, 1950, pp. 336–344 (copyright).

The underlying data were collected by the National Industrial Conference Board (NICB) from a sample of companies representing 25 industries (durable and nondurable goods) by means of a monthly mail questionnaire. The number of firms included in the sample, as well as the distribution of these firms by size and geographical location, varied somewhat from time to time. In 1936, the sample included 1,886 firms employing about one-third of all wage earners in the 25 industries covered and about one-fifth of all wage earners in all manufacturing industries. The average firm in the sample (in most of the 25 industries) was substantially larger (in terms of employment) than the average firm in the population from which the sample was taken. Although some tendency toward an upward bias in the level of earnings of the sample firms may exist, it is not clear that this bias also had a trend or varied with the business cycle.

Within each industry, average hourly earnings was obtained by dividing the aggregate payroll for reporting companies by the aggregate man-hours. Average weekly hours and average weekly earnings were obtained in a similar manner. The averages for all industries taken together were weighted means of the separate industry averages with fixed employment weights estimated for each industry with the help of the 1923 Census of Manufactures.

The distinction in classification between unskilled males and other male workers was not precisely stated by NICB and the classification was made by the reporting firms.

D 845–876. Average days in operation per year, average daily hours, and annual and hourly earnings, in manufacturing, by industry, 1889–1914.

Source: Albert Rees, *Real Wages in Manufacturing, 1890–1914*, National Bureau of Economic Research, New York, 1961, Princeton University Press, tables 10 and 13. (Copyright.)

Rees' estimates of hourly earnings of wage earners in all manufacturing begin with estimates of average annual earnings in census years (1889, 1899, 1904, 1909, and 1914 are considered census years). To obtain average annual earnings he divided total wage payments by the average number of wage earners after adjusting the data to conform to the definition of manufacturing in effect for the 1958 census. This meant deducting industries no longer considered manufacturing, the most important of which are railroad repair shop products, with 366,000 workers in 1914, and illuminating gas, with 44,000 workers. The effect of the adjustment was to reduce average annual earnings by $6 in each census year, except in 1889, when it reduced annual earnings by $4.

For 1889, Rees also had to adjust the original census figures to eliminate the hand and custom trades. This adjustment was made for each industry and was based on separate data on factory industries for 1899 given in the *Census of Manufactures* of 1904. When the 1899 data showed that an industry was partly a factory industry and partly a hand or custom trade, Rees applied the 1899 proportions to the 1889 figures.

The nature of the census employment concepts have an important effect on annual earnings figures for census years. The figures Rees would have preferred were total payrolls divided by the number of workers in average daily attendance when the plant was in operation because, at a later step, he divided annual earnings by the number of days in operation to get average daily earnings. The nature of the appropriate average employment concept can be seen more easily by reversing the order of the division: total payrolls divided by days in operation would give average daily payrolls, which, divided by the number of workers in average daily attendance, would give average daily earnings.

The actual census employment figures differ from this ideal in two opposite ways. In 1914 and 1909, employers were asked to report, from time or payroll records, the number of workers employed on the 15th day of each month or the nearest representative day. The employment figures for the 12 months were then added, employment in any month in which the plant was not in operation was counted as zero, and the sum was divided by 12. The first source of error was the inclusion of these zero figures, which resulted in too low an average employment and too high a daily earnings figure. In effect, time lost during whole months in which an establishment was not in operation was counted twice: once in employment and once in the number of days worked. In seasonal industries such as glass, where the error on this account is large, Rees made special corrections to allow for it.

The second source of error was that employers probably included in their count some workers who were on the payroll on the 15th day of the month but were not at work or receiving pay on that day. This source of error resulted in too high an average employment and too low an average daily wage. Checks of the hourly earnings figures against data built up from hourly wage rates did not suggest any consistent bias in the estimates and thus led Rees to conclude that the two sources of error were, in general, roughly offsetting.

Prior to 1909, the census employment concepts were somewhat different. In 1899 and 1904, employers reported average employment for each month without reference to a particular day. In 1889, the average employment concept was essentially average employment during the time the plant was in operation. Thus the first of the two sources of error is absent in 1889, while the second is not. For this reason, the earnings estimates for the early 1890's may be slightly too low.

For the intercensal years, Rees used data for Massachusetts, New

Jersey, and Pennsylvania as interpolators. The Massachusetts series covers the full period, the Pennsylvania series begins in 1892, and the New Jersey series in 1895. He linked the series at these points to prevent the changes in coverage from affecting the movement of the series.

The average number of days per year that establishments were in operation is a weighted average of data for the same States used in interpolating annual earnings. Within each State, Rees computed employment-weighted averages of days in operation by industries; the all-manufacturing averages published by some of the States are weighted by the number of establishments. The weights for combining States in census years were census employment in manufacturing; for other years, linear interpolations of the census weights. The full-time work year during the period 1889–1914 was apparently 312 days—365 minus 52 Sundays and one holiday.

Rees used the series on average full-time hours per day in all manufacturing again in deriving some of his industry data on hourly earnings, referring to it as the "general hours series." Throughout the study he converted weekly hours to daily hours by dividing by six. The daily hours figures for 1914 and 1909 were computed from the frequency distributions of full-time hours per week in the census of manufactures.

From 1903 to 1914 the movement of the "general hours series" was based on U.S. Bureau of Labor Statistics (BLS) data for seven industries, using Douglas' processing for six of them (Paul Douglas, *Real Wages in the United States, 1890–1926*, Boston, 1930). The industries are cotton, silk, hosiery and knit goods, woolen and worsted, boots and shoes, lumber, and iron and steel. These were combined by census employment weights, using linear interpolation of these weights for intercensal years. The resulting series was then adjusted to pass through the points computed from census data for 1909 and 1914.

This segment of the "general hours series" used the hours data for all of Douglas' payroll industries except clothing (for which Douglas interpolated the data for 1907–12) and slaughtering and meat-packing (for which he assumed a constant 60-hour week on the basis of information other than the BLS data). Rees added the silk industry, for which he computed average hours from the BLS bulletins following Douglas' method.

For 1890–1902, the movement of the "general hours series" was taken from Wolman's series for all manufacturing (*Hours of Work in American Industry*, Bulletin 71, NBER, 1938). This was linked to the segment of the general hours series for 1903–09 by means of an overlap of one year at 1903. The resulting change in the level of Wolman's series was an increase of 0.2 hour per week. Wolman's series uses all the hours data for manufacturing in the *Nineteenth Annual Report of the Commissioner of Labor*; it thus has much broader coverage (48 industries) than Douglas' series, which was derived from the same source for this period, but is confined to 14 industries.

Rees' estimates of money earnings for individual industries were derived in essentially the same way as the estimates for all manufacturing. However, he used data from several additional States to estimate the number of days in operation per year and to interpolate annual earnings between census years. These States provided usable data only for some industries or only for short periods of time. See source for additional detail.

The choice of industries was dictated by the availability of State data. None of the State sources provide definitions or descriptions of the industries to which their industry series refer, and the industry titles at times proved quite misleading. Large differences between State and census data in the movement of annual earnings from one census year to the next were often grounds for not using a series. Because it was possible for Rees to combine series given separately in his sources, but not to break them down, the industry coverage of his series is always that of the broadest of their components.

The levels of average daily hours for individual industries for 1909 and 1914 were computed from census data. In two industries, Rees made special assumptions about the means of the open-end classes

in the census distributions. For glass, short workweeks were common for part of the work force, apparently because of the heat and physical strain of some jobs. In this industry he assumed that the mean of the weekly-hours class "48 hours and under" was 44 hours. For iron and steel the means of the open-end class "over 72 hours" were computed from BLS data.

The movement of hours, except for the trend from 1909 to 1914, was based ultimately on BLS data, combined in several different ways. In five industries (cotton, woolens, hosiery and knit goods, boots and shoes, and iron and steel) Rees used the Douglas payroll series adjusted to the census levels of 1909 and 1914. For silk, he computed an hours series using Douglas' methods; this was then adjusted to census levels. The hours series for "all textiles" is the weighted averages of the series for cotton, woolen, silk, and hosiery and knit goods, with no new adjustment to census levels. In the remaining industries, except dyeing and finishing textiles, he used the general hours series to estimate the movement of hours from 1903 to 1914, adjusting it to the census levels of each industry. For dyeing and finishing textiles he used the "all textiles" series.

In five industries (dyeing and finishing textiles, leather, paper, glass, and foundries and machine shops) for the period before 1903, Rees used the data for individual industries in the *Nineteenth Annual Report of the Commissioner of Labor*. For the two remaining industries (rubber and electrical machinery) the data in that report covered four establishments or fewer, and were considered too unreliable to use. Therefore, he used the "general hours series" in these industries before 1903 as well as after.

D 877–892. Earnings and hours of construction and non-supervisory workers in selected nonmanufacturing industries, 1932–1970.

Source: See source for series D 802–810.

See also text for series D 802–810.

D 893–904. Average annual supplements to wages and salaries per full-time employee, by major industry, 1929–1970.

Source: Computed from the following: U.S. Office of Business Economics, 1929–1963, *The National Income and Product Accounts of the United States, 1929–1965, Statistical Tables*; 1964–1967, *U.S. National Income and Product Accounts, 1964–1967*; 1968–1970, U.S. Bureau of Economic Analysis, *Survey of Current Business*, July 1971, tables 6.4 and 6.7.

These figures were computed by dividing estimates of aggregate supplements to wages and salaries, by industry, by the corresponding estimates of the aggregate number of full-time equivalent employees. For discussion of estimates of full-time equivalent employees, see text for series D 739–764; for discussion of supplements to wages and salaries, see text for series D 905–912.

D 905–912. Average annual supplements to wages and salaries per full-time equivalent employee, by type of supplement, 1929–1970.

Source: See source for series D 893–904, tables 1.10, 3.8, and 6.4.

These figures were computed by dividing estimates of aggregate supplements to wages and salaries, by type, by estimates of full-time equivalent employees in all industries. For discussion of estimates of full-time equivalent employees, see text for series D 739–764. The source presents figures for a more detailed classification of supplements.

The averages shown for the different types of supplements may tend to be somewhat lower than they should be because the employment figures used to obtain the averages include employees for whom no contributions or payments were made and who would not therefore be recipients of supplemental compensation.

Data for "employer contributions for social insurance," series D 906–909, have a high degree of reliability since they are obtained almost exclusively from the accounting records of the agencies administering the programs. Estimates for "other labor income," series D 910–912, are less reliable.

Data on supplements to wages and salaries are obtained from a variety of sources. Reports filed by employers with the administrative agencies or with the U.S. Treasury are the sources of figures for employer contributions under old-age and survivors insurance, State unemployment insurance and cash sickness compensation, railroad retirement and unemployment insurance, and the Federal unemployment tax. Payments made by the Federal Government to its civilian employee retirement systems are obtained from U.S. Department of the Treasury records and the records of the administrative agencies. Estimates of Federal Government contributions made to Government life insurance programs are based on monthly reports of the Veterans Administration.

Contributions to State and local retirement systems are based on data supplied, since 1936, by the U.S. Department of Health, Education, and Welfare. Estimates for 1929–1935 are extrapolations from the 1936 figure based on a sample survey of State and local government units.

Estimates of compensation for injuries are based on data in the annual *Insurance Yearbook* (Spectator Company), on reports of State insurance funds, and on information furnished by State accident compensation commissions.

Employer contributions to private pension plans are estimated for 1945–1970 chiefly from tabulations prepared by the Internal Revenue Service. Contributions to health and welfare funds are estimated from data obtained from the Amalgamated Clothing Workers of America, the International Ladies' Garment Workers' Union, the United Mine Workers of America, and the American Telephone and Telegraph Company. Employer contributions for group insurance, series D 911, are based upon studies made by the U.S. Department of Health, Education, and Welfare and upon reports from the Institute of Life Insurance.

Data on the pay of military reservists were obtained from the Armed Services or from the annual *Budget of the United States Government*; data on Federal payments to enemy prisoners of war were obtained from the U.S. Department of Defense. Other items in "other labor income" have always been small in amount.

D 913. Annual salary of college teachers, 1929–1970.

Source: 1929–1952, George J. Stigler, *Trends in Employment in the Service Industries*, Princeton University Press, Princeton, 1956, p. 134, (copyright; reprinted by permission of Princeton University Press). 1956–1970, National Education Association (NEA), Research Report, 1960-R3, 1962-R2, and 1972-R5 (copyright © 1960, 1962, and 1972, respectively, by the National Education Association; all rights reserved).

The figures for 1929–1952 represent the average annual salary of college teachers in large public institutions. The average salary is the weighted arithmetic mean of median salaries estimated separately for the four ranks of instructional staff: Instructors, assistant professors, associate professors, and professors.

For 1929–1932, the median salaries by rank are based on Viva Boothe's *Salaries and the Cost of Living in Twenty-seven State Universities and Colleges, 1913–1932*, Ohio State University Press, 1932. For 1935–1942, 1950, and 1952, Stigler estimated median salaries by rank from data in various reports of the Office of Education. The weights used in calculating the weighted mean of the median salaries by rank were the relative numbers in each of the ranks in public universities, colleges, and professional schools in New York State as shown in annual reports of the University of the State of New York. For 1943–1949, the figures were interpolated by Stigler on the basis of expenditures on resident instruction per teacher.

Figures for 1908–1928 approximately comparable to those shown here and for median salaries for each of the four college teaching ranks for 1908–1942 appear in George J. Stigler, *Employment and Compensa-*

tion in Education, National Bureau of Economic Research, New York, 1950.

The NEA figures for 1956–1970 represent median annual salaries for all four ranks of instructional staff engaged in full-time teaching in four-year colleges and institutions. They cover the academic year of nine months—two semesters or three quarters—even when the compensation is paid over a 12-month period. The data exclude salaries paid to part-time employees and to administrative officers regardless of the amount of time they may have spent in teaching.

D 914 and D 917. Annual net income of nonsalaried lawyers, 1929–1954.

Source: U.S. Office of Business Economics, *Survey of Current Business*: 1929–1946, August 1949 issue, p. 18; 1947–1954, December 1956 issue, p. 27.

Nonsalaried lawyers are those who engage in private practice as entrepreneurs. The average shown, series D 914, is the arithmetic mean. Estimates of median net income are presented in series D 917. Net income is excess of gross receipts from legal practice over the total of the payroll, rent, and other costs of legal practice. Part-year incomes have been converted to full-year equivalents.

The estimates are based on a series of sample mail surveys of the legal profession made by the U.S. Department of Commerce. The results of the various surveys are reported in the *Survey of Current Business* for April 1938, August 1943, May 1944, August 1949, July 1952, and December 1956. These reports, particularly those of August 1949 and December 1956, contain the mean and median net income figures shown here and also, for selected years, detailed frequency distributions by size of income for nonsalaried, salaried, and part-salaried lawyers. Tabulations by various other characteristics are also shown.

D 915 and D 918. Annual net income of nonsalaried physicians, 1929–1970.

Source: 1929–1951, U.S. Office of Business Economics, *Survey of Current Business*: 1929–1949, July 1951 issue, p. 16; 1950–1951, July 1952 issue, p. 6. 1959–1970, Medical Economics Co., Oradell, N. J., *Medical Economics*, various issues (copyright © 1959–1970; reprinted by permission).

In the *Survey*, nonsalaried physician is defined as one whose sole source of medical income is from independent practice. The average shown, series D 915, is the arithmetic mean. The 1929–1951 *Survey* estimates of median net income, series D 918, are presented for linkage with the *Medical Economics* data for later years. Net income is the gross receipts from medical practice less the total of payroll, rent, supplies, equipment depreciation, and other expenses of medical practice. Part-year incomes have not been converted to full-year equivalents.

The 1929–1951 estimates of net income are based chiefly on a series of sample mail surveys of the medical profession made by the Department of Commerce. The results of the various surveys are reported in the *Survey of Current Business* for April 1938, October 1943, July 1951, and July 1952. These reports, particularly July 1951, show the mean and median net income figures shown here and also, for selected years, gross incomes and income distributions by size of income for nonsalaried, salaried, and part-salaried physicians. Tabulations by various other characteristics are also shown.

The 1959–1970 *Medical Economics* data in series D 918 relate to self-employed medical doctors under age 65; they represent income from practice after payment of tax-deductible professional expenses but before payment of income taxes.

D 916 and D 919. Annual net income of nonsalaried dentists, 1929–1970.

Source: 1929–1951, U.S. Office of Business Economics, *Survey of Current Business*: 1929–1948, January 1950 issue, p. 9; 1949–1951,

July 1952 issue, p. 6. 1952–1970, American Dental Association, Chicago, Ill., *The . . . Survey of Dental Practice* for the years 1953, 1956, 1959, 1962, 1965, 1968, and 1971 (copyright by the American Dental Association; reprinted by permission).

In the *Survey*, nonsalaried dentists are defined as those who engage in private practice as entrepreneurs. The average shown, series D 916, is the arithmetic mean. The 1929–1951 *Survey* estimates of median net income, series D 919, are presented for linkage with the American Dental Association data for later years. Net income is gross receipts from dental practice less the total of the payroll, rent, and other costs of dental practice. Part-year incomes have not been converted to full-year equivalent incomes.

The estimates of average annual net income are based on a series of sample mail surveys made by the Department of Commerce. The 1938 survey of dental incomes is reported in Herman Lasken, *Economic Conditions in the Dental Profession, 1929–37*, U.S. Department of Commerce, September 1939; the 1942 and 1949 surveys in the *Survey of Current Business*, April 1944 and January 1950, respectively. These reports contain, for selected years, mean and median net and gross incomes and detailed income distributions by size of income not only for nonsalaried dentists but also for salaried and part-salaried dentists. Tabulations by various other characteristics are also shown in the sources.

The 1952–1970 American Dental Association data cover gross income (total collected fees) minus professional expenses. Reports received from dentists who worked only part of the year are included in the survey results. In the source report, the term "independent dentists" is used for 1970 and is defined to include self-employed dentists and dentists who are shareowners of incorporated dental practices. The source states that, for practical purposes, the term "independent dentists" is equivalent to "nonsalaried dentists" used in previous dental practice surveys.

D 920. Median monthly salary rate, engineers, 1929–1970.

Source: 1929–1953, David M. Blank and George J. Stigler, *The Demand and Supply of Scientific Personnel*, National Bureau of Economic Research, New York, 1957, pp. 114 and 116 (copyright); 1956–1970, Engineering Manpower Commission of Engineers Joint Council, *Professional Income of Engineers, 1972*, New York, 1972, p. 13 (copyright).

Blank and Stigler's estimates for 1929, 1932, and 1934 were based on data obtained by the U.S. Bureau of Labor Statistics from a 1935 survey of all professional engineers in the United States who could be located. The survey placed heavy reliance on membership lists of engineering societies for its mailing list. Approximately 173,000 questionnaires were mailed and about one-third were returned with usable data. The estimates for 1939, 1943, and 1946 are for all engineers, both graduate and nongraduate, who were members of the six engineering societies of the Engineers Joint Council in May 1946. The Council obtained income data from a mail questionnaire sent to 87,000 member engineers. Approximately 47,000 questionnaires were returned. The tabulations made by the Council were based on returns from engineers who had maintained residence as civilians in the United States continuously during 1939–1946. The estimate for 1953 is for graduate engineers only and is the monthly equivalent of the annual rate given in the source used by Blank and Stigler. It is based on data obtained by the Engineers Joint Council from a sample survey of graduate engineers employed in industry and government.

Blank and Stigler give not only median monthly salary rates, but also first and third quartile monthly salary rates. In addition, other tables, particularly in appendix A, provide average income data for selected years (in some cases as far back as 1890) for engineers classified by years of experience and engineering specialization.

The data for 1956–1970 relate to salaries paid to graduate engineers 20 years after the baccalaureate degree. The 20-year medians were

selected arbitrarily as representative of engineers who had achieved a high level of experience and who were approaching their peak periods of professional activity and earning power. The annual medians shown in the source report were divided by 12 (and rounded to the nearest $10) to represent the monthly equivalent. These figures comprise base salary before deductions plus regular allowances including cost-of-living differential, if any, but not unpredictable payments for overtime work, stock options, etc.

The samples used in the biennial surveys conducted by the Engineering Manpower Commission may not be exactly comparable because of changes in the participating groups. However, according to the source report, the size of the total sample (1,109 establishments covering over 230,000 graduate engineers in 1970, or about 32 percent of all degree-holding engineers) and the consistency with which many companies and agencies have participated throughout the survey series suggest that changes in the composition of the survey group have not materially altered the reported medians.

Salary figures were reported by employers on two questionnaires designed to obtain information on earnings of all employed engineering graduates in both supervisory and nonsupervisory positions. All salary information was reported in relation to the year of baccalaureate degree as a measure of experience. The source report gives the U.S. annual medians at 2-year intervals up to 10 years after graduation and at 5-year intervals thereafter, terminating at 30 years after graduation.

D 921–926. Military annual pay rates, 1865–1970.

Source: 1865–1955, The President's Commission on Veterans' Pensions, *Veterans' Benefits in the United States*, vol. I, Staff Report No. IV, p. 79, 1956 (House Committee Print No. 261, 84th Congress, 2d session). 1960, U.S. Department of Defense, Office of the Secretary (based on the President's 1960 budget estimate); 1964 to 1970, U.S. Office of Management and Budget, unpublished data.

These rates are as of June 30 and are based on weighted averages. For enlisted men, basic pay represents only that part of the total compensation which is paid in cash. For officers, basic pay rates are supplemented by cash allowances for quarters and subsistence.

Basic pay plus allowances, series D 924–926, includes the value of quarters, food, and clothing, both in the form of cash allowances to officers and "in kind" to enlisted men. However, it does not include the value of medical care; income tax exemptions; recreational facilities; flight, combat, and other hazardous-duty pays; transportation; Government insurance benefits; etc. The omission of these latter items results in an understatement of the level of military compensation; also, to the extent that these subsidiary items have been introduced in recent years or improved in quality and extent, the upward trend in military compensation is not fully reflected. The data are not strictly comparable from year to year due to changes in coverage of allowances.

D 927–939. Labor union membership, by affiliation, 1935–1970.

Source: **Series D 927–934**, U.S. Bureau of Labor Statistics, *Handbook of Labor Statistics, 1972*, p. 332. **Series D 935–939**, Leo Troy, *Trade Union Membership, 1897–1962*, National Bureau of Economic Research, New York, 1965, p. 8 (copyright).

See also text for series D 940–951.

The following text is excerpted, with minor editorial changes, from the Troy study.

The Committee for Industrial Organization (CIO) was formed in November 1935 by eight unions affiliated with the American Federation of Labor (AFL). The new organization maintained its identity until it merged with the AFL in December 1955 as the American Federation of Labor and Congress of Industrial Organizations (AFL–CIO).

Although there are a variety of ways of defining union membership, Troy adhered, whenever possible, to the definition that only those paying dues to a union or for whom dues are paid to a federation such as the AFL, the CIO, or the AFL–CIO are members. Consequently, to the fullest possible extent, he reported union membership on a dues-paying basis.

This concept of membership has greater precision than some other concepts, but it is not ideal for all purposes. For example, to a union, total membership may include persons paying regular dues, whether in arrears or up to date in their payments; the unemployed, whether or not they pay any dues; those on strike, honorary members, persons in the Armed Forces, and retired, sick, disabled, or inactive persons. All or many of those categories may be regarded and reported by a union as membership in good standing.

Persons holding withdrawal cards are not counted as members in Troy's study. Withdrawal cards show that a member was in good standing when he left the union; therefore he is permitted to apply for reinstatement rather than required to apply as a new member.

For purposes of collective bargaining, a union may report on the number it represents. Typically, representation is larger than membership since it includes persons whom the union represents, but who are not members of the union. However, it also excludes members not in a represented unit and whom the union does include in its count of total membership.

Newly organized units may not be charged dues until a collective bargaining agreement is signed. This may show up as a lag in membership, as Troy measures it, but his count will include the newly organized once an agreement is signed and dues are collected.

For such vital purposes of determining voting rights at conventions, unions allot representation on the basis of membership dues received from locals. Thus, the International Ladies' Garment Workers, while defining a member as in good standing even though no dues are paid for 39 weeks, nevertheless changes its definition to a current dues-paying basis to count members for convention purposes.

For enumeration purposes at conventions, unions rely primarily on the average membership paying full per capita dues. The Steelworkers Union bases convention representation upon the average of the paid and exonerated membership of the local union. The United Automobile Workers allots representation at conventions by the *average* number of monthly per capita taxes paid by the local union to the international union.

For the concept of membership he adopted, Troy wanted to estimate the number of active members regularly paying either full-time or part-time dues, plus those who may temporarily not be required to pay dues because of a strike, unemployment, or other reasons recognized by the union. The method actually used, where dues receipts were available, was to divide the receipts by full-time dues per capita. This method can lead to an underestimate of a union's membership as defined above. Thus, should there be a prolonged strike during which dues are not collected, the estimate will underreport the membership for the period. Furthermore, union reports of dues receipts sometimes include amounts obtained at reduced rates from unemployed, retired, or honorary members, and also include dues paid for only part of a year. But, since the annual total is divided by the full-time rate, the estimate will be less than the total number of individuals who were members at some time during the year, though it will exceed the number who paid a full year's dues.

Two general methods of estimating total union membership have been used by the Bureau of Labor Statistics. Prior to 1951, the BLS derived its series by aggregating reports of the AFL and the CIO, to which were added estimates of independent membership derived from a number of sources. Membership by individual union in the BLS series is therefore not available before 1951. Since 1951, the BLS has compiled an annual series on total membership based primarily on replies of individual unions to biennial questionnaires. BLS figures of membership by union became available in 1951 and thereafter in alternate years beginning in 1954.

Basically, the BLS obtained its data from questionnaires which requested the correspondent union to report the average annual dues-paying membership, but it is likely that what was reported was not dues-paying as defined by Troy. If a union failed to respond, the BLS filled the gap with estimates taken from other sources. Troy

relied primarily on financial reports to obtain dues-paying membership but, like the BLS, used other sources when the necessary information was unavailable.

When the two methods of preparing membership figures are compared, the BLS figures are nearly always larger. It appears that the BLS often obtained membership figures that were rounded upward or inflated for prestige or strategic reasons, or that included members exempted from all or part of their dues because of unemployment, retirement, strikes, or other reasons. Representation figures, which include workers who are not members but are represented in collective bargaining by the union, also appear to be reported to the BLS, and these, too, usually exceed actual membership.

Differences in coverage account for only minor discrepancies between the BLS and NBER series. With the exception of one organization added to the BLS list of national unions in 1960, the Truck Drivers, Chauffeurs and Helpers Union of Chicago and Vicinity (membership for 1960 reported by the BLS as 9,770), both series include the same national and international unions. The new addition came too late for inclusion in the NBER series. On the other hand, Troy's totals include estimates for about fifty local and regional independent unions with a membership of about 140,000, and about half of these are not included in the BLS series.

Organizations excluded by the BLS are those which do not meet its definition of a national union. From time to time, a union qualifies or fails to qualify, and as a result is added to or dropped from the BLS directory. For example, the Industrial Trades Union was reported by the BLS as a national union in its directory covering the year 1951 and then dropped from subsequent directories, although the union continued to function. After 1951, it apparently lost contracts with employers outside the State of Rhode Island (where the union is largely concentrated), and did not meet the BLS definition of a national union.

In contrast, once Troy obtained information on a union and had some indication that it continued to function, it was retained in his series. Thus the Industrial Trades Union is included in the NBER series after 1951.

D 940–941. Total union membership, 1897–1934.

Source: See source for series D 942–945.

Series D 940 is the sum of series D 943 and D 945; series D 941 is the sum of series D 944 and D 945.

D 942–945. Unions and membership of American Federation of Labor, and membership in independent or unaffiliated unions, 1897–1934.

Source: *Proceedings*, 65th Convention of the American Federation of Labor (AFL), 1946, p. 43; Lewis L. Lorwin, *The American Federation of Labor*, Brookings Institution, Washington, 1933, p. 488 (copyright); *Proceedings* of the AFL. Conventions of 1897, 1898, and 1933–34; and Leo Wolman, *Ebb and Flow in Trade Unionism*, National Bureau of Economic Research, New York, 1936 (copyright).

D 943 represents "total paid membership of the affiliated national and international organizations and directly chartered trade and federal labor unions" based on "the actual per capita tax" remitted by affiliated unions. Such per capita tax payments can and frequently do cover either fewer or more members than the affiliated union reports in its own statements.

Total membership in series D 944 differs from that in series D 943 because series D 944 uses the direct reports of affiliated unions where available in preference to the membership indicated by per capita tax payments.

D 945, membership of independent and unaffiliated unions, covers national and international unions not affiliated with the AFL. It excludes independent unions that are purely local in character or whose jurisdiction is confined to the employees of a single employer. In most years about half the workers covered by this series were members of the four brotherhoods of workers in the railroad train and engine service.   This series is from Wolman, cited above, pp. 138–139, adjusted in 1929–1934 to include the membership of the Trade Union Unity League.   For 1932 and 1934, the membership of the Trade Union Unity League has been interpolated from figures for adjacent years.

For Wolman's estimates of union membership by industry, see series D 952–969.   Annual estimates of the membership of individual national and international unions for 1897–1934 may be found in Wolman's book cited above and in his *The Growth of American Trade Unions, 1880–1923*, National Bureau of Economic Research, 1924.

D 946–951.   Labor union membership and membership as percent of total labor force and of nonagricultural employment, 1930–1970.

Source: U.S. Bureau of Labor Statistics (BLS), *Handbook of Labor Statistics, 1972*, p. 333.

See also text for series D 940–945.

D 946, total union membership, is a continuation of series D 940. For 1935–1947, the membership of AFL–CIO unions is based on per capita taxes; the membership of independent unions was estimated by BLS from fragmentary data.   For 1948, 1949, and 1950, the figure shown is the midpoint of an estimated range of 14 million to 16 million. For 1951 and 1952, the figure shown is the midpoint of an estimated range of 16.5 million to 17 million.   These ranges are based on membership data from surveys of national and international unions made by BLS.   The level of the series may be more accurate during 1948–1952 than during 1939–1947.   Prior to 1947, the series seems to include substantially inflated membership claims of some unions. The year-to-year movement of this series from 1947–1953 and, in particular, the drop in membership from 1947–1948 should not be considered as reliable.

Beginning 1953, estimates are based on biennial surveys of national and international unions.   (See BLS *Directory of National and International Labor Unions in the United States*, for odd-numbered years from 1953 to 1971.)   The figures also include the members of directly chartered local labor unions affiliated with the AFL–CIO and members of unaffiliated national unions.   The *Directory* also gives membership by sex, white-collar occupations, industry, and State, and discusses aspects of union administration and activities.

The 1971 BLS *Directory of National Unions and Employee Associations* included, with its union membership count, members of professional and State employee associations engaging in collective bargaining.   Combined union and association membership for 1970 yields (for series D 946) 22,558,000, (D 947) 1,371,000, (D 948) 21,243,000, (D 949) 24.7 percent, (D 950) 70,644,000, and (D 951) 30.1 percent.

D 947, Canadian membership of U.S. unions, is from the Department of Labour of Canada, except for even-numbered years beginning in 1954 which are from the BLS directories as cited.

D 948–949, union membership, excluding Canada, is obtained by subtracting series D 947 from D 946.   The year-to-year movement for 1947–1953 is unreliable for the reasons given above for series D 946.   A better estimate might be obtained for these years by holding the percentage in series D 951 constant at 34.0 and by applying this figure to series D 950.

D 950, nonagricultural employment.   See series D 127–141.

D 951, union membership (excluding Canada) as a percent of employees in nonagricultural establishments is computed from series D 948 and D 950.   Wolman (see series D 940–945) has also estimated for three decennial census years the number of trade union members, exclusive of Canada, as a percentage of the total number of nonagricultural employees.   These percentages are 9.9 in 1910, 19.4 in 1920, and 10.2 in 1930.   The percentage shown for 1930 in series D 951 is larger than the corresponding percentage given by Wolman because his estimated union membership figure, exclusive of Canada (3,190,000), is smaller than that shown in series D 948, and also because his nonagricultural employment estimate (30,247,000), based on census data, is larger than the number of employees in nonagricultural establishments shown in series D 950.   Wolman's figure

excludes many salaried professional and managerial workers included in series D 950, and includes domestic servants, who are excluded from series D 950.

D 952–969.   Labor union membership, by industry, 1897–1934.

Source: Leo Wolman, *Ebb and Flow in Trade Unionism*, National Bureau of Economic Research, New York, 1936, pp. 172–193 (copyright).

These figures were obtained by classifying national and international unions into industrial categories and totaling the membership of the unions in each category in each year.

In the latter part of the period, series D 969, "Miscellaneous," consists largely of two unions, the Firemen and Oilers and the Operating Engineers.   The Industrial Workers of the World is included from 1905–1914, and is the largest union in the series for some years. The Horseshoers are important in the early years, declining rapidly in the 1920's.   Unions affiliated with the Trade Union Unity League in 1929–1934 are excluded.

Some errors of classification arise when a union has membership in more than one category.   For example, the Meat Cutters and Butcher Workmen, classified in food, liquor, and tobacco had many members in retail meat stores; the Operating Engineers, classified as miscellaneous, had many members in building construction.   These problems are less important in 1897–1934 than they would be in recent years.

The source gives annual estimates of the percentage distribution of union membership by industrial categories.   For 1910, 1920, and 1930, it gives estimates of the percentage of employees organized in each of the industrial categories shown here, and in more detailed categories.

D 970–985.   Work stoppages, workers involved, man-days idle, major issues, and average duration, 1881–1970.

Source: U.S. Bureau of Labor Statistics (BLS), *Handbook of Labor Statistics, 1972*.

Work stoppages include strikes and lockouts.   A strike is defined as a temporary stoppage of work by a group of employees to express a grievance or to enforce a demand.   A lockout is defined as a temporary withholding of work from a group of employees by an employer (or a group of employers) to enforce acceptance of the employer's terms.   Most work stoppages are strikes rather than lockouts. Strikes involving fewer than six workers or lasting less than a full shift, strikes of American seamen in foreign ports, and strikes of foreign crews on foreign ships in American ports are excluded.

Figures for workers involved include all workers made idle in the establishment where the stoppage occurs, even though they may not all be participants in the controversy.   The figures exclude indirect or secondary idleness in other establishments which suspend or curtail operations because of shortages of materials or services resulting from a stoppage.   The number of workers involved is the number on the day of maximum idleness; however, the figures for man-days idle, series D 973, take into account variations in the number idle during the strike and include all days on which work was scheduled.

The duration of stoppages, series D 981, is counted in calendar days rather than working days.   Strikes that are never formally settled are considered ended when a majority of vacant jobs are filled, whether by former strikers or by others, or when the establishment affected is permanently closed.

The classification of causes of strikes, series D 978–980 and D 983–985, necessarily lacks precision, since many strikes involve more than one issue.   In particular, strikes for union organization often involve demands concerning wages or hours.

In computing the number of workers involved in strikes as a percent of total employment and idleness as a percent of total working time, the following employment figures were used: From 1927 to 1950, all employees were counted, except those in occupations and professions in which little, if any, union organization existed or in which stoppages rarely, if ever, occurred. From 1951 to 1966, BLS estimates of total employment in nonagricultural establishments, exclusive of government, were used. Beginning in 1967, two measures of employment have been used. One is the former series of non-agricultural employment (exclusive of government), which is used to calculate "private nonfarm" working time. The second measure—working time in the "total economy"—is the BLS estimate of nonagricultural employment (including government) plus agricultural wage and salaried workers. The total economy measure was recomputed to 1939.

Estimated working time is computed by multiplying the average number of workers employed each year by the days worked by most employees during the year. To facilitate comparisons, the private nonfarm series was recalculated for all years beginning with 1950.

Unions are involved in the great majority of work stoppages. In 1970, no union was involved in 95 of 5,716 stoppages, accounting for 7,900 workers of the 3,305,000 involved in work stoppages during the year. For some purposes, therefore, workers involved in strikes as a percent of union membership is a more useful statistic than workers involved as a percent of all workers.

Data for 1881–1886 were first published in the *Third Annual Report of the Commissioner of Labor, 1887.* This report also gives fragmentary information for earlier years. Data for 1887–1894 are given in the *Tenth Annual Report, 1894*; for 1895–1900, in the *Sixteenth Annual Report, 1901*; and for 1900–1905, in the *Twenty-first Annual Report, 1906.* References to strikes and lockouts during 1881–1905 were located by the Bureau of Labor by examination of the daily and trade press. Agents of the Bureau then collected data from the parties involved.

No government agency collected data on work stoppages for 1906–1913. For 1914–1915, BLS collected data on the number of stoppages and major issues. For 1916–1926, the count of stoppages was made from press notices, and questionnaires were sent to determine the number of workers involved. This number was reported for only about two-thirds of the known stoppages.

Methods of compiling the series have been fairly uniform since 1927. Information on the existence of a stoppage is obtained from press clippings from a large number of newspapers throughout the country and from reports from unions, employers, and a number of Federal and State agencies. Improvement in the sources of these "leads," especially through State employment security agencies, increased the number of strikes reported over previous years and the number of workers involved and man-days idle. When the existence of a strike is known, a questionnaire is mailed to the parties reported as involved to obtain data on the number of workers involved, duration, issues, etc. In some instances, field representatives of the BLS call on the parties.

D 986–1021. Work stoppages, by major industry group, 1937–1970.

Source: U.S. Bureau of Labor Statistics, *Analysis of Work Stoppages*, annual issues.

See text for series D 970–985.

D 1022–1028. Average monthly labor turnover rates in manufacturing, by class of turnover, 1919–1970.

Source: U.S. Bureau of Labor Statistics (BLS), 1919–1929, *Monthly Labor Review*, July 1929, pp. 64–65; 1930–1970, *Employment and Earnings, United States, 1909–1971*, Bulletin 1312-8, table 8.

The figures for 1919–1929 are those of the Metropolitan Life Insurance Company which pioneered in collecting labor turnover data on a regular basis, beginning in January 1926. Subsequently, the Company secured data that enabled it to estimate turnover rates monthly back to January 1919.

The Company obtained its turnover data by means of a mail questionnaire sent monthly to reporting firms. (The sample of reporting firms, 160 in November 1926, had grown to 350 by mid-1929.) Each firm was asked to report each month: (1) The daily average number of employees on the payroll, and the total number of (2) accessions, (3) voluntary quits, (4) discharges, and (5) layoffs during the month. The accession rate for each company was computed by dividing the total number of accessions during the month by the daily average number on the payroll during the month. The composite or average accession rate for all reporting firms was the unweighted median of the accession rates computed for individual firms. The annual average was the arithmetic mean of the 12 monthly median accession rates. Discharges, quits, and layoffs were handled in a similar fashion. (The total separation rate, however, was computed as the sum of the median discharge rate, the median quit rate, and the median layoff rate.)

The figures for 1919–1929 are stated as equivalent annual rates rather than monthly rates. They have been converted in series D 1022–1027 to monthly rates by dividing by 12.

In July 1929, BLS took over the work of the Metropolitan Life Insurance Company. At that time approximately 350 large manufacturers employed 700,000 workers in the sample of reporting firms. Over the years the list of cooperating firms has grown greatly, the amount of industry detail has expanded, and methods of computation have been somewhat changed.

BLS turnover rate estimates are based on reports made monthly on a mail questionnaire by a sample of cooperating firms. In 1970, the sample covered approximately 38,000 establishments in manufacturing employing nearly 10.4 million workers. The reporting firms are considerably larger on the average than all firms within the population sampled. This large-firm bias may cause underestimation of turnover rates. Furthermore, the BLS sample of manufacturing firms and its estimates of turnover for manufacturing exclude printing, publishing, and allied industries (since April 1943); canning and preserving fruits, vegetables, and seafoods; women's and misses' outerwear; and fertilizers. The last three industries tend to have exceptionally high turnover rates seasonally. Plants experiencing work stoppages are excluded.

Each cooperating firm is asked to report each month: (1) Total accessions, (2) new hires, (3) other accessions, (4) total separations, (5) quits, (6) layoffs, (7) discharges, (8) other separations, and (9) the total number of employees who worked or received pay for any part of the payroll period which includes the 12th of the month. Prior to 1940, "miscellaneous" separations were included with "quits." Since January 1943 the labor turnover rates pertain to all employees; before that date the rates were for production workers only. Furthermore, before October 1945 the employment base was the average of the number of employees on the payroll the last day of the preceding month and the last day of the current month. The effect of changing the employment base to the number on the payroll for the period including the 12th of the month was negligible. Layoffs are terminations of employment for more than a week, initiated by management, without prejudice to the worker. Discharges are terminations of employment by management for cause (incompetence, laziness, etc.). Quits are terminations of employment initiated by employees; they include unauthorized absences of more than a week. Miscellaneous separations are terminations of employment for military duty of over 30 days and separations other than those itemized (deaths, retirements, etc.).

D 1029. Work-injury frequency rates in manufacturing, 1926–1970.

Source: U.S. Bureau of Labor Statistics (BLS), 1926–1949 and 1958–1970, *Handbook of Labor Statistics*, 1950 and 1972 editions; 1950–1952, *Work Injuries in the United States, 1950*, and subsequent annual issues; 1953–1957, U.S. Department of Labor, news releases.

The Bureau of Labor Statistics' first continuing compilation of injury-rate statistics began in 1910 for the iron and steel industry. In 1925, the injury-rate compilations were expanded to cover 24 industries. In 1952, the compilations covered over 200 manufacturing and nonmanufacturing industry classifications. At present (1970) the survey provides injury-frequency rates for 490 manufacturing and 180 nonmanufacturing categories.

Efforts to standardize the compilation of work-injury statistics were initiated by BLS in 1911 and resulted in 1920 in the first standardized procedures. In 1926, the American Engineering Standards Committee, later the American Standards Association, undertook a revision of these procedures. Their work led to the publication in 1937 of the first American Standard Method of Compiling Industrial Injury Rates. This standard was revised in 1954 and again in 1967.

The standard injury-frequency rate is the average number of disabling injuries per million man-hours worked. A disabling injury is an injury incurred in the course of and arising out of employment, which results in death or permanent physical impairment, or renders the injured person unable to perform any regularly established job, open and available to him, during the entire time interval corresponding to the hours of his regular shift on one or more days after the injury.

The BLS annual injury-rate estimates are based on a sample mail survey conducted once a year. Cooperating firms are asked to report for all employees (1) average employment, (2) aggregate man-hours worked by all employees, (3) aggregate number of disabling work injuries by extent of disability, and (4) time lost because of disabilities. The manufacturing sample covers approximately 50,000 establishments. The injury-rate series for manufacturing excludes petroleum refining, smelting and refining of nonferrous metals, cement and lime manufacturing, and coke production, which are covered in similar surveys conducted by the Bureau of Mines (see text for series D 1030–1034).

Prior to 1936, the data in series D 1029 are based on surveys covering only wage earners in 30 manufacturing industries. Since 1936 the data refer to all employees in all manufacturing industries. Separate injury-frequency rates have been computed since 1936 for component industries by dividing aggregate injuries by aggregate man-hours in reporting establishments. In computing the average rate for all manufacturing the separate averages for the component industries are weighted by estimated total employment in these industries. Before 1936 the weights implicitly were aggregate man-hours in the reporting firms in each industry.

D 1030–1034. Work-injury frequency rates in mining, 1924–1970.

Source: U.S. Bureau of Mines, *Minerals Yearbook*, 1970, and earlier annual issues.

Except for coal mining since 1941, the Bureau of Mines estimates of work-injury frequency rates in "mining" industries are based on reports made voluntarily by mining establishments. Coal mining firms since 1941 have been obliged by Federal law to report work-injury and related data to the Bureau of Mines.

D 1035–1036. Work-injury frequency rates on Class I railroads, 1922–1970.

Source: U.S. Federal Railroad Administration (prior to 1966, Interstate Commerce Commission), *Accident Bulletin*, various issues.

Both series exclude work injuries suffered by employees of Class I switching and terminal companies after 1932. They are based on monthly accident reports that the Class I railroads are required by Federal law to make to the Federal Railroad Administration. The two series thus result from essentially complete censuses of man-hours worked and of reportable work injuries.

Before 1936 a reportable work-injury was either a fatality or a nonfatal injury to an employee "sufficient to incapacitate him from performing his ordinary duties for more than 3 days in the aggregate in the 10 days immediately following the accident." Series D 1036 includes only such work-injuries. From 1936 through 1956, the railroads were required to report work injuries incapacitating employees for 1–3 days immediately following an accident as well as more serious injuries. Series D 1035 is series D 1036 plus the average work-injury frequency rate for "1–3 day" injuries.

In an effort to narrow the field of reportable accidents while conforming with the intent of the Accident Reports Act, significant changes, affecting the reportability of certain types of railroad accidents, were made in Rules Governing Monthly Reports of Railroad Accidents, effective January 1, 1957. Minor revisions of these rules have been made from time-to-time. Therefore, data for accidents occurring prior to 1957 are not necessarily comparable with those for later years.

The concept of "disabling injury" underlying series D 1029–1034 is essentially the same as that underlying series D 1035. Series D 1036, which excludes "1–3 day" injuries, is not comparable to series D 1029–1034 in level, and series D 1035 also tends to have a downward bias in trend relative to series D 1029–1034. It has been included to indicate at least crudely the trend in the average injury-frequency rates on Class I railroads before 1936.

Both series cover all employees of Class I railroads. The man-hour base of both series is the aggregate number of straight-time hours actually worked and overtime hours paid for in millions of man-hours. Days worked by daily-rated employees have been converted to man-hours worked by multiplying days worked by 8. The average injury-frequency rate is the ratio of the aggregate number of work-injuries to the man-hour base.

★ ★ ★ ★ ★ ★ ★ ★ ★   **More Recent Data for *Historical Statistics* Series**   ★ ★ ★ ★ ★ ★ ★ ★ ★

Statistics for more recent years in continuation of many of the still-active series shown here appear in annual issues of the *Statistical Abstract of the United States*, beginning with the 1975 edition. For direct linkage of the historical series to the tables in the *Abstract*, see Appendix I in the *Abstract*.

Series D 683–688. Indexes of Employee Output (NBER): 1869 to 1969

[NBER = National Bureau of Economic Research]

Year	1958 = 100				1958 dollars		Year	1958 = 100				1958 dollars	
	Output per man-hour [1]	Nonfarm output per man-hour [2]	Manufacturing output per man-hour	Farm output per man-hour	Output per employee [3]	Output per person engaged [4]		Output per man-hour [1]	Nonfarm output per man-hour [2]	Manufacturing output per man-hour	Farm output per man-hour	Output per employee [3]	Output per person engaged [4]
	683	684	685	686	687	688		683	684	685	686	687	688
1969	136.4	----------	145.7	177.5	----------	----------	1925	44.5	50.1	45.6	34.9	$4,218	$3,934
1968	135.3	----------	142.0	164.6	----------	----------	1924	44.6	50.5	42.8	33.7	4,256	3,950
1967	131.3	----------	135.0	163.5	----------	----------	1923	42.7	47.5	40.2	34.7	4,101	3,768
1966	129.5	127.1	134.2	149.4	$9,190	$9,435	1922	40.3	45.4	41.8	33.0	3,871	3,525
							1921	40.7	46.6	36.9	32.2	3,899	3,513
1965	125.7	123.8	131.0	144.2	8,930	9,190							
1964	121.6	120.3	125.6	131.7	8,635	8,855	1920	38.1	43.0	32.0	31.3	3,774	3,402
1963	117.4	116.3	121.5	128.7	8,386	8,522	1919	38.4	43.1	30.2	31.9	3,713	3,388
1962	113.5	113.0	116.6	118.2	8,188	8,247	1918	36.0	40.1	31.7	31.3	3,607	3,259
1961	108.5	107.8	112.6	115.8	7,841	7,845	1917	33.3	35.7	31.7	33.1	3,525	3,123
							1916	35.1	38.6	34.1	31.2	3,676	3,308
1960	104.9	104.7	108.8	106.5	7,705	7,647							
1959	103.5	103.5	106.2	101.1	7,640	7,535	1915	32.7	34.8	34.7	34.2	3,382	3,085
1958	100.0	100.0	100.0	100.0	7,367	7,196	1914	31.4	33.9	30.7	31.9	3,279	3,015
1957	97.2	97.6	98.8	89.8	7,292	7,068	1913	33.6	37.1	30.6	29.9	3,482	3,238
1956	94.6	95.6	96.5	84.6	7,207	6,976	1912	32.5	34.8	29.2	33.1	3,425	3,159
							1911	31.9	35.3	25.4	28.9	3,384	3,103
1955	94.2	95.9	94.9	81.0	7,236	6,976							
1954	89.9	91.2	88.3	80.1	6,924	6,587	1910	31.3	33.9	26.6	31.0	3,317	3,051
1953	87.4	88.8	86.9	76.6	6,830	6,467	1909	31.9	35.0	26.9	30.4	3,347	3,100
1952	83.5	85.6	83.0	68.0	6,586	6,246	1908	29.7	32.1	23.8	31.1	3,146	2,897
1951	82.0	85.1	81.3	62.3	6,497	6,132	1907	31.2	33.9	25.5	30.7	3,316	3,094
							1906	31.3	33.7	26.4	32.2	3,325	3,117
1950	80.1	83.8	81.4	61.9	6,308	6,000							
1949	74.0	78.4	74.9	54.3	5,958	5,601	1905	29.1	31.3	26.1	30.7	3,146	2,898
1948	71.4	74.8	72.1	56.2	5,955	5,430	1904	28.4	30.6	26.0	30.5	3,041	2,820
1947	68.7	72.8	69.6	49.6	5,920	5,292	1903	28.4	30.6	24.8	29.9	3,108	2,848
1946	68.7	73.3	65.8	51.4	6,060	5,418	1902	27.8	30.1	25.6	29.1	3,030	2,793
							1901	28.9	31.6	24.4	29.5	3,093	2,890
1945	70.7	76.8	71.5	47.9	6,807	5,892							
1944	67.2	72.7	72.5	47.6	6,439	5,800	1900	27.0	29.0	22.9	29.8	2,873	2,695
1943	63.0	67.4	73.4	47.9	5,769	5,395	1899	26.6	28.6	23.7	29.8	2,903	2,667
1942	62.0	66.7	72.4	49.9	5,487	5,168	1898	26.1	27.9	24.6	30.0	2,890	2,585
1941	61.8	67.2	71.2	47.7	5,355	5,003	1897	25.7	27.7	22.2	28.9	2,965	2,565
							1896	24.1	25.9	21.3	27.2	2,763	2,402
1940	58.5	66.1	68.7	42.7	4,998	4,695							
1939	56.9	63.6	65.4	44.2	4,803	4,490	1895	24.6	27.4	22.5	25.5	2,858	2,469
1938	54.7	61.4	59.9	43.3	4,587	4,241	1894	23.2	25.8	21.1	24.2	2,764	2,310
1937	53.1	59.7	60.7	40.3	4,603	4,282	1893	23.0	25.5	20.1	23.6	2,687	2,334
1936	53.2	60.2	61.6	37.0	4,560	4,194	1892	24.0	26.7	21.4	24.4	2,636	2,447
							1891	22.6	24.3	21.2	25.9	2,523	2,295
1935	50.6	57.7	61.2	39.2	4,230	3,852							
1934	49.0	55.9	57.4	36.2	3,998	3,609	1890	22.2	23.9	21.2	25.1		2,251
1933	44.5	50.4	54.9	38.9	3,891	3,539	1889	21.2	22.2	20.5	25.8		2,158
1932	45.4	51.6	50.5	39.8	3,935	3,616	1884 [5]	21.8	23.9	(NA)	(NA)	----------	2,183
1931	47.2	53.3	54.0	39.5	4,196	3,935	1879	(NA)	(NA)	16.2	23.9	----------	(NA)
							1874 [6]	16.0	15.8	(NA)	(NA)	----------	1,613
1930	46.8	52.5	52.3	35.6	4,215	3,994							
1929	48.6	54.1	52.0	37.3	4,444	4,260	1869	----------	----------	14.7	20.1	----------	----------
1928	46.5	52.0	49.7	36.3	4,422	4,118							
1927	46.5	51.6	47.6	37.2	4,398	4,113							
1926	45.7	51.4	46.5	34.8	4,359	4,079							

NA Not available.
[1] For total private domestic economy.
[2] For nonfarm business economy.
[3] Derived by dividing gross national product (in 1958 dollars) by total employment.
[4] Derived by dividing gross private domestic product by persons engaged in the private domestic economy.
[5] Decade average, 1879–1888.
[6] Decade average, 1869–1878.

Series D 689–704. Indexes of Output, Man-Hours, Compensation Per Man-Hour, and Unit Labor Cost (BLS): 1947 to 1970

[1967 = 100. BLS = Bureau of Labor Statistics]

Year	Output (GNP) [1]				Man-hours [2]				Compensation per man-hour [3]				Unit labor cost			
	Total	Nonfarm industries			Total	Nonfarm industries			Total	Nonfarm industries			Total	Nonfarm industries		
		Total	Manufacturing	Nonmanufacturing		Total	Manufacturing	Nonmanufacturing		Total	Manufacturing	Nonmanufacturing		Total	Manufacturing	Nonmanufacturing
	689	690	691	692	693	694	695	696	697	698	699	700	701	702	703	704
1970	106.8	107.1	105.7	107.8	102.4	103.5	98.1	106.0	124.0	122.7	121.6	123.9	118.9	118.6	112.9	121.9
1969	107.5	107.8	109.9	106.7	104.0	104.9	103.6	105.6	115.6	114.7	114.1	115.2	111.9	111.6	107.5	114.0
1968	104.8	105.1	106.7	104.2	101.8	102.1	101.9	102.2	107.6	107.3	107.2	107.3	104.6	104.3	102.3	105.3
1967	100.0	100.0	100.0	100.0	100.0	100.0	100.0	100.0	100.0	100.0	100.0	100.0	100.0	100.0	100.0	100.0
1966	97.7	97.9	100.1	96.7	99.7	99.5	100.2	99.1	94.5	94.6	95.3	94.2	96.5	96.2	95.5	96.5
1965	91.8	91.5	92.7	90.9	97.4	96.3	94.3	97.2	88.4	89.2	91.2	88.3	93.8	93.9	92.8	94.4
1964	86.2	85.9	84.5	86.6	94.5	92.9	89.4	94.6	84.9	86.1	89.0	84.8	93.1	93.2	94.1	92.7
1963	81.5	80.9	79.0	81.9	92.9	90.9	87.7	92.3	80.8	82.2	85.0	80.9	92.1	92.3	94.4	91.2
1962	78.2	77.6	75.2	78.9	92.4	89.8	86.9	91.2	77.7	79.3	82.3	77.9	91.8	91.8	95.0	91.2
1961	73.2	72.5	68.3	74.6	90.6	87.7	83.5	89.6	74.4	76.3	79.0	75.2	92.1	92.3	96.5	90.2

See footnotes at end of table.

Series D 689–704.   Indexes of Output, Man-Hours, Compensation Per Man-Hour, and Unit Labor Cost (BLS): 1947 to 1970—Con.

[1967 = 100.   BLS = Bureau of Labor Statistics]

Year	Output (GNP) [1]				Man-hours [2]				Compensation per man-hour [3]				Unit labor cost			
	Total	Nonfarm industries			Total	Nonfarm industries			Total	Nonfarm industries			Total	Nonfarm industries		
		Total	Manufacturing	Nonmanufacturing		Total	Manufacturing	Nonmanufacturing		Total	Manufacturing	Nonmanufacturing		Total	Manufacturing	Nonmanufacturing
	689	690	691	692	693	694	695	696	697	698	699	700	701	702	703	704
1960	71.9	71.1	68.6	72.5	92.0	88.6	85.8	89.9	71.7	73.9	76.6	72.6	91.8	92.0	95.9	90.0
1959	70.2	69.5	67.6	70.4	91.2	87.6	86.1	88.3	69.0	71.0	73.5	69.7	89.8	89.5	93.7	87.3
1958	65.6	64.8	60.2	67.2	88.4	84.5	80.9	86.1	66.0	68.1	70.6	67.0	88.9	88.7	94.9	85.9
1957	66.5	65.7	65.5	65.9	92.3	87.9	88.1	87.8	63.3	65.5	67.7	64.3	87.9	87.6	91.1	85.7
1956	65.6	64.7	65.3	64.4	93.7	88.4	89.5	87.9	59.5	62.0	63.9	60.8	85.0	84.7	87.6	82.9
1955	64.3	63.4	65.0	62.5	92.1	86.1	88.2	85.2	55.9	58.6	60.0	57.6	80.1	79.6	81.4	78.4
1954	59.3	58.3	58.2	58.3	88.6	82.6	83.7	82.2	54.5	56.6	57.8	55.9	81.5	80.3	83.2	78.8
1953	60.1	59.1	62.6	57.3	92.0	85.9	91.6	83.2	52.9	54.9	55.3	54.2	81.0	79.7	80.9	78.7
1952	57.2	56.3	57.8	55.5	91.2	84.1	87.3	82.6	49.8	52.0	52.4	51.5	79.4	77.6	79.1	76.6
1951	55.8	55.0	56.5	54.1	90.7	82.9	85.9	81.5	46.9	49.3	49.3	49.1	76.3	74.3	74.8	73.9
1950	52.5	51.3	51.3	51.4	87.9	79.0	79.8	78.6	42.8	45.3	44.7	45.7	71.7	69.7	69.5	69.9
1949	47.6	46.4	44.2	47.6	86.2	76.0	73.7	77.1	40.1	43.0	42.6	43.3	72.5	70.3	71.0	70.0
1948	47.8	46.5	46.9	46.3	89.2	79.1	80.9	78.2	39.5	41.8	40.7	42.3	73.7	71.0	70.3	71.4
1947	45.6	44.5	44.7	44.5	88.8	78.0	81.5	76.4	36.2	38.3	37.1	38.9	70.6	67.1	67.7	66.9

[1] Refers to gross national product in 1958 prices.
[2] Hours of all persons in private industry engaged in production; includes man-hours of proprietors and unpaid family workers.

[3] Wages and salaries of employees plus employers' contribution for social insurance and private benefit plans. Also includes an estimate of wages, salaries, and supplemental payments for the self-employed.

Series D 705–714.   Farm Laborers—Average Monthly Earnings With Board, by Geographic Divisions: 1818 to 1948

[For composition of divisions, see text for series A 172–194]

Year	United States	New England	Middle Atlantic	East North Central	West North Central	South Atlantic	East South Central	West South Central	Mountain	Pacific
	705	706	707	708	709	710	711	712	713	714
1948	$91.00	$104.00	$99.00	$101.00	$107.00	$57.00	$49.00	$73.00	$129.00	$158.00
1940	28.05	33.54	30.00	29.40	28.12	17.46	16.34	19.61	36.11	42.84
1929	40.40	50.93	45.72	41.73	42.10	25.23	23.28	27.67	49.96	59.90
1919	41.52	46.16	41.17	42.21	50.81	30.23	29.09	36.19	59.20	65.30
1909	21.30	25.82	22.21	23.59	26.47	14.64	15.05	17.33	34.34	34.28
1899	14.56	18.20	15.98	16.90	18.04	9.32	10.72	11.86	26.33	25.10
1890	13.93	17.78	15.76	15.92	15.84	9.46	10.58	12.84	21.67	22.64
1880	11.70	13.94	13.71	15.48	14.88	8.81	10.16	12.90	24.74	24.77
1870	16.57	19.84	17.89	16.94	17.10	9.95	12.78	14.05	-----	29.19
1860	13.66	14.73	12.75	13.79	13.76	11.08	14.06	15.53	-----	34.16
1850	10.85	12.98	11.17	11.44	12.00	8.20	9.60	11.28	-----	68.00
1830	8.85	11.60	8.52	8.73	10.15	7.16	9.37	-----	-----	-----
1826	8.83	11.65	8.38	8.73	10.15	7.18	9.39	-----	-----	-----
1818	9.45	11.90	9.82	8.86	10.15	8.10	10.36	-----	-----	-----

Series D 715–717.   Average Daily Wage Rates of Artisans, Laborers, and Agricultural Workers, in the Philadelphia Area: 1785 to 1830

Year	Artisans	Laborers	Agricultural workers, male	Year	Artisans	Laborers	Agricultural workers, male	Year	Artisans	Laborers	Agricultural workers, male
	715	716	717		715	716	717		715	716	717
1830	$1.73	$1.00	-----	1815	$1.91	$1.00	$.40	1800	$1.64	$1.00	-----
1829	1.80	1.00	$.50	1814	1.63	1.00	.50	1799	1.62	1.00	-----
1828	1.74	1.00	-----	1813	1.52	1.00	.40–.67	1798	1.57	1.00	$.40
1827	1.73	1.00	.40	1812	1.58	1.00	-----	1797	1.83	1.00	-----
1826	1.70	1.00	-----	1811	1.77	1.00	.365	1796	1.74	1.00	-----
1825	1.74	1.00	.40	1810	1.72	1.00	.40	1795	1.66	1.00	-----
1824	1.55	1.00	.40	1809	1.56	1.00	.40	1794	1.39	1.00	-----
1823	1.47	1.00	-----	1808	1.47	.75	.40	1793	1.25	.80	-----
1822	1.65	.75	.30–.40	1807	1.68	1.00	.40–.50	1792	1.00	.66	-----
1821	1.37	.75	.40	1806	1.66	1.00	.40	1791	1.05	.53	-----
1820	1.55	-----	.40	1805	1.57	1.00	-----	1790	1.01	.50	-----
1819	1.63	1.00	-----	1804	1.60	1.00	-----	1789	1.00	.50–.53	-----
1818	1.86	1.00	.40	1803	1.43	.75	-----	1788	.97	-----	-----
1817	1.71	1.00	-----	1802	1.31	.75	.40–.41	1787	1.00	.53	-----
1816	1.89	1.00	-----	1801	1.55	1.00	.40–.47	1786	1.00	-----	-----
								1785	1.33	.67–.72	-----

Series D 718–721. Daily Wage Rates on the Erie Canal: 1828 to 1881

Year	Common labor 718	Carpenters 719	Masons 720	Teamwork 721	Year	Common labor 718	Carpenters 719	Masons 720	Teamwork 721	Year	Common labor 718	Carpenters 719	Masons 720	Teamwork 721
1881	$1.25	$2.50	$2.25	$3.00	1863	$1.25	$2.00	$2.00	$3.50	1845	$.75	$1.00	$1.25	$1.75
1880	1.25	2.50	2.00	3.00	1862	1.00	1.50	1.88	3.00	1844	.75	1.25	1.25	2.00
1879	1.13	2.50	2.25	3.00	1861	1.00	1.63	1.50	3.00	1843	.75	1.25	1.25	1.75
1878	1.00	2.00	2.50	3.00						1842	.88	1.50	1.50	2.44
1877	1.25	2.00	2.50	3.00	1860	1.00	1.75	2.00	3.00	1841	.88	1.50	1.75	2.25
1876	1.50	2.50	2.00	4.00	1859	1.00	1.50	1.50	2.50					
					1858	1.00	1.50	1.50	2.50	1840	.88	1.50	1.75	2.40
1875	1.50	2.50	---	4.00	1857	1.00	1.75	1.50	2.50	1839	1.00	1.50	---	2.25
1874	1.50	2.50	---	4.00	1856	1.00	1.75	1.75	2.50	1838	.90	1.25	---	2.00
1873	1.75	2.50	---	4.00						1837	.88	1.25	---	2.25
1872	1.50	2.50	2.50	4.00	1855	1.00	1.75	2.00	2.50	1836	.88	1.25	1.50	2.00
1871	1.50	2.50	---	5.00	1854	1.00	1.75	1.75	2.50					
					1853	1.00	1.50	1.75	2.25	1835	.75	1.25	1.75	2.00
1870	1.75	2.50	3.00	5.00	1852	1.00	1.50	1.75	2.25	1834	.75	1.25	1.50	2.00
1869	1.75	3.00	---	4.00	1851	.88	1.50	---	2.25	1833	.75	1.25	1.50	1.75
1868	---	2.50	---	5.00						1832	.75	1.00	1.50	1.75
1867	---	2.75	---	4.00	1850	.88	1.50	1.50	2.00	1831	.75	1.25	1.50	1.75
1866	1.50	3.00	3.50	4.00	1849	.88	1.63	1.75	2.00					
					1848	.88	1.38	1.75	2.25	1830	.75	1.25	1.31	1.75
1865	1.50	2.50	2.50	4.00	1847	.88	1.25	1.50	2.00	1829	.75	1.25	1.25	1.50
1864	1.50	2.25	2.50	4.00	1846	.75	1.00	---	2.00	1828	.71	1.00	1.50	1.50

Series D 722–727. Average Annual Earnings of Employees: 1900 to 1970

Year	Full-time employees (OBE-BEA) [1] 722	Money earnings — After deduction for unemployment 723	Money earnings — When employed 724	Real earnings (1914 dollars) — After deduction for unemployment 725	Real earnings (1914 dollars) — When employed 726	Consumer price index (1914=100) 727
1970	$7,564	---	---	---	---	---
1969	7,095	---	---	---	---	---
1968	6,657	---	---	---	---	---
1967	6,230	---	---	---	---	---
1966	5,967	---	---	---	---	---
1965	5,710	---	---	---	---	---
1964	5,503	---	---	---	---	---
1963	5,243	---	---	---	---	---
1962	5,065	---	---	---	---	---
1961	4,884	---	---	---	---	---
1960	4,743	$4,780	$5,130	$1,620	$1,750	294.9
1959	4,594	4,626	4,965	1,592	1,709	290.5
1958	4,375	4,308	4,707	1,550	1,635	287.9
1957	4,230	4,301	4,546	1,534	1,622	280.3
1956	4,055	4,115	4,342	1,519	1,603	270.9
1955	3,851	3,899	4,128	1,461	1,547	266.9
1954	3,667	3,679	3,953	1,375	1,478	267.5
1953	3,581	3,710	3,852	1,391	1,444	266.7
1952	3,402	3,518	3,660	1,331	1,384	264.4
1951	3,217	3,305	3,452	1,279	1,335	258.5
1950	2,992	2,963	3,180	1,237	1,328	239.5
1949	2,844	2,769	3,000	1,167	1,265	237.2
1948	2,786	2,788	2,933	1,164	1,225	239.5
1947	2,589	2,468	2,602	1,108	1,168	222.7
1946	2,359	2,343	2,473	1,205	1,272	194.4
1945	2,190	2,303	2,364	1,284	1,318	179.3
1944	2,109	2,260	2,292	1,289	1,307	175.3
1943	1,951	2,053	2,107	1,190	1,221	172.5
1942	1,709	1,665	1,778	1,025	1,094	162.5
1941	1,443	1,261	1,492	861	1,018	146.5
1940	1,299	1,052	1,315	754	943	139.5
1939	1,264	967	1,266	699	915	138.4
1938	1,230	901	1,221	641	868	140.6
1937	1,258	1,008	1,259	704	880	143.1
1936	1,184	874	1,146	633	830	138.1
1935	1,137	799	1,115	584	816	136.7
1934	1,091	758	1,066	569	800	133.3
1933	1,048	678	1,045	526	811	128.8
1932	1,120	754	1,141	554	838	136.1
1931	1,275	995	1,298	657	857	151.5
1930	1,368	1,207	1,388	725	834	166.4
1929	1,405	1,356	1,425	793	834	170.9

Year	Money earnings — After deduction for unemployment 723	Money earnings — When employed 724	Real earnings (1914 dollars) — After deduction for unemployment 725	Real earnings (1914 dollars) — When employed 726	Consumer price index (1914=100) 727
1928	$1,297	$1,384	$759	$810	170.9
1927	1,312	1,380	759	799	172.8
1926	1,310	1,346	743	764	176.2
1925	1,253	1,317	717	753	174.8
1924	1,196	1,293	702	759	170.3
1923	1,231	1,278	725	753	169.7
1922	1,067	1,190	639	718	166.9
1921	1,009	1,227	566	689	178.1
1920	1,236	1,342	619	672	199.7
1919	1,117	1,142	648	662	172.5
1918	972	994	648	663	150.0
1917	748	807	586	632	127.7
1916	647	705	595	648	108.7
1915	547	635	541	628	101.1
1914	555	639	555	639	100.0
1913	587	633	594	640	98.9
1912	554	601	570	618	97.2
1911	520	587	546	616	95.2
1910	517	575	546	607	94.7
1909	496	545	543	597	91.3
1908	446	519	487	567	91.5
1907	502	529	535	564	93.8
1906	488	504	541	559	90.2
1905	451	490	510	554	88.5
1904	432	482	486	541	88.8
1903	441	477	501	542	88.0
1902	437	472	506	547	86.3
1901	401	438	470	513	85.4
1900	375	418	445	496	84.3

[1] OBE = Office of Business Economics (1929–1967); BEA = Bureau of Economic Analysis (1928–1970).   [2] Excludes Armed Forces.

Series D 728–734. Daily Wages of Five Skilled Occupations and of Laborers, in Manufacturing Establishments: 1860 to 1880

Year	Skilled occupations						Laborers
	Average daily wage [1]	Black-smiths	Carpen-ters	Engi-neers	Machin-ists	Painters	
	728	729	730	731	732	733	734
1880	$2.26	$2.31	$2.15	$2.17	$2.45	$2.21	$1.32
1879	2.16	2.21	2.05	2.08	2.35	2.08	1.27
1878	2.15	2.23	2.03	2.06	2.29	2.04	1.26
1877	2.18	2.27	2.06	2.11	2.29	2.09	1.28
1876	2.24	2.32	2.12	2.17	2.34	2.20	1.33
1875	2.39	2.41	2.42	2.33	2.47	2.35	1.39
1874	2.48	2.52	2.42	2.40	2.53	2.60	1.43
1873	2.62	2.70	2.52	2.50	2.73	2.68	1.52
1872	2.64	2.69	2.59	2.53	2.72	2.70	1.52
1871	2.58	2.66	2.57	2.38	2.72	2.67	1.50
1870	$2.61	$2.68	$2.64	$2.47	$2.67	$2.67	$1.52
1869	2.60	2.73	2.68	2.40	2.66	2.61	1.53
1868	2.58	2.73	2.67	2.35	2.66	2.52	1.51
1867	2.59	2.69	2.75	2.38	2.73	2.47	1.53
1866	2.62	2.74	2.77	2.44	2.73	2.40	1.53
1865	2.50	2.61	2.68	2.33	2.56	2.31	1.48
1864	2.33	2.42	2.58	2.19	2.28	2.25	1.39
1863	2.00	2.07	2.09	1.87	2.05	2.02	1.20
1862	1.78	1.77	1.97	1.72	1.77	1.76	1.08
1861	1.67	1.65	1.80	1.65	1.66	1.64	1.04
1860	1.62	1.64	1.65	1.61	1.61	1.62	1.03

[1] Weighted by number of establishments; unweighted within each occupation.

Series D 735–738. Average Annual and Daily Earnings of Nonfarm Employees: 1860 to 1900

Year	Annual earnings		Consumer price index (1914=100)	Daily earnings
	Money (when employed)	Real (1914=100)		
	735	736	737	738
1900	$483	$573	84.3	
1899	470	563	83.5	
1898	440	527	83.5	
1897	442	529	83.5	
1896	439	521	84.3	
1895	438	520	84.3	
1894	420	484	86.7	
1893	458	505	90.7	
1892	482	527	91.5	
1891	480	525	91.5	
1890	475	519	91.5	
1889	471	510	92.3	
1888	466	505	92.3	
1887	462	509	90.7	
1886	453	499	90.7	
1885	446	492	90.7	
1884	441	478	92.3	
1883	438	459	95.4	
1882	428	431	99.4	
1881	409	415	98.6	
1880	$386	$395	97.8	$1.16
1879	373	391	95.4	1.12
1878	379	397	95.4	1.14
1877	389	388	100.2	1.17
1876	403	393	102.6	1.21
1875	423	403	105.0	1.27
1874	439	403	109.0	1.32
1873	466	407	114.5	1.40
1872	486	416	116.9	1.46
1871	482	386	116.9	1.45
1870	489	375	124.9	1.47
1869	496	380	130.4	1.49
1868	499	367	136.0	1.50
1867	479	338	141.6	1.44
1866	489	322	151.9	1.47
1865	512	328	155.9	1.54
1864	506	421	150.3	1.52
1863	459	382	120.1	1.38
1862	383	398	96.2	1.15
1861	370	439	84.3	1.11
1860	363	457	79.5	1.09

Series D 739–764. Average Annual Earnings Per Full-Time Employee, by Industry: 1900 to 1970

[In current dollars]

Year	Agriculture, forestry, and fisheries [1]	Manufacturing	Mining Total	Anthracite coal	Bituminous coal	Metal	Construction	Transportation Total	Railroad	Water	Local	Communications and public utilities Total	Gas and electric	Telephone and telegraph
	739	740	741	742	743	744	745	746	747	748	749	750	751	752
1970	3,063	8,150	9,262	9,555		9,137	9,293	9,928	9,775	10,750	6,614	8,897	9,695	8,141
1969	2,848	7,775	8,619	8,522		8,615	8,615	9,318	9,230	9,990	6,296	8,388	9,013	7,721
1968	2,633	7,347	7,964	7,602		8,205	7,953	8,676	8,585	9,120	6,101	7,878	8,435	7,227
1967	2,434	6,880	7,556	7,326		7,700	7,417	8,129	8,034	8,619	5,801	7,413	7,964	6,796
1966	2,260	6,643	7,134	6,878		7,432	7,033	7,785	7,660	8,310	5,615	7,166	7,605	6,616
1965	2,053	6,389	6,785	6,444		7,212	6,595	7,485	7,415	7,770	5,438	6,899	7,292	6,379
1964	1,920	6,196	6,521	6,063		7,012	6,332	7,163	7,025	7,507	5,286	6,704	7,070	6,190
1963	1,771	5,920	6,240	5,669		6,667	6,018	6,852	6,762	7,317	5,120	6,440	6,751	5,888
1962	1,728	5,730	6,017	5,434		6,560	5,846	6,638	6,610	7,059	4,985	6,194	6,493	5,668
1961	1,678	5,507	5,828	5,289		6,337	5,618	6,361	6,392	6,597	4,854	5,928	6,236	5,402
1960	1,658	5,352	5,676	4,533	5,376	6,147	5,443	6,185	6,228	6,488	4,771	5,681	5,992	5,130
1959	1,596	5,221	5,518	4,368	5,322	5,845	5,213	5,995	6,054	6,014	4,646	5,445	5,753	4,902
1958	1,549	4,946	5,203	4,261	4,831	5,452	5,020	5,691	5,812	5,866	4,442	5,111	5,426	4,558
1957	1,518	4,786	5,197	4,345	5,162	5,504	4,881	5,432	5,416	5,912	4,332	4,883	5,212	4,344
1956	1,454	4,589	5,004	4,167	4,944	5,393	4,645	5,129	5,080	5,524	4,177	4,676	4,971	4,174
1955	1,376	4,356	4,689	3,871	4,550	5,076	4,388	4,823	4,697	5,299	4,030	4,471	4,704	4,046
1954	1,346	4,123	4,383	3,550	4,044	4,723	4,301	4,603	4,541	5,093	3,833	4,278	4,540	3,827
1953	1,412	4,053	4,361	3,389	4,194	4,972	4,207	4,476	4,415	5,142	3,746	4,087	4,356	3,654
1952	1,423	3,832	4,062	3,500	3,760	4,612	3,978	4,269	4,335	4,552	3,594	3,844	4,088	3,443
1951	1,387	3,608	3,885	3,386	3,831	4,147	3,702	4,044	4,161	4,141	3,462	3,583	3,803	3,220
1950	1,282	3,302	3,460	3,107	3,268	3,608	3,333	3,714	3,778	3,732	3,274	3,346	3,534	3,036
1949	1,312	3,095	3,216	2,896	2,930	3,421	3,209	3,568	3,703	3,421	3,155	3,180	3,344	2,911
1948	1,340	3,038	3,396	3,420	3,383	3,327	3,126	3,468	3,607	3,467	3,101	3,028	*3,187	2,776
1947	1,276	2,793	3,113	3,125	3,212	3,000	2,829	3,169	3,211	3,748	3,020	2,815	2,994	2,583
1946	1,200	2,517	2,719	2,890	2,724	2,636	2,537	2,973	3,049	3,415	2,886	2,582	2,697	2,413
1945	1,125	2,517	2,621	2,685	2,629	2,551	2,600	2,734	2,711	3,583	2,596	2,446	2,596	2,246
1944	1,021	2,517	2,499	2,525	2,458	2,458	2,602	2,679	2,714	3,624	2,280	2,275	2,467	2,035
1943	860	2,349	2,162	2,119	2,115	2,333	2,503	2,493	2,585	3,388	2,280	2,098	2,284	1,878
1942	669	2,023	1,796	1,753	1,715	2,045	2,191	2,183	2,303	2,729	1,990	1,891	2,040	1,715
1941	496	1,653	1,579	1,467	1,500	1,771	1,635	1,885	2,030	1,854	1,664	1,766	1,870	1,633
1940	407	1,432	1,388	1,297	1,235	1,610	1,330	1,756	1,906	1,648	1,559	1,717	1,795	1,610
1939	385	1,363	1,367	1,409	1,197	1,515	1,268	1,723	1,877	1,557	1,569	1,691	1,766	1,600
1938	369	1,296	1,282	1,315	1,050	1,453	1,193	1,676	1,849	1,299	1,529	1,673	1,749	1,580
1937	360	1,376	1,366	1,388	1,170	1,630	1,278	1,644	1,774	1,536	1,505	1,600	1,705	1,481
1936	308	1,287	1,263	1,408	1,103	1,380	1,178	1,582	1,724	1,373	1,433	1,520	1,615	1,420
1935	288	1,216	1,154	1,414	957	1,239	1,027	1,492	1,645	1,088	1,361	1,483	1,589	1,378
1934	253	1,153	1,108	1,500	900	1,133	942	1,393	1,505	1,055	1,310	1,424	1,510	1,338
1933	232	1,086	990	1,435	748	1,040	869	1,334	1,439	1,059	1,219	1,351	1,453	1,245
1932	250	1,150	1,016	1,452	723	1,060	907	1,373	1,461	1,038	1,328	1,440	1,542	1,335
1931	315	1,369	1,221	1,602	909	1,291	1,233	1,549	1,661	1,153	1,500	1,514	1,600	1,436
1930	388	1,488	1,424	1,750	1,119	1,551	1,526	1,610	1,717	1,214	1,587	1,499	1,603	1,410
1929	401	1,543	1,526	1,728	1,293	1,613	1,674	1,643	1,749	1,275	1,598	1,478	1,589	1,386
1928	385	1,534	1,478	1,825	1,342	1,516	1,719	1,607	1,720	1,255	1,553	1,474	1,591	1,378
1927	387	1,502	1,590	1,851	1,446	1,485	1,708	1,579	1,687	1,220	1,549	1,440	1,558	1,343
1926	386	1,476	1,597	2,124	1,434	1,463	1,664	1,562	1,671	1,238	1,530	1,427	1,571	1,317
1925	382	1,450	1,580	2,129	1,427	1,455	1,655	1,539	1,655	1,227	1,502	1,378	1,552	1,257
1924	375	1,427	1,703	2,117	1,621	1,378	1,620	1,509	1,627	1,219	1,472	1,371	1,544	1,250
1923	372	1,403	1,822	2,014	1,848	1,497	1,614	1,484	1,631	1,132	1,413	1,292	1,429	1,199
1922	331	1,283	1,300	1,814	1,165	1,345	1,297	1,461	1,630	1,088	1,394	1,265	1,423	1,176
1921	344	1,346	1,757	1,868	1,808	1,482	1,380	1,533	1,664	1,339	1,470	1,276	1,497	1,161
1920	528	1,532	1,684	1,777	1,633	1,639	1,710	1,645	1,807	1,499	1,499	1,238	1,489	1,115
1919	463	1,293	1,370	1,508	1,276	1,611	1,387	1,352	1,477	1,305	1,172	1,035	1,278	906
1918	401	1,107	1,399	1,426	1,427	1,499	1,191	1,265	1,393	1,086	938	866	1,081	753
1917	327	883	1,138	1,019	1,150	1,352	1,001	885	968	851	737	727	844	675
1916	259	751	889	711	884	1,152	882	768	848	669	674	640	672	647
1915	236	661	716	671	694	976	827	711	797	531	632	607	637	614
1914	234	696	666	636	640	923	838	695	778	484	623	579	644	557
1913	236	689	749	659	743	--------	827	667	743	467	595	560	654	515
1912	232	651	723	616	723	--------	791	634	705	437	570	527	635	467
1911	225	632	671	633	652	--------	779	624	690	417	579	558	641	488
1910	223	651	668	604	657	--------	804	607	662	420	575	516	616	461
1909	221	599	625	556	617	865	731	583	630	423	567	531	612	488
1908	220	548	590	553	574	--------	721	591	652	427	549	516	589	482
1907	220	598	697	633	683	--------	714	592	646	427	556	521	617	471
1906	219	577	636	550	633	--------	693	560	594	417	559	497	575	460
1905	199	561	610	579	589	--------	659	543	576	410	546	477	538	450
1904	221	538	599	638	554	--------	644	540	587	407	516	487	550	448
1903	191	548	619	544	615	--------	637	528	580	403	492	483	544	443
1902	191	537	532	289	577	794	611	472	550	400	487	473	518	444
1901	182	511	531	420	548	--------	590	505	537	393	508	496	506	433
1900	178	487	479	340	516	--------	593	505	536	390	510	470	506	433

See footnotes at end of table.

Series D 739–764. Average Annual Earnings Per Full-Time Employee, by Industry: 1900 to 1970—Con.

[In current dollars]

Year	Wholesale and retail trade	Finance, insurance, and real estate	Services Total	Personal [2]	Medical and other health services	Domestic	Nonprofit	Educational services	Government Total	State and local [3]	Public education	Federal civilian [4]
	753	754	755	756	757	758	759	760	761	762	763	764
1970	6,886	8,026	5,946	5,410	5,687	3,535	5,492	5,494	7,965	7,818	8,141	10,597
1969	6,540	7,680	5,505	5,177	5,043	3,307	5,177	5,083	7,189	7,231	7,529	9,442
1968	6,206	7,235	5,088	4,919	4,579	3,104	4,794	4,718	6,717	6,796	7,092	8,746
1967	5,870	6,717	4,770	4,653	4,197	2,952	4,537	4,410	6,222	6,324	6,605	7,985
1966	5,636	6,347	4,514	4,422	3,884	2,781	4,346	4,132	5,938	5,906	6,155	7,841
1965	5,436	6,055	4,295	4,253	3,736	2,655	4,171	3,887	5,717	5,616	5,847	7,614
1964	5,261	5,851	4,130	4,120	3,641	2,556	4,035	3,684	5,488	5,394	5,663	7,267
1963	5,071	5,595	3,924	3,935	3,452	2,470	3,843	3,465	5,205	5,180	5,448	6,792
1962	4,894	5,410	3,783	3,805	3,317	2,416	3,724	3,257	4,993	5,017	5,314	6,450
1961	4,719	5,260	3,642	3,664	3,184	2,363	3,640	3,078	4,859	4,787	5,097	6,274
1960	4,597	5,030	3,513	3,550	3,061	2,356	3,538	2,913	4,676	4,550	4,752	5,895
1959	4,442	4,882	3,364	3,414	2,907	2,213	3,475	2,802	4,499	4,345	4,522	5,682
1958	4,246	4,628	3,220	3,240	2,787	2,154	3,371	2,677	4,328	4,171	4,343	5,501
1957	4,109	4,432	3,110	3,122	2,660	2,075	3,239	2,599	4,045	3,980	4,085	4,960
1956	3,936	4,243	2,963	2,975	2,523	2,017	3,073	2,507	3,892	3,775	3,827	4,798
1955	3,755	4,051	2,831	2,827	2,497	1,956	3,004	2,380	3,708	3,599	3,608	4,589
1954	3,595	3,897	2,736	2,717	2,405	1,874	2,935	2,326	3,499	3,479	3,510	4,311
1953	3,470	3,716	2,623	2,609	2,338	1,805	2,801	2,265	3,385	3,317	3,314	4,217
1952	3,298	3,539	2,489	2,469	2,230	1,707	2,644	2,210	3,279	3,177	3,169	4,028
1951	3,178	3,390	2,321	2,336	2,099	1,588	2,524	2,169	3,113	2,981	2,998	3,768
1950	3,045	3,223	2,183	2,223	1,998	1,502	2,412	2,099	3,014	2,786	2,794	3,494
1949	2,899	3,038	2,138	2,158	1,912	1,498	2,319	2,056	2,862	2,700	2,671	3,348
1948	2,824	2,951	2,082	2,084	1,824	1,500	2,200	2,002	2,755	2,563	2,538	3,137
1947	2,632	2,740	1,996	1,978	1,821	1,463	2,077	2,113	2,575	2,327	2,261	3,065
1946	2,378	2,570	1,863	1,854	1,605	1,411	1,984	1,802	2,351	2,117	2,025	2,801
1945	2,114	2,347	1,688	1,709	1,401	1,312	1,876	1,641	2,052	1,962	1,882	2,646
1944	1,946	2,191	1,538	1,570	1,262	1,140	1,795	1,562	1,924	1,822	1,730	2,677
1943	1,781	2,041	1,347	1,384	1,127	919	1,679	1,469	1,777	1,713	1,608	2,628
1942	1,608	1,885	1,132	1,196	1,036	706	1,482	1,344	1,623	1,592	1,512	2,226
1941	1,478	1,777	1,020	1,075	955	601	1,379	1,264	1,388	1,534	1,462	1,970
1940	1,382	1,725	953	1,042	927	554	1,408	1,240	1,344	1,502	1,435	1,894
1939	1,360	1,729	952	1,034	908	544	1,546	1,234	1,337	1,476	1,403	1,843
1938	1,352	1,731	942	992	899	527	1,529	1,228	1,355	1,472	1,406	1,832
1937	1,352	1,788	938	978	876	558	1,497	1,211	1,355	1,441	1,367	1,797
1936	1,295	1,713	898	940	851	506	1,465	1,180	1,279	1,402	1,329	1,896
1935	1,279	1,632	873	915	829	485	1,435	1,162	1,292	1,290	1,293	1,759
1934	1,228	1,601	857	905	801	473	1,440	1,175	1,284	1,295	1,265	1,717
1933	1,183	1,555	854	889	810	460	1,442	1,189	1,328	1,338	1,300	1,673
1932	1,315	1,652	918	996	865	497	1,545	1,279	1,477	1,432	1,399	1,824
1931	1,495	1,858	1,008	1,136	919	584	1,653	1,323	1,547	1,500	1,463	1,895
1930	1,569	1,973	1,066	1,200	933	676	1,698	1,329	1,553	1,521	1,455	1,768
1929	1,594	2,062	1,079	1,219	925	731	1,712	1,312	1,551	1,504	1,445	1,933
1928	1,573	2,043	1,065	1,164	930	725	1,675	1,284	1,531	1,500	1,433	1,916
1927	1,480	2,019	1,046	1,095	931	756	1,647	1,252	1,531	1,488	1,393	1,907
1926	1,416	2,008	1,005	1,048	857	748	1,607	1,214	1,482	1,422	1,342	1,888
1925	1,359	1,997	984	1,006	916	741	1,578	1,173	1,425	1,377	1,299	1,762
1924	1,314	1,944	965	972	845	732	1,507	1,148	1,400	1,346	1,269	1,747
1923	1,272	1,896	942	941	845	711	1,454	1,130	1,378	1,336	1,239	1,704
1922	1,261	1,932	908	933	912	649	1,446	1,109	1,358	1,316	1,206	1,694
1921	1,260	1,860	905	932	983	649	1,392	1,022	1,317	1,296	1,109	1,683
1920	1,270	1,758	912	940	752	665	1,286	894	1,245	1,164	970	1,707
1919	1,070	1,589	757	780	606	538	1,104	784	1,156	1,022	852	1,609
1918	941	1,438	646	669	520	432	1,058	721	1,023	902	725	1,415
1917	828	1,439	571	580	451	389	953	679	880	832	682	1,318
1916	760	1,406	523	524	407	357	907	631	844	826	636	1,273
1915	720	1,399	493	490	381	342	876	623	753	804	608	1,224
1914	706	1,368	487	471	366	355	837	610	798	788	593	1,197
1913	685	1,349	479	459	357	357	802	603	788	779	575	1,169
1912	666	1,338	469	453	352	350	784	568	757	724	556	1,140
1911	666	1,355	462	453	352	343	763	560	739	712	535	1,113
1910	630	1,301	447	435	338	337	715	549	725	699	518	1,096
1909	609	1,263	439	420	326	331	741	546	710	696	501	1,071
1908	593	1,218	429	403	313	328	743	545	683	695	479	1,001
1907	580	1,180	420	394	306	316	741	544	675	694	453	1,014
1906	569	1,146	393	381	296	286	689	528	651	664	430	999
1905	561	1,115	385	376	292	278	677	511	628	646	412	976
1904	551	1,099	379	364	283	277	677	509	614	640	397	971
1903	537	1,078	370	354	275	270	679	532	602	621	377	1,009
1902	521	1,051	361	344	267	264	657	489	584	612	364	967
1901	510	1,037	344	332	258	243	651	483	572	605	354	974
1900	508	1,040	340	330	256	240	652	469	584	590	345	940

[1] Prior to 1929, agriculture only.
[2] Data prior to 1929 not comparable with later figures: 1900–1928, Lebergott estimates; 1929–1970, BLS estimates. See text.
[3] Prior to 1929, general government only.
[4] Prior to 1929, includes work relief.

Series D 765–778. Average Hours and Average Earnings in Manufacturing, in Selected Nonmanufacturing Industries, and for "Lower-Skilled" Labor 1890 to 1926

	Manufacturing industries						Bituminous coal mining		Railroads, full-time weekly earnings	Building trades (union)		Postal employees		"Lower-skilled" labor, full-time weekly earnings
	Total		Union		Payroll									
Year	Weekly hours	Hourly earnings	Weekly hours	Hourly earnings	Weekly hours	Hourly earnings	Weekly hours	Hourly earnings		Weekly hours	Hourly earnings	Weekly hours	Hourly earnings	
	765	766	767	768	769	770	771	772	773	774	775	776	777	778
1926	50.3	$0.647	45.9	$1.007	52.2	$0.488	48.4	$0.719	$32.16	43.8	$1.313	47.2	$0.867	
1925	50.3	.645	45.9	.989	52.2	.493	48.5	.724	31.80	43.9	1.229	47.2	.836	
1924	50.4	.656	46.1	.970	52.1	.502	48.5	.811	30.66	43.8	1.188	47.2	.788	
1923	51.0	.620	46.3	.913	53.0	.491	48.4	.864	30.24	43.9	1.107	47.2	.762	
1922	51.2	.574	46.2	.873	53.4	.443	48.4	.834	30.30	43.8	1.006	47.4	.748	
1921	50.7	.607	46.1	.921	52.7	.467	48.2	.846	31.14	43.8	1.076	47.4	.759	
1920	51.0	.663	45.7	.884	53.5	.561	48.2	.784	34.14	43.8	1.052	48.0	.739	$25.98
1919	52.3	.529	46.2	.706	55.1	.448	48.4	.699	27.66	44.0	.780	48.0	.648	23.83
1918	53.6	.448	47.2	.602	56.6	.374	48.7	.599	26.40	44.1	.684	48.0	.536	21.69
1917	54.6	.364	47.6	.499	57.9	.299	49.8	.484	18.84	44.4	.624	48.0	.484	17.18
1916	54.9	.320	48.0	.464	58.2	.250	51.6	.379	16.62	44.5	.587	48.0	.471	13.78
1915	55.0	.287	48.6	.459	58.2	.212	51.6	.337	15.78	44.8	.569	48.0	.466	10.65
1914	55.2	.287	48.8	.438	58.3	.213	51.6	.323	15.36	44.7	.567	48.0	.464	10.78
1913	55.5	.285	49.2	.430	58.8	.211	51.6	.316	15.12	44.9	.557	48.0	.450	10.84
1912	56.0	.274	49.5	.416	59.3	.200	51.6	.320	14.79	45.0	.544	48.0	.437	10.32
1911	56.4	.263	49.8	.411	59.6	.191	51.6	.305	14.49	45.0	.531	48.0	.429	10.13
1910	56.6	.260	50.1	.403	59.8	.188	51.6	.299	14.07	45.2	.520	48.0	.420	10.65
1909	56.8	.252	50.3	.392	60.2	.179	51.6	.292	13.59	45.6	.510	48.0	.409	10.37
1908	56.8	.250	50.4	.388	60.3	.175	51.6	.293	13.47	45.6	.505	48.0	.395	10.22
1907	57.3	.257	50.8	.396	60.6	.186	51.6	.288	13.35	45.7	.498	48.0	.378	10.76
1906	57.3	.248	51.0	.385	60.7	.176	51.6	.293	12.84	45.9	.481	48.0	.369	10.34
1905	57.7	.259	51.1	.378	61.1	.168	51.6	.276	12.45	46.1	.454	48.0	.375	9.91
1904	57.7	.256	51.1	.374	61.1	.164	51.6	.271	12.56	46.1	.443	48.0	.373	9.84
1903	57.9	.256	51.4	.372	61.2	.167	52.2	.267	12.12	46.3	.436	48.0	.372	9.64
1902	58.3	.227	51.8	.362	61.5	.162	52.3	.244	11.73	46.7	.413	48.0	.374	9.25
1901	58.7	.219	52.4	.350	61.9	.153	52.4	.231	11.49	47.5	.391	48.0	.375	9.05
1900	59.0	.216	53.0	.341	62.1	.152	52.6	.204	11.43	48.3	.374	48.0	.371	8.83
1899	59.1	.209	53.0	.338	62.1	.146	52.7	.185	11.37	48.9	.361	48.0	.370	8.70
1898	59.3	.204	53.4	.331	62.2	.143	52.8	.170	11.31	49.5	.348	48.0	.376	8.53
1897	59.1	.203	53.4	.330	61.9	.141	60.0	.138	11.25	49.8	.346	48.0	.381	8.40
1896	59.2	.205	53.5	.350	62.1	.143	60.0	.147	11.22	50.1	.343	48.0	.378	8.46
1895	59.5	.200	53.5	.327	62.3	.141	60.0	.158	11.22	50.3	.341	48.0	.375	7.45
1894	59.1	.200	53.6	.326	61.7	.140	60.0	.171	11.25	50.5	.339	48.0	.368	8.34
1893	59.7	.205	53.9	.331	62.2	.151	60.0	.188	11.37	50.4	.347	48.0	.361	8.73
1892	59.8	.203	54.0	.333	62.3	.147	60.0	.179	11.46	50.6	.348	48.0	.360	8.75
1891	59.7	.202	54.0	.328	62.1	.148	60.0	.169	11.27	51.0	.341	48.0	.358	9.74
1890	60.0	.199	54.4	.324	62.2	.149	60.0	.180	11.38	51.3	.341	48.0	.352	8.71

Series D 779–793. Average Annual Earnings in All and Selected Industries and in Occupations: 1890 to 1926

| | All industries | | Wage earners, manufacturing | Wage earners, steam railroads | Street railways | Telephones | Telegraphs | Gas and electricity | Clerical workers, mfg. and steam railroads | Bituminous coal mining | Farm labor | Federal employees [1] | Postal employees | Public school teachers | Ministers |
| Year | Incl. farm labor | Excl. farm labor | | | | | | | | | | | | | |
	779	780	781	782	783	784	785	786	787	788	789	790	791	792	793
1926	$1,376	$1,473	$1,309	$1,613	$1,566	$1,117	$1,215	$1,477	$2,310	$1,247	$593	$1,809	$2,128	$1,277	$1,826
1925	1,336	1,434	1,280	1,597	1,565	1,108	1,161	1,448	2,239	1,141	587	1,776	2,051	1,263	1,769
1924	1,303	1,402	1,240	1,570	1,544	1,104	1,150	1,436	2,196	1,120	574	1,708	1,934	1,247	1,678
1923	1,299	1,393	1,254	1,585	1,493	1,069	1,133	1,355	2,126	1,246	572	1,658	1,870	1,224	1,620
1922	1,201	1,305	1,149	1,591	1,436	1,064	1,110	1,343	2,067	954	508	1,625	1,844	1,188	1,622
1921	1,233	1,349	1,180	1,632	1,539	1,038	1,159	1,364	2,134	1,013	522	1,593	1,870	1,082	1,556
1920	1,407	1,489	1,358	1,817	1,608	980	1,145	1,432	2,160	1,386	810	1,648	1,844	936	1,428
1919	1,201	1,272	1,158	1,509	1,387	844	967	1,291	1,914	1,097	706	1,520	1,618	810	1,238
1918	1,047	1,115	980	1,424	1,111	690	831	1,092	1,697	1,211	604	1,380	1,339	689	1,186
1917	830	887	774	989	872	616	769	853	1,477	976	481	1,295	1,207	648	1,069
1916	708	765	651	867	798	567	806	679	1,359	750	388	1,211	1,175	605	1,017
1915	633	687	568	815	748	529	792	644	1,267	589	355	1,152	1,162	578	984
1914	627	682	580	795	737	476	742	651	1,257	543	351	1,140	1,157	564	938
1913	621	675	578	760	704	438	717	661	1,236	631	360	1,136	1,124	547	899
1912	592	646	550	721	674	438	669	641	1,209	614	348	1,128	1,091	529	879
1911	575	629	537	705	685	419	670	648	1,213	553	338	1,116	1,071	509	856
1910	574	630	558	677	681	417	649	622	1,156	558	336	1,108	1,049	492	802
1909	543	594	518	644	671	430	622	618	1,136	524	328	1,106	1,021	476	831
1908	516	563	475	667	650	420	639	595	1,111	487	324	1,102	987	455	833
1907	542	595	522	661	658	412	635	623	1,091	580	319	1,094	944	431	831
1906	520	569	506	607	662	412	592	581	1,074	537	315	1,084	921	409	773
1905	503	554	494	589	646	401	581	543	1,076	500	302	1,072	935	392	759
1904	490	540	477	600	610	392	601	556	1,056	470	290	1,066	931	377	759
1903	489	543	486	593	582	397	573	--------	1,037	522	277	1,067	928	358	761
1902	467	519	473	562	576	408	544	--------	1,025	490	264	1,061	934	346	737
1901	454	508	456	549	601	--------	--------	615	1,009	465	255	1,047	936	337	730
1900	438	490	435	548	604	--------	--------	620	1,011	438	247	1,033	925	328	731
1899	428	480	426	543	591	--------	--------	612	1,004	379	239	1,017	924	318	722
1898	417	468	412	542	558	--------	--------	698	1,010	316	228	1,025	939	306	739
1897	411	462	408	543	552	--------	--------	703	970	270	224	1,057	950	298	750
1896	411	462	406	544	531	--------	--------	665	954	282	220	1,084	944	294	764
1895	415	468	416	546	509	--------	--------	640	941	307	216	1,104	935	289	787
1894	400	448	386	546	508	--------	--------	670	928	292	214	1,110	919	283	824
1893	430	480	420	563	526	--------	--------	627	923	383	232	1,101	902	276	809
1892	445	495	446	563	535	--------	--------	625	885	393	238	1,096	899	270	793
1891	438	487	442	554	529	--------	--------	587	882	377	236	---------	894	264	786
1890	438	486	439	560	557	--------	--------	687	848	406	233	---------	878	256	794

[1] Executive departments.

Series D 794–801. Indexes of Wages, Hours, and Earnings in Manufacturing and in the Building Trades: 1890 to 1907

[1890–1899 = 100]

Year	All manufacturing				Building trades				Year	All manufacturing				Building trades			
	Average hourly wages [1]	Average full-time weekly earnings [1]	Average full-time weekly hours		Average hourly wages	Average full-time weekly earnings	Average full-time weekly hours			Average hourly wages [1]	Average full-time weekly earnings [1]	Average full-time weekly hours		Average hourly wages	Average full-time weekly earnings	Average full-time weekly hours	
			Bureau of Labor [1]	Wolman			Bureau of Labor	Wolman				Bureau of Labor [1]	Wolman			Bureau of Labor	Wolman
	794	795	796	797	798	799	800	801		794	795	796	797	798	799	800	801
1907	128.8	122.4	95.0	--------	144.6	131.0	90.6	87.8	1898	100.2	99.9	99.7	100.0	102.8	100.8	98.1	98.7
1906	124.2	118.5	95.4	--------	140.2	127.4	90.9	--------	1897	99.6	99.2	99.6	99.6	101.3	99.9	98.6	99.2
									1896	99.7	99.5	99.8	99.8	99.9	99.1	99.2	99.6
1905	118.9	114.0	95.9	--------	132.2	120.6	91.2	--------									
1904	117.0	112.2	95.9	--------	129.7	118.4	91.3	--------	1895	98.3	98.4	100.1	100.0	98.4	98.7	100.3	100.0
1903	116.3	112.3	96.6	97.3	126.8	116.4	91.8	93.1	1894	97.9	97.7	99.5	99.5	97.6	98.3	100.7	100.5
1902	112.2	109.2	97.3	98.1	121.1	112.1	92.6	92.9	1893	100.9	101.2	100.3	100.1	100.0	100.5	100.5	100.4
1901	108.0	105.9	98.1	98.6	114.5	108.1	94.4	94.4	1892	100.8	101.3	100.5	100.6	99.9	100.6	100.7	100.5
									1891	100.3	100.8	100.5	100.3	97.9	99.7	101.8	101.5
1900	105.5	104.1	98.7	99.1	109.9	105.0	95.5	96.3	1890	100.3	101.0	100.7	100.5	97.0	99.4	102.5	102.2
1899	102.0	101.2	99.2	99.6	105.3	102.7	97.5	97.4									

[1] Includes the building trades and other hand and neighborhood trades.

Series D 802–810. Earnings and Hours of Production Workers in Manufacturing: 1909 to 1970

Year	All manufacturing			Durable goods			Nondurable goods		
	Average hourly earnings	Average weekly hours	Average weekly earnings	Average hourly earnings	Average weekly hours	Average weekly earnings	Average hourly earnings	Average weekly hours	Average weekly earnings
	802	803	804	805	806	807	808	809	810
1970	$3.36	39.8	$133.73	$3.56	40.3	$143.47	$3.08	39.1	$120.43
1969	3.19	40.6	129.51	3.38	41.3	139.59	2.91	39.7	115.53
1968	3.01	40.7	122.51	3.19	41.4	132.07	2.74	39.8	109.05
1967	2.83	40.6	114.90	3.00	41.2	123.60	2.57	39.7	102.03
1966	2.72	41.3	112.34	2.90	42.1	122.09	2.45	40.2	98.49
1965	2.61	41.2	107.53	2.79	42.0	117.18	2.36	40.1	94.64
1964	2.53	40.7	102.97	2.71	41.4	112.19	2.29	39.7	90.91
1963	2.46	40.5	99.63	2.63	41.1	108.09	2.22	39.6	87.91
1962	2.39	40.4	96.56	2.56	40.9	104.70	2.17	39.6	85.93
1961	2.32	39.8	92.34	2.49	40.3	100.35	2.11	39.3	82.92
1960	2.26	39.7	89.72	2.43	40.1	97.44	2.05	39.2	80.36
1959*	2.19	40.3	88.26	2.36	40.7	96.05	1.98	39.7	78.61
1958	2.11	39.2	82.71	2.26	39.5	89.27	1.91	38.8	74.11
1957	2.05	39.8	81.59	2.19	40.3	88.26	1.85	39.2	72.52
1956	1.95	40.4	78.78	2.08	41.0	85.28	1.77	39.6	70.09
1955	1.86	40.7	75.70	1.99	41.3	82.19	1.67	39.9	66.63
1954	1.78	39.6	70.49	1.90	40.1	76.19	1.62	39.0	63.18
1953	1.74	40.5	70.47	1.86	41.2	76.63	1.58	39.6	62.57
1952	1.65	40.7	67.16	1.75	41.5	72.63	1.51	39.7	59.95
1951	1.56	40.6	63.34	1.65	41.5	68.48	1.44	39.5	56.88
1950	1.44	40.5	58.32	1.52	41.1	62.43	1.35	39.7	53.48
1949	1.38	39.1	53.88	1.45	39.4	57.25	1.30	38.9	50.38
1948	1.33	40.0	53.12	1.40	40.4	56.36	1.25	39.6	49.50
1947	1.22	40.4	49.17	1.28	40.5	51.76	1.15	40.2	46.03
1946	1.08	40.3	43.32	1.14	40.4	46.22	1.00	40.5	40.30
1945	1.02	43.5	44.20	1.10	44.0	48.36	.89	42.3	37.48
1944	1.01	45.2	45.70	1.11	46.5	51.38	.84	43.1	36.38
1943	.96	45.0	43.07	1.05	46.5	48.73	.79	42.5	33.45
1942	.85	43.1	36.68	.94	45.0	42.17	.71	40.3	28.57
1941	.73	40.6	29.48	.80	42.0	33.56	.63	38.9	24.39
1940	.66	38.1	24.96	.72	39.2	28.07	.59	37.0	21.83
1939	.63	37.7	23.64	.69	37.9	26.19	.57	37.4	21.36
1938	.62	35.6	22.07	.68	34.9	23.70	.57	36.1	20.65
1937	.62	38.6	23.82	.67	39.9	26.61	.57	37.4	21.17
1936	.55	39.2	21.56	.58	40.9	23.72	.52	37.7	19.57

* Denotes first year for which figures include Alaska and Hawaii.

Series D 802–810. Earnings and Hours of Production Workers in Manufacturing: 1909 to 1970—Con.

Year	All manufacturing			Durable goods			Nondurable goods		
	Average hourly earnings	Average weekly hours	Average weekly earnings	Average hourly earnings	Average weekly hours	Average weekly earnings	Average hourly earnings	Average weekly hours	Average weekly earnings
	802	803	804	805	806	807	808	809	810
1935	$0.54	36.6	$19.91	$0.57	37.2	$21.24	$0.52	36.1	$18.77
1934	.53	34.6	18.20	.55	33.8	18.59	.51	35.1	17.73
1933	.44	38.1	16.65	.47	34.7	16.20	.42	40.0	16.76
1932	.44	38.3	16.89	.49	32.5	15.99	.41	41.9	17.26
1931	.51	40.5	20.64			20.98			20.09
1930	.55	42.1	23.00			24.42			21.40
1929	.56	44.2	24.76			26.84			22.47
1928	.56	44.4	24.70			26.86			22.42
1927	.54	45.0	24.47			26.28			22.55
1926	.54	45.0	24.38			26.23			22.29
1925	.54	44.5	24.11			26.02			21.99
1924	.54	43.7	23.67			25.48			21.63
1923	.52	45.6	23.56			25.42			21.50
1922	.48	44.2	21.28						
1921	.51	43.1	21.94						
1920	.55	47.4	26.02						
1919	.47	46.3	21.84						
1918			19.12						
1917			14.97						
1916			12.63						
1915			11.22						
1914	.22	49.4	10.92						
1909	.19	51.0	9.74						

Series D 811–817. Earnings and Hours for Bituminous Coal–Lignite Mining and Class I Steam Railroads: 1890 to 1970

Year	Bituminous coal–lignite mining (BLS) [1]			Bituminous coal mining—average hourly compensation (Lewis)	Class I railroads [2]			Year	Bituminous coal–lignite mining (BLS) [1]			Bituminous coal mining—average hourly compensation (Lewis)	Year	Bituminous coal mining—average hourly compensation (Lewis)
	Average weekly earnings	Average weekly hours	Average hourly earnings		Average weekly earnings	Average weekly hours	Average hourly earnings		Average weekly earnings	Average weekly hours	Average hourly earnings			
	811	812	813	814	815	816	817		811	812	813	814		814
1970	$186.41	[3] 40.8	[3] $4.58		$171.94	44.2	$3.89	1938	$19.78	23.3	$0.85	$0.87	1908	$0.28
1969	169.18	[3] 40.1	[3] 4.24		162.66	44.2	3.68	1937	22.94	27.7	.83	.82	1907	.28
1968	155.17	[3] 40.2	[3] 3.86		151.02	43.9	3.44	1936	21.89	28.5	.77	.74	1906	.29
1967	153.28	[3] 40.7	[3] 3.75		139.97	43.2	3.24							
1966	149.74	[3] 40.8	[3] 3.66		135.65	43.9	3.09	1935	18.86	26.2	.72	.70	1905	.27
								1934	17.45	26.8	.65	.63	1904	.27
1965	140.26	[3] 40.2	[3] 3.49		130.80	43.6	3.00	1933	14.21	29.3	.49	.47	1903	.27
1964	128.91	[3] 39.2	[3] 3.30		121.80	43.5	2.80	1932	13.58	27.0	.50	.51	1902	.24
1963	121.43	[3] 38.9	[3] 3.15		118.40	42.9	2.76	1931	17.59	28.1	.63	.61	1901	.24
1962	114.46	[3] 37.0	[3] 3.12		115.87	42.6	2.72							
1961	112.01	35.9	3.12		112.94	42.3	2.67	1930	22.04	33.3	.66	.65	1900	.21
								1929	25.11	38.1	.66	.66	1899	.19
1960	112.41	35.8	3.14		108.84	41.7	2.61	1928	24.46	35.3	.69	.67	1898	.17
1959	111.34	35.8	3.11		106.43	41.9	2.54	1927	24.18	33.3	.73	.69	1897	.14
1958	97.57	33.3	2.93		101.50	41.6	2.44	1926	28.42	37.4	.76	.72	1896	.15
1957	106.00	36.3	2.92	$3.93	94.24	41.7	2.26							
1956	102.00	37.5	2.72	3.66	88.40	41.7	2.12	1925	26.24	33.9	.77	.72	1895	.16
								1924	23.42	29.8	.79	.81	1894	.17
1955	92.13	37.3	2.47	3.37	82.12	41.9	1.96	1923	25.41	31.1	.82	.92	1893	.19
1954	77.52	32.3	2.40	3.20	78.74	40.8	1.93	1922				.90	1892	.18
1953	81.84	34.1	2.40	3.14	76.33	40.6	1.88	1921				.92	1891	.17
1952	75.04	33.8	2.22	2.84	74.30	40.6	1.83							
1951	74.69	34.9	2.14	2.73	70.93	41.0	1.73	1920	25.84	35.2	.73	.94	1890	.18
								1919				.70		
1950	67.46	34.7	1.94	2.46	64.14	40.8	1.57	1918				.60		
1949	60.63	32.3	1.88	2.29	62.36	43.7	1.43	1917				.48		
1948	69.18	37.7	1.84	2.20	60.11	46.2	1.30	1916				.37		
1947	63.75	40.3	1.58	1.81	55.03	46.4	1.19							
1946	56.04	41.3	1.36	1.48	50.00	46.0	1.09	1915				.33		
								1914	12.11	34.9	.35	.32		
1945	50.36	42.0	1.20	1.28	46.32	48.5	.96	1913				.31		
1944	49.32	43.0	1.15	1.20	46.36	48.9	.95	1912				.31		
1943	39.97	36.3	1.10	1.10	41.49	48.7	.85	1911				.29		
1942	33.37	32.4	1.03	1.01	39.34	47.0	.84							
1941	29.47	30.7	.96	.94	34.03	45.8	.74	1910				.29		
								1909	11.70	37.5	.31	.28		
1940	23.74	27.8	.85	.83	32.47	44.3	.73							
1939	22.99	26.8	.86	.83	31.90	43.7	.73							

[1] Data relate to production workers.
[2] Hours and earnings based upon monthly data and relate to all employees except executives, officials, and staff assistants. For 1939–1955, data for railroads with operating revenues of $4 million or more; 1956–1964, $3 million or more; thereafter, $5 million or more.
[3] 11-month average.

Series D 818–829. Indexes of Union Hourly Wage Rates and Weekly Hours, Building and Printing Trades: 1907 to 1970

[1967 = 100]

Year	Building trades						Printing trades					
	All trades		Journeymen		Helpers and laborers		All printing		Book and job		Newspaper	
	Hourly wage rate	Weekly hours	Hourly wage rate	Weekly hours	Hourly wage rate	Weekly hours	Hourly wage rate	Weekly hours	Hourly wage rate	Weekly hours	Hourly wage rate	Weekly hours
	818	819	820	821	822	823	824	825	826	827	828	829
1970	128.8	99.9	128.9	99.9	128.1	99.9	121.2	99.6	121.0	99.7	120.8	99.7
1969	115.4	100.1	115.7	100.1	113.9	100.0	111.9	99.7	111.8	99.7	112.0	99.8
1968	106.6	100.0	106.7	100.0	105.9	100.0	[1]105.0	[1]99.9	105.2	99.9	105.1	100.0
1967	100.0	100.0	100.0	100.0	100.0	100.0	100.0	100.0	100.0	100.0	100.0	100.0
1966	94.7	100.1	94.7	100.2	94.6	100.1	96.1	100.2	96.6	100.2	95.4	100.3
1965	90.9	100.2	90.9	100.4	90.8	100.1	93.0	100.4	93.5	100.5	92.5	100.6
1964	87.3	100.3	87.4	100.5	86.8	100.1	90.4	100.6	90.7	100.8	90.1	100.6
1963	84.2	100.3	84.4	100.5	83.2	100.1	88.1	100.7	88.2	100.8	88.1	100.9
1962	81.3	100.5	81.4	100.7	80.3	100.2	85.6	100.8	85.6	100.9	85.7	101.0
1961	78.4	100.6	78.4	100.8	77.5	100.2	83.2	100.9	83.1	101.0	83.4	101.1
1960	75.4	100.7	75.5	100.9	74.0	100.2	80.6	101.1	80.3	101.2	81.1	101.2
1959	72.4	100.8	72.7	101.0	70.7	100.2	78.3	101.2	77.8	101.4	79.4	101.2
1958	69.0	100.8	69.5	101.0	66.5	100.2	75.8	101.5	75.1	101.8	77.1	101.3
1957	66.0	100.9	66.5	101.1	63.4	100.2	73.3	101.8	72.6	102.1	74.6	101.5
1956	62.8	100.9	63.3	101.1	59.9	100.2	70.8	102.1	70.0	102.5	72.3	101.7
1955	60.0	100.9	60.6	101.1	56.5	100.2	69.0	102.2	68.1	102.7	70.5	101.8
1954	58.0	100.9	58.6	101.1	54.2	100.2	67.1	102.4	66.2	103.0	68.9	101.9
1953	55.9	100.9	56.5	101.1	52.0	100.2	65.2	102.5	64.3	103.1	66.9	102.0
1952	53.2	100.9	53.9	101.1	48.6	100.2	62.7	102.5	61.9	103.1	64.4	102.0
1951	50.1	100.9	50.8	101.1	45.6	100.0	59.4	102.7	58.2	103.4	61.7	102.1
1950	47.0	101.0	47.8	101.2	42.7	100.1	56.9	102.8	56.1	103.7	58.7	102.2
1949	45.1	100.9	45.9	101.1	40.5	100.1	55.8	102.9	54.8	103.8	57.8	102.4
1948	43.3	100.8	44.0	101.0	39.1	100.1	49.8	103.1	48.9	104.0	51.6	103.0
1947	39.1	100.8	39.9	100.9	34.6	100.2	(NA)	(NA)	(NA)	(NA)	(NA)	(NA)
1946	34.2	100.9	35.0	101.1	29.6	100.2	39.2	105.2	38.5	106.4	40.7	104.1
1945	30.7	101.9	31.6	102.2	25.5	100.9	33.5	107.8	32.8	110.3	35.1	104.5
1944	30.1	101.9	31.0	102.2	24.3	100.9	33.1	107.8	32.3	110.3	34.6	104.5
1943	29.8	101.7	30.8	102.0	24.1	100.9	32.2	107.8	31.5	110.3	33.9	104.5
1942	29.6	101.8	30.7	101.8	23.8	101.6	31.3	107.5	30.7	110.0	32.5	104.5
1941	27.9	101.0	29.0	100.5	21.7	102.5	30.0	107.8	29.4	110.0	31.1	104.6
1940	26.9	100.6	28.0	100.0	20.7	102.2	29.6	107.8	29.1	110.0	30.7	105.1
1939	26.5	100.7	27.6	100.0	20.3	102.8	29.3	108.0	28.8	110.2	30.1	105.4
1938	26.3	100.9	27.5	100.1	20.1	103.0	29.0	108.3	28.6	111.5	29.7	105.9
1937	24.1	102.6	25.2	101.9	18.3	104.7	28.1	108.9	27.6	111.0	28.9	106.4
1936	22.5	102.2	23.6	101.5	16.8	104.3	27.2	109.4	26.7	111.2	27.9	107.4
1935	21.8	102.2	22.9	101.5	15.9	104.1	26.5	109.8	26.1	111.1	27.5	108.7
1934	21.6	103.0	22.6	102.3	15.8	104.8	25.6	111.8	25.5	112.7	25.9	110.5
1933	21.4	107.0	22.5	106.2	15.3	108.2	25.1	117.8	24.8	116.9	25.6	120.2
1932	22.0	107.3	23.1	106.6	16.1	108.7	26.7	118.8	26.2	118.0	27.3	120.8
1931	25.7	109.3	27.0	108.5	18.8	111.2	26.8	122.8	26.5	122.8	27.4	123.9
1930	25.7	110.6	26.9	110.0	18.9	112.1	26.7	122.9	26.4	122.8	27.3	123.9
1929	24.6	113.8	25.8	113.3	18.0	114.7	26.3	123.0	25.9	122.9	27.1	124.1
1928	24.3	114.8	25.5	114.0	17.7	117.0	25.9	123.1	25.5	123.0	26.6	124.3
1927	24.2	115.5	25.3	114.8	17.5	117.1	25.5	123.1	25.2	123.0	25.9	124.6
1926	23.4	115.7	24.5	115.2	17.2	117.1	24.7	123.2	24.6	123.0	25.3	124.9
1925	21.9	115.9	22.9	115.4	15.8	117.4	24.2	123.4	24.0	123.2	24.7	124.7
1924	21.1	115.9	22.1	115.4	15.3	117.6	23.8	123.4	23.8	123.1	24.2	125.0
1923	19.6	115.9	20.5	115.4	14.1	117.6	22.7	123.9	22.9	123.1	22.9	126.7
1922	17.7	115.8	18.6	115.3	13.3	117.4	22.1	124.5	22.0	123.8	22.6	127.1
1921	18.9	115.8	19.7	115.2	14.6	117.7	21.8	124.9	21.9	125.5	22.4	124.6
1920	18.5	115.9	19.3	115.3	14.5	117.7	19.9	133.0	19.9	136.4	20.6	124.9
1919	13.8	116.4	14.5	115.8	10.0	118.5	15.5	137.0	15.3	141.6	16.9	125.0
1918	12.0	117.0	12.7	116.2	8.6	119.6	12.7	137.0	12.4	141.8	13.9	124.8
1917	10.8	117.6	11.5	116.9	7.5	120.0	11.7	137.0	11.1	141.8	13.3	124.8
1916	10.2	117.9	10.8	117.1	6.8	120.5	11.3	137.0	10.8	141.8	12.9	124.8
1915	9.9	118.3	10.5	117.6	6.6	120.8	11.2	137.0	10.7	141.8	12.9	124.9
1914	9.8	118.4	10.4	117.7	6.5	120.9	11.1	137.0	10.6	141.8	12.9	125.0
1913	9.5	119.0	10.2	118.0	6.4	121.6	10.9	137.1	10.4	141.8	12.7	125.3
1912	9.3	119.2	9.9	118.3	6.2	121.6	10.7	137.2	10.1	141.8	12.5	125.4
1911	9.1	119.6	9.7	118.7	6.2	122.0	10.5	137.3	10.0	141.9	12.2	125.6
1910	9.0	120.0	9.6	119.1	6.2	122.2			9.8	141.9	12.0	125.6
1909	8.6	121.5	9.2	120.5	6.0	124.4			9.2	142.3	11.6	125.9
1908	8.2	123.2	8.8	122.0	5.8	127.1			8.6	143.5	11.2	126.2
1907	7.7	125.1	8.2	123.8	5.6	129.8			7.8	150.5	10.6	127.0

NA   Not available.

[1] Lithography workers were included in the indexes for the first time in 1968. The wage rate index excluding those workers was 138.7; the weekly hours index was not affected.

Series D 830–844. Earnings and Hours of Production Workers in 25 Manufacturing Industries, by Sex and by Degree of Skill: 1914 to 1948

Year	All production workers			Male			Female			Unskilled, male			Skilled and semiskilled, male		
	Average hourly earnings	Average weekly hours	Average weekly earnings	Average hourly earnings	Average weekly hours	Average weekly earnings	Average hourly earnings	Average weekly hours	Average weekly earnings	Average hourly earnings	Average weekly hours	Average weekly earnings	Average hourly earnings	Average weekly hours	Average weekly earnings
	830	831	832	833	834	835	836	837	838	839	840	841	842	843	844
1948 [1]	$1.431	40.3	$57.22	$1.503	40.7	$60.98	$1.090	38.4	$41.86	$1.227	40.7	$49.88	$1.567	40.6	$63.52
1947	1.342	40.4	54.27	1.414	40.9	57.77	1.007	38.7	38.99	1.147	40.9	46.80	1.478	40.9	60.35
1946	1.190	40.1	47.55	1.260	40.4	50.72	.876	39.0	34.14	1.015	40.4	40.86	1.320	40.3	53.10
1945	1.097	44.2	48.46	1.185	45.2	53.47	.787	40.8	32.18	.917	44.8	41.03	1.248	45.2	56.39
1944	1.067	45.6	48.83	1.164	46.9	54.65	.752	41.3	31.21	.892	46.0	41.07	1.227	47.1	57.85
1943	1.014	45.0	45.88	1.103	46.2	51.05	.699	41.1	28.83	.854	45.4	38.86	1.164	46.4	54.10
1942	.924	43.0	40.03	.987	43.9	43.46	.609	39.2	23.95	.773	43.1	33.49	1.043	44.3	46.31
1941	.814	41.2	33.62	.867	41.8	36.18	.533	38.0	20.29	.682	41.4	28.19	.914	42.0	38.32
1940	.739	38.6	28.54	.784	39.2	30.64	.491	35.5	17.43	.611	39.3	23.91	.827	39.2	32.41
1939	.720	37.6	27.05	.765	38.0	28.96	.475	35.8	17.02	.594	38.6	22.82	.808	37.9	30.53
1938	.716	34.3	24.43	.758	34.6	26.07	.482	32.6	15.69	.586	35.5	20.67	.802	34.4	27.49
1937	.695	38.7	26.80	.735	39.3	28.72	.473	36.1	17.02	.570	39.6	22.41	.777	39.3	30.39
1936	.619	39.5	24.39	.651	40.1	26.02	.434	36.2	15.74	.501	40.0	20.00	.689	40.1	27.58
1935	.599	37.2	22.23	.628	37.5	23.49	.437	35.2	15.37	.495	37.0	18.32	.665	37.7	24.98
1934	.580	34.7	20.06	.607	34.8	21.07	.427	34.0	14.50	.479	34.4	16.46	.643	35.0	22.45
1933	.491	36.4	17.71	.518	36.3	18.69	.340	36.6	12.35	.401	37.4	14.91	.550	37.1	20.27
1932	.498	34.8	17.05	.526	34.4	17.96	.325	36.3	11.73	.400	36.4	14.48	.559	35.1	19.48
1931	.564	40.4	22.62	.597	40.4	24.00	.371	39.8	14.69	.460	41.8	19.18	.634	39.7	25.05
1930	.589	43.9	25.84	.622	44.5	27.66	.395	40.5	15.98	.478	45.9	21.90	.663	44.0	29.17
1929	.590	48.3	28.55	.625	49.1	30.64	.398	44.2	17.61	.486	50.2	24.40	.668	48.8	32.60
1928	.579	47.9	27.80	.614	48.8	29.95	.396	43.4	17.15	.474	50.4	23.89	.659	48.5	31.94
1927	.576	47.7	27.53	.610	48.5	29.59	.398	43.7	17.37	.471	49.9	23.54	.656	48.1	31.51
1926	.568	48.1	27.42	.601	49.1	29.51	.398	43.5	17.27	.461	50.2	23.21	.652	48.5	31.61
1925	.561	48.2	27.08	.592	49.0	29.00	.389	44.1	17.17	.455	50.3	22.93	.644	48.6	31.29
1924	.562	46.9	26.43	.592	47.8	28.27	.393	42.6	16.75	.458	48.9	22.41	.644	47.5	30.55
1923	.541	49.2	26.61	.570	50.0	28.39	.383	45.0	17.24	.443	50.3	22.28	.619	49.9	30.81
1922 [2]	.494	49.2	24.29	.520	50.0	25.90	.352	45.0	15.84	.402	50.5	20.30	.566	49.8	28.11
1921	.524	45.6	23.77	.554	46.0	25.35	.362	43.2	15.63	.437	46.5	20.28	.599	45.9	27.36
1920 [3]	.606	48.2	29.39	.642	49.2	31.69	.414	43.0	17.71	.529	49.2	26.06	.687	49.4	34.10
1914 [4]	.247	51.5	12.68	.262	52.2	13.65	.155	50.1	7.75	.203	52.9	10.71	.291	51.7	14.99

[1] Average of 7 months, January–July.
[2] Average of 6 months, July–December.
[3] Average of 7 months, June–December.
[4] July.

Series D 845–876. Average Days in Operation Per Year, Average Daily Hours, and Annual and Hourly Earnings, in Manufacturing, by Industry: 1889 to 1914

Year	All industries				All textiles		Cotton		Wool		Silk		Hosiery and knit goods		Dyeing and finishing textiles	
	Average annual earnings [1]	Average days in operation per year	Average daily hours	Average hourly earnings (cents)	Average daily hours	Average hourly earnings (cents)	Average daily hours	Average hourly earnings (cents)	Average daily hours	Average hourly earnings (cents)	Average daily hours	Average hourly earnings (cents)	Average daily hours	Average hourly earnings (cents)	Average daily hours	Average hourly earnings (cents)
	845	846	847	848	849	850	851	852	853	854	855	856	857	858	859	860
1914	$574	281	9.28	22.0	9.35	16.0	9.50	14.1	9.23	19.0	9.18	16.9	9.18	16.0	9.31	
1913	585	283	9.36	22.1	9.48	15.9	9.60	14.1	9.37	17.3	9.36	17.9	9.27	14.6	9.43	19.1
1912	564	290	9.39	20.7	9.49	15.0	9.57	13.6	9.38	17.1	9.40	15.5	9.43	14.0	9.43	18.2
1911	545	284	9.47	20.2	9.63	14.3	9.72	13.0	9.51	16.1	9.48	15.0	9.57	13.3	9.56	17.5
1910	538	286	9.49	19.8	9.60	14.1	9.69	13.0	9.48	16.1	9.51	14.3	9.54	13.0	9.52	18.0
1909	512	289	9.56	18.6	9.76	13.4	9.90	11.8	9.63	15.6	9.53	13.8	9.70	12.4	9.66	17.4
1908	482	274	9.55	18.4	9.75	13.2	9.90	12.1	9.63	15.5	9.55	12.4	9.68	12.2	9.65	16.7
1907	538	294	9.60	19.1	9.83	13.4	10.01	12.4	9.66	15.4	9.57	13.8	9.73	12.3	9.73	16.6
1906	526	297	9.63	18.4	9.89	12.7	10.11	11.0	9.70	14.9	9.57	13.0	9.75	12.7	9.76	16.8
1905	487	292	9.70	17.2	9.93	11.9	10.16	10.3	9.73	13.9	9.57	13.0	9.80	11.2	9.82	16.4
1904	471	288	9.68	16.9	9.92	11.8	10.16	10.7	9.66	13.7	9.55	12.0	9.82	10.7	9.79	15.4
1903	481	291	9.71	17.0	9.95	12.2	10.18	10.9	9.73	13.9	9.63	12.3	9.82	11.0	9.77	15.7
1902	474	294	9.79	16.5	9.99	11.6	10.20	10.4	9.75	13.5	9.65	11.6	9.92	10.4	9.77	15.7
1901	446	287	9.84	15.8	10.05	11.2	10.25	10.1	9.86	13.2	9.68	10.8	9.92	10.2	9.77	15.0
1900	432	289	9.89	15.1	10.06	11.0	10.26	10.0	9.86	13.0	9.70	10.9	9.92	10.2	9.77	14.9
1899	420	290	9.94	14.6	10.10	10.6	10.30	9.2	9.86	12.4	9.70	11.4	10.05	10.2	9.77	14.8
1898	394	288	9.97	13.7	10.09	10.4	10.30	9.1	9.86	12.3	9.68	11.3	10.05	9.6	9.77	15.1
1897	395	284	9.94	14.0	9.99	10.5	10.16	9.7	9.73	12.0	9.67	11.5	10.05	9.5	9.60	15.0
1896	393	274	9.96	14.4	10.05	10.8	10.21	9.7	9.88	12.3	9.65	12.3	10.05	10.0	9.75	15.8
1895	392	284	9.97	13.8	10.06	10.5	10.25	9.5	9.88	11.8	9.60	11.2	10.05	9.9	9.75	15.4
1894	376	272	9.92	13.9	9.83	11.0	10.01	10.4	9.78	11.7	9.60	12.3	9.47	10.3	9.57	16.2
1893	410	271	9.99	15.1	10.06	11.7	10.26	10.4	9.83	13.3	9.63	13.2	10.07	10.6	9.74	16.8
1892	431	296	10.04	14.5	10.20	10.7	10.40	9.8	9.96	11.9	9.92	11.7	10.13	10.1	9.89	15.5
1891	429	297	10.01	14.4	10.19	10.7	10.37	9.9	9.96	11.8		11.8	10.02	12.2	9.96	15.7
1890	425	294	10.02	14.4	10.16	10.6	10.31	9.9	9.98	11.6	9.95	12.0	10.13		9.4	9.96	15.4
1889	417															

[1] Per full-time equivalent worker.

Series D 845–876. Average Days in Operation Per Year, Average Daily Hours, and Annual and Hourly Earnings, in Manufacturing, by Industry: 1889 to 1914—Con.

Year	Boots and shoes Average daily hours	Boots and shoes Average hourly earnings (cents)	Leather Average daily hours	Leather Average hourly earnings (cents)	Electrical machinery Average daily hours	Electrical machinery Average hourly earnings (cents)	Paper and paper products Average daily hours	Paper and paper products Average hourly earnings (cents)	Rubber Average daily hours	Rubber Average hourly earnings (cents)	Glass Average daily hours	Glass Average hourly earnings (cents)	Foundry and machine shops Average daily hours	Foundry and machine shops Average hourly earnings (cents)	Iron and steel Average daily hours	Iron and steel Average hourly earnings (cents)
	861	862	863	864	865	866	867	868	869	870	871	872	873	874	875	876
1914	9.15	21.2	9.50	21.4	9.03	24.0	9.51	20.5	9.18	23.9	8.91	26.3	9.20	25.3	10.12	26.6
1913	9.21	21.0	9.56	22.3	9.09	24.1	9.59	19.5	9.25	22.2	8.99	26.2	9.27	25.1	10.29	27.4
1912	9.27	20.4	9.56	18.9	9.10	23.5	9.61	18.9	9.27	21.7	9.01	25.0	9.29	24.1	10.31	24.8
1911	9.39	19.8	9.63	19.4	9.18	22.3	9.70	18.1	9.35	21.0	9.08	24.4	9.36	23.5	10.39	24.7
1910	9.40	19.4	9.62	18.8	9.18	22.1	9.71	17.3	9.36	20.8	9.09	23.9	9.37	23.0	10.58	23.2
1909	9.42	18.4	9.67	18.2	9.23	20.8	9.78	16.7	9.42	19.5	9.17	22.3	9.43	22.0	10.64	22.0
1908	9.44	18.4	9.66	17.8	9.22	21.0	9.76	17.7	9.41	19.6	9.16	23.5	9.42	21.9	10.53	21.4
1907	9.44	18.5	9.71	17.8	9.27	20.9	9.81	15.8	9.46	18.0	9.21	22.8	9.47	21.8	10.67	21.5
1906	9.46	17.6	9.70	17.2	9.30	20.6	9.50	14.2	9.50	18.1	9.26	22.1	9.50	21.3	10.67	20.3
1905	9.51	17.2	9.70	15.9	9.37	19.8	10.27	14.2	9.57	16.6	9.23	22.5	9.54	20.2	10.69	19.4
1904	9.52	16.3	9.67	16.1	9.35	19.6	10.17	14.1	9.55	16.4	9.15	21.4	9.52	20.0	10.57	19.2
1903	9.51	16.5	9.70	15.7	9.38	20.5	10.22	13.3	9.57	16.1	9.11	19.9	9.57	20.2	10.67	20.2
1902	9.62	15.4	9.71	15.4	9.45	18.7	10.13	13.6	9.65	16.0	8.92	21.0	9.69	19.4	10.66	20.3
1901	9.74	15.1	9.71	15.3	9.50	18.3	10.20	13.0	9.70	16.3	8.94	20.4	9.81	18.3	10.66	19.6
1900	9.72	14.8	9.71	15.2	9.55	17.4	10.38	12.7	9.75	15.7	9.01	19.5	9.96	18.0	10.74	18.7
1899	9.76	14.5	9.70	15.1	9.60	17.2	10.38	12.3	9.80	15.8	9.00	18.1	10.01	17.3	10.57	17.9
1898	9.76	14.2	9.74	15.5	9.63	17.4	10.99	11.2	9.83	15.9	___	___	10.05	17.5	10.69	15.8
1897	9.76	14.7	9.72	16.0	9.60	16.5	10.94	11.9	9.80	15.7	___	___	10.01	17.3	10.66	15.4
1896	9.79	15.0	9.69	16.2	9.62	16.3	10.87	12.1	9.82	16.0	___	___	10.03	17.8	10.59	15.8
1895	9.79	15.4	9.69	16.1	___	___	10.89	11.9	9.83	15.2	___	___	10.05	18.0	10.74	15.3
1894	9.79	16.0	9.67	15.9	___	___	10.89	12.3	9.78	15.4	___	___	10.01	18.6	10.75	15.8
1893	9.79	16.4	9.67	17.1	___	___	10.83	12.5	9.85	16.3	___	___	10.03	18.8	10.67	17.2
1892	9.81	16.1	9.65	17.3	___	___	10.87	12.2	9.90	15.3	___	___	10.06	18.6	10.67	17.0
1891	9.84	15.9	9.67	17.5	___	___	10.87	11.9	9.87	15.5	___	___	10.10	19.0	___	___
1890	9.81	16.1	9.67	16.9	___	___	10.90	12.0	9.88	15.8	___	___	10.10	18.5	___	___

Series D 877–892. Average Earnings and Average Hours of Construction and Nonsupervisory Workers in Selected Nonmanufacturing Industries: 1932 to 1970

Year	Contract construction[1] Hourly earnings	Contract construction[1] Weekly hours	Contract construction[1] Weekly earnings	Wholesale trade Hourly earnings	Wholesale trade Weekly hours	Wholesale trade Weekly earnings	Retail trade[2] Hourly earnings	Retail trade[2] Weekly hours	Retail trade[2] Weekly earnings	Electric company systems[3] Hourly earnings	Electric company systems[3] Weekly hours	Electric company systems[3] Weekly earnings	Finance, insurance, and real estate[4] Hourly earnings	Finance, insurance, and real estate[4] Weekly hours	Finance, insurance, and real estate[4] Weekly earnings	Insurance carriers, weekly earnings[5]
	877	878	879	880	881	882	883	884	885	886	887	888	889	890	891	892
1970	$5.25	37.4	$196.35	$3.44	40.0	$137.60	$2.44	33.8	$82.47	$4.22	41.8	$176.40	$3.08	36.8	$113.34	[4]121.40
1969	4.79	37.9	181.54	3.23	40.2	129.85	2.30	34.2	78.66	3.95	41.9	165.51	2.93	37.1	108.70	[4]114.02
1968	4.41	37.4	164.93	3.05	40.1	122.31	2.16	34.7	74.95	3.71	41.6	154.34	2.75	37.0	101.75	[4]107.16
1967	4.11	37.7	154.95	2.88	40.3	116.06	2.01	35.3	70.95	3.50	41.5	145.25	2.58	37.0	95.46	[4]103.14
1966	3.89	37.6	146.26	2.73	40.7	111.11	1.91	35.9	68.57	3.35	41.7	139.70	2.47	37.3	92.13	[4]99.32
1965	3.70	37.4	138.38	2.61	40.8	106.49	1.82	36.6	66.61	3.22	41.4	133.31	2.39	37.2	88.91	[4]95.86
1964	3.55	37.2	132.06	2.52	40.6	102.31	1.75	37.0	64.75	3.09	41.3	127.62	2.30	37.3	85.79	[4]92.01
1963	3.41	37.3	127.19	2.45	40.6	99.47	1.68	37.3	62.66	2.97	41.2	122.36	2.25	37.5	84.38	96.21
1962	3.31	37.0	122.47	2.37	40.6	96.22	1.63	37.4	60.96	2.87	41.2	118.24	2.17	37.3	80.94	93.45
1961	3.20	36.9	118.08	2.31	40.5	93.56	1.56	37.6	58.66	2.75	41.0	112.75	2.09	36.9	77.12	89.75
1960	3.08	36.7	113.04	2.24	40.5	90.72	1.52	38.0	57.76	2.66	41.3	109.86	2.02	37.2	75.14	87.37
1959*	2.93	37.0	108.41	2.18	40.6	88.51	1.47	38.2	56.15	2.55	41.1	104.81	1.95	37.3	72.74	85.28
1958	2.82	36.8	103.78	2.09	40.2	84.02	1.42	38.1	54.10	2.43	41.0	99.63	1.89	37.1	70.12	82.93
1957	2.71	37.0	100.27	2.02	40.3	81.41	1.37	38.1	52.20	2.30	41.4	95.22	1.84	36.7	67.53	80.83
1956	2.57	37.5	96.38	1.94	40.5	78.57	1.30	38.6	50.18	2.20	41.6	91.52	1.78	36.9	65.68	77.59
1955	2.45	37.1	90.90	1.83	40.7	74.48	1.25	39.0	48.75	2.09	41.3	86.32	1.70	37.6	63.92	73.39
1954	2.39	37.2	88.91	1.76	40.5	71.28	1.20	39.2	47.04	2.01	41.4	83.21	1.65	37.6	62.04	70.17
1953	2.28	37.9	86.41	1.70	40.6	69.02	1.16	39.1	45.36	1.93	41.5	80.10	1.58	37.7	59.57	67.38
1952	2.13	38.9	82.86	1.61	40.7	65.53	1.09	39.8	43.38	1.80	41.5	74.70	1.51	37.8	57.08	63.46
1951	2.02	38.1	76.96	1.52	40.8	62.02	1.06	40.4	42.82	1.70	42.0	71.40	1.45	37.7	54.67	61.39
1950	1.86	37.4	69.68	1.43	40.7	58.08	.98	40.4	39.71	1.58	41.6	65.85	1.34	37.7	50.52	58.57
1949	1.79	37.7	67.56	1.36	40.8	55.49	.95	40.4	38.42	1.53	41.6	63.73	1.26	37.8	47.63	56.54
1948	1.71	38.1	65.27	1.31	41.0	53.63	.90	40.2	36.22	1.44	42.1	60.54	1.20	37.9	45.48	55.00
1947	1.54	38.2	58.87	1.22	41.1	50.14	.84	40.3	33.77	1.34	42.0	56.41	1.14	37.9	43.21	52.65
1946	1.48	38.1	56.24	1.11	41.6	46.05	.80	41.3	32.92	1.26	41.6	52.04	___	___	___	50.94
1945	1.38	39.0	53.73	.99	42.8	42.37	.70	40.9	28.59	1.14	43.5	50.05	___	___	___	47.13
1944	1.32	39.6	52.18	.95	43.0	40.76	.65	41.0	26.77	1.11	43.1	48.04	___	___	___	44.87
1943	1.25	38.4	48.13	.90	42.3	37.99	.61	40.9	24.79	1.05	41.6	44.16	___	___	___	41.87
1942	1.15	36.4	41.80	.83	41.4	34.28	.56	41.8	23.37	.98	40.1	39.60	___	___	___	38.37
1941	1.01	34.8	35.14	.76	41.1	31.36	.52	42.8	22.17	.92	39.8	36.54	___	___	___	37.54
1940	.96	33.1	31.70	.71	41.3	29.36	.49	43.2	21.34	.88	39.7	35.10	___	___	___	36.55
1939	.93	32.6	30.39	.69	41.8	28.76	.48	43.4	21.01	.87	39.6	34.38	___	___	___	36.32
1938	.91	32.1	29.19	.67	42.3	28.51	___	___	___	.86	39.9	34.15	___	___	___	36.30
1937	.90	33.4	30.14	.66	43.1	28.36	___	___	___	.85	40.3	34.22	___	___	___	39.29
1936	.82	32.8	27.01	.63	42.9	26.96	___	___	___	.80	40.1	32.22	___	___	___	37.99
1935	.82	30.1	24.51	.61	41.6	25.38	___	___	___	.79	39.3	31.07	___	___	___	36.22
1934	.80	28.9	22.97	___	___	25.44	___	___	___	.78	38.8	29.98	___	___	___	35.02
1933	___	___	___	___	___	25.19	___	___	___	.69	42.0	29.23	___	___	___	34.29
1932	___	___	___	___	___	26.75	___	___	___	.70	44.0	30.78	___	___	___	36.99

* Denotes first year for which figures include Alaska and Hawaii.
[1] Beginning 1947, data cover both on-site and off-site workers on both private and public projects; prior to 1947, they refer only to on-site workers on privately financed construction.   [2] Beginning 1947, includes eating and drinking places.

[3] Beginning 1947, includes only companies engaged exclusively in producing and distributing electricity; prior to 1947, includes combined gas and electric utilities whose income results primarily from sale of electricity.   [4] Excludes nonoffice salemen.   [5] Beginning 1947, data are for "insurance carriers"; prior to 1947, for "insurance."

Series D 893–904.   Average Annual Supplements to Wages and Salaries Per Full-Time Employee, by Major Industry: 1929 to 1970

Year	All industries	Private industries										Government and government enterprises
		Total	Agriculture, forestry, and fisheries	Mining	Contract construction	Manufacturing	Wholesale and retail trade	Finance, insurance, and real estate	Transportation	Communications and public utilities	Services	
	893	894	895	896	897	898	899	900	901	902	903	904
1970	$845	$852	$220	$1,140	$948	$1,202	$569	$1,085	$1,203	$1,464	$384	$814
1969	779	797	206	1,067	871	1,113	536	1,014	1,113	1,301	358	708
1968	712	732	162	979	775	1,032	486	948	1,030	1,153	319	636
1967	650	667	150	880	723	928	443	879	928	1,084	293	586
1966	620	641	132	821	704	894	423	826	900	1,036	276	537
1965	556	571	98	744	611	822	366	733	800	963	227	496
1964	528	538	90	750	573	769	355	704	756	909	215	486
1963	504	515	81	738	563	723	350	714	726	802	212	458
1962	471	482	68	708	498	682	327	665	685	769	191	423
1961	431	436	58	659	471	607	293	616	654	726	169	410
1960*	410	411	56	618	422	579	272	552	612	653	157	401
1959	372	375	46	582	381	534	243	468	564	617	134	359
1958	326	324	40	511	319	475	204	395	466	536	113	334
1957	307	308	37	508	298	441	195	345	431	482	109	302
1956	271	276	32	503	258	396	168	316	383	448	96	245
1955	241	250	28	452	243	354	156	294	343	419	89	196
1954	214	228	19	401	231	316	142	280	308	408	85	156
1953	196	207	16	392	209	284	125	246	286	372	74	147
1952	188	196	15	349	193	271	122	228	274	367	69	155
1951	180	186	13	348	188	255	120	210	255	350	66	156
1950	159	158	8	305	168	210	112	190	235	315	53	167
1949	138	127	7	212	147	160	91	170	218	267	45	199
1948	118	116	6	205	141	141	84	152	202	243	42	135
1947	124	113	6	160	133	134	86	134	224	235	42	191
1946	123	99	6	117	120	117	77	132	176	221	41	229
1945	104	102	5	106	137	129	72	120	164	221	37	109
1944	81	97	4	100	134	120	68	130	157	194	34	44
1943	69	85	3	97	128	102	59	128	151	152	30	28
1942	66	73	3	87	120	87	55	105	139	132	26	36
1941	63	67	2	83	98	81	55	105	117	131	25	43
1940	60	61	3	79	87	75	54	103	110	127	23	55
1939	60	61	2	81	85	74	56	104	108	123	24	53
1938	58	60	2	80	84	72	56	102	106	123	25	49
1937	50	50	2	66	74	58	44	88	99	97	20	51
1936	28	26	1	32	45	27	19	59	59	61	10	40
1935	20	16	1	19	36	15	10	42	40	47	5	45
1934	19	15	1	19	36	12	8	35	55	39	5	41
1933	20	15	1	20	40	13	9	35	45	40	5	48
1932	21	16	2	22	44	16	10	42	41	31	6	55
1931	20	17	2	22	43	16	10	45	40	31	5	50
1930	19	16	2	24	42	15	10	47	36	28	5	49
1929	18	15	1	24	38	14	9	50	33	28	4	49

* Denotes first year for which figures include Alaska and Hawaii.

Series D 905–912.   Average Annual Supplements to Wages and Salaries Per Full-Time Equivalent Employee, by Type of Supplement: 1929 to 1970

Year	Total supplements	Employer contributions for social insurance				Other labor income		
		Total	Public retirement systems [1]	Unemployment insurance [2]	Other [3]	Total	Employer contributions to private pension and welfare funds	Compensation for injuries and other [4]
	905	906	907	908	909	910	911	912
1970	$845	$414	$365	$48	$1	$431	$361	$70
1969	779	387	339	47	(Z)	393	330	63
1968	712	349	300	48	(Z)	364	306	58
1967	650	322	272	50	(Z)	328	273	55
1966	620	307	249	57	(Z)	313	261	52
1965	556	258	197	60	(Z)	298	249	50
1964	528	254	192	62	(Z)	274	225	49
1963	504	254	185	68	(Z)	251	205	45
1962	471	234	162	71	(Z)	237	194	43
1961	431	207	153	54	(Z)	224	182	42

See footnotes at end of table.

Series D 905–912. Average Annual Supplements to Wages and Salaries Per Full-Time Equivalent Employee, by Type of Supplement: 1929 to 1970—Con.

Year	Total supplements	Employer contributions for social insurance				Other labor income		
		Total	Public retirement systems [1]	Un-employment insurance [2]	Other [3]	Total	Employer contributions to private pension and welfare funds	Compensation for injuries and other [4]
	905	906	907	908	909	910	911	912
1960*	$410	$199	$150	$44	(Z)	$210	$170	$41
1959	372	172	127	45	(Z)	200	161	39
1958	326	145	110	35	(Z)	181	143	37
1957	307	138	104	34	(Z)	168	133	35
1956	271	120	87	33	(Z)	150	118	33
1955	241	108	78	28	$2	133	104	30
1954	214	97	70	26	1	118	90	28
1953	196	88	57	29	1	108	83	25
1952	188	90	58	30	3	98	74	24
1951	180	90	55	33	3	90	67	23
1950	159	81	49	30	2	78	56	22
1949	138	74	38	27	10	64	43	21
1948	118	63	36	25	2	56	37	19
1947	124	75	33	29	13	49	33	16
1946	123	84	28	26	30	40	26	14
1945	104	71	23	25	24	34	21	12
1944	81	53	22	27	5	28	17	10
1943	69	49	20	29	(Z)	20	11	9
1942	66	48	19	28	1	18	8	10
1941	63	46	18	28	(Z)	17	7	9
1940	60	42	17	26	(Z)	18	7	11
1939	60	42	16	26	(Z)	17	7	10
1938	58	41	15	25	(Z)	17	7	11
1937	50	34	15	18	(Z)	16	6	10
1936	28	12	5	7	(Z)	16	7	9
1935	20	5	5	(Z)	(Z)	15	6	9
1934	19	5	5	(Z)	(Z)	14	5	9
1933	20	5	5		(Z)	15	5	10
1932	21	5	4		(Z)	17	5	11
1931	20	4	3		(Z)	17	5	11
1930	19	3	3		(Z)	16	5	12
1929	18	3	3		(Z)	16	5	11

* Denotes first year for which figures include Alaska and Hawaii.
Z   Less than $0.50.
[1] Old-age, survivors, and disability insurance; railroad retirement insurance; Federal civilian employee retirement systems; and State and local employee retirement systems, which include hospital insurance beginning 1966.
[2] State unemployment insurance, Federal unemployment tax, and railroad unemployment insurance.
[3] Cash sickness compensation funds and government life insurance.
[4] Includes pay of military reservists, directors' fees, jury and witness fees, compensation of prison inmates, and marriage fees to justices of the peace.

Series D 913–926.   Earnings in Selected Occupations: 1865 to 1970

Year	Average annual salary, college teachers [1]	Average annual net income			Annual median net income			Median monthly salary rate, engineers	Military annual pay rates					
		Non-salaried lawyers	Non-salaried physicians	Non-salaried dentists	Non-salaried lawyers	Non-salaried physicians	Non-salaried dentists		Basic pay			Basic pay plus allowances		
									All personnel	Officers	Enlisted personnel	All personnel	Officers	Enlisted personnel
	913	914	915	916	917	918	919	920	921	922	923	924	925	926
1970	$11,745			$30,770		$41,500	$28,100	$1,480	$4,205	$9,861	$3,399	$5,759	$12,947	$4,734
1969						40,550			3,539	8,425	2,867	5,016	11,341	4,146
1968	10,235					37,620		1,360	3,227	7,813	2,621	4,658	10,684	3,862
1967				24,740		34,730	22,850		3,055	7,765	2,473	4,399	10,684	3,622
1966	9,081					32,170		1,250	3,088	7,526	2,472	4,640	10,286	3,856
1965						28,960			2,917	7,130	2,301	4,368	9,763	3,567
1964	8,163			14,852		28,380	12,650	1,160	2,749	6,763	2,182	4,165	9,334	3,439
1963						25,050								
1962	7,486					24,300		1,060						
1961				*16,020			*14,747							
1960	*6,711							1,000	2,512	5,972	2,013	3,743	8,734	3,034
1959						22,100								
1958	6,015			14,311			13,366	900						
1957														
1956	5,243							820						
1955				12,480			11,533		2,067	5,004	1,672	3,222	6,787	2,742
1954		$10,258			$7,382									
1953		9,392			6,780			[2] 518						
1952	5,106	9,021		10,873	6,383		9,961		1,776	4,453	1,473	2,940	6,234	2,584
1951		8,855	$13,432	7,820	6,112	11,191	6,684							

See footnotes at end of table.

Series D 913–926.   Earnings in Selected Occupations: 1865 to 1970—Con.

Year	Average annual salary, college teachers [1]	Average annual net income			Annual median net income			Median monthly salary rate, engineers	Military annual pay rates					
									Basic pay			Basic pay plus allowances		
		Non-salaried lawyers	Non-salaried physicians	Non-salaried dentists	Non-salaried lawyers	Non-salaried physicians	Non-salaried dentists		All personnel	Officers	Enlisted personnel	All personnel	Officers	Enlisted personnel
	913	914	915	916	917	918	919	920	921	922	923	924	925	926
1950	$4,354	$8,349	$12,324	$7,436	$5,722	$10,518	$6,342							
1949	4,234	7,971	11,744	7,146		9,561	6,140							
1948	4,123	8,003	11,327	7,039	5,719	8,939	5,939							
1947	3,736	7,437	10,726	6,610	5,199	8,256	5,544							
1946	3,465	6,951	10,202	6,381	4,696	7,523	5,142	$409						
1945	3,277	6,861	10,975	6,922	4,660	8,073	5,439		$1,017	$2,442	$856	$1,811	$3,777	$1,587
1944	3,331	6,504	9,802	6,649	4,273		5,353							
1943	3,039	5,945	8,370	5,715	3,892			334						
1942	2,914	5,527	6,735	4,625										
1941		4,794	5,047	3,782	2,960	3,756	3,281							
1940	2,906	4,507	4,441	3,314		3,245								
1939		4,391	4,229	3,096	2,704	3,083		277						
1938	2,861	4,273	4,093	2,870		3,027								
1937	2,843	4,483	4,285	2,883	2,757	3,229	2,462							
1936	2,732	4,394	4,204	2,726	2,665	3,234	[3]2,371							
1935	2,666	4,272	3,695	2,485			[3]2,173							
1934		4,218	3,382	2,391			2,391	210						
1933		3,868	2,948	2,188			[3]1,880							
1932	3,111	4,156	3,178	2,479				235						
1931	3,134	5,090	4,178	3,422										
1930	3,065	5,194	4,870	4,020										
1929	3,056	5,534	5,224	4,267		3,758	[3]3,676	289						
1918									510	2,141	417	968	2,698	870
1898									282	2,101	205	528	2,489	444
1865									231	717	202	510	1,912	427

* Denotes first year for which figures include Alaska and Hawaii.
[1] Beginning 1956, represents median salaries.   For salary data for public elementary and secondary instructional staff, see series H 524.

[2] The 1953 figure comparable with data for later years is $646.
[3] For all dentists rather than for nonsalaried only.   However, the differences are probably quite minor; they amount to less than 1 percent in 1937 and 1948.

Series D 927–939.   Labor Union Membership, by Affiliation: 1935 to 1970

[Membership in thousands.   Includes members outside the United States, primarily in Canada. AFL = American Federation of Labor; CIO = Congress of Industrial Organizations]

Year	All unions, membership	Labor unions (BLS)							Labor union membership (NBER)				
		AFL		CIO		AFL-CIO		Independent or un-affiliated, membership [1]	All unions	AFL [2]	CIO [2]	AFL-CIO [2]	Independent or un-affiliated, membership [1]
		Number of affiliated unions	Member-ship	Number of affiliated unions	Member-ship	Number of affiliated unions	Member-ship						
	927	928	929	930	931	932	933	934	935	936	937	938	939
1970	20,752					120	15,978	4,773					
1969	20,382					120	15,642	4,740					
1968	20,258					126	15,608	4,650					
1967	19,712					128	16,638	3,074					
1966	19,181					129	16,198	2,983					
1965	18,519					128	15,604	2,915					
1964	17,976					129	15,150	2,825					
1963	17,586					130	14,818	2,768					
1962	17,630					130	14,835	2,794	15,928	9,238	3,958	13,576	2,352
1961	17,328					131	14,572	2,756	16,143	9,312	3,866	13,568	2,575
1960	18,117					134	15,072	3,045	16,607	9,378	4,134	13,881	2,726
1959	18,169					135	15,124	3,044	16,501	9,338	3,983	13,715	2,787
1958	18,081					137	14,993	3,088	16,702	9,417	4,060	13,891	2,812
1957	18,431					139	16,954	1,476	17,687	11,226	4,640	16,078	1,609
1956	18,477					137	16,904	1,573	17,383	11,015	4,624	15,639	1,744
1955	17,749					139	16,062	1,688	16,990	10,593	4,608		1,788
1954	17,955	109	10,929	32	[3]5,200			1,826	16,612	10,258	4,494		1,860
1953	17,860	110	10,778	35	5,252			1,830	17,316	10,438	4,838		2,040
1952	(4)	109	9,500	33	5,000			(5)	16,310	9,977	4,261		2,071
1951	(4)	108	9,500	33	5,000			(5)	15,772	9,497	4,183		2,092

See footnotes at end of table.

Series D 927–939. Labor Union Membership, by Affiliation: 1935 to 1970—Con.

[Membership in thousands]

Year	Labor unions (BLS)						Labor union membership (NBER)			
	All unions, membership	AFL		CIO		Independent or un-affiliated, membership [1]	All unions	AFL	CIO	Independent or un-affiliated, membership [1]
		Number of affiliated unions	Membership	Number of affiliated unions	Membership					
	927	928	929	930	931	934	935	936	937	939
1950	(4)	107	7,143	30	(NA)	(5)	14,823	8,494	3,713	2,616
1949	(4)	107	7,241	39	(NA)	(5)	14,695	8,143	4,314	2,238
1948	(4)	105	7,221	40	(NA)	(5)	15,020	8,095	4,451	2,474
1947	15,414	105	7,578	40	6,000	1,836	14,595	8,467	4,451	1,677
1946	14,974	102	7,152	40	6,000	1,822	13,263	7,652	3,847	1,764
1945	14,796	102	6,931	40	6,000	1,865	12,562	6,890	3,928	1,744
1944	14,621	100	6,807	41	5,935	1,879	12,628	6,877	3,937	1,814
1943	13,642	99	6,564	40	5,285	1,793	11,812	6,779	3,303	1,729
1942	10,762	102	5,483	39	4,195	1,084	10,200	6,076	2,493	1,631
1941	10,489	106	4,569	41	5,000	920	8,698	5,179	2,654	865
1940	8,944	105	4,247	42	3,625	1,072	7,282	4,343	2,154	785
1939	8,980	104	4,006	45	4,000	974	6,556	3,878	1,838	840
1938	8,265	102	3,623	42	4,038	604	6,081	3,547	1,958	575
1937							5,780	3,180	1,991	609
1936							4,107	3,516		591
1935							3,753	3,218		535

NA Not available.
[1] Excludes members of single-firm and local unaffiliated unions.
[2] New unions are included in merged Federation only. Beginning 1956, AFL and CIO show membership of unions affiliated with the AFL and CIO in 1955.

[3] Estimate.
[4] Source gives following estimates: 1948–1950, 14–16 million each year; 1951 and 1952, 16.5–17 million each year.
[5] Source gives following estimates: 1948, 2.2–2.5 million; 1949, 2–2.3 million; 1950, 2.4–2.8 million; 1951 and 1952, 2–2.5 million each year.

Series D 940–945. Labor Union Membership, by Affiliation: 1897 to 1934

[Includes Canadian members of labor unions with headquarters in U.S. BLS = U.S. Bureau of Labor Statistics]

Year	Total union membership (1,000)		American Federation of Labor			Inde-pendent or un-affiliated unions, total member-ship (1,000), Wolman	Year	Total union membership (1,000)		America Federation of Labor			Inde-pendent or un-affiliated unions, total member-ship (1,000), Wolman
			Number of affiliated unions, BLS	Total membership (1,000)						Number of affiliated unions, BLS	Total membership (1,000)		
	BLS	Wolman		BLS	Wolman			BLS	Wolman		BLS	Wolman	
	940	941	942	943	944	945		940	941	942	943	944	945
1934	3,728	3,713	109	3,045	3,030	683	1915	2,560	2,583	110	1,946	1,968	614
1933	2,857	3,048	108	2,127	2,318	730	1914	2,647	2,687	110	2,021	2,061	626
1932	3,226	3,191	106	2,532	2,497	694	1913	2,661	2,716	111	1,996	2,051	665
1931	3,526	3,379	105	2,890	2,743	636	1912	2,405	2,452	112	1,770	1,818	635
							1911	2,318	2,343	115	1,762	1,787	556
1930	3,632	3,416	104	2,961	2,745	671	1910	2,116	2,140	120	1,562	1,587	554
1929	3,625	3,461	105	2,934	2,770	691	1909	1,965	2,006	119	1,483	1,524	482
1928	3,567	3,480	107	2,896	2,809	671	1908	2,092	2,131	116	1,587	1,625	505
1927	3,600	3,546	106	2,813	2,759	787	1907	2,077	2,080	117	1,539	1,542	538
1926	3,592	3,502	107	2,804	2,715	788	1906	1,892	1,907	119	1,454	1,469	438
1925	3,566	3,519	107	2,877	2,831	689	1905	1,918	2,022	118	1,494	1,598	424
1924	3,549	3,536	107	2,866	2,853	683	1904	2,067	2,073	120	1,676	1,682	391
1923	3,629	3,622	108	2,926	2,919	703	1903	1,824	1,914	113	1,466	1,556	358
1922	3,950	4,027	112	3,196	3,273	754	1902	1,335	1,376	97	1,024	1,065	311
1921	4,722	4,781	110	3,907	3,967	815	1901	1,058	1,125	87	788	854	270
1920	5,034	5,048	110	4,079	4,093	955	1900	791	868	82	548	625	243
1919	4,046	4,125	111	3,260	3,339	786	1899	550	611	73	349	410	201
1918	3,368	3,467	111	2,726	2,825	642	1898	467	501	67	278	312	189
1917	2,976	3,061	111	2,371	2,457	605	1897	440	447	58	265	272	175
1916	2,722	2,773	111	2,073	2,124	649							

Series D 946–951. Labor Union Membership and Membership as Percent of Total Labor Force and of Nonagricultural Employment: 1930 to 1970

[In thousands, except percent]

Year	Union membership Total	Canadian members of U. S. unions	Excluding Canadian members Number	Percent of total labor force	Nonagricultural employment Total	Membership as percent of total [1]	Year	Union membership Total	Canadian members of U. S. unions	Excluding Canadian members Number	Percent of total labor force	Nonagricultural employment Total	Membership as percent of total [1]
	946	947	948	949	950	951		946	947	948	949	950	951
1970	20,752	1,371	19,381	22.6	70,644	27.4	1950	15,000	733	[2] 14,300	22.3	45,222	31.5
1969	20,382	1,346	19,036	22.6	70,274	27.1	1949	15,000	718	[2] 14,300	22.7	43,778	32.6
1968	20,258	1,342	18,916	23.0	67,915	27.9	1948	15,000	681	[2] 14,300	23.1	44,891	31.9
1967	19,712	1,343	18,367	22.7	65,857	27.9	1947	15,414	627	14,787	23.9	43,881	33.7
1966	19,181	1,241	17,940	22.7	63,955	28.1	1946	14,974	579	14,395	23.6	41,674	34.5
1965	18,519	1,220	17,299	22.4	60,815	28.4	1945	14,796	474	14,322	21.9	40,394	35.5
1964	17,976	1,135	16,841	22.2	58,331	28.9	1944	14,621	475	14,146	21.4	41,883	33.8
1963	17,586	1,062	16,524	22.2	56,702	29.2	1943	13,642	429	13,213	20.5	42,452	31.1
1962	17,630	1,044	16,586	22.6	55,596	29.8	1942	10,762	382	10,380	17.2	40,125	25.9
1961	17,328	1,025	16,303	22.3	54,042	30.2	1941	10,489	288	10,201	17.7	36,554	27.9
1960	18,117	1,068	17,049	23.6	* 54,234	* 31.4	1940	8,944	227	8,717	15.5	32,376	26.9
1959	18,169	1,052	17,117	24.1	53,313	32.1	1939	8,980	217	8,763	15.8	30,618	28.6
1958	18,081	1,052	17,029	24.2	51,363	33.2	1938	8,265	231	8,034	14.6	29,209	27.5
1957	18,431	1,062	17,369	24.9	52,894	32.8	1937	7,218	217	7,001	12.9	31,026	22.6
1956	18,477	987	17,490	25.2	52,408	33.4	1936	4,164	175	3,989	7.4	29,082	13.7
1955	17,749	947	16,802	24.7	50,675	33.2	1935	3,728	144	3,584	6.7	27,053	13.2
1954	17,955	933	17,022	25.4	49,022	34.7	1934	3,249	161	3,088	5.9	25,953	11.9
1953	17,860	912	16,948	25.5	50,232	33.7	1933	2,857	168	2,689	5.2	23,711	11.3
1952	16,750	858	[2] 15,900	24.2	48,825	32.5	1932	3,226	176	3,050	6.0	23,628	12.9
1951	16,750	804	[2] 15,900	24.5	47,849	33.3	1931	3,526	216	3,310	6.5	26,649	12.4
							1930	3,632	231	3,401	6.8	29,424	11.6

* Denotes first year for which figures include Alaska and Hawaii.
[1] Excludes Canadian members.
[2] Rounded to nearest hundred thousand.

Series D 952–969. Labor Union Membership, by Industry: 1897 to 1934

[In thousands]

Year	Total	Mining, quarrying, and oil	Building construction	Metals, machinery, shipbuilding	Textiles	Leather and shoes	Clothing	Lumber and woodworking	Paper, printing, and bookbinding	Chemicals, clay, glass, stone	Food, liquor, tobacco	Transportation and communication	Public service	Theaters and music	Trade	Hotel and restaurant services	Domestic and personal service	Miscellaneous
	952	953	954	955	956	957	958	959	960	961	962	963	964	965	966	967	968	969
1934	[1] 3,609	579	605	222	40	117	405	10	162	47	82	645	299	127	6	53	64	137
1933	2,973	355	583	180	16	76	336	8	153	27	58	609	296	127	5	32	55	57
1932	3,144	357	806	173	29	29	211	8	160	29	56	699	300	128	9	31	63	57
1931	3,358	309	890	191	34	38	224	12	166	33	60	816	276	132	10	38	70	60
1930	3,393	230	904	203	35	44	230	13	165	35	62	882	264	134	10	44	73	64
1929	3,443	271	919	211	35	47	218	13	162	38	65	892	247	135	10	45	67	67
1928	3,480	333	905	205	35	45	239	13	162	39	66	890	224	132	10	46	66	69
1927	3,546	397	903	204	35	49	267	13	162	41	70	889	212	113	10	47	66	68
1926	3,502	386	867	202	36	55	292	11	158	42	75	884	204	112	10	46	63	61
1925	3,519	439	837	205	36	54	292	10	156	42	75	893	193	110	10	46	60	60
1924	3,536	493	814	218	38	47	282	11	154	45	76	893	185	108	10	46	57	61
1923	3,622	530	790	257	37	56	295	11	151	50	76	907	180	104	10	45	56	67
1922	4,027	387	826	506	37	90	310	12	160	50	99	1,039	171	107	17	60	61	95
1921	4,781	470	869	728	88	96	323	20	182	53	146	1,240	172	106	21	69	55	143
1920	5,048	439	888	859	149	113	374	24	164	52	181	1,256	161	99	21	60	51	157
1919	4,125	419	802	618	60	104	324	16	148	48	168	959	137	88	15	61	42	119
1918	3,467	433	701	396	49	75	258	14	144	51	137	777	105	87	15	65	44	114
1917	3,061	373	606	310	41	73	222	18	137	52	120	695	102	82	15	65	44	105
1916	2,773	338	553	267	29	61	210	18	126	52	117	623	96	87	15	59	40	82
1915	2,583	332	533	224	22	53	174	21	116	53	119	576	90	87	15	61	38	69
1914	2,687	380	542	226	30	58	158	25	111	58	145	562	91	92	15	72	37	86
1913	2,716	432	553	219	29	55	164	25	107	56	141	557	86	82	15	69	34	92
1912	2,452	343	509	204	23	56	131	26	102	60	137	530	67	77	15	48	32	94
1911	2,343	311	479	210	21	50	145	29	97	59	128	513	66	69	15	43	31	76
1910	2,140	275	459	196	21	47	98	28	90	60	123	480	58	60	15	37	29	64
1909	2,006	307	426	178	14	40	80	19	83	57	119	438	44	52	15	37	29	66
1908	2,131	290	445	200	17	40	73	20	87	55	112	470	39	47	50	39	30	118
1907	2,080	312	433	212	16	40	65	27	86	55	110	460	31	45	50	36	27	73
1906	1,907	265	389	187	14	40	54	36	88	55	103	422	26	43	50	34	29	72
1905	2,022	297	373	166	14	41	63	42	91	51	104	446	24	38	50	39	27	158
1904	2,073	279	392	213	15	43	78	52	92	49	136	444	23	28	50	49	30	100
1903	1,914	280	369	205	19	42	77	48	88	46	122	339	22	20	50	39	29	119
1902	1,376	197	263	137	15	24	59	34	70	39	93	258	19	15	30	19	20	84
1901	1,125	218	192	104	7	15	38	32	55	33	77	216	18	13	25	10	14	59
1900	868	131	153	81	8	10	25	26	48	30	69	189	15	9	20	5	7	42
1899	611	75	97	59	7	8	15	16	43	27	51	158	11	9	8	2	4	22
1898	501	44	74	46	8	12	15	12	39	25	46	130	11	8	6	2	3	18
1897	447	21	67	50	8	15	15	6	38	23	46	116	11	7	4	2	2	17

[1] Includes 11,000 union members in the professional service industry, not shown separately.

Series D 970–985. Work Stoppages, Workers Involved, Man-Days Idle, Major Issues, and Average Duration: 1881 to 1970

Year	Work stoppages and man-days idle							Major issues and average duration								
	Stoppage beginning in year			Man-days idle				Stoppages[1]				Average duration of stoppages (days)	Workers involved (1,000)			
	Total	Workers involved		Number (1,000)	Percent of estimated total working time		Per worker involved	Total	Major issues				Total	Major issues		
		Number (1,000)	Percent of total employed		Total economy	Private nonfarm			Wages and hours[2]	Union organization	Other and not reported[2]			Wages and hours[2]	Union organization[3]	Other and not reported[2]
	970	971	972	973	974	975	976	977	978	979	980	981	982	983	984	985
1970	5,716	3,305	4.7	66,414	0.37	0.44	20.1	5,716	3,132	587	1,997	25.0	3,305	2,147	106	1,053
1969	5,700	2,481	3.5	42,869	.24	.28	17.3	5,700	3,199	593	1,908	22.5	2,481	1,425	250	806
1968	5,045	2,649	3.8	49,018	.28	.32	18.5	5,045	2,891	513	1,641	24.5	2,649	1,676	112	861
1967	4,595	2,870	4.3	42,100	.25	.30	14.7	4,595	2,433	586	1,576	22.8	2,870	1,966	114	790
1966	4,405	1,960	3.0	25,400	.15	.18	12.9	4,405	2,259	596	1,550	22.2	1,960	1,114	130	718
1965	3,963	1,550	2.5	23,300	.15	.18	15.1	3,963	1,923	594	1,446	25.0	1,550	821	154	571
1964	3,655	1,640	2.7	22,900	.15	.18	14.0	3,655	1,700	556	1,399	22.9	1,640	699	87	854
1963	3,362	941	1.1	16,100	.11	.13	17.1	3,362	1,573	531	1,258	23.0	941	470	94	376
1962	3,614	1,230	2.2	18,600	.13	.16	15.0	3,614	1,824	582	1,208	24.6	1,230	725	106	403
1961	3,367	1,450	2.6	16,300	.11	.12	11.2	3,367	1,664	518	1,185	23.7	1,450	565	92	795
1960	3,333	1,320	2.4	19,100	.14	.17	14.5	3,333	1,592	538	1,203	23.4	1,320	568	246	504
1959*	3,708	1,880	3.3	69,000	.50	.61	36.7	3,708	1,872	664	1,172	24.6	1,880	1,320	154	400
1958	3,694	2,060	3.9	23,900	.18	.22	11.6	3,694	1,875	583	1,236	19.7	2,060	1,380	73	603
1957	3,673	1,390	2.6	16,500	.12	.14	11.4	3,673	1,730	751	1,192	19.2	1,390	752	72	563
1956	3,825	1,900	3.6	33,100	.24	.29	17.4	3,825	1,821	774	1,230	18.9	1,900	1,270	183	447
1955	4,320	2,650	5.2	28,200	.22	.26	10.7	4,320	2,154	844	1,322	18.5	2,650	1,780	244	625
1954	3,468	1,530	3.1	22,600	.18	.19	14.7	3,468	1,726	588	1,154	22.5	1,530	886	54	591
1953	5,091	2,400	4.7	28,300	.22	.26	11.8	5,091	2,825	745	1,521	20.3	2,400	1,460	162	781
1952	5,117	3,540	7.3	59,100	.48	.57	16.7	5,117	2,447	839	1,831	19.6	3,540	1,450	841	1,244
1951	4,737	2,220	4.5	22,900	.18	.21	10.3	4,737	2,102	888	1,747	17.4	2,220	1,180	136	904
1950	4,843	2,410	5.1	38,800	.33	.40	16.1	4,843	2,559	919	1,365	19.2	2,410	1,460	130	819
1949	3,606	3,030	6.7	50,500	.44	.59	16.7	3,606	1,682	781	1,143	22.5	3,030	1,540	82	1,410
1948	3,419	1,960	4.2	34,100	.28	.37	17.4	3,419	1,737	780	902	21.8	1,960	1,210	228	518
1947	3,693	2,170	4.7	34,600	.30	.41	15.9	3,693	1,707	1,102	884	25.6	2,170	805	931	431
1946	4,985	4,600	10.5	116,000	1.04	1.43	25.2	4,990	2,238	1,617	1,135	24.2	4,940	3,710	568	663
1945	4,750	3,470	8.2	38,000	.31	.47	11.0	4,616	1,956	946	1,714	9.9	3,070	1,340	671	1,060
1944	4,956	2,120	4.8	8,720	.07	.09	4.1	4,958	2,146	808	2,004	5.6	2,130	810	395	922
1943	3,752	1,980	4.6	13,500	.10	.15	6.8	3,734	1,906	585	1,243	5.0	1,970	1,220	226	523
1942	2,968	840	2.0	4,180	.04	.05	5.0	3,036	1,423	943	670	11.7	852	429	191	232
1941	4,288	2,360	6.1	23,000	.23	.32	9.8	4,314	1,535	2,138	641	18.3	2,360	1,110	744	512
1940	2,508	577	1.7	6,700	.08	.10	11.6	2,493	753	1,243	497	20.9	573	235	190	148
1939	2,613	1,170	3.5	17,800	.21	.28	15.2	2,639	699	1,411	529	23.4	1,180	352	641	185
1938	2,772	688	2.8	9,150	--------	.15	13.3	2,772	776	1,385	611	23.6	688	252	224	211
1937	4,740	1,860	7.2	28,400	--------	.43	15.3	4,720	1,410	2,728	582	20.3	1,950	436	1,160	347
1936	2,172	789	3.1	13,900	--------	.21	17.6	2,156	756	1,083	317	23.3	710	251	365	94
1935	2,014	1,120	5.2	15,500	--------	.29	13.8	2,003	760	945	298	23.8	1,102	663	288	151
1934	1,856	1,470	7.2	19,600	--------	.38	13.4	1,817	717	835	265	19.5	1,480	346	762	372
1933	1,695	1,170	6.3	16,900	--------	.36	14.4	1,672	926	533	213	16.9	1,144	544	465	135
1932	841	324	1.8	10,500	--------	.23	32.4	852	560	162	130	19.6	325	234	73	18
1931	810	342	1.6	6,890	--------	.11	20.2	796	447	221	128	18.8	346	155	116	74
1930	637	183	.8	3,320		.05	18.1	651	284	207	160	22.3	182	73	76	33
1929	921	289	1.2	5,350		.07	18.5	924	373	382	169	22.6	286	104	102	80
1928	604	314	1.3	12,600		.17	40.2	620	222	226	172	27.6	323	140	95	88
1927	707	330	1.4	26,200		.37	79.5	666	273	240	153	26.5	319	232	45	43

Year	Stoppages[1]				Workers involved (1,000)				Year	Stoppages[1]				Workers involved (1,000)			
	Total	Major issues			Total	Major issues				Total	Major issues			Total	Major issues		
		Wages and hours	Union organization	Other and not reported		Wages and hours	Union organization[3]	Other and not reported			Wages and hours	Union organization	Other and not reported		Wages and hours	Union organization[3]	Other and not reported
	977	978	979	980	982	983	984	985		977	978	979	980	982	983	984	985
1926	1,035	478	206	351	---------	---------	---------	---------	1899	1,838	1,014	471	353	432	288	66	79
1925	1,301	537	219	545	---------	---------	---------	---------	1898	1,098	645	236	217	263	184	30	49
1924	1,249	537	244	468	---------	---------	---------	---------	1897	1,110	680	193	237	416	335	36	45
1923	1,553	721	308	524	---------	---------	---------	---------	1896	1,066	547	297	222	249	160	53	36
1922	1,112	583	208	321	---------	---------	---------	---------									
1921	2,385	1,501	373	511	---------	---------	---------	---------	1895	1,255	810	217	228	407	305	51	51
									1894	1,404	865	206	333	690	469	25	196
1920	3,411	2,038	622	751	---------	---------	---------	---------	1893	1,375	783	257	335	288	162	59	66
1919	3,630	2,036	869	725	---------	---------	---------	---------	1892	1,359	693	261	405	239	122	59	57
1918	3,353	1,869	584	900	---------	---------	---------	---------	1891	1,786	867	334	585	330	221	55	54
1917	4,450	2,268	799	1,383	---------	---------	---------	---------									
1916	3,789	2,036	721	1,032	---------	---------	---------	---------	1890	1,897	1,039	318	540	373	276	32	66
1915	1,593	770	312	511	---------	---------	---------	---------	1889	1,111	662	173	276	260	207	29	24
1914	1,204	403	253	548	---------	---------	---------	---------	1888	946	540	163	243	163	100	23	41
									1887	1,503	836	299	368	439	249	91	99
1906–13									1886	1,572	1,073	210	289	610	445	79	87
1905	2,186	942	800	444	302	191	57	54									
1904	2,419	944	964	511	574	272	210	92	1885	695	486	67	142	258	214	14	30
1903	3,648	1,778	1,200	670	788	396	235	156	1884	485	341	50	94	165	145	4	16
1902	3,240	1,604	1,051	585	692	279	279	134	1883	506	372	55	79	170	131	28	12
1901	3,012	1,413	1,016	583	564	288	161	115	1882	476	353	38	85	159	133	12	14
1900	1,839	931	414	494	568	210	282	76	1881	477	382	32	63	130	118	5	7

* Denotes first year for which figures include Alaska and Hawaii.
[1] For 1881–1927 and 1947–1970, data for stoppages beginning in calendar years; 1928–1946, data for those ending in calendar years.
[2] Beginning 1961, other contractual matters included under "Other and not reported" rather than "Wages and hours" as in previous years.
[3] Wages and hours were important issues in many of these stoppages also.

Series D 986–1021.　Work Stoppages, by Major Industry Group: 1937 to 1970

[Workers and man-days idle in thousands]

Year	MANUFACTURING				FABRICATED METAL PRODUCTS EXCEPT ORDNANCE, MACHINERY, AND TRANSPORTATION EQUIPMENT				MACHINERY, EXCEPT ELECTRICAL			
	Stoppages beginning in year		Man-days idle during year (all stoppages)		Stoppages beginning in year		Man-days idle during year (all stoppages)		Stoppages beginning in year		Man-days idle during year (all stoppages)	
	Number	Workers involved	Number	Percent of estimated working time	Number	Workers involved	Number	Percent of estimated working time	Number	Workers involved	Number	Percent of estimated working time
	986	987	988	989	990	991	992	993	994	995	996	997
1970	2,481	1,128	38,006	0.77	323	118.0	3,444	0.97	292	119.0	3,603	0.72
1969	2,822	1,308	24,107	.47	381	74.0	1,378	.37	361	148.0	3,168	.62
1968	2,664	1,180	24,000	.47	349	78.4	2,040	.57	414	180.0	3,940	.79
1967	2,328	1,350	27,800	.57	274	107.0	2,270	.66	260	177.0	4,010	.80
1966	2,296	922	13,700	.28	277	76.1	1,290	.37	301	136.0	2,440	.51
1965	2,080	913	14,300	.31	269	86.8	1,430	.45	266	113.0	1,870	.43
1964	1,794	994	15,700	.35	228	79.9	1,550	.50	191	120.0	1,140	.27
1963	1,685	555	10,400	.24	193	40.8	516	.18	171	58.5	845	.22
1962	1,789	638	10,100	.24	220	42.5	651	.23	196	63.3	1,200	.32
1961	1,677	897	9,780	.24	191	96.6	1,130	.41	176	89.1	1,240	.34
1960	1,598	707	11,200	.27	195	44.2	597	.21	144	68.5	1,240	.30
1959	2,043	1,280	55,500	1.34	276	100.0	3,150	1.14	217	82.7	2,820	.68
1958	1,955	1,490	15,400	.39	256	147.0	1,220	.46	223	152.0	2,760	.72
1957	1,965	778	9,390	.22	237	58.5	713	.25	231	89.9	1,380	.32
1956	1,986	1,360	12,700	.63	229	87.7	1,420	.50	211	113.0	2,630	.83
1955	2,406	2,000	18,800	.45	282	131.0	1,590	.57	306	230.0	3,800	.95
1954	1,703	772	13,700	.33	175	42.0	1,200	.45	175	64.0	1,350	.34
1953	2,612	1,320	15,600	.36	291	102.0	1,690	.57	286	126.0	2,150	.50
1952	2,665	1,880	42,300	1.03	282	111.0	2,430	.95	323	167.0	3,990	.96
1951	2,548	1,370	17,500	.43	242	84.2	1,300	.51	268	158.0	3,370	.83
1950	2,705	1,450	22,900	.66	278	85.8	969	.45	317	224.0	4,410	1.40
1949	1,661	1,220	24,200	.73	134	54.0	1,050	.52	176	116.0	2,720	.89
1948	1,675	959	17,600	.46	151	37.0	496	----------	189	152.0	2,090	.59
1947	1,993	801	15,700	.43	218	51.3	883	----------	252	114.0	2,910	.59
1946	2,887	2,210	81,700	2.42	----------	----------	----------	----------	324	244.0	13,700	4.51
1945	3,185	2,510	28,800	.78	----------	----------	----------	----------	335	228.0	2,970	.91
1944	3,257	1,680	6,150	.14	----------	----------	----------	----------	311	141.0	508	.13
1943	2,491	1,220	3,430	.07	----------	----------	----------	----------	210	62.1	139	.04
1942	1,879	616	2,680	.08	----------	----------	----------	----------	87	46.8	104	----------
1941	2,652	1,270	12,500	.49	----------	----------	----------	----------	199	102.0	1,680	----------
1940	1,410	352	4,400	.17	----------	----------	----------	----------	87	24.3	396	----------
1939	1,389	394	7,180	.31	----------	----------	----------	----------	63	20.4	337	----------
1938	1,436	410	5,820	.27	----------	----------	----------	----------	55	13.9	333	----------
1937	2,779	1,230	20,000	.79	----------	----------	----------	----------	175	48.3	546	----------

Year	TRANSPORTATION EQUIPMENT [1]				NONMANUFACTURING				MINING			
	998	999	1000	1001	1002	1003	1004	1005	1006	1007	1008	1009
1970	158	327.0	14,034	3.02	3,241	2,177	28,407	0.21	544	211.0	850	0.54
1969	202	264.0	4,500	.87	2,893	1,174	18,763	.14	495	220.0	1,157	.72
1968	241	255.0	2,990	.58	2,396	1,470	25,000	.20	301	213.0	2,550	1.60
1967	165	347.0	5,530	1.13	2,267	1,530	14,300	.15	254	102.0	3,030	1.95
1966	162	150.0	1,330	.27	2,110	1,040	11,700	.14	194	96.1	794	.50
1965	140	196.0	2,630	.60	1,886	633	9,020	.11	188	71.6	431	.27
1964	120	386.0	6,410	1.53	1,865	646	7,210	.09	155	83.4	808	.49
1963	101	71.5	678	.16	1,678	386	5,730	.07	153	45.8	481	.30
1962	100	81.5	1,410	.34	1,825	596	8,460	.11	159	51.8	983	.60
1961	98	297.0	2,500	.65	1,694	555	6,500	.08	154	37.7	310	.18
1960	122	189.0	3,550	.85	1,740	610	7,900	.11	154	48.5	700	.41
1959	108	76.5	1,390	.32	1,672	600	13,500	.19	187	120.0	5,650	3.26
1958	210	551.0	4,310	1.06	1,739	574	8,520	.12	168	38.6	302	.16
1957	154	167.0	1,170	.24	1,711	610	7,080	.10	198	56.3	240	.11
1956	145	123.0	1,800	.40	1,856	544	6,020	.09	321	129.0	1,320	.65
1955	200	440.0	1,910	.40	1,913	646	9,390	.14	343	114.0	1,080	.57
1954	84	107.0	656	.15	1,762	761	8,900	.14	248	111.0	845	.44
1953	179	300.0	2,730	.55	2,479	1,090	12,700	.19	460	156.0	846	.40
1952	199	216.1	2,230	.53	2,452	1,660	16,800	.27	650	547.0	4,310	1.92
1951	194	230.0	2,600	.68	2,189	844	5,470	.11	622	284.0	1,290	.55
1950	171	368.0	8,540	2.88	2,138	959	15,900	.30	508	196.0	9,700	4.37
1949	89	230.0	2,190	.78	1,945	1,820	26,300	.39	476	1,380.0	19,200	8.39
1948	107	278.0	3,170	.89	1,744	996	16,500	.31	614	651.0	10,400	4.51
1947	106	171.0	4,200	1.18	1,700	1,370	18,900	.39	478	517.0	2,440	1.12
1946	193	222.0	17,300	----------	2,108	2,360	34,100	.72	570	974.0	21,400	10.35
1945	407	834.0	9,740	----------	1,569	958	9,270	.21	670	678.0	6,230	2.88
1944	549	752.0	2,260	----------	1,700	434	2,570	.05	893	278.0	1,410	.56
1943	345	341.0	823	----------	1,261	763	10,100	.21	463	610.0	9,370	4.25
1942	115	97.1	211	----------	1,089	224	1,500	.03	156	83.3	516	.31
1941	185	394.0	2,290	----------	1,642	1,090	10,600	.23	143	737.0	7,230	----------
1940	51	49.6	270	----------	1,098	225	2,300	.05	65	42.3	269	----------
1939	56	134.0	2,660	----------	1,224	777	10,600	.25	64	383.0	7,460	----------
1938	49	82.7	318	----------	1,336	278	3,330	.08	63	37.5	529	----------
1937	165	372.0	4,720	----------	1,961	663	8,450	.20	111	163.0	2,620	----------

[1] For 1937–1958, includes municipally operated utilities.

Series D 986–1021. Work Stoppages, by Major Industry Group: 1937 to 1970—Con.

[Workers and man-days idle in thousands]

Year	Stoppages beginning in year		Man-days idle during year (all stoppages)		Stoppages beginning in year		Man-days idle during year (all stoppages)		Stoppages beginning in year		Man-days idle during year (all stoppages)	
	Number	Workers involved	Number	Percent of estimated working time	Number	Workers involved	Number	Percent of estimated working time	Number	Workers involved	Number	Percent of estimated working time
	1010	1011	1012	1013	1014	1015	1016	1017	1018	1019	1020	1021
	CONTRACT CONSTRUCTION				TRANSPORTATION, COMMUNICATIONS, ELECTRIC, GAS, AND SANITARY SERVICES				WHOLESALE AND RETAIL TRADE			
1970	1,137	621.0	15,240	1.79	400	858.0	7,208	0.63	487	74.0	1,876	0.05
1969	973	433.0	10,386	1.19	320	212.0	4,031	.36	470	93.0	1,310	.04
1968	912	364.0	8,720	1.05	303	571.0	9,310	.84	417	75.1	972	.03
1967	867	305.0	5,160	.62	345	866.0	3,450	.32	431	87.2	994	.03
1966	977	455.0	6,140	.73	240	312.0	3,390	.32	365	42.3	508	.02
1965	943	301.0	4,630	.57	216	185.0	3,000	.29	336	42.6	570	.02
1964	944	248.0	2,790	.35	257	205.0	1,900	.19	309	61.6	1,340	.04
1963	840	208.0	1,930	.25	205	63.4	2,540	.25	293	34.1	498	.02
1962	913	284.0	4,150	.60	213	182.0	2,490	.25	364	29.7	535	.02
1961	824	217.0	3,490	.50	243	211.0	1,710	.17	308	62.4	716	.02
1960	773	269.0	4,470	.63	266	200.0	1,750	.18	290	32.6	451	.02
1959	771	251.0	4,120	.58	233	140.0	1,910	.19	311	72.2	1,570	.05
1958	844	326.0	4,790	.71	242	132.0	2,270	.23	358	57.0	942	.03
1957	785	308.0	3,970	.51	209	169.0	2,010	.19	372	63.0	654	.02
1956	784	231.0	2,680	.35	243	130.0	1,170	.11	336	37.1	558	.02
1955	733	204.0	1,810	.28	275	253.0	4,860	.47	409	52.3	1,090	.04
1954	804	437.0	4,800	.71	282	146.0	1,410	.14	298	53.4	1,690	.06
1953	1,039	574.0	8,000	1.22	372	256.0	2,380	.22	408	71.2	1,050	.04
1952	794	634.0	6,700	1.03	406	372.0	4,170	.39	397	75.8	1,050	.04
1951	651	232.0	1,190	.18	387	231.0	1,790	.17	277	40.0	289	.01
1950	611	237.0	2,460	.44	386	405.0	2,380	.25	381	70.1	927	.04
1949	615	197.0	2,760	.53	347	154.0	2,320	.25	329	46.2	1,440	.07
1948	380	108.0	1,430	.29	293	160.0	3,290	.34	241	30.2	557	.03
1947	382	175.0	2,770	.66	282	468.0	11,500	1.19	336	60.6	1,010	.05
1946	351	146.0	1,450	.40	479	1,020.0	9,020	.94	385	64.1	882	.05
1945	206	45.8	447	.20	342	157.0	1,550	.15	182	34.8	336	.02
1944	168	22.5	120	.06	335	73.4	345	.03	139	31.5	270	.01
1943	188	35.7	141	.04	284	55.6	183	---------	119	25.5	90	---------
1942	239	31.0	164	.04	221	42.3	171	---------	260	30.0	304	---------
1941	395	186.0	923	---------	280	51.5	433	---------	---------	---------	---------	---------
1940	310	71.3	493	---------	185	45.4	596	---------	---------	---------	---------	---------
1939	320	70.1	633	---------	256	87.4	867	---------	---------	---------	---------	---------
1938	315	44.4	405	---------	216	76.7	730	---------	---------	---------	---------	---------
1937	328	71.9	848	---------	379	138.0	1,890	---------	---------	---------	---------	---------

Series D 1022–1028. Average Monthly Labor Turnover Rates in Manufacturing, by Class of Turnover: 1919 to 1970

[Monthly rate per 100 employees. Beginning 1930, averages are arithmetic means; prior to that, unweighted medians. See text for further discussion]

Year	Accession rates		Separation rates			Year	Accession rates	Separation rates		
	Total	New hires	Total	Quits	Layoffs			Total	Quits	Layoffs
	1022	1023	1024	1025	1026		1022	1024	1025	1026
1970	4.0	2.8	4.8	2.1	1.8	1949	4.3	5.0	1.9	2.9
1969	4.7	3.7	4.9	2.7	1.2	1948	5.4	5.4	3.4	1.6
1968	4.6	3.5	4.6	2.5	1.2	1947	6.2	5.7	4.1	1.1
1967	4.4	3.3	4.6	2.3	1.4	1946	8.1	7.2	5.2	1.4
1966	5.0	3.8	4.6	2.6	1.2					
						1945	7.7	9.6	6.1	2.6
1965	4.3	3.1	4.1	1.9	1.4	1944	7.4	8.1	6.2	.7
1964	4.0	2.6	3.9	1.5	1.7	1943 [2]	9.1	8.6	6.3	.7
1963	3.9	2.4	3.9	1.4	1.8	1942	9.3	7.8	4.6	1.3
1962	4.1	2.5	4.1	1.4	2.0	1941	6.5	4.7	2.4	1.6
1961	4.1	2.2	4.0	1.2	2.2					
						1940	5.4	4.0	[3] 1.1	2.6
1960	3.8	2.2	4.3	1.3	2.4	1939	5.0	3.7	1.0	2.6
1959 [1*]	4.2	2.6	4.1	1.5	2.0	1938	4.7	4.8	.8	3.9
1958	3.6	1.7	4.1	1.1	2.6	1937	4.3	5.2	1.5	3.5
1957	3.6	2.2	4.2	1.6	2.1	1936	5.3	4.0	1.3	2.4
1956	4.2	2.8	4.2	1.9	1.7					
						1935	5.1	4.3	1.1	3.0
1955	4.5	3.0	3.9	1.9	1.5	1934	5.7	4.9	1.1	3.7
1954	3.6	1.9	4.1	1.4	2.3	1933	6.5	4.5	1.1	3.2
1953	4.8	3.6	5.1	2.8	1.6	1932	4.1	5.2	.9	4.2
1952	5.4	4.1	4.9	2.8	1.4	1931	3.7	4.8	1.1	3.5
1951	5.3	4.1	5.3	2.9	1.4	1930	3.8	5.9	1.9	3.6
1950	5.3	---------	4.1	2.3	1.3					

See footnotes at end of table.

Series D 1022–1028. Average Monthly Labor Turnover Rates in Manufacturing, by Class of Turnover: 1919 to 1970—Con.

[Monthly rate per 100 employees. Beginning 1930, averages are arithmetic means; prior to that, unweighted medians. See text for further discussion]

Year	Accession rates 1022	Separation rates Total 1024	Layoffs 1026	Discharges 1027	Quits 1025	Miscellaneous 1028	Year	Accession rates 1022	Separation rates Total 1024	Layoffs 1026	Discharges 1027	Quits 1025	Miscellaneous 1028
1929 [4]	5.1	3.9	0.4	0.5	3.0		1923	9.0	7.5	0.3	1.0	6.2	
1928	3.7	3.1	.5	.4	2.2		1922	8.0	5.3	.4	.7	4.2	
1927	3.3	3.3	.7	.5	2.1		1921	2.8	4.4	1.8	.4	2.2	
1926	4.5	3.9	.5	.6	2.9		1920	10.1	10.3	.8	1.1	8.4	
1925	5.2	4.0	.4	.5	3.1		1919	10.1	7.5	.6	1.1	5.8	
1924	3.3	3.8	.6	.5	2.7								

* Denotes first year for which figures include Alaska and Hawaii.
[1] Beginning 1959, transfers between establishments of the same firm are included in total accessions and total separations; 1959–1970 figures therefore not strictly comparable with prior data.

[2] Beginning 1943, labor turnover rates refer to all employees; previously, to production workers only.
[3] Prior to 1940, quits include miscellaneous separations.
[4] January to May average.

Series D 1029–1036. Work-Injury Frequency Rates in Manufacturing, Mining, and Class I Railroads: 1922 to 1970

[Rate is average number of disabling injuries per million man-hours worked]

Year	Manufacturing [1] 1029	Mining Total 1030	Coal [2] 1031	Metals [3] 1032	Non-metals [4] 1033	Stone quarries [5] 1034	Class I railroads All injuries 1035	Excluding 1-3 day injuries 1036	Year	Manufacturing [1] 1029	Mining Total 1030	Coal [2] 1031	Metals [3] 1032	Non-metals [4] 1033	Stone quarries [5] 1034	Class I railroads All injuries 1035	Excluding 1-3 day injuries 1036
1970	15.2	28.9	42.6	25.6	26.1	19.8	11.5	--------	1945	18.6	55.5	60.7	44.9	47.2	32.8	20.5	11.9
1969	14.8	28.0	42.6	23.9	24.2	18.4	12.2	--------	1944	18.4	57.2	60.3	55.4	50.5	34.9	20.6	11.8
1968	14.0	27.8	42.5	23.1	25.3	17.8	12.5	--------	1943	20.0	59.4	63.8	56.9	53.4	34.0	20.3	11.9
1967	14.0	28.0	42.8	24.8	24.0	17.8	12.2	--------	1942	19.9	61.2	66.8	56.6	55.5	35.7	17.6	10.2
1966	13.6	28.4	43.8	25.1	23.3	19.1	12.0	--------	1941	18.1	63.2	67.6	64.2	51.6	40.1	14.6	8.3
1965	12.8	28.3	45.8	23.8	23.0	17.3	12.1	--------	1940	15.3	65.2	70.4	66.8	44.2	35.7	11.5	6.7
1964	12.3	28.8	44.8	25.0	23.4	18.2	12.6	--------	1939	14.9	64.8	69.5	69.4	42.2	36.5	11.1	6.7
1963	11.9	28.8	45.1	25.1	21.8	18.2	12.0	--------	1938	15.1	67.5	73.0	71.3	41.1	38.2	11.1	6.8
1962	11.9	28.6	45.1	25.0	21.9	17.4	11.7	--------	1937	17.8	70.5	74.2	78.9	48.7	40.6	13.6	8.2
1961	11.8	29.5	45.0	26.6	21.5	22.4	12.0	--------	1936	16.6	70.2	74.4	76.3	48.6	39.5	13.7	8.3
1960	12.0	29.8	43.4	25.2	23.4	23.3	7.3	--------	1935	17.9	72.7	79.0	65.8	50.7	38.2	--------	6.7
1959	12.4	29.2	42.1	26.7	25.6	24.3	7.2	--------	1934	20.2	73.8	78.1	71.5	52.4	41.8	--------	7.0
1958	[6] 11.4	[7] 31.9	45.1	26.7	23.3	24.7	6.7	--------	1933	19.3	71.7	75.9	65.8	53.3	42.1	--------	6.9
1957	11.4	35.8	47.2	28.0	27.1	23.3	[8] 5.3	--------	1932	19.6	74.8	82.2	57.2	45.2	38.5	--------	7.4
1956	12.0	37.1	46.7	32.9	29.7	21.3	14.7	7.7	1931	18.9	79.9	89.9	58.0	47.5	41.0	--------	7.5
1955	12.1	38.3	46.0	38.0	32.0	22.0	13.9	7.2	1930	23.1	--------	--------	--------	--------	40.3	--------	9.4
1954	11.9	37.7	46.7	34.3	32.6	22.0	12.6	6.5	1929	24.0	--------	--------	--------	--------	46.9	--------	13.8
1953	13.4	40.3	48.1	34.8	47.3	23.7	13.6	6.7	1928	22.5	--------	--------	--------	--------	47.5	--------	16.2
1952	14.3	43.6	51.6	38.3	40.9	24.5	13.7	7.0	1927	22.6	--------	--------	--------	--------	59.2	--------	19.4
1951	15.5	45.1	52.1	38.8	45.4	26.2	14.7	7.5	1926	24.2	--------	--------	--------	--------	58.0	--------	23.9
1950	14.7	46.3	53.3	41.0	44.2	25.4	14.2	7.3	1925	--------	--------	--------	--------	--------	61.4	--------	26.1
1949	14.5	48.3	56.0	43.6	42.1	26.8	13.7	7.0	1924	--------	--------	--------	--------	--------	62.9	--------	27.3
1948	17.2	53.2	60.6	43.4	44.2	28.3	16.2	8.5	1923	--------	--------	--------	--------	--------	--------	--------	30.9
1947	18.8	55.8	61.9	48.1	45.8	32.4	18.2	9.7	1922	--------	--------	--------	--------	--------	--------	--------	27.1
1946	19.9	58.0	64.0	51.2	51.9	32.8	19.0	10.5									

[1] Excludes petroleum refining, smelting and refining of nonferrous metals, cement and lime manufacturing, and coke production.
[2] Includes data on coal-mine mechanical-cleaning plants and mill data for metal, non-metal, and stone quarries. Excludes coke production.
[3] Copper, gold-silver, iron, lead-zinc, uranium, and miscellaneous.
[4] Clay-shale, gypsum, phosphate rock, potash, salt, sulfur, and miscellaneous.

[5] Cement, granite, lime, limestone, marble, sandstone, slate, traprock, and miscellaneous.
[6] Industry definition revised to conform to the 1957 edition of the Standard Industrial Classification Manual. Comparisons to prior years should be made with caution.
[7] Beginning 1958, includes data on sand and gravel operations.
[8] Beginning 1957, accidents reported on different basis; data not comparable with prior years.

Prices and Price Indexes

E 1–214. General note.

An early interest in the statistics of prices was evident at the beginning of the 19th century, with the appearance in 1806 of Samuel Blodgett, Jr.'s *Economica: A Statistical Manual for the United States of America*, which included a collection of prices for 16 important commodities in 5 markets for 1785–1805. Many other contemporary accounts contained references to prices, but the first serious attempt to summarize comprehensive price data for the United States in the form of index numbers was made by Horatio C. Burchard, Director of the Mint. His report to the Secretary of the Treasury in 1881 contained wholesale prices for many individual articles and an index number (which contains some serious inadequacies). In 1886, a special report containing retail prices of about 60 "necessaries of life" was included in volume 20 of the Tenth Census, *Report on the Statistics of Wages in Manufacturing Industries*, by Joseph D. Weeks (usually called the *Weeks Report*). No summary figures were included in this volume.

In 1891, a Senate Resolution led to the collection of a voluminous body of data which covered wholesale prices for 1840–1891 and retail prices for a 28-month period ending September 1891, for more than 200 commodities. The information assembled was summarized by Roland P. Falkner, whose indexes have been widely used as evidence of price changes for 1840–1891. These indexes were prepared as estimates of changes in wage earners' cost of living, but, in actuality, they were indexes of wholesale prices for one month of each year. Their technical adequacy was the subject of considerable controversy at the time, but the deficiencies in the indexes do not detract from the historical value of the basic price data collected for the Senate Committee and published in the "Aldrich Reports," including *Wholesale Prices, Wages, and Transportation* (4 parts), Senate Report No. 1394, 1893, and *Retail Prices and Wages* (3 parts), Senate Report No. 986, 1892.

In 1900, Roland Falkner extended his indexes to 1899 with quotations for 142 articles collected by the Department of Labor, with some adjustments in his methods. The results are published in Department of Labor Bulletin No. 27, *Wholesale Prices: 1890 to 1899*, pp. 237–313. In 1902, the Department of Labor began publication of its index of wholesale prices, which has continued since without interruption.

Interest in price measurements following the upturn in prices after 1897 led to the preparation of a number of wholesale price indexes for the United States, in addition to the official Department of Labor index series. John R. Commons published an index of wholesale prices of 66 commodities for 1878–1900 in the *Quarterly Bulletin of the Bureau of Economic Research* for July and October 1900. Bradstreet's indexes of wholesale prices of about 96 commodities were established in 1897 and carried back to 1890. Dun's index numbers of wholesale prices for about 350 commodities were published in *Dun's Review* on a continuous basis beginning in 1901 and gradually extended back to 1860. These last 2 series were expressed as sums of actual prices rather than in the conventional index number form. Several other relatively short-lived series were also compiled during the next 10 to 20 years.

After 1902, when the Department of Labor's wholesale price index was continuously available, additions to wholesale price index numbers were mainly to obtain a better historical perspective. In 1932, the series of wholesale price indexes for 1720–1932 were completed by

G. F. Warren and F. A. Pearson (see series E 52–63). Part of this work was done under the auspices of the International Scientific Committee on Price History referred to below.

Walter B. Smith and Arthur H. Cole computed wholesale commodity price indexes covering 1792–1862 for *Fluctuations in American Business, 1790–1860*, Harvard Economic Studies, Harvard University Press, Cambridge, 1935. The series include wholesale commodity price indexes for Boston, 1792–1820; for Boston, New York, and Philadelphia, 1815–1845; and New York (primarily), 1843–1862.

Wholesale prices in Cincinnati were assembled from newspapers for 1844–1914 and an index published by Henry E. White in *Wholesale Prices at Cincinnati and New York*, Cornell University Agricultural Experiment Station, *Memoir 182*, Ithaca, 1935.

The most extensive historical price investigations, however, were undertaken under the auspices of the International Scientific Committee on Price History. The results for 6 important marketing centers were summarized by Arthur H. Cole in *Wholesale Commodity Prices in the United States, 1700–1861*, Harvard University Press, Cambridge, 1938. The historical indexes are given in series E 90–122.

Wholesale price indexes were compiled by Frederick C. Mills for commodities grouped according to economically significant factors. Mills' studies of price relationships and price movements contain a number of special indexes which he derived by recombining price relatives for commodities in the Bureau of Labor Statistics (BLS) indexes. These indexes include some special commodity groupings not used by BLS, e.g., crops, as well as classifications by stage of processing and by durability. Some series were first published by the National Bureau of Economic Research (NBER) for 1890–1931 in *Economic Tendencies in the United States*, No. 21, New York, 1932, pp. 584–588. Additional indexes for 1913–1935 appeared in *Prices in Recession and Recovery*, NBER, No. 31, New York, 1936, pp. 491–547. Indexes through June 1943 were included in an appendix to *Prices in a War Economy*, NBER, Occasional Paper No. 12, October 1943, and through March 1948 in *The Structure of Postwar Prices*, NBER, Occasional Paper No. 27, July 1948.

The volume of information available for wholesale prices is not matched at the retail level, especially for the early years. The official Consumer Price Index of the BLS was initiated in 1904 with a food index. The *Eighteenth Annual Report of the Commissioner of Labor, 1903: Cost of Living and Retail Prices of Food* contained an index of retail prices of food for 1890–1903 weighted by family consumption in 1901. This food index was continued until the end of World War I, when it became one component group of a comprehensive "cost-of-living" index, originated as part of a study of cost of living in shipbuilding cities in 1918 and 1919. Supplementary price information had been collected by the BLS over the years, and a comprehensive index was compiled back to 1913. Since World War I, the index has undergone a number of changes in coverage and methodology, most of them in the direction of improvement in the quantity and quality of data. At present, the index is issued monthly under the official title Consumer Price Index, in brief press releases, in detailed reports, and in the *Monthly Labor Review* (see text for series E 135–173).

The National Industrial Conference Board also compiled a Consumer Price Index from 1918 to 1958. This index was similar to the BLS Consumer Price Index but the collection of data was primarily by mail instead of by personal visit. A description of the NICB index as it was compiled before discontinuance is included in the August 1954 issue of *Management Record*.

The index numbers of prices received and paid by farmers compiled by the Department of Agriculture were also initiated after World War I; see chapter K, series K 344–353.

. Prior to 1913, except for the data in the *Weeks Report* and the *Aldrich Reports*, readily available retail price data are extremely spotty and inadequate. As a result, many of the indexes widely used to approximate changes in retail prices, rest entirely or partially on changes in wholesale prices. A serious limitation in these indexes is that allowance was not made for the slow-moving rents and services nor was account always taken of the difference in movement between wholesale and retail prices of commodities. Falkner's indexes referred to above, for example, were calculated entirely from wholesale price information. Adjustments to wholesale price movements combined with available BLS retail prices formed the basis for Douglas' index of the cost of living (series E 185). The only "cost-of-living" indexes now available for any years before 1913, computed from retail price data, are Wesley C. Mitchell's *Relative Cost of Living for 1860 to 1880*, the *Consumer Price Index for 1851 to 1880* compiled by Ethel Hoover (series E 174–182), and Rees' cost-of-living index, 1890–1914 (series E 186). The cost-of-living index computed by Wesley C. Mitchell for *Gold, Prices, and Wages Under the Greenback Standard*, University of California Publications in Economics, vol. 1, Berkeley, March 1908, p. 91, utilized a portion of the retail data in the *Weeks Report* for 1860–1880. The Mitchell series was included as one of the links in the cost-of-living index estimate of the Federal Reserve Bank of New York (series E 183). The Hoover Consumer Price Index for 1851–1880 was based largely on a summarization of all of the usable retail price information from the *Weeks Report*, with some additions from other sources. The Rees' cost-of-living index utilized some components of the Douglas' index, but most of the data were compiled from mail-order catalogs, newspapers, and other sources.

Over the years there has been considerable improvement in the quality of the price reporting, in the scope of the data, and in the construction of index numbers. The lists of commodities that are now included in the price collection program cover a wider range of goods in the market, and services are represented in the consumer price indexes. Commodities and services are now defined fairly precisely and the current collection methods give the opportunity of securing supplementary data on discounts, terms of delivery, and other necessary information to measure price change. Data for weighting systems for index numbers can now be taken from the greatly improved expenditure studies, censuses, and other official statistics.

As the indexes and price reports were extended to earlier years, many of these advantages making for better price measures were not present. The range of commodities and services for which information could be obtained from surviving records was very limited. At the wholesale level, the commodity coverage was limited primarily to raw materials and goods in the early stages of processing. The limited coverage of finished goods, especially after the Civil War, is an important factor in the interpretation of price changes. At retail, the available price data were relatively scant and the emphasis was on food and dry goods prices, with little information for other less important commodities and for rents and services. The perennial problem of changes in qualities, changes in consumer tastes, and demographic and other changes which are still present to some extent in the current indexes, become accentuated as price comparisons are made over longer periods of time.

The newspapers and other sources from which prices were assembled for the early years give only brief or vague descriptions for the commodities quoted and the compiler could not always be assured that quotations over time were for the same quality. Incomplete files, nominal prices, and nonpublication in some issues were among the many other problems encountered. Data obtained from records of surviving firms raise the further question of how well these surviving firms represented the movement of prices for all firms for the period under consideration.

E 1–22.   Implicit price deflators for gross national product, 1929–1970.

Source: 1929–1963, U.S. Office of Business Economics, *The National Income and Product Accounts of the United States, 1929–1965*; 1964–1967, *U.S. National Income and Product Accounts, 1964–67*, tables 8.1 and 8.4; 1968–1970, U.S. Bureau of Economic Analysis, *Survey of Current Business*, July 1972, tables 8.1 and 8.4.

The implicit deflator for total gross national product (GNP) is the ratio of GNP in current prices to GNP in constant prices. It is a weighted average of the price indexes used to deflate the components of GNP; the implicit weights are expenditures in the current period valued in prices of the base year 1958. The implicit deflator measures the price change of a particular "market basket" since 1958. However, the market basket for any other period is not necessarily the same as for the base year 1958. Consequently, a comparison of the deflator for the current period with any period other than the base year measures both the effect of the difference between the weights in the two periods and the change in the price of a fixed market basket.

The deflation is not performed at the level of individual commodities; components that encompass expenditures on an array of commodities are deflated. On a quarterly basis, 142 components of GNP are deflated as shown below.

Gross national product	142
Personal consumption expenditures	41
Private fixed investment	42
Change in business inventories	10
Exports	3
Imports	3
Government purchases of goods and services	43

The components are deflated with conventional, fixed weighted price indexes that combine price relatives for individual types of commodities included in the expenditure component. Therefore, the implicit deflator involves current period weighting among the component price indexes, and fixed weighting within the components.

Differences between changes in the implicit deflator and the fixed weighted indexes are due to the shift in the weights in the implicit deflator. If the composition of expenditures shifts toward those components that have increased in price at an above-average rate since the price base period of 1958, the implicit deflator increases more than a fixed weighted index. If the composition shifts in the other direction, the implicit deflator increases less than a fixed weighted index.

Strictly speaking, the implicit deflator increases more (less) than a fixed weighted price index that has as its weight base the initial or terminal period of the span being compared if there is a positive (negative) correlation between the shifts in the weights in the implicit deflator and the changes since 1958 in the component price indexes. When the fixed weighted index has another period as its weight base, the difference also depends on the shift in the composition of real GNP between the weight base period and the initial or terminal period of the span being compared.

E 23–122.   General note.

Wholesale price indexes are compiled from prices in primary markets; that is, prices pertaining to the first major commercial transaction for each commodity. The quotations are usually selling prices of manufacturers or producers. A few prices are reported by trade associations and organized exchanges, and some are taken from trade publications or from other Government agencies which collect quotations as part of their regular work. They are not prices received by wholesalers, distributors, or jobbers.

In addition to the indexes presented here, brief descriptions of the coverage and calculation techniques for other indexes may be found in G. F. Warren and F. A. Pearson, *Wholesale Prices for 213 Years, 1720–1932*, Cornell University Agricultural Experiment Station, Memoir 142, Ithaca, 1932, pp. 167–196; and in BLS Bulletin No. 284, *Index Numbers of Wholesale Prices in the United States and Foreign*

Countries, 1921, pp. 115–175. This bulletin also contains Wesley C. Mitchell's "The Making and Using of Index Numbers."

See also general note for series E 1–214.

E 23–39. Wholesale price indexes (BLS), by major product groups, 1890–1970.

Source: U.S. Bureau of Labor Statistics, *Handbook of Labor Statistics, 1971*, Bulletin 1705, p. 276.

The current BLS wholesale price indexes were begun in 1952 but calculated to 1947, using new samples of items and new weights. However, the official index begins with January 1952, and does not replace the 1926 base series as the official index for 1947–1951. The new series of indexes was spliced to the former series (converted) by linking as of January 1947. The former group indexes were spliced with the new ones when the value aggregate of commodities in the former group represented 50 percent or more of the value of shipments in 1947 for all commodities (priced and unpriced) in the group. The index has been shown with 1967 as the base year since 1971. Prior to 1971, the 1957–59 period was the base from 1962 and the 1947–49 period from 1952 to 1961.

With the revision in 1952, the conceptual definition of the index was not altered, but major changes in coverage and methods were adopted. The list of priced commodities was expanded from 947 to approximately 1,800, embracing nearly 5,000 separate series. By 1970, the sample of priced commodities numbered approximately 2,450 and the number of separate price series totaled 7,725. The classification scheme in effect from 1952 to 1970 was revised somewhat in January 1967, providing a more meaningful and flexible structure without changing the basic concept of the structure. The 1967 scheme substituted an 8-digit coding system for the former 6- and 7-digit system permitting a number of special group indexes to be included in the regular classification of the index.

The weighting factors for each commodity represent the value of shipments for the specific commodity priced and for all others in the same group which are known (or assumed) to have price movements similar to those for the commodity priced. By this method of weighting, values for all commodities in a group are accounted for and the group automatically has its proper representation in the all-commodities index. The weight universe includes the net selling value of all commodities included in the producing and processing sector of the economy *including* sales for exports and imports for consumption but *excluding* interplant transfers, military goods, construction, real estate, transportation, securities, printing and publishing, and transactions for services.

The indexes are calculated as averages of relatives weighted by values of shipments. This is algebraically equivalent to quantity weighted aggregative indexes but allows for more flexibility in processing. As in all the official indexes, the linking process is used when there are changes in lists of commodities, changes in weighting factors, or other changes making for noncomparability. In the case of quality changes, adjustments are made to obtain month-to-month relatives for the same quality insofar as possible. If the change in description is minor, direct comparisons are made between the price of the old and the new items. For major quality changes, efforts are made to secure from the producer an estimate of the proportion of the gross price change due to quality differences and to a price change. When such information cannot be obtained, the new quality is linked into the index, thus assuming that the full price change is due to quality change.

Since the revised index was initiated in 1952, there have been four changes in the weighting factors. Value of shipments in 1952 and 1953 were introduced in 1955 and only relatively minor changes were made in the list of items priced. Another revision in the weighting factors to represent value of shipments in 1954 was introduced beginning 1958. Other revisions include introduction of 1958 value of shipments in 1961 and 1963 values in 1967. Policy has been to revise the weighting structure of the index periodically when data from industrial censuses become available, generally at 5-year intervals.

Most of the prices in the index are collected by mail directly from the manufacturer or other producer. A few are reported by trade associations or organized exchanges and some are obtained from authoritative trade publications or from other government agencies that collect price data for their regular work.

The indexes shown here are annual averages of monthly figures. Before 1952, the monthly prices used were averages of 1-day-a-week prices. From 1952 to 1966, prices were, for the most part, those of Tuesday of the week including the 15th of the month. From 1967 to 1970, the pricing date was Tuesday of the week including the 13th of the month. However, for some commodities another day may have been used as a more representative day.

Whenever possible, prices are obtained at the production point or at the central marketing point. Delivered prices are used only when it is the practice of the industry to quote prices on this basis. Prices obtained from manufacturers or other producers are subject to the applicable trade and quantity discounts. Cash discounts are deducted from the price when it is determined that most buyers avail themselves of the reduced prices. Excise taxes are excluded from the price. Closeout sales prices are usually not used. Free deals or allowances are used when possible in arriving at the net price to be used for index calculation. Nominal prices are used when they are indicative of the market situation and no other price is available.

For a more complete description of techniques used in compiling the index, see BLS Bulletin No. 1458, *Handbook of Methods for Surveys and Studies, 1966*, chap. 11.

See also general note for series E 23–122.

E 40–51. Wholesale price indexes (BLS), by major product groups, 1890–1951.

Source: 1890–1950, BLS, *Handbook of Labor Statistics*, 1950 edition, p. 118; 1951, 1951 supplement to the *Handbook*, p. 42.

Since 1902, when BLS began regular publication of wholesale price indexes, there have been a number of changes in lists of items, weighting factors, base periods, and methods of computing the indexes. Detailed descriptions of the early unweighted index numbers, and later the weighted indexes, are included in various annual bulletins on wholesale prices beginning with the Bulletin No. 39, issued in March 1902. The figures shown in series E 40–51 are weighted index numbers of the fixed base weighted aggregative type.

In 1914, BLS recalculated its series back to 1890 using as weights the quantity of each priced item marketed in 1909 but retained the base 1890–99. The system of classification for group indexes was generally according to origin rather than end use and each commodity was included in only one group index. For 1914–1921, the index series were continued with little change except for expanding the list of priced items and rebasing the indexes several times. In 1920 the year 1913 was adopted as the base period in order to provide a prewar standard for measuring price changes.

In 1921, a revision of the indexes extended the commodity coverage to include about 400 items as compared with 250 to 325 in previous years. The weighting factors were changed to represent the quantity of each priced item marketed in 1919. At this time an important change was made in the method of grouping commodities. Articles properly classified in more than one major group were included in the appropriate groups with their total weights but, in the all-commodities index, the weights for such articles were counted only once. In addition, a rearrangement of commodities within groups was made to provide separate indexes for 37 subgroups.

When the 1926 base period was adopted in 1927, the indexes were recalculated back to 1913 with new sets of weights (see BLS Bulletin No. 473, *Wholesale Prices, 1913 to 1927*, pp. 2–5). The figures for 1890–1912 were converted, not recalculated in detail.

In subsequent years, the weighting factors were brought up to date from time to time. Major additions to the lists of priced items in 1931 and again in 1940 provided better coverage of manufactured articles than in earlier indexes. By 1951, when these indexes were discontinued, the number of subgroups for which separate series were available had been enlarged to 49. The indexes shown here are annual averages of monthly figures.

Because of changes in the list of commodities and in the weighting factors, the indexes were calculated by the chain relative method. In this way, comparisons between any two periods were based on the same commodities with the same weights. Throughout the whole period, the weight used for each priced commodity was the quantity marketed for that class of commodity. Classes of commodities not represented by an item in the list priced were not represented in the weighting factors.

Table I contains a summary of the number of commodities and the weights used for the indexes in series E 40.

Table I. Number of Price Series and Weighting Factors Used in BLS Wholesale Price Index (All Commodities, Series E 40): 1890 to 1951

Year	Number of series	Weights used
1949–1951	900–947	Quantities marketed 1929 and 1931
1940–1948	881–890	
1938–1939	813	
1934–1937	784	
1932–1933	784	Quantities marketed 1927 and 1929
1931	784	Quantities marketed 1925 and 1927
1930	550	
1926–1929	404–550	Quantities marketed 1923 and 1925
1924–1925	526–528	
1922–1923	450–478	Quantities marketed 1921 and 1923
1920–1921	390–450	Quantities marketed 1919 and 1921
1914–1919	296–371	Quantities marketed 1914 and 1919
1913	252	Quantities marketed 1909 and 1914
1890–1912	251–261	Quantities marketed 1909

The price quotations on which the indexes were based were obtained by mail from leading manufacturers or selling agents or from such other sources as standard trade publications, reports of boards of trade, and produce exchanges. Before 1913, most of the data referred to the New York market, but after 1913, quotations were obtained in several major markets for a number of important commodities.

For articles subject to frequent fluctuations in price, monthly averages were made up of quotations for one day in each week and for a portion of the period from daily quotations. For other articles, monthly, quarterly, or semiannual quotations were secured.

Considerable attention was devoted to obtaining descriptive details so that price comparisons were based on the same or comparable commodities. By 1931, BLS had developed a specification for each commodity in the index. These specifications defined quality as precisely as possible, including the principal price-determining characteristics, terms of sale, and other details. These specifications were refined and improved over the years.

The prices used in the index were usually net cash prices, f.o.b., for the article described by the specification. Delivered prices were included only when it was customary for an industry to quote on the delivered basis.

See also general note for series E 23–122.

E 52–63. Wholesale price indexes (Warren and Pearson), by major product groups, 1749–1890.

Source: George F. Warren and Frank A. Pearson, *Prices*, John Wiley and Sons, New York, 1933, pp. 11–13, 25–27 (copyright).

The indexes are also presented in *Wholesale Prices for 213 Years, 1720–1932* (see general note, series E 23–122), *Memoir 142*, part 1, pp. 7–10 and 84–111. The "all-commodities" index for 1749–1889, converted to the base of 1926, is included in Bureau of Labor Statistics (BLS) Bulletin No. 572, *Wholesale Prices, 1931, 1933*, appendix, pp. 111–114.

The primary aim of Warren and Pearson was to present monthly comprehensive index numbers for the 19th century corresponding to those of BLS for 1890 and later years. The full series constitutes the longest index now available for 1720–1932. For 1890–1932, Warren and Pearson used the BLS indexes (series E 40–51) converted to the base 1910–14. Their work covered the period 1797–1890; the index was extended back to 1720 by Herman M. Stoker.

The bulk of the prices on which the index is based relate to New York City and were obtained from newspapers, supplemented with prices published in the *Report of the Secretary of the Treasury on the State of the Finances* (usually referred to as the *U. S. Finance Report*) for 1863. The number of products included in the all-items index numbers for 1797–1890 varied from a low of 113 in 1830 to 146 in 1880. For the extension back to 1720, Stoker encountered some serious gaps in the available source materials, especially for years prior to 1749. For 1720–1748, the price data were scarce and irregular, and an index could be computed only for certain months in each year. For 1749–1782, the number of commodities included generally varied from 11 to 19; and for 1783–1796, 71 series were available for most years.

The index numbers for 1797–1890 are weighted arithmetic averages of relatives, computed first on the 1876–91 base, then converted to the 1910–14 base using the relationship with BLS index numbers for 1890–1893. When one commodity was substituted for another, a linking procedure was employed. Two all-commodity indexes were prepared, one with fixed group weights throughout the whole period, and one with varying group weights. The latter is presented here as series E 52.

Separate subindexes (series E 53–63) were computed by Warren and Pearson for the 10 groups of commodities formerly used by BLS with a supplemental index for spirits. Within each group, weights representing the importance of the priced commodities in the total trade of the United States were varied over the years to represent, insofar as possible, changes in importance. (Specific mention should be made of the reduction in the importance of cotton during the Civil War period. Cotton was scarce and prices very high so weights were based on the amount available for consumption for 1861–1866 and on production for 1867–1871.) Censuses, imports, exports, and similar official figures were used as weighting factors. However, data were meager for the early years and some arbitrary weight assignments were necessary.

For 1787–1800, Stoker constructed a "71-commodity index" with the same commodity group classification and methods of calculation as those employed by Warren and Pearson. These all-commodity and group indexes were linked to the Warren-Pearson indexes. His "15-commodity index" for 1720–1787 based on the 11–19 items (practically all farm products and foods) was in turn linked to the 71-commodity index.

There are discrepancies between *Prices* and *Memoir 142* for farm products (series E 53) for 1807, 1808, and 1827. The figures shown in series E 53 are averages of monthly data in *Memoir 142*.

E 64–72. Wholesale price indexes (BLS), by durability of product, 1947–1970.

Source: U.S. Bureau of Labor Statistics, *Handbook of Labor Statistics, 1971*, Bulletin 1705, p. 285.

These indexes were constructed by recombining commodity segments of the regular BLS Wholesale Price Index according to durability. The basic weights, the price data, and the calculation methods were the same as for the regular indexes (see text for series E 23–39). The commodity groups included in each of these special indexes are listed in BLS Bulletins, *Wholesale Prices and Price Indexes*, annually for 1957–1963, and in *Wholesale Prices and Price Indexes* for January 1967 (final) and February 1967 (final).

Manufactured commodities were generally classified on the same basis as that used by the Federal Reserve Board for its Index of Industrial Production. The classification of the "raw or slightly processed goods" was based for the most part on that used by Frederick C. Mills in *Prices in Recession and Recovery*, National Bureau of Economic Research, New York, 1936, pp. 472–474.

E 73–86. Wholesale price indexes (BLS), for economic sectors, by stage of processing, 1913–1970.

Source: U.S. Bureau of Labor Statistics, 1913–1946, Bulletin 1235, *Wholesale Prices and Price Indexes*, 1957, p. 26 (these series on a 1926 base appear in the following publications: 1913–1941, *Handbook of Labor Statistics*, 1941 edition, p. 733; 1942–1946, Bulletin 947, *Wholesale Prices, 1947*, p. 6); 1947–1970, Bulletin 1705, *Handbook of Labor Statistics*, 1971, p. 286.

Although the basic weights, the price data, and the calculation methods for these indexes were the same as those used for the regular indexes, the series shown comprise two parts, one for 1903–1946 and the second for 1947–1970. Prior to the revision of the regular Wholesale Price Index (WPI) in 1952 (which was carried back to 1947), each commodity in the WPI was classified in one of three groups: Raw, semimanufactured, or manufactured. The prices were weighted using quantities as specified for series E 40–51. The list of commodities included in each classification is shown in BLS Bulletin 473, p. 62.

The more refined economic sector classification used for 1947–1970 required adjustments to these procedures. Many commodities were considered to fall appropriately in more than one category. For 1947–1966, the base weight for each such article was, therefore, distributed among the economic sectors on the basis of percentage distributions by end use, derived from the BLS interindustry studies for 1947. From 1967 to 1970, the 1958 interindustry study of the Commerce Department's Office of Business Economics was used as a guide. The same price series was used in several sectors when a commodity was classified in more than one sector. It was recognized that this procedure had some disadvantages, but it was believed to have little effect on the measurement of price trend.

In splicing the two parts, the index for "raw materials" was considered as most nearly comparable with the new "crude materials for further processing"; "semimanufactured" with "intermediate materials, supplies, and components"; and "manufactured" with "finished goods."

E 87–89. Wholesale price indexes (BLS), by 2 levels of processing, for identical commodities, 1890–1926.

Source: U.S. Bureau of Labor Statistics, Bulletin No. 440, *Wholesale Prices, 1890 to 1926*, pp. 28–29, 1926.

These series were calculated for the first time in 1915, were extended back to 1890, and continued through 1926. The items in each of the indexes were selected from those included in the BLS regular wholesale price index (see series E 40). The indexes are fixed weight aggregative indexes, derived by weighting the price series with the estimated quantity of each article marketed in 1919. Similar figures for 1890–1914 on the 1914 base, using 1909 quantity weights may be found in BLS Bulletin No. 181, *Wholesale Prices, 1890–1914*, pp. 28–29.

E 90–122. General note.

The inadequacy of the available statistics on commodity-price and wage movements over long periods of time led to the formation of the International Scientific Committee on Price History in 1929. In the United States, the attention of this Committee was directed to providing long series of prices for important commodities for pre-Civil War years. Price history research was initiated or expanded for 6 important markets—Philadelphia, Charleston, S.C., Cincinnati, New Orleans, New York City, and Boston. Information is presented here only for the first 4 of these markets.

The results of the investigations in all 6 areas were summarized in the form of wholesale price index numbers by the individual research directors and presented by Arthur H. Cole in *Wholesale Commodity Prices in the United States, 1700 to 1861*, Harvard University Press, Cambridge, 1938. A statistical supplement to Cole's report contains the actual monthly quotations for approximately 45 commodities for the years covered in each market.

The source materials for the price data included newspapers, merchants price lists, account books, and similar records that could be located. Differences in the availability of price and weighting data from area to area contributed to differences in the indexes derived, particularly with respect to the appropriate base periods, the length of the series, and the classifications of commodities for subindexes.

E 90–96. Wholesale price indexes (Taylor), for Charleston, S.C., 1732–1861.

Source: Arthur H. Cole, *Wholesale Commodity Prices in the United States, 1700–1861*, Harvard University Press, Cambridge, 1938, pp. 153, 155–157, and 159–167 (copyright).

See also articles by George Rogers Taylor, "Wholesale Commodity Prices at Charleston, S. C., 1732–1791," *Journal of Economic History*, February 1932, pp. 356–377, and "Wholesale Commodity Prices at Charleston, S.C., 1796–1861," August 1932 supplement to the *Journal*, pp. 848–868.

See also general note for series E 90–122.

Taylor's research in commodity prices was summarized in separate index numbers for 8 different periods. The choice of time periods was made partly to reflect business conditions in Charleston and partly to take account of availability of data. Newspapers and original manuscript materials produced price series for a maximum of 32 items for 1818–1842 and a minimum of 6 for 1732–1747. Gaps were relatively frequent and no quotations at all appeared for 1792–1795.

Indexes for each period were weighted arithmetic averages of price relatives, with weights representing the approximate importance of each commodity in South Carolina commerce. The weights were unchanged for all years within each time period but were changed from period to period. An all-commodities series was made up of prices for 6 articles for 1732–1747, 10 articles for 1748–1761, and 16 articles for 1762–1775. In each period, rice represented 50 to 64 percent of the total weight. For the 5 later time intervals, weighted sub-indexes were combined with group weights based on the following total number of price series: 1780–1791, 20; 1796–1812, 18; 1813–1822, 13; 1818–1842, 32; 1843–1861, 20. During these years, the importance of rice declined from about 37 percent of the total weight to 5 to 7 percent, while the importance of cotton increased from zero in 1791 to almost 35 percent in 1843–1861.

The all-commodity series (E 90) was obtained by splicing the indexes for the separate periods.

E 97–110. Wholesale price indexes (Bezanson), for Philadelphia, unweighted geometric average, 1784–1861.

Source: Anne Bezanson, Robert D. Gray, and Miriam Hussey, *Wholesale Prices in Philadelphia, 1784–1861*, part I, Industrial Research Study No. 29, Philadelphia, 1936, p. 392. (Copyright, University of Pennsylvania; reprinted by permission.)

See also general note for series E 90–122.

Records of prices for Philadelphia provided continuous price reports for 186 series covering 140 different commodities for 1784–1861 and 205 series for 157 commodities for 1819–1861. Monthly relative prices for the individual commodities and changes in the description of the commodities quoted are included in part II of the source, published as Industrial Research Study No. 30. Bezanson and her associates have also computed indexes for 1852–1896, corresponding to those for the earlier part of the century, which are available in a Bureau of Labor Statistics (BLS) pamphlet, *Wholesale Price Indexes for Philadelphia, 1852–96: Annual Group Totals*.

Indexes for all commodities and for subindexes using different modes of classification were computed as unweighted geometric averages of price relatives. Two all-commodities indexes were prepared, one based on 140 commodities (series E 97) and one for a more limited period for 157 commodities.

In addition to the subindexes selected for inclusion here, other subindexes for commodity groupings generally comparable to those of the BLS were also calculated. All indexes are available on a monthly basis.

E 111. Wholesale price indexes (Bezanson), for Philadelphia, unweighted arithmetic average, 1720–1861.

Source: See source for series E 97–110.

For the colonial period, Bezanson and her associates obtained some price data for 82 series. Because of the gaps in the data, however, indexes for the early years were based on prices for many fewer commodities.

Indexes for 1720–1861 were computed as unweighted arithmetic averages of relatives of prices for the same 12 commodities for the full period. The source also includes an unweighted geometric index of 20 commodities for 1731–1861.

E 112–114. Wholesale price indexes (Berry), for Cincinnati, 1816–1861.

Source: **Series E 112**, 1816–1860, Arthur H. Cole, *Wholesale Commodity Prices in the United States, 1700–1861*, Harvard University Press, Cambridge, 1938, p. 185 (averages of the monthly data were computed from the source); 1861, estimated by Ethel Hoover from series E 113 and E 114 with weights shown in Cole (cited above), p. 81. **Series E 113–114**, Thomas S. Berry, *Western Prices Before 1861*, Harvard University Press, Cambridge, 1943, p. 564. (Copyright.)

See also general note for series E 90–122.

These indexes were weighted arithmetic averages of price relatives, computed for 3 separate time periods which were spliced to obtain the continuous series. For 1816–1825, prices for 21 commodities were assembled, 13 "identified with northern agriculture" and 8 "not identified with northern agriculture." For 1824–1846, the total was 37 with 20 in the first category and 17 in the second. For 1846–1861, the total was 50, with 29 for northern agriculture, and 21 for other. The weighting factors for the first period were estimated from New Orleans receipts in 1825, while those for the 2 later periods were based on receipts at Cincinnati for 1845–1848 and 1852–1856. Berry's analysis is accompanied by many tabulations of supplementary data, including actual prices for individual articles.

E 115–117. Wholesale price indexes (Berry), for Ohio River Valley, 1788–1817.

Source: Thomas S. Berry, *Western Prices Before 1861*, Harvard University Press, Cambridge, 1943, pp. 563–564 (copyright).

See also general note for E 90–122.

In his study of Cincinnati prices, Berry encountered considerable difficulty in obtaining price information for years before 1816. He enlarged his geographical coverage for the market to include Lexington and Louisville, Ky., and Pittsburgh, Pa., and was successful in constructing 14 commodity price series for 1788–1816 from data in "account books of backwoods merchants" and from local journals.

The indexes were computed as unweighted averages of price relatives. The annual prices used to obtain the relatives were medians of all Ohio Valley quotations for each item each year.

E 118–122. Wholesale price indexes (Taylor), for New Orleans, 1800–1861.

Source: Arthur H. Cole, *Wholesale Commodity Prices in the United States, 1700–1861*, Harvard University Press, Cambridge, 1938, pp. 170–179 (copyright).

See also general note for series E 90–122.

A considerable difference was found in the volume of information available for New Orleans from decade to decade. Therefore, New Oreleans indexes were prepared for 4 separate time periods. Data for 8 commodities, primarily agricultural, were combined into an index for "Louisiana" products for 1800–1812 (July). For a part of this period, 1804–1812 (April), 2 series were constructed, 1 for

29 domestic products and the other for 15 imported goods. For 2 later periods, the volume of data was sufficient to set up 3 subindexes, classifying the commodities by origin. The number of articles included was: For 1815–1842, 5 Louisiana products, 34 other domestic products, and 11 foreign imports; for 1840–1861, the corresponding numbers of articles were 4, 37, and 8.

All of the index numbers were calculated using the method of weighted averages of relatives. The weights in the several time periods represented the importance of the various commodities in the trade of New Orleans.

The all-commodities index (series E 118) was obtained by splicing the "all-commodities" indexes for the different periods.

E 123–134. General note.

The wholesale prices for selected commodities from 1800 through 1970 provide an indication of price levels (in current dollars) for selected basic commodities at a particular point in time. Due to the changes in descriptions (specifications) for the commodities, in markets from which prices were obtained, in quality of the product which takes place over time, and other factors which affect prices, these series provide only a general indication of price trends.

From among the several hundred commodities for which wholesale prices have been published in various reports, 12 were selected for publication in the form of actual prices. Generally, consideration was given to representation of commodities in different product groups, importance in U.S. trade, and the length of the series available.

The descriptions for each commodity insofar as they could be determined and the sources from which the prices were compiled are shown below in the detailed notes for each series. When annual averages were not available in the original source, they were computed for this publication. If 12 monthly figures were presented, a simple average was calculated, but if only quarterly figures were given, straight line interpolation was used to estimate missing months.

It was not possible to obtain one continuously comparable series for the full period. The data were assembled from several sources for each commodity and there were, frequently, changes in the basis of quotation even in the same source. Two prices are shown for years in which a change in the series occurred, if it was possible to obtain the information. In some series, mostly prior to 1890, changes in the basis of quotation occurred and no overlapping prices were available. Such changes are noted below in the text for each series.

Prices for earlier years for some commodities are available in the same sources as those indicated for 1800, and in other publications. Because of limitations of time and space, however, figures prior to 1800 were not included in this chapter. For example, prices of wheat back to 1700 may be found in the publication by Cole, cited as the source for wheat prices for 1800–1825. Wheat prices in the New England colonies at 10-year intervals for 1630–1750 are included with prices for several other commodities in Bureau of Labor Statistics Bulletin 604, *History of Wages in the United States From Colonial Times to 1928*, p. 19.

The *Annual Report of the Director of the Mint*, cited as the source for practically all series for some part of the period 1825–1880, was used despite the lack of commodity descriptions. The prices included in this report were summaries of the New York prices included in the *U.S. Finance Reports* of 1863, 1873, and 1874 which had been compiled from the newspaper, *The New York Shipping and Commercial List*. Prices for 1875–1880 were also compiled from this source. Such descriptions as appear in the notes for each series of prices taken from *U.S. Finance Reports* were obtained from the report for 1863.

An alternate source for many of the price series included in the *Aldrich Reports* (cited for data prior to 1890) is *Monthly Summary of Commerce and Finance in the United States*, 57th Congress, 2d Session, House Doc. No. 15, part 1, 1902, pp. 59–100. The *Summary* covers not only the years included in the *Aldrich Report*, but also extends the data through July 1902.

E 123. Wheat, 1800–1970.

Source: A.—1800–1825, Arthur H. Cole, *Wholesale Commodity Prices in the United States, 1700–1861*, Statistical Supplement, Harvard University Press, Cambridge, 1938 (copyright); B.—1825–1880, *Annual Report of the Director of the Mint to the Secretary of the Treasury for the Fiscal Year Ended June 30, 1881*, p. 50; C.—1880–1890, *Wholesale Prices, Wages, and Transportation*, Senate Report No. 1394, 52d Congress, 2d Session, part 2, 1893, p. 61 (one of the reports usually referred to as the *Aldrich Reports*); D.—1890–1970, compiled from Bureau of Labor Statistics reports and records. In general, annual average prices, when available, were taken from annual reports, *Wholesale Prices and Price Indexes*, through the year 1963. Thereafter, annual average prices were computed from monthly prices as published in monthly reports, *Wholesale Prices and Price Indexes*.

For 1800–1825, prices are for Philadelphia (commodity description not available). For 1825–1880, prices are for New York, "Northern" wheat; the *1863 U.S. Finance Report* (from which these prices were partially compiled) shows prices for "genesee" for most years, 1825–1863, but for a few years prices refer to "North River," "prime white," "western," "western red," or "mixed and red." For 1880–1890, prices are for "wheat No. 2, Winter, Chicago." For 1890–1913, prices are for Chicago "Range No. 1 Northern Spring and No. 2 Red Winter" in carlots. For 1913–1948, prices are for Kansas City, "No. 2, hard (ordinary)" in carlots. For 1949–1961, prices are for Kansas City, "No. 2, hard winter, closing spot market price, carlots, f.o.b. track." From 1962 to 1970, prices are for Kansas City, "No. 1, hard winter."

See also general note for series E 123–134.

E 124. Wheat flour, 1800–1970.

Source: See sources cited for series E 123; 1800–1825, source A; 1825–1870, source B; 1870–1890, source C, p. 79; 1890–1970, source D.

For 1800–1825, prices are for Philadelphia, "Superfine" flour, per barrel of 196 pounds. For 1825–1870, prices are for New York, "Superfine" flour, per barrel. For 1870–1890, prices were provided by a New York firm (commodity description not available). For 1890–1913, prices are for "winter straights, f.o.b., New York," per barrel. For 1913–1943, prices are for "Straights, hard winter, white, in carlots, f.o.b., Kansas City," per barrel. During 1943, the basis of quotation was changed from per barrel to flour in sacks, per 100 pounds. For 1950–1970, prices are for "hard winter, bakery, short patents, plain or enriched, in 100-pound sacks, carlots, f.o.b. mill, Kansas City," per 100 pounds. During 1918 and a part of 1946, prices were quoted on the standard provided under government regulation.

See also general note for series E 123–134.

E 125. Sugar, 1800–1970.

Source: See sources for series E 123; 1800–1825, source A; 1825–1860, source B; 1860–1890, source C, p. 114; 1890–1970, source D.

For 1800–1825, prices are for the Philadelphia market. Prices for 1800 refer to "Muscovado, brown"; 1801–1802 (Oct.), "Muscovado"; 1802 (Nov.)–1813 (Oct.), "Muscovado, first quality"; 1813 (Nov.)–1815 (Apr.), "Muscovado, unspecified"; 1815 (May)–1825, "Muscovado, prime." For 1825–1860, prices are for New York, "Cuba" sugar; the *1863 U.S. Finance Report* (from which the data were compiled) quoted "Muscovado" for 1825–1829 and 1845–1860, "Cuba Muscovado" for 1830–1836 and "Cuba" for 1837–1844. For 1860–1890, prices are for "Refined, granulated" sugar (no market specified). For 1890–1946, prices are for New York, "Granulated" sugar. Prices were quoted for sugar in barrels until 1955 when the basis of quotation was changed to 100-pound paper bags. For 1947–1970, the description was amplified to "granulated, domestic, cane, refined, New York," per pound. Prices for 1934–1970 include the excise tax of 53½ cents per 100 pounds, effective in May 1934.

See also general note for series E 123–134.

E 126. Cotton, raw, 1800–1970.

Source: 1800–1890, Mathew B. Hammond, *The Cotton Industry, an Essay in American Economic History*, American Economic Association, New Series No. I, Macmillan, New York, 1897, p. 358; 1890–1970, see source D for series E 123.

For 1800–1890, prices refer to "Middling uplands" cotton for the New York market and are available back to 1790. For 1800–1820, prices are estimates made by merchants or government officials. For 1821–1890, prices were taken from James L. Watkin, *Production and Price of Cotton for One Hundred Years*, published by the Department of Agriculture, 1895. For 1890–1941, prices are for New York, "Upland, Middling" cotton, spot. In 1936, "7/8 inch" was added to the description. For 1941–1954 (July), prices are for "Middling, 15/16 inch," 10 spot market average. For 1954 (July)–1956 (Aug.), the number of markets included in the average was increased from 10 to 14. The July 1954 average for 10 markets was $0.342 per pound and for 14 markets, $0.341 per pound. For 1956 (Aug.)–1957, prices are for "Middling, 1-inch," 14 spot market average. In Aug. 1956, the average for 15/16-inch staple was $0.348 per pound and for 1-inch staple $0.357 per pound. Beginning Sept. 1962, prices are for 15-market average. Beginning July 1968, prices are for "1 1/16 middling," 12 spot market average.

See also general note for series E 123–134.

E 127. Wool, 1813–1970.

Source: See sources cited for series E 123; 1813–1825, source A; 1825–1850, source B, p. 60; 1850–1890, source C, p. 387; 1890–1970, source D.

For 1813–1825, prices are for Philadelphia, "Merino clean" wool except for 1819 and 1820 when description was "Merino" wool. For 1825–1850, prices are for New York, "Merino" wool. For 1850–1890, prices are for Boston, "Ohio, fine fleece, scoured." For 1890–1913, prices are for, "Domestic, Ohio, fine fleece (x and xx grades), scoured"; for 1913–1945, for Boston, "Domestic, Territory, staple, fine and fine medium, scoured"; for 1946–1949 for Boston, "Domestic, Territory, staple, fine combing, graded, scoured." For 1950–1970, the description was changed with no difference in price level to "Domestic, fine, good French combing and staple, clean basis."

See also general note for series E 123–134.

E 128. Cotton sheeting, 1800–1969.

Source: See sources cited for series E 123; 1800–1847, source A; 1847–1890, source C, p. 155; 1890–1969, source D.

Prices are for Philadelphia, "Russian, unspecified" for 1800–1804, "Russian, brown" for 1805–1814 and 1824–1847, and "Russian, half bleached" for 1815–1823. Prices were shown "per piece" (approximately 100 yards). For 1847–1890, prices are for "sheeting, brown, 4-4, Atlantic A," per yard (no market specified). For 1890–1912, prices are for "brown, Indian head, 4-4, 2.85 yards to pound, factory." For 1913–1941, description same except that the width designation was changed in 1913 to "36-inch" instead of "4-4," and "48×48, carded yarn" was added in 1923. For 1941–1943 (May), prices are for "Unbleached, 36-inch, 48×48, 2.85 yards per pound, Class A, non-feeler, f.o.b. mill." For 1943 (May)–1947, description same except for change from "48×48" to "48×44." For 1948–1969, prices are for "Unbleached (series 1), 40-inch, 48×48, 2.85 yards per pound, Class A, nonfeeler, f.o.b. mill." The January 1948 price for the former description (36-inch, 48×44) was $0.279 and for the new description (40-inch, 48×48) was $0.289 per pound.

See also general notes for series E 123–134.

E 129. Coal, anthracite, 1800–1970.

Source: See sources cited for series E 123; 1800–1825, source A; 1825–1833, source B; 1890–1970, source D. For 1833–1890, American Iron and Steel Association, *Statistics of the American and Foreign Iron Trades for 1896*, Philadelphia, 1897, p. 91.

Prices are for Philadelphia, "Virginia" coal for 1800–1811 and 1814–1825, and "Domestic" for 1812 and 1813. There was no description for 1826–1833. For 1825–1833, prices are for New York, "anthracite coal (Schuylkill)." For 1833–1890, prices are for "Schuylkill white ash lump" coal, by the cargo, at Philadelphia, per gross ton. For 1890–1970, prices are for "Pennsylvania anthracite, chestnut," but the basis of quotation was changed several times. For 1890–1928, the basis was "New York Tidewater," per gross ton; for 1928–1931, "destination on tracks," per gross ton; for 1931–1947, per net ton (2000 pounds); and 1947–1970, "f.o.b. cars" per net ton.

See also general note for series E 123–134.

E 130.   Steel rails, 1847–1970.

Source: 1847–1890, American Metal Market and Daily Iron and Steel Report, *Metal Statistics*, 1921, p. 91. (Reprinted with permission of American Metal Market, Fairchild Publications, Inc., N.Y., N.Y., copyright.) For 1891–1970, see source D for series E 123.

For 1847–1867, prices are for "Iron rails, Eastern Pennsylvania mill" (production of steel rails did not exceed production of iron rails until 1877). The source also shows prices of iron rails of this description for 1868–1882. For 1867–1870, prices are for New York "Steel rails, Bessemer," per gross ton. For 1871–1890, prices are for "Steel rails, Pennsylvania mill." For 1891–1913, prices are for "Bessemer, Standard, f.o.b. mill, Pittsburgh," per long ton; for 1913–1946, for "Open hearth, standard, f.o.b. mill"; for 1947–1953 (April), for "Standard, heavier than 60 pounds, No. 1 open hearth, f.o.b. mill" (refinement of previous specification and quoted per 100 pounds—no break in series); thereafter, for "Standard, carbon steel, No. 1 open hearth, 115 pounds per linear yard, control cooled, base quantity, f.o.b. mill."

See also general note for series E 123–134.

E 131.   Nails, 1800–1969.

Source: See sources cited for series E 123; 1800–1828, source A; 1828–1834, source B, p. 54; 1890–1969, source D. For 1835–1890, see source for series E 129, 1833–1890, p. 87. (For 1835–1849, prices were compiled from the *Report of the Secretary of the Treasury*, 1849; for 1850–1859, by the American Iron and Steel Association from the books of the Duncannon Iron Company; and for 1860–1890, by an official of the Duncannon Iron Company.)

For 1800–1828, prices are for the Philadelphia market. For 1814–1827, prices are for "Cut nails, all sizes"; for other years, "assorted sizes." For 1828–1834, prices are for New York, "Nails, cut." For 1835–1890, prices are for "Cut nails." For 1890–1953, prices refer to "wire, 8 penny, fence and common, 100-pound keg, f.o.b. Pittsburgh." "Base price" was added to the description in 1926 and fence nails were not included after 1947. For 1953–1959, prices refer to "wire, carbon steel 8d, common, carload lots, f.o.b. mill." The April 1953 price for the former specification was $7.41, and for the new specification, $7.33 per 100 pounds. "Packed in fiberboard boxes" was added to the description for 1955. "Carload lots" was changed to "in lots of 30,000 lb. or over" in Oct. 1960. Change was not considered to affect comparability of prices before or after.

See also general note for series E 123–134.

E 132.   Copper, 1800–1969.

Source: See sources cited for series E 123; 1800–1825, source A; 1825–1860, source B, p. 52; 1890–1970, source D. For 1860–1889, see source for series E 130, 1847–1890, p. 299.

For 1800–1825, prices are for the Philadelphia market. Prices are for "Copper in sheets," 1800–1801 (Apr.) and 1805 (June)–1809 (June); "Sheathing unspecified," 1801 (May)–1802 (Dec.), 1809 (July)–1818 (Apr.), and 1824 (Sept.)–1825; "Sheathing, cold rolled,"

1803–1805 (May); and "Sheathing unspecified," 1818 (May)–1824 (Aug.). For 1825–1860, prices are for New York, "Sheathing." For 1860–1889, prices are for New York, "Lake Copper." The price shown for 1890 is the same as that in *Metal Statistics, 1921*. For 1890–1907, prices are for New York, "Lake Copper"; for 1907–1927, for "Copper ingot, electrolytic, early delivery, refinery in New York"; for 1927–1953, for "Copper, electrolytic, delivered, Connecticut Valley"; and for 1954–1969, for "Copper ingot, electrolytic.

See also general note for series E 123–134.

E 133.   Turpentine, 1800–1969.

Source: See sources cited for series E 123; 1800–1825, source A; 1825–1840, source B, p. 56; 1840–1890, source C, p. 240; 1890–1969, source D.

For 1800–1825, prices are for the Philadelphia market, per barrel (31½ gallons per barrel). No description was available, but a comparison of prices indicates that they may be for "soft" turpentine. For 1825–1840, prices are for the New York market (no description is available). For 1840–1890, prices are for New York, "Spirits of turpentine." For 1890–1942, prices are for "Southern, barrels, at New York." The description was amplified in 1936 by the addition of "carlots, ex dock, gum spirits." For 1942–1951, prices refer to "Gum spirits, bulk, f.o.b. Savannah, Ga." For 1952–1956 (Oct.), quotations are for "Spirits of turpentine, tank cars, at New York." The Jan. 1952 price for the former specification (Savannah) was $0.80 per gallon and for the new (New York), $0.76 per gallon. For 1956 (Nov.)–1958 (Jan.) prices are for "gum, tank cars" at New York. For 1959 (Mar.)–1969 prices are for carlots or truckload quantities f.o.b. car or trucks at processing plants in Georgia and Florida. "Midpoint of range for week" was added in 1961.

See also general note for series E 123–134.

E 134.   Brick, 1849–1969.

Source: See sources cited for series E 123; 1849–1890, source C, p. 222; 1890–1969, source D.

For 1849–1890, prices are for "common domestic building" (market not indicated). For 1890–1933, prices are for "Common, Red, Domestic, at New York"; 1933–1947, for "Common building, f.o.b. plant" (composite of approximately 50 firms); for 1947–1961, for "Building brick, f.o.b. plant or New York dock" (composite of approximately 25 firms); and for 1962–1969, for "Building brick, f.o.b. plant." Changes in list of firms from time to time did not result in any significant differences in the annual average prices.

See also general note for series E 123–134.

E 135–186.   General note.

An appropriate name for indexes of retail price changes has been the subject of considerable discussion. Most indexes that have at some time been called "cost-of-living" indexes measure changes in retail prices for the goods and services families buy. Insofar as possible, the retail prices are for the same list of items in the same localities, the same qualities, and the same quantities from one period to the next. The indexes, therefore, measure changes in costs for living in the same way and in the same place.

Generally, people tend to think of the amount of money they spend for commodities and services as their cost of living. Changes in total expenditures reflect changes in costs resulting from differences in the place or manner of living, such as shifts in the kinds of goods and services bought, and may represent a better or a worse standard than at some earlier date.

The term "Consumer Price Index" was adopted by the Bureau of Labor Statistics (BLS) and the National Industrial Conference Board after much controversy during World War II regarding the BLS *Cost of Living Index*. For a discussion of differences in concept and measurement of the cost of living, see the *Report of the President's Committee on Cost of Living*, Office of Economic Stabilization, 1945.

E 135–166. Consumer price indexes (BLS)—all items, 1800 to 1970, and by groups, 1913–1970.

Source: U.S. Bureau of Labor Statistics (BLS), 1800–1912, series E 135 only, *Handbook of Labor Statistics 1973*, Bulletin 1790; 1913–1970, *Consumer Price Indexes for Urban Wage Earners and Clerical Workers; U.S. City Averages* (1967 = 100), Historical Series A through I.

See also general note for series E 135–186.

The BLS Consumer Price Index measures changes in retail prices of the goods and services bought by city wage earners and clerical workers. The indexes from 1800 through 1912 are estimates, based on price data from sources other than BLS. It was originated on a comprehensive basis at the end of World War I when data were in demand for wage negotiations in shipbuilding cities. A Department of Labor study of the cost of living in 92 shipbuilding and other industrial centers was made in 1918–19, as reported in BLS Bulletin 357, *Cost of Living in the United States*. The first publication of changes in the "cost of living" was in the BLS *Monthly Labor Review* for October 1919 and regular publication has continued since February 1921. The frequency of publication was increased from semiannually to quarterly in 1935. Since September 1940, the index has been computed and published monthly. The index is published each month in a press release, a detailed report, and in the *Monthly Labor Review*. The indexes shown here are annual averages.

All retail price data are collected with the use of specifications to ensure comparisons from period to period of prices for the same or similar qualities insofar as possible. These specifications include the quality factors associated with price differences and other physical characteristics needed for identification from store to store and from one pricing period to the next. A discussion of the use of specifications is contained in BLS Bulletin 1182, *Average Retail Prices: Collection and Calculation Techniques and Problems*. Every effort is made to obtain the prices paid by the customer, not list prices from which discounts normally are given. Sales, excise, and other taxes related to the purchase or continued ownership of consumer goods and services are reflected wherever applicable.

A number of changes in coverage, method, classification, and base periods have been made since these indexes were first issued in 1919 with index numbers back to 1913. Until 1935, the "cost-of-living" indexes were calculated using quantity weights derived from the BLS family expenditure study in 1917–19. The weights related to the individual items priced and to geographic areas rather than to individual cities. Group indexes were combined with percentages representing the importance of the group in total expenditures. The goods and services included were described in general terms only. The measurement of price change for comparable articles was accomplished by careful attention on the part of the field representative in obtaining price quotations for the same quality from one period to the next from the same respondents.

A major improvement in the index calculation method was introduced in 1935 and is described in Faith M. Williams, Margaret H. Hogg, and Ewan Clague, "Revision of Index of Cost of Goods Purchased by Wage Earners and Lower-Salaried Workers," *Monthly Labor Review*, September 1935, pp. 819–837. In the 1935 revision, consumption weights for individual cities were derived from the 1917–19 expenditure study, and population weights (average population in 1920 and 1930) were used to combine city data. At this time, indexes back to 1913 were recalculated based on the prices collected for the former indexes. "Specification pricing" was also introduced in 1935; see John H. Cover, *Retail Price Behavior*, University of Chicago Press, 1935.

Another revision was completed in 1940 to take into account the results of a study of family expenditures in 1934–36. At this time, indexes back to 1935 were recalculated with weights derived from this study. Indexes for earlier years were not recalculated completely, but the former group indexes were recombined with revised weights. Other improvements introduced are described in the

Table II. Number of Cities Included in BLS Consumer Price Index (CPI) for All Items (E 135) and for Foods (E 136–137), and Weights Used: 1913 to 1970

Period	Number of cities		Weights used	
	All items	Food	Family expenditures in—	Population in—
1913–1917	19	40–45	1917–19	none
1918–1924	32	45–51	1917–19	1920 and 1930
1925–1930	32	51	1917–19 [1] 1934–36	1920 and 1930
1930–1934	33	51	[1] 1934–36	1930
1935–1942	33–34	56–64	1934–36	1930
1943–1949	34	56	1934–36	May 1942
1950–1952	34	56	[2] 1947–49	1950
1953–1963	46	46	[3] 1950	1950
1964–1965	50	50	[4] 1960–61	1960
1966–1970	56	56	[5] 1960–61	1960

[1] Individual item weights for 1913–1935 were derived from the 1917–19 study. Group weights as shown.
[2] Family expenditures in 7 cities. [3] Adjusted to 1952 for price change.
[4] Adjusted to 1963 for price change. [5] Adjusted to 1965 for price change.

Bureau of Labor Statistics' New Index of Cost of Living, Serial No. R. 1156, reprinted from the August 1940 issue of the *Monthly Labor Review*.

During World War II, shortages and rationing imposed many measurement problems. The adjustments made by BLS in weights and in pricing are described in Faith M. Williams, "Bureau of Labor Statistics Cost of Living Index in Wartime," *Monthly Labor Review*, July 1943.

Before the comprehensive revision in 1953, when numerous changes in index procedures and coverage were introduced, an "interim adjustment" was made in 1951. This adjustment included a correction for "new unit bias" in the rent index (resulting from wartime rent controls) for 1940–1950 and the introduction of revised commodity weights based on expenditure surveys in 7 cities during 1947–1949. The revised commodity weights were used to recalculate indexes back to 1950 but not earlier years. A description of the adjustment is in BLS Bulletin 1039, *Interim Adjustment of Consumer Price Index*. The "interim adjustment" resulted in the publication of two index series for 1940–1952—the "old series" and the "adjusted series." When the comprehensive revision was completed in 1953, the revised indexes were linked to the "adjusted series."

In the 1953 revision, the city sample was changed to include small and medium-sized cities and the expenditure concept was broadened to include the purchase price of a house. (See February and April 1956 issues of *Monthly Labor Review* for a discussion of housing costs in the CPI.) Pricing of restaurant meals and home repair and maintenance items was begun and several other items were added. Items were regrouped into 8 major groups.

A later revision of the CPI was completed in 1963 and incorporated into the historical index series in 1964. The revised index is based on prices of about 400 goods and services; the goods and services priced for the index were chosen to represent price trends for all goods and services bought by families of urban wage earners and clerical workers. The selection was made on the basis of a detailed study of expenditures of 4,912 urban wage earner and clerical worker families and 585 single workers in 1960–61. The probability an item had of being selected for pricing in the index was proportional to its importance in index-family consumption expenditures in the 1960–61 base period. The average size of the families covered by the index was estimated to be about 3.7 persons and their average family income after taxes was estimated at about $6,250 in 1960–61.

In 1966, the CPI program was extended to six additional large areas as a result of a decision that indexes would be published for all standard metropolitan statistical areas (SMSA's) having a population of 1 million or more in 1960. Currently (1973), the sample of 56 areas on which the national index is based was chosen to represent all urban places that have population of 2,500 or more in 1960, including Alaska and Hawaii. Prices for foods and fuels and some other goods and services are obtained monthly in all cities. Prices for most other goods and services are obtained monthly in the 5 largest areas and every three months in the remaining 51 SMSA's or small urban places. Rents are surveyed bimonthly in the 5 largest areas and every 3 months in other areas. Separate indexes are computed for 23 large areas. A comprehensive discussion of these and other improvements is contained in BLS Bulletin 1517, *The Consumer Price Index: History and Techniques.*

Food prices are obtained from about 1,800 food stores, including all important types of food retailers in each city. Rent figures are collected from tenants for approximately 40,000 rental units selected from block listings of the total rental housing market in each city. Prices for other goods and services are obtained from about 16,000 retail and service establishments patronized by wage earner and clerical families and including department stores, specialty shops, etc., with a minimum of 4 quotations per item per SMSA or urban place in most cases. Retail stores and service establishments are stratified by type of outlet and by area of the SMSA, i.e., central business district, neighborhood, and suburban pricing areas.

Price collection for the majority of goods and services is made by personal visit of BLS field representatives. Food prices are collected by local agents; for some items mail or telephone collection is supplemented by occasional personal visits.

The indexes are calculated using a variation of the base quantity weighted index formula. In practice, the aggregates are obtained by applying price relatives to "value weights" representing the cost of 1960–61 quantities as determined from the 1960–61 Consumer Expenditure Survey. The base period importance of an item selected with certainty for pricing in the index represents the annual average expenditure made for the item by the index population in the 1960–61 period. The base period importance of other items represents the expenditure made for that item and in addition a "pro rata" share of the weight of items not selected for pricing. Indexes for individual areas are computed using the expenditure weights for each area. National indexes are calculated by combining area data with weights representing 1960 population.

The standard reference base of the Consumer Price Index presented here is 1967=100. The index was changed to this base from its previous base of 1957–59=100 effective with release of the index for January 1971. The official standard reference base of the CPI was 1957–59=100 from 1962 through 1970, 1947–49=100 from 1953 through 1961, 1935–39=100 from 1940 through 1952, 1923–25=100 from 1935 through 1939, and 1913=100 from 1913 through 1934.

For a more complete description of the Consumer Price Index, see *Handbook of Methods for Surveys and Studies,* BLS Bulletin 1458, Chapter 10, or BLS Bulletin 1517 cited above.

See also general note for series E 135–186.

E 167–173.   Consumer price indexes (BLS), for special groups, 1935–1970.

Source: U.S. Bureau of Labor Statistics, *1971 Handbook of Labor Statistics,* p. 255.

These indexes are based on a reclassification of the items priced for the Consumer Price Indexes (series E 135–166). The basic weights, price data, and calculation methods were the same as those used for the regular CPI. For a more complete description of the index, see BLS Bulletin 1517 cited above (E 135–166).

See also general note for series E 135–186.

E 174–182.   Consumer price index (Hoover), 1851–1880.

Source: Ethel D. Hoover, "Prices in the 19th Century," *Studies in Income and Wealth,* vol. 24, 1960, National Bureau of Economic Research, New York (copyright).

See also general note for series E 135–186.

The basic price data for these series are from Joseph D. Weeks, "The Average Retail Prices of Necessaries of Life," *Report on Statistics of Wages in Manufacturing Industries,* Tenth Census, vol. 20,

1886. Averages of retail prices for 58 commodities were calculated by making simple averages of the prices reported for each item by one or two storekeepers in approximately 40 cities. The consistency of price movement and price level between prices identified as of "June 1" and those as "year" averages led to the inclusion of all prices to calculate an all-city average for each year. In calculating the relative prices for each commodity, a comparability procedure was used; that is, for each year two average prices were calculated—one comparable with the preceding year and the other comparable with the following year. Data for these 58 commodities were supplemented with estimates of price change for services (shoe repairs and medical care) as well as some additional items important in family spending estimated from other sources. The number of price series included in each of the index groups was food, 40; clothing, 12; rents, 2; fuel and light, 5; and other, 7.

Relative prices for the individual commodities were combined with value weights derived from the study of family expenditures in Massachusetts in 1875, supplemented by detailed expenditures of 232 families as given in the *Aldrich Reports (Wholesale Prices,* part 1, pp. 62–63). The formula for calculation of the index was the algebraic equivalent of the Laspeyre index.

E 183.   Cost-of-living indexes (Federal Reserve Bank of N.Y.), 1820–1913.

Source: Federal Reserve Bank of New York, *Index of Estimated Cost of Living in the United States* (1938 revision, mimeographed).

Indexes for 1820–1952 converted to the 1947–49 base and figures showing purchasing power of the dollar "in terms of retail prices" for the same period are available in a mimeographed release with same title dated March 17, 1953.

See also general note for series E 135–186.

This index was obtained by splicing together parts of indexes already available to approximate a continuous series. No adjustments were made to the original series other than those necessary to convert to a common base period. Indexes for 1820–1839 were taken from Alvin H. Hansen's cost-of-living indexes which were based on wholesale prices for these years. For 1840–1859, the indexes used were also obtained from Hansen's index which had in turn utilized the weighted index of wholesale prices (assuming all unpriced items moved with all priced items) computed by Roland P. Falkner for the Senate Committee on Finance. The Falkner indexes for 1840–1891 may be found in Senate Report No. 1394 (*Aldrich Report*), *Wholesale Prices, Wages, and Transportation,* U. S. Senate Committee on Finance, 1893, p. 93. For 1860–1879, the Federal Reserve Bank used the relative cost-of-living series prepared by Wesley C. Mitchell, who calculated his index from retail price data for 60 of the "necessaries of life" included in the *Weeks Report.* The original series may be found in Mitchell's *Gold, Prices, and Wages Under the Greenback Standard,* University of California Publications in Economics, vol. 1, Berkeley, March 1908, p. 91. For 1880–1889, the indexes were those of W. Randolph Burgess in *Trends of School Costs* (see series E 184). For 1890–1909, Paul Douglas' "Most Probable Index of the Total Cost of Living for Workingmen" (see series E 185) as published in *American Economic Review,* March 1926 supplement, p. 22, was used. Indexes for 1920–1912 were derived from the cost-of-living index for Massachusetts appearing in the Department of Labor and Industries of the Commonwealth of Massachusetts, *Report of the Commission on the Necessaries of Life,* February 1920, p. 118.

E 184.   Cost-of-living index (Burgess), 1841–1920.

Source: *The Review of Economics and Statistics,* February 1934, vol. XVI, No. 2, p. 26 (copyright, Harvard College, Cambridge).

For original data in dollars, see W. Randolph Burgess, *Trends of School Costs,* Russell Sage Foundation, New York City, 1920, p. 54.

See also general note for series E 135–186.

To determine changes in the purchasing power of teacher's salaries for his study of *Trends in School Costs,* Burgess compiled the series,

"Cost of Living Per Week for a Small Family Using the Same Amount of the Same Commodities Over the Entire Period." This series is based on prices for 10 foods important in wage earners' spending. Quantity weights, derived from BLS 1901–1902 consumer expenditure studies, were used to combine prices of the 10 foods. On the assumption that other less important items fluctuated with food prices, the total food cost was adjusted upward to approximate the total weekly cost for all items for a typical wage earners' family of man, wife, and two children. The factor used for adjustment was based on the ratio of food costs to total costs in 1901. The source of the price data is indicated by general reference to BLS, the Massachusetts Bureau of Statistics of Labor, the *Aldrich Reports*, records of purchases by the Army and Navy, and miscellaneous publications.

E 185.   Cost-of-living index (Douglas), 1890–1926.

Source: Paul H. Douglas, *Real Wages in the United States, 1890–1926*, Houghton Mifflin Company, Boston and New York, 1930, p. 60 (copyright).

See also general note for series E 135–186.

This index was called the "Most Probable Index of the Movement of the Total Cost of Living for Workingmen" by Douglas, who constructed the series for his study of real wages during this period. The all-item indexes are available for two base periods, 1890–1899 and 1914.

For 1890–1914, the sources of the price data were BLS wholesale and retail reports. The available retail prices for foods were supplemented with wholesale prices for additional foods. These wholesale data were adjusted for the variation in movement between retail and wholesale prices for identical foods. Wholesale prices were also adjusted to approximate retail prices for clothing, fuel and light, furniture, tobacco, and spirits. The combined index for all items is a weighted arithmetic average of price relatives, using weights derived from the BLS consumer expenditure study of 1901–1902. No estimates were made for rent movements because of lack of data. For 1913–1926, the individual city indexes in the BLS "Cost-of-Living Index" were combined with city population weights.

E 186.   Cost-of-living index (Rees), 1890–1914.

Source: National Bureau of Economic Research, *Thirty-eighth Annual Report*, New York, May 1958, pp. 59–60 (copyright).

Rees' cost-of-living index was based largely on retail prices. Douglas' estimates were adopted for food at retail, and tobacco and spirits at wholesale prices (see text for series E 185), but retail data were assembled to compute new components for fuel, rent, clothing, and housefurnishings. Prices for gas obtained from utility companies, and retail prices of kerosene as used for the New Jersey State cost-of-living index, were included in fuels. Wholesale prices of coal were included before 1907 and for kerosene before 1898. Rents for six cities were compiled from newspaper advertisements. Prices for clothing and housefurnishings were compiled from mail-order catalogs.

The index is a weighted average of price relatives, using weights derived largely from the BLS consumer expenditure study of 1901–1902.

E 187–202.   Retail prices of selected foods in U.S. cities (BLS), 1890–1970.

Source: U.S. Bureau of Labor Statistics (BLS), 1890–1922, Bulletin 396, *Retail Prices, 1890 to 1924*, pp. 8–10; 1923–1934, BLS Bulletin 635, *Retail Prices of Food 1923–36*, pp. 77–89; 1935–1939, Serial No. R. 1172 (August 1940), *Retail Prices*, pp. 28–35; 1940–1970, annual or biennial bulletins, *Retail Prices of Food* (including Serial No. R. 1264, and Bulletins 707, 799, 899, 938, 965, 1032, 1055, 1141, 1183, 1217, 1254, 1301, 1446, and 1632).

While there were scattered statistics of prices of many individual commodities in various publications, it was not until 1901, when BLS began the collection of food prices on a regular basis, that a regular price collection program was initiated by the Federal Government. At that time, information was secured from dealers' books for 1890–1901. Since then, retail prices of food have been obtained by BLS, first at annual intervals, then monthly or semimonthly.

As the pricing program was expanded to other commodities and services purchased by families for daily living, the available resources and review of data requirements for the over-all Consumer Price Index (CPI) resulted in sampling and methodology changes for foods. The growth in importance of some foods and declines for others, changes in kinds and sizes of packages, different methods of preparation of foods for retail stores, and similar developments were taken into consideration in the adjustments made to the list of foods priced. Of the many foods included for most of the period since 1890, only 16 were selected for publication here.

The list of cites in which food prices were collected changed over the years. In the main, the cities covered were industrial localities in 30 to 40 States up to 1952. Beginning in 1953, the collection of food prices was restricted to the 46 cities included in the CPI. In 1964, pricing was extended to 50 areas. Six additional metropolitan areas were added in 1966 making the sample 56 metropolitan areas or urban places. See text for series E 135–166.

The number of stores in each city reporting food prices, after the initial collections through 1904, generally ranged from 25 in the larger cities to 15 in the smaller cities until 1932. Average prices for the United States were obtained by making simple averages of quotations from the total number of firms reporting for each food for 1915–1932. Average relative prices for each commodity were applied to prices in 1915 to estimate national averages for 1890–1914. Some chain stores were added to the samples as their sales volumes became significant in each city.

During 1932–1934 the store samples were expanded, particularly in the larger cities, and the method of averaging prices was adjusted to reflect food sales by chain and independent stores in each city. National averages were obtained by combining weighted city averages with the use of consumption and population weights. Refinements to the sampling and the weighting system have been introduced from time to time (see "Store Samples for Retail Food Prices," *Monthly Labor Review*, January 1947).

During the revision of the CPI in the late 1930's, comparable revised national averages were calculated back to 1923. The national averages shown here are those estimated by price relatives for 1890–1915, simple averages of quotations from all cities for 1916–1922, and weighted city averages beginning with 1923.

Food price data were collected by use of mail schedules and occasional personal visits until 1934. Since that year, all prices have been collected by personal visit of BLS representatives. Changes in descriptions for the foods priced, the cities covered, sizes and designs of samples of stores, and methods of processing introduce some non-comparabilities into the series.

Before the comprehensive CPI revision in 1964 BLS had published monthly city average retail food prices which were simply weighted means of the quotations used in the calculation of index numbers. However, the implementation of two recommendations of the Price Statistics Review Committee of the National Bureau of Economic Research concerning use of broader, less detailed specifications and the introduction of replicated samples resulted in data which could not be processed to meaningful average prices. Therefore, an estimating technique was adopted which takes advantage of the improved coverage resulting from broader specifications and those well-defined prices available. A set of average prices, called "benchmarks," is computed periodically, usually once a year, through the exclusion of all prices of items not meeting the exact requirements of a narrowly-defined specification. Once established, these benchmark prices are adjusted each month by the change in prices reflected in the index. A more detailed and technical explanation of this estimating procedure is available in "Calculation of Average Retail Food Prices," *Monthly Labor Review*, January 1965.

E 187, flour.   Prices are for general all-purpose white wheat flour.

The size of package on which quotations were secured were: 1890–1928, 1/8 or 1/4 of a barrel although some smaller units were also included; 1929–1938, 12 or 24 lb. sack; 1939–1942, 5–12 lb. sack; 1943–1970, 5 lb. sack.

E 188, bread. Prices are for white bread, pan style, excluding all specialty type bread. For 1913–1936, prices were obtained from bakeries for 16 or 18 ounces in the dough and converted to 16 ounces baked weight. Both wrapped and unwrapped breads were included. Beginning in 1937, prices have been obtained primarily from grocery stores for the volume-selling size loaf of wrapped bread. The baked weight as given on the wrapper or reported by the store was converted to 16 ounces.

National averages have not been computed for 1890–1912. Prices for individual firms are available in the early retail price bulletins.

E 189, round steak. For 1890–1939, the averages include quotations for the best cut of the best grade handled in each store for whole round or top round, mostly bone-in. For 1940–1970, prices were for top round, bone-in, U.S. choice grade (comparable to U.S. good grade prior to the changes in grades by the Department of Agriculture in 1950).

E 190, chuck roast. For 1913–1939, quotations were reported for the best cut of the best grade handled in each store and include both bone-in and boneless. Since then, all quotations have been for "bone-in" roasts. The grade priced for 1940–1970 was the same as for round steak. Beginning in 1951, the more precise description of the cut was "blade pot-roast cut from upper part of shoulder before rib roast and behind neck, U. S. choice, bone-in."

National averages have not been computed for 1890–1912. Prices for individual firms are available in the early retail price bulletins.

E 191, pork chops. For 1890–1935, quotations were for loin chops of the best grade handled. Rib chops and chops from the thick end of the loin were excluded. From 1935 through May 1970, prices were obtained for center cut loin chops of U.S. No. 1 grade. Since May 1970, no grade has been specified.

E 192, bacon. Most of the quotations included in the average were for sliced bacon for all years. In the early years (probably before 1930) bacon was sliced when sold and prices for slab bacon may be included. Sliced and packaged bacon has been priced since about 1930 in 1 pound or two ½ pound packages of cellophane or similar material. Grade descriptions were: 1890–1942, best but not fancy grade; 1943–1945, first quality or fancy grade; 1946–1963, standard Grade A; since 1964, best quality.

E 193, butter. All prices refer to creamery butter, 92 to 93 score or better for 1890–1942 and 92 score for 1943–1970. Tub or print butter was priced up to 1940, roll or print in 1941 and 1942, package of 4 sticks or quarters for 1943–1946, and package print or roll, including quarters for 1947–1970.

E 194, eggs. Averages are for fresh eggs for all years. For 1890–1942, prices are for the highest grade sold in volume in each store; for 1943–1944, U.S. extras or Grade A; for 1945–1952, the highest grade and size sold in volume in each store; since 1953, large Grade A eggs in most cities, although some ungraded eggs included in some small cities.

E 195, milk, delivered. Until 1935, prices are for fresh fluid milk, raw or pasteurized, no grade designation, in quart bottle or in bulk, delivered to homes; for 1935–1946, raw or pasteurized milk of the dominant grade in each city in quart bottles or cartons; for 1947–1949, same grades, but sizes included 1-quart, 2-quart, and 4-quart containers in many cities: for 1950–1956, pasteurized milk, homogenized or nonhomogenized, without Vitamin D, of the volume-selling grade in each city in quart or half-gallon cartons or bottles; for 1957–September 1966, pasteurized, homogenized milk with Vitamin D added, 3.25 percent or over butterfat content in quart or half-gallon cartons or bottles; beginning in October 1966, prices are for half-gallon containers; since May 1970, prices are for fresh whole milk, pasteurized, homogenized, Vitamin D added.

E 196, oranges. California and Florida oranges of the variety and size constituting the bulk of sales each month were quoted from 1919 to about 1935. After that time, the size range was narrowed to include only size 176–220 in standard box of U.S. No. 1 grade (good quality).

E 197, potatoes. White or Irish potatoes, excluding large baking types, have been priced consistently for all years in the quantities in which sales have customarily been made. The designation of U.S. No. 1 grade was added in 1935.

E 198, tomatoes, canned. The volume selling brands of canned tomatoes, standard grade, in No. 2 can were priced for 1919–1954. For 1955–1970, the description was expanded to specify "small and large pieces, with a maximum of 50 percent liquid, standard grade (C)" and the can size was changed to No. 303. Prices for 1919–1954 have been converted to No. 303 can.

E 199, navy beans. Dried beans, white, navy, or pea beans, No. 1 choice, hand picked, packaged or bulk were priced for 1915–1970. For 1949–1952, California small white beans were also included and for 1953–1970, Great Northern beans.

E 200, coffee. For 1913–1970, whole bean or ground roasted coffee was priced. Bulk or packaged coffee was quoted up to 1938. For 1939–1955, coffee in cans, glass, cardboard, or paper containers were averaged. For 1956–1970, prices are for ground roasted coffee in airtight cans only.

E 201, margarine. Prices are for uncolored oleomargarine, animal and vegetable, in 1-pound cartons for 1919–1948. For 1949 and 1950, uncolored vegetable margarine in 1-pound cartons was quoted. For 1951–1970, averages are for colored vegetable margarine in 1-pound cartons.

E 202, sugar. Prices are for white granulated cane or beet sugar but the size package has varied over the years. For 1890–1916, prices for the volume-selling quantity were quoted; for 1917–1928, 1 pound; for 1929–1942, 10 pounds; and for 1943–1970, 5 pounds. For a short period during World War II, the 2-pound unit was the only one available.

E 203–213. General note.

The collection of retail prices for fuel and light was initiated in 1911 with coal and gas data for 1907–1911. After that time, the program was expanded to include gas, electricity, and the heating fuels used in important quantities in the cities covered. Prices were collected semiannually up to 1920 and at quarterly or monthly intervals from 1920 on. The indexes shown here are annual averages.

The number of cities for which prices for this group have been compiled has varied widely. Before 1947, city coverage had gradually been extended until fuels prices and utility rates were obtained in 51 cities. In 1947, this program was cut back to the 34 cities in the Consumer Price Index (CPI). The CPI revision in 1952 resulted in changing the city sample and enlarging the number to 46 cities. Another revision, effective in 1964, enlarged the sample to 50 urban areas. In 1966, six additional areas were included.

The changing importance of particular kinds of fuel in particular localities, coupled with the overall change in the area sample over the years, produced many changes in the volume of data for the indexes. The amount of supplementary information for deriving weights has varied also. In order to produce continuous index numbers, all changes in samples and methods of averaging were handled by the linking process.

All prices have been collected by mail from retailers and utility companies in each city, except reports for electricity which have been secured through the Federal Power Commission since 1937.

The terms of sale for the quotations were net cash payment basis, delivered to the residential consumer in specified quantities. Charges for special services were excluded, but all applicable sales taxes were included. Annual averages were computed using standard Bureau of Labor Statistics (BLS) procedures.

The following BLS bulletins contain the history of the collection and publication of prices for this group: Bulletin 664, *Changes in Retail Prices of Electricity, 1923–38*, pp. 17–19; Bulletin 628, *Changes in Retail Prices of Gas, 1923–36*, pp. 48–52; Bulletin 950, *Residential Heating Fuels; Retail Prices, 1941–48*, pp. 1–4. These reports contain references to earlier bulletins and include other index and price series.

E 203. Retail price indexes of electricity for residential use, composite, 1913–1970.

Source: U.S. Bureau of Labor Statistics (BLS), *Retail Price Indexes of Fuels and Utilities* (formerly *Fuels and Electricity*) *January 1972*.

See also general note for series E 203–213.

This composite is an extension backward of a current BLS series. For 1913–1934, the index is based on the average price per kilowatt-hour for the average amount of electricity used by families in each of the 32 cities included in the Consumer Price Index (CPI). Average prices for the 32 cities were combined as simple averages.

In 1938, a new method of computation for the revised CPI was inaugurated, and data were extended back to 1935. Net monthly bills for typical residential services were calculated from rate schedules for each city. The number of cities in the composite included 34 cities for 1935–1952, 46 cities for 1953–1963, 50 cities for 1964–1965, and 56 cities for 1966–1970.

Changes also have been made in the typical services. For the period 1935–1952, 25, 40, 100, and 250 kilowatt-hour monthly net bills were priced. From December 1952 to December 1963, three services were priced—40, 100, and 200 kilowatt-hours. With the revision of the CPI in 1964, the composite of services priced was changed to 100, 250, and 500 kilowatt-hours. The new composite included the entire 50-city sample for 1964 and 1965, and the entire 56-city sample for 1966–1970.

The net monthly bills for the typical services were first combined into an index for each city by using weights approximating the importance of each of the services in that city. The city indexes were then combined with the consumption and population weights of the CPI.

E 204. Retail price indexes of electricity for residential use, 100 kilowatt-hours, 1923–1970.

Source: See source for series E 203.

See also general note for series E 203–213.

This index is based on net monthly bills for one of the typical services included in the composite, series E 203. When the new method of calculation was inaugurated in 1938, net monthly bills were obtained from rate schedules supplied by the companies or in BLS files. Originally, the indexes were calculated on the 1923–25 base and converted to later base periods when the CPI was revised.

For 1923–June 1947, the cities in the series totaled 51 (including the 34 CPI cities). Thereafter, only CPI cities were included. The weights used for 1923–June 1947 represented the number of residential customers as of December 31, 1935. Since July 1947, the weights have been the CPI consumption and population factors.

E 205. Retail price indexes of gas for residential use, composite, 1935–1970.

Source: See source for series E 203.

See also general note for series E 203–213.

This composite is another backward extension of a current BLS series. It combines data used to produce the indexes for "residential heating" and "other than residential heating."

When price collection for gas was begun by the BLS in 1911, the majority of the cities were served with manufactured gas. As a result of the increasing trend to use of natural gas, the number of cities for which the BLS obtained prices for manufactured gas declined from 35 of 39 cities in 1911 and 42 of 51 cities in 1923, to none of the CPI cities since 1957. While manufactured gas was being phased out, the use of natural gas increased. In 1913, only 8 or 9 of 50 cities were using natural gas; 18 of 50 cities were using natural gas in 1935, 33 of 46 cities in 1957, 49 of 50 cities in 1964, and 55 of the 56 CPI cities from 1966 to 1970.

The use of natural gas for residential heating grew in importance as additional pipelines made natural gas available to more and more cities. Although gas for residential heating was not included in the CPI before 1953, a special study in 1943 provided information on the volume of sales for residential heating as of 1940 and rate schedule data back to 1935 for cities in which natural gas was an important heating fuel.

In 1935, the BLS adopted the method of computing net monthly bills based on a definite number of heat units (therms of 100,000 British Thermal Units each) for each of 4 services—10.6, 19.6, 30.6, and 40.6 therms. These services were for use other than residential heating.

E 206. Retail price indexes of gas for residential heating, 1935–1970.

Source: See source for series E 203.

See also general note for series E 203–213.

For the period 1935–1946, 27 of the 51 cities used for utility pricing were included in residential heating. For 1947–1952, 16 of 34 cities were included; for 1953–1963, 28 of 46 cities; for 1964–1965, 45 of 50 CPI urban areas; and, from 1966–1970, 50 of the 56 areas.

The price for each city was calculated as an average of the rates per therm in all of the heating rate blocks of the rate schedule, weighted by the total number of therms sold by the gas company in that rate block for residential heating. For 1935–1952, the average rates per therm for the various cities were then combined, using total thermal sales for residential heating in each city as weights. For 1953–1970, they were combined with consumption and population weights in the CPI.

E 207. Retail price indexes of gas for other than residential heating, composite, 1935–1970.

Source: See source for series E 203.

See also general note for series E 203–213.

In 1935, BLS began pricing net monthly bills based upon a definite number of heat units (therms of 100,000 BTU each) for each of 4 selected services—10.6, 19.6, 30.6, and 40.6 therms. These 4 typical services were continued from 1935 through 1952. For 1953–1963, net monthly bills for 10 and 25 therms were used and, for 1964–1970, net monthly bills of 10, 25, and 40 therms. This method of calculating prices has provided a better measure of price changes since differences in heating values over time could be taken into account.

Indexes based on 10.6 and 30.6 therms back to 1923 and a description of the methods adopted in 1935 are included in BLS Bulletin 628, *Changes in Retail Prices of Gas*.

The number of cities included was 34 for 1935–1952 and 46 for 1953–1963. With the revised CPI of 1964, 49 of 50 cities were priced for gas other than residential heating, and, in 1966, this went to 55 of 56 CPI cities. For the methods of combining monthly bills used, see text for series E 203.

E 208. Retail price indexes of gas for other than residential heating, 10 therms, 1935–1970.

Source: See source for series E 203.

See also general note for series E 203–213, and text for E 207.

For 1935–June 1947, the net monthly bill for 10.6 therms was computed for each city, and cities were combined on the basis of number of residential customers as of December 1945. For July 1947–1970, prices were obtained for 10 therms and city averages were combined with the consumption and population weights of the CPI.

Annual averages were estimated from quarterly figures for 1935–1951, and from monthly figures beginning in 1952.

E 209.   Retail price indexes of gas for other than residential heating, 25 therms, 1935–1970.

Source: See source for series E 203.

See also general note for series E 203–213 and text for series E 207. With the revision of January 1964, pricing of 25 and 40 therm net bills was initiated. Pricing occurred in 40 of the 50 CPI cities in December 1963 and was increased to 55 of 56 CPI cities when the CPI was expanded in December 1965. For frequency of collection and methods employed to combine city data, see text for series E 208.

E 210.   Retail price indexes of fuel oil and coal for residential use, 1935–1970.

Source: See source for series E 203.

See also general note for series E 203–213.

This is a composite index combining consumption and population weights of fuel oil and coal used for the individual CPI commodities. In addition to fuel oil No. 2, the commodities priced for this index included, for varying periods of time, fuel oils No. 3 and No. 4, kerosene, anthracite, and bituminous coal. Pricing of petroleum fuels, other than fuel No. 2, was discontinued in 1964.

E 211.   Retail price indexes of No. 2 fuel oil for residential use, 1935–1970.

Source: See source for series E 203.

See also general note for series E 203–213.

Retail prices of petroleum fuels were first collected in 24 cities in 1937 and data were obtained back to 1935. Thereafter, the number of cities was increased as fuel oil for heating became more important. Beginning in 1947, the city coverage was restricted to those included in the CPI and, through 1963, usually covered about 20 cities. For 1964 and 1965, 30 of the 50 CPI cities were covered and, from 1966 to 1970, 32 of 56 CPI cities were covered.

The prices from which the index was computed refer to prices per 100 gallons delivered in "the amount usually delivered at one time." No. 2 fuel oil has been priced continuously and, for 1939–1947, No. 3 oil also was priced and included. Average prices for each city were simple averages of quotations from a sample of dealers. For 1935–1938, city averages were combined with CPI consumption and population weights. For 1939–1946, weighting factors to combine city averages were obtained from 1941 shipments to each city as measured by Office of Price Administration rationing authorities. CPI weights were again employed after 1946 to obtain the U.S. averages.

E 212.   Retail price indexes of Pennsylvania anthracite for residential use, stove size, 1913–1962.

Source: U.S. Bureau of Labor Statistics, *Retail Prices and Indexes of Fuels and Electricity*, December issues.

See also general note for series E 203–213.

Data for the early years by type of coal for each firm reporting were published in BLS Bulletin 105, *Retail Prices, 1890–1911*. Similar data for 1912–1917 are included in later issues of *Retail Prices*. Since the first collection, BLS has continuously obtained retail prices for all locally important fuels.

This index was based on average prices per net ton delivered at the curb or in the bin if there was no extra charge. Prices from dealers in each city always have been combined as a simple average for each city. For 1913–1928, city averages were combined also on an unweighted basis. Through a revision of method in 1936, city average prices for 1929–1952 were weighted by fixed weights based on anthracite shipments to each city by rail during the year ending July 1936. For 1953–1962, the city averages were combined with consumption and population weights of the CPI.

Cities for which anthracite prices were obtained varied partly because of change in consumer demand and partly due to CPI revisions. Generally the number of cities has declined until, with the revision of January 1964, indexes of retail prices for anthracite coal were no longer published.

E 213.   Retail price indexes of bituminous coal for residential use, all domestic sizes, 1913–1962.

Source: See source for series E 212.

See also general note for series E 203–213.

For methods of collection and averaging of prices, see text for series E 212. Generally, the index was based on unweighted averages of all prices for all sizes and types of bituminous coal for 1913–June 1947, and on city averages weighted with CPI weighting factors for July 1947–1962. Publication of this series also was discontinued effective with the January 1964 revision of the CPI.

E 214.   Rent indexes (Warren and Pearson) for dwelling units in 5 large cities, 1860–1880.

Source: George F. Warren and Frank A. Pearson, *Prices*, John Wiley and Sons, New York, 1933, p. 267 (copyright).

See also G. F. Warren and F. A. Pearson, *Wholesale Prices for 213 Years, 1720–1932*, Cornell University Agricultural Experiment Station, *Memoir 142*, Ithaca, New York, 1932, p. 27.

The method of calculating this index was not indicated. The rental data were obtained from the special report by J. D. Weeks, "Report on the Average Retail Prices of Necessaries of Life in the United States" in volume 20 of the Tenth Census of the United States, pp. 104–107.

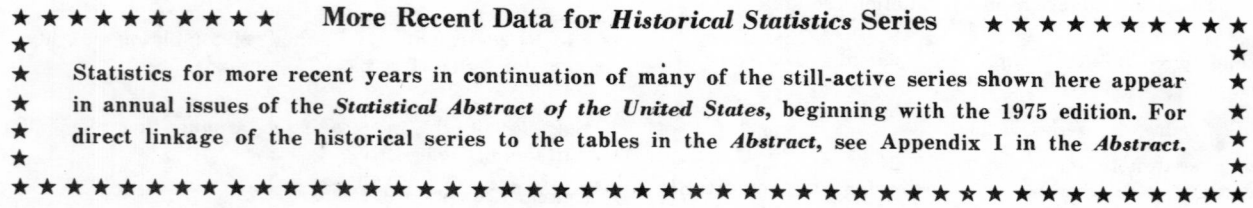

★ ★ ★ ★ ★ ★ ★ ★ ★   **More Recent Data for *Historical Statistics* Series**   ★ ★ ★ ★ ★ ★ ★ ★ ★

★ Statistics for more recent years in continuation of many of the still-active series shown here appear in annual issues of the *Statistical Abstract of the United States*, beginning with the 1975 edition. For direct linkage of the historical series to the tables in the *Abstract*, see Appendix I in the *Abstract*.

Series E 1–22. Implicit Price Deflators for Gross National Product: 1929 to 1970

[Index numbers, 1958=100. See series F 5 for GNP price deflator data for 1869–1928]

Year	Gross national product	Personal consumption expenditures				Gross private domestic investment						
						Total	Fixed investment					
							Nonresidential			Residential		
		Total	Durable goods	Non-durable goods	Services		Total	Structures	Producers' durable equipment	Total	Nonfarm	Farm
	1	2	3	4	5	6	7	8	9	10	11	12
1970	135.2	129.3	108.9	127.7	140.1	132.2	130.0	152.6	120.1	140.0	140.0	134.9
1969	128.2	123.5	106.1	122.2	133.2	126.4	123.0	141.0	115.2	137.7	137.8	132.9
1968	122.3	118.4	103.4	117.1	126.9	120.4	117.5	129.8	112.0	129.7	129.8	125.6
1967	117.6	114.4	100.3	113.0	122.2	115.9	113.8	124.0	109.3	123.1	123.1	122.6
1966	113.9	111.5	98.7	110.7	118.3	111.8	110.2	118.9	106.0	117.4	117.4	116.1
1965	110.9	108.8	99.6	106.9	115.1	109.3	107.5	114.7	103.9	114.2	114.3	110.1
1964	108.8	107.4	110.4	104.9	113.1	107.6	105.7	111.1	103.0	112.3	112.4	108.2
1963	107.2	106.1	100.4	104.0	110.9	106.0	104.5	108.9	102.3	108.9	109.0	107.2
1962	105.8	104.9	100.8	102.8	109.0	104.9	104.1	107.1	102.3	106.7	106.8	104.6
1961	104.6	103.9	100.6	101.9	107.6	103.9	103.4	105.6	102.1	105.0	105.0	104.9
1960	103.3	102.9	100.9	101.2	105.8	103.4	102.9	104.0	102.2	104.5	104.4	105.0
1959	101.6	101.3	101.4	99.9	103.0	102.6	102.2	102.7	102.0	103.1	103.1	103.0
1958	100.0	100.0	100.0	100.0	100.0	100.0	100.0	100.0	100.0	100.0	100.0	100.0
1957	97.5	97.7	98.4	97.7	97.3	98.5	97.9	98.6	97.5	99.8	99.8	100.5
1956	94.0	94.8	94.9	94.9	94.6	94.0	92.4	93.4	91.8	97.4	97.4	97.7
1955	90.9	92.8	91.9	93.6	92.0	89.0	86.7	88.1	85.9	92.9	92.9	93.4
1954	89.6	92.5	92.9	94.2	90.0	86.8	84.8	86.0	84.0	90.4	90.3	91.9
1953	88.3	91.7	94.3	93.9	87.7	86.6	84.0	84.9	83.5	91.9	91.8	93.3
1952	87.5	90.5	95.4	94.3	83.6	85.3	82.6	83.2	82.2	90.8	91.0	86.8
1951	85.6	88.6	94.2	93.3	80.0	83.1	80.4	79.3	80.9	88.6	88.4	92.2
1950	80.2	82.9	87.8	86.0	76.3	77.5	74.4	72.9	75.2	82.5	82.5	82.9
1949	79.1	81.7	86.8	85.6	74.3	74.7	72.8	71.2	73.6	78.5	78.2	82.7
1948	79.6	82.3	86.3	88.5	72.1	73.9	70.7	71.5	70.3	80.8	80.5	85.7
1947	74.6	77.9	82.7	83.6	67.9	66.7	64.5	64.4	64.6	71.7	71.3	78.6
1946	66.7	70.5	76.8	74.3	62.7	58.5	56.3	54.4	57.5	59.7	59.4	63.5
1945	59.7	65.4	75.9	68.7	58.7	51.5	51.0	49.2	51.7	54.9	54.6	58.5
1944	58.2	63.2	71.5	66.2	57.5	51.1	51.0	48.6	51.9	51.6	51.1	55.8
1943	56.8	59.9	64.2	62.5	55.3	49.3	49.9	46.8	51.1	47.0	46.8	48.8
1942	53.0	54.8	59.3	55.6	52.7	46.5	47.8	41.3	51.5	43.3	43.4	42.0
1941	47.2	48.7	50.4	47.7	49.8	42.0	42.7	36.4	46.3	40.3	40.6	36.3
1940	43.9	45.5	46.5	43.8	47.9	39.0	40.0	33.9	43.4	36.9	37.2	32.3
1939	43.2	45.1	46.0	43.2	47.7	37.7	38.7	33.1	42.2	35.7	35.9	32.0
1938	43.9	45.6	46.7	44.0	47.7	38.2	39.3	33.9	43.0	34.3	34.4	33.3
1937	44.5	46.5	45.8	46.4	46.8	37.8	38.8	34.4	41.4	31.3	31.2	32.2
1936	42.7	44.7	43.6	44.8	45.0	34.6	35.6	30.2	38.5			
1935	42.6	44.4	43.7	44.5	44.4	34.3	35.9	30.6	38.7	29.8	29.7	30.7
1934	42.2	43.5	44.7	42.7	44.3	33.7	34.9	28.9	38.8	30.1	30.1	30.8
1933	39.3	40.6	41.9	38.0	43.6	30.6	31.6	27.9	34.5	27.1	27.1	26.7
1932	40.2	42.3	43.2	37.7	48.3	31.6	32.9	27.6	39.1	27.3	27.4	26.2
1931	44.8	47.9	49.1	44.1	52.7	35.2	35.8	31.1	41.1	33.6	33.7	32.1
1930	49.3	53.6	55.3	51.6	55.7	37.9	38.1	34.0	43.0	37.1	37.1	38.0
1929	50.6	55.3	56.4	54.5	56.1	39.4	39.9	35.7	44.6	38.1	38.0	39.1

PRICES AND PRICE INDEXES

Series E 1–22. Implicit Price Deflators for Gross National Product: 1929 to 1970—Con.

[Index numbers, 1958 = 100]

Year	Government purchases of goods and services			Final sales			By sector			
								Private		
	Total	Federal	State and local	Goods output	Services	Structures	Total	Business	Households and institutions	General government
	13	14	15	16	17	18	19	20	21	22
1970	157.6	149.2	165.0	122.3	150.1	149.7	130.3	129.0	185.5	188.8
1969	144.0	134.5	153.6	117.3	140.9	140.9	124.3	123.2	172.5	171.0
1968	135.1	126.5	144.8	113.1	133.4	131.1	118.9	118.0	159.4	159.1
1967	128.5	121.5	136.4	109.9	127.1	124.7	114.8	114.0	147.5	147.7
1966	124.0	118.8	129.4	107.4	122.3	119.3	111.6	110.9	138.1	140.3
1965	119.4	115.5	123.5	105.0	118.5	114.7	108.8	108.3	131.7	133.5
1964	115.7	112.2	119.5	103.5	115.8	111.6	107.0	106.6	126.4	128.4
1963	111.8	108.0	116.3	103.0	112.6	108.7	105.8	105.4	120.9	121.5
1962	109.0	105.6	113.2	102.6	110.1	106.4	104.7	104.4	116.2	116.6
1961	107.1	105.2	109.4	101.9	108.4	104.4	103.7	103.5	112.3	113.6
1960	105.0	104.2	105.9	101.4	106.1	103.3	102.8	102.6	108.8	108.6
1959	102.4	102.2	102.6	100.6	102.9	102.2	101.4	101.3	104.0	104.2
1958	100.0	100.0	100.0	100.0	100.0	100.0	100.0	100.0	100.0	100.0
1957	96.4	95.8	97.3	97.9	96.3	99.3	97.9	97.9	96.2	93.3
1956	92.1	91.7	92.7	94.3	93.0	95.4	94.5	94.5	92.4	88.7
1955	87.1	86.9	87.5	91.6	89.9	90.2	91.6	91.6	89.8	84.0
1954	84.1	83.5	85.3	91.6	87.1	88.1	90.8	90.8	87.9	79.5
1953	81.8	81.4	82.8	90.6	84.7	88.6	89.6	89.7	85.4	76.6
1952	81.0	81.2	80.6	91.4	81.2	87.4	89.0	89.1	82.0	74.4
1951	78.5	79.4	76.9	91.0	77.5	84.4	87.4	87.5	78.1	70.5
1950	71.8	72.9	70.8	84.3	74.0	78.2	81.4	81.6	74.4	67.1
1949	71.0	73.0	68.9	84.6	71.9	75.3	80.6	80.8	72.6	64.7
1948	68.1	69.8	66.4	86.4	69.3	76.7	81.4	81.7	71.0	60.8
1947	62.9	65.6	60.4	81.1	65.9	68.7	76.3	76.5	68.1	58.5
1946	55.8	57.3	53.2	72.6	60.1	57.3	68.2	68.4	63.1	55.4
1945	52.6	53.1	48.6	65.1	53.1	50.6	62.6	62.7	58.0	48.3
1944	53.1	53.8	46.1	64.6	49.8	48.7	62.0	62.3	52.2	43.3
1943	53.9	54.9	44.6	64.2	47.4	48.5	60.9	61.3	45.2	39.7
1942	50.9	52.5	42.3	59.2	46.7	44.0	55.5	56.1	37.6	37.3
1941	44.0	46.6	39.2	50.5	44.9	38.5	48.7	49.2	33.7	34.7
1940	38.5	40.2	37.3	45.2	44.2	35.7	44.7	45.2	32.1	36.0
1939	37.9	40.8	36.3	44.2	44.2	34.6	43.9	44.4	32.0	36.8
1938	38.3	40.5	36.8	45.1	44.4	35.0	44.6	45.3	31.6	37.4
1937	38.4	40.7	37.1	46.7	43.7	35.1	45.3	45.9	32.0	36.5
1936	37.6	40.5	35.9	44.8	42.3	32.2	43.4	44.1	30.2	36.5
1935	37.0	37.0	37.0	45.0	41.6	31.5	43.5	44.2	29.4	34.7
1934	36.8	37.4	36.6	44.2	41.5	31.6	43.0	43.8	29.2	34.8
1933	34.5	33.1	35.0	39.2	40.8	29.5	39.9	40.6	29.2	33.5
1932	33.4	31.9	33.8	38.9	44.5	27.9	40.9	41.5	31.4	33.7
1931	36.3	34.5	36.6	45.0	48.1	33.2	45.7	46.2	34.5	34.5
1930	37.9	34.1	38.7	51.9	50.6	36.4	50.4	51.1	37.3	34.1
1929	38.6	36.0	39.1	53.9	51.4	37.7	51.7	52.2	38.9	34.1

Series E 23–39. Wholesale Price Indexes (BLS), by Major Product Groups: 1890 to 1970

[1967 = 100]

Year	All commodities	Industrial commodities	Farm products	Processed foods and feeds	Textile products and apparel	Hides, skins, leather, and related products	Fuels and related products and power	Chemicals and allied products	Rubber and plastic products	Lumber and wood products	Pulp, paper, and allied products	Metals and metal products	Machinery and equipment	Furniture and household durables	Nonmetallic mineral products	Motor vehicles and equipment	Miscellaneous products
	23	24	25	26	27	28	29	30	31	32	33	34	35	36	37	38	39
1970	110.4	110.0	111.0	112.0	107.2	110.1	105.9	102.2	108.6	113.7	108.2	116.7	111.4	107.5	113.3	108.5	109.9
1969	106.5	106.0	108.8	107.3	105.9	108.6	101.0	99.9	105.4	125.2	104.2	108.5	106.4	104.9	108.1	104.7	104.9
1968	102.5	102.5	102.5	101.2	103.7	103.2	98.9	99.8	103.4	113.3	101.1	102.6	103.2	102.8	103.7	102.8	102.2
1967	100.0	100.0	100.0	100.0	100.0	100.0	100.0	100.0	100.0	100.0	100.0	100.0	100.0	100.0	100.0	100.0	100.0
1966	99.8	98.5	105.9	101.2	100.1	103.4	97.8	99.4	97.8	100.2	98.8	98.8	96.8	98.0	98.4	98.6	97.7
1965	96.6	96.4	98.7	95.5	99.8	94.3	95.5	99.0	95.9	95.9	96.2	96.4	93.9	96.9	97.5	98.5	95.9
1964	94.7	95.2	94.6	92.3	99.2	90.3	93.7	98.3	95.5	95.4	95.4	93.8	92.8	97.4	97.3	98.3	95.2
1963	94.5	94.7	96.0	92.5	98.5	90.0	96.3	97.9	96.8	93.5	95.6	91.3	92.2	97.0	97.1	97.8	94.5
1962	94.8	94.8	98.0	91.9	98.6	92.7	96.7	99.1	96.3	91.6	96.3	91.2	92.0	97.7	97.6	98.6	93.7
1961	94.5	94.8	96.3	91.0	97.7	91.7	97.2	100.7	99.2	91.0	95.2	91.9	91.9	98.4	97.6	98.6	93.3
1960	94.9	95.3	97.2	89.5	99.5	90.8	96.1	101.8	103.1	95.3	98.1	92.4	92.0	99.0	97.2	98.8	93.0
1959	94.8	95.3	97.5	89.4	98.4	94.2	95.3	101.6	102.9	98.8	97.3	92.3	91.3	99.3	97.0	100.3	92.2
1958	94.6	93.6	103.9	91.8	97.0	82.9	95.3	102.0	103.3	92.4	96.4	90.4	89.4	99.1	95.8	98.1	92.0
1957	93.3	93.3	99.5	87.4	98.8	82.0	99.1	101.2	103.4	93.5	95.4	91.0	87.6	98.3	94.8	95.1	90.2
1956	90.7	90.8	96.9	84.9	98.7	81.9	94.0	99.1	103.8	98.5	93.6	89.2	81.8	95.8	91.3	91.2	87.6
1955	87.8	86.9	98.2	85.0	98.7	77.3	91.2	98.5	102.4	97.1	87.8	82.1	75.7	93.3	87.5	86.3	86.5
1954	87.6	85.0	104.7	88.9	98.6	77.6	91.3	98.9	90.4	92.6	85.5	76.9	73.4	92.9	85.1	83.8	86.4
1953	87.4	84.8	106.2	87.4	100.8	81.3	92.6	97.7	89.1	94.3	85.5	76.3	72.2	91.9	83.3	83.6	85.6
1952	88.6	84.1	117.2	91.6	103.4	80.1	90.1	96.5	95.5	94.4	85.7	73.9	70.6	90.1	80.1	84.0	83.4
1951	91.1	86.1	124.2	92.7	114.6	99.1	90.3	101.7	105.4	97.2	88.0	73.8	70.5	91.8	80.1	79.4	83.9
1950	81.8	78.0	106.7	83.4	102.7	86.3	87.1	88.9	85.9	89.3	74.3	66.3	63.1	84.7	75.4	75.3	79.2
1949	78.7	75.3	101.6	80.6	98.9	79.9	86.2	87.6	70.5	77.7	72.4	63.0	61.0	82.9	73.5	75.7	78.0
1948	82.8	76.9	117.5	88.7	108.1	84.2	90.5	95.9	72.8	84.0	75.7	54.9	58.2	81.6	71.6	70.8	76.5
1947	76.5	70.8	109.4	82.9	103.6	83.3	76.9	93.7	70.5	73.4	72.5	54.9	53.7	77.0	66.3	64.1	73.5
1946	62.3	58.0	90.9	--------	--------	61.1	64.4	70.5	70.8	47.2	--------	44.3	46.4	67.1	59.3	56.0	--------
1945	54.6	53.0	78.5	--------	--------	52.9	60.1	65.2	70.5	41.2	--------	39.6	42.2	63.2	55.7	48.3	--------
1944	53.6	52.3	75.5	--------	--------	52.2	59.5	64.8	72.7	40.6	--------	39.0	42.1	63.5	53.5	47.5	--------
1943	53.3	51.5	75.0	--------	--------	52.7	57.8	64.1	73.6	37.7	--------	39.0	42.4	61.4	52.4	47.2	--------
1942	50.9	50.7	64.8	--------	--------	52.8	56.2	63.3	71.6	35.6	--------	39.1	42.8	61.8	52.3	47.2	--------
1941	45.1	47.3	50.3	--------	--------	48.4	54.6	57.0	61.5	32.7	--------	38.5	42.1	57.2	50.2	43.2	--------
1940	40.5	44.0	41.4	--------	--------	45.2	51.4	52.4	57.1	27.4	--------	37.8	41.4	53.8	49.1	40.4	--------
1939	39.8	43.3	40.0	--------	--------	42.8	52.3	51.5	61.2	24.8	--------	37.6	41.3	52.6	49.1	39.1	--------
1938	40.5	43.4	42.0	--------	--------	41.6	54.6	51.8	58.9	24.1	--------	38.0	--------	52.8	50.0	39.9	--------
1937	44.5	45.2	52.9	--------	--------	46.9	55.5	54.5	60.0	26.5	--------	39.4	--------	54.1	51.7	37.4	--------
1936	41.7	42.2	49.5	--------	--------	42.7	54.5	52.0	51.0	22.4	--------	34.5	--------	48.8	50.5	34.9	--------
1935	41.3	41.4	48.1	--------	--------	40.2	52.6	47.3	47.0	21.4	--------	33.8	--------	48.1	50.4	35.2	--------
1934	38.6	41.6	40.0	--------	--------	38.8	52.4	49.6	47.0	22.3	--------	33.9	--------	48.5	50.4	36.7	--------
1933	34.0	37.8	31.4	--------	--------	36.3	47.6	47.4	40.2	19.0	--------	30.7	--------	44.6	47.2	34.8	--------
1932	33.6	37.3	29.5	--------	--------	32.8	50.3	--------	38.3	16.0	--------	29.9	--------	44.5	44.6	36.5	--------
1931	37.6	39.9	39.7	--------	--------	38.6	48.3	--------	44.2	18.6	--------	32.6	--------	50.5	47.7	37.5	--------
1930	44.6	45.2	54.2	--------	--------	44.9	56.2	--------	52.0	22.9	--------	36.2	--------	54.9	51.0	39.4	--------
1929	49.1	48.6	64.1	--------	--------	48.9	59.4	--------	59.4	25.0	--------	40.2	--------	55.8	51.2	41.9	--------
1928	50.0	49.3	64.8	--------	--------	54.4	60.4	--------	68.2	24.1	--------	38.8	--------	56.3	51.8	40.7	--------
1927	49.3	50.0	60.8	--------	--------	48.3	63.2	--------	86.2	25.0	--------	38.8	--------	57.7	50.3	40.2	--------
1926	51.6	53.2	61.3	--------	--------	44.8	71.5	--------	113.6	26.5	--------	41.4	--------	59.1	52.5	41.9	--------

Year	All commodities	Industrial commodities	Farm products	Year	All commodities	Year	All commodities
	23	24	25		23		23
1925	53.3	54.6	67.1	1912	35.6	1899	26.9
1924	50.5	53.1	61.1	1911	33.5	1898	25.0
1923	51.9	55.6	60.4	1910	36.4	1897	24.0
1922	49.9	54.4	57.4	1909	34.9	1896	23.9
1921	50.3	55.7	54.1	1908	32.4	1895	25.2
1920	79.6	85.7	92.2	1907	33.6	1894	24.7
1919	71.4	68.6	96.4	1906	32.0	1893	27.5
1918	67.6	65.9	90.6	1905	31.0	1892	26.9
1917	60.6	61.0	78.9	1904	30.8	1891	28.8
1916	44.1	46.8	51.7	1903	30.7	1890	28.9
1915	35.8	36.1	43.7	1902	30.4		
1914	35.2	35.2	43.5	1901	28.5		
1913	36.0	37.2	43.7	1900	28.9		

Series E 40–51. Wholesale Price Indexes (BLS), by Major Product Groups: 1890 to 1951

[1926 = 100]

Year	All commodities	All commodities other than farm products and foods	Farm products	Foods	Hides and leather products	Textile products	Fuel and lighting	Metals and metal products	Building materials	Chemicals and allied products	House-furnishing goods	Miscellaneous
	40	41	42	43	44	45	46	47	48	49	50	51
1951	180.4	169.4	196.1	186.9	221.4	172.2	138.2	189.2	225.5	143.3	176.0	141.0
1950	161.5	153.2	170.4	166.2	191.9	148.0	133.2	173.6	206.0	122.7	153.2	120.9
1949	155.0	147.3	165.5	161.4	180.4	140.4	131.7	170.2	193.4	118.6	145.3	112.3
1948	165.1	151.0	188.3	179.1	188.8	149.8	134.2	163.6	199.1	135.7	144.5	120.5
1947	152.1	135.2	181.2	168.7	182.4	141.7	108.7	145.0	179.7	127.3	131.1	115.5
1946	121.1	109.5	148.9	130.7	137.2	116.3	90.1	115.5	132.6	101.4	111.6	100.3
1945	105.8	99.7	128.2	106.2	118.1	100.1	84.0	104.7	117.8	95.2	104.5	94.7
1944	104.0	98.5	123.3	104.9	116.7	98.4	83.0	103.8	115.5	95.2	104.3	93.6
1943	103.1	96.9	122.6	106.6	117.5	97.4	80.8	103.8	111.4	94.9	102.7	92.2
1942	98.8	95.5	105.9	99.6	117.7	96.9	78.5	103.8	110.2	95.5	102.4	89.7
1941	87.3	89.0	82.4	82.7	108.3	84.8	76.2	99.4	103.2	84.4	94.3	82.0
1940	78.6	83.0	67.7	71.3	100.8	73.8	71.7	95.8	94.8	77.0	88.5	77.3
1939	77.1	81.3	65.3	70.4	95.6	69.7	73.1	94.4	90.5	76.0	86.3	74.8
1938	78.6	81.7	68.5	73.6	92.8	66.7	76.5	95.7	90.3	77.0	86.8	73.3
1937	86.3	85.3	86.4	85.5	104.6	76.3	77.6	95.7	95.2	82.6	89.7	77.8
1936	80.8	79.6	80.9	82.1	95.4	71.5	76.2	87.0	86.7	78.7	81.7	70.5
1935	80.0	77.9	78.8	83.7	89.6	70.9	73.5	86.4	85.3	79.0	80.6	68.3
1934	74.9	78.4	65.3	70.5	86.6	72.9	73.3	86.4	86.2	75.3	81.5	69.7
1933	65.9	71.2	51.4	60.5	80.9	64.8	66.3	79.8	77.0	72.1	75.8	62.5
1932	64.8	70.2	48.2	61.0	72.9	54.9	70.3	80.2	71.4	73.9	75.1	64.4
1931	73.0	75.0	64.8	74.6	86.1	66.3	67.5	84.5	79.2	79.3	84.9	69.8
1930	86.4	85.2	88.3	90.5	100.0	80.3	78.5	92.1	89.9	88.7	92.7	77.7
1929	95.3	91.6	104.9	99.9	109.1	90.4	83.0	100.5	95.4	94.0	94.3	82.6
1928	96.7	92.9	105.9	101.0	121.4	95.5	84.3	97.0	94.1	95.0	95.1	85.4
1927	95.4	94.0	99.4	96.7	107.7	95.6	88.3	96.3	94.7	96.1	97.5	91.0
1926	100.0	100.0	100.0	100.0	100.0	100.0	100.0	100.0	100.0	100.0	100.0	100.0
1925	103.5	102.6	109.8	100.2	105.3	108.3	96.5	103.2	101.7	101.8	103.1	109.0
1924	98.1	99.7	100.0	91.0	101.5	106.7	92.0	106.3	102.3	98.9	104.9	93.6
1923	100.6	104.3	98.6	92.7	104.2	111.3	97.3	109.3	108.7	101.1	108.9	99.7
1922	96.7	102.4	93.8	87.6	104.6	100.2	107.3	102.9	97.3	100.3	103.5	92.8
1921	97.6	104.9	88.4	90.6	109.2	94.5	96.8	117.5	97.4	115.0	113.0	109.2
1920	154.4	161.3	150.7	137.4	171.3	164.8	163.7	149.4	150.1	164.7	141.8	167.5
1919	138.6	128.8	157.6	129.5	174.1	135.3	104.3	130.9	115.6	157.0	105.9	139.1
1918	131.3	124.6	148.0	119.1	125.7	137.2	109.2	136.5	98.6	182.3	93.3	134.4
1917	117.5	114.2	129.0	104.5	123.8	98.7	105.4	150.6	88.2	165.0	74.2	122.1
1916	85.5	88.3	84.4	75.7	93.4	70.4	74.3	116.5	67.6	160.7	61.4	100.6
1915	69.5	68.0	71.5	65.4	75.5	54.1	51.8	86.3	53.5	112.0	56.0	86.9
1914	68.1	66.4	71.2	64.7	70.9	54.6	56.6	80.2	52.7	81.4	56.5	89.9
1913	69.8	70.0	71.5	64.2	68.1	57.3	61.3	90.8	56.7	80.2	56.1	93.1
1912	69.1	--------	72.6	66.8	64.5	55.7	51.4	89.5	55.9	80.7	53.0	106.4
1911	64.9	--------	66.8	62.0	58.8	55.5	46.7	80.8	55.3	81.6	52.7	108.6
1910	70.4	--------	74.3	64.9	60.2	58.4	47.6	85.2	55.3	82.0	54.0	152.7
1909	67.6	--------	69.6	62.6	61.5	56.5	51.6	84.5	53.7	79.9	51.7	129.6
1908	62.9	--------	62.2	58.7	55.6	54.8	53.7	86.3	52.0	79.6	51.6	97.8
1907	65.2	--------	62.2	57.0	58.0	63.5	54.4	109.8	56.8	78.5	55.0	108.2
1906	61.8	--------	57.3	53.4	57.7	58.7	52.0	102.4	54.0	76.8	51.3	115.3
1905	60.1	--------	56.4	55.1	53.9	54.1	49.6	89.1	48.1	82.3	49.7	117.4
1904	59.7	--------	58.5	54.0	49.7	52.9	53.3	79.9	45.0	84.1	50.3	109.5
1903	59.6	--------	55.6	52.0	49.9	52.8	60.3	90.2	46.7	84.1	50.9	98.9
1902	58.9	--------	58.4	53.3	50.8	49.4	51.8	91.0	45.3	86.5	49.2	88.1
1901	55.3	--------	52.8	50.5	48.9	48.1	44.6	93.1	44.3	84.2	48.9	93.4
1900	56.1	--------	50.5	50.8	49.4	53.3	46.3	98.0	46.2	82.1	48.9	102.0
1899	52.2	--------	45.8	47.7	49.4	47.7	41.2	100.0	43.6	81.1	45.0	97.4
1898	48.5	--------	44.9	47.8	48.3	44.9	34.5	65.3	39.6	77.4	44.0	93.4
1897	46.6	--------	42.5	45.5	45.9	42.9	33.9	65.0	37.4	70.9	42.5	92.5
1896	46.5	--------	39.6	44.1	45.2	43.1	39.5	71.2	38.9	65.0	43.4	90.2
1895	48.8	--------	43.9	47.3	49.4	44.3	40.3	70.4	38.8	64.7	43.5	88.9
1894	47.9	--------	44.6	48.2	43.0	46.1	34.3	65.7	39.8	65.5	45.3	86.4
1893	53.4	--------	51.3	54.7	45.1	54.1	35.3	76.8	41.6	72.7	48.1	89.0
1892	52.2	--------	49.5	51.0	47.2	55.2	34.8	84.0	41.7	74.6	48.1	86.6
1891	55.8	--------	54.2	54.8	47.9	54.6	37.0	92.2	44.2	74.0	50.4	94.3
1890	56.2	--------	50.4	55.5	47.5	57.8	38.1	105.3	46.5	73.2	49.9	97.9

Series E 52–63. Wholesale Price Indexes (Warren and Pearson), by Major Product Groups: 1749 to 1890

[1910–14 = 100]

Year	All commodities	Farm products	Foods	Hides and leather products	Textile products	Fuel and lighting	Metals and metal products	Building materials	Chemicals and drugs	House-furnishing goods	Spirits	Miscellaneous
	52	53	54	55	56	57	58	59	60	61	62	63
1890	82	71	86	74	103	72	123	84	90	91	--------	89
1889	81	67	79	80	99	71	116	81	101	94	74	80
1888	86	75	86	86	98	72	121	80	103	94	80	73
1887	85	71	86	92	98	70	119	81	97	92	77	75
1886	82	68	78	101	100	70	110	82	99	94	79	74
1885	85	72	84	105	105	72	109	81	100	99	79	78
1884	93	82	93	111	109	77	124	84	105	105	81	78
1883	101	87	103	107	116	89	144	85	110	110	83	93
1882	108	99	114	108	119	92	157	88	114	109	80	93
1881	103	89	106	109	119	91	150	83	120	109	81	90
1880	100	80	96	113	128	92	166	81	120	117	83	91
1879	90	72	90	100	114	80	134	74	120	105	82	90
1878	91	72	93	95	115	93	126	72	127	109	82	88
1877	106	89	115	109	125	108	141	80	136	118	86	95
1876	110	89	113	104	138	127	157	84	140	123	86	98
1875	118	99	120	123	141	128	175	90	149	134	88	98
1874	126	102	126	128	151	135	194	101	176	149	78	111
1873	133	103	122	132	175	148	243	106	181	160	75	115
1872	136	108	121	130	177	153	257	107	175	159	73	125
1871	130	102	130	126	170	152	203	102	177	154	74	120
1870	135	112	139	128	179	134	200	101	199	164	78	128
1869	151	128	154	134	194	166	227	110	227	178	86	136
1868	158	138	171	126	197	149	225	116	204	178	117	153
1867	162	133	167	132	220	144	248	120	229	196	146	162
1866	174	140	173	146	245	160	278	128	283	220	154	170
1865	185	148	180	152	266	214	306	118	300	214	150	175
1864	193	162	189	164	264	197	354	114	297	222	106	189
1863	133	113	123	133	206	125	236	88	234	165	45	146
1862	104	86	107	108	147	87	180	69	206	124	28	122
1861	89	75	89	90	120	80	152	63	174	110	21	98
1860	93	77	96	102	119	98	149	65	175	117	23	98
1859	95	82	99	115	120	93	150	64	168	118	24	98
1858	93	76	97	110	123	90	154	67	168	121	23	102
1857	111	95	123	139	138	97	173	73	171	130	27	107
1856	105	84	116	121	129	97	174	73	176	128	30	114
1855	110	98	126	104	125	102	176	71	178	129	31	103
1854	108	93	117	100	124	121	191	70	174	129	27	103
1853	97	83	98	84	119	102	186	67	169	128	22	96
1852	88	77	95	70	113	93	144	64	156	118	19	89
1851	83	71	84	65	115	87	141	61	153	117	20	86
1850	84	71	84	67	116	95	147	61	154	114	21	88
1849	82	62	88	64	111	93	155	58	152	110	21	92
1848	82	59	87	56	113	93	170	61	153	111	22	99
1847	90	72	96	66	117	90	186	61	156	117	24	99
1846	83	58	84	57	122	88	191	64	164	110	20	86
1845	83	58	84	63	125	96	189	64	178	107	21	85
1844	77	52	72	66	125	90	179	59	187	108	20	96
1843	75	48	77	69	114	87	172	58	188	99	19	109
1842	82	53	80	72	132	94	183	62	203	113	17	111
1841	92	64	90	86	140	111	204	67	220	121	19	113
1840	95	65	102	80	146	105	204	65	238	128	21	108
1839	112	86	126	90	159	122	220	70	250	---------	25	122
1838	110	82	128	80	157	121	219	70	257	---------	25	120
1837	115	84	132	80	167	130	243	70	264	---------	25	119
1836	114	89	128	78	177	130	241	53	251	---------	25	130
1835	100	75	107	74	170	111	206	52	225	---------	23	126
1834	90	64	93	70	161	101	201	52	212	---------	19	109
1833	95	69	100	76	162	111	205	51	220	---------	22	105
1832	95	63	99	85	161	137	212	49	226	---------	22	110
1831	94	61	98	91	179	112	209	49	211	---------	23	111
1830	91	58	94	85	181	116	209	47	207	---------	19	111
1829	96	59	100	85	182	133	227	49	222	---------	19	117
1828	97	58	99	90	190	138	234	51	251	---------	19	113
1827	98	59	100	87	186	137	243	51	287	---------	21	112
1826	99	62	98	91	188	138	269	52	298	---------	21	110
1825	103	67	100	99	198	131	279	50	313	---------	22	114
1824	98	61	99	97	191	133	242	48	304	---------	19	119
1823	103	64	108	97	209	131	247	49	320	---------	20	119
1822	106	70	109	93	218	138	257	50	342	---------	21	118
1821	102	64	102	89	215	142	261	50	306	---------	21	129
1820	106	68	109	83	211	157	270	53	300	---------	22	124
1819	125	87	140	101	233	162	285	55	306	---------	24	144
1818	147	117	172	113	275	149	279	56	318	---------	29	149
1817	151	126	184	95	268	141	277	60	327	---------	31	156
1816	151	119	172	86	274	190	310	68	376	---------	34	177
1815	170	117	187	85	300	318	399	76	538	---------	41	202
1814	182	112	181	96	300	525	464	69	814	---------	48	246
1813	162	104	172	77	291	334	419	63	848	---------	37	251
1812	131	81	141	72	257	185	356	58	735	---------	34	234
1811	126	82	140	73	243	166	325	57	570	---------	31	204

Series E 52–63. Wholesale Price Indexes (Warren and Pearson), by Major Product Groups: 1749 to 1890—Con.

[1910–14 = 100]

Year	All commodities	Farm products	Foods	Hides and leather products	Textile products	Fuel and lighting	Metals and metal products	Building materials	Chemicals and drugs	Spirits	Miscellaneous	Year	All commodities
	52	53	54	55	56	57	58	59	60	62	63		52
1810	131	90	139	75	278	167	332	59	483	29	208	1778	140
1809	130	83	129	73	323	147	350	60	538	27	197	1777	123
1808	115	71	113	79	279	148	336	57	455	23	164	1776	86
1807	130	92	142	82	274	161	327	59	440	22	173	1775	75
1806	134	95	150	85	280	153	328	58	519	23	179	1774	76
1805	141	106	162	85	270	196	309	58	511	24	165	1773	84
1804	126	89	142	84	252	182	300	56	493	23	149	1772	89
1803	118	83	135	83	232	152	290	53	431	25	138	1771	79
1802	117	84	132	80	230	153	301	55	377	24	145		
1801	142	113	177	71	236	167	348	55	445	27	173	1770	77
1800	129	99	157	62	225	159	322	51	427	25	194	1769	77
1799	126	98	147	62	227	150	310	51	523	24	206	1768	74
1798	122	93	145	65	226	131	304	51	442	26	177	1767	77
1797	131	98	163	--------	--------	144	299	54	--------	26	177	1766	73
1796	146	116	186			150	284	58		31	204		
1795	131	102	163			155	259	56		25	220	1764	74
1794	108	76	135			125	258	40		23	158	1763	79
1793	102	75	125			122	240	39		22	163	1762	87
1791	85	57	99			100	240	34		19	148	1761	77
1790	90	68	104			95	247	35		17	141		
1789	86	68	94			99	250	35		16	152	1760	79
1787	90	78	103			127	236	36		15	148	1759	79
1786	90	75	--------									1758	70
												1757	65
												1756	66
1785	92											1755	66
1784	--------											1754	65
1783	--------											1753	65
1782	--------											1752	66
1781		216										1751	65
1780		225											
1779		226										1750	60
												1749	68

Series E 64–72. Wholesale Price Indexes (BLS), by Durability of Product: 1947 to 1970

[1967 = 100]

Year	All commodities			Manufactures			Raw or slightly processed goods		
	Total	Durable	Nondurable	Total	Durable	Nondurable	Total	Durable	Nondurable
	64	65	66	67	68	69	70	71	72
1970	110.4	112.4	108.9	110.2	112.0	108.2	111.4	123.6	110.7
1969	106.5	107.9	105.3	106.2	107.7	104.6	108.0	114.1	107.6
1968	102.5	103.4	101.7	102.6	103.5	101.5	102.2	99.6	102.3
1967	100.0	100.0	100.0	100.0	100.0	100.0	100.0	100.0	100.0
1966	99.8	98.1	100.9	99.1	97.9	100.0	103.7	107.4	103.5
1965	96.6	95.9	96.9	96.3	95.8	96.8	98.1	103.2	97.8
1964	94.7	94.7	94.7	94.8	94.6	93.7	94.9	96.6	94.8
1963	94.5	93.4	95.1	94.3	93.5	94.8	95.9	88.3	96.4
1962	94.8	93.4	95.6	94.5	93.5	95.1	96.9	87.9	97.4
1961	94.5	93.7	95.1	94.4	93.6	95.0	95.7	93.8	95.8
1960	94.9	94.1	95.4	94.8	94.1	95.2	96.2	92.1	96.4
1959	94.8	94.2	95.1	94.6	94.0	94.8	96.5	97.8	96.4
1958	94.6	92.1	96.5	93.8	92.2	95.4	99.1	92.9	99.4
1957	93.3	91.2	94.9	92.8	90.9	94.7	96.5	104.9	96.0
1956	90.7	88.3	92.6	90.0	87.5	92.4	94.6	116.8	93.4
1955	87.8	82.8	91.8	86.6	82.2	91.2	94.3	104.3	93.7
1954	87.6	79.6	93.7	85.7	79.4	92.2	96.9	86.5	97.6
1953	87.4	78.8	93.9	85.0	78.4	91.9	98.6	94.9	98.9
1952	88.6	77.3	97.1	85.1	76.7	93.8	104.7	99.5	105.0
1951	91.1	77.0	101.8	87.0	76.3	98.4	109.7	102.6	110.1
1950	81.8	70.2	90.6	78.4	69.6	87.7	97.5	90.8	97.9
1949	78.7	67.5	87.2	75.5	67.3	84.3	93.3	78.1	94.2
1948	82.8	66.1	95.5	78.2	65.4	91.8	103.8	97.1	104.2
1947	76.5	59.9	89.2	72.3	59.4	86.0	95.7	82.0	96.6

Series E 73–86.   Wholesale Price Indexes (BLS), for Economic Sectors, by Stage of Processing: 1913 to 1970

Year	All commod-ities	Crude materials for further processing				Intermediate materials, supplies and components						Finished goods [1]		
		Total	Food-stuffs and feed-stuffs	Nonfood materials, except fuel	Fuel	Total	Materials and components for—		Processed fuels and lubricants	Containers	Supplies	Total	Consumer	Producer
							Manufac-turing	Construc-tion						
	73	74	75	76	77	78	79	80	81	82	83	84	85	86
						1967 = 100								
1970	110.4	112.2	112.1	109.8	122.3	109.8	110.0	112.6	104.2	111.4	107.9	110.4	109.9	111.9
1969	106.5	108.3	109.1	106.8	106.4	105.9	105.8	110.9	98.7	106.3	102.7	106.6	106.5	106.9
1968	102.5	101.6	101.3	102.1	102.3	102.3	102.2	104.9	97.7	102.4	101.2	102.9	102.7	103.5
1967	100.0	100.0	100.0	100.0	100.0	100.0	100.0	100.0	100.0	100.0	100.0	100.0	100.0	100.0
1966	99.8	105.7	105.9	106.7	96.3	99.2	99.3	98.8	99.2	98.4	99.4	98.8	99.4	96.8
1965	96.6	99.3	97.1	104.5	93.5	96.8	97.4	96.2	97.4	95.8	95.2	95.7	96.1	94.4
1964	94.7	94.5	90.8	102.4	92.8	95.5	95.9	95.4	96.0	94.0	94.3	94.1	94.3	93.3
1963	94.5	95.4	92.9	100.7	93.2	95.2	94.9	94.5	98.1	94.7	95.2	93.7	94.1	92.4
1962	94.8	97.5	95.7	102.0	92.1	94.9	94.7	94.2	99.0	95.9	93.8	94.0	94.6	92.2
1961	94.5	96.5	93.8	102.5	92.6	95.0	95.3	94.6	99.4	94.7	91.8	93.7	94.3	91.8
1960	94.9	97.0	95.1	101.4	92.8	95.6	96.5	95.9	98.2	95.5	90.7	93.7	94.5	91.7
1959	94.8	99.4	96.2	105.8	91.9	95.6	96.5	96.6	95.6	94.2	91.2	93.0	93.6	91.5
1958	94.6	102.0	103.0	102.2	90.3	94.3	95.2	94.0	96.0	94.7	90.0	93.2	94.4	89.8
1957	93.3	99.8	97.2	106.2	89.2	94.1	94.8	94.0	101.9	92.5	88.0	91.1	92.4	87.5
1956	90.7	97.6	93.1	107.6	84.4	92.0	92.6	93.5	96.3	88.6	87.1	87.9	89.8	82.4
1955	87.8	97.1	95.1	103.8	78.8	88.1	88.4	88.9	93.3	82.6	84.8	85.5	89.1	74.5
1954	87.6	101.0	104.9	98.2	79.0	86.5	86.3	85.5	93.3	81.5	86.3	85.3	89.2	73.6
1953	87.4	101.9	104.9	100.1	82.7	86.0	86.2	85.1	93.4	80.0	84.3	85.1	90.7	72.4
1952	88.6	110.3	117.2	104.6	79.9	85.5	84.8	83.7	92.8	79.9	88.8	86.0	91.8	71.2
1951	91.1	120.1	124.5	120.7	79.4	88.1	88.5	84.3	93.9	84.5	88.8	86.5	91.8	71.2
1950	81.8	104.6	107.6	104.7	77.9	78.6	78.1	77.0	89.9	72.0	78.9	79.0	83.9	64.9
1949	78.7	96.0	100.3	91.6	78.3	75.2	74.5	73.2	88.2	70.1	76.3	77.6	82.5	63.4
1948	82.8	110.9	120.8	100.7	78.7	78.3	77.8	73.1	96.9	69.8	81.0	79.9	86.5	60.4
1947	76.5	101.2	111.7	90.6	66.6	72.4	72.1	66.0	85.5	66.8	77.5	74.0	80.5	55.4

Year	All commod-ities	Crude materials for further processing	Inter-mediate materials, supplies and com-ponents	Finished goods [1]	Year	All commod-ities	Crude materials for further processing	Inter-mediate materials, supplies and com-ponents	Finished goods [1]	Year	All commod-ities	Crude materials for further processing	Inter-mediate materials, supplies and com-ponents	Finished goods [1]
	73	74	78	84		73	74	78	84		73	74	78	84
					1947–49 = 100									
1951	114.8	116.9	116.9	112.1	1938	51.1	42.8	49.4	55.7	1925	67.3	63.4	69.0	68.2
1950	103.1	101.8	104.3	102.4	1937	56.1	50.4	55.9	59.1	1924	63.8	58.0	71.2	65.3
1949	99.2	93.4	99.9	100.6	1936	52.5	47.5	49.7	55.6	1923	65.4	58.5	77.7	67.3
1948	104.4	108.0	104.0	103.5						1922	62.8	57.0	64.8	65.4
1947	96.4	98.6	96.2	95.9	1935	52.0	45.8	48.2	55.7	1921	63.4	52.5	62.9	70.0
1946	78.7	80.0	(NA)	78.7	1934	48.7	40.8	47.7	53.0					
					1933	42.8	33.6	42.8	47.8	1920	100.3	90.2	129.8	101.6
1945	68.8	69.4	62.8	69.0	1932	42.1	32.7	38.8	47.7	1919	90.1	86.7	103.3	88.6
1944	67.6	67.3	61.6	68.4	1931	47.4	39.0	45.2	52.2	1918	85.3	80.7	100.7	84.6
1943	67.0	66.6	60.8	67.9						1917	76.4	72.9	98.5	74.0
1942	64.2	59.8	60.6	66.9	1930	56.1	50.1	53.6	59.7	1916	55.6	49.1	77.5	55.8
1941	56.8	49.6	56.9	60.4	1929	61.9	57.9	61.5	64.1					
					1928	62.9	58.9	61.9	65.0	1915	45.2	39.9	53.2	46.7
1940	51.1	42.7	51.8	55.3	1927	62.0	57.3	61.8	64.4	1914	44.3	40.2	45.8	46.0
1939	50.1	41.7	50.4	54.5	1926	65.0	59.4	65.5	67.8	1913	45.4	40.9	49.0	47.1

NA   Not available.   [1] Goods to users, including raw foods and fuel.

Series E 87–89.   Wholesale Price Indexes (BLS), by 2 Levels of Processing, for Identical Commodities: 1890 to 1926
[1913 = 100]

Year	All commod-ities (97 series)	Raw commod-ities (27 series)	Manu-factured commod-ities (70 series)	Year	All commod-ities (97 series)	Raw commod-ities (27 series)	Manu-factured commod-ities (70 series)	Year	All commod-ities (97 series)	Raw commod-ities (27 series)	Manu-factured commod-ities (70 series)
	87	88	89		87	88	89		87	88	89
1926	145.3	139.4	154.6	1914	99.6	98.7	101.0	1901	75.8	72.2	81.5
				1913	100.0	100.0	100.0				
1925	154.1	150.7	159.6	1912	96.9	95.1	99.7	1900	76.8	72.8	83.0
1924	142.6	139.1	148.2	1911	88.9	86.3	92.9	1899	71.7	67.4	78.5
1923	142.0	138.2	148.1					1898	66.1	61.2	73.6
1922	133.5	130.0	139.1	1910	97.8	95.4	101.4	1897	62.7	57.2	71.2
1921	131.6	121.2	147.7	1909	93.7	91.1	97.8	1896	61.7	56.2	70.1
				1908	87.3	83.7	92.8				
1920	225.3	220.3	233.2	1907	89.6	86.6	94.2	1895	65.2	60.5	72.5
1919	215.4	216.0	214.6	1906	83.7	81.3	87.5	1894	63.0	56.8	72.4
1918	205.9	208.0	202.6					1893	71.7	64.2	83.2
1917	183.3	184.0	182.1	1905	82.3	78.2	88.5	1892	69.7	62.0	81.5
1916	127.6	125.4	131.0	1904	81.9	79.1	86.2	1891	75.1	68.3	85.6
				1903	80.2	76.5	85.9				
1915	102.9	101.0	105.9	1902	81.0	77.1	86.9	1890	76.1	69.3	86.6

Series E 90–96.   Wholesale Price Indexes (Taylor), for Charleston, South Carolina: 1732 to 1861

Left panel

Year	All commodities (1818–42 = 100) [90]	All commodities [91]	S. C. export staples [92]	U. S. products, other than S. C. export staples [93]	Foreign imports [94]
1843–61 = 100					
1861	113	133	105	144	166
1860	94	111	116	113	96
1859	94	111	120	112	92
1858	90	106	120	99	94
1857	106	125	135	123	109
1856	97	114	116	116	109
1855	98	115	108	132	95
1854	88	103	100	111	93
1853	84	99	108	96	89
1852	77	91	96	91	79
1851	78	92	97	90	84
1850	87	102	123	88	91
1849	73	86	85	85	90
1848	67	79	66	86	92
1847	90	105	110	100	107
1846	75	88	83	85	105
1845	70	82	72	82	102
1844	68	80	73	74	106
1843	66	77	66	74	106
1818–42 = 100					
1842	74	74	67	80	75
1841	85	85	81	88	86
1840	83	83	75	90	83
1839	107	107	108	114	90
1838	103	103	88	123	92
1837	108	108	92	133	90
1836	121	121	129	124	100
1835	108	108	123	100	91
1834	93	93	97	91	91
1833	93	93	94	93	89
1832	86	86	78	91	89
1831	81	81	70	88	86
1830	82	82	78	80	93
1829	82	82	72	85	97
1828	85	85	80	81	103
1827	87	87	77	87	104
1826	92	92	83	96	104
1825	109	109	133	84	110
1824	93	93	99	82	102
1823	98	98	94	94	111
1822	108	108	100	108	122
1821	101	101	103	92	113
1820	110	110	121	97	114
1819	133	133	131	138	128
1818	179	179	220	160	135

Right panel

Year	All commodities (1818–42 = 100) [90]	All commodities [91]	S. C. export staples [92]	Other than S. C. export staples [93, 94]
1813–22 = 100				
1822	108	77	75	79
1821	101	71	74	67
1820	110	78	86	71
1819	133	98	96	99
1818	179	135	160	110
1817	189	138	145	131
1816	172	125	134	116
1815	149	109	102	115
1814	123	90	70	110
1813	109	79	57	101
1796–1812 = 100				
1812	95	84	63	106
1811	96	85	70	100
1810	96	85	80	91
1809	90	79	74	85
1808	87	76	70	83
1807	107	94	100	88
1806	109	97	101	92
1805	126	111	116	105
1804	114	101	100	102
1803	112	98	106	90
1802	106	93	96	91
1801	136	120	122	118
1800	123	108	114	103
1799	133	117	125	110
1798	129	114	123	106
1797	122	108	108	108
1796	145	128	134	122

Year	All commodities (1818–42 = 100) [90]	S. C. products (1762–74 = 100) [95]	Imported [2] (1781, 1784–91 = 100) [96]
1791	92	110	106
1790	97	119	106
1789	88	113	86
1788	97	128	87
1787	108	142	97
1786	108	142	98
1785	100	135	84
1784	110	150	86
1782	[3] 192	[3] 250	[3] 178
1781	138	170	150
1780	[3] 118	[3] 137	[3] 146

Bottom panel

Year	All commodities (1818–42 = 100) [90]	S. C. products (1762–74 = 100) [95]	Year	All commodities (1818–42 = 100) [90]	S. C. products (1762–74 = 100) [95]	Year	All commodities (1818–42 = 100) [90]	S. C. products (1762–74 = 100) [95]	Year	All commodities (1818–42 = 100) [90]	S. C. products (1762–74 = 100) [95]
1775	[3] 80	[3] 102	1764	67	86	1753	88	112	1742	66	85
1774	81	104	1763	72	92	1752	76	97	1741	76	97
1773	91	116	1762	60	77	1751	65	83			
1772	107	137	1761	62	80				1740	60	77
1771	84	108				1750	78	100	1739	65	84
			1760	72	92	1749	75	96	1738	[3] 98	[3] 125
1770	72	93	1759	87	112	1748	68	88	1737	92	117
1769	81	104	1758	67	86	1747	54	69	1736	75	96
1768	80	102	1757	61	78	1746	35	45			
1767	74	94	1756	60	77				1735	82	105
1766	78	100				1745	36	46	1734	84	108
			1755	67	86	1744	50	64	1733	62	80
1765	68	87	1754	67	86	1743	54	70	1732	62	79

[1] Combination for 1796 to 1822 designated as "Other than South Carolina export staples."
[2] Includes goods imported from abroad and from other parts of the United States.
[3] Based on part of year only.

Series E 97–111.   Wholesale Price Indexes (Bezanson), for Philadelphia: 1720 to 1861

Year	Unweighted geometric average (1821–25 = 100)														Un-weighted arithmetic average (1741–45 = 100)
	All commodities	Source		Type		Major groups									
		Domestic	Imported	Agricultural	Industrial	Farm		Imported foods	Lumber products and naval stores	Industrial		Fish	Furs	Wine	
						Crops	Derivatives			Raw	Consumption				
	97	98	99	100	101	102	103	104	105	106	107	108	109	110	111
1861	88.2	94.7	85.3	111.6	79.9	117.9	106.4	67.3	125.0	82.5	76.2	118.5	50.6	125.0	167.5
1860	88.8	95.7	84.9	118.0	83.2	113.8	121.7	64.7	100.0	87.0	77.8	150.8	47.6	122.2	164.3
1859	89.4	98.7	83.0	123.3	84.0	124.3	122.4	63.1	103.3	87.1	79.6	152.4	49.9	108.5	176.5
1858	89.7	94.8	88.0	115.4	85.3	115.6	115.2	66.0	97.2	86.9	82.9	136.5	49.4	127.2	165.3
1857	100.9	106.1	99.9	134.8	92.5	136.8	133.1	86.5	99.9	93.8	90.5	161.9	54.3	130.8	198.4
1856	99.1	103.7	99.2	128.8	93.9	129.9	127.9	83.0	92.5	94.3	93.4	156.8	51.4	126.4	194.6
1855	99.3	107.6	96.5	142.5	93.1	147.7	138.2	75.1	100.2	92.7	93.6	153.4	44.4	125.6	234.9
1854	95.8	105.6	91.5	131.8	90.7	135.5	128.7	75.1	111.0	92.1	88.8	156.7	45.4	90.4	211.6
1853	87.7	96.8	82.3	117.4	82.8	116.4	118.3	71.8	101.2	86.8	77.2	146.5	54.5	74.2	171.9
1852	80.4	89.5	74.8	107.7	75.1	107.6	107.7	65.4	92.9	78.2	70.7	135.7	57.1	70.3	152.8
1851	80.3	86.4	76.7	102.2	75.9	110.0	95.9	71.3	87.9	78.9	71.6	118.7	56.0	70.3	144.8
1850	79.9	85.2	76.7	98.6	77.1	109.2	90.3	71.5	79.1	80.1	72.8	126.1	56.0	70.6	147.3
1849	76.5	81.6	72.9	94.0	76.1	100.1	89.1	64.3	73.2	78.1	73.1	104.0	56.0	68.7	146.8
1848	78.5	84.2	74.9	97.4	78.7	103.7	92.4	64.8	72.6	80.6	75.9	118.4	56.0	69.9	149.3
1847	83.5	90.7	78.4	112.8	80.6	123.1	104.6	72.2	75.3	82.6	77.7	123.1	57.3	71.9	177.5
1846	80.1	83.4	78.3	93.2	78.9	101.7	86.4	71.7	78.4	80.9	76.1	119.6	64.5	71.1	144.1
1845	79.7	82.3	78.4	90.1	78.6	94.2	86.6	73.1	75.5	81.4	74.7	128.3	65.5	73.4	142.5
1844	76.9	77.4	77.3	81.1	79.0	87.7	75.9	68.6	70.2	82.4	74.2	126.5	56.6	73.6	129.3
1843	75.4	77.2	74.6	81.1	78.7	88.0	75.5	64.3	75.7	81.7	74.3	107.7	45.4	66.5	131.4
1842	79.1	85.1	74.1	89.0	83.2	97.1	82.6	60.8	83.0	87.2	77.5	109.3	61.1	64.7	135.7
1841	85.2	93.6	77.5	102.2	87.1	111.8	94.6	65.0	88.6	90.9	81.8	131.8	70.2	68.0	152.3
1840	87.4	96.8	78.2	107.6	89.8	109.5	106.0	63.7	90.1	93.1	85.2	139.7	74.3	68.7	165.4
1839	95.9	110.8	82.0	136.6	95.6	146.7	128.5	67.2	95.0	99.3	90.5	177.5	72.0	70.6	203.8
1838	91.9	103.2	80.2	123.3	92.6	123.9	122.9	67.4	94.0	94.7	89.6	130.7	66.1	71.2	211.4
1837	95.3	109.7	80.5	131.0	95.3	132.0	130.3	68.5	97.6	97.2	92.6	120.3	88.8	72.4	233.8
1836	97.6	113.0	82.4	135.7	93.8	142.8	129.8	75.0	105.2	97.4	88.6	124.9	92.2	77.3	217.7
1835	90.7	99.9	81.4	115.4	87.3	126.6	106.5	74.8	99.0	89.9	83.6	111.5	83.2	80.2	181.9
1834	85.8	91.6	79.1	97.6	86.4	101.3	94.6	68.0	94.1	90.1	81.3	91.8	88.4	81.6	163.0
1833	88.1	91.8	81.6	101.9	88.3	102.2	101.7	71.7	91.6	90.1	85.7	92.8	85.4	85.9	171.2
1832	89.3	91.8	86.6	99.7	88.2	99.6	99.8	84.4	87.4	88.7	87.5	86.3	84.9	84.8	166.7
1831	87.7	89.7	87.1	97.0	87.1	94.3	99.4	81.2	84.7	88.6	84.9	97.1	86.8	83.3	165.2
1830	84.0	84.7	85.4	87.3	84.2	84.3	89.9	80.7	80.9	85.3	82.7	88.0	85.2	82.5	150.2
1829	88.8	90.2	88.6	90.9	88.7	91.1	90.7	84.9	89.8	89.9	87.0	91.4	97.6	87.6	172.4
1828	91.0	90.7	91.6	89.5	90.2	86.5	92.2	90.1	96.2	91.8	87.9	96.4	101.4	90.9	165.4
1827	93.0	93.2	92.3	95.0	92.2	96.8	93.4	91.9	95.5	94.4	89.0	95.4	93.1	92.2	161.5
1826	95.9	96.3	94.7	100.3	94.0	106.7	95.1	96.1	98.0	97.2	89.4	84.1	101.0	96.4	160.4
1825	98.5	97.4	99.9	97.0	97.0	100.5	94.1	102.4	102.8	101.0	91.4	89.3	111.8	99.1	163.6
1824	94.3	94.4	93.8	92.6	94.9	91.4	93.7	92.3	97.8	95.5	93.9	99.4	99.0	92.1	163.0
1823	98.6	99.7	97.3	101.5	98.2	101.8	101.3	95.3	100.1	97.6	99.1	105.0	101.0	95.4	179.3
1822	104.2	105.4	102.9	107.9	103.3	107.7	108.1	103.0	102.5	102.2	104.9	106.8	103.8	103.4	183.4
1821	102.0	100.5	103.8	97.5	104.7	95.3	99.4	103.5	95.6	101.8	109.3	99.2	82.6	109.3	160.2
1820	106.6	108.6	104.7	109.2	105.7	112.9	106.2	107.7	109.1	101.8	111.8	108.5	73.4	114.0	180.7
1819	119.4	123.8	116.4	132.9	113.5	136.7	129.6	126.1	121.5	109.6	119.4	137.9	75.0	122.8	223.2
1818	130.6	138.8	125.0	160.3	121.8	162.5	158.4	136.6	126.9	118.3	127.0	164.4	80.3	123.0	276.2
1817	132.6	145.1	122.9	178.0	121.8	183.5	173.5	133.0	123.4	117.2	128.8	155.1	93.7	122.7	307.6
1816	151.9	159.5	146.6	177.8	143.2	185.0	171.8	157.8	146.3	141.8	145.1	196.8	107.0	147.9	298.3
1815	173.1	160.8	186.4	161.1	175.1	154.1	167.3	194.8	165.8	175.1	175.0	220.5	111.5	167.1	337.1
1814	189.7	159.0	223.4	151.5	205.6	147.5	154.9	217.7	176.6	209.5	199.9	227.8	89.6	192.0	371.3
1813	161.0	135.5	187.8	133.4	175.9	133.2	133.7	182.4	132.9	177.0	174.2	174.7	90.7	164.5	286.3
1812	142.3	125.6	158.6	126.3	153.7	120.5	131.6	143.8	120.7	158.3	147.0	165.0	93.5	151.9	257.3
1811	135.3	134.2	139.4	129.4	141.8	122.2	135.9	127.0	132.5	146.1	135.7	157.7	97.6	137.0	260.2
1810	138.7	131.6	147.3	133.4	146.2	130.3	136.1	134.2	138.6	151.3	138.9	140.2	90.7	128.9	249.6
1809	135.6	121.9	151.1	119.3	145.9	115.7	122.5	146.8	131.3	148.1	142.6	136.9	83.8	113.0	224.0
1808	123.1	112.4	133.6	109.4	132.6	108.7	110.0	135.7	113.9	136.3	127.4	128.1	78.5	97.7	192.6
1807	123.7	121.9	123.7	126.0	128.4	125.9	126.0	128.3	114.8	133.9	120.7	167.6	82.7	89.1	217.9
1806	128.1	125.8	128.8	135.5	131.7	132.3	138.2	138.3	114.8	135.3	126.4	171.7	75.0	89.4	233.1
1805	131.5	131.6	130.8	142.0	131.9	145.5	139.0	142.8	124.7	130.9	133.3	163.0	81.7	96.7	262.9
1804	128.1	123.9	132.6	126.9	129.5	130.9	123.4	142.2	126.6	131.6	126.5	147.9	85.3	103.5	241.0
1803	120.2	115.9	124.9	114.7	123.1	120.6	109.9	130.8	125.0	126.1	118.9	138.2	72.9	98.7	212.1
1802	122.5	118.1	129.5	120.5	124.0	121.7	119.4	137.3	115.2	125.7	121.4	167.1	72.4	103.6	211.2
1801	131.9	129.5	137.4	140.8	131.6	142.7	144.8	144.2	120.5	132.1	130.9	169.4	77.6	101.7	274.4
1800	128.3	121.1	138.0	129.6	130.5	129.0	130.1	155.3	116.2	131.5	129.1	124.6	74.4	93.9	(NA)
1799	127.3	115.6	142.2	123.3	133.4	127.4	120.0	158.7	104.8	132.9	134.2	146.2	60.5	89.9	(NA)
1798	127.1	123.4	131.9	128.8	129.0	136.6	122.4	152.3	122.7	125.4	134.6	189.5	58.1	81.5	(NA)
1797	133.5	134.4	135.8	135.9	130.0	142.8	130.2	169.3	133.9	125.4	137.1	226.3	75.1	85.7	266.7
1796	139.1	140.7	142.6	144.6	136.0	147.8	141.8	178.3	130.7	126.1	152.0	211.0	85.7	87.1	295.8
1795	130.7	125.3	141.3	129.6	130.4	124.1	134.6	173.3	114.2	124.9	138.9	200.3	70.1	86.5	257.8
1794	109.6	101.6	120.7	108.7	110.7	104.6	112.3	143.7	86.6	104.2	121.0	141.9	59.3	83.3	(NA)
1793	96.3	91.2	103.0	97.8	92.8	98.8	96.9	133.3	79.1	91.7	94.4	113.8	61.9	78.6	174.9
1792	91.5	85.5	99.3	88.0	89.4	88.4	87.7	132.5	72.4	88.7	90.6	116.5	62.2	71.3	156.5
1791	89.7	84.7	96.5	88.4	87.0	88.3	88.4	128.7	74.2	87.3	86.5	117.1	57.7	67.1	149.2
1790	86.5	83.4	89.9	93.5	85.4	96.6	90.8	109.3	67.0	89.9	79.2	105.5	58.9	64.0	160.3
1789	82.4	76.5	88.8	80.7	85.2	84.6	77.4	102.7	60.5	91.1	77.1	103.5	55.8	62.7	128.6
1788	83.3	78.1	88.7	84.5	85.4	89.3	80.6	107.5	56.5	91.7	76.8	116.2	52.8	65.2	120.5
1787	88.4	85.4	92.7	97.5	88.3	104.2	92.1	110.9	59.9	93.7	80.8	117.8	55.3	69.1	135.8
1786	91.0	90.0	93.8	101.6	88.6	106.1	97.9	113.0	69.6	95.9	78.7	121.9	65.4	69.1	145.0
1785	94.1	97.0	93.5	101.8	90.9	105.9	98.4	110.7	92.4	100.6	78.3	121.9	72.4	66.0	158.0
1784	100.1	104.8	97.7	107.0	96.9	101.7	111.8	122.0	104.3	103.9	87.4	127.9	76.9	59.1	172.6

NA   Not available.

Series E 97–111. Wholesale Price Indexes (Bezanson), for Philadelphia: 1720 to 1861—Con.

Year	Un-weighted arithmetic average (1741–45 = 100) [111]	Year	Un-weighted arithmetic average (1741–45 = 100) [111]	Year	Un-weighted arithmetic average (1741–45 = 100) [111]	Year	Un-weighted arithmetic average (1741–45 = 100) [111]	Year	Un-weighted arithmetic average (1741–45 = 100) [111]
1774	127.5	1763	136.4	1752	111.9	1741	112.6	1730	98.0
1773	133.7	1762	133.4	1751	112.8			1729	92.5
1772	141.0	1761	121.2			1740	87.3	1728	92.8
1771	126.7			1750	113.0	1739	82.2	1727	97.6
		1760	125.7	1749	121.5	1738	91.1	1726	101.0
1770	121.6	1759	125.0	1748	124.7	1737	91.1		
1769	115.9	1758	109.6	1747	110.6	1736	83.6	1725	96.6
1768	119.7	1757	107.1	1746	99.7			1724	88.9
1767	123.7	1756	109.6			1735	87.8	1723	84.3
1766	124.7			1745	92.7	1734	87.2	1722	81.6
		1755	107.3	1744	90.9	1733	90.0	1721	78.6
1765	118.4	1754	109.1	1743	95.6	1732	83.6		
1764	119.4	1753	109.9	1742	108.3	1731	87.1	1720	86.2

Series E 112–117. Wholesale Price Indexes (Berry), for Cincinnati, 1816 to 1861, and Ohio River Valley, 1788 to 1817

Year	Cincinnati, weighted (1824–46 = 100)		
	All commodities [112]	Identified with northern agriculture [113]	Not identified with northern agriculture [114]
1861	103	123	76
1860	110	133	80
1859	114	140	79
1858	102	120	77
1857	128	154	94
1856	121	141	93
1855	123	153	81
1854	110	128	85
1853	104	118	84
1852	93	112	68
1851	90	107	68
1850	86	98	72
1849	77	87	65
1848	75	83	65
1847	90	102	76
1846	76	81	69
1845	87	97	68
1844	77	81	71
1843	72	73	70
1842	72	70	76
1841	89	91	87
1840	104	111	91
1839	138	150	116
1838	129	137	115
1837	131	142	112
1836	145	159	121
1835	117	125	102
1834	95	93	97
1833	102	101	102
1832	101	103	98
1831	99	100	98
1830	93	86	106
1829	98	91	112
1828	92	81	113
1827	91	79	114
1826	93	81	115
1825	100	85	127
1824	98	85	122
1823	101	87	129
1822	98	78	166
1821	86	68	160
1820	140	112	237
1819	193	164	265
1818	190	160	264
1817	205	175	272
1816	196	164	289

Year	Ohio River Valley, unweighted (1788–1817 = 100)		
	All commodities [115]	Identified with northern agriculture [116]	Not identified with northern agriculture [117]
1817	125	145	75
1816	116	131	75
1815	108	117	86
1814	122	134	90
1813	106	114	86
1812	77	84	60
1811	79	78	82
1810	87	88	85
1809	90	87	97
1808	95	89	110
1807	95	92	104
1806	95	95	96
1805	86	86	89
1804	87	85	90
1803	84	82	88
1802	88	84	99
1801	90	89	94
1800	93	88	106
1799	97	89	117
1798	109	108	113
1797	133	134	129
1796	127	125	132
1795	111	110	114
1794	96	95	100
1793	106	110	96
1792	98	101	92
1791	92	88	104
1790	98	90	118
1789	102	87	139
1788	104	93	130

Series E 118–122. Wholesale Price Indexes (Taylor), for New Orleans: 1800 to 1861

Year	All commodities (1824–42 =100) [118]	All commodities [119]	Louisiana products [120]	U.S. products, other than Louisiana [121]	Foreign imports [122]
1843–61 = 100					
1861	117	125	102	138	206
1860	105	112	113	110	110
1859	107	114	118	110	106
1858	104	111	118	104	106
1857	136	144	156	136	115
1856	114	121	121	124	107
1855	103	110	96	129	107
1854	90	96	82	114	101
1853	91	97	94	101	96
1852	85	90	91	91	84
1851	89	95	98	93	86
1850	103	110	123	95	95
1849	80	85	85	85	81
1848	68	73	66	81	80
1847	93	99	108	90	82
1846	78	83	88	77	83
1845	74	79	77	80	85
1844	75	80	84	74	84
1843	70	74	75	70	89
1842	75	78	76	79	93
1841	93	100	102	97	104
1840	91	97	88	106	105
1824–42 = 100					
1842	75	75	73	78	75
1841	93	93	89	100	85
1840	91	91	78	110	82
1839	116	116	105	136	93
1838	107	107	98	123	96
1837	108	108	103	118	98
1836	132	132	140	129	103
1835	123	123	133	114	95
1834	96	96	99	95	87
1833	99	99	103	95	95
1832	88	88	84	92	102
1831	80	80	74	86	97
1830	86	86	85	82	103
1829	90	90	84	94	108
1828	91	91	92	86	110

Year	All commodities (1824–42 =100) [118]	All commodities [119]	Louisiana products [120]	U.S. products, other than Louisiana [121]	Foreign imports [122]
1824–42 = 100—Con.					
1827	90	90	88	87	112
1826	95	95	97	88	116
1825	130	130	155	96	123
1824	110	110	122	90	123
1823	105	105	112	90	132
1822	124	124	140	94	152
1821	115	115	130	83	160
1820	119	119	126	98	190
1819	151	151	160	127	200
1818	200	200	224	146	220
1817	197	197	218	150	151
1816	214	214	227	184	182
1815	170	170	178	142	----
1805–11 = 100 [1] (cols. 120 and 121 = "Domestic products")					
1811	110	87	87		89
1810	119	95	91		108
1809	120	95	91		112
1808	112	89	90		83
1807	133	106	109		92
1806	142	113	114		106
1805	147	117	118		111
1804	126	100	100		101
1805–11 = 100					
1811	110	----	83	----	----
1810	119	----	87	----	----
1809	120	----	88	----	----
1808	112	----	89	----	----
1807	133	----	112	----	----
1806	142	----	118	----	----
1805	147	----	124	----	----
1804	126	----	99	----	----
1803	115	----	95	----	----
1802	130	----	106	----	----
1801	146	----	120	----	----
1800 [2]	138	----	114	----	----

[1] Combination of series E 120 and E 121 designated as "Domestic products."   [2] Based on part of year only.

Series E 123–134. Wholesale Prices of Selected Commodities: 1800 to 1970

[In dollars per unit. Where 2 prices are shown for a single year, those in *italics* are comparable with preceding years, and those in regular type comparable with following years; see text for detailed explanation]

Year	Wheat [123]	Wheat flour [124]	Sugar [125]	Cotton, raw [126]	Wool [127]	Cotton sheeting [128]	Coal, anthracite [129]	Steel rails [130]	Nails [131]	Copper [132]	Turpentine [133]	Brick [134]
	Bu.	100 lb.[1]	Lb.	Lb.	Lb.	Yd.[2]	Ton[3]	100 lb.[4]	50 lb.[5]	Lb.	Gallon[6]	1,000
1970	1.483	5.569	0.112	0.251	1.031	(NA)	16.57	6.800	(NA)	(NA)	(NA)	36.17
1969	1.392	5.438	.107	.255	1.223	0.235	15.02	6.575	4.674	0.476	1.090	(NA)
1968	1.468	(NA)	.101	(NA)	1.205	.241	[7]13.71	6.325	4.339	(NA)	.717	(NA)
1967	1.669	5.620	.099	.230	1.217	.255	[7]12.89	6.075	4.335	.381	.570	33.68
1966	1.789	5.994	.096	.263	1.348	.247	(NA)	5.894	4.351	.360	.563	31.32
1965	1.560	5.465	.095	.303	1.251	.225	12.98	5.825	4.646	.354	.545	30.46
1964	1.879	5.390	.100	.322	1.393	.230	13.90	5.825	4.646	.323	.433	(NA)
1963	2.178	5.365	.112	.335	1.323	.224	13.36	5.825	4.621	.310	.314	(NA)
1962	(NA)	5.621	.089	(NA)	1.245	.226	13.05	5.825	4.715	.310	.197	(NA)
1961	2.014	5.167	.087	.322	1.181	.215	13.35	5.825	(NA)	.303	.332	(NA)
1960	1.993	4.992	.087	.314	1.163	.223	13.95	5.825	9.596	.325	.489	(NA)
1959	1.978	5.080	.086	.333	1.217	.213	14.18	5.825	9.825	.311	.535	31.67
1958	2.026	5.423	.086	.347	1.185	.198	14.24	5.675	9.828	.263	.633	(NA)
1957	2.201	5.680	.090	.338	1.608	.205	14.67	5.442	9.596	.303	.662	30.86
1956	2.219	5.676	.086	{ [8].335 / [9]*.351* }	1.373	.229	13.53	4.946	8.917	.418	.645	30.61
1955	2.256	5.935	.084	.336	1.423	.213	12.93	4.663	8.180	.373	.640	29.15
1954	2.307	6.133	.086	.341	1.705	.210	14.01	4.463	7.651	.300	.653	28.22
1953	2.238	5.649	.086	.329	1.729	.222	15.45	{ [10]4.086 / [11]*3.775* }	7.440	.290	.594	27.85
1952	2.387	5.477	.084	.387	1.665	.226	14.30	3.672	7.123	.245	.632	27.35
1951	2.403	5.750	.082	.416	2.702	.275	14.19	3.600	6.930	.245	.812	27.33
1950	2.226	{ 5.427 / *5.215* }	.078	.362	1.981	.259	12.58	3.417	6.343	.216	.531	25.67
1949	2.149	5.036	.078	.316	1.662	.212	12.04	3.208	6.136	.195	.387	24.73
1948	2.409	5.445	.076	.338	1.646	.243	11.57	2.938	5.823	.223	.481	23.65
1947	2.602	6.200	.081	.345	1.242	.264	{ 10.33 / *14.11* }	2.606	{ 4.467 / *3.971* }	.213	.751	{ 20.98 / *20.50* }
1946	1.895	4.487	.064	.305	1.025	.201	13.06	47.90	3.477	.141	.953	18.13

See footnotes at end of table.

Series E 123–134. Wholesale Prices of Selected Commodities: 1800 to 1970—Con.
[In dollars per unit]

Year	Wheat	Wheat flour	Sugar	Cotton, raw	Wool	Cotton sheeting	Coal, anthracite	Steel rails	Nails	Copper	Turpentine	Brick
	123	124	125	126	127	128	129	130	131	132	133	134
	Bu.	100 lb.¹	Lb.	Lb.	Lb.	Yd.²	Ton³	100 lb.⁴	50 lb.⁵	Lb.	Gallon⁶	1,000
1945	1.664	3.181	0.054	0.226	1.192	0.153	11.89	42.94	2.850	0.120	0.794	15.89
1944	1.604	3.184	.055	.212	1.188	.145	11.47	40.00	2.550	.120	.776	14.29
1943	1.440	3.170	.055	.206	1.183	.142	10.89	40.00	2.550	.120	.668	13.43
1942	1.189	5.448	.055	.193	1.195	.141	10.31	40.00	2.550	.120	{ .619 .706 }	13.21
1941	.992	4.752	.049	{ .139 .146 }	1.091	{ .115 .121 }	10.01	40.00	2.550	.120	.617	12.59
1940	.871	4.307	.044	.104	.966	.085	9.55	40.00	2.550	.115	.371	12.13
1939	.755	3.872	.046	.095	.823	.079	9.14	40.00	2.461	.112	.314	12.05
1938	.777	4.364	.045	.087	.691	.076	9.44	41.79	2.575	.102	.294	12.00
1937	1.201	5.606	.047	.114	.971	.107	9.37	41.89	2.773	.131	.387	12.05
1936	1.123	5.441	.048	.121	.881	.097	9.74	36.63	2.229	.097	.438	11.74
1935	1.040	6.197	.049	.119	.723	.110	9.59	36.38	2.628	.089	.500	11.77
1934	.932	5.755	.044	.123	.817	.109	9.64	36.38	2.623	.087	.529	12.00
1933	.724	4.633	.043	.087	.663	.088	10.06	39.33	2.089	.073	.463	10.53 9.19
1932	.494	3.104	.040	.064	.459	.062	10.88	42.38	2.050	.058	.431	9.54
1931	.606	3.570	.044	.085	.621	.072	{ 11.40 12.77 }	43.00	1.978	.084	.447	10.02
1930	.900	4.865	.047	.135	.763	.105	12.72	43.00	2.191	.132	.473	10.10
1929	1.180	5.794	.051	.191	.987	.125	12.89	43.00	2.667	.184	.550	10.73
1928	1.324	6.406	.056	.200	1.159	.135	{ 13.00 10.93 }	43.00	2.676	.148	.565	13.00
1927	1.372	6.686	.058	.176	1.107	.120	10.95	43.00	2.638	{ .132 .130 }	.621	13.88
1926	1.496	7.252	.055	.175	1.152	.123	11.48	43.00	2.750	.138	.930	16.46
1925	1.670	7.678	.055	.235	1.392	.147	11.19	43.00	2.820	.141	1.013	14.70
1924	1.232	5.980	.074	.287	1.407	.161	11.37	43.00	2.989	.131	.912	17.04
1923	1.112	5.353	.084	.293	1.379	.163	10.88	43.00	3.035	.145	1.171	19.81
1922	1.213	6.130	.059	.212	1.238	.129	10.60	40.69	2.610	.134	1.150	17.34
1921	1.326	7.034	.062	.151	.828	.131	10.53	45.65	3.056	.126	.681	15.21
1920	2.455	11.580	.127	.339	1.604	.288	9.50	53.83	4.187	.180	1.734	21.85
1919	2.418	10.695	.089	.325	1.775	.232	8.27	49.26	3.518	.191	1.210	15.96
1918	2.159	10.302	.078	.318	1.815	.235	6.86	56.00	3.600	.247	.594	11.93
1917	2.296	10.551	.077	.235	1.568	.145	5.94	40.00	3.633	.294	.488	8.89
1916	1.329	6.091	.069	.145	.845	.088	5.57	33.33	2.596	.275	.491	8.04
1915	1.290	5.612	.056	.102	.707	.068	5.33	30.00	1.746	.173	.459	6.05
1914	.939	4.125	.047	.121	.593	.080	5.32	30.00	1.679	.134	.473	5.53
1913	{ .877 .953 }	{ 3.847 4.308 }	.043	.128	{ .562 .589 }	.084	5.31	{ 30.00 28.00 }	1.819	.157	.428	6.56
1912	1.049	4.686	.051	.115	.647	.081	5.28	28.00	1.740	.164	.470	6.76
1911	.984	3.984	.053	.130	.647	.088	5.00	28.00	1.804	.125	.679	5.89
1910	1.097	4.691	.050	.151	.686	.084	4.81	28.00	1.888	.129	.683	5.72
1909	1.200	5.451	.048	.121	.738	.075	4.82	28.00	1.917	.131	.491	6.39
1908	.990	4.291	.049	.105	.716	.078	4.82	28.00	2.100	.133	.453	5.10
1907	.907	3.988	.047	.119	.718	.084	4.82	28.00	2.117	{ .208 .213 }	.634	6.16
1906	.793	3.615	.045	.110	.718	.080	4.86	28.00	1.958	.196	.665	8.55
1905	1.010	4.543	.053	.096	.759	.076	4.82	28.00	1.896	.158	.628	8.10
1904	1.039	4.826	.048	.121	.686	.080	4.83	28.00	1.906	.131	.576	7.49
1903	.790	3.592	.046	.112	.655	.068	4.83	28.00	2.075	.137	.572	5.91
1902	.741	3.489	.045	.089	.577	.063	4.46	28.00	2.104	.120	.474	5.39
1901	.719	3.309	.051	.086	.545	.063	4.33	27.33	2.365	.169	.373	5.77
1900	.704	3.349	.053	.096	.659	.062	3.92	32.29	2.633	.166	.477	5.25
1899	.711	3.382	.049	.066	.623	.054	3.65	28.13	2.388	.177	.458	5.69
1898	.885	4.145	.050	.060	.615	.054	3.55	17.63	1.438	.119	.322	5.75
1897	.795	4.361	.045	.072	.496	.059	3.74	18.75	1.485	.113	.292	4.94
1896	.641	3.620	.045	.079	.394	.062	3.56	28.00	2.925	.110	.274	5.06
1895	.600	3.231	.042	.073	.377	.059	2.98	24.33	2.118	.108	.292	5.31
1894	.559	2.750	.041	.070	.445	.060	3.54	24.00	1.652	.095	.293	5.00
1893	.677	3.283	.048	.083	.564	.068	4.17	28.13	1.992	.109	.300	5.83
1892	.788	4.122	.044	.077	.612	.065	3.94	30.00	2.190	.115	.323	5.77
1891	.962	4.905	.047	.086	.686	.073	3.46	29.92	2.467	.131	.380	5.71
1890	{ .893 .865 }	{ 4.652 6.039 }	{ .062 .063 }	{ .111 .115 }	{ .716 .733 }	{ .073 .067 }	{ 3.35 3.92 }	31.78	{ 2.965 2.00 }	.158	{ .408 .414 }	6.56
1889	.895	6.540	.080	.107	.735	.067	4.04	29.25	2.00	.138	.461	7.00
1888	.886	6.120	.071	.103	.680	.069	4.21	29.83	2.03	.168	.398	6.52
1887	.769	5.817	.059	.103	.733	.068	4.05	37.08	2.30	.113	.358	7.40
1886	.797	6.119	.062	.094	.740	.064	4.00	34.52	2.27	.110	.395	7.58
1885	.864	6.275	.064	.105	.713	.067	4.10	28.52	2.33	.111	.351	6.36
1884	.913	7.043	.068	.106	.805	.069	4.42	30.75	2.39	.138	.328	6.52
1883	1.038	7.735	.087	.106	.860	.075	4.54	37.75	3.06	.159	.432	8.14
1882	1.198	9.020	.095	.122	.905	.079	4.61	48.50	3.47	.185	.518	¹² 7.58
1881	1.154	8.895	.097	.113	.955	.080	4.53	61.08	3.09	.183	.476	¹³ 7.50
1880	{ 1.057 1.253 }	8.895	.099	.120	1.028	.081	4.53	67.52	3.68	.215	.383	6.94
1879	1.223	8.632	.086	.104	.718	.076	2.70	48.21	2.69	.186	.315	5.26
1878	1.252	9.101	.092	.113	.748	.074	3.22	42.21	2.31	.166	.298	4.89
1877	1.685	10.806	.111	.117	.910	.080	2.59	45.58	2.57	.190	.362	4.94
1876	1.320	9.898	.106	.130	.870	.084	3.87	59.25	2.98	.210	.371	5.71
1875	1.403	10.218	.107	.150	1.045	.099	4.39	68.75	3.42	.227	.345	7.00
1874	1.517	10.728	.106	.170	1.153	.109	4.55	94.28	3.99	.220	.396	7.44
1873	1.787	11.498	.112	.182	1.198	.128	4.27	120.58	4.90	.280	.497	8.02
1872	1.780	12.141	.124	.205	1.568	.135	3.74	111.94	5.46	.356	.618	9.96
1871	1.581	10.245	.131	.170	1.068	.125	4.46	102.52	4.52	.241	.549	9.31

See footnotes at end of table.

Series E 123-134. Wholesale Prices of Selected Commodities: 1800 to 1970—Con.

[In dollars per unit]

Year	Wheat	Wheat flour	Sugar	Cotton, raw	Wool	Cotton sheeting	Coal, anthracite	Steel rails	Nails	Copper	Turpentine	Brick
	123	124	125	126	127	128	129	130	131	132	133	134
	Bu.	100 lb.[1]	Lb.	Lb.	Lb.	Yd.[2]	Ton [3]	100 lb.[4]	50 lb.[5]	Lb.	Gallon [6]	1,000
1870	1.373	9.281 / 5.029	0.135	0.240	0.898	0.140	4.39	106.79	4.40	0.212	0.427	8.40
1869	1.651	5.725	.162	.290	.905	.153	5.31	132.25	4.87	.243	.458	11.33
1868	2.541	7.912	.163	.249	.888	.160	3.86	158.50	5.17	.230	.510	12.08
1867	2.844	9.164	.159	.316	1.133	.174	4.37	166.00 / 83.12	5.92	.254	.639	10.85
1866	2.945	7.920	.166	.432	1.313	.236	5.80	86.75	6.97	.343	.810	11.44
1865	2.160	7.706	.207	.834	1.660	.370	7.86	98.62	7.08	.393	1.525	9.67
1864	1.942	8.062	.235	1.015	1.770	.513	8.39	126.00	7.85	.470	2.978	8.27
1863	1.640	5.690	.146	.672	1.515	.342	6.06	76.87	5.13	.339	2.924	6.41
1862	1.390	5.165	.113	.313	.938	.176	4.14	41.75	3.47	.219	1.574	4.16
1861	1.425	4.965	.090	.130	.828	.093	3.39	42.37	2.75	.223	.833	3.88
1860	1.495	5.190	.096 / .085	.110	1.025	.082	3.40	48.00	3.13	.229 / .262	.423	4.49
1859	1.435	5.110	.088	.121	1.093	.080	3.25	49.37	3.86	.261	.481	5.00
1858	1.325	4.295	.087	.122	.825	.078	3.43	50.00	3.53	.260	.460	3.96
1857	1.675	5.785	.118	.135	1.020	.085	3.87	64.25	3.72	.301	.453	4.21
1856	1.755	6.420	.098	.103	1.048	.072	4.11	64.37	3.92	.312	.401	4.29
1855	2.435	8.760	.072	.104	.858	.072	4.49	62.87	4.10	.297	.427	4.31
1854	2.210	8.945	.067	.110	.913	.075	5.19	80.12	4.76	.302	.556	4.89
1853	1.390	5.780	.072	.110	1.070	.074	3.70	77.25	4.85	.291	.593	5.42
1852	1.105	5.005	.070	.095	.818	.066	3.46	48.37	3.13	.235	.452	4.63
1851	1.075	4.520	.075	.121	.855	.066	3.34	45.62	3.28	.205	.353	4.69
1850	1.275	5.550	.074	.123	.833 / .400	.073	3.64	47.87	3.71	.215	.334	4.85
1849	1.240	4.510	.069	.076	.361	.064	3.62	53.87	4.00	.215	.333	3.85
1848	1.175	5.960	.067	.080	.343	.066	3.50	62.25	4.25	.215	.370	---------
1847	1.365	6.685	.077	.112	.352	.078 / 8.50	3.80	69.34	4.50	.232	.402	---------
1846	1.085	5.060	.085	.079	.323	8.45	3.90	---------	4.50	.235	.450	---------
1845	1.040	4.935	.059	.056	.351	8.10	3.46	---------	4.75	.227	.405	---------
1844	.975	4.670	.062	.077	.400	7.67	3.20	---------	4.50	.215	.335	---------
1843	.981	4.855	.057	.073	.305	7.92	3.27	---------	4.25	.212	.338	---------
1842	1.140	5.570	.046	.079	.320	8.57	4.18	---------	4.75	.227	.338	---------
1841	1.185	5.585	.060	.095	.442	8.92	5.79	---------	5.25	.250	.319	---------
1840	1.055	5.295	.058	.089	.391	9.26	4.91	---------	5.50	.245	.266 / .276	---------
1839	1.245	7.300	.068	.134	.512	9.22	5.00	---------	6.12	.245	.335	---------
1838	1.920	7.956	.069	.101	.381	9.60	5.27	---------	6.00	.255	.320	---------
1837	1.775	9.140	.070	.133	.424	10.56	6.72	---------	6.00	.270	.390	---------
1836	1.780	7.495	.090	.165	.586	10.50	6.64	---------	6.00	.270	.550	---------
1835	1.220	5.855	.078	.175	.539	8.62	4.84	---------	6.00	.235	.548	---------
1834	1.058	4.980	.071	.129	.488	8.53	4.84	---------	5.50	.235	.471	---------
1833	1.193	5.565	.072	.123	.490	8.74	5.23 / 6.82	---------	5.00	.230	.415	---------
1832	1.260	5.770	.065	.094	.475	9.28	10.21	---------	5.80	.225	.365	---------
1831	1.185	5.710	.058	.097	.535	10.00	7.08	---------	5.60	.222	.292	---------
1830	1.070	4.985	.070	.100	.390	10.24	9.05	---------	5.50	.220	.292	---------
1829	1.245	6.452	.076	.099	.345	9.44	10.72	---------	7.10	.235	.360	---------
1828	1.218	5.580	.086	.103	.370	8.99	10.92	---------	7.50 / 7.08	.247	.376	---------
1827	.992	5.140	.085	.093	.390	9.17	11.34	---------	6.76	.262	.365	---------
1826	.940	4.810	.082	.122	.495	9.94	10.92	---------	7.21	.297	.302	---------
1825	.920 / .998	5.130 / 5.11	.093 / .115	.186	.585 / .530	10.52	9.16 / .250	---------	7.33	.304 / .303	[12] 2.619 / .405	---------
1824	1.103	5.61	.118	.148	.550	9.80	.300	---------	8.87	.252	2.556	---------
1823	1.354	6.84	.120	.114	.717	14.50	.325	---------	9.80	.260	2.692	---------
1822	1.248	6.58	.122	.143	.750	15.00	.325	---------	9.80	.282	2.543	---------
1821	.880	4.78	.114	.143	.750	16.00	.325	---------	9.80	.300	2.219	---------
1820	.928	4.71	.123	.170	.750	16.00	.317	---------	9.80	.290	2.368	---------
1819	1.344	6.89	.153	.240	.825	16.50	.338	---------	9.67	.302	2.877	---------
1818	1.981	9.97	.148	.240	.892	16.99	.327	---------	9.60	.293	3.542	---------
1817	2.406	11.72	.158	.265	.750	17.96	.322	---------	10.90	.273	2.902	---------
1816	1.942	9.80	.184	.295	.975	19.47	.360	---------	12.83	.364	3.688	---------
1815	1.565	8.57	.215	.210	1.333	20.00	.597	---------	12.50	.449	4.478	---------
1814	1.482	8.11	.220	.150	3.312	22.68	1.134	---------	11.25	.600	6.665	---------
1813	1.622	8.94	.205	.125	[14] 2.750	21.60	.919	---------	8.50	.504	3.083	---------
1812	1.774	9.34	.142	.105	---------	19.04	.412	---------	8.50	.463	2.425	---------
1811	1.846	10.06	.129	.155	---------	19.04	.370	---------	9.33	.356	3.228	---------
1810	1.796	9.65	.125	.160	---------	21.58	.369	---------	9.50	.428	3.937	---------
1809	1.248	6.86	.127	.160	---------	25.17	.295	---------	9.50	.449	3.835	---------
1808	1.000	5.53	.120	.190	---------	22.50	.276	---------	9.50	.456	3.052	---------
1807	1.308	7.12	.120	.215	---------	20.69	.297	---------	9.50	.508	2.548	---------
1806	1.379	7.27	.125	.220	---------	21.83	.323	---------	9.50	.520	2.979	---------
1805	1.953	10.07	.140	.230	---------	21.27	.399	---------	10.50	.505	3.610	---------
1804	1.357	8.21	.138	.200	---------	19.21	.293	---------	10.50	.480	3.500	---------
1803	1.1:3	6.85	.122	.190	---------	16.00	.290	---------	10.52	.430	3.625	---------
1802	1.193	6.90	.114	.190	---------	16.00	.290	---------	11.65	.409	2.981	---------
1801	1.835	10.40	.118	.440	---------	17.35	.303	---------	10.67	.500	2.667	---------
1800	[15] 1.819	10.03	.134	.240	---------	17.38	.309	---------	10.67	.526	[15] 2.500	---------

NA Not available.
[1] Beginning 1943, per 100 pounds; for prior years, per 196-lb. barrel.
[2] Beginning 1847 (in regular type), per yard; for prior years, "per piece"; see text.
[3] Beginning 1825 (in regular type), per ton; for prior years, per 80-lb. bushel.
[4] Beginning 1947, per 100 pounds; for prior years, per gross ton.
[5] Beginning 1961, per 50 lb.; for prior years per 100 lb.
[6] Beginning 1825 (in regular type), per gallon; for prior years, per 31½-gal. barrel.
[7] 11-month average.

[8] July through December.
[9] January through July.
[10] May through December.
[11] January through April.
[12] July price.
[13] January price.
[14] December price.
[15] June through December.

Series E 135–166. Consumer Price Indexes (BLS)—All Items, 1800 to 1970, and by Groups, 1913 to 1970

[1967 = 100]

Year	All items	All foods	Food at home — Total	Cereals and bakery products	Meat	Poultry	Fish	Dairy products	Eggs	Fruits and vegetables — Fresh	Processed	Sugar and sweets	Beverages	Food away from home	Housing — Total	Rent
	135	136	137	138	139	140	141	142	143	144	145	146	147	148	149	150
1970	116.3	114.9	113.7	108.9	117.6	108.4	118.0	111.8	125.6	116.3	109.2	115.1	117.4	119.9	118.9	110.1
1969	109.8	108.9	108.2	103.3	111.4	109.0	107.2	106.7	126.8	111.1	106.5	109.1	104.6	111.6	110.8	105.7
1968	104.2	103.6	103.2	100.4	102.3	103.1	101.6	103.3	107.8	109.4	105.6	103.4	101.9	105.2	104.2	102.4
1967	100.0	100.0	100.0	100.0	100.0	100.0	100.0	100.0	100.0	100.0	100.0	100.0	100.0	100.0	100.0	100.0
1966	97.2	99.1	100.3	97.7	102.6	106.7	96.7	95.8	119.6	99.7	100.0	97.0	100.0	95.1	97.2	98.2
1965	94.5	94.4	95.5	93.8	93.9	101.2	90.8	90.0	105.0	97.9	98.3	99.0	100.9	90.9	94.9	96.9
1964	92.9	92.4	93.2	92.5	87.3	98.2	88.2	89.7	107.5	95.9	101.5	100.7	102.3	88.9	93.8	95.9
1963	91.7	91.2	92.2	92.1	88.7	100.4	90.3	88.9	108.6	90.6	99.2	96.0	91.2	87.3	92.7	95.0
1962	90.6	89.9	91.0	90.8	90.1	102.0	90.5	89.2	107.0	85.5	94.0	88.4	90.1	85.4	91.7	94.0
1961	89.6	89.1	90.4	88.9	88.3	96.5	86.9	89.8	113.2	83.3	96.7	88.4	91.5	83.2	90.9	92.9
1960	88.7	88.0	89.6	87.1	87.2	106.9	85.0	88.4	113.2	84.6	92.9	90.1	91.5	81.4	90.2	91.7
1959	87.3	87.1	88.8	85.4	88.8	105.2	84.9	86.5	105.1	79.7	96.2	89.7	92.1	79.3	88.6	90.4
1958	86.6	88.5	91.0	84.7	92.2	115.4	83.4	85.9	120.0	83.7	92.3	87.8	101.4	77.2	87.7	89.1
1957	84.3	84.9	87.2	83.0	82.8	116.8	78.0	84.7	114.1	78.0	86.3	84.0	109.1	74.9	86.2	87.5
1956	81.4	82.2	84.4	79.9	74.5	119.8	77.0	82.3	119.8	77.5	88.2	81.6	109.9	72.2	83.6	85.9
1955	80.2	81.6	84.1	78.8	77.1	136.7	77.1	80.2	120.5	73.2	85.5	83.5	105.1	70.8	82.3	84.3
1954	80.5	82.8	85.8	77.6	83.7	131.3	78.7	80.3	116.6	71.8	84.8	81.8	117.4	70.1	81.7	83.2
1953	80.1	83.0	86.2	75.8	84.2	145.4	78.2	82.9	139.4	73.3	85.3	80.1	98.6	68.9	80.8	80.3
1952	79.5	84.3	87.8	74.3	90.2	149.2	81.3	84.4	131.6	77.7	83.3	79.3	96.2	------	80.7	76.2
1951	77.8	------	82.8	72.6	91.0	148.6	83.4	81.0	144.1	66.9	84.6	78.6	95.6	------	78.7 / 77.2	73.2
1950	72.1	------	74.5	66.5	80.3	141.8	73.1	72.6	118.4	61.6	74.8	75.8	86.7	------	72.8	70.4
1949	71.4	------	73.5	65.4	76.2	148.1	74.5	75.4	137.1	65.4	77.2	74.3	61.3	------	70.9	68.0
1948	72.1	------	76.6	65.8	81.0	157.1	74.1	80.5	142.3	63.6	81.0	73.2	56.8	------	69.8	65.1
1947	66.9	------	70.6	59.8	71.3	141.7	64.3	73.2	136.9	60.3	85.2	75.8	51.8	------	65.2	61.1
1946	58.5	------	58.1	48.1	50.1	134.5	56.0	64.9	115.0	57.0	68.6	60.6	------	------	60.6	59.2
1945	53.9	------	50.7	41.9	39.2	119.5	51.5	52.6	112.0	56.3	63.0	53.3	------	------	59.1	58.8
1944	52.7	------	49.6	41.8	39.1	116.8	49.2	52.5	105.0	53.0	62.5	53.3	------	------	58.1	58.6
1943	51.8	------	50.3	41.4	41.3	113.0	48.9	52.9	110.3	53.3	62.3	53.5	------	------	56.8	58.5
1942	48.8	------	45.1	40.5	40.7	94.9	38.6	49.3	93.0	39.7	57.2	53.3	------	------	56.2	58.5
1941	44.1	------	38.4	37.6	35.3	79.0	29.6	44.0	76.5	31.1	45.8	44.8	------	------	53.7	57.2
1940	42.0	------	35.2	37.3	31.4	73.3	26.2	39.8	64.0	29.1	43.2	40.8	------	------	52.4	56.2
1939	41.6	------	34.6	36.4	32.1	72.6	23.9	37.7	62.0	28.5	42.5	42.4	------	------	52.2	56.0
1938	42.2	------	35.6	38.5	32.5	80.9	24.0	39.2	68.4	27.6	44.4	41.2	------	------	52.6	56.0
1937	43.0	------	38.4	39.7	35.3	81.2	23.9	41.4	69.0	32.5	48.6	42.5	------	------	51.7	54.2
1936	41.5	------	36.9	38.7	32.8	78.2	23.3	39.9	70.4	31.8	46.0	41.9	------	------	50.0	51.9
1935	41.1	------	36.5	39.2	33.4	73.9	23.2	38.3	71.0	29.5	48.4	42.5	------	------	49.3	50.6

Year	Housing—Con. Fuel and utilities — Total	Gas and electricity	Fuel oil and coal	Household furnishings and operation	House furnishings	Apparel — Total	Men's and boys'	Women's and girls'	Footwear	Transportation — Total	Private	Public	Medical care	Personal care	Reading and recreation	Other goods and services
	151	152	153	154	155	156	157	158	159	160	161	162	163	164	165	166
1970	107.6	107.3	110.1	113.4	111.4	116.1	117.1	116.0	117.7	112.7	111.1	128.5	120.6	113.2	113.4	116.0
1969	103.6	102.8	105.6	109.0	108.1	111.5	112.4	111.7	111.8	107.2	106.5	112.7	113.4	110.8	109.3	109.1
1968	101.3	100.9	103.1	104.4	103.9	105.4	105.7	105.9	105.3	103.2	103.0	104.6	106.1	104.2	104.7	104.6
1967	100.0	100.0	100.0	100.0	100.0	100.0	100.0	100.0	100.0	100.0	100.0	100.0	100.0	100.0	100.0	100.0
1966	98.8	99.6	97.0	97.0	98.0	96.1	96.5	95.6	95.3	97.2	97.5	95.2	93.4	95.2	97.1	97.2
1965	98.3	99.4	94.6	95.3	97.1	93.7	94.0	93.8	90.0	95.9	96.3	91.9	89.5	89.5	95.9	94.2
1964	98.4	99.4	92.7	95.0	97.6	92.7	92.7	92.8	88.4	94.3	94.7	90.1	87.3	89.5	95.2	92.0
1963	98.2	99.4	93.2	94.6	97.7	91.9	91.6	92.5	88.0	93.0	93.4	88.5	85.6	87.3	94.5	90.6
1962	97.3	99.4	91.5	93.8	98.1	90.9	90.4	91.8	87.1	92.5	93.0	87.4	83.5	85.6	92.8	90.6
1961	98.1	99.4	91.0	93.7	98.7	90.4	89.9	91.9	85.9	90.6	91.3	84.6	81.4	83.5	91.3	89.1
1960	95.9	98.6	89.2	93.8	99.3	89.6	88.9	91.6	85.1	89.6	90.6	81.0	79.1	81.0	90.1	87.8
1959	93.8	94.7	89.8	93.1	99.0	88.2	87.2	91.2	82.2	89.6	91.1	78.3	76.4	79.1	87.3	87.8
1958	91.7	92.4	88.7	92.3	99.0	87.5	87.4	90.8	79.0	86.0	87.4	76.1	73.2	78.3	86.9	86.1
1957	89.9	89.3	90.3	91.9	99.7	87.3	87.8	90.9	77.8	83.3	84.7	72.7	69.9	76.1	86.9	84.4
1956	87.3	88.4	85.9	89.9	98.1	85.8	86.4	90.4	75.4	78.8	80.1	70.0	67.2	74.8	81.1	83.3
1955	85.1	87.5	82.3	89.9	99.2	84.1	85.0	90.4	75.4	77.4	78.9	67.4	64.8	67.2	77.9	79.8
1954	83.5	85.3	81.2	90.9	101.1	84.5	86.0	90.6	70.8	78.3	80.3	65.5	63.4	63.4	76.9	79.8
1953	83.0	84.2	81.5	91.3	102.9	84.6	86.4	91.4	70.0	79.5	82.4	61.3	61.4	------	76.9	79.8
1952	------	82.6	78.0	91.1	106.0	85.3	87.1	92.4	70.1	77.3	80.8	57.5	59.3	76.3	77.7	78.5
1951	------	81.5	76.5	------	106.0	86.1	86.7	93.6	71.6	72.5	75.8	54.0	56.3	59.3	74.7	76.6
1950	------	81.2	72.7	------	95.5	79.0	80.1	86.9	63.3	68.2	72.5	48.9	53.7	68.3	74.4	69.9
1949	------	81.0	70.3	------	94.9	80.1	80.5	89.9	62.3	66.4	72.3	45.2	52.7	68.3	74.9	68.7
1948	------	79.1	68.6	------	98.3	83.3	82.7	95.1	62.8	61.8	68.2	40.7	51.1	68.5	72.2	66.8
1947	------	77.1	58.4	------	92.7	78.2	78.3	89.8	57.5	55.5	61.5	36.0	48.1	66.0	68.7	63.8
1946	------	77.4	51.3	------	80.0	67.5	66.1	77.5	46.0	50.3	54.3	34.4	44.4	59.0	64.5	58.8
1945	------	79.6	48.0	------	73.3	61.5	58.3	72.2	41.0	47.8	51.3	33.5	42.1	55.1	62.4	56.9
1944	------	80.3	47.1	------	68.6	58.5	55.9	68.5	40.0	47.9	51.4	33.5	41.1	53.4	60.0	54.7
1943	------	80.6	45.2	------	63.1	54.6	53.4	63.6	38.4	47.9	51.4	33.4	39.9	49.9	54.1	53.3
1942	------	81.0	43.1	------	61.4	52.3	50.9	60.9	36.4	48.1	52.3	33.3	38.0	45.2	51.0	53.3
1941	------	81.4	40.5	------	54.0	44.8	43.7	52.7	32.3	44.2	45.9	33.1	37.0	38.0	45.2	49.2
1940	------	82.1	38.2	------	50.5	42.8	41.6	50.4	31.3	42.7	43.6	33.1	36.8	40.2	46.1	48.3
1939	------	82.9	37.1	------	50.9	42.4	40.9	50.0	30.6	43.0	44.2	33.1	36.7	40.2	45.3	46.9
1938	------	83.0	37.8	------	52.0	43.0	41.6	50.7	31.0	44.0	45.8	32.9	36.7	40.4	45.2	46.1
1937	------	83.0	38.1	------	52.4	43.2	41.8	51.0	31.0	43.7	45.5	32.9	36.6	40.4	43.7	45.7
1936	------	84.5	37.4	------	48.4	41.1	39.7	48.6	29.4	43.0	44.2	32.9	36.3	39.6	43.7	45.7
1935	------	86.2	36.8	------	47.6	40.8	39.2	48.2	29.0	42.6	43.3	33.2	36.1	37.4	42.5	44.6

Series E 135–166. Consumer Price Indexes (BLS)—All Items, 1800 to 1970, and by Groups, 1913 to 1970—Con.

[1967 = 100]

Year	All items (135)	Food at home, total (137)	Rent (150)	House furnishings (155)	Apparel, total (156)	Year	All items (135)	Year	All items (135)	Year	All items (135)	Year	All items (135)	Year	All items (135)
1934	40.1	34.1	50.7	46.6	40.4	1912	29	1890	27	1868	40	1846	27	1823	36
1933	38.8	30.6	54.1	42.4	36.9	1911	28	1889	27	1867	42	1845	28	1822	40
1932	40.9	31.5	62.8	42.9	38.2			1888	27	1866	44	1844	28	1821	40
1931	45.6	37.8	70.0	49.3	43.2	1910	28	1887	27			1843	28	1820	42
						1909	27	1886	27	1865	46	1842	29	1819	46
1930	50.0	45.9	73.9	54.7	47.5	1908	27			1864	47	1841	31	1818	46
1929	51.3	48.3	76.0	56.2	48.5	1907	28	1885	27					1817	48
1928	51.3	47.7	77.8	56.8	49.0	1906	27	1884	27	1863	37	1840	30	1816	51
1927	52.0	48.2	79.7	58.2	49.7			1883	28	1862	30	1839	32		
1926	53.0	50.0	81.0	59.6	50.8	1905	27	1882	29	1861	27	1838	32	1815	55
						1904	27	1881	29			1837	34	1814	63
1925	52.5	48.4	81.8	61.0	51.6	1903	27			1860	27	1836	33	1813	58
1924	51.2	44.7	81.5	62.3	52.6	1902	26	1880	29	1859	27			1812	51
1923	51.1	45.1	78.6	63.4	53.1	1901	25	1879	28	1858	26	1835	31	1811	50
1922	50.2	43.7	76.7	59.0	53.0			1878	29	1857	28	1834	30	1810	47
1921	53.6	46.7	74.5	69.5	65.2	1900	25	1877	32	1856	27	1833	29	1809	47
						1899	25	1876	32			1832	30	1808	48
1920	60.0	61.5	64.9	82.7	84.6	1898	25			1855	28	1831	32	1807	44
1919	51.8	54.6	55.2	67.4	71.1	1897	25	1875	33	1854	27			1806	47
1918	45.1	49.0	51.0	53.5	53.6	1896	25	1874	34	1853	25	1830	32		
1917	38.4	42.6	50.1	41.6	39.6			1873	36	1852	25	1829	32	1805	45
1916	32.7	33.1	50.5	35.6	33.0	1895	25	1872	36	1851	25	1828	33	1804	45
						1894	26	1871	36	1850	25	1827	34	1803	45
1915	30.4	29.4	49.9	31.9	30.1	1893	27			1849	25	1826	34	1802	43
1914	30.1	29.8	49.6	30.5	29.4	1892	27	1870	38	1848	26	1825	34	1801	50
1913	29.7	29.2	49.6	29.8	29.2	1891	27	1869	40	1847	28	1824	33	1800	51

Series E 167–173. Consumer Price Indexes (BLS), for Special Groups: 1935 to 1970

[1967 = 100]

Year	All items, excluding food (167)	All items, excluding shelter (168)	Commodities Total (169)	Commodities Excluding food Total (170)	Commodities Excluding food Nondurable (171)	Services Total (172)	Services Excluding rent (173)
1970	116.7	114.4	113.5	112.5	113.1	121.6	123.7
1969	110.1	109.0	108.4	108.1	108.8	112.5	113.8
1968	104.4	104.1	103.7	103.7	104.1	105.2	105.7
1967	100.0	100.0	100.0	100.0	100.0	100.0	100.0
1966	96.7	97.4	98.2	97.5	97.0	95.8	95.3
1965	94.5	94.6	95.7	96.2	94.8	92.2	91.5
1964	93.2	93.2	94.6	95.6	93.5	90.2	89.2
1963	92.0	92.1	93.6	94.8	92.7	88.5	87.3
1962	90.8	90.9	92.8	94.1	91.8	86.8	85.5
1961	89.7	89.9	92.0	93.4	91.2	85.2	83.9
1960	88.8	88.9	91.5	93.1	90.7	83.5	81.9
1959	87.3	87.6	90.7	92.7	89.3	80.8	79.0
1958	85.7	86.9	90.6	91.5	88.2	78.5	76.4
1957	83.8	84.4	88.6	90.5	87.6	75.6	73.3
1956	81.1	81.7	85.9	87.8	85.3	72.7	70.1
1955	79.7	80.6	85.1	86.9	83.5	70.9	68.2
1954	79.5	81.0	85.9	87.5	83.5	69.5	66.7
1953	79.0	81.0	86.7	88.5	83.1	67.3	64.8
1952	77.5	80.8	87.0	88.3	82.4	64.5	62.2
1951	75.7	79.2	85.9	87.5	82.0	61.8	59.3
1950	71.1	73.1	78.8	81.4	76.2	58.7	56.0
1949	70.3	72.6	78.3	81.5	76.3	56.9	54.5
1948	69.6	73.9	80.4	82.7	77.8	54.3	51.9
1947	64.9	68.5	75.0	76.8	72.2	51.1	49.0
1946	59.4	59.0	62.4	68.1	62.9	49.1	46.7
1945	56.9	53.6	56.3	64.1	58.6	48.2	45.1
1944	55.7	52.2	54.7	61.6	56.6	47.5	44.2
1943	53.6	51.3	54.0	58.4	53.8	46.4	42.1
1942	52.1	47.7	49.6	56.0	51.6	45.6	40.3
1941	48.7	42.4	43.3	50.4	46.7	44.2	38.6
1940	47.3	39.9	40.6	48.0	44.7	43.6	38.1
1939	47.2	39.7	40.2	47.7	44.3	43.5	38.1
1938	47.5	40.4	41.0	48.5	45.0	43.4	38.1
1937	47.0	41.6	42.6	48.5	45.3	42.6	37.8
1936	45.4	40.3	41.0	46.5	43.5	41.3	37.4
1935	44.9	39.8	40.5	46.0	43.1	40.9	37.6

Series E 174–182. Consumer Price Index (Hoover): 1851 to 1880

[1860 = 100]

Year	All items Total	All items Less food	All items Less rent	All items Less food and rent	Food	Cloth-ing	Rent	Fuel and light	Other
	174	175	176	177	178	179	180	181	182
1880	110	108	106	96	111	94	127	95	133
1879	108	105	105	95	110	94	122	92	134
1878	111	107	108	96	113	95	124	93	135
1877	118	109	117	101	125	99	123	98	138
1876	119	118	118	106	124	104	123	106	138
1875	123	116	122	108	129	105	129	110	140
1874	129	122	128	116	134	115	133	114	141
1873	133	128	131	122	136	122	139	120	142
1872	135	132	133	125	136	126	144	122	141
1871	135	133	134	127	137	128	144	125	142
1870	141	137	141	135	143	141	142	126	143
1869	147	141	148	141	151	148	141	132	145
1868	154	141	157	143	164	148	138	133	144
1867	157	149	161	157	163	166	135	140	144
1866	167	163	172	178	169	194	138	152	146
1865	175	181	183	209	170	238	134	159	147
1864	176	187	185	222	167	261	130	155	141
1863	139	151	144	173	129	197	113	136	115
1862	113	120	115	131	107	143	101	112	105
1861	101	103	102	107	99	110	95	103	102
1860	100	100	100	100	100	100	100	100	100
1859	100	99	101	98	102	98	100	98	99
1858	99	100	99	100	99	99	100	103	98
1857	105	102	106	102	108	100	100	109	98
1856	102	102	102	101	102	100	103	106	96
1855	104	102	104	102	105	99	103	109	97
1854	101	103	101	103	103	100	102	113	96
1853	93	100	92	100	88	100	100	102	95
1852	93	100	91	100	87	100	100	99	95
1851	92	99	90	99	86	100	100	99	95

Series E 183–186. Cost-of-Living Indexes (Federal Reserve Bank of N.Y., Burgess, Douglas, Rees): 1820 to 1926

Year	1913 = 100 Federal Reserve Bank	1913 = 100 Burgess	Douglas [1] (1890–99 = 100)	Rees (1914 = 100)	Year	1913 = 100 Federal Reserve Bank	1913 = 100 Burgess	Rees (1914 = 100)	Year	1913 = 100 Federal Reserve Bank	1913 = 100 Burgess
	183	184	185	186		183	184	186		183	184
1926			241		1890	78	67.8	91	1855	67	64.1
1925			240		1889	78	67.8		1854	64	60.9
1924			234		1888	78	67.5		1853	64	53.9
1923			234		1887	76	65.4		1852	60	53.7
1922			229		1886	76	65.3		1851	60	53.0
1921			246								
					1885	75	64.6		1850	54	58.4
1920		203.7	286		1884	77	66.4		1849	51	61.1
1919		188.7	247		1883	81	71.7		1848	54	63.1
1918		171.1	218		1882	86	76.1		1847	58	63.4
1917		147.8	179		1881	83	73.8		1846	58	59.0
1916		113.4	149								
					1880	80	71.3		1845	54	56.3
1915		101.1	136		1879	79	68.8		1844	52	54.9
1914		102.5	139	100	1878	80	69.6		1843	51	53.6
1913	100	100.0	137	99	1877	80	77.2		1842	55	53.5
1912	102	92.8	133	97	1876	81	78.0		1841	60	55.9
1911	96	91.5	132	95							
					1875	86	81.2		1840	60	
1910	96	93.1	128	95	1874	88	83.1		1839	71	
1909	91	88.6	121	91	1873	88	84.7		1838	71	
1908	91	84.4	121	92	1872	90	86.3		1837	72	
1907	95	82.0	126	94	1871	89	86.9		1836	68	
1906	90	78.2	119	90							
					1870	91	92.5		1835	60	
1905	87	76.0	115	89	1869	95	97.8		1834	51	
1904	87	76.1	115	89	1868	98	104.2		1833	58	
1903	88	74.8	116	88	1867	102	103.5		1832	57	
1902	84	74.8	111	86	1866	103	107.4		1831	56	
1901	82	70.6	108	85							
					1865	102	108.1		1830	54	
1900	80	67.7	106	84	1864	95	104.6		1829	58	
1899	77	66.1	102	83	1863	78	80.0		1828	57	
1898	75	65.9	100	83	1862	69	66.0		1827	57	
1897	75	63.9	100	83	1861	63	61.2		1826	55	
1896	74	62.9	99	84							
					1860	61	63.0		1825	58	
1895	73	64.2	97	84	1859	63	63.7		1824	57	
1894	73	65.3	97	86	1858	69	61.2		1823	61	
1893	75	69.1	100	90	1857	70	67.3		1822	64	
1892	77	67.5	102	91	1856	68	63.9		1821	62	
1891	76	68.8	101	92					1820	65	

[1] Douglas' index for 1890 is 104.

Series E 187–202. Retail Prices of Selected Foods in U.S. Cities (BLS): 1890 to 1970

[In cents per unit indicated]

Year	Flour	Bread	Meats				Dairy products and eggs			Fruits and vegetables				Other		
			Round steak	Chuck roast	Pork chops	Bacon	Butter	Eggs	Milk, delivered	Oranges	Potatoes	Tomatoes, canned	Navy beans	Coffee	Margarine	Sugar
	187	188	189	190	191	192	193	194	195	196	197	198	199	200	201	202
	5 lb.	Lb.	Lb.	Lb.	Lb.	Lb.	Lb.	Doz.	½ gal.	Doz.	10 lb.	303 can	Lb.	Lb.	Lb.	5 lb.
1970	58.9	24.3	130.2	72.5	116.2	94.9	86.6	61.4	65.9	86.4	89.7	21.3	19.2	91.1	29.8	64.8
1969	58.1	23.0	126.7	70.4	112.2	87.8	84.6	62.1	62.9	83.8	81.6	19.7	19.6	76.5	27.8	62.0
1968	58.4	22.4	114.3	63.5	102.9	81.4	83.6	52.9	60.6	96.6	76.3	20.4	19.6	76.4	27.9	60.9
1967	59.6	22.2	110.3	60.7	100.4	83.7	83.0	49.1	57.4	76.6	74.7	19.5	18.2	76.9	28.4	60.5
1966	59.4	22.2	110.7	62.2	106.3	95.4	82.2	59.9	55.5	79.9	74.9	17.7	19.8	82.3	28.7	60.2
1965	58.1	20.9	108.4	59.5	97.3	81.3	75.4	52.7	52.6	77.8	93.7	16.1	17.5	83.3	27.9	59.0
1964	56.7	20.7	103.9	56.8	88.0	66.7	74.4	53.9	52.8	88.1	75.7	16.0	16.7	81.6	26.1	64.0
1963	57.0	21.6	106.4	60.3	88.2	68.3	75.0	55.1	52.0	90.4	65.1	15.5	17.8	69.4	27.5	67.9
1962	57.0	21.2	107.8	62.3	89.8	70.3	75.2	54.0	52.2	79.3	63.2	15.7	17.4	70.8	28.4	58.5
1961	56.0	20.9	103.6	59.4	87.9	71.2	76.3	57.3	52.4	77.7	62.9	16.0	17.0	73.6	28.6	58.9
1960	55.4	20.3	105.5	61.6	85.8	65.5	74.9	57.3	52.0	74.8	71.8	15.9	16.7	75.3	26.9	58.2
1959	54.5	19.7	107.3	64.1	85.3	66.5	75.3	53.0	50.6	66.4	63.3	15.5	17.2	78.0	28.0	57.2
1958	55.2	19.3	104.2	63.3	91.8	79.3	74.2	60.4	50.6	76.0	62.6	17.0	18.0	90.7	29.4	56.3
1957	54.6	18.8	93.6	52.5	86.6	73.8	74.3	57.3	50.0	57.9	57.1	15.0	16.1	101.7	29.9	55.2
1956	53.3	17.9	88.2	48.4	78.2	57.3	72.1	60.2	48.4	58.3	67.7	15.2	16.3	103.4	28.9	52.8
1955	53.8	17.7	90.3	50.1	79.3	65.9	70.9	60.6	46.2	52.8	56.4	15.1	(NA)	93.0	28.9	52.1
1954	53.6	17.2	90.7	51.4	86.3	81.7	72.4	58.5	46.0	55.4	52.6	[1] 14.6	17.6	110.8	29.9	52.6
1953	52.3	16.4	91.5	52.9	82.7	78.5	79.0	69.8	46.8	49.0	53.8	14.8	17.0	89.2	29.4	52.8
1952	52.3	16.0	111.2	73.5	80.3	64.9	85.5	67.3	48.4	50.6	76.0	14.8	16.1	86.8	29.4	51.5
1951	51.9	15.7	109.3	74.1	79.4	67.2	81.9	73.7	46.2	48.7	50.8	15.8	16.7	86.8	34.7	50.6
1950	49.1	14.3	93.6	61.6	75.4	63.7	72.9	60.4	41.2	49.3	46.1	12.4	15.3	79.4	30.8	48.7
1949	47.9	14.0	85.3	55.5	74.3	66.5	72.5	69.6	42.2	51.8	54.6	12.8	16.4	55.4	30.8	47.6
1948	49.0	13.9	90.5	64.4	77.2	76.9	86.7	72.3	43.6	44.7	55.9	13.9	22.0	51.4	41.4	47.0
1947	48.2	12.5	75.6	51.5	72.1	77.7	80.5	69.6	39.2	43.4	50.3	16.3	21.3	46.9	40.8	48.6
1946	35.4	10.4	52.1	36.6	48.5	53.3	71.0	58.6	35.2	49.9	46.8	12.6	14.0	34.4	28.3	38.4
1945	32.1	8.8	40.6	28.1	37.1	41.1	50.7	58.1	31.2	48.5	49.3	10.3	11.4	30.5	24.1	33.4
1944	32.4	8.8	41.4	28.8	37.3	41.1	50.0	54.5	31.2	46.0	46.5	10.1	10.7	30.1	24.1	33.6
1943	30.6	8.9	43.9	30.2	40.3	43.1	52.7	57.2	31.0	44.3	45.6	10.6	10.1	30.0	23.6	34.2
1942	26.4	8.7	43.5	29.3	41.4	39.4	47.3	48.4	30.0	35.7	34.2	9.9	9.0	28.3	22.1	34.1
1941	22.6	8.1	39.1	25.5	34.3	34.3	41.1	39.7	27.2	31.0	23.5	7.7	7.4	23.6	17.1	28.6
1940	21.5	8.0	36.4	23.5	27.9	27.3	36.0	33.1	25.6	29.1	23.9	7.2	6.6	21.2	15.9	26.0
1939	19.0	7.9	36.0	23.4	30.4	31.9	32.5	32.1	24.4	28.9	24.7	7.2	6.2	22.4	16.7	27.2
1938	19.8	8.6	34.9	22.8	32.9	36.7	34.7	35.5	25.0	26.7	21.3	7.5	6.3	23.2	17.5	26.6
1937	24.0	8.6	39.1	25.7	36.7	41.3	40.7	36.2	25.0	38.9	27.9	7.9	9.6	25.5	19.2	28.2
1936	23.8	8.2	34.1	22.3	34.1	40.7	39.5	37.1	24.0	33.6	31.9	8.0	6.7	24.3	18.5	27.9
1935	25.3	8.3	36.0	24.0	36.1	41.3	36.0	37.6	23.4	22.0	19.1	8.6	6.2	25.7	18.8	28.2
1934	24.5	8.3	28.1	17.5	25.5	29.1	31.5	32.5	22.4	31.9	23.0	8.8	6.1	26.9	13.5	27.5
1933	19.5	7.1	25.7	16.0	19.8	22.6	27.8	28.8	20.8	27.3	23.0	7.7	5.3	26.4	13.2	26.5
1932	16.0	7.0	29.7	18.5	21.5	24.2	27.8	30.2	21.4	30.2	17.0	7.8	5.2	29.4	15.4	25.0
1931	18.0	7.7	35.4	22.7	29.6	36.6	35.8	35.0	25.2	35.0	24.0	8.5	8.1	32.8	19.9	28.0
1930	23.0	8.6	42.6	28.6	36.2	42.5	46.4	44.5	28.2	57.1	36.0	10.2	11.7	39.5	25.0	30.5
1929	25.5	8.8	46.0	31.4	37.5	43.9	55.5	52.7	28.8	44.7	32.0	10.8	14.1	47.9	27.0	32.0
1928	26.5	8.9	43.7	29.6	35.2	44.4	56.9	50.3	28.4	58.6	27.0	9.9	11.8	48.2	27.3	34.5
1927	27.5	9.2	38.7	25.2	37.2	47.8	56.3	48.7	28.2	52.0	38.0	10.0	9.4	47.4	28.3	36.0
1926	30.0	9.3	37.1	23.7	39.9	50.8	53.6	51.9	28.0	51.6	49.0	9.9	9.4	50.2	30.1	34.0
1925	30.5	9.3	36.2	22.8	37.0	47.1	55.2	55.4	27.8	57.1	36.0	11.1	10.3	50.4	30.2	35.0
1924	24.5	8.9	34.8	21.6	31.0	38.4	52.2	51.0	26.8	44.8	28.0	10.8	9.9	42.6	29.3	45.0
1923	23.5	8.8	34.3	20.8	30.3	39.7	55.8	49.9	27.8	49.7	30.0	10.5	10.9	36.9	28.1	49.5
1922	25.5	8.7	32.3	19.7	33.0	39.8	47.9	44.4	26.2	57.4	28.0	11.3	9.9	36.1	28.0	36.5
1921	29.0	9.9	34.4	21.2	34.9	42.7	51.7	50.9	29.2	49.6	31.0	10.2	8.2	36.3	31.6	40.0
1920	40.5	11.5	39.5	26.2	42.3	52.3	70.1	68.1	33.4	63.2	63.0	12.5	11.4	47.0	42.3	97.0
1919	36.0	10.0	38.9	27.0	42.3	55.4	67.8	62.8	31.0	53.2	38.0	13.6	12.6	43.3	41.3	56.5
1918	33.5	9.8	36.9	26.6	39.0	52.9	57.7	56.9	27.8	-------	32.0	-------	17.3	30.5	-------	48.5
1917	35.0	9.2	29.0	20.9	31.9	41.0	48.7	48.1	22.4	-------	43.0	-------	17.9	30.2	-------	46.5
1916	22.0	7.3	24.5	17.1	22.7	28.7	39.4	37.5	18.2	-------	27.0	-------	11.0	29.9	-------	40.0
1915	21.0	7.0	23.0	16.1	20.3	26.9	35.8	34.1	17.6	-------	15.0	-------	7.8	30.0	-------	33.0
1914	17.0	6.3	23.6	16.7	22.0	27.5	36.2	35.3	17.8	-------	18.0	-------	-------	29.7	-------	29.5
1913	16.5	5.6	22.3	16.0	21.0	27.0	38.3	34.5	17.8	-------	17.0	-------	-------	29.8	-------	27.5
1912	17.5	-------	19.9	-------	19.2	24.4	37.4	34.1	17.4	-------	22.0	-------	-------	-------	-------	31.5
1911	17.0	-------	17.5	-------	17.9	24.7	33.7	32.3	17.0	-------	22.0	-------	-------	-------	-------	30.5
1910	18.0	-------	17.4	-------	19.2	25.5	35.9	33.7	16.8	-------	17.0	-------	-------	-------	-------	30.0
1909	18.0	-------	16.4	-------	17.4	22.4	34.5	31.9	16.2	-------	19.0	-------	-------	-------	-------	29.5
1908	16.5	-------	15.9	-------	16.0	20.7	32.8	29.7	16.0	-------	19.0	-------	-------	-------	-------	29.5
1907	15.5	-------	15.2	-------	15.6	20.1	32.7	29.0	15.6	-------	18.0	-------	-------	-------	-------	29.0
1906	14.5	-------	14.5	-------	15.2	19.6	30.4	27.8	14.8	-------	17.0	-------	-------	-------	-------	28.5
1905	16.0	-------	14.0	-------	13.9	18.1	29.0	27.2	14.4	-------	17.0	-------	-------	-------	-------	30.0
1904	16.0	-------	14.1	-------	13.7	18.0	28.0	27.1	14.4	-------	18.0	-------	-------	-------	-------	29.5
1903	13.5	-------	14.0	-------	14.0	18.2	28.5	25.9	14.4	-------	17.0	-------	-------	-------	-------	28.0
1902	12.5	-------	14.7	-------	14.1	17.7	28.7	24.7	14.0	-------	18.0	-------	-------	-------	-------	28.0
1901	12.5	-------	13.8	-------	13.0	15.8	26.5	21.9	13.6	-------	18.0	-------	-------	-------	-------	30.0
1900	12.5	-------	13.2	-------	11.9	14.3	26.1	20.7	13.6	-------	14.0	-------	-------	-------	-------	30.5
1899	12.5	-------	12.9	-------	11.2	13.4	25.1	20.9	13.4	-------	15.0	-------	-------	-------	-------	29.5
1898	14.0	-------	12.7	-------	10.9	13.1	24.4	19.9	13.4	-------	16.0	-------	-------	-------	-------	29.5
1897	14.0	-------	12.5	-------	10.8	12.7	23.9	18.9	13.4	-------	14.0	-------	-------	-------	-------	28.0
1896	12.5	-------	12.4	-------	10.7	12.6	23.8	19.2	13.6	-------	12.0	-------	-------	-------	-------	28.0
1895	12.0	-------	12.3	-------	11.0	13.0	24.9	20.6	13.6	-------	14.0	-------	-------	-------	-------	26.5
1894	11.5	-------	12.2	-------	11.2	13.5	26.1	19.9	13.6	-------	15.0	-------	-------	-------	-------	27.5
1893	12.5	-------	12.4	-------	11.8	14.2	28.3	22.4	13.6	-------	17.0	-------	-------	-------	-------	29.5
1892	14.0	-------	12.4	-------	11.1	12.9	27.5	22.1	13.6	-------	14.0	-------	-------	-------	-------	28.0
1891	15.0	-------	12.4	-------	10.9	12.6	27.4	22.1	13.6	-------	18.0	-------	-------	-------	-------	30.0
1890	14.5	-------	12.3	-------	10.7	12.5	25.5	20.8	13.6	-------	16.0	-------	-------	-------	-------	34.5

NA Not available.   [1] Average of January–September.

Series E 203–213. Retail Price Indexes (BLS) of Electricity, Gas, and Fuel for Residential Use: 1913 to 1970

[1967 = 100 except as otherwise indicated]

Year	Electricity Composite[1]	Electricity 100 Kwh	Gas Composite[2]	Gas Residential heating	Gas Other than residential heating Composite[2]	Gas Other than residential heating 10 Therms[3]	Gas Other than residential heating 25 Therms[4]	Fuel oil and coal	Fuel oil, No. 2[5]	Coal (1957–59 = 100) Pennsylvania anthracite, stove size	Coal (1957–59 = 100) Bituminous, all domestic sizes
	203	204	205	206	207	208	209	210	211	212	213
1970	106.2	104.3	108.5	107.4	109.4	107.4	108.4	110.1	109.3	----	----
1969	102.8	101.3	102.8	102.6	103.1	102.6	102.3	105.6	105.4	----	----
1968	100.9	100.4	101.0	101.1	100.8	100.7	100.7	103.1	103.2	----	----
1967	100.0	100.0	100.0	100.0	100.0	100.0	100.0	100.0	100.0	----	----
1966	99.1	98.5	100.2	100.4	100.0	100.3	100.1	97.0	96.9	----	----
1965	99.1	98.2	99.6	99.9	99.3	100.2	99.7	94.6	94.4	----	----
1964	99.6	98.0	99.3	100.2	98.6	99.3	99.7	92.7	92.5	----	----
1963*	100.1	98.1	99.0	99.9	98.3	99.4	98.9	93.2	94.6	----	----
1962	100.1	98.0	98.9	100.0	98.1	99.3	98.9	91.5	92.7	101.5	103.2
1961	100.1	98.0	99.0	100.7	97.7	99.1	98.3	91.0	92.6	99.8	102.8
1960	99.8	97.6	97.7	100.1	96.1	97.3	96.8	89.2	89.0	98.1	102.4
1959	98.5	96.1	91.6	92.3	91.1	94.6	91.0	89.8	90.6	98.9	101.6
1958	97.1	94.5	88.6	89.3	88.1	92.4	87.5	88.7	89.4	100.0	99.8
1957	95.9	93.3	83.7	84.4	83.1	88.6	82.6	90.3	94.8	101.1	98.4
1956	95.5	92.8	82.3	83.5	81.5	87.7	80.7	85.9	90.2	94.5	94.6
1955	95.2	92.4	81.0	82.9	79.7	85.6	78.9	82.3	86.0	88.6	91.3
1954	94.0	91.4	77.9	78.7	77.2	83.4	76.2	81.2	83.2	89.2	90.3
1953	93.6	90.5	76.4	76.6	76.0	82.4	74.8	81.5	82.7	93.1	90.4
1952	92.4	89.7	74.1	72.7	74.6	81.6	72.9	78.0	78.6	87.8	88.6
1951	91.5	89.5	72.7	70.5	73.4	81.1	71.5	76.5	76.7	86.6	86.9
1950	90.8	88.9	73.1	69.9	73.6	81.6	71.6	72.7	72.6	78.1	85.0
1949	90.6	88.9	72.8	69.5	73.5	84.0	71.4	70.3	71.9	74.3	82.0
1948	89.7	90.2	69.8	68.6	70.5	78.8	67.6	68.6	75.8	70.3	79.1
1947	88.9	89.1	67.4	68.0	68.2	74.6	63.5	58.4	59.6	62.8	66.4
1946	90.0	89.8	66.9	67.3	67.6	72.6	61.9	51.3	49.9	57.9	56.2
1945	93.7	91.6	68.0	68.0	68.7	73.7	62.6	48.0	49.5	52.1	53.4
1944	94.2	91.7	68.8	68.5	69.6	74.0	62.9	47.1	51.9	50.3	52.2
1943	94.4	92.3	69.2	68.9	69.9	74.3	63.3	45.2	51.8	47.6	50.4
1942	94.5	92.3	69.9	69.1	70.6	74.6	64.8	43.1	47.7	45.0	48.3
1941	95.0	92.7	70.1	70.4	70.9	74.9	65.0	40.5	41.6	43.2	45.9
1940	95.7	93.9	70.9	71.6	71.6	75.7	65.9	38.2	40.5	41.1	43.3
1939	96.7	95.2	71.4	72.3	72.1	76.3	66.8	37.1	38.6	39.1	42.9
1938	98.3	96.4	70.6	72.5	71.3	75.6	66.5	37.8	42.4	39.8	43.2
1937	99.8	97.7	69.7	75.0	70.5	74.2	66.1	38.1	44.5	40.0	42.9
1936	102.0	99.9	70.4	81.4	71.2	74.4	67.9	37.4	38.5	42.6	42.0
1935	105.3	104.3	70.9	83.4	71.6	74.6	69.4	36.8	36.9	41.4	41.2
1934	110.9	107.3	----	----	----	----	----	----	----	44.2	40.9
1933	119.9	110.4	----	----	----	----	----	----	----	44.0	38.0
1932	121.2	111.4	----	----	----	----	----	----	----	45.5	38.2
1931	122.4	115.5	----	----	----	----	----	----	----	49.6	41.2
1930	124.4	119.6	----	----	----	----	----	----	----	50.8	43.8
1929	126.7	123.4	----	----	----	----	----	----	----	51.3	43.9
1928	131.4	128.6	----	----	----	----	----	----	----	51.6	44.5
1927	133.8	133.4	----	----	----	----	----	----	----	52.1	46.0
1926	135.7	137.7	----	----	----	----	----	----	----	53.2	46.3
1925	137.6	140.5	----	----	----	----	----	----	----	52.5	45.0
1924	139.1	144.1	----	----	----	----	----	----	----	52.4	45.6
1923	140.1	147.3	----	----	----	----	----	----	----	52.4	51.3
1922	143.1	----	----	----	----	----	----	----	----	51.3	50.3
1921	144.7	----	----	----	----	----	----	----	----	51.6	53.0
1920	142.1	----	----	----	----	----	----	----	----	49.0	52.9
1919	142.3	----	----	----	----	----	----	----	----	41.0	40.6
1918	137.5	----	----	----	----	----	----	----	----	34.9	38.9
1917	137.0	----	----	----	----	----	----	----	----	31.7	35.9
1916	140.8	----	----	----	----	----	----	----	----	28.3	29.1
1915	144.5	----	----	----	----	----	----	----	----	26.2	27.7
1914	149.2	----	----	----	----	----	----	----	----	26.2	28.1
1913	[6]152.2	----	----	----	----	----	----	----	----	26.1	27.4

* Denotes first year for which figures include Alaska and Hawaii.
[1] Combination of 100, 250, and 500 kw.-hrs. from 1964 to 1970; 40, 100, and 200 kw.-hrs. from 1953 to 1963; 25, 40, 100, and 250 kw.-hrs. from 1935 to 1952; and the "average consumption" in each component city prior to 1935.
[2] Combination of 10, 25, and 40 therms from 1964 to 1970; 10 and 25 therms from 1953 to 1963; and 10.6, 19.6, 30.6, and 40.6 therms prior to 1953.

[3] 10 therms, 1953–1970; 10.6 therms, prior to 1953.
[4] 25 therms, 1953–1963; 30.6 therms, prior to 1953.
[5] Includes fuel oils No. 2 and 3 from 1939 through 1947.
[6] December only.

Series E 214. Rent Indexes (Warren and Pearson) for Dwelling Units in 5 Large Cities: 1860 to 1880

[1860 = 100. Covers Boston, Philadelphia, Cincinnati, Louisville, and St. Louis]

Year	Index 214	Year	Index 214	Year	Index 214	Year	Index 214
1880	151	1875	162	1870	180	1865	175
1879	148	1874	166	1869	187	1864	168
1878	152	1873	173	1868	179	1863	123
						1862	101
1877	148	1872	173	1867	167	1861	101
1876	147	1871	173	1866	187	1860	100

National Income and Wealth

National Product and Income (Series F 1-348)

F 1–348. General note.

In broad terms, national product or its equivalent, national income, is a comprehensive measure of the Nation's total annual production of commodities and services. Only the end products of a year's economic activity are included. For example, since the output of bread is included, the output of wheat used in producing the bread is excluded. At any given time, national product may be measured as the sum of the value added in various forms of economic activity (agriculture, mining, manufacturing, etc.); as the total of the incomes accruing to persons supplying different productive factors (wages and salaries, profits, including undistributed corporate profits, etc.); or as the aggregate value of the final products of the economy (food, clothing, shelter, etc.). While each of these approaches yields the same total (given a consistent scheme of valuation), the component detail illuminates different facets of the process of production, distribution, and consumption of the Nation's output, and, hence, serves different uses. These three approaches, of course, do not exhaust the possibilities.

Changes in national product may be measured either in current prices or in prices of a given year. In the latter case, the change ideally reflects only the change in the real volume of commodities and services. Each of these two forms of valuation has its particular uses. For example, in a study of financial developments or market trends, the current price series is often preferable, while for analysis of consumer levels of living or national productivity, the constant price series is more appropriate.

It may be useful to indicate briefly some of the more general conceptual limitations of national product estimates. First, national product is primarily a measure of the output of the market economy. Only a few items of "income in kind" are included. The most important are the value of food and fuel produced and consumed by farm families and the rental value of owner-occupied dwellings. No account is taken of items such as the value of the housewife's services or of home repairs, home dressmaking, or noncommercial recreation. Since economic growth generally involves a progressive commercialization of such activities, the increase of national product reflects to some extent a transfer of production from the nonmarket to the market sector rather than a real growth in the total volume of production.

Second, there is no complete agreement on all of the goods that may properly be considered end products of the economy. National product, as ordinarily constituted, includes, among other things, all items of consumer expenditure. This leads to the inclusion of such things as expenditures on transportation to work and payments to labor unions, which the consumer may not consider end products in themselves, but rather a necessary means under modern industrial organization to secure the money income needed to obtain goods that do constitute the goal of economic activity, such as food, clothing, and recreation. Also, since national product typically includes all government expenditure for commodities and services, criticism has been voiced regarding the inclusion of war and defense goods and government services to business, such as police and fire protection for factories and warehouses. If this argument is accepted, national product measures would be viewed as overstating the growth of the final product of the economy over time, since these items tend on balance to increase in relative importance as the economy develops.

Third, because of the techniques used in adjusting for price changes, national product in constant prices fails to reflect fully changes in the quality of goods during economic growth. In contrast to the foregoing limitation, this one would tend to understate the growth of national product, since, on the average, quality of products probably tends to improve over time.

Finally, national product may fail to measure accurately changes in the material level of living provided by economic activity, even when placed on a per capita basis, since the aggregate figures do not reflect changes in the distribution of income between rich and poor, in consumption needs arising from changes in the age composition of the population, or in man-hours spent in economic activity.

Despite these shortcomings of national product measures for historical analysis, there are wide areas of agreement on the proper means of constructing and interpreting such measures. Their usefulness in providing insights into the nature and growth of the economy is attested to by the wide acceptance of the figures.

The primary source for national income and product information is the *Survey of Current Business*, published monthly by the U.S. Department of Commerce, Bureau of Economic Analysis (formerly the Office of Business Economics). The most recent sources of the data presented here are the July 1973 issue of the *Survey; U.S. National Income and Product Accounts, 1964–1967;* and *The National Income and Product Accounts of the United States, 1929–1965.* Other principal works of a comprehensive nature that were used are: Simon Kuznets, *Capital in the American Economy: Its Formation and Financing*, National Bureau of Economic Research, New York, 1961, and "Long-Term Changes in the National Income of the United States of America Since 1870," in International Association for Research in Income and Wealth, *Income and Wealth of the United States: Trends and Structure*, Income and Wealth Series II, Bowes and Bowes, Cambridge, England, 1952; John W. Kendrick, *Productivity Trends in America*, National Bureau of Economic Research, New York, 1961; and Raymond W. Goldsmith, Dorothy S. Brady, and Horst Mendershausen, *A Study of Saving in the United States*, vol. III, Princeton University Press, 1956. Earlier works of historical nature are: Robert F. Martin, *National Income in the United States, 1799–1938*, National Industrial Conference Board, New York, 1939; Simon Kuznets, *National Income and Its Composition, 1919–1938*, National Bureau of Economic Research, New York, 1941, and *National Product Since 1869*, National Bureau of Economic Research, New York, 1946; *Enterprise and Social Progress*, National Industrial Conference Board, New York, 1939; Willford I. King, *The Wealth and Income of the People of the United States*, Macmillan, New York, 1915. A basic source for discussion of conceptual issues in the field is Conference on Research in Income and Wealth, *Studies in Income and Wealth*, vols. 1–38, National Bureau of Economic Research, New York, 1937–1960.

The extent of detail presented is limited by space requirements; greater detail is frequently available in the original source. No attempt was made to utilize estimates of contemporaries available for the 19th century, since these figures have not been subjected to critical review in the light of modern concepts and techniques. (See George Tucker, *Progress of the United States in Population and Wealth in Fifty Years*, Press of Hunt's Merchants' Magazine, New York,

1843; Ezra C. Seaman, *Essays on the Progress of Nations*, Charles Scribner, New York, 1868; *Annual Report of the Commissioner of Patents for the Year 1848;* David A. Wells, *Our Burden and Our Strength*, Loyal Publication Society, New York, 1864; Edward Atkinson, *The Distribution of Products*, New York, 1885; and Michael G. Mulhall, *Industries and Wealth of Nations*, Longmans, Green, London, 1896.)

The basic reference sources for concepts and methodology are *National Income, 1954 Edition; U.S. Income and Output, 1958;* the August 1965 issue of the *Survey of Current Business;* and *Readings in Concepts and Methods of National Income Statistics*, available from the U.S. National Technical Information Service, Springfield, Va.

F 1–5. Gross national product, total and per capita, in current and 1958 prices, 1869–1970.

Source: **Series F 1** and **F 3**, U.S. Bureau of Economic Analysis: 1869–1908, derived from Kendrick-Kuznets estimates published by John W. Kendrick in *Productivity Trends in the United States*, National Bureau of Economic Research, New York, 1961; 1909–1963, *The National Income and Product Accounts of the United States, 1929–65;* 1964–1970, *Survey of Current Business*, July issues, and later revisions by the Bureau of Economic Analysis. **Series F 2** and **F 4**, computed by dividing gross national product by population estimates in series A 1–2. **Series F 5**, computed by dividing the current price series of gross national product by the constant price series.

Gross national product, as defined by the Department of Commerce, is the market value of the output of goods and services produced by the Nation's economy, before deduction of depreciation charges and other allowances for business and institutional consumption of durable capital goods. Other business products used up by business in the accounting period are excluded. The Nation's economy in this context refers to the labor and property supplied by residents of the Nation. Gross national product comprises the purchase of goods and services by consumers and government, gross private domestic investment (including the change in business inventories), and net exports. See also general note for series F 1–348.

The current price estimates for 1909–1970 are the official estimates prepared by the Department of Commerce. For earlier years, gross national product estimates prepared by John W. Kendrick in terms of 1929 prices (see source cited above) were converted to 1958 prices by the Bureau of Economic Analysis (BEA) of the Department of Commerce. This was done by (1) taking the BEA 1958-base deflator for 1909 as a ratio of the Kendrick 1929-base deflator for 1909, (2) multiplying the Kendrick deflator series for 1869–1908 by the ratio, and (3) using the resulting 1958-base deflator series to deflate the Kendrick current dollar estimates into 1958 prices. For the years prior to 1909, the underlying estimates are those of Simon Kuznets, adjusted for 1889–1908 by John W. Kendrick to the same conceptual basis as the Commerce figures. The estimates for years before 1889 are in terms of the somewhat different Kuznets concept of gross national product. The specific nature of the conceptual differences is indicated below in connection with the discussion of series F 71–97. The constant price estimates at all dates are basically those of Simon Kuznets (see text for series F 98–124), but they have been adjusted to the Department of Commerce concept for 1889–1908 by Kendrick, who prepared constant dollar estimates for reconciliation items between the two series. The implicit price deflator is the ratio of gross national product in current prices to gross national product in constant prices. It is a weighted average of the price indexes used to deflate the components of gross national product, the implicit weights being expenditures in the current period.

With regard to statistical reliability, the Commerce estimates are considered to be "subject to only a small percentage of error." The same is very likely true of the estimates for 1919–1928, but for the years prior to 1919 the margin of error widens noticeably. For further discussion of the margin of error in the early estimates, see text for series F 71–97.

F 6–9. Net national product, national income, personal income, and disposable personal income, in current prices, 1897–1970.

Source: 1897–1928, computed by adjusting the gross national product totals (as shown in series F 1) by the estimated values of the items accounting for the difference between gross national product and the given aggregate. (See the reconciliation among the aggregates in series F 144–162.) The values of the reconciliation items are given in Raymond W. Goldsmith, Dorothy S. Brady, and Horst Mendershausen, *A Study of Saving in the U.S.*, vol. III, NBER, copyright by Princeton University Press, 1956, pp. 435 and 441. 1929–1970, U.S. Bureau of Economic Analysis: 1929–1963, *The National Income and Product Accounts of the U.S., 1929–1965;* 1964–1970, *Survey of Current Business*, July issues.

The following are definitions used by the Department of Commerce:

Net national product is the market value of the net output of goods and services produced by the Nation's economy. All business products used up by business in the accounting period are excluded. Net national product comprises the purchases of goods and services by consumers and government, net private domestic investment (including the change in business inventories), and net exports.

National income (sometimes called net national product at factor cost) represents the aggregate earnings of labor and property which arise from the current production of goods and services by the Nation's economy. Thus, it measures the total factor costs of the goods and services produced by the economy. Earnings are recorded in the forms in which they accrue to residents of the Nation, inclusive of taxes on those earnings. As such, they consist of the compensation of employees, the profits of corporate and unincorporated enterprises, net interest, and the rental income flowing to persons.

Personal income represents the current income received by persons from all sources, inclusive of transfers from government and business but exclusive of transfers among persons. Not only individuals (including owners of unincorporated enterprises), but also nonprofit institutions, private trust funds, and private health and welfare funds are classified as "persons." Personal income is measured on a before-tax basis, as the sum of wage and salary disbursements, other labor income, proprietors' and rental income, interest and dividends, and transfer payments, minus personal contributions for social insurance.

Disposable personal income is the income remaining to persons after the deduction from personal income of personal tax and nontax payments to general government.

Theoretically, net national product and national income are superior to gross national product as measures of the final output of the economy, since some duplication is involved by the inclusion in the latter of the production of fixed capital which serves merely for replacement purposes. However, the depreciation charges, taken as an approximation of the value of capital currently consumed in deriving net national product and national income, are largely in terms of original cost, and hence are on a basis of valuation not comparable to that of the gross production of fixed capital (see *National Income: 1954 Edition*, p. 43). In practice, therefore, the measures of the net product of the economy which are obtained are not fully satisfactory.

While net national product and national income are both measures of current national production (ideally, free from the duplication involved in gross national product), they differ in the manner in which this production is valued. Conceptually, in net national product, current production is valued at market prices, while in national income, it is valued at factor costs, that is, at the cost of the capital and labor used in producing it. In practice, as series F 144–162 shows, the principal difference between these two forms of valuation is indirect business taxes.

Personal income, which measures the actual current income receipts of persons from all sources, differs from the national income in that it excludes certain types of income which accrue in production but are not received by persons (for instance, the undistributed part of corporate profits) and, on the other hand, includes certain types of income which do not arise in current productive activity but constitute personal receipts (such as relief and unemployment benefits).

Hence, personal income, unlike the national product and national income aggregates, is not a measure of national production. Personal income net of taxes (i.e., disposable personal income) is the closest over-all statistical approximation to consumer purchasing power derived from current incomes.

The Department of Commerce figures (1929–1970) are believed to be subject to only a small percentage error. Personal income figures are more reliable than those for national income because the major items included in personal income (but not in national income) are reliable, and the exclusions either do not affect reliability or actually increase it.

For the years prior to 1929, the underlying estimates of gross national product are those of Simon Kuznets, adjusted by John W. Kendrick to the same conceptual basis as the Commerce figures for later years. The estimates for adjustments needed to move from gross national product to the series F 6–9 aggregates were made in a manner and from sources as closely comparable as possible with the Commerce figures. However, the estimates for these adjusting items "are probably affected by a larger margin of error for the period before 1929 . . . ." (*A Study of Saving* . . . vol. III, p. 424.)

F 10–16.   Growth rates (percent) of gross national product and output per employee for the United States and six countries, 1870–1969.

Source: U.S. Bureau of Economic Analysis, *Long Term Economic Growth, 1860–1970.*

These growth rates are average annual percentage rates of change computed over the indicated periods by use of the compound interest rate formula. The gross national product (GNP) data from which the growth rates were computed are from two sources. Real GNP data for 1950–1969 are from the Organisation for Economic Cooperation and Development (OECD). The OECD defines GNP as the market value of the output of goods and services, free of duplication, produced by a country's economy before deduction of depreciation and other operating provisions. Where possible, the OECD has adjusted published country statistics to standard concepts and definitions, thereby obtaining better intercountry comparability. The GNP data used were published in *National Accounts of OECD Countries, 1953–1969* and *National Accounts of OECD Countries, 1950–1968* (Paris: OECD).

Gross national product data for 1870–1950 are from *Economic Growth in the West*, by Angus Maddison (Twentieth Century Fund, New York, 1964) and unpublished data supplied by the same author. Maddison adjusted data from various government and private sources to conform as closely as possible to the OECD definitions and to reflect present geographic boundaries. Wherever possible, Maddison based his data on gross domestic product, but both net and gross domestic and national product were used.

The data used to compute growth rates of output per employee were derived by dividing the GNP data by total civilian employment. Employment data for 1950–1969 are from *Labour Force Statistics, 1958–1969* and earlier editions of *Labour Force Statistics* (formerly *Manpower Statistics*) (OECD, Paris). The OECD defines a person as employed if he is above a specified age (varying among countries) and is either working or temporarily absent from his job. Employment data for 1870–1950 are from Maddison's *Economic Growth in the West.*

The per capita gross national product data used to compute growth rates were derived by dividing the GNP data by population. The population data for 1950–1969 are from the OECD, which defines population to include all nationals present in or temporarily absent from the country and aliens permanently settled in the country. These data are from the same OECD publications as the employment data above. Population data for 1870–1950 are from Maddison's *Economic Growth in the West.* Maddison adjusted country estimates to refer to constant territory.

F 17–30.   Per capita income and product for selected items, in current and constant (1958) prices, 1929–1970.

Source: 1929–1970, U.S. Bureau of Economic Analysis, *Survey of Current Business*, July 1973, table 7.6.

See text for series F 1–5, F 6–9, and F 47–70 for definitions of major aggregates. Personal income and disposable personal income in constant prices are derived by deflating the totals in current prices by the implicit price deflator for personal consumption expenditures.

F 31.   Average annual growth rates of gross national product (percent), 1909–1970.

Source: U.S. Bureau of Economic Analysis, *Long Term Economic Growth, 1860–1970*, and unpublished data.

This series represents average annual percentage rates of change, or growth rates, in real (constant dollar) gross national product for all combinations of years in the period 1909 to 1970. These growth rates were computed from Department of Commerce estimates of real gross national product (in 1958 dollars) by means of the compound interest rate formula.

See general note for series F 1–348 and text for series F 1–5.

F 32–46.   Gross national product—summary in current and constant (1958) prices, 1929–1970.

Source: U.S. Bureau of Economic Analysis, 1929–1963, *The National Income and Product Accounts of the United States, 1929–1965;* 1964–1970, *Survey of Current Business*, July issues, tables 1.3, 1.5, 1.7, and 1.8.

The gross national product classifications shown in series F 32–46 are of output by major type of product—durable goods, nondurable goods, services, and structures; and output by sector of origin—business (farm and nonfarm), households and institutions, general government, and the rest of the world.

Output by major type of product provides type-of-product information on a consistent basis for the gross national product as a whole and represents regroupings of the estimates of expenditures by the major market groups.

The categories shown are defined as follows:

Durable goods—Sum of purchases of durable goods by business (producers' durable equipment), persons, government (Federal, State and local), of exports minus imports of these goods, plus an allowance for change in business inventories of durable goods.

Nondurable goods—Sum of purchases of nondurable goods by persons and general government, of exports minus imports of these goods, and an allowance for change in business inventories of nondurable goods.

Services—Sum of purchases of services by persons, of public purchases from business and from government employees (as measured by their compensation), and of exports minus imports of services.

Structures—Sum of new private construction and new public construction.

The classification by sector of origin shows the same total of gross national product derived by summing the gross product originating in the particular sectors of the Nation's economy: farm and nonfarm business and three nonbusiness groups—households, government, and the rest of the world. For the current dollar estimates, the output of the three nonbusiness sectors is measured by the incomes originating in them. The contribution of the farm business sector is estimated as the total value of farm products less farmers' cost purchases from nonfarm business. The resulting measure of output is, in principle, equal to the sum of income derived from farm production plus certain other charges, mainly indirect business taxes and depreciation. The total of these measures of output originating is deducted from the total gross national product as measured by the sum of final expenditures to obtain nonfarm business gross product as a residual.

The constant dollar measures are derived in the same general framework. The real gross product of farming is estimated by the separate deflation of product values and cost purchases, each in considerable detail. The real output of government is measured in terms of deflated labor input, without allowance for changes in productivity. Real income from foreign investment is obtained by deflating the current-dollar flows by composite price indexes that measure changes in the purchasing power of these flows in foreign trade transactions. The real product of households and institutions reflects labor input. The nonfarm business component is then derived as a residual.

F 47–143. General note.

These series provide a summary view of the end products of the economy. From these data one can determine, among other things, to what extent the annual flow of production took the form of consumers' goods, on the one hand, and capital goods, on the other. In addition, one can examine the composition of the flow of goods to consumers (in terms of broad categories such as services, nondurable goods, and durable goods), and of capital formation, classified according to types such as construction, producers' durable equipment, etc.

F 47–70. Gross national product, by type of expenditure, in current and constant (1958) prices, 1929–1970.

Source: U.S. Bureau of Economic Analysis, 1929–1963, *National Income and Product Accounts of the United States, 1929–1965;* 1964–1970, *Survey of Current Business,* July issues, tables 1.2 and 1.8.

The following are definitions used by the Department of Commerce (for the definition of gross national product, see text for series F 1–5):

Personal consumption expenditures (series F 48–51) represent the market value of purchases of goods and services by individuals and nonprofit institutions and the value of food, clothing, housing, and financial services received by them as income in kind. It includes the rental value of owner-occupied houses but does not include purchases of dwellings, which are classified as capital goods. Consumer durable commodities are generally defined as those having an average life of 3 years or longer.

Gross private domestic investment (series F 52–62) consists of net acquisitions of fixed capital goods by private business and nonprofit institutions including commissions arising in sale and purchase of new and existing fixed assets, principally real estate, and of the value of the change in the volume of inventories held by business. It covers all private new dwellings, including those acquired by owner occupants. Producers' durable equipment is defined in terms of items having an average life of one or more years.

Net exports of goods and services (series F 63–65) measures the balance on goods and services, excluding transfers under military grants, as reported in the U.S. balance of payments statistics.

Government purchases of goods and services (series F 66–70) are made up of the net expenditures on goods and services by the three levels of government—Federal, State, and local—and the gross investment of government enterprises. Among the items included in government purchases of goods and services are: Compensation of government employees; construction expenditures on highways, bridges, and schools; and net purchases of equipment and supplies from business and abroad. Excluded from this category are purchases for the acquisition of land, current outlays of government enterprises, transfer payments, government interest, subsidies, and transactions in financial claims.

National defense purchases (series F 68) include Department of Defense military functions, military assistance to other nations, development and control of atomic energy, and stockpiling of strategic materials.

The figures are official Department of Commerce estimates. With regard to the relative accuracy of the different product series, the Department states that government purchases of goods and services, particularly Federal Government purchases, is highest on the scale of reliability, while the change in business inventories (which includes an inventory valuation adjustment) is lowest. Lying between these extremes are, in order of decreasing accuracy: Producers' purchases of durable equipment and personal consumption expenditures for durables and nondurables; personal consumption expenditures for

services; and new construction. While the estimate of net exports is based on a good deal of statistical information, it is nevertheless liable to substantial percentage error because it is derived as the difference between much larger numerical values.

Constant prices.—These data represent estimates in 1958 prices for the current price series presented in series F 47–70. The general procedure followed by the Department of Commerce was to divide the current price figures (organized in a product breakdown much finer than that shown) by appropriate price indexes based on 1958 = 100. The price indexes used in deriving the 1958 price estimates do not generally allow for quality change. Therefore, the constant price figures do not reflect part of the secular quality improvement in the economy. Also, the constant-price series overstate somewhat short-run fluctuations in output, because available price information understates effective short-run fluctuations in prices. The choice of a recent year price base rather than an earlier year base (for example, 1929) to derive the constant price estimates tends to reduce somewhat the magnitude of the long-term growth in gross national product.

F 71–97. Gross and net national product, by major type of product, in current prices, 1869–1931.

Source: Simon Kuznets, *Capital in the American Economy: Its Formation and Financing,* National Bureau of Economic Research, New York, 1961 (copyright).

The difference between the gross national product series presented in series F 71 and the Department of Commerce series in series F 1 and F 32 is primarily conceptual, and relates almost wholly to the treatment of government in the estimation of national product. In series F 71, government purchases of goods and services is omitted as a component of gross national product. However, an estimate of government services to consumers is added to personal consumption expenditures to obtain an estimate of "flow of goods to consumers" and government capital formation (consisting of both war and nonwar public construction, purchases of durable equipment including durable munitions, and the change in the stock of monetary metals) is added to private capital formation. In addition, series F 71 excludes from flow of goods to consumers and from gross national product the imputed value of unpaid services of financial intermediaries.

The effect of these adjustments is to yield a lower aggregate for gross national product, chiefly because government expenditures which are considered not to take the form of services to consumers or capital formation are omitted from the total. In effect, these omitted expenditures are treated as yielding intermediate services that facilitate the flow of goods to consumers or capital formation, but do not in themselves constitute final products, just as the production of wheat contributes to the production of bread but is not counted as a final product in addition to bread. For the earlier years, the quantitative difference between the two series (F 1 and F 71) arising from this conceptual difference is fairly small, but for the most recent decades (since 1940) it would be quite large, because of the great relative expansion in Government expenditures for military and defense purposes, which in the Kuznets concept are largely excluded from the total.

Net national product differs from gross national product in that an allowance for capital consumed during the year in the process of production has been deducted from the gross national product total. In the present case, capital consumption, both private and public, is valued at reproduction cost. Thus, a piece of equipment used up during the current year is valued at the current cost of replacement irrespective of the original cost of the equipment. In addition, the capital consumption estimate includes an allowance for depletion of natural resources.

The differences between the present series and the Department of Commerce series with regard to the major components (that is, between personal consumption expenditures and flow of goods to consumers, and between gross private domestic investment and private and public capital formation) have been indicated above in the discussion of the differences in the gross national product concepts. Consumer perishables, semidurables, and durables are commodities that, without marked change and retaining their essential physical identity are ordinarily employed less than 6 months, from 6 months to 3 years, and more than 3 years, respectively.

With regard to the statistical reliability of the estimates, the following quotation, relating to decade rather than the quinquennial averages presented here, is relevant:

> For the comprehensive totals of national product and their major components, such as flow of goods to consumers, gross value of producer durables, gross construction, the maximum error in the estimates for the decades before 1919 can be said to be 15 percent; for the later three decades [1919–28, 1924–33, 1929–38] less than 10 percent. The maximum errors may be somewhat larger for the various categories of the flow of goods to consumers; and, on a percentage basis, much larger for the net totals—net producer durables, net construction, changes in inventories, changes in claims against foreign countries, particularly the last two.
> Owing to possible shortages in the underlying data or errors inherent in some of the assumptions, the comprehensive totals for the 1869–78 decade may be understated by as much as 10 percent; for the 1874–83 decade by as much as 5 percent; for the subsequent decades through 1899–1908 by as much as 2 to 3 percent. (Simon Kuznets, *National Product Since 1869*, National Bureau of Economic Research, New York, 1946, pp. 85–86.)

This statement, though made with respect to an earlier set of estimates, is also applicable to the revised figures presented here, but since the present estimates refer to quinquennial periods, the allowance for maximum error should be increased.

F 98–124.   Gross and net national product, by major type of product, in 1929 prices, 1869–1931.

Source: See source for series F 71–97.

See also text for series F 71–97.

These series are exact counterparts of series F 71–97, except that the estimates are expressed in 1929 prices instead of current prices.

The estimates were derived as follows: For commodity production, the current dollar estimates used in deriving series F 71–97, but in the narrowest categories that production statistics permitted, and at producers' prices, were deflated by price indexes for corresponding product groups. The resulting estimates of commodity output in 1929 prices were then adjusted upward by a constant ratio to allow for transportation and distributive margins, thus yielding commodity output at final cost to consumers. The current dollar estimates of services included in series F 71–97 were deflated by the implicit average price index for all consumer commodities, except in the case of rent, which was deflated by a specific rent index.

The discussion of margins of error with regard to series F 71–97 applies here also, except that the deflation procedure increases the possible error somewhat. In particular, since the price indexes used for deflation do not adequately allow for quality change or new goods, an element of downward bias is introduced that is not present in the current dollar estimates.

F 125–129.   Gross domestic product originating in private farm and nonfarm sectors and government, in 1929 prices, 1869–1960.

Source: John W. Kendrick, 1869–1955, *Productivity Trends in the United States*, National Bureau of Economic Research, New York, 1961 (copyright); 1956–1960, unpublished data.

Gross domestic product in series F 125 differs from gross national product in series F 3 in that the former excludes net factor income from abroad. Thus the return on capital located abroad but owned by United States residents is excluded, while the income from capital owned abroad but located in this country is included. Quantitative differences in the two series are also due to the valuation periods used.

Kendrick derived these estimates as follows: His gross national product series in 1929 prices was adjusted by a constant price estimate of net factor income from abroad to obtain gross domestic product. A constant dollar estimate of gross farm product was derived as the difference between constant dollar estimates of the total value of farm output and of the value of intermediate products consumed. This procedure is preferable to the more common one of taking the

physical outputs of an industry and weighting them by unit values in the base year. The latter procedure yields a measure that includes purchases from other industries, and the figures for a number of industries cannot be summed without duplication. For example, assume that the output of artificial fertilizers was to increase and to cause higher yields in agriculture; the effect on the combined output of agriculture and manufacturing (which would include the manufacture of artificial fertilizers) would be exaggerated if the individual sector estimates were derived without allowance for changes in the constant dollar value of purchases from other sectors.

"Farm," as used in series F 127, differs slightly from "agriculture" in series F 227 in that F 127 excludes agricultural services, forestry, and fisheries.

Gross government product, in accordance with present Department of Commerce concepts, consists of a deflated series on compensation of general government employees. The deflation procedure used does not allow for changes in the productivity of these employees.

Gross private domestic product was obtained as the difference between gross domestic product and gross government product. Gross nonfarm product is the difference between gross private domestic product and gross farm product.

The reliability of gross domestic product is essentially the same as that of gross national product, from which it was derived (see text for series F 1–5). While the estimates for farm and government product, the two directly estimated components, are probably less accurate, they are nevertheless based on fairly satisfactory sources, even for the earlier dates.

F 130–143.   Gross national product, by type of industry, in current and constant (1958) prices, 1947–1970.

Source: U.S. Bureau of Economic Analysis, 1947–1966, *U.S. National Income and Product Accounts, 1964–67*, tables 1.21, 1.22, 1, and 2; 1967–1970, *Survey of Current Business*, July issues, tables 1.21 and 1.22.

As indicated in the general note for series F 1–348, the national output total (GNP) may be obtained by several methods. The gross national product by industry series, in contrast to others, emphasizes the industrial origin of the gross product and shows an industry's (agriculture, manufacturing, retail trade, etc.) contribution to the Nation's total output of goods and services, as measured within the framework of the national income and product accounts.

Gross product originating in an industry, its value added, may be measured as the difference between the value of an industry's total output in producers' prices and the cost of materials and business services purchased by the industry at delivered prices. The same total may also be calculated by summing the industry's payments to the factors of production (employee compensation, profits, etc.) and its nonfactor costs (depreciation, property tax, sales tax, etc.). The sum of the gross products of all industries is equal to the Nation's total output of goods and services or GNP.

The current-price measures of gross national product by industry given in series F 130–143 are obtained by distributing and summing by industry the income payments to the factors of production and the nonfactor costs of production. In these distributions profit-type income and capital consumption allowances are adjusted to represent establishment totals. The estimates are valued at market prices and are consistent with other measures of GNP. The industry classification used conforms to the 1957 edition of the *Standard Industrial Classification (SIC) Manual*.

The statistical discrepancy entry in the current dollar series is the excess of the value of the estimated gross national product as computed by adding the expenditure components over its independently estimated value as computed by adding the factor income shares and the various nonfactor charges. This discrepancy is also included in the "residual" appearing in the constant price series and is a partial explanation of the reason why total real GNP measured by final purchases differs from the total real GNP measured by the gross product originating in industry.

Two methods were used in deriving industry gross product in constant prices. In one, implicit price deflators for industry gross product were calculated and applied to the current price gross product for the industry. Under the second method, a series was developed representing the annual index of the industry's real gross product. This index was then used to extrapolate the industry gross product for the base year—1958.

These alternative methods were used because, in general, it was not possible to calculate current price measures of industry total output and intermediate purchases that are necessary in order to apply the traditional "double-deflation" technique.

The methods employed to calculate real product by industry are described in detail in *GNP by Major Industries, Concepts and Methods*, a pamphlet available upon request from the Interindustry Economics Division, Bureau of Economic Analysis. The article "GNP by Major Industries" in the October 1962 *Survey of Current Business* also discusses in detail special qualifications applicable to deflators for the construction, services, and government industries. The latter article also discusses how the data shown in these tables may be used to examine the cost-profit structure underlying the industry and its overall price indexes.

F 144–162. Relation of gross national product, national income, and personal income and saving, 1929–1970.

Source: U.S. Bureau of Economic Analysis, 1929–1963, *The National Income and Product Accounts of the United States, 1929–1965*; 1964–1970, *Survey of Current Business*, July issues, tables 1.9 and 2.1.

Series F 144–162 is designed to show the precise relationship among the various national account aggregates. The major aggregates of gross national product, net national product, national income, personal income, and disposable personal income are defined in the text for series F 1–5 and F 6–9. *Personal saving* (series F 162) is defined as the excess of personal income over the sum of personal outlays and personal tax and nontax payments. It consists of the current saving of individuals (including owners of unincorporated businesses), nonprofit institutions, and private health, welfare, and trust funds. Personal saving equals the change in the net worth of persons which may be further viewed as the acquisition of financial claims (such as cash and deposits, securities and reserves of life insurance companies and non-insured pension funds) less the net increase in indebtedness, plus the acquisition of physical assets net of capital consumption allowances.

F 163–185. National income, by type of income, 1929–1970.

Source: U.S. Bureau of Economic Analysis, 1929–1963, *The National Income and Product Accounts of the United States, 1929–1965*; 1964–1970, *Survey of Current Business*, July issues, table 1.10.

For the definition of national income, see text for series F 6–9. Other definitions used by the Department of Commerce are as follows:

Compensation of employees is the income accruing to persons in an employee status as remuneration for their work. It is the sum of wages and salaries and supplements to wages and salaries. *Wages and salaries* consists of the monetary remuneration of employees, inclusive of executives' compensation, commissions, tips, and bonuses, and of payments in kind which represent income to the recipients. *Supplements to wages and salaries* consists of employer contributions for social insurance and of other labor income. Employer contributions for social insurance comprises employer payments under the social security, Federal and State unemployment insurance, railroad retirement and unemployment insurance, government retirement, and a few other minor social insurance programs. Other labor income comprises employer contributions to private pension, health, unemployment, and welfare funds; compensation for injuries; directors' fees; pay of the military reserve; and a few other minor items.

Proprietors' income measures the monetary earnings and income

in kind of sole proprietorships, partnerships, and producers' cooperatives from their current business operations—other than the supplementary income of individuals derived from renting property. It includes the inventory valuation adjustment and the other adjustments to taxable income described under corporate profits.

Rental income of persons consists of the monetary earnings of persons from the rental of real property, except the earnings of persons primarily engaged in the real estate business; the imputed net rental returns to owner-occupants of nonfarm dwellings; and the royalties received by persons from patents, copyrights, and rights to natural resources.

Corporate profits (before tax) and inventory valuation adjustment is the earnings of corporations organized for profit which accrue to residents of the Nation, measured before Federal and State profits taxes, without deduction of depletion charges, exclusive of capital gains and losses and intercorporate dividends, and including inventory valuation adjustment (the inventory valuation adjustment adjusts book cost of goods sold to replacement cost of goods sold in the computation of profits). It includes the profits of stock life insurance companies and of mutual financial institutions. Bad debt expenses are measured by actual losses, not additions to reserves; and the profit or loss of bankrupt firms includes the gain from unsatisfied debt. Corporate profits includes net receipts of dividends and branch profits from abroad, as reflected in the balance of payments statistics, in addition to profits earned in domestic operations. In other major respects, the definition of profits is in accordance with Federal income tax regulations.

Net interest measures the excess of interest payments of the domestic business system over its interest receipts, plus net interest received from abroad. In addition to monetary interest flows, net interest includes imputed interest arising in connection with the operations of financial intermediaries.

The figures are official Department of Commerce estimates. The relative accuracy of the various series as evaluated by the Department is, in terms of decreasing reliability: Employee compensation, corporate profits, net interest, proprietors' income, and rental income. In particular, the entrepreneurial income estimates (including rental income) are subject to significant shortcomings when compared with the other income shares.

F 186–191. Percent distribution of national income, by type of income, in current prices, 1900–1969.

Source: 1900–1939, D. Gale Johnson, "The Functional Distribution of Income in the United States, 1850–1952," *Review of Economics and Statistics*, vol. XXXVI, No. 2, May 1954, p. 178 (copyright, Harvard College); 1930–1969, U.S. Bureau of Economic Analysis, unpublished data.

The Commerce data for series F 186–191 were compiled by the Bureau of Economic Analysis from data published in the *National Income and Product Accounts of the United States, 1929–1965*, and subsequent July issues of the *Survey of Current Business*. The definitions for these series are the same as those given for series F 163–185.

D. Gale Johnson carried the Department of Commerce estimates (series F 163–185) back to 1900 on the basis of Kuznets' estimates for 1919–1928; King's for 1909–1918; Martin's for 1899–1908; and certain other sources. (Simon Kuznets, *National Income and Its Composition, 1919–1938*, National Bureau of Economic Research, New York, 1941; Willford I. King, *The National Income and Its Purchasing Power*, National Bureau of Economic Research, New York, 1930; and Robert F. Martin, *National Income in the United States, 1799–1938*, National Industrial Conference Board, New York, 1939.)

The procedures followed are summarized by Johnson as follows:

For the period 1910–1928, the Bureau of Agricultural Economics estimates of farm operators income is used. The estimate of corporate profits is taken from a series of net profits after taxes published by the National Industrial Conference Board to which is added the amount of corporate taxes paid. Kuznets series for wages and salaries, nonfarm entrepreneurial income, and rent were accepted as published for 1919–1928. His interest series is substantially below that of the Department of Commerce after interest paid by governments is eliminated. It was linked with the Department of Commerce series in terms of average relationship for the period 1929–1933. The estimates of King for 1909–1918 and Martin for 1899–1908 were adjusted in a similar fashion.

Definitions for the Johnson data are the same as those for F 163–185, except that prior to 1929 corporate profits before taxes (series F 190) does not include an inventory valuation adjustment, and income of unincorporated enterprises (series F 188) includes one only for farm income. Also, imputed interest is not included in the series used to extrapolate the Department of Commerce estimates of net interest prior to 1929.

See text for series F 163–185 for reliability estimate of the Department of Commerce data. For the years prior to 1929, and particularly before 1919, the general level of reliability of all series is less than for the later period.

F 192–209. National income, by sector and legal form of organization, 1929–1970.

Source: U.S. Bureau of Economic Analysis, 1929–1963, *The National Income and Product Accounts of the United States, 1929–1965;* 1964–1970, *Survey of Current Business,* July issues, table 1.13.

These series present an allocation of national income by type of income among seven legal forms of organization. These include three groupings of private business enterprises, namely, corporations, sole proprietorships and partnerships, and other private business; two major groupings related to government activities, government enterprises (covering the essentially commercial enterprises of the government, such as the U.S. Postal Service) and general government; private households and nonprofit institutions; and a sector that provides a measure of the net income originating in the rest of the world which accrues to U.S. residents.

Certain types of income, by definition, fall into one of the seven legal forms of organization distinguished in these series, such as corporate profits, proprietors' income, and rental income of persons. Net interest is estimated separately for each of the relevant legal forms, and a breakdown of compensation of employees among the three forms of private business enterprises is derived for benchmark years by applying distributions for each industry developed largely from economic censuses. A description of the various types of income may be found in the text for series F 163–185.

F 210–215. Percent distribution of aggregate payments, by type of income, in current prices, 1870–1968.

Source: Department of Commerce estimates, U.S. Bureau of Economic Analysis, unpublished data; other estimates, Simon Kuznets, "Long-Term Changes in the National Income of the United States of America Since 1870," in International Association for Research in Income and Wealth, *Income and Wealth of the United States: Trends and Structure,* Income and Wealth Series II, Bowes and Bowes, Cambridge, England, 1952, p. 136.

The Department of Commerce estimates were compiled by the Bureau of Economic Analysis from national income data published in *The National Income and Product Accounts of the United States, 1929–1965,* and subsequent July issues of the *Survey of Current Business.*

See text for series F 163–185 for definitions underlying the Department of Commerce series. Two modifications have been introduced to maintain comparability with the Martin and Kuznets series— corporate profits other than dividends have been deducted and government interest has been added.

These series provide a somewhat longer historical perspective than do series F 163–185 and F 186–191 on the distribution of income by type, chiefly by drawing on an earlier study by Willford I. King,

The Wealth and Income of the People of the United States, Macmillan, New York, 1919. However, the reliability of these earlier figures is uncertain, as is clear from the following statement accompanying presentation of the table in the source:

> [The following table] assembles the information available on [the] distribution of aggregate payments by type for the period under consideration. W. I. King's figures are of somewhat doubtful usefulness in this connection, since the treatment of corporate and government savings is not clear from his analysis, and the statistical basis for the estimates is quite thin. Although Martin's figures are on a somewhat more secure basis, the differences in level between [the overlap values for 1909–1918] indicate lack of comparability with the more acceptable estimates for recent decades. One must, therefore, pick one's way with caution in any attempt to infer long-term changes in the distribution of income payments by type.

These series are based on a somewhat different aggregate than those in series F 163–185 and F 186–191, the most important difference being that the "aggregate payments" concept includes only corporate dividends rather than corporate profits before taxes. Hence, corporate profits tax liability, undistributed corporate profits, and the corporate inventory valuation adjustment are all excluded from the total underlying series F 210. In addition, the interest series includes government interest and excludes imputed interest (though in bringing the National Bureau of Economic Research series up to date by means of the Department of Commerce data, a series including imputed interest was used). With regard to the remaining three series (employee compensation, entrepreneurial income, and rent), the underlying concepts correspond closely to their counterparts in series F 164, F 174, and F 177, though the statistical procedures followed differ somewhat.

F 216–225. Percent distribution of national income or aggregate payments, by industry, in current prices, 1869–1968.

Source: See series F 210–215, p. 89.

The basic estimates used in deriving the earlier series are those of Robert F. Martin, *National Income in the United States, 1799–1938,* National Industrial Conference Board, New York, 1939; and Simon Kuznets, *National Income and Its Composition, 1919–1938,* National Bureau of Economic Research, New York, 1941. The Kuznets series was extended through 1948 on the basis of appropriately adjusted Department of Commerce figures. The Department of Commerce estimates were compiled by the Bureau of Economic Analysis from national income data published in *The National Income and Product Accounts of the United States, 1929–1965,* and subsequent July issues of the *Survey of Current Business.*

The Kuznets measure of income originating in an industry differs somewhat from that employed in the published Department of Commerce estimates, series F 226–237, corporate taxes having been excluded and interest on government debt included. Also, in the Martin series on "aggregate payments," undistributed corporate profits are not included. Hence, aside from variations in statistical technique and sources, the income totals differ somewhat for the years where the three sets of estimates overlap.

Also, there is some variation in industrial classification. The finance and miscellaneous category in the National Bureau of Economic Research estimates includes items such as income originating in fisheries and in bus, truck, and air transportation, and dividend and interest flows from the rest of the world. In the Martin estimates this category also includes income from fisheries and the net international flow of interest and dividends, as well as income from miscellaneous professional occupations, such as the clergy, and from the hand trades. (In the other two sets of estimates these last two categories are classified in the service sector.) Also, in the Martin estimates shown in the last three lines of series F 216–225, rents are distributed among the various industries, whereas, in the estimates for all other years, they are classified under the "finance" sector.

The Department of Commerce series shown for the period 1929 through 1968 has been adjusted to conform to the Kuznets series, i.e., government debt interest has been included, corporate profits taxes have been excluded, and the industry classifications have been adjusted somewhat.

The comments made in connection with series F 226–237 regarding variations in the statistical reliability of the estimates for the different sectors are relevant here. (See also *National Income and Its Composition, 1919–1938*, pp. 509–523.) Also, the Martin estimates, particularly for the dates prior to 1899, should be considered of a definitely lower order of reliability.

F 226–237. National income, by industrial origin, in current prices, 1929–1970.

Source: U.S. Bureau of Economic Analysis, 1929–1963, *The National Income and Product Accounts of the United States, 1929–1965*; 1964–1970, *Survey of Current Business*, July issues, table 1.12.

The income total used in this distribution is that of national income (see text for series F 6–9). The industrial classification for 1929–1948 follows closely that of the 1942 Standard Industrial Classification System (for a comparison applicable to this period, see *National Income: 1954 Edition*). The classification for 1948–1970 is based upon the 1957 Standard Industrial Classification. Estimates for 1948 are provided by both classifications so that users may gauge the comparability of data for the earlier and later periods. It should be noted that all establishments operated by government agencies or corporations are classified in the government and government enterprises industrial division, regardless of their classification in the Standard Industrial Classification System.

In the discussion of series F 163–185, it is noted that there are differences in the reliability of the estimates for various *types* of income, and, in particular, that the estimates for proprietors' income and for rental income are of a much lower order of accuracy. This information may be used to draw some inferences concerning the relative accuracy of the industry estimates, since, generally speaking, the estimates for those sectors in which the least reliable types of income bulk large will be lowest in statistical accuracy. Accordingly, the estimates for the construction, trade, and service sectors should be considered least reliable, since in each of these, proprietors' income accounts for a disproportionately large share. The estimate for the sector labeled "finance, insurance, and real estate" should also be included in this category, because rental income is of preponderant importance. The most reliable estimates are those for mining, manufacturing, transportation, communications and public utilities, and government, while those for agriculture would probably rank somewhat below these, but noticeably above the least reliable group.

F 238–249. Value added by selected industries, and value of output of fixed capital, in current and 1879 prices, 1839–1899.

Source: Robert E. Gallman, "Commodity Output in the United States, 1839–1899," Conference on Research in Income and Wealth, *Studies in Income and Wealth*, vol. 24, National Bureau of Economic Research, New York, 1960 (copyright).

Value added in agriculture, mining, manufacturing, and construction, though narrower in scope than national product, is the most reliable output series of fairly comprehensive coverage for the period prior to 1870. "Value added" is the value of output, at producers' prices, less the value of commodities consumed in production, at delivered prices. Viewed from the income side, it comprises for any given sector the sum of payments to factors of production (net income originating), payments made to noncommodity producing firms (including government, but excluding transportation), and depreciation. Generally speaking, the coverage of the total for the four sectors combined is fairly close to that for finished commodity output plus construction materials (see also text for series P 318–374). It differs from gross national product primarily in that it excludes the value of transportation and distributive services and of services to ultimate consumers, such as medical and educational services, and refers to the product produced within a given area rather than that accruing to the residents of the area.

The series for agriculture includes the value of food, fuel, and

manufactures produced and consumed on the farm; that for mining excludes the output of precious metals mining; and that for manufacturing excludes home manufactures and the products of the independent hand trades. Forestry and fisheries are not covered in any of the series.

Estimates in constant prices were obtained for each sector as the difference between the constant price estimates of the total value of the output of the sector and of the value of intermediate products consumed.

The series on value of output of fixed capital covers the value of construction, manufactured producers' durables, and farm improvements. The value of repairs and maintenance is included only in the estimates for construction. Fixed capital produced by the independent hand trades—chiefly artisans' tools and agricultural implements—is not included. The figures relate to output, not domestic use. Constant price estimates were obtained for construction by deflating the current price series by an index of the cost of labor and construction materials. For producers' durables, an index of selling prices was chiefly used, and for farm improvements, use was made of a series on acres of land improved.

In general, the principal sources were the Federal and State censuses of the period, but a wide range of additional materials was used either directly for the estimates or to test the results. Compared with the national product estimates for the late 19th century, the present series might be considered less reliable, because of the greater scarcity of materials at the earlier dates and the lower reliability of the census returns. On the other hand, restriction of scope to the commodity sectors would tend to improve reliability relative to the national product estimates, since the basic sources for the service estimates included in the latter are much less satisfactory than those for commodity output. The estimates for the different commodity producing sectors are believed about equally reliable, except that for construction which is substantially inferior to the others. Also, because of the greater relative importance of construction in the fixed capital series, it is less reliable than the value-added series for all sectors combined.

F 250–261. National income and persons engaged in production, by industry divisions, 1869–1970.

Source: U.S. Bureau of Economic Analysis, *Long Term Economic Growth, 1860–1970*.

National income by industry of origin measures the income accruing to the various factors of production involved in producing each industry's output. This income is the sum of employee compensation, proprietors' income, rental income, corporate profits, and net interest. The national income data used to construct this table are from several sources. One set of data, covering 1869–1937, is from Robert F. Martin, *National Income in the United States, 1799–1938* (National Industrial Conference Board, New York, 1939). Another set, for 1919–1938, is from Simon Kuznets, *National Income and Its Composition, 1919–1938* (National Bureau of Economic Research, New York, 1941). A third set, for 1929–70, is from *The National Income and Product Accounts of the United States, 1929–1965* and the *Survey of Current Business* (U.S. Bureau of Economic Analysis).

The Martin data and the Kuznets data exclude corporate profits taxes and include interest on government debt, while the Commerce data include corporate profits taxes and exclude interest on government debt. Also, undistributed corporate profits are not included in the Martin data but are in the Kuznets and Commerce data.

Persons engaged in production, by industry, measures the number of persons engaged in producing each industry's output. Included are all persons working for wages or salaries and active proprietors of unincorporated enterprises who devote most of their time to the business. The data on persons engaged are from two sources. Data for the early period, 1869–1929, are from John W. Kendrick, *Productivity Trends in the United States* (Princeton University Press, 1961). Data for 1929–1970 are Bureau of Economic Analysis series from *The National Income and Product Accounts of the United States, 1929–1965*, and the *Survey of Current Business*.

F 262–286. Personal income and outlay, 1929–1970.

Source: U.S. Bureau of Economic Analysis, 1929–1963, *The National Income and Product Accounts of the United States, 1929–1965;* 1964–1970, *Survey of Current Business*, July issues, table 2.1.

For definitions of personal income and outlay components, see text for series F 6–9 and F 47–70. Transfer payments to persons consist of income received by persons, generally in monetary form, for which no services are rendered currently. Personal transfer payments to foreigners consist of personal remittances in kind and in cash to abroad, net of such remittances from abroad.

F 287–296. Personal income—percent distribution and per capita income as percent of U.S. total, by regions, 1840–1970.

Source: 1840–1950, Richard A. Easterlin, "Interregional Differences in Per Capita Income, Population, and Total Income, 1840–1950" in *Trends in the American Economy in the Nineteenth Century, Studies in Income and Wealth*, vol. 24, Princeton University Press, 1960, p. 137 (copyright by National Bureau of Economic Research, New York); 1960–1970, U.S. Bureau of Economic Analysis.

For definition of personal income, see text for series F 6–9.

Regional classification. The following regional classification, adopted by Easterlin, is used in this table: *New England*—Maine, New Hampshire, Vermont, Massachusetts, Rhode Island, Connecticut; *Middle Atlantic*—New York, New Jersey, Pennsylvania, Delaware, Maryland, and the District of Columbia; *East North Central*—Ohio, Indiana, Illinois, Michigan, Wisconsin; *West North Central*—Minnesota, Iowa, Missouri, North Dakota, South Dakota, Nebraska, Kansas; *South Atlantic*—Virginia, West Virginia, North Carolina, South Carolina, Georgia, Florida; *East South Central*—Kentucky, Tennessee, Alabama, Mississippi; *West South Central*—Arkansas, Louisiana, Oklahoma, Texas; *Mountain*—Montana, Idaho, Wyoming, Colorado, New Mexico, Arizona, Utah, Nevada; *Pacific*—Washington, Oregon, California.

Data for 1930–1970 are averages for, respectively, 1927–32, 1937–44, 1948–53, 1957–62, 1963–67, and 1968–71.

F 297–348. Personal income, by States: 1929–1970.

Source: U.S. Bureau of Economic Analysis, 1929, 1940, 1949, and 1956, *Survey of Current Business*, April 1969, tables 3 and 5; 1948, 1950–1955, and 1957–1970, *Survey of Current Business*, August 1973, tables 1 and 2.

See text for series F 262–286.

★ ★ ★ ★ ★ ★ ★ ★ ★ **More Recent Data for *Historical Statistics* Series** ★ ★ ★ ★ ★ ★ ★ ★ ★

Statistics for more recent years in continuation of many of the still-active series shown here appear in annual issues of the *Statistical Abstract of the United States*, beginning with the 1975 edition. For direct linkage of the historical series to the tables in the *Abstract*, see Appendix I in the *Abstract*.

Series F 1–5. Gross National Product, Total and Per Capita, in Current and 1958 Prices: 1869 to 1970

Year	Current prices Total (Bil. dol.)	Current prices Per capita (Dollars)	1958 prices Total (Bil. dol.)	1958 prices Per capita (Dollars)	Implicit price index (1958 = 100)
	1	2	3	4	5
1970	977.1	4,808	722.5	3,555	135.2
1969	930.3	4,590	725.6	3,580	128.2
1968	864.2	4,306	706.6	3,521	122.3
1967	793.9	3,995	675.2	3,398	117.6
1966	749.9	3,815	658.1	3,348	113.9
1965	684.9	3,525	617.8	3,180	110.9
1964	632.4	3,296	581.1	3,028	108.8
1963	590.5	3,120	551.0	2,912	107.2
1962	560.3	3,004	529.8	2,840	105.8
1961	520.1	2,831	497.2	2,706	104.6
1960 *	503.7	2,788	487.7	2,699	103.3
1959	483.7	2,731	475.9	2,688	101.6
1958	447.3	2,569	447.3	2,569	100.0
1957	441.1	2,576	452.5	2,642	97.5
1956	419.2	2,492	446.1	2,652	94.0
1955	398.0	2,408	438.0	2,650	90.9
1954	364.8	2,247	407.0	2,506	89.6
1953	364.6	2,285	412.8	2,587	88.3
1952	345.5	2,201	395.1	2,517	87.5
1951	328.4	2,129	383.4	2,485	85.6
1950	284.8	1,877	355.3	2,342	80.2
1949	256.5	1,719	324.1	2,172	79.1
1948	257.6	1,757	323.7	2,208	79.6
1947	231.3	1,605	309.9	2,150	74.6
1946	208.5	1,475	312.6	2,211	66.7
1945	211.9	1,515	355.2	2,538	59.7
1944	210.1	1,518	361.3	2,611	58.2
1943	191.6	1,401	337.1	2,465	56.8
1942	157.9	1,171	297.8	2,208	53.0
1941	124.5	934	263.7	1,977	47.2
1940	99.7	754	227.2	1,720	43.9
1939	90.5	691	209.4	1,598	43.2
1938	84.7	651	192.9	1,484	43.9
1937	90.4	701	203.2	1,576	44.5
1936	82.5	643	193.0	1,506	42.7
1935	72.2	567	169.5	1,331	42.6
1934	65.1	514	154.3	1,220	42.2
1933	55.6	442	141.5	1,126	39.3
1932	58.0	465	144.2	1,154	40.2
1931	75.8	611	169.3	1,364	44.8
1930	90.4	734	183.5	1,490	49.3
1929	103.1	847	203.6	1,671	50.6
1928	97.0	805	190.9	1,584	50.8
1927	94.9	797	189.8	1,594	50.0
1926	97.0	826	190.0	1,619	51.1
1925	93.1	804	179.4	1,549	51.9
1924	84.7	742	165.5	1,450	51.2
1923	85.1	760	165.9	1,482	51.3
1922	74.1	673	148.0	1,345	50.1
1921	69.6	641	127.8	1,177	54.5
1920	91.5	860	140.0	1,315	65.4
1919	84.0	804	146.4	1,401	57.4
1918	76.4	740	151.8	1,471	50.3
1917	60.4	585	135.2	1,310	44.7
1916	48.3	473	134.3	1,317	36.0
1915	40.0	398	124.5	1,238	32.1
1914	38.6	389	125.6	1,267	30.7
1913	39.6	407	131.4	1,351	30.1
1912	39.4	413	130.2	1,366	30.3
1911	35.8	382	123.2	1,313	29.1
1910	35.3	382	120.1	1,299	29.4
1909	33.4	369	116.8	1,290	28.6
1908	27.7	312	100.2	1,130	27.6
1907	30.4	349	109.2	1,255	27.8
1906	28.7	336	107.5	1,258	26.7
1905	25.1	299	96.3	1,149	26.1
1904	22.9	279	89.7	1,092	25.5
1903	22.9	284	90.8	1,126	25.2
1902	21.6	273	86.5	1,093	24.9
1901	20.7	267	85.7	1,105	24.1
1900	18.7	246	76.9	1,011	24.3
1899	17.4	233	74.8	1,000	23.2
1898	15.4	210	68.6	933	22.4
1897	14.6	202	67.1	930	21.8
1896	13.3	188	61.3	865	21.7
1895	13.9	200	62.6	900	22.3
1894	12.6	185	55.9	819	22.6
1893	13.8	206	57.5	859	24.1
1892	14.3	218	60.4	920	23.6
1891	13.5	210	55.1	856	24.6
1890	13.1	208	52.7	836	24.9
1889	12.5	202	49.1	795	25.4
1879–1888 [1]	11.2	205	42.4	774	26.5
1869–1878 [1]	7.4	170	23.1	531	32.1

* Denotes first year for which figures include Alaska and Hawaii.   [1] Decade average.

Series F 6–9. Net National Product, National Income, Personal Income, and Disposable Personal Income, in Current Prices: 1897 to 1970

[In billions of dollars. 5-year periods are annual averages]

Year or period	Net national product (6)	National income (7)	Personal income (8)	Disposable personal income (9)
1970	889.8	800.5	808.3	691.7
1969	848.7	766.0	750.9	634.4
1968	789.7	711.1	688.9	591.0
1967	725.0	653.6	629.3	546.3
1966	685.9	620.6	587.2	511.9
1965	625.1	564.3	538.9	473.2
1964	576.3	518.1	497.5	438.1
1963	537.9	481.9	465.5	404.6
1962	510.4	457.7	442.6	385.3
1961	474.9	427.3	416.8	364.3
1960 *	460.3	414.5	401.0	350.0
1959	442.3	400.0	383.5	337.3
1958	408.4	367.8	361.2	318.8
1957	404.0	366.1	351.1	308.5
1956	385.2	350.8	333.0	293.2
1955	366.5	331.0	310.9	275.3
1954	336.6	303.1	290.1	257.4
1953	338.9	304.7	288.2	252.6
1952	322.3	291.4	272.5	238.4
1951	307.2	278.0	255.6	226.6
1950	266.4	241.1	227.5	206.9
1949	239.9	217.5	207.2	188.6
1948	243.1	244.2	210.2	189.1
1947	219.1	199.0	191.2	169.8
1946	198.6	181.9	178.7	160.0
1945	200.7	181.5	171.1	150.2
1944	199.1	182.6	165.3	146.3
1943	181.3	170.3	151.3	133.5
1942	148.1	137.1	122.9	116.9
1941	116.3	104.2	96.0	92.7
1940	92.2	81.1	78.3	75.7
1939	83.2	72.6	72.8	70.3
1938	77.4	67.4	68.3	65.5
1937	83.3	73.7	74.1	71.2
1936	75.4	65.0	68.6	66.3
1935	65.4	57.2	60.4	58.5
1934	58.2	49.5	54.0	52.4
1933	48.6	40.3	47.0	45.5
1932	50.7	42.8	50.2	48.7
1931	68.0	59.7	65.9	64.0
1930	82.4	75.4	77.0	74.5
1929	95.2	86.8	85.9	83.3
1928	89.7	82.8	79.8	77.5
1927	88.2	81.7	79.6	77.4
1926	89.9	83.7	79.5	77.4
1925	84.0	78.2	75.0	73.0
1924	80.7	75.2	73.2	71.4
1923	79.5	74.3	71.5	69.7
1922	67.9	63.1	62.0	60.3
1921	68.1	64.0	62.1	60.2
1920	83.0	79.1	73.4	71.5
1919	73.8	70.2	65.0	63.3
1917–1921	70.3	66.9	62.5	61.0
1912–1916	36.9	34.8	33.7	33.3
1907–1911	28.9	27.2	26.7	26.4
1902–1906	22.1	20.7	20.2	20.0
1897–1901	15.8	14.6	14.3	14.1

* Denotes first year for which figures include Alaska and Hawaii.

Series F 10–16. Growth Rates (Percent) of GNP and Output per Employee for the U.S. and 6 Countries: 1870 to 1969

Period	United States	Japan	Germany	United Kingdom	France	Italy	Canada
	10	11	12	13	14	15	16
	ANNUAL GROWTH RATES OF GROSS NATIONAL PRODUCT						
1960–1969	4.5	11.1	4.7	2.8	5.8	5.6	1 5.2
1950–1960	3.2	2 8.2	8.6	2.7	4.9	3 5.6	4.0
1950–1969	3.9	2 9.7	6.8	2.7	5.3	3 5.6	1 4.5
1929–1950	2.9	.6	1.9	1.6	–	1.0	3.2
1929–1969	3.3	4.9	4.2	2.2	2.5	3.2	1 3.8
1913–1929	3.1	3.9	.4	.8	1.7	1.8	2.4
1870–1913	4 4.3	5 3.3	2.8	2.1	1.6	1.4	3.8
1870–1969	4 3.7	5 4.2	3.0	1.9	2.0	2.2	1 3.6
	ANNUAL GROWTH RATES OF OUTPUT PER EMPLOYEE						
1960–1969	2.6	9.5	4.6	2.5	5.0	6.4	1 2.2
1950–1960	2.1	6 6.7	6.0	1.9	7 5.4	7 4.5	2.1
1950–1969	2.3	6 8.3	5.3	2.2	7 5.2	7 5.6	1 2.2
1929–1950	1.7		1.2	1.1	.3	1.0	2.0
1929–1969	2.0		3.1	1.6	2.5	3.1	1 2.1
1913–1929	1.5		–.2	.4	2.0	1.5	.7
1870–1913	4 1.9		4 1.6	1.0	1.4	.8	1.7
1870–1969	4 1.9		4 1.9	1.2	1.9	1.8	1 1.7
	ANNUAL GROWTH RATES OF PER CAPITA GROSS NATIONAL PRODUCT						
1960–1969	3.2	9.9	3.7	2.1	4.7	4.7	1 3.3
1950–1960	1.4	2 7.0	7.1	2.3	3.9	3 4.8	1.3
1950–1969	2.3	2 8.6	5.4	2.2	4.3	3 4.8	1 2.2
1929–1950	1.8		.7	1.2	–.1	.3	1.8
1929–1969	2.0		2.9	1.7	2.0	2.4	1 2.0
1913–1929	1.7		–.1	.3	1.8	1.2	.7
1870–1913	4 2.2		4 1.7	1.2	1.4	.7	2.0
1870–1969	4 2.0		4 1.9	1.3	1.7	1.5	1 1.8

– Represents zero.   1 Final year is 1968.   4 Initial year is 1871.   5 Initial year is 1879.
2 Initial year is 1952.   3 Initial year is 1951.   6 Initial year is 1953.   7 Initial year is 1954.

Series F 17–30. Per Capita Income and Product for Selected Items in Current and Constant (1958) Prices: 1929 to 1970

[In dollars. Based on Bureau of the Census estimated population as of July 1, including Armed Forces abroad]

Year	Current prices							Constant (1958) prices						
	Gross national product	Personal income	Disposable personal income	Personal consumption expenditures				Gross national product	Personal income	Disposable personal income	Personal consumption expenditures			
				Total	Durable goods	Non-durable goods	Services				Total	Durable goods	Non-durable goods	Services
	17	18	19	20	21	22	23	24	25	26	27	28	29	30
1970	4,769	3,945	3,376	3,015	446	1,288	1,282	3,526	3,050	2,610	2,331	409	1,008	914
1969	4,590	3,705	3,130	2,859	448	1,213	1,198	3,580	2,999	2,534	2,315	422	993	899
1968	4,306	3,433	2,945	2,671	419	1,150	1,103	3,521	2,898	2,486	2,256	405	982	869
1967	3,995	3,167	2,749	2,476	368	1,082	1,027	3,398	2,768	2,403	2,164	367	957	840
1966	3,815	2,987	2,604	2,372	360	1,053	960	3,348	2,678	2,335	2,127	365	951	811
1965	3,525	2,773	2,436	2,228	341	983	903	3,180	2,549	2,239	2,047	343	919	785
1964	3,296	2,592	2,283	2,091	309	931	851	3,028	2,443	2,126	1,948	307	888	753
1963	3,120	2,460	2,138	1,981	285	891	805	2,912	2,318	2,015	1,867	284	857	726
1962	3,004	2,373	2,065	1,903	266	871	766	2,840	2,262	1,969	1,814	264	848	703
1961	2,831	2,269	1,984	1,825	241	849	735	2,706	2,184	1,909	1,756	239	833	684
1960*	2,788	2,219	1,937	1,800	251	837	712	2,699	2,157	1,883	1,749	248	828	673
1959	2,731	2,166	1,905	1,758	250	828	679	2,688	2,138	1,881	1,735	247	829	660
1958	2,569	2,074	1,831	1,666	218	805	643	2,569	2,074	1,831	1,666	218	805	643
1957	2,576	2,050	1,801	1,643	238	792	613	2,642	2,098	1,844	1,683	242	810	631
1956	2,492	1,980	1,743	1,585	231	768	585	2,652	2,088	1,839	1,673	244	810	619
1955	2,408	1,881	1,666	1,539	240	746	553	2,650	2,027	1,795	1,659	261	797	601
1954	2,247	1,787	1,585	1,456	202	728	526	2,506	1,932	1,714	1,575	218	773	584
1953	2,285	1,806	1,583	1,441	208	732	501	2,587	1,969	1,726	1,572	221	780	571
1952	2,201	1,736	1,518	1,381	187	726	468	2,517	1,918	1,678	1,525	196	770	559
1951	2,129	1,657	1,469	1,337	192	705	440	2,485	1,870	1,657	1,509	204	755	550
1950	1,877	1,501	1,364	1,259	201	647	412	2,342	1,810	1,646	1,520	229	752	539
1949	1,719	1,389	1,264	1,185	165	634	386	2,172	1,700	1,547	1,451	190	741	520
1948	1,757	1,434	1,290	1,184	155	656	373	2,208	1,742	1,567	1,438	179	741	517
1947	1,605	1,327	1,178	1,115	142	628	346	2,150	1,703	1,513	1,431	171	751	509
1946	1,475	1,264	1,132	1,014	111	583	320	2,211	1,793	1,606	1,439	145	784	510
1945	1,515	1,223	1,074	855	57	514	284	2,538	1,870	1,642	1,308	76	748	484
1944	1,518	1,194	1,057	782	49	465	269	2,611	1,889	1,673	1,238	68	703	467
1943	1,401	1,106	976	726	48	429	250	2,465	1,847	1,629	1,213	75	685	452
1942	1,171	911	867	656	52	376	228	2,208	1,663	1,582	1,197	87	677	434
1941	934	719	695	604	72	321	210	1,977	1,477	1,427	1,240	143	674	422
1940	754	593	573	536	59	280	197	1,720	1,303	1,259	1,178	126	640	412
1939	691	555	537	510	51	268	191	1,598	1,232	1,190	1,131	111	620	401
1938	651	526	504	492	44	261	187	1,484	1,153	1,105	1,079	94	593	392
1937	701	575	552	516	54	273	189	1,576	1,236	1,187	1,110	117	589	403
1936	643	535	518	483	49	256	177	1,506	1,198	1,158	1,080	113	573	394
1935	567	474	459	437	40	230	167	1,331	1,068	1,035	985	92	517	376
1934	514	427	414	406	33	211	162	1,220	981	952	934	74	494	364
1933	442	374	362	364	28	177	160	1,126	981	893	897	66	466	366
1932	465	401	390	389	29	182	178	1,154	949	921	919	67	483	367
1931	611	531	516	487	44	233	210	1,364	1,108	1,077	1,016	90	528	398
1930	734	625	605	567	58	276	233	1,490	1,167	1,128	1,059	105	535	418
1929	846	705	683	634	76	309	249	1,671	1,274	1,236	1,145	134	569	443

* Denotes first year for which figures include Alaska and Hawaii.

Series **F 31.** Average Annual Growth Rates of

[To find growth rate between any two years shown, locate the column for the initial year at the

Terminal year	Initial year																														
	1909	1910	1911	1912	1913	1914	1915	1916	1917	1918	1919	1920	1921	1922	1923	1924	1925	1926	1927	1928	1929	1930	1931	1932	1933	1934	1935	1936	1937	1938	1939
1910	2.8																														
1911	2.7	2.6																													
1912	3.7	4.1	5.7																												
1913	3.0	3.0	3.3	.9																											
1914	1.5	1.1	.7	-1.7	-4.3																										
1915	1.1	.7	.3	-1.4	-2.6	-.8																									
1916	2.0	1.9	1.7	.8	.7	3.4	7.9																								
1917	1.9	1.7	1.6	.8	.7	2.5	4.2	-.7																							
1918	3.0	3.0	3.0	2.6	2.9	4.9	6.8	6.3	12.3																						
1919	2.3	2.2	2.2	1.7	1.8	3.1	4.1	2.9	4.1	-3.5																					
1920	1.7	1.5	1.4	.9	.9	1.8	2.4	1.0	1.2	-3.9	-4.3																				
1921	.8	.6	.4	-.1	-.3	.3	.4	-.9	-1.3	-5.5	-6.5	-8.6																			
1922	1.8	1.8	1.7	1.3	1.3	2.1	2.5	1.6	1.8	-.5	.4	2.8	15.8																		
1923	2.5	2.5	2.5	2.2	2.4	3.1	3.7	3.1	3.5	1.8	3.2	5.8	13.9	12.1																	
1924	2.4	2.3	2.3	2.0	2.1	2.8	3.2	2.7	2.9	1.5	2.5	4.3	9.0	5.8	-.2																
1925	2.7	2.7	2.7	2.5	2.6	3.3	3.7	3.3	3.6	2.4	3.5	5.1	8.9	6.6	4.0	8.4															
1926	2.9	2.9	2.9	2.7	2.9	3.5	3.9	3.5	3.9	2.9	3.8	5.2	8.3	6.4	4.6	7.2	5.9														
1927	2.7	2.7	2.7	2.5	2.7	3.2	3.6	3.2	3.5	2.5	3.3	4.4	6.8	5.1	3.4	4.7	2.9	.0													
1928	2.6	2.6	2.6	2.4	2.5	3.0	3.3	3.0	3.2	2.3	3.0	4.0	5.9	4.3	2.9	3.6	2.1	.2	.6												
1929	2.8	2.8	2.8	2.7	2.8	3.3	3.6	3.3	3.5	2.7	3.4	4.3	6.0	4.7	3.5	4.2	3.2	2.3	3.6	6.7											
1930	2.2	2.1	2.1	1.9	2.0	2.4	2.6	2.3	2.4	1.6	2.1	2.7	4.1	2.7	1.5	1.7	.5	-.8	-1.0	-1.9	-9.8										
1931	1.7	1.7	1.6	1.4	1.4	1.8	1.9	1.6	1.6	.8	1.2	1.7	2.9	1.5	.3	.3	-.9	-2.2	-2.7	-3.8	-8.7	-7.6									
1932	.9	.8	.8	.5	.5	.9	.9	.5	.4	-.3	-.0	.3	1.1	-.2	-1.5	-1.6	-3.0	-4.4	-5.3	-6.7	-10.8	-11.3	-14.7								
1933	.8	.7	.6	.4	.4	.6	.7	.3	.3	-.4	-.1	.1	.9	-.3	-1.5	-1.6	-2.8	-4.0	-4.7	-5.7	-8.6	-8.2	-8.5	-1.8							
1934	1.1	1.1	1.0	.8	.8	1.0	1.1	.8	.8	.1	.4	.7	1.5	.4	-.6	-.6	-1.6	-2.5	-2.8	-3.4	-5.3	-4.1	-3.0	3.4	9.1						
1935	1.4	1.4	1.3	1.2	1.2	1.4	1.6	1.2	1.3	.7	.9	1.3	2.0	1.1	.2	.2	-.5	-1.2	-1.3	-1.6	-2.9	-1.5	.0	5.5	9.5	9.9					
1936	1.9	1.8	1.8	1.7	1.7	2.0	2.1	1.8	1.9	1.3	1.6	2.0	2.8	1.9	1.2	1.3	.7	.2	.2	.1	-.7	.8	2.7	7.6	10.9	11.8	13.9				
1937	2.0	2.0	1.9	1.8	1.8	2.1	2.3	2.0	2.1	1.6	1.8	2.2	2.9	2.1	1.5	1.6	1.0	.6	.7	.7	.0	1.5	3.1	7.1	9.5	9.6	9.5	5.3			
1938	1.7	1.7	1.7	1.5	1.5	1.8	1.9	1.7	1.7	1.2	1.5	1.8	2.5	1.7	1.0	1.1	.6	.1	.1	.1	-.5	.6	1.9	5.0	6.4	5.7	4.4	.0	-5.0		
1939	2.0	1.9	1.9	1.8	1.8	2.1	2.2	2.0	2.0	1.5	1.8	2.1	2.8	2.1	1.5	1.6	1.1	.8	.8	.8	.3	1.5	2.7	5.5	6.8	6.3	5.4	2.8	1.5	8.6	
1940	2.2	2.2	2.1	2.0	2.1	2.3	2.4	2.2	2.3	1.9	2.1	2.5	3.1	2.4	1.9	2.0	1.6	1.3	1.4	1.5	1.0	2.2	3.3	5.9	7.0	6.7	6.0	4.2	3.8	8.5	8.5
1941	2.6	2.6	2.6	2.5	2.5	2.8	2.9	2.7	2.8	2.4	2.7	3.1	3.7	3.1	2.6	2.8	2.4	2.2	2.4	2.5	2.2	3.4	4.5	6.9	8.1	8.0	7.6	6.4	6.7	11.0	12.2
1942	2.9	2.9	2.9	2.8	2.9	3.1	3.3	3.1	3.2	2.9	3.1	3.5	4.1	3.6	3.1	3.3	3.0	2.9	3.1	3.2	3.0	4.1	5.3	7.5	8.6	8.6	8.4	7.5	7.9	11.5	12.5
1943	3.2	3.2	3.2	3.1	3.2	3.5	3.6	3.5	3.6	3.2	3.5	3.9	4.5	4.0	3.6	3.8	3.6	3.4	3.7	3.9	3.7	4.8	5.9	8.0	9.1	9.1	9.0	8.3	8.8	11.8	12.6
1944	3.3	3.3	3.3	3.2	3.3	3.6	3.7	3.6	3.7	3.4	3.7	4.0	4.6	4.1	3.8	4.0	3.8	3.6	3.9	4.1	3.9	5.0	6.0	8.0	8.9	8.9	8.8	8.2	8.6	11.0	11.5
1945	3.1	3.2	3.2	3.1	3.2	3.4	3.6	3.4	3.5	3.2	3.5	3.8	4.4	3.9	3.5	3.7	3.5	3.4	3.5	3.7	3.5	4.5	5.4	7.2	8.0	7.9	7.7	7.0	7.2	9.1	9.2
1946	2.7	2.7	2.7	2.6	2.7	2.9	3.0	2.9	2.9	2.6	2.9	3.1	3.6	3.2	2.8	2.9	2.7	2.5	2.7	2.8	2.6	3.4	4.2	5.7	6.3	6.1	5.7	4.9	4.9	6.2	5.9
1947	2.6	2.6	2.6	2.5	2.6	2.8	2.9	2.7	2.8	2.5	2.7	3.0	3.5	3.0	2.6	2.8	2.5	2.4	2.5	2.6	2.4	3.1	3.9	5.2	5.8	5.5	5.2	4.4	4.3	5.4	5.0
1948	2.7	2.6	2.7	2.6	2.6	2.8	2.9	2.8	2.9	2.6	2.8	3.0	3.5	3.1	2.7	2.8	2.6	2.5	2.6	2.7	2.5	3.2	3.9	5.2	5.7	5.4	5.1	4.4	4.3	5.3	5.0
1949	2.6	2.6	2.6	2.5	2.5	2.8	2.9	2.7	2.8	2.5	2.7	2.9	3.4	3.0	2.6	2.7	2.5	2.4	2.5	2.6	2.4	3.0	3.7	4.9	5.3	5.1	4.7	4.1	4.0	4.8	4.5
1950	2.8	2.8	2.8	2.7	2.7	2.9	3.0	2.9	3.0	2.7	2.9	3.2	3.6	3.2	2.9	3.0	2.8	2.6	2.8	2.9	2.7	3.4	4.0	5.1	5.6	5.4	5.1	4.5	4.4	5.2	4.9
1951	2.9	2.9	2.9	2.8	2.9	3.1	3.2	3.0	3.1	2.9	3.1	3.3	3.7	3.3	3.0	3.2	3.0	2.9	3.0	3.1	2.9	3.6	4.2	5.3	5.7	5.5	5.2	4.7	4.6	5.4	5.2
1952	2.9	2.9	2.9	2.8	2.9	3.1	3.2	3.0	3.1	2.9	3.1	3.3	3.7	3.3	3.0	3.2	3.0	2.9	3.0	3.1	2.9	3.6	4.1	5.2	5.6	5.4	5.1	4.6	4.5	5.3	5.0
1953	2.9	2.9	2.9	2.9	2.9	3.1	3.2	3.1	3.2	2.9	3.1	3.3	3.7	3.3	3.1	3.2	3.0	2.9	3.0	3.1	3.0	3.6	4.1	5.1	5.5	5.3	5.1	4.6	4.5	5.2	5.0
1954	2.8	2.8	2.8	2.8	2.8	3.0	3.1	3.0	3.0	2.8	3.0	3.2	3.6	3.2	2.9	3.0	2.9	2.8	2.9	3.0	2.8	3.4	4.1	4.8	5.2	5.0	4.7	4.2	4.2	4.8	4.5
1955	2.9	2.9	2.9	2.9	2.9	3.1	3.2	3.1	3.1	2.9	3.1	3.3	3.7	3.3	3.1	3.2	3.0	2.9	3.0	3.1	3.0	3.5	4.0	5.0	5.3	5.1	4.9	4.4	4.4	4.9	4.7
1956	2.9	2.9	2.9	2.8	2.9	3.1	3.2	3.0	3.1	2.9	3.1	3.3	3.6	3.3	3.0	3.2	3.0	2.9	3.0	3.1	3.0	3.5	4.0	4.8	5.1	4.9	4.7	4.3	4.2	4.8	4.6
1957	2.9	2.9	2.9	2.8	2.9	3.0	3.1	3.0	3.1	2.8	3.0	3.2	3.6	3.2	3.0	3.1	2.9	2.8	2.9	3.0	2.9	3.4	3.9	4.7	5.0	4.8	4.6	4.1	4.1	4.6	4.4
1958	2.8	2.8	2.8	2.7	2.8	2.9	3.0	2.9	3.0	2.7	2.9	3.1	3.4	3.1	2.9	3.0	2.8	2.7	2.8	2.9	2.8	3.2	3.7	4.5	4.7	4.5	4.3	3.9	3.8	4.3	4.2
1959	2.9	2.9	2.9	2.8	2.8	3.0	3.1	3.0	3.0	2.8	3.0	3.2	3.5	3.2	3.0	3.1	2.9	2.8	2.9	3.0	2.9	3.3	3.8	4.5	4.8	4.7	4.5	4.3	3.9	4.3	4.2
1960	2.8	2.8	2.9	2.8	2.8	3.0	3.1	3.0	3.0	2.8	3.0	3.2	3.5	3.2	3.0	3.1	2.9	2.8	2.9	3.0	2.9	3.3	3.8	4.5	4.8	4.6	4.4	4.0	3.9	4.3	4.1
1961	2.8	2.8	2.8	2.8	2.8	3.0	3.1	3.0	3.0	2.8	3.0	3.1	3.5	3.2	2.9	3.0	2.9	2.8	2.9	3.0	2.9	3.3	3.7	4.5	4.7	4.5	4.3	3.9	3.9	4.2	4.1
1962	2.9	2.9	2.9	2.8	2.9	3.0	3.1	3.0	3.0	2.9	3.0	3.2	3.5	3.2	3.0	3.1	3.0	2.9	3.0	3.1	2.9	3.4	3.8	4.4	4.6	4.5	4.3	3.9	3.8	4.2	4.1
1963	2.9	2.9	2.9	2.9	2.9	3.1	3.2	3.1	3.1	2.9	3.1	3.2	3.5	3.3	3.1	3.1	3.0	2.9	3.0	3.1	3.0	3.4	3.8	4.4	4.6	4.5	4.3	4.0	3.9	4.3	4.1
1964	3.0	3.0	3.0	2.9	3.0	3.1	3.2	3.1	3.2	3.0	3.1	3.3	3.6	3.3	3.1	3.2	3.1	3.0	3.1	3.1	3.0	3.5	3.8	4.5	4.7	4.5	4.3	4.0	4.0	4.3	4.2
1965	3.0	3.0	3.0	3.0	3.0	3.4	3.4	3.2	3.3	3.0	3.2	3.4	3.7	3.4	3.2	3.3	3.1	3.1	3.2	3.2	3.1	3.5	3.9	4.5	4.7	4.6	4.4	4.1	4.1	4.4	4.3
1966	3.1	3.1	3.1	3.1	3.1	3.2	3.3	3.2	3.3	3.1	3.3	3.4	3.7	3.5	3.3	3.3	3.2	3.1	3.2	3.3	3.2	3.6	4.0	4.6	4.8	4.6	4.5	4.2	4.1	4.5	4.3
1967	3.1	3.1	3.1	3.0	3.1	3.2	3.3	3.2	3.3	3.1	3.2	3.4	3.7	3.4	3.2	3.3	3.2	3.1	3.2	3.3	3.2	3.6	4.0	4.5	4.7	4.6	4.4	4.1	4.1	4.4	4.3
1968	3.1	3.1	3.1	3.1	3.1	3.3	3.3	3.2	3.3	3.1	3.3	3.4	3.7	3.5	3.3	3.4	3.2	3.2	3.3	3.3	3.2	3.6	3.9	4.5	4.7	4.6	4.4	4.1	4.1	4.4	4.3
1969	3.1	3.1	3.1	3.1	3.1	3.2	3.3	3.2	3.3	3.1	3.3	3.4	3.7	3.4	3.3	3.3	3.2	3.2	3.3	3.3	3.2	3.6	3.9	4.5	4.6	4.5	4.4	4.1	4.1	4.4	4.3
1970	3.0	3.0	3.0	3.0	3.0	3.2	3.2	3.2	3.2	3.0	3.2	3.3	3.6	3.4	3.2	3.3	3.1	3.1	3.2	3.2	3.1	3.5	3.8	4.3	4.5	4.4	4.2	4.0	3.9	4.2	4.1

Gross National Product (Percent): 1909 to 1970

top of the table and read the figures in that column opposite the desired terminal year at the left]

1940	1941	1942	1943	1944	1945	1946	1947	1948	1949	1950	1951	1952	1953	1954	1955	1956	1957	1958	1959	1960	1961	1962	1963	1964	1965	1966	1967	1968	1969	Terminal year
																														1910
																														1911
																														1912
																														1913
																														1914
																														1915
																														1916
																														1917
																														1918
																														1919
																														1920
																														1921
																														1922
																														1923
																														1924
																														1925
																														1926
																														1927
																														1928
																														1929
																														1930
																														1931
																														1932
																														1933
																														1934
																														1935
																														1936
																														1937
																														1938
																														1939
																														1940
16.1																														1941
14.5	12.9																													1942
14.1	13.1	13.2																												1943
12.3	11.1	10.1	7.2																											1944
9.4	7.7	6.1	2.7	-1.7																										1945
5.5	3.4	1.2	-2.5	-7.0	-11.9																									1946
4.5	2.7	.8	-2.0	-5.0	-6.5	-.9																								1947
4.5	3.0	1.4	-.7	-2.7	-3.0	1.8	4.5																							1948
4.0	2.6	1.2	-.6	-2.1	-2.2	1.2	2.3	.1																						1949
4.6	3.4	2.2	.8	-.2	.0	3.3	4.7	4.8	9.6																					1950
4.9	3.8	2.9	1.6	.9	1.3	4.2	5.5	5.8	8.8	7.9																				1951
4.7	3.7	2.9	1.8	1.1	1.5	4.0	5.0	5.1	6.8	5.5	3.1																			1952
4.7	3.8	3.0	2.0	1.5	1.9	4.1	4.9	5.0	6.2	5.1	3.8	4.5																		1953
4.3	3.4	2.6	1.7	1.2	1.5	3.4	4.0	3.9	4.7	3.5	2.0	1.5	-1.3																	1954
4.5	3.7	3.0	2.2	1.8	2.1	3.8	4.4	4.4	5.2	4.3	3.4	3.5	3.0	7.6																1955
4.3	3.6	2.9	2.2	1.8	2.1	3.6	4.1	4.1	4.7	3.9	3.1	3.1	2.6	4.7	1.9															1956
4.1	3.4	2.8	2.1	1.8	2.0	3.4	3.9	3.8	4.3	3.5	2.8	2.8	2.3	3.6	1.6	1.4														1957
3.8	3.2	2.6	1.9	1.5	1.8	3.0	3.4	3.3	3.6	2.9	2.2	2.1	1.6	2.4	.7	.1	-1.1													1958
4.0	3.3	2.8	2.2	1.9	2.1	3.3	3.6	3.6	3.9	3.3	2.7	2.7	2.4	3.2	2.1	2.2	2.6	6.4												1959
3.9	3.3	2.8	2.2	1.9	2.1	3.2	3.5	3.5	3.8	3.2	2.7	2.7	2.4	3.1	2.2	2.3	2.5	4.4	2.5											1960
3.8	3.2	2.7	2.2	1.9	2.1	3.1	3.4	3.4	3.6	3.1	2.6	2.6	2.4	2.9	2.1	2.2	2.4	3.6	2.2	2.0										1961
3.9	3.4	2.9	2.4	2.2	2.4	3.4	3.6	3.6	3.9	3.4	3.0	3.0	2.8	3.4	2.8	2.9	3.2	4.3	3.6	4.2	6.6									1962
3.9	3.4	3.0	2.5	2.3	2.5	3.4	3.7	3.6	3.9	3.4	3.1	3.1	2.9	3.4	2.9	3.1	3.3	4.3	3.7	4.5	5.3	4.0								1963
4.0	3.5	3.1	2.6	2.4	2.6	3.5	3.8	3.7	4.0	3.6	3.3	3.3	3.2	3.6	3.2	3.4	3.6	4.5	4.1	4.5	5.3	4.7	5.5							1964
4.1	3.6	3.2	2.8	2.6	2.8	3.7	3.9	3.9	4.1	3.8	3.5	3.5	3.4	3.9	3.5	3.7	4.0	4.7	4.5	4.8	5.6	5.3	5.9	6.3						1965
4.2	3.7	3.4	3.0	2.8	3.0	3.8	4.0	4.0	4.3	3.9	3.7	3.6	3.6	4.0	3.8	4.0	4.3	4.9	4.7	5.1	5.8	5.6	6.1	6.4	6.5					1966
4.1	3.7	3.3	2.9	2.8	3.0	3.7	4.0	4.0	4.2	3.9	3.6	3.6	3.6	4.0	3.7	3.8	4.1	4.7	4.5	4.8	5.2	5.0	5.2	5.1	4.5	2.6				1967
4.1	3.7	3.4	3.0	2.8	3.0	3.8	4.0	4.0	4.2	3.9	3.7	3.7	3.7	4.0	3.8	3.9	4.1	4.7	4.5	4.5	5.2	4.9	5.1	5.0	4.6	3.6	4.7			1968
4.1	3.7	3.4	3.0	2.8	3.0	3.7	3.9	3.9	4.1	3.8	3.6	3.6	3.6	3.9	3.7	3.8	4.0	4.5	4.3	4.5	4.8	4.6	4.7	4.5	4.1	3.3	3.6	2.6		1969
3.9	3.5	3.2	2.9	2.7	2.9	3.5	3.7	3.7	3.9	3.6	3.4	3.4	3.3	3.6	3.4	3.5	3.6	4.1	3.8	4.0	4.2	3.9	3.9	3.6	3.1	2.3	2.2	1.1	-.6	1970

Initial year (column headings across the top). *Terminal year* (at the right).

Series F 32–46. Gross National Product—Summary in Current and Constant (1958) Prices: 1929 to 1970

[In billions of dollars]

Year	Gross national product — Total	Final sales	Change in business inventories	Goods output — Total	Durable goods	Non-durable goods	Services	Structures	Gross private product — Total	Business — Total	Nonfarm[1]	Farm	Households and institutions	Rest of world	Gross government product[1]
	32	33	34	35	36	37	38	39	40	41	42	43	44	45	46
CURRENT PRICES															
1970	977.1	972.6	4.5	471.2	183.7	287.5	410.3	95.6	862.4	827.0	797.9	29.0	30.8	4.6	114.7
1969	930.3	922.5	7.8	457.5	187.3	270.2	377.9	94.9	826.5	794.1	766.2	27.9	28.1	4.3	103.8
1968	864.2	857.1	7.1	429.5	174.5	255.0	346.6	88.1	769.3	739.0	713.9	25.2	25.5	4.7	94.9
1967	793.9	785.7	8.2	398.9	161.1	237.7	316.5	78.6	708.8	681.6	657.0	24.6	22.8	4.5	85.1
1966	749.9	735.1	14.8	383.3	156.7	226.6	289.1	77.5	673.3	648.9	624.0	24.9	20.2	4.1	76.6
1965	684.9	675.3	9.6	347.2	139.6	207.6	262.9	74.8	617.1	594.4	570.8	23.7	18.5	4.2	67.8
1964	632.4	626.6	5.8	319.4	127.0	192.4	244.2	68.8	569.4	548.2	527.6	20.6	17.3	4.0	63.0
1963	590.5	584.6	5.9	298.6	116.1	182.5	226.2	65.7	532.4	513.0	491.5	21.5	16.0	3.4	58.1
1962	560.3	554.3	6.0	284.5	109.0	175.5	213.3	62.6	505.7	487.4	466.2	21.2	15.0	3.3	54.7
1961	520.1	518.1	2.0	262.3	96.5	165.8	199.5	58.3	469.2	452.3	431.4	20.9	14.0	2.9	50.9
1960*	503.7	500.2	3.6	259.6	99.5	160.1	187.3	56.8	456.3	440.7	420.2	20.5	13.2	2.4	47.5
1959	483.7	478.9	4.8	249.1	95.6	153.6	176.2	58.3	439.4	425.0	405.3	19.6	12.2	2.2	44.3
1958	447.3	448.8	−1.5	230.8	83.6	147.2	163.4	53.1	405.2	391.7	370.9	20.8	11.4	2.0	42.1
1957	441.1	439.8	1.3	234.6	94.4	140.2	154.2	52.3	402.0	389.3	370.9	18.4	10.5	2.2	39.1
1956	419.2	414.5	4.7	225.4	90.3	135.1	143.3	51.5	382.6	370.8	352.2	18.6	9.8	2.1	36.6
1955	398.0	392.0	6.0	216.4	85.7	130.7	132.6	49.0	363.8	352.9	334.1	18.8	9.1	1.8	34.2
1954	364.8	366.4	−1.5	197.1	72.1	125.0	123.5	44.2	332.4	322.7	303.1	19.6	8.1	1.6	32.5
1953	364.6	364.1	.4	204.1	79.4	124.8	118.8	41.7	332.7	323.6	303.3	20.3	7.8	1.3	31.9
1952	345.5	342.4	3.1	195.6	74.6	121.0	110.8	39.1	314.3	305.8	283.7	22.2	7.2	1.3	31.2
1951	328.4	318.1	10.3	189.7	73.7	116.0	101.2	37.5	301.0	292.8	269.9	22.9	6.9	1.3	27.4
1950	284.8	278.0	6.8	162.4	60.4	102.0	87.0	35.4	263.9	256.3	236.3	20.0	6.4	1.2	20.9
1949	256.5	259.6	−3.1	147.5	47.8	99.7	80.8	28.3	237.0	230.1	211.4	18.8	5.9	1.0	19.4
1948	257.6	252.9	4.7	154.2	48.7	105.5	75.7	27.7	240.1	233.5	210.2	23.3	5.6	1.0	17.4
1947	231.3	231.8	−.5	139.7	46.0	93.7	70.2	21.4	214.6	208.6	188.5	20.2	5.1	.8	16.7
1946	208.5	202.1	6.4	124.9	36.9	88.0	68.0	15.6	187.7	182.7	163.9	18.8	4.5	.6	20.8
1945	211.9	213.0	−1.0	128.9	48.9	80.0	76.5	6.5	176.8	172.3	156.4	15.9	4.1	.4	35.2
1944	210.1	211.1	−1.0	132.3	57.9	74.4	71.8	6.1	177.9	173.8	158.5	15.3	3.7	.4	32.2
1943	191.6	192.2	−.6	120.4	54.2	66.2	62.5	8.7	166.0	162.4	147.2	15.3	3.2	.4	25.6
1942	157.9	156.2	1.8	93.6	35.5	58.1	50.3	14.0	142.8	139.5	126.5	13.0	2.9	.4	15.1
1941	124.5	120.1	4.5	72.5	26.8	45.6	40.3	11.8	115.1	112.2	103.3	8.9	2.5	.4	9.4
1940	99.7	97.5	2.2	56.0	16.6	39.3	35.4	8.3	91.9	89.1	82.6	6.5	2.4	.4	7.8
1939	90.5	90.1	.4	49.0	12.7	36.3	34.0	7.5	82.9	80.3	74.0	6.3	2.3	.3	7.6
1938	84.7	85.6	−.9	45.3	9.9	35.4	33.2	6.2	77.0	74.5	67.9	6.6	2.2	.3	7.7
1937	90.4	87.9	2.5	51.5	13.9	37.6	32.3	6.7	83.5	81.0	72.7	8.3	2.2	.3	6.9
1936	82.5	81.2	1.3	45.8	12.2	33.6	31.0	5.6	75.2	72.9	66.5	6.4	2.0	.3	7.3
1935	72.2	71.2	1.1	39.9	9.3	30.6	28.3	4.0	66.3	64.1	57.1	7.0	2.0	.3	5.9
1934	65.1	65.8	−.7	34.4	7.4	27.0	27.1	3.5	59.5	57.2	52.7	4.7	1.9	.4	5.6
1933	55.6	57.2	−1.6	27.0	4.9	22.1	25.7	2.9	50.9	48.9	44.3	4.6	1.8	.3	4.7
1932	58.0	60.5	−2.5	26.7	3.6	23.1	27.5	3.8	53.6	51.3	46.8	4.5	1.9	.4	4.4
1931	75.8	77.0	−1.1	37.4	7.7	29.7	31.7	6.7	71.2	68.3	62.0	6.3	2.3	.5	4.6
1930	90.4	90.7	−.4	46.9	11.4	35.5	34.2	9.2	85.8	82.4	74.8	7.7	2.7	.7	4.6
1929	103.1	101.4	1.7	56.1	17.5	38.5	35.6	11.4	98.8	95.1	85.4	9.7	2.9	.8	4.3
CONSTANT (1958) PRICES															
1970	722.5	718.5	3.9	385.4	159.0	226.4	273.3	63.8	661.7	641.1	616.4	24.8	16.6	4.0	60.7
1969	725.6	718.9	6.7	390.0	167.5	222.5	268.2	67.3	664.9	644.6	620.5	24.1	16.3	4.0	60.7
1968	706.6	700.2	6.4	379.7	160.7	219.0	259.7	67.2	647.0	626.5	603.1	23.4	16.0	4.5	59.7
1967	675.2	667.5	7.7	363.1	152.2	210.9	249.1	63.0	617.5	597.8	573.9	23.9	15.4	4.3	57.6
1966	658.1	644.2	13.9	356.6	151.8	205.1	236.3	65.0	603.5	584.9	562.5	22.4	14.6	3.9	54.6
1965	617.8	608.8	9.0	330.7	136.5	194.2	221.9	65.2	567.0	548.9	525.2	23.7	14.0	4.1	50.8
1964	581.1	575.2	5.8	308.6	124.6	184.1	210.8	61.6	532.0	514.4	492.1	22.3	13.7	3.9	49.1
1963	551.0	545.2	5.8	289.7	114.2	175.6	200.9	60.4	503.2	486.6	463.8	22.8	13.2	3.4	47.8
1962	529.8	523.8	6.0	277.3	107.0	170.3	193.7	58.8	482.9	466.7	444.6	22.1	12.9	3.4	46.9
1961	497.2	495.2	2.0	257.3	94.9	162.3	184.0	55.8	452.3	436.9	414.8	22.2	12.4	2.9	44.8
1960*	487.7	484.2	3.5	256.0	97.8	158.2	176.6	55.0	444.0	429.5	407.6	21.9	12.2	2.3	43.7
1959	475.9	471.1	4.8	247.7	94.0	153.7	171.2	57.0	433.4	419.4	398.8	21.1	11.7	2.2	42.5
1958	447.3	448.8	−1.5	230.8	83.6	147.2	163.4	53.1	405.2	391.7	370.9	20.8	11.4	2.0	42.1
1957	452.5	451.2	1.2	239.8	96.2	143.6	160.1	52.6	410.5	397.5	377.2	20.3	10.9	2.0	42.1
1956	446.1	441.2	4.8	239.0	96.5	142.5	153.0	54.0	404.8	392.2	371.4	20.8	10.6	2.1	41.3
1955	438.0	431.6	6.4	236.1	96.5	139.7	147.5	54.3	397.2	385.4	364.4	20.9	10.1	2.0	40.7
1954	407.0	409.0	−2.0	215.1	81.9	133.2	141.8	50.2	366.2	355.4	335.0	20.4	9.2	1.6	40.9
1953	412.8	411.8	.9	225.4	91.0	134.4	140.3	47.0	371.1	360.7	340.7	20.0	9.1	1.3	41.7
1952	395.1	391.8	3.3	214.0	84.6	129.4	136.3	44.7	353.2	343.2	324.2	19.0	8.8	1.2	41.8
1951	383.4	372.5	10.9	208.4	84.1	124.3	130.5	44.4	344.6	334.5	316.2	18.4	8.8	1.2	38.8
1950	355.3	347.0	8.3	192.6	73.4	119.1	117.5	45.2	324.2	314.2	294.9	19.4	8.7	1.3	31.1
1949	324.1	328.0	−3.9	174.2	58.0	116.2	112.4	37.5	294.1	284.7	266.2	18.4	8.2	1.2	30.1
1948	323.7	319.1	4.6	178.4	61.3	117.1	109.3	36.1	295.0	286.0	267.0	19.0	7.9	1.2	28.7
1947	309.9	310.1	−.2	172.2	60.1	112.2	106.5	31.2	281.4	272.8	255.8	17.0	7.5	1.1	28.6
1946	312.6	302.6	10.0	172.1	54.7	117.4	113.3	27.2	275.1	267.0	248.6	18.5	7.1	.9	37.5
1945	355.2	358.2	−2.9	198.0	84.3	113.7	144.3	12.9	282.5	274.6	256.5	18.1	7.1	.8	72.8
1944	361.3	363.2	−1.9	204.8	95.9	108.8	144.0	12.4	286.9	278.9	259.5	19.4	7.1	.8	74.4
1943	337.1	337.3	−.2	187.4	85.6	101.7	131.8	17.9	272.8	264.9	245.3	19.6	7.2	.8	64.3
1942	297.8	293.8	4.0	158.1	57.2	100.9	107.7	31.9	257.3	248.7	228.0	20.6	7.8	.8	40.5
1941	263.7	254.1	9.6	143.4	50.0	93.4	89.8	30.5	236.6	228.1	209.3	18.8	7.5	.9	27.2
1940	227.2	222.3	4.9	124.0	35.6	88.4	80.0	23.2	205.6	197.1	179.6	17.5	7.6	1.0	21.6
1939	209.4	208.2	1.2	110.7	27.6	83.0	76.9	21.8	188.7	180.7	162.5	18.2	7.1	.9	20.6
1938	192.9	195.3	−2.4	100.5	21.1	79.4	74.8	17.7	172.6	164.6	146.8	17.8	6.8	1.1	20.4
1937	203.2	197.8	5.5	110.2	31.0	79.2	73.9	19.1	184.3	176.4	158.5	17.9	7.1	.8	18.9
1936	193.0	189.9	3.1	102.2	28.7	73.5	73.3	17.5	173.1	165.4	150.5	14.9	6.8	1.0	19.9
1935	169.5	167.1	2.4	88.6	21.5	67.1	68.1	12.8	152.4	144.9	128.4	16.5	6.4	1.1	17.1
1934	154.3	157.0	−2.7	77.9	16.9	61.0	65.3	11.1	138.3	131.1	116.6	14.6	6.2	1.0	16.0
1933	141.5	145.9	−4.3	68.8	11.7	57.1	63.0	9.8	127.5	120.6	103.0	17.5	5.7	1.2	14.0
1932	144.2	150.5	−6.2	68.7	8.3	60.4	61.9	13.7	131.0	123.8	105.8	18.0	6.0	1.3	13.2
1931	169.3	171.7	−2.4	83.2	16.3	67.0	65.8	20.2	155.8	147.7	129.2	18.5	6.6	1.4	13.3
1930	183.5	184.1	−.6	90.5	22.4	68.0	67.7	25.3	170.1	161.4	145.4	16.1	7.1	1.6	13.3
1929	203.6	200.1	3.5	103.9	33.6	70.4	69.3	30.3	190.9	182.1	165.1	17.0	7.4	1.4	12.7

* Denotes first year for which figures include Alaska and Hawaii.

[1] GNP originating in government enterprises (e.g., the Tennessee Valley Authority) is included in the nonfarm business sector.

Series F 47–70. Gross National Product, by Type of Expenditure, in Current and Constant (1958) Prices: 1929 to 1970

[In millions of dollars]

Year	Gross national product	Personal consumption expenditures				Gross private domestic investment							
		Total	Durable goods	Nondurable goods	Services	Total	Fixed investment						
							Total	Nonresidential			Residential structures		
								Total	Structures	Producers' durable equipment	Total	Nonfarm	Farm
	47	48	49	50	51	52	53	54	55	56	57	58	59
					CURRENT PRICES								
1970	977.1	617.6	91.3	263.8	262.6	136.3	131.7	100.6	36.1	64.4	31.2	30.7	0.5
1969	930.3	579.5	90.8	245.9	242.7	139.0	131.1	98.5	34.2	64.3	32.6	32.0	.6
1968	864.2	536.2	84.0	230.8	221.3	126.0	118.9	88.8	30.3	58.5	30.1	29.5	.5
1967	793.9	492.1	73.1	215.0	204.0	116.6	108.4	83.3	28.0	55.3	25.1	24.5	.6
1966	749.9	466.3	70.8	206.9	188.6	121.4	106.6	81.6	28.5	53.1	25.0	24.5	.5
1965	684.9	432.8	66.3	191.1	175.5	108.1	98.5	71.3	25.5	45.8	27.2	26.7	.5
1964	632.4	401.2	59.2	178.7	163.3	94.0	88.2	61.1	21.2	39.9	27.1	26.6	.5
1963	590.5	375.0	53.9	168.6	152.4	87.1	81.3	54.3	19.5	34.8	27.0	26.4	.6
1962	560.3	355.1	49.5	162.6	143.0	83.0	77.0	51.7	19.2	32.5	25.3	24.8	.6
1961	520.1	335.2	44.2	155.9	135.1	71.7	69.7	47.0	18.4	28.6	22.6	22.0	.6
1960*	503.7	325.2	45.3	151.3	128.7	74.8	71.3	48.4	18.1	30.3	22.8	22.2	.6
1959	483.7	311.2	44.3	146.6	120.3	75.3	70.5	45.1	16.7	28.4	25.5	24.8	.6
1958	447.3	290.1	37.9	140.2	112.0	60.9	62.4	41.6	16.6	25.0	20.8	20.1	.6
1957	441.1	281.4	40.8	135.6	105.0	67.9	66.5	46.4	18.0	28.4	20.2	19.5	.6
1956	419.2	266.7	38.9	129.3	98.5	70.0	65.3	43.7	17.2	26.5	21.6	20.9	.7
1955	398.0	254.4	39.6	123.3	91.4	67.4	61.4	38.1	14.3	23.8	23.3	22.7	.6
1954	364.8	236.5	32.8	118.3	85.4	51.7	53.3	33.6	13.1	20.6	19.7	19.0	.7
1953	364.6	230.0	33.2	116.8	79.9	52.6	52.1	34.2	12.7	21.5	18.0	17.2	.8
1952	345.5	216.7	29.3	114.0	73.4	51.9	48.8	31.6	11.4	20.2	17.2	16.4	.8
1951	328.4	206.3	29.6	108.8	67.9	59.3	49.0	31.8	11.2	20.7	17.2	16.4	.8
1950	284.8	191.0	30.5	98.1	62.4	54.1	47.3	27.9	9.2	18.7	19.4	18.6	.8
1949	256.5	176.8	24.6	94.5	57.6	35.7	38.8	25.1	8.5	16.6	13.7	12.8	.9
1948	257.6	173.6	22.7	96.2	54.7	46.0	41.3	26.9	8.8	18.1	14.4	13.6	.9
1947	231.3	160.7	20.4	90.5	49.8	34.0	34.4	23.4	7.5	15.9	11.1	10.4	.7
1946	208.5	143.4	15.8	82.4	45.3	30.6	24.2	17.0	6.8	10.2	7.2	6.7	.5
1945	211.9	119.7	8.0	71.9	39.8	10.6	11.6	10.1	2.8	7.3	1.5	1.4	.1
1944	210.1	108.3	6.7	64.3	37.2	7.1	8.1	6.8	1.8	5.0	1.3	1.1	.1
1943	191.6	99.3	6.6	58.6	34.2	5.7	6.4	5.0	1.3	3.7	1.4	1.2	.2
1942	157.9	88.5	6.9	50.8	30.8	9.8	8.1	6.0	1.9	4.1	2.1	1.9	.2
1941	124.5	80.6	9.6	42.9	28.1	17.9	13.4	9.5	2.9	6.6	3.9	3.7	.2
1940	99.7	70.8	7.8	37.0	26.0	13.1	11.0	7.5	2.3	5.3	3.4	3.2	.2
1939	90.5	66.8	6.7	35.1	25.0	9.3	8.9	5.9	2.0	4.0	2.9	2.8	.1
1938	84.7	63.9	5.7	34.0	24.3	6.5	7.4	5.4	1.9	3.5	2.0	1.9	.1
1937	90.4	66.5	6.9	35.2	24.4	11.8	9.2	7.3	2.4	4.9	1.9	1.8	.1
1936	82.5	61.9	6.3	32.9	22.8	8.5	7.2	5.6	1.6	4.0	1.6	1.5	.1
1935	72.2	55.7	5.1	29.3	21.3	6.4	5.3	4.1	1.2	2.9	1.2	1.1	.1
1934	65.1	51.3	4.2	26.7	20.4	3.3	4.1	3.2	1.1	2.2	.9	.8	(Z)
1933	55.6	45.8	3.5	22.3	20.1	1.4	3.0	2.4	.9	1.5	.6	.5	(Z)
1932	58.0	48.6	3.6	22.7	22.2	1.0	3.4	2.7	1.2	1.5	.7	.7	.1
1931	75.8	60.5	5.5	29.0	26.0	5.6	6.8	5.0	2.3	2.7	1.7	1.6	.1
1930	90.4	69.9	7.2	34.0	28.7	10.1	10.6	8.3	4.0	4.3	2.3	2.2	.1
1929	103.1	77.2	9.2	37.7	30.3	16.2	14.5	10.6	5.0	5.6	4.0	3.8	.2
					CONSTANT (1958) PRICES								
1970	722.5	477.5	83.8	206.5	187.2	103.4	99.5	77.2	23.7	53.5	22.2	21.9	0.4
1969	725.6	469.1	85.6	201.3	182.2	110.5	103.8	80.1	24.3	55.8	23.7	23.2	.5
1968	706.6	452.7	81.3	197.1	174.4	105.2	98.8	75.6	23.4	52.2	23.2	22.8	.4
1967	675.2	430.1	72.9	190.2	167.0	101.2	93.5	73.2	22.6	50.6	20.4	19.9	.5
1966	658.1	418.1	71.7	187.0	159.4	109.3	95.4	74.1	24.0	50.1	21.3	20.9	.5
1965	617.8	397.7	66.6	178.6	152.5	99.2	90.1	66.3	22.3	44.0	23.8	23.4	.5
1964	581.1	373.7	59.0	170.3	144.4	87.8	81.9	57.8	19.1	38.7	24.2	23.7	.5
1963	551.0	353.3	53.7	162.2	137.4	82.5	76.7	51.9	17.9	34.0	24.8	24.2	.5
1962	529.8	338.4	49.2	158.2	131.1	79.4	73.4	49.7	17.9	31.7	23.8	23.2	.6
1961	497.2	322.5	43.9	153.0	125.6	69.0	67.0	45.5	17.4	28.1	21.6	21.0	.6
1960*	487.7	316.1	44.9	149.6	121.6	72.4	68.9	47.1	17.4	29.6	21.9	21.3	.6
1959	475.9	307.3	43.7	146.8	116.8	73.6	68.8	44.1	16.2	27.9	24.7	24.1	.6
1958	447.3	290.1	37.9	140.2	112.0	60.9	62.4	41.6	16.6	25.0	20.8	20.1	.7
1957	452.5	288.2	41.5	138.7	108.0	68.8	67.6	47.4	18.2	29.1	20.2	19.5	.7
1956	446.1	281.4	41.0	136.2	104.1	74.3	69.5	47.3	18.5	28.8	22.2	21.5	.7
1955	438.0	274.2	43.2	131.7	99.3	75.4	69.0	43.9	16.2	27.7	25.1	24.4	.7
1954	407.0	255.7	35.4	125.5	94.8	59.4	61.4	39.6	15.2	24.5	21.7	21.0	.8
1953	412.8	250.8	35.3	124.4	91.1	61.2	60.2	40.7	14.9	25.8	19.6	18.8	.8
1952	395.1	239.4	30.8	120.8	87.8	60.5	57.2	38.3	13.7	24.6	18.9	18.1	.9
1951	383.4	232.8	31.5	116.5	84.8	70.0	59.0	39.6	14.1	25.5	19.5	18.6	.9
1950	355.3	230.5	34.7	114.0	81.8	69.3	61.0	37.5	12.7	24.8	23.5	22.6	.9
1949	324.1	216.5	28.4	110.5	77.6	48.0	51.9	34.5	11.9	22.6	17.4	16.4	1.0
1948	323.7	210.8	26.3	108.7	75.8	60.4	55.9	38.0	12.3	25.7	17.9	16.9	1.0
1947	309.9	206.3	24.7	108.3	73.4	51.5	51.7	36.2	11.6	24.6	15.4	14.5	.9
1946	312.6	203.5	20.5	110.8	72.1	52.3	42.3	30.2	12.5	17.7	12.1	11.3	.8
1945	355.2	183.0	10.6	104.7	67.7	19.6	22.6	19.8	5.7	14.1	2.8	2.5	.2
1944	361.3	171.4	9.4	97.3	64.7	14.0	15.9	13.4	3.8	9.6	2.5	2.2	.3
1943	337.1	165.8	10.2	93.7	61.8	12.7	12.9	10.0	2.9	7.2	2.9	2.6	.3
1942	297.8	161.4	11.7	91.3	58.5	21.4	17.3	12.5	4.6	7.9	4.9	4.5	.4
1941	263.7	165.4	19.1	89.9	56.3	41.6	32.0	22.2	8.1	14.2	9.8	9.1	.6
1940	227.2	155.7	16.7	84.6	54.4	33.0	28.1	18.9	6.8	12.1	9.2	8.6	.6
1939	209.4	148.2	14.5	81.2	52.5	24.7	23.5	15.3	5.9	9.4	8.2	7.8	.4
1938	192.9	140.2	12.2	77.1	50.9	17.0	19.4	13.7	5.6	8.1	5.7	5.4	.3
1937	203.2	143.1	15.1	76.0	52.0	29.9	24.5	18.8	7.1	11.8	5.6	5.3	.4
1936	193.0	138.4	14.5	73.4	50.5	24.0	20.9	15.8	5.4	10.3	5.1	4.8	.3
1935	169.5	125.5	11.7	65.9	47.9	18.0	15.6	11.5	4.0	7.5	4.0	3.8	.3
1934	154.3	118.1	9.4	62.5	46.1	9.4	12.1	9.2	3.6	5.6	2.9	2.7	.2
1933	141.5	112.8	8.3	58.6	46.0	5.3	9.7	7.6	3.3	4.3	2.1	1.9	.2
1932	144.2	114.8	8.4	60.4	45.9	4.7	10.9	8.2	4.4	3.8	2.7	2.5	.1
1931	169.3	126.1	11.2	65.6	49.4	16.8	19.2	14.1	7.5	6.6	5.1	4.9	.2
1930	183.5	130.4	12.9	65.9	51.5	27.4	28.0	21.7	11.8	9.9	6.3	6.0	.3
1929	203.6	139.6	16.3	69.3	54.0	40.4	36.9	26.5	13.9	12.6	10.4	9.9	.4

* Denotes first year for which figures include Alaska and Hawaii.   Z   Less than $50 million.

Series F 47–70. Gross National Product, by Type of Expenditure, in Current and Constant (1958) Prices: 1929 to 1970—Con.

[In billions of dollars]

Year	Gross private domestic investment—Con. Net change in business inventories			Net exports of goods and services			Government purchases of goods and services				
	Total	Nonfarm	Farm	Total	Exports	Imports	Total	Federal Total	Federal National defense	Federal Other	State and local
	60	61	62	63	64	65	66	67	68	69	70
CURRENT PRICES											
1970	4.5	4.3	0.2	3.6	62.9	59.3	219.5	96.2	74.6	21.6	123.3
1969	7.8	7.7	.1	2.0	55.5	53.6	210.0	98.8	78.4	20.4	111.2
1968	7.1	6.9	.1	2.5	50.6	48.1	199.6	98.8	78.3	20.5	100.8
1967	8.2	7.5	.7	5.2	46.2	41.0	180.1	90.7	72.4	18.4	89.4
1966	14.8	15.0	-.2	5.3	43.4	38.1	156.8	77.8	60.7	17.1	79.0
1965	9.6	8.6	1.0	6.9	39.2	32.3	137.0	66.9	50.1	16.8	70.1
1964	5.8	6.4	-.6	8.5	37.1	28.6	128.7	65.2	50.0	15.2	63.5
1963	5.9	5.1	.8	5.9	32.3	26.4	122.5	64.2	50.8	13.5	58.2
1962	6.0	5.3	.7	5.1	30.3	25.1	117.1	63.4	51.6	11.8	53.7
1961	2.0	1.7	.3	5.6	28.6	23.0	107.6	57.4	47.8	9.6	50.2
1960*	3.6	3.3	.2	4.0	27.2	23.2	99.6	53.5	44.9	8.6	46.1
1959	4.8	4.8	(Z)	.1	23.5	23.3	97.0	53.7	46.0	7.6	43.3
1958	-1.5	-2.3	.8	2.2	23.1	20.9	94.2	53.6	45.9	7.7	40.6
1957	1.3	.8	.5	5.7	26.5	20.8	86.1	49.5	44.2	5.3	36.6
1956	4.7	5.1	-.4	4.0	23.6	19.6	78.6	45.6	40.3	5.3	33.0
1955	6.0	5.5	.5	2.0	19.8	17.8	74.2	44.1	38.6	5.5	30.1
1954	-1.5	-2.1	.6	1.8	17.8	15.9	74.8	47.4	41.2	6.2	27.4
1953	.4	1.1	-.6	.4	16.9	16.6	81.6	57.0	48.7	8.4	24.6
1952	3.1	2.1	1.0	2.2	18.0	15.8	74.7	51.8	45.9	5.9	22.9
1951	10.3	9.1	1.2	3.7	18.7	15.1	59.1	37.7	33.6	4.1	21.5
1950	6.8	6.0	.8	1.8	13.8	12.0	37.9	18.4	14.1	4.3	19.5
1949	-3.1	-2.2	-.9	6.1	15.8	9.6	37.8	20.1	13.3	6.8	17.7
1948	4.7	3.0	1.7	6.4	16.8	10.3	31.6	16.5	10.7	5.8	15.0
1947	-.5	1.3	-1.8	11.5	19.7	8.2	25.1	12.5	9.1	3.5	12.6
1946	6.4	6.4	(Z)	7.5	14.7	7.2	27.0	17.2	14.7	2.5	9.8
1945	-1.0	-.6	-.4	-.6	7.2	7.9	82.3	74.2	73.5	.7	8.1
1944	-1.0	-.6	-.4	-1.8	5.3	7.1	96.5	89.0	87.4	1.6	7.5
1943	-.6	-.6	-.1	-2.0	4.4	6.5	88.6	81.1	79.7	1.4	7.4
1942	1.8	.7	1.1	(Z)	4.8	4.8	59.6	51.9	49.4	2.5	7.7
1941	4.5	4.0	.4	1.3	5.9	4.6	24.8	16.9	13.8	3.1	7.9
1940	2.2	1.9	.3	1.7	5.4	3.6	14.0	6.0	2.2	3.8	8.0
1939	.4	.3	.1	1.1	4.4	3.4	13.3	5.1	1.2	3.9	8.2
1938	-.9	-1.0	.1	1.3	4.3	3.0	13.0	5.4	------	------	7.6
1937	2.5	1.7	.8	.3	4.6	4.3	11.9	4.7	------	------	7.2
1936	1.3	2.1	-.8	.1	3.5	3.4	12.0	4.9	------	------	7.0
1935	1.1	.4	.7	.1	3.3	3.1	10.0	2.9	------	------	7.1
1934	-.7	.2	-.9	.6	3.0	2.4	9.8	3.0	------	------	6.8
1933	-1.6	-1.4	-.2	.4	2.4	2.0	8.0	2.0	------	------	6.0
1932	-2.5	-2.6	.1	.4	2.5	2.1	8.1	1.5	------	------	6.6
1931	-1.1	-1.6	.5	.5	3.6	3.1	9.2	1.5	------	------	7.7
1930	-.4	-.1	-.3	1.0	5.4	4.4	9.2	1.4	------	------	7.8
1929	1.7	1.8	-.1	1.1	7.0	5.9	8.5	1.3	------	------	7.2
CONSTANT (1958) PRICES											
1970	3.9	3.7	0.1	2.3	52.2	50.0	139.3	64.3	------	------	75.0
1969	6.7	6.7	.0	.2	48.4	48.3	145.9	73.5	------	------	72.4
1968	6.4	6.3	.1	1.0	45.7	44.7	147.7	78.1	------	------	69.6
1967	7.7	7.0	.7	3.6	42.1	38.5	140.2	74.7	------	------	65.5
1966	13.9	14.1	-.2	4.2	40.2	36.1	126.5	65.4	------	------	61.1
1965	9.0	8.1	.9	6.2	37.4	31.2	114.7	57.9	------	------	56.8
1964	5.8	6.4	-.6	8.3	36.5	28.2	111.2	58.1	------	------	53.2
1963	5.8	5.1	.8	5.6	32.1	26.6	109.6	59.5	------	------	50.1
1962	6.0	5.2	.7	4.5	30.0	25.5	107.5	60.0	------	------	47.5
1961	2.0	1.8	.2	5.1	28.0	22.9	100.5	54.6	------	------	45.9
1960*	3.5	3.2	.2	4.3	27.3	23.0	94.9	51.4	------	------	43.5
1959	4.8	4.8	(Z)	.3	23.8	23.5	94.7	52.5	------	------	42.2
1958	-1.5	-2.3	.8	2.2	23.1	20.9	94.2	53.6	------	------	40.6
1957	1.2	.7	.5	6.2	26.2	19.9	89.3	51.7	------	------	37.6
1956	4.8	5.4	-.6	5.0	24.2	19.1	85.3	49.7	------	------	35.6
1955	6.4	6.0	.4	3.2	20.9	17.7	85.2	50.7	------	------	34.4
1954	-2.0	-2.6	.5	3.0	18.8	15.8	88.9	56.8	------	------	32.1
1953	.9	1.4	-.4	1.1	17.8	16.7	99.8	70.0	------	------	29.7
1952	3.3	2.5	.7	3.0	18.2	15.2	92.1	63.8	------	------	28.4
1951	10.9	9.9	1.0	5.3	19.3	14.1	75.4	47.4	------	------	27.9
1950	8.3	7.5	.8	2.7	16.3	13.6	52.8	25.3	------	------	27.5
1949	-3.9	-3.2	-.8	6.4	18.1	11.7	53.3	27.6	------	------	25.7
1948	4.6	3.6	1.0	6.1	18.1	12.0	46.3	23.7	------	------	22.7
1947	-.2	1.4	-1.6	12.3	22.6	10.3	39.9	19.1	------	------	20.8
1946	10.0	10.2	-.2	8.4	19.6	11.2	48.4	30.1	------	------	18.4
1945	-2.9	-2.1	-.9	-3.8	10.2	13.9	156.4	139.7	------	------	16.7
1944	-1.9	-1.4	-.5	-5.8	7.6	13.4	181.7	165.4	------	------	16.3
1943	-.2	-.4	.2	-5.9	6.8	12.6	164.4	147.8	------	------	16.6
1942	4.0	2.1	2.0	-2.1	7.8	9.9	117.1	98.9	------	------	18.3
1941	9.6	8.6	1.1	.4	11.2	10.8	56.3	36.2	------	------	20.1
1940	4.9	4.2	.7	2.1	11.0	8.9	36.4	15.0	------	------	21.4
1939	1.2	.7	.5	1.3	10.0	8.7	35.2	12.5	------	------	22.7
1938	-2.4	-2.6	.2	1.9	9.9	8.0	33.9	13.3	------	------	20.6
1937	5.5	3.7	1.8	-.7	9.8	10.5	30.8	11.5	------	------	19.4
1936	3.1	4.7	-1.6	-1.2	8.2	9.3	31.8	12.2	------	------	19.6
1935	2.4	1.0	1.4	-1.0	7.7	8.7	27.0	7.9	------	------	19.2
1934	-2.7	.3	-3.0	.3	7.3	7.1	26.6	8.0	------	------	18.6
1933	-4.3	-3.8	-.5	(Z)	7.1	7.1	23.3	6.0	------	------	17.3
1932	-6.2	-7.0	.8	.6	7.1	6.6	24.2	4.6	------	------	19.6
1931	-2.4	-3.9	1.5	.9	8.9	7.9	25.4	4.3	------	------	21.1
1930	-.6	-.4	-.2	1.4	10.4	9.0	24.3	4.0	------	------	20.2
1929	3.5	3.6	(Z)	1.5	11.8	10.3	22.0	3.5	------	------	18.5

* Denotes first year for which figures include Alaska and Hawaii.　　Z Less than $50 million.

Series F 71–97. Gross and Net National Product, by Major Type of Product, in Current Prices: 1869 to 1931

[In billions of dollars. 5-year periods are annual averages]

Period	Gross national product	Net national product	Flow of goods to consumers						Private and public capital formation						
			Total	Commodities			Services		Total		Gross construction				
				Perishable	Semi-durable	Durable			Gross	Net	Total	Private		Public	
												Nonfarm residential	Other	Nonwar	War
	71	72	73	74	75	76	77		78	79	80	81	82	83	84
1927–1931	89.9	79.4	73.0	25.1	9.46	7.76	30.7		16.8	6.35	10.3	3.22	4.46	2.56	0.02
1922–1926	84.8	75.1	66.8	23.3	9.31	7.56	26.7		18.0	8.30	10.6	4.50	4.21	1.88	.01
1917–1921	71.6	62.6	54.9	22.9	8.33	5.15	18.5		16.7	7.68	5.85	1.19	2.98	.99	.69
1912–1916	38.9	34.6	30.8	12.5	3.93	2.72	11.7		8.05	3.80	4.17	1.26	2.27	.64	.01
1907–1911	30.4	27.2	24.1	10.0	3.20	1.97	8.90		6.35	3.15	4.25	1.19	2.56	.50	--------
1902–1906	23.5	21.2	18.2	7.68	2.49	1.52	6.53		5.29	2.96	3.29	.93	2.05	.31	--------
1897–1901	16.8	15.0	12.9	5.60	1.79	1.03	4.44		3.89	2.13	2.26	.65	1.43	.18	--------
1892–1896	13.1	11.8	10.1	4.44	1.48	.84	3.38		3.01	1.63	2.21	.72	1.35	.14	--------
1887–1891	12.3	11.0	9.58	4.09	1.54	.87	3.08		2.69	1.44	1.91	.81	.98	.12	--------
1882–1886	11.3	10.3	9.10	4.09	1.41	.74	2.85		2.21	1.23	1.40	.57	.74	.10	--------
1877–1881	9.18	8.48	7.33	3.24	1.20	.56	2.33		1.86	1.16	.91	.31	.52	.07	--------
1872–1876	7.53	6.92	5.94	2.58	1.05	.53	1.78		1.59	.97	.90	.25	.59	.07	--------
1869–1873	6.71	6.20	5.38	2.29	1.01	.50	1.59		1.34	.82	.77	.22	.50	.06	--------

Private and public capital formation—Con.

Period	Gross producers' durables			Net construction					Net producers' durables			Net change in—	
	Total	Nonwar	War	Total	Private		Public		Total	Nonwar	War	Inventories	Claims against foreign countries
					Nonfarm residential	Other	Nonwar	War					
	85	86	87	88	89	90	91	92	93	94	95	96	97
1927–1931	5.85	5.68	0.17	3.69	1.59	0.72	1.56	-0.17	1.94	1.96	-0.02	0.04	0.68
1922–1926	5.54	5.44	.10	4.95	3.16	.90	1.08	-.19	1.49	1.99	-.50	1.21	.65
1917–1921	5.57	4.53	1.04	.88	.09	-.14	.38	.55	1.50	.93	.57	2.54	2.75
1912–1916	2.28	--------	--------	1.71	.64	.69	.37	.01	.49	--------	--------	.67	.93
1907–1911	1.62	--------	--------	2.28	.66	1.31	.32	--------	.39	--------	--------	.46	.02
1902–1906	1.36	--------	--------	1.81	.56	1.07	.18	--------	.50	--------	--------	.47	.17
1897–1901	.84	--------	--------	1.14	.36	.69	.10	--------	.20	--------	--------	.47	.31
1892–1896	.60	--------	--------	1.31	.50	.74	.07	--------	.13	--------	--------	.22	-.03
1887–1891	.64	--------	--------	1.10	.63	.40	.06	--------	.20	--------	--------	.24	-.10
1882–1886	.53	--------	--------	.78	.45	.28	.05	--------	.18	--------	--------	.33	-.06
1877–1881	.45	--------	--------	.46	.23	.20	.03	--------	.19	--------	--------	.44	-.06
1872–1876	.41	--------	--------	.54	.18	.33	.03	--------	.16	--------	--------	.39	-.11
1869–1873	.39	--------	--------	.46	.16	.28	.02	--------	.18	--------	--------	.35	-.18

Series F 98–124. Gross and Net National Product, by Major Type of Product, in 1929 Prices: 1869 to 1931

[In billions of dollars. 5-year periods are annual averages]

Period	Gross national product	Net national product	Flow of goods to consumers						Private and public capital formation						
			Total	Commodities			Services		Total		Gross construction				
				Perishable	Semi-durable	Durable			Gross	Net	Total	Private		Public	
												Nonfarm residential	Other	Nonwar	War
	98	99	100	101	102	103	104		105	106	107	108	109	110	111
1927–1931	93.4	82.6	76.0	26.6	9.77	8.18	31.5		17.4	6.58	10.6	3.34	4.57	2.66	0.02
1922–1926	84.4	74.6	66.4	24.1	8.40	7.55	26.3		18.0	8.19	10.8	4.70	4.34	1.75	.01
1917–1921	67.7	59.0	52.4	20.0	6.44	4.85	21.1		15.2	6.58	6.0	1.31	2.99	.92	.74
1912–1916	59.7	52.6	46.6	18.5	6.72	4.33	17.0		13.1	6.05	7.4	2.34	3.92	1.12	.02
1907–1911	52.5	46.6	40.9	16.5	5.79	3.74	14.9		11.7	5.71	8.0	2.30	4.73	.95	--------
1902–1906	45.0	40.2	34.3	14.1	5.02	3.27	11.8		10.8	5.94	7.0	2.10	4.21	.65	--------
1897–1901	35.4	31.4	26.7	11.4	3.96	2.62	8.7		8.7	4.73	5.5	1.72	3.30	.54	--------
1892–1896	28.3	24.9	20.9	9.0	3.21	2.11	6.6		7.4	3.98	5.5	2.02	3.14	.34	--------
1887–1891	24.0	21.3	18.1	7.5	2.92	1.95	5.7		5.9	3.24	4.4	2.09	2.01	.27	--------
1882–1886	20.7	18.7	16.2	7.1	2.49	1.50	5.1		4.5	2.52	3.1	1.41	1.47	.21	--------
1877–1881	16.1	14.6	12.4	5.4	1.96	1.07	4.0		3.7	2.23	2.1	.82	1.14	.16	--------
1872–1876	11.2	10.1	8.5	3.5	1.37	.77	2.9		2.6	1.62	1.8	.55	1.13	.13	--------
1869–1873	9.1	8.3	7.0	2.8	1.22	.64	2.4		2.1	1.30	1.5	.47	.92	.11	--------

Series F 98–124.   Gross and Net National Product, by Major Type of Product, in 1929 Prices: 1869 to 1931—Con.

[In billions of dollars.   5-year periods are annual averages]

	Private and public capital formation—Con.												
	Gross producers' durables			Net construction					Net producers' durables			Net change in—	
Period	Total	Nonwar	War	Total	Private		Public		Total	Nonwar	War	Inventories	Claims against foreign countries
					Nonfarm resi- dential	Other	Nonwar	War					
	112	113	114	115	116	117	118	119	120	121	122	123	124
1927–1931	6.05	5.87	0.18	3.80	1.64	0.71	1.62	−0.17	1.98	2.00	−0.02	0.11	0.69
1922–1926	5.58	5.48	.10	5.06	3.31	.93	1.00	−.18	1.50	2.01	−.51	1.00	.64
1917–1921	5.09	4.09	1.00	.95	.09	−.10	.34	.61	1.44	.86	.58	1.60	2.60
1912–1916	3.57			3.11	1.19	1.24	.66	.02	.76			.85	1.33
1907–1911	2.98			4.31	1.29	2.41	.61		.72			.65	.03
1902–1906	2.72			3.85	1.24	2.22	.40		1.01			.75	.32
1897–1901	1.75			2.80	.96	1.60	.23		.41			.87	.66
1892–1896	1.47			3.29	1.40	1.70	.19		.32			.42	−.05
1887–1891	1.82			2.61	1.63	.84	.14		.42			.41	−.20
1882–1886	1.00			1.79	1.11	.57	.11		.32			.51	−.10
1877–1881	.77			1.13	.60	.45	.08		.33			.66	.10
1872–1876	.51			1.11	.40	.65	.07		.19			.46	−.16
1869–1873	.46			.93	.34	.54	.05		.22			.39	−.24

Series F 125–129.   Gross Domestic Product Originating in Private Farm and Nonfarm Sectors and Government, in 1929 Prices: 1869 to 1960

[In billions of dollars.   5-year periods are annual averages]

Year	Gross domestic product	Gross private domestic product			Gross Govern- ment product	Year or period	Gross domestic product	Gross private domestic product			Gross Govern- ment product
		Total	Farm	Nonfarm				Total	Farm	Nonfarm	
	125	126	127	128	129		125	126	127	128	129
1960*	254.4	239.7	14.7	225.0	14.7	1933	73.8	68.8	11.0	57.8	5.0
1959	247.2	233.0	14.0	219.0	14.2	1932	75.9	71.4	10.7	60.7	4.5
1958	231.6	217.5	14.1	203.4	14.1	1931	88.8	84.2	11.2	73.0	4.6
1957	235.5	221.6	13.8	207.8	13.9	1930	94.4	89.8	10.0	79.8	4.6
1956	231.1	217.4	14.0	203.4	13.7	1929	103.6	99.3	10.7	88.6	4.3
1955	226.2	212.9	14.1	198.8	13.3	1928	97.7	93.5	10.4	83.1	4.2
1954	210.5	197.0	13.5	183.5	13.5	1927	96.6	92.5	10.6	81.9	4.1
1953	213.1	199.3	13.1	186.2	13.8	1926	95.7	91.7	10.3	81.4	4.0
1952	204.9	191.1	12.2	178.9	13.9	1925	89.8	85.9	10.4	75.5	3.9
1951	198.5	185.5	12.1	173.4	13.0	1924	87.7	84.0	9.7	74.3	3.7
1950	186.6	176.2	12.9	163.3	10.4	1923	85.1	81.5	10.2	71.3	3.6
1949	169.9	159.8	12.7	147.1	10.1	1922	75.2	71.7	9.6	62.1	3.5
1948	172.3	162.7	12.8	149.9	9.6	1921	71.3	67.7	9.0	58.7	3.6
1947	163.5	153.9	11.9	142.0	9.6	1920	72.9	69.3	9.5	59.8	3.7
1946	165.2	152.7	12.4	140.3	12.5	1919	73.6	68.7	9.7	59.0	5.0
1945	180.6	157.2	12.2	145.0	23.4	1917–1921	71.6	67.0	9.7	57.3	4.6
1944	183.2	159.2	12.7	146.5	24.0	1912–1916	62.5	59.9	10.1	49.8	2.6
1943	169.9	148.9	12.6	136.3	21.0	1907–1911	55.1	52.9	9.2	43.7	2.2
1942	154.3	140.6	13.2	127.4	13.7	1902–1906	46.9	45.2	8.9	36.3	1.8
1941	138.3	128.7	12.3	116.4	9.6	1897–1901	37.3	35.8	8.4	27.4	1.5
1940	120.6	112.7	11.4	101.3	7.9	1892–1896	29.8	28.5	6.8	21.7	1.3
1939	110.6	103.0	11.5	91.5	7.6	1889–1893	27.5	26.3	6.6	19.7	1.2
1938	102.8	95.2	11.4	83.8	7.6	1879–1888	21.2	20.2	5.8	14.4	1.0
1937	108.8	101.8	10.9	90.9	7.0	1869–1878	11.6	10.9	4.1	6.8	.7
1936	100.5	93.0	9.8	83.2	7.5						
1935	91.0	84.7	10.4	74.3	6.3						
1934	80.4	74.5	9.5	65.0	5.9						

* Denotes first year for which figures include Alaska and Hawaii.

Series **F 130–143.** Gross National Product, by Type of Industry, in Current and Constant (1958) Prices: 1947 to 1970

[In billions of dollars]

Year	Gross national product, total	Agriculture, forestry, and fisheries	Mining	Contract construction	Manufacturing	Transportation	Communication	Electric, gas, and sanitary services	Wholesale and retail trade	Finance, insurance, and real estate	Services	Government and government enterprises	Rest of the world	Statistical discrepancy/residual [1]
	130	131	132	133	134	135	136	137	138	139	140	141	142	143
CURRENT PRICES														
1970	977.1	31.6	16.9	46.6	252.3	38.5	22.7	22.6	166.4	137.8	114.0	129.4	4.6	−6.4
1969	930.3	30.3	15.3	44.4	255.4	36.8	21.0	21.4	156.5	128.6	105.0	117.4	4.3	−6.1
1968	864.2	27.4	14.8	39.5	244.3	34.3	18.9	19.8	143.6	116.9	94.9	107.8	4.7	−2.7
1967	793.9	26.7	13.9	36.1	223.7	32.0	17.6	18.4	129.9	108.8	87.0	95.8	4.5	−.7
1966	749.9	26.9	14.0	34.7	218.0	31.3	16.2	17.4	122.1	101.0	79.2	86.0	4.1	−1.0
1965	684.9	25.4	13.5	31.6	198.5	29.0	14.9	16.5	112.2	93.5	71.9	76.8	4.2	−3.1
1964	632.4	22.2	13.2	28.7	180.3	26.6	13.8	15.7	104.9	86.7	66.4	71.2	4.0	−1.3
1963	590.5	23.0	13.1	26.4	167.0	25.1	12.9	14.9	97.2	80.9	60.9	66.0	3.4	−.3
1962	560.3	22.6	13.0	24.9	158.8	24.0	11.9	14.2	92.7	76.2	56.9	61.5	3.3	.5
1961	520.1	22.1	12.9	23.4	144.2	22.7	11.0	13.4	87.0	71.5	52.9	57.0	2.9	−.8
1960	503.7	21.7	12.7	22.7	144.4	22.5	10.4	12.7	84.3	67.5	49.9	53.7	2.4	−1.0
1959	483.7	20.8	12.2	22.3	141.1	22.1	9.7	11.7	82.0	63.5	46.7	50.1	2.2	−.8
1958	447.3	22.0	12.4	20.7	123.7	21.0	8.9	10.7	75.1	59.2	42.9	47.3	2.0	1.6
1957	441.1	19.6	13.5	20.9	131.4	21.9	8.3	10.0	73.8	54.9	40.8	43.8	2.2	(Z)
1956	419.2	19.7	13.4	20.0	126.8	21.2	7.7	9.4	70.4	51.2	37.9	40.7	2.1	−1.1
1955	398.0	19.8	12.3	18.0	120.8	19.9	7.1	8.7	66.2	48.1	34.5	38.6	1.8	2.1
1954	364.8	20.7	10.8	16.7	106.2	18.2	6.5	8.0	60.8	44.7	31.0	36.8	1.6	2.7
1953	364.8	21.3	10.6	16.6	112.0	19.4	6.3	7.2	59.7	40.9	29.9	36.3	1.3	3.0
1952	345.5	23.1	10.1	16.2	102.9	18.8	5.6	6.6	58.5	37.0	28.0	35.1	1.3	2.2
1951	328.4	23.8	10.2	15.0	98.6	18.0	5.1	6.1	56.4	33.8	26.3	30.5	1.3	3.3
1950	284.8	20.8	9.2	12.7	83.8	16.0	4.5	5.3	51.3	30.7	24.3	23.7	1.2	1.5
1949	256.5	19.5	8.1	11.2	72.0	14.5	4.1	4.8	48.0	27.7	22.9	22.4	1.0	.3
1948	257.6	24.0	9.3	11.2	74.7	15.1	3.8	4.3	48.4	25.5	22.2	20.2	1.0	−2.0
1947	231.3	20.8	6.8	8.8	66.9	13.6	3.1	3.8	43.4	22.7	20.4	19.2	.8	.9
CONSTANT (1958) PRICES														
1970	722.5	26.2	17.2	23.6	217.5	33.9	22.3	21.2	126.5	96.4	69.2	70.0	4.0	−5.4
1969	725.6	25.4	16.8	24.1	228.6	34.6	20.3	20.5	124.2	95.5	67.7	70.3	4.0	−6.5
1968	706.6	24.8	16.3	23.8	219.2	33.2	18.5	19.2	120.8	95.2	65.8	68.6	4.5	−3.2
1967	675.2	25.2	16.0	23.1	205.4	31.4	17.2	17.9	113.9	91.6	63.4	65.5	4.3	.3
1966	658.1	23.7	15.8	24.7	205.7	31.2	15.8	17.0	111.6	86.8	60.6	61.8	3.9	−.3
1965	617.8	25.0	14.8	23.5	190.5	28.6	14.5	16.1	104.8	83.1	57.7	58.0	4.1	−3.1
1964	581.1	23.6	14.4	23.3	173.7	26.2	13.2	15.3	98.9	78.3	54.7	56.1	3.9	−0.5
1963	551.0	24.0	13.9	21.9	162.4	25.2	12.3	14.4	92.8	74.4	52.2	53.9	3.4	.1
1962	529.8	23.3	13.6	21.7	154.6	23.8	11.5	13.6	88.9	71.2	50.8	52.6	3.4	.9
1961	497.2	23.4	13.3	21.4	140.4	22.5	10.6	12.9	83.5	67.1	48.3	50.6	2.9	.1
1960	487.7	23.1	13.1	21.7	140.9	22.5	10.0	12.4	82.3	64.1	46.7	49.2	2.3	−.7
1959	475.9	22.3	12.8	22.0	138.9	22.2	9.5	11.6	80.8	61.4	45.1	47.9	2.2	−.9
1958	447.3	22.0	12.4	20.7	123.7	21.0	8.9	10.7	75.1	59.2	42.9	47.3	2.0	1.6
1957	452.5	21.5	13.6	21.1	134.6	22.5	8.5	10.3	75.1	57.0	41.8	46.9	2.1	−2.6
1956	446.1	22.0	13.6	21.8	134.1	22.8	8.0	9.7	73.8	54.8	40.2	46.2	2.0	−2.9
1955	438.0	22.1	12.8	20.8	133.6	22.0	7.5	9.1	71.6	52.7	38.2	46.0	1.8	−.2
1954	407.0	21.6	11.7	19.3	119.5	21.0	6.8	8.6	65.5	49.8	35.4	46.1	1.6	.2
1953	412.8	21.2	12.0	18.9	128.6	21.2	6.7	7.8	64.9	46.8	35.3	47.1	1.3	1.0
1952	395.1	20.2	11.7	18.3	118.7	21.2	6.1	7.3	62.9	44.7	34.5	47.2	1.2	1.1
1951	383.4	19.5	11.7	18.2	116.2	21.7	5.8	6.8	61.4	42.9	34.0	43.9	1.2	.1
1950	355.3	20.4	10.7	16.2	105.5	19.7	5.2	5.9	60.4	41.0	33.1	35.9	1.3	.1
1949	324.1	19.4	9.6	14.7	90.9	18.3	4.9	5.5	55.2	37.8	32.1	34.7	1.2	−.2
1948	323.7	20.0	10.7	14.1	96.3	20.7	4.7	5.0	54.2	36.5	31.9	33.2	1.2	−4.8
1947	309.9	17.9	10.2	12.9	91.8	21.1	4.1	4.4	52.7	35.6	30.6	32.4	1.1	−4.6

Z   Less than $50 million.

[1] "Residual" applies to constant dollar figures and represents the difference between GNP measured as sum of final products and GNP measured as the sum of gross product originating, by industries. It also includes "statistical discrepancy." See text for series F 130–143.

Series F 144–162. Relation of Gross National Product, National Income, and Personal Income and Saving: 1929 to 1970

[In billions of dollars]

Series No.	Item	1970	1969	1968	1967	1966	1965	1964	1963	1962	1961	1960*	1959	1958	1957
144	Gross national product	977.1	930.3	864.2	793.9	749.9	684.9	632.4	590.5	560.3	520.1	503.7	483.7	447.3	441.1
145	Less: Capital consumption allowances	87.3	81.6	74.5	68.9	63.9	59.8	56.1	52.6	50.0	45.2	43.4	41.4	38.9	37.1
146	Equals: Net national product	889.8	848.7	789.7	725.0	685.9	625.1	576.3	537.9	510.4	474.9	460.3	442.3	408.4	404.0
147	Plus: Subsidies less current surplus of government enterprises	1.7	1.0	.7	1.4	2.3	1.3	1.3	.8	1.4	1.4	.2	.1	.9	.9
148	Less: Indirect business tax and nontax liability	93.5	85.9	78.7	70.4	65.7	62.5	58.4	54.7	51.5	47.7	45.2	41.5	38.5	37.3
149	Business transfer payments	4.0	3.8	3.4	3.1	3.0	2.7	2.5	2.3	2.1	2.0	1.9	1.7	1.6	1.5
150	Statistical discrepancy	−6.4	−6.1	−2.7	−.7	−1.0	−3.1	−1.3	−.3	.5	−.8	−1.0	−.8	1.6	(Z)
151	Equals: National income	800.5	766.0	711.1	653.6	620.6	564.3	518.1	481.9	457.7	427.3	414.5	400.0	367.8	366.1
152	Plus: Government transfer payments to persons	75.1	61.9	56.1	48.7	41.1	37.2	34.2	33.0	31.2	30.4	26.6	24.9	24.1	19.9
153	Interest paid by government (net) and by consumers	31.0	28.7	26.1	23.6	22.2	20.5	19.1	17.6	16.1	15.0	15.1	13.6	12.1	12.0
154	Dividends	24.7	24.3	23.6	21.4	20.8	19.8	17.8	16.5	15.2	13.8	13.4	12.6	11.6	11.7
155	Business transfer payments	4.0	3.8	3.4	3.1	3.0	2.7	2.5	2.3	2.1	2.0	1.9	1.7	1.6	1.5
156	Less: Corporate profits and inventory valuation adjustment	69.2	79.8	84.3	78.7	82.4	76.1	66.3	58.9	55.7	50.3	49.9	51.7	41.1	45.6
157	Contributions for social insurance	57.7	54.2	47.1	42.4	38.0	29.6	27.9	26.9	24.0	21.4	20.7	17.6	14.8	14.5
158	Equals: Personal income	808.3	750.9	688.9	629.3	587.2	538.9	497.5	465.5	442.6	416.8	401.0	383.5	361.2	351.1
159	Less: Personal tax and nontax payments	116.6	116.5	97.9	83.0	75.4	65.7	59.4	60.9	57.4	52.4	50.9	46.2	42.3	42.6
160	Equals: Disposable personal income	691.7	634.4	591.0	546.3	511.9	473.2	438.1	404.6	385.3	364.4	350.0	337.3	318.8	308.5
161	Less: Personal outlays	635.5	596.2	551.2	506.0	479.3	444.8	411.9	384.7	363.7	343.3	333.0	318.3	296.6	287.8
162	Equals: Personal saving	56.2	38.2	39.8	40.4	32.5	28.4	26.2	19.9	21.6	21.2	17.0	19.1	22.3	20.7

Series No.	Item	1956	1955	1954	1953	1952	1951	1950	1949	1948	1947	1946	1945	1944	1943
144	Gross national product	419.2	398.0	364.8	364.6	345.5	328.4	284.8	256.5	257.6	231.3	208.5	211.9	210.1	191.6
145	Less: Capital consumption allowances	34.1	31.5	28.2	25.7	23.2	21.2	18.3	16.6	14.5	12.2	9.9	11.3	11.0	10.3
146	Equals: Net national product	385.2	366.5	336.6	338.9	322.3	307.2	266.4	239.9	243.1	219.1	198.6	200.7	199.1	181.3
147	Plus: Subsidies less current surplus of government enterprises	.8	−.1	−.2	−.4	−.1	.2	.2	−.1	−.1	−.2	.9	.8	.7	.2
148	Less: Indirect business tax and nontax liability	34.9	32.1	29.4	29.6	27.6	25.2	23.3	21.3	20.1	18.4	17.1	15.5	14.1	12.7
149	Business transfer payments	1.4	1.2	1.1	1.2	1.0	.9	.8	.8	.7	.6	.5	.5	.5	.5
150	Statistical discrepancy	−1.1	2.1	2.7	3.0	2.2	3.3	1.5	.3	−2.0	.9	1.0	3.9	2.5	−2.0
151	Equals: National income	350.8	331.0	303.1	[1] 304.7	[1] 291.4	[1] 278.0	[1] 241.1	[1] 217.5	[1] 224.2	[1] 199.0	[1] 181.9	[1] 181.5	[1] 182.6	[1] 170.2
152	Plus: Government transfer payments to persons	17.1	16.1	14.9	12.8	12.0	11.5	14.3	11.6	10.5	11.1	10.8	5.6	3.1	2.5
153	Interest paid by government (net) and by consumers	11.2	10.1	9.5	9.0	8.1	7.6	7.2	6.5	6.1	5.5	5.2	4.2	3.3	2.6
154	Dividends	11.3	10.5	9.3	8.9	8.6	8.6	8.8	7.2	7.0	6.3	5.6	4.6	4.6	4.4
155	Business transfer payments	1.4	1.2	1.1	1.2	1.0	.9	.8	.8	.7	.6	.5	.5	.5	.5
156	Less: Corporate profits and inventory valuation adjustment	46.1	46.9	38.0	39.6	39.9	42.7	37.7	30.8	33.0	25.6	19.3	19.2	23.8	24.4
157	Contributions for social insurance	12.6	11.1	9.8	8.8	8.7	8.3	6.9	5.7	5.2	5.7	6.0	6.1	5.2	4.5
158	Equals: Personal income	333.0	310.9	290.1	288.2	272.5	255.6	227.6	207.2	210.2	191.3	178.7	171.1	165.3	151.3
159	Less: Personal tax and nontax payments	39.8	35.5	32.7	35.6	34.1	29.0	20.7	18.6	21.1	21.4	18.7	20.9	18.9	17.8
160	Equals: Disposable personal income	293.2	275.3	257.4	252.6	238.3	226.6	206.9	188.6	189.1	169.8	160.0	150.2	146.3	133.5
161	Less: Personal outlays	272.6	259.5	241.0	234.3	220.2	209.3	193.9	179.2	175.8	162.5	144.8	120.7	109.1	100.1
162	Equals: Personal saving	20.6	15.8	16.4	18.3	18.1	17.3	13.1	9.4	13.4	7.3	15.2	29.6	37.3	33.4

Series No.	Item	1942	1941	1940	1939	1938	1937	1936	1935	1934	1933	1932	1931	1930	1929
144	Gross national product	157.9	124.5	99.7	90.5	84.7	90.4	82.5	72.2	65.1	55.6	58.0	75.8	90.4	103.1
145	Less: Capital consumption allowances	9.8	8.2	7.5	7.3	7.3	7.2	7.0	6.9	6.8	7.0	7.4	7.9	8.0	7.9
146	Equals: Net national product	148.1	116.3	92.2	83.2	77.4	83.3	75.4	65.4	58.2	48.6	50.7	68.0	82.4	95.2
147	Plus: Subsidies less current surplus of government enterprises	.2	.1	.4	.5	.2	.1	(Z)	.4	.3	(Z)	(Z)	(Z)	−.1	−.1
148	Less: Indirect business tax and nontax liability	11.8	11.3	10.0	9.4	9.2	9.2	8.7	8.2	7.8	7.1	6.8	6.9	7.2	7.0
149	Business transfer payments	.5	.5	.4	.5	.4	.6	.6	.6	.6	.7	.7	.6	.5	.6
150	Statistical discrepancy	−1.1	.4	1.0	1.3	.6	(Z)	1.2	−.2	.5	.6	.3	.7	−.8	.7
151	Equals: National income	137.1	104.2	81.1	72.6	67.4	73.7	65.0	57.2	49.5	40.3	42.8	59.7	75.4	86.8
152	Plus: Government transfer payments to persons	2.6	2.6	2.7	2.5	2.4	1.9	2.9	1.8	1.6	1.5	1.4	2.1	1.0	.9
153	Interest paid by government (net) and by consumers	2.2	2.2	2.1	1.9	1.9	1.9	1.7	1.7	1.7	1.6	1.7	1.8	1.8	2.5
154	Dividends	4.3	4.4	4.0	3.8	3.2	4.7	4.5	2.8	2.6	2.0	2.5	4.1	5.5	5.8
155	Business transfer payments	.5	.5	.4	.5	.4	.6	.6	.6	.6	.7	.7	.6	.5	.6
156	Less: Corporate profits and inventory valuation adjustment	20.3	15.2	9.8	6.3	4.9	6.8	5.6	3.4	1.7	−1.2	−1.3	2.0	7.0	10.5
157	Contributions for social insurance	3.5	2.8	2.3	2.1	2.0	1.8	.6	.3	.3	.3	.3	.3	.3	.2
158	Equals: Personal income	122.9	96.0	78.3	72.8	68.3	74.1	68.6	60.4	54.0	47.0	50.2	65.9	77.0	85.9
159	Less: Personal tax and nontax payments	6.0	3.3	2.6	2.4	2.9	2.9	2.3	1.9	1.6	1.5	1.5	1.9	2.5	2.6
160	Equals: Disposable personal income	116.9	92.7	75.7	70.3	65.5	71.2	66.3	58.5	52.4	45.5	48.7	64.0	74.5	83.3
161	Less: Personal outlays	89.3	81.7	71.8	67.7	64.8	67.4	62.7	56.4	52.0	46.5	49.3	61.4	71.1	79.1
162	Equals: Personal saving	27.6	11.0	3.8	2.6	.7	3.8	3.6	2.1	.4	−.9	−.6	2.6	3.4	4.2

* Denotes first year for which figures include Alaska and Hawaii.
Z   Less than $50 million or −$50 million.

[1] Includes "wage accruals less disbursements," not shown separately.

Series F 163–185. National Income, by Type of Income: 1929 to 1970

[In billions of dollars]

Year	National income	Compensation of employees									
		Total	Wages and salaries				Supplements to wages and salaries				
			Total	Private	Military	Government civilian ¹	Total	Employer contributions for social insurance	Other labor income		
									Total	Employer contributions ²	Other
	163	164	165	166	167	168	169	170	171	172	173
1970	800.5	603.9	542.0	426.9	19.6	95.5	61.9	29.7	32.2	27.2	5.0
1969	766.0	566.0	509.7	405.6	19.0	85.1	56.3	27.8	28.4	23.9	4.5
1968	711.1	514.6	464.9	369.2	17.9	77.8	49.7	24.3	25.4	21.4	4.0
1967	653.6	467.2	423.1	337.3	16.2	69.5	44.2	21.9	22.3	18.5	3.8
1966	620.6	435.5	394.5	316.8	14.6	63.1	41.0	20.3	20.7	17.2	3.5
1965	564.3	393.8	358.9	289.6	12.1	57.1	35.0	16.2	18.7	15.6	3.1
1964	518.1	365.7	333.7	269.4	11.7	52.6	32.0	15.4	16.6	13.7	3.0
1963	481.9	341.0	311.1	251.6	10.8	48.6	29.9	15.0	14.9	12.2	2.7
1962	457.7	323.6	296.1	240.1	10.8	45.2	27.5	13.7	13.9	11.4	2.5
1961	427.3	302.6	278.1	225.9	10.2	42.0	24.6	11.8	12.7	10.4	2.4
1960*	414.5	294.2	270.8	222.1	9.9	38.8	23.4	11.4	12.0	9.7	2.3
1959	400.0	279.1	258.2	212.5	9.9	35.8	20.9	9.7	11.3	9.1	2.2
1958	367.8	257.8	239.9	196.4	9.8	33.8	17.9	8.0	9.9	7.9	2.0
1957	366.1	256.0	238.7	198.2	9.6	30.8	17.3	7.8	9.5	7.5	2.0
1956	350.8	243.1	227.8	189.6	9.7	28.6	15.2	6.8	8.5	6.6	1.8
1955	331.0	224.5	211.3	175.1	9.8	26.4	13.2	5.9	7.3	5.7	1.6
1954	303.1	208.0	196.5	161.9	10.0	24.6	11.5	5.2	6.3	4.8	1.5
1953	304.7	209.1	198.3	164.2	10.3	23.7	10.9	4.9	6.0	4.6	1.4
1952	291.4	195.3	185.1	151.9	10.5	22.7	10.2	4.9	5.3	4.0	1.3
1951	278.0	180.7	171.1	142.1	8.7	20.3	9.6	4.8	4.8	3.6	1.2
1950	241.1	154.6	146.8	124.4	5.0	17.4	7.8	4.0	3.8	2.7	1.1
1949	217.5	141.0	134.5	113.9	4.2	16.4	6.5	3.5	3.0	2.0	1.0
1948	224.2	141.1	135.4	116.5	4.0	14.9	5.8	3.0	2.7	1.8	.9
1947	199.0	128.9	123.0	105.6	4.1	13.4	5.9	3.6	2.3	1.6	.8
1946	181.9	117.9	112.0	91.3	7.8	12.9	5.9	4.0	1.9	1.2	.7
1945	181.5	123.1	117.5	82.6	21.8	13.1	5.6	3.8	1.8	1.1	.7
1944	182.6	121.2	116.7	83.8	20.0	12.9	4.5	2.9	1.5	.9	.6
1943	170.3	109.5	105.8	79.2	14.1	12.5	3.8	2.7	1.1	.6	.5
1942	137.1	85.3	82.1	66.1	6.2	9.8	3.2	2.3	.9	.4	.5
1941	104.2	64.8	62.1	51.9	1.9	8.3	2.7	2.0	.7	.3	.4
1940	81.1	52.1	49.8	41.4	.6	7.9	2.3	1.6	.7	.3	.4
1939	72.6	48.1	45.9	37.7	.4	7.8	2.2	1.5	.6	.2	.4
1938	67.4	45.0	43.0	34.8	.4	7.9	2.0	1.4	.6	.2	.4
1937	73.7	47.9	46.1	38.6	.4	7.1	1.8	1.2	.6	.2	.4
1936	65.0	42.9	41.9	34.1	.3	7.5	1.0	.4	.6	.2	.3
1935	57.2	37.3	36.7	30.2	.3	6.2	.7	.2	.5	.2	.3
1934	49.5	34.3	33.7	27.6	.3	5.8	.6	.1	.4	.2	.3
1933	40.3	29.5	29.0	23.9	.3	4.9	.5	.1	.4	.1	.3
1932	42.8	31.1	30.5	25.5	.3	4.7	.6	.1	.5	.1	.3
1931	59.7	39.8	39.1	33.9	.3	5.0	.6	.1	.5	.2	.4
1930	75.4	46.8	46.2	41.0	.3	4.8	.7	.1	.6	.2	.4
1929	86.8	51.1	50.4	45.5	.3	4.6	.7	.1	.6	.2	.4

* Denotes first year for which figures include Alaska and Hawaii.
¹ Includes also the pay of employees of government enterprises and of permanent United States residents employed in the United States by foreign governments and international organizations.

² Employer contributions to private pension and welfare funds.

Series F 163–185. National Income, by Type of Income: 1929 to 1970—Con.

[In billions of dollars]

Year	Proprietors' income — Total	Business and professional	Farm	Rental income of persons	Corporate profits and inventory valuation adjustment — Total	Profits before tax	Profits tax liability	Profits after tax — Total	Dividends	Undistributed profits	Inventory valuation adjustment	Net interest
	174	175	176	177	178	179	180	181	182	183	184	185
1970	67.0	50.0	16.9	23.9	69.2	74.0	34.8	39.3	24.7	14.6	-4.8	36.5
1969	67.2	50.5	16.7	22.6	79.8	84.9	40.1	44.8	24.3	20.5	-5.1	30.5
1968	64.2	49.5	14.7	21.2	84.3	87.6	39.9	47.8	23.6	24.2	-3.3	26.9
1967	62.1	47.3	14.8	21.1	78.7	79.8	33.2	46.6	21.4	25.3	-1.1	24.4
1966	61.3	45.2	16.1	20.0	82.4	84.2	34.3	49.9	20.8	29.1	-1.8	21.4
1965	57.3	42.4	14.8	19.0	76.1	77.8	31.3	46.5	19.8	26.7	-1.7	18.2
1964	52.3	40.2	12.1	18.0	66.3	66.8	28.3	38.4	17.8	20.6	-.5	15.8
1963	51.0	37.9	13.1	17.1	58.9	59.4	26.3	33.1	16.5	16.6	-.5	13.8
1962	50.1	37.1	13.0	16.7	55.7	55.4	24.2	31.2	15.2	16.0	.3	11.6
1961	48.4	35.6	12.8	16.0	50.3	50.3	23.1	27.2	13.8	13.5	-.1	10.0
1960 *	46.2	34.2	12.0	15.8	49.9	49.7	23.0	26.7	13.4	13.2	.2	8.4
1959	46.6	35.1	11.4	15.6	51.7	52.1	23.7	28.5	12.6	15.9	-.5	7.1
1958	46.6	33.2	13.4	15.4	41.1	41.4	19.0	22.3	11.6	10.8	-.3	6.8
1957	44.1	32.8	11.3	14.8	45.6	47.2	21.2	26.0	11.7	14.2	-1.5	5.6
1956	42.7	31.3	11.4	14.3	46.1	48.8	21.7	27.2	11.3	15.9	-2.7	4.6
1955	41.7	30.3	11.4	13.9	46.9	48.6	21.6	27.0	10.5	16.5	-1.7	4.1
1954	40.0	27.6	12.4	13.6	38.0	38.3	17.7	20.6	9.3	11.3	-.3	3.6
1953	40.5	27.5	13.0	12.7	39.6	40.6	20.3	20.4	8.9	11.5	-1.0	2.8
1952	42.1	27.1	15.0	11.5	39.9	38.9	19.4	19.6	8.6	11.0	1.0	2.6
1951	42.0	26.1	15.8	10.3	42.7	43.9	22.3	21.6	8.6	13.0	-1.2	2.3
1950	37.5	24.0	13.5	9.4	37.7	42.6	17.8	24.9	8.8	16.0	-5.0	2.0
1949	35.3	22.6	12.7	8.4	30.8	28.9	10.4	18.5	7.2	11.3	1.9	1.9
1948	40.2	22.7	17.5	8.0	33.0	35.2	12.5	22.7	7.0	15.6	-2.2	1.8
1947	35.5	20.3	15.2	7.1	25.6	31.5	11.3	20.2	6.3	13.9	-5.9	1.9
1946	36.5	21.6	14.9	6.6	19.3	24.6	9.1	15.5	5.6	9.9	-5.3	1.5
1945	31.4	19.2	12.2	5.6	19.2	19.7	10.7	9.0	4.6	4.4	-.6	2.2
1944	29.8	18.2	11.6	5.4	23.8	24.1	12.9	11.2	4.6	6.5	-.3	2.3
1943	28.6	17.0	11.7	5.1	24.4	25.1	14.1	11.1	4.4	6.6	-.8	2.7
1942	23.8	14.0	9.8	4.5	20.3	21.5	11.4	10.1	4.3	5.9	-1.2	3.1
1941	17.5	11.1	6.4	3.5	15.2	17.7	7.6	10.1	4.4	5.7	-2.5	3.2
1940	13.0	8.6	4.5	2.9	9.8	10.0	2.8	7.2	4.0	3.2	-.2	3.3
1939	11.8	7.4	4.4	2.7	6.3	7.0	1.4	5.6	3.8	1.8	-.7	3.5
1938	11.3	6.9	4.4	2.6	4.9	4.0	1.0	2.9	3.2	-.2	1.0	3.6
1937	13.2	7.2	6.0	2.1	6.8	6.8	1.5	5.3	4.7	.6	(Z)	3.7
1936	11.0	6.7	4.3	1.8	5.6	6.3	1.4	4.9	4.5	.4	-.7	3.8
1935	10.8	5.5	5.3	1.7	3.4	3.6	1.0	2.6	2.8	-.2	-.2	4.1
1934	7.7	4.7	3.0	1.7	1.7	2.3	.7	1.6	2.6	-1.0	-.6	4.1
1933	5.9	3.3	2.6	2.0	-1.2	1.0	.5	.4	2.0	-1.6	-2.1	4.1
1932	5.7	3.6	2.1	2.7	-1.3	-2.3	.4	-2.7	2.5	-5.2	1.0	4.6
1931	9.2	5.8	3.4	3.8	2.0	-.4	.5	-.9	4.1	-4.9	2.4	5.0
1930	11.9	7.6	4.3	4.8	7.0	3.7	.8	2.9	5.5	-2.6	3.3	4.9
1929	15.1	9.0	6.2	5.4	10.5	10.0	1.4	8.6	5.8	2.8	.5	4.7

* Denotes first year for which figures include Alaska and Hawaii.   Z Less than −$50 million.

Series F 186–191. Percent Distribution of National Income, by Type of Income, in Current Prices: 1900 to 1969

[Percents based on annual averages for periods shown]

Period	Total	Compensation of employees	Income of unincorporated enterprises	Rental income of persons	Corporate profits before tax	Net interest	Period	Total	Compensation of employees	Income of unincorporated enterprises	Rental income of persons	Corporate profits before tax	Net interest
	186	187	188	189	190	191		186	187	188	189	190	191
1960–1969	100.0	71.1	10.0	3.3	12.4	3.2	1930–1939 [2]	100.0	66.8	15.0	5.0	4.9	8.2
1955–1964	100.0	70.0	11.4	3.8	12.6	2.1	1925–1934	100.0	63.0	15.8	6.6	6.4	8.1
1950–1959	100.0	68.0	13.0	4.0	13.6	1.3	1920–1929	100.0	60.5	17.6	7.6	8.2	6.2
1945–1954	100.0	65.5	15.6	3.8	14.1	.9	1915–1924	100.0	57.2	21.0	7.6	8.9	5.3
1940–1949	100.0	64.0	17.2	3.4	14.1	1.4	1910–1919	100.0	53.2	24.2	7.7	9.7	5.2
1935–1944	100.0	64.3	16.8	3.2	12.4	3.3	1905–1914	100.0	55.2	22.9	9.1	6.9	5.8
1930–1939 [1]	100.0	67.1	16.4	4.3	5.3	6.9	1900–1909	100.0	55.0	23.6	9.1	6.8	5.5

[1] Source: U.S. Bureau of Economic Analysis; see text.   [2] Source: D. Gale Johnson; see text.

Series F 192–209. National Income, by Sector and Legal Form of Organization: 1929 to 1970

[In billions of dollars]

Column legend (Originating in business):
- 192 — National income
- 193 — Total
- Corporate business, including mutual financial institutions: 194 Total; 195 Compensation of employees; 196 Corporate profits and inventory valuation adjustment; 197 Net interest
- Sole proprietorships and partnerships: 198 Total; 199 Compensation of employees; 200 Income of unincorporated enterprises and inventory valuation adjustment; 201 Net interest
- Other private business: 202 Total; 203 Compensation of employees and proprietors; 204 Rental income of persons; 205 Net interest
- 206 — Government commercial enterprises
- 207 — Originating in general government
- 208 — Originating in private households and nonprofit institutions
- 209 — Originating in the rest of the world

Year	192	193	194	195	196	197	198	199	200	201	202	203	204	205	206	207	208	209
1970	800.5	650.3	438.7	369.0	64.5	5.1	147.1	74.2	66.4	6.5	52.4	3.4	23.9	25.0	12.1	114.7	30.8	4.6
1969	766.0	629.8	428.4	351.5	75.3	1.7	141.6	69.4	66.7	5.5	49.3	3.1	22.6	23.6	10.5	103.8	28.1	4.3
1968	711.1	586.0	400.1	319.5	80.3	.2	130.8	62.4	63.8	4.5	45.4	2.9	21.2	21.4	9.8	94.9	25.5	4.5
1967	653.6	541.2	366.7	291.8	75.1	-.2	122.5	56.6	61.7	4.2	43.3	2.7	21.1	19.5	8.7	85.1	22.8	4.5
1966	620.6	519.7	353.7	275.5	79.2	-1.2	117.5	52.9	60.9	3.7	40.3	2.5	20.0	17.9	8.1	76.6	20.2	4.1
1965	564.3	473.9	320.5	249.8	72.8	-2.0	108.4	48.4	56.9	3.1	37.6	2.4	19.0	16.3	7.4	67.8	18.5	4.2
1964	518.1	433.8	292.2	231.6	63.2	-2.5	99.7	45.0	51.9	2.8	34.9	2.2	18.0	14.7	7.0	63.0	17.3	4.0
1963	481.9	404.4	270.4	216.3	56.4	-2.4	95.0	42.2	50.6	2.2	32.5	2.1	17.1	13.2	6.6	58.1	16.0	3.4
1962	457.7	384.4	256.4	205.5	53.1	-2.5	92.0	40.4	49.7	1.9	30.4	2.1	16.7	11.7	6.0	54.7	15.0	3.3
1961	427.3	359.5	237.3	191.8	48.0	-2.5	88.3	38.6	48.0	1.6	28.3	2.0	16.0	10.4	5.7	50.9	14.0	2.9
1960*	414.5	351.4	234.1	188.8	48.0	-2.8	85.0	37.7	46.2	1.5	26.9	1.9	15.8	9.2	5.4	47.5	13.2	2.4
1959	400.0	341.3	226.8	179.6	49.4	-2.6	84.0	36.5	46.2	1.3	25.5	1.8	15.6	8.1	5.0	44.3	12.2	2.0
1958	367.0	312.3	201.5	163.9	39.4	-1.8	81.5	34.3	46.2	1.2	24.9	1.8	15.4	7.2	4.3	42.1	11.4	2.2
1957	366.1	314.3	208.0	166.4	43.8	-2.1	79.0	34.1	43.7	1.0	22.9	1.7	14.8	6.4	4.3	39.1	10.5	2.2
1956	350.8	302.3	200.2	158.1	44.3	-2.2	76.4	33.1	42.4	.9	21.6	1.7	14.3	5.6	4.1	36.6	9.8	2.1
1955	331.0	286.0	188.0	144.6	45.3	-1.9	73.6	31.5	41.4	.8	20.4	1.6	13.9	4.9	3.9	34.2	9.1	1.8
1954	303.1	261.0	167.1	132.1	36.5	-1.5	70.9	30.5	39.7	.7	19.4	1.5	13.6	4.2	3.6	32.5	8.8	1.6
1953	304.7	263.7	170.7	133.9	38.5	-1.7	71.6	30.7	40.2	.7	17.9	1.4	12.7	3.7	3.6	31.9	7.8	1.3
1952	291.4	251.7	160.2	123.0	38.8	-1.6	71.8	29.3	41.8	.7	16.2	1.4	11.5	3.3	3.3	31.2	7.2	1.3
1951	278.0	242.4	154.6	114.5	41.6	-1.5	70.1	27.7	41.7	.7	14.6	1.3	10.3	3.0	3.0	27.4	6.9	1.3
1950	241.1	212.6	134.0	98.6	36.7	-1.3	62.7	24.9	37.2	.5	13.1	1.2	9.4	2.5	2.7	20.9	6.4	1.2
1949	217.5	191.1	117.8	88.8	30.0	-.9	59.0	23.4	35.1	.5	11.7	1.1	8.4	2.2	2.6	19.4	5.9	1.0
1948	224.2	200.2	122.5	91.0	32.2	-.8	64.3	23.9	40.0	.4	11.0	.9	8.0	2.0	2.3	17.4	5.6	.8
1947	199.0	176.3	106.6	82.0	24.9	-.3	58.0	22.3	35.3	.3	9.8	.9	7.1	1.8	2.0	16.7	5.1	.8
1946	181.9	156.0	88.1	69.7	18.9	-.5	56.9	20.3	36.3	.3	9.0	.8	6.6	1.6	1.9	20.8	4.5	.6
1945	181.5	141.8	83.3	64.1	18.9	.2	49.1	17.6	31.3	.3	7.8	.7	5.6	1.5	1.6	35.2	4.1	.4
1944	182.6	146.3	91.0	67.1	23.5	.3	46.1	16.1	29.7	.3	7.7	.7	5.4	1.5	1.5	32.2	3.7	.4
1943	170.3	141.2	88.8	64.2	24.1	.5	43.5	14.6	28.5	.4	7.4	.6	5.1	1.7	1.5	25.6	3.2	.4
1942	137.1	118.7	73.7	52.9	20.1	.7	36.9	12.7	23.7	.5	6.9	.5	4.5	1.8	1.2	15.1	2.9	.4
1941	104.2	91.9	57.4	41.6	15.0	.8	27.7	9.8	17.4	.5	5.7	.4	3.5	1.8	1.1	9.4	2.5	.4
1940	81.1	70.6	43.3	32.9	9.6	.9	21.3	7.8	13.0	.5	5.0	.3	2.9	1.8	1.0	7.8	2.4	.4
1939	72.6	62.4	37.1	29.8	6.1	1.1	19.5	7.2	11.8	.5	4.7	.3	2.7	1.8	.9	7.6	2.3	.4
1938	67.4	57.2	33.1	27.3	4.7	1.2	18.5	6.8	11.3	.5	4.7	.3	2.6	1.8	.9	7.6	2.2	.3
1937	73.7	64.2	38.4	30.6	6.6	1.2	20.7	7.1	13.2	.5	4.3	.3	2.1	1.8	.9	6.9	2.3	.3
1936	65.0	55.4	33.0	26.3	6.5	1.3	17.6	6.2	10.9	.5	3.9	.3	1.8	1.8	.8	7.3	2.0	.3
1935	57.2	49.0	27.8	23.1	3.2	1.5	16.7	5.5	10.7	.5	3.8	.2	1.7	1.9	.8	5.9	1.9	.4
1934	49.5	41.8	24.2	21.1	1.7	1.5	13.2	5.0	7.7	.6	3.8	.2	1.7	1.9	.7	5.6	1.8	.3
1933	40.3	33.6	18.0	18.0	-1.2	1.2	10.9	4.4	5.9	.6	4.1	.2	2.0	1.9	.6	4.7	1.7	.4
1932	42.8	36.1	19.0	19.0	-1.2	1.5	11.2	4.8	5.6	.7	4.9	.2	2.7	2.0	.7	4.4	1.9	.4
1931	59.7	52.2	29.0	25.4	2.0	1.6	16.4	6.4	9.1	.8	6.1	.3	3.8	2.1	.8	4.7	2.3	.5
1930	75.4	67.4	39.2	30.8	6.8	1.5	20.4	7.8	11.8	.8	7.1	.3	4.8	2.0	.8	4.5	2.7	.7
1929	86.8	78.8	45.9	34.3	10.2	1.4	24.3	8.6	15.1	.6	7.8	.3	5.4	2.1	.8	4.3	2.9	.8

* Denotes first year for which figures include Alaska and Hawaii.

Series F 210–215. Percent Distribution of Aggregate Payments, by Type of Income, in Current Prices: 1870 to 1968

[Percents based on annual averages for periods shown]

Period	Total	Employee compensation	Entrepreneurial income	Dividends	Interest	Rent	Period	Total	Employee compensation	Entrepreneurial income	Dividends	Interest	Rent
	210	211	212	213	214	215		210	211	212	213	214	215
Based on Dept. of Commerce estimates:							**Based on Martin's estimates of aggregate payments:[2]**						
1959–1968	100.0	75.0	10.9	3.6	3.5	7.0	1909–1918	100.0	59.7	23.3	6.5	4.9	5.7
1954–1963	100.0	74.3	12.4	4.2	3.4	5.7	1904–1913	100.0	59.6	23.3	5.7	5.1	6.3
1949–1958	100.0	73.1	14.5	4.4	3.4	4.6	1899–1908	100.0	59.5	23.8	5.3	5.1	6.4
1944–1953	100.0	71.2	17.5	4.0	3.3	4.0	**Based on King's estimates of value of product:**						
1939–1948	100.0	69.8	18.9	3.6	3.4	4.3	1900 and 1910	100.0	47.1	28.8	15.9		8.3
1934–1943	100.0	67.7	17.7	3.4	4.6	6.6	1890 and 1900	100.0	50.4	27.3	14.7		7.7
1929–1938	100.0	64.0	16.0	4.5	5.9	9.6	1880 and 1890	100.0	52.5	23.0	16.5		8.2
Based on NBER[1] estimates of aggregate payments:							1870 and 1880	100.0	50.0	26.4	15.8		7.8
1929–1938	100.0	64.9	15.9	6.6	8.4	4.3							
1924–1933	100.0	63.1	16.6	6.5	7.8	5.9							
1919–1928	100.0	61.7	19.5	5.6	6.1	7.1							
1914–1923	100.0	59.2	22.5	5.6	5.6	7.2							
1909–1918	100.0	56.2	24.6	6.1	5.4	7.6							

[1] National Bureau of Economic Research.

[2] Excluding entrepreneurial savings.

Series F 216–225. Percent Distribution of National Income or Aggregate Payments, by Industry, in Current Prices: 1869 to 1968

[Percents based on annual averages for periods shown]

Period	Total	Agriculture	Mining	Manufacturing	Contract construction	Transportation and other public utilities	Trade	Services	Government	Finance and miscellaneous
	216	217	218	219	220	221	222	223	224	225
Based on Dept. of Commerce estimates of national income (adjusted):[1]										
1959–1968	100.0	3.8	1.1	28.4	5.2	7.5	15.2	11.7	15.9	11.2
1954–1963	100.0	4.5	1.5	28.8	5.2	7.8	15.6	10.7	14.9	11.0
1949–1958	100.0	5.9	1.8	29.3	5.3	8.0	16.0	9.7	13.9	10.2
1939–1948	100.0	9.2	1.9	28.0	3.7	8.2	16.4	8.6	15.7	8.4
1934–1943	100.0	9.1	2.1	26.7	3.4	9.2	16.1	9.4	14.4	9.7
1929–1938	100.0	9.3	2.1	22.4	3.2	10.6	16.1	11.1	12.1	13.1
Based on NBER estimates of national income:										
1939–1948	100.0	9.4	1.6	27.1	3.4	7.3	13.3	10.5	17.2	10.2
1934–1943	100.0	9.2	1.7	24.2	2.9	8.5	13.2	12.1	15.4	12.7
1929–1938	100.0	8.5	1.7	19.4	2.9	10.0	13.6	13.9	14.4	15.6
1924–1933	100.0	8.7	1.9	19.6	4.2	10.4	13.3	13.4	11.8	16.7
1919–1928	100.0	10.5	2.5	21.9	4.4	9.8	13.6	11.6	9.6	16.1
Based on Martin's estimates of aggregate payments:										
1919–1928	100.0	12.2	3.1	22.2	3.9	11.3	13.7	9.4	8.6	15.7
1914–1923	100.0	15.2	3.3	22.2	3.0	11.0	14.0	8.3	7.9	15.0
1909–1918	100.0	17.7	3.3	20.8	3.2	10.7	14.5	8.2	6.3	15.4
1904–1913	100.0	17.0	3.3	18.9	4.3	11.0	15.0	8.9	5.4	16.2
1899–1908	100.0	16.7	3.1	18.4	4.5	10.7	15.3	9.6	5.6	16.0
1889 and 1899	100.0	17.1	2.5	18.2	4.9	10.7	16.8	11.8	6.0	12.0
1879 and 1889	100.0	16.1	2.1	16.6	5.5	11.9	16.6	13.6	4.9	12.6
1869 and 1879	100.0	20.5	1.8	13.9	5.3	11.9	15.7	14.7	4.4	11.7

[1] See text for explanation.

Series F 226–237. National Income, by Industrial Origin, in Current Prices: 1929 to 1970

[In billions of dollars]

Year	Total	Agriculture, forestry, and fisheries	Mining	Contract construction	Manufacturing	Wholesale and retail trade	Finance, insurance, and real estate	Transportation	Communications and public utilities	Services	Government and government enterprises	Rest of the world
	226	227	228	229	230	231	232	233	234	235	236	237
1970	800.5	25.6	7.7	42.8	217.5	121.3	89.9	29.8	31.5	102.9	126.9	4.6
1969	766.0	24.8	6.8	40.9	222.3	114.8	84.5	28.7	30.0	94.7	114.3	4.3
1968	711.1	22.1	6.7	36.3	212.7	106.1	77.8	26.9	27.5	85.7	104.7	4.7
1967	653.6	21.6	6.3	33.2	195.2	97.5	71.9	25.2	25.7	78.5	93.8	4.5
1966	620.6	22.7	6.3	32.0	191.5	91.4	67.4	24.9	24.6	71.1	84.7	4.1
1965	564.3	21.0	6.1	29.1	172.6	84.3	61.9	23.2	22.7	64.1	75.2	4.2
1964	518.1	18.0	5.9	26.5	155.6	79.3	57.1	21.2	21.5	59.1	70.0	4.0
1963	481.9	18.6	6.0	24.2	143.8	73.4	53.6	20.0	20.2	54.1	64.7	3.4
1962	457.7	18.5	5.7	22.8	137.0	70.3	50.7	19.1	19.0	50.7	60.7	3.3
1961	427.3	17.9	5.7	21.5	125.1	66.2	48.0	18.3	18.0	47.2	56.6	2.9
1960 *	414.5	16.9	5.7	20.8	125.8	64.4	45.8	18.2	17.2	44.5	52.9	2.4
1959	400.0	16.0	5.5	20.5	124.0	63.3	43.7	17.9	15.8	41.8	49.3	2.2
1958	367.8	17.9	5.7	19.0	107.7	58.2	40.9	16.6	14.4	38.4	46.9	2.0
1957	366.1	15.5	6.5	19.3	116.3	57.2	38.2	17.4	13.6	36.5	43.4	2.2
1956	350.8	15.5	6.6	18.5	113.1	54.8	35.9	17.0	12.8	33.9	40.7	2.1
1955	331.0	15.4	5.9	16.6	107.9	52.3	34.1	15.9	11.9	31.1	38.1	1.8
1954	303.1	16.4	5.3	15.6	94.6	48.3	32.0	14.6	11.0	27.8	36.1	1.6
1953	304.7	17.2	5.4	15.6	100.4	47.3	29.3	15.8	10.2	26.8	35.5	1.3
1952	291.4	19.2	5.5	15.2	92.5	46.7	26.5	15.5	9.3	25.1	34.7	1.3
1951	278.0	20.1	5.7	14.1	90.0	45.1	24.1	14.9	8.4	23.5	30.4	1.3
1950	241.1	17.6	5.2	11.9	76.2	40.9	22.0	13.4	7.3	21.8	23.6	1.2
1949	217.5	16.6	4.5	10.5	64.8	39.0	19.8	12.1	6.7	20.5	22.0	1.0
1948 [1]	224.2	21.6	5.4	10.6	68.7	39.9	18.4	12.8	6.0	20.0	19.8	1.0
1948 [2]	224.2	21.5	5.4	10.6	67.6	41.7	18.3	12.8	6.0	19.5	19.8	1.0
1947	199.0	18.9	4.2	8.4	59.5	37.6	16.1	11.6	5.1	18.1	18.7	.8
1946	181.9	18.2	3.0	6.5	49.1	34.6	15.3	10.3	4.8	16.7	22.7	.6
1945	181.5	15.2	2.8	4.3	52.2	28.0	13.0	10.5	4.2	14.1	36.8	.4
1944	182.6	14.5	3.0	4.1	60.3	25.8	12.3	11.2	4.0	13.2	33.7	.4
1943	170.3	14.4	2.8	5.5	58.3	23.9	11.6	10.8	3.9	11.8	27.0	.4
1942	137.1	12.2	2.6	6.5	45.4	20.4	10.7	8.6	3.7	10.3	16.3	.4
1941	104.2	8.4	2.4	4.2	33.2	17.4	9.3	6.3	3.3	8.9	10.5	.4
1940	81.1	6.1	1.9	2.6	22.5	14.5	8.3	5.0	3.0	8.0	8.8	.4
1939	72.6	6.0	1.6	2.3	18.1	12.6	8.0	4.6	2.8	7.6	8.5	.3
1938	67.4	5.9	1.5	2.0	15.2	12.1	7.7	4.1	2.7	7.2	8.5	.4
1937	73.7	7.6	2.0	2.1	19.5	12.4	7.3	4.6	2.7	7.5	7.8	.3
1936	65.0	5.7	1.5	2.0	16.3	10.8	6.7	4.3	2.4	6.8	8.1	.3
1935	57.2	6.7	1.2	1.3	13.4	9.4	6.0	3.7	2.2	6.2	6.7	.4
1934	49.5	4.2	1.1	1.1	11.1	8.3	5.6	3.4	2.2	5.8	6.3	.3
1933	40.3	3.9	.6	.8	7.7	5.6	5.9	3.0	2.0	5.1	5.3	.3
1932	42.8	3.5	.7	1.1	7.3	6.5	7.0	3.2	2.3	5.7	5.2	.4
1931	59.7	5.2	1.0	2.2	12.5	9.9	8.8	4.4	2.6	7.2	5.4	.5
1930	75.4	6.4	1.7	3.2	18.3	12.4	10.7	5.6	2.7	8.4	5.3	.7
1929	86.8	8.5	2.1	3.8	21.9	13.5	12.8	6.6	2.8	8.8	5.1	.8

* Denotes first year for which figures include Alaska and Hawaii.
[1] Based on 1957 Standard Industrial Classification System; comparable with later years.
[2] Based on 1942 Standard Industrial Classification System; comparable with earlier years.

Series F 238–249. Value Added by Selected Industries, and Value of Output of Fixed Capital, in Current and 1879 Prices: 1839 to 1899

[In billions of dollars]

Year	Current prices						1879 prices					
	Total	Agriculture	Mining	Manufacturing	Construction	Value of output of fixed capital	Total	Agriculture	Mining	Manufacturing	Construction	Value of output of fixed capital
	238	239	240	241	242	243	244	245	246	247	248	249
1899	10.20	3.40	0.47	5.04	1.29	3.47	11.75	3.92	0.55	6.26	1.02	3.35
1894	7.83	2.64	.29	3.60	1.30	--------	10.26	3.27	.39	5.48	1.12	--------
1889	7.87	2.77	.28	3.73	1.10	2.82	8.66	3.24	.35	4.16	.92	2.72
1884	7.09	2.84	.20	3.05	1.01	--------	7.30	3.00	.23	3.22	.86	--------
1879	5.30	2.60	.15	1.96	.59	1.64	5.30	2.60	.15	1.96	.59	1.64
1874	5.40	2.53	.15	2.07	.65	--------	4.30	1.98	.11	1.69	.52	--------
1869	4.83	2.54	.13	1.63	.54	1.51	3.27	1.72	.07	1.08	.40	1.09
1859	2.57	1.50	.03	.82	.23	.62	2.69	1.49	.03	.86	.30	.73
1854	2.39	1.46	.03	.66	.23	--------	2.32	1.32	.03	.68	.30	--------
1849	1.40	.83	.02	.45	.11	.31	1.66	.99	.02	.49	.16	.39
1844	1.09	.69	.01	.31	.08	--------	1.37	.94	.01	.29	.13	--------
1839	1.04	.71	.01	.24	.08	.20	1.09	.79	.01	.19	.11	.25

Series F 250–261. National Income and Persons Engaged in Production, by Industry Divisions: 1869 to 1970

[Series F 250 figures shown for grouped years are annual averages; for series F 251–261, percents shown for grouped years are based on annual averages]

NATIONAL INCOME

Year or period	Total	Agriculture	Mining	Contract construction	Manufacturing	Transportation, communications, public utilities	Trade	Finance, insurance, and real estate	Services	Government Federal	State and local	Rest of the world
	250	251	252	253	254	255	256	257	258	259	260	261
	Mil. dol.					Percent distribution						
Commerce estimates:												
1970	795,887	3.1	.9	5.3	27.4	7.6	15.3	10.9	13.0	6.7	9.2	0.6
1960–1969	558,195	3.6	1.1	5.1	30.0	8.1	15.1	11.0	11.5	6.2	7.6	.7
1957–1960	386,032	4.3	1.5	5.1	30.5	8.4	15.7	10.9	10.4	6.2	6.2	.6
1953–1957	330,092	4.8	1.8	5.2	32.1	8.5	15.7	10.3	9.4	6.4	5.3	.5
1948–1953	258,476	7.2	2.0	5.0	31.6	8.5	16.7	9.0	8.8	6.2	4.5	.5
1944–1948	191,442	9.2	1.9	3.5	29.4	8.3	17.5	7.8	8.5	10.1	3.6	.3
1937–1944	108,684	8.4	2.0	3.5	30.6	9.2	15.8	8.6	8.4	8.9	4.3	.3
1929–1937	58,763	9.3	2.1	3.1	22.8	11.2	16.1	12.9	11.4	3.7	6.6	.8
Kuznets estimates:												
1929–1937	57,460	8.6	1.7	3.0	19.6	10.2	13.5	[1] 15.7	13.9	13.9		----------
1926–1929	82,818	9.0	2.2	4.9	21.4	9.7	12.9	[1] 17.0	12.8	10.2		----------
1923–1926	76,168	9.7	2.5	5.0	21.6	9.7	13.5	[1] 16.4	11.9	9.7		----------
1920–1923	63,021	10.2	2.7	3.8	21.5	10.3	13.5	[1] 16.3	11.4	10.2		----------
Martin estimates:												
1929–1937	58,943	9.0	2.3	2.6	21.0	11.6	13.7	[2] 13.8	10.8	15.1		----------
1926–1929	75,460	11.5	3.0	4.2	22.2	11.2	14.5	[2] 14.3	10.4	8.7		----------
1923–1926	68,882	12.5	3.4	4.3	22.1	11.3	14.8	[2] 13.3	9.7	8.5		----------
1920–1923	60,303	13.2	3.6	3.5	22.2	11.8	15.1	[2] 12.8	9.1	8.9		----------
1918–1920	62,820	18.9	3.4	2.6	23.3	10.7	14.4	10.9	7.2	8.5		----------
1913–1918	38,613	19.0	3.5	2.8	21.6	10.6	16.0	12.2	7.9	6.4		----------
1910–1913	29,111	18.9	3.5	4.1	19.9	11.1	15.8	12.7	8.6	5.5		----------
1907–1910	25,400	19.4	3.4	4.1	18.3	10.9	16.4	13.0	9.1	5.4		----------
1903–1907	21,670	17.5	3.5	4.7	18.6	10.8	17.0	13.7	8.9	5.3		----------
1899–1903	17,313	18.2	2.9	4.3	18.6	10.3	16.6	12.7	10.3	6.0		----------
1889	10,701	14.2	2.2	5.9	18.9	11.2	16.8	13.1	12.5	5.2		----------
1879	7,227	19.0	2.1	5.0	13.3	12.9	16.1	12.0	15.2	4.5		----------
1869	6,827	22.2	1.5	5.7	14.6	10.9	15.2	11.5	14.2	4.2		----------

PERSONS ENGAGED IN PRODUCTION

Year or period	Total	Agriculture	Mining	Contract construction	Manufacturing	Transportation, communications, public utilities	Trade	Finance, insurance, and real estate	Services	Government Federal	State and local	Rest of the world
	1,000					Percent distribution						
Commerce estimates:												
1970	79,750	4.3	0.8	5.3	24.8	5.5	19.1	4.6	17.4	7.4	10.7	----------
1960–1969	71,375	5.8	.9	5.4	25.8	5.7	18.4	4.3	16.4	7.8	9.4	----------
1957–1960	64,798	7.6	1.2	5.5	26.1	6.3	18.6	4.1	15.0	7.6	8.0	----------
1953–1957	64,496	8.8	1.3	5.6	27.0	6.5	18.0	3.8	13.5	8.4	6.9	----------
1948–1953	61,110	10.6	1.6	5.6	26.7	6.9	18.1	3.4	13.1	7.7	6.2	----------
1944–1948	59,952	11.8	1.5	4.0	25.9	6.8	16.7	2.9	11.8	13.5	5.1	----------
1937–1944	53,002	15.1	1.8	4.0	24.4	6.3	16.3	3.0	12.4	11.4	5.4	----------
1929–1937	42,214	21.3	2.0	4.1	20.5	7.5	16.9	3.5	13.9	3.7	6.4	----------
1929	46,216	19.9	2.2	5.0	22.8	8.8	16.9	3.4	14.0	6.9		----------
Kendrick estimates:												
1929	47,611	21.2	2.2	5.0	22.2	8.6	16.9	3.3	13.9	6.7		----------
1919	42,313	24.6	2.7	3.6	25.1	9.4	13.2	2.1	10.7	8.6		----------
1909	34,785	30.4	3.1	5.0	22.1	8.8	11.8	1.6	12.5	4.8		----------
1899	26,861	36.9	2.5	4.9	20.0	7.7	10.8	1.2	11.9	4.1		----------
1889	21,620	41.6	2.3	4.5	18.7	7.1	9.7	.8	11.5	3.8		----------
1879	15,639	48.9	1.8	4.1	18.0	5.2	7.9	.4	9.9	3.9		----------
1869	11,910	48.3	1.3	4.9	17.6	5.1	7.8	.4	11.1	3.5		----------

[1] Includes income originating in fisheries and in bus, truck, and air transportation.
[2] Includes income from fisheries, miscellaneous income of private origin, net international transfer of dividends and interest, as well as income from miscellaneous professional occupations and the hand trades.

Series F 262–286. Personal Income and Outlay: 1929 to 1970

[In billions of dollars]

Year	Personal income	Wage and salary disbursements					Other labor income	Proprietors' income			Rental income of persons	Dividends	Personal interest income
		Total	Commodity-producing industries	Distributive industries	Service industries	Government		Total	Business and professional	Farm			
	262	263	264	265	266	267	268	269	270	271	272	273	274
1970	808.3	542.0	200.9	129.3	96.6	115.1	32.2	66.9	50.0	16.9	23.9	24.7	67.5
1969	750.9	509.7	197.5	120.0	88.1	104.1	28.4	67.2	50.5	16.7	22.6	24.3	59.3
1968	688.9	464.9	181.5	109.2	78.5	95.7	25.4	64.2	49.5	14.7	21.2	23.6	52.9
1967	629.3	423.1	166.5	100.3	70.5	85.8	22.3	62.1	47.3	14.8	21.1	21.4	48.0
1966	587.2	394.5	159.3	93.8	63.7	77.7	20.7	61.3	45.2	16.1	20.0	20.8	43.6
1965	538.9	358.9	144.5	86.9	58.3	69.3	18.7	57.3	42.4	14.8	19.0	19.8	38.7
1964	497.5	333.7	134.1	81.2	54.1	64.3	16.6	52.3	40.2	12.1	18.0	17.8	34.9
1963	465.5	311.1	125.7	76.0	49.9	59.5	14.9	51.0	37.9	13.1	17.1	16.5	31.4
1962	442.6	296.1	120.8	72.5	46.8	56.0	13.9	50.1	37.1	13.0	16.7	15.2	27.7
1961	416.8	278.1	112.8	69.1	44.0	52.2	12.7	48.4	35.6	12.8	16.0	13.8	25.0
1960*	401.0	270.8	112.5	68.1	41.5	48.7	12.0	46.2	34.2	12.0	15.8	13.4	23.4
1959	383.5	258.2	109.1	64.8	38.7	45.6	11.3	46.6	35.1	11.4	15.6	12.6	20.7
1958	361.2	239.9	99.7	60.8	35.9	43.5	9.9	46.6	33.2	13.4	15.4	11.6	18.9
1957	351.1	238.7	103.8	60.5	33.9	40.5	9.5	44.1	32.8	11.3	14.8	11.7	17.6
1956	333.0	227.8	100.2	57.7	31.6	38.3	8.5	42.7	31.3	11.4	14.3	11.3	15.7
1955	310.9	211.3	92.8	53.4	28.9	36.2	7.3	41.7	30.3	11.4	13.9	10.5	14.2
1954	290.1	196.5	85.4	50.2	26.4	34.6	6.3	40.0	27.6	12.4	13.6	9.3	13.1
1953	288.2	198.3	89.4	49.8	25.1	34.1	6.0	40.5	27.5	13.0	12.7	8.9	11.8
1952	272.5	185.1	81.8	46.9	23.3	33.1	5.3	42.1	27.1	15.0	11.5	8.6	10.6
1951	255.6	171.0	76.1	44.3	21.7	28.9	4.8	42.0	26.1	15.8	10.3	8.6	9.9
1950	227.6	146.7	64.6	39.9	19.9	22.4	3.8	37.5	24.0	13.5	9.4	8.8	9.2
1949	207.2	134.6	57.7	37.7	18.6	20.6	3.0	35.3	22.6	12.7	8.4	7.2	8.5
1948	210.2	135.3	61.0	37.6	17.9	18.9	2.7	40.2	22.7	17.5	8.0	7.0	7.9
1947	191.3	123.0	54.3	35.2	16.1	17.4	2.3	35.5	20.3	15.2	7.1	6.3	7.5
1946	178.7	112.0	46.0	31.0	14.4	20.7	1.9	36.5	21.6	14.9	6.6	5.6	6.8
1945	171.1	117.5	45.8	24.8	12.0	34.9	1.8	31.4	19.2	12.2	5.6	4.6	6.3
1944	165.3	116.9	50.3	22.7	10.9	33.0	1.5	29.8	18.2	11.6	5.4	4.6	5.6
1943	151.3	105.6	48.9	20.1	9.9	26.6	1.1	28.6	17.0	11.7	5.1	4.4	5.3
1942	122.9	82.1	39.1	18.0	9.0	16.0	.9	23.8	14.0	9.8	4.5	4.3	5.3
1941	96.0	62.1	27.5	16.3	8.1	10.2	.7	17.5	11.1	6.4	3.5	4.4	5.5
1940	78.3	49.8	19.7	14.2	7.5	8.4	.7	13.0	8.6	4.5	2.9	4.0	5.4
1939	72.8	45.9	17.4	13.3	7.1	8.2	.6	11.8	7.4	4.4	2.7	3.8	5.5
1938	68.3	43.0	15.3	12.6	6.8	8.2	.6	11.3	6.9	4.4	2.6	3.2	5.5
1937	74.1	46.1	18.4	13.2	7.1	7.5	.6	13.2	7.2	6.0	2.1	4.7	5.6
1936	68.6	41.9	15.8	11.8	6.5	7.9	.6	11.0	6.7	4.3	1.8	4.5	5.5
1935	60.4	36.7	13.5	10.7	5.9	6.5	.5	10.8	5.5	5.3	1.7	2.8	5.7
1934	54.0	33.7	12.1	9.9	5.7	6.1	.4	7.7	4.7	3.0	1.7	2.6	5.8
1933	47.0	29.0	9.8	8.8	5.2	5.1	.4	5.9	3.3	2.6	2.0	2.0	5.7
1932	50.2	30.5	9.9	9.8	5.8	5.0	.5	5.7	3.6	2.1	2.7	2.5	6.3
1931	65.9	39.1	14.3	12.5	7.1	5.3	.5	9.2	5.8	3.4	3.8	4.1	6.7
1930	77.0	46.2	18.5	14.5	8.0	5.2	.6	11.9	7.6	4.3	4.8	5.5	6.8
1929	85.9	50.4	21.5	15.6	8.4	4.9	.6	15.1	9.0	6.2	5.4	5.8	7.2

* Denotes first year for which figures include Alaska and Hawaii.

Series F 262–286. Personal Income and Outlay: 1929 to 1970—Con.

[In billions of dollars]

Year	Transfer payments to persons					Personal contributions for social insurance[1]	Personal tax and nontax payments	Disposable personal income	Personal outlays			
	Total	Old-age and survivors insurance benefits	State unemployment insurance benefits	Veterans benefits	Other				Total	Personal consumption expenditures	Interest paid by consumers	Personal transfer payments to foreigners
	275	276	277	278	279	280	281	282	283	284	285	286
1970	79.1	38.5	3.9	9.7	27.1	28.0	116.6	691.7	635.5	617.6	16.8	1.0
1969	65.8	33.0	2.1	8.3	22.4	26.3	116.5	634.4	596.2	579.5	15.8	.9
1968	59.6	30.3	2.1	7.3	20.0	22.8	97.9	591.0	551.2	536.2	14.3	.8
1967	51.8	25.7	2.1	6.6	17.5	20.5	83.0	546.3	506.0	492.1	13.2	.7
1966	44.1	20.8	1.8	5.7	15.7	17.7	75.4	511.9	479.3	466.3	12.4	.6
1965	39.9	18.1	2.2	5.6	14.0	13.4	65.7	473.2	444.8	432.8	11.3	.7
1964	36.7	16.0	2.6	5.3	12.9	12.5	59.4	438.1	411.9	401.2	10.1	.6
1963	35.3	15.2	2.8	5.0	12.2	11.8	60.9	404.6	384.7	375.0	9.1	.6
1962	33.3	14.3	2.9	4.8	11.2	10.3	57.4	385.3	363.7	355.1	8.1	.5
1961	32.4	12.6	4.0	4.8	10.9	9.6	52.4	364.4	343.3	335.2	7.6	.5
1960*	28.5	11.1	2.8	4.6	10.0	9.3	50.9	350.0	333.0	325.2	7.3	.5
1959	26.6	10.2	2.5	4.6	9.4	7.9	46.2	337.3	318.3	311.2	6.5	.6
1958	25.7	8.5	3.9	4.6	8.7	6.9	42.3	318.8	296.6	290.1	5.9	.6
1957	21.4	7.3	1.8	4.4	7.9	6.7	42.6	308.5	287.8	281.4	5.8	.6
1956	18.5	5.7	1.4	4.3	7.2	5.8	39.8	293.2	272.6	266.7	5.4	.6
1955	17.3	4.9	1.4	4.3	6.8	5.2	35.5	275.3	259.5	254.4	4.7	.5
1954	16.0	3.6	2.0	3.9	6.5	4.6	32.7	257.4	241.0	236.5	4.0	.5
1953	14.0	3.0	1.0	3.7	6.3	4.0	35.6	252.6	234.3	230.0	3.8	.5
1952	13.0	2.2	1.0	3.9	6.0	3.8	34.1	238.3	220.2	216.7	3.0	.5
1951	12.5	1.9	.8	3.9	5.9	3.4	29.0	226.6	209.3	206.3	2.7	.4
1950	15.1	1.0	1.4	4.9	7.9	2.9	20.7	206.9	193.9	191.0	2.4	.5
1949	12.4	.7	1.7	5.1	4.9	2.2	18.6	188.6	179.2	176.8	1.9	.5
1948	11.2	.6	.8	5.8	4.1	2.2	21.1	189.1	175.8	173.6	1.5	.7
1947	11.7	.5	.8	6.7	3.7	2.1	21.4	169.8	162.5	160.7	1.1	.7
1946	11.3	.4	1.1	6.7	3.1	2.0	18.7	160.0	144.8	143.4	.8	.7
1945	6.2	.3	.4	2.8	2.7	2.3	20.9	150.2	120.7	119.7	.5	.5
1944	3.6	.2	.1	.9	2.4	2.2	18.9	146.3	109.1	108.3	.5	.4
1943	3.0	.2	.1	.5	2.2	1.8	17.8	133.5	100.1	99.3	.5	.2
1942	3.1	.1	.3	.5	2.2	1.2	6.0	116.9	89.3	88.5	.7	.2
1941	3.1	.1	.3	.5	2.2	.8	3.3	92.7	81.7	80.6	.9	.2
1940	3.1	(Z)	.5	.5	2.0	.7	2.6	75.7	71.8	70.8	.8	.2
1939	3.0	(Z)	.4	.5	2.0	.6	2.4	70.3	67.7	66.8	.7	.2
1938	2.8	(Z)	.4	.5	1.9	.6	2.9	65.5	64.8	63.9	.7	.2
1937	2.4	(Z)	(Z)	.6	1.8	.6	2.9	71.2	67.4	66.5	.7	.2
1936	3.5	--------	--------	1.9	1.6	.2	2.3	66.3	62.7	61.9	.6	.2
1935	2.4	--------	--------	.5	1.9	.2	1.9	58.5	56.4	55.7	.5	.2
1934	2.2	--------	--------	.4	1.8	.2	1.6	52.4	52.0	51.3	.5	.2
1933	2.1	--------	--------	.5	1.6	.2	1.5	45.5	46.5	45.8	.5	.2
1932	2.2	--------	--------	.8	1.4	.2	1.5	48.7	49.3	48.6	.5	.2
1931	2.7	--------	--------	1.6	1.1	.2	1.9	64.0	61.4	60.5	.7	.3
1930	1.5	--------	--------	.6	.9	.1	2.5	74.5	71.1	69.9	.9	.3
1929	1.5	--------	--------	.6	.9	.1	2.6	83.3	79.1	77.2	1.5	.3

* Denotes first year for which figures include Alaska and Hawaii.   Z Less than $50 million.   [1] Deduct from total personal income.

Series F 287–296. Personal Income—Percent Distribution and Per Capita Income as Percent of U.S. Total, by Regions: 1840 to 1970

Year	United States	New England	Middle Atlantic	East North Central	West North Central	South Atlantic	East South Central	West South Central	Mountain	Pacific
	287	288	289	290	291	292	293	294	295	296
PERCENT DISTRIBUTION OF PERSONAL INCOME										
1970	100	6	24	21	8	11	5	8	4	14
1965	100	6	24	21	8	10	5	8	4	14
1960	100	6	25	22	8	9	5	8	4	13
1950	100	7	26	23	9	9	5	8	3	12
1940	100	8	28	23	8	8	4	7	3	11
1930	100	9	32	23	9	6	4	6	2	9
1920	100	9	30	22	10	7	4	7	3	7
1900	100	10	31	22	13	5	4	5	3	5
1880	100	11	33	23	11	6	5	5	3	4
1840	100	17	41	12	2	14	11	4	----------	----------
RATIO OF PER CAPITA INCOME TO U.S. PER CAPITA										
1970	100	108	113	105	95	86	74	85	90	110
1965	100	108	114	108	95	81	71	83	90	115
1960	100	109	116	107	93	77	67	83	95	118
1950	100	106	116	112	94	74	63	81	96	121
1940	100	121	124	112	84	69	55	70	92	138
1930	100	129	140	111	82	56	48	61	83	130
1920	100	124	134	108	87	59	52	72	100	135
1900	100	134	139	106	97	45	49	61	139	163
1880	100	141	141	102	90	45	51	60	168	204
1840	100	132	136	67	75	70	73	144	----------	----------

Series F 297–348. Personal Income, by States: 1929 to 1970

Year	United States	Alabama	Alaska	Arizona	Arkansas	California	Colorado	Connecticut	Delaware	District of Columbia	Florida	Georgia	Hawaii	Idaho	Illinois	Indiana	Iowa	Kansas
	297	298	299	300	301	302	303	304	305	306	307	308	309	310	311	312	313	314
	TOTAL INCOME (millions of dollars)																	
1970	803,521	10,053	1,404	6,507	5,527	89,312	8,541	14,803	2,466	4,016	25,275	15,269	3,476	2,352	50,023	19,539	10,609	8,635
1969	746,449	9,163	1,250	5,765	5,004	83,067	7,623	13,819	2,271	3,740	22,542	14,347	3,044	2,148	47,233	19,110	9,907	8,138
1968	684,745	8,369	1,111	5,062	4,597	76,720	6,855	12,674	2,070	3,540	19,791	12,784	2,700	1,885	43,653	17,413	9,132	7,528
1967	625,576	7,659	1,022	4,516	4,236	69,807	6,122	11,703	1,882	3,320	17,451	11,541	2,414	1,790	40,627	16,002	8,509	6,902
1966	583,828	7,245	916	4,110	3,999	65,002	5,697	10,657	1,790	3,112	15,683	10,568	2,220	1,681	38,266	15,278	8,315	6,599
1965	535,948	6,713	855	3,773	3,577	60,104	5,295	9,765	1,704	2,969	14,182	9,531	2,014	1,668	35,070	14,067	7,559	6,030
1964	494,912	6,108	788	3,529	3,387	56,471	4,984	9,004	1,561	2,827	12,976	8,635	1,907	1,459	32,188	12,640	6,643	5,581
1963	463,054	5,666	702	3,362	3,104	52,522	4,745	8,449	1,453	2,675	11,859	7,895	1,772	1,409	30,174	11,869	6,347	5,327
1962	440,189	5,274	664	3,177	2,899	48,948	4,559	7,999	1,350	2,540	11,050	7,280	1,676	1,410	28,948	11,214	6,001	5,183
1961	414,411	5,025	633	2,905	2,704	45,601	4,294	7,447	1,275	2,380	10,248	6,746	1,595	1,310	27,486	10,542	5,742	4,945
1960	398,726	4,887	647	2,681	2,461	42,913	4,018	7,122	1,244	2,313	9,739	6,477	1,476	1,238	26,689	10,271	5,473	4,714
1959	[1] 380,964	4,699	562	2,455	2,421	40,955	3,752	6,785	1,202	2,228	9,303	6,211	1,315	1,227	25,751	9,817	5,317	4,484
1958	[1] 358,474	4,442	528	2,220	2,210	37,321	3,524	6,446	1,135	2,132	8,453	5,767	1,178	1,161	24,353	9,192	5,200	4,443
1957	[1] 348,460	4,261	537	2,028	2,091	35,497	3,365	6,398	1,125	2,061	7,730	5,531	1,114	1,104	24,056	9,187	5,077	4,006
1956	[1] 330,479	4,005	548	1,861	2,035	33,177	3,066	6,029	1,124	2,019	6,972	5,350	1,041	1,047	23,024	8,875	4,580	3,804
1955	[1] 308,266	3,761	505	1,655	1,970	30,378	2,804	5,552	980	1,949	6,070	5,000	972	951	21,167	8,265	4,307	3,626
1954	[1] 287,607	3,314	495	1,514	1,810	27,682	2,566	5,160	857	1,917	5,328	4,536	908	902	19,933	7,653	4,525	3,597
1953	[1] 285,456	3,432	511	1,478	1,842	27,002	2,528	5,087	835	1,914	5,050	4,581	896	899	19,812	8,073	4,200	3,434
1952	[1] 269,769	3,287	494	1,399	1,823	25,214	2,498	4,710	782	1,978	4,554	4,447	865	932	18,608	7,326	4,338	3,524
1951	[1] 253,232	3,077	448	1,230	1,763	22,756	2,313	4,335	731	1,921	4,048	4,122	793	850	17,711	6,938	4,127	3,077
1950	[1] 226,214	2,691	322	1,006	1,575	19,774	1,970	3,779	684	1,790	3,599	3,574	692	764	15,948	5,998	3,897	2,765
1949	[1] 205,793	2,446	----	906	1,474	17,878	1,820	3,374	586	1,700	3,177	3,150	685	712	14,607	5,388	3,392	2,477
1948	[1] 208,876	2,571	----	879	1,597	17,633	1,810	3,450	537	1,644	3,043	3,154	723	725	15,521	5,624	4,042	2,523
1940	[1] 78,122	792	----	251	496	5,802	615	1,511	275	827	971	1,047	----	235	5,958	1,889	1,274	756
1929	[1] 85,803	852	----	255	567	5,505	649	1,585	245	624	758	1,014	----	225	7,291	1,983	1,449	1,013
	PER CAPITA INCOME (dollars)																	
1970	3,943	2,913	4,603	3,631	2,869	4,467	3,839	4,871	4,483	5,333	3,692	3,318	4,562	3,280	4,492	3,752	3,749	3,841
1969	3,708	2,664	4,223	3,319	2,616	4,214	3,519	4,606	4,205	4,908	3,394	3,153	4,097	3,038	4,279	3,716	3,532	3,639
1968	3,436	2,429	3,899	3,010	2,417	3,956	3,233	4,276	3,876	4,551	3,077	2,852	3,755	2,712	3,970	3,419	3,258	3,397
1967	3,170	2,215	3,675	2,743	2,228	3,640	2,982	3,987	3,585	4,198	2,796	2,618	3,409	2,602	3,711	3,167	3,047	3,141
1966	2,987	2,092	3,380	2,547	2,106	3,447	2,839	3,671	3,469	3,934	2,569	2,413	3,185	2,440	3,531	3,056	3,011	3,000
1965	2,770	1,950	3,154	2,382	1,888	3,234	2,668	3,418	3,362	3,725	2,382	2,200	2,885	2,431	3,280	2,858	2,757	2,733
1964	2,590	1,799	2,997	2,268	1,785	3,111	2,530	3,218	3,141	3,542	2,245	2,028	2,813	2,145	3,042	2,603	2,419	2,527
1963	2,458	1,687	2,744	2,210	1,655	2,973	2,451	3,098	3,009	3,353	2,107	1,892	2,641	2,062	2,901	2,473	2,310	2,403
1962	2,370	1,587	2,699	2,160	1,564	2,867	2,401	3,022	2,879	3,223	2,025	1,782	2,567	2,038	2,816	2,368	2,182	2,323
1961	2,265	1,515	2,659	2,065	1,497	2,764	2,329	2,880	2,765	3,059	1,955	1,680	2,481	1,916	2,713	2,229	2,083	2,232
1960	2,216	1,493	2,824	2,030	1,376	2,704	2,271	2,800	2,772	3,023	1,946	1,637	2,366	1,846	2,646	2,198	1,986	2,159
1959	[1] 2,161	1,467	2,507	1,947	1,378	2,648	2,194	2,689	2,725	2,927	1,935	1,606	2,156	1,867	2,579	2,128	1,948	2,076
1958	[1] 2,068	1,405	2,357	1,861	1,280	2,508	2,114	2,635	2,621	2,817	1,826	1,516	1,981	1,797	2,463	2,006	1,920	2,074
1957	[1] 2,045	1,371	2,323	1,802	1,207	2,489	2,023	2,712	2,641	2,701	1,768	1,469	1,944	1,720	2,488	2,028	1,869	1,882
1956	[1] 1,975	1,304	2,446	1,767	1,194	2,419	1,887	2,603	2,754	2,660	1,723	1,445	1,900	1,667	2,416	1,991	1,694	1,795
1955	[1] 1,876	1,233	2,273	1,677	1,142	2,313	1,814	2,414	2,519	2,483	1,620	1,375	1,838	1,539	2,243	1,894	1,608	1,732
1954	[1] 1,785	1,099	2,300	1,623	1,044	2,172	1,718	2,294	2,328	2,423	1,520	1,259	1,802	1,503	2,154	1,795	1,723	1,762
1953	[1] 1,804	1,124	2,492	1,654	1,035	2,204	1,767	2,346	2,379	2,363	1,526	1,288	1,795	1,509	2,186	1,930	1,598	1,722
1952	[1] 1,733	1,071	2,612	1,662	992	2,167	1,830	2,263	2,293	2,457	1,442	1,241	1,748	1,588	2,078	1,766	1,652	1,783
1951	[1] 1,652	1,006	2,836	1,566	927	2,044	1,745	2,137	2,209	2,378	1,359	1,167	1,580	1,443	2,015	1,694	1,577	1,578
1950	[1] 1,496	880	2,384	1,330	825	1,852	1,487	1,875	2,132	2,221	1,281	1,034	1,386	1,295	1,825	1,512	1,485	1,443
1949	[1] 1,384	815	----	1,270	800	1,730	1,406	1,660	1,853	2,106	1,191	947	1,354	1,249	1,685	1,361	1,316	1,287
1948	[1] 1,430	866	----	1,274	875	1,752	1,433	1,713	1,720	1,958	1,180	968	1,407	1,315	1,815	1,451	1,590	1,333
1940	[1] 592	278	----	502	254	835	544	885	1,023	1,198	507	336	----	450	754	550	502	423
1929	[1] 705	322	----	593	306	995	644	994	1,037	1,292	525	349	----	502	959	615	589	543
	TOTAL INCOME, PERCENT OF U.S.																	
1970	100.00	1.25	0.17	0.81	0.69	11.12	1.06	1.84	0.31	0.50	3.15	1.90	0.43	0.29	6.23	2.43	1.32	1.07
1969	100.00	1.23	.17	.77	.67	11.13	1.02	1.85	.30	.50	3.02	1.92	.41	.29	6.33	2.56	1.33	1.09
1968	100.00	1.22	.16	.74	.67	11.20	1.00	1.85	.30	.52	2.89	1.87	.39	.28	6.38	2.54	1.33	1.10
1967	100.00	1.22	.16	.72	.68	11.16	.98	1.87	.30	.53	2.79	1.84	.39	.29	6.49	2.56	1.36	1.10
1966	100.00	1.24	.16	.70	.68	11.13	.98	1.83	.31	.53	2.69	1.81	.38	.29	6.55	2.62	1.42	1.13
1965	100.00	1.25	.16	.70	.67	11.21	.99	1.82	.32	.55	2.65	1.78	.38	.31	6.54	2.62	1.41	1.13
1964	100.00	1.23	.16	.71	.68	11.41	1.01	1.82	.32	.57	2.62	1.74	.39	.29	6.50	2.55	1.34	1.13
1963	100.00	1.22	.15	.73	.67	11.34	1.02	1.82	.31	.58	2.56	1.71	.38	.30	6.52	2.56	1.37	1.15
1962	100.00	1.20	.15	.72	.66	11.12	1.04	1.82	.31	.58	2.51	1.65	.38	.32	6.58	2.55	1.36	1.18
1961	100.00	1.21	.15	.70	.65	11.00	1.04	1.80	.31	.57	2.47	1.63	.38	.32	6.63	2.54	1.39	1.19
1960	100.00	1.23	.16	.67	.62	10.76	1.01	1.79	.31	.58	2.44	1.62	.37	.31	6.69	2.58	1.37	1.18
1959	[1] 100.00	1.23	.15	.64	.64	10.75	.98	1.78	.32	.58	2.44	1.63	.35	.32	6.76	2.58	1.40	1.18
1958	[1] 100.00	1.24	.15	.62	.62	10.41	.98	1.80	.32	.59	2.36	1.61	.33	.32	6.79	2.56	1.45	1.24
1957	[1] 100.00	1.22	.15	.58	.60	10.19	.97	1.84	.32	.59	2.22	1.59	.32	.32	6.90	2.64	1.46	1.15
1956	[1] 100.00	1.21	.17	.56	.62	10.04	.93	1.82	.34	.61	2.11	1.62	.31	.32	6.97	2.69	1.39	1.15
1955	[1] 100.00	1.22	.16	.54	.64	9.85	.91	1.80	.32	.63	1.97	1.62	.32	.31	6.87	2.68	1.40	1.18
1954	[1] 100.00	1.15	.17	.53	.63	9.62	.89	1.79	.30	.67	1.85	1.58	.32	.31	6.93	2.66	1.57	1.25
1953	[1] 100.00	1.20	.18	.52	.65	9.46	.89	1.78	.29	.67	1.77	1.60	.31	.32	6.94	2.83	1.47	1.20
1952	[1] 100.00	1.22	.18	.52	.68	9.35	.93	1.75	.29	.73	1.69	1.65	.32	.35	6.90	2.72	1.61	1.31
1951	[1] 100.00	1.22	.18	.49	.70	8.99	.91	1.71	.29	.76	1.60	1.63	.31	.34	6.99	2.74	1.63	1.22
1950	[1] 100.00	1.19	.14	.44	.70	8.74	.87	1.67	.30	.79	1.59	1.58	.31	.34	7.05	2.65	1.72	1.22
1949	[1] 100.00	1.19	----	.44	.72	8.69	.88	1.64	.28	.83	1.54	1.53	.33	.35	7.10	2.62	1.65	1.20
1948	[1] 100.00	1.23	----	.42	.76	8.44	.87	1.65	.26	.79	1.46	1.51	.35	.35	7.43	2.69	1.94	1.21
1940	[1] 100.00	1.01	----	.32	.64	7.43	.79	1.93	.35	1.06	1.24	1.34	----	.30	7.63	2.42	1.63	.97
1929	[1] 100.00	.99	----	.30	.66	6.42	.76	1.85	.29	.73	.88	1.18	----	.26	8.50	2.31	1.69	1.18

[1] Prior to 1960, U. S. total does not include Alaska and Hawaii.

Series F 297–348.   Personal Income, by States: 1929 to 1970—Con.

TOTAL INCOME (millions of dollars)

Year	Kentucky 315	Louisiana 316	Maine 317	Maryland 318	Massachusetts 319	Michigan 320	Minnesota 321	Mississippi 322	Missouri 323	Montana 324	Nebraska 325	Nevada 326	New Hampshire 327	New Jersey 328	New Mexico 329	New York 330	North Carolina 331
1970	10,008	11,180	3,255	16,856	24,731	36,993	14,709	5,753	17,682	2,438	5,653	2,195	2,779	33,347	3,173	86,070	16,383
1969	9,214	10,364	2,986	15,437	22,926	35,782	13,509	5,262	16,140	2,200	5,297	2,047	2,475	30,423	2,908	80,923	15,036
1968	8,518	9,887	2,762	14,020	21,049	32,831	12,205	4,848	15,074	2,029	4,653	1,792	2,286	27,987	2,656	75,041	13,566
1967	7,772	9,052	2,544	12,590	19,286	29,667	11,150	4,425	13,832	1,915	4,413	1,581	2,079	25,638	2,463	68,657	12,288
1966	7,202	8,247	2,431	11,668	17,715	28,206	10,366	4,122	12,874	1,875	4,242	1,510	1,905	23,862	2,380	63,717	11,341
1965	6,553	7,412	2,262	10,681	16,421	25,860	9,523	3,743	11,975	1,722	3,851	1,434	1,728	22,105	2,269	59,487	10,092
1964	5,996	6,799	2,090	9,749	15,392	23,005	8,604	3,420	11,028	1,592	3,481	1,353	1,601	20,515	2,115	55,987	9,292
1963	5,751	6,298	1,923	8,959	14,514	21,039	8,303	3,289	10,407	1,587	3,340	1,265	1,510	19,372	2,031	52,559	8,606
1962	5,444	5,908	1,876	8,342	13,878	19,568	7,858	2,976	9,896	1,581	3,274	1,122	1,442	18,430	1,969	50,535	8,154
1961	5,139	5,589	1,808	7,800	13,220	18,243	7,570	2,819	9,415	1,371	3,046	911	1,356	17,333	1,871	47,821	7,596
1960	4,807	5,417	1,788	7,285	12,657	18,318	7,227	2,630	9,142	1,383	2,988	829	1,300	16,526	1,799	46,178	7,123
1959	4,667	5,361	1,696	6,952	12,123	17,588	6,787	2,569	8,936	1,344	2,757	770	1,237	15,849	1,759	44,301	6,712
1958	4,441	5,105	1,637	6,567	11,438	16,603	6,585	2,349	8,461	1,370	2,713	711	1,132	14,823	1,618	41,715	6,263
1957	4,291	5,028	1,583	6,314	11,074	16,870	6,135	2,172	8,053	1,297	2,615	673	1,102	14,550	1,442	40,818	5,980
1956	4,107	4,547	1,534	5,976	10,497	16,529	5,778	2,141	7,844	1,241	2,274	625	1,035	13,719	1,254	38,608	5,935
1955	3,866	4,114	1,449	5,467	9,891	15,900	5,483	2,102	7,450	1,178	2,191	604	983	12,688	1,181	36,453	5,571
1954	3,692	3,881	1,314	5,069	9,293	14,354	5,202	1,875	6,974	1,079	2,253	519	915	11,957	1,077	34,275	5,120
1953	3,752	3,858	1,298	5,041	9,179	14,741	5,079	1,943	6,948	1,096	2,125	480	884	11,750	1,048	33,206	5,040
1952	3,587	3,636	1,291	4,721	8,675	13,050	4,823	1,907	6,576	1,075	2,187	440	833	10,934	1,004	31,396	4,851
1951	3,361	3,336	1,188	4,318	8,344	12,176	4,660	1,796	6,245	1,049	2,067	378	792	10,151	936	30,009	4,691
1950	2,881	3,021	1,087	3,772	7,654	10,895	4,227	1,643	5,672	962	1,978	327	704	8,934	811	27,841	4,219
1949	2,659	2,857	1,060	3,392	6,971	9,627	3,846	1,441	5,196	788	1,697	286	671	8,131	719	26,046	3,675
1948	2,788	2,679	1,084	3,331	7,012	9,691	4,106	1,639	5,338	876	1,909	283	668	8,063	655	26,051	3,732
1940	908	852	437	1,304	3,367	3,595	1,475	470	1,974	316	573	101	281	3,406	198	11,724	1,155
1929	1,026	863	476	1,265	3,855	3,809	1,548	573	2,287	315	827	81	320	3,705	160	14,171	1,044

PER CAPITA INCOME (dollars)

Year	Kentucky 315	Louisiana 316	Maine 317	Maryland 318	Massachusetts 319	Michigan 320	Minnesota 321	Mississippi 322	Missouri 323	Montana 324	Nebraska 325	Nevada 326	New Hampshire 327	New Jersey 328	New Mexico 329	New York 330	North Carolina 331
1970	3,104	3,068	3,272	4,281	4,340	4,156	3,848	2,596	3,768	3,498	3,794	4,452	3,745	4,635	3,117	4,714	3,218
1969	2,881	2,864	3,010	3,991	4,058	4,075	3,595	2,370	3,478	3,170	3,594	4,264	3,418	4,288	2,877	4,470	2,989
1968	2,666	2,744	2,779	3,675	3,747	3,775	3,296	2,185	3,300	2,899	3,172	3,862	3,224	3,995	2,672	4,157	2,711
1967	2,450	2,528	2,534	3,351	3,448	3,438	3,047	1,986	3,047	2,731	3,029	3,521	2,982	3,701	2,463	3,828	2,481
1966	2,288	2,323	2,433	3,158	3,200	3,314	2,866	1,836	2,846	2,652	2,914	3,385	2,797	3,483	2,364	3,571	2,316
1965	2,087	2,120	2,269	2,967	2,985	3,094	2,651	1,667	2,681	2,439	2,618	3,229	2,556	3,267	2,242	3,354	2,075
1964	1,916	1,973	2,105	2,792	2,825	2,810	2,418	1,526	2,483	2,255	2,349	3,177	2,414	3,089	2,102	3,183	1,935
1963	1,857	1,865	1,937	2,646	2,716	2,611	2,351	1,466	2,370	2,258	2,263	3,185	2,326	2,966	2,053	3,010	1,829
1962	1,768	1,766	1,887	2,556	2,637	2,467	2,237	1,327	2,271	2,264	2,236	3,188	2,282	2,890	2,011	2,921	1,815
1961	1,683	1,700	1,817	2,456	2,533	2,311	2,182	1,278	2,165	1,969	2,107	2,893	2,193	2,767	1,939	2,803	1,732
1960	1,581	1,662	1,834	2,340	2,453	2,338	2,110	1,205	2,113	2,036	2,108	2,848	2,135	2,708	1,886	2,742	1,629
1959	1,556	1,671	1,772	2,268	2,369	2,264	2,016	1,202	2,099	2,009	1,974	2,760	2,076	2,635	1,914	2,655	1,558
1958	1,500	1,618	1,734	2,202	2,283	2,165	1,988	1,126	2,021	2,021	1,962	2,645	1,948	2,517	1,826	2,513	1,506
1957	1,465	1,614	1,679	2,198	2,247	2,229	1,874	1,040	1,922	1,944	1,876	2,588	1,927	2,536	1,702	2,493	1,431
1956	1,417	1,500	1,635	2,126	2,146	2,214	1,783	1,026	1,884	1,891	1,628	2,502	1,829	2,443	1,593	2,396	1,377
1955	1,328	1,396	1,552	1,994	2,026	2,183	1,729	1,020	1,802	1,852	1,594	2,549	1,765	2,306	1,504	2,283	1,313
1954	1,272	1,346	1,417	1,888	1,893	2,031	1,671	908	1,715	1,729	1,681	2,437	1,651	2,231	1,412	2,167	1,239
1953	1,293	1,346	1,421	1,964	1,910	2,161	1,665	923	1,728	1,779	1,612	2,462	1,616	2,167	1,412	2,139	1,223
1952	1,229	1,279	1,411	1,888	1,866	1,962	1,592	886	1,656	1,786	1,668	2,429	1,557	2,134	1,386	2,067	1,181
1951	1,143	1,205	1,297	1,769	1,793	1,874	1,548	830	1,556	1,761	1,571	2,249	1,497	2,028	1,367	2,015	1,139
1950	981	1,120	1,186	1,602	1,633	1,701	1,410	755	1,431	1,622	1,490	2,018	1,323	1,834	1,306	1,873	1,037
1949	933	1,084	1,174	1,456	1,470	1,520	1,310	691	1,339	1,385	1,304	1,823	1,259	1,663	1,177	1,749	940
1948	990	1,032	1,235	1,467	1,500	1,560	1,431	790	1,389	1,616	1,509	1,814	1,284	1,689	1,084	1,797	973
1940	317	360	515	709	780	676	529	216	521	566	436	890	571	816	373	871	323
1929	394	414	597	780	912	794	602	287	631	601	602	896	685	929	381	1,164	333

TOTAL INCOME, PERCENT OF U.S.

Year	Kentucky 315	Louisiana 316	Maine 317	Maryland 318	Massachusetts 319	Michigan 320	Minnesota 321	Mississippi 322	Missouri 323	Montana 324	Nebraska 325	Nevada 326	New Hampshire 327	New Jersey 328	New Mexico 329	New York 330	North Carolina 331
1970	1.25	1.39	0.41	2.10	3.08	4.60	1.83	0.72	2.20	0.30	0.70	0.27	0.35	4.15	0.39	10.71	2.04
1969	1.23	1.39	.40	2.07	3.07	4.79	1.81	.71	2.16	.29	.71	.27	.33	4.08	.39	10.84	2.01
1968	1.24	1.44	.40	2.05	3.07	4.79	1.78	.71	2.20	.30	.71	.27	.33	4.09	.39	10.96	1.98
1967	1.24	1.45	.41	2.01	3.08	4.74	1.78	.71	2.21	.31	.71	.25	.33	4.10	.39	10.97	1.96
1966	1.23	1.41	.42	2.00	3.03	4.83	1.78	.71	2.21	.32	.73	.26	.33	4.09	.41	10.91	1.94
1965	1.22	1.38	.42	1.99	3.06	4.83	1.78	.70	2.23	.32	.72	.27	.32	4.12	.42	11.10	1.88
1964	1.21	1.37	.42	1.97	3.11	4.65	1.74	.69	2.23	.32	.70	.27	.32	4.15	.43	11.31	1.88
1963	1.24	1.36	.42	1.93	3.13	4.54	1.79	.71	2.25	.34	.72	.27	.32	4.18	.44	11.35	1.86
1962	1.24	1.34	.43	1.90	3.15	4.45	1.79	.68	2.25	.36	.74	.25	.33	4.19	.45	11.48	1.85
1961	1.24	1.35	.44	1.88	3.19	4.40	1.83	.68	2.27	.33	.74	.22	.33	4.18	.45	11.54	1.83
1960	1.21	1.36	.45	1.83	3.17	4.59	1.81	.66	2.29	.35	.75	.21	.33	4.14	.45	11.58	1.79
1959	1.23	1.41	.45	1.82	3.18	4.62	1.78	.67	2.35	.35	.72	.20	.32	4.16	.46	11.63	1.76
1958	1.24	1.42	.46	1.83	3.19	4.63	1.84	.66	2.36	.38	.76	.20	.32	4.14	.45	11.64	1.75
1957	1.23	1.44	.45	1.81	3.18	4.84	1.76	.62	2.31	.37	.75	.19	.32	4.18	.41	11.71	1.72
1956	1.24	1.38	.46	1.81	3.18	5.00	1.75	.65	2.37	.38	.69	.19	.31	4.15	.39	11.68	1.80
1955	1.25	1.33	.47	1.77	3.21	5.16	1.78	.68	2.42	.38	.71	.20	.32	4.12	.38	11.83	1.81
1954	1.28	1.35	.46	1.76	3.23	4.99	1.81	.65	2.42	.38	.78	.18	.32	4.16	.37	11.92	1.78
1953	1.31	1.35	.45	1.77	3.22	5.16	1.78	.68	2.43	.38	.74	.17	.31	4.12	.37	11.63	1.77
1952	1.33	1.35	.48	1.75	3.22	4.84	1.79	.71	2.44	.40	.81	.16	.31	4.05	.37	11.64	1.80
1951	1.33	1.32	.47	1.71	3.30	4.81	1.84	.71	2.47	.41	.82	.15	.31	4.01	.37	11.85	1.85
1950	1.27	1.34	.48	1.67	3.38	4.82	1.87	.73	2.51	.43	.87	.14	.31	3.95	.36	12.31	1.87
1949	1.29	1.39	.52	1.65	3.39	4.68	1.87	.70	2.53	.38	.82	.14	.33	3.95	.35	12.66	1.79
1948	1.33	1.28	.52	1.59	3.36	4.64	1.97	.78	2.56	.42	.91	.14	.32	3.86	.31	12.47	1.79
1940	1.16	1.09	.56	1.67	4.31	4.60	1.89	.60	2.53	.40	.73	.13	.36	4.36	.25	15.01	1.48
1929	1.20	1.01	.55	1.47	4.49	4.44	1.80	.67	2.67	.37	.96	.09	.37	4.32	.19	16.52	1.22

Series F 297–348. Personal Income, by States: 1929 to 1970—Con.

Year	North Dakota	Ohio	Oklahoma	Oregon	Pennsyl-vania	Rhode Island	South Carolina	South Dakota	Tennessee	Texas	Utah	Vermont	Virginia	Wash-ington	West Virginia	Wiscon-sin	Wyo-ming
	332	333	334	335	336	337	338	339	340	341	342	343	344	345	346	347	348
TOTAL INCOME (millions of dollars)																	
1970	1,928	42,665	8,617	7,765	46,593	3,748	7,691	2,080	12,118	40,240	3,451	1,480	17,000	13,730	5,320	16,818	1,268
1969	1,867	40,424	7,827	7,276	43,301	3,453	6,985	1,995	11,231	36,678	3,116	1,426	15,461	13,118	4,780	15,299	1,112
1968	1,656	37,098	7,224	6,631	39,938	3,270	6,353	1,886	10,214	33,309	2,892	1,305	14,123	12,067	4,487	14,208	997
1967	1,596	33,788	6,675	6,096	37,062	2,988	5,728	1,731	9,280	30,019	2,672	1,178	12,741	10,890	4,251	13,094	932
1966	1,568	32,201	6,154	5,760	34,783	2,740	5,303	1,681	8,663	27,676	2,517	1,089	11,684	9,876	3,994	12,442	893
1965	1,505	29,383	5,668	5,333	31,943	2,504	4,702	1,528	7,850	24,956	2,356	956	10,718	8,627	3,728	11,345	854
1964	1,288	26,878	5,231	4,892	29,936	2,346	4,253	1,320	7,138	23,116	2,220	856	9,905	8,058	3,492	10,449	825
1963	1,292	25,189	4,889	4,553	27,876	2,193	3,928	1,350	6,640	21,646	2,156	798	8,983	7,736	3,266	9,665	813
1962	1,370	24,208	4,698	4,287	26,918	2,110	3,733	1,407	6,255	20,576	2,071	777	8,443	7,599	3,124	9,396	795
1961	964	23,008	4,561	4,046	25,747	1,964	3,450	1,227	5,881	19,615	1,910	731	7,777	7,051	3,031	8,885	776
1960	1,087	22,762	4,358	3,939	25,451	1,895	3,283	1,218	5,521	18,588	1,774	715	7,340	6,680	2,987	8,619	750
1959	949	22,035	4,137	3,804	24,719	1,844	3,119	981	5,394	18,047	1,678	672	6,995	6,514	2,968	8,376	717
1958	1,030	20,637	4,000	3,556	23,594	1,748	2,885	1,094	5,025	17,175	1,549	626	6,591	6,114	2,887	7,755	677
1957	905	20,959	3,744	3,416	23,414	1,701	2,810	1,068	4,872	16,538	1,482	619	6,349	5,912	2,967	7,547	645
1956	881	19,992	3,591	3,422	22,295	1,674	2,697	914	4,671	15,472	1,381	598	6,084	5,583	2,768	7,211	605
1955	848	18,762	3,390	3,198	20,669	1,614	2,599	857	4,374	14,438	1,272	549	5,638	5,306	2,492	6,682	570
1954	766	17,397	3,193	2,961	19,515	1,523	2,434	916	4,105	13,504	1,165	526	5,338	5,035	2,347	6,212	533
1953	757	17,423	3,201	2,990	19,938	1,531	2,615	892	4,080	13,196	1,166	521	5,292	4,934	2,473	6,265	549
1952	740	15,942	3,087	2,966	18,617	1,446	2,527	828	3,810	12,837	1,116	496	5,150	4,697	2,462	6,093	547
1951	794	14,894	2,837	2,784	17,752	1,384	2,321	942	3,645	11,914	1,053	482	4,763	4,414	2,365	5,837	556
1950	782	12,930	2,547	2,482	16,189	1,262	1,886	814	3,295	10,486	911	425	4,070	3,995	2,136	5,078	484
1949	674	11,749	2,460	2,251	14,553	1,151	1,724	689	3,001	9,839	835	396	3,648	3,600	1,994	4,633	445
1948	813	12,269	2,390	2,278	14,716	1,175	1,779	916	3,037	9,142	810	407	3,624	3,608	2,126	4,701	429
1940	218	4,575	851	671	6,408	531	572	231	982	2,762	266	183	1,245	1,140	767	1,734	151
1929	246	5,179	1,076	652	7,546	596	467	288	976	2,764	283	224	1,053	1,165	790	2,007	152
PER CAPITA INCOME (dollars)																	
1970	3,120	3,992	3,350	3,694	3,943	3,941	2,963	3,124	3,082	3,576	3,228	3,311	3,653	4,022	3,047	3,794	3,796
1969	3,006	3,827	3,088	3,528	3,688	3,705	2,718	2,987	2,882	3,321	2,976	3,262	3,351	3,924	2,738	3,495	3,380
1968	2,667	3,528	2,886	3,309	3,402	3,546	2,483	2,819	2,634	3,079	2,810	3,035	3,098	3,690	2,545	3,270	3,077
1967	2,549	3,245	2,682	3,081	3,173	3,287	2,261	2,580	2,405	2,832	2,622	2,785	2,826	3,431	2,403	3,043	2,895
1966	2,424	3,117	2,508	2,925	2,982	3,048	2,104	2,461	2,267	2,638	2,495	2,638	2,622	3,231	2,250	2,911	2,765
1965	2,319	2,880	2,323	2,753	2,749	2,804	1,885	2,208	2,067	2,405	2,377	2,365	2,430	2,908	2,087	2,681	2,571
1964	1,985	2,666	2,138	2,591	2,599	2,650	1,719	1,883	1,893	2,251	2,270	2,146	2,273	2,721	1,943	2,509	2,435
1963	2,006	2,522	2,004	2,457	2,440	2,504	1,597	1,906	1,786	2,131	2,213	2,010	2,101	2,618	1,819	2,350	2,419
1962	2,151	2,438	1,936	2,358	2,371	2,422	1,541	1,996	1,703	2,047	2,162	1,976	2,020	2,583	1,727	2,321	2,386
1961	1,504	2,335	1,917	2,264	2,260	2,289	1,432	1,770	1,624	1,997	2,041	1,875	1,899	2,447	1,658	2,216	2,304
1960	1,714	2,338	1,865	2,223	2,247	2,216	1,372	1,783	1,544	1,931	1,971	1,839	1,842	2,340	1,612	2,175	2,267
1959	1,536	2,278	1,807	2,179	2,200	2,152	1,329	1,471	1,532	1,919	1,929	1,736	1,770	2,309	1,600	2,153	2,239
1958	1,699	2,150	1,764	2,070	2,134	2,038	1,252	1,668	1,448	1,856	1,833	1,648	1,684	2,205	1,565	2,018	2,148
1957	1,479	2,227	1,641	1,996	2,137	1,998	1,236	1,603	1,419	1,823	1,794	1,647	1,652	2,170	1,610	1,991	2,054
1956	1,437	2,171	1,580	2,016	2,032	1,993	1,210	1,365	1,368	1,752	1,707	1,586	1,634	2,092	1,491	1,927	1,938
1955	1,378	2,081	1,507	1,927	1,889	1,962	1,181	1,293	1,281	1,667	1,625	1,463	1,571	2,038	1,326	1,816	1,857
1954	1,254	1,961	1,445	1,821	1,804	1,866	1,119	1,398	1,222	1,611	1,554	1,501	1,501	2,001	1,232	1,722	1,818
1953	1,244	2,028	1,467	1,867	1,870	1,878	1,199	1,376	1,229	1,583	1,578	1,374	1,488	2,001	1,282	1,787	1,892
1952	1,217	1,926	1,391	1,875	1,773	1,804	1,160	1,272	1,137	1,544	1,542	1,324	1,470	1,919	1,258	1,757	1,866
1951	1,314	1,848	1,284	1,789	1,697	1,765	1,071	1,438	1,081	1,469	1,491	1,275	1,387	1,821	1,192	1,697	1,911
1950	1,263	1,620	1,143	1,620	1,541	1,605	893	1,242	994	1,349	1,309	1,121	1,228	1,674	1,065	1,477	1,668
1949	1,130	1,474	1,169	1,573	1,401	1,437	850	1,091	927	1,291	1,244	1,074	1,108	1,569	1,033	1,366	1,805
1948	1,401	1,558	1,144	1,621	1,431	1,493	891	1,497	944	1,199	1,241	1,133	1,130	1,600	1,120	1,418	1,595
1940	340	660	366	618	648	739	301	360	334	430	482	505	458	655	402	552	606
1929	365	782	454	689	776	871	269	417	375	480	558	625	434	749	460	684	683
TOTAL INCOME, PERCENT OF U.S.																	
1970	0.24	5.31	1.07	0.97	5.80	0.47	0.96	0.26	1.51	5.01	0.43	0.18	2.12	1.71	0.66	2.09	0.15
1969	.25	5.42	1.05	.97	5.80	.46	.94	.27	1.50	4.91	.42	.19	2.07	1.76	.64	2.05	.15
1968	.24	5.42	1.05	.97	5.83	.48	.93	.28	1.49	4.86	.42	.19	2.06	1.76	.66	2.07	.15
1967	.26	5.40	1.07	.97	5.92	.48	.92	.28	1.48	4.80	.43	.19	2.04	1.74	.68	2.09	.15
1966	.27	5.52	1.05	.99	5.96	.47	.91	.29	1.48	4.74	.43	.19	2.00	1.69	.68	2.13	.15
1965	.28	5.48	1.06	1.00	5.96	.47	.88	.29	1.46	4.66	.44	.18	2.00	1.61	.70	2.12	.16
1964	.26	5.43	1.06	.99	6.05	.47	.86	.27	1.44	4.67	.45	.17	2.00	1.63	.71	2.11	.17
1963	.28	5.44	1.06	.98	6.02	.47	.85	.29	1.43	4.67	.47	.17	1.94	1.67	.71	2.09	.18
1962	.31	5.50	1.07	.97	6.12	.48	.85	.32	1.42	4.67	.47	.18	1.92	1.73	.71	2.13	.18
1961	.23	5.55	1.10	.98	6.21	.47	.83	.30	1.42	4.73	.46	.18	1.88	1.70	.73	2.14	.19
1960	.27	5.71	1.09	.99	6.38	.48	.82	.31	1.38	4.66	.44	.18	1.84	1.68	.75	2.16	.19
1959	.25	5.78	1.09	1.00	6.49	.48	.82	.26	1.42	4.74	.44	.18	1.84	1.71	.78	2.20	.19
1958	.29	5.76	1.12	.99	6.58	.49	.80	.31	1.40	4.79	.43	.17	1.84	1.71	.81	2.16	.19
1957	.26	6.01	1.07	.98	6.72	.49	.81	.31	1.40	4.75	.43	.18	1.82	1.70	.85	2.17	.19
1956	.27	6.05	1.09	1.04	6.75	.51	.82	.28	1.41	4.68	.42	.18	1.84	1.69	.84	2.18	.18
1955	.27	6.09	1.10	1.04	6.70	.52	.84	.28	1.42	4.68	.41	.18	1.83	1.72	.81	2.17	.18
1954	.27	6.05	1.11	1.03	6.79	.53	.85	.32	1.43	4.70	.41	.18	1.86	1.75	.82	2.16	.19
1953	.27	6.10	1.12	1.05	6.98	.54	.92	.31	1.43	4.62	.41	.18	1.85	1.73	.87	2.19	.19
1952	.27	5.91	1.14	1.10	6.90	.54	.94	.31	1.41	4.76	.41	.18	1.91	1.74	.91	2.26	.20
1951	.31	5.88	1.12	1.10	7.01	.55	.92	.37	1.44	4.70	.42	.19	1.88	1.74	.93	2.31	.22
1950	.35	5.72	1.13	1.10	7.16	.56	.83	.36	1.46	4.64	.40	.19	1.80	1.77	.94	2.24	.21
1949	.33	5.71	1.20	1.09	7.07	.56	.84	.33	1.46	4.78	.41	.19	1.77	1.75	.97	2.25	.22
1948	.39	5.87	1.14	1.09	7.05	.56	.85	.44	1.45	4.38	.39	.19	1.73	1.73	1.02	2.25	.21
1940	.28	5.86	1.09	.86	8.20	.68	.73	.30	1.26	3.54	.34	.23	1.59	1.46	.98	2.22	.19
1929	.29	6.04	1.25	.76	8.79	.69	.54	.34	1.14	3.22	.33	.26	1.23	1.36	.92	2.34	.18

National Wealth and Saving (Series F 349-667)

F 349-469. General note.

The national balance sheet is derived by summing similar balance sheets for sectors in the economy—nonfarm households, agriculture, unincorporated business, corporations, etc. The balance sheet of each group is in turn derived by summing the balance sheets of the constituent units, based as far as possible on a comparable valuation of assets and liabilities. In deriving the balance sheet, no creditor-debtor or owner-issuer relationships among units are eliminated; for example, the debts of households to corporations appear on one side as assets of corporations and on the other as liabilities of households. When all relationships among constituent units are canceled, whether these units be in the same or different groups, the balance sheet reduces to a national wealth statement. (In the series shown, the estimate for total tangible assets in the national balance sheet differs very slightly from that in the statements of national wealth and national tangible assets because of a minor disparity in the treatment of monetary metals.) Thus, the national balance sheet adds to the national wealth statement a comprehensive summary of the various types of financial obligations outstanding at a particular date, and provides perspective on the magnitude of financing activities in the Nation's economy.

The national balance sheet falls somewhat short of the goal of a comprehensive summary of the assets, liabilities, and net worth of all transactors in the economy, since, for lack of data, obligations among households are not included, and in the case of corporations with subsidiaries, the balance sheet of the parent company is used, thus eliminating relationships among the subsidiary units. In addition, intangibles such as goodwill and patent rights are excluded from the balance sheet. Finally, and this limits the comprehensiveness of the national wealth statement as well, inventories of nondurable goods in the hands of consumers, expenditures on soil improvement, subsoil assets, and military and naval equipment held by the government are omitted.

The value for "equity" in the national balance sheet exceeds total national wealth, that is, consolidated net national worth. This is primarily because, in the balance sheet, the net worth of the various constituent units are added together. For example, the net worth of a corporation is added to the net worth of the stockholders. In the national wealth statement, however, they are consolidated. That is, the outstanding stock of the corporation is canceled against the holdings of the owners, leaving only the net worth of the stockholders and the undistributed earnings of the corporations. Stated differently, the "equity" entry in the balance sheet includes the equity of intermediaries as well as of ultimate owners.

F 349-364. National tangible assets, in current prices, 1952-1968.

Source: U.S. Congress, *Institutional Investor Study Report of the Securities and Exchange Commission, Supplementary Volume I*, House Document 92-64, Part 6, March 10, 1971.

Estimates of reproducible assets shown in series F 349-364 and F 365-376 were made using the perpetual inventory method. This method involves the computation of a weighted sum of a time series of gross investments in the asset; the weights are determined by the particular life and depreciation assumptions employed in the calculation. The difference between the gross investment of a given year and the change in stock during that year is, by definition, the depreciation which has occurred. To derive the replacement cost estimates used in series F 349-364, the calculation was first made in terms of constant dollars (series F 365-376), and then the stock and depreciation estimates were reflated to current year prices.

The gross investment series used for the estimates of the private stock of depreciable assets are in all cases those used in the gross investment component of the income and product accounts produced by the U.S. Bureau of Economic Analysis (BEA). For public sector estimates, the construction data and equipment series were taken from the income and product accounts wherever possible. Such data are published regularly in the *Survey of Current Business*, although the two government sectors are not credited with capital formation in the BEA accounts.

For a detailed description of the method used to obtain estimates for the various components of depreciable assets, see the source publication cited above, pp. 252-259.

Land estimates shown in series F 349-364 and F 365-376, with few exceptions, are those given in Appendix II, "Estimates of the Value of Land in the United States Held by Various Sectors of the Economy, Annually, 1952 to 1968," of the source publication. The land of financial corporations was estimated by multiplying the Internal Revenue Service estimates of the book value of land of all financial institutions by the market-to-book ratio developed in Appendix II for "finance, insurance, and real estate." No adjustment was made for unincorporated financial institutions, which tend to be brokerage houses, as the land holdings of the finance, insurance, and real estate aggregate for partnerships and proprietorships are accounted for primarily by the holdings of real estate firms.

The estimated value of farmland shown in these series was derived by subtracting the value of buildings from the U.S. Department of Agriculture's estimate of the value of farm real estate.

Transactions were measured by first differences in the holdings.

F 365-376. National reproducible tangible assets in constant (1958) prices, 1952-1968.

Source: See source for series F 349-364.

See also general note for series F 349-469 and text for series F 349-364.

F 377-421. National balance sheet, in current prices, 1900-1968.

Source: Raymond W. Goldsmith, et al., *Studies in the National Balance Sheet of the United States*, vol. II, Princeton University Press, tables I and Ia (copyright 1963 by National Bureau of Economic Research, New York); and unpublished data.

The national balance sheet is derived by summing similar balance sheets for various transactor groups in the economy—nonfarm households, agriculture, unincorporated business, etc. (see general note for series F 349-469). For most of these groups, however, balance sheets of the constituent units are nonexistent, so that in practice the group balance sheet is compiled from separate estimates of the various categories of assets and liabilities, net worth being derived as a residual. Only in the case of corporations and the Federal Government does a substantial proportion of the items come from their own financial statements. Military assets, i.e., military structures and equipment and the assets of the Atomic Energy Commission, are excluded from these balance sheets.

The estimates presented are in current prices rather than original cost. Essentially, this means that reproducible tangible assets are valued at reproduction cost, and nonreproducible tangible assets and intangibles at market value, though some intangibles, particularly short-term claims, are valued at par or face value.

In deriving the estimates, a problem sometimes arose because of a difference between two groups in the value at which the same item is carried on the balance sheet, a difference not attributable to bad debt reserves alone. Where this was the case, no attempt was made to force consistency. Both valuations were carried over into the national balance sheet on the appropriate sides. This, together with the treatment of net holdings of foreign assets and liabilities, principally accounts for differences between the asset and liability totals for certain intangible items—differences which are generally small compared with the balance sheet totals.

The source provides considerable additional detail—in particular, balance sheets for separate transactor groups, such as nonfarm households, agriculture, etc., and makes it possible to trace the patterns of claims and counterclaims among the various groups.

Figures for 1958–1968 have been derived principally from the Federal Reserve Board's flow-of-funds data and differ from earlier data mainly because of statistical revisions in the basic data. However, differences in the following items are the result of conceptual differences.

F 381, monetary metals. Data for 1900–1958 include all gold and silver coin; data for 1958–1968 include gold and official foreign exchange reserves.

F 382, other currency and demand deposits. The earlier estimates include cash items in process of collection and other interbank claims within the private financial sector which are not included in the flow-of-funds data. These items amounted to $35.1 billion in 1958.

F 397, U.S. Government securities, long-term. Data for 1900–1958 include special issues held by U.S. Government pension and trust funds; data for 1958–1968 do not. Data for 1958–1968 include issues of U.S. Government credit agencies, while 1900–1958 estimates include these in "other bonds and notes" below.

F 401, other bonds and notes. See above.

F 405, equity in other business. Data for 1900–1958 include equity in unincorporated broker-dealers; 1958–1968 data cover non-farm, nonfinancial business only.

F 410, private life insurance reserves. The 1900–1958 data include the pension reserves of life insurance companies and the policy reserves of fraternal insurance organizations which are not included in the flow-of-funds figures. However, the policy reserve estimates are available in Appendix I of the *Institutional Investor Study* (see source for series F 349–364).

F 411, private pension and retirement funds. Data for 1958–1968 include the pension reserves of life insurance companies which are included in F 410 for 1900–1958.

F 412, Government pension and insurance funds. Data for 1900–1958 include the reserves of Old Age Survivors Insurance, about $21.9 billion in 1958; data for 1958–1968 omit these, although data are available in the *Monthly Treasury Statement.*

F 422–445. National wealth, by type of asset, in current prices, 1850–1958.

Source: Raymond W. Goldsmith, 1850–1900, "The Growth of Reproducible Wealth of the United States of America From 1805 to 1950," International Association for Research in Income and Wealth, *Income and Wealth of the United States: Trends and Structure,* Income and Wealth Series II, Bowes and Bowes, Cambridge, England, 1952, p. 306 (estimates for 1805 presented in this publication have not been reproduced here because of questionable reliability); 1900–1958, *The National Wealth of the United States in the Postwar Period,* Princeton University Press, App. A and B (copyright 1962 by National Bureau of Economic Research, New York).

The estimates for 1900 to 1958 were constructed by Goldsmith by means of the "perpetual inventory method." In this method, the stock of an asset in existence at a given point in time is estimated from annual output totals extending back over a period equal to the average life of the asset, the output total for every year being depreciated to the end of the period, and the results summed. (See also text for series F 349–364.) Military assets are excluded.

The underlying estimates for 1850 appear in the Census Office, *Preliminary Report of the Eighth Census,* 1862, p. 195; and those for 1880, 1890, and 1900 in Simon Kuznets, *National Product Since 1869,*

National Bureau of Economic Research, New York, 1946, pp. 202–215. In every case, the original estimates were adjusted by Goldsmith (for 1880 substantially) to improve comparability with the estimates for 1900–1958. The basic sources for these earlier estimates were returns on stocks of various assets in the industrial censuses and censuses of wealth. Hence, there is a sharp break in the method of derivation between the earlier and later estimates. However, the figures for the overlap year, 1900, agree reasonably well. The figures for 1850 exclude the value of slaves.

The estimates for 1900–1958 are in "current prices," that is, each asset is valued at its replacement cost in the given year. This is preferable to valuation at original cost, whether depreciated or undepreciated. Assets appearing in the wealth statement for any given date were produced in different years, and since prices change from year to year, summation of original cost values would often result in an arithmetic aggregate without economic meaning.

For the estimates for 1850 to 1900, which are primarily from the Federal censuses, the basis of valuation is not always certain, and is not uniform among types of assets and among industries. It is possible that the figures may approximate either current market values or original cost, depreciated or undepreciated, or some combination of the two. Some assurance as to the comparability of the earlier and later sets of figures on this score is provided, however, by the overlapping values for 1900, though this comparison applies only to a single year.

As to the reliability of the estimates for 1850 to 1900, the source (*Income and Wealth of the United States: Trends and Structure*) states that the margin of error amounts to hardly less than 10 to 20 percent at any date, that this relative margin increases going back in time, and that it is not certain that comparability is impaired by as much as the size of the margin may imply because the error probably tends in the same direction for most if not all benchmarks, although the understatement is probably more pronounced in the early part of the period than in the latter. Concerning the estimates for 1900 to 1958, derived by the perpetual inventory method, the most important source of error is considered to reside in the estimates of construction expenditures. For some of the components of total wealth, reliability is strengthened because of the availability of checks against alternative estimates, as is the case for residential real estate, farm structures, inventories, and international assets. Checks are less satisfactory for nonfarm business structures and equipment but the information in corporate balance sheets submitted to the Internal Revenue Service gives assurance that the perpetual inventory estimates are not too far off for recent years. The only sectors of reproducible tangible wealth in which the perpetual inventory estimates are not subject to checks, or only to very unsatisfactory checks, are consumers' durables and government fixed assets.

The source also presents considerably greater detail than given here (for example, annual estimates for 1896–1949). Estimates of national wealth by contemporaries are also available for various dates during the 19th century. See, for example, Samuel Blodget, Jr., *Economica; A Statistical Manual for the United States,* 1806 edition, and *Annual Report of the Director of the Mint, 1881.*

F 446–469. National wealth, by type of asset, in 1929 and 1947–49 prices, 1850–1958.

Source: See source for series F 422–445.

These estimates were derived by adjusting the current dollar figures for a given class of assets in series F 422–445 for the change in price or cost of construction of that type of asset between each year and the base year. Thus, conceptually, changes over time in the constant price value of a category of assets reflect changes in the physical stock of that asset and not in its value. For 1945–1958, a different base year was necessary because estimates in 1929 prices for the most recent years were not available. This shift in base years introduces some element of incomparability, since the relative weights of individual assets in the price index differ between the two years.

For 1900–1958, an attempt was made to adjust for price changes by fairly narrow classes of assets, using construction cost or price indexes referring specifically to the assets in each class. For 1880, 1890, and 1900, a more summary adjustment was used. Only three separate deflators were employed for construction (residential, other private, and farm), and a single deflator was used for all types of equipment. For 1850, the same price index (Snyder's index of the general price level) was applied to all types of structures and equipment, although for the adjustment of inventories the wholesale price index was used.

Goldsmith states that the conceptual significance of a constant price estimate for land is open to question. If land is carried for all dates at its absolute value in the base year, the relation to the constant price value of reproducible assets tends to become unrealistic, particularly at dates fairly far removed from the base year. In the present estimate, an alternative procedure is followed, a constant price value of land being derived, generally speaking, as a fixed proportion of the constant price value of structures. This permits derivation of a constant price series for aggregate national wealth, but it should be recognized that the deflated estimates of land values included in the totals cannot be conceived as reflecting changes in physical units alone.

The adjustment for price changes introduces errors in the estimates in addition to those discussed in connection with series F 422–445. On balance, any error is likely to lead towards an overstatement of the price rise over the period and hence an understatement of growth rates because the techniques used in adjusting for price change fail to make adequate allowance for improvement in the quality of the assets, and there is no evidence that the error is larger for one part of the period than for another, although the possibilities of error are certainly greater in the 19th century than the 20th. In addition, it is likely that the failure to allow for quality improvement has a differential effect on the different components of wealth. In particular, it leads to a more serious understatement in the growth of components such as producer and consumer durables than for structures and inventories.

F 470–534.   General note.

Although estimates of capital stocks are less well developed than those of economic flows, in recent years a number of capital stock estimates have been prepared and published by the U.S. Bureau of Economic Analysis (formerly the U.S. Office of Business Economics), as part of a project to measure the entire tangible wealth of the Nation. BEA estimates have been published for (1) residential capital, (2) fixed nonresidential business capital, (3) provisional estimates of consumer durable goods, and (4) stocks of business inventories. References for these studies are as follows: (1) John C. Musgrave, "New Estimates of Residential Capital in the United States, 1925–73," *Survey of Current Business*, October 1974; (2) Bureau of Economic Analysis, *Fixed Nonresidential Business Capital in the United States, 1925–73*, 1974; (3) Henry Shavell, "The Stocks of Durable Goods in the Hands of Consumers, 1946–1969," *1970 Proceedings of the Business and Economics Section of the American Statistical Association*, 1971; (4) Shirley F. Loftus, "Stocks of Business Inventories in the United States, 1928–71," *Survey of Current Business*, December 1972, with updating in August 1974 *Survey of Current Business*. Also, estimates of inventories owned by nonfinancial corporations, as of midyear for the years 1948–71, in constant (1958) prices and the current prices of each year, appeared in "Nonfinancial Corporations: New Measures of Output and Input," by John A. Gorman, *Survey of Current Business*, March 1972.

Series F 470–479, F 480–515, F 516–527, and F 528–534 provide selected series from these BEA capital stock studies. Series F 470–479 is a summary table providing series on gross and net stocks of nonresidential structures and equipment, residential structures and equipment, and inventories in both current and constant prices. Greater detail on nonresidential structures and equipment and residential structures is provided in series F 480–515, F 516–527, and F 528–534.

Fixed nonresidential structures and equipment estimates are computed by the perpetual inventory method, which derives capital stock estimates for a given year by cumulating past investment and deducting the cumulated value of the investment that is used up. The data used to implement this method are taken from the national income and product accounts since 1929 and from various private studies prior to that time. Included are all privately owned nonresidential structures and producers' durable equipment. Estimates shown are on the secondhand price method of valuing business purchases of government surplus assets, variant 1 deflators for structures, straight-line depreciation, and 85 percent of service lives given in Bulletin F, Internal Revenue Service. The series published here is just one of a number of variants of capital stock estimates reflecting different valuations, service lives, and depreciation techniques. (See source for additional estimates.)

The residential capital estimates are also computed by the perpetual inventory method. The data used to implement this method are taken from the national income and product accounts since 1929 and from various private studies prior to that time. Included are all residential structures, both privately and publicly owned. Depreciation is estimated by a declining balance formula.

The stocks of business inventories shown in series F 470–479 were calculated by cumulating the annual inventory changes, in book values and in constant (1958) prices, respectively, that are estimated in the national income and product account. An estimate of the level of each book value and constant price stock series was made for some single point in time for which appropriate data were available; that stock was then moved forward through time by adding the estimated annual changes and backward through time by substracting the annual changes.

Series F 516–527 and F 528–534 give information on the age structure of the capital stock. Such information is essential for gauging the extent to which capital is up-to-date in terms of both physical condition and technological characteristics. Two measures of age structure are presented in the publications cited above: an average age series of the capital stock and the ratios of the net stock of the capital to the gross.

These two measures of age can be used interchangeably for many purposes, but each provides specific information. The net-gross ratios show the extent to which the services initially embodied in capital goods remains intact, on the assumption that the purchase price is a measure of the value of the services bought initially and that depreciation reflects the value of the services that have been used up. The average age measures, which are given in series F 516–527 and F 534, provide information on absolute age.

F 470–479.   Private capital stocks, current and constant (1958) cost valuation, 1925–1970.

Source: **Series F 470**, sum of series F 471–474; **series F 475**, sum of series F 476–479. **Series F 471, 472, 476,** and **477**, U.S. Bureau of Economic Analysis, *Fixed Nonresidential Business Capital in the United States, 1925–1973*, 1974, pp. 1–12 and unpublished data. **Series F 473** and **478**, "New Estimates of Residential Capital in the United States, 1925–73," *Survey of Current Business*, October 1974. **Series F 474** and **479**, "Stocks of Business Inventories in the United States, 1928–71," *Survey of Current Business*, December 1972, pp. 29–32, and August 1974.

For a description of the conceptual framework and estimating techniques used to derive these data, see the general note for series F 470–534.

F 480–515.   Fixed nonresidential business capital—current and constant (1958) cost valuation, 1925–1970.

Source: U.S. Bureau of Economic Analysis, *Fixed Nonresidential Business Capital in the United States, 1925–1973*, 1974, pp. 1–12 and 48–51, and unpublished data.

For a description of the conceptual framework and estimating techniques used to derive these data, see the general note for series F 470–534.

F 516–527. Fixed nonresidential business capital—average age of gross stocks, constant (1958) cost valuation, 1925–1970.

Source: U.S. Bureau of Economic Analysis, *Fixed Nonresidential Business Capital in the United States, 1925–73*, 1974, pp. 1–12.

For a description of the conceptual framework and estimating techniques used to derive these data, see the general note for series F 470–534.

F 528–534. Residential capital, current and constant (1958) cost valuation, 1925–1970.

Source: U.S. Bureau of Economic Analysis, "New Estimates of Residential Capital in the United States, 1925–73," *Survey of Current Business*, October 1974.

For a description of the conceptual framework and estimating techniques used to derive these data, see the general note for series F 470–534.

F 535–539. Value of stock of structures and equipment in specified sectors, in 1929 prices, 1880–1948.

Source: Simon Kuznets, *Capital in the American Economy: Its Formation and Financing*, National Bureau of Economic Research, New York, 1961 (copyright).

These estimates fall somewhat short of the value of all reproducible wealth in each sector, since the value of inventories is omitted, and considerably short of total wealth, since land is excluded. Also, data are not available for other business sectors; for example, trade and the service industries are omitted. However, it is estimated that the four sectors included here accounted for about 80 percent of the stock of structures and equipment in 1880.

The underlying sources of the estimates are three monographs prepared in connection with the National Bureau of Economic Research Study of Capital Formation and Financing: Alvin S. Tostlebe, *Capital in Agriculture: Its Formation and Financing Since 1870*, Princeton University Press, 1957; Daniel Creamer, Israel Borenstein, and Sergei P. Dobrovolsky, *Capital Formation and Financing in Manufacturing and Mining*, 1960; and Melville J. Ulmer, *Capital in Transportation, Communication, and Public Utilities: Its Formation and Financing*, 1960. With the exception of the last monograph, the approach followed in deriving the estimates of capital stock differed rather noticeably from that chiefly employed in obtaining the figures presented in series F 422–469, since the basic data, such as census returns on capital or balance sheet items in *Statistics of Income*, related to stocks rather than output flows. Further detail on capital investment by type and/or minor industrial sector is given in these monographs.

F 540–667. General note.

Statistics of saving provide the link between the statements of national income or product, on the one hand, and the national wealth statement and balance sheet, on the other. Generally speaking, for the Nation as a whole, aggregate saving, which equals national income less national consumption, is identical with net national investment, and the latter, in turn, is equal to the change in real national wealth. For the individual economic unit, however, saving is equal not to the change in holdings of real assets, but to the difference between the change in total assets (both tangible and intangible) and total liabilities. The national balance sheet registers the effect of saving on the stock of intangibles as well as tangibles.

The link provided by the saving statistics is imperfect for both conceptual and statistical reasons. To note only some of the principal conceptual differences, there are, first, variations in the treatment of government. In the Department of Commerce estimates of income and saving, government investment and government saving are excluded, while in the Kuznets income estimates, and the Gold-

smith saving and wealth estimates, government saving and investment are included, though the Goldsmith estimates exclude military assets. Another important difference is in the treatment of consumer durables, which in both the Department of Commerce and Kuznets income estimates is not considered investment, but in the Goldsmith estimates of saving and wealth is so considered. Finally, there are important differences in the scope and valuation of capital consumption allowances. Beyond the conceptual differences, there are variations in the sources and techniques employed by the different estimators. The broad outlines of the relationships among the different social accounts can, nevertheless, be distinguished. In addition, the saving statistics throw important light on the nature of the different groups of savers in the economy and the forms that saving takes.

F 540–551. National saving, by major saver groups, in current prices, 1897–1945.

Source: Raymond W. Goldsmith, *A Study of Saving in the United States*, vol. I, 1955, p. 345 (saving, excluding consumer durables, computed by subtraction of estimates of saving in consumer durables for nonagricultural individuals, p. 359, and for agriculture, p. 756). Reprinted by permission of Princeton University Press.

These series provide an estimate of saving by government (thus permitting the derivation of aggregate national saving), and estimates of personal saving subdivided among three major groups—nonagricultural individuals (including private nonprofit institutions and personal trust funds), agriculture, and unincorporated business.

The saving concept underlying these estimates differs somewhat from the concept represented by series F 552–565. While these estimates include all forms of saving covered in series F 552–565, they also cover saving in the form of consumer durables, and of brokers' and dealers' commissions and profits on change of hands of existing assets. In addition, in deriving these estimates of net saving, capital consumption allowances have been valued at replacement cost. Neither set of figures, however, includes saving in the form of soil improvement or additions to military assets. An important difference also exists between the two sets of estimates in the technique of derivation. The estimates in series F 552–565 were derived by the income approach; these figures, with the exception of those for corporate saving, were obtained by the balance sheet method. In this respect, they are similar to the estimates of personal saving presented in series F 638–667, though differences in techniques and in concept cause the actual estimates to differ between the two tables, e.g. because of inclusion in series F 659 (but not in series F 623) of stock issues of small corporations not distributed by security dealers.

The following statement from the source (pp. 40–41) provides an indication of the reliability of the estimates:

Evaluation of the possible errors in the individual series from which the estimates of group and national saving have been constructed indicates that the margin of error is hardly under 10 percent for any given year or for the average annual figure in any series, that it is probably in the order of magnitude of 20 to 30 percent in many of them, that it may run even higher in not a few cases, but that the relative margin of error in most cases is reduced for sequences of several years and generally the smaller the longer the period . . .

Most of the components utilized in building the estimates of saving of any of the major saver groups are statistically independent; and the estimates for the major saver groups are very largely independent of each other except for those on nonfarm households and unincorporated business enterprises. Accordingly since the number of components of saving is large for each of the groups, running to several dozen even if only those of substantial quantitative importance are taken into account, there is reason to assume that errors in one direction, i.e. overstatements or underestimates of saving, made in any one year in some of the component series will be offset by errors in the opposite direction in other series. As a result, the relative error in the estimates of saving by the major groups, and still more the estimates of broad aggregates such as national or personal saving, may be expected to be considerably lower than the average of the relative errors in the component series. Indeed, it is quite possible that, if we take account of the number of independent component series and their relative size, and even take a pessimistic view of errors in constituent series, the relative error of national or personal saving in any one year does not on the average exceed something like 10 percent.

The quality of most of the individual series used in the measurement of saving has undoubtedly improved. It would seem to be substantially poorer for the period before the thirties than for the last two decades, and within the earlier period, in turn, to be particularly poor for the years before approximately 1905. Nevertheless, there is no statistical evidence, such as might be provided by the difference between estimates of saving and investment, that the estimates of aggregate saving have larger relative errors in the earlier part of the period than in the later part. Indeed, from that point of view, the relative error in the estimates would have to be regarded as substantially the same through the thirties, and as considerably lower only for the last decade. There is, however, evidence . . . that the error is . . . in the direction of an overstatement of saving in the first three decades and an understatement during the thirties.

F 552–565.   Sources and uses of gross saving, 1929–1970.

Source: U.S. Bureau of Economic Analysis, 1929–1963, *The National Income and Product Accounts of the United States, 1929–1965*; 1964–1967, *U.S. National Income and Product Accounts, 1964–67*; and 1968–1970, *Survey of Current Business*, July issues, table 5.1.

The following are definitions used by the source:

Gross private saving is the total of household and business saving. Saving through government, including government insurance funds, is excluded.   Household expenditures for consumer durables, except on residential construction, are not treated as saving.   The series is "gross" in that it includes business capital consumption allowances and depreciation on residences.

Personal saving represents the excess of personal income over the sum of personal consumption expenditures and personal tax and nontax payments.   It includes the current saving of individuals (including owners of unincorporated business), nonprofit institutions, and private health, welfare, and trust funds.   Personal saving may be in such forms as changes in cash and deposits, security holdings, indebtedness, and reserves of life insurance companies and mutual savings institutions, the net investment of unincorporated enterprises, and the acquisition of real property net of depreciation.   Inventory profits and other capital gains are excluded.

Gross business saving includes undistributed corporate profits, corporate inventory valuation adjustment and capital consumption allowances, and, for 1943–1953, the excess of wage accruals over disbursements.

Undistributed corporate profits represent the difference between corporate profits after taxes and dividends.   Corporate profits after taxes are the earnings of corporations organized for profit which accrue to the residents of the Nation, measured after Federal and State profit taxes, without deduction of depletion charges and exclusive of capital gains and losses.   Dividends measure cash dividend disbursements by corporations organized for profit to stockholders who are residents of the United States.

Corporate inventory valuation adjustment is the excess of the value of the change in the volume of nonfarm corporate business inventories, valued at average prices during the period, over the change in the book value of nonfarm corporate inventories.

Capital consumption allowances represent the sum of business depreciation charges and accidental damage to fixed business capital. Business depreciation charges are charges made by private business against receipts for the current consumption of durable capital goods and comparable allowances for nonprofit institutions.   They include depreciation charges against owner-occupied houses.   Depreciation reported by business is not adjusted for changes in the replacement value of capital goods, except for farm enterprises.   Accidental damage to fixed business capital represents the value of the physical losses by fire, natural events, and other accidents to fixed capital of private business not covered by depreciation charges.

Government surplus or deficit is the excess of government receipts over government expenditures as defined in the national income and product accounts.   As such, it equals the acquisition of financial assets less borrowing by general government and government enterprises.   It also includes new government purchases of land.   Net acquisitions of reproducible assets are excluded here because they are included in government purchases of goods and services.

Capital grants received by the United States in 1970 are the Special Drawing Rights allocated to the United States by the International Monetary Fund.   These allocations represent additions to the foreign assets of the United States that are not matched by corresponding liabilities.   They are considered part of the U.S. net foreign investment and are shown as a source by means of this special entry.

Gross private domestic investment consists of the net acquisitions of fixed capital goods by private business and nonprofit institutions; including commissions arising in the sale and purchase of new and existing fixed assets, principally real estate; and the value of the change in the volume of inventories held by business.   It covers all private dwellings including those acquired by persons for their own occupancy.

Net foreign investment is numerically equal to the balance on goods, services, and unilateral transfers as measured in the balance of payments statistics.   As such, it is equal to the acquisition of foreign assets by U.S. residents less the acquisition of U.S. assets by foreign residents.   It also includes the "errors and omissions" item in the balance of payments statistics.

With respect to reliability of these estimates, the Department of Commerce notes that the margin of error in the estimates of gross private saving and its components tends generally to be high.   Because personal saving is derived as the difference between two much larger totals, it is subject to large percentage error in both level and movement.   Undistributed corporate profits is more accurate, but the corporate inventory valuation adjustment is liable to considerable error, so that the reliability of the two items combined is not high.   Furthermore, while approximately half of the estimate for capital consumption allowances is based on fairly solid data, the remainder is estimated on the basis of a variety of sources and methods, and some of these are subject to a wide margin of error.

Series F 566–594.   Individuals' saving, by components, in current prices, 1946–1970.

Source: Board of Governors of the Federal Reserve System, *Flow of Funds Accounts: Annual Flows, 1946–1971*, August 1972, pp. 69–71.

Series F 566–594 presents an estimate of personal saving that is conceptually equivalent to the amounts derived in national income accounts (NIA), series F 553, but statistically it is almost entirely independent of NIA data.   The NIA series for personal saving is calculated as a residual in current transactions: Personal income less personal taxes less consumption and other current outlays.   That residual measures the net flow of funds from current activities of persons and is used for acquisition of capital assets, both tangible and financial, and for repayment of personal debt.   Series F 566–594 is a direct measure of those capital acquisitions and debt flows and is thus an estimate of the same net flow of personal saving in terms of the capital uses to which it is put.   The basic identity relationship reflected in series F 566–594 is that personal saving equals net acquisition of capital assets less net increase in debt, or alternatively that total sources of funds from saving and net borrowing equals total uses of funds for capital asset purchases.

Series F 566–594 divides these capital account transactions into three sections: Net increase in financial assets, net investment in tangible assets, and increase in debt owed by individuals.   Financial assets consist of claims on others (including other individuals), mainly in the form of money, deposits, securities, corporate equities, and equities in insurance and pension reserves.   The amounts shown are net transaction flows, the excess of acquisitions over liquidations; and changes in values of holdings through market price movements. Unrealized capital gains are not included in the figures.

Investment in tangible assets (series F 583) appears net of capital consumption allowances, which are mainly book depreciation charges. These charges are reflected in personal consumption in NIA and personal saving is thus smaller because of them.   Increases in personal debt, in the third section, are offsets to asset acquisitions. Funds acquired from borrowing are used either for the asset purchases shown in the table or for consumption or tax payments, both of which decrease saving.

The table on p. 251 compares this capital-account calculation of net investment—which is equal to saving—with the NIA estimate.

The capital account version differs in a few conceptual aspects from the NIA definition, and adjustments are made for these differences. The adjustments allow for equities in government life insurance and retirement fund reserves, which are included in assets in this table but not in NIA personal saving; investment in consumer durables, which are treated as capital goods in this table but as current consumption in NIA; and investment company capital gains dividends,

Table 1.   Relation Between Individuals' Saving and Personal
Saving in the National Income Accounts

[In millions of dollars]

Item	1966–1970, average	1961–1965, average	1956–1960, average	1951–1955, average	1946–1950, average
Individuals' saving	61,839	41,073	32,555	29,606	23,243
Less—					
Government insurance and pension reserves	6,368	3,950	2,696	1,784	1,703
Net investment in consumer durables	13,631	8,894	4,387	6,052	7,537
Capital gains, dividends from investment companies	1,785	594	347	119	40
Net saving from farm corporations	−5	−44	−27	−19	45
Equals—					
Personal saving, flow of funds basis	40,060	27,679	25,152	21,669	13,918
Personal saving, national income accounts	40,921	23,461	19,943	17,196	11,682
Statistical difference	−862	4,218	5,208	4,473	2,236

which are excluded from NIA personal income but are reflected in
either current or capital outlays of individuals receiving the dividends. The allowance for retained earnings of farm corporations is
needed because their asset and liability transactions are unavoidably
included in the earlier parts of the table. With these adjustments
the net total for saving is conceptually equal to the NIA estimate,
and as a statistically independent measure is compared with the NIA
series at the end of the table. For most years the estimates of asset
acquisitions less borrowing are several billion dollars higher than the
NIA residual estimate of saving. One probable source for these
differences is net sales of land and existing real estate by individuals
to corporations and government. No data are available to estimate
land transactions, but if in fact there are net sales they should be
included as a negative investment among tangible assets. Beyond
the land item, sources of the statistical discrepancy are not known,
and the errors and omissions that it reflects cannot be distributed on
any basis between the NIA and capital account estimates.

The data in series F 566–594 are from the Federal Reserve's flow
of funds accounts which appear in broader form in Chapter X.

Series F 566–594 is a consolidation of capital accounts for households, personal trust funds, nonprofit organizations, farms, and nonfarm noncorporate business. In Chapter X, the farm and nonfarm
business components are included with corporate business in a statement for all business together, while the nonbusiness components here
appear there as a household group. In the consolidation, flows of
proprietors' equity funds to business activity have been eliminated.

**F 595–637.   Individuals' saving, by components, in current prices,
1929–1962.**

Source: 1929–1932, Irwin Friend and Vito Natrella, *Individuals'
Saving*, John Wiley & Sons, New York, 1954, pp. 85 and 91 (copyright) (except series F 627 for 1929–1932, see source for series F
540–551, p. 354); 1933–1962, U.S. Securities and Exchange Commission, unpublished data.

Conceptually, individual saving in series F 595 is identical with
personal saving in series F 553. However, the total is derived in an
entirely different way. In the procedure followed in obtaining series
F 595, referred to as the direct or balance sheet method of estimating
saving, the total is derived by summing the changes in the various
assets and liabilities of the economic units included in the personal
sector. Since the reliability of the underlying components varies
widely, it is not possible to state unequivocally that the total in series
F 595 is subject to a smaller margin of error than that in series F 553.
Rather, the two series should be viewed as providing a reciprocal
check, with the present series also presenting detail on the various
types of saving. While the difference between the two series is substantial for a few dates, they are generally in fair agreement with
regard to absolute amount.

The estimates for saving in the form of currency and deposits
(including deposits in savings and loan associations) have a relatively
small margin of error, while those for saving in the form of corporate
and State and local securities probably have a greater margin of error.
Generally speaking, the estimates for the earlier years, particularly
1929–1932, are subject to greater error than those for the later years.
For a discussion of the limitations of the estimates for a number of
the components, see the source (Friend and Natrella).

**F 638–667.   Personal saving, by major components, in current prices,
1897–1945.**

Source: See source for series F 540–551, pp. 353–355.

See text for series F 540–551 regarding concept and reliability of
personal saving estimates.

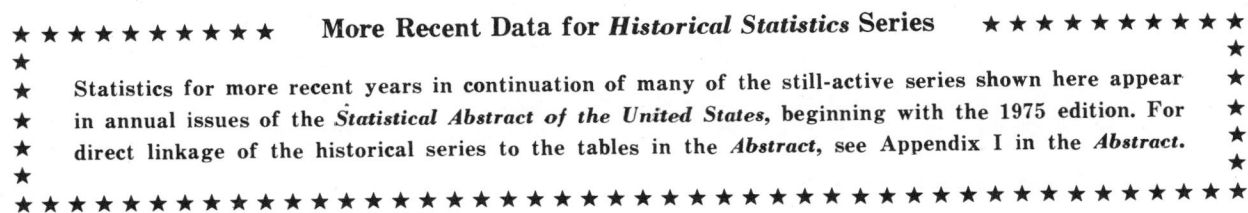

★ ★ ★ ★ ★ ★ ★ ★ ★   **More Recent Data for *Historical Statistics* Series**   ★ ★ ★ ★ ★ ★ ★ ★ ★

Statistics for more recent years in continuation of many of the still-active series shown here appear
in annual issues of the *Statistical Abstract of the United States*, beginning with the 1975 edition. For
direct linkage of the historical series to the tables in the *Abstract*, see Appendix I in the *Abstract*.

Series F 349–364. National Tangible Assets, in Current Prices: 1952 to 1968

[In billions of dollars. Excludes Alaska and Hawaii. Data should be regarded as approximate only. Consult source for methods and sources used to derive these estimates]

Year	Total tangible assets	Reproducible assets Total	Structures Total [1]	Nonfarm Public nonresidential	Nonfarm Institutional	Nonfarm Other private nonresidential	Nonfarm Residential	Farm structures	Equipment [1] Producer durables	Equipment [1] Consumer durables	Inventories [2] Private Farm	Inventories [2] Private Nonfarm	Inventories [2] Public	Land [3] Private Farm	Land [3] Private Nonfarm	Land [3] Public
	349	350	351	352	353	354	355	356	357	358	359	360	361	362	363	364
1968	3,079.4	2,364.0	1,537.0	459.8	55.7	288.7	682.7	50.0	377.0	233.8	29.5	172.7	14.0	152.6	418.6	144.2
1967	2,868.9	2,192.8	1,4 5.5	431.5	50.3	263.8	641.6	48.3	345.1	211.5	26.5	161.3	12.9	144.8	395.5	135.8
1966	2,670.8	2,035.0	1,329.4	395.8	45.8	244.2	597.6	46.0	314.3	196.9	28.4	153.1	12.9	136.5	371.9	127.4
1965	2,474.8	1,880.5	1,233.7	361.8	41.5	224.2	562.6	43.5	285.1	183.2	26.6	136.0	15.9	129.0	347.9	117.4
1964	2,309.4	1,755.1	1,155.9	332.8	37.8	208.9	534.7	41.8	264.1	169.8	23.2	125.2	16.9	119.2	325.0	110.1
1963	2,174.3	1,658.9	1,089.9	308.8	34.7	199.5	506.0	40.8	249.7	158.6	24.9	118.1	17.7	111.3	302.2	101.9
1962	2,019.6	1,573.6	1,027.3	286.9	32.0	191.9	476.6	39.9	240.2	150.3	25.5	112.1	18.2	103.9	248.1	94.0
1961	1,942.6	1,495.3	970.4	266.5	29.4	183.4	451.8	39.9	232.6	143.3	24.3	107.1	17.6	98.7	261.7	86.9
1960	1,851.3	1,439.6	924.4	249.2	27.2	176.1	433.1	38.9	227.4	140.8	23.0	105.4	18.6	92.9	239.8	79.0
1959	1,776.3	1,384.3	884.9	236.0	25.5	170.7	415.1	37.6	220.2	136.4	22.7	102.2	17.9	92.5	226.5	73.0
1958	1,675.3	1,319.1	837.3	222.6	24.2	165.2	388.8	36.5	212.1	129.1	26.2	96.8	17.6	87.9	201.7	66.6
1957	1,586.0	1,263.0	797.0	209.7	22.8	159.9	369.3	35.4	204.5	126.5	21.2	98.8	15.0	80.6	181.5	60.9
1956	1,480.8	1,188.2	752.4	195.2	21.0	149.7	352.1	34.3	189.1	117.3	18.5	96.4	15.1	76.1	161.9	54.0
1955	1,350.1	1,090.1	688.9	176.5	18.7	135.3	326.1	32.3	170.0	107.9	17.9	88.1	17.3	70.6	141.3	48.1
1954	1,231.3	1,001.2	631.8	161.8	16.9	124.8	297.7	30.6	155.6	99.1	18.5	80.7	15.5	67.6	120.8	41.7
1953	1,173.7	958.8	601.3	153.0	15.8	120.3	282.3	29.8	147.9	95.6	18.6	82.5	12.9	65.2	110.7	41.7
1952	1,115.4	916.0	576.3	145.2	15.0	115.7	271.1	29.3	138.5	90.3	23.2	80.2	7.5	67.3	97.6	34.5

[1] Estimates obtained by multiplying the *constant dollar* figures shown in series F 365–376 by the appropriate price index for current year. See also footnote 1 in that table.
[2] Estimates are based on book values.

[3] Estimates are based on census or similar data. For other private land, estimates are derived by application of rough ratios of land to structure values for different types of real estate. Excludes subsoil assets.

Series F 365–376. National Reproducible Tangible Assets, in Constant (1958) Prices: 1952 to 1968

[In billions of 1958 dollars. Excludes Alaska and Hawaii. Data should be regarded as approximate only. Consult source for methods and sources used to derive these estimates]

Year	Total reproducible assets	Structures Total [1]	Nonfarm Public nonresidential	Nonfarm Institutional	Nonfarm Other private nonresidential	Nonfarm Residential	Farm	Equipment [1] Producer durables	Equipment [1] Consumer durables	Inventories [2] Private Farm	Inventories [2] Private Nonfarm	Inventories [2] Public
	365	366	367	368	369	370	371	372	373	374	375	376
1968	1,935.8	1,177.7	343.6	43.6	231.8	519.2	39.5	327.2	227.0	27.1	163.9	12.9
1967	1,849.2	1,142.6	332.1	41.6	223.1	506.5	39.3	307.7	210.6	25.0	151.1	12.2
1966	1,787.1	1,110.4	320.8	39.6	214.4	496.6	39.0	288.3	199.3	26.8	150.1	12.2
1965	1,701.4	1,071.6	306.5	37.2	203.9	485.3	38.7	268.2	183.9	26.0	136.1	15.6
1964	1,621.3	1,032.4	292.6	34.9	194.8	471.6	38.5	252.0	169.1	23.0	128.0	16.8
1963	1,557.5	995.5	278.9	32.9	188.6	457.0	38.1	240.1	157.9	24.8	121.5	17.7
1962	1,500.0	959.6	265.9	31.1	183.2	441.7	37.7	231.4	149.1	25.3	116.5	18.1
1961	1,444.4	925.2	254.5	29.1	177.7	426.6	37.3	223.8	142.4	24.2	111.3	17.5
1960	1,394.0	892.9	243.2	27.3	172.2	413.4	36.8	218.6	139.6	14.9	109.5	18.5
1959	1,350.8	860.8	232.6	25.7	166.4	399.8	36.3	211.7	131.6	22.6	106.3	17.8
1958	1,306.3	826.0	221.4	24.2	161.7	382.9	35.8	206.1	129.1	26.1	101.4	17.6
1957	1,267.1	795.3	211.0	22.7	156.7	369.7	35.2	202.9	128.6	21.4	103.7	15.2
1956	1,221.4	764.8	202.0	21.3	149.9	357.1	34.5	195.1	123.6	19.2	103.0	15.7
1955	1,172.1	733.0	193.9	20.1	142.7	342.5	33.8	186.2	117 4	19.2	97.7	18.6
1954	1,111.1	699.7	185.7	19.0	137.2	324.7	33.1	177.9	106.6	18.5	91.7	16.7
1953	1,070.9	669.6	177.1	17.8	132.7	309.8	32.2	171.6	101.4	20.1	94.2	14.0
1952	1,024.7	642.4	169.3	17.0	128.2	296.7	31.2	162.2	94.6	24.7	92.8	8.0

[1] Estimates derived by "perpetual inventory" method which is intended to reflect reproduction cost of different types of assets. Estimates are obtained by: (a) reducing each year's gross capital expenditures in current prices to 1958 price level by means of appropriate construction cost or wholesale price indexes; (b) depreciating gross capital expenditures in accordance with an assumed length of life for different types of assets, thus obtaining net capital expenditures for each year in 1958 prices; (c) cumulating net capital expenditures for as many years backwards as corresponds to the assumed length of life of the type of asset involved.
[2] Estimates reflect book values reduced by means of wholesale price indexes.

Series F 377–421.　National Balance Sheet, in Current Prices: 1900 to 1968
[In billions of dollars. As of end of year]

Year	Total assets or liabilities and equities	Tangible assets	Intangible assets												
			Total	Currency and demand deposits			Other bank deposits and shares	Life insurance reserves	Pension and retirement funds, private	Pension and insurance funds, government	Consumer credit	Trade credit	Loans on securities	Bank loans, not elsewhere classified	Other loans
				Total	Monetary metals	Other									
	377	378	379	380	381	382	383	384	385	386	387	388	389	390	391
1968	6,989.0	3,079.4	3,909.6	270.0	15.7	254.3	405.7	112.9	136.4	77.0	113.2	178.0	26.9	139.0	98.6
1967	6,401.4	2,868.9	3,532.5	250.2	14.8	235.3	372.0	108.2	121.4	71.0	102.1	163.0	22.9	122.9	86.2
1966	5,823.6	2,670.8	3,152.8	233.5	14.9	218.6	332.5	103.5	105.2	65.0	97.5	153.0	17.4	115.2	79.8
1965	5,552.3	2,474.8	3,077.5	228.1	15.5	212.7	313.7	98.9	100.9	59.8	90.3	139.8	17.0	106.1	70.1
1964	5,120.1	2,309.4	2,810.7	221.4	16.7	204.7	281.1	94.2	89.2	55.0	80.3	126.1	16.2	89.5	63.3
1963	4,745.4	2,174.3	2,571.1	212.8	16.8	196.0	251.8	89.9	78.7	50.9	71.7	117.2	16.3	79.6	55.6
1962	4,364.1	2,019.6	2,344.5	208.3	17.2	191.1	223.1	85.8	68.9	47.2	63.8	110.4	13.8	71.6	49.5
1961	4,234.6	1,942.6	2,292.0	204.0	18.8	185.3	194.9	82.1	66.5	43.5	58.0	105.6	13.0	66.0	44.2
1960	3,916.3	1,851.3	2,065.0	198.5	19.4	179.1	174.2	78.8	57.0	40.1	56.1	99.5	10.8	62.5	40.6
1959	3,770.6	1,776.3	1,994.3	201.1	21.5	179.6	159.2	75.6	51.7	36.8	51.5	95.6	10.4	58.9	35.9
1958 [1]	3,543.8	1,675.3	1,868.5	200.8	22.5	178.3	148.4	72.3	44.8	33.8	45.1	89.7	10.3	51.7	32.6
1958 [2]	3,735.3	1,653.0	2,082.3	221.9	25.4	196.5	150.2	106.4	27.8	66.1	46.1	100.4	9.2	53.8	31.6
1957	3,461.7	1,579.4	1,882.3	219.5	27.5	192.0	134.6	100.2	22.3	64.9	45.9	92.1	7.7	52.1	29.3
1956	3,318.5	1,473.7	1,844.8	217.5	26.5	191.0	122.5	95.2	20.0	62.0	43.1	88.8	8.0	50.0	27.3
1955	3,114.3	1,360.4	1,753.9	214.2	26.1	188.1	113.3	89.9	17.4	58.4	39.4	80.4	8.7	44.4	27.2
1954	2,859.2	1,264.9	1,594.3	213.1	26.0	187.0	104.9	84.0	14.3	55.2	32.9	68.8	7.6	37.6	25.0
1953	2,669.2	1,217.0	1,452.2	208.7	26.3	182.4	95.2	78.1	11.4	52.5	31.8	63.9	5.8	37.0	24.2
1952	2,570.5	1,171.9	1,398.6	210.0	27.4	182.6	86.8	73.0	9.5	49.1	27.9	64.0	5.0	36.6	23.3
1951	2,438.9	1,123.5	1,315.4	204.2	26.8	177.4	79.0	68.0	7.8	44.8	23.1	58.3	4.3	33.6	22.3
1950	2,248.0	1,026.8	1,221.2	192.9	26.8	166.1	74.5	63.7	6.2	40.7	21.8	53.5	4.6	28.9	21.1
1949	2,008.1	889.7	1,118.3	189.6	28.5	161.2	72.3	59.5	5.3	39.4	17.6	40.2	3.8	23.4	19.2
1948	1,965.2	887.2	1,078.0	193.1	28.2	164.9	69.6	55.4	4.6	36.9	14.7	41.0	3.0	25.0	18.3
1947	1,839.8	805.9	1,033.9	189.1	26.7	162.4	67.1	51.7	3.9	33.4	11.8	38.0	2.8	22.9	16.1
1946	1,648.9	673.7	975.2	178.9	24.4	154.5	63.4	48.2	3.3	29.5	8.5	31.8	3.9	18.3	11.6
1945 [1]	1,532.9	554.6	978.3	194.4	23.9	170.5	56.5	44.5	2.7	25.8	5.7	28.1	8.3	13.3	7.9
1945 [2]	1,519.1	550.4	968.7	195.6			54.9	44.3	2.9	25.5	5.8	24.9	8.1	13.0	4.9
1939	863.3	376.1	487.2	94.2			31.9	29.2	1.1	6.2	7.8	14.7	2.7	9.8	5.8
1933	721.8	318.5	403.3	38.8			29.3	20.9	.7	3.0	4.3	18.2	5.2	10.0	7.8
1929	973.4	422.5	550.9	39.8			34.5	17.5	.5	1.5	8.6	25.7	16.3	20.5	4.0
1922	644.8	321.9	322.9	35.5			20.8	8.7	.1	.3	5.7	14.9	6.7	18.2	1.7
1912	306.2	164.8	141.5	16.4			9.2	4.1		(Z)	2.9	8.1	2.3	9.0	.8
1900	156.8	88.4	68.4	8.9			3.7	1.6		(Z)	1.0	5.7	1.3	3.9	.2

Year	Intangible assets—Con.													
	Mortgages				Securities								Equity in—		
	Nonfarm			Farm	U.S. Government				State and local governments	Other bonds and notes	Preferred stock	Common stock	Mutual finance organizations	Other business	Other
	Total	Residential	Nonresidential		Total	Short-term	Savings bonds	Other long term							
	392	393	394	395	396	397	398	399	400	401	402	403	404	405	406
1968	370.0	298.6	71.4	27.5	299.7	113.5	51.5	134.7	124.4	167.4	1,016.3		15.6	166.9	164.2
1967	344.8	280.0	64.8	25.5	282.5	111.3	51.1	120.1	114.4	152.4	874.1		14.5	154.5	150.0
1966	324.1	264.0	60.1	23.3	272.1	103.5	50.2	118.4	106.0	135.9	688.1		14.0	144.2	142.4
1965	304.6	250.1	54.5	21.2	261.0	101.2	49.6	110.2	100.3	125.0	763.4		13.4	131.4	132.4
1964	281.2	231.1	50.0	18.9	257.1	97.3	49.0	110.9	93.0	115.7	670.3		12.3	124.1	121.8
1963	257.4	211.2	46.2	16.8	251.0	92.4	48.0	110.5	87.3	108.3	584.5		11.4	118.1	111.8
1962	233.4	192.3	41.1	15.2	246.1	90.6	46.9	108.7	81.4	101.7	495.3		10.5	114.2	104.3
1961	212.3	176.0	36.4	13.9	239.1	91.9	46.4	100.8	76.1	95.9	562.2		9.5	108.8	96.3
1960	194.0	161.6	32.4	12.8	232.0	80.5	45.6	105.8	70.8	90.2	441.7		8.5	106.3	90.5
1959	178.7	149.5	29.2	12.1	234.3	77.3	45.9	111.1	65.6	84.5	444.6		7.8	105.2	84.8
1958 [1]	160.7	134.5	26.1	11.1	228.3	74.0	47.7	106.6	59.5	80.2	409.7		7.1	104.7	77.6
1958 [2]	160.7	133.0	27.6	11.3	274.3	66.0	51.9	156.4	61.1	88.8	18.3	447.2	8.0	98.7	100.6
1957	146.1	121.3	24.8	10.5	266.4	67.2	53.2	146.0	55.1	82.9	17.8	329.7	7.4	97.6	100.3
1956	134.8	112.1	22.7	9.9	268.1	61.7	57.0	149.4	50.3	73.0	17.4	364.2	6.7	92.1	93.8
1955	120.9	100.6	20.3	9.1	272.7	55.3	58.6	158.9	47.0	67.2	16.9	347.4	6.1	86.6	86.9
1954	105.4	87.2	18.2	8.3	272.1	63.1	58.4	150.6	43.5	61.5	16.9	281.7	5.5	83.2	72.9
1953	93.6	77.1	16.5	7.8	268.8	75.0	57.9	135.9	39.3	58.0	16.4	201.5	5.0	83.0	70.3
1952	84.2	68.9	15.3	7.3	261.8	59.2	58.1	144.5	35.7	53.2	16.1	203.4	4.6	80.8	66.4
1951	75.6	61.4	14.2	6.7	254.9	53.4	57.7	143.7	32.5	48.0	15.6	187.6	4.3	79.4	65.6
1950	66.7	53.6	13.1	6.1	252.4	64.2	58.3	129.9	30.2	43.4	15.0	163.9	4.0	72.3	59.3
1949	57.1	44.9	12.2	5.6	254.2	62.4	56.9	135.0	27.0	40.4	14.8	132.5	3.7	65.7	47.1
1948	50.9	39.6	11.3	5.3	250.0	52.1	55.2	142.7	24.7	37.2	14.4	117.5	3.3	65.8	47.4
1947	43.9	33.8	10.1	5.1	254.5	55.1	52.2	147.3	22.5	32.0	14.1	117.0	2.9	59.8	45.6
1946	36.9	28.1	8.8	4.9	257.4	59.0	49.9	148.6	21.0	28.7	13.6	119.4	2.7	53.8	39.7
1945 [1]	30.8	23.3	7.5	4.8	275.7	77.5	48.2	150.0	21.2	27.5	13.5	133.2	2.3	44.5	37.9
1945 [2]	30.8	23.3	7.5	4.7	274.4				15.9	25.9	150.8		2.2	45.7	38.4
1939	28.9	20.8	8.1	6.6	47.0				19.8	32.5	100.1		1.7	28.3	18.8
1933	30.5	21.1	9.4	7.7	23.9				19.1	37.7	101.7		1.7	18.6	24.4
1929	36.9	24.9	11.9	9.6	16.2				16.9	38.1	186.7		1.6	29.5	46.5
1922	16.7	11.1	5.6	10.8	23.0				10.4	23.7	76.1		.8	21.6	27.3
1912	7.7	5.0	2.7	4.3	1.2				4.4	14.5	38.0		.4	9.8	8.2
1900	4.5	3.0	1.5	2.3	1.2				2.0	5.2	13.9		.2	6.7	6.1

See footnotes at end of table.

Series F 377–421.   National Balance Sheet, in Current Prices: 1900 to 1968—Con.

[In billions of dollars.   As of end of year]

Year	Total	Currency and demand deposits	Other bank deposits and shares	Life insurance reserves, private	Pension and retirement funds, private	Pension and insurance funds, government	Consumer debt	Trade debt	Loans on securities	Bank loans, n.e.c.	Other loans	Mortgages	Bonds and notes	Other	Equity
	407	408	409	410	411	412	413	414	415	416	417	418	419	420	421
1968	2,203.4	258.2	412.9	112.9	136.4	77.0	113.2	134.2	27.0	132.2	74.1	397.5	156.5	171.2	4,785.6
1967	2,009.4	238.5	379.6	108.2	121.4	71.0	102.1	123.2	22.9	115.8	63.2	370.2	142.6	150.7	4,392.0
1966	1,846.0	221.2	338.8	103.5	105.2	65.0	97.5	115.0	17.5	107.9	59.7	347.4	126.6	140.7	3,977.6
1965	1,722.7	214.7	319.7	98.9	100.9	59.8	90.3	103.1	17.1	98.4	50.6	325.8	115.5	128.0	3,827.6
1964	1,572.0	206.5	286.5	94.2	89.2	55.0	80.3	93.2	16.2	82.2	44.7	300.1	107.4	116.3	3,548.1
1963	1,447.7	196.8	256.1	89.9	78.7	50.9	71.7	90.2	16.3	75.1	38.8	274.3	100.8	108.2	3,297.7
1962	1,329.7	191.7	226.5	85.8	68.9	47.2	63.8	85.9	13.8	67.7	34.2	248.6	95.2	100.3	3,034.4
1961	1,231.2	185.7	197.8	82.1	66.5	43.5	58.0	82.5	13.0	62.3	30.0	226.2	90.4	93.0	3,003.4
1960	1,153.0	178.7	177.1	78.8	57.0	40.1	56.1	79.1	10.8	59.5	27.5	206.8	85.2	96.3	2,763.3
1959	1,085.8	179.2	161.8	75.6	51.7	36.8	51.5	76.3	10.4	55.9	23.3	190.8	80.2	92.1	2,684.8
1958 [1]	1,010.0	177.8	151.9	72.3	44.8	33.8	45.1	72.8	10.4	49.0	20.0	171.8	76.1	84.1	2,533.8
1958 [2]	1,488.4	225.8	152.8	108.5	27.8	66.1	46.1	87.0	9.6	51.2	19.4	171.9	428.4	93.8	2,246.9
1957	1,405.9	221.5	136.1	102.2	22.3	64.9	45.9	80.0	8.0	50.0	17.8	156.6	409.0	91.7	2,055.8
1956	1,346.0	222.2	124.1	97.1	20.0	62.0	43.1	76.9	8.3	48.3	16.2	144.7	396.3	86.9	1,972.5
1955	1,280.7	218.2	114.9	91.7	17.4	58.4	39.4	69.7	9.0	43.0	16.1	129.9	391.6	81.3	1,833.7
1954	1,192.1	211.5	106.7	85.7	14.3	55.2	32.9	60.7	7.9	36.6	14.0	113.7	380.1	72.7	1,667.2
1953	1,130.5	208.7	96.5	79.6	11.4	52.5	31.8	53.9	6.0	36.3	13.0	101.3	368.7	70.7	1,538.7
1952	1,074.2	209.1	87.5	74.5	9.5	49.1	27.9	52.9	5.2	35.8	12.4	91.4	352.4	66.7	1,496.3
1951	1,007.9	202.0	79.6	69.3	7.8	44.8	23.1	48.4	4.5	32.8	11.8	82.3	335.9	65.7	1,431.0
1950	945.1	191.1	74.9	65.0	6.2	40.7	21.8	44.8	4.8	28.2	10.8	72.9	326.7	57.4	1,302.9
1949	879.7	181.7	72.5	60.7	5.3	39.4	17.6	34.5	4.0	22.7	9.1	62.7	321.5	48.1	1,128.4
1948	853.2	184.5	69.6	56.5	4.6	36.9	14.7	35.3	3.2	24.4	8.6	56.2	311.5	47.3	1,112.0
1947	819.3	182.4	67.1	52.7	3.9	33.4	11.8	33.6	3.0	22.3	7.6	48.9	308.3	44.6	1,020.5
1946	774.2	172.8	63.4	49.1	3.3	29.5	8.5	29.7	4.1	17.7	6.7	41.8	306.1	41.7	874.7
1945 [1]	778.3	187.6	56.5	45.3	2.7	25.8	5.7	27.6	8.5	13.0	6.2	35.5	324.0	39.8	754.6
1945 [2]	756.9	182.6	56.0	44.3	2.9	25.5	5.8	23.7	8.1	12.1	4.5	35.6	323.8	31.9	762.1
1939	346.1	79.2	31.7	29.2	1.1	6.2	7.6	16.2	2.7	9.2	5.7	35.5	108.4	13.4	517.2
1933	272.2	37.0	28.1	20.9	.7	3.0	3.4	14.5	5.2	9.8	7.9	38.2	84.5	19.2	449.6
1929	315.7	41.3	34.9	17.5	.5	1.5	6.9	20.4	16.3	19.7	4.8	46.5	75.6	29.9	657.7
1922	216.6	34.3	21.1	8.7	.1	.3	3.1	17.7	6.7	17.8	2.1	27.4	59.3	18.0	428.3
1912	91.2	14.6	9.3	4.1	--------	(Z)	1.6	7.4	2.3	8.8	1.1	12.0	23.8	6.1	215.1
1900	44.6	7.5	3.7	1.6	--------	(Z)	.6	5.1	1.3	3.8	.3	6.8	10.3	3.5	112.2

Z   Less than $50 million.
[1] Comparable with later years.   The relatively small differences between the two series of data given for 1945 are due primarily to use of more recent data for the series comparable with later years and to different methods of estimation; there are no conceptual differences.
[2] Comparable with earlier years.

Series F 422–445. National Wealth, by Type of Asset, in Current Prices: 1850 to 1958

[In billions of dollars. As of end of year except as noted]

Year	Total national wealth	Reproducible tangible assets — Total	Structures Total	Nonfarm Residential	Nonfarm Nonresidential	Farm	Institutional	Government	Equipment Total	Producer durables	Consumer durables
	422	423	424	425	426	427	428	429	430	431	432
1958	1,702.8	1,367.6	833.7	385.0	211.2	36.0	26.3	175.2	378.6	199.8	178.8
1957	1,629.8	1,311.3	790.2	367.2	200.6	35.2	24.3	163.0	366.8	193.1	173.6
1956	1,518.1	1,226.2	736.6	351.4	177.2	34.4	22.3	151.3	340.8	177.4	163.4
1955	1,401.9	1,130.4	683.6	328.2	163.7	33.0	20.4	138.4	307.4	156.6	150.8
1954	1,306.3	1,052.6	631.3	302.5	150.8	31.7	18.8	127.5	288.2	149.5	138.7
1953	1,259.3	1,015.3	605.7	291.9	144.4	31.0	17.6	121.0	275.5	140.8	134.8
1952	1,214.1	972.9	578.7	280.7	135.4	30.3	16.5	115.8	259.6	132.0	127.6
1951	1,164.6	928.6	545.4	266.2	127.9	29.3	15.2	106.9	246.1	123.6	122.5
1950	1,067.1	851.8	507.3	249.0	118.5	26.8	13.9	98.6	221.3	110.0	111.3
1949	932.0	742.2	446.1	215.0	105.2	24.6	12.4	88.9	188.1	96.9	91.2
1948	928.4	736.5	449.5	217.9	104.9	24.2	12.5	90.1	172.8	87.5	85.3
1947	843.5	668.4	414.7	200.8	95.4	22.9	11.5	83.9	147.1	73.7	73.4
1946	700.9	556.2	345.4	165.0	81.4	19.3	9.3	70.4	118.2	58.5	59.6
1945 [1]	576.2	457.0	285.6	141.1	63.8	16.3	7.0	57.4	94.9	48.6	46.2
1945 [2]	571.4	442.3	265.1	124.6	67.6	15.7	6.4	50.7	101.3	50.3	51.0
1939	396.8	307.4	188.5	86.3	54.1	9.0	5.4	33.8	66.8	34.2	32.5
1933	330.5	241.3	159.4	69.6	50.1	8.7	4.8	26.2	54.9	29.2	25.7
1929	439.4	313.5	189.8	89.5	59.1	12.2	5.6	23.4	80.6	38.4	42.2
1922	334.5	233.4	134.5	56.6	45.9	12.4	4.1	15.5	61.8	30.8	31.0
1912	165.4	109.1	62.5	25.4	23.5	5.6	2.0	5.9	27.3	13.8	13.6
1900 [1]	87.9	59.3	35.0	15.8	12.9	3.3	1.1	2.0	12.6	6.5	6.1
1900 [2][3]	---------	63.8	35.0	15.0	14.3	3.6	2.1		15.3	9.3	6.0
1890 [3]	---------	46.1	25.0	10.8	10.3	2.7	1.2		10.3	5.8	4.5
1880 [3]	---------	25.8	13.3	4.9	5.8	2.0	.6		5.4	3.0	2.4
1850 [3]	---------	4.5	---------	.8	[4]1.1	.7	.1		---------	[4].2	.3

Year	Inventories Total	Private Livestock	Private Crops	Private Nonfarm	Public	Monetary gold and silver	Land Total	Private Agricultural	Private Nonfarm Residential	Private Nonfarm Nonresidential	Forests	Public	Net foreign assets
	433	434	435	436	437	438	439	440	441	442	443	444	445
1958	129.9	18.1	8.0	95.7	8.1	25.4	310.8	87.6	60.7	108.0	13.7	40.8	24.3
1957	126.8	14.1	6.5	100.1	6.1	27.5	295.7	79.9	57.9	101.8	15.0	41.0	22.8
1956	122.3	11.1	7.1	97.1	7.1	26.5	274.1	74.0	55.4	90.3	14.7	39.7	17.9
1955	113.3	10.7	6.7	88.8	7.1	26.1	256.2	68.9	51.8	82.0	15.0	38.4	15.4
1954	107.1	11.2	7.5	81.4	7.0	26.0	238.3	66.4	47.8	75.0	12.6	36.5	15.4
1953	107.8	11.8	7.2	83.1	5.7	26.3	228.1	64.2	46.2	69.7	12.0	36.0	15.9
1952	106.9	14.8	8.4	80.9	2.8	27.4	226.7	66.9	44.4	65.5	13.3	36.6	14.7
1951	110.4	19.5	8.6	79.9	2.4	26.8	221.6	66.3	42.2	61.2	14.3	37.6	14.4
1950	96.5	17.1	7.3	69.3	2.8	26.8	201.8	58.4	39.6	56.4	11.9	35.5	13.4
1949	79.6	12.9	6.0	57.3	3.4	28.5	176.0	50.9	34.2	53.0	8.3	29.6	13.8
1948	86.0	14.4	7.8	61.8	2.0	28.2	178.9	51.9	34.6	54.4	7.6	30.4	12.9
1947	80.0	13.3	9.2	56.3	1.2	26.7	164.2	49.8	31.9	46.7	6.1	29.7	10.9
1946	68.2	11.9	7.2	47.6	1.5	24.4	141.9	46.5	26.3	39.4	3.8	25.9	2.8
1945 [1]	52.6	9.7	6.0	34.3	2.7	23.9	121.6	43.5	22.6	31.9	3.1	20.5	-2.3
1945 [2]	52.3	9.7	5.6	34.2	2.7	22.9	128.1	44.5	31.1	24.9	3.6	24.0	1.7
1939	30.5	5.1	2.2	22.2	1.0	19.6	88.6	23.2	22.9	22.2	2.9	17.4	1.7
1933	21.9	3.2	1.8	16.9	.1	4.7	81.2	22.8	18.7	22.1	2.2	15.4	8.1
1929	38.0	6.5	3.0	28.4	.1	4.8	113.5	34.9	24.1	36.1	3.1	15.3	12.4
1922	32.6	5.4	3.1	24.0	.1	4.4	92.8	41.5	15.4	19.8	3.5	12.6	8.2
1912	16.7	5.7	2.6	8.4	(Z)	2.5	58.3	31.6	7.0	10.2	2.0	7.5	-2.1
1900 [1]	10.0	3.1	1.4	5.4	(Z)	1.6	31.0	14.6	4.4	6.5	1.5	4.0	-2.3
1900 [2][3]	11.8	3.3	---------	8.5	---------	1.7	---------	---------	---------	---------	---------	---------	-1.1
1890 [3]	9.6	2.6	---------	7.0	---------	1.2	---------	---------	---------	---------	---------	---------	-1.6
1880 [3]	6.6	2.0	---------	4.6	---------	.6	---------	---------	---------	---------	---------	---------	-.5
1850 [3]	1.1	.5	.2	.5	---------	.2	---------	---------	---------	---------	---------	---------	-.2

Z Less than $50 million.
[1] Comparable with later years. See footnote 1 for series F 377–421.
[2] Comparable with earlier years.
[3] As of June 1.
[4] Producer durables in the hands of nonagricultural business included with nonfarm nonresidential construction.

Series F 446–469.   National Wealth, by Type of Asset, in 1929 and 1947–49 Prices: 1850 to 1958

[In billions of dollars.   As of end of year, except as noted]

Year	Total national wealth	Reproducible tangible assets Total	Structures Total	Nonfarm Residential	Nonfarm Nonresidential	Farm	Institutional	Government	Equipment Total	Producer durables	Consumer durables
	446	447	448	449	450	451	452	453	454	455	456
1947–49 PRICES											
1958	1,244.4	1,022.3	592.8	283.6	136.4	28.2	17.8	126.8	297.0	137.4	159.7
1957	1,216.3	998.9	572.9	275.9	132.4	27.9	17.0	119.7	292.0	135.7	156.3
1956	1,174.6	965.2	533.4	268.0	127.3	27.7	16.1	114.0	279.4	129.9	149.5
1955	1,131.6	928.2	553.4	258.7	122.5	27.4	15.5	109.4	265.1	123.8	141.3
1954	1,086.3	887.0	512.3	248.2	117.5	27.1	14.8	104.7	249.6	119.8	129.8
1953	1,055.3	858.9	495.5	240.5	113.7	26.7	14.1	100.5	239.0	115.7	123.3
1952	1,022.5	828.0	479.9	233.2	109.9	26.2	13.6	97.0	225.2	109.4	115.8
1951	990.8	798.2	465.6	226.6	106.8	25.5	13.2	93.6	213.5	103.4	110.2
1950	949.2	761.9	451.4	219.8	103.7	24.8	12.6	90.6	199.7	96.8	102.9
1949	910.4	726.4	437.0	211.9	101.4	24.2	12.1	87.5	181.0	90.6	90.4
1948	882.6	702.3	426.5	206.8	99.4	23.6	11.7	85.0	167.0	84.8	82.2
1947	845.9	669.2	416.7	200.9	97.0	23.0	11.5	84.4	149.4	75.6	73.8
1946	812.7	644.1	411.1	197.4	95.1	22.5	11.6	84.6	131.4	66.7	64.7
1945 [1]	788.1	622.3	407.9	195.6	92.8	22.2	11.6	85.6	118.9	61.3	57.5
1945 [2]	763.7	591.1	365.6	172.6	94.5	20.1	8.8	69.6	128.6	67.3	61.3
1939	748.4	572.0	378.0	177.3	103.3	20.7	10.2	66.5	112.4	54.8	57.6
1933	742.2	546.5	382.9	179.4	113.4	22.5	11.4	56.3	102.6	52.8	49.8
1929	778.0	572.3	382.7	186.2	116.0	24.7	11.2	44.5	118.4	61.1	57.3
1922	588.2	428.5	277.3	125.0	91.6	23.9	8.6	28.2	87.8	50.1	37.8
1912	464.7	335.6	223.6	99.0	77.3	18.8	7.5	21.0	70.3	37.6	32.7
1900	314.6	221.9	144.7	68.1	48.9	13.6	4.7	9.5	42.1	20.5	21.7
1929 PRICES											
1945	435.6	331.5	185.3	84.0	49.7	10.1	4.4	37.2	89.4	42.6	46.9
1939	424.8	317.8	191.7	86.3	54.3	10.4	5.1	35.5	78.8	34.7	44.1
1933	421.5	301.5	194.1	87.4	59.6	11.3	5.7	30.1	72.0	33.9	38.1
1929	445.8	318.7	193.5	90.6	61.0	12.5	5.6	23.8	83.0	39.1	43.8
1922	336.6	238.0	140.4	60.8	48.1	12.0	4.3	15.1	60.7	31.8	28.9
1912	265.3	186.3	113.2	48.2	40.7	9.4	3.8	11.2	49.6	24.6	25.0
1900 [1]	179.5	122.6	73.0	33.1	25.7	6.8	2.3	5.1	30.0	13.5	16.6
1900 [2][3]	139.0	—	81.5	35.4	32.9	8.5	4.7		36.5	19.9	16.6
1890 [3]	99.7	—	58.4	26.0	23.2	6.5	2.7		24.3	11.7	12.6
1880 [3]	53.7	—	31.1	11.6	13.2	4.9	1.4		11.2	4.7	6.5
1850 [3]	10.8	—	—	2.1	[4]3.0	1.7	.3		—	[4].4	.8

Year	Inventories Total	Private Livestock	Private Crops	Private Nonfarm	Public	Monetary gold and silver	Land Total	Private Agricultural	Private Nonfarm Residential	Private Nonfarm Nonresidential	Forests	Public	Net foreign assets
	457	458	459	460	461	462	463	464	465	466	467	468	469
1947–49 PRICES													
1958	110.0	14.9	10.7	75.4	8.9	22.7	203.2	52.9	44.6	64.6	6.9	34.2	18.9
1957	109.2	14.3	9.0	79.5	6.5	24.8	199.3	51.6	43.4	63.0	6.9	34.5	18.0
1956	108.9	14.7	8.3	78.1	7.9	23.9	194.8	50.9	42.2	61.0	6.8	34.0	14.5
1955	106.2	15.0	8.4	74.4	8.5	23.6	190.9	50.1	40.7	58.9	6.8	34.4	12.5
1954	101.6	14.8	8.2	70.9	7.6	23.6	186.5	50.2	39.1	57.1	6.8	33.2	12.8
1953	100.9	14.6	7.8	72.5	6.0	23.9	183.1	50.2	38.0	55.6	6.7	32.6	13.4
1952	97.5	14.8	8.3	71.7	2.8	25.0	182.1	50.7	36.9	54.5	6.7	33.3	12.5
1951	94.5	14.6	8.0	69.7	2.2	24.5	180.5	51.3	35.9	53.5	6.6	33.2	12.3
1950	86.4	14.0	7.9	62.0	2.5	24.5	175.3	50.9	34.8	51.7	6.6	31.3	12.0
1949	82.1	13.6	7.5	57.2	3.8	26.2	171.2	49.6	33.6	51.2	6.6	30.3	12.9
1948	83.0	13.4	8.9	58.7	2.1	26.0	168.1	49.3	32.8	50.1	6.5	29.4	12.2
1947	78.6	13.6	7.1	56.8	1.1	24.5	166.1	50.3	32.0	48.6	6.5	28.7	10.6
1946	79.4	14.3	8.3	55.3	1.6	22.2	165.7	50.9	31.5	48.6	6.4	28.2	3.0
1945 [1]	74.2	14.9	7.9	47.8	3.6	21.7	168.7	53.8	31.3	47.7	6.4	29.5	-2.7
1945 [2]	73.8	15.1	7.3	47.7	3.7	22.3	170.0	53.5	43.0	33.3	4.6	35.5	1.2
1939	61.4	14.0	6.0	38.6	3.0	19.0	174.2	47.4	47.0	39.0	5.7	35.0	3.1
1933	53.2	15.0	5.5	32.6	.1	7.3	180.5	51.5	48.0	42.0	4.8	34.1	15.8
1929	63.3	13.7	5.5	44.0	.1	7.5	188.1	52.1	49.9	54.7	5.1	26.2	18.2
1922	56.0	15.2	6.0	34.6	.1	7.1	146.9	52.9	34.0	33.6	5.3	21.1	12.0
1912	37.8	13.7	6.6	17.4	.1	3.7	132.5	54.1	27.2	29.8	4.5	16.9	-4.8
1900	32.6	13.6	4.8	14.2	(Z)	2.3	98.8	41.7	19.0	22.4	4.2	11.5	-6.9
1929 PRICES													
1945	44.0	7.2	3.9	30.8	2.1	12.7	103.3	35.9	20.9	22.5	3.1	20.8	.8
1939	36.4	6.6	3.2	24.9	1.6	10.9	105.0	31.8	22.9	26.4	3.4	20.4	2.1
1933	31.2	7.1	3.0	21.1	.1	4.2	109.2	34.5	23.4	28.5	2.9	20.0	10.8
1929	38.0	6.5	3.0	28.4	.1	4.3	114.7	34.9	24.4	37.0	3.1	15.3	12.4
1922	32.9	7.2	3.2	22.4	.1	4.0	90.4	35.5	16.6	22.7	3.2	12.4	8.2
1912	21.3	6.5	3.6	11.2		2.1	82.2	36.3	13.3	20.2	2.6	9.9	-3.2
1900 [1]	18.2	6.4	2.6	9.2		1.3	61.6	28.0	9.2	15.2	2.5	6.7	-4.7
1900 [2][3]	19.3	6.4	2.6	10.3		1.7	—	—	—	—	—	—	-3.1
1890 [3]	15.6	6.2	2.3	7.1		1.2	—	—	—	—	—	—	-3.6
1880 [3]	10.8	4.5	2.0	4.3		.6	—	—	—	—	—	—	-1.0
1850 [3]	2.2	1.1	.3	.8		.3	—	—	—	—	—	—	-.3

Z Less than $50 million.   [1] Comparable with later years.
[2] Comparable with earlier years.   [3] As of June 1.   [4] Producer durables in the hands of nonagricultural business included with nonfarm nonresidential construction.

Series F 470–479.　Private Capital Stocks, Current and Constant (1958) Cost Valuation: 1925 to 1970

[In billions of dollars.　Stocks as of December 31]

Year	Gross private capital stocks					Net private capital stocks				
	Total	Nonresidential structures	Equipment	Residential structures	Inventories	Total	Nonresidential structures	Equipment	Residential structures	Inventories
	470	471	472	473	474	475	476	477	478	479
CURRENT COST										
1970	2,855.7	728.3	639.1	1,246.7	241.6	1,815.5	436.7	362.7	774.5	241.6
1969	2,630.2	647.3	585.5	1,166.3	231.4	1,678.3	386.7	335.0	725.2	231.4
1968	2,392.2	578.3	531.5	1,069.9	212.5	1,525.1	344.3	303.5	664.8	212.5
1967	2,199.4	525.4	486.3	988.4	199.3	1,403.8	311.6	276.4	616.5	199.3
1966	2,046.1	489.4	445.0	921.4	190.3	1,306.0	287.9	250.5	577.3	190.3
1965	1,902.2	454.0	407.0	870.4	170.8	1,205.3	264.6	225.1	544.8	170.8
1964	1,789.6	424.7	380.0	830.0	154.9	1,126.3	245.3	207.4	518.7	154.9
1963	1,705.5	404.9	360.6	790.5	149.5	1,068.6	232.5	195.2	491.4	149.5
1962	1,630.5	388.8	347.5	749.5	144.7	1,018.9	222.3	187.6	464.3	144.7
1961	1,564.4	373.4	336.0	716.7	138.3	974.6	212.5	181.8	442.0	138.3
1960	1,522.3	359.9	327.3	699.6	135.5	948.8	203.8	179.2	430.3	135.5
1959	1,471.3	347.3	316.1	675.9	132.0	915.9	195.1	174.1	414.7	132.0
1958	1,399.7	333.7	304.0	633.2	128.8	869.7	186.2	168.6	386.1	128.8
1957	1,343.8	319.5	290.0	607.6	126.7	835.6	176.7	164.0	368.2	126.7
1956	1,272.4	300.0	267.1	583.5	121.8	788.9	163.3	152.5	351.3	121.8
1955	1,173.2	275.0	238.9	547.1	112.2	724.3	146.6	137.7	327.8	112.2
1954	1,090.3	257.4	217.5	508.2	107.2	668.7	134.7	126.0	300.8	107.2
1953	1,052.8	248.0	204.4	490.3	110.1	645.0	127.6	120.5	286.8	110.1
1952	1,018.0	239.6	191.2	477.8	109.4	620.7	120.9	113.5	276.9	109.4
1951	974.7	228.2	177.6	456.8	112.1	593.9	113.0	107.0	261.8	112.1
1950	889.8	211.5	157.4	422.1	98.8	535.3	102.3	95.1	239.1	98.8
1949	797.1	199.0	136.7	380.5	80.9	469.5	94.4	82.6	211.6	80.9
1948	772.6	194.6	123.3	364.1	90.6	455.5	90.7	73.5	200.7	90.6
1947	713.0	182.5	106.0	337.6	86.9	414.1	83.2	60.5	183.5	86.9
1946	600.2	156.5	87.4	282.6	73.7	343.0	69.9	47.1	152.3	73.7
1945	501.0	131.9	75.8	240.1	53.2	279.0	57.3	39.2	129.3	53.2
1944	468.4	122.4	69.6	223.0	53.4	264.2	53.5	35.2	122.1	53.4
1943	449.0	120.3	67.5	208.0	53.2	255.8	53.5	34.2	114.9	53.2
1942	428.6	117.5	66.7	192.5	51.9	246.8	53.2	34.4	107.3	51.9
1941	395.8	108.1	63.8	178.3	45.6	228.7	49.7	33.2	100.2	45.6
1940	352.5	97.7	57.6	162.4	34.8	199.6	45.1	28.5	91.2	34.8
1939	331.0	93.4	54.4	151.1	32.1	186.2	43.5	25.9	84.7	32.1
1938	324.3	94.0	53.9	146.2	30.2	182.2	44.3	25.5	82.2	30.2
1937	325.2	96.2	53.8	142.1	33.1	185.2	45.9	25.6	80.6	33.1
1936	306.7	92.4	50.6	132.1	31.6	175.3	44.4	23.4	75.9	31.6
1935	286.6	87.2	48.5	121.8	29.1	164.5	42.5	22.0	70.9	29.1
1934	279.8	86.0	48.7	119.3	25.8	160.7	42.7	22.0	70.2	25.8
1933	269.9	83.2	48.5	114.2	24.0	157.0	42.3	22.7	68.0	24.0
1932	262.5	81.9	49.5	109.1	22.0	154.7	42.7	24.1	65.9	22.0
1931	297.2	89.6	53.2	127.2	27.2	177.3	47.8	27.2	75.1	27.2
1930	330.8	99.8	57.0	140.5	33.5	205.0	54.1	30.1	87.3	33.5
1929	351.2	104.6	59.2	147.4	40.0	222.5	57.0	32.7	92.8	40.0
1928	344.5	103.9	57.9	143.6	39.1	217.1	56.4	30.9	90.7	39.1
1927	----	101.4	56.0	136.3	----	----	54.9	30.0	86.0	----
1926	----	99.4	54.7	132.6	----	----	53.6	29.5	83.2	----
1925	----	97.4	52.4	127.8	----	----	52.2	28.2	79.5	----
CONSTANT (1958) COST										
1970	2,023.2	462.0	511.4	849.2	200.6	1,295.6	273.0	291.4	530.6	200.6
1969	1,960.9	448.7	487.9	827.6	196.7	1,259.0	264.7	280.3	517.3	196.7
1968	1,889.8	434.5	460.0	805.3	190.0	1,210.8	255.3	263.6	501.9	190.0
1967	1,823.7	420.9	434.4	784.9	183.5	1,167.4	246.4	247.7	489.8	183.5
1966	1,763.3	408.0	409.8	769.7	175.8	1,125.4	237.9	231.5	480.2	175.8
1965	1,693.4	393.5	384.6	753.4	161.9	1,073.0	227.5	213.3	470.3	161.9
1964	1,631.7	380.5	364.6	733.8	152.8	1,028.3	218.3	199.5	457.6	152.8
1963	1,580.8	370.9	349.2	713.7	147.0	992.7	212.0	189.4	444.3	147.0
1962	1,534.8	362.2	337.7	693.7	141.2	960.6	206.5	182.7	430.2	141.2
1961	1,491.8	353.1	326.9	676.6	135.2	930.0	200.6	177.2	417.0	135.2
1960	1,463.3	344.8	318.8	666.4	133.3	911.5	195.0	174.7	408.5	133.3
1959	1,426.3	336.5	308.6	651.4	129.8	887.1	188.9	170.0	398.4	129.8
1958	1,378.3	329.5	300.7	623.2	124.9	854.4	183.8	166.8	379.0	124.9
1957	1,349.5	322.0	293.8	607.3	126.4	837.4	178.1	166.2	366.7	126.4
1956	1,311.7	313.0	282.5	591.0	125.2	812.6	170.3	161.3	355.8	125.2
1955	1,267.0	303.8	268.9	574.0	120.3	780.0	161.9	155.0	342.8	120.3
1954	1,222.6	296.8	256.7	555.2	113.9	743.8	155.4	148.6	325.9	113.9
1953	1,189.2	290.8	245.5	536.9	116.0	723.3	149.6	144.6	313.1	116.0
1952	1,154.4	285.4	232.6	521.4	115.0	698.5	143.9	137.9	301.7	115.0
1951	1,119.8	281.2	219.4	507.4	111.8	674.3	139.1	132.0	291.4	111.8
1950	1,074.4	276.7	204.2	492.7	100.8	637.1	133.8	123.2	279.3	100.8
1949	1,027.4	273.3	188.5	473.1	92.5	598.3	129.7	113.6	262.5	92.5
1948	1,003.0	270.7	176.5	459.3	96.5	578.7	126.2	105.0	251.0	96.5
1947	965.5	267.7	161.0	444.9	91.9	547.5	122.1	92.0	241.5	91.9
1946	935.9	265.3	145.5	433.0	92.1	521.4	118.6	78.5	232.2	92.1
1945	910.9	262.1	138.0	428.7	82.1	494.1	114.2	71.4	226.4	82.1
1944	911.0	265.3	132.2	428.5	85.0	497.9	116.5	66.5	229.9	85.0
1943	916.5	270.4	130.6	428.6	86.9	507.5	120.8	65.7	234.1	86.9
1942	923.6	276.4	131.5	428.6	87.1	517.9	126.2	67.3	237.3	87.1
1941	922.9	280.5	131.6	427.6	83.2	521.0	130.1	68.2	239.5	83.2

Series F 470–479. Private Capital Stocks, Current and Constant (1958) Cost Valuation: 1925 to 1970—Con.

[In billions of dollars]

Year	Gross private capital stocks					Net private capital stocks				
	Total	Nonresidential structures	Equipment	Residential structures	Inventories	Total	Nonresidential structures	Equipment	Residential structures	Inventories
	470	471	472	473	474	475	476	477	478	479
	CONSTANT (1958) COST—Con.									
1940	903.5	280.9	127.5	421.6	73.5	503.6	130.5	63.1	236.5	73.5
1939	892.8	282.5	125.5	416.2	68.6	494.6	132.3	60.0	233.7	68.6
1938	889.0	284.7	125.9	411.0	67.4	493.6	135.0	59.5	231.7	67.4
1937	891.4	287.1	126.8	407.7	69.8	499.8	138.0	60.3	231.7	69.8
1936	880.5	287.7	124.1	404.4	64.3	492.9	139.6	57.4	231.6	64.3
1935	875.1	289.9	122.4	401.6	61.2	491.7	142.9	55.4	232.2	61.2
1934	876.4	293.4	123.7	400.5	58.8	497.0	147.7	56.2	234.3	58.8
1933	886.2	296.8	127.3	400.7	61.4	511.4	153.0	59.2	237.9	61.4
1932	899.8	300.5	132.7	400.8	65.8	530.7	158.7	64.1	242.1	65.8
1931	913.6	302.9	138.1	400.6	72.0	551.5	163.5	70.0	245.6	72.0
1930	914.1	301.8	140.5	397.4	74.4	560.0	165.2	73.6	246.8	74.4
1929	904.2	296.3	139.9	392.9	75.1	558.7	162.5	74.1	247.0	75.1
1928	880.9	288.5	136.1	384.8	71.5	543.7	157.5	71.8	242.9	71.5
1927	--------	281.3	133.2	373.0	--------	153.1	70.8	235.1	--------
1926	--------	273.6	130.8	360.1	--------	148.2	70.1	226.1	--------
1925	--------	266.0	126.3	346.3	--------	143.4	67.6	215.5	--------

Series F 480–515. Fixed Nonresidential Business Capital—Current and Constant (1958) Cost Valuation: 1925 to 1970

[In billions of dollars. Stocks as of December 31; depreciation for calendar year]

Year	All industries									Manufacturing								
	Gross stocks			Net stocks			Depreciation			Gross stocks			Net stocks			Depreciation		
	Total	Equipment	Structures	Total	Equipment	Structures	Total	Equipment	Structures	Total	Equipment	Structures	Total	Equipment	Structures	Total	Equipment	Structures
	480	481	482	483	484	485	486	487	488	489	490	491	492	493	494	495	496	497
	CURRENT COST																	
1970	1,367.4	639.1	728.3	799.0	362.7	436.3	73.8	51.0	22.8	320.9	184.1	136.8	177.8	103.0	74.9	18.2	13.3	4.8
1969	1,232.8	585.5	647.3	721.6	335.0	386.7	66.5	46.1	20.4	291.4	169.6	121.8	162.5	95.6	66.9	16.4	12.1	4.3
1968	1,109.8	531.5	578.3	647.8	303.5	344.3	60.0	41.7	18.2	263.1	154.8	108.3	146.7	87.2	59.5	14.9	11.0	3.8
1967	1,011.8	486.3	525.4	587.0	275.4	311.6	54.7	37.8	16.9	241.2	143.0	98.2	134.0	80.1	53.9	13.6	10.1	3.6
1966	933.7	445.0	489.4	538.4	250.5	287.9	49.9	34.2	15.7	221.8	130.6	91.3	121.5	71.9	49.7	12.4	9.0	3.3
1965	861.0	407.0	454.0	489.6	225.1	264.6	45.9	31.3	14.6	203.8	118.4	85.4	109.7	63.5	46.2	11.3	8.2	3.1
1964	804.6	380.0	452.7	452.7	207.4	245.3	43.2	29.4	13.9	190.2	109.7	80.6	101.2	57.7	43.5	10.6	7.7	3.0
1963	765.5	360.6	404.9	427.7	195.2	232.5	41.2	27.9	13.3	181.2	104.2	77.1	96.3	54.4	41.8	10.2	7.3	2.8
1962	736.3	347.5	388.8	409.9	187.6	222.3	39.7	26.9	12.8	175.2	101.0	74.2	93.5	53.0	40.5	9.9	7.2	2.7
1961	709.4	336.0	373.4	394.4	181.8	212.5	38.3	26.0	12.3	170.2	98.3	71.9	91.7	52.0	39.7	9.6	7.0	2.7
1960	687.2	327.3	359.9	382.9	179.2	203.8	37.1	25.3	11.8	165.8	95.7	70.0	90.6	51.6	39.0	9.4	6.8	2.6
1959	663.4	316.1	347.3	369.2	174.1	195.1	35.6	24.5	11.4	161.2	92.5	68.7	89.1	50.6	38.5	9.1	6.6	2.6
1958	637.7	304.0	333.7	354.8	168.6	186.2	34.3	23.5	10.8	156.7	89.1	67.6	88.0	49.9	38.1	8.8	6.3	2.5
1957	609.5	290.0	319.5	340.7	164.0	176.7	32.6	22.3	10.3	150.4	84.8	65.6	85.6	48.7	36.9	8.3	5.9	2.4
1956	567.2	267.1	300.0	315.8	152.5	163.3	29.6	20.2	9.4	138.4	76.8	61.6	78.6	44.4	34.2	7.4	5.2	2.2
1955	513.9	238.9	275.0	284.3	137.7	146.6	26.7	18.1	8.6	122.7	66.7	55.9	69.3	38.7	30.6	6.5	4.6	2.0
1954	474.9	217.5	257.4	260.7	126.0	134.7	25.0	16.9	8.1	112.0	59.3	52.7	63.5	35.0	28.5	6.1	4.2	1.9
1953	452.4	204.4	248.0	248.2	120.5	127.6	23.8	16.0	7.8	106.3	54.2	52.1	60.4	32.5	28.0	5.8	3.9	1.9
1952	430.8	191.2	239.6	234.4	113.5	120.9	22.3	14.9	7.4	101.2	49.8	51.4	57.4	30.2	27.3	5.4	3.5	1.9
1951	405.8	177.6	228.2	220.0	107.0	113.0	20.5	13.6	6.9	95.3	45.6	49.6	53.9	28.0	25.9	5.0	3.2	1.8
1950	368.9	157.4	211.5	197.5	95.1	102.3	17.6	11.3	6.3	85.5	39.6	45.9	47.9	24.4	23.5	4.3	2.7	1.6
1949	335.8	136.7	199.0	177.0	82.6	94.4	16.1	10.0	6.1	77.8	34.4	43.4	43.6	21.5	22.1	3.9	2.4	1.6
1948	318.0	123.3	194.6	164.2	73.5	90.7	14.6	8.7	5.9	73.8	30.7	43.1	41.0	19.3	21.8	3.6	2.0	1.6
1947	288.4	106.0	182.5	143.8	60.5	83.2	12.3	7.1	5.2	66.1	25.8	40.3	35.7	15.7	20.0	3.0	1.6	1.4
1946	243.9	87.4	156.5	117.0	47.1	69.9	10.0	5.7	4.3	55.1	21.2	33.9	28.3	12.2	16.1	2.4	1.3	1.1
1945	207.7	75.8	131.9	96.4	39.2	57.3	8.8	5.0	3.8	44.8	18.2	26.7	21.5	9.9	11.6	2.0	1.1	.9
1944	192.0	69.6	122.4	88.7	35.2	53.5	8.4	4.7	3.7	40.3	16.5	23.8	18.9	8.7	10.3	1.9	1.1	.9
1943	187.8	67.5	120.3	87.7	34.2	53.5	8.2	4.5	3.7	40.1	16.0	24.1	19.0	8.3	10.7	1.9	1.0	.9
1942	184.2	66.7	117.5	87.7	34.4	53.2	8.0	4.5	3.5	40.2	15.8	24.3	19.3	8.2	11.1	1.9	1.0	.9
1941	171.9	63.8	108.1	83.0	33.2	49.7	7.1	4.0	3.1	37.9	15.4	22.5	18.4	7.9	10.5	1.7	1.0	.8
1940	155.3	57.6	97.7	73.6	28.5	45.1	6.6	3.7	2.9	34.1	14.2	19.9	16.1	7.0	9.1	1.6	.9	.7
1939	147.8	54.4	93.4	69.4	25.9	43.5	6.5	3.7	2.8	31.9	13.2	18.6	14.8	6.3	8.5	1.5	.8	.7
1938	147.9	53.9	94.0	69.8	25.5	44.3	6.6	3.7	2.9	31.7	13.0	18.7	14.8	6.2	8.6	1.6	.9	.7
1937	150.0	53.8	96.2	71.5	25.6	45.9	6.5	3.6	3.0	32.4	13.0	19.4	15.3	6.2	9.1	1.5	.8	.7
1936	143.0	50.6	92.4	67.7	23.4	44.4	5.9	3.2	2.7	30.6	12.2	18.5	14.4	5.7	8.7	1.4	.8	.6
1935	135.7	48.5	87.2	64.4	22.0	42.5	5.8	3.2	2.6	28.8	11.6	17.2	13.6	5.3	8.3	1.4	.7	.6
1934	134.8	48.7	86.0	65.0	22.0	42.7	5.8	3.2	2.6	28.6	11.7	17.0	13.7	5.4	8.3	1.4	.8	.6
1933	131.6	48.5	83.2	65.0	22.7	42.3	5.7	3.2	2.5	27.3	11.3	15.9	13.4	5.4	8.0	1.3	.7	.6
1932	131.5	49.5	81.9	66.8	24.1	42.7	6.1	3.5	2.5	26.2	11.1	15.0	13.3	5.5	7.8	1.3	.7	.6
1931	142.8	53.2	89.6	75.0	27.2	47.8	6.9	3.9	2.9	28.5	12.0	16.6	15.0	6.2	8.9	1.5	.8	.7
1930	156.8	57.0	99.8	84.3	30.1	54.1	7.3	4.2	3.1	32.0	12.9	19.1	17.3	6.9	10.5	1.6	.9	.8
1929	163.8	59.2	104.6	89.7	32.7	57.0	7.5	4.3	3.2	34.4	13.6	20.8	18.8	7.3	11.5	1.7	.9	.8
1928	161.8	57.9	103.9	87.3	30.9	56.4	7.2	4.1	3.1	34.3	13.5	20.8	18.5	7.2	11.3	1.7	.9	.8
1927	157.4	56.0	101.4	84.9	30.0	54.9	7.0	4.0	3.0	33.3	12.9	20.3	17.9	7.0	10.9	1.6	.9	.7
1926	154.2	54.7	99.4	83.1	29.5	53.6	6.8	3.8	2.9	32.5	12.6	19.9	17.4	6.8	10.6	1.6	.8	.7
1925	149.8	52.4	97.4	80.4	28.2	52.2	6.5	3.6	2.9	31.6	12.1	19.5	16.8	6.5	10.3	1.5	.8	.7

Series F 480–515. Fixed Nonresidential Business Capital—Current and Constant (1958) Cost Valuation: 1925 to 1970—Con.

[In billions of dollars]

CONSTANT (1958) COST

Year	All industries									Manufacturing								
	Gross stocks			Net stocks			Depreciation			Gross stocks			Net stocks			Depreciation		
	Total	Equip-ment	Struc-tures	Total	Equip-ment	Struc-tures	Total	Equip-ment	Struc-tures	Total	Equip-ment	Struc-tures	Total	Equip-ment	Struc-tures	Total	Equip-ment	Struc-tures
	480	481	482	483	484	485	486	487	488	489	490	491	492	493	494	495	496	497
1970	973.4	511.4	462.0	564.3	291.4	273.0	57.7	42.3	15.4	224.2	140.6	83.4	124.9	78.9	46.0	13.7	10.6	3.1
1969	936.6	487.9	448.7	544.9	280.3	264.7	54.7	39.8	14.9	217.1	134.8	82.3	121.6	76.3	45.4	13.1	10.0	3.1
1968	894.5	460.0	434.5	519.0	263.6	255.3	51.6	37.1	14.5	208.2	128.0	80.1	116.6	72.3	44.3	12.4	9.4	3.0
1967	855.3	434.4	420.9	494.1	247.7	246.4	48.7	34.7	14.0	199.9	121.9	78.0	111.5	68.5	43.0	11.7	8.8	2.9
1966	817.8	409.8	408.0	469.3	231.5	237.9	45.8	32.3	13.6	190.0	114.7	75.4	104.5	63.3	41.2	11.0	8.2	2.8
1965	778.1	384.6	393.5	440.8	213.3	227.5	43.2	30.1	13.1	180.3	107.4	72.9	97.3	57.8	39.5	10.3	7.6	2.7
1964	745.1	364.6	380.5	417.8	199.5	218.3	41.2	28.5	12.7	173.1	102.0	71.1	92.4	53.8	38.6	9.9	7.3	2.7
1963	720.0	349.2	370.9	401.4	189.4	212.0	39.6	27.2	12.4	168.6	98.5	70.1	89.8	51.5	38.2	9.6	7.0	2.6
1962	699.9	337.7	362.2	389.2	182.7	206.5	38.3	26.2	12.1	165.5	96.1	69.3	88.5	50.5	38.0	9.4	6.8	2.6
1961	680.1	326.9	353.1	377.8	177.2	200.6	37.2	25.4	11.7	162.6	94.1	68.5	87.8	49.8	38.0	9.3	6.7	2.6
1960	663.5	318.8	344.8	369.6	174.7	195.0	36.1	24.7	11.4	159.9	92.1	67.8	87.5	49.6	37.9	9.1	6.6	2.5
1959	645.2	308.6	336.5	358.9	170.0	188.9	35.1	24.0	11.1	156.9	89.7	67.2	86.7	49.1	37.6	8.9	6.4	2.5
1958	630.3	300.7	329.5	350.7	166.8	183.8	34.3	23.5	10.8	154.9	88.0	66.9	87.0	49.3	37.8	8.8	6.3	2.5
1957	615.9	293.8	322.0	344.2	166.2	178.1	33.4	22.9	10.5	151.5	85.8	65.7	86.2	49.3	36.9	8.5	6.1	2.4
1956	595.5	282.5	313.0	331.6	161.3	170.3	32.1	22.0	10.1	145.1	81.1	63.9	82.3	46.9	35.5	8.1	5.7	2.4
1955	572.7	268.9	303.8	316.9	155.0	161.9	30.7	21.0	9.7	138.3	75.9	62.4	78.2	44.0	34.1	7.7	5.4	2.3
1954	553.5	256.7	296.8	304.0	148.6	155.4	29.5	20.1	9.4	133.3	71.8	61.5	75.6	42.4	33.3	7.4	5.1	2.3
1953	536.3	245.5	290.8	294.2	144.6	149.6	28.3	19.1	9.2	128.2	67.5	60.8	73.0	40.4	32.6	7.0	4.8	2.2
1952	518.1	232.6	285.4	281.8	137.9	143.9	27.0	18.0	8.9	123.2	63.1	60.1	70.1	38.2	31.8	6.7	4.5	2.2
1951	500.6	219.4	281.2	271.1	132.0	139.1	25.5	16.7	8.7	118.3	58.8	59.5	67.1	36.0	31.0	6.3	4.1	2.2
1950	480.9	204.2	276.7	257.0	123.2	133.8	23.8	15.2	8.6	112.8	54.1	58.7	63.4	33.3	30.0	6.0	3.8	2.2
1949	461.8	188.5	273.3	243.3	113.6	129.7	22.3	13.8	8.4	109.6	50.7	58.9	61.7	31.6	30.0	5.7	3.5	2.2
1948	447.2	176.5	270.7	231.2	105.0	126.2	20.8	12.5	8.3	106.3	47.4	58.9	59.4	29.7	29.7	5.3	3.2	2.1
1947	428.7	161.0	267.7	214.1	92.0	122.1	19.2	11.0	8.1	100.6	42.6	57.9	54.6	26.0	28.6	4.8	2.8	2.1
1946	410.8	145.5	265.3	197.2	78.5	118.6	17.9	9.9	8.0	93.9	37.5	56.4	48.2	21.6	26.7	4.4	2.4	2.0
1945	400.0	138.0	262.1	185.5	71.4	114.2	17.2	9.2	8.0	87.6	34.3	53.2	41.8	18.6	23.2	4.1	2.2	1.9
1944	397.5	132.2	265.3	183.0	66.5	116.5	16.9	8.8	8.1	86.2	32.6	53.6	40.2	17.0	23.2	4.1	2.1	2.0
1943	401.0	130.6	270.4	186.5	65.7	120.8	17.0	8.8	8.3	87.4	32.0	55.4	41.1	16.5	24.6	4.1	2.1	2.1
1942	407.9	131.5	276.4	193.5	67.3	126.2	17.2	8.8	8.5	89.3	32.0	57.4	42.7	16.5	26.2	4.2	2.1	2.1
1941	412.1	131.6	280.5	198.3	68.2	130.1	17.2	8.7	8.5	90.4	31.9	58.6	43.6	16.3	27.2	4.2	2.0	2.1
1940	408.5	127.5	280.9	193.6	63.1	130.5	17.1	8.6	8.5	88.9	31.0	57.9	41.7	15.3	26.4	4.1	2.0	2.1
1939	408.0	125.5	282.5	192.2	60.0	132.3	17.2	8.6	8.6	88.6	30.4	58.1	41.1	14.6	26.6	4.1	2.0	2.1
1938	410.6	125.9	284.7	194.5	59.5	135.0	17.4	8.7	8.7	89.5	30.5	59.0	41.8	14.4	27.3	4.2	2.0	2.2
1937	413.9	126.8	287.1	198.4	60.3	138.0	17.3	8.6	8.7	90.8	30.8	60.0	43.1	14.7	28.4	4.2	2.0	2.2
1936	411.8	124.1	287.7	197.0	57.4	139.6	17.0	8.3	8.7	90.3	30.4	60.0	42.6	14.1	28.5	4.2	2.0	2.2
1935	412.3	122.4	289.9	198.3	55.4	142.9	16.9	8.1	8.8	90.8	30.1	60.7	43.0	13.7	29.3	4.2	1.9	2.3
1934	417.1	123.7	293.4	203.9	56.2	147.7	17.2	8.3	8.9	92.3	30.4	61.9	44.7	14.0	30.6	4.3	2.0	2.3
1933	424.1	127.3	296.8	212.2	59.2	153.0	17.8	8.7	9.1	94.0	31.2	62.8	46.6	14.8	31.9	4.4	2.1	2.3
1932	433.2	132.7	300.5	222.8	64.1	158.7	18.5	9.3	9.2	95.8	32.2	63.7	48.9	15.9	33.1	4.5	2.1	2.4
1931	441.0	138.1	302.9	233.5	70.0	163.5	19.0	9.8	9.2	98.4	33.2	65.2	52.1	17.1	35.0	4.6	2.2	2.4
1930	442.3	140.5	301.8	238.8	73.6	165.2	19.1	10.0	9.1	99.4	33.5	65.9	54.0	17.8	36.2	4.7	2.2	2.4
1929	436.2	139.9	296.3	236.6	74.1	162.5	18.8	9.9	8.9	98.3	33.3	65.0	53.8	17.9	35.9	4.6	2.2	2.4
1928	424.6	136.1	288.5	229.3	71.8	157.5	18.2	9.6	8.6	94.7	32.2	62.4	51.1	17.3	33.9	4.4	2.1	2.3
1927	414.5	133.2	281.3	223.9	70.8	153.1	17.7	9.4	8.4	91.8	31.4	60.5	49.3	16.8	32.4	4.3	2.1	2.2
1926	404.4	130.8	273.6	218.3	70.1	148.2	17.2	9.0	8.1	89.6	30.6	59.0	47.9	16.5	31.4	4.2	2.0	2.2
1925	392.3	126.3	266.0	211.0	67.6	143.4	16.4	8.5	7.9	87.0	29.6	57.4	46.1	15.8	30.3	4.0	1.9	2.1

CURRENT COST

Year	Nonfarm nonmanufacturing									Farm								
	Gross stocks			Net stocks			Depreciation			Gross stocks			Net stocks			Depreciation		
	Total	Equip-ment	Struc-tures	Total	Equip-ment	Struc-tures	Total	Equip-ment	Struc-tures	Total	Equip-ment	Struc-tures	Total	Equip-ment	Struc-tures	Total	Equip-ment	Struc-tures
	498	499	500	501	502	503	504	505	506	507	508	509	510	511	512	513	514	515
1970	952.3	391.0	561.3	569.5	224.8	344.6	50.4	33.2	17.2	94.2	64.0	30.2	51.7	34.9	16.8	5.3	4.5	0.8
1969	853.4	356.5	496.9	510.7	207.0	303.8	45.1	29.8	15.3	88.0	59.4	28.6	48.4	32.3	16.1	4.9	4.2	.8
1968	764.0	321.3	442.7	455.6	186.3	269.3	40.5	26.8	13.7	82.6	55.4	27.2	45.5	30.0	15.5	4.6	3.9	.7
1967	692.9	291.5	401.4	411.3	168.4	242.8	36.7	24.1	12.6	77.7	51.9	25.9	42.8	27.9	14.9	4.3	3.6	.7
1966	638.7	266.1	372.6	377.2	153.2	223.9	33.5	21.8	11.7	73.1	48.3	24.8	39.7	25.4	14.3	4.0	3.4	.6
1965	587.9	242.9	345.0	342.7	138.1	204.7	30.8	19.9	10.9	69.3	45.7	23.6	37.2	23.5	13.8	3.9	3.2	.6
1964	547.8	226.3	321.5	316.1	127.5	188.5	28.8	18.5	10.3	66.6	44.0	22.6	35.4	22.1	13.3	3.7	3.1	.6
1963	519.2	213.3	305.9	297.0	119.3	177.7	27.3	17.5	9.8	65.0	43.1	21.9	34.4	21.5	13.0	3.7	3.1	.6
1962	497.4	204.4	293.0	282.9	114.0	168.9	26.2	16.7	9.5	63.7	42.1	21.6	33.5	20.7	12.8	3.6	3.0	.6
1961	476.0	196.0	279.9	269.3	109.3	160.0	25.1	16.0	9.1	63.2	41.6	21.5	33.3	20.5	12.8	3.6	3.0	.6
1960	458.8	190.3	268.5	259.1	107.1	152.0	24.1	15.5	8.7	62.6	41.3	21.4	33.2	20.5	12.7	3.6	3.0	.6
1959	440.2	182.6	257.6	246.8	102.7	144.1	23.2	14.9	8.3	62.0	41.0	21.0	33.3	20.8	12.5	3.6	3.0	.6
1958	421.3	175.3	246.0	234.6	98.4	136.2	22.1	14.3	7.8	59.7	39.6	20.1	32.3	20.4	11.9	3.4	2.9	.5
1957	402.3	167.7	234.6	224.1	95.7	128.4	21.0	13.6	7.4	56.8	37.4	19.4	31.0	19.6	11.4	3.3	2.8	.5
1956	374.6	155.1	219.5	207.1	89.1	118.0	19.1	12.4	6.7	54.2	35.3	18.9	30.2	19.1	11.1	3.1	2.6	.5
1955	340.3	139.0	201.3	186.1	80.4	105.7	17.2	11.1	6.1	50.9	33.1	17.8	28.9	18.6	10.4	2.9	2.4	.5
1954	315.0	127.2	187.7	169.6	73.1	96.5	16.2	10.4	5.8	47.9	31.0	16.9	27.6	17.9	9.7	2.7	2.3	.4
1953	300.1	120.8	179.3	160.8	70.6	90.2	15.4	9.9	5.5	46.0	29.4	16.6	26.9	17.5	9.4	2.6	2.2	.4
1952	285.2	114.1	171.1	150.8	66.7	84.1	14.5	9.3	5.1	44.4	27.4	17.0	26.1	16.6	9.5	2.5	2.0	.5
1951	268.8	106.7	162.1	141.5	63.4	78.1	13.3	8.6	4.8	41.7	25.3	16.4	24.6	15.7	8.9	2.2	1.8	.4

NATIONAL INCOME AND WEALTH

Series F 480-515. Fixed Nonresidential Business Capital—Current and Constant (1958) Cost Valuation: 1925 to 1970—Con.

[In billions of dollars]

Year	Nonfarm nonmanufacturing									Farm								
	Gross stocks			Net stocks			Depreciation			Gross stocks			Net stocks			Depreciation		
	Total	Equipment	Structures	Total	Equipment	Structures	Total	Equipment	Structures	Total	Equipment	Structures	Total	Equipment	Structures	Total	Equipment	Structures
	498	499	500	501	502	503	504	505	506	507	508	509	510	511	512	513	514	515
CURRENT COST—Con.																		
1950	246.7	95.6	151.1	128.0	56.9	71.1	11.5	7.2	4.3	36.7	22.1	14.6	21.5	13.8	7.8	1.9	1.5	0.4
1949	225.4	83.1	142.2	114.7	49.4	65.3	10.5	6.3	4.1	32.6	19.2	13.4	18.7	11.7	6.9	1.7	1.3	.3
1948	214.7	76.1	138.5	107.0	44.5	62.5	9.6	5.6	4.0	29.5	16.5	13.0	16.2	9.8	6.5	1.4	1.1	.3
1947	196.6	66.6	130.0	94.7	37.2	57.5	8.1	4.5	3.6	25.7	13.6	12.2	13.4	7.6	5.8	1.2	.9	.3
1946	167.4	55.1	112.4	78.2	29.1	49.2	6.6	3.6	3.0	21.4	11.1	10.3	10.5	5.9	4.6	1.0	.7	.2
1945	144.6	47.7	96.9	66.2	24.1	42.2	5.9	3.2	2.7	18.4	10.0	8.4	8.7	5.2	3.5	.9	.7	.2
1944	134.7	43.8	90.9	61.8	21.8	40.0	5.6	3.0	2.6	17.1	9.4	7.7	8.0	4.8	3.2	.9	.7	.2
1943	131.6	42.6	89.1	61.2	21.4	39.8	5.4	2.8	2.6	16.1	8.9	7.2	7.5	4.5	3.0	.8	.6	.2
1942	128.7	42.0	86.8	61.0	21.5	39.5	5.3	2.8	2.4	15.2	8.9	6.3	7.3	4.7	2.6	.8	.6	.1
1941	120.1	40.0	80.2	57.8	20.7	37.1	4.7	2.5	2.2	13.8	8.5	5.3	6.7	4.5	2.2	.7	.6	.1
1940	109.1	35.9	73.2	51.7	17.6	34.1	4.4	2.3	2.1	12.0	7.5	4.6	5.8	3.9	1.9	.6	.5	.1
1939	104.3	34.0	70.3	49.1	15.9	33.1	4.4	2.3	2.0	11.7	7.2	4.5	5.6	3.7	1.9	.6	.5	.1
1938	104.2	33.8	70.4	49.3	15.7	33.6	4.4	2.4	2.1	12.0	7.1	4.9	5.7	3.6	2.1	.6	.5	.1
1937	105.4	33.7	71.6	50.4	15.8	34.6	4.4	2.3	2.1	12.2	7.0	5.2	5.7	3.6	2.2	.6	.5	.1
1936	100.6	31.8	68.8	48.0	14.5	33.5	3.9	2.1	1.9	11.7	6.6	5.2	5.4	3.2	2.2	.6	.4	.1
1935	95.5	30.7	64.8	45.7	13.8	32.0	3.9	2.0	1.9	11.4	6.2	5.2	5.2	2.9	2.2	.6	.4	.1
1934	94.6	30.7	63.9	46.0	13.9	32.1	3.9	2.0	1.8	11.6	6.3	5.2	5.2	3.0	2.3	.6	.4	.1
1933	93.0	30.5	62.4	46.2	14.1	32.1	3.9	2.1	1.8	11.4	6.6	4.8	5.3	3.2	2.1	.6	.5	.1
1932	94.0	31.7	62.3	48.0	15.2	32.8	4.2	2.3	1.8	11.3	6.7	4.6	5.5	3.4	2.1	.6	.5	.1
1931	102.2	34.4	67.7	53.9	17.4	36.5	4.7	2.6	2.1	12.1	6.8	5.3	6.1	3.6	2.5	.6	.5	.1
1930	111.5	37.1	74.5	60.1	19.4	40.7	5.0	2.8	2.2	13.3	7.0	6.2	6.9	3.9	3.0	.7	.5	.2
1929	115.4	38.7	76.7	62.6	20.5	42.1	5.1	2.9	2.2	14.0	6.9	7.1	7.3	3.9	3.4	.7	.5	.2
1928	113.6	37.9	75.8	61.5	20.0	41.6	4.9	2.7	2.1	13.8	6.6	7.3	7.2	3.7	3.5	.7	.5	.2
1927	110.6	36.8	73.7	59.9	19.5	40.4	4.8	2.7	2.1	13.6	6.2	7.3	7.1	3.5	3.6	.7	.5	.2
1926	108.3	36.2	72.1	58.7	19.4	39.3	4.6	2.6	2.0	13.4	6.0	7.4	7.0	3.4	3.7	.6	.4	.2
1925	105.0	34.7	70.3	56.7	18.5	38.2	4.4	2.4	2.0	13.1	5.6	7.5	6.9	3.2	3.7	.6	.4	.2
CONSTANT (1958) COST																		
1970	678.6	322.9	355.7	400.7	186.4	214.3	39.9	28.2	11.7	70.5	47.9	22.6	38.7	26.1	12.6	4.1	3.5	0.6
1969	650.7	306.6	344.1	385.4	178.7	206.7	37.7	26.4	11.3	68.9	46.5	22.4	37.9	25.3	12.6	4.0	3.4	.6
1968	619.0	286.7	332.2	365.3	166.8	198.5	35.3	24.4	10.9	67.3	45.2	22.1	37.1	24.5	12.6	3.9	3.3	.6
1967	589.6	268.6	321.1	346.4	155.6	190.8	33.3	22.7	10.6	65.8	44.0	21.8	36.2	23.7	12.5	3.8	3.2	.6
1966	563.9	252.8	311.1	330.1	145.9	184.2	31.3	21.0	10.2	63.9	42.3	21.5	34.7	22.3	12.5	3.6	3.1	.6
1965	535.5	236.1	299.4	310.0	134.5	175.5	29.3	19.5	9.8	62.3	41.0	21.3	33.5	21.1	12.4	3.5	3.0	.6
1964	510.8	222.4	288.4	292.9	125.5	167.4	27.8	18.3	9.5	61.2	40.2	21.0	32.6	20.2	12.4	3.5	2.9	.6
1963	490.9	210.9	280.0	279.5	118.0	161.5	26.5	17.3	9.2	60.6	39.8	20.7	32.1	19.8	12.2	3.4	2.9	.6
1962	474.6	202.2	272.4	269.2	112.9	156.4	25.4	16.5	8.9	59.8	39.3	20.5	31.5	19.3	12.1	3.4	2.9	.5
1961	457.8	193.5	264.4	258.6	108.0	150.6	24.5	15.8	8.6	59.6	39.4	20.2	31.4	19.4	12.0	3.4	2.9	.5
1960	444.3	187.3	257.0	250.7	105.5	145.2	23.6	15.2	8.3	59.4	39.4	20.0	31.4	19.6	11.9	3.5	2.9	.5
1959	429.0	179.4	249.6	240.4	100.9	139.6	22.7	14.7	8.1	59.3	39.5	19.7	31.8	20.0	11.7	3.4	2.9	.5
1958	416.9	173.8	243.1	232.0	97.5	134.5	22.1	14.3	7.8	58.4	39.0	19.5	31.6	20.0	11.6	3.4	2.9	.5
1957	407.1	169.9	237.2	226.8	97.0	129.8	21.5	14.0	7.5	57.3	38.1	19.2	31.3	20.0	11.3	3.4	2.9	.5
1956	394.2	164.0	230.2	217.9	94.2	123.7	20.7	13.5	7.2	56.3	37.4	18.9	31.3	20.2	11.1	3.3	2.8	.5
1955	379.2	156.4	222.8	207.4	90.4	117.0	19.8	12.8	6.9	55.2	36.6	18.5	31.3	20.5	10.8	3.2	2.7	.5
1954	366.6	149.7	217.0	197.5	85.9	111.6	19.0	12.3	6.7	53.5	35.2	18.3	30.8	20.3	10.5	3.1	2.6	.5
1953	356.5	144.4	212.1	191.0	84.2	106.8	18.3	11.9	6.5	51.6	33.7	17.9	30.2	20.0	10.2	2.9	2.5	.5
1952	345.6	138.0	207.7	182.7	80.5	102.2	17.5	11.2	6.3	49.2	31.6	17.6	29.0	19.1	9.8	2.8	2.3	.5
1951	335.3	130.8	204.5	176.2	77.5	98.7	16.6	10.5	6.1	47.0	29.8	17.2	27.8	18.5	9.4	2.6	2.2	.4
1950	323.8	122.7	201.1	167.6	72.8	94.8	15.4	9.5	6.0	44.3	27.4	16.9	26.0	17.1	9.0	2.4	2.0	.4
1949	310.8	112.9	197.9	157.9	66.7	91.2	14.4	8.6	5.8	41.3	24.9	16.5	23.7	15.2	8.5	2.2	1.7	.4
1948	302.6	106.8	195.8	150.6	62.1	88.5	13.5	7.8	5.7	38.3	22.3	16.1	21.2	13.2	8.0	1.9	1.5	.4
1947	292.8	98.6	194.2	141.0	54.8	86.2	12.6	6.9	5.7	35.4	19.8	15.6	18.5	11.1	7.4	1.8	1.4	.4
1946	283.8	89.9	193.9	132.6	47.4	85.2	11.8	6.2	5.6	33.1	18.0	15.1	16.4	9.6	6.7	1.7	1.3	.4
1945	280.5	86.2	194.3	128.5	43.5	85.0	11.4	5.8	5.7	32.0	17.4	14.5	15.2	9.2	6.0	1.6	1.2	.4
1944	279.7	82.8	196.9	127.9	40.8	87.1	11.3	5.5	5.7	31.6	16.8	14.8	14.8	8.7	6.1	1.6	1.2	.4
1943	282.4	82.3	200.0	130.9	40.9	90.0	11.3	5.5	5.8	31.3	16.3	15.0	14.6	8.4	6.2	1.6	1.2	.4
1942	286.9	83.1	203.8	135.9	42.2	93.7	11.4	5.5	5.9	31.7	16.5	15.2	15.0	8.7	6.3	1.6	1.2	.4
1941	289.9	83.4	206.4	139.6	43.1	96.4	11.5	5.5	6.0	31.8	16.4	15.5	15.1	8.8	6.4	1.5	1.2	.4
1940	288.5	81.2	207.3	137.4	39.8	97.6	11.5	5.5	6.0	31.1	15.4	15.7	14.5	8.0	6.5	1.5	1.1	.4
1939	288.4	80.1	208.3	136.7	37.7	99.0	11.6	5.6	6.0	31.0	15.0	16.0	14.4	7.7	6.7	1.5	1.1	.4
1938	290.1	80.6	209.4	138.3	37.5	100.8	11.7	5.7	6.0	31.0	14.7	16.3	14.3	7.5	6.8	1.5	1.0	.4
1937	292.0	81.4	210.5	140.9	38.3	102.7	11.6	5.6	6.1	31.1	14.5	16.5	14.4	7.4	7.0	1.4	1.0	.4
1936	290.8	79.8	211.0	140.5	36.5	104.0	11.4	5.3	6.1	30.7	14.0	16.8	14.0	6.8	7.1	1.4	1.0	.4
1935	291.0	78.8	212.2	141.7	35.3	106.4	11.3	5.2	6.1	30.5	13.5	17.0	13.6	6.4	7.3	1.4	1.0	.4
1934	294.1	80.0	214.1	145.5	35.9	109.5	11.5	5.3	6.2	30.7	13.3	17.4	13.8	6.2	7.5	1.4	1.0	.5
1933	298.9	82.7	216.3	151.3	38.0	113.3	11.9	5.7	6.3	31.2	13.4	17.8	14.3	6.4	7.9	1.5	1.0	.5
1932	305.2	86.6	218.6	158.6	41.2	117.4	12.4	6.1	6.3	32.1	13.9	18.2	15.3	7.0	8.3	1.5	1.0	.5
1931	309.6	90.6	219.0	165.1	45.3	119.8	12.8	6.5	6.3	33.0	14.3	18.7	16.3	7.6	8.7	1.6	1.1	.5
1930	309.5	92.7	216.9	167.9	47.9	120.0	12.9	6.7	6.2	33.4	14.4	19.1	16.9	7.9	9.0	1.6	1.1	.5
1929	304.6	92.8	211.9	165.8	48.5	117.3	12.7	6.6	6.0	33.3	13.9	19.4	17.0	7.7	9.3	1.6	1.1	.5
1928	297.2	90.6	206.5	161.4	47.3	114.2	12.3	6.5	5.8	32.8	13.3	19.5	16.8	7.3	9.5	1.5	1.0	.5
1927	290.4	89.2	201.2	158.1	47.0	111.1	12.0	6.3	5.6	32.2	12.6	19.5	16.5	7.0	9.6	1.5	1.0	.5
1926	283.0	88.1	194.9	154.0	46.9	107.2	11.6	6.1	5.4	31.8	12.1	19.6	16.4	6.7	9.6	1.4	1.0	.5
1925	274.1	85.2	188.9	148.7	45.3	103.3	11.0	5.8	5.3	31.3	11.5	19.8	16.2	6.4	9.8	1.4	1.0	.5

Series F 516–527. Fixed Nonresidential Business Capital—Average Age of Gross Stocks, Constant (1958) Cost Valuation: 1925 to 1970

[In years. As of December 31]

Year	All industries			Manufacturing			Nonfarm nonmanufacturing			Farm		
	Total	Equipment	Structures	Total	Equipment	Structures	Total	Equipment	Structures	Total	Equipment	Structures
	516	517	518	519	520	521	522	523	524	525	526	527
1970	9.9	6.1	14.0	8.8	6.6	12.6	10.2	5.8	14.2	10.1	6.8	17.2
1969	9.9	6.1	14.1	8.8	6.6	12.5	10.3	5.3	14.3	10.1	6.8	17.0
1968	10.1	6.2	14.3	9.0	6.7	12.5	10.5	5.8	14.6	10.2	6.9	16.9
1967	10.3	6.3	14.4	9.0	6.8	12.5	10.7	5.9	14.7	10.3	7.0	16.7
1966	10.5	6.4	14.6	9.2	7.0	12.6	11.0	6.1	14.9	10.4	7.2	16.6
1965	10.8	6.6	14.9	9.5	7.2	12.7	11.3	6.2	15.3	10.5	7.4	16.5
1964	11.0	6.8	15.1	9.6	7.4	12.7	11.6	6.4	15.6	10.6	7.5	16.4
1963	11.2	6.8	15.3	9.6	7.4	12.7	11.9	6.4	15.9	10.6	7.5	16.4
1962	11.3	6.9	15.5	9.6	7.4	12.7	12.0	6.5	16.2	10.6	7.6	16.3
1961	11.5	6.9	15.7	9.5	7.3	12.6	12.3	6.5	16.5	10.5	7.5	16.4
1960	11.6	6.8	16.0	9.4	7.1	12.5	12.5	6.4	16.9	10.4	7.4	16.4
1959	11.7	6.7	16.3	9.3	7.0	12.5	12.8	6.5	17.3	10.3	7.1	16.5
1958	11.8	6.6	16.5	9.2	6.7	12.5	13.0	6.5	17.7	10.2	7.0	16.6
1957	11.9	6.4	16.9	9.1	6.5	12.6	13.2	6.3	18.1	10.1	6.8	16.8
1956	12.1	6.4	17.3	9.3	6.4	12.8	13.5	6.3	18.6	10.0	6.5	17.0
1955	12.4	6.3	17.9	9.4	6.4	13.1	13.9	6.3	19.2	10.0	6.2	17.3
1954	12.7	6.3	18.3	9.5	6.2	13.4	14.3	6.3	19.8	10.0	6.1	17.6
1953	13.0	6.2	18.7	9.6	6.1	13.5	14.6	6.3	20.3	10.1	5.8	18.0
1952	13.4	6.2	19.2	9.8	6.0	13.8	15.1	6.4	20.8	10.3	5.8	18.4
1951	13.7	6.2	19.6	10.0	6.0	14.0	15.5	6.4	21.3	10.5	5.6	19.0
1950	14.2	6.4	20.0	10.3	6.1	14.3	16.0	6.7	21.8	11.0	5.7	19.6
1949	14.8	6.6	20.4	10.5	6.1	14.3	16.7	7.0	22.2	11.6	5.9	20.2
1948	15.3	6.9	20.7	10.7	6.1	14.5	17.2	7.4	22.6	12.5	6.3	21.0
1947	16.0	7.5	21.1	11.3	6.5	14.8	17.9	8.0	22.9	13.5	6.8	21.9
1946	16.7	8.2	21.4	12.1	7.2	15.3	18.5	8.7	23.1	14.5	7.3	23.0
1945	17.3	8.7	21.8	13.1	7.8	16.4	18.8	9.2	23.1	15.1	7.5	24.3
1944	17.5	9.0	21.7	13.4	8.3	16.4	19.0	9.6	22.9	15.4	7.7	24.3
1943	17.4	9.2	21.3	13.3	8.4	16.1	18.8	9.8	22.5	15.7	7.8	24.3
1942	17.1	9.2	20.9	13.1	8.5	15.6	18.5	9.7	22.1	15.6	7.6	24.3
1941	17.0	9.2	20.6	13.0	8.6	15.4	18.3	9.8	21.8	15.7	7.6	24.2
1940	17.1	9.6	20.5	13.3	8.9	15.6	18.4	10.2	21.6	16.1	8.0	24.1
1939	17.1	9.9	20.4	13.4	9.2	15.6	18.4	10.5	21.4	16.3	8.2	23.9
1938	17.0	10.0	20.1	13.3	9.3	15.3	18.2	10.6	21.2	16.4	8.3	23.8
1937	16.8	10.0	19.8	13.1	9.2	15.0	18.0	10.6	20.9	16.5	8.3	23.6
1936	16.8	10.3	19.6	13.1	9.4	15.0	18.0	11.0	20.7	16.7	8.6	23.4
1935	16.7	10.5	19.3	13.0	9.5	14.8	17.8	11.2	20.3	16.9	8.9	23.2
1934	16.4	10.4	18.9	12.7	9.4	14.4	17.5	11.1	19.9	16.9	8.9	23.0
1933	16.0	10.2	18.4	12.4	9.2	14.0	17.0	10.8	19.4	16.6	8.7	22.6
1932	15.4	9.7	17.9	12.0	8.8	13.7	16.4	10.3	18.9	16.1	8.2	22.1
1931	14.9	9.2	17.5	11.5	8.4	13.2	16.0	9.8	18.5	15.6	7.7	21.6
1930	14.6	8.9	17.2	11.2	8.1	12.8	15.6	9.4	18.2	15.3	7.4	21.2
1929	14.5	8.8	17.2	11.1	8.0	12.7	15.5	9.3	18.2	15.2	7.3	20.9
1928	14.6	8.8	17.3	11.3	8.0	13.0	15.6	9.3	18.3	15.3	7.4	20.7
1927	14.6	8.8	17.4	11.4	8.0	13.1	15.6	9.3	18.3	15.4	7.4	20.6
1926	14.6	8.7	17.5	11.4	8.0	13.2	15.6	9.2	18.4	15.5	7.3	20.5
1925	14.7	8.8	17.6	11.5	8.1	13.3	15.6	9.3	18.6	15.6	7.4	20.3

Series F 528–534. Residential Capital, Current and Constant (1958) Cost Valuation: 1925 to 1970

[Stocks and depreciation in billions of dollars; average age in years. Stocks and average age as of December 31; depreciation for the calendar year]

Year	Residential structures, current cost			Residential structures, constant (1958) cost			Average age, gross stocks [1]
	Gross stocks	Net stocks	Depreciation	Gross stocks	Net stocks	Depreciation	
	528	529	530	531	532	533	534
1970	1,284.7	804.2	18.2	870.3	544.6	13.1	27.6
1969	1,197.3	749.5	17.1	843.3	526.9	12.7	27.6
1968	1,094.4	682.6	15.6	823.2	514.5	12.3	27.6
1967	1,010.6	633.3	14.5	802.2	502.2	11.9	27.7
1966	941.8	593.0	13.5	786.4	492.3	11.6	27.7
1965	888.9	559.7	12.8	769.6	482.2	11.3	27.7
1964	848.0	533.1	12.2	749.5	469.2	10.9	28.0
1963	807.5	505.1	11.6	729.7	455.7	10.6	28.1
1962	765.7	477.6	10.9	709.5	441.5	10.1	28.3
1961	731.6	453.4	10.4	690.5	427.5	10.0	28.5
1960	713.5	440.9	10.1	679.5	419.6	9.7	28.7
1959	689.0	424.9	9.6	663.8	408.1	9.4	28.9
1958	645.1	395.4	9.0	634.7	388.0	9.0	29.2
1957	618.4	376.7	8.7	618.0	375.1	8.8	29.4
1956	593.7	359.4	8.2	601.2	363.9	8.4	29.6
1955	556.7	335.5	7.5	583.9	350.8	8.1	30.0
1954	517.1	308.3	7.0	564.8	333.8	7.8	30.5
1953	498.8	293.9	6.8	546.1	320.8	7.5	30.9
1952	486.8	283.7	6.5	530.0	309.0	7.2	31.3
1951	465.0	268.0	6.1	515.3	298.2	6.9	31.6
1950	428.4	244.5	5.5	500.1	285.6	6.6	32.1
1949	386.2	216.4	4.9	480.2	268.5	6.2	32.8
1948	369.3	205.2	4.8	466.2	256.9	6.0	33.2
1947	342.6	187.9	4.1	451.6	247.4	5.8	33.7
1946	286.7	155.9	3.3	439.4	237.9	5.6	34.1
1945	243.4	132.3	3.0	434.5	231.7	5.5	34.2
1944	226.2	124.9	2.9	434.2	235.1	5.6	33.6
1943	211.5	117.3	2.6	433.9	239.0	5.7	33.0
1942	195.1	108.9	2.5	432.3	241.2	5.7	32.5
1941	179.3	101.2	2.3	429.9	241.8	5.6	32.1
1940	162.9	91.7	2.1	422.9	237.8	5.6	32.0
1939	151.4	85.0	2.0	417.0	234.5	5.5	31.9
1938	146.4	82.4	1.9	411.6	232.3	5.5	31.6
1937	142.3	80.9	1.9	408.2	232.2	5.4	31.3
1936	132.2	76.0	1.7	404.6	231.8	5.4	30.9
1935	121.8	70.9	1.6	401.6	232.2	5.4	30.4
1934	119.3	70.2	1.7	400.5	234.3	5.5	29.9
1933	114.2	68.0	1.4	400.7	237.9	5.5	29.2
1932	109.1	65.9	1.5	400.8	242.1	5.6	28.5
1931	122.2	75.1	1.9	400.6	245.6	5.6	27.8
1930	140.5	87.3	2.1	397.4	246.8	5.6	27.3
1929	147.4	92.8	2.1	392.9	247.0	5.5	26.8
1928	143.6	90.7	2.0	384.8	242.9	5.2	26.6
1927	136.3	86.0	1.9	373.0	235.1	5.0	26.6
1926	131.6	83.2	1.9	360.1	226.1	4.9	26.8
1925	127.8	79.5	1.8	346.3	215.5	4.7	27.0

[1] Constant (1958) cost valuation.

Series F 535–539.   Value of Stock of Structures and Equipment in Specified Sectors, in 1929 Prices: 1880 to 1948

[In billions of dollars.   Figures in *italics* for 1900 are comparable with earlier years; those in regular type are comparable with later years]

Year	Total, specified sectors	Agri-culture [1]	Mining	Manu-facturing	Trans-portation and other public utilities	Year	Total, specified sectors	Agri-culture [1]	Mining	Manu-facturing	Trans-portation and other public utilities
	535	536	537	538	539		535	536	537	538	539
1948, Dec. 31	103.9	18.5	5.3	34.8	45.3	1912, Dec. 31	65.1	13.4	3.4	15.3	33.0
1940, April 1	85.2	13.5	4.7	25.3	41.6	1900, June 1	38.5 / *39.0*	8.8	1.6	7.2 / *7.6*	21.0
1930, April 1	92.9	15.5	6.2	27.0	44.2	1890, June 1	29.1	7.3	.8	4.5	16.5
1922, Dec. 31	78.0	15.3	5.3	22.0	35.4	1880, June 1	20.6	6.6	.4	1.9	11.8

[1] Includes value of farm residences.

Series F 540–551.   National Saving, by Major Saver Groups, in Current Prices: 1897 to 1945

[In billions of dollars]

Year	National saving		Personal saving								Unincor-porated business	Corpo-rate saving	Government saving	
			Total		Nonagricultural individuals		Agriculture							
	Including consumer durables	Excluding consumer durables	Including consumer durables	Excluding consumer durables	Including consumer durables	Excluding consumer durables	Including consumer durables	Excluding consumer durables					State and local	Federal
	540	541	542	543	544	545	546	547	548	549	550	551
1945	−7.31	−6.56	36.41	37.15	29.31	29.92	3.61	3.75	3.48	2.51	2.59	−48.81
1944	−7.28	−5.61	39.30	40.96	30.78	32.21	4.22	4.44	4.31	4.79	3.17	−54.53
1943	−3.64	−2.14	36.17	37.67	27.85	29.37	4.40	4.38	3.92	4.23	2.72	−46.76
1942	4.50	5.81	33.24	34.55	23.80	25.15	5.04	5.01	4.39	2.86	1.82	−33.42
1941	14.31	11.23	13.97	10.89	10.54	7.71	2.74	2.49	.69	1.70	1.72	−3.08
1940	10.98	8.76	8.54	6.31	6.54	4.39	.95	.86	1.06	1.62	1.85	−1.02
1939	4.84	3.47	6.85	5.49	6.08	4.86	.83	.69	−.06	−.09	.80	−2.73
1938	2.00	1.87	3.72	3.58	3.95	3.78	.39	.43	−.63	−.57	1.50	−2.64
1937	7.29	5.32	7.32	5.35	6.32	4.50	1.29	1.14	−.29	−.55	1.31	−.79
1936	1.56	−.21	5.28	3.51	4.26	2.67	−.02	−.20	1.04	−1.41	1.23	−3.54
1935	.24	−.33	2.35	1.79	.62	.18	1.25	1.13	.48	−1.29	.75	−1.58
1934	−4.42	−3.76	−.95	−.29	−1.45	−.80	−1.13	−1.12	1.63	−2.72	1.41	−2.16
1933	−8.85	−7.34	−3.81	−2.30	−3.38	−2.06	.02	.20	−.44	−4.69	.77	−1.12
1932	−10.49	−8.39	−3.27	−1.17	−.72	1.08	.19	.50	−2.75	−5.03	−.95	−1.23
1931	−3.31	−2.21	2.47	3.56	6.01	6.85	.01	.26	−3.55	−3.36	−.48	−1.93
1930	5.82	5.89	5.62	5.67	7.99	7.92	−.18	−.05	−2.20	−.51	.90	−.19
1929	15.97	14.02	11.49	9.53	10.98	9.16	.13	−.01	−.38	2.14	1.25	1.10
1928	10.91	9.25	6.01	4.35	6.28	4.72	.11	.01	−.38	2.11	1.75	1.04
1927	13.69	12.02	10.07	8.40	10.17	8.44	−.11	−.06	.02	1.37	1.11	1.14
1926	15.89	13.18	10.10	7.40	9.30	6.69	−.04	−.14	.85	3.39	1.22	1.17
1925	15.45	12.82	10.74	8.11	10.52	8.09	.07	−.14	.16	2.37	1.32	1.02
1924	12.13	10.29	8.62	6.77	7.74	5.88	.58	.59	.30	1.46	1.27	.80
1923	13.61	11.42	9.88	7.70	9.81	7.67	.33	.29	−.26	2.35	.41	.96
1922	7.95	7.05	6.30	5.40	5.96	4.89	−.20	−.03	.54	.95	.50	.20
1921	2.26	2.57	1.29	1.59	3.01	2.76	−1.84	−1.29	.12	1.34	.09	−.45
1920	9.97	9.46	6.57	6.06	6.50	5.77	−1.63	−1.42	1.71	3.44	−.19	.15
1919	6.57	6.10	9.76	9.30	10.33	10.08	−1.76	−1.97	1.19	2.48	.13	−5.81
1918	1.61	1.91	12.69	12.99	10.92	11.29	1.50	1.43	.27	.42	.06	−11.56
1917	9.93	9.26	10.07	9.40	8.65	8.30	1.22	.90	.20	2.53	.16	−2.83
1916	9.58	8.74	5.56	4.72	5.85	5.14	−1.10	−1.23	.81	3.19	.22	.61
1915	6.27	6.07	4.68	4.47	4.47	4.34	.21	.12	.01	1.25	.20	.15
1914	3.51	3.35	2.55	2.38	2.07	1.95	.40	.36	.07	.74	.20	.03
1913	4.14	3.69	2.67	2.22	2.85	2.44	−.66	−.70	.48	.92	.45	.10
1912	5.23	4.76	4.24	3.76	3.88	3.48	.27	.19	.09	.57	.30	.13
1911	2.93	2.58	2.09	1.74	2.78	2.50	−.65	−.72	−.04	.58	.20	.06
1910	4.60	4.11	3.24	2.76	2.79	2.41	−.01	−.11	.46	1.10	.16	.09
1909	3.69	3.24	3.00	2.55	3.08	2.72	.10	.00	−.17	.42	.22	.05
1908	2.45	2.35	2.00	1.90	2.30	2.24	.03	−.01	−.33	.41	.08	−.04
1907	3.13	2.70	2.10	1.67	2.25	1.87	−.27	−.32	.12	.77	.16	.10
1906	4.21	3.70	3.24	2.73	2.90	2.44	.10	.04	.25	.73	.12	.12
1905	4.31	3.94	3.46	3.08	2.87	2.53	.10	.06	.49	.68	.14	.04
1904	2.04	1.82	1.42	1.19	1.56	1.36	.08	.05	−.22	.40	.23	−.00
1903	2.77	2.49	1.50	1.22	1.61	1.35	−.14	−.16	.03	1.07	.14	.06
1902	3.95	3.67	2.94	2.67	2.21	1.97	.48	.45	.25	.72	.22	.06
1901	2.20	1.98	1.36	1.14	1.78	1.58	−.35	−.37	−.07	.65	.12	.09
1900	2.10	1.92	1.27	1.10	1.07	.91	−.03	−.05	.24	.67	.12	.03
1899	2.82	2.59	2.19	1.96	1.72	1.52	.11	.08	.36	.55	.07	.01
1898	1.62	1.49	1.29	1.16	.82	.72	.23	.21	.23	.37	.07	−.00
1897	.93	.79	.55	.41	.66	.54	.04	.02	−.15	.29	.07	.02

Series F 552–565. Sources and Uses of Gross Saving: 1929 to 1970

[In billions of dollars]

Year	Gross saving and statistical discrepancy											Gross investment		
	Private saving						Government surplus or deficit (−)			Capital grants received by the United States	Statistical discrepancy	Total	Gross private domestic investment	Net foreign investment
	Total	Personal saving	Gross business saving				Total	Federal	State and local					
			Total	Undistributed corporate profits	Corporate inventory valuation adjustment	Capital consumption allowances								
	552	553	554	555	556	557	558	559	560	561	562	563	564	565
1970	153.2	56.2	97.0	14.6	−4.8	87.3	−10.1	−11.9	1.8	0.9	−6.4	137.6	136.3	1.3
1969	135.2	38.2	97.0	20.5	−5.1	81.6	8.8	8.1	.7	---------	−6.1	137.9	139.0	−1.0
1968	135.2	39.8	95.4	24.2	−3.3	74.5	−6.8	−6.5	−.3	---------	−2.7	125.6	126.0	−.4
1967	133.4	40.4	93.0	25.3	−1.1	68.9	−13.9	−12.4	−1.6	---------	−.7	118.8	116.6	2.2
1966	123.8	32.5	91.3	29.1	−1.8	63.9	1.1	−.2	1.3	---------	−1.0	123.9	121.4	2.4
1965	113.1	28.4	84.7	26.7	−1.7	59.8	2.2	1.2	1.0	---------	−3.1	112.2	108.1	4.1
1964	102.4	26.2	76.2	20.6	−.5	56.1	−1.4	−3.0	1.7	---------	−1.3	99.7	94.0	5.7
1963	88.7	19.9	68.8	16.6	−.5	52.6	1.8	.7	1.2	---------	−.3	90.3	87.1	3.1
1962	87.9	21.6	66.3	16.0	.3	50.0	−2.9	−3.8	.9	---------	.5	85.5	83.0	2.5
1961	79.8	21.2	58.7	13.5	−.1	45.2	−4.3	−3.8	−.5	---------	−.8	74.7	71.7	3.0
1960	73.9	17.0	56.8	13.2	.2	43.4	3.7	3.5	.2	---------	−1.0	76.5	74.8	1.7
1959	75.9	19.1	56.8	15.9	−.5	41.4	−2.1	−1.2	−.8	---------	−.8	73.0	75.3	−2.3
1958	71.7	22.3	49.4	10.8	−.3	38.9	−12.5	−10.2	−2.3	---------	1.6	60.7	60.9	−.2
1957	70.5	20.7	49.8	14.2	−1.5	37.1	.7	2.1	−1.4	---------	(Z)	71.2	67.9	3.4
1956	67.8	20.6	47.3	15.9	−2.7	34.1	4.9	5.7	−.9	---------	−1.1	71.6	70.0	1.5
1955	62.1	15.8	46.3	16.5	−1.7	31.5	2.7	4.0	−1.3	---------	2.1	66.9	67.4	−.5
1954	55.6	16.4	39.2	11.3	−.3	28.2	−7.0	−5.9	−1.1	---------	2.7	51.3	51.7	−.5
1953	54.4	18.3	36.1	11.5	−1.0	25.7	−6.9	−7.0	.1	---------	3.0	50.5	52.6	−2.1
1952	53.3	18.1	35.1	11.0	1.0	23.2	−3.8	−3.8	(Z)	---------	2.2	51.6	51.9	−.3
1951	50.3	17.3	33.1	13.0	−1.2	21.2	5.8	6.2	−.4	---------	3.3	59.5	59.3	.2
1950	42.5	13.1	29.4	16.0	−5.0	18.3	7.9	9.1	−1.2	---------	1.5	51.8	54.1	−2.2
1949	39.0	9.4	29.7	11.3	1.9	16.6	−3.2	−2.4	−.7	---------	.3	36.2	35.7	.5
1948	41.4	13.4	28.0	15.6	−2.2	14.5	8.5	8.4	.1	---------	−2.0	47.9	46.0	1.9
1947	27.5	7.3	20.2	13.9	−5.9	12.2	14.4	13.4	1.0	---------	.9	42.9	34.0	8.9
1946	29.7	15.2	14.5	9.9	−5.3	9.9	5.4	3.5	1.9	---------	.1	35.2	30.6	4.6
1945	44.7	29.6	15.1	4.4	−.6	11.3	−39.5	−42.1	2.6	---------	3.9	9.1	10.6	−1.4
1944	54.3	37.3	17.1	6.5	−.3	11.0	−51.8	−54.5	2.7	---------	2.5	5.0	7.1	−2.1
1943	49.7	33.4	16.3	6.6	−.8	10.3	−44.1	−46.6	2.5	---------	−2.0	3.5	5.7	−2.2
1942	42.0	27.6	14.5	5.9	−1.2	9.8	−31.4	−33.1	1.8	---------	−1.1	9.6	9.8	−.2
1941	22.4	11.0	11.4	5.7	−2.5	8.2	−3.8	−5.1	1.3	---------	.4	19.0	17.9	1.1
1940	14.3	3.8	10.5	3.2	−.2	7.5	−.7	−1.3	.6	---------	1.0	14.6	13.1	1.5
1939	11.0	2.6	8.4	1.8	−.7	7.3	−2.2	−2.2	(Z)	---------	1.3	10.2	9.3	.9
1938	8.7	.7	8.0	−.2	1.0	7.3	−1.8	−2.1	.4	---------	.6	7.6	6.5	1.1
1937	11.5	3.8	7.7	.6	(Z)	7.2	.3	−.4	.7	---------	(Z)	11.8	11.8	.1
1936	10.3	3.6	6.7	.4	−.7	7.0	−3.1	−3.6	.5	---------	1.2	8.4	8.5	−.1
1935	8.6	2.1	6.4	−.2	−.2	6.9	−2.0	−2.6	.6	---------	−.2	6.4	6.4	−.1
1934	5.6	.4	5.2	−1.0	−.6	6.8	−2.4	−2.9	.5	---------	.5	3.8	3.3	.4
1933	2.3	−.9	3.2	−1.6	−2.1	7.0	−1.4	−1.3	−.1	---------	.6	1.6	1.4	.2
1932	2.5	−.6	3.2	−5.2	1.0	7.4	−1.8	−1.5	−.3	---------	.3	1.1	1.0	.2
1931	8.0	2.6	5.3	−4.9	2.4	7.9	−2.9	−2.1	−.8	---------	.7	5.8	5.6	.2
1930	12.1	3.4	8.6	−2.6	3.3	8.0	−.3	.3	−.6	---------	−.8	11.0	10.3	.7
1929	15.3	4.2	11.2	2.8	.5	7.9	1.0	1.2	−.2	---------	.7	17.0	16.2	.8

Z   Less than $50 million or −$50 million.

Series F 566–594. Individuals' Saving, by Components, in Current Prices: 1946 to 1970

[In billions of dollars. Combined statement for households, farms, and nonfarm noncorporate business]

Year	Individual savings	Increase in financial assets — Total	Currency and demand accounts	Savings accounts	Securities — Total	U.S. savings bonds	Other U.S. Treasury	Other U.S. Government	State and local government	Corporate and foreign bonds	Investment company shares	Other corporate stock	Life insurance reserves	Insured pension reserves	Non-insured pension reserves
	566	567	568	569	570	571	572	573	574	575	576	577	578	579	580
1970	71.4	74.6	4.8	32.2	8.4	.3	−4.2	4.2	−1.5	12.2	2.4	−5.0	4.8	3.1	6.6
1969	56.1	60.9	6.0	13.3	16.2	−.4	9.1	4.5	1.5	5.7	5.3	−9.5	4.8	2.9	6.3
1968	63.5	69.6	11.3	28.6	4.0	.4	3.5	1.4	.9	5.4	5.7	−9.5	4.6	2.9	6.4
1967	62.0	65.9	9.5	33.7	−.9	1.0	−1.3	1.2	−1.3	3.6	4.7	−12.2	4.7	2.6	6.4
1966	56.1	54.4	3.1	19.1	10.5	.6	2.6	4.2	2.1	3.6	2.0	−4.7	4.5	2.1	6.1
1965	52.5	56.0	7.3	26.4	3.3	.6	1.3	.2	2.3	.7	3.1	−5.0	4.7	2.1	5.6
1964	45.2	51.3	6.5	23.9	3.6	.9	.5	.8	2.0	−.5	1.9	−1.9	4.2	2.0	4.9
1963	38.9	44.9	5.5	23.0	1.0	1.2	1.9	.4	.8	−.6	1.2	−4.0	4.0	1.7	4.5
1962	37.3	39.3	2.9	23.4	−1.7	.4	−.7	.3	.8	−.6	1.8	−3.9	3.6	1.4	4.2
1961	31.3	34.9	1.3	17.4	1.4	.8	−1.4	−.1	1.4	.3	1.9	−1.5	3.3	1.4	4.0
1960*	28.7	27.7	−1.9	12.4	2.6	−.3	.1	−.3	3.4	.2	1.5	−1.9	3.1	1.3	4.0
1959	33.2	34.9	.4	11.4	9.1	−1.8	5.3	1.5	3.1	.3	1.7	−1.1	2.8	2.0	3.7
1958	32.5	31.1	3.3	14.0	.7	−.5	−1.8	−.4	.8	1.1	1.4	.1	2.9	1.5	3.2
1957	33.5	28.0	−.5	12.1	4.4	−1.9	1.3	.7	1.8	1.0	1.2	.3	2.6	1.6	3.1
1956	34.9	28.9	1.2	9.5	6.3	−.1	.9	.3	2.3	.9	1.1	.9	3.1	1.2	2.7
1955	33.6	27.9	.8	8.8	8.1	.3	1.6	.6	3.4	1.1	.9	.2	3.0	1.3	2.3
1954	27.9	22.3	1.9	9.2	1.3	.6	−1.9	−.1	2.3	−.4	.5	.2	3.0	1.2	2.1
1953	29.9	22.1	.5	8.3	3.3	.2	(Z)	.1	2.1	(Z)	.4	.5	2.9	1.1	2.0
1952	26.3	21.4	1.7	7.7	2.4	.1	−.2	−.1	1.0	(Z)	.4	.5	2.7	1.1	1.8
1951	30.3	18.0	4.6	4.5	.9	−.5	−.7	.3	.4	−.2	.5	1.3	2.5	1.0	1.1
1950	27.3	13.7	2.2	2.5	.2	.3	−.5	(Z)	.6	−.8	.2	.5	2.6	.8	1.7
1949	19.2	10.0	−1.9	2.6	2.1	1.5	−.4	−.1	.7	−.4	.3	.4	2.6	.6	.6
1948	23.6	9.2	−2.5	2.3	2.0	1.6	−1.6	.1	1.1	−.2	.1	.9	2.6	.6	.6
1947	20.7	13.3	−.5	3.4	2.7	2.1	−.3	.1	.4	−.8	.2	.9	2.5	.5	.6
1946	25.4	18.4	4.8	6.3	−.9	1.2	−2.5	.1	(Z)	−.9	.3	.8	2.6	.4	.5

Year	Increase in financial assets—Con. Government insurance and pension reserves	Miscellaneous	Net investment in tangible assets — Total	Nonfarm homes	Noncorporate business construction and equipment	Consumer durables	Inventories	Increase in debt — Total	Mortgage debt on nonfarm homes	Noncorporate business mortgage debt	Consumer credit	Security credit	Policy loans	Other debt
	581	582	583	584	585	586	587	588	589	590	591	592	593	594
1970	9.0	5.7	25.8	9.7	7.5	8.4	.2	29.0	12.5	8.0	4.3	−1.9	2.3	3.7
1969	6.2	5.1	36.4	12.8	7.1	15.5	.9	41.1	16.2	6.9	9.3	−2.5	2.6	8.5
1968	5.9	5.9	37.2	12.8	7.1	16.7	.6	43.3	14.9	6.6	11.1	2.1	1.3	7.4
1967	5.3	4.7	29.8	9.2	7.3	12.4	.9	33.7	10.5	7.0	4.6	3.3	1.0	7.3
1966	5.3	3.7	33.9	11.5	6.8	15.2	.4	32.2	12.3	5.8	7.2	−.2	1.5	5.6
1965	4.8	1.9	35.8	12.0	7.3	14.8	1.7	39.2	15.2	6.6	10.0	.8	.6	5.9
1964	4.2	2.0	29.9	12.5	6.2	11.2	(Z)	36.0	16.0	6.5	8.5	−.2	.5	4.6
1963	3.7	1.5	28.5	12.6	5.4	8.9	1.5	34.5	14.8	5.4	7.9	2.0	.5	4.0
1962	3.6	2.0	25.0	12.8	4.3	6.7	1.3	27.0	12.7	4.5	5.8	−.1	.5	3.6
1961	3.5	2.7	18.0	12.0	2.7	2.9	.5	21.6	10.9	3.9	1.8	1.3	.6	3.0
1960*	3.3	3.0	21.7	14.5	1.6	5.1	.5	20.7	10.8	2.4	4.6	−.1	.7	2.4
1959	3.0	2.6	25.1	16.5	2.6	5.5	.6	26.9	12.6	3.0	6.4	(Z)	.5	4.4
1958	2.5	3.0	16.5	12.7	2.3	.6	1.0	15.2	8.8	2.7	.2	1.2	.4	1.9
1957	2.2	2.6	21.1	13.8	1.6	4.9	.8	15.6	8.8	1.6	2.6	−.4	.4	2.6
1956	2.6	2.3	24.2	16.4	2.1	5.9	−.2	18.2	11.2	1.8	3.5	(Z)	.2	1.5
1955	1.8	1.9	31.1	17.7	2.5	9.9	1.0	25.4	12.2	2.1	6.4	.7	.2	3.8
1954	1.6	2.2	21.3	13.7	2.3	4.9	.4	15.7	8.6	1.9	1.1	1.1	.2	2.8
1953	1.9	2.1	21.5	13.5	2.0	6.4	−.4	13.6	7.7	1.3	3.9	.5	.2	.1
1952	2.0	2.0	18.9	12.8	1.6	3.6	.9	14.1	6.4	1.7	4.8	.2	.1	.9
1951	1.6	1.9	23.6	13.5	2.8	5.5	1.7	11.2	7.1	1.5	1.2	−.2	.2	1.3
1950	1.8	1.9	30.3	13.7	4.4	10.2	2.0	16.7	7.4	1.8	4.1	.7	.2	2.5
1949	1.7	1.6	18.5	9.0	3.8	7.0	−1.4	9.3	4.1	1.5	2.9	.3	.2	.4
1948	1.5	2.1	25.0	10.5	4.7	7.1	2.7	10.5	5.0	1.1	2.8	−.3	.2	1.7
1947	1.8	2.4	17.6	6.9	4.9	7.5	−1.7	10.2	4.3	1.2	3.2	−.4	(Z)	1.8
1946	1.8	2.9	13.3	4.2	2.9	5.8	.4	6.3	3.8	.9	2.7	−2.7	−.1	1.7

* Denotes first year for which figures include Alaska and Hawaii.   Z Less than $50 million or −$50 million.

Series F 595–637.　Individuals' Saving, by Components, in Current Prices: 1929 to 1962

[In billions of dollars]

Year	Individuals' saving (F 610 + F 613 minus F 628)	Investment in tangible assets													
		Gross investment									Depreciation³				
		Total	Nonfarm homes	Other construction and producers' durable equipment				Inventories of noncorporate and farm enterprises			Total	Nonfarm homes	Noncorporate nonfarm enterprises	Farm enterprises	Nonprofit institutions
				Total	Nonfarm enterprises¹	Farm enterprises²	Nonprofit institutions	Total	Nonfarm	Farm					
	595	596	597	598	599	600	601	602	603	604	605	606	607	608	609
1962	26.27	39.47	17.63	20.29	11.93	4.71	3.64	1.55	.86	.69	17.66	6.54	6.16	4.17	.79
1961	24.31	35.08	16.72	18.27	10.22	4.66	3.39	.10	−.24	.34	16.75	6.15	5.76	4.11	.74
1960 *	17.74	36.79	18.90	17.09	9.69	4.20	3.20	.80	.47	.33	16.49	5.76	5.90	4.15	.70
1959	23.53	36.86	19.20	17.20	9.67	4.65	2.87	.46	.37	.09	15.90	5.32	5.78	4.16	.65
1958	24.40	31.21	15.35	15.20	8.03	4.44	2.73	.67	−.25	.91	15.19	4.95	5.68	3.97	.59
1957	23.32	31.12	15.63	14.51	8.07	3.97	2.47	.98	.22	.76	14.68	4.70	5.53	3.89	.55
1956	22.01	30.86	16.26	14.82	8.86	3.84	2.12	−.22	.19	−.42	13.49	4.26	5.00	3.74	.50
1955	18.15	32.99	17.34	14.80	8.60	4.19	2.01	.86	.56	.30	12.81	3.92	4.68	3.74	.48
1954	16.64	27.61	14.24	13.09	7.02	4.19	1.87	.29	−.20	.49	12.14	3.61	4.46	3.63	.45
1953	21.09	25.53	12.75	13.14	6.91	4.70	1.53	−.36	.26	−.62	11.58	3.32	4.31	3.53	.43
1952	19.16	25.24	11.96	12.44	6.32	4.71	1.41	.84	−.08	.92	10.89	3.02	4.07	3.42	.39
1951	19.93	26.29	11.61	12.99	6.48	4.99	1.53	1.68	.50	1.18	10.26	2.83	3.85	3.24	.33
1950	10.01	27.73	12.70	13.04	6.96	4.65	1.44	1.99	1.18	.82	9.01	2.53	3.45	2.74	.29
1949	8.09	18.36	8.23	11.49	5.76	4.52	1.21	−1.35	−.49	−.86	8.21	2.29	3.22	2.44	.26
1948	11.19	22.41	9.00	10.76	5.53	4.28	.95	2.66	.92	1.73	7.15	2.12	2.72	2.07	.24
1947	7.05	14.97	6.76	9.91	6.01	3.33	.57	−1.70	.06	−1.76	6.15	1.94	2.37	1.62	.23
1946	12.13	11.49	4.42	6.66	4.34	1.86	.45	.41	.38	.03	5.04	1.84	1.76	1.23	.22
1945	29.52	4.31	1.09	3.25	2.05	1.08	.12	−.03	.43	−.46	5.57	1.81	1.51	2.04	.20
1944	35.14	3.18	.98	2.15	.96	1.13	.06	.05	.50	−.44	5.38	1.80	1.47	1.91	.20
1943	33.73	2.68	1.14	1.84	.78	1.02	.03	−.30	−.12	−.18	5.14	1.79	1.45	1.71	.20
1942	29.99	5.62	1.90	2.38	1.16	1.11	.11	1.34	.18	1.16	4.84	1.76	1.37	1.51	.20
1941	11.12	8.96	3.67	4.10	2.55	1.31	.24	1.18	.73	.45	4.33	1.68	1.16	1.29	.19
1940	5.13	6.92	3.15	3.18	2.04	.93	.21	.59	.32	.27	3.94	1.62	1.02	1.13	.18
1939	4.03	5.54	2.79	2.63	1.68	.73	.22	.12	.06	.06	3.81	1.56	.95	1.12	.17
1938	.41	4.08	1.83	2.28	1.36	.69	.22	−.02	−.13	.10	3.84	1.58	.96	1.12	.18
1937	4.06	5.45	1.63	3.09	2.03	.87	.19	.73	.21	.52	3.77	1.54	.97	1.09	.17
1936	3.96	3.05	1.27	2.42	1.68	.60	.14	−.64	.48	−1.11	3.65	1.53	.95	1.00	.17
1935	1.64	3.02	.54	1.78	1.26	.44	.09	.70	.16	.54	3.45	1.47	.90	.91	.16
1934	.42	.07	.19	1.19	.94	.17	.08	−1.31	.01	−1.32	3.37	1.47	.87	.87	.16
1933	−3.17	.10	.09	.78	.70	(Z)	.08	−.76	−.50	−.26	3.32	1.48	.83	.84	.16
1932	1.57	.62	.35	1.01	.69	.12	.20	−.75	−.78	.04	3.26	1.42	.79	.89	.16
1931	5.64	3.23	1.25	2.19	1.25	.54	.40	−.21	−.52	.31	3.48	1.46	.82	1.05	.16
1930	5.19	4.73	1.52	3.68	2.02	1.14	.53	−.47	−.22	−.25	3.66	1.46	.82	1.23	.16
1929	5.82	7.78	3.20	4.57	2.43	1.58	.56	(Z)	.26	−.25	3.68	1.44	.81	1.27	.16

Year	Investment in tangible assets—Con.			Increase in financial assets⁴										
	Net investment in tangible assets			Total	Currency and bank deposits				Savings and loan association shares	Securities				
	Total (F 596 minus F 605)	Nonfarm homes	Other		Total	Currency	Demand deposits	Time deposits⁵		Total	U.S. savings bonds⁶	Other U.S. Government	State and local government	Corporate and other
	610	611	612	613	614	615	616	617	618	619	620	621	622	623
1962	21.81	11.09	10.72	38.68	19.07	.91	3.19	14.97	10.09	−.66	.42	.50	−.12	−1.46
1961	18.33	10.57	7.76	29.74	9.34	.58	−.07	8.83	9.35	1.18	.80	−1.36	.98	.76
1960*	20.30	13.16	7.14	20.09	2.77	−.01	−2.22	4.99	8.25	−.10	−.20	−2.68	1.69	1.09
1959	20.96	13.88	7.08	30.38	4.42	.71	−.41	4.11	7.16	9.91	−1.80	9.06	1.75	.90
1958	16.02	10.40	5.62	26.08	10.24	.29	2.21	7.74	6.36	1.06	−.52	−1.84	.82	2.60
1957	16.44	10.93	5.51	22.71	4.92	−0.03	−1.30	6.26	5.18	4.61	−1.91	1.54	2.23	2.75
1956	17.36	12.00	5.36	23.25	4.67	.04	.88	3.75	5.37	5.06	−.09	1.78	1.48	1.89
1955	20.18	13.42	6.76	22.46	3.81	.37	−.06	3.50	4.79	6.29	.26	1.62	1.68	2.73
1954	15.47	10.63	4.84	17.40	5.41	−.36	1.08	4.68	4.45	.23	.60	−1.60	.66	.57
1953	13.94	9.44	4.50	18.85	4.93	.58	−.21	4.56	3.64	3.41	.20	.06	1.83	1.32
1952	14.34	8.94	5.40	20.06	7.14	1.11	1.52	4.51	3.05	3.48	.09	.35	.96	2.07
1951	16.03	8.78	7.25	14.06	6.00	.77	3.08	2.14	2.07	.58	−.47	−1.00	.38	1.67
1950	18.72	10.17	8.55	11.09	3.74	−.06	3.20	.59	1.54	.99	.25	−.46	.49	.71
1949	10.15	5.94	4.21	6.94	−1.38	−.79	−1.56	.97	1.51	2.51	1.46	−.10	.41	.73
1948	15.26	6.88	8.38	6.98	−1.78	−.46	−2.23	.91	1.19	3.42	1.60	−.28	.98	1.12
1947	8.82	4.83	3.99	9.47	2.07	−.43	.22	2.28	1.20	2.26	2.08	−.85	.33	.69
1946	6.45	2.58	3.86	13.48	10.61	.12	5.12	5.37	1.18	−2.03	1.22	−3.10	−.15	(Z)
1945	−1.26	−.72	−.54	34.38	19.01	2.96	7.19	8.86	1.06	9.93	6.85	4.44	−.20	−1.16
1944	−2.20	−.81	−1.38	37.90	17.57	4.55	5.87	7.15	.81	15.71	11.80	4.64	−.05	−.68
1943	−2.46	−.65	−1.81	33.94	16.20	4.72	7.12	4.36	.25	14.14	11.14	3.37	−.12	−.26
1942	.79	.14	.64	24.14	10.95	4.12	6.05	.78	.25	10.33	7.98	2.56	−.22	.01
1941	4.63	1.98	2.64	10.04	4.84	2.18	2.54	.11	.36	2.64	2.75	.66	−.28	−.50
1940	2.97	1.53	1.44	4.60	2.93	.77	1.45	.71	.20	−.43	.86	−.39	−.46	−.44
1939	1.73	1.22	.51	4.02	3.04	.45	1.90	.69	.04	−.83	.66	−.64	−.23	−.62
1938	.24	.24	(Z)	1.60	.42	.04	.36	.02	(Z)	−.42	.41	−.61	−.23	.02
1937	1.68	.09	1.59	2.74	.46	.20	−.49	.74	−.11	.57	.42	.71	−.05	−.51
1936	−.60	−.27	−.33	5.01	3.66	.52	2.04	1.09	−.06	−.34	.28	.58	−.47	−.73
1935	−.43	−.93	.50	2.12	2.47	.23	1.02	1.22	−.20	−1.76	.13	−.56	−.12	−1.20
1934	−3.29	−1.27	−2.02	2.80	1.81	−.10	.24	1.67	−.29	−.09	----------	1.09	−.79	−.39
1933	−3.21	−1.39	−1.82	−1.47	−1.28	.16	1.21	−2.65	−.58	−.23	----------	.60	−.67	−.16
1932	−2.64	−1.06	−1.59	−1.39	−1.70	.28	−.54	−1.44	−.59	.61	----------	.70	−.29	.20
1931	−.25	−.20	−.05	.45	−1.58	1.01	−.31	−2.27	−.38	1.54	----------	.84	.58	.12
1930	1.07	.07	1.00	1.03	−1.46	.03	−2.18	.69	.06	1.28	----------	−.49	.78	.98
1929	4.10	1.76	2.34	2.37	−3.57	−.12	−2.54	−.92	.48	4.25	----------	−1.27	.88	4.64

See footnotes at end of table.

Series F 595–637. Individuals' Saving, by Components, in Current Prices: 1929 to 1962—Con.

[In billions of dollars]

Year	Increase in financial assets—Con.				Increase in debt to corporations and financial intermediaries									
	Private insurance and pension reserves							Mortgage debt						
	Total	Insurance reserves	Insured pension reserves	Non-insured pension funds	Total	Consumer debt	Securities loans	Total	On nonfarm homes	On nonfarm enterprises [1]	On farms	Net trade debt of nonfarm enterprises [1]	Non-real estate farm debt	Bank debt, not elsewhere classified
	624	625	626	627	628	629	630	631	632	633	634	635	636	637
1962___	10.18	4.80	1.40	3.98	34.22	5.33	1.10	20.53	15.44	4.23	.86	5.18	1.01	1.08
1961___	9.87	4.46	1.40	4.01	23.76	1.45	1.05	16.13	12.49	3.02	.62	2.27	.72	2.13
1960*__	9.18	4.18	1.28	3.73	22.64	4.21	.25	13.94	10.95	2.51	.48	1.75	.46	2.03
1959___	8.89	3.49	1.98	3.43	27.81	6.07	.17	16.28	13.17	2.51	.60	.02	1.15	4.12
1958___	8.41	3.76	1.58	3.08	17.70	.20	.43	12.09	9.32	2.37	.40	1.20	.94	2.83
1957___	8.00	3.54	1.58	2.88	15.84	2.53	−.07	9.76	7.95	1.44	.37	1.56	.64	1.42
1956___	8.15	4.34	1.20	2.61	18.60	3.14	−.75	12.23	10.20	1.53	.50	2.03	.23	1.72
1955___	7.57	4.19	1.30	2.08	24.49	6.09	.60	13.98	11.93	1.48	.57	−.18	.54	3.46
1954___	7.31	4.21	1.18	1.93	16.24	.96	.86	10.54	9.01	1.20	.34	1.57	.34	1.97
1953___	6.88	3.94	1.10	1.84	11.70	3.65	.40	8.58	7.30	1.00	.29	−.47	−.37	−.09
1952___	6.39	3.76	1.12	1.51	15.25	4.36	.60	7.89	6.52	1.02	.35	2.17	.30	−.08
1951___	5.41	3.09	.98	1.35	10.16	.99	−.30	8.36	6.59	1.48	.30	.35	.96	−.21
1950___	4.82	3.92		.90	19.81	3.64	.22	8.86	7.29	1.30	.27	2.42	.81	3.85
1949___	4.31	3.71		.60	9.00	2.64	.32	5.34	4.12	1.03	.19	−.96	.41	1.25
1948___	4.15	3.75		.40	11.05	2.41	.43	5.87	4.72	1.07	.08	1.84	.70	−.20
1947___	3.94	3.64		.30	11.24	2.81	−.76	5.54	4.62	.81	.11	1.25	.60	1.80
1946___	3.72	3.42		.30	7.79	2.32	−2.34	4.37	3.60	.79	−.02	1.11	.45	1.87
1945___	4.38	3.46		.93	3.61	.48	1.48	.14	.22	.16	−.25	.86	.03	.61
1944___	3.81	3.21		.60	.57	.14	1.38	−.54	−.05	−.13	−.36	−.32	−.10	.01
1943___	3.05	2.85		.20	−2.26	−1.03	.58	−1.05	−.38	−.20	−.48	−.64	−.04	−.15
1942___	2.61	2.49		.12	−5.07	−2.96	.27	−.37	.10	−.15	−.31	−2.01	−.01	.01
1941___	2.22	2.14		.08	3.55	.69	−.11	.93	.82	.16	−.06	1.28	.29	.47
1940___	1.90	1.85		.05	2.44	1.01	−.20	.86	.85	.04	−.03	.53	.21	.03
1939___	1.77	1.72		.05	1.72	.81	−.23	.48	.50	.11	−.13	.33	.26	.07
1938___	1.60	1.54		.06	1.43	−.62	−.12	.16	.17	.08	−.09	1.77	.20	.04
1937___	1.82	1.76		.06	.36	.58	−.49	.07	.01	.15	−.08	.43	.10	−.34
1936___	1.75	1.67		.08	.45	1.29	.06	−.44	−.09	−.28	−.07	−.43	−.04	.01
1935___	1.60	1.55		.05	.04	.83	−.04	−.32	−.13	−.24	.06	−.55	.19	−.06
1934___	1.38	1.33		.05	−.91	.40	−.47	.98	.55	−.04	.47	−1.38	−.30	−.14
1933___	.62	.57		.05	−1.50	−.10	−.25	−.22	−.62	.66	−.26	−.31	−.26	−.35
1932___	.29	.24		.05	−5.60	−1.13	−1.06	−1.44	−.89	−.24	−.31	−.98	−.41	−.58
1931___	.87	.82		.05	−5.45	−1.22	−2.10	−.64	−.34	−.17	−.13	−.32	−.46	−.71
1930___	1.15	1.10		.05	−3.09	−.57	−2.20	.40	.11	.41	−.12	−.16	−.22	−.34
1929___	1.21	1.05		.16	.64	.84	−1.66	1.11	.86	.37	−.12	.06	−.10	.38

* Denotes first year for which figures include Alaska and Hawaii.
Z Less than $5 million.   [1] Noncorporate.
[2] Includes farm dwellings.   [3] Includes accidental damage to fixed property.
[4] Includes changes in assets of noncorporate enterprises of the types specified. Ex- cludes changes in government insurance and pension reserves, and small amounts of Armed Forces leave bonds.
[5] Includes shares and deposits in credit unions and the Postal Saving System.
[6] Includes increases in redemption value of outstanding bonds.

Series F 638–667. Personal Saving, by Major Components, in Current Prices: 1897 to 1945

[In billions of dollars]

Year	Total		Nonfarm construction		Farm construction	Consumer durables	Producer durables	Inventories	Currency	Commercial bank deposits	Savings bank deposits	Credit unions and cooperatives	Savings and loan associations	Mortgage holdings	Life insurance reserves
	Incl. consumer durables	Excl. consumer durables	Residential	Nonresidential											
	638	639	640	641	642	643	644	645	646	647	648	649	650	651	652
1945_____	36.41	37.16	−1.33	−.30	−.17	−.75	.67	.05	2.87	13.26	2.75	.21	1.11	.65	3.38
1944_____	39.30	40.97	−1.44	−.44	−.11	−1.67	.46	.35	4.58	10.59	2.32	.17	.83	.02	3.19
1943_____	36.17	37.68	−1.19	−.50	−.05	−1.51	−.18	−.17	4.67	9.98	1.57	.11	.61	−.24	2.87
1942_____	33.24	34.55	−.26	−.39	−.04	−1.31	.15	1.64	4.21	6.26	.28	.11	.30	−.23	2.50
1941_____	13.97	10.89	1.78	−.10	.09	3.08	.83	.79	2.13	2.54	.03	.15	.40	.08	2.20
1940_____	8.54	6.31	1.29	−.16	.02	2.23	.49	.56	.89	2.00	.25	.11	.29	−.28	1.84
1939_____	6.85	5.50	.95	−.19	−.02	1.35	.20	.13	.45	2.44	.36	.08	.17	−.29	1.72
1938_____	3.72	3.58	.14	−.21	−.09	.14	.09	−.02	−.01	.34	.19	.07	−.00	−.20	1.61
1937_____	7.32	5.36	−.06	−.17	−.04	1.96	.52	.90	.20	.35	.23	.07	−.09	−.09	1.62
1936_____	5.28	3.51	−.31	−.25	−.10	1.77	.33	−.67	.53	2.77	.35	.06	−.18	.10	1.69
1935_____	2.35	1.79	−.99	−.44	−.14	.56	.00	.80	.18	2.48	.21	.06	−.30	.13	1.51
1934_____	−.95	−.29	−1.50	−.44	−.26	−.66	−.35	−1.31	−.01	2.14	.34	.05	−.24	−.53	1.13
1933_____	−3.81	−2.31	−1.60	−.41	−.26	−1.50	−.59	−.82	.19	−1.83	.02	.00	−.36	−.90	.54
1932_____	−3.27	−1.17	−1.45	−.24	−.29	−2.10	−.70	−.54	.31	−1.98	.31	−.00	−.42	−.23	.27
1931_____	2.47	3.57	−.51	.04	−.23	−1.10	−.44	−.23	.75	−3.66	1.03	−.00	−.23	−.18	.77
1930_____	5.62	5.69	−.07	.45	−.13	−.07	.03	−.73	−.00	−.90	.76	−.00	.20	.78	1.01
1929_____	11.49	9.54	1.45	.65	.05	1.95	.36	.13	.20	−.80	.16	.03	.53	1.89	1.12
1928_____	6.01	4.34	2.73	.69	.10	1.67	.18	−.26	−.06	−1.75	.59	.03	.69	1.65	1.29
1927_____	10.07	8.39	3.17	.81	.15	1.68	.20	−.23	−.05	2.64	.66	.03	.74	1.32	1.25
1926_____	10.10	7.40	3.79	.85	.06	2.70	.31	.03	−.04	−.36	.54	.03	.63	.68	1.14
1925_____	10.74	8.11	4.00	.72	.08	2.63	.23	.10	−.10	1.58	.47	.03	.60	.43	1.02
1924_____	8.62	6.78	3.75	.51	.06	1.84	.07	−.92	−.03	2.08	.51	.03	.60	−.46	.82
1923_____	9.88	7.70	3.16	.47	.09	2.18	.18	.47	.09	1.25	.44	.03	.45	.18	.79
1922_____	6.30	5.40	2.19	.40	.04	.90	−.12	.11	.13	2.47	.40	.03	.35	−.18	.66
1921_____	1.29	1.59	.90	.27	−.04	−.30	−.37	−.80	−.91	−1.36	.28	.03	.28	.28	.53

Series F 638–667. Personal Saving, by Major Components, in Current Prices: 1897 to 1945—Con.

[In billions of dollars]

Year	Total Incl. consumer durables	Total Excl. consumer durables	Nonfarm construction Residential	Nonfarm construction Nonresidential	Farm construction	Consumer durables	Producer durables	Inventories	Currency	Commercial bank deposits	Savings bank deposits	Credit unions and cooperatives	Savings and loan associations	Mortgage holdings	Life insurance reserves
	638	639	640	641	642	643	644	645	646	647	648	649	650	651	652
1920	6.57	6.06	.54	.24	.39	.51	.36	1.97	.37	−1.02	.51	.03	.28	2.24	.52
1919	9.76	9.30	.75	.07	.64	.46	.23	.56	−.02	4.06	.44	.03	.17	1.14	.53
1918	12.69	12.99	−.06	−.01	.41	−.30	.25	−.17	.96	1.46	.18	.03	.11	.51	.37
1917	10.07	9.40	.38	.13	.44	.67	.28	1.19	.61	2.85	.15	.03	.13	1.11	.39
1916	5.56	4.72	.69	.17	.29	.84	.13	−.82	.33	2.92	.35	.02	.09	.55	.35
1915	4.68	4.47	.61	.06	.17	.21	−.00	.41	.30	1.73	.17	.02	.10	.27	.27
1914	2.55	2.38	.60	.09	.17	.17	.06	.50	−.14	.21	.13	.02	.08	.47	.20
1913	2.67	2.23	.73	.20	.17	.44	.16	−.21	.05	.50	.19	.02	.08	.62	.23
1912	4.24	3.76	.72	.15	.18	.48	.15	.51	.09	.76	.20	.01	.09	.26	.23
1911	2.09	1.74	.65	.10	.16	.35	.07	−.45	−.07	.79	.16	.01	.08	.25	.25
1910	3.24	2.75	.73	.13	.18	.49	.11	.47	.04	.46	.15	.01	.06	.22	.21
1909	3.00	2.55	.73	.14	.16	.45	.10	−.06	.06	.67	.17	.01	.06	.06	.21
1908	2.00	1.90	.55	.14	.13	.10	.05	−.03	−.28	−.10	.06	.01	.04	.08	.18
1907	2.10	1.67	.68	.24	.12	.43	.18	−.24	.12	−.28	.07	.01	.04	.07	.17
1906	3.24	2.72	.61	.18	.12	.52	.17	.25	.06	.47	.17	.01	.03	.04	.21
1905	3.46	3.09	.55	.13	.12	.37	.10	.27	.22	1.12	.18	.01	.02	.07	.19
1904	1.42	1.18	.36	.11	.12	.24	.07	−.13	−.07	.14	.13	.01	.02	.07	.17
1903	1.50	1.22	.40	.15	.12	.28	.09	−.04	.06	.22	.12	.01	.01	.07	.15
1902	2.94	2.67	.27	.23	.12	.27	.14	.54	.06	.45	.15	.01	.01	.06	.15
1901	1.36	1.14	.14	.19	.11	.22	.06	−.57	.04	.63	.13	.01	.01	.05	.14
1900	1.27	1.09	.00	.20	.10	.18	.03	.19	.06	.29	.19	.01	.01	.05	.11
1899	2.19	1.96	.07	.12	.08	.23	.02	.21	.12	.59	.12	.01	.01	.06	.10
1898	1.29	1.17	.04	.13	.09	.12	−.01	.27	.04	.33	.12	.01	.01	.06	.10
1897	.55	.40	.07	.15	.07	.15	−.04	−.10	.03	.18	.09	.01	.00	.06	.08

Year	Pension and retirement funds U.S. Government	Pension and retirement funds State and local	Pension and retirement funds Private	Securities U.S. Government	Securities State and local	Securities Corporate and foreign bonds	Securities Stocks	Share in saving of foreign corporations other than U.S. subsidiaries	Nonfarm mortgage debt on structures Residential	Nonfarm mortgage debt on structures Nonresidential	Farm mortgage debt	Debt to banks and other institutions	Borrowing on securities	Consumer and other debt	Tax liabilities
	653	654	655	656	657	658	659	660	661	662	663	664	665	666	667
1945	4.80	.25	.80	11.84	−.31	−1.58	1.25	.05	.39	.04	−.25	.48	1.38	1.46	−.41
1944	4.41	.26	.60	17.80	−.08	−1.14	.52	.04	−.11	−.09	−.46	.05	1.57	.31	.70
1943	3.71	.24	.20	14.67	−.15	−.65	.47	.04	−.55	−.19	−.56	−.04	.56	−1.51	.61
1942	2.42	.22	.13	10.57	−.18	.06	.19	.04	−.23	−.14	−.42	−.55	.06	−4.20	−1.09
1941	1.68	.20	.08	3.40	−.15	−.96	.63	.04	.96	−.06	−.11	.82	−.09	.98	2.44
1940	1.14	.19	.05	.29	−.13	−.42	.49	.04	.78	−.08	−.09	.49	−.28	1.30	.49
1939	1.11	.18	.05	−.08	−.12	−.67	.57	.03	.57	−.11	−.18	.28	−.15	1.10	.08
1938	.96	.16	.06	.00	−.05	−.05	.23	.03	.20	−.06	−.16	−.10	−.10	.42	−.54
1937	1.25	.16	.06	1.03	.10	−1.06	.83	.03	.11	−.06	−.15	.28	−.52	1.22	−.22
1936	.45	.13	.08	.98	−.36	−.92	.19	.03	−.20	.02	−.19	.15	−.03	1.10	.55
1935	.14	.12	.05	−.90	−.01	−.94	−.07	.03	−.23	−.10	−.09	.17	−.11	.23	.26
1934	.05	.11	.05	−.23	−.86	.04	.42	.03	.01	−.09	−.03	−.23	−.28	−.85	.39
1933	.03	.09	.05	1.11	−.91	−.10	.44	.03	−1.26	−.08	−.71	−.95	−.04	−.46	.48
1932	−.04	.07	.05	.69	.13	−.40	.23	.03	−1.15	−.14	−.60	−.88	−1.03	.44	.33
1931	−.40	.07	.05	.72	1.78	.56	.60	.03	−.56	.07	−.28	−1.22	−2.01	1.14	−.19
1930	.13	.07	.05	−.23	.59	.67	1.28	.03	.57	.21	−.22	−.99	−2.05	1.28	−.51
1929	.16	.07	.16	−.47	.51	.66	4.79	.04	1.95	.39	−.12	.05	−1.33	1.09	−.03
1928	.13	.07	.08		.38	1.63	3.41	.04	2.50	.55	.01	.19	1.65	.98	.40
1927	.13	.06	.07	−2.26	.45	2.02	2.08	.03	2.39	.54	.11	−.23	1.33	.35	.38
1926	.16	.05	.04	−.64	.15	1.90	1.76	.03	2.60	.54	−.05	−.04	−.00	.45	.19
1925	.16	.04	.03	−.30	.23	1.94	2.09	.03	2.18	.80	−.19	.21	1.48	.64	.15
1924	.09	.04	.02	−1.52	.20	1.44	1.25	.02	1.74	.55	−.74	−.83	.84	.15	.08
1923	.04	.04	.01	−.28	.62	1.57	1.23	.02	1.70	.55	−.11	.64	−.10	.30	.18
1922	.04	.03	.03	−2.69	.75	1.26	1.35	.01	1.00	.30	.09	−.21	.66	.13	−.10
1921	.03	.03	.01	−.61	.70	1.40	.96	.01	.81	.20	.49	−1.48	−.08	−.15	.25
1920	.02	.02		−.67	.68	1.67	1.82	.01	1.17	.35	1.77	.92	−.67	.57	−.19
1919	.01	.01		3.15	.03	.52	2.00	.01	.36	.15	1.31	1.78	.79	.65	−.02
1918	.01	.01		8.67	.50	1.01	.96	.01	.27	.10	.60	.41	.37	.15	.30
1917		.01		3.40	.21	.69	.96	.01	.62	.19	.71	1.04	.14	.26	.61
1916		.01		−.12	.22	1.09	1.38	.01	.33	.12	.57	.63	.28	.32	.68
1915		.01		−.00	.30	1.46	.69	.01	.25	.10	.27	.64	.40	.19	.24
1914				−.00	.23	.47	.46		.36	.13	.28	.01	.11	.10	.18
1913				−.00	.01	.20	.54		.41	.14	.36	.11	−.02	.14	.14
1912				.00	.14	.67	.93		.22	.08	.42	.32	.10	.16	.04
1911				.02	.11	.41	.25		.20	.08	.41	.14	.05	.14	.02
1910				.01	.14	−.03	.80		.24	.09	.31	.16	.01	.12	.02
1909				−.03	.01	.53	.75		.23	.08	.12	.30	.11	.17	.02
1908				.00	.21	.61	.66		.13	.06	.11	.03	.04	.01	.02
1907				−.08	.12	.08	.69		.14	.06	.11	−.03	−.05	.09	.02
1906				.01	.07	.42	.81		.19	.07	.10	.34	.04	.13	.02
1905				−.01	.05	.66	.35		.17	.07	.10	.33	.14	.11	.02
1904				−.02	.02	.30	.36		.13	.06	.10	.04	.03	.06	.02
1903				−.02	.02	.08	.48		.11	.05	.09	.28	.07	.07	.02
1902				−.02	.00	.47	.72		.10	.05	.09	.27	.08	.08	.02
1901				−.03	.03	.39	.56		.06	.04	.09	.30	.15	.07	.02
1900				−.05	.02	.24	.26		.06	.04	.08	.23	.11	.06	.02
1899				.13	.06	.29	.54		.03	.03	.08	.22	.11	.06	.02
1898				.09	.03	.12	.10		.02	.03	.08	.07	.07	.05	.02
1897				−.02	.03	.06	.11			.02	.07	.14	.07	.03	.02

Chapter F

Input-Output Structure of the U.S. Economy (Series F 668-723)

F 668–723. General Note.

This section of chapter F presents input-output tables for the United States which portray the interindustry structure of the economy for five selected post World War II years: 1947, 1958, 1961, 1963, and 1967. The input-output tables show the dollar value of transactions that took place among producing industries and between producing industries and the final markets of the economy.

Periodic preparation of national input-output tables was begun by the Bureau of Economic Analysis (formerly Office of Business Economics) in the late 1950's with the development of a table for 1958. The program was undertaken in response to a recommendation of the National Accounts Review Committee that input-output accounts be prepared regularly as an important and integral component of the national accounts. The findings of this committee, set up at the request of the Bureau of the Budget to evaluate the national accounts work, were published in *The National Economic Accounts of the United States*, Hearings before the Subcommittee on Economic Statistics of the Joint Economic Committee, U.S. Congress, 1957.

Benchmark input-output tables fully integrated into the national accounts have been prepared for 1958, 1963, and 1967; updated tables for the years between benchmarks were made for 1961 and for 1966 (the latter of which is not included in this volume). In addition, the input-output table for 1947, prepared by the Bureau of Labor Statistics in the early 1950's, has been reworked to reflect the concepts and conventions of the current series of I-O tables and to make the data conform to the national accounts. The set of historical input-output tables presented in series F 668–723, are substantially comparable and can be used to observe structural and other changes in interindustry relationships which occur over time. The development of the input-output tool of economic analysis and the actual construction of the first input-output tables for the United States were the work of Wassily W. Leontief. Professor Leontief constructed such tables for 1919, 1929, and 1939. These tables appear in his book, *The Structure of American Economy: 1919-1939*, Oxford University Press, 1951. The tables, however, were not integrated with the national income and product accounts and it has not been possible to rework them into a format directly comparable with the later set of tables.

The relationship between the national income and product accounts, discussed at the beginning of chapter F, and the input-output flow tables presented in this section, are illustrated in the three tables below. The national income and product account is presented in table I. The output of the Nation is shown both in terms of final product flows and in terms of the income types generated in its production. The final product flows appear in the right-hand column of table I. They consist of sales to consumers (personal consumption expenditures), sales to business on capital account and change in business inventories (gross private domestic investment), sales to government (government purchases of goods and services), and net sales to foreigners (net exports). The sum of these final product flows equals the gross national product (GNP). This same total can be derived also by summing the income types (referred to in these series as value added) shown in the left-hand column. The first five items are factor payments that make up national income; the remaining items are nonfactor charges that are added to arrive at GNP.

Table I. The Gross National Product, National Income and Product Account

Types of income	Final product flows
Factor payments:	10. Personal consumption expenditures
1. Compensation of employees	11. Gross private domestic investment
2. Proprietors' income	12. Net export of goods and services
3. Rental income of persons	13. Government purchases of goods and services
4. Corporate profits and inventory valuation adjustment	
5. Net interest	
Nonfactor charges:	
6. Business transfer payments	
7. Indirect business tax and nontax liability	
8. Less: Subsidies less current surplus of government enterprises	
9. Capital consumption allowances	

Table II displays the same components of GNP as shown in table I, but they are rearranged in an input-output format—a matrix or table containing data arranged in rows and columns. The row labeled "producers" shows the sales of these producers to the same final markets which appear in the right-hand column of table I. The column headed "producers" enumerates the income types which make up GNP—grouped here as payments to employees, to owners of business and capital, and to government. The column sum, like the row sum, equals GNP.

Table II. The Gross National Product In Input-Output Format

	Producers	Persons	Investors	Foreigners	Government	
Producers	///////	Personal consumption expenditures item 10	Gross private domestic investment item 11	Net exports of goods and services item 12	Government purchases of goods and services item 13	Gross national product
Employees	Employee compensation, item 1					
Owners of business and capital	Profit-type income and capital consumption allowances, items 2, 3, 4, 5, 6, 9					
Government	Indirect business taxes and current surplus of government enterprises, etc., items 7 and 8					
	Gross national product					

The shaded box, which represents sales by producers to other producers of the goods and services used in production, is blank in table II. These producer-to-producer sales are already included in the value of the final products that add up to the total GNP. Accordingly, they are omitted to avoid duplication.

For input-output analysis, however, these sales by producers to producers must be measured separately, because this analysis focuses on the way the industries of the Nation interact with each other in producing their output and contributing to GNP. These sales are revealed in table III, which provides an elaboration of the producers portion of table II. Again, sales by producers to final markets are shown, as well as income payments by producers. However, the previously empty shaded box has been expanded into a large shaded area with many boxes in order to display separately the industries producing (as well as consuming) raw materials, semifinished products, and intermediate services.

These industry-to-industry flows depict the input-output structure of the economy. For example, the manufacturing row shows the sales by manufacturing industries to each of their industrial customers (intermediate markets) as well as to the final markets; the column for manufacturing shows the industrial sources of the goods and services used in production, and also the value added by manufacturers.

Because the interindustry account is conceptually and statistically integrated with the national income and product account, the value of total GNP as well as of the flows to each of the final markets (personal consumption, gross private domestic investment, government purchases, and net exports) is the same in the two sets of accounts. However, the breakdown of the flows differs in the two accounts. In the interindustry account, the detail in the final demand columns is classified by industry. For the national income and product account, other types of breakdowns are shown.

Value added is shown by component in the national income and product account. In the input-output tables presented in this chapter the components are combined into "value added" totals. Although the sum of value added for all industries is identical in the two accounts, the industrial distribution of value added in the I-O tables differs from that of the national income and product account due to certain statistical and conceptual differences.

Table III. Input-Output Flow

		Producers								Final markets			
		Agri-culture	Mining	Con-struction	Manufac-turing	Trade	Transpor-tation	Services	Other	Persons	Investors	Foreigners	Govern-ment
Producers	Agriculture												
	Mining												
	Construction												Government purchases of goods and services
	Manufacturing									Personal consumption expenditures	Gross private domestic investment	Net exports of goods and services	
	Trade												
	Transportation												
	Services												
	Other												
Value added	Employees	Employee compensation											
	Owners of business and capital	Profit-type income and capital consumption allowances									Gross national product		
	Government	Indirect business taxes and current surplus of government enterprises, etc.											

F 668–696. Value of input-output transactions among industries in the U.S. economy, 1947–1967.

Source: U.S. Bureau of Economic Analysis (formerly Office of Business Economics), 1947, "The Input-Output Structure of the United States Economy: 1947," March 1970 (duplicated); 1958, "The Transactions Table of the 1958 Input-Output Study and Revised Direct and Total Requirements Data," *Survey of Current Business*, September 1965; 1961, "Input-Output Transactions: 1961," Staff Working Paper in Economics and Statistics, No. 16, 1968; 1963, "The Input-Output Structure of the U.S. Economy: 1963," *Survey of Current Business*, November 1969; 1967, "The Input-Output Structure of the U.S. Economy: 1967," *Survey of Current Business*, February 1974.

The interindustry transactions table shows the value in current dollars of transactions among the various industries for a given year. Each row displays the distribution to every industry and to final users of the output of goods or services of that industry. The columns show the values of each industry's consumption (inputs) of raw materials, semifinished products and services, and its value added.

The industrial classification used to present the data in series F 668–696 combines all production activities of the U.S. economy into 23 industries. This is a condensation of the industrial classification used for the original basic tables. The condensation represents combinations of industries as defined in the *Standard Industrial Classification (SIC) Manual*, 1957 edition. A list of the industrial categories and their composition in terms of both the SIC and the I-O industry classification is given in table IV.

Table IV. Industry Classification of the Input-Output Tables

Industry number and title	Related SIC codes (1957 edition)	Detailed I–O industry numbers
1. Agriculture, forestry, and fisheries__	01–09 (ex. 0722)	1–4
2. Metal mining_____	10	5, 6
3. Petroleum and natural gas mining__	13 (ex. 138)	8
4. Other mining_____	11, 12, 14	7, 9, 10
5. Construction_____	15–17, 138, pt. 6561	11, 12
6. Food, feed, and tobacco products__	20, 21	14, 15
7. Textile products and apparel_____	22, 23, 3992	16–19
8. Wood products and furniture_____	24, 25	20–23
9. Paper, printing, and publishing____	26, 27	24–26
10. Chemicals and chemical products__	28 (ex. 28195)	27–30
11. Petroleum and coal products_____	29	31
12. Rubber, plastics, and leather_____	30, 31	32–34
13. Stone, clay and glass products_____	32	35, 36
14. Primary and fabricated metals____	33, 34, 28195	37–42
15. Machinery, except electrical_____	35	43–52
16. Electrical equipment and supplies__	36	53–58
17. Transport equipment and ordnance__	37, 19	59–61, 13
18. Other manufacturing_____	38, 39	62–64, 82
19. Transportation and trade_____	40–47, 50, 52–59, 7396	65, 69
20. Electric, gas, water, and sanitary services_____	49	68
21. Other services_____	48, 60–89 (ex. 7396, pt. 6561), 0722	66, 67, 70–77, 81
22. Government enterprises_____	----	78, 79
23. Scrap and secondhand goods_____	----	83
Directly allocated imports_____	----	80a
Transferred imports_____	----	80b
Value added_____	----	(1)
Final demand:		
Personal consumption expenditures		
Gross private domestic investment		
Exports		
Government purchases		

[1] For the condensed tables shown here in Chapter F, industries 84–87 in the detailed I–O classification are shown as value added originating in the appropriate final demand sector; thus, compensation paid household employees reflects value added resulting from personal consumption expenditures; the inventory valuation adjustment originates in gross private domestic investment; factor payments received by U.S. residents from foreign sources are part of exports; and the compensation of government employees is a government purchase.

The definitions and conventions used in constructing the input-output data for this series are as follows:

Trade. To show the links between producing industries and consuming industries or final markets, the input-output data reflect commodities as moving directly from producer to user, by-passing trade. If trade were shown as buying and reselling commodities, the detailed connections would be between trade and the producing industries, while the consuming industries and final users would make most of their purchases from a single source, trade, and the relationship between producer and consumer would be lost. The output of trade is measured in terms of total margins—that is, operating expense plus profit.

Valuation of transactions. The valuation underlying the data in these series is based on producers' prices. Such prices exclude the distribution costs which make up the difference between producers' and purchasers' prices. Under a system of producers' valuations, the individual inputs into a consuming industry are valued at producers' prices and the trade and transportation margin costs associated with delivery of these inputs appear as inputs to the consuming industry from the trade industry and transportation industry, respectively.

Secondary products or activities. In most cases, secondary products are treated as if sold by the producing industry to the primary industry and added to the output of the primary industry for distribution to users.

The basic unit of classification in the SIC is the establishment. An establishment is classified in an industry according to its principal activity. However, once an establishment is classified in an industry, its entire output, subsidiary as well as principal, is counted as part of the output of the industry. Its principal output, that which determines its industry classification, is called primary output; its subsidiary output is called secondary. In several industries for which secondary production is large and, at the same time, considerably different from the primary output, the secondary products, and their associated inputs, are subtracted from the producing industries and added to the primary industry. For example, self

performed new and maintenance construction are shifted from the industries where they occur to the appropriate construction industry.

Imports. Imports used in production (intermediate goods and services) which are substitutable for domestically produced goods and services are treated like secondary products; they are shown as if purchased by the industry producing the substitutable item and added to that industry's output. Substitutability was determined on a judgmental basis, using the following guide: the import should be interchangeable with a domestically produced item and not require any changes in the technology of the consuming industry or the resultant product.

Imports used in production which have no domestic counterparts, and imports purchased by final users in substantially the same form in which they were imported, are shown as purchased directly by the consuming industry or final market.

Gross output and gross input. Gross output of an industry represents the sum of the values of the following elements: (a) The total production by the industry, including both primary and secondary products or services; (b) the producers' value of the secondary products or services of other industries which are primary to the given industry; and (c) the domestic port value of substitutable imports, which are distributed as part of the output of the given industry.

Gross input of an industry is equal to the sum of the values of the following elements: (a) Total consumption of goods and services required for the industry's total production; (b) value added by the industry; (c) the producers' value of the secondary products or services of other industries which are primary to the given industry; and (d) the domestic port value of substitutable imports. Thus, secondary products and substitutable imports are added to both the inputs and outputs. Gross output, the row total, equals gross input, the column total.

Inventories. Inventory change, which is part of gross private domestic investment, series F 692, is defined as the change in inventories of the industry's primary products regardless of which industry actually owns or holds the inventories. (This is different from the customary inventory data, which represent inventories held by each industry.) Inventories are so classified in the input-output table in order to provide the balance between the output of each industry and the total consumption of its products. Current production includes products which end up in inventories and are therefore not reflected in consumption. On the other hand, consumption may come from inventories of the producer, of the consumer, or of trade companies as well as current output. To the extent it comes from inventories, it is not included in current production. Therefore, adding increases in inventories of products of the industry to, and subtracting depletions from, the consumption of that industry's products achieves the balance with gross output of the industry.

The source for 1967 shows the I-O data in 85-industry detail and eight final demand sectors. The data are also published in 367-industry detail and ten final demand sectors in a supplement to the *Survey of Current Business*. The 1967 transactions table provides benchmark data which will be used in revising the national income and product accounts.

The source for 1963 shows the I-O data in 85-industry detail and six final demand sectors. The data were also published in 1969 in 367-industry detail and ten final demand sectors in *Input-Output Structure of the U.S. Economy: 1963*, a three volume supplement to the *Survey of Current Business*. The 1963 data provide benchmarks for the national income and product accounts, but they have not yet been incorporated into the series.

Other articles containing data relating to the 1963 I-O study and published in the issues of the *Survey of Current Business* noted below are as follows: Allan H. Young and Claiborne M. Ball, "Industrial Impact of Residential Construction and Mobile Homes," October 1970; "Personal Consumption Expenditures in the 1963 Input-Output Study," January 1971; Allan H. Young, Leo C. Maley, Jr., Sally R. Reed, and Roy A. Seaton II, "Interindustry Transactions in New Structures and Equipment," August 1971; Albert J. Walderhaug, "The Composition of Value Added in the 1963 Input-Output Study," April 1973; and Philip M. Ritz and Eugene P. Roberts, "Industry Inventory Requirements: An Input-Output Analysis," November 1973.

The 1961 I-O data were developed as part of a program to maintain input-output data on as current a basis as possible. The interindustry transactions data for 1961 were obtained by updating BEA's 1958 input-output data. They incorporate a mixture of actual data for 1961 and summary updating of the base year relationships contained in the 1958 benchmark data.

In the updated data for 1961, the total output of each industry and a major portion of the final market purchases were based directly on 1961 statistics. In addition, the updated data incorporate allowances for changes from 1958 to 1961 in the relative prices of the inputs to each industry and for the average change in the use of a product as a result, for example, of changes in technology, scale of operation, and product mix within an industry. The allowances for changes in relative prices involved a much more detailed repricing of inputs than that which has been contained in updated data prepared by others. However, in general, the data do not incorporate allowances for variation from the average change in the use of a product among industries.

The 1958 Input-Output Study provided the benchmarks for the national income and product accounts series. The transactions data are, therefore, completely integrated with the national accounts and the published totals for the major component of GNP in the two sets of data agree. The 1958 study presents data for 86 intermediate industries and six final demand sectors.

Other articles appearing in issues of the *Survey of Current Business* relating to the 1958 study are: Morris R. Goldman, Martin L. Marimont, and Beatrice N. Vaccara, "The Interindustry Structure of the United States," November 1964; Norman Frumkin, "Construction Activity in the 1958 Input-Output Study," May 1965; Nancy W. Simon, "Personal Consumption Expenditures in the 1958 Input-Output Study," October 1965; and "Additional Industry Detail for the 1958 Input-Output Study," April 1966.

The 1947 data shown here represent a reworking of the 1947 input-output figures originally prepared by the U.S. Bureau of Labor Statistics. The data were revised to be integrated with the national income and product accounts and to be conceptually and statistically consistent with the input-output data for 1958 and 1963 developed by the Office of Business Economics.

This reworking involved the reorganization of the basic information, which reflected the 1945 and 1949 Standard Industrial Classifications, to make it conform to the revised 1957 Standard Industrial Classification and the sectoring scheme of the 1958 data. It also required numerous adjustments to the output and input data to change the original 1947 definitions of the various intermediate industries and final demand sectors to reflect those used for the 1958 data. Unfortunately, it was not possible to reconcile completely the final demand estimates of the input-output data with the already predetermined GNP components. As a consequence, the 1947 GNP total of $233.367 billion yielded by the input-output data was $2 billion higher than the published GNP total of $231 billion. The bulk of this $2 billion difference is accounted for by differences of $1 billion in personal consumption expenditures, primarily for food, and $800 million in Federal Government purchases.

F 697-719. Direct requirements per dollar of gross output, 1947-1967.

Source: See source for series F 668-696.

The direct requirements data for each year are derived from the respective interindustry transactions table. They relate each of the inputs of an industry to its total output. Each column shows the inputs that the industry named at the top of that column requires from each of the industries named at the beginning of the rows to produce a dollar of its output. For example, to produce a dollar of output in 1967, the chemical manufacturing industry, series F 706, required 22 cents of its own production, 4 cents from the petroleum and coal products industry (11), 2 cents of other mining products (4), etc.

The data in series F 697-719 permit the tracing of the interconnections among the various industries and final demand in a systematic way. For example, assume that in 1967 the wood products and furniture industry produces $1 million of products for sale to consumers. By use of series F 704 it can be established that the industry would require slightly more than $220,000 ($1,000,000 × 0.22089) of the products supplied by other producers in the same industry. Thus, the wood products and furniture industry would have to produce a minimum of $1,220,000. Continuing the calculation, this output would require almost $29,400 ($1,220,000 × 0.02408) of textile products from industry 7, about $68,000 ($1,220,000 × 0.05574) of primary and fabricated metal products from industry 14, and so on down the column.

The next calculation is that of the output required by each of the supplying industries to meet the requirement that has been placed on it. For example, the wood products and furniture industry has so far required $29,400 of textile products from industry 7. To meet this requirement, industry 7 (series F 703) needs another $12,000 ($29,400 × 0.40880) of its own products for a total of $41,400. To produce this, it will require $2,900 ($41,400 × 0.07112) of chemical products from industry 10.

This chain of calculations of the output requirements which spread through the economy can be continued, and the total output required from each industry to produce $1 million of wood products and furniture for consumers can thus be derived. This is a very laborious and time-consuming procedure when done by hand, but it can be performed rapidly on an electronic computer with established programs. Although not shown here, this calculation has been carried out for each of the I-O tables at the more detailed level of industry classification. The sources cited for each year for series F 668-696 also contain a table of *total requirements* (direct and indirect) per dollar of an industry's product delivered to final demand—in addition to the interindustry transactions data and the direct requirements data.

The relationship among inputs required to produce one unit of an industry's product is mainly technical, particularly if one abstracts from price changes. Assuming that these technical requirements do not change rapidly over time one can use the relationships described in the input-output data to examine the likely impact of projected or hypothetical situations on producing industries in the nation.

F 720-723. Industrial composition per dollar of purchases, by final demand categories, 1947-1967.

Source: See source for series F 668-696.

The ratios in series F 720-723 relate each industry's sales for a particular end use to total sales to (purchases in) the final demand category. The differing industrial composition of the purchases in each of the final demand categories highlights the varying impacts on the producing industries of the economy that a dollar of each type of final expenditure can have.

However, there is no structural relationship, in a technological sense, between the purchases from individual industries and total purchases in a final demand category. Accordingly, there is no reason to expect the same sort of stability over time in these ratios as in the case of input ratios for the producing industries shown in series F 697-719.

Series F 668–696. Value of Input-Output Transactions Among

[In millions of dollars at producers' prices. For the distribution of output of an industry, read the

Industry No.	Consuming industry / Producing industry	Agriculture, forestry, and fisheries	Metal mining	Petroleum and natural gas mining	Other mining	Construction	Food, feed, and tobacco products	Textile products and apparel	Wood products and furniture	Paper, printing, and publishing	Chemicals and chemical products	Petroleum and coal products	Rubber, plastics, and leather	Stone, clay, and glass products
		668	669	670	671	672	673	674	675	676	677	678	679	680
	1967													
1	Agriculture, forestry, and fisheries	18,542	–	–	–	263	28,505	1,603	1,125	–	122	–	14	–
2	Metal mining	–	320	–	9	–	–	–	–	–	118	–	–	22
3	Petroleum and natural gas mining	–	–	374	1	–	–	–	–	–	49	11,556	–	–
4	Other mining	138	17	(Z)	535	930	53	20	8	154	807	73	30	943
5	Construction	603	46	476	50	30	264	91	94	224	274	363	57	130
6	Food, feed, and tobacco products	3,762	–	–	–	–	16,493	47	6	135	627	31	268	6
7	Textile products and apparel	201	2	5	31	279	145	18,954	511	352	96	3	1,157	85
8	Wood products and furniture	123	14	(Z)	23	5,528	124	28	4,683	1,212	66	1	100	88
9	Paper, printing, and publishing	161	1	2	26	295	3,225	402	216	11,213	1,178	162	414	493
10	Chemicals and chemical products	2,451	78	173	125	1,477	874	3,298	379	1,477	9,712	726	2,940	386
11	Petroleum and coal products	1,113	10	33	112	2,024	220	51	118	172	2,019	1,831	27	111
12	Rubber, plastics, and leather	216	23	34	64	749	739	324	404	434	692	58	1,898	217
13	Stone, clay, and glass products	33	4	83	131	7,128	1,002	99	198	34	302	58	104	1,522
14	Primary and fabricated metals	192	101	230	201	15,192	2,438	81	1,203	614	1,520	155	434	324
15	Machinery, except electrical	322	118	276	222	1,842	250	169	137	200	432	88	153	240
16	Electrical equipment and supplies	55	3	171	17	2,509	6	19	35	27	36	12	25	49
17	Transport equipment and ordnance	38	8	–	1	5	4	4	45	6	33	3	70	15
18	Other manufacturing	12	2	16	3	535	84	448	97	341	141	30	184	74
19	Transportation and trade	4,144	214	321	203	10,839	5,970	1,960	1,374	2,293	2,304	1,691	977	1,166
20	Electric, gas, and sanitary services	304	89	172	187	74	645	331	180	514	885	461	182	494
21	Other services	5,235	318	2,886	606	7,824	5,730	1,795	991	3,794	5,238	1,733	1,179	1,007
22	Government enterprises	9	3	6	5	66	94	76	20	301	74	17	29	23
23	Scrap and secondhand goods	–	14	86	21	14	1	–	39	239	69	11	16	10
DI	Directly allocated imports	36				101	1,318	62	2	3	87	2	198	1
TrI	Transferred imports	1,025	858	1,076	203		1,355	825	791	1,387	875	1,018	279	271
I	Intermediate inputs, total	38,716	2,244	6,420	2,776	57,705	69,590	30,727	12,616	25,127	27,755	20,085	10,738	7,675
VA	Value added	24,382	1,117	8,611	3,762	45,575	27,852	15,638	8,584	19,402	17,244	6,889	8,331	7,133
T	Total inputs	63,097	3,362	15,031	6,538	103,280	97,391	46,365	21,200	44,529	44,999	26,975	19,069	14,808
Tr	Transfers [5]	1,189	1,024	1,298	365		2,922	1,358	1,443	2,003	3,924	1,969	1,205	750
	1963													
1	Agriculture, forestry, and fisheries	17,034	–	–	7	326	23,826	1,700	1,086	–	57	–	57	7
2	Metal mining	–	322	–	7	–	–	–	–	–	168	–	–	17
3	Petroleum and natural gas mining	–	–	297	–	–	–	–	–	–	32	9,813	–	–
4	Other mining	128	18	–	467	737	53	17	5	145	610	89	22	945
5	Construction	567	8	379	28	25	156	57	44	83	136	349	32	56
6	Food, feed, and tobacco products	3,635	(Z)	–	(Z)	29	14,652	54	1	137	684	25	242	4
7	Textile products and apparel	212	(Z)	2	(Z)	207	162	15,262	385	164	37	4	872	65
8	Wood products and furniture	115	12	(Z)	17	4,808	102	15	4,130	853	66	4	77	116
9	Paper, printing, and publishing	118	1	2	9	286	2,674	394	138	9,056	888	164	291	325
10	Chemicals and chemical products	1,571	77	105	93	1,425	648	2,460	307	1,222	6,844	667	2,275	406
11	Petroleum and coal products	1,162	18	64	80	1,660	212	49	58	183	1,332	1,622	28	120
12	Rubber, plastics, and leather	154	17	16	104	627	257	294	367	272	436	4	1,632	166
13	Stone, clay, and glass products	46	5	41	119	6,396	777	49	151	56	240	55	100	1,323
14	Primary and fabricated metals	267	57	61	105	11,997	2,063	37	1,018	306	1,184	196	247	288
15	Machinery, except electrical	244	111	65	299	1,489	51	104	64	109	193	7	33	109
16	Electrical equipment and supplies	71	2	101	35	2,131	7	5	26	6	35	1	27	41
17	Transport equipment and ordnance	47	7	3	33	60	15	2	9	14	3	1	40	9
18	Other manufacturing	7	3	9	2	473	69	471	70	252	133	14	186	48
19	Transportation and trade	2,795	205	426	245	9,789	5,154	1,858	1,014	1,709	1,865	1,364	665	945
20	Electric, gas, and sanitary services	301	67	141	163	294	503	230	123	389	707	390	128	421
21	Other services	4,461	249	2,570	311	5,431	4,184	1,248	794	2,753	2,882	1,199	701	638
22	Government enterprises	10	4	8	8	64	90	70	17	205	66	16	25	23
23	Scrap and secondhand goods	5	6	–	7	38	–	45	–	240	41	17	4	16
DI	Directly allocated imports	216	–	–	–		1,258	171	1	–	85	–	246	13
TrI	Transferred imports	822	635	1,046	198		1,271	783	680	1,112	460	735	142	167
I	Intermediate inputs, total	33,988	1,824	5,338	2,329	48,292	58,185	25,374	10,487	19,267	19,184	16,736	8,073	6,269
VA	Value added	22,702	1,101	6,926	3,023	37,022	23,503	11,651	6,421	14,589	14,052	5,100	6,168	6,201
T	Total inputs	56,690	2,925	12,265	5,352	85,313	81,688	37,025	16,908	33,856	33,236	21,837	14,241	12,469
Tr	Transfers [5]	946	769	1,365	372		2,581	1,138	1,221	1,546	2,608	1,378	865	507

See footnotes at end of table.

Industries in the U.S. Economy: 1947 to 1967

row for that industry; for the composition of inputs to an industry, read the column for that industry]

	Intermediate markets—Con.									Final markets						
Primary and fabricated metals	Machinery, except electrical	Electrical equipment and supplies	Transport equipment and ordnance	Other manufacturing	Transportation and trade	Electric, gas, and sanitary services	Other services	Government enterprises	Scrap and second-hand goods	Personal consumption expenditures	Gross private domestic investment [1]	Net exports [2]	Government purchases [3]	Total output	Transfers [4]	Industry No.
681	682	683	684	685	686	687	688	689	690	691	692	693	694	695	696	
																1967
–	–	–	–	21	196	–	3,014	392	–	6,152	1,162	3,301	–1,314	63,097	4,006	1
2,611	–	8	–	3	1	1	14	–	–	–	38	158	60	3,362	25	2
–	–	–	–	–	25	2,521	165	–	–	–	257	82	–	15,031	1,138	3
772	13	9	22	9	16	896	89	145	–	128	145	538	47	6,538	366	4
478	165	142	216	62	1,833	1,137	9,191	1,771	–	–	54,338	15	31,231	103,280	–	5
10	7	–	–	31	1,067	2	3,797	121	10	66,244	1,089	2,507	1,131	97,391	4,397	6
105	61	67	879	358	433	17	434	25	72	20,227	640	583	645	46,365	605	7
373	137	369	572	199	252	1	54	–	–	4,293	2,017	413	528	21,200	467	8
641	265	542	228	2,694	2,103	44	11,395	75	129	5,694	564	924	1,442	44,529	12,410	9
1,266	152	668	600	693	679	58	2,628	165	–	7,867	607	2,863	2,656	44,999	1,609	10
262	211	100	203	43	3,374	275	1,644	141	12	10,194	541	765	1,370	26,975	2,509	11
407	568	762	1,214	618	1,042	23	1,434	43	14	5,928	187	385	589	19,069	913	12
361	385	696	566	136	340	1	456	7	–	562	166	322	111	14,808	562	13
25,721	9,048	5,226	12,249	1,883	1,134	78	2,163	25	588	1,232	2,636	2,253	983	87,906	3,834	14
2,851	6,748	1,272	4,246	262	746	39	2,020	33	108	812	22,108	5,249	2,648	53,593	3,242	15
884	3,470	7,621	2,709	809	554	74	1,723	24	96	8,566	7,312	1,989	7,964	46,759	3,537	16
698	983	752	18,611	179	1,022	3	1,545	18	168	17,271	16,828	4,300	20,221	82,831	3,258	17
318	320	522	822	1,422	959	31	3,492	29	35	6,047	2,919	1,222	2,181	22,288	2,032	18
5,119	2,318	1,843	2,968	998	11,447	765	14,285	1,440	58	120,763	8,108	6,506	6,091	216,165	10,201	19
1,571	312	311	402	101	2,757	6,888	3,242	1,268	–	13,935	–	74	1,942	37,321	188	20
4,044	3,514	3,346	4,334	1,601	30,671	1,002	51,351	1,392	11	178,786	3,142	1,599	12,459	335,588	132	21
67	57	61	95	35	3,931	5,610	3,660	23	–	2,148	–	106	819	17,337	9,768	22
1,761	60	3	213	–	16	–	40	(Z)	–	1,286	–3,042	580	554	1,991	–	23
63	29	86	80	182	942	–	290	341	689	9,870	558	–18,221	3,967	–	–	DI
3,870	1,364	1,181	985	870	1,363	145	376	–	–	–2,047	–20,807	2,908	–861	–	20,807	TrI
54,254	30,189	25,589	52,214	13,210	66,904	19,609	118,502	7,480	1,991	122,320	–	–	–	795,388	–	I
33,651	23,404	21,170	30,617	9,078	149,261	17,712	217,087	9,857	1,991	4,701	–1,843	4,517	81,654	–	–	VA
87,906	53,593	46,759	82,831	22,288	216,165	37,321	335,588	17,337	1,991	490,660	120,477	5,132	179,119	–	–	T
6,665	5,270	3,100	2,770	4,283	8,466	5,947	28,062									Tr
																1963
–	–	–	–	19	260	–	2,771	639	–	5,065	1,003	3,012	–173	56,690	3,937	1
2,076	–	5	–	(Z)	2	4	14	(Z)	–	–	–59	119	251	2,925	32	2
–	–	–	–	–	28	1,948	82	39	–	–	16	12	–	12,265	622	3
591	12	8	22	7	16	636	43	150	–	182		405	46	5,352	316	4
255	60	39	106	27	1,556	889	8,667	1,349	–	–	46,151	2	24,290	85,313	–	5
11	8	(Z)	–	27	868	2	2,654	214	9	54,864	606	2,156	806	81,688	3,286	6
128	46	57	641	244	213	9	306	30	104	16,819	284	493	279	37,025	490	7
233	90	241	292	193	184	2	41	(Z)	–	3,387	1,406	226	297	16,908	353	8
476	129	385	74	2,056	1,666	25	8,438	57	136	4,475	231	634	729	33,856	9,110	9
1,200	180	474	379	563	490	57	1,734	92	–	5,858	313	2,079	1,718	33,236	1,234	10
320	127	109	144	36	2,902	223	1,206	72	10	8,232	177	678	1,012	21,837	1,651	11
259	456	685	1,157	522	544	6	654	16	21	4,895	68	334	277	14,241	788	12
283	253	492	522	128	203	1	308	20	–	455	139	224	81	12,469	607	13
18,490	5,937	4,167	9,331	1,251	728	75	412	15	372	956	1,296	1,563	189	62,608	2,757	14
1,507	4,776	1,015	3,280	170	437	3	963	2	107	659	12,892	3,507	1,565	33,762	2,554	15
589	1,885	4,586	2,365	614	476	27	1,328	27	104	5,869	4,686	1,197	5,902	32,142	2,429	16
550	764	567	16,605	157	811	3	970	19	200	16,591	8,555	2,605	15,296	63,935	2,465	17
279	254	453	690	975	650	25	2,543	21	39	4,333	1,629	716	1,231	15,575	1,574	18
3,730	1,436	1,454	2,304	722	7,244	735	9,317	1,475	78	89,737	5,909	4,775	2,845	159,794	6,801	19
1,155	213	202	308	72	2,321	5,529	2,724	765	–	11,358	–	30	1,124	29,660	132	20
2,460	1,690	1,876	2,531	1,031	21,348	1,121	35,117	816	–	132,082	1,716	1,052	7,427	237,685	84	21
61	50	53	82	32	2,719	4,361	2,986	14	–	1,526	–	90	517	13,100	7,225	22
1,296	49	–	44	13	7	–	24	–	–	–	–250	–866	329	452	1,518	23
6	27	9	–	115	784	–	302	244	–	6,004	187	–12,320	2,652	–	–	DI
2,035	468	420	249	446	1,017	105	266	–	336	[6]–1,382	–13,394	[6]2,025	[6]–643	–	13,394	TrI
37,989	18,910	17,295	41,127	9,418	47,473	15,787	83,867	6,076	1,518	86,341						I
24,619	14,852	14,847	22,808	6,157	112,321	13,874	153,818	7,024	–	3,824	–502	[7]3,259	55,029	590,389	–	VA
62,608	33,762	32,142	63,935	15,575	159,794	29,660	237,685	13,100	1,518	375,540	85,839	5,812	123,198	–	–	T
4,098	2,980	2,023	1,605	3,186	6,247	4,632	20,253	–	1,518							Tr

Series F 668–696.　Value of Input–Output Transactions Among

[In millions of dollars at producers' prices.　For the distribution of output of an industry, read the

Industry No.	Consuming industry (Producing industry)	Intermediate markets												
		Agriculture, forestry, and fisheries	Metal mining	Petroleum and natural gas mining	Other mining	Construction	Food, feed, and tobacco products	Textile products and apparel	Wood products and furniture	Paper, printing, and publishing	Chemicals and chemical products	Petroleum and coal products	Rubber, plastics, and leather	Stone, clay, and glass products
		668	669	670	671	672	673	674	675	676	677	678	679	680
	1961													
1	Agriculture, forestry, and fisheries	15,142	–	–	–	257	23,175	1,751	1,004	–	51	–	66	4
2	Metal mining	–	357	–	2	–	–	–	(Z)	–	129	3	–	14
3	Petroleum and natural gas mining	–	–	310	2	(Z)	–	–	–	–	31	9,498	–	–
4	Other mining	112	7	(Z)	508	876	54	18	4	133	508	77	29	679
5	Construction	616	2	5	5	8	249	17	18	110	43	28	8	5
6	Food, feed, and tobacco products	3,308	–	–	(Z)	18	13,240	46	28	94	437	11	269	7
7	Textile products and apparel	135	2	3	2	7	187	13,109	287	155	5	903	49	85
8	Wood products and furniture	98	9	6	18	4,414	114	27	3,220	831	76	5	903	24
9	Paper, printing, and publishing	58	1	7	30	423	1,693	357	250	8,680	910	102	211	475
10	Chemicals and chemical products	1,340	74	62	90	1,641	655	1,878	283	786	6,662	677	1,706	438
11	Petroleum and coal products	986	23	58	87	1,501	316	43	94	178	1,087	1,435	26	101
12	Rubber, plastics, and leather	202	6	40	62	430	174	257	225	236	295	8	1,611	96
13	Stone, clay, and glass products	32	9	5	125	5,332	674	35	169	66	280	42	109	1,239
14	Primary and fabricated metals	124	106	80	111	11,160	2,042	54	757	246	982	356	196	206
15	Machinery, except electrical	224	67	162	250	1,108	19	82	84	134	230	5	50	38
16	Electrical equipment and supplies	35	11	54	17	1,975	40	5	30	41	32	11	44	53
17	Transport equipment and ordnance	90	5	10	27	10	–	3	15	25	2	(Z)	26	3
18	Other manufacturing	9	2	5	7	440	79	441	82	187	133	17	90	42
19	Transportation and trade	3,004	230	443	275	9,337	5,799	1,830	1,301	1,804	1,800	1,265	679	959
20	Electric, gas, and sanitary services	292	62	95	139	215	428	219	95	319	510	327	113	368
21	Other services	4,570	227	2,328	252	4,675	4,158	1,267	668	2,615	2,822	875	739	596
22	Government enterprises	12	3	6	8	21	96	57	17	155	102	50	25	30
23	Scrap and secondhand goods	–	1	79	7	58	–	24	2	113	3	2	3	27
DI	Directly allocated imports	220					1,322	166	1	1	69		221	30
TrI	Transferred imports	704	561	941	178	–	1,190	643	535	1,115	405	622	115	168
I	Intermediate inputs, total	31,313	1,765	4,697	2,201	43,910	55,704	22,330	9,169	18,024	17,657	15,419	7,289	5,686
VA	Value added	21,597	1,121	7,185	2,841	32,683	21,875	10,630	5,173	12,960	10,890	4,942	5,284	5,513
T	Total inputs	52,910	2,887	11,882	5,041	76,593	77,579	32,961	14,342	30,983	28,547	20,361	12,573	11,199
Tr	Transfers [5]	798	689	1,174	357	–	2,820	996	1,022	1,444	2,320	1,318	575	465
	1958													
1	Agriculture, forestry, and fisheries	14,806	–	–	2	237	22,467	1,502	998	–	36	–	53	4
2	Metal mining	–	317	–	2	–	–	–	(Z)	–	113	3	–	13
3	Petroleum and natural gas mining	–	–	242	1	(Z)	–	–	–	–	24	9,291	–	–
4	Other mining	102	7	(Z)	528	756	54	19	4	126	464	71	27	609
5	Construction	613	2	4	5	8	234	16	18	99	35	25	7	4
6	Food, feed, and tobacco products	2,999	–	–	(Z)	17	11,743	39	28	77	407	11	210	6
7	Textile products and apparel	106	2	6	2	6	148	11,964	282	128	52	4	767	21
8	Wood products and furniture	104	7	6	19	4,215	113	21	3,095	678	44	3	767	21
9	Paper, printing, and publishing	55	1	6	29	400	1,529	322	237	7,670	765	91	188	428
10	Chemicals and chemical products	1,210	55	54	80	1,513	571	1,716	258	664	5,381	593	1,400	385
11	Petroleum and coal products	968	19	52	81	1,361	286	38	89	157	794	1,242	21	92
12	Rubber, plastics, and leather	192	4	31	55	377	155	227	208	193	228	7	1,419	87
13	Stone, clay, and glass products	30	7	4	108	4,800	609	29	156	57	221	37	84	1,079
14	Primary and fabricated metals	121	85	72	109	10,754	1,846	46	700	208	836	318	159	176
15	Machinery, except electrical	205	58	144	249	969	17	72	76	109	173	4	36	32
16	Electrical equipment and supplies	30	8	46	16	1,766	34	4	26	32	24	8	31	44
17	Transport equipment and ordnance	81	4	9	25	9	–	2	14	26	1	(Z)	20	3
18	Other manufacturing	8	1	4	7	356	66	360	68	150	89	14	72	34
19	Transportation and trade	2,842	217	417	255	8,446	5,183	1,612	1,195	1,533	1,410	1,092	561	834
20	Electric, gas, and sanitary services	265	47	78	128	175	362	187	85	262	364	262	88	293
21	Other services	4,073	172	1,942	226	4,086	3,442	1,055	587	2,117	2,132	700	579	492
22	Government enterprises	10	2	2	6	15	73	45	14	118	75	38	20	23
23	Scrap and secondhand goods	–	1	110	10	85	–	32	3	170	4	3	3	34
DI	Directly allocated imports	253					1,517	134	1	2	62		240	11
TrI	Transferred imports	777	603	952	163	–	1,176	470	450	996	346	571	71	126
I	Intermediate inputs, total	29,850	1,618	4,182	2,106	40,354	51,625	19,910	8,592	15,572	14,078	14,389	6,097	4,906
VA	Value added	22,110	914	6,671	2,831	28,937	19,485	9,431	4,921	10,993	9,811	3,608	4,786	4,900
T	Total inputs	51,960	2,532	10,852	4,936	69,291	71,109	29,341	13,513	26,565	23,889	17,997	10,883	9,805
Tr	Transfers [5]	891	739	1,183	315	–	2,844	776	931	1,260	1,784	1,127	421	385

See footnotes at end of table.

Industries in the U.S. Economy: 1947 to 1967—Con.

row for that industry; for the composition of inputs to an industry, read the column for that industry]

Intermediate markets—Con. (columns 681–690); Final markets (columns 691–694)

Primary and fabricated metals	Machinery, except electrical	Electrical equipment and supplies	Transport equipment and ordnance	Other manufacturing	Transportation and trade	Electric, gas, and sanitary services	Other services	Government enterprises	Scrap and second-hand goods	Personal consumption expenditures	Gross private domestic investment [1]	Net exports [2]	Government purchases [3]	Total output	Transfers [4]	Industry No.
681	682	683	684	685	686	687	688	689	690	691	692	693	694	695	696	
																1961
-	3	-	-	16	226	-	2,497	1,082	-	4,971	519	2,714	-570	52,910	4,042	1
2,072	1	13	-	2	(Z)	3	10	2	-	-	-22	106	195	2,887	28	2
-	-	-	-	-	(Z)	1,733	194	28	-	-	61	24	-	11,882	736	3
539	23	6	19	5	38	627	78	132	-	164	-2	313	92	5,041	300	4
156	33	26	118	19	2,145	640	7,935	1,477	-	-	40,634	2	22,296	76,593	-	5
9	2	(Z)	(Z)	24	695	2	2,625	84	4	53,343	811	1,951	571	77,579	3,135	6
90	34	41	393	224	188	2	780	8	142	15,438	-32	415	340	32,961	490	7
197	79	203	202	148	209	2	56	(Z)	-	2,823	1,022	185	286	14,342	336	8
403	136	359	216	1,894	1,277	29	8,049	119	33	4,029	279	556	407	30,983	8,121	9
797	113	420	350	408	389	19	1,518	33	-	4,746	224	1,884	1,353	28,547	1,113	10
328	121	50	118	30	2,445	298	986	58	-	8,114	43	626	1,208	20,361	1,144	11
231	329	469	1,125	385	581	11	765	9	8	4,451	58	287	222	12,573	611	12
583	200	437	512	132	272	30	291	19	-	363	43	187	12	11,199	463	13
16,516	4,725	3,581	7,211	1,218	413	266	385	33	394	790	1,245	1,387	726	55,312	2,353	14
1,524	3,140	727	2,325	280	434	16	1,664	3	180	595	10,145	3,143	1,377	28,006	2,720	15
641	1,515	3,883	1,888	520	439	23	2,217	3	175	5,040	4,064	1,092	3,185	27,034	3,014	16
339	674	385	12,233	294	963	3	5,230	29	198	12,514	5,502	1,958	10,009	50,547	5,923	17
248	209	409	656	803	629	30	2,741	70	96	4,062	1,115	554	1,615	14,771	1,638	18
3,836	1,489	1,543	2,298	901	5,682	753	8,689	1,286	46	80,672	5,010	4,490	2,464	147,884	6,702	19
1,008	161	155	269	60	2,576	4,895	1,945	615	-	10,047	-	29	1,030	25,974	69	20
2,081	1,597	1,896	1,966	945	22,527	708	29,976	594	4	114,746	1,842	1,011	10,660	216,343	72	21
80	40	81	88	26	2,507	3,765	2,408	18	-	1,159	-	71	329	11,157	6,164	22
803	24	7	18	4	76	-	88	(Z)	-	-24	-681	431	551	1,616	-	23
24	47	24	(Z)	150	637	-	292	182	336	4,606	-164	-10,357	2,527	-	-	DI
1,587	418	286	559	466	891	55	212	-	-	-	-11,987	-	-	-	11,987	TrI
34,094	15,113	15,004	32,565	8,952	46,241	13,910	81,632	5,885	1,616	[6]-1,230	-	[6]1,613	[6]-383	-	-	I
21,218	12,893	12,031	17,982	5,819	101,644	12,064	134,711	5,272	-	3,733	-19	[7]2,932	47,123	520,097	-	VA
55,312	28,006	27,034	50,547	14,771	147,884	25,974	216,343	11,157	1,616	335,152	71,699	5,621	107,625	-	-	T
3,265	2,397	1,390	1,543	2,849	5,167	3,959	24,997	-	1,616	-	-	-	-	-	-	Tr
																1958
-	3	-	-	15	190	-	2,304	624	-	4,821	1,068	1,884	948	51,960	3,901	1
1,876	1	10	-	1	(Z)	3	10	2	-	-	-55	45	192	2,532	27	2
-	-	-	-	-	(Z)	1,166	121	20	-	-	-40	28	-	10,852	535	3
596	18	5	20	4	37	546	67	126	-	280	-20	410	81	4,936	253	4
145	29	20	103	17	2,024	551	7,291	1,206	-	-	36,957	2	19,877	69,291	-	5
8	1	(Z)	(Z)	20	633	1	2,357	260	3	50,009	222	1,734	325	71,109	2,830	6
82	31	33	336	196	166	2	688	6	92	13,720	-210	415	300	29,341	383	7
179	70	205	199	127	202	3	54	(Z)	-	2,695	978	146	232	13,513	305	8
361	116	283	186	1,573	1,164	22	6,913	85	80	3,331	7	373	347	26,565	6,961	9
686	98	332	298	354	333	12	1,263	27	-	3,949	-16	1,368	1,302	23,889	899	10
290	108	39	105	26	2,246	245	847	47	10	7,259	-186	655	1,107	17,997	857	11
194	285	346	888	324	518	9	658	7	7	3,916	54	275	217	10,883	549	12
511	179	325	415	111	235	24	228	12	-	344	22	168	10	9,805	378	13
14,317	4,222	2,860	6,124	984	377	226	324	27	357	728	545	1,371	720	48,612	2,087	14
1,334	2,789	570	2,015	209	388	12	1,302	2	144	490	9,001	2,446	1,318	24,165	2,196	15
540	1,229	2,628	1,679	399	342	17	1,763	2	101	4,516	2,484	871	2,051	20,694	2,301	16
335	638	337	10,430	239	852	2	4,054	22	166	10,112	4,330	1,792	10,210	43,715	4,714	17
213	163	313	528	611	521	23	2,209	50	68	3,354	1,004	389	1,207	11,879	1,219	18
3,344	1,281	1,141	1,990	730	5,041	612	7,505	905	84	70,223	4,477	3,722	2,669	129,322	5,755	19
827	136	114	219	46	2,063	3,380	1,530	449	-	8,060	-	-	34	20,289	59	20
1,737	1,306	1,345	1,576	727	18,754	540	24,877	422	3	95,123	1,593	865	8,066	178,536	57	21
61	31	54	65	19	2,132	2,946	1,875	12	-	945	-	64	243	8,889	5,003	22
1,021	33	7	23	5	105	-	119	(Z)	-	-	-14	-1,028	209	459	1,394	23
14	19	12	(Z)	88	562	-	271	184	-	3,855	23	-9,967	2,719	-	-	DI
1,200	265	112	648	345	829	36	172	-	277	-	-10,584	-	-	-	10,584	TrI
29,872	13,051	11,092	27,846	7,166	39,716	10,375	68,802	4,497	1,394	[6]-1,153	-	[6]1,460	[6]-307	-	-	I
18,739	11,114	9,602	15,868	4,713	89,606	9,914	109,734	4,392	-	3,503	-311	[7]2,030	39,029	447,334	-	VA
48,612	24,165	20,694	43,715	11,879	129,322	20,289	178,536	8,889	1,394	290,069	60,901	2,206	94,158	-	-	T
2,685	1,990	1,037	1,455	2,320	4,550	3,112	20,653	-	1,394	-	-	-	-	-	-	Tr

Series F 668–696. Value of Input-Output Transactions Among

[In millions of dollars at producers' prices. For the distribution of output of an industry, read the

Industry No.	Consuming industry / Producing industry	Agriculture, forestry, and fisheries	Metal mining	Petroleum and natural gas mining	Other mining	Construction	Food, feed, and tobacco products	Textile products and apparel	Wood products and furniture	Paper, printing, and publishing	Chemicals and chemical products	Petroleum and coal products	Rubber, plastics, and leather	Stone, clay, and glass products
		668	669	670	671	672	673	674	675	676	677	678	679	680
	1947													
1	Agriculture, forestry, and fisheries	14,741	–	–	–	92	21,096	2,236	437	7	89	–	63	(Z)
2	Metal mining	–	130	–	3	–	–	–	–	–	32	1	–	9
3	Petroleum and natural gas mining	–	–	55	–	8	–	–	–	–	26	3,960	–	–
4	Other mining	47	4	–	618	269	65	36	8	83	260	29	22	326
5	Construction	568	1	8	6	7	90	41	17	43	27	14	26	25
6	Food, feed, and tobacco products	2,541	–	–	1	13	7,662	149	29	62	1,043	23	445	2
7	Textile products and apparel	112	(Z)	7	2	18	223	9,404	310	109	51	2	585	47
8	Wood products and furniture	150	22	6	63	2,472	126	41	1,581	289	57	16	37	34
9	Paper, printing, and publishing	7	(Z)	33	22	170	805	224	113	3,775	470	162	185	230
10	Chemicals and chemical products	628	21	63	77	623	380	941	148	280	1,974	186	523	114
11	Petroleum and coal products	519	8	28	36	592	120	69	86	117	244	755	39	50
12	Rubber, plastics, and leather	140	(Z)	10	5	77	65	119	83	65	71	18	1,285	29
13	Stone, clay, and glass products	27	2	19	13	1,665	256	12	65	20	113	39	31	331
14	Primary and fabricated metals	118	19	80	118	4,601	656	60	434	119	530	160	123	113
15	Machinery, except electrical	74	13	59	144	314	60	42	113	102	40	10	26	36
16	Electrical equipment and supplies	21	(Z)	21	14	499	16	8	18	23	33	9	17	25
17	Transport equipment and ordnance	93	1	10	28	23	21	22	30	16	18	13	15	12
18	Other manufacturing	5	(Z)	4	3	65	11	218	48	57	33	6	67	6
19	Transportation and trade	2,617	111	155	91	3,884	2,133	1,094	706	851	678	676	391	411
20	Electric, gas, and sanitary services	56	34	17	77	36	177	116	49	99	112	76	52	118
21	Other services	2,925	73	615	181	1,824	1,297	596	429	734	764	348	291	186
22	Government enterprises	5	1	3	3	–	25	25	10	58	32	21	14	10
23	Scrap and secondhand goods	–	–	–	–	32	100	21	–	243	11	–	7	11
DI	Directly allocated imports	2	–	–	–	–	972	204	17	–	34	–	318	5
TrI	Transferred imports	560	232	162	116	–	1,211	115	186	630	124	85	18	27
I	Intermediate inputs, total	25,955	673	1,352	1,621	17,284	37,568	15,792	4,918	7,780	6,868	6,608	4,578	2,156
VA	Value added	20,903	648	3,088	2,999	12,047	13,216	8,703	3,938	5,737	3,834	1,501	2,710	1,985
T	Total inputs	46,858	1,322	4,441	4,619	29,331	50,785	24,496	8,856	13,517	10,701	8,108	7,288	4,141
Tr	Transfers [5]	690	318	231	135	–	3,292	247	515	714	440	228	77	97

– Represents zero.   Z Less than $500,000.

[1] The industrial distribution of inventory change included in this column represents the change in inventories of primary products of an industry (wherever held), rather than change in all inventories held by an industry. For input-output table, the inventory valuation adjustment has been made in total only and appears on the value-added row.

[2] The detailed entries reflect gross exports of goods and services from each producing industry. Imports in total are shown as negative entries in this column on the import rows. Therefore, the sum of the column equals GNP component "net exports of goods and services."

[3] Final purchases are shown net of sales; this can result in negative entries where sales exceed purchases.

Industries in the U.S. Economy: 1947 to 1967—Con.

row for that industry; for the composition of inputs to an industry, read the column for that industry]

Intermediate markets—Con.										Final markets				Total output	Transfers [4]	Industry No.
Primary and fabricated metals	Machinery, except electrical	Electrical equipment and supplies	Transport equipment and ordnance	Other manufacturing	Transportation and trade	Electric, gas, and sanitary services	Other services	Government enterprises	Scrap and secondhand goods	Personal consumption expenditures	Gross private domestic investment [1]	Net exports [2]	Government purchases [3]			
681	682	683	684	685	686	687	688	689	690	691	692	693	694	695	696	
																1947
(Z)	–	–	–	18	16	–	2,048	15	–	6,193	−1,989	1,700	96	46,858	3,856	1
1,063	(Z)	5	–	1	–	194	5	–	–		18	58	−2	1,322	8	2
(Z)	–	–	–	–	6	375	53	–	–	33		104		4,441	139	3
577	18	12	19	50	507	105		25	–	630		409	97	4,619	78	4
105	34	22	49	16	1,489	217	3,980	503	–		16,831		5,211	29,331	–	5
11	(Z)	(Z)	–	40	237	1	1,567	(Z)	30	34,014	361	2,104	449	50,785	1,490	6
49	20	32	193	108	95	2	141	3	19	11,194	283	1,288	199	24,496	104	7
191	77	179	132	160	52	2	123	2	11	1,963	727	208	136	8,856	112	8
245	115	171	83	171	1,044	6	3,108	33	28	1,842	−22	236	260	13,517	2,344	9
393	90	214	203	146	197	9	425	18	15	1,970	118	751	193	10,701	210	10
299	58	43	56	27	1,263	164	245	21	1	2,308	136	558	266	8,108	108	11
88	262	189	663	192	254	1	202	8	16	2,870	225	276	74	7,288	171	12
249	76	190	174	44	113	14	59	4	3	314	114	16	16	4,141	29	13
7,385	2,497	1,672	3,000	518	434	118	201	19	233	770	1,087	1,271	125	26,459	848	14
492	1,194	326	802	83	117	2	294	18	36	156	5,971	1,625	208	12,346	526	15
273	522	1,006	311	94	152	18	383	7	38	2,812	2,328	563	247	9,457	417	16
72	83	36	3,704	8	671	10	859	8	84	3,511	4,320	1,471	1,262	16,399	540	17
63	54	59	107	408	114	2	687	10	16	2,414	403	351	242	5,451	438	18
1,908	550	482	508	346	3,617	216	4,245	374	4	43,446	2,944	3,372	836	76,644	3,499	19
359	84	63	78	25	682	766	638	70	–	2,910	–	–	179	6,878	38	20
710	441	418	412	266	9,269	217	9,462	122	1	39,539	1,129	359	1,767	74,376	24	21
29	19	31	31	10	803	1,066	872	6	–	343	8	62		3,485	1,742	22
1,318	34	2	(Z)	3							30	957	−2,163	606	–	23
47	–	2	10	60	358	–	39	–	–	866	−85	−3,327	479	–	–	DI
388	49	4	17	126	262	5	198	–	71		−4,587			–	4,587	TrI
16,315	6,276	5,158	10,554	2,919	21,753	3,406	29,942	1,252	606	[6]−718		[6]768	[6]−50		–	I
10,144	6,070	4,299	5,845	2,531	54,892	3,472	44,435	2,233	–	2,348	−764	[7]824	15,730	233,367	–	VA
26,459	12,346	9,457	16,399	5,450	76,644	6,878	74,376	3,485	606	161,726	34,195	11,528	25,918	–	–	T
874	426	240	203	307	927	1,104	9,639	–	606		–	–	–	–	–	Tr

[4] Entry in each row represents the value of the secondary output of the industry named at the beginning of the row which has been transferred to primary producing industries.

[5] Entry in each column represents the sum of the value of transferred imports at domestic port value and the value of the secondary output of other industries which has been transferred to the industry named at the head of the column. See text.

[6] The subtotal for intermediate inputs is not relevant in the final demand sector. These entries are overall adjustments to the respective columns to reflect purchases by foreigners in the U.S. and aid in kind sent abroad which were shifted from the personal consumption expenditures and government sectors of final demand without adjusting the detailed entries in the respective column.

[7] Entry reflects net factor receipts; i.e., earnings of foreigners from their investments in the U.S. have been deducted from gross earnings from abroad of U.S. citizens.

Series F 697–719. Direct Requirements Per

[In dollars, producers' prices. For composition of

Industry No.	Producing industry	Agriculture, forestry, and fisheries (697)	Metal mining (698)	Petroleum and natural gas mining (699)	Other mining (700)	Construction (701)	Food, feed, and tobacco products (702)	Textile products and apparel (703)	Wood products and furniture (704)	Paper, printing, and publishing (705)
	1967									
1	Agriculture, forestry, and fisheries	.29386	—	—		.00254	.29268	.03458	.05306	—
2	Metal mining	—	.09527		.00136		—	—	—	—
3	Petroleum and natural gas mining	—		.02487	.00017	—	—	—	—	—
4	Other mining	.00219	.00497	.00002	.08189	.00901	.00055	.00043	.00036	.00345
5	Construction	.00956	.01359	.03168	.00760	.00029	.00271	.00196	.00442	.00503
6	Food, feed, and tobacco products	.05962					.16935	.00101	.00029	.00303
7	Textile products and apparel	.00319	.00062	.00032	.00477	.00270	.00148	.40880	.02408	.00790
8	Wood products and furniture	.00194	.00428		.00352	.05353	.00127	.00060	.22089	.02723
9	Paper, printing, and publishing	.00255	.00033	.00011	.00396	.00286	.03311	.00868	.01018	.25182
10	Chemicals and chemical products	.03885	.02317	.01149	.01918	.01430	.00898	.07112	.01787	.03318
11	Petroleum and coal products	.01764	.00289	.00220	.01708	.01960	.00226	.00109	.00555	.00386
12	Rubber, plastics, and leather	.00343	.00687	.00227	.00982	.00725	.00759	.00699	.01908	.00976
13	Stone, clay, and glass products	.00052	.00110	.00552	.01999	.06902	.01028	.00214	.00936	.00077
14	Primary and fabricated metals	.00304	.03019	.01534	.03077	.14709	.02503	.00175	.05674	.01378
15	Machinery, except electrical	.00510	.03507	.01839	.03394	.01784	.00257	.00366	.00646	.00450
16	Electrical equipment and supplies	.00088	.00104	.01136	.00255	.02429	.00007	.00040	.00164	.00061
17	Transport equipment and ordnance	.00060	.00235	—	.00011	.00005	.00004	.00009	.00210	.00013
18	Other manufacturing	.00018	.00074	.00105	.00054	.00518	.00087	.00966	.00458	.00766
19	Transportation and trade	.06568	.06371	.02134	.03105	.10495	.06130	.04228	.06483	.05149
20	Electric, gas, and sanitary services	.00482	.02659	.01145	.02854	.00071	.00662	.00715	.00847	.01155
21	Other services	.08297	.09468	.19198	.09275	.07576	.05883	.03871	.04676	.08520
22	Government enterprises	.00014	.00080	.00042	.00076	.00064	.00097	.00165	.00094	.00677
23	Scrap and secondhand goods	—	.00422	.00573	.00315	.00014	.00001	.00084	—	.00536
DI	Directly allocated imports	.00058	—	—	—	.00098	.01353	.00134	.00011	.00006
TrI	Transferred imports	.01624	.25512	.07159	.03108	—	.01391	.01779	.03731	.03115
VA	Value added	.38641	.33237	.57287	.57542	.44128	.28598	.33728	.40490	.43572
T	Total inputs	1.00000	1.00000	1.00000	1.00000	1.00000	1.00000	1.00000	1.00000	1.00000
	1963									
1	Agriculture, forestry, and fisheries	.30048	—	—		.00383	.29167	.04592	.06422	—
2	Metal mining	—	.11010	.00002	.00123		—	—	—	—
3	Petroleum and natural gas mining	—		.02418		—	—	—	—	—
4	Other mining	.00225	.00616	(Z)	.08716	.00864	.00065	.00045	.00027	.00429
5	Construction	.01000	.00284	.03093	.00527	.00029	.00191	.00155	.00262	.00246
6	Food, feed, and tobacco products	.06412			.00004	.00034	.17937	.00145	.00004	.00406
7	Textile products and apparel	.00373	.00016	.00017	.00008	.00243	.00198	.41221	.02278	.00485
8	Wood products and furniture	.00203	.00420	.00001	.00320	.05635	.00125	.00040	.24427	.02519
9	Paper, printing, and publishing	.00209	.00025	.00017	.00168	.00336	.03273	.01063	.00816	.26749
10	Chemicals and chemical products	.02771	.02637	.00859	.01732	.01670	.00793	.06643	.01813	.03608
11	Petroleum and coal products	.02049	.00600	.00523	.01499	.01945	.00260	.00132	.00341	.00542
12	Rubber, plastics, and leather	.00272	.00565	.00128	.01947	.00735	.00315	.00795	.02172	.00803
13	Stone, clay, and glass products	.00081	.00181	.00333	.02228	.07497	.00952	.00133	.00892	.00166
14	Primary and fabricated metals	.00471	.01951	.00501	.01954	.14062	.02526	.00099	.06020	.00903
15	Machinery, except electrical	.00431	.03798	.00532	.05585	.01745	.00063	.00281	.00380	.00323
16	Electrical equipment and supplies	.00125	.00078	.00827	.00653	.02498	.00009	.00012	.00153	.00018
17	Transport equipment and ordnance	.00083	.00223	.00027	.00614	.00070	.00019	.00005	.00052	.00041
18	Other manufacturing	.00012	.00091	.00077	.00041	.00555	.00085	.01272	.00412	.00743
19	Transportation and trade	.04931	.06999	.03472	.04583	.11474	.06309	.05019	.05997	.05049
20	Electric, gas, and sanitary services	.00531	.02308	.01148	.03042	.00345	.00616	.00621	.00728	.01148
21	Other services	.07869	.08520	.20952	.05804	.06366	.05121	.03371	.04698	.08130
22	Government enterprises	.00018	.00130	.00068	.00152	.00075	.00110	.00188	.00103	.00607
23	Scrap and secondhand goods	.00010	.00197	—	.00123	.00045	—	.00120	—	.00708
DI	Directly allocated imports	.00381	—	—	—	—	.01540	.00463	.00003	—
TrI	Transferred imports	.01451	.21727	.08531	.03694	—	.01556	.02115	.04021	.03284
VA	Value added	.40046	.37626	.56475	.56484	.43395	.28772	.31469	.37978	.43091
T	Total inputs	1.00000	1.00000	1.00000	1.00000	1.00000	1.00000	1.00000	1.00000	1.00000

— Represents zero.   Z Less than $0.000005.

Dollar of Gross Output: 1947 to 1967

inputs to an industry, read the column for that industry]

Chemicals and chemical products	Petroleum and coal products	Rubber, plastics, and leather	Stone, clay, and glass products	Primary and fabricated metals	Machinery except electrical	Electrical equipment and supplies	Transport equipment and ordnance	Other manu-facturing	Transpor-tation and trade	Electric, gas, and sanitary services	Other services	Govern-ment enter-prises	Scrap and second-hand goods	Industry No.
706	707	708	709	710	711	712	713	714	715	716	717	718	719	
														1967
.00270	–	.00076	–	–	–	–	–	.00094	.00091	–	.00898	.02262	–	1
.00262	–	–	.00149	.02971	–	.00017	–	.00012	(Z)	.00003	.00004	–	–	2
.00109	.42840	–	–	–	.00024	.00020	.00027	.00041	.00012	.06756	.00049	.00836	–	3
.01794	.00272	.00158	.06365	.00878	.00543	.00308	.00304	.00260	.00276	.00008	.02400	.00027	.02739	4
.00609	.01347	.00302	–	–	–	–	–	–	.00848	.03047	–	.10216	–	5
.01393	.00114	.01408	.00041	.00012	.00014	–	–	.00141	.00494	.00005	.01131	.00696	.00502	6
.00212	.00010	.06070	.00571	.00120	.00113	.00144	.01061	.01607	.00200	.00045	.00129	.00147	.03631	7
.00147	.00006	.00527	.00597	.00424	.00256	.00789	.00691	.00895	.00116	.00003	.00016	.00042	–	8
.02618	.00602	.02171	.03329	.00729	.00495	.01159	.00276	.12089	.00973	.00118	.03395	.00435	.06493	9
.21582	.02691	.15420	.02606	.01441	.00283	.01429	.00725	.03110	.00314	.00156	.00783	.00949	–	10
.04486	.06787	.00144	.00750	.00299	.00394	.00213	.00245	.00195	.01561	.00737	.00490	.00812	.00583	11
.01539	.00216	.09955	.01467	.00463	.01061	.01629	.01465	.02771	.00482	.00061	.00427	.00248	.00718	12
.00671	.00215	.00547	.10276	.00411	.00718	.01489	.00684	.00609	.00157	.00002	.00136	.00042	–	13
.03378	.00575	.02276	.02187	.29260	.16884	.11176	.14788	.08449	.00525	.00210	.00645	.00145	.29533	14
.00961	.00325	.00801	.01619	.03243	.12591	.02720	.05127	.01175	.00345	.00105	.00602	.00189	.05409	15
.00079	.00044	.00131	.00329	.01006	.06476	.16299	.03270	.03628	.00256	.00198	.00514	.00140	.04801	16
.00073	.00010	.00367	.00101	.00794	.01835	.01608	.22469	.00804	.00473	.00008	.00460	.00106	.08422	17
.00313	.00110	.00964	.00500	.00362	.00597	.01117	.00992	.06381	.00444	.00083	.01041	.00168	.01778	18
.05271	.06270	.05121	.07871	.05823	.04325	.03943	.03583	.04480	.05295	.02049	.04257	.08305	.02938	19
.01967	.01711	.00955	.03334	.01787	.00582	.00664	.00485	.00452	.01276	.18456	.00966	.07313	–	20
.11639	.06425	.06181	.06800	.04600	.06558	.07156	.05232	.07183	.14189	.02684	.15302	.08028	.00567	21
.00164	.00062	.00150	.00154	.00077	.00107	.00131	.00115	.00158	.01819	.15031	.01091	.00134	–	22
.00153	.00042	.00084	.00068	.02003	.00112	.00005	.00257	–	.00007	–	.00012	.00001	–	23
.00193	.00007	.01040	.00005	.00072	.00055	.00185	.00096	.00818	.00436	–	.00087	.01970	–	DI
.01945	.03774	.01463	.01829	.04403	.02545	.02527	.01189	.03903	.00631	.00389	.00112	–	.34626	TrI
.38321	.25541	.43688	.48171	.38281	.43670	.45275	.36964	.40729	.69050	.47458	.64688	.56858	–	VA
1.00000	1.00000	1.00000	1.00000	1.00000	1.00000	1.00000	1.00000	1.00000	1.00000	1.00000	1.00000	1.00000	1.00000	T
														1963
.00172	–	.00400	.00056	–	–	–	–	.00124	.00162	–	.01166	.04875	–	1
.00504	–	–	.00137	.03317	–	.00014	–	.00001	.00001	.00012	.00006	.00001	–	2
.00097	.44937	–	–	–	–	–	–	–	.00017	.06568	.00034	.00294	–	3
.01836	.00409	.00155	.07575	.00944	.00034	.00023	.00035	.00042	.00010	.02145	.00018	.01145	–	4
.00408	.01600	.00226	.00451	.00407	.00179	.00123	.00166	.00171	.00974	.02997	.03646	.10300	–	5
.02058	.00116	.01696	.00033	.00018	.00024	.00001	–	.00171	.00543	.00007	.01116	.01631	.00598	6
.00110	.00017	.06123	.00520	.00204	.00135	.00176	.01003	.01567	.00133	.00029	.00129	.00232	.06844	7
.00199	.00020	.00543	.00928	.00373	.00268	.00748	.00456	.01238	.00115	.00007	.00017	(Z)	–	8
.02672	.00749	.02043	.02608	.00761	.00382	.01197	.00115	.13201	.01042	.00083	.03550	.00438	.08986	9
.20592	.03055	.15978	.03253	.01916	.00532	.01475	.00593	.03614	.00307	.00193	.00730	.00704	–	10
.04009	.07430	.00195	.00965	.00511	.00375	.00340	.00225	.00228	.01816	.00753	.00507	.00552	.00675	11
.01311	.00017	.11463	.01332	.00413	.01351	.02130	.01810	.03353	.00341	.00020	.00275	.00123	.01402	12
.00723	.00252	.00704	.10613	.00452	.00749	.01531	.00817	.00820	.00127	.00003	.00129	.00155	–	13
.03563	.00896	.01733	.02311	.29533	.17584	.12964	.14595	.08031	.00455	.00252	.00173	.00114	.24537	14
.00581	.00031	.00230	.00877	.02407	.14147	.03158	.05130	.01094	.00273	.00011	.00405	.00016	.07081	15
.00104	.00003	.00191	.00327	.00940	.05583	.14266	.03699	.03942	.00298	.00090	.00559	.00204	.06874	16
.00010	.00004	.00278	.00072	.00878	.02262	.01764	.25972	.01005	.00508	.00011	.00408	.00147	.13144	17
.00399	.00062	.00062	.01307	.00384	.00753	.01409	.01080	.06260	.00407	.00084	.01070	.00162	.02578	18
.05611	.06246	.04667	.07579	.05957	.04254	.04525	.03604	.04635	.04533	.02479	.03920	.11257	.05167	19
.02128	.01787	.00899	.03374	.01845	.00632	.00629	.00482	.00462	.01452	.18641	.01146	.05842	–	20
.08671	.05491	.04925	.05115	.03929	.05004	.05837	.03959	.06619	.13359	.03778	.14775	.06226	–	21
.00200	.00075	.00179	.00187	.00097	.00147	.00165	.00128	.00204	.01702	.14705	.01256	.00104	–	22
.00122	.00080	.00025	.00128	.02070	.00146	–	.00069	.00084	.00005	–	.00010	–	–	23
.00257	–	.01728	.00105	.00009	.00080	.00027	–	.00741	.00491	–	.00127	.01860	–	DI
.01383	.03366	.00998	.01339	.03250	.01386	.01307	.00390	.02862	.00637	.00355	.00112	–	.22115	TrI
.42278	.23357	.43313	.49729	.39322	.43991	.46191	.35674	.39531	.70291	.46775	.64715	.53620	–	VA
1.00000	1.00000	1.00000	1.00000	1.00000	1.00000	1.00000	1.00000	1.00000	1.00000	1.00000	1.00000	1.00000	1.00000	T

Series **F 697–719.** Direct Requirements Per

[In dollars, producers' prices. For composition of

Industry No.	Consuming industry / Producing industry	Agriculture, forestry, and fisheries 697	Metal mining 698	Petroleum and natural gas mining 699	Other mining 700	Construction 701	Food, feed and tobacco products 702	Textile products and apparel 703	Wood products and furniture 704	Paper, printing, and publishing 705
	1961									
1	Agriculture, forestry, and fisheries	.28619	–	–	–	.00336	.29873	.05313	.07002	–
2	Metal mining	–	.12362	–	.00049	–	–	–	.00002	–
3	Petroleum and natural gas mining	–	–	.02612	.00033	(Z)	–	–	–	–
4	Other mining	.00211	.00240	.00001	.10073	.01144	.00069	.00056	.00029	.00428
5	Construction	.01163	.00077	.00038	.00093	.00011	.00321	.00051	.00127	.00354
6	Food, feed, and tobacco products	.06252	–	–	.00001	.00023	.17067	.00140	.00192	.00303
7	Textile products and apparel	.00255	.00085	.00021	.00040	.00009	.00241	.39772	.01999	.00499
8	Wood products and furniture	.00185	.00309	.00053	.00351	.05763	.00147	.00081	.22449	.02682
9	Paper, printing, and publishing	.00109	.00043	.00055	.00603	.00553	.02182	.01082	.01746	.28014
10	Chemicals and chemical products	.02533	.02556	.00520	.01792	.02142	.00844	.05698	.01972	.02537
11	Petroleum and coal products	.01864	.00808	.00484	.01723	.01960	.00408	.00132	.00653	.00574
12	Rubber, plastics, and leather	.00382	.00192	.00335	.01233	.00562	.00224	.00780	.01572	.00761
13	Stone, clay, and glass products	.00061	.00318	.00043	.02474	.06962	.00869	.00106	.01175	.00214
14	Primary and fabricated metals	.00235	.03686	.00674	.02196	.14571	.02632	.00163	.05280	.00794
15	Machinery, except electrical	.00423	.02309	.01362	.04950	.01447	.00024	.00250	.00584	.00433
16	Electrical equipment and supplies	.00066	.00379	.00452	.00346	.02579	.00051	.00016	.00212	.00134
17	Transport equipment and ordnance	.00170	.00186	.00085	.00534	.00013	–	.00008	.00104	.00080
18	Other manufacturing	.00017	.00056	.00039	.00131	.00574	.00101	.01337	.00569	.00604
19	Transportation and trade	.05678	.07977	.03725	.05451	.12190	.07475	.05552	.09071	.05822
20	Electric, gas, and sanitary services	.00552	.02148	.00797	.02765	.00280	.00551	.00666	.00666	.01031
21	Other services	.08638	.07847	.19593	.05002	.06104	.05360	.03845	.04658	.08439
22	Government enterprises	.00023	.00110	.00052	.00158	.00028	.00124	.00174	.00121	.00501
23	Scrap and secondhand goods	–	.00030	.00665	.00135	.00076	–	.00074	.00011	.00365
DI	Directly allocated imports	.00416	–	–	–	–	.01704	.00505	.00008	.00004
TrI	Transferred imports	.01330	.19435	.07919	.03525	–	.01534	.01950	.03728	.03599
VA	Value added	.40819	.38848	.60473	.56344	.42671	.28197	.32251	.36070	.41828
T	Total inputs	1.00000	1.00000	1.00000	1.00000	1.00000	1.00000	1.00000	1.00000	1.00000
	1958									
1	Agriculture, forestry, and fisheries	.28494	–		–	.00342	.31595	.05117	.07382	–
2	Metal mining	–	.12504		.00041	–	–	–	.00002	–
3	Petroleum and natural gas mining	–	–	.02225	.00024	(Z)	–	–	–	–
4	Other mining	.00197	.00285	.00002	.10701	.01092	.00076	.00064	.00030	.00473
5	Construction	.01181	.00074	.00039	.00096	.00012	.00329	.00053	.00132	.00372
6	Food, feed, and tobacco products	.05772	–		.00001	.00024	.16514	.00133	.00208	.00289
7	Textile products and apparel	.00204	.00078	.00020	.00042	.00009	.00209	.40776	.02085	.00481
8	Wood products and furniture	.00200	.00290	.00053	.00386	.06084	.00158	.00071	.22906	.02552
9	Paper, printing, and publishing	.00105	.00039	.00055	.00591	.00578	.02151	.01097	.01754	.28874
10	Chemicals and chemical products	.02329	.02176	.00502	.01629	.02184	.00803	.05848	.01912	.02499
11	Petroleum and coal products	.01863	.00733	.00478	.01641	.01965	.00403	.00130	.00656	.00590
12	Rubber, plastics, and leather	.00369	.00175	.00287	.01110	.00545	.00218	.00773	.01542	.00725
13	Stone, clay, and glass products	.00057	.00274	.00040	.02184	.06927	.00856	.00100	.01156	.00214
14	Primary and fabricated metals	.00233	.03360	.00665	.02199	.15520	.02596	.00156	.05182	.00782
15	Machinery, except electrical	.00395	.02272	.01330	.05045	.01398	.00024	.00247	.00561	.00411
16	Electrical equipment and supplies	.00059	.00320	.00427	.00332	.02549	.00048	.00015	.00194	.00122
17	Transport equipment and ordnance	.00157	.00157	.00083	.00505	.00013	–	.00008	.00106	.00099
18	Other manufacturing	.00015	.00048	.00036	.00134	.00513	.00092	.01225	.00504	.00565
19	Transportation and trade	.05469	.08582	.03842	.05171	.12190	.07289	.05493	.08844	.05772
20	Electric, gas, and sanitary services	.00510	.01842	.00723	.02602	.00253	.00508	.00637	.00631	.00987
21	Other services	.07839	.06777	.17899	.04585	.05897	.04840	.03595	.04341	.07969
22	Government enterprises	.00020	.00088	.00052	.00131	.00022	.00102	.00153	.00101	.00445
23	Scrap and secondhand goods	–	.00043	.01015	.00206	.00123	–	.00109	.00019	.00639
DI	Directly allocated imports	.00487	–	–	–	–	.02133	.00455	.00007	.00007
TrI	Transferred imports	.01496	.23802	.08770	.03302	–	.01654	.01601	.03329	.03750
VA	Value added	.42551	.36079	.61468	.57342	.41762	.27401	.32142	.36417	.41382
T	Total inputs	1.00000	1.00000	1.00000	1.00000	1.00000	1.00000	1.00000	1.00000	1.00000

– Represents zero.   Z Less than $0.000005.

Dollar of Gross Output: 1947 to 1967—Con.

inputs to an industry, read the column for that industry]

Chemicals and chemical products	Petroleum and coal products	Rubber, plastics, and leather	Stone, clay, and glass products	Primary and fabricated metals	Machinery except electrical	Electrical equipment and supplies	Transport equipment and ordnance	Other manu-facturing	Transpor-tation and trade	Electric, gas, and sanitary services	Other services	Govern-ment enter-prises	Scrap and second-hand goods	In-dustry No.
706	707	708	709	710	711	712	713	714	715	716	717	718	719	
														1961
.00178	–	.00529	.00036	–	.00011	–	–	.00112	.00153	–	.01154	.09696	–	1
.00452	.00016	–	.00121	.03746	.00003	.00046	–	.00011	(Z)	.00013	.00005	.00022	–	2
.00110	.46647	–	–	–	–	–	–	–	(Z)	.06673	.00089	.00253	–	3
.01781	.00378	.00231	.06065	.00974	.00082	.00024	.00038	.00034	.00026	.02414	.00036	.01187	–	4
.00151	.00137	.00067	.00043	.00282	.00116	.00096	.00233	.00127	.01450	.02464	.03668	.13234	–	5
.01532	.00053	.02139	.00066	.00017	.00006	(Z)	(Z)	.00160	.00470	.00007	.01213	.00757	.00261	6
.00268	.00024	.07181	.00218	.00164	.00122	.00153	.00778	.01520	.00127	.00007	.00361	.00074	.08789	7
.00194	.00013	.00392	.00758	.00357	.00284	.00751	.00399	.00999	.00141	.00008	.00026	(Z)	–	8
.03189	.00500	.01681	.04238	.00729	.00486	.01329	.00427	.12821	.00864	.00111	.03720	.01064	.02020	9
.23336	.03327	.13571	.03913	.01442	.00402	.01555	.00693	.02764	.00263	.00073	.00702	.00297	–	10
.03808	.07046	.00206	.00902	.00594	.00434	.00184	.00234	.00202	.01654	.01146	.00456	.00518	–	11
.01034	.00039	.12814	.00854	.00417	.01174	.01736	.02225	.02606	.00393	.00040	.00353	.00084	.00481	12
.00983	.00208	.00863	.11061	.01055	.00714	.01617	.01013	.00894	.00184	.00114	.00134	.00169	–	13
.03440	.01748	.01560	.01841	.29860	.16871	.13246	.14266	.08248	.00279	.01024	.00178	.00293	.24371	14
.00805	.00024	.00400	.00342	.02755	.11214	.02688	.04600	.01894	.00294	.00061	.00769	.00024	.11119	15
.00114	.00055	.00346	.00474	.01159	.05408	.14363	.03736	.03523	.00297	.00088	.01025	.00024	.10799	16
.00006	.00001	.00207	.00023	.00613	.02406	.01426	.24202	.01987	.00651	.00012	.02417	.00258	.12282	17
.00467	.00084	.00716	.00377	.00448	.00748	.01513	.01298	.05439	.00426	.00116	.01267	.00627	.05964	18
.06306	.06211	.05399	.08559	.06936	.05316	.05709	.04545	.06097	.03842	.02900	.04016	.11528	.02868	19
.01785	.01605	.00902	.03283	.01823	.00575	.00574	.00533	.00405	.01742	.18848	.00899	.05513	–	20
.09886	.04296	.05875	.05319	.03763	.05701	.07013	.03889	.06396	.15233	.02728	.13856	.05328	.00235	21
.00356	.00247	.00199	.00270	.00144	.00144	.00300	.00174	.00175	.01696	.14496	.01113	.00162	–	22
.00011	.00012	.00020	.00242	.01451	.00087	.00027	.00036	.00025	.00051	–	.00041	(Z)	–	23
.00243	–	.01755	.00265	.00044	.00167	.00090	(Z)	.01013	.00431	–	.00135	.01631	–	DI
.01418	.03057	.00919	.01505	.02869	.01492	.01058	.01106	.03153	.00602	.00211	.00098	–	.20810	TrI
.38148	.24272	.42026	.49224	.38360	.46037	.44501	.35576	.39396	.68732	.46446	.62267	.47256	–	VA
1.00000	1.00000	1.00000	1.00000	1.00000	1.0000	1.00000	1.00000	1.00000	1.00000	1.00000	1.00000	1.00000	1.00000	T
														1958
.00149	–	.00488	.00040	–	.00013	–	–	.00122	.00147	–	.01291	.07019	–	1
.00472	.00015	–	.00134	.03860	.00002	.00049	–	.00013	(Z)	.00014	.00006	.00020	–	2
.00099	.51624	–	–	–	–	–	–	–	(Z)	.05747	.00068	.00224	–	3
.01941	.00393	.00244	.06210	.01225	.00076	.00026	.00046	.00032	.00029	.02691	.00037	.01423	–	4
.00146	.00141	.00064	.00045	.00299	.00120	.00095	.00235	.00140	.01565	.02715	.04084	.13569	–	5
.01704	.00061	.01928	.00064	.00016	.00006	(Z)	(Z)	.00168	.00490	.00003	.01320	.02924	.00246	6
.00216	.00025	.07045	.00219	.00169	.00126	.00161	.00769	.01647	.00128	.00009	.00385	.00066	.06634	7
.00185	.00014	.00401	.00759	.00368	.00290	.00989	.00455	.01065	.00156	.00014	.00030	(Z)	–	8
.03203	.00505	.01724	.04369	.00744	.00480	.01369	.00426	.13240	.00900	.00108	.03872	.00959	.05743	9
.22524	.03298	.12860	.03930	.01411	.00406	.01605	.00681	.02980	.00258	.00061	.00707	.00302	–	10
.03324	.06902	.00194	.00941	.00596	.00448	.00186	.00239	.00215	.01737	.01206	.00474	.00524	.00749	11
.00954	.00038	.13039	.00888	.00400	.01181	.01671	.02032	.02727	.00401	.00042	.00369	.00082	.00489	12
.00924	.00205	.00774	.11000	.01052	.00740	.01572	.00949	.00931	.00182	.00118	.00128	.00140	–	13
.03500	.01767	.01463	.01798	.29452	.17470	.13821	.14009	.08281	.00292	.01112	.00181	.00300	.25641	14
.00726	.00024	.00335	.00322	.02745	.11540	.02754	.04610	.01757	.00300	.00060	.00729	.00020	.10348	15
.00100	.00046	.00281	.00450	.01110	.05088	.12698	.03841	.03359	.00265	.00082	.00988	.00022	.07269	16
.00006	.00001	.00180	.00025	.00689	.02642	.01630	.23858	.02015	.00659	.00011	.02270	.00244	.11923	17
.00372	.00075	.00660	.00343	.00439	.00673	.01513	.01207	.05145	.00403	.00113	.01237	.00561	.04871	18
.05903	.06067	.05153	.08510	.06879	.05301	.05515	.04552	.06147	.03898	.03015	.04204	.10182	.06017	19
.01523	.01458	.00810	.02983	.01702	.00563	.00552	.00500	.00384	.01595	.16659	.00857	.05052	–	20
.08925	.03890	.05318	.05017	.03573	.05403	.06499	.03606	.06117	.14501	.02660	.13934	.04751	.00221	21
.00313	.00213	.00181	.00234	.00125	.00130	.00259	.00149	.00158	.01649	.14518	.00150	.00132	–	22
.00015	.00018	.00027	.00347	.02100	.00135	.00035	.00053	.00042	.00081	–	.00067	(Z)	–	23
.00258	–	.02201	.00117	.00028	.00080	.00059	(Z)	.00738	.00435	–	.00152	.02073	–	DI
.01448	.03171	.00653	.01283	.02469	.01097	.00542	.01482	.02906	.00641	.00177	.00096	–	.19849	TrI
.41070	.20050	.43975	.49971	.38549	.45991	.46401	.36300	.39671	.69289	.48865	.61463	.49411	–	VA
1.00000	1.00000	1.00000	1.00000	1.00000	1.00000	1.00000	1.00000	1.00000	1.00000	1.00000	1.00000	1.00000	1.00000	T

Series F 697–719. Direct Requirements Per

[In dollars, producers' prices. For composition of

Industry No.	Producing industry	Agriculture, forestry, and fisheries	Metal mining	Petroleum and natural gas mining	Other mining	Construction	Food, feed, and tobacco products	Textile products and apparel	Wood products and furniture	Paper, printing, and publishing
		697	698	699	700	701	702	703	704	705
	1947									
1	Agriculture, forestry, and fisheries	.31459	–	–	–	.00314	.41539	.09130	.04939	.00049
2	Metal mining	–	.09824	–	.00059	–	–	–	–	–
3	Petroleum and natural gas mining	–	–	.01238	–	.00028	–	–	–	–
4	Other mining	.00100	.00324	–	.13387	.00918	.00127	.00145	.00091	.00611
5	Construction	.01213	.00095	.00170	.00135	.00024	.00177	.00169	.00190	.00321
6	Food, feed, and tobacco products	.05423	–	–	.00015	.00043	.15087	.00608	.00331	.00458
7	Textile products and apparel	.00238	.00002	.00150	.00044	.00061	.00440	.38389	.03501	.00810
8	Wood products and furniture	.00321	.01702	.00134	.01353	.08429	.00247	.00167	.17850	.02135
9	Paper, printing, and publishing	.00015	.00001	.00740	.00483	.00580	.01586	.00916	.01279	.27925
10	Chemicals and chemical products	.01341	.01617	.01410	.01670	.02125	.00748	.03842	.01676	.02070
11	Petroleum and coal products	.01108	.00640	.00626	.00771	.02017	.00236	.00283	.00972	.00862
12	Rubber, plastics, and leather	.00298	.00014	.00215	.00101	.00263	.00129	.00486	.00939	.00478
13	Stone, clay, and glass products	.00057	.00156	.00429	.00286	.05676	.00505	.00047	.00731	.00147
14	Primary and fabricated metals	.00251	.01421	.01809	.02561	.15688	.01292	.00245	.04903	.00877
15	Machinery, except electrical	.00158	.00979	.01340	.03109	.01070	.00119	.00171	.01273	.00758
16	Electrical equipment and supplies	.00045	.00012	.00474	.00292	.01700	.00032	.00031	.00199	.00171
17	Transport equipment and ordnance	.00199	.00089	.00227	.00609	.00077	.00042	.00091	.00334	.00115
18	Other manufacturing	.00010	(Z)	.00086	.00059	.00223	.00022	.00890	.00537	.00420
19	Transportation and trade	.05585	.08377	.03487	.01975	.13242	.04200	.04465	.07977	.06298
20	Electric, gas, and sanitary services	.00119	.02594	.00378	.01674	.00122	.00348	.00474	.00558	.00735
21	Other services	.06243	.05490	.13842	.03925	.06219	.02554	.02434	.04846	.05433
22	Government enterprises	.00010	.00068	.00063	.00065	–	.00049	.00101	.00115	.00426
23	Scrap and secondhand goods	–	–	–	–	.00109	.00197	.00086		.01796
DI	Directly allocated imports	.00004	–	–	–		.01915	.00833	.00189	
TrI	Transferred imports	.01195	.17525	.03637	.02510	–	.02385	.00470	.02104	.04661
VA	Value added	.44609	.49069	.69545	.64917	.41072	.26024	.35530	.44465	.42443
T	Total inputs	1.00000	1.00000	1.00000	1.00000	1.00000	1.00000	1.00000	1.00000	1.00000

– Represents zero.   Z Less than $0.000005.

Series F 720–723. Industrial Composition Per Dollar of

[In dollars,

Industry No.	Producing industry	1967				1963			
		Personal consumption expenditures	Gross private domestic investment	Gross exports [1]	Government purchases	Personal consumption expenditures	Gross private domestic investment	Gross exports [1]	Government purchases
		720	721	722	723	720	721	722	723
1	Agriculture, forestry, and fisheries	.01254	.00965	.07475	−.00733	.01349	.01169	.09555	−.00140
2	Metal mining	–	.00031	.00358	.00034	–	−.00068	.00378	.00204
3	Petroleum and natural gas mining	–	.00213	.00186	–	–	.00018	.00038	–
4	Other mining	.00026	.00120	.01218	.00026	.00048	.00001	.01285	.00038
5	Construction	–	.45102	.00034	.17436	–	.53765	.00006	.19716
6	Food, feed, and tobacco products	.13501	.00904	.05677	.00631	.14609	.00706	.06840	.00654
7	Textile products and apparel	.04122	.00531	.01320	.00360	.04479	.00331	.01564	.00226
8	Wood products and furniture	.00875	.01674	.00935	.00295	.00902	.01638	.00717	.00241
9	Paper, printing, and publishing	.01160	.00468	.02092	.00805	.01192	.00269	.02011	.00592
10	Chemicals and chemical products	.01603	.00504	.06483	.01483	.01560	.00364	.06595	.01395
11	Petroleum and coal products	.02078	.00449	.01732	.00765	.02192	.00206	.02151	.00822
12	Rubber, plastics, and leather	.01208	.00155	.00872	.00329	.01304	.00080	.01060	.00225
13	Stone, clay, and glass products	.00114	.00138	.00729	.00062	.00121	.00162	.00711	.00066
14	Primary and fabricated metals	.00251	.02188	.05102	.00549	.00255	.01510	.04958	.00153
15	Machinery, except electrical	.00166	.18350	.11886	.01478	.00176	.15018	.11126	.01270
16	Electrical equipment and supplies	.01746	.06069	.04504	.04446	.01563	.05460	.03797	.04791
17	Transport equipment and ordnance	.03520	.13968	.09737	.11289	.04418	.09967	.08264	.12416
18	Other manufacturing	.01233	.02423	.02767	.01218	.01154	.01898	.02271	.00999
19	Transportation and trade	.24612	.06730	.14733	.03400	.23895	.06884	.15148	.02309
20	Electric, gas, and sanitary services	.02840	–	.00168	.01084	.03024	–	.00095	.00912
21	Other services	.36438	.02608	.03621	.06956	.35171	.01999	.03337	.06028
22	Government enterprises	.00438	–	.00240	.00457	.00406	–	.00286	.00419
23	Scrap and secondhand goods	.00262	−.02525	.01313	.00309	−.00066	−.01009	.01044	.00367
DI	Directly allocated imports	.02011	.00463			.01599	.00218		.02153
TrI	Transferred imports	[2]−.00417	–	[2].06585	[2]−.00481	[2]−.00368		[2].06424	[2]−.00521
VA	Value added	−.00958	−.01530	.10229	.45586	.01018	−.00585	.10339	.44667
T	Total inputs	1.00000	1.00000	1.00000	1.00000	1.00000	1.00000	1.00000	1.00000

– Represents zero.
[1] Ratios are calculated on the basis of gross exports. Negative entries for gross imports have been excluded.
[2] Adjustment entries; see footnote 7, series F 668–696.

Dollar of Gross Output: 1947 to 1967—Con.

inputs to an industry, read the column for that industry]

Chemicals and chemical products (706)	Petroleum and coal products (707)	Rubber, plastics, and leather (708)	Stone, clay, and glass products (709)	Primary and fabricated metals (710)	Machinery except electrical (711)	Electrical equipment and supplies (712)	Transport equipment and ordnance (713)	Other manufacturing (714)	Transportation and trade (715)	Electric, gas, and sanitary services (716)	Other services (717)	Government enterprises (718)	Scrap and secondhand goods (719)	Industry No.
														1947
.00833	.00009	.00861	.00005	(Z)	.00001	–	.00052	–	.00336	.00020	.02754	.00429	–	1
.00296	–	.00229	–	.04016	–	–	–	.00012	–	–	–	.00007	–	2
.00246	.48846	–	–	(Z)	–	–	–	–	.00008	.02823	–	.00071	–	3
.02428	.00356	.00300	.07877	.02182	.00143	.00131	.00912	.00295	.00661	.05451	.00141	.05351	.00716	4
.00251	.00176	.00357	.00598	.00396	.00275	.00234	.00301	.01943	.03155	.14420	–	–	–	5
.09750	.00282	.06106	.00049	.00040	.00001	.00004	–	.00735	.00310	.00014	.02107	.00004	.04969	6
.00480	.00020	.08029	.01138	.00185	.00160	.00337	.01180	.01983	.00124	.00033	.00190	.00082	.03076	7
.00533	.00193	.00502	.00817	.00721	.00627	.01896	.00806	.02930	.00068	.00023	.00166	.00045	.01816	8
.04393	.01994	.02541	.05548	.00927	.00929	.01811	.00507	.03143	.01362	.00084	.04179	.00947	.04685	9
.18446	.02299	.07170	.02753	.01486	.00732	.02263	.01236	.02677	.00257	.00132	.00572	.00515	.02532	10
.02283	.09310	.00533	.01196	.01130	.00473	.00453	.00341	.00495	.01648	.02391	.00329	.00599	.00192	11
.00660	.00222	.17629	.00693	.00334	.02118	.02001	.04045	.03521	.00332	.00019	.00272	.00242	.02657	12
.01056	.00478	.00432	.07986	.00616	.00616	.02008	.01600	.00799	.00148	.00203	.00080	.00129	.00424	13
.04951	.01970	.01684	.02724	.27911	.20224	.17678	.18293	.09502	.00566	.01713	.00270	.00551	.38395	14
.00376	.00125	.00359	.00866	.01861	.09669	.03451	.04890	.01526	.00153	.00034	.00395	.00138	.05997	15
.00309	.00115	.00233	.00612	.01030	.04229	.10643	.01896	.01732	.00198	.00268	.00515	.00193	.06245	16
.00166	.00166	.00200	.00287	.00273	.00670	.00378	.22584	.00149	.00875	.00145	.01155	.00230	.13794	17
.00309	.00075	.00914	.00142	.00237	.00434	.00620	.00653	.07482	.00149	.00023	.00923	.00291	.02693	18
.06336	.08335	.05365	.09917	.07212	.04452	.05093	.03098	.06349	.04719	.03140	.05708	.10722	–	19
.01051	.00935	.00720	.02850	.01359	.00684	.00661	.00475	.00466	.00890	.11139	.00858	.02004	–	20
.07142	.04287	.03987	.04488	.02684	.03573	.04415	.02514	.04873	.12094	.03156	.12722	.03497	.00112	21
.00300	.00254	.00191	.00239	.00109	.00152	.00330	.00190	.00180	.01047	.15493	.01172	.00172	–	22
.00105	–	.00095	.00278	.04980	.00272	.00025	.00001	.00055	–	–	–	–	–	23
.00317	–	.04368	.00124	.00179	–	.00017	.00061	.01101	.00467	–	.00052	–	–	DI
.01158	.01047	.00241	.00659	.01467	.00400	.00040	.00106	.02310	.00342	.00079	.00267	–	.11697	TrI
.35825	.18506	.37184	.47924	.38339	.49164	.45458	.35644	.46438	.71619	.50482	.59743	.64073	–	VA
1.00000	1.00000	1.00000	1.00000	1.00000	1.00000	1.00000	1.00000	1.00000	1.00000	1.00000	1.00000	1.00000	1.00000	T

Purchases, by Final Demand Categories: 1947 to 1967

producers' prices]

1961				1958				1947				Industry No.
Personal consumption expenditures (720)	Gross private domestic investment (721)	Gross exports [1] (722)	Government purchases (723)	Personal consumption expenditures (720)	Gross private domestic investment (721)	Gross exports [1] (722)	Government purchases (723)	Personal consumption expenditures (720)	Gross private domestic investment (721)	Gross exports [1] (722)	Government purchases (723)	
.01483	.00724	.09705	−.00530	.01662	.01754	.08279	.01007	.03829	−.05816	.08744	.00370	1
–	−.00031	.00379	.00181	–	−.00091	.00198	.00203	–	–	.00299	−.00009	2
–	.00085	.00086	–	–	−.00066	.00123	–	.00021	–	.00535	–	3
.00049	−.00003	.01119	.00085	.00096	−.00033	.01802	.00086	.00390	–	.00085	.00373	4
–	.56673	.00007	.20716	–	.60684	.00009	.21110	–	.49221	–	.20106	5
.15916	.01131	.06977	.00530	.17240	.00365	.07620	.00345	.21032	.01056	.10822	.01732	6
.04606	−.00045	.01484	.00316	.04730	−.00345	.01824	.00319	.06921	.00828	.06625	.00768	7
.00842	.01426	.00662	.00266	.00929	.01605	.00642	.00247	.01214	.02126	.01070	.00523	8
.01202	.00390	.01988	.00378	.01148	.00011	.01639	.00369	.01139	−.00065	.01214	.01003	9
.01416	.00313	.06737	.01257	.01361	−.00026	.06011	.01383	.01218	.00344	.03863	.00746	10
.02421	.00060	.02239	.01122	.02503	−.00305	.02878	.01176	.01427	.00398	.02870	.01028	11
.01328	.00081	.01026	.00206	.01350	−.00089	.01209	.00231	.01775	.00658	.01420	.00287	12
.00108	.00060	.00669	.00011	.00119	.00036	.00738	.00011	.00194	.00332	.00921	.00060	13
.00236	.01737	.04963	.00675	.00251	.00895	.06025	.00765	.00476	.03179	.06538	.00483	14
.00178	.14150	.11243	.01279	.00169	.14779	.10748	.01400	.00097	.17463	.08358	.00803	15
.01504	.05669	.03908	.02959	01557	.04079	.03824	.02178	.01738	.06809	.02896	.00952	16
.03734	.07674	.07002	.09300	.03486	.07110	.07875	.10844	.02171	.12634	.07566	.04868	17
.01212	.01556	.01981	.01501	.01156	.01649	.01709	.01282	.01492	.01180	.01806	.00935	18
.24070	.06987	.16059	.02290	.24209	.07352	.16566	.02835	.26864	.08610	.17344	.03224	19
.02998	–	.00104	.00957	.02779	–	.00150	.00886	.01800	–	.00005	.00691	20
.34237	.02569	.03615	.09905	.32794	.02615	.03801	.08566	.24448	.03302	.01847	.06818	21
.00346	–	.00254	.00306	.00326	–	.00281	.00258	.00212	–	.00041	.00241	22
−.00007	−.00950	.01541	.00512	−.00005	−.01687	.00919	.00487	–	.00088	.04923	−.08346	23
.01374	−.00228	–	.02348	.01329	.00039	–	.02888	.00536	−.00250	–	.01847	DI
[2]−.00367	–	[2].05768	[2]−.00356	[2]−.00397	–	[2].06416	[2]−.00326	[2]−.00443	–	[2].03950	[2]−.00193	TrI
.01114	−.00026	.10485	.43784	.01208	−.00511	.08921	.41451	.01451	−.02234	.04238	.60691	VA
1.00000	1.00000	1.00000	1.00000	1.00000	1.00000	1.00000	1.00000	1.00000	1.00000	1.00000	1.00000	T

Chapter G

Consumer Income and Expenditures

Family and Individual Income (Series G 1-415)

G 1-415. General note.

The development of reasonably reliable nationwide estimates of income distribution for families and individuals was dependent on the availability of comprehensive basic source material from Federal individual income tax returns and from representative sample field surveys of family incomes. Annual tabulations of tax-return data originated during World War I, but until the 1940's, when the minimum income requirement for filing returns was substantially lowered, these tabulations provided information for only a small fraction of the upper-income population. Sample field surveys of family incomes that were designed to cover all income and occupation groups in the Nation were not introduced until the 1930's.

Reflecting the lack of adequate source data, the early estimators of income distribution had to piece together various sets of sample income statistics that were available for selected occupation groups or local areas, and combine these figures with income data from State or Federal income tax returns or with income distribution series derived by applying yield rates to estimated size-class distributions of wealth. Among the early estimators were Charles B. Spahr who constructed a family income distribution in 1896, Willford I. King who developed income distribution estimates by size-class for families for 1910, and for individuals for 1921 and 1928, Frederick R. Macaulay who constructed income distributions for individuals for 1918, and Maurice Leven who did the same for families and individuals for 1929.

The following publications relate to these early efforts:

C. L. Merwin, "American Studies of the Distribution of Wealth and Income by Size," *Studies in Income and Wealth*, vol. 3, Conference on Research in Income and Wealth, National Bureau of Economic Research, New York, 1939.

Charles B. Spahr, *The Present Distribution of Wealth in the United States*, New York, 1896.

Willford I. King, *Wealth and Income of the People of the United States*, New York, 1915; also unpublished manuscript at the National Bureau of Economic Research, New York.

W. C. Mitchell, W. I. King, F. R. Macaulay, and O. W. Knauth, *Income in the United States*, National Bureau of Economic Research, New York, 1921 and 1922.

Maurice Leven, H. G. Moulton, and Clark Warburton, *America's Capacity to Consume*, The Brookings Institution, Washington, D.C., 1934.

The Consumer Purchases Study of 1935-36 was the first sample field survey in the United States in which income data were collected from all types of families without restriction as to occupation or earnings group. Based largely on the 300,000 family income schedules collected in that study and on tax returns for upper incomes, the National Resources Committee constructed estimates of family income, by income size-class, for a 12-month period during 1935 and 1936. Aside from their firmer statistical basis, the figures developed by Dr. Hildegarde Kneeland and her staff represented a marked improvement over earlier estimates by providing separate income distributions for numerous subgroups, e.g., for families classified by major occupation of the head, type and size of community, region, color, and family size. (See National Resources Committee, *Consumer Incomes in the United States: Their Distribution in 1935-36*, Washington, D.C., 1938.)

The Survey of Spending and Saving in Wartime provided the only other pre-World War II statistics on the distribution of families, by total income brackets, on a nationwide basis. This survey for 1941, though much smaller in size than the 1935-36 study, represented a further advance in that the sample of families selected for interview was designed specifically for the purpose of "inflating" the results to produce nationwide estimates of family income distribution. (See Bureau of Labor Statistics, *Family Spending and Saving in Wartime*, BLS Bulletin 822, 1945; also Bureau of Human Nutrition and Home Economics, *Rural Family Spending and Saving in Wartime*, U.S. Department of Agriculture Misc. Publication No. 520, 1943.)

Detailed distributions of families, and of persons 14 years old and over, by size-class of their money wage and salary income in 1939, were provided by the 1940 Census of Population, the first decennial census to include income questions. For items of income other than wages or salaries, the census obtained only a "yes" or "no" response as to the receipt of $50 or more, so that over-all size-class distributions on a total income basis are not available. A 5-percent sample of these returns was tabulated with extensive cross-classifications. For many types of analysis, e.g., for studying occupational differentials in wage-salary earnings distribution, these tabulations for 1939 comprise the best available data for comparisons between the prewar and postwar periods. (See Bureau of the Census, *Population—The Labor Force (Sample Statistics): Wage or Salary Income in 1939*; and *Population—Families: Family Wage or Salary Income in 1939*. For other decennial census reports that include income data, and for list of available tabulations, see Edwin D. Goldfield, "Decennial Census and Current Population Survey Data on Income," *Studies in Income and Wealth*, vol. 23, Conference on Research in Income and Wealth, National Bureau of Economic Research, Princeton, 1958.)

For post-World War II years, annual nationwide sample survey data are available from two sources: The annual current population surveys of the Census Bureau which present distributions by total money income brackets for families and for persons 14 years old and over for 1944-1970; and the annual surveys of consumer finances conducted by the Survey Research Center of the University of Michigan, which furnish distributions by total money income brackets for families and for "spending units" for 1945-1969. Income size-class distributions from both these sets of sample survey data are available for numerous subgroups of the population. (See Bureau of the Census, *Current Population Reports: Consumer Income*, series P-60, Nos. 1-80, and series P-S, Nos. 22 and 22-S; and Board of Governors of the Federal Reserve System, "1958 Survey of Consumer Finances: The Financial Position of Consumers," *Federal Reserve Bulletin*, September 1958, and corresponding articles for earlier years.)

A historical and analytical summary of the income data collected in the Current Population Survey appears in Technical Paper No. 17, *Trends in the Income of Families and Persons in the United States: 1947 to 1964*, published in 1967. This report contains detailed tables showing income distributions in constant (1964) dollars, mean incomes, fifths, and Gini Ratios of families and unrelated individuals cross-classified by various characteristics, for the United States, nonfarm and farm. Similar data are also shown for males and females classified by the amount of their own income and various personal characteristics.

Also available for the postwar years are data published from the

1950, 1960, and 1970 censuses of population. These three censuses provide detailed cross-classifications for large areas and less detailed data for smaller areas. Moreover, they provide data on the level of total money income for families and persons 14 years old and over in addition to data on wage and salary income, whereas the 1940 Census of Population provided data covering primarily wage and salary income only. (For a discussion of the 1970 census publication program, see Bureau of the Census, *1970 Census of Population and Housing*, "Publication and Computer Tape Program"; for the 1960 census, see Bureau of the Census, *1960 Censuses of Population and Housing: Procedural History* or *Guide to Census Bureau Data Files and Special Tabulations*.

In the 1950 Census of Population the income questions covered all items of money income, not just wages and salaries. The tabulations based on this census show separate money income distributions for families for local areas, and for persons 14 years old and over, classified by demographic and socioeconomic characteristics. (See Bureau of the Census, *1950 Census of Population*, vol. II; see also article by Goldfield, cited above.) Comparative distributions for 1939 and 1949 of persons classified by money wage or salary brackets and cross-classified by sex and detailed occupation and industry groups have been compiled from the census material by H. P. Miller. (See Herman P. Miller, *Income of the American People*, John Wiley and Sons, New York, 1955; and "Changes in the Industrial Distribution of Wages in the United States, 1939–1949," *Studies in Income and Wealth*, vol. 23, Conference on Research in Income and Wealth, National Bureau of Economic Research, Princeton, 1958.)

In addition to these nationwide surveys and censuses, other surveys providing income data for selected population groups are the income-expenditure surveys conducted by the Bureau of Labor Statistics, which show urban family income distributions for 1944, 1950, and 1960, several studies of farm family incomes by the Department of Agriculture, and a number of surveys in individual localities conducted by the Bureau of the Census. (See Bureau of Labor Statistics, "Expenditures and Savings of City Families in 1944," *Monthly Labor Review*, January 1946; "City Family Composition in Relation to Income, 1941 and 1944," *Monthly Labor Review*, February 1946; and *Study of Consumer Expenditures, Incomes and Savings, Statistical Tables, Urban U.S.—1950*, vol. XI, *Details of Family Accounts for Incomes, Savings, Insurance and Gifts and Contributions*, tabulated by the Bureau of Labor Statistics for the Wharton School of Finance and Commerce, University of Pennsylvania, 1957; Department of Agriculture and Department of Commerce, *Farms and Farm People, A Special Cooperative Report*, 1953; and *Farmers' Expenditures, A Special Cooperative Survey*, 1956.)

Since 1937, income distributions are also available for workers covered under the old-age, survivors, disability, and health insurance (OASDHI) program. These figures show workers classified by size brackets of "covered" wages and salaries (and, since 1951, "covered" self-employment income). The group of workers covered by these series was substantially expanded in the post-World War II period, but the usefulness of the series is limited by the upper limit for "covered" earnings. The upper limit was $3,000 prior to 1951, $3,600 for 1951–1954, $4,200 for 1955–1958, $4,800 for 1959–1965, $6,600 for 1966–1967, and $7,800 for 1968–1970. (See Social Security Administration, *Social Security Bulletin, Annual Statistical Supplement, 1971*, and earlier issues.)

Distributions of Federal individual income tax returns by income bracket are available annually since 1913. Until World War II, the minimum filing requirements were relatively high so that the tabulations covered only a small fraction of the population. Successive lowering of the filing limit coupled with the rise in incomes after the depression of the 1930's led to a very marked expansion in coverage so that very few groups of the population are excluded in the postwar tabulations. (See Internal Revenue Service, *Statistics of Income, Individual Income Tax Returns*, annual.)

Tax-return data have been used in several studies to measure changes in relative income distribution over time. Rufus Tucker applied measures of dispersion to tax-return distributions for 1863–1935. He included in his series some less reliable tax data for the Civil War period. (See Rufus S. Tucker, "The Distribution of Income Among Income Taxpayers in the United States, 1863–1935," *Quarterly Journal of Economics*, vol. LII, 1938, pp. 547–587.) The most detailed study of the tax-return statistics is that by Simon Kuznets (see text for series G 337–352).

A number of the family income distribution estimates for the pre-World War II period were developed by integrating tax-return and survey data. Among them are the estimates of The Brookings Institution for 1929 and the National Resources Committee for 1935–36, both cited earlier, and the Survey of Spending and Saving in Wartime distribution for 1941 as subsequently adjusted in the light of tax-return data by Joseph Pechman. (See Joseph Pechman, "Distribution of Income Before and After Federal Income Tax, 1941 and 1947," *Studies in Income and Wealth*, vol. 13, Conference on Research in Income and Wealth, National Bureau of Economic Research, New York, 1951.) In developing these prewar distributions, data from Federal individual income tax returns could be used only to construct estimates for the top ranges of the family income scale, which were then linked directly to field survey data for the low and middle income brackets.

The much broader coverage of Federal individual income tax returns introduced in World War II, coupled with the availability of annual postwar sample survey data, made possible the construction of family income distributions for the postwar period that are more firmly based statistically than the earlier estimates. As part of its national income work, the former Office of Business Economics, now the Bureau of Economic Analysis, developed distributions of families and family income by brackets of family personal income for 1944, 1946, 1947, and for each year, 1950–1964, by combining the two sets of source data and adjusting the results so that they accord statistically and definitionally with the personal income series prepared in that office. (See Office of Business Economics, *Income Distribution in the United States by Size, 1944–1950*, 1953; revised and brought up to date in articles on income distribution in the *Survey of Current Business*, March 1955, June 1956, April 1958, 1959, and 1964.)

In order to derive meaningful comparisons over time, the family distributions for the prewar period required adjustment to make them consistent with postwar series. Adjusted family income distributions reasonably comparable with the postwar series of the Office of Business Economics were developed for 1935–36 and 1941 by Selma Goldsmith, et al (see source cited for series G 269–296 for 1935–36 and 1941). Mrs. Goldsmith also adjusted the figures in The Brookings Institution study for 1929 to remove the major elements of incomparability. (See Selma F. Goldsmith, "The Relation of Census Income Distribution Statistics to Other Income Data," *Studies in Income and Wealth*, vol. 23, Conference on Research in Income and Wealth, National Bureau of Economic Research, Princeton, 1958.)

Direct comparability among income distribution series is frequently precluded by variations in definition or coverage which are due in many instances to the different purposes for which the data were collected. Definitional differences may apply to the basic unit of classification, to the definition of the income measure, or to the time period to which the income data or the definition of the family unit refers. (See Simon Kuznets, "The Why and How of Distributions of Income by Size," *Studies in Income and Wealth*, vol. 5, Conference on Research in Income and Wealth, National Bureau of Economic Research, New York, 1943, and "Economic Growth and Income Inequality," *American Economic Review*, March 1955, vol. XLV, No. 1; Dorothy S. Brady, "Research on the Size Distribution of Income," *Studies in Income and Wealth*, vol. 13, Conference on Research in Income and Wealth, National Bureau of Economic Research, New York, 1951; and *Income Distribution in the United States . . .*, cited above.) For measures of the effect of alternative income definitions on changes observed over time in relative income shares of top income groups, see Selma F. Goldsmith, "Changes in the Size Distribution of Income," *American Economic Review*, May 1957, vol. XLVII, No. 2.

The income data presented here are not directly comparable with estimates of aggregate personal income prepared by the Bureau of Economic Analysis (BEA), nor with the distributions of families and unrelated individuals by family personal income brackets published by that Bureau. The lack of correspondence stems from the following differences in definition and coverage:

(1) *Income definition.* The personal income series include, among other items, the following types of nonmoney income which are not included in the census definition. Wages received in kind, the value of food and fuel produced and consumed on farms, the net rental value of owner-occupied homes, the property income received by mutual life insurance companies, and the value of the services of banks and other financial intermediaries rendered to persons without the assessment of specific charges. These items of income in kind account for about 4 percent of total personal income. The Census Bureau definition of income includes such items as regular contributions for support received from persons who do not reside in the same living quarters, income received from roomers and boarders residing in households, and employee contributions for social insurance, which are not included in the personal income series. These items, however, represent a much smaller income total than the nonmoney items included in personal income.

(2) *Source of data.* The personal income series is estimated largely on the basis of data derived from business and governmental sources. These sources include the industrial and population censuses, employers' wage reports under the Social Security programs, and records of disbursements to individuals by governmental agencies. The income data presented in the census reports are based directly on field surveys of households.

(3) *Coverage.* The Bureau of the Census excluded from its sample inmates of institutions and military personnel overseas or living on post in the United States (except for a few families living on post). In addition, the income of persons who died or emigrated prior to the date of interview was not reported in the census inquiry. The income of these groups is included in the aggregate personal income series released by BEA but is excluded from the BEA family income distributions.

Furthermore, income data obtained in household interviews are subject to various types of reporting errors which tend to produce an understatement of income. It is estimated that the income surveys conducted by the Bureau of the Census during the past few years have obtained about 89 percent of the comparable total money income aggregates derived from the personal income series prepared by BEA.

Additional information concerning comparability with other data sources can be found in *Current Population Reports,* Consumer Income series P-60, No. 85.

For the pre-World War II period, also, direct comparison is not warranted between certain sets of income distribution statistics. For example, for 1941, the income classification in series G 813–827 is in terms of family money income brackets, and in series G 269–296, it is in terms of family personal income brackets. For 1929 and 1935–36, the income for series G 828–848 and for series G 269–296 are not directly comparable because of adjustments incorporated in the latter as noted above.

G 1–268. General note.

Estimates for these series are based on sample data obtained in the Current Population Survey (CPS) of the Bureau of the Census. Most of the data were collected in March of the year following the year stated. For 1967–1970, the sample was spread over 449 areas comprising 863 counties and independent cities, with coverage in each of the 50 States and the District of Columbia. Approximately 50,000 households are designated in the CPS for interview each month. In addition, there are about 8,500 sample units in an average month which are visited but are found to be vacant or otherwise not

enumerated. Prior to 1967, the sample was spread over fewer households. Prior to the March 1966 survey, income data were collected from only 75 percent of the households included in the CPS.

For each person, 14 years old and over, in the sample, questions were asked concerning money income received in the preceding calendar year from each of the following sources: (1) Money wages or salary; (2) net income from nonfarm self-employment; (3) net income from farm self-employment; (4) Social Security payments; (5) dividends, or trusts, or net rental income; (6) public assistance or welfare payments; (7) unemployment compensation, government employee pensions, or veterans' payments; (8) private pensions, annuities, alimony, regular contributions from persons not living in the household, and other periodic income. See also *Current Population Reports,* series P-23, No. 22, "Concepts and Methods Used in Manpower Statistics from the Current Population Survey," June 1967, pp. 7–10.

See general note for series G 1–415 and text for series G 269–296. See also data and text for series A 288–358.

G 1–15. Percent distribution of families and unrelated individuals, by race of head, by money income levels, 1947–1970.

Source: U.S. Bureau of the Census, Current Population Reports, series P-60, No. 90.

See general note for series G 1–268. For definitions of race, family head, and families and unrelated individuals, see text for series A 91–104, G 146–157, and G 269–296, respectively.

G 16–30. Percent distribution of families and unrelated individuals, by race of head, by money income levels in constant (1967) dollars, 1947–1970.

Source: U.S. Bureau of the Census, unpublished data.

See general note for series G 1–268. For definitions of race, family head, and families and unrelated individuals, see text for series A 91–104, G 146–157, and G 269–296, respectively.

G 31–138. Distribution of money income of families and unrelated individuals ranked by fifths according to income received, by race of head, 1947–1970.

Source: U.S. Bureau of the Census, *Current Population Reports,* series P-60, No. 90, and unpublished data.

See general note for series G 1–268. For definitions of race, family head, and families and unrelated individuals, see text for series A 91–104, G 146–157, and G 269–296, respectively.

G 139–178. Percent distribution of families ranked by fifths according to money income received, by selected family characteristics, 1950, 1960, and 1970.

Source: U.S. Bureau of the Census, *Current Population Reports,* series P-60, No. 80, and unpublished data.

For composition of regions, see text for series A 172–194; for definition of race, see text for series A 91–104.

G 140–141. The farm population refers to rural residents living on farms. The method of determining farm-nonfarm residence in the 1970 survey is the same as that used in the 1960 census and in the Current Population Surveys since 1960, but differs from that used in earlier surveys and censuses. For definitions, see text for series A 73–81.

G 146–157 and G 175–178. One person in each family was designated as the head. The head of a family is usually the person regarded as the head by members of the family. Women are not classified as heads if their husbands are resident members of the family at the time of the survey. Married couples related to the head of a family are included in the head's family and are not classified as separate families.

See also general note for series G 1–268.

G 179–188. Number and median money income of families and unrelated individuals, 1947–1970.

Source: See source for series G 1–15.

Median income is the amount which divides the distribution into two equal groups, one having incomes above the median, and the other having incomes below the median.   The medians for families and individuals are based on all families and individuals.

The base figures for 1961 to 1970 were prepared by inflating weighted sample results to agree with independent estimates of the population based on statistics updated from the 1960 Census of Population.   The data for years prior to 1961 were based on the 1950 census.

See also general note for series G 1–268.   For definitions of family head, and families and unrelated individuals, see text for series G 146–157 and G 269–296, respectively.

G 189–204. Median money income of families and unrelated individuals in current and constant (1967) dollars, by race of head, 1947–1970.

Source: U.S. Bureau of the Census, *Current Population Reports*, series P-60, No. 90, and unpublished data.

See general note for series G 1–268 and text for series G 179–188.

G 205–256. Median money income of families, by States, 1949, 1959, and 1969.

Source: U.S. Bureau of the Census.   1949, *U.S. Census of Population: 1960*, vol. I; 1959 and 1969, *U.S. Census of Population: 1970*, vol. I.

The income data collected in the 1950 and 1960 censuses are basically similar to the 1970 census data, but there are variations in the detail of the questions.   In 1960, information on income was obtained from all members in every fourth housing unit and from every fourth person 14 years old and over living in group quarters. Each person was required to report (a) wage or salary income, (b) net self-employment income, and (c) income other than earnings received in 1959. Between the 1960 and 1970 censuses, there were also some changes in the processing of the data.   In the 1960 census, an assumption was made in the editing process that no other type of income was received by a person who reported the receipt of either wage and salary income or self-employment income but who had failed to report the receipt of other money income.   This person was considered as unallocated.   In the 1970 census, this assumption was not made.   Generally, all missing values were imputed either as "none" or as a dollar amount.   If a person reported a dollar amount in (a) wage or salary income, (b) net nonfarm self-employment income, or (c) net farm self-employment income, he was designated as unallocated only if no further dollar amounts were imputed for any additional missing entries.

In both the 1960 and 1970 censuses, all nonrespondents on income (whether heads of families or other persons) were assigned the reported income of persons with similar characteristics.

In 1950, information on income was obtained from every fifth person 14 years old and over.   If the sample person was the head of the family, the income questions were repeated for the other family members as a group in order to obtain the income of the whole family. In the tabulations of family income for the 1950 census, if only the head's income was reported, it was assumed that there was no other income in the family.

For definition of median income, see text for series G 179–188.

G 257–268. Percent distribution of persons, by sex, by money income levels, 1944–1970.

Source: U.S. Bureau of the Census, *Current Population Reports*, series P-60, Nos. 35 and 90.

See general note for series G 1–268 and text for series G 179–188.

G 269–296. Percent distribution of families and unattached individuals and of aggregate personal income among families and unattached individuals, by family personal income levels, 1929–1964.

Source: 1929, Selma F. Goldsmith, "The Relation of Census Income Distribution Statistics to Other Income Data," *Studies in Income and Wealth*, vol. 23, National Bureau of Economic Research, New York, 1958 (copyright); 1935–1936 and 1941, Selma F. Goldsmith, George Jaszi, Hyman Kaitz, and Maurice Liebenberg, "Size Distribution of Income Since the Mid-Thirties," *Review of Economics and Statistics*, February 1954 (copyright, Harvard College); 1944–1962, U.S. Office of Business Economics, *Survey of Current Business*, April 1958 and April 1964; 1964, Edward C. Budd, Daniel B. Radner, and John C. Hinrichs, "Size Distribution of Family Personal Income: Methodology and Estimates for 1964," *Bureau of Economic Analysis, Staff Paper No. 21*, June 1973.

The definitions of families and unattached individuals in these series conform with those used by the Census Bureau.   Families are units of two or more persons related by blood, marriage, or adoption, and residing together; unattached (unrelated) individuals are persons (age 14 or over) other than institutional inmates who are not living with any relatives.   For years prior to 1964, the total number of families and unattached individuals was estimated as of the end of the calendar year to which the income data pertained (for 1935–36, the estimate refers to July 1, 1936).   It was derived, for most years, by interpolating between Census Bureau figures after adjustment to exclude certain minor groups of individuals.   For 1964, the total number of families and unattached (unrelated) individuals was estimated as of the middle of March 1965, the date of the Current Population Survey from which the estimates were obtained.

Personal income represents the current income received by families and unattached individuals from all sources.   For years prior to 1964, it included wage and salary receipts and proprietors' income (both net of social insurance contributions), other labor income, rental income, dividends, personal interest income, and transfer payments. For 1964, the definition differed slightly in that employer contributions to private pension, health, and welfare funds (a component of other labor income) were excluded and private pension and annuity payments received were included.   In addition to monetary income, family personal income for all years includes certain nonmoney items such as wages in kind, the value of food and fuel produced and consumed on farms, the net imputed rental value of owner-occupied homes, and imputed interest.   Total personal income is a somewhat smaller amount in each year than the personal income aggregate from which it is derived, because it excludes the income received by certain types of recipients, such as institutional residents (including military personnel not living with their families) and nonprofit institutions.

For discussion of the earlier definitions, see Office of Business Economics, *Income Distribution in the United States by Size, 1944–1950*, 1953.   The 1964 definitions are discussed in Budd, Radner, and Hinrichs, cited above for 1964.   For limitations of the pre-World War II distributions affecting comparability with the postwar series (excluding 1964), see source for prewar figures.   1964 data are of limited comparability with 1962 and earlier data because a different estimating methodology (described in Budd, Radner, and Hinrichs) was used for 1964.

See also general note for series G 1–415.

G 297–305. Percent distribution of families and unattached individuals and family personal income, by income level in 1950 dollars, 1929–1957.

Source: 1929, see first source for series G 269–296, p. 93; 1935–36 to 1944, see second source for series G 269–296; 1950, U.S. Office of Business Economics, *Survey of Current Business*, April, 1959, p. 14; 1957, unpublished data.

1957 data were computed by applying the OBE price index used for deflating personal consumption expenditures (of the national income accounts) to the income distribution expressed in current dollars for that year; the latter appears in the *Survey of Current Business*, April 1959, p. 11. For definitions of terms, see text for series G 269–296.

The price-deflated income size distributions such as are shown here represent only approximate measures of real income distribution because separate price indexes applicable to the various income brackets are not available. It is therefore necessary to use the same index throughout the income range even though all brackets may not have been affected by the price rise in the same way. Moreover, available price indexes which refer to consumer expenditures for goods and services must be applied to income totals that include income taxes and saving as well as outlays for consumption. For interpolation procedures used in deflating income size distributions, see Office of Business Economics, *Income Distribution in the United States by Size, 1944–1950*, p. 38.

Because of inadequacies in the basic source data, the estimates for 1929 are less reliable than for other years in the series. For limitations of the prewar data, see the sources.

G 306–318. Number and average size of families, number of unattached individuals, and average family personal income before and after Federal individual income tax liability, 1929–1964.

Source: 1929–1941, unpublished tabulations underlying estimates shown in source for 1935–36, series G 269–296. U.S. Office of Business Economics, 1944–1954, *Survey of Current Business*, April 1958, pp. 11 and 16–19 (except series G 315, G 317, and G 318, for the following years: 1944–1947, *Income Distribution in the United States by Size, 1944–1950*, 1953, pp. 82–84; 1950–1951, *Survey of Current Business*, March 1955, pp. 25–26; 1952, *Survey of Current Business*, June 1956, p. 13; series G 309 and G 311, 1944–1954, and series G 310, 1944–1946, unpublished data; 1955–1957, *Survey of Current Business*, April 1959, pp. 10 and 15–16, and unpublished data; 1964, Edward C. Budd, Daniel B. Radner, and John C. Hinrichs, "Size Distribution of Family Personal Income: Methodology and Estimates for 1964," *Bureau of Economic Analysis, Staff Paper No. 21*, June 1973, and U.S. Bureau of Economic Analysis, unpublished data).

For definitions of terms, see text for series G 269–296.

Farm-operator families cover all families operating farms as defined in the census of agriculture; the total number is estimated annually by the Agricultural Marketing Service. (See general note for series K 1–203.) Nonfarm families include all multiperson units other than farm-operator families.

G 319–336. Family personal income received by each fifth and top 5 percent of families and unattached individuals, 1929–1964.

Source: 1929, **series G 319–324**, see source for 1929, series G 297–305, p. 92; 1929, **series G 325–336**, unpublished tabulations underlying estimates shown in source for 1929, series G 297–305; 1935–36 and 1941, see source for same years, series G 269–296, p. 9; 1944–1947, U.S. Office of Business Economics, *Income Distribution in the United States by Size, 1944–50*, 1953, p. 81; 1950–1954, *Survey of Current Business*, April 1958, p. 17; 1955–1962, *Survey of Current Business*,

April 1964, p. 16; 1964, Edward C. Budd, Daniel B. Radner, and John C. Hinrichs, "Size Distribution of Family Personal Income: Methodology and Estimates for 1964," *Bureau of Economic Analysis, Staff Paper No. 21*, June 1973, and U.S. Bureau of Economic Analysis, unpublished data.

For definitions of terms, see text for series G 269–296.

G 337–352. Percent shares of total income received by top 1 percent and 5 percent of total population, 1913–1948.

Source: Simon Kuznets, *Shares of Upper Income Groups in Income and Savings*, National Bureau of Economic Research, New York, 1953, pp. 582, 585, 635, 637, 646, and 649 (copyright).

The top percentiles in these series represent the 1 or 5 percent of men, women, and children covered on those individual income tax returns reporting the largest per capita incomes in each year. The basic variant is the total of employee compensation, entrepreneurial income, rent, interest, and dividends; the economic variant represents the basic variant adjusted to allow for such factors as the nonreporting of State and local government salaries prior to 1938, the omission of imputed rent on owner-occupied houses, and, most important, the effects of classifying the tax data by an inappropriate base and unit; the disposable income variant is derived by deducting from the economic income variant Federal income taxes paid, and adding the net balance of realized gains and losses from sales of assets.

G 353–371. Median money wage or salary income of primary families and unrelated individuals with wage or salary income, by selected characteristics, 1939–1970.

Source: U.S. Bureau of the Census, *Current Population Reports*, series P-60, Nos. 5, 7, 9, 12, 24, 27, 30, 33, 35, 37, 39, 41, 43, 47, 51, 53, 59, 66, 75, and 80; and unpublished data.

The term "primary family" refers to the head of a household and all other persons in the household related to the head by blood, marriage, or adoption. If no one in the household is related to the head, then the head himself constitutes a "primary individual."

Money wages or salaries are defined as total money earnings received for work performed as an employee during the calendar year, including wages, salary, commissions, tips, piece-rate payments, and cash bonuses earned, before deductions were made for taxes, bonds, pensions, union dues, etc.

For definitions of race and family head, see text for series A 91–104 and series G 146–157, respectively.

G 372–415. Median money wage or salary income of all workers with wage or salary income, and of year-round full-time workers, by sex, race, and major occupation group, 1939–1970.

Source: U.S. Bureau of the Census, *Current Population Reports*, series P-60, Nos. 9, 11, 14, 16, 19, 23, 27, 30, 33, 35, 37, 39, 41, 43, 47, 51, 53, 60, 66, 75, and 80.

See text for series G 353–371.

★ ★ ★ ★ ★ ★ ★ ★ ★ **More Recent Data for *Historical Statistics* Series** ★ ★ ★ ★ ★ ★ ★ ★ ★

★ Statistics for more recent years in continuation of many of the still-active series shown here appear ★
★ in annual issues of the *Statistical Abstract of the United States*, beginning with the 1975 edition. For ★
★ direct linkage of the historical series to the tables in the *Abstract*, see Appendix I in the *Abstract*. ★

Series G 1–15. Percent Distribution of Families and Unrelated Individuals, by Race of Head, by Money Income Levels: 1947 to 1970

[Families and unrelated individuals as of March following year shown]

Race of head and year	Families								Unrelated individuals						
	Number (1,000)	Percent distribution by income level							Number (1,000)	Percent distribution by income level					
		Under $3,000	$3,000 to $4,999	$5,000 to $6,999	$7,000 to $9,999	$10,000 to $11,999	$12,000 to $14,999	$15,000 and over		Under $1,500	$1,500 to $2,999	$3,000 to $4,999	$5,000 to $6,999	$7,000 to $9,999	$10,000 and over
	1	2	3	4	5	6	7	8	9	10	11	12	13	14	15
TOTAL															
1970	51,948	8.9	10.3	11.8	19.9	12.7	14.1	22.3	15,357	23.2	25.4	17.7	12.2	12.3	9.3
1969	51,237	9.3	10.7	12.3	21.7	13.0	13.7	19.3	14,452	26.5	24.3	17.9	12.8	10.5	8.0
1968	50,510	10.3	12.1	14.5	23.4	12.5	12.4	14.7	13,803	28.8	23.3	19.0	12.0	10.2	6.7
1967	49,834	12.6	12.9	16.2	24.4	11.9	10.7	11.4	13,114	34.6	22.3	17.3	12.6	7.9	5.2
1966	49,065	14.1	13.7	17.7	24.6	11.5	9.3	9.3	12,271	59.5		18.5	11.2	6.8	3.8
1965	48,279	16.1	15.6	18.8	24.2	10.1	7.6	7.6	12,132	38.2	21.9	17.8	12.0	6.9	3.5
1964	47,835	17.6	17.0	19.8	23.2	9.5	6.9	6.3	12,057	42.2	20.3	17.4	11.1	5.8	3.1
1963	47,436	18.5	17.7	21.3	22.5	8.3	6.2	5.4	11,182	44.1	21.7	15.9	10.2	5.4	2.6
1962	46,998	19.9	19.1	22.4	21.0	7.6	5.3	4.9	11,013	45.1	21.8	15.8	9.9	5.0	2.4
1961	46,341	21.4	19.9	21.9	20.7	6.6	4.6	4.6	11,163	45.6	21.4	17.6	9.8	3.3	2.4
1960	45,456	21.7	20.3	23.7	20.0	6.2	4.4	3.7	11,081	46.8	20.0	19.5	9.3	3.2	1.2
1959	45,111	22.7	21.8	24.2	18.9	5.4	3.7	3.1	10,879	49.0	21.6	17.9	7.5	2.7	1.4
1958	44,232	24.1	24.6	24.4	16.8	4.7	2.9	2.4	10,884	50.4	20.0	18.8	7.0	2.2	1.7
1957	43,696	24.5	25.9	24.8	16.4	4.0	2.5	1.9	10,435	50.1	21.6	18.4	6.5	2.0	1.1
1956	43,497	25.6	27.4	23.5	15.6	3.5	2.5	2.0	9,779	51.7	22.2	18.9	5.3	1.3	.7
1955	42,889	28.5	30.1	22.2	13.0	3.0	1.8	1.4	9,889	54.6	22.0	17.4	4.3	1.0	.7
1954	41,951	31.7	31.0	20.4	11.1	2.7	1.6	1.4	9,724	55.9	22.9	15.5	4.2	.7	.6
1953	41,202	30.2	31.7	21.3	11.6	2.5	1.6	1.3	9,514	52.1	25.7	17.0	3.4	.7	.9
1952	40,832	33.4	33.9	19.4	9.0	1.7	1.2	1.3	9,705	52.2	25.7	17.2	3.4	1.0	.5
1951	40,578	35.9	35.3	17.6	7.6	1.5	.9	1.2	9,142	55.3	25.3	16.1	2.6	.5	.2
1950	39,929	42.5	34.3	14.2	5.8		3.3		9,366	59.5	24.8	13.3	1.6	.6	.4
1949	39,303	47.6	32.0	12.6	5.0		2.6		8,995	60.3	27.0	10.4	1.5		.3
1948	38,624	45.7	33.6	12.5	5.4		2.9		8,361	63.2	24.7	10.2	1.7		.4
1947	37,237	49.4	31.3	11.7	4.9		2.7		8,165	63.6	25.9	7.6	1.9		1.0
WHITE															
1970	46,535	7.5	9.6	11.3	20.1	13.1	14.8	23.7	13,413	21.4	25.5	17.8	12.4	12.7	10.1
1969	46,022	8.1	9.7	11.8	21.9	13.6	14.5	20.6	12,473	24.6	24.6	18.0	13.0	11.1	8.8
1968	45,437	8.9	11.0	14.3	24.0	13.0	13.1	15.7	11,955	27.2	23.3	19.1	12.2	10.6	7.5
1967	44,814	10.7	12.0	16.0	25.1	12.5	11.2	12.2	11,318	33.2	22.5	17.3	12.8	8.5	5.7
1966	44,110	12.2	12.6	17.7	25.4	12.2	10.0	10.1	10,686	58.0		18.7	11.8	7.3	4.3
1965	43,497	14.0	14.4	19.1	25.5	10.7	8.1	8.3	10,477	36.6	22.0	17.9	12.4	7.5	3.8
1964	43,081	15.4	15.9	20.1	24.4	10.0	7.3	6.8	10,416	40.5	20.3	17.9	11.6	6.2	3.5
1963	42,663	15.8	17.0	21.8	23.8	9.0	6.6	5.9	9,725	42.3	21.7	16.2	10.9	5.9	2.9
1962	42,437	17.1	18.4	23.1	22.3	8.1	5.7	5.3	9,494	42.8	21.6	16.5	10.7	5.5	2.9
1961	41,888	18.6	19.4	22.7	22.1	7.1	5.0	5.1	9,597	43.1	22.0	18.1	10.4	3.7	2.7
1960	41,123	19.2	19.9	24.5	21.3	6.6	4.6	4.1	9,559	44.6	20.1	20.4	10.0	3.5	1.3
1959	40,872	19.8	21.4	25.4	20.1	5.9	4.1	3.4	9,306	47.2	21.1	18.9	8.2	3.0	1.6
1958	40,236	21.1	24.6	25.7	18.0	5.0	3.1	2.6	9,237	48.5	19.6	19.8	7.6	2.3	1.9
1957	39,676	21.6	25.9	26.0	17.4	4.4	2.6	2.0	8,940	48.4	21.6	19.1	7.5	2.3	1.4
1956	39,498	22.6	27.5	24.7	16.7	3.8	2.6	2.2	8,468	50.8	21.3	19.7	5.8	1.4	.8
1955	38,982	25.7	30.3	23.3	14.0	3.2	2.0	1.5	8,457	52.4	21.7	19.1	4.8	1.0	.9
1954	38,185	28.9	31.3	21.6	12.0	3.0	1.8	1.5	8,282	54.1	23.0	16.3	5.0	.9	.7
1953	(NA)	27.2	32.1	22.5	12.3	2.7	1.6	1.4	(NA)	50.4	25.3	18.1	4.2	.9	1.0
1952	(NA)	29.3	35.1	20.9	10.0	1.8	1.3	1.5	(NA)	49.6	25.6	19.4	3.5	1.0	.7
1951	(NA)	32.5	36.6	18.7	8.1	1.7	.9	1.3	(NA)	54.1	24.1	18.2	2.8	.4	.3
1950	(NA)	39.4	35.7	15.1	6.1		3.5		(NA)	57.8	25.1	14.4	1.6	.7	.4
1949	(NA)	44.6	33.7	13.4	5.4		2.8		(NA)	58.2	27.6	11.6	1.8		.4
1948	35,345	42.6	35.2	13.3	5.8		3.1		7,346	61.5	25.4	10.8	1.9		.4
1947	34,120	46.2	33.2	12.4	5.2		3.0		7,191	61.4	27.2	8.2	2.1		1.1
NEGRO AND OTHER RACES															
1970	5,413	20.1	16.9	16.4	18.2	8.9	8.4	10.8	1,944	35.1	24.0	17.5	11.0	9.6	2.7
1969	5,215	20.4	19.3	17.0	19.5	8.1	7.5	8.2	1,979	38.2	22.8	17.4	11.5	7.5	2.8
1968	5,074	22.8	21.9	16.5	17.7	8.1	6.6	6.3	1,848	39.5	22.9	17.8	10.7	7.1	2.0
1967	5,020	27.6	21.7	17.8	17.0	6.6	5.3	4.2	1,796	43.6	21.4	17.4	11.2	4.2	2.0
1966	4,954	30.2	23.3	17.8	16.5	5.9	4.0	2.4	1,585	70.8		17.4	7.7	3.2	.9
1965	4,782	35.3	25.6	16.3	13.7	4.4	3.3	1.4	1,655	47.6	22.0	16.7	9.9	3.2	.6
1964	4,754	37.3	25.9	16.4	12.1	4.1	2.4	1.8	1,641	52.2	20.8	15.1	8.3	3.1	.4
1963	4,773	43.1	24.4	16.0	10.8	2.5	1.6	1.6	1,457	56.2	22.3	13.9	5.3	2.2	.2
1962	4,561	44.8	26.5	15.4	8.1	2.7	1.6	.8	1,519	58.6	22.5	11.3	4.9	2.0	.9
1961	4,453	47.5	24.4	13.8	9.0	2.7	1.7	1.2	1,566	60.4	17.7	14.2	6.3	.8	.8

NA Not available.

Series G 1–15.　Percent Distribution of Families and Unrelated Individuals, by Race of Head, by Money Income Levels: 1947 to 1970—Con.

[Families and unrelated individuals as of March following year shown]

Race of head and year	Families								Unrelated individuals						
	Number (1,000)	Percent distribution by income level							Number (1,000)	Percent distribution by income level					
		Under $3,000	$3,000 to $4,999	$5,000 to $6,999	$7,000 to $9,999	$10,000 to $11,999	$12,000 to $14,999	$15,000 and over		Under $1,500	$1,500 to $2,999	$3,000 to $4,999	$5,000 to $6,999	$7,000 to $9,999	$10,000 and over
	1	2	3	4	5	6	7	8	9	10	11	12	13	14	15
NEGRO AND OTHER RACES— Con.															
1960	4,333	46.5	24.5	15.4	8.7	2.7	1.6	0.6	1,522	60.8	19.4	13.7	4.8	0.7	0.5
1959	4,239	51.4	25.8	12.3	8.1	1.3	.8	.3	1,573	60.1	23.6	12.2	2.8	1.2	–
1958	3,996	54.0	25.7	12.1	5.8	1.2	.7	.3	1,647	61.8	22.0	12.9	2.6	.6	.1
1957	4,020	53.3	25.8	13.3	6.2	.8	.4	–	1,495	61.5	22.2	14.5	1.3	.3	–
1956	3,999	56.4	26.3	11.6	4.7	.5	.3	.1	1,311	57.1	27.2	13.2	1.7	.7	–
1955	3,907	57.3	28.3	10.6	3.1	.3	.3		1,432	66.5	24.6	7.5	1.0	.3	
1954	3,766	60.2	27.8	8.1	3.0	.5	.3	.1	1,442	65.7	23.1	10.8			
1953	(NA)	60.2	25.7	8.8	4.6	.5	.3	–	(NA)	59.4	27.7	12.7	–	–	.5
1952	(NA)	66.7	23.8	7.1	1.9	.3	.2	.2	(NA)	66.8	25.4	4.8	2.6	–	.3
1951	(NA)	70.9	21.6	5.9	1.0	–	–	.3	(NA)	61.9	32.8	4.0	.6	.4	–
1950	(NA)	76.9	17.8	3.4	1.6		.3		(NA)	70.6	22.1	6.3	.9	–	–
1949	(NA)	81.6	13.8	3.8	.6		.2		(NA)	72.9	23.4	3.7	–	–	–
1948	3,279	78.1	16.3	4.1	1.0		.5		1,015	75.0	19.4	5.2	.4		–
1947	3,117	81.1	12.8	4.4	1.7		.1		974	79.0	17.4	2.9	.7		–

–　Represents zero.　　　　　　　　　　　　　　　　　NA　Not available.

Series G 16–30.　Percent Distribution of Families and Unrelated Individuals, by Race of Head, by Money Income Levels in Constant (1967) Dollars: 1947 to 1970

[Families and unrelated individuals as of March following year shown]

Race of head and year	Families								Unrelated individuals						
	Number (1,000)	Percent distribution by income level							Number (1,000)	Percent distribution by income level					
		Under $3,000	$3,000 to $4,999	$5,000 to $6,999	$7,000 to $9,999	$10,000 to $11,999	$12,000 to $14,999	$15,000 and over		Under $1,500	$1,500 to $2,999	$3,000 to $4,999	$5,000 to $6,999	$7,000 to $9,999	$10,000 and over
	16	17	18	19	20	21	22	23	24	25	26	27	28	29	30
TOTAL															
1970	51,948	11.4	12.5	14.4	23.3	12.5	8.2	18.0	15,357	28.6	25.2	17.7	12.8	9.6	6.1
1969	51,237	10.8	12.0	14.4	23.9	12.4	9.5	17.0	14,452	29.6	24.3	18.1	12.9	8.9	6.2
1968	50,510	11.1	12.7	15.4	23.9	12.2	10.7	14.0	13,803	30.2	23.5	18.7	12.0	9.5	6.1
1967	49,834	12.5	12.8	16.1	24.3	11.8	10.5	12.0	13,114	34.6	22.3	17.3	12.6	7.9	5.1
1966	49,065	13.4	13.2	16.8	24.4	11.9	9.9	10.2	12,271	(NA)	(NA)	(NA)	(NA)	(NA)	(NA)
1965	48,279	14.8	14.6	17.2	24.4	10.9	8.8	9.2	12,132	35.7	22.8	17.1	12.3	8.1	4.1
1964	47,835	15.8	15.8	17.8	23.6	10.6	8.3	8.2	12,057	38.8	21.6	16.7	11.8	7.5	3.4
1963	47,436	16.7	16.0	19.0	23.8	9.6	7.7	8.0	11,182	40.1	23.4	15.1	11.0	7.2	3.2
1962	46,998	17.6	16.7	19.9	23.2	8.8	7.0	7.3	11,013	40.6	23.5	15.4	11.1	6.2	3.3
1961	46,341	18.8	17.2	19.8	22.9	8.1	6.4	6.9	11,163	41.4	22.2	17.1	10.8	5.4	3.2
1960	45,456	18.9	17.2	21.1	22.9	7.9	6.2	6.6	11,081	42.4	20.8	18.5	11.5	5.0	1.9
1959	45,111	19.1	18.0	21.8	22.7	7.6	5.6	5.7	10,879	44.0	22.2	17.3	10.0	4.4	2.0
1958	44,232	20.4	19.5	23.3	21.8	6.2	4.9	5.1	10,884	45.0	21.2	18.2	9.3	3.9	2.4
1957	43,696	20.4	19.0	24.1	22.0	6.4	4.4	4.0	10,435	44.2	22.5	17.8	9.8	3.8	1.9
1956	43,497	20.0	19.2	23.3	22.3	6.4	4.4	3.6	9,779	45.3	22.5	17.9	9.6	3.4	1.3
1955	42,889	22.0	21.3	23.2	20.9	5.4	4.0	4.2	9,889	47.1	22.2	18.5	7.6	3.2	1.1
1954	41,951	24.5	23.3	22.7	18.6	4.6	3.6	3.2	9,724	49.6	21.1	19.1	6.5	2.7	1.1
1953	41,202	23.0	22.9	23.7	19.1	4.9	3.4	2.9	9,514	46.2	21.6	21.6	6.8	2.4	1.4
1952	40,832	24.5	27.0	22.6	17.0	4.0	2.4	2.8	9,705	44.8	24.2	21.1	6.5	2.5	1.1
1951	40,578	25.7	27.8	22.6	15.7	3.6	2.3	2.6	9,142	49.5	21.2	20.9	5.9	1.9	.6
1950	39,929	27.8	28.4	21.1	14.4	8.4		2.3	9,366	50.8	20.1	20.6	6.1	1.6	.9
1949	39,303	29.9	30.2	19.6	13.0	7.3			8,995	50.4	22.5	19.2	5.5	1.6	.7
1948	38,624	28.4	30.6	20.5	12.6	7.7			8,361	52.3	23.5	17.7	4.5	1.3	.7
1947	37,237	27.4	29.7	20.6	13.5	8.9			8,165	50.8	23.5	17.5	4.8	1.7	1.7

NA　Not available.

Series G 16–30. Percent Distribution of Families and Unrelated Individuals, by Race of Head, by Money Income Levels in Constant (1967) Dollars: 1947 to 1970—Con.

[Families and unrelated individuals as of March following year shown]

Race of head and year	Families								Unrelated individuals						
	Number (1,000)	Percent distribution by income level							Number (1,000)	Percent distribution by income level					
		Under $3,000	$3,000 to $4,999	$5,000 to $6,999	$7,000 to $9,999	$10,000 to $11,999	$12,000 to $14,999	$15,000 and over		Under $1,500	$1,500 to $2,999	$3,000 to $4,999	$5,000 to $6,999	$7,000 to $9,999	$10,000 and over
	16	17	18	19	20	21	22	23	24	25	26	27	28	29	30
WHITE															
1970	46,535	9.7	11.7	14.1	23.8	13.1	8.5	19.1	13,413	26.9	25.3	17.8	13.2	10.1	6.8
1969	46,022	9.4	11.0	14.0	24.4	13.0	9.9	18.1	12,473	27.8	24.4	18.2	13.2	9.5	6.8
1968	45,437	9.6	11.7	15.3	24.7	12.8	11.2	14.9	11,955	28.6	23.6	18.9	12.3	10.1	6.7
1967	44,814	10.7	11.9	16.0	25.1	12.4	11.2	12.8	11,318	33.2	22.5	17.3	12.8	8.5	5.7
1966	44,110	11.7	12.2	16.7	25.2	12.5	10.5	11.1	10,686	(NA)	(NA)	(NA)	(NA)	(NA)	(NA)
1965	43,497	12.8	13.5	17.3	25.5	11.5	9.3	9.9	10,477	34.2	22.8	17.1	12.6	8.6	4.6
1964	43,081	13.7	14.7	18.0	24.7	11.2	8.9	8.6	10,416	37.2	21.6	17.0	12.3	8.0	4.0
1963	42,663	14.3	15.1	19.3	24.8	10.3	8.3	8.0	9,725	38.2	23.5	15.3	11.6	7.7	3.7
1962	42,437	15.3	15.8	20.3	24.5	9.4	7.4	7.5	9,494	38.4	23.3	15.9	11.9	6.8	3.6
1961	41,888	16.2	16.5	20.4	24.3	8.6	6.8	7.3	9,597	39.1	22.7	17.5	11.4	5.9	3.4
1960	41,123	16.4	16.5	21.7	24.1	8.5	6.5	6.2	9,559	40.1	21.0	19.1	12.1	5.6	2.1
1959	40,872	16.4	17.4	22.4	24.0	8.1	6.0	5.5	9,306	42.1	22.1	17.7	11.0	4.8	2.5
1958	40,236	17.6	19.1	24.2	23.1	6.6	5.3	4.3	9,237	43.2	21.0	18.5	10.3	4.3	2.6
1957	39,676	17.6	18.6	24.9	23.3	6.7	4.8	3.9	8,940	42.2	22.3	18.0	10.9	4.4	2.1
1956	39,498	17.3	18.7	24.1	23.7	6.9	4.9	4.6	8,468	44.3	22.2	18.1	10.4	3.8	1.4
1955	38,982	19.4	20.7	24.0	22.1	5.9	4.3	3.5	8,457	45.2	21.8	19.6	8.4	3.6	1.5
1954	38,185	21.8	22.6	23.7	19.8	5.0	3.8	3.2	8,282	47.6	20.8	19.9	7.2	3.1	1.2
1953	(NA)	20.5	22.5	24.8	20.3	5.2	3.7	3.1	(NA)	45.1	20.8	21.8	7.9	3.0	1.7
1952	(NA)	21.3	26.3	24.2	18.5	4.3	2.7	2.8	(NA)	43.0	23.3	22.6	7.1	2.7	1.3
1951	(NA)	22.6	28.0	23.7	16.8	3.9	2.5	2.5	(NA)	48.5	19.8	22.3	6.7	2.3	.6
1950	(NA)	25.0	28.4	22.4	15.3	9.0			(NA)	49.4	19.7	21.5	6.7	1.7	1.1
1949	(NA)	26.9	30.6	20.7	13.8	7.9			(NA)	48.6	22.0	20.5	6.3	1.8	.8
1948	35,345	25.4	31.2	21.6	13.5	8.3			7,346	50.7	23.4	18.8	4.9	1.4	.8
1947	34,120	24.1	30.3	21.8	14.3	9.5			7,191	49.3	22.9	19.0	5.2	1.9	1.9
NEGRO AND OTHER RACES															
1970	5,413	25.0	19.5	16.8	17.9	7.6	4.5	8.5	1,944	40.6	24.0	17.0	10.6	6.4	1.5
1969	5,215	23.6	20.4	17.8	19.0	7.0	4.9	7.2	1,979	40.9	23.0	17.8	11.3	5.1	2.2
1968	5,074	24.5	22.1	16.6	17.7	7.6	5.5	6.0	1,848	40.8	23.3	17.5	10.5	6.1	1.6
1967	5,020	27.2	21.5	17.7	16.9	6.5	5.2	5.0	1,796	43.6	21.4	17.4	11.2	4.2	2.0
1966	4,954	29.0	23.1	17.5	16.8	6.3	4.4	2.7	1,585	(NA)	(NA)	(NA)	(NA)	(NA)	(NA)
1965	4,782	33.0	25.0	16.6	14.6	4.9	3.8	2.0	1,655	44.8	23.3	16.3	10.6	4.4	.8
1964	4,754	34.3	25.1	16.5	13.7	4.9	3.2	2.4	1,641	48.8	22.4	14.9	8.6	4.4	.8
1963	4,773	39.2	24.1	16.1	13.6	2.9	2.1	2.0	1,457	52.3	23.0	14.4	6.9	3.1	.3
1962	4,561	40.0	26.7	15.7	10.6	3.2	2.4	1.4	1,519	53.7	25.0	12.4	5.4	2.4	1.2
1961	4,453	42.8	23.3	15.0	11.0	3.3	2.5	1.8	1,566	55.6	20.1	14.5	6.6	2.1	.9
1960	4,333	42.0	23.1	15.9	11.9	3.1	2.6	1.4	1,522	56.6	19.8	14.0	7.3	1.7	.7
1959	4,239	45.4	23.7	15.8	10.2	2.7	1.3	.7	1,573	55.6	23.6	14.5	3.9	2.0	.3
1958	3,996	48.3	24.1	15.1	8.4	2.0	1.3	.8	1,647	56.2	22.1	16.5	3.7	1.2	.3
1957	4,020	46.7	24.0	16.4	9.3	2.4	.9	.4	1,495	55.9	22.9	16.3	3.9	.7	.2
1956	3,999	46.5	25.7	15.6	8.9	2.0	.8	.5	1,311	52.2	25.1	16.5	4.8	.9	.4
1955	3,907	47.5	27.3	14.6	8.6	1.3	.5	.3	1,432	58.6	25.0	12.7	3.1	.5	.2
1954	3,766	50.1	28.5	12.5	6.7	1.3	.7	.4	1,442	60.8	22.5	14.3	2.0	–	.5
1953	(NA)	48.6	27.2	13.8	7.6	1.9	.8	.3	(NA)	51.2	25.6	20.8	2.1	–	.3
1952	(NA)	51.1	33.3	8.5	5.5	.8	.4	.4	(NA)	55.3	28.8	11.8	2.7	1.3	.2
1951	(NA)	57.0	26.4	11.0	4.6	.5	.2	.3	(NA)	55.9	29.4	13.1	.8	.6	.4
1950	(NA)	57.7	29.1	8.0	3.5	1.8			(NA)	60.1	22.1	14.2	2.7	.9	–
1949	(NA)	63.0	24.6	7.7	3.9	.9			(NA)	61.3	25.9	11.9	.8	–	.2
1948	3,279	60.5	25.6	8.5	4.0	1.5			1,015	63.2	23.9	10.5	2.1	.2	.2
1947	3,117	62.4	22.3	7.9	5.1	2.2			974	61.6	27.9	7.3	2.5	.8	–

– Represents zero.   NA Not available.

Series G 31–138. Distribution of Money Income of Families and Unrelated Individuals Ranked by Fifths According to Income Received, by Race of Head: 1947 to 1970

Series No.	Income rank	1970	1969	1968	1967	1966	1965	1964	1963	1962	1961	1960	1959	1955	1950	1947
		PERCENT DISTRIBUTION OF AGGREGATE INCOME														
	FAMILIES AND UNRELATED INDIVIDUALS															
	All races:															
31	Lowest fifth	3.6	3.7	3.8	3.6	3.8	3.6	3.4	3.4	3.4	3.1	3.2	3.2	3.3	3.1	3.5
32	Second fifth	10.3	10.5	10.7	10.6	10.7	10.6	10.4	10.4	10.4	10.2	10.6	10.6	10.5	10.5	10.6
33	Third fifth	17.2	17.4	17.4	17.5	17.5	17.5	17.3	17.5	17.5	17.2	17.6	17.7	17.4	17.3	16.7
34	Fourth fifth	24.7	24.7	24.7	24.8	24.7	24.8	24.8	24.8	24.8	24.6	24.7	24.7	24.5	24.1	23.6
35	Highest fifth	44.1	43.7	43.5	43.4	43.4	43.6	44.1	43.9	43.9	44.9	44.0	43.9	44.3	45.0	45.6
36	Top 5 percent	16.9	16.8	16.8	16.5	16.7	16.6	17.2	16.9	16.8	17.7	17.0	17.1	18.0	18.2	18.7
	White:															
37	Lowest fifth	3.8	3.9	4.0	3.8	4.0	3.8	3.6	3.6	3.7	3.4	3.4	3.5	3.5	3.3	3.7
38	Second fifth	10.7	10.9	11.1	11.1	11.1	11.1	10.9	11.0	11.0	10.8	11.1	11.2	11.1	11.0	11.1
39	Third fifth	17.4	17.6	17.6	17.7	17.6	17.7	17.5	17.6	17.7	17.4	17.8	17.8	17.5	17.4	16.9
40	Fourth fifth	24.5	24.5	24.5	24.6	24.6	24.6	24.6	24.6	24.6	24.4	24.5	24.4	24.2	23.9	23.3
41	Highest fifth	43.6	43.1	42.9	42.8	42.8	42.9	43.4	43.1	43.1	44.1	43.2	43.1	43.6	44.4	45.0
42	Top 5 percent	16.8	16.7	16.7	16.3	16.6	16.4	17.0	16.6	16.5	17.5	16.7	16.8	17.8	18.1	18.6
	Negro and other races:															
43	Lowest fifth	3.3	3.4	3.5	3.4	3.5	3.5	3.2	3.3	3.3	2.8	2.7	2.9	3.1	2.7	3.3
44	Second fifth	8.9	9.2	9.2	9.2	9.4	9.4	9.1	9.2	8.8	8.4	8.2	8.6	8.8	8.8	9.4
45	Third fifth	15.9	16.1	15.8	16.0	16.1	16.3	15.7	15.6	15.8	15.3	15.7	15.5	16.4	16.7	15.7
46	Fourth fifth	25.1	25.0	25.0	25.0	25.3	25.0	24.7	25.0	25.1	25.0	25.5	25.5	26.1	25.9	23.8
47	Highest fifth	46.8	46.3	46.5	46.4	45.7	45.9	47.3	46.9	47.0	48.6	47.9	47.5	45.6	45.8	47.8
48	Top 5 percent	17.1	16.8	16.9	17.0	16.1	16.5	18.1	17.7	17.5	18.5	17.8	17.1	15.8	17.4	18.4
		AVERAGE (MEAN) MONEY INCOME														
	All races:															
49	Total	$9,612	$9,184	$8,452	$7,702	$7,386	$6,795	$6,478	$6,200	$5,921	$5,719	$5,522	$5,306	$4,467	$3,422	$3,215
50	Lowest fifth	1,745	1,694	1,606	1,398	1,403	1,216	1,111	1,063	1,018	889	870	854	737	530	563
51	Second fifth	4,969	4,831	4,505	4,090	3,933	3,584	3,356	3,227	3,082	2,911	2,921	2,799	2,345	1,797	1,704
52	Third fifth	8,286	7,976	7,353	6,755	6,452	5,946	5,603	5,413	5,172	4,924	4,857	4,688	3,886	2,960	2,685
53	Fourth fifth	11,861	11,351	10,421	9,550	9,114	8,433	8,029	7,697	7,336	7,037	6,825	6,553	5,472	4,124	3,794
54	Highest fifth	21,199	20,067	18,375	16,721	16,031	14,796	14,290	13,600	12,997	12,833	12,137	11,639	9,894	7,700	7,330
55	Top 5 percent	32,565	30,895	28,466	25,370	24,714	22,573	22,310	20,906	19,847	20,291	18,786	18,125	16,081	12,456	12,024
	White:															
56	Total	9,986	9,563	8,787	8,018	7,710	7,106	6,771	6,499	6,217	5,996	5,776	5,571	4,694	3,582	3,369
57	Lowest fifth	1,897	1,846	1,753	1,523	1,538	1,336	1,229	1,176	1,141	1,007	991	983	821	591	623
58	Second fifth	5,352	5,226	4,864	4,438	4,283	3,926	3,680	3,584	3,429	3,223	3,214	3,114	2,605	1,970	1,870
59	Third fifth	8,683	8,392	7,719	7,096	6,793	6,289	5,935	5,729	5,490	5,226	5,129	4,964	4,107	3,116	2,847
60	Fourth fifth	12,243	11,724	10,747	9,874	9,425	8,740	8,332	8,007	7,638	7,306	7,061	6,797	5,680	4,280	3,925
61	Highest fifth	21,755	20,623	18,853	17,159	16,507	15,239	14,683	13,999	13,388	13,218	12,482	11,997	10,233	7,952	7,580
62	Top 5 percent	33,513	31,864	29,349	26,091	25,536	23,279	22,954	21,538	20,466	20,962	19,338	18,730	16,711	12,967	12,533
	Negro and other races:															
63	Total	6,568	6,104	5,678	5,099	4,676	4,186	4,050	3,702	3,404	3,369	3,353	2,977	2,486	1,878	1,772
64	Lowest fifth	1,074	1,038	988	869	821	735	656	609	557	475	453	436	385	254	292
65	Second fifth	2,919	2,808	2,615	2,348	2,200	1,965	1,833	1,699	1,505	1,407	1,380	1,277	1,094	826	833
66	Third fifth	5,235	4,917	4,491	4,079	3,767	3,401	3,181	2,895	2,689	2,572	2,632	2,303	2,039	1,568	1,391
67	Fourth fifth	8,249	7,639	7,095	6,361	5,917	5,224	4,996	4,626	4,265	4,206	4,268	3,800	3,244	2,432	2,109
68	Highest fifth	15,363	14,119	13,199	11,835	10,675	9,605	9,586	8,683	8,003	8,183	8,032	7,069	5,668	4,301	4,235
69	Top 5 percent	22,502	20,509	19,192	17,347	15,085	13,814	14,669	13,120	11,914	12,459	11,910	10,163	7,856	6,535	6,521
		LOWER INCOME LIMIT														
	All races:															
70	Second fifth	$3,300	$3,200	$3,020	$2,700	$2,600	$2,360	$2,200	$2,075	$2,000	$1,900	$1,900	$1,820	$1,475	$1,114	$1,138
71	Third fifth	6,642	6,433	6,000	5,460	5,200	4,850	4,500	4,400	4,160	4,000	3,979	3,800	3,179	2,409	2,211
72	Fourth fifth	10,000	9,542	8,775	8,000	7,640	7,080	6,710	6,487	6,100	5,929	5,750	5,500	4,598	3,460	3,189
73	Highest fifth	14,212	13,500	12,388	11,393	10,815	10,000	9,609	9,140	8,800	8,437	8,100	7,800	6,498	4,939	4,568
74	Top 5 percent	22,700	21,260	19,410	17,965	17,000	15,910	15,040	14,475	14,000	13,638	12,850	12,130	10,141	8,103	7,775
	White:															
75	Second fifth	3,600	3,530	3,306	3,000	2,900	2,603	2,455	2,327	2,250	2,100	2,105	2,079	1,690	1,264	1,282
76	Third fifth	7,056	6,918	6,350	5,900	5,600	5,132	4,907	4,800	4,543	4,300	4,218	4,100	3,412	2,588	2,364
77	Fourth fifth	10,260	10,000	9,075	8,316	8,000	7,412	7,000	6,790	6,467	6,112	6,000	5,800	4,822	3,616	3,320
78	Highest fifth	14,650	13,950	12,700	11,751	11,100	10,254	10,000	9,500	9,100	8,706	8,400	8,014	6,704	5,118	4,736
79	Top 5 percent	23,210	21,900	19,892	18,295	17,450	16,190	15,406	14,916	14,356	14,137	13,124	12,500	10,461	8,382	7,967
	Negro and other races:															
80	Second fifth	1,947	1,828	1,765	1,564	1,487	1,320	1,200	1,164	1,024	960	872	852	737	519	575
81	Third fifth	4,000	3,804	3,500	3,064	3,000	2,650	2,470	2,259	2,010	1,966	1,980	1,720	1,499	1,163	1,100
82	Fourth fifth	6,508	6,100	5,600	5,045	4,700	4,155	4,000	3,611	3,378	3,268	3,400	3,000	2,597	1,995	1,703
83	Highest fifth	10,200	9,500	8,900	8,000	7,403	6,500	6,200	5,816	5,290	5,232	5,265	4,720	3,983	2,495	2,660
84	Top 5 percent	17,100	15,798	14,767	13,195	11,950	10,933	10,600	9,295	9,000	9,400	9,163	8,000	6,386	4,683	4,969

Series G 31–138. Distribution of Money Income of Families and Unrelated Individuals Ranked by Fifths According to Income Received, by Race of Head: 1947 to 1970—Con.

Series No.	Income rank	1970	1969	1968	1967	1966	1965	1964	1963	1962	1961	1960	1959	1955	1950	1947
							PERCENT DISTRIBUTION OF AGGREGATE INCOME									
	FAMILIES															
	All races:															
85	Lowest fifth	5.4	5.6	5.6	5.5	5.6	5.2	5.1	5.0	5.0	4.7	4.8	4.9	4.8	4.5	5.0
86	Second fifth	12.2	12.4	12.4	12.4	12.4	12.2	12.0	12.1	12.1	11.9	12.2	12.3	12.2	11.9	11.8
87	Third fifth	17.6	17.7	17.7	17.9	17.8	17.8	17.7	17.7	17.6	17.5	17.8	17.9	17.7	17.4	17.0
88	Fourth fifth	23.8	23.7	23.7	23.9	23.8	23.9	24.0	24.0	24.0	23.8	24.0	23.8	23.4	23.4	23.1
89	Highest fifth	40.9	40.6	40.5	40.4	40.5	40.9	41.2	41.2	41.3	42.2	41.3	41.1	41.8	42.8	43.2
90	Top 5 percent	15.6	15.6	15.6	15.2	15.6	15.5	15.9	15.8	15.7	16.6	15.9	15.9	16.8	17.3	17.5
	White:															
91	Lowest fifth	5.8	5.9	6.0	5.8	5.9	5.6	5.5	5.4	5.4	5.0	5.2	5.4	5.1	4.8	5.4
92	Second fifth	12.5	12.7	12.7	12.8	12.8	12.6	12.4	12.5	12.6	12.3	12.7	12.7	12.6	12.3	12.2
93	Third fifth	17.7	17.8	17.8	17.9	17.8	17.8	17.8	17.7	17.7	17.5	17.8	17.8	17.9	17.4	17.0
94	Fourth fifth	23.6	23.5	23.5	23.7	23.5	23.7	23.8	23.8	23.8	23.6	23.7	23.6	23.3	23.2	22.8
95	Highest fifth	40.5	40.1	40.1	39.9	40.1	40.3	40.5	40.6	40.6	41.6	40.7	40.5	41.1	42.3	42.6
96	Top 5 percent	15.5	15.4	15.5	15.1	15.4	15.4	15.7	15.6	15.4	16.4	15.7	15.7	16.7	17.2	17.4
	Negro and other races:															
97	Lowest fifth	4.5	4.8	4.8	4.8	4.9	4.7	4.4	4.5	4.2	4.0	3.7	4.0	4.0	3.5	4.3
98	Second fifth	10.6	10.9	10.7	10.6	10.9	10.8	10.5	10.4	10.6	9.9	9.7	9.7	10.3	10.2	10.3
99	Third fifth	16.8	16.9	16.6	16.8	16.9	16.6	16.2	16.3	16.8	16.1	16.5	16.6	17.8	16.0	16.0
100	Fourth fifth	24.8	24.7	24.8	24.6	25.0	24.7	24.2	24.6	24.5	24.5	25.2	25.3	25.5	25.2	23.8
101	Highest fifth	43.4	42.7	43.2	43.2	42.3	43.2	44.7	44.3	43.9	45.6	44.9	44.4	42.4	43.6	45.6
102	Top 5 percent	15.4	15.2	15.4	15.5	14.6	15.1	16.9	16.5	15.8	16.9	16.2	15.6	14.3	16.6	17.2
							AVERAGE (MEAN) MONEY INCOME									
	All races:															
103	Total	$11,106	$10,577	$9,670	$8,801	$8,395	$7,704	$7,336	$6,998	$6,670	$6,471	$6,227	$5,976	$5,010	$3,832	$3,566
104	Lowest fifth	3,021	2,951	2,722	2,411	2,330	2,011	1,882	1,763	1,674	1,505	1,479	1,473	1,202	862	892
105	Second fifth	6,775	6,552	6,000	5,461	5,205	4,699	4,409	4,230	4,042	3,844	3,798	3,663	3,056	2,280	2,104
106	Third fifth	9,795	9,377	8,572	7,855	7,451	6,860	6,489	6,176	5,880	5,659	5,536	5,334	4,434	3,334	3,031
107	Fourth fifth	13,216	12,550	11,464	10,504	9,973	9,214	8,807	8,391	7,997	7,707	7,457	7,117	5,862	4,483	4,119
108	Highest fifth	22,723	21,461	19,587	17,769	17,017	15,739	15,094	14,426	13,757	13,644	12,868	12,293	10,471	8,200	7,703
109	Top 5 percent	34,584	32,894	30,190	26,773	26,125	23,929	23,372	22,156	20,917	21,497	19,789	19,040	16,834	13,259	12,481
	White:															
110	Total	11,495	10,953	10,002	9,116	8,726	8,021	7,625	7,306	6,962	6,741	6,483	6,235	5,228	3,991	3,717
111	Lowest fifth	3,311	3,220	2,986	2,653	2,570	2,230	2,082	1,987	1,883	1,699	1,686	1,690	1,333	958	1,004
112	Second fifth	7,196	6,955	6,361	5,821	5,567	5,061	4,743	4,577	4,369	4,152	4,100	3,962	3,294	2,454	2,267
113	Third fifth	10,150	9,721	8,877	8,141	7,749	7,155	6,775	6,477	6,165	5,912	5,757	5,559	4,679	3,472	3,159
114	Fourth fifth	13,558	12,892	11,747	10,784	10,262	9,497	9,066	8,676	8,274	7,938	7,682	7,342	6,091	4,483	4,237
115	Highest fifth	23,266	21,977	20,039	18,182	17,478	16,162	15,456	14,813	14,119	14,004	13,190	12,620	10,744	8,441	7,917
116	Top 5 percent	35,520	33,823	31,046	27,439	26,928	24,641	23,958	22,809	21,499	22,124	20,370	19,628	17,462	13,729	12,935
	Negro and other races:															
117	Total	7,759	7,255	6,689	5,985	5,450	4,827	4,726	4,259	3,948	3,937	3,873	3,463	2,890	2,128	2,015
118	Lowest fifth	1,754	1,748	1,599	1,439	1,346	1,127	1,042	950	835	780	711	691	578	372	433
119	Second fifth	4,093	3,939	3,569	3,160	2,959	2,602	2,488	2,215	2,085	1,943	1,882	1,676	1,488	1,085	1,038
120	Third fifth	6,498	6,138	5,549	5,024	4,611	4,014	3,816	3,463	3,306	3,167	3,201	2,867	2,572	1,873	1,612
121	Fourth fifth	9,621	8,971	8,281	7,371	6,807	5,959	5,723	5,239	4,842	4,819	4,876	4,384	3,685	2,681	2,398
122	Highest fifth	16,829	15,482	14,448	12,934	11,527	10,434	10,560	9,432	8,670	8,974	8,695	7,695	6,127	4,639	4,594
123	Top 5 percent	23,913	22,012	20,602	18,530	15,925	14,597	15,955	14,055	12,484	13,276	12,533	10,825	8,265	7,065	6,932
							LOWER INCOME LIMIT									
	All races:															
124	Second fifth	$5,100	$5,000	$4,544	$4,097	$3,935	$3,500	$3,250	$3,096	$3,000	$2,800	$2,784	$2,677	$2,221	$1,661	$1,584
125	Third fifth	8,320	8,000	7,300	6,700	6,398	5,863	5,500	5,200	5,000	4,820	4,800	4,565	3,780	2,856	2,566
126	Fourth fifth	11,299	10,800	9,960	9,000	8,563	7,950	7,500	7,134	6,800	6,560	6,364	6,081	5,105	3,822	3,472
127	Highest fifth	15,531	14,751	13,400	12,270	11,640	10,800	10,201	9,969	9,500	9,035	8,800	8,380	6,909	5,355	4,929
128	Top 5 percent	24,250	22,703	20,590	19,025	18,000	16,695	15,788	15,144	14,900	14,600	13,536	12,800	10,679	8,666	8,141
	White:															
129	Second fifth	5,500	5,360	5,000	4,500	4,270	3,870	3,586	3,480	3,300	3,086	3,025	3,000	2,464	1,836	1,757
130	Third fifth	8,727	8,375	7,640	7,000	6,700	6,100	5,802	5,502	5,281	5,041	5,000	4,872	4,005	3,025	2,714
131	Fourth fifth	11,691	11,090	10,097	9,301	8,924	8,123	7,800	7,481	7,040	6,862	6,585	6,300	5,307	3,961	3,603
132	Highest fifth	15,929	15,021	13,700	12,528	12,000	11,013	10,500	10,093	9,800	9,292	9,000	8,600	7,104	5,502	5,071
133	Top 5 percent	24,941	23,298	21,000	19,500	18,514	17,067	16,056	15,525	15,159	15,000	13,964	13,050	10,917	8,877	8,384
	Negro and other races:															
134	Second fifth	2,972	2,959	2,705	2,340	2,175	1,927	1,857	1,674	1,476	1,421	1,310	1,207	1,043	723	759
135	Third fifth	5,246	5,000	4,490	4,011	3,750	3,300	3,100	2,787	2,474	2,502	2,180	2,013	1,479	1,320
136	Fourth fifth	7,900	7,356	6,800	6,000	5,520	4,900	4,630	4,200	4,000	3,952	3,900	3,567	3,129	2,254	1,927
137	Highest fifth	11,700	10,920	10,089	9,000	8,120	7,300	7,000	6,400	5,942	6,000	6,000	5,300	4,423	3,178	2,940
138	Top 5 percent	18,521	17,238	15,800	14,076	12,510	11,800	11,400	10,376	10,000	10,268	9,892	8,722	6,735	5,200	5,393

Series G 139–178. Percent Distribution of Families Ranked by Fifths According to Money Income Received, by Selected Family Characteristics: 1950, 1960, and 1970

Series No.	Selected characteristics	Total			Family income								
					Lowest fifth			Second fifth			Third fifth		
		1970	1960	1950	1970	1960	1950	1970	1960	1950	1970	1960	1950
139	Number_____1,000__	51,948	45,456	39,929	10,390	9,091	7,986	10,390	9,091	7,986	10,390	9,091	7,986
							PERCENT DISTRIBUTION						
	Residence:												
140	Nonfarm_____	95.5	91.9	85.4	91.6	80.2	68.2	94.5	90.2	82.8	96.4	95.5	89.4
141	Farm [1]_____	4.5	8.1	14.6	8.4	19.8	31.7	5.5	9.8	17.3	3.6	4.5	10.6
	Region: [2]												
142	Northeast_____	23.8	25.3	30.4	19.2	16.7	15.4	22.0	24.5	26.4	24.5	28.0	30.3
143	North Central_____	28.0	27.8	33.7	24.8	26.2	24.6	26.5	26.3	26.9	29.1	28.7	30.3
144	South_____	30.8	29.7	19.7	40.1	46.2	48.8	35.1	35.0	33.2	28.9	26.1	26.0
145	West_____	17.3	17.2	16.2	15.9	10.9	11.2	16.4	14.2	13.5	17.5	17.2	13.4
	Race of head:												
146	White_____	89.6	90.5	91.6	79.9	78.6	81.2	87.3	87.6	87.7	91.9	93.2	93.7
147	Negro and other races_____	10.4	9.5	8.4	20.1	21.4	18.8	12.7	12.4	12.3	8.1	6.8	6.3
	Type of family:												
148	Male head_____	88.5	90.0	90.1	71.1	76.2	77.6	86.2	88.2	88.6	92.7	93.6	93.6
149	Married, wife present_____	86.1	87.4	87.1	68.1	72.7	74.0	83.7	85.4	85.6	90.4	91.2	90.7
150	Wife in paid labor force___	33.8	26.3	19.8	12.5	13.0	11.4	26.1	21.2	15.8	36.1	25.1	18.6
151	Wife not in paid labor force_____	52.3	61.1	67.3	55.6	59.7	62.6	57.5	64.2	69.8	54.4	66.1	72.1
152	Other marital status_____	2.4	2.6	3.0	3.0	3.5	3.6	2.5	2.8	3.0	2.3	2.4	2.9
153	Female head_____	11.4	10.1	10.0	28.9	23.8	22.5	13.8	11.9	11.3	7.4	6.5	6.4
	Age of head:												
154	25–44 years_____	41.4	44.7	46.8	27.2	27.9	32.6	41.1	43.4	47.3	48.1	54.1	55.8
155	45–64 years_____	37.6	36.8	36.4	26.2	32.7	34.1	32.8	32.9	42.8	48.1	54.1	55.8
156	65 years and over__	13.8	13.0	11.9	35.1	31.4	27.2	15.1	14.7	33.5	36.0	33.4	31.9
157	Median age of head_	45.7	44.9	44.3	54.3	53.8	51.7	43.8	43.8	11.7	7.7	6.8	7.2
	Size of family:												
158	2 persons_____	35.2	32.3	32.8	56.1	52.2	48.4	38.8	35.0	35.0	30.5	26.4	29.8
159	3 persons_____	20.6	20.7	24.9	18.1	16.7	20.6	22.0	21.6	25.4	21.4	21.7	26.1
160	4 persons_____	19.1	20.8	20.8	10.9	12.1	12.7	17.3	18.8	19.1	21.4	23.4	23.1
161	5 persons_____	12.6	13.2	11.4	6.6	7.4	8.1	10.4	11.2	10.3	13.8	14.5	11.5
162	6 persons or more__	12.5	13.1	10.2	8.4	11.5	10.2	11.6	13.4	10.2	12.9	14.0	9.5
163	Mean size of family_	3.60	3.73	3.54	3.03	3.31	3.26	3.47	3.67	3.48	3.71	3.86	3.57
	Number of related children under 18 years:												
164	No children_____	42.3	39.4	41.8	54.2	52.5	49.9	42.2	39.5	40.5	36.9	31.7	36.9
165	1 child_____	19.3	19.5	23.4	16.9	15.8	19.5	20.4	20.3	23.7	19.9	21.0	24.2
166	2 children_____	17.8	18.8	18.4	12.2	12.0	13.6	17.6	17.9	17.8	20.3	22.1	20.8
167	3 children_____	10.7	11.6	9.1	7.7	8.5	7.7	9.6	10.1	9.5	11.9	13.3	10.7
168	4 children or more__	9.9	10.7	7.3	9.0	11.3	9.4	10.3	12.3	8.4	11.0	11.9	7.3
169	Mean number of children_____	1.34	1.47	1.23	1.09	1.29	1.17	1.33	1.50	1.29	1.48	1.63	1.33
	Number of earners:												
170	No earners_____	9.0	6.9	6.4	34.8	27.7	24.0	6.7	4.9	4.8	1.8	.8	1.2
171	1 earner_____	37.1	46.6	54.5	43.4	46.4	52.5	49.8	57.3	65.3	40.7	54.2	65.0
172	2 earners_____	39.4	35.8	30.4	18.9	20.7	19.5	36.7	31.9	25.1	46.6	37.4	28.6
173	3 earners or more__	14.6	10.7	8.7	2.9	5.2	3.9	6.7	5.9	4.7	11.3	7.5	5.1
174	Mean number of earners_____	1.68	1.57	1.47	.92	1.07	1.05	1.48	1.42	1.32	1.74	1.56	1.41
	Occupation of employed head:												
175	Professional workers, managers, and proprietors__	30.9	26.8	20.4	15.1	13.1	11.1	19.8	15.6	14.8	26.6	19.8	14.8
176	Sales and clerical workers_____	13.8	13.5	11.4	12.0	7.0	4.4	14.1	12.6	12.6	14.8	17.0	12.6
177	Craftsmen and operatives_____	37.5	38.7	42.1	34.1	22.9	24.3	46.4	41.2	51.6	45.1	47.7	51.5
178	Other_____	17.7	21.0	26.1	38.8	56.8	60.5	19.6	30.7	20.7	13.4	15.5	21.1

See footnotes at end of table.

Series **G 139–178.**   Percent Distribution of Families Ranked by Fifths According to Money Income Received, by Selected Family Characteristics: 1950, 1960, and 1970—Con.

Series No.	Selected characteristics	Family income—Con.								
		Fourth fifth			Highest fifth			Top 5 percent		
		1970	1960	1950	1970	1960	1950	1970	1960	1950
139	Number_____1,000__	10,390	9,091	7,986	10,390	9,091	7,986	2,597	2,273	1,996
		PERCENT DISTRIBUTION								
	Residence:									
140	Nornfarm_____	97.3	96.3	93.2	97.6	97.2	93.4	98.0	97.4	91.5
141	Farm [1]_____	2.7	3.7	6.8	2.4	2.8	6.6	2.0	2.5	8.7
	Region: [2]									
142	Northeast_____	25.9	27.4	29.6	27.5	29.8	29.7	29.0	30.4	28.2
143	North Central_____	30.3	30.7	32.9	29.4	27.2	34.9	27.2	24.0	34.7
144	South_____	25.7	22.5	22.7	24.3	18.5	18.5	24.7	19.0	18.2
145	West_____	18.1	19.4	14.8	18.8	24.5	16.9	19.1	26.6	18.9
	Race of head:									
146	White_____	93.7	95.1	97.2	95.0	96.5	98.0	96.5	98.2	98.9
147	Negro and other races_____	6.3	4.9	2.8	5.0	3.5	2.0	3.5	1.8	1.1
	Type of family:									
148	Male head_____	95.5	95.2	95.4	97.3	96.7	95.1	98.2	98.0	96.7
149	Married, wife present_____	93.4	93.1	92.9	95.1	94.7	92.2	95.7	95.4	93.0
150	Wife in paid labor force___	45.1	33.1	25.4	49.3	39.2	27.6	41.4	28.0	16.1
151	Wife not in paid labor force_	48.3	60.0	67.5	45.8	55.5	64.6	54.3	67.4	76.9
152	Other marital status_____	2.1	2.1	2.5	2.2	2.0	2.9	2.6	2.6	3.7
153	Female head_____	4.4	4.9	4.7	2.7	3.3	4.9	1.8	1.9	3.3
	Age of head:									
154	25–44 years_____	49.6	53.9	54.3	40.8	43.9	43.6	33.6	37.7	33.3
155	45–64 years_____	40.4	37.0	35.8	52.6	48.1	46.9	58.6	52.7	55.3
156	65 years and over_____	5.6	5.6	5.6	5.6	6.8	7.8	7.2	9.5	11.2
157	Median age of head_____	43.4	42.4	41.9	47.5	46.5	46.8	49.3	48.6	50.4
	Size of family:									
158	2 persons_____	26.7	24.1	26.0	23.9	23.7	24.6	25.0	23.2	24.1
159	3 persons_____	21.5	22.0	27.9	20.3	21.5	24.4	18.9	17.5	22.9
160	4 persons_____	22.9	24.8	23.9	22.9	24.7	24.9	23.0	24.8	25.8
161	5 persons_____	14.9	15.9	12.5	17.1	16.8	14.4	17.6	19.1	14.1
162	6 persons or more_____	14.1	13.3	9.6	15.8	13.2	11.7	15.6	15.4	13.2
163	Mean size of family_____	3.82	3.88	3.62	3.96	3.90	3.79	3.95	4.05	3.87
	Number of related children under 18 years:									
164	No children_____	36.9	33.3	37.3	41.1	40.3	44.5	44.0	44.2	48.3
165	1 child_____	19.8	20.4	25.7	19.3	19.8	24.1	19.3	14.8	22.3
166	2 children_____	20.4	22.2	21.0	18.7	19.7	18.5	17.5	18.7	17.7
167	3 children_____	12.5	13.8	9.5	11.9	12.5	8.0	11.0	13.5	7.7
168	4 children or more_____	10.3	10.2	6.5	9.0	7.7	4.8	8.3	8.9	4.0
169	Mean number of children___	1.46	1.58	1.26	1.34	1.34	1.08	1.25	1.34	.99
	Number of earners:									
170	No earners_____	1.0	.5	.7	.8	.7	1.1	.9	1.2	1.9
171	1 earner_____	29.2	42.2	50.8	22.3	32.1	39.0	28.4	41.9	51.1
172	2 earners_____	50.3	44.5	40.2	44.4	44.5	38.7	37.6	31.7	23.4
173	3 earners or more_____	19.5	12.7	8.3	32.5	22.8	21.2	33.1	25.3	23.6
174	Mean number of earners____	2.00	1.77	1.61	2.29	2.03	1.93	2.23	1.98	1.87
	Occupation of employed head:									
175	Professional workers, managers, and proprietors_____	38.7	27.4	22.0	54.6	50.5	38.6	76.0	72.3	61.4
176	Sales and clerical workers____	14.2	14.6	13.8	13.7	13.5	13.5	11.4	10.1	11.3
177	Craftsmen and operatives____	37.3	46.7	50.7	24.7	28.6	36.6	9.0	13.3	16.3
178	Other_____	10.0	11.4	13.6	6.9	7.5	11.5	3.9	4.4	11.0

[1] Data for 1950 may not be strictly comparable with those for 1960 and 1970.   [2] In 1950 column, data for 1953; 1950 regional data not available.

Series G 179–188. Number and Median Money Income of Families and Unrelated Individuals: 1947 to 1970

[Number of families and unrelated individuals as of March following year shown; income for calendar year shown]

Year	Families Total	Male head Total	Married, wife present Total	Wife in paid labor force	Wife not in paid labor force	Other marital status	Female head	Unrelated individuals Total	Male	Female
	179	180	181	182	183	184	185	186	187	188
NUMBER (1,000)										
1970	51,948	45,998	44,739	17,568	27,172	1,258	5,950	15,357	5,963	9,394
1969	51,237	45,657	44,436	17,464	26,972	1,221	5,580	14,452	5,441	9,011
1968	50,510	45,070	43,841	16,638	27,203	1,229	5,439	13,803	5,202	8,600
1967	49,834	44,501	43,292	15,845	27,447	1,210	5,333	13,114	4,845	8,269
1966	49,065	43,864	42,723	15,061	27,662	1,141	5,202	12,271	4,486	7,785
1965	48,279	43,287	42,108	14,183	27,925	1,179	4,992	12,132	4,475	7,657
1964	47,835	42,829	41,647	13,647	28,000	1,182	5,006	12,057	4,600	7,457
1963	47,436	42,554	41,311	13,398	27,913	1,243	4,882	11,182	4,275	6,907
1962	46,998	42,257	40,923	13,028	27,895	1,334	4,741	11,013	4,253	6,760
1961	46,341	41,698	40,405	12,366	28,039	1,293	4,643	11,163	4,388	6,775
1960	45,435	40,826	39,624	12,007	27,617	1,202	4,609	10,900	4,196	6,704
1959	45,062	40,568	39,335	11,265	28,070	1,233	4,494	10,702	4,217	6,485
1958	44,202	39,870	38,585	11,014	27,571	1,285	4,332	10,751	4,332	6,419
1957	43,714	39,404	38,112	10,696	27,416	1,292	4,310	10,313	4,161	6,152
1956	43,445	39,079	37,849	10,266	27,583	1,230	4,366	9,658	3,929	5,729
1955	42,843	38,604	37,200	9,786	27,414	1,404	4,239	9,766	4,071	5,695
1954	41,934	37,709	36,395	9,005	27,390	1,314	4,225	9,623	4,039	5,584
1953	41,202	(NA)	(NA)	(NA)	(NA)	(NA)	(NA)	9,514	(NA)	(NA)
1952	41,020	37,178	35,782	9,154	26,628	1,396	3,842	9,774	4,316	5,458
1951	40,442	36,412	35,196	8,044	27,152	1,216	4,030	9,015	3,945	5,070
1950	39,822	35,782	34,556	----	----	1,226	4,040	9,194	4,032	5,162
1949	39,193	35,556	34,291	----	----	1,265	3,637	8,835	4,072	4,763
1948	38,537	34,825	33,538	----	----	1,287	3,713	8,136	3,862	4,274
1947	37,279	33,522	32,288	----	----	1,234	3,757	8,056	3,720	4,337
MEDIAN MONEY INCOME (DOLLARS)										
1970	9,867	10,480	10,516	12,276	9,304	9,012	5,093	3,137	4,540	2,483
1969	9,433	9,965	10,001	11,629	8,879	8,340	4,822	2,931	4,134	2,397
1968	8,633	9,096	9,144	10,686	8,215	7,321	4,477	2,786	4,086	2,239
1967	7,933	8,358	8,398	9,917	7,570	6,804	4,269	2,379	3,514	1,917
1966	7,532	7,910	7,944	9,279	7,256	6,373	4,074	2,290	3,181	1,908
1965	6,957	7,310	7,330	8,633	6,706	6,515	3,535	2,153	3,194	1,767
1964	6,569	6,883	6,932	8,170	6,338	5,792	3,458	1,983	2,965	1,555
1963	6,249	6,561	6,593	7,789	6,039	5,710	3,211	1,800	2,424	1,476
1962	5,956	6,237	6,263	7,461	5,764	5,711	3,131	1,753	2,351	1,461
1961	5,737	6,019	6,037	7,188	5,592	5,069	2,993	1,755	2,638	1,407
1960	5,620	5,857	5,873	6,900	5,520	4,860	2,968	1,720	2,480	1,377
1959	5,417	5,628	5,662	6,705	5,317	4,613	2,764	1,556	2,118	1,318
1958	5,087	5,292	5,315	6,214	4,983	4,260	2,741	1,486	2,114	1,268
1957	4,971	5,158	5,157	6,141	4,833	4,581	2,763	1,496	2,102	1,264
1956	4,783	4,965	4,973	5,957	4,645	4,167	2,754	1,426	1,980	1,160
1955	4,421	4,592	4,599	5,622	4,326	4,190	2,471	1,316	1,831	1,054
1954	4,173	4,322	4,333	5,336	4,051	4,014	2,294	1,224	1,696	966
1953	4,233	4,371	4,371	5,405	4,117	4,113	2,455	1,394	2,177	972
1952	3,890	4,050	4,061	4,900	3,812	3,615	2,235	1,409	2,002	1,019
1951	3,709	3,829	3,837	4,631	3,634	3,452	2,220	1,195	1,909	917
1950	3,319	3,435	3,446	----	----	3,115	1,922	1,045	1,539	846
1949	3,107	3,187	3,195	----	----	2,821	2,103	1,050	1,437	856
1948	3,187	3,273	3,272	----	----	3,295	2,064	996	1,244	861
1947	3,031	3,104	3,109	----	----	2,936	2,172	980	1,349	792

NA   Not available.

Series G 189–204. Median Money Income of Families and Unrelated Individuals in Current and Constant (1967) Dollars, by Race of Head: 1947 to 1970

Year	Families and unrelated individuals	Median income (current dollars)						Median income (constant 1967 dollars)							Ratio: Negro and other races compared with white	
		Families			Unrelated individuals			Families and unrelated individuals	Families			Unrelated individuals			Families	Unrelated individuals
		Total	White	Negro and other races	Total	White	Negro and other races		Total	White	Negro and other races	Total	White	Negro and other races		
	189	190	191	192	193	194	195	196	197	198	199	200	201	202	203	204
1970	8,335	9,867	10,236	6,516	3,137	3,283	2,243	7,167	8,473	8,772	5,617	2,702	2,825	1,943	0.64	0.69
1969	8,017	9,433	9,794	6,190	2,930	3,078	2,170	7,301	8,598	8,922	5,652	2,682	2,815	1,981	.63	.70
1968	7,434	8,632	8,937	5,590	2,786	2,952	1,999	7,134	8,295	8,592	5,378	2,661	2,809	1,939	.63	.69
1967	6,852	7,933	8,234	5,094	2,379	2,470	1,825	6,852	7,933	8,234	5,094	2,379	2,470	1,825	.62	.74
1966	6,546	7,532	7,825	4,691	2,290	2,408	1,514	6,735	7,749	8,050	4,826	2,356	2,477	1,558	.60	.63
1965	6,032	6,957	7,251	3,994	2,153	2,246	1,639	6,383	7,355	7,668	4,254	2,288	2,382	1,769	.55	.74
1964	5,696	6,569	6,858	3,839	1,983	2,088	1,430	6,131	7,070	7,385	4,132	2,143	2,260	1,568	.56	.69
1963	5,490	6,249	6,548	3,465	1,800	1,887	1,294	5,987	6,825	7,149	3,799	1,970	2,072	1,419	.53	.68
1962	5,264	5,956	6,237	3,330	1,753	1,876	1,251	5,810	6,588	6,889	3,682	1,946	2,083	1,391	.53	.67
1961	5,009	5,737	5,981	3,191	1,755	1,885	1,160	5,590	6,417	6,701	3,563	1,963	2,113	1,316	.53	.62
1960	4,970	5,620	5,835	3,233	1,720	1,860	1,064	5,603	6,347	6,599	3,644	1,953	2,098	1,276	.55	.61
1959	4,759	5,417	5,643	2,917	1,556	1,663	1,075	5,451	6,207	6,471	3,335	1,820	1,924	1,297	.52	.67
1958	4,454	5,087	5,300	2,711	1,486	1,592	1,080	5,143	5,872	6,123	3,137	1,778	1,878	1,293	.51	.69
1957	4,353	4,971	5,166	2,764	1,496	1,592	1,013	5,164	5,888	6,129	3,278	1,817	1,917	1,307	.54	.68
1956	4,226	4,783	4,993	2,628	1,426	1,466	1,087	5,192	5,884	6,147	3,242	1,767	1,820	1,414	.53	.78
1955	3,909	4,421	4,605	2,549	1,316	1,402	935	4,874	5,531	5,767	3,187	1,656	1,770	1,217	.55	.69
1954	3,664	4,173	4,339	2,410	1,224	1,317	875	4,552	5,187	5,414	3,000	1,519	1,643	1,133	.55	.69
1953	3,733	4,233	4,392	2,461	1,394	1,473	1,161	4,660	5,312	5,518	3,091	1,756	1,854	1,460	.56	.79
1952	3,435	3,890	4,114	2,338	1,409	1,519	1,051	4,321	4,894	5,183	2,941	1,787	1,922	1,335	.57	.69
1951	3,348	3,709	3,859	2,032	1,195	1,258	929	4,303	4,766	4,959	2,615	1,535	1,618	1,256	.53	.78
1950	2,990	3,319	3,445	1,869	1,045	1,115	817	4,147	4,612	4,796	2,592	1,472	1,546	1,147	.54	.74
1949	2,739	3,107	3,232	1,650	1,050	1,134	819	3,836	4,349	4,528	2,317	1,482	1,588	1,165	.51	.73
1948	2,840	3,187	3,310	1,768	996	1,053	789	3,939	4,418	4,597	2,456	1,423	1,474	1,107	.53	.75
1947	2,685	3,031	3,157	1,614	980	1,035	746	4,013	4,531	4,720	2,418	1,467	1,546	1,119	.51	.72

Series G 205–256. Median Money Income of Families, by States: 1949, 1959, and 1969

Series No.	State	1969	1959	1949	Series No.	State	1969	1959	1949	Series No.	State	1969	1959	1949
205	U.S.	$9,586	$5,660	[1]$3,083	222	Kansas	$8,690	$5,295	$2,834	240	North Dakota	$7,836	$4,530	$2,939
					223	Kentucky	7,439	4,051	2,037	241	Ohio	10,309	6,171	3,412
206	Alabama	7,263	3,937	1,820	224	Louisiana	7,527	4,272	2,140	242	Oklahoma	7,720	4,620	2,429
207	Alaska	12,441	7,305	(NA)	225	Maine	8,205	4,873	2,616	243	Oregon	9,487	5,892	3,403
208	Arizona	9,185	5,568	2,861	226	Maryland	11,057	6,309	3,307	244	Pennsylvania	9,554	5,719	3,214
209	Arkansas	6,271	3,184	1,547	227	Massachusetts	10,833	6,272	3,399					
210	California	10,729	6,726	3,603						245	Rhode Island	9,733	5,589	3,136
					228	Michigan	11,029	6,256	3,588	246	South Carolina	7,620	3,821	1,924
211	Colorado	9,552	5,780	3,079	229	Minnesota	9,928	5,573	3,184	247	South Dakota	7,490	4,251	2,787
212	Connecticut	11,808	6,887	3,609	230	Mississippi	6,068	2,884	1,228	248	Tennessee	7,446	3,949	1,984
213	Delaware	10,209	6,197	3,193	231	Missouri	8,908	5,127	2,647	249	Texas	8,486	4,884	2,716
214	District of Columbia	9,576	5,993	3,832	232	Montana	8,509	5,403	3,292	250	Utah	9,320	5,899	3,297
215	Florida	8,261	4,722	2,429	233	Nebraska	8,562	4,862	2,829					
										251	Vermont	8,928	4,890	2,595
216	Georgia	8,165	4,208	1,902	234	Nevada	10,687	6,736	3,623	252	Virginia	9,044	4,964	2,644
217	Hawaii	11,552	6,366	3,568	235	New Hampshire	9,682	5,636	2,875	253	Washington	10,404	6,225	3,523
218	Idaho	8,380	5,259	3,054	236	New Jersey	11,403	6,786	3,720	254	West Virginia	7,414	4,572	2,597
219	Illinois	10,957	6,566	3,667	237	New Mexico	7,845	5,371	2,695	255	Wisconsin	10,065	5,926	3,284
220	Indiana	9,966	5,798	3,223	238	New York	10,609	6,371	3,559	256	Wyoming	8,944	5,877	3,523
221	Iowa	9,016	5,069	3,079	239	North Carolina	7,770	3,956	2,141					

NA Not available.   [1] Excludes Alaska and Hawaii.

CONSUMER INCOME AND EXPENDITURES

Series G 257–268. Percent Distribution of Persons, by Sex, by Money Income Levels: 1944 to 1970

[Persons 14 years old and over as of March following year shown]

Sex and year	Total persons		Persons with income									Median income
	With income	Without income	$1–$999 or loss	$1,000–$1,999	$2,000–$2,999	$3,000–$3,999	$4,000–$4,999	$5,000–$5,999	$6,000–$6,999	$7,000–$9,999	$10,000 and over	
	257	258	259	260	261	262	263	264	265	266	267	268
MALE												
1970	92.1	7.9	10.4	8.3	6.9	6.8	6.2	6.7	7.0	21.0	26.7	$6,670
1969	92.5	7.5	10.9	8.6	7.5	6.6	6.2	7.0	7.6	21.6	24.1	6,429
1968	92.4	7.6	11.5	8.9	7.3	7.2	7.1	8.2	8.6	21.6	19.7	5,980
1967	92.4	7.6	12.3	9.5	7.8	7.7	7.6	9.1	9.5	20.5	16.0	5,553
1966	92.4	7.6	13.2	10.3	8.1	8.2	7.9	9.6	9.8	19.0	14.0	5,242
1965	91.5	8.5	13.5	10.3	8.6	8.6	8.9	10.6	9.8	18.1	11.8	5,023
1964	91.4	8.6	14.2	10.9	8.9	9.4	9.8	10.6	9.9	16.0	10.3	4,647
1963	91.4	8.6	14.7	11.0	9.5	9.5	9.9	11.7	9.9	14.7	9.0	4,511
1962	91.1	8.9	14.7	11.7	9.6	9.9	10.6	12.3	9.8	13.2	7.9	4,372
1961	91.4	8.6	15.8	11.3	9.9	10.6	11.2	12.2	8.9	12.5	7.5	4,189
1960	91.4	8.6	16.2	11.3	10.3	11.1	12.0	12.7	8.9	11.3	6.1	4,081
1959	91.4	8.6	16.2	11.7	10.4	11.8	13.3	12.7	8.5	10.0	5.4	3,996
1958	91.7	8.3	16.9	12.3	11.2	13.0	14.5	12.1	7.6	8.1	4.4	3,742
1957	91.8	8.2	17.3	11.7	11.6	13.7	15.3	12.5	7.0	7.1	3.7	3,684
1956	91.9	8.1	17.2	11.7	12.1	14.8	15.9	11.9	6.2	6.5	3.6	3,608
1955	92.1	7.9	18.2	12.8	13.2	16.5	15.8	10.3	5.4	5.1	2.9	3,354
1954	90.2	9.8	18.4	13.8	14.1	18.4	14.6	9.2	4.4	4.4	2.7	3,199
1953	91.3	8.7	18.1	12.4	15.0	19.3	14.8	9.5	4.3	4.2	2.3	3,223
1952	91.3	8.7	16.5	13.9	16.8	22.9	13.5	8.0	3.2	3.2	1.9	3,105
1951	90.1	9.9	17.5	13.9	19.4	22.6	12.7	6.4	2.8	2.6	1.9	2,952
1950	90.1	9.9	20.7	16.4	21.6	20.9	9.6	4.6	2.0	2.0	2.0	2,570
1949	89.9	10.1	23.1	18.7	23.3	19.2	7.7	3.4	1.6	1.4	1.4	2,346
1948	89.9	10.1	20.5	19.1	24.7	19.5	8.0	3.6		3.1	1.6	2,396
1947	88.9	11.1	21.3	21.8	26.2	16.8	6.4	3.0		3.0	1.6	2,230
1945	89.5	10.5	28.7	26.0	23.9	13.2	3.8	2.4		1.3	.8	1,811
1944	88.9	11.1	25.7	23.0	25.7	15.1	5.0	2.2		2.0	1.2	2,046
FEMALE												
1970	66.5	33.5	27.6	19.2	11.8	10.3	8.8	6.9	4.9	7.5	3.0	2,237
1969	65.8	34.2	29.1	19.0	12.0	10.9	8.8	6.9	4.8	5.9	2.4	2,132
1968	64.8	35.2	30.8	18.9	12.1	12.1	8.7	6.4	4.4	5.0	1.8	2,019
1967	63.7	36.3	34.1	18.8	12.5	11.7	8.2	6.1	3.8	3.6	1.3	1,801
1966	63.0	37.0	35.6	19.3	12.5	12.2	8.1	5.7	3.0	2.8	1.0	1,675
1965	59.4	40.6	38.4	18.6	13.0	11.1	7.8	5.1	2.6	2.4	.8	1,521
1964	59.7	40.3	40.0	18.8	13.3	10.6	7.6	4.8	2.1	2.1	.7	1,449
1963	58.7	41.3	41.6	19.2	13.2	10.5	7.1	4.4	1.7	1.6	.6	1,372
1962	57.7	42.3	41.8	19.8	13.4	10.8	6.8	3.9	1.6	1.4	.5	1,342
1961	57.3	42.7	43.9	19.0	13.2	10.4	6.8	3.4	1.5	1.2	.5	1,279
1960	56.0	44.0	44.4	18.4	14.0	11.1	6.7	3.1	1.2	.9	.2	1,262
1959	53.7	46.3	45.2	19.0	14.0	11.1	5.9	2.6	1.1	.7	.4	1,222
1958	52.9	47.1	46.3	19.1	14.2	11.0	5.4	2.2	1.0	.6	.3	1,176
1957	52.6	47.4	45.7	19.9	14.9	11.3	4.9	1.9	.7	.5	.3	1,199
1956	51.9	48.1	46.9	19.3	15.7	11.0	4.3	1.5	.5	.4	.2	1,146
1955	49.3	50.7	47.3	20.6	15.8	10.7	3.4	1.2	.4	.4	.3	1,116
1954	46.4	53.6	46.4	21.4	16.8	10.7	2.6	1.0	.5	.4	.2	1,161
1953	46.4	53.6	46.2	21.4	18.1	9.9	2.3	1.0	.3	.2	.4	1,168
1952	46.5	53.5	46.8	21.8	18.0	10.0	1.9	.7	.3	.2	.1	1,147
1951	43.7	56.3	49.0	23.2	18.2	7.1	1.5	.5	.2	.2	.1	1,045
1950	43.2	56.8	51.8	23.6	18.1	4.5	1.2	.3	.1	.2	.2	953
1949	41.8	58.2	51.6	26.2	16.4	4.1	1.2	.2	.2	.1	.1	960
1948	40.9	59.1	49.6	28.4	16.8	3.4	.7	.3		.3	.2	1,009
1947	39.2	€0.8	49.5	31.6	14.2	3.0	.9	.3		.3	.3	1,017
1945	45.1	54.9	54.7	33.2	9.7	1.4	.4	.1		.1	.1	901
1944	47.9	52.1	54.3	32.2	10.2	1.8	.7	.3		.3	.3	909

Series G 269–282. Percent Distribution of Families and Unattached Individuals, by Income Levels: 1929 to 1964

Item and year	Total (1,000)	Under $1,000	$1,000–$1,999	$2,000–$2,999	$3,000–$3,999	$4,000–$4,999	$5,000–$5,999	$6,000–$7,499	$7,500–$9,999	$10,000–$14,999	$15,000–$19,999	$20,000–$24,999	$25,000–$49,999	$50,000 and over
	269	270	271	272	273	274	275	276	277	278	279	280	281	282
FAMILIES AND UNATTACHED INDIVIDUALS														
1964	59,836	11.9		8.0	8.5	8.8	8.6	12.8	17.1	16.0	4.4	1.6	1.8	0.5
1962	57,890	12.0		8.5	9.8	10.2	10.2	14.1	15.7	12.3	7.2			
1961	57,290	12.9		9.1	10.3	10.8	10.5	14.1	14.7	11.1	3.7	1.2	1.3	.3
1960*	56,060	13.1		9.2	10.6	11.0	10.7	14.1	14.5	10.6	3.5	1.2	1.2	.3
1959	55,300	13.6		9.6	11.1	11.4	10.9	14.1	14.0	9.6	3.1	1.1	1.2	.3
1958	54,620	14.1		10.1	12.1	12.5	11.4	13.9	12.6	8.5	2.5	.9	1.1	.3
1957	53,650	14.2		10.0	12.1	12.7	11.6	14.1	12.6	8.0	2.4	.9	1.1	.3
1956	52,850	14.6		10.2	12.9	14.0	11.8	13.6	11.6	7.2	2.1	.8	1.0	.2
1955	52,170	15.8		11.3	14.1	14.0	12.1	13.3	10.0	5.9	1.7	.7	.9	.2
1954	51,150	6.0	11.5	12.7	14.3	13.9	11.8	12.3	9.2	5.2	1.5	.6	.8	.2
1953	50,510	5.9	11.0	12.6	14.0	14.1	12.2	12.6	9.4	5.2	1.4	.6	.8	.2
1952	50,210	6.5	11.3	13.0	15.2	15.2	12.1	11.6	8.2	4.1	1.2	.6	.8	.2
1951	49,480	6.5	12.2	14.5	16.5	15.1	11.3	10.7	6.8	3.8	1.1	.6	.7	.2
1950	48,890	7.9	15.3	16.6	17.6	14.4	9.6	7.9	5.6	3.1	.8	.4	.6	.2
1947	44,740	8.4	16.5	18.9	19.3	12.8	7.8	7.0	4.8	2.7	.8	.4	.5	.1
1946	43,330	8.8	17.6	20.3	19.8	12.4	7.1	5.9	4.0	2.5	.8	.3	.4	.1
1944	40,880	10.7	19.8	21.4	18.9	11.1	6.2	5.5	3.4	1.7	.6	.3	.3	.1
1941	41,370	29.0	29.9	22.3	9.8	4.0	2.8		.9			1.3		
1935–1936	38,410	43.5	34.2	13.1	4.4	1.7	1.6		.6			.9		
1929	36,100	65.0		17.0	8.0	4.0	2.0	3.0				1.0		
FAMILIES														
1964	47,779	5.3		6.4	7.8	8.4	9.0	14.3	20.0	19.1	5.4	2.0	2.0	.5
1962	46,890	6.9		6.2	8.2	9.8	10.8	16.0	18.6	14.8	8.7			
1961	46,190	7.5		6.7	8.9	10.5	11.3	16.2	17.5	13.5	4.5	1.5	1.5	.4
1960*	45,370	7.4		6.8	9.2	10.9	11.7	16.3	17.4	12.8	4.2	1.4	1.5	.4
1959	44,780	7.8		7.1	9.8	11.6	12.0	16.5	16.7	11.6	3.8	1.3	1.4	.4
1958	44,120	8.0		7.6	11.1	13.0	12.7	16.4	15.1	10.3	3.0	1.2	1.3	.3
1957	43,670	8.2		7.5	11.1	13.3	13.0	16.6	15.1	9.7	2.9	1.1	1.2	.3
1956	43,350	8.4		7.7	12.2	15.1	13.4	16.0	13.7	8.6	2.5	1.0	1.1	.3
1955	42,670	9.3		8.9	13.7	15.4	13.9	15.7	11.9	7.0	2.0	.9	1.0	.3
1954	41,750	2.5	8.2	10.5	14.2	15.4	13.7	14.6	11.1	6.3	1.7	.7	.9	.2
1953	41,110	2.3	7.6	10.3	13.8	15.6	14.2	15.1	11.3	6.3	1.7	.7	.9	.2
1952	40,770	2.9	7.8	10.8	15.4	17.1	14.2	13.8	9.8	4.9	1.4	.8	.9	.2
1951	40,420	2.7	8.6	12.5	17.3	17.0	13.3	12.8	8.2	4.6	1.3	.7	.8	.2
1950	39,790	3.7	11.9	15.1	19.0	16.6	11.3	9.4	6.8	3.8	1.0	.5	.7	.2
1947	37,025	4.1	13.2	18.2	21.3	14.8	9.1	8.3	5.8	3.2	1.0	.4	.5	.1
1946	35,860	4.2	14.3	20.1	22.1	14.4	8.3	6.9	4.8	2.9	.9	.4	.5	.2
1944	33,300	5.6	16.4	21.9	21.5	13.0	7.3	6.6	4.1	2.1	.7	.3	.4	.1
1941	32,920	24.0	29.2	24.4	11.8	4.6	3.4		1.1			1.5		
1935–1936	30,430	38.3	35.8	15.1	5.2	2.0	1.8		.7			1.1		

* Denotes first year for which figures include Alaska and Hawaii.

Series **G 283–296.**   Percent Distribution of Aggregate Personal Income Among Families and Unattached Individuals, by Income Levels: 1929 to 1964

Item and year	Total (mil. dol.)	Percent distribution by income level (before taxes)												
		Under $1,000	$1,000–$1,999	$2,000–$2,999	$3,000–$3,999	$4,000–$4,999	$5,000–$5,999	$6,000–$7,499	$7,500–$9,999	$10,000–$14,999	$15,000–$19,999	$20,000–$24,999	$25,000–$49,999	$50,000 and over
	283	284	285	286	287	288	289	290	291	292	293	294	295	296
AGGREGATE FAMILY AND UNATTACHED INDIVIDUALS PERSONAL INCOME														
1964	470,597	1.6		2.6	3.8	5.0	6.0	10.9	18.9	24.3	9.6	4.6	7.4	5.2
1962	420,412	1.8		3.0	4.7	6.4	7.7	13.0	18.6	20.2		24.6		
1961	396,992	2.1		3.3	5.2	7.0	8.3	13.6	18.2	19.2	9.1	3.9	6.1	4.0
1960*	382,251	2.1		3.4	5.5	7.3	8.6	13.9	18.3	18.6	8.7	3.8	6.0	3.8
1959	365,795	2.3		3.6	5.9	7.8	9.1	14.4	18.1	17.3	8.1	3.6	5.7	4.1
1958	343,257	2.5		4.0	6.8	8.9	10.0	14.8	17.2	16.3	6.8	3.4	5.6	3.7
1957	334,647	2.6		4.0	6.8	9.1	10.1	15.1	17.4	15.5	6.6	3.3	5.7	3.8
1956	317,448	2.7		4.3	7.5	10.5	10.8	15.2	16.5	14.4	6.0	3.0	5.4	3.7
1955	294,239	3.2		5.1	8.8	11.2	11.8	15.8	15.1	12.5	5.1	2.8	5.1	3.5
1954	273,956	.6	3.3	6.0	9.4	11.7	12.1	15.3	14.7	11.6	4.6	2.5	4.8	3.4
1953	272,186	.6	3.1	5.9	9.1	11.8	12.4	15.6	14.9	11.6	4.6	2.5	4.7	3.2
1952	257,162	.7	3.3	6.4	10.4	13.3	12.9	15.1	13.5	9.4	4.0	2.7	4.9	3.4
1951	242,652	.7	3.7	7.4	11.8	13.8	12.6	14.7	11.8	9.3	3.7	2.5	4.6	3.4
1950	217,262	.9	5.2	9.3	13.8	14.5	11.8	11.8	10.8	8.4	3.3	2.2	4.5	3.5
1947	184,598	1.1	6.1	11.5	16.3	13.8	10.2	11.3	10.0	7.7	3.6	2.0	3.7	2.7
1946	170,705	1.2	6.8	12.9	17.5	14.0	9.8	9.9	8.7	7.5	3.3	1.9	3.7	2.8
1944	147,721	1.6	8.4	14.9	18.3	13.7	9.3	10.1	8.0	5.7	2.9	1.6	3.1	2.4
1941	91,406	7.6	20.3	24.8	15.3	7.9	7.6		3.5		13.0			
1935–1936	62,654	15.4	30.0	19.5	9.2	4.5	5.8		3.2		12.4			
1929	84,300	31.0		17.0	11.0	7.0	5.0	10.0			19.0			
AGGREGATE FAMILY PERSONAL INCOME														
1964	422,294	.6		1.8	3.1	4.3	5.6	10.9	19.7	25.9	10.3	4.9	7.7	5.2
1962	382,215	1.0		1.9	3.5	5.4	7.3	13.2	19.7	21.7		26.3		
1961	360,125	1.2		2.2	4.0	6.1	8.0	14.0	19.3	20.6	9.8	4.2	6.5	4.1
1960*	347,830	1.2		2.3	4.2	6.4	8.4	14.3	19.4	20.0	9.4	4.1	6.3	4.0
1959	332,942	1.3		2.4	4.7	7.0	8.9	14.9	19.3	18.5	8.7	3.9	6.1	4.3
1958	311,727	1.4		2.7	5.6	8.3	9.9	15.5	18.4	17.5	7.4	3.6	5.9	3.8
1957	305,336	1.5		2.7	5.6	8.6	10.2	15.8	18.5	16.6	7.1	3.5	6.0	3.9
1956	290,696	1.6		2.9	6.4	10.1	10.9	16.0	17.6	15.4	6.4	3.2	5.7	3.8
1955	268,939	1.8		3.6	7.7	11.0	12.1	16.7	16.1	13.5	5.5	3.0	5.4	3.6
1954	250,255	.2	2.1	4.4	8.3	11.6	12.6	16.3	15.7	12.5	5.0	2.7	5.4	3.5
1953	248,350	.2	1.9	4.3	8.1	11.6	12.9	16.7	16.0	12.4	4.9	2.7	5.1	3.3
1952	233,896	.3	2.1	4.7	9.5	13.4	13.6	16.1	14.4	10.1	4.2	2.9	5.2	3.5
1951	221,379	.3	2.4	5.8	11.1	14.0	13.3	15.6	12.5	10.0	3.9	2.7	4.8	3.6
1950	197,724	.4	3.7	7.6	13.4	15.0	12.5	12.5	11.5	9.0	3.5	2.4	4.8	3.7
1947	169,340	.5	4.5	10.0	16.2	14.4	10.8	12.0	10.7	8.3	3.8	2.1	3.9	2.8
1946	156,670	.6	5.0	11.6	17.7	14.7	10.3	10.5	9.3	8.0	3.5	1.9	3.9	3.0
1944	134,102	.8	6.2	13.7	18.7	14.5	9.9	10.9	8.6	6.2	3.0	1.7	3.3	2.5
1941	80,238	6.1	18.1	24.8	16.6	8.5	8.2		3.8		13.9			
1935–1936	54,275	12.5	29.0	20.5	10.0	4.8	6.1		3.4		13.7			

* Denotes first year for which figures include Alaska and Hawaii.

Series **G 297–305.**   Percent Distribution of Families and Unattached Individuals and Family Personal Income, by Income Level in 1950 Dollars: 1929 to 1957

Series No.	Income level in 1950 dollars (before income taxes)	Families and unattached individuals (1,000)						Family personal income in 1950 dollars ($1,000,000)					
		1957	1950	1944	1941	1935–36	1929	1957	1950	1944	1941	1935–36	1929
297	Total	53,510	48,890	40,880	41,370	38,410	36,100	283,808	217,262	190,093	151,586	112,809	121,387
298	Under $1,000	17.3	7.9	7.3	15.1	19.5	15.9	3.7	0.9	0.8	2.7	4.0	2.0
299	$1,000 to $1,999		15.3	13.7	19.9	29.2	25.6		5.2	4.5	8.2	14.9	11.4
300	$2,000 to $2,999	12.8	16.6	15.5	18.5	20.7	25.7	6.1	9.3	8.3	12.6	17.4	19.0
301	$3,000 to $3,999	15.3	17.6	17.6	15.7	12.3	12.2	10.1	13.8	13.1	14.9	14.4	12.5
302	$4,000 to $4,999	14.5	14.4	14.7	12.3	7.3	7.2	12.3	14.5	14.2	14.9	11.1	9.5
303	$5,000 to $7,499	22.8	17.5	18.4	12.0	6.7	7.4	26.1	23.6	23.8	19.6	13.6	13.1
304	$7,500 to $9,999	8.6	5.6	7.0	3.1	1.8	3.1	13.8	10.8	12.8	7.2	5.2	8.0
305	$10,000 and over	8.7	5.1	5.8	3.4	2.5	2.9	27.9	21.9	22.5	19.9	19.4	24.5

Series G 306–318. Number and Average Size of Families, Number of Unattached Individuals, and Average Family Personal Income Before and After Federal Individual Income Tax Liability: 1929 to 1964

Year	Number of consumer units (mil.)	Average (mean) number of persons per consumer unit	Before tax — In current dollars	Before tax — In 1954 dollars	After tax — In current dollars	After tax — In 1954 dollars	Number of families (mil.)	Average (mean) number of persons per family	Average (mean) family personal income per family, in current dollars	Farm-operator — Number of families (mil.)	Farm-operator — Average (mean) family personal income per family, in current dollars	Nonfarm — Number of families (mil.)	Nonfarm — Average (mean) family personal income per family, in current dollars
	306	307	308	309	310	311	312	313	314	315	316	317	318
1964	59.8	3.17	7,865	6,774	----	----	47.8	3.71	8,838	----	5,015	42.6	8,469
1962	57.9	3.18	7,262	6,490	6,507	5,815	46.9	3.69	8,151	4.3	4,752	41.8	8,120
1961	57.3	3.16	6,930	6,243	6,222	5,605	46.2	3.68	7,797	4.4	4,752	41.8	8,120
1960*	56.1	3.19	6,819	6,193	6,132	5,570	45.4	3.71	7,667	4.5	4,531	40.8	8,015
1959	55.3	3.17	6,615	6,097	5,939	5,474	44.8	3.67	7,435	4.6	4,264	40.1	7,802
1958	54.6	3.15	6,284	5,857	5,669	5,284	44.1	3.66	7,065	4.7	4,521	39.4	7,372
1957	53.6	3.15	6,238	5,935	5,608	5,335	43.7	3.64	6,992	4.9	4,111	38.8	7,352
1956	52.8	3.14	6,007	5,883	5,403	5,292	43.4	3.60	6,706	5.0	4,015	38.4	7,054
1955	52.2	3.12	5,640	5,618	5,090	5,070	42.7	3.59	6,303	5.1	3,917	37.6	6,626
1954	51.2	3.12	5,356	5,356	4,842	4,842	41.8	3.60	5,994	5.2	3,881	36.5	6,295
1953	50.5	3.10	5,389	5,443	4,809	4,857	41.1	3.58	6,041	5.3	3,905	35.8	6,358
1952	50.2	3.06	5,122	5,226	4,570	4,663	40.8	3.54	5,737	5.4	4,147	35.4	6,013
1951	49.5	3.06	4,904	5,108	4,417	4,601	40.4	3.52	5,477	5.6	4,114	34.8	5,721
1950	48.9	3.05	4,444	4,943	4,069	4,526	39.8	3.52	4,969	5.7	3,498	34.1	5,232
1947	44.7	3.19	4,126	4,877	3,719	3,947	37.0	3.64	4,574	5.9	3,583	31.1	4,775
1946	43.3	3.22	3,940	5,150	3,575	4,167	35.9	3.68	4,369	5.9	3,385	30.0	4,573
1944	40.9	3.07	3,614	5,268	3,212	4,133	33.3	3.54	4,027	5.9	2,860	27.4	4,267
1941	41.4	3.15	2,209	4,161	2,108	3,496	32.9	3.70	2,437	6.1	1,552	26.8	2,638
1935–1936	38.4	3.28	1,631	3,343	1,608	2,895	30.4	3.88	1,784	6.7	951	23.7	2,020
1929	36.1	3.34	2,335	3,791	2,318	3,339	27.9	4.03	----	----	----	----	----

* Denotes first year for which figures include Alaska and Hawaii.

Series G 319–336. Family Personal Income Received by Each Fifth and Top 5 Percent of Families and Unattached Individuals: 1929 to 1964

Year	Lowest fifth	Second fifth	Third fifth	Fourth fifth	Highest fifth	Top 5 percent	Total	Lowest fifth	Second fifth	Third fifth	Fourth fifth	Highest fifth	Top 5 percent
	319	320	321	322	323	324	325	326	327	328	329	330	331
1964	4.2	10.6	16.4	23.2	45.5	20.0	7,865	1,652	4,180	6,465	9,130	17,896	31,393
1962	4.6	10.9	16.3	22.7	45.5	19.6	7,262	1,662	3,966	5,938	8,241	16,505	28,482
1961	4.6	10.9	16.3	22.7	45.5	19.6	6,930	1,572	3,769	5,660	7,869	15,777	27,212
1960*	4.6	10.9	16.4	22.7	45.4	19.6	6,819	1,562	3,731	5,577	7,731	15,493	26,721
1959	4.6	10.9	16.3	22.6	45.6	20.0	6,615	1,513	3,615	5,396	7,474	15,076	26,408
1958	4.7	11.0	16.3	22.5	45.5	20.0	6,284	1,472	3,480	5,115	7,063	14,292	25,124
1957	4.7	11.1	16.3	22.4	45.5	20.2	6,238	1,462	3,471	5,087	6,983	14,185	25,139
1956	4.8	11.3	16.3	22.3	45.3	20.2	6,007	1,437	3,403	4,898	6,691	13,604	24,210
1955	4.8	11.3	16.4	22.3	45.2	20.3	5,640	1,355	3,200	4,634	6,290	12,722	22,893
1954	4.8	11.1	16.4	22.5	45.2	20.3	5,356	1,289	2,975	4,401	6,019	12,096	21,761
1953	4.9	11.3	16.6	22.5	44.7	19.9	5,389	1,322	3,038	4,471	6,072	12,041	21,481
1952	4.9	11.4	16.6	22.4	44.7	20.5	5,122	1,249	2,918	4,255	5,732	11,455	21,028
1951	5.0	11.3	16.5	22.3	44.9	20.7	4,904	1,221	2,775	4,034	5,473	11,016	20,287
1950	4.8	10.9	16.1	22.1	46.1	21.4	4,444	1,056	2,418	3,579	4,911	10,254	19,066
1947	5.0	11.0	16.0	22.0	46.0	20.9	4,126	1,023	2,275	3,308	4,542	9,483	17,226
1946	5.0	11.1	16.0	21.8	46.1	21.3	3,940	982	2,178	3,156	4,290	9,091	16,796
1944	4.9	10.9	16.2	22.2	45.8	20.7	3,614	882	1,979	2,920	4,014	8,272	14,963
1941	4.1	9.5	15.3	22.3	48.8	24.0	2,209	450	1,044	1,694	2,463	5,396	10,617
1935–1936	4.1	9.2	14.1	20.9	51.7	26.5	1,631	337	749	1,146	1,708	4,216	8,654
1929		12.5	13.8	19.3	54.4	30.0	2,335	725		1,606	2,252	6,327	13,960

* Denotes first year for which figures include Alaska and Hawaii.

Series G 319–336. Family Personal Income Received by Each Fifth and Top 5 Percent of Families and Unattached Individuals: 1929 to 1964—Con.

Year	Second fifth (332)	Third fifth (333)	Fourth fifth (334)	Highest fifth (335)	Top 5 percent (336)
1964	3,010	5,320	7,660	10,850	18,110
1962	2,940	4,950	6,960	9,900	17,230
1961	2,790	4,710	6,650	9,460	16,460
1960*	2,770	4,660	6,530	9,270	16,240
1959	2,690	4,500	6,320	8,910	15,740
1958	2,610	4,290	5,970	8,450	14,700
1957	2,590	4,280	5,940	8,320	14,580
1956	2,540	4,170	5,680	7,960	13,960
1955	2,390	3,920	5,370	7,410	13,070
1954	2,200	3,700	5,120	7,100	12,350
1953	2,260	3,770	5,180	7,160	12,320
1952	2,170	3,610	4,910	6,760	11,480
1951	2,090	3,420	4,680	6,450	11,110
1950	1,810	3,020	4,160	5,850	10,200
1947	1,730	2,800	3,830	5,470	9,560
1946	1,660	2,680	3,650	5,130	9,180
1944	1,510	2,450	3,410	4,800	8,240
1941	740	1,370	2,040	2,940	5,010
1935–1936	560	930	1,380	2,120	3,910
1929		1,340	1,860	2,810	5,690

* Denotes first year for which figures include Alaska and Hawaii.
[1] Rounded to nearest $10.

Series G 337–352. Percent Shares of Total Income Received by Top 1 Percent and 5 Percent of Total Population: 1913 to 1948

Year	Basic income variant Top 1 pct (337)	Basic income variant Top 5 pct (338)	Economic income variant Top 1 pct (339)	Economic income variant Top 5 pct (340)	Disposable income variant Top 1 pct (341)	Disposable income variant Top 5 pct (342)	Employee compensation Top 1 pct (343)	Employee compensation Top 5 pct (344)	Entrepreneurial income Top 1 pct (345)	Entrepreneurial income Top 5 pct (346)	Dividends Top 1 pct (347)	Dividends Top 5 pct (348)	Interest Top 1 pct (349)	Interest Top 5 pct (350)	Rent Top 1 pct (351)	Rent Top 5 pct (352)
1948	8.38	17.63	---	---	---	---	3.78	10.87	15.16	30.72	53.56	69.84	15.76	26.47	12.77	22.60
1947	8.49	17.41	---	---	---	---	3.90	10.61	15.16	30.04	50.23	65.43	17.20	27.95	10.98	20.39
1946	8.98	18.20	9.58	19.96	7.71	17.66	3.76	10.37	18.28	34.39	50.90	67.94	19.17	31.94	10.15	19.20
1945	8.81	17.39	9.37	19.27	7.27	16.65	3.33	9.73	23.00	38.94	[1]	[1]	[1]	[1]	9.11	16.82
1944	8.58	16.62	8.98	18.68	6.61	15.75	3.33	9.92	22.00	34.83	[1]	[1]	[1]	[1]	8.94	15.79
1943	9.38	17.75	9.95	20.86	6.44	16.66	3.75	10.86	23.35	35.68	52.30	65.54	22.70	33.03	9.76	17.47
1942	10.06	18.94	10.70	22.47	7.81	19.03	4.89	13.07	18.84	29.27	52.72	65.26	25.98	37.04	9.96	18.24
1941	11.39	21.89	12.32	25.67	9.89	22.98	6.00	15.60	16.88	28.52	57.81	72.85	25.30	38.35	11.35	22.85
1940	11.89	22.71	12.87	26.83	11.39	25.44	6.41	16.86	14.81	26.02	63.23	75.99	23.65	36.44	13.01	23.35
1939	11.80	23.45	13.12	27.77	12.14	26.81	6.36	17.80	14.21	25.92	62.02	75.21	24.27	36.22	12.78	24.51
1938	11.45	22.80	12.75	27.62	12.01	26.85	6.57	17.75	13.17	24.32	61.33	75.69	22.61	33.16	13.26	24.99
1937	12.84	23.80	13.96	28.20	12.81	27.06	6.55	17.46	12.69	23.01	67.55	80.29	25.37	35.87	13.00	24.29
1936	13.14	24.35	14.46	28.82	13.52	27.92	6.43	17.08	15.27	27.73	65.41	77.40	25.17	36.93	12.68	26.09
1935	12.05	23.73	13.58	28.77	12.74	27.89	6.77	18.86	11.70	21.80	68.00	80.04	23.92	34.23	12.54	26.38
1934	12.48	24.88	14.08	30.26	12.84	28.95	6.79	19.00	15.26	29.98	66.59	78.14	22.63	32.49	12.84	28.10
1933	12.48	25.34	14.76	31.73	13.01	30.21	7.23	20.06	15.30	29.62	66.25	78.55	19.66	29.83	13.94	32.06
1932	13.25	26.71	15.65	32.99	12.62	30.40	7.45	20.55	14.82	31.24	67.32	79.17	21.01	33.76	15.83	34.50
1931	13.31	26.27	15.57	32.03	14.56	31.23	6.82	18.40	14.03	31.12	65.44	79.34	22.32	36.63	15.54	37.65
1930	14.12	26.19	15.88	31.34	15.38	30.95	6.64	17.25	14.23	31.15	67.05	78.61	26.11	40.72	14.58	30.81
1929 [2]	14.65	26.36	17.31	32.19	19.08	33.81	6.26	16.37	17.12	32.47	71.26	83.37	28.41	43.26	13.42	29.21
1929 [3]	14.50	26.09	17.15	31.88	18.92	33.49	6.17	16.13	16.16	30.65	66.02	77.24	31.13	47.40	17.17	37.39
1928	14.94	26.78	17.18	32.06	19.12	34.06	6.41	16.67	17.16	32.10	71.35	81.80	32.02	49.39	16.08	33.95
1927	14.39	25.96	16.46	31.19	17.22	31.92	6.23	15.71	15.79	31.03	72.86	85.18	31.70	49.08	16.75	36.56
1926	13.93	25.25	15.77	30.21	16.26	30.78	6.08	14.85	15.11	30.80	73.26	85.66	30.77	48.18	17.86	40.18
1925	13.73	25.20	15.74	30.24	16.54	31.09	6.24	15.24	15.60	31.49	67.89	78.91	28.73	45.08	17.22	38.73
1924	12.91	24.29	14.69	29.06	14.28	28.73	6.05	14.28	14.47	31.71	68.83	81.08	27.83	45.64	14.84	36.15
1923	12.28	22.89	14.02	28.08	13.08	27.05	5.81	13.38	13.04	29.70	64.60	77.49	28.97	45.74	14.62	32.41
1922	13.38	24.79	15.58	30.39	14.39	29.04	6.33	16.56	14.80	27.89	71.66	85.26	30.66	45.09	15.43	29.77
1921	13.50	25.47	16.15	31.70	14.20	29.32	6.82	17.29	15.73	28.94	65.33	82.00	29.90	45.66	16.12	34.30
1920	12.34	22.07	13.64	25.76	11.80	23.96	5.82	14.40	13.78	24.93	72.40	84.47	32.55	45.69	14.86	28.54
1919 [2]	12.84	22.91	14.04	26.10	12.21	24.27	6.14	14.92	12.68	23.76	74.09	86.23	37.34	51.09	14.23	29.48
1919 [3]	12.96	23.13	---	---	---	---	6.58	16.01	11.47	21.48	66.55	77.45	42.35	57.96	14.23	29.48
1918	12.69	22.69	---	---	---	---	5.96	15.10	10.63	20.45	61.74	70.25	47.01	66.69	14.90	30.73
1917	14.16	24.60	---	---	---	---	6.64	16.90	9.15	19.29	72.39	78.77	44.59	53.01	14.89	33.21
1916	15.58	---	---	---	---	---										
1915	14.32	---	---	---	---	---										
1914	13.07	---	---	---	---	---										
1913	14.98	---	---	---	---	---										

[1] Data on dividends and interest are not separately available for 1944 and 1945. The combined data for 1944 and 1945 are, respectively: Top 1 percent, 38.88 and 37.80; top 5 percent, 52.30 and 52.24.
[2] Comparable with later years.
[3] Comparable with earlier years.

Series G 353–371. Median Money Wage or Salary Income of Primary Families and Unrelated Individuals With Wage or Salary Income, by Selected Characteristics: 1939 to 1970

Series No.	Selected characteristics	1970	1969	1968	1967	1966	1965	1964	1963	1962	1961	1960	1959*	1958
	RACE													
353	**Total**	$8,933	$8,547	$7,844	$7,305	$6,899	$6,469	$6,080	$5,807	$5,556	$5,315	$5,199	$5,016	$4,650
354	White families and individuals	9,284	8,892	8,147	7,589	7,183	6,767	6,362	6,088	5,808	5,570	5,424	5,252	4,882
355	Negro and other races, families and individuals	6,073	5,701	5,150	4,746	4,344	3,863	3,673	3,268	3,088	2,908	3,058	2,672	2,437
	SEX, MARITAL STATUS, AND AGE OF HEAD													
356	Families with male head, married, wife present	10,169	9,674	8,834	8,177	7,658	7,157	6,722	6,378	6,047	5,830	5,688	5,478	5,107
	Age of head:													
357	Under 35 years	9,316	8,925	8,214	7,658	7,218	6,756	6,207	5,938	5,604	5,516	5,377	5,221	4,843
358	35–44 years	11,448	10,879	9,966	9,215	8,569	7,907	7,384	6,979	6,761	6,479	6,344	6,088	5,593
359	45–54 years	11,807	11,196	10,043	9,379	8,609	8,024	7,606	7,190	6,814	6,374	6,256	5,896	5,594
360	55 years and over	8,402	7,981	7,339	6,737	6,298	5,933	5,574	5,366	5,038	4,850	4,719	4,449	4,221
361	Other families with male head	8,692	7,718	6,819	6,677	6,090	6,088	5,599	5,140	5,325	5,019	4,439	4,258	3,987
362	Families with female head	4,797	4,510	4,113	3,984	3,699	3,461	3,362	3,286	3,052	3,006	2,983	2,966	2,865
	SIZE OF FAMILY													
363	2 persons					6,277	5,913	5,562	5,281	5,029	4,972	4,754	4,548	4,362
364	3 persons					7,313	6,860	6,431	6,144	5,807	5,578	5,429	5,176	4,897
365	4 persons					7,890	7,469	7,062	6,776	6,353	6,056	5,932	5,744	5,344
366	5 persons					8,017	7,416	6,996	6,541	6,282	6,094	5,975	5,813	5,252
367	6 persons or more					7,502	6,934	6,482	6,082	5,726	5,463	5,271	5,132	4,592
	FAMILIES, BY NUMBER OF RELATED CHILDREN UNDER 18 YEARS OF AGE													
368	No children					6,938	6,515	6,172	5,812	5,522	5,403	5,235	5,028	4,732
369	1 child					7,396	6,982	6,446	6,156	5,933	5,619	5,421	5,202	4,961
370	2 children					7,629	7,259	6,798	6,536	6,176	5,883	5,794	5,630	5,203
371	3 children or more					7,379	6,820	6,435	6,047	5,727	5,559	5,428	5,272	4,724

Series No.	Selected characteristics	1957	1956	1955	1954	1953	1951	1950	1949	1947	1945	1944	1939
	RACE												
353	**Total**	$4,594	$4,454	$4,137	$3,960	$4,011	$3,515	$3,216	$2,959	$2,854	$2,390	$2,378	$1,231
354	White families and individuals	4,831	4,685	4,331	4,150	4,201	3,673	3,390	3,138	2,999	--------	--------	1,325
355	Negro and other races, families and individuals	2,536	2,429	2,418	2,333	2,357	1,943	1,671	1,533	1,448	--------	--------	489
	SEX, MARITAL STATUS, AND AGE OF HEAD												
356	Families with male head, married, wife present	5,033	4,858	4,467	4,286	4,324	3,773	3,486	3,194	3,042	--------	--------	1,319
	Age of head:												
357	Under 35 years	4,890	4,700	4,279	4,118	4,189	3,665	3,305	2,998	2,733	--------	--------	1,171
358	35–44 years	5,500	5,312	4,872	4,719	4,640	4,111	3,805	3,418	3,398	--------	--------	1,449
359	45–54 years	5,489	5,308	4,944	4,633	4,660	3,957	3,752	3,564	3,514	--------	--------	1,481
360	55 years and over	4,045	3,985	3,757	3,570	3,722	3,303	3,031	2,848	2,788	--------	--------	1,243
361	Other families with male head	4,244	4,321	3,857	3,636	4,009	3,412	3,092	2,972	2,909	--------	--------	1,159
362	Families with female head	2,902	2,780	2,651	2,546	2,750	2,407	2,122	2,185	2,195	--------	--------	909
	SIZE OF FAMILY												
363	2 persons	4,296	4,148	3,835	3,709	3,788	3,365	3,002	2,777	2,587	--------	--------	1,219
364	3 persons	4,868	4,754	4,417	4,172	4,320	3,694	3,394	3,116	2,897	--------	--------	1,297
365	4 persons	5,234	5,045	4,646	4,468	4,419	3,891	3,619	3,361	3,232	--------	--------	1,374
366	5 persons	5,208	5,043	4,506	4,535	4,565	3,952	3,632	3,376	3,403	--------	--------	1,322
367	6 persons or more	4,664	4,500	4,146	3,894	4,024	3,556	3,182	3,100	3,284	--------	--------	1,134
	FAMILIES, BY NUMBER OF RELATED CHILDREN UNDER 18 YEARS OF AGE												
368	No children	4,697	4,558	4,227	4,006	4,163	3,662	3,349	3,113	2,942	--------	--------	1,363
369	1 child	4,855	4,644	4,343	4,188	4,285	3,662	3,421	3,120	2,964	--------	--------	1,315
370	2 children	5,047	4,911	4,518	4,450	4,389	3,761	3,493	3,261	3,122	--------	--------	1,288
371	3 children or more	4,783	4,605	4,157	3,933	4,009	3,554	3,082	2,858	2,812	--------	--------	956

* Denotes first year for which figures include Alaska and Hawaii.

Series G 372–415. Median Money Wage or Salary Income of All Workers With Wage or Salary Income, and of Year-Round Full-Time Workers, by Sex, Race, and Major Occupation Group: 1939 to 1970

	All male workers											
	Race [1]		Major occupation group [2]									
Year	White	Negro and other races	Professional, technical, and kindred workers	Farmers and farm managers	Managers, officials, and proprietors, except farm	Clerical and kindred workers	Sales workers	Craftsmen, foremen, and kindred workers	Operatives and kindred workers	Service workers, except private household	Farm laborers and foremen	Laborers, except farm and mine
	372	373	374	375	376	377	378	379	380	381	382	383
1970	$8,254	$5,485	$10,722	$1,105	$11,430	$7,585	$7,992	$8,580	$6,671	$5,027	$1,911	$4,337
1969	7,859	5,237	10,257	1,151	10,874	7,135	7,570	8,231	6,473	4,545	1,855	4,091
1968	7,291	4,839	9,368	1,215	9,904	6,755	7,245	8,066	6,066	4,462	1,775	3,850
1967	6,833	4,369	8,882	968	9,357	6,193	6,644	7,142	5,702	4,251	1,432	3,764
1966	6,510	3,864	8,204	1,179	8,730	5,893	6,337	6,819	5,528	3,830	1,454	3,323
1965	6,188	3,563	7,798	696	8,444	5,617	6,097	6,493	5,258	3,864	1,284	3,234
1964	5,853	3,426	7,460	710	7,560	5,549	5,620	6,133	4,985	3,684	1,128	3,126
1963	5,663	3,217	7,182	703	7,411	5,318	5,581	5,875	4,830	3,581	1,051	2,869
1962	5,462	3,023	6,870	486	7,099	5,187	5,267	5,737	4,601	3,372	1,205	2,895
1961	5,287	3,015	6,716	521	6,957	4,990	5,122	5,527	4,344	3,238	1,002	2,730
1960	5,137	3,075	6,343	500	6,864	4,800	4,742	5,443	4,275	3,155	893	2,559
1959*	4,902	2,844	6,287	645	6,670	4,691	4,660	5,272	4,101	3,192	968	2,834
1958	4,569	2,652	5,956	498	6,034	4,398	4,291	4,970	3,909	3,090	750	2,486
1957	4,396	2,436	5,601	469	5,872	4,252	4,379	4,777	3,984	2,894	940	2,763
1956	4,260	2,396	5,465	455	5,589	4,150	4,275	4,619	3,824	2,946	892	2,635
1955	3,986	2,342	5,055	461	5,290	3,870	4,315	4,356	3,586	2,778	971	2,387
1954	3,754	2,131	4,905	577	5,234	3,735	3,823	4,246	3,349	2,818	923	2,358
1953	3,760	2,233	4,816	493	5,071	3,716	3,716	4,156	3,415	2,806	817	2,406
1952	3,507	2,038	4,691	479	4,696	3,421	3,576	3,756	3,216	2,374	847	2,244
1951	3,345	2,060	4,071	482	4,143	3,366	3,539	3,601	3,064	2,426	982	2,170
1950	2,982	1,828	3,874	711	4,171	3,002	3,148	3,405	2,736	2,299	986	1,850
1939	1,112	460	1,809	373	2,136	1,421	1,277	1,309	1,007	833	309	673

	All female workers									
	Race [1]		Major occupation group [2]							
Year	White	Negro and other races	Professional, technical, and kindred workers	Managers, officials, and proprietors, except farm	Clerical and kindred workers	Sales workers	Craftsmen, foremen, and kindred workers	Operatives and kindred workers	Private household workers	Service workers, except private household
	384	385	386	387	388	389	390	391	392	393
1970	$3,870	$3,285	$6,589	$5,741	$4,467	$1,972	$4,053	$3,637	$527	$2,248
1969	3,640	2,884	6,012	5,469	4,124	1,896	4,358	3,544	513	2,053
1968	3,465	2,497	5,564	4,840	3,882	2,073	4,040	3,383	546	2,029
1967	3,254	2,288	5,225	4,724	3,719	1,870	3,717	3,088	512	1,904
1966	3,079	1,981	4,801	4,151	3,515	1,896	3,432	2,839	526	1,696
1965	2,994	1,722	4,720	3,830	3,444	1,933	3,408	2,764	555	1,588
1964	2,841	1,652	4,374	3,675	3,420	1,761	3,074	2,630	518	1,449
1963	2,723	1,448	4,163	3,370	3,285	1,521	3,008	2,518	477	1,369
1962	2,630	1,396	4,150	3,640	3,190	1,606	3,141	2,430	476	1,378
1961	2,538	1,302	3,991	3,182	3,112	1,528	3,095	2,322	458	1,384
1960	2,537	1,276	3,868	3,500	3,039	1,359	(3)	2,368	473	1,427
1959*	2,422	1,289	3,615	3,556	2,955	1,474	(3)	2,267	502	1,287
1958	2,364	1,055	3,501	3,313	2,943	1,604	(3)	2,075	467	1,255
1957	2,240	1,019	3,344	3,118	2,802	1,342	(3)	2,130	459	1,249
1956	2,179	970	3,114	2,976	2,699	1,204	(3)	2,130	486	1,151
1955	2,065	894	2,963	3,158	2,597	1,182	(3)	2,048	502	1,135
1954	2,046	914	3,008	(3)	2,468	1,348	(3)	1,852	495	1,154
1953	2,049	994	2,929	2,548	2,420	1,158	(3)	1,901	554	1,223
1952	1,976	814	2,695	2,705	2,270	1,075	2,075	1,908	433	1,128
1951	1,855	781	2,495	2,679	2,147	1,176	(3)	1,739	447	996
1950	1,698	626	2,264	2,089	2,064	1,148	(3)	1,616	448	895
1939	676	246	1,023	1,107	966	636	827	582	296	493

See footnotes at end of table.

Series G 372–415. Median Money Wage or Salary Income of All Workers With Wage or Salary Income, and of Year-Round Full-Time Workers, by Sex, Race, and Major Occupation Group: 1939–1970—Con.

Male year-round full-time workers

Year	Race [1]		Major occupation group [2]									
	White	Negro and other races	Professional, technical, and kindred workers	Farmers and farm managers	Managers, officials, and proprietors, except farm	Clerical and kindred workers	Sales workers	Craftsmen, foremen, and kindred workers	Operatives and kindred workers	Service workers, except private household	Farm laborers and foremen	Laborers, except farm and mine
	394	395	396	397	398	399	400	401	402	403	404	405
1970	$9,373	$6,598	$11,806	$1,260	$12,117	$8,617	$9,790	$9,254	$7,623	$6,955	$3,519	$6,563
1969	8,876	6,158	11,266	1,180	11,467	7,966	9,135	8,757	7,307	6,373	2,985	6,150
1968	8,014	5,603	10,151	1,275	10,340	7,351	8,549	7,978	6,738	6,058	3,069	5,504
1967	7,512	5,069	9,523	993	9,817	6,757	7,744	7,484	6,316	5,439	2,489	5,182
1966	7,164	4,528	8,945	1,229	9,103	6,487	7,569	7,197	6,112	5,078	2,489	4,946
1965	6,814	4,367	8,464	750	8,856	6,231	7,188	6,877	5,830	4,986	2,458	4,445
1964	6,497	4,285	8,004	754	7,870	6,134	6,733	6,538	5,659	4,701	2,160	4,436
1963	6,277	4,104	7,713	750	7,639	5,838	6,493	6,315	5,480	4,399	1,655	4,449
1962	6,025	3,799	7,357	587	7,454	5,589	6,193	6,251	5,319	4,406	1,984	4,380
1961	5,880	3,883	7,339	558	7,343	5,387	6,163	6,067	5,108	4,203	1,793	4,330
1960	5,662	3,789	6,848	499	7,241	5,247	5,755	5,868	4,977	4,089	1,731	3,872
1959*	5,456	3,339	6,835	683	6,910	5,130	5,545	5,654	4,607	4,002	1,637	3,930
1958	5,186	3,368	6,513	490	6,431	4,839	5,332	5,365	4,460	3,898	1,406	3,672
1957	4,950	3,137	5,990	454	6,110	4,564	5,143	5,216	4,397	3,605	1,518	3,710
1956	4,710	2,912	5,847	479	5,967	4,388	5,005	4,981	4,235	3,521	1,526	3,410
1955	4,458	2,831	5,382	414	5,584	4,162	4,937	4,712	4,046	3,565	(3)	3,105
1939	1,419	639	2,100	430	2,254	1,564	1,451	1,562	1,268	1,019	365	991

Female year-round full-time workers

Year	Race [1]		Major occupation group [2]							
	White	Negro and other races	Professional, technical, and kindred workers	Managers, officials, and proprietors, except farm	Clerical and kindred workers	Sales workers	Craftsmen, foremen, and kindred workers	Operatives and kindred workers	Private household workers	Service workers, except private household
	406	407	408	409	410	411	412	413	414	415
1970	$5,490	$4,674	$7,878	$6,834	$5,551	$4,188	$5,089	$4,510	$2,101	$3,953
1969	5,168	4,231	7,309	6,091	5,187	3,704	4,992	4,317	1,851	3,755
1968	4,700	3,677	6,691	5,635	4,789	3,461	4,625	3,991	1,523	3,332
1967	4,394	3,363	6,307	5,341	4,537	3,283	4,284	3,649	1,298	3,071
1966	4,152	2,949	5,826	4,919	4,316	3,103	4,345	3,416	1,297	2,815
1965	3,960	2,713	5,634	4,593	4,154	2,961	4,023	3,327	1,150	2,607
1964	3,859	2,674	5,150	4,369	4,060	2,719	(3)	3,271	1,082	2,525
1963	3,723	2,368	4,998	4,219	3,951	2,531	(3)	3,143	1,108	2,528
1962	3,601	2,278	4,863	4,311	3,832	2,699	(3)	3,157	1,107	2,283
1961	3,480	2,325	4,961	3,910	3,743	2,409	(3)	2,925	1,045	2,357
1960	3,410	2,372	4,384	4,173	3,586	2,428	(3)	2,970	1,133	2,418
1959*	3,306	2,196	4,385	3,934	3,493	2,340	(3)	2,916	1,146	2,241
1958	3,225	1,988	4,146	3,771	3,388	2,333	(3)	2,745	1,161	2,073
1957	3,107	1,866	3,810	3,890	3,287	2,289	(3)	2,611	980	1,995
1956	2,958	1,637	3,650	3,525	3,145	2,090	(3)	2,632	879	1,950
1955	2,870	1,637	3,500	(3)	3,065	(3)	(3)	2,489	(3)	1,759
1939	863	327	1,277	1,218	1,072	745	995	742	339	607

* Denotes first year for which figures include Alaska and Hawaii.
[1] For wage or salary workers at time of survey.
[2] For experienced civilian labor force. 1939 excludes public emergency workers and persons having less than $100 of wage or salary income, but includes members of the Armed Forces; 1950 excludes persons having less than $100 of wage or salary income.
[3] Fewer than 100 cases in the sample reporting with $1 or more of wage or salary income.

Chapter G

Consumer Expenditure Patterns (Series G 416-915)

G 416–469. Personal consumption expenditures, by type of product, 1929–1970.

Source: U.S. Office of Business Economics, 1929–1963, *The National Income and Product Accounts of the United States, 1929–1965, Statistical Tables*, table 2.5; 1964–1967, *U.S. National Income and Product Accounts, 1964–67*, table 2.5; 1968–1970, U.S. Bureau of Economic Analysis, *Survey of Current Business*, July 1972, table 2.5.

Detailed estimates by the Department of Commerce of consumer expenditures for commodities and services since 1929 were first published in the *Survey of Current Business*, June 1944. The figures on personal consumption expenditures for commodities were calculated by the "commodity flow methods" developed by Simon Kuznets, *Commodity Flow and Capital Formation*, National Bureau of Economic Research, New York, 1938. Estimates of personal consumption expenditures for services are based on a variety of source materials which cannot be summarized briefly. For further detail, see *National Income: 1954 Edition*.

As defined by the Department of Commerce, personal consumption expenditures represent the market value of purchases of goods and services by individuals and nonprofit institutions and the value of food, clothing, housing, and financial services received by them as income in kind. Rental value of owner-occupied houses is included; purchases of dwellings, which are classified as capital goods, are excluded.

G 470–494. Personal consumption expenditures, by type of product, 1909–1929.

Source: J. Frederic Dewhurst and Associates, *America's Needs and Resources, A New Survey*, pp. 965–980, © 1955 by The Twentieth Century Fund, New York.

The first detailed estimates of aggregate consumer expenditures for goods and services in the United States over a period of time appeared in William H. Lough (with the assistance of Martin Gainsbrugh), *High-Level Consumption*, McGraw-Hill, New York, 1935. These pioneer estimates covered the years 1909, 1914, 1919, 1921, 1923, 1925, 1927, 1929, and 1931. The data for the later years were revised and extended by Harold Barger, *Outlay and Income in the United States, 1921–1938*, National Bureau of Economic Research, New York, 1942. In the 1940's, J. Frederic Dewhurst and Associates (*America's Needs and Resources*, 1947) revised these various estimates and expanded those on recreational expense to take account of estimates by Julius Weinberger, "The Economic Aspects of Recreation," *Harvard Business Review*, summer issue, 1937.

G 495–848. General note.

Collection of data on consumer expenditures, and especially wage earners' expenditures, began in the United States in the 1870's. It was undertaken on a small scale by a number of different State agencies using a great variety of methods. The most substantial of these studies was the one made for Massachusetts by Carroll D. Wright, Bureau of Statistics of Labor, Massachusetts. He undertook a carefully planned survey of the earnings and expenditures of 397 families of skilled and unskilled workers in 1875. The usefulness of the data gathered in this study led the Congress to request further studies of this type on a broader base by the newly formed U.S. Bureau of Labor of which Wright had become Commissioner.

Some of the results of the large-scale studies made by the U.S. Bureau of Labor for 1888–91 and 1901 are given in series G 554–572. The data on food expenditures obtained in the 1901 survey were used to provide the design for an index of prices of food purchased by workingmen. This index was used generally as a deflator for workers' incomes and expenditures for all kinds of goods until World War I.

During that period, the need for a more inclusive index of retail prices became clearer because food prices rose so much faster than those of many other commodities and of rents. A nationwide study of the expenditures of wage earners and clerical workers was undertaken in 1918 to provide a list of items to be priced for such an index and also to provide data on the relative importance of each item. Because of the number of wage disputes in the shipbuilding centers, the survey was first undertaken in seacoast cities. It was later expanded into what was regarded as a representative sample of industrial centers in the United States.

The first study made in this country of the over-all consumer expenditures of a group of farm families was made in Livingston County, N.Y., in 1909. In the early 1920's, the U.S. Department of Agriculture initiated a cooperative project on the subject with the State Agricultural Experiment Stations under the direction of E. L. Kirkpatrick. In 1925, it was decided, for lack of any other data on farm family expenditures extending across State lines, to average the data that had been collected in 11 States covering one year in the period 1923–1925. The resulting averages given in series G 778–797 have been widely used, but other State studies made in the next few years indicated that the averages for the 2,886 families were too high to be representative of the expenditures of farm-operator families throughout the country at that time.

Dramatic increases in productivity in industry and agriculture during the 1920's and the economic collapse which began in 1929 led a number of economists to study the factors affecting consumer expenditures and to estimate changes in consumption patterns over time. The pioneer investigation in this field was made by Simon Kuznets, *Commodity Flow and Capital Formation*, National Bureau of Economic Research, New York, 1938. This study shows national aggregates for four types of consumer goods and services. The Brookings Institution published, in 1934, estimates of expenditure patterns at different income levels of farm and nonfarm families and single individuals in 1929 (see M. Leven, H. G. Moulton, and C. Warburton, *America's Capacity to Consume*, The Brookings Institution, Washington, D. C., 1934). The figures were prepared by Clark Warburton on the basis of scattered sample studies made during the 1920's and early 1930's and correlated with national income estimates made by Maurice Leven (see text for series G 772–777 and G 843–848). In 1935, estimates of aggregate consumer expenditures in detail for 1909 and 1929 and selected years between were prepared by Martin Gainsbrugh and published in William H. Lough, *High-Level Consumption* (see text for series G 470–494). This book included a comparison with The Brookings Institution's aggregates for 1929, showing that the two estimates were very close for food expense, and reasonably close for attire and home maintenance; but the estimates by Lough and Gainsbrugh of expenditures for all other items were much higher than the Brookings' figures.

In the middle 1930's, two national cross-section studies of consumer expenditure patterns were undertaken. The first, conducted by the Bureau of Labor Statistics, covered employed city wage and clerical workers and was initiated to provide a new list of items and weights for the Consumer Price Index of the Bureau of Labor Statistics. The second, the Study of Consumer Purchases, conducted jointly by the BLS and the Bureau of Home Economics in the Department of Agriculture, related to families (with native-born heads) who were not on public relief rolls during the survey year, and was initiated to provide data relating the effect on expenditure patterns of income, occupation of the head, race, family composition, and type of community. The results of the second study were used by the National Resources Planning Board as the basis for a national estimate of consumer expenditures (see text for series G 679–696, G 754–771, and G 828–842). The data from this study were supplemented by information from the Bureau of Internal Revenue (now Internal Revenue Service) on income distribution and receipts from excise taxes, and from a few studies of the expenditures of families on public relief rolls and of those with foreign-born heads.

A small nationwide survey covering 1941 conducted by the Bureau of Labor Statistics and the Bureau of Home Economics (see text for series G 661–678 and G 735–753) provides detailed data on the expenditure patterns of rural and urban families in the same year. BLS also conducted a sample national study of urban family expenditures in 1944 (see text for series G 643–660). Another BLS urban study covering 1950, intended primarily to serve as a basis for revision of the Consumer Price Index, subsequently provided detailed tabulations of consumer expenditures, income, and savings (see text for series G 495–514). The Department of Agriculture, in cooperation with the Bureau of the Census, conducted a survey of farm family expenditures in 1955 (see text for series G 717–734) to obtain data to revise the Parity Index and improve the basis for estimating farm operators' production expenses, which provides detailed data on farm family expenditures.

In recent years, there have been a number of nationwide surveys of consumer expenditures by income level for specified types of goods. See, for example, individual reports in the series published by the Department of Agriculture, *Household Food Consumption Survey,* 1965–66. The reports of this survey provide detailed data for farm and nonfarm households on quantities and values of food consumed and on dietary levels by money income after taxes in the United States as a whole and in four major regions.

The Surveys of Consumer Finances, conducted annually from 1946–1971 for the Board of Governors of the Federal Reserve System by the Survey Research Center of the University of Michigan, yield data on consumer purchases of selected durable goods by income level of all "spending units" in the United States. Reports of these surveys appear in the *Federal Reserve Bulletin.*

Other national sample surveys conducted for use in marketing research have covered a very large proportion, but not all types, of consumer goods and services. The most comprehensive of these is the study of consumer expenditures conducted for Life Magazine by Alfred Politz Research, Inc., which is based on a sample designed to represent all individuals, 20 years of age and over, in conterminous United States. The study provides an unusual amount of detailed material on expenditures for commodities along with data on buying habits of households of different types.

The lack of continuity in the tables shown here which present data by income level is, at least in part, due to the fact that the coverage and definitions used in obtaining the data differ so greatly from study to study. The chief differences in population coverage and in the classification and definition of goods and services purchased are briefly specified in the tables and in the text which follows. Differences in definition primarily affect the figures on income, expenditures for housing, and for "sundries" or "miscellaneous goods and services."

The figures on income represent annual income before deduction of direct personal taxes, i.e., income, poll, and personal property, except the following, which represent annual income after deduction of taxes: Urban families in 1917–19, series G 534–553; 1944, series G 643–660; and 1950, series G 495–514 and G 623–642; and farm-operator families in 1955, series G 717–734; and urban and farm families in 1960–61, series G 602–622 and G 697–716.

Direct personal taxes, as well as indirect taxes, were generally

tabulated as an item of current expenditure in the consumer expenditure surveys made before the 1930's. Since the Consumer Purchases Study of 1935–36, such taxes have been presented separately and have not been included in consumer expenditures. For the series presented here, direct personal taxes were deducted from expenditure figures in the earlier surveys, wherever possible, to insure greater comparability with the most recent surveys.

Social Security taxes paid by the worker (first collected in 1937) were treated as savings in the 1941 and 1944 surveys, and handled with personal insurance as a separate class of disbursements in the 1950 urban, the 1955 farm, and the 1960–61 urban and farm surveys.

In the early studies of wage earners' incomes and expenditures, no attempt was made to evaluate the products received by a family from its garden, poultry, hogs, or cows. Most studies of the incomes and expenditures of farm-operator families include data on the value of food and fuel produced by the family for its own use, sometimes valued at prices which would have been paid for them had they been purchased through nearby trade channels, and sometimes at prices which would have been received if the products had been sold.

The treatment of imputed income resulting from expenditures for owned homes varies considerably from one series to another. Series G 416–494 include rental value of owned homes, but not capital expenditures for housing. In the early studies of wage earners' expenditures, the statistical difficulties of handling homeowners' housing expenditures were avoided by excluding homeowners from the "normal" family group and including only renters. In studies made since the middle-1930's, emphasis has been laid on homeowners' current year expenditures for housing and for investments in their homes, but in some surveys data on rental value is also available in the original sources.

Conceptually, premiums paid on life insurance policies may be classified wholly as current expenditures or partly as savings and partly current expenditures, depending on the type of policy; but in sample surveys it is difficult to obtain from respondents information on the type of policies on which premiums are paid.

Series G 416–494 include as consumer expenditures the part of insurance premiums paid which covers the expense of handling life insurance, but not the part which will eventually be returned to the consumer buyer or his beneficiaries. In sample surveys of consumer expenditures made before the 1930's, the difficulty of obtaining information on the types of policies held resulted in classifying payments on such premiums in the sundries or miscellaneous group as current expenditures. In expenditure surveys made since 1930, it has been the practice to exclude insurance premiums from current expenditure data, handling them either as savings or as a separate class of disbursements.

Until the 1960–61 survey, farm studies included operator families only, in some cases defined to cover nonresident operators and resident operators of urban farms as well as those living on rural farms. In the 1960–61 survey, the three population groups were defined by place of residence. Farm families in that survey are limited to those living on rural farms, and include other than operator families.

In addition to the sources of the individual series, students of the history of the subject are referred to the following:

Dorothy S. Brady and Faith M. Williams, "Advances in the Techniques of Measuring and Estimating Consumer Expenditures," *Journal of Farm Economics,* May 1945, vol. 27, No. 2.

"Consumer Survey Statistics, Report of Consultant Committee on Consumer Survey Statistics, organized by the Board of Governors of the Federal Reserve System at the request of the Subcommittee on Economic Statistics of the Joint Committee on the Economic Report, July 1955," *Hearings Before the Subcommittee on Economic Statistics,* 84th Congress, July 19 and 26, October 4 and 5, 1955, pp. 251–372.

Solomon Fabricant, "Measuring National Consumption," *Studies in Income and Wealth,* vol. 8, National Bureau of Economic Research, New York, 1946.

Helen Humes Lamale, *Methodology of the Survey of Consumer Expenditures in 1950*, Wharton School of Finance and Commerce, University of Pennsylvania, 1959.

William H. Shaw, "Consumption Expenditures, 1929–1943," *Survey of Current Business*, June 1944.

Bureau of Home Economics, *Study of Consumer Purchases, Urban, Village, and Farm Series*, 1935–1936 (22 volumes).

Agricultural Research Service, *Farm Family Spending and Saving in Illinois*, Agricultural Information Bulletin, No. 101.

Agricultural Research Service, *Condensed vs. Detailed Schedule for Collection of Family Expenditure Data*, FE-51, March 1954.

Bureau of Labor Statistics, *Money Disbursements of Wage Earners and Clerical Workers, 1934–1936*, Bulletin Nos. 636–641, inclusive. (No. 638 is the summary volume.)

Bureau of Labor Statistics, *Study of Consumer Purchases, Urban Series, 1935–1936*, Bulletin Nos. 642–649, inclusive.

Clark Warburton, "Three Estimates of the Value of the Nation's Output of Commodities and Services," *Studies in Income and Wealth*, vol. 3, National Bureau of Economic Research, New York, 1939.

Faith M. Williams, "International Comparisons of Patterns of Family Consumption," in *Consumer Behavior: Research on Consumer Reactions*, Harper and Brothers, 1958.

Faith M. Williams and Carle C. Zimmerman, *Family Living Studies in the United States and Other Countries*, Department of Agriculture, Miscellaneous Publication No. 223.

Chase Going Woodhouse and Faith M. Williams, *Comparison of Schedule and Account Methods of Collecting Data on Family Living*, Department of Agriculture, Technical Bulletin 386.

G 495–581.   General note.

Data on the consumption expenditures of city wage- and clerical-worker families of two or more persons were collected at irregular intervals and for a variety of purposes. Only the 1950 BLS Study of Consumer Expenditures was based on a sample representing families of all types in these occupational groups in cities of all sizes throughout the entire country. Insofar as the original publications make it possible, the figures from the earlier studies have been adjusted as to definition and classification of consumer expenditures so as to conform to those used in 1950.

See also general note for series G 495–848.

G 495–514.   Consumption expenditures, in current prices, of city wage- and clerical-worker families of 2 or more persons, by income class, 1950.

Source: U.S. Department of Labor, *How American Buying Habits Change*, 1959.

These series are based on a *Study of Consumer Expenditures, Incomes and Savings; Statistical Tables: Urban U.S.—1950*, a joint study by the U.S. Bureau of Labor Statistics (BLS) and the Wharton School of Finance and Commerce, University of Pennsylvania, 1956, vols. I, II, III, IX, and X.

The survey of consumer expenditures in 1950 was conducted by BLS to provide the basis for revising its Consumer Price Index (CPI). The survey was undertaken during the first half of 1951 in 91 urban areas throughout the United States ranging in size from places of 2,500 inhabitants to the greater New York area with a population of 9 million. Complete and usable reports were obtained from 12,489 consumer units. Since the study was directed toward the determination of expenditure weights for the revised CPI, the data for family expenditures for individual consumption goods and services purchased by the 7,007 wage-earner and clerical-worker families of two or more persons were tabulated and averaged for each of the 91 cities surveyed.

Subsequently, the same data were tabulated in considerable detail and published as part of the study of consumer expenditures, income,

and savings, which was made by the Wharton School of Finance and Commerce in cooperation with BLS under a grant from the Ford Foundation.

To obtain data for wage-earner and clerical-worker families of two or more, the following groups were excluded: Single consumers; self-employed; salaried professionals; officials, etc.; and persons not gainfully employed. Within the nine classes of cities averaged for the Wharton School publications (large cities, suburbs, and small cities in the North, South, and West), averages were based on the sample families as weights; in combining the resulting averages, universe (total consumer units, i.e., families and single consumers) weights were used.

G 515–533.   Consumption expenditures, in current prices, of employed city wage- and clerical-worker families of 2 or more persons, by income class, 1934–36.

Source: U.S. Bureau of Labor Statistics, unpublished data.

These series are based on Faith M. Williams and Alice C. Hanson, *Money Disbursements of Wage Earners and Clerical Workers*, Bureau of Labor Statistics, Bulletin No. 638, summary volume, 1941.

The data in this 1934–36 study were gathered to provide the basis for revising the BLS Consumer Price Index. The survey (conducted in a period of mass unemployment) was restricted to families of two or more in large cities, who had an income of at least $500 and who had not been on public relief during the survey year. These limits precluded from the pattern on which the CPI was to be based the irregular spending of workers on "relief" and those employed so irregularly that their purchases could not have been typical of long-range consumption patterns. The survey covered 12,903 white families and 1,566 Negro families in 42 cities with population 50,000 or more.

These series, derived from Bulletin No. 638, have been adjusted for comparability with definitions and classifications of the 1950 *Study of Consumer Expenditures* . . . (see text for series G 495–514), as follows: "Vocation" outlays shown in table 1 were deducted from both "average annual current expenditures" in table 1 and from "average annual amount" of total net family income in table 7. "Community welfare" and "gifts and contributions to persons outside the economic family" were deducted from "average annual current consumption expenditures" in table 7.

G 534–553.   Consumption expenditures, in current prices, of city wage- and clerical-worker families with at least 1 child, by income class, 1917–19.

Source: U.S. Bureau of Labor Statistics, Bulletin No. 357, *Cost of Living in the United States, 1917–19*.

These data were collected from white city worker families consisting of husband and wife and at least one child, who was not a boarder or lodger. The families could have no boarders and not over three lodgers; at least 75 percent of family income had to come from the principal breadwinner or others who contributed all earnings to the family fund; slum or charity families or non-English speaking families who had been in the United States less than five years were excluded.

This survey was first undertaken in shipbuilding centers for the purpose of providing market baskets which could be used in computing consumer price indexes for cities most affected by the inflation which occurred during and just after World War I. It was later broadened to cover 92 cities and localities throughout the entire country.

The income and expenditure figures presented in Bulletin No. 357 were adjusted for comparability with definitions and classifications used in the 1950 *Study of Consumer Expenditures* . . . (see text for series G 495–514). Thus, average money income after taxes (see series G 536) was derived by deducting dues to labor organizations, personal property and poll taxes, and expenditures for tools (Bulletin

No. 357, pp. 448 and 454) from total average income per family (Bulletin No. 357, p. 4). Average expenditures for current consumption (see series G 537) were derived by deducting from total average yearly expenses per family (Bulletin No. 357, p. 5) the same items deducted from income and, in addition, life insurance premiums; contributions to church, charity, and patriotic purposes; and gifts (Bulletin No. 357, pp. 447 and 448). Each consumption group was adjusted for maximum comparability with the corresponding groups as classified in the 1950 *Study* (when they differed from the original published table).

G 554–563. Consumption expenditures, in current prices, of normal city wage- and clerical-worker families of 2 or more persons, by income class, 1901.

Source: See source for series G 495–514.

These series are based on 18th Annual Report of the Commissioner of Labor, Document No. 23, Bureau of Labor, 1903, *Cost of Living and Retail Prices of Food*, pp. 581, 592, and 593.

Earnings and expenditure data from this report covered families with wage and salary incomes not exceeding $1,200 a year, and were collected through personal interviews by experienced special agents of the Bureau of Labor. About 15 percent of these families had incomes from boarders and lodgers and other sources. The latter income raised total income above $1,200 for a few families. Therefore their expenditures could be, and were, above $1,200. Altogether, data were collected from 25,440 families of all types but only those from the 11,156 families defined as "normal" were summarized by income levels. These "normal" families had a husband at work, a wife, not more than five children and none over 14 years of age; no dependents, boarders, lodgers, or servants; and provided data on expenditures for rent, fuel, lighting, food, clothing, and sundries.

The 1901 study had a wide city and industry coverage in 32 States and the District of Columbia, and appears to have provided a very good picture of "normal" families in wage and salaried occupations. The selection of the number of persons interviewed in each geographical area was roughly apportioned in accordance with the number of persons employed in the manufacturing industries of the States.

G 564–572. Consumption expenditures, in current prices, of normal city wage- and clerical-worker families of 2 or more persons in 9 basic industries, by income class, 1888–91.

Source: See source for series G 495–514.

These series are based on Sixth Annual Report of the Commissioner of Labor, 1890, *Cost of Production*, part III; and Seventh Annual Report of the Commissioner of Labor, 1891, *Cost of Production*, vol. II, part III. Only data for so-called "normal" families in all industries (identified by budget numbers, Seventh Annual Report, pp. 1826–1839, 1887–1898) were used for comparative purposes. Family size, income, and expenditures were tabulated from the Sixth Annual Report (pp. 790–801, 914–925, 984–989, 1076–1085, 1128–1131, 1160–1162), and the Seventh Annual Report (pp. 1170–1206, 1374–1390, and 1552–1569). Those data provided the basis for calculation of average family size, income, and total expenditures for all "normal" families by income class. The percentage distributions of total expenditures for "normal" families, in the Seventh Annual Report (pp. 2012 and 2013), were applied to the appropriate averages to estimate the dollar expenditure by income class.

Earnings and expenditure data in the study covered 2,562 "normal" families. "Normal" families had both a husband and wife, not more than five children, no one of whom was over 14 years of age; no dependents or boarders; did not own its own dwelling place; and had expenditures for rent, fuel, lighting, clothing, and food. The study covered workers in the following industries: Pig iron, bar iron, steel, bituminous coal, coke, iron ore, cotton, woolen, and glass.

G 573–581. Consumption expenditures, in current prices, of Massachusetts city wage- and clerical-worker families of 2 or more persons, by income class, 1874–75.

Source: See source for series G 495–514.

These data are based on Massachusetts Bureau of Statistics of Labor, Sixth Annual Report, March 1875, Public Document No. 31, pp. 221–354, 372, 373, and 441. The data were collected from families of wage earners in 15 cities and 21 towns by trained agents of the Bureau of Statistics of Labor who approached 1,000 families before they were able to find 397 who had enough information about their affairs to answer the questions put to them and who were also willing to "having their private life inquired into." The families included about equal numbers of skilled and unskilled workers, and were those who, with comparatively few exceptions, had children dependent on them for support.

Series G 573–581 were computed from data in the Massachusetts report which show, by income class, the number of families from whom figures were received, their aggregate earnings and expenses in each class, and percentages of expenditure as regards income, by income class, for five major categories of expense. The resulting weighted averages for all families' earnings and expenses were found to check with all family averages shown elsewhere in the report. Average figures on money earnings, expenses for all goods and services and for fuel also checked with such averages in the report. The figures on expenses for food, rent, and sundries checked within a few dollars (differences probably caused by rounding of the percentages).

In this report, the items of expenditure not specifically for subsistence, clothing, rent, and fuel were listed as sundries. The report states that sundry items of expense are those which "although . . . not absolutely necessary for the life of the body, are, in their way, imperative necessity in a man's social life." Some specified sundries include furniture, carpets, books and papers, societies, religion, charity, sickness, care of parents, care of house, recreation, housegirl, travel to work, and life insurance.

G 582–601. Consumption expenditures of city wage- and clerical-worker families of 2 or more persons, 1888–91 to 1960–61.

Source: 1888–91, 1901, and 1917–19, see source for series G 495–514. For 1934–36 and 1950, U.S. Bureau of Labor Statistics, "Standards and Levels of Living of City-Worker Families," *Monthly Labor Review*, September 1956, p. 1018. Averages for 1960–61 compiled from unpublished tabulations from the Bureau's survey of consumer expenditures, 1960–61.

Figures on average money receipts and outlays of wage and clerical-workers' families of two or more persons in large cities have been converted into dollars of 1950 purchasing power for each of the survey years since 1888–91. The BLS Consumer Price Index was used to convert current expenditures and average income into dollars of 1950 purchasing power for the surveys of 1917–19, 1934–36, and 1960–61. The cost-of-living index developed by Paul Douglas (see *American Economic Review*, Supplement, March 1926, p. 22) was used to convert income and total consumption expenditures for the 1888–91 and 1901 studies; the BLS Retail Food Index was used to convert the expenditures for food and drink. Other categories of expenditures were not converted into 1950 dollars because no indexes are available for these categories prior to 1913.

Series G 582–601 for 1917–19, 1934–36, and 1950 relate to expenditures of wage and clerical workers' families in large cities, i.e. with populations of 50,000 and over in 1917–19 and 1934–36 and 30,500 and over in 1950. For 1960–61, they relate to expenditures of wage and clerical workers' families in urban places of 2,500 and over. Populations of the large industrial centers surveyed in 1888–91 and 1901 were not specified.

G 602–696. General note.

For discussion of the surveys from which these series were taken, see general note for series G 495–848 and the following text for certain series grouped by survey.

G 602–622. Consumption expenditures, in current prices, of all families of 2 or more persons in cities of 2,500 and over, by income class, 1960–61.

Source: U.S. Bureau of Labor Statistics, *Survey of Consumer Expenditures, 1960–61.*

The 1961 survey coverage was extended to rural areas so, for the first time since 1941, information was available on spending habits for a cross-section of the total noninstitutional population in urban and rural areas of the United States.

See also text for series G 495–514 and series G 798–812.

G 623–642. Consumption expenditures, in current prices, of all families of 2 or more persons in cities of 2,500 and over, by income class, 1950.

Source: *Study of Consumer Expenditures, Incomes and Savings; Statistical Tables: Urban U.S.—1950*, cited in text for series G 495–514, vol. XVIII, pp. 14–23.

For a description of this survey, see text for series G 495–514. To obtain the data for all families of two or more persons, only single consumers were excluded; all occupational groups were included. Within the nine classes of cities averaged for the Wharton School publications (large cities, suburbs, and small cities in the North, South, and West), averages were based on the sample families as weights. In combining the resulting averages, universe (total consumer units) weights were used.

G 643–660. Consumption expenditures, in current prices, of all families of 2 or more persons in cities of 2,500 and over, by income class, 1944.

Source: U.S. Bureau of Labor Statistics, *Monthly Labor Review*, January 1946, p. 4; and Bulletin No. 838, *Wartime Food Purchases*, pp. 1–4 and appendix.

A study of expenditures and savings in 1944 of city families was undertaken by BLS for the primary purpose of comparing prices reported by city consumers with prices indicated by urban store reports. The survey was made in two parts. The first part, made in the fall of 1944, provided detailed information on food purchases during one week, purchases of clothing and household textiles during the first eight months of the year, tenure and rental in August 1944, and sufficient information on family composition, living arrangements, and income to provide a basis for classification. The second part provided data on purchases of food during one week early in 1945, of clothing and other textiles during the last four months of 1944, and of other goods and services throughout 1944.

The sample used in this survey was very similar to that used in the 1941 survey (see text for series G 661–678) and related to the civilian noninstitutional population in cities of 2,500 or more scattered throughout the country. The sample included approximately 1,700 families and single persons in 28 metropolitan districts and 20 cities with a population under 50,000 outside of metropolitan districts. These places were selected to represent, with respect to region, State, and city size, all cities in the United States with a population of 2,500 or more.

Family income represents the sum of all types of income received by family members during 1944; included are wage and salary earnings after payroll deductions of income taxes, entrepreneurial net income or withdrawals, and nonearned income from all sources except inheritances, large gifts, and lump-sum insurance settlements.

Although the figures were originally published as preliminary and subject to slight revisions, no revisions were subsequently issued.

G 661–678. Consumption expenditures, in current prices, of all families of 2 or more persons in cities of 2,500 and over, by income class, 1941.

Source: U.S. Bureau of Labor Statistics, Bulletin No. 822, *Family Spending and Saving in Wartime*, pp. 68, 70, 71, 76, 102, and 109.

The survey of family spending and saving in wartime (World War II) is the only survey which was conducted for the primary purpose of providing national estimates of expenditures and savings by income class.

The method of drawing the sample used for this survey differed in several important respects from that followed in earlier surveys of family incomes and expenditures. A description of these changes appears in part I, "Scope and Method," of the source. The coverage of population was more complete than in any previous survey and included such segments of the population as families on public relief rolls, foreign-born and broken families, single consumers, occupational groups, and city-size classes; but it excluded inmates of institutions, residents of military camps, and persons in labor camps.

The sample was smaller than in any previous survey on which national estimates have been based. The sample for urban areas covered about 1,300 families and single persons in 62 cities of 2,500 or more scattered throughout the country. The cities were so selected as to give proper representation to (1) each city-size group; (2) proximity to a metropolis (for cities under 50,000); (3) each region and State; (4) low, medium, and high rent cities; and (5) cities of differing racial composition.

Information was obtained on both money and nonmoney income, although only money income figures are shown here. Expenditures for family living were reported in detail under 14 categories of expense. All purchases of durable goods made during the year, except payments on homes and improvements on homes, were considered current expenditures. Financing charges, interest on installment and other credit purchases, and shipping and delivery charges were considered as part of the expenditure. Discounts and trade-in allowances were deducted from the gross price. Sales and excise taxes were included in the expenditure for each article except in the case of the details for food expenditure.

Sample data for the $5,000 to $10,000 and the $10,000 and over classes are included, although the averages for these classes are based on a small number of cases and are therefore quite irregular and subject to a wide margin of error. They should be considered as statements of sample results only, and not as estimates of actual expenditures by the entire group of families in those income groups.

G 679–696. Consumption expenditures, in current prices, of all families of 2 or more persons in cities of 2,500 and over, by income class, 1935–36.

Source: U.S. National Resources Planning Board, *Family Expenditures in the United States, Statistical Tables and Appendixes*, 1941, pp. 61, 120, and 157.

The study of family expenditures is part of the *Study of Consumer Purchases*, conducted by the Bureau of Labor Statistics and the Bureau of Home Economics, in cooperation with the National Resources Committee, the Central Statistical Board, and the Works Progress Administration. The Bureau of Home Economics conducted the survey in rural-farm and rural-nonfarm areas and in the majority of the small cities covered, and the Bureau of Labor Statistics conducted the surveys in the other small cities and all of the larger urban communities.

The study of consumer purchases was the most detailed analysis of family expenditures in the United States made up to that time. Data were published on over 90 categories of outlays. They are classified to permit study of differences between the farm, rural-nonfarm, and urban population, of regional variations, of differences with respect to size of family and between white and Negro families, as well as of differences between income levels.

Detailed information on expenditures and savings during a 12-month period between January 1935 and December 1936 was secured from a sample of about 60,000 families living in cities of different sizes, in villages, and on farms in 30 States, of which 54,000 were used in preparing the family expenditure data. The urban sample covered 51 cities and approximately 30,000 expenditure schedules. Both the sample expenditure data and the population weights used in preparing the estimates (shown in these series) of family expenditures by income class exclude families receiving any direct or work-relief assistance (however little) at any time during the year.

Income was defined to include total net money income received during the year by all members of the economic family, plus the value of certain items of nonmoney income such as net value of owner-occupied homes and rent received as pay. Consumption data were collected only from native white families in most sample communities and from native Negro families in the Southeast, in New York City, and Columbus, Ohio.

G 697–797. General note.

For discussion of the surveys from which these series were obtained, see general note for series G 495–848 and the following text for series grouped by survey.

G 697–716. Consumption expenditures, in current prices, of farm families of 2 or more persons, by income class, 1961.

Source: U.S. Department of Agriculture, Consumer Expenditure Survey Report No. 20, *Consumer Expenditures and Income, Rural Farm Population*, United States, 1961, p. 6.

These data are from a cooperative undertaking of the U.S. Bureau of Labor Statistics and the U.S. Department of Agriculture in which the USDA had responsibility for the farm population. They are based on a sample of 1,967 families and single consumers in 41 States selected by a three-stage sampling technique utilizing stratification of counties by State Economic Areas.

Classification is by income from which Federal, State, and local personal taxes and occupational expenses have been deducted. The value of food and rent received as pay are included in both income and expenditures. The rental value of dwellings rented by farm operators and the share of ownership expenses (taxes, insurance, and mortgate interest payments) attributed to the family dwelling by farm owners are included in shelter expenses and deducted from farm operating expenses. Shelter also includes expenses for lodging away from home and for vacation homes. Automobile expenses include the estimated family share of cars and trucks also used on the farm or other business. Expenditures for other goods and services include expense for funerals of family members, legal fees, bank charges for service and deposit box, rental of post office box, money lost or stolen, interest paid on borrowings for family use, poll taxes, and personal property taxes.

In addition to the data shown in these series, data have been published on net change in assets and liabilities; disbursements for gifts, contributions, and personal insurance; the value of food produced for home use; and the value of food, shelter and other items received without direct expenditure.

G 717–734. Consumption expenditures, in current prices, of farm families of 2 or more persons, by income class, 1955.

Source: Derived from U.S. Department of Agriculture, Statistical Bulletin No. 224, *Farmers' Expenditures in 1955 by Regions*, 1958, and from unpublished data of the Agricultural Research Service.

These data are based on a weighted sample of approximately 4,000 schedules, selected on the basis of the 1954 Census of Agriculture distribution of farms by economic class of farm (value of all products sold). The number of families included a small number not reporting income. Federal and State personal taxes have been deducted from money income. Expenditures for dwelling upkeep included, for owned homes, an assigned share of real estate taxes and special assessments, insurance premiums, mortgage interest charges, legal and settlement charges; and, for both owned and rented homes, expense for repairs, replacements, alterations and improvements, and cash rent for off-farm rented dwellings. Expense for lodging away from home and for vacation homes was also included. Expenditures for automobile and truck transportation include family share of purchase and upkeep. Expenditures for other goods and services include expense for funerals for family members, legal fees, bank charges for service and deposit box, rental of post office box, money lost or stolen, interest paid on borrowing for family use, occupational expense, union dues, poll taxes, and personal property taxes.

G 735–753. Consumption expenditures, in current prices, of farm families of 2 or more persons, by income class, 1941.

Source: U.S. Department of Agriculture, Miscellaneous Bulletin No. 520, *Rural Family Spending and Saving in Wartime*, June 1943, pp. 156 and 159.

These data were obtained from a study conducted in 1942 by the Bureau of Home Economics in areas representing the entire rural population of the country. The survey was paralleled by a study of the income and expenditures of urban families and single consumers conducted by the Bureau of Labor Statistics (see text for series G 661–678). The study was based on a sample of 1,000 rural-non-farm families and single consumers and 760 farm families and single consumers in 45 counties, stratified to give representation to all regions and to economic groups in the rural population.

The data collected included nonmoney as well as money income; the former was limited to that received in the form of food, housing, fuel, ice, clothing, or household furnishings. However, classification in these series is by money income only. Expenditures for family living were reported in detail under 15 categories of expense. All purchases of durable goods made during the year, except payments on homes and improvements on homes, were considered as current expenditures. Financing charges and interest on installment and other credit purchases, shipping and delivery charges were considered as part of the expenditure. Discounts and trade-in allowances were deducted from the gross price. Sales and excise taxes were included in the expenditures for each article except in the case of the details for food expenditure. Although the survey included expenditures of families and single consumers, these series cover farm families only.

G 754–771. Consumption expenditures, in current prices, of farm families, by income class, 1935–36.

Source: U.S. National Resources Planning Board, *Family Expenditures in the United States, Statistical Tables and Appendixes*, June 1941, pp. 51, 120, and 157.

These data are based on information obtained as part of the Works Progress Administration study (see text for series G 679–696) and summarized for the United States by the National Resources Planning Board. The definition of income used in this study includes, in addition to money income, the nonmoney income items of net rental value of owner-occupied homes and housing received as pay and the net imputed value of food produced at home for the family's own use. For farm families, it also includes the net imputed value of certain other farm-produced goods used by the family, i.e., fuel, ice, tobacco, and wool, plus or minus the value of any increase or decrease in the amount of livestock owned or of crops stored for sale.

311

Estimates for approximately 15,000 native farm families (excluding those on public relief rolls) living in rural areas are presented in these series. For the main categories of disbursement, 140 villages and 66 farm counties in 30 States were surveyed. The farm sample represents the more important types of farming. Farm families operating part-time farms were excluded from the consumption sample (except in Oregon).

G 772–777. Consumption expenditures, in current prices, of farm families, by income class, 1929.

Source: Computed from M. Leven, H. G. Moulton, and C. Warburton, *America's Capacity to Consume*, The Brookings Institution, Washington, D.C., 1934, p. 260 (copyright).

Aggregates presented in the original source were divided by the number of families in each income class to derive average expenditures per family.

The number of families is based on the distribution of families by income estimated by Maurice Leven. The estimates of consumer expenditures were made by Clark Warburton on the basis of six sample studies of the value of consumer goods and services used by farm families in one year between 1924 and 1930.

The income figures shown here represent both annual money and nonmoney income. Included in nonmoney income are imputed value of home-produced food and fuel, and of owned homes. The expenditure for "other" items includes direct taxes and contributions.

G 778–797. Consumption expenditures of farm families, by income class, 1922–1924.

Source: Computed from E. I. Kirkpatrick, *The Farmer's Standard of Living: A Socio-Economic Study of 2,886 White Farm Families of Selected Localities in 11 States*, U.S. Department of Agriculture, Bulletin 1466, pp. 29 and 34.

These data were derived from a number of special studies made by the Department of Agriculture in cooperation with 12 colleges or universities. The studies were planned to show the following items among others: Tenure, acres per farm, and value of land per acre; quantities and value of food, fuel, and other materials furnished during the year; quantities and costs of food, fuel, furniture and furnishings, household supplies, and household labor purchased during the year; and expenditures for other items such as clothing, health, education, recreation, personal care, etc.

The economic level of farm business resources and of farm family living was the chief consideration in the selection of the localities represented in this study. The localities were situated in 11 States (New Hampshire, Vermont, Massachusetts, Connecticut, Kentucky, South Carolina, Alabama, Missouri, Kansas, Iowa, and Ohio). Of the 2,886 families represented in the study, 1,950 were owners, 867 were cash and share tenants including croppers, and 69 were hired men or managers. The study was limited to families who had an adult man operating the farm and an adult woman as homemaker; generally the operator and homemaker were man and wife.

Total expenditures for current consumption and expenditures for each consumption category were derived from figures in the source showing percentage distribution of the value of all goods. Expenditures for life and health insurance were deducted from the total. Consumer goods and services purchased include food, fuel, and housing furnished by the farm. Food and fuel provided by the farm were valued at prices halfway between what they would have brought and what they would have cost in the open market; housing provided was valued at 10 percent of the estimated value of the house occupied.

The class intervals shown in series G 778–797 as value of goods purchased and goods furnished in kind are ambiguously referred to in the original as "total value or income" groups. A comparison with other studies by the author indicates that the classes are not repre-

sentative of income. Series G 778–797 therefore differs in this respect from the other series in this chapter.

G 798–848. General note.

For discussion of the surveys from which these series were obtained, see general note for series G 495–848 and the following text for series separately grouped by survey.

G 798–812. Consumption expenditures, in current prices, of families and single consumers combined, by income class, 1960–61.

Source: U.S. Bureau of Labor Statistics, *Consumer Expenditure and Income Survey—Total United States, Urban and Rural*, Report No. 237–93, 1965.

About 73 percent of the families in the universe for the 1960–61 survey lived in urban places, 21 percent in rural nonfarm areas, and 6 percent in rural farm areas of the 50 States and the District of Columbia. The urban segment includes persons living in incorporated or unincorporated areas of 2,500 population or more and in densely settled areas immediately adjacent to cities of 50,000 population or more. The rural population is subdivided into the rural-farm population, which constitutes all rural residents living on farms, and the rural-nonfarm population, composed of the remaining rural population.

The survey was planned to represent a year's income, expenditure, and saving experience of all noninstitutional consumer units living in the United States (including military posts, camps, reservations, homes for the aged, asylums, jails, and similar "long stay" institutions).

G 813–827. Consumption expenditures, in current prices, of families and single consumers combined, by income class, 1941.

Source: See source for series G 661–678, p. 75.

For a description of this study, see text for series G 661–678 and G 735–753.

The expenditure data in these series represent expenditures of all families and single consumers including families with negative incomes and incomes of $5,000 and over not shown separately, for the country as a whole. Nonmoney income is not included. The expenditure patterns are based on a sample of 3,100 families and single consumers in 62 cities and 45 rural counties.

G 828–842. Consumption expenditures, in current prices, of families and single consumers combined, by income class, 1935–36.

Source: U.S. National Resources Committee, *Consumer Expenditures in the United States, Estimates for 1935–36*, pp. 77 and 84.

The study from which these series were derived was part of the Works Progress Administration study already described in the text for series G 679–696 and G 754–771, supplemented by data from other sources on expenditures of families with foreign-born heads, and of families having received public relief assistance. The expenditure data were secured from a sample of more than 60,000 families living in cities of different size, in villages, and on farms in 30 States. Similar patterns for single men and women were built up from less extensive sample data available from the study of Consumer Purchases and from various supplementary sources. Average consumption patterns for broad groups of the population and for the Nation as a whole were obtained by weighting the patterns for the component groups of families and single individuals according to their relative importance at each income level. The population weights for this purpose and for estimating the aggregate consumption of the Nation in 1935–36 were derived from the study of consumer incomes (see National Resources Committee, *Consumer Incomes in the United States, Their Distribution in 1935–36*).

G 843–848.   Consumption expenditures, in current prices, of families and single consumers combined, by income class, 1929.

Source: Computed from M. Leven, H. G. Moulton, and C. Warburton, *America's Capacity to Consume*, The Brookings Institution, Washington, D.C., 1934, pp. 260, 261, and 265 (copyright).

For the purpose of presenting these series in a form roughly comparable with those from other sources for earlier years, average consumption expenditures of all families and single consumers were derived by combining aggregate consumption expenditures (in millions of dollars), by income class, of farm and urban families and single consumers, as given in the report, and dividing these by the total number of consumers (in thousands) in each income class.

The estimates of consumer expenditures presented in *America's Capacity to Consume* were made by Clark Warburton who based his figures on sample surveys of expenditures of nonfarm families for 1918–1930, of farm families for 1924–1930 (see text for series G 772–777), and of single persons for 1918–1933 from a variety of sources. In addition, he used the results of a questionnaire concerning incomes, expenditures, and savings in 1929 circulated by The Brookings Institution to families of business and professional men.

G 849.   Index of volume of food marketings and home consumption, 1910–1970.

Source: U.S. Department of Agriculture, Economic Research Service, *Farm Income Situation*, July 1971, *Agricultural Statistics, 1971*, and unpublished data.

This index was derived for various time periods by weighting the quantities of the major farm-produced foodstuffs sold or used in farm households by average farm prices. The following average prices were used: For 1910–1939, prices for 1935–1939; for 1940–1955, prices for 1947–1949; for 1956–1970, prices for 1957–1959. The series were "spliced" on the basis of overlapped calculations for 1940 and 1955. This index, as well as others including nonfood commodities, is described in *Major Statistical Series of the U.S. Department of Agriculture*, Agriculture Handbook No. 365, vol. 2, pp. 17–19.

G 850.   Index of food consumption per capita, 1909–1970.

Source: U.S. Department of Agriculture, Economic Research Service, *National Food Situation*, February 1971; and *Food Consumption, Prices, and Expenditures*, Agricultural Economics Report No. 138, and supplements.

This index was derived by weighting per capita consumption of food, retail weight equivalents, by average retail prices in 1957–1959. Details of the construction of this index are described in *U.S. Food Consumption—Sources of Data and Trends*, 1909–63, Statistical Bulletin No. 364. The retail weight data were derived from such series as those on per capita food consumption, series G 881–915, by means of average conversion factors for nonprocessed and partially processed items which allow for waste and losses in distribution between the particular primary distribution level at which each series is measured and the retail store level.

This index measures, primarily, changes in quantity, although it also reflects certain changes in quality of foods consumed, such as the shift from lower-priced to higher-priced foods. It does not reflect price changes as such, because base-period prices are used throughout.

G 851–856.   Nutrients available per capita, per day, 1909–1970.

Source: See source for series G 850.

These figures are averages for the total population, 1909–1940, and for the civilian population only, 1941–1970. Data were computed on the basis of estimates of apparent civilian consumption (retail basis) including estimates of consumption from home gardens. No deductions were made in the nutrient estimates for the loss or

waste of food in the home or for the destruction or loss of nutrients during the preparation of food. Deductions were made for inedible refuse.

The computations were made by multiplying the estimated per capita quantity of each food consumed by appropriate food composition figures. The composition values are those published in Department of Agriculture, *Composition of Foods . . . Raw, Processed, Prepared*, Agriculture Handbook No. 8, supplemented by a few unpublished values.

Since the early 1940's, there has been enrichment or fortification of several types of foods with minerals and vitamins. Included here are estimated quantities of iron, thiamine, riboflavin, and niacin added to flour and cereal products; quantities of vitamin A value added to margarine and milk of all types; and quantities of ascorbic acid added to fruit juices and drinks.

The consumption of vitamins and mineral preparations, other than those used in the enrichment or in the fortification of foods, is not included here. Quantities of calcium or other minerals added to flour to make it self-rising or phosphated are not included nor is the nutritive content of baking powder, yeast, or dough conditioner.

G 857–865 and G 866–880.   General note.

Surveys of household food consumption provide information about the kinds and quantities of food that families with different characteristics eat, as well as the amount of money they spend for food. Dietary levels of different groups within the population are then computed from the nutrient content of the reported food. The results are used by Congress and Federal agencies to develop and administer programs and policies related to food, by the food industry for information on needs and wants of consumers, and by educators and others to assess the nutritional situation and to develop programs for improving nutritional levels in the United States.

The survey data presented here are limited to housekeeping households in the spring of the survey year. Housekeeping households are those with at least one person eating 10 or more meals from household food supplies during the preceding seven days.

The Department of Agriculture has made five nationwide surveys of food consumption over the past 35 years—in 1936, 1942, 1948 (urban only), 1955, and 1965. The 1955 and 1965 surveys were more comprehensive than their predecessors. Both obtained information on patterns of food consumption, expenditures, dietary levels, and household food practices. Data for households were classified (1) by regions—Northeast, North Central, South, and West (according to Census of Population classifications); (2) by urbanization—rural farm, rural nonfarm, and urban, within regions; and (3) by several household income classes within region-urbanization categories. The 1936, 1942, 1948, and 1955 surveys covered only the spring. The 1965–66 survey covered the four seasons, but only data for the spring are shown here.

G 857–865.   Nutritive value of city diets—average per person per day from food used at home: 1936, 1942, 1948, 1955, and 1965.

Source: H. K. Stiebeling, D. Monroe, E. F. Phipard, and others, 1936, *Consumer Purchases Study*. (Urban and Village Series.) *Family Food Consumption and Dietary Levels. Five Regions*. U.S. Department of Agriculture (USDA) Miscellaneous Publication 452; U.S. Bureau of Human Nutrition and Home Economics, 1942, *Family Food Consumption in the United States, Spring 1942*. USDA Miscellaneous Publication 550; 1948, *Nutritive Value of Diets of Urban Families, Spring 1948 and Comparison With Diets in 1942*. USDA 1948 Food Consumption Surveys, Preliminary Report No. 12; 1955, *Dietary Levels of Households in the United States*. USDA Household Food Consumption Survey 1955, Report No. 6. 1965, U.S. Department of Agriculture, *Dietary Levels of Households in the United States, Spring 1965*, Report No. 6.

Nutritive value data from the surveys relate only to urban housekeeping households for the spring in each year. Data for 1936,

313

1942, 1948, and 1955 exclude single person households; 1965 data include them, but they have only a minor effect on the average use of most foods. The number of persons in a household is the number of household meals divided by 21, the theoretical number of meals eaten by one person during a week. Thus a person eating 14 meals at home and 7 meals away is counted as .67 person.

G 866–880. Food used at home—average annual income, household size, and quantity of food per person per week: 1942, 1948, 1955, and 1965.

Source: See source for series G 857–865.

See general note for series G 857–865 and G 866–880.

G 881–915. Apparent civilian per capita consumption of food, 1849–1970.

Source: See source for G 850.

Department of Agriculture estimates of the consumption of major foods are based on a great variety of information pertaining to supplies moving through trade channels for use by the civilian population. All estimates for foods other than cane and beet sugar are derived from data obtained primarily for other purposes. This accounts (1) for the lesser degree of reliability which should be placed on data in many of the series for earlier years, particularly before 1924 and (2) for the several levels in distribution at which the official estimates of consumption of individual foods are measured.

From the annual supply of each food (production plus beginning stocks, plus imports) are deducted feed, seed, industrial, and other nonfood use, exports and shipments, government purchases, and ending stocks. The residual is taken as a measure of the quantities moving into domestic civilian consumption during a given calendar year. Data used are from the following sources:

Item	Source of data
Stocks	U.S. Department of Agriculture, Statistical Reporting Service; U.S. Department of Commerce, trade reports.
Production	Statistical Reporting Service; National Marine Fishery Service.
Foreign trade	Department of Commerce; Statistical Reporting Service.
Nonfood use	Statistical Reporting Service.
Military procurement	Special reports submitted to Department of Agriculture.

Data on military takings during World War I were so incomplete that they could not be used. Accordingly, data on total domestic food "disappearance" for 1909–1940 were divided by the total population. For 1941–1970, the total food supplies available for civilian consumption were divided by the number of people eating from civilian supplies. For 1941–1945, adjustments were made for members of the Armed Forces who were on leave or were, for other reasons, eating in homes or restaurants in this country.

The basic disappearance data are in varied terms, such as the carcass weight of meats at the slaughter level and the farm weight of fresh fruits and vegetables. However, such variation does not impede comparisons for a given food through time. Although disappearance data are not the same as consumption data, since they measure the quantities of food going into the distribution system instead of the quantities bought or consumed by consumers, they are the only available estimates of consumption. All disappearance data are on a national basis and no regional or State estimates can be made without the collection of much additional statistical information.

Some scattered data that are basic to estimates of apparent consumption have been gathered from decennial censuses prior to 1900. The food production data from the Census of Agriculture for 1910 were more complete, and are the first important benchmark for most food consumption estimates. The completeness and accuracy of the data have been greatly improved as the crop reporting system has developed.

Extensive descriptions of methodology, sources, and inherent limitations for all series are given in *U.S. Food Consumption . . .* (cited in the text for series G 850) and are summarized in *Major Statistical Series of the U.S. Department of Agriculture*, Agriculture Handbook No. 365, vol. 5.

G 881–884, meat. Consumption is measured at the wholesale level in terms of weights of dressed carcass, excluding offal. Carcass weight of pork includes head meat, but excludes cuts rendered into lard. Quantities slaughtered under the Emergency Government Relief Purchase Program in 1934 and 1935 are included.

G 886, total fats and oils. Data are measurements at wholesale level and include fat content of butter, margarine, lard, shortening, and "other edible fats and oils" (those used in cooking and salad oils and for minor uses such as fish canning, etc.).

G 890, fresh fruit. Consumption is measured at the farm level. Includes apples (from commercial areas only, 1934–1970), apricots, avocados, bananas, cherries, cranberries, figs, grapes, nectarines, papayas, peaches, pears, pineapples, plums and prunes, strawberries, and citrus fruits. Excludes supplies used in processing.

G 891, citrus fruits. Includes oranges, tangerines, lemons, limes, and grapefruit.

G 893, canned fruit. Includes apples and applesauce, apricots, berries, cherries, cranberries, figs, fruit salad and cocktail, peaches (including spiced), pears, pineapple, plums and prunes, olives, citrus segments, and, beginning 1956, chilled fruit sections and salads. Data in terms of net weight reflect disappearance from the wholesale level of distribution.

G 894, canned fruit juice. Consumption is measured at wholesale level. It includes grapefruit, orange, blended citrus and lemon juices (single strength juices, 1930–1970; concentrated juices converted to single strength basis, 1941–1970), and apple, berry, fruit nectars, grape, pineapple, prune, tangerine juices, and, beginning 1955, chilled citrus juices. Prior to 1928 only grape juice was covered.

G 895, dried fruit. Includes apples, apricots, dates (pits-in basis), figs, peaches, pears, prunes (excluding quantities used for juice), and raisins and currants. Disappearance or consumption since 1941 has been measured at the wholesale level.

G 896, frozen fruits and fruit juices. Includes blackberries, blueberries, raspberries, strawberries, other berries, apples, apricots, cherries, grapes and pulp, peaches, citrus juices (product weight), and miscellaneous frozen fruits. Disappearance is measured at the wholesale level.

G 897, potatoes. Consumption is measured at the farm level. It excludes quantities supplied by nonfarm home gardens and quantities frozen or canned because they are counted in processed form, but includes quantities used for other purposes, such as for potato chips.

G 898, sweetpotatoes. Consumption is measured at the farm level. It excludes quantities canned and supplies from nonfarm home gardens.

G 899, fresh vegetables. Consumption is measured in terms of farm weights at the farm level, and includes tomatoes, artichokes, asparagus, lima beans, snap beans, broccoli, brussels sprouts, cabbage, carrots, kale, lettuce and escarole, green peas, peppers, spinach, beets, cauliflower, celery, corn, cucumbers, eggplant, garlic, onions and shallots, and minor vegetables. Beginning 1968, beets, green peas (in shell), kale, and lima beans are included in minor vegetables. It excludes quantities produced in home gardens and all supplies going into commercial processing.

G 900, canned vegetables. Excludes soups, baby food, and baked beans; but includes asparagus, lima beans, snap beans, carrots, peas, pumpkin and squash, spinach, tomatoes, tomato catsup and chili sauce, paste and sauce, and pulp and puree, tomato and other vegetable juices, beets, corn, pickles, sauerkraut, potatoes, sweetpotatoes, miscellaneous greens, pimientos, and mixed vegetables. Information on January 1 stocks was not available before 1943. Disappearance measured at wholesale level.

G 901, frozen vegetables. Includes asparagus, snap beans, lima beans, carrots, peas, pumpkin and squash, broccoli, brussels sprouts, spinach, cauliflower, corn (cut basis), rhubarb, potato products, and miscellaneous frozen vegetables. Disappearance measured at wholesale level.

G 902, melons. Consumption is measured at the farm level and includes watermelons, cantaloups, and honeydew and honey-ball melons. Excludes quantities produced in home gardens.

G 903, dry beans. Disappearance is measured at the farm level, includes quantities used for canned baked beans and soups, and excludes supplies produced in home gardens.

G 904, total milk for human consumption. The total is measured in terms of whole milk equivalent, on fat solids basis, of all dairy products.

G 905, fluid milk and cream. Includes fluid cream on a whole milk equivalent basis (about 4 percent butterfat) and covers fresh use only; excludes fluid skim and buttermilk.

G 906, condensed and evaporated milk. Evaporated milk is unskimmed, unsweetened, case goods; the condensed milk is unsweetened (plain condensed), unskimmed bulk goods; and sweetened condensed milk, unskimmed, case and bulk goods. Data are measured at the processing level.

G 907, cheese. Includes all whole and part whole milk cheeses; excludes cottage, pot, and bakers' cheese and full-skimmed American.

G 908, ice cream. Data measured at the processing level in terms of product weight. Figures exclude frozen dairy product desserts such as sherbet, frozen custard and malted, and ice milk and mellorine (which is made from skim milk products and vegetable fats).

G 909, eggs. Consumption is measured at approximately the wholesale level of distribution and includes all eggs used in processed foods. Eggs were assumed to weigh approximately 1.5 pounds per dozen through 1946. To adjust for the increasing size of eggs, this factor was increased, beginning in 1947, by 0.01 pound each year through 1952, continued at 1.56 for 1953–1956, and raised to 1.57 in 1957.

G 910, chicken and turkey. Consumption is measured at the wholesale level. The entire series is on a ready-to-cook basis, which includes the weight of giblets. Prior to 1947, the factor used to derive ready-to-cook weight from dressed weight for chicken was 0.75; for turkey, 0.824; beginning in 1947, data were computed using differing factors for the various items of supply and distribution.

G 911, sugar, cane and beet. Represents sugar used for all purposes, including quantities in processed fruit and vegetable items and ice cream. Data for 1875–1908 were obtained from Henry Schultz, *Theory and Measurement of Demand* (based on data in *Concerning Sugar*, a looseleaf service by United States Sugar Manufacturers Association, which had been derived from Willett and Gray, *Weekly Statistical Sugar Trade Journal*).

G 912, wheat flour. Includes white, whole wheat, and semolina flour (which is used primarily for macaroni and spaghetti); excludes use in breakfast cereals, but includes use in all other processed foods.

G 913, corn flour and meal. Estimates are based on census data. Approximately 50 percent of cornmeal is degermed.

G 914, peanuts. Excludes quantities crushed for oil; includes commercially cleaned and shelled peanuts plus quantities used on farms and farm sales for food use.

G 915, coffee. Consumption is measured in terms of greenbean equivalent of all types of coffee, reflecting disappearance from the wholesale roasting level.

★ ★ ★ ★ ★ ★ ★ ★ ★ **More Recent Data for *Historical Statistics* Series** ★ ★ ★ ★ ★ ★ ★ ★ ★

Statistics for more recent years in continuation of many of the still-active series shown here appear in annual issues of the *Statistical Abstract of the United States,* beginning with the 1975 edition. For direct linkage of the historical series to the tables in the *Abstract,* see Appendix I in the *Abstract.*

Series G 416–469. Personal Consumption Expenditures, by Type of Product: 1929 to 1970

[In millions of dollars]

Series No.	Products	1970	1969	1968	1967	1966	1965	1964	1963	1962	1961
416	Total	617,644	579,457	536,178	492,066	466,334	432,839	401,221	374,982	355,057	335,152
417	Commodities	355,077	336,713	314,844	288,088	277,688	257,367	237,920	222,560	212,097	200,083
418	Services	262,567	242,744	221,334	203,978	188,646	175,472	163,301	152,422	142,960	135,069
419	Food and beverages	129,989	120,585	115,327	108,451	105,756	98,783	92,938	88,232	85,676	82,878
420	Purchased meals and beverages	29,286	26,749	25,038	23,233	21,981	20,068	18,766	17,545	17,020	16,365
421	Food, excluding alcoholic beverages	112,112	104,108	99,737	93,921	92,005	85,828	80,528	76,512	74,381	72,073
422	Alcoholic beverages	17,877	16,477	15,590	14,530	13,751	12,955	12,410	11,720	11,295	10,805
423	Tobacco products	11,192	10,122	9,807	9,293	8,865	8,400	7,863	7,776	7,378	7,248
424	Clothing, accessories, and jewelry	62,834	59,924	55,474	50,995	48,360	43,318	40,431	37,049	35,700	33,836
425	Women's and children's	29,010	27,293	25,315	23,112	22,162	19,742	18,338	16,709	16,071	15,115
426	Men's and boys'	15,651	14,938	13,785	12,742	11,934	10,687	9,906	9,026	8,683	8,228
427	Jewelry and watches	4,298	4,107	3,790	3,501	3,308	2,855	2,638	2,397	2,262	2,155
428	Personal care	10,420	9,760	9,049	8,558	8,068	7,578	7,065	6,530	6,248	5,792
429	Housing	90,926	84,141	77,311	71,848	67,506	63,509	59,298	55,410	51,950	48,717
430	Owner-occupied nonfarm	59,585	54,991	50,753	47,057	44,385	41,735	39,337	37,095	34,745	32,493
431	Tenant-occupied nonfarm	25,253	23,203	21,142	19,706	18,479	17,357	15,857	14,435	13,535	12,702
432	Farmhouses, rental value	2,907	2,863	2,586	2,481	2,352	2,300	2,215	2,153	2,072	2,005
433	Household operation	87,360	82,294	76,215	70,514	66,786	61,789	58,046	54,127	51,170	48,258
434	Furniture, equipment, and supplies	44,251	42,178	38,868	35,410	33,920	30,789	28,827	26,238	24,745	23,167
435	Household utilities	24,325	22,447	20,945	19,831	18,912	17,845	16,861	16,096	15,237	14,400
436	Electricity	9,824	8,905	8,141	7,496	7,027	6,608	6,294	5,960	5,688	5,340
437	Gas	5,262	4,938	4,613	4,432	4,242	4,075	3,939	3,770	3,644	3,415
438	Telephone	9,879	9,092	8,178	7,532	6,905	6,423	5,914	5,509	5,101	4,822
439	Domestic service	4,830	4,685	4,629	4,477	4,028	3,964	3,908	3,824	3,803	3,733
440	Medical care expenses	47,401	42,814	37,767	34,491	31,142	28,082	25,803	23,340	22,002	20,321
441	Physicians and dentists [1]	17,236	15,389	13,508	12,585	11,352	10,498	9,667	8,720	8,257	7,620
442	Hospitals, privately controlled [2]	16,851	14,640	12,323	10,744	9,294	8,309	7,729	6,751	6,100	5,581
443	Drug preparations and sundries	6,945	6,429	5,873	5,433	5,133	4,720	4,331	4,137	4,012	3,759
444	Health insurance	2,565	2,770	2,541	2,421	2,215	1,960	1,775	1,654	1,672	1,558
445	Personal business	35,314	33,277	29,532	26,182	24,287	21,879	20,055	18,422	16,481	16,021
446	Transportation	77,776	77,772	71,983	62,588	60,489	58,154	51,437	49,140	45,975	41,455
447	User-operated	72,250	72,639	67,265	58,163	56,446	54,356	47,842	45,695	42,516	38,135
448	New cars and used cars [3]	31,595	35,087	32,979	26,646	26,805	27,153	22,822	21,549	19,486	15,991
449	Gasoline and oil	22,211	20,894	18,992	17,619	16,562	15,261	14,023	13,457	12,908	12,386
450	Purchased local transport	2,505	2,386	2,266	2,216	2,099	2,017	1,988	1,977	1,981	1,953
451	Purchased intercity transport	3,021	2,747	2,452	2,209	1,944	1,781	1,607	1,468	1,478	1,367
452	Recreation	40,653	36,901	33,623	30,758	28,850	26,298	24,571	22,213	20,474	19,506
453	Radio and television sets, records, and musical instruments [4]	9,439	8,274	7,715	7,328	6,905	6,013	5,409	4,539	3,935	3,668
454	Toys and sport supplies, nondurable	5,918	5,311	4,701	3,975	3,743	3,436	3,174	2,986	2,792	2,702
455	Wheel goods, durable toys, sport equipment [5]	4,916	4,517	3,937	3,422	3,248	2,933	2,805	2,538	2,269	2,129
456	Books, maps, magazines, newspapers, sheet music	7,679	6,976	6,333	5,896	5,424	4,929	4,704	4,141	3,938	3,744
457	Private education and research	10,363	9,536	8,690	7,576	6,608	5,927	5,199	4,736	4,392	4,028
458	Religious and welfare activities	8,601	8,084	7,605	6,948	6,421	5,972	5,678	5,262	5,082	4,926
459	Foreign travel and other, net	4,815	4,247	3,795	3,864	3,196	3,150	2,837	2,745	2,529	2,166
	PERCENT DISTRIBUTION										
460	Food, beverages, and tobacco	23.2	22.6	23.3	23.9	24.6	24.8	25.1	25.6	26.2	26.9
461	Clothing, accessories, and jewelry	10.0	10.3	10.3	10.4	10.4	10.0	10.1	9.9	10.1	10.1
462	Personal care	1.7	1.7	1.7	1.7	1.7	1.8	1.8	1.7	1.8	1.7
463	Housing	14.7	14.5	14.4	14.6	14.5	14.7	14.8	14.8	14.6	14.5
464	Household operations	14.0	14.2	14.2	14.3	14.3	14.3	14.5	14.4	14.4	14.4
465	Medical care expenses	7.6	7.4	7.0	7.0	6.7	6.5	6.4	6.2	6.2	6.1
466	Personal business	5.7	5.7	5.5	5.3	5.2	5.1	5.0	4.9	4.6	4.8
467	Transportation	12.6	13.4	13.4	12.7	13.0	13.4	12.8	13.1	12.9	12.4
468	Recreation	6.5	6.4	6.3	6.3	6.2	6.1	6.1	5.9	5.8	5.8
469	Other	3.9	3.8	3.7	3.7	3.5	3.5	3.4	3.4	3.4	3.3

See footnotes at end of table.

Series G 416–469. Personal Consumption Expenditures, by Type of Product: 1929 to 1970—Con.

[In millions of dollars]

Series No.	Products	1960*	1959	1958	1957	1956	1955	1954	1953	1952	1951
416	**Total**	**325,241**	**311,207**	**290,069**	**281,432**	**266,675**	**254,381**	**236,494**	**229,969**	**216,679**	**206,266**
417	**Commodities**	**196,589**	**190,929**	**178,033**	**176,384**	**168,182**	**162,948**	**151,114**	**150,040**	**143,284**	**138,401**
418	**Services**	**128,652**	**120,278**	**112,036**	**105,048**	**98,493**	**91,433**	**85,380**	**79,929**	**73,395**	**67,865**
419	Food and beverages	80,543	78,597	76,381	73,555	69,907	67,188	65,402	64,365	63,447	60,358
420	Purchased meals and beverages	16,182	15,894	15,321	15,171	14,528	13,848	13,363	13,350	13,093	12,467
421	Food, excluding alcoholic beverages	70,113	68,437	66,631	63,890	60,437	58,073	56,532	55,455	54,702	52,123
422	Alcoholic beverages	10,430	10,160	9,750	9,665	9,470	9,115	8,870	8,910	8,745	8,235
423	Tobacco products	6,967	6,554	5,982	5,687	5,303	5,048	4,939	5,095	4,910	4,535
424	Clothing, accessories, and jewelry	33,032	31,911	29,868	29,517	29,230	27,982	26,786	26,668	26,416	25,485
425	Women's and children's	14,769	14,332	13,356	13,152	12,967	12,444	11,965	11,912	11,608	10,843
426	Men's and boys'	7,976	7,706	7,164	7,288	7,327	6,971	6,711	6,675	6,782	6,608
427	Jewelry and watches	2,094	2,016	1,850	1,817	1,812	1,743	1,631	1,560	1,523	1,412
428	Personal care	5,324	5,031	4,604	4,284	3,892	3,461	3,162	2,976	2,782	2,617
429	Housing	46,305	43,654	41,127	38,506	36,020	33,738	31,664	29,315	26,476	23,853
430	Owner-occupied nonfarm	30,685	28,674	26,809	24,805	22,959	21,178	19,534	17,734	15,763	13,980
431	Tenant-occupied nonfarm	12,220	11,724	11,273	10,772	10,309	9,901	9,574	9,022	8,243	7,592
432	Farmhouses, rental value	1,975	1,957	1,861	1,787	1,734	1,741	1,711	1,765	1,736	1,607
433	Household operation	46,906	45,285	42,274	41,171	39,765	37,322	33,727	33,119	31,673	31,399
434	Furniture, equipment, and supplies	22,779	22,581	20,844	20,925	20,641	19,534	17,648	17,688	17,102	17,508
435	Household utilities	13,749	12,986	12,267	11,588	10,913	10,180	9,328	8,707	8,272	7,876
436	Electricity	5,071	4,721	4,381	4,097	3,802	3,496	3,213	2,932	2,652	2,395
437	Gas	3,211	2,901	2,685	2,403	2,259	2,027	1,800	1,589	1,469	1,345
438	Telephone	4,515	4,188	3,892	3,648	3,341	3,061	2,789	2,683	2,421	2,170
439	Domestic service	3,799	3,553	3,503	3,322	3,266	3,051	2,570	2,690	2,614	2,661
440	Medical care expenses	19,116	17,924	16,472	15,187	13,853	12,755	12,046	11,150	10,225	9,488
441	Physicians and dentists [1]	7,299	6,950	6,450	5,870	5,418	4,985	4,779	4,300	3,959	3,690
442	Hospitals, privately controlled [2]	5,096	4,601	4,202	3,775	3,426	3,135	2,878	2,647	2,406	2,171
443	Drug preparations and sundries	3,607	3,462	3,195	2,981	2,661	2,362	2,163	2,137	2,058	1,979
444	Health insurance	1,377	1,277	1,130	1,143	1,013	1,056	1,022	906	704	611
445	Personal business	14,974	13,872	12,768	11,862	10,985	10,049	9,194	8,445	7,791	7,443
446	Transportation	43,134	41,184	35,634	37,909	34,811	35,574	29,732	29,739	25,097	24,508
447	User-operated	39,825	37,980	32,572	34,755	31,725	32,589	26,768	26,647	22,037	21,548
448	New cars and used cars [3]	17,748	17,154	13,258	16,281	14,686	16,840	12,295	12,761	9,501	10,125
449	Gasoline and oil	12,252	11,571	10,951	10,642	9,783	9,000	8,177	7,715	6,833	6,128
450	Purchased local transport	2,001	1,971	1,917	1,987	1,971	1,933	1,938	2,008	1,990	1,965
451	Purchased intercity transport	1,308	1,233	1,145	1,167	1,115	1,052	1,026	1,084	1,070	995
452	Recreation	18,295	17,381	15,817	15,333	14,979	14,078	13,077	12,720	12,102	11,564
453	Radio and television sets, records, and musical instruments [4]	3,412	3,330	2,836	2,825	2,938	2,869	2,726	2,588	2,349	2,236
454	Toys and sport supplies, nondurable	2,417	2,306	2,115	2,047	1,951	1,803	1,624	1,694	1,708	1,662
455	Wheel goods, durable toys, sport equipment [5]	2,106	2,038	1,845	1,720	1,573	1,386	1,174	1,090	989	897
456	Books, maps, magazines, newspapers, sheet music	3,497	3,269	3,083	2,956	2,831	2,736	2,631	2,606	2,477	2,349
457	Private education and research	3,718	3,417	3,140	2,853	2,574	2,339	2,130	1,999	1,870	1,748
458	Religious and welfare activities	4,748	4,434	4,178	3,860	3,677	3,257	3,154	2,929	2,784	2,437
459	Foreign travel and other, net	2,179	1,963	1,824	1,708	1,679	1,590	1,481	1,449	1,106	831
	PERCENT DISTRIBUTION										
460	Food, beverages, and tobacco	26.9	27.4	28.4	28.2	28.2	28.4	29.7	30.2	31.5	31.5
461	Clothing, accessories, and jewelry	10.2	10.3	10.3	10.5	11.0	11.0	11.3	11.6	12.2	12.4
462	Personal care	1.6	1.6	1.6	1.5	1.5	1.4	1.3	1.3	1.3	1.3
463	Housing	14.2	14.0	14.2	13.7	13.5	13.3	13.4	12.7	12.2	11.6
464	Household operations	14.4	14.6	14.6	14.6	14.9	14.7	14.3	14.4	14.6	15.2
465	Medical care expenses	5.9	5.8	5.7	5.4	5.2	5.0	5.1	4.8	4.7	4.6
466	Personal business	4.6	4.5	4.4	4.2	4.1	4.0	3.9	3.7	3.6	3.6
467	Transportation	13.3	13.2	12.3	13.5	13.1	14.0	12.6	12.9	11.6	11.9
468	Recreation	5.6	5.6	5.5	5.4	5.6	5.5	5.5	5.5	5.6	5.6
469	Other	3.3	3.2	3.2	3.0	3.0	2.8	2.9	2.8	2.7	2.4

See footnotes at end of table.

Series G 416–469. Personal Consumption Expenditures, by Type of Product: 1929 to 1970—Con.

[In millions of dollars]

Series No.	Products	1950	1949	1948	1947	1946	1945	1944	1943	1942	1941	1940
416	**Total**	**191,009**	**176,803**	**173,555**	**160,704**	**143,400**	**119,701**	**108,255**	**99,336**	**88,501**	**80,575**	**70,824**
417	**Commodities**	**128,587**	**119,173**	**118,892**	**110,865**	**98,131**	**79,947**	**71,066**	**65,169**	**57,700**	**52,500**	**44,783**
418	**Services**	**62,422**	**57,630**	**54,663**	**49,839**	**45,269**	**39,754**	**37,189**	**34,167**	**30,801**	**28,075**	**26,041**
419	Food and beverages	53,869	52,484	54,177	52,345	47,368	40,649	36,667	33,220	28,358	23,358	20,162
420	Purchased meals and beverages	11,092	10,848	11,029	10,861	10,895	9,503	8,129	7,138	5,670	4,611	3,888
421	Food, excluding alcoholic beverages	45,979	44,789	46,277	43,725	39,008	33,164	29,892	27,380	23,278	19,173	16,562
422	Alcoholic beverages	7,890	7,695	7,900	8,620	8,360	7,485	6,775	5,840	5,080	4,185	3,600
423	Tobacco products	4,251	4,109	4,009	3,744	3,353	2,871	2,636	2,615	2,337	2,080	1,870
424	Clothing, accessories, and jewelry	23,709	23,333	24,201	22,760	22,007	19,645	17,466	15,993	13,061	10,509	8,852
425	Women's and children's	10,002	10,191	10,899	9,945	9,711	8,796	7,838	6,940	5,341	4,348	3,766
426	Men's and boys'	6,026	5,801	5,913	5,630	5,352	4,313	3,809	3,546	3,196	2,784	2,387
427	Jewelry and watches	1,318	1,298	1,374	1,395	1,427	1,182	1,004	935	722	550	409
428	Personal care	2,438	2,306	2,287	2,225	2,058	1,982	1,834	1,616	1,354	1,162	1,036
429	Housing	21,286	19,252	17,535	15,665	13,879	12,479	12,049	11,485	10,957	10,167	9,446
430	Owner-occupied nonfarm	12,305	10,902	9,679	8,428	7,343	6,492	6,060	5,588	5,192	4,706	4,310
431	Tenant-occupied nonfarm	6,910	6,371	5,786	5,289	4,851	4,596	4,729	4,737	4,692	4,438	4,154
432	Farmhouses, rental value	1,464	1,408	1,505	1,447	1,303	1,052	955	879	821	767	744
433	Household operation	29,461	25,938	26,395	23,989	20,113	15,530	14,032	13,110	12,727	11,951	10,479
434	Furniture, equipment, and supplies	16,571	14,334	14,874	13,582	10,868	6,917	6,136	5,887	6,071	6,026	4,897
435	Household utilities	7,293	6,520	6,600	5,780	5,023	4,507	4,242	4,079	3,875	3,582	3,391
436	Electricity	2,138	1,879	1,668	1,473	1,328	1,194	1,125	1,045	1,017	965	910
437	Gas	1,185	1,038	963	865	754	705	667	648	623	575	573
438	Telephone	1,942	1,731	1,569	1,376	1,288	1,142	1,077	973	825	695	615
439	Domestic service	2,572	2,356	2,363	2,348	2,120	2,142	1,887	1,598	1,477	1,237	1,218
440	Medical care expenses	8,788	8,110	7,821	6,897	6,175	5,042	4,705	4,189	3,735	3,298	3,018
441	Physicians and dentists [1]	3,530	3,383	3,350	2,903	2,578	1,990	1,894	1,631	1,553	1,416	1,332
442	Hospitals, privately controlled [2]	1,979	1,734	1,596	1,401	1,170	925	846	752	649	555	527
443	Drug preparations and sundries	1,719	1,555	1,466	1,313	1,271	1,138	1,072	1,014	848	725	635
444	Health insurance	602	531	528	487	422	374	315	279	231	196	165
445	Personal business	6,858	6,210	5,950	5,426	5,069	4,656	4,348	3,968	3,599	3,501	3,326
446	Transportation	24,672	20,793	17,659	15,172	11,946	6,845	5,848	5,539	5,529	8,438	7,143
447	User-operated	21,866	17,910	14,670	12,270	9,017	3,992	3,045	2,859	3,581	7,031	5,872
448	New cars and used cars [3]	11,521	8,637	6,144	4,843	2,563	357	322	410	415	2,706	2,217
449	Gasoline and oil	5,431	5,031	4,446	3,630	3,034	1,809	1,384	1,339	2,090	2,649	2,273
450	Purchased local transport	1,934	1,951	1,989	1,927	1,908	1,746	1,726	1,646	1,294	978	907
451	Purchased intercity transport	872	932	1,000	975	1,021	1,107	1,077	1,034	654	429	364
452	Recreation	11,147	10,010	9,692	9,249	8,539	6,139	5,422	4,961	4,677	4,239	3,761
453	Radio and television sets, records, and musical instruments [4]	2,421	1,675	1,450	1,398	1,116	344	311	403	634	607	494
454	Toys and sport supplies, nondurable	1,394	1,170	1,076	907	840	553	459	393	404	362	306
455	Wheel goods, durable toys, sport equipment [5]	869	836	965	955	793	400	323	271	306	314	254
456	Books, maps, magazines, newspapers, sheet music	2,169	2,081	1,958	1,774	1,688	1,485	1,330	1,204	994	891	823
457	Private education and research	1,618	1,507	1,387	1,243	1,026	936	943	936	801	692	632
458	Religious and welfare activities	2,282	2,150	2,150	1,984	1,943	1,735	1,667	1,428	1,207	1,060	1,012
459	Foreign travel and other, net	630	601	292	5	−76	1,192	638	276	159	120	87
	PERCENT DISTRIBUTION											
460	Food, beverages, and tobacco	30.4	32.0	33.5	34.9	35.4	36.4	36.3	36.1	34.7	31.6	31.1
461	Clothing, accessories, and jewelry	12.4	13.2	13.9	14.2	15.3	16.4	16.1	16.1	14.8	13.0	12.5
462	Personal care	1.3	1.3	1.3	1.4	1.4	1.7	1.7	1.6	1.5	1.4	1.5
463	Housing	11.1	10.9	10.1	9.7	9.7	10.4	11.1	11.6	12.4	12.6	13.3
464	Household operations	15.4	14.7	15.2	14.9	14.0	13.0	13.0	13.2	14.4	14.8	14.8
465	Medical care expenses	4.6	4.6	4.5	4.3	4.3	4.2	4.3	4.2	4.2	4.1	4.3
466	Personal business	3.6	3.5	3.4	3.4	3.5	3.9	4.0	4.0	4.1	4.3	4.7
467	Transportation	12.9	11.8	10.2	9.4	8.3	5.7	5.4	5.6	6.2	10.5	10.1
468	Recreation	5.8	5.7	5.6	5.8	6.0	5.1	5.0	5.0	5.3	5.3	5.3
469	Other	2.4	2.4	2.2	2.0	2.0	3.2	3.0	2.7	2.4	2.3	2.4

See footnotes at end of table.

Series G 416–469. Personal Consumption Expenditures, by Type of Product: 1929 to 1970—Con.

[In millions of dollars]

Series No.	Products	1939	1938	1937	1936	1935	1934	1933	1932	1931	1930	1929
416	Total	66,834	63,920	66,507	61,912	55,699	51,335	45,795	48,589	60,464	69,880	77,222
417	Commodities	41,786	39,639	42,149	39,161	34,433	30,904	25,726	26,387	34,441	41,177	46,898
418	Services	25,048	24,281	24,358	22,751	21,266	20,431	20,069	22,202	26,023	28,703	30,324
419	Food and beverages	19,149	18,857	19,919	18,441	16,190	14,217	11,530	11,365	14,741	17,976	19,544
420	Purchased meals and beverages	3,633	3,392	3,528	2,985	2,610	2,248	1,816	2,102	2,541	2,788	2,911
421	Food, excluding alcoholic beverages	15,729	15,587	16,454	15,266	13,635	12,217	10,865	11,365	14,741	17,976	19,544
422	Alcoholic beverages	3,420	3,270	3,465	3,175	2,555	2,000	665	- - - -	- - - -	- - - -	- - - -
423	Tobacco products	1,767	1,697	1,673	1,535	1,434	1,367	1,233	1,322	1,489	1,450	1,695
424	Clothing, accessories, and jewelry	8,406	7,991	8,092	7,661	7,010	6,562	5,438	6,042	8,217	9,713	11,193
425	Women's and children's	3,607	3,337	3,277	3,226	3,080	2,801	2,254	2,446	3,528	4,100	4,662
426	Men's and boys'	2,286	2,158	2,269	2,177	1,902	1,784	1,477	1,576	2,185	2,559	3,020
427	Jewelry and watches	355	323	333	265	233	198	172	252	328	513	560
428	Personal care	1,004	951	961	864	802	760	660	817	979	1,039	1,116
429	Housing	9,139	8,936	8,533	8,011	7,702	7,602	7,907	9,011	10,291	11,050	11,530
430	Owner-occupied nonfarm	4,179	4,104	3,950	3,759	3,646	3,643	3,844	4,416	5,101	5,552	5,868
431	Tenant-occupied nonfarm	3,994	3,870	3,639	3,365	3,199	3,158	3,296	3,753	4,200	4,397	4,500
432	Farmhouses, rental value	741	745	733	693	683	640	614	664	775	865	913
433	Household operation	9,624	8,865	9,525	8,821	7,737	7,209	6,466	6,779	8,425	9,585	10,735
434	Furniture, equipment, and supplies	4,444	3,992	4,426	4,016	3,286	2,931	2,498	2,594	3,592	4,161	5,090
435	Household utilities	3,128	2,971	3,042	2,979	2,792	2,729	2,561	2,615	2,844	3,058	3,044
436	Electricity	849	810	766	726	697	671	645	662	674	660	616
437	Gas	538	523	528	516	503	494	495	537	556	560	542
438	Telephone	576	542	542	511	472	443	436	482	554	577	569
439	Domestic service	1,129	1,023	1,187	1,016	911	850	732	835	1,146	1,483	1,716
440	Medical care expenses	2,848	2,688	2,672	2,493	2,288	2,164	1,983	2,127	2,549	2,835	2,937
441	Physicians and dentists [1]	1,252	1,189	1,204	1,151	1,033	973	893	973	1,227	1,387	1,441
442	Hospitals, privately controlled [2]	492	467	454	422	406	369	363	386	395	404	403
443	Drug preparations and sundries	612	578	558	509	474	468	427	449	517	568	604
444	Health insurance	153	134	123	106	93	85	70	72	92	110	108
445	Personal business	3,313	3,265	3,430	3,231	3,043	2,860	2,832	2,875	3,311	3,704	4,158
446	Transportation	6,365	5,633	6,517	6,131	5,281	4,596	3,987	3,981	5,003	6,147	7,612
447	User-operated	5,128	4,453	5,288	4,956	4,217	3,584	3,035	2,935	3,747	4,662	5,960
448	New cars and used cars [3]	1,679	1,228	1,988	1,921	1,508	1,024	779	635	1,144	1,642	2,588
449	Gasoline and oil	2,181	2,145	2,143	1,945	1,743	1,640	1,466	1,476	1,540	1,749	1,814
450	Purchased local transport	878	842	871	845	790	761	720	786	921	1,053	1,117
451	Purchased intercity transport	359	338	358	330	274	251	232	260	335	432	535
452	Recreation	3,452	3,241	3,381	3,020	2,630	2,441	2,202	2,442	3,302	3,990	4,331
453	Radio and television sets, records, and musical instruments [4]	420	339	385	333	248	229	195	268	478	921	1,012
454	Toys and sport supplies, nondurable	285	268	269	242	216	200	181	207	266	281	336
455	Wheel goods, durable toys, sport equipment [5]	228	210	210	171	136	118	93	110	159	172	219
456	Books, maps, magazines, newspapers, sheet music	780	735	761	698	639	606	571	581	732	776	847
457	Private education and research	620	612	594	541	503	480	479	570	665	683	664
458	Religious and welfare activities	938	923	900	899	862	870	872	973	1,125	1,209	1,196
459	Foreign travel and other, net	209	261	310	264	217	207	206	285	367	499	511
	PERCENT DISTRIBUTION											
460	Food, beverages, and tobacco	31.3	32.2	32.5	32.3	31.6	30.4	27.9	26.1	26.8	27.8	27.5
461	Clothing, accessories, and jewelry	12.6	12.5	12.2	12.4	12.6	12.8	11.9	12.4	13.6	13.9	14.5
462	Personal care	1.5	1.5	1.4	1.4	1.4	1.5	1.4	1.7	1.6	1.5	1.4
463	Housing	13.7	14.0	12.8	12.9	13.8	14.8	17.3	18.5	17.0	15.8	14.9
464	Household operations	14.4	13.9	14.3	14.2	13.9	14.0	14.1	14.0	13.9	13.7	13.9
465	Medical care expenses	4.3	4.2	4.0	4.0	4.1	4.2	4.3	4.4	4.2	4.1	3.8
466	Personal business	5.0	5.1	5.2	5.2	5.5	5.6	6.2	5.9	5.5	5.3	5.4
467	Transportation	9.5	8.8	9.8	9.9	9.5	9.0	8.7	8.2	8.3	8.8	9.9
468	Recreation	5.2	5.1	5.1	4.9	4.7	4.8	4.8	5.0	5.5	5.7	5.6
469	Other	2.6	2.8	2.7	2.8	2.8	3.0	3.4	3.8	3.6	3.4	3.1

* Denotes first year for which figures include Alaska and Hawaii.
[1] Includes other professional services.
[2] Includes sanitariums.

[3] Net purchases of used cars.
[4] Includes radio and television repair.
[5] Includes boats and pleasure aircraft.

Series G 470–494. Personal Consumption Expenditures, by Type of Product: 1909 to 1929

[In millions of dollars]

Year	Total consumption expenditures	Food and non-alcoholic beverages	Alcoholic beverages	Tobacco products [1]	Clothing and related products		Personal care	Rent and imputed rent [2]	Household equipment and operation				
					Purchases	Cleaning, repair, and maintenance			Furniture and furnishings	Mechanical appliances	Fuel, ice, and lighting supplies	Electricity, gas, and water	Domestic services [3]
	470	471	472	473	474	475	476	477	478	479	480	481	482
1929	80,761	19,674	2,000	1,700	9,832	965	1,116	11,421	3,698	768	1,694	1,397	1,501
1927	74,569	18,318	1,800	1,617	9,894	851	1,042	11,319	3,630	667	1,882	1,230	1,429
1925	71,750	17,919	1,700	1,521	9,422	734	903	11,454	3,668	548	1,646	1,137	1,327
1923	66,594	16,138	1,500	1,476	9,575	672	873	10,613	3,589	511	2,160	1,004	1,191
1921	55,766	13,908	1,400	1,481	8,162	572	602	9,682	2,474	294	1,817	828	1,005
1919	60,573	18,554	2,000	1,429	8,413	539	615	8,045	2,841	400	1,492	707	967
1914	33,395	8,954	2,000	732	4,059	344	305	6,222	1,333	167	1,190	460	697
1909	28,814	7,369	1,800	627	3,735	281	261	5,563	1,229	145	985	362	712

Year	Household operation—Con.			Medical care	Insurance [5]	Transportation			Recreation [7]	Education (private)	Religious and welfare activities	Occupational and miscellaneous expenses
	Communication	Cleaning, repair, and maintenance	Financial, legal, and insurance [4]			New cars and net purchases of used cars (private)	Other private transportation [6]	Public carrier				
	483	484	485	486	487	488	489	490	491	492	493	494
1929	860	805	5,645	2,915	108	2,588	3,216	2,203	3,836	1,170	1,469	180
1927	721	754	3,770	2,599	91	1,995	3,114	2,081	3,141	1,007	1,447	170
1925	641	681	3,166	2,411	80	2,411	3,214	1,953	2,840	894	1,310	170
1923	557	656	2,482	2,130	65	2,289	2,406	1,819	2,624	813	1,291	160
1921	466	535	1,948	1,483	53	1,157	1,972	1,679	2,068	746	1,364	70
1919	427	625	2,073	2,019	41	1,300	2,172	1,411	2,157	751	1,455	140
1914	214	307	977	881	24	417	673	1,042	997	493	837	70
1909	174	259	870	782	17	167	493	829	859	416	819	60

[1] Includes smoking supplies.
[2] Includes rent of transient accommodations.
[3] Excludes practical nurses.
[4] Includes death expenses.
[5] Accident, health, and prepayment. 1909–1927, estimated at 11 percent of life insurance expenditures.

[6] Includes expenditures for automobile parts, repair, and maintenance, gasoline and oil, luggage, and 1909–1927 for horse-drawn vehicles and equipment, and blacksmiths' services.
[7] Figures differ from comparable estimates shown in series H 878. See text for series H 878–893 for explanation.

Series G 495–581. Consumption Expenditures, in Current Prices, of City Wage- and Clerical-Worker Families of 2 or More Persons, by Income Class: 1874–75 to 1950

Series No.	Item	All income classes	Income class (after taxes)								
			Under $1,000	$1,000–$2,000	$2,000–$3,000	$3,000–$4,000	$4,000–$5,000	$5,000–$6,000	$6,000–$7,500	$7,500–$10,000	$10,000 and over
	1950										
	FAMILIES IN CITIES OF 2,500 AND OVER										
495	Number of families in sample	7,007	64	498	1,423	2,180	1,453	749	427	164	49
496	Average family size persons	3.4	2.3	2.9	3.1	3.4	3.5	3.7	3.9	4.2	4.5
497	Average income after taxes	$3,923	$651	$1,629	$2,564	$3,487	$4,454	$5,434	$6,606	$8,394	$13,292
498	**Average expenditures for current consumption**	**$3,925**	**$1,683**	**$1,924**	**$2,795**	**$3,573**	**$4,408**	**$5,262**	**$6,187**	**$7,161**	**$10,342**
499	Food	1,205	540	690	946	1,139	1,324	1,514	1,691	1,992	2,656
500	Alcoholic beverages	70	8	25	41	58	82	102	134	158	289
501	Tobacco	79	29	50	66	73	88	96	107	130	126
502	Housing	415	283	249	336	390	454	511	590	606	976
503	Fuel, light, and refrigeration	163	122	111	140	158	174	194	208	228	287
504	Household operation	155	77	71	108	135	169	213	245	304	814
505	Furnishings and equipment	278	86	117	193	242	331	388	462	435	805
506	Clothing	453	131	197	286	385	508	648	822	1,026	1,588
	Transportation:										
507	Automobile	472	107	131	248	421	561	737	887	1,052	1,002
508	Other	69	25	37	53	56	73	98	113	158	202
509	Medical care	200	112	102	150	194	221	246	294	333	411
510	Personal care	91	35	51	69	84	99	118	132	161	212
511	Recreation	177	33	46	93	155	219	256	324	397	605
512	Reading	34	14	17	26	33	38	44	50	55	80
513	Education	17	1	6	7	14	20	29	39	43	84
514	Miscellaneous	47	81	25	34	37	49	70	89	84	206

Series G 495–581. Consumption Expenditures, in Current Prices, of City Wage- and Clerical-Worker Families of 2 or More Persons, by Income Class: 1874–75 to 1950—Con.

Series No.	Item	All income classes	Income class (after taxes)									
			$500–$600	$600–$900	$900–$1,200	$1,200–$1,500	$1,500–$1,800	$1,800–$2,100	$2,100–$2,400	$2,400–$2,700	$2,700–$3,000	$3,000 and over
	1934–36											
	FAMILIES OF EMPLOYED WORKERS IN CITIES (50,000 INHABITANTS OR MORE)											
515	Number of families in sample	14,469	116	1,215	2,952	3,444	2,937	2,185	810	391	188	231
516	Average family size____persons	3.6	3.1	3.2	3.4	3.5	3.6	3.8	4.0	4.3	4.4	4.8
517	Average income	$1,518	$550	$775	$1,062	$1,348	$1,634	$1,928	$2,241	$2,507	$2,867	$3,450
518	**Average expenditures for current consumption**	**$1,463**	**$637**	**$832**	**$1,081**	**$1,332**	**$1,576**	**$1,804**	**$2,075**	**$2,305**	**$2,590**	**$3,093**
519	Food and alcoholic beverages	508	250	315	398	472	540	597	683	756	837	1,021
520	Tobacco	29	11	15	20	26	31	36	44	51	58	75
521	Housing	259	132	169	215	246	281	300	324	346	370	411
522	Fuel, light, and refrigeration	108	64	76	94	106	114	123	136	131	131	148
523	Household operation	58	20	30	38	49	63	77	92	102	119	142
524	Furnishings and equipment	60	13	28	39	55	70	77	90	96	83	112
525	Clothing	160	49	74	102	136	173	211	258	309	388	471
	Transportation:											
526	Automobile	87	9	20	40	73	99	137	162	161	197	212
527	Other	38	17	25	29	33	40	43	52	65	78	115
528	Medical care	59	22	33	42	53	64	78	81	97	109	115
529	Personal care	30	13	17	22	27	32	37	43	51	59	71
530	Recreation	38	11	15	23	32	40	49	62	73	88	116
531	Reading	15	6	8	11	14	16	19	23	28	31	41
532	Education	7	2	2	4	5	7	11	14	19	17	22
533	Miscellaneous	7	18	5	4	5	6	9	11	20	25	21

Series No.	Item	All income classes	Income class (after taxes)						
			Under $900	$900–$1,200	$1,200–$1,500	$1,500–$1,800	$1,800–$2,100	$2,100–$2,500	$2,500 and over
	1917–19								
	FAMILIES WITH AT LEAST 1 CHILD								
534	Number of families in survey	12,096	332	2,423	3,959	2,730	1,594	705	353
535	Average family size____persons	4.9	4.3	4.5	4.7	5.0	5.1	5.7	6.4
536	Average income after taxes	$1,505	$810	$1,070	$1,336	$1,622	$1,914	$2,261	$2,777
537	**Average expenditures for current consumption**	**$1,352**	**$804**	**$1,016**	**$1,234**	**$1,452**	**$1,656**	**$1,937**	**$2,331**
538	Food	549	372	456	516	572	627	712	860
539	Alcoholic beverages	7	4	7	7	7	7	9	16
540	Tobacco	17	12	14	15	17	20	21	28
541	Housing [1]	187	122	150	180	207	232	248	260
542	Household operation	37	18	14	32	41	51	61	63
543	Fuel, light, and refrigeration	74	57	64	73	79	87	93	102
544	Furnishings and equipment	62	28	43	54	71	79	93	105
545	Clothing	238	112	156	206	257	307	384	503
	Transportation:								
546	Automobile	16	1	4	9	18	31	50	58
547	Other	26	11	18	23	29	32	43	54
548	Medical care	64	36	46	58	71	78	87	102
549	Personal care	14	9	11	13	15	17	19	24
550	Recreation	33	8	15	25	38	52	69	97
551	Reading	11	6	8	10	11	13	15	16
552	Education	7	4	3	5	8	11	16	22
553	Miscellaneous	10	4	7	8	11	12	17	21

Series No.	Item	All income classes	Income class (before taxes)											
			Under $200	$200–$300	$300–$400	$400–$500	$500–$600	$600–$700	$700–$800	$800–$900	$900–$1,000	$1,000–$1,100	$1,100–$1,200	$1,200 and over
	1901													
	NORMAL FAMILIES													
554	Number of families	11,156	32	115	545	1,676	2,264	2,336	2,094	806	684	340	96	168
555	Average family size persons	4.0	3.2	3.4	3.8	3.8	3.9	3.9	4.0	4.2	4.1	4.3	4.0	3.8
556	Average income	$651	(NA)	(NA)	(NA)	(NA)	(NA)	(NA)	(NA)	(NA)	(NA)	(NA)	(NA)	(NA)
557	**Average expenditures for current consumption**	**$618**	**$196**	**$312**	**$389**	**$466**	**$540**	**$612**	**$693**	**$771**	**$816**	**$900**	**$973**	**$1,052**
558	Food	266	100	148	187	218	249	266	287	319	326	349	367	384
559	Rent	112	33	56	73	87	100	113	126	132	144	158	161	183
560	Fuel	28	13	19	23	26	27	28	29	30	31	34	35	41
561	Light	7	2	4	4	5	6	7	8	8	9	10	11	12
562	Clothing	80	17	27	39	53	65	79	94	105	117	136	145	165
563	Sundries	124	31	59	63	77	93	119	150	177	189	213	254	267

NA Not available.   [1] Excludes 301 families whose rent included the cost of heat or light, or both.

Series G 495–581. Consumption Expenditures, in Current Prices, of City Wage- and Clerical-Worker Families of 2 or More Persons, by Income Class: 1874–75 to 1950—Con.

Series No.	Item	All income classes	Income class (before taxes)						
			Under $200	$200–$400	$400–$600	$600–$800	$800–$1,000	$1,000–$1,200	$1,200 and over
	1888–91								
	NORMAL FAMILIES OF WORKERS IN 9 BASIC INDUSTRIES								
564	Number of families in sample	2,562	24	500	1,168	492	206	86	86
565	Average family size _____persons	3.9	3.4	3.7	3.9	3.9	4.1	4.2	4.3
566	Average money income	$573	$156	$335	$486	$674	$883	$1,064	$1,450
567	**Average expenditures for current consumption**	**$534**	**$233**	**$363**	**$476**	**$608**	**$746**	**$878**	**$1,128**
568	Food	219	116	165	212	245	271	295	323
569	Housing	80	36	54	73	95	116	126	142
570	Fuel and light	32	18	26	31	34	37	38	34
571	Clothing	82	30	51	70	97	119	151	177
572	Sundries	121	33	67	90	137	203	268	452

Series No.	Item	All income classes	Income class (before taxes)				
			$300–$450	$450–$600	$600–$750	$750–$1,200	$1,200 and over
	1874–75						
	MASSACHUSETTS—FAMILIES OF WAGE EARNERS IN 15 CITIES AND 21 TOWNS						
573	Number of families in sample	397	6	52	143	188	8
574	Average family size _____persons	5.1	5.0	5.2	4.8	5.3	6.9
575	Average money income	$763	$395	$549	$679	$871	$1,383
576	**Average expenditures for goods and services**	**$738**	**$410**	**$555**	**$668**	**$832**	**$1,212**
577	Subsistence [1]	427	262	350	401	466	618
578	Clothing	106	29	58	94	125	230
579	Rent	117	82	86	94	141	182
580	Fuel	44	25	33	40	50	60
581	Sundry expenses	44	12	28	40	50	121

[1] Includes kerosene.

Series G 582–601. Consumption Expenditures of City Wage- and Clerical-Worker Families of 2 or More Persons: 1888–91 to 1960–61

Series No.	Item	1960–61	1950	1934–36	1917–19	1901	1888–91
582	Families covered _____number	[1] 19,455	5,994	14,469	12,096	11,156	2,562
583	Average family size _____persons	3.6	3.3	3.6	4.9	4.0	3.9
584	Average money income before taxes _____current dol	6,763	4,299	1,518	1,505	651	573
		In constant 1950 dollars [2]					
585	Money income after personal taxes	4,877	4,005	2,659	2,408	1,914	1,793
	AVERAGE OUTLAYS						
586	**Current outlays for goods and services, total**	**4,604**	**4,076**	**2,564**	**2,163**	**1,817**	**1,671**
587	Food and drink	1,297	1,335	1,030	854	952	797
588	Clothing	541	473	309	343		
589	Shelter (current expense)	539	448	356	252		
590	Fuel, light, refrigeration, and water	207	153	158	126		
591	Housefurnishings and equipment	297	281	119	109		
592	Household operation	225	167	80			
593	Automobile purchase and operation	635	457	150			
594	Other transportation	50	81	57			
595	Medical care	243	213	88			
596	Personal care	130	93	55			
597	Recreation	194	191	67		479	
598	Reading	34	36	27			
599	Education	42	19	11			
600	Tobacco	88	80	46			
601	Miscellaneous goods and services	82	49	11			

[1] Estimated number of families, in thousands, represented by sample.
[2] The cost of living index developed by Paul Douglas (*American Economic Review*, Supplement, March 1926, p. 22) was used to convert the 1888–91 and 1901 expenditures into 1950 dollars. The Consumer Price Index of the Bureau of Labor Statistics was used for the surveys thereafter.

Series G 602–696. Consumption Expenditures, in Current Prices, of All Families of 2 or More Persons in Cities of 2,500 and Over, by Income Class: 1935–36 to 1960–61

Series No.	Item	All income classes	Income class (after taxes)								
			Under $1,000	$1,000–$2,000	$2,000–$3,000	$3,000–$4,000	$4,000–$5,000	$5,000–$6,000	$6,000–$7,500	$7,500–$10,000	$10,000 and over
	1960–61										
	FAMILIES										
602	Estimated number of families____1,000__	33,370	158	1,546	2,663	3,505	4,519	4,905	6,245	5,865	3,965
603	Average family size [1]_____persons__	3.5	2.9	2.5	2.9	3.1	3.4	3.6	3.7	3.8	4.0
604	Average income after taxes_____	$6,509	$394	$1,575	$2,522	$3,531	$4,517	$5,501	$6,712	$8,578	$14,127
605	**Average expenditures for current consumption**_____	**$5,954**	**$2,389**	**$2,038**	**$2,840**	**$3,884**	**$4,624**	**$5,288**	**$6,282**	**$7,580**	**$10,960**
606	Food_____	1,451	611	627	833	1,056	1,195	1,344	1,531	1,825	2,334
607	Alcoholic beverages_____	95	29	22	30	51	66	78	100	129	206
608	Tobacco_____	106	51	48	63	85	98	106	119	129	132
609	Housing_____	1,723	781	691	950	1,187	1,377	1,565	1,823	2,094	3,040
610	Shelter [2]_____	790	377	349	493	570	654	733	835	946	1,302
611	Fuel, light, refrigeration, water_____	270	166	143	175	201	229	260	289	320	399
612	Household operation_____	348	128	121	167	226	260	289	345	418	749
613	Furnishings and equipment_____	315	110	78	115	190	234	283	354	410	590
614	Clothing_____	626	145	131	221	347	444	523	655	849	1,317
	Transportation:										
615	Automobile_____	790	91	99	194	452	630	737	871	1,097	1,454
616	Other_____	98	78	36	48	61	67	65	85	113	260
617	Medical care_____	394	246	171	240	296	299	346	416	483	677
618	Personal care_____	172	78	64	94	122	138	160	180	217	285
619	Recreation_____	243	77	43	74	127	164	194	259	338	529
620	Reading_____	53	23	19	25	33	40	45	57	67	102
621	Education_____	70	29	10	13	25	28	40	60	86	254
622	Miscellaneous_____	133	150	77	55	62	78	85	126	153	371
	1950										
	FAMILIES										
623	Number of families in sample_____	10,791	284	982	1,962	2,807	2,058	1,191	793	425	289
624	Average family size_____persons__	3.3	2.4	2.7	3.1	3.3	3.5	3.7	3.7	4.0	3.7
625	Average income after taxes_____	$4,224	$622	$1,556	$2,549	$3,492	$4,464	$5,449	$6,638	$8,432	$15,932
626	**Average expenditures for current consumption**_____	**$4,119**	**$1,863**	**$1,892**	**$2,809**	**$3,613**	**$4,469**	**$5,277**	**$6,062**	**$7,160**	**$10,808**
627	Food_____	1,221	605	679	944	1,135	1,313	1,498	1,648	1,925	2,423
628	Alcoholic beverages_____	67	15	20	37	55	74	96	112	140	223
629	Tobacco_____	74	25	41	60	71	85	88	95	103	112
630	Housing_____	455	278	262	343	408	485	536	620	704	1,146
631	Fuel, light, and refrigeration_____	172	137	126	146	161	179	196	211	242	306
632	Household operation_____	191	89	79	114	144	184	235	281	389	968
633	Furnishings and equipment_____	290	105	103	190	242	334	383	438	456	906
634	Clothing_____	476	131	168	282	388	511	649	776	971	1,535
	Transportation:										
635	Automobile_____	490	133	120	252	422	572	728	841	973	1,172
636	Other_____	69	22	35	51	57	70	89	103	140	199
637	Medical care_____	215	142	111	154	202	227	256	302	378	453
638	Personal care_____	92	37	46	68	84	99	116	129	150	203
639	Recreation_____	185	40	45	92	155	217	251	317	365	598
640	Reading_____	37	19	18	27	34	40	45	52	59	83
641	Education_____	26	9	4	9	15	26	35	48	70	166
642	Miscellaneous_____	60	76	34	41	39	53	76	88	95	316

Series No.	Item	All income classes	Income class (after taxes)								
			Under $500	$500–$1,000	$1,000–$1,500	$1,500–$2,000	$2,000–$2,500	$2,500–$3,000	$3,000–$4,000	$4,000–$5,000	$5,000 and over
	1944										
	FAMILIES										
643	Percent of families in each class_____	100.0	1.5	5.2	5.3	10.7	14.0	14.7	23.0	11.2	14.4
644	Average number of persons per family [1]____	3.42	2.45	2.45	2.78	3.03	3.10	3.13	3.69	4.01	4.13
645	Average income after taxes_____	$3,411	$313	$776	$1,243	$1,779	$2,259	$2,757	$3,480	$4,408	$7,595
646	**Average expenditures for current consumption**_____	**$2,633**	**$887**	**$1,053**	**$1,407**	**$1,788**	**$2,051**	**$2,410**	**$2,838**	**$3,439**	**$4,305**
647	Food and beverages [3]_____	947	374	434	555	701	797	913	1,043	1,150	1,386
648	Tobacco_____	52	16	15	21	41	41	48	59	71	76
649	Clothing_____	430	42	80	163	234	283	364	462	623	848
650	Housing, fuel, light, and refrigeration [2]____	450	257	251	298	341	394	430	488	547	616
651	Household operation_____	138	56	47	66	83	93	110	140	166	295
652	Furnishings and equipment_____	89	5	25	39	49	60	88	95	132	157
	Transportation:										
653	Automobile_____	104	16	19	29	42	69	105	119	177	171
654	Other_____	61	7	20	26	44	50	51	63	84	109
655	Medical care_____	148	62	88	94	105	104	123	149	190	265
656	Personal care_____	63	21	19	33	41	48	56	65	84	110
657	Recreation_____	75	3	15	28	46	55	63	82	105	137
658	Reading_____	28	14	13	14	18	22	27	31	37	43
659	Education, formal_____	17	1	2	2	11	9	15	13	29	42
660	Other_____	32	13	25	39	32	26	17	29	44	50

See footnotes at end of table.

Series G 602–696.   Consumption Expenditures, in Current Prices, of All Families of 2 or More Persons in Cities of 2,500 and Over, by Income Class: 1935–36 to 1960–61—Con.

Series No.	Item	All income classes	Income class (before taxes)								
			Under $500	$500–$1,000	$1,000–$1,500	$1,500–$2,000	$2,000–$2,500	$2,500–$3,000	$3,000–$5,000	$5,000–$10,000	$10,000 and over
	1941										
	FAMILIES										
661	Estimated number of families ___1,000__	20,419	750	2,237	2,703	3,735	3,472	2,816	3,384	524	798
662	Average family size [1] ___persons__	3.44	2.64	3.17	3.05	3.39	3.30	3.70	3.71	4.43	4.62
663	Average money income	$2,672	$323	$736	$1,257	$1,756	$2,240	$2,745	$3,726	$6,208	$14,196
664	**Average expenditures for current consumption**	**$2,290**	**$457**	**$781**	**$1,288**	**$1,662**	**$2,137**	**$2,572**	**$3,234**	**$4,717**	**$8,731**
665	Food and beverages [3]	706	183	324	468	575	666	839	949	1,330	1,943
666	Tobacco	48	9	15	34	40	49	52	71	108	97
667	Housing, fuel, light, and refrigeration	423	123	185	290	354	418	458	526	696	1,433
668	Household operation	120	20	31	44	70	84	104	162	262	890
669	Furnishings and equipment	122	9	30	67	80	116	163	210	202	329
670	Clothing	278	26	69	139	191	233	310	432	663	1,146
	Transportation:										
671	Automobile	223	23	39	78	112	239	264	353	495	996
672	Other	53	5	12	27	31	36	62	62	138	356
673	Personal care	50	8	17	27	36	45	55	74	106	188
674	Medical care	107	33	29	58	85	113	90	154	244	399
675	Recreation	101	9	14	32	51	78	105	155	297	633
676	Reading	23	6	7	13	19	21	26	32	51	82
677	Education	18	1	5	2	6	16	18	34	89	174
678	Other	18	2	4	9	12	23	26	20	36	65

Series No.	Item	Income class (money plus nonmoney, before taxes)											
		Under $500	$500–$750	$750–$1,000	$1,000–$1,250	$1,250–$1,500	$1,500–$1,750	$1,750–$2,000	$2,000–$2,500	$2,500–$3,000	$3,000–$4,000	$4,000–$5,000	$5,000–$10,000
	1935–1936												
	FAMILIES												
679	Number of families	780	1,448	2,284	3,009	3,310	3,168	3,270	5,299	2,617	2,635	1,036	878
680	Average family size ___persons__	3.1	3.4	3.5	3.6	3.6	3.6	3.7	3.7	3.9	4.0	4.2	4.1
681	Average family income	$329	$649	$886	$1,134	$1,374	$1,626	$1,875	$2,235	$2,733	$3,454	$4,438	$6,912
682	**Average expenditures for current consumption**	**$593**	**$739**	**$934**	**$1,152**	**$1,350**	**$1,567**	**$1,769**	**$2,043**	**$2,411**	**$2,882**	**$3,523**	**$5,050**
683	Food and beverages	232	290	354	414	472	519	568	627	706	793	899	1,143
684	Tobacco	11	15	21	26	30	34	37	42	46	51	56	68
685	Housing	147	167	198	236	268	308	342	385	447	538	643	963
686	Housing operation	77	96	116	138	155	174	198	225	272	346	439	676
687	Furnishings	10	16	30	41	51	59	72	79	91	99	115	176
688	Clothing	39	54	73	100	122	152	174	215	266	342	430	601
	Transportation:												
689	Automobile	11	18	35	62	80	112	143	187	235	281	371	543
690	Other	7	9	13	15	19	22	23	26	31	36	46	67
691	Medical care	26	30	39	47	61	74	81	98	115	142	186	284
692	Personal care	13	17	21	26	30	35	39	45	53	63	72	98
693	Recreation	8	12	18	26	35	44	54	67	87	113	151	245
694	Education	2	3	3	5	7	10	12	17	27	36	59	104
695	Reading	6	8	10	12	15	17	19	21	25	27	36	45
696	Other items	4	4	3	4	5	7	7	9	10	13	20	37

[1] Family size is based on equivalent persons, with 52 weeks of family membership considered equivalent to 1 person; 26 weeks equivalent to 0.5 person, etc.

[2] Includes rent for tenant-occupied dwellings and for lodging away from home, and current operation expenses of homeowners. Excludes principal payment on mortgages on owned homes.

[3] Includes alcoholic beverages.

Series G 697–797. Consumption Expenditures, in Current Prices, of Farm Families, by Income Class: 1922–1924 to 1961

Series No.	Item	All income classes	Income class (after taxes)									
			Under $1,000	$1,000–$1,999	$2,000–$2,999	$3,000–$3,999	$4,000–$4,999	$5,000–$5,999	$6,000–$7,499	$7,500–$9,999	$10,000–$14,999	$15,000 and over
	1961											
	FAMILIES OF 2 OR MORE PERSONS											
697	Estimated number of families 1,000	3,290	219	491	517	503	375	351	355	271	143	65
698	Average family size____persons__	4.0	3.1	3.3	3.6	4.2	3.9	4.2	4.6	4.8	4.9	4.2
699	**Average expenditure for current consumption**	**$3,738**	**$2,390**	**$2,057**	**$2,612**	**$3,370**	**$3,791**	**$4,371**	**$5,123**	**$5,653**	**$6,234**	**$7,949**
700	Food	897	631	557	703	813	910	1,033	1,209	1,275	1,284	1,606
701	Alcohol	28	14	15	22	27	25	31	42	36	41	69
702	Tobacco	66	40	49	56	78	67	74	72	83	79	98
703	Housing	949	609	536	657	865	954	1,116	1,285	1,387	1,594	2,113
704	Shelter	320	216	171	210	271	316	369	455	481	582	806
705	Housefurnishings and equip___	230	109	115	158	223	229	287	319	347	399	481
706	Fuel, light, refrig., water___	239	179	163	184	223	246	269	311	317	341	415
707	Household operations	160	105	87	105	148	163	191	200	242	272	411
708	Clothing, materials, services___	449	259	222	288	400	417	520	659	739	837	1,077
709	Automobile transportation	612	336	260	353	537	691	772	877	987	1,174	1,245
710	Other travel and transportation_	26	7	9	17	28	26	28	31	68	31	49
711	Medical care	322	233	210	253	298	338	338	425	430	503	610
712	Personal care	112	74	66	81	108	109	133	147	168	169	204
713	Recreation	129	69	55	73	114	128	167	172	219	261	342
714	Reading	26	20	14	19	21	26	30	34	44	43	62
715	Education	41	22	11	14	23	34	49	71	100	104	165
716	Other expenditures	81	76	53	76	58	66	80	99	117	114	309

Series No.	Item	All income classes [1]	Income class (after taxes)							
			Under $1,000			$1,000–$1,499	$1,500–$1,999	$2,000–$2,999	$3,000–$3,999	$4,000–$7,499	$7,500 and over
			Total	Under $250	$250–$499	$500–$999					
	1955										
	FAMILIES OF 2 OR MORE PERSONS										
717	Number of families represented by sample____1,000__	4,534	1,111	399	193	519	480	469	822	594	663	173
718	Average family size_____persons__	4.0	3.5	3.6	3.6	3.4	3.7	3.9	4.2	4.3	4.4	4.4
719	**Average expenditures for current consumption**	**$2,984**	**$1,887**	**$2,238**	**$1,716**	**$1,680**	**$2,077**	**$2,513**	**$2,952**	**$3,395**	**$4,459**	**$6,560**
720	Food and beverages	868	612	690	598	558	653	781	857	982	1,204	1,592
721	Tobacco	51	38	43	38	34	44	50	52	57	66	70
722	Dwelling upkeep	195	119	160	91	98	124	143	173	204	324	552
723	Housefurnishings and equip_____	213	122	126	105	125	145	183	219	244	330	505
724	Fuel, light, refrigeration, water_	193	136	169	114	118	148	179	201	222	256	321
725	Other household operation_____	114	69	83	70	58	79	92	111	123	172	312
726	Clothing	419	249	290	232	224	281	369	430	459	630	973
727	Auto and truck transportation_	370	175	204	159	157	207	258	352	466	669	976
728	Other transportation_____	17	6	6	5	6	9	12	18	21	24	78
729	Medical care	248	196	262	162	157	196	213	252	274	322	437
730	Personal care	71	44	50	42	41	52	63	71	76	107	158
731	Recreation	126	64	77	59	57	77	96	126	158	202	323
732	Reading	19	11	14	9	10	14	17	19	22	28	46
733	Education	25	11	15	5	9	15	22	24	29	42	80
734	Other goods and services_____	52	36	51	25	28	35	34	47	59	83	137

Series No.	Item	All income classes [2]	Income class (before taxes)							
			0–$250	$250–$499	$500–$749	$750–$999	$1,000–$1,499	$1,500–$1,999	$2,000–$2,999	$3,000–$4,999
	1941									
	FAMILIES OF 2 OR MORE PERSONS									
735	Farm families_____number__	733	104	135	102	85	110	79	64	28
736	Average family size_____persons__	4.15	3.93	3.95	4.11	4.16	4.74	4.39	3.56	4.54
737	Average money income_____	$1,163	$139	$378	$628	$866	$1,226	$1,701	$2,441	$3,776
738	**Average expenditures for current consumption**___	**$841**	**$313**	**$451**	**$617**	**$806**	**$921**	**$1,207**	**$1,562**	**$1,836**
739	Food and beverages_____	254	114	152	193	258	295	340	444	467
740	Tobacco	17	9	14	13	17	17	22	27	24
741	Housing	22	4	12	19	22	25	26	45	44
742	Fuel, light, and refrigeration____	53	16	26	40	55	60	77	97	109
743	Other household operation_____	35	12	15	22	33	37	47	72	94
744	Furnishings and equipment_____	67	15	30	44	62	74	117	138	144
745	Clothing	139	58	83	112	128	152	180	234	308
746	Automobile transportation_____	104	16	42	74	98	103	187	220	307
747	Other transportation_____	7	5	4	8	3	7	9	12	4
748	Medical care	62	30	35	41	60	65	96	116	126
749	Personal care	20	7	11	15	19	21	29	37	50
750	Recreation	27	8	12	16	19	32	40	48	109
751	Reading	8	3	4	5	8	8	11	15	16
752	Formal education_____	9	2	5	6	7	9	11	10	20
753	Miscellaneous	17	14	6	9	17	16	15	47	14

[1] Includes families not classified by income.
[2] Includes a small number of families with negative incomes and incomes of $5,000 or more, not shown separately.

Series G 697–797. Consumption Expenditures, in Current Prices, of Farm Families, by Income Class: 1922–1924 to 1961—Con.

Series No.	Item	Income class (money plus nonmoney, before taxes)											
		Under $500	$500–$750	$750–$1,000	$1,000–$1,250	$1,250–$1,500	$1,500–$1,750	$1,750–$2,000	$2,000–$2,500	$2,500–$3,000	$3,000–$4,000	$4,000–$5,000	$5,000–$10,000
	1935–1936												
	FAMILIES												
754	Farm families_____number__	2,548	2,616	2,390	1,821	1,510	1,111	761	1,011	538	466	143	108
755	Average family size_____persons__	4.0	4.4	4.4	4.5	4.6	4.5	4.5	4.6	4.6	4.6	4.7	4.8
756	Average income per family_____	$339	$633	$878	$1,127	$1,374	$1,620	$1,864	$2,218	$2,716	$3,390	$4,396	$6,587
757	**Average expenditures for current consumption____**	**$537**	**$720**	**$919**	**$1,113**	**$1,266**	**$1,404**	**$1,528**	**$1,704**	**$1,881**	**$2,149**	**$2,395**	**$2,946**
758	Food and beverages_____	288	393	474	537	585	610	635	681	729	788	850	868
759	Tobacco_____	10	13	14	16	16	17	17	20	22	20	24	33
760	Housing_____	51	67	96	128	152	188	212	244	256	319	376	488
761	Household operation_____	54	65	79	97	111	123	135	146	163	182	205	302
762	Furnishings_____	12	16	21	29	38	43	51	58	73	86	90	117
763	Clothing_____	47	64	83	104	125	137	148	174	191	221	280	348
	Transportation:												
764	Automobile_____	31	40	65	88	106	132	158	181	217	253	254	395
765	Other_____	1	2	2	2	3	3	4	5	6	6	11	14
766	Medical care_____	22	29	40	50	55	64	77	83	90	111	106	152
767	Personal care_____	7	9	13	17	20	22	23	27	30	35	42	48
768	Recreation_____	6	9	14	21	26	32	33	43	51	60	78	87
769	Education_____	2	4	8	11	12	15	16	23	30	37	46	57
770	Reading_____	3	4	5	7	8	9	9	11	12	13	16	20
771	Other items_____	3	5	5	6	9	9	10	8	11	18	17	17

Series No.	Item	All income classes	Income class (money plus nonmoney, before taxes)							
			Under $1,000	$1,000–$1,500	$1,500–$2,000	$2,000–$3,000	$3,000–$4,000	$4,000–$5,000	$5,000–$7,000	$7,000–$10,000
	1929									
	FAMILIES									
772	Estimated number of families_____1,000__	5,796	3,164	1,005	607	614	230	102	59	15
773	**Average expenditures for current consumption_____**	**$990**	**$602**	**$1,130**	**$1,359**	**$1,634**	**$1,983**	**$2,216**	**$2,407**	**$2,800**
774	Food_____	439	336	491	550	611	665	706	729	800
775	Home_____	234	119	260	339	435	570	637	678	733
776	Attire_____	146	75	180	209	261	322	363	373	467
777	Other_____	171	73	200	260	327	426	510	627	800

Series No.	Item	All families	Value of goods purchased and goods furnished in kind								
			Under $600	$600–$899	$900–$1,199	$1,200–$1,499	$1,500–$1,799	$1,800–$2,099	$2,100–$2,399	$2,400–$2,699	$2,700–$2,999	$3,000 and over
	1922–1924											
	VALUE OF CURRENT CONSUMPTION OF FARM-OPERATOR FAMILIES IN 11 STATES											
778	Farm families_____number__	2,886	58	280	579	614	492	332	196	116	83	136
779	Average family size____persons__	4.4	3.0	3.4	3.7	4.1	4.8	4.8	5.3	5.4	5.7	6.2
780	Average size of household persons__	4.8	3.3	3.6	4.0	4.5	5.1	5.3	5.9	6.0	6.5	7.0
781	Average value, all goods_____	$1,598	$486	$779	$1,055	$1,339	$1,639	$1,932	$2,240	$2,529	$2,854	$3,779
782	**Average expenditures for current consumption_____**	**$1,556**	**$484**	**$769**	**$1,038**	**$1,315**	**$1,597**	**$1,884**	**$2,171**	**$2,446**	**$2,771**	**$3,609**
783	Food_____	658	264	406	502	606	705	769	833	916	959	1,160
784	Clothing_____	235	56	93	133	185	248	298	354	392	457	620
785	Rent_____	200	61	90	137	170	200	261	282	311	374	412
786	Furniture and furnishings_____	40	7	12	22	31	48	48	63	71	80	110
787	Operation goods_____	212	64	110	150	182	211	257	302	344	354	472
788	Maintenance_____	61	10	20	32	47	56	75	103	96	191	181
789	Advancement_____	105	9	21	38	59	90	122	168	248	277	506
790	Personal_____	42	11	16	24	32	38	48	58	63	77	144
791	Unclassified_____	3	----------	1	----------	3	2	6	7	5	3	4
	Proportion of living (percent):											
792	Furnished by farm_____	42.8	55.6	52.9	48.9	46.3	44.0	42.1	39.5	38.2	38.1	31.7
793	Purchased_____	57.2	44.4	47.1	51.1	53.7	56.0	57.9	60.5	61.8	61.9	68.3
	Proportion of food (percent):											
794	Furnished by farm_____	66.9	69.0	70.6	67.9	67.5	67.5	66.0	65.5	64.7	67.8	63.2
795	Purchased_____	33.1	31.0	29.4	32.1	32.5	32.5	34.0	34.5	35.3	32.2	36.8
	Number of rooms:											
796	Per household_____	6.8	4.4	5.4	6.2	6.6	7.0	7.5	7.9	8.2	8.2	8.6
797	Per person_____	1.4	1.3	1.5	1.5	1.5	1.4	1.4	1.3	1.4	1.3	1.2

Series G 798–848. Consumption Expenditures, in Current Prices, of Families and Single Consumers Combined, by Income Class: 1929 to 1960–61

1960–61

Series No.	Item	All income classes	Income class (after taxes)									
			Under $1,000	$1,000–$1,999	$2,000–$2,999	$3,000–$3,999	$4,000–$4,999	$5,000–$5,999	$6,000–$7,499	$7,500–$9,999	$10,000–$14,999	$15,000 and over
798	Average expenditure for current consumption	$5,047	$1,276	$1,781	$2,670	$3,636	$4,428	$5,172	$6,125	$7,416	$9,521	$14,208
799	Food and beverages	1,313	377	550	782	1,003	1,192	1,367	1,580	1,887	2,273	2,979
800	Tobacco	91	22	36	60	79	94	103	115	125	121	140
801	Housing, fuel, light, and refrigeration	907	343	449	582	706	807	947	1,081	1,229	1,487	2,260
802	Household operation	288	71	105	148	205	239	277	335	407	572	1,180
803	Furnishings and equipment	266	48	72	117	179	225	284	340	407	522	765
804	Clothing	518	79	119	222	328	420	508	641	830	1,133	1,745
	Transportation:											
805	Automobile	693	67	113	251	465	664	768	892	1,117	1,390	1,589
806	Other	77	18	26	43	54	62	58	75	105	181	459
807	Medical care	340	130	156	218	267	293	341	399	469	600	878
808	Personal care	145	32	52	86	114	130	155	175	212	256	336
809	Recreation	200	27	38	73	121	161	190	254	327	471	665
810	Reading	45	11	16	23	31	37	45	55	65	90	121
811	Education	53	14	5	10	20	26	39	59	83	183	395
812	Other	111	37	44	55	64	78	90	124	153	242	696

1941

Series No.	Item	All income classes [1]	Income class (before taxes)					
			Under $500	$500–$1,000	$1,000–$1,500	$1,500–$2,000	$2,000–$3,000	$3,000–$5,000
813	Average expenditures for current consumption	$1,666	$374	$740	$1,173	$1,566	$2,214	$3,088
814	Food and beverages	516	144	272	402	521	693	894
815	Tobacco	35	9	18	27	37	47	65
816	Housing, fuel, light, and refrigeration	290	63	135	221	295	394	494
817	Household operation	85	16	30	46	67	92	158
818	Furnishings and equipment	93	14	37	68	87	135	201
819	Clothing	205	45	85	137	184	262	410
	Transportation:							
820	Automobile	171	21	56	100	141	248	359
821	Other	34	5	12	20	27	43	55
822	Medical care	84	27	40	63	86	102	152
823	Personal care	36	8	16	26	34	47	70
824	Recreation	69	12	19	33	50	85	144
825	Reading	16	3	7	12	17	22	29
826	Education	15	2	5	4	7	18	33
827	Other	17	5	8	14	13	26	24

1935–36

Series No.	Item	All income classes	Income class (money plus nonmoney, before taxes)													
			Under $500	$500–$750	$750–$1,000	$1,000–$1,250	$1,250–$1,500	$1,500–$1,750	$1,750–$2,000	$2,000–$2,500	$2,500–$3,000	$3,000–$4,000	$4,000–$5,000	$5,000–$10,000	$10,000–$15,000	$15,000 and over
828	Average expenditures for current consumption	$1,273	$420	$673	$886	$1,099	$1,285	$1,480	$1,652	$1,925	$2,269	$2,681	$3,219	$4,369	$6,060	$12,563
829	Food and beverages	428	187	285	357	415	466	510	543	601	677	753	831	1,010	1,195	2,044
830	Tobacco	24	7	13	19	24	29	31	34	39	42	49	53	63	78	118
831	Housing	241	94	135	170	208	237	272	306	352	406	489	584	807	1,258	2,437
832	Household operation	134	40	66	89	114	131	150	170	195	246	296	368	531	697	1,612
833	Furnishings	36	6	11	20	30	37	47	57	64	76	90	98	139	201	342
834	Clothing	133	32	62	84	105	129	150	169	208	254	314	406	551	821	1,775
	Transportation:															
835	Automobile	96	9	20	37	63	84	113	142	186	232	277	363	502	675	1,460
836	Other	22	9	14	17	19	22	24	26	30	30	38	46	63	131	421
837	Medical care	56	16	24	33	43	53	67	75	88	107	131	159	248	255	724
838	Personal care	26	9	15	19	23	27	31	34	41	48	53	64	85	108	197
839	Recreation	42	4	13	20	29	38	48	55	69	87	112	142	215	350	781
840	Reading	14	5	8	11	13	15	16	18	21	23	28	32	42	56	101
841	Education	13	1	3	5	7	9	11	14	18	28	34	51	72	198	444
842	Other items	8	1	4	5	6	8	10	9	13	13	17	22	41	37	107

1929

Series No.	Item	All income classes	Income class (money plus nonmoney, before taxes)								
			Under $1,000	$1,000–$1,500	$1,500–$2,000	$2,000–$3,000	$3,000–$4,000	$4,000–$5,000	$5,000–$7,000	$7,000–$10,000	$10,000 and over
843	Estimated number of families ... 1,000	36,462	10,020	7,782	5,993	6,059	2,695	1,350	1,190	626	747
844	Average expenditures for current consumption	$2,062	$767	$1,218	$1,596	$2,124	$2,885	$3,624	$4,583	$6,054	$18,284
845	Food	544	298	448	552	671	788	859	901	974	1,359
846	Home	590	198	334	448	600	847	1,120	1,493	1,998	5,051
847	Attire	304	118	201	265	329	422	515	639	850	2,194
848	Other	624	152	235	331	524	828	1,130	1,550	2,232	9,680

[1] Includes a small number of families with negative incomes and incomes of $5,000 or more, not shown separately.

Series G 849–856. Food Marketings and Consumption Indexes and Nutrients Available: 1909 to 1970

Year	Index (1967=100)		Nutrients available per capita, per day						Year	Index (1967=100)		Nutrients available per capita, per day					
	Food marketings and home consumption	Food consumption per capita	Food energy	Calcium	Vitamin A value	Thiamine	Ascorbic acid	Protein		Food marketings and home consumption	Food consumption per capita	Food energy	Calcium	Vitamin A value	Thiamine	Ascorbic acid	Protein
	849	850	851	852	853	854	855	856		849	850	851	852	853	854	855	856
			Calories	Grams	I.U.	Mgs.	Mgs.	Grams				Calories	Grams	I.U.	Mgs.	Mgs.	Grams
1970	103	102.5	3,300	0.94	7,800	1.84	109	100	1939	57	89.1	3,340	0.91	8,600	1.50	116	92
1969	103	101.5	3,280	.94	7,900	1.84	108	100	1938	55	86.2	3,260	.90	8,400	1.44	114	90
1968	101	101.2	3,260	.95	7,900	1.84	106	99	1937	51	86.0	3,260	.89	8,400	1.42	110	90
1967	100	100.0	3,210	.94	7,700	1.83	108	98	1936	51	86.0	3,290	.89	8,000	1.42	109	91
1966	97	98.3	3,170	.95	7,600	1.77	102	97	1935	47	83.0	3,200	.87	8,300	1.39	112	88
1965	96	97.2	3,140	.95	7,700	1.78	101	96	1934	53	84.8	3,260	.86	8,300	1.48	108	91
1964	95	97.6	3,190	.97	7,700	1.84	100	97	1933	52	83.7	3,280	.86	8,100	1.50	105	90
1963	93	96.6	3,150	.96	7,900	1.84	102	96	1932	51	83.5	3,320	.86	8,400	1.53	107	91
1962	89	96.3	3,120	.96	7,800	1.83	107	94	1931	52	85.6	3,390	.86	8,200	1.55	109	92
1961	89	96.0	3,120	.96	7,800	1.84	107	95	1930	51	86.2	3,440	.87	8,000	1.54	103	93
1960	*87	*96.4	3,140	.97	8,000	1.85	108	95	1929	52	86.7	3,460	.88	8,300	1.57	111	94
1959	86	96.8	3,170	.98	8,100	1.88	106	95	1928	52	86.5	3,490	.86	7,900	1.57	105	94
1958	83	94.8	3,120	.97	8,000	1.82	102	94	1927	51	86.5	3,470	.86	8,200	1.55	105	95
1957	81	96.1	3,110	.98	8,100	1.83	107	95	1926	50	87.6	3,460	.85	8,000	1.51	104	94
1956	84	98.1	3,180	.99	8,200	1.87	105	96	1925	49	86.4	3,450	.85	7,700	1.54	106	95
1955	80	96.9	3,180	1.00	8,200	1.87	106	95	1924	52	87.1	3,460	.85	7,800	1.60	108	96
1954	78	96.3	3,150	.98	8,000	1.81	105	95	1923	53	86.5	3,440	.84	8,100	1.62	109	96
1953	77	96.4	3,170	.98	8,100	1.85	106	95	1922	50	84.7	3,430	.84	8,300	1.53	104	94
1952	76	95.4	3,190	1.00	8,000	1.90	105	94	1921	47	80.3	3,200	.83	7,800	1.50	104	91
1951	73	93.6	3,160	.98	8,000	1.90	107	93	1920	46	82.6	3,290	.84	7,900	1.52	104	93
1950	72	95.3	3,260	.99	8,400	1.90	105	94	1919	49	83.5	3,440	.84	8,000	1.55	100	97
1949	72	94.1	3,200	.98	8,500	1.89	109	94	1918	49	82.6	3,380	.86	7,700	1.60	102	97
1948	72	94.1	3,200	.99	8,700	1.89	112	94	1917	44	80.7	3,330	.81	7,800	1.54	98	96
1947	74	97.2	3,290	1.02	9,100	1.94	119	97	1916	45	81.3	3,380	.79	7,500	1.57	96	96
1946	74	99.2	3,320	1.08	9,600	2.15	123	102	1915	44	82.3	3,430	.80	7,600	1.60	105	97
1945	75	96.8	3,300	1.06	10,000	2.06	125	102	1914	42	82.7	3,440	.80	7,300	1.58	100	98
1944	75	96.0	3,350	1.00	9,700	2.09	125	99	1913	41	82.8	3,460	.83	7,400	1.63	103	100
1943	72	93.0	3,360	.99	9,500	2.05	115	100	1912	42	84.5	3,470	.85	7,600	1.65	104	102
1942	67	91.7	3,320	.98	9,100	1.83	117	97	1911	41	84.0	3,470	.78	7,500	1.63	99	101
1941	62	92.7	3,410	.93	8,700	1.64	115	94	1910	39	83.3	3,490	.80	7,600	1.63	107	102
1940	60	90.9	3,350	.92	8,500	1.55	115	93	1909	--------	84.7	3,530	.83	7,800	1.68	105	104

* Denotes first year for which figures include Alaska and Hawaii.

Series G 857–865. Nutritive Value of City Diets—Average Per Person Per Day from Food Used at Home: 1936, 1942, 1948, 1955, and 1965

[Urban housekeeping households of two or more persons in the United States for 1936, 1942, 1948, and 1955; of one or more persons for 1965]

Year and income third	Energy value	Protein	Calcium	Iron	Vitamin A value	Thiamine [1]	Riboflavin [1]	Niacin [1]	Ascorbic acid [1]
	857	858	859	860	861	862	863	864	865
	Calories	Grams	Grams	Milligrams	I.U.	Milligrams	Milligrams	Milligrams	Milligrams
1965 [2]									
All households [3]	3,110	106	1.04	17.8	7,930	1.48	2.15	21.3	102
Lowest income third	2,960	98	.96	17.2	7,670	1.44	2.02	19.7	86
Middle income third	3,130	107	1.05	18.0	8,060	1.50	2.19	21.5	100
Highest income third	3,210	110	1.10	17.9	8,030	1.51	2.21	22.1	114
1955									
All households [3]	3,040	103	1.11	17.0	9,060	1.48	2.22	18.6	111
Lowest income third	2,910	94	1.00	16.4	8,700	1.42	2.04	17.4	94
Middle income third	3,040	103	1.12	17.0	8,830	1.51	2.25	18.7	108
Highest income third	3,170	109	1.18	17.6	9,430	1.52	2.35	19.5	124
1948									
All households [3]	3,010	91	1.09	15.9	8,910	1.28	2.19	15.6	125
Lowest income third	2,930	86	1.02	15.6	8,200	1.26	2.07	14.8	116
Middle income third	3,040	91	1.11	15.8	8,580	1.29	2.19	15.5	121
Highest income third	3,040	95	1.15	16.2	9,840	1.29	2.30	16.3	137
1942									
All households	2,840	85	.96	13.6	8,760	1.06	1.85	13.2	125
Lowest income third	2,670	76	.86	12.8	7,810	.97	1.64	11.5	103
Middle income third	2,870	85	.98	13.5	8,690	1.06	1.88	13.4	126
Highest income third	2,920	89	1.01	13.8	9,250	1.10	1.95	14.5	143
1936									
All households	2,790	77	.78	11.8	6,940	.94	1.48	11.1	80
Lowest income third	2,580	66	.64	10.2	5,520	.79	1.20	9.4	58
Middle income third	2,790	78	.83	11.8	7,180	.96	1.56	11.2	82
Highest income third	3,130	90	.95	14.0	8,900	1.16	1.86	14.0	110

[1] Cooking losses deducted.
[2] Nutritive averages adjusted for comparability with earlier studies.
[3] Includes 147 households in 1948, 274 in 1955, and 245 in 1965 that were not classified by income.

Series G 866–880.　Food Used at Home—Income, Household Size, and Food Per Person: 1942, 1948, 1955, and 1965

[Urban housekeeping households of two or more persons in the United States for 1942, 1948, and 1955; of one or more persons for 1965]

Year and income third	Average annual income	Persons per house-hold	Milk, cream, ice cream, cheese		Meat, poultry, fish, eggs, dry legumes, nuts			Vegetables		Fruits		Grain products	Fats and oils		Sugars and sweets
			Total	Milk, fresh and processed	Total	Meat, poultry, fish	Eggs	Total	Potatoes	Total	Citrus		Total	Butter and mar-garine	
	866	867	868	869	870	871	872	873	874	875	876	877	878	879	880
	Dollars		Quarts	Quarts	Pounds	Pounds	Number	Pounds	Pounds	Pounds	Pounds	Pounds	Pounds	Pounds	Pounds
1965															
All houholds [1]	6,460	3.16	4.05	3.08	5.90	4.45	6.5	5.32	1.45	3.81	1.34	2.46	0.79	0.36	1.26
Lowest income third	2,610	2.64	3.56	2.79	5.56	4.01	7.1	4.86	1.32	3.05	1.03	2.67	.80	.35	1.28
Middle income third	5,850	3.42	4.11	3.13	5.97	4.51	6.6	5.31	1.51	3.65	1.26	2.47	.80	.36	1.29
Highest income third	10,870	3.54	4.36	3.26	6.04	4.66	6.1	5.65	1.50	4.48	1.61	2.34	.78	.38	1.25
1955															
All households [1]	5,163	3.34	4.34	3.62	5.54	4.10	7.0	5.96	1.64	3.98	1.41	2.42	.83	.40	1.22
Lowest income third	2,507	3.20	3.77	3.14	5.15	3.71	6.6	5.52	1.60	3.22	1.05	2.65	.83	.36	1.24
Middle income third	4,473	3.50	4.50	3.79	5.39	4.01	6.8	5.91	1.71	3.85	1.36	2.41	.81	.38	1.23
Highest income third	8,526	3.46	4.71	3.88	5.93	4.42	7.4	6.26	1.63	4.73	1.75	2.30	.86	.44	1.25
1948															
All households [1]	3,606	3.42	4.33	3.66	4.38	2.95	6.8	6.60	2.03	3.95	1.43	2.73	.88	.40	1.42
Lowest income third	1,772	3.28	3.95	3.39	4.05	2.61	6.4	6.13	1.98	3.35	1.25	2.98	.88	.36	1.41
Middle income third	3,125	3.59	4.44	3.77	4.30	2.90	6.7	6.65	2.21	3.86	1.34	2.78	.89	.41	1.49
Highest income third	5,921	3.55	4.64	3.88	4.69	3.25	7.2	6.94	1.94	4.57	1.65	2.52	.87	.44	1.37
1942															
All households	2,758	3.34	3.68	3.14	3.90	2.70	5.0	6.91	2.50	3.35	1.26	2.69	.87	.42	.98
Lowest income third	1,074	3.00	3.31	2.89	3.33	2.06	4.8	6.35	2.41	2.62	.83	2.95	.83	.37	.91
Middle income third	2,214	3.31	3.82	3.29	3.98	2.75	5.4	7.07	2.62	3.35	1.26	2.65	.88	.42	1.01
Highest income third	4,985	3.72	3.88	3.20	4.31	3.21	5.0	7.25	2.47	3.92	1.59	2.55	.90	.47	1.00

[1] Includes 147 households in 1948, 274 in 1955, and 245 in 1965, that were not classified by income.

Series G 881–915.　Apparent Civilian Per Capita Consumption of Foods: 1849 to 1970

[In pounds, except eggs.　Calendar years, except as noted]

Year	Meats (carcass weight)				Fish (edible weight)	Edible fats and oils				Fruits							Pota-toes (farm weight)	Sweet-pota-toes (farm weight)
	Total	Beef and veal	Pork, exclud-ing lard	Lamb and mutton		Total [1] (fat con-tent)	Lard [2]	Marga-rine [3] (actual weight)	Butter, farm and factory (actual weight)	Fresh (farm weight)		Apples	Processed					
										Total [1]	Citrus [5]		Canned fruit [6]	Canned fruit juice [7]	Dried fruit [8]	Frozen fruits and juices (prod-uct weight)		
	881	882	883	884	885	886	887	888	889	890	891	892	893	894	895	896	897	898
1970	186.3	116.6	66.4	3.3	14.8	53.2	4.6	11.0	5.3	81.0	28.6	18.3	22.9	18.5	2.7	9.8	91	4.4
1969	182.5	114.1	65.0	3.4	14.2	51.9	5.1	10.8	5.4	79.0	28.3	14.9	24.4	18.8	2.7	9.3	92	4.1
1968	183.2	113.3	66.2	3.7	14.0	51.2	5.6	10.8	5.7	78.3	26.3	15.7	22.3	16.4	2.8	9.3	94	4.3
1967	178.3	110.3	64.1	3.9	13.6	49.4	5.4	10.5	5.5	80.9	31.6	16.2	23.1	16.1	2.8	10.1	92	4.5
1966	170.9	108.8	58.1	4.0	13.9	49.7	5.5	10.5	5.7	81.4	29.1	16.1	23.4	14.8	3.0	8.1	96	5.0
1965	167.1	104.7	58.7	3.7	13.9	47.8	6.4	9.9	6.4	81.1	29.1	16.3	23.8	12.8	3.0	8.5	93	4.7
1964	174.7	105.1	65.4	4.2	13.5	47.6	6.3	9.7	6.9	78.7	26.2	17.9	23.4	12.8	2.9	7.4	96	4.4
1963	169.7	99.4	65.4	4.9	13.7	46.3	6.4	9.6	6.9	74.5	22.1	16.7	23.3	14.1	2.9	8.0	100	5.7
1962	163.1	94.4	63.5	5.2	13.6	45.7	7.2	9.3	7.3	83.4	29.5	17.4	23.2	13.9	3.0	9.7	98	5.2
1961	160.5	93.4	62.0	5.1	13.7	45.1	7.7	9.4	7.4	88.6	30.8	16.4	23.6	13.4	3.1	8.8	102	5.3
1960*	160.9	91.2	64.9	4.8	13.2	45.3	7.6	9.4	7.5	93.4	33.7	18.3	23.0	15.1	3.1	9.1	101	6.1
1959	159.5	87.1	67.6	4.8	13.7	46.2	8.8	9.2	7.9	95.7	34.0	21.1	22.3	14.0	3.2	8.8	101	7.4
1958	151.6	87.2	60.2	4.2	13.3	45.3	9.6	9.0	8.3	94.0	31.0	22.5	22.9	16.1	3.0	8.0	101	6.5
1957	158.7	93.4	61.1	4.2	12.8	44.4	9.4	8.6	8.3	96.7	37.1	19.3	22.6	15.6	3.6	9.0	106	7.6
1956	166.7	94.9	67.3	4.5	12.9	45.2	9.8	8.2	8.7	98.9	39.1	18.9	[9]21.9	14.8	3.7	8.8	99	7.8
1955	162.8	91.4	66.8	4.6	12.9	45.9	10.1	8.2	9.0	99.4	41.8	19.6	22.5	[10]14.0	3.6	8.7	106	8.4
1954	154.7	90.1	60.0	4.6	13.5	45.5	10.2	8.5	8.9	105.1	42.0	20.0	21.2	13.2	3.9	7.4	106	8.1
1953	155.3	87.1	63.5	4.7	13.6	44.1	11.4	8.1	8.5	109.4	44.1	20.9	21.0	13.4	3.8	7.1	106	8.0
1952	146.0	69.4	72.4	4.2	13.3	44.1	11.8	7.9	8.6	114.4	45.1	21.6	20.8	14.1	3.8	6.6	101	7.3
1951	138.0	62.7	71.9	3.4	13.2	42.1	12.3	6.6	9.6	118.0	45.8	25.7	19.0	15.0	3.8	4.8	113	8.1

See footnotes at end of p. 330.

Series G 881–915. Apparent Civilian Per Capita Consumption of Foods: 1849 to 1970—Con.

[In pounds, except eggs]

Year	Meats (carcass weight) Total	Beef and veal	Pork, excluding lard	Lamb and mutton	Fish (edible weight)	Edible fats and oils Total [1] (fat content)	Lard [2]	Margarine [3] (actual weight)	Butter, farm and factory (actual weight)	Fruits—Fresh (farm weight) Total [4]	Citrus [5]	Apples	Processed Canned fruit [6]	Canned fruit juice [7]	Dried fruit [8]	Frozen fruits and juices (product weight)	Potatoes (farm weight)	Sweet potatoes (farm weight)
	881	882	883	884	885	886	887	888	889	890	891	892	893	894	895	896	897	898
1950	144.6	71.4	69.2	4.0	13.8	45.9	12.6	6.1	10.7	108.8	41.7	22.7	21.6	13.5	4.1	4.3	106	12.1
1949	144.6	72.8	67.7	4.1	12.9	42.5	11.8	5.8	10.5	122.9	47.9	24.7	19.4	15.1	4.1	3.5	110	11.7
1948	145.5	72.6	67.8	5.1	13.1	42.6	12.7	6.1	10.0	131.6	54.4	26.3	18.9	17.1	3.9	3.0	105	11.5
1947	155.3	80.4	69.6	5.3	12.3	42.0	12.6	5.0	11.2	143.7	62.2	25.4	18.2	15.6	3.7	3.2	125	14.5
1946	154.1	71.6	75.8	6.7	12.8	40.0	11.8	3.9	10.5	133.9	59.1	23.0	22.3	17.8	4.5	3.2	123	17.2
1945	145.2	71.3	66.6	7.3	11.9	39.1	11.7	4.1	10.9	139.9	66.6	22.9	14.4	10.9	6.0	2.3	122	18.3
1944	154.2	68.0	79.5	6.7	10.7	40.9	12.3	3.9	11.9	140.1	68.2	25.5	9.3	10.3	6.1	2.0	136	19.7
1943	146.8	61.5	78.9	6.4	9.9	41.5	13.0	3.9	11.8	118.4	60.3	24.9	12.6	7.4	5.9	1.1	125	21.4
1942	140.3	69.4	63.7	7.2	10.7	44.9	12.8	2.8	15.9	130.0	57.7	28.1	17.3	8.5	4.2	1.4	127	20.4
1941	143.7	68.5	68.4	6.8	13.2	47.6	13.8	2.8	16.1	146.0	57.7	31.7	17.8	8.5	4.3	1.3	128	18.4
1940	142.4	62.3	73.5	6.6	13.0	46.4	14.4	2.4	17.0	139.1	56.7	29.7	19.1	7.2	6.0	1.3	123	16.2
1939	133.6	62.3	64.7	6.6	12.7	46.4	12.7	2.3	17.4	148.2	61.4	30.7	16.1	5.9	6.4	1.1	122	19.7
1938	127.1	62.0	58.2	6.9	12.8	45.3	11.1	3.0	16.6	131.7	49.1	28.2	15.4	4.6	5.5	1.0	129	21.3
1937	126.2	63.8	55.8	6.6	13.8	45.5	10.5	3.1	16.8	138.6	44.5	33.6	13.5	4.5	5.8	.5	126	21.5
1936	130.6	68.9	55.1	6.6	13.7	45.7	11.3	3.1	16.8	125.6	46.2	27.6	16.7	2.4	5.4	.7	130	19.8
1935	117.4	61.7	48.4	7.3	12.5	44.1	9.6	3.0	17.6	133.2	44.6	32.9	13.4	2.0	5.9	.5	142	25.6
1934	143.9	73.2	64.4	6.3	11.2	44.5	13.0	2.1	18.6	116.3	39.8	25.3	12.5	.5	5.1	.5	135	24.4
1933	136.1	58.6	70.7	6.8	10.7	43.0	14.0	1.9	18.2	124.8	39.4	40.0	11.8	.5	5.2	.5	132	24.0
1932	131.1	53.3	70.7	7.1	10.4	42.9	14.4	1.6	18.5	125.9	36.7	39.2	10.2	.5	5.4	.6	134	27.7
1931	130.7	55.2	68.4	7.1	10.8	44.4	13.6	1.9	18.3	160.3	42.3	51.7	10.9	.4	4.7	.4	136	20.6
1930	129.0	55.3	67.0	6.7	12.2	------	12.7	2.6	17.6	129.9	31.2	42.1	12.8	.3	5.4	.5	132	18.3
1929	131.2	56.0	69.6	5.6	13.9	------	12.7	2.9	17.6	139.2	39.8	39.7	12.3	.3	5.3	.6	159	22.4
1928	131.6	55.2	70.9	5.5	14.1	------	13.2	2.6	17.6	146.1	29.5	48.9	12.6	.1	6.2	.5	147	20.7
1927	134.9	61.9	67.7	5.3	14.2	------	12.7	2.3	18.3	126.0	32.2	37.4	12.6	.3	6.3	.3	141	25.0
1926	138.0	68.5	64.1	5.4	13.4	------	12.2	2.0	18.3	160.8	31.4	62.3	12.0	.2	6.1	.1	128	21.1
1925	140.1	68.1	66.8	5.2	13.1	------	12.3	2.0	18.1	132.2	28.9	46.3	11.1	.2	6.3	.2	157	17.7
1924	147.3	68.1	74.0	5.2	13.0	------	14.2	2.0	17.8	148.0	33.9	54.1	8.9	.1	6.4		154	17.6
1923	147.3	67.8	74.2	5.3	12.7	------	14.3	2.0	17.8	144.5	32.5	54.7	9.0	.3	5.5	------	174	24.8
1922	137.7	66.9	65.7	5.1	13.3	------	13.3	1.7	17.1	144.8	24.6	57.5	7.5	.2	6.6	------	143	28.9
1921	134.0	63.1	64.8	6.1	12.5	------	10.8	2.0	16.3	112.8	30.5	36.1	8.2	.3	5.5		156	27.2
1920	136.0	67.1	63.5	5.4	13.8	------	12.0	3.4	14.9	142.6	26.0	63.0	9.4	.6	6.7		140	29.1
1919	138.9	69.3	63.9	5.7	13.6	------	10.7	3.4	15.2	122.3	23.5	45.2	9.7	.3	6.9		152	29.3
1918	141.6	75.8	61.0	4.8	12.9	------	11.8	3.3	14.1	119.6	16.5	56.9	7.5	.4	4.4		174	26.7
1917	135.3	71.9	58.9	4.5	12.9	------	10.0	2.7	15.7	129.8	22.0	56.1	7.7	.3	6.3		146	27.9
1916	140.1	65.3	69.0	5.8	13.0	------	11.6	1.8	17.3	133.7	22.0	63.9	7.1	.4	5.1	------	143	24.5
1915	134.9	62.3	66.5	6.1	13.2	------	11.5	1.4	17.2	154.5	23.1	69.0	5.6	.6	5.0	------	185	25.3
1914	140.0	67.8	65.1	7.1	13.7	------	10.6	1.4	17.0	160.4	24.1	71.8	5.7	.1	4.1	------	157	22.1
1913	143.7	69.6	66.9	7.2	13.5	------	10.7	1.5	16.5	130.2	16.6	59.3	4.2	.3	3.7	------	189	23.6
1912	145.9	71.5	66.7	7.7	13.3	------	11.2	1.5	16.6	156.5	18.5	74.6	4.2	.5	4.5	------	179	24.0
1911	151.9	75.6	69.0	7.3	13.3	------	12.1	1.1	18.6	152.6	19.8	73.5	3.9	.2	4.3	------	157	24.0
1910	146.4	77.6	62.3	6.5	13.2	------	12.5	1.6	18.3	134.7	17.8	59.4	3.6	.5	3.5		198	26.2
1909	155.5	81.5	67.0	6.7	13.0	------	12.5	1.2	17.8	135.0	16.2	62.2	3.0	------	4.2		187	26.2
1908	163.3	79.3	77.7	6.3			14.4	1.0	19.7									
1907	158.2	77.8	74.1	6.3			13.2	.9	17.6									
1906	155.6	78.3	71.0	6.3			11.7	.8	17.8									
1905	155.2	77.9	71.0	6.3			11.8	.6	19.9									
1904	152.7	75.6	70.6	6.6			12.5	.6	18.5									
1903	152.1	77.0	68.2	6.9			11.8	.6	18.3									
1902	144.8	71.0	66.7	7.1			12.1	.9	17.6									
1901	151.1	73.3	70.8	7.0			12.8	1.6	20.0									
1900	150.7	72.3	71.9	6.5			13.2	1.3	20.1									
1899	150.7	72.4	71.8	6.5			12.8	1.4	19.6									

Year	Butter (actual weight) 889	Year	Butter (actual weight) 889	Year	Butter (actual weight) 889	Year	Butter (actual weight) 889	Year	Butter (actual weight) 889	Year	Butter (actual weight) 889
1898	19.8	1892	15.9	1886	16.8	1880	15.5	1875	12.4	1870	10.7
1897	20.8	1891	16.7	1885	16.1	1879	15.6	1874	13.4	1869	13.6
1896	22.2	1890	18.2	1884	15.3	1878	14.6	1873	13.4		
1895	18.4	1889	20.5	1883	15.2	1877	14.4	1872	10.6	1859	14.8
1894	15.4	1888	16.0	1882	13.9	1876	14.5	1871	11.7	1849	13.7
1893	15.5	1887	16.3	1881	15.2						

* Denotes first year for which figures include Alaska and Hawaii.
[1] Computed from unrounded numbers.
[2] Includes small quantity of lard used in other fats and oils products, 1899–1908; beginning 1909, excludes quantities so used.
[3] Prior to 1909, data are for year beginning July.
[4] Beginning 1934, excludes apples from noncommercial areas. Citrus fruits on crop year basis, 1941 to date.
[5] Beginning 1941, year begins October or November prior to year indicated.
[6] Data on pack-year basis, 1909–1942, beginning early June of year indicated.
[7] Citrus juice, all years, and grape juice, 1909–1933 and 1948–1970, on pack-year basis beginning November prior to year indicated.
[8] Pack-year data, beginning middle of year indicated.
[9] Beginning 1956, includes chilled sections and salads.
[10] Beginning 1955, includes chilled citrus juices.

Series G 881–915. Apparent Civilian Per Capita Consumption of Foods: 1849 to 1970—Con.

[In pounds, except eggs]

Year	Vegetables Fresh (farm weight)	Canned [1]	Frozen	Melons (farm weight)	Dry beans [2]	Total milk for human consumption	Fluid milk and cream [3]	Condensed and evaporated milk	Cheese	Ice cream (product weight)	Eggs (number)	Chicken and turkey [4] (ready-to-cook)	Sugar, cane and beet (refined)	Wheat flour	Corn flour and meal	Peanuts (shelled)[5]	Coffee (green-bean basis)
	899	900	901	902	903	904	905	906	907	908	909	910	911	912	913	914	915
1970	98.9	53.1	20.8	23.3	5.9	564	264	7.1	11.5	17.7	319	49.5	102.5	110	7.4	5.9	13.8
1969	98.9	53.4	18.9	23.1	6.8	570	272	7.9	11.0	18.0	318	47.4	100.1	112	7.4	5.9	14.2
1968	98.7	52.3	18.2	22.4	6.3	577	280	8.9	10.6	18.4	321	45.4	100.1	112	7.4	5.8	14.9
1967	98.1	50.5	16.6	22.4	6.9	581	285	9.0	10.1	17.8	324	45.8	97.3	112	7.2	5.7	14.8
1966	96.0	49.1	15.8	22.0	6.3	604	297	9.7	9.8	18.2	314	43.9	97.6	112	6.9	5.5	14.5
1965	98.6	48.7	13.8	23.6	6.6	620	302	10.6	9.6	18.5	314	40.9	96.6	113	6.6	5.6	14.8
1964	98.6	47.2	13.5	23.0	7.6	632	304	11.3	9.4	18.3	318	38.5	96.6	114	6.2	5.3	15.3
1963	101.4	47.5	11.6	24.5	7.6	632	307	11.6	9.2	18.0	318	37.5	96.7	114	5.9	5.0	15.7
1962	101.4	46.9	11.3	23.1	7.6	641	308	12.5	9.2	17.9	327	37.0	97.3	115	6.1	4.9	15.9
1961	103.8	45.0	9.9	24.8	7.9	641	312	13.3	8.9	18.0	329	37.4	97.8	118	6.3	4.9	15.8
1960*	105.9	44.7	9.7	25.8	7.3	653	322	13.7	8.3	18.3	335	34.2	97.6	118	6.6	4.9	15.8
1959	102.3	45.2	8.9	24.5	7.7	667	330	14.4	8.0	18.7	352	35.2	96.4	120	7.0	4.7	15.9
1958	103.7	45.0	8.1	26.4	7.7	682	337	14.8	8.1	17.8	354	34.0	96.8	121	7.4	4.5	15.5
1957	106.4	44.1	7.5	24.4	7.6	687	344	15.4	7.7	18.0	362	31.4	95.0	119	7.9	4.5	15.7
1956	107.0	43.9	7.3	27.4	8.0	702	348	15.8	8.0	18.0	369	29.6	97.8	121	8.3	4.4	15.8
1955	105.2	43.4	6.6	29.6	7.5	706	348	16.2	7.9	18.0	371	26.3	96.3	123	8.7	4.1	15.3
1954	107.2	41.9	5.9	29.0	8.0	697	346	16.8	7.9	17.4	376	28.1	95.6	126	9.3	4.2	14.7
1953	109.1	43.3	5.4	28.2	7.6	689	346	17.4	7.5	18.0	379	26.7	97.2	128	9.8	4.4	16.9
1952	111.6	42.0	5.3	25.7	8.1	698	350	17.6	7.6	17.9	390	26.8	97.1	131	10.4	4.4	16.9
1951	111.9	42.1	4.3	26.1	8.1	712	350	18.3	7.2	17.4	393	26.1	94.0	133	10.8	4.6	16.6
1950	115.2	42.1	3.4	24.8	8.6	740	348	20.1	7.7	17.2	389	24.7	100.6	135	11.8	4.5	16.1
1949	116.2	39.0	3.0	26.9	6.9	734	352	19.8	7.3	17.6	383	22.9	96.4	136	12.7	4.1	18.7
1948	123.0	37.9	3.0	27.3	6.8	723	355	20.2	6.9	18.5	389	21.4	94.1	137	12.8	4.6	18.4
1947	122.4	40.5	2.6	28.0	6.5	768	369	20.4	6.9	20.1	383	21.7	95.1	139	13.1	4.5	17.4
1946	129.9	46.8	2.0	30.6	8.7	786	389	18.6	6.7	23.1	379	23.1	75.1	156	15.2	5.3	20.1
1945	134.3	43.2	1.9	29.7	7.8	788	399	18.3	6.7	15.7	403	25.1	73.9	161	17.6	6.6	16.4
1944	123.9	34.4	1.6	28.0	8.1	763	381	15.7	4.9	14.3	354	23.1	89.5	149	19.2	6.0	15.8
1943	116.7	37.0	.7	21.8	8.9	750	371	18.8	4.9	13.1	347	25.7	80.7	163	20.5	5.7	12.9
1942	119.0	39.7	1.1	22.5	11.1	832	354	18.4	6.4	15.8	318	20.7	81.8	157	19.8	6.2	13.6
1941	113.8	36.9	.7	24.5	8.8	803	334	18.5	5.9	13.6	311	18.3	104.3	156	20.6	4.8	15.9
1940	116.9	34.4	.6	26.5	8.4	818	331	19.3	6.0	11.4	319	17.0	95.7	155	21.8	5.0	15.5
1939	116.6	31.8	.5	25.4	9.3	824	332	17.8	6.0	11.0	313	16.6	100.8	158	21.7	4.4	14.9
1938	114.5	31.1	.4	27.2	9.6	796	329	17.2	5.9	10.4	310	15.0	95.2	160	22.1	4.3	14.9
1937	111.0	29.4	.4	28.8	7.8	797	331	16.7	5.5	10.6	308	15.9	96.4	159	22.8	4.4	13.3
1936	112.5	27.7	--------	26.4	9.0	792	330	15.9	5.4	9.5	289	15.9	97.3	163	24.2	4.6	13.7
1935	111.2	26.2	--------	27.2	8.4	800	326	16.2	5.3	8.1	280	14.8	97.8	158	24.7	4.0	13.4
1934	115.2	23.3	--------	25.6	9.1	813	322	15.0	4.9	7.1	289	15.3	93.7	157	25.3	3.3	12.3
1933	104.5	22.0	--------	25.3	7.1	814	337	13.8	4.6	6.1	296	16.7	93.7	162	25.7	3.6	12.8
1932	108.8	22.1	--------	27.1	7.4	832	339	14.0	4.4	6.3	313	16.0	94.7	170	26.5	4.1	12.4
1931	108.3	25.3	--------	32.8	8.8	838	335	13.4	4.5	8.6	333	15.5	100.5	169	26.6	4.4	13.0
1930	111.9	28.4	--------	33.0	9.5	819	337	13.6	4.7	9.8	331	17.2	109.6	171	28.3	3.2	12.5
1929	112.6	25.9	--------	32.1	7.8	811	340	13.6	4.7	10.7	334	15.7	96.9	177	30.5	4.1	12.2
1928	104.2	23.0	--------	30.6	8.6	804	337	12.3	4.4	9.9	338	14.6	103.7	179	29.9	3.8	11.9
1927	106.0	22.3	--------	30.8	8.7	813	336	11.7	4.6	9.9	342	15.2	102.4	181	28.8	3.9	12.2
1926	100.6	25.9	--------	36.4	7.6	818	338	11.8	4.6	9.5	339	14.2	104.5	182	28.9	3.4	12.4
1925	101.3	25.7	--------	34.4	7.3	802	337	11.7	4.7	9.7	318	14.3	104.3	180	29.4	3.6	10.6
1924	100.9	23.0	--------	35.7	7.8	796	336	11.9	4.6	8.8	324	13.7	99.5	180	32.4	3.5	12.2
1923	90.1	21.5	--------	29.1	5.9	787	328	11.4	4.5	9.0	326	14.6	90.5	180	35.8	3.2	12.6
1922	92.8	17.1	--------	37.3	5.1	783	342	10.9	4.3	8.2	316	14.2	104.4	180	36.4	2.7	11.8
1921	82.2	16.9	--------	34.9	4.8	768	346	9.9	4.2	7.6	300	13.4	87.3	167	34.4	2.7	12.0
1920	95.0	18.5	--------	31.8	5.7	736	348	8.6	4.0	7.6	299	13.7	85.5	179	35.2	3.0	11.7
1919	76.6	21.3	--------	24.8	5.4	733	335	9.8	4.2	6.8	303	14.2	86.6	192	35.4	4.6	11.8
1918	--------	22.3	--------		7.4	725	361	10.3	3.9	6.4	284	13.3	74.6	179	49.7	2.8	10.0
1917	--------	18.9	--------		7.5	729	328	9.4	3.7	4.8	281	13.3	78.0	191	46.5	4.2	12.1
1916	--------	16.1	--------		5.1	747	315	9.6	3.8	4.3	299	13.8	76.8	204	45.1	2.8	11.5
1915	--------	18.0	--------		5.8	751	318	9.5	4.1	3.9	313	14.4	77.6	205	44.3	2.8	10.6
1914	--------	19.2	--------		6.4	747	321	8.9	4.2	3.4	295	14.5	81.0	207	45.0	2.5	9.2
1913	--------	19.8	--------		6.1	754	342	7.9	4.2	3.0	303	14.5	81.3	209	45.9	2.5	9.0
1912	--------	18.7	--------		6.8	763	355	7.1	3.9	2.7	312	14.9	75.9	211	47.8	2.3	10.8
1911	--------	15.6	--------		6.3	749	301	6.4	4.0	2.3	329	15.6	77.4	213	49.6	2.3	8.3
1910	--------	14.5	--------		6.5	759	315	5.8	4.3	1.9	306	15.5	75.4	214	51.1	2.5	9.2
1909	--------	15.3	--------		6.8	770	343	5.5	3.8	1.6	293	14.7	73.7	217	53.0	2.4	--------

Year	Condensed and evaporated milk 906	Cheese 907	Sugar, cane and beet (refined) 911	Year	Condensed and evaporated milk 906	Cheese 907	Sugar, cane and beet (refined) 911	Year	Cheese 907	Sugar, cane and beet (refined) 911	Year	Cheese 907	Sugar, cane and beet (refined) 911	Year	Cheese 907	Sugar, cane and beet (refined) 911	Year	Cheese 907
1908	5.1	3.8	81.2	1901	3.0	4.5	68.7	1894	2.9	66.7	1887	3.2	52.7	1880	2.7	42.7	1873	2.9
1907	4.7	3.5	77.5	1900	2.7	3.7	65.2	1893	2.9	64.4	1886	2.8	56.9	1879	2.2	38.1	1872	3.0
1906	4.4	3.5	76.1	1899	2.5	3.7	62.6	1892	3.7	63.8	1885	3.0	51.8	1878	3.5	38.6	1871	2.4
1905	4.1	4.1	70.5	1898	--------	3.4	61.5	1891	3.5	66.3	1884	3.1	53.4	1877	2.7	46.1	1870	3.2
1904	3.8	4.1	75.3	1897	--------	3.6	64.8	1890	3.8	52.8	1883	3.3	51.1	1876	2.6	38.5	1869	3.0
1903	3.5	4.0	70.9	1896	--------	2.9	62.5	1889	3.5	51.8	1882	3.1	48.4	1875	3.1	40.3	1859	2.9
1902	3.2	4.0	72.8	1895	--------	2.9	63.4	1888	3.5	56.7	1881	3.2	44.2	1874	2.6	--------	1849	4.1

[1] For 1909–1942, calendar-year data were derived from pack-year data by combining proportional parts of each pack-year involved.
[2] Cleaned basis.
[3] Cream included on whole-milk equivalent basis.
[4] Chicken only, 1909–1928, but turkey consumption very small during that time.
[5] September-August year through 1939; August-July year, thereafter.

Social Statistics

Social Security and Welfare (Series H 1-411)

H 1-411. General note.

The concept of social welfare used in these series, and more particularly in series H 1-47, includes all governmental programs directed specifically toward promoting the well-being of individuals and families. Except for the veterans' program, social welfare activities in the United States remained largely a local responsibility throughout most of the 19th century. Following the passage of the first compulsory attendance law in Massachusetts in 1852, the movement for tax-supported public schools received increasing support. State governments began to establish separate State institutions for the mentally ill and other dependent groups in the late 1850's and State boards of health were in operation in a number of States by 1900. State laws authorizing pensions for the blind, for orphans and their mothers, and for the aged were adopted in a number of States during the period 1900-1930. Workmen's compensation spread rapidly between 1911 and 1920. Special retirement systems for State and local government employees, principally teachers, policemen, and firemen, were in existence in a few localities before 1900. The civil service retirement system for Federal employees was established in 1920.

It was not until the Social Security Act of 1935, however, that the Federal Government participated in any major way in permanent welfare programs for the general population. The Social Security Act established a national system of old-age insurance (old-age, survivors, disability, and health insurance—OASDHI, since July 1966) and a Federal-State system of unemployment insurance, and provided Federal grants-in-aid to the States for public assistance, maternal and child health and welfare services, general public health services, and vocational rehabilitation services.

Since 1936, a substantial volume of statistical data relating to OASDHI, unemployment insurance, and public assistance is available from the operating records of the administering agencies. Statistics based on operating data can also be obtained for the railroad retirement program, the Federal employee retirement programs, and the State temporary disability insurance programs. Estimates of expenditures under State workmen's compensation programs and State and local employee retirement systems have been made by the Social Security Administration.

The principal source of statistics of social insurance and welfare programs is the Social Security Administration, which presents annual figures in the *Annual Statistical Supplement* to the monthly *Social Security Bulletin* (for the years 1939-1948 in the *Social Security Yearbook;* for 1949-1954, in the September 1950-1955 issues of the *Bulletin;* since 1956, issued separately), and in annual articles in the October issues of the *Social Security Bulletin,* 1955-1965, and the December issues generally since 1966.

Figures shown for recent years are subject to revision. All figures represent the latest estimates available and may differ from those shown in the sources cited. In all such cases, the revised figures were obtained from the Social Security Administration's unpublished data or estimates.

H 1-31. Social welfare expenditures under public programs, 1890-1970.

Source: 1929-1964, U.S. Social Security Administration, *Social Welfare Expenditures Under Public Programs in the United States,* 1929-1966, Research Report Number 25; 1965-1970, *Social Security Bulletin,* December 1971 and January 1974.

Estimates presented for 1890 and 1913 were primarily based on the following: R. A. Musgrave and J. J. Culbertson, "The Growth of Public Expenditures in the U.S., 1890-1948," *National Tax Journal,* June 1953; and J. Frederic Dewhurst and Associates, *America's Needs and Resources,* Twentieth Century Fund, New York, 1955; and reports of official agencies.

Scattered data relating to social welfare programs in particular localities or States may be found in other sources. The definitions used in these sources, however, are highly variable and the original source of the data is frequently not indicated. No data comparable to those shown for 1929-1970 are readily available.

Social welfare expenditures under public programs represent payments (but not loans) from Federal, State, and local revenues (general and special) and trust funds. Capital outlay for hospitals, schools, and other facilities are included as well as administrative expenses.

Data on Federal programs include expenditures in Alaska and Hawaii for all years; State and local data include expenditures in Alaska and Hawaii from the year of their admission to the Union. Data include Federal expenditures (and matching local expenditures under grant programs) in Puerto Rico, the Virgin Islands, Guam, Trust Territory of the Pacific, American Samoa, and the Panama Canal Zone, as well as expenditures to beneficiaries of some of the income-maintenance programs residing in foreign countries, and that part of Defense Department education and health expenses incurred abroad.

Wherever possible, data for Federal, Federal-State, and Federal-local programs were drawn from published and unpublished materials of the appropriate Federal agencies, and from the annual *Budget of the United States Government.* The principal source for State, State-local, and local program statistics has been the census of governments. To bridge gaps, especially for early years of the series, and to augment fragmentary data, the Social Security Administration has estimated expenditures for certain years for some programs, e.g., State and local public employee retirement benefits and administration.

In the social insurance category, data for old-age, survivors, disability and health insurance, series H 6, include the health insurance for the aged program (Medicare). The public employee retirement figures, series H 8, exclude refunds of contributions to employees leaving public service; they include payments to retired military personnel and to their survivors. Data on unemployment insurance and employment services, series H 9, include benefits under the regular State programs, programs for Federal employees and ex-servicemen, trade adjustment and cash training allowances, and payments under the extended unemployment insurance programs of 1958 and 1961. The data for State temporary disability insurance, series H 12, which exists in only a few States, include cash and medical benefits. Also included are benefits provided by private plans where the State law permits such insurance in lieu of the government protection. The data include the State costs of administering State plans and of supervising private plans; administrative expenses of the private plans are not available. Similarly, workmen's compensation data, series H 13, include cash and medical benefits paid under

Federal and State laws by private insurance carriers, State funds, and self-insurers; administrative costs of private carriers and self-insurers are not available. "Black Lung" benefits are included under workmen's compensation, beginning 1970.

Total public aid expenditures, series H 14, include public assistance, work relief, other emergency aid, surplus food for the needy, food stamps, repatriate and refugee assistance, and the Job Corps, Neighborhood Youth Corps, and work-experience training programs under the Economic Opportunity Act and related laws. Certain other economic opportunity programs are included under total "other social welfare," series H 28, as anti-poverty programs. The figures on public assistance, series H 15, include payments under the categorical cash and medical programs established by the Social Security Act, as amended, and general assistance payments from State and local funds only. Beginning 1969, work incentive program expenditures are included.

The estimates for health and medical programs, series H 16, are derived from the Census of Governments and the U.S. *Budget* (cited above). They include net public expenditures for hospital and medical care (after deduction of fee payments), hospital construction, school health, community and related public health services, and maternal and child health services. Through 1966 they exclude expenditures for domiciliary care (other than in mental and tuberculosis institutions) which are included under institutional care, series H 30. They include Federal domiciliary care beginning 1967 because Federal hospital and domiciliary care expenditures are no longer separable in the source document for this portion of the series, the Special Analyses on Health of the U.S. *Budget*. They also exclude expenditures for health and medical services provided in connection with OASDHI, State temporary disability insurance, workmen's compensation, public assistance, vocational rehabilitation, and veterans' and antipoverty programs; these are included in the total expenditures shown for those programs. Also excluded are international health activities. Omitted from the health category, but included under education, series H 17–20, are expenditures for medical schools and other health training institutions.

The estimates for veterans programs, series H 21–26, were obtained from the *Annual Report of the Veterans Administration*, supplemented by unpublished data. Pension and compensation expenditures, series H 22, include burial awards and, beginning 1965, subsistence payments to disabled veterans undergoing training and special allowances for survivors of veterans who did not qualify under OASDHI. The life insurance figures, series H 25, exclude the Servicemen's Group Life Insurance program. Administrative expenses are included in each of the five categories of veterans' program expenditures shown. However, these expenditures are reported in the series on a somewhat different basis in three time periods: (1) Before 1947, only unallocated administrative costs are available; these were distributed among the programs by the Social Security Administration, in accordance with the historical relation (derived from later-year data) that administrative expenses bore to program expenditures for each of the veterans' programs; (2) for 1947–1964, part of the administrative expenses were allocated by the Veterans Administration to each program and the remainder was allocated among the programs by the Social Security Administration in the same ratio that allocated costs for each is to total allocated costs; (3) beginning 1965, only the allocated administration is added to the program figures; all the unallocated administration is added to the residual category, welfare and other, series H 26.

The education data, series H 17–20, include expenditures for support, maintenance, and operation of local, State, and Federal elementary-secondary, vocational, adult, and higher education institutions. Included are expenditures for the support of students, the construction of educational facilities, and the administrative operations of State and local departments of education and the U.S. Office of Education.

The primary basis for the education estimates are the various Federal and State expenditures series compiled by the U.S. Office of

Education and appearing in the annual editions of the *Digest of Educational Statistics*. Data from these sources, however, are adjusted to fit the conceptual framework for these social welfare expenditures series. For example, the latter omit the various student and school construction loan programs and certain research and development expenditures that have subordinate educational objectives. Also excluded are in-house training programs conducted outside of educational institutions and expenditures for international education (except for U.S.-operated schools abroad).

In addition, certain programs included in the Office of Education series, such as veterans' benefits, manpower and training programs, school meals, and health-related research facilities, are included elsewhere in the social welfare expenditures series and are therefore not included as education expenditures.

The data on Federal housing expenditures, series H 27, are supplied principally by the Department of Housing and Urban Development and confined to outlays for housing owned or operated by a public body ("public housing") and to programs designed to provide subsidized housing for low- and moderate-income families (e.g. rent supplements, homeownership and rental housing assistance, rehabilitation grants). Excluded from the series are urban renewal and city demonstration programs as well as mortgage and loan insurance programs and programs providing credit facilities for home-financing institutions.

Total expenditures for other social welfare, series H 28, include, in addition to the programs listed separately, expenditures for child welfare and such miscellaneous social welfare programs as Indian welfare and guidance; aging, juvenile delinquency, and certain manpower activities; anti-poverty programs; and some overall Federal social welfare administrative costs not attributable to specific operating programs. Anti-poverty expenditures include the community action program (except for Headstart, included in education, series H 17–20); migrant workers and VISTA programs; and all administrative expenses of the Office of Economic Opportunity. Data on Federal institutional care represent primarily surplus food for institutions; State and local expenditures include some amounts for anti-poverty programs, foster care, legal assistance to the needy, and the care of transients. Surplus food for schools appears with programs under the National School Lunch and Child Nutrition Acts in series H 31, child nutrition.

See also general note for series H 1–411.

H 32–47. Social welfare expenditures under public programs, by source of funds, 1890–1970.

Source: See source for series H 1–31.

Federal grants-in-aid are classified as expenditures from Federal funds (contrary to the practice in the national income accounts which includes them as expenditures from State and local funds). Benefit payments under the State unemployment insurance programs are classified as expenditures from State funds (in the national income accounts they are classified as Federal expenditures, based on the fact that the State unemployment insurance trust funds are held and invested by the Secretary of the Treasury). Federal grants to the States for the administration of unemployment insurance and the employment service are classified as expenditures from Federal funds as are also the benefits paid under the temporary extended unemployment insurance acts of 1958 and 1961.

See also general note for series H 1–411 and text for series H 1–31.

H 48–50. Civilian labor force, 1934–1970.

Source: 1934 and 1939, **series H 48**, U.S. Bureau of Labor Statistics, *Monthly Labor Review*, July 1948, p. 50; **series H 49–50**, U.S. Social Security Administration, unpublished data; 1944–1957, U.S. Bureau of the Census, *Current Population Reports*, series P-50, Nos. 2, 19, 59, 67, 72, and 85; 1958–1970, U.S. Social Security Administration, *Social Security Bulletin*, various issues.

H 51–56. Workers covered under government social insurance programs, 1934–1970.

Source: U.S. Social Security Administration, 1934, unpublished data; 1939–1970, *Social Security Bulletin, Annual Statistical Supplement,* various issues.

See general notes for series H 1–411 and series H 172–252, and text for series H 57–69.

H 57–69. Estimated payrolls in employment covered by selected government social insurance programs, 1937–1970.

Source: U.S. Social Security Administration, 1937–1939, unpublished data; 1940–1970, *Social Security Bulletin, Annual Statistical Supplement, 1971,* table 6.

The Bureau of Economic Analysis (formerly Office of Business Economics) is the original source for total earnings and wage and salary disbursements, series H 57–59. The Social Security Administration is the original source for payrolls covered by State and local government retirement systems and by workmen's compensation, series H 64 and H 69. See also text for series H 332–345. Figures for series H 60–63 and H 65–68 are based on reports of the agencies administering the programs specified.

Annual estimates of the number of workers and the amount of payrolls covered by workmen's compensation laws are based on data compiled by the Social Security Administration for certain benchmark years—usually at 4-year intervals. For the intervening years, coverage estimates have been projected on the basis of the percentage change under the unemployment insurance laws, with adjustments, where necessary, for changes in coverage under the two programs. Coverage estimates for the benchmark years are based primarily on payroll data provided by the National Council on Compensation Insurance, the major rate-making organization in the country. The number covered is the average of the number of workers in covered employment in the pay period ending nearest the 15th of each month.

H 70–114. Employee-benefit plans—estimated coverage, contributions, and benefits, 1950–1970.

Source: U.S. Social Security Administration, *Social Security Bulletin,* April 1969, April 1972, and April 1973, and unpublished data.

An "employee-benefit plan," as defined here, is any type of plan sponsored or initiated unilaterally or jointly by employers or employees and providing benefits that stem from the employment relationship and are not underwritten or paid directly by government (Federal, State, or local). In general, the intent is to include plans that provide in an orderly predetermined fashion (1) income maintenance when regular earnings are cut off because of death, accident, sickness, retirement, or unemployment and (2) benefits to meet medical expenses associated with illness or injury.

Government employees who are covered by plans underwritten by nongovernment organizations are included in the series, whether or not the government unit contributes (as an employer) to the financing of the program. Specifically included here are plans providing government employees with group life insurance, accidental death and dismemberment insurance, and hospital, surgical, regular medical, and major-medical expense insurance. Retirement and sick-leave plans for government employees, which are financed and administered directly by government, are excluded from the series.

Estimates of coverage, contributions, and benefits are based primarily on reports of insurers and other nongovernmental bodies. For life insurance, accidental death and dismemberment, and health benefits, major sources are Institute of Life Insurance and Health Insurance Association of America, *Group Insurance Coverages in the United States,* annual issues; Institute of Life Insurance, *Life Insurance Fact Book,* annual issues; reports of Blue Cross Association and the National Association of Blue Shield plans; and reports of self-insured (independent) trade-union, mutual benefit association and company-administered health and life insurance plans. (For further detail

regarding health insurance estimates, see *Social Security Bulletin,* "Private Health Insurance in 1972, Health Care Services, Enrollment, and Finance," February 1974.) For temporary disability, data derived mainly from Health Insurance Council, *Extent of Voluntary Coverage in the United States,* annual issues, and unpublished data. (For further detail, see *Social Security Bulletin,* "Cash Benefits for Short-Term Sickness, 1948–1972," January 1974.) For retirement, estimates made by Social Security Administration based on data from Institute of Life Insurance, *Tally,* and *Life Insurance Fact Book,* annual editions, and Securities and Exchange Commission, *Survey of Private Non-insured Pension Plans,* annual issues.

Coverage data are generally based on the number of active participants (those currently employed) and may include in addition persons who have been temporarily laid off or retired. The practice of continuing coverage for a retired worker is particularly prevalent in group life insurance. Many group life and health plans permit a person on layoff to continue coverage in the group for 3 to 6 months, and, in some cases, even longer. In addition, workers who have terminated employment may carry vested pension rights; these persons are often included in the total coverage group. No attempt has been made to correct the coverage data for such limitations. Therefore, the proportion that covered employees represent of all employed workers and that contributions represent of aggregate payrolls have some overstatement. Nevertheless, longrun growth patterns for the various types of plans remain valid.

Employee-benefit plans are now (1970) the predominant way through which most workers and their families obtain basic medical care protection and they provide many services and protections not originally included. The increasing dollar amounts of benefits paid under employee-benefit plans, however, do not necessarily represent real gains—in terms of increased quality of care and adequacy of protection provided—for individual employees. Some of the rise in aggregate expenditures is the result of growth in the number of employees and dependents covered, the increased per unit cost of providing specific services and benefits, and the increased utilization of services.

Measuring the magnitude of real gain in health care benefits is particularly difficult. See Herbert E. Klarman, Dorothy P. Rice, Barbara S. Cooper, and H. Louis Stettler III, *Sources of Increase in Selected Medical Care Expenditures, 1929–1969* (Staff Paper No. 4), Social Security Administration, Office of Research and Statistics, 1970. The extent of utilization of medical and hospital services is influenced by a number of factors such as age distribution of the work force, variations in incidence of sickness, shifts in types of services used, and the tendency for private plans to provide supplemental rather than basic protection to the elderly, as the result of Medicare.

H 115–124. Protection against income loss from short-term sickness, 1948–1970.

Source: U.S. Social Security Administration, *Social Security Bulletin,* January 1974, pp. 20 and 26.

Protection against loss of earnings in periods of nonoccupational disability is provided in a number of ways. For wage and salary workers in private industry, the most common method is through group or individual insurance policies sold by commercial insurance companies that pay cash amounts during specified periods of disability. Employers may also self-insure, providing either cash benefits or paid sick leave. Some unions, union management trust funds, fraternal societies, and mutual benefit associations also pay cash disability benefits. In addition, employers often use a paid-sick-leave plan to supplement benefits under insurance plans, and workers may, as individuals, purchase insurance policies to supplement the protection provided through their jobs. Private insured protection may be obtained through voluntary action by the employer or the employee, or it may come about as the result of compulsory programs. (For discussion of such programs, see source.)

H 125–171. Monthly cash benefits and beneficiaries under social insurance and related programs, by risk and program, 1940–1970.

Source: U.S. Social Security Administration, *Social Security Bulletin, Annual Statistical Supplement, 1971,* and earlier issues.

Lump-sum payments are excluded. Data for workmen's compensation and State and local retirement systems exclude Alaska and Hawaii, 1940–1958; data for other programs include benefits paid and beneficiaries in outlying areas or in other countries for all years.

Most of the data are derived from operating statistics of the administering agencies. For the basis of estimates of workmen's compensation payments, see text for series H 332–345.

Estimates of the operations of State and local government retirement systems, series H 130 and H 155, prior to 1950 are based primarily on the Bureau of the Census *Annual Compendium of State Government Finances* and *Compendium of City Government Finances.* These present fiscal year data (which were averaged to secure calendar year figures) for State-administered and city-administered systems. Data on county-administered systems (not reported, and not many in that period) were estimated by the Social Security Administration.

After 1950 extensive use was made of the 1957, 1962, and 1967 Census of Governments reports, *Employee-Retirement Systems of State and Local Governments,* for benchmark purposes. Beginning 1959, data from the Census Bureau's annual *Finances of Employee-Retirement Systems of State and Local Governments* were used, with certain adjustments through the year 1966 (no adjustments thereafter). Two fiscal years are averaged to approximate calendar year data.

H 172–259. General note.

The national system of old-age, survivors, disability, and health insurance (OASDHI) originally covered employees in industry and commerce. Beginning 1951, coverage was extended to regularly employed agricultural and domestic workers, to most urban self-employed persons, and, on a voluntary group basis, to employees of nonprofit organizations and to employees of State and local governments not covered by separate retirement programs. During the 1950's, coverage was further extended to self-employed farmers and additional farmworkers, to most professional self-employed persons and, on a voluntary basis, to most State and local government employees covered by their own retirement system. As of January 1957, military personnel were covered on a compulsory basis. Free wage credits for military service from September 1940 through December 1956 are reflected in benefits paid during the years covered by the series (primarily in benefits to young survivors) but do not enter into the count of covered workers or taxable earnings. The additional cost of benefits paid as a result of these credits is met by transfers to the trust funds from general revenues. In 1965, self-employed doctors of medicine were covered, and in 1967 the previous elective coverage of ministers became compulsory unless exemption was claimed on grounds of conscience or religious principle.

When the OASDHI program began in 1937, less than 60 percent of all persons who worked in paid employment during an average week were covered. Following the 1950 amendments, the proportion rose to 75 percent and by 1970 was more than 90 percent. Major groups still excluded from coverage are: (1) Workers covered under Federal civilian employee staff retirement systems; (2) most railroad employees; (3) household workers and farmworkers whose earnings are below certain minimum levels; and (4) persons with very low net earnings from self-employment. Federal civil servants and railroad employees are covered, separately, by compulsory, contributory retirement systems of their own. The railroad system is closely coordinated with OASDHI.

A worker may be covered, and receive wage credits toward his benefits, for less than the full amount of his earnings. Contributions were payable only on the first $3,000 earned annually during 1937–1950, the first $3,600 for 1951–1954, $4,200 for 1955–1958, $4,800 for 1959–1965, $6,600 for 1966–1967, and $7,800 for 1968–1970.

Contributions were payable on taxable earnings at the following rates (percent):

Year	Employer-employee (each)	Self-employed
1937–49	1	–
1950	1.5	–
1951–53	1.5	2.25
1954–56	2	3
1957–58	2.25	3.375
1959	2.5	3.75
1960–61	3	4.5
1962	3.125	4.7
1963–65	3.625	5.4
1966	4.2	6.15
1967–68	4.4	6.4
1969–70	4.8	6.9

– Represents zero.

These rates include disability insurance contributions for 1957–1970 and hospital insurance contributions for 1966–1970.

An employer deducts social security contributions from a worker's pay and adds an equal amount for his tax as employer. The money is forwarded to the Internal Revenue Service and deposited into Federal trust funds from which the benefits and administrative expenses are paid. Self-employed persons pay their social security contributions with their Federal income tax.

To qualify for cash benefits, a worker must have worked a sufficient time in covered employment to have acquired an insured status. Under the 1939 amendments, a worker was generally "fully insured" for benefits if he had worked in covered employment half the time after 1936 and before age 65 and had a minimum of six calendar quarters of coverage. Subsequent liberalizations permitted a person to become fully insured if he had been in covered work roughly equal to one-fourth of the time between 1950 (or age 21, if later) and retirement age or death. If a worker dies before acquiring a fully insured status but is "currently insured"—1½ years employment out of the three years preceding death—survivor benefits may be paid to his young widow with children. To be insured for disability benefits, a worker must generally have worked for at least 5 out of the 10 years before onset of disability.

The 1965 amendments eased the eligibility requirements for persons 72 years old and over who were not eligible for cash benefits by introducing a transitional insured status under which a special flat monthly benefit may be paid to persons with three to five quarters of coverage. A 1966 amendment extended these special monthly benefits to certain persons 72 years old and over who could not meet even these minimal requirements.

Lump-sum payments became payable in 1937, monthly benefits in 1940. The original Social Security Act provided for monthly old-age benefits only. Amendments adopted in 1939 added benefits for dependents and survivors of the insured worker. Benefits for disabled persons were added in 1956, and benefits for the dependents of disabled persons in 1958. Beginning 1966, the cost of rehabilitation services furnished to disability beneficiaries was also paid by the program.

In 1965, a comprehensive health insurance program (Medicare) for persons 65 years old and over was established. The program consists of a compulsory hospital insurance plan covering hospital and related services and a voluntary supplementary medical insurance plan covering physicians' and related medical services. The hospital insurance plan is financed through contributions made while the individual is working (except that Federal general revenues are used to finance the benefits for certain elderly persons who reach retirement age without becoming insured under the Social Security Act). The supplementary medical insurance plan is financed through voluntary contributions by the elderly matched by the Federal Government general revenues.

Each person working in covered employment or self-employment must obtain a social security number, which is used to identify the earnings record from which his benefits are calculated. Benefits are based on the worker's average monthly earnings as computed under the law. For most workers, at present, monthly earnings are averaged over a period of years beginning with 1951, or age 22 if later, up to the year in which the worker reaches age 65 (62 for a woman), becomes disabled, or dies. Generally, the 5 years of lowest earnings are disregarded in computing this average. After the worker's average monthly earnings have been figured, the monthly benefit amount payable at age 65 or upon disablement—the primary insurance amount—is then obtained from a table in the law. Benefits for dependents and survivors are calculated as a percentage of the primary insurance amount.

H 172–185. Old-age, survivors, disability, and health insurance— covered workers, earnings, and selected trust fund transactions, 1937–1970.

Source: U.S. Social Security Administration, *Social Security Bulletin, Annual Statistical Supplement, 1971*, pp. 24, 26, 47, 50–52, 54, 66.

See general note for series H 172–259.

H 186–196. Old-age, survivors, disability, and health insurance— estimated paid employment and coverage status, 1940–1970.

Source: See source for series H 172–185, p. 46.

The figures are annual averages based on data for the calendar week in March, June, September, and December during which the Bureau of the Census' Current Population Survey was taken. Total paid employment, series H 186, relates to persons 14 years old and over for 1940–1966 and to persons 16 years old and over thereafter; all members of the Armed Forces are included.

H 197–208. Old-age, survivors, disability, and health insurance— number of monthly cash benefits, by type of beneficiary, 1940–1970.

Source: See source for series H 172–185, pp. 49 and 96, and unpublished data.

See general note for series H 172–259.

H 209–229. Old-age, survivors, disability, and health insurance— benefits, by type of beneficiary, 1940–1970.

Source: See source for series H 172–185, pp. 70, 95, 103, 104, 119, 120, and unpublished data.

See general note for series H 172–259.

H 230–237. Old-age, survivors, disability, and health insurance— number and average monthly benefits in current-payment status, by selected family groups, 1940–1970.

Source: See source for series H 172–185, p. 48.

See general note for series H 172–259.

H 238–244. Old-age and survivors insurance trust fund, 1937–1970.

Source: U.S. Social Security Administration, *Social Security Bulletin, Annual Statistical Supplement, 1971*, p. 50, except series H 258–259, *Social Security Bulletin*, April issues.

Original sources of the data are the *Daily Statement of the United States Treasury* and, beginning 1954, the *Monthly and Final Statement of Receipts and Expenditures of the United States Government*, also issued by the Department of the Treasury.

H 245–259. Old-age, survivors, disability, and health insurance— benefits in current-payment status for retired-worker beneficiaries, by sex, 1940–1970.

Source: See source for series H 172–185, pp. 95, 96, and 101.

See general note for series H 172–259.

H 260–270. Civil Service retirement, 1921–1970.

Source: U.S. Civil Service Commission, *Civil Service Retirement, Federal Employees Group Life Insurance, Federal Employees Health Benefits, Retired Federal Employees Health Benefits*, various annual issues.

The original retirement act (Public Law 66-215) was signed May 22, 1920, and initially covered about 330,000 employees in the classified civil service. The act provided only for mandatory and disability retirement after 15 years of service with annual annuities ranging from $180 to $720 based on length of service and the average salary for the ten years preceding retirement.

The present retirement law (1973) provides optional retirement on full annuity at age 55 with 30 years service, age 60 with 20 years service, or age 62 with 5 years service; disability retirement is permitted at any age with 5 years service; involuntary retirement at any age after 25 years service or at age 50 with 20 years service. Deferred annuities are payable at age 62 with 5 years service. Mandatory retirement remains age 70 with 15 years service. The average salary is now the highest three years of salary. The annuity formula provides $1\frac{1}{2}\%$ of average salary for the first 5 years service, $1\frac{3}{4}\%$ for the next 5 years, and 2% for any remaining service, up to a maximum of 80% of average salary. Disability annuitants receive the greater of the preceding computation or a guaranteed minimum of 40% of average salary or regular formula using service projected to age 60, whichever is less. The law also contains special eligibility and computation requirements for certain hazardous duty positions and for legislative branch employees.

The major provisions under various laws follow:

Law and effective date	Age-service requirements to receive annuity				
	Optional	Disability	Involuntary	Deferred	Mandatory
1920 8–20–20	No provision	Any–15	No provision	No provision	70–15 65–15[1] 62–15[1]
1930 7–1–30	68–30 63–30[1] 60–30[1]	Any–5	55–15[2] (1922 Act)	No provision	Same
1942 1–24–42	62–15 60–30 55–30[2]	Any–5	62–5 55–5[2]	Any–5 (Payable at 62)[2]	70–15
1948 4–1–48	Same	Any–5	Any–25[2]	Same	70–15
1956 10–1–56	62–5 60–30 55–30[2]	Any–5	Any–25[2] 50–20[2]	Same	70–15
1962 10–12–62	Same	Any–5	Same	Same	70–15
1969 10–20–69	62–5 60–20 55–30 (1966 Act)	Any–5	Same	Same	70–15

[1] Limited to occupations involving overseas or arduous duty.
[2] Annuity reduced for age.

Law	Employee contribution as percent of pay	General formula	Average salary for—	Survivor benefit election	Average annual annuity for issues in year following enactment	Estimated number of employees covered
1920	2½	30 to 60% of salary by schedule	10 years	No provision	$568	330,000
1930	3½	$30 x service plus amount purchasable from contributions, various maxima and minima	5 years	No provision	952	415,000
1942	5	Same, plus minimum 1/70 x salary x service (maximum 35 years)	5 years	Election by retiree [1] (1939 law)	986	2,000,000 (3,000,000 in 1944)
1948	6	1½% x salary x service or (1% x salary + $25) x service. Maximum 80% of salary	5 years	Widow and children	1,121	1,735,000
1956	6½	Same, but 1¾% for 5–10 years and 2% for 10 years and over	5 years	Same but deferred could elect	1,920	2,133,000
1962	6½	Same	5 years	Same	2,700	2,300,000
1969	7	Same	3 years	Same	4,920	2,700,000

[1] Public Law 85–465 provided benefits to widows whose husbands had died before February 29, 1948, since the law before that time did not provide a liberal survivor benefit.

The number of annuities certified refers to the number of employee and survivor annuitants added to the roll during the year. The number terminated refers to the employee and survivor annuitants dropped from the roll during the year; it is derived by adding the prior year "number in force" to the current year "number certified" and subtracting the current year "number in force." The number in force represents total employee and survivor annuitants in active annuity status as of June 30. The annual value is the average monthly annuity as of June 30 projected to an annual basis.

Lump-sum payments or refunds are paid to persons leaving the Federal service and withdrawing contributions and to survivors of deceased employees and of deceased annuitants. In the case of deceased employees with no survivor annuity payable, accumulated deductions (contributions) are paid. In the case of deceased annuitants whose annuity paid has not equaled contributions, the unexpended balance is paid.

H 271–286. Railroad retirement benefits—number and amount, by type of beneficiary, 1937–1970.

Source: U.S. Railroad Retirement Board, *Annual Report*, 1950, 1960, and 1971 editions, and unpublished data.

The social insurance programs administered by the Railroad Retirement Board cover employees of railroads and of companies and organizations affiliated with railroad transportation. The Railroad Retirement Act provides retirement annuities for aged and disabled workers and for wives of retired employees, and benefits to survivors of deceased workers. Wage credits of workers with less than 10 years of railroading are transferred to, and counted with, social security covered employment at retirement. Supplemental annuities have also been provided for career employees since 1966. In addition, Federal health insurance protection is available to railroad workers on the same basis as to workers covered by social security. Funds for the regular railroad retirement and survivor benefit program come primarily from a tax, divided equally between employer and employee, on specified amounts of earnings, which have varied over time.

For a review of amendment activities, employer and employee contributions, benefit adjustments, etc., see source.

H 287–304. Private pension and deferred profit-sharing plans—estimated coverage, contributions, reserves, beneficiaries, and benefit payments, 1930–1970.

Source: U.S. Social Security Administration, *Social Security Bulletin*, March 1959, p. 12; April 1966, p. 11; and April 1972, p. 20.

These series were compiled by the Social Security Administration

from releases of the Institute of Life Insurance, Securities and Exchange Commission, Department of Labor, and Internal Revenue Service, supplemented by various other reports, such as those of nonprofit organizations and the annual statements of the leading life insurance companies writing group annuities. Information was also received from various industrial concerns. In addition, for the earlier years, M. W. Latimer's studies were utilized (see M. W. Latimer, *Industrial Pension Systems in the United States and Canada*, Industrial Relations Counselors, Inc., New York, 1932).

These series present estimates with respect to formal private pension and deferred profit-sharing plans. Included are plans covering employees of industrial and nonprofit organizations. Most of them are funded although some of the noninsured plans are on a pay-as-you-go basis. The majority are single-employer plans with an increasing number of industry- or area-wide multiemployer plans.

Under insured plans, insurance carriers are the medium through which benefits are provided; sponsors of the plans pay premiums to these carriers. Under noninsured plans, the sponsors themselves perform the functions of insurance carriers.

Series H 287–289 exclude annuitants and potential members who have not yet met the entrance requirements (age and/or service). Employees under both insured and noninsured plans are included only once—under the insured plans. The larger groups under insured plans are covered by group annuity contracts, whereas individual-policy pension trusts cover smaller groups.

Contributions to insured plans, series H 291 and H 294, are on a net basis with dividends and refunds deducted. Those of noninsured plans, series H 292 and H 295, are for the most part on a gross basis, refunds appearing as benefit payments. For pay-as-you-go plans, contributions have been assumed to equal benefit payments.

Reserves for insured plans, series H 297, were furnished by the Institute of Life Insurance. Reserves for noninsured plans, series H 298, include those of corporate pension plans, obtained from releases of the Securities and Exchange Commission; to these were added estimated reserves of noninsured nonprofit organization and multiemployer plans.

The number of beneficiaries, series H 299–301, relate to those in receipt of periodic payments at the end of the year, thus excluding those receiving lump sums during the year. Payments under insured plans, series H 303, are net amounts. Payments for the noninsured plans, series H 304, were obtained by adding to the Securities and Exchange Commission data the estimated payments under formal pay-as-you-go plans and under noninsured multiemployer and nonprofit organization plans. The data from SEC include lump sums and refunds from corporate pension funds (types not segregated). Therefore, dividing the payments of the year by the mean number of beneficiaries results in an overstatement of the average annual periodic payment.

H 305–317. Unemployment insurance—coverage, benefits, and financing under State programs, 1941–1970.

Source: U.S. Manpower Administration, monthly *Unemployment Insurance Statistics*, and quarterly *Employment and Wages*.

Most of these series also appear in the *Social Security Bulletin, Annual Statistical Supplement*. Data relate only to State programs under Title IX of the Social Security Act. Note that data in series H 1–171 include, in addition, the railroad unemployment insurance system, unemployment allowances for veterans, reconversion unemployment benefits for seamen, and unemployment benefits for Federal employees paid by the States as agents of the Federal Government.

In all States, covered employment represents employment in industrial and commercial establishments of 8 or more for 1941–1955, and 4 or more for 1956–1970 (coverage required under the Federal statute); in some States, covered employment also represents employment in smaller establishments and employment for additional groups of workers, such as State and local employees or seamen. Taxable wages, which are that part of wages subject to the State unemployment insurance tax, and the contributions paid on such wages are also reported on quarterly contribution reports from covered employers. An employer pays contributions on only the first $3,000 of an employee's annual wage in all but 22 States. The limit is $3,300 in Tennessee; $3,600 in Arizona, Connecticut, Delaware, Idaho, Massachusetts, Michigan, New Jersey, Oregon, Pennsylvania, Rhode Island, Vermont, West Virginia, Wisconsin, and Wyoming; $3,800 in California, North Dakota, and Nevada; $4,200 in Utah; $4,800 in Minnesota; $5,500 in Hawaii; and $7,200 in Alaska. Workers' contributions are included in the data for States whose laws provide for such contributions. Contributions payable by employers to the Federal Government (0.4 percent of taxable wages), and used primarily for Federal grants to the States for the cost of administering unemployment insurance and employment services, are not included in these series. Employer contributions to States for unemployment insurance vary in rate depending on the individual employer's experience (in earlier years not all States permitted variable rates), ranging generally from 0.1 percent or less to 4.0 percent or more of taxable payrolls. In 1941, 5 States also collected contributions for this program from employees; by 1970, only Alabama, Alaska, and New Jersey did so.

In most States, a waiting period of 1 week must be served before payments begin. Benefits are payable for a maximum number of weeks, ranging from 20 to 36 weeks among the States; maximum weekly benefits without dependents' allowances range from $40 to $86 under the several State laws. In 11 States, maximum allowances for dependents ranging from $12 to $38 raise the range of maximum augmented benefits to $65 to $114.

H 318–331. Railroad unemployment insurance benefits, 1940–1970.

Source: See source for series H 271–286.

The Railroad Unemployment Insurance Act provides benefits for unemployment and sickness financed by contributions from covered employers.

For a review of amendment activities, contributions, benefit adjustments, etc., see source.

H 332–345. Workmen's compensation—payments, by type of benefit and type of insurance, 1939–1970.

Source: U.S. Social Security Administration, 1939–1967, *Social Security Bulletin*, October 1970; 1968–1970, *Social Security Bulletin*, January issues.

The figures include estimated payments under State workmen's compensation laws (46 States in 1939; 48 States, 1948–1957; 50 States, 1959–1970) and under Federal workmen's compensation laws covering employees of the Federal Government, private employees in the District of Columbia, and longshoremen and harbor workers. Be-

ginning 1970, includes the Federal "Black Lung" benefits program for disabled coal miners and their dependents. Most of the State workmen's compensation laws exempt employment in agriculture, domestic service, and casual labor; about half exempt employers who have fewer than a specified number of employees. Occupational diseases, or at least specified diseases, are compensable under all laws. To make certain that benefit payments will be made when due, the covered employer is required by law to obtain insurance from a private insurance carrier, from a State insurance fund, or to give proof of his qualifications to carry his own risk, which is known as self-insurance.

Estimates of workmen's compensation payments depend on a variety of sources of published information, supplemented by correspondence with State agencies. Data on payments by private insurance companies and some of the competitive State funds are obtained from annual issues of *Spectator: Insurance by States of Fire, Marine, Casualty, Surety and Miscellaneous Lines* and from the A. M. Best Company. Data on payments made by the remaining State funds are obtained from annual or biennial reports issued by State Workmen's Compensation Bureaus or Divisions, or State Insurance Departments, and from the annual publication of the Bureau of the Census, *State Government Finances*. Data on payments by self-insurers in some States are obtained directly from State reports. For most States, however, estimates are calculated using one of several ratios (e.g., reported accidents, claims filed, taxes paid, etc.) that exist between firms which are insured with private carriers, or State funds, and firms which self-insure.

See also text for series H 57–69 and for series B 256.

H 346–367. Public assistance—payments, recipients, and average monthly payments, 1936–1970.

Source: U.S. Social Security Administration, *Social Security Bulletin, Annual Statistical Supplement, 1971*, tables 143 and 145. Data from U.S. Social and Rehabilitation Service.

Assistance programs financed in part by Federal grants-in-aid were in effect on a State-wide basis in 1936 in 42 States for old-age assistance, 27 States for aid to dependent children, and 25 States for aid to the blind. Programs have been in effect in the 48 conterminous States and the District of Columbia beginning 1938 for old-age assistance, 1955 for aid to dependent children, and 1953 for aid to the blind. Approval of the first plans for aid to the permanently and totally disabled was effective October 1950 and, in 1957, 44 States and the District of Columbia were participating. Assistance payments for all above programs are still financed in part from Federal funds and, with the exception of Nevada (aid to the permanently and totally disabled), these programs are currently in effect in all 50 States, the District of Columbia, Guam, Puerto Rico, and Virgin Islands. General assistance, provided from State or local funds or both, is available to certain other categories of needy persons in all 54 jurisdictions. See also text for series B 255.

H 368–375. Emergency public assistance and Federal work programs —recipients and assistance, 1933–1943.

Source: See source for series H 346–367, various issues.

The estimates shown here for 1933–1939 are very similar to those in the National Resources Planning Board report on *Security, Work, and Relief Policies*, 1942, appendixes 9 and 10.

See also text for series H 1–31 and H 32–47.

H 376–381. Old-age assistance recipients and insurance beneficiaries per 1,000 population 65 years old and over; and children receiving aid, and child insurance beneficiaries per 1,000 population under age 18, 1936–1970.

Source: U.S. Social and Rehabilitation Service, **series H 380**, *Trend Report, A-4*; **series H 376–379** and **H 381**, *Concurrent Receipt of Public Assistance Money Payments and OASDHI Cash Benefits by Persons Aged 65 or Over* (G-2).

H 382–391. Services under public child health and welfare service programs, 1937–1970.

Source: Series H 382–389, 1937–1969, U.S. Children's Bureau, *Statistical Series*, and U.S. Social Security Administration, unpublished data; 1970, U.S. Health Services Administration, unpublished data; series H 390–391, U.S. Social and Rehabilitation Service, *Child Welfare Statistics, 1969*, and *Children Served by Public Welfare Agencies and Voluntary Child Welfare Agencies and Institutions*, Report CW-1 and E-9.

H 392–397. Vocational rehabilitation—caseload and expenditures, 1921–1970.

Source: U.S. Social and Rehabilitation Service, *Caseload Statistics of State Vocational Rehabilitation Agencies in Fiscal Years and State Vocational Rehabilitation Agency Program Data in Fiscal Years*, annual issues.

Vocational rehabilitation of the disabled is defined as the restoration, preservation, or development of the ability to function in productive activity. The rehabilitation services provided by State agencies with matching State and Federal funds include medical restoration, training, guidance, and placement services.

Eligibility of an individual for vocational rehabilitation services requires that all three of the following conditions be shown to exist: (a) The presence of a physical or mental disability; (b) the existence of a substantial handicap to employment; and (c) a reasonable expectation that vocational rehabilitation services may render the individual fit to engage in a gainful occupation. For a detailed discussion of these conditions, see *An Introduction to the Vocational Rehabilitation Process*, prepared by John F. McGowan and Thomas L. Porter, 1967.

H 398–411. Private philanthropy—estimated fund flows, by donors and recipients, 1929–1970.

Source: Ralph L. Nelson, Professor of Economics, Queens College of the City University of New York, 1973.

The estimates shown here differ from those presented in the *Statistical Abstract of the United States* (1973 edition, table 510). Reasons for the differences include differences in estimating procedures, definition and scope of particular categories, and the need to make projections. The source of the *Statistical Abstract* table is American Association of Fund-Raising Counsel, Inc., New York, *Giving USA*. In the annual *Giving USA*, the objective is to present contemporary estimates, which requires projection of historical data. According to Nelson, his estimates reflect a greater opportunity to use historical benchmarks and the availability of the time and research resources required to handle more thoroughly problems of data refinement and estimation.

H 399, living donors. 1929–1954, based on C. Harry Kohn, *Personal Deductions in the Federal Income Tax*, Princeton University Press, 1960, table 17, p. 66; 1955–1967, based on unpublished memoranda prepared for the Carnegie Corporation by Nelson; 1968–1970, estimates prepared for the Commission on Private Philanthropy and Public Needs, also by Nelson. All estimates originally based on contributions itemized on personal income tax returns as tabulated in U.S. Internal Revenue Service, *Statistics of Income: Individual Income Tax Returns*. Base figures, adjusted for overreporting of contributions, were increased by estimates of the contributions of individuals and families using the standard deduction or not required to file a return.

H 400, charitable bequests. Based on charitable bequests reported on estate tax returns as tabulated in U.S. Internal Revenue Service, *Statistics of Income: Estate and Gift Tax Returns*. For years in which no tabulations were made, estimates were based on linear interpolation between years for which tabulations were available.

H 401, corporation contributions. Based on contributions reported on corporation income tax returns as tabulated in U.S. Internal Revenue Service, *Statistics of Income: Corporation Income Tax Returns*, not adjusted for contribution flows through company-sponsored foundations. For such adjustment, see Ralph L. Nelson, *Economic Factors in the Growth of Corporation Giving*, National Bureau of Economic Research and Russell Sage Foundation, New York, 1970, chapter 4.

H 402, foundation grants. Based on editions 1 through 5 of *The Foundation Directory*, Russell Sage Foundation, 1960, 1964, 1967, and the Foundation Center, 1971 and 1975, New York; U.S. Department of the Treasury, *Treasury Department Report on Private Foundations*, 1965; Ralph L. Nelson "Estimates of Balance Sheets and Income Statements of Foundations and Colleges and Universities," supplementary vol. I of *Institutional Investor Study Report of the Securities and Exchange Commission*, 1965, Appendix A-III; Nelson, *The Investment Policies of Foundations*, Russell Sage Foundation, New York, 1967, chapter 2; Nelson, *Private Giving in the American Economy, 1960–1972*, Commission on Private Philanthropy and Public Needs (forthcoming).

H 403, higher education endowment income. For 1950–1970, estimates based on U.S. Office of Education, *Biennial Survey of Higher Education* (biennial 1951–52 through 1963–64, annual survey thereafter). See also Nelson, "Estimates of Balance Sheets and Income Statements . . . of Colleges and Universities," cited above.

H 404, hospitals endowment income. Based on data on the capital funds of voluntary short term hospitals as reported by the American Hospital Association. A current investment return (rate of interest) was applied to the capital funds to obtain a measure of investment income.

H 406 and **H 407**, religious organizations and parochial schools. For description of data sources, estimation procedures, and 1929–1959 estimates, see Frank G. Dickinson, *The Changing Position of Philanthropy in the American Economy*, National Bureau of Economic Research, New York, 1970, chapter 3. 1960–1970 estimates (and also 1929–1959) prepared by Ralph L. Nelson for Carnegie Corporation and for Commission on Private Philanthropy and Public Needs.

H 408, higher education. See source note for series H 403. The Council on Financial Aid to Education also has published survey data on giving to higher education since the 1954–55 academic year.

H 409, hospitals and health. Based on estimates made by Research and Statistics staff of U.S. Social Security Administration and published in *Social Security Bulletin* and on estimates made by the American Association of Fund Raising Counsel and published in *Giving USA*. These estimates were verified for general trend from a variety of data sources (federated campaign allocations, national health agencies, church benevolences distributions, etc.).

H 410, youth services, welfare, race relations. This has been the most profoundly changing category over this 4-decade period, reflecting changing social needs, government programs, and support patterns. Many sources of information were used, the most comprehensive being "Expenditures from public and private funds for organized income maintenance and welfare service programs" presented in the *Social Security Bulletin*.

H 411, other. Includes philanthropic receipts of (1) independent nonsectarian primary and secondary schools, (2) church foreign missions and private foreign relief, (3) foundations' net endowment increase, project and administrative expense, (4) civic and cultural support, and (5) charity raffles.

Series H 1–31. Social Welfare Expenditures Under Public Programs: 1890 to 1970

[In millions of dollars. Years ending June 30 for Federal Government, most States, and some localities]

Year	Total expenditures: Total	Percent of gross national product	Percent of all government expenditures[1]	Per capita (actual prices)	Social insurance: Total	Old-age, survivors, disability, and health insurance	Railroad retirement	Public employee retirement	Unemployment insurance and employment services	Railroad unemployment insurance	Railroad temporary disability insurance	State temporary disability insurance	Workmen's compensation	Public aid: Total	Public assistance	Health and medical programs
	1	2	3	4	5	6	7	8	9	10	11	12	13	14	15	16
1970	145,893	15.3	47.8	701	54,676	36,835	1,610	8,659	3,819	38	61	718	2,936	16,488	14,434	9,753
1969	127,149	14.1	44.7	617	48,772	33,389	1,551	7,494	2,947	44	58	648	2,641	13,439	11,926	9,006
1968	113,840	13.8	43.2	558	42,740	28,748	1,417	6,582	2,929	46	36	574	2,409	11,092	9,887	8,459
1967	99,710	12.9	42.4	494	37,339	24,581	1,278	5,904	2,752	38	38	530	2,217	8,811	7,832	7,628
1966	88,000	12.2	43.4	441	31,934	20,295	1,212	5,145	2,662	52	43	508	2,017	7,301	6,497	6,938
1965	77,175	11.8	42.4	391	28,123	16,998	1,128	4,529	3,003	77	46	484	1,859	6,283	5,875	6,246
1964	71,491	11.7	40.0	368	26,971	16,201	1,107	4,057	3,274	93	50	468	1,722	5,642	5,381	6,004
1963	66,766	11.6	39.5	349	25,614	15,345	1,077	3,569	3,391	123	53	444	1,612	5,296	5,029	5,594
1962	62,659	11.6	39.4	332	24,194	13,985	1,037	3,190	3,854	163	57	407	1,501	4,945	4,675	5,230
1961	58,236	11.5	39.3	314	22,365	12,161	996	2,870	4,280	213	58	385	1,401	4,444	4,301	4,927
1960	52,293	10.6	38.0	286	19,307	11,032	935	2,570	2,830	215	69	348	1,309	4,101	4,042	4,464
1959	49,821	10.6	(2)	278	18,287	9,616	790	2,343	3,731	200	57	327	1,223	3,998	3,891	4,401
1958	45,457	10.3	(2)	258	15,957	8,221	730	2,026	3,303	176	55	304	1,142	3,615	3,540	4,091
1957	39,350	9.1	(2)	227	12,472	6,666	686	1,785	1,842	88	52	270	1,084	3,309	3,231	3,776
1956	35,131	8.6	(2)	206	10,646	5,485	608	1,577	1,624	60	52	233	1,008	3,115	3,024	3,307
1955	32,640	8.6	32.7	195	9,835	4,436	556	1,389	2,081	159	54	218	943	3,003	2,941	3,103
1954	29,547	8.2	(2)	179	8,265	3,364	518	1,251	1,872	100	47	211	903	2,788	2,776	3,099
1953	27,045	7.5	(2)	167	6,607	2,717	467	1,124	1,143	58	45	198	856	2,728	2,728	3,190
1952	25,576	7.6	(2)	160	5,671	2,067	400	999	1,189	26	28	175	787	2,585	2,584	3,331
1951	24,055	7.7	(2)	154	4,772	1,569	322	920	1,063	28	29	143	699	2,592	2,585	2,783
1950	23,508	8.9	37.6	153	4,947	784	306	818	2,190	120	31	72	625	2,496	2,490	2,064
1949	21,165	8.1	(2)	140	4,186	661	288	649	1,876	51	32	50	580	2,089	2,089	1,753
1948	18,652	7.6	(2)	126	3,603	559	230	580	1,601	36	29	33	536	1,702	1,702	1,416
1947	17,337	7.8	(2)	119	4,160	466	178	510	2,454	51	---	16	485	1,442	1,442	1,367
1946	12,798	6.1	(2)	90	3,652	358	157	413	2,256	24	---	5	440	1,151	1,148	1,904
1945	9,205	4.4	8.4	65	1,409	267	145	355	217	4	---	5	417	1,031	1,029	2,354
1944	8,228	4.1	(2)	59	1,256	217	138	332	174	4	---	5	387	1,032	1,015	2,225
1943	8,283	4.7	(2)	60	1,259	177	134	305	281	4	---	1	357	1,550	1,012	1,886
1942	8,609	6.1	(2)	63	1,376	137	130	322	452	11	---	---	324	2,777	1,062	949
1941	8,953	8.0	(2)	66	1,330	91	125	298	507	21	---	---	288	3,524	1,108	724
1940	8,795	9.2	49.0	66	1,272	40	117	283	553	19	---	---	259	3,597	1,124	616
1939	9,213	10.5	(2)	70	1,181	37	110	270	517	2	---	---	247	4,230	1,102	575
1938	7,924	9.0	(2)	60	849	26	86	257	236	---	---	---	244	3,233	991	540
1937	7,858	9.1	(2)	60	545	6	20	244	45	---	---	---	231	3,436	780	500
1936	10,184	13.2	(2)	79	456	1	1	233	18	---	---	---	204	3,079	656	454
1935	6,548	9.5	48.6	51	406	---	---	209	9	---	---	---	188	2,998	624	427
1934	5,832	9.7	(2)	46	362	---	---	186	3	---	---	---	173	2,531	436	400
1933	4,462	7.9	(2)	35	344	---	---	164	---	---	---	---	180	689	344	418
1932	4,303	6.4	(2)	34	355	---	---	146	---	---	---	---	209	256	190	435
1931	4,201	5.1	(2)	33	368	---	---	136	---	---	---	---	233	164	145	406
1930	4,085	4.2	(2)	33	361	---	---	122	---	---	---	---	239	78	78	378
1929	3,921	3.9	36.3	32	342	---	---	113	---	---	---	---	229	60	60	351
1913	1,000	2.5	34.0	15	---	---	---	---	---	---	---	---	---	(3)	---	150
1890	318	2.4	38.0	---	---	---	---	---	---	---	---	---	---	(3)	---	18

Year	Education: Total[4]	Elementary-secondary	Higher education	Vocational and adult	Veterans programs: Total	Pensions and compensation	Health and medical programs	Education	Life insurance	Welfare and other	Housing	Other social welfare: Total[5]	Vocational rehabilitation	Institutional care	Child nutrition
	17	18	19	20	21	22	23	24	25	26	27	28	29	30	31
1970	50,848	38,632	9,914	2,146	9,018	5,394	1,784	1,019	502	320	701	4,409	704	1,307	896
1969	43,673	33,705	8,174	1,648	7,934	4,987	1,531	679	493	243	532	3,792	583	1,115	743
1968	40,590	31,675	7,328	1,435	7,247	4,644	1,439	466	504	194	428	3,285	466	888	706
1967	35,808	27,742	6,629	1,296	6,898	4,499	1,359	297	548	195	378	2,848	410	860	589
1966	32,825	25,566	6,023	1,108	6,358	4,409	1,285	34	442	187	335	2,309	299	737	537
1965	28,108	22,358	4,826	854	6,031	4,141	1,229	41	434	186	318	2,066	211	790	617
1964	24,989	20,688	3,740	513	5,862	4,002	1,173	70	472	146	278	1,746	182	693	522
1963	22,671	18,916	3,300	421	5,751	3,913	1,113	101	489	136	248	1,593	149	669	480
1962	21,005	17,744	2,878	354	5,654	3,749	1,041	157	499	207	217	1,415	129	550	464
1961	19,337	16,448	2,546	317	5,624	3,665	1,020	258	493	189	196	1,343	109	590	406
1960	17,626	15,109	2,191	298	5,479	3,403	954	410	494	219	177	1,139	96	421	399
1959	16,498	14,139	2,063	283	5,472	3,304	905	609	486	170	156	1,010	87	359	368
1958	15,313	13,151	1,893	261	5,427	3,127	844	737	490	229	134	920	78	332	325
1957	13,732	11,857	1,629	241	5,119	2,886	787	816	477	153	120	823	67	225	364
1956	12,154	10,579	1,350	222	5,061	2,805	760	810	476	210	112	735	56	232	294
1955	11,157	9,734	1,214	205	4,834	2,690	761	706	490	187	89	619	42	195	240
1954	10,084	8,816	1,082	184	4,631	2,507	740	596	538	249	67	612	37	203	240
1953	9,231	8,034	1,013	179	4,735	2,449	739	707	539	301	51	503	35	149	192
1952	8,246	7,115	948	179	5,256	2,184	767	1,381	555	370	35	451	33	144	154
1951	7,415	6,330	912	170	5,996	2,114	696	2,019	515	652	37	462	31	150	166
1950	6,674	5,596	915	161	6,866	2,092	748	2,692	476	858	15	448	30	146	160
1949	5,807	4,890	769	146	6,927	1,980	718	2,818	452	958	8	396	27	131	132
1948	4,897	4,130	634	132	6,638	1,911	564	2,630	433	1,101	27	369	25	126	117
1947	4,089	3,479	497	111	5,683	1,834	578	2,273	441	556	281	316	20	114	100
1946	3,297	2,834	364	98	2,403	1,280	244	369	376	135	46	233	14	98	57
1945	3,076	2,621	314	139	1,126	767	102	10	201	46	11	198	10	83	47

See footnotes at end of table.

Series H 1–31. Social Welfare Expenditures Under Public Programs: 1890 to 1970—Con.

[In millions of dollars]

Year	Education Total[4] (17)	Elementary–secondary (18)	Higher education (19)	Vocational and adult (20)	Veterans Total (21)	Pensions and compensation (22)	Health and medical programs (23)	Education (24)	Life insurance (25)	Welfare and other (26)	Housing (27)	Other social welfare Total[5] (28)	Vocational rehabilitation (29)	Institutional care (30)	Child nutrition (31)
1944	2,800	2,392	262	144	720	513	87	----	94	26	13	182	7	86	34
1943	2,793	2,324	269	198	623	458	75	----	67	23	14	159	6	79	23
1942	2,694	2,263	251	179	645	446	72	----	60	67	14	154	5	78	23
1941	2,617	2,255	226	135	613	448	70	----	69	26	9	136	5	72	14
1940	2,561	2,267	218	75	629	443	76	----	77	33	4	116	4	62	4
1939	2,504	2,221	209	73	606	430	69	----	76	31	3	114	4	62	1
1938	2,563	2,297	199	67	627	415	65	----	108	40	4	108	4	56	1
1937	2,376	2,144	178	54	893	409	62	----	113	308	3	105	3	66	(Z)
1936	2,228	2,021	155	51	3,826	411	55	----	118	3,241	42	101	3	72	(Z)
1935	2,008	1,820	148	39	597	387	51	----	123	38	13	99	2	71	
1934	1,914	1,733	143	37	530	333	42	----	125	30	(Z)	96	2	94	
1933	2,104	1,911	153	39	819	565	70	----	145	39	----	89	2	87	
1932	2,352	2,144	164	42	825	562	78	----	146	39	----	81	2	79	
1931	2,440	2,218	180	41	744	504	68	----	138	34	----	79	2	77	
1930	2,523	2,288	196	38	668	433	59	----	140	35	----	78	2	76	
1929	2,434	2,216	182	35	658	435	51	----	136	36	----	76	2	75	
1913	525	----	----	----	196	----	----	----	----	----	----	³114			
1890	146	----	----	----	113	----	----	----	----	----	----	³41			

Z Less than $500,000.　¹ Government expenditures exclude workmen's compensation and temporary disability insurance payments made through private insurance carriers and self-insurers, although these (payable under statutory provisions) are included as social welfare expenditures, series H 1.　² Not computed.　³ "Public aid" included with "Other social welfare."　⁴ Includes administrative costs and research, not shown separately.　⁵ Includes child welfare, anti-poverty programs, and miscellaneous social welfare expenditures, not shown separately.

Series H 32–47. Social Welfare Expenditures Under Public Programs, by Source of Funds: 1890 to 1970

[In millions of dollars]

Year	From Federal funds Total (32)	Social insurance (33)	Public aid (34)	Health and medical programs (35)	Veterans programs (36)	Education (37)	Housing (38)	Other social welfare (39)	From State and local funds[1] Total (40)	Social insurance[2] (41)	Public aid (42)	Health and medical programs (43)	Veterans programs (44)	Education (45)	Housing (46)	Other social welfare (47)
1970	77,337	45,245	9,649	4,775	8,952	5,873	582	2,262	68,557	9,431	6,839	4,978	67	44,975	120	2,147
1969	68,355	40,847	7,829	4,543	7,883	4,923	425	1,905	58,794	7,925	5,610	4,463	51	38,750	107	1,888
1968	60,314	35,390	6,455	4,233	7,214	5,000	325	1,697	53,526	7,350	4,637	4,226	33	35,589	103	1,589
1967	53,267	30,545	5,244	3,681	6,875	5,279	283	1,360	46,444	6,794	3,567	3,947	23	30,529	95	1,489
1966	45,379	25,663	4,366	3,146	6,337	4,580	251	1,035	42,622	6,271	2,935	3,792	21	28,244	84	1,274
1965	37,712	21,807	3,594	2,781	6,011	2,470	238	812	39,464	6,316	2,690	3,466	20	25,638	80	1,254
1964	34,928	20,646	3,208	2,749	5,843	1,620	212	650	36,563	6,325	2,434	3,254	19	23,370	66	1,096
1963	32,675	19,417	2,999	2,441	5,731	1,323	193	571	34,091	6,196	2,297	3,153	20	21,348	56	1,022
1962	30,624	18,290	2,741	2,242	5,559	1,090	173	530	32,034	5,904	2,204	2,988	95	19,915	43	885
1961	27,403	15,966	2,337	1,949	5,539	1,001	159	451	30,833	6,399	2,107	2,978	84	18,337	37	892
1960	24,957	14,307	2,117	1,737	5,367	868	144	417	27,337	4,999	1,984	2,727	112	16,758	33	723
1959	23,550	13,054	2,082	1,717	5,411	767	128	392	26,271	5,233	1,916	2,684	61	15,732	28	618
1958	20,631	10,857	1,835	1,567	5,305	608	111	349	24,826	5,100	1,781	2,524	121	14,705	24	571
1957	18,130	8,926	1,690	1,410	5,080	541	101	381	21,221	3,545	1,619	2,365	39	13,192	19	442
1956	16,212	7,534	1,555	1,256	4,972	476	92	327	18,919	3,112	1,559	2,051	89	11,679	20	409
1955	14,623	6,385	1,504	1,150	4,772	485	75	252	18,017	3,450	1,499	1,953	62	10,672	15	367
1954	12,990	5,094	1,420	1,210	4,528	419	54	267	16,557	3,171	1,369	1,890	103	9,666	14	345
1953	12,244	4,224	1,361	1,380	4,621	429	38	191	14,801	2,383	1,367	1,810	114	8,802	13	312
1952	11,730	3,342	1,211	1,586	5,113	308	25	145	13,847	2,329	1,373	1,746	143	7,938	12	306
1951	11,126	2,724	1,196	1,170	5,661	180	22	173	12,929	2,049	1,395	1,613	335	7,235	13	289
1950	10,541	2,103	1,103	604	6,386	157	15	174	12,967	2,844	1,393	1,460	479	6,517	--------	274
1949	10,252	2,103	942	522	6,400	139	8	140	10,913	2,083	1,148	1,231	527	5,668	--------	256
1948	9,482	2,040	724	421	6,001	141	27	128	9,171	1,563	978	995	637	4,757	--------	241
1947	9,794	2,605	617	555	5,504	129	281	103	7,543	1,555	825	812	178	3,960	--------	213
1946	6,343	1,913	449	1,273	2,349	127	159	75	6,455	1,740	702	631	54	2,889	--------	158
1945	3,759	735	420	1,801	1,119	187	11	66	4,866	675	610	553	7	2,608	--------	132
1944	4,339	631	428	1,725	713	193	13	56	4,469	625	604	500	7	2,542	--------	126
1943	3,684	565	818	1,383	617	251	14	36	4,599	694	731	503	7	2,476	--------	123
1942	3,605	532	1,698	471	637	218	14	36	5,004	844	1,079	478	9	2,482	--------	118
1941	3,660	470	2,188	232	605	136	9	22	5,293	860	1,336	493	8	2,482	--------	114
1940	3,443	394	2,243	97	620	75	4	11	5,351	878	1,353	519	9	2,487	--------	106
1939	3,987	358	2,871	79	596	73	3	7	5,226	823	1,359	496	10	2,431	--------	107
1938	3,255	295	2,075	73	615	188	4	5	4,669	553	1,158	467	12	2,376	--------	103
1937	3,788	193	2,494	70	880	143	3	4	4,070	352	942	430	12	2,232	--------	101
1936	6,506	133	2,310	55	3,826	139	42	3	3,678	323	770	399	--------	2,089	--------	97
1935	3,207	119	2,374	50	598	53	13	2	3,341	287	624	378	--------	1,955	--------	97
1934	2,771	95	2,004	48	530	93	(Z)	2	3,061	267	527	352	--------	1,821	--------	94
1933	1,339	81	345	52	819	41	--------	2	3,123	263	344	366	--------	2,063	--------	87
1932	1,002	75	--------	55	825	46	--------	2	3,301	281	256	379	--------	2,306	--------	79
1931	911	69	--------	51	744	45	--------	2	3,290	299	164	355	--------	2,394	--------	77
1930	817	60	--------	47	668	40	--------	2	3,268	301	78	331	--------	2,483	--------	76
1929	798	56	--------	47	658	37	--------	1	3,123	286	60	304	--------	2,397	--------	75
1913	196	--------	--------	--------	--------	--------	--------	--------	804	--------	--------	--------	--------	--------	--------	--------
1890	115	--------	--------	--------	--------	--------	--------	--------	203	--------	--------	--------	--------	--------	--------	--------

Z Less than $500,000.　¹ Includes expenditures from State accounts in unemployment trust fund; excludes Federal grants-in-aid.　² Includes payments by private insurance carriers and self-insurers of benefits payable under State workmen's compensation and temporary disability insurance laws.

Series H 48–56. Civilian Labor Force and Workers Covered Under Government Social Insurance Programs: 1934 to 1970

[In millions. As of December, except as indicated. OASDHI = Old-age, survivors, disability, and health insurance]

Year	Civilian labor force			Retirement systems			Workmen's compensation	Unemployment insurance [4]	Temporary disability insurance [5]
	Total [1]	Paid employees	Self-employed	OASDHI [2]	Railroad retirement	Public employee [3]			
	48	49	50	51	52	53	54	55	56
1970	83.2	70.8	6.9	69.2	0.6	4.8	58.7	55.8	14.6
1969	81.4	71.0	6.9	68.6	.7	4.6	60.0	57.0	14.8
1968	79.1	68.8	7.1	67.1	.7	4.5	58.3	55.5	14.2
1967	78.1	67.3	7.1	65.7	.7	4.6	56.3	53.8	14.0
1966	77.3	65.7	7.9	64.9	.7	4.6	55.1	52.8	13.7
1965	75.6	63.6	8.0	62.8	.8	4.1	52.5	50.3	13.3
1964	73.8	60.8	8.5	60.1	.8	3.9	50.0	47.9	12.7
1963	72.5	59.1	8.5	58.5	.8	3.7	48.2	46.3	12.5
1962	71.4	58.0	8.4	57.3	.8	4.0	46.8	45.4	12.3
1961	70.6	56.3	9.0	56.1	.8	4.0	46.0	44.6	11.8
1960 *	70.5	55.3	9.3	55.7	.9	3.9	44.6	43.7	11.3
1959	69.3	55.1	9.3	55.4	.9	3.8	45.1	44.1	11.4
1958	68.1	53.7	9.0	53.4	1.0	3.9	42.7	42.6	11.0
1957	67.8	53.9	9.2	53.7	1.1	3.9	43.1	43.2	11.2
1956	67.0	54.1	9.1	53.2	1.2	4.5	44.1	43.8	11.5
1955	66.6	53.4	9.4	51.8	1.3	4.7	42.9	41.7	11.2
1954	63.5	50.0	9.5	45.3	1.2	4.6	40.4	37.2	10.7
1954 (monthly average)	64.5	49.8	9.7	45.3	1.2	4.5	39.7	36.6	10.6
1949 (monthly average)	62.1	45.9	10.8	34.3	1.4	4.4	35.3	33.1	5.3
1944 (monthly average)	54.6	41.9	9.3	30.8	1.7	4.7	33.0	31.6	.2
1939 (monthly average)	55.2	33.2	10.4	24.0	1.2	2.0	22.0	22.4	---
1934 (monthly average)	52.2	28.9	10.0	---	---	1.4	17.0	---	---

* Denotes first year for which figures include Alaska and Hawaii. [1] Bureau of the Census total of persons 14 years old and over (16 and over, beginning December 1967) in the civilian labor force; includes unpaid family members and the unemployed, not shown separately. [2] Beginning 1955, includes persons covered under both a government retirement system and OASDHI (about 5.3 million in December 1970); excludes persons whose coverage was authorized on an elective or optional basis but not in effect (about 3.5 million in December 1970); also excludes railroad employees jointly covered by OASDHI and their own retirement program. [3] Excludes persons covered under both a government retirement system and OASDHI; see footnote 2. [4] State, railroad, and Federal employee programs. [5] State and railroad programs. Excludes government employees covered by sick-leave provisions.

Series H 57–69. Estimated Payrolls in Employment Covered by Selected Government Social Insurance Programs: 1937 to 1970

[In millions of dollars. Conterminous United States, except as noted. Earnings and payroll data are gross, before deduction of social insurance contributions]

Year	Total earnings [1]	Wages and salaries [2]		Payrolls in employment covered by retirement programs					Net earnings of self-employed covered by OASDHI [8]	Payrolls in employment covered by unemployment insurance programs			Payrolls in employment covered by workmen's compensation program [10]
		Total	Civilian	Total [3]	Old-age, survivors, and disability insurance [4][5]	Railroad retirement [4][6]	Federal civil service retirement [7]	State and local government retirement		Total [9]	State unemployment insurance [9]	Railroad unemployment insurance [4][6]	
	57	58	59	60	61	62	63	64	65	66	67	68	69
1970	608,727	541,927	522,366	534,916	484,100	6,281	26,335	52,700	48,200	420,033	413,751	6,281	433,000
1969	576,881	509,690	490,642	503,419	456,500	6,092	23,127	47,900	48,100	398,773	392,681	6,092	414,000
1968	529,076	464,862	446,928	454,715	410,500	5,878	21,537	43,500	46,300	362,432	356,554	5,878	376,000
1967	485,222	423,075	406,865	413,439	372,900	5,734	19,105	38,600	44,700	330,807	325,073	5,734	342,000
1966	455,798	394,499	379,939	381,916	343,900	5,676	17,640	34,700	43,900	310,941	305,265	5,676	321,000
1965	416,138	358,885	346,742	342,944	308,600	5,590	16,254	31,300	39,900	282,773	277,143	5,590	292,000
1964	385,998	333,683	321,991	321,135	288,400	5,446	15,789	28,500	33,500	262,785	257,339	5,446	272,000
1963	362,108	311,095	300,246	298,770	268,200	5,350	14,620	26,100	31,600	245,449	240,099	5,350	254,000
1962	346,202	296,091	285,335	284,838	255,700	5,381	13,557	24,100	31,500	233,930	228,549	5,381	241,000
1961	326,514	278,080	267,895	266,872	238,800	5,345	13,227	22,200	29,900	219,482	214,137	5,345	226,500
1960 *	317,053	270,844	260,950	260,600	234,300	5,648	11,952	20,300	29,100	215,313	209,665	5,648	220,000
1959	304,737	258,187	248,314	246,957	222,500	5,751	11,406	18,600	29,700	206,412	200,661	5,751	209,000
1958	286,533	239,926	230,159	229,624	205,600	5,722	11,102	17,000	28,300	189,658	183,936	5,722	192,000
1957	282,758	238,695	229,051	227,893	203,100	6,177	10,116	15,500	28,200	191,226	185,049	6,177	190,000
1956	270,577	227,842	218,179	210,166	186,200	6,206	9,560	13,700	28,100	181,548	175,342	6,206	181,500
1955	252,967	211,266	201,488	193,291	169,400	5,801	8,290	12,400	24,400	164,240	158,439	5,801	168,000
1954	236,462	196,474	186,523	176,660	153,200	5,630	6,980	11,650	16,700	142,224	136,594	5,630	153,000
1953	238,847	198,335	187,998	177,447	154,000	6,147	6,950	10,670	16,900	144,804	138,657	6,147	153,500
1952	227,209	185,098	174,626	164,734	141,800	6,185	6,929	9,820	16,300	133,505	127,320	6,185	141,500
1951	212,982	171,019	162,335	152,576	131,200	6,101	6,395	8,880	16,300	124,344	118,243	6,101	131,500
1950	184,223	146,748	141,749	128,795	109,400	5,327	6,068	8,000	---	108,092	102,765	5,327	113,500
1949	169,836	134,551	130,303	117,780	99,600	5,133	5,707	7,340	---	98,653	93,520	5,133	103,000
1948	175,559	135,341	131,371	118,458	101,900	5,539	4,469	6,550	---	101,270	95,731	5,539	105,000
1947	158,466	122,978	118,911	107,462	92,100	5,113	4,809	5,440	---	91,347	86,234	5,113	91,500
1946	148,544	112,020	104,202	93,618	79,000	4,883	5,195	4,540	---	78,028	73,145	4,883	80,000
1945	148,901	117,479	95,660	85,438	71,300	4,530	5,840	3,768	---	70,941	66,411	4,530	74,000
1944	146,763	116,942	96,909	86,443	73,100	4,523	5,600	3,220	---	73,409	68,886	4,523	(NA)
1943	[11] 134,159	[11] 105,527	[11] 91,394	81,640	69,400	4,100	5,100	3,040	---	69,971	65,871	4,100	(NA)
1942	[11] 105,347	[11] 81,516	[11] 75,348	67,714	58,000	3,394	3,600	2,720	---	57,942	54,548	3,394	(NA)
1941	[11] 78,369	[11] 60,862	[11] 58,590	52,499	45,300	2,697	1,912	2,590	---	44,682	41,985	2,697	(NA)
1940	[11] 81,272	[11] 48,227	[11] 47,664	41,660	35,600	2,280	1,430	2,350	---	34,632	32,352	2,280	35,500
1939	[11] 55,901	[11] 44,056	43,668	36,892	31,488	2,149	1,221	2,034	---	31,218	29,069	2,149	---
1938	[11] 52,157	[11] 40,860	40,495	33,755	28,635	2,010	1,139	1,971	---	28,210	26,200	2,010	---
1937	[11] 57,624	[11] 44,421	44,067	37,943	32,770	2,265	1,050	1,858	---	---	---	2,265	---

* Denotes first year for which figures include Alaska and Hawaii. NA Not available. [1] Includes earnings of self-employed. [2] Wage and salary disbursements paid in cash and in kind. Includes pay of Federal personnel (civilian and military) in all areas. [3] Beginning 1953, adjusted for duplication of payrolls covered by both OASDHI and State and local retirement systems. [4] Taxable plus estimated nontaxable wages and salaries in employment covered by programs. [5] Beginning 1957, includes Armed Forces in all areas. [6] Includes a small amount of taxable wages for Alaska and Hawaii, all years. [7] Includes Alaska and Hawaii, all years. [8] Old-age, survivors, disability, and health insurance. [9] Beginning 1955, includes payrolls of Federal civilian employees in all areas. [10] Payrolls of employers insuring with private carriers, State funds, or self-insured, and Federal programs; excludes railroads (covered by Employers' Liability Act). [11] Excludes earnings under work relief programs.

Series H 70–114. Employee-Benefit Plans—Estimated Coverage, Contributions, and Benefits: 1950 to 1970

Year	Total coverage (including dependents of employees) — Life insurance and death [1]	Accidental death and dismemberment	Health benefits — Hospitalization [2][3]	Surgical [2]	Regular medical [2]	Major medical [4]	Covered employees — Life insurance and death [1]	Accidental death and dismemberment	Health benefits — Hospitalization [2][3]	Surgical [2]	Regular medical [2]	Major medical [4]	Private employees covered (millions) — Temporary disability [5]	Retirement [6]
	70	71	72	73	74	75	76	77	78	79	80	81	82	83
1970	60.4	38.7	152.8	150.8	133.4	72.3	51.6	38.7	59.6	58.9	52.9	26.6	31.2	29.7
1969	56.6	36.5	147.1	144.8	124.3	66.6	48.5	36.5	57.4	56.5	49.2	24.6	30.9	29.0
1968	55.7	33.7	139.8	136.4	116.5	61.7	48.2	33.7	54.6	53.1	46.1	22.8	29.5	28.0
1967	52.8	30.4	133.8	130.3	111.5	57.4	45.7	30.4	52.1	50.8	43.9	21.2	27.4	27.5
1966	50.0	28.5	128.2	124.0	104.2	52.0	43.5	28.5	50.1	48.6	41.2	19.0	26.9	26.3
1965	47.4	28.4	123.9	119.9	99.4	47.3	41.9	28.4	48.5	47.0	39.4	17.5	27.6	25.3
1964	45.2	26.5	119.6	114.9	92.9	42.6	40.1	26.5	46.5	44.8	36.6	15.6	26.4	24.6
1963	42.8	24.7	116.2	111.3	87.2	38.7	37.8	24.7	45.3	43.5	34.9	14.6	25.7	23.8
1962	40.6	22.6	110.9	105.9	82.0	35.1	36.4	22.6	43.3	41.4	32.8	12.9	25.2	23.1
1961	39.1	21.3	107.3	102.3	78.2	31.5	35.5	21.3	42.0	40.2	31.5	11.6	24.6	22.2
1960	37.3	20.9	103.9	98.3	73.3	25.6	34.2	20.9	40.6	38.6	29.5	9.7	24.5	21.2
1959	36.5	19.7	98.1	92.0	67.0	20.4	33.5	19.7	38.3	36.1	27.0	7.8	24.4	19.9
1958	34.5	18.7	95.3	88.5	62.4	16.2	31.7	18.7	37.3	34.8	25.3	6.3	23.8	18.8
1957	33.9	18.4	94.0	86.7	59.5	12.4	31.2	18.4	37.1	34.5	24.4	5.1	24.9	18.1
1956	32.1	17.3	89.4	81.5	54.0	8.3	29.8	17.3	35.4	32.7	22.3	3.6	24.7	16.9
1955	29.6	15.6	81.4	73.1	47.0	4.8	28.0	15.6	33.1	30.2	20.4	2.3	23.5	15.4
1954	26.9	14.0	75.0	65.9	39.1	1.9	25.7	14.0	31.1	27.8	17.5	.8	22.9	14.2
1953	25.0	12.3	72.5	61.6	34.0	1.0	24.3	12.3	31.0	26.9	15.8	.5	23.4	13.2
1952	22.9	10.7	65.9	53.7	26.5	.5	22.3	10.7	28.8	24.2	12.8	.2	22.4	11.7
1951	21.2	9.5	60.9	46.9	21.3	.1	20.8	9.5	27.1	21.7	10.7	(Z)	21.7	11.0
1950	19.6	8.1	54.5	37.5	15.6	--------	19.4	8.1	24.3	17.7	8.2	--------	20.1	9.8

Year	Contributions — Private and public employees — Total [7]	Life insurance and death [1]	Accidental death and dismemberment	Health benefits — Hospitalization [2][3]	Surgical and regular medical [2]	Major medical [4]	Private employees only — Temporary disability [5]	Retirement [6]	Benefits paid — Private and public employees — Total [7]	Life insurance and death [1]	Accidental death and dismemberment	Health benefits — Hospitalization [2][3]	Surgical and regular medical [2]	Major medical [4]	Private employees only — Temporary disability [5]	Retirement [6]
	84	85	86	87	88	89	90	91	92	93	94	95	96	97	98	99
1970	34,678	3,523	224	7,569	3,998	2,310	2,924	14,000	25,799	2,435	151	7,344	3,564	2,415	2,405	7,360
1969	30,481	3,224	190	6,341	3,363	1,890	2,582	12,780	22,119	2,386	129	6,128	2,934	1,922	2,070	6,450
1968	26,720	2,937	169	5,539	2,915	1,621	2,244	11,170	19,154	2,137	121	5,289	2,468	1,658	1,847	5,530
1967	23,367	2,538	142	4,703	2,552	1,294	1,845	10,180	16,389	1,899	101	4,526	2,142	1,306	1,506	4,790
1966	21,651	2,376	131	4,547	2,300	1,195	1,722	9,250	14,939	1,707	97	4,312	1,980	1,136	1,436	4,190
1965	19,892	2,233	116	4,333	2,109	1,078	1,547	8,360	13,544	1,550	90	4,161	1,848	1,004	1,310	3,520
1964	17,635	2,044	99	3,885	1,876	965	1,375	7,280	12,012	1,430	88	3,731	1,642	869	1,201	2,990
1963	15,861	1,867	92	3,472	1,684	837	1,341	6,420	10,831	1,342	83	3,312	1,472	752	1,183	2,590
1962	14,744	1,667	80	3,159	1,596	753	1,297	6,030	9,949	1,237	69	3,005	1,411	667	1,129	2,330
1961	13,472	1,557	75	2,834	1,440	651	1,205	5,610	8,798	1,122	58	2,676	1,244	562	1,036	1,970
1960	12,522	1,416	70	2,505	1,282	470	1,171	5,490	7,805	1,018	47	2,355	1,116	427	1,030	1,720
1959	11,707	1,292	66	2,230	1,187	357	1,090	5,360	6,992	919	43	2,108	1,024	332	952	1,540
1958	10,513	1,179	61	1,945	1,076	266	1,041	4,820	6,267	851	42	1,893	929	233	894	1,290
1957	10,036	1,077	57	1,806	1,021	169	1,017	4,720	5,589	779	37	1,714	877	131	891	1,140
1956	8,905	1,002	50	1,603	898	94	908	4,225	4,823	650	31	1,495	758	67	818	1,000
1955	7,852	881	43	1,385	770	39	854	3,840	4,071	582	26	1,242	637	24	710	850
1954	6,985	732	34	1,221	684	18	781	3,515	3,527	509	25	1,080	553	10	640	710
1953	6,626	694	31	1,071	593	--------	762	3,475	3,179	463	22	954	492	--------	628	620
1952	5,673	620	27	881	493	--------	683	2,970	2,743	405	20	791	411	--------	596	520
1951	4,983	524	23	727	412	--------	637	2,660	2,382	363	17	660	352	--------	542	450
1950	3,937	480	18	562	294	--------	502	2,080	1,813	310	16	478	231	--------	408	370

Z   Less than 50,000 or less than 0.05 percent.

[1] Includes group and wholesale life insurance but excludes Servicemen's Group Life Insurance program.

[2] Includes persons covered by group comprehensive major-medical insurance as well as those with basic benefits.

[3] Includes private hospital plans written in compliance with State temporary disability insurance law in California.

[4] Group supplementary and comprehensive major-medical insurance written by commercial insurance companies.

[5] Includes private plans written in compliance with State temporary disability insurance laws in California, New Jersey, and New York, and formal sick-leave plans, but excludes credit accident and health insurance. Starting with 1966, temporary disability coverage estimates exclude long-term disability policies.

[6] Includes pay-as-you-go and deferred profit-sharing plans, plans for non-profit organizations, union pension plans, and railroad plans supplementing the Federal railroad retirement program. Excludes plans for the self-employed. Retirement coverage estimates exclude annuitants.

[7] Includes data for supplemental unemployment insurance benefits, not shown separately.

Series H 70–114. Employee-Benefit Plans—Estimated Coverage, Contributions, and Benefits: 1950 to 1970—Con.

Covered employees as percent of all wage and salary workers[2] — Private and public employees (cols. 100–105), Private employees only (cols. 106–107). Contributions as percent of total wages and salaries[2] — Private and public employees (cols. 108–112), Private employees only (cols. 113–114).

Year	Life insurance and death[1]	Accidental death and dismemberment	Health benefits: Hospitalization[2][3]	Surgical[2]	Regular medical[2]	Major medical[4]	Temporary disability[5]	Retirement[6]	Life insurance and death[1]	Accidental death and dismemberment	Health benefits: Hospitalization[2][3]	Surgical and regular medical[2]	Major medical[4]	Temporary disability[5]	Retirement[6]
	100	101	102	103	104	105	106	107	108	109	110	111	112	113	114
1970	69.4	52.1	80.2	79.2	71.1	35.8	50.7	48.3	0.67	0.04	1.45	0.77	0.44	0.69	3.28
1969	65.3	49.1	77.2	76.0	66.2	33.1	50.2	47.1	.66	.04	1.29	.69	.38	.64	3.15
1968	66.9	46.7	75.7	73.6	63.9	31.6	49.3	46.8	.66	.04	1.23	.65	.36	.61	3.03
1967	65.2	43.4	74.3	72.5	62.6	30.2	47.1	47.2	.62	.03	1.16	.63	.32	.55	3.03
1966	63.4	41.5	73.0	70.8	60.1	27.7	46.9	45.9	.62	.03	1.20	.61	.31	.54	2.92
1965	64.2	43.5	74.3	72.0	60.3	26.8	50.4	46.2	.64	.03	1.25	.61	.31	.54	2.89
1964	63.8	42.1	73.8	71.2	58.3	24.8	49.9	46.5	.63	.03	1.21	.58	.30	.51	2.70
1963	61.5	40.2	73.5	70.7	56.7	23.7	49.6	45.9	.62	.03	1.16	.56	.28	.53	2.55
1962	60.4	37.4	71.5	68.5	54.5	21.2	49.4	45.3	.59	.03	1.11	.56	.26	.54	2.51
1961	60.4	36.2	71.3	68.4	53.6	19.7	49.4	44.6	.58	.03	1.06	.54	.24	.53	2.48
1960	58.2	35.5	68.9	65.5	50.2	16.5	49.0	42.4	.54	.03	.96	.49	.18	.53	2.47
1959	58.1	34.1	66.4	62.6	46.6	13.5	49.5	40.4	.52	.03	.90	.48	.14	.51	2.52
1958	56.5	33.3	66.5	62.0	44.9	11.2	49.7	39.2	.51	.03	.85	.47	.12	.53	2.45
1957	54.4	32.1	64.6	60.1	42.5	8.9	50.4	36.6	.47	.02	.79	.45	.07	.53	2.45
1956	52.4	30.4	62.2	57.5	39.2	6.3	50.2	34.3	.46	.02	.73	.41	.04	.51	2.38
1955	50.7	28.3	60.0	54.7	37.0	4.0	49.2	32.2	.44	.02	.69	.38	.02	.49	2.23
1954	48.2	26.3	58.3	52.2	32.8	1.5	49.7	30.8	.39	.02	.65	.37	.01	.48	2.19
1953	44.4	22.5	56.7	49.2	28.9	.9	49.1	27.7	.36	.02	.57	.32	-------	.44	2.17
1952	41.7	20.0	53.8	45.2	23.9	.4	48.2	25.2	.35	.02	.50	.28	-------	.42	2.00
1951	39.5	18.0	51.4	41.2	20.3	(Z)	47.2	23.9	.33	.01	.45	.26	-------	.45	1.85
1950	38.9	16.2	48.7	35.5	16.4	-------	46.2	22.5	.34	.01	.40	.21	-------	.40	1.67

See footnotes at end of p. 343.

Series H 115–124. Protection Against Income Loss From Short-Term Sickness: 1948 to 1970

[In millions of dollars, except percent. "Short-term sickness" refers to short-term or temporary nonwork-connected disability (lasting not more than 6 months) and the first 6 months of long-term disability]

Year	Income loss from short-term sickness	Protection provided: Total	Percent of loss	Individual insurance	Benefits provided by protection: Total	Group benefits provided as protection — Workers in private employment: Total	Private cash sickness insurance and self-insurance[1]	Publicly operated cash sickness funds	Sick leave	Sick leave for government employees
	115	116	117	118	119	120	121	122	123	124
1970	16,741	5,791.2	34.6	693.7	5,097.5	2,893.5	1,442.9	410.6	1,040	2,204
1969	15,227	5,020.3	33.0	635.4	4,384.9	2,507.9	1,221.2	373.7	913	1,877
1968	14,528	4,591.1	31.6	609.1	3,982.0	2,213.0	1,102.8	320.2	790	1,769
1967	12,836	3,864.1	30.1	527.4	3,336.7	1,803.7	850.0	284.7	669	1,533
1966	12,205	3,616.9	29.6	512.9	3,104.0	1,709.0	829.8	273.2	606	1,395
1965	11,278	3,330.8	29.5	482.6	2,848.2	1,579.2	757.1	269.1	553	1,269
1964	10,248	3,085.8	30.1	483.9	2,601.9	1,464.9	708.5	264.4	492	1,137
1963	10,178	2,984.4	29.3	447.2	2,537.2	1,427.2	670.3	243.9	513	1,110
1962	9,622	2,757.7	28.7	418.5	2,339.2	1,341.2	668.2	212.0	461	998
1961	8,639	2,556.8	29.6	425.9	2,130.9	1,230.9	625.7	195.2	410	900
1960 *	8,555	2,422.3	28.3	392.8	2,029.5	1,202.5	638.4	172.1	392	827
1959	7,724	2,229.8	28.9	389.6	1,840.2	1,115.2	600.5	163.7	351	725
1958	7,458	2,084.5	27.9	353.4	1,731.1	1,035.1	555.7	141.4	338	696
1957	7,363	1,952.6	26.5	307.2	1,645.4	1,018.4	567.2	127.2	324	627
1956	7,031	1,800.3	25.6	278.0	1,522.3	931.3	524.5	113.8	293	591
1955	6,546	1,614.8	24.7	250.0	1,364.8	819.8	442.4	109.4	268	545
1954	6,094	1,473.2	24.2	230.0	1,243.2	743.2	399.1	103.1	241	500
1953	6,144	1,409.7	22.9	209.0	1,200.7	718.7	397.2	90.5	231	482
1952	5,814	1,300.6	22.4	177.0	1,123.6	670.6	382.1	74.5	214	453
1951	5,473	1,149.7	21.0	157.0	992.7	602.8	343.8	60.9	198	390
1950	4,795	938.9	19.6	153.0	785.9	470.9	230.8	63.1	177	315
1949	4,424	846.1	19.1	150.0	696.1	396.1	172.0	62.1	162	300
1948	4,568	756.9	16.6	141.0	615.9	359.9	145.8	57.1	157	256

* Denotes first year for which figures include Alaska and Hawaii.

[1] Includes a small but undetermined amount of group disability insurance benefits paid to government workers and to self-employed persons through farm, trade, or professional associations.

Series H 125–171. Monthly Cash Benefits and Beneficiaries Under Social Insurance and Related Programs, by Risk and Program: 1940 to 1970

[Includes benefits to dependents where applicable. Refunds of employee contributions excluded for public employee retirement systems. Disability data exclude payments for medical care]

Series No.	Risk and program	1970	1969	1968	1967	1966	1965	1964	1963	1962	1961	1960
	AMOUNT OF BENEFITS (mil. dol.)											
125	Total	54,886	45,682	41,971	37,243	34,554	32,151	29,571	28,342	26,806	25,790	22,311
126	Old-age retirement	29,357	24,710	22,726	19,822	18,276	16,787	15,121	14,239	13,239	11,867	10,755
127	OASDHI [1]	21,075	17,698	16,533	14,361	13,417	12,542	11,281	10,795	10,162	9,032	8,196
128	Railroad retirement	1,113	966	936	817	739	705	667	654	638	617	594
129	Federal Government retirement [2]	4,550	3,787	3,285	2,896	2,549	2,130	1,891	1,628	1,396	1,241	1,076
130	State and local government retirement	2,615	2,250	1,960	1,735	1,555	1,390	1,260	1,135	1,011	940	845
131	Veterans' programs [3]	4	9	11	13	16	20	22	27	32	37	43
132	Disability	10,959	9,775	8,725	8,042	7,622	7,041	6,473	6,187	5,851	5,415	4,860
133	OASDHI [1]	3,067	2,542	2,294	1,939	1,781	1,573	1,309	1,210	1,105	887	568
134	Workmen's compensation	1,664	1,519	1,374	1,284	1,170	1,074	1,007	932	879	804	755
135	Veterans' programs [3]	3,931	3,706	3,265	3,198	3,173	3,026	2,846	2,819	2,724	2,647	2,530
136	Railroad retirement	219	193	188	172	165	149	162	159	156	150	147
137	Federal Government [2]	1,057	905	813	747	682	596	553	500	457	425	397
138	State and local government retirement	300	255	220	195	175	155	140	125	114	105	95
139	State temporary disability insurance [4]	665	598	531	472	443	426	410	393	365	342	311
140	Railroad temporary disability insurance	56	57	41	35	39	41	46	49	51	55	57
141	Survivorship—Monthly benefits only	10,266	8,774	8,192	7,015	6,620	5,872	5,176	4,869	4,566	4,150	3,672
142	OASDHI [1]	7,428	6,219	5,840	4,854	4,613	3,979	3,416	3,216	3,011	2,659	2,316
143	Railroad retirement	424	367	351	308	291	278	255	244	234	217	201
144	Federal Government retirement [2]	445	369	322	288	242	199	181	161	137	123	110
145	State and local government retirement	220	195	175	165	140	125	115	105	92	85	75
146	Veterans' programs [3]	1,545	1,439	1,340	1,245	1,184	1,150	1,074	1,018	977	956	865
147	Workmen's compensation [5]	205	185	165	155	150	140	135	125	115	110	105
148	Unemployment [6]	4,304	2,423	2,328	2,364	2,031	2,452	2,801	3,047	3,150	4,358	3,025
149	State unemployment insurance [7]	4,135	2,262	2,151	2,183	1,852	2,283	2,671	2,926	3,013	4,156	2,867
150	Railroad unemployment insurance	39	37	40	41	39	60	78	99	133	202	158
151	Veterans' allowances [8]											(Z)
	NUMBER OF BENEFICIARIES (1,000) [9]											
	Old-age retirement:											
152	OASDHI [1]	16,870	16,430	16,062	15,665	14,670	13,918	13,589	13,038	12,248	11,128	10,310
153	Railroad retirement	553	550	542	531	525	498	495	489	474	464	444
154	Federal Government retirement [2]	1,120	1,044	975	900	832	747	687	618	550	497	442
155	State and local government retirement	1,060	978	903	832	775	725	685	645	600	575	535
156	Veterans' programs [3]	3	6	7	9	11	14	17	21	24	29	33
	Disability:											
157	OASDHI [1]	2,573	2,416	2,257	2,057	1,883	1,654	1,519	1,380	1,161	892	543
158	Veterans' programs [3]	3,178	3,155	3,157	3,173	3,190	3,203	3,180	3,160	3,126	3,078	2,976
159	Railroad retirement	95	97	99	100	101	103	102	101	100	99	97
160	Federal Government [2]	333	315	298	287	274	257	244	231	219	205	192
161	State and local government retirement	95	87	80	75	72	69	66	63	61	58	55
162	State temporary disability insurance [4]	181	172	164	157	151	149	146	142	134	129	121
163	Railroad temporary disability insurance	25	25	20	20	22	24	25	27	25	27	28
	Survivorship—Monthly beneficiaries only:											
164	OASDHI [1]	6,369	6,115	5,824	5,511	5,228	4,681	4,459	4,227	3,966	3,701	3,446
165	Railroad retirement	324	319	315	306	295	288	283	275	265	259	251
166	Federal Government retirement [10]	307	291	276	258	242	227	212	195	181	167	154
167	State and local government retirement [10]	125	115	110	108	98	92	89	85	78	76	70
168	Veterans' programs [3]	2,284	2,176	2,253	2,041	1,970	1,900	1,815	1,707	1,596	1,493	1,262
	Unemployment:											
169	State unemployment insurance [7]	1,617	976	987	1,057	933	1,189	1,449	1,623	1,729	2,582	1,723
170	Railroad unemployment insurance	18	17	21	26	23	31	39	50	66	96	74
171	Veterans' allowances											2

Series No.	Risk and program	1959	1958	1957	1956	1955	1954	1953	1952	1951	1950
	AMOUNT OF BENEFITS (mil. dol.)										
125	Total	20,574	19,704	15,617	13,097	11,971	10,996	8,795	7,619	6,737	6,235
126	Old-age retirement	9,916	8,514	7,503	5,965	5,157	3,983	3,325	2,589	2,201	1,423
127	OASDHI [1]	7,607	6,474	5,688	4,361	3,748	2,698	2,175	1,539	1,321	651
128	Railroad retirement	523	449	420	380	336	325	282	267	187	177
129	Federal Government retirement [2]	966	849	725	628	538	466	414	370	346	287
130	State and local government retirement	770	685	606	525	460	415	368	325	293	250
131	Veterans' programs [3]	50	57	64	71	76	79	86	88	54	58
132	Disability	4,528	4,087	3,590	3,345	3,185	2,980	2,850	2,632	2,495	2,441
133	OASDHI [1]	457	249	57	----						
134	Workmen's compensation	700	647	617	577	521	498	491	460	416	360
135	Veterans' programs [3]	2,425	2,326	2,116	2,031	1,982	1,842	1,754	1,634	1,593	1,674
136	Railroad retirement	134	121	118	111	103	104	92	94	82	77
137	Federal Government [2]	374	343	309	298	280	256	248	211	202	189
138	State and local government retirement	85	76	68	62	55	45	35	30	28	24
139	State temporary disability insurance [4]	287	273	254	216	193	186	185	168	148	89
140	Railroad temporary disability insurance	66	52	51	50	52	49	45	35	26	28
141	Survivorship—Monthly benefits only	3,325	2,893	2,611	2,247	2,068	1,741	1,569	1,354	1,179	902
142	OASDHI [1]	2,063	1,720	1,521	1,244	1,108	880	744	592	507	277
143	Railroad retirement	181	154	144	133	122	93	83	74	50	44
144	Federal Government retirement [2]	97	76	61	51	41	34	27	20	14	8
145	State and local government retirement	65	59	51	45	40	35	32	30	29	26
146	Veterans' programs [3]	819	794	749	699	688	629	613	573	519	492
147	Workmen's compensation [5]	100	90	85	75	70	70	70	65	60	55
148	Unemployment [6]	2,805	4,210	1,913	1,540	1,560	2,292	1,051	1,044	862	1,468
149	State unemployment insurance [7]	2,563	3,899	1,766	1,409	1,379	2,027	962	998	840	1,373
150	Railroad unemployment insurance	225	229	94	70	93	157	47	42	20	60
151	Veterans' allowances [8]	17	82	53	61	88	108	42	4	2	35

See footnotes at end of table.

Series H 125–171. Monthly Cash Benefits and Beneficiaries Under Social Insurance and Related Programs, by Risk and Program: 1940 to 1970—Con.

Series No.	Risk and program	1959	1958	1957	1956	1955	1954	1953	1952	1951	1950
	NUMBER OF BENEFICIARIES (1,000) [9]										
	Old-age retirement:										
152	OASDHI [1]	9,631	8,738	7,623	6,191	5,443	4,590	3,889	3,187	2,757	1,918
153	Railroad retirement	405	383	364	347	329	308	289	269	182	175
154	Federal Government retirement [2]	402	370	332	297	271	249	232	218	210	184
155	State and local government retirement	505	465	424	375	335	310	280	260	240	222
156	Veterans' programs [3]	39	44	50	56	60	66	72	79	51	54
	Disability:										
157	OASDHI [1]	378	205	124							
158	Veterans' programs [3]	2,895	2,812	2,746	2,682	2,609	2,524	2,434	2,339	2,223	2,314
159	Railroad retirement	96	93	91	90	87	85	82	80	79	76
160	Federal Government [2]	181	170	157	154	147	139	130	117	107	99
161	State and local government retirement	51	47	44	43	42	41	40	38	35	32
162	State temporary disability insurance [4]	119	116	114	101	96	103	102	93	89	55
163	Railroad temporary disability insurance	29	31	31	30	32	32	33	32	29	31
	Survivorship—Monthly beneficiaries only:										
164	OASDHI [1]	3,189	2,912	2,633	2,282	2,097	1,892	1,688	1,485	1,287	1,094
165	Railroad retirement	242	231	221	211	197	167	158	150	147	136
166	Federal Government retirement [10]	140	109	95	83	72	62	50	40	30	18
167	State and local government retirement [10]	63	61	55	53	50	48	46	44	42	40
168	Veterans' programs [3]	1,210	1,188	1,184	1,176	1,154	1,130	1,089	1,042	1,012	991
	Unemployment:										
169	State unemployment insurance [7]	1,763	2,772	1,250	1,037	1,100	1,615	812	874	797	1,305
170	Railroad unemployment insurance	82	130	60	48	63	111	40	43	29	76
171	Veterans' allowances	14	67	45	51	72	89	34	15	3	32

Series No.	Risk and program	1949	1948	1947	1946	1945	1944	1943	1942	1941	1940
	AMOUNT OF BENEFITS (mil. dol.)										
125	**Total**	6,468	5,194	5,314	5,684	2,539	1,562	1,329	1,511	1,432	1,504
126	Old-age retirement	1,227	1,035	890	739	592	516	457	418	378	331
127	OASDHI [1]	437	352	288	222	148	113	93	76	51	17
128	Railroad retirement	169	150	139	118	106	99	95	92	88	83
129	Federal Government retirement [2]	356	278	232	185	141	122	110	104	104	103
130	State and local government retirement	203	190	175	158	143	134	125	115	107	103
131	Veterans' programs [3]	62	65	56	56	53	48	34	31	28	24
132	Disability	2,176	2,131	2,019	1,537	954	701	562	536	506	477
134	Workmen's compensation	329	309	280	250	241	225	203	185	157	129
135	Veterans' programs [3]	1,630	1,646	1,620	1,213	644	409	297	294	293	294
136	Railroad retirement	72	58	39	31	31	31	31	31	31	31
137	Federal Government [2]	35	31	25	22	19	17	16	15	14	13
138	State and local government retirement	22	20	18	16	14	14	12	11	11	10
139	State temporary disability insurance [4]	58	36	26	5	5	5				
140	Railroad temporary disability insurance	30	31	11							
141	Survivorship—Monthly benefits only	794	696	619	529	418	278	229	207	189	162
142	OASDHI [1]	197	172	149	128	100	73	55	40	24	6
143	Railroad retirement	39	36	19	2	2	2	2	2	2	1
144	Federal Government retirement [2]	4	1	(Z)	(Z)	(Z)	(Z)	(Z)	(Z)	(Z)	(Z)
145	State and local government retirement	25	23	22	21	20	19	18	18	17	16
146	Veterans' programs [3]	477	414	383	334	254	144	116	111	112	106
147	Workmen's compensation [5]	52	50	46	44	42	40	38	36	34	32
148	Unemployment	2,271	1,332	1,786	2,879	575	67	81	350	359	535
149	State unemployment insurance [7]	1,737	793	776	1,095	446	62	80	344	344	519
150	Railroad unemployment insurance	104	29	39	40	2	1	1	6	15	16
151	Veterans' allowances [8]	430	510	971	1,744	127	4				
	NUMBER OF BENEFICIARIES (1,000) [9]										
	Old-age retirement:										
152	OASDHI [1]	1,575	1,295	1,068	843	592	463	386	323	221	77
153	Railroad retirement	164	156	147	140	129	122	117	114	113	102
154	Federal Government retirement [2]	209	168	148	124	101	90	86	87	84	81
155	State and local government retirement	200	190	180	167	155	146	136	127	117	113
156	Veterans' programs [3]	58	61	63	64	60	54	49	45	39	34
	Disability:										
158	Veterans' programs [3]	2,256	2,254	2,292	2,067	1,084	759	573	579	580	576
159	Railroad retirement	70	63	51	39	39	39	40	40	40	39
160	Federal Government [2]	40	36	32	27	24	21	20	18	18	16
161	State and local government retirement	29	27	25	23	21	20	18	16	15	14
162	State temporary disability insurance [4]	38	30	26	6	5					
163	Railroad temporary disability insurance	34	33	23							
	Survivorship—Monthly beneficiaries only:										
164	OASDHI [1]	984	872	767	661	534	403	304	217	128	36
165	Railroad retirement	122	102	41	5	4	4	4	4	4	3
166	Federal Government retirement [10]	9	2	(Z)	(Z)	(Z)	(Z)	(Z)	(Z)	(Z)	(Z)
167	State and local government retirement [10]	38	36	35	34	32	30	29	28	26	25
168	Veterans' programs [3]	960	934	897	790	537	337	315	317	319	323
	Unemployment:										
169	State unemployment insurance [7]	1,666	821	852	1,150	465	79	116	542	621	982
170	Railroad unemployment insurance	120	38	53	53	3	1	2	12	22	42
171	Veterans' allowances	388	435	761	1,359	89	10				

Z Less than $500,000 or less than 50 beneficiaries. [1] Old-age, survivors, disability, and health insurance. [2] Includes Federal civil service and other contributory systems and Federal noncontributory systems. Prior to 1954, retirement data include unknown amount and number of disability and survivor payments. [3] Retirement data are for veterans of the Civil War, the Indian Wars, the Spanish-American War, the Boxer Rebellion, and the Philippine Insurrection; beginning October 1951, includes all service pensions. Disability data include pensions and compensation, and subsistence payments to disabled veterans undergoing training. Survivor data include special allowances for survivors of veterans who did not qualify under OASDHI. [4] Cash benefits payable in Calif., N.J., N.Y., R.I. and P.R., under public and private plans. Beneficiary data exclude private-plan beneficiaries in N.J. [5] Small but unknown amount of lump-sum death payments included with monthly survivor payments. [6] Beginning 1962, includes training allowances not shown separately. [7] Includes payments made by the States as agents of the Federal Government under the Federal employees' unemployment compensation program and under the Ex-Servicemen's Compensation Act of 1958 and payments under extended unemployment insurance programs; beginning 1961, includes program in P. R. and also payments under the Automotive Products Trade Act of 1965 and the Trade Expansion Act of 1962, from January 1970. [8] Under the Servicemen's Readjustment Act of 1944 (terminated July 1949) and the Veterans' Readjustment Assistance Act of 1952 (terminated January 1960). Amount but not number includes self-employment allowances. [9] For OASDHI, average monthly number; for the railroad retirement program, public employee retirement systems, and the veterans' programs, number on rolls June 30; for State unemployment and temporary disability insurance and for veterans' unemployment allowances, average weekly number; for railroad unemployment and temporary disability insurance, average number during 14-day registration period. Beneficiary data for workmen's compensation not available. [10] For Federal military retirement programs and for State and local government retirement systems, number represents families.

Series H 172–185. Old-Age, Survivors, Disability, and Health Insurance—Covered Workers, Earnings, and Selected Trust Fund Transactions: 1937 to 1970

Year	Living covered workers at beginning of year [1]		New entrants into covered employment [3]	Workers with taxable earnings during year [4]	Taxable earnings				Employers reporting taxable wages	Contribution rates	
	With insured status [2]	With uninsured status			Amount	Percent of total earnings [5]	Maximum taxable per worker [6]	Average per worker		Employers and employees (each)	Self-employed
	172	173	174	175	176	177	178	179	180	181	182
	Millions	Millions	1,000	1,000	Mil. dol.		Dol.	Dol.	1,000	Percent	Percent
1970	106.8	26.7	[7] 4,400	[7] 93,500	[7] 418,200	78.0	7,800	4,473	[7] 5,380	4.80	6.90
1969	104.0	26.8	5,160	92,946	405,617	79.9	7,800	4,364	5,420	4.80	6.90
1968	101.2	26.7	4,826	89,377	375,865	81.7	7,800	4,205	5,470	4.40	6.40
1967	98.3	26.7	4,526	87,035	330,003	78.1	6,600	3,792	5,520	4.40	6.40
1966	95.8	25.5	5,076	84,602	312,561	80.0	6,600	3,694	5,540	4.20	6.15
1965	93.6	24.5	4,623	80,681	250,727	71.3	4,800	3,108	5,590	3.625	5.4
1964	92.0	23.6	3,887	77,432	236,396	72.8	4,800	3,053	5,510	3.625	5.4
1963	90.4	22.9	3,520	75,537	225,548	74.6	4,800	2,986	5,450	3.625	5.4
1962	89.1	22.1	3,358	74,285	219,084	75.8	4,800	2,949	5,370	3.125	4.7
1961	85.4	24.0	2,993	72,819	209,610	77.4	4,800	2,879	5,320	3.0	4.5
1960	79.7	27.7	3,126	72,530	206,981	78.0	4,800	2,854	5,270	3.0	4.5
1959	78.9	26.4	3,183	71,695	202,314	79.3	4,800	2,822	5,200	2.5	3.75
1958	77.0	26.8	2,452	69,774	180,729	76.4	4,200	2,590	5,100	2.25	3.375
1957	74.3	27.1	3,383	70,590	181,382	77.5	4,200	2,570	5,100	2.25	3.375
1956	71.4	27.2	3,655	67,612	170,738	78.8	4,200	2,525	5,100	2.0	3.0
1955	70.6	24.1	4,756	65,203	157,541	80.3	4,200	2,416	5,050	2.0	3.0
1954	71.0	22.1	2,357	59,610	133,524	77.7	3,600	2,240	4,350	2.0	3.0
1953	68.2	22.6	3,094	60,839	135,865	78.5	3,600	2,233	4,350	1.5	2.25
1952	62.8	25.2	3,495	59,576	128,642	80.5	3,600	2,159	4,450	1.5	2.25
1951	59.8	22.9	5,999	58,120	120,767	81.1	3,600	2,078	4,440	1.5	2.25
1950	45.7	35.1	2,520	48,283	87,498	79.7	3,000	1,812	3,345	1.5	-----
1949	44.8	34.6	1,958	46,796	81,808	81.8	3,000	1,748	3,316	1.0	-----
1948	43.4	34.0	2,635	49,018	84,122	82.3	3,000	1,716	3,298	1.0	-----
1947	41.8	33.4	2,685	48,908	78,372	84.8	3,000	1,602	3,246	1.0	-----
1946	40.3	32.1	3,078	48,845	69,088	87.2	3,000	1,414	3,017	1.0	-----
1945	38.6	31.0	3,477	46,392	62,945	88.0	3,000	1,357	2,614	1.0	-----
1944	34.9	30.5	4,691	46,296	64,426	87.8	3,000	1,392	2,469	1.0	-----
1943	31.2	27.3	7,337	47,656	62,423	89.6	3,000	1,310	2,394	1.0	-----
1942	27.5	23.4	7,965	46,363	52,939	90.9	3,000	1,142	2,655	1.0	-----
1941	24.9	19.9	6,436	40,976	41,848	92.0	3,000	1,021	2,646	1.0	-----
1940	22.9	17.8	4,430	35,393	32,974	92.4	3,000	932	2,500	1.0	-----
1939	-----	-----	4,450	33,751	29,745	92.3	3,000	881	2,366	1.0	-----
1938	-----	-----	3,930	31,822	26,502	93.0	3,000	833	2,239	1.0	-----
1937	-----	-----	32,904	32,904	29,615	92.0	3,000	900	2,421	1.0	-----

Year	Contributions and transfers [8]	Total benefits paid [9]	Trust fund assets at end of year [10]	Year	Contributions and transfers [8]	Total benefits paid [9]	Trust fund assets at end of year [10]	Year	Contributions and transfers [8]	Total benefits paid [9]	Trust fund assets at end of year [10]
	183	184	185		183	184	185		183	184	185
	Mil. dol.	Mil. dol.	Mil. dol.		Mil. dol.	Mil. dol.	Mil. dol.		Mil. dol.	Mil. dol.	Mil. dol.
1970	43,209	38,982	41,458	1958	8,531	8,576	23,243	1946	1,295	378	8,150
1969	38,988	33,371	36,887	1957	7,527	7,404	23,042				
1968	34,352	30,651	31,233	1956	6,172	5,715	22,519	1945	1,285	274	7,121
1967	30,598	25,967	27,735					1944	1,316	209	6,005
1966	24,912	21,070	23,374	1955	5,713	4,968	21,663	1943	1,239	166	4,820
				1954	5,163	3,670	20,576	1942	1,012	131	3,688
1965	17,205	18,311	19,841	1953	3,945	3,006	18,707	1941	789	88	2,762
1964	16,843	16,223	21,172	1952	3,819	2,194	17,442				
1963	15,640	15,427	20,715	1951	3,367	1,885	15,540	1940	325	35	2,031
1962	13,105	14,461	20,705					1939	580	14	1,724
1961	12,323	12,749	22,162	1950	2,671	961	13,721	1938	360	10	1,132
				1949	1,670	667	11,816	1937	765	1	766
1960	11,876	11,245	22,613	1948	1,688	556	10,722				
1959	8,943	10,298	21,966	1947	1,558	466	9,360				

[1] Estimated number of persons who had covered employment at any time during the period 1937 to year shown; not adjusted to reflect effect of (a) provisions that coordinate the OASDHI and railroad retirement programs and (b) wage credits for military service. Only partially adjusted to eliminate duplicate count of persons with taxable earnings reported on more than 1 account number; effect of such duplication is substantially less significant for the insured than for the uninsured.
[2] Fully or currently insured.
[3] Workers with first taxable earnings under program in specified year. There have been 166.3 million different persons reported with taxable earnings during 1937–70.
[4] Relates to wage and salary workers for 1937–50. Beginning 1951, includes self-employment.
[5] Total earnings in covered employment, including estimated amounts above the taxable limit.

[6] Beginning 1951, includes reported taxable net earnings of self-employed persons; amount taxable may not exceed amounts specified above from a combination of wages and self-employed earnings.
[7] Preliminary estimate.
[8] Includes insurance contributions of employers, employees, and self-employed, adjusted for refunds, and transfers from general funds to meet cost arising from noncontributory military wage credits, special age-72 cash benefits, and hospital insurance coverage of elderly persons not insured for cash benefits. Includes premiums paid by enrollees for supplementary medical insurance and Federal matching funds.
[9] Starting 1966, includes hospital and medical insurance benefits under Medicare and rehabilitation services.
[10] Before 1940, represents operations of old-age reserve account.

Series H 186–196. Old Age, Survivors, Disability, and Health Insurance—Estimated Paid Employment and Coverage Status: 1940 to 1970

[In millions, except percent]

Year	Total paid employment	Total, covered	Percent of paid employment	Covered [1] Wage and salary	Covered [1] Self-employed [2]	Total, not covered	Excluded by Federal law Federal civilian employment	Excluded by Federal law Nonfarm self-employed	Excluded by Federal law Domestic service	Excluded by Federal law Other [3]	Permitted by Federal law [4]
	186	187	188	189	190	191	192	193	194	195	196
1970	80.6	72.1	89.5	66.2	5.9	8.5	2.5	.9	.5	1.2	3.4
1969	80.5	72.0	89.4	66.0	6.0	8.5	2.5	.9	.5	1.2	3.4
1968	78.6	70.7	89.9	64.7	6.0	7.9	2.5	.9	.5	1.1	2.9
1967	76.9	68.9	89.6	63.0	6.0	8.0	2.5	.9	.7	1.2	2.6
1966	76.0	68.0	89.5	62.0	6.0	8.0	2.4	1.0	.7	1.2	2.6
1965	73.6	65.6	89.1	59.4	6.2	8.0	2.2	1.0	.9	1.4	2.3
1964	71.7	63.3	88.3	57.1	6.2	8.5	2.2	1.1	.9	1.4	2.4
1963	70.2	61.9	88.2	55.6	6.3	8.4	2.1	1.2	1.0	1.5	2.7
1962	69.3	61.0	88.0	54.6	6.4	8.2	2.1	1.2	.9	1.5	2.7
1961	67.9	59.7	87.9	53.0	6.8	8.1	2.1	1.3	1.0	1.3	2.6
1960 *	67.5	59.4	88.0	52.6	6.8	8.1	2.1	1.3	1.0	1.2	2.5
1959	66.6	58.5	87.8	51.6	6.9	8.1	2.0	1.3	.9	1.3	2.6
1958	64.9	56.8	87.5	50.1	6.7	8.1	2.0	1.3	.9	1.4	2.5
1957	66.0	57.4	87.0	50.6	6.8	8.6	2.1	1.2	.9	1.4	2.6
1956	66.0	57.2	86.7	50.3	6.9	8.8	1.9	1.2	.9	1.6	2.8
1955	64.5	55.0	85.3	48.3	6.7	9.5	1.8	1.2	.9	1.6	3.2
1954	62.8	49.8	79.3	45.7	4.1	13.0	1.8	1.5	.8	1.7	3.7
1953	63.8	51.1	80.1	47.1	4.0	12.8	1.7	1.4	.9	8.7	.3
1952	63.3	50.5	79.8	46.4	4.1	12.8	1.6	1.4	.9	8.6	.3
1951	62.5	49.5	79.5	45.2	4.2	13.0	1.8	1.2	.9	8.7	.3
1950	60.0	38.7	64.5	38.7	----------	21.3	1.7	6.2	2.0	11.4	----------
1949	58.4	37.4	64.0	37.4	----------	21.0	1.7	6.2	1.8	11.3	----------
1948	59.0	38.5	65.3	38.5	----------	20.5	1.7	6.0	1.7	11.1	----------
1947	57.7	37.3	64.6	37.3	----------	20.4	1.7	6.0	1.7	11.0	----------
1946	56.2	36.4	64.8	36.4	----------	19.8	2.0	5.7	1.6	10.5	----------
1945	61.0	42.0	68.9	42.0	----------	19.0	2.5	5.2	1.6	9.7	----------
1944	62.6	44.0	70.3	44.0	----------	18.6	2.6	5.0	1.7	9.3	----------
1943	60.8	42.0	69.1	42.0	----------	18.8	2.7	4.7	1.9	9.5	----------
1942	55.8	36.3	65.1	36.3	----------	19.5	2.1	4.8	2.3	10.3	----------
1941	50.4	31.3	62.1	31.3	----------	19.1	1.3	4.9	2.2	10.7	----------
1940	46.4	26.8	57.8	26.8	----------	19.6	.9	5.2	2.3	11.2	----------

* Denotes first year for which figures include Alaska and Hawaii.
[1] Includes railroad employees and all persons covered by Federal law except those on a group-elective or individual voluntary basis for whom coverage has not been arranged.
[2] Estimates based on number expected to report earnings at end of year.
[3] Farmworkers, self-employed farmers, State and local government employees, employees of nonprofit organizations, and some additional small groups.
[4] Persons whose coverage was authorized but not arranged on a group-elective or individual voluntary basis.

Series H 197–208. Old-Age, Survivors, Disability, and Health Insurance—Number of Monthly Cash Benefits, by Type of Beneficiary: 1940 to 1970

[In thousands. Number in current payment status at end of year. Data contain some duplication arising from dual entitlement]

Year	Total benefits [1]	Payable to beneficiaries 65 or over	Payable to beneficiaries Under 65 years	Retired workers [2] Total	Retired workers [2] Male	Retired workers [2] Female	Disabled workers [3]	Wives and husbands [2][4]	Widows and widowers [2][5]	Parents [2]	Children [6]	Widowed mothers [7]
	197	198	199	200	201	202	203	204	205	206	207	208
1970	26,229	17,517	8,712	13,349	7,688	5,661	1,493	2,952	3,227	29	4,122	523
1969	25,314	17,031	8,283	12,822	7,459	5,363	1,394	2,908	3,092	30	3,952	512
1968	24,560	16,635	7,925	12,421	7,309	5,111	1,295	2,899	2,938	32	3,796	505
1967	23,705	16,202	7,503	12,019	7,160	4,859	1,193	2,879	2,770	33	3,585	496
1966	22,767	15,614	7,153	11,658	7,034	4,624	1,097	2,860	2,602	33	3,393	488
1965	20,867	14,278	6,589	11,101	6,825	4,276	988	2,807	2,371	35	3,093	472
1964	19,800	13,678	6,122	10,669	6,657	4,011	894	2,783	2,159	35	2,787	471
1963	19,035	13,159	5,877	10,263	6,497	3,766	827	2,749	2,011	36	2,687	462
1962	18,053	12,537	5,517	9,739	6,244	3,494	741	2,679	1,859	37	2,547	452
1961	16,495	11,714	4,781	8,925	5,765	3,160	618	2,510	1,697	37	2,279	428
1960	14,845	10,921	3,924	8,061	5,217	2,845	455	2,346	1,544	36	2,000	401
1959	13,704	10,176	3,528	7,526	4,937	2,589	334	2,208	1,394	35	1,832	376
1958	12,430	9,364	3,066	6,921	4,617	2,303	238	2,031	1,233	30	1,624	354
1957	11,129	8,391	2,738	6,198	4,198	1,999	150	1,827	1,095	29	1,502	328
1956	9,128	7,089	2,039	5,112	3,572	1,540	----------	1,434	913	27	1,341	301
1955	7,961	6,335	1,625	4,474	3,252	1,222	----------	1,192	701	25	1,276	292
1954	6,886	5,405	1,482	3,775	2,803	972	----------	1,016	638	25	1,161	272
1953	5,981	4,633	1,348	3,222	2,438	784	----------	888	541	24	1,053	254
1952	5,026	3,824	1,202	2,644	2,052	592	----------	738	455	21	939	229
1951	4,379	3,300	1,079	2,278	1,819	459	----------	647	384	19	846	204
1950	3,477	2,599	878	1,771	1,469	302	----------	508	314	15	700	169
1949	2,743	1,951	792	1,286	1,100	186	----------	391	261	13	639	152
1948	2,315	1,591	723	1,048	900	148	----------	321	210	12	581	142
1947	1,978	1,318	660	875	756	119	----------	269	164	10	525	135
1946	1,642	1,051	590	702	610	92	----------	216	127	7	462	128
1945	1,288	777	511	518	447	71	----------	159	94	6	390	121
1944	955	567	388	378	323	55	----------	116	68	5	298	90
1943	748	448	299	306	261	45	----------	92	46	4	229	70
1942	598	368	230	260	224	36	----------	77	29	3	173	57
1941	434	274	160	200	175	25	----------	57	15	2	117	42
1940	222	147	75	112	99	13	----------	30	4	1	55	20

[1] Beginning 1966, includes special age-72 beneficiaries, not shown separately. [2] Persons aged 65 and over (and 62–64, beginning 1956 for women and 1961 for men). [3] July 1957–Oct. 1960, disabled workers aged 50–64; thereafter, disabled workers under 65. [4] Beginning 1950, includes wife beneficiaries under age 65 with entitled children in their care and, beginning Sept. 1965, entitled divorced wives. [5] Beginning Sept. 1965, includes widows, 60–61, and surviving divorced wives, 60 and over, and, beginning Mar. 1968, disabled widows and widowers, 50 and over. [6] Beginning 1957, includes disabled persons aged 18 and over whose disability began before age 18 and, beginning Jan. 1965, entitled full-time students aged 18–21. [7] Beginning 1950, includes surviving divorced mothers with entitled children in care.

Series H 209–229. Old-Age, Survivors, Disability, and Health Insurance—Benefits, by Type of Beneficiary: 1940 to 1970

Year	Benefit payments during year (mil. dol.)								Lump-sum death payments
	Total	Monthly benefits							
		Total [1]	Retired workers	Disabled workers	Wives and husbands	Children	Widowed mothers	Widows and widowers	
	209	210	211	212	213	214	215	216	217
1970	31,863	31,570	18,435	2,448	2,194	3,517	574	4,055	294
1969	26,751	26,460	15,383	2,014	1,889	2,971	490	3,371	291
1968	24,936	24,667	14,277	1,804	1,804	2,821	478	3,117	269
1967	21,406	21,154	12,371	1,519	1,569	2,383	420	2,545	252
1966	20,048	19,811	11,727	1,394	1,537	2,307	415	2,351	237
1965	18,311	18,094	10,984	1,246	1,478	1,922	388	2,041	217
1964	16,223	16,007	9,854	1,044	1,356	1,611	354	1,754	216
1963	15,427	15,221	9,391	965	1,331	1,540	348	1,612	206
1962	14,461	14,278	8,813	888	1,284	1,454	336	1,470	183
1961	12,749	12,577	7,802	724	1,178	1,295	316	1,232	171
1960	11,245	11,081	7,053	489	1,083	1,085	286	1,057	164
1959	10,299	10,127	6,548	390	1,011	969	263	921	171
1958	8,576	8,443	5,567	246	852	778	223	757	133
1957	7,404	7,266	4,888	57	756	694	198	653	139
1956	5,715	5,605	3,793	----------	536	614	177	469	109
1955	4,968	4,855	3,253	----------	466	561	163	396	113
1954	3,670	3,578	2,340	----------	338	451	133	304	92
1953	3,006	2,919	1,884	----------	275	385	114	248	87
1952	2,194	2,131	1,328	----------	200	310	92	191	63
1951	1,885	1,828	1,135	----------	175	271	82	156	57
1950	961	928	557	----------	88	142	49	89	33
1949	667	634	373	----------	60	100	39	60	33
1948	556	524	300	----------	49	90	36	48	32
1947	466	437	245	----------	40	80	34	37	29
1946	378	350	189	----------	31	68	32	28	28
1945	274	248	126	----------	21	54	27	20	26
1944	209	187	97	----------	16	40	20	14	22
1943	166	148	79	----------	13	31	16	9	18
1942	131	116	65	----------	10	22	13	5	15
1941	88	75	44	----------	7	14	8	2	13
1940	32	24	15	----------	2	4	2	(Z)	9

Year	Benefits awarded during year (1,000)							Average monthly benefit (in current payment status, end of year)				
	Number of beneficiaries [1]	Retired workers	Disabled workers	Wives and husbands	Children	Widowed mothers	Widows and widowers	Retired workers	Disabled workers	Wives and husbands	Widowed mothers	Widows
	218	219	220	221	222	223	224	225	226	227	228	229
1970	3,722	1,338	350	436	1,091	112	363	$118.10	$131.29	$59.40	$86.51	$102.02
1969	3,700	1,273	345	430	1,112	117	376	100.40	112.74	50.63	75.06	87.48
1968	3,620	1,240	323	420	1,065	114	375	98.86	111.86	50.08	74.93	86.54
1967	3,597	1,161	301	407	985	111	356	85.37	98.43	43.43	65.86	74.99
1966	4,722	1,648	278	478	1,056	107	404	84.35	98.09	43.10	65.59	74.11
1965	3,072	1,183	253	390	783	100	359	83.92	97.76	43.04	65.46	73.75
1964	2,552	1,042	208	376	534	106	283	77.57	91.12	39.72	59.40	67.85
1963	2,730	1,146	224	412	561	105	279	76.88	90.59	39.94	59.43	66.85
1962	3,005	1,347	251	463	573	100	267	76.19	89.99	39.62	59.38	65.88
1961	3,047	1,362	280	472	580	98	251	75.65	89.59	39.45	59.38	64.92
1960	2,336	982	208	394	416	93	239	74.04	89.31	38.72	59.29	57.69
1959	2,502	1,090	178	445	427	102	253	72.78	89.00	38.15	57.37	56.73
1958	2,123	1,042	131	379	287	81	199	66.35	82.10	35.07	50.53	51.91
1957	2,832	1,425	179	578	313	88	245	64.58	72.76	34.37	49.05	51.09
1956	1,855	934	----------	385	212	67	254	63.09	----------	33.71	47.35	50.14
1955	1,658	910	----------	289	239	76	141	61.90	----------	33.07	45.91	48.70
1954	1,402	750	----------	237	213	71	128	59.14	----------	31.77	44.52	46.28
1953	1,419	772	----------	247	212	72	113	51.10	----------	27.05	37.49	40.88
1952	1,053	531	----------	178	183	65	92	49.25	----------	25.99	36.13	40.67
1951	1,336	703	----------	229	231	78	90	42.14	----------	22.74	33.25	36.04
1950	963	567	----------	163	123	41	67	43.86	----------	23.60	34.24	36.54
1949	682	337	----------	117	119	43	63	26.00	----------	13.76	21.08	20.82
1948	596	276	----------	99	119	44	56	25.35	----------	13.42	20.80	20.60
1947	573	271	----------	94	116	43	45	24.90	----------	13.17	20.44	20.40
1946	547	259	----------	89	115	44	39	24.55	----------	12.99	20.07	20.22
1945	462	185	----------	63	128	55	30	24.19	----------	12.82	19.83	20.19
1944	319	110	----------	40	100	43	25	23.73	----------	12.63	19.80	20.17
1943	263	89	----------	32	86	35	20	23.42	----------	12.49	19.72	20.15
1942	258	100	----------	33	77	32	15	23.02	----------	12.28	19.57	20.15
1941	269	115	----------	36	76	31	11	22.70	----------	12.11	19.50	20.22
1940	255	132	----------	35	59	23	5	22.60	----------	12.13	19.61	20.28

Z Less than $500,000.

[1] Includes parents and special age-72 beneficiaries, not shown separately.

Series H 230–237. Old-Age, Survivors, Disability, and Health Insurance—Number and Average Monthly Benefits in Current-Payment Status, by Selected Family Groups: 1940 to 1970

[Estimated for 1940–43; based on sample thereafter]

	Families (1,000)								Average monthly benefits (dollars)							
	Retired-worker families [1]				Survivor families				Retired-worker families [1]				Survivor families			
	Worker only			Worker and wife [2]	Aged widow only [1]	Widowed mother and—			Worker only			Worker and wife [2]	Aged widow only [1]	Widowed mother and—		
End of year	Total	Men	Women			1 child	2 children	3 or more children	Total	Men	Women			1 child	2 children	3 or more children
	230	231	232	233	234	235	236	237	230	231	232	233	234	235	236	237
1970	10,533	4,904	5,629	2,457	3,080	183	155	182	114.20	128.70	101.60	198.90	102.40	213.00	291.10	289.90
1969	10,039	4,707	5,332	2,440	2,984	180	148	178	96.60	109.00	85.70	168.90	87.80	182.20	255.80	253.60
1968	9,641	4,558	5,082	2,430	2,836	181	144	177	95.00	107.10	84.20	166.30	86.80	175.00	257.10	253.40
1967	9,247	4,416	4,831	2,429	2,696	181	140	172	81.70	92.50	71.90	144.20	75.20	155.90	224.40	221.70
1966	8,897	4,301	4,596	2,418	2,541	180	140	164	80.60	91.20	70.70	142.50	74.30	154.30	221.90	218.80
1965	8,386	4,137	4,249	2,400	2,332	182	135	153	80.10	90.50	70.00	141.50	73.90	153.00	219.80	218.10
1964	7,982	3,998	3,984	2,392	2,129	191	134	142	73.90	83.60	64.30	130.70	67.90	141.60	193.40	192.10
1963	7,606	3,867	3,739	2,368	1,984	191	131	137	73.20	82.60	63.40	129.40	66.90	139.40	192.50	190.40
1962	7,134	3,666	3,468	2,324	1,835	191	128	131	72.50	81.80	62.60	127.90	65.90	137.30	190.70	186.80
1961	6,470	3,336	3,134	2,214	1,677	185	120	121	71.90	81.20	62.00	126.60	64.90	135.00	189.30	182.80
1960	5,742	2,922	2,820	2,122	1,527	172	113	114	69.90	79.90	59.60	123.90	57.70	131.70	188.00	181.70
1959	5,321	2,755	2,565	2,029	1,380	160	106	108	68.70	78.00	58.70	121.60	56.70	129.70	170.70	178.60
1958	4,872	2,587	2,285	1,902	1,224	156	105	99	62.60	70.70	53.50	111.20	51.90	117.00	151.70	150.70
1957	4,344	2,361	1,983	1,726	1,089	142	97	92	60.90	68.30	52.20	108.40	51.10	114.30	146.30	144.80
1956	3,662	2,133	1,528	1,359	912	128	88	83	59.90	66.10	51.10	105.90	50.10	109.90	141.00	138.70
1955	3,266	2,054	1,212	1,124	700	126	86	80	59.10	64.60	49.80	103.50	48.70	106.80	135.40	133.20
1954	2,744	1,780	964	958	637	116	82	72	56.50	61.60	47.00	99.10	46.30	103.90	130.50	126.80
1953	2,321	1,543	778	839	540	113	74	64	48.80	52.90	40.60	85.00	40.90	90.10	111.90	109.00
1952	1,894	1,306	588	699	454	103	68	56	47.10	50.70	39.10	81.60	40.70	87.50	106.00	101.30
1951	1,618	1,162	456	614	384	92	61	49	40.30	43.20	33.00	70.20	36.00	77.30	93.80	92.00
1950	1,240	939	301	498	314	82	53	33	42.20	44.60	34.80	71.70	36.50	76.90	93.90	92.40
1949	872	687	186	390	261	78	44	26	25.30	26.50	20.60	41.40	20.80	36.50	50.40	54.00
1948	708	560	148	321	210	73	41	24	24.60	25.80	20.10	40.40	20.60	36.00	49.80	53.00
1947	590	471	119	269	164	69	39	23	24.20	25.30	19.90	39.60	20.40	35.40	48.80	52.20
1946	473	381	92	216	127	66	37	22	23.90	24.90	19.60	39.00	20.20	34.60	48.20	51.40
1945	416	338	78	181	95	86	48	24	23.50	24.50	19.50	38.50	20.20	34.10	47.70	50.40
1944	315	253	62	135	69	67	36	20	23.00	24.10	19.30	37.90	20.20	34.40	47.30	50.10
1943	206	161	45	92	46	34	20	11	22.90	23.80	19.10	37.50	20.20	34.20	46.90	50.40
1942	176	146	30	77	29	29	17	7	22.50	23.30	18.70	36.80	20.20	33.90	46.50	50.70
1941	136	114	22	57	15	20	13	4	22.20	22.90	18.50	36.30	20.20	33.90	46.60	51.00
1940	78	65	12	30	4	10	6	3	22.10	22.80	18.40	36.40	20.30	33.90	46.60	51.30

[1] Averages reflect benefits to individuals entitled under the transitionally insured status provisions in effect since 1965.   [2] Wife's entitlement not dependent on having entitled children in her care.

Series H 238–244. Old-Age and Survivors Insurance Trust Fund: 1937 to 1970

[In millions of dollars]

Year	Net contribution income (238)	Net interest received (239)	Benefit payments (240)	Administrative expenses (241)	Total (242)	Invested in U.S. Government securities (243)	Cash balances (244)	Year	Net contribution income (238)	Net interest received (239)	Benefit payments (240)	Administrative expenses (241)	Total (242)	Invested in U.S. Government securities (243)	Cash balances (244)
1970	30,256	1,515	28,796	471	32,454	29,935	2,519	1953	3,945	414	3,006	88	18,707	18,291	416
1969	27,947	1,165	24,209	474	30,082	27,886	2,197	1952	3,819	365	2,194	88	17,442	16,960	481
1968	23,719	939	22,642	476	25,704	23,258	2,446	1951	3,363	417	1,885	81	15,540	15,017	522
1967	23,138	818	19,468	406	24,222	22,513	1,708	1950	2,667	257	961	61	13,721	13,331	391
1966	20,580	644	18,267	256	20,570	18,789	1,781	1949	1,666	146	667	54	11,816	11,728	88
1965	16,017	593	16,737	328	18,235	16,643	1,592	1948	1,685	281	556	51	10,722	10,556	166
1964	15,689	569	14,914	296	19,125	17,758	1,367	1947	1,557	164	466	46	9,360	9,268	92
1963	14,541	521	14,217	281	18,480	17,154	1,327	1946	1,295	152	378	40	8,150	8,079	71
1962	12,059	526	13,356	256	18,337	17,060	1,277	1945	1,285	134	274	30	7,121	7,054	66
1961	11,285	548	11,862	239	19,725	18,404	1,321	1944	1,316	107	209	29	6,005	5,967	38
1960	10,866	516	10,677	203	20,324	19,128	1,196	1943	1,239	88	166	29	4,820	4,779	42
1959	8,052	532	9,842	184	20,141	19,151	990	1942	1,012	72	131	28	3,688	3,655	33
1958	7,566	552	8,327	194	21,864	20,953	911	1941	789	56	88	26	2,762	2,736	26
1957	6,825	556	7,347	162	22,393	21,566	827	1940	325	43	35	26	2,031	2,017	14
1956	6,172	526	5,715	132	22,519	21,831	689	1939	580	27	14	--------	1,724	1,435	289
1955	5,713	454	4,968	119	21,663	21,102	561	1938	360	15	10	--------	1,132	862	269
1954	5,163	447	3,670	92	20,576	19,863	713	1937	765	2	1	--------	766	513	253

[1] Excludes transfers from general revenue amounting to $16 million for 1947–1951 and $1,429 million for 1966–1970.

[2] Excludes expenditures for rehabilitation services for the disabled amounting to $4 million, 1966–1970; and transfers to railroad retirement account amounting to $5,103 million, 1954–1970.

Series H 245–259. Old-Age, Survivors, Disability, and Health Insurance—Benefits in Current-Payment Status for Retired-Worker Beneficiaries, by Sex, 1940 to 1970

[Excludes persons 72 years old and over with special benefits paid]

End of year	Number of retired workers					Age of retired workers [4] (percent distribution)						Average monthly amount received by retired workers			
	Total [1] (1,000)	Full benefits [2] (1,000)	Reduced benefits [3]		Average age	Total	62–64 years	65–69 years	70–74 years	75–79 years	80 and over	All benefits [1] (dol.)	Full benefits [2] (dol.)	Reduced benefits [3]	
			Number (1,000)	Percent of total										Before reduction (dol.)	After reduction [5] (dol.)
	245	246	247	248	249	250	251	252	253	254	255	256	257	258	259
MALE															
1970	7,688	4,930	2,759	35.9	72.6	100.0	7.5	30.1	26.9	19.6	15.9	130.53	139.05	128.89	115.30
1969	7,459	5,002	2,457	32.9	73.2	100.0	7.1	29.9	27.3	20.0	15.8	110.96	117.78	109.16	97.06
1968	7,309	5,108	2,202	30.1	73.1	100.0	7.0	29.5	28.0	20.0	15.5	109.08	115.02	106.95	95.29
1967	7,160	5,215	1,946	27.2	73.1	100.0	6.8	29.5	28.5	20.2	14.9	94.49	99.33	92.53	81.53
1966	7,034	5,345	1,689	24.0	73.1	100.0	6.9	29.5	29.2	19.8	14.5	93.26	97.37	90.98	80.26
1965	6,825	5,389	1,436	21.0	72.9	100.0	6.9	29.7	29.5	19.9	14.0	92.59	96.12	90.14	79.35
1964	6,657	5,460	1,197	18.0	72.8	100.0	7.2	30.0	29.7	19.8	13.3	85.58	88.37	82.72	72.85
1963	6,497	5,552	945	14.5	72.7	100.0	7.0	30.9	29.8	19.7	12.6	84.69	86.81	81.63	72.21
1962	6,244	5,587	657	10.5	72.7	100.0	6.5	31.4	30.4	19.4	12.3	83.79	85.26	80.03	71.24
1961	5,765	5,491	273	4.7	72.8	100.0	4.1	32.7	31.0	20.2	11.9	83.13	83.84	76.94	69.01
1960	5,217	5,217	-----	-----	73.2	100.0	-----	33.8	33.1	21.1	12.1	81.87	81.87	-----	-----
1959	4,937	4,937	-----	-----	73.1	100.0	-----	34.0	33.7	20.9	11.5	80.11	80.11	-----	-----
1958	4,617	4,617	-----	-----	73.0	100.0	-----	33.9	34.3	20.6	11.2	72.74	72.74	-----	-----
1957	4,198	4,198	-----	-----	72.9	100.0	-----	34.9	34.2	20.4	10.5	70.47	70.47	-----	-----
1956	3,572	3,572	-----	-----	72.9	100.0	-----	34.2	35.2	20.3	10.3	68.23	68.23	-----	-----
1955	3,252	3,252	-----	-----	72.7	100.0	-----	35.7	34.8	20.0	9.5	66.40	66.40	-----	-----
1954	2,803	2,803	-----	-----	72.6	100.0	-----	37.2	32.8	20.6	9.4	63.34	63.34	-----	-----
1953	2,438	2,438	-----	-----	72.6	100.0	-----	37.3	32.5	21.3	8.9	54.46	54.46	-----	-----
1952	2,052	2,052	-----	-----	72.6	100.0	-----	36.9	32.9	21.7	8.5	52.16	52.16	-----	-----
1951	1,819	1,819	-----	-----	72.3	100.0	-----	38.8	32.4	21.2	7.6	44.44	44.44	-----	-----
1950	1,469	1,469	-----	-----	72.2	100.0	-----	39.1	33.7	20.2	7.1	45.67	45.67	-----	-----
1949	1,100	1,100	-----	-----	72.3	100.0	-----	36.3	37.0	19.8	6.8	26.92	26.92	-----	-----
1948	900	900	-----	-----	72.3	100.0	-----	35.6	39.1	18.9	6.4	26.21	26.21	-----	-----
1947	756	756	-----	-----	72.1	100.0	-----	36.5	40.4	17.4	5.8	25.68	25.68	-----	-----
1946	610	610	-----	-----	71.9	100.0	-----	38.0	41.1	15.7	5.2	25.30	25.30	-----	-----
1945	447	447	-----	-----	71.7	100.0	-----	39.9	40.2	15.1	4.7	24.94	24.94	-----	-----
1944	323	323	-----	-----	71.5	100.0	-----	42.7	38.6	14.2	4.6	24.48	24.48	-----	-----
1943	261	261	-----	-----	71.1	100.0	-----	49.2	34.1	12.7	4.0	24.17	24.17	-----	-----
1942	224	224	-----	-----	70.5	100.0	-----	57.3	28.6	10.9	3.3	23.71	23.71	-----	-----
1941	175	175	-----	-----	69.8	100.0	-----	65.6	23.0	8.9	2.6	23.32	23.32	-----	-----
1940	99	99	-----	-----	68.8	100.0	-----	74.4	17.4	6.4	1.8	23.17	23.17	-----	-----
FEMALE															
1970	5,661	2,352	3,309	58.5	72.0	100.0	11.5	30.1	25.4	18.7	14.3	101.22	111.71	105.60	93.77
1969	5,363	2,321	3,042	56.7	72.4	100.0	11.4	30.3	25.8	18.8	13.8	85.71	94.51	90.18	78.99
1968	5,111	2,345	2,766	54.1	72.3	100.0	11.3	30.4	26.5	18.8	13.1	84.24	91.89	88.90	77.75
1967	4,859	2,338	2,521	51.9	72.2	100.0	11.4	30.7	27.1	18.7	12.1	71.92	78.28	76.46	66.01
1966	4,624	2,307	2,317	50.1	72.1	100.0	11.8	31.0	27.7	18.1	11.4	70.79	76.40	75.47	65.21
1965	4,276	2,192	2,083	48.7	71.8	100.0	12.2	31.6	28.1	17.6	10.5	70.07	75.36	73.82	64.50
1964	4,011	2,138	1,873	46.7	71.6	100.0	12.9	32.3	28.1	17.1	9.5	64.28	69.01	67.88	58.87
1963	3,766	2,111	1,655	44.0	71.4	100.0	13.0	33.5	28.3	16.4	8.8	63.42	67.48	67.11	58.23
1962	3,494	2,060	1,434	41.0	71.2	100.0	13.3	34.3	28.5	15.7	8.2	62.61	66.10	66.41	57.59
1961	3,160	1,977	1,183	37.4	71.1	100.0	13.0	35.4	28.5	15.4	7.6	62.00	64.87	65.84	57.20
1960	2,845	1,896	949	33.4	71.0	100.0	12.6	36.3	29.0	15.0	7.2	59.67	61.61	64.19	55.78
1959	2,589	1,825	764	29.5	70.8	100.0	12.9	37.5	28.8	14.4	6.6	58.81	60.34	63.18	55.16
1958	2,303	1,735	569	24.7	70.7	100.0	13.0	38.3	28.7	13.9	6.1	53.55	54.62	57.06	50.27
1957	1,999	1,613	386	19.3	70.5	100.0	13.3	39.7	28.2	13.4	5.5	52.23	52.98	55.33	49.08
1956	1,540	1,425	115	7.5	70.9	100.0	7.3	42.5	30.7	14.0	5.5	51.16	51.41	53.64	48.17
1955	1,222	1,222	-----	-----	71.3	100.0	-----	47.8	32.3	14.6	5.2	49.93	49.93	-----	-----
1954	972	972	-----	-----	71.2	100.0	-----	49.0	31.2	14.8	5.0	47.05	47.05	-----	-----
1953	784	784	-----	-----	71.1	100.0	-----	49.8	30.9	14.8	4.6	40.66	40.66	-----	-----
1952	592	592	-----	-----	71.0	100.0	-----	50.2	30.9	14.7	4.1	39.17	39.17	-----	-----
1951	459	459	-----	-----	70.8	100.0	-----	51.5	30.6	14.2	3.7	33.03	33.03	-----	-----
1950	302	302	-----	-----	71.1	100.0	-----	48.4	32.9	15.0	3.7	35.05	35.05	-----	-----
1949	186	186	-----	-----	71.7	100.0	-----	39.8	39.0	17.0	4.2	20.58	20.58	-----	-----
1948	148	148	-----	-----	71.6	100.0	-----	39.9	41.3	15.0	3.7	20.11	20.11	-----	-----
1947	119	119	-----	-----	71.4	100.0	-----	41.2	42.6	13.0	3.3	19.91	19.91	-----	-----
1946	92	92	-----	-----	71.1	100.0	-----	43.3	42.5	11.2	3.0	19.64	19.64	-----	-----
1945	71	71	-----	-----	70.8	100.0	-----	47.1	40.0	10.2	2.6	19.51	19.51	-----	-----
1944	55	55	-----	-----	70.5	100.0	-----	52.6	36.1	9.1	2.3	19.35	19.35	-----	-----
1943	45	45	-----	-----	70.0	100.0	-----	60.4	29.8	7.8	1.9	19.06	19.06	-----	-----
1942	36	36	-----	-----	69.5	100.0	-----	68.4	23.5	6.5	1.6	18.73	18.73	-----	-----
1941	25	25	-----	-----	68.9	100.0	-----	75.2	18.2	5.4	1.2	18.48	18.48	-----	-----
1940	13	13	-----	-----	68.1	100.0	-----	82.6	12.8	3.9	.6	18.37	18.37	-----	-----

[1] Includes beneficiaries and benefits paid on reduced benefits basis for early retirement, beginning 1961 for male workers and 1956 for female.
[2] Benefits payable without reduction for early retirement.
[3] Benefits payable with reduction for early retirement, beginning 1956 for women and 1961 for men.

[4] Age at birthday in stated year.
[5] Benefits reduced by 5/9 of 1 percent for each month of entitlement before age 65 (maximum reduction of 20 percent).

SOCIAL STATISTICS

Series H 260–270. Civil Service Retirement: 1921 to 1970

[For years ending June 30]

Year	Annuities					Lump-sum payments (refunds)					
	Number certified (1,000)	Number terminated (1,000)	Number in force (1,000)		Annual value (mil. dol.)	Separated employees		Deceased employees		Deceased annuitants	
			Total	Disability		Number (1,000)	Amount (mil. dol.)	Number (1,000)	Amount (mil. dol.)	Number (1,000)	Amount (mil. dol.)
	260	261	262	263	264	265	266	267	268	269	270
1970	99	50	959	185	2,660	215	197.5	5	12.8	19	10.0
1969	86	48	910	178	2,315	207	198.8	5	12.3	15	8.2
1968	83	42	872	173	2,089	190	160.1	5	12.0	18	8.5
1967	77	42	831	167	1,881	164	157.1	5	10.5	16	7.6
1966	105	38	796	161	1,688	129	139.2	5	11.2	15	7.5
1965	78	37	729	149	1,354	121	112.5	5	10.2	15	7.3
1964	79	34	688	139	1,240	128	108.2	4	9.7	16	6.0
1963	73	32	643	130	1,127	131	105.8	4	9.0	13	6.1
1962	73	30	602	122	975	137	108.6	4	8.7	11	6.2
1961	72	28	559	112	883	131	103.7	4	8.7	9	3.6
1960	65	26	515	102	792	153	114.2	4	7.8	9	3.6
1959	81	23	476	93	723	144	95.4	4	7.3	9	3.6
1958	70	21	418	84	635	199	114.7	4	7.4	9	3.7
1957	61	19	369	73	516	184	99.3	4	6.7	8	3.9
1956	47	17	327	66	441	164	84.2	4	6.0	8	3.7
1955	42	14	297	61	358	101	73.3	4	5.7	8	3.6
1954	41	13	269	56	324	123	89.0	4	5.4	8	3.6
1953	38	13	241	52	289	136	81.4	4	5.2	8	3.4
1952	31	12	216	48	227	147	71.0	4	4.3	8	3.8
1951	36	11	197	46	206	167	64.9	4	4.0	8	3.6
1950	33	9	172	43	182	239	88.2	5	3.7	7	4.2
1949	31	9	148	39	154	229	61.4	6	3.9	5	4.7
1948	22	7	126	35	134	432	112.8	11	9.4	4	3.5
1947	22	7	111	32	103	943	178.9	17	10.4	4	3.7
1946	16	5	96	27	93	(NA)	¹179.8	(NA)	(NA)	(NA)	2.6
1945	12	5	85	23	82	901	62.4	16	7.4	3	2.5
1944	10	6	78	21	76	390	21.5	9	5.2	3	2.3
1943	10	5	74	20	71	111	7.2	6	5.0	3	2.0
1942	8	5	69	18	66	46	5.6	4	3.9	3	1.7
1941	8	4	66	17	63	21	3.6	4	4.3	3	1.7
1940	7	3	62	15	60	15	2.9	3	3.7	2	1.5
1939	6	4	58	14	57	15	2.7	3	3.2	2	1.4
1938	6	3	56	13	55	18	3.8	3	3.1	2	1.4
1937	5	3	53	12	52	14	3.1	3	2.9	2	1.3
1936	6	4	51	11	50	12	2.6	3	2.7	2	1.2
1935	7	3	49	10	48	²16	²5.8	-----	-----	-----	-----
1934	14	2	45	9	44	22	8.0	-----	-----	-----	-----
1933	9	2	33	7	32	17	4.8	-----	-----	-----	-----
1932	5	2	26	6	24	21	3.9	-----	-----	-----	-----
1931	7	2	23	5	22	24	4.2	-----	-----	-----	-----
1930	3	2	18	4	13	28	5.0	-----	-----	-----	-----
1929	3	1	17	4	12	26	4.1	-----	-----	-----	-----
1928	3	2	15	3	11	28	3.8	-----	-----	-----	-----
1927	3	2	14	3	10	32	3.9	-----	-----	-----	-----
1926	2	1	13	2	7	34	3.4	-----	-----	-----	-----
1925	2	1	12	2	6	37	2.7	-----	-----	-----	-----
1924	2	(Z)	11	2	6	45	2.9	-----	-----	-----	-----
1923	3	2	9	1	5	58	2.8	-----	-----	-----	-----
1922	2	–	8	1	4	71	2.2	-----	-----	-----	-----
1921	7	1	6	1	4	26	.3	-----	-----	-----	-----

– Represents zero.   NA Not available.   Z Less than 500.

¹ Includes amount paid to beneficiaries of deceased employees.

² Only total lump-sum payments available prior to September 1934 when administration of the Retirement Act was transferred to the Civil Service Commission.

Series H 271–286. Railroad Retirement Benefits—Number and Amount, by Type of Beneficiary: 1937 to 1970

[For years ending June 30]

Year	Average number of employees (1,000)	Number of recipients (1,000)	Retirement and survivor monthly benefits awarded [1] (1,000) Total	Retirement	Spouse	Survivor	Number of monthly benefits in current payment status [2] (1,000) Total	Retirement	Spouse	Survivor	Number of lump-sum death benefits awarded [1] (1,000)	Amount of benefit payments (mil. dol.) Total	Retirement	Spouse	Survivor Monthly	Survivor Lump-sum
	271	272	273	274	275	276	277	278	279	280	281	282	283	284	285	286
1970	652	1,051	99	48	24	27	1,036	501	210	324	19	1,594	963	214	391	26
1969	670	1,050	114	55	26	33	1,016	489	208	319	21	1,536	941	208	362	25
1968	696	1,040	115	60	25	29	989	470	204	314	20	1,403	869	183	327	24
1967	731	1,022	103	50	24	29	950	445	200	306	20	1,266	780	162	299	24
1966	747	1,002	104	35	41	28	921	429	197	294	20	1,200	737	148	293	23
1965	762	980	85	36	19	29	889	426	174	288	23	1,118	716	118	259	24
1964	785	970	91	40	21	30	879	423	174	282	23	1,096	704	119	250	24
1963	796	951	94	42	22	30	861	416	173	272	23	1,068	686	119	240	23
1962	832	932	93	41	23	29	838	405	168	265	22	1,027	661	118	227	21
1961	861	906	98	43	26	29	821	397	166	259	23	987	641	118	207	21
1960	930	873	115	45	42	28	794	384	157	254	22	926	602	110	195	20
1959	971	824	94	44	21	28	746	369	132	245	22	781	519	81	164	18
1958	1,063	798	92	42	21	29	710	350	126	234	24	721	482	73	149	18
1957	1,186	757	83	37	20	26	679	336	119	224	21	678	455	69	139	15
1956	1,252	730	89	38	20	31	651	323	114	214	23	601	396	62	127	15
1955	1,222	696	106	38	21	47	616	310	107	200	24	550	376	49	110	16
1954	1,334	638	77	36	19	22	562	294	99	169	29	512	362	46	85	19
1953	1,416	609	77	33	23	20	531	279	91	161	27	460	324	41	79	16
1952	1,452	568	137	30	85	21	503	268	81	154	26	394	296	23	62	13
1951	1,480	484	57	32	-------	24	408	261	-------	147	31	317	259	-------	45	13
1950	1,360	461	65	38	-------	27	387	251	-------	137	33	302	248	-------	42	12
1949	1,590	427	67	36	-------	31	356	234	-------	122	34	283	234	-------	38	12
1948	1,574	376	121	43	-------	78	320	218	-------	102	21	225	188	-------	31	7
1947	1,609	265	63	29	-------	34	231	194	-------	37	15	173	159	-------	7	7
1946	1,649	224	28	27	-------	1	185	181	-------	4	20	154	143	-------	2	9
1945	1,682	210	22	21	-------	1	171	167	-------	4	20	143	133	-------	2	8
1944	1,635	197	19	18	-------	1	164	160	-------	4	15	135	128	-------	2	6
1943	1,548	191	17	16	-------	1	160	156	-------	4	15	131	124	-------	2	5
1942	1,402	186	18	16	-------	1	157	153	-------	4	13	127	122	-------	2	4
1941	1,239	182	22	21	-------	2	153	150	-------	3	13	122	117	-------	2	3
1940	1,177	173	25	23	-------	2	144	141	-------	3	13	114	111	-------	1	2
1939	1,110	163	38	35	-------	3	132	130	-------	3	15	107	104	-------	1	1
1938	1,175	117	110	107	-------	2	108	107	-------	1	1	83	82	-------	1	(Z)
1937	-------	7	8	7	-------	(Z)	7	7	-------	(Z)	-------	5	4	-------	(Z)	-------

Z Less than 500 or less than $500,000.
[1] Benefits awarded refers to favorable action on application for monthly benefits or for lump-sum death payments. They include supplemental annuities.
[2] Refers to benefit payments actually being made during period stated.

Series H 287–304. Private Pension and Deferred Profit-Sharing Plans—Estimated Coverage, Contributions, Reserves, Beneficiaries, and Benefit Payments: 1930 to 1970

[Includes pay-as-you-go plans, nonprofit organization plans, multiemployer, union-administered, and deferred profit-sharing plans. Excludes railroad plans other than those supplementing Federal Railroad Retirement Act. In 1930 and 1935, respectively, private railroad plans covered an average of 1.3 and 1.1 million employees; had about 50,000 and 60,000 beneficiaries; and paid about $30 million and $40 million in benefits]

Year	Coverage [1][2] (1,000) Total	Insured plans	Noninsured plans	Employer contributions (mil. dol.) Total	Insured plans	Noninsured plans	Employee contributions (mil. dol.) Total	Insured plans	Noninsured plans
	287	288	289	290	291	292	293	294	295
1970	29,700	9,300	20,400	12,580	2,860	9,720	1,420	350	1,070
1969	29,000	8,700	20,300	11,520	3,030	8,490	1,360	350	1,010
1968	28,000	7,900	20,100	9,940	2,240	7,700	1,230	340	890
1967	27,500	7,700	19,800	9,050	2,010	7,040	1,130	340	790
1966	26,300	6,900	19,400	8,210	1,850	6,360	1,040	330	710
1965	25,300	6,200	19,100	7,370	1,770	5,600	990	320	670
1964	24,600	6,000	18,600	6,370	1,520	4,850	910	310	600
1963	23,800	5,400	18,400	5,560	1,390	4,170	860	300	560
1962	23,100	5,200	17,900	5,200	1,240	3,960	830	310	520
1961	22,200	5,100	17,100	4,830	1,180	3,650	780	290	490
1960	21,200	4,900	16,300	4,710	1,190	3,520	780	300	480
1959	19,900	4,800	15,100	4,590	1,330	3,260	770	330	440
1958	18,800	4,500	14,300	4,100	1,250	2,850	720	310	410
1957	18,100	4,400	13,700	4,030	1,220	2,810	690	300	390
1956	16,900	4,100	12,800	3,600	1,110	2,490	625	290	335
1955	15,400	3,800	11,600	3,280	1,100	2,180	560	280	280
1954	14,200	3,600	10,600	3,000	1,030	1,970	515	270	245
1953	13,200	3,400	9,800	2,990	1,010	1,980	485	260	225
1952	11,700	3,200	8,500	2,540	910	1,630	430	240	190
1951	11,000	2,900	8,100	2,280	820	1,460	380	210	170
1950	9,800	2,600	7,200	1,750	720	1,030	330	200	130
1945	6,400	-------	-------	830	-------	-------	160	-------	-------
1940	4,100	-------	-------	180	-------	-------	130	-------	-------
1935	2,700	-------	-------	140	-------	-------	90	-------	-------
1930	2,700	-------	-------	130	-------	-------	70	-------	-------

See footnotes at end of table.

Series H 287–304. Private Pension and Deferred Profit-Sharing Plans—Estimated Coverage, Contributions, Reserves, Beneficiaries, and Benefit Payments: 1930 to 1970—Con.

Year	Reserves [2] (bil. dol.)			Number of monthly beneficiaries [2] (1,000)			Amount of benefit payments [3] (mil. dol.)		
	Total	Insured plans	Noninsured plans	Total	Insured plans	Noninsured plans	Total	Insured plans	Noninsured plans
	296	297	298	299	300	301	302	303	304
1970	137.1	40.1	97.0	4,720	1,220	3,500	7,360	1,330	6,030
1969	127.8	37.2	90.6	4,180	1,070	3,110	6,450	1,160	5,290
1968	117.8	34.8	83.1	3,770	1,010	2,760	5,530	1,030	4,500
1967	106.2	31.9	74.2	3,410	930	2,480	4,790	910	3,880
1966	95.5	29.3	66.2	3,110	870	2,240	4,190	810	3,380
1965	86.5	27.3	59.2	2,750	790	1,960	3,520	720	2,800
1964	77.7	25.2	52.4	2,490	740	1,750	2,990	640	2,350
1963	69.9	23.3	46.6	2,280	690	1,590	2,590	570	2,020
1962	63.5	21.6	41.9	2,100	630	1,470	2,330	510	1,820
1961	57.8	20.2	37.5	1,910	570	1,340	1,970	450	1,520
1960	52.0	18.8	33.1	1,780	540	1,240	1,720	390	1,330
1959	46.6	17.6	29.1	1,590	500	1,090	1,540	340	1,200
1958	40.9	15.6	25.2	1,400	430	970	1,290	290	1,000
1957	36.1	14.1	22.1	1,240	370	870	1,140	240	900
1956	31.4	12.5	18.9	1,090	320	770	1,000	210	790
1955	27.5	11.3	16.1	980	290	690	850	180	670
1954	23.8	10.0	13.8	880	270	610	710	160	550
1953	20.5	8.8	11.7	750	230	520	620	140	480
1952	17.3	7.7	9.7	650	200	450	520	120	400
1951	14.5	6.6	8.0	540	170	370	450	100	350
1950	12.1	5.6	6.5	450	150	300	370	80	290
1945	5.4			310			220		
1940	2.4			160			140		
1935	1.3			110			100		
1930	.8			100			90		

[1] Excludes annuitants.   [2] As of end of the year.   [3] Includes refunds to employees and their survivors, and lump-sum payments under deferred profit-sharing plans.

Series H 305–317. Unemployment Insurance—Coverage, Benefits, and Financing Under State Programs: 1941 to 1970

[Includes Alaska and Hawaii]

Year	Average covered employment [1]	Average weekly insured unemployment	First payments	Average weekly initial claims [2]	Average weekly benefits [3]	Percent of average weekly wage	Average actual duration of benefit payments	Claimants exhausting benefits [4]	Duration of benefits for exhaustees [5]	Total benefits paid [6]	Contributions collected [7]	Taxable wages [8]	Reserves [9] (end of year)
	305	306	307	308	309	310	311	312	313	314	315	316	317
	1,000	1,000	1,000	1,000	Dollars		Weeks	1,000	Weeks	Mil. dol.	Mil. dol.	Mil. dol.	Mil. dol.
1970	52,814	1,805	6,402	296	50.34	35.6	12.3	1,295	24.4	3,848	2,507	182,320	11,896
1969	52,915	1,101	4,214	200	46.17	34.4	11.4	812	19.8	2,128	2,545	181,535	12,638
1968	50,867	1,111	4,198	201	43.43	34.3	11.6	848	19.6	2,032	2,552	171,335	11,717
1967	49,272	1,205	4,628	226	41.25	34.6	11.4	867	19.3	2,092	2,678	161,097	10,778
1966	48,112	1,061	4,140	203	39.75	34.7	11.2	781	21.1	1,771	3,030	156,673	9,828
1965	45,495	1,328	4,813	232	37.19	33.8	12.2	1,086	21.3	2,166	3,053	143,969	8,357
1964	43,575	1,605	5,498	268	35.92	33.7	13.0	1,371	21.7	2,522	3,047	136,326	7,296
1963	42,371	1,806	6,040	298	35.27	34.5	13.3	1,569	21.6	2,775	3,019	129,557	6,648
1962	41,629	1,783	6,074	302	34.56	34.9	13.1	1,638	21.6	2,675	2,952	125,477	6,273
1961	40,407	2,290	7,066	350	33.80	35.4	14.7	2,371	21.8	3,423	2,450	119,371	5,802
1960	40,523	1,908	6,753	331	32.87	35.2	12.7	1,603	21.4	2,727	2,288	119,260	6,643
1959	39,852	1,684	5,867	277	30.41	33.5	13.1	1,703	21.7	2,279	1,956	115,272	6,892
1958	38,406	2,526	7,941	369	30.58	35.3	14.8	2,599	21.7	3,513	1,471	109,133	6,953
1957	39,670	1,474	5,071	278	28.21	33.5	11.6	1,191	20.5	1,734	1,544	112,826	8,662
1956	38,929	1,212	4,729	235	27.02	33.3	11.4	1,020	20.0	1,381	1,463	109,879	8,574
1955	36,590	1,254	4,508	235	25.04	32.1	12.4	1,272	20.3	1,350	1,209	101,575	8,264
1954	35,372	1,865	6,590	315	24.93	33.5	12.8	1,769	20.0	2,027	1,136	96,539	8,219
1953	36,667	995	4,228	225	23.58	32.3	10.1	764	19.2	962	1,348	99,630	8,913
1952	35,577	1,024	4,384	222	22.79	33.0	10.4	931	19.3	998	1,368	94,670	8,328
1951	34,858	969	4,127	218	21.09	32.2	10.1	811	17.9	840	1,493	90,252	7,782
1950	32,887	1,503	5,212	252	20.76	34.4	13.0	1,853	19.3	1,373	1,191	81,545	6,972
1949	31,695	1,976	7,364	340	20.48	36.0	11.8	1,935	18.7	1,736	987	76,268	7,010
1948	33,088	1,002	4,008	210	19.03	34.1	10.7	1,028	[10] 18.0	790	1,000	78,536	7,603
1947	32,278	1,009	3,984	187	17.83	34.6	11.1	1,272	17.8	775	1,096	72,981	7,303
1946	30,234		4,461	189	18.50	39.6	13.4	1,986	18.5	1,095	912	63,690	6,860
1945	28,407		[5] 2,823	116	18.77	41.6	8.5	[11] 254	14.5	446	1,162	58,545	6,914
1944	30,044		533	29	15.90	35.9	7.7	[11] 102	13.8	62	1,317	60,637	6,072
1943	30,828		664	36	13.84	33.6	9.0	[11] 194	14.3	80	1,325	59,049	4,716
1942	29,349		2,815	122	12.66	35.3	10.0	[11] 1,078	12.6	344	1,139	49,721	3,388
1941	26,814		3,439	164	11.06	36.6	9.4	[11] 1,544	12.1	344	1,006	38,677	2,524

[1] Before 1945, average of workers in last pay period of each type (weekly, semi-monthly, etc.) ending within the month; thereafter, ending nearest 15th of each month. Beginning January 1964, represents the number of workers earning wages during the pay period including the 12th of the month. Includes Puerto Rico beginning Jan. 1961.   [2] Includes initial transitional claims.   [3] For total unemployment; includes dependents' allowance.   [4] Based on date final payments were issued.   [5] Excludes Wisconsin prior to 1964; in addition, excludes data as follows: 1941, for 5 States; 1942–1943, 3 States; 1944, 7 States; 1945, 11 States; 1948–1949, 1 State.   [6] Excludes reconversion unemployment benefits for seamen from 1947–1950.   [7] Includes contributions, penalties, and interest from employers; employee contributions in States which tax workers; and $40.6 million deposited by Federal Government in 1938 to trust funds of 15 States, representing payroll taxes collected by the former in 1936.   [8] Wages subject to State unemployment insurance taxes.   [9] Funds available for benefits. Excludes transfers to: Railroad unemployment insurance program, $8 million in 1941; to States' temporary disability funds, $200,000 in 1946, $15 million in 1947, and $64 million in 1948. Includes, in 1955, $3 million advance to Alaska from Federal account in Unemployment Insurance Trust Fund, which advance was repaid in Dec. 1956. Includes $33.4 million allocation to the States in July 1956, based on 1955 taxable wages (Employment Security Administrative Financing Act of 1954).   [10] Excludes Jan.-Mar. 1948 data for all States.   [11] Excludes Indiana, Wisconsin, and Wyoming in 1941–1943; Wisconsin and Wyoming in 1944; and Wisconsin in January-November 1945.

Series H 318–331. Railroad Unemployment Insurance Benefits: 1940 to 1970

[In thousands, except as indicated. For years ending June 30. Covers program activities during year regardless of when unemployment or sickness occurred. Average payments for 2-week claim period and number of beneficiaries based on sample]

Year	Unemployment benefits							Sickness benefits [2]						
	Applications received	Claims received	Bene-ficiaries	Accounts exhausted	Benefit payments, number [1]	Total payments ($1,000)	Average payment	Applications received	Claims received	Bene-ficiaries	Accounts exhausted	Benefit payments, number [1]	Total payments ($1,000)	Average payment
	318	319	320	321	322	323	324	325	326	327	328	329	330	331
1970	98	438	79	6	407	35,028	$91.84	121	707	91	17	674	57,927	$112.87
1969	112	516	96	8	485	40,840	88.85	128	684	93	16	646	55,747	110.63
1968	275	751	233	9	711	41,698	61.45	121	560	88	14	523	34,052	90.80
1967	98	525	81	8	496	34,413	74.44	127	591	92	16	553	36,477	91.00
1966	175	727	153	10	696	47,673	71.26	134	631	101	18	595	40,447	91.15
1965	153	979	127	19	927	71,260	78.97	142	688	106	20	648	43,984	91.37
1964	172	1,188	152	24	1,137	86,563	77.42	150	727	114	20	693	47,349	91.30
1963	213	1,572	191	34	1,506	116,789	78.38	156	751	121	21	718	50,035	91.55
1962	231	2,048	215	50	1,995	156,788	78.79	168	798	125	22	764	54,120	91.75
1961	359	2,663	319	68	2,546	206,651	80.40	169	828	128	24	788	54,974	91.44
1960	254	2,026	221	51	(NA)	208,554	79.49	190	880	142	26	847	66,080	90.42
1959	265	2,765	300	90	2,636	193,118	67.09	171	876	139	26	842	54,757	76.28
1958	391	2,746	312	67	2,595	169,214	65.42	204	942	153	25	896	52,544	73.05
1957	279	1,553	221	28	1,434	83,154	58.23	194	915	145	25	875	50,028	71.29
1956	177	1,123	149	22	1,022	55,456	54.98	200	930	150	26	889	50,040	69.40
1955	371	2,785	320	77	2,594	152,668	59.06	205	961	151	27	912	52,388	68.63
1954	316	2,118	265	34	1,981	95,541	48.68	203	942	154	26	902	44,904	60.47
1953	264	1,305	224	15	1,202	53,849	45.26	207	918	158	24	878	43,526	58.87
1952	220	905	162	11	823	22,741	28.06	192	801	143	20	758	25,898	41.35
1951	233	1,028	181	17	912	24,780	27.53	186	826	143	22	783	27,003	40.96
1950	562	3,731	506	83	3,475	113,769	32.72	197	896	160	22	852	29,487	41.16
1949	347	1,706	286	20	1,531	46,745	30.70	214	922	179	21	873	29,823	40.29
1948	267	1,347	210	22	1,146	32,426	28.57	235	800	150	16	734	26,604	39.66
1947	257	1,763	225	48	1,583	46,617	29.41							
1946	201	847	157	15	731	20,517	28.01							
1945	9	35	6	1	27	728	26.47							
1944	7	27	5	(Z)	21	547								
1943	22	101	18	3	79	1,753								
1942	90	517	80	11	448	8,890								
1941	181	1,258	164	27	999	17,699								
1940	211	1,441	161	29	1,001	14,810								

NA Not available.   Z Less than 500.   [1] Not adjusted for recoveries or settlements of underpayments.   [2] Includes maternity benefits for claims prior to July 1968.

Series H 332–345. Workmen's Compensation—Payments, by Type of Benefit and Type of Insurance: 1939 to 1970

[In millions of dollars, except as indicated]

Year	Estimated number of workers covered per month (millions)	Total payments	Medical and hospitali-zation payments	Compensation payments			Insurance losses paid by private insurance carriers [1]		State fund disbursements [2]		Self-insurance payments [3]		Percent of payroll covered	
				Total	Disability	Survivor	Amount	Percent of total	Amount	Percent of total	Amount	Percent of total	Work-men's compen-sation costs [4]	Benefits
	332	333	334	335	336	337	338	339	340	341	342	343	344	345
1970	59.0	3,011	1,040	1,971	1,741	230	1,843	61.2	755	25.1	413	13.7	1.13	0.66
1969	59.0	2,624	920	1,704	1,519	185	1,641	62.5	607	23.1	376	14.3	1.07	.62
1968	56.9	2,369	830	1,539	1,374	165	1,482	62.6	557	23.5	331	14.0	1.07	.62
1967	55.1	2,189	750	1,439	1,284	155	1,363	62.3	524	23.9	303	13.8	1.02	.63
1966	53.8	2,000	680	1,320	1,170	150	1,239	62.0	486	24.3	275	13.8	1.00	.61
1965	50.9	1,814	600	1,214	1,074	140	1,124	62.0	445	24.5	244	13.5	1.00	.63
1964	48.9	1,707	565	1,142	1,007	135	1,070	62.7	412	24.1	226	13.2	.99	.62
1963	47.4	1,582	525	1,057	932	125	988	62.5	388	24.5	207	13.1	.96	.62
1962	46.3	1,489	495	994	879	115	924	62.1	371	24.9	194	13.0	.95	.61
1961	45.1	1,374	460	914	804	110	851	61.9	347	25.3	176	12.8	.93	.59
1960	45.0	1,295	435	860	755	105	810	62.5	325	25.1	160	12.4	.89	.58
1959 *	44.1	1,210	410	800	700	100	753	62.2	316	26.1	141	11.7	.91	.58
1958	42.6	1,112	375	737	647	90	694	62.4	285	25.6	132	11.9	.91	.56
1957	43.4	1,062	360	702	617	85	661	62.2	271	25.5	130	12.2	.92	.55
1956	43.1	1,002	350	652	577	75	618	61.7	259	25.8	125	12.5	.91	.55
1955	41.6	916	325	591	521	70	563	61.5	238	25.9	115	12.5	.98	.57
1954	40.0	876	308	568	498	70	540	61.7	225	25.7	110	12.6	.97	.55
1953	41.0	841	280	561	491	70	524	62.3	210	25.0	107	12.7	.94	.55
1952	39.7	785	260	525	460	65	491	62.5	193	24.6	101	12.9	.90	.54
1951	39.0	709	233	476	416	60	444	62.7	170	24.0	94	13.3		
1950	37.2	615	200	415	360	55	381	62.0	149	24.2	85	13.8	.89	.54
1949	35.7	566	185	381	329	52	353	62.4	132	23.3	81	14.4	.98	.55
1948	36.3	534	175	359	309	50	335	62.7	121	22.7	78	14.6	.96	.51
1947		486	160	326	280	46	302	62.1	110	22.7	74	15.2		
1946	33.2	434	140	294	250	44	270	62.1	96	22.1	68	15.8	.91	.54
1945		408	125	283	241	42	253	61.9	91	22.3	65	15.8		
1944		385	120	265	225	40	237	61.4	86	22.3	63	16.3		
1943		353	112	241	203	38	213	60.4	81	22.8	59	16.8		
1942		329	108	221	185	36	190	57.9	81	24.7	57	17.4		
1941		291	100	191	157	34	160	55.0	77	26.6	54	18.4	1.19	.72
1940	25.0	256	95	161	129	32	135	52.7	73	28.4	48	18.9		
1939		235	85	150	120	30	122	52.0	68	29.2	44	18.8		

* Denotes first year for which figures include Alaska and Hawaii.
[1] Net cash and medical benefits paid under standard workmen's compensation policies.
[2] Net cash and medical benefits paid by State funds, and Federal workmen's compensation programs; and starting 1970, cash benefits paid by Federal black lung program. Data for fiscal years for some funds.

[3] Cash and medical benefits paid by self-insurers, plus value of medical benefits paid by employers carrying workmen's compensation policies that exclude standard medical coverage. Estimated from available State data.
[4] Premiums written by private carriers and State funds, and benefits paid by self-insurers increased 5–10 percent to allow for administrative costs. Also includes benefits paid and administrative costs of Federal system for government employees.

Series H 346–367.　Public Assistance—Payments, Recipients, and Average Monthly Payments: 1936 to 1970

[As of December. Through 1942, conterminous U.S. only; thereafter, data include Alaska and Hawaii; beginning 1950, Puerto Rico and Virgin Islands; beginning 1959, Guam]

Year	Payments for year [1] (mil. dol.)									Number of recipients (1,000)	
	Total	Federal	State	Local	Old-age assistance	Aid to the blind	Aid to the permanently and totally disabled	Aid to families with dependent children	General assistance [4]	Old-age assistance	Aid to the blind
	346	347	348	349	350	351	352	353	354	355	356
1970	14,467	7,494	[2] 6,973	([2])	1,866	98	1,000	4,853	705	2,082	81
1969	11,547	6,003	4,260	1,285	1,850	94	827	3,565	558	2,074	81
1968	9,768	5,135	3,391	1,242	1,779	91	692	2,851	496	2,027	81
1967	7,804	4,213	2,618	973	1,859	90	612	2,280	389	2,073	83
1966	6,313	3,498	2,038	777	1,908	90	566	1,924	336	2,073	84
1965	5,476	2,959	1,865	652	2,046	90	561	1,809	382	2,087	85
1964	5,073	2,791	1,686	596	2,039	98	473	1,634	381	2,120	95
1963	4,713	2,627	1,543	542	2,023	96	415	1,466	381	2,152	97
1962	4,437	2,411	1,527	499	1,955	94	359	1,386	392	2,183	99
1961	4,099	2,177	1,439	483	1,886	93	316	1,228	462	2,229	103
1960	3,785	1,958	1,376	451	1,922	94	287	1,056	422	2,305	107
1959	3,658	1,909	1,306	443	1,875	90	259	995	438	2,370	108
1958	3,426	1,728	1,261	438	1,824	87	228	891	396	2,438	110
1957	3,090	1,586	1,143	362	1,768	83	200	750	289	2,480	108
1956	2,853	1,411	1,101	341	1,671	77	176	660	269	2,499	107
1955	2,748	1,358	1,054	337	1,606	71	156	633	282	2,538	104
1954	2,643	1,337	989	316	1,590	68	137	590	258	2,553	102
1953	2,540	1,318	963	259	1,597	66	116	559	203	2,582	100
1952	2,451	1,183	1,005	264	1,527	61	91	551	221	2,635	98
1951	2,383	1,134	991	257	1,469	56	58	559	241	2,701	97
1950	2,406	1,084	1,066	256	1,485	53	8	556	353	2,786	97
1949	2,175	986	982	207	1,373	48	----------	472	281	2,736	93
1948	1,731	759	788	184	1,128	41	----------	363	199	2,498	86
1947	1,481	650	673	158	986	36	----------	294	164	2,332	81
1946	1,179	478	568	133	820	31	----------	208	120	2,196	77
1945	988	402	463	123	726	27	----------	150	86	2,056	71
1944	940	389	430	121	691	25	----------	135	89	2,066	72
1943	926	379	412	135	650	25	----*-----	140	111	2,149	76
1942	957	365	415	176	593	25	----------	158	180	2,230	79
1941	989	336	441	213	540	23	----------	153	273	2,238	77
1940	1,020	294	479	247	473	22	----------	133	392	2,070	73
1939	1,051	243	532	276	434	20	----------	115	482	1,912	70
1938	987	219	496	271	395	19	----------	98	476	1,779	67
1937	803	173	396	234	310	16	----------	71	407	1,579	56
1936	655	88	336	231	156	13	----------	50	437	1,108	45

Year	Number of recipients (1,000)—Con.					Average monthly payment per recipient (dollars)					
	Aid to the permanently and totally disabled	Aid to families with dependent children			General assistance [4]	Old-age assistance	Aid to the blind	Aid to the permanently and totally disabled	Aid to families with dependent children		General assistance [4]
		Families	Total recipients [3]	Children					Per family	Per recipient	
	357	358	359	360	361	362	363	364	365	366	367
1970	935	2,552	9,659	7,033	1,056	77.65	104.35	97.65	187.95	49.65	57.85
1969	803	1,875	7,313	5,413	860	73.90	98.75	90.15	176.05	45.15	50.25
1968	702	1,522	6,086	4,555	826	69.55	92.15	82.65	168.15	42.05	44.70
1967	646	1,297	5,309	3,986	782	70.15	90.45	80.60	161.70	39.50	39.40
1966	588	1,127	4,666	3,526	663	68.05	86.85	74.75	150.10	36.25	36.20
1965	557	1,054	4,396	3,316	677	63.10	81.35	66.50	136.95	32.85	31.65
1964	509	1,012	4,219	3,170	779	63.65	76.15	62.25	131.30	31.50	30.50
1963	464	954	3,930	2,951	872	62.80	73.95	59.85	122.40	29.70	27.45
1962	428	932	3,789	2,844	900	61.55	71.95	58.50	119.10	29.30	26.30
1961	389	916	3,566	2,753	1,069	57.60	68.05	57.05	114.65	29.45	26.15
1960	369	803	3,073	2,370	1,244	58.90	67.45	56.15	108.35	28.35	24.85
1959	346	776	2,946	2,265	1,107	56.70	65.60	54.15	103.70	27.30	25.05
1958	325	755	2,486	2,181	1,246	56.95	63.55	53.80	100.40	26.65	24.05
1957	290	667	2,497	1,912	907	55.50	62.20	52.35	95.15	25.40	22.70
1956	266	615	2,270	1,731	731	53.25	60.00	50.70	91.50	24.80	23.45
1955	241	602	2,192	1,661	743	50.05	55.55	48.75	85.50	23.50	23.30
1954	222	604	2,173	1,639	880	48.70	54.35	48.35	83.70	23.25	22.85
1953	192	547	1,941	1,464	618	48.90	54.05	47.90	82.30	23.20	22.05
1952	161	596	1,991	1,495	587	48.80	53.50	48.40	82.10	23.45	23.30
1951	124	592	2,041	1,523	664	44.55	48.05	46.45	75.80	22.00	22.90
1950	69	651	2,233	1,661	866	43.05	46.00	44.10	71.45	20.85	22.25
1949	–	599	2,048	1,521	1,337	44.75	46.10	–	74.20	21.70	21.25
1948	–	475	1,632	1,214	842	42.00	43.55	–	71.90	20.90	22.40
1947	–	416	1,426	1,060	739	37.40	39.60	–	63.00	18.40	20.60
1946	–	346	1,190	885	673	35.30	36.65	–	62.25	18.10	18.45
1945	–	274	943	701	507	30.90	33.50	–	52.05	15.15	16.55
1944	–	254	862	639	477	28.45	29.30	–	45.60	13.40	15.60
1943	–	272	916	676	558	26.65	27.95	–	41.55	12.35	14.55
1942	–	349	1,158	851	1,000	23.35	26.55	–	36.25	10.95	11.65
1941	–	391	1,288	944	2,068	21.25	25.80	–	33.65	10.20	9.40
1940	–	372	1,222	895	3,618	20.25	25.35	–	32.40	9.85	8.30
1939	–	316	1,042	764	4,675	19.30	25.45	–	31.75	9.65	8.30
1938	–	281	935	688	5,177	19.55	25.20	–	31.95	9.60	7.90
1937	–	229	769	568	4,840	19.45	27.20	–	31.50	9.35	8.50
1936	–	162	546	404	4,545	18.80	26.10	–	29.85	8.80	8.00

– Represents zero. [1] Beginning 1950, includes vendor payments for medical care. [2] Local included with State. [3] Children and one or both parents or one adult caretaker relative other than a parent in families in which the requirements of such adults were considered in determining the amount of assistance; before 1950, partly estimated. [4] Data incomplete.

Series H 368–375. Emergency Public Assistance and Federal Work Programs—Recipients and Assistance: 1933 to 1943

[In thousands. Data through 1942 refer to conterminous United States only; 1943 public assistance data include Alaska and Hawaii]

Year	Federal Emergency Relief Administration	Farm Security Administration	Civilian Conservation Corps	National Youth Administration		Work Projects Administration	Civilian Works Administration	Other Federal projects
				Student program	Out-of-school program			
	368	369	370	371	372	373	374	375
RECIPIENTS (OR PERSONS EMPLOYED), DECEMBER								
1943				86		300		
1942				333	283	1,023		2
1941		26	126					
1940		45	246	449	326	1,826		22
1939		96	266	434	296	2,109		141
1938		115	275	372	240	3,156		167
1937		109	284	304	136	1,594		235
1936	11	135	328	411	178	2,243		506
1935	96	130	459	283		2,667		408
1934	459		330					331
1933	101		290				3,597	264
ASSISTANCE (OR EARNINGS) DURING YEAR								
1943				[1] $3,794		[1] $46,737		$730
1942		$6,271	$34,030	11,328	$32,009	503,055		
1941		12,281	155,604	25,118	94,032	937,366		12,904
1940		18,282	215,846	26,864	65,211	1,269,617		92,604
1939		19,055	230,513	22,707	51,538	1,565,515		247,285
1938		22,579	230,318	19,598	41,560	1,751,053		186,505
1937	$467	35,894	245,756	24,287	32,664	1,186,266		324,639
1936	3,873	20,365	292,397	26,329	28,883	1,592,039		498,415
1935	114,996	2,541	332,851	6,364		238,018		289,897
1934	61,069		260,957				$503,060	275,161
1933	5,753		140,736				214,956	30,718

[1] Program discontinued before end of 1943.

Series H 376–381. Old-Age Assistance Recipients and Insurance Beneficiaries Per 1,000 Population 65 Years Old and Over; and Children Receiving Aid and Child Insurance Beneficiaries Per 1,000 Population Under Age 18: 1936 to 1970

[June of each year. For 1936–1950, 51 jurisdictions, States, and Territories; 1951–1957, 53 jurisdictions, States, and Territories. OAA denotes old-age assistance; OASDHI, old-age, survivors, disability and health insurance; and AFDC, aid to families with dependent children]

Year	Number per 1,000 population 65 years old and over receiving—				Number per 1,000 child population under 18 years old receiving [1]—		Year	Number per 1,000 population 65 years old and over receiving—				Number per 1,000 child population under 18 years old receiving [1]—	
	OAA, OASDHI, or both	OAA	OASDHI	Both OAA and OASDHI	AFDC	OASDHI		OAA, OASDHI, or both	OAA	OASDHI	Both OAA and OASDHI	AFDC	OASDHI
	376	377	378	379	380	381		376	377	378	379	380	381
1970	[2] 896	[2] 104	[2] 855	[2] 63	85	45	1953	464	189	307	32	28	19
1969	890	104	847	61	68	43	1952	424	199	256	31	30	17
1968	886	105	841	60	58	41	1951	418	213	233	28	32	16
1967	878	109	828	59	52	40	1950	374	225	170	21	34	14
1966	837	111	782	56	47	38	1949	350	218	149	17	29	13
1965	814	115	752	53	45	37	1948	318	205	126	13	25	12
1964	805	118	737	50	43	36	1947	298	202	106	10	23	11
1963	794	122	719	47	41	35	1946	274	194	87	7	19	10
1962	768	126	686	44	41	33	1945	251	194	62	5	15	8
1961	746	132	656	42	39	30	1944	251	205	50	4	16	6
1960	721	139	623	41	35	27	1943	257	219	41	3	18	5
1959	700	146	594	40	35	26	1942	265	234	34	3	23	4
1958	669	153	554	38	34	24	1941	254	233	23	2	23	2
1957	625	160	502	37	30	23	1940	223	217	7	1	20	1
1956	568	166	437	35	29	22	1939	210	210			18	
1955	539	172	401	34	30	21	1938	194	194			15	
1954	496	181	348	33	29	20	1937	156	156			11	
							1936	81	81			9	

[1] A small number of children were in families receiving both OASDHI and AFDC.   [2] February 1970 data.

Series H 382–391.   Services Under Public Child Health and Welfare Service Programs: 1937 to 1970

Year	Crippled children's program [1]		Maternal and child health program [2]						Child welfare program	
			Maternity medical clinic		Child health clinic service					
					Infants		Other children			
	Children served	Rate per 10,000 children	Mothers served [3]	Rate per 1,000 live births	Number served	Rate per 1,000 infants	Number served	Rate per 1,000 children 1 to 4 years old	Children served	Rate per 10,000 children under 21
	382	383	384	385	386	387	388	389	390	391
1970	492,000	61	331,499	89	622,708	167	851,081	----------	652,000	80
1969	483,000	59	346,000	97	515,000	144	871,000	----------	694,000	85
1968	475,000	59	292,000	83	591,000	169	1,019,000	----------	656,000	80
1967	476,000	60	366,373	98	603,661	161	1,028,225	----------	607,900	74
1966	437,000	54	282,432	77	679,688	184	1,084,318	----------	573,800	71
1965	(4)	(4)	(4)	(4)	(4)	(4)	(4)		531,600	67
1964	423,000	54	276,187	70	605,480	147	902,013	----------	487,500	62
1963	396,000	51	271,084	65	593,362	142	915,868	----------	457,300	60
1962	385,000	50	267,741	63	606,015	143	893,745	----------	422,800	56
1961	372,000	50	276,771	64	598,736	138	898,919	----------	403,900	56
1960	355,000	49	253,754	59	614,883	142	865,494	----------	382,500	54
1959	339,000	49	235,638	54	629,258	145	854,210	----------	344,500	49
1958	325,000	47	250,630	58	607,291	140	812,371	----------	328,300	48
1957	313,000	47	240,630	(5)	557,801	140	768,476	----------	318,000	48
1956	296,000	46	225,624	(5)	517,243	139	769,102	(6)	297,500	46
1955	278,000	45	188,988	46	448,058	121	576,896	39	289,400	46
1954	271,000	45	190,667	47	446,772	123	576,966	39	289,000	48
1953	252,000	43	177,580	44	411,907	117	591,959	41	282,000	48
1952	238,000	42	180,265	45	433,911	126	576,260	41	279,000	49
1951	229,000	41	188,541	48	402,279	120	580,344	41	277,000	50
1950	214,000	39	175,270	47	302,892	94	420,334	31	270,000	49
1949	207,000	39	168,234	45	294,998	91	398,582	31	265,000	50
1948	195,000	37	152,691	41	263,819	81	379,472	31	260,000	50
1947	175,000	34	151,117	38	245,514	69	320,263	28	255,000	50
1946	155,000	32	130,909	37	187,045	75	275,969	25	250,000	51
1945	130,000	27	116,961	31	169,965	67	256,815	24	241,000	51
1944	125,000	27	129,596	43	169,799	66	266,774	26	----------	----------
1943	115,000	24	147,599	46	185,729	67	264,817	28	----------	----------
1942	133,000	27	161,367	52	185,562	78	307,344	33	----------	----------
1941	147,000	30	167,002	61	185,139	85	314,238	36	----------	----------
1940	127,000	26	146,440	55	175,357	84	299,174	34	----------	----------
1939	127,000	26	125,667	51	138,280	69	277,703	33	----------	----------
1938	114,000	24	119,623	48	156,749	80	266,466	32	----------	----------
1937	110,000	24	75,193	31	127,365	66	200,022	25	----------	----------

NA   Not available.
[1] General coverage of State reports: 1937–1947, services administered or financed in whole or in part by official State agencies under the Social Security Act; 1948–1949, services provided or purchased by official State agencies exclusive of prediagnostic services; 1950–1956, "physician's services" consisting of clinic service, hospital care, convalescent home care, and other services by physicians. Data for 1937 are for 45 States, the District of Columbia, Alaska, Hawaii (Georgia, Louisiana, Oregon not participating); for 1938, Georgia and Oregon also included and, for 1939, Louisiana as well (except for first quarter).   Puerto Rico excluded beginning with the last half of 1940, and Virgin Islands beginning the last half of 1947; prior to these dates they were included.   Arizona, which did not participate 1950–1956, excluded for these years.   Rates for each year are based on the population of States participating in those years.

[2] Includes services administered or supervised by official State health agencies. Reports were received each year except 1941 from 48 States, the District of Columbia, Alaska, and Hawaii.   Missouri was not participating in 1941.   Puerto Rico is included beginning with 1940, and the Virgin Islands beginning with the last half of 1947.
[3] Prior to 1956, antepartum service only.
[4] Through 1964, data on calendar year basis; beginning 1966, on fiscal year basis. Data for 1965 omitted.
[5] Rates not computed.
[6] Beginning 1956, rates no longer computed as older children are included.

Series H 392–397. Vocational Rehabilitation—Caseload and Expenditures: 1921 to 1970

[Expenditures in thousands of dollars. For years ending June 30. Includes Puerto Rico, Guam, and Virgin Islands]

Year	Number of cases: Served	Number of cases: Rehabilitated	Rehabilitation rate per 100,000 population[1]	Expenditures[2]: Total	Expenditures[2]: Federal	Expenditures[2]: State
	392	393	394	395	396	397
1970	875,911	266,975	130	557,707	431,764	125,943
1969	781,614	241,390	119	455,865	340,858	115,007
1968	680,415	207,918	104	377,646	282,337	95,309
1967	569,907	173,594	87	303,846	225,268	78,578
1966	499,464	154,279	78	213,639	144,629	69,009
1965	441,332	134,859	70	154,140	94,713	59,427
1964	399,852	119,708	63	133,259	82,195	51,065
1963	368,696	110,136	58	113,111	69,325	43,786
1962	345,635	102,377	55	101,390	61,986	39,404
1961	320,963	92,501	51	88,150	53,898	34,252
1960	297,950	88,275	49	78,711	48,144	30,567
1959	280,384	80,739	46	71,206	43,932	27,274
1958	258,444	74,317	43	63,727	39,365	24,362
1957	238,582	70,940	41	54,282	33,648	20,634
1956	221,128	65,640	39	46,221	28,830	17,391
1955	209,039	57,981	35	38,629	23,812	14,818
1954	211,219	55,825	34	35,366	22,965	12,402
1953	221,849	61,308	39	34,583	22,948	11,636
1952	228,490	63,632	41	32,689	22,122	10,567
1951	231,544	66,193	43	30,273	21,001	9,271
1950	225,724	59,597	39	29,347	20,340	9,007
1949	216,997	58,020	39	25,819	18,216	7,603
1948	191,063	53,131	36	24,569	17,707	6,862
1947	170,143	43,880	30	19,313	14,189	5,124
1946	169,796	36,106	26	13,749	10,002	3,747
1945	161,050	41,925	32	9,856	7,135	2,720
1944	145,059	43,997	34	6,372	4,052	2,320
1943	129,297	42,618	33	5,630	2,762	2,868
1942	91,572	21,757	16	5,205	2,557	2,648
1941	78,320	14,579	11	4,711	2,282	2,429
1940	65,624	11,890	9	4,108	1,972	2,136
1939	63,575	10,747	8	3,992	1,833	2,159
1938	63,666	9,844	8	3,862	1,791	2,071
1937	----	11,091	9	3,319	1,513	1,806
1936	----	10,338	8	2,603	1,230	1,373
1935	----	9,422	7	2,248	1,032	1,216
1934	----	8,062	6	2,080	916	1,164
1933	----	5,613	5	2,176	999	1,177
1932	----	5,592	5	2,186	998	1,187
1931	----	5,184	4	2,043	933	1,110
1930	----	4,605	4	1,700	739	960
1929	----	4,645	4	1,490	665	825
1928	----	5,012	4	1,541	654	887
1927	----	5,092	6	1,407	631	775
1926	----	5,604	5	1,274	579	695
1925	----	5,825	5	1,187	520	668
1924	----	5,654	5	1,243	551	691
1923	----	4,530	4	1,188	525	663
1922	----	1,898	2	736	312	424
1921	----	523	(Z)	285	93	191

Z Less than one person.
[1] Based on U.S. Bureau of the Census population estimates.
[2] Authorized for basic support under Section 2 of the Vocational Rehabilitation Act.

Series H 398–411. Private Philanthropy—Estimated Fund Flows, by Donors and Recipients: 1929 to 1970

[In millions of dollars]

Year	Payments by donors: Total	Living donors	Charitable bequests	Corporation contributions	Foundation grants	Higher education endowment income	Hospital endowment income	Revenues of recipients: Total	Religious organizations	Parochial schools	Higher education	Hospitals and health	Youth services, welfare, race relations	Other
	398	399	400	401	402	403	404	405	406	407	408	409	410	411
1970	19,241	14,004	2,087	797	1,460	668	225	18,052	6,854	1,422	2,487	2,400	2,050	2,839
1969	18,595	13,265	2,132	1,055	1,320	633	190	16,947	6,464	1,391	2,423	2,305	1,950	2,414
1968	17,374	12,495	1,927	1,005	1,200	580	167	15,985	6,283	1,293	2,265	2,080	1,825	2,239
1967	15,712	11,325	1,721	830	1,155	527	154	15,254	6,390	1,235	2,037	1,907	1,621	2,064
1966	14,660	10,612	1,515	805	1,100	485	143	14,011	5,937	1,239	1,982	1,685	1,484	1,684
1965	13,714	9,983	1,309	785	1,060	445	132	13,468	5,866	1,154	1,938	1,602	1,335	1,573
1964	13,011	9,546	1,164	729	1,042	408	122	12,552	5,273	1,203	1,786	1,546	1,296	1,448
1963	11,930	8,927	1,020	657	839	374	113	12,008	5,029	1,180	1,632	1,349	1,256	1,562
1962	11,277	8,576	876	595	780	345	105	11,295	4,835	1,120	1,476	1,246	1,218	1,400
1961	10,705	8,134	913	512	728	321	97	10,663	4,764	1,058	1,343	1,087	1,163	1,248
1960	10,394	7,891	951	482	677	303	90	9,996	4,550	993	1,232	947	1,108	1,166
1959	9,606	7,349	810	482	626	257	82	(NA)	(NA)	(NA)	(NA)	(NA)	(NA)	(NA)
1958	9,165	7,221	669	395	575	231	74	8,613	4,036	896	1,057	750	1,116	758
1957	8,695	6,652	602	417	740	218	66	(NA)	(NA)	(NA)	(NA)	(NA)	(NA)	(NA)
1956	8,136	6,338	534	418	599	189	58	7,537	3,497	801	936	900	900	503
1955	7,161	5,775	466	415	283	172	50	6,751	3,166	697	795	632	850	611
1954	6,478	5,346	398	314	219	157	44	(NA)	(NA)	(NA)	(NA)	(NA)	(NA)	(NA)
1953	6,389	5,191	355	495	164	146	38	(NA)	(NA)	(NA)	(NA)	(NA)	(NA)	(NA)
1952	5,779	4,772	328	399	110	138	32	(NA)	(NA)	(NA)	(NA)	(NA)	(NA)	(NA)
1951	5,238	4,344	301	343	107	117	26	(NA)	(NA)	(NA)	(NA)	(NA)	(NA)	(NA)
1950	4,546	3,782	274	252	105	113	20	4,429	1,962	428	447	515	685	392
1949	4,130	3,476	206	223	103	122		(NA)	(NA)	(NA)	(NA)	(NA)	(NA)	(NA)
1948	4,104	3,352	296	239	101	116		(NA)	(NA)	(NA)	(NA)	(NA)	(NA)	(NA)
1947	3,734	3,061	223	241	99	110		(NA)	(NA)	(NA)	(NA)	(NA)	(NA)	(NA)
1946	3,265	2,656	186	214	97	112		(NA)	(NA)	(NA)	(NA)	(NA)	(NA)	(NA)
1945	3,042	2,375	192	266	95	114		2,611	1,009	146	246	330	675	205
1944	2,842	2,208	202	234	93	105		(NA)	(NA)	(NA)	(NA)	(NA)	(NA)	(NA)
1943	2,637	2,106	186	159	91	95		(NA)	(NA)	(NA)	(NA)	(NA)	(NA)	(NA)
1942	2,109	1,672	155	98	89	95		(NA)	(NA)	(NA)	(NA)	(NA)	(NA)	(NA)
1941	1,721	1,307	175	58	87	94		(NA)	(NA)	(NA)	(NA)	(NA)	(NA)	(NA)
1940	1,436	1,078	143	38	85	92		1,212	612	115	179	56	150	100
1939	1,395	1,012	179	31	83	90		(NA)	(NA)	(NA)	(NA)	(NA)	(NA)	(NA)
1938	1,259	861	200	27	81	90		(NA)	(NA)	(NA)	(NA)	(NA)	(NA)	(NA)
1937	1,238	909	127	33	79	90		(NA)	(NA)	(NA)	(NA)	(NA)	(NA)	(NA)
1936	1,167	847	128	30	77	85		(NA)	(NA)	(NA)	(NA)	(NA)	(NA)	(NA)
1935	1,001	712	106	28	75	80		969	534	75	141	36	120	63
1934	1,001	679	146	27	74	75		(NA)	(NA)	(NA)	(NA)	(NA)	(NA)	(NA)
1933	868	602	96	27	73	70		(NA)	(NA)	(NA)	(NA)	(NA)	(NA)	(NA)
1932	1,010	646	191	31	72	70		(NA)	(NA)	(NA)	(NA)	(NA)	(NA)	(NA)
1931	1,102	692	220	40	71	79		(NA)	(NA)	(NA)	(NA)	(NA)	(NA)	(NA)
1930	1,244	833	223	35	70	83		1,474	787	153	210	97	167	60
1929	1,277	932	154	32	70	72		(NA)	(NA)	(NA)	(NA)	(NA)	(NA)	(NA)

NA Not available.

Education (Series H 412-787)

H 412–787. General note.

Nationwide statistics on education have been collected and published primarily by the U.S. Office of Education and the U.S. Bureau of the Census. Data on education have also been collected and published by other Federal and State and local governmental agencies, and by independent research organizations.

The Office of Education generally obtains data from reports of State and local school systems and institutions of higher learning. These data relate to school enrollment and attendance, graduates, instructional staff, curricula, school district organization, receipts, and expenditures for elementary and secondary schools, and enrollment, faculty, degrees conferred, income, expenditures, property, and plant fund operations for institutions of higher education.

Data from the Bureau of the Census are obtained through household interviews in decennial censuses and current sample surveys, and relate essentially to school enrollment, literacy, and educational attainment of the general population.

H 412–601. General note.

The Office of Education has issued statistical reports on elementary and secondary education since 1870. For 1870–1917, statistics were included as part of the *Annual Report of the United States Commissioner of Education*. From 1918–1958, a report had been issued for each even-numbered school year under the title, *Biennial Survey of Education in the United States*. Chapter 1 of the *Biennial Survey*, "Statistical Summary of Education," and chapter 2, "Statistics of State School Systems," are primary sources for some derived measures relating to education. Beginning with 1941 and ending with 1951, chapter 2 was supplemented by an abridged report issued as a circular for each odd-numbered school year. Data from the odd-year biennial circulars have not been included in the present compilation. Biennial survey data are based on report forms completed by State departments of education (a copy of the report form appears in the *Biennial Survey* of 1952–1954). Beginning with the *Biennial Survey* of 1952–1954, these forms have been completed by education officials in accordance with detailed instructions contained in the Office of Education, *Handbook I, the Common Core of State Educational Information*. Prior to that date, the forms were completed in accordance with various circulars of information distributed by the Office of Education. Since 1962, the annual publication, *Digest of Educational Statistics*, has provided an abstract of statistical information covering the broad field of American education from kindergarten through the graduate school. The *Digest* utilizes materials from numerous sources, including the statistical surveys and estimates of the Office of Education and other appropriate agencies, both governmental and nongovernmental. It is divided into five chapters: (1) All levels of education; (2) elementary and secondary education; (3) higher education; (4) Federal programs of education; and (5) selected statistics related to education in the United States.

One of the major factors in presenting accurate statistical data on a national basis is the uniformity with which all recording units use standard terms, definitions, and procedures. Prior to 1909, this was controlled only by definitions on the questionnaires requesting information. Since 1909, the Office of Education in cooperation with other national and State organizations has improved uniform recording and reporting through the means of national committees, publications, and national and regional conferences.

A major problem in the collection and processing of comprehensive nationwide school statistics is that of getting all the schools to respond within reasonable time limits. The school authorities are not compelled to report to the Office of Education. There is some evidence that the proportion of schools reporting has increased through the years. This increase is most evident in the data for secondary schools. Prior to 1930, a complete list of public secondary day schools had not been compiled, and consequently there is no way to measure the degree of response in the earlier years. In 1930, there were 23,930 public secondary day schools on file, and reports were received from 22,237. In 1938, the number of schools on file increased to 25,308, and the number reporting was 25,091. In 1952, there were 23,757 schools, and replies were received from all but 12 schools. The data for the missing schools were estimated, and the published totals for 1952 cover all public secondary day schools.

Since 1870, there have been both major and minor changes in the collection patterns with changes in the administration of the program. Some patterns lasted for many years. With voluntary response and no field service (until 1924), response rates varied in their completeness for both reporting in general and for specific items. The completeness of the coverage is not always made evident in the publication. Field service supplemented returns by mail for the 1923–1924 biennial chapters. Visits were made to State departments of education and colleges and universities to complete the coverage from basic or secondary records that were available in the State departments of education or at individual schools and institutions. The introduction of sampling in recent years has also insured adequate coverage.

The data in these historical tables will not always agree with similar data in the publications cited as sources for a specific year because tabulations were "kept open" for many years and as data came in they were added and reflected in future historical tables.

H 412–432. Kindergarten, elementary, and secondary schools and enrollment, 1870–1970.

Source: **Series H 412, H 414–418, H 420–422, H 424, H 426–427, H 429,** and **H 431–432,** U.S. Office of Education, 1870–1916, *Annual Report of the United States Commissioner of Education*, various issues; 1917–1956, *Biennial Survey of Education in the United States*, Statistics of State School Systems, various issues; 1958–1970, *Digest of Educational Statistics*, annual issues. **Series H 413, H 419, H 423, H 425, H 428,** and **H 430,** (except for 1968 and 1970) Abbott L. Ferriss, *Indicators of Trends in American Education*, appendix A and C, © Russell Sage Foundation, New York, 1969, reprinted with permission; 1968 and 1970, U.S. Bureau of the Census, unpublished data.

A school is defined as a division of the school system consisting of a group of pupils composed of one or more grade groups, organized as one unit with one or more teachers to give instruction of a defined type, and housed in a school plant of one or more buildings. More than one school may be housed in one school plant, as is the case when the elementary and secondary programs are housed in the same school plant. The actual operation of schools is generally the responsibility of local school systems in the various States. The local basic administrative unit or school district, series H 412, is an area organized as a quasi-corporation under the jurisdiction of a board of education responsible for the administration of all public schools in the area. School districts provide the machinery through which local control of schools is exercised, and are largely responsible for the location and size of schools, the types of educational programs and services offered, and the amount of financial support to be provided locally.

One-teacher public schools, series H 417, are schools in which one teacher is employed to teach all grades authorized in the school, regardless of the number of rooms in the building.

A public school is defined as one operated by publicly elected or appointed school officials in which the program and activities are under the control of these officials and which is supported by public funds. School enrollment and other figures, prior to 1960, are for public elementary and secondary day schools in conterminous United States. Excluded are public schools in the outlying areas of the United States, public schools operated directly by the Federal Government on military reservations and schools for Indians, public residential schools for exceptional children, and subcollegiate departments of institutions of higher education. Only regular day school pupils are included; pupils enrolled in night schools and summer schools are excluded.

Nonpublic schools, while subject to certain regulatory controls of the State, are under the operational control of private individuals or church-affiliated or nonsectarian institutions. Whether operated on a profit or nonprofit basis, nonpublic schools are generally supported by private funds as distinguished from public funds.

Nonpublic school figures are not strictly comparable. For example, in some of the earlier years, the figures include enrollment of secondary pupils in subcollegiate departments of institutions of higher education, normal schools, etc. Enrollment figures do not include private schools for exceptional children or private vocational or trade schools. They cover only regular day school pupils; they exclude summer school pupils.

Other schools, series H 431–432, include subcollegiate departments of institutions of higher education, residential schools for exceptional children, Federal schools for Indians, and Federal schools on Federal installations.

It should be noted that the enrollment information in the *Biennial Survey of Education* is collected on a State-by-State basis, and represents a cumulative count of the total number of different pupils registered at any time during the school year in each State. Pupils enrolled in two or more States at any time during the school year are, therefore, counted more than once, resulting in a tendency to increase the total enrollment figure for the Nation.

The number of pupils per classroom teacher, otherwise known as the "pupil-teacher ratio," series H 423, H 425, H 428, and H 430, has often been used as a measure of teacher workload. However, precise data of this type have never actually been available either nationally or for the individual States. In the first place, it has been difficult to obtain accurate information on the number of classroom teachers. The available figures on "teachers" have generally included librarians and guidance and psychological personnel as well as classroom teachers. In the second place, the meaning of the term "pupils" has not always been uniform, since "pupils" may refer to the number *enrolled*, the number in *average daily attendance*, or the number in *average daily membership*. Even if valid pupil-teacher ratios could be computed from satisfactory data, they lose meaning when applied to the whole Nation or to an entire State. National averages tend to obscure the significant differences in pupil-teacher ratios, such as those between urban and rural areas, between large and small schools, and between elementary and secondary schools.

H 433–441. School enrollment rates per 100 population, by sex and race, 1850–1970.

Source: U.S. Bureau of the Census. Annual data, *Current Population Reports*, series P-20, Nos. 54, 66, 74, 80, 93, 101, 110, 117, 126, 129, 148, 162, 167, 206, and 222. Decennial data, 1850–1930, Fifteenth Census Reports, *Population*, vol. II, pp. 1094 and 1095; 1940–1950, *U.S. Census of Population: 1950*, vol. II, part 1, p. 1–206; 1960, *U.S. Census of Population: 1960*, PC(1)-1D, table 165, pp. 1–369 to 1–371; 1970, *U.S. Census of Population: 1970*.

For decennial census years, the statistics refer to the total population within the specified age group; figures from the Current Population Survey refer to the civilian noninstitutional population. Persons not covered in the CPS (Armed Forces and institutional population) are known to have low enrollment rates.

In the Census of Population for 1940, 1950, 1960, and 1970, and in the Current Population Survey, 1954–1970, enrollment was defined as enrollment in "regular" schools only—that is, schools where enrollment may lead to an elementary or high school diploma, or to a college, university, or professional school degree. Such schools are public, private, or parochial schools; colleges, universities, or professional schools, either day or night. Enrollment was either full time or part time.

If a person was receiving regular instruction at home from a tutor and if the instruction was considered comparable to that of a regular school or college, the person was counted as enrolled. Enrollment in a correspondence course was counted only if the course was given by a regular school, such as a university, and the person received credit thereby in the regular school system.

Children enrolled in kindergarten were included in the "regular" school enrollment figures in the Current Population Survey beginning in 1950; children enrolled in nursery school were included beginning in 1967. Children enrolled in kindergarten were not included in the "regular" school enrollment figures in the 1950 Census of Population; however, they have been included here to make the data comparable with earlier years and with current practice. In censuses prior to 1950, no attempt was made to exclude children in kindergarten so that the statistics for those years include varying proportions attending kindergarten. Also, in censuses prior to 1940, the data were not restricted as to type of school or college the person was attending.

In addition to differences in definitions of school enrollment and in population coverage, the enrollment data for different years may differ because of variations in the dates when the questions were asked and time periods to which enrollment referred. Data from the current surveys were obtained in October and refer to enrollment in the current school term. In 1940, 1950, 1960, and 1970, the censuses were taken as of April 1, but enrollment related to any time after March 1 in 1940 and any time after February 1 in 1950, 1960, and 1970. The corresponding question in the censuses from 1850 to 1930 applied to a somewhat longer period: In 1850 to 1900, to the 12 months preceding the census date; and in 1910, 1920, and 1930, to the period between the preceding September 1 and the census date (April 15 in 1910, January 1 in 1920, and April 1 in 1930).

Information on school enrollment is also collected and published by the Office of Education (see series H 418–432 and H 700–715). These data are obtained from reports of school surveys and censuses. They are, however, only roughly comparable with data collected by the Bureau of the Census through household interviews, because of differences in definitions, time references, population coverage, and enumeration methods.

See also general note for series H 412–787.

H 442–476. School enrollment, by age, race, and sex, 1953–1970, and by age and sex, 1940–1952.

Source: U.S. Bureau of the Census, *Current Population Reports*, series P-20, Nos. 19, 24, 30, 34, 45, 52, 54, 66, 74, 80, 93, 101, 110, 117, 126, 129, 148, 162, 167, 190, 206, and 222.

The estimates are based on data obtained in October in the Current Population Survey of the Bureau of the Census, except that data shown for 1940 are based on complete enumeration of the population and were published in volumes II and IV of the 1940 census reports on population. Except for 1940, data are for the civilian population excluding the relatively small number in institutions. Data shown for 1940 relate to the total population, including those in institutions and all members of the Armed Forces (about 267,000) enumerated on April 1.

The school enrollment statistics from the current surveys are based on replies to the enumerator's inquiry as to whether the person was enrolled in school. Enumerators were instructed to count as enrolled anyone who had been enrolled at any time during the current term of the school year in any type of graded public, parochial, or other private school in the regular school system. Such schools include nursery schools, kindergartens, elementary schools, high schools, colleges, universities, and professional schools. Attendance may be on either a full-time or part-time basis and during the day or night. Thus, regular schooling is that which may advance a person toward an elementary or high school diploma, or a college, university, or professional school degree. Children enrolled in nursery schools and kindergarten are included in the enrollment figures for "regular" schools.

"Special" schools are those which are not in the regular school system, such as trade schools or business colleges. Persons attending "special" schools are not included in the enrollment figures.

Persons enrolled in classes which do not require physical presence in school, such as correspondence courses or other courses of independent study, and in training courses given directly on the job, are also excluded from the count of those enrolled in school, unless such courses are being counted for credit at a "regular" school.

Since the estimates are based on a sample, they may differ somewhat from the figures that would have been obtained if a complete census had been taken using the same schedules, instructions, and enumerators. As in any survey work, the results are subject to errors of response and reporting as well as to sampling variability.

H 477–485. Enrollment of exceptional children in special programs, 1922–1970.

Source: U.S. Office of Education, 1922–1948, *Biennial Survey of Education in the United States, 1946–1948*, chapter 5, Statistics of Special Schools and Classes for Exceptional Children; 1953, same report, *1952–1954*; 1958–1970, *Digest of Educational Statistics*, various issues.

"Exceptional children" applies to pupils who need special adjustive services, referred to as "special education," because of their physical, intellectual, or personal-social differences from other children. Included are the unusually bright or gifted children; the mentally retarded; the crippled, including the cerebral-palsied; those with special health problems such as cardiac involvement, epilepsy, and other debilitating conditions; the blind and partially seeing; the deaf and hard-of-hearing; those with speech defects; and the socially and emotionally maladjusted.

Pupils are reported according to the major type of exceptionality for which they were receiving special education.

H 486–491. Public elementary and secondary schools—receipts, by source, 1890–1970.

Source: U.S. Office of Education, 1890–1916, *Annual Report of the United States Commissioner of Education*, various issues; 1918–1958, *Biennial Survey of Education in the United States*, various issues, except for series H 487–489 for 1940–1958, see source citation for 1960–1970; 1960–1970, *Digest of Educational Statistics*, various issues, except for series H 486 for 1960 and series H 490–491 for 1960 and 1962, see *Statistics of State School Systems*, various issues.

Revenue receipts represent additions to assets (cash) from taxes, appropriations, and other funds which do not incur an obligation that must be met at some future date and do not represent exchanges of property for money. Receipts from county and other intermediate sources are included with local receipts. Other sources of revenue, series H 491, include gifts and tuition, and transportation fees from patrons.

Nonrevenue receipts represent amounts which either incur an obligation that must be met at some future date or change the form of an asset from property to cash and therefore decrease the amount and the value of school property. Money received from loans, sale of bonds, sale of property purchased from capital funds, and proceeds from insurance adjustments constitute most of the nonrevenue receipts.

See also general note for series H 412–601 and text for series H 412–432.

H 492–507. Public elementary and secondary schools—expenditures, by purpose, 1870–1970.

Source: All series except as noted, U.S. Office of Education, 1870–1916, *Annual Report of the United States Commissioner of Education*, various issues; 1918–1956, *Biennial Survey of Education in the United States*, various issues; 1958–1970, *Digest of Educational Statistics*, annual issues. **Series H 502–503**, gaps in Office of Education series computed at U.S. Bureau of the Census on basis of series A 29, H 492, and H 520. **Series H 505–507**, 1914–1948, Office of Education, unpublished data. **Series H 493**, Abbott L. Ferriss, *Indicators of Trends in American Education*, appendix C, © Russell Sage Foundation, New York, 1969, reprinted with permission.

Expenditures for administration, series H 495, include those for the central office staff for administrative functions and all general control which is systemwide and not confined to one school, subject, or narrow phase of school services. Instruction expenditures, series H 496, include salaries of instructional staff and clerical assistants, and expenditures for free textbooks, school library books, and supplies and other expenditures for instruction. Plant operation and maintenance expenditures, series H 497, include salaries of custodians, engineers, carpenters, painters, etc.; fuel, light, water, and power; and supplies, expenses, and contractual service. Other current expenditures, series H 498, include those for fixed charges and for attendance, health, transportation, food, and miscellaneous services.

Capital outlay, series H 499, includes expenditures for the acquisition of fixed assets or additions to fixed assets (such as land or existing buildings, improvement of grounds, construction of buildings, additions to buildings, remodeling of buildings, and initial or additional equipment). Interest, series H 500, includes interest payments on short-term and current loans from current funds, and on bonds from current and sinking funds. Other expenditures, series H 501, include expenditures, when separately reported, for summer schools, community colleges, and adult education.

See also general note for series H 412–601 and text for series H 412–432.

H 508–519. Private schools—receipts and expenditures, by level of instruction and by purpose, 1930–1970.

Source: U.S. Office of Education, 1930–1958, *Biennial Survey of Education in the United States*, various issues; 1960–1970, *Digest of Educational Statistics* and *Projections of Educational Statistics*, annual issues.

See text for series H 486–491 and H 492–507.

H 520–530. Public elementary and secondary day schools—attendance and instructional staff, 1870–1970.

Source: U.S. Office of Education, 1870–1916, *Annual Report of the United States Commissioner of Education*, various issues; 1918–1958, *Biennial Survey of Education in the United States*, various issues; 1960–1970, *Digest of Educational Statistics*, annual issues.

Figures for average daily attendance in public schools were computed by dividing the total number of days attended by all pupils enrolled by the number of days school was actually in session. Only days when the pupils were under the guidance and direction of teachers are considered as days in session.

"Instructional staff" refers to personnel who render direct and personal services which are in the nature of teaching or the improvement of the teacher-learning situation. Included, therefore, are supervisors of instruction, principals, teachers, guidance personnel, librarians, and psychological personnel. The duty of supervisors of instruction, including consultants, is to assist teachers in improving the learning situation and instructional methods at a particular level or in a particular subject. Principals are the administrative heads of schools. They usually administer a building or a group of buildings with or without the aid of supervisors.

The term "teacher" may be defined as a person employed to instruct pupils or students. At the elementary and secondary levels it does not include supervisors and principals, or librarians and guidance and psychological personnel when separately reported; at the higher education level it does not include administrative and research staff members.

Beginning with the school year ending in 1920, the Office of Education has collected data on salaries of total instructional staff (supervisors, principals, teachers, librarians, and guidance and psychological personnel). Salary information for prior years is available for teachers only. Average annual salaries of instructional staff members were obtained by dividing total expenditures for salaries by the number of such personnel.

H 531–534. Pupil transportation—public elementary and secondary schools, 1930–1970.

Source: U.S. Office of Education, *Digest of Educational Statistics, 1972*, p. 37.

Pupil transportation services are generally the result of State legislation for reorganization of school systems and consolidation of widely scattered school attendance areas and the objective of school districts to achieve equalization of educational opportunity.

Expenditures of public funds for transportation include salaries, vehicle replacement, supplies and maintenance for vehicles and garages, transportation insurance, contracted services, fares for public transportation, and payments in lieu of transportation.

Prior to 1960, the cost per pupil transported was based on pupils in average daily membership; thereafter, on pupils in average daily attendance.

H 535–544. Catholic elementary and secondary schools, 1920–1970.

Source: 1920–1948 (except 1947), U.S. Office of Education, *Biennial Survey of Education in the United States, 1930–1932, 1934–1936*, and *1946–1948*, and *Digest of Educational Statistics, 1972*; 1947 and 1952–1963, National Catholic Welfare Conference, Washington, D.C., *Summary of Catholic Education*, biennial issues; 1950 and 1964–1970, National Catholic Educational Association, Washington, D.C., *A Statistical Report on Catholic Elementary and Secondary Schools for the Years 1967–68 to 1969–70* and *A Report on U.S. Catholic Schools, 1970–71* (copyright).

The elementary division of the Catholic school system includes five types of schools: (1) Parochial schools are operated in connection with parishes; (2) inter-parochial schools are under the administrative control of two or more parishes; (3) archdiocesan or diocesan schools are under the direct administration of an ordinary and serve the parishes designated by him; (4) private schools are conducted independently of parishes by religious communities; (5) institutional schools include industrial schools; schools for blind, deaf, delinquent, or subnormal children; and schools conducted in orphanages.

In Catholic secondary education, there are, broadly, three types of administrative control, defined generally as for the elementary above: (1) Central or diocesan; (2) parochial; and (3) private. However, many parochial and private schools really function as diocesan schools.

The data for elementary school teachers exclude priests serving as part-time teachers of religion.

H 545–571. Public secondary day schools—percent of pupils enrolled in specified subjects, 1890–1965.

Source: U.S. Office of Education, 1890–1949, *Biennial Survey of Education in the United States, 1948–1950*; 1955–1965, *Digest of Educational Statistics, 1972*, and unpublished data.

For 1910–1934, the percentages are based on the number of pupils enrolled in the last 4 years of all schools that returned usable questionnaires. For 1890, 1900, and 1949–1965, the figures are based on the total number of pupils enrolled in the last 4 years of all schools. The source for 1890–1949 states that "when necessary, the subjects

reported in previous surveys were analyzed, and appropriate components were either recombined, separately listed, or eliminated (with corresponding changes in the number and percentage enrolled) in a manner to yield as close comparability as possible with the data in the current (1948–49) survey."

H 572–586. Vocational programs, federally aided, 1918–1970.

Source: U.S. Office of Education, *Vocational & Technical Education* (previously titled *Digest of Annual Reports of State Boards for Vocational Education*), annual issues.

These series include Alaska, Hawaii, and Puerto Rico for all years; Virgin Islands beginning 1951; Guam beginning 1960; and American Samoa and the Trust Territory of the Pacific Islands in 1970.

H 587–597. School retention rates—fifth grade through college entrance, 1924–1932 to 1962–1970.

Source: U.S. Office of Education, *Digest of Educational Statistics, 1972*, p. 14.

The Office of Education bases its school retention rates on fifth-grade enrollment because the high rate of retardation in the early elementary grades tends to inflate the enrollment figures for these grades. Fifth-grade enrollment is regarded as a better measure of the number of persons entering the first grade for the first time 4 years earlier than is total first-grade enrollment for that year. Compulsory attendance laws keep virtually all children in school at least until the fifth grade.

Retention rates are based on enrollments in public elementary and secondary schools and are adjusted to include estimates for nonpublic schools. The computations include all college students, full-time and part-time, who are enrolled in degree-credit programs.

H 598–601. High school graduates, by sex, 1870–1970.

Source: U.S. Office of Education. 1870–1938, *Statistical Summary of Education, 1937–38*, table 15; 1940–1952, *Biennial Survey of Education in the United States*, various issues; 1954–1970, *Projections of Educational Statistics*, annual issues. **Series H 599**, computed on basis of U.S. Bureau of the Census estimates in *Current Population Reports*, series P-25, Nos. 310, 311, and 511, and unpublished data.

Figures for high school graduates include graduates from public and nonpublic schools and exclude persons granted equivalency certificates.

H 602–617. Years of school completed, by race and sex, 1940–1970.

Source: U.S. Bureau of the Census, *Current Population Reports*, series P-20, Nos. 15, 45, 77, 99, 121, 138, 158, 169, 182, 194, and 207.

These data are based on sample surveys and relate to the resident population, including inmates of institutions and members of the Armed Forces living off post or with their families on post; all other members of the Armed Forces are excluded. Except for 1940, the data were derived from the combination of answers to two questions: (a) "What is the highest grade of school he has ever attended?" and (b) "Did he finish this grade?" In 1940, a single question was asked on highest grade of school completed.

The questions on educational attainment apply only to progress in "regular" schools; for definition, see text for series H 442–476.

The median years of school completed, series H 609 and H 617, is defined as the value which divides the population into two equal parts—one-half having completed more, and the other half less, schooling than the median. The median was computed after the statistics on years of school completed had been converted to a continuous series of numbers (e.g., completion of the first year of high school was treated as completion of the 9th year and completion of the first year of college as completion of the 13th year). The persons completing a given school year were assumed to be distributed evenly within the interval from .0 to .9 of the year (e.g., persons completing the 12th year were assumed to be distributed evenly between 12.0 and 12.9). The effect of the assumption is to place the median for younger persons slightly below, and for older persons slightly above, the true median. Because of the inexact assumption as to the distribution within an interval, this median is more appropriately used for comparing groups and the same group at different dates than as an absolute measure of educational attainment.

H 618–647. Median years of school completed, by age, sex, and race, 1940–1970.

Source: U.S. Bureau of the Census, 1940 and 1950, *U.S. Census of Population: 1950*, vol. II, part 1, pp. 1–236 to 1–239; 1960, *U.S. Census of Population: 1960*, series PC(1)–1D, pp. 1–404 to 1–407; 1970, *Current Population Reports*, series P–20, No. 207, pp. 11–15.

The data for 1940, 1950, and 1960 are based on the decennial censuses—complete count in 1940, 20-percent sample in 1950, and 25-percent sample in 1960. The data for 1970 are based on the March 1970 Current Population Survey and may differ from census data for the following reasons: (1) Only those members of the Armed Forces in the United States living off post or with their families on post are included in the CPS whereas all members of the Armed Forces in the United States are included in the census data; (2) there are differences between the CPS and the censuses in coverage, enumeration techniques, and methods of allocating responses.

In general, the data refer to education received in "regular" schools. For definition, see text for series H 442–476.

For definition of median years of school completed, see text for series H 602–617. The procedure used both in 1940 and 1950 for calculating the median years of school completed made allowance for the fact that many persons reported as having completed a given full school year had also completed a part of the next higher grade. Thus, it is assumed that persons who reported 12 full years of school completed had actually completed 12.5 years, on the average.

Differences in the quality of education data for the two censuses may have resulted in part from changes in the way the information was requested. In 1940, a single question was asked on highest grade of school completed. In the 1950 and 1960 censuses and the 1970 survey, data on years of school completed were obtained from a combination of responses to two questions, one asking for the highest grade of school attended and another whether that grade was finished. Analysis of data from the 1940 census returns and from surveys conducted by the Bureau of the Census based on the same question wording as in 1940 indicated that respondents frequently reported the year or grade they had last attended, instead of the one completed. There is evidence that, as a result of the change in the questions in 1950, there was relatively less exaggeration in reporting educational attainment than in 1940. Hence, the indicated increases in attainment between 1940 and 1950 tend slightly to understate the true increase.

Although the statistics on median years of school completed have been available only since 1940, the data by age give further indication of time trends.

See also general note for series H 412–787.

H 648–663. Income of males 25 years old and over, by years of school completed, 1939–1970.

Source: 1939–1949, Herman P. Miller, "Annual and Lifetime Income in Relation to Education: 1939–1959," in American Economic Association, *The American Economic Review*, December 1960, pp. 966 and 981 (copyright); 1956–1970, U.S. Bureau of the Census, *Current Population Reports*, series P–60, No. 74, and unpublished data.

Data for 1939 were derived from *1940 Census of Population, Education: Educational Attainment by Economic Characteristics and Marital Status*, tables 29 and 31; for 1946, from *Current Population Reports*, series P–60, No. 5; and for 1949, from *1950 Census of Population*,

series P–E, No. 5B, *Education*, tables 12 and 13. For details of methodology, see the source.

Neither the income concept nor the universe covered is directly comparable for all years shown. Most of the differences, however, are relatively small and are not believed to seriously distort the relationships. The figures for 1939 are based on the 1940 census and are restricted to males 25–64 years of age with $1 or more of wage or salary income and less than $50 of nonwage income. For this group the averages represent total money income; however, the universe has been restricted to those persons who received only wage or salary income. Only about three-fifths of all men 25–64 years old in 1940 were in this category. The effects of this restriction cannot be measured, but it is undoubtedly more important than restrictions cited for other years. It is also possible that this restriction affects college graduates more than persons with less schooling and for them tends to create an adverse selection since college graduates are more likely to have income other than earnings.

The 1946 figures are based on the Current Population Survey and represent the total money earnings (not total income) of the civilian noninstitutional male population 25 years old and over. Although the conceptual differences between income and earnings are substantial, the actual differences in the averages are quite small, primarily because the amount of nonearned income is small relative to the total and this type of income tends to be seriously underreported in household surveys of income. The 1949 figures are based on the 1950 census and also represent the total money income of all males 25 years old and over, including a relatively small number of institutional inmates.

The 1956–1970 figures are entirely comparable since they are based on the Current Population Survey and represent the total money income of the civilian noninstitutional population of the United States and members of the Armed Forces in the United States living off post or with their families on post, but excluding all other members of the Armed Forces. For each person in the sample 14 years old and over questions were asked on the amount of money income received during the preceding calendar year from each of the following sources: (1) Money wages or salary; (2) net income from nonfarm self-employment; (3) net income from farm self-employment; (4) Social Security; (5) dividends, interest (on savings or bonds), income from estates or trusts or net rental income; (6) public assistance or welfare payments; (7) unemployment compensation, government employee pensions, or veterans' payments; (8) private pensions, annuities, alimony, regular contributions from persons not living in this household, royalties, and other periodic income. The amounts received represent income before deductions for personal taxes, Social Security, bonds, etc.

Mean income represents the amount obtained by dividing the total income of a group by the number of income recipients in that group. In the derivation of aggregate amounts based on grouped data for 1956–1968, the number of males in each income interval was multiplied by an estimated mean income. For income intervals below $8,000, the midpoint of each class interval was used; $8,900 was used for the interval $8,000 to $9,999; $12,000 for the interval $10,000 to $14,999; and $19,000 for the interval $15,000 to $24,999. For the $25,000 and over interval, the interpolation was from a Pareto Curve fitted to the data for the upper income range.

H 664–668. Percent illiterate in the population, by race and nativity, 1870–1969.

Source: U.S. Bureau of the Census, 1870–1930, Fifteenth Census Reports, *Population*, vol. II, p. 1223; 1940–1969, *Current Population Reports*, series P–20, Nos. 20, 45, and 217.

Persons were regarded as illiterate who could not read and write, either in English or some other language. Information on illiteracy of the population was obtained from direct questions in the censuses of 1870–1930. The data for 1947, 1952, 1959, and 1969 were obtained from sample surveys; they exclude the Armed Forces and inmates of institutions. The statistics for the census years 1940 and 1950 were derived by estimating procedures. In 1947, the literacy question was asked only of persons who had completed less than 5 years of school; in 1952, 1959, and 1969, the same general procedure was used but the question was asked of those who had completed less than 6 years of school.

Some variation has existed over the years in the way the question on illiteracy was asked. Since 1930, reference has been made as to whether or not the person was able to read and write. In censuses of 1870–1930, two questions were asked, one on whether the person was able to read and one on whether he could write. Illiteracy was defined as inability to write "regardless of ability to read." Since the data showed that nearly all persons who were able to write could also read, the earlier statistics should be generally comparable with data obtained through the consolidated question used in later years.

Ability to read and write cannot be defined so precisely in a census as to cover all cases with certainty. No specific test of ability to read and write was used, but enumerators were instructed not to classify a person as literate simply because he was able to write his name. Analysts of earlier census data assumed that the illiterate population comprised only those persons who had no education whatever. Information on the educational attainment of illiterates obtained in recent sample surveys indicates, however, that some persons cannot read and write even though they have had some formal schooling. For example, data from the Current Population Survey of October 1952 show that among persons 14 years old and over the proportion reported as illiterate ranged from 77.8 percent of those who had not completed a year of school to 1.3 percent of those who had completed 5 years. Comparable figures from the November 1969 survey were 57.4 percent and 2.3 percent, respectively.

Data on illiteracy were also collected in the censuses of 1840, 1850, and 1860, but are not included here because they are not comparable with statistics for subsequent years, and because of limitations in the quality of data for those early years. In 1840, the head of the family was asked for the total number of illiterates in each family, a method which undoubtedly led to some understatement. Beginning with 1850, the individual entry system was used, the question being asked regarding each member of the family. By 1870, another change in census methods was introduced, separate questions being asked on ability to read and ability to write. In addition to changes in the form of the inquiry, the statistics on illiteracy for 1840, 1850, and 1860 related to the population 20 years old and over, whereas in the 1870 and later censuses they referred to the population 10 years old and over.

The percentages of illiterates in the total population 20 years old and over, as recorded in those earlier censuses, were as follows: 1840, 22.0 percent; 1850, 22.6 percent; and 1860, 19.7 percent. The comparable percentages for the white population 20 years old and over in those years were 9.0, 10.7, and 8.9 percent, respectively. The apparent increases in illiteracy of white persons in 1850 and 1870 may be due, in part, to the large influx of immigrants during those periods, many of whom could not read and write in any language. It is more likely, however, that the apparent increases resulted from improvements in the way the information was obtained at those census dates.

See also general note for series H 412–787.

H 669–688. Illiteracy, by age and race, 1947–1969.

Source: U.S. Bureau of the Census, *Current Population Reports*, series P-20, Nos. 45, 99, 112, and 217.

See text for series H 664–668.

H 689–765. General note.

The Office of Education has issued statistical reports on higher education on a periodic basis since 1870. Until 1916, these statistics appeared in the *Annual Report of the United States Commissioner of Education*. There was no report for 1917. For 1918–1958, statistical reports were issued biennially, as chapters of the *Biennial Survey of Education in the United States*. Since 1962, data have appeared in the annual publication, *Digest of Educational Statistics*. In addition, an annual report on conferral of earned degrees has been issued since 1948 and one on early fall enrollments since 1946. An annual report on current income and expenditures and other finance items was also issued from 1933 to 1940, first under the title *The Economic Outlook in Higher Education* and later under the title *College Income and Expenditures*.

Among the major problems involved in the collecting and processing of nationwide statistics of higher education have been those of uniformity and promptness of reporting and completeness of coverage of the field. The problem of uniformity of reporting was attacked in 1930 with the formation of the National Committee on Standard Reports for Institutions of Higher Education; this committee was disbanded in 1935. Its successor, the Financial Advisory Service of the American Council on Education, carried on the work until 1940, when it, too, was discontinued. These two organizations, voluntary in character and operating with no official status, did much to conventionalize finance accounting and reporting procedures in universities and colleges.

The problems of promptness of reporting and completeness of coverage stem from the fact that only the land-grant institutions (fewer than 4 percent of all the institutions in the Nation) are under legal obligation to submit financial or statistical reports to the Office of Education. The percent of institutions supplying usable reports within a reasonable time, however, has increased materially in the last two or three decades, in spite of the fact that inquiries emanating from the Office of Education have increased in number and scope.

Another problem in the compilation of historical statistics of higher education is the double counting of data for some institutions. Until 1916, the tabulations of the Office of Education were built largely around the various professional curricula, with the result that in many instances the data of a professional school within a university were included both in the over-all tabulations of universities and colleges and in those of the profession involved. With the inception of the *Biennial Survey of Education* in 1918, the emphasis in tabulation was shifted to the administrative organization and the data relating to certain professional schools were so tabulated that any possible duplication was identifiable without too much difficulty. Since 1932, the Office of Education has maintained a master list of all institutions in the Nation; thus, the problem of duplicate tabulation is no longer an important one.

H 689–699. Institutions of higher education—number and faculty, 1870–1970.

Source: **Series H 689–692**, and **series H 696–699**, U.S. Office of Education, 1870–1916, *Annual Report of the United States Commissioner of Education*, various issues; 1918–1956, *Biennial Survey of Education in the United States*, various issues; 1958–1970, *Digest of Educational Statistics*, annual issues. **Series H 693–695**, Abbott L. Ferriss, *Indicators of Trends in American Education*, appendix E, © Russell Sage Foundation, New York, 1969, reprinted with permission; and National Center for Health Statistics, *Health Resources Statistics*, DHEW Pub. 73–1509.

Institutions reporting include universities, colleges, professional schools, junior colleges, teachers colleges, and normal schools, both privately and publicly controlled, regular session. The figures for institutions represent administrative organizations rather than individual campuses, i.e., a university operating one or more branches away from the main campus is counted as one institution. There is probably some (undeterminable) underreporting in some of the earlier years. Since 1946, this underreporting has been corrected by the use of estimated reports prepared from secondary sources for nonrespondent institutions.

The term "junior college" is used comprehensively to designate all institutions, of whatever curricular organization, which offer at least 2 but fewer than 4 years of college-level work immediately beyond the high school.

Although the first medical school in the United States was established in 1765, the accuracy of data recorded for years prior to 1900 is questionable. Inspection and classification of medical schools was initiated by the American Medical Association Council on Medical Education in 1904; by 1929 there was only one unapproved school. As far as the data permit, only approved medical and basic science schools are included. Data for 1964 and 1966 show only schools granting M.D. degrees, as reported to the U.S. Office of Education.

Before the founding of the first dental school in 1840, dental work was done by medical doctors or by persons who were self-taught or apprentice-trained. By 1880, most States required dental practitioners to be dental school graduates. For 1840 and 1926–1930, schools offering courses in dentistry are included; for 1850–1924, schools conferring degrees; for other years through 1962, schools in operation. Data for 1964 and 1966 show only schools granting D.D.S. degrees, as reported to the U.S. Office of Education.

Faculty figures include full-time and part-time faculty members. Except in 1932, no attempt has been made to evaluate these services on a full-time equivalent basis. Faculty figures also include the administrative, instructional, research, and other professional personnel. Resident instructional staff, however, excluded administrative and other professional personnel not engaged in instructional activities.

H 700–715. Institutions of higher education—degree-credit enrollment, 1870–1970.

Source: U.S. Office of Education, series H 700–710 and H 712–713, 1946–1970, *Digest of Educational Statistics, 1973*, tables 87–89, 91, and 99; series H 706–709, 1870–1916, *Annual Report of the United States Commissioner of Education*, various issues; 1918–1944, *Biennial Survey of Education in the United States*, various issues. (Also, for series H 707, scattered years, U.S. Bureau of the Census, unpublished data.) Series H 711, 1946–1968, and series H 714–715, 1946–1960, Abbott L. Ferriss, *Indicators of Trends in American Education*, appendix D, © Russell Sage Foundation, New York, 1969, reprinted with permission. Series H 711, 1950, U.S. Bureau of the Census, unpublished data. Series H 714–715, 1962–1970, U.S. Office of Education, *Projections of Educational Statistics*, 1972 and 1973 editions.

The term "degree-credit enrollment" refers to students whose current program in an institution of higher education consists wholly or principally of work which is creditable toward a bachelor's or higher degree, either in the student's own institution or by transfer to another institution.

See also text for series H 689–699.

H 716–727. Institutions of higher education—current income, 1890–1970.

Source: U.S. Office of Education. 1890–1910, *Annual Report of the United States Commissioner of Education*, various issues; 1920–1960, *Biennial Survey of Education in the United States*, various issues; 1962–1964, *Higher Education Finances*, OE 52009, and unpublished data; 1966–1970, *Financial Statistics of Institutions of Higher Education*, various issues. (Most of these data appear also in the annual *Digest of Educational Statistics*.)

Total current income represents funds accruing to, or received by, higher educational institutions, usable for their recurring day-to-day activities.

Educational and general funds, series H 717–725, are those available for the regular or customary activities of an institution which are part of, contributory to, and/or necessary to its instructional or research program. These include salaries and travel of faculty and administrative or other employees; purchase of supplies or materials

for current use in classrooms, libraries, laboratories, or offices; and operation and maintenance of the educational plant.

Income from students, series H 718, represents fees (matriculation, tuition, laboratory, library, health, and other fees, but not charges for rooms or meals) regularly paid by students themselves or for them by their relatives or philanthropic groups. Payments of tuition and fees by the Federal Government for veterans are not included.

Endowment and other nonexpendable funds, series H 719, are those funds the principal of which is to be invested and only the income of which is to be used for the current purposes of the institution. If funds are merely temporarily placed in the endowment fund, the right to withdraw them being reserved by the donor or the governing board of the institution concerned, they are known as "funds functioning as endowment" and are not subject to the principal of "once endowment, always endowment."

Private gifts and grants, series H 723, are voluntary contributions from philanthropically-minded individuals and organizations to the various institutions of higher education.

Sales and services of instructional departments and of organized activities related to them, series H 724, are frequently referred to briefly as "related activities." The term includes all the incidental earnings of an institution, such as sales of livestock or dairy products of an agricultural school; tuition and other income of a laboratory school, a demonstration school, or a museum; fees for care at a medical or dental clinic; and other income of this nature derived from services directly connected with the instructional program of the institution.

Other sources of income, series H 725, include annuity funds and plant funds. Annuity funds are funds acquired subject to the condition that the recipient institution pay a stipulated sum of money annually or at other regular intervals to a designated beneficiary or beneficiaries, not necessarily the same person as the donor. These payments continue until the death of the beneficiary (the last beneficiary, if more than one), at which time the principal of the fund becomes the property of the institution.

Plant funds are funds which have been or are to be invested in buildings, grounds, furniture, scientific equipment, or other permanent physical property of the institution. Real estate held for direct educational or auxiliary use by the institution is thus part of the plant-fund group. See also series H 739–746.

Income from auxiliary enterprises and activities, series H 726, includes income of dormitories, dining halls, cafeterias, union buildings, college bookstores, university presses, student hospitals, faculty housing, intercollegiate athletic programs, concerts, industrial plants operated on a student self-help basis, and other enterprises conducted primarily for students and staff and intended to be self-supporting without competing with the industries of the community in which the institution is located.

Student-aid funds, series H 727, are funds having to do with the provision of scholarships, fellowships, prizes, and student financed aid of any type not involving employment by or repayment to the institution. Student-aid funds may be lent to students to help them defray their expenses while in school.

The "other income" account of an institution of higher education includes income which is either so incidental in its nature, so irregular in its frequency, or so minor in its amount as to make its classification difficult or impractical. The most common types of other income are probably (1) interest on current funds; (2) rent of institutional property for noninstitutional purposes; (3) transcript fees of students; (4) library fines; and possibly other minor items.

See general note for series H 689–765.

H 728–738. Institutions of higher education—current expenditures, 1930–1970.

Source: U.S. Office of Education. 1930–1960, *Biennial Survey of Education in the United States*, various issues; 1962–1964, *Higher Education Finances*, OE 52009, and unpublished data; 1966–1970, *Financial Statistics of Institutions of Higher Education*, various issues.

(Most of these data appear also in the annual *Digest of Educational Statistics*.)

Expenditure data were not tabulated for all institutions of higher education until 1930. Prior to that time they were collected from land-grant institutions and teacher-education institutions only. Other professional schools and non-land-grant institutions were omitted from the surveys.

Organized research expenditures, series H 732, cover research programs of sufficient magnitude to warrant carrying them separately in the finance budget.

Plant operation and maintenance expenditures, series H 734, include wages of janitors and other caretakers; cost of fuel, light, trucking of materials about the campuses, and repairs to buildings; and other costs connected with keeping the physical plant in good order.

Expenditures for conducting laboratory or demonstration schools, medical-school hospitals, dental clinics, home-economics cafeterias, agricultural-college creameries, college-operated industries, and other activities closely connected with the instructional program but not actually integral parts of it are frequently referred to briefly as "related activities," series H 735.

Extension and public service expenditures, series H 736, cover correspondence courses, radio and television courses, adult study courses and other non-degree-credit courses, institutes, public lectures, cooperative extension in land-grant institutions, radio and television stations, and similar media for carrying the work of an institution beyond its traditional and customary campus activities.

H 739–746. Institutions of higher education—plant fund operations, 1920–1966.

Source: U.S. Office of Education. 1920–1958, *Biennial Survey of Education in the United States*, various issues; 1960, *Statistics of Higher Education—Receipts, Expenditures, and Property, 1959–60*; 1962–1964, *Higher Education Finances*, OE 52009; 1966, *Higher Education Finances*. (Most of these data appear also in the annual *Digest of Educational Statistics*.)

Data represent moneys received and spent by higher educational institutions for expanding their physical holdings (land, buildings, equipment of various sorts) held or utilized primarily for instructional, recreational, or student residence purposes. Real estate held and operated for investment purposes is not included.

See also text for series H 716–727.

H 747–750. Institutions of higher education—property, 1890–1970.

Source: See source for series H 716–727.

Data represent value of all permanent or quasi-permanent assets which include lands, buildings, and equipment; funds held for investment purposes only (the income from such funds being available for current use); funds subject to annuity or living trust agreements; and funds the principal of which may be lent to students to help defray their living expenses or tuition bills. The term "fund" is used in its accounting sense of cash or other valuable assets (real estate, bonds, stock certificates, and other evidences of ownership or equity).

See also text for series H 716–727.

H 751–765. Institutions of higher education—degrees conferred, by sex, 1870–1970.

Source: **Series H 751–754, H 757–759,** and **H 761–763,** U.S. Office of Education, 1870–1953, *Biennial Survey of Education in the United States*, Statistics of Higher Education, biennial issues, and unpublished data; 1954–1970, *Projections of Educational Statistics*, annual issues. Series **H 755–756, H 760, H 764,** and **H 765,** Abbott L. Ferriss, *Indicators of Trends in American Education*, appendix D, © Russell Sage Foundation, New York, 1969, reprinted with permission, except series H 756 and H 760, 1968–1970, from U.S. Office of Education, unpublished data.

The first-level degree (designated as "bachelor's or first professional") is defined as the first degree granted upon completion of a course of study in a given field. The degree must be based on at least 4 years of college work or the equivalent thereof. The same classification (namely, "first level") is given to a degree, e.g., LL.B., regardless of whether the degree is based on 7 years' preparation, 6 years' preparation, or less; and regardless of whether the student had previously earned a degree in another field. The first-level degree is ordinarily a bachelor's degree, but important exceptions occur in certain of the professional fields. The second-level degree is a degree beyond the first level but below the doctorate; ordinarily, a master's degree. The doctorate (the highest level of earned degrees) includes such advanced degrees as Ph.D., Ed.D., D.Eng., and Dr. P.H.; it includes only earned degrees, not honorary.

H 766–787. Number of doctorates, by field, 1920–1970.

Source: National Research Council, Commission on Human Resources, Washington, D.C., Doctorate Records File.

The Doctorate Records File is a virtually complete source of data about persons receiving doctorates since 1920. The doctoral degrees reported are those earned at regionally accredited U.S. universities and include such degree titles as Doctor of Philosophy (Ph.D.), Doctor of Science (Sc.D.), Doctor of Education (Ed.D.), Doctor of Engineering (D.Eng.), etc. Professional degrees such as Doctor of Medicine (M.D.), Doctor of Dental Surgery (D.D.S.), and Doctor of Veterinary Medicine (D.V.M.) are excluded.

Information about the doctorate recipients of 1920 to 1957 was obtained from the graduate schools and is limited to the following: Sex, baccalaureate institution and year, master's institution and year, and doctoral institution, year, and field of degree. Since 1957 the information has been obtained from the Survey of Earned Doctorates questionnaire which is given to the doctoral candidates by the graduate schools at the time all requirements for the degree have been met. The questionnaires are completed by the doctorate recipients who provide data about their birth date and place, sex, citizenship, marital status, and racial or ethnic group. Information is also provided about their educational background from high school to doctorate, sources of financial support in graduate school, and postgraduation employment plans.

Some of the fields included in the groupings shown in this table are:

H 769, Earth sciences: mineralogy, geochemistry, stratigraphy, paleontology, geophysics, hydrology, oceanography, meteorology, applied geology, fuel technology, etc.

H 772, Basic medical sciences: biochemistry, biophysics, anatomy, cytology, embryology, immunology, microbiology and bacteriology, animal physiology, and molecular biology.

H 773, Medical sciences: medicine and surgery, public health, parasitology, pathology, pharmacology, hospital administration, veterinary medicine, pharmacy, etc.

H 774, Agricultural sciences: agronomy, agricultural economics, food science and technology, fish and wildlife, animal sciences, forestry, horticulture, phytopathology, etc.

H 775, Other biological sciences: biometrics and biostatistics, botany, ecology, hydrobiology, plant physiology, zoology, genetics, entomology, etc.

H 780, Other social sciences: communications, statistics, geography, area studies, urban and regional planning, etc.

H 784, Other arts and humanities: applied art, history and criticism of art, music, archaeology, religion, philosophy, linguistics, speech as a dramatic art, etc.

H 785, Professional fields: business administration, journalism, law and jurisprudence, theology, social work, home economics, library and archival science, speech and hearing sciences, etc.

Series H 412–432. Kindergarten, Elementary, and Secondary Schools and Enrollment: 1870 to 1970

Schools [1]

School year ending—	School districts [2]	Elementary Total	Elementary Public	Secondary Total	Secondary Public	One-teacher public schools (1,000)
	412	413	414	415	416	417
1970 [3]	17,995	80,172	65,800	29,122	25,352	1.8
1968	22,010	85,779	70,879	31,311	27,011	4.1
1966	26,983	88,556	73,216	31,203	26,597	6.5
1964	31,705	(NA)	77,584	30,882	26,431	9.9
1962	35,676	96,672	81,910	29,479	25,350	13.3
1960 *	40,520	105,427	91,853	29,845	25,784	20.2
1958	47,594	108,511	95,446	29,501	25,507	25.3
1956	54,859	116,799	104,427	29,933	26,046	35.0
1954	63,057	122,614	110,875	29,550	25,637	42.8
1952	71,094	134,429	123,763	27,068	23,746	50.7
1950	83,718	138,600	128,225	27,873	24,542	59.7
1948	94,926	156,831	146,760	28,776	25,484	75.1
1946	101,382	170,090	160,227	27,608	24,314	86.6
1944	111,383	180,190	169,905	31,984	28,973	96.3
1942	115,493	193,397	183,112	28,134	25,123	107.7
1940	117,108	(NA)	(NA)	(NA)	(NA)	113.6
1938	119,001	231,652	221,660	28,794	25,467	121.2
1936	(NA)	242,166	232,174	28,979	25,652	131.1
1934	(NA)	246,228	236,236	28,041	24,714	139.2
1932	127,531	242,484	232,750	29,698	26,409	143.4
1930		247,581	238,306	27,188	23,930	149.3
1928						156.1
1926						162.8
1924						169.7
1922						180.8
1920						190.7
1918						196.0
1916						200.1

Enrollment

School year ending—	Total [4]	Per 100 persons, 5–17 years old	Public day schools Total	Public Kindergarten	Public Elementary Pupils	Public Elementary Pupil/teacher ratio	Public Secondary Pupils	Public Secondary Pupil/teacher ratio	Nonpublic schools [1] Total [5]	Nonpublic Elementary Pupils	Nonpublic Elementary Pupil/teacher ratio	Nonpublic Secondary Pupils	Nonpublic Secondary Pupil/teacher ratio	Other schools Elementary	Other schools Secondary
	418	419	420	421	422	423	424	425	426	427	428	429	430	431	432
	1,000		1,000	1,000	1,000		1,000		1,000	1,000		1,000		1,000	1,000
1970	51,319	97.8	45,619	2,601	29,996	27.1	13,022	14.4	5,700	4,100	28.3	1,400	18.9	195	97
1968	50,742	97.6	44,742	2,479	29,775	28.6	12,488	15.3	6,000	4,600	30.9	1,400	18.2	190	96
1966	48,479	95.9	42,174	2,262	28,315	31.0	11,597	15.2	6,304	4,763	33.5	1,329	18.1	187	95
1964	46,674	94.8	40,187	2,132	27,172	31.8	10,883	15.7	6,487	4,796	35.9	1,287	17.6	180	85
1962	44,285	94.9	38,269	2,081	26,622	32.4	9,566	15.4	6,016	4,521	36.9	1,120	17.7	179	83
1960 *	41,762	95.0	36,087	1,923	25,679	32.2	8,485	15.4	5,675	4,286	38.8	1,035	18.4	154	80
1958	38,756	93.5	33,529	1,772	23,897	31.5	7,860	16.0	5,228	3,944	38.6	931	17.9	151	79
1956	35,872	93.1	31,163	1,564	22,726	33.6	6,873	16.8	4,709	3,623	41.5	823	16.2	145	79
1954	33,175	92.5	28,836	1,474	21,072	34.3	6,290	16.8	4,339	3,275	42.3	747	15.2	131	71
1952	30,372	91.5	26,563	1,272	19,409	33.4	5,882	17.1	3,809	2,922	38.3	656	15.7	112	59
1950	28,492	92.3	25,111	1,034	18,353	32.9	5,725	17.7	3,380	2,575	35.6	672	15.9	105	56
1948	26,998	91.1	23,945	989	17,302	33.0	5,653	18.5	3,054	2,269	36.4	602	14.4	82	49
1946	26,124	91.2	23,300	773	16,905	32.6	5,622	19.4	2,825	2,213	35.0	565	15.5	(NA)	40
1944	25,758	89.7	23,267	697	17,016	32.9	5,554	19.2	2,491	2,022	(NA)	421	(NA)	(NA)	46
1942	27,179	93.5	24,562	626	17,549	32.5	6,388	21.3	2,617	2,085	32.6	483	15.3	(NA)	53
1940	28,045	94.2	25,434	595	18,237	32.7	6,601	22.0	2,611	2,096	33.2	458	15.2	133	71
1938	28,663	93.7	25,975	607	19,141	33.2	6,227	22.0	2,687	2,252	33.4	437	16.0	(NA)	63
1936	29,006	92.9	26,367	607	19,786	33.8	5,975	22.3	2,639	2,253	34.0	387	15.3	(NA)	63
1934	29,163	92.6	26,434	602	20,163	33.5	5,669	24.9	2,729	2,371		360	(NA)	(NA)	63
1932	29,061	91.8	26,275	701	20,434	33.0	5,140	22.2	2,786	2,384		403	(NA)	(NA)	49
1930	28,329	89.5	25,678	723	20,556	33.2	4,399	20.6	2,651	2,255		341		143	71
1928	27,810	89.1	25,180	695	20,573	33.1	3,911	20.7	2,631	2,235		341	14.0		71
1926	27,180	88.8	24,741	673	20,311	32.6	3,757	22.2	2,439						
1924	26,016	87.3	24,289	610	20,289	33.9	3,390	23.5	1,727						
1922	24,820	85.8	23,239	529	19,837	34.3	2,873	22.2	1,581						
1920	23,278	83.2	21,578	481	18,897	33.6	2,200	21.6	1,699	1,456		214	12.3	99	86
1918	22,516	81.8	20,854		18,920	32.6	1,934	23.0	1,662						
1916	22,172	83.0	20,352		18,896		1,456		1,820						
1915	21,474	81.5	19,704		18,375		1,329		1,770						
1914	20,935	80.6	19,154		17,935		1,219		1,781						
1913	20,348	79.8	18,609		17,474		1,135		1,739						
1912	19,830	79.2	18,183		17,078		1,105		1,647						
1911	19,636	79.5	18,035		17,050		985		1,601						
1910	19,372	79.4	17,814		16,899	34.4	915	27.8	1,558	1,440		117	10.5	71	83
1909	18,995	79.1	17,506		16,665		841		1,489						
1908	18,609	78.6	17,062		16,292		770		1,547						
1907	18,200	77.8	16,891		16,140		751		1,309						
1906	18,056	78.0	16,642		15,919		723		1,414						
1905	17,806	77.9	16,468		15,789		680		1,338						
1904	17,560	77.8	16,256		15,620		636		1,304						
1903	17,205	77.1	16,009		15,417		592		1,196						
1902	17,126	77.6	15,917		15,367		551		1,209						
1901	17,072	78.3	15,703		15,161		542		1,370						

See footnotes at end of table.

Series H 412–432. Kindergarten, Elementary, and Secondary Schools and Enrollment: 1870 to 1970—Con.

School year ending—	Total [4]	Per 100 persons, 5–17 years old	Public day schools			Nonpublic schools [1]				Other schools	
			Total	Elementary pupils	Secondary pupils	Total [5]	Elementary pupils	Secondary		Elementary	Secondary
								Pupils	Pupil/ teacher ratio		
	418	419	420	422	424	426	427	429	430	431	432
	1,000		*1,000*	*1,000*	*1,000*	*1,000*	*1,000*	*1,000*		*1,000*	*1,000*
1900	16,885	78.3	15,503	14,984	519	1,382	1,147	111	10.9	37	69
1899	16,474	78.2	15,176	14,700	476	1,298					
1898	16,459	79.2	15,104	14,654	450	1,355					
1897	16,140	78.8	14,823	14,414	409	1,317					
1896	15,834	78.4	14,499	14,118	380	1,335					
1895	15,455	77.6	14,244	13,894	350	1,211					
1894	15,314	78.0	13,995	13,706	289	1,319					
1893	14,826	76.6	13,483	13,229	254	1,343					
1892	14,556	76.3	13,256	13,016	240	1,300					
1891	14,541	77.3	13,050	12,839	212	1,491					
1890	14,479	78.1	12,723	12,520	203	1,757	1,662	95	13.2		60
1889	13,661	75.2	12,392			1,269					
1888			12,183								
1887			11,885								
1886			11,664								
1885			11,398								
1884			10,982								
1883			10,652								
1882			10,212								
1881			10,001								
1880			9,868	9,757	110						
1879			9,504								
1878			9,439								
1877			8,965								
1876			8,869								
1875			8,786								
1874			8,444								
1873			8,004								
1872			7,815								
1871			7,562	7,481	80						
1870			6,872								

* Denotes first year for which figures include Alaska and Hawaii.
NA Not available.
[1] Data for nonpublic schools for most years are partly estimated.
[2] Includes operating and nonoperating districts.
[3] Statistics are for 1970–71.
[4] Partially estimated.
[5] Data for 1890 and 1932–1938 exclude kindergarten enrollment; all other years include it.

Series H 433–441. School Enrollment Rates Per 100 Population, by Sex and Race: 1850 to 1970

[1954–1970, Current Population Survey estimates based on Survey sample; 1950, 1960, and 1970 census data based on 20-percent, 25-percent, and 15-percent samples, respectively. For 1890 and 1940–1970, figures refer to population 5 to 19 years old; 1850–1880, enrollment refers to all ages and population base to persons 5 to 19 years old; 1900–1930, figures refer to population 5 to 20 years old]

Year	Both sexes			Male			Female		
	Total	White	Negro and other races	Total	White	Negro and other races	Total	White	Negro and other races
	433	434	435	436	437	438	439	440	441
CURRENT POPULATION SURVEY									
1970	90.6	90.8	89.4	91.6	91.9	89.6	89.6	89.7	89.1
1969	90.9	91.1	89.5	92.1	92.5	90.0	89.5	89.7	88.9
1968	90.8	91.0	89.4	92.2	92.5	90.5	89.3	89.5	88.4
1967	90.5	90.8	88.6	91.9	92.2	89.8	89.0	89.3	87.4
1966	89.7	89.9	88.5	91.2	91.5	89.9	88.2	88.4	87.2
1965	89.6	89.8	88.5	91.0	91.2	89.8	88.3	88.5	87.2
1964	89.6	89.8	88.4	91.1	91.4	89.2	88.1	88.2	87.6
1963	89.6	89.8	88.0	91.1	91.5	88.7	88.0	88.1	87.3
1962	89.1	89.6	86.3	90.8	91.3	87.6	87.4	87.8	85.0
1961	88.5	88.9	86.3	90.2	90.5	87.7	86.9	87.2	84.9
1960*	88.6	89.0	86.1	90.0	90.6	86.6	87.1	87.3	85.7
1959	88.5	88.8	85.9	89.7	90.2	86.8	87.1	87.5	85.0
1958	88.4	88.9	85.1	90.1	90.5	87.2	86.7	87.2	82.9
1957	87.8	88.2	85.3	89.4	90.0	85.6	86.2	86.4	85.0
1956	87.2	87.8	83.6	88.6	89.4	83.6	85.8	86.1	83.5
1955	86.5	87.0	82.9	88.4	88.9	84.6	84.5	85.0	81.2
1954	86.2	87.0	80.8	87.5	88.4	80.9	84.8	85.4	80.7

See footnotes at end of table.

Series H 433–441.   School Enrollment Rates Per 100 Population, by Sex and Race: 1850 to 1970—Con.

Year	Both sexes			Male			Female		
	Total	White	Negro and other races	Total	White	Negro and other races	Total	White	Negro and other races
	433	**434**	**435**	**436**	**437**	**438**	**439**	**440**	**441**
DECENNIAL CENSUS									
1970	87.9	88.3	85.3	88.5	89.0	85.5	87.2	87.6	85.2
1960*	84.4	84.8	81.5	84.9	85.4	81.7	83.8	84.2	81.2
1950	78.7	79.3	74.8	79.1	79.7	74.7	78.4	78.9	74.9
1940	74.8	75.6	68.4	74.9	75.9	67.5	74.7	75.4	69.2
1930 [1]	69.9	71.2	60.3	70.2	71.4	59.7	69.7	70.9	60.8
1920	64.3	65.7	53.5	64.1	65.6	52.5	64.5	65.8	54.5
1910	59.2	61.3	44.8	59.1	61.4	43.1	59.4	61.3	46.6
1900	50.5	53.6	31.1	50.1	53.4	29.4	50.9	53.9	32.8
1890	54.3	57.9	32.9	54.7	58.5	31.8	53.8	57.2	33.9
1880	57.8	62.0	33.8	59.2	63.5	34.1	56.5	60.5	33.5
1870	48.4	54.4	9.9	49.8	56.0	9.6	46.9	52.7	10.0
1860	50.6	59.6	1.9	52.6	62.0	1.9	48.5	57.2	1.8
1850	47.2	56.2	1.8	49.6	59.0	2.0	44.8	53.3	1.8

* Denotes first year for which figures include Alaska and Hawaii.   [1] Revised to include Mexicans as white persons.

Series H 442–476.   School Enrollment, by Age, Race, and Sex, 1953 to 1970, and by Age and Sex, 1940 to 1952

[As of October, except as noted.   Relates to civilian noninstitutional population 5–34 years of age, except as noted.   Percentages are based on population for specified age, not total population]

Series No.	Age, race, and sex	1970		1969		1968		1967		1966		1965		1964	
		Number (1,000)	Percent of population	Number (1,000)	Percent of population	Number (1,000)	Percent of population	Number (1,000)	Percent of population	Number (1,000)	Percent of population	Number (1,000)	Percent of population	Number (1,000)	Percent of population
442	Total enrolled, 5–34 years old	58,896	59.0	58,718	60.1	57,564	60.1	56,511	60.2	55,070	60.0	53,769	59.7	51,660	58.7
443	5 and 6 years old	7,000	89.5	7,155	88.4	7,241	87.6	7,352	87.4	7,156	85.1	6,995	84.4	6,842	83.3
444	7–13 years old	28,943	99.2	28,844	99.1	28,620	99.1	28,286	99.3	27,895	99.3	27,450	99.3	26,725	99.0
445	14–17 years old	14,796	94.1	14,452	94.0	14,118	94.2	13,638	93.7	13,293	93.7	13,033	93.2	13,014	93.1
446	18 and 19 years old	3,322	47.7	3,351	50.2	3,317	50.4	3,026	47.6	3,176	47.2	2,930	46.3	2,196	41.6
447	20–24 years old	3,359	21.5	3,380	23.0	2,988	21.4	3,002	22.0	2,547	19.9	2,360	19.0	2,048	16.8
448	25–34 years old	1,477	6.0	1,536	6.4	1,280	5.5	1,207	5.4	1,003	4.6	1,001	4.7	835	3.9
449	White persons enrolled	50,538	58.7	50,531	59.8	49,631	59.9	48,816	60.1	47,715	59.9	46,681	59.6	44,851	58.6
450	5 and 6 years old	5,899	90.3	6,056	89.2	6,149	88.5	6,260	88.2	6,106	85.7	6,016	85.3	5,888	84.0
451	7–13 years old	24,564	99.2	24,571	99.2	24,435	99.1	24,223	99.3	23,913	99.3	23,582	99.4	22,966	99.0
452	14–17 years old	12,769	94.5	12,489	94.3	12,226	94.5	11,838	94.1	11,537	94.0	11,327	93.4	11,390	93.5
453	18 and 19 years old	2,924	48.7	2,934	50.9	2,898	50.9	2,663	48.4	2,845	48.2	2,628	47.1	1,948	42.3
454	20–24 years old	3,055	22.5	3,072	23.9	2,748	22.4	2,747	22.9	2,387	21.3	2,206	20.2	1,914	17.9
455	25–34 years old	1,326	6.1	1,408	6.7	1,174	5.7	1,086	5.5	927	4.9	922	4.9	745	4.0
456	Negro and other persons enrolled	8,359	60.8	8,187	61.6	7,934	61.6	7,694	61.3	7,355	60.5	7,088	60.0	6,808	59.5
457	5 and 6 years old	1,101	85.4	1,099	84.3	1,091	83.3	1,092	82.9	1,050	81.6	979	79.3	954	79.6
458	7–13 years old	4,380	99.4	4,273	98.9	4,185	99.0	4,063	98.8	3,982	97.8	3,868	99.2	3,759	99.1
459	14–17 years old	2,027	92.1	1,962	92.4	1,892	92.2	1,800	90.8	1,756	91.6	1,706	91.7	1,624	90.7
460	18 and 19 years old	398	41.9	416	45.5	418	46.7	363	42.7	331	40.0	302	40.1	248	37.1
461	20–24 years old	303	15.2	308	16.7	240	14.0	255	15.4	160	10.2	154	10.2	133	9.1
462	25–34 years old	150	5.2	128	4.6	107	4.0	121	4.6	76	3.0	79	3.1	90	3.6
463	Males enrolled	30,642	62.6	30,583	64.1	30,051	64.3	29,368	64.1	28,733	64.1	28,059	63.5	26,851	62.3
464	5 and 6 years old	3,545	88.9	3,623	87.7	3,683	87.3	3,719	86.6	3,619	84.5	3,555	84.4	3,478	83.4
465	7–13 years old	14,688	99.0	14,620	98.9	14,513	98.9	14,342	99.1	14,139	99.2	13,932	99.3	13,548	98.8
466	14–17 years old	7,531	94.8	7,374	95.0	7,199	95.0	6,975	94.7	6,770	94.4	6,613	93.6	6,658	94.4
467	18 and 19 years old	1,821	54.4	1,886	59.4	1,892	60.4	1,637	56.3	1,841	57.8	1,689	55.6	1,238	50.9
468	20–24 years old	2,062	29.3	2,070	32.0	1,867	30.5	1,862	30.6	1,667	29.2	1,559	27.6	1,332	23.8
469	25–34 years old	996	8.4	1,011	8.9	897	8.1	832	7.8	697	6.8	711	7.0	597	5.9
470	Females enrolled	28,254	55.5	28,135	56.3	27,513	56.1	27,144	56.5	26,337	56.1	25,710	56.0	24,809	55.3
471	5 and 6 years old	3,455	90.2	3,532	89.1	3,558	88.0	3,632	88.2	3,537	85.7	3,440	84.4	3,364	83.2
472	7–13 years old	14,255	99.4	14,223	99.5	14,106	99.3	13,944	99.4	13,756	99.5	13,518	99.4	13,177	99.2
473	14–17 years old	7,265	93.4	7,078	93.1	6,919	93.4	6,662	92.6	6,523	92.9	6,420	92.8	6,356	91.8
474	18 and 19 years old	1,501	41.6	1,465	41.8	1,425	41.3	1,390	40.3	1,335	37.7	1,241	37.7	958	33.7
475	20–24 years old	1,297	15.2	1,310	16.0	1,121	14.3	1,139	15.1	880	12.4	801	11.8	716	10.9
476	25–34 years old	480	3.8	526	4.2	383	3.2	375	3.2	306	2.7	290	2.6	238	2.1

Series H 442-476. School Enrollment, by Age, Race, and Sex, 1953 to 1970, and by Age and Sex, 1940 to 1952—Con.

Series No.	Age, race, and sex	1963 Number (1,000)	1963 Percent of population	1962 Number (1,000)	1962 Percent of population	1961 Number (1,000)	1961 Percent of population	1960 Number (1,000)	1960 Percent of population	1959 Number (1,000)	1959 Percent of population	1958 Number (1,000)	1958 Percent of population	1957 Number (1,000)	1957 Percent of population
442	Total enrolled, 5–34 years old	50,356	58.5	48,704	57.8	47,708	56.8	46,259	56.4	44,370	55.5	42,900	54.8	41,166	53.6
443	5 and 6 years old	6,768	82.7	6,651	82.2	6,638	81.7	6,438	80.7	6,222	80.0	6,101	80.4	5,829	78.6
444	7–13 years old	26,203	99.3	25,634	99.3	25,801	99.3	25,621	99.5	24,626	99.4	23,623	99.5	22,705	99.5
445	14–17 years old	12,517	92.9	11,740	92.0	11,163	91.4	10,240	90.3	9,839	90.2	9,446	89.2	9,067	89.5
446	18 and 19 years old	2,061	40.9	2,144	41.8	1,952	38.0	1,817	38.4	1,601	36.8	1,564	37.6	1,409	34.9
447	20–24 years old	2,014	17.3	1,725	15.6	1,468	13.7	1,350	13.1	1,283	12.7	1,307	13.4	1,336	14.0
448	25–34 years old	793	3.7	810	3.8	686	3.2	792	3.6	799	3.8	858	3.8	820	3.6
449	White persons enrolled	43,815	58.4	42,501	57.9	41,498	56.9	40,348	56.4	38,857	55.5	37,662	54.9	36,132	53.7
450	5 and 6 years old	5,863	83.7	5,761	83.2	5,673	82.2	5,574	82.0	5,402	81.0	5,321	81.4	5,065	79.3
451	7–13 years old	22,551	99.4	22,083	99.4	22,234	99.5	22,149	99.6	21,399	99.5	20,572	99.6	19,849	99.7
452	14–17 years old	10,999	93.3	10,387	92.8	9,848	92.0	9,027	90.8	8,722	90.8	8,398	90.0	8,026	90.1
453	18 and 19 years old	1,805	41.0	1,936	43.0	1,759	39.0	1,606	38.9	1,412	37.3	1,377	38.1	1,214	34.6
454	20–24 years old	1,871	18.3	1,590	16.5	1,342	14.4	1,248	13.9	1,173	13.4	1,200	14.1	1,230	14.7
455	25–34 years old	726	3.9	744	3.9	642	3.3	742	3.8	746	3.8	793	4.0	748	3.7
456	Negro and other persons enrolled	6,541	58.8	6,203	57.1	6,210	56.8	5,910	55.9	5,513	55.1	5,238	54.0	5,034	53.5
457	5 and 6 years old	905	76.6	890	76.0	965	79.1	864	73.3	820	74.3	779	73.9	764	74.3
458	7–13 years old	3,652	99.0	3,551	98.7	3,567	98.2	3,472	99.1	3,228	99.0	3,052	98.8	2,856	98.2
459	14–17 years old	1,518	90.4	1,353	86.6	1,315	86.9	1,213	86.8	1,115	85.3	1,047	82.8	1,041	84.8
460	18 and 19 years old	256	39.8	208	33.4	193	30.6	210	34.6	189	33.6	188	34.3	195	36.7
461	20–24 years old	143	10.2	135	9.9	126	9.1	102	7.5	110	8.5	108	8.7	106	8.8
462	25–34 years old	67	2.7	66	2.6	44	1.7	49	1.9	51	2.1	65	2.6	72	2.9
463	Males enrolled	26,243	62.3	25,452	61.7	24,944	60.4	24,234	60.0	23,192	59.1	22,497	58.7	21,509	57.5
464	5 and 6 years old	3,440	82.7	3,399	82.6	3,402	82.0	3,292	80.8	3,292	79.5	3,123	80.6	2,963	78.3
465	7–13 years old	13,280	99.1	13,003	99.2	13,167	99.3	13,074	99.5	12,556	99.3	12,059	99.5	11,584	99.5
466	14–17 years old	6,402	94.2	6,032	93.7	5,705	92.2	5,247	91.3	5,041	91.4	4,854	90.7	4,646	91.1
467	18 and 19 years old	1,180	51.0	1,212	51.2	1,170	48.6	1,063	47.8	918	45.6	898	47.5	780	43.3
468	20–24 years old	1,365	25.6	1,177	23.4	989	20.2	936	19.9	892	19.6	915	21.0	897	21.3
469	25–34 years old	576	5.7	629	6.2	511	4.9	621	5.9	627	5.9	648	6.0	639	5.9
470	Females enrolled	24,113	54.9	23,252	54.0	22,764	53.4	22,025	52.8	21,178	52.0	20,404	51.0	19,657	50.0
471	5 and 6 years old	3,328	82.6	3,252	81.7	3,236	81.4	3,146	80.6	3,064	80.5	2,978	80.2	2,866	79.0
472	7–13 years old	12,923	99.6	12,631	99.4	12,634	99.3	12,547	99.6	12,070	99.6	11,564	99.4	11,121	99.5
473	14–17 years old	6,115	91.6	5,708	90.3	5,458	90.5	4,993	89.2	4,798	89.0	4,591	87.6	4,421	87.8
474	18 and 19 years old	881	32.3	932	33.7	782	28.6	754	30.0	683	29.2	666	29.4	629	28.1
475	20–24 years old	649	10.3	548	9.1	479	8.3	414	7.4	391	7.1	392	7.3	439	8.2
476	25–34 years old	217	1.9	181	1.6	175	1.5	171	1.7	172	1.5	210	1.8	181	1.5

Series No.	Age, race, and sex	1956 Number (1,000)	1956 Percent of population	1955 Number (1,000)	1955 Percent of population	1954 Number (1,000)	1954 Percent of population	1953 Number (1,000)	1953 Percent of population	1952 Number (1,000)	1952 Percent of population	1951 Number (1,000)	1951 Percent of population	1950 Number (1,000)	1950 Percent of population
442	Total enrolled, 5–34 years old	39,353	52.3	37,426	50.8	36,083	50.0	32,796	46.4	31,980	45.4	30,466	52.8	30,073	51.6
443	5 and 6 years old	5,597	77.6	5,520	78.1	5,443	77.3	4,038	55.7	3,732	54.7	3,196	54.5	3,304	58.2
444	7–13 years old	21,946	99.3	21,028	99.2	19,952	99.4	18,525	99.4	18,414	98.8	17,946	99.1	17,222	98.7
445	14–17 years old	8,413	88.2	7,970	86.9	7,784	87.1	7,538	85.9	7,440	85.2	7,216	85.2	6,988	83.4
446	18 and 19 years old	1,407	35.4	1,232	31.5	1,268	32.4	1,180	31.2	1,062	28.8	974	26.2	1,199	29.7
447	20–24 years old	1,192	12.8	1,010	11.1	999	11.2	981	11.1	904	9.7	846	8.6	1,001	9.2
448	25–34 years old	798	3.5	667	2.9	635	2.7	534	2.3	428	1.8	[1]288	[1]2.5	[1]360	[1]3.0
449	White persons enrolled	34,641	52.5	32,929	50.8	31,895	50.2	29,009	46.6	—	—	—	—	—	—
450	5 and 6 years old	4,868	78.4	4,834	79.2	4,802	78.6	3,621	57.1	—	—	—	—	—	—
451	7–13 years old	19,243	99.4	18,485	99.3	17,562	99.6	16,292	99.7	—	—	—	—	—	—
452	14–17 years old	7,447	89.2	7,007	87.5	6,888	88.3	6,621	86.4	—	—	—	—	—	—
453	18 and 19 years old	1,242	35.9	1,091	32.1	1,149	33.6	1,049	31.7	—	—	—	—	—	—
454	20–24 years old	1,090	13.4	927	11.6	935	12.0	924	11.9	—	—	—	—	—	—
455	25–34 years old	751	3.7	585	2.8	559	2.7	503	2.4	—	—	—	—	—	—
456	Negro and other persons enrolled	4,712	51.5	4,498	50.7	4,188	48.6	3,787	45.5	—	—	—	—	—	—
457	5 and 6 years old	729	72.8	687	71.1	642	68.8	416	46.3	—	—	—	—	—	—
458	7–13 years old	2,703	98.4	2,543	98.2	2,389	98.0	2,233	97.3	—	—	—	—	—	—
459	14–17 years old	966	81.2	962	82.8	897	78.8	918	82.3	—	—	—	—	—	—
460	18 and 19 years old	165	31.8	141	27.6	120	24.0	132	27.6	—	—	—	—	—	—
461	20–24 years old	102	8.7	82	7.2	64	5.8	58	5.4	—	—	—	—	—	—
462	25–34 years old	47	1.9	83	3.3	76	3.0	31	1.3	—	—	—	—	—	—
463	Males enrolled	20,552	56.3	19,573	54.9	18,759	54.0	16,974	50.2	16,644	49.4	15,774	56.8	15,736	54.8
464	5 and 6 years old	2,839	77.1	2,821	78.1	2,746	76.3	2,035	55.0	1,912	54.8	1,648	55.1	1,649	56.8
465	7–13 years old	11,179	99.1	10,725	99.2	10,138	99.2	9,405	99.2	9,382	98.7	9,148	99.1	8,773	98.7
466	14–17 years old	4,275	89.1	4,096	88.6	4,002	88.7	3,844	86.8	3,758	85.4	3,614	85.2	3,568	84.4
467	18 and 19 years old	809	45.1	752	42.5	730	40.6	642	37.7	612	37.2	534	32.4	680	35.7
468	20–24 years old	830	20.6	686	18.1	677	19.1	636	18.5	630	16.9	602	14.3	733	16.0
469	25–34 years old	620	5.7	494	4.5	465	4.2	414	3.7	350	3.2	[1]228	[1]4.2	[1]333	[1]5.9
470	Females enrolled	18,801	48.7	17,853	47.0	17,324	46.3	15,822	43.0	15,336	41.9	14,692	49.1	14,337	48.4
471	5 and 6 years old	2,758	78.2	2,700	78.1	2,697	78.3	2,003	56.6	1,820	54.6	1,548	54.0	1,655	59.5
472	7–13 years old	10,767	99.4	10,304	99.1	9,813	99.6	9,120	99.6	9,032	98.9	8,798	98.9	8,449	98.7
473	14–17 years old	4,138	87.3	3,873	85.2	3,782	85.4	3,695	85.0	3,682	85.0	3,602	85.2	3,420	82.3
474	18 and 19 years old	598	27.4	480	22.5	538	25.4	538	25.4	450	22.1	440	21.3	519	24.3
475	20–24 years old	362	6.8	324	6.1	322	6.0	346	6.4	274	4.9	244	4.3	268	4.6
476	25–34 years old	178	1.5	173	1.4	171	1.4	120	.9	78	.6	[1]60	[1]1.0	[1]27	[1].4

[1] 25–29 years old.

Series H 442-476. School Enrollment, by Age, Race, and Sex, 1953 to 1970, and by Age and Sex, 1940 to 1952—Con.

Series No.	Age, race, and sex	1949 Number (1,000)	1949 Percent of population	1948 Number (1,000)	1948 Percent of population	1947 Number (1,000)	1947 Percent of population	1946 Number (1,000)	1946 Percent of population	1945 Number (1,000)	1945 Percent of population	1940[2] Number (1,000)	1940[2] Percent of population
442	Total enrolled, 5-34 years old	29,283	42.4	28,390	41.5	27,746	41.1	26,924	61.1	25,515	64.0	26,759	57.7
443	5 and 6 years old	3,487	59.3	3,237	56.0	3,069	58.0	3,030	62.0	2,833	60.4	1,805	43.0
444	7-13 years old	16,374	98.6	15,688	98.1	15,302	98.5	14,966	98.3	14,747	98.1	15,035	95.0
445	14-17 years old	6,778	81.6	6,824	81.8	6,737	79.3	6,900	79.6	6,956	78.4	7,709	79.3
446	18 and 19 years old	1,028	25.3	1,134	26.9	1,007	24.3	884	22.5	668	20.7	1,449	28.9
447	20-24 years old	1,041	9.2	1,103	9.7	1,183	10.2	1,144	10.1	311	3.9	761	6.6
448	25-34 years old	576	2.5	405	1.8	448	2.0	--------		--------		--------	
463	Males enrolled	15,489	45.8	14,991	44.8	14,635	44.3	13,941	64.9	12,660	72.7	13,615	58.6
464	5 and 6 years old	1,807	60.2	1,628	55.1	1,549	57.4	1,514	60.8	1,423	59.6	901	42.3
465	7-13 years old	8,330	98.5	7,990	98.3	7,781	98.6	7,585	98.0	7,456	97.7	7,607	94.8
466	14-17 years old	3,447	82.5	3,436	81.9	3,364	78.9	3,435	79.2	3,475	78.0	3,870	78.9
467	18 and 19 years old	593	31.6	682	34.3	587	31.4	469	29.0	192	21.6	770	30.8
468	20-24 years old	827	15.4	898	16.5	947	17.0	938	17.7	114	5.6	467	8.2
469	25-34 years old	487	4.5	358	3.3	407	3.8	--------		--------		--------	
470	Females enrolled	13,794	39.2	13,399	38.4	13,111	38.0	12,983	57.5	12,855	57.3	13,145	56.9
471	5 and 6 years old	1,679	58.4	1,608	56.8	1,520	58.7	1,516	63.3	1,410	61.3	904	43.7
472	7-13 years old	8,045	98.7	7,698	98.0	7,521	98.5	7,381	98.5	7,291	98.4	7,428	95.2
473	14-17 years old	3,331	80.7	3,388	81.7	3,373	79.8	3,465	80.1	3,481	78.7	3,840	79.7
474	18 and 19 years old	435	19.9	452	20.3	420	18.5	415	18.0	476	20.3	680	26.9
475	20-24 years old	215	3.7	206	3.4	236	3.9	206	3.4	197	3.3	294	5.0
476	25-34 years old	89	.7	48	.4	41	.3	--------		--------		--------	

[2] As of April 1.

Series H 477-485. Enrollment of Exceptional Children in Special Programs: 1922 to 1970

[In thousands]

Year [1]	Total	Visually handicapped	Aurally handicapped	Speech impaired	Crippled and special health problems	Emotionally and socially maladjusted	Mentally retarded	Other handicapping conditions	Gifted
	477	478	479	480	481	482	483	484	485
1970[2]	3,158	24	78	1,237	269	113	830	126	481
1966	2,106	23	51	990	69	88	540	33	312
1963[3]*	1,682	22	46	802	65	80	432	22	215
1958	890	12	20	490	52	29	223	12	52
1953	497	9	16	307	29	(NA)	114	--------	23
1948	378	[4] 8	[4] 14	182	[4] 50	15	[4] 87	--------	21
1940	314	9	13	126	53	10	98	--------	3
1936	297	7	9	117	48	13	100	--------	3
1932	164	5	4	23	40	14	75	--------	2
1930	--------	(NA)	(NA)	--------		32	10	(NA)	--------	--------
1927	--------	4		4	--------		--------	52	--------	--------
1922	--------			3	--------		--------	23	--------	--------

* Denotes first year for which figures include Alaska and Hawaii.
NA Not available.
[1] Beginning 1958, data as of February; earlier years, data for school year ending.
[2] Estimated on the basis of State reports to the U.S. Office of Education. (See *Digest of Educational Statistics, 1972*, table 34.)
[3] Beginning 1963, includes residential schools.
[4] Includes Hawaii.

Series H 486–491. Public Elementary and Secondary Schools—Receipts, by Source: 1890 to 1970

[In millions of dollars]

School year ending—	Total receipts	Sources of revenue receipts					School year ending—	Sources of revenue receipts		
		Total [1]	Federal	State [2]	Local [3]	Other		Total [1]	State [2]	Local [3]
	486	487	488	489	490	491		487	489	490
1970	48,891	40,267	3,219.6	16,063	[4] 20,985	[4]	1916	634	95	488
1968 [5]	40,385	31,903	2,806.5	12,276	[4] 16,821	[4]	1915	590	91	457
1966	28,688	25,357	[6] 1,997.0	9,920	13,314	125.3	1914	562	88	425
1964	23,065	20,544	[6] 897.0	8,078	11,481	88.6	1913	507	78	376
1962	20,041	17,528	761.0	6,789	9,905	73.0	1912	469	76	347
							1911	451	69	334
1960*	17,362	14,747	651.6	5,768	8,257	69.8				
1958	14,696	12,182	486.5	4,800	6,858	36.9	1910	433	65	312
1956	12,043	9,687	441.4	3,829	5,394	22.3	1909	404	64	289
1954	9,691	7,867	355.2	2,944	4,547	20.3	1908	382	58	259
1952	7,637	6,424	227.7	2,479	3,716	1.1	1907	355	45	232
							1906	322	48	223
1950	6,401	5,437	155.8	2,166	3,115	.1				
1948	4,869	4,312	120.3	1,676	2,515	.3	1905	302	44	210
1946	3,318	3,060	41.4	1,062	1,956	.3	1904	279	43	193
1944	2,699	2,604	35.9	859	1,709	.3	1903	252	40	174
1942	2,594	2,417	34.3	760	1,622	.2	1902	245	39	173
							1901	235	36	164
1940	2,521	2,261	39.8	684	1,536	.3				
1938	2,493	2,223	26.5	656	1,540	.3	1900	220	38	149
1936	[7] 2,178	[7] 1,971	[7] 9.9	578	1,383	.3	1899	203	35	145
1934	1,940	1,811	21.5	423	1,366	.4	1898	200	35	136
1932	2,229	2,068	8.3	411	1,649	.5	1897	192	34	130
							1896	182	35	125
1930	2,469	2,089	7.3	354	1,727	.8				
1928	2,325	2,026	6.2	333	1,685	1.0	1895	177	35	119
1926	2,172	1,830	5.6	285	1,540	---------	1894	170	33	113
1924	1,959	1,618	4.0	262	1,290	---------	1893	165	34	108
1922	1,743	1,444	2.9	231	1,185	---------	1892	157	30	106
							1891	148	28	100
1920	1,156	970	2.5	160	808	---------				
1918	803	737	1.7	122	613	---------	1890	143	26	97

* Denotes first year for which figures include Alaska and Hawaii.
[1] For 1922, 1924, and years prior to 1918, includes receipts undistributed by source.
[2] Prior to 1918, excludes receipts from sources other than State taxes and appropriations.
[3] Includes county and other intermediate sources of income. Prior to 1918, excludes receipts from sources other than local taxes and appropriations.
[4] "Other sources of revenue receipts" included with "Local."
[5] Estimated.
[6] Includes value of commodities distributed under the school lunch and milk programs.
[7] Includes only Federal aid for vocational education.

Series H 492–507. Public Elementary and Secondary Schools—Expenditures, by Purpose: 1870 to 1970

[In millions of dollars, except as noted]

School year ending—	Expenditures, all schools		Current expenditures, day schools					Capital outlay [4]	Interest	Other expend-itures [5]	Expenditures in current dollars			Expenditures in constant (1970) dollars		
	Total	Per pupil enrolled	Total [1]	Admin-istration	Instruc-tion [2]	Plant opera-tion and main-tenance	Other [3]				Total		Current, per pupil in aver-age daily attend-ance	Total		Current, per pupil in aver-age daily attend-ance
											Per capita	Per pupil in aver-age daily attend-ance		Per capita	Per pupil in aver-age daily attend-ance	
	492	493	494	495	496	497	498	499	500	501	502	503	504	505	506	507
1970	40,683	877	34,218	1,607	23,270	3,512	5,829	4,659	1,171	636	200.20	955.00	815.98	200	955	816
1968	32,977	737	26,877	1,249	18,376	2,864	4,388	4,256	978	866	166.67	786.44	658.26	185	873	731
1966	26,248	613	21,053	938	14,445	2,386	3,284	3,755	792	648	135.44	653.81	537.35	160	773	636
1964	21,325	519	17,218	745	11,750	1,985	2,738	2,978	701	428	113.04	558.59	460.24	138	684	563
1962	18,373	480	14,729	648	10,016	1,760	2,304	2,862	588	194	100.37	529.73	419.00	126	665	526
1960*	15,613	433	12,329	528	8,351	1,508	1,943	2,662	490	133	87.07	472.17	375.14	112	607	482
1958	13,569	405	10,252	443	6,901	1,302	1,605	2,853	342	123	79.68	448.62	341.14	105	593	451
1956	10,955	352	8,251	373	5,502	1,072	1,304	2,387	216	101	66.68	388.06	294.22	94	545	413
1954	9,092	315	6,791	311	4,552	908	1,020	2,055	154	92	57.43	350.90	264.76	81	493	372
1952	7,344	276	5,722	266	3,782	757	917	1,477	114	30	47.88	312.68	244.24	69	449	351
1950	5,838	232	4,687	220	3,112	642	713	1,014	101	36	39.27	258.85	208.83	63	413	333
1948	4,311	180	3,795	170	2,572	526	527	412	76	28	29.51	202.81	179.43	48	329	291
1946	2,907	125	2,707	133	1,854	372	349	111	77	11	20.78	144.62	136.41	43	300	283
1944	2,453	105	2,293	111	1,591	316	276	54	97	9	17.76	124.67	116.99	39	270	254
1942	2,323	95	2,068	101	1,458	289	220	138	109	9	17.23	110.46	98.31	42	268	238
1940	2,344	92	1,942	92	1,403	268	179	258	131	13	17.77	105.74	88.09	48	286	238
1938	2,233	86	1,870	86	1,360	260	164	239	114	10	17.15	99.70	83.87	45	263	221
1936	1,969	75	1,657	67	1,214	233	142	171	133	8	15.38	88.30	74.30	42	243	204
1934	1,720	65	1,516	64	1,121	203	127	59	137	8	13.54	76.22	67.48	54	217	192
1932	2,175	83	1,810	75	1,333	257	144	211	140	13	17.42	97.77	81.36	46	256	213

See footnotes at end of table.

Series H 492–507. Public Elementary and Secondary Schools—Expenditures, by Purpose: 1870 to 1970—Con.

[In millions of dollars, except as noted]

School year ending—	Expenditures, all schools		Current expenditures, day schools					Capital outlay [4]	Interest	Other expenditures [5]	Expenditures in current dollars			Expenditures in constant (1970) dollars		
	Total	Per pupil enrolled	Total [1]	Administration	Instruction [2]	Plant operation and maintenance	Other [3]				Total		Current, per pupil in average daily attendance	Total		Current, per pupil in average daily attendance
											Per capita	Per pupil in average daily attendance		Per capita	Per pupil in average daily attendance	
	492	493	494	495	496	497	498	499	500	501	502	503	504	505	506	507
1930	2,317	90	1,844	79	1,318	295	152	371	93	10	18.87	108.49	86.70	42	239	191
1928	2,184	87	1,706	77	1,220	278	130	383	92	4	18.12	105.98	82.76	40	231	182
1926	2,026	82	1,538	68	1,127	244	99	411	72	5	17.26	102.03	77.45	28	216	164
1924	1,821	75	1,369	55	1,001	221	92	388	59	5	16.25	95.17	71.53	36	209	157
1922	1,581	68	[6] 1,235	51	903	203	69	306	36	4	14.37	85.77	66.98	32	189	148
1920	1,036	48	861	37	633	146	46	154	18	3	9.91	64.16	53.52	20	127	106
1918	764	37	629	25	444	133	27	119	15		7.40	49.13	40.48	20	135	111
1916	641	31	537	15	378		144	104			6.29	41.73	34.98	23	151	127
1915	605	31	503	13	358		131	103			6.03	40.43	33.55	23	151	125
1914	555	29	463	12	335		116	92			5.60	39.04	32.60	21	148	123
1913	522	28	438	10	316		112	84			5.37	38.34	32.17			
1912	483	27	405	9	295		101	78			5.07	36.31	30.44			
1911	447	25	371	6	273		91	76			4.76	34.73	28.84			
1910	426	24	356	7	260		89	70			4.64	33.23	27.85			
1909	401	23	320		237		83	82			4.43	31.61	25.19			
1908	371	22	298		220		78	74			4.18	30.52	24.49			
1907	337	20	272		202		70	65			3.87	28.26	22.77			
1906	308	18	247		186		61	61			3.60	26.30	21.10			
1905	292	18	235		177		58	56			3.53	25.40	20.49			
1904	273	17	224		168		56	49			3.32	24.12	19.77			
1903	251	16	205		157		48	46			3.11	22.70	18.56			
1902	238	15	198		151		47	40			3.01	21.51	17.92			
1901	228	14	188		143		44	40			2.94	21.28	17.51			
1900	215	14	180		138		42	35			2.84	20.21	16.67			
1899	200	13	169		129		40	31				19.25	16.26			
1898	194	13	163		124		39	31				18.73	15.73			
1897	188	13	155		119		36	32				18.76	15.45			
1896	183	13	151		117		34	33				18.71	15.43			
1895	176	12	146		114		33	29			2.55	18.41	15.33			
1894	173	12	142		109		33	30				18.83	15.51			
1893	164	12	134		105		29	30				18.52	15.12			
1892	156	12	126		100		26	29				18.22	14.77			
1891	147	11	121		96		25	26				17.65	14.53			
1890	141	11	114		92		22	26			2.24	17.23	13.99			
1889	133	11	109		88		22	23				16.61	13.63			
1888	124	10			83							15.68				
1887	116	10			79							15.10				
1886	113	10			76							15.01				
1885	110	10			73							15.07				
1884	103	9			68							14.60				
1883	97	9			65							14.58				
1882	89	9			61							14.06				
1881	84	8			58							13.67				
1880	78	8			56						1.56	12.71				
1879	76	8			55							12.93				
1878	79	8			56							13.66				
1877	79	9			55							14.56				
1876	83	9			55							15.69				
1875	84	10			55							16.01				
1874	80	9			51							15.84				
1873	76	10			48							16.02				
1872	74	9			46							15.88				
1871	69	9			43							15.18				
1870	63	9			38						1.64	15.55				

* Denotes first year for which figures include Alaska and Hawaii.
[1] Prior to 1918, includes expenditures for interest.
[2] Prior to 1910, includes only expenditures for salaries of teachers and superintendents.
[3] Prior to 1918, includes plant operation and maintenance; prior to 1910, includes all current expenditures except salaries of teachers and superintendents.

[4] Beginning 1966, includes capital outlay by State and local school building authorities.
[5] Beginning 1954, includes expenditures for community services, previously included in "current expenditures, day schools."
[6] Includes $7,816,000 in undistributed expenses.

Series H 508–519. Private Schools—Receipts and Expenditures, by Level of Instruction and by Purpose: 1930 to 1970

[In millions of dollars]

School year ending—	Receipts					Expenditures						
	Total	Elementary and secondary	Higher education			Total	Current expenditures and interest			Capital outlay or plant expansion		
			Total	Government funds	Other sources		Total	Elementary and secondary	Higher education	Total	Elementary and secondary	Higher education
	508	509	510	511	512	513	514	515	516	517	518	519
1970	13,998	4,500	9,498	2,056	7,443	13,300	11,500	3,900	7,600	1,800	500	1,300
1968	12,535	4,200	8,335	1,972	6,364	11,600	9,700	3,500	6,200	1,900	500	1,400
1966	10,544	3,600	6,944	1,922	5,022	9,800	8,100	2,900	5,200	1,700	500	1,200
1964	8,468	3,070	5,398	1,359	4,039	7,800	6,400	2,500	3,900	1,400	400	1,000
1962	6,659	2,457	4,201	866	3,335	6,100	5,000	1,900	3,100	1,100	400	700
1960	5,707	2,412	3,295	564	2,731	5,275	4,464	1,993	2,471	812	419	393
1958	4,630	2,079	2,551	362	2,189	4,100	3,300	1,500	1,800	800	400	400
1956	3,753	1,627	2,127	265	1,861	3,500	2,800	1,300	1,500	700	400	300
1954	¹2,876	1,354	1,512	230	1,282	(NA)	(NA)	1,000	(NA)	(NA)	400	(NA)
1952	¹2,408	1,028	1,372	274	1,098	(NA)	(NA)	(NA)	(NA)	(NA)	(NA)	(NA)
1950	¹1,656	783	854	307	547	1,739	1,462	654	808	277	136	141
1948	¹1,271	530	727	293	434	(NA)	(NA)	205	(NA)	(NA)	25	(NA)
1940	----	----	----	----	----	503	457	205	252	46	25	21
1930	----	----	----	----	----	578	467	200	267	111	37	74

NA Not available.   ¹ Includes income in addition to that reported for other sources.

Series H 520–530. Public Elementary and Secondary Day Schools—Attendance and Instructional Staff: 1870 to 1970

School year ending—	School attendance			Instructional staff							
	Average daily attendance	Average length of school term (days)	Average number of days attended per enrolled pupil	Total	Average annual salary ¹		Classroom teachers and other nonsupervisory staff ²			Principals	Other supervisory staff or consultants
					In current dollars	In constant (1970) dollars	Total	Male	Female		
	520	521	522	523	524	525	526	527	528	529	530
	1,000			*1,000*			*1,000*	*1,000*	*1,000*	*1,000*	*1,000*
1970	41,934	178.9	161.7	2,253	8,840	8,840	2,131	729	1,402	90.6	31.5
1968	40,828	178.8	163.2	2,071	7,885	8,751	1,957	616	1,341	85.5	29.0
1966	39,154	178.9	163.5	1,885	6,935	8,199	1,786	568	1,218	77.3	21.6
1964	37,405	179.0	163.2	1,717	6,240	7,635	1,625	506	1,119	72.6	18.7
1962	34,682	179.1	162.3	1,588	5,700	7,157	1,504	451	1,053	67.2	16.2
1960*	32,477	178.0	160.2	1,464	5,174	6,648	1,387	402	985	63.6	13.8
1958	29,722	177.6	157.4	1,333	4,702	6,211	1,261	340	921	59.0	14.0
1956	27,740	178.0	158.5	1,213	4,156	5,837	1,149	³294	³839	51.0	13.3
1954	25,644	178.6	158.9	1,098	3,825	5,368	1,042	³254	³779	45.7	10.3
1952	23,257	178.2	156.0	1,012	3,450	4,954	963	235	728	39.7	9.8
1950	22,284	177.9	157.9	962	3,010	4,799	914	195	719	39.3	9.2
1948	20,910	177.6	155.1	907	2,639	4,274	861	162	699	37.1	9.2
1946	19,849	176.8	150.6	867	1,995	4,131	831	138	693	29.4	6.8
1944	19,603	175.5	147.9	865	1,728	3,748	828	127	701	31.6	5.5
1942	21,031	174.7	149.6	898	1,507	3,652	859	183	676	33.1	6.1
1940	22,042	175.0	151.7	912	1,441	3,893	875	195	681	31.5	4.8
1938	22,298	173.9	149.3	919	1,374	3,625	877	185	692	36.4	5.0
1936	22,299	173.0	146.3	906	1,283	3,526	871	179	692	29.6	5.8
1934	22,458	171.6	145.8	880	1,227	3,500	847	162	685	28.1	5.0
1932	22,245	171.2	144.9	901	1,417	3,710	872	154	718	23.9	5.7
1930	21,265	172.7	143.0	892	1,420	3,131	854	142	712	30.9	6.9
1928	20,608	171.5	140.4	868	1,364	----	832	138	694	28.8	7.7
1926	19,856	169.3	135.9	850	1,277	----	814	139	675	26.9	8.4
1924	19,132	168.3	132.5	787	1,227	----	761	129	633	17.9	7.9
1922	18,432	164.0	130.6	756	1,166	----	723	118	605	18.6	14.1
1920	16,150	161.9	121.2	700	871	1,725	⁴680	96	584	13.6	6.6
1918	15,549	160.7	119.8	----	635	----	651	105	546	----	----
1916	15,359	160.3	120.9	----	563	----	622	123	499	----	----
1915	14,986	159.4	121.2	----	543	----	604	118	486	----	----
1914	14,216	158.7	117.8	----	525	----	580	115	465	----	----
1913	13,614	158.1	115.6	----	512	----	565	113	452	----	----
1912	13,302	158.0	115.6	----	492	----	547	115	433	----	----
1911	12,872	156.8	111.8	----	466	----	534	110	423	----	----
1910	12,827	157.5	113.0	----	485	----	523	110	413	----	----
1909	12,685	155.3	112.6	----	----	----	506	108	398	----	----
1908	12,154	154.1	109.8	----	----	----	495	104	391	----	----
1907	11,926	151.8	107.3	----	----	----	481	104	377	----	----
1906	11,712	150.6	106.0	----	----	----	466	109	357	----	----

See footnotes at end of table.

Series H 520–530. Public Elementary and Secondary Day Schools—Attendance and Instructional Staff: 1870 to 1970—Con.

School year ending—	School attendance			Instructional staff			
	Average daily attendance	Average length of school term (days)	Average number of days attended per enrolled pupil	Average annual salary in current dollars [1]	Classroom teachers and other nonsupervisory staff [2]		
					Total	Male	Female
	520	521	522	524	526	527	528
	1,000				1,000	1,000	1,000
1905	11,482	150.9	105.2	386	460	111	350
1904	11,318	146.7	102.1		455	114	341
1903	11,055	147.2	101.7		449	117	332
1902	11,064	144.7	100.6		442	121	321
1901	10,716	143.7	98.0		432	126	306
1900	10,633	144.3	99.0	325	423	127	296
1899	10,389	143.0	97.9		414	131	283
1898	10,356	143.0	98.0		411	132	279
1897	10,053	142.0	96.3		405	131	274
1896	9,781	140.5	94.8		400	130	270
1895	9,549	139.5	93.5	286	398	130	268
1894	9,188	139.5	91.6		389	125	264
1893	8,856	136.3	89.6		383	122	261
1892	8,561	136.9	88.4		374	122	253
1891	8,329	135.7	86.6		368	123	245
1890	8,154	134.7	86.3	252	364	126	238
1889	8,006	133.7	86.4		357	124	232
1888	7,907	132.3	85.9		347	126	221
1887	7,682	131.3	84.9		339	127	212
1886	7,526	130.4	84.1		331	124	208
1885	7,298	130.7	83.6	224	326	122	204
1884	7,056	129.1	82.9		314	119	195
1883	6,652	129.8	81.1		304	116	188
1882	6,331	131.2	81.3		299	119	180
1881	6,146	130.1	80.0		294	123	171
1880	6,144	130.3	81.1	195	287	123	164
1879	5,876	130.2	80.5		280	121	159
1878	5,783	132.0	80.9		277	119	158
1877	5,427	132.1	80.0		267	114	153
1876	5,291	133.1	79.4		260	110	150
1875	5,248	134.4	77.9		258	109	149
1874	5,051	128.8	77.0		248	103	145
1873	4,745	129.1	76.5		238	98	140
1872	4,659	133.4	79.5		230	95	135
1871	4,545	132.1	79.4		220	90	130
1870	4,077	132.2	78.4	189	201	78	123

* Denotes first year for which figures include Alaska and Hawaii.
[1] Prior to 1920, computed for teaching positions only; beginning 1920, also includes supervisors and principals.

[2] Prior to 1938, number of different persons employed rather than number of positions. Includes librarians and guidance and psychological personnel.
[3] Classroom teachers only. Excludes other nonsupervisory instructional staff.
[4] Includes 231 part-time teachers not classified by sex.

Series H 531–534. Pupil Transportation—Public Elementary and Secondary Schools: 1930 to 1970

School year ending—	Pupils transported		Expenditures of public funds [2]		School year ending—	Pupils transported		Expenditures of public funds [2]	
	At public expense [1] (1,000)	Percent of enrollment	Total (mil. dol.)	Cost per pupil transported [1] (dol.)		At public expense [1] (1,000)	Percent of enrollment	Total (mil. dol.)	Cost per pupil transported [1] (dol.)
	531	532	533	534		531	532	533	534
1970	18,199	43.4	1,219	66.96	1950	6,947	27.7	215	30.88
1968	17,131	42.0	981	57.27	1948	5,854	24.4	176	30.11
1966	15,537	39.7	787	50.68	1946	5,057	21.7	130	25.66
1964	14,476	38.7	674	46.55	1944	4,512	19.4	108	23.88
1962	13,223	38.1	576	43.59	1942	4,503	18.3	93	20.64
1960	12,225	37.6	486	39.78	1940	4,144	16.3	83	20.10
1958	10,862	36.5	416	38.34	1938	3,769	14.5	76	20.07
1956	9,696	35.0	354	36.51	1936	3,251	12.3	63	19.27
1954	8,412	32.8	307	36.55	1934	2,795	10.6	54	19.29
1952	7,697	29.0	269	34.93	1932	2,419	9.2	58	24.01
					1930	1,903	7.4	55	28.81

[1] Beginning 1960, relates to pupils in average daily attendance.

[2] Excludes capital outlay.

Series H 535–544. Catholic Elementary and Secondary Schools: 1920 to 1970

[In thousands, except number of schools]

Year [1]	Elementary schools					Secondary schools				
	Number	Pupils enrolled	Teachers			Number	Pupils enrolled	Teachers		
			Total	Religious	Lay			Total	Religious	Lay
	535	536	537	538	539	540	541	542	543	544
1970	9,362	3,355	112	52	60	1,981	1,008	54	27	26
1969	9,695	3,607	110	56	54	2,076	1,051	53	29	23
1968	10,113	3,860	[2]126	68	58	2,192	1,081	[2]57	33	23
1967	10,350	4,106	[2]124	70	53	2,277	1,093	[2]55	34	21
1966	10,769	4,375	120	74	46	2,463	1,110	56	36	20
1965	10,879	4,492	120	76	44	2,413	1,082	57	38	19
1964	10,832	4,534	118	76	42	2,417	1,067	53	36	18
1963	10,775	4,546	115	77	38	2,430	1,044	51	35	16
1962	10,676	4,485	112	77	36	2,502	1,009	47	34	13
1961	10,631	4,445	111	78	33	2,376	938	47	34	14
1960	10,501	4,373	108	79	29	2,392	880	44	33	11
1956	9,615	3,571	85	71	14	2,311	705	35	28	7
1954	9,279	3,235	77	67	9	2,296	624	32	26	6
1952	8,880	2,842	72	66	6	2,180	549	29	24	5
1950	8,589	2,561	67	62	5	2,189	506	28	23	5
1948	8,285	2,305	62	59	3	2,150	483	27	23	4
1947	(NA)	(NA)	(NA)	(NA)	(NA)	2,111	467	27	23	4
1940	7,944	2,035	60	(NA)	(NA)	2,105	361	21	(NA)	(NA)
1936	7,929	2,103	59	55	3	1,946	285	17	14	3
1930	7,923	2,223	58	53	5	(NA)	(NA)	(NA)	---	---
1920	6,551	1,796	42	---	---	1,552	130	8	---	---

NA Not available.   [2] Includes part-time teachers.
[1] Prior to 1958, data for school year ending; thereafter, for October of year shown.

Series H 545–571. Public Secondary Day Schools—Percent of Pupils Enrolled in Specified Subjects: 1890 to 1965

[Covers enrollment in last 4 years of school. For school years ending in year indicated]

Series No.	Specified subject	1965	1963	1959	1955	1949	1934	1928	1922	1915	1910	1900	1890
545	Total enrollment 1,000	11,628	10,372	8,077	6,480	5,399	4,497	2,897	2,155	1,165	739	519	203
546	General science	18.7	17.6	19.6	(NA)	20.8	17.8	17.5	18.3	----	----		
547	Biology	23.2	24.0	20.8	20.0	18.4	14.6	13.6	8.8	6.9	1.1	7.7	10.1
548	Chemistry	9.3	8.3	8.1	7.5	7.6	7.6	7.1	7.4	7.4	6.9	19.0	22.8
549	Physics	4.5	3.8	4.7	4.7	5.4	6.3	6.8	8.9	14.2	14.6	15.3	27.4
550	Physiology					1.0	1.8	2.7	5.1	9.5	15.3	29.8	
551	Earth science					0.4	1.7	2.8	4.5	15.3	21.0		
552	Algebra	28.5	30.4	29.9	25.3	26.8	30.4	35.2	40.2	48.8	56.9	56.3	45.4
553	General mathematics	15.4	11.7	12.7	12.3	13.1	7.4	7.9	12.4	----			
554	Geometry	13.9	14.7	13.4	12.5	12.8	17.1	19.8	22.7	26.5	30.9	27.4	21.3
555	Trigonometry	2.0	2.0	2.7	2.6	2.0	1.3	1.3	1.5	1.5	1.9	1.9	
556	Spanish	14.5	(NA)	(NA)	(NA)	8.2	6.2	9.4	11.3	2.7	.7		
557	French	12.4	(NA)	(NA)	(NA)	4.7	10.9	14.0	15.5	8.8	9.9	7.8	5.8
558	German	2.7	(NA)	(NA)	(NA)	.8	2.4	1.8	.6	24.4	23.7	14.3	10.5
559	English					92.9	90.5	93.1	76.7	58.4	57.1	38.5	
560	Latin					7.8	16.0	22.0	27.5	37.3	49.0	50.6	34.7
561	U.S. and English history					22.8	17.8	18.8	18.2	[1]50.5	[1]55.0	[1]38.2	[1]27.3
562	Civil and community government					[2]8.0	16.4	20.0	19.3	15.7	15.6	21.7	
563	Industrial subjects					26.6	21.0	13.5	13.7	11.2			
564	Bookkeeping					8.7	9.9	10.7	12.6	3.4			
565	Typewriting					22.5	16.7	15.2	13.1				
566	Shorthand					7.8	9.0	8.7	8.9				
567	Home economics					24.2	16.7	16.5	14.3	12.9	3.8		
568	Agriculture					6.7	3.6	3.7	5.1	7.2	4.7		
569	Physical education					69.4	50.7	15.0	5.7				
570	Music					30.1	25.5	26.0	25.3	31.5			
571	Art					9.0	8.7	11.7	14.7	22.9			

NA Not available.   [2] Civil government only.
[1] Includes ancient history and medieval and modern history.

Series H 572–586. Vocational Programs, Federally Aided: 1918 to 1970

[For years ending June 30]

Students enrolled (1,000) — columns 572–577. Expenditures (mil. dol.) — columns 578–586.

Year	Total	Home economics	Distributive occupations	Trades and industry	Agriculture	Other[1]	Total	Federal	State	Local	Home economics	Distributive occupations	Trades and industry	Agriculture	Other[1]
	572	573	574	575	576	577	578	579	580	581	582	583	584	585	586
1970	8,794	2,570	529	1,906	853	2,935	1,842	300	1,542		----	----	----	----	----
1969	7,979	2,449	563	1,721	851	2,395	1,369	255	467	647	182	58	318	118	475
1968	7,534	2,283	575	1,629	851	2,196	1,193	262	400	530	161	48	268	110	317
1967	7,048	2,187	481	1,491	935	1,954	1,004	260	305	439	125	47	236	103	242
1966	6,070	1,898	420	1,269	907	1,576	800	234	217	350	113	28	186	89	173
1965	5,431	2,099	333	1,088	888	1,023	605	157	187	261	98	22	145	87	136
1964	4,566	2,022	334	1,069	861	280	333	55	125	153	90	15	103	77	47
1963	4,217	1,839	310	1,002	828	238	309	55	113	142	83	13	94	74	44
1962	4,073	1,726	321	1,005	823	198	284	51	104	128	80	11	85	73	34
1961	3,856	1,610	306	964	805	171	254	48	89	117	73	11	75	70	26
1960	3,768	1,588	304	938	796	142	239	45	82	111	69	10	73	67	20
1959	3,701	1,586	311	968	757	79	228	41	80	107	67	10	74	67	12
1958	3,629	1,560	283	984	776	27	210	39	72	99	63	9	69	65	4
1957	3,522	1,508	280	952	775	7	191	37	68	86	57	8	64	60	1
1956	3,413	1,487	257	884	786	----	176	33	62	81	53	6	60	57	----
1955	3,314	1,432	235	871	776	----	165	30	58	77	49	6	56	54	----
1954	3,165	1,380	221	827	738	----	151	25	55	71	45	5	51	50	----
1953	3,100	1,327	209	809	755	----	146	25	52	68	43	5	51	47	----
1952	3,166	1,391	235	793	746	----	146	26	48	73	43	5	53	45	----
1951	3,363	1,459	341	792	771	----	137	27	44	66	39	6	51	41	----
1950	3,365	1,430	365	805	765	----	129	27	41	62	37	5	48	39	----
1949	3,096	1,329	313	802	652	----	115	26	30	58	32	4	44	33	----
1948	2,836	1,140	293	763	641	----	103	26	26	51	28	4	41	30	----
1947	2,509	969	235	720	585	----	83	21	22	40	22	3	34	25	----
1946	2,228	912	175	631	510	----	73	21	19	34	20	2	29	21	----
1945	2,013	890	153	523	447	----	66	20	15	30	18	2	26	19	----
1944	2,001	807	182	543	470	----	64	20	15	29	17	1	25	20	----
1943	2,282	874	298	618	492	----	63	20	14	29	17	1	26	19	----
1942	2,625	954	215	851	605	----	59	21	14	24	15	1	23	20	----
1941	2,429	872	157	805	596	----	58	21	13	24	14	1	23	19	----
1940	2,291	819	129	758	584	----	55	20	12	23	13	1	23	18	----
1939	2,084	742	88	715	539	----	53	19	11	22	13	1	22	17	----
1938	1,810	627	36	686	461	----	45	18	9	18	10	1	19	15	----
1937	1,345	377	----	581	386	----	36	10	9	17	7	----	18	12	----
1936	1,256	375	----	537	344	----	33	10	9	15	7	----	16	11	----
1935	1,179	349	----	504	326	----	29	9	7	13	(NA)	----	(NA)	(NA)	----
1934	1,051	298	----	467	286	----	28	7	7	14	5	----	14	9	----
1933	1,034	280	----	490	264	----	30	8	8	14	(NA)	----	(NA)	(NA)	----
1932	1,078	265	----	560	252	----	33	8	9	16	6	----	16	11	----
1931	1,048	220	----	592	235	----	32	8	9	15	(NA)	----	(NA)	(NA)	----
1930	982	175	----	619	188	----	30	7	8	14	5	----	15	10	----
1929	887	155	----	564	168	----	27	7	7	13	(NA)	----	(NA)	(NA)	----
1928	858	176	----	538	145	----	26	7	7	12	5	----	13	8	----
1927	785	164	----	496	125	----	25	7	7	11	(NA)	----	(NA)	(NA)	----
1926	753	177	----	467	110	----	23	7	7	10	4	----	11	8	----
1925	677	154	----	429	93	----	21	6	6	10	(NA)	----	(NA)	(NA)	----
1924	653	157	----	410	86	----	19	5	5	9	4	----	9	6	----
1923	537	139	----	326	71	----	17	4	5	8	(NA)	----	(NA)	(NA)	----
1922	476	119	----	297	60	----	15	4	5	6	3	----	7	5	----
1921	324	63	----	218	43	----	13	3	4	6	(NA)	----	(NA)	(NA)	----
1920	265	49	----	185	31	----	9	2	3	3	2	----	4	3	----
1919	195	39	----	136	20	----	5	2	2	2	(NA)	----	(NA)	(NA)	----
1918	164	31	----	118	15	----	3	1	1	1	1	----	2	1	----

NA Not available.
[1] Health and technical occupations.
[2] Beginning 1965, expenditures include construction and work-study programs, not shown separately.

Series H 587–597. School Retention Rates—Fifth Grade Through College Entrance: 1924–1932 to 1962–1970

| School year of entrance into 5th grade [1] | Retention per 1,000 pupils who entered 5th grade | | | | | | | | High school graduates | Year of high school graduation | First-time college students |
| | 5th grade | 6th grade | 7th grade | 8th grade | 9th grade | 10th grade | 11th grade | 12th grade | | | |
	587	588	589	590	591	592	593	594	595	596	597
1962	1,000	990	983	976	963	931	863	793	752	1970	465
1960	1,000	980	973	967	952	913	858	787	749	1968	452
1958	1,000	983	979	961	946	908	842	761	732	1966	384
1956–57	1,000	985	984	948	930	871	790	728	676	1964	362
1954–55	1,000	980	979	948	915	855	759	684	642	1962	343
1952–53	1,000	974	965	936	904	835	746	667	621	1960	328
1950–51	1,000	981	968	921	886	809	709	632	582	1958	308
1948–49	1,000	984	956	929	863	795	706	619	581	1956	301
1946–47	1,000	954	945	919	872	775	641	583	553	1954	283
1944–45	1,000	952	929	858	848	748	650	549	522	1952	234
1942–43	1,000	954	909	847	807	713	604	539	505	1950	205
1940–41	1,000	968	910	836	781	697	566	507	481	1948	(NA)
1938–39	1,000	955	908	853	796	655	532	444	419	1946	(NA)
1936–37	1,000	954	895	849	839	704	554	425	393	1944	121
1934–35	1,000	953	892	842	803	711	610	512	467	1942	129
1932–33	1,000	935	889	831	786	664	570	510	455	1940	160
1930–31	1,000	943	872	824	770	652	529	463	417	1938	148
1928–29	1,000	939	847	805	736	624	498	432	378	1936	137
1926–27	1,000	919	824	754	677	552	453	400	333	1934	129
1924–25	1,000	911	798	741	612	470	384	344	302	1932	118

NA Not available.
[1] Beginning 1958, data are based on fall enrollment and exclude ungraded pupils.

The net effect of these changes is to increase high school graduation and college entrance rates slightly.

Series H 598–601. High School Graduates, by Sex: 1870 to 1970

[In thousands, except percent]

| Year of graduation | Total | | Sex | |
| | Number | Percent of persons 17 years old [1] | Male | Female |
	598	599	600	601
1970	2,906	75.6	1,439	1,467
1969	2,839	75.9	1,408	1,431
1968	2,702	74.2	1,341	1,360
1967	2,680	76.5	1,332	1,348
1966	2,672	76.2	1,326	1,346
1965	2,665	76.3	1,314	1,351
1964	2,290	60.9	1,123	1,167
1963	1,950	71.5	959	991
1962	1,925	69.9	941	984
1961	1,971	70.8	958	1,013
1960	1,864	63.4	898	966
1959	1,639	63.4	790	849
1958	1,506	62.3	726	780
1957	1,446	63.0	696	750
1956	1,415	62.5	680	735
1954	1,276	59.7	613	664
1952	1,197	55.3	569	627
1950	1,200	57.4	571	629
1948	1,190	52.9	563	627
1946	1,080	47.4	467	613
1944	1,019	42.7	424	595
1942	1,242	51.3	577	666
1940	1,221	49.0	579	643
1938	1,120	45.6	524	596
1937	1,068	44.2	505	563
1936	1,015	42.7	486	530
1935	965	41.1	459	506
1934	915	39.2	432	483
1933	871	37.3	403	468
1932	827	35.5	375	452
1931	747	32.1	337	409
1930	667	28.8	300	367
1929	632	27.5	283	349
1928	597	26.2	266	330
1927	579	25.8	256	323
1926	561	25.5	246	315
1925	528	24.4	230	298
1924	494	23.4	213	281
1923	426	20.8	181	244
1922	357	17.8	150	207
1921	334	17.1	137	198
1920	311	16.3	124	188
1919	298	16.0	118	180
1918	285	15.1	112	173
1917	272	14.5	110	162
1916	259	13.8	108	151
1915	240	12.8	99	140
1914	219	11.7	90	129
1913	200	10.8	82	117
1912	181	9.8	74	106
1911	168	9.2	69	99
1910	156	8.6	64	93
1909	142	8.0	57	84
1908	129	7.4	52	77
1907	127	7.4	51	76
1906	126	7.5	50	76
1905	119	7.2	47	72
1904	112	6.9	44	68
1903	105	6.6	41	64
1902	99	6.3	39	61
1901	97	6.3	37	60
1900	95	6.3	38	57
1899	90	------	36	53
1898	84	------	34	50
1897	80	------	32	47
1896	76	------	31	45
1895	72	------	29	43
1894	65	------	27	39
1893	59	------	24	35
1892	53	------	21	32
1891	48	------	20	28
1890	44	3.5	19	25
1889	39	------	16	22
1888	33	------	14	19
1887	32	------	14	18
1886	33	------	15	18
1885	32	------	14	18
1884	31	------	14	17
1883	28	------	13	16
1882	27	------	12	15
1881	25	------	11	14
1880	24	2.5	11	13
1879	23	------	10	13
1878	22	------	10	12
1877	21	------	9	11
1876	20	------	9	11
1875	20	------	9	11
1874	19	------	8	11
1873	18	------	8	10
1872	17	------	8	10
1871	17	------	7	9
1870	16	2.0	7	9

[1] Population as of July 1, including Armed Forces overseas.

Series H 602–617.   Years of School Completed, by Race and Sex: 1940 to 1970

[As of March, except as noted.   Covers persons 25 years old and over]

Year and race	Percent of male population completing—							Median school years completed	Percent of female population completing—							Median school years completed
	Elementary school			High school		College			Elementary school			High school		College		
	0–4 years	5–7 years	8 years	1–3 years	4 years	1–3 years	4 years or more		0–4 years	5–7 years	8 years	1–3 years	4 years	1–3 years	4 years or more	
	602	603	604	605	606	607	608	609	610	611	612	613	614	615	616	617
TOTAL																
1970	5.9	9.5	13.6	16.1	30.1	10.8	14.1	12.2	4.7	8.7	13.1	17.9	37.5	9.7	8.2	12.1
1969	6.1	9.9	14.0	16.4	29.7	10.3	13.5	12.1	5.1	9.0	13.5	17.9	36.9	9.4	8.2	12.1
1968	6.5	10.3	14.3	16.9	28.9	9.8	13.3	12.1	5.3	9.4	13.9	18.1	35.7	9.5	8.0	12.1
1967	6.8	10.5	15.1	17.0	28.2	9.6	12.8	12.0	5.4	9.8	14.5	18.5	34.8	9.4	7.6	12.0
1966	7.3	10.7	15.6	17.4	27.7	8.8	12.5	11.8	5.7	10.2	14.6	18.8	34.4	9.0	7.4	12.0
1964	8.1	11.4	16.1	17.4	26.3	9.0	11.7	11.5	6.3	10.8	15.6	18.5	33.4	8.8	6.8	11.8
1962	8.7	12.2	16.7	17.4	24.7	8.9	11.4	11.1	6.9	11.2	16.5	17.9	31.6	9.3	6.7	11.6
1959 [1]	9.1	12.6	17.2	17.7	23.1	8.1	10.1	10.7	7.0	12.1	16.6	18.2	30.4	8.1	5.9	11.2
1957 [1]	10.0	13.2	18.4	17.3	22.1	7.2	9.4	10.3	8.0	12.3	17.4	18.1	29.5	7.4	5.7	10.9
1952 [1][2]	10.3	14.9	20.2	16.6	20.7	7.5	8.2	9.7	7.8	14.0	19.5	17.8	26.8	7.7	5.7	10.4
1950 [1]	11.9	16.4	20.7	16.4	17.6	6.8	7.1	9.0	9.8	15.4	19.8	17.4	22.6	7.5	5.0	9.7
1947 [1][3]	[4][5]11.4	[4]9.1	[4]30.6	16.1	18.2	6.5	6.1	8.9	[4]9.5	[4]8.5	[4]30.0	16.5	22.7	6.9	5.8	9.3
1940 [1][3]	[4][5]14.8	[4]11.7	[4]35.3	14.2	12.0	4.9	5.4	8.3	[4]12.2	[4]11.0	[4]33.9	15.7	16.2	6.0	3.7	8.5
WHITE																
1970	4.5	8.8	13.9	15.6	30.9	11.3	15.0	12.2	3.9	7.8	13.4	17.3	39.0	10.1	8.6	12.2
1969	4.8	9.1	14.3	16.1	30.6	10.8	14.3	12.2	4.2	8.1	13.7	17.3	38.5	9.8	8.4	12.2
1968	4.9	9.5	14.7	16.6	29.9	10.3	14.1	12.1	4.3	8.5	14.1	17.7	37.2	9.9	8.2	12.1
1967	5.3	9.7	15.4	16.8	29.1	10.0	13.7	12.1	4.4	8.8	14.9	18.0	36.2	9.7	7.9	12.1
1966	5.7	10.1	15.8	17.1	28.8	9.2	13.3	12.0	4.7	9.1	14.9	18.2	35.9	9.4	7.7	12.1
1965	6.1	10.3	16.4	17.0	28.2	9.3	12.7	12.0	4.9	9.3	15.4	18.2	35.6	9.3	7.3	12.1
1964	6.5	10.5	16.5	17.1	27.6	9.4	12.3	11.9	5.2	9.7	15.9	18.1	34.8	9.2	7.1	12.0
1962	6.9	11.4	17.0	17.3	25.8	9.4	12.2	11.6	5.6	10.3	16.8	17.4	33.1	9.9	7.0	12.0
1960	7.4	13.7	18.4	18.9	22.2	9.1	10.3	10.6	6.0	11.9	17.8	19.6	29.2	9.5	6.0	11.0
1947 [1][3]	[4]9.1	[4]8.4	[4]31.6	16.6	19.2	6.9	6.5	9.0	[4]7.6	[4]7.4	[4]30.6	16.9	24.1	7.3	4.8	9.7
1940 [1][3]	[4]11.8	[4]10.9	[4]37.0	14.9	12.8	5.2	5.8	8.4	[4]9.7	[4]9.9	[4]35.2	16.3	17.3	6.4	4.0	8.7
NEGRO AND OTHER																
1970	17.9	15.3	10.9	20.6	22.4	6.2	6.8	9.8	11.9	16.7	11.3	23.5	24.6	6.4	5.6	10.3
1969	17.5	17.5	10.8	19.8	21.8	6.0	6.7	9.6	13.3	17.4	11.8	23.0	23.5	5.6	5.5	10.0
1968	20.4	17.3	10.6	20.2	20.3	5.6	5.7	9.2	14.6	17.5	12.6	22.0	22.5	5.3	5.3	9.7
1967	21.2	18.2	12.0	18.9	19.3	5.2	5.2	8.9	14.1	18.5	11.7	22.7	22.3	6.1	4.8	9.8
1966	22.5	16.6	13.1	20.1	17.4	5.3	5.0	8.8	14.0	19.4	11.5	24.0	21.2	5.4	4.4	9.6
1964	22.2	19.7	12.2	20.1	15.3	4.9	5.6	8.7	15.4	20.7	12.9	22.0	20.2	4.9	3.7	9.1
1962	26.1	19.3	13.2	18.2	14.5	4.8	4.0	8.3	18.5	19.3	13.9	22.1	18.2	4.0	4.0	8.9
1960	27.7	23.0	12.3	17.0	12.1	4.4	3.5	7.9	19.7	23.7	13.3	20.2	15.2	4.4	3.6	8.5
1959 [1]	28.1	23.4	11.1	14.7	11.5	3.7	3.6	7.6	19.4	24.6	13.0	19.6	14.7	3.5	2.9	8.4
1957 [1]	30.3	23.2	11.1	15.1	10.6	3.0	2.6	7.3	23.8	24.0	13.3	17.7	13.1	3.3	2.9	8.1
1952 [1][2]	34.1	25.1	12.7	12.3	8.4	3.3	2.0	6.8	27.2	27.9	13.2	15.2	9.6	3.2	2.7	7.4
1950 [1]	35.3	26.0	10.8	11.6	7.2	2.8	2.0	6.4	27.8	28.4	12.1	14.4	8.9	3.1	2.3	7.2
1947 [1][3]	[4]35.0	[4]16.9	[4]20.6	11.9	8.0	2.0	2.3	6.6	[4]27.9	[4]19.2	[4]24.2	12.7	9.0	2.6	2.6	7.2
1940 [1][3]	[4]45.3	[4]20.1	[4]18.5	7.3	3.8	1.6	1.4	5.4	[4]37.0	[4]22.1	[4]21.3	9.8	5.0	2.1	1.2	6.1

[1] Excludes population for whom school years not reported.
[2] As of October.
[3] As of April.

[4] Elementary school years completed are: Less than 5 years, 5 and 6 years, 7 and 8 years, respectively.
[5] Includes population for whom school years not reported.

Series H 618–647. Median Years of School Completed, by Age, Sex, and Race: 1940 to 1970

Series No.	Year, sex, and race	Total	25–29 years	30–34 years	35–39 years	40–44 years	45–49 years	50–54 years	55–59 years	60–64 years	65–69 years	70–74 years	75 years and over
	1970												
618	Total	12.2	12.6	12.5	12.4		12.2		10.7		8.8		8.5
619	Male	12.2	12.7	12.6	12.4		12.2		10.5		8.7		8.3
620	White	12.2	12.7	12.6	12.5		12.3		10.9		8.8		8.4
621	Negro and other	9.8	12.2	11.9	10.9		9.5		7.6		5.2		3.7
622	Negro	9.6	12.1	11.4	10.7		9.1		7.6		4.9		3.6
623	Female	12.1	12.5	12.5	12.3		12.2		10.9		8.9		8.6
624	White	12.2	12.5	12.5	12.4		12.3		11.6		9.1		8.6
625	Negro and other	10.3	12.2	12.2	11.7		9.5		8.1		6.8		5.5
626	Negro	10.2	12.2	12.1	11.4		9.4		8.1		6.8		5.7
	1960*												
627	Total	10.5	12.3	12.2	12.1	11.8	10.6	9.7	8.8	8.6	8.4	8.3	8.2
628	Male	10.3	12.3	12.1	12.1	11.6	10.3	9.4	8.7	8.5	8.3	8.1	8.0
629	White	10.6	12.4	12.2	12.2	12.0	10.7	9.8	8.8	8.6	8.4	8.2	8.1
630	Negro and other	7.9	10.5	9.7	8.9	8.3	7.4	6.8	6.0	5.5	4.7	4.4	3.9
631	Female	10.7	12.3	12.2	12.2	12.0	10.8	10.1	9.0	8.7	8.5	8.4	8.3
632	White	11.0	12.3	12.3	12.2	12.1	11.2	10.4	9.2	8.8	8.6	8.5	8.4
633	Negro and other	8.5	11.1	10.5	9.7	8.7	8.1	7.6	6.9	6.4	5.6	5.2	4.5
	1950												
634	Total	9.3	12.1	11.6	10.7	9.8	8.9	8.7	8.5	8.4	8.2	8.2	8.1
635	Male	9.0	12.0	11.4	10.3	9.4	8.9	8.6	8.4	8.3	8.1	8.0	7.9
636	White	9.3	12.4	11.9	10.7	9.9	8.9	8.7	8.5	8.3	8.2	8.1	8.1
637	Negro and other	6.4	8.4	7.8	7.1	6.5	6.0	5.6	5.1	4.7	4.0	3.9	3.1
638	Female	9.6	12.1	11.8	10.7	10.1	9.0	8.8	8.6	8.4	8.3	8.3	8.2
639	White	10.0	12.2	12.1	11.2	10.5	9.5	8.9	8.7	8.5	8.4	8.4	8.3
640	Negro and other	7.2	8.9	8.4	7.8	7.2	6.7	6.1	5.8	5.3	4.5	4.2	3.4
	1940												
641	Total	8.6	10.3	9.5	8.8	8.6	8.5	8.4	8.3	8.3	8.2	8.1	8.0
642	Male	8.6	10.1	9.2	8.7	8.6	8.4	8.3	8.2	8.2	8.1	8.0	7.7
643	White	8.7	10.5	9.7	8.8	8.7	8.5	8.4	8.3	8.3	8.2	8.1	8.0
644	Negro and other	5.4	6.5	6.2	5.8	5.5	5.2	4.8	4.6	4.3	3.7	2.9	1.5
645	Female	8.7	10.5	9.9	8.9	8.7	8.5	8.4	8.4	8.3	8.2	8.2	8.1
646	White	8.8	10.9	10.3	9.1	8.8	8.6	8.5	8.5	8.4	8.3	8.3	8.2
647	Negro and other	6.1	7.5	7.0	6.5	6.1	5.7	5.2	4.9	4.5	3.8	2.8	1.0

* Denotes first year for which figures include Alaska and Hawaii.

Series H 648–663. Income of Males 25 Years Old and Over, by Years of School Completed: 1939 to 1970

[In dollars]

	Lifetime income								Annual mean income							
	Elementary school		High school		College				Elementary school		High school		College			
						4 years or more								4 years or more		
Year	Less than 8 years	8 years	1–3 years	4 years	1–3 years	Total	4 years	5 years or more	Less than 8 years	8 years	1–3 years	4 years	1–3 years	Total	4 years	5 years or more
	648	649	650	651	652	653	654	655	656	657	658	659	660	661	662	663
UNGROUPED DATA:[1]																
1970	219,454	286,744	331,600	394,516	478,913	637,822	588,755	697,285	4,434	6,035	7,629	9,185	10,891	14,434	13,372	15,732
1969	208,689	276,079	316,133	375,932	451,153	626,112	585,626	679,428	4,242	5,809	7,279	8,827	10,387	14,079	13,258	15,097
1968	196,014	257,500	294,160	350,228	411,003	586,047	561,631	615,242	3,981	5,467	6,769	8,148	9,397	12,938	12,418	13,555
1967	173,724	233,106	271,415	320,989	377,675	521,554	486,296	561,410	3,540	5,002	6,258	7,515	8,713	11,753	11,022	12,639
GROUPED DATA:[2]																
1968	201,888	265,198	303,663	361,082	422,156	579,653	543,308	621,906	4,093	5,624	6,983	8,430	9,692	12,888	12,236	13,672
1967	179,561	242,357	280,380	333,305	393,888	543,244	503,631	587,249	3,648	5,195	6,476	7,821	9,105	12,295	11,521	13,237
1966	173,692	228,325	270,394	320,159	380,710	520,347	485,623	566,554	3,520	4,867	6,294	7,494	8,783	11,739	11,135	12,563
1964	158,650	208,736	242,752	293,772	343,752	459,832	438,858	488,114	3,298	4,520	5,653	6,738	7,907	10,284	9,757	11,004
1963	148,856	203,192	230,047	284,782	333,009	441,920	423,174	465,490	3,078	4,410	5,348	6,557	7,633	9,811	9,392	10,353
1961	142,480	191,955	223,201	257,434	324,809	436,932	414,049	459,042	2,998	4,206	5,161	5,946	7,348	9,817	9,342	9,987
1958	120,051	166,248	191,615	226,658	276,861	386,050	·346,649	429,595	2,530	3,677	4,452	5,257	6,272	8,643	7,565	9,178
1956	121,975	165,870	188,761	228,189	268,038	358,538	--------	--------	2,574	3,631	4,367	5,183	5,997	7,877	--------	--------
1949	91,095	122,787	141,870	174,740	201,938	286,833	--------	--------	2,062	2,829	3,226	3,784	4,423	6,179	--------	--------
1946 [3]	74,369	98,702	107,940	135,852	161,699	201,731	--------	--------	1,738	2,327	2,449	2,939	3,654	4,527	--------	--------
1939 [4]	--------	--------	--------	--------	--------	--------	--------	--------	1,036		1,379	1,661	1,931	2,607	--------	--------

[1] Improved methodology introduced in 1967 permits the computation of data based on actual reported amounts.
[2] Estimates based on a series of estimated mean values for specific income class intervals.
[3] Total money earnings.
[4] Restricted to persons reporting $1 or more of wage or salary income and less than $50 of other income for native white and Negro males 25 to 64 years old only.

Series H 664–668. Percent Illiterate in the Population, by Race and Nativity: 1870 to 1969

[1870 to 1940, data are for population 10 years old and over; thereafter, for population 14 years old and over]

Year	Total	White			Negro and other	Year	Total	White			Negro and other
		Total	Native	Foreign born				Total	Native	Foreign born	
	664	665	666	667	668		664	665	666	667	668
1969*	1.0	0.7	--------	--------	[1] 3.6	1920	6.0	4.0	2.0	13.1	23.0
1959	2.2	1.6	--------	--------	7.5	1910	7.7	5.0	3.0	12.7	30.5
1952	2.5	1.8	--------	--------	10.2	1900	10.7	6.2	4.6	12.9	44.5
1950	[2] 3.2	(NA)	--------	--------	(NA)	1890	13.3	7.7	6.2	13.1	56.8
1947	2.7	1.8	--------	--------	11.0	1880	17.0	9.4	8.7	12.0	70.0
1940	2.9	2.0	1.1	9.0	11.5	1870	20.0	11.5	--------	--------	79.9
1930	4.3	3.0	1.6	10.8	16.4						

* Denotes first year for which figures include Alaska and Hawaii.
NA Not available.

[1] Based on Negro population only.
[2] See source, pp. 6 and 7, for explanation of this figure.

Series H 669–688. Illiteracy, by Age and Race: 1947 to 1969

[In thousands, except percent. Relates to civilian noninstitutional population 14 years old and over]

Series No.	Year and item	14 years old and over	14–24 years old	25–44 years old	45–64 years old	65 years old and over	Series No.	Year and item	14 years old and over	14–24 years old	25–44 years old	45–64 years old	65 years old and over
	1969, November*							**1952, October**					
669	Population, total	143,137	36,853	46,501	40,985	18,798	679	Population, total	110,074	21,716	44,358	31,740	12,260
670	Number illiterate	1,433	97	237	449	650	680	Number illiterate	2,780	250	564	1,120	846
	Percent illiterate:							Percent illiterate:					
671	Total	1.0	.3	.5	1.1	3.5	681	Total	2.5	1.2	1.3	3.5	6.9
672	White	.7	.2	.4	.7	2.3	682	White	1.8	.8	(NA)	(NA)	5.0
673	Negro	3.6	.5	1.3	5.5	16.7	683	Negro and other	10.2	3.9	(NA)	(NA)	33.3
	1959, March							**1947, October**					
674	Population, total	121,373	25,118	46,143	35,205	14,907	684	Population, total	106,428	24,257	42,379	29,277	10,515
675	Number illiterate	2,619	144	575	929	971	685	Number illiterate	2,838	232	730	1,168	709
	Percent illiterate:							Percent illiterate:					
676	Total	2.2	.6	1.2	2.6	6.5	686	Total	2.7	1.0	1.7	4.0	6.7
677	White	1.6	.5	.8	1.8	5.1	687	White	1.8	.6	(NA)	(NA)	4.9
678	Negro	7.5	1.2	5.1	11.3	25.5	688	Negro and other	11.0	4.4	(NA)	(NA)	32.4

* Denotes first year for which figures include Alaska and Hawaii.   NA Not available.

Series H 689–699. Institutions of Higher Education—Number and Faculty: 1870 to 1970

School year ending—	Number of institutions							Faculty			
	Total	Junior colleges [1]			4-year colleges	Medical schools	Dental schools	Total	Male	Female	Resident instructional staff
		Total	Public	Private							
	689	690	691	692	693	694	695	696	697	698	699
1970	2,525	[2] 886	634	252	1,639	101	53	[3] 729,000	--------	--------	551,000
1968	2,374	[2] 786	520	266	1,588	95	50	[3] 674,000	--------	--------	484,000
1966	2,230	[2] 622	392	230	1,608	85	49	596,400	464,000	132,400	412,000
1964	2,139	[2] 644	381	263	1,495	83	47	494,514	385,405	109,109	331,000
1962	2,003	524	329	195	1,479	92	47	424,862	332,006	92,856	292,000
1960*	1,959	508	310	198	1,451	91	47	380,554	296,773	83,781	281,506
1958	1,894	490	283	207	1,404	85	47	344,525	267,482	77,043	258,184
1956	1,850	467	275	192	1,383	82	43	298,910	230,342	68,568	228,188
1954	1,862	518	293	225	1,344	80	43	265,911	204,871	61,040	207,365
1952	1,891	511	294	217	1,380	79	42	244,488	187,136	57,352	183,758
1950	1,863	518	275	243	1,345	79	41	246,722	186,189	60,533	190,353
1948	1,788	472	242	230	1,316	77	40	223,660	164,616	59,044	174,204
1946	1,768	464	242	222	1,304	77	39	165,324	116,134	49,190	125,811
1944	1,650	413	210	203	1,237	77	39	150,980	106,254	44,726	105,841
1942	1,769	461	231	230	1,308	77	39	151,066	109,309	41,757	114,693
1940	1,708	456	217	239	1,252	77	39	146,929	106,328	40,601	110,885
1938	1,690	453	209	244	1,237	77	39	135,989	97,362	38,627	102,895
1936	1,628	415	187	228	1,213	77	39	121,036	86,567	34,469	92,580
1934	1,418	322	152	170	1,096	77	39	108,873	78,369	30,504	86,914
1932	1,478	342	159	183	1,136	76	38	[4] 100,789	[4] 71,680	[4] 29,109	88,172

See footnotes at end of table.

Series H 689–699.　Institutions of Higher Education—Number and Faculty: 1870 to 1970—Con.

School year ending—	Number of institutions							Faculty			
	Total	Junior colleges [1]			4-year colleges	Medical schools	Dental schools	Total	Male	Female	Resident instructional staff
		Total	Public	Private							
	689	690	691	692	693	694	695	696	697	698	699
1930	1,409	277	129	148	1,132	76	38	82,386	(NA)	(NA)	82,386
1928	1,410	248	114	134	1,162	80	40	(NA)	(NA)	(NA)	76,080
1926	1,377	153	47	106	1,224	79	44	(NA)	(NA)	(NA)	70,674
1924	1,295	132	39	93	1,163	79	43	(NA)	(NA)	(NA)	63,999
1922	1,162	80	17	63	1,082	81	45	(NA)	(NA)	(NA)	56,486
1920	1,041	52	10	42	989	85	46	48,615	35,807	12,808	------
1918	980	46	14	32	934	90	46	(NA)	(NA)	(NA)	------
1916	(NA)	------	------	------	------	95	49	(NA)	(NA)	(NA)	------
1910	951	------	------	------	------	131	54	36,480	29,132	7,348	------
1900	977					160	57	23,868	19,151	4,717	------
1890	998					133	31	15,809	5 12,704	5 3,105	------
1880	811					100	14	11,552	5 7,358	5 4,194	------
1870	563					75	10	5,553	5 4,887	5 666	------

* Denotes first year for which figures include Alaska and Hawaii.
NA Not available.
1 Beginning 1950, includes 2-year normal schools.
2 Includes institutions which do not offer courses creditable toward a bachelor's degree.
3 Estimated.
4 Full-time equivalent; total number of different persons not tabulated.
5 Distributions estimated.

Series H 700–715.　Institutions of Higher Education—Degree–Credit Enrollment: 1870 to 1970

[In thousands, except percent]

Year	Total degree-credit enrollment [1]						Resident [3]				First-time [1]				Junior college	
	Number	Percent of population 18–24 years old [2]	Male	Female	4-year institution	2-year institution	Number [4]	Percent of population 18–24 years old [2]	Undergraduate [4]	Graduate [4]	Number	Percent of population 18 years old	Male	Female	Male	Female
	700	701	702	703	704	705	706	707	708	709	710	711	712	713	714	715
1970	7,920	32.1	4,637	3,284	6,290	1,630	7,545	30.6	6,645	900	1,780	47.1	984	796	275	279
1968	6,928	30.3	4,119	2,809	5,639	1,289	6,659	29.2	5,851	808	1,630	46.8	925	705	333	221
1966	5,928	27.7	3,577	2,351	4,984	945	(NA)	(NA)		682	1,378	42.7	787	591	232	157
1964	4,950	26.3	3,033	1,917	4,239	711	4,296	22.9	3,756	540	1,225	44.5	702	523	193	129
1962	4,175	23.6	2,587	1,588	3,585	590	3,726	22.0	3,328	398	1,031	37.4	598	432	156	104
1960*	3,583	22.2	2,257	1,326	3,131	451	3,216	20.5	2,874	342	923	35.7	540	384	129	86
1958	3,226	21.2	2,092	1,134	2,840	386	2,900	19.2	2,622	278	772	33.8	464	308	102	67
1956	2,918	19.5	1,911	1,007	2,571	347	2,619	17.6	2,348	271	715	32.2	442	273	77	53
1954	2,446	16.2	1,563	883	2,164	282	2,515	16.5	2,238	277	625	29.6	383	242	64	46
1952	2,134	13.8	1,380	754	1,896	238	2,302	14.7	2,069	233	532	26.1	321	211	65	41
1950	2,281	14.2	1,560	721	2,064	217	2,659	16.5	2,422	237	512	23.9	317	195	65	39
1948	2,403	14.7	1,709	694	2,192	211	2,616	15.9	2,442	174	567	25.2	369	198	78	41
1946	2,078	12.5	1,418	661	------	------	1,677	10.0	1,556	121	696	30.4	500	197		

Year	Resident [3]				Year	Resident [3]				Year	Resident [3]			
	Number [4]	Percent of population 18–24 years old	Undergraduate [4]	Graduate [4]		Number [4]	Percent of population 18–24 years old	Undergraduate [4]	Graduate [4]		Number [4]	Percent of population 18–24 years old	Undergraduate [4]	Graduate [4]
	706	707	708	709		706	707	708	709		706	707	708	709
1944	1,155	6.8	5 1,100	5 59	1920	598	4.7	582	16	1910	355	2.9	346	9
1942	1,404	8.4	5 1,319	5 85	1918	441	3.6	(NA)	(NA)	1905	264	2.3	(NA)	(NA)
1940	1,494	9.1	1,388	106	1916	441	3.3	(NA)	(NA)	1900	238	2.3	232	6
1938	1,351	8.3	1,270	91	1915	404	3.1	(NA)	(NA)	1890	157	1.8	154	2
1936	1,208	7.5	1,129	79	1914	379	2.9	(NA)	(NA)	1880	116	1.6	------	------
1934	1,055	6.6	983	71	1913	361	2.8	(NA)	(NA)	1870	52	1.1	------	------
1932	1,154	7.4	1,082	78	1912	356	2.7	(NA)	(NA)					
1930	1,101	7.2	1,054	47	1911	354	2.8	(NA)	(NA)					
1928	1,054	7.1	(NA)	(NA)										
1926	941	6.6	(NA)	(NA)										
1924	6 823	5.9	(NA)	(NA)										
1922	681	5.1	(NA)	(NA)										

* Denotes first year for which figures include Alaska and Hawaii.
NA Not available.
1 Data for fall of year shown.
2 Percentages for 1910, 1920, 1930, and 1940–1970 are based on population, 18 to 24 years old, as of July 1 prior to the opening of school; for all other years, based on July 1 population after the closing of school in June.
3 Data for 1870–1954 for academic year; 1956–1964 for 1st term of academic year; thereafter, for fall of year shown.
4 In some instances, a student may be enrolled simultaneously as both a graduate and an undergraduate, with the result that the total, series H 706 (different individuals), is less than the sum of series H 708 and H 709.
5 Distributions estimated.
6 Data for 1924 and previous years taken from U.S. Office of Education, *Education for Victory*, vol. 3, No. 6, 1944.

Series H 716–727. Institutions of Higher Education—Current Income: 1890 to 1970

[In millions of dollars]

School year ending—	Total income	Education and general income									Auxiliary enterprises and activities	Student-aid and other current income
		Total	Student fees	Endowment earnings	Government			Private gifts and grants [1]	Organized activities related to instructional departments	Other sources		
					Federal	State	Local					
	716	717	718	719	720	721	722	723	724	725	726	727
1970	21,515	16,486	4,420	447	2,682	5,788	775	1,001	613	760	2,900	[2]2,129
1969	18,875	14,330	3,814	413	2,505	4,812	614	916	549	706	2,691	[2]1,854
1968	16,825	13,846	3,380	364	3,348	4,181	504	848	808	411	2,482	[3]498
1966	12,734	10,285	2,641	289	2,588	2,895	303	614	624	332	2,139	[3]310
1964	9,544	7,788	1,893	266	2,161	2,111	240	551	428	139	1,607	[3]148
1962	7,429	6,040	1,500	232	1,538	1,668	191	450	356	105	1,271	[3]118
1960*	5,786	4,688	1,157	207	1,037	1,374	152	383	290	88	1,004	[3]93
1958	4,641	3,733	934	182	707	1,138	129	324	246	71	839	[3]70
1956	3,603	2,859	722	145	490	878	107	245	192	80	692	[3]52
1954	2,946	2,339	551	127	417	740	88	191	165	59	575	[3]32
1952	2,562	2,021	447	113	451	611	72	150	136	41	510	[3]32
1950	2,375	1,834	395	96	524	492	61	119	112	35	511	30
1948	2,027	1,538	305	87	526	352	48	91	93	36	465	24
1946	1,169	925	214	90	197	225	31	78	67	23	244	(NA)
1944	1,047	864	154	75	308	175	26	50	54	20	184	(NA)
1942	784	626	201	74	58	167	27	46	40	15	157	(NA)
1940	715	571	201	71	39	151	24	40	33	11	144	(NA)
1938	653	522	179	71	29	141	22	37	28	15	131	(NA)
1936	598	491	158	60	43	120	21	37	25	27	106	(NA)
1934	486	389	138	56	20	[4]118	(4)	27	18	12	88	10
1932	566	452	151	61	(5)	[4][5]175	(4)	30	21	15	103	11
1930	555	483	144	69	21	[4]151	(4)	26	----------	73	60	11
1920	200	173	42	26	[6]13	[4][7]62	(4)	8	----------	22	27	----------
1910	77	68										
1900		35										
1890		21										

* Denotes first year for which figures include Alaska and Hawaii.
NA Not available.
[1] Beginning 1968, private grants represent nongovernmental revenue for sponsored research and other sponsored programs.
[2] Includes "Major public service," previously included in "Educational and general income" items, series H 717–725.
[3] Student-aid income only.
[4] Local included with State.
[5] Federal included with State.
[6] Universities, colleges, and professional schools only; teachers colleges and normal schools omitted.
[7] May also include Federal funds for teachers colleges and normal schools.

Series H 728–738. Institutions of Higher Education—Current Expenditures: 1930–1970

[In millions of dollars]

School year ending—	Total expenditures	Educational and general expenditures								Auxiliary enterprises and activities	Student-aid and other expenditures
		Total	Administration and general expense	Instruction and departmental research	Organized research	Libraries	Plant operation and maintenance	Organized activities related to instructional departments	Extension and public services		
	728	729	730	731	732	733	734	735	736	737	738
1970	21,043	15,789	2,628	7,653	2,144	653	1,542	648	521	2,769	[1]2,485
1969	18,482	13,835	2,278	6,610	2,034	572	1,338	535	468	2,539	[1]2,107
1968	16,481	13,190	1,739	5,653	2,699	493	1,127	881	598	2,302	988
1966	12,509	9,951	1,251	3,911	2,448	346	845	711	438	1,888	671
1964	9,178	7,425	958	2,802	1,973	237	686	472	297	1,452	300
1962	7,155	5,768	730	2,202	1,474	177	564	375	244	1,158	229
1960*	5,601	4,513	583	1,793	1,022	135	470	303	206	916	172
1958	4,510	3,604	474	1,466	728	110	406	246	175	775	130
1956	3,499	2,766	355	1,141	501	86	324	222	138	638	95
1954	2,883	2,271	288	961	373	73	278	187	112	538	74
1952	2,471	1,921	234	823	318	61	240	148	97	478	72
1950	2,246	1,706	213	781	225	56	225	119	87	476	63
1948	1,883	1,392	172	658	159	44	202	85	71	439	53
1946	1,088	820	105	375	87	27	111	61	55	242	26
1944	974	657	70	334	58	20	81	48	44	199	[2]118
1942	738	572	67	299	34	20	73	38	43	137	28
1940	675	522	63	280	27	19	70	27	35	124	29
1938	614	473	56	253	25	18	63	24	34	116	[3]26
1936	541	417	48	225	22	16	57	20	29	95	[3]29
1934	469	362	43	203	17	13	51	14	20	79	[3]28
1932	537	415	47	233	22	11	57	21	24	91	[3]30
1930	507	378	43	221	18	10	61	(4)	25	3	126

* Denotes first year for which figures include Alaska and Hawaii.
[1] Includes "Major public service," previously included in "Educational and general expenditures" items, series H 729–736.
[2] Includes $97 million for Federal contract courses.
[3] Includes unitemized educational and general expenditures as follows, in thousands of dollars: 2,020 in 1938; 2,580 in 1936; 7,502 in 1934; and 5,239 in 1932.
[4] Not tabulated separately; probably included in series H 738.

Series H 739-750. Institutions of Higher Education—Plant Fund Operations and Property: 1890 to 1970

[In millions of dollars]

School year ending—	Plant fund operations								Property (at end of year)			
	Receipts by source							Expend-itures	Physical plant [1]	Nonexpendable funds		
	Total	Government			Private gifts and grants	Loans	Other sources			Endow-ment [2]	Annuities	Student loans
		Federal	State	Local								
	739	740	741	742	743	744	745	746	747	748	749	750
1970									42,094	10,854		
1968									34,506	(NA)		
1966	3,484	332.5	738	80.7	365.9	1,590	376	2,920	26,851	8,766		
1964	2,532	134.2	630	62.7	314.6	808	582	2,293	21,279	6,953	208	135
1962	1,817	69.8	514	35.5	226.5	548	423	1,582	16,682	6,079	168	105
1960*	1,309	57.6	320	36.3	196.4	393	306	1,191	13,449	5,322	123	126
1958	1,221	61.4	373	45.5	157.1	345	239	1,008	11,124	4,646	91	71
1956	821	13.3	219	17.3	143.0	191	237	681	8,859	3,702	75	58
1954	469	8.4	132	14.0	103.8	133	78	531	7,523	3,194	67	49
1952	356	12.7	144	16.1	71.6	48	63	403	6,756	2,869	75	47
1950	529	12.4	284	19.4	72.6		140	417	5,273	[3] 2,601	([3])	43
1948	365	(NA)			(NA)			306	3,996	2,384	69	44
1946	122	3.5	71	1.8	45.0			71	(NA)	(NA)	(NA)	(NA)
1944	23	(NA)	(NA)	(NA)	(NA)			27	(NA)	(NA)	(NA)	(NA)
1942	30	1.6	12	1.1	15.0			50	2,759	[4] 1,767	(NA)	(NA)
1940	66	23.0	18	2.2	22.7		(NA)	84	2,754	1,686	50	29
1938	58		(NA)	(NA)	20.7		[5] 38	70	2,556	1,653	44	25
1936	(NA)		(NA)	(NA)	(NA)		(NA)	47	2,359	1,554	42	27
1934	42		(NA)	(NA)	10.2		[5] 32	30	2,253	1,473	44	23
1932	56		(NA)	(NA)	(NA)			98	2,207	1,372		91
1930	82		[6] 31	([6])	51.5			125	2,065	1,372		
1920	19		[6] 11	([6])	7.9				741	569		
1910									461	[4] 324		
1900									254	[4] 195		
1890									95	[4] 79		

* Denotes first year for which figures include Alaska and Hawaii.
NA Not available.
[1] 1890 to 1952, includes unexpended plant funds.
[2] Includes funds functioning as endowment (book value).
[3] Annuities included with endowment funds.
[4] Includes annuity and student loan funds.
[5] Includes items not tabulated separately.
[6] Local included with State.

Series H 751-765. Institutions of Higher Education—Degrees Conferred, by Sex: 1870 to 1970

School year ending—	Total, all degrees	Bachelor's or first professional					Master's or second professional				Doctor's or equivalent				Lapse time in years, bachelor's-to-doctor's
		Total	Male	Female	Per 1,000 persons 23 years old	Per 100 high school graduates 4 years earlier	Total	Male	Female	Per 100 bachelor's degrees 2 years earlier	Total	Male	Female	Per 1,000 bachelor's degrees x-years earlier [1]	
	751	752	753	754	755	756	757	758	759	760	761	762	763	764	765
1970	1,065,391	827,234	484,174	343,060	223	31	208,291	125,624	82,667	31	29,866	25,890	3,976	72.1	7.9
1969	984,129	764,185	444,380	319,805	282	29	193,756	121,531	72,225	33	26,188	22,752	3,436	66.3	8.0
1968	866,548	666,710	390,507	276,203	243	29	176,749	113,519	63,230	32	23,089	20,183	2,906	59.2	8.1
1967	768,871	590,547	353,349	237,198	212	30	157,707	103,092	54,615	30	20,617	18,163	2,454	55.5	8.1
1966	709,832	551,047	328,853	222,194	186	29	140,548	93,063	47,485	28	18,237	16,121	2,116	57.4	10.0
1965	663,622	530,003	316,286	213,717	203	27	117,152	77,544	39,608	26	16,467	14,692	1,775	56.7	10.0
1964	614,194	494,153	296,676	197,477	206	27	105,551	70,339	35,212	25	14,490	12,955	1,535	48.9	10.0
1963	551,810	443,518	271,882	171,636	195	27	95,470	64,198	31,272	24	12,822	11,448	1,374	41.8	10.2
1962	514,323	414,287	259,507	154,780	184	27	88,414	59,710	28,704	23	11,622	10,377	1,245	34.7	10.2
1961	487,513	395,248	253,077	142,171	178	27	81,690	55,267	26,423	22	10,575	9,463	1,112	27.1	10.3
1960*	476,704	389,183	252,996	136,187	182	27	77,692	51,965	25,727	21	9,829	8,801	1,028	22.4	10.4
1959	461,823	379,931	252,517	127,414	178	28	72,532	48,360	24,172	21	9,360	8,371	989	25.1	10.3
1958	438,030	363,502	241,560	121,942	167	28	65,586	44,229	21,357	21	8,942	7,978	964	32.3	10.2
1957	409,132	338,436	221,650	116,786	163	28	61,940	41,329	20,611	22	8,756	7,817	939	64.3	10.3
1956	377,698	309,514	198,615	110,899	147	26	59,281	39,393	19,888	20	8,903	8,018	885	62.2	10.3
1955	352,881	285,841	182,839	103,002	151	24	58,200	38,739	19,461	19	8,840	8,014	826	70.2	9.9
1954	357,327	291,508	186,884	104,624	129	24	56,823	38,147	18,676	17	8,996	8,181	815	69.2	9.7
1953	372,315	303,049	199,793	103,256	132	25	60,959	40,946	20,013	16	8,307	7,515	792	44.8	9.7
1952	401,203	329,986	225,981	104,005	143	28	63,534	43,557	19,977	15	7,683	6,969	714	41.6	9.8
1951	454,960	382,546	278,240	104,306	161	35	65,077	46,196	18,881	18	7,337	6,663	674	39.6	9.8
1950	496,874	432,058	328,841	103,217	182	40	58,183	41,220	16,963	22	6,633	5,990	643	34.9	10.2
1949	421,282	365,492	263,608	101,884	154	36	50,741	35,212	15,529	37	5,049	4,527	522	30.6	10.2
1948	317,607	271,186	175,615	95,571	113	27	42,432	28,931	13,501	37	3,989	3,496	493	25.3	10.8
1946	157,349	136,174	58,664	77,510	56	11	19,209	9,484	9,725	10	1,966	1,580	386	14.2	11.0
1944	141,582	125,863	55,865	69,998	52	10	13,414	5,711	7,703	7	2,305	1,880	425	13.8	9.4
1942	213,491	185,346	103,889	81,457	78	16	24,648	14,179	10,469	15	3,497	3,036	461	24.9	8.8

See footnotes at end of table.

Series H 751–765. Institutions of Higher Education—Degrees Conferred, by Sex: 1870 to 1970—Con.

School year ending	Total, all degrees	Bachelor's or first professional — Total	Male	Female	Per 1,000 persons 23 years old	Per 100 high school graduates 4 years earlier	Master's or second professional — Total	Male	Female	Per 100 bachelor's degrees 2 years earlier	Doctor's or equivalent — Total	Male	Female	Per 1,000 bachelor's degrees x-years earlier [1]	Lapse time in years, bachelor's-to-doctor's
	751	752	753	754	755	756	757	758	759	760	761	762	763	764	765
1940	216,521	186,500	109,546	76,954	81	18	26,731	16,508	10,223	19	3,290	2,861	429	23.5	9.4
1938	189,503	164,943	97,678	67,265	72	18	21,628	13,400	8,228	16	2,932	2,502	430	22.3	9.5
1936	164,197	143,125	86,067	57,058	63	17	18,302	11,503	6,799	13	2,770	2,370	400	24.7	9.2
1934	157,279	136,156	82,341	53,815	61	20	18,293	11,516	6,777	15	2,830	2,456	374	27.7	9.2
1932	160,084	138,063	83,271	54,792	63	23	19,367	12,210	7,157	17	2,654	2,247	407	29.0	8.5
1930	139,752	122,484	73,615	48,869	57	22	14,969	8,925	6,044	15	2,299	1,946	353	33.4	8.7
1928	124,995	111,161	67,659	43,502	55	22	12,387	7,727	4,660	15	1,447	1,249	198	33.2	8.4
1926	108,407	97,263	62,218	35,045	49	27	9,735	6,202	3,533	16	1,409	1,216	193	37.3	8.6
1924	92,097	82,783	54,908	27,875	43	27	8,216	5,515	2,701	17	1,098	939	159	24.8	8.4
1922	68,488	61,668	41,306	20,362	33	22	5,984	4,304	1,680	16	836	708	128	17.6	7.8
1920	53,516	48,622	31,980	16,642	26	19	4,279	2,985	1,294	9	615	522	93	14.2	7.7
1918	42,041	38,585	26,269	12,316	22	18	2,900	1,806	1,094	7	556	491	65	15.0	
1916	49,823	45,250	31,852	13,398	24	25	3,906	2,934	972	9	667	586	81	18.1	
1915	48,100	43,912	31,417	12,495	23	26	3,577	2,638	939	8	611	549	62	17.2	
1914	48,097	44,268	32,183	12,085	24	28	3,270	2,256	1,014	8	559	486	73	15.7	
1913	45,959	42,396	31,312	11,084	23	30	3,025	2,021	1,004	8	538	481	57	14.9	
1912	42,943	39,408	29,560	9,848	21	30	3,035	2,215	820	8	500	436	64	15.9	
1911	40,434	37,481	28,547	8,934	20	30	2,456	1,821	635	6	497	449	48	14.9	
1910	39,755	37,199	28,762	8,437	20	30	2,113	1,555	558	6	443	399	44	12.5	
1909	40,531	37,892	29,433	8,459	21	32	2,188	1,713	475	7	451	397	54	13.6	
1908	36,162	33,800	26,376	7,424	19	30	1,971	1,511	460	6	391	339	52	13.8	
1907	34,202	32,234	25,269	6,965	19	31	1,619	1,215	404	5	349	320	29	12.6	
1906	34,189	32,019	25,215	6,804	19	32	1,787	1,366	421	6	383	358	25	13.0	
1905	33,813	31,519	24,934	6,585	19	32	1,925	1,538	387	6	369	341	28	12.9	
1904	32,514	30,501	24,237	6,264	19	32	1,679	1,340	339	6	334	302	32	11.8	
1903	31,962	29,907	23,872	6,035	19	33	1,718	1,385	333	6	337	302	35	11.2	
1902	31,117	28,966	23,225	5,741	19	34	1,858	1,464	394	7	293	264	29	10.2	
1901	30,790	28,681	23,099	5,582	19	36	1,744	1,405	339	7	365	334	31	13.7	
1900	29,375	27,410	22,173	5,237	19	36	1,583	1,280	303	6	382	359	23	14.2	
1899	27,867	25,980	21,064	4,916		36	1,542	1,275	267	6	345	327	18	13.3	
1898	26,816	25,052	20,358	4,694		37	1,440	1,188	252	6	324	285	39	15.2	
1897	26,963	25,231	20,550	4,681		43	1,413	1,163	250	6	319	299	20	19.8	
1896	26,342	24,593	20,076	4,517		46	1,478	1,213	265	7	271	236	35	16.0	
1895	25,712	24,106	19,723	4,383		56	1,334	1,124	210	7	272	247	25	18.3	
1894	23,352	21,850	17,917	3,933		50	1,223	1,013	210	7	279	261	18	18.5	
1893	19,989	18,667	15,342	3,325		49	1,104	—	—	7	218	—	—	13.2	
1892	17,722	16,802	13,840	2,962		51	730	—	—	5	190	—	—	13.0	
1891	17,803	16,840	13,902	2,938		53	776	—	—	5	187	—	—	9.2	
1890	16,703	15,539	12,857	2,682		47	1,015	—	—	7	149	147	2	9.0	
1889	16,305	15,020	12,397	2,623		47	1,161	—	—	9	124	—	—	8.1	
1888	16,383	15,256	12,562	2,694		49	987	—	—	8	140	—	—	6.1	
1887	14,402	13,402	11,008	2,394		48	923	—	—	6	77	—	—	6.4	
1886	14,040	13,097	10,731	2,366		48	859	—	—	7	84	—	—	2.9	
1885	15,882	14,734	12,043	2,691		59	1,071	—	—	7	77	—	—	5.8	
1884	13,732	12,765	10,408	2,357		53	901	—	—	6	66	—	—	3.8	
1883	16,029	15,116	12,294	2,822		—	863	—	—	6	50	—	—	4.2	
1882	15,928	14,998	12,168	2,830		—	884	—	—	7	46	—	—	3.7	
1881	15,830	14,871	12,035	2,836		—	922	—	—	8	37	—	—	3.7	
1880	13,829	12,896	10,411	2,485		—	879	—	—	8	54	51	3	5.7	
1879	13,036	12,081	9,808	2,273		—	919	—	—	9	36	—	—	2.9	
1878	12,381	11,533	9,416	2,117		—	816	—	—	7	32	—	—	3.4	
1877	10,915	10,145	8,329	1,816		—	731	—	—	6	39	—	—		
1876	12,871	12,005	9,911	2,094		—	835	—	—	7	31	—	—		
1875	12,616	11,932	9,905	2,027		—	661	—	—	6	23	—	—		
1874	12,366	11,493	9,593	1,900		—	860	—	—	11	13	—	—		
1873	11,723	10,807	9,070	1,737		—	890	—	—	7	26	—	—		
1872	8,660	7,852	6,626	1,226		—	794	—	—	8	14	—	—		
1871	12,370	12,357	10,484	1,873		—	—	—	—	—	13	—	—		
1870	9,372	9,371	7,993	1,378		—	—	—	—	—	1	1	—		

* Denotes first year for which figures include Alaska and Hawaii.

[1] Number of years from the receipt of the bachelor's (or first professional) degree to the receipt of the doctorate degree.

Series H 766-787. Number of Doctorates, by Field: 1920 to 1970

Year [1]	Total, all fields	Physics– astronomy	Chemistry	Earth sciences	Mathematics	Engineering	Basic medical sciences	Medical sciences	Agricultural sciences	Other biological sciences	Psychology
	766	767	768	769	770	771	772	773	774	775	776
1970	29,479	1,655	2,235	510	1,225	3,433	1,746	487	918	1,423	1,888
1969	25,728	1,454	1,953	503	1,065	3,251	1,662	425	811	1,229	1,756
1968	22,916	1,432	1,792	442	970	2,847	1,490	396	681	1,131	1,464
1967	20,584	1,311	1,773	418	830	2,604	1,324	340	606	874	1,295
1966	17,953	1,061	1,594	404	769	2,301	1,148	318	576	844	1,139
1965	16,340	1,046	1,444	375	685	2,074	1,053	280	576	775	954
1964	14,324	866	1,351	310	589	1,664	890	263	517	691	1,012
1963	12,724	817	1,288	322	483	1,357	772	199	466	645	891
1962	11,505	710	1,138	249	388	1,216	724	205	470	576	856
1961	10,412	597	1,150	246	332	940	654	172	438	519	820
1960	9,732	530	1,078	253	291	793	622	133	414	559	772
1959	9,212	515	1,054	232	289	699	582	153	342	504	786
1958	8,773	497	965	190	238	629	621	143	339	519	743
1957 [1]	6,187	378	777	147	199	455	450	114	233	369	502
1956	8,501	484	980	157	228	579	486	193	352	487	628
1955	8,904	510	1,013	180	243	651	574	164	368	539	735
1954	8,706	524	1,018	160	247	562	539	150	370	595	665
1953	8,378	522	1,008	167	225	568	549	115	332	599	656
1952	7,716	519	1,063	149	204	570	439	113	309	496	581
1951	7,331	501	1,033	148	205	585	403	95	271	437	490
1950	6,519	422	1,050	130	176	467	323	97	252	441	360
1949	5,421	319	942	121	147	450	289	86	182	388	276
1948	3,898	224	607	67	117	257	214	61	101	312	181
1947	2,958	146	427	61	115	119	147	41	81	259	122
1946	1,989	71	323	37	54	102	92	31	44	149	82
1945	1,621	43	288	23	36	68	121	31	54	96	64
1944	1,954	64	474	18	43	64	173	38	46	128	68
1943	2,585	131	511	43	44	53	227	43	75	218	92
1942	3,402	157	589	66	76	98	271	60	101	297	126
1941	3,481	179	647	64	95	122	244	53	93	273	113
1940	3,276	144	534	59	103	107	260	47	94	303	129
1939	2,948	160	467	62	93	69	242	36	69	266	117
1938	2,756	156	409	70	61	75	220	51	68	258	116
1937	2,749	155	504	54	74	98	162	26	59	255	112
1936	2,712	138	444	71	76	70	150	45	60	274	114
1935	2,521	132	365	66	75	111	126	47	80	233	112
1934	2,696	124	415	68	91	119	175	64	91	246	128
1933	2,460	133	382	74	75	92	153	44	75	203	92
1932	2,401	115	328	55	74	68	132	40	83	202	105
1931	2,340	112	333	42	82	67	130	52	62	225	118
1930	2,071	106	302	66	76	64	103	46	61	169	101
1929	1,913	97	251	48	68	41	107	38	60	164	122
1928	1,628	95	255	31	42	51	97	20	56	154	84
1927	1,539	81	216	45	51	33	103	24	42	121	76
1926	1,442	87	252	42	48	27	78	33	29	120	74
1925	1,206	51	211	27	28	16	69	30	36	110	71
1924	1,133	62	224	44	29	14	50	34	32	100	54
1923	1,062	60	185	40	34	14	67	28	45	102	65
1922	780	55	140	22	17	15	42	19	27	69	34
1921	661	37	125	12	15	10	34	27	15	57	28
1920	560	31	76	21	19	7	38	12	17	66	35

[1] From 1920–1956, calendar year basis; thereafter fiscal year basis. Only the first half of 1957 is shown.

SOCIAL STATISTICS

Series H 766–787. Number of Doctorates, by Field: 1920 to 1970—Con.

Year[1]	Economics	Anthropology and sociology	Political science	Other social sciences	History	English and American language and literature	Foreign language and literature	Other arts and humanities	Professional fields	Education	Other and unspecified fields
	777	778	779	780	781	782	783	784	785	786	787
1970	853	721	635	466	1,092	1,097	733	1,138	1,203	5,859	162
1969	706	588	558	357	880	1,026	665	995	1,006	4,648	190
1968	746	505	580	195	740	929	629	911	930	4,026	80
1967	891	478	501	136	733	797	541	801	825	3,478	28
1966	627	357	408	88	645	671	451	752	734	3,043	23
1965	560	321	391	101	607	667	413	649	628	2,736	5
1964	526	284	337	97	530	528	345	589	565	2,351	19
1963	450	293	290	104	389	492	264	525	533	2,132	12
1962	418	265	278	73	366	463	252	485	468	1,899	6
1961	413	222	254	69	375	373	237	515	403	1,679	4
1960	352	231	238	75	364	386	213	491	382	1,549	6
1959	327	238	230	62	331	340	220	391	363	1,553	1
1958	332	211	211	71	317	333	189	389	344	1,491	1
1957	214	126	155	38	264	266	169	245	249	834	3
1956	316	220	247	88	266	347	221	310	275	1,636	1
1955	375	229	213	53	333	327	216	340	269	1,572	—
1954	350	250	186	50	364	344	216	347	260	1,509	—
1953	311	214	164	58	349	333	202	338	241	1,425	2
1952	313	178	157	37	298	263	180	286	247	1,314	—
1951	299	189	165	54	339	297	201	256	250	1,113	—
1950	243	168	164	41	274	236	211	213	219	1,032	—
1949	185	117	147	41	225	179	155	151	174	847	—
1948	141	82	109	19	171	166	134	154	141	666	—
1947	136	92	61	17	145	165	120	111	116	450	—
1946	84	60	40	9	117	114	71	79	80	349	1
1945	59	33	26	5	71	72	70	62	107	291	1
1944	61	39	36	14	60	74	69	66	103	316	—
1943	82	58	48	13	122	124	115	81	105	399	1
1942	138	77	70	13	168	177	150	126	148	493	1
1941	158	91	71	13	182	189	178	127	111	478	—
1940	125	73	81	25	167	174	180	107	94	470	—
1939	112	75	60	14	177	173	164	106	109	377	—
1938	125	61	56	10	159	159	172	84	83	363	—
1937	108	73	64	10	144	161	169	80	80	357	4
1936	103	56	53	12	135	144	185	98	103	354	27
1935	90	52	59	26	156	136	174	81	133	250	17
1934	113	52	65	24	148	137	166	74	103	280	13
1933	108	52	68	27	148	114	140	109	103	261	7
1932	122	58	58	20	123	129	137	115	123	309	5
1931	119	50	57	18	118	108	102	125	107	303	10
1930	107	44	33	27	128	96	95	96	74	268	9
1929	103	58	37	24	107	69	94	113	85	211	16
1928	85	25	51	11	94	70	68	83	77	173	6
1927	91	29	45	17	88	63	64	88	88	170	4
1926	81	26	33	13	71	71	55	76	64	161	1
1925	64	29	28	13	63	55	57	60	56	128	4
1924	52	20	29	5	60	57	65	47	52	102	1
1923	40	15	22	8	61	44	48	69	45	68	2
1922	33	14	17	3	56	34	45	44	32	59	3
1921	38	13	24	7	38	30	42	40	34	33	2
1920	22	15	12	3	23	23	42	31	18	48	1

— Represents zero.

[1] From 1920–1956, calendar year basis; thereafter, fiscal year basis. Only the first half of 1957 is shown.

Chapter H

Religious Affiliation (Series H 788-805)

H 788-805. General note.

National statistics for all religious bodies, on an interdenominational basis, have been compiled at intervals since 1850 and until 1936 by the Bureau of the Census and, during the past few decades by the *Christian Herald*, a periodical published in New York, and by the National Council of the Churches of Christ in the United States of America, which, in its *Yearbook of American and Canadian Churches*, presents statistical data furnished by all faiths.

Practically all national religious bodies compile reports or estimates from time to time based on records kept by local churches (congregations or parishes), or from estimates furnished by the local churches. Probably about half the national bodies receive reports from their local churches annually and then issue the figures to their constituencies or to the public. The bodies which report annually the figures systematically received from their local churches are mainly the larger denominations. The other national bodies report their statistics at irregular intervals.

For those denominations which have standard forms, the records are kept locally as determined by the national body. For other denominations, the records are kept in accordance with the wishes of the local churches. The statistics are gathered by the denominations for their own, often different, purposes, thus leading to variety in the forms used and in the nature of the information gathered. In addition, local church records are usually kept by persons untrained in the keeping of statistical records, or persons with only the most elementary instruction or experience.

All denominations make their own definitions of membership or affiliation and, accordingly, there are also variations in the basis of compilation. However, the bodies reporting have made no major changes in their definitions since the Census of Religious Bodies, 1926. The definitions used since that date for the larger bodies are as follows:

The Eastern Churches report estimates of the total number of persons within the cultural or nationality group served.

The Jewish Congregations report on the number of Jews in communities having congregations.

The Roman Catholic Church, the Lutheran bodies, and the Protestant Episcopal Church report as members the total number of baptized persons, including infants.

Most Protestant bodies report as members those persons who have attained full membership, usually at about age 13.

Variations in definitions for years prior to 1926 are noted below in the text for specific series.

One relatively large body, the Church of Christ, Scientist, with headquarters in Boston, Mass., now forbids the enumeration of its members and the publication of statistics of affiliation. The local churches of this body reported a total membership of 268,915 in the Census of Religious Bodies for 1936, but have made no public report since then. A few relatively small bodies also do not report membership figures to compilers of national data. However, it is believed that the figures presented here cover all but a fraction of one percent of total religious affiliation.

H 788-792. Church denominations, members, and edifices, 1850-1936.

Source: U.S. Bureau of the Census, 1850-1890 and 1916, *Religious Bodies, 1916*, part I; 1906-1936, *Religious Bodies*, 1906, 1926, and 1936 volumes.

Data presented are not directly comparable from census period to census period. Special note must be taken in the case of the data

for 1936 in relation to other years. The compilation for that year was less complete than those of other years for reasons noted below.

Limited information on religious bodies (number of congregations and buildings, and value of edifices) was first published in the census report for 1850 and similar information was included in the reports for 1860 and 1870. In 1880, the figures gathered by the Census Office were not published. In 1890, the Census Office collected figures from religious organizations concerning membership, number and value of edifices, number of ministers, etc.

The 1906 Census of Religious Bodies (2 parts) was the first to be compiled by means of a questionnaire mailed to the pastors or clerks of the local churches. The Jewish Congregations reported heads of families only (101,457, principally male, persons). It is indicated that, in most denominations, 99 percent of the local churches to which forms were mailed made returns.

The 1916 census reported 41,926,854 members, a figure adjusted in the 1926 report to read 43,311,648 persons, for reasons there given. The Jewish Congregations reported only heads of families (357,135 persons). The methods used in the 1916 and 1926 censuses were essentially the same as those used in the 1936 census (see below).

Students of church statistics regard the compilation of 1926 as probably the most adequate one ever made. In this census, every local organization was classed as a church whether it was commonly known as a church, a congregation, a meeting, a society, a mission, a station, a chapel, or by some other term. "A local church may have had officers and an enrolled membership, or it may have been little more than an association or fellowship, but to be included in this enumeration it must have had a religious purpose and a distinctive membership."

For all denominations except the Jewish Congregations, the 1926 census reported 50,495,104 members, compared with a corrected total figure, partly estimated, of 42,954,512 persons in 1916. The Jewish Congregations reported "all Jews in communities where there is a congregation," whereas in 1916 they reported only "heads of families, seat holders, and other contributors." The figures for Jews were admittedly incomplete. With this census also, the Lutheran bodies, the Protestant Episcopal Church, and the Christian Reformed Church began to report on a more inclusive basis than in previous censuses.

The data for the 1936 census were obtained by means of a schedule for local church organizations mailed to the clergyman or the lay clerk of the local parish or congregation. The data collected were for the year 1936, "or to the church record year most nearly conforming to the end of that year." The Census Bureau established contact with persons in authority in the various religious bodies in order to secure lists of pastors or clerks of the local religious organizations. Special agents were employed for the purpose of securing data from "some loosely organized denominations, or those averse to publishing the statistics of their organizations." The census received only halfhearted support from a few denominations and undoubtedly the total membership figures would have been much larger if all churches had furnished statistics. The incompleteness of returns is also reflected by the fact that total value of church edifices (series H 792) is lower in 1936 than in 1926. A private compilation for 1936, published in the *Christian Herald*, New York, July 1937, based on official reports of the religious bodies, listed 244,147 local churches. It seems probable that about 20 percent of the officers of active local churches in 1936 did not report to the Bureau of the Census. The *Christian Herald* stated, for example, that the *Southern Baptist Handbook* for 1937 reported 4,482,315

389

members for 1936, while the Bureau of the Census reported only 2,700,155 members.

Differences among the religious bodies in defining the term "member" were noted. The Jewish Congregations, continuing a basis begun in 1926, reported "all persons of the Jewish faith living in communities in which local congregations are situated. . . . Among the Roman Catholic and Eastern churches, all persons, even infants, are considered members, provided they have been baptized according to the rites of the church. . . . The Protestant Episcopal Church, and the Lutheran bodies, because they also count as members all baptized persons in the congregation, tend toward the more inclusive definition of the term." In the large majority of Protestant bodies, the term "member" is applied only to "communicants," or to persons who have attained to full membership, usually at age 13.

H 793–799. Membership of religious bodies, 1890–1970, and by major groups, 1951–1970.

Source: 1890–1926 and 1936, U.S. Bureau of the Census, *Religious Bodies*, various issues; 1931–1935, 1937, and 1945–1949, The Christian Herald Association, New York, *Christian Herald*, various issues (copyright); 1938–1944 and 1950–1970, National Council of the Churches of Christ, New York, *Yearbook of American Churches*, various issues (copyright).

The Bureau of the Census usually secured information for the year indicated, but it also accepted a figure for the church year nearest to that for which data were sought. In the compilations of private agencies the "latest information" is published for each denomination; in a number of instances, the actual figures of a denomination are for a previous period. For 1956, e.g., most bodies reported figures for that year, but many others had available only the data compiled for previous years. The lag is usually only of several years duration, but in a few instances (for small bodies) the actual figures are from the 1936 Census of Religious Bodies. Data for certain years, which do not appear in these series, appear in the *Christian Herald*; these data are not comparable as they include only the "communicant" or adult membership.

For definition of membership used by the larger groups (Eastern, Jewish Congregations, Roman Catholic, and Protestant bodies), see general note for series H 788–805. See also text for series H 788–792.

H 800. Roman Catholic members, 1891–1970.

Source: P. J. Kenedy & Sons, *The Official Catholic Directory*, New York (copyright), and unpublished data.

The continuous history of the Roman Catholic Church in this country began in Maryland in 1634.

Certain of the typographical errors appearing in the annual published reports issued by the source have been corrected in this series. Figures are compiled from reports by dioceses and parishes. For definition of membership, see general note for series H 788–805.

H 801. Presbyterian members, 1826–1970.

Source: Presbyterian Church in the U.S.A., 1826–1926, *Presbyterian Statistics Through One Hundred Years, 1826 to 1926*, Philadelphia (copyright); 1927–1957, unpublished data; 1958–1970, The United Presbyterian Church in the United States of America, annual *Minutes of the General Assembly* (copyright).

Figures include persons who have attained full membership, usually at age 13. Foreign members are excluded.

In 1958, The United Presbyterian Church of North America merged with The Presbyterian Church in the United States of America to form

The United Presbyterian Church in the United States of America. This is the largest of 8 Presbyterian Churches in the United States. The other large Presbyterian Church, located primarily in the South, is the Presbyterian Church in the U.S.

H 802. Protestant Episcopal members, 1927–1970.

Source: *The Episcopal Church Annual*, Morehouse-Gorham Co. (previously Morehouse Barlow), New York (copyright).

This body entered the Colonies with the earliest settlers (1607) as the Church of England. It became autonomous as the Protestant Episcopal Church in the U.S.A. and adopted its present name in 1789. In 1967, the General Convention adopted "The Episcopal Church" as an alternate name.

Data include "communicants" residing abroad, numbering less than one-half of one percent of the total communicants during the period covered by the figures. For definition of membership, see general note for series H 788–805.

H 803. Methodist members, 1790–1970.

Source: Statistical Office of the Methodist Church, 1790–1948, *Methodist History as Revealed in Statistical Form* (loose insert in *The Methodist Fact Book*), Chicago, 1949; 1949–1955, *The Methodist Fact Book*, 1957; 1956–1970, *The General Minutes of The United Methodist Church*. (Copyright.)

The Methodist Church was formed in 1939 by a merger of the Methodist Episcopal Church; the Methodist Episcopal Church, South; and the Methodist Protestant Church. Figures include all three bodies prior to 1939. Members are persons who have attained full membership, usually at age 13.

The Evangelical United Brethren Church was formed in 1946 with the merger of the Evangelical Church and The Church of the United Brethren in Christ.

The United Methodist Church was formed in 1968 by a merger of The Methodist Church and The Evangelican United Brethren Church. The United Methodist Church is the largest of nearly 20 separate Methodist denominations. Three large black Methodist denominations, for which there are no annual statistical reports, are African Methodist Episcopal Church, African Methodist Episcopal Zion Church, and Christian Methodist Episcopal Church.

H 804. Seventh-day Adventist members, 1907–1970.

Source: Statistical Secretary of the Seventh-day Adventist Church, Tacoma Park, Washington, D.C., unpublished data.

This Protestant body developed out of an interdenominational movement in the early decades of the 19th century but was not formally organized until 1863.

The members of this body are mainly 13 years old and over. The latest year for which age grouping was reported was 1936, when the local churches of the body reported that only about 3 percent of their members were less than 13 years of age.

H 805. Southern Baptist members, 1845–1970.

Source: Southern Baptist Convention, *Southern Baptist Handbook, 1970*, Convention Press, Nashville (copyright).

In 1845, Southern Baptist withdrew from The General Missionary Convention over the question of slavery and other matters and formed the Southern Baptist Convention.

Membership in the Southern Baptist Convention consists only of individuals who present themselves to the church, request membership, and are baptized. Infant baptism is not practiced.

Series H 788–792. Church Denominations, Members, and Edifices: 1850 to 1936

Year	Denominations reporting	Local organizations	Members [1]	Church edifices Number	Church edifices Value [2]	Year	Denominations reporting	Local organizations	Members [1]	Church edifices Number	Church edifices Value [2]
	788	789	790	791	792		788	789	790	791	792
			1,000		$1,000				1,000		$1,000
1936	256	199,302	55,807	179,742	3,411,875	1890	145	165,151	21,699	142,487	679,426
1926	212	232,154	54,576	210,924	3,839,501	1870		72,459		63,082	354,484
1916	200	227,487	41,927	203,432	1,676,601	1860		54,009			171,398
1906	186	212,230	35,068	192,795	1,257,576	1850		38,061			87,329

[1] Represents members as defined by each denomination. Figures do not furnish an adequate basis for computing membership growth, not only because of organic denominational changes, but also because of basic changes in the definition of "member" by certain denominations.
[2] For churches reporting.

Series H 793–799. Membership of Religious Bodies, 1890 to 1970, and by Major Groups: 1951 to 1970

[In thousands]

Year	Total membership	Buddhist	Old Catholic and Polish National Catholic [1]	Eastern churches	Jewish	Roman Catholic	Protestant [2]	Year	Total membership	Year	Total membership
	793	794	795	796	797	798	799		793		793
1970	131,046	100	848	3,850	5,870	48,215	72,162	1950	86,830	1936	[6] 55,807
1969	128,505	100	818	3,745	5,780	47,872	70,189	1949	81,862	1935	62,678
1968	128,470	100	599	2,660	5,725	47,873	71,513	1948	79,436	1934	62,007
1967	126,445	(3)	580	2,651	5,725	47,468	70,021	1947	77,386	1933	60,813
1966	123,826	(3)	(3)	(3)	5,725	46,865	71,236	1946 [5]	73,673	1932	60,157
										1931	59,798
1965	124,682	92	484	3,172	5,600	46,246	69,088	1945 [5]	71,700		
1964	123,307	110	491	3,167	5,600	45,641	68,299	1944	72,493	1926	54,576
1963	120,965	60	498	3,094	5,585	44,874	66,854	1942	68,501		
1962	117,946	60	597	3,002	5,509	43,848	64,930			1916	41,927
1961	116,110	60	573	2,800	5,365	42,877	64,435	1940	64,502	1906	35,068
1960	114,449	20	590	2,699	5,367	42,105	63,669	1938	64,157	1890	21,699
1959 *	112,227	20	484	2,808	5,500	40,871	62,544	1937	63,848		
1958 [4]	109,558	10	488	2,545	5,500	39,510	61,505				
1957	104,190	10	469	2,540	5,500	35,847	59,824				
1956	103,225	63	351	2,598	5,500	34,564	60,149				
1955	100,163	63	368	2,387	5,500	33,397	58,449				
1954	97,483	63	368	2,024	5,500	32,403	57,124				
1953	94,843	63	366	2,100	5,000	31,476	55,837				
1952	92,277	73	367	2,354	5,000	30,253	54,230				
1951	88,673	73	337	1,859	5,000	29,242	52,162				

* Denotes first year for which figures include Alaska and Hawaii.
[1] Beginning 1957, includes Armenian Church of North America.
[2] Includes non-Protestant bodies such as "Latter Day Saints" and "Jehovah's Witnesses"; non-Christian bodies such as "Spiritualists," "Ethical Culture Movement," and "Unitarian-Universalists"; in 1966 and 1967, "Buddhists"; and in 1966, "Old Catholic and Polish National Catholic," and "Eastern churches."

[3] Included in "Protestant" category; not available separately.
[4] Includes Alaska.
[5] Includes only bodies with memberships over 50,000.
[6] The *Christian Herald* reported 1936 membership as 63,222,000.

Series H 800–805. Membership of Selected Religious Bodies: 1790 to 1970

[In thousands]

Year	Roman Catholic [1]	Presbyterian [2]	Protestant Episcopal	Methodist	Seventh-day Adventist [3]	Southern Baptist [4]	Year	Roman Catholic [1]	Presbyterian [2]	Protestant Episcopal	Methodist	Seventh-day Adventist [3]	Southern Baptist [4]
	800	801	802	803	804	805		800	801	802	803	804	805
1970	47,872	3,096	3,475	10,672	420	11,629	1960	40,871	3,259	3,444	9,884	318	9,731
1969	47,873	3,173	3,536	10,790	408	11,489	1959	39,505	*3,210	3,359	*9,815	312	9,485
1968	47,468	3,230	3,588	[5] 10,991	396	11,332	1958	36,024	3,160	3,275	9,692	305	9,207
1967	46,864	3,269	3,585	10,289	385	11,142	1957	34,564	2,775	3,163	9,567	292	8,966
1966	46,246	3,298	3,647	10,311	374	10,949	1956	33,574	2,743	3,111	9,445	283	8,709
1965	45,640	3,309	3,616	10,332	365	10,772	1955	32,576	2,645	3,014	9,313	277	8,475
1964	44,874	3,303	3,591	10,304	355	10,601	1954	31,648	2,567	2,907	9,223	270	*8,169
1963	43,847	3,292	3,587	10,235	346	10,395	1953	30,425	2,492	2,791	9,152	261	7,886
1962	42,882	3,278	3,565	10,153	336	10,193	1952	29,408	2,438	2,716	9,180	254	7,634
1961	42,105	3,249	3,520	10,046	329	9,978	1951	28,635	2,360	2,643	9,066	246	7,373

See footnotes at end of table.

Series H 800–805. Membership of Selected Religious Bodies: 1790 to 1970—Con.

[In thousands]

Year	Roman Catholic [1]	Presbyterian [2]	Protestant Episcopal	Methodist	Seventh-day Adventist [3]	Southern Baptist [4]	Year	Roman Catholic [1]	Presbyterian [2]	Methodist	Seventh-day Adventist [3]	Southern Baptist [4]
	800	801	802	803	804	805		800	801	803	804	805
1950	27,766	2,364	2,541	8,936	237	7,080	1926	18,879	1,868	6,830	105	3,617
1949	26,718	2,319	2,512	8,793	230	6,761	1925	18,654	1,829	7,066	103	3,649
1948	26,076	2,266	2,437	8,651	223	6,489	1924	18,560	1,787	6,604	102	3,575
1947	25,268	2,203	2,350	8,568	216	6,271	1923	18,261	1,760	6,522	98	3,494
1946	24,402	2,115	2,301	8,430	208	6,079	1922	18,105	1,718	6,444	96	3,366
1945	23,964	2,104	2,270	8,084	201	5,866	1921	17,886	1,686	6,289	94	3,220
1944	23,420	2,040	2,228	8,046	196	5,668						
1943	22,945	1,996	2,189	7,979	190	5,493	1920	17,736	1,603	6,140	91	3,149
1942	22,556	1,986	2,168	7,838	186	5,367	1919	17,549	1,571	5,937	91	2,961
1941	22,293	1,961	2,162	7,683	181	5,238	1918	17,416	1,604	6,006	*88	2,887
							1917	17,023	1,579	5,970	83	2,844
1940	21,403	1,971	2,172	7,360	175	5,104	1916	16,584	1,541	5,829	76	2,744
1939	21,407	1,930	2,157	7,590	167	4,949						
1938	21,167	1,906	2,110	7,507	162	4,770	1915	16,309	1,493	5,698	74	2,686
1937	20,959	1,928	2,095	7,387	155	4,596	1914	16,068	1,428	5,394	69	2,589
1936	20,735	1,915	2,068	7,346	152	4,482	1913	15,154	1,388	5,402	69	2,523
							1912	15,016	1,353	5,261	66	2,446
1935	20,523	1,921	2,038	7,320	149	4,389	1911	14,619	1,331	5,168	65	2,421
1934	20,323	1,934	2,040	7,254	143	4,277						
1933	20,268	1,917	2,015	7,153	136	4,174	1910	14,347	1,315	5,073	64	2,332
1932	20,236	1,958	1,986	7,301	128	4,066	1909	14,235	1,299	4,977	65	2,219
1931	20,215	1,950	1,957	7,247	121	3,945	1908	13,877	1,276	4,851	65	2,139
							1907	13,089	1,305	4,735	65	2,015
1930	20,204	1,937	1,939	7,319	114	3,850	1906	12,652	1,127	4,612	....	1,947
1929	20,113	1,959	1,876	7,245	112	3,771						
1928	19,689	1,919	1,878	7,248	108	3,706						
1927	*19,483	1,886	1,789	7,171	107	3,674						

Year	Roman Catholic	Presbyterian [2]	Methodist	Southern Baptist [4]	Year	Presbyterian [2]	Methodist	Southern Baptist [4]	Year	Methodist
	800	801	803	805		801	803	805		803
1905	12,463	1,090	4,518	1,899	1865	232	1,381	(NA)	1825	342
1904	11,887	1,068	4,477	1,833	1864	231	1,438	(NA)	1824	330
1903	11,290	1,044	4,389	1,806	1863	227	1,581	(NA)	1823	314
1902	10,977	1,024	4,354	1,737	1862	303	1,549	(NA)	1822	299
1901	10,775	1,000	4,302	1,683	1861	300	1,617	(NA)	1821	282
1900	10,130	983	4,226	1,658	1860	292	1,661	650	1820	258
1899	9,907	961	4,186	1,608	1859	279	1,561	639	1819	242
1898	9,857	955	4,230	1,587	1858	259	1,510	618	1818	230
1897	9,596	939	4,134	1,569	1857	244	1,372	580	1817	226
1896	9,411	924	4,086	1,529	1856	233	1,348	569	1816	215
1895	9,078	903	3,990	1,469	1855	231	1,326	542	1815	212
1894	8,902	877	3,841	1,431	1854	225	1,187	519	1814	212
1893	8,806	837	3,705	1,363	1853	219	1,121	496	1813	215
1892	8,618	812	3,619	1,322	1852	210	1,254	467	1812	196
1891	8,277	790	3,511	1,282	1851	210	1,223	424	1811	185
1890	....	761	3,442	1,236	1850	207	1,186	(NA)	1810	175
1889	....	739	3,290	1,195	1849	201	1,158	405	1809	164
1888	....	706	3,168	1,166	1848	192	1,196	386	1808	153
1887	....	681	3,104	1,126	1847	179	1,102	377	1807	145
1886	....	648	3,059	1,072	1846	175	1,168	367	1806	131
1885	....	627	2,974	1,013	1845	172	995	352	1805	120
1884	....	607	2,907	975	1844	166	1,143	....	1804	114
1883	....	593	2,794	935	1843	159	1,175	....	1803	104
1882	....	585	2,727	915	1842	140	1,072	....	1802	87
1881	....	575	2,665	961	1841	134	917	....	1801	73
1880	....	573	2,694	1,673	1840	127	856	....		
1879	....	568	2,633	1,516	1839	128	798	....	1800	65
1878	....	563	2,412	1,484	1838	178	744	....	1799	62
1877	....	553	2,346	1,418	1837	221	700	....	1798	60
1876	....	531	2,224	1,342	1836	219	651	....	1797	59
1875	....	503	2,185	1,249	1835	....	655	....	1796	57
1874	....	493	2,118	1,200	1834	248	641	....	1795	61
1873	....	470	2,026	1,099	1833	234	602	....	1794	67
1872	....	466	1,987	956	1832	217	551	....	1793	68
1871	....	454	1,915	(NA)	1831	182	515	....	1792	66
1870	....	445	1,822	(NA)	1830	173	478	....	1791	76
1869	....	258	1,748	(NA)	1829	163	450	....		
1868	....	251	1,667	(NA)	1828	146	423	....	1790	58
1867	....	245	1,565	(NA)	1827	135	384	....		
1866	....	238	1,428	(NA)	1826	127	362	....		

* Denotes first year for which figures include Alaska and Hawaii.
NA Not available.
[1] Beginning 1923, includes membership in Alaska, and beginning 1927, in Hawaii. Beginning 1959, includes membership within jurisdiction of military ordinariate.
[2] In 1958, United Presbyterian Church of North America merged with Presbyterian Church in United States of America. Data for earlier years cover only the latter. See text.
[3] Beginning 1907, includes membership in Alaska and, beginning 1918, in Hawaii.
[4] Beginning 1951, includes membership in Alaska and, beginning 1954, in Hawaii. Excludes membership of Baptist Missionary Association beginning 1925; included prior to that time.
[5] Denotes first year of data for The United Methodist Church. See text.

Recreation (Series H 806-951)

H 806-951. General note.

The Department of the Interior issues various reports relating to recreation. The National Park Service publishes information on national parks in its monthly report (also issued cumulatively), *Public Use of the National Parks*, which gives visits; its semiannual report, *Areas Administered by the National Park Service*, which gives acreage; and its *National Parks and Landmarks*, which gives a brief description of each area and also covers sites eligible for registry as natural or national historic landmarks and non-federally owned national historic sites.

Data for municipal parks and playgrounds, as well as for other outdoor recreational activities, are compiled by the National Recreation and Park Association, Arlington, Va., which issues its *Recreation and Park Yearbook* at 5-year intervals, and its official publication, *Parks & Recreation*, monthly.

The Department of Agriculture's Forest Service, in its *Annual Report of the Chief*, issues data on recreational uses of the national forests.

Statistics on recreation have not been generally compiled and published in a systematic way. One major difficulty is that recreation, as a field of human activity and of social science research, has not been clearly defined in a manner accepted by all students. This general problem, and some of the consequent statistical problems, have been explored in the study by Marion Clawson, "Statistical Data Available for Economic Research on Certain Types of Recreation," *Journal of the American Statistical Association*, March 1959.

In general, many more data are available in the files of public agencies or private groups than have been published; and much of the publication is in forms not physically permanent nor likely to be preserved in libraries and other reference sources. The series presented here represent only the more readily available data. For many of these series, more detail for years prior to 1958, particularly for individual States and other geographic areas, may be found in a report by Marion Clawson, *Statistics on Outdoor Recreation*, Resources for the Future, Inc., Washington, D.C., 1958.

H 806-828. National parks, monuments, and allied areas—number, area, and visits, 1850-1970.

Source: 1850-1903, Marion Clawson, *Statistics on Outdoor Recreation*, Resources for the Future, Inc., Washington, D.C., 1958 (copyright); 1904-1970, U.S. National Park Service, *Areas Administered by the National Park Service*, annual issues, and *Public Use of the National Parks, A Statistical Report*, summary issues covering 1904-1940, 1941-1953, 1954-1964, and 1960-1970.

For 1850-1966, the estimates cover all areas administered by the National Park Service, some of which had previously been administered by the Department of Agriculture or by the War Department. These areas were established by congressional authority or by Executive order. Beginning 1967, estimates also cover areas authorized, but not yet in operation. Areas are tabulated according to their legal designation at the time of original tabulation. When designations were changed, numbers of areas and acreages in each series were shifted accordingly from that date forward but not retroactively.

Data do not include areas which are named national historic sites administered by States. Furthermore, a number of non-federally owned units in the United States and in the International Park north of Maine, which are deemed to be "administered" by the National Park Service by virtue of its involvement in their support, are included only in the count of areas.

Gross acres are reported for 1850-1934; federally owned acreage

thereafter. Data on acreage are compiled from both official and unofficial reports, internal records, and memoranda, among which are many unresolved inconsistencies, particularly for the early years.

In many areas, visitors are required to pay an entrance fee, and an actual count of visitors or of cars is obtained. In other areas, visits must be estimated. Each person is counted each time he enters any area of the system. Hence, the number of visits is substantially in excess of the number of different individuals. No data are available on the latter. Data do not include visits to parts of the system which were not under National Park Service administration. After 1936, all areas which were a part of the system were administered by the National Park Service. In general, the use of these areas prior to 1936 was not extensive.

H 821-823, national recreation areas, exclude national seashore recreational areas, which are listed in series H 824-826, "national seashores." Also excluded (from both) are recreation demonstration areas which existed from about 1933 until 1952. In 1932, there were 46 such areas with a total acreage of 395,844. By 1952, all had been disposed of to States or absorbed into the national park system.

The records of the National Park Service also contain data on area and visits to each of the units of the national park system, at least for recent years and, in some cases, for years before 1904.

H 829-835. Recreational use of national forest lands, 1924-1970.

Source: 1924-1956, Marion Clawson, *Statistics on Outdoor Recreation*, Resources for the Future, Inc., Washington, D.C., 1958 (copyright); 1957-1965, U.S. Forest Service, *Report of the Chief*, annual issues, and unpublished data; 1966-1970, U.S. Department of Agriculture, *Agricultural Statistics*, annual issues.

A recreational use includes a stop of at least 15 minutes. Data do not include a count of persons who drove over highways through national forests but made no other use of the areas. For 1924-1964, use of a national forest area for recreation for a period of $\frac{1}{4}$ to 3 hours was counted as $\frac{1}{4}$ day; of 3-5 hours as $\frac{1}{2}$ day; of 5-7 hours as $\frac{3}{4}$ day; and of 7-24 hours as a full-day use.

Beginning 1965, all Federal agencies responsible for administration of recreation use on public lands have reported on the volume of that use in terms of visitor-days, under the direction of the President's Advisory Council on Recreation and Natural Beauty. A *visitor-day* represents use of national forest land and water which aggregates 12 person-hours. It may entail 1 person for 12 hours, 12 persons for 1 hour, or any equivalent combination of individual or group use, either continuous or intermittent.

The downward trend of the data between 1965 and 1967 is believed to reflect more intensive standards of measurement rather than an actual reduction in use of the forest lands. Recreation specialists feel that estimates for those years would show a trend of increasing outdoor recreation use if the same standards of measurement had been consistently used during the first few years under the new system of use measurement.

As with the National Park Service data, series H 806-828, a visitor was counted each time he visited an area. Therefore, the number of different persons involved is substantially fewer than number of visits.

H 836-848. State parks—acreage, expenditures, funds, revenue, employees, and attendance, 1939-1970.

Source: 1939-1953 (except 1941 and 1946), U.S. National Park Service, *State Park Statistics*, annual issues; 1941, 1946, and 1954-

1962, U.S. Bureau of Outdoor Recreation, *State Outdoor Recreation Statistics—1962*; 1967 and 1970, The National Conference on State Parks, National Recreation and Park Association, Arlington, Va., *State Park Statistics, 1970* (copyright).

Many different kinds of areas and names are used to describe State-owned areas open for public recreation. The areas as defined in these studies exclude State forests and wildlife areas, some of which have important recreational facilities, and also exclude wayside areas if administered by State highway departments. The areas included vary in size from less than one acre each to well over 100,000 acres each.

Acreage data are based upon reports from most but not all States, the extent of the coverage increasing in more recent years. Total acreage, series H 836, refers to the land in State-owned recreation areas at the time of each State's reporting. Land acquired, series H 837, represents purchases, gifts, transfers from other State or Federal agencies, and other means of acquisition occurring during each State's fiscal year.

Funds available for expenditure include not only current appropriations, but also carryovers from previous appropriations; revenues from operations of concessions, entrance and parking fees; and revenues from other sources when these are available for expenditure.

Attendance data at recreational areas are often estimated, sometimes on various bases. Comparability of figures in series H 846–848 is somewhat marred by the transfer in California of numerous very popular beaches from State to county control. This accounts for the apparent drop in total attendance from 1947 to 1948, when, in fact, attendance was rising rather rapidly.

The data are based upon voluntary reports by State agencies; however, the same park agencies have not reported each year. The 1970 data were obtained through a questionnaire survey completed by 67 agencies that administer parks, recreation areas, historic sites, and related facilities in 47 States. Three State park agencies and three historical sites failed to report; in those instances, 1967 data were used. A number of State agencies throughout the nation that administer only one relatively small area are not included. Although the extent of the reporting has been variable, the more important States and agencies in terms of State park development have usually reported.

H 849–861. Municipal and county park and recreation areas—number, acreage, professional personnel, and selected facilities, 1910–1970.

Source: 1910–1955, Marion Clawson, *Statistics on Outdoor Recreation*, Resources for the Future, Inc., Washington, D.C., 1958 (copyright). National Recreation and Park Association, Arlington, Va., 1960 and 1965, *Recreation and Park Yearbook, 1961* and *1966*; 1970, *Parks & Recreation*, August 1971. (Copyright.)

Statistics on municipal and county park and recreation areas have been collected for many years by the National Recreation and Park Association (formerly National Recreation Association) of Arlington, Virginia, a private organization. Questionnaires are sent to all cities of 2,500 and over, to many smaller communities, and to all counties which are believed to have county park systems; and within each, to all agencies known or believed to have administration over parks or recreational programs. Provision of information is voluntary, and in spite of the best efforts of the Association, there is apparently a large degree of underreporting. In the 1940 and 1955 park surveys, for example, between 50 and 60 percent of all cities reported; however, the reporting was complete for the largest cities, fair for middle-size ones, and low for small ones. Many of the latter had no parks, but it is not possible to differentiate between those with no parks and those making no report. Perhaps as many as 90 percent or more of all parks are reported. In 1965, reports were received from 3,142 municipal and county agencies; in 1970, from 1,119.

Data from these surveys have been published in U.S. Bureau of Labor Statistics, *Park Recreation Areas in the United States*, Misc.

Series Bulletin No. 462, 1928, and No. 565, 1932; George D. Butler, *Municipal and County Parks in the United States, 1935*, National Park Service and National Recreation Association; and the following National Recreation and Park Association publications: *Municipal and County Parks in the United States, 1940; Recreation and Park Yearbook—Midcentury Edition—A Review of Local and County Recreation and Park Developments, 1900–1950; Recreation and Park Yearbook*, published quinquennially since 1956; and other *Yearbooks* published annually for 1910–1940 and biennially for 1942–1950. In the published reports, no effort was made to correct for underreporting, but the number of cities reporting is shown.

H 862–877. General note.

The items included here were selected because they are of some importance, and data are available for them. Other items of perhaps equal importance have been omitted for lack of data or have been included in other chapters. For data on radio and television, for example, see series R 93–105.

H 862–864. Bowling, 1896–1970.

Source: American Bowling Congress, Milwaukee, Wis., *Bowling Magazine* (copyright), and unpublished data.

The data cover organized tenpin bowling leagues of the American Bowling Congress, the Women's International Bowling Congress, and the American Junior Bowling Congress.

H 865–867. Horseracing, 1949–1970.

Source: The National Association of State Racing Commissioners, Lexington, Kentucky, *Statistical Reports on Horse Racing in the United States*, annual issues (copyright).

The data cover thoroughbred, harness, and quarter horse racing as well as races at fairs. The source presents data separately for each category and also gives detailed breakdowns, by State, of revenue to States, parimutuel takeout and breakage, and money distributed in stakes and purses.

For data on attendance at thoroughbred racing only, 1940–1957, see *Historical Statistics of the United States, Colonial Times to 1957*, series H 518.

H 868–870. Major league baseball attendance, 1901–1970.

Source: **Series H 868–869**, The National League of Professional Baseball Clubs, San Francisco, *1971 National League Green Book*, p. 28, and The American League of Professional Baseball Clubs, Boston, *American League Red Book, 1971*, p. 49; **series H 870**, The Sporting News Publishing Company, St. Louis, *Official World Series Records, 1971*.

H 871. Number of golfers, 1947–1970.

Source: National Golf Foundation, Inc., Chicago, *Golf Facilities in the United States*, annual information sheets (copyright).

H 872. Boxing, gross receipts, 1944–1970.

Source: *The Ring*, Nat Loubet (publisher), New York (copyright).

The basic data are compiled from reports of State boxing commissions.

H 873. Motion pictures—average weekly attendance, 1922–1965.

Source: The Film Daily, New York, 1922–1957, *The Film Daily Yearbook of Motion Pictures*, 1959 edition, p. 105; 1958–1965, same report, various annual issues. (Copyright.)

H 874. Motion pictures—box office receipts, 1929–1970.

Source: Motion Picture Association of America, Inc., New York, unpublished data.

H 875–876. Paid hunting and fishing license holders, 1923–1970.

Source: 1923–1956, see source for series H 806–828; 1957–1970, U.S. Fish and Wildlife Service, mimeographed releases and *Federal Aid in Fish and Wildlife Restoration*, annual reports.

Additional data on number of nonresident licenses and amounts paid for licenses, by States, are shown in the source. The original data for 1923–1956 are from reports made by the various State game commissions or departments of the Fish and Wildlife Service, and released annually in mimeographed statements.

H 877. Outboard motors sold, 1919–1970.

Source: Boating Industry Association, Chicago, unpublished data.

These and other data on outboard motors, boats, and trailers, including some data by States for years prior to 1958 are summarized in *Statistics on Outdoor Recreation*.

H 878–893. Personal consumption expenditures for recreation, 1909–1970.

Source: Twentieth Century Fund, 1909–1927, unpublished data (prepared for *Survey of Time, Work, and Leisure*); U.S. Bureau of Economic Analysis (formerly Office of Business Economics), 1929–1963, *The National Income and Product Accounts of the United States, 1929–1965*; 1964–1970, *Survey of Current Business*, July issues.

For more detailed definitions of the specific series, see the BEA publications defining these series. The data represent market value of purchases of goods and services by individuals and nonprofit institutions. They exclude expenditures for clothing, transportation, food and drink, shelter, and other items, even though they were made primarily for the purpose of recreation. However, expenditures for most of these items are included in chapter G, the section on Consumer Expenditure Patterns.

The data for 1909–1927 are based on J. Frederic Dewhurst and Associates, *America's Needs and Resources: A New Survey*, Twentieth Century Fund, New York, 1955. Dewhurst in turn drew his data on recreation from William H. Lough, *High-Level Consumption*, McGraw-Hill, New York, 1935; and Julius Weinberger, "Economic Aspects of Recreation," *Harvard Business Review*, summer 1937.

H 894–898. Expenditures of U.S. tourists to foreign countries, 1861–1900.

Source: Matthew Simon, "The United States Balance of Payments, 1861–1900," National Bureau of Economic Research, New York, *Trends in the American Economy in the Nineteenth Century*, Studies in Income and Wealth, vol. 24, Princeton University Press, 1960, p. 673 (copyright).

Underlying assumptions and derivations of the estimates are discussed in detail in the source, p. 658 ff.

H 899–920. Passports, by characteristics of travel and travelers, 1905–1970.

Source: **Series H 899**, 1905–1911, U.S. Passport Office, unpublished data; 1912–1948, U.S. Senate Committee on Government Operations, *Reorganization of the Passport Office*, 84th Congress, 2d session, Report No. 1604, p. 25. All series, 1948–1970, U.S. Passport Office, *Summary of Passport Statistics*, various issues.

The number of passports issued and renewed represents an actual count for calendar years. Comparable data are available for fiscal years in source publications.

Data by characteristics of travel and travelers, compilation of which began in 1948, are based on a sampling of the passports processed. The figures have been adjusted, wherever practicable, to reflect, primarily, the travel characteristics of the non-Government traveler. No adjustments have been made for persons changing their travel plans after receiving their passports, nor for travel restrictions to any area listed on the application.

Users of these data are cautioned that, while the Passport Office tries to ensure that the selection of applications for sampling is a truly random process, the size of the sample has diminished markedly over the past 15 years in relation to the volume of passport applications from which it is drawn. This is true because the size of the sample has not changed appreciably over that period while the volume of issuances has more than quadrupled. Also, it should be noted that the volume of applications received varies throughout the year so that in June there may be four times the volume received in November while the number included in the sample remains fairly constant.

H 921–940. Travel to foreign countries—travelers and expenditures, 1919–1970.

Source: U.S. Office of Business Economics, **series H 921** and **H 924–927**, 1919–1946, *The Balance of International Payments of the United States, 1946–1948*, p. 72; **series H 931**, 1919–1939, *Survey of Current Business*, July 1954, pp. 14 and 15; **series H 932–938**, 1920–1938, same report, March 1950, p. 18, and May 1951, p. 21; **series H 931–938**, 1940–1944, *International Transactions of the United States During the War, 1940–45*, p. 61. U.S. Bureau of Foreign and Domestic Commerce, **series H 928**, 1919–1938, sum of series H 929–931; **series H 929–930**, 1919–1938, *Oversea Travel and Travel Expenditures in the Balance of International Payments of the United States, 1919–38*, p. 77; **series H 939–940**, 1919–1938, same report, p. 62. All other data, U.S. Bureau of Economic Analysis (formerly Office of Business Economics), *Survey of Current Business*, various issues (usually June or July).

H 941–951. Foreign visitors to the United States—number and receipts, 1919–1970.

Source: **Series H 941–944**, U.S. Immigration and Naturalization Service, special tabulation. **Series H 945**, 1919–1946, and **series H 946**, 1946, U.S. Office of Business Economics, *Survey of Current Business*, July 1954; **series H 946–951**, 1940–1944, same agency, *International Transactions of the United States During the War, 1940–45*, p. 61; **series H 948–951**, 1919–1938, U.S. Bureau of Foreign and Domestic Commerce, *Oversea Travel and Travel Expenditures in the Balance of International Payments of the United States, 1919–38*, p. 73; **series H 945–951**, 1947–1970, U.S. Bureau of Economic Analysis (formerly Office of Business Economics), *Survey of Current Business*, various issues (usually June or July).

H 941–944, visitors. The data for 1919–1932 include all classes of nonimmigrants except aliens returning to the United States to resume residence after a temporary stay abroad of less than one year. The data for 1933–1970 include only nonimmigrant aliens admitted as temporary visitors for business or pleasure, foreigners in transit through the United States, and students. The "area of origin" refers to the country of last residence.

H 945–951, receipts. The data cover essentially the same classes of travelers as the visitors data except that they include Canada and Mexico. They include receipts from foreign government personnel and foreign businessmen employed in the United States.

Series H 806–828. National Parks, Monuments, and Allied Areas—Number, Area, and Visits: 1850 to 1970

[For years ending Sept. 30 prior to 1941; thereafter, for years ending Dec. 31, or as of Jan. 1 of the following year. Includes areas in Alaska, Hawaii, Virgin Islands, and Puerto Rico]

Year	Total, enumerated areas [1]			National parks			National monuments			National historical and military areas [3]			National parkways		
	Number	Area	Visits [2]	Number	Area	Visits	Number	Area	Visits	Number	Area	Visits	Number	Area	Visits
	806	807	808	809	810	811	812	813	814	815	816	817	818	819	820
		1,000 acres	1,000		1,000 acres	1,000		1,000 acres	1,000		1,000 acres	1,000		1,000 acres	1,000
1970	282	28,543	172,005	35	14,307	[4]45,879	85	9,970	17,304	120	163	46,593	5	130	27,818
1969	277	28,460	163,990	35	14,275	42,519	85	9,950	14,610	118	162	47,052	5	130	26,678
1968	273	27,971	150,836	35	14,212	42,515	83	9,509	14,206	115	160	43,838	5	130	23,919
1967	263	27,187	139,676	33	13,664	39,641	82	9,484	13,741	113	156	40,403	5	116	21,130
1966	258	26,551	133,081	33	13,628	38,556	81	8,945	13,144	109	153	43,030	5	114	15,925
1965	214	26,549	121,312	32	13,619	36,566	77	8,942	12,286	83	151	39,022	3	106	12,977
1964	203	26,102	111,386	32	13,566	34,047	77	8,939	12,164	80	148	34,847	3	103	11,478
1963	201	25,869	102,711	31	13,338	33,438	77	8,935	11,676	80	147	30,786	3	100	12,523
1962	191	26,003	97,045	31	13,333	32,191	80	8,926	11,752	71	145	27,958	3	97	11,835
1961	192	25,958	86,663	30	13,211	27,906	83	9,005	10,922	70	144	26,356	3	95	9,733
1960	187	25,704	79,229	29	13,208	26,630	83	8,981	10,738	66	144	21,820	3	94	8,983
1959	183	24,497	68,901	29	13,205	22,392	83	8,984	10,696	63	139	15,437	3	91	8,952
1958	180	24,398	65,461	29	13,106	21,672	83	8,988	9,734	60	137	14,076	3	90	8,131
1957	180	24,410	68,016	29	13,136	20,903	83	8,975	9,351	60	132	15,582	3	86	7,890
1956	181	24,398	61,602	29	13,131	20,055	83	8,957	8,769	60	137	13,543	3	85	7,438
1955	182	23,924	56,573	28	12,670	18,830	84	8,976	7,953	59	116	12,605	5	82	6,700
1954	180	23,908	54,210	28	12,641	17,969	83	8,999	7,805	59	113	12,587	4	78	6,067
1953	181	23,902	52,268	28	12,640	17,372	85	9,000	7,540	58	112	12,593	4	76	5,693
1952	178	23,840	47,379	28	12,589	17,143	85	9,010	6,807	56	106	11,979	4	76	3,558
1951	178	23,702	37,106	28	12,557	15,079	85	8,964	6,187	58	103	10,590	4	69	2,449
1950	179	23,836	33,253	28	12,222	13,919	86	9,439	5,310	58	102	9,476	4	64	1,996
1949	177	22,976	31,736	28	11,420	12,968	86	9,383	4,923	57	102	8,778	3	61	1,422
1948	178	22,955	29,859	28	11,347	11,293	86	9,279	4,438	56	102	7,849	3	59	1,510
1947	175	22,824	25,534	28	11,347	10,674	85	9,279	4,027	54	66	7,575	3	55	1,247
1946	172	22,424	21,752	27	11,062	8,991	86	9,284	3,603	52	44	6,734	3	55	1,262
1945	168	22,126	11,714	27	11,061	4,538	84	9,286	2,512	53	44	3,694	3	55	383
1944	169	22,107	8,340	27	11,055	2,646	84	9,274	1,851	54	44	3,310	3	55	268
1943	167	21,061	6,828	26	10,303	2,054	84	9,186	1,578	53	44	2,851	3	49	131
1942	165	20,886	9,371	26	10,300	3,815	83	9,015	1,832	52	44	3,130	3	49	256
1941	163	20,817	21,237	26	10,285	8,459	82	9,008	3,745	51	38	7,292	3	46	896
1940	160	20,762	16,755	26	10,258	7,358	82	8,994	2,817	48	33	5,924	3	36	———
1939	153	19,892	15,531	27	9,459	6,854	78	8,944	2,592	44	31	5,472	3	18	———
1938	143	18,647	16,331	27	9,409	6,619	73	7,498	2,364	41	30	6,784	1	10	———
1937	133	16,537	15,133	26	8,750	6,705	67	7,756	1,966	38	29	6,073	1	1	———
1936	132	15,433	11,990	26	8,692	5,791	67	6,714	1,681	38	26	4,518	1	1	———
1935	129	15,115	7,676	24	8,486	4,056	68	6,609	1,332	37	20	2,288	———	———	———
1934	114	15,244	6,337	22	8,532	3,517	67	6,687	1,386	25	24	1,434	———	———	———
1933	113	15,140	3,482	22	8,435	2,867	66	6,681	523	25	24	91	———	———	———
1932	108	12,968	3,755	22	8,417	2,949	61	4,527	406	25	24	400	———	———	———
1931	105	12,523	3,545	22	8,027	3,153	60	4,473	392	23	23	———	———	———	———
1930	99	10,581	3,247	22	7,797	2,775	59	2,766	472	18	17	———	———	———	———
1929	96	10,538	3,248	21	7,755	2,757	57	2,766	491	18	17	———	———	———	———
1928	92	10,359	3,025	20	7,581	2,569	57	2,761	456	15	17	———	———	———	———
1927	89	10,320	2,798	20	7,570	2,381	57	2,733	417	12	17	———	———	———	———
1926	86	10,249	2,315	20	7,501	1,942	57	2,733	373	9	14	———	———	———	———
1925	82	9,987	2,055	20	7,286	1,762	55	2,687	292	7	14	———	———	———	———
1924	73	8,813	1,671	19	7,278	1,424	47	1,520	247	7	14	———	———	———	———
1923	71	8,790	1,494	19	7,278	1,281	45	1,497	213	7	14	———	———	———	———
1922	64	8,781	1,216	19	7,278	1,045	38	1,489	172	7	14	———	———	———	———
1921	63	8,452	1,172	19	6,950	1,007	37	1,488	164	7	14	———	———	———	———
1920	63	8,452	1,058	19	6,950	920	37	1,488	139	7	14	———	———	———	———
1919	60	8,372	811	18	6,873	757	35	1,485	54	7	14	———	———	———	———
1918	59	7,554	455	16	6,255	452	36	1,285	3	7	14	———	———	———	———
1917	60	7,491	491	17	6,254	488	36	1,223	2	7	14	———	———	———	———
1916	54	5,984	358	15	4,742	356	34	1,229	2	5	14	———	———	———	———
1915	49	5,880	335	14	4,666	335	30	1,200	1	5	14	———	———	———	———
1914	48	5,986	240	13	4,437	240	30	1,535	1	5	14	———	———	———	———
1913	46	5,984	252	13	4,437	252	28	1,533	(Z)	5	14	———	———	———	———
1912	46	5,977	230	13	4,431	229	28	1,533	(Z)	5	14	———	———	———	———
1911	46	5,978	224	13	4,431	224	28	1,533	(Z)	5	14	———	———	———	———
1910	44	5,998	199	13	4,431	199	26	1,553	———	5	14	———	———	———	———
1909	38	5,013	86	12	3,449	86	21	1,550	———	5	14	———	———	———	———
1908	32	4,363	69	12	3,449	69	15	900	———	5	14	———	———	———	———
1907	24	3,547	61	12	3,444	61	7	89	———	5	14	———	———	———	———
1906	17	3,265	31	12	3,251	31	———	———	———	5	14	———	———	———	———
1905	15	3,471	141	10	3,457	141	———	———	———	5	14	———	———	———	———
1904	15	3,471	121	10	3,457	121	———	———	———	5	14	———	———	———	———
1903	14	3,470	———	9	3,456	———	———	———	———	5	14	———	———	———	———
1902	13	3,459	———	8	3,445	———	———	———	———	5	14	———	———	———	———
1901	12	3,300	———	7	3,286	———	———	———	———	5	14	———	———	———	———
1900	12	3,300	———	7	3,286	———	———	———	———	5	14	———	———	———	———
1899	12	3,300	———	7	3,286	———	———	———	———	5	14	———	———	———	———
1898	10	3,287	———	6	3,274	———	———	———	———	5	14	———	———	———	———
1897	10	3,287	———	6	3,274	———	———	———	———	4	13	———	———	———	———
1896	10	3,287	———	6	3,274	———	———	———	———	4	13	———	———	———	———
1895	10	3,287	———	6	3,274	———	———	———	———	4	13	———	———	———	———
1894	8	3,058	———	6	3,052	———	———	———	———	4	13	———	———	———	———
1893	8	3,058	———	6	3,052	———	———	———	———	2	7	———	———	———	———
1892	8	3,058	———	6	3,052	———	———	———	———	2	7	———	———	———	———
1891	7	3,058	———	5	3,051	———	———	———	———	2	7	———	———	———	———
1890	3	2,889	———	3	2,889	———	———	———	———	———	———	———	———	———	———
1872–1889 [5]	2	1,921	———	2	1,921	———	———	———	———	———	———	———	———	———	———
1850–1871 [6]	1	1	———	1	1	———	———	———	———	———	———	———	———	———	———

See footnotes at end of table.

Series H 806–828. National Parks, Monuments, and Allied Areas—Number, Area, and Visits: 1850 to 1970—Con.

Year	National recreation areas			National seashores			National Capital Parks (1 area) [7]		Year	National recreation areas—Con.		
	Number	Area	Visits	Number	Area	Visits	Area	Visits		Number	Area	Visits
	821	822	823	824	825	826	827	828		821	822	823
		1,000 acres	*1,000*		*1,000 acres*	*1,000*	*1,000 acres*	*1,000*			*1,000 acres*	*1,000*
1970	13	3,628	[4] 11,544	7	237	9,111	8	9,012	1950	3	2,010	2,551
1969	13	3,609	12,701	7	232	8,616	8	9,399	1949	3	2,010	3,646
1968	13	3,592	10,385	7	232	7,044	8	7,138	1948	5	2,167	4,769
1967	12	3,496	8,954	7	214	5,911	8	7,503	1947	5	2,077	2,012
1966	12	3,479	8,438	7	202	4,527	8	7,165	1946	4	1,979	1,162
1965	11	3,497	6,222	6	198	3,395	35	9,171	1945	1	1,680	587
1964	4	3,234	5,178	5	77	2,920	35	8,911	1944	1	1,680	264
1963	4	3,234	4,797	4	79	873	35	8,618	1943	1	1,478	214
1962	4	3,443	4,072	1	25	649	35	8,588	1942	1	1,478	338
1961	4	3,443	3,575	1	25	547	35	7,623	1941	1	1,440	845
1960	4	3,214	3,650	1	25	467	37	6,941	1940	1	1,440	656
1959	3	2,014	4,864	1	25	472	40	6,089	1939	1	1,440	612
1958	3	2,014	4,717	1	25	348	39	6,784	1938	1	1,700	565
1957	3	2,014	5,235	1	25	324	39	8,731	1937	1	(NA)	389
1956	4	2,025	4,817	1	25	302	38	6,679				
1955	4	2,020	3,655	1	25	264	35	6,565				
1954	4	2,020	3,407	1	22		35	6,376				
1953	4	2,020	3,026	1	15		39	6,043				
1952	4	2,020	2,814				39	5,080				
1951	3	2,010	2,801									

NA Not available. Z Less than 500.

[1] Not the same as the "national park system." Definition of the latter has changed from time to time. For 1850–1962, series H 806–808 are merely totals of the other items listed; thereafter, totals include other national parks and allied areas not shown separately, as follows (as of year end or Jan. 1 of following year): 1970, 16 areas, 100 thousand acres, and 4,742 thousand visits; 1969, 13 areas, 13 thousand acres, and 2,415 thousand visits; 1968, 14 areas, 128 thousand acres, and 1,790 thousand visits; 1967, 10 areas, 48 thousand acres, and 2,393 thousand visits; 1966, 10 areas, 23 thousand acres, and 2,296 thousand visits; 1965, 1 area, 18 acres, and 1,673 thousand visits; 1964, 1 area, 18 acres, and 1,840 thousand visits; 1963, 1 area, 18 acres, and no reported visits.

[2] Beginning 1964, includes visits to the White House. Beginning 1965, series also available on visitor-day basis; see text, series H 829–835.

[3] Includes national historical parks, national military parks, national battlefields, national battlefield parks, national battlefield sites, national cemeteries, national historic sites, national memorials, and one national memorial park. Does not include historical areas established under the Antiquities Act of 1906 and designated national monuments, nor the White House.

[4] Includes visits to two National Recreation Areas adjacent to North Cascades National Park.

[5] Yellowstone National Park, the first national park, established 1872.

[6] Hot Springs Reservation set aside by the Federal Government in 1832 and established as a national park in 1921. Initial Federal acreage was much greater than indicated, but over a period of years was subdivided into tracts and sold, some 900-odd acres being permanently reserved to the Federal Government. These series begin with 1850, the first year following the establishment of the Department of the Interior.

[7] Beginning 1966, comprises approximately 700 units in and around Washington, D.C. Prior years also include 2 parkways as well as Catoctin Mountain Park and Prince William Forest Park.

Series H 829–835. Recreational Use of National Forest Lands: 1924 to 1970

[In thousands. Calendar-year data, except 1933–1938 for fiscal years. Includes U.S. outlying areas and Puerto Rico. For definition of "visitor-days," see text]

Year	Visitor-days			Year	Visitor-days		
	Total use	Developed sites	Dispersed areas [1]		Total use	Developed sites	Dispersed areas [1]
	829	830	831		829	830	831
1970	172,555	67,655	104,900	1967	149,647	60,875	88,772
1969	162,838	63,740	99,098	1966	150,729	63,875	86,854
1968	156,655	62,462	94,193	1965	[2] 160,336	68,879	88,873

Year	Total use		Visits to areas improved by Federal funds	Visits to all other areas [3]	Year	Total use		Visits to areas improved by Federal funds	Visits to all other areas [3]
	Man-days	Visits				Man-days	Visits		
	832	833	834	835		832	833	834	835
1964	135,015	133,762	43,641	90,121	1943	11,322	6,274	3,412	2,862
1963	126,502	122,582	41,893	80,689	1942	17,036	10,407	6,066	4,341
1962	119,388	112,762	39,882	72,880	1941	26,077	18,005	10,688	7,317
1961	109,900	101,913	36,856	65,057	1940	42,421	16,163	13,062	3,101
1960	101,841	92,595	35,504	57,091	1939	39,480	14,332	11,466	2,866
1959	95,535	81,521	33,542	47,979	1938		14,496	10,810	3,686
1958	86,365	68,450	31,428	37,022	1937		11,833	8,810	3,021
1957	80,224	60,957	27,770	33,187	1936		10,781	8,233	2,548
1956	69,714	52,556	25,053	27,503	1935		9,719	7,722	1,996
1955	62,103	45,713	22,317	23,396	1934		8,581	6,953	1,628
1954	54,847	40,304	19,747	20,557	1933		8,166	6,576	1,590
1953	48,750	35,403	17,199	18,204	1932		7,896	6,227	1,669
1952	45,861	33,007	15,929	17,078	1931		8,074	5,959	2,115
1951	43,789	29,950	14,857	15,093	1930		6,911	5,253	1,658
1950	38,932	27,368	13,061	14,307	1929		7,132	4,959	2,173
1949	37,538	26,080	13,277	12,803	1928		6,550	4,783	1,767
1948	35,190	24,011	12,391	11,620	1927		6,136	4,469	1,667
1947	34,576	21,331	10,506	10,825	1926		6,044	4,460	1,584
1946	33,561	18,241	8,763	9,478	1925		5,623	4,217	1,406
1945	24,480	10,074	5,072	5,002	1924		4,660	3,460	1,200
1944	16,364	7,152	3,585	3,567					

[1] Represents unimproved areas and all areas officially designated as "national recreation areas."

[2] Includes 2,584,000 visitor-days undistributed.

[3] Represents unimproved areas and a few public areas improved by non-Federal funds.

Series H 836–848. State Parks—Acreage, Expenditures, Funds, Revenue, Employees, and Attendance: 1939 to 1970

Year	Acreage[1] Total	Land acquired	Land disposed of	Expenditures[2] Total	Operation and maintenance	Capital expenditures[3]	Funds available for expenditure	Revenue from operations	Employees Total, year round	Total, seasonal	Attendance[2] Total	Day visitors	Overnight use
	836	837	838	839	840	841	842	843	844	845	846	847	848
	1,000 acres	1,000 acres	1,000 acres	1,000 dol.	1,000 dol.	1,000 dol.	1,000 dol.	1,000 dol.			1,000	1,000	1,000
1970	8,555	1,100	(NA)	386,752	186,825	197,478	619,194	70,956	13,313	21,021	482,536	431,964	50,572
1967	7,352	(NA)	(NA)	279,520	114,022	165,334	472,467	50,084	11,477	17,777	391,063	354,819	36,244
1962	5,763	(NA)	(NA)	108,881	61,115	46,300	144,611	26,466	7,075	10,546	284,795	260,745	[4]24,050
1961	5,799	156	4.0	110,101	60,981	49,120	133,673	23,364	7,984	10,142	273,484	249,186	22,999
1960	5,602	68	9.5	87,373	56,269	31,103	131,419	22,641	7,412	10,125	259,001	238,432	20,569
1959 *	5,681	252	9.9	88,268	50,932	37,266	139,341	20,773	6,966	9,724	255,310	237,316	17,994
1958	5,406	159	.9	73,222	46,990	26,187	135,060	18,235	6,691	9,982	237,329	220,206	17,123
1957	5,248	63	1.7	74,008	41,623	32,335	124,077	15,987	6,302	9,141	216,780	201,881	14,899
1956	5,165	62	4.0	65,844	38,047	27,508	88,255	14,928	6,048	8,884	200,705	185,325	12,642
1955	5,086	70	3.0	55,093	34,024	20,816	69,075	13,817	5,657	7,980	183,188	169,123	11,057
1954	5,005	92	1.0	49,134	31,621	17,360	64,059	13,099	5,105	7,299	166,427	155,817	9,472
1953	4,876	21	8.6	49,565	30,158	19,407	68,791	10,776	5,030	7,906	159,116	148,189	8,347
1952	4,928	54	4.0	40,469	26,139	14,329	60,886	9,349	4,753	7,363	149,255	139,578	7,812
1951	4,877	48	12.7	38,545	22,841	15,704	62,859	6,652	4,376	6,937	120,722	114,024	6,698
1950	4,657	62	---------	36,399	21,384	15,015	52,283	6,646	4,191	6,435	114,291	108,212	6,079
1949	(NA)	68	---------	31,921	19,122	12,780	44,176	6,089	4,004	6,245	106,792	100,105	6,687
1948	(NA)	73	---------	32,059	17,279	14,781	42,497	5,794	3,987	6,238	105,248	100,222	5,026
1947	(NA)	101	---------	25,991	13,844	12,147	36,813	4,731	3,489	5,900	109,995	105,624	4,231
1946	4,634	122	---------	15,445	8,717	5,508	20,711	4,118	2,771	3,879	92,507	88,923	3,139
1945	(NA)	88	---------	10,564	7,115	3,449	11,973	2,595	2,433	4,800	57,649	51,619	2,622
1944	(NA)	154	---------	6,466	5,755	710	9,788	1,979	2,233	2,754	39,668	33,991	2,069
1943	(NA)	105	---------	6,570	5,406	1,164	7,684	1,910	2,186	2,547	38,306	35,190	2,312
1942	(NA)	40	---------	9,373	6,774	2,599	9,993	2,488	1,518	2,107	70,359	50,496	2,188
1941	4,260	82	---------	10,022	6,942	3,009	10,372	3,177	2,630	2,856	97,489	94,570	2,918
1940	---------	---------	---------	9,443	6,226	3,195	9,078	---------	---------	---------	---------	---------	---------
1939	---------	---------	---------	7,429	4,524	2,635	8,169	---------	---------	---------	---------	---------	---------

* Denotes first year for which figures include Alaska and Hawaii.
NA Not available.
[1] Excludes State forests, wildlife refuges, and waysides not administered by State park agencies.
[2] Detail may not add to total because some States did not report detail.
[3] In recent years, roughly three-quarters spent for improvements; the rest for land acquisition.
[4] Includes 836,086 camper days for primitive camps (few if any facilities) not previously included.

Series H 849–861. Municipal and County Park and Recreation Areas—Number, Acreage, Professional Personnel, and Selected Facilities: 1910 to 1970

Year	Areas Number	Acreage	Professional personnel	Playgrounds under leadership	Baseball diamonds (90-foot)	Softball diamonds (60-foot)	Tennis courts	Bathing beaches	Swimming pools Total	Outdoor	Golf courses (9 and 18 hole)	Recreation buildings	Indoor recreation centers
	849	850	851	852	853	854	855	856	857	858	859	860	861
1970	31,235	965,785	87,717	11,691	4,486	14,808	12,343	760	2,555	2,194	518	9,212	14,237
1965	30,509	1,496,378	119,515	24,298	9,335	17,467	19,926	1,261	4,745	4,277	1,005	6,486	16,041
1960	24,710	1,015,461	99,696	20,107	7,044	14,832	15,676	951	2,846	2,513	585	3,828	13,142
1955	20,417	748,701	76,878	18,224	5,542	11,834	13,188	830	2,233	1,813	478	4,097	13,142
1950	17,142	644,067	58,029	14,747	5,502	12,266	13,085	780	1,616	1,289	454	2,987	6,630
1948	(NA)	(NA)	48,548	13,520	4,576	11,143	11,964	638	1,395	1,062	355	8,561	
1946	(NA)	(NA)	41,159	11,559	4,323	10,034	11,847	618	1,449	1,116	340	5,843	
1944	(NA)	(NA)	35,503	10,022	(NA)	(NA)	(NA)	564	1,447	1,095	409	4,536	
1942	(NA)	(NA)	26,244	8,739	3,645	9,207	11,516	529	1,190	925	380	4,449	
1941	(NA)	(NA)	26,096	9,646	3,951	10,061	12,262	583	1,278	948	366	5,143	
1940	20,145	641,471	24,533	9,921	3,904	10,042	12,075	572	1,200	898	387	5,736	
1939	(NA)	(NA)	25,042	9,749	3,846	8,995	11,617	548	1,181	866	358	5,789	
1938	(NA)	(NA)	23,975	9,712	3,902	8,833	11,310	564	1,162	838	354	5,612	
1937	(NA)	(NA)	22,160	9,618	3,923	8,384	11,031	569	1,063	842	354	5,234	
1936	(NA)	(NA)	20,052	9,490	3,568	7,369	10,029	516	1,142	828	354	5,294	
1935	15,631	540,758	18,496	8,062	3,669	6,896	9,313	488	1,038	710	332	4,682	
1934	(NA)	(NA)	20,245	8,384	3,838	5,313	9,420	496	1,016	716	343	4,719	
1933	(NA)	(NA)	21,085	7,434	5,572	(NA)	9,921	530	1,148	751	370	3,502	
1932	(NA)	(NA)	23,037	6,990	4,161	(NA)	9,267	472	1,094	778	374	2,822	
1931	(NA)	(NA)	25,508	7,685	4,396	(NA)	8,804	470	1,093	775	323	2,687	

See footnotes at end of table.

Series H 849–861. Municipal and County Park and Recreation Areas—Number, Acreage, Professional Personnel, and Selected Facilities: 1910 to 1970—Con.

Year	Areas Number	Areas Acreage	Professional personnel	Playgrounds under leadership	Baseball diamonds (90-foot)	Softball diamonds (60-foot)	Tennis courts	Bathing beaches	Swimming pools Total	Swimming pools Outdoor	Golf courses (9 and 18 hole)	Recreation buildings	Indoor recreation centers
	849	850	851	852	853	854	855	856	857	858	859	860	861
1930	12,101	417,290	24,949	7,677	4,322	(NA)	8,422	457	1,042	724	312		2,708
1929		(NA)	22,920	7,681	4,024	(NA)	7,960	409	1,010	700	299		3,019
1928		(NA)	20,762	6,930	3,303	(NA)	7,186	353	937		267		2,693
1927		(NA)	19,825	6,301	2,917	(NA)	6,977	403	840		263		2,505
1926		(NA)	17,090	5,868	2,972	(NA)	6,254	276	708		194		2,116
1925		316,092	17,177	5,121	2,831	[1] 1,256	6,110	273	534		153		1,878
1924			15,871	5,006	2,522		4,865	293	626		131		2,051
1923			12,282	5,309				261	536		118		1,620
1922			10,867	4,601				223	465				1,392
1921			11,079	4,584				246	456				1,627
1920			10,218	4,293				260	359				1,197
1919			8,043	3,969				241	359				1,130
1918			8,137	3,871				175	309				1,034
1917			8,748	3,944				192	328				(NA)
1916			7,122	3,140				173	243				805
1915			7,507	3,294					306				758
1913			6,318	2,402									
1912			5,320	2,094									
1911			4,132	1,543									
1910			3,345	1,244									

NA Not available.
[1] Facilities reported by cities of 20,000 and over.

Series H 862–877. Participation in Selected Recreational Activities: 1896 to 1970

Year	Bowling Number of bowlers	Bowling Number of teams [1]	Bowling Number of alley beds	Horseracing Racing days	Horseracing Attendance [2]	Horseracing Parimutuel turnover	Major league baseball attendance [2] American League	National League	World Series	Number of golfers	Boxing, gross receipts [3]
	862	863	864	865	866	867	868	869	870	871	872
	1,000				*1,000*	*Mil. dol.*	*1,000*	*1,000*	*1,000*	*1,000*	*$1,000*
1970	7,623		141,492	9,962	69,704	5,977	12,085	16,662	253	9,700	6,200
1969	7,608		143,929	9,539	68,099	5,723	12,135	15,095	272	9,500	5,422
1968	7,584		147,526	9,051	65,460	5,310	11,317	11,785	380	9,300	7,264
1967	7,525		151,731	8,621	63,373	4,922	11,337	12,971	304	9,100	6,310
1966	7,546		156,219	8,384	63,577	4,784	10,167	15,015	221	8,525	5,188
1965	7,617		159,079	8,051	62,887	4,615	8,861	13,581	364	7,750	8,264
1964	7,496		158,996	7,561	60,595	4,402	9,235	12,045	322	7,000	7,948
1963	7,405	1,128,300	157,713	7,136	55,754	3,975	9,095	11,382	247	6,250	7,828
1962	6,930	1,018,047	148,535	6,532	50,582	3,669	10,015	11,360	377	5,500	7,225
1961	6,316		130,805	6,280	49,560	3,467	10,163	8,732	223	5,000	5,650
1960	*5,374	858,869	*107,908	6,099	46,879	3,358	9,227	10,685	350	*4,400	5,902
1959	4,449	*714,395	87,475	5,963	45,451	3,246	9,149	9,995	421	4,125	4,101
1958	3,686	571,457	73,081	5,348	43,373	3,039	7,296	10,165	394	3,970	5,624
1957	3,222	492,249	65,127	5,187	41,365	2,937	8,196	8,820	395	3,812	5,185
1956	2,787	425,089	60,654	5,052	39,871	2,791	7,894	8,650	346	3,680	4,448
1955	2,514	386,912	58,203	4,899	38,503	2,592	8,943	7,674	362	3,500	6,335
1954	2,363	368,231	56,861	4,734	38,637	2,515	7,922	8,014	252	3,400	4,285
1953	2,238	351,506	55,739	4,656	38,249	2,556	6,964	7,420	307	3,336	4,183
1952	2,096	333,300	55,272	4,397	35,065	2,326	8,294	6,339	341	3,265	3,988
1951	1,999	322,277	54,943	4,114	31,865	1,934	8,883	7,244	342	3,237	5,100
1950	1,937	320,878	52,488	4,018	29,291	1,638	9,142	8,321	196	3,215	3,800
1949	1,821	310,299	49,555	3,702		1,599	10,731	9,485	237	3,112	5,001
1948	1,635	284,777	45,296				11,150	9,771	358	2,742	11,240
1947	1,415	250,117	44,028				9,486	10,388	390	2,517	13,500
1946	1,060	184,000	40,146				9,621	8,902	250		14,000
1945	1,048	172,000	38,023				5,580	5,261	333		13,000
1944	910	151,000	37,104				4,798	3,975	207		10,840
1943	895	150,000	38,582				3,697	3,769	277		
1942	1,059	190,000	39,812				4,200	4,353	277		
1941	874	163,000	34,195				4,912	4,778	236		
1940	684	132,000	26,382				5,434	4,390	282		
1939	535	103,000	22,866				4,271	4,707	184		
1938	482	93,000	18,238				4,446	4,561	201		
1937	329	64,000	16,285				4,736	4,204	238		
1936	267	52,000	11,655				4,179	3,904	303		
1935	216	41,000	11,473				3,688	3,657	287		
1934	168	32,000	9,760				3,764	3,200	282		
1933	148	29,000	9,473				2,926	3,163	163		
1932	197	39,000	9,277				3,133	3,841	192		
1931	224	44,000	8,897				3,883	4,584	232		

See footnotes at end of table.

Series H 862–877. Participation in Selected Recreational Activities: 1896 to 1970—Con.

Year	Bowling — Number of bowlers (862)	Bowling — Number of teams [1] (863)	Bowling — Number of alley beds (864)	Major league baseball attendance [2] — American League (868)	National League (869)	World Series (870)
	1,000			1,000	1,000	1,000
1930	219	43,000	10,796	4,686	5,447	213
1929	147	27,000	9,366	4,662	4,926	190
1928	116	22,000	8,426	4,221	4,881	199
1927	99	18,000	7,419	4,613	5,310	202
1926	81	15,000	6,818	4,913	4,920	328
1925	68	12,000	6,299	5,187	4,354	283
1924	54	10,000	5,776	5,255	4,341	284
1923	60	11,000	----	4,603	4,070	301
1922	32	7,500	----	4,874	3,942	186
1921	26	4,800	----	4,620	3,987	270
1920	27	5,100	----	5,084	4,037	174
1919	14	2,700	----	3,654	2,878	237
1918	16	3,100	----	1,708	1,372	186
1917	17	3,300	----	2,859	2,361	129
1916	16	3,200	----	3,452	3,052	163
1915	11	2,100	----	2,435	2,430	143
1914	9	1,500	----	2,748	1,707	111
1913	8	1,700	----	3,527	2,832	151
1912	6	1,700	----	3,264	2,736	252
1911	7	1,200	----	3,340	3,232	180
1910	7	1,400		3,271	3,495	124
1909	7	1,300		3,740	3,496	145
1908	7	1,320		3,611	3,512	62
1907	6	1,266		3,399	2,640	78
1906	5	970		2,938	2,781	100
1905	3	630		3,121	2,734	92
1904	2	470		3,024	2,664	(NA)
1903	2	400		2,345	2,390	100
1902	1	220		2,206	1,683	----
1901	1	200		1,684	1,920	----
1900	1	150		----	----	----
1899	1	120		----		
1898	1	100		----		
1897	(Z)	75		----		
1896	(Z)	60		----		

Year	Motion pictures [2] — Average weekly attendance (873)	Box office receipts (874)	Paid hunting and fishing license holders [4] — Hunting (875)	Fishing (876)	Outboard motors sold (877)
	Millions	Mil. dol.	1,000	1,000	1,000
1970		1,162	22,184	31,136	430
1969		1,099	21,622	29,855	510
1968		1,045	20,859	28,787	500
1967		989	20,225	27,072	444
1966		964	19,587	26,302	440
1965	44	927	19,372	24,976	393
1964	44	913	19,059	24,472	390
1963	42	904	18,679	23,976	362
1962	43	903	18,175	23,084	360
1961	42	921	[5] 18,202	23,136	343
1960	40	951	*[5] 18,440	*23,323	*468
1959	42	958	[5] 11,924	19,914	540
1958	40	992	14,764	20,178	504
1957	45	1,126	14,918	19,277	550
1956	47	1,394	14,462	18,702	647
1955	46	1,326	14,192	18,855	515
1954	49	1,228	14,073	18,581	[6] 479
1953	46	1,187	14,803	17,652	463
1952	51	1,246	13,902	17,128	337
1951	54	1,310	12,661	16,027	[7] 284
1950	60	1,376	12,638	15,338	367
1949	70	1,451	12,759	15,479	329
1948	90	1,506	11,392	14,078	499
1947	90	1,594	12,067	12,620	584
1946	90	1,692	9,854	11,069	398
1945	85	1,450	8,191	8,280	(NA)
1944	85	1,341	7,491	7,830	(NA)
1943	85	1,275	8,081	8,029	(NA)
1942	85	1,022	8,521	8,423	(NA)
1941	85	809	7,913	8,004	170
1940	80	735	7,646	7,931	130
1939	85	659	7,511	7,858	120
1938	85	663	6,903	7,436	100
1937	88	676	6,860	6,902	100
1936	88	626	6,658	5,832	50
1935	80	556	5,988	5,121	41
1934	70	518	5,918	4,856	23
1933	60	482	5,742	4,858	15
1932	60	527	5,777	----	12
1931	75	719	6,368	----	14
1930	90	732	6,901	----	44
1929	80	720	6,429	----	59
1928	65	----	6,463	----	54
1927	57	----	5,998	----	42
1926	50	----	5,332	----	33
1925	46	----	4,905	----	27
1924	46	----	4,395	----	21
1923	43	----	4,341	----	21
1922	40	----	----	----	16
1921		----	----	----	12
1920		----	----	----	17
1919		----	----	----	12

* Denotes first year for which figures include Alaska and Hawaii.
NA Not available.   Z Less than 500.
[1] Covers only men's bowling teams in leagues sanctioned by American Bowling Congress.
[2] Excludes Alaska and Hawaii for all years.
[3] Includes Hawaii for all years. Beginning 1963, includes Alaska and Guam. Excludes closed circuit TV receipts.
[4] Beginning 1960, includes multiple counting of license holders who bought 1 or more non-resident licenses as well as a license for their own home State.
[5] Excludes Colorado, Michigan, Minnesota, and Wisconsin.
[6] Production disrupted due to labor arbitration.
[7] Production disrupted due to material allocation under the Controlled Material Plan.

Series H 878–893. Personal Consumption Expenditures for Recreation: 1909 to 1970

[In millions of dollars]

Columns 883–886 fall under the group heading **Admission to specified spectator amusements**.

Year	Total [878]	Nondurable toys and sport supplies [879]	Wheel goods, durable toys, sport equipment, boats, and pleasure aircraft [880]	Radio and television receivers, records, and musical instruments [881]	Radio and television repair [882]	Admission — Total [883]	Motion picture theaters [884]	Theater entertainment (plays, operas, etc.) of nonprofit institutions, except athletics [885]	Spectator sports [886]	Clubs and fraternal organizations, except insurance [887]	Commercial participant amusements [888]	Parimutuel, net receipts [889]	Books and maps [890]	Magazines, newspapers, and sheet music [891]	Flowers, seeds, and potted plants [892]	Other [893]
1970	39,049	5,726	4,873	8,328	1,322	2,413	1,162	735	516	1,158	1,819	1,018	3,441	4,097	1,436	3,418
1969	36,284	5,250	4,434	7,838	1,266	2,260	1,099	674	487	1,112	1,733	952	3,172	3,798	1,368	3,101
1968	33,623	4,701	3,937	7,715	1,227	2,130	1,045	632	453	1,047	1,662	861	2,825	3,508	1,251	2,759
1967	30,758	3,975	3,422	7,328	1,143	2,030	989	605	436	988	1,600	795	2,689	3,207	1,107	2,474
1966	28,850	3,743	3,248	6,905	1,072	1,923	964	545	414	934	1,555	765	2,365	3,059	1,078	2,203
1965	26,298	3,436	2,933	6,013	1,032	1,811	927	495	389	879	1,509	734	2,061	2,868	983	2,039
1964	24,571	3,174	2,805	5,409	954	1,762	913	484	365	854	1,486	694	1,969	2,735	870	1,859
1963	22,213	2,986	2,538	4,539	906	1,692	904	446	342	808	1,443	626	1,620	2,521	842	1,692
1962	20,474	2,792	2,269	3,935	882	1,646	903	417	326	773	1,366	564	1,523	2,415	739	1,570
1961	19,506	2,702	2,129	3,668	839	1,625	921	398	306	763	1,299	536	1,396	2,348	702	1,499
1960 *	18,295	2,417	2,106	3,412	801	1,606	951	365	290	733	1,161	517	1,304	2,193	641	1,404
1959	17,381	2,306	2,038	3,330	735	1,571	958	344	269	721	991	493	1,159	2,110	599	1,328
1958	15,817	2,115	1,845	2,836	681	1,538	992	297	249	692	848	454	1,022	2,061	544	1,181
1957	15,333	2,047	1,720	2,825	628	1,655	1,126	287	242	653	738	438	983	1,973	587	1,086
1956	14,979	1,951	1,573	2,938	573	1,899	1,394	268	237	611	654	414	951	1,880	554	981
1955	14,078	1,803	1,386	2,869	516	1,801	1,326	245	230	569	584	381	867	1,869	546	887
1954	13,077	1,624	1,174	2,726	482	1,672	1,228	220	224	539	528	368	806	1,825	540	793
1953	12,720	1,694	1,090	2,588	434	1,605	1,187	197	221	517	514	372	830	1,776	545	755
1952	12,102	1,708	989	2,349	393	1,655	1,246	189	220	498	489	327	788	1,689	526	691
1951	11,564	1,662	897	2,236	353	1,716	1,310	186	220	477	472	255	776	1,573	495	652
1950	11,147	1,394	869	2,421	283	1,781	1,376	183	222	462	448	239	674	1,495	457	624
1949	10,010	1,170	836	1,675	202	1,872	1,451	182	239	454	428	247	627	1,454	451	594
1948	9,692	1,076	965	1,450	174	1,918	1,506	180	232	435	425	257	584	1,374	440	594
1947	9,249	907	955	1,398	140	2,003	1,594	187	222	397	404	255	531	1,243	442	574
1946	8,539	840	793	1,116	115	2,066	1,692	174	200	359	379	241	589	1,099	416	526
1945	6,139	553	400	344	88	1,714	1,450	148	116	281	284	153	520	965	378	459
1944	5,422	459	323	311	72	1,563	1,341	142	80	236	241	131	450	880	327	429
1943	4,961	393	271	403	60	1,455	1,275	118	62	217	215	79	366	838	274	390
1942	4,677	404	306	634	46	1,204	1,022	92	90	205	213	69	291	703	241	361
1941	4,239	362	314	607	36	995	809	79	107	203	210	65	255	636	229	327
1940	3,761	306	254	494	32	904	735	71	98	203	197	55	234	589	201	292
1939	3,452	285	228	420	28	821	659	64	98	199	183	41	226	554	191	276
1938	3,241	268	210	339	25	816	663	58	95	200	164	44	221	514	176	264
1937	3,381	269	210	385	23	818	676	53	89	203	194	38	243	518	186	294
1936	3,020	242	171	333	21	759	626	50	83	198	165	29	208	490	159	245
1935	2,630	216	136	248	21	672	556	44	72	197	141	26	183	456	130	204
1934	2,441	200	118	229	17	625	518	42	65	199	135	19	165	441	116	177
1933	2,202	181	93	195	14	573	482	41	50	208	121	6	152	419	90	150
1932	2,442	207	110	268	19	631	527	57	47	242	132	4	153	428	89	159
1931	3,302	266	159	478	24	854	719	78	57	277	175	6	253	479	134	197
1930	3,990	281	172	921	27	892	732	95	65	294	203	7	264	512	190	227
1929	4,331	336	219	1,012	26	913	720	127	66	283	207	8	309	538	221	240
1927	[1]3,120	470		713		769	526	195	48	275	159			[2]349	183	------
1925	[1]2,835	411		739		588	367	174	47	242	145			[2]318	182	------
1923	[1]2,620	455		637		528	336	146	46	242	148			[2]270	176	------
1921	[1]2,055	338		439		412	301	81	30	242	128			[2]239	135	------
1919	[1]2,189	377		667		336				242	55			[2]204	128	------
1914	[1]1,000	186		193		191				140	25			[2]131	56	------
1909	[1]860	143		166		167				121	22			[2]104	70	------

* Denotes first year for which figures include Alaska and Hawaii.
[1] Includes estimates for "Other" recreational expenditures.
[2] Represents only 42 percent of the national estimated expenditures for books and maps, and magazines, newspapers, and sheet music; the remaining 58 percent was classified as educational rather than recreational outlay.

Series H 894–898. Expenditures of U.S. Tourists to Foreign Countries: 1861 to 1900

[Persons in thousands; expenditures in millions of dollars, except per capita. For fiscal years]

Year	Total expenditures	Expenditures of tourists in Canada and Mexico	Ocean-bound tourists: Number	Expenditures: Total	Per capita
	894	895	896	897	898
1900	97.8	4.7	124.1	93.1	$750
1899	77.2	3.7	98.1	73.5	750
1898	75.9	3.6	96.4	72.3	750
1897	68.5	3.3	98.8	65.2	660
1896	70.6	3.4	101.3	67.2	660
1895	75.1	3.6	103.7	71.5	690
1894	45.3	2.2	68.7	43.1	628
1893	62.4	3.0	93.4	59.4	637
1892	68.9	3.3	95.1	65.6	690
1891	68.9	3.3	91.9	65.6	713
1890	67.6	3.2	90.7	64.4	711
1889	61.7	2.9	83.7	58.8	702
1888	66.7	3.2	98.4	63.5	645
1887	64.8	3.1	95.1	61.7	649
1886	59.5	2.8	89.0	56.7	638
1885	57.6	2.7	100.2	54.9	548
1884	56.0	2.7	91.6	53.3	582
1883	45.4	2.2	69.3	43.2	623
1882	38.9	1.9	54.5	37.0	680
1881	34.4	1.6	50.0	32.8	656
1880	35.1	1.7	51.8	33.4	$645
1879	36.0	1.7	56.9	34.3	603
1878	28.5	1.4	42.9	27.1	631
1877	22.8	1.1	42.7	21.7	507
1876	28.7	1.4	49.4	27.3	552
1875	30.2	1.4	51.6	28.8	558
1874	29.5	1.4	49.2	28.1	571
1873	25.0	1.2	49.2	23.8	483
1872	31.8	1.5	50.5	30.3	600
1871	28.4	1.4	45.0	27.0	600
1870	22.0	1.1	34.9	20.9	600
1869	17.3	.8	27.6	16.5	600
1868	26.0	1.2	41.3	24.8	600
1867	25.4	1.2	40.3	24.2	600
1866	24.5	1.2	38.9	23.3	600
1865	21.8	1.0	34.7	20.8	600
1864	16.8	.8	26.6	16.0	600
1863	14.9	.7	23.7	14.2	600
1862	14.1	.7	22.3	13.4	600
1861	15.2	.7	24.1	14.5	600

Series H 899–920. Passports, by Characteristics of Travel and Travelers: 1905 to 1970

[In thousands. Except as noted, data refer to number of passports issued, not travelers. Covers new and renewed passports except, effective August 26, 1968, passports became valid for 5 years and renewals were eliminated. A single passport may cover more than one trip and more than one person]

Year	Total passports	Government	Object of travel [1] — Nongovernment: Total	Personal reasons [2]	Pleasure [3]	Business [4]	Education	Religion	Health	Other
	899	900	901	902	903	904	905	906	907	908
1970	2,219	146	2,073	1,791	217	40	20	3	1	1
1969	1,820	167	1,653	1,476	131	25	16	2	—	3
1968	1,748	210	1,538	912	443	104	69	7	2	2
1967	1,686	161	1,524	639	671	141	61	8	2	3
1966	1,548	216	1,332	483	651	135	52	8	1	2
1965	1,330	191	1,139	487	535	76	31	7	1	2
1964	1,133	180	953	367	470	78	30	5	1	1
1963	1,056	145	910	436	353	86	26	7	1	1
1962	907	107	800	428	268	74	23	5	1	1
1961	858	100	758	376	298	46	28	7	1	1
1960	853	116	737	322	351	25	31	7	1	1
1959	732	122	610	252	291	31	29	5	2	1
1958	677	100	577	88	400	54	26	6	2	1
1957	586	97	489	19	368	72	23	5	2	1
1956	559	85	474	37	366	40	25	4	2	1
1955	528	528	(NA)	(NA)	(NA)	(NA)	(NA)	(NA)	(NA)	(Z)
1954	452	452		180	171	67	23	6	3	2
1953	418	418		177	150	58	22	4	4	2
1952	395	395		162	144	56	29	1	4	2
1951	290	290		116	106	48	18	2	2	1
1950	300	300		142	108	27	14	5	1	3
1949	269	269		148	66	28	19	4	2	2
1948 [5]	171	171		94	24	32	13	4	1	3

See footnotes at end of table.

Series H 899–920. Passports, by Characteristics of Travel and Travelers: 1905 to 1970—Con.

[In thousands]

Year	First area destination [6]						Mode of travel-departure[6]		Sex of traveler		Citizenship of traveler	
	Africa	Australia and Oceania	Europe	Far East	North, Central, and South America	Middle East	Ship	Air	Male	Female	Native	Naturalized
	909	910	911	912	913	914	915	916	917	918	919	920
1970	19	51	1,910	117	72	49	(7) 3	(7) 1,817	1,124	1,096	2,073	147
1969	20	68	1,460	125	92	55	15	1,733	945	875	1,702	118
1968	21	61	1,295	160	129	82	38	1,648	903	845	1,603	145
1967	20	56	1,265	157	126	61	50	1,498	870	815	1,535	150
1966	23	58	1,116	166	121	64	39	1,291	811	737	1,374	174
1965	20	51	993	111	100	56	39	1,291	699	631	1,237	93
1964	16	37	865	96	73	47	115	1,019	580	554	1,012	122
1963	12	33	795	102	71	42	165	890	534	521	918	137
1962	13	29	687	85	64	29	162	745	455	452	777	130
1961	10	48	646	71	58	26	176	682	431	427	752	106
1960	8	35	670	56	59	25	226	627	420	433	710	143
1959	8	32	562	47	60	23	241	491	353	379	560	172
1958	7	17	537	39	56	16	269	408	[8] 404	[8] 471	503	174
1957	7	5	461	46	46	12	299	287	[8] 381	[8] 412	426	160
1956	7	5	421	45	46	13	335	224	[8] 320	[8] 413	416	143
1954	14	6	355	10	51	16	253	195	237	215	292	160
1953	10	5	335	9	45	14	241	173	217	201	269	149
1952	5	3	329	8	43	7	243	148	215	180	257	138
1951	7	2	229	5	41	6	184	104	159	131	181	109
1950	5	2	244	6	33	10	201	97	156	144	175	125
1949	6	2	211	7	32	11	--------	--------	149	120	147	122
1948 [5]	3	2	122	9	31	4	--------	--------	107	64	104	67

Year	Total passports	Year	Total passports	Year	Total passports	Year	Total passports	Year	Total passports	Year	Total passports	Year	Total passports
	899		899		899		899		899		899		899
1948	230	1941	50	1934	112	1927	182	1920	160	1913	23		
1947	202	1940	26	1933	107	1926	176	1919	98	1912	22		
1946	[9] 189	1939	90	1932	153	1925	172	1918	57	1911	23		
1945	[9] 155	1938	135	1931	163	1924	146	1917	38	1910	24		
1944	[9] 141	1937	168	1930	203	1923	126	1916	23				
1943	[9] 138	1936	142	1929	197	1922	138	1915	23	1905	17		
1942	[9] 130	1935	118	1928	189	1921	138	1914	20				

– Represents zero.   NA Not available.   Z Less than 500.
[1] Data not entirely comparable because of changes in classifications.
[2] Includes "Personal business," "Join husband," "Accompany husband," and "Visit family"; through 1965, also includes "Business and pleasure."
[3] Includes "Sightseeing," "Vacation," "Visit," and "Tourist."
[4] Includes applicants formerly listed under "Employment" and "Commercial business"; beginning 1966, includes "Business and pleasure."

[5] Compilation of material by characteristics began on April 1, 1948; therefore, only 9 months information is available for calendar year 1948.
[6] Excludes small number not stated and world travel.
[7] Data not compiled; 99 percent of all applicants indicate air as mode of departure.
[8] Represents all travelers covered by passports issued or renewed.
[9] Includes passports issued to American seamen.

Series H 921–940. Travel to Foreign Countries—Travelers and Expenditures: 1919 to 1970

[Travelers in thousands; expenditures in millions of dollars.   Covers residents of United States and Puerto Rico]

Year	Overseas travelers [1]							Expenditures [2]		
	Total	Means of transportation		Region of destination				Total	Transportation [3]	
		Sea	Air	Europe and Mediterranean	West Indies and Central America	South America	Other		Foreign flag carriers [4]	U.S. flag carriers [4]
	921	922	923	924	925	926	927	928	929	930
1970	5,260	120	5,140	2,898	1,663	249	450	6,173	1,215	985
1969	4,623	151	4,472	2,363	1,700	245	315	5,382	1,080	895
1968	3,885	147	3,738	1,937	1,461	223	264	4,730	885	815
1967	3,425	167	3,258	1,800	1,220	175	230	4,752	830	715
1966	2,975	220	2,755	1,570	1,050	130	225	4,047	755	635
1965	2,623	237	2,386	1,405	891	127	200	3,768	720	610
1964	2,220	277	1,943	1,250	701	107	162	3,376	645	520
1963	1,990	318	1,672	1,102	634	97	160	3,219	615	490
1962	1,767	280	1,487	931	609	85	142	2,929	575	415
1961	1,575	268	1,307	826	550	83	116	2,650	507	358
1960	1,634	317	1,317	832	641	71	90	2,623	513	360
1959	1,516	279	1,237	705	677	59	75	2,380	380	390
1958	1,398	292	1,106	637	645	52	64	2,140	320	360
1957	1,369	303	1,066	556	704	51	58	1,955	261	322
1956	1,239	327	912	521	631	42	45	1,814	238	301

See footnotes at end of table.

Series H 921–940. Travel to Foreign Countries—Travelers and Expenditures: 1919 to 1970—Con.

[Travelers in thousands; expenditures in millions of dollars, except as indicated]

Year	Overseas travelers [1]							Expenditures [2]		
	Total	Means of transportation		Region of destination				Total	Transportation [3]	
		Sea	Air	Europe and Mediterranean	West Indies and Central America	South America	Other		Foreign flag carriers [4]	U.S. flag carriers [4]
	921	922	923	924	925	926	927	928	929	930
1955	1,075	318	757	482	522	34	37	1,612	201	258
1954	912	307	605	420	432	36	24	1,401	183	209
1953	827	300	527	376	396	33	22	1,306	179	198
1952	772	(NA)	(NA)	332	382	39	19	1,188	172	176
1951	684	(NA)	(NA)	255	375	42	12	1,028	132	139
1950	676	298	378	302	323	38	13	1,022	145	123
1949	573			250	271	38	14	933	107	126
1948	495			192	253	36	14	828	80	117
1947	435			149	245	27	14	716	55	88
1946	329			101	176	52		(NA)	(NA)	(NA)
1945	117			40	48	29		(NA)	(NA)	(NA)
1944	75			20	32	22		(NA)	(NA)	(NA)
1943	57			6	32	19		(NA)	(NA)	(NA)
1942	71			6	49	15		(NA)	(NA)	(NA)
1941	170			7	142	21		(NA)	(NA)	(NA)
1940	156			11	119	27		(NA)	(NA)	(NA)
1939	282			120	133	30		378	60	28
1938	370			196	149	26		411	81	27
1937	435			248	153	9	24	470	95	27
1936	381			209	139	33		400	74	29
1935	314			185	99	30		333	65	23
1934	302			178	96	29		302	63	21
1933	300			191	84	25		278	60	19
1932	393			266	102	25		353	75	19
1931	438			280	129	29		471	101	29
1930	538			359	146	33		655	154	38
1929	517			350	136	8	23	688	164	41
1928	518			343	144	30		638	150	40
1927	471			326	115	30		569	137	32
1926	433			293	111	29		528	125	31
1925	408			271	109	28		495	118	30
1924	351			230	93	28		434	107	24
1923	291			183	82	26		378	91	27
1922	320			205	89	26		361	91	27
1921	294			186	88	20		292	70	22
1920	302			196	82	24		281	70	21
1919	152			91	45	16		170	36	11

Year	Expenditures [2]—Con.								Average expenditure per trip, Europe and Mediterranean [6] (dollars)
	Abroad								
	Total	Canada	Mexico	Overseas areas					
				Total	Europe and Mediterranean [5]	West Indies and Central America	South America	Other [5]	
	931	932	933	934	935	936	937	938	939
1970	3,973	1,049	740	2,184	1,310	390	90	394	490
1969	3,407	900	692	1,815	1,075	375	92	273	490
1968	3,030	820	638	1,572	925	325	87	235	512
1967	3,207	1,070	602	1,535	944	295	70	226	563
1966	2,657	678	575	1,404	920	259	65	160	583
1965	2,438	600	540	1,298	795	220	68	215	611
1964	2,211	550	490	1,171	800	190	57	124	637
1963	2,114	522	472	1,120	755	180	56	129	680
1962	1,939	479	449	1,011	652	178	55	125	692
1961	1,785	425	420	940	618	160	48	114	738
1960	1,750	380	383	987	692	166	45	84	830
1959	1,610	365	350	895	604	174	41	76	851
1958	1,460	323	319	818	560	156	37	65	876
1957	1,372	340	305	727	483	153	37	54	867
1956	1,275	316	279	680	473	134	29	44	905

See footnotes at end of table.

Series H 921–940. Travel to Foreign Countries—Travelers and Expenditures: 1919 to 1970—Con.

[Travelers in thousands; expenditures in millions of dollars, except as indicated]

Columns below fall under **Expenditures[2]—Con.** The columns 931–938 are under **Abroad** (with 934–938 under **Overseas areas**); columns 939–940 are under **Average expenditure per trip[6] (dollars)**.

Year	Abroad, Total	Canada	Mexico	Overseas areas, Total	Europe and Mediterranean	West Indies and Central America	South America	Other	Avg. exp. per trip, Europe and Mediterranean	Avg. exp. per trip, All areas
	931	932	933	934	935	936	937	938	939	940
1955	1,153	306	255	592	430	107	22	33	889	---
1954	1,009	284	233	492	360	87	22	23	857	---
1953	929	282	226	421	306	76	20	19	814	---
1952	840	257	209	374	256	78	25	15	767	---
1951	757	255	194	308	195	75	25	13	(NA)	---
1950	754	261	172	321	225	61	22	13	742	---
1949	700	265	155	280	185	57	21	17	740	---
1948	631	267	147	217	128	52	22	15	(NA)	---
1947	573	241	140	192	107	56	16	13	742	---
1946	457	209	125	123	63	35	25		(NA)	---
1945	298	149	81	67	(7)	5	8	[7] 54	(NA)	---
1944	225	106	79	40	(7)	2	7	[7] 31	(NA)	---
1943	173	79	71	23	(7)	3	10	[7] 10	(NA)	---
1942	155	72	60	23	(7)	4	8	[7] 11	(NA)	---
1941	212	97	69	46	(7)	18	12	[7] 16	(NA)	---
1940	190	89	57	44	(7)	16	10	[7] 18	(NA)	---
1939	290	(NA)	(NA)	(NA)	(NA)	(NA)	(NA)	(NA)	734	---
1938	303	(NA)	(NA)	(NA)	79	(NA)	(NA)	(NA)	735	586
1937	348	156	44	148	97	35	16		710	577
1936	297	(NA)	(NA)	(NA)	85	(NA)	(NA)	(NA)	720	579
1935	245	(NA)	(NA)	(NA)	70	(NA)	(NA)	(NA)	691	579
1934	218	(NA)	(NA)	(NA)	(NA)	(NA)	(NA)	(NA)	665	561
1933	199	71	33	95	67	19	9		633	546
1932	259	(NA)	(NA)	(NA)	(NA)	(NA)	(NA)	(NA)	615	535
1931	341	(NA)	(NA)	(NA)	(NA)	(NA)	(NA)	(NA)	799	671
1930	463	(NA)	(NA)	(NA)	(NA)	(NA)	(NA)	(NA)	1,017	854
1929	483	178	36	269	213	37	5	14	1,125	935
1928	448	(NA)	(NA)	(NA)	(NA)	(NA)	(NA)	(NA)	1,108	898
1927	400	(NA)	(NA)	(NA)	(NA)	(NA)	(NA)	(NA)	1,067	879
1926	372	(NA)	(NA)	(NA)	(NA)	(NA)	(NA)	(NA)	1,103	892
1925	347	(NA)	(NA)	(NA)	(NA)	(NA)	(NA)	(NA)	1,110	896
1924	303	(NA)	(NA)	(NA)	(NA)	(NA)	(NA)	(NA)	1,149	911
1923	260	(NA)	(NA)	(NA)	(NA)	(NA)	(NA)	(NA)	1,197	941
1922	243	(NA)	(NA)	(NA)	(NA)	(NA)	(NA)	(NA)	1,133	903
1921	200	(NA)	(NA)	(NA)	(NA)	(NA)	(NA)	(NA)	1,025	819
1920	190	52	6	132	102	19	11		1,023	807
1919	123	---	---	---	---	---	---	---	1,004	783

NA Not available.

[1] Excludes the following: Travel to Canada and Mexico; travel between conterminous United States and Alaska, Hawaii, Puerto Rico, and Virgin Islands; cruise travelers; military personnel and other Government employees and their dependents stationed abroad, and U.S. citizens residing abroad.

[2] Includes shore expenditures of cruise travelers; excludes travel expenditures of military personnel and other Government employees and their dependents stationed abroad, and U.S. citizens residing abroad.

[3] Excludes passenger fares of emigrant aliens.

[4] Beginning 1960, new series; not comparable with earlier years.

[5] Beginning 1965, Mediterranean Asia and Africa, and Eastern Europe included with "Other."

[6] Excludes transatlantic passenger fares. For 1919–1938, refers to expenditures by U.S. citizens; thereafter, by U.S. residents.

[7] Europe and Mediterranean included in "Other."

Series H 941–951. Foreign Visitors to the United States—Number and Receipts: 1919 to 1970

[Visitors data are for years ending June and, except for 1933 and 1934, exclude Canada and Mexico. Receipts data exclude transocean fares]

Year	Visitors (1,000)				Receipts (mil. dol.)						
	Total	Area of origin			Total	Area of origin					
		Europe	West Indies, Central and South America	Other		Canada	Mexico	Overseas			
								Total	Europe and Mediterranean [1]	West Indies, Central and South America	Other [1]
	941	942	943	944	945	946	947	948	949	950	951
1970	2,193	953	799	441	2,330	896	545	889	318	334	237
1969	1,894	850	693	351	2,058	815	530	713	264	276	172
1968	1,825	875	644	306	1,775	650	493	632	226	262	144
1967	1,431	662	542	227	1,646	575	457	614	227	263	124
1966	1,274	597	478	199	1,590	586	458	546	210	226	110
1965	1,130	537	414	179	1,380	490	390	500	205	200	95
1964	937	429	360	148	1,207	448	342	417	165	161	91
1963	780	359	303	118	1,015	372	313	330	113	147	70
1962	671	311	255	105	957	392	296	269	105	110	54
1961	602	270	240	92	885	449	200	236	93	90	53
1960	572	243	245	84	919	469	226	224	90	86	48
1959	520	207	239	74	902	462	160	280	98	133	49
1958	447	177	211	59	825	425	144	256	86	125	45
1957	419	186	183	50	785	419	135	231	87	107	37
1956	345	133	171	41	705	390	123	192	68	96	28
1955	328	119	172	37	654	364	110	180	61	93	26
1954	307	111	165	31	595	322	99	174	48	103	23
1953	287	100	158	29	574	307	101	166	42	90	34
1952	296	107	158	31	550	294	89	167	40	96	31
1951	255	89	139	27	473	246	75	152	51	75	26
1950	242	87	130	25	419	193	69	157	56	77	24
1949	258	102	131	25	392	165	68	159	54	82	23
1948	282	126	126	30	334	113	71	150	57	72	21
1947	229	103	101	25	342	152	42	148	64	63	22
1946	117	35	70	12	257	130	(NA)	(NA)	(NA)	(NA)	(NA)
1945	102	15	75	12	162	(NA)	(NA)	(NA)	(NA)	(NA)	(NA)
1944	70	20	46	4	117	52	34	32	(2)	3	2 29
1943	50	18	27	5	84	31	31	22	(2)	2	2 20
1942	42	14	20	8	82	22	31	29	(2)	2	2 26
1941	46	16	23	7	70	16	33	21	(2)	7	2 14
1940	81	41	29	11	95	36	31	27	(2)	8	2 20
1939	100	57	28	15	135	---------	---------	(NA)	(NA)	(NA)	(NA)
1938	98	56	27	15	130	---------	---------	74	45	29	
1937	96	58	25	13	135	---------	---------	78	49	29	
1936	81	49	20	12	117	---------	---------	70	45	25	
1935	69	41	18	10	101	---------	---------	54	34	20	
1934	75	(NA)	(NA)	(NA)	81	---------	---------	45	28	17	
1933	60	(NA)	(NA)	(NA)	66	---------	---------	36	22	14	
1932	49	29	14	6	65	---------	---------	36	21	15	
1931	66	39	17	10	94	---------	---------	58	38	20	
1930	83	51	21	11	129	---------	---------	86	56	31	
1929	78	45	20	13	139	---------	---------	91	58	33	
1928	78	43	22	13	121	---------	---------	83	53	30	
1927	73	39	21	13	114	---------	---------	73	46	27	
1926	70	37	21	12	110	---------	---------	80	49	31	
1925	65	32	21	12	83	---------	---------	65	39	26	
1924	79	37	27	15	77	---------	---------	74	43	31	
1923	65	30	25	10	71	---------	---------	73	45	28	
1922	53	23	20	10	61	---------	---------	62	37	24	
1921	75	28	25	22	76	---------	---------	86	61	25	
1920	81	36	27	18	67	---------	---------	81	42	39	
1919	47	19	18	10	56	---------	---------	64	37	27	

NA Not available.
[1] Beginning 1966, Mediterranean Asia and Africa, and Eastern Europe, included in "Other."

[2] Europe and Mediterranean included in "Other."

Crime and Correction (Series H 952-1170)

H 952-1170. General note.

In the United States there are many difficulties in drawing together national statistics on crime and correction. There is no one body of criminal law or procedure that relates to the United States as a whole. Under the U.S. Constitution, the police powers are reserved to the States. Thus, there are 50 sovereign jurisdictions of crime control in the 50 States in this country and a 51st in the District of Columbia which has a penal code and a criminal enforcement system provided by Act of Congress.

Federal criminal jurisdiction is something quite apart from State jurisdiction. Federal crimes are defined by Acts of Congress in connection with enforcing laws relating primarily to customs, taxation, and interstate matters. Therefore, except for offenses committed within the limited geographical area of a Federal reservation, crimes such as murder, robbery, burglary, larceny, rape, arson, etc., are juridically State crimes rather than Federal.

Within each State, the enforcement of the criminal law is predominantly the responsibility of local agencies. Police departments, prosecutors, and courts are in most instances either municipal or county agencies. To a large extent, even the correctional processes such as probation and misdemeanant imprisonment are functions administered by local authorities. Direct State responsibility is largely confined to providing penal institutions for those offenders convicted and committed to long-term imprisonment.

The inherent difficulties of collecting only the basic information about crime from hundreds of independent police departments, prosecutors, courts, and correctional agencies within a single State, not to mention the difficulties encountered in attempting to synthesize such information for the 50 States and the District of Columbia, have limited the development of adequate national compilations of criminal statistics.

Statistics on prisoners were collected by the Bureau of the Census in connection with each decennial Census of Population from 1850 to 1890. Independent enumerations of prisoners were made in 1904, 1910, 1923, and 1933. The first nationwide collection of criminal data on an annual basis was made in 1926 by the Bureau of the Census (a compilation of prisoners received and released from State and Federal prisons and reformatories). This agency published an annual summary and an analysis of these data from 1926 to 1946, and a very brief summary in 1947. Subsequently, the Federal Bureau of Prisons assumed this responsibility.

These annual reports have, from the beginning, covered most of the States, never less than 44 of the 51 jurisdictions plus reports from the Federal prison system, and have been consistent and complete enough to offer historical data that have some acceptable comparability (see series H 1135-1154).

The second annual nationwide collection began in 1930. Summary reports on serious offenses known to the police and arrests made by them were collected from a large number of police departments by the Federal Bureau of Investigation. Annual and semiannual statistics have been regularly issued ever since in *Uniform Crime Reports for the United States*. Because the sources of data for this series are cooperating individual police departments in all of the States, there have never been data available which represented complete reporting from all police departments in any one State. Further, the variability in procedure and practice in the reporting of crimes known to the police and the lack of uniformity in the definition of offenses are serious obstacles in compiling valid historical series on crimes and arrests in the United States as a whole.

A third collection of data on a national basis was made under the auspices of the Bureau of the Census in 1932 when reports were obtained from a number of States accounting for defendants prosecuted and convicted and sentenced in courts of general trial jurisdiction. The usual pattern throughout the country is that there is one such court in each county and there are over 3,000 counties in the 50 States. This series was continued for 15 years, and reports summarizing these data were issued annually by the Bureau of the Census under the title, *Judicial Criminal Statistics*. However, at no time were there more than 32 States involved in this reporting system. Partly because of its limited existence and incomplete coverage, its inclusion here is not justified. In addition, the variations from State to State and even within States from county to county that occurred in the reporting of the data created many unresolved questions of comparability and completeness.

H 952-961. Crimes and crime rates, by type, 1957-1970.

Source: U.S. Federal Bureau of Investigation, *Uniform Crime Reports for the United States*, annual issues.

The Uniform Crime Reporting Program is the outgrowth of a need for a national and uniform compilation of law enforcement statistics. A national program of collection of crime counts was initiated in 1930 by the Committee on Uniform Crime Records of the International Association of Chiefs of Police (IACP). In that same year, the Federal Bureau of Investigation was authorized as the national clearinghouse for statistical information on crime. Crime reports are solicited from law enforcement agencies throughout the Nation based on uniform classifications and procedures of reporting.

In the national Uniform Crime Reporting Program, contributing law enforcement agencies are wholly responsible for compiling their own crime reports and submitting them to the FBI. The FBI, in an effort to maintain quality and uniformity in the data received, furnishes training in Uniform Crime Reporting procedures to contributing agencies upon request. All contributors are furnished with the Uniform Crime Reporting Handbook which outlines, in detail, procedures for scoring and classifying offenses. The Handbook illustrates and discusses the monthly and annual reporting forms as well as the numerous tally sheets made available to facilitate the periodic tabulation of desired data.

On a monthly basis, law enforcement agencies (police, sheriffs, and State police) report the number of offenses that became known to them during the month in the following crime categories: Murder and nonnegligent manslaughter, manslaughter by negligence, forcible rape, robbery, assault, burglary, larceny, and auto theft. This count is taken from a record of all complaints of crime received by the law enforcement agency from victims, other sources, and/or discovered by officers. Whenever complaints of crime are determined through investigation to be unfounded or false they are eliminated from the actual count. The number of "actual offenses known" in these crime categories is reported to the FBI without regard to whether anyone is arrested for the crime, to whether the stolen property is recovered, to the local prosecutive policy, or to any other restrictive consideration. Law enforcement agencies report, on a monthly basis, the total number of these reported crimes which they clear either by arrest or exceptional means. A separate count of crimes cleared which involve only persons under the age of 18 is shown. The number of law enforcement officers killed and assaulted and the value of property stolen and recovered during the month are also reported.

Arrests are reported on an annual basis for all criminal acts except traffic violations, by crime category, including the age, sex, and race of each person arrested. A report is also submitted, by crime classification, concerning the number of persons formally charged and the disposition of such charges.

Uniformity of crime data collected under this program is of primary concern to the FBI as the national clearinghouse. With the receipt of reports covering approximately 10,000 jurisdictions, prepared on a voluntary basis, the problems of attaining uniformity are readily apparent. It is standard procedure to examine each incoming report for arithmetical accuracy, and for reasonableness, as a possible indication of errors.

Variations in the level and ratios among the crime classes established by previous reports of each agency are used as a measure of possible or probable incompleteness or changes in reporting policy. Necessary arithmetical adjustments or unusual variations are brought to the attention of the submitting agency by correspondence, which is the principal tool for supervision of quality. Not only are the individual reports studied, but also periodic trends for individual reporting units are prepared. Crime rates for all units are grouped for general comparability to assist in detecting variations and fluctuations possibly due to some reason other than chance.

The elimination of duplication of crime reporting by the various agencies is given constant attention. In addition to detailed instructions as to the limits of reporting jurisdictions between sheriffs and police in urban places, lists of urban places by county are furnished to sheriffs, county police, and, in some instances, State police organizations.

In 1958, a special committee was appointed by the FBI to study the 28-year old program. The consultant committee made 22 recommendations, most of which were incorporated in *Uniform Crime Reports for the United States*, beginning with the 1958 issue. The completed changes involved three major revisions in the presentation of data but no change in information collected from contributors. Broadly, format changes were (1) elimination of manslaughter by negligence and minor thefts from crime classes used as a crime index; (2) crime index totals for standard metropolitan statistical areas and for States; (3) crime rates based on current estimates of population for individual areas prepared by the FBI in line with suggestions by the U.S. Bureau of the Census. The entire report of the committee was published by the FBI in *Uniform Crime Reports for the United States*, Special Issue—1958.

Offenses in Uniform Crime Reporting are divided into two groupings designated as Part I and Part II offenses. Crime Index offenses are included among the Part I offenses. Offense and arrest information is reported for the Part I offenses on a monthly basis whereas only arrest information is reported for Part II offenses.

The Part I offenses are:

1. Criminal homicide.—(a) Murder and nonnegligent manslaughter: All willful felonious homicides as distinguished from deaths caused by negligence. Excludes attempts to kill, assaults to kill, suicides, accidental deaths, or justifiable homicides. Justifiable homicides are limited to the killing of a person by a peace officer in line of duty and the killing of a person in the act of committing a felony by a private citizen. (b) Manslaughter by negligence: Any death which was determined by police investigation as primarily attributable to gross negligence of some individual other than the victim.

2. Forcible rape.—Rape by force, assault to rape, and attempted rape. Beginning 1958, excludes statutory offenses (no force used—victim under age of consent).

3. Robbery.—Stealing or taking anything of value from the care, custody, or control of a person by force or violence or by putting in fear, such as strong-arm robbery, stickups, armed robbery, assaults to rob, and attempts to rob.

4. Aggravated assault.—Assault with intent to kill or for the purpose of inflicting severe bodily injury by shooting, cutting,

stabbing, maiming, poisoning, scalding, or by the use of acids, explosives, or other means. Excludes simple assaults.

5. Burglary—breaking or entering.—Burglary, housebreaking, safecracking, or any breaking or unlawful entry of a structure with the intent to commit a felony or a theft. Includes attempted forcible entry.

6. Larceny—theft (except auto theft).—(a) Fifty dollars and over in value; (b) under $50 in value. Thefts of bicycles, automobile accessories, shoplifting, pocket-picking, or any stealing of property or article which is not taken by force and violence or by fraud. Excludes embezzlement, "con" games, forgery, worthless checks, etc.

7. Auto theft.—Unlawful taking or stealing of a motor vehicle.

The Part II offenses are: Other assaults; arson; forgery and counterfeiting; fraud; embezzlement; buying, receiving, or possessing stolen property; vandalism; carrying or possessing weapons; prostitution and commercialized vice; sex offenses; violations of narcotic drug laws; gambling; offenses against family and children; driving while intoxicated; violations of liquor laws; drunkenness; disorderly conduct; vagrancy; all violations of State or local laws except as mentioned above; suspicion; curfew and loitering (juveniles); and runaways (juveniles).

See also data and text for series H 962–970.

H 962–970. Urban crime, by type of major offense, 1937–1957.

Source: U.S. Federal Bureau of Investigation, *Uniform Crime Reports for the United States*, Annual Bulletin, 1957, vol. XXVIII, No. 2, p. 85.

Figures are from the same 353 cities for each year. Their total population was 36.5 million in 1940 and 42.7 million in 1950. If a police department was known to have made major changes in its records procedures during the period covered, its reports were excluded.

Interpretation of these figures as reflecting a relatively exact measure of crime is somewhat questionable for the following reasons: The data came from 353 individual reporting areas scattered over the 48 conterminous States; there were differences among the States in the definition of some of these offenses; and there was improvement in reporting procedures on the part of some police agencies over this period of years. It is likely that the reports on murder and robbery are more reliable than those for other offenses because these two offenses were more clearly and consistently defined throughout the various States than were the other types of offenses shown.

See also data and text for series H 952–961.

H 971–986. Homicides and suicides, 1900–1970.

Source: U.S. National Center for Health Statistics, *Vital Statistics of the United States* and *Mortality Statistics*, annual issues.

Deaths were classified by cause according to the *Revision of the International Lists of Diseases and Causes of Death* that was in use for the years shown. Data for the entire United States were not available until 1933. For the years prior to 1933 this series includes deaths only for the death registration States of the respective years. For 1900, 10 States and the District of Columbia are included, comprising 26 percent of the population of the United States. As States were added, the registration area gradually grew to include approximately 50 percent of the population of the United States in 1910, about 80 percent in 1920, and the entire United States in 1933.

H 987–998. Police officers killed, by geographic divisions, 1945–1970.

Source: See source for series H 952–961.

See also text for series H 952–961.

H 999–1011. Persons arrested, by race, sex, and age, 1932–1970.

Source: See source for series H 952–961.

Arrest practices, policies, and enforcement emphasis vary from place to place and within a community from time to time. The volume of police arrests for certain unlawful conduct such as drunkenness, disorderly conduct, and violations of certain local ordinances is particularly influenced by such variations. Arrests for robbery, burglary, and other serious crimes are more likely the result of standard procedures. Although arrests are primarily a measure of police activity as it relates to crime, they also provide a useful index to indicate involvement in criminal acts by the age, sex, and race of the perpetrators, particularly for those crimes which have a high solution rate. Procedures used in the Uniform Crime Reporting Program require that an arrest be counted on each separate occasion that a person is taken into custody, notified, or cited. Arrests do not measure the number of individuals taken into custody since one person may be arrested several times during the year for the same or different offenses. This happens frequently for certain types of offenses against public order such as drunkenness, vagrancy, disorderly conduct, and related violations.

As a result of an expanded program beginning in 1960 to increase reporting areas, the number of agencies reporting arrests by sex and age exceeds the number reporting arrests by race. Consequently, the two sets of totals for arrests differ from 1960 on.

See also text for series H 952–961.

H 1012–1027. Criminal justice system—public expenditures, by level of government, 1902–1970.

Source: U.S. Bureau of the Census. Compiled from *Governmental Finances*, annual issues; *State Government Finances*, annual issues; *U.S. Census of Governments: Historical Statistics on Governmental Finances and Employment, 1957, 1962,* and *1967; Criminal Justice Expenditure & Employment for Selected Large Governmental Units, 1967–1968;* and (jointly with the U.S. Law Enforcement Assistance Administration) *Expenditure and Employment Data for the Criminal Justice System, 1969–1970.*

These statistics are the products of the Bureau of the Census governmental statistics program, which consists of a quinquennial census, recurrent surveys, and special studies done either as inhouse research or on a contractual basis. The data are obtained through a combination of field compilation, office compilation, and mail canvass. Field compilation is used for States and for large counties and cities; mail canvass and office compilation for the Federal Government, counties under 100,000 population, and cities under 50,000 population.

Definitions of the criminal justice functions have changed somewhat over the years. A classification scheme developed for use in the 1952 Census of Governments narrowed the scope of many functions. Beginning in 1967, public expenditure data for criminal justice activities were published separately for the first time. In 1969, expanded definitions of criminal justice functions were developed and, with some further refinement, are still in use.

Police protection is the function of enforcing the law, preserving order, and apprehending those who violate the law, whether these activities are performed by a police department, a sheriff's department, or a special police force maintained by an agency whose prime responsibility is outside the criminal justice system, but which has a police force to perform these activities in its specialized area (geographic or functional).

Included in this activity are regular police services, the maintenance of buildings used for police purposes and such specialized police forces (including public and private contract forces) as airport police, free and toll highway police, free and toll bridge and tunnel police, housing police, maritime police, park police, transit and other utility system police, college and university campus police, and alcoholic beverage control agents. Coroners and medical examiners are also included. Excluded are vehicular inspection and licensing, traffic safety and engineering, fish and game wardens, fire marshals, and the like.

The special police forces included in the data are only those which are part of general purpose governments. Security forces and building guards without the power to make a police arrest were excluded. Special police forces which are part of independent school districts or special districts are not included in the data, inasmuch as these districts are not general purpose governments.

At the county government level, both county police agencies and sheriffs' departments, where such departments exist, are included in the police protection sector, unless research has indicated that sheriffs have no substantial responsibility for police activities. The lack of needed information has prevented the consistent proration of expenditure or employment of sheriffs' departments where those departments are multifunctional.

Short-term custody and detention have traditionally been considered part of the "police protection" function and, prior to 1969, were treated as such. However, beginning 1969, the concept was modified on the basis of information obtained from the *1970 National Jail Census.* Data for institutions with authority to hold prisoners 48 hours or more are included in the "corrections" sector. Data for lockups or "tanks" holding prisoners less than 48 hours are included in the "police protection" sector.

Judicial activities encompass all courts and activities associated with courts such as law libraries, grand juries, petit juries, and the like.

In many States, statutes either require or permit local governments to supplement the salary of State-paid judges of major trial courts. In 1969, an attempt was made to count these judges and their total payroll only at the State level. However, this effort was not uniformly successful; nor was a similar adjustment attempted for prosecutors or public defenders who are also frequently paid by more than one government. For these reasons, the judges were counted in 1970 as part-time employees at both the State and local levels when actually receiving a check from both governments.

Correction is that function of government involving the confinement and rehabilitation of adults and juveniles convicted of offenses against the law, and the confinement of persons suspected of a crime and awaiting adjudication. Data for institutions with authority to hold prisoners 48 hours or more are included in this sector. Data for lockups or "tanks" holding prisoners less than 48 hours are included in "Police protection." Correction includes the operation of prisons, reformatories, jails, houses of correction, and other institutions. It also includes institutions, facilities and programs exclusively for the confinement of the criminally insane or for the examination, evaluation, classification, and assignment of inmates; institutions and programs for the confinement, treatment, and rehabilitation of drug addicts and alcoholics if the institution or program is administered by a correction agency of the criminal justice system; and pardon boards and parole and probation agencies, including resettlement or halfway houses for those not in need of institutionalization.

When a correctional institution maintains a prison industry or agricultural program, data on the cost of production or the value of prison labor used by agencies of the same government, if identifiable, are excluded (and classed as expenditure for the function using the products or services). Expenditure for the manufacture, production, sale, and distribution of goods produced for sale or use outside the government are included under this heading.

Legal services and prosecution includes the civil and criminal justice activities of the attorneys general; district attorneys, State's attorneys and their variously named equivalents; corporation counsels, solicitors, and legal departments with various names. It includes providing legal advice to the chief executives and subordinate departmental officers, representation of the government in lawsuits, and the prosecution of accused violators of criminal law. These activities are included whether performed by one office or several, since in some jurisdictions a single officer provides all legal services, while in others a prosecutor's office handles only criminal matters and a separate attorney's office performs all civil legal services. The operations of various investigative agencies having full arrest powers and attached to offices of attorneys general, district attorneys or their variously named equivalents are also included.

Indigent defense includes activities associated with the right of persons to have legal counsel and representation, office of the public defender, and other government programs which pay the fees of court-appointed counsel. These include court-paid fees to individually retained counsel, fees paid by the court to court-appointed counsel, government contributions to private legal aid societies and bar association sponsored programs, and the activities of an established public defender office or program.

H 1028–1062. Lawyers—selected characteristics, 1948–1970.

Source: American Bar Foundation, Chicago, *The 1971 Lawyer Statistical Report*, tables 1–6 (copyright).

The source report is the sixth in the series of reports on the legal profession published by the American Bar Foundation. It includes the national statistics compiled by Martindale-Hubbell for the previous five American Bar Foundation reports and for two reports of the Survey of the Legal Profession which preceded the current series. Previous reports have been issued triennially since 1949. In making preparations for the sixth report, it was decided to postpone the 1969 report to take advantage of the 1970 decennial census. Future reports will be issued at appropriate intervals, probably every five years.

Martindale-Hubbell acquires its data in a variety of ways. The principal source of information is the questionnaire completed by thousands of members of the legal profession. In addition to the questionnaire, Martindale-Hubbell relies upon reports by its traveling field representatives, newspaper clippings, bar association rosters and publications, correspondence, and reports by the National Conference of Bar Examiners to maintain current information.

A lawyer, as defined by the *Martindale-Hubbell Law Directory*, is a person who has been admitted to practice law in one of the States or the District of Columbia, even though he may not be practicing.

All lawyers, series H 1028, is the closest available approximation of the actual number of lawyers. Lawyers reporting, series H 1029, represents lawyers listed in the *Law Directory*. A lawyer is listed if he, or someone closely identified with him, i.e., a partner or associate, provides the basic listing information or completes and returns a questionnaire to Martindale-Hubbell.

Lawyers not reporting, included in series H 1028, covers those lawyers failing to respond to the questionnaire. Since 1950, Martindale-Hubbell has endeavored to maintain accurate records for this category, but for various reasons these figures are undoubtedly in excess of the actual number of individuals who have been admitted to the Bar but who are unlisted in the *Law Directory*. Presumably the figures also reflect a number of deceased individuals.

Cities were classified into population groupings on the basis of official figures from the Census Bureau. Since the Census Bureau does not regularly supply estimated population figures for cities, the classification for 1963 and 1966 was based upon unofficial estimates from *Editor and Publisher Yearbook*.

A lawyer was classified as female if listed as "Miss" or "Mrs." or the given name indicated the individual to be a woman.

If a lawyer attended college and received a degree, he is included in both series H 1041 and H 1042. If the listing disclosed college but not a degree, he is counted in series H 1041. The same applies to law school, series H 1043 and H 1044. If the listing disclosed no educational data, the lawyer was tabulated in series H 1045.

Because some lawyers may engage in private practice and work for the government at the same time, the total for lawyers under "Status in practice" may exceed the total number of lawyers listed. From 1948 through 1954, all judges who maintained a private practice were tabulated in both categories; from 1957 through 1966, this practice was followed only for judges in cities of under 200,000 population, and, for 1970, cities under 250,000. U.S. Attorneys and Assistant U.S. Attorneys who also practiced law were tabulated in both categories in 1948 and 1951, but from 1954, they have been listed only in the Government category. Lawyers serving in the Armed Forces were tabulated in both categories from 1948 through 1954; from 1957, they have appeared only in the Government cate-

gory. The criteria for classification of lawyers by status in practice follow:

Government. *Federal:* A lawyer who is either an elected or an appointed Federal official or employee other than a judge. Members of Congress were almost the only ones who were also tabulated under a private practice subdivision. *State:* A lawyer who is either an elected or appointed State official or employee other than a judge. Many individuals in this category were also tabulated under the appropriate private practice subdivision. *City or County:* A lawyer who is a county or local official or employee other than a judge. Except for officials in cities over 500,000, all individuals in this category who also practiced privately were listed in the appropriate private practice subdivision.

Judicial. *Federal:* A lawyer who is a Federal judicial officer, i.e., Justice of the Supreme Court, judge of a district court or a court of appeal, U.S. Commissioner, or referee in bankruptcy. *County or State:* A lawyer who is a judicial officer of a county or State, i.e., probate judge, circuit court commissioner, appellate court judge, or supreme court judge. *City:* A lawyer whose listing indicates that he is a local judicial officer, i.e., city judge, police magistrate, recorder, or justice of the peace. Judges and other judicial officers in cities under 200,000 population (under 250,000 in 1970) were also tabulated in the appropriate private practice subdivision.

Private practice. *Individual:* A lawyer who is practicing without partners. *Partner:* A lawyer who is a partner in a law firm. *Associate:* A lawyer employed by a law firm or an individual practitioner. An individual is listed as an associate in the *Law Directory* only if his employer publishes a professional card and identifies him as such. Some of the growth in this category reflects the continuing trend of subscribers to identify their associates.

Salaried. *Private industry:* A lawyer employed in either a legal or a non-legal capacity by a business concern. *Educational institutions:* A lawyer who is a dean, full-time faculty member, or employee in some other capacity of a college, university, or law school. *Other private employment:* A lawyer connected with a religious, charitable, trade, or other organization not within either of the two preceding subdivisions. Since lawyers in these subdivisions generally devote full time to their listed positions, they were not also tabulated under any private practice subdivision.

Retired or inactive. A lawyer who is actually retired or who could not be identified within the above categories.

H 1063–1124. General note.

Court statistics on criminal offenses and the outcome of prosecutions are incomplete for the country as a whole although data are available for many States individually. The only national compilations of such statistics were made by the Bureau of the Census from 1932 to 1945. At no time, however, were there more than 32 States involved in the reporting system.

Comprehensive information on the business of the Federal courts is collected by the Administrative Office of the U.S. Courts and is published in the *Annual Report of the Director* and in *Juror Utilization in United States Courts*. The bulk of civil and criminal litigation in the country is commenced and determined in the various State courts. Only when the U.S. Constitution and acts of Congress specifically confer jurisdiction upon the Federal courts may civil litigation be heard and decided by these courts. Whether a State court or a Federal court has jurisdiction over a particular action is often difficult to determine. Generally, the Federal courts have jurisdiction over the following types of cases: Suits or proceedings by or against the United States; civil actions between private parties arising under the Constitution, laws, or treaties of the United States; civil actions between private litigants who are citizens of different States; civil cases involving admiralty, maritime, or prize jurisdiction; all matters and proceedings in bankruptcy.

The Federal courts of original jurisdiction are known as the U.S. district courts. One or more of these courts is established in every

State and one each in Puerto Rico, the Virgin Islands, the Canal Zone, and Guam. Appeals from the district courts are taken to intermediate appellate courts of which there are 11, known as U.S. courts of appeals. The Supreme Court of the United States is the final and highest appellate court in the Federal system of courts.

H 1063–1078. U.S. Supreme Court—cases filed and disposed of during October terms, 1940–1969.

Source: U.S. Administrative Office of the United States Courts, *Annual Report of the Director*, various issues.

See general notes for series H 952–1170 and H 1063–1124.

H 1079–1096. U.S. Courts of Appeals, 1942–1970.

Source: See source for series H 1063–1078.

See general notes for series H 952–1170 and H 1063–1124.

H 1097–1118. U.S. District Courts—civil and criminal cases, 1941–1970, and trials, 1944–1970.

Source: See source for series H 1063–1078.

Data on criminal cases exclude Juvenile Delinquency Act.
See also general notes for series H 952–1170 and H 1063–1124.

H 1119–1124. Juvenile court—cases handled, 1940–1970.

Source: U.S. Social and Rehabilitation Service, *Juvenile Court Statistics, 1969* and *1970*.

From 1957 through 1969, national estimates on the number of juvenile delinquency cases disposed of by juvenile courts were based on data derived from a national sample of juvenile courts which, drawn from the Current Population Survey sample of the Bureau of the Census, was considered to be representative of the country as a whole. In 1970, taking advantage of the extremely high percentage of reporting coverage and in anticipation of developing a new national sample utilizing more current information from the 1970 decennial census, data from all courts reporting both for 1969 and 1970 provided the basis for the national estimates. All courts in the United States and those reporting for both years were stratified by the size of the population served by the courts. Estimates were made for each stratum, with the ratio of the population served by the reporting courts to the population served by all courts in the stratum used as an inflation factor. Prior to 1957, data were estimated by the Children's Bureau, based on reports from a comparable group of courts.

Dependency and neglect cases cover neglect or inadequate care on the part of parents or guardians; e.g., lack of adequate care or support resulting from death, absence, or physical or mental incapacity of the parents, abandonment or desertion, abuse or cruel treatment, and improper or inadequate conditions in the home.

Juvenile delinquency cases are those referred for acts defined in the statutes of the State as the violation of a State law or municipal ordinance by children or youth of juvenile court age, or for conduct so seriously antisocial as to interfere with the rights of others or to menace the welfare of the delinquent himself or of the community. This broad definition of delinquency includes conduct which violates the law only when committed by children; e.g., truancy, ungovernable behavior, and running away.

H 1125–1134. Persons in custody in training schools for juvenile delinquents and in detention homes, 1950, 1960, and 1970.

Source: U.S. Bureau of the Census, 1950, *U.S. Census of Population: 1950*, vol. IV, part 2, Institutional Population; 1960, *U.S. Census of Population: 1960*, Final Report PC(2)-8A, *Inmates of Insti-*

tutions; 1970, *U.S. Census of Population: 1970*, Final Report PC(2)-4E, *Persons in Institutions and Other Group Quarters.*

Persons under care or custody in institutions at the time of enumeration are classified as "inmate of institution" regardless of their length of stay in the place and regardless of the number of people there.

Institutions are a subcategory of group quarters. All persons not living in households are classified by the Bureau of the Census as living in group quarters. The nature of the service provided by an institution was the determinant for classifying inmates by type of institution.

Training schools for juvenile delinquents (including forestry camps for juveniles) are classified by the nature of their control into public or private institutions.

Public training schools for juvenile delinquents are readily identifiable institutions. The majority of them are State institutions operated by a State agency (i.e., departments of welfare, corrections, or institutions, or a youth authority). Some are operated by county and city governments. These public training schools are specialized institutions serving delinquent children, generally between the ages of 10 and 17, all of whom are committed to them by the courts.

Private training schools are those operated under private auspices. Some of the children they serve are committed to them by the courts as delinquents; others are referred by parents or social agencies because of delinquent behavior. A distinguishing factor between private and public training schools is that, by their administrative policy, the former can control their selection and intake.

Detention homes are institutions providing temporary care primarily for delinquent children pending disposition of their cases by a court. In practice, such institutions may be caring for both delinquent and neglected children pending court disposition.

In the 1960 census, the definition of "inmate of institution" was similar to that used in 1970 with the exception of the use of "length of stay" as a criterion for defining inmates in 1960. Differences in the classification and definition of inmates between the 1950 and 1960 censuses are minimal and the estimates for both dates are comparable.

H 1135–1167. General note.

Statistics of prisoners committed to penal institutions have been collected and published for a longer period of time than have other criminal statistics. Data on prisoners in Federal and State prisons and reformatories were collected annually by the Bureau of the Census until 1950. This work was transferred to the Bureau of Prisons in 1950 (and to the Law Enforcement Assistance Administration in 1971). Summary statistics covering persons received and discharged from State prisons and reformatories and from Federal prisons and persons executed in the United States under civilian authority are now published periodically by the Law Enforcement Assistance Administration in *National Prisoner Statistics*. Nearly every State publishes annual data either for its whole prison system or for each separate State institution.

H 1135–1143. Federal and State institutions—prisoners, 1926–1970.

Source: 1926–1938, U.S. Bureau of the Census, *Prisoners in State and Federal Prisons and Reformatories;* 1939–1970, U.S. Bureau of Prisons, **series H 1135–1140**, *National Prisoner Statistics*, Bulletin No. 47, April 1972; **series H 1141–1143**, same report, annual issues.

These data, as well as those shown in series H 1144–1154, are based on information reported for State prisons and reformatories and for Federal prisons with the following exceptions: No data were reported for Delaware or the District of Columbia prior to 1931. The New Castle County Workhouse was the only reporting institution for Delaware for 1931–1956 except for 1933 when no data were reported; beginning 1957, all State prisoners in Delaware were included, except for 1968 when no data were reported. No data were reported in 1926 for Alabama, Florida, Idaho; in 1927 for Alabama; in 1928 for Mississippi, Idaho; in 1929 for Alabama, Georgia, Mississippi; in 1930 for Alabama, Georgia, Idaho. For 1931–1937, inclusive, no data were reported for Alabama, Georgia, or Mississippi. South Carolina was omitted in 1932. The Milwaukee House of Correction in Wisconsin is excluded in series H 1137 and H 1140 for 1937–1939; it is also excluded in series H 1143 for 1937–1946. In 1938 and 1939, all States except Alabama and Georgia were included. Rhode Island data include both misdemeanant and felony prisoners for all years except 1957 when only felony prisoners were included; no data were reported for Rhode Island in 1968, 1969, and 1970. Although there have been years since 1939 when two or three States did not report, the published data have been adjusted to include estimates for these missing States, 1939–1967. Hawaii has been included beginning 1960; Alaska has been excluded for all years. State figures were not adjusted for 1968–1970. No data were reported in 1968 for Arkansas; in 1969 for Arkansas, Indiana Reformatory, and District of Columbia Women's Detention Center; in 1970 for Arkansas and the Indiana Reformatory. A significant change was introduced in the series in 1940 by the addition of reports for nine Federal correctional institutions and two detention headquarters to the Federal totals. Also for 1939–1970, except in 1968 when no data were reported for North Carolina, series H 1137 and H 1140 include felony prisoners present at the end of the year and received from court for North Carolina Road Camps; series H 1143 excludes such prisoners except for 1957.

Institutions for adult offenders may include a sizable number of juveniles for certain States.

H 1144–1154. Federal and State institutions—prisoners released, by type of release, 1926–1970.

Source: U.S. Bureau of the Census, 1926–1946, *Prisoners in State and Federal Prisons and Reformatories*. U.S. Bureau of Prisons, 1947–1948, unpublished data; 1949–1970, *National Prisoner Statistics*, annual issues.

Data are for live releases. From 1935 to 1970, 2,306 prisoners died in Federal institutions; 33 of these were executions carried out during 1930 to 1967. In State institutions, there were 39,206 deaths from 1926 to 1970. Of these, 4,291 were executions. Most of these executions were carried out by State authorities; some by local authorities. The data on executions by State and local authorities are incomplete for 1926–1929.

All the limitations on completeness of coverage of series H 1135–1143 are also applicable for these series.

Series H 1144–1154 exclude escapees, temporary releases, etc.

H 1155–1167. Prisoners executed under civil authority, by race and offense, 1930–1970.

Source: U.S. Bureau of Prisons, *National Prisoner Statistics*, Bulletin No. 46, *Capital Punishment, 1939–1970*, August 1971.

Figures represent all executions occurring within the States whether they were carried out in a State institution or by local agencies. Executions by military authorities are excluded. The Army (including Air Force) carried out 160 executions (148 between 1942 and 1950; 3 each in 1954, 1955, and 1957; and 1 each in 1958, 1959, and 1961); 106 of the 160 were executed for murder (including 21 involving rape), 53 for rape, and 1 for desertion. The Navy carried out no executions during the period.

H 1168–1170. Persons lynched, by race, 1882–1970.

Source: 1882–1951, *1952 Negro Year Book*, William H. Wise and Co., p. 278 (copyright); 1952–1970, Tuskegee Institute, Alabama, Department of Records and Research, unpublished estimates.

Additional information and more detailed figures can be found in Arthur F. Raper, *The Tragedy of Lynching*, University of North Carolina Press, Chapel Hill, 1933, pp. 480–484, and James E. Cutler, *Lynch Law: An Investigation Into the History of Lynching in the United States*, Longmans-Green, New York, 1905, pp. 160–161. Raper presents statistics of lynchings for whites and Negroes for 1889–1932, based on the *Negro Year Book*, 1931–1932, and on material obtained from the Department of Records and Research, Tuskegee Institute. For 1916–1932, Raper's estimates agree with those shown here; but for all earlier years there are differences which are due to subsequent revisions made in the series by Tuskegee Institute. Cutler's estimates are based on the annual record kept by the Chicago Tribune (daily newspaper). Estimates shown here are for whites and Negroes only. During the period 1882–1903, Cutler found that 45 Indians, 12 Chinese, 1 Japanese, and 20 persons of Mexican ancestry had been lynched.

The *1952 Negro Year Book* presents a detailed discussion concerning the difficulty of defining the term "lynching." According to this source, "... agencies concerned about the lynching problem have not been able to come to a conclusive agreement even when using the same criteria in classifying cases of lynching." The same source refers to a conference held on December 11, 1940, at Tuskegee Institute which established the following criteria to cover persons considered as victims of lynching:

1. There must be legal evidence that a person was killed;
2. The person must have met death illegally;
3. A group must have participated in the killing;
4. The group must have acted under pretext of service to justice, race, or tradition.

★ ★ ★ ★ ★ ★ ★ ★ ★ **More Recent Data for *Historical Statistics* Series** ★ ★ ★ ★ ★ ★ ★ ★ ★ ★

★ Statistics for more recent years in continuation of many of the still-active series shown here appear in annual issues of the *Statistical Abstract of the United States*, beginning with the 1975 edition. For direct linkage of the historical series to the tables in the *Abstract*, see Appendix I in the *Abstract*. ★

Series H 952–961. Crimes and Crime Rates, by Type: 1957 to 1970

[In thousands, except rate. Data refer to offenses known to the police. Rates are based on Bureau of the Census population data, excluding Armed Forces abroad]

Item and year	Total	Violent crime					Property crime			
		Total	Murder and non-negligent manslaughter	Forcible rape	Robbery	Aggravated assault	Total	Burglary	Larceny, $50 and over	Auto theft
	952	953	954	955	956	957	958	959	960	961
	NUMBER OF OFFENSES									
1970	5,581	733	16	38	348	331	4,848	2,177	1,750	922
1969	5,013	657	15	37	297	308	4,357	1,956	1,528	872
1968	4,477	590	14	31	262	283	3,887	1,835	1,274	778
1967	3,811	496	12	27	202	254	3,316	1,611	1,049	655
1966	3,272	426	11	26	157	233	2,846	1,392	897	557
1965	2,937	384	10	23	138	213	2,553	1,266	794	493
1964	2,762	361	9	21	130	201	2,401	1,198	734	470
1963	2,442	314	9	17	116	172	2,128	1,072	650	405
1962	2,219	299	8	17	110	163	1,920	982	574	364
1961	2,088	287	9	17	106	155	1,801	937	530	334
1960*	2,020	286	9	17	107	153	1,734	900	507	326
1959	1,630	223	9	15	75	124	1,408	698	416	294
1958	1,573	212	8	15	75	114	1,362	685	394	283
1957	1,422	199	8	[1] 13	67	111	1,224	604	355	265
	RATE PER 100,000 INHABITANTS									
1970	2,747	361	8	19	171	163	2,386	1,071	861	454
1969	2,483	325	7	18	147	152	2,158	969	757	432
1968	2,240	295	7	16	131	142	1,945	918	637	389
1967	1,926	251	6	14	102	129	1,676	814	530	331
1966	1,671	218	6	13	80	119	1,453	711	458	285
1965	1,516	198	5	12	71	110	1,317	653	410	255
1964	1,443	189	5	11	68	105	1,255	626	383	245
1963	1,295	167	5	9	62	91	1,129	569	345	215
1962	1,194	161	5	9	59	88	1,033	528	309	196
1961	1,141	157	5	9	58	85	984	512	290	182
1960*	1,126	160	5	10	60	85	967	502	283	182
1959	918	126	5	9	42	70	792	393	234	165
1958	904	121	5	8	43	65	781	393	226	162
1957	835	117	5	[1] 8	39	65	719	355	208	156

* Denotes first year for which figures include Alaska and Hawaii.　　　　[1] Includes statutory cases.

Series H 962–970. Urban Crime, by Type of Major Offense: 1937 to 1957

[Offenses known to police in 353 cities with 25,000 inhabitants or more, and having a total 1950 population of 42,719,693, based on 1950 Census of Population]

Year	Total	Criminal homicide		Rape	Robbery	Aggravated assault	Burglary— breaking or entering	Larceny— theft	Auto theft
		Murder, non-negligent manslaughter	Manslaughter by negligence						
	962	963	964	965	966	967	968	969	970
1957	1,096,337	2,533	1,722	6,752	34,641	39,833	247,845	632,215	130,796
1956	1,003,641	2,502	1,766	6,502	31,471	39,439	218,248	586,969	116,744
1955	884,682	2,410	1,643	5,910	30,675	38,785	202,660	505,011	97,588
1954	876,275	2,352	1,573	5,339	34,139	37,976	206,426	497,201	91,269
1953	845,208	2,439	1,599	5,449	31,813	38,064	191,339	476,771	97,734
1952	809,267	2,471	1,688	5,302	28,644	36,136	181,216	460,921	92,889
1951	779,458	2,302	1,557	5,306	26,086	31,884	169,209	457,977	85,137
1950	736,721	2,370	1,544	4,994	25,909	32,350	170,708	425,325	73,521
1949	734,925	2,332	1,308	5,137	29,693	32,144	173,312	422,583	68,416
1948	704,410	2,533	1,450	4,987	27,850	31,014	163,965	402,543	70,068
1947	708,014	2,535	1,481	5,268	29,395	31,004	164,709	396,798	76,824
1946	745,282	2,629	1,724	5,225	31,028	30,228	171,029	405,829	97,590
1945	702,720	2,361	1,723	5,042	27,671	28,026	156,835	375,488	105,574
1944	621,925	2,141	1,424	4,592	22,301	25,698	132,768	346,060	86,941
1943	604,554	2,030	1,428	4,349	22,636	22,126	127,368	342,337	82,280
1942	619,165	2,278	1,698	3,903	22,903	22,914	123,642	372,664	69,163
1941	661,132	2,295	1,852	3,513	24,212	20,736	138,043	393,615	76,866
1940	661,988	2,208	1,469	3,207	25,269	20,312	146,361	391,812	71,350
1939	637,514	2,223	1,229	3,235	26,347	19,063	145,208	369,442	70,767
1938	613,062	2,133	1,428	2,967	27,836	18,765	138,939	346,178	74,816
1937	605,447	2,479	1,978	3,047	26,696	19,841	137,757	325,974	87,675

Series H 971–986. Homicides and Suicides: 1900 to 1970

[Refers only to deaths occurring within the United States. Rates per 100,000 resident population; for population bases used in computing rates, see series A 7]

Year	Homicides — Number	Rate	Male	Female	Assault by — Firearms and explosives	Cutting and piercing instruments	Intervention of police	Other means	Suicides — Number	Rate	Male	Female	By — Poisoning	Hanging or strangulation	Firearms and explosives	Other
	971	972	973	974	975	976	977	978	979	980	981	982	983	984	985	986
1970	16,848	8.3	13,278	3,570	11,213	2,780	333	2,522	23,480	11.6	16,629	6,851	6,584	3,253	11,772	1,871
1969	15,477	7.7	12,166	3,311	10,174	2,726	354	2,223	22,364	11.1	15,857	6,507	6,118	3,158	11,304	1,784
1968	14,686	7.3	11,523	3,163	9,425	2,626	350	2,285	21,372	10.7	15,379	5,993	5,684	3,099	10,911	1,678
1967	13,425	6.8	10,236	3,189	8,332	2,467	387	2,239	21,325	10.8	15,187	6,138	5,695	2,778	10,550	2,302
1966	11,606	5.9	8,729	2,877	6,855	2,330	298	2,123	21,281	10.9	15,416	5,865	5,588	2,863	10,407	2,423
1965	10,712	5.5	8,148	2,564	6,158	2,292	271	1,991	21,507	11.1	15,490	6,017	5,995	3,197	9,898	2,417
1964	9,814	5.1	7,367	2,447	5,474	2,108	278	1,954	20,588	10.8	15,092	5,496	5,541	3,005	9,806	2,236
1963	9,225	4.9	6,921	2,304	5,126	1,990	246	1,863	20,825	11.0	15,276	5,549	5,785	3,057	9,595	2,388
1962	9,013	4.8	6,707	2,306	4,954	1,978	187	1,894	20,207	10.9	15,062	5,145	5,126	3,154	9,487	2,440
1961	8,578	4.7	6,346	2,232	4,753	1,819	237	1,769	18,999	10.4	14,460	4,539	4,501	3,157	9,037	2,304
1960*	8,464	4.7	6,269	2,195	4,627	1,836	245	1,756	19,041	10.6	14,539	4,502	4,330	3,366	9,017	2,328
1959 ¹	8,159	4.6	6,068	2,091	4,457	1,804	227	1,671	18,633	10.6	14,441	4,192	4,048	3,525	8,788	2,272
1958	7,815	4.5	5,804	2,011	4,230	1,765	229	1,591	18,519	10.7	14,366	4,153	3,958	3,562	8,871	2,128
1957	7,641	4.5	5,739	1,902	4,010	1,867	228	1,536	16,632	9.8	12,951	3,681	3,559	3,562	7,841	1,885
1956	7,629	4.6	5,705	1,924	4,039	1,854	226	1,510	16,727	10.0	12,968	3,759	3,367	3,638	7,817	1,905
1955	7,418	4.5	5,630	1,788	3,807	1,826	227	1,558	16,760	10.2	12,961	3,799	3,429	3,591	7,763	1,977
1954	7,735	4.8	5,886	1,849	4,115	1,793	244	1,583	16,356	10.1	12,964	3,392	3,516	3,370	7,539	1,931
1953	7,640	4.8	5,828	1,812	4,013	1,837	255	1,535	15,947	10.1	12,534	3,413	3,269	3,397	7,293	1,988
1952	8,054	5.2	6,202	1,852	4,244	1,986	256	1,568	15,567	10.0	12,115	3,452	3,187	3,358	7,013	2,009
1951	7,495	4.9	5,669	1,826	3,898	1,787	227	1,583	15,909	10.4	12,300	3,609	3,664	3,360	6,873	2,012
1950	7,942	5.3	6,089	1,853	4,179	1,879	282	1,602	17,145	11.4	13,297	3,848	3,969	3,592	7,377	2,207
1949	8,033	5.4	6,214	1,819	4,235	1,869	277	1,652	16,993	11.4	13,209	3,784	3,834	3,641	7,215	2,303
1948	8,654	5.9	6,769	1,885	4,894	2,074	—	1,686	16,354	11.2	12,505	3,849	3,830	3,577	6,660	2,287
1947	8,708	6.1	6,858	1,850	4,922	1,981	—	1,805	16,538	11.5	12,560	3,978	3,690	3,750	6,691	2,407
1946	8,913	6.4	7,012	1,901	4,966	2,159	—	1,788	16,152	11.5	12,074	4,078	3,859	3,599	6,276	2,418
1945	7,547	5.7	5,969	1,578	4,029	1,837	—	1,681	14,782	11.2	10,754	4,028	3,718	3,301	5,321	2,442
1944	6,675	5.0	5,251	1,424	3,449	1,741	—	1,485	13,231	10.0	9,497	3,734	3,205	3,062	4,808	2,156
1943	6,823	5.1	5,363	1,460	3,444	1,849	—	1,530	13,725	10.2	10,014	3,711	3,434	3,045	5,076	2,170
1942	7,890	5.9	6,266	1,624	4,204	2,120	—	1,566	16,117	12.0	12,189	3,928	4,136	3,433	6,117	2,431
1941	8,048	6.0	6,408	1,640	4,525	2,034	—	1,489	17,102	12.8	12,903	4,199	4,892	3,340	6,385	2,485
1940	8,329	6.3	6,647	1,682	4,655	2,064	—	1,610	18,907	14.4	14,466	4,441	5,623	3,554	7,073	2,657
1939	8,394	6.4	6,657	1,737	4,799	2,048	—	1,547	18,511	14.1	14,259	4,252	5,405	3,504	6,944	2,658
1938	8,799	6.8	6,935	1,864	5,055	2,018	—	1,726	19,802	15.3	15,376	4,426	5,756	3,756	7,357	2,933
1937	9,811	7.6	7,731	2,080	5,701	2,192	—	1,918	19,294	15.0	14,793	4,501	5,485	3,795	7,073	2,941
1936	10,232	8.0	8,134	2,098	6,016	2,151	—	2,065	18,294	14.3	13,971	4,323	5,241	3,528	6,771	2,754
1935	10,587	8.3	8,554	2,033	6,506	2,018	—	2,063	18,214	14.3	13,942	4,272	5,247	3,399	6,830	2,738
1934	12,055	9.5	9,850	2,205	7,702	2,122	—	2,231	18,828	14.9	14,564	4,264	5,334	3,517	7,296	2,681
1933	12,124	9.7	9,874	2,250	7,863	2,065	—	2,196	19,993	15.9	15,785	4,208	5,835	3,543	7,798	2,817
1932	10,722	9.0	8,646	2,076	7,252	1,578	—	1,892	20,646	17.4	16,453	4,193	6,225	3,615	7,940	2,866
1931	10,862	9.2	8,761	2,101	7,335	1,662	—	1,865	19,807	16.8	15,662	4,145	5,972	3,560	7,409	2,866
1930	10,331	8.8	8,233	2,098	6,995	1,553	—	1,783	18,323	15.6	14,319	4,004	5,541	3,268	6,735	2,779
1929	9,637	8.4	7,644	1,993	6,362	1,539	—	1,736	16,045	13.9	12,305	3,740	5,074	2,901	5,565	2,505
1928	9,780	8.6	7,889	1,891	6,668	1,409	—	1,703	15,390	13.5	11,905	3,485	4,794	2,851	5,366	2,379
1927	8,997	8.4	7,168	1,829	6,004	1,376	—	1,617	14,096	13.2	10,831	3,265	4,505	2,516	4,864	2,211
1926	8,740	8.4	7,057	1,683	6,035	1,239	—	1,466	13,082	12.6	9,894	3,188	4,046	2,371	4,469	2,196
1925	8,440	8.3	6,823	1,617	5,908	1,130	—	1,402	12,209	12.0	9,297	2,912	3,628	2,259	4,209	2,113
1924	8,014	8.1	6,408	1,606	5,736	920	—	1,358	11,846	11.9	9,100	2,746	3,544	2,102	4,197	2,003
1923	7,557	7.8	6,096	1,461	5,422	884	—	1,251	11,096	11.5	8,344	2,752	3,229	2,049	3,825	1,993
1922	7,381	8.0	5,996	1,385	5,430	763	—	1,188	10,876	11.7	8,259	2,617	3,231	1,880	3,831	1,934
1921	7,090	8.1	5,682	1,408	5,178	687	—	1,225	10,906	12.4	8,430	2,476	3,045	1,934	4,015	1,912
1920	5,815	6.8	4,661	1,154	4,178	587	—	1,050	8,790	10.2	6,364	2,426	1,368	1,611	3,078	2,733
1919	5,973	7.2	4,820	1,153	4,247	632	—	1,094	9,543	11.5	6,968	2,575	1,500	1,716	3,204	3,123
1918	5,113	6.5	4,107	1,006	3,475	603	—	1,035	9,685	12.3	7,223	2,462	1,411	1,624	3,372	3,278
1917	4,864	6.9	3,904	960	3,205	621	—	1,038	9,157	13.0	6,880	2,277	1,645	1,488	3,057	2,967
1916	4,237	6.3	3,419	818	2,708	546	—	983	9,181	13.7	7,069	2,112	1,814	1,434	3,066	2,867
1915	3,633	5.9	2,829	804	2,213	483	—	937	10,011	16.2	7,712	2,299	2,178	1,634	3,266	2,933
1914	3,776	6.2	3,000	776	2,366	511	—	899	9,802	16.1	7,522	2,280	2,657	1,468	2,950	2,727
1913	3,521	6.1	2,818	703	2,123	492	—	906	8,932	15.4	6,914	2,018	2,469	1,300	2,609	2,554
1912	2,938	5.4	2,305	633	1,775	417	—	746	8,549	15.6	6,603	1,946	2,419	1,341	2,462	2,327
1911	2,978	5.5	2,385	593	1,743	478	—	757	8,612	16.0	6,637	1,975	2,567	1,291	2,559	2,195
1910	2,161	4.6	1,670	491	1,174	289	—	698	7,283	15.3	5,621	1,662	1,955	1,160	2,173	1,995
1909	1,857	4.2	1,400	457	—	—	—	—	7,061	16.0	5,481	1,580	1,989	1,092	2,017	1,963
1908	1,858	4.8	1,421	437	—	—	—	—	6,506	16.8	5,045	1,461	1,803	1,016	1,931	1,756
1907	1,701	4.9	1,334	367	—	—	—	—	5,027	14.5	3,861	1,166	1,454	780	1,522	1,271
1906	1,310	3.9	1,013	297	—	—	—	—	4,323	12.8	3,368	955	1,257	692	1,230	1,144
1905	463	2.1	339	124	—	—	—	—	2,940	13.5	2,208	732	843	541	741	815
1904	283	1.3	193	90	—	—	—	—	2,611	12.2	1,976	635	838	518	585	670
1903	236	1.1	175	61	—	—	—	—	2,371	11.3	1,807	564	791	413	520	649
1902	255	1.2	168	87	—	—	—	—	2,124	10.3	1,589	535	626	382	449	667
1901	233	1.2	150	83	—	—	—	—	2,105	10.4	1,567	538	636	411	439	667
1900	230	1.2	167	63	—	—	—	—	2,036	10.2	1,568	468	619	409	449	559

* Denotes first year for which figures include Alaska and Hawaii.   ¹ Includes Alaska.

Series H 987–998. Police Officers Killed, by Geographic Divisions: 1945 to 1970

[Covers law enforcement officers killed in line of duty. For composition of divisions, see text for series A 172–194]

Year	Total killed	By felons	In accidents	New England	Middle Atlantic	East North Central	West North Central	South Atlantic	East South Central	West South Central	Mountain	Pacific
	987	988	989	990	991	992	993	994	995	996	997	998
1970	146	100	46	2	29	38	6	23	5	15	4	24
1969	125	86	39	3	15	31	10	15	9	19	6	17
1968	123	64	59	3	10	19	12	34	9	15	4	17
1967	123	76	47	4	15	29	8	20	9	14	6	18
1966	99	57	42	1	16	20	11	16	11	8	5	11
1965	83	53	30	3	10	10	3	15	9	14	7	12
1964	88	57	31	4	12	12	5	25	5	13	2	10
1963	88	55	33	3	13	10	7	20	5	17	3	10
1962	78	48	30	4	13	14	4	19	4	9	3	8
1961	71	37	34	–	11	12	6	12	3	8	3	16
1960	48	--------	--------	3	7	9	3	13	2	6	–	5
1959	49	--------	--------	1	8	5	4	13	–	7	3	8
1958	49	--------	--------	4	3	6	1	10	4	7	5	9
1957	45	--------	--------	2	9	9	4	4	3	5	–	9
1956	46	--------	--------	2	9	10	4	8	1	5	–	7
1955	55	--------	--------	2	5	13	3	11	4	5	2	10
1954	61	--------	--------	1	11	10	2	10	5	11	4	7
1953	63	--------	--------	2	14	13	4	7	2	10	3	8
1952	63	--------	--------	1	6	15	2	10	11	6	2	10
1951	64	--------	--------	2	8	13	3	12	6	9	4	7
1950	36	--------	--------	2	8	9	1	4	3	2	–	7
1949	55	--------	--------	1	14	6	10	6	3	6	1	8
1948	64	--------	--------	1	7	17	7	13	3	10	1	5
1947	67	--------	--------	2	15	15	6	10	1	6	3	9
1946	82	--------	--------	5	15	16	5	18	7	5	1	10
1945	59	--------	--------	1	11	13	6	8	1	7	3	9

– Represents zero.

Series H 999–1011. Persons Arrested, by Race, Sex, and Age: 1932 to 1970

[In thousands]

Year	Persons arrested [1]	White	Negro	Other	Persons arrested [1]	Male	Female	Under 18 years	18–24 years	25–34 years	35–44 years	45–54 years [2]	55 years and over [3]
	999	1000	1001	1002	1003	1004	1005	1006	1007	1008	1009	1010	1011
1970	6,257	4,373	1,688	196	6,570	5,624	947	1,661	1,785	1,128	887	685	425
1969	5,577	3,843	1,559	175	5,862	5,058	804	1,500	1,514	990	823	635	398
1968	5,349	3,700	1,472	178	5,617	4,891	725	1,457	1,372	931	828	627	401
1967	5,265	3,631	1,463	172	5,518	4,830	689	1,340	1,274	928	882	667	426
1966	4,798	3,329	1,316	152	5,016	4,407	610	1,149	1,089	858	857	641	413
1965	4,743	3,235	1,348	160	5,031	4,432	600	1,074	1,050	891	917	670	421
1964	4,381	3,054	1,194	133	4,685	4,138	547	961	959	858	877	664	364
1963	4,259	2,943	1,187	129	4,511	3,997	514	789	881	875	911	357	696
1962 [4]	3,923	2,602	1,196	126	4,117	3,645	472	653	749	833	869	343	668
1961	3,608	2,425	1,073	110	3,852	3,418	434	567	703	806	818	329	626
1960 [4]	3,499	2,321	1,065	113	3,679	3,272	406	527	654	787	793	321	595
1959 [4]	2,613	1,742	789	82	2,613	2,334	279	321	452	587	580	240	430
1958 [4]	2,340	1,583	696	61	2,340	2,092	248	284	401	540	515	212	387
1957 [4]	2,069	1,406	616	47	2,069	1,849	220	254	346	482	457	186	343
1956 [4]	2,071	1,391	634	46	2,071	1,845	226	234	341	500	466	187	340
1955 [4]	1,862	1,310	510	41	1,862	1,657	205	196	300	460	418	170	318
1954 [4]	1,689	1,206	440	43	1,689	1,503	185	164	272	423	383	154	292
1953 [4]	1,791	1,270	481	40	1,791	1,597	194	150	297	460	416	165	303
1952 [4]	1,111	808	281	21	1,111	991	120	86	171	284	264	108	196
1951	831	599	219	14	831	746	85	37	203	254	185	63	89
1950	794	576	206	12	794	717	77	35	208	239	171	58	83
1949	792	582	199	11	792	713	79	33	214	235	171	59	80
1948	760	557	192	11	760	683	77	32	210	223	163	54	78
1947	734	537	188	10	734	659	75	34	210	214	152	49	71
1946	645	478	159	8	645	577	69	38	183	188	133	44	59
1945	544	390	146	8	544	460	84	50	144	144	115	39	53
1944	489	352	129	8	489	405	84	47	130	129	104	32	47
1943	491	358	125	7	491	412	79	48	129	128	102	34	50
1942	586	432	147	7	586	516	70	38	152	159	129	43	64
1941	631	475	148	7	631	573	58	37	161	182	140	43	66
1940	609	463	139	7	609	557	52	35	164	183	129	39	59
1939	577	445	126	6	577	533	44	36	164	174	115	34	51
1938	554	428	121	6	554	517	38	36	164	169	108	31	46
1937	520	400	114	6	520	484	36	33	148	157	105	30	45
1936	462	350	105	6	462	428	34	26	133	141	94	27	40
1935	392	296	91	5	392	365	27	23	122	123	75	21	28
1934	344	258	81	5	344	320	24	19	109	112	63	17	22
1933	320	236	76	8	320	297	23	18	105	105	57	15	19
1932 [5]	--------	--------	--------	--------	278	257	21	15	93	90	48	13	17

[1] Each person arrested is counted rather than the number of charges filed against one person. Includes persons for whom age was not known. Prior to 1952, arrest data determined by examination of fingerprint cards.
[2] Prior to 1964, age breakdown 45–49 years.
[3] Prior to 1964, age breakdown 50 years and over.
[4] City arrest data.
[5] February 1 through December 31.

Series H 1012–1027. Criminal Justice System—Public Expenditures, by Level of Government: 1902 to 1970

[In millions of dollars]

Year	All governments				Federal Government				State government				Local government			
	Total [1]	Police protection	Judicial activities	Correction	Total [1]	Police protection	Judicial activities	Correction	Total [1]	Police protection	Judicial activities	Correction	Total [1]	Police protection	Judicial activities	Correction
	1012	1013	1014	1015	1016	1017	1018	1019	1020	1021	1022	1023	1024	1025	1026	1027
1970	8,571	5,081	1,190	1,706	978	589	129	83	2,134	689	282	1,051	5,454	3,803	779	572
1969	7,340	4,430	1,002	1,462	800	492	106	71	1,849	621	236	914	4,691	3,317	660	477
1968	6,070	3,725	976	1,369	445	290	90	65	1,622	541	209	872	4,003	2,894	677	432
1967	5,424	3,331	894	1,199	429	282	87	60	1,381	441	193	747	3,615	2,609	614	392
1966	4,903	3,033	793	1,077	393	257	79	57	1,224	385	175	664	3,286	2,391	539	356
1965	4,574	2,792	748	1,034	377	243	75	59	1,135	348	155	632	3,062	2,201	518	343
1964	4,222	2,586	697	939	342	220	66	56	1,042	315	141	586	2,838	2,051	490	297
1963	4,009	2,440	693	876	358	209	94	55	960	297	127	536	2,691	1,934	472	285
1962	3,795	2,326	628	841	304	196	57	51	902	276	118	508	2,589	1,854	453	282
1961	3,613	2,210	593	810	298	193	58	47	849	261	109	479	2,466	1,756	426	284
1960	3,349	2,030	597	722	291	173	74	44	769	245	99	425	2,289	1,612	424	253
1959	3,149	1,880	561	708	275	170	68	37	733	228	92	413	2,141	1,482	401	258
1958	2,861	1,769	519	573	261	159	63	39	671	214	87	370	1,929	1,396	369	164
1957	2,655	1,624	481	550	252	155	62	35	584	179	77	328	1,819	1,290	342	187
1956	2,434	1,487	447	500	250	156	61	33	526	159	72	295	1,658	1,172	314	172
1955	2,231	1,359	409	463	206	129	49	28	475	139	68	268	1,550	1,091	292	167
1954	2,080	1,254	399	427	210	124	56	30	446	130	66	250	1,424	1,000	277	147
1953		1,160		(NA)		122		(NA)	418	119	61	238		919		(NA)
1952		1,080		365		141		28	386	106	57	223		833		
1951		(NA)				104			365	97	53	215		(NA)		114
1950		864				88			332	85	49	198		691		
1948		724				80				65		153		579		
1947												107				
1946		549				70				45		97		434		
1945												82				
1944		497				83			159	41	35	83		373		
1942		444				50				40		80		354		
1940		386				21				34		86		331		
1938		378				19				30		85		329		
1936		331				17				19		73		295		
1932		349				31				15		87		303		
1927		290				20				7		64		263		
1922		204				14				4		64		186		
1913		92				3				1		28		88		
1902		50				–				–		14		50		

– Represents zero.   NA Not available.

[1] Beginning 1969, legal services and prosecution and indigent defense included in totals; for definitions, see text.

Series H 1028–1062. Lawyers—Selected Characteristics: 1948 to 1970

[Data based on editions of *Martindale-Hubbell Law Directory*. Represents all persons who are members of the bar]

Series No.	Characteristic	1970	1966	1963	1960	1957	1954	1951	1948
1028	All lawyers [1]	355,242	316,856	296,069	285,933	262,320	241,514	221,605	
1029	Lawyers reporting [2]	324,818	289,404	268,782	252,385	235,783	221,600	204,111	171,110
	In cities with population [3]—								
1030	Less than 200,000	159,291	135,515	124,092	115,453	111,543	105,709	96,960	83,480
1031	200,000–499,999	37,411	41,205	39,279	37,388	33,001	30,651	27,693	19,983
1032	500,000 or more	128,116	112,684	105,411	99,544	91,239	85,240	79,458	67,647
1033	Male	315,715	281,336	261,639	245,897	229,433	216,564	199,052	168,113
1034	Female	9,103	8,068	7,143	6,488	6,350	5,036	5,059	2,997
	Year of birth:								
1035	1904 and earlier	42,454	52,026	60,346	69,017	76,479	83,582	91,833	93,732
1036	1905–1914	52,956	56,378	58,055	59,327	59,491	58,526	56,909	50,998
1037	1915–1924	63,077	63,944	63,566	62,704	60,235	54,793	48,966	18,937
1038	1925–1934	79,679	76,651	70,692	57,082	36,225	19,100		
1039	1935 and later	85,980	38,559	14,345	1,891				
1040	Not reported	672	1,846	1,778	2,364	3,353	5,599	6,403	7,443
	Education:								
1041	Attended college	296,572	256,823	232,617	211,711	191,198	171,687	149,320	111,836
1042	College degree	238,213	194,120	168,179	146,359	122,767	107,617	88,938	62,935
1043	Attended law school	314,458	276,327	253,250	233,600	214,019	194,273	170,977	129,471
1044	Law degree	301,076	259,402	234,684	213,178	188,883	170,597	145,467	104,239
1045	Unknown	6,078	8,597	10,052	12,358	14,893	18,695	23,337	31,254
	Status in practice:[4]								
1046	Government	35,803	31,280	29,314	25,621	24,245	21,279	19,910	14,143
1047	Federal	18,710	16,284	15,113	13,045	12,458	9,040	8,314	(NA)
1048	State	9,293	7,416	6,486	4,316	4,000	3,561	3,577	(NA)
1049	City or county	7,800	7,580	7,715	8,260	7,787	8,678	8,019	8,013
1050	Judicial	10,349	9,712	8,748	8,180	7,910	7,903	7,471	7,130
1051	Federal	878	800	707	599	769	621	675	(NA)
1052	State or county	7,548	6,823	5,712	5,301	5,056	5,041	4,561	(NA)
1053	City	1,923	2,089	2,329	2,280	2,085	2,241	2,235	(NA)
1054	Private practice	236,085	212,662	200,586	192,353	188,955	189,423	176,995	152,649
1055	Individual	118,963	113,273	113,127	116,911	122,389	127,389	120,340	104,687
1056	Partner	92,442	78,544	70,064	60,709	54,966	51,668	47,311	40,448
1057	Associate [5]	24,680	20,845	17,395	14,733	11,600	10,366	9,344	7,514
1058	Salaried	40,486	33,222	29,510	25,198	21,054	16,648	12,997	5,555
1059	Private industry	33,593	29,405	26,492	22,533	18,911	15,063	11,274	(NA)
1060	Educational institutions	3,732	2,717	2,100	1,798	1,504	1,351	1,213	(NA)
1061	Other private employment	3,161	1,100	918	867	639	234	510	(NA)
1062	Retired or inactive	16,812	14,881	12,024	10,887	7,661	6,581	6,974	6,043

NA Not available.
[1] Includes lawyers not reporting and an adjustment (subtraction) for duplications.
[2] Includes duplicatons: 1948, 3,242; 1951, 4,147; 1954, 4,440; 1957, 4,506; 1960, 4,504; 1963, 5,918; 1966, 6,787; 1970, 8,834.
[3] 1948, 1940 Census of Population; 1951–1957, 1950 Census of Population; 1960, 1960 Census of Population; 1963 and 1966, unofficial estimates, *Editor & Publisher*

Yearbook; and 1970, 1970 Census of Population. For 1970, refers to cities with population of less than 250,000, 250,000–499,999, and 500,000 or more, respectively.
[4] In some cases, if more than one subentry was applicable, the person was counted in each.
[5] Lawyers employed by individual practitioners or partnerships.

Series H 1063–1078. U.S. Supreme Court—Cases Filed and Disposed of During October Terms: 1940 to 1969

[For years beginning in June. Statutory term of Court begins first Monday in October but, for statistical purposes, new term begins upon adjournment of preceding term, usually in June]

Year	Total cases				Original cases filed	Appeals filed	Pauper appeals filed	Petitions for review			Pauper petitions for review			Motions for leave to file various writs		
	Filed	Disposed of		Remaining on docket				Filed	Granted	Denied or dismissed	Filed	Granted	Denied or dismissed	Filed	Granted	Denied or dismissed
		Total	Opinions													
	1063	1064	1065	1066	1067	1068	1069	1070	1071	1072	1073	1074	1075	1076	1077	1078
1969	3,405	3,379	347	793	6	204	51	1,253	108	1,121	1,772	38	1,759	119	3	121
1968	3,271	3,117	346	767	1	192	40	1,131	101	983	1,744	62	1,603	163	2	168
1967	3,106	2,946	462	613	2	162	36	1,114	166	979	1,610	84	1,337	182	5	166
1966	2,752	2,890	402	453	5	144	48	1,058	121	922	1,319	56	1,371	178	2	188
1965	2,774	2,665	338	591	8	158	42	1,030	124	900	1,388	43	1,271	148	1	147
1964	2,288	2,173	275	482	4	118	29	920	116	791	1,025	21	927	192	1	178
1963	2,294	2,401	393	367	1	147	28	870	118	733	1,069	69	1,093	179	1	180
1962	2,373	2,327	388	474	2	134	36	823	115	690	1,213	88	1,086	165	7	156
1961	2,185	2,142	264	428	2	110	36	778	103	665	1,138	38	1,093	121	1	120
1960	1,940	1,911	282	385	–	124	28	718	87	628	950	22	871	120	–	125
1959	1,862	1,787	249	356	–	90	22	767	122	645	836	55	743	147	–	146
1958	1,819	1,763	275	281	3	126	25	760	108	641	772	24	716	133	1	123
1957	1,639	1,765	323	225	2	110	17	716	110	670	680	34	648	114	–	119
1956	1,802	1,670	266	351	3	123	24	851	139	664	639	38	584	162	–	153
1955	1,644	1,630	246	219	4	104	17	787	123	643	583	16	579	149	2	155
1954	1,397	1,352	196	205	–	87	8	626	108	532	543	12	494	133	–	126
1953	1,302	1,293	170	160	–	81	--------	603	78	522	528	10	507	90	–	92
1952	1,283	1,278	193	151	2	87	--------	655	104	541	434	11	429	105	–	104
1951	1,234	1,207	197	146	1	104	--------	612	94	518	413	19	386	104	1	102
1950	1,181	1,202	191	119	–	77	--------	582	89	495	404	17	386	118	–	121
1949	1,270	1,301	202	140	–	85	--------	633	85	556	441	7	436	111	–	108
1948	1,465	1,425	238	171	2	86	--------	687	144	523	447	18	425	243	2	241
1947	1,295	1,322	208	131	–	69	--------	647	97	555	426	17	400	153	--------	150
1946	1,510	1,520	256	158	–	97	--------	731	148	586	528	8	520	154	--------	154
1945	1,316	1,292	215	168	1	64	--------	727	155	565	393	15	378	131	--------	131
1944	1,237	1,249	274	144	2	93	--------	803	176	642	339	10	329	--------	--------	--------
1943	997	962	210	156	1	82	--------	700	127	547	214	12	202	--------	--------	--------
1942	984	997	259	121	5	105	--------	727	158	592	147	8	139	--------	--------	--------
1941	1,178	1,168	376	134	3	213	--------	784	150	623	178	16	162	--------	--------	--------
1940	977	985	281	124	4	84	--------	769	174	592	120	19	101	--------	--------	--------

– Represents zero.

Series H 1079–1096. U.S. Courts of Appeals: 1942 to 1970

[For years ending June 30]

Year	Cases commenced						Cases terminated		
	Total	Criminal	U.S. civil	Private civil	Administrative appeals	Other	Total	Criminal	U.S. civil
	1079	1080	1081	1082	1083	1084	1085	1086	1087
1970	11,662	2,660	2,167	4,834	1,522	479	10,699	2,581	1,912
1969	10,248	2,508	1,823	4,197	1,345	375	9,014	2,022	1,559
1968	9,116	2,098	1,500	3,569	1,545	404	8,264	1,754	1,356
1967	7,903	1,665	1,372	3,101	1,385	380	7,527	1,524	1,378
1966	7,183	1,458	1,338	2,809	1,254	324	6,571	1,214	1,309
1965	6,766	1,223	1,387	2,677	1,106	373	5,771	1,014	1,229
1964	6,023	1,043	1,309	2,299	983	389	5,700	917	1,183
1963	5,437	965	1,054	2,030	1,141	247	5,011	862	1,049
1962	4,823	773	1,066	1,692	1,024	268	4,167	622	936
1961	4,204	616	903	1,617	846	222	4,049	628	881
1960	3,899	623	788	1,534	737	217	3,713	580	750
1959	3,754	616	802	1,501	606	229	3,753	633	831
1958	3,694	599	836	1,447	625	187	3,704	596	878
1957	3,701	535	895	1,464	618	189	3,687	544	905
1956	3,588	557	872	1,361	609	189	3,734	573	865
1955	3,695	677	811	1,363	576	268	3,654	670	893
1954	3,481	550	875	1,124	659	273	3,192	460	809
1953	3,226	454	815	1,106	639	212	3,043	398	700
1952	3,079	391	724	1,133	610	221	3,048	362	687
1951	2,982	298	677	1,172	566	269	2,829	291	688
1950	2,830	308	708	1,114	485	215	3,064	342	783
1949	2,989	309	791	1,171	491	227	2,753	318	665
1948	2,758	359	677	1,118	381	223	2,577	356	702
1947	2,615	370	770	861	400	214	2,654	383	780
1946	2,627	400	690	894	418	225	2,621	418	640
1945	2,730	486	651	758	511	324	2,848	469	633
1944	3,072	437	621	954	717	343	3,039	395	599
1943	3,093	363	581	950	826	373	3,197	319	529
1942	3,228	339	510	(1)	835	[1] 1,544	2,999	287	486

[1] Private civil included in other.

Series H 1079–1096. U.S. Courts of Appeals: 1942 to 1970—Con.

Year	Cases terminated—Con.				Cases disposed of after hearing or submission				
	Private civil	Administrative appeals	Other	Median time ² (months)	Total	Affirmed or granted	Reversed or denied		Other
							Total	Percent of total	
	1088	1089	1090	1091	1092	1093	1094	1095	1096
1970	4,367	1,407	432	8.2	6,139	4,626	1,280	20.9	233
1969	3,679	1,394	360	8.3	5,121	3,838	1,072	20.9	211
1968	3,268	1,512	374	7.8	4,668	3,499	1,009	21.6	160
1967	2,968	1,257	400	8.8	4,468	3,340	954	21.5	174
1966	2,552	1,141	355	8.3	4,087	3,026	866	21.7	195
1965	2,183	1,004	341	8.0	3,546	2,635	773	22.0	138
1964	2,159	1,105	336	7.4	3,552	2,660	765	21.5	127
1963	1,894	962	244	7.3	3,172	2,261	791	24.9	120
1962	1,508	855	246	7.1	2,895	2,101	680	23.5	114
1961	1,483	825	232	6.8	2,806	2,023	692	24.7	91
1960	1,517	660	206	6.8	2,681	1,924	656	24.5	101
1959	1,473	601	215	6.7	2,705	1,935	648	24.0	122
1958	1,482	567	181	7.0	2,831	2,013	689	24.7	129
1957	1,388	666	184	7.1	2,709	1,949	621	23.1	139
1956	1,445	626	225	7.4	2,973	2,082	743	25.1	148
1955	1,289	523	279	7.3	2,809	1,907	777	26.9	125
1954	986	689	248	7.1	2,427	1,632	668	26.4	127
1953	1,124	621	200	7.0	2,436	1,710	641	26.3	85
1952	1,141	598	260	7.3	2,308	1,629	588	25.5	91
1951	1,119	481	250	6.7	2,136	1,438	572	26.8	126
1950	1,184	541	214	7.1	2,355	1,700	528	22.4	127
1949	1,132	418	220	7.1	2,045	1,421	544	26.6	80
1948	925	359	235	6.3	1,821	1,269	483	26.5	69
1947	853	412	226	6.9	1,887	1,317	509	27.0	61
1946	829	503	231	6.8	1,805	1,299	477	26.4	29
1945	836	566	344	7.0	1,992	1,413	556	27.9	23
1944	967	738	340	6.5	2,148	1,568	547	25.5	33
1943	1,089	841	419	6.5	2,226	1,563	600	27.0	63
1942	(¹)	830	¹ 1,396	7.7	2,292	--------	573	24.9	--------

¹ Private civil included in other.
² Median time interval from filing of complete record to final disposition in cases terminated after hearing or submission, except, prior to 1948, median interval is from time of docketing to final disposition.

Series H 1097–1111. U.S. District Courts—Civil and Criminal Cases: 1941 to 1970

[For years ending June 30]

Year	Civil cases		Criminal cases												
	Total cases commenced	Total cases terminated	Cases commenced ¹	Defendants disposed of											
				Total	Not convicted				Convicted						
					Total	Dismissed	Acquitted		Total	By guilty plea or nolo contendere	By court or jury	Imprisonment	Probation ²	Fine	Other
							Court	Jury							
	1097	1098	1099	1100	1101	1102	1103	1104	1105	1106	1107	1108	1109	1110	1111
1970	87,321	80,435	39,959	36,356	8,178	6,608	703	867	28,178	24,111	4,067	12,415	11,387	1,935	2,441
1969	77,193	73,354	35,413	32,796	5,993	4,867	483	643	26,803	23,138	3,665	12,847	9,991	1,682	2,283
1968	71,449	68,873	32,571	31,843	6,169	4,981	484	704	25,674	22,055	3,619	12,610	9,820	1,816	1,428
1967	70,961	70,172	32,207	31,535	5,191	4,196	409	586	26,344	23,131	3,213	13,085	9,435	2,293	1,531
1966	70,906	66,184	31,494	31,975	4,661	3,570	397	694	27,314	24,127	3,187	13,282	10,256	2,356	1,420
1965	67,678	65,478	33,334	33,718	4,961	3,789	463	709	28,757	25,923	2,834	13,668	10,779	2,477	1,833
1964	66,930	63,954	30,268	33,381	4,211	2,936	559	716	29,170	26,273	2,897	13,273	11,634	2,689	1,574
1963	63,630	62,379	39,920	34,845	5,042	3,735	544	763	29,803	25,924	3,879	13,639	12,047	2,847	1,270
1962	61,836	57,996	37,665	33,110	4,599	3,374	390	835	28,511	24,639	3,872	14,042	11,071	2,618	780
1961	58,293	55,416	28,460	32,671	4,046	2,887	291	868	28,625	24,830	3,795	14,462	10,714	2,772	677
1960	59,284	61,829	28,137	30,512	3,784	2,596	329	859	26,728	24,245	2,483	13,433	10,391	2,904	--------
1959	57,800	62,172	28,729	30,729	3,696	2,638	310	748	27,033	24,793	2,240	13,648	10,726	2,659	--------
1958	67,115	61,285	28,897	30,469	3,661	2,571	357	733	26,808	24,256	2,552	13,288	10,903	2,617	--------
1957	62,380	63,568	28,120	29,725	3,471	2,366	335	770	26,254	23,867	2,387	12,986	10,760	2,508	--------
1956	62,394	67,700	28,739	31,811	4,244	3,068	406	770	27,567	25,029	2,538	12,854	11,759	2,954	--------
1955	59,375	58,974	35,310	38,990	5,135	3,792	441	902	33,855	31,148	2,707	16,889	14,021	2,945	--------
1954	59,461	57,903	41,808	42,989	4,848	3,571	492	785	38,141	35,560	2,581	18,483	16,856	2,802	--------
1953	64,001	57,490	37,291	37,762	4,289	3,167	402	720	33,473	31,336	2,137	15,637	15,118	2,718	--------
1952	58,428	53,150	37,950	38,622	3,834	2,891	282	661	34,788	32,734	2,054	15,379	17,018	2,391	--------
1951	51,600	52,119	38,670	41,066	4,066	3,180	303	583	37,000	35,271	1,729	14,963	19,271	2,766	--------
1950	54,622	53,259	36,383	37,675	4,173	3,237	270	666	33,502	31,739	1,763	14,435	16,046	3,021	--------
1949	53,421	48,396	34,432	36,264	4,190	3,280	295	615	32,074	30,447	1,627	14,204	14,690	3,180	--------
1948	46,725	48,791	32,097	34,242	4,862	3,948	218	696	29,380	27,833	1,547	12,961	13,422	2,997	--------
1947	58,956	54,515	33,652	36,635	5,527	4,452	274	801	31,108	29,138	1,970	14,375	12,612	4,121	--------
1946	67,835	61,000	33,203	36,482	6,597	5,519	243	835	29,885	27,385	2,500	14,353	11,446	4,086	--------
1945	60,965	52,300	39,429	41,653	7,536	6,369	319	848	34,117	30,817	3,300	16,311	13,153	4,653	--------
1944	38,499	37,086	39,621	--------	--------	--------	--------	--------	--------	--------	--------	--------	--------	--------	--------
1943	36,789	36,044	36,588	--------	--------	--------	--------	--------	--------	--------	--------	--------	--------	--------	--------
1942	38,140	38,352	33,294	--------	--------	--------	--------	--------	--------	--------	--------	--------	--------	--------	--------
1941	38,477	38,561	31,823	--------	--------	--------	--------	--------	--------	--------	--------	--------	--------	--------	--------

¹ Excludes transfers.
² Includes probation and suspended sentence.

Series H 1112–1118. U.S. District Courts—Trials: 1944 to 1970

[For years ending June 30. Through 1960, trials commenced; thereafter, trials completed]

Year	Total trials	Civil trials Total	Civil Nonjury	Civil Jury	Criminal trials Total	Criminal Nonjury	Criminal Jury
	1112	1113	1114	1115	1116	1117	1118
1970	16,032	9,449	6,078	3,371	6,583	2,357	4,226
1969	14,397	8,834	5,619	3,215	5,563	1,883	3,680
1968	14,221	8,688	5,478	3,210	5,533	1,800	3,733
1967	12,500	8,095	4,742	3,353	4,405	1,345	3,060
1966	12,193	7,783	4,607	3,176	4,410	1,239	3,171
1965	11,485	7,613	4,459	3,154	3,872	1,143	2,729
1964	11,079	7,155	4,063	3,092	3,924	1,076	2,848
1963	10,960	7,095	3,925	3,170	3,865	1,159	2,706
1962	10,048	6,260	3,335	2,925	3,788	1,090	2,698
1961	9,594	6,156	3,245	2,911	3,438	982	2,456
1960	9,998	6,488	3,453	3,035	3,510	1,008	2,502
1959	10,293	6,896	3,566	3,330	3,397	1,033	2,364
1958	10,888	7,057	3,666	3,391	3,831	1,326	2,505
1957	10,443	6,884	3,595	3,289	3,559	1,214	2,345
1956	11,198	7,341	3,811	3,530	3,857	1,319	2,538
1955	11,138	7,049	4,110	2,939	4,089	1,351	2,738
1954	11,275	6,958	4,182	2,776	4,317	1,493	2,824
1953	10,768	6,861	4,272	2,589	3,907	1,361	2,546
1952	10,073	6,668	4,179	2,489	3,405	1,167	2,238
1951	9,878	6,962	4,492	2,470	2,916	1,035	1,881
1950	9,572	6,539	4,276	2,263	3,033	961	2,072
1949	9,282	6,426	4,149	2,277	2,856	997	1,859
1948	8,905	6,156	4,204	1,952	2,749	892	1,857
1947	8,818	5,850	3,989	1,861	2,968	1,112	1,856
1946	9,030	5,220	3,633	1,587	3,810	1,250	2,560
1945	9,779	5,265	3,561	1,704	4,514	1,503	3,011
1944	9,951	5,025	2,702	2,323	4,926	1,819	3,107

Series H 1119–1124. Juvenile Court—Cases Handled: 1940 to 1970

[In thousands, except rate]

Year	Population under 18 years old Total [1]	Dependency and neglect cases Total	Dependency and neglect cases Rate per 1,000 population	Population, 10–17 years old Total [1]	Delinquency cases Total [2]	Delinquency cases Rate per 1,000 population
	1119	1120	1121	1122	1123	1124
1970	69,669	133	1.9	32,614	1,052	32.3
1969	69,694	127	1.8	32,157	989	30.7
1968	69,831	141	2.0	31,566	900	28.5
1967	69,878	154	2.2	30,837	811	26.3
1966	69,851	161	2.3	30,124	745	24.7
1965	69,699	157	2.3	29,536	697	23.6
1964	69,625	150	2.2	29,244	686	23.5
1963	68,371	146	2.1	28,056	601	21.4
1962	67,092	141	2.1	26,989	555	20.6
1961	65,789	140	2.1	26,056	503	19.3
1960	64,516	131	2.0	25,368	510	20.1
1959	63,038	128	2.0	24,607	483	19.6
1958	61,238	124	2.0	23,443	470	20.0
1957	59,336	114	1.9	22,173	440	19.8
1956	57,377	105	1 8	20,623	520	25.2
1955	55,568	106	1.9	20,111	431	21.4
1954	53,737	103	1.9	19,551	395	20.2
1953	51,987	103	2.0	18,980	374	19.7
1952	50,296	98	1.9	18,201	332	18.2
1951	48,598	97	2.0	17,705	298	16.8
1950	47,017	93	2.0	17,397	280	16.1
1949	45,775	98	2.1	17,365	272	15.6
1948	44,512	103	2.3	17,314	254	14.9
1947	43,301	104	2.4	17,344	262	15.1
1946	41,759	101	2.4	17,419	295	16.9
1945	41,313	(NA)	--------	17,512	344	19.6
1944	(NA)	--------	--------	17,738	330	18.6
1943	(NA)	--------	--------	18,309	344	18.7
1942	(NA)	--------	--------	18,648	250	13.4
1941	(NA)	--------	--------	18,916	224	11.8
1940	40,365	--------	--------	19,138	200	10.5

NA Not available.
[1] U.S. Bureau of the Census estimates of civilian population as of July 1, except 1940, 1950, 1960, and 1970, as of April 1.
[2] For 1940–1956, includes traffic cases.

Series H 1125–1134. Persons in Custody in Training Schools for Juvenile Delinquents and in Detention Homes: 1950, 1960, and 1970

[1970 based on 20-percent sample, 1960 on 25-percent sample, and 1950 on complete count. Comparability of figures is affected by differences in classification]

Series No.	Characteristic	1970 Training schools Total	1970 Public	1970 Private	1970 Detention homes	1960 Training schools Total	1960 Public	1960 Private	1960 Detention homes	1950 Training schools Total	1950 Public	1950 Private	1950 Detention homes
1125	Total	66,457	57,691	8,766	10,272	45,695	38,359	7,336	10,821	36,986	29,042	7,944	3,894
1126	Male	52,769	46,867	5,902	6,590	33,765	29,681	4,084	7,680	23,968	21,679	2,289	3,018
1127	Female	13,688	10,824	2,864	3,682	11,930	8,678	3,252	3,141	13,018	7,363	5,655	876
1128	White	39,757	33,428	6,329	6,754	31,294	24,900	6,394	7,342	28,578	21,342	7,236	2,847
1129	Negro and other	26,700	24,263	2,437	3,518	14,401	13,459	942	3,479	8,408	7,700	708	1,047
1130	Under 10 years	1,006	647	359	481	476	327	149	785	735	507	228	334
1131	10–13 years	7,291	5,581	1,710	1,986	6,131	4,858	1,273	2,468	5,170	3,908	1,262	527
1132	14 years	8,272	6,873	1,399	1,656	6,078	5,067	1,011	1,625	4,859	3,825	1,034	342
1133	15–19 years	42,767	37,929	4,838	5,937	31,316	26,676	4,640	4,988	23,978	19,360	4,618	1,244
1134	20 years and over	7,121	6,661	460	212	1,694	1,431	263	955	2,244	1,442	802	1,447

Series H 1135–1143. Federal and State Institutions—Prisoners: 1926 to 1970

[Prisoners in institutions for adult offenders only. For geographic coverage, see text]

Year	Prisoners present (at end of year)			Prisoners received from courts (during year)			Conditional-release violators returned to prison (during year) [1]		
	Total	Federal institutions	State institutions	Total	Federal institutions	State institutions	Total	Federal institutions	State institutions
	1135	1136	1137	1138	1139	1140	1141	1142	1143
1970	196,429	20,038	176,391	79,351	12,047	67,304	17,294	1,530	15,764
1969	196,007	19,623	176,384	75,277	11,589	63,688	16,844	1,607	15,237
1968	187,914	19,703	168,211	72,058	11,120	60,938	17,780	1,855	15,925
1967	194,896	19,579	175,317	77,850	11,447	66,403	17,583	1,774	15,809
1966	199,654	19,245	180,409	77,857	11,508	66,349	17,662	1,746	15,916
1965	210,895	21,040	189,855	87,505	12,781	74,724	19,393	1,823	17,570
1964	214,336	21,709	192,627	87,578	12,482	75,096	19,558	1,691	17,867
1963	217,283	23,128	194,155	87,826	12,882	74,944	18,909	1,650	17,259
1962	218,830	23,944	194,886	89,082	13,514	75,568	17,247	1,643	15,604
1961	220,149	23,696	196,453	93,513	13,517	79,996	16,409	1,587	14,822
1960	212,957	23,218	189,739	88,575	13,723	74,852	15,042	1,456	13,586
1959	207,446	22,492	184,954	87,192	13,872	73,320	13,418	1,362	12,056
1958	205,493	21,549	183,944	88,633	13,803	74,830	12,815	1,275	11,540
1957	195,256	20,420	174,836	80,482	13,305	67,177	12,096	1,092	11,004
1956	189,421	20,134	169,287	77,924	13,454	64,470	11,720	1,032	10,688
1955	185,780	20,088	165,692	78,414	15,286	63,128	11,002	980	10,022
1954	182,848	20,003	162,845	80,900	16,685	64,215	10,355	902	9,453
1953	173,547	19,363	154,184	74,240	16,376	57,864	10,036	956	9,080
1952	168,200	18,014	150,186	70,892	15,305	55,587	9,465	995	8,470
1951	165,640	17,395	148,245	67,165	14,120	53,045	9,124	1,226	7,898
1950	166,123	17,134	148,989	69,473	14,237	55,236	8,692	1,371	7,321
1949	163,749	16,868	146,881	68,925	13,130	55,795	9,079	1,529	7,550
1948	155,977	16,328	139,649	63,777	12,430	51,347	8,226	1,099	7,127
1947	151,304	17,146	134,158	64,804	12,948	51,856	8,263	946	7,317
1946	140,079	17,622	122,457	61,338	14,950	46,388	7,324	688	6,636
1945	133,649	18,638	115,011	53,212	14,171	39,041	6,792	632	6,160
1944	132,456	18,139	114,317	50,162	14,047	36,115	7,087	599	6,488
1943	137,220	16,113	121,107	50,082	12,203	37,879	6,728	708	6,020
1942	150,384	16,623	133,761	58,858	13,725	45,133	7,007	742	6,265
1941	165,439	18,465	146,974	68,700	15,350	53,350	7,252	898	6,354
1940	173,706	19,260	154,446	73,104	15,109	57,995	6,655	834	5,821
1939	179,818	19,730	160,088	64,816	12,027	52,789	5,899	645	5,254
1938	159,382	17,083	142,299	66,890	12,538	54,352	5,964	558	5,406
1937	149,357	15,309	134,048	62,069	11,171	50,898	5,928	437	5,491
1936	143,573	15,373	128,200	60,925	11,459	49,466	4,575	348	4,227
1935	144,665	14,777	129,888	65,723	11,837	53,886	4,795	292	4,503
1934	138,220	12,080	126,140	62,251	9,275	52,976	4,154	161	3,993
1933	136,947	10,851	126,096	62,801	8,333	54,468	4,073	177	3,896
1932	137,183	12,282	124,901	67,477	9,652	57,825	4,257	172	4,085
1931	137,082	12,964	124,118	71,520	10,615	60,905	3,658	120	3,538
1930	127,495	12,181	115,314	66,013	9,800	56,213	3,158	79	3,079
1929	120,496	12,964	107,532	58,906	9,734	49,172	2,820	42	2,778
1928	116,626	8,204	108,422	55,746	5,570	50,176	2,750	63	2,687
1927	106,517	7,722	98,795	51,936	5,021	46,915	2,393	36	2,357
1926	96,125	6,803	89,322	48,108	5,010	43,098	2,228	26	2,202

[1] Beginning 1963, figures do not include some violators who were returned with new or additional sentences and were included as "court commitments."

Series H 1144–1154. Federal and State Institutions—Prisoners Released, by Type of Release: 1926 to 1970

[Prisoners in institutions for adult offenders only. For geographic coverage, see text for series H 1135–1143]

Year	Total, Federal and State institutions	Released from Federal institutions					Released from State institutions				
		Total	Conditional		Unconditional		Total	Conditional		Unconditional	
			Parole	Other	Expiration of sentence	Other		Parole	Other	Expiration of sentence	Other
	1144	1145	1146	1147	1148	1149	1150	1151	1152	1153	1154
1970	91,732	11,689	5,696		5,993		80,043	56,181		23,862	
1969	89,060	11,406	6,881		4,525		77,654	52,030		25,624	
1968	85,968	12,175	4,400		7,775		73,793	50,309		23,484	
1967	96,377	12,361	5,297	2,740	¹ 4,324		84,016	52,424	4,369	¹ 27,223	
1966	102,335	14,695	6,029	3,244	² 5,422		87,640	53,678	3,957	² 30,005	
1965	106,161	14,874	5,109	3,587	³ 6,178		91,287	55,606	3,742	³ 31,939	
1964	106,633	15,100	5,178	3,742	⁴ 6,180		91,533	55,024	4,008	⁴ 32,501	
1963	105,050	15,181	5,127	3,747	6,307	–	89,869	53,934	3,658	28,599	3,678
1962	106,143	14,814	4,915	3,603	6,296	–	91,329	54,420	3,849	29,159	3,901
1961	100,724	14,519	4,380	3,855	6,284	–	86,205	51,445	3,403	27,859	3,498
1960	96,362	14,196	4,344	3,368	6,484	–	82,166	48,457	3,229	27,144	3,336
1959	96,530	14,215	4,220	3,089	6,906	–	82,315	48,278	2,949	27,552	3,536
1958	88,679	13,970	3,587	3,308	7,072	3	74,709	42,320	2,493	26,682	3,214
1957	85,356	14,029	3,822	3,258	6,941	8	71,327	39,535	2,147	26,467	3,178
1956	83,099	14,285	3,975	3,087	7,209	14	68,814	38,288	1,888	25,489	3,149
1955	82,924	15,776	3,823	2,617	9,328	8	67,148	37,631	1,842	24,678	2,997
1954	78,184	16,743	4,410	2,507	9,825	1	61,441	33,551	1,779	23,276	2,835
1953	75,125	15,813	3,793	2,361	9,659	–	59,312	32,525	1,508	22,693	2,586
1952	74,268	15,524	3,642	2,121	9,761	–	58,744	32,712	1,387	22,037	2,608
1951	73,937	14,974	3,495	4,049	7,422	8	58,963	32,936	1,466	22,064	2,497
1950	72,179	15,187	3,294	6,172	5,710	11	56,992	31,428	1,342	22,147	2,075
1949	69,051	13,999	3,051	5,596	5,317	35	55,052	28,267	2,590	22,368	1,827
1948	65,978	14,243	3,822	5,124	5,146	151	51,735	27,062	3,206	19,798	1,669
1947	60,080	14,246	4,020	4,893	5,317	16	45,834	25,107	2,766	17,107	854
1946	59,289	15,544	5,362	5,191	4,869	122	43,745	24,571	3,641	14,959	574
1945	57,500	13,598	3,101	5,242	5,229	26	43,902	24,255	4,145	14,935	567
1944	59,860	12,457	3,272	4,784	4,263	138	47,403	26,029	4,574	16,520	280
1943	69,723	13,190	3,101	5,853	4,223	13	56,533	30,526	5,331	20,426	250
1942	81,630	16,032	3,079	7,162	5,776	15	65,598	30,980	7,849	26,143	626
1941	86,887	16,998	2,723	7,583	6,669	23	69,889	32,246	6,372	30,500	771
1940	88,640	16,280	2,572	7,988	5,702	18	72,360	30,360	8,081	32,092	1,827
1939	66,303	11,794	2,315	6,932	2,538	9	54,509	25,568	5,554	22,898	489
1938	62,771	11,102	2,416	6,795	1,876	15	51,669	25,220	4,300	21,754	395
1937	60,462	11,477	2,944	6,566	1,950	17	48,985	24,331	3,521	20,766	367
1936	62,750	10,965	2,445	6,256	2,263	1	51,785	28,686	407	21,778	914
1935	60,475	9,010	2,369	4,294	2,345	2	51,465	28,039	391	20,990	2,045
1934	60,732	8,310	2,709	2,887	2,709	5	52,422	29,747	184	20,761	1,730
1933	63,640	10,206	4,242	1,203	4,756	5	53,434	30,597	----------	21,194	1,643
1932	66,863	10,394	5,050	----------	5,314	30	56,469	32,087	----------	20,530	3,852
1931	60,930	9,749	4,643	----------	5,105	1	51,181	30,339	----------	20,321	521
1930	54,925	8,926	4,157	----------	4,764	5	45,999	25,352	----------	20,112	535
1929	45,986	5,610	1,347	----------	4,261	2	40,376	22,791	----------	16,931	654
1928	45,124	4,983	1,082	----------	3,900	1	40,141	22,887	----------	16,575	679
1927	41,356	4,179	688	----------	3,491	–	37,177	20,964	----------	14,964	1,249
1926	39,044	4,248	834	----------	3,413	1	34,796	19,083	----------	14,418	1,295

– Represents zero.
¹ Includes 12 full pardons, Federal and State institutions.
² Includes 16 full pardons, Federal and State institutions.
³ Includes 13 full pardons, Federal and State institutions.
⁴ Includes 20 full pardons, Federal and State institutions.

Series H 1155–1167. Prisoners Executed Under Civil Authority, by Race and Offense: 1930 to 1970

[Prior to 1960, excludes Alaska and Hawaii except for 3 Federal executions in Alaska: 1939, 1948, and 1950]

Year	All offenses				Murder[2]			Rape			Other offenses		
	Total	White	Negro	Other[1]	Total[3]	White	Negro	Total	White	Negro	Total[4]	White[5]	Negro
	1155	1156	1157	1158	1159	1160	1161	1162	1163	1164	1165	1166	1167
1970	–	–	–	–	–	–	–	–	–	–	–	–	–
1969	–	–	–	–	–	–	–	–	–	–	–	–	–
1968	–	–	–	–	–	–	–	–	–	–	–	–	–
1967	2	1	1	–	2	1	1	–	–	–	–	–	–
1966	1	1	–	–	1	1	–	–	–	–	–	–	–
1965	7	6	1	–	7	6	1	–	–	–	–	–	–
1964	15	8	7	–	9	5	4	6	3	3	–	–	–
1963	21	13	8	–	18	12	6	2	–	2	1	1	–
1962	47	28	19	–	41	26	15	4	2	2	2	–	2
1961	42	20	22	–	33	18	15	8	1	7	1	1	–
1960	56	21	35	–	44	18	26	8	–	8	4	3	1
1959	49	16	33	–	41	15	26	8	1	7	–	–	1
1958	49	20	28	1	41	20	20	7	–	7	1	–	1
1957	65	34	31	–	54	32	22	10	2	8	1	–	1
1956	65	21	43	1	52	20	31	12	–	12	1	1	–
1955	76	44	32	–	65	41	24	7	1	6	4	2	2
1954	81	38	42	1	71	37	33	9	1	8	1	–	1
1953	62	30	31	1	51	25	25	7	1	6	4	4	–
1952	83	36	47	–	71	35	36	12	1	11	–	–	–
1951	105	57	47	1	87	55	31	17	2	15	1	–	1
1950	82	40	42	–	68	36	32	13	4	9	1	–	1
1949	119	50	67	2	107	49	56	10	–	10	2	1	1
1948	119	35	82	2	95	32	61	22	1	21	2	2	–
1947	153	42	111	–	129	40	89	23	2	21	1	–	1
1946	131	46	84	1	107	45	61	22	–	22	2	1	1
1945	117	41	75	1	90	37	52	26	4	22	1	–	1
1944	120	47	70	3	96	45	48	24	2	22	–	–	–
1943	131	54	74	3	118	54	63	13[3]	–	11	–	–	–
1942	147	67	80	–	115	57	58	25	4	21	7	6	1
1941	123	59	63	1	102	55	46	20	4	16	1	–	1
1940	124	49	75	–	105	44	61	15	2	13	4	3	1
1939	160	80	77	3	145	79	63	12	–	12	3	1	2
1938	190	96	92	2	154	89	63	25	1	24	11	6	5
1937	147	69	74	4	133	67	62	13	2	11	1	–	1
1936	195	92	101	2	181	86	93	10	2	8	4	4	–
1935	199	119	77	3	184	115	66	13	2	11	2	2	–
1934	168	65	102	1	154	64	89	14	1	13	–	–	–
1933	160	77	81	2	151	75	74	7	1	6	2	1	1
1932	140	62	75	3	128	62	63	10	–	10	2	–	2
1931	153	77	72	4	137	76	57	15	1	14	1	–	1
1930	155	90	65	–	147	90	57	6	–	6	2	–	2

– Represents zero.
[1] All were for murder except 2 for rape in 1943.
[2] Includes 32 females: 20 white, 12 Negro.
[3] Total includes other races, not shown separately.
[4] Includes 25 armed robbery, 20 kidnaping, 11 burglary, 6 sabotage, 6 aggravated assault, and 2 espionage.
[5] Includes 2 females.

Series H 1168–1170. Persons Lynched, by Race: 1882 to 1970

[No lynchings occurred in 1952–1954, 1956, 1958, 1960, 1962, and 1965–1970]

Year	Total	White	Negro	Year	Total	White	Negro	Year	Total	White	Negro	Year	Total	White	Negro	Year	Total	White	Negro
	1168	1169	1170		1168	1169	1170		1168	1169	1170		1168	1169	1170		1168	1169	1170
1964[1]	3	2	1	1940	5	1	4	1925	17	–	17	1910	76	9	67	1895	179	66	113
1963	1	–	1	1939	3	1	2	1924	16	–	16	1909	82	13	69	1894	192	58	134
1961	1	–	1	1938	6	–	6	1923	33	4	29	1908	97	8	89	1893	152	34	118
1959	1	–	1	1937	8	–	8	1922	57	6	51	1907	60	2	58	1892	230	69	161
1957	1	1	–	1936	8	–	8	1921	64	5	59	1906	65	3	62	1891	184	71	113
1955	8	–	8	1935	20	2	18	1920	61	8	53	1905	62	5	57	1890	96	11	85
1951	1	–	1	1934	15	–	15	1919	83	7	76	1904	83	7	76	1889	170	76	94
1950	2	1	1	1933	28	4	24	1918	64	4	60	1903	99	15	84	1888	137	68	69
1949	3	–	3	1932	8	2	6	1917	38	2	36	1902	92	7	85	1887	120	50	70
1948	2	1	1	1931	13	1	12	1916	54	4	50	1901	130	25	105	1886	138	64	74
1947	1	–	1	1930	21	1	20	1915	69	13	56	1900	115	9	106	1885	184	110	74
1946	6	–	6	1929	10	3	7	1914	55	4	51	1899	106	21	85	1884	211	160	51
1945	1	–	1	1928	11	1	10	1913	52	1	51	1898	120	19	101	1883	130	77	53
1944	2	–	2	1927	16	–	16	1912	63	2	61	1897	158	35	123	1882	113	64	49
1943	3	–	3	1926	30	7	23	1911	67	7	60	1896	123	45	78				
1942	6	–	6																
1941	4	–	4																

– Represents zero.   [1] No lynchings, 1965–1970.

Land, Water, and Climate

Land and Water Utilization (Series J 1-109)

J 1–2. Territorial expansion and land and water area of the United States, 1790–1970.

Source: U.S. Bureau of the Census, Reports of Fourteenth, Fifteenth, Sixteenth, Seventeenth, Eighteenth, and Nineteenth Censuses, *Population*, vol. I, and unpublished data.

Boundaries of territories listed under United States were indefinite, at least in part, at the time of acquisition. Area figures shown here represent precise determinations of specific territories which have been marked upon maps, based upon interpretations of the several treaties of cession, which are necessarily debatable. These determinations were made by a committee consisting of representatives of various governmental agencies in 1912. Subsequently, these figures were adjusted to bring them into agreement with remeasurements made in 1960.

Area measurements within the United States began with the country as a whole and developed, as mapping progressed, to measurements for the States. The annual report of the U.S. General Land Office for 1850 contained the first reference to the areas of the States and Territories, although there was no indication of the method used in obtaining the measurements. In 1881, as part of the 1880 Census of Population, the Bureau of the Census laid the foundation for accurate and detailed area measurement in the United States. For the first time an account was given of the method and maps employed, the water bodies included, and the outer limits of the United States used as a basis for measurement. As part of the 1940 census, the Bureau published *Areas of the United States: 1940*, presenting data on the total land and water areas of the States, counties, cities, and minor civil divisions. For reports of the 1950 and 1960 censuses, adjustments in selected area figures were made for reasons of changes in boundaries, development of water reservoirs, or improvement in maps from which measurements are made.

"All other" (series J 1) includes the following islands with gross areas as indicated: Midway (2), Wake (3), Palmyra (4), Canton and Enderbury (combined area, 27), Swan (1), Navassa (2), Baker, Howland, and Jarvis (combined area, 3), Johnston and Sand (combined area, less than 0.5), Kingman Reef, Quita Sueno Bank, Roncador Cay, and Serrana Bank (each less than 0.5). Other possessions include the following islands for which area figures are not available: Caroline, Christmas, Danger (Pukapuka), Flint, Funafuti, Malden, Manahiki, Nukufetau, Nukulailai, Nurakita, Penrhyn, Rakahanga, Starbuck, Vostok, Phoenix Group (except Canton and Enderbury), and Union (Tokelau) Group, not enumerated in decennial censuses. See also data and text for series A 1–5.

J 3–7. General note.

The U.S. Government acquired sovereignty over its present area through a series of international agreements and treaties. However, the Federal Government did not gain title to all of the lands covered by such agreements; title to much of the land was retained by individual States and their political subdivisions or by private owners.

"Original public-domain land" embraces all of the area to which title was vested in the U.S. Government by virtue of its sovereignty. Any of such lands which the Government has not disposed of under the public-land laws are generally referred to as "public-domain lands."

In addition to public-domain lands, the Federal Government has acquired by purchase, condemnation, and gift, tracts of land needed for various public purposes, such as sites for public buildings, defense installations, and natural resources conservation activities. Such lands are referred to as "acquired lands."

J 3. Public domain plus acquired land, 1802–1970.

Source: 1802–1950, U.S. Bureau of Land Management; 1955–1970, U.S. General Services Administration, *Inventory Report on Real Property Owned by the United States Throughout the World*, annual.

Series J 3 presents the total of public domain and acquired lands owned by the United States from 1802 through 1970, exclusive of any federally owned lands outside the United States. About 55 million acres of acquired lands are included in the 1970 estimate.

J 4–7. Acquisition of the public domain, 1781–1867.

Source: U.S. Bureau of Land Management, *Public Land Statistics, 1970*, p. 4.

Series J 5 presents the original public-domain lands acquired from 1781 through 1867. During the period from 1781 through 1802, seven of the original 13 States relinquished to the Federal Government, by acts of cession, their claims to what was then described as "western lands." Roughly, the western lands covered the area north of the Ohio River and east of the Mississippi River and the area embraced by the present States of Alabama and Mississippi. The State of Maryland ceded the present area of the District of Columbia in 1788. In 1850, the State of Texas sold its land outside its present boundaries to the United States. During the period from 1803 through 1867, title to the remaining area west of the Mississippi River (except the State of Texas) and to Florida passed to the Federal Government. With the exception of land in the District of Columbia, the total of 1,808 million acres of land is vested in the United States Government as original public-domain land.

Series J 6 presents the areas of inland waters which were acquired with the original public-domain lands.

Series J 7, cost for State cessions, 1781–1802, is only for the purchase of the Georgia cession (56,689,920 acres) in 1802; see Thomas Donaldson, *The Public Domain, Its History, with Statistics*, 1884. Other cost data were obtained from U.S. Geological Survey, *Boundaries, Areas, Geographic Centers*, 1939.

J 8–15. General note.

Data shown are for fiscal years. For definition of public-domain lands and acquired lands, see text for series J 3–7. The laws which govern the management, use, and sale or other disposal of public-domain lands are known as the *public-land laws*. The policy of the Federal Government in the early years was to pass the public lands into private ownership as rapidly as possible. Congress passed thousands of laws providing for the disposal of the original public domain to States and their subdivisions and to private owners. Initially this was done to raise revenue and later to hasten the settlement and development of the country. Special laws provide for the disposal of surplus *acquired lands*, as, for example, the Surplus Property Act of 1944. By 1970, approximately 287 million acres of public lands had been patented to homesteaders, 328 million acres had been granted to States for various public purposes, 94 million acres had been granted to railroad corporations to aid in financing the construction of railroads, and about 434 million acres had been sold or otherwise disposed of.

J 8. Vacant public lands, 1904–1970.

Source: U.S. Bureau of Land Management, *Public Land Statistics* (*Annual Report of the Director* prior to 1962), various issues, and unpublished data.

Data are estimates as of June 30 of each year.

The vacant public lands of the United States are public-domain lands (see text for series J 3–7) which are not reserved for any purpose other than for reclassification and which are not covered by any non-Federal right or claim other than permits, leases, right-of-ways, or unreported mining claims. They are subject to acquisition by applicants under appropriate laws, such as the laws governing homesteads or grants to States. It is upon these laws for the most part that entries and selections (see text for series J 10–12) are made. The Bureau of Land Management administers the public-land laws relating to such entries and selections, a function transferred to it from the General Land Office as a part of Reorganization Plan No. 3 of 1946 (U.S. Congress).

Data prior to 1959 exclude Alaska. Unreserved lands in Alaska were withdrawn from any form of disposition under the public land laws by Public Land Order 4582 (January 17, 1969) which reserved the lands and resources until December 31, 1970, for the rights of native Aleuts, Eskimos, and Indians in Alaska.

J 9. Land granted by the United States to the several States, 1802–1959.

Source: U.S. Bureau of Land Management, *Annual Report of the Commissioner of the General Land Office, 1946, Statistical Appendix*, pp. 108–119, and *Public Land Statistics, 1970*, p. 7.

See also *General Land Office Information Bulletin No. 1, 1939 series*.

Includes grants for such public purposes as the following: Educational, penal, and other public institutions and buildings; bridges, reservoirs, and other internal improvements; reclamation of swamp and arid lands; experiment stations; recreational areas; wildlife and forestry areas; military camps; and payment of bonds issued by local governments. Excludes 46,600,000 acres granted to States for aid in construction of railroads, wagon roads, canals, etc. (see series J 21–25). Does not include acreage of swamplands lost to the States, for which the States received indemnity in cash.

The data on land grants to the States for various public purposes are presented according to the calendar year in which the granting legislation was passed by the Congress. Some variation in the series is possible since the language of some of the statutes, including that of amendatory legislation, offers alternatives in the selection of the year to which individual grants could be assigned. As with the land grants for the construction of canals and other transportation improvements (series J 21–25), many of these grants were satisfied through delivery of evidence of legal title throughout the years.

J 10–12. Original entries and selections, final entries, and patents and certifications, 1869–1970.

Source: 1869–1919, U.S. Department of Commerce, *Statistical Abstract of the United States*, various issues, 1879–1919; 1920–1970, U.S. Bureau of Land Management, *Public Land Statistics* (*Annual Report of the Director* prior to 1962), various issues.

The data on entries, selections, patents, and certifications refer to transactions which involve the disposal, under the public-land laws (including the homestead laws), of Federal public-domain lands to non-Federal owners. In general terms, *original entries* and *selections* are applications to secure title to public-domain lands which have been accepted as properly filed. Some types of applications, however, are not reported until the final certificate is issued and are, therefore, not included in series J 10.

Applications become *final entries* upon issuance of a *final certificate* which is given to the applicant after he has complied fully with the requirements of the laws relating to his application. These requirements may include, in particular cases, settlement upon and improvement of the lands entered, or payment of statutory fees or purchase money. A *final certificate* passes equitable title to the land to the applicant. With respect to certain State selections, no final certificate is issued. Such selections are, therefore, not included in series J 11 (final entries). *Patents* are instruments which pass legal title to the lands to the applicant. *Certifications* are issued in lieu of patents in connection with certain State selections.

The data do not include the area of certain lands which have been granted to the States to aid in the support of common schools. Title to such lands usually passes to the States upon survey of the lands by the Federal Government. Owing to legal complexities, detailed statistical records were not kept of these lands. Figures published here have been subjected to minor adjustments to improve comparability. They have not been checked, however, for internal accuracy or for strict comparability which would require analysis of supporting records. Data include disposals of lands in Alaska for all years.

J 13–15. Homestead entries, except on ceded Indian lands, 1863–1970.

Source: **Series J 13**, 1863–1883, Thomas Donaldson, *The Public Domain, Its History, with Statistics*, 1884, pp. 351–355 (reprinted, Johnson Reprint Corporation); 1884–1970, U.S. Bureau of Land Management, *Public Land Statistics* (*Annual Report of the Director* prior to 1962), various issues. **Series J 14**, 1881–1945, U.S. Department of Commerce, *Statistical Abstract of the United States*, various issues; 1946–1970, U.S. Bureau of Land Management, *Public Land Statistics* (*Annual Report of the Director* prior to 1962), various issues. **Series J 15**, U.S. Department of the Interior, 1868–1940, *Annual Report of the Commissioner of the General Land Office, 1946*; 1941–1960, *Annual Report of the Director, 1961 Statistical Appendix*; 1961–1970, *Public Land Statistics, 1969 and 1970*.

For definitions of the terms *original entries* and *final entries*, see text for series J 10–12.

Figures for original homestead entries exclude applications which were accepted for lands ceded by the Indians to the United States with the provision that proceeds from their disposal would be covered into the Treasury to the credit of the Indians. Detailed statistics on such homestead entries were not published in the reports of the Commissioner of the General Land Office prior to 1924. Such reports contain general information as to the disposal of ceded Indian lands. The records upon which the reports were based are for the most part on file in the National Archives.

Acreage figures of final entries (series J 15) do not include commuted homesteads. A *commuted homestead entry* is a homestead entry not exceeding 160 acres in connection with which the entryman pays the minimum statutory price for the land in consideration for reduction in residence and other requirements. Only certain classes of homestead entries can be commuted.

J 16–19. Lands under jurisdiction of Bureau of Indian Affairs, 1881–1970.

Source: U.S. Department of the Interior: 1881–1897, 1900, 1903, 1910–1920, 1953–1958, *Annual Report of the Secretary of the Interior*, various issues; 1901, 1902, 1904–1909, 1939, 1940, 1942–1946, 1949, *Annual Report of the Commissioner of Indian Affairs* and *Statistical Supplements*, various issues; 1921–1930, 1932–1937, 1941, compiled by the Commissioner of Indian Affairs; 1959–1970, *Annual Real Property Management Report*, various issues.

Indian lands are the private landholdings of individual Indians or Indian tribes that are subject to special restrictive provisions of Federal law administered by the Bureau of Indian Affairs. They have been set aside for Indian use by treaties, congressional acts, and executive orders. Although most of these lands are in reservations for specific tribes, there are groups of scattered off-reservation allotments in individual ownership and other small tracts of land occupied by Indian groups.

J 20. Public land sales, 1800–1860.

Source: Walter B. Smith and Arthur H. Cole, *Fluctuations in American Business, 1790–1860*, Harvard University Press, Cambridge, 1935 (copyright).

Data were derived from Hibbard, *A History of the Public Land Policies*, 1924, pp. 100, 103, 106, and from *Annual Report of the Commissioner of the General Land Office*, various issues. The data differ from those presented by Hibbard (p. 106) for the years after 1850, when Hibbard's data shift from calendar years to fiscal years ending June 30.

J 21–25. Public land grants by United States to aid in construction of railroads, wagon roads, canals, etc., 1823–1871.

Source: U.S. Bureau of Land Management, *Annual Report of the Commissioner of the General Land Office, 1946, Statistical Appendix*, pp. 100–107.

Figures include only the area of lands for which title passed to the grantee States and corporations. The exact extent of practically all of these grants was, owing to their terms, indeterminate at the time the granting acts were passed by the Congress. The procedures for the satisfaction of the grants generally required the grantees to submit lists of lands to which they requested evidence of legal title on the basis of the provisions of the authorizing legislation. This process of issuance of instruments of title has not been fully completed by the Department of the Interior; a relatively small area remains to be adjudicated.

For the series presented, the areas shown in the instruments of title which were issued for each grant over the years were totaled and shown as of the fiscal year in which the grant was *originally enacted*, even though in certain instances grants were revived at a later date after the expiration of statutory time limits while others were enlarged by subsequent legislation. Because the tabulation is based on instruments of title, the data do not reflect the area of those portions of grants which could not be satisfied under the law for various reasons or of those grants or portions of grants which were forfeited.

J 26–32. Revenues from public-domain, revested, and acquired land, 1785–1970.

Source: U.S. General Land Office, 1785–1939, *Annual Report of the Commissioner, 1946, Statistical Appendix*, table 90. U.S. Bureau of Land Management, 1940–1946, *Annual Report of the Director, 1958, Statistical Appendix*, table 116; 1947–1960, *Public Land Statistics, 1962*, table 111; 1961–1970, *Public Land Statistics, 1970*, table 112.

Data for 1785 to 1956 are also available in a publication by Marion Clawson and Burnell Held, *The Federal Lands: Their Use and Management*, The Johns Hopkins Press, Baltimore, 1957, text table 8 and appendix tables 25 and 27.

Original data for 1785–1880 are from J. R. Mahoney, *Natural Resources Activity of the Federal Government*, Public Affairs Bulletin No. 76, Library of Congress, 1950.

Figures are for fiscal years and represent the total receipts of the General Land Office and Bureau of Land Management transferred to the Treasury for 1785–1970 and include the relatively small receipts from land and resources in Alaska. They do not include the receipts which other Government agencies realized from their operations on Federal lands, although they do include some receipts from lands under the administration of such agencies. For example, mineral leases for public-domain lands within areas administered by the National Forest Service were issued by the General Land Office, which also collected the mineral rentals, royalties, and bonuses from such lands. Also, for 1935 through part of 1940, the General Land Office collected grazing fees for lands within grazing districts; and, for 1908 through the first half of 1913, it collected water-right charges in connection with the Bureau of Reclamation irrigation projects. Other examples of multiple jurisdiction exist.

O & C lands are those areas granted to the Oregon and California Railroad Company in 1866. Later the Federal Government repossessed this land because the terms of the grant were not carried out. Sale of timber from the O & C lands amounted to $58.8 million in 1970.

J 33–34. Livestock permitted to graze on National Forest System lands, 1905–1970.

Source: U.S. Forest Service, 1905–1965, annual reports and unpublished data; 1966–1970, *Annual Grazing Statistical Report*, annual issues.

Data are for the number of animals under paid permit (excluding "exempt provision" and "other paid permit" shown in the second source cited) and not necessarily the actual number grazed. Includes data for some Title III (Bankhead–Jones Act) lands transferred to the Forest Service for administration in 1954. In 1960, most of these lands were incorporated into the National Forest System.

J 35–40. Grazing on public-domain lands, 1935–1970.

Source: U.S. Bureau of Land Management, *Public Land Statistics (Annual Report of the Director*, prior to 1962), various issues.

Data on grazing exclude grazing on reclamation land, land utilization projects where not part of a grazing district, O & C lands (see text for series J 26–32 for definition of O & C lands), and Alaskan grazing; they include lands rented and sublet under the Pierce Act (43 U.S.C. 315M). Amount of grazing in districts (series J 38–40) includes free-use, crossing, and trailing permits in addition to regular paid use. Beginning 1964, it does not include nonuse permits or exchange-of-use permits for grazing district lands.

Grazing receipts are credited to the year received even though part of the period covered extends into the following year. An animal-unit month represents the forage required to maintain five sheep or goats or one horse or one cow for a month.

J 41–49. Oil and gas leases of public-domain land—acreage, receipts, and output, 1920 to 1970.

Source: **Series J 41–43**, U.S. Bureau of Land Management, *Public Land Statistics*, annual issues. **Series J 44**, U.S. Geological Survey estimates derived by subtracting series J 45 from J 43. **Series J 45 and J 47–49**, U.S. Geological Survey, 1920–1944, unpublished data; 1945–1970, *Federal and Indian Lands Oil and Gas Production, Royalty Income*, and *Related Statistics*, June 1972. **Series J 46**, U.S. Geological Survey estimates based on computations of gasoline and butane on an equal basis with petroleum (42 gallons per barrel), and 6,000 cubic feet of natural gas equal to 1 barrel of petroleum.

Of the total public-domain acreage owned by the Federal Government in 1970 (706 million acres) about 9 percent was leased for oil and gas operations under the Mineral Leasing Act of February 25, 1920, as amended. Of the total number of leases under the supervision of the U.S. Geological Survey about 8 percent were in a producible status, producing oil, gas, and associated liquid products.

30 U.S.C. 226 specifies a minimum royalty rate of $12\frac{1}{2}$ percent of the value of production removed or sold from oil and gas leases. Rates vary upward as high as 25 percent depending upon the royalty rate specified in the lease issued. Royalty on liquid products is net after an allowance for the cost of manufacture. The rental for nonproducing oil and gas leases varies from 50 cents per acre or fraction thereof for each lease year to $2 per acre. The minimum royalty which is paid in lieu of rental at the expiration of each lease year after discovery is $1 per acre or fraction thereof.

J 50–80. General note.

Area measurements in the United States are performed in connection with the decennial censuses of population. They began with measurements for the country as a whole; and, as mapping progressed, included measurements for the States and later for counties and minor civil divisions. Differences in the land area figures over time are due primarily to the more accurate determination of the outer limits of the United States, improvements in mapping and map measuring techniques, omission of certain bodies of water included in the earlier measurements, and increases in the area of artificial reservoirs. For total figures (land, water, and gross area) in square miles, 1790–1970, and sources of data, see series J 2.

Collection of land utilization statistics began with the census of 1850, when farmland was enumerated as "improved land" or "unimproved land." In 1890 and later census years, these inquiries were expanded and revised. After the turn of the century, collection of various land utilization statistics was begun by branches of the Department of Agriculture, while other contributions to the literature on this subject were made by numerous agencies, State universities, and individuals.

The census of agriculture is the primary source of data concerning land in farms in census years. Statistics concerning land not in farms are less complete, except for forest land, and have been collected by various interested agencies for individual items and for local areas by Federal, State, and private agencies and individuals. During the 1930's, studies by the National Resources Planning Board and assisting agencies contributed greatly to the available statistics on total land utilization. Since 1920, the Department of Agriculture's Economic Research Service and its predecessor agencies have prepared periodic inventories of land use.

Data on the utilization of farmland refer to the land use in preceding years except for 1954, 1959, 1964, and 1969. For 1850–1925, the data are chiefly estimates made by the former Bureau of Agricultural Economics based on the censuses of agriculture conducted by the Bureau of the Census. The estimates for 1930–1969 are from the census of agriculture, except for an adjustment made by the Economic Research Service in cropland harvested and other land in farms for 1950 through 1969. This adjustment was made to compensate for normal underenumeration of cropland and to obtain greater conformity with the total acreage of crops harvested as reported by the Department of Agriculture's Statistical Reporting Service and its predecessor agencies.

Acreages of nonfarm uses of land were estimated by the Economic Research Service and predecessor agencies from records and reports of State and Federal agencies concerned with management of public land, conservation of land, public services, and assessment of land for taxation.

Changes in total farmland for 1850–1969 represent in part changes in agricultural activity and in part more complete census enumeration and changes in census definition of *land in farms*. Land uses not reported by the Bureau of the Census and additions to census data for 1930–1969 are based largely on agricultural statistics assembled by the Department of Agriculture. Forest land inventories and grazing land studies during this period are believed to have improved the reliability of the estimates of these items for this period as contrasted with earlier years. Estimates for 1925 and prior census years for land not in farms are based on more limited evidence, such as available charts, maps, records, and reports on land areas and uses.

J 50–65. Land utilization, by type, 1850–1969.

Source: U.S. Department of Agriculture, 1850–1900, *Major Uses of Land in the United States: Summary for 1954*, Agriculture Information Bulletin No. 168, 1957, pp. 36 and 37; 1910–1968, *Agricultural Statistics, 1972*, p. 506; 1969, *Major Uses of Land in the United States, Summary for 1969*, Agricultural Economics Report No. 247.

These data are based on estimates from Department of Agriculture publications as follows: *Major Uses of Land and Water in the United States, Summary for 1964*, Agricultural Economics Report 149, 1968; *Major Uses of Land and Water in the United States: Summary for 1959*, Agricultural Economics Report No. 13, 1962; *Major Uses of Land in the United States*, Technical Bulletin No. 1082, and Supplement, *Basic Land Use Statistics, 1950*; *Inventory of Major Land Uses, United States, 1945*, Miscellaneous publication 663, 1948; *Pasture*

Land on Farms in the United States, Bulletin No. 626, 1918; *Agricultural Yearbook, 1923*, 1924; and National Resources Board, *A Report on National Planning and Public Works . . ., 1934*.

Total land area, as defined by the Census Bureau in 1940 and subsequent years includes "dry land and land temporarily or partially covered by water, such as marshland, swamps and river flood plains . . . (except tidal flats) . . . streams, sloughs, estuaries, and canals less than 1/8 of a statute mile in width; and lakes, reservoirs, and ponds having less than 40 acres of area."

See also U.S. Bureau of the Census reports, *U.S. Census of Population*, vol. I, for 1920, 1930, 1940, 1950, and 1960; *Areas of the United States, 1940*; and *Area Measurement Reports* (for individual States, 1960 area), Series GE-20, 1964–1967.

Cropland used for crops includes cropland harvested, crop failure, and cultivated summer fallow. *Cropland idle or in cover crops* includes temporarily idle land as well as some poorer cropland abandoned for crop purposes and soil-improvement crops not harvested and not pastured. *Grassland pasture* includes cropland used only for pasture in the year indicated and all other nonforested pasture in farms. *Farm woodland* includes grazed or ungrazed farm wood lots or timber tracts, natural or planted, and cutover land with young growth, which has or will have value as wood or timber. Chaparral and woody shrubs are omitted. *Special uses in farms* includes farmsteads, farm roads, and farm lanes. *Other land in farms* includes miscellaneous unclassified uses and wasteland.

Nonfarm grazing land comprises the open grassland and shrub grazing lands and the woodland and forest area grazed. *Nonfarm forest land not used for grazing* excludes forested areas in parks, wildlife refuges, military areas, recreation sites, and arid woodland, brushland, and forest land used for grazing. *Special uses not in farms* includes urban areas, highways and roads, railroads, airports, parks and related recreational areas, wildlife refuges, and military reservations. *Other nonfarm land* includes various unclassified uses and unused areas such as desert, rock, swamp, and tundra.

J 66–80. Private and public land ownership, by major uses, 1920–1969.

Source: U.S. Department of Agriculture, Economic Research Service. 1920, unpublished data; 1930–1954, *Major Uses of Land in the United States: Summary for 1954*, Agricultural Information Bulletin 168, 1957; 1959, *Major Uses of Land and Water in the United States: Summary for 1959*, Agricultural Economics Report 13, 1962; 1964, *Major Uses of Land and Water in the United States: Summary for 1964*, Agricultural Economics Report 149, 1968; 1969, see source for series J 50–65.

The figures were compiled from a number of Federal and State reports and records which reflect varying degrees of reliability. The figures used are applicable for different dates. All of them were assembled for some other purpose than that for which they are used here. The areas of all unsurveyed lands are estimated, and the areas of many lands based on surveys are subject to correction. Some of the data are not complete and are used merely for comparison. Therefore, although they are the best available, the figures given here are not strictly accurate, often not complete, and are not comparable among themselves. Nevertheless, they give some idea of the major features of land use and control for the country as a whole.

Private land is land held or owned by private individuals, groups, and corporations, and is generally used for private purposes. Indian lands held in trust and administered by the Federal Government for the benefit and use of groups or tribes of the Indian people are included in private land, as more than three-fourths of this land is used directly for farming and grazing by Indian farmers and stockmen. Much of the rest is leased for farming and grazing to other farmers and ranchers and the proceeds are received by the Indian owners.

Public land as used here is land owned or administered by Federal, State, county, municipal, or other governments for common or public purposes (e.g., highways, airports, national defense, flood control, water supply, forests, and parks). Public land frequently is used for farming and grazing by private parties under a system of permits or leases. However, most of it is dry, rough, rocky, swampy, or otherwise unsuited for farming. When used by individuals, public land is sometimes included in reporting statistics on acreages in farms. More often, when public land is used in common by several persons, it is not reported as in farms.

See also text for series J 50–65.

J 81–91. Agricultural land drainage and irrigation, 1890–1969.

Source: U.S. Bureau of the Census. **Series J 81–84**, 1920–1969, 1969 Census of Agriculture, vol. VI, *Drainage of Agricultural Lands, 1969*, p. X. **Series J 85–91**, 1890–1954, *Irrigation of Agricultural Lands, 1950*, and *1959*; 1959–1969, 1969 Census of Agriculture, vol. IV, *Irrigation*, p. 2.

Drainage and irrigation are the two major reclamation means by which additional land can be brought under cultivation. Land that is drained greatly exceeds land that is irrigated in terms of acreage already developed. Drainage activities are concentrated in the North Central States and lower Mississippi Valley. Other highly drained areas are the Gulf Coast area of Texas, Southern Florida, and the Sacramento and San Joaquin River areas of California. Irrigation is practiced predominantly in the arid and semi-arid areas of the West. In recent years the acreage of irrigated land has stabilized in the Southwest and California because of the full utilization of existing water supplies whereas rapid expansion has occurred in Nebraska, Kansas, Oklahoma, Texas, and Florida. In irrigated areas, particularly areas where water is applied by flooding or by furrows and ditches, drainage is necessary to carry away excess water.

The Bureau of the Census has collected drainage and irrigation statistics by means of three censuses: (1) The censuses of agriculture which represent a direct enumeration of farms; (2) the special censuses of drainage projects; and (3) the special censuses of irrigation organizations. The censuses of agriculture have collected statistics on drainage on farms for 1920, 1930, and 1969, and statistics on irrigation on farms since 1890. The special censuses of drainage projects were taken decennially from 1920 to 1960 and collected information in only those States where projects existed. Changes in the method for collecting drainage statistics shifted the census year from 1970 to 1972 for the most recent census of drainage projects. The special censuses of irrigation organizations have been taken decennially since 1910 and collect information from irrigation organizations in those States where organizations exist. In addition, a special census of irrigation was taken in 1902; the statistics were published in 1904 in *Bulletin 16* of the Census Bureau.

Drainage on farms. Statistics were collected from all farms in the 48 States and the District of Columbia in the censuses of agriculture for 1920 and 1930. For 1969, statistics were collected from all 50 States for farms with sales of $2,500 and over.

Drainage projects. The date of each special census of drainage projects was January 1, of the census year. The number of States covered in the five censuses of drainage projects taken between 1920 and 1960 has varied from census to census. The New England States, Pennsylvania, and West Virginia have never been included. The number of States included in each census are: 1920, 34 States; 1930, 35 States; 1940, 38 States; 1950, 40 States; and 1960, 39 States.

The special census of drainage projects has always been primarily a census of community or public drainage undertakings and of the larger private drainage undertakings. Variation in the methods employed and the scope of the census have had most effect on the number of projects covered but have not greatly affected the comparability of other items. The major changes have been, beginning with 1950,

(1) the exclusion of projects of under 500 acres, (2) elimination in the enumeration of numerous projects which had been taken over by a later project, and (3) the consolidation into a single report of undertakings under common management; and in 1960, the elimination of drainage undertakings required solely because of the irrigation of the land.

Irrigation. For reasons of comparability, the irrigation data presented here are from the censuses of agriculture.

The States included for series J 87–89 are: Arizona, California, Colorado, Idaho, Kansas, Montana, Nebraska, Nevada, New Mexico, North Dakota, Oklahoma, Oregon, South Dakota, Texas, Utah, Washington, and Wyoming.

For series J 90–91, the 31 States included prior to 1959 are: Alabama, Arkansas, Connecticut, Delaware, Florida, Georgia, Illinois, Indiana, Iowa, Kentucky, Louisiana, Maine, Maryland, Massachusetts, Michigan, Minnesota, Mississippi, Missouri, New Hampshire, New Jersey, New York, North Carolina, Ohio, Pennsylvania, Rhode Island, South Carolina, Tennessee, Vermont, Virginia, West Virginia, and Wisconsin.

J 92–103. Estimated water use, 1900–1960.

Source: U.S. Department of Commerce, Business and Defense Services Administration, *Water Use in the United States, 1900–1980*, March 1960, and Bureau of Domestic Commerce, unpublished data.

These estimates of water use are based on estimates developed initially in 1948 but revised on the basis of information available from Federal surveys and censuses in 1954 and later years. The source publication (cited above) includes estimates of future requirements for 1965, 1970, 1975, and 1980.

The year 1954 was used as a benchmark because of the availability of detailed data on water use during that year, such as the 1954 censuses of manufactures and mineral industries; Inventory of Major Public Water Utilities; Survey of Water Use in Steam Generation of Electric Power by Public Electric Utilities; and Survey of Water Use by the Department of Defense. Adjustments were also made after comparison with surveys of water use by the U.S. Geological Survey in 1950 and 1955, and studies of projections of water requirements by several river basin committees and State water survey commissions.

Related data resulting from later studies have been published by the U.S. Water Resources Council in *The Nation's Water Resources*, 1968, and by the U.S. Geological Survey in a series of quinquennial reports, *Estimated Use of Water in the United States* (circulars 115, 398, 456, 556, and 676) covering the years 1950 through 1970.

J 104–109. Water wells in use, 1900–1962.

Source: U.S. Bureau of Domestic Commerce (formerly Business and Defense Services Administration), unpublished data. (Estimates for 1900–1955 are shown in chart form in Walter L. Picton, "The Water Picture Today," *Water Well Journal*, April 1956.)

In the formulation of these estimates, due consideration has been given to growth in population, the population served by public water supplies, the rural-farm and nonfarm self-served population, and the relative essential water facility requirements to serve them. In addition to population growth, the increase in per capita domestic water use, irrigation requirements, and industrial demands have been considered.

In the absence of measurable data, the level of activity in the field has been gauged by the process of deduction, utilizing the populations of rural and other areas not serviced by public water supplies.

Series J 1–2. Territorial Expansion and Land and Water Area of the United States: 1790 to 1970
[In square miles]

Accession	Territorial expansion		Year	Area		
	Date	Gross area (land and water)		Gross area	Land	Water
		1		2	2a	2b
Total	1970	3,628,066	UNITED STATES			
United States		3,615,122	1970 (Apr. 1)	3,615,122	3,536,855	78,267
Territory in 1790 [1]		888,685	1960 (Apr. 1)	3,615,123	3,540,911	74,212
Louisiana Purchase	1803	827,192	1950 (Apr. 1)	3,615,211	3,552,206	63,005
By treaty with Spain:						
Florida	1819	58,560	CONTERMINOUS U.S. [6]			
Other areas	1819	13,443				
			1960 (Apr. 1)	3,002,261	2,968,054	54,207
Texas	1845	390,143	1950 (Apr. 1)	3,022,387	2,974,726	47,661
Oregon	1846	285,580	1940 (Apr. 1)	3,022,387	2,977,128	45,259
Mexican Cession	1848	529,017	1930 (Apr. 1)	3,022,387	2,977,128	45,259
Gadsden Purchase	1853	29,640	1920 (Jan. 1)	3,022,387	2,969,451	52,936
Alaska	1867	586,412	1910 (Apr. 15)	3,022,387	2,969,565	52,822
Hawaii	1898	6,450				
			1900 (June 1)	3,002,387	2,969,834	52,553
Other areas:			1890 (June 1)	3,022,387	2,969,640	52,747
The Philippines [2]	1898	115,600	1880 (June 1)	3,022,387	2,969,640	52,747
Puerto Rico	1899	3,435	1870 (June 1)	3,022,387	2,969,640	52,747
Guam	1899	212	1860 (June 1)	3,022,387	2,969,640	52,747
American Samoa	1900	76	1850 (June 1)	2,992,747	2,940,042	52,705
Canal Zone [3]	1904	553				
Corn Islands [4]	1914	4	1840 (June 1)	1,788,006	1,749,462	38,544
Virgin Islands of the U.S	1917	133	1830 (June 1)	1,788,006	1,749,462	38,544
Trust Territory of the Pacific Islands [5]	1947	8,489	1820 (Aug. 7)	1,788,006	1,749,462	38,544
All other		42	1810 (Aug. 6)	1,716,003	1,681,828	34,175
			1800 (Aug. 4)	888,811	864,746	24,065
			1790 (Aug. 2)	888,811	864,746	24,065

[1] Includes that part of drainage basin of Red River of the North, south of 49th parallel, sometimes considered part of Louisiana Purchase. [2] Not included in total. Ceded by Spain in 1898, the Philippines constituted a territorial possession of the United States until 1946. Granted independence July 4, 1946. [3] Under jurisdiction of United States in accordance with treaty of Nov. 18, 1903, with Republic of Panama.

[4] Included in total for 1970. Leased (1914) from Republic of Nicaragua for 99 years, but returned April 25, 1971. [5] Under trusteeship with the United States as administering authority. See *Trusteeship Agreement for the Former Japanese Mandated Islands (Documentary Supplement No. 1)* of the Security Council of the United Nations which became effective on July 18, 1947. [6] Excludes Alaska and Hawaii.

Series J 3–7. Area and Acquisition of the Public Domain, United States: 1781 to 1970
[Area in thousands of acres. All areas except Alaska are as computed in 1912 and have not been adjusted for subsequent recomputation of the area of the United States]

Year	Public domain plus acquired land	Year	Public domain plus acquired land	Year and acquisition	Area			Cost ($1,000)
	3		3		Total	Land	Inland water	7
					4	5	6	
1970	761,301	1960 [1]	771,512	Aggregate	1,837,763	1,807,682	30,081	85,079
1969	762,514	1959 [2]	768,640					
1968	755,345	1958	408,553	1867, Alaska Purchase	375,296	365,482	9,814	7,200
1967	760,364	1955	407,896	1853, Gadsden Purchase	18,989	18,962	27	10,000
1966	764,762	1950	[3] 412,000	1850, Purchase from Texas	78,927	78,843	84	15,496
				1848, Mexican Cession [4]	338,681	334,479	4,202	16,295
1965	765,797	1946	[3] 413,000	1846, Oregon Compromise	183,386	180,644	2,742	
1964	770,514	1912	[3] 600,000	1819, Cession from Spain	46,145	43,343	[5] 2,802	6,674
1963	769,903	1880	[3] 900,000	Red River Basin [6]	29,602	29,067	535	
1962	770,797	1850	[3] 1,200,000	1803, Louisiana Purchase [4]	529,912	523,446	6,465	23,214
1961	767,766	1802	[3] 200,000	1781–1802 State cessions	236,826	233,416	3,410	[7] 6,200

[1] Beginning 1960, includes acquired land in Hawaii. [2] Beginning 1959, includes Alaska. [3] Estimated from limited data available. [4] Data for Louisiana Purchase exclude areas eliminated by Treaty of 1819 with Spain. Such areas are included in figures for Mexican Cession. [5] Includes 33,920 acres subsequently recognized as part of State of Texas which is not a public-domain State. [6] Represents drainage basin of Red River of the North, south of 49th parallel. Authorities differ as to method and exact date of its acquisition. Some hold it as part of Louisiana Purchase; others maintain it was acquired from Great Britain. [7] See text.

Series J 8–15. Vacant Lands and Disposal of Public Lands: 1802 to 1970

Year	Vacant public lands	Land granted to States	All entries, selections, patents, etc. [1]			Homestead entries [3]		Final entries [4]
			All original entries and selections [2]	All final entries	Patents and certifications	Original entries		
						Number	Acreage	
	8	9	10	11	12	13	14	15
	Million acres	*1,000 acres*	*1,000 acres*	*1,000 acres*	*1,000 acres*	*Number*	*1,000 acres*	*1,000 acres*
1970	159		124	298	582	13	2	6
1969	417		319	264	821	26	4	8
1968	425		1,171	405	906	33	4	10
1967	426		474	942	1,622	51	7	23
1966	427		1,787	214	3,407	115	16	33
1965	428		2,403	220	768	182	22	30
1964	434		5,696	507	1,224	291	31	63
1963	437		880	254	835	383	46	57
1962	439		2,453	622	756	674	83	51
1961	441		2,211	451	482	615	77	57
1960	438		1,295	270	512	1,077	148	45
1959	438	104,569	303	280	850	1,181	147	42
1958	168		146	257	915	524	70	43
1957	169		180	279	561	662	79	66
1956	170		151	267	629	455	57	42

See footnotes at end of table.

Series J 8–15. Vacant Lands and Disposal of Public Lands: 1802 to 1970—Con.

Year	Vacant public lands	Land granted to States	All entries, selections, patents, etc.[1]			Homestead entries[3]		
			All original entries and selections[2]	All final entries	Patents and certifications	Original entries — Number	Original entries — Acreage	Final entries[4]
	8	9	10	11	12	13	14	15
	Million acres	*1,000 acres*	*1,000 acres*	*1,000 acres*	*1,000 acres*	*Number*	*1,000 acres*	*1,000 acres*
1955	170	------	251	250	539	482	60	37
1954	171	------	306	239	416	474	60	43
1953	171	------	310	177	364	482	61	39
1952	172	------	113	165	374	458	59	38
1951	174	------	121	198	388	363	49	63
1950	170	------	142	150	492	523	73	46
1949	170	------	134	116	390	681	82	40
1948	171	------	117	56	287	635	78	18
1947	170	------	76	53	403	474	55	26
1946	170	------	27	61	154	143	18	29
1945	170	------	40	61	217	182	22	35
1944	168	------	91	85	402	157	20	51
1943	169	------	63	168	637	211	29	102
1942	174	------	135	252	1,055	283	37	188
1941	172	------	76	491	1,039	400	51	390
1940	(NA)	------	54	756	1,904	349	46	652
1939	(NA)	------	302	1,198	1,982	378	66	1,089
1938	(NA)	2	131	1,478	1,944	447	78	1,362
1937	(NA)	1	125	2,026	2,184	561	111	1,915
1936	(NA)	200	426	1,938	1,359	1,209	357	1,765
1935	(NA)	(Z)	1,759	1,772	1,610	3,297	1,166	1,640
1934	166	3	3,585	1,225	1,362	7,507	2,787	1,124
1933	172	193	3,118	980	1,866	7,527	2,642	907
1932	173	77	4,552	1,333	2,013	10,639	3,914	1,210
1931	177	2	5,219	1,537	2,126	12,640	4,757	1,353
1930	179	1	5,435	1,577	2,253	12,708	4,723	1,371
1929	190	100	4,613	2,030	2,648	11,598	4,178	1,701
1928	194	252	3,726	2,168	2,519	10,429	3,367	1,816
1927	194	55	3,595	3,011	4,586	10,500	3,237	2,584
1926	5 196	------	3,243	3,962	4,600	10,354	2,875	3,451
1925	185	1	3,641	4,489	5,627	11,010	3,041	4,049
1924	187	(Z)	4,564	5,229	9,082	13,886	3,873	4,791
1923	186	------	6,415	6,201	10,352	18,942	5,524	5,594
1922	183	------	10,367	8,074	13,761	29,263	8,980	7,307
1921	190	(Z)	15,632	8,772	10,930	43,813	13,662	7,727
1920	200	------	16,437	9,778	13,327	48,532	13,511	8,373
1919	213	------	11,871	------	------	39,341	10,204	6,525
1918	222	------	10,147	------	------	35,875	7,420	8,236
1917	231	(Z)	16,202	------	------	58,896	12,021	8,497
1916	255	4	18,708	------	------	65,282	13,628	7,278
1915	280	2	16,861	------	------	62,360	12,440	7,181
1914	291	------	16,523	------	------	62,229	12,117	9,291
1913	298	------	15,867	------	------	57,800	11,222	10,009
1912	315	(6)	14,575	------	------	52,991	13,624	4,306
1911	327	------	19,211	------	------	70,720	17,639	4,620
1910	344	17,150	26,391	------	------	98,598	18,329	3,796
1909	363	(Z)	19,893	------	------	75,445	12,302	3,699
1908	387	16	19,090	------	------	87,057	13,586	4,243
1907	406	(Z)	20,998	------	------	93,957	14,755	3,741
1906	424	3,114	19,431	------	------	89,600	13,975	3,527
1905	449	(Z)	17,057	------	------	70,344	12,896	3,419
1904	474	20	16,332	------	------	69,175	10,171	3,233
1903	------	------	22,824	------	------	80,188	11,193	3,577
1902	------	(Z)	19,372	------	------	98,829	14,033	4,343
1901	------	------	15,453	------	------	68,648	9,497	5,241
1900	------	8	13,391	------	------	61,270	8,478	3,478
1899	------	50	9,091	------	------	45,776	6,178	3,134
1898	------	5,600	8,422	------	------	44,980	6,207	3,095
1897	------	(Z)	7,754	------	------	33,250	4,452	2,778
1896	------	------	13,174	------	------	36,548	4,831	2,790
1895	------	69	8,364	------	------	37,336	5,009	2,981
1894	------	8,470	10,377	------	------	56,632	8,047	2,930
1893	------	------	11,802	------	------	48,436	6,809	3,477
1892	------	8	13,567	------	------	55,113	7,716	3,260
1891	------	(Z)	10,357	------	------	37,602	5,040	3,955
1890	------	7,678	12,666	------	------	40,244	5,532	4,061
1889	------	15,367	17,026	------	------	42,183	6,029	3,682
1888	------	(Z)	24,161	------	------	46,236	6,677	3,175
1887	------	------	25,111	------	------	52,028	7,594	2,749
1886	------	------	20,992	------	------	61,638	9,145	2,664
1885	------	------	20,114	------	------	60,877	7,416	3,033
1884	------	46	26,834	------	------	54,982	7,832	2,946
1883	------	------	19,031	------	------	56,565	8,172	2,504
1882	------	------	13,999	------	------	45,331	6,348	2,219
1881	------	276	10,763	------	------	36,999	5,028	1,928

Year	Land granted to States	All original entries and selections[1][2]	Homestead Original entries — Number	Homestead Final entries[4]
	9	10	13	15
	1,000 acres	*1,000 acres*	*Number*	*1,000 acres*
1880	(Z)	9,152	47,293	1,938
1879	------	8,724	41,005	2,071
1878	------	7,210	35,630	2,663
1877	------	3,495	18,675	2,408
1876	------	4,292	25,104	2,591
1875	3,842	3,792	20,668	2,069
1874	------	4,784	29,126	1,586
1873	------	6,386	31,561	1,225
1872	------	7,248	38,742	707
1871	------	7,119	39,768	629
1870	------	6,663	33,972	520
1869	------	6,678	25,628	504
1868	------	------	23,746	355
1867	4	------	16,957	------
1866	226	------	15,355	------
1865	------	------	8,924	------
1864	4,955	------	9,405	------
1863	------	------	8,223	------
1862	9,420	------	------	------
1861	3,052	------	------	------
1859	3,498	------	------	------
1857	2,974	------	------	------
1855	46	------	------	------
1853	5,587	------	------	------
1850	55,401	------	------	------
1849	9,491	------	------	------
1846	1,081	------	------	------
1845	2,076	------	------	------
1841	7,807	------	------	------
1836	2,146	------	------	------
1832	24	------	------	------
1831	6	------	------	------
1827	46	------	------	------
1826	25	------	------	------
1823	92	------	------	------
1820	1,317	------	------	------
1819	986	------	------	------
1818	1,186	------	------	------
1817	824	------	------	------
1816	740	------	------	------
1812	807	------	------	------
1803	793	------	------	------
1802	24	------	------	------

NA Not available.   Z Less than 1,000 acres.   [1] Includes homesteads. [2] Previous to 1911 the data included, in addition to original entries and selections, some classes of final entries and patents.   [3] Except on ceded Indian lands.   [4] Exclusive of commuted homesteads.   [5] The increase in area over 1925 was reported as the result of a "special check" of field office records which was "used as a basis for a complete revision of the vacant land statistics."   [6] Grants of unsurveyed lands to Wisconsin for forestry purposes; area not determined.

Series J 16–19. Lands Under Jurisdiction of Bureau of Indian Affairs: 1881 to 1970

[In thousands of acres]

Year	Total	Indian Trust allotted	Indian Tribal	Government owned	Year	Total	Indian Trust allotted	Indian Tribal	Year	Total	Indian Trust allotted	Indian Tribal
	16	17	18	19		16	17	18		16	17	18
1970	55,408	10,698	39,642	5,068	1937	34,620	....	34,620	1909	49,566	....	49,566
1969	55,351	10,757	39,641	4,952	1936	51,057	....	51,057	1908	52,013	....	52,013
1968	55,427	10,894	39,586	4,947					1907	53,549	....	53,549
1967	55,413	11,019	39,443	4,951	1935	50,696	....	50,696	1906	55,831	....	55,831
1966	55,294	11,121	39,251	4,922	1934	49,388	....	49,388				
					1933	52,651	....	47,398	1905	58,202	....	58,202
1965	55,319	11,287	39,097	4,935	1932	46,795	....	46,795	1904	72,392	....	72,392
1964	55,134	11,450	38,975	4,709					1903	83,426	8,823	74,603
1963	55,196	11,607	38,877	4,713	1930	32,097	....	32,097	1902	75,149	....	75,149
1962	55,247	11,763	38,814	4,669	1929	32,015	....	32,015	1901	76,117	....	....
1961	57,107	11,958	40,538	4,612	1928	30,262	....	30,262				
					1927	31,420	....	31,420	1900	84,602	6,737	77,865
1960	58,080	12,235	41,226	4,618	1926	31,791	....	31,791	1897	82,770	....	82,770
1959	56,870	12,560	39,676	4,634					1896	83,405	....	83,405
1958	57,023	12,896	42,304	1,823	1925	31,582	....	31,582				
1957	53,331	13,223	39,549	558	1924	34,948	....	34,948	1895	84,571	....	84,571
1956	53,376	13,328	39,465	583	1923	34,988	....	34,988	1894	85,581	....	85,581
					1922	34,979	....	34,979	1893	85,873	....	85,873
1955	53,771	13,662	39,487	622	1921	35,502	....	35,502	1892	92,478	....	92,478
1954	54,108	13,652	39,882	574					1891	91,146	....	91,146
1953	55,406	14,251	40,178	977	1920	72,661	37,159	35,502				
1949	56,005	16,534	38,608	863	1919	72,564	36,986	35,560	1890	104,314	....	104,314
1946	56,567	17,143	37,524	1,901	1918	71,094	36,861	34,233	1889	116,386	....	116,386
					1917	71,306	35,740	35,566	1888	118,484	....	118,484
1945	55,363	16,796	37,251	1,317	1916	71,978	35,565	36,413	1887	136,395	....	136,395
1944	56,577	17,474	37,233	1,869					1886	135,978	....	135,978
1943	55,657	17,441	36,957	1,258	1915	68,103	34,768	33,334				
1942	55,410	17,503	36,602	1,305	1914	69,900	34,072	35,828	1885	137,725	....	137,725
1941	55,392	17,762	36,276	1,354	1913	72,147	33,571	38,576	1884	137,767	....	137,767
					1912	71,917	32,414	39,503	1882	143,526	....	143,526
1940	55,406	17,574	36,047	1,786	1911	72,535	32,272	40,263	1881	155,632	....	155,632
1939	54,839	17,594	35,402	1,842								
					1910	72,146	31,094	41,052				

Series J 20. Public Land Sales: 1800 to 1860

[In thousands]

Year	Acres 20	Year	Acres 20	Year	Acres 20	Year	Acres 20	Year	Acres 20	Year	Acres 20
1860	2,543.4	1847	2,521.3	1835	12,564.5	1822	710.0	1810			285.8
1859	4,011.7	1846	2,263.7	1834	4,658.2	1821	782.5	1809			275.0
1858	3,663.6			1833	3,856.2			1808			209.2
1857	4,220.1	1845	1,843.5	1832	2,462.3	1820	814.0	1807			320.9
1856	5,247.0	1844	1,754.8	1831	2,777.9	1819	2,968.4	1806			506.0
		1843	1,605.3			1818	3,491.0				
1855	11,959.8	1842	1,129.2	1830	1,929.7	1817	1,886.2	1805			582.0
1854	12,823.0	1841	1,164.8	1829	1,244.9	1816	1,742.5	1804			398.2
1853	3,787.1			1828	965.6			1803			174.2
1852	894.8	1840	2,236.9	1827	926.7	1815	1,306.4	1802			271.1
1851	2,055.9	1839	4,976.4	1826	848.1	1814	1,176.1	1801			497.9
		1838	3,414.9			1813	505.6				
1850	1,405.8	1837	5,601.1	1825	999.0	1812	386.1	1800			67.8
1849	1,329.9	1836	20,074.9	1824	737.0	1811	575.1				
1848	1,887.6			1823	652.1						

Series J 21–25. Public Land Grants by United States to Aid in Construction of Railroads, Wagon Roads, Canals, etc.: 1823 to 1871

[In thousands of acres]

Year	Total grants	Railroads	Wagon roads	Canals	River improvements	Year	Total grants	Railroads	Wagon roads	Canals	River improvements
	21	22	23	24	25		21	22	23	24	25
1871	3,253	3,253	....	....	....	1853	3,379	2,629	....	750	....
1870	129	129	....	....	....	1852	1,773	1,773	....	....	....
1869	105	....	105	....	....	1851	3,752	3,752	....	....	....
1867	25,173	23,535	1,538	100	....						
1866	200	....	....	200	....	1847	1,845	840	....	....	1,005
1865	42,794	41,452	941	401	....	1838	139	....	....	139	....
1864	2,349	2,349	....	....	....						
1863	31,401	30,877	524	....	....	1828	1,338	....	....	938	400
1857	6,689	6,689	....	....	....	1827	2,273	....	202	2,071	....
1856	14,085	14,085	....	....	....	1823	49	....	49	....	....

Series J 26–32. Revenues From Public-Domain, Revested, and Acquired Land: 1785 to 1970

[In millions of dollars. For years ending June 30]

Period	Total (26)	Sales of public domain (27)	Fees and commissions (28)	Timber sales [1] (O & C, and public domain) (29)	Mineral leases [2] (30)	Outer Continental Shelf leases (31)	Miscellaneous [3] (32)
Total	7,033.2	253.5	109.1	703.1	1,976.6	3,352.5	638.5
1970	407.4	2.1	4.5	65.4	127.1	186.9	21.4
1969	651.1	1.8	4.9	69.7	123.3	428.3	23.1
1968	1,158.9	2.5	3.9	56.2	113.8	961.3	21.3
1967	821.5	2.6	3.3	47.1	110.2	637.3	21.1
1966	433.7	2.3	3.9	47.6	108.0	248.3	23.6
1965	234.4	3.1	3.8	44.9	107.3	53.5	21.9
1964	199.1	3.2	3.7	47.2	107.1	16.5	21.4
1963	530.7	3.4	3.0	33.6	102.6	366.8	21.3
1962	173.5	3.6	2.8	34.7	105.2	11.6	15.6
1961	159.2	4.3	2.5	32.1	89.2	7.3	23.9
1960	371.1	5.1	1.8	36.4	84.1	229.5	14.3
1959	136.7	4.2	1.3	31.8	83.5	3.4	12.5
1958	127.4	3.0	1.2	24.6	81.4	3.5	13.7
1957	112.1	3.4	1.0	21.4	72.3	2.2	11.7
1956	154.8	2.3	.8	24.9	61.6	53.8	11.4
1955	239.5	1.9	.7	25.0	60.0	142.4	9.6
1954	77.5	1.2	.6	13.4	52.5	---------	9.8
1953	66.8	1.0	.4	13.8	43.5	---------	8.0
1952	64.5	.7	.8	9.6	41.9	---------	11.6
1951	49.1	.5	.4	7.8	35.0	---------	5.5
1950	36.2	.5	.4	4.3	27.0	---------	4.1
1949	37.1	.5	.3	3.9	29.0	---------	3.5
1948	33.3	.3	.2	4.7	24.4	---------	3.9
1947	21.0	.1	.1	3.0	15.1	---------	2.6
1946	13.8	.1	.1	---------	10.0	---------	3.6
1945	14.1	.2	.1	---------	10.1	---------	3.9
1944	15.2	.1	.1	---------	10.9	---------	4.2
1943	10.5	.1	(Z)	---------	7.2	---------	3.2
1942	9.9	.1	(Z)	---------	6.9	---------	2.8
1941	8.7	.2	.1	---------	5.7	---------	2.8
1940	7.5	.1	.1	---------	5.2	---------	2.2
1939	7.8	.2	.1	---------	5.7	---------	1.7
1938	8.4	.1	.1	---------	6.5	---------	1.7
1937	7.4	.1	.1	---------	5.6	---------	1.6
1936	5.2	.1	.1	---------	4.4	---------	.6
1935	4.8	.1	.2	---------	3.9	---------	.6
1934	4.0	.1	.3	---------	3.2	---------	.5
1933	3.9	.1	.3	---------	3.3	---------	.2
1932	4.1	.2	.3	---------	3.2	---------	.4
1931	4.8	.3	.4	---------	3.5	---------	.6
1930	6.8	.4	.4	---------	4.7	---------	1.2
1929	6.2	.3	.5	---------	3.9	---------	1.5
1928	6.7	.4	.4	---------	4.7	---------	1.2
1927	9.2	.6	.5	---------	6.7	---------	1.4
1926	11.4	.7	.4	---------	8.4	---------	1.9
1925	10.8	0.6	0.6	---------	8.3	---------	1.3
1924	16.4	.6	.7	---------	13.6	---------	1.5
1923	10.7	.6	.8	---------	7.6	---------	1.6
1922	11.8	.9	1.1	---------	8.8	---------	1.0
1921	14.5	2.0	1.7	---------	9.7	---------	1.5
1920	6.1	2.0	1.6	---------	---------	---------	2.6
1919	4.3	1.5	1.2	---------	---------	---------	1.6
1918	5.4	2.1	1.2	---------	---------	---------	2.2
1917	6.1	1.9	1.6	---------	---------	---------	2.6
1916	5.4	1.8	1.7	---------	---------	---------	2.0
1915	5.4	2.2	1.6	---------	---------	---------	1.6
1914	6.1	2.6	1.7	---------	---------	---------	1.9
1913	7.0	2.7	1.5	---------	---------	---------	2.7
1912	10.0	5.4	1.2	---------	---------	---------	3.3
1911	11.1	5.8	1.5	---------	---------	---------	3.8
1910	11.5	6.3	2.0	---------	---------	---------	3.1
1909	12.2	7.7	1.5	---------	---------	---------	3.0
1908	12.7	9.8	1.7	---------	---------	---------	1.2
1907	11.6	7.7	1.8	---------	---------	---------	2.0
1906	7.6	4.9	1.6	---------	---------	---------	1.1
1905	7.0	4.8	1.3	---------	---------	---------	.9
1904	9.3	7.4	1.3	---------	---------	---------	.5
1903	11.0	9.0	1.6	---------	---------	---------	.5
1902	6.3	4.1	1.7	---------	---------	---------	.4
1901	5.0	3.0	1.3	---------	---------	---------	.7
1900	4.4	2.9	1.2	---------	---------	---------	.3
1899	3.1	1.7	.9	---------	---------	---------	.5
1898	2.3	1.3	.9	---------	---------	---------	.1
1897	2.1	.9	.7	---------	---------	---------	.5
1896	2.1	1.1	.8	---------	---------	---------	.3
1895	2.0	1.1	.8	---------	---------	---------	.2
1894	2.8	1.7	1.0	---------	---------	---------	.1
1893	4.5	3.2	1.0	---------	---------	---------	.3
1892	4.9	3.3	1.1	---------	---------	---------	.5
1891	5.4	4.2	.9	---------	---------	---------	.3
1890	7.8	6.3	1.1	---------	---------	---------	.3
1889	9.7	8.0	1.3	---------	---------	---------	.4
1888	13.5	11.2	1.5	---------	---------	---------	.8
1887	12.3	9.2	1.5	---------	---------	---------	1.5
1886	9.0	5.8	1.7	---------	---------	---------	1.6
1885	8.6	6.2	1.5	---------	---------	---------	.9
1884	12.8	10.3	1.5	---------	---------	---------	.9
1883	11.7	9.7	1.4	---------	---------	---------	.6
1882	8.4	6.6	1.1	---------	---------	---------	.6
1881	5.4	3.5	.9	---------	---------	---------	1.0
May 20, 1785 to June 30, 1880	208.1	---------	---------	---------	---------	---------	208.1

Z Less than $50,000.

[1] Excludes revenues of earlier years totaling $21.4 million, which are included under "Miscellaneous." Annual data for years prior to 1947 are not available separately; cumulative totals are as follows (in millions): 1941–46, $8.8; 1931–40, $4.3; 1921–30, $7.5; and 1911–20, $0.8.

[2] Act of Feb. 25, 1920.

[3] Represents sales of Indian lands, grazing revenues, rental of land, mineral leasing under special laws, and other miscellaneous revenues. Also includes sales of timber for years prior to 1947 (see note 1).

Series J 33–34. Livestock Permitted to Graze on National Forest System Lands: 1905–1970

[In thousands. Excludes animals under 6 months of age. Data are for fiscal years prior to 1921, calendar years thereafter]

Year	Cattle, horses, and swine (33)	Sheep and goats (34)
1970	1,340	1,775
1969	1,338	1,861
1968	1,330	1,904
1967	1,313	1,969
1966	1,301	2,061
1965	1,280	2,102
1964	1,268	2,196
1963	1,243	2,270
1962	1,239	2,357
1961	1,219	2,479
1960	1,241	2,567
1959	1,238	2,614
1958	1,296	2,689
1957	1,304	2,703
1956	1,340	2,821
1955	1,350	2,916
1954	1,356	3,011
1953	1,108	2,964
1952	1,096	3,000
1951	1,088	3,013
1950	1,092	3,006
1949	1,126	3,092
1948	1,153	3,322
1947	1,162	3,403
1946	1,203	3,713
1945	1,206	3,889
1944	1,225	4,280
1943	1,212	4,539
1942	1,191	4,758
1941	1,176	4,787
1940	1,177	4,949
1939	1,209	5,132
1938	1,250	5,307
1937	1,284	5,485
1936	1,311	5,645
1935	1,345	5,691
1934	1,419	6,161
1933	1,399	6,162
1932	1,397	6,321
1931	1,376	6,608
1930	1,358	6,714
1929	1,399	6,964
1928	1,415	6,784
1927	1,486	6,704
1926	1,559	6,503
1925	1,621	6,432
1924	1,753	6,597
1923	1,864	6,712
1922	1,987	6,892
1921	2,080	6,980
1920	2,217	7,881
1919	2,234	7,996
1918	2,243	8,512
1917	2,054	7,636
1916	1,861	7,886
1915	1,727	7,284
1914	1,620	7,619
1913	1,557	7,868
1912	1,503	7,552
1911	1,448	7,449
1910	1,498	7,649
1909	1,586	7,820
1908	1,382	7,087
1907	1,200	6,657
1906	1,015	5,762
1905	692	1,710

Series J 35–40.   Grazing on Public-Domain Lands: 1935 to 1970

[In thousands.   Data are for fiscal years except as noted]

Year	Receipts			Animal-unit-months of use [2]		
	Total [1]	In grazing districts	Outside grazing districts	Total	Cattle and horses	Sheep and goats
	35	36	37	38	39	40
1970	$5,380	$4,647	$733	10,981	8,626	2,354
1969	5,257	4,663	594	11,238	8,821	2,416
1968	4,326	3,788	538	11,665	9,060	2,605
1967	4,287	3,718	569	11,635	8,948	2,686
1966	4,371	3,817	554	11,801	9,064	2,738
1965	3,990	3,467	523	11,773	8,830	2,943
1964	4,142	3,611	531	11,861	8,713	3,148
1963	3,772	3,355	418	12,051	8,710	3,341
1962	2,780	2,190	590	12,000	8,557	3,443
1961	2,982	2,311	671	12,097	8,478	3,619
1960	3,488	2,729	759	12,454	8,738	3,716
1959	3,228	2,713	515	14,750	9,898	4,852
1958	2,763	2,388	376	14,797	9,919	4,878
1957	2,286	1,902	384	14,661	9,725	4,936
1956	2,386	2,050	355	15,301	10,223	5,078
1955	2,219	1,879	339	15,367	10,186	5,181
1954	2,039	1,678	359	15,686	10,371	5,315
1953	2,095	1,764	328	15,780	10,483	5,297
1952	$1,985	$1,658	$322	15,403	10,157	5,246
1951	1,694	1,382	306	14,331	9,211	5,120
1950	1,534	1,146	383	14,461	9,205	5,256
1949	1,239	1,060	173	14,522	9,117	5,405
1948	1,415	1,165	244	14,726	9,078	5,648
1947	1,046	819	221	14,993	9,195	5,798
1946	964	736	228	15,254	---------	---------
1945	996	765	231	15,572	---------	---------
1944	1,015	813	202	15,745	---------	---------
1943	979	785	194	15,061	---------	---------
1942	1,095	900	195	15,271	---------	---------
1941	1,113	922	191	15,369	---------	---------
1940	747	595	152	13,832	---------	---------
1939	1,038	886	152	13,789	---------	---------
1938	850	800	49	13,376	---------	---------
1937	488	415	73	14,383	---------	---------
1936	48	48	---------	11,106	---------	---------
1935	1	1	---------	6,507	---------	---------

[1] Includes minor receipts from grazing on privately owned lands within grazing districts (Pierce Act) which were administered by Bureau of Land Management.

[2] Beginning 1960, data are for calendar years.

Series J 41–49.   Oil and Gas Leases of Public–Domain Lands—Acreage, Receipts, and Output: 1920 to 1970

[Excludes acquired lands, military and naval oil reserves, and submerged lands.   Data are for fiscal years, except as noted]

Year or period	Number in effect	Acreage under lease	Receipts			Volume of output [2]			
			Total	Rentals [1]	Royalties [2]	Total petroleum equivalent [3]	Petroleum	Natural gas	Gasoline and butane
	41	42	43	44	45	46	47	48	49
	1,000	Mil. acres	Mil. dol.	Mil. dol.	Mil. dol.	Mil. bbl.	Mil. bbl.	Bil. cu. ft.	Mil. gal.
1970	99.0	63.0	124.5	34.0	90.5	364.6	196	934	542
1969	97.4	61.8	122.3	32.9	89.4	363.7	201	903	513
1968	93.0	56.4	111.5	25.7	85.8	369.2	201	942	470
1967	91.3	53.9	109.8	26.8	83.0	372.6	193	976	712
1966	98.2	61.3	108.2	30.4	77.8	333.3	187	807	493
1965	100.3	64.1	109.3	34.9	74.4	310.0	181	711	438
1964	104.5	67.4	109.8	36.6	73.2	301.7	180	665	457
1963	114.0	75.5	107.4	35.9	71.5	285.9	178	588	414
1962	129.9	93.3	107.2	39.8	67.4	267.7	171	518	436
1961	132.8	101.7	101.5	32.9	68.6	268.4	169	539	401
1960	139.5	113.7	85.9	25.4	60.5	249.7	156	513	344
1959 [4]	132.0	107.1	84.3	26.5	57.8	231.0	147	460	304
1958	110.0	73.7	78.9	24.3	54.6	213.3	137	418	280
1957	104.1	72.0	72.5	17.6	54.9	209.9	135	418	218
1956	98.5	70.3	62.3	15.9	46.4	184.2	127	313	211
1955	95.9	71.7	59.7	18.2	41.5	168.5	118	274	203
1954	86.6	64.2	53.4	14.2	39.2	159.5	111	261	211
1953	78.0	58.5	43.4	8.3	35.1	146.9	105	223	197
1952	63.0	48.4	46.7	18.0	28.7	127.2	94	173	184
1951	42.5	32.9	34.3	6.8	27.5	121.6	92	152	179
1950	28.9	23.6	26.7	2.8	23.9	107.6	84	121	142
1949	21.3	19.0	28.4	5.8	22.6	98.2	74	125	141
1948	13.4	10.7	24.1	—.5	24.6	102.5	78	125	156
1947	12.5	7.9	14.5	—1.4	15.9	89.2	70	95	142
1946	8.8	6.0	9.3	—.6	9.9	78.4	62	81	120
1945	7.0	4.6	9.4	1.8	7.6	75.7	58	88	126
1944	5.3	3.1	10.3	3.3	7.0	71.4	54	92	85
1943	4.5	2.8	6.6	----------	6.6	69.7	53	88	87
1942	4.3	3.3	6.3	.8	5.5	62.1	45	91	82
1941	5.3	5.5	5.3	—.1	5.4	62.0	46	87	61
1931–1940	----------	----------	----------	----------	44.4	462.4	328	698	759
1920–1930	----------	----------	----------	----------	61.1	302.3	260	198	390

[1] Includes bonuses.   Rentals are estimates derived by deducting royalties from total receipts.

[2] Calendar year data.

[3] Includes gasoline and butane on an equal basis with petroleum (42 gallons per barrel), and 6,000 cubic feet of natural gas equal to 1 barrel of petroleum.

[4] Beginning 1959, includes Alaska.

Series J 50–65. Land Utilization, by Type: 1850 to 1969

[In millions of acres]

		Land in farms										Land not in farms				
Year	Total land area	Total	Cropland			Grass-land pasture	Farm woodland			Special uses	Other	Total	Grazing land	Forest land not used for grazing	Special uses	Other
			Total	Used for crops	Idle or in cover crops		Total	Pastured	Not pastured							
	50	51	52	53	54	55	56	57	58	59	60	61	62	63	64	65
1969	2,264	1,064	384	333	51	540	112	62	50	9	19	1,200	288	475	169	268
1964	2,266	1,110	387	335	52	547	146	82	64	9	21	1,156	293	443	158	262
1959 *	2,271	1,124	392	359	33	532	163	93	70	10	27	1,147	319	438	141	249
1954	1,904	1,158	399	380	19	526	197	121	76	13	23	746	353	238	87	68
1950	1,904	1,159	409	387	22	485	220	135	85	21	24	745	400	201	81	63
1945	1,905	1,142	403	379	24	529	166	95	71	20	24	763	428	186	76	73
1940	1,905	1,061	399	363	36	461	157	100	57	44		844	504	203	137	
1935	1,903	1,055	416	375	41	410	185	108	77	44		848	533	184	131	
1930	1,903	987	413	379	34	379	150	85	65	21	24	916	578	208	53	77
1925	1,903	924	391	365	26	331	144	77	67	58		979	646	203	130	
1920	1,903	956	402	374	28	328	168	77	91	58		947	661	160	126	
1910	1,903	879	347	324	23	284	191	98	93	57		1,024	739	162	123	
1900	1,903	839	319			276	191	87	103	54		1,064	768	175	121	
1890	1,903	623	248			144	190			41		1,280	818	344	118	
1880	1,903	536	188			122	190			36		1,367	883	368	116	
1870	1,903	408	189				219					1,495				
1860	1,903	407	163				244					1,496				
1850	1,884	294	113				181					1,590				

* Denotes first year for which figures include Alaska and Hawaii.

Series J 66–80. Private and Public Land Ownership, by Major Uses: 1920 to 1969

[In millions of acres]

	Total land area					Private land					Public land [1]				
Year	All land	Crop-land	Pasture and grazing land	Forest and wood-land not grazed	Other land	Total	Crop-land	Pasture and graz-ing land	Forest and wood-land not grazed	Other land	Total	Crop-land	Pasture and graz-ing land	Forest and wood-land not grazed	Other land
	66	67	68	69	70	71	72	73	74	75	76	77	78	79	80
1969	2,264	384	890	525	465	1,367	381	621	271	94	897	3	269	254	371
1964	2,266	387	922	507	450	1,378	384	660	253	81	888	3	262	254	369
1959*	2,271	392	944	501	434	1,385	389	659	255	82	886	3	285	246	352
1954	1,904	399	1,000	314	191	1,399	396	704	211	88	505	3	296	103	103
1950	1,904	409	1,020	286	189	1,399	405	724	184	86	505	4	296	102	103
1945	1,905	403	1,052	265	185	1,396	401	748	156	91	509	2	304	109	94
1940	1,905	399	1,065	260	181	1,404	398	766	150	90	501	1	299	110	91
1930	1,903	413	1,042	273	175	1,409	411	745	168	85	494	2	297	105	90
1920	1,903	402	1,066	251	184	1,404	401	766	145	92	499	1	300	106	92

* Denotes first year for which figures include Alaska and Hawaii.   [1] Includes land owned by State, county, municipal, or other local governments as well as Federal lands.

Series J 81–91. Agricultural Land Drainage and Irrigation: 1890 to 1969

[In thousands of acres, except number of farms and projects]

	Drainage				Irrigation						
	Drainage on farms [1]		Drainage projects [2]		Total		17 Western States			All other States [3]	
Year	Number of farms with artificial drainage	Acreage drained	Number of projects	Acreage in drainage projects	Number of farms with irrigated land	Acreage irrigated	Number of farms with irrigated land	Land in irrigated farms	Total acreage irrigated	Number of farms with irrigated land	Total acreage irrigated
	81	82	83	84	85	86	87	88	89	90	91
1969	[4] 338,696	59,551	(⁵)	(⁵)	257,147	39,122	205,848	216,189	34,786	51,299	4,336
1964					297,387	37,056	233,040	226,334	33,208	64,347	3,848
1959			[6] 8,461	[6] 101,870	307,783	33,163	262,614	211,564	30,738	45,169	2,425
1954					320,236	29,552	279,896	188,898	26,971	40,340	2,581
1950			14,533	[7] 102,688	305,061	25,787	281,476	166,074	24,271	23,585	1,516
1945					288,195	20,539	270,629		19,431	17,566	1,108
1940			39,597	86,967	299,604	17,983	283,089	110,942	17,243	16,515	740
1930	651,172	44,524	67,927	84,408		14,689	258,463	77,083	14,086		603
1920	924,810	53,025	56,949	65,495		14,482	215,152		[8] 13,883		599
1910						11,667	159,801		[8] 11,259		408
1900						7,789	109,298		7,543		246
1890						3,717	54,136		3,632		85

[1] Data are from the censuses of agriculture, which represent direct enumeration of farms. Acreage drained figures in series J 82 are largely duplicated in series J 84.
[2] Data are from the special censuses of drainage projects.
[3] For 1910, 1920, and 1930, Arkansas and Louisiana only. For 1940, 1945, and 1950, 31 States and D.C. For 1954, 31 States. For 1959, 32 States including Hawaii. For 1964 and 1969, 33 States including Alaska and Hawaii.
[4] Data are for farms with sales of $2,500 and over (Classes 1–5).
[5] Recent changes in census procedures for collecting drainage project statistics have shifted the census year from 1969 to 1971 and limited the projects enumerated to publicly organized projects.
[6] Census date for Census of Drainage Projects is January 1, 1960.
[7] Includes 4,110,000 acres reported drained by irrigation organizations.
[8] Data interpolated from the special censuses of irrigation organizations for 1910 and 1920.

Series J 92–103. Estimated Water Use: 1900 to 1970

[In billions of gallons, daily average]

Year	Total water use		Irrigation [1]		Public water utilities		Self-supplied use					
							Rural domestic [2]		Industrial and miscellaneous [3]		Steam electric utilities	
	Total	Ground	Total	Ground	Total	Ground	Total	Ground	Total	Ground	Total	Ground
	92	93	94	95	96	97	98	99	100	101	102	103
1970	327.30	54.27	119.18	33.13	27.03	6.65	4.34	4.13	55.95	10.24	120.80	0.12
1969	403.30	71.87	156.82	43.39	26.60	6.56	6.82	6.47	83.44	15.32	129.62	.13
1968	395.40	70.48	154.64	42.57	26.20	6.49	6.74	6.39	80.88	14.90	126.94	.13
1967	387.50	69.08	152.46	41.76	25.80	6.42	6.66	6.31	78.32	14.47	124.26	.12
1966	379.60	67.68	150.28	40.95	25.40	6.35	6.58	6.22	75.76	14.04	121.58	.12
1965	269.62	48.57	110.85	30.04	23.74	5.96	4.08	3.86	46.41	8.63	84.54	.08
1964	361.94	64.67	145.48	39.16	24.40	6.16	6.40	6.03	70.80	13.21	114.86	.11
1963	352.18	63.04	142.86	38.18	23.80	6.04	6.30	5.91	68.40	12.80	110.82	.11
1962	344.48	62.09	141.16	37.58	23.31	6.00	6.22	5.81	66.62	12.55	107.17	.15
1961	334.72	60.46	138.54	36.60	22.71	5.88	6.12	5.70	64.22	12.14	103.13	.14
1960*	322.90	58.17	135.00	35.24	22.00	5.68	6.00	5.58	61.20	11.57	98.70	.10
1958	299.26	54.02	127.52	32.78	19.72	5.12	5.76	5.31	56.40	10.72	89.86	.09
1955	263.80	47.79	116.30	29.08	16.30	4.27	5.40	4.91	49.20	9.45	76.60	.08
1950	202.70	35.19	100.00	19.80	14.10	3.78	4.60	4.09	38.10	7.47	45.90	.05
1946	165.74	27.88	86.44	15.04	12.00	3.25	3.50	3.06	33.00	6.50	30.80	.03
1945	170.46	28.33	83.06	14.12	12.00	3.28	3.20	2.78	41.00	8.12	31.20	.03
1944	178.43	29.19	80.65	13.55	12.00	3.30	3.18	2.76	48.00	9.55	34.60	.03
1940	136.43	22.56	71.03	11.22	10.10	2.82	3.10	2.64	29.00	5.86	23.20	.02
1930	110.50	18.18	60.20	9.09	8.00	2.30	2.90	2.40	21.00	4.37	18.40	.02
1920	91.54	15.78	55.94	8.17	6.00	1.79	2.40	1.94	18.00	3.87	9.20	.01
1910	66.44	11.68	39.04	5.27	4.70	1.49	2.20	1.76	14.00	3.15	6.50	.01
1900	40.19	7.28	20.19	2.22	3.00	1.05	2.00	1.60	10.00	2.40	5.00	.01

* Denotes first year for which figures include Alaska and Hawaii.
[1] Total take, including delivery losses but not including reservoir evaporation.
[2] Rural farm and nonfarm household and garden use, and water for farm stock and dairies.

[3] For 1900–1960, includes manufacturing industries, mineral industries, rural commercial industries, air conditioning, resorts, hotels, motels, military and other State and Federal agencies, and other miscellaneous uses; thereafter, includes manufacturing, mining and mineral processing, ordnance, and construction.

Series J 104–109. Water Wells in Use: 1900 to 1962

[In thousands]

Year	Total	Domestic wells		Public water supplies	Industrial and miscellaneous	Irrigation	Year	Total	Domestic wells		Public water supplies	Industrial and miscellaneous	Irrigation
		Farm	Non-farm						Farm	Non-farm			
	104	105	106	107	108	109		104	105	106	107	108	109
1962	14,751	5,354	8,831	36	347	183	1940	10,362	5,935	4,200	18	144	65
1961	14,651	5,336	8,770	35	334	176	1935	9,843	5,457	4,195	16	115	60
1960	14,554	5,317	8,709	34	323	171	1930	9,601	5,220	4,200	15	110	56
1959*	14,395	5,307	8,574	33	315	166	1925	9,265	5,139	3,952	13	105	55
1958	14,216	5,290	8,433	32	301	160	1920	8,844	5,080	3,600	12	100	53
1957	14,059	5,280	8,300	31	293	155	1915	8,104	4,712	3,244	10	92	45
1956	13,915	5,260	8,190	30	285	150	1910	7,336	4,305	2,900	9	84	38
1955	13,730	5,248	8,035	28	278	142	1905	7,046	4,038	2,898	9	75	26
1950	12,766	5,620	6,800	23	216	107	1900	6,866	3,975	2,800	7	67	17
1945	11,273	6,063	4,943	22	170	75							

* Denotes first year for which figures include Alaska and Hawaii.

Chapter J

Climate (Series J 110-278)

J 110–267. General note.

Climate may be defined as the statistical summary of the state of the atmosphere at a given place for a given period of time. The "state" of the atmosphere properly includes many weather elements in addition to such influential ones as temperature, precipitation, and wind. Not all of them are given much attention, nor have they been adequately measured throughout the United States.

In view of the significance of ranges of climatic elements, mere arithmetic averages are usually unsatisfactory in specifying the state of the atmosphere, although the description of climate in much of the Nation has had to be so limited. Fully as significant, if less convenient to summarize, are the probability distribution and extreme values of individual weather elements, the joint frequency distributions of two or more elements, and certain specialized indices involving many elements. Such detailed information is available at cost from the U.S. Environmental Data Service, National Climate Center, Asheville, North Carolina, 28801.

Monthly and annual values of average temperature and total precipitation can be found in the following official Weather Service publications of the U.S. Weather Service (formerly the Weather Bureau):

Local Climatological Data, annual summary. This is issued annually for each of approximately 300 stations. With few exceptions, these are first-ordered Weather Service city and/or airport stations. The contents partially include normal values of temperature and precipitation, and comparative data for each month and year back to 1900 or the beginning of record, whichever is later. They also include a station history giving the various station locations and elevations of instruments.

Climatological Data, annual summary. This bulletin is issued annually by climatological sections. In most instances, a section is a State. Nearly all cooperative climatological stations as well as first-order Weather Service stations are included. This publication was founded in the 1880's, but was included as part of the Weather Bureau *Monthly Weather Review* from 1911 to 1913, inclusive.

Climatic Summary of the United States (Bulletin "W"). Monthly and annual series of total precipitation at all stations and mean temperature at selected (first-order) stations are also contained in this publication. Values from the beginning of record up through 1930 are given by geographical sections in the earlier Bulletin, published in the early 1930's. Values for later years are given in *Climatic Summary of the United States—Supplement for 1931 through 1952*, by States, and in the *Supplement for 1951 through 1960*.

Length-of-record series of monthly and annual temperature, pressure, and precipitation up to 1940 may also be found in H. H. Clayton (ed.), *World Weather Records*, Smithsonian Miscellaneous Collections, vol. 79 (1944), vol. 90 (1944), and vol. 105 (1947). This series has been extended and published by the Weather Bureau in *World Weather Records, 1941 to 1950* (1959) and *World Weather Records, 1951 to 1960* (1965). Temperature data are corrected for differences in daily observation time, and, being reduced to 24-hour means, differ somewhat in value from the same data appearing in Weather Service publications.

For daily data on extreme values, or on elements other than temperature and precipitation, see monthly editions of *Climatological Data* and, since 1948, *Local Climatological Data*.

"*Reference climatological network.*" Since less than one percent of the total reporting network, suitably distributed, would be sufficient for sampling historical variations of climate in the Nation, it is potentially possible to select a network in which each station not only (1) possesses fairly long and unbroken records, but also (2) has suffered few if any relocations of instruments, (3) has a good ground exposure little influenced by environmental changes such as city growth or sheltering trees, and (4) is preferably operated by a public or private agency which, by reason of its own interest in the data, will ensure future perpetuation of the station.

A network which comes as nearly as possible to meeting these requirements is the "Reference climatological network." The latitude, longitude, and altitude of the climatological stations are given in table I.

Table I. Reference Climatological Stations

[Abbreviations: A. C.—Agricultural College; E. F.—Experiment Farm; E. S.—Experiment Station; N. P.—National Park; and Obs.—Observatory]

Station	Latitude	Longitude	Altitude
Northeast:			
Blue Hill Obs., Mass	42° 13'	71° 07'	640
Geneva E. S., N. Y	42° 53'	77° 00'	615
Presque Isle E. S., Maine	46° 39'	68° 00'	606
North Central:			
Chatham E. F., Mich	46° 21'	86° 56'	875
Cottonwood E. F., S. Dak	43° 58'	101° 52'	2,414
Crete (Doane College), Nebr	40° 37'	96° 57'	1,368
Dickinson E. F., N. Dak	46° 53'	102° 48'	2,460
Itasca State Park School, Minn	47° 13'	95° 13'	1,500
Urbana (U. of Ill.), Ill	40° 06'	88° 14'	743
Wooster E. F., Ohio	40° 47'	81° 56'	1,030
The South:			
Beeville E. S., Tex	28° 27'	97° 42'	225
Calhoun E. S., La	32° 31'	92° 20'	180
Fayetteville E. S., Ark	36° 06'	94° 10'	1,270
Goodwell A. C., Okla	36° 36'	101° 39'	3,300
Lewisburg E. S., Tenn	35° 27'	86° 48'	787
St. Leo's Abbey, Fla	28° 20'	82° 15'	178
Winthrop College, S. C	34° 57'	81° 03'	690
Woodstock, Md	39° 20'	76° 52'	415
The West:			
Agricultural College, N. Mex	32° 17'	106° 45'	3,909
Bozeman A. C., Mont	45° 40'	111° 00'	4,856
Davis A. C., Calif	38° 32'	121° 45'	51
Grand Canyon N. P. Hdq., Ariz	36° 03'	112° 08'	6,890
Indio U.S. Date Garden, Calif	33° 43'	116° 15'	11
Logan (Utah State A. C.), Utah	41° 44'	111° 49'	4,775
Medford E. S., Oreg	42° 18'	122° 52'	1,457
Montrose No. 2, Colo	38° 29'	107° 53'	5,830
Union E. S., Oreg	45° 13'	117° 53'	2,765

J 110–136. Reference climatological stations—normal monthly, seasonal, and annual temperature.

Source: U.S. National Weather Service, unpublished data (figures computed from monthly temperature data in *Climatological Data*). (Data for series J 111 appear in *Local Climatological Data*, but the temperatures there have been adjusted to values based on 24 daily observations and so are incompatible with other temperature data for that station given here.)

Nearly all weather stations have been moved several times in their history. Consequently, the Weather Service has adopted the practice of using "normal" values of temperature and precipitation for comparative purposes rather than long-term means which are derived from records taken at the several different locations the stations may have had over the years.

Normal values of temperature and precipitation are based on records for the 30-year period 1941 to 1970, inclusive. Where a station had a record for the entire 30 years from the same instrument site, monthly precipitation normals are the mean of the monthly values for the 30 years. For such stations, the temperature normals were obtained in a similar manner, using normal maximum and normal minimum values to obtain monthly normals. The annual normal temperature is obtained by dividing the sum of the annual normal maximum value and the annual normal minimum value for temperature by 2.

For stations that did not have continuous records from the same instrument site for the entire 30 years, 1941 to 1970, the means have been adjusted to the record at the present site. In these adjustments, a "difference factor" was used for temperature and a "ratio factor" for precipitation. These factors were determined by parallel comparison, either between records at the actual station sites or through a second station that had a continuous record to compare against both sites for obtaining the resultant adjusting factors. Normals were thereafter obtained as outlined above.

This system of normals has three characteristics: (1) The 30-year period (1941 to 1970) adopted for the computations is consistent with the term of years accepted by the World Meteorological Organization for climatic normals; (2) where the station and exposure for records in a given locality have been changed, the whole record has been carefully studied and adjusted to the latest source of records and reports; (3) the normals for maximum and minimum temperatures are separately tabulated.

See also general note for series J 110–267.

J 137–163. Reference climatological stations—normal monthly, seasonal, and annual precipitation.

Source: See source for series J 110–136.

See also text for series J 110–136.

J 164–247. Reference climatological stations—temperature, precipitation, and description of year, 1884–1970.

Source: U.S. National Weather Service, *Climatological Data*, annual summaries.

The description of the year is given by three digits; the first digit applies to the year as a whole, the second applies to the summer season (June, July, and August), and the third applies to the winter season (December of the previous year, January, and February). The following code defines the meaning of each digit:

Code	Temperature	Precipitation
1	In warmest quartile	In wettest quartile
2	Near normal	In wettest quartile
3	In coldest quartile	In wettest quartile
4	In warmest quartile	Near normal
5	Near normal	Near normal
6	In coldest quartile	Near normal
7	In warmest quartile	In driest quartile
8	Near normal	In driest quartile
9	In coldest quartile	In driest quartile

For example, a code 5–1–9 indicates that, for a particular year and station, the annual mean temperature and annual total precipitation were both near normal (i.e., not within either extreme quartile of their distributions in the normal 1941–1970 period); but that the summer season was unusually warm and wet, while the winter season was unusually cold and dry.

Smoothed ogives of the distribution of average values in the 30-year normal period were used to obtain the upper and lower quartile limits of temperature and precipitation for each season and for the year as a whole. Any given quartile therefore separates approximately one-quarter of the number of years in the normal period, but probably more or less than one-quarter of the total years in any full length-of-record series owing to the presence of climatic trends or variations.

J 248–267. Long-record city stations—annual mean temperature and annual total precipitation, 1780–1970.

Source: **Series J 248, J 249, J 252–257, J 259–267**, 1780–1940, H. H. Clayton (ed.), *World Weather Records*, Smithsonian Miscellaneous Collections, vol. 79 (1944), vol. 90 (1944), vol. 105 (1947); 1941–1960, U.S. National Weather Service, *World Weather Records*, 1941 to 1950 (1959) and 1951 to 1960 (1965; 1961–1970, U.S. Environmental Data

Service, *Local Climatological Data* (corrected to 24-hour means), annual editions. **Series J 250, J 251**, and **J 258**, *Local Climatological Data* and *Climatic Summary of the United States*, annual editions.

The series for city stations selected for presentation here are among the longest existing climatological series for the United States. They were selected with the realization that they are not homogeneous, but have comparative value in the earlier years and have been less frequently affected by changes of station location. The series, however, are not adjusted for known station changes, and coming as they do from growing cities, they contain climatic trends which in part are typical only of major metropolitan centers.

Each long-record station has suffered several changes of location and exposure of instruments. The following station history notes are extracted from the annual editions of *Local Climatological Data*, and indicate all known changes likely to have affected the temperature and/or precipitation records. The history of each station prior to the date of establishment by the Federal weather service is essentially unknown; occasional exposure changes in earlier years undoubtedly occurred whose effects, although significant, may never be discovered.

Records for two of the 10 stations shown refer in recent years to airport locations; the observation program in New Haven city terminated in 1943, and that in St. Paul-Minneapolis terminated in 1937. With one exception, all other records are continuously available from city locations although the major part of National Weather Service activities in each case has been transferred to airport stations. The exception is Santa Fe, where interpolations have been required to complete the city record in recent years.

In the following notes, "temperature means" indicate the combination of hourly temperature readings each day which were averaged together to form means. For example, 1/3 (7, 15, 21) indicates an average of readings at 7 a.m., 3 p.m., and 9 p.m. local standard time. The formula 1/3 (7:35, 16:35, 23) was in general use for 1870–1879 (Nov.), and the formula 1/3 (7, 15, 23) for 1879–1888, the times referring to the 75th meridian (Washington). Since about 1888, however, daily maximum and minimum temperatures, observed with special registering thermometers, have been averaged to obtain means.

Numbers in parentheses refer to elevations of the thermometers and rain gauge, respectively; the example (51/70) indicates the thermometers were 51 feet above ground, and the rain gauge funnel was 70 feet above ground (roof exposures). Asterisks (*) indicate that heights are estimated from circumstantial information; a question mark (?) indicates unknown.

Albany, N.Y. Temperature means: 1795–1796, unknown; 1813–1814, 1/3 (7, 15, 21); 1820–1870, 1/3 (7, 14, 21). Station established by Army Signal Service in Dudley Heights December 1873 (11/?); instruments moved July 1874 (17/1). Station moved 1.3 miles W March 1880 (51/70), 400 feet E October 1884 (80/100). Exposure changed July 1888 (84/99), October 1901 (102/100), October 1928 (107/100). Station moved 100 feet N April 1935 (97/88).

Baltimore, Md. Temperature means: 1817–1870, unknown. Station established December 1870 (34/69); thermometers relocated October 1885 (76/69). Station moved 0.1 mile January 1889 (86/78), 0.8 mile June 1891 (87/80), 0.7 mile September 1895 (120/116), 0.6 mile August 1896 (69/73), 0.8 mile January 1908 (100/91). Recording instruments only after July 1949 (100/90).

Charleston, S.C. 1738–1861, discontinuous records by various doctors. Temperature means: 1823–1872, unknown. Station established January 1871 (40/57); thermometers moved January 1886 (60/55). Station moved 0.2 mile N February 1897 (11/76); rain gauge moved July 1932 (11/3); thermometers moved August 1949 (6/3).

New Haven, Conn. Temperature means: 1780–1865, unknown but corrected to 24 hours; 1866–1872, unknown, monthly temperatures available to whole degrees only. Station established December 1872 (85/109); instruments moved February 1881 (118/110). Station moved 600 feet E March 1919 (74/68). City station closed and observations taken over by airport station 4 miles SE July 1943 (4/3).

New York, N.Y. (Central Park). 1822–1864, records from Jamaica, N.Y.; 1865–1868, records from 86th St. Reservoir, N.Y. Temperature means: 1822–1842, 1/3 (7, 14, 21); 1843–1870, 1/4 (Sunrise, 9, 15, 21). Station established December 1868 (61/64); moved 1 mile N January 1920 (6/22).

Philadelphia, Pa. Temperature means: 1825–1870, unknown. Station established December 1870 (?/?); moved 0.3 mile E September 1871 (100*/91), 0.7 mile W February 1882 (54*/106*), 0.1 mile E April 1884 (169/167). Instruments moved February 1904 (117/114); thermometers moved January 1914 (124/114). Station moved 0.6 mile E December 1934 (175/166), and 0.7 mile W May 15, 1959 (155/166).

San Francisco, Calif. Temperature means: 1851–1853, 1/4 (Sunrise, 9, 15, 21); 1854, 1/3 (9, 12, 21); 1857–1859, 1/3 (7, 14, 21); 1861–1868, 1/4 (7, 14, 21 weighted twice). Station established February 1871 (48/75); moved 0.5 mile SW September 1890 (109/101), 0.3 mile NE November 1892 (161/154), 3.1 miles W May 1906 (29/40), 3.0 miles E October 1906 (200/191). Instruments moved October 1914 (209/200). Station moved 1.0 mile SW May 1936 (112/104). Temperature probably affected at times by nearby ventilators April 1919–May 1936.

Santa Fe, N. Mex. Temperature means: 1849–1854, 1/4 (Sunrise, 9, 15, 21); 1855–1872, 1/3 (7, 14, 21). Station established November 1871 (30*/27*); moved March 1878 (5*/2*), March 1882 (50*/50*), November 1884 (35*/32*), January 1892 (53*/50*), March 1893 (42*/39*), July 1907 (5*/2*), April 1912 (52*/49*) March 1922 (34*/31*). Continued as cooperative station 0.5 mile NE September 1941 (39*/36*). Instruments moved May 1942 (5*/2*), October 1942 (23*/20*). Station moved about 1 mile SE May 1944, few hundred feet NW July 1947, 1 mile SE October 1950, about 0.3 mile NW October 1951, few hundred feet March 1954, 1.5 miles SE May 1955, and 2 miles SSE July 1960. Ground exposures, approximately (5/3), at last seven locations.

St. Louis, Mo. Temperature means: 1836–1870, unknown but corrected to 24 hours. Station established October 1870 (70/93). Several suspected changes of thermometer exposure; station then moved 0.2 mile WNW March 1873 (105/100), 250 feet E August 1903 (208/199), 300 feet E September 1913 (264/258), 0.4 mile SW November 1935 (179/172), and 1 mile SE July 1968 (6/4).

St. Paul, Minn. Records from Fort Snelling 1820–1855, from Minneapolis 1856–1858. Temperature means: 1820–1858, unknown; 1859–1870, 1/4 (7, 14, 21 weighted twice). Station established November 1870 (30/36); moved 0.2 mile WSW December 1871 (34/44), 0.2 mile ENE April 1878 (33/58), 0.2 mile NE April 1883 (45/61),

0.2 mile NNW July 1885 (103/92), 0.1 mile SE July 1904 (171/162). Instruments moved January 1911 (201/195), July 1918 (237/227). Station moved 0.3 mile W April 1931 (114/106). Record July 1933–April 1937 8.8 miles WNW at Minneapolis city (102/91); April 1937–December 1959 7.5 miles SSE at Minneapolis-St. Paul International Airport (43/41), January 1960–October 1962 (5/41), and November 1962–December 1970 (5/4).

J 268–278. Tornadoes, floods, and tropical cyclones, 1886 to 1970.

Source: U.S. National Oceanic and Atmospheric Administration, *Climatological Data National Summary, Annual 1970,* pp. 55, 68, 94, and *Annual 1971,* pp. 740, 752, 789.

The National Weather Service (formerly the Weather Bureau) issues warnings of tornadoes, floods, and tropical cyclones that threaten the United States mainland. "Tropical cyclone" is a general term for storms that form in the tropics. If the winds of a tropical cyclone are known to be 39 miles per hour or more, the circulation is called a tropical storm; when its winds reach 74 miles per hour, the storm is considered a hurricane. These winds are accompanied by heavy rains, high waves, and tides, and sometimes tornadoes, which are local storms of short duration formed of winds rotating at very high speeds, usually in a counter-clockwise direction. These storms are visible as a vortex, a whirlpool structure of winds rotating about a hollow cavity in which centrifugal forces produce a partial vacuum.

Whenever an area is likely to experience severe thunderstorms or tornadoes, the National Weather Service issues a *watch* bulletin. A severe thunderstorm or tornado *warning* bulletin is issued only when a severe thunderstorm or tornado has actually been sighted in the area or indicated by radar.

From 1916 to 1952, fewer than 300 tornadoes were reported in any one year. In 1953, however, when the U.S. Department of Commerce initiated its tornado forecasting effort, 437 tornadoes were observed and reported, beginning the first period of reliable statistical history. Since 1953, essentially complete tornado records have been available.

Through its special river and rainfall reporting network, the National Weather Service also issues flood warnings which provide time to evacuate low-lying areas, to move property and livestock to higher ground, and to take necessary emergency action. River forecasts based on atmosphere and hydrologic data are prepared by River Forecast Centers from reports of river stages and precipitation provided by a network of observing stations in each district.

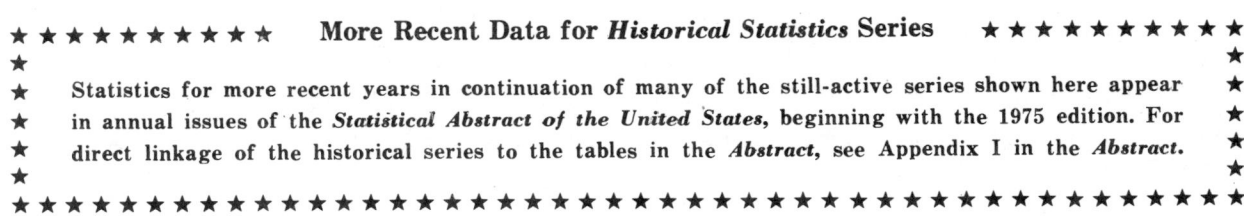

★ ★ ★ ★ ★ ★ ★ ★ ★   **More Recent Data for *Historical Statistics* Series**   ★ ★ ★ ★ ★ ★ ★ ★ ★

★ Statistics for more recent years in continuation of many of the still-active series shown here appear ★
★ in annual issues of the *Statistical Abstract of the United States*, beginning with the 1975 edition. For ★
★ direct linkage of the historical series to the tables in the *Abstract*, see Appendix I in the *Abstract*. ★

Series J 110–136. Reference Climatological Stations—Normal Monthly, Seasonal, and Annual Temperatures

[In Fahrenheit degrees. Figures are "normal" values based on records for the 30-year period 1941–1970; see text]

Series No.	Station	January	February	March	April	May	June	July	August	September	October	November	December	Summer	Winter	Annual
	NORTHEAST															
110	Blue Hill Observatory, Mass	25.8	27.0	34.6	45.5	55.8	64.9	70.4	68.6	61.7	52.6	41.7	29.4	68.0	27.4	48.2
111	Geneva Experiment Station, N.Y	24.3	25.1	33.7	46.5	56.5	66.7	71.4	69.5	62.6	52.3	41.0	28.4	69.2	26.0	48.2
112	Presque Isle Experiment Station, Maine	12.6	14.7	25.3	38.2	51.1	61.0	66.1	63.6	55.7	45.2	32.8	17.5	63.6	14.9	40.3
	NORTH CENTRAL															
113	Chatham Experiment Farm, Mich	16.8	18.1	25.6	39.6	50.0	59.8	65.1	64.2	56.3	47.4	33.4	21.9	63.0	18.9	41.5
114	Cottonwood Experiment Farm, S. Dak	19.4	24.5	31.4	46.4	56.9	66.1	74.3	73.5	61.9	50.3	34.7	24.1	71.3	22.8	46.9
115	Crete (Doane College), Nebr	23.7	29.5	37.8	52.4	62.8	72.0	77.4	76.0	66.3	56.1	40.0	28.5	75.2	27.2	51.9
116	Dickinson Experiment Farm, N. Dak	10.4	15.1	24.2	40.8	52.2	61.1	68.5	67.6	55.8	45.2	28.4	17.1	65.7	14.3	40.5
117	Itasca State Park School, Minn	5.7	10.6	22.8	39.6	51.4	61.6	67.1	65.2	55.1	45.4	27.5	12.3	64.6	9.5	38.7
118	Urbana (U. of Ill.), Ill	26.9	30.3	39.3	52.4	62.6	72.1	75.3	73.5	66.8	56.3	41.6	30.3	73.6	29.2	52.3
119	Wooster Experiment Farm, Ohio	26.3	27.9	36.6	48.3	58.1	67.6	71.0	69.4	62.8	52.3	40.2	29.0	69.3	27.7	49.1
	THE SOUTH															
120	Beeville Experiment Station, Tex	53.9	57.3	63.1	71.5	76.8	81.8	84.3	87.8	80.1	72.3	63.0	56.6	83.6	55.9	70.7
121	Calhoun Experiment Station, La	46.9	50.1	56.4	65.9	72.9	79.7	82.3	82.0	76.2	66.2	55.7	48.8	81.3	48.6	65.3
122	Fayetteville Experiment Station, Ark	37.0	41.1	47.3	59.4	66.5	74.4	78.6	77.6	70.5	60.5	48.2	39.9	76.9	39.3	58.4
123	Goodwell Agricultural College, Okla	35.3	39.4	44.4	56.1	65.3	74.6	79.0	78.0	70.2	59.2	45.1	37.2	77.2	37.3	57.0
124	Lewisburg Experiment Station, Tenn	38.0	40.5	47.6	58.8	66.9	74.8	77.8	76.9	70.7	59.7	47.9	40.0	76.5	39.5	58.3
125	St. Leo's Abbey, Fla	60.5	62.0	66.5	72.2	77.3	80.8	81.7	82.0	80.4	74.2	66.6	61.7	81.5	61.4	72.2
126	Winthrop College, S.C	43.3	45.4	52.1	62.3	70.1	76.6	78.9	77.8	72.3	62.7	52.5	43.9	77.8	44.2	61.5
127	Woodstock, Md	32.3	34.0	41.9	53.0	62.8	70.7	74.8	73.1	66.3	55.6	44.5	34.1	(NA)	(NA)	53.6
	THE WEST															
128	Agricultural College, N. Mex	41.7	46.0	51.3	60.0	68.0	76.9	80.0	78.1	71.7	61.2	48.9	42.4	78.3	43.4	60.5
129	Bozeman Agricultural College, Mont	20.8	26.5	29.9	41.9	50.8	57.6	66.4	65.0	55.3	45.5	32.5	25.1	63.0	24.1	43.1
130	Davis Agricultural College, Calif	45.0	49.6	52.8	58.2	64.3	70.6	74.6	73.1	71.0	63.1	53.2	46.0	72.8	46.9	60.1
131	Grand Canyon National Park Headquarters, Ariz	30.5	33.3	37.6	45.8	54.5	63.3	69.4	67.1	61.7	51.0	39.2	32.2	66.6	33.8	48.8
132	Indio U.S. Date Garden, Calif	54.4	58.9	63.6	71.4	78.4	85.7	91.8	90.8	86.0	75.7	63.3	55.5	89.4	56.3	73.0
133	Logan (Utah State Agricultural College), Utah	24.0	28.9	36.1	46.9	56.2	63.1	72.9	71.4	62.0	50.7	36.7	27.5	69.1	26.9	48.0
134	Medford Experiment Station, Oreg	37.3	41.9	45.3	50.6	57.0	63.2	69.6	68.4	63.0	52.9	43.6	38.2	67.0	39.2	52.6
135	Montrose No. 2, Colo	26.4	31.6	38.1	48.0	57.5	66.1	72.5	69.9	62.3	51.1	37.4	28.5	69.5	28.8	49.1
136	Union Experiment Station, Oreg	30.0	35.2	39.5	46.4	53.1	59.0	66.3	64.9	58.0	48.8	39.4	33.2	63.4	32.9	47.8

NA   Not available.

Series J 137–163. Reference Climatological Stations—Normal Monthly, Seasonal, and Annual Precipitation

[In inches. T = trace. Figures are "normal" values based on records for the 30-year period 1941–1970; see text]

Series No.	Station	January	February	March	April	May	June	July	August	September	October	November	December	Summer	Winter	Annual
	NORTHEAST															
137	Blue Hill Observatory, Mass	4.12	3.97	4.51	3.64	3.62	3.15	2.95	3.83	3.65	3.62	5.06	4.70	9.93	12.79	46.82
138	Geneva Experiment Station, N.Y	2.02	2.09	2.64	2.88	3.02	3.10	3.06	2.82	2.59	2.97	2.78	2.35	8.98	6.43	32.32
139	Presque Isle Experiment Station, Maine	2.16	2.13	2.15	2.26	2.93	3.29	3.89	3.59	3.38	3.27	3.47	2.59	10.77	6.88	35.11
	NORTH CENTRAL															
140	Chatham Experiment Farm, Mich	1.75	1.63	1.71	2.45	3.11	3.65	3.22	3.35	4.14	3.18	3.29	2.21	10.22	5.59	33.69
141	Cottonwood Experiment Farm, S. Dak	.45	.45	.79	1.79	2.97	3.62	1.71	1.38	1.24	.91	.40	.35	6.71	1.24	16.06
142	Crete (Doane College), Nebr	.74	1.11	1.70	2.72	4.04	5.76	3.31	3.87	3.41	1.71	1.06	.87	12.94	2.72	30.30
143	Dickinson Experiment Farm, N. Dak	.41	.41	.66	1.51	2.51	4.01	2.29	1.86	1.37	.72	.51	.30	8.17	1.12	16.56
144	Itasca State Park School, Minn	.82	.60	1.33	2.63	3.35	4.48	3.69	3.67	2.68	1.65	1.20	1.08	11.84	2.50	27.18
145	Urbana (U. of Ill.), Ill	2.13	2.02	3.13	4.06	4.15	4.38	3.89	2.97	2.98	2.93	2.56	2.22	11.24	6.37	37.42
146	Wooster Experiment Farm, Ohio	2.51	1.95	2.99	3.28	4.18	3.78	4.07	3.16	2.73	2.04	2.39	2.19	11.00	6.66	35.27
	THE SOUTH															
147	Beeville Experiment Station, Tex	1.67	2.01	1.40	2.57	3.53	2.76	2.33	2.27	4.14	3.03	1.85	1.66	7.36	5.47	29.22
148	Calhoun Experiment Station, La	4.73	4.65	4.75	5.00	5.31	3.58	4.00	2.69	3.12	2.97	4.15	4.73	10.27	14.11	49.68
149	Fayetteville Experiment Station, Ark	2.13	2.89	3.16	4.76	6.22	4.90	3.65	3.85	3.72	3.66	2.87	2.60	12.40	7.62	44.41
150	Goodwell Agricultural College, Okla	.31	.49	.67	1.14	2.50	2.70	3.45	2.76	1.53	1.48	.54	.40	8.91	1.21	17.97
151	Lewisburg Experiment Station, Tenn	5.32	5.62	5.62	4.86	4.36	3.42	4.65	3.30	3.50	2.62	4.10	4.76	11.37	15.68	52.13
152	St. Leo's Abbey, Fla	2.55	3.13	4.53	3.10	3.79	8.02	8.68	8.86	7.08	2.93	1.87	2.36	25.56	8.04	56.90
153	Winthrop College, S. C	3.98	4.10	4.62	3.50	3.13	3.49	5.76	4.86	3.79	2.80	2.92	3.73	14.11	11.86	46.68
154	Woodstock, Md	2.85	2.70	3.62	3.27	3.83	3.65	4.01	3.87	3.67	2.93	3.31	3.27	10.53	8.82	40.98
	THE WEST															
155	Agricultural College, N. Mex	.44	.48	.33	.15	.23	.62	1.34	1.65	1.18	.68	.31	.48	3.61	1.40	7.89
156	Bozeman Agricultural College, Mont	.92	.65	1.44	1.78	2.67	3.22	1.30	1.37	1.76	1.46	1.26	.83	5.89	2.40	18.66
157	Davis Agricultural College, Calif	3.88	2.79	1.95	1.50	.51	.16	.01	.03	.16	1.04	2.04	3.21	.20	9.88	17.28
158	Grand Canyon National Park Headquarters, Ariz	1.35	1.28	1.47	1.00	.54	.48	1.50	2.15	1.22	1.07	8.2	1.59	4.13	4.22	14.47
159	Indio U.S. Date Garden, Calif	.46	.21	.29	.11	.02	T	.14	.40	.23	.21	.41	.52	.54	1.19	3.00
160	Logan (Utah State Agricultural College), Utah	1.63	1.45	1.74	2.12	1.86	1.78	.34	.87	.94	1.43	1.79	1.64	2.99	4.69	17.59
161	Medford Experiment Station, Oreg	3.43	2.16	1.74	1.14	1.53	1.09	.26	.36	.65	2.09	3.04	3.77	1.71	9.26	21.27
162	Montrose No. 2, Colo	.63	.57	.63	1.03	.74	.64	.82	1.36	.99	1.07	.60	.59	2.82	1.79	9.67
163	Union Experiment Station, Oreg	1.05	.94	1.14	1.30	2.04	1.90	.48	.74	.87	1.24	1.31	1.32	3.13	3.30	14.33

Series J 164–247. Reference Climatological Stations—Temperature, Precipitation, and Description of Year: 1884 to 1970

[*Italicized* figures are based on interpolated monthly values.   Standard error of interpolated figures: For temperature, less than 1° F.; for precipitation, less than 0.5 inch]

Year	Northeast — Blue Hill Observatory, Mass.			Northeast — Geneva Experiment Station, N.Y.			Northeast — Presque Isle Experiment Station, Maine			North Central — Chatham Experiment Farm, Mich.			North Central — Cottonwood Experiment Farm, S. Dak.		
	Annual mean temperature	Annual total precipitation	Description of year	Annual mean temperature	Annual total precipitation	Description of year	Annual mean temperature	Annual total precipitation	Description of year	Annual mean temperature	Annual total precipitation	Description of year	Annual mean temperature	Annual total precipitation	Description of year
	164	165	166	167	168	169	170	171	172	173	174	175	176	177	178
	°F.	Inches		°F.	Inches		°F.	Inches		°F.	Inches		°F.	Inches	
1970	48	48.3	5-1-3	47	34.6	5-2-5	40	35.6	5-4-5	41	36.5	5-5-3	46	15.8	6-4-5
1969	49	58.4	1-7-2	47	31.4	5-5-5	41	42.4	2-2-1	42	35.5	5-5-2	47	20.1	2-2-3
1968	48	49.9	5-5-5	47	37.9	2-3-9	40	29.8	8-9-4	42	42.9	2-5-2	47	15.9	5-2-5
1967	48	54.1	2-1-8	47	29.7	5-5-8	39	37.7	3-4-5	41	32.0	5-5-2	47	20.2	2-2-5
1966	49	41.1	4-4-5	47	28.7	8-8-5	41	30.0	8-8-1	42	35.5	5-4-5	46	15.3	6-5-6
1965	48	27.0	8-7-5	47	25.8	8-9-5	39	28.5	9-5-5	41	31.6	5-9-6	47	17.4	5-5-5
1964	49	40.2	7-8-5	48	26.7	8-8-5	40	31.1	5-5-8	43	40.3	1-2-2	47	15.4	5-5-8
1963	48	41.6	5-7-6	46	31.1	6-6-9	39	40.0	3-2-5	41	27.0	8-5-6	49	17.4	4-4-5
1962	47	51.6	3-6-2	47	29.8	9-6-9	39	35.4	5-3-5	41	27.4	8-8-6	47	14.9	5-5-5
1961	49	50.7	2-7-5	48	33.1	6-6-6	40	44.4	2-2-3	42	31.8	5-8-8	48	14.1	5-5-7
1960	49	46.7	4-8-4	47	27.1	9-9-2	41	37.9	2-9-1	41	44.4	2-2-7	47	15.2	5-5-2
1959	49	48.3	5-2-9	49	40.2	2-2-9	40	35.5	5-5-9	41	40.2	2-1-9	47	15.5	5-7-2
1958	46	59.9	3-6-2	46	37.7	3-3-5	39	37.7	2-3-1	41	27.5	8-6-4	48	16.4	5-2-4
1957	50	35.5	7-7-5	48	26.1	8-8-8	40	31.3	5-9-5	41	30.2	8-8-8	47	22.5	2-2-5
1956	48	59.2	2-8-2	47	34.2	6-6-6	39	30.8	5-6-4	41	25.2	8-5-7	48	14.6	5-4-2
1955	49	64.4	1-1-5	49	42.4	2-4-6	40	34.2	5-4-1	43	26.5	7-7-8	48	12.9	4-7-5
1954	49	57.4	2-6-4	48	29.2	8-8-7	40	52.4	2-3-1	42	32.2	5-8-4	49	13.0	4-8-4
1953	51	59.6	1-7-1	50	26.3	7-5-4	42	35.4	4-8-4	44	36.0	1-4-1	49	18.6	1-5-1
1952	50	39.8	7-7-1	49	31.6	5-8-4	41	36.4	4-4-1	43	31.7	4-1-7	47	16.7	5-5-3
1951	50	50.9	1-5-4	48	31.3	6-6-6	41	40.2	2-2-1	40	39.8	2-3-5	43	20.9	3-3-2
1950	49	42.0	8-8-4	47	36.9	6-6-1	41	37.4	2-2-4	38	33.3	6-6-5	44	11.9	6-9-6
1949	51	33.7	7-7-7	50	22.8	7-4-7	42	33.5	4-4-4	43	37.7	1-1-4	46	14.8	5-7-3
1948	48	47.8	5-5-3	49	32.9	5-5-9	40	31.0	5-8-9	40	27.3	8-8-9	46	17.0	5-3-8
1947	49	44.9	5-5-7	49	35.7	5-2-5	41	34.1	4-4-1	41	34.5	5-5-5	47	13.0	5-5-5
1946	50	42.0	7-3-3	50	29.6	7-6-8	41	31.2	4-8-5	42	29.0	8-6-5	49	17.8	1-5-7
1945	49	54.4	1-5-6	49	40.4	2-8-6	41	37.1	1-4-5	40	32.4	6-9-6	47	11.4	5-6-7
1944	49	45.6	4-4-8	50	32.1	5-4-8	41	30.4	7-7-8	42	33.1	5-5-7	45	12.9	6-6-5
1943	48	34.9	8-7-5	48	37.1	6-4-3	39	33.8	5-2-5	40	33.6	6-1-5	46	11.0	8-5-8
1942	48	46.3	5-6-5	50	38.9	2-8-5	41	28.0	7-5-4	42	32.8	4-8-7	47	19.3	2-6-8
1941	49	32.6	8-5-8	50	30.2	7-5-5	40	33.0	5-5-2	44	40.9	1-4-1	49	18.6	1-2-4
1940	46	45.0	6-9-6	47	36.9	6-5-3	39	36.9	3-2-5	41	38.4	2-5-1	47	9.8	8-5-2
1939	48	37.8	8-7-5	50	28.9	8-8-2	39	36.6	6-1-5	41	36.5	2-5-5	50	8.4	7-7-5
1938	49	58.5	1-1-5	50	35.2	4-1-5	38	33.4	6-2-9	42	34.1	4-5-2	48	14.9	4-8-5
1937	49	46.1	5-7-1	49	38.2	2-4-1	41	31.8	4-4-4	41	32.7	5-4-5	46	14.6	5-1-6
1936	47	59.1	3-6-3	49	30.1	8-8-6	39	44.0	2-6-2	40	25.5	9-8-3	47	7.1	8-7-3
1935	47	43.7	6-5-3	48	35.5	6-2-6	39	28.4	6-4-6	40	31.8	6-5-5	48	15.7	5-5-4
1934	47	41.2	9-9-6	48	23.4	9-8-6	38	36.4	6-3-3	39	32.6	6-9-6	51	12.0	4-4-4
1933	48	52.8	2-6-7	50	26.9	7-4-7	39	32.5	5-8-7	40	29.8	8-7-2	49	14.5	4-7-5
1932	49	48.9	4-5-4	50	40.5	1-5-1	40	34.0	5-5-7	41	40.9	2-2-4	46	17.3	5-5-2
1931	50	49.3	4-2-5	52	31.7	4-7-5	42	37.1	1-5-8	45	32.0	4-4-7	50	9.6	7-7-7
1930	49	41.3	7-4-5	50	26.8	8-5-5	41	29.1	8-1-5	41	26.9	8-5-6	48	23.0	2-2-2
1929	48	47.0	9-8-5	49	35.5	5-9-8	39	29.7	8-6-7	39	32.7	6-6-6	44	18.2	3-5-6
1928	48	46.8	5-2-5	49	33.5	5-2-2	39	36.7	2-6-2	40	36.1	2-6-5	47	14.0	5-3-5
1927	49	51.6	1-3-5	49	42.8	2-6-5	39	36.8	2-6-3	40	31.0	8-9-8	44	21.0	3-3-8
1926	46	48.9	6-6-5	46	36.2	6-3-5	37	35.4	6-9-2	38	37.8	3-6-5	47	13.5	5-5-1
1925	49	50.4	1-4-8	48	36.8	6-6-5	38	43.6	7-8-6	40	21.7	8-8-9	47	10.4	8-5-2
1924	47	42.8	9-5-2	46	32.2	6-6-8	38	24.6	9-9-5	42	35.6	1-3-2	44	11.2	9-6-5
1923	47	44.9	6-9-3	47	31.2	6-6-3	37	29.5	9-9-6	40	30.8	9-2-9	46	22.3	3-3-6
1922	48	54.0	2-1-9	49	39.8	2-2-5	39	33.7	5-2-5	42	34.7	4-5-2	44	22.4	3-2-3
1921	49	51.8	2-2-5	52	29.4	7-7-4	40	31.1	5-5-2	43	32.0	4-4-8	49	10.9	7-4-7
1920	46	63.8	3-3-3	49	37.2	6-2-5	39	43.6	2-2-6	39	32.6	6-5-9	46	19.4	3-5-5
1919	47	56.2	3-3-5	49	35.4	5-5-7	38	29.2	9-9-5	40	27.8	9-8-4	45	16.0	6-5-5
1918	47	44.9	6-6-6	48	34.4	6-6-6	37	35.9	6-3-3	39	36.4	3-6-9	46	15.0	5-5-6
1917	45	48.8	6-5-5	45	35.4	6-2-6	36	41-3	3-1-_	34	30.3	9-6-9	44	13.2	6-8-3
1916	46	45.5	6-3-5	48	42.0	5-5-2				38	41.9	3-5-3	44	12.3	6-5-6
1915	48	44.0	5-3-2	48	29.0	5-6-5				40	42.2	3-5-3	44	27.6	3-3-3
1914	46	40.3	9-6-5	48	33.4	5-5-9				38	33.0	6-3-5	48	15.0	5-8-2
1913	49	45.1	4-8-4	51	33.5	4-8-4				39	26.7	9-9-9	48	10.5	8-7-8
1912	47	40.4	9-9-9							36	27.0	9-9-6	46	14.1	6-5-2
1911	48	44.6	5-2-9							40	37.2	3-2-5	49	12.3	4-8-5
1910	48	34.3	8-8-5												
1909	48	43.6	6-9-5							40	27.9	9-8-3	48	10.0	8-8-3
1908	49	37.7	8-4-2							39	30.2	9-2-5	47	6.6	8-1-_
1907	46	47.6	6-9-6							41	27.6	8-8-5			
1906	48	45.5	5-6-4							37	29.3	9-9-3			
1905	46	39.4	9-6-6							40	30.7	9-5-2			
1904	45	46.2	6-9-6							38	33.4	6-6-6			
1903	47	46.8	6-6-2							37	32.5	6-6-6			
1902	48	42.7	6-9-2							40	39.1	2-6-2			
1901	47	54.0	3-4-9							40	34.8	5-6-2			
1900	49	48.1	5-7-5							41	42.0	2-5-8			
1899	48	40.6	8-8-5							41	33.4	5-_-_			
1898	48	58.7	2-2-2												
1897	47	45.4	6-6-8												
1896	47	47.4	6-6-5												
1895	47	46.2	6-9-9												
1894	48	35.8	8-8-5												
1893	46	45.1	6-6-8												
1892	47	39.7	9-5-4		36.7										
1891	48	50.3	5-6-3		33.8										
1890	47	50.8	3-9-7		44.3										
1889	48	54.6	2-3-2		40.0										
1888	45	55.8	3-6-6												
1887	46	43.7	6-6-3												
1886	47	47.0	6-9-_												

See footnotes at end of table.

Series J 164–247. Reference Climatological Stations—Temperature, Precipitation, and Description of Year: 1884 to 1970—Con.

[*Italicized* figures are based on interpolated monthly values. Standard error of interpolated figures: For temperature, less than 1° F.; for precipitation, less than 0.5 inch]

North Central—Con.

Year	Crete (Doane College), Nebr. Annual mean temperature	Annual total precipitation	Description of year	Dickinson Experiment Farm, N. Dak. Annual mean temperature	Annual total precipitation	Description of year	Itasca State Park School, Minn. Annual mean temperature	Annual total precipitation	Description of year	Urbana (U. of Ill.), Ill. Annual mean temperature	Annual total precipitation	Description of year	Wooster Experiment Farm, Ohio Annual mean temperature	Annual total precipitation	Description of year
	179	180	181	182	183	184	185	186	187	188	189	190	191	192	193
	°F.	Inches		°F.	Inches		°F.	Inches		°F.	Inches		°F.	Inches	
1970	53	28.7	4-4-4	39	20.2	3-4-2	38	22.7	9-7-5	52	36.5	5-5-9	49	38.4	5-5-9
1969	51	29.0	6-8-2	40	16.4	5-2-3	39	28.2	5-5-2	51	37.1	5-8-5	48	41.4	3-2-5
1968	52	36.4	2-5-9	40	15.7	5-6-5	40	32.6	1-5-5	51	39.7	5-2-3	48	36.3	6-5-6
1967	52	35.8	2-3-4	40	14.2	5-8-5	37	23.8	6-8-2	51	34.8	9-9-2	49	29.9	2-8-8
1966	52	20.4	8-5-5	39	16.7	6-2-5	36	29.7	6-5-1	51	35.8	9-8-5	48	30.2	9-8-5
1965	52	36.1	2-6-1	39	21.6	3-5-6	37	33.4	3-5-4	53	44.4	2-3-2	49	34.9	5-6-2
1964	53	21.1	7-5-5	41	18.7	5-2-7	38	31.3	3-6-5	53	35.5	8-5-6	49	39.0	5-6-9
1963	53	28.7	4-4-9	43	18.9	4-4-5	40	22.6	7-4-9	51	26.9	9-8-9	46	24.2	9-6-9
1962	52	29.9	2-3-3	42	18.3	1-5-8	39	31.3	2-2-2	51	38.0	5-2-3	48	27.9	9-9-6
1961	51	31.8	3-6-8	43	13.9	4-4-7	41	23.8	4-4-7	52	42.1	5-5-9	48	35.7	6-3-6
1960	50	33.3	3-3-3	41	10.2	8-5-8	39	27.3	2-2-7	51	32.9	9-5-5	48	27.4	9-6-5
1959	51	37.1	3-5-6	40	13.5	8-7-5	39	26.4	5-1-9	53	36.6	5-7-6	50	44.3	2-5-3
1958	51	30.9	3-6-2	42	12.2	7-6-4	40	20.3	7-6-7	51	36.6	6-3-6	47	36.4	6-3-6
1957	51	33.0	3-2-8	41	22.2	2-2-8	39	33.9	2-2-5	52	41.6	5-5-5	50	44.6	2-3-5
1956	53	24.4	5-5-9	42	12.7	7-4-8	39	20.7	8-5-5	53	27.3	8-5-8	49	*43.4*	3-3-5
1955	53	15.9	8-8-5	42	14.6	4-4-5	40	20.4	7-7-4	54	38.5	4-5-5	50	38.2	5-5-6
1954	54	33.7	1-1-1	42	16.3	4-2-4	40	25.4	4-5-1	55	29.7	7-4-4	50	32.0	5-9-4
1953	54	21.5	7-7-4	44	19.4	1-5-7	41	31.7	1-2-7	55	26.1	7-7-4	51	25.9	8-8-4
1952	*51*	35.1	*3-3-2*	42	12.0	7-5-2	40	21.8	4-2-2	54	33.9	8-4-4	50	32.0	5-7-1
1951	49	44.4	3-3-2	37	16.7	6-6-5	36	30.9	3-6-5	51	38.4	6-6-3	49	41.0	6-8-3
1950	50	30.7	3-6-5	36	15.1	6-9-6	35	29.9	3-6-3	51	43.0	3-6-1	48	49.1	2-3-1
1949	*51*	38.8	*3-3-3*	40	10.8	8-7-3	*38*	23.5	5-5-5	53	41.4	5-2-6	50	35.1	5-5-9
1948	52	28.6	5-5-3	40	16.1	5-5-5	38	24.2	5-2-5	52	36.9	5-2-8	50	45.4	2-2-5
1947	53	27.6	5-2-8	40	17.2	5-3-5	38	27.7	2-5-5	54	35.5	4-5-6	51	34.6	4-6-9
1946	55	27.8	4-5-4	42	14.5	4-5-8	39	22.3	5-6-5	51	48.0	3-5-8	50	39.1	5-5-9
1945	*51*	25.4	6-6-5	39	12.2	9-9-8	37	32.6	1-2-7	53	40.7	5-4-5	49	30.2	9-8-8
1944	52	38.5	2-3-4	40	20.6	2-3-7	40	23.5	5-4-6	52	35.5	5-7-9	48	30.2	9-5-6
1943	52	24.2	5-1-5	39	15.0	6-5-6	38	29.5	1-2-3	52	42.4	5-5-5	49	29.8	9-9-5
1942	52	29.5	2-5-2	40	19.8	2-3-4	40	27.4	1-4-3	54	42.9	1-5-8	51	29.9	8-1-8
1941	52	30.9	*2-8-5*	42	31.2	1-2-7	41	21.9	5-8-3	51	30.6	8-5-9	47	39.7	6-2-6
1940	*50*	21.2	9-8-6	41	17.1	5-5-8	38	20.7	3-5-2	54	38.0	4-2-1	51	30.7	5-5-5
1939	*54*	18.3	7-5-5	42	15.8	4-5-5	40	25.4	4-4-5	54	42.8	1-2-5	51	36.7	4-5-5
1938	*54*	28.3	4-5-5	42	16.6	4-5-2	40	24.6	6-4-3	51	37.6	6-5-2	50	42.2	2-5-1
1937	51	21.7	9-4-6	39	16.3	6-2-6	36	17.6	9-7-6	52	35.1	8-7-6	50	36.9	5-1-6
1936	53	12.4	8-7-6	40	6.7	8-7-6	36	28.7	2-2-5	52	37.2	5-5-5	50	46.3	2-2-8
1935	53	26.8	5-7-7	40	15.0	5-5-7	38	18.6	8-6-5	53	35.2	8-4-8	50	29.9	8-4-8
1934	56	17.2	7-7-1	44	7.9	7-5-7	39	22.6	5-7-5	54	34.5	7-7-4	52	33.5	4-7-4
1933	55	26.8	4-4-8	42	11.5	7-7-5	38	20.8	8-8-7	53	30.5	8-5-4	50	34.6	4-8-1
1932	51	27.3	6-2-2	40	17.2	4-8-1	38	20.4	7-5-7	53	36.5	4-4-7	51	35.7	4-4-7
1931	55	36.3	1-4-7	44	16.2	4-4-4	43	21.4	5-8-2	55	25.1	8-8-2	53	28.8	7-8-1
1930	*54*	22.5	7-4-5	41	13.8	8-4-2	39	13.9	9-8-6	53	44.1	3-3-6	51	44.4	2-5-2
1929	*50*	24.4	6-9-6	37	17.2	6-8-3	36	27.0	2-3-2	50	33.0	6-6-2	49	33.5	6-2-2
1928	*52*	28.2	5-6-8	41	15.3	5-3-3	*38*	21.4	6-6-5	51	55.6	2-3-8	51	43.3	2-6-5
1927	52	26.4	5-6-5	38	19.6	3-6-5	36	21.0	8-9-4	52	43.5	3-5-5	48	39.4	6-5-6
1926	*52*	26.4	5-2-3	41	13.1	8-8-4	38	28.8	2-3-6	50	29.4	8-3-3	50	30.4	5-8-5
1925	*52*	26.3	5-2-3	41	12.2	8-5-6	*38*	22.2	6-9-5	52	40.4	6-3-2	48	38.9	6-3-2
1924	*50*	22.5	9-6-8	37	15.1	6-5-8	*36*	19.7	8-5-3	49	40.4	5-5-5	50	36.3	5-8-2
1923	*52*	31.2	2-3-7	41	19.7	5-2-5	38	24.9	5-5-2	52	36.7	5-3-5	51	34.4	4-5-5
1922	*53*	23.0	8-5-6	39	18.2	3-6-3	39	24.3	4-4-4	53	41.7	4-7-4	53	41.9	1-7-4
1921	*54*	20.3	4-2-7	42	15.8	1-4-7	*41*	23.6	5-2-6	55	29.3	9-9-9	49	39.7	6-3-9
1920	*51*	23.0	9-6-9	41	15.8	2-2-5	*38*	27.5	2-1-1	51	35.2	5-5-4	51	43.1	1-1-4
1919	*51*	33.4	3-5-4	41	8.4	8-7-4	*37*	18.9	8-8-9	52	43.2	3-5-9	50	33.8	5-8-6
1918	53	26.2	5-7-6	41	12.4	8-5-6	39	16.3	9-8-6	48	32.2	9-5-9	46	31.9	9-5-6
1917	*49*	24.8	6-6-8	38	9.2	6-5-7	35	26.5	6-2-3	51	29.7	9-8-3	49	34.9	6-5-2
1916	*50*	23.9	6-6-3	38	18.4	3-5-5	35	23.6	5-3-5	51	34.2	9-3-6	49	42.1	3-3-6
1915	50	36.0	3-3-3	40	20.0	2-3-8	*38*	28.0	2-2-8	52	24.7	8-7-5	49	37.4	6-2-5
1914	*52*	29.6	2-5-2	42	22.7	1-2-7	38	22.4	5-5-9	53	38.2	5-8-5	51	51.2	2-5-2
1913	47	27.0	6-7-6	42	14.9	4-5-8	*38*	17.8	8-8-9	50	31.5	9-9-6	48	46.6	3-3-6
1912	50	23.8	6-9-3	39	19.1	3-6-8		24.2	—1—	53	32.3	8-8-5	51	47.2	2-5-5
1911	53	25.4	5-7-6	40	15.6	5-5-5				51	28.0	9-9-6	49	35.4	6-9-3
1910	52	*25.3*	5-6-3	42	13.3	7-5-3				50	47.0	3-3-2	50	44.2	2-2-1
1909	*51*	33.6	3-8-5	40	21.3	2-2-5				52	33.3	3-3-3	51	33.9	5-5-2
1908	52	38.1	2-3-4	42	19.5	1-5-4				50	40.2	6-3-2	48	40.0	6-6-2
1907	51	29.6	3-3-5	39	13.7	9-6-3				52	34.2	8-5-5	51	42.8	2-1-7
1906	52	29.7	2-6-7	41	20.5	2-3-8				50	29.6	9-5-6	49	42.9	3-2-6
1905	50	33.0	3-6-6	42	16.6	4-5-5				49	29.8	9-9-6	47	41.3	3-9-3
1904	50	30.2	3-6-6	40	15.2	5-5-2				50	32.5	9-6-6	49	40.4	3-3-3
1903	50	33.5	3-6-3	*42*	16.9	4-5-6							50	33.0	5-3-9
1902	*50*	42.9	*3-3-6*	*44*	16.1	*4-9-2*							49	35.9	6-4-9
1901	52	24.0	5-4-5	44	12.9	7-4-7									
1900	53	34.0	2-3-6	45	11.8	7-4-4							51	36.6	5-1-5
1899	50	30.3	3-3-6	38	17.2	6-5-6							50	32.9	5-8-6
1898	51	22.8	9-6-5	40	11.9	8-8-7							50	47.8	2-1-5
1897	51	30.3	3-6-4	*40*	13.5	8-8-2							49	36.8	5-6-5
1896	52	41.0	2-3-7	38	18.5	3-8-2							50	39.1	5-3-5
1895	*51*	20.7	9-9-4	*38*	11.8	9-6-8							48	30.9	9-8-6
1894	52	*22.4*	8-6-6	*40*	15.5	5-7-5							51	30.6	8-8-5
1893		*22.1*		*38*	11.6	9-7-_							48	40.6	*3-8-3*

See footnotes at end of table.

Series J 164–247. Reference Climatological Stations—Temperature, Precipitation, and Description of Year: 1884 to 1970—Con.

[*Italicized* figures are based on interpolated monthly values. Standard error of interpolated figures: For temperature, less than 1° F.; for precipitation, less than 0.5 inch]

The South

Year	Beeville Experiment Station, Tex.			Calhoun Experiment Station, La.			Fayetteville Experiment Station, Ark.			Goodwell Agricultural College, Okla.			Lewisburg Experiment Station, Tenn.			St. Leo's Abbey, Fla.		
	Annual mean temperature	Annual total precipitation	Description of year[1]	Annual mean temperature	Annual total precipitation	Description of year[1]	Annual mean temperature	Annual total precipitation	Description of year[1]	Annual mean temperature	Annual total precipitation	Description of year[1]	Annual mean temperature	Annual total precipitation	Description of year[1]	Annual mean temperature	Annual total precipitation	Description of year[1]
	194	195	196	197	198	199	200	201	202	203	204	205	206	207	208	209	210	211
	°F.	Inches		°F.	Inches		°F.	Inches		°F.	Inches		°F.	Inches		°F.	Inches	
1970	69	28.0	6-3-5	64	44.6	5-6-6	59	41.6	5-7-6	57	12.9	8-5-8	57	47.5	5-6-6	71	52.9	6-8-3
1969	70	29.5	5-5-5	64	39.2	9-8-5	59	44.4	5-7-2	57	20.1	5-5-5	56	54.6	6-5-6	71	65.8	3-5-9
1968	68	31.5	6-6-6	62	74.0	3-3-3	58	48.7	5-5-6	57	17.6	5-8-5	56	47.9	6-8-5	70	46.3	6-6-5
1967	71	42.1	2-5-5	64	37.1	9-6-5	59	38.4	5-9-8	58	16.5	4-3-8	57	57.1	6-3-5	72	43.5	8-3-5
1966	69	26.2	6-5-3	63	49.2	6-5-8	58	37.1	8-5-2	56	14.0	6-2-3	56	47.8	6-5-9	71	53.5	6-6-2
1965	71	32.8	5-8-2	65	41.4	5-5-5	60	39.8	4-5-4	57	16.4	5-5-5	58	51.6	5-3-8	72	57.8	5-3-4
1964	70	21.9	5-5-6	64	40.3	5-8-9	59	36.5	7-5-9	57	11.5	7-7-6	58	63.2	2-2-6	72	59.7	5-4-3
1963	71	*17.8*	8-5-6	64	36.9	8-2-9	60	21.6	7-7-9	59	12.8	7-4-5	57	45.3	9-2-9	72	61.0	5-4-3
1962	70	27.2	5-2-8	65	45.5	9-2-3	58	48.2	5-2-5	57	21.5	5-3-8	58	57.7	6-6-2	72	45.9	8-4-4
1961	67	36.7	9-6-3	63	72.4	3-3-6	57	56.7	3-3-6	56	16.7	6-6-5	58	56.4	6-6-6	73	36.6	8-7-6
1960	68	43.4	3-3-6	64	41.5	9-5-9	57	42.8	6-2-9	56	21.7	6-5-3	56	42.1	9-6-6	71	75.3	2-5-6
1959	68	30.9	6-6-6	66	45.5	8-2-9	57	*38.9*	9-6-9	56	20.6	5-2-5	59	54.8	6-9-9	73	70.4	1-5-2
1958	69	33.1	6-7-3	64	53.5	6-2-9	57	45.8	6-2-9	56	21.0	5-5-4	57	45.0	6-5-9	71	56.2	5-7-3
1957	70	40.1	3-8-4	66	69.1	2-6-4	57	62.5	3-6-4	56	15.4	5-5-8	60	65.3	2-8-1	73	58.8	4-5-4
1956	71	19.3	8-7-8	66	43.3	8-8-5	59	38.7	8-5-9	59	10.3	7-4-8	60	52.3	5-5-5	72	45.4	8-8-5
1955	72	19.4	7-5-8	66	50.1	5-6-8	57	42.6	5-6-2	57	14.5	5-4-8	59	59.8	2-9-6	72	43.1	8-8-6
1954	72	15.4	7-7-8	68	30.9	7-7-7	60	35.3	7-7-8	60	10.1	7-4-4	60	47.3	4-7-5	72	45.0	8-4-5
1953	72	19.3	7-7-8	67	54.6	4-7-5	60	35.6	8-7-8	60	12.2	7-4-7	60	48.1	5-5-5	73	81.1	1-4-5
1952	71	32.2	5-7-4	64	34.0	9-7-1	59	34.8	8-4-7	58	9.2	7-7-7	60	48.9	5-4-1	72	42.6	8-7-1
1951	73	25.5	7-7-8	66	48.4	5-5-7	57	48.1	6-5-6	56	16.2	5-5-5	59	52.9	5-8-6	72	50.1	8-7-6
1950	73	13.9	7-5-4	67	67.2	1-3-1	57	50.7	6-3-2	57	26.9	2-2-7	58	66.6	3-6-1	72	57.4	4-4-7
1949	72	35.5	4-2-4	68	53.0	4-5-1	58	47.0	6-6-2	56	22.2	5-2-2	60	59.4	2-2-2	74	50.8	7-8-4
1948	71	19.9	8-7-6	66	39.2	8-7-6	58	48.3	5-3-6	56	24.0	2-2-3	59	63.7	3-8-6	74	51.3	7-4-5
1947	70	19.3	8-8-9	68	57.1	4-4-6	58	40.0	9-5-9	56	23.0	2-2-7	58	41.4	9-6-5	72	68.5	2-3-5
1946	72	37.1	5-5-5	68	71.5	1-2-2	60	52.6	2-5-5	58	26.0	1-5-5	60	54.7	5-9-3	74	51.8	4-5-2
1945	72	25.7	7-5-8	68	61.9	1-3-3	58	64.7	3-3-2	57	15.5	5-5-2	59	52.6	3-9-3	72	81.9	1-2-5
1944	71	27.4	5-4-5	66	56.6	5-5-5	59	48.0	5-2-5	56	21.6	6-5-3	60	58.1	5-7-5	72	54.3	5-4-5
1943	71	33.6	5-5-7	66	32.2	8-4-8	59	40.7	5-7-5	57	15.0	5-4-4	59	42.1	8-4-8	72	63.3	2-1-5
1942	70	40.0	2-2-5	65	44.5	8-5-9	59	56.9	2-2-6	57	27.0	2-2-4	59	44.8	6-2-6	72	60.1	5-1-3
1941	70	47.5	2-3-2	66	54.6	5-5-6	60	50.5	5-5-2	56	26.2	2-3-5	60	38.6	8-2-8	72	60.0	5-4-2
1940	70	33.0	5-2-8	64	62.2	3-3-6	57	40.5	5-6-9	56	16.2	5-8-5	57	43.8	6-6-8	70	43.9	9-5-6
1939	73	16.7	7-4-5	67	45.0	7-4-5	61	36.4	7-7-4	58	13.6	7-5-2	59	59.4	2-2-2	73	50.1	7-2-7
1938	73	21.1	7-7-1	67	47.1	4-5-7	61	48.3	4-5-1	59	14.9	4-7-7	61	46.8	4-5-5	72	49.2	8-8-8
1937	71	23.3	8-7-8	65	62.1	2-5-2	58	42.4	5-4-5	57	11.3	8-7-5	59	64.4	3-2-1	72	60.7	5-5-1
1936	68	34.9	6-3-6	65	32.9	8-8-9	60	29.3	7-7-9	57	9.7	5-7-6	59	51.1	5-4-9	72	55.8	5-8-3
1935	70	33.2	6-6-5	66	48.4	5-8-5	59	48.5	2-2-8	58	11.7	7-7-7	59	46.8	5-5-5	70	57.6	6-3-9
1934	71	32.1	5-8-1	67	54.8	4-4-4	61	40.0	7-7-7	60	14.3	4-7-1	60	41.3	8-4-5	71	69.8	3-3-5
1933	72	29.7	4-3-5	68	62.8	1-2-2	61	54.2	2-4-2	58	12.6	7-4-6	61	49.6	4-5-5	72	65.0	2-3-4
1932	70	42.7	3-5-1	66	51.8	5-7-1	60	45.1	5-5-1	55	14.7	6-8-2	60	41.5	1-4-1	73	40.5	7-7-7
1931	70	37.8	3-3-2	66	58.6	5-6-6	60	41.9	4-5-5	57	16.2	5-8-5	61	41.3	7-8-8	70	45.2	9-8-3
1930	70	26.9	6-8-3	66	44.9	8-8-8	59	40.2	5-8-5	52	18.5	6-5-9	60	41.7	8-7-4	69	51.9	6-9-6
1929	70	38.4	3-6-3	65	43.1	9-5-6	58	52.8	3-5-3	50	18.4	6-3-6	59	58.0	5-5-8	72	52.3	5-6-4
1928	70	36.8	5-4-5	65	49.8	6-5-9	59	52.9	2-6-5	55	24.3	3-6-5	59	43.0	9-2-8	70	64.8	3-2-6
1927	73	20.6	7-4-4	67	49.8	4-9-1	60	66.6	2-3-4	57	16.3	5-5-3	61	54.5	4-6-4	71	48.5	8-5-8
1926	69	31.6	6-6-6	64	49.8	6-2-8	58	42.5	5-6-8	56	17.3	5-5-8	59	63.5	2-2-8	71	55.4	6-5-3
1925	70	31.2	5-5-5	67	54.6	4-4-5	60	27.0	8-7-5	57	15.9	5-5-6	59	42.4	7-7-5	71	55.4	6-5-3
1924	70	21.8	9-8-3	64	29.5	9-7-5	57	38.8	8-5-8	55	12.1	9-8-5	57	45.8	6-8-5	73	53.8	4-4-4
1923	71	46.4	2-5-1	65	72.8	3-6-2	60	46.3	5-7-4	56	24.1	2-5-7	59	59.2	3-3-2	72	62.2	2-7-5
1922	71	37.7	2-2-8	65	60.8	3-6-2	60	35.6	7-5-4	58	14.8	4-5-5	61	55.2	4-8-5	71	53.9	6-6-8
1921	72	27.5	4-7-8	66	49.5	5-3-5	62	39.3	7-5-4	59	16.9	4-6-1	62	50.1	4-4-5	71	61.8	5-9-5
1920	70	22.3	9-5-6	63	71.1	3-3-9	58	44.0	5-5-9	56	14.8	5-9-5	59	57.3	6-6-5	69	50.3	9-6-6
1919	69	47.4	3-3-3	64	59.6	6-6-9	57	45.5	5-2-4	54	14.9	6-9-3	60	55.1	5-5-5	71	63.3	3-3-3
1918	70	29.6	6-8-9	64	44.0	9-2-9	60	39.5	8-7-8	56	20.1	5-4-9	60	49.1	5-5-6	71	54.4	6-6-6
1917	70	12.1	8-7-8	63	39.0	8-6-8	57	40.0	8-6-5	55	16.6	6-6-5	57	52.8	6-5-5	70	54.0	6-3-2
1916	72	23.4	7-1-7	65	36.4	9-5-6	60	43.0	4-7-2	58	11.7	4-5-8	59	57.6	5-3-4	71	50.6	6-8-8
1915	72	13.1	8-7-9	64	48.8	6-6-6	59	58.2	2-3-6	50	26.8	3-2-5	59	57.4	6-3-6	70	53.5	6-8-3
1914	70	46.6	3-1-8	65	48.2	6-2-9	60	38.8	8-4-2	58	22.5	1-2-2	59	46.8	5-1-8	71	51.9	6-6-4
1913	69	32.8	6-6-9	64	62.7	3-6-2	59	47.3	5-4-6	51	19.0	6-5-6	60	53.1	4-5-2	72	50.6	8-6-4
1912	70	30.0	6-8-3	64	50.6	6-6-3	57	40.4	6-5-6	47	17.5	6-5-3	58	61.0	3-3-6	72	54.9	4-2-9
1911	73	23.5	7-7-7	67	54.4	4-5-7	61	38.9	7-5-7	59	15.5	4-4-4	62	60.3	1-2-5	73	64.1	2-9-3
1910	71	29.8	5-5-5	65	41.7	8-6-6	59	33.4	8-6-6				59	46.7	6-6-6	70	53.8	6-3-6
1909	72	30.8	4-2-7	66	44.7	8-5-4	61	34.0	7-7-7	59	*11.4*	7-4-2	60	50.5	5-5-4	72	53.3	5-2-8
1908	72	35.7	4-1-8	65	64.0	2-3-5	60	50.5	5-3-5	---	---	---	60	50.4	4-5-6	72	41.7	8-8-3
1907	72	19.1	7-7-7	65	47.5	6-8-7	60	40.7	4-5-4	---	---	---	60	51.5	5-2-4	72	46.6	8-8-8
1906	70	31.2	5-5-6	64	57.8	6-3-9	58	51.6	6-3-6	---	---	---	60	57.1	5-2-5	71	60.0	5-2-5
1905	69	39.6	3-5-6	63	65.3	2-3-3	56	54.7	3-3-6	---	---	---	60	62.8	2-2-6	71	62.3	2-2-5
1904	---	---	---	65	49.1	6-3-9	58	*43.5*	6-3-6	---	---	---	60	37.4	8-8-9	71	50.7	6-9-2
1903	---	---	---	63	50.3	6-3-6	56	45.3	6-6-3	---	---	---	59	51.1	6-6-5	70	54.9	
1902	---	---	---	64	52.1	6-5-9	58	48.2	5-5-6	---	---	---	60	52.3	5-4-6	72	*45.5*	8-7-6
1901	---	---	---	62	36.7	9-5-9	58	28.9	8-7-8	---	---	---	58	45.0	6-1-8	---	---	---
1900				64	57.7	6-3-6	59	37.7	8-5-6							---	---	---
1899				64	30.7	9-8-9	58	40.2	5-5-9				60	53.6	4-2-6	---	---	---
1898				67	53.6	4-3-5	58	66.1	2-3-5				59	47.4	5-7-6	---	---	---
1897				65	45.5	8-5-9	59	37.2	8-5-5					49.8	-5-			
1896				66	37.3	8-7-9	61	38.5	7-7-5									
1895				62	48.4	6-3-9	57	41.6	5-2-9									
1894				64	55.2	6-6-6	59	47.1	5-5-5									
1893				64	43.5	9-6-6	58	58.5	3-3-9									
1892					65.5		57	51.3	6-6-6									
1891					52.5		56	34.6	9-6-8									
1890																		-5-
1889													60	53.0	5-6-			
1888													58	48.6	6-3-			
1884								51.9						53.3				

See footnotes at end of table.

Series J 164–247. Reference Climatological Stations—Temperature, Precipitation, and Description of Year: 1884 to 1970—Con.

[*Italicized* figures are based on interpolated monthly values. Standard error of interpolated figures: For temperature, less than 1° F.; for precipitation, less than 0.5 inch]

	The South—Con.						The West										
	Winthrop College, S.C.			Woodstock, Md. [2]			Agricultural College, N. Mex.			Bozeman Agricultural College, Mont.			Davis Agricultural College, Calif.			Grand Canyon National Park Headquarters, Ariz.		
Year	Annual mean temperature	Annual total precipitation	Description[1] of year	Annual mean temperature	Annual total precipitation	Description[1] of year	Annual mean temperature	Annual total precipitation	Description[1] of year	Annual mean temperature	Annual total precipitation	Description[1] of year	Annual mean temperature	Annual total precipitation	Description[1] of year	Annual mean temperature	Annual total precipitation	Description[1] of year
	212	213	214	215	216	217	218	219	220	221	222	223	224	225	226	227	228	229
	°F.	Inches		°F.	Inches		°F.	Inches		°F.	Inches		°F.	Inches		°F.	Inches	
1970	62	46.4	5-7-9	-----	41.3	------	61	3.4	8-8-4	44	19.6	4-4-4	61	22.4	1-2-3	48	14.0	6-6-7
1969	60	41.9	6-5-6	-----	36.9	------	62	11.9	1-1-4	43	23.4	2-1-6	61	25.1	2-6-3	47	16.8	6-6-2
1968	60	40.0	9-5-6	-----	40.0	------	61	13.2	2-2-5	43	23.6	2-3-2	60	15.6	5-5-5	47	13.5	6-3-5
1967	61	50.8	2-4-8	-----	36.7	------	62	8.4	4-2-8	44	22.9	1-4-4	60	19.7	5-1-2	49	12.6	5-5-2
1966	60	43.0	6-5-5	-----	37.0	------	60	9.8	2-2-6	45	14.6	7-4-8	60	15.0	5-5-9	49	17.5	2-4-6
1965	62	40.2	8-5-4	53	31.1		61	8.3	5-5-5	43	19.2	5-5-4	59	15.6	6-3-5	47	20.7	3-9-5
1964	61	60.4	2-2-3	54	32.1	------	60	3.6	8-7-8	43	19.9	5-2-5	59	15.4	6-3-9	48	11.5	9-8-9
1963	60	41.0	6-9-9	52	34.7		62	6.1	5-5-5	45	17.9	4-4-5	58	21.8	3-5-5	50	13.9	4-2-5
1962	61	47.4	6-9-3	52	38.8	6-9-6	62	6.4	4-8-1	44	20.0	1-2-5	59	20.7	3-6-6	49	11.4	8-9-5
1961	60	53.2	3-3-6	54	37.6	5-5-6	61	10.1	1-1-2	45	16.1	4-7-7	59	13.1	5-4-8	48	14.4	6-2-8
1960	60	48.6	6-5-2	52	46.5	3-2-4	61	7.7	4-4-5	43	14.6	8-7-5	61	14.1	5-4-4	49	16.2	5-7-3
1959	62	69.5	2-2-5	55	41.0	4-4-9	61	5.9	7-4-7	43	19.6	5-4-4	63	12.9	4-4-4	49	13.8	5-8-8
1958	61	50.4	6-2-6	52	43.4	6-3-3	61	14.0	1-1-1	45	18.1	4-2-4	63	24.7	1-4-1	49	16.7	5-5-4
1957	63	50.0	5-8-4	54	41.1	5-8-4	61	9.3	4-4-1	43	16.5	5-1-8	61	15.3	4-7-8	48	20.9	3-3-4
1956	63	36.7	8-8-8	54	44.1	5-2-8	60	4.8	7-4-4	43	11.3	7-7-5	60	13.0	5-8-1	50	7.6	7-8-7
1955	63	43.9	5-5-5	54	46.8	2-1-8	61	7.3	4-6-9	41	17.2	5-8-5	60	13.6	5-5-6	48	11.9	9-2-6
1954	63	35.7	4-7-2	54	30.5	8-8-7	62	5.8	7-8-8	44	12.7	5-5-4	60	18.3	5-5-4	51	12.5	4-5-7
1953	61	42.1	5-5-5	55	47.2	1-9-1	60	3.8	7-7-5	46	16.4	5-4-4	61	10.0	7-2-1	50	10.9	4-2-8
1952	62	49.5	5-2-5	54	60.8	2-1-1	60	6.2	5-4-4	43	19.6	5-5-2	60	21.5	2-5-2	48	17.8	3-5-3
1951	62	37.2	5-5-9	54	41.4	5-5-5	61	5.0	7-7-8	40	20.2	5-6-5	60	12.9	5-5-4	49	17.2	5-5-7
1950	62	44.5	5-3-7	53	48.8	2-3-4	62	5.3	7-5-4	42	18.2	5-3-5	61	20.0	1-8-6	50	10.3	7-6-5
1949	62	58.9	2-3-4	56	39.0	4-4-1	60	9.0	4-7-3	43	17.1	5-4-3	59	10.6	9-5-6	47	17.9	3-6-3
1948	62	49.8	5-8-9	54	53.5	2-5-3	58	5.2	9-7-3	42	19.5	5-2-5	58	16.0	6-2-8	49	13.5	6-2-5
1947	61	51.1	6-6-5	54	36.5	8-3-5	59	6.1	6-5-5	44	23.6	1-2-4	60	11.3	8-2-9	49	11.8	8-6-7
1946	63	41.3	4-9-6	54	38.5	4-3-5	60	7.1	4-7-6	43	18.6	4-8-2	59	10.8	9-5-6	49	18.7	2-2-5
1945	63	45.2	5-5-5	54	53.9	2-3-3	59	5.8	9-5-8	42	19.5	5-5-8	60	19.9	2-4-5	49	12.6	5-5-7
1944	62	47.0	5-8-2	53	41.1	5-4-8	58	9.8	3-3-2	42	20.9	2-3-8	60	19.5	2-6-5	48	10.9	9-8-5
1943	62	39.9	8-4-5	54	35.4	8-7-5	61	7.6	4-4-4	42	17.2	6-6-6	61	15.6	4-6-1	51	12.3	4-5-4
1942	62	53.1	2-2-6	54	47.2	2-2-5	60	9.8	2-2-5	41	17.2	6-9-3	60	18.4	5-7-1	50	9.7	7-4-5
1941	62	45.2	5-2-9	54	29.9	8-5-5	60	19.6	2-3-1	43	22.9	2-5-4	61	28.8	1-5-1	48	24.6	2-5-1
1940	60	41.1	6-5-6	51	41.4	6-9-9	60	9.2	5-6-5	44	18.6	4-4-2	62	29.4	1-8-1	50	22.7	1-4-4
1939	63	46.9	4-1-1	54	38.8	5-5-2	59	5.8	8-8-6	44	14.0	7-5-8	60	5.9	8-5-8	50	17.7	2-7-6
1938	63	40.1	7-5-4	54	33.2	7-7-8	59	9.3	6-3-4	43	20.4	1-8-4	59	20.6	3-5-2	49	17.2	5-5-2
1937	62	55.3	2-4-1	53	48.7	2-4-1	60	7.0	5-8-5	41	18.0	6-5-3	60	21.6	2-5-3	49	19.3	2-8-3
1936	61	63.3	3-5-3	53	39.1	6-5-3	60	9.5	4-5-2	43	12.8	5-7-6	61	18.2	4-2-1	50	15.8	5-5-5
1935	61	39.3	9-8-8	52	39.5	6-8-3	60	12.7	2-1-7	42	15.5	8-4-4	59	16.6	5-5-5	49	14.1	5-1-5
1934	61	45.1	6-7-8	53	46.2	3-7-6	61	4.6	7-7-8	47	10.5	4-7-4	62	11.2	7-2-4	52	10.5	7-5-7
1933	63	32.6	7-5-4	55	50.1	1-1-4	59	4.7	9-5-6	44	15.9	4-4-6	60	12.5	5-4-9	51	10.6	7-4-6
1932	63	51.4	4-4-1	55	45.6	4-5-4	59	8.8	6-5-3	42	17.3	6-2-5	60	8.4	8-5-5	50	12.7	5-7-3
1931	63	50.0	5-2-9	56	35.6	7-1-8	60	13.3	2-2-2	44	15.3	7-7-5	61	16.1	4-1-7	49	15.0	5-4-8
1930	62	36.2	8-8-8	55	20.1	7-7-7	60	6.9	5-5-8	42	14.2	8-4-8	59	12.1	6-6-4	48	14.7	6-2-7
1929	61	60.8	3-6-5	54	40.3	5-9-5	59	9.2	6-6-8	41	15.8	6-4-6	59	8.6	8-3-9	49	10.8	8-2-6
1928	61	48.8	6-2-5	53	41.0	6-8-5	60	9.4	5-6-5	42	16.2	5-6-6	60	13.9	5-8-8	50	13.1	4-4-5
1927	63	43.8	4-6-4	54	38.1	5-9-5	60	9.5	5-3-4	41	21.8	3-6-2	59	18.1	6-2-5	50	22.9	2-3-2
1926	62	38.4	8-4-5	52	43.2	6-6-5	59	14.4	3-9-6	43	19.8	2-5-1	61	23.0	1-4-5	50	17.4	5-5-8
1925	63	32.6	7-7-2	54	35.0	8-5-5	60	7.8	5-2-8	44	19.4	4-5-8	60	15.4	5-4-5	49	17.6	3-3-6
1924	60	58.4	3-8-5	52	52.4	3-6-1	59	4.8	9-4-5	40	20.9	3-9-2	59	13.8	6-8-8	48	18.6	3-3-4
1923	62	48.0	5-5-5	54	39.1	5-5-5	60	10.4	2-5-1	42	15.3	8-5-8	60	7.8	8-5-5	48	16.4	6-5-3
1922	62	52.9	2-5-2	55	38.9	4-2-5	62	5.6	7-7-7	40	17.7	6-2-6	59	22.6	2-7-3	48	15.8	6-3-9
1921	63	40.1	7-4-5	56	38.3	4-5-4	62	7.6	4-5-8	42	15.2	8-4-4	60	13.4	5-7-5			
1920	61	51.6	5-2-3	53	49.9	3-2-6	60	8.2	5-2-4	40	19.2	3-6-5	60	15.4	5-4-8	47	12.6	6-9-1
1919	63	54.2	2-2-2	55	42.3	4-5-1	60	8.0	5-8-6	42	11.0	9-7-8	59	14.6	5-5-3	48	18.4	3-5-6
1918	62	47.8	5-5-9	54	40.9	5-5-6	60	7.2	5-4-8	42	18.9	6-5-2	60	16.7	5-7-7	48	19.9	3-3-8
1917	58	40.6	9-6-8	52	38.2	6-2-6	60	5.6	8-5-8	41	15.7	6-8-3	61	9.5	7-7-2	47	10.7	9-8-6
1916	61	43.8	6-3-8	54	39.9	5-2-5	61	7.8	4-8-7	38	21.2	3-6-6	60	20.1	2-5-1	46	14.5	6-6-2
1915	62	48.0	5-5-2	54	47.6	2-3-2	59	7.4	6-8-2	42	25.0	2-3-8	60	21.0	2-7-2	46	13.9	6-9-6
1914	61	45.8	6-1-5	54	36.1	8-4-2	61	11.8	1-2-5	43	16.5	5-6-8	59	22.2	6-3-2	48	13.0	6-6-2
1913	62	52.4	2-5-4	56	39.0	4-4-4	58	11.7	3-2-6	40	18.7	6-6-6	59	17.9	5-5-9	47	15.8	6-6-3
1912	61	47.4	6-3-6	53	40.8	6-5-6	58	9.2	6-2-9	40	21.6	3-6-5	58	11.0	9-3-8	43	9.6	9-9-9
1911	63	40.0	7-4-8	55	44.7	4-2-9	60	5.8	7-8-4	40	18.1	6-6-5	57	22.4	3-6-2	46	21.7	3-3-1
1910	61	42.5	6-3-5	53	29.6	8-9-6	63	4.0	7-4-8	43	18.7	5-8-6	------	7.0	------	48	12.0	6-3-3
1909	62	40.9	8-2-7	53	33.7	9-4-4	61	4.9	7-7-7	40	22.3	3-5-8	------	25.8	------	45	26.1	3-3-2
1908	62	55.0	2-2-3	54	35.7	5-2-3	60	6.0	7-5-4	41	25.3	3-6-5				45	22.5	3-3-5
1907	61	49.3	6-3-7	52	47.5	6-3-6	63	6.4	4-4-4	41	17.2	6-3-5				49	36.7	2-3-1
1906	62	55.6	2-2-3	54	53.1	2-1-8	61	8.8	4-8-2	41	16.9	6-6-5				48	22.3	3-3-6
1905	61	45.5	6-2-6	52	42.9	6-4-6	60	17.1	1-5-1	41	14.7	9-6-5				48	29.6	3-3-2
1904	60	35.4	9-3-9	50	34.4	9-6-9	60	10.1	1-5-8	42	16.2	5-9-2				50	17.6	5-2-3
1903	61	43.6	6-5-6	53	41.6	6-3-3	59	10.3	3-2-2	41	17.6	6-6-5						
1902	61	48.8	6-5-3	53	51.6	3-6-3	60	10.9	1-2-7	42	15.5	8-6-5						
1901	59	64.1	3-3-6	52	39.7	6-4-9	61	12.0	1-1-4	44	15.5	7-8-5						
1900	62	44.9	5-4-6	53	32.5	8-4-8	61	8.4	4-7-4	44	14.2	7-8--						
1899		------		51	40.8	6-5-3	57	9.7	3-3-6									
1898				53	36.8	9-4-6	53	14.4	3-3-9									
1897				51	49.3	3-3-6	58	9.0	6-6-8									
1896				51	33.3	9-6-3	59	------	-6--									
1895				50	28.0	9-9-9												
1894				52	35.4	9-9-9												
1893				50	39.0	6-9-6												

See footnotes at end of table.

Series J 164–247. Reference Climatological Stations—Temperature, Precipitation, and Description of Year: 1884 to 1970—Con.

[*Italicized* figures are based on interpolated monthly values. Standard error of interpolated figures: For temperature, less than 1° F.; for precipitation, less than 0.5 inch]

The West—Con.

Year	Indio U.S. Date Garden, Calif. — Annual mean temp.	Indio — Annual total precip.	Indio — Description of year [1]	Logan (Utah State Agricultural College), Utah — Annual mean temp.	Logan — Annual total precip.	Logan — Description of year [1]	Medford Experiment Station, Oreg. — Annual mean temp.	Medford — Annual total precip.	Medford — Description of year [1]	Montrose No. 2, Colo. — Annual mean temp.	Montrose — Annual total precip.	Montrose — Description of year [1]	Tatoosh Island (Weather Bureau Office), Wash. — Annual mean temp.	Tatoosh — Annual total precip.	Tatoosh — Description of year [1]	Union Experiment Station, Oreg. — Annual mean temp.	Union — Annual total precip.	Union — Description of year [1]
	230	231	232	233	234	235	236	237	238	239	240	241	242	243	244	245	246	247
	°F.	Inches		°F.	Inches		°F.	Inches		°F.	Inches		°F.	Inches		°F.	Inches	
1970	73	4.7	2-2-4	48	20.9	2-4-4	54	24.2	4-4-1	47	10.1	6-6-8	[3]	[3]	[3]			
1969	74	2.6	4-5-5	48	16.9	5-2-2	53	23.2	5-1-2	48	11.2	3-3-5	[3]	[3]	[3]	48	19.2	4-1-1
1968	74	2.2	5-2-5	47	22.5	3-3-3	54	18.0	7-4-5	46	7.7	9-6-3	[3]	[3]	[3]	48	13.4	5-2-5
1967	73	3.3	5-2-5	48	21.1	2-5-5	54	18.2	4-7-5	48	10.9	6-3-5	[3]	[3]	[3]	48	13.7	5-5-5
1966	74	2.1	5-5-5	48	10.6	8-7-9	54	18.8	4-5-5	49	6.8	8-5-8	[3]	[3]	[3]	49	11.2	3-3-2
1965	72	5.9	3-9-8	47	*19.8*	5-3-1	53	17.5	8-5-2	48	14.0	3-3-2	[3]	[3]	[3]	49	12.3	3-5-6
1964	71	1.7	6-5-9	46	19.1	6-3-9	52	28.9	2-5-8	47	11.2	3-3-6	49	76.9	(NA)	48	13.4	5-4-4
1963	73	4.7	2-6-4	49	19.7	4-5-7	53	18.4	5-5-8	50	8.6	4-5-5	48	71.5	(NA)	46	12.7	8-7-6
1962	74	0.8	7-8-8	49	15.1	5-6-2	53	24.8	2-5-9	50	8.6	5-9-5	50	79.2	(NA)	48	13.1	5-5-5
1961	74	1.4	4-1-7	50	14.8	4-4-7	54	21.7	4-4-7	48	11.3	3-8-2	49	76.8	5-6-8	47	11.0	5-9-5
1960	75	1.3	4-7-5	48	14.2	8-8-5	54	21.2	4-4-5	49	9.4	5-7-3	49	92.8	2-4-1	49	11.7	4-7-7
1959	75	2.7	4-4-7	49	16.4	5-2-4	53	11.7	8-5-4	49	8.7	5-4-7	49	75.5	5-5-5	47	16.3	2-5-8
1958	75	3.0	4-4-4	50	13.4	7-5-4	55	25.1	4-1-1	52	6.2	7-7-1	52	77.5	5-5-5	47	14.2	5-5-1
1957	74	3.0	4-4-4	48	17.8	5-5-5	52	23.2	5-8-6	50	15.4	2-2-2	52	78.2	4-7-1	50	20.8	1-1-1
1956	73	0.4	8-5-8	46	11.7	8-8-2	52	26.7	2-5-2	50	6.7	7-4-4	50	71.6	5-1-6	47	15.6	2-8-6
1955	72	1.7	6-6-6	50	17.0	5-5-6	52	15.8	5-8-8	48	7.8	6-5-6	48	79.4	6-2-6	46	15.8	2-2-2
1954	74	2.7	4-6-7	50	12.5	7-5-4	52	18.1	5-6-5	52	8.6	4-5-7	49	80.8	6-3-8	48	11.8	4-3-4
1953	73	0.8	8-5-5	50	*14.0*	7-5-7	52	28.7	2-6-1	50	10.8	2-4-5	50	86.2	2-3-2	48	12.5	4-3-4
1952	73	6.5	2-8-3	48	12.8	8-5-3	52	20.7	5-2-3	49	9.7	5-4-2	50	92.2	1-8-1	49	18.3	1-6-1
1951	72	3.2	6-2-8	47	18.9	6-6-4	53	20.9	5-8-4	49	5.8	8-4-4	48	68.7	6-6-6	48	11.7	5-2-6
1950	74	0.7	8-6-8	48	19.9	2-6-2	52	28.4	2-5-6	50	6.8	7-9-2	47	80.0	6-9-2	48	13.9	5-5-4
1949	72	2.3	6-8-6	47	19.8	2-5-3	51	11.5	9-8-6	49	8.4	5-4-7	48	101.6	3-6-9	48	13.0	5-5-8
1948	72	2.0	6-6-5	47	17.3	5-5-8	49	25.7	3-3-6	48	10.8	6-3-2	*48*	*73.6*	*6-5-6*	47	10.0	8-8-6
1947	73	1.0	8-5-4	48	18.8	5-2-4	52	16.2	8-3-8	50	12.5	2-3-7	50	77.3	4-4-5	46	16.9	3-3-5
1946	72	1.8	6-8-5	49	20.5	2-5-8	51	17.1	9-8-9	50	9.1	4-4-8	49	82.2	5-3-5	48	14.6	4-3-4
1945	72	5.0	6-3-8	47	24.6	2-3-5	52	23.0	5-8-5	49	8.2	5-5-5	49	83.7	2-6-4	48	15.4	2-5-5
1944	71	3.0	6-8-3	47	18.9	6-3-8	51	17.5	5-6-8	50	10.4	2-5-6	50	72.7	4-9-4	48	14.4	5-6-4
1943	73	8.1	2-2-5	50	18.1	4-2-5	52	19.3	5-3-2	51	9.7	4-2-5	49	58.6	8-5-5	48	10.6	5-3-8
1942	73	3.2	5-1-5	47	18.0	6-5-3	52	23.8	5-5-5	50	8.5	5-8-5	50	58.9	7-1-4	47	12.4	5-3-2
1941	72	8.3	3-3-2	48	19.6	2-2-4	53	24.7	5-2-5	49	16.9	2-2-2	50	64.7	7-4-7	48	17.2	2-2-2
1940	74	4.9	4-7-4	52	17.0	4-7-4	54	22.0	------	50	10.1	4-7-5	52	78.1	4-4-7	50	21.3	1-2-4
1939	73	10.8	2-8-2	50	12.4	7-5-5	53	17.9	------	50	6.6	8-4-6	50	75.0	5-5-5	49	6.1	8-3-8
1938	73	4.1	6-5-4	50	17.8	4-5-4	53	19.3	------	48	13.3	2-8-2	49	60.9	8-9-2	49	11.8	5-4-1
1937	74	1.3	4-7-6	48	20.4	2-5-3	53	*26.6*	------	47	7.0	8-9-6	49	75.8	5-2-6	47	12.8	5-5-6
1936	74	6.8	1-2-5	50	18.3	4-4-2				50	7.6	7-4-5	50	63.4	8-1-8	48	9.8	8-4-9
1935	73	3.5	6-4-2	49	13.5	8-7-5				50	7.2	7-4-4	49	80.4	5-5-8	47	8.0	8-5-7
1934	76	0.5	7-5-7	*53*	*11.8*	7-4-4				53	7.9	4-7-4	51	82.1	1-4-9	51	10.8	4-5-4
1933	73	0.8	9-7-6	49	11.9	8-7-6				49	7.5	8-7-6	48	88.4	3-6-3	46	12.7	6-5-6
1932	72	3.5	6-5-6	46	16.4	6-2-3				48	8.9	6-5-6	49	93.2	2-2-5	46	11.3	6-9-6
1931	73	4.6	5-5-5	*48*	*12.3*	8-7-9				49	7.6	8-4-8	50	89.5	2-2-4	*48*	*9.9*	*8-7-8*
1930	73	3.3	5-5-4	47	20.3	3-2-5				47	9.1	6-2-6	49	69.3	5-5-3	47	13.5	6-5-2
1929	73	1.5	5-4-8	48	16.0	5-5-6				46	10.4	6-5-9	48	49.6	9-5-6	46	11.0	6-1-9
1928	73	0.7	8-8-2	48	*10.8*	8-6-8				49	11.3	2-5-8	50	73.1	5-8-5	48	9.4	8-8-9
1927	72	7.9	3-3-2	49	18.4	5-5-5				49	12.7	2-2-2	49	82.7	2-5-6	46	16.5	3-5-2
1926	74	6.2	1-5-7	50	16.0	4-5-4				49	10.8	2-8-8	51	71.8	4-7-4	48	15.9	2-4-4
1925	73	3.6	5-5-8	50	16.3	4-3-5				49	10.0	5-2-3	49	71.4	5-5-5	49	11.6	4-4-5
1924	74	0.7	7-7-7	47	12.4	9-8-8				47	9.1	6-5-3	48	79.1	6-9-2	46	9.4	9-6-5
1923	73	0.5	8-5-7	46	16.9	6-6-2				49	9.0	6-5-4	49	71.1	5-7-3	48	17.5	2-2-2
1922	73	1.7	5-4-3	47	15.2	6-4-3				49	7.6	8-4-8	48	60.3	9-9-3	46	8.3	9-7-9
1921	74	6.6	2-2-9	49	18.3	5-8-5				51	10.6	1-2-5	48	100.4	3-3-5	48	13.8	5-7-2
1920	72	6.8	3-2-5	47	19.2	3-6-8				48	10.1	6-5-8	48	89.8	3-3-8	46	14.8	6-5-9
1919	73	3.1	5-1-9	48	15.7	5-7-7				48	9.9	6-8-3	49	73.9	6-9-2	46	9.5	9-4-5
1918	73	2.0	5-4-8	49	16.9	5-4-1				48	11.0	3-5-2	49	82.6	2-6-5	48	12.4	5-4-1
1917	73	2.1	5-4-6	46	18.1	6-8-3				47	7.8	6-5-6	48	82.4	6-4-6	46	15.0	6-5-3
1916	72	5.1	6-5-2	47	18.8	5-8-2				49	13.1	2-5-1	47	77.8	6-5-3	45	13.3	6-6-6
1915	72	5.2	6-5-3	50	15.2	4-9-8				48	9.0	6-5-3	50	72.2	4-7-5	49	11.6	4-4-5
1914	74	2.7	4-4-5	48	19.6	2-2-2				48	13.2	2-2-3	49	83.4	2-9-5	49	16.9	1-5-8
1913	72	2.0	6-6-6	47	17.8	5-3-8				47	8.1	6-9-6	48	78.3	6-1-9	49	11.6	4-5-4
1912	72	4.5	6-5-8	46	18.9	6-3-8				48	10.9	3-2-8	49	72.8	5-2-5	46	17.3	3-3-9
1911	72	2.5	6-5-5	46	19.1	3-9-2				49	11.8	2-5-1	47	52.6	9-9-6	46	17.7	3-3-2
1910	75	1.0	7-4-6	50	11.7	7-8-3				47	4.7	9-9-6	48	67.1	9-9-6			
1909	72	4.1	6-2-5	*48*	*22.3*	*2-4-2*				45	11.2	3-3-2	47	74.9	6-6-9			
1908	73	3.6	6-5-5	46	18.8	6-3-8				*46*	*9.9*	*6-3-8*	48	72.4	6-9-8			
1907	73	3.9	5-8-2	48	22.0	2-3-1				*48*	*11.5*	*3-3-7*	48	61.1	9-9-6			
1906	73	7.1	2-2-5	*48*	*26.4*	*2-3-6*				48	13.4	3-6-5	49	69.2	5-5-5			
1905	*73*	*5.4*	*3-7-1*	49	12.5	8-5-8				45	11.2	3-6-2	50	63.7	8-8-5			
1904				49	13.5	8-5-5				*45*	*7.5*	*9-6-3*	49	78.7	5-6-8			
1903				46	14.0	9-8-6				*45*	*8.1*		49	68.9	5-5-5			
1902				48	13.3	8-6-7					6.5		49	91.6	3-6-5			
1901				50	14.5	7-5-7					6.2		48	101.3	2-6-5			
1900											6.2							
1899				50	15.1	4-8-8					5.9		50	101.4	1-1-2			
1898				47	12.6	9-6-9					9.2		50	114.0	2-9-3			
1897				46	13.2	9-8-9					7.8		*49*	*86.4*	*2-4-2*			
1896				47	17.4	6-6-5					15.6	-6-2	48	95.2	3-2-2			
1895				48	16.2	5-2-8					6.5	-7-2	48	100.8	3-4-2			
1894				45	13.5	9-9-6					12.3		48	93.0	3-5-5			
1893				*46*	*14.4*	*9-6-5*							47	114.3	5-5-3			
1892				*46*	*14.5*	*9-9-6*				48	9.5	6-5-2	47	104.2	3-2-6			
1891										48	9.0	6-9-3						
1890											11.4	-6-						
1889											9.1							
1888											7.2	—-6						
1887										*48*	*8.5*	*6-6-*						
1886											9.6							
1885											9.9							
1884											10.9							

NA Not available.
[1] For definition of codes, see text.
[2] Figures corrected for station move about Jan. 1914.
[3] Tatoosh Island (WBO), Wash. closed July 1966.

Series J 248–267. Long-Record City Stations—Annual Mean Temperature and Annual Total Precipitation: 1780 to 1970

[*Italicized figures are based on interpolated monthly values*]

Year	Albany, N.Y. Annual mean temperature 248 (°F)	Albany, N.Y. Annual total precipitation 249 (Inches)	Baltimore, Md. Annual mean temperature 250 (°F)	Baltimore, Md. Annual total precipitation 251 (Inches)	Charleston, S.C. Annual mean temperature 252 (°F)	Charleston, S.C. Annual total precipitation 253 (Inches)	New Haven, Conn. Annual mean temperature 254 (°F)	New Haven, Conn. Annual total precipitation 255 (Inches)	New York, N.Y. Annual mean temperature 256 (°F)	New York, N.Y. Annual total precipitation 257 (Inches)	Philadelphia, Pa. Annual mean temperature 258 (°F)	Philadelphia, Pa. Annual total precipitation 259 (Inches)	San Francisco, Calif. Annual mean temperature 260 (°F)	San Francisco, Calif. Annual total precipitation 261 (Inches)	Sante Fe, N. Mex. Annual mean temperature 262 (°F)	Sante Fe, N. Mex. Annual total precipitation 263 (Inches)	St. Louis, Mo. Annual mean temperature 264 (°F)	St. Louis, Mo. Annual total precipitation 265 (Inches)	St. Paul, Minn. Annual mean temperature 266 (°F)	St. Paul, Minn. Annual total precipitation 267 (Inches)
1970	49	30.5	58	35.4	66	43.0	51	29.4	54	35.3	55	39.1	57	24.3	49	11.6	¹58	¹37.0	44	30.5
1969	49	39.9	58	33.2	65	54.5	51	41.3	55	48.5	55	43.4	57	27.0	50	*19.6*	¹57	¹39.2	45	19.4
1968	49	35.3	59	40.1	66	45.5	51	40.1	54	43.6	54	35.5	57	18.0	48	15.2	¹57	¹39.1	45	37.9
1967	49	35.6	57	40.6	66	42.6	50	40.6	53	49.1	53	44.8	57	26.5	49	*15.1*	56	38.7	43	25.4
1966	49	34.4	58	39.8	66	48.1	50	32.1	54	39.9	53	40.0	57	16.5	49	*12.3*	58	30.2	43	24.3
1965	48	26.7	58	30.8	66	52.2	50	27.7	54	26.1	53	29.3	57	19.9	49	20.7	58	33.0	43	39.9
1964	50	20.7	58	37.2	66	73.4	50	33.5	54	33.0	54	35.0	57	17.7	48	13.4	58	28.2	46	26.0
1963	48	25.0	57	34.1	65	48.3	49	38.2	53	34.3	52	42.6	57	18.8	50	14.2	57	28.2	44	19.6
1962	48	28.8	56	38.1	65	49.7	49	36.6	53	37.2	52	42.6	56	20.6	50	11.3	57	40.4	42	28.8
1961	50	34.0	58	40.0	66	48.9	51	41.3	55	39.3	53	41.0	57	14.6	48	14.8	56	44.7	44	25.7
1960	50	47.9	57	43.9	65	46.5	50	41.6	54	46.4	53	41.2	56	17.8	49	17.6	56	28.2	44	21.5
1959	51	32.5	59	35.8	66	58.6	51	43.1	55	38.8	56	38.4	59	12.5	50	12.9	57	30.8	46	26.9
1958	48	38.0	56	50.7	65	44.4	49	51.9	52	40.9	53	47.9	56	28.6	51	14.6	55	37.3	46	16.2
1957	51	29.1	59	37.8	66	51.8	51	38.1	56	36.2	²56	²35.0	56	22.8	49	17.6	57	52.7	45	27.8
1956	49	32.6	58	37.8	66	35.1	51	48.4	55	39.9	56	33.7	54	15.1	49	6.7	58	33.0	45	26.8
1955	50	41.5	57	47.9	66	40.5	52	51.3	55	35.6	56	36.9	55	21.0	49	10.8	58	30.0	46	21.1
1954	50	41.0	59	30.5	67	31.0	52	48.5	57	45.2	56	50.5	56	19.8	52	14.1	59	23.0	47	23.7
1953	52	41.0	59	41.0	67	44.0	54	56.7	57	41.5	58	45.2	56	12.6	50	12.8	60	26.7	46	27.9
1952	51	39.2	58	55.9	66	39.2	53	49.7	55	41.5	57	51.1	54	31.5	49	11.4	58	38.6	46	23.7
1951	50	43.6	57	46.9	66	38.2	53	50.5	55	44.4	56	42.0	54	22.9	50	9.3	55		42	34.6
1950	49	37.8	57	44.0	66	43.4	51	42.5	54	36.9	55	45.4	55	26.3	51	10.4	55	43.2	42	21.6
1949	52	28.5	59	37.7	67	46.0	54	39.9	57	36.2	58	43.3	54	16.2	49	17.7	57	46.3	46	25.1
1948	49	39.9	57	54.7	65	61.3	51	50.7	54	46.9	55	49.5	56	14.4	49	16.9	56	34.5	45	17.0
1947	50	33.0	57	46.2	67	67.4	51	47.6	54	40.8	55	52.1	56	12.3	50	11.0	56	37.1	44	21.1
1946	50	40.0	58	37.6	66	49.0	52	40.6	55	38.4	56	40.9	55	25.6	49	13.5	59	57.1	44	29.0
1945	49	47.3	57	46.6	66	74.9	52	50.4	55	45.0	56	47.0	55	17.7	48	12.9	55	49.8	47	27.2
1944	49	39.6	57	45.5	66	51.2	51	49.1	54	36.7	55	36.8	55	24.9	50	14.6	56	33.5	47	29.1
1943	48	36.5	57	36.8	66	36.4	51	37.9	54	43.5	55	36.7	56	17.0	49	9.6	57	33.6	45	22.7
1942	50	38.2	58	46.0	67	41.4	51	45.4	54	39.0	56	43.5	56	24.9	49	13.0	57	45.1	45	30.6
1941	50	28.0	57	34.7	66	62.6	52	36.7	55	39.0	56	32.2	58	35.2	49	17.7	58	32.1	51	27.0
1940	45	35.9	55	44.3	64	45.5	49	48.7	52	39.0	53	45.1	57	34.8	50	16.4	56	25.0	44	28.5
1939	47	31.2	58	40.9	67	49.0	51	46.4	55	40.4	56	45.4	56	11.2	49	13.4	58	40.2	46	24.5
1938	49	40.2	58	43.4	65	31.1	52	57.8	54	45.6	56	46.9	56	22.2	50	15.6	59	41.2	45	22.6
1937	50	38.5	57	50.8	65	48.8	51	53.2	53	56.1	55	37.4	57	25.8	50	14.4	55	26.1	44	22.6
1936	49	40.0	56	44.6	65	40.2	50	59.6	53	47.8	54	46.4	58	22.4	49	12.9	56	39.4	43	18.5
1935	48	33.7	56	51.5	66	54.1	48	37.0	52	41.7	54	38.4	55	20.6	52	13.3	56	29.2	42	27.5
1934	47	31.4	56	50.9	65	38.8	51	49.0	53	41.7	55	44.1	56	15.9	49	13.1	56	34.8	45	22.7
1933	50	30.5	57	53.0	66	46.6	49	45.4	55	40.6	55	39.2	56	17.0	49	13.4	59	38.0	46	23.5
1932	50	34.1	58	49.6	67	44.8	50	43.6	55	44.7	56	29.3	55	12.0	48	15.9	58	37.4	46	23.6
1931	51	33.2	59	39.6	67	28.8	51	44.2	56	37.8	58	35.4	57	22.9	49		60		48	22.6
1930	50	25.5	58	21.6	64	32.4	52	34.7	54	39.0	57	34.0	57	16.7	48	13.2	56	23.2	46	20.0
1929	49	31.7	57	42.5	67	45.0	51	43.1	54	40.4	56	41.6	56	10.0	48	21.5	55	46.3	42	24.4
1928	49	33.6	56	43.4	65	42.8	51	45.0	54	45.6	55	39.4	56	19.0	49	13.1	57	38.6	45	24.8
1927	49	39.9	57	36.2	64	29.9	51	52.0	53	56.1	56	43.2	57	24.3	50	14.2	56	50.8	43	26.4
1926	46	30.8	55	45.2	66	35.1	48	43.8	51	47.8	54	32.4	56	26.7	49	13.0	54	33.4	44	27.3
1925	48	31.4	56	32.7	64	33.4	49	44.4	52	38.5	56	36.5	56	23.1	49	12.6	56	32.2	42	20.9
1924	47	30.5	56	45.0	64	51.1	51	38.3	52	56.1	54	39.1	55	20.2	48	8.9	54	36.5	42	30.6
1923	47	34.1	57	36.7	66	46.6	49	44.6	53	44.2	55	29.3	56	20.4	47	14.2	58	41.7	44	20.2
1922	50	32.1	57	42.5	65	50.6	52	43.3	55	46.5	57	35.4	55	11.0	47	13.3	54	32.3	46	25.0
1921	51	29.7	58	37.7	67	45.6	52	41.8	55	37.8	58	33.4	56	19.7	50	17.8	57	41.1	48	24.8
1920	47	40.5	55	48.4	64	46.8	49	53.2	52	53.8	54	46.2	55	18.3	48	13.2	56	31.5	45	24.7
1919	49	35.5	57	47.2	67	36.7	51	52.6	54	50.8	56	49.1	55	19.0	48	20.8	57	40.8	44	30.4
1918	48	30.1	56	37.9	65	31.3	50	44.9	53	36.9	55	37.7	56	20.8	48	15.2	57	35.9	45	30.2
1917	46	28.7	53	36.0	64	33.6	48	39.3	50	36.7	53	39.4	55	9.0	49	6.4	54	25.0	40	24.5
1916	47	33.9	55	46.4	66	42.5	49	40.5	52	43.1	54	32.3	56	28.1	48	16.4	56	41.8	43	30.8
1915	49	37.6	56	46.3	64	46.6	51	45.8	53	38.5	55	44.8	56	24.0	47	17.9	57	49.3	45	24.0
1914	47	29.8	56	36.1	64	44.3	49	43.8	52	41.7	55	39.1	56	19.0	47	17.3	56	35.6	46	24.0
1913	50	26.4	58	36.4	66	41.5	52	46.3	55	44.7	57	47.4	56	15.6	48	15.0	58	38.7	46	24.2
1912	47	32.1	55	45.1	65	51.3	50	44.8	52	44.2	54	47.0	54	26.0		10.3	54	44.6	43	21.2
1911	49	32.1	57	48.6	67	31.7	50	46.9	53	46.5	55	51.4	54			17.1	57	36.1	45	40.4

See footnotes at end of table.

Series J 248–267. Long-Record City Stations—Annual Mean Temperature and Annual Total Precipitation: 1780 to 1970—Con.

[Italicized figures are based on interpolated monthly values]

Year	Albany, N.Y. 248 Temp °F.	249 Precip In.	Baltimore, Md. 250 Temp °F.	251 Precip In.	Charleston, S.C. 252 Temp °F.	253 Precip In.	New Haven, Conn. 254 Temp °F.	255 Precip In.	New York, N.Y. 256 Temp °F.	257 Precip In.	Philadelphia, Pa. 258 Temp °F.	259 Precip In.	San Francisco, Calif. 260 Temp °F.	261 Precip In.	Santa Fe, N. Mex. 262 Temp °F.	263 Precip In.	St. Louis, Mo. 264 Temp °F.	265 Precip In.	St. Paul, Minn. 266 Temp °F.	267 Precip In.
1910	48	28.5	56	35.0	64	39.7	50	39.9	53	32.7	55	39.6	54	12.4	50	8.6	55	37.3	46	10.2
1909	48	28.0	56	34.7	65	43.0	50	43.1	53	39.9	55	37.4	54	31.4	47	12.3	56	47.5	44	31.8
1908	49	28.4	56	35.4	66	31.4	51	45.3	55	39.4	56	38.1	54	16.4	48	12.8	57	34.2	44	31.6
1907	47	32.5	54	49.1	66	31.7	48	46.2	52	43.8	53	38.7	55	22.5	49	15.2	55	41.4	42	23.1
1906	48	33.2	56	46.8	65	43.6	50	51.3	54	39.4	55	51.9	55	26.3	49	16.6	55	35.5	45	33.2
1905	47	27.0	55	46.6	65	34.8	49	43.3	53	39.8	54	41.6	55	16.2	47	17.2	55	38.5	44	30.8
1904	45	31.3	53	36.1	64	37.9	47	41.7	50	35.5	54	39.8	55	24.7	48	14.2	54	33.6	43	34.1
1903	48	34.1	55	46.3	64	42.9	49	41.2	52	39.5	54	41.5	54	18.3	48	9.8	56	33.4	44	37.9
1902	48	37.5	55	50.1	65	37.2	49	44.3	53	55.5	54	55.5	54	19.2	48	13.4	56	38.4	45	31.8
1901	48	40.5	54	43.0	64	32.7	49	52.6	52	47.0	54	45.5	54	19.8	50	17.4	57	24.8	46	25.8
1900	50	30.6	57	31.6	66	38.1	51	34.8	54	39.4	56	40.9	55	15.3	50	15.9	58	29.5	46	34.2
1899	49	28.8	55	40.6	66	44.3	49	44.3	53	36.8	54	40.0	54	23.2	49	10.0	56	34.6	44	27.5
1898	50	38.8	56	36.5	66	[2]46.4	50	55.3	54	46.2	55	49.2	54	9.3	48	13.0	57	49.2	45	25.3
1897	49	40.8	55	47.5	66	50.6	49	57.9	53	42.4	55	42.0	54	16.4	48	20.4	57	40.2	44	25.3
1896	48	27.9	56	38.6	66	47.8	49	38.4	53	40.1	54	32.0	55	28.2	50	14.3	58	37.6	44	30.5
1895	44	29.8	54	40.5	64	55.2	47	36.0	52	33.7	54	31.0	55	17.1	47	13.3	55	31.2	44	34.7
1894	49	35.1	56	46.9	66	56.8	49	37.7	52	39.3	54	37.6	54	24.3	49	13.3	57	27.4	46	24.8
1893	49	38.9	54	45.5	66	71.0	50	46.7	50	46.6	53	39.2	53	17.9	49	13.3	55	39.3	44	25.8
1892	47	34.8	54	45.0	65	53.3	48	44.7	52	34.1	54	34.8	55	22.1	49	11.6	55	41.6	41	26.0
1891	48	41.7	56	54.2	64	45.5	49	44.7	54	37.6	54	38.2	56	21.1	47	16.8	56	30.5	44	32.6
1890	48	44.9	57	47.0	67	47.8	49	49.0	52	43.7	55	34.0	55	25.4	50	12.9	56	37.7	44	21.8
1889	50	39.5	56	62.4	65	52.2	50	59.8	52	54.4	55	50.6	57	36.9	50	7.9	56	33.2	45	23.4
1888	46	44.7	55	43.6	65	49.5	47	60.3	49	51.0	53	34.5	56	23.0	50	12.0	54	41.2	41	17.0
1887	48	39.7	55	43.2	64	44.7	49	44.1	51	41.7	55	42.2	55	19.0	49	13.4	58	35.3	43	25.8
1886	46	36.1	54	46.7	64	35.9	47	54.1	51	38.3	54	37.2	56	20.0	48	15.9	55	44.3	43	22.9
1885	44	34.4	54	45.3	66	[2]67.9	46	38.3	51	33.5	53	33.4	56	24.9	50	14.9	53	45.6	42	23.1
1884	47	38.2	56	46.9	66	60.2	48	49.3	52	49.7	50	39.3	55	38.8	48	19.7	55	40.6	44	26.1
1883	48	37.9	55	40.5	65	51.0	49	39.5	50	39.3	53	39.2	54	15.4		14.4	57	40.1	41	26.7
1882	48	39.4	56	42.1	67	57.0	49	47.9	52	34.4	52	45.6	54	18.7		11.4	54	43.2	46	32.6
1881	50	36.3	56	49.1	66	[2]43.2	50	51.3	52	35.0	55	30.2	55	23.7	49	[2]22.2	56	37.4	45	39.2
1880	49	32.5	56	41.9	67	46.7	52	46.5	53	34.7	57	33.6	54	30.1	46	9.9	55	34.7	44	29.8
1879	46	38.7	55	36.0	66	50.3	51	55.5	52	37.1	55	36.6	56	30.8	51	11.4	56	25.7	46	32.4
1878	49	49.4	57	50.1	66	77.4	53	58.1	53	46.0	53	34.5	56	33.3	48	19.6	58	40.8	48	22.8
1877	48	36.1	56	43.1	66	78.4	52	51.4	52	38.7	54	37.3	57	11.9	49	15.1	57	41.4	47	28.8
1876	47	38.2	54	46.7	65	51.0	51	54.1	52	40.6	54	47.4	56	23.5	48	15.0	56	48.5	42	30.7
1875	44	45.3	54	45.3	67	62.5	48	43.5	49	38.6	50	40.2	56	22.6	48	19.0	53	43.0	39	35.5
1874	47	37.9	57	33.6	67	62.2	49	55.8	51	44.2	56	46.2	55	22.5	49	19.9	57	37.9	44	33.7
1873	48	39.1	55	34.8	67	33.1	49	57.3	51	45.5	55	55.3	55	18.6	49	9.7	54	37.6	42	29.8
1872	*50*	36.0	54	42.7	66	52.3	48		51	40.3	54	48.4	55	22.4	50	9.9	54	45.5	43	30.6
1871	*50*	56.8	55		66	[2]63.4	48		51	49.2	55	47.3	56	27.5	48	[2]11.2	58	23.4	44	
1870	50	55.8	58	37.5	66	48.3	49		53	37.8	54	44.1		16.2	53	13.9	56	27.1	46	30.5
1869	47	44.2	56	55.6	67	43.1	47		52	48.6	54	48.4	56	22.6	48	12.1	54	47.0	42	31.8
1868	46	41.9	55	46.1	66	61.1	47		50	57.4	54	51.4	54	[2]30.6	49	7.8	54	45.6	42	31.0
1867	47	38.0	56	38.4	66	61.1	48	45.4	51	53.4	53	61.2	57			*7.8*	55	37.8	40	33.3
1866	48	34.3	58	27.5	67	36.3	48	47.0	52	38.3	52	45.8		[2]30.6		23.2	56	43.2	40	27.5
1865	48	36.4	56	33.2	67	57.2	49	41.9	53	45.0	54	56.3	54	14.1	49	21.6	55	46.6	45	38.0
1864	46	43.2	57	23.0	67	57.2	50		52	39.5	55	45.0	54	21.6	50	27.8	56	37.6	43	15.5
1863	46	27.9	55	43.0	66	33.1	50		52	43.4	55	49.2	54	15.1	51	7.8	54	40.4	43	28.2
1862	46	37.8	56	34.8	67	52.3	50		51	46.8	53	45.0	55	38.5		*11.3*	54	44.0	41	30.1
1861	*50*	36.0	55	42.7	66	44.5	50		53	37.2	54	46.3	56		52	*15.8*	57	38.0	42	
1860	48	32.2	54	37.5	68	44.4	49		52	31.1	54	44.2	55	21.2	51	8.8	56	29.4	43	29.3
1859	51	32.0	56	55.6	66	50.2	48		52	59.7	54	58.1	56	21.4	48	9.5	54	61.4	41	29.4
1858		34.0	57	46.1	66	48.1	48		51	36.7	54	39.8	57	23.5	49	11.4	56	68.8	44	27.6
1857	*47*	41.9	55	38.4	65	38.1	48		50	38.7	53	48.3		21.0	50	8.5	53	39.0	42	32.1
1856	47	39.1	54	29.3	64	49.1	47		50	35.0	52	34.0		22.3	50	23.1	52	42.6	44	22.6
1855	50	42.5	57	59.2	66	34.8	49		51	43.2	54	44.1		26.4	51	24.2	57	50.4	43	24.8
1854	49	34.1	57	36.0	66	37.6	50		51	46.4	55	40.2	56	22.2	50	24.8	57	57.0	45	26.6
1853	49	45.8	56	51.5	67	43.5	49		52	46.3	55	40.7	55	21.2	50	21.8	56	30.9	45	20.5
1852	48	32.0	55	51.5	66	49.7	49		51	35.3	53	45.8		27.3		*21.7*	55	47.0	44	15.1
1851	47	34.6	57	38.1	66	33.1			52	38.8	54	35.5	56	15.6		*13.2*	55	46.8	47	23.4

See footnotes at end of table.

Series J 248–267. Long-Record City Stations—Annual Mean Temperature and Annual Total Precipitation: 1780 to 1970—Con.

[Italicized figures are based on interpolated monthly values]

Year	Albany, N.Y. mean temp (248)	Albany, N.Y. precip (249)	Baltimore, Md. mean temp (250)	Baltimore, Md. precip (251)	Charleston, S.C. mean temp (252)	Charleston, S.C. precip (253)	New Haven, Conn. mean temp (254)	New Haven, Conn. precip (255)	New York, N.Y. mean temp (256)	New York, N.Y. precip (257)	Philadelphia, Pa. mean temp (258)	Philadelphia, Pa. precip (259)	San Francisco, Calif. mean temp (260)	San Francisco, Calif. precip (261)	Santa Fe, N. Mex. mean temp (262)	Santa Fe, N. Mex. precip (263)	St. Louis, Mo. mean temp (264)	St. Louis, Mo. precip (265)	St. Paul, Minn. mean temp (266)	St. Paul, Minn. precip (267)
	°F.	Inches	°F.	Inches	°F.	Inches	°F.	Inches	°F.	Inches	°F.	Inches	°F.	Inches	°F.	Inches	°F.	Inches	°F.	Inches
1850	48	51.8	58	44.8	66	23.7	49		51	44.6	54	54.6		17.4		9.1	55	50.5	44	25.5
1849	48	36.7	56	30.6	66	30.7	48		50	40.1	53	42.1			52		54	45.7	42	49.7
1848	50	48.2	57	34.4	65	43.4	49		52	32.8	55	35.0					54	65.4	42	23.2
1847	49	41.4	56	33.0	65	47.8	49		52	44.5	54	45.1					57	52.7	48	21.8
1846	50	39.8	55	40.7	65	44.3	50		52	35.9	54	44.4					56	45.4	46	26.1
1845	50	39.4	55	28.4	64	46.4	50		53	33.7	53	40.2					57	38.0	43	25.3
1844	48	35.0	54	32.5	66	36.4	47		52	39.8	53	46.9					54	45.8	40	30.2
1843	47	48.4	54	48.8	64	54.7	50		51	35.7	53	48.5					56	34.8	43	23.8
1842	48	46.0	55	35.1	66	42.1	50		53	41.6	52	55.5					56	32.3	44	25.2
1841	48	38.0	53	43.9	66	53.9			51	44.6								42.7		21.7
1840	49	44.4	54	37.5	67	46.1	49		51	35.5	53	47.4					56	41.6	45	23.2
1839	48	38.1	56	51.7	67	53.0	49		51	33.4	52	43.7					55	47.4	47	21.2
1838	47	42.0	54	47.1	67	58.9	48		50	33.7	51	45.3					53	31.5	42	27.7
1837	46	41.2	54	45.0	67	²56.4	46		49	32.1	51	39.0					53	27.0	44	24.0
1836	45	44.6	52	54.6	66	40.9	45		47	36.6	50	42.7							43	
1835	46	40.5	54	34.1	67	49.0	47		50	28.8	54	39.3							43	
1834	48	32.4	57	29.5	68	68.6	49		51	33.6	55	34.2							47	
1833	48	41.8	57	41.3	66	48.4	48		52	37.7	54	48.6							48	
1832	48	44.4	57	34.3	67	45.0	48	51.4	52	39.2	54	39.5							46	
1831	49	39.5	55	37.4	66		49			38.8		43.9							43	
1830	51	41.8	58	39.0	70		51	44.6	55	43.3	55	45.1							48	
1829	48	38.1	55	52.3	66		49		52	45.8	53	41.9							46	
1828	51	37.7	58	33.0	71		52		54	48.9	56	38.0							46	
1827	49	49.8	58	32.7	67		49		52	51.1	52	38.5							45	
1826	51	33.1	58	30.7	66		50		52	55.7	54	35.2							48	
1825	50		57	26.2	67		51		54		54	29.7							43	
1824	48		56	42.3	67		50		51			49.9							44	
1823	47		59	44.6	65		48		54			44.5							44	
1822	49		56	29.2			50					30.6							43	
1821	48			50.2			48					36.2								
1820	49		55	42.5			48	46.2				49.4							43	
1819			57	28.8			49	33.9												
1818			55	32.6			47	38.0												
1817			55	49.0			46	43.4												
1816							47	38.0												

Year	Albany, N.Y. mean temp (248)	New Haven, Conn. mean temp (254)
	°F.	°F.
1797		48
1796	47	48
1795		50
1794	50	50
1793		48
1792		50
1791		50
1790		50
1789		48
1788		48
1787		48
1786		47
1785		48
1784		49
1783		50
1782		50
1781		
1780		

Year	New Haven, Conn. mean temp (254)	New Haven, Conn. precip (255)	Charleston, S.C. precip (253)	Albany, N.Y. mean temp (248)
	°F.	Inches	Inches	°F.
1815	47	50.6		
1814	49	56.1		50
1813	49	53.4		48
1812	47	44.2		
1811	50	47.7	49.3	
1810	50	²39.4	45.4	
1809	49	44.6	66.0	
1808	50		40.8	
1807	49	45.3	42.2	
1806	50	38.6		
1805	52			
1804	50	40.8		
1803	51	43.3		
1802	51			
1801				
1800	50			50
1799	48			48
1798	49			

[1] St. Louis City closed June 1968; data are for Gateway Arch.

[2] Value corrected for typographical errors in *World Weather Record*.

Series J 268–278. Tornadoes, Floods, and Tropical Cyclones: 1886 to 1970

Year	Tornadoes — Number	Tornadoes — Number of tornado days	Tornadoes — Lives lost, Total	Tornadoes — Lives lost, Most in a single tornado	Tornadoes — Property loss $50,000 to $500,000	Tornadoes — Property loss $500,000 and over	Floods — Lives lost	Floods — Property loss ($1,000)	N. Atl. tropical cyclones — Reaching U.S. coast, Total	N. Atl. tropical cyclones — Hurricanes only	Lives lost in United States
	268	269	270	271	272	273	274	275	276	277	278
1970	649	171	73	26	97	30	135	225,453	4	1	11
1969	604	155	66	32	98	19	297	902,654	3	2	256
1968	661	171	131	34	82	32	31	339,399	3	2	9
1967	912	173	116	33	125	41	34	375,218	2	2	18
1966	570	150	99	58	79	17	31	117,004	2	2	54
1965	899	181	298	44	126	41	119	788,046	2	1	75
1964	713	156	73	22	113	22	100	651,642	6	4	49
1963	461	141	31	5	77	16	39	177,946	1	1	11
1962	658	152	28	17	51	10	19	75,237	1	---	4
1961	682	169	51	16	103	22	52	154,033	3	2	46
1960	618	172	47	16	65	12	32	92,976	5	2	65
1959	589	156	58	21	70	5	25	141,255	7	3	24
1958	565	166	66	19	70	9	47	218,255	1	---	2
1957	864	154	191	44	129	29	82	360,303	5	1	395
1956	532	155	83	25	83	25	42	64,688	2	1	21
1955	593	153	125	80	74	14	302	995,491	5	3	218
1954	549	159	35	6	63	9	55	106,842	4	2	193
1953	437	136	516	116	63	25	40	122,204	6	2	2
1952	236	98	230	57	53	19	54	254,064	2	1	3
1951	272	113	34	6	35	13	51	1,028,741	1	---	---
1950	199	88	70	18	47	9	93	176,050	4	3	19
1949	249	80	212	58	54	13	48	93,931	3	2	4
1948	183	68	140	33	62	13	82	229,959	4	3	3
1947	165	78	313	169	46	8	55	272,328	7	3	53
1946	106	65	78	15	29	7	28	70,813	4	1	---
1945	121	66	210	69	21	11	91	165,798	5	3	7
1944	169	68	275	100	50	9	33	101,079	4	3	64
1943	152	61	58	5	28	8	107	199,732	4	1	16
1942	167	66	384	65	42	10	68	98,507	3	2	8
1941	118	57	53	25	24	1	47	39,524	4	2	10
1940	124	62	65	18	13	2	60	40,467	3	2	51
1939	152	75	87	27	21	3	83	13,834	3	1	3
1938	213	76	183	32	29	6	180	101,098	4	2	600
1937	147	75	29	5	24	---	142	440,738	4	---	---
1936	151	71	552	216	17	6	142	282,549	7	3	9
1935	180	77	70	11	29	---	236	127,127	2	2	414
1934	147	77	47	6	10	3	88	10,362	7	3	17
1933	258	96	362	34	46	9	33	36,679	7	5	63
1932	151	67	394	37	23	2	11	10,295	5	2	---
1931	94	57	36	6	14	1	---	2,808	2	---	---
1930	192	72	179	41	38	6	14	15,850	1	---	---
1929	197	74	274	40	48	4	89	68,098	2	2	3
1928	203	79	92	14	40	7	15	44,611	3	2	1,836
1927	163	62	540	92	42	10	423	347,656	1	---	---
1926	111	57	144	23	28	---	16	23,468	4	4	269
1925	119	65	794	689	34	3	36	9,923	2	1	6
1924	130	57	376	85	26	12	---	---	3	2	2
1923	102	59	109	23	21	1	---	---	4	2	---
1922	108	64	135	16	27	5	---	---	1	---	---
1921	105	55	202	61	22	3	---	---	2	2	5
1920	87	50	498	87	14	10	---	---	3	2	2
1919	64	35	206	59	10	2	---	---	2	1	287
1918	81	45	135	36	20	5	---	---	2	1	34
1917	121	38	509	101	21	9	---	---	1	1	5
1916	90	36	150	30	7	1	---	---	8	6	107
1915									4	3	600
1914									1	---	(1)
1913									3	2	(1)
1912									4	2	12
1911									2	2	17
1910									2	2	13
1909									7	3	404
1908									2	1	(1)
1907									3	---	(1)
1906									6	4	285
1905									2	---	(1)
1904									3	2	(1)
1903									2	2	9
1902									2	1	(1)
1901									6	2	10
1900									3	1	---
1899									4	3	---
1898									6	3	---
1897									4	1	---
1896									4	4	---
1895									4	1	---
1894									3	2	---
1893									7	6	---
1892									3	---	---
1891									4	2	---
1890											---
1889									4	2	---
1888									6	3	---
1887									4	3	---
1886									7	6	---

[1] Not reported, believed to be small number.

Agriculture

Farms (Series K 1-203)

K 1–203. General note.

Basic statistics on agriculture are, for the most part, prepared by the U.S. Bureau of the Census, which conducts the census of agriculture, and by the Statistical Reporting Service and the Economic Research Service of the U.S. Department of Agriculture, which prepare current estimates.

Annual agricultural statistics have been issued by the Department of Agriculture since May 1, 1863. Statistics compiled by the Statistical Reporting Service on crops, livestock and livestock products, agricultural prices, farm employment, and related subjects are based mainly on data obtained by mail and by personal interview of farmers and ranchers. Mailed questionnaires are returned from nearly three-quarters of a million respondents, mostly farmers. More than 50,000 farmers are interviewed to obtain agricultural data. They are located in almost all the counties in the United States and usually report on one or more items during a year.

Beginning 1840, a census of agriculture has been taken every 10 years and, beginning 1925, a mid-decade census of agriculture has also been taken. Census information was obtained by a personal canvass of individual farms until 1969, when for the first time the Census Bureau shifted to a questionnaire mailed to persons or organizations associated with agricultural operations in the Nation to be completed by them and returned by mail.

The first census was limited in scope. It included such items as an inventory of the principal classes of domestic animals, the production of wool, the value of poultry, the value of dairy products, and the production of principal crops. The number of farms and the acreage and value of farmland were first included in 1850 and information on farm tenure was first obtained in 1880. A detailed classification of farmland according to use was first obtained in 1925; in earlier censuses, farmland was classified only as improved land, woodland, and other unimproved land (see Chapter J). For brief discussions of the comparability of various agricultural data, census to census, see Bureau of the Census, *U.S. Census of Agriculture: 1969*, vol. II, chapter 1.

For each decade from 1840 through 1900, the census of agriculture was taken as of June 1. The five decennial censuses since then have been taken as of April 15, 1910; January 1, 1920; April 1, 1930, 1940, and 1950. The 1925, 1935, and 1945 quinquennial censuses of agriculture were taken as of January 1; the 1954, 1959, and 1964 censuses were taken during October and November. For the 1969 census the report forms were mailed to farm operators in the last week of December, 1969. The reports covered production and sales for the 1969 calendar year, with livestock inventories as of December 31, 1969. For 1969, data for farms with less than $2,500 are based on a 50-percent sample of these farms.

The definition of a farm has varied as follows from census to census: For the 1959, 1964, and 1969 censuses, census farms comprised places on which agricultural operations were conducted at any time under the control or supervision of one person, a partnership, or a manager. Places of less than 10 acres were counted as farms if the estimated sales of agricultural products for the year amounted or normally would amount to at least $250. Places of 10 or more acres were counted as farms if the estimated sales of agricultural products for the year amounted or normally would amount to at least $50.

For the 1954 Census of Agriculture, places of 3 or more acres were counted as farms if the annual value of agricultural products for sale or home use (exclusive of home-garden products) amounted to $150 or more. Places of less than 3 acres were counted as farms only if the annual value of sales of agricultural products amounted to $150 or more. Places for which the value of agricultural products for 1954 was less than these minimums because of crop failure or other unusual conditions and places operated for the first time in 1954 were counted as farms if normally they could be expected to produce these minimum quantities of agricultural products.

If a place had croppers or other tenants, the land assigned each one was considered a separate farm, even though the landlord handled the entire holding as one operating unit in respect to supervision, equipment, rotation practice, purchase of supplies, or sale of products. Land retained by the landlord and worked by him with the help of his family and/or hired labor was likewise considered a farm.

For the 1950 Census of Agriculture, the definition of a farm was the same as for 1954. For the 1945 and earlier censuses, the definition of a farm was somewhat more inclusive. For 1925–1945, farms included (1) places of 3 or more acres on which there were agricultural operations and (2) places of less than 3 acres if the agricultural products for home use or for sale were valued at $250 or more. The only reports excluded from the 1925–1940 tabulations were those taken in error and those with very limited agricultural production, such as only a small home garden, a few fruit trees, a very small flock of chickens, etc. In 1945, reports for places of 3 acres or more with limited agricultural operations were retained only if (1) there were 3 or more acres of cropland and pasture or (2) the value of products in 1944 amounted to $150 or more.

The definition of a farm in the 1910 and 1920 censuses was similar to that used from 1925 to 1940 but was even more inclusive. In those years, farms of less than 3 acres with products valued at less than $250 were to be included provided they required the continuous services of at least one person. In 1900, there were no acreage or production limits. Market, truck, and fruit gardens, orchards, nurseries, cranberry marshes, greenhouses, and city dairies were to be included provided the entire time of at least one person was devoted to their care. For 1870, 1880, and 1890, no tract of less than 3 acres was to be reported as a farm unless $500 worth of produce was sold from it during the year. For 1860, no definition was given the enumerators. For 1850, no acreage qualification was given, but there was a lower limit of $100 for value of products.

K 1–3. Farm population, 1880–1970.

Source: 1880–1900, U.S. Bureau of the Census, Technical Paper No. 3, *Farm Population: 1880 to 1950*; 1910–1970, U.S. Department of Agriculture, Economic Research Service, *Farm Population Estimates, 1910–70*, Statistical Bulletin No. 523.

The estimates presented relate to the rural civilian population living on farms, regardless of occupation. For convenience, the term "farm population" is used without qualification, although the relatively few members of the Armed Forces living on farms are excluded. Beginning 1960, the farm population has been defined as all persons living in rural territory on places of 10 or more acres, if as much as $50 worth of agricultural products were sold from the place in the reporting year. It also includes those living on places of under 10 acres, if as much as $250 worth of agricultural products were sold from the place in the reporting year. Prior to 1960, no specific criteria of acreage operated or value of products sold from a place were used to classify farm population. The change in definition in 1960 was largely stimulated by the fact that an increasing number of families whose livelihood was not gained directly from agriculture were living in the open country.

In the farm population, where the flow of migrants is responsive to many influences such as employment opportunities, mechanization, and technological advancements, migration becomes the dominant factor in population change, rather than the balance of births and deaths. Net change through migration, series K 3, includes not only those persons who made a physical move from farm to nonfarm areas, but also the loss that occurred when agricultural operations ceased on a place, and the occupants of the related dwelling units were reclassified from farm to nonfarm. Although exact figures are not available, actual migration is considered to be the larger of these two components.

The farm population estimates are based on data obtained from three principal sources: (1) The Current Population Survey (CPS) of the Bureau of the Census, which provides the annual estimate of the U.S. farm population; (2) the censuses of population, from which benchmark data for States, geographic divisions, and regions are derived; and (3) annual surveys of the farm population, conducted for the Economic Research Service by the Statistical Reporting Service, on which annual estimates of geographic distributions are based for intercensal years, and from which estimates of components of farm population change are derived annually. The Economic Research Service and its predecessor agencies conducted an annual survey of the farm population and its components of change from 1923 to 1969. Utilizing USDA's crop reporting system, reports were collected through a mailed questionnaire. Respondents reported on the number of persons who were living on their own and neighboring farms at the beginning and end of a specified 12-month period. They also reported on births, deaths, and changes through migration which occurred during this period.

Farm population estimates are based on USDA mailed-questionnaire survey data, tied to benchmark figures from complete censuses, and adjusted to total estimates of farm population obtained from the CPS. The reliability of these estimates is dependent upon the reliability of the U.S. estimate and the mail survey data. Annual estimates of the U.S. total farm population are obtained from the CPS. As these estimates are based on a sample, they may differ somewhat from figures obtained if a complete census had been taken using the same schedules, instructions, and enumerators. As in any survey work, the results are subject to error of response and of reporting as well as to sampling variability. The reliability of data from the mail survey alone cannot be assessed in terms of sample error. Reliability depends in part upon State-to-State variations in the size and representativeness of the mailing list, as well as upon variations in rate, representativeness, and accuracy of returns. In general, it should be noted that small figures, small changes, and trends over a short period of time may have less reliability than larger numbers and changes and trends over a period of several years.

K 4. Number of farms, 1850–1970.

Source: Census years, U.S. Bureau of the Census, *U.S. Census of Agriculture, 1964, General Report*, vol. II, p. 15, and *U.S. Census of Agriculture, 1969*, vol. II, chapter 3, p. 23; intercensal years, U.S. Department of Agriculture, Statistical Reporting Service, *Number of Farms, 1910–1959—Land in Farms, 1950–1959, by States*, Statistical Bulletin No. 316, *Number of Farms and Land in Farms, 1959–1970*, Statistical Bulletin No. 507, and annual supplements.

Comparability of data for census years is affected by varying degrees of underenumeration and by changes in definition of a farm (see general note for series K 1–203). Estimates for intercensal years

are based on trend and indications of change in acreage and livestock surveys, in annual assessors' censuses in a number of States, in Agricultural Stabilization and Conservation records, and in other miscellaneous verifying data.

Data for Alaska and Hawaii are included except as noted.

K 5–9. Land in farms, 1850–1970.

Source: Census years, see source for series K 4; intercensal years, see source for series K 4 except 1911–1949, U.S. Department of Agriculture, unpublished data obtained by straight-line interpolations.

The acreage in each farm was allocated by the farm operator among the various land-use categories. Any acreage which had two or more uses during the year was classified according to the first use on the report form. For example, if a crop was harvested from an acreage and the same acreage was then pastured, the acreage was included as land from which crops were harvested but not as pasture.

Cropland includes cropland harvested, cropland used only for pasture, and all other cropland. Cropland harvested includes land from which crops were harvested; land from which hay (including wild hay) was cut; and land in small fruits, orchards, vineyards, nurseries, and greenhouses. Cropland used only for pasture includes all land used only for pasture or grazing that could have been used for crops without additional improvement, and all land planted to crops that was pastured before the crops reached maturity. All land used for rotation pasture and land in government diversion programs which was pastured is included. All other cropland includes cropland used only for soil improvement crops, land on which all crops failed, cultivated summer fallow, idle cropland, and land planted to crops to be harvested after the year covered by the census.

Pastureland includes land not classified as either cropland or woodland.

Information on farmland values in scattered local areas is found in P. W. Bidwell and J. I. Falconer, *History of Agriculture in the Northern United States, 1620–1860*, pp. 70–71, 242, and 328. Similar information for Southern States is found in L. C. Gray, *History of Agriculture in the Southern United States to 1860*, vol. I, pp. 403–406, and vol. II, pp. 640–645.

Data for Alaska and Hawaii are excluded except as noted.

K 10. Total value of selected items of farm property, 1850–1970.

Source: Census years, U.S. Bureau of the Census, *U.S. Census of Agriculture: 1935*, vol. III, chapter I, table 12, and chapter V, table 2; intercensal years, U.S. Department of Agriculture, Economic Research Service, compiled from *The Balance Sheet of Agriculture* and its successor, *The Balance Sheet of the Farming Sector*, annual issues, and *Farm Real Estate Market Developments*, annual issues and supplements.

Current market values of farm real estate, machinery and equipment, and livestock are combined in this series. Estimates of the value of farm real estate are based upon census reports and the annual index of farm real estate values, as described in series K 16. Inventory values for machinery and equipment and for livestock are based in part on census reports and supplemental estimates made by the Statistical Reporting Service and Economic Research Service.

K 11, 14, 15. Value of farmland and buildings, 1850–1970.

Source: Census years, U.S. Bureau of the Census, *U.S. Census of Agriculture, 1964, General Report*, vol. II, p. 22, and *U.S. Census of Agriculture, 1969*, vol. II, chapter 2, p. 20; intercensal years, U.S. Department of Agriculture, Economic Research Service, *Current Developments in the Farm Real Estate Market*, issued annually and sometimes biennially, and its successor, *Farm Real Estate Market Developments*, annual issues and supplements.

Figures for intercensal years are estimates derived by applying the change in the index of average value of land and buildings per acre to census benchmarks, recognizing changes in acres of land in farms. All farm operators were asked to estimate the market value of their farms in each census from 1850 through 1969. In the 1950, 1954, 1959, and 1964 censuses, data were obtained from all large farms and from a 20-percent sample of other farms. In the 1969 census, all operators who received a form were asked to estimate the present market value of land and buildings.

Average value of land and buildings per farm is obtained by dividing the total value shown by the number of farms, using rounded data.

Average value of land and buildings per acre is obtained by dividing the total value shown by the acres of land in farms, using unrounded data.

Data for Alaska and Hawaii are excluded except as noted.

K 12. Value of farm implements and machinery, 1850–1970.

Source: 1850–1900, U.S. Bureau of the Census, *Thirteenth Census, 1910, Agriculture*, vol. V, p. 51; 1910–1939, U.S. Department of Agriculture, Agricultural Marketing Service, unpublished data; 1940–1970, Economic Research Service, *The Balance Sheet of Agriculture, 1957, 1967*, and *1968*, and *The Balance Sheet of the Farming Sector, 1971*.

Figures for 1910–1970 represent inventory value at the beginning of the year. They are closely tied to the values presented in the censuses of agriculture, the figures for intercensal years being estimated from information on manufacture and sales with due allowance for wear and tear and then adjusted for changes in price levels.

The data for 1850–1900 are not entirely comparable. They covered periods of vastly different price levels and attendant investment values, including the period of expansion into the West. According to the source, however, "the data are sufficiently comparable to indicate in a broad way the agricultural progress of the country . . . ."

K 13. Value of farm livestock, 1870–1970.

Source: U.S. Department of Agriculture, Statistical Reporting Service, *Agricultural Statistics, 1952, 1967*, and *1972* editions.

Data cover all cattle, hogs and pigs, and stock sheep.

K 16. Index of average value of farm real estate per acre, 1912–1970.

Source: U.S. Department of Agriculture, Economic Research Service, *Farm Real Estate Market Developments*, August 1971, p. 48.

See also *Major Statistical Series of the U.S. Department of Agriculture*, Agriculture Handbook No. 365, vol. 6, for a more complete description of methods used and limitations.

This index, which is available also by States, is designed to measure changes in the market value of farm real estate, including land, buildings, and such other permanent improvements as are customarily included when farms are sold. The index is constructed from estimates of average value of farm real estate per acre obtained from the regular crop reporters of the Department of Agriculture. It is not based upon the value of farm real estate obtained in the census. Between 15,000 and 20,000 reporters supply estimates of the market value of farms per acre in their localities as of March 1 and November 1. Although they undoubtedly base their estimates in part upon actual sales, no sales data are used directly in computing the index. Averages for crop-reporting districts are weighted by acres of land in farms as taken from the 1945, 1950, 1954, 1959, 1964, and 1969 censuses to obtain weighted State averages which are, in turn, weighted by acres of land in farms to obtain regional and national averages. The weighted dollar values per acre are then expressed as index numbers.

Data for Alaska and Hawaii are excluded.

K 17–81. Farm population, farms, land in farms, and value of farm property and farm products sold, by State, 1850–1969.

Source: Farm population and number of farms, see source for series K 1–3. All other items, U.S. Bureau of the Census, *U.S. Census of Agriculture: 1925*, Summary Statistics, by States; *1945*, vol. II; *1950*, vol. II; *1954*, vol. II; *1959*, vol. II; *1964*, vol. II; and *1969*, vol. II.

See text for series K 4–16.

Data for the value of farm products sold in 1969 were obtained by direct questioning. This procedure was a departure from the one used in previous censuses, in which data on value of sales were obtained by enumeration for some products and by estimation for others.

For 1969, value of farm products sold excludes income which the farm operator and members of his family received from providing hunting, fishing, picnicking, camping, boarding and lodging, or other recreational services on his farm; for 1964 and prior censuses, recreation income was included. The value of farm products sold does not include government payments received by farm operators for participation in wheat, feed grains, and other government programs.

K 82–108. Characteristics of farm operators, 1880–1969.

Source: U.S. Bureau of the Census, *U.S. Census of Agriculture: 1964*, vol. II, chapter 5, and *1969*, vol. II, chapter 3.

The term "farm operator" is used to designate a person who operates a farm, either doing the work himself or directly supervising the work. He may be the owner, a member of the owner's household, a salaried manager, or a tenant, renter, or sharecropper. If he rents land to others or has land worked on shares by others, he is considered as operator only of the land which he retains for his own operation. In the case of a partnership, only one partner is counted as an operator. For census purposes the number of farm operators is the same as the number of farms. A farm operator may spend a few hours a week on a "farm" producing only a few hundred dollars worth of farm products while partly or fully employed elsewhere, or be working full time as operator of a "farm" producing hundreds of thousands of dollars worth of farm products a year.

Classification by race of the farm operator was first made in the census of 1900. Since 1900, the race classification has consisted of two major groups, "white" and "all other," and for a limited number of items, a more detailed breakdown by race. The detailed breakdown, since 1954, has provided for a separate count of Negro and other races. For decennial censuses prior to 1954, separate totals are available for Negro, Indian, Chinese, Japanese, Filipino, and other races.

Farm operators were classified by residence on the basis of their reporting whether or not they lived on the farm operated. Data as to residence of the farm operators have been collected for the last seven censuses of agriculture, beginning with 1940. Except for 1964, when the instructions were to include operators who lived on the farm "any time" during the year, the inquiries have been similar and no time limitations were used. The instructions used for 1964 did not have a significant effect on the comparability of the 1964 data with other censuses.

Data on age of farm operators have been obtained in each of the decennial censuses beginning with 1910 and also in the censuses of agriculture for 1945, 1954, 1959, 1964, and 1969. No data on age of operators were obtained in the censuses of 1925 and 1935. For both 1964 and 1969, the operator's age was imputed if it was not reported. Tabulated data for 1964 and 1969, therefore, show an age for each farm operator. The number of operators for which age was not reported are shown for prior censuses. Average age of operators was tabulated in 1945 and 1954 through 1969.

The data for years on present farm reflect the continuity of operators on particular farms. They do not refer to years of farm experience. Information for years on farm has been obtained for each census of agriculture beginning with 1910. In the censuses of 1925, 1930, and

1950 through 1964, the inquiry called for the month as well as the year of occupancy. For 1935, 1940, and 1945, only the year of occupancy was asked. The report forms for 1910 and 1920 asked for the number of years and months the operator had operated the farm occupied at the time of the census. For each census, the data for years on farm have been summarized by groups of "years on present farm." The number of years or months comprising these groups of "years on present farm" have not always been the same, largely due to changes in the date of census enumeration. The group "less than 5 years" has been subdivided for some censuses. The difference between censuses in elapsed time from the beginning of the calendar year to the date the census reports were completed affects the data for the year-on-present-farm group "less than 5" years more than for groups "5 to 9" years and "10 or more" years.

Information on work off the farm by farm operators has been obtained for each agriculture census beginning with 1930. Farm operators reporting off-farm work vary from those who supplement their farm incomes with odd or spare-time jobs to those operators who have regular nonfarm jobs and use the farm to supplement their regular income or as a residence. The operators with odd or spare-time jobs usually consider their nonfarm employment to be of secondary importance; they may work part time on someone else's farm or work at seasonal nonfarm jobs. Many persons who may be employed in cities or have other regular nonfarm jobs live in rural areas and conduct sufficient agricultural operations for their places to meet the definition of a farm. Some use the farm income to supplement their regular nonfarm income. Some farm operators working off their farms may be using their nonfarm income as a source of capital for expanding their farming operations. For 1964 and 1969, data are tabulated only for those operators reporting one or more days of work off the farm. For 1959, farm operators reporting "none" for days of work off farm and those not reporting off-farm work were not tabulated separately. For 1930 through 1954, data are given separately for farm operators reporting "none" for days of work off farm.

For the most part, data from the 1969 census and earlier censuses are comparable. However, a difference in timing and the change from personal interview to mail enumeration affect the comparability of some of the 1969 data with those from earlier censuses. The 1969 census forms were mailed just prior to January 1, 1970. Extensive mail, telephone, and enumerator followup procedures extended the data-collection phase through September 1970. Prior censuses were taken by enumerators, each assigned to a specific geographic area. Field work for the 1964 census was completed largely in November and December 1964, while most of the field work for 1959 was accomplished during October and November. In censuses prior to 1959, the time of enumeration varied from late fall to April 1 to January 1 and even to June 1.

K 109–153. Farms, by race and tenure of operator, and acreage and value, by tenure of operator, 1880–1969.

Source: U.S. Bureau of the Census, *U.S. Census of Agriculture: 1954*, vol. II, pp. 956 and 958; and *1969*, vol. II, chapter 3, pp. 11 and 14.

See also text for series K 17–81.

Data on farm-operator status were not obtained until the census of 1880. Studies of land tenure before 1860 are based, necessarily, upon fragments of information. See Bidwell and Falconer's *History of Agriculture. . .*, and Gray's *History of Agriculture. . .* (see text for series K 5).

The 1900 Census of Agriculture covered the ownership of rented farms, with particular reference to absentee ownership and the concentration of ownership. On a sample basis, the Department of Agriculture made a study of ownership of rented farms in 1920; the results were published as *Bulletins 1432* and *1433*. The Bureau of the Census and the Department of Agriculture cooperated on sample

surveys in 1945, 1950, and 1954 which were designed to show the portion of all farmland owned by each major class of owner. The results of these studies were published in Department of Agriculture, *Agricultural Economics Research*, vol. V, No. 4, 1953, and in Agricultural Research Service and Bureau of the Census, *Graphic Summary of Tenure, 1954*. A complete study of farmland ownership in the United States was made in 1945 and published as Department of Agriculture, *Miscellaneous Publication No. 699*.

In 1916, the Bureau of the Census published *Plantation Farming in the United States* from a 1910 census study of plantations in 325 selected counties in 11 Southern States. In the selected plantation area, 39,073 plantations were reported as having 5 or more tenants. Another study of plantations was made in connection with the 1940 census, but the results were not published. In 1947, the Bureau of the Census published *Multiple Unit Operations* from a study made in connection with the 1945 Census of Agriculture. The Bureau has also published volumes on multiple unit operations from the 1950 and 1954 censuses of agriculture. In 1924, the Bureau of Agricultural Economics issued *Department Bulletin 1269*, the results of a study by C.O. Brannen, *Relation of Land Tenure to Plantation Organization*.

For the censuses of 1880 and 1890 only the number of farms was classified by tenure. Classifications by the race of the farm operator and crossclassifications by race and tenure were first made in the census of 1900.

A farm operator, according to the census definition, is a person who operates a farm, either performing the labor himself or directly supervising it. The census definition of a farm is based on operating units, rather than ownership tracts. A farm may consist of a number of separate tracts held under different tenures, some owned and some rented. Similarly, when a landowner has several tenants, renters, or croppers, the land operated by each is considered a separate farm. Therefore, the number of farm operators, for all practical purposes, is identical with the number of farms, series K 8, and these items are used interchangeably.

In the race classification of farm operators, Mexicans are reported as white. The Negro and other race group includes Negroes, Indians, Chinese, Japanese, and other races not classified as white.

Each farm was classified according to the tenure under which the operator controlled the land. Land was considered owned if the operator or his wife held it under title, homestead law, purchase contract, or as one of the heirs or as trustee of an undivided estate. If both an owned and a rented tract were farmed by the same operator, the tracts were to be considered as one farm even though they were not contiguous and each was locally called a farm. Farm operators were classified as (a) full owners who own all the land they operate; (b) part owners who own a part and rent from others the rest of the land they operate; (c) managers who operate farms for others and receive wages or salaries for their services (persons acting merely as caretakers or hired laborers were not classed as managers, and farms operated for institutions or corporations were considered to be managed even where no person was specifically indicated as being employed as the farm manager); in the 1969 census, managers were no longer classified separately because of the difficulty in identifying managed farms in the mail enumeration procedures used; farms which may have had a manager were classified by tenure based on the tenure of the individual, partnership, or firm which hired the manager and controlled the land; (d) tenants who operate hired or rented land only. Croppers are share tenants to whom landlords furnish all of the work animals or tractor power in lieu of work animals. Croppers were first classified separately in the 1920 census.

In the 1920, 1925, and 1930 censuses, croppers were defined as share tenants whose landlords furnished the work animals. The 1935 census schedule carried no inquiry on the method of paying rent and, therefore, croppers for that year included all tenants whose landlords furnished the work animals. The furnishing of tractor power was not taken into account in classifying croppers until the 1940 census.

The greatest difficulties in making a classification by tenure resulted from the sharecropper system. Briefly, the question involved was whether the sharecropper should be considered merely a type of laborer or a farm operator. In reality, croppers had some of the characteristics of both laborers and tenants. Because of the decreasing importance of the cropper system in the South, croppers have not been classified separately since 1959.

K 154–161. Mortgaged farms—number, acreage, value, and amount of indebtedness, by tenure of operator, 1930–1966.

Source: U.S. Bureau of the Census and U.S. Department of Agriculture, Agricultural Research Service, *U.S. Census of Agriculture: 1954*, vol. III, pt. 5; *1959*, vol. V, pt. 4; and *1964*, vol. III, pt. 4.

Information on the number of mortgaged farms has been collected by both the Bureau of the Census and the Agricultural Research Service, or more recently, the Economic Research Service. Generally speaking, such data have been published with the data on amount of debt in census years, except in 1900 when no information on amount of debt was obtained. For a historical summary and an analysis of the data on number of mortgaged owner-operated farms for 1890–1935, see "Number and Percentage of Farms Under Mortgage," *Agricultural Finance Review*, vol. 1, No. 2, November 1938. The sources cited above also include State data on the number of mortgaged farms in each tenure class for 1940, 1945, 1950, 1956, and 1961.

Farm-mortgage debt includes the unpaid principal of mortgages, deeds of trust, sales contracts, vendors' liens, and all other debt for which farm real estate is pledged as security. Any farm which has a real estate mortgage is classified as a mortgaged farm even though only a portion of it is mortgaged.

Estimates for 1930–1961 are based on information obtained in the Census of Agriculture for owner-operated farms, mail surveys of samples of farm owners (including both operators and landlords), and reports from farm-mortgage lenders.

For each of the years shown, mortgage information was obtained from full-owner farm operators in the census of agriculture. Similar information was obtained by the Bureau of the Census for part owners for 1940, 1945, 1950, 1956, and 1961. This information was supplemented by data obtained in mail surveys for land operated by part owners, tenants, and managers. The 1930 mail survey was conducted by the Bureau of Agricultural Economics. Later surveys were cooperative undertakings of the Bureau of the Census and the Bureau of Agricultural Economics or the Agricultural Research Service.

Data for 1966 were collected in a supplementary survey for the 1964 Census of Agriculture of approximately 16,000 farms. The survey was taken in 1966 and the farms included in the survey were selected from the 1964 Census of Agriculture and from the records of the coverage evaluation survey for the 1964 Census. Comparable data for the tenure breakdown for 1966 are not available because of procedures used in the processing of the data.

For information by States and geographic divisions and descriptions of procedures, see the sources cited, and *U.S. Census of Agriculture: 1950*, vol. V, pt. 8, and *1959*, vol. V, pt. 4.

See also text for series K 109–153 for definition of tenure.

K 162–173. Farms and land in farms, by size of farm, 1880–1969.

Source: U.S. Bureau of the Census, *U.S. Census of Agriculture: 1954*, vol. II, pp. 352–354, *1959*, vol. II, pp. 390 and 392, and *1969*, vol. II, chapter 2, pp. 65–69.

See general note for series K 1–203 for changes in definition of farm.

K 174–176. Farm employment, 1910–1970.

Source: U.S. Department of Agriculture, Statistical Reporting Service (SRS), 1910–1928, *Farm Employment*, Statistical Bulletin No. 334, July 1963; 1929–1969, *Agricultural Statistics*, *1967* and *1971* issues; 1970, *Farm Labor*, January 1972.

For detailed descriptions of farm employment concepts, see *Major Statistical Series of the U.S. Department of Agriculture*, Agriculture Handbook No. 365, vol. 7, pp. 7–12. See source publications for regional, State, and monthly data.

These data are based on (1) data from the census of population used as benchmarks for 1910, 1920, and 1930, and data from the census of agriculture used for 1940, 1950, 1954, and 1959; (2) nationwide annual sample surveys made by SRS since 1965; (3) estimates of farm employment from nationwide enumerative sample surveys made at intervals during 1945–1948, together with historical data on the seasonal distributions of man-hour labor requirements in farm production, used to develop measures of seasonal variation; (4) returns from the crop reporters of the monthly mailed questionnaire on employment on farms, available since 1925; and (5) annual estimates of the number of farms by States and regions used to expand "adjusted" average employment per farm to obtain regional and national estimates of total farm employment and of the family and hired worker components of the total.

Family workers include working farm operators, plus members of their families who did unpaid farmwork or chores for 15 hours or more during the survey week. All persons working one hour or more during the survey week for pay at farmwork or chores are classified as hired farmworkers. Members of the operator's family receiving wages for work on their farms are counted as hired workers. Sharecroppers are considered family workers when working on their own crops but are classified as hired workers when doing farmwork for pay off their tracts. A person employed as both a family worker and a hired worker during the survey week on the same farm is counted as a hired worker. The survey week is the last complete calendar week in the month, but when that week includes the last day of the month the survey week is the next to the last full calendar week.

The average number of hired and family workers per farm is computed for the reporting farms for conterminous United States. The averages are then adjusted by factors based on comparisons with the last census level, labor requirements data, and the estimated seasonal pattern of employment based on the latest census and special studies in selected States. The adjusted averages are then multiplied by the estimated number of farms in each State to estimate the number of family and hired workers employed. Data from the census, State assessors' reports, Agricultural Stabilization and Conservation records, and indications of change from the larger acreage and livestock surveys are used in estimating the number of farms. Annual averages of employment are simple averages of last-of-month employment estimates.

Farm employment data were first collected through crop reporters in October 1923. In 1938, the National Research Project of the Works Progress Administration developed monthly farm employment estimates for 1925–1936 from the crop reporter data. See E. C. Shaw and J. A. Hopkins, *Trends in Employment in Agriculture, 1909–1936*, Works Progress Administration, Philadelphia, November 1938. Monthly estimates have been made by the Agricultural Marketing Service and the former Bureau of Agricultural Economics from crop reporter data for 1936–1970, using the methods developed in the Works Progress Administration project, plus certain recent refinements. Following the 1950 Census of Agriculture, the entire historical series was reexamined and revised. Data for 1950–1970 reflect revisions following the 1959 and 1964 censuses of agriculture and enumerative area surveys made by SRS.

K 177–181. Farm wage rates, 1866–1970.

Source: U.S. Department of Agriculture, 1866–1909, Bureau of Agricultural Economics, *Farm Wage Rates, Farm Employment, and Related Data*, January 1943 (processed); 1910–1947, Agricultural Marketing Service, *Farm Labor*, January 1958; 1948–1969, Statistical Reporting Service (SRS), *Agricultural Statistics*, *1967* and *1971* issues; 1970, *Farm Labor*, January 1972.

Information on farm wages prior to 1866 is scattered; it consists of individual records or covers only certain States rather than the entire country. See Department of Agriculture, Bureau of Statistics, *Wages of Farm Labor in the United States*, Miscellaneous Series, Report No. 4, 1892; same agency's *Wages of Farm Labor*, by George K. Holmes, Bulletin 99, 1912; and T. M. Adams, *Prices Paid by Vermont Farmers for Goods and Services and Received by Them for Farm Products, 1790–1940*; see also Vermont Agricultural Experiment Station Bulletin 507, *Wages of Vermont Farm Labor, 1780–1940*, Burlington, February 1944.

The first investigation made by the Department of Agriculture of wage rates for hired farm workers was in 1866. In the next 44 years, 18 similar studies were made at irregular intervals. Then, for 1909–1923, inquiries were made annually and, since 1923, quarterly. In these surveys, questionnaires were sent to the voluntary crop reporters.

For 1866–1909, crop reporters were requested to estimate the average wages in the locality for the year. Sometimes the inquiry was made in the spring and sometimes in the fall or winter. When it was made in the spring, the year to which the annual average refers is uncertain. For this reason, a dual date is designated for certain of these years as, for example, "1874 or 1875." In each of these 19 investigations, wage rates per day were obtained separately for harvest work and other work. The data published here for 1866–1909 are the day rates for "other than harvest work."

The monthly wage rates, series K 178–179, shown for 1866–1909 are not strictly comparable throughout this period. For 1866–1890, monthly wage rates shown are for workers hired by the year. In addition, in the first three of the aforementioned inquiries, crop reporters were asked for monthly rates paid to workers hired for the season, which are published by Holmes (see above). For 1891–1909, the monthly rate requested was on a combined annual and seasonal basis. In 1909, the distinction was again made, but the two types of monthly rates were averaged. The weighted average (revised) is published here. For the original averages of the monthly rates for workers hired by the year and for those hired by the season, see Holmes, *Wages of Farm Labor*, referred to above. For 1866–1909, wage rates requested were those paid to men doing outdoor work. In 1902, 1906, and 1909, rates paid women for domestic work on farms were also requested.

Data from the 19 wage inquiries were published in 4 bulletins by the Bureau of Statistics of the Department of Agriculture—Nos. 4 (1892), 22 (1901), and 26 (1903) of the "Miscellaneous" series, and Bulletin 99 (1912) of the Bureau of Statistics series. In the first 3 bulletins, the rates were published without reducing currency to gold values, since the monetary system was not on a gold basis; but in Bulletin 99 and in subsequent reports the wage rates for the period of inflated currency values following the Civil War were reduced to gold values. In Bulletin 99 the weighting system, which was not uniform for all previous surveys, was revised and wage-rate data for all 19 surveys were recomputed. The number of male agricultural laborers in each State, as reported by the census of occupations, was used as the weight to obtain United States and major region averages from State average wage rates.

For 1909–1923, annual inquiries on farm wage rates in their localities were made of crop reporters. They were asked about monthly rates with and without board; and about daily rates with and without board "at harvest" and for "other than harvest labor." In 1923, to give an overlap for linking purposes, a quarterly inquiry was initiated. The new quarterly series eliminated the distinction between day rates for harvest work and for nonharvest work; it changed the time reference of day rates to "average wage rates being paid to hired labor at the present time in your locality," with an additional instruction to include in the estimates of day rates "average daily earnings of piece workers." The new rates obtained after 1923 are probably more nearly comparable with the old daily wage rates for "other than harvest work" than they are with either the old daily rates for harvest work or with a combination of the two types of daily rates.

For 1923–1948, the questions asked crop reporters on wage rates continued in almost exactly the same form. In 1948, the wage rate series was changed to include more different kinds of rates and to specify more clearly the perquisites received in addition to cash wages. Value of perquisites is not included in wage rates obtained—they are cash rates only. The types of rates currently obtained are as follows: Per month with board and room, per month with house (no meals), per week with board and room, per week without board or room, per day with board and room, per day with house (no meals), per day without board or room, per hour with house (no meals), and per hour without board or room.

Rates for 1949–1970 are not exactly comparable with rates for previous years. They only approximate the rates denoted in the series headings and represent averages for each type of rate obtained.

Average rates based on data reported by crop reporters are published quarterly and annually in Statistical Reporting Service, *Farm Labor*, but annually only in the Department of Agriculture, *Agricultural Statistics*. The annual average rates are averages of the quarterly averages weighted by the number of hired farm workers employed each quarter.

Since employment data are for approximately the last week of the month and wage rates are usually reported a few days before the end of the month, they must be weighted to center on July 1 (the midpoint in the calendar year) in computing an annual average. The annual average is a 5-quarter average based on data for January of the current year and January of the following year. The use of only the January current year data would not properly weight the changes after October 1, especially when rates are rising or falling significantly.

K 182. Farmers' expenditures for hired labor, 1910–1970.

Source: U.S. Department of Agriculture. 1910–1924, Agricultural Marketing Service, *The Farm Income Situation*, July 1958 (No. 174); 1925–1928, Economic Research Service, same publication, July 1968 (No. 211); 1929–1970, Statistical Reporting Service, *Agricultural Statistics, 1967* and *1971* issues.

Data for census years are from the Bureau of the Census; intercensal year figures are Economic Research Service estimates. For a detailed description of concepts and methods, see *Major Statistical Series of the U.S. Department of Agriculture*, Agriculture Handbook No. 365, vol. 3.

Estimates of farmers' total expenditures for hired labor are available for 1929 and since 1949 for individual States. The total farm labor bill is divided between cash, which accounts for about nine-tenths of the total, and the value of board and lodging and other wages in kind. Such perquisites of hired workers are valued at the estimated cost to operators, not at prices that workers would have to pay if the same items were purchased elsewhere. It is also necessary to distinguish wages paid to hired workers who live on farms from those paid to nonresident hired workers.

K 183. Index, man-hours of labor used for farmwork, 1910–1970.

Source: U.S. Department of Agriculture, Economic Research Service (ERS). 1910–1949, compiled by ERS; 1950–1970, *Changes in Farm Production and Efficiency*, Statistical Bulletin No. 233, 1971 issue.

Man-hours of labor used in farming are estimated by applying regional average man-hours per acre of crops and per head or unit of production of livestock to the official estimates of acreages and numbers made by the Statistical Reporting Service.

Time for farm maintenance or general overhead work is calculated separately and added to the direct hours for crops and livestock to obtain the total number of man-hours. Annual man-hours per acre or per head are estimated by interpolating between or extrapolating from benchmarks.

Benchmarks are estimates of labor used per acre and per head in each State converted to a geographic-division basis.

The interpolation of numbers of man-hours per acre or per animal between benchmarks and extrapolation beyond benchmarks are modified by several factors. For crops, these include such items as yields per acre, utilization of the crop, methods of harvest, and source of power as indicated by numbers of tractors and work stock on farms. For livestock, the modifiers include such factors as size of enterprise, production per animal, and extent of different methods and practices followed.

For more detailed explanation, for the aggregate man-hours upon which the indexes are based, and for other more detailed data, see *Major Statistical Series of the U.S. Department of Agriculture*, Agriculture Handbook No. 365, vol. 2.

K 184-191. Farm machinery and equipment, 1910-1970.

Source: U.S. Department of Agriculture, Economic Research Service, *Changes in Farm Production and Efficiency*, Statistical Bulletin No. 233, July 1964 and June 1971 issues.

Census counts of tractors, automobiles, and motortrucks were first made in the 1920 Census of Agriculture; of grain combines and farms with milking machines in the 1945 census; of cornpickers and pickup balers in the 1950 census; and of field forage harvesters in the 1954 census. Estimates for intercensal years and before census data were available are as of January 1.

Before 1950, figures of machines shipped by manufacturers for farm use, with an allowance for disappearance, were used mainly as the basis for these estimates. Figures for automobiles and motortrucks were based on annual registrations for a limited number of agricultural States, and a few special sample surveys that were nationwide. Since 1950, the annual series is based on census counts, production, imports and shipments of machines, survey data (mainly a questionnaire to Statistical Reporting Service crop reporters in February), trends in census data, and estimated annual discard rates.

K 192. Farmers' expenditures for fertilizer and lime, 1909-1970.

Source: U.S. Department of Agriculture. 1909-1929, Agricultural Marketing Service, *The Farm Income Situation*, July 1958 (No. 174); 1930-1970, Economic Research Service, *Farm Income Situation*, July 1971 (No. 218).

For a detailed discussion of concepts, coverage, and methods, see *Major Statistical Series of the U.S. Department of Agriculture*, Agriculture Handbook No. 365, vol. 3.

K 193. Commercial fertilizer consumed in U.S., 1850-1970.

Source: U.S. Department of Agriculture, 1850-1944, Agricultural Research Service, *Statistics on Fertilizers and Liming Materials in the United States*, Statistical Bulletin No. 191, April 1957; 1945-1969, Statistical Reporting Service, *Consumption of Commercial Fertilizer and Primary Plant Nutrients in the United States*, Statistical Bulletins No. 375 and No. 472, June 1966 and June 1971; 1970, Statistical Reporting Service, *Commercial Fertilizers—Consumption in the United States*, Sp. Cr. 7 October 1971.

Commercial fertilizer includes any substance containing nitrogen (N), phosphoric acid (P_2O_5), potash (K_2O), or any other recognized plant-food element or compound, such as lime (CaO), magnesia (MgO), boron (B), etc., which is consumed primarily for the purpose of supplying plant food to crops, excluding barnyard manures but including dried animal manures sold commercially. Ground phosphate rock, gypsum, sulfur, borax, copper sulfate, manganese sulfate, zinc sulfate, cottonseed meal, dried blood, animal tankage, etc., are included when sold to farmers for plant food, but are excluded when sold as fungicides, animal feeds, or for any other purpose than for plant food. Limestone, dolomite, magnesia, etc., are included when used as components of mixed fertilizers but excluded when sold as soil amendments (materials used to change the physical properties or the acidity of the soil rather than to supply plant food).

The data refer to all commercial plant food, including that dis-

tributed by the Agricultural Stabilization and Conservation Service in its soil-building program and that used by the Tennessee Valley Authority in test demonstrations.

For 1920 to 1944, the data relate to consumption only in conterminous United States; for 1850-1919 and 1945-1970, they include consumption in Alaska, Hawaii, and Puerto Rico. The total consumption in these outlying areas increased from about 3,000 tons in 1890 to 52,000 in 1900, 93,000 in 1910, 120,000 in 1920, 254,000 in 1930, 321,000 in 1940, 366,000 in 1950, 376,000 in 1960, and 351,000 in 1970. Most of this consumption occurred in Puerto Rico and Hawaii.

The earliest data on fertilizers were collected by State fertilizer control officials. The first volume of *American Fertilizer*, 1894, presents figures for Georgia for 1875-1892. In 1945, 36 States had a Fertilizer Control Office or similar agency which published tonnages of fertilizers consumed in the State. Now, all States have a Fertilizer Control Office or similar agency. A bibliography of such reports is given in U.S. Department of Agriculture, Circular No. 756, 1946, which also gives considerable detail on fertilizer consumption.

Since 1965, annual estimates of consumption have been made by the Statistical Reporting Service, using reports from State fertilizer control officials and voluntary reports from fertilizer manufacturers.

Annual estimates of consumption made by the National Fertilizer Association (now a part of the Fertilizer Institute) were discontinued in 1955. *The Fertilizer Review*, vol. XXI, No. 2, pp. 11-14, presents figures for conterminous United States by decades from 1880 to 1910, and annually to 1945.

K 194. Lime consumed on farms, 1910-1970.

Source: U.S. Department of Agriculture, Economic Research Service, *Changes in Farm Production and Efficiency*, Statistical Bulletin No. 233, July 1964; June 1966; and June 1973.

This series links two series not quite alike in coverage. For 1929-1945, the tonnage is in terms of ground limestone, materials in other forms being converted to that basis, except for some coarser materials used in Illinois. These figures were based on surveys made by State agricultural college agronomists and include county surveys of producers, and data from county extension agents and AAA offices, assembled by C. E. Carter of the Production and Marketing Administration. The data for 1910, 1920, and 1925-1928, however, were assembled by A. L. Mehring of the Bureau of Plant Industry, Soils, and Agricultural Engineering. The intervening years were interpolated. Mehring's figures, with the interpolations, were carried through 1939 in the Bureau of Agricultural Economics series, *Income Parity for Agriculture*, pt. II, sec. 2; hence, the figures given there for 1929-1939 differ from those presented here. Lime used by fertilizer manufacturers in their mixed goods is not included. Data for recent years are from National Agricultural Limestone Institute, Inc.

K 195-203. Farmers' marketing and purchasing cooperatives— number, memberships, and business, 1913-1970.

Source: U.S. Farmer Cooperative Service, 1913-1950, *Statistics of Farmer Cooperatives, 1954-1955*; 1951-1970, *Statistics of Farmer Cooperatives, 1969-70*.

These data were first compiled in 1913-1915 from questionnaires collected by mail from all cooperatives known to exist in the period 1912-1915. In 1919, data on the extent of cooperative marketing and farm supply purchasing were collected as a part of the census of agriculture. Other nationwide surveys were conducted in 1922 and for the fiscal years 1925-1926 and 1927-1928. Beginning with 1929-1930, annual nationwide surveys have been taken of farmer marketing, farm supply, and related services cooperatives. Data were collected by mail in each of these surveys except for 1936-1937 when information was collected in the field by Farm Credit Administration in cooperation with the banks for cooperatives and 33 State agricultural colleges.

A farmer cooperative is defined as one which meets the following requirements: (1) Farmers or associations of agricultural producers hold the controlling interest; (2) each member is limited to one vote regardless of the amount of stock or membership capital he owns therein, unless dividends on stock or membership capital are limited to 8 percent a year or less, in which case the number of votes per member can vary; and (3) the value of products handled for non-members is not greater in value than the amount handled for members. All active farmer cooperatives that meet the above criteria, and that provide information indicating they market farm products, handle farm supplies, or perform related services, are included in the annual survey.

As cooperatives tended increasingly to diversify their operations, the annual survey figures became less satisfactory. Therefore, beginning with the survey covering fiscal 1951, revised questionnaires were used to develop information on a functional and commodity basis. The questionnaires were further revised in 1960 to limit the scope of questions on service organizations.

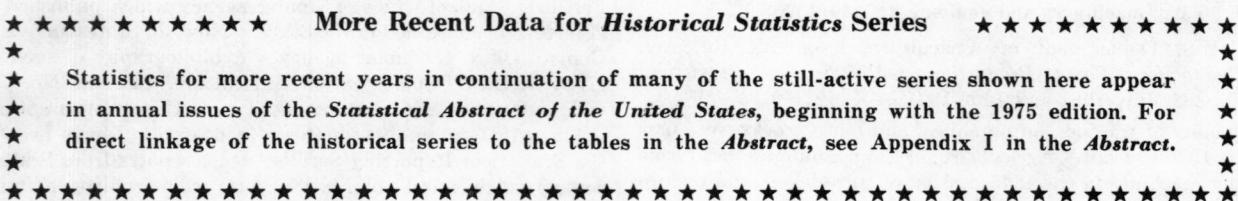

★ ★ ★ ★ ★ ★ ★ ★ ★ ★   **More Recent Data for *Historical Statistics* Series**   ★ ★ ★ ★ ★ ★ ★ ★ ★ ★
★   ★
★   Statistics for more recent years in continuation of many of the still-active series shown here appear   ★
★   in annual issues of the *Statistical Abstract of the United States*, beginning with the 1975 edition. For ★
★   direct linkage of the historical series to the tables in the *Abstract*, see Appendix I in the *Abstract*. ★
★   ★
★ ★

Series K 1–16. Farm Population, Farms, Land in Farms, and Value of Farm Property and Real Estate: 1850 to 1970

[Census figures in *italics*]

Year	Farm population Total (1,000)	Percent of total population	Net change through migration (1,000)	Number of farms (1,000)	Land in farms Total (1,000 acres)	Percent of total land area	Average acreage per farm (acres)	Cropland (1,000 acres)	Pasture-land (1,000 acres)	Value of all farm property (mil. dol.) Total	Land and buildings [2]	Implements and machinery	Live-stock [3]	Average value per farm of land and buildings (dol.)	Average value per acre of land and buildings (dol.)	Index of average value of farm real estate per acre (1967=100)
	1	2	3	4	5	6	7	8	9	10	11	12	13	14	15	16
1970	9,712	4.8	−330	2,954	1,102,769		373			265,744	208,214	34,052	22,810	70,485	193.23	117
1969	10,307	5.1	−642	*2,730*	*1,063,346*	47.0	390	459,048	389,493		[4] 206,751	32,964	19,649	75,725	194.43	113
1968	10,454	5.3	−198	3,071	1,115,231		363			243,222	193,703	31,366	18,247	63,075	177.54	107
1967	10,875	5.5	−481	3,162	1,123,456		355			230,291	182,456	28,917	18,343	57,703	167.05	100
1966	11,595	5.9	−793	3,257	1,131,844		348			217,170	172,532	27,093	17,009	52,973	157.28	94
1965	12,363	6.4	−858	3,356	1,139,597		340			200,913	160,942	25,522	13,950	47,956	146.18	87
1964	12,954	6.8	−703	*3,158*	*1,110,185*	49.0	*352*	434,232	490,307		[4] 159,932	24,075	15,344	50,646	143.81	82
1963	13,367	7.1	−533	3,572	1,151,572		322			183,802	143,834	22,704	16,779	40,267	129.75	77
1962	14,313	7.7	−1,086	3,685	1,161,383		314			176,672	137,956	22,499	15,914	37,437	124.12	78
1961	14,803	8.1	−646	3,821	1,169,899		306			169,177	131,752	21,977	*15,052*	34,481	118.23	74
1960	*15,635	*8.7	*−1,000	3,962	1,176,946		297			167,564	130,169	22,189	14,719	32,854	116.49	72
1959	16,592	9.4	−1,142	*3,711	*1,123,508	*49.5	*303	*448,087	466,225		[4] 129,005	22,059	16,730	*34,763	*115.08	71
1958	17,128	9.9	−740	4,233	1,184,944		280			149,936	115,934	20,230	12,998	27,388	102.80	65
1957	17,656	10.4	−748	4,372	1,191,340		273			141,658	110,422	20,240	10,183	25,257	97.25	61
1956	18,712	11.2	−1,295	4,514	1,197,070		265			132,901	102,934	19,339	9,810	22,803	90.06	57
1955	19,078	11.6	−627	4,654	1,201,900		258			127,977	98,172	18,595	10,463	21,094	85.32	57
1954	19,019	11.8	−210	*4,782	*1,158,192	60.8	*242	459,649	459,879		97,583	16,279	10,829	*20,405	84.25	53
1953	19,874	12.5	−1,151	4,984	1,205,740		242			128,711	96,535	15,627	13,830	19,369	83.34	55
1952	21,748	13.9	−2,201	5,198	1,204,930		232			131,279	95,078	15,161	18,395	18,291	82.08	55
1951	21,890	14.2	−483	5,428	1,203,500		222			117,817	86,586	13,017	15,969	15,952	74.74	49
1950	23,048	15.3	−1,531	[4] 5,388	[4] 1,161,420	[4] 51.1	[4] 216	[4] 478,315	[4] 416,802	101,117	[4] 75,462	12,166	11,696	[4] 14,005	[4] 64.97	43
1949	24,194	16.3	−1,537	5,722	1,155,174		202			94,287	76,623	9,420	12,996	13,391	66.33	44
1948	24,383	16.7	−586	5,803	1,151,784		199			85,717	73,664	6,969	11,780	12,694	63.96	43
1947	25,829	18.0	−1,889	5,871	1,148,394		196			76,151	68,463	5,083	10,294	11,661	59.62	39
1946	25,403	18.0	−44	5,926	1,145,003		193			76,151	61,046	5,174	8,072	10,301	53.31	35
1945	24,420	17.5	671	*5,859	*1,141,615	59.9	195	450,694	481,017	69,369	*46,389	6,474	7,281	*7,918	40.63	31
1944	24,815	18.0	−748	6,003	1,125,461		187			63,323	48,200	5,346	7,687	8,029	42.83	28
1943	26,186	19.2	−1,740	6,089	1,109,308		182			56,195	41,604	4,906	7,754	6,833	37.50	25
1942	28,914	21.5	−3,145	6,202	1,093,155		176			48,608	37,547	3,981	5,552	6,054	34.35	23
1941	30,118	22.6	−1,587	6,293	1,077,002		171			42,979	34,400	3,254	3,877	5,466	31.94	21
1940	30,547	23.2	−788	*6,102	*1,065,114	[4] 46.8	*175	*530,556	*393,544	41,829	*33,758	3,060	3,540	*5,532	*31.69	21
1939	30,840	23.6	−703	6,441	1,059,582		165			42,213	34,074	3,036	3,359	5,290	32.17	23
1938	30,980	23.9	−545	6,527	1,058,315		162			43,202	35,170	2,998	3,164	5,388	33.23	23
1937	31,266	24.3	−661	6,636	1,057,047		159			42,926	35,213	2,648	3,036	5,306	33.31	23
1936	31,737	24.8	−834	6,739	1,055,780		157			41,803	34,260	2,359	3,145	5,084	32.45	22
1935	32,161	25.3	−799	6,812	*1,054,515	55.4	155	513,914	311,226	38,959	32,859	2,217	1,837	4,823	31.16	21
1934	32,305	25.6	−527	6,776	1,040,963		154			37,538	32,201	2,168	1,743	4,752	30.93	20
1933	32,393	25.8	−463	6,741	1,027,415		152			36,249	30,802	2,464	1,787	4,569	29.98	19
1932	31,388	25.2	607	6,687	1,013,865		152			43,651	37,180	2,915	2,264	5,560	36.67	24
1931	30,845	24.9	156	6,608	1,000,317		151			51,806	43,730	3,217	3,337	6,618	43.72	28
1930	30,529	24.9	−61	*6,295	*990,112	[4] 43.6	*157	*522,396	*269,673	57,689	*47,994	3,302	4,598	*7,624	*48.47	31
1929	30,580	25.2	−477	6,512	974,277		150			57,738	47,985	3,178	4,672	7,369	49.25	32
1928	30,548	25.4	−422	6,470	961,787		149			56,727	47,532	3,088	4,139	7,347	49.42	22
1927	30,530	25.7	−457	6,458	949,297		147			56,393	47,680	3,126	3,653	7,383	50.23	33
1926	30,979	26.5	−907	6,462	936,806		145			57,412	49,000	3,042	3,421	7,583	52.31	34
1925	31,190	27.0	−702	6,372	924,319	48.6	145	505,027	217,687	57,439	49,468	2,955	3,075	7,764	53.52	35
1924	31,177	27.5	−487	6,480	930,628		144			58,519	50,487	2,985	3,066	7,791	54.25	36
1923	31,490	28.2	−807	6,492	936,941		144			60,902	52,629	2,832	3,235	8,107	56.17	37
1922	32,109	29.3	−1,137	6,500	943,253		145			61,982	54,050	2,900	2,884	8,315	57.30	39
1921	32,123	29.7	−564	6,511	949,566		146			71,401	61,523	3,551	3,713	9,449	64.79	44
1920	31,974	30.1	−336	[4] 6,454	[4] 958,677	[4] 42.2	[4] 149	[5] 348,604		78,386	[4] 66,446	3,595	5,304	[4] 10,295	[4] 69.31	48
1919	31,200	29.7		6,506	948,169		146			66,863	54,533	3,345	5,807	8,382	57.51	39
1918	31,950	30.6		6,488	940,461		145			61,466	49,980	2,965	5,324	7,703	53.14	36
1917	32,430	31.5		6,478	932,752		144			54,902	45,524	2,338	4,006	7,027	48.80	33
1916	32,530	32.0		6,463	925,044		143			50,651	42,264	2,046	3,403	6,539	45.69	30
1915	32,440	32.4		6,458	917,335		142			47,715	39,590	1,849	3,319	6,130	43.16	28
1914	32,320	32.8		6,447	909,627		141			47,429	39,579	1,719	3,021	6,139	43.51	28
1913	32,270	33.4		6,437	901,918		140			45,720	38,456	1,630	2,560	5,974	42.64	28
1912	32,210	33.9		6,430	894,209		139			43,842	37,298	1,522	2,131	5,801	41.71	27
1911	32,110	34.3		6,425	886,501		138			42,693	36,042	1,401	2,251	5,610	40.66	
1910	32,077	34.9		[4] 6,366	[4] 881,431	[4] 38.8	[4] 139	[5] 311,293		40,959	[4] 34,885	1,265	2,074	[4] 5,480	[4] 39.58	
1900	29,875	41.9		[4] 5,740	[4] 841,202	[4] 37.0	[4] 147	[5] 283,218		20,365	[4] 16,614	750	1,991	[4] 2,895	[4] 19.82	
1890	24,771	42.3		4,565	623,219	32.7	137	[5] 219,706		16,439	13,279	494	1,346	2,909	21.31	
1880	21,973	43.8		4,009	536,082	28.2	134	[5] 166,187		12,404	10,197	406	1,064	2,544	19.02	
1870				2,660	407,735	21.4	153			9,412	7,444	271	968	2,799	18.26	
1860				2,044	407,213	21.4	199			7,980	6,645	246		3,251	16.32	
1850				1,449	293,561	15.6	203			3,967	3,272	152		2,258	11.14	

* Except as indicated by footnote 4, denotes first year for which figures include Alaska and Hawaii.
[1] Intercensal estimates derived from straight-line interpolation. Excludes District of Columbia.
[2] Census years as of date of enumeration. All other years as of March 1. Excludes District of Columbia.

[3] Estimates as of January 1, except hog and pig inventory, beginning 1969, estimated as of December 1.
[4] Includes Alaska and Hawaii.
[5] Cropland harvested only.

Series K 17–81. Farm Population, Farms, Land in Farms, and Value of Farm Property and Farm Products Sold, by State: 1850 to 1969

Farm population (1,000)

Series No.	Division, region, and State	1890	1900	1910	1920	1925	1930	1935	1940	1945	1950	1954	1959	1964	1969
17	United States	24,771	29,875	32,077	31,974	31,190	30,529	32,161	30,547	24,420	23,048	19,019	16,592	12,954	10,307
18	Northeast	3,194	3,364	2,901	2,537	2,435	2,287	2,633	2,411	1,906	1,791	1,397	1,175	929	741
19	New England	878	892	764	633	617	575	718	623	446	403	301	246	183	138
20	Maine	283	267	247	200	190	171	187	176	125	122	86	66	46	33
21	New Hampshire	130	131	102	77	72	63	77	71	51	47	32	23	17	12
22	Vermont	148	152	142	127	122	113	123	107	75	81	66	60	45	34
23	Massachusetts	167	183	140	120	125	124	165	147	111	80	61	52	39	30
24	Rhode Island	26	28	20	15	17	16	22	17	12	10	6	6	6	4
25	Connecticut	123	131	112	94	92	87	144	105	71	63	47	39	30	25
26	Middle Atlantic	2,317	2,472	2,137	1,904	1,818	1,712	1,915	1,788	1,460	1,388	1,095	929	747	603
27	New York	1,076	1,113	922	806	768	722	789	730	601	578	467	408	321	254
28	New Jersey	155	176	165	145	138	131	145	143	112	105	85	75	61	50
29	Pennsylvania	1,085	1,183	1,050	953	912	859	981	915	746	705	543	446	365	300
30	North Central	9,995	11,094	10,714	10,158	9,805	9,583	9,951	9,349	7,767	7,433	6,732	6,191	5,246	4,496
31	East North Central	5,144	5,653	5,275	4,953	4,637	4,501	4,808	4,638	3,866	3,703	3,276	2,974	2,519	2,147
32	Ohio	1,241	1,354	1,245	1,149	1,060	1,016	1,136	1,089	893	853	717	607	515	434
33	Indiana	998	1,071	997	914	848	815	860	816	696	667	606	569	493	432
34	Illinois	1,289	1,341	1,219	1,107	1,033	1,002	1,026	979	808	763	694	652	565	492
35	Michigan	843	982	912	856	807	785	847	871	704	695	590	510	410	324
36	Wisconsin	773	904	902	927	889	883	939	883	765	725	668	636	537	464
37	West North Central	4,851	5,441	5,440	5,205	5,168	5,082	5,143	4,711	3,901	3,729	3,457	3,217	2,727	2,349
38	Minnesota	641	856	903	903	908	898	934	915	753	740	698	671	572	502
39	Iowa	1,047	1,139	1,053	991	990	981	974	931	783	783	767	755	645	565
40	Missouri	1,318	1,475	1,352	1,219	1,172	1,118	1,192	1,125	882	863	747	630	515	417
41	North Dakota	139	239	369	398	397	398	389	328	277	254	235	220	187	161
42	South Dakota	240	274	371	364	380	391	360	307	261	254	238	228	201	178
43	Nebraska	615	619	631	588	588	587	585	498	417	391	370	349	301	263
44	Kansas	851	838	830	742	733	709	709	607	495	444	401	364	306	263
45	South	10,723	14,226	16,657	17,063	16,762	16,364	17,162	16,400	12,740	11,896	9,139	7,613	5,513	4,058
46	South Atlantic	4,209	5,271	6,212	6,496	6,215	5,914	6,283	6,060	4,891	4,633	3,573	2,984	2,106	1,483
47	Delaware	47	50	58	52	49	47	50	46	39	34	29	26	21	16
48	Maryland	221	254	297	283	261	238	245	246	201	183	150	135	108	84
49	District of Columbia	2	1	1	1	—	—	—	—	—	—	—	—	—	—
50	Virginia	748	952	1,065	1,078	1,020	953	1,066	986	831	732	579	502	356	259
51	West Virginia	429	535	544	484	466	450	569	533	445	411	264	165	117	84
52	North Carolina	998	1,258	1,409	1,520	1,566	1,604	1,645	1,659	1,360	1,377	1,126	1,006	710	507
53	South Carolina	628	835	970	1,088	1,001	919	1,052	917	709	701	543	455	282	165
54	Georgia	950	1,183	1,594	1,706	1,566	1,423	1,424	1,368	1,052	962	697	530	371	251
55	Florida	185	203	285	285	286	280	324	305	254	233	186	165	140	117
56	East South Central	3,833	4,860	5,291	5,257	5,163	5,109	5,409	5,283	4,271	4,048	3,146	2,641	1,933	1,433
57	Kentucky	1,024	1,267	1,286	1,324	1,286	1,180	1,326	1,261	1,038	974	768	652	550	474
58	Tennessee	1,007	1,246	1,278	1,290	1,249	1,219	1,326	1,276	1,046	1,016	818	715	538	412
59	Alabama	909	1,166	1,383	1,355	1,343	1,344	1,405	1,343	1,068	960	708	553	367	240
60	Mississippi	892	1,181	1,344	1,288	1,322	1,366	1,352	1,403	1,119	1,097	852	721	477	308
61	West South Central	2,681	4,095	5,154	5,310	5,384	5,341	5,470	5,057	3,578	3,215	2,420	1,988	1,474	1,141
62	Arkansas	804	956	1,107	1,165	1,153	1,122	1,198	1,113	802	802	595	483	327	245
63	Louisiana	431	804	732	798	823	833	872	854	608	567	414	326	240	173
64	Oklahoma	44	587	1,022	1,033	1,045	1,027	1,031	930	651	553	404	318	258	219
65	Texas	1,401	1,943	2,293	2,314	2,363	2,359	2,369	2,160	1,520	1,292	1,007	860	650	503
66	West	859	1,192	1,805	2,216	2,188	2,295	2,415	2,387	2,008	1,929	1,751	1,613	1,265	1,011
67	Mountain	312	502	918	1,179	1,119	1,143	1,199	1,118	905	859	780	719	577	471
68	Montana	32	67	111	228	209	205	197	176	134	136	128	123	106	94
69	Idaho	39	81	148	203	189	189	201	203	161	165	159	158	128	107
70	Wyoming	18	30	52	68	67	74	76	73	53	57	54	52	41	35
71	Colorado	97	115	203	268	267	284	278	253	191	198	175	154	122	99
72	New Mexico	43	61	184	163	154	159	192	178	149	132	103	76	60	48
73	Arizona	11	33	83	92	92	99	101	114	101	77	74	73	55	37
74	Utah	66	106	122	141	124	116	139	105	101	81	74	69	53	41
75	Nevada	7	9	15	16	15	16	15	16	14	13	13	13	11	10
76	Pacific	546	690	887	1,037	1,069	1,152	1,216	1,270	1,102	1,070	971	894	689	541
77	Washington	123	171	260	289	291	306	342	340	304	274	242	216	170	140
78	Oregon	141	180	210	219	217	224	253	259	233	228	200	176	145	124
79	California	283	339	417	529	561	622	621	670	565	568	529	502	362	268
80	Alaska	—	—	—	—	—	—	—	—	—	—	—	—	2	2
81	Hawaii	—	—	—	—	—	—	—	—	—	—	—	—	9	7

Series K 17-81. Farm Population, Farms, Land in Farms, and Value of Farm Property and Farm Products Sold, by State: 1850 to 1969—Con.

Number of farms (1,000)

Series No.	Division, region, and State	1850	1860	1870	1880	1890	1900	1910	1920	1925	1930	1935	1940	1945	1950	1954	1959	1964	1969
17	United States	1,449	2,044	2,660	4,009	4,565	5,740	6,366	6,454	6,372	6,295	6,812	6,102	5,859	5,388	4,782	3,711	3,158	2,730
18	Northeast	490	565	602	696	659	678	657	582	578	483	556	483	498	400	339	255	202	152
19	New England	168	184	181	207	190	192	187	157	159	125	158	135	150	103	82	57	42	29
20	Maine	47	56	60	64	62	59	60	48	50	39	42	39	41	30	23	17	13	8
21	New Hampshire	29	31	30	32	29	29	27	21	21	15	18	17	19	13	10	7	5	3
22	Vermont	30	32	34	36	33	33	33	29	28	25	27	24	26	19	16	12	9	7
23	Massachusetts	34	36	27	38	34	38	37	32	33	26	35	32	37	22	17	11	8	6
24	Rhode Island	5	5	5	6	5	5	5	4	3	3	4	3	4	2	2	1	1	1
25	Connecticut	22	25	26	31	26	27	27	23	23	17	32	21	22	16	13	8	6	4
26	Middle Atlantic	322	381	421	489	469	486	468	425	419	358	398	348	347	297	257	198	160	123
27	New York	171	197	216	241	226	227	216	193	189	160	177	153	149	125	106	82	67	52
28	New Jersey	24	28	31	34	31	35	33	30	30	25	29	26	26	25	23	15	11	8
29	Pennsylvania	128	156	174	214	212	224	219	202	200	172	191	169	172	147	129	100	83	63
30	North Central	438	772	1,125	1,698	1,924	2,197	2,233	2,182	2,163	2,079	2,264	2,097	1,986	1,868	1,704	1,461	1,277	1,152
31	East North Central	368	587	762	985	1,009	1,136	1,123	1,085	1,052	967	1,084	1,006	954	885	799	666	574	513
32	Ohio	144	180	196	247	251	277	272	257	245	219	255	234	221	199	177	140	120	111
33	Indiana	94	132	161	194	198	222	215	205	196	182	201	185	176	167	154	128	108	101
34	Illinois	76	143	203	256	241	264	252	237	226	214	231	213	204	195	176	155	133	124
35	Michigan	34	62	99	154	172	203	207	197	192	169	197	188	175	156	139	112	94	78
36	Wisconsin	20	69	103	134	146	170	177	189	193	182	200	187	178	169	154	131	119	99
37	West North Central	69	185	363	713	915	1,061	1,110	1,097	1,111	1,113	1,180	1,091	1,032	983	905	795	704	639
38	Minnesota	(Z)	18	47	92	117	155	156	178	188	185	203	197	189	179	165	146	131	111
39	Iowa	15	61	116	185	202	229	217	213	213	215	222	213	209	203	193	175	154	140
40	Missouri	54	93	148	216	238	285	277	263	260	256	278	256	243	230	202	169	147	137
41	North Dakota			[1]2	14	28	45	74	78	76	78	85	74	70	65	62	55	49	46
42	South Dakota		3	10	14	50	53	78	75	80	83	134	72	69	66	63	56	50	46
43	Nebraska			12	63	114	122	130	124	128	129	134	121	112	107	101	90	80	72
44	Kansas			38	139	167	173	178	165	166	166	175	156	141	131	120	104	92	86
45	South	515	672	885	1,531	1,836	2,620	3,098	3,207	3,131	3,224	3,422	3,007	2,881	2,652	2,317	1,646	1,373	1,161
46	South Atlantic	248	302	374	644	750	962	1,112	1,159	1,108	1,058	1,147	1,019	1,043	959	859	592	468	371
47	Delaware	6	7	7	9	9	10	11	10	10	10	10	9	9	7	6	5	4	4
48	Maryland	22	25	27	41	41	46	49	48	49	43	44	42	41	36	33	25	21	17
49	District of Columbia	(Z)	(Z)	(Z)	(Z)		(Z)	(Z)											
50	Virginia	77	93	74	119	128	168	184	186	194	171	198	175	173	151	136	98	80	65
51	West Virginia			40	63	73	93	97	87	90	83	105	99	98	81	69	44	35	23
52	North Carolina	57	75	94	158	178	225	254	270	283	280	301	278	287	289	268	191	148	119
53	South Carolina	30	33	52	94	115	155	176	193	173	158	166	138	148	139	124	78	56	40
54	Georgia	52	62	70	139	171	225	291	311	249	256	251	216	226	198	166	106	83	67
55	Florida	4	7	10	23	34	41	50	54	59	59	73	62	61	57	58	45	41	36
56	East South Central	223	271	372	570	656	903	1,042	1,052	1,006	1,062	1,137	1,023	960	913	790	563	468	392
57	Kentucky	75	91	118	166	179	235	259	271	259	246	278	253	239	218	193	151	133	125
58	Tennessee	73	82	118	166	174	225	246	253	253	246	274	248	234	232	203	158	133	121
59	Alabama	42	55	68	136	158	223	263	256	238	257	273	232	223	212	177	116	93	72
60	Mississippi	34	43	68	102	144	221	274	272	257	313	312	291	264	251	216	138	109	73
61	West South Central	43	99	139	317	431	755	943	996	1,017	1,103	1,138	964	878	780	668	491	436	399
62	Arkansas	18	39	49	94	125	179	215	233	232	242	253	217	199	182	145	95	80	60
63	Louisiana	13	17	28	48	69	116	121	135	132	161	170	150	129	124	111	74	62	42
64	Oklahoma					[3]9	[2]108	190	192	197	204	213	180	165	142	119	95	89	83
65	Texas	12	43	61	174	228	352	418	436	466	495	501	418	385	332	293	227	205	214
66	West	7	35	48	84	146	245	378	484	499	510	571	515	494	468	423	349	306	265
67	Mountain	5	9	14	25	49	101	183	244	233	241	271	233	213	195	180	149	134	120
68	Montana			1	2	6	13	26	58	47	47	51	42	38	35	33	29	27	25
69	Idaho			1	2	7	17	31	42	41	42	45	44	41	40	39	34	30	25
70	Wyoming			(Z)	(Z)	3	6	11	16	16	16	17	15	13	13	11	10	9	9
71	Colorado				5	16	25	46	60	58	60	64	51	48	46	41	33	30	28
72	New Mexico	4	5	4	5	4	12	36	30	32	31	41	34	30	24	21	16	14	12
73	Arizona				1	1	5	9	10	11	14	19	18	13	10	9	7	6	6
74	Utah	1	4	5	9	11	19	22	26	26	27	31	25	26	24	23	18	16	13
75	Nevada			(Z)	1	1	2	3	3	4	4	4	4	3	3	3	2	2	2
76	Pacific	2	26	34	59	96	144	194	240	266	268	300	282	282	273	243	200	171	145
77	Washington		1	3	6	18	33	56	66	66	71	84	82	80	60	54	43	40	34
78	Oregon	1	6	8	16	26	36	46	50	56	55	65	62	63	54	54	43	40	29
79	California	1	19	24	36	53	73	88	118	136	136	150	133	139	137	123	99	81	78
80	Alaska												1		1		(Z)	(Z)	(Z)
81	Hawaii						2	4	5	5	6		5		6	6	6	5	4

See footnotes at end of table.

Series K 17–81. Farm Population, Farms, Land in Farms, and Value of Farm Property and Farm Products Sold, by State: 1850 to 1969—Con.

Land in farms (1,000 acres)

Series No.	Division, region, and State	1850	1860	1870	1880	1890	1900	1910	1920	1925	1930	1935	1940	1945	1950	1954	1959	1964	1969
17	United States	293,561	407,213	407,735	536,082	623,219	841,202	881,431	958,677	924,319	990,112	1,054,515	1,065,114	1,141,615	1,161,420	1,158,192	1,123,508	1,110,187	1,063,346
18	Northeast	55,163	61,082	62,744	67,986	62,744	65,409	62,906	57,564	53,349	49,330	51,919	47,010	48,903	44,402	41,019	36,047	31,979	25,683
19	New England	18,367	20,111	19,570	21,484	19,756	20,549	19,715	16,991	15,858	14,283	15,463	13,371	14,497	12,547	11,121	9,316	7,744	5,599
20	Maine	4,555	5,728	5,838	6,553	6,180	6,300	6,297	5,426	5,161	4,640	4,722	4,223	4,613	4,182	3,614	3,082	2,590	1,760
21	New Hampshire	3,392	3,745	3,606	3,721	3,459	3,610	3,249	2,604	2,262	1,960	2,116	1,809	2,017	1,714	1,457	1,124	903	613
22	Vermont	4,126	4,274	4,529	4,883	4,396	4,724	4,664	4,236	3,926	3,896	4,043	3,667	3,931	3,527	3,318	2,945	2,524	1,916
23	Massachusetts	3,356	3,339	2,730	3,359	2,998	3,147	2,876	2,494	2,368	2,005	2,196	1,938	2,078	1,660	1,439	1,142	902	701
24	Rhode Island	554	521	502	515	469	456	443	332	309	279	308	222	265	191	155	138	104	69
25	Connecticut	2,384	2,504	2,364	2,454	2,253	2,312	2,186	1,899	1,832	1,502	2,080	1,512	1,593	1,272	1,138	884	721	541
26	Middle Atlantic	36,795	40,971	43,175	46,502	42,988	44,860	43,191	40,573	37,491	35,047	36,455	33,639	34,406	31,855	29,898	26,730	24,235	20,085
27	New York	19,119	20,975	22,190	23,781	21,962	22,648	22,030	20,633	19,270	17,980	18,686	17,170	17,568	16,017	15,071	13,490	12,275	10,148
28	New Jersey	2,753	2,984	2,990	2,980	2,662	2,841	2,574	2,283	1,925	1,758	1,914	1,874	1,818	1,725	1,665	1,379	1,156	1,036
29	Pennsylvania	14,923	17,012	17,994	19,791	18,364	19,371	18,587	17,658	16,296	15,309	15,855	14,594	15,020	14,113	13,162	11,862	10,804	8,901
30	North Central	62,686	107,900	139,215	206,982	256,587	317,349	350,577	374,708	360,834	376,379	390,034	388,078	398,812	396,427	393,458	385,394	383,090	373,369
31	East North Central	50,189	72,697	87,449	105,785	105,787	116,341	117,735	116,957	117,752	116,891	116,957	113,655	115,564	112,098	109,024	103,386	99,486	94,507
32	Ohio	17,997	20,472	21,712	24,529	23,352	24,502	24,106	23,516	22,219	21,514	22,858	21,908	21,928	20,969	19,992	18,507	17,619	17,111
33	Indiana	12,793	16,388	18,120	20,421	21,620	21,620	21,300	21,063	21,300	20,519	20,519	21,908	20,027	19,659	19,659	18,613	17,933	17,573
34	Illinois	12,037	20,912	25,883	31,674	30,498	32,795	32,523	31,975	30,732	30,695	31,661	31,033	31,602	30,978	30,399	30,327	29,958	29,913
35	Michigan	4,384	7,031	10,019	13,807	14,786	17,562	18,941	19,033	19,033	17,119	18,460	18,038	18,392	17,270	16,467	14,783	13,599	11,901
36	Wisconsin	2,977	7,894	11,715	15,353	15,531	19,863	21,060	21,370	21,851	21,874	23,459	22,876	23,615	23,221	22,507	21,156	18,109	18,109
37	West North Central	12,498	35,203	51,766	101,198	150,800	201,009	232,648	257,752	243,081	259,488	273,077	274,423	283,248	284,329	284,861	282,007	283,603	278,761
38	Minnesota	29	2,712	6,484	13,403	18,664	26,248	27,676	30,222	30,059	30,913	32,818	32,607	32,883	32,052	32,285	30,796	30,805	28,845
39	Iowa	2,736	10,070	15,542	24,753	30,492	34,574	33,931	33,475	33,281	34,019	34,359	34,149	34,265	34,045	34,045	33,831	33,758	33,570
40	Missouri	9,733	19,985	21,707	27,879	30,780	33,998	34,591	34,775	34,327	33,743	35,055	34,740	34,195	35,123	34,195	33,155	32,692	32,420
41	North Dakota				1,028	7,660	15,543	28,427	36,215	36,215	38,658	39,118	37,936	41,001	41,194	41,877	41,466	42,717	43,118
42	South Dakota				2,773	11,396	19,071	26,017	34,636	34,327	36,470	37,102	39,474	43,032	44,786	44,949	43,155	45,567	45,584
43	Nebraska		631	2,074	9,945	21,593	29,912	38,622	42,225	42,025	44,709	46,616	47,344	47,753	47,467	47,487	47,793	47,793	45,834
44	Kansas		1,778	5,657	21,417	30,214	41,663	43,385	45,425	43,729	46,976	48,010	48,174	48,589	48,611	50,024	50,153	50,271	49,390
45	South	171,047	225,514	189,556	234,920	256,606	362,036	354,453	350,122	324,189	343,086	376,206	370,168	377,795	393,215	386,289	357,448	346,228	332,808
46	South Atlantic	93,402	106,521	90,121	101,420	100,158	104,298	103,782	97,775	88,571	86,363	95,987	92,555	96,601	102,170	98,259	83,339	76,959	68,031
47	Delaware	956	1,004	1,052	1,090	1,056	1,066	1,039	1,020	900	901	921	896	923	851	814	763	717	674
48	Maryland	4,634	4,836	4,513	5,120	4,952	5,170	5,057	4,758	4,433	4,374	4,384	4,198	4,200	4,056	3,897	3,457	3,181	2,803
49	District of Columbia	27	34	18	18	13	(Z)	6	6	4	2	2	2						
50	Virginia	26,152	31,117	18,146	19,836	19,105	19,908	19,496	18,561	17,210	16,729	17,645	16,445	16,358	15,572	14,686	13,126	12,002	10,650
51	West Virginia			8,146	10,194	10,321	10,655	10,321	8,980	8,980	8,055	9,424	8,909	8,720	8,215	7,352	6,063	5,279	4,341
52	North Carolina	20,997	23,763	19,835	22,364	22,652	22,749	22,439	20,022	18,594	18,055	19,936	18,845	18,618	19,318	18,260	15,888	14,382	12,734
53	South Carolina	16,218	16,196	12,105	13,458	13,185	13,985	13,512	12,427	10,639	10,393	12,330	11,339	11,022	11,069	11,069	9,149	8,101	6,992
54	Georgia	22,821	26,650	23,648	26,043	25,200	26,392	26,953	25,441	21,945	22,079	25,297	23,684	23,676	25,751	24,019	19,658	17,887	15,806
55	Florida	1,595	2,920	2,374	3,297	3,674	4,364	5,254	6,047	5,865	5,027	6,048	8,338	8,162	18,162	15,411	15,237	15,411	14,032
56	East South Central	58,562	74,777	66,324	76,873	79,163	81,248	81,521	78,897	70,607	73,058	76,198	77,086	76,198	79,576	77,202	68,285	64,509	60,159
57	Kentucky	16,950	19,163	18,660	21,495	21,412	21,979	22,189	21,613	19,913	19,927	20,699	20,294	19,725	19,442	18,034	17,031	16,265	15,968
58	Tennessee	18,984	20,669	19,581	20,667	20,167	20,342	20,042	19,511	17,901	18,003	19,086	18,493	17,789	18,534	18,081	16,081	15,266	15,057
59	Alabama	12,138	19,105	14,861	18,855	19,853	20,685	20,732	19,577	16,739	17,555	19,661	19,143	19,617	20,889	20,810	16,543	15,226	13,654
60	Mississippi	10,490	15,840	13,121	15,855	17,731	18,241	18,558	18,197	16,053	17,555	19,655	19,156	19,617	20,711	20,702	18,630	17,752	16,040
61	West South Central	19,084	44,216	33,020	56,627	77,491	176,491	169,150	173,449	165,013	183,906	201,118	200,527	204,995	211,469	210,828	205,824	204,760	204,058
62	Arkansas	2,598	9,574	7,597	12,062	14,891	16,637	17,416	17,457	15,632	16,053	17,742	18,045	17,456	18,871	17,944	16,457	16,565	15,695
63	Louisiana	4,989	9,299	7,026	8,274	9,544	11,059	10,439	10,020	9,355	9,996	9,086	9,996	10,040	11,202	11,441	10,411	10,411	9,789
64	Oklahoma					1,606	22,988	28,859	31,952	30,352	33,791	35,335	34,803	36,162	36,007	35,630	35,801	36,077	36,000
65	Texas	11,496	25,344	18,397	36,292	51,407	125,807	112,435	114,021	109,674	124,066	137,597	137,803	141,338	145,389	145,813	143,218	141,706	142,567
66	West	4,664	12,718	16,219	26,194	47,282	96,407	113,495	176,283	185,947	221,316	236,356	259,857	316,105	327,377	337,426	344,620	348,890	331,486
67	Mountain	337	1,561	1,754	3,976	14,766	46,397	59,533	117,337	131,689	157,450	173,881	191,901	244,577	250,213	260,942	264,429	268,003	256,525
68	Montana			834	406	1,964	11,844	13,546	35,071	32,736	44,659	44,512	46,452	58,787	59,247	61,469	64,081	65,834	62,918
69	Idaho			4	328	1,302	3,205	5,284	8,376	8,116	8,526	9,952	10,298	12,503	13,224	13,224	15,232	15,302	14,417
70	Wyoming		77		124	1,830	8,125	8,543	11,809	13,542	23,525	28,162	31,527	33,117	34,421	34,989	36,200	37,053	35,476
71	Colorado		140	140	1,165	4,179	9,475	13,532	24,462	24,167	28,876	29,978	31,527	36,218	37,953	38,787	38,787	38,259	36,697
72	New Mexico	291	1,415	320	631	5,131	5,131	11,270	24,410	27,850	30,822	34,397	38,860	49,608	47,522	49,451	46,293	47,647	46,792
73	Arizona			22	135	788	1,985	1,270	5,050	11,065	10,527	14,019	25,651	37,856	39,916	41,790	40,203	40,559	38,203
74	Utah	47	90	148	656	1,297	4,117	3,398	5,050	5,001	5,613	6,239	7,302	10,309	10,865	12,262	12,689	12,867	11,313
75	Nevada		56	209	531	1,661	2,666	2,715	2,357	4,091	4,081	3,622	3,785	6,178	7,064	8,231	10,943	10,483	10,708
76	Pacific	4,327	11,157	14,465	22,218	32,516	50,009	53,962	58,946	54,258	63,866	62,476	67,956	71,529	77,164	76,484	80,191	80,887	74,962
77	Washington		366	649	1,409	6,910	8,499	11,712	13,245	12,610	13,534	14,680	17,988	16,720	17,369	17,641	18,717	19,053	17,559
78	Oregon	433	2,061	2,389	4,215	4,179	10,071	11,685	13,542	14,131	20,328	17,358	17,988	19,754	20,328	21,047	20,509	20,509	18,103
79	California	3,894	8,730	11,427	16,594	21,427	28,829	27,931	29,366	27,517	30,443	30,438	30,524	35,054	36,613	37,795	36,888	37,011	35,722
80	Alaska										526		91	43	422	422	1,776	1,959	1,604
81	Hawaii					2,610	2,610	2,591	2,702		2,815		2,486	2,432	2,432	2,354	2,461	2,354	2,058

See footnotes at end of table.

Series **K 17–81.** Farm Population, Farms, Land in Farms, and Value of Farm Property and Farm Products Sold, by State: 1850 to 1969—Con.

Average acreage per farm (acres)

Series No.	Division, region, and State	1850	1860	1870	1880	1890	1900	1910	1920	1925	1930	1935	1940	1945	1950	1954	1959	1964	1969
17	United States	203	199	153	134	137	147	139	149	145	157	155	175	195	216	242	303	352	390
18	Northeast	113	108	104	98	95	97	96	99	92	102	93	97	98	112	121	142	158	169
19	New England	110	109	108	104	104	107	104	109	99	114	98	99	96	122	136	164	185	195
20	Maine	97	103	98	102	100	106	105	113	103	119	113	108	109	138	155	178	201	221
21	New Hampshire	116	123	122	116	119	123	120	127	107	132	120	109	107	128	140	172	194	211
22	Vermont	139	136	134	138	135	143	143	146	141	157	149	156	148	185	208	243	273	279
23	Massachusetts	99	94	103	88	85	83	78	78	71	78	63	61	56	75	83	102	113	123
24	Rhode Island	103	96	93	80	86	86	82	84	79	87	65	72	74	82	77	99	94	98
25	Connecticut	106	100	103	99	92	92	92	95	90	113	92	97	99	107	116	135	151	121
26	Middle Atlantic	114	107	103	99	95	100	102	107	102	113	106	112	118	128	145	135	185	163
27	New York	112	107	103	99	97	100	105	107	102	113	106	112	118	128	145	211	151	196
28	New Jersey	115	108	98	85	86	82	77	77	65	69	65	73	69	70	73	89	109	122
29	Pennsylvania	117	109	103	93	87	86	85	87	81	89	83	86	87	96	102	119	130	142
30	North Central	143	140	124	122	133	145	157	172	167	181	172	185	201	212	231	264	300	324
31	East North Central	136	124	115	107	105	102	105	109	107	115	108	113	121	127	136	155	146	154
32	Ohio	125	114	111	99	93	89	89	92	91	98	90	94	102	105	113	132	146	173
33	Indiana	136	124	112	105	103	97	103	103	102	108	102	107	114	114	125	145	166	163
34	Illinois	158	146	128	124	127	124	129	135	136	143	137	145	155	159	173	196	226	242
35	Michigan	129	113	101	90	86	86	92	97	94	101	94	96	105	111	119	132	145	153
36	Wisconsin	148	114	114	114	115	117	119	117	113	120	117	123	133	138	147	161	172	183
37	West North Central	180	190	143	142	165	190	210	234	223	239	231	252	275	289	315	355	403	437
38	Minnesota	184	149	139	145	160	170	177	169	160	167	161	165	175	184	195	211	235	261
39	Iowa	185	165	134	134	151	151	156	157	156	158	155	160	165	169	177	194	219	239
40	Missouri	179	215	131	129	129	119	125	132	125	132	126	136	145	153	170	197	222	237
41	North Dakota	—	—	[1]176	271	277	343	382	466	452	496	462	513	590	630	676	755	875	930
42	South Dakota	—	—	169	203	277	362	335	464	403	439	445	545	626	674	719	805	917	997
43	Nebraska	—	226	169	157	190	246	298	339	329	345	349	391	427	443	471	528	596	634
44	Kansas	—	171	148	155	181	241	244	275	264	283	275	308	344	370	416	481	544	574
45	South	332	335	214	153	140	138	114	109	104	106	110	123	131	148	167	217	252	287
46	South Atlantic	376	353	241	157	134	108	93	84	80	82	84	91	107	114	141	155	164	182
47	Delaware	158	151	138	125	121	112	96	93	91	101	99	100	102	112	129	146	153	163
48	Maryland	212	190	167	126	124	112	103	99	102	108	99	100	102	114	120	132	166	165
50	Virginia	340	336	246	167	150	119	106	100	89	108	89	94	103	103	108	135	149	188
51	West Virginia	—	—	214	163	142	115	104	110	99	107	90	90	89	101	107	138	153	165
52	North Carolina	369	316	212	142	127	101	88	74	66	65	66	68	65	67	68	83	97	107
53	South Carolina	541	488	233	143	115	90	77	65	62	66	75	82	75	85	89	117	144	177
54	Georgia	441	430	338	188	147	118	93	82	88	86	101	110	105	130	145	185	215	234
55	Florida	371	276	232	141	107	107	105	112	99	85	83	134	179	290	316	338	380	394
56	East South Central	262	251	178	135	121	90	78	80	70	69	74	80	79	87	98	121	138	155
57	Kentucky	227	261	158	129	121	94	86	77	71	73	70	80	83	89	93	113	122	128
58	Tennessee	261	251	166	125	116	91	82	76	71	73	72	83	85	80	87	102	114	128
59	Alabama	289	347	222	139	126	93	79	76	70	68	63	66	85	99	118	143	165	188
60	Mississippi	309	370	193	156	122	83	68	67	62	55	70	82	99	82	96	135	163	221
61	West South Central	440	446	238	179	180	234	179	174	162	167	177	208	234	271	316	419	469	511
62	Arkansas	146	245	154	128	138	93	81	75	67	66	70	83	88	103	124	173	207	260
63	Louisiana	372	537	247	171	138	95	87	74	67	58	61	67	78	90	103	139	167	232
64	Oklahoma	—	—	301	208	[3]182	[2]213	152	166	157	166	166	194	219	253	300	378	407	434
65	Texas	943	591	301	208	225	357	269	262	236	252	275	329	367	439	498	631	691	668
66	West	695	367	336	313	324	393	300	364	373	434	414	504	639	700	798	987	1,142	1,250
67	Mountain	—	177	127	159	299	458	325	481	564	653	641	822	1,151	1,284	1,450	1,774	1,998	2,139
68	Montana	—	—	164	267	351	886	517	608	698	940	940	1,111	1,557	1,689	1,859	2,213	2,437	2,522
69	Idaho	—	—	186	174	183	183	172	199	200	224	221	236	301	328	371	332	516	566
70	Wyoming	—	—	25	272	586	1,333	778	750	1,203	1,469	1,610	1,866	2,533	2,729	3,069	3,715	4,100	4,014
71	Colorado	—	—	184	259	281	384	293	408	417	482	832	1,139	761	833	942	1,162	1,284	1,313
72	New Mexico	78	278	186	125	910	417	316	818	879	982	745	1,139	1,671	2,014	2,347	2,908	3,354	4,020
73	Arizona	—	25	127	69	910	333	135	582	1,024	743	745	1,287	2,881	1,834	4,483	5,558	6,262	6,486
74	Utah	51	617	30	201	337	212	157	197	192	207	203	287	392	449	537	712	817	867
75	Nevada	—	432	201	378	1,301	1,175	1,010	745	1,054	1,186	980	1,059	1,802	2,271	2,881	4,649	4,862	5,070
76	Pacific	2,125	275	420	379	337	348	278	246	(NA)	238	241	186	(NA)	2,283	(NA)	401	472	516
77	Washington	—	355	208	216	271	256	208	200	172	191	174	186	209	249	271	363	418	620
78	Oregon	372	466	315	260	281	281	257	270	253	300	268	291	313	340	387	499	516	459
79	California	4,466	—	482	462	405	397	317	250	202	224	202	230	252	267	307	372	458	4,832
80	Alaska	—	—	—	—	—	—	192	249	—	1,052	—	2,850	—	803	—	2,421	5,129	528
81	Hawaii	—	—	—	—	—	1,148	600	511	—	428	—	498	—	423	—	394	484	—

See footnotes at end of table.

Series K 17–81. Farm Population, Farms, Land in Farms, and Value of Farm Property and Farm Products Sold, by State: 1850 to 1969—Con.

Value of farmland and buildings (mil. dol.)

Series No.	Division, region, and State	1850	1860	1870	1880	1890	1900	1910	1920	1925	1930	1935	1940	1945	1950	1954	1959	1964	1969
17	United States	3,272	6,645	7,444	10,197	13,279	16,675	34,885	66,446	49,468	47,994	32,859	33,758	46,389	75,462	97,583	129,005	159,932	206,751
18	Northeast	1,455	2,122	2,527	2,803	2,539	2,477	3,161	3,920	3,705	3,758	3,043	2,780	3,328	4,708	5,409	6,293	6,901	9,025
19	New England	372	476	468	581	490	528	719	917	906	941	901	741	939	1,222	1,253	1,414	1,459	1,803
20	Maine	55	79	82	102	99	97	160	204	197	194	144	124	160	227	219	256	257	283
21	New Hampshire	55	70	76	109	66	70	86	90	87	77	67	62	80	125	125	118	118	146
22	Vermont	63	94	111	109	80	83	113	159	137	146	116	111	135	196	202	240	275	429
23	Massachusetts	109	123	93	146	128	158	194	248	255	261	256	212	265	315	322	354	349	396
24	Rhode Island	17	20	17	26	22	23	28	26	28	35	35	26	36	44	53	52	51	50
25	Connecticut	73	91	99	121	95	97	138	190	202	227	284	205	263	315	331	393	409	499
26	Middle Atlantic	1,083	1,646	2,059	2,223	2,050	1,949	2,443	3,002	2,800	2,818	2,141	2,039	2,389	3,485	4,156	4,879	5,442	7,222
27	New York	555	803	1,018	1,056	968	888	1,185	1,425	1,367	1,316	1,045	947	1,088	1,467	1,675	1,971	2,181	2,772
28	New Jersey	120	180	206	191	159	163	217	250	263	299	234	228	293	505	672	717	782	1,131
29	Pennsylvania	408	662	835	976	922	898	1,041	1,327	1,170	1,203	862	864	1,009	1,513	1,809	2,190	2,479	3,319
30	North Central	752	2,130	3,452	5,129	7,070	9,564	20,489	39,407	27,555	24,495	15,982	16,130	22,074	33,748	42,616	55,469	64,182	86,394
31	East North Central	672	1,736	2,647	3,629	4,101	4,913	8,874	14,938	11,024	9,337	6,597	7,334	9,959	14,704	18,942	24,737	27,909	36,683
32	Ohio	359	678	844	1,127	1,050	1,037	1,654	2,661	1,946	1,693	1,278	1,444	1,868	2,859	3,707	4,573	5,221	6,819
33	Indiana	136	357	508	635	755	842	1,594	2,654	1,696	1,416	1,040	1,251	1,794	2,691	3,733	4,933	5,582	7,136
34	Illinois	96	409	736	1,010	1,263	1,766	3,523	5,998	4,199	3,336	2,206	2,537	3,663	5,395	7,036	9,580	10,744	14,643
35	Michigan	52	161	319	499	556	583	901	1,437	1,284	1,161	826	913	1,200	1,701	2,195	2,855	3,182	3,883
36	Wisconsin	29	131	240	358	478	686	1,202	2,188	1,899	1,732	1,247	1,189	1,434	2,057	2,271	2,796	3,180	4,201
37	West North Central	80	394	804	1,500	2,968	4,651	11,615	24,469	16,531	15,159	9,385	8,796	12,115	19,044	23,673	30,732	36,272	49,711
38	Minnesota	(Z)	28	78	194	340	670	1,262	3,301	2,394	2,125	1,383	1,443	1,834	2,777	3,478	4,749	5,125	6,512
39	Iowa	17	120	314	567	858	1,498	3,257	7,602	4,954	4,225	2,462	2,691	3,611	5,507	6,770	8,587	9,181	13,150
40	Missouri	63	231	314	376	626	844	1,716	3,063	2,003	1,796	1,099	1,107	1,527	2,236	2,785	3,727	4,928	7,269
41	North Dakota	—	—	12[1]	14[1]	75	199	823	1,489	1,020	951	707	490	708	1,189	1,493	2,141	2,854	4,045
42	South Dakota	—	—	[1]	[1]	107	220	1,005	2,473	1,437	1,285	692	505	764	1,402	1,767	2,277	2,814	3,815
43	Nebraska	—	4	24	106	402	578	1,813	3,712	2,523	2,495	1,563	1,138	1,699	2,735	3,400	4,234	5,232	7,076
44	Kansas	—	12	72	235	560	644	1,738	2,830	2,198	2,281	1,479	1,421	1,971	3,199	3,980	5,017	6,138	7,843
45	South	1,056	2,323	1,289	1,873	2,575	3,279	7,353	15,157	11,539	12,344	8,737	9,716	13,149	22,955	29,549	39,011	52,068	69,664
46	South Atlantic	577	1,009	610	892	1,135	1,206	2,486	5,202	4,099	3,852	2,792	3,160	4,239	7,160	9,555	12,832	16,151	20,513
47	Delaware	19	31	37	37	40	34	53	65	60	67	51	55	73	97	128	180	235	336
48	Maryland	87	146	136	166	175	175	242	387	341	356	243	274	355	507	691	982	1,349	1,793
49	District of Columbia	2	3	3	3	4	6	8	6	5	7	7	6	5	5	—	—	—	—
50	Virginia	216	372	170	216	254	272	532	1,024	887	856	594	675	869	1,277	1,551	1,819	2,215	3,047
51	West Virginia	—	—	81	133	152	168	264	411	356	342	238	270	341	487	497	450	478	589
52	North Carolina	68	143	63	136	184	195	457	1,076	926	844	623	737	1,003	1,906	2,346	2,949	3,622	4,244
53	South Carolina	82	140	36	69	99	127	333	813	458	379	286	338	441	820	965	1,226	1,403	1,826
54	Georgia	96	157	76	112	152	183	479	1,138	588	577	430	480	654	1,115	1,442	1,908	2,431	3,701
55	Florida	6	16	8	20	73	41	118	281	479	424	321	324	498	946	1,935	3,317	4,423	4,976
56	East South Central	372	929	544	678	828	934	1,738	3,664	2,481	2,685	1,915	2,325	3,094	5,169	6,086	7,855	10,251	14,540
57	Kentucky	155	291	249	299	346	382	635	1,305	847	871	620	776	1,016	1,572	1,722	2,305	2,958	4,041
58	Tennessee	98	271	175	207	243	265	481	1,025	759	743	556	664	871	1,432	1,635	2,095	2,737	4,028
59	Alabama	64	176	54	79	111	135	288	544	415	502	368	409	560	1,017	1,206	1,480	1,902	2,725
60	Mississippi	55	191	65	93	127	152	334	790	459	568	371	475	648	1,148	1,523	1,974	2,655	3,746
61	West South Central	108	385	135	304	613	1,139	3,129	6,291	4,959	5,806	4,030	4,232	5,816	10,626	13,908	18,324	25,660	34,611
62	Arkansas	15	92	32	74	119	135	238	753	541	548	376	457	663	1,136	1,378	1,797	2,935	4,081
63	Louisiana	76	205	55	59	85	141	309	474	325	418	296	354	472	921	1,278	1,766	2,413	3,145
64	Oklahoma	—	—	—	—	9[3]	171[2]	739	1,364	1,049	1,243	784	831	1,106	1,851	2,256	3,002	4,366	6,214
65	Texas	17	88	48	170	400	692	1,843	3,700	3,045	3,597	2,574	2,590	3,575	6,718	8,997	11,759	15,945	21,170
66	West	9	70	177	391	1,095	1,355	3,881	7,963	6,668	7,397	5,097	5,133	7,839	14,052	20,009	28,233	36,781	41,668
67	Mountain	2	4	9	58	199	339	1,319	3,163	2,173	2,458	1,772	1,780	2,756	5,513	7,775	10,878	13,650	17,444
68	Montana	—	—	1	3	26	62	252	777	455	528	376	350	518	999	1,476	2,791	2,931	3,748
69	Idaho	—	—	3	3	17	42	245	582	373	417	307	339	493	923	1,296	1,701	2,022	2,545
70	Wyoming	—	—	(Z)	1	14	27	98	235	173	207	167	159	232	455	535	774	1,043	1,445
71	Colorado	—	—	2	25	85	106	409	866	592	629	419	388	565	1,212	1,529	2,053	2,687	3,471
72	New Mexico	—	3	2	6	7	21	112	222	175	208	170	188	327	713	1,055	1,086	1,663	1,960
73	Arizona	—	—	(Z)	1	7	14	47	172	192	184	133	154	288	604	1,075	1,384	2,001	2,664
74	Utah	2	1	1	14	28	51	118	244	144	221	158	154	262	471	586	755	910	1,040
75	Nevada	—	—	(Z)	5	12	16	40	66	72	64	43	48	72	136	223	334	393	571
76	Pacific	7	66	168	333	896	1,016	2,562	4,800	4,495	4,939	3,325	3,353	5,083	8,538	12,234	17,355	23,131	24,224
77	Washington	—	2	4	14	83	116	572	920	727	774	551	593	900	1,276	2,022	2,455	2,931	3,930
78	Oregon	3	15	22	57	116	132	456	675	616	634	449	481	698	1,612	1,643	1,857	2,349	2,707
79	California	4	49	141	262	697	708	1,451	3,074	3,152	3,419	2,325	2,166	3,485	5,650	8,569	13,026	17,352	16,956
80	Alaska	—	—	—	—	—	—	—	—	—	—	—	—	—	7	—	18	18	20
81	Hawaii	—	—	—	—	—	60	83	129	—	112	—	113	—	195	—	—	481	611

[1] For 1870 and 1880, North and South Dakota are combined (Dakota Territory).

See footnotes at end of table.

Series K 17–81. Farm Population, Farms, Land in Farms, and Value of Farm Property and Value of Farm Property and Farm Products Sold, by State: 1850 to 1969—Con.

Average value per farm (dollars)

Series No.	Division, region, and State	1850	1860	1870	1880	1890	1900	1910	1920	1925	1930	1935	1940	1945	1950	1954	1959	1964	1969
17	United States	2,258	3,251	2,799	2,544	2,909	2,905	5,480	10,295	7,764	7,624	4,823	5,532	7,917	14,005	20,405	34,768	50,646	75,725
18	Northeast	2,971	3,756	4,201	4,027	3,856	3,656	4,811	6,738	6,407	7,789	5,473	5,751	6,685	11,771	15,950	24,702	34,130	59,426
19	New England	2,221	2,589	2,591	2,802	2,577	2,753	3,806	5,860	5,678	(NA)	(NA)	5,478	6,244	11,839	15,303	24,860	34,762	62,937
20	Maine	1,173	1,413	1,377	1,589	1,592	1,627	2,660	4,232	3,943	4,981	3,425	3,183	3,785	7,462	9,392	14,756	19,979	35,496
21	New Hampshire	1,890	2,285	2,175	2,356	2,270	2,391	3,176	4,385	4,113	5,190	3,783	3,758	4,080	10,314	11,989	18,046	25,402	50,418
22	Vermont	2,129	2,988	3,296	3,078	2,469	2,509	3,442	5,473	4,940	5,861	4,286	4,712	5,080	10,163	12,662	19,887	25,733	62,347
23	Massachusetts	3,202	3,462	3,515	3,807	3,710	4,190	5,260	7,737	7,611	10,205	7,285	6,647	7,167	14,163	18,552	31,692	43,492	69,362
24	Rhode Island	3,129	3,616	3,897	3,957	3,977	4,206	5,158	8,463	7,139	10,388	8,144	8,737	11,826	17,062	26,475	37,571	46,030	72,033
25	Connecticut	3,170	3,607	3,892	4,164	4,374	3,615	5,278	6,463	8,689	13,226	8,828	8,828	11,826	20,189	25,971	47,372	67,429	111,071
26	Middle Atlantic	3,361	4,319	4,709	4,546	4,374	4,013	5,216	7,061	7,243	8,234	5,905	5,858	6,875	11,747	16,156	24,657	33,964	58,609
27	New York	3,250	4,078	4,892	4,709	4,280	3,917	5,495	7,376	8,428	8,234	5,977	6,180	7,275	11,742	15,844	23,936	32,797	58,399
28	New Jersey	5,030	6,520	6,721	5,564	5,166	4,692	6,484	8,428	8,848	8,428	5,977	8,818	11,171	20,343	29,635	46,397	73,487	133,202
29	Pennsylvania	3,197	4,234	4,796	4,569	4,359	4,006	4,747	6,560	5,838	6,977	4,505	5,113	5,872	10,299	14,039	21,892	29,836	52,829
30	North Central	2,051	3,455	3,068	3,021	3,675	4,354	9,174	18,063	12,740	11,781	7,061	7,693	11,116	18,065	25,010	37,974	50,244	75,002
31	East North Central	3,114	3,770	3,475	3,683	4,065	4,325	7,899	13,771	10,483	(NA)	(NA)	7,289	10,441	16,607	23,717	37,132	48,656	71,465
32	Ohio	2,854	2,706	4,305	4,561	3,809	3,746	6,080	10,368	7,951	7,720	5,007	6,176	8,470	13,341	20,937	32,583	43,373	70,316
33	Indiana	1,261	2,577	3,225	3,948	5,247	3,793	5,986	12,937	8,661	7,796	5,180	6,506	10,197	16,151	24,303	32,489	48,489	51,645
34	Illinois	1,453	2,854	3,631	4,085	5,289	6,684	13,986	25,289	18,615	16,853	11,887	11,887	17,933	40,083	40,083	61,946	80,894	118,507
35	Michigan	1,414	1,893	2,335	2,663	3,262	4,041	4,354	11,558	6,676	6,853	4,205	4,865	6,453	10,935	15,535	25,535	43,027	49,821
36	Wisconsin	1,153	2,126	2,215	2,097	2,663	2,866	6,784	11,558	9,830	9,526	6,238	6,365	8,069	12,203	14,789	21,309	26,765	42,448
37	West North Central	1,032	1,513	1,683	2,105	2,910	4,329	10,464	22,307	14,875	11,471	6,803	8,065	9,379	15,507	26,151	38,680	51,539	77,845
38	Minnesota	1,125	1,960	2,701	3,061	4,247	4,385	10,464	22,817	12,717	19,655	11,092	8,065	9,705	15,379	26,151	32,605	39,075	58,803
39	Iowa	1,161	2,485	2,119	3,061	6,550	6,550	15,008	35,616	23,207	19,655	12,614	11,739	17,284	27,105	35,090	49,150	59,553	93,694
40	Missouri		1,742	1,683	2,629	6,163	6,163	15,616	22,496	12,717	17,018	6,285	8,965	9,705	9,722	13,815	33,451	33,451	53,034
41	North Dakota		784[1]	1,970[1]	2,263	4,247	6,550	15,646	35,616	19,160	19,655	3,948	12,614	6,285	18,178	24,110	38,978	58,450	87,222
42	South Dakota				2,143	2,629	4,183	11,063	19,162	18,071	15,455	8,358	6,628	11,124	18,263	28,263	38,852	58,615	83,427
43	Nebraska		1,391	1,967	1,671	3,542	4,753	12,945	29,836	19,760	19,274	8,305	6,399	11,205	21,095	33,713	46,796	65,268	97,931
44	Kansas		1,179	1,892	1,697	3,359	3,718	9,770	17,122	13,250	13,738	8,469	9,092	13,962	24,344	33,117	48,084	66,397	91,131
45	South	2,051	3,455	1,456	1,224	1,402	1,251	2,374	4,727	3,685	3,829	2,553	3,231	4,564	8,654	12,755	23,702	37,931	59,983
46	South Atlantic	3,114	3,340	1,632	1,384	1,254	1,254	2,236	4,488	3,699	3,099	4,959	3,099	4,062	7,466	11,123	21,671	34,496	35,355
47	Delaware	2,810	3,770	4,907	4,205	4,291	3,807	4,905	6,386	5,818	6,244	5,465	6,104	7,820	13,043	20,287	34,551	53,443	90,632
48	Maryland	6,481	5,726	5,048	8,350	4,085	41,911	4,941	8,070	6,966	8,244	5,180	6,506	8,596	14,048	21,258	39,095	64,999	104,370
49	District of Columbia		12,560	14,546	8,350	16,940	41,911	37,932	27,340	34,500	68,690	80,709	91,429	24,034	166,643				
50	Virginia	2,810	4,014	2,043	2,124	1,994	1,618	2,891	5,016	3,941	3,860	3,005	3,860	5,021	8,458	11,369	18,635	27,572	47,191
51	West Virginia		1,906	669	1,031	1,823	1,812	2,735	4,706	3,018	4,138	2,069	2,647	3,490	5,983	11,123	10,230	24,442	25,450
52	North Carolina	1,192	2,751	1,081	862	867	867	1,800	3,990	3,267	2,401	1,715	2,461	2,982	6,605	8,758	15,475	24,948	35,551
53	South Carolina	1,850	2,533	691	732	816	816	1,887	3,663	2,359	2,259	1,725	2,223	2,896	5,886	7,769	15,685	29,155	46,171
54	Georgia	1,469	2,502	777	807	889	816	1,647	3,663	5,212	2,211	4,407	5,211	8,149	5,623	8,710	17,944	29,155	54,883
55	Florida	1,665	3,428	1,081	866	1,034	1,000	1,668	2,362	8,088	7,179	4,407	5,224	8,224	16,617	33,627	73,554	109,053	139,818
56	East South Central	1,345	3,210	1,461	1,190	1,262	1,628	1,953	3,484	3,278	3,025	2,229	2,272	3,259	1,662	7,709	13,962	21,897	37,135
57	Kentucky	1,533	3,294	1,481	1,932	1,798	1,180	1,953	4,055	3,006	3,025	2,030	3,070	4,259	7,196	8,900	15,269	20,235	32,309
58	Tennessee	1,345	3,189	804	1,248	1,392	603	1,096	2,123	1,785	1,818	1,347	2,683	3,715	6,182	8,049	15,288	20,509	33,176
59	Alabama	1,612	4,453	961	581	883	688	1,218	2,903	1,785	1,818	1,190	1,764	2,506	4,809	6,816	12,780	20,552	37,596
60	Mississippi	2,481	3,876	969	912	883	1,509	3,317	6,316	4,875	4,388	1,486	1,632	2,457	4,566	7,053	14,292	24,322	51,611
61	West South Central	2,481	2,350	648	958	950	757	1,440	2,436	2,451	2,108	1,736	2,108	3,334	13,616	20,817	37,306	38,826	86,681
62	Arkansas	860	2,350	691	786	950	757	1,971	3,499	2,590	2,359	1,715	2,359	3,653	6,225	9,496	18,915	36,734	67,532
63	Louisiana	5,649	11,818	1,916	1,222	232	21,582[2]	1,217	3,884	5,318	2,096	3,677	4,625	6,713	13,016	11,497	23,719	38,636	74,414
64	Oklahoma					3,972[3]		1,440	3,884	5,318	2,590	3,677	4,625	6,713	13,016	11,497	23,719	38,636	74,838
65	Texas	1,357	2,054	787	979	1,753	1,964	4,412	8,486	6,540	7,260	5,677	6,196	9,286	20,263	30,711	51,787	49,212	99,133
66	West	1,295	2,033	3,662	4,669	7,506	5,329	10,271	16,455	13,364	14,518	8,928	9,962	15,853	30,029	47,334	80,870	120,383	157,179
67	Mountain	420	493	651	2,319	4,019	3,342	7,192	12,958	9,310	(NA)	7,623	7,623	12,969	28,294	43,191	72,967	101,780	145,486
68	Montana			685	2,129	4,553	4,639	7,899	12,958	9,709	(NA)	7,433	8,373	13,720	28,475	43,191	76,761	103,271	150,222
69	Idaho			952	1,503	2,640	2,422	7,955	13,811	9,197	7,796	6,814	7,768	11,888	22,920	44,653	50,528	68,178	99,916
70	Wyoming				1,829	4,627	4,424	8,912	13,811	11,132	12,919	9,537	10,585	17,746	36,060	46,935	69,447	115,355	163,529
71	Colorado		532	1,558	5,572	5,189	4,305	8,848	14,449	10,211	10,497	6,580	7,550	11,855	26,588	46,935	61,494	90,183	124,180
72	New Mexico	441	404	750	1,091	5,065	1,697	5,125	17,432	5,520	12,999	4,113	6,580	11,004	30,228	50,078	68,233	117,042	168,336
73	Arizona		375	1,483	1,471	9,663	2,619	14,730	9,499	13,332	12,999	5,157	8,321	21,905	57,996	25,652	330,549	330,549	452,241
74	Utah	337	367	1,434	3,852	9,291	7,150	13,050	20,947	17,512	18,626	5,157	9,947	20,985	19,492	25,652	42,391	57,747	79,705
75	Nevada			1,272	5,672	4,622	7,630	13,885	19,941	19,941	10,911	6,527	13,321	18,028	43,700	78,162	141,974	182,436	270,507
76	Pacific	3,302	2,559	2,946	2,120	4,537	3,482	10,012	13,449	11,019	11,438	6,922	11,720	17,264	31,266	50,406	43,608	64,304	166,834
77	Washington	1,668	3,509	1,272	4,622	9,663	3,693	16,447	26,122	23,111	25,203	15,466	7,712	11,054	21,057	51,018	59,079	64,304	115,487
78	Oregon	2,448	2,618	2,946	3,509	4,537	3,693	10,012	13,449	11,019	11,438	6,922	7,712	11,054	20,327	30,178	47,590	59,079	93,134
79	California	4,443	2,603	5,953	7,293	13,180	26,410	19,770	17,122	23,111	25,084	15,466	16,331	25,084	41,192	69,620	131,212	214,650	217,730
80	Alaska								3,329		5,714		6,165		12,465		48,379		61,541
81	Hawaii							19,197	24,438		18,771		22,580		33,961		(NA)	98,936	156,800

See footnotes at end of table.

Series K 17–81. Farm Population, Farms, Land in Farms, and Value of Farm Property and Farm Products Sold, by State: 1850 to 1969—Con.

Value of farm products sold (mil. dol.)

Series No.	Division, region, and State	1925⁴	1930	1940	1945	1950	1954	1959	1964	1969
17	United States	858	9,610	6,682	16,231	22,217	24,645	30,493	35,292	45,609
18	Northeast	71	978	723	1,490	1,922	2,049	2,292	2,575	2,822
19	New England	21	278	208	425	532	535	593	716	683
20	Maine	4	81	42	96	126	140	171	256	198
21	New Hampshire	(Z)	24	19	39	46	45	48	49	49
22	Vermont	4	48	34	70	87	86	109	115	136
23	Massachusetts	4	68	63	115	135	125	126	139	139
24	Rhode Island	1	9	6	15	16	18	18	19	16
25	Connecticut	8	48	44	89	121	123	120	139	146
26	Middle Atlantic	50	699	515	1,065	1,391	1,514	1,699	1,859	2,138
27	New York	38	343	242	503	631	668	755	853	979
28	New Jersey	2	83	74	166	214	242	231	216	214
29	Pennsylvania	10	273	198	396	546	604	713	791	945
30	North Central	437	4,140	2,923	7,047	9,733	10,647	13,002	14,838	20,097
31	East North Central	145	1,608	1,302	2,953	4,044	4,594	5,203	6,105	7,544
32	Ohio	28	315	254	533	712	844	863	1,013	1,246
33	Indiana	17	265	217	492	732	906	946	1,105	1,400
34	Illinois	53	455	415	954	1,362	1,506	1,811	2,123	2,612
35	Michigan	20	227	178	366	474	545	623	766	829
36	Wisconsin	27	346	239	608	765	793	961	1,097	1,455
37	West North Central	292	2,531	1,620	4,094	5,689	6,053	7,799	8,733	12,553
38	Minnesota	73	361	301	637	961	984	1,212	1,376	1,748
39	Iowa	81	621	512	1,152	1,635	1,840	2,284	2,597	3,656
40	Missouri	33	329	215	506	720	734	1,012	1,053	1,460
41	North Dakota	17	194	100	365	401	376	469	629	749
42	South Dakota	19	212	96	286	430	436	514	570	958
43	Nebraska	33	398	192	543	778	881	1,198	1,334	2,165
44	Kansas	37	418	204	604	765	802	1,111	1,175	1,818
45	South	199	2,903	1,921	4,632	6,359	7,025	8,884	10,586	13,354
46	South Atlantic	73	922	700	1,735	2,125	2,631	3,248	4,142	4,874
47	Delaware	(Z)	18	16	62	76	82	86	108	129
48	Maryland	7	77	55	137	172	195	231	276	340
49	District of Columbia	--	(Z)	1	1	1	1	1	--	--
50	Virginia	21	155	108	248	310	364	424	470	570
51	West Virginia	1	53	30	63	82	90	92	90	106
52	North Carolina	13	221	199	489	557	733	797	1,068	1,195
53	South Carolina	9	117	87	192	214	252	303	349	362
54	Georgia	9	197	122	302	375	448	607	826	1,040
55	Florida	13	83	80	240	339	466	700	954	1,132
56	East South Central	50	727	428	1,082	1,371	1,542	1,972	2,382	2,749
57	Kentucky	28	170	128	338	417	425	518	592	770
58	Tennessee	7	162	107	247	341	353	475	529	623
59	Alabama	8	165	77	213	274	304	414	537	670
60	Mississippi	7	230	115	284	340	460	566	724	685
61	West South Central	76	1,255	793	1,815	2,863	2,853	3,664	4,063	5,731
62	Arkansas	7	187	118	269	393	492	639	830	973
63	Louisiana	9	137	90	178	246	310	335	407	496
64	Oklahoma	21	264	146	369	471	409	581	601	969
65	Texas	39	666	439	1,000	1,753	1,642	2,109	2,225	3,293
66	West	151	1,589	1,115	3,062	4,203	4,924	6,315	7,293	9,337
67	Mountain	35	672	449	1,068	1,631	1,810	2,356	2,537	3,839
68	Montana	3	129	84	223	279	339	377	390	576
69	Idaho	3	127	84	215	281	332	438	478	650
70	Wyoming	1	59	46	83	122	115	162	151	249
71	Colorado	21	177	102	251	426	380	580	612	1,101
72	New Mexico	3	56	43	82	155	155	197	227	359
73	Arizona	3	47	39	95	204	328	388	469	611
74	Utah	2	59	40	97	130	127	156	159	218
75	Nevada	--	19	11	23	34	34	57	51	81
76	Pacific	116	916	666	1,994	2,571	3,113	3,959	4,756	5,498
77	Washington	21	184	117	354	365	506	569	637	771
78	Oregon	8	125	99	239	298	346	412	428	531
79	California	87	608	452	1,400	1,742	2,261	2,822	3,499	3,904
80	Alaska	--	--	--	--	--	2	3	4	4
81	Hawaii	--	--	--	--	165	--	152	188	288

NA Not available.
Z Less than 500 or $500,000.
¹ Dakota Territory.
² Oklahoma Territory and Indian Territory.
³ Oklahoma Territory only.
⁴ Products sold through cooperative marketing organizations only.

Series K 82–108. Characteristics of Farm Operators: 1880 to 1969

[In thousands, except as indicated]

Series No.	Item	1969	1964	1959	1954 [1]	1950	1945 [1]	1940	1935 [1]	1930	1925 [1]	1920	1910 [1]	1900	1890	1880
82	**Total**	**2,730**	**3,158**	**3,711**	**4,782**	**5,388**	**5,859**	**6,102**	**6,812**	**6,295**	**6,372**	**6,454**	**6,362**	**5,740**	**4,565**	**4,009**
	Race and residence:															
83	White	2,626	2,958	3,420	4,299	4,803	5,170	5,379	5,957	5,374	(NA)	5,500	5,441	4,970		
84	Negro and other races	104	200	291	484	586	689	724	856	921	(NA)	954	921	770		
85	North	1,304	1,480	1,715	2,043	2,268	2,484	2,580	2,819	2,562	2,741	2,763	2,891	2,874	2,582	2,394
86	South	1,161	1,373	1,646	2,317	2,652	2,881	3,007	3,422	3,224	3,131	3,207	3,098	2,620	1,836	1,531
87	White	1,071	1,188	1,374	1,851	2,093	2,216	2,327	2,606	2,342	2,300	2,284	2,207	1,880		
88	Negro and other races	90	185	272	465	559	665	680	816	882	831	923	890	741		
89	West	265	306	349	423	468	494	515	571	510	499	484	373	245	146	84
	Residence:															
90	On farm operated	1,983	2,774	3,236	4,392	4,987	5,460	[1] 5,506								
91	Off farm operated	458	291	267	290	270	337	[1] 314								
92	Not reporting	290	93	207	100	132	62	[1] 277								
	Age:															
93	Under 25 years	53	53	62	91	164	147	233		[1] 372		[1] 384	419	[1][2] 275	[2] 219	
94	25–34 years	274	309	403	620	792	854	950		[1] 1,049		[1] 1,333	1,414	[1][2] 1,194	[2] 1,083	
95	35–44 years	523	654	806	1,100	1,188	1,324	1,252		[1] 1,452		[1] 1,588	1,571	[1][2] 1,410	[2] 1,182	
96	45–54 years	724	851	980	1,154	1,159	1,432	1,429		[1] 1,460		[1] 1,482	1,433	[1][2] 1,296	[2] 1,035	
97	55–64 years	704	742	803	951	1,002	1,173	1,148		[1] 1,064		[1] 994	948	[1][2] 865	} [2] 1,249	
98	65 years or more	453	548	617	779	745	867	829		[1] 676		[1] 584	555	[1][2] 595		
99	Average age—years	51.2	51.3	50.5	49.6	(NA)	48.7									
100	Not reporting age			37	87	335	61	261		[1] 215		[1] 84	22	[1][2] 13		
	Years on present farm:															
101	Less than 5	429	612	639	1,011	1,858	2,433	2,149	2,909	2,710	2,985	[1] 2,957	3,000			
102	5–9	331	469	630	1,172	1,012	957	945	1,080	939	1,215	[1] 1,086	992			
103	10 or more	1,385	1,906	2,340	2,487	2,194	2,336	2,517	2,688	2,394	2,019	[1] 2,184	1,803			
104	Not reporting	585	171	100	113	321	132	492	135	252	153	[1] 221	567			
	Days working off farm:															
105	Less than 100	392	449	556	820	836	491	804	1,317	[1] 1,180						
106	100–199	220	189	230	306	313	244	379	348	[1] 327						
107	200 or more	871	824	878	1,027	944	835	566	413	[1] 397						
108	None or not reporting	1,248	1,696	2,044	2,629	3,293	4,289	4,352	4,735	[1] 4,386						

NA Not available.
[1] Excludes Alaska and Hawaii.

[2] Occupants of farm homes. In 1900, the number of occupants of farm homes was 88,364 less than the number of farm operators, while in 1890, the number of occupants exceeded the number of operators by 202,358.

Series K 109–153. Farms, by Race and Tenure of Operator, and Acreage and Value, by Tenure of Operator: 1880 to 1969

Series No.	Race and tenure of operator	1969	1964 [1]	1959 [1][2]	1954 [1][2]	1950	1945 [2]	1940	1930	1920	1910 [3]	1900	1890	1880
	NUMBER OF FARMS													
109	U.S.	2,730,250	3,157,857	3,707,973	4,783,021	5,388,437	5,859,169	6,102,417	6,295,103	6,453,991	6,365,822	5,739,657	4,564,641	4,008,907
110	Full owner	1,705,720	1,818,254	2,116,594	2,744,708	3,091,666	3,301,361	3,085,491	[4] 2,913,052	[4] 3,368,146	3,355,731	3,202,643	} 3,269,728	2,984,306
111	Part owner	671,607	781,884	834,470	868,180	825,670	660,502	615,502	657,109	558,759	593,954	451,515		
112	Manager			17,798	21,060	20,894	23,646	38,885	36,501	56,131	68,583	58,353	59,213	
113	Tenant	352,923	539,921	735,849	1,149,239	1,447,455	1,858,421	2,364,923	2,668,811	2,458,554	2,357,784	2,026,286	1,294,913	1,024,601
114	White	2,626,403	2,957,905	[5] 3,423,361	4,301,420	4,802,520	5,169,954	5,378,913	[5] 5,373,703	[5] 5,499,707	5,441,372	4,970,129		
115	Full owner	1,642,253	1,739,721	2,016,808	2,604,730	2,936,960	3,126,212	2,917,255	[6] 2,753,187	3,174,675	3,159,560	3,026,214		
116	Part owner	652,512	747,051	792,422	814,112	769,751	629,734	581,678	612,887	517,820	548,457	420,916		
117	Manager			17,402	20,457	20,236	23,140	38,263	35,750	52,890	66,317	56,679	57,353	
118	Tenant	331,638	453,731	592,417	862,342	1,072,669	1,375,745	1,844,230	1,954,247	1,740,534	1,676,676	1,465,646		
119	Negro and other	103,847	199,952	[5] 284,612	481,601	585,917	689,215	723,504	[5] 921,400	[5] 954,284	924,450	769,528		
120	Full owner	63,467	78,533	97,388	139,978	154,706	175,149	168,236	159,894	193,126	196,171	176,429		
121	Part owner	19,095	34,833	40,733	54,068	55,919	30,768	33,824	43,863	40,888	45,497	30,599		
122	Manager			396	489	658	506	622	751	3,202	2,258	1,674	1,860	
123	Tenant	21,285	86,190	141,017	286,897	374,786	482,676	520,693	714,433	718,009	681,108	560,640		
124	**South**	**1,161,399**	**1,372,732**	**1,645,028**	**2,317,296**	**2,652,423**	**2,881,135**	**3,007,170**	**3,223,816**	**3,206,664**	**3,097,547**	**2,620,391**	**1,836,372**	**1,531,077**
125	Full owner	779,731	808,500	946,613	1,275,226	1,411,123	1,509,056	1,327,690	1,190,683	1,405,762	1,329,390	1,237,114	} 1,130,029	977,229
126	Part owner	245,280	303,612	322,952	351,016	325,999	193,607	216,607	224,992	191,463	215,121	133,368		
127	Manager			7,120	9,196	9,571	9,979	13,193	13,580	17,358	18,318	16,284	18,765	
128	Tenant	136,388	253,500	366,267	681,483	905,322	1,165,279	1,449,293	1,790,783	1,591,121	1,536,752	1,231,144	706,343	553,848
129	Croppers			121,037	267,662	346,765	446,556	541,291	776,278	561,091				
130	White	1,071,258	1,188,154	1,379,407	1,853,820	2,093,333	2,215,722	2,326,904	2,342,129	2,283,750	2,207,406	1,879,721		
131	Full owner	724,131	737,701	856,864	1,145,372	1,269,641	1,348,076	1,185,788	1,050,187	1,227,204	1,154,100	1,078,635		
132	Part owner	228,974	272,349	285,418	300,280	274,135	165,355	185,246	183,469	152,432	171,944	105,171		
133	Manager			6,975	8,906	9,190	9,740	12,751	13,215	16,548	15,084	17,172		
134	Tenant	118,153	171,129	228,219	398,978	539,817	689,540	942,655	1,091,944	887,566	866,278	678,743		
135	Croppers			47,650	107,416	148,708	176,290	242,173	383,381	227,378				
136	Negro and other	90,141	184,578	265,621	463,476	559,090	665,413	680,266	881,687	922,914	890,141	740,670		
137	Full owner	55,600	70,799	89,749	129,854	141,482	160,980	141,902	140,496	178,558	175,290	158,479		
138	Part owner	16,306	31,263	37,534	50,736	51,864	28,252	31,361	41,523	39,031	43,177	28,197		
139	Manager			145	290	381	239	442	365	829	1,770	1,200	1,593	
140	Tenant	18,235	82,371	138,048	282,505	365,505	475,739	506,638	698,839	703,555	670,474	552,401		
141	Croppers			73,387	160,246	198,057	270,296	299,118	392,897	333,713				

See footnotes at end of table.

Series K 109–153. Farms, by Race and Tenure of Operator, and Acreage and Value, by Tenure of Operator: 1880 to 1969—Con.

Series No.	Tenure of operator	1969	1964 [1]	1959 [1]	1954 [1][2]	1950 [1]	1945 [2]	1940	1930	1920 [7]	1910 [2]	1900 [2]
	LAND IN FARMS (1,000 acres)											
142	All farms	1,063,346	1,110,185	1,123,378	1,160,044	1,161,420	1,141,615	1,065,114	990,112	955,974	878,798	838,592
143	Full owner	375,092	318,876	346,483	397,214	419,109	412,358	382,184	[8]372,575	[8]461,327	464,923	431,261
144	Part owner	550,649	533,044	503,682	472,465	422,812	371,251	300,782	246,605	175,525	133,681	124,779
145	Manager		113,361	109,990	100,003	107,296	106,372	68,939	63,626	54,141	53,731	87,518
146	Tenant	137,605	144,906	163,223	190,362	212,204	251,634	313,209	307,306	264,982	226,513	195,034
147	Croppers (South)			5,097	9,413	14,166	18,922	23,313	31,605	22,531		
	AVERAGE VALUE PER FARM OF FARMLAND AND BUILDINGS (dollars)											
148	All farms	75,725	50,646	[9]33,175	19,761	13,932	7,917	5,532	7,623	10,284	5,471	2,896
149	Full owner			[9]22,478	14,511	10,719	6,393	4,959	[4]7,253	[4]9,122	5,160	2,851
150	Part owner			[9]56,660	35,764	25,137	15,184	9,936	12,400	16,387	8,515	4,347
151	Manager			[9]244,714	165,800	153,043	60,552	42,208	41,307	38,936	25,075	13,114
152	Tenant			[9]36,159	19,464	12,926	6,941	4,566	6,143	9,689	4,662	2,345
153	Croppers (South)			[9]7,040	3,972	3,333	1,981	1,433	1,802	2,633		

[1] Data for subclass of tenants for 1964, all data for 1959 and 1954, and average value per farm of farmland and buildings for 1950, are based on sample reports.
[2] Excludes Alaska and Hawaii.
[3] 49 States; no classification by tenure for Alaska.
[4] Full owners for 1930 include 330 "Owners" and, for 1920, 345 "Owners" for Alaska, for whom no differentiation was made between full and part owners.
[5] Totals by race include 1,257 white and 4,985 Negro and other race operators for 1959 for Hawaii, 492 white and 8 Negro and other race operators for 1930 for Alaska, and 361 white and 3 Negro and other race operators for 1920 for Alaska, for whom tenure distribution is not available.

[6] Full owners by race for 1930 include 359 part owners for Hawaii; tenure distribution by race for Hawaii for that year was for "Owners" with no differentiation between full and part owners.
[7] 49 States; data not distributed by race or tenure for Hawaii.
[8] Data for full owners for 1930 include 63,626 acres and, for 1920, 77,288 acres for "Owners" for Alaska, for which there was no differentiation between full and part owners.
[9] Excludes Hawaii.

Series K 154–161. Mortgaged Farms—Number, Acreage, Value, and Amount of Indebtedness, by Tenure of Operator: 1930 to 1966

Year	Number of farms	Land in farms	Value of farmland and buildings	Mortgage debt				Equity per mortgaged farm
				Total	Ratio of mortgage debt to total value	Debt per acre	Debt per farm	
	154	155	156	157	158	159	160	161
	1,000	Mil. acres	Mil. dol.	Mil. dol.	Percent	Dollars	Dollars	Dollars
ALL TENURES								
1966	1,434	597	108,371	24,660				
1961		361	48,623	12,812	26.3	35.53		
1956		349	36,282	9,066	25.0	26.00		
1950	1,480	304	22,049	5,579	25.3	18.38	3,769	11,125
1945	1,714	373	16,376	4,941	30.2	13.24	2,883	6,672
1940	2,364	457	15,874	6,586	41.5	14.40	2,786	3,929
1935	2,350			7,584			3,227	
1930	2,523			9,631			3,817	
FULL OWNER								
1961	732	138	21,450	5,899	27.5	42.70	8,058	21,240
1956	909	149	17,626	4,720	26.8	31.65	5,191	14,194
1950	894	135	11,273	3,116	27.6	23.03	3,485	9,123
1945	997	149	8,166	2,690	32.9	18.04	2,697	5,492
1940	1,278	180	7,887	3,353	42.5	18.58	2,623	3,547
1935	1,270	182	7,338	3,682	50.2	20.25	2,899	2,879
1930	1,232	182	10,955	4,337	39.6	23.82	3,521	5,373
PART OWNER [1]								
1961	388	137	14,221	3,970	27.9	29.08	10,228	26,412
1956	368	117	9,087	2,312	25.4	19.75	6,278	18,397
1950	281	90	4,585	1,179	25.7	13.08	4,187	12,103
1945	274	90	2,863	875	30.6	9.73	3,194	7,256
1940	336	94	2,358	1,106	46.9	11.78	3,287	3,724
1935	349							
1930	360							
MANAGER AND TENANT [2]								
1961 [3]		86	12,952	2,943	22.7	34.26		
1956 [3]		82	9,570	2,034	21.3	24.66		
1950 [3]	305	78	6,190	1,284	20.7	16.43	(4)	16,095
1945 [3]	443	134	5,347	1,376	25.7	10.26	(4)	8,969
1940 [3]	749	183	5,628	2,127	37.8	11.62	(4)	4,674
1935	731							
1930	932							

[1] Acres, value, and debt are for owned portion only.
[2] Acres, value, and debt include the rented portion of part-owner farms.
[3] Except for number of farms, includes figures for the rented portion of part-owner farms.
[4] Not shown because data for mortgage debt include rented portion of part-owner farms.

Series K 162–173. Farms and Land in Farms, by Size of Farm: 1880 to 1969

[Farms in thousands; land in farms in thousands of acres]

Year	Total	Under 10 acres — Total	Under 3 acres	3–9 acres	10–29 acres	30–49 acres	50–99 acres	100–179 acres	180–259 acres	260–499 acres	500–999 acres	1,000 acres and over
	162	163	164	165	166	167	168	169	170	171	172	173
NUMBER OF FARMS												
1969	2,730	162	79	83	473		460	542	307	419	216	151
1964	3,158	183	60	123	637		542	633	355	451	210	145
1959	3,711	244	79	165	813		658	773	415	472	200	136
1954[1]	4,782	484	100	384	713	499	864	953	464	482	192	130
1950	5,388	489	78	410	855	625	1,048	2,068			182	121
1945[1]	5,859	595	99	496	946	709	1,157	1,200	493	473	174	113
1940	6,102	509	37	472	1,782		1,291	2,255			164	101
1935[1]	6,812	571	36	535	1,241	882	1,444	1,438	507	473	167	89
1930	6,295	362	44	318	2,002		1,375	2,315			160	81
1925[1]	6,372	379	15	363	2,039		1,421	1,887		440	144	63
1920	6,454	[2]292	[2]21	[2]270	2,014		1,475	2,457			150	67
1910[1]	6,362	335	18	317	1,918		1,438	2,051		444	125	50
1900	5,740	268	42	227	1,665		1,366	2,291			103	47
1890	4,565	150	(NA)	(NA)	1,168		1,122	2,009			84	32
1880	4,009	139	4	135	1,036		1,033	1,696			76	29
LAND IN FARMS												
1969	1,063,346	568	93	474	13,253		33,620	74,005	66,378	149,309	147,801	578,412
1964	1,110,185	778	(NA)	(NA)	17,327		39,590	86,588	76,854	159,597	144,598	584,847
1959	1,123,508	1,053	(NA)	(NA)	21,850		47,950	105,732	89,503	165,438	137,351	554,631
1954[1]	1,158,192	2,260	(NA)	(NA)	12,704	19,165	62,725	130,120	99,863	168,368	131,505	531,482
1950	[3]1,162,643	2,443	(NA)	(NA)	39,372		75,647	149,991	105,403	168,944	125,988	494,856
1945[1]	1,141,615	2,805	141	2,664	16,864	27,074	83,206	162,375	105,802	164,647	118,836	460,006
1940	1,065,114	2,679	52	2,627	47,538		93,336	177,558	104,289	161,995	111,946	365,772
1935[1]	1,054,515	3,057	51	3,006	22,272	33,691	104,016	194,804	108,462	164,268	114,244	309,701
1930	990,112	1,922	63	1,859	54,085		98,700	290,525		159,273	108,940	276,667
1925[1]	924,319	2,097	23	2,074	54,465		101,906	292,180		151,731	97,468	224,472
1920	[4]958,677	1,600	33	1,567	55,553		105,631	307,244		164,244	100,976	220,636
1910	[4]881,431	(NA)	(NA)	(NA)	(NA)		103,121	470,770			83,653	167,082
1900	841,202	1,482	80	1,402	47,253		98,600	295,978		129,686	67,878	200,324

NA Not available.
[1] Excludes Alaska and Hawaii.   [2] Excludes Alaska.
[3] Based on sample; therefore differs from series K 5 and K 17.
[4] Total includes Alaska and Hawaii.

Series K 174–183. Farm Employment, Wages, and Indexes of Man-Hours Used for Farmwork: 1866 to 1970

[Excludes Alaska and Hawaii except as indicated]

Year	Total farm	Family workers[2]	Hired workers	Index, composite farm wage rates (1967 = 100)	Per month[3] — With board and room	Per month[3] — With house	Per day[3] — With board and room	Per day[3] — Without board or room	Farmers' expenditures for hired labor[4]	Index, man-hours of labor used for farmwork (1967 = 100)
	174	175	176	177	178	179	180	181	182	183
	1,000	*1,000*	*1,000*		*Dollars*	*Dollars*	*Dollars*	*Dollars*	*Mil. dol.*	
1970	4,523	3,348	1,175	129	251.00	328.00	10.70	11.70	3,394	90
1969	4,596	3,420	1,176	121	234.00	307.00	10.10	10.90	3,196	92
1968	4,749	3,535	1,213	110	216.00	283.00	9.30	9.90	3,047	96
1967	4,903	3,650	1,253	100	200.00	262.00	8.60	9.00	2,878	100
1966	5,214	3,854	1,360	94	184.00	243.00	8.00	8.20	2,889	102
1965	5,610	4,128	1,482	86	170.00	223.00	7.40	7.60	2,849	107
1964	6,110	4,506	1,604	82	162.00	212.00	7.10	7.30	2,913	113
1963	6,518	4,738	1,780	80	159.00	206.00	6.90	7.10	2,990	119
1962	6,700	4,873	1,827	78	155.00	200.00	6.70	6.90	2,961	124
1961	6,919	5,029	1,890	76	151.00	195.00	6.50	6.60	2,977	129
1960	7,057	5,172	1,885	74	149.00	192.00	6.50	6.60	*2,923	135
1959	7,342	5,390	1,952	72	144.00	186.00	6.30	6.40	2,882	142
1958	7,503	5,521	1,982	69	137.00	176.00	6.10	6.00	2,842	145
1957	7,600	5,660	1,940	66	133.00	168.00	5.80	5.80	2,734	152
1956	7,852	5,900	1,953	64	128.00	161.00	5.60	5.60	2,641	165
1955	8,381	6,345	2,036	61	123.00	154.00	5.40	5.30	2,615	176
1954	8,651	6,570	2,081	60	120.00	151.00	5.30	5.30	2,596	183
1953	8,864	6,775	2,089	61	122.00	151.00	5.40	5.30	2,736	192
1952	9,149	7,005	2,144	60	119.00	146.00	5.30	5.30	2,857	200
1951	9,546	7,310	2,236	57	113.00	137.00	5.00	5.00	2,921	209

See footnotes at end of table.

Series K 174–183. Farm Employment, Wages, and Indexes of Man-Hours Used for Farmwork: 1866 to 1970—Con.

Year	Employment [1] Total farm	Family workers [2]	Hired workers	Index, composite farm wage rates (1967 = 100)	Wage rates Per month [3] With board and room	With house	Per day [3] With board and room	Without board or room	Farmers' expenditures for hired labor [4]	Index, man-hours of labor used for farmwork (1967 = 100)
	174	175	176	177	178	179	180	181	182	183
	1,000	*1,000*	*1,000*		*Dollars*	*Dollars*	*Dollars*	*Dollars*	*Mil. dol.*	
1950	9,926	7,597	2,329	51	99.00	121.00	4.45	4.50	2,811	208
1949	9,964	7,712	2,252	51	99.00	121.00	4.45	4.45	2,806	223
1948	10,363	8,026	2,337	53	101.00	122.00	4.50	4.45	2,990	232
1947	10,382	8,115	2,267	50	92.00	117.00	4.50	5.10	2,783	237
1946	10,295	8,106	2,189	47	86.00	108.00	4.20	4.80	2,532	249
1945	10,000	7,881	2,119	43	79.00	101.00	3.85	4.35	2,299	259
1944	10,219	7,988	2,231	39	71.00	91.00	3.50	3.95	2,202	277
1943	10,446	8,010	2,436	32	59.00	77.00	2.90	3.30	2,027	279
1942	10,504	7,949	2,555	25	45.50	59.00	2.20	2.55	1,631	283
1941	10,669	8,017	2,652	19	34.50	44.50	1.65	1.95	1,249	276
1940	10,979	8,300	2,679	15	27.50	37.50	1.30	1.60	1,029	282
1939	11,338	8,611	2,727	15	27.00	36.00	1.25	1.55	988	284
1938	11,622	8,815	2,807	15	27.00	36.00	1.30	1.55	979	283
1937	11,978	9,054	2,924	16	27.50	36.50	1.35	1.65	988	304
1936	12,331	9,350	2,981	14	24.00	32.50	1.20	1.45	868	281
1935	12,733	9,855	2,878	13	22.00	30.50	1.10	1.35	775	290
1934	12,627	9,765	2,862	12	20.00	28.00	1.00	1.25	679	278
1933	12,739	9,874	2,865	11	18.00	25.50	.90	1.15	617	310
1932	12,816	9,922	2,894	12	20.50	29.00	.95	1.20	669	311
1931	12,745	9,642	3,103	16	28.50	38.00	1.30	1.65	914	322
1930	12,497	9,307	3,190	21	37.50	48.00	1.80	2.15	1,177	315
1929	12,763	9,360	3,403	22	40.00	51.00	2.00	2.30	1,300	319
1928	12,691	9,340	3,351	22	39.50	50.00	2.00	2.30	1,290	321
1927	12,642	9,278	3,364	22	39.50	50.00	2.00	2.35	1,302	316
1926	12,976	9,526	3,450	22	39.50	50.00	2.00	2.40	1,330	328
1925	13,036	9,715	3,321	22	38.50	49.00	2.00	2.35	1,267	327
1924	13,031	9,705	3,326	21	38.00	49.00	1.95	2.40	1,248	321
1923	13,162	9,798	3,364	21	37.50	47.50	1.95	2.35	1,251	317
1922	13,337	9,936	3,401	18	33.00	43.50	1.65	2.00	1,127	315
1921	13,398	10,001	3,397	18	33.50	44.50	1.65	2.05	1,170	305
1920	13,432	10,041	3,391	28	51.00	65.00	2.80	3.30	1,790	330
1919	13,243	9,968	3,275	24	43.00	56.00	2.40	2.90	1,515	325
1918	13,391	10,053	3,338	21	37.50	48.50	2.05	2.45	1,337	331
1917	13,568	10,121	3,447	17	31.00	40.50	1.55	1.90	1,127	327
1916	13,632	10,144	3,488	13	25.00	33.00	1.25	1.50	904	318
1915	13,592	10,140	3,452	12	22.50	30.00	1.10	1.40	815	320
1914	13,580	10,147	3,433	12	22.50	29.50	1.10	1.35	804	326
1913	13,572	10,158	3,414	12	22.50	30.00	1.15	1.40	804	317
1912	13,559	10,162	3,397	12	22.00	29.50	1.10	1.40	789	321
1911	13,539	10,169	3,370	12	21.50	28.00	1.05	1.40	758	317
1910	13,555	10,174	3,381	11	21.00	28.00	1.05	1.35	755	310

Year	Wage rates Per month [3] With board and room	With house	Per day [3] With board and room	Without board or room	Year	Wage rates Per month [3] With board and room	With house	Per day [3] With board and room	Without board or room
	178	179	180	181		178	179	180	181
	Dollars	*Dollars*	*Dollars*	*Dollars*		*Dollars*	*Dollars*	*Dollars*	*Dollars*
1909	22.00	28.00	1.00	1.25	1887 or 1888	13.50	19.50	0.70	1.00
1906	18.50	26.00	1.05	1.30	1884 or 1885	13.00	19.00	.70	.95
1902	15.50	22.00	.85	1.10	1881 or 1882	13.00	19.00	.70	.95
1899	14.00	20.00	.75	1.00	1880 or 1881	12.50	18.50	.65	.90
1898	13.50	19.00	.70	.95	1879 or 1880	11.50	17.50	.65	.90
					1877 [5]	11.00	17.00	.60	.85
1895	12.50	18.50	.65	.85					
1894	12.50	18.50	.65	.85					
1893	14.00	20.00	.70	.90	1874 or 1875	11.00	17.00	.70	.95
1891 or 1892	13.50	20.00	.75	1.00	1869	10.00	15.50	.65	.85
1889 or 1890	13.50	19.50	.70	.95	1866 [6]	10.00	15.50	.65	.90

* Denotes first year for which figures include Alaska and Hawaii.
[1] These annual averages are simple averages of last-of-month employment estimates.
[2] Includes farm operators and members of their families doing farm work without wages.
[3] Annual averages are weighted averages of wage rates as reported quarterly by crop reporters. Different wage rate categories used after 1948. See text.
[4] Cash wages and value of perquisites.
[5] 1877 or 1878, 1878 or 1879 (combined).
[6] For years 1866 to 1878, paid in gold.

Series K 184–191. Farm Machinery and Equipment: 1910 to 1970

[In thousands]

Year	Tractors [1] 184	Motor-trucks 185	Auto-mobiles 186	Grain combines 187	Corn-pickers 188	Farms with milking machines 189	Pickup balers 190	Field forage harvesters 191
1970	4,790	3,185	--------	850	620	--------	795	331
1969	4,810	3,160	--------	860	630	--------	790	328
1968	4,822	3,130	--------	870	640	--------	785	325
1967	4,815	3,100	--------	880	655	--------	775	322
1966	4,800	3,060	--------	895	675	--------	765	320
1965	2 4,783	2 3,023	2 3,587	2 910	2 690	2 500	2 751	2 316
1964	4,755	2,970	--------	920	705	--------	734	312
1963	4,730	2,925	--------	940	720	--------	718	307
1962	4,710	2,885	--------	960	730	--------	703	300
1961	4,695	2,850	--------	980	740	--------	685	291
1960	2 4,685	2 2,825	2 3,629	2 1,042	2 792	2 666	2 680	2 291
1959	4,673	2,800	--------	1,045	775	--------	645	270
1958	4,620	2,775	--------	1,030	755	--------	600	258
1957	4,570	2,745	--------	1,015	740	--------	560	240
1956	4,480	2,707	--------	1,005	715	--------	505	220
1955	2 4,345	2,675	4,140	2 980	2 688	2 712	2 448	2 202
1954	4,243	2,610	--------	965	660	705	395	175
1953	4,100	2,535	--------	930	630	690	345	148
1952	3,907	2,430	--------	887	588	675	298	124
1951	3,678	2,325	--------	810	522	655	240	102
1950	2 3,394	2 2,207	2 4,100	2 714	2 456	2 636	2 196	81
1949	3,123	2,065	--------	620	372	610	135	60
1948	2,821	1,900	--------	535	299	575	90	45
1947	2,613	1,700	--------	465	236	525	65	30
1946	2,480	1,550	--------	420	203	440	54	25
1945	2 2,354	2 1,490	2 4,148	2 375	168	2 365	42	20
1944	2,160	1,385	--------	345	146	300	34	--------
1943	2,055	1,280	--------	320	138	275	31	--------
1942	1,860	1,160	--------	275	130	255	25	--------
1941	1,665	1,095	--------	225	120	210	--------	--------

Year	Tractors [1] 184	Motor-trucks 185	Auto-mobiles 186	Grain combines 187	Corn-pickers 188	Farms with milking machines 189
1940	2 1,567	2 1,047	2 4,144	190	110	175
1939	1,445	1,020	4,030	--------	--------	--------
1938	1,370	1,042	4,109	--------	--------	--------
1937	1,230	990	3,962	--------	--------	--------
1936	1,125	923	3,735	--------	--------	--------
1935	1,048	890	3,642	--------	--------	--------
1934	1,016	875	3,399	--------	--------	--------
1933	1,019	865	3,399	--------	--------	--------
1932	1,022	910	3,798	--------	--------	--------
1931	997	920	4,077	--------	--------	--------
1930	2 920	2 900	2 4,135	61	50	100
1929	827	840	3,970	--------	--------	--------
1928	782	753	3,820	--------	--------	--------
1927	693	662	3,820	--------	--------	--------
1926	621	559	3,605	--------	--------	--------
1925	549	459	3,283	--------	--------	--------
1924	496	363	3,004	--------	--------	--------
1923	428	316	2,618	--------	--------	--------
1922	372	263	2,425	--------	--------	--------
1921	343	207	2,382	--------	--------	--------
1920	2 246	2 139	2 2,146	4	10	55
1919	158	111	1,760	--------	--------	--------
1918	85	89	1,502	--------	--------	--------
1917	51	60	966	--------	--------	--------
1916	37	40	687	--------	--------	--------
1915	25	25	472	--------	--------	--------
1914	17	15	343	--------	--------	--------
1913	14	10	258	--------	--------	--------
1912	8	5	175	--------	--------	--------
1911	4	2	100	--------	--------	--------
1910	1	--------	50	1	--------	12

[1] Excludes steam or garden type.

2 Census of agriculture data. Census dates: January 1, 1920 and 1945; April 1, 1930, 1940, and 1950; November 1954, 1959, and 1964.

Series K 192–194. Expenditures for, and Consumption of, Fertilizer and Lime: 1850 to 1970

Year	Farmers' expenditures for fertilizer and lime 192 (Mil. dol.)	Commercial fertilizer consumed in U.S. [1] 193 (1,000 short tons)	Lime consumed on farms 2 194 (1,000 short tons)
1970	2,222	39,591	25,901
1969	2,084	38,948	28,803
1968	2,130	38,743	30,536
1967	2,124	37,081	29,202
1966	1,952	34,532	30,461
1965	1,754	31,836	28,075
1964	1,701	30,681	27,002
1963	1,570	28,844	26,119
1962	1,474	26,615	23,616
1961	1,373	25,567	22,612
1960	* 1,315	24,877	22,614
1959	1,291	25,313	22,726
1958	1,206	22,516	23,215
1957	1,166	22,709	22,476
1956	1,166	22,194	22,021
1955	1,185	22,726	20,659
1954	1,209	22,773	18,975
1953	1,178	23,413	20,669
1952	1,184	22,432	27,252
1951	1,064	20,991	27,583
1950	975	18,343	29,842
1949	895	18,542	27,902
1948	826	17,818	25,686
1947	755	16,839	30,283
1946	683	15,128	29,462

Year	192 (Mil. dol.)	193 (1,000 short tons)	194 (1,000 short tons)
1945	657	15,128	23,055
1944	576	13,045	24,568
1943	505	11,516	19,935
1942	417	10,125	19,838
1941	334	9,296	15,916
1940	306	9,360	14,406
1939	273	7,728	9,066
1938	258	7,471	7,859
1937	279	8,139	7,199
1936	261	6,956	6,566
1935	188	6,275	3,505
1934	176	5,547	2,748
1933	120	4,872	1,548
1932	118	4,336	1,811
1931	202	6,306	2,611
1930	297	8,171	3,588
1929	300	7,982	3,907
1928	318	7,989	3,806
1927	267	6,844	3,798
1926	298	7,326	3,330
1925	299	7,329	3,359
1924	264	6,833	3,217
1923	263	6,435	3,076
1922	234	5,680	2,935
1921	249	4,854	2,794

Year	192 (Mil. dol.)	193 (1,000 short tons)	194 (1,000 short tons)
1920	390	7,176	2,653
1919	358	6,751	2,476
1918	311	6,580	2,306
1917	232	6,087	2,136
1916	193	5,214	1,966
1915	165	5,418	1,796
1914	195	7,194	1,626
1913	175	6,416	1,456
1912	161	5,852	1,286
1911	168	6,108	1,116
1910	152	5,547	946
1909	120	4,821	--------
1908	--------	4,449	--------
1907	--------	4,307	--------
1906	--------	4,249	--------
1905	--------	3,913	--------
1904	--------	3,704	--------
1903	--------	3,382	--------
1902	--------	3,084	--------
1901	--------	3,044	--------
1900	--------	2,730	--------
1899	--------	2,603	--------
1898	--------	2,333	--------
1897	--------	2,131	--------
1896	--------	1,888	--------

Year	Commercial fertilizer consumed in U.S. [1] 193 (1,000 short tons)
1895	1,578
1894	1,773
1893	1,715
1892	1,504
1891	1,584
1890	1,390
1880	753
1870	321
1860	164
1850	53

* Denotes first year for which figures include Alaska and Hawaii.

[1] Includes Puerto Rico, Hawaii, and Alaska for all years except 1920–1944; see text. Prior to 1944, data for a calendar year; thereafter, for years ending June 30.

2 Excludes Alaska and Hawaii for all years.

Series K 195–203. Farmers' Marketing and Purchasing Cooperatives—Number, Memberships, and Business: 1913 to 1970

[Fiscal-year data]

Year	Cooperatives listed			Estimated memberships (1,000)			Estimated business [1] (mil. dol.)			Year	Cooperatives listed			Estimated memberships (1,000)			Estimated business [1] (mil. dol.)		
	Total	Marketing	Purchasing	Total	Marketing	Purchasing	Total	Marketing [2]	Purchasing		Total	Marketing	Purchasing	Total	Marketing	Purchasing	Total	Marketing [2]	Purchasing
	195	196	197	198	199	200	201	202	203		195	196	197	198	199	200	201	202	203
1970	7,790	5,015	2,775	6,355	3,133	3,222	19,080	15,207	3,873	1950	10,035	6,922	3,113	6,584	4,075	2,509	8,726	7,083	1,643
1969	7,747	4,954	2,793	6,364	3,175	3,189	17,396	13,796	3,600	1949	10,075	6,993	3,082	6,384	3,973	2,411	9,320	7,700	1,620
1968	7,940	5,105	2,835	6,445	3,259	3,186	17,034	13,513	3,521	1948	10,135	7,159	2,976	5,890	3,630	2,260	8,635	7,195	1,440
1967	8,125	5,254	2,871	6,502	3,333	3,169	16,557	13,218	3,339	1947	10,125	7,268	2,857	5,436	3,378	2,058	7,116	6,005	1,111
1966	8,329	5,380	2,949	6,826	3,672	3,154	15,608	12,523	3,085	1946	10,150	7,378	2,772	5,010	3,150	1,860	6,070	5,147	923
1965	8,583	5,498	3,085	7,082	3,831	3,251	14,742	11,832	2,910	1945	10,150	7,400	2,750	4,505	2,895	1,610	5,645	4,835	810
1964	8,847	5,621	3,226	7,080	3,655	3,425	14,354	11,522	2,832	1944	10,300	7,522	2,778	4,250	2,730	1,520	5,160	4,430	730
1963	8,907	5,696	3,211	7,219	3,623	3,596	13,842	11,138	2,704	1943	10,450	7,708	2,742	3,850	2,580	1,270	3,780	3,180	600
1962	9,039	5,833	3,206	7,099	3,464	3,635	13,024	10,463	2,561	1942	10,550	7,824	2,726	3,600	2,430	1,170	2,840	2,360	480
1961	9,163	5,941	3,222	7,203	3,523	3,680	12,409	9,937	2,472	1941	10,600	7,943	2,657	3,400	2,420	980	2,280	1,911	369
1960	9,345	6,048	3,297	7,273	3,673	3,600	12,036	9,628	2,408	1936	10,500	8,388	2,112	3,660	2,710	950	1,840	1,586	254
1959*	9,658	6,271	3,387	7,559	3,915	3,644	11,747	9,376	2,371	1931	11,950	10,362	1,588	3,000	2,608	392	2,400	2,185	215
1958	9,735	6,352	3,383	7,486	3,943	3,543	10,753	8,566	2,187	1926	10,803	9,586	1,217	2,700	2,453	247	2,400	2,265	135
1957	9,891	6,518	3,373	7,673	4,184	3,489	10,379	8,233	2,146	1921	7,374	6,476	898	(NA)	(NA)	(NA)	1,256	1,198	58
1956	9,894	6,519	3,375	7,732	4,288	3,444	9,756	7,710	2,046	1915	5,424	5,149	275	651	592	59	636	624	12
1955	9,903	6,557	3,346	7,604	4,281	3,323	9,642	7,620	2,022	1913	3,099	2,988	111	------	------	------	310	304	6
1954	10,072	6,698	3,374	7,608	4,355	3,252	9,475	7,497	1,978										
1953	10,128	6,750	3,378	7,475	4,336	3,139	9,521	7,508	2,013										
1952	10,179	6,855	3,324	7,364	4,331	3,033	9,410	7,491	1,919										
1951	10,064	6,781	3,283	7,091	4,212	2,879	8,147	6,462	1,685										

* Denotes first year for which figures include Alaska and Hawaii.
NA Not available.

[1] Data for years prior to 1951 are not entirely comparable due to revisions in statistical procedures in 1951.
[2] Includes services related to marketing or supply purchasing.

Chapter K

Agricultural Income and Finances (Series K 204-383)

K 204–219. Balance sheet of the farming sector, 1940–1970.

Source: U.S. Department of Agriculture, *The Balance Sheet of the Farming Sector* (formerly *The Balance Sheet of Agriculture*), annual issues.

The balance sheet of the farming sector is a statement of the dollar value, at a point in time, of major assets and debts of farm operators and landlords directly related to farming and farm family living. The balancing item is the equity of proprietors in those assets.

The balance sheet which originated in 1944 in the Bureau of Agricultural Economics as the "balance sheet of agriculture" provides aggregate estimates for the United States excluding Alaska and Hawaii. It is not a consolidation of the balance sheets of individual farm operators and landlords.

Balance sheets were constructed as of January 1, for each of the five years 1940–1944. The immediate aim was to provide benchmarks from which to measure changes in the farm economy in the years following World War II. The balance sheet along with an analysis of trends has been published annually since 1945. In 1969, the name was changed to "balance sheet of the farming sector" because "agriculture" had come to denote more than farm interests of operators and nonfarm landlords.

Certain assets and debts of farmers and farm landlords are not included in the accounting, due to lack of adequate data. For example, farmers' financial assets such as cash value of life insurance, savings in savings and loan associations, ownership of corporate stocks, and the value of farmer owned crops stored off farms and not under CCC loans are not included. Another limitation is the estimate of farm debt held by individuals, merchants, dealers, and other miscellaneous lenders. They are based on census surveys taken every 5 or 10 years and are less accurate than the amount of debt held by lenders who report at least annually to the Department of Agriculture (USDA).

The methodology used in constructing the balance sheet series is presented in detail in *Major Statistical Series of the U.S. Department of Agriculture, How They Are Constructed and Used*, Agriculture Handbook No. 365, vol. 6.

K 205, farm real estate. These are estimates as of March 1. They include buildings and improvements and are published annually by the Economic Research Service in "Farm Real Estate Market Developments." The index of average value per acre is used to calculate the annual dollar value per acre. The average dollar value per acre multiplied by the number of acres in farms results in the total dollar value of farmland. Estimates are made by States. Census surveys each five years serve as benchmarks. Changes in the index of value per acre based on USDA annual surveys are used to interpolate between census years.

K 206, livestock and poultry. These estimates are derived by multiplying the value per head of the various species by the number on hand at the beginning of the year. The Statistical Reporting Service supplies the basic data, which are obtained through their surveys. Commercial broilers, assumed not to be owned by farm operators or landlords, are not included.

K 207, machinery and motor vehicles. The data include the value of automobiles, trucks, tractors, combines, hay balers, forage harvesters, corn pickers, and miscellaneous other items. The value of the individual classes is obtained by adding value of purchases during the year and subtracting depreciation. The annual survey of manufactures and sample surveys of agriculture, both conducted by the Bureau of the Census, supply basic data.

K 208, crops stored on and off farms. These estimates are derived by multiplying the quantity of the various farmer-owned crops stored on farms, by States, January 1, by the average price, by States, as of the previous December 15. Crops under CCC loan are included. Quantity and price data are from the Statistical Reporting Service. Farmer-owned crops stored off farms are limited to crops under CCC loan. The value is estimated as the higher of (1) the value of the CCC loan or (2) the market value of the crop. Data are not available for value of farmer-owned crops stored off farms and not under CCC loan.

K 209, household equipment and furnishings. The Agricultural Research Service provides these estimates. Basically, the inventory value for the previous January 1 is increased by expenditures for such items and decreased by the amount of depreciation during the year. Changes in the number of farm households are considered in the calculations.

K 210, deposits and currency. Until 1961, the Board of Governors of the Federal Reserve System estimated the demand deposits of farmers in commercial banks. Farmers' time deposits in banks were estimated as a certain percentage of demand deposits based on data of insured banks in a selected sample of about 600 predominantly agricultural counties. Since 1961, the Economic Research Service has made the estimates based on (1) changes in bank demand and time deposits in the 600 selected agricultural counties and (2) changes in the index of demand and time deposits in "country banks" (members of the Federal Reserve System with head offices located in towns of under 15,000 population). The estimate of currency owned by farmers is based on a percentage of demand deposits as determined by a survey of the total U.S. population in 1960, by the Securities and Exchange Commission.

Estimates of demand and time deposits and currency of farmers may not be very accurate. Basic data used are from samples of banks which could be outdated. The measure of currency is based on assumptions and fragmentary data.

K 211, U.S. savings bonds. Farmers' holdings of U.S. savings bonds are estimated by adding purchases and interest accrued during the year to holdings at the beginning of the year and subtracting redemptions. There are no separate records of bond sales and redemptions for farmers as a group. Estimates are partially based on total sales data of series E and H bonds in about 600 selected agricultural counties which essentially are the same counties used in estimating farmers' bank deposits. Farmers' rate of redemption is assumed to be half the rate of the total population. Changes in the number of farmers are also considered. These estimates are admittedly weak.

K 212, investment in cooperatives. The net worth of farmer cooperatives is compiled from data furnished by the service or supervisory agencies for some of the various types of cooperatives, such as marketing and purchasing cooperatives, Federal land banks, production credit associations, and rural electric cooperatives. For other cooperatives, estimates are made by the Economic Research Service. A major limitation of the estimate of farmers' investment in cooperatives is that the cooperatives are not used exclusively by farmers, and all of the net worth cannot be claimed by farmers. No reliable data are available of the farmer portion of the net worth of cooperatives.

K 214, liabilities. Farm loans or farm related debts owed by farmers and farm landlords are classified for balance sheet purposes into (1) farm real estate loans and (2) farm nonreal estate loans. Data are for loans outstanding January 1.

K 215, real estate debt.   These are loans owed by farmers and farm landlords and secured by mortgages or other liens on farm real estate regardless of the purpose of the loan.   Terms are relatively long, usually ranging from 10 to 30 years or longer.

Farm loans held by Federal land banks, life insurance companies, commercial banks, and Farmers Home Administration are reported directly to USDA.   Loans held by miscellaneous nonreporting lenders are estimated from information obtained from Bureau of the Census sample surveys every 5 or 10 years.   For intercensal years it is assumed that loans held by miscellaneous lenders changed at the same rate as loans held by reporting lenders.   A limitation in estimating debt held by miscellaneous lenders is the time lag between Census Bureau reports during which the rate of change may vary.

K 216–218, nonreal estate debt.   These are loans owed by farmers not secured by real estate.   Most such debt is for operating expenses, purchases of livestock, machinery, and repairs.   Some loans are secured by crop or other chattel liens but many are unsecured.   Terms are usually 12 months or less but some which involve machinery and livestock purchases or farmstead improvements may have maturities of 5 to 7 years.

Loans held by commercial banks, production credit associations, Federal intermediate credit banks, Farmers Home Administration, and Commodity Credit Corporations are reported directly to USDA. Loans held by miscellaneous lenders are estimated.   Based on Census Bureau sample surveys, the percent that loans held by the miscellaneous lenders is of loans held by reporting lenders is applied annually to debt held by reporting lenders to give an estimate of debt held by miscellaneous lenders.   Recent estimates are that debt held by miscellaneous lenders is equivalent to 70 percent of the non-real-estate debt held by the reporting lenders.

An important limitation of these data is the questionable accuracy of the miscellaneous debt.   Except for census data and results of a few less extensive special surveys, little is known of total farm loans held by miscellaneous lenders such as individuals, merchants, dealers, and small loan companies.

K 219, proprietors' equities.   These figures are the residual after subtracting total debt from total value of assets—estimated net worth or the value of unencumbered farm assets.

K 220–239.   Value of gross farm product in current and constant (1958) dollars, 1929–1970.

Source: U.S. Office of Business Economics, 1929–1963, *The National Income and Product Accounts of the United States, 1929–1965*, tables 1.17 and 1.18; 1964–1967, *U.S. National Income and Product Accounts, 1964–1967*, tables 1.17 and 1.18.   U.S. Bureau of Economic Analysis (formerly Office of Business Economics), 1968–1970, *Survey of Current Business*, July issues, tables 1.17 and 1.18.

The Department of Agriculture series on gross and net farm income is the basis of the agricultural components of the national income and product accounts maintained by the Bureau of Economic Analysis.

The estimates of farm income and expenditures in general refer to income from commodities and services produced on farms as defined in the Census of Agriculture, to the expenses associated with such production, and to nonfarm income received by persons living on these farms.   The net income of farm operators from farming is not directly comparable with incomes in nonfarm industries, since farm operators in the main are not only involved in management (including investment decisions) but are actively working on their farms.

For bases of these data, see text for series K 256–285, K 286–302 and K 326–329.

K 240–250.   Value of farm gross output and product, in current and constant (1910–14) dollars, 1800–1900.

Source: M. W. Towne and W. E. Rasmussen, "Farm Gross Product and Gross Investment During the 19th Century," *Studies in Income and Wealth*, vol. 24, National Bureau of Economic Research, 1960 (copyright).

These estimates are designed to measure the output of agriculture from 1800 to 1900 on a gross product, or "value-added" basis.   The series for 1870–1900 are more reliable than for earlier years, and those for 1840–1860 are more reliable than for 1800–1830.

K 241–243, sales and home consumption of farm products, are totals of commodity values estimated separately from price and quantity estimates for individual commodities and groups of commodities.   The data for 1870–1900 are based primarily on Department of Agriculture, *Gross Farm Income and Indices of Farm Production in the United States, 1869–1937*, Technical Bulletin No. 703, December 1940.   Production estimates for 1840–1860 are based mostly on the Census of Agriculture. For 1800–1830, output is generally derived as the product of population and per capita production rates suggested by data for 1840–1860, although independent estimates were employed for the major cash crops, which amounted to about one-eighth of the total.   Prices for current dollar valuation were obtained by extrapolating the 1870 farm price estimates of Technical Bulletin No. 703 to earlier years by changes in related wholesale prices and average prices received by farmers.

K 244, livestock inventory changes, is based on Department of Agriculture inventory and value-per-head data for 1870–1900.   Inventory data from the Census of Agriculture were used for 1840–1860. For 1800–1830, the inventory estimates were projected backward from 1840 by population changes.   Average values per head were projected to earlier years from 1870 by related wholesale price series.

K 245, gross rent from farm dwellings, represents imputed income from home ownership.   Figures were obtained by multiplying the 1910–1914 average gross rent per farm (from the current farm income series) by the estimated number of farms in the decade years 1800–1900, and by inflating to current dollars by an index of construction costs.   Estimates for number of farms were obtained from the censuses of agriculture for 1850–1900, and were extrapolated from 1850 to 1820 by the estimated number of persons engaged in agriculture, and from 1820 to 1800 by population figures.

K 247, intermediate products consumed, represents the cost of goods and services purchased for production purposes by farms from the nonfarm sector.   It is deducted from gross output to derive the net contribution of the agricultural sector, or farm gross product, series K 246.   The intermediate products and services originating off farms include fertilizer, cotton ginning, horseshoeing, repairs, and rent paid to nonfarm landlords.   For most items, estimates for 1800–1900 were constructed by extrapolating the 1910–14 average costs in the current series backward by changes in series closely related with respect to quantity or price.   The estimates of intermediate products have as a whole less foundation in census or other contemporary benchmark sources and are less reliable than the gross output estimates.

K 249 and **K 250**, farm-produced improvements and home manufactures, although not included in current official measurements of gross farm output, are presented here because of their greater relative importance in the earlier years.   The land improvement estimates were derived as the product of average annual number of acres improved and estimated per acre labor cost of improvement.   The value of home manufactures series is based on survey and census estimates for 1810 and 1840–1870, with other decades estimated on the basis of trends in real output indicated by these benchmarks; a textiles price index was used for deflation.

Estimates of data in 1910–14 dollars were derived in nearly all cases by multiplying estimated quantities of individual products by average prices for 1910–14.

K 251–255.   Exports and imports of farm products, 1901–1970.

Source: U.S. Department of Agriculture, *Agricultural Statistics, 1937*, table 463; *1952*, table 817; *1957*, table 808; and *1972*, table 817.

U.S. foreign agricultural trade statistics include official U.S. data based on compilations of the Bureau of the Census.   Agricultural commodities consist of (1) nonmarine food products and (2) other products of agriculture which have not passed through complex processes of manufacture such as rawhides and skins, fats and oils, and wine. Such manufactured products as textiles, leather, boots and shoes, cigarettes, naval stores, forestry products, and distilled alcoholic beverages are not considered agricultural.

The trade statistics exclude shipments between the 50 States and Puerto Rico, between the 50 States and the outlying areas, between Puerto Rico and the outlying areas, among the outlying areas, and in transit through the United States from one foreign country to another when documented as such through U.S. Customs.

The export value, the value at the port of exportation, is based on the selling price (or cost if not sold) and includes inland freight, insurance, and other charges to the port. Except for Canada, export shipments valued $251–$499 ($100–$499 prior to October 1969) are included on the basis of sampling estimates; shipments to Canada valued $251–$1,999 ($100–$1,999 prior to October 1969) are sampled.

The export statistics also exclude shipments to the U.S. Armed Forces and diplomatic missions abroad for their own use and supplies for vessels and planes engaged in foreign trade. Data on shipments valued at less than $251 ($100 prior to October 1969) are not compiled by commodity and are excluded from agricultural statistics but are reflected in nonagricultural and overall export totals. The agricultural export statistics include shipments under P.L. 83-480 (Agricultural Trade Development and Assistance Act), and related laws; under P.L. 87-195 (Act for International Development); and involving Government payments to exporters. (USDA payments are excluded from the export value.) Separate statistics on Government program exports are compiled by the U.S. Department of Agriculture from data obtained from operating agencies.

Imports for consumption are a combination of entries for immediate consumption and withdrawals from warehouses for consumption. The import value, defined generally as the market value in the foreign country, excludes import duties, ocean freight, and marine insurance. Low-valued shipments under $251 are reflected in nonagricultural and overall import totals.

K 256–285. Farm income and expenses, 1910–1970.

Source: U.S. Department of Agriculture, Economic Research Service, *The Farm Income Situation*, annual issues, and unpublished data.

These estimates refer to calendar-year income arising from commodities and services produced on farms, as defined in the Census of Agriculture, to the expenses associated with such production, and to other income received by persons living on farms.

Estimates of farm income were started in 1924 on a crop-year basis. In 1936, a legislative formula for income parity for agriculture, based on a 1910–1914 comparison of farm and nonfarm per capita incomes, resulted in an extensive project of research designed to extend the estimates back to 1910, to put them on a full calendar-year basis comparable with estimates of nonagricultural income, and to improve and expand the data in other respects.

No adequate statistics are available on farm income and expenses before 1910. Willford I. King's early estimates of the total value produced in agriculture go back to 1850, but for census years only (published in *The Wealth and Income of the People of the United States*, Macmillan Co., 1915). They were based on inadequate information and are not comparable with any of the current series. Without data for intercensal years, King's decennial figures may be misleading even as an indication of the long-term trend. The decennial projections back to 1800 prepared by the National Industrial Conference Board, *National Income in the United States, 1799–1938*, 1939, are in much the same category, and must be regarded only as very rough approximations. Annual estimates of gross farm income extending back to 1869, and covering a substantial part of total farm production, are given in Department of Agriculture, *Gross Farm Income and Indices of Farm Production and Prices in the United States, 1869–1937*, Technical Bulletin No. 703, December 1940. Although not comparable with any of the current series, these estimates are probably fairly reliable as an indication of trends in the gross value of farm production.

In the absence of any direct reporting of farm income on an adequate scale, estimates have been developed by indirect methods using available data on production, disposition, prices, and costs. The procedure followed has been to treat agriculture as one tremendous enterprise, and to derive its net income by first computing "gross income," series K 264–270, and then deducting aggregate expenses of production.

K 256–258, personal income of the farm population. Personal income of the farm population is the sum from farm and nonfarm sources. Personal income from farm sources, series K 257, is the total net income of farm operators, including government payments, *less* the net income of nonresident farm operators, *plus* wages and salaries and other labor income of farm resident workers, *less* contributions of farm resident operators and workers to social insurance. Personal income of the farm population from nonfarm sources, series K 258, consists of income received from nonfarm wages and salaries, business and professional income, interest, and transfer payments, such as unemployment compensation, social security, and veterans benefits. Also included is rental income from nonfarm sources and an estimate of income from items such as dividends and royalties. The figures for series K 256–258 are generally comparable throughout the period shown and are believed to be fairly complete and reliable despite the indirect methods of estimation. For a more detailed discussion and for other series, see *Major Statistical Series of the U.S. Department of Agriculture*, Agriculture Handbook No. 365, vol. 3.

K 259, farm operators' total net income. It is their realized income plus or minus the value of the net change in inventories. It is the figure included in the national income estimates of the U.S. Department of Commerce as farm proprietors' income. Series **K 260**, average per farm, is derived by dividing total net income by the number of farms as of January 1 each year.

K 264–270, realized gross income from farming. Figures for series K 264–270 are estimates of realized gross farm income and its principal components. These estimates are "gross" in the sense that they represent the total value of commodities and services produced by farms without any deduction for costs incurred in their production, and without any consideration of who reaps the ultimate benefit from their sale or use, whether it be a farm operator, a landlord, a farm laborer, or a bank. Cash receipts from farm marketings, in the case of crops, include all sales of crops by farmers, series K 266; purchases by other farmers for use as feed or seed are later deducted as production expenses. Similarly, in the case of livestock and products, series K 267, the estimates include all sales by farmers, with purchases of livestock by other farmers included as a production expense in series K 271–283.

For 1933–1970, realized gross farm income includes Government payments to farmers, series K 268. Indirect financial aid to farmers through commodity prices or loan values is covered in cash receipts from marketings. Government payments to landlords, as well as farm operators, are included but the former are also covered under farm production expense, series K 283, as rental payments to nonfarm landlords.

Realized gross farm income, series K 264, represents total cash farm income, series K 265; Government payments, series K 268; the value of farm-produced food and fuel consumed in farm households, series K 269; and an imputed rental value for all farm dwellings, series K 270. Farm-household consumption of farm products is valued at prices received for the sale of similar products. It includes food and fuel furnished to hired farm laborers, later deducted as a part of total labor costs to farm operators. The rental value of dwellings is on a gross basis; later deductions of rent, interest, taxes, insurance, maintenance, and depreciation are for farms as a whole with their buildings and equipment, and include shares allocable to farm dwellings.

The figures for cash receipts from marketings have been derived, commodity by commodity, from the periodic Crop Reporting Board estimates of production, disposition, price, and value. These estimates in turn are generally based on periodic census enumerations supplemented by regular reports from field statisticians, long lists of farmers, and special crop, livestock, and price correspondents, and by records and reports of public and private agencies concerned with the inspection, storage, marketing, transportation, or processing of farm products. Separate commodities or groups are shown in series K 286–302.

K 271–283, expenses of agricultural production. The figures for total farm-production expenses, series K 271–283, comprise the aggregate cost to farm operators, or all of that part of gross farm income not retained by farm operators. It includes (1) purchases of feed, livestock, seed, fertilizer, and lime; (2) outlays for the operation of tractors, trucks, and automobiles (excluding the portion assigned to family use); (3) a large number of other current farm operating expenses; (4) charges for maintenance and depreciation of farm buildings, motor vehicles, machinery, and equipment; (5) taxes levied on farm property; (6) wages paid for hired labor, both in cash and in kind; (7) interest paid on farm-mortgage loans; and (8) net rents paid to landlords not living on farms, including that part of Government payments that goes to such landlords and not to farm operators. Other farm rents paid to landlords who are also farm operators are not included, as they constitute offsetting items of income and cost for farm operators as a group.

The estimates of production expenses are generally based on the censuses of agriculture, supplemented by special surveys. For years other than census or survey years, estimates for a specific item have for the most part been derived from relative changes in similar or related series. A combination of two series is frequently used, one indicating changes in quantity, and the other, changes in price. For a few types of costs, however, the records of public or private agencies provide the basis for direct annual estimates.

K 284, realized net income of farm operators from farming. The figures are obtained by subtracting total production expenses from realized gross farm income. The term "realized" is used because the estimates include the value only of farm products sold.

K 285, net change in farm inventories. This series measures the change in physical quantities of livestock and crops on farms, valued at average prices prevailing during the year. For some purposes, particularly for combining with the national income estimates of the nonfarm economy, which measure the net value of production during the calendar year, it is necessary to take into account changes in farm inventories. However, it should be kept in mind that the value of a buildup in inventories is "unrealized" until sold and that prices realized at the time of sale may be considerably different from those prevailing during the year of accumulation.

K 286–302.　Farm income—cash receipts from farm marketings, 1910–1970.

Source: U.S. Department of Agriculture, Economic Research Service, *The Farm Income Situation*, annual issues.

Approximately 150 different commodities or commodity groups are included in the data on cash receipts from marketings. Only major groups are shown here. For crops under the Commodity Credit Corporation (CCC) loan program, a CCC loan is treated as a cash receipt. If the crop is later redeemed, the outlay required is treated as an offset to cash receipts.

See also text for series K 264–270.

K 303–325.　Farm marketings, by price support status, 1930–1970.

Source: See source for series K 286–302.

The Department of Agriculture has conducted price support programs for a number of agricultural products since 1933 when supports and production controls were authorized by the Agricultural Adjustment Act of 1933. The purpose of these programs is to provide farmers certain dollars-and-cents prices for specified products as an adjunct to orderly production and marketing practices. Price support is provided primarily through nonrecourse loans and purchase agreements with farmers or by purchases from processors and others. Sup-

plies acquired by the Department of Agriculture under such programs are stored and returned to commercial channels when needs arise.

Over the years subsequent legislation has often changed the number of commodities under support, the means of supporting prices, and the rules for determining the level of support. Mandatory commodities are those for which the Secretary of Agriculture must provide support; support for nonmandatory commodities is discretionary with the Secretary. Series K 303–325 lists farmers' cash receipts from marketings, by commodity, under legislation in effect in 1969. Marketings include gross receipts from commercial market sales as well as unredeemed loans and purchases under price support programs.

K 326–329.　Direct Government payments to farmers, by program, 1933–1970.

Source: See source for series K 286–302.

Direct Government payments to farmers are those made in connection with the farm programs shown in series K 326–329 (Conservation, Sugar Act, and Cotton), as well as those included in the total but not shown: Soil bank, wool, feed grain, wheat, rental and benefits, price adjustment and parity; wartime production subsidy; and cropland adjustment. These payments do not involve commodity transactions in the form of nonrecourse loans but are made directly to farmers who participate in specified farm programs.

K 330–343.　Commodity Credit Corporation—summary, 1934–1970.

Source: U.S. Department of Agriculture, Agricultural Stabilization and Conservation Service, *Commodity Credit Corporation Report of Financial Condition and Operations*, annual issues.

The Commodity Credit Corporation (CCC) is a wholly-owned Government corporation. Its purpose is stabilizing, supporting, and protecting farm income and prices; assisting in the maintenance of balanced and adequate supplies of agricultural commodities; and facilitating their orderly distribution. Originally incorporated October 17, 1933, with a capitalization of $3 million, CCC was initially managed and operated in close affiliation with the Reconstruction Finance Corporation, which funded its on-going operations. On July 1, 1939, it was transferred to the Department of Agriculture by the President's Reorganization Plan I; and on July 1, 1948, it was reincorporated as a Federal corporation within the Department of Agriculture by the Commodity Credit Corporation Charter Act. Management of CCC is vested in a Board of Directors, subject to the general supervision and direction of the Secretary of Agriculture. The Board consists of six members, in addition to the Secretary as chairman, who are appointed by the President of the United States by and with the advice and consent of the Senate.

CCC has an authorized capital stock of $100 million held by the United States and authority to borrow up to $14.5 billion from the U.S. Treasury and from private lending agencies. Each year CCC submits, in the budget of the United States, the programs it expects to carry out in the coming year. Upon approval of the budget by the Congress, this becomes its basic operating plan for the fiscal year.

CCC's price support programs, and domestic acquisition and disposal activities for price support commodities, are carried out entirely through the Agricultural Stabilization and Conservation Service (ASCS).

Commodity support programs include (1970) those for wheat, corn, cotton (upland and extra long staple), rice, tobacco, milk and milk products, wool, mohair, tung nuts, barley, oats, grain sorghum, rye, flaxseed, soybeans, dry edible beans, honey, crude pine gum, and peanuts. These support operations are handled primarily through loan, purchase, and payment programs.

CCC is directed to utilize, to the maximum extent practicable, the customary channels, facilities, and arrangements of trade and commerce in carrying on purchasing and selling activities, and in conducting warehousing, transporting, processing, and handling operations.

CCC may contract for the use of plants and facilities for the handling, storing, processing, servicing, and transporting of agricultural commodities subject to its control; it has authority to acquire personal property and to rent or lease office space necessary for the conduct of its business.

Commodities from the price support inventory are moved into consumption outlets in various ways. Some commodities are sold for domestic uses in the United States, and some are sold for export, including those under the CCC Export Sales Program and programs authorized under Title I of Public Law 480. Some commodities are bartered for goods and services to fill U.S. Government needs abroad, and for foreign produced strategic and critical materials for stockpiling. In addition, commodities are donated through Federal, State, and private agencies for use in child nutrition programs and in the assistance of needy persons in the United States; commodities are transferred for donation through U.S. welfare organizations and intergovernmental organizations to needy persons and child feeding programs abroad; and dairy products are transferred for use by the Veterans Administration and by the Department of Defense. Some grains are donated to aid livestock producers in declared acute economic distress and major disaster areas; some grains are sold at reduced prices to livestock producers in areas where feed is short due to drought, flood, hurricane, or other catastrophe.

K 344–353. Indexes of prices received and paid by farmers, and parity ratio, 1910–1970.

Source: U.S. Department of Agriculture, Statistical Reporting Service, *Agricultural Prices: Annual Summary*, various issues.

The indexes of prices received and paid by farmers are compiled from the series of prices received by farmers for commodities sold and the series of prices paid by farmers for commodities bought.

The basic concept involved in series K 344–346 is that of a price which, if multiplied by the total quantity of the commodity sold, would give the total amount received by all farmers for that commodity. That is, prices received by farmers are estimated to reflect sales of all classes and grades of the commodity being sold. They reflect discounts for poor quality and premiums for high quality. Estimates relate generally to average prices farmers receive for their products at the point of first sale, usually at a local market, or at the point to which farmers deliver their products.

The Statistical Reporting Service (SRS) estimates midmonth or monthly average prices each month for about 95 of the more important crop and livestock items, and for 17 seasonal items in season. Prices of about 100 additional items are estimated on an annual or season average basis only. These crops have either relatively short marketing seasons, are of relatively minor importance, or are used for processing and sold mainly on contracts covering the entire season.

Prices received by farmers for products they sell were collected from various primary sources, but mostly from voluntary reporters. In general, price reporters were classified in the following broad groups: (1) Country merchants; (2) farm produce dealers at local shipping points; (3) country mill and elevator operators; (4) Federal Milk Market Administrators; (5) State milk control agencies; (6) managers of milk distributing or manufacturing plants; (7) cooperative marketing organizations; (8) country bankers; and (9) well-informed farmers.

Most of the data on prices received were collected by means of a mailed questionnaire supplemented by enumerative checks of various types, depending on the commodities in question. Prices of beef cattle were collected by enumeration of actual sales by commission firms and to buyers at auctions in a number of States.

Estimates of prices paid by farmers, series K 347 and K 348, relate to average prices paid for a wide variety of items. The prices were obtained from the sellers and considered as being at the seller's location, unless otherwise specified. Since prices received were estimated to reflect sales of all classes and grades of the commodity being sold, a comparable concept was used in connection with prices paid, so

as to reflect changes in items bought by farmers, such as grade, quality, and size of container; that is, to reflect the average price of things farmers bought under the economic conditions existing at the time of purchase.

Ideally, to maintain conceptual similarity to prices received, the price paid for a given item should be the average price which results from dividing the total amount farmers spent for the item in a given period by the number of items bought. However, it was impossible to obtain the data needed for such a computation, and in pricing most items emphasis was placed on the kind "most commonly bought by farmers," or the "volume seller," as the closest approximation.

The commodity coverage of the prices paid series embraced most, but not all, of the major areas of expenditure and each area was represented by a sample of items. The areas covered were divided into two main groups, those bought for family living (food, clothing, household furnishings, household operation, autos and auto supplies, and building materials bought for farm home construction and repair), and those bought for production purposes (feed, feeder livestock, motor supplies, motor vehicles, farm machinery, building materials for service buildings, fencing materials, fertilizer, farm supplies, and seed). Farm family expenditures excluded medical, dental, and hospital services; a variety of personal and financial services; and services performed on a custom or fee basis such as hay baling, threshing, plowing, spraying, fertilizing, and the like.

Prices paid information was collected from samples consisting mainly of stores handling commodities purchased by farmers. Farmers comprise the data source for certain commodities or services such as feeder pigs purchased and cost of electric or telephone service.

The index of prices received by farmers is a measure of the changes in average prices that farmers receive for agricultural commodities that they sell. The parity index (index of prices paid by farmers for commodities and services, including interest, taxes, and wage rates) is a measure of changes in average prices paid by farmers for goods and services used in family living and in production, together with interest, taxes, and farm wage rates. The base period for both is 1910–14, by law. A third important measure, known as the parity ratio, consists of the relationship between these two indexes, series K 353. The parity ratio measures the purchasing power of products sold by farmers in terms of things they buy compared to their purchasing power in the base period 1910–14. As of any given date it is computed by dividing the index of prices received by farmers by the parity index. If the result is above 100, products sold by farmers have an average per unit purchasing power higher than in 1910–14. When the result is below 100, the average per unit purchasing power of commodities sold by farmers is less than in the base period.

The parity ratio approximates a weighted average of the percentages of parity for individual farm commodities, but is not exact, mostly for the reason that the index of prices received by farmers is based on 56 of the most important commodities sold by farmers, but not all of them. The parity ratio is a price comparison. It is not a measure of cost of production, standard of living, or income parity.

The last general revision of these indexes was made January 1, 1959, at which time a detailed description of the weighting structure and sources was published in *The January 1959 Revision of the Price Indexes*. For the parity index the weighting pattern for the 450-price series in the index was derived from a survey of farmers' expenditure patterns in 1955. The quantity weights applied to the various price series represent the average quantities of each commodity bought by farmers during 1955. For the index of prices received by farmers the quantity weights were the average quantities of farm products sold by farmers over the 5-year period centered on 1955, that is 1953–57. Since 1955, only minor shifts in commodities have been made as certain new items have replaced older ones. The description of the indexes published in 1959 is still applicable. However, the 1910–14 base required by law is now over 50 years distant. To provide comparability with other national indexes, the index of prices received by farmers and the parity index were converted to the 1967 base prescribed by the Office of Management and Budget, for use by Federal agencies generally. However, mere arithmetic conversion to a different reference base is no substitute for initial computation of the indexes on a modern base.

To find any extensive list of commodities commonly bought both now and a half-century ago is obviously impossible. What has been done as the best possible alternative is to construct these indexes in three links. The first link covers the period 1910 to March 1935, and uses commodities common to that period and weights based on data representing an average for 1924–29. The second link covers the period March 1935 to September 1952, using commodities common to that period and weights representative of 1937–41. The third link runs from September 1952 to the present (1970), and uses weights representing 1955 for the parity index and 1953–57 for prices received. Each of these links provides reasonable homogeneity in commodity structure and a reasonably good measure of price relationships over the period covered. By linking the three indexes together, a comparison of the present with 1910–14 is provided as required by law.

K 354–357. Farm-to-retail price spreads of farm food products, 1913–1970.

Source: U.S. Department of Agriculture, Economic Research Service, *Farm-Retail Spreads for Food Products*, Miscellaneous Publication No. 741, 1972.

The market basket contains the average quantities of domestic farm-originated food products purchased annually per household in 1960–1961 by wage earners, clerical-worker families, and workers living alone. To maintain comparability, the 1961–1962 market basket was linked at 1957 to a market basket containing the quantity of farm food purchased annually by wage earner and clerical-worker families in 1952. The series was also linked at 1947 to a market basket containing the quantities of food purchased annually by a family in 1935–1939. Dollar values for 1913–1946 were derived from index numbers published in the source. Current data are published by the Economic Research Service in *The Marketing and Transportation Situation*.

Retail costs are calculated from retail prices published by the Bureau of Labor Statistics. The retail cost of market basket foods is less than the cost of all foods bought per household because it does not include the cost of meals in eating places, imported foods, and seafood or other foods not of farm origin. Farm value represents payments to farmers, exclusive of government subsidies, for unprocessed products equivalent to the foods in the market basket. The farm-retail spread is the difference between retail cost and farm value. It represents the total gross margin received by marketing firms for assembling, processing, transporting, and distributing the products of the market basket.

K 358–360. Consumer expenditures, farm value, and marketing bill, for all farm food products purchased by domestic civilian consumers, 1913–1970.

Source: U.S. Department of Agriculture, Agricultural Marketing Service, 1913–1947, *Farm-Retail Spreads for Food Products*, Miscellaneous Publication No. 741, 1957; Economic Research Service, revised figures for 1929, 1935, and 1939, *The Farm Food Marketing Bill and Its Components*, AER No. 105, 1967; 1947–1970, *Marketing and Transportation Situation*, August 1971.

Consumer expenditures for farm foods, series K 358, represent the market value of foods originating on U.S. farms and purchased by or for civilian consumers in this country. Included are expenditures for food in retail stores and for food bought directly from farmers, processors, and wholesalers and served in restaurants and other away-from-home eating establishments; the value of food served by schools, hospitals, and other institutions, and of food furnished by employers to civilian employees; and sales taxes and tips. Excluded are expenditures for imported foods, fish and other foods not originating on U.S. farms, and alcoholic beverages; the value of food furnished by

the Government to members of the Armed Services; and the value of food consumed on farms where it is produced.

Farm value, series K 359, is the value at the point of sale by the farmer of the farm products equivalent to foods purchased by or for civilian consumers. It does not include the imputed values of nonfood byproducts derived from processing farm food products.

The marketing bill, series K 360, is an estimate of the total cost of transporting, processing, and distributing U.S. farm-originated foods purchased by civilian consumers. It is the difference between consumer expenditures and farm value. Unlike the farm food market basket statistics, series K 354–357, the marketing bill statistics are affected by changes in the volume and type of products marketed and in the quantity of marketing services per unit of product marketed. For example, marketing services per unit of product change when the volume of foods served in eating establishments increases or decreases relative to the volume moving through retail food stores. They may also change when the volume of processed products changes relative to the volume of unprocessed products.

Benchmark estimates of consumer expenditures, farm value, and the marketing bill have been made for census years back to 1929 for the revised series by the commodity flow method. Annual estimates, derived by a less comprehensive method, have been used to interpolate for interbenchmark years back to 1947 and to extrapolate for years since the last benchmark estimate (1958). See *Major Statistical Series of the U.S. Department of Agriculture*, Agriculture Handbook No. 365, vol. 4.

K 361–369. Farm-mortgage debt outstanding and loans closed, 1910–1970.

Source: 1910–1928, U.S. Department of Agriculture, Agricultural Research Service and Economic Research Service; U.S. Bureau of the Census; Farm Credit Administration; and Federal Deposit Insurance Corporation. For specific sources, see below. 1929–1970, U.S. Department of Agriculture, Statistical Reporting Service, *Agricultural Statistics, 1967* and *1972* issues. See also *Major Statistical Series of the U.S. Department of Agriculture*, Agriculture Handbook No. 365, vol. 6.

Farm-mortgage credit has been referred to as farm-real-estate credit, long-term credit, or capital credit. The data presented here, however, merely represent the amount of credit secured by farm real estate, whether it is extended for a short term or a long term, whether it is used for purchasing the farm, operating the farm, or financing nonagricultural activities, and whether the loan instrument is a mortgage, deed of trust, vendor's lien, or sales contract.

Estimates of farm-mortgage debt outstanding at the beginning of each year, series K 361, are based upon census data and special surveys. Data on mortgage debt on farms operated by full owners appear in each census back to 1890, except that for 1900. In 1890, 1940, 1945, 1950, 1956, 1961, and 1966, similar information was collected on the owned part of part-owner farms.

Mortgage data may be found in the following reports of the Bureau of the Census: Eleventh Census, 1890, *Report on Real Estate Mortgages*; Thirteenth Census, 1910, *Agriculture*, vol. V, chap. 3; Fourteenth Census, 1920, *Agriculture*, vol. V, chap. 7; Census of Agriculture, 1925, *Summary Statistics by States*; Fifteenth Census, 1930, *Agriculture*, vol. IV, chap. 6; Sixteenth Census, 1940, *Agriculture*, vol. III, chap. 4; *Census of Agriculture, 1964*, vol. III, Special Reports, pt. 4, Farm Debt. Data for 1935, 1945, 1950, 1956, and 1961 are in three cooperative publications—Bureau of the Census and Bureau of Agricultural Economics, *U.S. Census of Agriculture: 1950*, vol. V, pt. 8; Bureau of the Census and Agricultural Research Service, *U.S. Census of Agriculture: 1954*, vol. III, pt. 5; and Bureau of the Census and Economic Research Service, *U.S. Census of Agriculture: 1959*, vol. V, pt. 4.

In 1920, 1928, and 1930 the Bureau of Agricultural Economics conducted surveys on which estimates of debt on farms operated by part owners, tenants, and managers were based. The Bureau of the Census and the Bureau of Agricultural Economics cooperated in the 1935, 1940, 1945, 1950, 1956, and 1961 surveys. The Bureau of the Census conducted the 1966 survey. The results of the 1928 survey, which included 1925 data, were published in Department of Agriculture, *Farm-Mortgage Credit*, Technical Bulletin No. 288, February 1932. Results of the later surveys appear in the three cooperative publications and *Census of Agriculture: 1964*, Special Report, referred to above. Some earlier census-year estimates were revised on the basis of relationships established by the more recent surveys to make estimates for all census years more comparable.

Estimates for intercensal years are based on data for mortgages held by certain lending agencies, on estimates of farm mortgages recorded annually by major lender groups, and on the distribution by lenders of farm-mortgage debt in the last preceding census. Whenever a new census-year benchmark was established, the intercensal-year estimates were revised to reflect the new trend. For the years prior to 1935, the data on mortgages recorded were compiled from the records of selected counties through a nationwide Works Progress Administration project sponsored by the Bureau of Agricultural Economics. For 1935–1970, this information was collected by the Farm Credit Administration. Revisions of annual debt estimates for 1950–1957 appear in Agricultural Research Service, *Farm-Mortgage Debt Rises in 1957*, ARS 43–59, September 1957. A number of publications of the Bureau of Agricultural Economics contain annual estimates of farm-mortgage debt revised to the last census-year benchmark preceding the date of publication: *Revised Annual Estimates of Farm-Mortgage Debt by States, 1930–1943*, April 1944; *Distribution by Lender Groups of Farm-Mortgage and Real Estate Holdings, January 1, 1930–1945*, August 1945; *Farm-Mortgage Loans and Their Distribution by Lender Groups, 1940–1948*, USDA Circular No. 812, August 1949; *Agricultural Finance Review*, vol. 15 supplement I, May 1953, which has annual data by States for 1945–1953; *Farm Mortgage Debt*, FMD-1, May 1963, which has annual data by States for 1950–1962; *Farm Mortgage Debt*, FMD-3, October 1964, which has annual data by States for 1963–1964; *Farm Mortgage Debt*, FMD-5, October 1966, which has annual data by States for 1965–1966; *Farm Mortgage Debt*, FMD-7, December 1968, which has annual data by States for 1967–1968; *Farm Mortgage Debt*, FMD-9, November 1970, which has annual data by States for 1960–1970.

K 362 and **K 368**, Federal land banks and FFMC. The Federal land banks were organized pursuant to the Federal Farm Loan Act of 1916 and became important lenders in the farm-mortgage field, particularly after 1933. The data on loans outstanding and loans closed are from publications of the Farm Credit Administration or its predecessor, the Federal Farm Loan Board. Land Bank Commissioner loans, first made under the authority of the Emergency Farm-Mortgage Act of 1933, were taken over by the Federal Farm Mortgage Corporation upon its creation in 1934 and were continued until July 1, 1947, when authority to make new loans, except those incidental to liquidation, expired. In 1955, the remaining outstanding loans of the Corporation were sold to the Federal land banks. For a discussion of these agencies, see Department of Agriculture, *Farm-Mortgage Credit Facilities in the United States*, Miscellaneous Publication No. 478, 1942, and annual reports of the Farm Credit Administration.

K 363, life insurance companies. Figures on farm-mortgage debt held by life insurance companies are estimates of the Bureau of Agricultural Economics, the Agricultural Research Service, and the Economic Research Service, and refer to unpaid principal owed to the companies. The estimates are compiled from reports of life insurance companies, "Best's Life Insurance Reports," "Spectator Life Insurance Yearbook," and data from the Life Insurance Association of America and the Institute of Life Insurance. The data for 1910–1929 include the unpaid principal of regular mortgages only; for 1930–1970, they also include the unpaid principal of purchase-money mortgages and, prior to 1965, farm real estate sales contracts. Beginning 1965, they exclude sales contracts. See also the following Department of Agriculture publications: *Farm-Mortgage Loans Held by Life Insurance Companies*, ARS 43–58, October 1957; *Farm Investments of Life Insurance Companies, 1956*, ARS 43–57, October 1956; and *Farm-Mortgage Investments of Life Insurance Companies*, December 1943.

K 364, commercial and savings banks. Figures on farm-mortgage debt held by commercial and savings banks for 1910–1947 do not cover all banks, but they do represent a very large proportion of all bank loans on farm real estate. For 1910–1934, the data include only open State and national banks, and are estimates prepared by the Bureau of Agricultural Economics from special surveys and reports of bank supervisory authorities. (See *Agricultural Loans of Commercial Banks*, USDA Technical Bulletin No. 521, July 1936, for a discussion of these special surveys.) For 1935–1947, the data include only farm-mortgage loans of insured commercial banks as summarized in reports of the Federal Deposit Insurance Corporation. For 1948–1970, the data include farm-mortgage debt held by all operating banks—commercial, savings, and private—as compiled by the Federal Deposit Insurance Corporation and published in annual reports of the Comptroller of the Currency, and also bank holdings of soil and water loans and farm-ownership loans insured by the Farmers Home Administration. Sales contracts on farm real estate may or may not be included in the figures, because banks often classify such contracts with the real estate owned. The figures do not include loans of closed banks, of mutual savings banks before 1948, nor of noninsured commercial banks for 1935–1947.

K 365 and **K 369**, joint-stock land banks. The joint-stock land banks also authorized under the Federal Farm Loan Act of 1916, were under Federal supervision and regulation, but differed from the Federal land banks in that they were privately owned. Their organization and growth are discussed in C. H. Schwartz, Jr., *Financial Study of the Joint-Stock Land Banks*, Washington College Press, Takoma Park, Md., 1938, as well as in the publications cited above for Federal land banks. Liquidation of the joint-stock banks was called for in the Emergency Farm Mortgage Act of 1933 and was completed in 1951. For several Federal and federally sponsored agencies, "loans closed" include only their regular loans as distinct from purchase-money mortgages and sales contracts, and they are not necessarily comparable with "loans recorded" by other lender groups.

K 366, Farmers Home Administration. Data from the Farmers Home Administration, formerly Farm Security Administration, include farm-purchase, farm-enlargement, farm-development, project-liquidation, and direct soil and water loans to individuals, loans for these purposes from State Corporation trust funds, and rural-housing loans to farmers.

K 367, individuals and others. Individuals are by far the most important holders of farm mortgages. Because of its residual nature, this general lender group also includes many miscellaneous sources of farm-mortgage credit, including mortgage, real estate, finance, and investment companies; State and local governmental agencies; religious, educational, civic, and fraternal organizations; mercantile firms dealing largely in farm supplies; lending agencies operating chiefly in the urban mortgage field but sometimes lending on farmland; corporations and associations chiefly engaged in making production loans but sometimes requiring real estate as security. In addition to these are the loans of mutual savings banks, for 1910–1947; closed commercial banks; noninsured commercial banks for 1935–1947; insurance companies other than life insurance companies; and certain types of loans not specifically included in the figures for the major lending groups.

K 370–372. Interest payable on farm mortgages, 1910–1970.

Source: 1910–1948, U.S. Department of Agriculture, Agricultural Research Service and Farm Credit Administration, unpublished data; **series K 370**, 1949–1964, Economic Research Service, annual releases with various titles; 1965–1969, *Agricultural Finance Review* and supplements, annual volumes; **series K 371–372**, 1949–1970, Statistical Reporting Service, *Agricultural Statistics, 1967* and *1972* issues, and Economic Research Service, *Agricultural Finance Review*, vol. 32 supplement, January 1972.

These data represent average contract rates. They are averages of the rates charged by the various types of lenders weighted by the amount of mortgages recorded or held by each. Furthermore, they are averages of rates on all farm mortgages regardless of their priority. Year-to-year changes in the average rates do not necessarily reflect changes in the level of interest rates charged by the different lenders but may represent changes in the distribution among the lender groups of loans recorded or held. The averages are based on the rates specified in the mortgage contract and payable by borrowers during the calendar year; they do not necessarily represent averages of the rates actually paid, except that for rates on outstanding mortgages, they do reflect the temporarily reduced rates of the Federal land banks for 1934–1944 and of the Federal Farm Mortgage Corporation for 1938–1945.

Some information either on interest rates or interest charges on outstanding mortgages was obtained in the censuses of agriculture for 1890, 1920, 1930, and 1940.

K 370, interest rates on loans recorded. Interest rates on mortgages recorded come from two sources. Rates for 1910–1935 were developed from data obtained in a nationwide Works Progress Administration project sponsored by the Bureau of Agricultural Economics (see that agency's *Average Rates of Interest Charged on Farm-Mortgage Recordings of Selected Lender Groups,* November 1940).

The averages for odd-numbered years from 1941 to 1953 are estimates of the Farm Credit Administration based on mortgages recorded during the month of March in approximately one-third of the counties in the United States. For 1955–1965, the average interest rates are based on mortgages recorded in the first quarter of the year. For 1967 and 1969, the average interest rates are based on mortgages recorded in the first half of the year.

K 371, interest rates on loans outstanding. Average interest rates on outstanding mortgages for 1937–1970 are based on data obtained by the Bureau of Agricultural Economics, the Economic Research Service, the Agricultural Research Service, and the Bureau of the Census in special surveys made in census years and from Farm Credit Administration surveys of farm-mortgage recordings made in selected months of intercensal years. For 1910–1936, the rates are based on the WPA data mentioned above. Rates on mortgages recorded as reported in the WPA project were converted to rates on outstanding mortgages by assuming that all mortgages recorded remained in effect for a period equal to the average of the terms of years specified in the mortgage contracts. This procedure was used for all lender groups except the Federal land banks and Federal Farm Mortgage Corporation for which averages were computed from information on the amount of loans outstanding at various interest rates. (See Bureau of Agricultural Economics, *Interest Charges Payable on Farm Indebtedness in the United States, 1910–40,* August 1942.) Some of the data for years after 1930 were later revised; see Bureau of Agricultural Economics, *Revised Annual Estimates of Interest Charges and Interest Rates on Farm-Mortgage Debt, 1930–43,* October 1944, and USDA Circular No. 821, *Farm-Mortgage Interest Charges and Interest Rates, 1940–48,* October 1949.

K 372, interest charges payable. Figures for interest charges payable were developed from the estimates of farm-mortgage debt outstanding at the beginning of each year and the average interest rates charged thereon, except in the case of the Federal land banks and the Federal Farm Mortgage Corporation. Calendar-year estimates were computed by averaging the charges payable on debts outstanding at the beginning of each year and the beginning of the succeeding year. For the Federal land banks and the Federal Farm Mortgage Corporation, the actual amounts of interest charges payable on their outstanding loans during the calendar year were obtained from the Farm Credit Administration. These amounts, of course, excluded those charges no longer payable because of the interest reductions granted to borrowers.

K 373–375. Taxes levied on farm property, 1890–1970.

Source: U.S. Department of Agriculture, Economic Research Service, **series K 373–374,** *Farm Real Estate Taxes, Recent Trends and De-*

velopments, January 1972; **series K 375,** 1924–1967, *Personal Property Taxes Levied on Farmers, 1950 to 1967,* Statistical Bulletin No. 447, March 1970; 1968–1970, unpublished data.

These data cover all ad valorem taxes levied upon farm property by State and local governments. They do not cover special assessments such as those levied by drainage, irrigation, or other special districts. Farm real estate comprises all land defined by the Bureau of the Census as land in farms, and structures thereon (see general note for series K 1–203). Farm personal property covers all livestock, machinery, automobiles, trucks, produce, and household and personal effects. Much personal property on farms is not taxed, either because of statutory exemptions or through faulty assessment.

Taxes include those levied on farm property whether owned by the operator or not. They do not necessarily represent taxes paid by farmers. "Levies" rather than "payments" are shown because the timing of actual payments is uncertain.

Real estate tax figures are developed from data for sample farms obtained from local tax officials and from data in the censuses of agriculture for 1930, 1940, 1950, and 1960. The acreages used in computing taxes per acre are census data for farmland in private ownership, with interpolations for intercensal years. The values used in computing taxes per $100 of value are based on census data of operator estimates of value, with interpolations for intercensal years based on the ERS index of farmland values. For a more detailed discussion, see U.S. Department of Agriculture, *Major Statistical Series of the U.S. Department of Agriculture,* Agriculture Handbook 365, vol. 6.

Personal property tax figures are developed from statistical data on assessed values and taxes published by State tax commissions, boards of equalization, or similar bodies.

K 376–380. Non-real-estate agricultural loans outstanding, 1910–1970.

Source: **Series K 376–379,** 1910–1934 and 1936–1938, Federal Farm Loan Board and Farm Credit Administration, unpublished data; 1939 and 1941–1944, U.S. Department of Agriculture, Statistical Reporting Service, *Agricultural Statistics, 1967*; 1935, 1940, and 1945–1970, Economic Research Service, *Agricultural Finance Review,* vol. 32 supplement, January 1972. **Series K 380,** 1934–1938, see source for series K 376–379; 1939–1970, *Agricultural Statistics, 1967* and *1972* issues.

See also specific sources mentioned below.

Non-real-estate credit, variously called short-term credit, personal and collateral credit, or production credit, is obtained by farmers from many sources including banks, Federal and federally sponsored credit agencies, merchants, dealers, commission men, finance companies, landlords, and other individuals. Commercial banks have provided the bulk of this type of credit extended by credit institutions although, since the early 1930's, Federal and federally sponsored agencies and finance companies have become important in this lending field. The volume of non-real-estate credit extended by sources other than banks and Federal agencies is believed to have been about $3½ billion in recent years; however, data for precise estimates are lacking.

Since 1939, non-real-estate agricultural loan data of all operating commercial banks have been available from the Comptroller of the Currency and the Federal Deposit Insurance Corporation. Since 1936, similar loans of insured commercial banks, whose loans comprise about 97 percent of the loans of all banks, have been regularly reported by the Federal Deposit Insurance Corporation. For earlier years, the only data of this type available are from Department of Agriculture surveys made in 1914, 1918, 1921, 1924, 1931, 1934, and 1936, all of which (except for 1936) are discussed in that Department's *Agricultural Loans of Commercial Banks,* Technical Bulletin No. 521, July 1936. Upon the basis of these survey data and of data on all loans of "country" national banks for intervening years, estimates have been made back to 1910. See *Agricultural Finance Review,* "Short-Term Agricultural Loans of Commercial Banks, 1910–1945," vol. 8, November 1945; and *Major Statistical Series of the U.S. Department of Agriculture,* Agriculture Handbook No. 365, vol. 6.

The Federal Government first entered the non-real-estate agricultural credit field in 1918 when it made available $5 million for direct loans to farmers in the Northwest and Southwest where there had been two successive crop failures. During the 1920's, seed and feed loans were made available from time to time in certain "distressed" areas by special Acts of Congress. In the early 1930's, the basis for lending was broadened and the Emergency Crop and Feed Loan Office came to be the more-or-less permanent source of credit for farmers in distress. The Farmers Home Administration Act of 1946 transferred the activities of the Emergency Crop and Feed Loan Office from the Farm Credit Administration to the newly created Farmers Home Administration (successor to the Farm Security Administration) and provided for the liquidation of these loans. Thereafter, any loans of this character were made by the Farmers Home Administration under the provisions of the new law and are not included in this series. For a further discussion of the crop and feed loan program, see Department of Agriculture, *Federal Seed-Loan Financing and Its Relation to Agricultural Rehabilitation and Land Use*, Technical Bulletin No. 539, October 1936; and reports of the Farm Credit Administration.

The Agricultural Credits Act of 1923 created the Federal intermediate credit banks, the first permanent federally sponsored credit agencies making non-real-estate loans available to farmers. These banks make no loans directly to farmers, but they do make loans to and discount loans for private financing institutions (agricultural credit corporations and livestock loan companies). Loans discounted by the Federal intermediate credit banks for the production credit associations since their organization in 1933 are not included here. See Frieda Baird and Claude L. Benner, *Ten Years of Federal Intermediate Credits*, The Brookings Institution, Washington, D.C., 1933; and reports of the Farm Credit Administration.

The same 1923 Act also authorized the Federal intermediate credit banks to provide loans to and discounts for agricultural cooperatives; that is, direct loans to marketing cooperatives on the security of commodities. In 1933, special legislation authorized the creation of the "banks for cooperatives," which, by 1936, had largely taken over the function of the intermediate credit banks in making loans to cooperatives. A part of the loan funds of the "banks for cooperatives," however, is supplied by the Federal intermediate credit banks.

K 381–383. Indexes of deposits of country banks, 1925–1970.

Source: 1926–1929, 1931–1934, 1936–1939, 1941–1944, data compiled by U.S. Department of Agriculture, Economic Research Service, and are unpublished; 1925, 1930, 1935, 1940, 1945–1970, Statistical Reporting Service, *Agricultural Statistics, 1972*.

The indexes for demand, time, and total deposits are based upon deposits of member banks of the Federal Reserve System, located in places of less than 15,000 inhabitants in the 20 leading agricultural States. Prior to 1966, annual indexes are simple averages of monthly indexes, which are based on average amounts of daily deposits. Beginning 1966, data available were as of June 30 and December 31. In preparing indexes for groups of States, the amount of deposits for each State were weighted by the cash farm income of each State in the base period. Beginning December 1959, U.S. Government deposits are excluded from the base data for demand deposits. See Department of Agriculture, *Demand Deposits of Country Banks*, Technical Bulletin No. 575, August 1937; *Agricultural Finance Review Supplement*, vol. 32 supplement, January 1972; and *Major Statistical Series of the U.S. Department of Agriculture*, Agriculture Handbook No. 365, vol. 6.

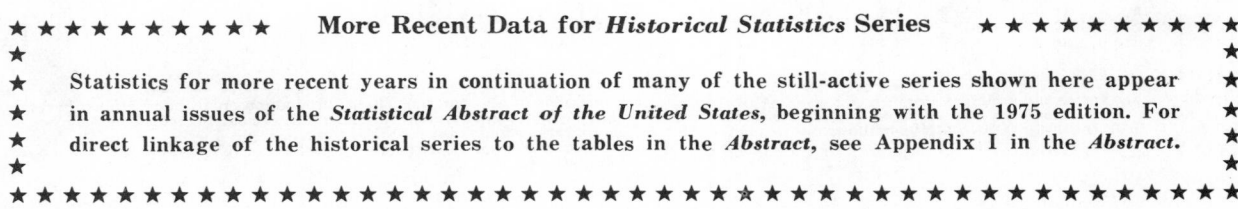

★ ★ ★ ★ ★ ★ ★ ★ ★   **More Recent Data for *Historical Statistics* Series**   ★ ★ ★ ★ ★ ★ ★ ★ ★

Statistics for more recent years in continuation of many of the still-active series shown here appear in annual issues of the *Statistical Abstract of the United States*, beginning with the 1975 edition. For direct linkage of the historical series to the tables in the *Abstract*, see Appendix I in the *Abstract*.

Series K 204–219. Balance Sheet of the Farming Sector: 1940 to 1970

[In billions of dollars. As of January 1. Excludes Alaska and Hawaii]

	Total	Assets								Claims					
		Physical					Financial			Total	Liabilities				Propri-etors' equities
		Real estate	Nonreal estate				Deposits and currency	U.S. savings bonds	Invest-ment in coopera-tives		Total	Real estate debt	Nonreal estate debt		
Year			Live-stock and poultry [1]	Ma-chinery and motor vehicles	Crops stored on and off farms [2]	House-hold equip-ment and furnish-ings							Com-modity Credit Corpora-tion (CCC) [3]	Other report-ing institu-tions [4]	Non-institu-tional credi-tors [5]	
	204	205	206	207	208	209	210	211	212	213	214	215	216	217	218	219
1970	305.8	207.1	23.5	31.8	10.9	9.7	11.9	3.7	7.2	305.8	58.1	28.4	2.7	15.8	11.2	247.7
1969	294.8	201.5	20.2	30.9	10.6	9.6	11.5	3.7	6.8	294.8	54.6	27.1	2.7	14.5	10.3	240.2
1968	280.1	192.0	18.8	29.5	9.6	9.0	10.9	3.8	6.5	280.1	50.4	25.5	1.4	13.7	9.8	229.7
1967	266.8	181.8	18.9	27.3	10.0	8.4	10.3	3.9	6.2	266.8	45.7	23.3	1.2	12.4	8.8	221.1
1966	253.8	172.2	17.6	25.8	9.7	8.6	10.0	4.0	5.9	253.8	41.6	21.2	1.4	11.1	7.9	212.2
1965	237.2	160.9	14.4	24.7	9.2	8.6	9.6	4.2	5.6	237.2	37.6	18.9	1.5	10.0	7.2	199.6
1964	229.2	152.1	15.8	23.9	9.8	8.8	9.2	4.2	5.4	229.2	34.9	16.8	1.9	9.5	6.7	194.3
1963	221.4	143.8	17.3	23.4	9.3	9.0	9.2	4.4	5.0	221.4	31.7	15.2	2.0	8.5	6.0	189.7
1962	212.8	138.0	16.4	22.5	8.8	9.1	8.8	4.4	4.8	212.8	28.7	13.9	1.9	7.5	5.4	184.1
1961	204.2	131.8	15.5	22.2	8.0	8.9	8.7	4.6	4.5	204.2	26.2	12.8	1.4	7.0	5.0	178.0
1960	203.5	130.2	15.2	22.7	7.7	9.6	9.2	4.7	4.2	203.5	24.8	12.1	1.1	6.7	4.9	178.7
1959	202.1	124.4	17.7	21.8	9.3	9.8	10.0	5.2	3.9	202.1	23.6	11.1	2.5	5.7	4.3	178.5
1958	185.8	115.9	13.9	20.2	7.6	9.9	9.5	5.1	3.7	185.8	20.4	10.4	1.2	5.0	3.8	165.4
1957	177.9	110.4	11.0	20.2	8.3	10.0	9.4	5.1	3.5	177.9	19.3	9.8	1.5	4.5	3.5	158.6
1956	169.6	102.9	10.6	19.3	8.4	10.5	9.5	5.2	3.2	169.6	18.8	9.0	1.9	4.4	3.5	150.8
1955	165.1	98.2	11.2	18.6	9.6	10.0	9.4	5.0	3.1	165.1	17.6	8.2	2.2	4.0	3.2	147.5
1954	161.2	95.0	11.7	18.4	9.2	9.9	9.4	4.7	2.9	161.2	16.9	7.7	2.4	3.7	3.1	144.3
1953	164.3	96.5	14.8	17.4	9.0	9.9	9.4	4.6	2.7	164.3	16.1	7.2	1.2	4.2	3.5	148.2
1952	167.0	95.1	19.5	16.7	8.8	10.3	9.4	4.7	2.5	167.0	14.7	6.7	.6	4.1	3.3	152.3
1951	151.5	86.6	17.1	14.1	7.9	9.7	9.1	4.7	2.3	151.5	13.1	6.1	.8	3.4	2.8	138.4
1950	132.5	75.3	12.9	12.2	7.6	8.6	9.1	4.7	2.1	132.5	12.4	5.6	1.7	2.8	2.3	120.1
1949	134.9	76.6	14.4	10.1	8.6	9.1	9.6	4.6	1.9	134.9	11.4	5.3	1.2	2.7	2.2	123.5
1948	127.9	73.7	13.3	7.4	9.0	8.5	9.9	4.4	1.7	127.9	9.3	5.1	.1	2.3	1.8	118.6
1947	116.4	68.5	11.9	5.3	7.1	7.7	10.2	4.2	1.5	116.4	8.5	4.9	.1	2.0	1.5	107.9
1946	103.5	61.0	9.7	5.4	6.3	6.1	9.4	4.2	1.4	103.5	8.0	4.8	.3	1.7	1.2	95.5
1945	94.2	53.9	9.0	6.5	6.7	5.6	7.9	3.4	1.2	94.2	8.3	4.9	.7	1.6	1.1	85.9
1944	84.6	48.2	9.7	5.4	6.1	5.3	6.6	2.2	1.1	84.6	8.9	5.4	.6	1.7	1.2	75.7
1943	73.7	41.6	9.6	4.9	5.1	5.0	5.4	1.1	1.0	73.7	10.0	6.0	.8	1.7	1.5	63.7
1942	62.9	37.5	7.1	4.0	3.8	4.9	4.2	.5	.9	62.9	10.5	6.4	.6	1.8	1.7	52.4
1941	55.0	34.4	5.3	3.3	3.0	4.2	3.5	.4	.9	55.0	10.4	6.5	.6	1.6	1.7	44.6
1940	52.9	33.6	5.1	3.1	2.7	4.2	3.2	.2	.8	52.9	10.0	6.6	.4	1.5	1.5	42.9

[1] Beginning 1961, excludes horses and mules.
[2] Includes crops held on farms and crops held off farms by farmers as security for CCC loans. On Jan. 1, 1970, the latter totaled $1,184 million.
[3] Nonrecourse CCC loans secured by crops owned by farmers and included as assets.
[4] Loans of all operating banks, production credit associations, Farmers Home Administration, and discounts of Federal intermediate credit banks for agricultural credit corporations and livestock loan companies.
[5] Loans and credit extended by dealers, merchants, finance companies, individuals, and others.

Series K 220–239. Value of Gross Farm Product in Current and Constant (1958) Dollars: 1929 to 1970

[For explanation of concepts of gross product and national income, and current and constant dollars, see text for series F 1–5, F 6–9, and F 47–70]

Series No.	Item	1970	1969	1968	1967	1966	1965	1964	1963	1962	1961	1960
	CURRENT DOLLARS (mil. dol.)											
220	Total value of farm output	54,226	51,821	47,571	46,578	46,382	43,457	39,373	40,997	39,928	38,443	37,564
221	Cash receipts from farm marketings and CCC loans	50,352	48,105	44,136	42,615	43,371	39,371	36,823	37,046	36,068	34,985	34,108
222	Farm products consumed directly in farm households	745	750	732	745	817	929	813	1,014	1,074	1,174	1,248
223	Change in farm inventories	222	103	117	737	−158	973	−594	785	714	279	233
224	Gross rental value of farm homes	2,907	2,863	2,586	2,481	2,352	2,300	2,215	2,153	2,072	2,005	1,975
225	Less: Value of intermediate products consumed	24,906	23,668	22,203	21,817	21,296	19,622	18,689	19,291	18,642	17,516	17,011
226	Plus: Other items	−305	−275	−218	−203	−184	−169	−74	−161	−63	−68	−71
227	Equals: Gross farm product	29,015	27,878	25,150	24,558	24,902	23,666	20,610	21,545	21,223	20,859	20,482
228	Less: Capital consumption allowances	6,349	6,162	5,802	5,396	4,953	4,658	4,398	4,201	4,095	3,979	4,007
229	Indirect business taxes	2,376	2,215	2,042	1,860	1,720	1,589	1,506	1,457	1,384	1,317	1,246
230	Plus: Government payments to farm landlords	3,349	3,417	3,119	2,782	2,954	2,211	1,947	1,517	1,557	1,335	628
231	Equals: National income originating in farming	23,639	22,918	20,425	20,084	21,183	19,630	16,653	17,404	17,301	16,898	15,857
	CONSTANT (1958) DOLLARS (bil. dol.)											
232	Total value of farm output	47.5	46.4	45.0	45.1	42.9	43.3	41.2	42.0	40.7	39.9	39.2
233	Cash receipts from farm marketings and CCC loans	45.1	44.0	42.4	41.8	40.5	39.7	38.9	38.3	37.0	36.5	35.8
234	Farm products consumed directly in farm households	.6	.6	.7	.7	.7	.8	1.0	1.1	1.1	1.3	1.3
235	Change in farm inventories	.1	–	.1	.7	−.2	.9	−.6	.8	.7	.2	.2
236	Gross rental value of farm homes	1.7	1.8	1.8	1.8	1.9	1.9	1.9	1.9	1.9	1.9	1.9
237	Less: Value of intermediate products consumed	22.5	22.1	21.4	21.0	20.3	19.4	18.8	19.1	18.6	17.6	17.2
238	Plus: Other items	−.3	−.2	−.2	−.2	−.2	−.2	−.2	−.1	−.2	−.1	−.1
239	Equals: Gross farm product	24.8	24.1	23.4	23.9	22.4	23.7	22.3	22.8	22.1	22.2	21.9

− Represents zero.

Series K 220–239. Value of Gross Farm Product in Current and Constant (1958) Dollars: 1929 to 1970—Con.

Series No.	Item	1959	1958	1957	1956	1955	1954	1953	1952	1951	1950	1949
	CURRENT DOLLARS (mil. dol.)											
220	Total value of farm output	36,878	37,647	33,603	33,264	33,124	33,823	34,150	37,406	37,953	32,800	30,577
221	Cash receipts from farm marketings and CCC loans	33,611	33,433	29,798	30,325	29,238	29,737	30,999	32,463	32,803	28,484	27,805
222	Farm products consumed directly in farm households	1,318	1,505	1,484	1,585	1,678	1,789	2,007	2,220	2,304	2,063	2,230
223	Change in farm inventories	-8	848	534	-380	467	586	-621	987	1,239	789	-866
224	Gross rental value of farm homes	1,957	1,861	1,787	1,734	1,741	1,711	1,765	1,736	1,607	1,464	1,408
225	Less: Value of intermediate products consumed	17,093	16,656	15,042	14,563	14,248	14,089	13,739	15,099	14,934	12,725	11,709
226	Plus: Other items	-140	-145	-128	-124	-120	-124	-126	-144	-131	-120	-111
227	Equals: Gross farm product	19,645	20,846	18,433	18,577	18,756	19,610	20,285	22,163	22,888	19,955	18,757
228	Less: Capital consumption allowances	4,001	3,793	3,692	3,520	3,481	3,377	3,262	3,141	2,958	2,511	2,223
229	Indirect business taxes	1,193	1,100	1,069	1,013	975	942	925	906	864	810	773
230	Plus: Government payments to farm landlords	619	988	891	486	200	224	186	240	250	249	161
231	Equals: National income originating in farming	15,070	16,941	14,563	14,530	14,500	15,515	16,284	18,356	19,316	16,883	15,922
	CONSTANT (1958) DOLLARS (bil. dol.)											
232	Total value of farm output	38.3	37.6	35.9	36.1	35.7	34.7	33.8	33.0	32.3	32.5	30.9
233	Cash receipts from farm marketings and CCC loans	35.0	33.4	31.9	33.1	31.6	30.5	30.6	28.5	27.5	27.9	27.8
234	Farm products consumed directly in farm households	1.4	1.5	1.6	1.8	1.8	1.9	2.0	2.1	2.1	2.3	2.3
235	Change in farm inventories	-	.8	.5	-.6	.4	.5	-.4	.7	1.0	.8	-.8
236	Gross rental value of farm homes	1.9	1.9	1.8	1.8	1.8	1.8	1.7	1.7	1.6	1.6	1.5
237	Less: Value of intermediate products consumed	17.1	16.7	15.4	15.2	14.6	14.1	13.7	13.9	13.8	13.0	12.4
238	Plus: Other items	-.2	-.1	-.1	-.1	-.1	-.1	-.1	-.1	-.1	-.1	-.1
239	Equals: Gross farm product	21.1	20.8	20.3	20.8	20.9	20.4	20.0	19.0	18.4	19.4	18.4

Series No.	Item	1948	1947	1946	1945	1944	1943	1942	1941	1940	1939	1938
	CURRENT DOLLARS (mil. dol.)											
220	Total value of farm output	36,197	32,072	28,796	24,632	23,262	22,699	19,243	13,727	10,617	9,917	9,835
221	Cash receipts from farm marketings and CCC loans	30,227	29,620	24,802	21,663	20,536	19,620	15,565	11,111	8,382	7,872	7,723
222	Farm products consumed directly in farm households	2,733	2,765	2,662	2,356	2,181	2,253	1,758	1,429	1,210	1,209	1,235
223	Change in farm inventories	1,732	-1,760	29	-439	-410	-53	1,099	420	281	95	132
224	Gross rental value of farm homes	1,505	1,447	1,303	1,052	955	879	821	767	744	741	745
225	Less: Value of intermediate products consumed	12,773	11,784	9,942	8,661	7,951	7,385	6,190	4,762	4,132	3,589	3,248
226	Plus: Other items	-109	-102	-86	-66	-56	-50	-50	-37	-20	-19	-19
227	Equals: Gross farm product	23,315	20,186	18,768	15,905	15,255	15,264	13,016	8,936	6,465	6,309	6,568
228	Less: Capital consumption allowances	1,854	1,421	1,086	1,224	1,340	1,290	1,265	811	742	734	791
229	Indirect business taxes	714	645	542	499	438	418	403	397	382	382	375
230	Plus: Government payments to farm landlords	227	277	683	659	687	563	563	472	626	661	377
231	Equals: National income originating in farming	20,974	18,397	17,823	14,841	14,164	14,119	11,911	8,200	5,967	5,854	5,779
	CONSTANT (1958) DOLLARS (bil. dol.)											
232	Total value of farm output	31.5	29.5	30.8	29.8	30.2	30.2	30.9	28.1	26.2	26.0	24.9
233	Cash receipts from farm marketings and CCC loans	26.5	27.1	26.8	26.5	26.7	25.7	24.8	22.9	21.2	21.2	20.4
234	Farm products consumed directly in farm households	2.5	2.6	2.9	2.7	2.7	2.8	2.7	2.7	2.9	2.9	2.8
235	Change in farm inventories	1.0	-1.6	-.2	-.9	-.5	.2	2.0	1.1	.7	.5	.2
236	Gross rental value of farm homes	1.5	1.4	1.4	1.4	1.4	1.4	1.4	1.4	1.4	1.4	1.4
237	Less: Value of intermediate products consumed	12.4	12.5	12.3	11.6	10.8	10.6	10.2	9.3	8.7	7.8	7.0
238	Plus: Other items	-.1	-.1	-.1	-.1	-.1	-.1	-.1	-.1	-.1	-.1	-.1
239	Equals: Gross farm product	19.0	17.0	18.5	18.1	19.4	19.6	20.6	18.8	17.5	18.2	17.8

Series No.	Item	1937	1936	1935	1934	1933	1932	1931	1930	1929
	CURRENT DOLLARS (mil. dol.)									
220	Total value of farm output	11,847	9,672	9,821	7,192	6,782	6,515	8,881	11,203	13,816
221	Cash receipts from farm marketings and CCC loans	8,864	8,391	7,120	6,357	5,332	4,748	6,381	9,055	11,312
222	Farm products consumed directly in farm households	1,434	1,394	1,320	1,125	1,030	993	1,265	1,552	1,713
223	Change in farm inventories	816	-806	698	-930	-194	110	460	-269	-122
224	Gross rental value of farm homes	733	693	683	640	614	664	775	865	913
225	Less: Value of intermediate products consumed	3,568	3,234	2,818	2,495	2,160	2,013	2,568	3,519	4,105
226	Plus: Other items	-22	-19	-16	-14	-11	-9	-13	-20	-31
227	Equals: Gross farm product	8,257	6,419	6,987	4,683	4,611	4,493	6,300	7,664	9,680
228	Less: Capital consumption allowances	750	687	624	615	613	702	818	911	864
229	Indirect business taxes	378	364	354	349	362	418	485	535	538
230	Plus: Government payments to farm landlords	283	242	498	397	113	--------	--------	--------	--------
231	Equals: National income originating in farming	7,412	5,610	6,507	4,116	3,749	3,373	4,997	6,218	8,278
	CONSTANT (1958) DOLLARS (bil. dol.)									
232	Total value of farm output	24.7	21.5	22.5	20.2	23.4	23.5	24.4	22.5	23.8
233	Cash receipts from farm marketings and CCC loans	18.7	18.9	16.9	18.8	19.4	18.4	18.6	18.4	19.6
234	Farm products consumed directly in farm households	2.8	2.8	2.8	3.0	3.1	2.9	2.9	2.7	2.7
235	Change in farm inventories	1.8	-1.6	1.4	-3.0	-.5	.8	1.5	-.2	1.5
236	Gross rental value of farm homes	1.4	1.4	1.4	1.4	1.4	1.4	1.5	1.5	1.5
237	Less: Value of intermediate products consumed	6.7	6.6	5.9	5.6	5.8	5.5	5.9	6.3	6.8
238	Plus: Other items	-	-	-	-	-	-	-	-	-.1
239	Equals: Gross farm product	17.9	14.9	16.5	14.6	17.5	18.0	18.5	16.1	17.0

\- Represents zero.

Series K 240–250. Value of Farm Gross Output and Product, in Current and Constant (1910–14) Dollars: 1800 to 1900

[In millions of dollars]

Year	Gross output						Farm gross product	Intermediate products consumed	Farm gross product, including improvements and manufactures			
	Total	Sales and home consumption of farm products			Livestock inventory changes	Gross rent from farm dwellings			Total	Farm gross product	Improvements to farms	Value of home manufactures
		Total	Livestock	Crops								
	240	241	242	243	244	245	246	247	248	246	249	250
CURRENT DOLLARS												
1900	4,298	3,912	2,047	1,865	79	307	3,799	499	3,857	3,799	55	3
1890	3,397	3,106	1,515	1,591	44	247	3,035	362	3,107	3,035	67	5
1880	3,263	3,021	1,498	1,523	39	203	2,967	296	3,045	2,967	68	10
1870	2,774	2,553	1,393	1,160	52	169	2,542	232	2,631	2,542	67	22
1860	1,579	1,469	700	769	21	89	1,484	95	1,556	1,484	47	25
1850	904	837	414	423	10	57	851	53	914	851	34	29
1840	757	699	431	268	14	44	720	37	769	720	22	27
1830	466	427	251	176	15	24	445	21	491	445	17	29
1820	338	308	178	130	10	20	323	15	364	323	12	29
1810	336	311	186	125	9	16	324	12	363	324	9	30
1800	236	220	127	93	6	10	230	6	255	230	7	18
CONSTANT (1910–14) DOLLARS												
1900	6,409	5,903	3,100	2,803	109	397	5,740	669	5,837	5,740	94	3
1890	4,990	4,604	2,612	1,992	70	316	4,527	463	4,638	4,527	106	5
1880	4,129	3,784	2,006	1,778	68	277	3,770	359	3,906	3,770	128	8
1870	2,694	2,436	1,436	1,000	74	184	2,479	215	2,597	2,479	106	12
1860	2,186	1,985	1,088	897	60	141	2,059	127	2,156	2,059	76	21
1850	1,521	1,379	826	553	42	100	1,442	79	1,536	1,442	69	25
1840	1,212	1,103	651	452	33	76	1,156	56	1,222	1,156	47	19
1830	854	764	462	302	34	56	819	35	879	819	44	16
1820	619	555	345	210	22	42	595	24	642	595	33	14
1810	463	415	260	155	16	32	448	15	485	448	26	11
1800	343	307	194	113	13	23	333	10	362	333	21	8

Series K 251–255. Exports and Imports of Farm Products: 1901 to 1970

[In millions of dollars, except percent. For years ending June 30]

Year	Exports, domestic products			Imports for consumption		Year	Exports, domestic products			Imports for consumption	
	Total	Percent of all exports	Percent under Government financed programs	Total	Percent of all imports		Total	Percent of all exports	Percent under Government financed programs	Total	Percent of all imports
	251	252	253	254	255		251	252	253	254	255
1970	6,721	16	15	5,592	15	1935	669	32	----------	934	52
1969	5,741	16	18	4,931	14	1934	787	39	----------	839	50
1968	6,311	20	21	4,656	16	1933	590	42	----------	614	52
1967	6,771	22	19	4,453	17	1932	752	39	----------	834	48
1966	6,676	23	21	4,454	19	1931	1,038	34	----------	1,162	48
1965	6,097	23	26	3,986	20						
1964	6,068	25	24	4,096	23	1930	1,496	32	----------	1,900	49
1963	5,078	23	29	3,907	24	1929	1,847	35	----------	2,177	51
1962	5,142	24	31	3,762	24	1928	1,815	38	----------	2,194	53
1961	4,946	24	30	3,645	26	1927	1,908	39	----------	2,281	54
						1926	1,892	41	----------	2,529	57
1960	4,519	24	28	4,010	26	1925	2,280	48	----------	2,057	54
1959	3,719	21	33	4,004	29	1924	1,867	44	----------	1,875	53
1958	4,003	21	30	3,929	31	1923	1,798	46	----------	2,077	55
1957	4,728	23	41	3,800	30	1922	1,915	52	----------	1,370	53
1956	3,496	21	38	4,086	34	1921	2,606	41	----------	2,059	56
1955	3,144	21	27	3,781	36						
1954	2,936	19	21	4,176	40	1920	3,850	48	----------	3,410	65
1953	2,819	19	16	4,303	40	1919	3,579	51	----------	1,930	62
1952	4,053	26	15	4,699	45	1918	2,279	39	----------	1,822	62
1951	3,411	27	35	5,147	48	1917	1,966	32	----------	1,592	60
						1916	1,516	35	----------	1,342	61
1950	2,986	30	66	3,177	45	1915	1,474	54	----------	992	59
1949	3,830	30	60	3,001	43	1914	1,112	48	----------	993	52
1948	3,505	25	45	2,862	45	1913	1,121	46	----------	909	50
1947	3,610	28	25	2,704	50	1912	1,048	48	----------	882	53
1946	2,857	34	63	1,878	45	1911	1,029	51	----------	767	50
1945	2,191	17	71	1,729	44						
1944	2,305	16	80	1,774	47	1910	869	51	----------	787	51
1943	1,497	15	82	1,342	45	1909	901	55	----------	696	53
1942	1,032	16	72	1,503	49	1908	1,016	55	----------	573	48
1941	350	9	----------	1,474	53	1907	1,053	57	----------	683	48
						1906	975	57	----------	597	49
1940	738	20	----------	1,239	51	1905	825	55	----------	601	54
1939	683	24	----------	999	48	1904	858	60	----------	499	50
1938	891	27	----------	1,155	50	1903	877	63	----------	484	47
1937	732	26	----------	1,537	53	1902	855	63	----------	436	48
1936	766	32	----------	1,141	52	1901	949	65	----------	418	51

Series K 256–285. Farm Income and Expenses: 1910 to 1970

[In millions of dollars, except as indicated]

Year	Personal income of farm population			Net income of farm operators from farming		Per capita personal income of farm population (dollars)			Realized gross income from farming						
									Realized gross farm income	Cash receipts from marketings			Government payments	Value of farm products consumed in farm households	Gross rental value of farm dwellings
	From all sources	From farm sources	From nonfarm sources	Total net income	Average per farm (dollars)	From all sources	From farm sources	From nonfarm sources		Total	Crops	Livestock and livestock products			
	256	257	258	259	260	261	262	263	264	265	266	267	268	269	270
1970	28,193	15,019	13,174	16,825	5,754	2,832	1,462	1,370	57,925	50,522	20,907	29,615	3,717	773	2,913
1969	27,553	14,862	12,691	16,856	5,674	2,691	1,446	1,245	55,550	48,143	19,541	28,602	3,794	750	2,863
1968	25,118	13,237	11,881	14,825	4,854	2,400	1,263	1,137	50,897	44,117	18,620	25,497	3,462	732	2,586
1967	24,030	13,149	10,881	14,882	4,730	2,210	1,209	1,001	48,998	42,693	18,434	24,259	3,079	745	2,481
1966	24,878	14,414	10,464	16,253	5,019	2,146	1,243	903	49,740	43,294	18,373	24,921	3,277	817	2,352
1965	23,591	13,546	10,045	14,987	4,487	1,908	1,096	812	44,926	39,350	17,392	21,958	2,463	813	2,300
1964	20,639	11,334	9,305	12,266	3,564	1,593	875	718	42,567	37,233	17,377	19,856	2,181	930	2,223
1963	20,619	12,109	8,510	13,206	3,708	1,543	906	637	42,271	37,398	17,435	19,963	1,696	1,016	2,161
1962	20,449	12,254	8,195	13,215	3,586	1,429	856	573	41,258	36,356	16,294	20,062	1,747	1,076	2,079
1961	19,738	12,195	7,543	12,987	3,399	1,333	824	509	39,771	35,089	15,660	19,429	1,493	1,176	2,012
1960	18,679	11,526	7,153	12,079	3,049	1,195	737	458	38,088	34,154	15,208	18,946	702	1,250	1,981
1959	18,059	11,009	7,050	11,454	2,795	1,089	664	425	37,468	33,511	14,648	18,863	682	1,318	1,957
1958	19,481	12,800	6,681	13,500	3,189	1,137	747	390	37,911	33,456	14,229	19,227	1,089	1,505	1,861
1957	17,657	11,041	6,616	11,325	2,590	1,000	625	375	34,001	29,714	12,338	17,376	1,016	1,484	1,787
1956	17,803	11,219	6,584	11,444	2,535	952	600	352	34,274	30,401	14,038	16,363	554	1,585	1,734
1955	17,579	11,382	6,197	11,464	2,463	922	597	325	33,138	29,490	13,523	15,967	229	1,678	1,741
1954	18,443	12,509	5,934	12,503	2,606	970	658	312	33,589	29,832	13,556	16,276	257	1,789	1,711
1953	19,790	13,353	6,437	13,088	2,626	996	672	324	34,986	31,001	14,078	16,923	213	2,007	1,765
1952	22,078	15,352	6,726	15,051	2,896	1,015	706	309	36,759	32,528	14,290	18,238	275	2,220	1,736
1951	22,701	16,190	6,511	15,987	2,946	1,037	740	297	37,055	32,858	13,239	19,619	286	2,304	1,607
1950	20,366	14,103	6,263	13,673	2,421	884	612	272	32,271	28,461	12,356	16,105	283	2,063	1,464
1949	19,476	13,284	6,192	12,780	2,233	805	549	256	31,628	27,805	12,396	15,409	185	2,230	1,408
1948	23,792	17,977	5,815	17,664	3,044	976	737	239	34,722	30,227	13,098	17,129	257	2,733	1,505
1947	21,133	15,836	5,297	15,354	2,615	818	613	205	34,146	29,620	13,093	16,527	314	2,765	1,447
1946	20,026	15,475	4,551	15,068	2,543	788	609	179	29,539	24,802	11,016	13,786	772	2,662	1,303
1945	17,212	12,807	4,405	12,312	2,063	705	524	181	25,813	21,663	9,655	12,008	742	2,356	1,052
1944	16,636	12,201	4,435	11,705	1,950	671	492	179	24,448	20,536	9,185	11,351	776	2,181	955
1943	16,481	12,120	4,361	11,736	1,927	629	463	166	23,397	19,620	8,127	11,493	645	2,253	879
1942	14,090	10,149	3,941	9,853	1,588	487	351	136	18,794	15,565	6,526	9,039	650	1,758	821
1941	10,080	6,823	3,257	6,490	1,031	335	227	108	13,851	11,111	4,619	6,492	544	1,429	767
1940	7,597	4,838	2,759	4,482	706	249	158	91	11,059	8,382	3,469	4,913	723	1,210	744
1939	7,361	4,751	2,610	4,414	685	239	154	85	10,585	7,872	3,336	4,536	763	1,209	741
1938	7,177	4,702	2,475	4,361	668	232	152	80	10,149	7,723	3,200	4,523	446	1,235	745
1937	8,976	6,228	2,748	6,005	905	287	199	88	11,367	8,864	3,924	4,940	336	1,434	733
1936	7,232	4,592	2,640	4,308	639	228	145	83	10,756	8,391	3,649	4,742	278	1,394	693
1935	7,730	5,423	2,307	5,278	775	241	169	72	9,696	7,120	2,977	4,143	573	1,320	683
1934	5,374	3,188	2,186	2,923	431	167	99	68	8,568	6,357	3,021	3,336	446	1,125	640
1933	---	---	---	2,555	379	---	---	---	7,107	5,332	2,486	2,846	131	1,030	614
1932	---	---	---	2,032	304	---	---	---	6,405	4,748	1,996	2,752	---	993	664
1931	---	---	---	3,344	506	---	---	---	8,421	6,381	2,540	3,841	---	1,265	775
1930	---	---	---	4,259	651	---	---	---	11,472	9,055	3,868	5,187	---	1,552	865
1929	---	---	---	6,152	945	---	---	---	13,938	11,312	5,130	6,182	---	1,713	913
1928	---	---	---	5,981	924	---	---	---	13,598	10,991	4,956	6,035	---	1,724	883
1927	---	---	---	5,699	883	---	---	---	13,336	10,733	5,125	5,608	---	1,725	878
1926	---	---	---	5,937	919	---	---	---	13,302	10,558	4,875	5,683	---	1,875	869
1925	---	---	---	6,734	1,041	---	---	---	13,716	11,021	5,545	5,476	---	1,827	868
1924	---	---	---	4,855	749	---	---	---	12,785	10,225	5,413	4,812	---	1,706	854
1923	---	---	---	5,068	781	---	---	---	12,167	9,545	4,865	4,680	---	1,772	850
1922	---	---	---	4,343	668	---	---	---	11,059	8,575	4,300	4,275	---	1,717	767
1921	---	---	---	3,370	517	---	---	---	10,573	8,058	4,106	3,952	---	1,746	769
1920	---	---	---	7,795	1,196	---	---	---	15,944	12,600	6,644	5,956	---	2,509	835
1919	---	---	---	9,078	1,395	---	---	---	17,918	14,538	7,603	6,935	---	2,556	824
1918	---	---	---	8,887	1,370	---	---	---	16,547	13,467	6,974	6,493	---	2,341	739
1917	---	---	---	8,304	1,282	---	---	---	13,410	10,736	5,642	5,094	---	2,003	671
1916	---	---	---	4,570	707	---	---	---	9,744	7,746	4,035	3,711	---	1,384	614
1915	---	---	---	4,307	667	---	---	---	8,147	6,392	3,263	3,129	---	1,192	563
1914	---	---	---	4,181	649	---	---	---	7,793	6,036	2,899	3,137	---	1,228	529
1913	---	---	---	3,738	581	---	---	---	7,978	6,238	3,077	3,161	---	1,222	518
1912	---	---	---	4,456	693	---	---	---	7,710	6,008	3,095	2,913	---	1,204	498
1911	---	---	---	3,371	525	---	---	---	7,213	5,584	2,905	2,679	---	1,165	464
1910	---	---	---	4,176	652	---	---	---	7,495	5,780	2,929	2,851	---	1,270	445

Series K 256–285. Farm Income and Expenses: 1910 to 1970—Con.

[In millions of dollars, except as indicated]

Year	Total	Operating expenses (excluding hired labor)							Depreciation [3]	Taxes on farm property	Wages paid hired farm labor [4]	Interest on farm mortgage debt	Net rent to nonfarm landlords	Realized net income of farm operators from farming	Net change in farm inventories
		Total	Feed purchased	Livestock purchased	Seed purchased [1]	Fertilizer and lime	Repairs	Miscellaneous [2]							
	271	272	273	274	275	276	277	278	279	280	281	282	283	284	285
1970	41,091	24,748	7,189	4,345	829	2,222	5,031	5,132	6,724	2,957	3,643	1,717	1,302	16,834	−9
1969	38,759	23,270	6,602	4,219	737	2,084	4,896	4,732	6,562	2,732	3,299	1,599	1,297	16,791	65
1968	36,209	21,654	5,894	3,676	672	2,130	4,831	4,451	6,209	2,515	3,047	1,477	1,307	14,688	137
1967	34,775	21,228	6,472	3,391	678	2,124	4,495	4,068	5,746	2,275	2,878	1,343	1,305	14,223	659
1966	33,406	20,481	6,324	3,498	626	1,952	4,227	3,854	5,281	2,108	2,889	1,205	1,442	16,334	−81
1965	30,933	18,754	5,749	2,913	637	1,754	4,073	3,628	4,982	1,943	2,849	1,077	1,328	13,993	994
1964	29,481	17,857	5,715	2,420	566	1,701	3,940	3,515	4,703	1,833	2,913	952	1,223	13,086	−820
1963	29,688	18,425	6,128	2,917	553	1,570	3,942	3,315	4,471	1,763	2,990	846	1,193	12,583	623
1962	28,639	17,755	5,575	3,106	521	1,474	3,944	3,135	4,348	1,684	2,961	759	1,132	12,619	596
1961	27,125	16,539	5,121	2,730	521	1,373	3,858	2,936	4,217	1,597	2,977	686	1,109	12,646	341
1960	26,352	16,045	4,923	2,502	510	1,315	3,966	2,829	4,244	1,502	2,923	628	1,010	11,736	343
1959	26,106	16,012	4,744	2,693	491	1,291	4,069	2,724	4,228	1,401	2,882	572	1,011	11,362	92
1958	25,236	15,395	4,541	2,702	508	1,206	3,921	2,517	4,011	1,306	2,842	521	1,161	12,675	825
1957	23,294	13,894	4,035	1,934	510	1,166	3,917	2,332	3,913	1,242	2,734	482	1,029	10,707	618
1956	22,374	13,281	3,894	1,610	519	1,166	3,785	2,307	3,723	1,178	2,641	442	1,109	11,900	−456
1955	21,889	12,974	3,880	1,539	566	1,185	3,600	2,204	3,700	1,141	2,615	402	1,057	11,249	215
1954	21,577	12,786	3,906	1,563	525	1,209	3,506	2,077	3,581	1,084	2,596	371	1,159	12,012	491
1953	21,275	12,466	3,770	1,320	551	1,178	3,541	2,106	3,454	1,060	2,736	345	1,214	13,711	−623
1952	22,630	13,675	4,331	1,918	594	1,184	3,506	2,142	3,326	1,033	2,857	318	1,421	14,129	922
1951	22,252	13,542	4,144	2,437	551	1,064	3,282	2,064	3,147	983	2,921	291	1,368	14,803	1,184
1950	19,410	11,518	3,283	2,004	518	975	2,975	1,763	2,665	919	2,811	264	1,233	12,861	812
1949	17,982	10,589	3,024	1,529	543	895	2,896	1,702	2,365	872	2,806	243	1,107	13,646	−866
1948	18,790	11,390	3,996	1,589	581	826	2,818	1,580	2,002	806	2,990	232	1,370	15,932	1,732
1947	17,032	10,283	3,746	1,379	514	755	2,468	1,421	1,553	733	2,783	225	1,455	17,114	−1,760
1946	14,500	8,542	3,022	1,170	428	683	2,054	1,185	1,189	617	2,532	219	1,401	15,039	29
1945	13,062	7,611	2,738	1,011	435	657	1,689	1,081	1,310	557	2,299	221	1,064	12,751	−439
1944	12,333	6,934	2,427	812	440	576	1,608	1,071	1,425	499	2,202	230	1,043	12,115	−410
1943	11,608	6,445	2,135	908	406	505	1,465	1,026	1,369	477	2,027	246	1,044	11,789	−53
1942	10,040	5,446	1,625	877	301	417	1,289	937	1,335	466	1,631	272	890	8,754	1,099
1941	7,781	4,268	1,089	635	203	334	1,132	875	870	463	1,249	284	647	6,070	420
1940	6,858	3,840	998	517	197	306	1,038	784	797	451	1,029	293	448	4,201	281
1939	6,266	3,357	732	465	169	273	959	759	781	456	988	305	379	4,319	95
1938	5,920	3,022	557	368	206	258	907	726	833	448	979	320	318	4,229	132
1937	6,178	3,221	805	332	194	279	879	732	796	452	988	341	380	5,189	816
1936	5,642	2,859	755	283	147	261	749	664	728	440	868	364	383	5,114	−806
1935	5,116	2,500	528	312	108	188	717	647	664	434	775	396	347	4,580	698
1934	4,715	2,276	542	183	104	176	608	663	650	424	679	430	256	3,853	−930
1933	4,358	2,029	422	199	65	120	554	669	644	438	617	472	158	2,749	−194
1932	4,483	1,989	348	193	79	118	521	730	734	510	669	526	55	1,922	110
1931	5,537	2,489	448	253	117	202	635	834	856	589	914	553	136	2,884	460
1930	6,944	3,273	791	362	124	297	785	914	955	648	1,177	570	321	4,528	−269
1929	7,664	3,729	919	504	122	300	886	998	916	651	1,300	582	486	6,274	−122
1928	7,757	3,845	977	588	134	318	827	1,001	900	636	1,290	590	496	5,841	140
1927	7,462	3,537	892	465	140	267	787	986	890	620	1,302	593	520	5,874	−175
1926	7,372	3,534	891	396	142	298	774	1,033	886	599	1,330	598	425	5,930	7
1925	7,347	3,537	988	382	136	299	711	1,021	872	589	1,267	612	470	6,369	365
1924	7,447	3,497	1,116	313	120	264	654	1,030	952	583	1,248	647	520	5,338	−483
1923	7,054	3,161	819	304	111	263	637	1,027	943	590	1,251	679	430	5,113	−45
1922	6,614	2,922	676	319	109	234	557	1,027	934	583	1,127	680	368	4,445	−102
1921	6,638	2,886	710	202	123	249	550	1,052	1,039	586	1,170	653	304	3,935	−565
1920	8,837	4,202	1,254	422	178	390	695	1,263	1,211	556	1,790	574	504	7,107	688
1919	8,331	3,918	1,097	567	138	358	615	1,143	1,040	454	1,515	476	928	9,587	−509
1918	7,507	3,631	1,106	522	132	311	536	1,024	902	361	1,337	417	859	9,040	−153
1917	6,092	2,709	614	414	122	232	464	863	714	339	1,127	378	825	7,318	986
1916	4,836	2,156	517	260	76	193	395	715	597	304	904	341	534	4,908	−338
1915	4,167	1,827	411	207	62	165	343	639	524	284	815	314	403	3,980	327
1914	4,029	1,831	414	215	62	195	297	648	482	261	804	296	355	3,764	417
1913	3,974	1,816	406	250	62	175	289	634	481	257	804	276	340	4,004	−266
1912	3,833	1,755	419	217	74	161	278	606	469	225	789	252	343	3,877	579
1911	3,582	1,610	350	188	65	168	251	588	443	215	758	225	331	3,631	−260
1910	3,531	1,642	426	199	56	152	251	558	416	195	755	203	320	3,964	212

[1] Includes bulbs, plants, and trees.
[2] Includes interest on non-real-estate debt, marketing charges, net insurance premiums (crop, fire, wind, and hail), and miscellaneous supplies and services purchased.
[3] Includes other consumption of farm capital.
[4] Includes value of perquisites.

Series K 286–302. Farm Income—Cash Receipts from Farm Marketings: 1910 to 1970

[In millions of dollars]

Year	Crops								Livestock and livestock products								
	Cotton (lint and seed)	Tobacco	Food grains	Oil-bearing crops	Feed crops	Vegetables [1]	Fruits and tree nuts [2]	Other [3]	Hogs	Cattle and calves	Sheep and lambs	Wool	Dairy products	Eggs	Broilers and farm chickens	Turkeys and other poultry [4]	Other [5]
	286	287	288	289	290	291	292	293	294	295	296	297	298	299	300	301	302
1970	1,254	1,388	2,564	3,567	5,067	3,024	2,090	2,152	4,475	13,695	327	57	6,533	2,166	1,564	575	223
1969	1,403	1,296	2,229	3,045	4,507	2,803	2,197	2,066	4,745	12,566	333	69	6,206	2,262	1,643	531	247
1968	1,316	1,173	2,105	2,842	4,264	2,850	2,071	1,999	3,819	11,241	315	72	5,955	1,921	1,417	490	267
1967	1,095	1,391	2,382	2,805	4,337	2,649	1,843	1,932	3,755	10,478	300	75	5,743	1,781	1,315	544	268
1966	1,588	1,211	2,379	2,700	4,306	2,559	1,758	1,872	4,093	10,431	334	101	5,532	2,114	1,472	563	281
1965	2,330	1,186	2,041	2,173	3,669	2,580	1,667	1,746	3,693	8,942	329	95	5,037	1,788	1,304	489	281
1964	2,521	1,414	1,994	2,126	3,412	2,300	1,797	1,813	3,034	7,785	318	113	5,027	1,770	1,156	448	205
1963	2,838	1,269	2,524	1,954	3,401	2,018	1,669	1,762	3,035	8,101	319	115	4,860	1,732	1,155	435	211
1962	2,552	1,321	2,445	1,803	2,960	2,035	1,562	1,616	3,154	8,187	324	115	4,854	1,685	1,143	412	188
1961	2,482	1,325	2,487	1,647	2,779	1,872	1,592	1,476	3,140	7,565	302	109	4,918	1,737	1,045	415	198
1960	2,340	1,154	2,460	1,364	3,025	1,941	1,514	1,410	2,873	7,398	327	108	4,753	1,738	1,127	427	195
1959	2,647	1,060	2,247	1,280	2,779	1,803	1,501	1,331	2,784	7,834	334	113	4,604	1,545	1,045	392	212
1958	2,138	1,020	2,442	1,410	2,904	1,736	1,394	1,185	3,367	7,322	358	72	4,557	1,833	1,147	373	198
1957	1,756	971	1,868	1,181	2,395	1,710	1,292	1,165	3,062	5,944	330	141	4,628	1,682	1,024	370	195
1956	2,500	1,162	2,148	1,155	2,648	1,873	1,358	1,194	2,638	5,353	330	104	4,485	1,834	1,023	397	199
1955	2,580	1,225	1,990	1,131	2,555	1,683	1,276	1,083	2,694	5,245	316	91	4,217	1,777	1,070	377	180
1954	2,702	1,161	2,327	942	2,549	1,548	1,220	1,107	3,455	5,088	325	129	4,114	1,627	1,000	386	152
1953	3,179	1,094	2,456	959	2,397	1,662	1,197	1,134	3,483	4,878	317	129	4,366	2,073	1,136	393	148
1952	2,976	1,091	2,558	1,081	2,271	2,023	1,097	1,193	3,464	6,206	391	123	4,567	1,801	1,118	411	157
1951	2,858	1,190	2,004	986	2,091	1,728	1,157	1,225	3,889	7,005	466	234	4,254	2,062	1,137	406	166
1950	2,434	1,061	1,941	935	2,143	1,436	1,188	1,218	3,214	5,680	387	130	3,719	1,579	946	314	136
1949	2,637	903	2,255	854	2,161	1,616	929	1,041	3,125	4,849	351	100	3,748	1,857	939	314	126
1948	2,553	945	2,629	1,053	2,026	1,712	1,128	1,052	3,660	5,285	409	110	4,389	1,884	948	303	141
1947	2,245	1,032	2,753	917	2,265	1,632	1,199	1,050	3,926	4,967	402	105	4,013	1,813	870	274	157
1946	1,473	969	1,841	715	1,679	1,591	1,759	989	2,917	3,761	363	119	3,709	1,508	928	318	163
1945	1,208	898	1,563	615	1,509	1,611	1,498	753	2,263	3,318	319	126	3,021	1,518	1,004	295	144
1944	1,548	690	1,375	590	1,271	1,484	1,528	699	2,800	2,605	300	144	2,915	1,365	862	241	119
1943	1,301	538	1,068	703	1,135	1,472	1,273	637	2,929	2,563	342	182	2,785	1,446	926	202	118
1942	1,272	476	977	525	839	1,028	844	565	2,198	2,263	306	133	2,330	1,018	538	170	83
1941	1,006	323	689	238	626	692	604	441	1,302	1,705	226	138	1,900	663	364	116	78
1940	638	242	479	126	600	559	446	379	836	1,375	180	106	1,521	468	268	92	67
1939	627	271	465	111	507	527	439	389	810	1,289	172	81	1,346	437	248	85	68
1938	655	294	468	92	444	471	403	373	870	1,163	157	69	1,388	485	235	79	77
1937	886	320	659	85	446	586	540	402	925	1,239	186	114	1,525	517	269	80	85
1936	904	243	500	77	473	597	473	382	991	1,114	166	95	1,478	481	262	74	81
1935	712	243	418	69	302	468	432	333	682	1,063	152	70	1,310	502	235	68	61
1934	863	236	348	53	355	468	398	300	520	813	132	81	1,146	373	190	54	27
1933	578	157	335	33	327	423	343	290	524	599	105	77	1,004	309	161	44	23
1932	461	115	220	30	245	347	321	257	445	620	93	30	986	324	190	45	19
1931	497	157	298	38	312	471	455	312	774	838	130	51	1,277	434	258	55	24
1930	826	244	500	73	557	687	577	404	1,135	1,184	162	68	1,608	606	333	59	32
1929	1,511	279	788	85	694	711	631	431	1,297	1,495	224	99	1,839	740	374	70	44
1928	1,453	247	840	84	757	514	633	428	1,218	1,556	221	114	1,755	709	350	64	48
1927	1,500	245	969	87	668	617	602	437	1,238	1,326	197	88	1,585	626	333	60	45
1926	1,222	240	901	65	668	708	618	453	1,407	1,271	205	92	1,566	696	340	59	47
1925	1,762	260	910	87	776	677	619	454	1,318	1,252	207	100	1,515	682	306	51	45
1924	1,664	260	889	100	906	572	561	461	1,064	1,119	181	87	1,405	585	278	46	47
1923	1,569	276	679	61	692	553	559	476	1,027	1,042	160	91	1,425	583	262	44	46
1922	1,148	249	749	42	613	488	584	427	1,024	1,037	143	62	1,171	506	250	40	42
1921	852	253	907	36	634	477	514	433	857	876	108	42	1,200	528	251	41	49
1920	1,476	295	1,535	68	1,220	712	702	636	1,385	1,528	166	114	1,529	781	317	50	86
1919	2,282	500	1,743	92	1,166	593	632	595	1,911	1,921	213	134	1,522	762	296	48	128
1918	1,784	343	1,703	94	1,428	603	505	514	1,866	2,029	196	147	1,250	599	232	41	133
1917	1,604	242	1,187	75	1,043	660	403	428	1,299	1,651	159	98	1,030	523	184	32	118
1916	1,148	139	912	48	715	412	330	331	949	1,132	127	64	764	375	152	27	121
1915	830	93	822	32	618	286	297	285	691	966	111	53	686	341	134	24	123
1914	602	99	716	31	555	318	300	278	713	985	116	42	667	336	138	26	114
1913	968	135	537	37	567	294	264	275	741	999	115	44	669	321	132	26	114
1912	852	108	532	49	621	363	295	275	647	885	109	48	630	338	120	24	112
1911	855	96	482	43	559	306	283	281	617	784	99	48	577	304	123	25	102
1910	880	102	532	38	601	271	243	262	670	851	105	66	597	330	127	27	78

[1] Beginning 1949, includes melons.
[2] Includes melons, 1910–1948.
[3] Sugar crops, greenhouse and nursery products, forest products, legume and grass seeds, hops, mint, broomcorn, popcorn, hemp fiber and seed, and flax fiber.
[4] Ducks, geese, guineas, pigeons, quail, pheasants, and turkey hatching eggs.
[5] Horses, mules, mohair, honey, beeswax, bees, goats, rabbits, and fur animals.

AGRICULTURE

Series K 303–325. Farm Marketings, by Price Support Status: 1930 to 1970

[**In millions of dollars.** Represents gross receipts from commercial market sales as well as net commodity credit corporation loans]

Year	Total market sales	Under price support									
		Total	Mandatory support								
			Total	Basic commodities							
				Total	Cotton (lint)	Wheat	Corn	Tobacco	Rice	Peanuts
	303	304	305	306	307	308	309	310	311	312
1970	50,539	20,667	17,075	8,627	1,037	2,068	3,317	1,388	447	370
1969	48,179	18,926	15,903	7,867	1,243	1,736	2,802	1,296	468	322
1968	44,183	17,854	14,952	7,296	1,093	1,568	2,637	1,173	515	310
1967	42,817	17,820	14,989	7,656	931	1,917	2,709	1,391	441	267
1966	43,435	17,795	14,957	7,785	1,322	1,948	2,629	1,211	406	269
1965	39,365	16,555	14,261	7,693	2,065	1,637	2,157	1,186	377	271
1964	37,326	16,692	14,391	7,871	2,246	1,617	2,017	1,414	350	227
1963	37,477	17,142	14,975	8,596	2,533	2,143	2,074	1,269	354	223
1962	36,468	16,184	14,173	7,977	2,275	2,110	1,773	1,321	304	194
1961	35,164	15,882	14,020	7,789	2,205	2,188	1,606	1,325	275	190
1960	34,248	15,262	13,715	7,696	2,116	2,195	1,817	1,154	244	170
1959	33,647	14,831	13,369	7,454	2,432	1,994	1,582	1,060	234	152
1958	33,456	14,683	13,148	7,083	1,932	2,199	1,512	1,020	218	202
1957	29,714	12,976	11,631	5,909	1,555	1,635	1,391	971	212	145
1956	30,401	14,234	12,860	7,320	2,229	1,888	1,645	1,162	239	157
1955	29,490	13,804	12,474	7,203	2,330	1,699	1,506	1,225	268	175
1954	29,832	14,003	12,738	7,503	2,391	2,046	1,527	1,161	261	117
1953	31,001	14,661	13,439	8,179	2,868	2,196	1,602	1,094	243	176
1952	32,528	14,617	13,176	7,682	2,585	2,244	1,328	1,091	290	144
1951	32,858	13,610	12,306	6,956	2,484	1,779	1,137	1,190	199	167
1950	28,461	12,428	11,299	6,563	2,143	1,732	1,232	1,061	189	206
1949	27,805	12,911	11,872	7,299	2,386	2,145	1,494	903	174	197
1948	30,227	13,824	12,515	7,189	2,214	2,500	1,134	945	170	226
1947	29,620	13,452	12,254	7,179	1,905	2,539	1,323	1,032	182	198
1946	24,802	10,493	9,614	5,019	1,258	1,659	827	969	140	166
1945	21,663	8,796	8,114	4,337	1,050	1,388	738	898	115	148
1944	20,536	8,376	7,634	4,064	1,296	1,200	615	690	111	152
1943	19,620	7,569	6,754	3,329	1,126	814	580	538	124	147
1942	15,565	6,459	5,857	3,026	1,048	837	461	476	91	113
1941	11,111	5,062	4,649	2,344	868	687	350	323	55	61
1940	8,382	3,733	3,533	1,712	564	428	387	242	40	51
1939	7,872	3,436	3,243	1,640	550	433	319	271	32	35
1938	7,723	3,408	3,235	1,601	558	401	269	294	34	45
1937	8,864	4,052	3,844	1,989	770	605	223	320	33	38
1936	8,391	3,787	3,563	1,789	763	451	265	243	32	35
1935	7,120	3,117	2,939	1,410	608	372	125	243	37	25
1934	6,357	3,058	2,896	1,556	759	317	191	236	24	29
1933	5,332	2,518	2,426	1,202	529	304	175	157	22	15
1932	4,748	2,078	2,003	874	419	200	110	115	15	15
1931	6,381	2,622	2,527	1,072	455	266	151	157	26	17
1930	9,055	3,879	3,667	1,786	727	451	305	244	33	26

Year	Under price support—Con.												Not under price support
	Mandatory support—Con.							Nonmandatory support					
	Nonbasic commodities [1]							Total	Soybeans	Cotton-seed	Flaxseed	Dry beans	
	Total	Dairy products	Oats	Barley	Sorghum grain	Sugar beets	Others [2]						
	313	314	315	316	317	318	319	320	321	322	323	324	325
1970	8,448	6,525	231	298	641	393	360	3,592	3,161	217	66	148	29,872
1969	8,036	6,196	209	265	642	353	371	3,023	2,647	161	75	140	29,253
1968	7,656	5,957	203	300	574	350	272	2,902	2,459	222	71	150	26,329
1967	7,333	5,742	186	289	584	260	272	2,831	2,474	164	60	133	24,997
1966	7,172	5,533	194	311	584	260	290	2,838	2,346	266	81	145	25,640
1965	6,568	5,038	194	305	496	250	285	2,294	1,812	265	86	131	22,810
1964	6,520	5,027	182	274	428	276	333	2,301	1,833	274	58	136	20,634
1963	6,379	4,861	181	257	453	285	342	2,167	1,637	305	90	135	20,335
1962	6,196	4,860	175	264	383	233	281	2,011	1,523	277	81	130	20,284
1961	6,231	4,933	187	266	370	198	277	1,862	1,375	277	73	137	19,282

See footnotes at end of table.

Series K 303–325. Farm Marketings, by Price Support Status: 1930 to 1970—Con.

[In millions of dollars]

Year	Under price support—Con.												Not under price support
	Mandatory support—Con.							Nonmandatory support					
	Nonbasic commodities [1]							Total	Soybeans	Cotton-seed	Flaxseed	Dry beans	
	Total	Dairy products	Oats	Barley	Sorghum grain	Sugar beets	Others [2]						
	313	314	315	316	317	318	319	320	321	322	323	324	325
1960	6,019	4,760	199	247	372	190	251	1,547	1,125	225	67	130	18,986
1959	5,915	4,604	189	262	401	191	268	1,462	1,042	214	80	126	18,816
1958	6,065	4,557	216	301	565	208	218	1,535	1,117	206	84	128	18,773
1957	5,722	4,628	204	245	237	171	237	1,345	948	200	83	114	16,738
1956	5,540	4,485	227	247	193	153	235	1,374	869	271	125	109	16,167
1955	5,271	4,217	246	242	211	136	219	1,330	832	250	124	124	15,686
1954	5,235	4,114	260	246	209	146	260	1,265	698	311	123	133	15,829
1953	5,260	4,366	220	185	86	141	262	1,222	661	311	113	137	16,340
1952	5,494	4,567	251	192	108	122	254	1,441	814	392	113	122	17,911
1951	5,350	4,254	253	218	144	128	353	1,304	702	374	112	116	19,248
1950	4,736	3,719	229	194	209	140	245	1,129	596	290	130	113	16,033
1949	4,573	3,748	236	179	104	106	200	1,039	489	246	155	149	14,894
1948	5,326	4,389	306	232	110	97	192	1,309	489	353	324	143	16,403
1947	5,075	4,013	332	275	106	152	197	1,198	506	337	200	155	16,168
1946	4,595	3,709	303	189	86	111	197	879	455	204	84	136	14,309
1945	3,777	3,021	214	155	97	101	189	682	365	149	94	74	12,867
1944	3,570	2,915	166	140	69	77	203	742	360	200	76	106	12,160
1943	3,425	2,785	155	151	61	53	220	815	365	189	142	119	12,051
1942	2,831	2,330	102	90	21	84	204	602	234	189	86	93	9,106
1941	2,305	1,900	83	62	17	59	184	413	117	177	54	65	6,049
1940	1,821	1,521	58	42	9	56	135	200	42	83	34	41	4,649
1939	1,603	1,346	46	40	7	49	115	193	51	77	26	39	4,436
1938	1,634	1,388	43	38	8	55	102	173	34	89	12	38	4,315
1937	1,855	1,525	67	43	8	52	160	208	31	113	13	51	4,812
1936	1,774	1,478	47	46	8	56	139	224	27	142	10	45	4,604
1935	1,529	1,310	45	32	3	43	96	178	22	103	18	35	4,003
1934	1,340	1,146	26	24	5	40	99	162	13	104	9	36	3,299
1933	1,224	1,004	36	19	5	58	102	92	6	49	11	26	2,814
1932	1,129	986	31	14	4	48	46	75	6	42	9	18	2,670
1931	1,455	1,277	42	15	4	51	66	95	7	42	15	31	3,759
1930	1,881	1,608	74	33	7	63	96	212	14	97	32	69	5,176

[1] Under legislation in effect in 1969. Prior to 1959, support was nonmandatory for oats, barley, sorghum grain, and rye.

[2] Includes wool, mohair, honey, tung nuts, rye, and sugarcane.

Series K 326–329. Direct Government Payments to Farmers, by Program: 1933 to 1970

[In millions of dollars]

Year	Total [1] (326)	Conservation [2] (327)	Sugar Act (328)	Cotton (329)
1970	3,717	208	88	919
1969	3,794	204	78	828
1968	3,462	229	75	787
1967	3,079	237	70	932
1966	3,277	231	71	773
1965	2,463	224	75	70
1964	2,181	236	79	39
1963	1,696	231	67	–
1962	1,747	230	64	–
1961	1,493	236	53	–
1960	702	223	59	–
1959	682	233	44	–
1958	1,089	215	44	–
1957	1,016	230	32	–
1956	554	220	37	–
1955	229	188	41	–
1954	257	217	40	–
1953	213	181	32	–
1952	275	242	33	–
1951	286	246	40	–
1950	283	246	37	–
1949	185	156	30	–
1948	257	218	39	–
1947	314	277	37	–
1946	772	285	31	–
1945	742	259	24	–
1944	776	378	27	–
1943	645	332	36	–
1942	650	450	25	–
1941	544	382	27	–
1940	723	496	27	–
1939	763	527	28	8
1938	446	309	22	114
1937	336	324	----	41
1936	278	24	----	
1935	573	----	----	15
1934	446	----	----	51
1933	131	----	----	----

– Represents zero.

[1] Includes programs not shown separately.

[2] Includes Great Plains and other conservation programs.

Series K 330–343. Commodity Credit Corporation—Summary: 1934 to 1970

[In millions of dollars. As of June 30]

Year	Value of loans made	Value of loans outstanding				Cost of acquisitions [1][2]				Value of commodities owned [1][2]				Cost of sales and donations, and other expenses [3]
		Total	Wheat	Corn	Cotton	Total	Wheat	Corn	Cotton	Total	Wheat	Corn	Cotton	
	330	331	332	333	334	335	336	337	338	339	340	341	342	343
1970	2,388	2,952	576	632	170	1,518	217	49	304	1,858	405	293	225	1,195
1969	2,964	3,493	583	656	324	939	96	179	7	1,244	225	306	27	821
1968	2,052	2,345	298	606	61	599	9	3	132	913	149	162	101	1,690
1967	1,411	1,536	96	296	153	1,351	24	111	742	1,858	195	168	1,051	2,816
1966	1,971	2,231	111	451	731	1,540	55	191	767	3,113	680	344	1,497	2,645
1965	2,144	2,534	136	616	775	2,005	169	140	952	3,892	1,297	595	1,123	2,880
1964	2,776	2,815	115	641	1,012	2,305	212	541	760	4,338	1,683	906	739	3,178
1963	3,070	2,602	161	1,044	751	2,771	454	709	566	4,726	2,168	604	719	3,070
1962	2,662	2,255	149	1,040	591	1,969	257	431	(Z)	4,474	2,143	737	249	3,691
1961	1,814	1,523	223	782	12	3,066	498	449	1,226	5,563	2,484	1,696	340	3,991
1960	1,507	1,347	163	646	9	4,020	371	361	2,507	6,021	2,452	1,700	880	3,790
1959	3,543	2,480	158	513	1,060	2,802	892	359	335	5,259	2,416	1,576	150	2,642
1958	2,135	1,600	68	511	366	2,999	378	695	604	4,703	1,862	1,609	179	3,380
1957	2,445	1,994	28	710	603	3,086	346	611	1,025	4,738	1,883	1,297	845	4,051
1956	3,024	2,319	90	654	979	3,150	552	461	1,166	5,384	2,205	1,136	1,184	2,689
1955	2,377	2,137	32	470	1,129	2,985	1,075	586	271	4,572	2,297	934	266	2,125
1954	3,355	2,368	198	641	1,157	2,396	965	516	(Z)	3,430	1,813	581	17	1,389
1953	2,129	1,163	97	468	290	1,598	855	8	78	2,158	1,090	324	31	513
1952	949	390	47	55	48	502	256	72	1	1,073	364	500	(Z)	905
1951	771	354	22	180	1	908	203	266	19	1,433	483	643	16	2,115
1950	2,023	923	65	554	122	2,716	601	601	633	2,624	760	506	580	1,184
1949	2,169	1,270	40	456	609	1,617	622	14	3	1,082	(Z)	(Z)	(Z)	685
1948	289	144	8	1	5	373	(Z)		(Z)	150	(Z)	(NA)	(Z)	524
1947	278	121	1	17	2	424			82	294	(NA)	(NA)	1	530
1946	185	48	4	(Z)	32					490	53	14	141	2,922
1945	534	309	31	17	252					922	154	20	448	3,188
1944	531	436	24	5	399					861	160	5	191	
1943	841	479	161	67	230					896	315	22	199	
1942	609	336	100	154	65					678	325	46	239	
1941	453	359	27	185	108					726	133	142	351	
1940	308	168	7	106	36					473	1	58	369	
1939	457	360	10	26	292					11	4	7		
1938	280	241		7	220					9		9		
1937	1	123		(Z)	114									
1936	29	243		5	226									
1935	311	152		1	139									
1934	260	205		117	88									

NA Not available.
Z Less than $500,000.
[1] Price support commodities only.

[2] Prior to 1953, inventory dollar transactions include costs incurred subsequent to acquisition of title, such as storage, handling, transportation, and cost of storing certain grains while under extended loan.

[3] Beginning 1953, includes storage and handling expense and reseal loan storage expense.

Series K 344–353. Indexes of Prices Received and Paid by Farmers, and Parity Ratio: 1910 to 1970

Year	Indexes of prices received and paid by farmers (1967 = 100)									Parity ratio [1]
	Prices received by farmers			Prices paid by farmers		Payable per acre		Wage rates	Prices paid, including interest, taxes, and wage rates	
	All farm products	Crops	Livestock and products	Living	Production	Interest payable	Taxes payable			
	344	345	346	347	348	349	350	351	352	353
1970	110	100	118	114	110	128	134	128	114	72
1969	108	97	116	109	106	119	124	119	109	74
1968	103	101	104	104	102	110	111	108	104	73
1967	100	100	100	100	100	100	100	100	100	74
1966	105	105	105	98	99	90	92	93	98	80
1965	98	103	94	95	96	80	85	86	94	77
1964	93	106	85	93	94	71	80	82	92	76
1963	96	106	89	92	95	63	77	80	91	78
1962	96	103	92	91	94	56	74	78	90	80
1961	94	100	91	90	93	51	70	76	88	79
1960*	94	99	91	90	92	46	66	74	88	80
1959	95	98	93	89	93	42	60	72	87	81
1958	98	99	99	89	92	38	56	68	84	81
1957	92	99	88	88	90	35	52	66	84	82
1956	91	104	82	85	87	32	49	63	81	83
1955	91	102	84	84	87	28	45	61	81	84
1954	97	107	90	84	89	26	43	60	81	89
1953	100	106	97	84	89	24	41	61	81	92
1952	113	118	110	84	95	23	39	59	84	100
1951	119	117	121	83	95	21	38	55	82	107

See footnotes at end of table.

Series K 344-353. Indexes of Prices Received and Paid by Farmers, and Parity Ratio: 1910 to 1970—Con.

Year	All farm products 344	Crops 345	Livestock and products 346	Living 347	Production 348	Interest payable 349	Taxes payable 350	Wage rates 351	Prices paid, including interest, taxes, and wage rates 352	Parity ratio[1] 353	Year	All farm products 344	Crops 345	Livestock and products 346	Living 347	Production 348	Interest payable 349	Taxes payable 350	Wage rates 351	Prices paid, including interest, taxes, and wage rates 352	Parity ratio[1] 353
1950	102	103	101	76	86	19	36	50	75	101	1930	49	55	48	45	47	43	32	21	44	83
1949	98	111	98	75	83	17	34	51	73	100	1929	58	65	57	48	51	45	31	22	47	92
1948	113	127	114	78	87	16	31	52	76	110	1928	58	65	56	48	52	46	31	22	47	91
1947	109	122	104	74	78	16	27	49	70	115	1927	55	62	53	48	49	47	31	22	46	88
1946	93	104	87	63	67	15	24	46	61	113	1926	57	64	55	49	49	48	30	22	47	91
1945	81	92	76	57	61	16	22	42	56	109	1925	61	69	54	50	51	49	30	21	48	95
1944	78	87	71	54	60	17	21	38	53	108	1924	56	63	46	48	49	52	30	21	47	89
1943	76	85	71	52	57	18	21	31	50	113	1923	56	63	46	48	48	55	29	20	46	89
1942	63	70	62	46	52	20	21	23	44	105	1922	52	58	45	48	44	54	29	18	44	87
1941	49	55	50	40	45	21	21	18	39	93	1921	49	55	46	51	45	52	27	18	45	80
1940	39	44	39	38	43	21	21	15	36	81	1920	83	93	69	71	68	45	23	28	63	99
1939	37	42	39	37	42	22	21	15	36	77	1919	85	96	74	63	68	38	18	24	58	110
1938	38	43	40	38	43	23	21	15	36	78	1918	81	91	70	53	63	33	17	21	51	119
1937	48	54	45	40	46	24	20	15	38	93	1917	70	79	60	44	54	30	15	17	43	120
1936	45	50	43	39	43	26	20	13	36	92	1916	47	53	42	36	40	28	14	13	34	103
1935	43	48	41	39	43	28	20	13	36	88	1915	39	44	37	32	36	26	13	12	31	94
1934	35	40	29	38	40	31	21	12	35	75	1914	40	45	39	32	36	24	13	12	30	98
1933	28	31	25	34	34	34	25	10	32	64	1913	40	45	38	31	35	23	12	12	30	101
1932	26	29	26	33	34	39	29	12	33	58	1912	39	44	35	31	36	21	11	12	30	98
1931	34	38	35	39	39	41	31	16	38	67	1911	37	42	32	31	34	19	10	12	29	96
											1910	41	46	37	31	34	17	10	11	28	107

* Denotes first year for which figures include Alaska and Hawaii.

[1] Ratio of prices received by farmers to prices paid, including interest, taxes, and wages rates.

Series K 354-357. Farm-to-Retail Price Spreads of Farm Food Products: 1913 to 1970

Year	Retail cost 354	Farm value[1] 355	Farm-retail spread 356	Farmer's share 357	Year	Retail cost 354	Farm value[1] 355	Farm-retail spread 356	Farmer's share 357	Year	Retail cost 354	Farm value[1] 355	Farm-retail spread 356	Farmer's share 357
	Dollars	Dollars	Dollars	Percent		Dollars	Dollars	Dollars	Percent		Dollars	Dollars	Dollars	Percent
1970	1,223	476	747	39	1950	878	415	463	47	1930	568	218	350	38
1969	1,176	480	696	41	1949	884	418	466	47	1929	587	245	342	42
1968	1,119	441	678	39	1948	935	477	458	51	1928	587	246	341	42
1967	1,081	419	662	39	1947	868	448	420	52	1927	585	237	348	41
1966	1,092	445	647	41	1946	711	373	338	53	1926	604	249	355	41
1965	1,037	416	621	40	1945	618	329	289	53	1925	595	249	346	42
1964	1,009	377	632	37	1944	608	312	296	51	1924	547	218	329	40
1963	1,007	378	629	38	1943	618	316	302	51	1923	556	220	336	39
1962	1,009	395	614	39	1942	551	261	290	47	1922	550	217	333	39
1961	999	386	613	39	1941	470	206	264	44	1921	575	228	347	40
1960	996	393	603	39	1940	430	170	260	40	1920	764	327	437	43
1959	991	385	606	39	1939	428	163	265	38	1919	688	331	357	48
1958	1,015	418	597	41	1938	443	170	273	38	1918	614	311	303	51
1957	960	388	572	40	1937	489	202	287	41	1917	594	277	317	47
1956	926	374	552	40	1936	471	189	282	40	1916	431	191	240	44
1955	923	379	544	41	1935	467	179	288	38	1915	360	158	202	44
1954	939	405	534	43	1934	420	142	278	34	1914	365	165	200	45
1953	956	428	528	45	1933	373	120	253	32	1913	354	163	191	46
1952	985	463	522	47	1932	384	120	264	31					
1951	975	477	498	49	1931	458	160	298	35					

[1] Payments to farmers, exclusive of government subsidies, for unprocessed products.

Series K 358–360. Consumer Expenditures, Farm Value, and Marketing Bill, for All Farm Food Products Purchased by Domestic Civilian Consumers: 1913 to 1970

[In billions of dollars]

Year	Consumer expenditures 358	Farm value 359	Marketing bill 360	Year	Consumer expenditures[1] 358	Farm value 359	Marketing bill 360	Year	Consumer expenditures[1] 358	Farm value 359	Marketing bill 360	Year	Consumer expenditures[1] 358	Farm value 359	Marketing bill 360
1970	101.6	68.5	33.1	1954	51.1	32.3	18.8	1939[4]	15.3	5.4	9.9	1926	16.4	7.0	9.4
1969	95.3	63.2	32.1	1953	51.0	31.5	19.5	1939	13.4	5.2	8.2	1925	15.7	6.8	8.9
1968	90.1	61.1	29.0	1952	50.9	30.5	20.4	1938	13.4	5.2	8.2	1924	14.5	5.9	8.6
1967	84.8	57.5	27.3	1951	49.2	28.7	20.5	1937	14.2	6.0	8.2	1923	14.0	5.6	8.4
1966	82.8	54.7	28.1	1950	44.0	26.0	18.0	1936	14.3	5.8	8.5	1922	12.9	5.2	7.7
												1921	12.6	5.1	7.5
1965	77.6	52.1	25.5	1949	43.4	26.0	17.4	1935[4]	13.8	5.2	8.6				
1964	74.6	51.2	23.4	1948	44.8	24.9	19.9	1935	12.9	5.0	7.9	1920	16.5	7.4	9.1
1963	71.5	48.9	22.6	1947[2]	41.9	22.6	19.3	1934	12.5	4.3	8.2	1919	15.2	7.6	7.6
1962	69.3	46.9	22.4	1947[3]	36.5	18.7	17.8	1933	10.9	3.6	7.3	1918	13.2	6.9	6.3
1961	67.1	45.1	22.0	1946	30.8	15.7	15.6	1932	10.6	3.4	7.2	1917	12.4	6.1	6.3
								1931	13.1	4.7	8.4	1916	9.5	4.4	5.1
1960	65.9	44.2	21.7	1945	24.4	12.6	12.5								
1959	63.1	42.2	20.9	1944	22.5	11.6	11.4	1930	16.2	6.3	9.9	1915	8.0	3.6	4.4
1958	61.0	39.5	21.5	1943	22.3	11.4	11.1	1929[4]	18.0	7.5	10.5	1914	7.9	3.6	4.3
1957	58.3	37.9	20.4	1942	19.8	9.3	10.5	1929	17.1	7.2	9.9	1913	7.4	3.5	3.9
1956	55.5	36.3	19.2	1941	16.3	7.1	9.2	1928	16.3	6.9	9.4				
1955	53.1	34.4	18.7	1940	14.1	5.6	8.5	1927	16.2	6.7	9.5				

[1] For 1913–1947, consumer expenditures for farm foods eaten away from home are based on retail food store prices.
[2] Comparable with later years. Beginning 1947, new series based on 1958 benchmark estimate (see text).
[3] Comparable with earlier years.
[4] Revised figures according to the commodity flow method; comparable to 1947–1970 data based on 1958 benchmark estimate.

Series K 361–375. Farm-Mortgage Debt, Loans, and Interest: 1890 to 1970

[In millions of dollars, except as indicated. Loans held by Federal Farm Mortgage Corporation (FFMC) are those made by Land Bank Commissioner. Land Bank Commissioner loans first made in 1933; in 1934 and thereafter made on behalf of FFMC. Authority to make new loans, except incidental to liquidation, expired July 1, 1947. On June 30, 1955, loans of the FFMC were sold to the 12 Federal land banks. Joint-stock land banks have been in liquidation since May 12, 1933; includes banks in receivership]

Year	Debt as of Jan. 1							Loans closed		Interest payable			Taxes levied on farm property		
	Total debt out-standing	Federal land banks and FFMC[1]	Life insurance com-panies[1]	Commer-cial and savings banks[2]	Joint-stock land banks[1]	Farmers Home Adminis-tration[3]	Indi-viduals and others	By Federal land banks and FFMC	By joint-stock land banks	Rates (percent)[4]		Total charges[5]	Real estate		Personal property
										Loans recorded	Loans outstand-ing, Jan. 1		Total	Amount per acre (dollars)	
	361	362	363	364	365	366	367	368	369	370	371	372	373	374	375
1970	28,407	6,671	5,733	4,113	--------	455	11,433	1,088	--------	(NA)	5.8	1,714	2,501	2.47	415
1969	27,139	6,081	5,763	3,856	--------	493	10,944	1,212	--------	[6] 6.8	5.7	1,597	2,295	2.27	408
1968	25,486	5,563	5,539	3,541	--------	536	10,305	1,123	--------	(NA)	5.6	1,475	2,067	2.05	415
1967	23,301	4,914	5,213	3,169	--------	585	9,418	1,266	--------	[6] 6.1	5.4	1,341	1,858	1.84	382
1966	21,186	4,240	4,801	2,939	--------	631	8,574	1,344	--------	(NA)	5.4	1,203	1,715	1.70	368
1965	18,894	3,686	4,287	2,668	--------	619	7,631	1,237	--------	[6] 5.6	5.4	1,075	1,583	1.57	338
1964	16,803	3,281	3,780	2,360	--------	605	6,775	1,014	--------	(NA)	5.3	951	1,487	1.47	331
1963	15,167	3,024	3,391	2,056	--------	588	6,106	759	--------	[6] 5.7	5.3	845	1,430	1.41	320
1962	13,899	2,803	3,161	1,789	--------	569	5,576	654	--------	(NA)	5.2	757	1,381	1.36	304
1961	12,820	2,539	2,974	1,691	--------	483	5,131	644	--------	[6] 5.8	5.1	684	1,315	1.29	298
1960	[7] 12,082	[7] 2,335	[7] 2,819	[7] 1,631	--------	[7] 439	[7] 4,857	520	--------	(NA)	5.0	627	1,244	1.22	286
1959	11,091	2,065	2,661	1,511	--------	388	4,464	626	--------	[6] 5.4	4.9	571	1,155	1.13	274
1958	10,382	1,897	2,578	1,414	--------	339	4,152	472	--------	(NA)	4.8	520	1,081	1.05	248
1957	9,821	1,722	2,476	1,386	--------	289	3,946	403	--------	[6] 5.2	4.7	482	1,032	.99	228
1956	9,012	1,480	2,271	1,346	--------	277	3,635	520	--------	(NA)	4.7	442	974	.92	219
1955	8,245	1,279	2,051	1,210	--------	287	3,415	482	--------	[6] 4.9	4.7	402	931	.88	223
1954	7,739	1,187	1,892	1,131	--------	282	3,246	301	--------	(NA)	4.6	371	878	.82	216
1953	7,240	1,095	1,716	1,105	--------	268	3,056	286	--------	[6] 5.0	4.6	345	847	.79	221
1952	6,662	1,026	1,541	1,046	--------	240	2,805	251	--------	(NA)	4.6	318	810	.76	229
1951	6,112	991	1,352	1,008	--------	220	2,539	211	--------	[6] 4.7	4.5	290	777	.73	209

See footnotes at end of table.

Series K 361–375. Farm-Mortgage Debt, Loans, and Interest: 1890 to 1970—Con.

[In millions of dollars, except as indicated]

Year	Debt as of Jan. 1							Loans closed		Interest payable			Taxes levied on farm property		
	Total debt out-standing	Federal land banks and FFMC [1]	Life insurance com-panies [1]	Commer-cial and savings banks [2]	Joint-stock land banks [1]	Farmers Home Adminis-tration	Indi-viduals and others	By Federal land banks and FFMC	By joint-stock land banks	Rates (percent) [4]		Total charges [5]	Real estate		Personal property
										Loans recorded	Loans outstand-ing, Jan. 1		Total	Amount per acre (dollars)	
	361	362	363	364	365	366	367	368	369	370	371	372	373	374	375
1950	5,579	964	1,172	937	0.3	193	2,311	203	_____	(NA)	4.5	263	742	.69	177
1949	5,288	946	1,036	900	.5	192	2,212	180	_____	[6] 4.7	4.5	243	706	.66	166
1948	5,064	995	959	840	.6	197	2,069	148	_____	(NA)	4.5	232	656	.62	150
1947	4,896	1,123	888	683	1.6	191	2,008	147	_____	[6] 4.5	4.5	224	605	.57	128
1946	4,760	1,318	891	507	3.2	184	1,856	143	_____	(NA)	4.6	218	519	.49	99
1945	4,940	1,556	938	449	5.5	195	1,795	120	(Z)	[6] 4.7	4.5	221	465	.44	92
1944	5,395	1,882	986	448	10.1	173	1,894	103	(NA)	(NA)	4.4	230	419	.40	80
1943	5,956	2,262	1,042	476	37.0	159	1,978	91	(Z)	[6] 4.8	4.4	246	400	.38	77
1942	6,376	2,515	1,063	535	55.9	115	2,090	81	.1	(NA)	4.4	272	400	.38	67
1941	6,493	2,642	1,016	543	73.5	65	2,151	102	(Z)	[6] 4.9	4.5	284	407	.39	56
1940	6,586	2,723	984	534	91.7	32	2,220	100	.1	(NA)	4.6	293	401	.39	50
1939	6,779	2,862	982	519	115.0	10	2,289	78	.4	(NA)	4.6	305	407	.39	49
1938	6,954	2,950	988	501	133.6	_____	2,380	80	.2	(NA)	4.7	320	400	.38	48
1937	7,153	2,989	1,015	487	162.8	_____	2,499	102	.4	(NA)	4.9	340	405	.39	47
1936	7,422	2,907	1,112	487	200.6	_____	2,714	185	.3	(NA)	5.1	364	394	.38	46
1935	7,584	2,564	1,301	498	277.0	_____	2,942	443	.3	5.4	5.5	396	392	.37	42
1934	7,685	1,328	1,697	710	412.3	_____	3,535	1,283	.2	5.3	5.8	430	384	.37	40
1933	8,466	1,147	1,898	889	475.0	_____	4,057	222	.7	5.8	6.0	472	398	.39	39
1932	9,093	1,180	2,036	940	552.2	_____	4,384	27	2.2	6.4	6.0	525	461	.45	49
1931	9,398	1,197	2,087	946	605.9	_____	4,561	41	5.4	6.4	6.0	553	526	.53	63
1930	9,630	1,201	2,118	997	637.8	_____	4,675	47	5.2	6.4	6.0	569	567	.57	81
1929	9,756	1,182	2,138	1,046	656.5	_____	4,731	63	18.2	6.3	6.0	581	568	.58	84
1928	9,756	1,144	2,172	1,097	669.8	_____	4,672	100	40.6	6.2	6.1	589	556	.58	80
1927	9,658	1,068	2,123	1,143	632.5	_____	4,690	138	83.7	6.2	6.1	593	545	.57	75
1926	9,713	998	2,030	1,178	545.6	_____	4,960	128	123.0	6.3	6.2	598	526	.56	73
1925	9,912	923	1,942	1,200	446.4	_____	5,400	124	131.4	6.3	6.3	611	517	.56	72
1924	10,664	797	1,792	1,388	392.6	_____	6,294	162	74.6	6.3	6.3	646	511	.55	72
1923	10,785	639	1,556	1,506	218.8	_____	6,864	190	189.7	6.3	6.4	679	516	.55	_____
1922	10,702	432	1,432	1,540	85.0	_____	7,212	224	138.7	6.7	6.3	679	509	.54	_____
1921	10,221	349	1,205	1,447	78.0	_____	7,140	91	9.3	7.0	6.2	652	510	.54	_____
1920	8,448	293	974	1,204	60.0	_____	5,915	66	19.3	6.4	6.1	574	483	.51	_____
1919	7,137	156	1,018	1,030	8.4	_____	4,924	144	53.0	6.4	6.1	476	393	.41	_____
1918	6,536	39	955	1,008	1.9	_____	4,531	118	6.6	6.3	6.1	417	311	.33	_____
1917	5,825	_____	861	933	_____	_____	4,030	39	1.9	6.2	6.1	378	292	.31	_____
1916	5,256	_____	765	776	_____	_____	3,714	_____	_____	6.3	6.2	340	260	.28	_____
1915	4,990	_____	669	746	_____	_____	3,574	_____	_____	6.4	6.1	314	243	.26	_____
1914	4,707	_____	597	723	_____	_____	3,386	_____	_____	6.4	6.1	296	222	.24	_____
1913	4,347	_____	550	673	_____	_____	3,123	_____	_____	6.4	6.1	276	218	.24	_____
1912	3,929	_____	479	580	_____	_____	2,869	_____	_____	6.4	6.1	251	191	.21	_____
1911	3,522	_____	423	477	_____	_____	2,621	_____	_____	6.4	6.0	225	183	.21	_____
1910	3,207	_____	386	406	_____	_____	2,414	_____	_____	6.4	6.0	203	166	.19	_____

Year	Taxes levied on farm real estate		Year	Taxes levied on farm real estate		Year	Taxes levied on farm real estate		Year	Taxes levied on farm real estate	
	Total	Amount per acre (dollars)		Total	Amount per acre (dollars)		Total	Amount per acre (dollars)		Total	Amount per care (dollars)
	373	374		373	374		373	374		373	374
1909	163	0.19	1904	125	0.15	1899	105	0.13	1894	93	0.13
1908	150	.17	1903	123	.15	1898	102	.13	1893	92	.13
1907	141	.16	1902	113	.14	1897	101	.13	1892	87	.13
1906	132	.16	1901	111	.13	1896	97	.13	1891	84	.13
1905	130	.15	1900	106	.13	1895	98	.14	1890	82	.13

NA Not available. Z Less than $50,000.
[1] Beginning 1930, includes purchase-money mortgages and sales contracts in addition to regular mortgages.
[2] Includes soil and water conservation loans and farm-ownership loans insured by Farmers Home Administration.
[3] Beginning October 1961, rural-housing loans were made on nonfarm tracts; these loans are included in amount outstanding reported for Jan. 1, 1962, but excluded beginning 1963.
[4] Average contract rates, except for temporarily reduced rates on outstanding loans of Federal land banks, 1934–1944, and Federal Farm Mortgage Corporation, 1938–1945.

[5] Payable during calendar year on outstanding loans. Excludes amounts paid by Secretary of the Treasury to Federal land banks, 1933–1944, and Federal Farm Mortgage Corporation, 1937–1945, as reimbursement for interest reductions granted borrowers.
[6] Average of rates on mortgages recorded during month of March except, beginning 1955, average rates on recordings during first quarter, and, beginning 1967, average rates on recordings during first half of year.
[7] Beginning 1960, includes data for reporting lending institutions in Alaska and Hawaii. No estimates of total farm-mortgage debt for these States are available.

Series K 376–383. Non-Real-Estate Agricultural Loans Outstanding and Indexes of Deposits of Country Banks: 1910 to 1970

[In millions of dollars, except indexes]

Year	All operating commercial banks [1]	Farmers Home Administration [2]	Agencies supervised by Farm Credit Administration — Production credit association	Federal intermediate credit banks [3]	Banks for cooperatives	Total deposits	Demand deposits	Time deposits
	376	377	378	379	380	381	382	383
1970	10,329	785	4,494	217	1,724	127	115	142
1969	9,719	821	3,825	180	1,567	118	111	129
1968	9,271	798	3,517	176	1,496	110	106	115
1967	8,533	737	3,015	156	1,277	100	100	100
1966	8,214	717	2,578	139	1,042	92	97	86
1965	7,506	643	2,277	124	944	83	93	73
1964	7,472	593	2,105	125	830	77	89	64
1963	7,099	556	1,838	109	723	72	87	56
1962	6,250	496	1,640	98	687	68	84	48
1961	5,677	419	1,479	88	639	63	81	40
1960	*5,019	*397	*1,361	*89	613	61	80	36
1959	4,910	405	1,114	83	500	62	85	34
1958	4,046	435	885	67	447	59	82	30
1957	4,101	430	699	60	450	56	80	26
1956	4,477	405	644	61	363	54	80	22
1955	4,659	417	576	58	359	54	79	21
1954	4,489	375	541	63	370	52	77	20
1953	3,920	337	599	82	416	50	76	18
1952	3,409	304	561	77	421	49	74	16
1951	2,906	329	450	62	343	46	71	14
1950	3,052	346	387	50	300	45	68	14
1949	2,861	342	366	55	303	43	66	14
1948	1,660	370	289	37	273	44	67	14
1947	1,333	400	230	31	177	44	66	13
1946	1,177	413	194	26	157	42	65	12
1945	1,377	452	188	29	212	35	54	10
1944	1,328	519	196	34	235	28	44	7
1943	1,490	525	182	38	144	21	34	6
1942	1,497	485	185	37	112	15	22	6
1941	1,326	459	170	33	74	13	17	6
1940	1,134	418	153	32	75	12	14	6
1939	1,109	351	146	32	87	11	13	6
1938	821	305	136	39	87	10	12	6
1937	620	321	104	40	69	10	13	6
1936	743	278	93	46	49	10	11	5
1935	840	203	60	55	27	8[5]	9[5]	5
1934	913	235	(Z)	60	18	7	8	5

Year	All operating commercial banks	Farmers Home Administration [2]	Federal intermediate credit banks [3]	Total deposits	Demand deposits	Time deposits
	376	377	379	381	382	383
1933	1,272	114	79	6	6	4
1932	1,649	49	71	8	7	6
1931	2,109	8[6]	62	10	10	7
1930	2,490	7[6]	47	11	11	8
1929	2,596	2[6]	43	12	13	8
1928	2,552	2[6]	42	12	13	8
1927	2,568	2[6]	38	12	13	8
1926	2,699	2[6]	25	12	13	8
1925	2,674	2[6]	18	12	13	8
1924	2,943	2[6]	9			
1923	3,088	3[6]				
1922	3,281	3[6]				
1921	3,869					
1920	3,453					
1919	2,661					
1918	2,489					
1917	2,033					
1916	1,747					
1915	1,605					
1914	1,596					
1913	1,520					
1912	1,379					
1911	1,338					
1910	1,350					

* Denotes first year for which figures include Alaska and Hawaii.
Z Less than $500,000.
[1] Data for 1935–1966 include loans guaranteed by Commodity Credit Corporation.
[2] Includes operating loans, emergency loans, emergency crop and feed loans, and, beginning 1966, economic opportunity loans; prior to 1933, only emergency crop and feed loans.
[3] Loans to, and discounts for, livestock loan companies and agricultural credit corporations.
[4] Based upon deposits of member banks of the Federal Reserve System located in places of less than 15,000 population: Ark., Ill., Ind., Iowa, Kans., Ky., Mich., Minn., Mo., Nebr., N.Y., N.C., N. Dak., Ohio, Okla., Pa., S. Dak., Tex., Wash., and Wis.
[5] Average of 7 months.
[6] July 1 of previous year.

Chapter K

Farm Productivity (Series K 384-495)

K 384–391. Index of supply and utilization of farm commodities as a percentage of total annual net utilization, 1924–1970.

Source: U.S. Department of Agriculture, Statistical Reporting Service, *Agricultural Statistics, 1967,* p. 542, and *1972,* p. 535.

This index is based on the disappearance data described in series G 881–915, converted to farm level, weighted by average 1957–59 farm prices to derive value aggregates in terms of constant dollars. Prices used are midmonth prices received by farmers in 1957–59 weighted by volume of monthly sales during that period. Both food and nonfood commodities are included.

Each part of the index includes processed and unprocessed commodities. Where processing of farm commodities yields byproducts or joint products, the relative economic importance of the various products is retained by apportioning the farm value of the unprocessed commodity according to the ratio of the wholesale value of the several resulting end products. For processed commodities where no byproduct or joint product is involved, direct conversion to the farm weight is made. See also Agriculture Handbook No. 91, *Measuring the Supply and Utilization of Farm Commodities,* 1955.

K 384, net production. Includes harvested crops (excluding amount used for feed and seed) and marketings of livestock products for consumption plus use on farms where produced.

K 385, net imports. Imports and inshipments from U.S. outlying areas include farm commodities similar to those produced in this country plus those not produced domestically but which are substitutes for U.S. products. Coffee, tea, cocoa, and bananas are included but rubber and silk are excluded. Dockside prices were used for commodities not produced in the United States. Imports include both processed and unprocessed commodities. Imports used for feed and seed are deducted from total imports.

Reports on shipments to and from Alaska and Hawaii were discontinued in April 1948. For foods for which such trade is significant, estimates of inshipments were made through 1959. Beginning 1960, Alaska and Hawaii are included as States.

K 388, civilian food. Figures are derived as a residual by deducting feed, seed, and other nonfood uses, exports and shipments, Government purchases for the military and for export, and ending stocks from total supply of each food available for the year.

K 389, military food. No reliable information on military food procurement is available before 1941, but such takings were relatively small between 1919 and 1940. Data from reports of the Armed Services are supplemented by estimates to cover local procurement of some fresh commodities and items supplied daily.

K 391, exports and shipments. Includes commercial and U.S. Department of Agriculture (USDA) exports and shipments. USDA export programs measure purchases by USDA from commercial sources for subsequent shipments under foreign supply and special export programs. Reports of trade with Alaska and Hawaii were discontinued in 1948 with estimates of some items being made through 1959; beginning 1960, Alaska and Hawaii are included as States.

K 392–406. Value of agricultural raw materials in constant (1967) dollars, 1900–1969.

Source: U.S. Bureau of the Census and U.S. Bureau of Mines, *Raw Materials in the United States Economy: 1900–1969* (Working Paper No. 35, 1972), tables A1–A4 and A7.

These series were obtained by multiplying the physical quantity of each raw material for a given year by the average unit dollar value of the material for 1967, then adding together for the given year all of these dollar values. For materials produced domestically, the unit-value weights represent averages at point of production for all of the specified materials which were produced in the United States in 1967. For materials which were not produced domestically in 1967, the weights usually represent comparable average unit values for materials imported during 1967.

For 1924–1969, the series for production, imports, exports, and consumption, K 392–395, are based primarily on data for supply and utilization of farm commodities developed by the Agricultural Marketing Service (AMS) and extended for 1962–1969 by the Economic Research Service (ERS). (See Major Statistical Series of the U.S. Department of Agriculture, vol. 5, *Consumption and Utilization of Agriculture Products,* Agriculture Handbook No. 118, December 1957, and U.S. Department of Agriculture, *Measuring the Supply and Utilization of Farm Commodities,* Agriculture Handbook No. 91, November 1955.) These data represent over 95 percent coverage and include essentially all farm commodities produced domestically and imported "complementary and supplementary commodities." The latter represent those that do not compete directly with commodities produced in the United States, such as coffee, tea, cocoa, bananas, and some oilseeds. They exclude rubber and other gum products, silk and vegetable fibers, such as sisal, hemp, and abaca, because they compete more directly with industrial products. They also exclude spices. Imports and consumption have been adjusted to include such foreign farm commodities.

The basic data are on a gross basis. They were adjusted to a net basis by excluding seed and feed consumed domestically from production and consumption.

For 1924–1954 the AMS data are in terms of 1947–1949 average farm prices. For 1955–1969, average farm prices for 1957–1959 were used in the AMS and ERS data. These prices represent receipts by farmers for their products sold at local markets or at the point to which they deliver their products in their own conveyances or in local conveyances hired for the purpose. For commodities not produced domestically, import prices for the first domestic transaction were used.

Consumption data include military takings but are adjusted, insofar as possible, to exclude from consumption and treat as exports quantities shipped for civilian use in liberated and occupied areas. Consumption data are also adjusted for changes in stocks and are, therefore, presented as actual rather than apparent consumption.

The AMS and ERS imports and exports data comprise the raw materials equivalent of the major manufactured products produced from agricultural materials.

For years prior to 1924, the AMS commodity group data were extrapolated back to 1900 by use of production, imports, and exports measures for major components of such series or for closely related series. These series are less precise than the measures for 1924 and later years and no attempt was made to adjust the derived apparent consumption figures for this early period for changes in stocks.

The AMS and ERS crop and livestock production data, K 396 and K 400, used for 1924–1969 measure crop production at the point of harvest and livestock products in terms of marketings for consumption. These data represent "gross production of all farm commodities." They have been adjusted to a net basis by excluding feed and seed. These production series were also adjusted to exclude the farm value of imported cattle and hogs.

For 1909–1923, the product group figures were extrapolated from 1924 by means of indexes of production for 12 groups of agricultural products taken from "Volume of Production of Crops and of Livestock Products for Sale and for Home Consumption, 1910–46," *The Farm*

Income Situation, U.S. Department of Agriculture FIS–83, December 1946.

For 1900–1908, production data used for extrapolation were taken from "Gross Farm Income and Indices of Farm Production and Prices in the United States, 1869–1937," by Frederick Strauss and Louis H. Bean, U.S. Department of Agriculture, Technical Bulletin No. 703, December 1940.

The basic source of imports and exports data compiled primarily by the AMS and ERS to measure the supply and utilization of farm commodities is Bureau of the Census imports and exports data. The AMS and ERS figures were supplemented by import figures for rubber, silk, vegetable fibers, and spices not covered by AMS and ERS and by certain imports and exports of cattle, hogs, live horses and mules, and live poultry for breeding.

For years prior to 1924, Bureau of the Census quantity series for imports and exports of commodities which are components of the AMS groups used for later years were combined to the AMS group level by use of unit-value weights.

K 407–409. Persons supplied per farmworker, 1820–1970.

Source: U.S. Department of Agriculture, *Agricultural Statistics*, annual issues.

The series is a ratio of all consumers of U.S. farm products to U.S. farmworkers. The series was designed to provide a simple, easily calculated measure of productivity of people employed in farming— farm operators, unpaid family workers, and hired workers. As a long-time measure, it appraises changes in farmworker efficiency. It is not intended to be a precise index of slight year-to-year variations in worker efficiency. Slight variations from year to year or during short periods merely denote changes in total yearly agricultural production and farm employment.

To attribute all of the increased productivity only to farmworkers would be a misuse of this series. Over the years, farms and farmworkers have become specialized. Many jobs and functions have been transferred from farms to nonfarm business firms. The classic example of this is the transfer of production of farm-power from farms to tractor manufacturing firms, from horses and mules to mechanized farming. More recently, functions transferred have taken other forms, such as feed preparation and management and custom services. Many nonfarm workers now perform functions formerly done by farmworkers. This series does not quantify their contributions.

As functions are transferred from farmworkers to non-farmworkers, the number used directly in farm production declines. However, the number of non-farmworkers engaged in production of goods and services used by farmers increases relative to farmworkers. Thus the series overstates the contribution of farmworkers and ignores the growing importance of non-farmworkers in agricultural production.

The meaning of "persons supplied" has changed over time. In the 19th century and early in the 20th century farmworkers did many things both on the farm and in the farm home which later were done by city workers. Furthermore, agricultural products supplied consumers are now greater in quantity and higher in quality than they were in early years.

The series covers the 48 conterminous States. Four sets of data are used in computing the series:

(1) The farm employment series is the annual average number of farm operators, unpaid family workers, and hired workers reported by the Statistical Reporting Service (SRS), rounded to the nearest 100,000.

(2) The total U.S. population is that reported by the Bureau of the Census for July 1, rounded to the nearest 100,000. Data are adjusted to 1940 definitions, and from 1940 include persons in U.S. military forces in this country and abroad.

(3) The value of agricultural exports and imports is obtained from the Economic Research Service (ERS) and the Foreign Agricultural Service.

(4) Data on the value of domestic production are from ERS.

The total supply available for consumption in this country is represented by the current dollar value of farm production minus the value of agricultural exports plus the value of agricultural imports. This value of supply, divided by the total U.S. population, gives the per capita level of all agricultural products available for any given year.

The value of U.S. farm production available for domestic use divided by the per capita level of all agricultural products available gives the number of persons in the United States who could be supplied at this level of support with agricultural products from U.S. farm production only.

The value of agricultural exports divided by the U.S. per capita level of agricultural products available gives the number of persons abroad who could be supplied at the same level with agricultural products from our farm production.

The domestic and foreign population that could be supplied by U.S. farm products is divided by total farm employment to obtain numbers of consumers supplied farm products by one farmworker.

K 410–413. Man-hours of labor required on farms, 1910–1970.

Source: See source for series K 407–409.

These series are used to establish the amount of, and to measure changes in, labor input in agriculture by various enterprises. The series were developed for each year by farm production regions beginning with 1939, and for the United States, beginning 1910. They are of help in determining the effects of technological advances, such as mechanization and new hybrids or varieties of crops and animals, on the quantity of farm labor used. They serve as the labor component of an index of total production inputs in agriculture. (See R. A. Loomis and G. T. Barton, *Productivity of Agriculture, United States, 1870–1959*, U.S. Department of Agriculture, Technical Bulletin 1238, 1961.)

The figures are derived for individual farm enterprises by applying average man-hours per acre of crops and per head or unit of production of livestock to the official estimates of acres and numbers reported by the Statistical Reporting Service. The man-hours per acre for each crop are divided into preharvest and harvest work. The hours for preharvest work are applied to the acres planted. They include time for hauling and spreading fertilizer, plowing and disking the land, planting or seeding, cultivating, irrigating, and spraying and dusting for pest control. The hours for harvest work are applied to the acres harvested. They include time for the main harvesting operations and for hauling the crop to storage and to the local market or processing plant.

Man-hours needed for the care and production of livestock include direct labor for such operations as feeding, hauling feed and bedding, cleaning barns and pens, moving animals to or from pasture or range, caring for animals, and disposing of the animals and their products.

Time for farm maintenance or general overhead work is calculated separately and added to the direct labor for crops and livestock in arriving at total man-hours for all farmwork. Maintenance labor includes time spent in constructing and maintaining fences, buildings, and irrigation and drainage structures; in repairing machinery and farm power units; in conservation work that is not part of a regular field operation; in work on permanent pastures and farm woodlots; in conducting the farm business; in making business trips; and in other miscellaneous overhead tasks.

K 414–429. Indexes of total output, and gross production of livestock and crops, by groups, 1870–1970.

Source: U.S. Department of Agriculture, 1870–1900, Statistical Reporting Service, *Gross Farm Income and Indices of Farm Production and Prices in the United States, 1869–1937*, Technical Bulletin No.703, December 1940; 1910–1933, Economic Research Service, *Changes in Farm Production and Efficiency*, Statistical Bulletin No. 233, August 1958 and July 1964; 1929–1970 (except for series K 425, 1929–1949, and K 429 [1967 = 100]), Council of Economic Advisers, *Economic Report of the President*, January 1972, p. 290 (data compiled by U.S. Department of Agriculture, Economic Research Service), and *Changes in Farm Production and Efficiency*, Statistical Bulletin No. 233, June 1972.

Series **K 425**, 1929–1949 (1967 = 100) and series **K 429**, compiled by Economic Research Service.

The index of farm output, series K 414, includes all crops produced during the crop year except hayseeds, pasture seeds, cover crop seeds, and hay and concentrates fed to horses and mules on farms. The index also includes "net" livestock production (gross livestock production minus hay and concentrates fed) other than horses and mules on a calendar-year basis. This calculation is made to eliminate counting of feed crops in both livestock and crop production. The farm output index is also available for each of the ten farm production regions from 1939 to 1970, and the U.S. data are available by decades from 1870 to 1910, and annually from 1910 to 1970. Although the indexes prior to 1910 are not strictly comparable with those for 1910–1970, they provide the best available measures for the early years.

The indexes for livestock production and crop production are measures of gross production, as they include items of production excluded in the index of farm output. They are subdivided into three livestock groups and nine crop groups. Meat animals, series K 416, includes cattle and calves, sheep and lambs, and hogs; dairy products, series K 417, includes butter, butterfat, wholesale milk, retail milk, and milk consumed on farms; and poultry and eggs, series K 418, includes chicken eggs, commercial broilers, chickens, and turkeys. Feed grains, series K 420, includes corn for grain, oats, barley, and sorghum grain; hay and forage, series K 421, includes all hay, sorghum forage, corn silage, and sorghum silage; food grains, series K 422, includes all wheat, rye, buckwheat, and rice; vegetables, series K 423, includes potatoes, sweetpotatoes, dry edible beans, dry field peas, truck crops for processing, and truck crops for fresh market having value; fruits and nuts, series K 424, includes fruits, berries, and tree nuts having value; sugar crops, series K 425, includes sugar beets, sugarcane for sugar and seed, sugarcane sirup, and maple sirup; cotton, series K 426, includes cotton lint and cottonseed; and oil crops, series K 428, includes soybeans, peanuts harvested for nuts, peanuts hogged, flaxseed, and tung nuts.

Weighted average prices per unit of each commodity are used in constructing these indexes. Separate sets of weights are calculated for each of the 10 farm production regions. Official reports of the Statistical Reporting Service are the chief sources of data on both production and prices. The omission of production from farm forests and other minor items probably accounts for less than 5 percent of the total output in recent years. Commodities of little importance are omitted in some regions for earlier years.

Three weight periods are used: 1935–39 prices for 1939 and prior years, 1947–49 prices for 1940 to 1954, and 1957–59 prices for the period beginning in 1955. The index series for the three subperiods are "spliced" together in 1939 and 1955 through the use of overlapped calculations for those years. Annual quantity-price aggregates for the United States are obtained by summing the regional data.

For more detail, see *Major Statistical Series of the United States Department of Agriculture*, Agriculture Handbook No. 365, vol. 2.

K 430–444. Indexes of farm output per man-hour, 1939–1970.

Source: U.S. Department of Agriculture, *Agricultural Statistics, 1972*, p. 540.

The index of farm labor productivity is the ratio of farm production to labor input. The index numbers are developed by relating the indexes of farm output and production of individual or groups of farm products to the appropriate index of labor input expressed in man-hours. The two basic series are explained in series K 414–429 and series K 445–485, respectively.

Indexes of farm labor productivity reflect the net effect of all factors that affect either farm production or the labor input. Labor is one of the more important inputs in agricultural production and changes in the ratio of production to labor provide a useful measure of changes in efficiency of farm production. These changes in production per man-hour must be evaluated in the light of changes in mechanization, yields of crops and livestock, and the other technological forces that operate on labor input and farm production.

K 445–485. Man-hours per unit and yield per unit of production of selected crops and livestock, 1800–1970.

Source: **Series K 445–472**, U.S. Department of Agriculture, 1800–1900, *Progress of Farm Mechanization*, Miscellaneous Publication No. 630, October 1947; 1910–14 to 1955–59, Economic Research Service, *Labor Used to Produce Field Crops*, Statistical Bulletin No. 346, May 1964, and unpublished data. **Series K 473–485**, U.S. Department of Agriculture, 1910–14 to 1945–49, *Gains in Productivity of Farm Labor*, Technical Bulletin No. 1020, December 1950; 1950–54 to 1955–59, *Labor Used to Produce Livestock*, Estimates by States, 1959, Statistical Bulletin No. 336, 1963. All series, U.S. Department of Agriculture, 1960–64 to 1965–69, *Agricultural Statistics, 1972*; 1970, unpublished data. (Before harvest and harvest data, unpublished compilations by Economic Research Service.)

For derivation of figures on man-hours of labor used in farming, see text for series K 410–413.

Estimates of annual man-hours per acre or per head are made by interpolating between or extrapolating from benchmarks. Benchmarks consist of estimates of labor used per acre and per head in each State converted to a farm production region basis. For livestock, interpolation of the labor hours between benchmarks takes into account changes in size of enterprise, such as cows per herd or chickens per flock; production per animal, such as milk per cow and eggs per hen; and extent of different methods and practices followed, such as proportion of farms with milking parlors.

State estimates for major benchmark years may be found in reports issued by the Bureau of Agricultural Economics and Agricultural Research Service, as well as the Economic Research Service.

For more detailed explanation, see *Major Statistical Series of the U.S. Department of Agriculture*, Agriculture Handbook, No. 365, vol. 2.

K 486–495. Indexes of total farm input and major input subgroups, 1910–1970.

Source: U.S. Department of Agriculture, 1910–1930, *Productivity of Agriculture*, Technical Bulletin No. 1238, April 1961; 1939–1970, *Changes in Farm Production and Efficiency*, Supplement V, Statistical Bulletin 233, July 1972.

The farm input index measures yearly changes in resources committed or used to produce farm output. It is also available for each of the 10 farm production regions from 1939 to 1970. Conceptually, the input series includes all inputs requiring annual cash expenditures, such as fertilizer, gasoline, and tires; in addition, it includes unpaid farm operator and family labor and a charge for the use of farmers' equity in capital investments.

The index is calculated by the weighted aggregate method. When possible, quantities of each input used during the year are multiplied by the weighted average prices paid by farmers in the weight period. When quantities are not available, current dollar values are deflated by appropriate indexes of prices paid. To compute the input index, the quantity-price aggregates are expressed as a percentage of average quantity-price aggregates in the reference period.

Three weight periods are used: 1935–39 for the years prior to 1939, 1947–49 for 1939 to 1954, and 1957–59 for 1955 and later years. The quantity-price aggregates are spliced at 1939 and 1955 to convert to one final series of index numbers. The 1967 quantity-price aggregate is used as the reference period. Annual quantity-price aggregates for the United States are obtained by summing the regional data for 1939 and later years. Only U.S. data were calculated for years prior to 1939.

In calculating total farm input, indexes for seven major groups of inputs, series K 489–495, are computed. In addition, inputs are divided into purchased and nonpurchased, series K 487 and K 488. The input index is revised following revision of the data from which it is derived. Most of these revisions are based on benchmarks established by the census of agriculture.

For more detail, see *Major Statistical Series of the United States Department of Agriculture*, Agriculture Handbook No. 365, vol. 2.

Series K 384–391. Index of Supply and Utilization of Farm Commodities as a Percentage of Total Annual Net Utilization: 1924 to 1970

[Domestic use estimated on the basis of value of processed products.   "Net" concept excludes domestic use of feed and seed to avoid double counting]

Year	Percent of supply, by source			Percent of annual net utilization, by type of use				
	Net production	Net imports	Stock change [1]	Domestic use				Exports and shipments
				Total	Food		Net nonfood use [3]	
					Civilian	Military [2]		
	384	385	386	387	388	389	390	391
1970	85.9	11.0	3.1	85.7	76.0	1.1	8.6	14.3
1969	89.6	11.1	−.7	87.8	76.9	1.4	9.5	12.2
1968	89.1	12.1	−1.2	86.5	75.1	1.6	9.8	13.5
1967	89.8	11.1	−.9	86.3	74.8	1.7	9.8	13.7
1966	85.0	11.3	3.7	85.1	72.9	1.6	10.6	14.9
1965	90.7	10.7	−1.4	85.6	73.5	1.5	10.6	14.4
1964	86.5	10.5	3.0	84.3	72.9	1.4	10.0	15.7
1963	89.7	12.0	−1.7	85.8	74.5	1.3	10.0	14.2
1962	88.4	12.2	−.6	86.9	74.4	1.4	11.1	13.1
1961	88.5	11.5	(NA)	86.5	74.8	1.3	10.4	13.5
1960	* 91.1	11.1	* −2.2	* 86.4	* 74.7	* 1.2	* 10.5	13.6
1959	89.4	12.7	−2.1	88.8	76.1	1.4	11.3	11.2
1958	93.2	11.4	−4.6	88.9	76.6	1.5	10.8	11.1
1957	88.4	10.7	.9	87.1	75.0	1.4	10.7	12.9
1956	90.1	10.8	−.9	88.4	75.3	1.6	11.5	11.6
1955	93.0	11.0	−4.0	90.7	77.1	1.7	11.9	9.3
1954	93.5	10.6	−4.1	91.1	77.5	2.0	11.6	8.9
1953	92.9	12.0	−4.9	92.0	77.0	2.3	12.7	8.0
1952	91.6	11.6	−3.2	90.8	75.8	2.5	12.5	9.2
1951	85.4	11.6	3.0	89.4	72.7	3.4	13.3	10.6
1950	87.3	12.4	.3	91.1	75.2	1.7	14.2	8.9
1949	91.4	11.6	−3.0	91.2	75.4	3.5	12.3	8.8
1948	96.2	12.2	−8.4	92.8	75.2	3.5	14.1	7.2
1947	86.8	10.8	2.4	90.9	74.7	2.9	13.3	9.1
1946	87.0	11.0	2.0	90.1	73.6	2.7	13.8	9.9
1945	86.4	10.6	3.0	92.2	67.9	10.5	13.8	7.8
1944	89.7	10.5	−.2	92.6	67.1	11.3	14.2	7.4
1943	84.8	9.9	5.3	91.8	68.6	8.0	15.2	8.2
1942	94.1	9.6	−3.7	94.3	72.9	5.2	16.2	5.7
1941	88.9	14.6	−3.5	95.4	77.7	1.6	16.1	4.6
1940	91.2	12.6	−3.8	95.0	81.3	----------	13.7	5.0
1939	88.3	12.8	−1.1	93.4	80.1	----------	13.3	6.6
1938	93.1	12.4	−5.5	92.1	80.1	----------	12.0	7.9
1937	97.0	14.7	−11.7	93.3	79.5	----------	13.8	6.7
1936	79.0	14.1	6.9	94.0	80.1	----------	13.9	6.0
1935	90.9	14.1	−5.0	93.3	80.8	----------	12.5	6.7
1934	81.2	10.9	7.9	93.1	81.6	----------	11.5	6.9
1933	84.1	11.6	4.3	91.2	79.6	----------	11.6	8.8
1932	91.4	10.4	−1.8	90.1	80.3	----------	9.8	9.9
1931	94.4	11.8	−6.2	90.9	80.1	----------	10.8	9.1
1930	88.8	12.9	−1.7	90.5	79.5	----------	11.0	9.5
1929	85.9	14.1	(NA)	89.2	76.8	----------	12.4	10.8
1928	88.3	12.7	−1.0	88.2	76.3	----------	11.9	11.8
1927	85.6	12.7	1.7	87.4	75.0	----------	12.4	12.6
1926	89.0	13.1	−2.1	88.2	76.4	----------	11.8	11.8
1925	87.1	12.8	.1	88.2	76.4	----------	11.8	11.8
1924	89.4	11.8	−1.2	87.6	76.9	----------	10.7	12.4

* Denotes first year for which figures include Alaska and Hawaii.
NA   Not available.
[1] Farm, commercial, and government holdings; excludes live animal inventory. Negative sign indicates stock increases; positive figures denote withdrawals.

[2] Includes civilian feeding in occupied areas.
[3] Includes alcoholic beverages, soap, and industrial uses.

Series K 392–406. Value of Agricultural Raw Materials in Constant (1967) Dollars: 1900 to 1969

[In millions of dollars]

Year	Total				Crops				Livestock				Used for feed and seed		
	Production, net	Imports	Exports	Consumption	Production, net	Imports	Exports	Consumption	Production, net	Imports	Exports	Consumption	Total	Crops	Livestock
	392	393	394	395	396	397	398	399	400	401	402	403	404	405	406
1969	35,552	4,272	4,797	35,002	13,662	3,118	4,020	12,664	21,890	1,154	777	22,338	10,449	9,736	713
1968	35,467	4,639	5,171	34,608	13,601	3,447	4,379	12,318	21,866	1,192	792	22,290	10,057	9,358	699
1967	35,162	4,134	5,113	33,744	13,481	3,122	4,358	12,009	21,681	1,012	755	21,735	9,737	9,001	736
1966	32,891	4,233	5,407	33,044	12,079	3,127	4,668	11,931	20,812	1,106	739	21,113	10,242	9,364	878
1965	33,973	3,958	5,127	32,394	13,502	2,953	4,252	11,781	20,471	1,005	875	20,613	9,163	8,325	838
1964	32,776	3,836	5,603	32,177	11,865	2,930	4,445	11,427	20,911	906	1,158	20,750	9,421	8,539	882
1963	32,494	4,213	4,840	31,474	12,641	3,051	3,915	11,374	19,853	1,162	925	20,100	9,426	8,564	862
1962	31,145	4,179	4,315	30,800	11,920	3,062	3,623	11,278	19,225	1,117	692	19,522	9,432	8,562	870
1961	30,563	3,871	4,259	30,215	11,448	2,944	3,565	11,123	19,115	927	694	19,092	9,343	8,418	925
1960	30,793	3,681	4,231	29,605	12,112	2,881	3,578	10,843	18,681	800	653	18,762	8,896	7,974	922
1959	29,621	4,084	3,435	29,549	11,287	3,117	2,789	10,852	18,334	967	646	18,697	9,215	8,322	893
1958	29,395	3,618	3,223	28,368	11,787	2,788	2,625	10,424	17,608	830	598	17,944	8,925	7,969	956
1957	28,886	3,452	3,828	28,649	10,728	2,846	3,131	10,463	18,158	606	697	18,186	8,288	7,291	997
1956	29,448	3,394	3,479	29,091	10,849	2,867	2,667	10,577	18,599	527	812	18,514	8,470	7,388	1,082
1955	28,604	3,313	2,678	28,224	10,799	2,761	1,928	10,254	17,805	552	750	17,970	8,402	7,248	1,154
1954	27,507	3,056	2,438	27,059	10,513	2,605	1,923	10,021	16,994	451	515	17,038	8,512	7,201	1,311
1953	27,160	3,521	2,173	27,065	10,410	2,973	1,718	10,166	16,750	548	455	16,899	8,605	7,437	1,168
1952	26,430	3,498	2,416	26,486	10,466	2,854	2,049	10,185	15,964	644	367	16,301	8,753	7,599	1,154
1951	25,028	3,454	2,841	26,312	9,610	2,798	2,349	10,453	15,418	656	492	15,859	8,990	7,715	1,275
1950	24,870	3,546	2,359	26,265	9,428	2,781	1,909	10,332	15,442	765	450	15,933	8,860	7,566	1,294
1949	25,238	3,252	2,280	24,936	10,044	2,778	1,902	9,591	15,194	474	378	15,345	8,630	7,354	1,276
1948	26,162	3,425	1,841	25,237	11,386	2,689	1,529	9,862	14,776	736	312	15,375	8,179	6,932	1,247
1947	25,062	3,051	2,421	26,021	9,174	2,614	1,860	10,211	15,888	437	561	15,810	8,592	7,267	1,325
1946	25,388	3,144	2,774	26,106	9,632	2,426	1,765	10,412	15,756	718	1,009	15,694	9,048	7,808	1,240
1945	24,839	2,951	2,193	25,998	8,719	2,381	1,244	10,287	16,120	570	949	15,711	9,211	7,847	1,364
1944	25,750	3,175	2,121	26,288	9,006	2,646	747	10,148	16,744	529	1,374	16,140	9,272	7,859	1,413
1943	23,190	2,716	2,225	24,788	7,163	2,131	822	9,615	16,027	585	1,403	15,173	10,340	8,764	1,576
1942	23,675	2,319	1,428	23,982	8,973	1,621	551	9,699	14,702	698	877	14,283	9,350	7,650	1,700
1941	21,552	3,716	1,065	23,406	8,280	2,848	641	9,770	13,272	868	424	13,636	8,622	6,811	1,811
1940	20,828	3,148	1,079	22,097	8,024	2,492	910	8,843	12,804	656	169	13,254	8,361	6,604	1,757
1939	19,922	3,093	1,392	21,425	7,907	2,406	1,227	8,779	12,015	687	165	12,646	8,115	6,367	1,748
1938	19,816	2,825	1,567	19,984	8,299	2,295	1,427	7,970	11,517	530	140	12,014	7,746	6,015	1,731
1937	20,709	3,531	1,381	20,352	9,594	2,789	1,268	8,343	11,115	742	113	12,009	6,993	5,355	1,638
1936	17,087	3,267	1,230	20,479	5,611	2,533	1,117	8,365	11,476	734	113	12,114	7,190	5,506	1,684
1935	18,338	3,152	1,302	19,302	7,921	2,488	1,179	8,049	10,417	664	123	11,253	7,043	5,339	1,704
1934	17,315	2,436	1,399	20,064	5,141	1,993	1,192	7,687	12,174	443	207	12,377	6,754	4,990	1,764
1933	17,759	2,568	1,747	19,444	6,022	2,009	1,540	7,402	11,737	559	207	12,042	8,031	6,187	1,844
1932	18,424	2,354	1,913	18,661	7,132	1,873	1,720	6,923	11,292	481	193	11,738	8,375	6,533	1,842
1931	19,479	2,756	1,811	19,190	8,162	2,151	1,578	7,383	11,317	605	233	11,807	7,764	5,921	1,843
1930	18,404	2,961	1,881	19,127	7,296	2,301	1,592	7,528	11,108	660	289	11,599	7,647	5,896	1,751
1929	18,331	3,395	2,204	19,561	7,310	2,440	1,858	7,816	11,021	955	346	11,745	8,020	6,297	1,723
1928	18,414	3,032	2,370	18,956	7,452	2,173	2,039	7,442	10,962	859	331	11,514	8,134	6,439	1,695
1927	17,996	3,021	2,531	18,989	7,032	2,205	2,202	7,378	10,964	816	329	11,561	8,266	6,545	1,721
1926	18,611	3,013	2,365	18,876	7,585	2,289	2,000	7,366	11,026	724	365	11,510	7,570	5,883	1,687
1925	17,931	2,847	2,340	18,493	7,027	2,159	1,906	7,155	10,904	688	434	11,338	8,000	6,376	1,624
1924	18,121	2,572	2,409	18,101	6,897	1,994	1,866	6,709	11,224	578	543	11,392	7,646	6,036	1,610
1923	17,433	2,734	2,137	18,030	6,416	2,037	1,493	6,960	11,017	697	644	11,070	————	————	————
1922	16,798	2,618	2,469	16,947	6,451	1,936	1,933	6,454	10,347	682	536	10,493	————	————	————
1921	15,144	2,278	2,846	14,576	5,507	1,671	2,218	4,960	9,637	607	628	9,616	————	————	————
1920	16,820	2,479	2,571	16,728	7,145	1,773	1,888	7,030	9,675	706	683	9,698	————	————	————
1919	16,855	2,560	3,295	16,120	6,551	1,716	2,055	6,212	10,304	844	1,240	9,908	————	————	————
1918	16,856	2,284	2,735	16,405	6,776	1,453	1,376	6,853	10,080	831	1,359	9,552	————	————	————
1917	15,851	2,301	2,102	16,050	6,340	1,617	1,280	6,677	9,511	684	822	9,373	————	————	————
1916	15,263	2,164	2,750	14,677	5,775	1,469	1,893	5,351	9,488	695	857	9,326	————	————	————
1915	15,828	2,164	3,087	14,905	6,627	1,367	2,215	5,779	9,201	797	872	9,126	————	————	————
1914	16,020	2,237	2,018	16,239	7,202	1,378	1,691	6,889	8,818	859	327	9,350	————	————	————
1913	15,286	1,893	2,170	15,009	6,265	1,336	1,845	5,756	9,021	557	325	9,253	————	————	————
1912	15,760	1,766	2,310	15,216	6,751	1,289	1,980	6,060	9,009	477	330	9,156	————	————	————
1911	15,443	1,595	2,036	15,002	6,287	1,236	1,640	5,883	9,156	359	396	9,119	————	————	————
1910	14,557	1,551	1,622	14,486	5,854	1,168	1,330	5,692	8,703	383	292	8,794	————	————	————
1909	14,552	1,731	1,886	14,397	5,782	1,269	1,476	5,575	8,770	462	410	8,822	————	————	————
1908	14,996	1,306	2,266	14,036	6,054	1,023	1,710	5,367	8,942	283	556	8,669	————	————	————
1907	14,480	1,416	2,389	13,507	5,779	1,124	1,745	5,158	8,701	292	644	8,349	————	————	————
1906	15,016	1,418	2,409	14,025	6,476	1,120	1,625	5,971	8,540	298	784	8,054	————	————	————
1905	14,255	1,416	2,329	13,342	5,815	1,046	1,544	5,317	8,440	370	785	8,025	————	————	————
1904	14,166	1,348	1,975	13,539	6,009	1,060	1,263	5,806	8,157	288	712	7,733	————	————	————
1903	13,563	1,271	2,330	12,504	5,573	1,016	1,635	4,954	7,990	255	695	7,550	————	————	————
1902	13,186	1,307	2,299	12,194	5,689	1,046	1,635	5,100	7,497	261	664	7,094	————	————	————
1901	13,212	1,140	2,920	11,432	5,381	915	1,900	4,396	7,831	225	1,020	7,036	————	————	————
1900	13,041	1,114	2,648	11,507	5,409	818	1,776	4,451	7,632	296	872	7,056	————	————	————

Series K 407–413. Farm Productivity—Persons Supplied Per Farmworker and Man-Hours of Labor: 1820 to 1970

[Excludes Alaska and Hawaii]

Year	Persons supplied per farmworker [1]			Man-hours (in billions) of labor required on farms [2]				Year	Persons supplied per farmworker [1]			Man-hours (in billions) of labor required on farms [2]			
	Total	Persons at home	Persons living abroad	Total	Livestock and livestock products	All crops	Farm maintenance [3]		Total	Persons at home	Persons living abroad	Total	Livestock and livestock products	All crops	Farm maintenance [3]
	407	408	409	410	411	412	413		407	408	409	410	411	412	413
1970	47.1	39.9	7.2	6.5	2.4	3.2	0.9	1935				21.1	5.7	10.9	4.4
1969	45.1	39.0	6.1	6.7	2.5	3.3	1.0	1934				20.2	6.1	9.9	4.3
1968	43.4	37.9	5.5	7.0	2.6	3.4	1.0	1933				22.6	6.2	11.6	4.7
1967	42.1	36.0	6.1	7.3	2.7	3.5	1.0	1932				22.6	6.0	11.9	4.7
1966	39.6	33.6	6.0	7.4	2.8	3.5	1.0	1931				23.4	5.9	12.6	4.9
1965	37.0	30.8	6.2	7.8	3.0	3.7	1.1	1930	9.8	8.8	1.0	22.9	5.7	12.3	4.9
1964	33.2	27.9	5.3	8.2	3.2	3.9	1.1	1929				23.2	5.6	12.6	5.0
1963	30.7	25.8	4.9	8.7	3.4	4.1	1.2	1928				23.4	5.5	12.7	5.1
1962	28.6	24.7	3.9	9.0	3.5	4.2	1.3	1927				22.9	5.5	12.4	5.1
1961	27.6	23.6	4.0	9.4	3.7	4.4	1.3	1926				23.9	5.4	13.1	5.3
1960	25.8	22.3	3.5	9.8	3.8	4.6	1.4	1925				23.8	5.4	13.0	5.3
1959	24.5	21.4	3.1	10.3	4.1	4.8	1.5	1924				23.3	5.4	12.6	5.3
1958	23.2	20.6	2.6	10.5	4.2	4.8	1.5	1923				23.1	5.4	12.3	5.3
1957	22.7	19.8	2.9	11.1	4.5	5.0	1.6	1922				22.9	5.3	12.3	5.4
1956	21.7	18.5	3.2	12.0	4.7	5.6	1.7	1921				22.1	5.1	11.8	5.3
1955	19.5	17.3	2.2	12.8	4.9	6.0	1.8	1920	8.3	6.8	1.4	24.0	5.0	13.4	5.6
1954	18.1	16.2	1.9	13.3	5.1	6.2	1.9	1919				23.6	5.1	13.0	5.5
1953	17.2	15.8	1.4	14.0	5.2	6.6	2.1	1918				24.1	5.2	13.2	5.6
1952	16.4	15.0	1.4	14.5	5.3	6.9	2.3	1917				23.8	5.1	13.1	5.5
1951	15.8	14.0	1.8	15.2	5.5	7.2	2.6	1916				23.1	5.1	12.6	5.4
1950	15.5	13.8	1.7	15.1	5.5	6.9	2.7	1915				23.2	5.0	12.8	5.4
1949	14.9	13.4	1.5	16.2	5.5	7.8	2.9	1914				23.7	5.0	13.3	5.5
1948	14.5	12.8	1.7	16.8	5.5	8.3	3.0	1913				23.0	4.9	12.8	5.3
1947	14.1	12.6	1.5	17.2	5.7	8.3	3.2	1912				23.3	4.8	13.2	5.4
1946	14.3	12.4	1.9	18.1	6.0	8.7	3.4	1911				23.0	4.8	13.0	5.3
1945	14.6	12.9	1.7	18.8	6.3	9.0	3.6	1910	7.1	6.1	1.0	22.5	4.8	12.6	5.2
1944	13.8	12.5	1.3	20.2	6.5	9.8	3.8	1900	7.0	5.2	1.7				
1943	13.5	12.1	1.4	20.3	6.6	9.8	3.9	1890	5.8	4.7	1.1				
1942	13.0	11.8	1.2	20.6	6.4	10.2	4.0	1880	5.6	4.5	1.1				
1941	12.0	11.0	1.0	20.0	6.2	9.9	3.9	1870	5.1	4.6	.5				
1940	10.7	10.3	.4	20.5	6.1	10.4	4.0	1860	4.5	4.1	.5				
1939				20.7	6.0	10.6	4.1	1850	4.2	4.0	.2				
1938				20.6	5.8	10.7	4.1	1840	4.0	3.7	.2				
1937				22.1	5.8	11.9	4.4	1830	4.0	3.8	.2				
1936				20.4	5.9	10.4	4.2	1820	4.1	3.8	.3				

[1] Refers to persons supplied farm products; includes farmworkers.
[2] Man-equivalent hours; represents overhead and time used by average adult males in performing farm operations on crops and livestock.
[3] Includes work on horses and mules.

Series K 414–429. Indexes of Total Output and Gross Production of Livestock and Crops, by Groups: 1870 to 1970

[Excludes Alaska and Hawaii]

Year	Farm output	Livestock and livestock products [1]				Crops										Feed used by farm horses and mules
		Total	Meat animals	Dairy products	Poultry and eggs	Total	Feed grains	Hay and forage	Food grains	Vege-tables	Fruits and nuts	Sugar crops	Cotton	Tobacco	Oil crops	
	414	415	416	417	418	419	420	421	422	423	424	425	426	427	428	429
						1967 = 100										
1970	102	106	108	100	106	100	90	99	91	101	107	119	137	97	117	
1969	103	101	102	99	101	104	99	100	97	103	113	120	135	91	115	
1968	102	100	102	99	98	103	95	100	105	103	93	116	148	87	112	
1967	100	100	100	100	100	100	100	100	100	100	100	100	100	100	100	
1966	96	97	96	101	96	95	89	96	87	97	97	100	129	95	96	100
1965	97	95	92	104	90	98	89	97	87	96	95	100	202	94	90	
1964	94	97	98	105	87	93	76	93	84	90	90	113	206	113	75	
1963	95	95	95	104	83	95	87	92	76	94	89	111	207	119	75	
1962	91	92	90	105	81	92	80	92	73	94	92	86	200	117	72	
1961	90	91	89	104	81	91	79	89	78	96	91	84	193	104	71	
1960	90	87	85	101	75	92	88	89	86	91	87	75	192	99	61	
1959	88	88	88	100	76	89	85	84	72	89	93	77	196	91	58	104
1958	86	85	82	101	73	89	82	88	90	90	91	70	154	88	65	117
1957	80	83	80	102	69	80	75	88	61	88	84	72	148	84	53	130
1956	82	84	83	101	68	82	69	81	65	91	92	63	180	110	54	143

[1] Production for human use; excludes horses and mules.

Series **K 414–429.**   Indexes of Total Output and Gross Production of Livestock and Crops, by Groups: 1870 to 1970—Con.

Year	Farm output	Livestock and livestock products [1]				Crops										Feed used by farm horses and mules
		Total	Meat animals	Dairy products	Poultry and eggs	Total	Feed grains	Hay and forage	Food grains	Vege-tables	Fruits and nuts	Sugar crops	Cotton	Tobacco	Oil crops	
	414	415	416	417	418	419	420	421	422	423	424	425	426	427	428	429
						1967 = 100										
1955	82	84	86	99	62	82	69	85	62	86	88	63	199	111	46	161
1954	79	82	81	98	63	79	66	80	66	83	88	69	188	114	41	187
1953	79	79	78	97	61	81	62	80	74	84	87	62	222	105	37	213
1952	78	78	79	92	59	81	64	78	81	81	86	55	205	114	37	252
1951	75	78	79	92	59	77	60	80	63	80	89	54	205	118	38	296
1950	73	75	74	93	56	76	65	77	64	85	87	68	135	103	41	335
1949	74	72	69	93	54	79	64	72	69	84	87	55	217	100	36	383
1948	75	68	66	90	48	83	73	73	80	87	82	54	202	100	39	430
1947	69	70	67	93	49	73	50	73	83	82	90	66	160	107	32	491
1946	71	71	68	94	50	76	66	76	71	93	94	62	118	117	30	557
1945	69	73	70	95	54	73	61	81	68	84	79	56	122	100	31	622
1944	70	73	73	93	51	75	63	78	66	82	87	50	166	99	29	683
1943	68	77	81	91	52	71	60	79	53	86	75	50	155	71	35	743
1942	69	71	73	92	45	76	66	81	62	80	87	68	173	71	33	796
1941	62	64	63	89	39	68	70	74	59	75	88	60	145	64	22	826
1940	60	60	60	85	36	66	53	75	52	74	83	64	170	74	20	852
1939	58	59	59	83	35	64	52	65	47	72	85	66	160	97	17	874
1938	57	56	52	82	33	65	52	70	57	72	75	71	162	70	13	896
1937	58	53	48	80	32	69	54	65	55	73	83	59	257	80	11	926
1936	47	54	50	80	32	50	31	57	40	67	62	59	168	60	9	948
1935	52	50	44	79	30	60	48	71	41	72	80	56	143	67	12	974
1934	43	52	49	79	30	46	27	56	33	71	63	52	130	55	8	991
1933	50	57	58	80	32	56	45	60	35	65	68	63	175	70	6	1,013
1932	54	56	56	80	32	62	59	64	47	68	67	56	175	51	8	1,043
1931	56	56	55	79	32	66	51	63	59	67	82	49	230	78	8	1,083
1930	52	55	52	77	33	59	45	57	55	66	65	52	188	83	8	1,122
1929	53	54	52	76	32	62	50	69	50	65	67	45	200	77	8	1,161
		1947–49 = 100				1957–59 = 100										
1933	70	82	86	87	62	65	56	69	47	73	76	87	105	80	11	863
1932	76	81	83	86	63	73	73	74	63	76	75	77	105	58	13	889
1931	79	80	82	86	63	77	63	72	79	75	92	66	138	89	14	922
1930	72	78	78	84	65	69	56	66	74	74	73	71	113	95	14	956
1929	74	77	77	82	63	73	62	79	69	73	75	61	120	88	13	989
1928	75	76	78	80	62	75	68	77	75	74	80	58	117	79	13	1,026
1927	72	76	78	79	64	72	63	86	73	71	67	60	105	71	15	1,067
1926	73	74	75	77	62	73	61	75	69	67	87	58	146	74	11	1,107
1925	70	71	73	76	58	72	69	73	57	66	66	62	130	78	13	1,141
1924	68	73	78	74	57	69	57	82	71	68	71	62	110	71	15	1,181
1923	69	74	81	72	58	70	68	83	64	65	77	65	82	86	10	1,222
1922	68	71	79	70	55	70	62	90	74	69	77	64	79	70	8	1,256
1921	62	66	71	68	51	65	68	77	69	59	47	82	65	57	8	1,289
1920	70	64	68	65	49	76	76	82	73	64	72	86	109	86	9	1,326
1919	66	66	73	66	50	70	65	82	82	58	62	72	93	81	7	1,370
1918	66	68	80	64	48	69	64	73	78	61	60	83	98	81	9	1,381
1917	65	67	77	64	47	69	73	78	55	63	55	82	92	75	8	1,378
1916	62	66	77	63	47	64	60	83	55	53	63	70	93	68	7	1,374
1915	68	67	77	63	49	72	72	80	84	56	70	65	91	65	6	1,370
1914	66	64	74	61	47	69	61	72	74	57	76	63	131	58	6	1,356
1913	60	63	71	61	47	62	56	67	63	54	52	69	115	56	7	1,330
1912	66	61	68	59	47	71	73	77	62	58	68	63	112	62	10	1,307
1911	59	61	66	59	49	62	58	60	52	51	64	71	128	53	8	1,285
1910	61	60	66	58	47	63	68	70	53	53	52	65	95	64	6	1,252
1900	56	--------	--------	--------	--------	--------	--------	--------	--------	--------	--------	--------	--------	--------	--------	--------
1890	43	--------	--------	--------	--------	--------	--------	--------	--------	--------	--------	--------	--------	--------	--------	--------
1880	37	--------	--------	--------	--------	--------	--------	--------	--------	--------	--------	--------	--------	--------	--------	--------
1870	23	--------	--------	--------	--------	--------	--------	--------	--------	--------	--------	--------	--------	--------	--------	--------

[1] Production for human use; excludes horses and mules.

Series K 430–444. Indexes of Farm Output Per Man-Hour: 1939 to 1970

[1967 = 100. Excludes Alaska and Hawaii]

Year	Farm output per man-hour	Livestock and products				Crops									
		Total	Meat animals	Milk cows	Poultry	Total	Feed grains	Hay and forage	Food grains	Vege-tables	Fruits and nuts	Sugar crops	Cotton	Tobacco	Oil crops
	430	431	432	433	434	435	436	437	438	439	440	441	442	443	444
1970	113	119	116	123	120	110	101	148	117	106	107	121	125	104	115
1969	112	112	110	115	112	112	109	145	113	106	109	115	117	98	114
1968	106	105	105	106	105	106	102	102	108	101	98	113	130	98	110
1967	100	100	100	100	100	100	100	100	100	100	100	100	100	100	100
1966	94	93	95	93	95	95	93	99	102	99	99	92	101	96	101
1965	91	87	90	87	87	92	92	96	101	99	95	88	101	95	100
1964	83	83	89	81	82	85	78	93	97	96	91	90	87	99	89
1963	80	77	83	74	73	82	77	92	90	97	87	97	78	97	94
1962	73	71	78	70	66	77	70	89	89	92	87	82	71	93	92
1961	70	67	74	65	61	73	64	89	86	93	78	32	61	88	90
1960	67	62	70	60	55	71	58	84	93	89	74	79	56	87	84
1959	62	59	68	57	50	66	52	81	77	88	74	75	52	81	82
1958	59	55	65	53	45	65	47	77	85	82	73	67	48	81	81
1957	53	50	63	49	39	56	40	71	62	80	69	67	44	77	69
1956	50	48	62	46	37	52	35	65	54	76	75	59	41	80	67
1955	47	46	62	43	32	48	31	63	50	70	75	53	39	75	60
1954	43	43	59	40	30	45	29	58	46	67	74	51	35	71	54
1953	41	41	58	39	27	43	27	63	43	64	70	49	33	67	51
1952	39	40	56	37	24	42	26	60	46	63	67	43	30	67	50
1951	36	39	56	36	23	38	23	58	38	59	65	39	28	67	46
1950	35	37	55	35	21	39	23	55	40	57	64	38	25	66	47
1949	33	36	54	35	21	36	20	50	34	55	62	34	27	64	40
1948	32	34	53	33	19	35	20	47	36	56	57	30	24	65	34
1947	29	33	52	33	18	31	14	43	35	50	59	30	22	61	26
1946	29	32	52	31	18	31	16	40	31	48	59	28	19	62	25
1945	27	31	53	30	18	29	14	37	28	45	53	25	19	58	23
1944	25	31	53	28	17	27	13	35	27	42	56	24	20	59	21
1943	24	32	55	27	18	26	12	33	24	43	50	23	18	54	20
1942	24	30	53	27	17	26	13	32	26	42	54	25	19	56	20
1941	22	28	50	26	16	24	13	30	23	40	53	26	16	54	20
1940	21	27	50	25	15	22	10	30	21	40	51	27	17	56	18
1939	20	27	49	25	15	21	10	28	18	39	51	24	16	53	17

Series K 445–485. Man-Hours Per Unit and Yield Per Unit of Production of Selected Crops and Livestock: 1800 to 1970

[Figures for 5-year periods are annual averages]

Year	Wheat					Corn for grain					Cotton				
	Man-hours per acre			Yield per acre [1] (bu.)	Man-hours per 100 bushels	Man-hours per acre			Yield per acre [1] (bu.)	Man-hours per 100 bushels	Man-hours per acre			Yield of limit per acre [1] (pounds)	Man-hours per bale [2]
	Total	Before harvest	Harvest			Total	Before harvest	Harvest			Total	Before harvest	Harvest		
	445	446	447	448	449	450	451	452	453	454	455	456	457	458	459
1970	2.9	1.8	1.1	31.0	9	5.2	2.9	2.3	71.6	7	24	21	3	438	26
1965–1969	2.9	1.8	1.1	27.5	11	5.8	3.3	2.5	77.4	7	30	22	8	485	30
1960–1964	3.0	1.9	1.1	25.2	12	7.0	4.3	2.7	62.2	11	47	23	24	475	47
1955–1959	3.8	2.3	1.5	22.3	17	9.9	6.5	3.4	48.7	20	66	25	41	428	74
1950–1954	4.6	2.6	2.0	17.3	27	13.3	8.9	4.4	39.4	34	66	30	36	296	107
1945–1949	5.7	2.9	2.8	16.9	34	19.2	12.2	7.0	36.1	53	83	38	45	273	146
1940–1944	7.5	3.8	3.7	17.1	44	25.5	16.0	9.5	32.2	79	99	46	53	260	182
1935–1939	8.8	4.3	4.5	13.2	67	28.1	17.9	10.2	26.1	108	99	47	52	226	209
1930–1934	9.4	4.6	4.8	13.5	70	28.2	17.6	10.6	23.0	123	97	53	44	184	252
1925–1929	10.5	5.1	5.4	14.1	74	30.3	17.9	12.4	26.3	115	96	59	37	171	268
1920–1924	12.4	6.0	6.4	13.8	90	32.7	19.2	13.5	26.8	122	96	59	37	155	296
1915–1919	13.6	6.6	7.0	13.9	98	34.2	20.0	14.2	25.9	132	105	62	43	168	299
1910–1914	15.2	7.0	8.2	14.4	106	35.2	20.4	14.8	26.0	135	116	64	52	201	276
1900	15.0	7.0	8.0	13.9	108	38.0	22.0	16.0	25.9	147	112	62	50	189	284
1880	20.0	8.0	12.0	13.2	152	46.0	28.0	18.0	25.6	180	119	67	52	188	303
1840	35.0	12.0	23.0	15.0	233	69.0	44.0	25.0	25.0	276	135	90	45	147	438
1800	56.0	16.0	40.0	15.0	373	86.0	56.0	30.0	25.0	344	185	135	50	147	601

See footnotes at end of table.

Series K 445–485. Man-Hours Per Unit and Yield Per Unit of Production of Selected Crops and Livestock: 1800 to 1970—Con.

Year	Hay			Potatoes					Tobacco				
	Man-hours per acre harvested	Yield per acre (tons)	Man-hours per ton	Man-hours per acre			Yield per acre (cwt.)	Man-hours per ton	Man-hours per acre			Yield per acre (pounds)	Man-hours per 100 pounds
				Total	Before harvest	Harvest			Total	Before harvest	Harvest		
	460	461	462	463	464	465	466	467	468	469	470	471	472
1970	3.5	2.03	1.7	44.1	17.6	26.5	229.0	4	496	106	390	2,121	23
1965–1969	3.8	1.94	1.9	45.1	18.7	26.4	212.8	4	489	116	373	1,957	25
1960–1964	5.0	1.77	2.8	48.0	20.0	28.0	194.9	5	493	131	362	1,879	26
1955–1959	6.0	1.61	3.7	53.1	23.0	30.1	178.1	6	475	146	329	1,541	31
1950–1954	6.3	1.43	4.4	63.1	27.5	35.6	151.2	8	464	159	305	1,292	36
1945–1949	8.4	1.35	6.2	68.5	32.7	35.8	117.8	12	460	164	296	1,176	39
1940–1944	11.0	1.35	8.1	68.5	36.7	31.8	82.1	17	442	161	281	1,026	43
1935–1939	11.3	1.24	9.1	69.7			70.3	20	415			886	47
1930–1934	10.3	1.08	9.5	67.9			64.6	21	370			784	47
1925–1929	12.0	1.22	9.8	73.1			68.4	21	370			772	48
1920–1924	12.5	1.22	10.2	75.2			64.6	23	353			773	46
1915–1919	13.0	1.25	10.4	73.8			56.9	26	353			803	44
1910–1914	11.9	1.15	10.3	76.0			59.8	25	356			816	44

Year	Milk cows			Cattle, man-hours per cwt. of beef produced [3][4]	Hogs, man-hours per cwt. produced [4]	Chickens (laying flocks and eggs)			Chickens (farm raised)		Chickens (broilers)		Turkeys, man-hours per cwt. produced [4]
	Man-hours per cow	Milk per cow (pounds)	Man-hours per cwt. of milk			Man-hours per 100 layers	Rate of lay per year	Man-hours per 100 eggs produced	Man-hours per 100 birds	Man-hours per cwt. produced [4]	Man-hours per 100 birds	Man-hours per cwt. produced [4]	
	473	474	475	476	477	478	479	480	481	482	483	484	485
1970	67.8	9,385.0	0.7	1.8	1.2	86.0	218.0	0.4	13.1	3.6	1.4	0.4	1.0
1965–1969	78.0	8,733.0	.9	2.1	1.4	98.0	219.0	.4	14.0	3.7	2.0	.5	1.3
1960–1964	93.0	7,507.0	1.2	2.6	1.9	126.0	212.0	.6	17.0	4.7	3.0	.8	2.4
1955–1959	109.0	6,307.0	1.7	3.2	2.4	175.0	200.0	.9	23.0	6.7	4.0	1.3	4.4
1950–1954	121.0	5,444.0	2.2	3.6	2.7	232.0	181.0	1.3	27.0	7.3	8.0	2.4	6.8
1945–1949	129.0	4,992.0	2.6	4.0	3.0	240.0	161.0	1.5	29.0	7.7	16.0	5.1	13.1
1940–1944	142.0	4,653.0	3.1	4.0	3.0	223.0	142.0	1.6	29.0	8.2	23.0	7.7	19.6
1935–1939	148.0	4,401.0	3.4	4.2	3.2	221.0	129.0	1.7	30.0	9.0	25.0	8.5	23.7
1930–1934	147.0	4,289.0	3.4	4.3	3.2	225.0	121.0	1.9	31.0	9.3			26.7
1925–1929	145.0	4,437.0	3.3	4.3	3.3	218.0	117.0	1.9	32.0	9.4			28.5
1920–1924	142.0	4,000.0	3.6	4.5	3.5				32.0	9.3			30.0
1915–1919	141.0	3,790.0	3.7	4.5	3.6				33.0	9.4			31.1
1910–1914	146.0	3,842.0	3.8	4.6	3.6				33.0	9.5			31.4

[1] Data for 1800 and 1840 are estimates by the authors. Data for 1880 and 1900 are 5-year averages of published data, centered on year shown. Data for 1970 are for single year.

[2] For statistical purposes, the bale of cotton is 500 pounds gross weight or 480 pounds net weight of lint. Prior to August 1, 1946, the net weight was estimated at 478 pounds.

Running bales reported prior to 1899 have been converted to bales of 478 pounds net weight. Actual bale weights vary considerably.

[3] Production includes beef produced as a byproduct of the milk cow enterprise.

[4] Live-weight production.

Series K 486–495. Indexes of Total Farm Input and Major Input Subgroups: 1910 to 1970

[1967 = 100]

Year	Total input			Farm labor	Farm real estate	Mechanical power and machinery	Fertilizer and liming materials	Feed, seed, and livestock purchases [3]	Taxes and interest	Miscellaneous
	All	Non-purchased [1]	Purchased [2]							
	486	487	488	489	490	491	492	493	494	495
1970	102	98	104	89	100	102	113	109	107	107
1969	102	100	104	94	100	103	110	105	105	107
1968	101	100	102	96	100	102	107	101	103	110
1967	100	100	100	100	100	100	100	100	100	108
1966	99	101	97	101	99	100	90	97	98	100
1965	98	103	94	109	100	96	80	91	95	98
1964	98	104	92	115	100	93	76	90	94	101
1963	97	105	90	120	99	92	70	89	92	99
1962	96	108	87	123	98	91	62	89	90	94
1961	96	111	85	129	99	90	58	87	89	89
1960	97	112	84	134	99	91	54	84	87	84
1959	98	118	82	139	100	92	54	84	86	80
1958	97	120	79	143	100	91	48	80	82	79
1957	97	124	77	149	102	90	46	75	81	74
1956	100	130	77	160	103	91	44	76	82	69
1955	102	136	76	170	106	91	45	73	82	70
1954	102	138	75	176	105	90	43	72	80	68
1953	103	140	75	184	105	90	42	70	80	64
1952	104	141	76	191	105	88	39	70	79	65
1951	104	144	74	200	106	84	36	68	77	67
1950	101	141	71	199	105	79	32	64	77	67
1949	102	143	72	212	104	75	31	62	77	63
1948	100	142	69	220	104	68	29	57	74	62
1947	99	142	68	226	103	60	28	56	76	59
1946	99	145	68	239	102	55	24	54	76	54
1945	100	151	65	249	99	56	23	55	75	54
1944	103	156	66	265	98	55	23	53	74	53
1943	102	155	65	267	98	53	19	53	72	54
1942	101	154	64	271	100	50	17	49	69	52
1941	98	147	63	265	102	44	15	46	68	49
1940	98	147	63	269	103	42	14	43	68	52
1939	97	147	61	270	101	40	12	41	67	51
1930	100	164	54	299	101	40	11	30	70	50
1920	96	166	46	313	102	32	8	26	57	51
1910	85	147	41	294	98	20	6	19	47	53
										45

[1] Includes operator and unpaid family labor, and operator-owned real estate and other capital inputs.

[2] Includes all inputs other than nonpurchased inputs.
[3] Nonfarm portion of feed, seed, and livestock purchases.

Chapter K

Crops and Livestock (Series K 496-623)

K 496–501. Acreages of harvested crops, by use, and indexes of cropland used for crops and crop production per acre, 1910–1970.

Source: U.S. Department of Agriculture. **Series K 496–499**, 1910–1949, Economic Research Service, *Changes in Farm Production and Efficiency*, Statistical Bulletin No. 233, July 1964; **series K 500–501**, 1910–1949, unpublished data. All series, 1950–1970, *Changes in Farm Production and Efficiency*, Statistical Bulletin No. 233, June 1971.

Acreages for harvested crops do not include pasture. The total crop acres harvested, series K 496, consists of acreages of the 59 crops harvested (excluding duplication) plus acreages in tree fruits, small fruits, tree nuts, and farm gardens. Acreages of several minor crops, which are not included, have accounted for about 0.5 million acres in recent years.

Acreages used for production of crop exports, series K 497, are determined by dividing the quantity exported by the average yield per acre. Two steps are necessary in computing the acreages of crops used to produce each of the livestock products exported. The first consists of estimating the quantities of each feed crop used to produce 100 pounds of pork, 100 pounds of milk, 100 dozen eggs, and so on. The second consists of determining the quantity of each feed crop used to produce the products exported, and then determining the acreages needed to produce each feed crop, at average yields per acre. Periodic 5-year average yields rather than yields for each year are used.

Yield data for the export estimates are from reports of the Crop Reporting Board. Data for volume of exports prior to 1940 are from *Agricultural Statistics*. For 1940–1970, export data are from reports and records of the Economic Research Service.

Estimates of feed consumed by horses and mules are based on the following average rations of corn, oats, and all hay: For 1910–1919, the calculations allow 800 pounds of oats, 1,600 pounds of shelled corn, and 1.8 tons of hay per head for farm horses and mules 3 years old and over and animal-unit equivalents for younger animals. For 1920–1940, it was assumed that as farm horses were worked less, they consumed less grain and more hay. Consequently, the rate of feeding corn was decreased 10 pounds per head per year and the rate of feeding hay was increased 20 pounds. Beginning with 1941, it was assumed that horses and mules would work less each year, and that on the average they would be fed less corn, oats, and hay and would consume more pasture.

For nonfarm horses and mules, it was assumed that, for 1910–1931, the quantities of grain and hay consumed per head per year were a third more than those consumed by farm work animals. Since 1932, the computations have rounded out to one million acres used in producing feed for nonfarm horses and mules.

Prior to 1960, basic data on horses and mules were from publications of the Economic Research Service. Estimates of horses and mules on farms were discontinued in 1960. The rations for horses and mules are based on data from many sources, especially from Bureau of Agricultural Economics, *Work Performed and Feed Utilized by Horses and Mules*, Farm Management 44, 1944, and on judgment of workers familiar with the subject.

The series on cropland used for crops, series K 500, is made up of three components—acres of harvested cropland (land from which one or more crops were harvested), crop failure, and summer fallow. The index excludes idle cropland and land in soil-improvement crops during the entire year and not harvested. These figures are based on estimates of principal crops harvested and crop losses prepared by the former Bureau of Agricultural Economics (BAE) and the Statistical Reporting Service (SRS) and on data from the 1925 to 1954 censuses of agriculture. Data from the 1950 to 1964 censuses of agriculture were adjusted to cover some of the underenumeration indicated by postenumeration surveys.

Acreages of crop failure were derived from the 1925 to 1945 censuses of agriculture, and interpolations for intervening years were based on BAE estimates of crop losses or differences between planted and harvested acreages of principal crops. Acreages of crop failure for recent years are based chiefly on crop losses as reported by SRS. Reported acreages of crop losses are adjusted for the replanting of part of the acreage on which winter wheat is abandoned. Hay land that produced nothing but pasture in some dry seasons is not included in crop failure in recent years.

Estimates of acreage of cultivated summer fallow were made only for the geographic divisions west of the Mississippi River.

Indexes of total crop production were divided by indexes of cropland used for crops to derive indexes of crop production per acre, series K 501. Indexes of crop production were developed as one step in the calculation of farm output; see series K 419–429.

For a more detailed explanation of these series, see *Major Statistical Series of the U.S. Department of Agriculture*, Agriculture Handbook No. 365, vol. 2.

K 502–563. General note.

For many crops, estimates of acreage, production, and prices begin in 1866, the year in which the Department of Agriculture began making regular reports. *Agricultural Statistics*, particularly the issues of 1941 and 1952, presents most of the available statistics, chiefly on a national basis, covering every phase, from acreage and production of individual commodities to utilization and consumption. *Crop Production* (Crop Reporting Board) presents monthly forecasts for the current season, beginning in March and carrying through the growing season. The December issue provides a summary for the current season, revisions for the previous season, and comparisons with previous years. These data appear also in *Crops and Markets*.

Census data shown are often not entirely comparable with the estimates shown, but furnish the benchmarks to establish the level of the estimates. For years before 1866, information from trade sources is available for some crops, such as cotton, tobacco, and rice.

Crop estimates are based chiefly upon reports from volunteer farmer-reporters who represent every part of every State. Check information is gathered from processors, from transportation and storage facilities, from buyers of farm products, from annual State farm enumerations, from various farm programs, and from other governmental agencies such as the Bureau of the Census, the Internal Revenue Service, and the Bureau of Customs.

Season average prices are averages of the midmonth prices weighted by the quantity sold each month in the crop-marketing season, which is the 12-month period following the harvesting of the crop. This season may vary for different crops, and for any crop it may vary by States. The season average price of any crop is the average of all the State prices, weighted by the production of each State. Thus, it may be applied to production in any given year to obtain a measure of the value of that production. State season average prices may be weighted by quantities sold in each State to obtain an average for the United States which may be applied to total quantities sold in the United States to measure value of sales in the crop season. In neither case, however, should the computed value be confused with calendar-year income from the crop. Monthly estimates of quantity sold are based upon reports of receipts by the chief purchasers of the commodity—in the case of grains, the interior mills and elevators.

Midmonth prices received by farmers are estimated by the Crop Reporting Board and are based upon reports from thousands of firms dealing directly with farmers (such as elevators, truckers, processors, produce dealers, etc.) and from farmers themselves.

Season average prices for each State and the United States are summed up in the December issue of *Crop Values* and in *Field and Seed Crops Farm Production, Farm Disposition, and Value* issued each May. Data for season average prices begins for most commodities in 1908, but is supplemented for preceding years by the December 1 price series based on farmers' estimates on December 1 of average prices for the season's sales.

K 502–505. Corn acreage, production, price, and stocks, 1839–1970.

Source: **Series K 502–504**, U.S. Department of Agriculture, Statistical Reporting Service, *Agricultural Statistics: 1967* and *1972* editions; census years, U.S. Bureau of the Census, *U.S. Census of Agriculture: 1964*, vol. II, table 5, p. 313; and *1969*, vol. II, chapter 6. **Series K 505**, U.S. Department of Agriculture, Statistical Reporting Service, *Agricultural Statistics: 1952, 1957, 1962, 1967*, and *1972* editions.

Corn figures include not only the production of corn on the acreage harvested for grain, but also an allowance for that harvested for silage and for forage, including some harvested by grazing farm animals (commonly called hogging off). Beginning 1961, production figures represent corn harvested for grain only. Census figures for 1919 and previous years for both acreage and production represent corn harvested for grain only. For 1924–1969, census data for acreage represent corn harvested for all purposes, but those for production represent corn harvested for grain only.

The Crop Reporting Board has estimated farm stocks, series K 505, by States, quarterly since 1926 from reports of a large number of farmers. Farm stocks represent the farm carryover for crops of previous years, which become a part of the feed supply for the new season. In addition to farm stocks of corn, stocks in all off-farm positions have been estimated since 1943. Comparison with the farm-stocks data indicates that the bulk of carryover stocks of corn on October 1 of any year is still on farms.

U.S. Department of Agriculture data exclude Hawaii, census data include Hawaii; corn is not grown in Alaska.

See also general note for series K 502–563.

K 506–510. Wheat acreage, production, price, and stocks, 1839–1970.

Source: **Series K 506–507**, see source for series K 502–504. **Series K 508**, see source for series K 502–504 and, for census years, *U.S. Census of Agriculture: 1954*, vol. II, p. 633; *1964*, vol. II, table 5, p. 313; and *1969*, vol. II, chapter 6. **Series K 509**, see source for series K 505. **Series K 510**, 1926–1933, U.S. Department of Agriculture, Statistical Reporting Service, *Agricultural Statistics, 1941* and *1946*; 1934, Agricultural Marketing Service, Statistical Bulletin No. 203, January 1957 (processed); 1935–1970, *Agricultural Statistics: 1957, 1962, 1967*, and *1972* editions.

Wheat figures are the combined estimates for winter, durum, and other spring wheat harvested for grain. The census data on acreage and production are regarded as comparable with the estimates in most cases. Wheat acreage harvested for hay is not included in these series.

Farm stocks of all wheat, by States, have been estimated quarterly since 1926 from reports of a large number of farmers. Farm stocks, series K 509, represent the farm carryover from previous crops at the beginning of a new crop year. The carryover added to the new crop is the supply for the new season.

U.S. Department of Agriculture data exclude Alaska, census data include Alaska; wheat is not grown in Hawaii.

See also general note for series K 502–563.

K 511–513. Oats acreage, production, and price, 1839–1970.

Source: See source for series K 502–504.

For 1866–1948, oats for grain figures include the acreage cut ripe and fed unthreshed; for 1949–1970, they include only the acreage and production combined or threshed. Estimates of harvested acreage exclude oats cut green for hay for all years, and oats cut ripe and fed unthreshed, 1949–1970. Census data are comparable only with the estimates beginning in 1949.

See also general note for series K 502–563.

K 514–516. Barley acreage, production, and price, 1839–1970.

Source: See source for series K 502–504.

The annual estimates of barley acreage and production and the census data are on a comparable basis. Barley cut for hay is excluded. Figures on farm stocks are available from 1933–1970, and stocks in off-farm positions have been estimated since 1943.

See also general note for series K 502–563.

K 517–519. Flaxseed acreage, production, and price, 1849–1970.

Source: **Series K 518**, 1866–1888, U.S. Department of Agriculture, Agricultural Marketing Service, *Revised Estimates of Flaxseed Production, 1866–1929*, July 1936 (processed). **Series K 517–519**, 1889–1970, Statistical Reporting Service, *Agricultural Statistics, 1941, 1942, 1952, 1957, 1962, 1967*, and *1971* editions; and for census years, see census source cited for series K 502–504.

Annual estimates and census data are on a comparable basis. Flax grown for fiber is not included in the acreage estimates; flaxseed deseeded from fiber flax is not included in the production estimates. Estimates of fiber flax are available in publications of the Crop Reporting Board. Farm-stocks data and stocks in off-farm positions, 1947–1970, are also available from the same source.

See also general note for series K 502–563.

K 520–522. Soybeans acreage, production, and price, 1909–1970.

Source: See source for series K 502–504.

Price figures are season average prices prepared by weighting the midmonth prices received by farmers. Figures for acreage grown for all purposes, alone and interplanted, and acreage and production of soybeans for hay are also estimated by the Crop Reporting Board. Data on farm stocks and stocks in off-farm positions, 1942–1970, are also available in publications of the same agency.

See also general note for series K 502–563.

K 523–525. Sorghum grain acreage, production, and price, 1919–1970.

Source: U.S. Department of Agriculture, Statistical Reporting Service, *Agricultural Statistics, 1937, 1972*, and *1973* editions.

Sorghum grain includes both grain sorghums for grain, and sweet sorghums for grain or seed. Price is based on the reported price of grain sorghums. It is obtained by weighting State prices by quantity sold and includes allowance for unredeemed loans and purchases by the Government valued at the average loan and purchase rate, by States.

See also general note for series K 502–563.

K 526–528. Rye acreage, production, and price, 1839–1970.

Source: **Series K 526–527**, 1866–1908, U.S. Department of Agriculture, Statistical Reporting Service, *Agricultural Statistics, 1941*; 1909–1961, see source for series K 505; 1962–1970, see source for series K 502–504. **Series K 528**, 1866–1908, *Agricultural Statistics, 1941*; 1909–1969, see source for series K 505; 1970 and census years, see source for series K 502–504.

Data on farm stocks are available from 1933–1970, and on stocks in off-farm positions from 1943.

See also general note for series K 502–563.

K 529–531.   Buckwheat acreage, production, and price, 1839–1969.

Source: 1866–1923, U.S. Department of Agriculture, Agricultural Marketing Service, *Rice, Popcorn and Buckwheat Acreage, Yield, Production, Price and Value, 1866–1953*, Statistical Bulletin No. 238, October 1958. **Series K 529–530** for 1924–1961, and **series K 531** for 1924–1964, U.S. Department of Agriculture, Statistical Reporting Service, *Agricultural Statistics, 1962, 1967*, and *1971*. **Series K 529–530**, 1962–1964, *Crop Production*, 1971 annual summary, January 14, 1972. **Series K 531**, 1966–1969, *Crop Values*, 1966 and subsequent annual issues. For census years, see source for series K 502–504.

See general note for series K 502–563.

K 532–537.   Irish potatoes and sweetpotatoes acreage, production, and price, 1849–1970.

Source: **Series K 532**, U.S. Department of Agriculture, 1866–1918, Agricultural Marketing Service, Statistical Bulletin No. 122, March 1933. **Series K 533** and **series K 536**, 1866–1918, U.S. Department of Agriculture, Crop Reporting Board, unpublished data. **Series K 534**, 1866–1908, see source for series K 533; 1909–1918, U.S. Department of Agriculture, Agricultural Marketing Service, *Agricultural Prices*, February 1957. **Series K 535**, 1868–1918, U.S. Department of Agriculture, Statistical Reporting Service, *Agricultural Statistics, 1941*. **Series K 537**, 1866–1908, see source for series K 533; 1909–1918, U.S. Department of Agriculture, Agricultural Marketing Service, *Agricultural Prices*, January 1957. For all series, 1919–1970, Statistical Reporting Service, *Agricultural Statistics, 1957, 1962*, and *1972* issues. Census years, U.S. Bureau of the Census, *U.S. Census of Agriculture: 1964*, vol. II, table 5, p. 313; and *1969*, vol. II, chapter 6, tables 46 and 47.

Estimates of potatoes and sweetpotatoes relate to the total crop harvested and include quantities used on farms where grown, and losses from shrinkage, cullage, and dumping after harvest. The potato crop is divided into six seasonal groups: Winter, early spring, late spring, early summer, late summer, and fall. The seasonal estimates are based on the usual time of harvest. The schedule of estimates and the classification of States are shown in Agriculture Handbook No. 127, June 1967.

In censuses prior to 1950, the acreage of sweetpotatoes was to be reported in all cases, even when the quantity harvested was small. Therefore, acres harvested for censuses prior to 1950 are not fully comparable with those of the last four censuses.

K 538–540.   Rice acreage, production, and price, 1895–1970.

Source: **Series K 538–539**, 1895–1908, U.S. Department of Agriculture, Agricultural Marketing Service, *Fluctuations in Crops and Weather*, Statistical Bulletin No. 101, June 1951 (processed); 1909–1961, see source for series K 505; 1962–1970, see source for series K 502–504. **Series K 540**, 1904–1908, Agricultural Marketing Service, unpublished data; 1909–1969, see source for series K 505; 1970 and census years, see source for series K 502–504.

See general note for series K 502–563.

K 541–543.   Sugarcane acreage, production, and price, 1909–1970.

Source: U.S. Department of Agriculture, Statistical Reporting Service, *Agricultural Statistics*, various issues. Census years, U.S. Bureau of the Census, *U.S. Census of Agriculture: 1964*, vol. II, chapter 4, table 5; and *1969*, vol. II, chapter 6, table 62.

See general note for series K 502–563.

K 544–549.   Sugar beets and peanuts acreage, production, and price, 1909–1970.

Source: U.S. Department of Agriculture, Statistical Reporting Service, *Agricultural Statistics, 1952, 1957, 1962, 1972*, and *1973* editions.

See general note for series K 502–563.

K 550–552.   Hay acreage, production, and price, 1839–1970.

Source: See source for series K 502–504.

Census data are comparable to annual estimates in the series in which they are included. Figures for stocks of hay are published in U.S. Department of Agriculture, Statistical Reporting Service, *Crop Production*.

See also general note for series K 502–563.

K 553–558.   Cotton and cottonseed acreage, production, price, and stocks, 1790–1970.

Source: **Series K 553**, see source for series K 502–504. **Series K 554**, 1790–1865, U.S. Department of Agriculture, Bureau of Statistics, Circular 32, August 1912; 1866–1970, see source for series K 502–504. **Series K 555** and **series K 557**, see source for series K 502–504. **Series K 556**, 1906–1970, U.S. Department of Agriculture, Statistical Reporting Service, *Agricultural Statistics, 1941, 1952, 1956, 1957, 1967*, and *1971* editions. **Series K 558**, 1909–1918, U.S. Department of Agriculture, Agricultural Marketing Service, Statistical Bulletin No. 164, June 1955 (processed); 1919–1970, *Agricultural Statistics, 1957, 1962*, and *1972*.

Cotton production estimates are defined by statute as cotton actually ginned. For 1913–1924, annual ginnings as published by the Bureau of the Census included some cotton produced in lower California and Mexico and ginned in California; however, it is not included in U.S. production for those years. For those years, also, cotton ginned in the United States exceeds production by the quantity of the cross-border movement of seed cotton into this country. For all other years, beginning in 1899, production of cotton is the quantity of census ginnings by States adjusted for cross-State movement of seed cotton and rounded to thousands of bales. U.S. production is obtained by adding rounded State estimates and therefore differs slightly from the Census Bureau report on ginnings.

Before 1899, production figures were compiled from various current sources including exports and imports, rail and water shipments, mill receipts, etc., together with the decennial enumerations of the Bureau of the Census. These production estimates are the same as those in Department of Agriculture, Bureau of Statistics, Circular 32, cited above, except for minor adjustments caused by rounding State estimates.

Figures for stocks, series K 556, are in running bales, except that any small quantity of foreign cotton which is included is in equivalent 500-pound gross-weight bales. Before 1914, stocks are as of September 1. Data for 1906–1922 are from the New York Cotton Exchange Service; those for 1923–1970 were compiled by the Bureau of the Census.

Cottonseed production, series K 557, for 1866–1927 was computed from net lint production using a uniform ratio of 65 pounds of cottonseed for each 35 pounds of net lint. Beginning in 1928, ratios were estimated from data collected from cotton ginners.

The season average prices from 1908 to 1970 for both cotton and cottonseed, series K 555 and series K 558, are the weighted averages of midmonth prices. Prior to 1909, cottonseed prices are not available; prior to 1908, cotton prices were based on farmers' estimates on December 1 of average prices for the season.

The crop-marketing season for both cotton and cottonseed begins August 1 for all States except Texas where it begins about mid-July.

See also general note for series K 502–563.

K 559–560.   Shorn wool production and price, 1869–1970.

Source: U.S. Department of Agriculture, **series K 559**, 1869–1908, *Agriculture Yearbook, 1923;* **series K 560**, 1869–1908, *Gross Farm Income and Indices of Farm Production and Prices in the United States, 1869–1937*, Technical Bulletin No. 703, December 1940; **series K 559–560**, 1909–1939, *Livestock and Meat Statistics*, Statistical Bulletin No. 230, July 1958; 1940–1970, Statistical Reporting Service, *Agricultural Statistics, 1967* and *1972* editions.

The original source of data for 1869–1908 was the National Association of Wool Manufacturers. Estimates have been made by the Department of Agriculture since 1909. Wool production is estimated by ascertaining the number of sheep and lambs shorn and the average weight per fleece, and using data from the censuses of agriculture as periodic benchmarks. Extensive revision of production estimates back through 1909 were made in 1936. The figures for 1869–1908 are not comparable to these revised estimates. To illustrate the lack of comparability, the unrevised production estimate of 287 million pounds for 1909, published in the *Agriculture Yearbook* for 1923, may be compared with the revised estimate of 310 million pounds.

K 561–563. Tobacco acreage, production, and price, 1866–1970.

Source: See source for series K 502–504.

Consumer and Marketing Service publications also present estimates of stocks of tobacco, 1929–1970, and of acreage and production of tobacco, by types, 1919–1970.

See also general note for series K 502–563.

K 564–574. Livestock on farms and value per head, and number of workstock, 1867–1970.

Source: Annual data, U.S. Department of Agriculture, Statistical Reporting Service, *Agricultural Statistics, 1957, 1962, 1967*, and subsequent annual editions. Census years, U.S. Bureau of the Census, *U.S. Census of Agriculture: 1959*, vol. III, chapter 6; *1964*, vol. II, chapter 2; and *1969*, vol. II, chapter 5.

These estimates have been made by the Department of Agriculture since 1867. The early estimates were based on reports of the percentage change in numbers from the previous year by field agents and crop reporters. At 10-year intervals, the census of agriculture furnished the basic figures to which these percentage changes were applied. Beginning 1920, a national agriculture census has been taken every 5 years. Since 1920, the Department of Agriculture annual estimates are based primarily on survey returns from livestock producers who reported on the number of livestock, by classes, on their own farms about December 1 each year. Records of livestock assessed for taxation in the various States have furnished indications of the annual percentage change in numbers, and records of marketings and slaughter have been used both by States and for the United States as check information.

Data from the census of agriculture have been used as periodic benchmarks for the January 1 estimates but there are few census years when the Department of Agriculture estimates and the census data are in close agreement. One of the main reasons for these differences is that there are only a few times when the census was taken as of January 1. In years when the census relates to a different date, adjustments are made to determine a January 1 equivalent number. In the midthirties, the Department of Agriculture undertook a general revision of all estimates prior to 1920 to correct for irregularities in the early series and to utilize more fully the records of numbers assessed for taxation and other information not considered in preparing the original estimates.

Prior to 1920, crop reporters provided a single estimate of the value per head for a given species. Since 1920, the estimates are weighted averages based on values per head reported separately for the different age and sex classes of a given species, using as weights the estimated number in the respective class.

K 575, 578, 580. Live weight production of livestock, 1909–1970.

Source: U.S. Department of Agriculture, 1909–1923, Bureau of Agricultural Economics, *Meat Animals, Farm Production, and Income, 1924–1944*, September 1947; 1924–1970, Statistical Reporting Service, *Agricultural Statistics, 1952, 1957, 1962, 1967*, and *1971* editions.

Production in live weight relates to the total poundage produced on farms and ranches during a calendar year. The estimate of production is derived by determining for each State a balance sheet which shows, as debit items, the inventory at the beginning of the year, the births, and inshipments; and, as credit items, the marketings, farm slaughter, death losses, and numbers on hand at the end of the year. Estimates of average live weight are based on reports from slaughterers, collected by the Department of Agriculture and in the census of manufactures, and on records obtained from stockyards. Reports have also been obtained from farmers on the average weight of livestock slaughtered on farms. The total live weight for beginning and end of year is obtained by multiplying estimates of the different age and sex classes for a species by an estimate of their respective average live weight. Live weight of marketings, farm slaughter, and inshipments is determined by multiplying the estimate for these items by the respective average live weight. To obtain production, the total weight of inshipments is subtracted from the combined weight of marketings and farm slaughter. Then the difference in the inventory weight between the beginning and end of year is added or subtracted as the case might be.

K 576, 577, 579, 581, 582. Annual average price received by farmers, per hundred pounds of livestock, 1909–1970.

Source: 1909–1923, U.S. Department of Agriculture, Agricultural Marketing Service, *Prices Received by Farmers, 1908–1955*, Statistical Bulletin No. 180, June 1956; 1924–1970, see source for series K 575, 578, 580.

Price information is obtained from voluntary price reporters who furnish average local market prices each month. The estimates of monthly prices are weighted by monthly estimates of marketings to obtain the annual average. The monthly marketings are based on reports from stockyards and packers on monthly receipts of livestock by State of origin.

K 583–594. Meat slaughtering, production, and price, 1899–1970.

Source: U.S. Department of Agriculture. 1899–1939, Production and Marketing Administration, *Livestock Market News, Statistics and Related Data, 1946*, September 1947; 1940–1970, Economic Research Service, *Livestock and Meat Statistics*, annual issues, and Statistical Reporting Service, *Agricultural Statistics*, annual issues.

Figures for slaughter include federally inspected slaughter and estimates of all other slaughter (other commercial slaughter and farm slaughter). Before 1944, this information was obtained largely on an annual basis from various sources; but, beginning in 1944, information was collected by months, first under the slaughter control program of the War Food Administration, and later under the slaughter and meat control programs of Office of Price Administration. Current data on federally inspected slaughter, which includes animals condemned as unfit for human food, are compiled by the Consumer and Marketing Service in connection with its regulatory functions on meat inspection. The number of animals slaughtered in other commercial channels is estimated by the Statistical Reporting Service from monthly reports made by slaughterers who are not under Federal inspection. Estimates of farm slaughter are based on annual voluntary reports from livestock producers with periodic data from the census of agriculture as benchmarks. Production of the different kinds of meat are computed from estimated average live weights and dressing yields and, except for pork, is shown on a carcass weight basis. Pork production represents carcass weight excluding the raw fat rendered into lard.

The data on production under Federal inspection are based on records of production and yields reported monthly by slaughterers operating under Federal inspection. Monthly estimates of production under Federal inspection are not available prior to 1921. Reports of the biennial census of manufactures on slaughter were used as a basis for annual production estimates for years for which they are available. In other years, the estimates were based on information obtained from market records and other sources. Currently, information on weights and yields for other commercial slaughter is based on monthly reports from commercial slaughterers who are not under Federal inspection.

Prices of the different species of livestock at Chicago for the early years are from records published in the *Drovers Journal Yearbook*. Beginning in 1922, the price of beef steers at Chicago is based on records of all steers sold out of first hands for slaughter. The number of head, live weight, and total value of steers, by grades, are compiled by weeks. The annual prices represent the weighted average of all grades of steers sold during the year for slaughter. Since 1919, the average price for veal calves is based on the average of daily quotations. The average price of hogs at Chicago has been obtained from different sources; since 1920, it is the weighted average of packer and shipper purchases at the Chicago market. Since 1921, the price of lambs at Chicago represents an average computed from the bulk of sales price data.

K 595–608.　General note.

Early development of the dairy industry in the United States is indicated by export statistics of 1790 which showed the New England States, New York, and Pennsylvania producing considerable amounts of butter and cheese in excess of their consumption requirements. The growth and spread of the industry between that time and 1849, when statistics on dairying were first available through the national census of agriculture, are described in the *Agriculture Yearbook*, 1922, pp. 297–306. At the middle of the 19th century, milk cows were rather generally distributed over the eastern half of the United States as far west as southern Wisconsin, eastern Iowa, western Missouri and Arkansas, and the eastern third of Texas. By 1860, there were appreciable numbers of milk cows in the Pacific Coast States. In later years, they gradually spread over the intervening territory.

Dairy products sold by farmers in the early period were limited mainly to whole milk, farm-made butter, and farm-made cheese. Prior to 1850, these products were produced mainly on farms. The 1850 Census showed the bulk of cheese production for 1849 coming from farms in the area extending from northeastern Ohio eastward through New York and New England. Factory cheese production was in an experimental stage shortly before 1850, and made considerable progress during the next two decades. Although some butter was made in early cheese plants, the first commercial creamery was not established until 1861. Since that time, factories have largely supplanted farms in the production of both cheese and butter.

The first condensery was established in 1856, but little interest was given the product until the Civil War. Unsweetened condensed milk was first produced in 1885; the canned unsweetened product (evaporated milk) now makes up about nine-tenths of all evaporated and condensed whole milk. Ice cream was produced and sold by some retail stores in the first half of the 19th century, and wholesale plant distribution to dealers began about the middle of the century.

K 595–596.　Cows and heifers kept for milk, 1850–1970.

Source: U.S. Department of Agriculture, Statistical Reporting Service, *Agricultural Statistics, 1967* and *1972* editions. Census years, U.S. Bureau of the Census, 1850–1920, Sixteenth Census Reports, *Agriculture*, vol. III, pp. 606–607; 1925–1945, *Census of Agriculture, 1945*, vol. II, p. 381; 1950–1954, *U.S. Census of Agriculture: 1954*, vol. II, p. 440; 1959–1964, *U.S. Census of Agriculture: 1964*, vol. II, p. 58; 1969, *U.S. Census of Agriculture: 1969*, vol. II, chapter 5, p. 146.

The estimates are based on interpretation of data from the census of agriculture, tax assessors, and other State agencies, together with the analysis of changes taking place in herds kept by a large sample of livestock reporters. With respect to the data on milk cow numbers obtained in the censuses of agriculture, the wording of the census questions has not necessarily been comparable with the definitions represented by the annual estimates and has varied somewhat from one census enumeration to another.

K 597.　Milk production on farms, 1889–1970.

Source: 1889–1919, U.S. Bureau of the Census, various census of agriculture reports. U.S. Department of Agriculture, 1924–1944, Agricultural Marketing Service, *Milk-Farm Production, Disposition, and Income*, Statistical Bulletin No. 175, April 1956; 1945–1970, Statistical Reporting Service, *Agricultural Statistics, 1967* and *1972* editions.

Beginning in 1924, the figures represent calendar-year estimates. The estimates are based on interpretations of census data, analysis of annual and monthly survey data on milk cows and milk production, and checks against information on milk utilization obtained from dairy plants and other sources. For 1919 and earlier years, the data are based on censuses of agriculture and converted from gallons to pounds by use of a conversion factor of 8.6 pounds per gallon. For 1889, the census totals are the reported figures. For 1899, they include estimates for incomplete reports; and for 1909 and 1919, they include estimates of production on farms that reported milk cows but failed to report milk produced. The 1889 and 1899 data were enumerated as of the following June, the 1909 data as of April 15, 1910, and the 1919 data as of January 1, 1920.

K 598–601.　Production of dairy products, 1849–1970.

Source: 1849–1916, E. E. Vial, *Production and Consumption of Manufactured Dairy Products*, U.S. Department of Agriculture, Technical Bulletin No. 722, April 1940. U.S. Department of Agriculture, Agricultural Marketing Service, 1917–1939, *Revisions in the Production of Creamery Butter, Cheese, and Ice Cream by States, 1916–1939*, and *Production and Utilization of Milk, United States, 1924–1952*; 1940–1949, *Production of Manufactured Dairy Products* (except for series K 601, 1940–1949, *Revisions of Ice Cream and Ice Milk Data, by States, 1940–1949*); 1950–1970, *Agricultural Statistics, 1964*, and subsequent annual issues except series K 598, 1970, unpublished data.

For 1940–1970, data are from the annual survey of output of dairy plants. For 1916–1939, data were based on the annual survey of dairy plants supplemented by estimates for incompleteness in some States based on data from the census of manufactures or from State sources. For the years prior to 1916 or 1917, the level of the figures was based mainly on the Census Bureau's survey of the output of dairy plants with interpolations for intervening years for some products (see E. E. Vial, cited above).

Butter production data represent farm and factory production combined. Factory butter figures for 1917–1970 are for production of creamery butter and include some estimates for incompleteness. Figures for factory production for 1849, 1859, 1869, 1879, 1899, 1904, 1909, and 1914 are from the census of manufactures. The 1889 census data were revised upward to allow for incompleteness. Annual figures on factory butter production for the intercensal years were interpolated on the basis of receipts of butter at major central markets for 1879–1919 and on factory production for 1917–1970.

Cheese production figures include both farm and factory cheese production prior to 1927. Since 1926, farm cheese was negligible and is excluded. For 1909–1917, cheese figures exclude full-skim American. For 1918–1970, data are from plant reports of all types of cheese manufactured except cottage, pot, and bakers' cheese and full-skim American. For 1849, 1859, 1869, 1879, 1889, and 1909 the figures for total cheese production are from the decennial censuses. The census data for 1889 were revised upward to allow for incompleteness. Estimates for the intercensal years 1869–1899 were interpolated on the basis of market receipts. Data on factory production of cheese for 1904 and 1914 are from the census of manufactures; data for the intercensal years 1869–1919 were interpolated on the basis of market receipts. Production of farm cheese for the intercensal years 1899–1926 was roughly projected on the basis of average change between census years and added to the factory product to obtain total cheese figures.

Evaporated and condensed milk production includes evaporated whole milk, bulk unsweetened condensed whole milk, and case and bulk sweetened condensed whole milk. Production figures for 1879, 1899, 1904, 1909, and 1914 are census totals for all condensed and evaporated milk. For 1889, the census data were revised upward to allow for incompleteness. Data for 1869 are estimated; those for the noncensus years before 1919 represent an estimated trend of production based on intervening census data.

Ice cream production figures for 1916–1970 are based on the annual survey of dairy manufacturing plants supplemented by estimates for incompleteness in some States based on data from the census of manufactures or State sources. For 1914, data were estimated from the census of manufactures. For 1909 and earlier years, the data represent merely an estimated trend of production.

K 602. Milk equivalent of manufactured dairy products, 1849–1970.

Source: See source for series K 598–601, except 1970, unpublished data.

For 1849–1923, the figures are based on national production of manufactured dairy products converted to milk equivalent on the basis of somewhat less refined conversion factors than those used for later years. As such they include no allowance for shifts in production between States or areas of high- or low-testing milk, and they assume standard butterfat content of the products for all years.

For 1930–1970, data were based on information of products made in each State and State conversion factors for each product. Duplication of milk usage involving the production of butter from whey fat recovered from cheese making and the use of butter and condensed milk in the production of ice cream were eliminated.

K 603–606. Dairy products—prices received by farmers, 1909–1970.

Source: U.S. Department of Agriculture. 1909–1944, Agricultural Marketing Service, *Prices Received by Farmers*, Statistical Bulletin No. 180, June 1956; 1945–1970, Statistical Reporting Service, *Agricultural Statistics, 1967* and *1972* issues.

Prices received by farmers for milkfat in cream, wholesale milk, and retail milk are estimates based on averages of survey data reported by dealers and farmers for their local market areas. Prices of milkfat in cream, series K 604, represent the butterfat in farm-skimmed cream sold by farmers; survey information was not collected prior to 1920, and estimates were extrapolated on the basis of trends in butter prices.

Wholesale milk prices, series K 605, are for milk sold by farmers to plants and dealers including such establishments as cheese factories, condenseries, creameries, or market milk plants. Prior to 1923, these prices were asked on a per-gallon basis and since that time on a per-100-pounds basis. Additional historic information on wholesale milk-price series was collected by direct plant contacts during the middle 1930's when the State estimates were revised.

Retail milk prices, series K 606, represent the milk retailed by farmers directly to consumers. Before 1923, survey information was collected on a price per-gallon rather than per-quart basis. Some of the increase in price between 1909 and 1945 probably represents additional services rendered in process of distributing the milk.

K 607–608. Cheese and butter—wholesale prices, 1830–1970.

Source: U.S. Department of Agriculture, Consumer and Marketing Service, unpublished data and Statistical Reporting Service, *Agricultural Statistics*, annual editions.

The wholesale prices of cheese represent averages of weekly quotations prior to 1950 on American twins and thereafter on cheddar cheese only, on the Wisconsin cheese exchange at Plymouth. The wholesale price of butter is for the New York City market. Since 1830, the data for butter differ somewhat in definition and source (see tabular footnote).

K 609–623. Poultry and eggs—number, production, and price, 1909–1970.

Source: U.S. Department of Agriculture, Statistical Reporting Service, *Agricultural Statistics, 1957, 1962, 1967, 1971, 1972,* and *1973* editions, except series K 611–613, 1909–1929, and series K 617–618, 1909–1919, Bureau of Agricultural Economics, *Farm Production, Disposition, and Income From Chickens and Eggs*, Statistical Bulletin No. 133, July 1953. Census years, for chickens: 1910, U.S. Bureau of the Census, *U.S. Census of Agriculture, 1940*, Special Poultry Report, p. 4, and *1945*, vol. II, p. 407; 1920–1964, *U.S. Census of Agriculture: 1964*, vol. II, chapter 2, table 5; 1969, *U.S. Census of Agriculture: 1969*, vol. II, chapter 5, table 20. Census data for turkeys: *U.S. Census of Agriculture, 1954*, vol. II, p. 556.

In census data, age limitations for chickens and turkeys are: 3 months old and over for the 1910, 1930, 1935, and 1969 censuses; no age limitation for the 1920 and 1925 censuses; and 4 months old and over for the 1940, 1945, 1950, 1954, 1959, and 1964 censuses. Broilers are young chickens of the heavy breeds and other meat-type birds, to be marketed at 2–5 pounds live weight, and from which no pullets are kept for egg production. These data are not included in farm production of chickens.

The estimates are believed to indicate, within reasonable limits of accuracy, the actual number of farm chickens and turkeys; the production of chickens, turkeys, and eggs; and, with greater accuracy, the direction and extent of the changes from year to year.

Complete surveys of the hatchery industry are made every year in all States. Monthly estimates of the production of baby chicks, based on returns from about 70 percent of total hatchery capacity, are also made. These figures of hatchery output give a dependable check on the actual level of chicken production.

Estimates of inventory numbers of chickens on farms January 1, series K 609, are based primarily upon census enumerations. Enumerations for 1910–1955 were adjusted for changes between January 1 and the average date of enumeration in each State, and cover only farm flocks as defined by the Census Bureau. Estimates of change in numbers from year to year through 1967 were based on annual surveys made in December of each year, covering about 150,000 livestock farms, and on changes in flocks belonging to about 30,000 crop reporters, plus assessor and State farm census data where available. Since 1967, estimates of change in numbers from year to year are based on annual surveys in December of each year covering about 40,000 flock owners (contractors and independents) which account for nearly half of all birds in the country.

Although census enumerations of chickens on farms were made in 1880, 1890, and 1900, the Department of Agriculture did not make annual estimates until 1909 because data showing annual changes were not available.

Estimates of inventory numbers of turkeys on farms January 1, series K 619, are based primarily upon the census enumerations of turkeys on farms January 1, 1935, and April 1, 1940, adjusted for changes in numbers between January 1 and the date of enumeration. Turkeys on farms were not reported in the 1945 census. The number on January 1, 1945, was estimated from the relationship between turkeys raised in 1944 and the number on hand January 1, 1945, as reported by crop and livestock reporters, using as a base the revised estimates of turkeys raised in 1944 based on the census enumeration. Annual changes in the estimates for intervening years are based mainly on the numbers on hand as reported on January 1 by crop and livestock reporters. Estimates of turkeys raised from 1954–1970 are based on poultry placement data secured from hatcheries. In recent years coverage has been virtually complete. Although census enumerations of turkeys on farms were made in 1890, 1900, 1910, and 1920, the Department of Agriculture did not make annual estimates for years prior to 1929 because data showing annual changes were not available.

Chickens, series K 611, and turkeys, series K 621, produced on farms are computed from the number raised during the year, minus the death loss of chickens and of turkeys that were on hand at the beginning of the year. Young chickens and young turkeys of the current year's hatchings that die are also excluded.

Egg production, series K 617, is estimated from returns from about 30,000 crop respondents and 5,000 commercial egg producers (contractors and independents) reporting on the first of each month for their own flocks, the number of layers on hand, and the eggs produced yesterday. Beginning with the estimated total number of layers on hand at the beginning of the year, the change in numbers from month to month is estimated from the changes shown by these survey operations. The monthly average number of layers and total egg production is revised at the end of the year if the change in number of layers shown by the annual survey in December differs from the change estimated from monthly returns. Adjustment is also made for change in the number of chicken farms on an annual basis.

★ ★ ★ ★ ★ ★ ★ ★ ★ ★ **More Recent Data for *Historical Statistics* Series** ★ ★ ★ ★ ★ ★ ★ ★ ★ ★

★   ★

★   Statistics for more recent years in continuation of many of the still-active series shown here appear   ★

★   in annual issues of the *Statistical Abstract of the United States,* beginning with the 1975 edition. For   ★

★   direct linkage of the historical series to the tables in the *Abstract,* see Appendix I in the *Abstract.*   ★

★   ★

★ ★

Series K 496–501.　Acreages of Harvested Crops, by Use, and Indexes of Cropland Used for Crops and Crop Production Per Acre: 1910 to 1970

[Excludes Alaska and Hawaii]

Year	Total (496)	Export products (497)	Feed for horses and mules (498)	Products for domestic use (499)	Cropland used for crops (500)	Crop production per acre (501)	Year	Total (496)	Export products (497)	Feed for horses and mules (498)	Products for domestic use (499)	Cropland used for crops (500)	Crop production per acre (501)
					Index (1967 = 100)							**Index (1967 = 100)**	
1970	297	72		225	98	102	1940	341	8	43	290	107	62
1969	294	61		233	97	107	1939	331	23	45	263	106	60
1968	303	54		249	99	104	1938	349	22	48	279	108	59
1967	308	69		239	100	100	1937	347	29	52	266	110	62
1966	295	69		226	96	99	1936	323	18	54	251	109	45
1965	298	76		222	98	100	1935	345	20	56	269	110	54
1964	301	74		227	98	95	1934	304	20	57	227	109	41
1963	300	77		223	98	97	1933	340	28	59	253	110	49
1962	295	66		229	97	95	1932	371	35	60	276	112	55
1961	303	67	4	232	99	92	1931	365	36	62	267	112	58
1960	324	64	5	255	104	88	1930	369	39	65	265	111	52
1959	324	61	6	257	104	86	1929	365	44	67	254	110	56
1958	324	44	7	273	103	86	1928	361	49	70	242	110	58
1957	324	48	8	268	104	77	1927	358	49	73	236	109	56
1956	324	60	9	255	107	77	1926	359	54	76	229	108	57
1955	340	47	10	283	110	74	1925	360	44	78	238	108	56
1954	346	37	11	298	111	71	1924	355	53	81	221	106	55
1953	348	31	13	304	111	73	1923	354	47	84	223	106	56
1952	349	36	15	298	111	73	1922	355	50	86	219	106	56
1951	344	59	18	267	111	69	1921	359	66	87	206	107	51
1950	345	50	19	276	110	69	1920	360	60	90	210	107	60
1949	360	45	22	293	113	70	1919	364	56	91	217	109	54
1948	356	52	24	280	110	75	1918	362	62	92	208	108	54
1947	355	42	26	287	109	67	1917	349	44	92	213	104	56
1946	352	45	29	278	108	70	1916	340	53	92	195	101	54
1945	354	42	32	280	108	68	1915	340	49	93	198	101	60
1944	362	25	36	301	110	68	1914	334	57	92	185	100	58
1943	357	21	37	299	110	64	1913	333	43	92	198	99	53
1942	348	13	39	296	108	70	1912	329	42	91	196	98	62
1941	344	12	40	292	107	64	1911	330	40	90	200	98	54
							1910	325	37	88	200	96	55

Series K 502–516.　Corn, Wheat, Oats, and Barley—Acreage, Production, Price, and Stocks: 1839 to 1970

[Census figures in *italics*]

Year	Corn for all purposes — Acreage harvested (502)	Production (503)	Price per bushel [1] (504)	Stocks on farms, Oct. 1 (505)	All wheat for grain — Acreage harvested (506)	Production (507)	Price per bushel [1] (508)	Stocks on farms, July 1 (509)	Wheat in all off-farm positions, July 1 (510)	Oats for grain — Acreage harvested (511)	Production (512)	Price per bushel [1] (513)	Barley for grain — Acreage harvested (514)	Production (515)	Price per bushel [1] (516)
	1,000 acres	*Million bushels*	*Dollars*	*Million bushels*	*1,000 acres*	*Million bushels*	*Dollars*	*Million bushels*	*Million bushels*	*1,000 acres*	*Million bushels*	*Dollars*	*1,000 acres*	*Million bushels*	*Dollars*
1970	66,222	[2]4,099	1.33	569.4	44,141	1,370	1.33	306.9	577.8	18,524	909	0.62	9,628	410	0.96
1969[3]	*60,402*	[2]*4,357*	------	------	*45,373*	*1,328*	*1.34*	------	------	*16,354*	*880*	*.58*	*8,925*	*394*	*.88*
1969	63,360	[2]4,583	1.16	728.2	47,577	1,460	1.24	327.8	490.7	17,930	950	.59	9,531	424	.87
1968	64,603	[2]4,393	1.08	781.8	55,262	1,576	1.24	230.4	309.0	17,533	939	.60	9,709	423	.91
1967	69,978	[2]4,760	1.03	569.2	58,771	1,522	1.39	145.5	279.5	16,017	789	.66	9,177	373	1.00
1966	65,828	[2]4,117	1.24	529.7	49,867	1,312	1.63	130.8	404.4	17,861	801	.67	10,205	393	1.05
1965	64,565	[2]4,084	1.16	581.4	49,560	1,316	1.35	132.5	684.7	18,479	927	.62	9,144	392	1.02
1964	*63,515*	[2]*3,361*	*1.16*		*47,958*	*1,218*	*1.37*			*18,936*	*808*	*.63*	*9,805*	*362*	*.93*
1964	65,388	[2]3,484	1.17	681.1	49,762	1,283	1.37	75.7	825.7	19,759	852	.63	10,277	386	.95
1963	68,317	[2]4,019	1.11	533.8	45,506	1,147	1.85	95.5	1,099.7	21,308	966	.62	11,236	393	.90
1962	64,474	[2]3,606	1.12	578.3	43,688	1,092	2.04	102.4	1,219.6	22,377	1,012	.62	12,214	428	.92
1961	65,405	[2]3,598	1.10	588.1	51,571	1,232	1.83	137.1	1,274.2	23,886	1,010	.64	12,806	392	.98
1960	80,678	4,314	1.00	452.0	51,879	1,355	1.74	95.9	1,217.6	26,588	1,153	.60	13,856	429	.84
1959[4]	*79,616*	[2]*3,697*	*1.05*		*49,567*	*1,056*	*1.77*			*26,573*	*1,001*	*.64*	*14,199*	*398*	*.86*
1959	81,902	4,197	1.05	325.0	51,716	1,118	1.76	114.9	1,180.2	27,758	1,050	.65	14,869	420	.86
1958	72,224	3,725	1.12	343.0	53,047	1,457	1.75	51.2	830.2	31,247	1,401	.58	14,791	477	.90
1957	71,864	3,400	1.11	418.9	43,754	956	1.93	59.9	848.9	34,065	1,290	.61	14,872	443	.89
1956	75,247	3,445	1.29	299.3	49,768	1,005	1.97	67.3	966.2	33,333	1,151	.69	12,852	377	.99
1955	79,367	3,220	1.35	313.8	47,290	935	1.98	40.6	995.5	39,027	1,496	.60	14,523	403	.92
1954	*78,123*	[2]*2,613*	*1.44*		*51,362*	*909*	*2.13*			*37,921*	*1,314*	*.71*	*12,556*	*355*	*1.08*
1954	80,186	3,058	1.43	359.4	54,356	984	2.12	103.2	830.3	40,551	1,410	.71	13,370	379	1.09
1953	80,459	3,210	1.48	330.0	67,840	1,173	2.04	79.2	526.4	37,536	1,153	.74	8,680	247	1.17
1952	80,940	3,292	1.52	172.0	71,130	1,306	2.09	63.4	192.6	37,012	1,217	.79	8,236	228	1.37
1951	80,729	2,926	1.66	313.1	61,873	988	2.11	76.3	323.6	35,233	1,278	.82	9,424	257	1.26

See footnotes at end of table.

Series K 502–516. Corn, Wheat, Oats, and Barley—Acreage, Production, Price, and Stocks: 1839 to 1970—Con.

[Census figures in *italics*]

Year	Corn for all purposes				All wheat for grain				Wheat in all off-farm positions, July 1	Oats for grain			Barley for grain		
	Acreage harvested	Production	Price per bushel [1]	Stocks on farms, Oct. 1	Acreage harvested	Production	Price per bushel [1]	Stocks on farms, July 1		Acreage harvested	Production	Price per bushel [1]	Acreage harvested	Production	Price per bushel [1]
	502	503	504	505	506	507	508	509	510	511	512	513	514	515	516
	1,000 acres	*Million bushels*	*Dollars*	*Million bushels*	*1,000 acres*	*Million bushels*	*Dollars*	*Million bushels*	*Million bushels*	*1,000 acres*	*Million bushels*	*Dollars*	*1,000 acres*	*Million bushels*	*Dollars*
1950	81,818	3,075	1.52	470.1	61,607	1,019	2.00	65.9	358.9	39,306	1,369	0.79	11,155	304	1.19
1949	*83,337*	*2 2,778*	*1.24*		*71,163*	*1,007*	*1.86*		*35,344*	*35,344*	*1,137*	*.65*	*9,180*	*221*	*1.05*
1949	85,595	3,238	1.24	696.1	75,910	1,098	1.88	66.5	240.8	37,794	1,220	.66	9,872	237	1.06
1948	84,778	3,605	1.28	112.1	72,418	1,295	1.99	94.5	101.5	39,280	1,450	.72	11,905	316	1.16
1947	82,888	2,355	2.16	251.8	74,519	1,359	2.29	40.5	43.3	37,855	1,176	1.05	10,995	282	1.73
1946	87,585	3,217	1.53	151.9	67,105	1,152	1.90	41.6	58.5	42,812	1,478	.81	10,380	265	1.38
1945	87,625	2,869	1.23	293.4	65,167	1,108	1.49	87.7	191.5	41,739	1,524	.67	10,454	267	1.01
1944	*92,259*	*2 2,788*	*1.08*		*58,286*	*1,033*	*1.41*		*35,425*	*35,425*	*1,041*	*.69*	*11,694*	*261*	*1.00*
1944	94,014	3,088	1.03	202.7	59,749	1,060	1.41	103.6	212.9	39,741	1,149	.71	12,301	276	1.01
1943	92,060	2,966	1.12	355.2	51,355	844	1.36	189.6	429.3	38,914	1,140	.72	14,900	323	.99
1942	87,367	3,069	.92	422.0	49,773	969	1.10	162.7	468.1	38,197	1,343	.49	16,958	429	.63
1941	85,357	2,652	.75	473.5	55,935	942	.94	86.7	298.1	38,161	1,183	.41	14,276	363	.53
1940	86,429	2,457	.62	541.4	53,273	815	.68	79.6	200.1	35,431	1,246	.30	13,525	311	.40
1939	*86,991*	*2 2,311*	*.56*		*50,527*	*709*	*.69*		*162.0*	*29,934*	*870*	*.31*	*12,025*	*261*	*.41*
1939	88,279	2,581	.57	553.8	52,669	741	.69	88.0	162.0	33,460	958	.31	12,739	278	.41
1938	92,160	2,549	.49	351.5	69,197	920	.56	58.9	94.3	36,042	1,089	.24	10,610	257	.37
1937	93,980	2,643	.52	60.0	64,169	874	.96	22.0	61.2	35,542	1,177	.30	9,969	222	.54
1936	93,154	1,506	1.04	171.6	49,125	630	1.02	43.1	97.3	33,654	793	.45	8,329	148	.78
1935	95,974	2,299	.66	61.4	51,305	628	.83	44.1	101.8	40,109	1,210	.26	12,436	289	.38
1934	*87,476*	*2 1,169*	*.82*		*41,943*	*513*	*.86*			*24,589*	*458*	*.47*	*6,193*	*110*	*.67*
1934	92,193	1,449	.82	274.0	43,347	526	.85	61.1	211.8	29,455	544	.48	6,577	117	.69
1933	105,918	2,398	.52	326.8	49,424	552	.74	82.7	295.1	36,528	736	.34	9,641	153	.43
1932	110,577	2,930	.32	251.7	57,851	756	.38	93.6	281.7	41,700	1,254	.16	13,206	299	.22
1931	106,866	2,576	.32	162.6	57,704	942	.39	37.1	275.4	40,193	1,124	.21	11,181	200	.33
1930	101,465	2,080	.60	134.4	62,637	887	.67	62.5	228.7	39,847	1,274	.32	12,629	302	.41
1929	*97,742*	*2 2,131*	*.77*		*62,000*	*801*	*1.05*			*33,466*	*993*	*.41*	*12,891*	*264*	*.53*
1929	97,805	2,516	.80	142.4	63,392	824	1.04	43.6	183.3	38,153	1,112	.42	13,564	281	.54
1928	100,336	2,666	.84	87.2	59,226	914	1.00	20.0	92.8	40,128	1,312	.41	12,735	328	.57
1927	98,357	2,616	.85	192.5	59,628	875	1.19	26.6	82.9	40,350	1,093	.47	9,465	239	.69
1926	99,452	2,547	.74	262.1	56,616	832	1.22	23.7	73.2	42,854	1,152	.40	7,917	166	.58

Year	Corn for all purposes			All wheat for grain			Oats for grain			Barley for grain		
	Acreage harvested	Production	Price per bushel [1]	Acreage harvested	Production	Price per bushel [1]	Acreage harvested	Production	Price per bushel [1]	Acreage harvested	Production	Price per bushel [1]
	502	503	504	506	507	508	511	512	513	514	515	516
	1,000 acres	*Million bushels*	*Dollars*	*1,000 acres*	*Million bushels*	*Dollars*	*1,000 acres*	*Million bushels*	*Dollars*	*1,000 acres*	*Million bushels*	*Dollars*
1925	101,331	2,798	0.70	52,443	669	1.44	44,240	1,405	0.39	8,186	192	0.61
1924	*98,402*	*2 1,824*	*1.02*	*50,862*	*801*	*1.30*	*37,650*	*1,305*	*.47*	*6,767*	*159*	*.77*
1924	100,420	2,223	1.06	52,463	842	1.25	41,857	1,416	.48	7,038	165	.74
1923	101,123	2,875	.81	56,920	759	.93	40,245	1,227	.41	7,151	159	.55
1922	100,345	2,707	.73	61,397	847	.97	40,324	1,148	.37	6,601	153	.50
1921	103,155	2,928	.52	64,566	819	1.03	45,539	1,045	.32	7,074	133	.48
1920	101,359	3,071	.64	62,358	843	1.83	42,732	1,444	.54	7,439	171	.84
1919	*87,778*	*2 2,346*	*1.50*	*73,099*	*945*	*2.19*	*37,991*	*1,055*	*.81*	*6,473*	*122*	*1.31*
1919	98,145	2,679	1.51	73,700	952	2.16	39,601	1,107	.77	6,579	131	1.24
1918	102,195	2,441	1.52	61,068	904	2.05	42,464	1,429	.69	9,198	225	.95
1917	110,893	2,908	1.46	46,787	620	2.05	41,604	1,443	.70	8,453	182	1.23
1916	100,561	2,425	1.14	53,510	635	1.43	39,098	1,139	.49	7,623	159	.80
1915	100,623	2,829	.68	60,303	1,009	.96	38,802	1,435	.38	7,279	207	.52
1914	97,796	2,524	.71	55,613	897	.98	37,213	1,066	.44	7,653	178	.54
1913	100,206	2,273	.70	52,012	751	.79	37,245	1,039	.39	7,673	159	.53
1912	101,451	2,948	.55	48,413	730	.81	37,244	1,353	.34	7,542	197	.51
1911	101,393	2,475	.68	49,894	618	.87	37,149	886	.45	7,613	145	.83
1910	102,267	2,853	.52	45,793	625	.91	36,844	1,106	.36	7,546	142	.61
1909	*98,386*	*2 2,552*	*.56*	*44,263*	*683*	*.96*	*35,159*	*1,007*	*.41*	*7,699*	*173*	*.53*
1909	100,200	2,611	.62	44,262	684	.99	35,062	1,014	.43	7,697	173	.56
1908	95,285	2,567	.65	45,102	643	.97	34,310	829	.49	7,409	171	.57
1907	96,094	2,614	.51	44,139	629	.87	34,439	801	.44	6,854	151	.67
1906	95,624	3,033	.39	46,230	741	.66	33,688	1,023	.32	6,744	179	.42
1905	95,746	2,954	41	46,306	706	.75	33,426	1,104	.29	6,658	172	.39
1904	95,228	2,687	44	43,155	556	.93	32,749	1,012	.31	6,579	166	.41
1903	93,555	2,515	.42	48,456	663	.69	32,187	885	.34	6,231	149	.45
1902	97,177	2,774	.40	46,244	687	.63	31,358	1,077	.31	5,474	146	.45
1901	94,422	1,716	.60	50,847	763	.63	30,891	800	.40	4,963	124	.45

See footnotes at end of table.

Series K 502–516. Corn, Wheat, Oats, and Barley—Acreage, Production, Price, and Stocks: 1839 to 1970—Con.

[Census figures in *italics*]

Year	Corn for all purposes			All wheat for grain			Oats for grain			Barley for grain		
	Acreage harvested	Production	Price per bushel [1]	Acreage harvested	Production	Price per bushel [1]	Acreage harvested	Production	Price per bushel [1]	Acreage harvested	Production	Price per bushel [1]
	502	503	504	506	507	508	511	512	513	514	515	516
	1,000 acres	*Million bushels*	*Dollars*	*1,000 acres*	*Million bushels*	*Dollars*	*1,000 acres*	*Million bushels*	*Dollars*	*1,000 acres*	*Million bushels*	*Dollars*
1900	94,852	2,662	0.35	49,203	599	0.62	31,049	945	0.25	4,703	97	0.41
1899	*[2] 94,917*	*[2] 2,666*	*.31*	*52,589*	*659*	*.56*	*29,540*	*943*	*.23*	*4,470*	*120*	*.35*
1899	94,591	2,646	.30	52,342	655	.59	29,254	937	.26	4,472	118	.39
1898	87,784	2,351	.29	50,506	768	.58	29,327	842	.25	4,113	98	.39
1897	89,965	2,288	.26	43,413	606	.81	28,829	830	.21	4,120	103	.34
1896	89,074	2,671	.21	40,828	523	.72	30,248	775	.18	4,131	97	.30
1895	90,479	2,535	.25	38,998	542	.51	30,905	925	.19	4,185	104	.33
1894	80,069	1,615	.45	40,167	542	.49	29,556	750	.32	3,639	74	.44
1893	79,832	1,900	.36	40,790	506	.53	29,266	707	.29	3,689	87	.40
1892	76,914	1,897	.39	42,979	612	.62	28,168	722	.32	3,857	95	.47
1891	78,855	2,336	.40	41,090	678	.83	27,756	837	.31	3,590	94	.52
1890	74,785	1,650	.50	36,686	449	.84	28,275	609	.42	3,250	70	.62
1889	*[2] 72,088*	*[2] 2,122*	--------	*33,580*	*468*	--------	*28,321*	*809*	--------	*3,221*	*78*	--------
1889	77,656	2,294	.28	36,098	504	.70	28,697	831	.22	3,352	81	.42
1888	77,474	2,251	.33	34,969	424	.93	27,807	773	.27	3,283	76	.59
1887	73,296	1,605	.43	36,873	491	.68	26,272	696	.30	3,258	72	.52
1886	73,911	1,783	.36	36,312	514	.69	24,426	682	.29	3,027	74	.53
1885	71,854	2,058	.32	35,095	400	.77	23,351	674	.28	2,862	64	.56
1884	68,834	1,948	.35	38,485	571	.65	21,974	641	.27	2,694	68	.48
1883	68,168	1,652	.42	35,587	439	.91	20,621	606	.32	2,474	57	.59
1882	66,157	1,755	.48	36,496	552	.89	19,075	540	.37	2,434	60	.63
1881	63,026	1,245	.63	36,795	406	1.20	16,916	446	.46	2,201	49	.82
1880	62,545	1,707	.39	38,096	502	.95	16,414	418	.35	1,990	45	.66
1879	*[2] 62,369*	*[2] 1,755*	--------	*35,430*	*459*	--------	*16,145*	*408*	--------	*1,998*	*44*	--------
1879	62,229	1,752	.36	35,347	459	1.11	15,955	415	.33	1,926	42	.60
1878	59,659	1,565	.31	33,379	449	.77	15,830	443	.24	1,848	37	.58
1877	58,799	1,516	.36	27,963	396	1.08	14,816	435	.29	1,962	39	.63
1876	55,277	1,478	.36	28,283	309	1.04	14,589	327	.35	1,973	41	.69
1875	52,446	1,450	.42	28,382	314	1.01	13,616	365	.37	1,702	33	.86
1874	47,640	1,059	.64	27,310	356	.95	12,775	273	.52	1,628	36	.96
1873	44,084	1,008	.48	24,866	322	1.17	12,010	307	.37	1,473	31	.96
1872	43,584	1,279	.38	22,962	271	1.24	11,789	327	.32	1,421	32	.74
1871	42,002	1,142	.46	22,230	272	1.25	11,061	306	.39	1,348	28	.77
1870	38,388	1,125	.52	20,945	254	1.04	10,348	268	.43	1,331	29	.85
1869		*[2] 761*			*288*			*282*			*30*	
1869	35,833	782	.73	21,194	290	.92	9,555	284	.46	1,238	29	.87
1868	35,116	920	.62	19,140	246	1.46	8,897	230	.54	1,064	23	1.49
1867	32,116	794	.78	16,738	211	2.01	8,176	223	.59	1,058	24	1.22
1866	30,017	731	.66	15,408	170	2.06	7,935	232	.47	754	18	.95
1859		*[2] 839*			*173*			*173*			*16*	
1849		*[2] 592*			*100*			*147*			*5*	
1839		*[2] 378*			*85*			*123*			*4*	

[1] December 1 price received by farmers prior to 1908; season average price thereafter.
[2] Corn harvested for grain only.
[3] Not comparable with previous censuses; data for farms with farm product sales of $2,500 or more.
[4] Beginning 1959, census data include Alaska and Hawaii.

Series K 517–531. Flaxseed, Soybeans, Sorghum Grain, Rye, and Buckwheat—Acreage, Production, and Price: 1839 to 1970

[Census figures in *italics*]

Year	Flaxseed			Soybeans for beans			Sorghum grain			Rye for grain			Buckwheat		
	Acreage harvested	Production	Price per bushel [1]	Acreage harvested	Production	Price per bushel [1]	Acreage harvested	Production	Price per bushel [1]	Acreage harvested	Production	Price per bushel [1]	Acreage harvested	Production	Price per bushel [1]
	517	518	519	520	521	522	523	524	525	526	527	528	529	530	531
	1,000 acres	*Million bushels*	*Dollars*	*1,000 acres*	*Million bushels*	*Dollars*	*1,000 acres*	*Million bushels*	*Dollars*	*1,000 acres*	*1,000 bushels*	*Dollars*	*1,000 acres*	*1,000 bushels*	*Dollars*
1970	2,888	30.0	2.40	42,056	1,123.7	2.85	13,568	684	1.14	1,495	38,819	.986			
1969 [3]	*2,490*	*32.0*	*2.63*	*38,550*	*1,041.5*	*2.35*	*13,437*	*730*	*1.07*	*1,115*	*25,703*	*1.00*	*38*	*680*	*1.00*
1969	2,616	35.1	2.65	40,982	1,126.3	2.35	--------	--------	--------	1,346	31,583	1.00	--------	--------	2.31
1968	2,098	27.1	2.81	41,104	1,103.1	2.43	13,890	731	.949	1,014	23,365	1.02	--------	--------	2.43
1967	1,975	20.0	2.95	39,767	976.1	2.49	14,988	755	.992	1,071	24,154	1.07	--------	--------	2.75
1966	2,576	23.4	2.89	36,546	928.5	2.75	12,813	715	1.03	1,275	27,775	1.07	--------	--------	2.49
1965	2,775	35.4	2.80	34,449	845.6	2.54	13,029	673	1.00	1,469	33,223	.975	--------	--------	(NA)
1964 [3]	*2,651*	*21.7*	*2.81*	*29,844*	*669.7*	*2.66*	*11,742*	*490*	*1.05*	*1,640*	*30,916*	*1.04*	*48*	*986*	*1.07*
1964	2,825	24.4	2.82	30,793	700.9	2.62	11,168	463	--------	1,696	32,476	1.04	50	1,020	1.08
1963	3,172	31.0	2.76	28,615	699.2	2.51	13,326	585	.977	1,588	29,178	1.08	45	952	1.42
1962	2,808	32.2	2.83	27,608	669.2	2.34	11,571	510	1.02	1,981	40,698	.947	41	828	1.31
1961	2,514	22.2	3.26	27,003	678.6	2.28	10,985	480	1.01	1,543	27,336	1.01	46	864	1.15

See footnotes at end of table.

Series K 517–531. Flaxseed, Soybeans, Sorghum Grain, Rye, and Buckwheat—Acreage, Production, and Price: 1839 to 1970—Con.

[Census figures in *italics*]

Year	Flaxseed Acreage harvested	Flaxseed Production	Flaxseed Price per bushel [1]	Soybeans Acreage harvested	Soybeans Production	Soybeans Price per bushel [1]	Sorghum Acreage harvested	Sorghum Production	Sorghum Price per bushel [1]	Rye Acreage harvested	Rye Production	Rye Price per bushel [1]	Buckwheat Acreage harvested	Buckwheat Production	Buckwheat Price per bushel [1]
	517	518	519	520	521	522	523	524	525	526	527	528	529	530	531
	1,000 acres	*Million bushels*	*Dollars*	*1,000 acres*	*Million bushels*	*Dollars*	*1,000 acres*	*Million bushels*	*Dollars*	*1,000 acres*	*1,000 bushels*	*Dollars*	*1,000 acres*	*1,000 bushels*	*Dollars*
1960	3,342	30.4	2.65	23,655	555.1	2.13	15,601	620	0.836	1,688	33,108	0.882	48	847	1.16
1959 [3]	*2,848*	*19.6*	*3.04*	*22,080*	*515.6*	*1.97*	*15,406*	*555*	*.858*	*1,392*	*21,809*	*1.02*	*56*	*923*	*1.08*
1959	2,932	21.2	3.00	22,631	532.9	1.96	14,561	508	--------	1,457	23,076	1.00	60	1,012	1.05
1958	3,679	37.4	2.69	23,993	580.3	2.00	16,524	581	.999	1,797	33,182	1.02	86	1,533	1.02
1957	4,793	25.1	2.94	20,857	483.4	2.07	19,682	568	.973	1,718	28,516	1.08	98	1,664	1.10
1956	5,473	47.0	2.99	20,620	449.3	2.18	9,209	205	1.15	1,624	21,288	1.16	100	1,832	1.19
1955	4,914	40.4	2.90	18,620	373.7	2.22	12,891	243	.977	2,049	29,089	1.06	107	1,822	1.16
1954	*5,179*	*35.5*	*3.04*	*16,444*	*324.1*	*2.52*	*11,718*	*236*	*1.26*	*1,450*	*21,844*	*1.22*	*128*	*2,277*	*.97*
1954	5,663	41.3	3.05	17,047	341.1	2.46	11,304	224	--------	1,795	25,963	1.21	150	2,692	1.24
1953	4,570	37.7	3.64	14,829	269.2	2.72	6,295	116	1.32	1,430	18,894	1.29	178	3,199	.897
1952	3,304	30.2	3.73	14,435	298.8	2.72	5,326	91	1.58	1,393	16,146	1.72	163	3,232	1.40
1951	3,904	34.7	3.72	13,615	283.8	2.73	8,544	163	1.32	1,722	21,517	1.52	199	3,296	1.39
1950	4,090	40.2	3.34	13,807	299.2	2.47	10,346	234	1.05	1,753	21,403	1.31	253	4,424	1.08
1949	*4,813*	*40.2*	*3.60*	*10,148*	*212.4*	*2.12*	*6,602*	*148*	*1.13*	*1,418*	*16,563*	*1.22*	*236*	*4,318*	*.94*
1949	5,048	43.0	3.63	10,482	234.2	2.16	6,325	141	--------	1,554	18,102	1.20	269	4,956	.915
1948	4,973	54.8	5.71	10,682	227.2	2.27	7,317	131	1.28	2,058	25,886	1.43	330	6,085	1.08
1947	4,129	40.6	6.15	11,411	186.5	3.33	5,480	93	1.83	1,991	25,497	2.28	505	7,177	1.90
1946	2,432	22.6	4.03	9,932	203.4	2.57	6,669	106	1.40	1,597	18,487	1.92	383	6,812	1.46
1945	3,785	34.6	2.89	10,740	193.2	2.08	6,324	96	1.20	1,850	23,708	1.36	401	6,467	1.16
1944	*2,477*	*20.8*	*2.91*	--------	*187.7*	*2.07*	*9,386*	*185*	*.914*	*2,023*	*21,349*	*1.09*	--------	--------	--------
1944	2,610	21.7	2.91	10,245	192.1	2.05	9,061	178	--------	2,132	22,525	1.09	508	8,956	9.64
1943	5,691	50.0	2.83	10,397	190.1	1.81	6,889	110	1.14	2,652	28,680	.982	505	8,830	1.26
1942	4,408	41.0	2.36	9,894	187.5	1.61	5,991	110	.777	3,792	52,929	.603	375	6,636	.846
1941	3,266	32.1	1.79	5,889	107.2	1.55	6,015	114	.549	3,573	43,878	.542	337	6,038	.674
1940	3,182	30.9	1.42	4,807	78.0	.90	6,374	86	.478	3,204	39,725	.420	388	6,476	.538
1939	*2,081*	*18.8*	*1.46*	*4,274*	*87.6*	*.81*	*4,760*	*53*	*.569*	*3,556*	*35,844*	*.440*	*361*	*5,589*	*.62*
1939	2,171	19.6	1.46	4,315	90.1	.81	4,693	52	--------	3,822	38,562	.439	370	5,736	.622
1938	905	8.0	1.59	3,035	61.9	.67	4,699	67	.391	4,087	55,984	.338	448	6,763	.539
1937	927	7.1	1.87	2,586	46.2	.85	4,915	70	.501	3,825	48,862	.686	421	6,808	.667
1936	1,125	5.3	1.90	2,359	33.7	1.27	2,793	30	.948	2,694	24,239	.812	379	6,440	.851
1935	2,126	14.9	1.42	2,915	48.9	.73	4,597	58	.553	4,066	56,938	.398	505	8,488	.548
1934	*998*	*5.6*	*1.70*	--------	*23.0*	*1.01*	*2,396*	*19*	*.948*	*1,914*	*16,234*	*.730*	--------	--------	--------
1934	1,002	5.7	1.70	1,556	23.2	.99	2,370	19	--------	1,921	16,285	.720	475	8,994	.585
1933	1,341	6.9	1.63	1,044	13.5	.94	4,354	54	.506	2,405	20,573	.627	460	7,816	.558
1932	1,988	11.5	.88	1,001	15.2	.54	4,400	66	.298	3,350	39,099	.280	454	6,727	.434
1931	2,431	11.8	1.17	1,141	17.3	.50	4,443	72	.300	3,159	32,777	.341	507	8,910	.423
1930	3,780	21.7	1.61	1,074	13.9	1.37	3,477	38	.553	3,646	45,383	.444	574	6,967	.788
1929	*2,966*	*15.0*	*2.86*	--------	*8.7*	*1.67*	*3,522*	*49*	--------	*3,033*	*34,303*	*.860*	*622*	*8,359*	*.96*
1929	3,049	15.9	2.81	708	9.4	1.88	3,523	50	.745	3,138	35,411	.857	629	8,710	.962
1928	2,611	19.1	1.94	579	7.9	1.88	4,115	77	--------	3,320	38,055	.836	679	10,117	.898
1927	2,763	25.2	1.93	568	6.9	1.81	4,260	81	--------	3,466	51,196	.835	764	12,820	.872
1926	2,736	18.5	2.03	466	5.2	2.01	4,211	71	--------	3,427	34,968	.830	679	10,976	.875
1925	3,022	22.3	2.26	415	4.9	2.34	3,917	57	--------	3,807	42,418	.791	742	12,559	.871
1924	*3,435*	*28.2*	*2.34*	--------	--------	--------	*3,519*	*61*	--------	*3,744*	*55,674*	*1.040*	*717*	*12,004*	*1.07*
1924	3,535	31.2	2.18	448	4.9	2.46	3,526	59	--------	3,943	58,470	.953	737	12,508	1.075
1923	2,015	16.6	2.12	--------	--------	--------	4,204	62	--------	4,946	56,091	.594	689	11,596	.958
1922	1,113	10.5	2.08	--------	--------	--------	3,369	50	--------	6,770	101,142	.639	729	11,776	.893
1921	1,143	8.1	1.66	--------	--------	--------	3,700	71	--------	4,865	61,205	.841	640	11,822	.881
1920	1,647	10.9	2.33	--------	--------	--------	4,027	88	--------	4,843	62,113	1.469	729	12,193	1.254
1919	*1,261*	*6.7*	*4.41*	*113*	*1.1*	*4.10*	*3,630*	*74*	--------	*7,679*	*75,992*	*1.530*	*743*	*12,690*	*1.55*
1919	1,293	6.8	4.41	--------	--------	--------	3,619	72	--------	7,187	78,849	1.459	733	12,707	1.590
1918	1,783	12.8	3.58	--------	--------	--------	--------	--------	--------	6,709	83,586	1.497	1,018	14,404	1.640
1917	1,881	8.4	3.11	--------	--------	--------	--------	--------	--------	5,064	60,381	1.733	926	13,605	1.674
1916	1,298	11.8	2.31	--------	--------	--------	--------	--------	--------	3,528	43,089	1.124	786	10,302	1.267
1915	1,116	11.3	1.68	--------	--------	--------	--------	--------	--------	3,417	46,752	.839	754	12,523	.815
1914	1,561	12.9	1.31	--------	--------	--------	--------	--------	--------	3,144	42,120	.819	752	12,919	.807
1913	1,954	15.1	1.23	--------	--------	--------	--------	--------	--------	3,089	40,390	.610	774	10,208	.763
1912	2,941	28.1	1.29	--------	--------	--------	--------	--------	--------	2,724	37,911	.651	804	15,095	.679
1911	2,631	18.5	1.97	--------	--------	--------	--------	--------	--------	2,452	31,396	.807	805	13,888	.758
1910	2,222	11.4	2.28	--------	--------	--------	--------	--------	--------	2,262	29,098	.729	840	14,536	.675
1909	*2,083*	*19.5*	*1.48*	*2*	*(Z)*	*1.25*	--------	--------	--------	*2,196*	*29,520*	*.690*	*878*	*14,849*	*.63*
1909	2,081	19.5	1.42	--------	--------	--------	--------	--------	--------	2,212	30,083	.730	871	14,762	.723
1908	2,351	20.6	1.16	--------	--------	--------	--------	--------	--------	2,130	28,650	.728	842	14,675	.777
1907	2,699	23.8	.96	--------	--------	--------	--------	--------	--------	2,073	28,247	.726	833	14,225	.699
1906	2,568	27.6	1.02	--------	--------	--------	--------	--------	--------	2,154	29,609	.585	821	14,806	.594
1905	2,439	28.7	.84	--------	--------	--------	--------	--------	--------	2,297	31,173	.603	825	15,997	.583
1904	2,092	22.6	.99	--------	--------	--------	--------	--------	--------	2,205	28,461	.692	831	15,489	.625
1903	3,180	25.4	.81	--------	--------	--------	--------	--------	--------	2,260	28,932	.535	824	14,263	.608
1902	3,878	36.1	1.05	--------	--------	--------	--------	--------	--------	2,444	33,862	.500	810	13,547	.595
1901	3,173	27.6	--------	--------	--------	--------	--------	--------	--------	2,409	30,773	.550	807	15,145	.563
1900	2,762	16.0	--------	--------	--------	--------	--------	--------	--------	2,127	27,413	.501	791	11,709	.558
1899	*2,111*	*20.0*	*.78*	--------	--------	--------	--------	--------	--------	*2,054*	*25,569*	*.480*	*807*	*11,234*	*.51*
1899	2,102	20.0	.98	--------	--------	--------	--------	--------	--------	2,059	26,001	.495	803	11,197	.561
1898	1,889	18.5	--------	--------	--------	--------	--------	--------	--------	2,204	29,044	.441	794	12,187	.448
1897	1,365	13.2	--------	--------	--------	--------	--------	--------	--------	2,323	31,129	.426	827	14,318	.419
1896	1,848	17.7	--------	--------	--------	--------	--------	--------	--------	2,599	31,852	.369	856	13,791	.390

See footnotes at end of table.

Series K 517–531. Flaxseed, Soybeans, Sorghum Grain, Rye, and Buckwheat—Acreage, Production, and Price: 1839 to 1970—Con.

[Census figures in *italics*]

Year	Flaxseed Acreage harvested 517	Flaxseed Production 518	Rye for grain Acreage harvested 526	Rye for grain Production 527	Rye for grain Price per bushel [1] 528	Buckwheat Acreage harvested 529	Buckwheat Production 530	Buckwheat Price per bushel [1] 531
	1,000 acres	*Million bushels*	*1,000 acres*	*1,000 bushels*	*Dollars*	*1,000 acres*	*1,000 bushels*	*Dollars*
1895	2,039	21.4	2,400	29,614	0.407	801	12,426	0.453
1894	1,457	10.5	2,166	26,758	.488	805	11,024	.551
1893	1,287	10.4	2,162	26,700	.496	806	10,330	.584
1892	1,423	11.8	2,239	28,718	.537	840	12,119	.522
1891	2,040	16.7	2,180	29,569	.772	829	12,863	.571
1890	2,283	19.2	2,116	26,378	.623	821	11,979	.573
1889	*1,319*	*10.3*	*2,172*	*28,421*	--------	*837*	*12,110*	--------
1889	1,344	10.6	2,248	29,524	.420	809	11,654	.509
1888	--------	10.0	2,181	28,440	.592	812	9,729	.629
1887	--------	9.8	1,985	22,530	.535	799	9,666	.566
1886	--------	10.0	1,918	23,854	.530	802	10,771	.543
1885	--------	9.3	1,897	21,714	.580	826	11,567	.560
1884	--------	9.5	2,100	26,627	.534	782	10,139	.584
1883	--------	8.6	2,123	25,407	.584	804	7,143	.820
1882	--------	8.6	2,080	26,747	.631	800	10,678	.728
1881	--------	7.8	1,749	19,181	.917	800	8,678	.867
1880	--------	7.5	1,752	19,306	.745	818	11,009	.592
1879	--------	*7.2*	*1,842*	*19,832*	--------	*848*	*11,817*	--------

Year	Flaxseed, production 518	Rye for grain Acreage harvested 526	Rye for grain Production 527	Rye for grain Price per bushel [1] 528	Buckwheat Acreage harvested 529	Buckwheat Production 530	Buckwheat Price per bushel [1] 531
	Million bushels	*1,000 acres*	*1,000 bushels*	*Dollars*	*1,000 acres*	*1,000 bushels*	*Dollars*
1879	7.2	1,825	19,789	0.674	842	11,742	0.596
1878	7.0	1,905	21,755	.545	838	12,000	.528
1877	7.0	1,844	21,860	.606	839	11,854	.693
1876	5.8	1,770	19,266	.680	815	9,613	.715
1875	5.4	1,647	16,927	.759	793	10,991	.695
1874	5.4	1,568	17,305	.856	747	10,031	.803
1873	4.8	1,553	16,141	.757	751	10,370	.815
1872	3.4	1,563	16,776	.744	769	10,337	.837
1871	2.8	1,588	16,975	.767	725	9,271	.824
1870	2.4	1,559	15,637	.805	739	9,249	.797
1869	*1.7*	--------	*16,919*	--------	--------	*9,822*	--------
1869	2.1	1,631	17,906	.873	761	10,437	.869
1868	2.0	1,620	17,218	1.202	781	10,520	1.038
1867	1.9	1,649	19,595	1.312	811	11,184	1.060
1866	1.8	1,509	17,619	1.058	772	11,861	.944
1859	*.6*	--------	*21,101*	--------	--------	*17,572*	--------
1849	*.6*	--------	*14,189*	--------	--------	*8,957*	--------
1839	--------	--------	*18,646*	--------	--------	*7,292*	--------

NA   Not available.
Z   Less than 50,000.
[1] December 1 price received by farmers prior to 1908; season average price thereafter.
[2] Not comparable with previous censuses; data for farms with farm products sales of $2,500 or more in 1969.
[3] Beginning 1959, census data include Alaska and Hawaii.

Series K 532–537.   Irish Potatoes and Sweetpotatoes—Acreage, Production, and Price: 1849 to 1970

[Census figures in *italics*.   Prices are those received by growers]

Year	Irish potatoes Acreage harvested 532	Irish potatoes Production 533	Irish potatoes Price per cwt. [1] 534	Sweetpotatoes Acreage harvested 535	Sweetpotatoes Production 536	Sweetpotatoes Price per cwt. [1] 537
	1,000 acres	*1,000 cwt.*	*Dollars*	*1,000 acres*	*1,000 cwt.*	*Dollars*
1970	1,420	325,588	2.21	135	13,792	4.36
1969 [2]	*1,261*	*273,644*	*2.00*	*99*	[3] *19,643*	[4] *2.49*
1969	1,413	311,908	2.23	146	14,654	4.16
1968	1,376	293,984	2.23	147	13,591	4.89
1967	1,457	305,334	1.86	147	13,658	4.49
1966	1,464	306,902	2.04	157	13,697	4.98
1965	1,384	291,169	2.52	169	15,524	4.21
1964	*1,174*	*221,874*	*3.43*	*112*	*10,123*	*5.11*
1964	1,272	241,076	3.50	151	12,969	5.09
1963	1,323	271,158	1.78	171	14,356	4.03
1962	1,347	264,810	1.67	203	17,120	3.54
1961	1,480	293,166	1.36	183	14,415	4.30
1960	1,386	257,104	2.00	191	14,858	4.09
1959	*1,200*	*224,140*	*2.14*	*218*	*16,162*	*3.33*
1959	1,331	245,272	2.27	257	18,865	3.25
1958	1,428	266,897	1.31	256	17,571	3.76
1957	1,359	242,522	1.91	274	18,057	4.18
1956	1,371	245,792	2.02	276	17,381	4.01
1955	1,405	227,696	1.77	342	21,608	3.27
1954	*1,211*	*204,113*	*2.16*	*261*	*15,068*	*4.53*
1954	1,413	219,547	2.15	332	17,198	4.20
1953	1,536	231,679	1.31	343	18,998	4.44
1952	1,397	211,095	3.21	322	16,040	5.99
1951	1,348	195,776	2.68	312	15,998	5.55
1950	1,698	259,112	1.50	489	27,269	2.99
1949	*1,515*	*219,917*	*2.13*	*393*	*23,654*	*3.85*
1949	1,755	240,950	2.10	472	24,804	3.87
1948	1,981	269,937	2.53	455	23,702	3.93
1947	2,001	233,391	2.67	547	27,303	3.85
1946	2,527	292,389	2.02	637	33,454	3.87

Year	Irish potatoes Acreage harvested 532	Irish potatoes Production 533	Irish potatoes Price per cwt. [1] 534	Sweetpotatoes Acreage harvested 535	Sweetpotatoes Production 536	Sweetpotatoes Price per cwt. [1] 537
	1,000 acres	*1,000 cwt.*	*Dollars*	*1,000 acres*	*1,000 cwt.*	*Dollars*
1945	2,664	251,639	2.30	646	33,692	3.64
1944	*2,537*	*213,928*	*2.43*	*673*	*37,973*	*3.40*
1944	2,780	230,356	2.40	726	37,538	3.40
1943	3,239	275,332	2.10	857	39,128	3.85
1942	2,671	221,339	1.90	687	36,008	2.22
1941	2,693	213,418	1.31	731	34,384	1.71
1940	2,832	226,152	8.50	648	28,434	1.59
1939	*2,645*	*190,999*	*1.14*	*697*	*35,195*	*1.35*
1939	2,813	205,423	1.16	728	33,959	1.35
1938	2,870	213,509	.897	793	37,732	1.31
1937	3,055	225,869	.837	768	37,479	1.41
1936	2,960	194,373	1.87	769	32,871	1.70
1935	3,469	227,337	.980	944	44,687	1.25
1934	*3,582*	*242,052*	*.800*	*967*	*42,891*	*1.47*
1934	3,599	243,889	.707	959	42,722	1.41
1933	3,423	205,922	1.34	907	41,040	1.29
1932	3,568	224,815	.627	1,059	47,627	.858
1931	3,490	230,590	.748	854	37,023	1.21
1930	3,139	206,290	1.47	670	30,017	2.02
1929	*3,945*	*193,480*	*2.14*	*650*	*35,856*	*1.89*
1929	3,030	200,035	2.17	647	35,758	2.15
1928	3,499	256,349	.887	636	32,548	2.07
1927	3,182	221,786	1.70	724	38,993	1.93
1926	2,811	192,964	2.18	645	34,815	2.07
1925	2,810	177,880	2.83	636	27,576	2.96
1924	*2,911*	*211,477*	*1.06*	*467*	*20,594*	*2.62*
1924	3,106	230,500	1.14	564	24,686	2.71
1923	3,378	219,814	1.54	674	35,129	2.18
1922	3,901	249,224	1.10	817	43,101	1.76
1921	3,598	195,187	1.88	817	40,539	2.02

See footnotes at end of table.

Series K 532–537. Irish Potatoes and Sweetpotatoes—Acreage, Production, and Price: 1849 to 1970—Con.

[Census figures in *italics*]

Year	Irish potatoes Acreage harvested (532)	Production (533)	Price per cwt.[1] (534)	Sweetpotatoes Acreage harvested (535)	Production (536)	Price per cwt.[1] (537)
	1,000 acres	1,000 cwt.	Dollars	1,000 acres	1,000 cwt.	Dollars
1920	3,301	221,342	2.08	767	42,349	2.53
1919	*3,253*	*174,293*	*3.67*	*803*	*42,951*	*2.91*
1919	3,300	178,405	3.23	791	43,050	2.96
1918	3,597	207,668	1.98	738	37,720	2.89
1917	3,801	239,192	2.08	725	40,022	2.36
1916	3,274	162,233	2.55	658	33,850	1.79
1915	3,433	202,056	1.14	627	34,783	1.38
1914	3,417	220,949	.932	572	29,780	1.59
1913	3,477	199,468	1.14	596	30,799	1.50
1912	3,505	243,729	.928	586	31,154	1.60
1911	3,532	181,628	1.57	603	30,407	1.72
1910	3,644	205,231	.970	634	33,170	1.41
1909	*3,669*	*233,527*	*.710*	*642*	*32,590*	*1.09*
1909	3,675	234,100	.945	639	32,447	1.41
1908	3,417	183,148	1.16	621	34,264	1.21
1907	3,333	199,875	1.01	596	31,533	1.28
1906	3,254	204,876	.845	585	31,762	1.13
1905	3,263	180,421	1.02	574	32,208	1.05
1904	3,208	209,695	.755	570	30,533	1.10
1903	3,079	165,770	1.02	565	29,079	1.06
1902	3,077	177,941	.790	558	26,936	1.05
1901	2,950	124,447	1.28	558	26,486	1.04
1900	2,997	155,813	.717	542	25,126	.918
1899	*2,939*	*163,997*	*.600*	*537*	*23,390*	*.854*
1899	2,939	163,541	.668	531	23,235	.960
1898	2,877	144,209	.703	547	27,909	---
1897	2,809	118,904	.922	531	22,873	.884
1896	2,968	157,641	.483	557	23,101	.784
1895	3,090	181,269	.443	545	24,687	.865
1894	2,869	118,614	.892	548	27,322	(NA)
1893	2,614	122,534	.983	545	25,088	(NA)
1892	2,519	114,120	1.10	544	25,500	(NA)
1891	2,633	158,170	.602	537	25,175	9.00
1890	2,557	102,065	1.26	531	24,730	0.956
1889	*2,601*	*130,528*	---	*525*	*24,173*	---
1889	2,603	130,760	.598	521	24,628	.945
1888	2,604	143,785	.652	515	24,661	.856
1887	2,466	95,769	1.15	494	21,190	1.02
1886	2,393	117,045	.758	481	21,484	.969
1885	2,335	118,286	.733	474	22,061	.925
1884	2,307	124,789	.637	476	17,807	1.04
1883	2,373	136,253	.688	470	17,103	1.02
1882	2,216	118,390	.908	469	22,958	1.09
1881	2,036	76,544	1.52	441	13,656	---
1880	1,968	99,095	.803	469	22,070	.918
1879	*(5)*	*101,675*	---	*(5)*	*18,358*	---
1879	1,961	101,663	.720	451	18,618	.998
1878	1,879	86,018	.975	479	21,287	(NA)
1877	1,878	104,221	.743	454	19,358	(NA)
1876	1,783	73,567	1.10	460	21,018	(NA)
1875	1,789	107,887	.638	425	17,885	1.34
1874	1,654	78,668	1.12	406	16,582	1.44
1873	1,543	77,698	1.16	392	18,298	1.42
1872	1,559	80,144	.997	379	14,931	1.52
1871	1,496	80,833	.963	375	15,451	1.52
1870	1,443	64,725	1.18	352	17,001	1.61
1869	---	*86,002*	---	---	*11,940*	---
1869	1,479	86,759	.848	351	12,492	2.12
1868	1,400	72,175	1.31	325	15,706	1.93
1867	1,289	59,798	1.51	---	---	---
1866	1,225	66,969	1.11	---	---	---
1859	---	*66,660*	---	---	*23,152*	---
1849	---	*39,479*	---	---	*21,047*	---

NA Not available.
[1] December 1 price, 1866–1908; season average price thereafter.
[2] Not comparable with previous censuses; data for farms with farm products sales of $2,500 or more.
[3] Bushels.
[4] Price per bushel.
[5] Acreage reporting incomplete: 13 States reported 911,325 acres of Irish potatoes; 23 States 444,817 acres of sweetpotatoes.

Series K 538–549. Rice, Sugarcane, Sugar Beets, and Peanuts—Acreage, Production, and Price: 1895 to 1970

[Census figures in *italics*]

Year	Rice Acreage harvested (538)	Production (539)	Price per 100 lb.[1] (540)	Sugarcane Acreage harvested for sugar (541)	Production, raw sugar (542)	Price per ton of sugarcane (543)	Sugar beets Acreage harvested (544)	Production (545)	Price per ton[2] (546)	Peanuts harvested for nuts Acreage harvested (547)	Production[3] (548)	Price per pound[4] (549)
	1,000 acres	1,000 cwt.	Dollars	1,000 acres	1,000 tons	Dollars	1,000 acres	1,000 tons	Dollars	1,000 acres	Million pounds	Cents
1970	1,815	83,754	5.17	551.1	2,416	10.50	1,413	26,378	14.82	1,467	2,979	12.8
1969 [5]	*2,131*	*91,544*	*4.91*	*519.2*	---	---	*1,541*	*27,736*	*12.70*	*1,456*	*2,535*	*12.3*
1969	2,128	90,838	4.95	502.8	2,254	9.94	1,410	25,363	13.80	1,438	2,547	11.9
1968	2,353	104,075	5.00	577.3	2,447	9.34	1,122	19,197	13.50	1,404	2,477	11.4
1967	1,970	89,379	4.97	596.2	2,648	9.38	1,161	20,342	12.80	1,421	2,416	11.3
1966	1,967	85,020	4.95	590.2	2,448	8.49	1,249	20,918	11.90	1,438	2,390	11.4
1965	1,793	76,281	4.93	583.3	2,322	7.90	1,249	20,918	11.90	1,438	2,390	11.4
1964	*1,815*	*74,824*	*4.93*	*643.4*	---	*8.15*	---	---	---	---	---	---
1964	1,786	73,166	4.90	655.9	2,326	6.93	1,395	23,389	11.80	1,397	2,099	11.2
1963	1,771	70,269	5.01	542.8	2,284	10.20	1,235	23,328	12.22	1,396	1,942	11.2
1962	1,773	66,045	5.04	477.2	1,972	8.40	1,103	18,251	12.78	1,401	1,719	11.0
1961	1,589	54,198	5.14	441.4	1,950	7.71	1,077	17,704	11.16	1,185	1,657	10.9
1960	1,595	54,591	4.55	407.5	1,566	7.41	957	16,421	11.58	1,395	1,718	10.0
1959 [6]	*1,617*	*54,403*	*4.58*	*408.4*	---	*7.32*	---	---	---	---	---	---
1959	1,586	53,647	4.59	[7]406.8	[7]1,591	[7]7.13	906	17,015	11.24	1,435	1,523	9.6
1958	1,415	44,760	4.68	337.5	1,344	7.48	891	15,150	11.74	1,516	1,814	10.6
1957	1,340	42,935	5.11	365.3	1,617	6.90	878	15,505	11.22	1,481	1,436	10.4
1956	1,569	49,459	4.86	341.1	1,661	8.04	785	12,995	11.94	1,384	1,607	11.2

See footnotes at end of table.

Series K 538–549.   Rice, Sugarcane, Sugar Beets, and Peanuts—Acreage, Production, and Price: 1895 to 1970—Con.

[Census figures in *italics*]

Year	Rice Acreage harvested	Rice Production	Rice Price per 100 lb.[1]	Sugarcane Acreage harvested for sugar	Sugarcane Production, raw sugar	Sugarcane Price per ton of sugarcane	Sugar beets Acreage harvested	Sugar beets Production	Sugar beets Price per ton[2]	Peanuts harvested for nuts Acreage harvested	Peanuts harvested for nuts Production[3]	Peanuts harvested for nuts Price per pound[4]
	538	539	540	541	542	543	544	545	546	547	548	549
	1,000 acres	*1,000 cwt.*	*Dollars*	*1,000 acres*	*1,000 tons*	*Dollars*	*1,000 acres*	*1,000 tons*	*Dollars*	*1,000 acres*	*Million pounds*	*Cents*
1955	1,826	55,902	4.81	373.0	1,714	6.51	740	12,231	11.16	1,669	1,548	11.7
1954	*2,498*	*65,284*	*4.53*	*278.6*		*6.70*						
1954	2,550	64,193	4.57	393.1	1,687	6.95	876	14,082	10.80	1,387	1,008	12.2
1953	2,159	52,834	5.19	432.8	1,729	7.25	745	12,084	11.60	1,515	1,574	11.1
1952	1,997	48,193	5.87	425.9	1,625	6.96	665	10,169	12.00	1,443	1,356	10.9
1951	1,996	46,089	4.82	406.4	1,415	6.37	691	10,482	11.70	1,982	1,659	10.4
1950	1,637	38,820	5.09	419.8	1,525	7.80	925	13,535	11.20	2,262	2,035	10.9
1949	*1,819*	*40,251*	*3.94*	*427.8*			687	10,196	10.80	2,308	1,865	10.4
1949	1,858	40,769	4.10	424.4	1,477	6.25	687	10,196	10.80	2,308	1,865	10.4
1948	1,804	38,275	4.88	309.2	477	5.76	694	9,424	10.60	3,296	2,336	10.5
1947	1,708	35,217	5.97	293.6	377	7.17	879	12,503	11.80	3,377	2,182	10.1
1946	1,582	32,497	5.00	286.8	425	6.62	802	10,582	11.10	3,141	2,038	9.1
1945	1,499	30,668	3.98	265.4	475	[8]5.67	713	8,616	10.20	3,160	2,042	8.3
1944	*1,394*	*29,270*	*3.90*	*269.1*		*5.05*						
1944	1,480	30,974	3.93	273.1	437	[8]4.95	555	6,718	10.60	3,068	2,081	8.0
1943	1,472	29,264	3.96	284.2	497	[8]4.57	550	6,547	8.81	3,528	2,175	7.1
1942	1,457	29,082	3.61	290.2	458	4.40	954	11,685	6.84	3,355	2,193	6.1
1941	1,214	23,095	3.01	254.8	416	3.95	755	10,342	6.43	1,900	1,475	4.7
1940	1,069	24,495	1.80	240.1	332	2.88	912	12,194	5.11	2,052	1,767	3.3
1939	*852*	*19,732*	*1.63*	*383.9*		*3.64*						
1939	1,045	24,328	1.62	254.1	506	2.84	918	10,781	4.76	1,908	1,213	3.4
1938	1,076	23,628	1.42	296.2	584	2.71	925	11,497	4.65	1,692	1,289	3.3
1937	1,099	24,040	1.46	285.2	459	2.90	753	8,759	5.26	1,538	1,233	3.3
1936	981	22,419	1.85	243.6	438	3.67	776	9,028	6.05	1,660	1,260	3.7
1935	817	17,753	1.60	253.1	382	3.15	763	7,908	5.76	1,497	1,153	3.1
1934	*706*	*14,831*	*1.72*									
1934	812	17,571	1.76	235.8	262	2.33	770	7,519	5.16	1,514	1,014	3.3
1933	798	16,943	1.73	211.4	250	3.14	983	11,030	5.13	1,217	820	2.9
1932	874	18,729	.93	220.6	265	2.98	764	9,070	5.26	1,501	941	1.6
1931	965	20,076	1.08	182.1	184	3.21	713	7,903	5.94	1,440	1,056	1.6
1930	966	20,218	1.74	187.2	215	3.31	776	9,199	7.14	1,073	697	3.5
1929	*743*	*15,137*	*2.18*	*341.3*								
1929	860	17,790	2.22	191.7	218	3.73	688	7,315	7.08	1,262	898	3.7
1928	972	19,725	2.03	130.7	136	3.86	644	7,101	7.11	1,213	844	4.9
1927	1,027	20,024	2.02	73.0	72	4.61	721	7,753	7.67	1,086	844	5.2
1926	1,016	18,911	2.51	128.0	48	4.92	677	7,223	7.61	860	662	5.0
1925	853	14,866	3.30	190.0	142	4.05	648	7,381	6.39	996	722	4.3
1924	*744*	*13,286*	*3.20*									
1924	838	14,689	2.99	163.0	90	5.58	816	7,508	7.95	1,084	713	5.8
1923	874	14,957	2.49	217.5	168	7.09	657	7,006	8.99	797	568	6.5
1922	1,053	18,748	2.19	242.5	302	5.83	530	5,183	7.91	821	523	5.3
1921	990	17,673	2.18	228.9	334	3.63	815	7,782	6.35	980	678	3.8
1920	1,299	23,242	2.48	189.3	180	5.76	872	8,538	11.63	995	696	4.8
1919	*917*	*16,195*	*6.10*									
1919	1,083	19,310	5.46	180.0	125	14.00	692	6,421	11.74	957	688	9.3
1918	1,101	17,999	3.99	234.1	290	7.28	594	5,949	10.00	1,326	946	6.5
1917	953	15,621	4.26	246.0	251	7.10	665	5,980	7.39	1,314	989	7.0
1916	843	17,795	2.19	227.3	317	5.29	665	6,228	6.12	878	666	4.8
1915	740	11,748	1.86	184.0	141	4.55	611	6,511	5.67	617	481	4.1
1914	646	10,565	1.98	216.5	252	3.75	483	5,585	5.45	526	421	4.2
1913	722	10,894	1.98	255.0	307	3.13	580	5,886	5.69	465	383	4.5
1912	643	10,665	1.98	205.0	166	3.73	555	5,648	5.82	480	362	4.4
1911	636	10,198	1.75	317.1	368	4.29	474	5,062	5.50	472	366	4.2
1910	666	11,129	1.47	311.0	362	3.69	398	4,138	5.45	464	384	4.0
1909	*620*	*10,246*	*1.67*									
1909	662	10,614	1.76	292.0	338	3.83	420	4,240	5.06	537	355	4.1
1908	596	10,079	1.80									
1907	563	9,338	1.91									
1906	505	7,999	2.01									
1905	457	7,217	2.10									
1904	574	8,647	1.46									
1903	547	8,590										
1902	545	6,541										
1901	423	5,702										
1900	361	4,407										
1899	*351*	*4,386*	*1.80*									
1899	338	4,029										
1898	314	3,737										
1897	290	3,084										
1896	270	2,340										
1895	292	3,341										

[1] December 1 price, 1895–1907; season average price thereafter.
[2] Prices do not include Government payments under the Sugar Act.
[3] Net weight basis.
[4] Obtained by weighting State prices by quantity sold.

[5] Not comparable with previous censuses; data for farms with farm products sales of $2,500 or more.
[6] Beginning 1959, census data include Alaska and Hawaii.
[7] Beginning 1959, annual data include Hawaii.
[8] Includes average support payments: 1945, $1.50; 1944, $.83; 1943, $.34.

Series K 550–563. Hay, Cotton, Cottonseed, Shorn Wool, and Tobacco—Acreage, Production, and Price: 1790 to 1970

[Census figures in *italics*]

Year	Hay [1] Acreage harvested	Production	Price per ton [2]	Cotton Acreage harvested	Production [3]	Price per pound [2]	Stocks, Aug. 1, running bales	Cottonseed Production	Price per ton [2]	Shorn wool Production [4]	Price per pound [5]	Tobacco Acreage harvested	Production	Price per pound [6]
	550	551	552	553	554	555	556	557	558	559	560	561	562	563
	1,000 acres	Million tons	Dollars	1,000 acres	1,000 bales	Cents	1,000 bales	1,000 tons	Dollars	Million pounds	Cents	1,000 acres	Million pounds	Cents
1970	62,911	127	26.10	11,160	10,166	21.98	5,760	4,093	56.50	162	35.4	899	1,908	72.8
1969	*53,204*	*112*	*24.70*	*11,496*	*10,360*	*20.94*								
1969	62,053	128	24.70	11,055	9,990	[7]21.09	6,521	4,068	41.10	166	41.9	920	1,804	71.8
1968	62,693	126	23.60	10,160	10,925	[8]22.15	6,448	4,640	50.50	178	40.5	880	1,710	69.5
1967	64,667	126	24.50	7,997	7,443	25.59	12,533	3,210	55.20	189	39.8	960	1,968	66.8
1966	65,140	121	25.00	9,552	9,555	20.84	16,862	3,960	65.90	195	52.1	974	1,887	66.4
1965	67,684	126	23.20	13,615	14,951	28.14	14,291	6,087	46.70	201	47.1	977	1,855	65.1
1964	*65,295*	*116*	*23.71*	*13,917*	*14,734*									
1964	67,375	119	23.90	14,055	15,144	29.76	12,378	6,237	47.10	212	53.2	1,078	2,228	59.2
1963	66,428	118	24.60	14,212	15,294	32.23	11,216	6,192	50.70	232	48.4	1,176	2,344	57.7
1962	67,563	122	21.80	15,569	14,827	31.90	7,831	6,139	47.90	247	47.7	1,224	2,315	58.9
1961	67,376	117	20.70	15,634	14,318	32.92	7,228	5,978	51.10	[9]259	[9]42.9	1,174	2,061	63.8
1960	67,313	118	21.70	15,309	14,272	30.19	7,559	5,886	42.60	265	42.0	1,142	1,944	60.9
1959	*63,549*	*107*	*20.46*	*14,649*	*13,914*			*5,745*	*38.71*					
1959	66,266	111	22.30	15,117	14,558	31.66	8,885	5,991	38.80	260	43.2	1,153	1,796	58.3
1958	70,547	120	18.80	11,849	11,512	33.23	8,737	4,798	43.80	244	36.4	1,078	1,736	59.9
1957	71,912	120	19.30	13,558	10,964	[8]29.65	11,323	4,609	51.10	239	53.4	1,122	1,668	56.1
1956	72,292	108	22.20	15,615	13,310	31.75	14,529	5,407	53.40	242	44.3	1,364	2,176	53.7
1955	74,956	113	22.50	16,928	14,721	32.33	11,205	6,043	44.60	241	42.7	1,495	2,193	53.2
1954	*69,940*	*104*	*22.22*	*18,858*	*12,921*	*33.85*		*5,413*	*60.55*					
1954	73,721	108	21.90	19,251	13,697	33.61	9,728	5,709	60.30	236	53.2	1,668	2,244	51.1
1953	74,997	108	21.90	24,341	16,465	32.25	5,605	6,748	52.70	232	[10]54.9	1,633	2,059	52.3
1952	75,147	106	26.90	25,921	15,139	34.59	2,789	6,190	69.60	233	54.1	1,772	2,256	49.9
1951	75,063	110	25.70	26,949	15,149	37.88	2,278	6,286	69.30	228	97.1	1,780	2,332	51.1
1950	75,150	104	21.10	17,843	10,014	40.07	6,846	4,105	86.60	217	62.1	1,599	2,030	51.7
1949	*67,470*	*89*	*21.62*	*26,599*	*15,419*	*28.70*		*6,410*	*43.43*					
1949	72,821	97	21.10	27,439	16,128	28.58	5,287	6,559	43.40	213	49.4	1,623	1,969	45.9
1948	71,817	96	24.30	22,911	14,877	30.38	3,080	5,945	67.20	232	49.2	1,554	1,980	48.2
1947	74,666	101	22.90	21,330	11,860	31.93	2,530	4,682	85.90	251	42.0	1,852	2,107	43.6
1946	73,741	100	22.70	17,584	8,640	32.64	7,326	3,514	72.00	281	42.3	1,960	1,315	45.1
1945	76,697	107	20.30	17,029	9,015	22.52	11,164	3,664	51.10	308	41.9	1,821	1,991	42.6
1944	*73,402*	*95*	*18.06*	*18,962*	*11,838*			*4,896*	*53.20*					
1944	77,639	103	21.40	19,617	12,230	20.73	10,744	4,902	52.70	338	42.3	1,750	1,951	42.0
1943	77,004	103	18.60	21,610	11,427	19.90	10,657	4,688	52.10	379	41.6	1,458	1,406	40.5
1942	74,827	108	13.70	22,602	12,817	19.05	10,640	5,202	45.60	388	40.1	1,377	1,408	36.9
1941	73,136	96	12.20	22,236	10,744	17.03	12,166	4,553	47.65	388	35.5	1,307	1,262	26.4
1940	73,058	96	9.82	23,861	12,566	9.89	10,564	5,286	21.72	372	28.4	1,410	1,460	16.1
1939	*61,229*	*74*	*8.74*	*22,811*	*11,481*			*5,259*	*21.10*					
1939	69,243	87	10.20	23,805	11,817	9.09	13,033	4,869	21.14	362	22.3	2,000	1,881	15.4
1938	68,175	91	6.78	24,248	11,943	8.60	11,533	4,950	21.79	360	19.1	1,601	1,386	19.6
1937	66,001	83	8.74	33,623	18,946	8.41	4,499	7,844	19.50	356	32.0	1,753	1,569	20.4
1936	67,732	70	1.20	29,755	12,399	12.36	5,409	5,472	33.30	353	26.9	1,441	1,163	23.6
1935	68,550	90	7.52	27,509	10,638	11.09	7,208	4,634	30.54	362	19.3	1,439	1,302	18.4
1934	*63,156*	*54*	*13.82*	*26,754*	*9,472*									
1934	65,387	60	13.20	26,866	9,636	12.36	7,744	4,256	33.03	369	21.9	1,273	[11]1,085	21.3
1933	68,439	75	8.09	29,383	13,047	10.17	8,165	5,511	12.91	374	20.6	1,739	1,372	13.0
1932	70,412	84	6.20	35,891	13,003	6.52	9,678	5,815	10.35	351	8.6	1,405	1,018	10.5
1931	68,160	75	8.73	38,704	17,097	5.66	6,370	7,310	8.98	376	13.6	1,988	1,565	8.2
1930	67,947	75	11.10	42,444	13,932	9.46	4,530	6,028	22.07	352	19.5	2,124	1,648	12.8
1929	*67,823*	*82*	*11.45*	*43,228*	*14,574*			*6,915*	*30.34*					
1929	69,531	87	10.90	43,232	14,825	16.78	2,312	6,406	30.93	328	30.2	1,980	1,533	18.3
1928	67,185	84	11.28	42,434	14,477	17.98	2,536	6,319	34.21	315	36.2	1,864	1,373	20.0
1927	72,131	98	10.29	38,342	12,956	20.20	3,762	5,758	34.86	289	30.3	1,556	1,211	20.7
1926	68,795	76	13.27	44,608	17,978	12.49	3,543	7,989	22.08	269	34.0	1,628	1,289	17.9
1925	70,105	79	12.80	44,386	16,105	19.62	1,610	7,150	31.69	253	39.5	1,751	1,376	16.8
1924	*74,692*	*88*	*12.18*	*39,204*	*13,683*									
1924	74,459	91	12.68	39,501	13,630	22.91	1,556	6,050	33.25	238	36.6	1,702	1,245	19.0
1923	73,545	89	13.08	35,550	10,140	28.69	2,325	4,503	41.21	230	39.4	1,855	1,518	19.0
1922	75,432	95	11.63	31,361	9,755	22.88	3,322	4,330	30.33	228	27.1	1,616	1,254	22.8
1921	73,070	85	11.61	28,678	7,945	17.00	6,896	3,528	29.07	242	17.3	1,340	1,005	19.5
1920	73,033	92	16.50	34,408	13,429	15.89	3,824	5,966	25.65	251	45.5	1,935	1,509	17.3
1919	*70,936*	*89*	*21.50*	*33,740*	*11,376*			*5,328*	*65.27*					
1919	73,156	92	20.92	32,906	11,141	35.34	4,445	5,069	65.59	270	49.5	1,959	1,444	31.2
1918	71,909	82	19.62	35,038	12,018	28.88	3,509	5,341	65.23	254	57.7	1,720	1,445	27.9
1917	71,017	85	16.53	32,245	11,284	27.09	2,720	5,012	64.28	237	41.6	1,616	1,326	24.0
1916	72,918	99	11.13	33,071	11,448	17.36	3,140	5,085	45.63	244	26.1	1,483	1,207	14.8
1915	69,518	91	10.26	29,951	11,172	11.22	3,936	4,963	30.15	241	22.1	1,419	1,157	9.0
1914	67,337	83	10.64	35,615	16,112	7.35	1,366	7,155	15.51	251	16.6	1,258	1,037	9.7
1913	66,873	77	11.37	35,206	14,153	12.47	1,511	6,286	21.96	266	16.7	1,284	992	12.8
1912	67,395	86	10.80	32,557	13,703	11.50	1,652	6,037	18.36	278	17.3	1,335	1,117	10.7
1911	65,885	65	14.11	34,916	15,694	9.65	1,275	6,970	17.18	302	15.8	1,133	941	9.3
1910	68,332	75	11.66	31,508	11,609	13.96	940	5,156	26.11	306	21.7	1,398	1,142	9.3
1909	*68,227*	*87*	*8.90*	*32,044*	*10,649*			*5,325*	*22.74*					
1909	68,703	87	10.20	30,555	10,005	13.52	1,469	4,442	24.35	310	22.2	1,292	1,054	10.1
1908	51,487	72	9.08	31,091	13,241	9.01	1,161	5,883	--------	270	16.3	1,009	836	10.2
1907	49,833	66	11.60	30,729	11,106	10.36	1,465	4,931	--------	256	20.5	1,042	886	10.0
1906	48,650	60	10.40	31,404	13,274	9.58	1,299	5,898	--------	257	23.1	1,123	973	9.6

See footnotes at end of table.

Series K 550–563. Hay, Cotton, Cottonseed, Shorn Wool, and Tobacco—Acreage, Production, and Price: 1790 to 1970—Con.

[Census figures in italics]

Year	Hay [1] Acreage harvested	Hay [1] Production	Hay [1] Price per ton [2]	Cotton Acreage harvested	Cotton Production [3]	Cotton Price per pound [2]	Cottonseed Production	Cottonseed Price per ton [2]	Shorn wool Production [4]	Shorn wool Price per pound [5]	Tobacco Acreage harvested	Tobacco Production	Tobacco Price per pound [6]
	550	551	552	553	554	555	557	558	559	560	561	562	563
	1,000 acres	Million tons	Dollars	1,000 acres	1,000 bales	Cents	1,000 tons	Dollars	Million pounds	Cents	1,000 acres	Million pounds	Cents
1905	48,333	67	8.49	27,753	10,576	10.78	4,700	---------	253	22.2	1,103	939	8.2
1904	47,480	66	8.82	30,077	13,438	8.98	5,967	---------	250	16.3	1,026	857	7.8
1903	46,650	64	9.18	27,762	9,851	10.49	4,379	---------	245	15.4	1,212	976	6.7
1902	44,716	59	9.05	27,561	10,630	7.60	4,729	---------	274	13.7	1,189	960	6.9
1901	43,555	53	9.88	27,050	9,508	7.03	4,226	---------	266	13.7	1,098	886	7.2
1900	42,488	50	9.78	24,886	10,124	9.15	4,500	---------	260	13.7	1,086	852	6.7
1899	*61,691*	*79*	*6.11*	*24,275*	*9,535*	---------	*4,767*	*9.85*					
1899	43,395	54	8.20	24,163	9,346	6.98	4,152	---------	272	14.5	1,102	870	7.1
1898	43,083	60	6.52	24,715	11,278	5.73	5,120	---------	267	13.7	1,116	909	6.1
1897	42,396	56	7.21	25,131	10,899	6.68	4,878	---------	259	11.1	978	703	7.4
1896	40,971	51	7.60	23,230	8,533	6.66	3,778	---------	272	10.3	1,038	760	5.5
1895	41,153	40	9.63	19,839	7,162	7.62	3,174	---------	294	10.3	1,006	745	6.8
1894	41,864	48	8.98	21,886	9,091	4.59	4,448	---------	325	11.1	993	767	6.6
1893	42,083	53	9.48	20,256	7,493	7.00	3,297	---------	349	14.5	1,096	767	7.9
1892	41,328	53	8.78	18,869	6,700	8.34	2,956	---------	294	16.3	1,039	757	8.9
1891	40,350	51	8.65	21,503	9,035	7.24	3,967	---------	285	16.3	955	747	8.2
1890	39,613	51	8.11	20,937	8,653	8.59	3,802	---------	276	17.1	851	648	8.0
1889	*52,949*	*67*	---------	*20,175*	*7,473*								
1889	38,867	50	7.74	20,191	7,473	8.55	3,318	---------	265	18.0	758	525	6.6
1888	37,411	47	9.24	19,520	6,938	8.50	3,074	---------	269	17.1	891	661	7.9
1887	36,480	42	10.09	18,793	7,047	8.55	3,056	---------	285	18.0	722	469	10.5
1886	35,771	45	8.72	18,370	6,505	8.06	2,802	---------	302	16.3	848	609	7.2
1885	34,507	43	10.07	17,922	6,576	8.39	2,828	---------	308	14.5	815	611	7.5
1884	33,448	43	8.99	16,849	5,682	9.19	2,427	---------	300	14.5	754	580	8.1
1883	32,077	44	8.77	16,295	5,713	9.13	2,450	---------	290	17.1	750	509	8.8
1882	30,373	39	9.99	15,638	6,949	9.12	3,033	---------	272	20.5	744	579	8.5
1881	28,619	35	12.25	16,483	5,456	10.66	2,280	---------	240	22.2	698	426	9.6
1880	27,011	33	11.82	15,921	6,606	9.83	2,822	---------	233	23.1	650	469	8.1
1879	*30,631*	*35*	---------	*14,480*	*5,755*								
1879	26,641	31	9.63	14,474	5,756	10.28	2,425	---------	211	18.0	633	472	6.1
1878	25,627	33	7.32	13,539	5,074	8.16	2,106	---------	208	18.8	651	455	5.8
1877	24,749	30	8.72	12,606	4,773	8.53	1,994	---------	200	21.4	789	621	5.4
1876	23,986	29	9.80	11,747	4,474	9.71	1,826	---------	192	19.7	625	466	7.3
1875	22,662	26	12.75	11,348	4,631	---------	1,909	---------	181	25.7	746	609	7.7
1874	21,861	25	13.85	10,753	3,836	---------	1,567	---------	170	25.7	378	217	13.7
1873	21,597	24	14.40	10,998	4,168	---------	1,718	---------	158	26.5	513	382	8.6
1872	21,081	24	15.35	9,580	3,933	---------	1,621	---------	150	31.7	492	385	10.7
1871	20,270	22	16.57	8,285	2,974	---------	1,223	---------	160	27.4	420	327	10.2
1870	19,719	21	14.45	9,238	4,352	---------	1,786	---------	162	22.2	424	345	9.7
1869		*27*	---------		*3,012*								
1869	19,310	25	12.76	7,751	3,011	---------	1,118	---------	162	22.2	395	264	10.9
1868	19,568	23	13.90	6,973	2,366	---------	974	---------	---------	---------	369	286	12.2
1867	18,641	23	14.30	7,864	2,520	---------	1,042	---------	---------	---------	370	260	11.6
1866	18,250	21	14.48	7,666	2,097	---------	864	---------	---------	---------	394	316	11.6

Year	Hay, production 551	Cotton, production 554	Year	Hay, production 551	Cotton, production 554	Year	Cotton, production 554	Year	Cotton, production 554	Year	Cotton, production 554	Year	Cotton, production 554
	Million tons	1,000 bales		Million tons	1,000 bales		1,000 bales		1,000 bales		1,000 bales		1,000 bales
1865		2,094	1850		2,136	1835	1,062	1820	335	1805	146	1795	17
1864		299	*1849*	*14*	*2,469*	1834	962	1819	349	1804	136	1794	17
1863		449	1849		2,066	1833	931	1818	262	1803	126	1793	10
1862		1,597	1848		2,615	1832	816	1817	272	1802	115	1792	6
1861		4,491	1847		2,128	1831	805	1816	259	1801	100	1791	4
			1846		1,604								
1860		3,841				1830	732	1815	209	1800	73	1790	3
1859	*19*	*5,387*	1845		1,806	1829	764	1814	146	1799	42		
1859		4,508	1844		2,079	1828	680	1813	157	1798	31		
1858		3,758	1843		1,750	1827	565	1812	157	1797	23		
1857		3,012	1842		2,035	1826	732	1811	167	1796	21		
1856		2,874	1841		1,398								
						1825	533	1810	178				
1855		3,221	1840		1,348	1824	450	1809	172				
1854		2,708	*1839*	*10*	*1,976*	1823	387	1808	157				
1853		2,766	1839		1,654	1822	439	1807	167				
1852		3,130	1838		1,093	1821	377	1806	167				
1851		2,799	1837		1,428								
			1836		1,129								

[1] All hay, 1909–1970; tame hay prior to 1909.
[2] December 1 average price prior to 1909; season average price thereafter. Loose hay price 1909–1938; baled hay price thereafter.
[3] Annual production estimates prior to 1962 are shown in 500-pound gross-weight bales; beginning 1962, 480-pound net-weight bales. Figures for census years are shown in running bales, and are not comparable with annual production estimates; the net weight per running bale was 383 pounds in 1839; 496.1 pounds in 1944; 482.0 pounds in 1954; 501.1 pounds in 1964; and 503.6 pounds in 1969.
[4] Includes shearing at commercial feeding yards.
[5] Average price relates to calendar year prior to 1943, April–March marketing season for 1943–1962, April–December for 1963, and calendar year thereafter.
[6] December 1 price prior to 1919; season average price thereafter.
[7] Average price to December 1, 1969, with no allowance for unredeemed loans.
[8] Includes allowance for unredeemed loans.
[9] Beginning 1961, includes Alaska; no estimates made for Hawaii.
[10] Beginning 1953, price includes allowance for unredeemed wool.
[11] Includes 26.5 million pounds that were not utilized due to Agricultural Adjustment Act.

Series K 564–582. Livestock—Number, Value Per Head, Production, and Price: 1867 to 1970

[Census figures in *italics*. All figures are as of January 1 except for 1870, 1880, 1890, 1900 (June 1); 1910 (April 15); 1930, 1940, 1950 (April 1); 1954, 1959 (October-November); 1964 (November-December); and 1969 (December 31)]

Year	Number on farms and value per head: All cattle, Number	All cattle, Value per head	Hogs, Number	Hogs, Value per head	Stock sheep, Number	Stock sheep, Value per head	Horses [1], Number	Horses [1], Value per head	Mules [1], Number	Mules [1], Value per head	Number of workstock, 2 years old and over	Live weight production and annual average price received by farmers, per 100 pounds: All cattle, Production [2]	All cattle, Price, beef cattle	All cattle, Price, veal calves	Hogs, Production [2]	Hogs, Price	Sheep, Production [2]	Sheep, Price, sheep	Sheep, Price, lambs
	564	565	566	567	568	569	570	571	572	573	574	575	576	577	578	579	580	581	582
	1,000 head	*Dollars*	*1,000 head*	*Dollars*	*1,000 head*	*Dollars*	*1,000 head*	*Dollars*	*1,000 head*	*Dollars*	*1,000 head*	*Million pounds*	*Dollars*	*Dollars*	*Million pounds*	*Dollars*	*Million pounds*	*Dollars*	*Dollars*
1970	112,303	180.00	[3] 56,655	[3] 39.00	17,411	24.70	---	---	---	---	---	39,450	27.10	34.50	21,851	22.70	1,082	7.64	26.40
1969	*106,381*	---	*55,455*	---	*21,611*	---	[4] *2,238*	---	---	---	---	---	---	---	---	---	---	---	---
1969	109,885	158.00	[3] 60,632	[3] 30.50	18,332	22.00	---	---	---	---	---	37,142	26.20	31.50	20,489	22.20	1,037	8.24	27.20
1968	109,152	149.00	58,777	28.30	19,105	19.20	---	---	---	---	---	36,368	23.40	27.60	21,102	18.50	1,130	6.55	24.40
1967	108,645	149.00	53,249	33.20	20,661	19.70	---	---	---	---	---	35,932	22.30	26.30	20,634	18.90	1,143	6.35	22.10
1966	108,862	133.00	47,414	45.20	21,456	19.70	---	---	---	---	---	35,020	22.29	26.00	19,107	22.80	1,251	6.84	23.40
1965	109,000	113.00	50,792	24.50	21,843	15.80	---		---	---	---	34,003	19.80	22.00	18,055	20.60	1,217	6.34	22.80
1964	*105,558*	---	*54,080*	---	*25,472*	---	---	---	---	---	---	---	---	---	---	---	---	---	---
1964	107,903	127.00	56,757	23.40	23,455	14.00	---	---	---	---	---	34,836	18.00	20.40	20,217	14.80	1,331	6.00	19.90
1963	104,488	142.00	57,993	27.50	25,122	14.40	---	---	---	---	---	32,777	19.90	24.00	20,960	14.90	1,403	5.76	18.10
1962	100,369	140.00	56,619	27.50	26,719	12.90	---	---	---	---	---	30,775	21.30	25.10	20,275	16.30	1,491	5.63	17.85
1961*	97,700	134.00	55,560	27.20	28,320	14.60	---	---	---	---	---	29,902	20.20	23.70	20,167	16.60	1,646	5.20	15.80
1960	96,236	137.00	59,026	18.50	28,849	16.50	3,089	113.00	---	---	2,883	28,796	20.40	22.90	19,203	15.30	1,628	5.60	17.90
1959	*92,534*	---	*67,949*	---	*33,945*	---	*2,955*	---	---	---	---	---	---	---	---	---	---	---	---
1959	93,322	153.00	58,045	32.00	28,108	20.30	3,189	102.00	---	---	2,988	28,280	22.60	26.70	21,273	14.10	1,713	6.00	18.70
1958	91,176	120.00	51,517	30.20	27,167	19.40	3,415	84.40	---	---	3,220	26,764	21.90	25.30	19,180	19.60	1,657	7.20	21.00
1957	92,860	91.60	51,897	24.70	26,348	14.90	3,632	71.80	---	---	3,436	26,555	17.20	18.70	18,413	17.80	1,534	6.05	19.90
1956	95,900	88.10	55,354	17.70	26,890	14.30	3,958	62.60	---	---	3,757	27,531	14.90	16.10	19,089	14.40	1,569	5.60	18.50
1955	96,592	88.20	50,474	30.60	27,137	14.90	4,309	56.20	---	---	4,101	28,099	15.60	16.80	20,154	15.00	1,618	5.78	18.40
1954	*95,027*	---	*57,093*	---	*31,619*	---	*4,141*	---	---	---	---	---	---	---	---	---	---	---	---
1954	95,679	92.00	45,114	36.60	27,079	13.80	4,791	52.90	---	---	4,572	27,580	16.00	16.50	18,218	21.60	1,607	6.14	19.10
1953	94,241	128.00	51,755	26.10	27,593	15.70	5,403	53.00	---	---	5,166	27,405	16.30	16.70	16,800	21.40	1,538	6.67	19.30
1952	88,072	179.00	62,117	29.90	27,944	28.00	6,150	53.90	---	---	5,887	24,933	24.30	25.80	19,727	17.80	1,471	10.00	24.30
1951	82,083	160.00	62,269	33.30	27,251	26.50	7,036	54.60	---	---	6,732	22,990	28.70	31.90	21,436	20.00	1,372	16.00	31.00
1950	*76,762*	---	*55,722*	---	*31,387*	---	*5,402*	---	*2,202*	*95.28*		---	---	---	---	---	---	---	---
1950	77,963	124.00	58,937	27.10	26,182	17.80	5,548	46.00	2,233	99.10	7,415	21,185	23.30	26.30	20,214	18.00	1,336	11.60	25.10
1949	76,830	135.00	56,257	38.30	26,940	17.00	6,096	52.50	2,402	116.00	8,074	19,274	19.80	22.60	19,457	18.10	1,278	9.27	22.40
1948	77,171	117.00	54,590	42.90	29,486	15.00	6,704	55.70	2,575	133.00	8,800	18,402	22.20	24.40	18,222	23.10	1,383	9.69	22.80
1947	80,554	97.50	56,810	36.00	31,805	12.20	7,340	59.30	2,789	141.00	9,578	19,130	18.40	20.40	18,159	24.10	1,567	8.39	20.50
1946	82,235	76.20	61,306	24.00	35,525	9.57	8,081	57.50	3,027	133.00	10,434	18,999	14.50	15.20	18,744	17.50	1,762	7.48	15.60
1945	*82,654*	---	*46,735*	---	*41,224*	---	*8,499*	---	*3,130*	---	---	---	---	---	---	---	---	---	---
1945	85,573	66.90	59,373	20.60	39,609	8.45	8,715	64.90	3,235	134.00	11,116	19,517	12.10	13.00	18,843	14.00	1,912	6.38	13.10
1944	85,334	68.40	83,741	17.50	44,270	8.68	9,192	78.60	3,421	143,00	11,668	19,708	10.80	12.40	20,584	13.06	1,938	6.01	12.50
1943	81,204	69.30	73,881	22.50	48,196	9.68	9,605	79.80	3,626	127.00	12,117	19,159	11.90	13.30	25,375	13.69	2,108	6.57	13.00
1942	76,025	55.00	60,607	15.60	49,346	8.66	9,873	64.70	3,782	107.00	12,346	18,568	10.70	12.30	21,105	13.04	2,313	5.80	11.70
1941	71,755	43.20	54,353	8.34	47,441	6.77	10,193	68.20	3,911	107.00	12,651	17,029	8.82	10.30	17,489	9.09	2,251	5.06	9.58
1940 [5]	*60,675*	---	*34,037*	---	*40,129*	---	*10,087*	---	*3,845*	---	[6] *13,029*	---	---	---	---	---	---	---	---
1940	68,309	40.60	61,165	7.78	46,266	6.35	10,444	77.30	4,034	116.00	13,000	15,702	7.56	8.83	17,043	5.39	2,101	3.95	8.10
1939	66,029	38.44	50,012	11.18	45,463	5.74	10,629	84.32	4,163	118.58	13,273	15,177	7.14	8.40	17,079	6.23	2,029	3.90	7.78
1938	65,249	36.58	44,525	11.26	44,972	6.13	10,995	90.89	4,250	123.39	13,690	14,047	6.54	7.90	14,372	7.74	2,038	3.58	7.05
1937	66,098	34.06	43,083	11.89	45,251	6.02	11,342	99.14	4,460	130.25	14,330	13,746	7.00	8.10	12,506	9.50	1,932	4.52	8.88
1936	67,847	34.06	42,975	12.71	45,435	6.35	11,598	96.73	4,628	120.63	14,839	14,438	5.82	7.20	12,976	9.37	1,852	3.77	8.05
1935	*68,284*	---	*37,213*	---	*48,358*	---	*11,858*	---	*4,818*	---	[6] 15,467	---	---	---	---	---	---	---	---
1935 [7]	68,846	20.20	39,066	6.31	46,139	4.33	11,861	77.05	4,822	99.34	15,473	13,651	6.04	7.16	10,673	8.65	1,835	3.75	7.28
1934 [7]	74,369	17.78	58,621	4.09	48,244	3.77	12,052	66.88	4,945	82.42	15,984	14,538	4.13	4.92	12,385	4.14	[8] 1,911	2.85	5.90
1933 [7]	70,280	19.74	62,127	4.21	47,303	2.91	12,291	54.12	5,046	60.42	16,404	15,405	3.75	4.64	16,566	3.53	1,860	2.38	5.04
1932	65,801	26.39	59,301	6.13	47,682	3.44	12,664	53.48	5,148	60.70	16,822	14,232	4.25	4.95	16,368	3.34	1,829	2.24	4.47
1931	63,030	38.99	54,835	11.35	47,720	5.40	13,195	60.64	5,273	69.23	17,375	13,386	5.53	6.95	16,541	5.73	2,052	3.11	5.64
1930 [5]	*63,896*	---	*56,288*	---	*56,975*	---	*13,511*	---	*5,354*	---	[6] 17,612	---	---	---	---	---	---	---	---
1930	61,003	56.36	55,705	13.45	45,577	9.00	13,742	69.98	5,382	83.93	17,981	13,263	7.71	9.68	15,176	8.84	1,965	4.74	7.76
1929	58,877	58.47	59,042	12.93	43,481	10.71	14,234	69.68	5,510	82.45	18,514	12,754	9.47	12.16	15,582	9.42	1,823	7.19	11.90
1928	57,322	50.63	61,873	13.17	40,689	10.36	14,792	66.71	5,656	79.84	19,120	12,327	9.52	11.75	16,189	8.54	1,773	7.65	12.20
1927	58,178	39.98	55,496	17.19	38,067	9.79	15,388	63.73	5,804	74.51	19,765	12,072	7.62	10.14	16,340	9.64	1,664	7.01	11.50
1926	60,576	36.80	52,105	15.66	35,719	10.53	16,083	65.31	5,903	81.51	20,491	12,605	6.75	9.34	14,909	11.79	1,609	7.20	11.70
1925	*60,760*	---	*50,854*	---	*35,590*	---	*16,401*	---	*5,681*	---	*20,619*	---	---	---	---	---	---	---	---
1925	63,373	31.72	55,770	13.15	34,469	9.63	16 651	64.28	5,918	82.91	21,038	12,953	6.53	8.59	14,168	10.91	1,508	7.56	12.40
1924	65,996	32.11	66,576	10.30	32,859	7.94	17,378	65.39	5,907	85.89	21,578	13,402	5.84	7.83	15,388	7.34	1,459	6.57	10.80
1923	67,546	31.66	69,304	12.29	32,597	7.50	18,125	70.49	5,893	86.87	22,050	13,174	5.84	7.90	17,008	6.94	1,253	6.55	10.52
1922	68,795	30.39	59,849	10.58	33,365	4.79	18,764	71.01	5,824	88.99	22,271	13,185	5.73	7.64	16,518	8.40	1,080	5.96	9.90
1921	68,714	39.07	58,942	13.63	35,426	6.34	19,369	84.48	5,768	117.37	22,348	12,817	5.63	7.85	14,132	7.63	1,146	4.55	7.13
1920	*66,640*	---	*59,346*	---	*35,034*	---	*19,767*	---	*5,432*	---	*21,873*	---	---	---	---	---	---	---	---
1920	70,400	52.64	60,159	20.00	37,328	10.59	20,091	96.45	5,651	148.29	22,386	12,403	8.71	11.80	13,533	12.92	926	8.17	11.64
1919	72,094	54.65	64,326	22.18	38,360	11.49	20,922	97.94	5,568	135.58	---	13,387	9.97	12.68	13,986	16.39	1,143	9.26	12.83
1918	73,040	50.01	62,931	19.69	36,704	11.76	21,238	103.97	5,485	128.97	---	15,658	9.88	11.73	14,792	16.14	1,238	10.75	13.96
1917	70,979	43.34	57,578	11.82	35,246	7.06	21,306	102.64	5,353	118.45	---	16,764	8.54	10.42	12,928	13.89	1,126	9.58	12.71
1916	67,438	40.10	60,596	8.48	36,260	5.10	21,334	101.45	5,200	113.78	---	15,933	6.76	8.37	13,582	8.37	1,118	6.28	8.34
1915	63,849	40.67	56,600	9.95	36,263	4.39	21,431	103.23	5,062	112.19	---	15,136	6.26	7.70	13,935	6.47	1,254	5.30	6.98
1914	59,461	38.97	52,853	10.51	38,059	3.91	21,308	109.27	4,870	123.47	---	15,562	6.52	7.85	12,594	7.52	1,271	4.83	6.36
1913	56,592	33.07	53,747	9.89	40,544	3.87	21,008	110.58	4,683	124.10	---	14,866	6.20	7.51	12,220	7.54	1,187	4.52	5.99
1912	55,675	27.68	55,394	7.99	42,972	3.42	20,726	105.58	4,551	120.33	---	13,807	5.43	6.49	11,945	6.73	1,275	4.25	5.62
1911	57,225	27.22	55,366	9.33	46,055	3.83	20,418	111.11	4,429	125.73	---	12,586	4.57	5.97	12,517	6.21	1,128	4.01	5.17
1910	*61,804*	---	*58,186*	---	*52,448*	---	*19,833*	---	*4,101*	---	---	---	---	---	---	---	---	---	---
1910	58,993	24.54	48,072	9.05	46,939	4.06	19,972	107.70	4,239	119.98	---	12,672	4.86	6.40	12,025	8.14	1,150	4.99	6.16
1909	60,774	21.99	52,508	6.45	47,098	3.42	19,731	95.13	4,085	108.20	---	13,081	---	---	11,027	6.62	1,272	---	---

See footnotes at end of table.

Series K 564–582. Livestock—Number, Value Per Head, Production, and Price: 1867 to 1970—Con.

[Census figures in *italics*]

Year	All cattle Number 564	All cattle Value per head 565	Hogs Number 566	Hogs Value per head 567	Stock sheep Number 568	Stock sheep Value per head 569	Horses[1] Number 570	Horses[1] Value per head 571	Mules[1] Number 572	Mules[1] Value per head 573
	1,000 head	*Dollars*	*1,000 head*	*Dollars*	*1,000 head*	*Dollars*	*1,000 head*	*Dollars*	*1,000 head*	*Dollars*
1908	61,989	20.92	58,388	5.99	45,095	3.87	19,444	92.76	3,949	107.81
1907	63,754	20.91	56,543	7.54	43,460	3.81	19,090	92.85	3,814	111.46
1906	65,009	19.65	53,633	6.07	41,965	3.51	18,806	79.77	3,680	97.75
1905	66,111	18.39	53,176	5.89	40,410	2.77	18,491	69.73	3,586	87.06
1904	66,442	19.69	51,623	6.08	41,908	2.55	18,331	67.59	3,465	78.02
1903	66,004	21.55	48,100	7.69	44,436	2.62	18,121	62.27	3,353	71.73
1902	64,418	21.48	47,858	6.95	46,196	2.62	17,968	58.52	3,264	67.23
1901	62,576	22.68	50,681	6.08	46,126	2.96	17,955	53.03	3,190	53.47
1900[9]	*67,719*	----	*62,868*	----	*61,504*	----	*16,965*	----	*3,039*	----
1900	59,739	26.50	51,055	5.36	45,065	2.97	17,856	43.56	3,139	51.46
1899	55,927	24.53	51,558	4.67	42,688	2.80	17,728	36.61	3,012	43.52
1898	52,868	22.79	53,282	4.70	40,097	2.51	17,698	33.35	2,918	42.31
1897	50,447	18.62	51,232	4.36	38,891	1.84	17,803	30.92	2,836	40.49
1896	49,205	17.86	49,154	4.50	39,609	1.71	17,876	32.34	2,782	44.08
1895	49,510	16.56	47,628	5.09	41,827	1.57	17,849	35.57	2,708	47.23
1894	51,713	16.84	46,522	6.06	43,414	1.97	17,709	46.63	2,632	60.65
1893	55,119	17.00	43,652	6.37	44,567	2.64	17,289	60.72	2,550	69.18
1892	58,126	16.81	45,165	4.65	44,628	2.60	16,846	64.56	2,459	74.31
1891	59,968	16.49	47,435	4.24	43,882	2.51	16,329	67.19	2,377	76.93
1890	*57,649*	----	*57,427*	----	*40,876*	----	*15,266*	----	*2,252*	----
1890	60,014	16.95	48,130	4.80	42,693	2.29	15,732	69.27	2,322	77.61
1889	59,178	18.77	44,508	5.80	42,365	2.14	15,064	72.39	2,295	78.95
1888	58,599	19.39	42,134	5.12	43,011	2.06	14,490	72.03	2,260	79.06

Year	All cattle Number 564	All cattle Value per head 565	Hogs Number 566	Hogs Value per head 567	Stock sheep Number 568	Stock sheep Value per head 569	Horses[1] Number 570	Horses[1] Value per head 571	Mules[1] Number 572	Mules[1] Value per head 573
	1,000 head	*Dollars*	*1,000 head*	*Dollars*	*1,000 head*	*Dollars*	*1,000 head*	*Dollars*	*1,000 head*	*Dollars*
1887	56,602	21.18	42,563	4.60	44,217	2.05	13,821	71.59	2,213	78.39
1886	54,868	22.20	45,457	4.30	46,654	1.95	13,276	70.62	2,162	78.96
1885	52,463	24.40	47,330	5.06	49,620	2.19	12,700	72.94	2,102	81.88
1884	49,804	25.26	45,961	5.64	51,101	2.40	12,215	73.80	2,047	83.53
1883	47,387	23.87	43,440	6.74	50,935	2.53	11,794	69.92	1,975	77.79
1882	45,738	20.93	42,566	6.00	48,883	2.35	11,444	58.75	1,928	71.69
1881	44,501	18.67	43,076	4.80	47,371	2.35	11,187	57.91	1,912	68.84
1880	*39,676*	----	*49,773*	----	*42,192*	----	*10,357*	----	*1,813*	----
1880	43,347	17.80	44,327	4.40	44,867	2.18	10,903	53.74	1,878	61.74
1879	41,420	17.80	43,767	3.15	41,678	2.01	10,574	51.55	1,816	57.08
1878	39,396	19.05	43,375	4.89	38,942	2.12	10,230	55.38	1,746	62.61
1877	37,333	18.38	39,333	5.68	38,147	2.03	9,910	55.11	1,674	63.16
1876	36,140	18.76	35,715	5.97	37,477	2.20	9,606	56.48	1,608	65.51
1875	35,361	18.96	35,834	4.65	37,237	2.39	9,333	60.10	1,548	71.64
1874	34,821	19.51	38,377	3.93	36,234	2.33	9,055	64.12	1,485	80.26
1873	33,830	20.50	39,794	3.60	35,782	2.60	8,767	65.52	1,419	83.49
1872	33,078	21.64	39,296	3.96	34,312	2.51	8,441	66.54	1,360	86.02
1871	32,107	24.71	36,688	5.48	34,063	2.10	8,054	70.02	1,305	91.47
1870	*23,821*	----	*25,135*	----	*28,478*	----	*7,145*	----	*1,125*	----
1870	31,082	22.84	33,781	5.64	36,449	1.87	7,633	66.99	1,245	89.71
1869	30,060	20.74	32,570	4.60	39,802	1.65	7,304	60.48	1,130	78.57
1868	29,238	18.30	33,304	3.23	43,808	1.83	7,051	52.54	1,057	56.70
1867	28,636	19.13	34,489	3.95	44,997	2.40	6,820	57.56	1,000	67.73

* Denotes first year for which figures include Alaska and Hawaii.
[1] Includes colts. Beginning 1951, horses and mules combined.
[2] Includes adjustment for livestock shipped in and inventory changes.
[3] December 1, preceding year.
[4] Horses and ponies.
[5] Excludes spring-born calves, pigs, lambs, and colts.
[6] Over 27 months old.
[7] Government purchases included in figures for all cattle, 1935 and 1934; for hogs, 1933.
[8] Includes Government purchases.
[9] Excludes spring-born colts.

Series K 583–594. Meat Slaughtering, Production, and Price: 1899 to 1970

[Prices are those at Chicago. Average price of all grades]

Year	Beef Cattle slaughtered[1] 583	Beef Production, dressed weight 584	Beef Price of beef steers per cwt. 585	Veal Calves slaughtered[1] 586	Veal Production, dressed weight 587	Veal Price of veal calves per cwt. 588	Pork Hogs slaughtered[1] 589	Pork Production, dressed weight 590	Pork Price of hogs per cwt.[2] 591	Lamb and mutton Lambs and sheep slaughtered[1] 592	Lamb and mutton Production, dressed weight 593	Lamb and mutton Price of lambs per cwt. 594
	1,000 head	*Mil. lb.*	*Dollars*	*1,000 head*	*Mil. lb.*	*Dollars*	*1,000 head*	*Mil. lb.*	*Dollars*	*1,000 head*	*Mil. lb.*	*Dollars*
1970	35,354	21,651	30.20	4,204	588	----	86,962	13,427	----	10,802	551	----
1969	35,574	21,126	30.48	5,010	673	----	84,958	12,946	23.09	10,923	550	28.35
1968	35,414	20,846	27.65	5,613	734	----	86,401	13,055	18.65	12,119	602	26.02
1967	34,295	20,184	25.97	6,107	792	----	83,421	12,572	18.88	13,034	646	23.48
1966	34,171	19,694	26.17	6,861	910	----	75,325	11,328	22.61	13,003	650	25.00
1965	33,171	18,699	25.81	7,788	1,020	----	76,394	11,132	20.78	13,300	651	24.29
1964	31,678	18,429	22.86	7,632	1,013	----	86,284	12,503	14.89	14,895	715	21.93
1963	28,070	16,428	23.79	7,204	929	----	87,117	12,419	15.03	16,147	770	18.69
1962	26,911	15,298	27.20	7,857	1,015	----	83,424	11,819	16.44	17,168	808	19.45
1961	26,471	15,300	24.46	8,080	1,044	----	81,970	11,399	16.71	17,537	832	17.07
1960	26,029	14,728	25.93	8,615	1,109	28.07	84,150	11,598	15.50	16,240	768	19.26
1959	23,723	13,580	27.53	8,072	1,008	31.91	87,606	11,993	14.12	15,528	738	20.93
1958	24,368	13,330	27.09	9,738	1,186	32.20	76,822	10,454	19.80	14,495	688	22.58
1957	27,068	14,202	23.48	12,353	1,526	25.93	78,636	10,424	17.89	15,292	707	22.37
1956	27,755	14,462	22.00	12,999	1,632	23.62	85,064	11,200	14.35	16,328	741	21.12
1955	26,587	13,569	22.59	12,864	1,578	24.80	81,051	10,990	14.80	16,553	758	20.95
1954	25,889	12,963	24.23	13,270	1,647	23.07	71,495	9,870	21.32	16,255	734	21.59
1953	24,465	12,407	23.62	12,200	1,546	25.04	74,368	10,006	21.65	16,321	729	22.46
1952	18,625	9,650	32.38	9,388	1,169	34.42	86,572	11,527	17.94	14,304	648	26.76
1951	17,084	8,837	35.72	8,902	1,059	37.19	85,540	11,481	20.12	11,416	521	34.31

See footnotes at end of table.

Series K 583–594. Meat Slaughtering, Production, and Price: 1899 to 1970—Con.

Year	Beef			Veal			Pork			Lamb and mutton		
	Cattle slaughtered [1]	Production, dressed weight	Price of beef steers per cwt.	Calves slaughtered [1]	Production, dressed weight	Price of veal calves per cwt.	Hogs slaughtered [1]	Production, dressed weight	Price of hogs per cwt. [2]	Lambs and sheep slaughtered [1]	Production, dressed weight	Price of lambs per cwt.
	583	584	585	586	587	588	589	590	591	592	593	594
	1,000 head	Mil. lb.	Dollars	1,000 head	Mil. lb.	Dollars	1,000 head	Mil. lb.	Dollars	1,000 head	Mil. lb.	Dollars
1950	18,614	9,534	29.35	10,501	1,230	31.08	79,263	10,714	18.20	13,244	597	27.54
1949	18,765	9,439	25.80	11,398	1,334	27.64	74,997	10,286	18.12	13,780	603	25.54
1948	19,177	9,075	30.88	12,378	1,423	29.02	70,869	10,055	23.14	17,371	747	25.04
1947	22,404	10,432	25.83	13,726	1,605	24.98	74,001	10,502	24.45	18,706	799	22.63
1946	19,824	9,373	19.16	12,176	1,443	16.87	76,115	11,136	18.40	22,788	968	18.40
1945	21,694	10,276	16.18	13,657	1,664	15.12	71,891	10,697	14.66	24,639	1,054	14.90
1944	19,844	9,112	15.44	14,242	1,738	14.86	98,068	13,304	13.57	25,355	1,024	14.52
1943	17,845	8,571	15.30	9,940	1,167	15.18	95,226	13,640	14.31	27,073	1,104	14.91
1942	18,033	8,843	13.79	9,718	1,151	14.48	78,547	10,876	13.70	25,585	1,042	13.82
1941	16,419	8,082	11.33	9,252	1,036	12.18	71,397	9,528	9.45	22,309	923	11.28
1940	14,958	7,175	10.43	9,089	981	10.61	77,610	10,044	5.71	21,571	876	9.66
1939	14,621	7,011	9.75	9,191	991	9.82	66,561	8,660	6.57	21,614	872	9.33
1938	14,822	6,908	9.39	9,306	994	9.00	58,927	7,680	8.09	22,423	897	8.50
1937	15,254	6,798	11.47	10,304	1,108	10.07	53,715	6,951	10.02	21,455	852	10.78
1936 [3]	15,897	7,358	8.82	10,008	1,075	9.30	58,730	7,474	9.89	21,555	854	9.91
1935 [3]	14,566	6,608	10.26	9,580	1,023	8.88	46,011	5,919	9.27	22,000	877	9.02
1934 [3]	15,071	[4]8,343	6.76	10,106	1,246	6.10	68,760	8,397	4.65	20,444	851	8.01
1933 [5]	13,107	6,440	5.42	8,564	891	5.88	73,270	9,234	3.94	21,833	852	6.65
1932	11,980	5,789	6.70	7,970	822	6.21	71,425	8,923	3.83	23,043	884	5.92
1931	12,096	6,009	8.06	8,057	823	8.33	69,233	8,739	6.16	23,133	885	7.26
1930	12,056	5,917	10.95	7,761	792	11.51	67,272	8,482	9.47	21,125	825	9.69
1929	12,038	5,871	13.43	7,406	761	14.76	71,012	8,833	10.16	17,483	682	14.62
1928	12,028	5,771	13.91	7,651	773	14.56	72,889	9,041	9.22	17,076	663	14.99
1927	13,413	6,395	11.36	8,478	867	12.90	66,195	8,430	9.95	16,113	629	14.12
1926	14,781	7,089	9.47	9,354	955	11.61	62,585	7,966	12.34	16,444	639	14.26
1925	14,704	6,878	10.16	9,936	989	10.87	65,508	8,128	11.81	15,430	603	15.66
1924	14,750	6,877	9.24	9,804	972	9.86	76,809	9,149	8.11	15,578	597	14.57
1923	14,283	6,721	9.40	9,327	916	9.66	77,508	9,483	7.55	15,146	588	13.89
1922	13,706	6,588	8.65	8,832	852	9.15	66,201	8,145	9.22	14,373	553	13.68
1921	12,428	6,022	8.20	8,394	820	9.36	61,818	7,697	8.51	16,742	639	9.86
1920	13,470	6,306	13.30	8,481	842	14.58	61,502	7,648	13.91	13,984	538	14.60
1919	15,027	6,756	15.50	8,201	819	16.83	65,795	8,477	17.85	15,784	590	16.00
1918	17,093	7,726	14.65	7,485	760	15.75	65,100	8,349	17.45	13,220	506	16.60
1917	15,741	7,239	11.60	7,372	744	13.78	56,500	7,055	15.10	12,128	463	15.60
1916	13,793	6,460	9.50	6,628	655	10.98	67,000	8,207	9.60	15,160	585	10.75
1915	12,901	6,075	8.40	6,054	590	10.08	62,000	7,616	7.10	15,576	605	9.00
1914	12,676	6,017	8.65	5,927	569	10.10	55,000	6,824	8.30	18,035	693	8.00
1913	12,939	6,182	8.25	6,305	608	10.20	57,000	6,979	8.35	18,375	706	7.70
1912	13,386	6,234	7.75	6,828	662	8.94	55,500	6,822	7.55	19,131	735	7.20
1911	13,817	6,549	6.40	6,855	666	7.91	57,000	6,961	6.70	18,177	693	5.95
1910	14,140	6,647	6.80	6,917	667	8.25	48,215	6,087	8.90	15,332	597	7.55
1909	14,135	6,915	6.35	6,864	660	7.10	54,986	6,557	7.35	15,464	608	7.40
1908	13,569	6,662	6.10	6,546	637	6.50	63,463	7,535	5.70	14,200	559	6.35
1907	13,886	6,544	5.80	6,395	626	6.40	56,527	7,059	6.10	13,799	553	7.05
1906	13,456	6,537	5.30	6,187	598	6.25	54,698	6,793	6.25	13,800	543	6.85
1905	13,096	6,504	5.05	5,731	556	5.75	54,433	6,629	5.25	13,100	530	6.80
1904	12,257	6,176	4.95	5,076	491	5.60	52,072	6,387	5.15	13,100	538	5.60
1903	12,266	6,240	4.80	5,044	492	6.20	48,548	6,067	6.00	13,800	563	5.45
1902	11,751	5,649	6.20	4,854	476	6.35	48,306	5,936	6.85	13,700	564	5.50
1901	11,526	5,814	5.25	4,318	422	5.61	53,898	6,357	5.85	13,200	548	4.80
1900	10,792	5,628	5.15	4,105	397	----------	51,885	6,329	5.05	12,000	493	----------
1899	----------	5,522	5.30	----------	387	----------	----------	6,310	4.05	----------	487	----------

[1] Includes inspected, noninspected, retail, and farm slaughter.
[2] Excludes processing tax of $0.50 per 100 pounds from Nov. 5–30, 1933; $1.00 from Dec. 1, 1933–Jan. 31, 1934; $1.50 from Feb. 1–28, 1934; and $2.25 from Mar. 1, 1934–Jan. 6, 1936.
[3] Excludes cattle and calves purchased for slaughter for Federal Surplus Relief Corporation from June 1934–Feb. 1935 and for Aug. 1936; excludes also cattle thus purchased for Sept. 1936.
[4] Includes slaughter under the Emergency Government Relief Purchase Program in 1934–1935.
[5] Excludes purchases on Government account for the Emergency Hog Production Control Program from Aug. 22–Oct. 7, 1933.

Series K 595–608. Cows Kept for Milk on Farms, Milk Produced, Manufactured Dairy Products, Prices Received by Farmers, and Wholesale Prices of Cheese and Butter: 1830 to 1970

[Census figures in *italics*]

Year	Cows and heifers 2 years old and over kept for milk, Jan. 1 — Number (1,000 head)	Value per head (Dollars)	Milk produced on farms during year (Million pounds)	Production of dairy products — Butter [1] (Million pounds)	Cheese [2] (Million pounds)	Evaporated and condensed milk [3] (Million pounds)	Ice cream (Million gallons)	Milk equivalent of manufactured dairy products [4] (Million pounds)	Prices received by farmers — Butter, per pound (Cents)	Milkfat in cream, per pound (Cents)	Whole milk — Wholesale, per 100 pounds (Dollars)	Retail, per quart (Cents)	Wholesale prices — Cheese, American twins, per pound [5] (Cents)	Butter at New York, per pound [6] (Cents)
	595	596	597	598	599	600	601	602	603	604	605	606	607	608
1970	13,838	300.00	117,149	1,143	2,204	1,517	763	60,330	--------	69.6	5.71	27.1	54.6	70.4
1969	*11,175*													
1969	14,152	270.00	116,345	1,129	1,990	1,776	766	58,499	--------	68.9	5.49	25.9	51.5	68.5
1968	14,644	251.00	117,234	1,175	1,938	1,800	773	59,664	--------	68.4	5.24	24.8	47.3	67.8
1967	15,198	247.00	118,769	1,238	1,919	1,886	745	60,062	--------	68.2	5.02	24.0	45.1	67.5
1966	15,987	208.00	119,892	1,128	1,854	2,196	751	58,234	--------	67.2	4.81	23.2	45.9	67.2
1965	16,981	188.00	124,173	1,346	1,755	2,178	757	62,240	--------	61.1	4.23	22.3	38.3	61.0
1964	*14,623*													
1964	17,647	194.00	126,967	1,469	1,724	2,395	739	65,133	--------	60.2	4.15	22.3	57.6	59.9
1963	18,379	206.00	125,202	1,454	1,632	2,369	718	63,410	--------	59.5	4.10	22.2	36.6	59.0
1962	18,963	212.00	126,251	1,579	1,592	2,409	704	65,056	--------	59.4	4.09	21.9	(NA)	59.4
1961	*19,271	*208.00	125,707	1,536	1,635	2,632	699	64,695	--------	61.5	4.22	21.7	37.2	61.2
1960	19,527	210.00	*123,109	*1,436	*1,478	*2,666	*700	61,088	--------	60.5	*4.21	*21.7	36.4	59.9
1959 [7]	*16,522*													
1959	20,132	221.00	121,989	1,411	1,383	2,743	699	60,010	--------	60.1	4.16	21.5	33.2	60.6
1958	21,265	177.00	123,220	1,486	1,399	2,752	658	60,847	--------	59.3	4.13	21.3	33.7	59.7
1957	22,325	147.00	124,628	1,533	1,407	2,872	651	61,640	--------	60.6	4.21	21.3	34.8	60.7
1956	22,912	139.00	124,860	1,553	1,388	2,953	641	62,220	--------	59.4	4.14	21.0	34.3	59.9
1955	23,462	134.00	122,945	1,545	1,367	2,922	629	61,272	--------	57.8	4.01	20.8	33.1	58.2
1954	*20,183*													
1954	23,896	147.00	122,094	1,628	1,383	2,845	597	62,266	--------	58.7	3.97	20.6	33.9	60.5
1953	23,549	203.00	120,221	1,607	1,344	2,875	605	61,492	--------	66.5	4.32	20.9	37.2	66.6
1952	23,060	252.00	114,671	1,402	1,170	3,165	593	55,783	--------	75.0	4.85	20.8	40.3	73.0
1951	23,568	219.00	114,681	1,443	1,161	3,228	569	56,349	60.8	71.2	4.58	19.9	38.9	69.9
1950	*21,233*													
1950	23,853	177.00	116,602	1,648	1,191	3,205	554	60,330	56.8	62.0	3.89	18.5	31.9	62.2
1949	23,862	193.00	116,103	1,688	1,199	3,106	558	60,764	58.0	61.6	3.95	18.6	30.4	61.5
1948	24,615	164.00	112,671	1,504	1,098	3,755	576	57,669	66.7	79.9	4.88	18.8	40.7	75.8
1947	25,842	145.00	116,814	1,640	1,183	3,630	631	61,716	63.3	71.8	4.27	17.5	36.0	71.3
1946	26,521	112.00	117,697	1,502	1,106	3,333	714	58,325	58.3	64.3	3.99	15.2	34.8	62.8
1945	*22,803*													
1945	27,770	99.40	119,828	1,699	1,117	4,126	477	61,859	45.3	50.3	3.19	13.4	23.2	42.8
1944	27,704	102.00	117,023	1,818	1,017	3,750	445	61,566	43.8	50.3	3.21	13.2	23.2	42.2
1943	27,138	99.50	117,017	2,015	993	3,344	412	63,724	43.7	49.9	3.12	12.7	23.2	44.8
1942	26,313	77.90	118,533	2,130	1,112	3,782	464	67,996	35.2	39.6	2.58	11.8	21.6	40.1
1941	25,453	60.90	115,088	2,268	956	3,555	390	67,832	30.4	34.2	2.19	10.8	19.4	34.3
1940	*21,937*													
1940	24,940	57.30	109,412	2,240	785	2,731	318	62,845	26.6	28.0	(NA)	10.3	14.3	29.5
1939	24,600	55.73	106,792	2,210	710	2,367	306	60,455	25.0	23.9	1.69	10.3	12.8	26.0
1938	24,466	54.52	105,807	2,252	726	2,322	286	60,989	26.6	26.3	1.73	10.3	12.6	28.0
1937	24,649	50.45	101,908	2,135	653	2,131	291	57,548	29.6	33.3	1.99	10.5	15.9	34.4
1936	25,196	49.32	102,410	2,168	650	2,270	259	58,250	28.8	32.2	1.88	10.1	15.3	33.1
1935	*24,582*													
1935	26,082	30.17	101,205	2,211	628	2,032	219	57,881	26.7	28.1	1.72	9.8	14.3	29.8
1934	26,931	27.00	101,621	2,286	587	1,908	192	58,479	22.7	22.7	1.55	9.4	11.8	25.7
1933	25,936	29.18	104,762	2,375	548	1,899	162	59,557	20.1	18.8	1.30	8.6	10.2	21.6
1932	24,896	39.51	103,810	2,307	491	1,780	168	57,433	20.8	17.9	1.28	8.9	10.0	21.0
1931	23,820	57.03	103,029	2,239	499	1,682	226	56,686	27.2	24.8	1.69	10.1	12.5	28.3
1930	*21,124*													
1930	23,032	82.70	100,158	2,149	510	1,761	255	55,581	36.3	34.5	2.21	11.3	16.4	36.5
1929	22,440	83.89	98,988	2,184	499	1,849	277	56,625	42.2	45.2	2.53	11.5	20.2	45.0
1928	22,231	73.38	95,843	2,120	479	1,604	254	54,261	42.6	46.1	2.52	11.5	22.1	47.4
1927	22,251	59.15	95,172	2,188	462	1,576	251	55,409	41.5	44.5	2.51	11.3	22.7	47.3
1926	22,410	54.65	93,325	2,132	468	1,456	238	53,902	40.9	41.6	2.38	11.3	20.1	44.4
1925	*20,900*													
1925	22,575	48.34	90,699	2,082	503	1,548	240	53,434	40.5	42.4	2.38	11.2	21.5	45.3
1924	22,331	49.91	89,240	2,066	474	1,507	213	52,417	39.5	40.4	2.22	11.1	18.2	42.6
1923	22,138	48.65	--------	1,993	471	1,585	214	52,204	40.4	42.2	2.49	10.9	22.1	46.9
1922	21,851	48.68	--------	1,870	432	1,281	191	48,629	35.3	35.9	2.11	10.4	19.3	40.6
1921	21,456	61.19	--------	1,748	434	1,324	175	45,759	37.0	37.0	2.30	11.2	18.3	43.3
1920	*19,675*													
1920	21,455	81.51	--------	1,574	423	1,416	171	42,446	54.3	55.5	3.22	12.8	24.9	61.4
1919	21,545	78.37	67,124	1,647	486	1,883	153	45,388	50.3	53.3	3.29	11.9	29.0	60.7
1918	21,536	70.63	--------	1,503	415	1,619	143	40,077	42.7	45.4	2.96	10.6	25.9	51.5
1917	21,212	59.51	--------	1,644	472	1,391	106	44,010	35.9	38.0	2.38	8.9	22.5	42.7
1916	20,752	53.81	--------	1,793	422	1,196	94	45,927	28.0	29.4	1.73	7.4	17.5	34.0
1915	20,270	55.30	--------	1,751	440	1,028	--------	44,677	25.7	25.9	1.58	7.1	14.2	29.8
1914	19,821	53.91	--------	1,685	367	883	72	42,101	25.1	25.5	1.60	7.2	14.6	29.8
1913	19,580	45.04	--------	1,608	359	787	--------	40,010	26.7	27.4	1.61	7.1	14.3	32.2
1912	19,517	39.42	--------	1,592	323	701	--------	38,963	25.7	26.7	1.59	6.9	15.6	31.6
1911	19,422	40.07	--------	1,762	345	624	--------	42,464	22.9	23.2	1.52	6.7	12.7	27.9

See footnotes at end of table.

Series **K 595–608.** Cows Kept for Milk on Farms, Milk Produced, Manufactured Dairy Products, Prices Received by Farmers, and Wholesale Prices of Cheese and Butter: 1830 to 1970—Con.

[Census figures in *italics*]

Year	Cows and heifers 2 years old and over kept for milk, Jan. 1 — Number	Value per head	Milk produced on farms during year	Production of dairy products — Butter [1]	Cheese [2]	Evaporated and condensed milk [3]	Ice cream	Milk equivalent of manufactured dairy products [4]	Prices received by farmers — Butter, per pound	Milkfat in cream, per pound	Whole milk — Wholesale, per 100 pounds	Retail, per quart	Wholesale prices — Cheese, American twins, per pound [5]	Butter at New York, per pound [6]
	595	596	597	598	599	600	601	602	603	604	605	606	607	608
	1,000 head	*Dollars*	*Million pounds*	*Million pounds*	*Million pounds*	*Million pounds*	*Million gallons*	*Million pounds*	*Cents*	*Cents*	*Dollars*	*Cents*	*Cents*	*Cents*
1910	*20,625*													
1910	19,450	35.40		1,706	355	556		41,132	25.5	26.4	1.58	6.6	14.7	31.1
1909	19,201	32.09	64,211	1,622	313	495	30	38,715	24.0	25.5		6.4	14.6	29.9
1908	18,992	30.48		1,763	313	450		41,439					12.2	27.6
1907	18,629	30.63		1,537	286	410		36,290					13.4	28.1
1906	18,230	29.34		1,545	292	373		36,403					11.8	24.6
1905	17,823	27.19		1,667	327	339		39,210					11.7	24.6
1904	17,485	29.00		1,540	331	308	12	36,468					9.3	21.7
1903	17,217	30.06		1,485	323	279		35,159					11.1	23.4
1902	16,992	29.08		1,401	318	252		33,248					11.2	24.7
1901	16,708	29.88		1,575	362	228		37,280					9.8	21.4
1900	*17,136*													
1900	16,544	31.30		1,540	324	207		36,106					10.0	22.2
1899	16,094	29.46	62,486	1,493	299	187	5	34,806					[8]10.6	21.3
1898	15,641	27.34		1,473	281			34,145					[8]7.6	19.6
1897	15,382	23.08		1,533	311			35,640					[8]8.5	19.0
1896	15,266	22.53		1,604	240			36,385					[8]7.7	18.5
1895	15,230	22.11		1,297	234			29,828					[8]7.4	21.2
1894	15,237	21.86		1,063	257			25,113					[8]10.2	23.0
1893	15,164	21.90		1,047	254			24,718					[8]9.6	27.1
1892	15,177	21.53		1,058	318			25,561					[8]9.3	26.3
1891	15,133	21.73		1,091	293			25,990					[8]8.9	26.2
1890	*16,512*													
1890	15,000	22.30		1,171	318			27,906					[8]9.0	23.7
1889	14,706	24.03	44,807	1,292	301	45	1	30,260					[8]8.7	24.4
1888	14,350	24.82		978	286			23,494					[8]8.1	27.5
1887	13,888	26.23		978	268			23,301					[8]10.8	26.7
1886	13,478	27.52		989	244			23,283					[8]9.6	26.8
1885	13,213	29.88		933	260			22,258					[8]8.7	26.6
1884	12,883	31.58		869	275			21,061					[8]11.1	30.3
1883	12,571	30.47		844	281			20,584					[8]11.0	31.2
1882	12,234	26.12		743	261			18,248					[8]11.9	35.6
1881	11,977	23.82		803	304			19,934					[8]12.4	31.8
1880	*12,443*													
1880	11,754	23.31		816	270			19,861					[8]12.5	30.5
1879	11,486	21.55		807	243	13	(Z)	19,402					[8]8.0	24.2
1878	11,222	25.70		726	303			18,307						27.3
1877	11,004	25.14		696	235			16,995						28.5
1876	10,821	25.20		677	214			16,390						31.3
1875	10,714	25.29		556	233			14,029						32.8
1874	10,562	25.20		585	206			14,347						36.2
1873	10,348	26.32		566	212			14,029						35.4
1872	10,191	29.18		434	187			10,997						32.0
1871	9,941	33.62		470	164			11,527						33.6
1870	*8,935*													
1870	9,672	31.89		412	181			10,472						38.1
1869	9,205	28.86		514	163	4	(Z)	12,434						43.3
1868	8,705	26.96												44.7
1867	8,263	29.40												34.8
1866														42.7
1865														39.8
1864														43.7
1863														28.2
1862														20.9
1861														19.4
1860	*8,586*													
1860														21.9
1859				460	104		(Z)	10,690						23.9
1858														23.8
1857														25.7
1856														25.8
1855														26.4
1854														23.0
1853														23.0
1852														23.6
1851														18.4

See footnotes at end of table.

Series K 595–608. Cows Kept for Milk on Farms, Milk Produced, Manufactured Dairy Products, Prices Received by Farmers, and Wholesale Prices of Cheese and Butter: 1830 to 1970—Con.

[Census figures in *italics*]

Year	Cows and heifers 2 years old and over kept for milk, Jan. 1, number	Production of dairy products		Milk equivalent of manufactured dairy products [4]	Wholesale price, butter at New York, per pound [6]	Year	Wholesale price, butter at New York, per pound [6]	Year	Wholesale price, butter at New York, per pound [6]	Year	Wholesale price, butter at New York, per pound [6]
		Butter [1]	Cheese [2]								
	595	598	599	602	608		608		608		608
	1,000 head	*Million pounds*	*Million pounds*	*Million pounds*	*Cents*		*Cents*		*Cents*		*Cents*
1850	*6,385*					1845	17.7	1840	17.4	1835	19.2
1850					19.6	1844	15.2	1839	22.9	1834	14.4
1849		313	106	7,636	18.9	1843	13.3	1838	23.4	1833	15.8
1848					20.1	1842	16.5	1837	21.6	1832	15.2
1847					20.7	1841	18.6	1836	23.9	1831	14.9
1846					16.7					1830	13.9

* Denotes first year for which figures include Alaska and Hawaii.
NA Not available.   Z Less than 500,000 gallons.
[1] Farm and factory production combined.
[2] Includes all types of cheese except cottage, pot, and bakers' cheese; full-skim American cheese excluded since 1908. Farm output not estimated since 1926.
[3] For 1919–1970 includes all evaporated and condensed whole milk as compiled by the former Bureau of Agricultural Economics and Agricultural Marketing Service. Prior to 1919, includes total production of all condensed and evaporated milk as interpolated from census enumerations.
[4] For 1849–1923, computed from data on estimated production of manufactured dairy products, using average milk equivalent factors; 1924–1970, as published by Agricultural Marketing Service. Data include farm butter.

[5] On Wisconsin cheese exchange, based on weekly prices established on Friday each week. Beginning 1950, data for cheddar cheese only.
[6] Annual averages of monthly figures from sources and for grades as follows: 1830–1879, average of high and low for 2 days each week, high grade, New York shipping and commercial list; 1880–1895 average of monthly range, creamery extras, annual reports of New York Chamber of Commerce; 1896–1920, average of daily quotations for extra fresh, specials, extras and firsts, or fresh extras, *New York Produce Review and American Creamery*, published by Urner-Barry Company; 1921–1970, 92 score creamery, daily market reports of U.S. Department of Agriculture.
[7] Beginning 1959, census figures include Alaska and Hawaii.
[8] September figure shown because annual averages were not available.

Series K 609–623. Poultry and Eggs—Number, Production, and Price: 1909 to 1970

[Census figures in *italics* and as of April 15, 1910; April 1, 1930, 1940, 1950, and 1954; January 1, 1920, 1925, 1935, and 1945; October–November, 1959; November–December, 1964; and December 31, 1969]

Year	Chickens					Broilers			Eggs		Turkeys				
	Number, Jan. 1	Value per head, Jan. 1	Number produced	Pounds produced	Price per pound [1]	Number produced	Pounds produced	Price per pound [1]	Number produced	Price per dozen [1]	Number, Jan. 1	Value per head, Jan. 1	Number produced	Pounds produced	Price per pound [1]
	609	610	611	612	613	614	615	616	617	618	619	620	621	622	623
	Millions	*Dollars*	*Millions*	*Millions*	*Cents*	*Millions*	*Millions*	*Cents*	*Millions*	*Cents*	*Millions*	*Dollars*	*Millions*	*Millions*	*Cents*
1970	434	1.35	267	1,197	8.8	2,987	10,819	13.6	70,312	37.6	6,769	5.50	116	2,184	22.7
1969	*371*	*1.31*													
1969	420	1.21	253	1,146	9.7	2,789	10,048	15.2	69,086	40.0	6,604	4.95	106	2,020	22.4
1968	425	1.14	248	1,158	8.2	2,620	9,326	14.2	69,270	34.0	7,301	4.65	106	2,010	20.5
1967	429	1.20	265	1,246	7.9	2,592	9,183	13.3	70,031	31.2	7,817	5.13	126	2,343	19.7
1966	393	1.21	282	1,278	9.7	2,571	8,989	15.3	66,484	39.1	6,905	5.26	116	2,123	23.1
1965	394	1.17	240	1,135	8.9	2,334	8,111	15.0	65,692	33.7	6,105	4.40	106	1,915	22.2
1964	*343*	*1.17*													
1964	382	1.16	255	1,170	9.2	2,161	7,521	14.2	65,215	33.8	5,996	4.28	101	1,826	21.0
1963	376	1.16	254	1,147	10.0	2,102	7,276	14.6	63,500	34.5	6,374	4.40	94	1,686	22.3
1962	377	1.15	257	1,157	10.2	2,023	6,907	15.2	63,569	33.8	6,423	3.79	92	1,626	21.6
1961	[2]366	[2]1.25	[2]275	[2]1,224	[2]10.1	1,991	6,832	13.9	[2]62,423	[2]35.6	7,008	4.91	107	1,871	18.9
1960	369	1.06	260	1,142	12.2	1,795	6,017	16.9	61,602	36.1	5,633	4.89	84	1,489	25.4
1959	*351* [3]	*1.06* [3]													
1959	387	1.26	311	1,346	11.0	1,737	5,763	16.1	63,335	31.4	6,105	4.65	84	1,433	23.9
1958	374	1.26	344	1,490	14.0	1,660	5,431	18.5	61,607	38.5	5,612	4.67	79	1,356	23.9
1957	391	1.17	310	1,339	13.7	1,448	4,683	18.9	61,026	35.9	5,828	5.05	81	1,356	23.4
1956	384	1.26	386	1,639	16.0	1,344	4,270	19.6	61,113	39.3	4,937	5.50	77	1,274	27.2
1955	391	1.05	375	1,623	18.6	1,092	3,350	25.2	59,526	39.5	4,917	5.33	65	1,091	30.2
1954	*376*	*1.04*									[4]*2,278*	[4]*3.76*			
1954	397	1.43	455	1,948	16.8	1,048	3,236	23.1	58,933	36.6	4,956	6.32	68	1,161	28.8
1953	398	1.41	464	2,046	22.1	947	2,904	27.1	57,891	47.7	5,086	6.15	60	1,008	33.7
1952	427	1.53	473	2,025	22.1	861	2,624	28.8	58,068	41.6	5,725	6.99	62	1,049	33.6
1951	431	1.46	540	2,312	25.0	789	2,415	28.5	58,063	47.7	5,037	6.48	53	950	37.5

See footnotes at end of table.

Series K 609–623. Poultry and Eggs—Number, Production, and Price: 1909 to 1970—Con.

[Census figures in *italics* and as of April 15, 1910; April 1, 1930, 1940, 1950, and 1954; January 1, 1920, 1925, 1935, and 1945; October-November, 1959; November-December, 1964; and December 31, 1969]

Year	Chickens					Broilers			Eggs		Turkeys				
	Number, Jan. 1	Value per head, Jan. 1	Number produced	Pounds produced	Price per pound [1]	Number produced	Pounds produced	Price per pound [1]	Number produced	Price per dozen [1]	Number, Jan. 1	Value per head, Jan. 1	Number produced	Pounds produced	Price per pound [1]
	609	610	611	612	613	614	615	616	617	618	619	620	621	622	623
	Millions	*Dollars*	*Millions*	*Millions*	*Cents*	*Millions*	*Millions*	*Cents*	*Millions*	*Cents*	*Millions*	*Dollars*	*Millions*	*Millions*	*Cents*
1950	*343*	*1.09*									*2,849*	*4.51*			
1950	457	1.36	535	2,310	22.2	631	1,945	27.4	58,954	36.3	5,124	6.34	44	817	32.9
1949	431	1.66	623	2,643	25.4	513	1,570	28.2	56,154	45.2	4,622	8.80	41	769	35.2
1948	500	1.44	536	2,289	30.1	371	1,127	36.0	54,899	47.2	3,959	6.97	31	574	46.8
1947	467	1.44	636	2,668	26.5	310	936	32.3	55,384	45.3	5,879	6.54	34	611	36.5
1946	523	1.27	646	2,715	27.6	293	884	32.7	55,962	37.6	7,862	5.75	40	714	36.3
1945	*433*	*1.23*													
1945	516	1.21	799	3,315	25.9	366	1,107	29.5	56,221	37.7	7,082	5.79	42	740	33.7
1944	582	1.18	725	3,009	23.7	274	818	28.8	58,537	32.5	7,294	5.35	35	584	33.9
1943	542	1.04	914	3,679	24.3	285	833	28.6	54,547	37.1	6,584	4.47	31	509	32.7
1942	477	.83	752	3,005	18.7	228	674	22.9	48,610	30.0	7,447	3.08	32	522	27.5
1941	423	.65	664	2,586	15.6	192	559	18.4	41,894	23.5	7,150	2.27	32	512	19.9
1940	*338*	*.56*									*4,362*	*1.71*			
1940	438	.60	556	2,158	13.0	143	413	17.3	39,707	18.0	8,569	2.14	33	502	15.2
1939	419	.70	621	2,338	13.2	106	306	17.0	38,843	17.4	6,489	2.56	33	494	15.7
1938	390	.76	583	2,185	14.8	82	239	19.0	37,356	20.3	6,096	2.49	27	395	17.5
1937	424	.66	533	2,032	16.0	68	196	21.4	37,564	21.3	6,358	2.06	25	376	18.1
1936	403	.75	651	2,410	15.0	53	152	20.6	34,534	21.8	5,731	2.82	28	405	15.6
1935	*372*	*.52*									*5,382*	*2.17*			
1935	390	.54	598	2,210	14.9	43	123	20.0	33,609	23.4	5,499	2.18	20	298	20.1
1934	434	.42	578	2,105	11.1	34	97	19.3	34,429	17.0	6,309	1.48	21	300	15.1
1933	445	.45	685	2,524	9.5				35,514	13.8	6,852	1.41	23	319	11.6
1932	437	.62	673	2,489	11.7				36,298	14.2	5,946	2.43	22	303	12.8
1931	450	.70	647	2,368	15.8				38,532	17.6	5,318	2.60	18	244	19.3
1930	*379*	*.85*													
1930	468	.93	714	2,553	18.4				39,067	23.7	5,969	3.00	17	228	20.2
1929	449	.91	692	2,506	22.8				37,921	29.8	5,541	3.55	18	239	24.5
1928	475	.86	640	2,316	21.4				38,659	28.1					
1927	461	.91	694	2,507	20.2				38,627	25.1					
1926	438	.89	665	2,409	22.1				37,248	28.9					
1925	*409*	*.93*													
1925	435	.79	626	2,275	20.5				34,969	30.4					
1924	435	.76	605	2,197	19.4				34,592	26.7					
1923	415	.75	610						35,000	26.5					
1922	395	.81	585						33,000	25.0					
1921	370	.89	556						30,800	28.3					
1920	*360*	*1.04*									*3,627*				
1920	381	.97	514						29,700	43.5					
1919	391	.96	527						30,500	41.3					
1918	363	.77	543						28,000	36.0					
1917	359	.59	509						27,700	31.8					
1916	369	.49	501						28,800	22.1					
1915	379	.46	514						29,900	19.4					
1914	367	.49	531						27,900	20.5					
1913	365	.47	514						28,100	19.4					
1912	367	.42	513						28,300	20.2					
1911	382	.46	517						29,400	17.5					
1910	*280*	*.50*									*3,689*				
1910	356	.47	543						27,000	20.9					
1909	340	.44	498						25,300	20.0					

[1] Average annual price received by farmers.
[2] Beginning 1961, Department of Agriculture data include Alaska and Hawaii.
[3] Beginning 1959, census data include Alaska and Hawaii.
[4] Data for October-November 1954.

Chapter L

Forestry and Fisheries

Forests and Forest Products (Series L 1-223)

L 1–223. General note.

Since 1900, several reports containing basic forest statistics have been published and the seven most noteworthy for inclusion of new data are listed below.

U.S. Forest Service, *Timber Depletion, Lumber Prices, Lumber Exports, and Concentration of Timber Ownership*, Report on Res. 311, 66th Congress, 2d session (The Capper Report), 1920; *A National Plan for American Forestry*, Senate Document 12, 73d Congress, 1st session, 2 vols. (The Copeland Report), 1933.

U.S. Congress Joint Committee on Forestry, *Forest Lands in the United States*, Senate Document 32, 77th Congress, 1st session (The J.C.C. Report), 1938.

U.S. Forest Service, *Forests and National Prosperity*, Agriculture Miscellaneous Publication No. 668 (The Reappraisal Report), 1948; *Timber Resources for America's Future*, 1958; *Timber Trends in the United States* (Forest Resource Report No. 17), 1965; *The Outlook for Timber in the United States* (Forest Resource Report No. 20), 1973.

All series from the Forest Service include Alaska and Puerto Rico for all years; there are no national forest areas in Hawaii.

L 1–9. Forest land—total and commercial timber area, net volume of sawtimber, and net volume of growing stock, 1953, 1963, and 1970.

Source: U.S. Forest Service, 1953, *Timber Resources for America's Future*, Forest Resource Report No. 14, 1958; 1963, *Timber Trends in the United States*, Forest Resource Report No. 17, 1965; 1970, *The Outlook for Timber in the United States*, Forest Resource Report No. 20, 1973.

To be classified as forest land, an area must be at least 10 percent stocked by forest trees of any size, or formerly having had such tree cover and not currently developed for nonforest use. Includes chaparral areas in the West and afforested acres. The minimum area for classification of forest land is 1 acre. Roadside, streamside, and shoulder belt strips of timber must have a crown width at least 120 feet wide to qualify as forest land. Unimproved roads and trails, streams, and clearings in forest areas are classed as forest if less than 120 feet in width.

Commercial timber land is forest land which is producing or is capable of producing crops of industrial wood and not withdrawn from timber utilization by statute or administrative regulation. Includes areas suitable for management to grow crops of industrial wood generally capable of producing in excess of 20 cubic feet per acre of annual growth. Includes both accessible and inaccessible areas.

Net volume of sawtimber is the net volume of the saw log portion of live sawtimber trees. A saw log is a log meeting minimum approved log-grade specifications; or for species for which approved log grades are lacking, at least 8 feet long, with a minimum diameter inside the bark of 6 inches, and with deduction for defect no greater than two-thirds the gross volume. Sawtimber trees are live trees of commercial species containing at least one saw log. Softwoods must be at least 9.0 inches in diameter breast height, except in California, Oregon, Washington, and coastal Alaska where minimum diameter is 11.0 inches. Hardwoods must be at least 11.0 inches in diameter in all States.

Net growing stock volume is the net volume in cubic feet of live

sawtimber and pole timber trees from stump to a minimum 4-inch top (of central stem) outside bark or to the point where the central stem breaks into limbs.

The data for 1953 and 1963 have been slightly revised from those shown in source documents to make them comparable with 1970 definitions.

L 10–11. Gross area of national forest system and other lands, 1905–1970.

Source: U.S. Forest Service, *National Forest System*, annual issues.

Data are prepared from individual land transactions of the Forest Service, such as transfers from other agencies, land exchanges, purchases, and other adjustments.

Gross area within unit boundaries (series L 10) prior to 1936 included the total land area within the authorized boundaries of the units formally designated or proclaimed as national forests. Since 1936, other lands administered by the Forest Service, including national forest purchase units, experimental areas, land utilization projects, and other land units have also been included.

The Federal Government seldom has complete ownership of all the land within the national forests and other units under administration of the Forest Service. Parts of such units are under private, State, county, and municipal ownership, or under the jurisdiction of a Federal agency other than the Forest Service. Gross area under Forest Service administration (series L 11) is thus the net area in the units owned by the United States and administered by the Forest Service. National forests comprise the largest part of this net area, accounting for 98 percent of the total in 1970. National grasslands, administered under Title III of the Bankhead-Jones Farm Tenant Act, account for most of the remainder.

The source also includes statistics for States on the gross and net area of each national forest, purchase unit, experimental area, and land utilization area under the jurisdiction of the Forest Service.

L 12–14. Gross area approved for national forest purchase, 1912–1970.

Source: U.S. National Forest Reservation Commission, *Annual Report*, annual issues.

The figures for gross area approved for purchase include the total area as of June 30 within purchase units that the Secretary of Agriculture had been authorized to purchase for national forest purposes by the National Forest Reservation Commission.

The source also includes statistics which show, by States and by national forests or purchase units, the area authorized by the Commission for purchase, the area purchased for national forests during each fiscal year, and the cost.

L 15–23. Volume and value of timber cut from national forest system areas, 1905–1970.

Source: U.S. Forest Service, unpublished data.

Commercial sales (series L 17–19) include all sales from the national forests for which a charge is made. Nearly all commercial sales are made on a competitive bid basis with the sale going to the highest bidder. Most sales are timber sales (series L 17–18) but some material not measurable in board feet is also sold from the national forests (series L 19). Some timber from the national forest is exchanged for land (series L 20–21) and some is disposed of under free- and administrative-use permits to settlers, miners, residents, and other similar users (series L 22–23).

Information on individual transactions involving national-forest timber is available from the Forest Service. Unpublished data of national-forest stumpage sales are also available for all sales in the form of quarterly compilations classified according to Forest Service regions, major species and product, e.g., pulpwood, saw logs, etc.

For a comparison of timber production on Forest Service lands and on lands administered by the Bureau of Land Management, see Robert S. Manthy, *Future Demands on the Public Lands*, vol. III: *Probable Future Demands on the Public Lands*, Washington, D.C., Public Land Law Review Commission, National Technical Information Service Publication, PB 195–043. Table 14 in that publication shows that production of timber products on Federal lands during the period 1947–1968 ranged from 7 percent to 23 percent of total U.S. production.

L 24–27. Receipts from national forest system lands, 1905–1970.

Source: U.S. Forest Service. Published in U.S. Dept. of Agriculture, *Agricultural Statistics*, *1957*, *1967*, and *1971* editions.

Receipts from the national forests are derived from timber and other forest product sales, settlement, and trespass; grazing and grazing trespass; and land uses such as power lines, resort and summer homesites, ski lifts, and mineral leases.

L 28–31. Payments to States and outlying areas, 1906–1970.

Source: U.S. Forest Service, unpublished data.

The "25-percent fund" (series L 29) consists of payments from gross receipts of the previous fiscal year from each national forest to the State or outlying area in which the forest is situated for the benefit of public roads and schools under an Act of May 23, 1908 (35 Stat. 260) as amended. Payments are also made from timber receipts from the Tongass National Forest to Alaska for public schools and public roads, under an Act approved July 24, 1956 (70 Stat. 605).

The "Arizona and New Mexico school fund" (series L 30) consists of payments made to the States of Arizona and New Mexico under an Act of June 20, 1910. From the gross receipts of the national forests in the two States, payments are made in the proportion that the area of land granted the States for school purposes within these national forests bears to the total area of all national forests within the two respective States.

"Payments to State of Minnesota" (series L 31) consist of payments made under an Act of June 22, 1948 (62 Stat. 568).

L 32–43. Forest tree distribution and forest management programs, 1939–1970.

Source: U.S. Dept. of Agriculture, *Agricultural Statistics*, *1967* and *1972*.

Under the forest tree distribution program, series L 32–36, the Federal Government cooperates with State forestry agencies to distribute forest tree seedlings for forestation and windbreak purposes.

Data for the forest management program, series L 37–43, are collected in the field as the tasks are accomplished, and summarized by the Forest Service.

L 37, woodland owners. Defined as any private nonindustrial owner who owns from 1 acre to 5,000 acres or more of woodlands (forest land).

L 38, woodland (or forest land). Defined as land bearing forest growth or land from which the forest has been removed but which shows evidence of past forest occupancy and which is not currently developed for nonforest uses. To qualify as forest, an area must be at least 120 feet wide and 1 acre in area; have a sufficient number of trees to provide 16.7 percent crown coverage; or, lacking 16.7 percent, be likely to remain in forest use.

L 39, products harvested. Includes any cut from which an income is derived from the sale of forest products—sawtimber, veneer, poles, piling, pulpwood, etc. This may be a sanitation cut, or a thinning or final cut at the end of rotation.

L 40, gross sale value. The known or estimated stump value; the selling price of the trees on the stump.

L 41–43, expenditures. The Federal expenditures are appropriated from the Cooperative Forest Management Act of 1950; the State expenditures, from State legislative appropriated funds. The Federal share may not exceed the net expenditures by a State in any fiscal year.

L 44–47. Expenditures for cooperative forest fire control on Federal, State, and private lands, 1912–1970.

Source: U.S. Dept. of Agriculture, *Agricultural Statistics*, various annual issues.

State and private expenditures (series L 46 and L 47) consist of expenditures for control under the Clarke-McNary section 2 program.

L 48–55. Forest fires and area burned over, 1926–1970.

Source: U.S. Forest Service. 1926–1967, *Forest Fire Statistics*, various annual issues; 1968–1970, *Wildfire Statistics*, annual issues.

Data are based upon reports submitted by the office of the State Foresters, by the Regional Foresters of the Forest Service, the Department of Interior, and the Tennessee Valley Authority. The statistics obtained are for forest land and nonforested watershed lands in Federal ownership, and for State and privately-owned lands which are included in the Cooperative Forest Fire Control Program as authorized by section 2 of the Clarke-McNary Act of 1924.

Protected area (series L 50–53) includes all forest lands that receive some organized fire protection. Unprotected area (series L 54–55) includes all forest lands not covered by organized fire protection.

The source publication also presents information by regions and States on areas needing protection, areas protected and unprotected, and areas burned on both protected and unprotected forest land by type of ownership, and size of fires on protected areas. No field organizations are available to report fires on unprotected areas and the statistics for these areas are generally the best estimates available. Beginning 1966, when Arizona entered the Cooperative Forest Fire Control Program, statistics became available for all 50 States.

L 56–71. Forest product raw materials production, imports, exports, and consumption in constant 1967 dollars, 1900–1969.

Source: U.S. Bureau of the Census and U.S. Bureau of Mines, *Raw Materials in the United States Economy: 1900–1969*, *Working Paper 35*, pp. 33, 35, 37, and 39.

The series is based on statistics compiled by the Forest Service and the Bureau of the Census. Forest products classes were combined into three major groups: Saw logs, pulpwood, and other forest products. The other forest products series include: Veneer logs, fuelwood (roundwood), other (except naval stores), turpentine, and rosin. These seven product classes, measured in physical quantity units were combined by means of unit-value weights. The basic unit values of forest products at first point of market were supplied by the Forest Service or, for naval stores, taken from reports of the Agricultural Marketing Service, Department of Agriculture. The quantity of production, imports, and exports series used were as compiled by the Forest Service and AMS, although the basic import and export series, and part of the production series were collected by the Bureau of the Census.

The production series represent about 99 percent of the total value of forest products from the United States (excluding Hawaii). The major item not included is Christmas trees. (Maple syrup and maple sugar are covered in the agricultural production series rather than in forest products.) Other minor forest products excluded are tanbark, holly, mistletoe, ferns, wild nuts, and balsam.

The import and export series, which represent nearly as high coverage of the total value of foreign trade in forest products, include the pulpwood equivalent of processed products, such as woodpulp, paper, and paperboard products, and such products as shingles and cork.

For the consumption series in terms of broad use classes, the Forest Service provided not only the series for roundwood fuelwood which is a part of the other forest products group, but also a series of estimates for residue, fuelwood which is implicitly included in the saw logs series, as well as appropriate unit-value weights for each of these series based on sample market values of such products in various States.

L 72–86.   General note.

Industrial timber products include all products, except fuelwood, commonly cut from round sections of trees.   Items such as Christmas trees, Christmas greens, naval stores, and other nontimber forest products are not included.

The production, imports, and exports of timber products as reported by the Bureau of the Census, the Forest Service, trade associations, and other sources are customarily shown in a wide variety of units, such as board feet, cubic feet, cords, pieces, linear feet, and variations of these units.   Appropriate factors have been used to convert the different measures of the various products to standard units of measure (cubic-feet roundwood) so that one product can be properly compared with another or that all can be combined and treated as a group.   Cubic-feet roundwood is a measure of the roundwood volume of a log or bolt (excluding bark) from which the various products such as lumber and veneer are cut.

L 72–74.   Domestic production, net imports, and apparent consumption of industrial timber products, in roundwood equivalent, 1900–1970.

Source: 1900–1949, U.S. Forest Service, *The Demand and Price Situation for Forest Products, 1964*, table 2; 1950–1970, *1973–74* edition, table 2. Data are sums of the series for different product groups; for production (L 75, L 78, L 81, L 84, L 86), net imports (L 76, L 79, L 82, L 85, L 86), and apparent consumption (L 77, L 80, L 83, L 84).

L 75–77.   Domestic production, net imports, and apparent consumption of lumber, 1900–1970.

Source: See source for series L 72–74.

Estimates have been converted to cubic-feet roundwood on the basis of 156 cubic feet per 1,000 board-feet softwoods and 153 cubic feet per 1,000 board-feet hardwoods lumber tally.

L 78–80.   Domestic production, net imports, and apparent consumption of plywood and veneer, 1900–1970.

Source: See source for series L 72–74.

Data on the volume of logs consumed in the manufacture of veneers were first reported by the Bureau of the Census in 1905.   Subsequently, the Bureau published data showing either log consumption or data with sufficient information on veneer or plywood production to permit the derivation of estimates of log consumption for 1905–1911, biennially for 1919–1939, 1942–1945, 1947, and annually 1951–1970.   Data for all other years represent estimates derived by the Forest Service.

Logs consumed in the manufacture of veneer have been assumed to equal domestic production although small quantities of logs, mostly hardwoods, are imported each year by the veneer industry.   Veneer logs commonly reported in board feet, log scale, have been converted to cubic-feet roundwood on the basis of 170 cubic feet per 1,000 board feet.

Net imports of plywood and veneer (series L 79) are converted to board feet, log scale, and then to cubic-feet roundwood.   The small volume of plywood and veneer imported is included under production (series L 78).

L 81–83.   Domestic production, net imports, and apparent consumption of pulp products, 1900–1970.

Source: See source for series L 72–74.

Domestic pulpwood production, net pulpwood imports, and the pulpwood equivalent of the net woodpulp and paper and board imports have been converted to cubic-feet roundwood on the basis of 77 cubic feet per cord.

L 84.   Apparent consumption of miscellaneous products, 1900–1970.

Source: See source for series L 72–74.

"Miscellaneous production" includes cooperage logs, poles and piling, fenceposts, hewn ties, round mine timbers, box bolts, excelsior bolts, turnery bolts, shingle bolts, chemical wood, and a miscellaneous assortment of similar items.   Fairly complete data are available for some of these items.   For example, the Forest Service and the Bureau of the Census, either separately or jointly, published data which could be used to estimate the annual production of cooperage logs for 1905–1911 and 1918–1919; biennially for 1919–1939; 1947 and 1952.   Similar information covering about the same years was published by these two agencies for hewn ties and poles.   For some products, particularly poles, data reported by the Forest Service in cooperation with the American Wood Preservers Association in *Wood Preservation Statistics* were used as an indicator of production.   Production estimates for mine timbers and other miscellaneous items have been based on periodic surveys made by the Forest Service or the Bureau of the Census.   Imports of these products are small.

L 85–86.   Imports and exports of logs, 1940–1970.

Source: See source for series L 72–74.

L 87–97.   Per capita consumption of timber products, by major product, 1900–1970.

Source: U.S. Forest Service, 1900–1949, *Demand and Price Situation for Forest Products, 1964*, Miscellaneous Publication No. 983, 1964; 1950–1970, *Demand and Price Situation for Forest Products, 1973–74*, Miscellaneous Publication No. 1292, 1973.

These figures were derived by dividing the apparent consumption of each product or group of products by total population, including Armed Forces overseas, as of July 1 each year.

L 98–100.   Lumber, domestic production, 1799–1970.

Source: U.S. Forest Service.   1799–1945, *Lumber Production in the United States, 1799–1946*; U.S. Bureau of the Census, 1946–1956, *Facts for Industry*, annual releases, "Lumber Production"; 1957–1970, *Current Industrial Reports*, "Lumber Production and Mill Stocks," series MA–24T, annual.

Data on lumber were first collected by the Census Office in the census of 1810 (for the year 1809).   Subsequently, this agency collected and published statistics on lumber production for 1819 and decennially for 1839–1899, and annually from 1904 through 1954 except in 1905, 1906, 1913, 1915–1918, 1920, and 1948.   The Bureau of Crop Estimates collected and published data for 1913, and the Forest Service for all other years.

For 1809–1859, only the value of lumber produced was included in the decennial reports of the Census Office, although some reference to number of mills or number of saws was often made.   For 1869, 1879, and 1889, the total quantity of lumber produced was reported by States.   Since 1899, lumber production has been reported in quantity terms by States and species, although in recent years such reporting, based on sampling of the industry, has been restricted to major species and principal producing States.

Prior to 1912, except for decennial censuses (when there was some field followup of nonreporting mills by field agents), lumber production figures were based upon a mail canvass of producers for the entire Nation. Since 1912, except for 1948, the census in the Western United States has been conducted by mail supplemented by a field canvass to obtain reports from nonrespondents. In the Eastern States, statistics were obtained by mail canvass for 1912–1941. Since 1941, except for 1948, statistics for the East have been based either upon a complete field canvass (1942 and 1947) or upon a mail canvass supplemented by area sampling. For 1948, lumber production figures for the West were obtained by the Forest Service in cooperation with the West Coast Lumbermen's Association and the Western Pine Association through a mail canvass, with field followup of nonrespondents. For the East, 1948 figures are Forest Service estimates based upon data published by the National Lumber Manufacturers Association and other associations.

Eastern field canvasses in the early 1940's disclosed thousands of small sawmills and many larger mills not previously included in the annual surveys. These mills collectively produced a substantial volume of lumber. Accordingly, the Forest Service prepared revised estimates of lumber production for 1904–1908, 1910–1918, and 1920–1941 designed to include the production of nonreporting mills as well as of reporting mills. The revised estimates and a description of the methodology employed in revising reported lumber production estimates also appear in the source cited above for 1799–1945. In addition, this source presents lumber production figures prior to 1946, by species and States, and data on average value per thousand board feet for years prior to 1944. Data on lumber production by species and States are also available for 1946, 1947, and 1949–1970 in the Bureau of the Census publications cited above.

Production figures for 1869–1919 as reported in the decennial censuses of 1870–1920 were accepted as substantially correct. The figures for 1809, 1819, and 1839–1859 are estimates by the Forest Service based on value data from the decennial reports of the Census Office (see above). The figures for 1799 and 1829 are also Forest Service estimates.

L 101–106. Lumber, imports and exports, 1899–1970.

Source: U.S. Bureau of the Census, 1899–1946, *Foreign Commerce and Navigation of the United States*, annual issues; 1947–1970, **series L 101–103**, *United States Imports of Merchandise for Consumption*, annual issues, and **series L 104–106**, *United States Exports of Domestic and Foreign Merchandise*, annual issues.

Figures are the summation of import entries and warehouse withdrawals prepared by importers or their brokers, and of export declarations prepared by shippers or their authorized agents or brokers. Series L 101–103 include lumber imports from all U.S. outlying areas; series L 104–106 include exports to all U.S. outlying areas.

Lumber imports and exports include sawn timbers, boards, planks, scantlings, joists, box shooks, and sawn railroad ties where quantities are given in board feet.

Supplementary statistics on the value of lumber imports and exports as well as value and volume of imports and exports of forest products, such as logs and bolts, poles, piling, Christmas trees, woodpulp, paper and paperboard, and other forest products, by country of origin and destination, also appear in the sources cited above.

L 107–109. Lumber, apparent consumption, 1899–1970.

Source: See sources for series L 98–100 and L 101–106.

Figures represent production plus imports minus exports.

L 110–112. Lumber, per capita consumption, 1899–1970.

Source: U.S. Forest Service, unpublished data.

These figures were derived by dividing the apparent consumption figures (series L 107–109) by total population (including Armed Forces overseas) as of July 1 of each year.

L 113–121. Lumber production, by region, 1869–1970.

Source: U.S. Forest Service, 1869–1945, *Lumber Production in the United States, 1799–1946*, Miscellaneous Publication No. 669; U.S. Bureau of the Census, 1946–1956, *Facts for Industry*, annual releases, "Lumber Production"; 1957–1970, *Current Industrial Reports*, annual releases, "Lumber Production and Mill Stocks," series MA-24T.

The States included in each region are as follows:

New England	South Atlantic
Connecticut	North Carolina
Maine	South Carolina
Massachusetts	Virginia
New Hampshire	South
Rhode Island	Alabama
Vermont	Arkansas
Middle Atlantic	Florida
Delaware	Georgia
Maryland	Louisiana
New Jersey	Mississippi
New York	Oklahoma
Pennsylvania	Texas
Lake	Rocky Mountain
Michigan	Arizona
Minnesota	Colorado
Wisconsin	Idaho
Central	Montana
Illinois	New Mexico
Indiana	South Dakota
Iowa	Utah
Kansas	Wyoming
Kentucky	West Coast
Missouri	Alaska
Nebraska	California
North Dakota	Hawaii
Ohio	Nevada
Tennessee	Oregon
West Virginia	Washington

Note: Production data for 1904–1908 and 1910–1914 are not adjusted for underreporting and therefore do not agree with the totals shown for series L 98.

L 122–137. Lumber production, by principal species, 1869–1970.

Source: See source for series L 113–121.

Production by species for the years 1904–1908, 1910–1918, and 1920–1941 are not adjusted for underreporting and, therefore, do not agree with the totals shown for L 98–100.

L 138–150. Exports and imports of logs, by major species, 1950–1970.

Source: U.S. Forest Service, *Demand and Price Situation for Forest Products, 1971–1972*, Miscellaneous Publication No. 1231, 1972, tables 13 and 15.

These data are from two reports published by the Bureau of the Census: Exports, *U.S. Exports—Commodity by Country*, FT 410, monthly and cumulative; and imports, *U.S. Imports—Commodity by Country*, FT 135, monthly and cumulative. These publications contain data on the volume and value of logs exported and imported, respectively, by major species and by country of origin and destination.

L 151–165. Plywood production, imports, exports, and consumption, by softwoods and hardwoods, 1950–1970.

Source: U.S. Forest Service, *Demand and Price Situation for Forest Products, 1971–1972*, Miscellaneous Publication No. 1231, 1972, table 31.

The basic source for these data is the Bureau of the Census in *Softwood Plywood*, Current Industrial Reports, series MA-24H, published annually since 1958; and *Softwood Plywood and Veneer*, in the *Facts for Industry* series M-24H, published annually in prior years; *Hardwood Plywood*, Current Industrial Reports series MA-24F, published annually since 1958, and in the *Facts for Industry* series

M-24F under various titles in prior years. In addition to total production, consumption of veneer and veneer logs, both domestic and imported, is shown in the reports for most recent years. Also included are data on production by State for softwood plywood and by region for hardwoods, as well as species and grade production. Data on imports and exports are from Bureau of the Census, *U.S. Imports—Commodity by Country*, FT 135, monthly and cumulative, and from *U.S. Exports—Commodity by Country*, FT 410, also monthly and cumulative. These publications contain data on the volume and value of plywood and veneer imported and exported, respectively. Data are shown by major species and by country of origin or destination.

Apparent consumption is production plus imports minus exports. Per capita consumption has been calculated by dividing apparent consumption by the total U.S. population including Armed Forces overseas.

L 166, L 169, and L 172. Domestic production of pulpwood, woodpulp, and paper and board, 1809–1970.

Source: 1809–1904, 1914, 1929, 1931, 1933, 1935, 1937–1970, U.S. Bureau of the Census, *Census of Manufactures*, various reports; various *Facts for Industry* reports, retitled *Current Industrial Reports*, series M26A; and other reports issued annually; 1905, 1916–1918, and 1920, U.S. Forest Service, unpublished data; all other years, joint reports of the Bureau of the Census and the Forest Service. The separate and joint annual releases of the Bureau of the Census and the Forest Service were issued under the general title, "Pulp, Paper, and Board."

These data are also published by the American Paper Institute, in *The Statistics of Paper*, 1960 and 1971 editions, and *Wood Pulp Statistics*, annual issues.

For nearly all years, statistics have been based upon a mail canvass of woodpulp and paper producers.

Pulpwood production figures (series L 166) were reported by the Bureau of the Census for 1869–1899 in the decennial census reports for 1870–1900. In most years since 1904, data have been published showing domestic receipts (production), imports, species, and average cost delivered at manufacturing plants. Domestic pulpwood receipts and domestic production are considered to be synonymous.

For 1946–1970, the Forest Service has published annual statistics in "Pulpwood Production in the South," which shows pulpwood production by county and by softwoods and hardwoods in Alabama, Arkansas, Florida, Georgia, Louisiana, Mississippi, North Carolina, Oklahoma, South Carolina, Tennessee, Texas, and Virginia. It has also published similar data showing pulpwood production by species in Michigan, Minnesota, and Wisconsin.

Woodpulp production figures (series L 169) were reported decennially for 1869–1889. In 1899, 1904, 1909, 1914, and annually since 1916, woodpulp production has been reported by major grades, i.e., mechanical, sulfite, soda, sulfate, and more recently semichemical, defibrated and exploded, and special alpha and dissolving grades.

Paper and board production figures (series L 172) for 1809, 1819, 1839, 1849, and 1869 are based on value data of paper production collected in the decennial censuses. Since 1870, for all years during which data were published, paper production was reported in quantity terms classified by newsprint, book paper, coarse paper, fine paper, container board, and other major grades.

In recent years the Bureau of the Census monthly report M26A (cited above) has presented data for domestic pulpwood receipts, imports, consumption, and inventories by hardwoods and softwoods and by region. The annual M26A summary presents these data by States. Figures for woodpulp production, inventories, and consumption, by grade are also shown in M26A. The same monthly report shows production data for nearly 60 grades of paper and paperboard for recent years; the annual summary over a longer period has shown production of the major grades of paper by States and total production for nearly 165 separate grades of paper and paperboard.

L 167, L 170, and L 173. Net imports of pulpwood, woodpulp, and paper and board, 1899–1970.

Source: Computed by the U.S. Forest Service from annual issues of the following U.S. Bureau of the Census publications: 1899–1946, *Foreign Commerce and Navigation of the United States*; 1947–1963, *U.S. Imports of Merchandise for Consumption* (FT 110) and *U.S. Exports of Domestic and Foreign Merchandise*; 1964–1970, *U.S. Imports—Commodity by Country* (FT 135) and *U.S. Exports—Commodity by Country* (FT 410).

Net imports represent gross imports minus gross exports.

L 168, L 171, and L 174. Apparent consumption of pulpwood, woodpulp, and paper and board, 1899–1970.

Source: U.S. Forest Service. Computed by U.S. Forest Service. See source notes for series L 166, L 169, and L 172; and L 167, L 170, and L 173.

Apparent consumption represents production plus net imports.

L 175. Waste paper consumption in paper and board, 1904–1970.

Source: American Paper Institute, Inc., New York, *Wood Pulp Statistics*, 36th and 32d editions (copyright).

L 176–177. Domestic production of turpentine and rosin, 1900–1970.

Source: U.S. Department of Agriculture. 1900–1943, Agricultural Marketing Service, *Naval Stores Statistics, 1900–1954*, and Commodity Stabilization Service, *World Trends in Supply, Distribution and Prices of Naval Stores*. 1944–1960, Statistical Reporting Service, *Agricultural Statistics, 1967*, table 805; 1961–1970, *Agricultural Statistics, 1971*, table 801. (1900–1931, figures derived from trade estimates published in *Gamble's International Naval Stores Yearbook*; 1932–1944, figures collected and published by Bureau of Agricultural and Industrial Chemistry; 1944–1970, issued by Statistical Reporting Service.)

Supplementary data showing naval stores consumption and stocks, production by type of extraction process, consumption of turpentine and rosin by type of industrial user (1922–1970), and average price and value of gum naval stores are also presented in *Naval Stores Statistics, 1900–1954*, cited above, and in *Annual Report of Naval Stores*.

Beginning with the 1948 crop year, the current AMS report, *Naval Stores Market News*, presents monthly production, stock, and export data for all naval stores except rosin oil. Information on consumption, prices, and stocks at consumption points which is not covered in the monthly or weekly report is included in the annual issue of this report.

L 178–191. Apparent consumption of paper and board, by principal grades, 1899–1970.

Source: American Paper Institute, 1899–1941, *The Statistics of Paper*, 1960 edition (copyright). U.S. Bureau of the Census, 1942–1958, *Facts for Industry*, "Pulp, Paper and Board," series M14A, annual; 1959–1970, *Current Industrial Reports*, "Pulp, Paper and Board," series M26A, annual.

Data shown are apparent consumption, i.e., production plus imports minus exports, except as noted in the footnotes. Paper and board exports are also shown in Bureau of the Census, *U.S. Exports Schedule B, Commodity and Country*, report FT 410 for December of each year. Paper and board imports are also shown in *U.S. Imports—TSUSA Commodity by Country*, annual, report FT-246.

The *Facts for Industry* and *Current Industrial Reports* series indicated above report production of paper and board by State and region each year as well as woodpulp and pulpwood consumption. Monthly production of paper and board by grade is also shown.

L 180, newsprint paper. A generic term used to describe paper generally used in the publication of newspapers. It does not include printing papers of types generally used for other purposes even though such papers may be to some extent used by newspapers.

L 181, groundwood paper. A general term applied to a variety of papers made with substantial proportions of mechanical woodpulp together with chemical wood pulps, and used mainly for printing and converting purposes.

L 182, book paper. A general term used to define a class or group of papers that are most suitable for the graphic arts, exclusive of newsprint. The physical characteristics of the paper are varied to meet the type of impress employed and the prospective use of the article produced.

L 183, fine paper. A general term including writing, bristols, cover, text, and thin papers. Most are made from chemical pulps although rag pulps are used in producing certain specialty grades, such as bond, currency, ledger, and maps.

L 184, course and industrial paper. A general term applied to various grades of paper used for industrial purposes such as bag papers, gummed types, towels, tabulating card stock, blotting paper, etc.

L 185, sanitary and tissue paper. A general term indicating a class of papers of characteristic gauzy texture. In addition to sanitary tissues they include wrapping tissue, waxing tissue, fruit and vegetable wrapping stock, etc.

L 186, construction paper. A general term applied to a class of paper used in building construction for sheathing and under flooring and may be converted to such products as roofing, sheathing, and tarred or asphalt–coated vapor barrier.

L 188, container board. A general term designating solid fiber or corrugated combined board used in the manufacture of shipping containers and related products and also the component materials used in the fabrication of corrugated board.

L 189, bending board. Includes folding boxboard used for the manufacture of collapsible or folding cartons and special food board used in the packaging of milk, frozen food, and other similar foods and as containers for hot and cold drinks.

L 190, building board. A general term describing paper boards used by the building trades. In this tabulation, both hardboard and insulating board are included.

L 192–198. Newsprint production, shipments, consumption, stocks, imports, and prices, 1935–1970.

Source: U.S. Bureau of Economic Analysis, *Survey of Current Business*, monthly issues.

L 192–193, 195, production, shipments, stocks at mills. Data are from the American Paper Institute, Newsprint Division, New York. They cover virtually the entire industry in the United States (including Alaska beginning 1961). Shipments include tonnage invoiced (whether shipped or not); stocks at mills include supplies at destination warehouses not yet invoiced to customers.

L 194, 196, consumption by publishers, stocks at and in transit to publishers. Data are from the American Newspaper Publishers Association, New York. Data for all years are as reported by publishers who, over the period covered here, accounted for over 70 percent of U.S. newsprint consumption. Beginning 1961, the consumption figures include data for Alaska and Hawaii. Stocks at and in transit to publishers are those on hand in the city of publication plus tonnage billed to the publishers by mills, but not received.

L 197, imports. Data are from the U.S. Bureau of the Census. They cover "imports for consumption" of standard newsprint paper, and are compiled from import entries filed with U.S. Customs officials. They show imports into the U.S. Customs area from foreign countries.

L 198, wholesale price. Data are from the U.S. Bureau of Labor Statistics. The prices quoted are for a ton of standard newsprint, rolls, contract, manufacturer to publisher, f.o.b. mill, freight allowed

or delivered. Beginning 1952, the prices are quotation averages for one day each month (usually in the week containing the 15th), based on data reported by various sellers (no fewer than three) of the commodity; prior to 1952, they are quotation averages for one day each week.

L 199–202. Stumpage prices for selected species, 1910–1970.

Source: U.S. Forest Service. 1910–1949, *The Demand and Price Situation for Forest Products, 1964* edition, table 5, and unpublished data; 1950–1970, *1972* edition, table 5, and unpublished data.

See also text for series L 15–23. All national-forest prices referred to are bid prices for timber sold on a Scribner Decimal-C log scale basis, except in the Northeastern States where international ¼-inch log rule is used. Prices exclude timber sold by land exchanges and from land utilization project lands.

Stumpage prices of private timber sales and log prices were compiled by major species and principal producing regions during the period 1900–1934 and published by the Department of Agriculture in Technical Bulletin No. 626, *Stumpage Prices of Privately Owned Timber in the United States*. Comparable data for 1935–1943 and 1945 were published by the same agency in Statistical Bulletin Nos. 57, 62, 66, 71, 75, 76, 78, 79, 80, and 82. Prices shown in these publications were obtained through a mail canvass of timber sellers and buyers, such as independent loggers, sawmill operators, and other wood-using industries. The unit prices reported are of variable accuracy since exact information was lacking on timber volume, quality, accessibility and other factors that determine stumpage and log prices. These data, however, constitute a comprehensive price series on private stumpage and log prices during earlier years and are considered useful in charting general trends and timber values.

Data on lumber values per thousand board feet, f.o.b. mill, are available for specified years in the Department of Agriculture Miscellaneous Publication No. 669, *Lumber Production in the United States, 1799–1946*. Data on lumber prices and price indexes have also been published by the Bureau of Labor Statistics since 1890. The publications of the Bureau of Labor Statistics vary in detail from year to year but, in general, give the average price, f.o.b. mill, or at some stated delivery point, for various species of lumber, by grade for major species. (For further detail on Bureau of Labor Statistics data, see text for series L 206–210).

Douglas-fir figures (series L 199) for 1910–1931 represent national-forest timber sales of all species in Washington and Oregon; for 1932–1941 and 1957–1970, all species in western Washington and western Oregon; and for 1944–1956, national forest and Bureau of Land Management sales, Douglas-fir only, in western Washington and western Oregon.

Southern pine figures (series L 200) for 1910–1934 are stumpage prices of privately owned second growth southern pine timber as reported in Department of Agriculture Technical Bulletin No. 626, *Stumpage Prices of Privately Owned Timber in the United States*; for 1935–1949, national-forest timber sales for all southern species (most of which, however, were southern pine); and for 1950–1970, national-forest timber sales for southern pine only.

Sugar and ponderosa pine figures (series L 201 and L 202) represents national-forest timber sales for these species in California.

L 203–204. Douglas fir log prices, 1910–1970.

Source: U.S. Forest Service. 1910–1949, *The Demand and Price Situation for Forest Products, 1964* edition, table 5; 1950–1970, *1972* edition, table 5.

For 1910–1932, data were derived from trade estimates as published in the magazine, *The Timberman*; for 1933–1962, data were derived from a compilation of average annual regional log values based on transactions shown in the Pacific Northwest Loggers Association report, *Composite Sale Analyses*; for 1963–1970, data are from the Industrial Forestry Association.

L 205.   **Douglas fir lumber prices (wholesale), 1910–1966.**

Source: U.S. Forest Service, unpublished data.

For 1910–1929, data were derived from Bureau of the Census or Forest Service reports (or both) on lumber; see text for series L 98–100. For 1930–1970, data were derived from publications of the Western Wood Products Association (formerly West Coast Lumberman's Association), which show average realization on lumber shipments f.o.b. mill.

L 206.   **Wholesale price index for lumber, 1900–1970.**

Source: For 1947–49 base, 1900–1925, U.S. Forest Service, unpublished data; 1926–1930, U.S. Bureau of Labor Statistics, unpublished data. For 1967 base, 1926–1970, U.S. Bureau of Labor Statistics, *Handbook of Labor Statistics, 1971,* p. 280.

Figures for 1900–1912 were converted to a 1947–49 base by the Forest Service from an index (1935–39 = 100) of wholesale lumber prices published in Bureau of the Census, *Raw Materials in United States Economy, 1900–1952.* Figures for 1913–1925 were similarly converted from an index (1926 = 100) published in Bureau of Labor Statistics, *Wholesale Price Indexes.*

The Bureau of Labor Statistics began publishing price data on lumber in 1890 with a series that showed wholesale prices per thousand board feet (with price indexes) for several important lumber species at designated points. In 1913, coverage was expanded and an index for all lumber was added.

L 207.   **Wholesale price index for plywood, 1947–1970.**

Source: U.S. Bureau of Labor Statistics, unpublished data.

Figures for 1936–1957 on a 1947–49 base are shown in Forest Service, *Price Trends and Relationships for Forest Products,* 1957.

L 208.   **Wholesale price index for woodpulp, 1926–1970.**

Source: See source for series L 207.

Woodpulp (sulfite domestic unbleached) figures were first published by the Bureau of Labor Statistics in 1913. In 1926, a more comprehensive series covering selected grades of woodpulp and an average wholesale price index was instituted. Between 1926 and 1970 a number of changes were made in coverage. In 1970, the Bureau of Labor Statistics coverage included wholesale prices and price indexes for five grades of woodpulp.

L 209.   **Wholesale price index for paper, 1926–1970.**

Source: See source for series L 207.

Wholesale prices and price indexes for newsprint and manila wrapping paper were first collected and published by the Bureau of

Labor Statistics in 1890. In 1926, a more comprehensive series along with an average wholesale price index covering selected grades of paper was instituted. Between 1926 and 1970 a number of minor changes were made in coverage. In 1970, the Bureau of Labor Statistics coverage included an all paper-price index, a price index for 10 grades of paper, and the average price for most of these grades.

L 210.   **Wholesale price index for paperboard, 1926–1970.**

Source: See source for series L 207.

L 211.   **Wholesale price index of lumber, 1798–1932.**

Source: *Memoir 142, Wholesale Prices for 213 Years, 1720 to 1932* (part 1), pp. 107–119, by G. F. Warren and F. A. Pearson, published by the N.Y.S. College of Agriculture and Life Sciences, a statutory unit of the State University at Cornell University.

Prior to 1915, various lumber species at different delivery points were used in constructing this index. See source for further detail. For 1915–1932, the index numbers are based on the lumber index published by the Bureau of Labor Statistics.

L 212–223.   **Average hourly earnings in timber-based industries, 1950–1970.**

Source: U.S. Bureau of Labor Statistics, *Employment and Earnings Statistics for the United States,* annual issues.

These data are derived from reports of payrolls and man-hours for production and related workers in manufacturing, and nonsupervisory employees in the remaining private nonagricultural components.

Production and related workers include working foremen and all nonsupervisory workers (including leadmen and trainees) engaged in fabricating, processing, assembling, inspection, receiving, storage, handling, packing, warehousing, shipping, maintenance, repair, janitorial and watchman services, product development, auxiliary production for plant's own use (e.g., power plant), and recordkeeping and other services closely associated with the above production operations.

Average hourly earnings are on a "gross" basis, reflecting not only changes in basic hourly and incentive wage rates but also such variable factors as premium pay for overtime and late-shift work and changes in output of workers paid on an incentive plan. Shifts in the volume of employment between relatively high-paid and low-paid work and changes in workers' earnings in individual establishments also affect the general earnings averages.

Averages of hourly earnings differ from wage rates. Earnings are the actual return to the worker for a stated period of time; rates are the amounts stipulated for a given unit of work or time.

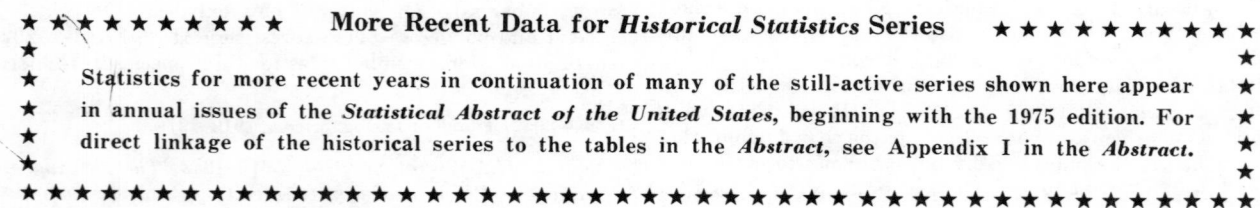

★ ★ ★ ★ ★ ★ ★ ★ ★ ★   **More Recent Data for** *Historical Statistics* **Series**   ★ ★ ★ ★ ★ ★ ★ ★ ★ ★

Statistics for more recent years in continuation of many of the still-active series shown here appear in annual issues of the *Statistical Abstract of the United States,* beginning with the 1975 edition. For direct linkage of the historical series to the tables in the *Abstract,* see Appendix I in the *Abstract.*

Series L 1–9. Forest Land—Total and Commercial Timber Area, Net Volume of Sawtimber and Net Volume of Growing Stock: 1953, 1963, and 1970

[As of January 1]

Year and region [1]	Total forest land (mil. acres)	Commercial timber land ownership (mil. acres)				Net volume of sawtimber (bil. bd. ft.)			Net volume of growing stock (bil. cu. ft.)
		All ownerships	Federally owned or managed	State, county, and municipal	Private	Total	Softwood	Hardwood	
	1	2	3	4	5	6	7	8	9
1970									
United States	754	500	107	29	364	2,420	1,905	515	649
North	186	178	12	20	146	332	80	252	156
South	212	193	14	3	175	484	276	208	160
West	355	129	81	6	42	1,605	1,549	56	334
1963									
United States	757	508	111	28	369	2,431	1,956	475	624
North	183	175	13	19	143	290	69	221	135
South	219	200	14	3	183	435	230	205	145
West	355	133	84	6	43	1,705	1,656	49	344
1953									
United States	748	495	111	28	356	2,412	1,979	433	583
North	178	170	13	19	138	246	59	187	110
South	214	192	14	3	175	391	186	205	131
West	356	133	84	6	43	1,774	1,734	40	342

[1] For composition of regions, see text for series L 113–121; North includes New England, Middle Atlantic, Lake (plus eastern South Dakota), and Central (minus Tennessee); South includes South Atlantic and South (plus Tennessee); West includes Rocky Mountain (minus eastern South Dakota) and West Coast.

Series L 10–14. National Forest System Areas and Purchases: 1905 to 1970

[Forest area data as of June 30; includes Alaska and Puerto Rico. Forest purchases for years ending June 30; includes Puerto Rico]

Year	Gross area of national forest and other lands [1]		Gross area approved for national forest purchase			Year	Gross area of national forest and other lands [1]		Gross area approved for national forest purchase		
	Within unit boundaries	Under Forest Service administration	Total area	Total price	Average price per acre		Within unit boundaries	Under Forest Service administration	Total area	Total price	Average price per acre
	10	11	12	13	14		10	11	12	13	14
	1,000 acres	1,000 acres	Acres	$1,000	Dollars		1,000 acres	1,000 acres	Acres	$1,000	Dollars
1970	226,064	186,900	92,437	11,539	124.83	1937	226,621	174,405	425,637	2,124	4.99
1969	226,045	186,632	126,341	12,353	97.77	1936	197,435	165,979	2,891,040	11,535	3.99
1968	226,502	186,921	112,767	9,413	83.47	1935	188,292	163,310	3,661,848	14,991	4.09
1967	227,721	186,799	104,507	7,037	67.34	1934	188,037	162,591	4,206,817	10,018	2.38
1966	226,519	186,497	171,947	13,307	77.39	1933	186,837	162,009	667,314	1,221	1.83
1965	226,434	186,577	28,507	1,364	47.86	1932	186,215	161,361	83,086	206	2.48
1964	225,743	186,476	40,873	1,600	39.14	1931	185,252	160,788	547,945	1,944	3.55
1963	225,584	186,316	24,698	1,795	72.69	1930	183,976	160,091	538,048	1,468	2.73
1962	225,613	186,324	22,556	964	42.74	1929	184,565	159,751	464,177	1,787	3.85
1961	226,110	186,385	10,355	236	22.75	1928	184,404	159,481	261,107	1,996	7.65
1960	226,623	185,772	7,845	114	14.76	1927	183,938	158,800	135,088	726	5.37
1959	227,359	185,805	8,716	224	25.67	1926	184,124	158,759	191,725	737	3.85
1958	231,080	188,042	10,463	722	69.40	1925	184,126	158,395	247,067	1,187	4.80
1957	231,293	188,013	17,519	416	23.74	1924	182,817	157,503	130,290	425	3.26
1956	232,118	188,117	21,376	372	17.42	1923	182,100	157,237	79,923	348	4.35
1955	235,728	188,120	18,665	192	10.30	1922	181,800	156,837	242,169	826	3.41
1954	235,694	188,138	7,761	109	14.02	1921	181,820	156,666	112,397	499	4.44
1953	229,112	181,568	7,969	99	12.46	1920	180,300	156,032	101,428	451	4.44
1952	229,165	181,293	10,181	106	10.42	1919	174,261	153,933	103,355	657	6.35
1951	229,258	181,255	25,317	265	10.46	1918	175,951	155,375	185,199	848	5.12
1950	229,341	181,205	61,078	532	8.71	1917	176,340	155,220	175,463	853	4.86
1949	229,175	180,895	60,719	464	7.65	1916	176,089	155,400	54,898	316	5.76
1948	228,936	180,528	103,490	739	7.15	1915	184,506	162,773	282,900	1,618	5.72
1947	228,810	180,264	380,471	2,190	5.76	1914	185,321	163,849	391,114	1,940	4.96
1946	228,760	179,726	------	------	------	1913	186,617	165,517	425,717	2,005	4.71
1945	228,703	179,381	5	1	194.00	1912	187,406	165,027	287,698	1,627	5.65
1944	228,643	179,101	9	1	66.02	1911	190,608	168,165	------	------	------
1943	228,633	178,508	8,759	38	4.31	1910	192,931	168,029	------	------	------
1942	228,725	178,340	243,522	1,103	4.53	1909	194,505	172,230	------	------	------
1941	228,309	177,653	195,818	805	4.11	1908	167,977	147,820	------	------	------
1940	228,174	176,779	553,077	2,203	3.98	1907	150,832	132,732	------	------	------
1939	228,784	176,494	534,138	2,275	4.26	1906	106,994	94,159	------	------	------
1938	227,280	175,238	800,113	2,713	3.39	1905	85,693	75,352	------	------	------

[1] On January 2, 1954, some 6,910,000 acres of land utilization project lands were transferred to the Forest Service for administration.

Series L 15–23. Volume and Value of Timber Cut From National Forest System Areas: 1905 to 1970

[Volume in millions of board feet; value in thousands of dollars. For years ending June 30 except as noted]

Year	Total Volume	Total Value [1]	Commercial sales [2][3] Timber Volume	Timber Value [4]	Miscellaneous forest products, value [1]	Land exchange [2] Volume	Value	Free use [5] Volume	Value [6]
	15	16	17	18	19	20	21	22	23
1970	11,706	308,638	11,527	307,610	695	--------	--------	179	333
1969	11,951	327,944	11,783	326,997	665	--------	--------	168	282
1968	12,304	240,226	12,129	239,311	622	--------	--------	175	293
1967	11,021	189,563	10,851	188,711	575	--------	--------	170	277
1966	12,319	196,427	12,138	195,590	572	--------	--------	181	265
1965	11,435	161,880	11,229	160,809	494	15	296	191	280
1964	11,140	151,880	10,911	150,711	529	43	363	186	276
1963	10,190	135,173	9,957	134,148	514	69	258	164	253
1962	9,181	129,654	8,946	128,514	522	86	392	149	226
1961	8,531	125,170	8,308	123,957	477	73	495	150	241
1960	9,490	157,094	9,302	156,132	454	65	292	123	216
1959	8,525	114,579	8,262	113,509	366	79	387	184	316
1958	6,542	94,762	6,335	93,777	346	85	411	121	228
1957	7,086	116,098	6,910	115,093	312	68	474	108	219
1956	7,011	98,107	6,813	96,865	268	94	755	104	219
1955	6,434	71,231	6,225	70,105	266	103	656	106	204
1954	5,474	65,887	5,180	64,149	255	185	1,259	109	224
1953	5,261	71,039	4,982	69,727	226	179	889	101	196
1952	4,516	59,759	4,232	58,275	193	186	1,066	98	225
1951	4,794	48,227	4,422	46,533	178	266	1,284	106	233
1950	3,623	31,140	3,195	29,084	211	307	1,630	121	215
1949	3,854	29,163	3,380	26,928	224	360	1,821	114	190
1948	3,875	21,389	3,451	19,842	145	307	1,212	116	189
1947	3,962	16,780	3,472	14,955	183	363	1,445	128	197
1946	2,868	11,811	2,470	10,494	150	260	997	138	170
1945	3,299	13,291	2,732	11,682	104	413	1,334	154	171
1944	3,514	14,517	2,840	12,416	150	493	1,739	181	213
1943	2,529	8,907	1,864	6,835	60	495	1,837	169	175
1942	2,424	6,429	1,560	4,523	79	645	1,586	219	241
1941	2,352	6,084	1,552	4,529	62	515	1,233	284	260
1940	2,066	5,168	1,371	3,825	57	369	982	326	304
1939	1,558	3,687	1,017	2,685	52	273	691	268	260
1938	1,589	3,539	1,075	2,662	52	213	547	301	279
1937	1,608	3,505	1,097	2,740	39	194	449	318	277
1936	1,314	2,892	815	2,119	30	206	471	293	272
1935	1,069	2,260	668	1,719	41	84	219	317	281
1934	923	1,845	599	1,397	26	76	213	248	210
1933	740	1,333	389	838	19	84	239	266	237
1932	882	1,767	545	1,326	21	67	193	270	227
1931	1,390	3,527	1,048	2,888	17	174	460	168	162
1930	1,769	4,930	1,488	4,340	23	165	449	116	117
1929	1,583	4,456	1,353	3,892	31	144	437	87	98
1928	1,354	3,610	1,168	3,209	12	104	299	82	90
1927	1,442	3,944	1,161	3,306	7	[7] 199	[7] 540	81	91
1926	1,281	3,477	1,193	3,371	10			88	97
1925	1,100	2,895	1,022	2,808	5	--------	--------	78	82
1924	1,233	3,203	1,144	3,095	14	--------	--------	89	94
1923	1,092	2,680	995	2,570	11	--------	--------	97	98
1922	812	1,859	723	1,752	8	--------	--------	90	99
1921	981	2,081	800	1,896	8	--------	--------	180	177
1920	893	1,887	805	1,764	10	--------	--------	88	113
1919	796	1,635	705	1,515	8	--------	--------	91	113

Year	Total Volume	Value [1]	Commercial sales, timber [3] Volume	Value	Free use Volume	Value	Year	Total Volume	Value [1]	Commercial sales, timber [3] Volume	Value	Free use Volume	Value
	15	16	17	18	22	23		15	16	17	18	22	23
1918	827	1,655	730	1,527	97	128	1911	498	1,040	375	843	123	197
1917	850	1,683	736	1,533	113	150							
1916	714	1,439	595	1,255	119	185	1910	484	1,082	380	906	105	176
							1909	458	847	352	678	105	169
1915	689	1,386	566	1,179	123	207	1908	525	964	393	794	132	169
1914	747	1,454	626	1,271	121	183	1907	195	338	195	338	--------	--------
1913	617	1,267	496	1,075	122	192	1906	139	[8] 203	139	[8] 203	--------	--------
1912	555	1,139	431	943	123	197	1905	68	[8] 86	68	[8] 86	--------	--------

[1] Includes materials not measurable in board feet, such as Christmas trees, tanbark, turpentine, seedlings, Spanish moss, etc.
[2] Land exchange included with commercial sales beginning 1966.
[3] Includes all sales for which a charge is made.
[4] Beginning 1960, includes collections for forest restoration under the Knutson-Vandenberg Act of 1930.
[5] Calendar-year data, 1922 to 1932. Figures for 1921 are for July 1, 1920, to Dec. 31, 1921. Figures for both 1932 and 1933 include data for July 1 to Dec. 1, 1932.

[6] Includes value of quantities not reducible to board feet, as follows, in dollars: 1934, 146; 1935, 870; 1937, 1,969; 1938, 3,643; 1940, 3,774; 1944, 7,304; 1945, 8,291; 1946, 8,394; 1947, 14,895; 1948, 20,968; 1949, 21,270; 1950, 20,468; 1951, 20,081; 1952, 15,477; 1953, 13,228; 1954, 23,281; 1955, 16,202; 1956, 15,501; 1957, 20,004; 1958, 19,873. For 1959–70, data not available.
[7] Includes land-exchange figures from beginning of exchange cuttings.
[8] Estimated.

Series L 24–31.   Receipts From National Forest System Lands, and Payments to States and Outlying Areas: 1905 to 1970

[In thousands of dollars.   For years ending June 30]

Year	Receipts from national forest system lands [1]				Payments to States and outlying areas [2]			
	Total receipts	Timber use	Grazing use	Other use	Total	25-percent fund [3]	Arizona and New Mexico school fund	State of Minnesota
	24	25	26	27	28	29	30	31
1970	299,703	283,907	4,371	11,425	72,239	71,897	84	258
1969	321,254	306,815	4,438	10,001	78,396	78,013	125	258
1968	218,323	205,627	4,083	8,613	52,562	52,326	90	146
1967	184,517	172,791	4,184	7,541	44,163	43,912	106	145
1966	175,616	164,940	3,861	6,816	42,190	41,942	103	145
1965	149,239	138,772	3,521	6,946	35,757	35,504	112	141
1964	137,514	127,962	3,790	5,763	33,083	32,837	108	138
1963	126,224	117,390	4,028	4,805	30,225	29,994	100	131
1962	114,174	106,160	3,806	4,207	27,440	27,235	80	125
1961	106,100	98,443	3,899	3,757	25,279	25,056	99	124
1960	148,213	140,126	4,507	3,579	35,672	35,409	140	123
1959	123,454	115,541	4,487	3,426	29,904	29,669	114	121
1958	93,461	86,473	3,711	3,276	22,370	22,205	117	48
1957	113,324	107,088	3,367	2,869	27,128	26,975	105	48
1956	116,997	110,583	3,729	2,685	28,665	28,490	129	46
1955	81,139	75,353	3,760	2,026	19,573	19,413	114	46
1954	68,993	63,146	3,930	1,917	16,543	16,394	103	46
1953	76,042	70,040	4,890	1,113	18,865	18,697	123	45
1952	71,452	65,407	5,023	1,023	17,536	17,359	132	45
1951	57,622	52,512	4,166	945	14,126	13,974	107	45
1950	34,551	30,269	3,385	896	8,479	8,363	72	44
1949	32,149	27,889	3,276	984	7,858	7,753	61	44
1948	25,013	21,243	2,898	872	6,069	6,012	57	----------
1947	18,721	15,745	2,294	682	4,596	4,547	49	----------
1946	14,168	10,802	2,060	1,306	3,463	3,424	39	----------
1945	16,302	11,813	2,159	2,330	4,039	4,003	36	----------
1944	15,879	12,872	2,459	548	4,177	4,139	38	----------
1943	10,095	7,634	1,973	488	2,503	2,476	27	----------
1942	7,177	5,100	1,595	482	1,693	1,670	23	----------
1941	6,638	4,737	1,429	471	1,556	1,533	23	----------
1940	5,863	3,943	1,463	456	1,456	1,433	23	----------
1939	4,908	2,857	1,574	477	1,216	1,192	24	----------
1938	4,671	2,518	1,696	457	1,167	1,136	31	----------
1937	4,936	2,924	1,580	431	1,243	1,215	28	----------
1936	4,063	2,203	1,441	418	1,028	996	32	----------
1935	3,289	1,729	1,151	408	838	817	21	----------
1934	3,315	1,522	1,359	434	844	821	23	----------
1933	2,626	783	1,498	345	679	651	28	----------
1932	2,294	1,049	830	415	589	568	21	----------
1931	4,993	2,608	1,961	425	1,272	1,241	31	----------
1930	6,752	4,390	1,943	419	1,719	1,678	41	----------
1929	6,300	4,109	1,740	451	1,606	1,565	41	----------
1928	5,442	3,325	1,714	403	1,387	1,351	36	----------
1927	5,167	3,253	1,531	382	1,311	1,285	26	----------
1926	5,156	3,367	1,422	367	1,300	1,286	14	----------
1925	5,000	2,940	1,725	334	1,271	1,243	28	----------
1924	5,252	3,036	1,916	300	1,347	1,302	45	----------
1923	5,336	2,722	2,341	272	1,371	1,321	50	----------
1922	3,422	1,813	1,316	292	882	846	36	----------
1921	4,152	1,770	2,132	250	1,083	1,023	60	----------
1920	4,793	2,045	2,486	263	1,253	1,180	73	----------
1919	4,358	1,535	2,609	214	1,149	1,070	79	----------
1918	3,575	1,630	1,726	219	946	876	70	----------
1917	3,457	1,640	1,550	267	911	849	62	----------
1916	2,824	1,422	1,210	192	737	696	41	----------
1915	2,481	1,183	1,130	168	649	611	38	----------
1914	2,438	1,311	1,002	124	640	599	41	----------
1913	2,392	1,271	999	122	633	587	46	----------
1912	2,109	1,028	961	120	554	518	36	----------
1911	1,969	952	928	89	515	485	30	----------
1910	2,041	1,011	970	60	511	510	1	----------
1909	1,766	702	1,023	42	442	442	----------	----------
1908	1,788	811	947	30	447	447	----------	----------
1907	1,530	654	857	19	153	153	----------	----------
1906	758	237	513	7	76	76	----------	----------
1905	73	73	----------	----------	----------	----------	----------	----------

[1] Beginning 1939, includes receipts from National Grasslands and Land Utilization Farm Tenant Act lands; beginning 1941, national-forest revested Oregon and California Railroad Grant Lands; and beginning 1948, Tongass (Alaska) Suspense Account.

[2] Payments made during years following collection of receipts.
[3] Beginning 1956, includes 25 percent of Tongass (Alaska) suspense account receipts; for all years, other 25-percent funds for Alaska are also included.

Series L 32–43. Forest Tree Distribution and Forest Management Programs: 1939 to 1970
[For years beginning July, except as noted]

Year	Forest tree distribution program [1]					Forest management program						
	Trees distributed	Area planted	Costs			Accomplishments				Expenditures		
			Total	Federal contributions	State expenditures	Woodland owners assisted	Woodland involved	Products harvested	Gross sale value	Total	Federal	State
	32	33	34	35	36	37	38	39	40	41	42	43
	1,000	1,000 acres	$1,000	$1,000	$1,000	Number	1,000 acres	1,000 bd. ft.	$1,000	$1,000	$1,000	$1,000
1970	598,762	790	5,840	165	5,675	127,828	7,937	860,950	27,398	13,443	4,363	9,080
1969	494,941	619	8,544	197	8,347	115,197	6,954	1,225,520	31,881	11,627	3,655	7,972
1968	523,986	655	10,114	203	9,911	109,835	7,184	855,336	31,429	9,486	3,130	6,356
1967	573,067	695	9,057	221	8,836	106,328	7,775	704,241	23,265	8,861	3,184	5,677
1966	572,088	693	7,989	220	7,769	107,654	6,232	517,368	22,005	8,178	3,157	5,021
1965	521,440	632	6,812	219	6,593	105,014	6,553	682,088	22,575	7,430	3,171	4,259
1964	508,651	617	6,865	216	6,649	99,074	6,165	716,950	17,442	6,839	2,730	4,109
1963	535,429	630	7,453	229	7,224	97,063	6,141	668,274	15,582	6,246	2,268	3,978
1962	587,647	691	6,543	234	6,309	101,823	5,762	588,046	13,744	5,577	2,255	3,322
1961	679,968	800	6,748	195	6,553	91,418	4,797	547,787	12,344	5,302	2,268	3,035
1960	774,159	911	7,135	194	6,941	89,254	4,613	495,325	11,776	4,317	1,363	2,954
1959	844,599	965	6,573	186	6,387	82,188	4,116	596,178	14,083	3,855	1,370	2,484
1958	945,464	1,080	6,949	658	6,291	76,546	4,146	659,850	13,254	3,744	1,353	2,391
1957	764,364	874	7,365	1,131	6,234	58,752	3,436	444,797	9,978	3,079	1,329	1,750
1956	712,272	814	5,769	820	4,949	44,494	3,086	538,958	11,896	2,369	866	1,503
1955	560,456	641	4,770	429	4,341	38,121	3,125	625,592	14,758	2,004	572	1,432
1954	496,571	568	3,929	372	3,557	34,828	2,914	549,373	11,757	1,919	534	1,386
1953	465,639	532	4,029	383	3,646	32,224	2,558	538,391	11,121	1,765	537	1,228
1952	434,982	497	3,988	386	3,602	32,474	2,828	527,419	12,590	1,717	541	1,176
1951	299,665	342	3,658	376	3,282	27,933	2,501	609,562	13,925	1,523	537	986
1950	291,875	324	3,021	377	2,644	25,352	2,558	721,938	15,942	1,435	549	886
1949	136,395	151	1,503	189	1,314	22,828	2,543	518,566	9,421	1,266	539	727
1948	102,903	114	1,406	113	1,293	17,140	1,769	437,903	7,722	923	349	574
1947	[2]77,324	85	1,178	113	1,065	14,220	1,400	503,641	7,668	820	353	467
1946	[2]42,347	47	886	117	769	13,531	1,577	502,312	7,805	794	345	450
1945	[2]43,588	48	637	113	524	12,083	1,322	452,367	6,092	685	315	369
1944	[2]37,743	41	572	114	458	8,093	831	411,330	4,476	431	200	231
1943	------	------	------	------	------	8,842	743	323,557	3,963	400	187	212
1942	------	------	------	------	------	3,242	359	75,600	1,044	213	101	112
1941	------	------	------	------	------	224	92	10,076	125	38	18	20
1940	------	------	------	------	------	165	49	2,667	31	32	15	17
1939	------	------	------	------	------					13	5	8

[1] Includes Hawaii and Puerto Rico; excludes Alaska.   [2] Calendar-year data.

Series L 44–47. Expenditures for Cooperative Forest Fire Control on Federal, State, and Private Lands: 1912 to 1970
[In thousands of dollars. Fiscal-year data. Excludes emergency funds]

Year	Expenditures				Year	Expenditures			
	Total	Federal [1]	State	Private		Total	Federal [1]	State	Private
	44	45	46	47		44	45	46	47
1970	113,549	16,440	95,293	1,816	1940	9,188	1,988	5,155	2,045
1969	100,955	14,396	85,222	1,337	1939	8,410	1,793	4,725	1,892
1968	96,070	14,357	80,464	1,249	1938	6,911	1,463	4,014	1,434
1967	90,950	12,834	76,612	1,504	1937	6,852	1,472	4,152	1,228
1966	85,858	12,803	71,812	1,243	1936	5,222	1,427	2,671	1,124
1965	76,537	12,758	62,612	1,167	1935	5,588	1,457	2,936	1,195
1964	72,411	11,589	59,751	1,071	1934	5,263	1,468	2,966	829
1963	65,828	11,632	52,586	1,610	1933	4,594	1,452	2,493	649
1962	64,314	11,675	51,194	1,445	1932	5,943	1,573	3,276	1,094
1961 *	59,813	9,384	48,511	1,918	1931	6,548	1,537	3,910	1,101
1960	56,641	9,401	45,059	2,181	1930	5,370	1,252	2,886	1,232
1959	54,385	9,401	43,071	1,913	1929	4,111	1,069	2,119	923
1958	52,238	9,410	40,918	1,910	1928	3,941	868	2,075	998
1957	45,337	9,386	33,802	2,149	1927	3,144	607	1,853	684
1956	42,393	9,485	30,637	2,271	1926	2,460	585	1,611	264
1955	39,216	8,945	28,168	2,103	1925	2,205	361	1,844	----------
1954	39,435	8,934	28,395	2,106	1924	1,837	364	1,473	----------
1953	37,716	8,946	26,460	2,310	1923	2,194	368	1,826	----------
1952	35,597	8,960	23,734	2,903	1922	2,270	373	1,897	----------
1951	33,160	8,996	21,885	2,279	1921	1,174	108	1,066	----------
1950	28,934	8,551	18,121	2,262	1920	948	87	861	----------
1949	27,875	8,572	17,201	2,102	1919	718	93	625	----------
1948	23,500	8,605	12,831	2,064	1918	658	92	566	----------
1947	19,603	7,890	9,477	2,236	1917	521	86	435	----------
1946	16,635	6,749	7,497	2,389	1916	493	85	408	----------
1945	13,673	4,998	6,562	2,113	1915	574	68	506	----------
1944	11,860	3,771	6,350	1,739	1914	493	78	415	----------
1943	8,985	2,268	5,407	1,310	1913	433	53	380	----------
1942	10,107	2,182	6,012	1,913	1912	403	53	350	----------
1941	9,278	1,979	5,087	2,212					

* Denotes first year for which figures include Alaska and Hawaii.   [1] Excludes administrative and inspection costs.

Series L 48–55.　Forest Fires and Area Burned Over: 1926 to 1970

Year	Total		Protected area				Unprotected area	
			Federal lands [1]		State and private lands		State and private lands [2]	
	Fires	Area burned over	Fires	Area burned over	Fires	Area burned over	Fires	Area burned over
	48	49	50	51	52	53	54	55
		1,000 acres		*1,000 acres*		*1,000 acres*		*1,000 acres*
1970	121,736	3,279	14,968	719	101,455	1,541	5,313	1,019
1969	113,351	6,689	10,112	4,112	97,393	1,582	5,846	995
1968	125,371	4,232	10,027	1,205	107,689	1,633	7,655	1,394
1967	125,025	4,659	11,495	342	102,267	1,926	11,263	2,390
1966	122,500	4,574	11,571	1,265	98,157	1,908	12,772	1,401
1965	113,684	2,652	9,073	146	91,495	1,206	13,116	1,300
1964	116,358	4,197	8,877	194	90,480	1,670	17,001	2,333
1963	164,183	7,121	11,493	209	134,427	3,108	18,263	3,804
1962	115,345	4,079	10,421	270	94,487	1,646	10,437	2,163
1961	98,517	3,036	14,122	303	72,247	1,125	12,148	1,608
1960	[3]103,387	[3]4,478	12,090	622	[3]77,537	[3]1,909	[4]13,760	[4]1,947
1959	104,662	4,156	[5]8,935	[5]897	77,802	1,681	17,925	1,578
1958	97,910	3,280	12,942	288	67,366	1,173	17,602	1,819
1957	83,392	3,410	6,219	188	59,483	1,099	17,690	2,123
1956	143,485	6,606	11,341	372	82,997	1,613	49,147	4,621
1955	145,180	[6]8,069	6,830	364	80,774	2,448	57,576	4,976
1954	[6]176,891	[6]8,833	8,592	176	118,681	2,787	49,614	5,830
1953	154,160	9,976	10,149	318	94,446	2,534	49,565	7,124
1952	188,277	14,187	9,634	281	118,363	6,347	60,280	7,559
1951	164,090	10,781	8,638	471	97,230	3,055	58,222	7,255
1950	[6]208,402	15,519	8,418	391	96,578	3,408	103,404	11,720
1949	193,774	15,397	9,592	317	78,649	2,320	105,533	12,760
1948	174,189	16,557	6,681	312	61,095	1,962	106,413	14,283
1947	200,799	23,226	8,928	318	71,442	2,814	120,429	20,094
1946	172,278	20,691	9,670	321	66,103	2,253	96,505	18,117
1945	124,728	17,681	8,539	445	48,176	2,456	68,013	14,780
1944	131,229	16,549	8,985	375	56,148	2,301	66,096	13,873
1943	210,326	32,333	9,892	702	78,815	3,860	121,619	27,771
1942	[6]208,218	31,854	9,940	576	75,849	3,863	122,428	27,415
1941	199,702	26,405	10,002	437	80,994	3,138	108,706	22,830
1940	195,427	25,848	14,076	482	73,527	2,934	107,824	22,432
1939	212,671	30,449	12,356	523	85,677	3,266	114,638	26,660
1938	232,229	33,815	9,873	316	76,326	2,623	146,030	30,876
1937	185,209	21,981	9,468	90	54,292	1,254	121,449	20,637
1936	226,285	43,207	11,144	425	73,709	3,792	141,432	38,990
1935	140,297	30,335	7,962	228	54,592	2,311	77,743	27,796
1934	162,663	41,821	8,064	658	61,254	3,515	93,345	37,648
1933	140,722	43,890	4,517	380	48,770	3,343	87,435	40,167
1932	166,399	42,063	4,933	419	55,567	3,234	105,899	38,410
1931	187,214	51,607	5,715	551	56,459	5,856	125,040	45,200
1930	190,980	52,266	(7)	(7)	[7]70,832	[7]5,809	120,148	46,457
1929	134,895	46,230	(7)	(7)	[7]44,076	[7]4,876	90,819	41,354
1928	175,934	43,542	(7)	(7)	[7]39,260	[7]4,111	136,674	39,431
1927	158,438	38,531	(7)	(7)	[7]35,300	[7]2,784	123,138	35,747
1926	91,793	24,316	(7)	(7)	[7]33,867	[7]4,755	57,926	19,561

[1] Includes Hawaii, beginning 1952.
[2] Includes Hawaii, beginning 1932.
[3] Includes Alaska and Hawaii beginning 1960.
[4] Includes Alaska beginning 1960.
[5] Includes Alaska beginning 1959.

[6] Includes data for unprotected Federal land:

Year	Fires	Acres burned		Year	Fires
1955	-----	281,000		1950	2
1954	4	40,000		1942	1

[7] Federal lands included in State and private lands.

Series L 56–71. Forest Product Raw Materials Production, Imports, Exports, and Consumption in Constant 1967 Dollars: 1900 to 1969

[In millions of dollars]

Year	Total				Saw logs				Pulpwood				Other forest products			
	Production	Imports	Exports	Consumption	Production	Imports	Exports	Consumption	Production	Imports	Exports	Consumption	Production	Imports	Exports	Consumption
	56	57	58	59	60	61	62	63	64	65	66	67	68	69	70	71
1969	3,210	676	309	3,577	1,731	310	56	1,985	781	286	122	945	698	80	131	647
1968	3,248	649	315	3,582	1,771	302	56	2,017	733	271	113	891	744	76	146	674
1967	3,105	573	273	3,405	1,687	252	55	1,884	693	266	99	860	725	55	119	661
1966	3,238	591	235	3,594	1,777	255	51	1,981	693	277	90	880	768	59	94	733
1965	3,236	563	210	3,589	1,785	256	46	1,995	667	253	82	838	784	54	82	756
1964	3,159	548	206	3,501	1,774	256	47	1,983	621	241	85	777	764	51	74	741
1963	3,000	536	188	3,348	1,685	261	43	1,903	575	228	73	730	740	47	72	715
1962	2,878	513	156	3,235	1,612	241	38	1,815	552	227	63	716	714	45	55	704
1961	2,803	466	155	3,114	1,557	209	38	1,728	527	215	63	679	719	42	54	707
1960	2,866	447	155	3,158	1,598	193	43	1,748	552	212	59	705	716	42	53	705
1959	3,045	458	142	3,361	1,809	200	39	1,970	501	209	42	668	735	49	61	723
1958	2,798	397	113	3,082	1,624	166	36	1,754	459	193	36	616	715	38	41	712
1957	2,829	392	123	3,098	1,605	146	40	1,711	508	207	40	675	716	39	43	712
1956	3,152	436	120	3,468	1,864	169	38	1,995	534	224	34	724	754	43	48	749
1955	3,052	438	120	3,370	1,821	176	40	1,957	470	210	38	642	761	52	42	771
1954	2,944	398	114	3,228	1,774	151	36	1,889	422	198	29	591	748	49	49	748
1953	2,964	380	83	3,261	1,797	135	31	1,901	411	201	15	597	756	44	37	763
1952	2,986	363	80	3,269	1,832	123	36	1,919	390	203	18	575	764	37	26	775
1951	3,023	392	107	3,308	1,819	125	48	1,896	393	221	19	595	811	46	40	817
1950	2,998	415	106	3,307	1,858	169	31	1,996	323	201	11	513	817	45	64	798
1949	2,736	289	84	2,941	1,576	78	33	1,621	278	183	12	449	882	28	39	871
1948	3,009	327	79	3,257	1,813	92	31	1,874	321	203	13	511	875	32	35	872
1947	2,923	288	124	3,087	1,735	64	66	1,733	298	193	16	475	890	31	42	879
1946	2,795	256	77	2,974	1,669	61	31	1,699	274	166	11	429	852	29	35	846
1945	2,493	223	54	2,662	1,377	52	21	1,408	247	142	15	374	869	29	18	880
1944	2,737	185	52	2,870	1,613	48	18	1,643	252	116	15	353	872	21	19	874
1943	2,769	185	67	2,887	1,679	42	15	1,706	223	127	18	332	867	16	34	849
1942	2,944	236	66	3,114	1,778	75	22	1,831	245	141	22	364	921	20	22	919
1941	3,056	242	97	3,201	1,789	66	34	1,821	233	141	23	351	1,034	35	40	1,029
1940	2,789	191	106	2,874	1,526	36	47	1,515	204	123	28	299	1,059	32	31	1,060
1939	2,673	200	120	2,753	1,408	35	54	1,389	161	139	11	289	1,104	26	55	1,075
1938	2,473	169	104	2,538	1,216	26	48	1,194	131	125	10	246	1,126	18	46	1,098
1937	2,676	238	147	2,767	1,420	34	71	1,383	147	173	16	304	1,109	31	60	1,080
1936	2,584	209	137	2,656	1,353	33	63	1,323	125	153	11	267	1,106	23	63	1,066
1935	2,347	172	140	2,379	1,123	21	64	1,080	109	132	11	230	1,115	19	65	1,069
1934	2,169	146	131	2,184	922	15	66	871	99	118	9	208	1,148	13	56	1,105
1933	2,114	147	134	2,127	840	18	63	795	99	111	5	205	1,175	18	66	1,127
1932	1,899	130	120	1,909	662	19	56	625	81	98	5	174	1,156	13	59	1,110
1931	2,171	162	150	2,183	978	37	83	932	99	109	6	202	1,094	16	61	1,049
1930	2,624	206	191	2,639	1,436	60	115	1,381	101	127	8	220	1,087	19	68	1,038
1929	3,059	238	240	3,057	1,896	75	156	1,815	107	133	8	232	1,056	30	76	1,010
1928	2,936	224	234	2,926	1,798	72	158	1,712	96	126	6	216	1,042	26	70	998
1927	2,981	228	222	2,987	1,824	85	151	1,758	91	117	5	203	1,066	26	66	1,026
1926	3,055	242	207	3,090	1,947	93	138	1,902	91	116	5	202	1,017	33	64	986
1925	3,121	218	192	3,147	2,009	91	128	1,972	83	101	4	180	1,029	26	60	995
1924	3,105	204	216	3,093	1,934	85	135	1,884	79	96	4	171	1,092	23	77	1,038
1923	3,195	217	188	3,224	2,009	97	121	1,985	76	94	4	166	1,110	26	63	1,073
1922	2,949	182	150	2,981	1,728	76	96	1,708	74	81	4	151	1,147	25	50	1,122
1921	2,702	110	108	2,704	1,420	42	65	1,397	62	53	4	111	1,220	15	39	1,196
1920	3,026	149	122	3,053	1,714	66	83	1,697	83	62	9	136	1,229	21	30	1,220
1919	2,990	122	124	2,988	1,690	56	73	1,673	73	48	10	111	1,227	18	41	1,204
1918	2,886	117	86	2,917	1,560	60	54	1,566	74	42	6	110	1,252	15	26	1,241
1917	3,070	120	101	3,089	1,753	60	57	1,756	77	42	6	113	1,240	18	38	1,220
1916	3,269	119	118	3,270	1,948	60	63	1,945	73	42	4	111	1,248	17	51	1,214
1915	3,101	105	114	3,092	1,811	52	64	1,799	68	39	2	105	1,222	14	48	1,188
1914	3,277	103	150	3,230	1,980	45	102	1,923	60	39	2	97	1,237	19	46	1,210
1913	3,459	95	232	3,322	2,152	47	148	2,051	59	36	2	93	1,248	12	82	1,178
1912	3,514	95	225	3,384	2,201	51	143	2,109	58	34	2	90	1,255	10	80	1,185
1911	3,445	86	214	3,317	2,103	42	133	2,012	56	32	2	86	1,286	12	79	1,219
1910	3,501	87	185	3,403	2,175	46	115	2,106	52	30	1	81	1,274	11	69	1,216
1909	3,476	81	164	3,393	2,175	48	97	2,126	53	24	2	75	1,248	9	65	1,192
1908	3,363	63	161	3,265	2,052	38	89	2,001	44	18	1	61	1,267	7	71	1,203
1907	3,569	75	198	3,446	2,249	44	111	2,182	51	24	2	73	1,269	7	85	1,191
1906	3,487	73	185	3,375	2,249	49	102	2,196	48	18	2	64	1,190	6	81	1,115
1905	3,336	60	160	3,236	2,127	39	88	2,078	42	15	1	56	1,167	6	71	1,102
1904	3,321	51	178	3,194	2,101	30	96	2,035	41	15	2	54	1,179	6	80	1,105
1903	3,250	50	168	3,132	2,029	31	93	1,967	38	13	1	50	1,183	6	74	1,115
1902	3,181	55	151	3,085	1,946	36	71	1,911	34	13	1	46	1,201	6	79	1,128
1901	3,119	46	165	3,000	1,867	29	75	1,821	32	11	2	41	1,220	6	88	1,138
1900	3,056	40	157	2,939	1,788	26	82	1,732	29	9	1	37	1,239	5	74	1,170

Series L 72–86. Production, Net Imports, and Apparent Consumption of Industrial Timber Products in Roundwood Equivalent: 1900 to 1970

[In millions of cubic feet, rounded to the nearest 5 million. Excludes fuelwood]

Year	Total Domestic production	Total Net imports	Total Apparent consumption	Lumber Domestic production	Lumber Net imports	Lumber Apparent consumption	Plywood and veneer Domestic production	Plywood and veneer Net imports	Plywood and veneer Apparent consumption	Pulp products Domestic production	Pulp products Net imports	Pulp products Apparent consumption	Miscellaneous products apparent consumption	Logs Imports	Logs Exports
	72	73	74	75	76	77	78	79	80	81	82	83	84	85	86
1970	11,115	1,065	12,180	5,355	755	6,110	1,065	155	1,220	3,835	565	4,405	425	25	430
1969	11,000	1,375	12,370	5,535	800	6,340	1,050	160	1,205	3,585	770	4,355	455	15	375
1968	11,025	1,275	12,305	5,630	780	6,405	1,120	155	1,275	3,385	735	4,120	485	15	405
1967	10,410	1,205	11,615	5,360	625	5,985	1,030	100	1,130	3,190	780	3,970	515	15	310
1966	10,645	1,430	12,075	5,645	650	6,295	1,030	110	1,140	3,190	870	4,060	565	15	220
1965	10,540	1,385	11,930	5,670	670	6,340	1,030	95	1,125	3,095	795	3,890	560	10	190
1964	10,170	1,315	11,485	5,635	665	6,300	960	85	1,045	2,865	725	3,585	540	10	170
1963	9,560	1,360	10,920	5,355	695	6,050	870	75	950	2,670	720	3,390	515	15	150
1962	9,035	1,415	10,450	5,120	640	5,765	800	75	875	2,565	760	3,330	465	20	85
1961	8,745	1,250	9,995	4,945	545	5,485	765	60	825	2,475	705	3,175	490	20	75
1960	8,920	1,220	10,145	5,080	475	5,560	705	60	765	2,575	710	3,290	510	20	45
1959	9,390	1,345	10,735	5,745	515	6,260	720	70	790	2,355	775	3,130	535	20	35
1958	8,530	1,185	9,715	5,160	415	5,575	615	50	665	2,165	730	2,895	560	15	30
1957	8,615	1,155	9,770	5,100	330	5,435	560	45	605	2,350	775	3,125	580	25	25
1956	9,620	1,330	10,950	5,920	410	6,330	590	45	630	2,475	880	3,355	605	30	30
1955	9,225	1,270	10,495	5,785	430	6,215	575	40	615	2,200	795	3,000	630	35	25
1954	8,755	1,190	9,945	5,635	370	6,000	480	30	505	1,960	785	2,745	655	35	25
1953	8,790	1,230	10,020	5,710	330	6,040	475	15	490	1,910	865	2,775	675	40	20
1952	8,775	1,160	9,935	5,820	270	6,095	435	10	440	1,810	860	2,665	700	30	10
1951	8,740	1,205	9,950	5,780	235	6,020	390	10	400	1,825	935	2,765	730	35	15
1950	8,525	1,380	9,910	5,905	455	6,360	345	5	350	1,500	885	2,385	770	45	10
1949	7,355	935	8,290	5,000	140	5,145	320	(Z)	320	1,275	775	2,050	745	30	10
1948	8,375	1,090	9,465	5,750	190	5,940	290	(Z)	295	1,470	865	2,335	850	45	10
1947	8,090	815	8,905	5,500	[1]5	5,495	275	[1]5	265	1,370	805	2,175	940	30	10
1946	7,705	810	8,515	5,295	90	5,390	255	[1]5	250	1,260	700	1,960	890	25	(Z)
1945	6,605	685	7,290	4,365	100	4,465	250	[1]10	240	1,140	575	1,715	845	25	5
1944	7,455	555	8,010	5,115	100	5,215	270	[1]10	260	1,160	445	1,605	905	25	5
1943	7,560	565	8,125	5,325	85	5,410	280	[1]15	265	1,030	480	1,510	920	20	5
1942	8,085	705	8,790	5,645	170	5,815	305	[1]5	300	1,130	515	1,645	1,000	30	5
1941	8,055	650	8,705	5,680	105	5,785	265	5	260	1,075	500	1,575	1,030	55	5
1940	6,990	420	7,410	4,845	[1]35	4,810	235	5	230	930	440	1,370	965	35	10
1939	6,370	535	6,905	4,470	[1]60	4,410	210	(Z)	210	725	595	1,320	965	------	------
1938	5,570	470	6,040	3,860	[1]70	3,790	195	(Z)	195	595	540	1,135	920	------	------
1937	6,360	610	6,980	4,505	[1]115	4,390	195	[1]5	195	640	730	1,375	1,020	------	------
1936	5,990	560	6,540	4,295	[1]95	4,195	165	[1]5	160	555	660	1,210	975	------	------
1935	5,090	420	5,515	3,565	[1]135	3,630	145	[1]5	140	485	560	1,050	895	------	------
1934	4,340	355	4,695	2,925	[1]165	2,760	130	[1]5	125	430	525	955	855	------	------
1933	4,040	345	4,385	2,665	[1]145	2,520	125	[1]5	120	415	495	910	835	------	------
1932	3,400	305	3,705	2,100	[1]120	1,980	120	(Z)	115	350	425	780	830	------	------
1931	4,600	335	4,945	3,105	[1]150	2,960	125	[1]5	120	400	490	895	970	------	------
1930	6,305	400	6,705	4,560	[1]175	4,385	155	[1]5	150	395	580	975	1,195	------	------
1929	8,045	330	8,375	6,020	[1]255	5,765	200	[1]5	195	445	590	1,035	1,380	------	------
1928	7,670	290	7,960	5,710	[1]275	5,435	175	[1]5	175	400	570	965	1,385	------	------
1927	7,780	340	8,115	5,790	[1]205	5,585	175	(Z)	170	380	545	925	1,435	------	------
1926	8,215	375	8,595	6,180	[1]145	6,035	145	---------	145	400	520	925	1,490	------	------
1925	8,350	360	8,710	6,375	[1]120	6,255	135	---------	135	345	480	825	1,495	------	------
1924	8,250	285	8,530	6,140	[1]155	5,980	115	---------	115	340	440	780	1,655	------	------
1923	8,535	345	8,880	6,375	[1]75	6,295	115	---------	115	340	420	765	1,705	------	------
1922	7,605	290	7,895	5,480	[1]60	5,420	90	---------	90	340	350	690	1,695	------	------
1921	6,560	165	6,730	4,505	[1]80	4,430	75	---------	75	260	245	505	1,720	------	------
1920	7,770	205	7,975	5,440	[1]55	5,380	80	---------	80	360	260	625	1,890	------	------
1919	7,725	125	7,850	5,370	[1]55	5,315	105	---------	105	330	180	510	1,915	------	------
1918	7,310	180	7,490	4,955	20	4,975	95	---------	95	335	160	500	1,920	------	------
1917	7,940	170	8,110	5,570	5	5,575	90	---------	90	345	165	515	1,930	------	------
1916	8,530	165	8,695	6,185	[1]10	6,175	90	---------	90	325	175	500	1,930	------	------
1915	8,020	[1]135	8,150	5,750	[1]35	5,715	85	---------	85	300	170	465	1,885	------	------
1914	8,565	[1]15	8,550	6,290	[1]185	6,110	85	---------	85	265	170	435	1,925	------	------
1913	9,170	[1]165	9,005	6,835	[1]320	6,510	80	---------	80	260	155	415	1,995	------	------
1912	9,330	[1]145	9,185	6,990	[1]295	6,695	80	---------	80	250	150	395	2,015	------	------
1911	9,020	[1]150	8,870	6,680	[1]290	6,385	80	---------	80	240	140	380	2,020	------	------
1910	9,295	[1]80	9,215	6,910	[1]215	6,695	90	---------	90	220	135	355	2,075	------	------
1909	9,275	[1]50	9,225	6,910	[1]155	6,760	80	---------	80	230	105	335	2,050	------	------
1908	8,725	[1]80	8,645	6,520	[1]160	6,360	70	---------	70	205	80	285	1,930	------	------
1907	9,555	[1]115	9,440	7,145	[1]215	6,930	65	---------	65	235	100	335	2,110	------	------
1906	9,225	[1]95	9,130	7,145	[1]170	6,975	60	---------	60	225	75	300	1,800	------	------
1905	8,625	[1]90	8,535	6,755	[1]155	6,600	35	---------	35	195	65	260	1,640	------	------
1904	8,490	[1]150	8,340	6,675	[1]205	6,470	20	---------	20	190	60	250	1,600	------	------
1903	8,215	[1]140	8,075	6,445	[1]195	6,255	15	---------	15	175	55	230	1,575	------	------
1902	7,880	[1]60	7,820	6,180	[1]110	6,070	10	---------	10	160	50	210	1,525	------	------
1901	7,580	[1]110	7,470	5,930	[1]150	5,780	5	---------	5	150	40	190	1,490	------	------
1900	7,285	[1]140	7,140	5,680	[1]175	5,505	5	---------	5	135	35	170	1,460	------	------

Z Less than 2.5 million cubic feet.

[1] Net exports.

Series L 87–97. Per Capita Consumption of Timber Products, by Major Product: 1900 to 1970

Year	All products	Industrial roundwood used for—								Fuelwood	
		Total	Lumber		Plywood and veneer		Pulp products		Miscellaneous products [1]		
	87	88	89	90	91	92	93	94	95	96	97
	Cubic feet	Cubic feet	Cubic feet	Board feet (lumber tally)	Cubic feet	Board feet (local log rule)	Cubic feet	Cords	Cubic feet	Cubic feet	Cords
1970	62.1	59.5	29.8	193	6.0	36.4	21.5	0.3	2.1	2.6	(Z)
1969	64.1	61.0	31.3	202	6.0	36.2	21.5	.3	2.2	3.1	(Z)
1968	64.8	61.3	31.9	207	6.4	38.6	20.5	.3	2.4	3.5	(Z)
1967	62.4	58.5	30.1	195	5.7	34.4	20.0	.3	2.6	3.9	0.1
1966	65.8	61.5	32.0	207	5.8	35.1	20.7	.3	2.9	4.3	.1
1965	66.1	61.4	32.7	212	5.8	34.9	20.0	.3	2.9	4.7	.1
1964	65.0	59.9	32.9	213	5.5	32.9	18.7	.2	2.8	5.1	.1
1963	63.3	57.7	32.0	207	5.0	30.3	17.9	.2	2.7	5.6	.1
1962	62.0	56.0	30.9	200	4.7	28.2	17.8	.2	2.5	6.0	.1
1961	61.0	54.4	29.9	193	4.5	26.9	17.3	.2	2.7	6.6	.1
1960	63.3	56.1	30.8	199	4.2	25.4	18.2	.2	2.8	7.2	.1
1959	68.2	60.4	35.2	228	4.4	26.6	17.6	.2	3.0	7.8	.1
1958	64.0	55.5	31.9	206	3.8	22.7	16.5	.2	3.2	8.5	.1
1957	65.9	56.8	31.6	204	3.5	20.8	18.2	.2	3.4	9.1	.1
1956	74.6	64.8	37.5	242	3.7	22.1	19.9	.3	3.6	9.8	.1
1955	73.8	63.3	37.5	242	3.7	21.9	18.1	.2	3.8	10.5	.1
1954	72.3	61.0	36.8	237	3.1	18.3	16.8	.2	4.0	11.3	.2
1953	74.5	62.6	37.7	243	3.1	18.1	17.3	.2	4.2	12.0	.2
1952	75.8	63.0	38.7	249	2.8	16.3	16.9	.2	4.4	12.7	.2
1951	78.6	64.2	38.9	250	2.6	14.9	17.8	.2	4.7	14.4	.2
1950	80.0	65.1	41.8	269	2.3	13.5	15.6	.2	5.1	14.9	.2
1949	74.6	55.7	34.5	221	2.1	12.6	14.1	.2	5.0	18.9	.3
1948	81.9	63.7	40.5	260	2.0	11.8	15.3	.2	5.8	18.2	.2
1947	79.8	61.2	38.1	244	1.8	10.6	14.7	.2	6.5	18.6	.2
1946	78.4	59.4	38.1	244	1.8	10.4	13.3	.2	6.3	18.9	.3
1945	73.2	51.9	31.9	205	1.7	9.7	12.3	.2	6.0	21.3	.3
1944	78.6	57.6	37.7	242	1.9	10.6	11.5	.2	6.5	21.1	.3
1943	79.9	59.5	39.6	254	1.9	11.1	11.3	.1	6.7	20.4	.3
1942	86.3	65.1	43.1	276	2.2	12.6	12.3	.2	7.4	21.2	.3
1941	91.9	65.0	43.4	279	1.9	11.5	11.9	.2	7.7	26.9	.4
1940	85.3	55.8	36.4	234	1.7	10.2	10.4	.1	7.3	29.4	.4
1939	84.8	52.8	33.7	217	1.6	9.1	10.1	.1	7.4	32.0	.4
1938	79.8	46.5	29.2	188	1.5	8.9	8.7	.1	7.1	33.3	.4
1937	85.8	54.2	34.1	219	1.5	8.5	10.7	.1	7.9	31.6	.4
1936	84.3	51.1	32.7	211	1.2	7.4	9.4	.1	7.6	33.3	.4
1935	78.8	43.4	27.0	173	1.1	6.3	8.3	.1	7.0	35.5	.5
1934	75.3	37.1	21.8	141	1.0	5.8	7.6	.1	6.8	38.2	.5
1933	74.8	34.9	20.1	130	1.0	5.4	7.2	.1	6.6	39.8	.5
1932	69.6	29.7	15.9	102	.9	5.5	6.3	.1	6.7	39.9	.5
1931	75.3	39.9	23.9	153	1.0	5.5	7.2	.1	7.8	35.4	.5
1930	85.3	54.5	35.6	229	1.2	7.2	7.9	.1	9.7	30.8	.4
1929	94.8	68.8	47.3	305	1.6	9.0	8.5	.1	11.3	26.0	.3
1928	92.8	66.1	45.1	290	1.5	8.5	8.0	.1	11.5	26.8	.4
1927	95.1	68.2	46.9	302	1.4	8.0	7.8	.1	12.1	26.9	.4
1926	99.3	73.2	51.4	330	1.2	7.2	7.9	.1	12.7	26.1	.3
1925	103.1	75.2	54.0	347	1.2	6.3	7.1	.1	12.9	27.8	.4
1924	104.4	74.7	52.4	337	1.0	6.0	6.8	.1	14.5	29.6	.4
1923	109.5	79.4	56.3	362	1.0	5.8	6.8	.1	15.2	30.2	.4
1922	105.9	71.7	49.2	317	.8	4.7	6.3	.1	15.4	34.2	.5
1921	101.4	62.0	40.8	263	.7	3.7	4.7	.1	15.9	39.4	.5
1920	113.1	74.9	50.5	325	.8	4.6	5.9	.1	17.7	38.2	.5
1919	113.5	74.7	50.6	325	1.0	5.5	4.9	.1	18.2	38.8	.5
1918	112.7	71.7	47.6	306	.9	5.4	4.8	.1	18.4	41.1	.5
1917	117.5	78.4	53.9	347	.9	5.2	5.0	.1	18.7	39.1	.5
1916	124.1	85.3	60.6	390	.9	5.2	4.9	.1	18.9	38.8	.5
1915	120.6	81.1	56.9	366	.8	5.1	4.6	.1	18.8	39.6	.5
1914	126.4	86.3	61.7	397	.9	5.0	4.4	.1	19.4	40.1	.5
1913	131.5	92.6	67.0	431	.8	4.9	4.3	.1	20.5	38.9	.5
1912	135.8	96.4	70.3	452	.8	4.8	4.1	.1	21.1	39.5	.5
1911	137.4	94.5	68.0	438	.9	4.7	4.0	.1	21.5	43.0	.6
1910	142.0	99.7	72.5	468	1.0	5.2	3.8	(Z)	22.5	42.3	.5
1909	144.2	101.9	74.7	481	.9	4.8	3.7	(Z)	22.7	42.3	.6
1908	142.3	97.5	71.7	462	.8	4.3	3.2	(Z)	21.8	44.8	.6
1907	152.5	108.5	79.7	513	.7	4.0	3.9	.1	24.3	44.0	.6
1906	152.6	106.9	81.7	526	.7	3.9	3.5	(Z)	21.1	45.7	.6
1905	150.2	101.8	78.8	507	.4	2.2	3.1	(Z)	19.6	48.3	.6
1904	152.6	101.5	78.7	507	.2	1.6	3.0	(Z)	19.5	51.1	.7
1903	154.2	100.2	77.6	----------	.2	1.1	2.9	(Z)	19.5	54.0	.7
1902	155.6	98.7	76.6	----------	.1	.8	2.7	(Z)	19.3	56.8	.8
1901	156.2	96.3	74.5	----------	.1	.5	2.4	(Z)	19.2	59.9	.8
1900	156.9	93.8	72.3	----------	.1	.4	2.2	(Z)	19.2	63.1	.8

Z Less than .05 cords.

[1] Includes cooperage logs, poles and piling, fenceposts, hewn ties, round mine timbers, box bolts, excelsior bolts, chemical wood, shingle bolts, and miscellaneous items.

Series L 98–112. Lumber Production, Imports, Exports, and Consumption, by Softwoods and Hardwoods: 1799 to 1970

[In billions of board feet, except per capita consumption in board feet]

Year	Domestic production			Imports			Exports			Apparent consumption			Per capita consumption		
	Total	Soft-woods	Hard-woods	Total	Soft-woods [1]	Hard-woods	Total	Soft-woods [1]	Hard-woods	Total	Soft-woods	Hard-woods	Total	Soft-woods	Hard-woods
	98	99	100	101	102	103	104	105	106	107	108	109	110	111	112
1970	34.7	27.5	7.1	6.1	5.8	0.3	1.3	1.2	0.1	39.5	32.1	7.3	193	157	36
1969	35.8	28.3	7.5	6.3	5.9	.4	1.1	1.0	.1	41.0	33.2	7.8	202	164	39
1968	36.5	29.3	7.2	6.2	5.8	.3	1.2	1.0	.1	41.5	34.0	7.4	207	170	37
1967	34.7	27.3	7.4	5.1	4.8	.3	1.1	1.0	.2	38.8	31.1	7.6	195	157	38
1966	36.6	28.8	7.7	5.2	4.8	.4	1.0	.9	.2	40.8	32.8	8.0	207	167	41
1965	36.8	29.3	7.5	5.2	4.9	.3	.9	.8	.1	41.1	33.4	7.7	212	172	39
1964	36.6	29.3	7.3	5.2	4.9	.3	1.0	.8	.1	40.8	33.4	7.4	213	174	39
1963	34.7	27.6	7.2	5.3	5.0	.3	.9	.7	.1	39.2	31.8	7.3	207	166	39
1962	33.2	26.8	6.4	4.9	4.6	.3	.8	.6	.1	37.3	30.8	6.5	200	165	35
1961	32.0	26.1	6.0	4.3	4.0	.2	.8	.6	.2	35.5	29.5	6.0	193	160	33
1960	32.9	26.7	6.3	3.9	3.6	.3	.9	.7	.2	36.0	29.6	6.4	199	164	35
1959	37.2	30.5	6.7	4.1	3.8	.3	.8	.6	.2	40.5	33.7	6.8	228	189	38
1958	33.4	27.4	6.0	3.4	3.2	.2	.7	.6	.2	36.1	30.0	6.1	206	171	35
1957	32.9	27.1	5.8	3.0	2.7	.2	.8	.6	.2	35.0	29.2	5.8	204	170	34
1956	38.2	30.2	8.0	3.4	3.2	.3	.8	.6	.2	40.9	32.8	8.1	242	194	48
1955	37.4	29.8	7.6	3.6	3.3	.3	.8	.7	.2	40.1	32.5	7.6	242	196	46
1954	36.4	29.3	7.1	3.1	2.9	.2	.7	.6	.1	38.7	31.5	7.1	237	194	44
1953	36.7	29.6	7.2	2.8	2.5	.2	.6	.5	.1	38.9	31.6	7.3	243	197	45
1952	37.5	30.2	7.2	2.5	2.3	.2	.7	.6	.2	39.2	31.9	7.3	249	203	46
1951	37.2	29.5	7.7	2.5	2.3	.3	1.0	.9	.1	38.7	30.9	7.8	250	199	51
1950	38.0	30.6	7.4	3.4	3.1	.3	.5	.4	.1	40.9	33.4	7.5	269	219	50
1949	32.2	26.5	5.7	1.6	1.4	.1	.7	.5	.1	33.1	27.4	5.7	221	184	38
1948	37.0	29.6	7.4	1.9	1.7	.2	.6	.6	.1	38.2	30.7	7.5	260	210	51
1947	35.4	27.9	7.5	1.3	1.1	.2	1.4	1.2	.2	35.4	27.9	7.5	244	194	51
1946	34.1	25.9	8.3	1.2	1.0	.2	.6	.6	.1	34.7	26.3	8.4	244	187	59
1945	28.1	21.1	7.0	1.1	.9	.2	.4	.3	.1	28.8	21.7	7.0	205	155	51
1944	32.9	25.2	7.8	1.0	.8	.1	.4	.3	.1	33.6	25.7	7.8	242	186	57
1943	34.3	26.9	7.4	.9	.7	.1	.3	.2	.1	34.8	27.4	7.4	254	200	54
1942	36.3	29.5	6.8	1.5	1.4	.1	.5	.4	.1	37.4	30.6	6.8	276	226	50
1941	36.5	29.9	6.7	1.4	1.2	.2	.7	.5	.1	37.2	30.5	6.7	278	228	51
1940	31.2	25.6	5.5	.7	.6	.1	1.0	.8	.2	31.0	25.4	5.5	234	193	41
1939	28.8	23.3	5.5	.7	.6	.1	1.1	.8	.3	28.4	23.1	5.3	217	176	41
1938	24.8	20.0	4.9	.5	.5	.1	1.0	.7	.3	24.4	19.7	4.7	188	151	36
1937	29.0	23.1	5.9	.7	.6	.1	1.4	1.1	.4	28.2	22.6	5.6	219	176	43
1936	27.6	22.0	5.6	.7	.6	.1	1.3	.9	.3	27.0	21.6	5.4	211	169	42
1935	22.9	18.2	4.7	.4	.4	.1	1.3	1.0	.3	22.1	17.6	4.5	173	138	35
1934	18.8	14.6	4.2	.3	.3	.1	1.3	1.1	.3	17.8	13.8	3.9	141	109	31
1933	17.2	13.8	3.4	.4	.3	(Z)	1.3	1.0	.3	16.2	13.1	3.1	130	104	25
1932	13.5	10.8	2.7	.4	.4	(Z)	1.2	.9	.2	12.7	10.3	2.5	102	83	19
1931	20.0	15.9	4.1	.7	.7	(Z)	1.7	1.4	.3	19.0	15.2	3.8	153	123	31
1930	29.4	23.2	6.1	1.2	1.2	(Z)	2.4	1.9	.4	28.2	22.5	5.8	229	183	46
1929	38.7	30.8	7.9	1.5	1.4	.1	3.2	2.7	.5	37.1	29.5	7.6	305	242	62
1928	36.8	29.9	6.9	1.5	1.4	.1	3.2	2.8	.5	35.0	28.5	6.5	290	237	54
1927	37.3	30.0	7.3	1.7	1.6	.1	3.1	2.6	.4	35.9	29.0	7.0	302	244	59
1926	39.8	32.1	7.7	1.9	1.8	.1	2.8	2.5	.4	38.8	31.4	7.4	330	268	63
1925	41.0	33.3	7.7	1.8	1.7	.1	2.6	2.2	.4	40.2	32.8	7.5	347	283	64
1924	39.5	31.5	8.0	1.7	1.7	.1	2.7	2.4	.3	38.5	30.8	7.7	337	269	68
1923	41.0	33.2	7.8	2.0	1.9	.1	2.5	2.2	.3	40.5	32.9	7.6	362	294	68
1922	35.2	28.9	6.3	1.6	1.5	(Z)	2.0	1.7	.3	34.9	28.8	6.1	317	261	55
1921	29.0	23.4	5.6	.8	.8	(Z)	1.3	1.2	.1	28.5	23.0	5.5	263	212	51
1920	35.0	27.6	7.4	1.4	1.3	(Z)	1.7	1.5	.2	34.6	27.4	7.2	325	257	68
1919	34.5	27.4	7.1	1.1	1.1	--------	1.5	1.1	.4	34.2	27.4	6.7	325	261	64
1918	31.9	25.7	6.2	1.2	1.2	--------	1.1	.9	.2	32.0	26.0	6.0	306	249	57

Year	Domestic production			Imports	Exports			Apparent consumption	Per capita consumption	Year	Domestic production		
	Total	Softwoods	Hardwoods	Total	Total	Softwoods [1]	Hardwoods				Total	Softwoods	Hardwoods
	98	99	100	101	104	105	106	107	110		98	99	100
1917	35.8	29.2	6.6	1.2	1.1	1.0	0.1	35.9	347	1889	27.0	20.0	7.0
1916	39.8	31.3	8.5	1.2	1.3	1.2	.1	39.7	390	1879	18.1	13.3	4.8
1915	37.0	29.5	7.5	1.1	1.3	1.1	.2	36.8	366	1869	12.8	9.3	3.5
1914	40.5	31.5	9.0	.9	2.1	1.9	.2	39.3	397	1859	8.0	5.8	2.2
1913	44.0	34.1	10.0	1.0	3.0	2.6	.4	41.9	431	1849	5.4	4.1	1.3
1912	45.0	34.7	10.3	1.0	2.9	2.5	.4	43.1	452	1839	1.6	1.3	.3
1911	43.0	33.0	10.0	.8	2.7	2.5	.2	41.1	438	1829	.8	.7	.1
1910	44.5	34.0	10.5	1.0	2.3	--------	--------	43.2	468	1819	.6	.5	.1
1909	44.5	33.9	10.6	1.0	2.0	--------	--------	43.5	481	1809	.4	.3	.1
1908	42.0	31.9	10.1	.8	1.8	--------	--------	41.0	462	1799	.4	.3	--------
1907	46.0	34.9	11.1	.9	2.3	--------	--------	44.6	513				
1906	46.0	34.9	11.0	1.0	2.1	--------	--------	44.9	526				
1905	43.5	33.0	10.5	.8	1.8	--------	--------	42.5	507				
1904	43.0	32.5	10.5	.6	2.0	--------	--------	41.7	507				
1903	(NA)	(NA)	(NA)	.6	1.9	--------	--------	(NA)	(NA)				
1902	(NA)	(NA)	(NA)	.7	1.4	--------	--------	(NA)	(NA)				
1901	(NA)	(NA)	(NA)	.6	1.5	--------	--------	(NA)	(NA)				
1900	(NA)	(NA)	(NA)	.5	1.7	--------	--------	(NA)	(NA)				
1899	35.1	26.2	8.9	.7	1.5	--------	--------	34.3	458				

NA Not available.   Z Less than 50 million board feet.   [1] Includes small volumes of mixed species (not classified as hardwoods or softwoods).

Series L 113–121. Lumber Production, by Region: 1869 to 1970

[In millions of board feet. For composition of regions, see text]

Year	Total	New England	Middle Atlantic	Lake	Central	South Atlantic	South	Rocky Mountain [1][2]	West Coast [2]
	113	114	115	116	117	118	119	120	121
1970	34,668	749	938	3,293		3,184	7,081	4,158	15,265
1969	35,824	750	1,059	3,437		3,103	7,398	4,406	15,671
1968	36,473	665	1,043	3,364		3,107	7,004	4,566	16,724
1967	34,741	654	1,013	3,367		3,112	6,790	4,192	15,613
1966	36,584	684	1,051	3,426		3,216	6,997	4,186	17,024
1965	36,762	656	1,019	3,325		3,155	7,010	4,143	17,454
1964	36,559	678	1,017	3,265		3,135	6,720	4,068	17,676
1963	34,706	609	1,054	3,114		3,197	6,417	3,758	16,557
1962	33,174	672	876	2,885		2,905	5,956	3,584	16,296
1961	*32,019	687	836	2,785		2,875	5,650	3,410	*15,776
1960	32,926	759	847	3,003		2,894	5,783	3,349	16,291
1959	37,166	776	990	3,116		3,471	6,798	3,990	18,025
1958	33,385	679	1,012	712	2,133	3,166	5,981	3,381	16,321
1957	32,901	980	(NA)	(NA)	2,966	3,599	(NA)	3,120	15,440
1956	38,199	1,074	(NA)	(NA)	(NA)	3,944	(NA)	3,587	16,876
1955	37,380	1,035	(NA)	3,251		3,857	(NA)	3,085	17,618
1954	36,356	991	1,154	865	2,277	3,775	7,314	2,960	17,020
1953	36,742	2,334		1,115	2,111	3,858	7,416	2,624	17,284
1952	37,462	2,244		1,279	2,033	3,886	8,300	2,498	17,222
1951	37,204	2,368		963	2,190	4,363	8,429	2,265	16,626
1950	38,007	1,073	1,030	1,065	2,396	4,502	9,383	2,449	16,108
1949	32,176	949	951	864	2,009	3,568	7,358	2,038	14,439
1948	37,000	(NA)	(NA)	(NA)	(NA)	(NA)	(NA)	2,366	15,472
1947	35,404	1,141	1,183	1,310	2,460	3,577	9,397	2,120	14,216
1946	34,112	1,147	1,016	1,117	2,567	3,832	10,033	1,969	12,432
1945	28,122	967	917	923	2,321	2,936	7,940	1,596	10,522
1944	32,938	1,087	986	1,228	2,875	3,560	8,207	1,854	13,141
1943	34,289	939	902	994	2,851	3,679	9,896	1,783	13,244
1942	36,332	1,035	860	1,247	2,690	3,989	10,886	1,841	13,786
1941	36,538	1,087	934	1,226	2,935	4,118	10,566	1,754	13,918
1940	31,159	930	798	1,015	2,507	3,285	9,393	1,533	11,698
1939	28,755	1,064	811	954	2,460	3,006	8,389	1,378	10,693
1938	24,825	805	715	880	1,910	3,040	7,645	1,229	8,601
1937	29,004	873	795	1,150	2,190	2,980	8,555	1,621	10,840
1936	27,626	848	750	1,110	2,155	2,760	8,265	1,441	10,297
1935	22,944	772	647	970	1,870	2,460	7,085	1,186	7,953
1934	18,826	721	591	740	1,710	2,150	5,540	916	6,459
1933	17,151	526	489	500	1,280	2,110	5,395	704	6,147
1932	13,524	499	473	430	1,100	1,760	4,125	572	4,565
1931	19,997	609	605	910	1,510	2,110	5,860	900	7,494
1930	29,358	836	720	1,500	2,030	2,800	9,280	1,522	10,670
1929	38,745	887	850	1,900	2,720	3,360	12,975	1,904	14,149
1928	36,750	765	497	1,859	2,454	3,166	12,448	1,844	13,717
1927	37,250	722	585	1,862	2,678	3,251	12,876	1,795	13,482
1926	39,750	834	675	2,127	2,885	3,476	13,739	1,725	14,289
1925	41,000	907	717	2,524	2,777	3,523	15,212	1,971	13,368
1924	39,500	1,050	773	2,447	3,066	3,635	14,748	1,758	12,024
1923	41,000	1,090	854	2,507	3,095	3,992	14,767	1,868	12,825
1922	35,250	959	836	2,052	2,729	3,417	13,169	1,474	10,613
1921	29,000	1,133	864	1,839	2,172	2,784	12,015	979	7,215
1920	35,000	1,206	1,105	2,414	3,044	3,218	11,914	1,744	10,355
1919	34,552	1,418	1,166	2,692	3,038	3,374	12,704	1,342	8,818
1918	31,890	1,412	962	3,220	2,513	2,640	11,135	1,419	8,590
1917	35,831	1,462	1,026	3,525	2,683	3,265	13,900	1,400	8,571
1916	39,807	1,823	1,292	4,050	3,336	4,292	15,325	1,553	8,136
1915	37,012	2,115	1,660	3,410	3,705	4,390	13,590	1,372	6,770
1914	37,346	1,966	1,587	3,918	3,634	4,417	13,384	1,359	7,082
1913	38,387	1,672	1,425	3,866	3,953	3,983	14,329	1,266	7,892
1912	39,158	1,981	1,732	4,424	4,387	4,580	13,538	1,277	7,239
1911	37,003	1,863	1,771	4,714	4,298	3,743	12,222	1,304	7,087
1910	40,018	1,969	1,985	5,030	4,752	4,184	13,249	1,402	7,448
1909	44,510	2,668	2,529	5,476	5,625	5,177	14,796	1,323	6,916
1908	33,224	2,393	2,229	4,378	4,098	2,896	10,711	1,130	5,390
1907	40,256	2,769	2,888	5,492	5,073	3,684	12,341	1,244	6,764
1906	37,551	2,458	2,732	6,220	3,972	2,853	10,996	1,062	7,259
1905	30,503	1,690	2,341	6,189	2,974	2,262	8,238	567	6,241
1904	34,127	2,040	2,562	6,572	4,254	2,878	10,499	761	4,562
1899	35,078	2,204	3,506	8,750	6,011	2,712	8,404	588	2,901
1889	27,039	1,717	3,679	9,970	4,130	1,207	3,875	310	2,151
1879	18,125	1,481	3,189	6,284	3,823	746	1,755	183	664
1869	12,756	1,401	3,157	3,592	2,698	364	923	63	558

* Denotes first year for which figures include Alaska and Hawaii.
NA Not available.
[1] South Dakota is included in the Rocky Mountain Region because its production is limited to western species.

[2] For 1955–1959, Nevada included in Rocky Mountain Region; all other years, in West Coast.

Series L 122-137. Lumber Production, by Principal Species: 1869 to 1970

[In millions of board feet. Figures for certain years not adjusted for underreporting; see text]

Year	Total production	Softwoods								Hardwoods						
		Total	Douglas fir	Southern pine	Western pine [1]	Hemlock	Redwood	Eastern white pine	Other softwoods [2]	Total	Oak	Yellow poplar	Sweetgum	Maple	Cottonwood and aspen	Other hardwoods
	122	123	124	125	126	127	128	129	130	131	132	133	134	135	136	137
1970	34,668	27,530	7,727	7,063	4,327	1,980	1,078	[3]	5,355	7,138	3,250	606	376	742	229	1,935
1969	35,824	28,342	8,059	7,181	4,523	1,902	1,083	[3]	5,594	7,482	3,410	644	390	746	220	2,072
1968	36,473	29,285	8,532	6,901	4,763	2,186	1,049	[3]	5,854	7,188	3,319	662	364	704	190	1,949
1967	34,741	27,311	7,822	6,511	4,469	2,257	939	[3]	5,313	7,430	3,424	666	385	715	202	2,038
1966	36,584	28,847	8,528	6,609	4,713	2,490	1,038	[3]	5,469	7,737	3,675	692	434	658	211	2,067
1965	36,762	29,295	8,783	6,628	4,666	2,576	1,087	[3]	5,555	7,467	3,356	681	387	786	198	2,059
1964	36,559	29,284	8,868	6,414	4,598	2,490	1,199	[3]	5,715	7,275	3,417	645	380	642	205	1,986
1963	34,706	27,552	8,353	6,055	4,305	2,486	1,138	[3]	5,215	7,154	3,170	644	418	556	192	2,174
1962	33,174	26,812	8,504	5,733	3,995	2,279	1,024	[3]	5,277	6,362	3,068	619	328	523	178	1,646
1961 *	32,019	26,066	8,378	5,622	3,824	2,031	1,011	[3]	5,200	5,953	2,817	541	316	526	167	1,586
1960	32,926	26,672	8,832	5,660	3,909	2,032	1,000	[3]	5,239	6,254	2,789	592	331	602	206	1,734
1959	37,166	30,509	10,265	6,716	4,075	1,658	1,221	[3]	6,574	6,657	3,369	655	432	450	149	1,602
1958	33,385	27,379	9,329	6,420	3,868	1,386	917	[3]	5,459	6,006	2,882	615	412	572	176	1,349
1957	32,901	27,100	9,094	6,568	3,262	1,242	953	[3]	5,981	5,801	2,796	539	346	487	173	1,460
1956	38,199	30,231	10,195	7,740	4,279	1,322	1,125	848	4,722	7,968	3,928	752	516	593	230	1,949
1955	37,380	29,815	10,414	7,360	4,362	1,568	991	796	4,324	7,565	3,716	690	529	568	327	1,735
1954	36,356	29,282	10,328	7,332	4,544	1,337	958	1,036	3,746	7,074	3,451	592	522	575	280	1,653
1953	36,742	29,562	10,367	7,581	2 4,506	1,441	969	1,064	2 3,634	7,180	3,339	709	530	551	406	1,645
1952	37,462	30,234	10,569	8,572	2 4,142	1,525	900	976	2 3,550	7,228	3,353	671	567	566	404	1,667
1951	37,204	29,493	10,372	8,495	[3]	1,502	860	[3]	8,264	7,711	3,590	753	792	584	241	1,751
1950	38,007	30,633	9,984	9,939	2 4,632	1,508	875	950	2 2,745	7,374	3,347	833	758	546	225	1,665
1949	32,178	26,472	9,074	8,259	4,491	1,177	744	820	1,907	5,704	2,518	556	515	508	217	1,390
1948 [4]	37,000	29,600	9,794	(NA)	4,926	(NA)	793	(NA)	(NA)	7,400	(NA)	(NA)	(NA)	(NA)	(NA)	(NA)
1947	35,404	27,937	9,043	9,473	4,534	1,244	530	1,119	1,995	7,467	3,193	636	803	630	381	1,824
1946	34,112	25,857	7,640	9,376	4,314	1,216	243	1,165	1,903	8,256	3,378	827	1,080	598	312	2,061
1945	28,122	5 21,140	6,237	7,210	3,596	1,039	444	1,023	1,589	5 6,982	2,859	578	971	522	209	1,759
1944 [6]	32,938	25,160	7,864	8,132	4,465	1,201	462	1,244	1,792	7,778	3,292	641	1,017	634	297	1,898
1943	34,289	26,917	7,951	9,962	4,568	1,213	461	1,045	1,718	7,371	3,038	589	1,044	581	244	1,875
1942	36,332	29,510	8,550	11,761	4,830	1,089	462	1,083	1,736	6,822	2,763	543	840	642	283	1,753
1941	33,613	28,032	8,532	10,339	5,196	1,005	456	916	1,589	5,581	2,208	433	589	619	231	1,501
1940	28,934	24,903	7,121	10,163	4,571	716	389	577	1,366	4,031	1,467	376	479	463	154	1,092
1939	25,148	5 21,408	6,494	7,749	4,214	665	345	514	1,261	5 3,741	1,432	276	383	445	130	1,067
1938	21,646	18,293	5,216	7,196	3,474	578	317	408	1,104	3,353	1,204	221	454	389	140	946
1937	25,997	21,589	6,555	7,691	4,264	862	436	449	1,331	4,408	1,582	299	578	525	146	1,278
1936	24,355	20,242	6,321	7,113	3,861	813	403	442	1,290	4,113	1,535	260	606	490	137	1,085
1935	19,539	16,248	4,772	5,960	3,209	578	329	383	1,016	3,291	1,195	182	482	404	98	931
1934	15,494	12,735	4,066	4,473	2,304	478	282	388	745	2,758	1,083	163	393	311	109	700
1933	13,961	11,899	3,969	4,446	2,082	416	164	236	586	2,062	698	111	386	221	108	539
1932	10,151	8,746	2,904	3,069	1,590	337	136	198	512	1,406	516	86	202	160	49	392
1931	16,523	13,852	4,648	4,430	2,364	960	211	305	933	2,671	954	172	343	328	77	796
1930	26,051	21,323	6,453	7,450	3,375	1,517	403	564	1,560	4,729	1,662	258	694	601	158	1,355
1929	36,886	29,813	8,689	11,630	4,207	2,099	486	709	1,994	7,073	2,574	436	1,104	824	165	1,970
1928	34,142	28,345	8,449	10,610	3,837	2,222	487	838	1,902	5,797	1,830	328	968	743	144	1,785
1927	34,532	28,443	8,443	10,891	3,614	2,071	570	824	2,029	6,090	2,013	335	1,101	774	104	1,764
1926	36,936	30,469	8,807	11,752	3,964	2,159	488	911	2,390	6,467	2,191	322	1,133	829	122	1,870
1925	38,339	31,710	8,154	13,236	3,949	2,140	511	1,031	2,690	6,628	2,129	376	1,101	922	142	1,959
1924	35,931	29,406	7,462	12,487	3,347	1,879	604	1,056	2,571	6,525	2,077	351	1,071	857	167	2,003
1923	37,166	30,904	8,223	12,949	3,511	1,873	592	1,109	2,647	6,262	2,028	353	1,016	842	158	1,864
1922	31,569	26,644	6,832	11,501	2,700	1,535	566	972	2,540	4,925	1,605	274	808	640	114	1,483
1921	26,961	22,186	4,642	10,960	1,853	1,201	468	998	2,064	4,775	1,592	235	683	610	122	1,532
1920	29,878	24,254	6,957	8,964	2,785	1,685	476	1,039	2,347	5,624	1,854	270	685	768	138	1,909
1919	34,552	27,407	5,902	13,063	2,203	1,755	410	1,425	2,648	7,145	2,708	329	851	857	144	2,255
1918	29,362	24,100	5,819	9,942	2,113	1,696	443	1,687	2,398	5,262	1,659	242	652	697	148	1,865
1917	33,193	27,130	5,351	12,483	2,267	1,968	487	1,794	2,779	6,063	1,968	326	731	802	179	2,058
1916	34,791	28,576	5,413	13,411	2,262	1,987	491	1,952	3,061	6,215	2,165	395	652	809	135	2,059
1915	31,242	25,441	4,122	12,177	1,810	2,026	419	1,872	3,015	5,801	2,070	377	478	771	138	1,966
1914	37,346	29,407	4,764	14,473	1,808	2,166	535	2,307	3,355	7,939	3,279	519	675	910	195	2,361
1913	38,387	30,303	5,556	14,839	1,768	2,320	510	2,229	3,080	8,084	3,212	620	773	901	209	2,370
1912	39,158	30,526	5,175	14,737	1,737	2,427	497	2,775	3,179	8,632	3,319	623	694	1,021	227	2,747
1911	37,003	28,902	5,054	12,897	1,808	2,555	490	2,904	3,194	8,101	3,098	659	583	952	199	2,610
1910	40,018	31,161	5,204	14,143	1,940	2,836	543	3,104	3,390	8,857	3,522	735	610	1,007	220	2,763
1909	44,510	33,897	4,856	16,277	1,826	3,051	522	3,695	3,669	10,613	4,414	858	707	1,107	266	3,261
1908	33,224	25,546	3,675	11,236	1,522	2,531	405	3,198	2,979	7,678	2,772	654	589	875	232	2,556
1907	40,256	31,001	4,749	13,215	1,747	3,373	569	4,088	3,260	9,255	3,719	863	689	939	293	2,752
1906	37,551	30,235	4,970	11,661	1,636	3,537	660	4,469	3,303	7,315	2,820	683	454	883	264	2,211
1905	30,503	24,915	4,319	8,772	1,227	2,804	412	4,868	2,512	5,588	1,834	583	317	609	236	2,010
1904	34,127	27,345	2,928	11,522	1,402	3,269	519	5,316	2,390	6,782	2,903	854	524	588	322	1,592
1899	35,078	26,179	1,739	9,670	1,011	3,421	360	7,747	2,231	8,898	4,553	1,118	299	662	417	1,850
1889	27,039	20,024	1,206	4,220	741	2,533	--------	9,409	1,915	7,015	3,804	783	69	636	--------	1,723
1879	18,125	13,334	289	2,379	366	1,200	--------	7,863	1,237	4,791	2,943	496	24	447	--------	881
1869	12,756	9,252	196	1,378	321	770	--------	5,770	817	3,504	2,014	320	4	410	--------	756

* Denotes first year for which figures include Alaska and Hawaii.
NA Not available.
[1] Includes Idaho white pine, ponderosa pine, and sugar pine; prior to 1957, also includes lodgepole pine.
[2] For 1950, 1952 and 1953, and beginning 1957, lodgepole pine included in other softwoods; for other years included in western pine.

[3] Separate data not available; included in series L 130, "other softwoods."
[4] Forest Service estimates.
[5] Includes some lumber not distributed by species.
[6] Data for eastern species represent Forest Service estimates; all other reported by Bureau of the Census.

Series L 138–150. Exports and Imports of Logs, by Major Species: 1950 to 1970

[In millions of board feet, log scale]

Year	Total	Exports							Imports				
		Softwoods				Hardwoods			Total	Softwoods	Hardwoods		
		Total	Douglas fir	Port Orford cedar	Other	Total	Walnut	Other			Total	Mahogany	Other
	138	139	140	141	142	143	144	145	146	147	148	149	150
1970	2,753.0	2,684.1	487.7	54.1	2,142.3	68.9	17.4	51.5	144.4	106.5	37.9	6.8	31.1
1969	2,397.0	2,316.8	380.6	40.7	1,895.6	80.2	20.6	59.5	81.8	41.7	40.2	6.5	33.7
1968	2,568.1	2,473.2	396.5	38.4	2,038.3	94.9	21.9	73.0	85.3	39.4	45.9	8.5	37.4
1967	1,970.7	1,873.6	272.0	34.6	1,567.0	97.1	16.4	80.7	76.9	33.9	43.1	10.5	32.5
1966	1,393.1	1,317.5	130.5	43.0	1,144.0	75.6	12.8	62.8	95.6	42.5	53.1	16.1	37.0
1965	1,192.8	1,111.4	111.3	39.1	961.0	81.4	23.6	57.9	68.1	13.5	54.6	12.8	41.8
1964	1,086.3	1,022.6	94.6	37.0	891.0	63.7	11.1	52.6	65.1	8.7	56.3	16.1	40.2
1963	951.3	879.6	71.6	63.9	744.1	71.8	16.5	55.3	97.9	44.1	53.9	13.7	40.2
1962	522.2	452.7	48.1	41.5	363.1	69.5	10.3	59.2	100.1	38.1	62.1	16.6	45.5
1961	481.8	432.2	66.8	61.2	304.2	49.5	7.2	42.4	105.7	57.1	48.6	15.5	33.1
1960	266.3	210.3	27.5	37.2	145.6	56.0	10.2	45.9	112.5	32.3	80.2	25.2	55.1
1959	204.6	167.6	20.8	39.2	107.7	37.0	3.7	33.2	98.2	25.4	72.8	22.5	50.3
1958	169.8	127.3	12.4	32.3	82.7	42.5	2.3	40.2	95.3	21.6	73.8	21.2	52.5
1957	139.3	107.3	8.1	22.8	76.4	32.0	1.4	30.6	131.3	40.5	90.9	27.8	63.1
1956	187.7	154.9	15.8	13.9	125.2	32.8	1.1	31.6	160.3	39.7	120.6	46.6	74.0
1955	166.2	144.2	9.8	10.7	123.7	22.0	1.2	20.8	198.8	79.4	119.3	50.8	68.5
1954	139.5	106.4	12.8	13.8	79.8	33.1	.6	32.5	220.9	128.2	92.6	37.8	54.9
1953	115.1	86.0	12.4	3.5	70.0	29.2	.5	28.6	227.1	115.5	111.6	47.7	63.9
1952	63.7	44.4	4.2	1.9	38.3	19.2	.3	18.9	190.8	113.8	77.1	34.8	42.3
1951	79.4	57.9	2.4	.6	54.9	21.5	1.0	20.5	212.0	84.8	127.2	48.4	78.8
1950	48.2	28.9	1.0	.3	27.6	19.3	1.0	18.3	268.5	156.5	111.9	56.5	55.4

Series L 151–165. Plywood Production, Imports, Exports, and Consumption, by Softwoods and Hardwoods: 1950 to 1970

[In millions of square feet, except as indicated. ⅜-inch basis]

Year	Total					Softwoods					Hardwoods				
	Domestic production	Imports	Exports	Apparent consumption	Per capita consumption (sq. ft.)	Domestic production	Imports	Exports	Apparent consumption	Per capita consumption (sq. ft.)	Domestic production	Imports	Exports	Apparent consumption	Per capita consumption (sq. ft.)
	151	152	153	154	155	156	157	158	159	160	161	162	163	164	165
1970	15,945	2,049	172	17,822	87	14,149	2	114	14,038	69	1,796	2,047	58	3,784	19
1969	15,407	2,121	215	17,314	85	13,538	15	199	13,354	66	1,869	2,107	58	3,960	20
1968	16,395	1,896	78	18,213	91	14,385	10	64	14,332	71	2,009	1,886	14	3,882	19
1967	14,756	1,247	93	15,909	80	12,840	3	85	12,758	64	1,916	1,244	8	3,152	16
1966	14,925	1,257	56	16,126	82	12,849	3	48	12,804	65	2,076	1,254	8	3,321	17
1965	14,477	1,052	37	15,492	80	12,428	5	30	12,402	64	2,049	1,047	6	3,090	16
1964	13,366	1,045	31	14,380	75	11,455	5	28	11,431	60	1,912	1,040	2	2,949	15
1963	12,058	945	19	12,984	69	10,375	10	18	10,367	55	1,683	935	1	2,617	14
1962	10,831	903	19	11,716	63	9,315	13	17	9,311	50	1,516	891	2	2,404	13
1961	9,801	739	17	10,523	57	8,496	13	14	8,495	46	1,305	727	3	2,028	11
1960	8,861	725	15	9,571	53	7,759	11	13	7,757	43	1,102	715	2	1,814	10
1959	9,082	938	75	9,945	56	7,736	(NA)	72	7,664	43	1,346	938	3	2,281	13
1958	7,638	643	14	8,267	47	6,487	(Z)	12	6,475	37	1,151	643	2	1,792	10
1957	6,830	597	15	7,412	43	5,653	(Z)	15	5,639	33	1,177	597	1	1,773	10
1956	6,780	498	16	7,262	43	5,432	(NA)	15	5,418	32	1,347	498	1	1,844	11
1955	6,639	443	10	7,071	43	5,284	(Z)	8	5,276	32	1,355	442	2	1,795	11
1954	5,106	306	7	5,405	33	3,989	(Z)	7	3,983	24	1,116	306	1	1,422	9
1953	5,076	156	10	5,222	33	3,848	(Z)	10	3,839	24	1,228	155	1	1,383	9
1952	4,403	60	13	4,450	28	3,178	1	13	3,166	20	1,224	60	(Z)	1,284	8
1951	4,192	53	4	4,241	27	2,995	4	4	2,995	19	1,197	49	1	1,246	8
1950	(NA)	45	4	(NA)	(NA)	2,676	(Z)	3	2,672	18	(NA)	45	(Z)	(NA)	(NA)

NA Not available.   Z Less than 500,000 square feet.

Series L 166-177. Pulpwood, Woodpulp, Paper and Board, Turpentine and Rosin Production, Net Imports, and Apparent Consumption: 1809 to 1970

[In thousands]

Year	Pulpwood			Woodpulp			Paper and board				Domestic production of turpentine and rosin [2]	
	Domestic production	Net imports	Apparent consumption	Domestic production	Net imports	Apparent consumption	Domestic production	Net imports	Apparent consumption [1]	Waste paper consumption	Turpentine	Rosin
	166	167	168	169	170	171	172	173	174	175	176	177
	Cords	Cords	Cords	Tons	Tons	Tons	Tons	Tons	Tons	Tons	50-gal. bbl.	Drums, 520 lb. net
1970	70,460	[3]700	69,760	43,546	423	44,969	53,516	4,541	58,057	10,594	576	1,656
1969	66,910	[3]680	66,225	42,813	1,937	44,751	54,187	4,815	59,003	10,939	617	1,741
1968	61,670	235	61,905	40,892	1,616	42,508	51,245	4,419	55,664	10,222	652	1,846
1967	57,470	945	58,420	36,677	1,445	38,122	46,926	5,019	51,945	9,888	628	1,869
1966	56,070	1,105	57,175	36,603	1,811	38,414	47,113	5,566	52,680	10,564	666	1,958
1965	52,320	1,150	53,470	33,993	1,735	35,728	44,080	5,022	49,102	10,231	701	2,067
1964	48,600	1,390	49,995	32,415	1,362	33,777	41,703	4,682	46,384	9,843	679	2,015
1963	44,710	1,545	46,255	30,121	1,353	31,474	39,230	4,485	43,715	9,613	674	2,085
1962	42,770	1,290	44,060	27,908	1,602	29,510	37,541	4,675	42,216	9,075	653	2,064
1961	40,270	1,160	41,430	26,523	1,289	27,812	35,749	4,563	40,312	9,018	637	2,051
1960	40,010	1,160	41,170	25,316	1,240	26,556	34,444	4,694	39,138	9,032	605	2,010
1959	36,715	1,055	37,770	24,383	1,779	26,162	34,015	4,710	38,725	9,414	637	1,916
1958	33,240	1,270	34,510	21,796	1,586	23,382	30,823	4,296	35,119	8,671	608	1,857
1957	34,420	1,665	36,085	21,800	1,478	23,278	30,666	4,602	35,268	8,493	627	1,865
1956	35,195	1,760	36,955	22,131	1,800	23,931	31,441	5,055	36,496	8,836	645	1,994
1955	30,950	1,705	32,655	20,740	1,579	22,319	30,178	4,541	34,719	9,041	656	1,947
1954	26,970	1,560	28,535	18,302	1,608	19,910	26,876	4,503	31,379	7,857	618	1,920
1953	26,320	1,540	27,860	17,537	1,996	19,533	26,605	4,756	31,360	8,531	538	1,780
1952	25,045	2,110	27,155	16,473	1,729	18,202	24,418	4,599	29,017	7,881	565	1,751
1951	25,130	2,495	27,625	16,524	2,159	18,683	26,047	4,514	30,561	9,071	684	2,084
1950	20,715	1,385	22,100	14,849	2,290	17,138	24,375	4,636	29,011	7,956	709	2,172
1949	17,620	1,410	19,030	12,207	1,641	13,848	20,315	4,379	24,694	6,600	673	2,028
1948	20,025	1,980	22,010	12,872	2,082	14,955	21,897	4,185	26,082	7,585	659	2,076
1947	18,545	1,750	20,295	11,946	2,192	14,138	21,102	3,647	24,749	8,009	641	1,991
1946	16,965	1,675	18,640	10,607	1,766	12,373	19,278	3,233	22,510	7,278	570	1,720
1945	15,255	1,520	16,775	10,167	1,619	11,786	17,371	2,295	19,665	6,800	488	1,452
1944	15,350	1,350	16,700	10,108	853	10,962	17,183	2,262	19,445	6,859	471	1,318
1943	13,580	1,355	14,935	9,680	1,005	10,685	17,036	2,401	19,437	6,368	508	1,463
1942	14,905	1,660	16,565	10,783	858	11,642	17,084	2,697	19,780	5,495	560	1,656
1941	14,175	1,560	15,735	10,375	829	11,205	17,762	2,659	20,421	6,075	549	1,708
1940	12,370	1,375	13,745	8,960	744	9,703	14,484	2,274	16,757	4,668	566	1,717
1939	9,735	1,080	10,815	6,993	1,887	8,880	13,510	2,439	15,949	4,366	605	1,814
1938	7,955	1,240	9,195	5,934	1,570	7,503	11,381	2,162	13,542	(NA)	709	2,077
1937	8,895	1,500	10,395	6,573	2,072	8,645	12,837	3,191	16,028	(NA)	700	2,031
1936	7,525	1,190	8,715	5,695	2,084	7,779	11,976	2,675	14,651	(NA)	635	1,866
1935	6,620	1,010	7,630	4,926	1,761	6,687	10,479	2,279	12,758	3,587	603	1,821
1934	5,840	960	6,795	4,436	1,663	6,099	9,187	2,102	11,289	(NA)	602	1,783
1933	5,870	710	6,580	4,276	1,862	6,139	9,190	1,726	10,916	(NA)	622	1,838
1932	5,015	620	5,635	3,760	1,434	5,194	7,998	1,729	9,727	(NA)	573	1,659
1931	5,780	940	6,725	4,409	1,543	5,952	9,382	1,965	11,347	(NA)	564	1,613
1930	5,745	1,450	7,195	4,630	1,782	6,412	10,169	2,149	12,319	(NA)	685	1,972
1929	6,345	1,300	7,645	4,863	1,827	6,690	11,140	2,271	13,411	3,842	724	2,070
1928	5,640	1,520	7,160	4,511	1,721	6,232	10,403	2,048	12,451	(NA)	649	1,867
1927	5,215	1,540	6,750	4,313	1,644	5,957	10,002	1,923	11,925	(NA)	737	2,093
1926	5,405	1,365	6,765	4,395	1,697	6,092	9,794	1,790	11,584	(NA)	589	1,680
1925	4,625	1,470	6,095	3,962	1,626	5,588	9,002	1,415	10,417	(NA)	545	1,516
1924	4,515	1,250	5,770	3,723	1,491	5,214	7,930	1,351	9,281	(NA)	586	1,610
1923	4,540	1,335	5,875	3,789	1,360	5,149	7,871	1,323	9,194	(NA)	616	1,695
1922	4,535	1,010	5,550	3,522	1,234	4,756	6,875	990	7,865	(NA)	558	1,542
1921	3,475	1,080	4,555	2,876	669	3,544	5,333	694	6,027	(NA)	500	1,365
1920	4,875	1,240	6,115	3,822	874	4,696	7,185	454	7,640	(NA)	510	1,358
1919	4,430	1,045	5,480	3,518	596	4,114	5,966	287	6,253	1,854	393	1,088
1918	3,880	1,370	5,250	3,314	556	3,870	5,938	337	6,275	(NA)	359	997
1917	4,450	1,030	5,480	3,510	639	4,149	5,804	250	6,054	(NA)	502	1,378
1916	4,130	1,100	5,230	3,435	644	4,079	(NA)	(NA)	(NA)	(NA)	626	1,697
1915	(NA)	(NA)	(NA)	(NA)	548	(NA)	(NA)	(NA)	(NA)	(NA)	537	1,443
1914	3,470	1,000	4,470	2,893	663	3,556	5,153	243	5,395	1,510	566	1,519
1913	(NA)	(NA)	(NA)	(NA)	522	(NA)	(NA)	(NA)	(NA)	(NA)	695	1,902
1912	(NA)	(NA)	(NA)	(NA)	526	(NA)	(NA)	(NA)	(NA)	(NA)	730	1,984
1911	3,440	890	4,330	2,686	553	3,239	(NA)	(NA)	(NA)	(NA)	664	1,777
1910	3,160	930	4,095	2,534	498	3,032	(NA)	(NA)	(NA)	(NA)	617	1,649
1909	3,095	910	4,000	2,496	361	2,857	4,121	[3]19	4,103	984	600	1,600
1908	2,652	695	3,347	2,119	239	2,358	(NA)	(NA)	(NA)	(NA)	750	2,000
1907	3,037	925	3,963	2,548	284	2,832	(NA)	(NA)	(NA)	(NA)	585	1,824
1906	2,922	739	3,661	(NA)	(NA)	(NA)	(NA)	(NA)	(NA)	(NA)	588	1,566
1905	2,547	645	3,192	(NA)	(NA)	(NA)	(NA)	(NA)	(NA)	(NA)	590	1,571
1904	2,477	574	3,051	1,922	169	2,091	3,107	[3]78	3,029	589	600	1,600
1903	(NA)	(NA)	(NA)	(NA)	(NA)	(NA)	(NA)	--------	(NA)	--------	545	1,452
1902	(NA)	(NA)	(NA)	(NA)	(NA)	(NA)	(NA)	--------	(NA)	--------	581	1,548
1901	(NA)	(NA)	(NA)	(NA)	(NA)	(NA)	(NA)	--------	(NA)	--------	600	1,600
1900	(NA)	(NA)	(NA)	(NA)	(NA)	(NA)	(NA)	--------	(NA)	--------	620	1,652
1899	1,617	369	1,986	1,180	37	1,216	2,168	--------	2,168	--------	--------	--------
1889	583	--------	--------	306	--------	--------	935	--------	--------	--------	--------	--------
1879	41	--------	--------	23	--------	--------	452	--------	--------	--------	--------	--------
1869	2	--------	--------	1	--------	--------	[4]386	--------	--------	--------	--------	--------
1859	--------	--------	--------	--------	--------	--------	127	--------	--------	--------	--------	--------
1849	--------	--------	--------	--------	--------	--------	[4]78	--------	--------	--------	--------	--------
1839	--------	--------	--------	--------	--------	--------	[4]38	--------	--------	--------	--------	--------
1819	--------	--------	--------	--------	--------	--------	[4]12	--------	--------	--------	--------	--------
1809	--------	--------	--------	--------	--------	--------	[4]3	--------	--------	--------	--------	--------

NA Not available.
[1] Beginning 1929, includes changes in newsprint stocks.
[2] Crop year beginning April 1.
[3] Net exports.
[4] Estimated from values reported by the Bureau of the Census.

Series L 178–191.　Apparent Consumption of Paper and Board, by Principal Grades: 1899 to 1970

[In thousands of tons]

Year	Total paper and board	Paper Total	News-print [1]	Ground-wood [2]	Book [3]	Fine [4]	Coarse and industrial [5]	Sanitary and tissue [6]	Construction	Board Total	Container [7]	Bending [8]	Building [9]	Other [10]
	178	179	180	181	182	183	184	185	186	187	188	189	190	191
1970	58,056	31,698	9,836	1,215	6,137	3,859	5,313	3,748	1,590	26,359	14,245	--------	2,829	--------
1969	59,004	31,794	9,915	1,208	6,168	3,967	5,388	3,556	1,592	27,210	14,580	--------	3,000	--------
1968	55,798	30,171	9,302	1,187	5,820	3,691	5,231	3,376	1,564	25,626	13,520	--------	2,831	--------
1967	52,075	28,836	9,153	1,163	5,499	3,462	4,865	3,195	1,498	23,240	12,140	--------	2,407	--------
1966	52,640	28,719	9,098	1,158	5,552	3,438	4,905	3,082	1,486	23,921	12,649	5,701	2,395	3,176
1965	49,244	26,793	8,442	1,038	4,984	3,130	4,766	2,866	1,567	22,451	11,375	5,352	2,566	3,158
1964	46,518	25,330	8,046	995	4,604	2,824	4,610	2,724	1,527	21,187	10,551	5,172	2,448	3,016
1963	43,965	24,028	7,557	956	4,288	2,677	4,536	2,566	1,448	19,937	9,846	4,902	2,255	2,934
1962	42,387	23,273	7,464	910	4,028	2,624	4,422	2,406	1,419	19,114	9,454	4,778	2,066	2,816
1961	40,488	22,501	7,408	907	3,785	2,427	4,292	2,305	1,377	17,987	8,794	4,474	1,933	2,786
1960	39,324	22,084	7,353	938	3,753	2,226	4,226	2,191	1,397	17,240	8,240	4,406	1,869	2,725
1959	38,793	21,540	7,030	909	3,588	2,190	4,285	2,116	1,422	17,255	8,108	4,352	2,018	2,777
1958	35,248	19,560	6,515	824	3,202	1,885	3,821	1,933	1,379	15,688	7,331	4,124	1,725	2,508
1957	35,280	19,757	6,778	846	3,180	1,849	3,884	1,902	1,318	15,523	7,394	4,149	1,610	2,371
1956	36,386	20,537	6,807	972	3,348	1,910	4,226	1,853	1,420	15,851	7,562	4,112	1,699	2,477
1955	34,979	19,422	6,491	886	3,045	1,711	3,942	1,755	1,593	15,557	7,356	3,929	1,668	2,606
1954	31,516	17,873	6,106	788	2,794	1,246	3,911	1,607	1,420	13,644	6,340	3,580	1,495	2,229
1953	31,520	17,724	6,111	771	2,800	1,268	3,907	1,500	1,366	13,796	6,576	3,544	1,379	2,297
1952	28,971	16,839	5,915	806	2,556	1,257	3,661	1,352	1,293	12,131	5,678	3,144	1,311	1,998
1951	30,530	17,630	5,872	790	2,719	1,320	4,086	1,466	1,378	12,900	6,191	3,272	1,274	2,164
1950	29,108	16,833	5,863	705	2,608	1,160	3,719	1,358	1,419	12,275	5,771	3,135	1,228	2,141
1949	24,781	14,859	5,533	675	2,289	969	3,065	1,186	1,143	9,922	4,625	2,613	837	1,848
1948	26,070	15,350	5,137	772	2,418	1,097	3,429	1,183	1,314	10,720	5,017	2,672	1,266	1,766
1947	24,775	14,445	4,660	821	2,228	1,105	3,270	1,080	1,281	10,329	4,886	2,758	1,064	1,621
1946	22,550	13,091	4,192	776	1,970	1,065	3,038	1,037	1,014	9,459	4,278	2,708	977	1,495
1945	19,827	11,004	3,452	636	1,481	916	2,680	971	868	8,823	4,057	2,270	890	1,606
1944	19,540	10,599	3,218	593	1,448	900	2,610	954	876	8,941	4,186	2,116	936	1,704
1943	19,644	11,043	3,559	586	1,604	953	2,513	957	871	8,601	4,054	2,047	907	1,593
1942	19,731	11,790	3,722	610	1,723	1,007	2,759	974	995	7,941	3,735	1,712	882	1,612
1941	20,386	12,084	3,923	643	2,013	906	2,792	899	909	8,302	4,120	1,842	623	1,716
1940	16,770	10,606	3,739	588	1,629	691	2,561	721	677	6,163	3,283	1,416	163	1,302
1939	15,982	10,029	3,543	568	1,533	712	2,379	642	653	5,953	3,305	1,360	102	1,185
1938	13,951	8,970	3,492	490	1,297	613	1,982	529	564	4,982	2,590	1,221	109	1,062
1937	15,653	9,969	3,868	596	1,510	690	2,181	521	602	5,684	3,135	1,289	98	1,162
1936	14,652	9,308	3,657	487	1,429	725	1,986	478	546	5,344	2,756	1,272	88	--------
1935	12,820	8,234	3,351	384	1,272	609	1,717	463	437	4,586	2,358	1,121	65	--------
1934	11,201	7,219	3,068	391	1,046	505	1,497	388	325	3,982	1,882	966	59	--------
1933	10,869	6,893	2,660	285	1,067	573	1,584	399	325	3,977	2,021	958	47	--------
1932	9,803	6,587	2,895	125	935	514	1,478	350	290	3,216	1,593	887	65	--------
1931	11,400	7,671	3,298	311	1,195	597	1,495	387	388	3,729	1,904	906	107	--------
1930	12,340	8,416	3,501	221	1,368	711	1,805	351	460	3,924	1,916	1,013	108	--------
1929	13,421	9,101	3,787	363	1,474	731	1,719	378	649	4,320	2,256	991	137	--------
1928	12,489	8,455	3,561	235	1,326	572	1,856	346	560	4,034	1,985	--------	80	--------
1927	11,954	8,188	3,492	296	1,326	537	1,603	314	620	3,766	2,100	--------	81	--------
1926	11,607	7,956	3,516	209	1,192	528	1,559	308	645	3,651	(NA)	--------	102	--------
1925	10,437	7,131	2,989	189	1,162	503	1,432	279	577	3,306	1,777	--------	83	--------
1924	9,298	6,435	2,821	170	1,054	427	1,374	241	348	2,863	--------	--------	--------	--------
1923	9,208	6,397	2,814	166	1,044	402	1,378	249	344	2,811	--------	--------	--------	--------
1922	7,878	5,717	2,451	150	826	378	1,279	214	419	2,162	--------	--------	--------	--------
1921	6,061	4,327	2,013	92	675	234	912	184	217	1,734	--------	--------	--------	--------
1920	7,744	5,448	2,196	170	910	387	1,220	190	375	2,296	--------	--------	--------	--------
1919	6,253	4,403	1,841	150	1,380		858	190	195	1,850	--------	--------	--------	--------
1918	6,275	4,371	1,760	133	1,267		891	150	311	1,904	--------	--------	--------	--------
1917	6,054	4,279	1,778	130	1,221		844	146	300	1,775	--------	--------	--------	--------
1914	5,395	4,103	1,547	104	1,163		911	115	244	1,292	--------	--------	--------	--------
1909	4,103	3,220	1,119	100	887		763	78	226	883	--------	--------	--------	--------
1904	3,029	2,469	861	63	738		644	44	145	560	--------	--------	--------	--------
1899	2,168	1,773	569	54	490		535	28	97	394	--------	--------	--------	--------

NA　Not available.
[1] Beginning 1929, includes changes in stocks.
[2] Production only.
[3] 1899–1919, production only. Includes absorbent paper. Includes a small amount of imported groundwood paper.
[4] 1899–1919, production only. 1955–1970, not strictly comparable with prior years due to reporting changes.
[5] 1899–1919, production only. 1920–1970, includes wrapping, shipping sack, bag, converting, special industrial, and other similar grades of paper and absorbent paper. 1955–1970, not strictly comparable with prior years due to reporting changes.
[6] 1899–1919, production only.
[7] 1925–1936, production only.
[8] Includes special food board.
[9] Includes hardboard and insulating board.
[10] Includes nonbending, special paperboard, cardboard, wet machine board, and other similar grades of board.

Series L 192–198. Newsprint Production, Shipments, Consumption, Stocks, Imports, and Price: 1935 to 1970

[In thousands of short tons, except price]

Year	Produc- tion	Shipments from mills	Consump- tion by publishers	Stocks, end of year		Imports	Wholesale price, average (dollars per ton)	Year	Produc- tion	Shipments from mills	Consump- tion by publishers	Stocks, end of year		Imports	Wholesale price, average (dollars per ton)
				At mills	At and in transit to pub- lishers							At mills	At and in transit to pub- lishers		
	192	193	194	195	196	197	198		192	193	194	195	196	197	198
1970	3,310	3,303	7,130	33	749	6,635	151	1952	1,147	1,143	4,551	12	612	5,036	120
1969	3,232	3,233	7,344	27	699	6,790	146	1951	1,125	1,125	4,511	8	522	4,963	110
1968	2,935	2,946	7,025	27	633	6,463	141	1950	1,015	1,017	4,542	8	425	4,864	102
1967	2,620	2,602	6,907	39	630	6,599	140	1949	900	898	4,257	11	446	4,640	101
1966	2,408	2,405	6,898	21	681	6,991	136	1948	867	867	4,010	9	458	4,395	98
1965	2,180	2,183	6,387	19	573	6,323	132	1947	826	832	3,565	8	377	3,958	89
1964	2,261	2,273	6,031	22	585	5,954	134	1946	771	762	3,136	15	293	3,492	72
1963	2,218	2,208	5,585	34	545	5,413	134	1945	724	725	2,455	6	266	2,669	60
1962	2,154	2,162	5,577	25	604	5,474	134	1944	720	723	2,351	7	342	2,491	58
1961	2,094	2,086	5,461	33	584	5,435	134	1943	805	803	2,720	11	367	2,637	55
1960	2,038	2,031	5,532	26	628	5,412	134	1942	953	951	2,835	10	479	2,921	50
1959	1,964	1,963	5,328	18	659	5,255	134	1941	1,015	1,021	2,947	8	385	2,982	50
1958	1,758	1,761	4,950	16	652	4,884	134	1940	1,013	1,013	2,856	13	356	2,763	50
1957	1,826	1,817	5,149	19	675	5,218	134	1939	939	945	2,730	13	328	2,615	50
1956	1,717	1,715	5,209	10	636	5,567	130	1938	820	817	2,653	19	315	2,275	50
1955	1,552	1,550	5,045	8	458	5,164	126	1937	946	945	2,956	16	613	3,317	42
1954	1,211	1,213	4,684	6	516	4,995	126	1936	921	917	2,939	15	305	2,752	41
1953	1,084	1,088	4,669	8	552	5,006	126	1935	912	917	2,663	10	295	2,383	40

Series L 199–205. Stumpage, Log, and Lumber Prices for Selected Species: 1910 to 1970

[In dollars per thousand board feet]

Year	Stumpage prices				Douglas fir log prices		Douglas fir lumber prices (whole- sale)	Year	Stumpage prices				Douglas fir log prices		Douglas fir lumber prices (whole- sale)
	Douglas fir	Southern pine	Sugar pine	Ponderosa pine	Saw logs	Peeler logs [1]			Douglas fir	Southern pine	Sugar pine	Ponderosa pine	Saw logs	Peeler logs [1]	
	199	200	201	202	203	204	205		199	200	201	202	203	204	205
1970	41.90	44.10	38.50	32.10	89.30	136.60	---------	1953	20.20	34.20	30.20	25.90	48.00	96.30	73.10
1969	82.20	51.70	75.20	71.00	98.70	137.70	---------	1952	25.80	38.50	36.40	27.40	50.60	96.00	78.80
1968	61.20	42.20	35.00	30.20	82.00	111.00	---------	1951	25.40	34.60	40.40	33.60	47.90	96.50	80.50
1967	41.70	38.30	23.50	22.20	68.90	105.90	---------	1950	16.40	26.70	25.00	18.30	44.70	89.40	73.30
1966	50.00	38.60	24.90	19.80	65.00	97.50	76.60	1949	11.10	19.70	18.90	17.60	39.00	74.90	61.20
1965	42.60	31.70	23.30	19.80	63.00	93.90	76.10	1948	19.90	16.40	16.20	14.60	39.30	79.70	77.20
1964	38.10	27.80	23.30	19.00	59.50	85.90	76.00	1947	9.90	10.90	12.50	8.30	33.70	56.40	70.60
1963	27.90	25.10	19.20	15.80	58.50	85.20	74.60	1946	6.60	8.90	7.20	5.80	(NA)	(NA)	45.50
1962	24.80	26.00	20.00	16.10	57.40	95.00	73.30	1945	5.00	9.30	7.30	5.60	(NA)	(NA)	39.00
1961	27.60	26.80	18.40	12.10	57.50	94.90	71.30	1944	5.20	10.90	5.20	4.00	(NA)	(NA)	38.30
1960	32.00	34.50	29.00	19.10	58.40	100.10	75.00	1943	(NA)	8.70	4.20	5.00	(NA)	(NA)	38.10
1959	36.80	35.20	26.70	20.60	57.70	97.10	78.90	1942	(NA)	8.90	4.80	2.70	(NA)	(NA)	35.30
1958	21.80	31.10	23.50	19.10	53.10	95.70	69.40	1941	3.60	10.80	3.40	2.60	17.00	32.00	29.40
1957	26.20	31.50	30.00	24.20	52.80	98.90	71.80	1940	2.30	4.50	3.00	2.20	15.50	28.00	22.20
1956	37.70	37.40	34.90	27.20	55.10	99.10	81.20	1939	(NA)	5.80	3.10	2.40	14.50	27.50	20.00
1955	28.90	32.00	30.00	26.10	52.20	96.30	80.90	1938	2.50	7.30	3.50	2.50	14.50	29.00	19.10
1954	16.20	29.70	31.20	27.20	48.10	94.80	72.20	1937	1.60	5.30	2.80	2.20	15.50	27.50	22.20
								1936	2.10	---------	2.80	2.20	14.00	25.00	19.50

Year	Stumpage prices				Douglas fir log prices, saw logs	Douglas fir lumber prices (whole- sale)	Year	Stumpage prices				Douglas fir log prices, saw logs	Douglas fir lumber prices (whole- sale)
	Douglas fir	Southern pine	Sugar pine	Ponderosa pine				Douglas fir	Southern pine	Sugar pine	Ponderosa pine		
	199	200	201	202	203	205		199	200	201	202	203	205
1935	1.70	4.50	3.10	2.40	11.50	17.30	1922	2.50	2.80	3.80	4.00	15.00	21.00
1934	1.50	2.90	3.50	2.50	11.00	17.20	1921	1.90	3.70	4.20	3.20	14.50	18.00
1933	1.20	2.70	(NA)	(NA)	9.50	14.60							
1932	1.70	2.80	3.70	2.60	9.50	11.50	1920	1.80	4.40	5.00	3.70	22.00	34.90
1931	2.90	3.40	4.60	4.20	11.00	13.60	1919	2.40	3.70	3.40	3.00	17.00	24.90
							1918	1.80	3.00	3.40	2.70	14.50	19.50
1930	3.30	3.20	6.30	3.60	15.50	17.80	1917	1.60	3.40	2.80	2.20	11.00	16.20
1929	2.70	3.50	4.60	3.60	16.00	20.60	1916	1.20	3.20	3.50	2.90	8.50	10.80
1928	2.90	3.60	3.20	2.50	15.50	19.40							
1927	2.50	3.50	4.00	3.40	15.00	19.80	1915	2.90	2.10	3.40	2.50	7.00	10.60
1926	2.20	3.60	4.50	3.70	16.00	20.40	1914	1.60	2.90	3.00	2.00	7.50	(NA)
							1913	1.70	1.70	3.30	2.20	8.50	(NA)
1925	2.10	3.20	4.40	3.60	15.00	21.10	1912	2.30	1.50	3.50	2.70	8.00	11.50
1924	2.20	3.50	4.20	3.50	16.00	22.40	1911	2.30	2.80	2.50	2.50	8.00	11.00
1923	2.50	3.00	4.40	3.90	18.50	27.30	1910	2.20	1.50	4.30	3.60	9.00	13.00

NA Not available.   [1] Includes logs used in manufacture of veneer.

Series L 206–210. Wholesale Price Indexes of Selected Timber Products: 1900 to 1970
[Beginning 1961, includes the value of shipments for Alaska and Hawaii]

Year	Lumber 206	Plywood[1] 207	Wood-pulp 208	Paper 209	Paperboard 210	Year	Lumber 206	Wood-pulp 208	Paper 209	Paperboard 210	Year	Lumber 206	Year	Lumber 206
	1967 = 100						1967 = 100					1947–49 = 100		1947–49 = 100
1970	113.7	116.4	109.3	111.0	101.1	1946	44.7	59.5	50.2	54.8	1930	28.5	1910	16.6
1969	131.6	140.3	100.0	105.5	99.4	1945	38.9	53.8	45.9	49.9			1909	16.7
1968	117.4	133.6	100.0	102.0	95.9	1944	38.5	53.3	45.5	47.9	1929	31.2	1908	16.7
1967	100.0	100.0	100.0	100.0	100.0	1943	35.5	49.3	44.5	46.8	1928	30.1	1907	18.0
1966	100.1	109.2	100.0	97.5	102.2	1942	33.4	49.3	43.4	43.4	1927	30.9	1906	17.9
1965	94.0	103.9	100.1	94.6	101.5	1941	30.8	47.4	42.3	42.2	1926	33.2		
1964	92.9	104.2	98.1	94.2	101.5								1905	14.7
1963	91.2	107.1	93.6	93.1	99.7	1940	25.8	43.0	40.3	37.6	1925	34.5	1904	13.8
1962	89.0	102.7	95.1	93.3	98.0	1939	23.4	28.2	38.5	32.9	1924	34.0	1903	14.7
1961	87.4	107.0	96.9	92.9	97.4	1938	22.0	32.8	39.4	32.0	1923	38.3	1902	13.8
						1937	25.1	44.6	38.6	37.8	1922	33.9	1901	13.1
1960	92.1	110.6	102.2	92.7	104.6	1936	21.9	28.8	36.4	32.1	1921	30.5		
1959	96.4	127.5	102.8	91.5	105.2	1935	20.6	27.7	36.2	32.0			1900	13.1
1958	89.5	120.0	102.8	90.7	105.3	1934	21.2	30.0	36.0	36.6	1920	56.6		
1957	90.9	118.8	100.7	90.5	105.4	1933	17.8	25.0	34.5	31.9	1919	38.7		
1956	96.5	130.4	99.8	87.6	104.2	1932	14.8	24.6	36.2	24.3	1918	28.6		
1955	94.5	142.1	95.7	82.8	98.2	1931	17.5	30.7	38.6	24.4	1917	24.7		
1954	88.9	138.1	93.0	80.8	96.2						1916	18.9		
1953	90.5	143.5	92.4	80.1	96.1	1930	21.5	33.1	39.9	28.8				
1952	91.3	143.6	94.5	79.1	98.5	1929	23.6	33.9	40.0	34.4	1915	16.7		
1951	93.7	157.1	96.9	76.0	101.9	1928	22.7	34.0	40.7	37.7	1914	17.1		
						1927	23.5	35.4	41.1	40.8	1913	18.5		
1950	86.6	150.1	81.0	67.9	81.2	1926	25.2	38.3	45.0	38.8	1912	17.5		
1949	74.3	130.3	82.2	66.3	76.4						1911	16.3		
1948	81.2	152.1	90.9	65.5	78.8									
1947	71.5	119.7	81.0	59.5	76.7									

[1] Soft plywood, interior grade A-D.

Series L 211. Wholesale Price Index of Lumber: 1798 to 1932
[1910–14 = 100]

Year	Index 211	Year	Index 211	Year	Index 211	Year	Index 211	Year	Index 211	Year	Index 211	Year	Index 211	Year	Index 211	Year	Index 211
1932	115	1915	95	1898	58	1881	63	1864	74	1847	41	1830	27	1813	25
1931	136	1914	98	1897	55	1880	59	1863	58	1846	42	1829	28	1812	24
1930	167	1913	103	1896	57	1879	55	1862	48	1845	43	1828	29	1811	25
1929	184	1912	102	1895	57	1878	54	1861	45	1844	39	1827	29	1810	26
1928	177	1911	98	1894	59	1877	59	1860	46	1843	37	1826	28	1809	26
1927	183	1910	98	1893	60	1876	62	1859	46	1842	40	1825	27	1808	26
1926	196	1909	98	1892	59	1875	66	1858	48	1841	43	1824	26	1807	27
		1908	94	1891	61	1874	72	1857	53			1823	26	1806	27
1925	197	1907	98			1873	75	1856	52	1840	42	1822	25		
1924	194	1906	92	1890	62	1872	74			1839	45	1821	26	1805	27
1923	219			1889	62	1871	72	1855	51	1838	45			1804	26
1922	193	1905	82	1888	62			1854	48	1837	45	1820	27	1803	24
1921	174	1904	78	1887	63	1870	71	1853	47	1836	32	1819	28	1802	27
1920	323	1903	76	1886	62	1869	75	1852	46	1835	31	1818	28	1801	27
1919	221	1902	71	1885	61	1868	80	1851	43	1834	31	1817	31	1800	24
1918	163	1901	66	1884	64	1867	83	1850	43	1833	30	1816	35	1799	23
1917	141	1900	69	1883	64	1866	87	1849	40	1832	29	1814	27	1798	24
1916	108	1899	64	1882	66	1865	79	1848	41	1831	29				

Series L 212–223. Average Hourly Earnings in Timber-Based Industries: 1950 to 1970
[Average hourly earnings for production or nonsupervisory workers]

Year	Lumber and wood products exc. furniture		Logging camps and logging contractors[1]		Sawmills and planing mills		Millwork, veneer, and plywood[2]		Paper and allied products		Furniture and fixtures	
	Hourly earnings	Index, 1967 = 100	Hourly earnings	Index, 1967 = 100	Hourly earnings	Index, 1967 = 100	Hourly earnings	Index, 1967 = 100	Hourly earnings	Index, 1967 = 100	Hourly earnings	Index, 1967 = 100
	212	213	214	215	216	217	218	219	220	221	222	223
	Dollars		Dollars		Dollars		Dollars		Dollars		Dollars	
1970	2.96	124.9	4.72	127.6	2.84	126.2	3.12	122.8	3.44	119.9	2.77	118.9
1969	2.74	115.6	4.23	114.3	2.63	116.9	2.90	114.2	3.24	112.9	2.62	112.4
1968	2.57	108.4	3.88	104.9	2.47	109.8	2.72	107.1	3.05	106.3	2.47	106.0
1967	2.37	100.0	3.70	100.0	2.25	100.0	2.54	100.0	2.87	100.0	2.33	100.0
1966	2.25	94.9	3.47	93.8	2.12	94.2	2.42	95.3	2.75	95.8	2.21	94.8
1965	2.17	91.6	3.34	90.3	2.03	90.2	2.33	91.7	2.65	92.3	2.12	91.0
1964	2.11	89.0	3.25	87.8	1.98	88.0	2.26	89.0	2.56	89.2	2.05	88.0
1963	2.04	86.1	3.09	83.5	1.88	83.6	2.18	85.8	2.48	86.4	2.00	85.8
1962	1.99	84.0	2.98	80.5	1.83	81.3	2.14	84.3	2.40	83.6	1.95	83.7
1961	1.95	82.3	2.96	80.0	1.76	78.2	2.09	82.3	2.34	81.5	1.91	82.0
1960	1.89	79.7	2.96	80.0	1.71	76.0	2.05	80.7	2.26	78.7	1.88	80.7
1959	1.87	78.9	2.87	77.6	1.69	75.1	2.01	79.1	2.18	76.0	1.83	78.5
1958	1.79	75.5	2.76	74.6	1.63	72.4	1.93	76.0	2.10	73.2	1.78	76.4
1957	1.74	73.4	2.68	72.4	1.61	71.6	1.86	73.2	2.02	70.4	1.75	75.1
1956	1.69	71.3	2.69	72.7	1.58	70.2	1.80	70.9	1.92	66.9	1.69	72.5
1955	1.62	68.4	2.58	69.7	1.50	66.7	1.74	68.5	1.81	63.1	1.62	69.5
1954	1.57	66.2	--------	--------	1.46	64.9	1.68	66.1	1.73	60.3	1.57	67.4
1953	1.55	65.4	--------	--------	1.44	64.0	1.63	64.2	1.67	58.2	1.54	66.1
1952	1.49	62.9	--------	--------	1.38	61.3	1.57	61.8	1.59	55.4	1.47	63.1
1951	1.41	59.5	--------	--------	1.30	57.8	1.49	58.7	1.51	52.6	1.39	59.7
1950	1.30	54.9	--------	--------	1.20	53.3	1.38	54.3	1.40	48.8	1.28	54.9

[1] Data for Washington State only.   [2] Figures also cover fabricated structural wood products.

Chapter L

Fisheries (Series L 224-370)

L 224–370. General note.

Fisheries data were largely compiled or derived from publications of the National Oceanic and Atmospheric Administration, National Marine Fisheries Service (NMFS). Additional detail can be found in these publications and in those of predecessor agencies (i.e., the Bureau of Fisheries, Department of Commerce, prior to July 1940; the Commission of Fish and Fisheries prior to 1904; and the Fish and Wildlife Service, Bureau of Commercial Fisheries, Department of Interior, prior to October 1970). Statistical canvasses relating to the fishing industry carried out in 1880 and 1908 were made in conjunction with the Bureau of the Census (and predecessor agencies) and were published as Senate Document No. 124, 47th Congress, 1887, and as a Bureau of the Census Special Report, 1911, respectively. Since 1941, preliminary figures on many present and historical aspects of the fisheries have been published by the NMFS in the form of leaflets entitled *Current Fishery Statistics*. Final and more detailed figures are published by the NMFS as comprehensive annual Statistical Digests and in *Annual Reports of Alaska Fishery and Fur-Seal Industries* (last printing was in 1955 for the latter).

The first comprehensive statistical study of the fisheries and fishery industries of nearly all the United States was made for the year 1880 by the U.S. National Museum with the cooperation of the Commission of Fisheries and the Superintendent of the Tenth Census. The first complete statistical canvass of the entire United States was made for 1908 by the Bureau of the Census. The next general survey of the entire United States was not made until 1931. Periodic general surveys of a limited number of States or areas were made for the years from 1881 to 1907 and from 1909 to 1930. Various sections were surveyed during the years 1932 to 1949. A complete survey of all sections of the country was made for 1950. Since then all of the coastal areas have been canvassed annually. Annual surveys of the Mississippi River and its tributaries have been continuous since 1962. Since 1954 all sections of the United States were canvassed to provide complete data on the wholesale and manufacturing segments of the fisheries industries.

While extended series for successive years are lacking for most regions of the United States, there are long continuous records available for landings at certain important ports or for certain species. The latter have been collected in connection with annual surveys of canned fish and industrial products. Data on the production of canned fishery products and industrial fishery products have been collected annually for all regions since 1921, while information was obtained on the production of packaged fish for 1926 and annually since 1928.

The coastal statistical surveys include canvasses of the commercial fisheries of the contiguous and noncontiguous ocean waters and bays of the United States and as far up the coastal rivers as commercial fishing is conducted. The Mississippi River region includes tributaries thereof. The Great Lakes region encompasses the bays thereof, the international lakes of northern Minnesota, and the rivers emptying into these waters.

Several methods for the collection of fishery statistics have been employed. Where data were not available from some central private or public source, canvassing both by interview and by correspondence has been used to secure the required information from fishing vessel owners and operators, wholesale dealers, and manufacturers of fishery products.

Since 1946, a growing number of State fishery agencies have developed independently, or in cooperation with the NMFS, relatively complete systems chiefly with respect to fish catch statistics which greatly facilitate the surveys in those States. In such instances, the NMFS conducts only supplementary surveys to make the catch statistics comparable with those of other States and to secure additional wholesale and manufacturing data. Securing fishery statistical data by the Federal fishery agencies has been on a nonmandatory basis.

Until 1951, all statistics of the Alaska fisheries were collected by canvass of the industry chiefly through correspondence. Subsequently, catch statistics have been compiled from copies of dealer invoices for fish and shellfish purchased from individual fishermen that are required by law to be furnished to the NMFS. This procedure, first instituted by California in 1917, is becoming more generally used in a number of coastal States, and is improving the source materials available for the compilation of national statistics by the Federal Government.

Statistics on commercial landed catches of fish are usually shown in the published reports as round salable weight, being converted to such a common basis by established conversion factors. In the Great Lakes States, catches are usually shown in weights as landed, which may be in the round or eviscerated condition. Oyster, clam, and clam-like shellfish data are usually expressed in amounts of recoverable meats. Crabs, shrimps, squid, and octopus landings are shown in round weights. Whaling production from land-based plants in the United States is included in the total of fish production in series L 224 and L 244. These land-based plants have not produced more than 17 million pounds of whale products in any year of record in this report. These series do not include the high-seas production of whale products either in this or in the previous century. The yield is expressed in terms of the weight of products produced, not the live weight of the whales.

The values of the landed catches are gross dollar returns to catching vessels and fishermen. The value of processed or manufactured items is that by the manufacturer. Data are usually collected and published on a calendar-year basis, although compilations for some States are on a fiscal-year basis.

Statistics of landed catches do not include either the marine or freshwater catches made for personal use including those by Indian populations, or for sport, or landings by foreign fishing vessels in U.S. ports, or imports. They include catches by U.S. fishing vessels landed in foreign ports for transshipment in bond to the United States.

Since 1942, the commercial catches have been credited to the port at which they were landed. Prior to that time the entire annual catch of a vessel was credited to the port out of which the majority of its yearly operations were conducted, regardless of the actual point of landing. Due to the generally broad regional grouping of the data shown here, the effect of the change in method of crediting yields upon the trends of landings has, for the most part, been insignificant. While neither method provides completely satisfactory information as to the approximate location of the fishing grounds producing the landed catches, the present practice permits closer estimates than the former.

All general references to fish include fish, shellfish, and other marine or freshwater products including those of the land-based segment of the U.S. whaling industry.

Fisheries outside the United States, some products of which enter the domestic market duty-free, are those of American Samoa and the Commonwealth of Puerto Rico. Fisheries of these areas are not subject to Federal control and are not included in the series shown here unless otherwise indicated. Total commercial production in these fisheries is of relatively small magnitude. Canned tuna for the U.S. market is the chief commercial item produced in American Samoa. Hawaiian fisheries statistics are presented annually since 1948 in *Fishery Statistics of the United States*, Statistical Digests.

L 224–235.   Yield and value of domestic fisheries, imports, and exports, 1880–1970.

Source: 1880, U.S. Commission of Fish and Fisheries, *The Fisheries and Fishery Industries of the United States*, 1887; 1889–1917, H. F. Taylor, *Economics of the Fisheries of North Carolina*, part III, "Survey of Marine Fisheries of North Carolina," University of North Carolina Press, Chapel Hill (copyright), 1951; 1921–1938, U.S. Bureau of Fisheries, *Fishery Industries of the United States*, annual issues; 1939–1970, U.S. National Oceanic and Atmospheric Administration and predecessor agencies, *Fishery Statistics of the United States*, annual Statistical Digests.

Since 1880, complete or partial surveys have been made of the various regions of the United States, except for the Mississippi River, with sufficient frequency to produce satisfactory annual estimates of the yield and value of the U.S. fisheries. Due to the relative stability and low magnitude of the Mississippi River production, the inclusion of interpolated estimates for that region do not significantly affect the national totals.

Prior to 1921, except for 1909–1914, Taylor provides a well validated and statistically satisfactory series of annual figures by summation of critically adjusted and interpolated data based upon various individual State and regional data published by the Bureau of Fisheries or its predecessor, the Commission of Fish and Fisheries. No statistically satisfactory national totals can be provided for 1909 to 1914 (Taylor). A satisfactory Alaska total is provided by J. N. Cobb, *Products of the Commercial Fisheries of the United States*, American Fisheries Society Transactions, XLVIII, which, added to Taylor's 1917 U.S. total, provides a combined total for that year.

Prior to 1908, records of salt fish were not converted to equivalent fresh round weights except for 1880. It was estimated (Taylor) that such salt fish in 1887 represented at least 20 percent of the national total catch of food-fish species. By 1920, this proportion had declined to about 1 percent. Estimated corrections back to 1908 (derived from Taylor, figure 7, p. 379) have been added to the estimates of national totals (Taylor, p. 480).

Statistics on foreign fishery trade are obtained from compilations made by the Bureau of the Census. Statistics on all known imported or exported fishery products have been assembled and published annually since 1924. For earlier years figures are available in reports of the Census Bureau and predecessor agencies.

See also general note for series L 224–370.

L 236–253.   Quantity and value of landed catches in the United States, by regions, 1880–1970.

Source: 1880–1903, U.S. Commission of Fish and Fisheries (in cooperation with the U.S. Bureau of the Census and its predecessor agencies), *Commissioner's Report and Appendices*, reports for 1880 and 1908; 1904–1939, U.S. Bureau of Fisheries, *Fishery Industries of the United States*, annual issues; 1940–1970, see publications by U.S. National Oceanic and Atmospheric Administration and its predecessor agencies, and H. F. Taylor, cited for series L 224–235.

The regions are composed as follows:

New England States	South Atlantic States
Maine	North Carolina
New Hampshire	South Carolina
Massachusetts	Georgia
Connecticut	East coast Florida
Rhode Island	Gulf States
Middle Atlantic States	West coast Florida
New York	Alabama
New Jersey	Mississippi
Delaware	Louisiana
Chesapeake Bay States	Texas
Maryland	
Virginia	

Pacific Coast States	Lakes Region
California	Great Lakes
Hawaii (beginning 1959)	International lakes of
Oregon	northern Minnesota
Washington	Mississippi River
	Including tributaries

Regional totals prior to 1909 include cured fish in terms of product weights and not round weights used for figures in series L 224.

In spite of deficiencies arising from interpolating values over periods during which no canvasses were made in some regions, it is probable that these figures provide statistically satisfactory estimates of the trends of quantity and value of landed catches of all species combined in the several regions.

The annual and secular changes for the various regions have resulted from changes in composition of the catches from time to time. These changes may be deduced from the figures for series L 262–293.

Since only seven surveys were made of the Mississippi River fisheries during the period from 1899 to 1955, no extended production records are available for the principal species of the Mississippi River region. During that period, buffalo fish, bullheads and catfish combined, and mussel shells for the button industry, provided an average of 15 percent, 12 percent, and 42 percent, respectively, of the total recorded average annual production in this region. After reaching a high point of 82 million pounds in 1908, freshwater mussel-shell production has shown a declining trend to 7 million pounds in 1969.

See also general note for series L 224–370.

L 254–261.   Fisheries—employment, fishing craft, and establishments, 1930–1970.

Source: U.S. National Oceanic and Atmospheric Administration, *Fishery Statistics of the United States*, annual Statistical Digests.

L 255, fishermen. Includes all persons engaged in commercial fishing operations.

L 257–260, craft utilized. Fishing craft having a capacity of five net tons or more are called vessels; those with less are called boats.

L 262–269.   Landed catches of principal species in New England States, 1876–1970.

Source: 1876–1886 (except for 1880), U.S. Bureau of Fisheries, *Statistics of the Mackerel Fishery of the East Coast of North America, 1804 to 1930*, Investigational Report No. 19, vol. 1, 1934; 1880, U.S. Commission of Fish and Fisheries, *The Fisheries and Fishery Industries of the United States*, 1887; 1887–1950, U.S. Fish and Wildlife Service, *Fishery Statistics of the United States, 1950*, Statistical Digest No. 27; 1951–1970, U.S. National Oceanic and Atmospheric Administration and predecessor agencies, *Fishery Statistics of the United States*, annual Statistical Digests.

The species shown here have accounted for between 65 percent and 87 percent of the total New England fish production (series L 236). The accuracy of these data has been enhanced by the fact that a long unbroken, annual detailed record of landings by individual vessels at the major New England ports has been available. The figures for 1908 and earlier years, not including 1880, have not been corrected for portions of the catches of some species that were recorded in those early years as product weights of cured fish.

See also general note for series L 224–370.

L 270–271.   Landed catches of menhaden and oysters in Middle Atlantic States, 1880–1970.

Source: See source for series L 262–269.

See also general note for series L 224–370.

L 272–274.   Landed catches of menhaden, oysters, and crabs in Chesapeake Bay States, 1880–1970.

Source: See source for series L 262–269.

See also general note for series L 224–370.

L 275–280. Landed catches of shrimp, menhaden, and mullet in South Atlantic States and Gulf States, 1880–1970.

Source: See source for series L 262–269.

Historically, these two regions were canvassed for statistics at infrequent intervals, and until recent years most State agencies in these regions maintained no statistical systems. The data on menhaden, however, are more complete because its use for reduction has resulted in the landings being recorded during the more frequent canvasses for manufactured fishery products by the National Marine Fisheries Service and its predecessor agencies.

See also general note for series L 224–370.

L 281–282. Landed catches of lake trout and whitefish in Lakes Region, 1885–1970.

Source: Except for 1885, see source for series L 262–269; 1885, *Fishery Statistics of the United States, 1950,* Statistical Digest No. 27.

See also general note for series L 224–370.

L 283–287. Landed catches of principal species in Pacific Coast States, 1888–1970.

Source: See source for series L 262–269 except for series L 286 for which—1888–1966, International Pacific Halibut Commission, published in U.S. Bureau of Commercial Fisheries, *Fishing Leaflet 602, Revised,* "United States and Canadian Halibut Landings, 1888–1966"; 1967–1970, International Pacific Halibut Commission, *Annual Report, 1969* and *1970.*

State and Federal agencies in this region, due in part to the consistent support by the fishing industry, have maintained the most continuous and probably the most accurate series of fisheries statistics of any region in the United States.

The landed catches include both those from waters contiguous to the coasts of California, Oregon, and Washington, and waters off foreign shores; tuna from waters off South and Central America; salmon and halibut from waters off Canada. Also, a large proportion of the landed catch of the halibut comes from waters off Alaska.

See also general note for series L 224–370.

L 288–292. Landed catches of salmon, halibut, and herring in Alaska, 1882–1970.

Source: **Series L 288,** 1927–1970, U.S. National Oceanic and Atmospheric Administration and predecessor agencies, *Fishery Industries of the United States,* annual issues, and *Fishery Statistics of the United States,* annual Statistical Digests. **Series L 289,** see source for series L 286. **Series L 290,** 1882–1956, O. E. Sette, *Historical Catch Statistics on Pacific Herring, Clupea pallasi,* 1955, Fish and Wildlife Service Ocean Research Note 4 (also amendments and O. E. Sette, 1957 addendum). **Series L 291–292,** 1884–1931, *Pacific Fisherman,* "Annual Statistical Number 30," Miller Freeman Publications, Seattle, January 1932 (copyright, Journal Publishing Co.); 1932–1956, *Pacific Fisherman,* "1957 Yearbook Number," January 1957 (copyright, Journal Publishing Co.). **Series L 290–292,** 1957–1970, see source for series L 288.

The halibut figures (series L 289) include catches landed by U.S. vessels in the railhead port of Prince Rupert, Canada, for shipment in bond to the United States, as has also been the practice in the published compilations by Federal fishery agencies.

The major portion of the Alaska herring catch has been used for reduction to meal and oil except during the period 1912 to 1922 when salting and canning predominated. Such direct use as a food fish has since declined and practically disappeared after 1948. The variety and changing emphasis in the products reported produced each year and the problem of converting such diverse products to a common raw fish value reduced the usefulness of the originally published total catch statistics. These have been revised from time to time (see Sette who appraised the revisions of such workers as Rounsefell up to 1928 and Skud more recently).

See also general note for series L 224–370.

L 293. Landed catches of tuna in Hawaii, 1946–1970.

Source: U.S. National Oceanic and Atmospheric Administration and predecessor agencies, *Fishery Statistics of the United States,* annual Statistical Digests.

Statistics were not collected for Hawaii prior to 1946.

L 294–304. Per capita consumption of fishery products, 1909–1970.

Source: U.S. National Oceanic and Atmospheric Administration, *Fisheries of the United States,* various issues.

Per capita consumption is based on the consumption of edible fishery products in the United States divided by estimates of the total civilian resident population as of July 1 of each year.

These estimates are from the Bureau of the Census, Current Population Reports, series P–25.

L 305–310. Disposition of landed catches, by major product groups, 1921–1970.

Source: U.S. National Oceanic and Atmospheric Administration, *Fishery Statistics of the United States,* annual Statistical Digests; and *Imports and Exports of Fishery Products, Annual Summary 1970,* p. 8.

The fresh and frozen catch figures (series L 307) should be considered only as rough estimates since they were derived as residuals of the total catch figures (series L 305, same as series L 224) and the canned, cured, and industrial catch figures (series L 308, L 309, and L 310).

Canned catch figures (series L 308) represent a computed amount of fish or other aquatic organisms that were heat processed in cans. Cured products figures (series L 309) represent an estimated amount of fish and other living aquatic animals that were dried or dehydrated, salted, smoked, or pickled. Industrial products figures (series L 310) represent the weights of fish and other aquatic products determined to have been manufactured into fish meal, oil, fish solubles, homogenized condensed fish, shell products, or used as bait or for animal food, and other miscellaneous items.

U.S. production may also be classified according to type of products whether crustacea such as crabs, shrimps, lobsters; mollusks such as oysters, clams, squid; fresh-water organisms; bottom or demersal marine fish; surface or pelagic marine fish; and such miscellaneous products as turtles, seaweeds, and other items, not including whale products. The percentage of total production contributed by the foregoing groups at various times has been as follows:

	1908	1930	1937	1945	1950	1955
Crustacea	5	6	6	7	8	9
Mollusks	13	7	4	4	4	4
Fresh-water	11	5	4	4	4	5
Marine demersal	21	22	17	23	19	19
Marine pelagic	50	60	69	62	65	63
Miscellaneous	(1)	(1)	(1)	(1)	(1)	(1)

¹ Less than 1 percent.

See also general note for series L 224–370.

L 311–318. Production and imports of selected fishery items, 1924–1970.

Source: **Series L 311,** 1939–1956, U.S. Fish and Wildlife Service, *Packaged Fish—1956,* Current Fishery Statistics, No. 1518; 1957–1970, U.S. National Oceanic and Atmospheric Administration, *Fishery Statistics of the United States,* annual Statistical Digests. **Series L 313, L 315,** and **L 317,** 1924–1939, U.S. Bureau of Fisheries, *Fishery Industries of the United States,* annual issues; 1940–1970, U.S. National Oceanic and Atmospheric Administration, *Fishery Statistics of the United States,* annual Statistical Digests. **Series L 312, L 314, L 316,** and **L 318,** 1924–1956, U.S. Customs Service, unpublished data; 1957–1970, see source for series L 311.

The import figures for groundfish fillets and steaks are based on Customs documents and Bureau of the Census data; all other import figures are from census data.

See also general note for series L 224–370.

L 319–320. Sponge sales at the Tarpon Springs (Fla.) Exchange, 1913–1970.

Source: 1913–1949, U.S. Fish and Wildlife Service, unpublished data; 1950–1970, U.S. National Oceanic and Atmospheric Administration, *Fishery Statistics of the United States*, annual Statistical Digests.

L 321–337. Prices received by fishermen, 1939–1970.

Source: 1939–1968, U.S. National Oceanic and Atmospheric Administration, *Prices Received by Fishermen*, H.S. No. 12; 1969–1970, *Fishery Statistics of the United States*, annual Statistical Digests.

These data represent prices received by fishermen from processors. The bases of weight measurement in pounds are as follows: Round, whole—flounder, American lobsters, menhaden, ocean perch, salmon (chum, pink, and sockeye), tuna (albacore, bluefin, skipjack, and yellowfin); dressed, scaled and eviscerated, usually with head, tail, and fins removed—salmon (chinook, troll and coho, troll); meat, edible weight—clams, soft, and sea scallops; drawn, eviscerated—cod and haddock.

The points of pricing are as follows: clams, soft and American lobster—Maine; cod, flounder, and haddock—Massachusetts; ocean perch—Maine and Massachusetts; sea scallops—New Bedford, Mass.; and for the other series—no specific point.

L 338–357. Production and value of canned fishery products, 1921–1970.

Source: 1921–1935, U.S. Bureau of Fisheries, *Fishery Industries of the United States*, annual issues. U.S. National Oceanic and Atmospheric Administration, 1936–1938 and 1969–1970, *Fishery Statistics of the United States*, annual Statistical Digests; 1939–1968, *Canned Fishery Products, Annual Summary 1970*.

See also general note for series L 224–370.

L 338–339, total, all products. In addition to the nine products for which figures are separately presented (series L 340–357) and which have represented over the period of record from 85 percent to 97 percent of production of all canned fishery products, these totals include very substantial packs of clams and clam products, large and valuable packs of crabs, and small but valuable packs of fish roes and of shrimp and oyster specialty products, and many other less important items. These data are the latest revised figures and all are equated to units of the latest defined standard case for each product. A history of conversion factors that have been used and their present definitions appear in *Fishery Statistics of the United States, 1970*, Statistical Digest No. 64.

L 340–341, Pacific Coast salmon. (Standard case, 48 cans of 16 ounces net weight each.) Includes Alaska salmon (also shown separately, series L 288) which account for the largest proportion of the total. Five species of the genus *Oncorhynchus* are included— sockeye (red), chinook (king), coho (silver), pink, and chum salmon— and also an extremely small proportion of steelhead trout of the genus *Salmo*.

L 342–343, Pacific sardines. (Standard case, 48 cans of 15 ounces net weight each.) The Pacific sardine is also known as the pilchard. Prior to 1937, the magnitude of the pack was determined in part by the proportion of the total catch that was permitted by California State law to be used for reduction to meal and oil. A California State law in 1967 established a two-year moratorium on the taking of sardines in California waters, excepting an allowable 15-percent tolerance for sardines taken incidentally in mixed catches of mackerel. In 1969, the moratorium was continued indefinitely.

L 344–345, Maine sardines. (Standard case, 100 cans 3–3/4 ounces net weight each.) The Maine sardine is also known as the Atlantic sea herring.

L 346–347, tuna. (Standard case, 48 cans of 6, 6½, or 7 ounces net weight per can for flakes or grated, chunks, and solid packs, re-

spectively.) Includes the canned pack of the true tuna species, albacore, yellowfin, bluefin, skipjack, and tonno.

L 348–349, oysters. (Standard case, 48 cans of 4–2/3 ounces drained weight each.)

L 350–351, shrimp. (Standard case, 24 cans of 4½ ounces net weight each.)

L 352–353, anchovies. (Standard case, 100 cans of 5 ounces net weight each.)

L 354–355, mackerel. (Standard case, 48 cans of 15 ounces net weight each.) The production consists of Jack and Chub (Pacific) mackerel of California.

L 356–357, animal food. (Standard case, 48 cans of 16 ounces net weight each.) Consists largely of pet and animal food derived from groundfish species and parts of other fish unsalable for human use or of species of low market value as human food.

L 358–361. Production of canned tuna, 1926–1970.

Source: U.S. National Oceanic and Atmospheric Administration and predecessor agencies. **Series L 358–359**, and **L 361**, 1926–1938 and 1941–1946, *Fishery Statistics of the United States*, annual Statistical Digests; 1939–1940 and 1947–1970, *Fisheries of the United States*, various annual issues. **Series L 360**, 1926–1938 and 1941–1948, unpublished data; 1939–1940 and 1949–1970, *Fisheries of the United States*.

Domestically canned tuna from domestic catch, series L 361, includes the pack from U.S. catch landed in Puerto Rico and American Samoa. Domestically canned tuna from frozen imports, series L 360, includes tuna canned in American Samoa from foreign-caught fish.

L 362–368. Production and value of dried fish meal and scrap, acidulated scrap, fish and other marine oils, and imports of fish meal, 1921–1970.

Source: 1921–1938, U.S. Bureau of Fisheries, *Fishery Industries of the United States*, annual issues; 1939–1970, U.S. National Oceanic and Atmospheric Administration and predecessor agencies, *Fishery Statistics of the United States*, annual Statistical Digests.

In contrast to series L 224, L 244, and others which included only the products of U.S. land-based whaling, series L 362 and L 364 include the meal and oil yields from the United States Antarctica and West Australia factory-ship whaling in 1935–1939.

Since 1941, the acidulated product of the menhaden fishery has been a negligible proportion of the total production of scrap and meal and it is not separated in the recorded statistics of the industry after 1946.

Acidulation of the wet menhaden press cake after removal of the oil was an alternative preservative process to drying. Since it was sometimes carried out as a temporary measure prior to drying at a later and more propitious time, it is probable that some of the tonnage of acidulated scrap may have been subsequently also reported as dried scrap leading to some duplication of reported tonnage in the earlier years.

See also general note for series L 224–370.

L 369. Sealskins obtained from the Pribilof Islands, 1910–1970.

Source: 1910–1938, U.S. Bureau of Fisheries, *Alaska Fishery and Fur-Seal Industries*, Administrative Reports; 1939–1957, U.S. Fish and Wildlife Service, *Alaska Fishery and Fur-Seal Industries*, Statistical Digest; 1958–1970, U.S. National Oceanic and Atmospheric Administration and predecessor agencies, *Fishery Statistics of the United States*, annual Statistical Digests.

Under the terms of the 1911 and succeeding treaties or agreements with Canada, Japan, and Russia, the take of fur seal on the Pribilof Islands in the Bering Sea has been under the exclusive and direct custodianship of the U.S. Government.

Sealskin figures represent the total take before the partitioning of the yield among the several countries involved.   The figures for 1910 and 1911 were pretreaty and represent skins taken directly by the U.S. Government, as the U.S. lease to the private company that had engaged in the operation since 1867 had expired early in 1910. The 1918 take was the first treaty take out of which Japan and Canada each received a 15-percent share for relinquishing all rights to pelagic sealing in the eastern North Pacific. Russia had not been previously engaged in pelagic sealing. With the abrogation of the treaty by Japan in 1940, Canada's share was increased to 20-percent under the Provisional Fur-Seal Agreement of 1942 as amended.

Management of the fur seal herd has been determined by a policy of taking pelts of those animals that are considered surplus to breeding requirements and that have highest quality skins. These desirable seals are principally the 3- and 4-year-old males. Scientists managing the herd believe that it can be maintained at an optimum level by keeping a male-female ratio which will produce about 500,000 pups each year. The present (1970) 1.5 million animals is large enough to sustain the seal population.

Available knowledge on the total size of the Pribilof Islands fur-seal herds, the high value of the skins and the fact that specified shares (15 percent) of the take were conveyed under treaty to Japan and Canada has ensured the accuracy of the record of annual takes. The U.S.S.R. does not share in the take even though it was a party to the treaty.

See also Fish and Wildlife Service, *A Population Study of the Alaska Fur-Seal Herd*, Special Scientific Report, Wildlife No. 12, 1954, for a history of the sealskin resource, 1786–1950.

L 370. Land-based production of whales, 1912–1970.

Source: 1912–1957, *Pacific Fisherman*, "Annual Statistical Numbers," 1910–1957, formerly Miller Freeman Publications, Seattle (copyright, Journal Publishing Co.); 1958–1970, U.S. National Oceanic and Atmospheric Administration, and predecessor agencies, *Fishery Statistics of the United States*, annual Statistical Digests. See also Norway Committee for Whaling Statistics, *International Whaling Statistics*, Nos. 1–15, Oslo, 1930–1941.

Present century participation by the United States in the whaling industry has been relatively inconsequential compared to that of other countries and to the American high-seas whaling of the past century. It has been largely restricted to land-based operations chiefly in Alaska and to a lesser extent in Washington, terminating in each in 1939 and 1925, respectively, and to operations in California from time to time for 1918–1970.

In 1969, the International Whaling Commission recommended that all member countries establish quotas for the commercial catch of fin and sei whales because of the danger of extinction. The U.S. quota was set at 44 fin whales and 60 sei whales; no quota was set for sperm whales, the other important whale in the U.S. catch.

See also general note for series L 224–370.

★ ★ ★ ★ ★ ★ ★ ★ ★ **More Recent Data for *Historical Statistics* Series** ★ ★ ★ ★ ★ ★ ★ ★ ★
★   ★
★   Statistics for more recent years in continuation of many of the still-active series shown here appear   ★
★   in annual issues of the *Statistical Abstract of the United States*, beginning with the 1975 edition. For   ★
★   direct linkage of the historical series to the tables in the *Abstract*, see Appendix I in the *Abstract*.   ★
★   ★
★ ★

Series L 224–235.　Yield and Value of Domestic Fisheries, Imports, and Exports: 1880 to 1970

Year	Yield (mil. lb.)					Value (mil. dol.)						
	Domestic			Imports for human use	Exports for human food	Domestic, total	Imports [1]			Exports [1]		
	Total	For human food	For industrial use				Total	For human food	For industrial use	Total	For human food	For industrial use
	224	225	226	227	228	229	230	231	232	233	234	235
1970	4,917	2,537	2,380	1,873	140	613.1	1,037.4	812.5	224.9	117.5	93.9	23.6
1969	4,337	2,321	2,016	1,707	141	526.5	844.3	704.8	139.5	104.5	86.5	18.1
1968	4,160	2,347	1,814	1,741	91	497.3	822.7	643.2	179.5	67.8	56.8	10.9
1967	4,055	2,368	1,687	1,470	108	439.6	707.9	538.3	169.6	82.2	67.5	14.7
1966	4,366	2,573	1,794	1,594	110	472.3	719.7	568.1	151.6	84.8	62.9	21.9
1965	4,777	2,587	2,190	1,399	96	445.7	600.9	479.4	121.5	69.5	49.3	20.2
1964	4,541	2,497	2,044	1,318	95	389.5	564.2	433.7	130.6	64.2	42.9	21.3
1963	4,847	2,556	2,291	1,197	65	377.2	500.7	399.9	100.8	56.6	30.4	26.2
1962	5,354	2,540	2,814	1,256	57	396.4	489.8	405.8	84.0	35.7	22.5	13.3
1961	5,187	2,490	2,697	1,087	40	362.2	400.6	339.3	61.3	34.7	19.6	15.1
1960	4,942	2,498	2,444	1,095	61	353.6	363.3	310.6	52.7	44.2	25.6	18.5
1959	5,122	2,369	2,753	1,141	81	346.1	370.1	314.7	55.5	44.2	26.7	17.5
1958	4,747	2,651	2,096	1,020	65	373.3	330.8	283.8	47.0	31.0	19.4	11.6
1957	4,789	2,475	2,314	900	85	353.7	299.3	252.8	46.5	36.0	20.5	15.4
1956	5,268	2,690	2,578	802	102	372.2	282.7	234.7	48.0	39.5	22.9	16.6
1955	4,809	2,579	2,230	780	110	338.9	258.9	209.0	49.9	40.0	24.9	15.1
1954	4,762	2,705	2,057	804	63	359.3	252.4	203.7	48.7	31.5	16.2	15.3
1953	4,487	2,519	1,968	726	69	356.1	245.5	195.9	49.6	27.9	17.1	10.8
1952	4,432	2,778	1,654	705	62	363.6	240.4	183.1	57.3	21.9	15.5	6.4
1951	4,433	3,048	1,385	647	166	364.8	212.5	158.4	54.1	35.7	27.1	8.7
1950	4,901	3,307	1,594	640	122	347.4	198.3	158.4	39.9	27.5	18.9	8.6
1949	4,804	3,305	1,499	471	147	342.7	151.6	113.8	37.9	35.1	29.2	5.8
1948	4,513	3,146	1,367	473	95	371.1	156.6	111.7	45.0	24.4	21.0	3.4
1947	4,349	3,020	1,329	408	207	312.0	110.0	83.3	26.7	52.8	49.3	3.6
1946	4,467	3,049	1,418	474	200	313.0	129.7	90.0	39.7	40.0	38.4	1.6
1945	4,598	3,167	1,431	405	136	269.9	101.3	76.4	24.8	38.5	30.9	7.7
1944	4,533	2,865	1,668	339	112	213.0	78.4	53.4	25.0	35.9	31.9	4.0
1943	4,162	2,737	1,425	324	239	204.0	67.2	43.7	23.5	48.5	43.2	5.3
1942	3,875	2,683	1,192	277	167	170.3	39.6	29.0	10.6	31.9	27.9	4.0
1941	4,900	3,062	1,838	306	216	129.0	41.0	28.0	12.9	22.0	21.5	.5
1940	4,060	2,675	1,385	303	145	96.1	41.8	29.1	12.8	17.8	17.1	.7
1939	4,445	2,713	1,732	346	125	97.6	46.0	32.4	13.6	14.2	13.6	.6
1938	4,254	2,639	1,615	303	118	94.2	39.3	28.3	11.0	14.4	13.8	.6
1937	4,353	2,703	1,650	365	119	101.4	50.6	33.9	16.7	14.6	13.7	.8
1936	4,826	2,854	1,972	371	111	94.8	41.9	30.4	11.5	13.2	12.3	1.0
1935	4,135	2,583	1,552	325	120	82.8	36.2	27.5	8.7	14.4	12.9	1.5
1934	4,104	2,434	1,670	287	116	76.8	30.8	23.2	7.6	13.8	12.0	1.8
1933	2,997	2,087	911	284	80	61.1	30.5	21.8	8.7	8.3	7.4	1.0
1932	2,612	1,864	748	260	87	56.0	29.6	21.7	7.9	7.8	7.7	.2
1931	2,630	2,129	501	277	114	77.0	43.0	28.9	14.1	11.6	11.4	.2
1930	3,224	2,478	746	338	167	109.0	50.8	35.0	15.8	17.3	17.0	.3
1929	3,491	2,601	890	357	213	125.8	66.6	38.8	27.8	23.8	23.5	.3
1928	3,061	2,370	691	361	171	114.3	58.9	37.4	21.5	21.2	20.8	.4
1927	2,806	2,172	634	312	158	111.5	55.6	34.9	20.8	18.7	18.3	.4
1926	2,871	2,198	673	309	164	106.7	50.1	32.5	17.6	20.3	19.9	.4
1925	2,891	2,029	862	263	161	105.1	49.0	29.1	20.0	21.3	20.7	.5
1924	2,461	1,874	587	285	165	----------	46.3	29.3	17.1	20.9	20.3	.5
1923	2,726	1,807	919	----------	----------	----------	----------	----------	----------	----------	----------	----------
1922	2,619	1,677	942	----------	----------	----------	----------	----------	----------	----------	----------	----------
1921	2,255	1,451	804	----------	----------	----------	----------	----------	----------	----------	----------	----------
1917	2,676	----------	----------	----------	----------	71.1	----------	----------	----------	----------	----------	----------
1908	2,053	----------	----------	----------	----------	62.7	----------	----------	----------	----------	----------	----------
1907	1,930	----------	----------	----------	----------	60.9	----------	----------	----------	----------	----------	----------
1906	2,046	----------	----------	----------	----------	59.3	----------	----------	----------	----------	----------	----------
1905	2,002	----------	----------	----------	----------	57.3	----------	----------	----------	----------	----------	----------
1892	1,652	----------	----------	----------	----------	40.7	----------	----------	----------	----------	----------	----------
1891	1,709	----------	----------	----------	----------	42.3	----------	----------	----------	----------	----------	----------
1890	1,758	----------	----------	----------	----------	41.3	----------	----------	----------	----------	----------	----------
1889	1,685	----------	----------	----------	----------	39.0	----------	----------	----------	----------	----------	----------
1880	1,706	----------	----------	----------	----------	39.1	----------	----------	----------	----------	----------	----------

[1] Includes Puerto Rico; beginning 1955, imports also include landings of tuna by foreign vessels in American Samoa, and imports of tuna into U.S. outlying areas.

Series L 236–253. Quantity and Value of Landed Catches in the United States, by Regions: 1880 to 1970

[For composition of regions, see text]

Year	Catch (mil. lb.)									Value (mil. dol.)								
	New England States (236)	Middle Atlantic States (237)	Chesapeake Bay States (238)	South Atlantic States (239)	Gulf States (240)	Lakes Region (241)	Mississippi River and tributaries (242)	Pacific Coast States (243)	Alaska (244)	New England States (245)	Middle Atlantic States (246)	Chesapeake Bay States (247)	South Atlantic States (248)	Gulf States (249)	Lakes Region (250)	Mississippi River and tributaries (251)	Pacific Coast States (252)	Alaska (253)
1970	531	140	630	280	1,698	72	75	945	545	91	30	41	30	167	6	10	143	96
1969	568	138	354	319	1,615	69	69	819	386	81	26	36	36	152	6	9	110	70
1968	635	187	438	339	1,289	69	73	681	450	76	25	37	33	139	6	8	95	79
1967	625	163	422	353	1,181	84	81	785	361	70	24	35	25	127	6	8	96	48
1966	684	168	502	368	1,196	69	112	685	582	78	22	35	27	123	6	11	91	81
1965	702	356	592	357	1,463	56	85	674	492	75	25	40	27	114	6	8	82	70
1964	682	370	537	336	1,318	57	77	672	493	68	21	36	21	99	6	7	76	56
1963	829	550	430	371	1,400	59	80	737	392	68	21	30	19	99	5	7	81	46
1962	872	944	521	305	1,437	66	69	710	429	66	25	34	23	95	6	7	85	57
1961	760	825	478	402	1,377	71	76	784	413	61	24	37	20	76	7	7	84	46
1960	852	784	436	379	1,266	68	86	714	358	61	22	35	20	85	7	8	74	41
1959	933	760	589	469	1,155	66	78	[1] 748	324	66	23	38	19	78	7	8	[1] 79	29
1958	998	625	503	376	809	72	75	899	379	65	23	37	20	87	9	7	90	33
1957	1,031	928	447	335	692	76	77	821	371	61	28	32	21	84	10	7	76	32
1956	1,015	1,054	376	444	900	81	91	862	428	59	31	33	20	85	10	8	85	38
1955	955	871	496	347	830	77	103	800	315	57	29	32	17	76	10	8	80	27
1954	966	887	473	326	755	81	90	826	338	58	31	32	18	73	10	8	96	31
1953	864	964	343	327	759	77	------	734	297	60	30	26	20	85	10	------	84	26
1952	955	593	284	436	760	82	------	832	374	67	29	27	20	68	11	------	91	37
1951	917	555	331	311	650	70	------	1,067	408	67	29	25	18	64	11	------	97	39
1950	1,007	492	381	261	571	71	106	1,515	482	61	29	25	19	50	11	10	108	31
1949	1,000	521	335	------	525	86	------	1,365	473	59	27	25	------	50	11	------	100	39
1948	998	501	364	------	427	84	------	1,135	567	68	29	28	------	------	13	------	114	31
1947	803	632	408	------	------	70	------	1,043	614	56	28	28	------	------	11	------	94	28
1946	806	518	360	------	------	78	------	1,162	651	62	14	27	------	------	12	------	76	29
1945	845	494	304	405	341	79	------	1,428	596	57	23	30	15	39	14	------	63	22
1944	714	423	267	------	------	76	------	1,676	561	42	21	20	------	------	11	------	60	20
1943	646	321	------	------	------	78	------	1,453	595	43	18	------	------	------	12	------	57	21
1942	705	319	202	------	------	75	------	1,375	522	36	12	10	------	------	9	------	49	18
1941			328			78		1,813	736			9			6		40	15
1940	626	356	321	326	250	79	------	1,456	564	20	8	7	4	11	6	------	30	11
1939	664	280	324	388	240	85	------	1,714	666	20	7	7	4	10	7	------	27	11
1938	632	217	295	414	208	82	------	1,526	799	18	8	8	4	9	6	------	26	12
1937	671	265	292	316	231	84	------	1,577	835	20	8	6	4	10	6	------	29	15
1936			314	370	187	94		1,925	932			6	6	8	6		25	14
1935	655	279	266			90	------	1,676	649	18	6	6	------	------	6	------	23	9
1934			289	261	187	96		1,546	819			6	4	6	5		20	12
1933	500	170	272	------	------	75	------	860	631	13	5	5	------	------	4	------	14	9
1932	481	141	359	154	146	84	------	561	607	14	5	6	2	4	4	------	9	7
1931	540	165	293	150	139	92	82	597	598	20	9	7	3	5	6	3	14	10
1930	701	194	316	276	142	95	------	833	621	27	13	11	4	7	6	------	23	13
1929	689	165	265	338	177	85	------	1,034	651	29	14	12	6	9	7	------	25	17
1928	599	------	------	259	172	63	------	705	699	26	------	------	6	10	6	------	21	18
1927	------	------	------	262	176	81	------	663	470	------	------	------	------	------	7	------	22	14
1926		153				75		538										
1925			321			69		627	616								25	10
1924	403					78		488										
1923				226	146	79		416										
1922			323			79	106	287				12						
1921						83												
1920			523			77						13						
1919	460					92				20								
1918				331	118	107							5	7				
1917						96												
1916						88												
1915						109		305										
1914						99												
1913						68												
1908	512	205	411	158	95	107	148	193		15	8	8	4	5	4	3	7	
1905	461																	
1904		368	420					191								2		
1903						86	93											
1902	525			101	95					12			3	3				
1901		347	458								9	8						
1899				114	97			207							3	2	6	
1898	394																	
1897		218	363	78	58													
1895								136										
1894							53											
1893						97												
1892								108										
1891		259	321															
1890		294	325	65	59	114												
1889	654	270		57	55	117											4	
1888	573	282	213	54	41			87										
1887	521	219	203	56	39											3		
1885						100												
1880	726	412	250	43	24	65		73		13	9	8		1	1			

[1] Beginning 1959, includes Hawaii.

Series L 254–261. Fisheries—Employment, Fishing Craft, and Establishments: 1930 to 1970

Year	Persons employed (1,000)			Craft utilized				Fishery shore establishments
	Total	Fishermen	Shore workers	Total	Vessels [1]	Motorboats	Other boats	
	254	255	256	257	258	259	260	261
1970	227	140	87	88,400	13,300	73,100	2,000	3,735
1969	220	132	88	77,057	12,018	56,889	8,150	4,207
1968	217	128	89	81,614	13,150	66,654	1,810	3,967
1967	220	132	89	81,328	12,874	66,075	2,379	4,053
1966	224	136	89	82,122	12,677	66,941	2,504	4,187
1965	215	129	87	79,532	12,311	63,828	3,393	4,189
1964	212	128	84	76,412	11,808	60,945	3,659	4,121
1963	216	128	87	77,973	11,928	62,090	3,955	4,194
1962	217	126	91	70,733	11,511	54,406	4,816	4,135
1961	222	130	92	77,487	11,964	60,118	5,405	4,138
1960	224	130	94	77,057	12,018	56,889	8,150	4,207
1959	222	129	93	75,301	12,109	54,735	8,457	4,372
1958	227	129	98	75,291	11,496	54,821	8,974	4,402
1957	235	138	97	77,970	11,671	56,434	9,865	4,322
1956	248	145	103	82,300	11,300	52,000	19,000	4,000
1955	241	144	97	83,292	11,796	58,218	13,278	4,124
1954	246	145	101	82,090	11,179	51,814	19,097	4,012
1953	254	153	101	86,681	10,621	48,067	27,993	3,904
1952	254	152	102	88,136	11,065	46,291	30,780	3,843
1951	(NA)	155	(NA)	89,791	11,242	45,749	32,800	(NA)
1950	263	161	102	92,310	11,496	46,067	34,747	3,883
1940	215	125	90	71,810	5,562	31,055	35,193	3,055
1930	199	120	79	77,772	4,374	35,437	37,961	2,995

NA Not available. [1] 5 net tons and over.

Series L 262–293. Landed Catches of Principal Species, by Regions: 1876 to 1970

[In millions of pounds, except as noted. For composition of regions, see text for series L 236–253]

Year or period	New England States								Middle Atlantic States		Chesapeake Bay States			South Atlantic States		
	Whiting	Cod	Flounder	Haddock	Herring	Lobster	Mackerel	Ocean perch	Menhaden	Oysters	Menhaden	Oysters	Crabs	Shrimp	Menhaden	Mullet
	262	263	264	265	266	267	268	269	270	271	272	273	274	275	276	277
1970	40	53	104	27	66	30	6	55	31	1	450	25	70	21	136	4
1969	39	57	100	46	69	31	8	56	44	1	182	22	61	27	165	5
1968	72	49	95	71	92	30	6	61	86	2	274	23	56	24	191	5
1967	60	44	98	98	69	25	7	71	47	1	223	26	83	21	194	5
1966	84	37	105	132	66	28	4	82	22	1	278	21	97	21	215	8
1965	75	35	112	134	75	29	3	84	151	1	360	21	86	26	192	7
1964	88	38	112	133	63	29	4	89	139	1	336	22	79	17	190	5
1963	87	40	107	124	155	29	3	108	373	1	259	18	66	16	216	8
1962	98	44	87	134	158	28	2	124	782	2	328	20	87	26	157	8
1961	94	42	67	134	58	26	2	132	715	2	299	28	75	20	255	8
1960	104	35	62	119	155	29	2	141	671	1	249	27	71	31	215	8
1959	110	41	57	113	121	27	4	137	653	1	415	33	46	26	331	8
1958	107	38	59	120	178	26	4	149	526	4	323	38	49	23	244	8
1957	126	32	54	133	161	29	2	134	822	8	268	34	58	29	196	7
1956	90	33	48	152	146	25	4	151	954	8	190	37	51	26	315	8
1955	111	32	50	135	104	28	3	157	764	10	315	39	45	29	228	8
1954	90	35	47	155	129	26	3	181	782	13	289	42	55	29	206	8
1953	85	32	47	139	111	27	7	154	858	14	162	37	63	33	199	8
1952	106	42	55	161	154	24	13	189	480	17	92	34	65	26	315	11
1951	118	47	61	153	65	26	10	258	442	17	127	30	71	28	188	14
1950	65	54	67	158	195	23	14	208	373	18	171	30	80	36	147	11
1949	90	59	67	134	168	24	18	237	392	17	138	32	68	--------	262	--------
1948	80	68	72	155	192	20	41	238	389	16	152	34	68	--------	249	--------
1947	62	64	68	162	124	23	47	147	509	16	178	34	65	--------	[1] 281	--------
1946	51	89	67	147	82	24	43	178	381	14	149	33	57	--------	[1] 292	--------

See footnotes at end of table.

Series L 262–293. Landed Catches of Principal Species, by Regions: 1876 to 1970—Con.

[In millions of pounds, except as noted. For composition of regions, see text for series L 236–253]

Year or period	New England States								Middle Atlantic States		Chesapeake Bay States			South Atlantic States		
	Whiting	Cod	Floun-der	Had-dock	Her-ring	Lobster	Mack-erel	Ocean perch	Men-haden	Oysters	Men-haden	Oysters	Crabs	Shrimp	Men-haden	Mullet
	262	263	264	265	266	267	268	269	270	271	272	273	274	275	276	277
1945	78	141	61	147	94	22	50	132	368	14	89	33	41	44	256	12
1944	52	94	58	133	83	17	64	120	304	13	78	30	45		[1]304	
1943	54	66	66	117	60	16	53	115	196	13		29	36		[1]332	
1942	47	65	75	137	100	12	47	128	205	12	64	29	36		[1]215	
1941											182	35	30			
1940	41	82	58	141	44	11	36	85	245	14	143	37	42	23	225	7
1939	28	105	46	158	75	11	28	77	149	12	128	37	57	28	287	8
1938	25	118	47	158	21	11	39	65	87	16	95	33	55	28	303	8
1937	22	135	48	169	53	11	23	58	149	15	122	32	49	27	205	8
1936											168	30	44	34	230	13
1935	17	120	39	195	54	11	62	17	180	15	121	30	41			
1934											144	36	40	26	155	9
1933	9	100	38	160	48	9	41		80	14	116	25	56	22	77	5
1932	7	86	37	150	38	10	60		43	15	195	28	62	25	72	6
1931	8	93	42	181	64	11	47		41	22	113	32	65			
1930	10	102	49	265	83	12	51		52	22	116	37	69	26	193	6
1929	10	87	49	256	107	10	62		41	29	99	33	60	31	234	9
1928	8	90	50	238	71	12	43							33	151	9
1927														30	158	11
1926									40	25						
1925											150	48	30			
1924	8	93	31	94	62	10	27							24	148	9
1923																
1921									228	26						
1920											366	52	23			
1919	16	89	16	90	98	11	16									
1918													50	16	258	12
1915							12									
1914																
1908	6	95	10	60	122	15	11		85	23	202	64	45	6	57	15
1905	5	94	6	78	86	12	18									
1904									254	33	258	67	31			
1902	3	124	5	48	201	15	23							4	19	16
1901									213	32	281	79	22			
1900							16									
1898	(Z)	125	4	47	66	15	10									
1897					46		17		91	29	179	96	16	1	11	7
1892					53	23	21									
1891							19		126	30	137	108	10			
1890							11		159	29	135	111	9	1	12	7
1889	(Z)	164	3	46	43	30	10		138	27				1	9	6
1888	(Z)	196	3	47	53	28	20		152	38	85	82			14	
1887	(Z)	207	2	41	43	29	33		88	39	85	75			15	
1886							30									
1885							124									
1884							179									
1883							85									
1882							142									
1881							147									
1880							131		319	28	92	117		1		4
1876–1879							306									

Year	Gulf States			Lakes Region		Pacific Coast States					Alaska			Canned salmon		Hawaii
	Shrimp	Men-haden	Mullet	Lake trout	White-fish	Tuna	Salm-on	Sar-dine	Hali-but	Mack-erel	Salm-on	Hali-but	Her-ring	Standard cases (millions)	Value (mil. dol.)	Tuna
	278	279	280	281	282	283	284	285	286	287	288	289	290	291	292	293
1970	230	1,209	27	(Z)	3	386	397	(Z)	6	1	333	28	16	3.9	142.7	9
1969	200	1,155	30	(Z)	3	315	267	(Z)	10	2	219	23	13	2.5	97.2	7
1968	204	823	25	(Z)	2	281	328	(Z)	12	3	285	13	8	3.4	118.0	10
1967	226	700	29	(Z)	2	315	217	(Z)	13	39	139	27	11	1.5	52.1	9
1966	179	763	30	(Z)	2	256	388	2	7	46	333	33	19	4.0	120.6	11
1965	195	1,023	34	(Z)	2	296	327	2	10	74	275	31	26	3.3	107.7	17
1964	179	904	37	(Z)	1	286	352	13	12	117	312	23	48	3.6	87.6	10
1963	203	968	35	(Z)	1	297	294	7	16	136	223	30	31	2.7	67.4	10
1962	142	1,057	35		1	294	315	15	17	139	278	37	34	3.5	94.4	11
1961	134	1.020	35		1	311	310	43	20	142	265	33	49	3.2	98.3	12

See footnotes at end of table.

Series L 262–293.   Landed Catches of Principal Species, by Regions: 1876 to 1970—Con.

[In millions of pounds, except as noted.   For composition of regions, see text for series L 236–253]

Year or period	Gulf States — Shrimp	Gulf States — Menhaden	Gulf States — Mullet	Lakes Region — Lake trout	Lakes Region — Whitefish	Pacific Coast — Tuna	Pacific Coast — Salmon	Pacific Coast — Sardine	Pacific Coast — Halibut	Pacific Coast — Mackerel	Alaska — Salmon	Alaska — Halibut	Alaska — Herring	Alaska — Canned salmon, Standard cases (millions)	Alaska — Canned salmon, Value (mil. dol.)	Hawaii — Tuna
	278	279	280	281	282	283	284	285	286	287	288	289	290	291	292	293
1960	206	841	33		1	288	235	58	23	112	207	28	78	2.6	76.5	9
1959	194	752	33	1	1	286	[2]202	74	24	76	147	30	107	1.8	49.5	14
1958	173	443	35	1	1	316	66	207	22	50	241	26	89	3.0	66.1	9
1957	168	363	33	1	1	295	62	46	21	144	203	27	118	2.5	62.9	8
1956	194	560	29	2	1	329	54	70	23	126	270	33	107	3.0	78.6	14
1955	212	481	28	1	3	269	86	146	23	59	204	27	64	2.5	56.8	12
1954	237	401	26	2	2	321	78	137	25	42	247	33	35	3.2	63.3	17
1953	225	437	26	2	3	301	93	9	21	64	220	26	32	2.9	58.2	16
1952	198	460	26	3	4	321	69	14	19	168	283	32	46	3.6	76.4	10
1951	194	358	25	3	3	317	98	329	16	124	277	31	88	3.5	79.2	16
1950	152	326	24	3	5	391	64	715	13	166	265	39	168	3.3	82.4	12
1949	127	277	32	3	9	330	96	634	15	101	388	34	35	4.4	81.3	11
1948	120	192		4	12	316	65	373	15	112	338	35	171	4.0	96.5	9
1947		(1)		5	12	254	116	272	10	175	382	33	195	4.3	88.7	7
1946		(1)		7	5	215	87	531	20	69	392	36	217	4.0	53.2	7
1945	145	65	30	9	4	181	96	850	18	63	403	34	153	4.3	44.5	
1944		(1)		11	3	167	50	1,147	17	97	393	36	139	4.9	51.2	
1943		(1)		10	3	126	49	997	19	88	457	35	90	5.4	57.8	
1942		(1)		10	4	118	78	975	21	58	431	31	46	5.1	48.3	
1941				11	5	124	86	1,328	28	80	543	26	156	6.9	56.2	
1940	128	25	30	10	5	205	61	914	27	122	439	28	111	5.0	31.5	
1939	120	12	29	10	4	171	75	1,241	29	85	452	22	230	5.2	34.4	
1938	113		28	9	3	136	64	1,110	29	84	590	21	231	6.8	36.5	
1937	114	6	28	9	3	155	96	1,140	30	68	593	21	261	6.7	45.0	
1936	85	3	30	9	4	125	64	1,503	32	106	727	20	209	8.5	44.8	
1935				10	5	117	99	1,168	31	156	434	18	226	5.2	25.8	
1934	93	10	22	10	6	94	87	1,136	29	116	625	21	203	7.5	37.6	
1933				10	8	68	107	510	31	71	467	21	173	5.2	28.4	
1932	66	12	20	11	10	60	76	312	30	13	453	20	149	5.3	21.7	
1931	71	4	21	11	11	57	133	300	21	15	468	27	120	5.4	29.1	
1930	62	6	22	10	10	99	100	494	18	17	426	38	189	5.0	29.7	
1929	78	19	25	11	8	72	142	652	19	59	443	45	186	5.4	40.5	
1928	82	6	26	9	6	62	81	420	19	36	517	39	163	6.1	45.4	
1927	69	13	29	10	5	69	132	342	17	5	301	45	128	3.6	30.0	
1926				12	5	43	85	287	14	4		45	179	6.7	46.1	
1925				11	4	53	140	315	14	4		44	182	4.5	32.0	
1924				11	4	28	102	243	11	3		47	101	5.3	33.0	
1923	47	19	31	10	4	38	106	159	12	4		44	86	5.1	32.9	
1922				12	4	35	63	93	14	2		31	83	4.5	29.8	
1921				15	3	20		59	16	3		40	38	2.6	19.6	
1920				10	3	39		119	17	3		34	54	4.4	35.6	
1919				12	4	36		154	16	3		28	38	4.6	43.3	
1918	32	14	30	11	6	16		158	14	4		28	48	5.7	51.0	
1917				11	6	32			21			31	28	5.9	46.3	
1916				10	5	43			22			29	23	4.9	23.3	
1915				11	4	22	127	4	38			29	14	4.5	18.7	
1914				10	5	18			49			12	17	4.1	18.9	
1913				11	4	7			41			18	27	3.7	13.5	
1912						3			38			14	33	4.1	18.7	
1911						1			44			11	24	2.8	14.6	
1910													14	2.4	11.1	
1909													17	2.3	9.4	
1908	13		19	13	7		86	5					12	2.6	10.2	
1907								[2]49				(2)	10	2.2	8.8	
1906													10	2.2	7.9	
1905													15	1.9	6.3	
1904							107	1					16	2.0		
1903				16	5								14	2.2		
1902	12	(Z)	27										10	2.5		
1901													15	2.0		
1900													13	1.5		
1899				10	6		129	2					8	1.1		
1898													9	1.0		
1897	7		16	13	7								7	.9		
1896													6	1.0		
1895						1	78	1	[2]2			(2)	7	.6		
1894													15	.7		
1893				16	8								14	.6		
1892							47	1	[2]2			(2)	19	.5		
1891												(3)	18	.8		
1890	7		15	13	11				[2]1			(2)	11	.7		
1889	8		13	11	16				[2]1			(2)	11	.7		
1888			8						[2]2			(2)	6	.4		
1887													22	.3		
1886													22	.1		
1885				13	18								17	.1		
1884													13	.1		
1883													8			
1882													3			
1881																
1880			2													
1876–1879																

Z   Less than 500,000 pounds.

[1] Gulf States included with South Atlantic States.
[2] Production in Alaska included with Pacific Coast States.

Series L 294–304. Per Capita Consumption of Fishery Products: 1909 to 1970

[Pounds of edible meat]

Year	Total	Fresh and frozen			Canned						Cured
		Total	Fish	Shellfish	Total	Salmon	Sardines	Tuna	Shellfish	Other	
	294	**295**	**296**	**297**	**298**	**299**	**300**	**301**	**302**	**303**	**304**
1970	11.8	6.9	4.5	2.4	4.5	0.7	0.3	2.5	0.5	0.5	0.4
1969	11.2	6.6	4.4	2.2	4.2	.7	.3	2.4	.4	.4	.4
1968	11.0	6.2	4.0	2.2	4.3	.7	.4	2.4	.5	.3	.5
1967	10.6	5.8	3.6	2.2	4.3	.7	.4	2.4	.5	.3	.5
1966	10.9	6.1	3.9	2.2	4.3	.8	.4	2.3	.4	.4	.5
1965	10.9	6.0	3.8	2.2	4.4	.9	.3	2.3	.5	.4	.5
1964	10.5	5.9	3.8	2.1	4.1	.7	.3	2.0	.5	.6	.5
1963	10.7	5.8	3.8	2.0	4.4	.9	.4	2.0	.5	.6	.5
1962	10.6	5.8	3.9	1.9	4.3	.9	.3	2.1	.4	.6	.5
1961	10.7	5.9	3.9	2.0	4.3	.8	.5	2.1	.4	.5	.5
1960	10.3	5.7	3.8	1.9	4.0	.7	.4	2.0	.4	.5	.6
1959	10.9	5.9	4.1	1.8	4.4	.9	.6	1.9	.5	.5	.6
1958	10.6	5.7	4.1	1.6	4.3	1.1	.6	1.8	.4	.4	.6
1957	10.2	5.5	3.8	1.7	4.0	1.0	.4	1.6	.4	.6	.7
1956	10.4	5.7	4.0	1.7	4.0	1.1	.4	1.6	.4	.5	.7
1955	10.5	5.9	4.2	1.7	3.9	1.0	.6	1.4	.4	.5	.7
1954	11.2	6.2	4.5	1.7	4.3	1.1	.8	1.4	.4	.6	.7
1953	11.4	6.4	4.7	1.7	4.3	1.3	.7	1.4	.4	.5	.7
1952	11.2	6.2	4.5	1.7	4.3	1.4	.5	1.3	.3	.8	.7
1951	11.2	6.3	4.6	1.7	4.3	1.4	.8	1.2	.4	.5	.6
1950	11.8	6.3	4.7	1.6	4.9	1.4	1.4	1.1	.4	.6	.6
1949	10.9	5.8	4.3	1.5	4.5	1.6	1.2	.9	.3	.5	.6
1948	11.1	6.0	4.4	1.6	4.4	1.6	1.1	.9	.3	.5	.7
1947	10.3	5.8	4.2	1.6	3.8	1.3	.9	.8	.2	.6	.7
1946	10.8	5.9	4.3	1.6	4.2	1.4	1.1	.7	.4	.6	.7
1945	9.9	6.6	5.0	1.6	2.6	.9	.8	.6	.1	.2	.7
1944	8.7	5.5	4.1	1.4	2.6	.8	.9	.5	.1	.3	.6
1943	7.9	5.5	4.2	1.3	1.8	.7	.4	.4	.2	.1	.6
1942	8.7	5.2	4.0	1.2	2.9	1.2	.8	.4	.2	.3	.6
1941	11.2	6.3	5.0	1.3	4.2	2.3	.9	.5	.2	.3	.7
1940	11.0	5.7	4.5	1.2	4.6	2.0	1.0	.6	.5	.5	.7
1939	10.7	5.3	4.1	1.2	4.7	2.1	1.1	.6	.5	.4	.7
1938	10.8	5.2	4.0	1.2	4.8	2.4	1.0	.5	.4	.5	.8
1937	11.8	5.6	4.4	1.2	5.3	2.6	1.3	.5	.4	.5	.9
1936	11.7	5.2	4.1	1.1	5.8	3.0	1.3	.4	.4	.7	.7
1935	10.5	5.1	4.1	1.0	4.7	2.2	1.0	.5	.2	.8	.7
1934	9.2	4.3	3.3	1.0	4.2	2.3	.8	.4	.2	.5	.7
1933	8.7	4.2	3.4	.8	3.9	2.3	.7	.3	.2	.4	.6
1932	8.4	4.3	3.4	.9	3.4	2.3	.5	.3	.2	.1	.7
1931	8.8	4.9	3.9	1.0	3.2	2.1	.5	.2	.2	.2	.7
1930	10.2	5.8	4.6	1.2	3.4	2.1	.6	.3	.2	.2	1.0
1929	11.9	6.9	5.5	1.4	3.9	2.1	1.0	.3	.3	.2	1.1
1928	12.1	7.1	--------	--------	3.9	2.4	1.1	.2	.2	(Z)	1.1
1927	12.2	7.0	--------	--------	3.9	2.6	.8	.2	.2	.1	1.3
1926	11.4	6.6	--------	--------	3.4	2.1	.8	.2	.2	.1	1.4
1925	11.1	6.3	--------	--------	3.2	2.0	.8	.2	.2	(Z)	1.6
1924	11.0	6.1	--------	--------	3.2	2.1	.8	.1	.2	(Z)	1.7
1923	10.7	6.0	--------	--------	2.9	1.9	.6	.2	.2	(Z)	1.8
1922	11.3	6.1	--------	--------	3.2	2.1	.7	.1	.2	.1	2.0
1921	10.5	6.2	--------	--------	2.2	1.1	.7	.1	.2	.1	2.1
1920	11.8	6.3	--------	--------	3.2	--------	--------	--------	--------	--------	2.3
1919	11.6	6.4	--------	--------	2.8	--------	--------	--------	--------	--------	2.4
1918	10.9	6.4	--------	--------	2.0	--------	--------	--------	--------	--------	2.5
1917	10.9	6.2	--------	--------	2.0	--------	--------	--------	--------	--------	2.7
1916	11.0	6.0	--------	--------	2.2	--------	--------	--------	--------	--------	2.8
1915	11.2	5.8	--------	--------	2.4	--------	--------	--------	--------	--------	3.0
1914	11.7	5.6	--------	--------	3.0	--------	--------	--------	--------	--------	3.1
1913	11.5	5.3	--------	--------	2.9	--------	--------	--------	--------	--------	3.3
1912	11.3	5.0	--------	--------	2.9	--------	--------	--------	--------	--------	3.4
1911	11.3	4.8	--------	--------	2.8	--------	--------	--------	--------	--------	3.7
1910	11.2	4.5	--------	--------	2.8	--------	--------	--------	--------	--------	3.9
1909	11.0	4.3	--------	--------	2.7	--------	--------	--------	--------	--------	4.0

Z Less than 0.05 pound.

Series L 305–310. Disposition of Landed Catches, by Major Product Groups: 1921 to 1970

[In millions of pounds]

Year	Total	Edible — Total edible	Edible — Fresh and frozen	Edible — Canned	Edible — Cured	Industrial products
	305	306	307	308	309	310
1970	4,917	2,537	1,316	1,150	71	2,380
1969	4,337	2,321	1,320	933	68	2,016
1968	4,160	2,347	1,263	1,017	67	1,813
1967	4,055	2,368	1,290	1,001	77	1,687
1966	4,366	2,573	1,490	1,006	77	1,793
1965	4,777	2,587	1,469	1,042	76	2,190
1964	4,541	2,497	1,393	1,033	71	2,044
1963	4,847	2,556	1,405	1,073	78	2,291
1962	5,354	2,540	1,486	974	80	2,814
1961	5,187	2,490	1,439	970	81	2,697
1960	4,942	2,498	1,373	1,043	82	2,444
1959	5,122	2,369	1,309	977	83	2,753
1958	4,747	2,651	1,356	1,210	85	2,096
1957	4,789	2,475	1,270	1,117	88	2,314
1956	5,268	2,690	1,401	1,202	87	2,578
1955	4,809	2,579	1,454	1,039	86	2,230
1954	4,762	2,705	1,461	1,159	85	2,057
1953	4,487	2,519	1,441	993	85	1,968
1952	4,432	2,778	1,445	1,248	85	1,654
1951	4,433	3,048	1,638	1,326	84	1,385
1950	4,901	3,307	1,487	1,720	100	1,594
1949	4,804	3,305	1,542	1,663	100	1,499
1948	4,513	3,146	1,558	1,488	100	1,367
1947	4,349	3,020	1,536	1,384	100	1,329
1946	4,467	3,049	1,672	1,277	100	1,418
1945	4,598	3,167	1,827	1,230	110	1,431
1944	4,533	2,865	1,530	1,225	110	1,668
1943	4,162	2,737	1,458	1,165	114	1,425
1942	3,875	2,683	1,338	1,230	115	1,192
1941	4,900	3,062	1,292	1,645	125	1,838
1940	4,060	2,675	1,264	1,280	130	1,385
1939	4,445	2,713	1,302	1,281	130	1,732
1938	4,254	2,639	1,275	1,234	130	1,615
1937	4,353	2,703	1,217	1,356	130	1,650
1936	4,826	2,854	1,260	1,459	135	1,972
1935	4,135	2,583	1,233	1,220	130	1,552
1934	4,104	2,434	1,011	1,293	130	1,670
1933	2,997	2,087	961	991	135	911
1932	2,612	1,864	937	787	140	748
1931	2,630	2,129	1,037	962	130	501
1930	3,224	2,478	1,256	1,077	145	746
1929	3,491	2,601	1,165	1,286	150	890
1928	3,061	2,370	1,125	1,095	150	691
1927	2,806	2,172	1,119	878	175	634
1926	2,871	2,198	1,085	938	175	673
1925	2,891	2,029	990	864	175	862
1924	2,461	1,874	900	799	175	587
1923	2,726	1,807	845	782	180	919
1922	2,619	1,677	801	696	180	942
1921	2,255	1,451	788	483	180	804

Series L 311–318. Production and Imports of Selected Fishery Items: 1924 to 1970

[In millions of pounds of product weight. Production includes Alaska for all years and, beginning 1959, Hawaii; imports include Alaska, Hawaii, Puerto Rico, and outlying areas]

Year	Groundfish fillets and steaks — Production	Groundfish fillets and steaks — Imports	Shrimp — Production	Shrimp — Imports	American lobsters (northern) — Production	American lobsters (northern) — Imports	Lobsters, spiny — Production	Lobsters, spiny — Imports
	311	312	313	314	315	316	317	318
1970	43	459	367	219	34	17	10	38
1969	47	427	319	194	34	17	9	45
1968	55	390	299	189	33	17	8	43
1967	71	284	308	186	27	16	5	35
1966	75	315	239	179	30	17	6	37
1965	77	295	244	163	30	19	6	38
1964	75	247	212	155	31	20	4	35
1963	83	232	240	152	30	22	4	34
1962	94	221	191	141	29	22	4	36
1961	93	195	175	126	28	21	3	33
1960	94	156	249	113	31	21	3	32
1959	91	185	240	107	29	21	4	28
1958	99	147	214	85	27	21	4	26
1957	97	141	204	70	30	22	5	28
1956	107	135	224	69	27	22	4	25
1955	105	128	244	53	29	23	3	22
1954	122	138	268	41	27	22	3	20
1953	112	90	260	43	28	23	3	20
1952	133	107	227	38	25	23	2	16
1951	149	88	224	42	26	24	4	15
1950	137	65	191	40	23	22	2	13
1949	140	47	173	30	25	21	3	9
1948	138	54	167	22	21	21	1	8
1947	116	35	192	13	24	18	1	6
1946	127	49	192	12	24	20	1	6
1945	126	43	191	8	23	20	1	3
1944	109	25	152	6	18	15	1	3
1943	87	16	152	6	16	13	1	3
1942	105	17	152	4	12	13	1	3
1941	123	10	153	3	12	21		2
1940	91	10	153	5	12	19		2
1939	99	9	150	4	12	16		2
1938	---	---	143	3	12	15		2
1937	---	---	143	2	12	16		2
1936	---	---	122	1	11	12		2
1935	---	---	124	2	11	11		2
1934	---	---	122	1	10	11		2
1933	---	---	91	1	10	12		1
1932	---	---	92	---	11	13		1
1931	---	---	99	---	12	12		2
1930	---	---	92	---	14	11		2
1929	---	---	113	---	12	10		2
1928	---	---	102	---	11	8		2
1927	---	---	---	---		8		1
1926	---	---	---	---		8		1
1925	---	---	---	---		8		1
1924	---	---	---	---		6		1

Series L 319–320. Sponge Sales at the Tarpon Springs (Fla.) Exchange: 1913 to 1970

Year	Pounds (319)	Value ($1,000) (320)
1970	32,000	253
1969	37,000	293
1968	42,000	342
1967	43,000	386
1966	26,000	217
1965	33,000	307
1964	44,000	363
1963	55,000	387
1962	48,000	416
1961	36,900	367
1960	39,000	314
1959	28,000	290
1958	29,700	216
1957	44,500	247
1956	29,600	242
1955	34,700	251
1954	15,100	120
1953	17,300	127
1952	25,000	142
1951	15,800	110
1950	22,000	130
1949	83,947	471
1948	[2]74,464	466
1947	158,304	1,742
1946	156,916	2,946
1945	203,447	2,716
1944	186,027	2,552
1943	217,355	2,305
1942	184,280	1,700
1941	201,126	1,365
1940	232,164	847
1939	423,682	1,036
1938	530,183	952
1937	561,943	1,097
1936	628,226	1,035
1935	388,888	620
1934	499,635	671
1933	373,178	420
1932	430,641	518
1931	386,219	610
1930	475,294	803
1929	413,763	707
1928	451,034	730
1927	474,200	866
1926	423,061	666
1925	494,183	715
1924	508,954	715
1923	519,582	734
1922	556,097	699
1921	404,729	540
1920	412,597	678
1919	456,558	708
1918	355,695	593
1917	487,943	870
1914	468,457	566
1913	513,434	685

[1] For 1950–1970, includes sponges sold outside the Exchange.   [2] Drop in catch caused by serious outbreak of sponge disease.

Series L 321–337. Prices Received By Fishermen: 1939 to 1970

[Annual average price in cents per pound]

Year	Clams, soft	Cod	Flounder	Haddock	American lobsters (northern)	Menhaden	Ocean perch	Salmon Chinook	Chum	Coho	Pink	Sockeye	Sea scallops	Tuna Albacore	Bluefin	Skipjack	Yellowfin
	321	322	323	324	325	326	327	328	329	330	331	332	333	334	335	336	337
1970	47.5	13.1	15.3	25.8	94.7	1.8	4.9	70.3	12.7	45.2	13.2	25.7	135.6	25.0	17.4	15.9	18.4
1969	42.4	10.1	13.7	19.4	80.9	1.5	4.2	59.4	14.3	43.0	15.0	27.3	110.8	21.9	15.3	13.4	16.2
1968	41.7	8.4	11.4	15.0	72.8	1.3	3.9	49.6	13.6	39.5	13.8	27.8	111.9	20.6	14.2	12.9	15.5
1967	46.6	9.6	11.5	12.9	82.5	1.2	3.9	47.1	11.2	40.8	12.1	24.4	77.2	18.9	12.6	11.1	14.1
1966	46.1	10.5	12.7	10.5	78.4	1.7	4.2	49.6	11.8	33.3	13.6	22.5	49.2	18.5	15.2	13.8	18.0
1965	49.1	9.4	9.5	10.2	75.2	1.6	4.1	48.3	8.9	30.1	10.4	22.2	67.5	15.7	13.6	10.8	13.9
1964	46.0	8.9	8.0	10.1	66.2	1.4	4.1	51.3	8.0	31.7	10.6	23.5	54.6	15.8	12.0	10.2	12.9
1963	42.8	8.3	8.4	10.8	55.4	1.2	4.2	50.1	9.3	27.2	11.7	23.8	45.7	15.9	11.2	10.7	13.2
1962	45.2	7.9	9.7	9.3	50.7	1.1	4.8	50.9	8.8	30.4	14.2	22.1	40.7	16.3	14.1	13.1	15.2
1961	43.0	7.3	10.6	8.4	53.2	1.1	4.3	52.6	8.8	30.6	10.1	19.6	38.0	18.2	12.8	11.1	12.8
1960	39.7	7.6	12.2	9.0	45.7	1.0	4.0	50.8	8.8	40.8	13.0	21.4	34.9	15.7	12.0	10.5	12.5
1959	37.8	8.2	12.8	11.1	50.4	1.2	3.8	40.9	9.1	28.4	11.4	21.4	48.4	18.6	12.4	10.6	13.0
1958	36.7	8.8	11.8	11.2	49.0	1.4	4.1	42.0	7.4	30.6	9.2	23.0	48.4	20.5	13.0	11.7	13.5
1957	37.6	7.0	13.0	8.3	36.7	1.3	4.2	32.5	8.2	22.4	11.7	18.2	48.5	14.4	12.0	11.0	13.3
1956	36.3	7.1	12.8	7.2	44.3	1.4	3.8	35.3	7.1	27.3	9.1	16.2	54.0	17.1	13.1	11.5	13.5
1955	36.1	6.8	12.6	6.8	38.4	1.3	3.8	33.8	7.8	24.5	10.3	14.8	52.3	16.6	14.3	13.4	15.3
1954	36.6	6.9	12.0	7.3	37.3	1.4	4.1	30.2	7.5	21.5	8.9	18.6	44.8	20.1	16.9	15.2	17.2
1953	33.2	7.8	12.4	8.6	37.7	1.1	3.9	25.4	6.7	18.2	9.5	14.0	44.0	19.9	15.5	14.0	16.0
1952	30.3	8.4	13.6	8.7	42.5	1.0	4.3	26.8	8.4	19.7	9.4	13.1	59.5	17.3	15.5	13.0	16.0
1951	23.2	8.2	13.8	8.8	34.8	1.2	4.9	30.1	9.2	24.4	12.4	14.0	44.8	15.7	15.0	14.5	15.5
1950	17.2	7.2	11.1	8.5	34.9	1.0	4.4	28.7	7.9	27.5	7.9	10.1	46.6	-------	-------	-------	-------
1949	16.5	6.8	10.0	7.8	34.8	1.0	4.1	26.0	6.1	19.4	8.8	9.1	36.7				
1948	20.1	7.4	10.7	9.1	40.4	1.1	4.0	28.8	7.1	25.2	6.3	7.6	52.4				
1947	19.0	6.6	9.3	7.6	37.3	1.1	4.0	24.6	4.6	21.7	6.9	5.4	49.1				
1946	18.5	7.6	8.7	9.6	38.3	.9	4.5	-------	-------	-------	-------	-------	55.8				
1945	14.3	7.1	7.5	7.8	40.1	.8	3.9						32.9				
1944	11.8	6.9	7.2	7.6	28.8	.5	3.9						32.5				
1943	13.0	8.0	7.6	9.2	25.6	.6	4.0						42.4				
1942	7.7	6.5	5.4	6.8	21.7	.6	3.0						31.8				
1941	5.7	3.6	4.0	4.1	17.7	.5	2.0						22.2				
1940	4.0	3.4	3.3	3.7	16.2	.4	1.5						13.0				
1939	4.2	2.5	3.1	2.7	15.6	.4	1.4						14.3				

Series L 338–357. Production and Value of Canned Fishery Products: 1921 to 1970

[Production in thousands of cases, value in thousands of dollars. Includes production of U.S. outlying areas]

Year	Total, all products Production	Value	Salmon (Pacific) Production	Value	Sardines (Pacific) Production	Value	Sardines (Maine) Production	Value	Tuna Production	Value
	338	339	340	341	342	343	344	345	346	347
1970	46,188	741,760	3,822	138,673	---------	---------	807	11,227	22,063	380,574
1969	40,744	575,533	2,551	90,286	---------	---------	1,043	11,512	20,098	297,456
1968	43,006	583,908	3,448	118,015	(1)	(1)	1,730	19,297	20,012	268,731
1967	41,241	525,563	2,072	76,121	(1)	(1)	1,250	13,862	19,681	261,527
1966	40,784	563,708	4,358	136,075	3	25	1,333	12,262	19,954	270,239
1965	38,349	495,231	3,634	122,744	8	71	1,267	10,868	18,099	232,976
1964	35,752	436,660	3,759	95,761	121	1,030	866	7,584	17,689	217,585
1963	34,571	421,607	3,295	87,963	57	685	1,619	13,244	16,556	201,588
1962	36,843	456,866	3,801	106,712	137	1,300	2,147	20,077	17,018	209,821
1961	33,395	422,836	3,697	116,955	419	3,664	754	7,560	15,768	189,173
1960	34,917	387,595	2,834	88,197	616	4,659	1,998	16,700	15,305	172,679
1959	31,781	348,251	2,465	71,827	755	5,399	1,753	14,902	14,332	159,143
1958	34,483	388,582	3,731	92,822	2,222	16,497	2,100	15,874	14,094	161,793
1957	31,063	335,829	3,207	86,149	498	4,721	2,218	14,733	11,891	135,813
1956	30,962	349,516	3,505	95,101	755	5,734	2,231	16,692	11,827	140,287
1955	26,315	303,165	3,289	81,356	1,415	10,014	1,269	9,333	9,934	125,223
1954	28,166	331,018	4,163	92,255	1,338	9,818	2,935	18,153	10,811	141,504
1953	26,007	306,874	3,912	82,240	64	653	2,782	16,954	9,407	124,744
1952	26,260	305,829	4,464	98,264	107	918	3,531	21,503	8,894	111,076
1951	24,563	301,210	4,646	108,626	2,865	19,363	1,677	14,635	8,131	98,102
1950	29,837	331,335	4,310	109,541	5,071	26,346	3,844	21,209	8,945	112,136
1949	25,650	295,504	5,525	103,431	3,768	21,335	3,075	21,052	7,130	96,040
1948	23,734	336,181	4,825	120,537	2,654	21,893	3,682	29,359	6,664	107,981
1947	21,868	310,679	5,642	120,635	1,653	16,538	3,014	28,311	5,448	85,093
1946	20,486	227,629	4,510	70,160	2,977	19,896	3,276	20,276	4,597	57,343
1945	18,555	152,801	4,908	52,586	3,766	15,346	2,725	12,077	4,442	46,713
1944	18,521	152,914	5,139	56,383	3,651	15,226	3,262	14,820	3,531	40,615
1943	16,716	141,189	5,704	62,935	3,355	14,352	2,505	11,105	2,580	30,542
1942	18,077	144,997	5,835	61,974	3,745	15,510	2,873	12,162	2,405	30,009
1941	23,555	138,684	7,832	67,417	5,007	18,092	3,165	12,591	2,557	17,605
1940	18,909	94,182	5,605	38,050	2,946	8,975	1,118	3,736	3,994	22,926
1939	19,487	96,628	5,992	41,781	3,108	9,554	2,210	7,075	3,643	19,147
1938	17,004	83,446	7,280	42,366	2,262	7,102	672	2,367	2,512	14,143
1937	19,531	105,175	7,555	52,934	2,812	8,592	1,680	4,998	2,929	17,915
1936	20,098	94,564	8,965	50,061	2,617	7,302	1,846	5,740	2,681	13,559

See footnotes at end of table.

Series L 338–357. Production and Value of Canned Fishery Products: 1921 to 1970—Con.

[Production in thousands of cases, value in thousands of dollars. Includes production of U.S. outlying areas]

Year	Total, all products		Salmon (Pacific)		Sardines (Pacific)		Sardines (Maine)		Tuna	
	Production	Value	Production	Value	Production	Value	Production	Value	Production	Value
	338	339	340	341	342	343	344	345	346	347
1935	17,435	74,999	6,028	32,475	2,420	6,237	1,656	5,143	2,272	11,848
1934	17,379	80,021	8,383	45,818	1,970	5,481	1,143	3,315	1,897	9,731
1933	13,117	59,800	6,362	36,242	1,539	3,805	981	2,397	1,357	6,601
1932	10,495	43,749	5,909	26,460	954	2,358	546	1,370	1,152	5,961
1931	12,581	62,949	6,740	38,083	1,713	4,715	885	2,647	1,160	7,031
1930	14,767	82,858	6,086	42,836	2,979	8,742	1,399	4,459	1,876	12,377
1929	17,310	101,065	6,991	56,086	3,831	11,997	2,026	6,898	1,448	9,585
1928	15,630	95,872	6,927	54,638	2,772	9,659	2,056	8,077	1,178	8,171
1927	12,282	81,384	5,077	45,729	2,563	9,269	1,262	5,249	1,195	8,056
1926		86,193	7,489	56,219	2,093	7,807	1,718	6,727	777	4,924
1925		80,577	6,019	47,370	1,715	6,381	1,871	6,717	1,079	8,368
1924		72,165	6,254	42,402	1,367	5,446	1,900	7,191	623	5,581
1923		72,445	6,403	45,534	1,100	4,608	1,272	5,289	793	6,781
1922		60,465	5,235	38,421	715	3,361	1,870	5,750	657	4,434
1921		46,635	3,600	28,857	399	2,346	1,400	3,961	549	3,074

Year	Oysters		Shrimp		Anchovies		Mackerel [2]		Animal food	
	Production	Value	Production	Value	Production	Value	Production	Value	Production	Value
	348	349	350	351	352	353	354	355	356	357
1970	272	2,102	3,722	37,277	(Z)	(Z)	189	1,536	11,244	105,232
1969	286	2,164	2,836	27,730	(Z)	(Z)	386	3,317	9,416	82,474
1968	651	5,624	2,810	29,444	(Z)	(Z)	495	4,098	10,103	84,621
1967	660	6,152	2,496	24,332	(Z)	(Z)	283	2,363	10,398	78,256
1966	400	3,201	2,104	21,973	(Z)	(Z)	413	3,346	7,596	54,614
1965	576	3,701	2,315	20,655	(Z)	(Z)	703	4,997	7,737	46,848
1964	845	5,292	1,443	12,986	(Z)	(Z)	1,071	6,760	7,342	43,471
1963	893	5,633	2,356	19,531	(Z)	(Z)	1,275	7,603	6,379	39,042
1962	643	4,557	1,963	18,973	16	(Z)	1,220	7,560	7,827	45,866
1961	891	5,776	1,375	11,742	73	(Z)	1,378	8,529	6,945	39,072
1960	821	5,640	2,114	17,233	(NA)	(NA)	935	5,804	8,787	43,979
1959	842	5,721	2,049	16,948	4	(Z)	587	4,235	7,210	37,077
1958	797	5,445	2,120	20,791	54	(Z)	404	2,657	7,503	41,959
1957	997	7,008	1,351	13,136	440	2	1,327	7,404	7,223	34,153
1956	930	6,257	2,020	16,421	612	3,361	1,116	6,435	6,688	32,715
1955	1,119	7,004	2,002	13,562	415	2,431	564	3,334	5,337	27,517
1954	932	5,829	2,007	13,691	506	2,773	366	2,509	4,027	18,420
1953	978	6,559	2,258	18,947	1,062	7,661	596	5,039	3,881	17,348
1952	1,058	7,047	1,818	12,999	674	4,737	1,525	11,363	3,498	15,668
1951	933	5,931	1,936	12,187	63	489	1,049	6,259	2,342	11,676
1950	985	7,096	1,747	12,773	38	227	1,457	7,492	2,721	13,871
1949	906	6,525	1,477	11,203	6	34	1,050	6,849	1,932	8,663
1948	714	4,778	1,242	7,791	103	755	1,281	9,851	1,324	6,971
1947	820	4,259	1,050	8,192	200	1,377	1,755	15,019	910	3,950
1946	782	5,249	1,160	8,429			962	7,575		
1945	452	2,030	478	1,919			693	4,047		
1944	548	2,283	1,248	4,855			1,225	7,034		
1943	692	2,822	1,468	5,361	(Z)	1	937	5,271	2	5
1942	1,046	3,599	2,141	7,347	(Z)	6	721	3,693	105	375
1941	1,314	2,997	1,966	4,883			935	3,504	1,010	2,624
1940	1,382	2,527	2,481	4,318			1,422	4,101	722	1,862
1939	1,298	2,379	3,059	5,398			889	2,589	567	1,109
1938	1,034	1,886	2,683	4,872			966	2,896	413	888
1937	1,520	2,933	3,189	7,131			841	2,674	377	840
1936	1,136	2,181	2,276	4,672			1,237	3,543	267	744
1935	1,074	2,045	2,701	4,722			1,812	4,976	476	1,304
1934	940	1,871	2,515	4,403			1,275	3,245	302	823
1933	746	1,076	2,130	3,479			749	1,868	214	588
1932	842	1,008	1,869	2,595			95	254	117	286
1931	656	964	2,038	3,982			102	247	53	143
1930	848	1,837	1,997	4,961			132	468	17	50
1929	1,112	2,732	2,233	5,529			602	2,516	19	60
1928	1,080	2,761	2,052	5,182			399	1,714	5	17
1927	958	2,368	2,068	5,322			23	152		
1926	886	2,027	1,627	4,122			13	114		
1925	1,404	3,721	1,635	3,783			14	116		
1924	958	2,478	1,597	4,609			1	3		
1923	1,124	2,720	1,557	4,382			1	8		
1922	1,084	2,424	1,288	3,064			10	93		
1921	948	2,179	1,456	3,805			2	16		

NA Not available.
Z Less than $500 or 500 cases.

[1] Less than three plants in operation, therefore included with miscellaneous fishery products.
[2] Includes Pacific mackerel, jack mackerel, and small proportion of Atlantic mackerel.

Series L 358–361. Production of Canned Tuna: 1926 to 1970

[In millions of pounds of net product weight. Canned imports include bonito and yellowtail for 1932 to 1948]

Year	Domestically canned — Total (358)	Domestic catch (359)	Frozen imports (360)	Canned imports (361)
1970	437.6	203.5	234.1	72.3
1969	398.4	181.8	216.7	73.1
1968	396.0	176.7	219.4	67.2
1967	388.8	183.2	205.6	65.3
1966	394.3	153.2	241.0	61.6
1965	358.4	161.5	196.9	51.0
1964	349.8	154.2	195.6	54.6
1963	326.7	160.8	165.9	57.5
1962	335.5	147.6	187.9	56.7
1961	310.6	163.9	146.8	58.7
1960	301.4	142.6	158.8	51.8
1959	282.2	132.2	150.0	56.1
1958	277.1	149.8	127.3	46.2
1957	232.5	140.2	92.3	44.4
1956	229.4	152.7	76.7	38.2
1955	196.4	113.6	82.8	35.6
1954	213.0	148.9	64.1	31.6
1953	185.5	135.9	49.6	34.6
1952	175.2	140.2	35.0	23.3
1951	155.4	125.8	29.6	13.0
1950	173.5	152.7	20.8	36.8
1949	138.6	134.0	4.6	4.6
1948	132.2	129.6	2.6	8.3
1947	108.5	107.4	1.1	6.1
1946	90.2	89.6	.6	4.7
1945	87.3	86.5	.8	5.3
1944	69.1	68.4	.7	3.2
1943	51.2	51.0	.2	.5
1942	48.2	47.8	.4	.4
1941	52.2	51.7	.5	3.3
1940	81.8	80.4	1.4	7.7
1939	70.2	66.7	3.5	10.1
1938	52.1	47.1	5.0	7.2
1937	60.7	55.2	5.5	11.1
1936	50.2	48.0	2.2	6.8
1935	47.2	44.7	2.5	8.2
1934	39.4	36.9	2.5	8.3
1933	28.2	25.8	2.4	14.4
1932	23.8	21.5	2.3	6.0
1931	24.1	21.0	3.1	--------
1930	39.0	23.2	15.8	--------
1929	30.1	16.7	13.4	--------
1928	24.6	15.9	8.7	--------
1927	25.0	16.4	8.6	--------
1926	16.3	13.0	3.3	--------

Series L 362–368. Production and Value of Dried Fish Meal and Scrap, Acidulated Scrap, Fish and Other Marine Oils, and Imports of Fish Meal: 1921 to 1970

[Includes Alaska]

Year	Meal and scrap [1] Quantity [2] (362)	Value (363)	Marine oils Quantity (364)	Value (365)	Meal imports [3] (366)	Acidulated scrap Quantity (367)	Value (368)
	1,000 tons	Mil. dol.	Mil. gal.	Mil. dol.	1,000 tons	1,000 tons	Mil. dol.
1970	269	46.4	27	18.2	251		
1969	253	39.8	22	9.3	358		
1968	235	30.3	22	7.3	855		
1967	211	26.0	16	6.1	651		
1966	224	32.3	21	12.5	448		
1965	254	35.7	25	14.9	271		
1964	235	28.0	23	13.3	439		
1963	256	30.2	24	10.8	376		
1962	312	35.6	33	11.0	252		
1961	311	31.9	34	14.4	218		
1960	290	25.3	28	13.4	132		
1959	307	35.9	25	13.1	133		
1958	248	31.8	22	12.3	100		
1957	264	32.6	20	12.6	81		
1956	296	37.9	27	17.3	90		
1955	265	34.7	25	14.9	98		
1954	257	32.8	22	12.8	146		
1953	239	29.6	20	11.5	132		
1952	221	27.2	16	9.4	204		
1951	210	25.4	18	16.6	128		
1950	240	29.3	22	17.5	64		
1949	237	35.7	18	17.4	52		
1948	200	23.1	17	31.0	41		
1947	187	22.4	17	31.8	9		
1946	200	20.4	20	34.7	9	2	0.1
1945	199	14.3	25	27.2	3	2	.1
1944	210	15.1	28	31.0	9	3	.1
1943	189	13.6	23	29.8	3	2	.1
1942	168	11.5	21	22.6	3	3	.1
1941	226	12.9	29	29.6	33	11	.3
1940	178	7.6	25	12.0	46	16	.3
1939	210	8.8	36	14.7	61	16	.3
1938	183	7.0	35	13.5	40	22	.4
1937	188	6.9	36	16.4	93	32	.6
1936	220	7.3	40	15.3	44	23	.4
1935	183	5.2	32	13.1	28	30	.5
1934	175	5.7	30	6.4	36	22	.4
1933	121	3.7	18	2.6	27	9	.2
1932	95	2.3	12	1.4	24	7	.1
1931	75	2.9	9	1.6	38	9	.1
1930	124	5.7	15	4.2	--------	16	.4
1929	120	6.2	15	6.8	--------	23	.6
1928	84	4.9	12	5.2	--------	20	.5
1927	72	3.8	11	4.9	--------	20	.6
1926	69	3.1	11	5.0	--------	24	.5
1925	77	3.5	13	6.5	--------	42	1.1
1924	57	2.4	9	4.3	--------	25	.5
1923	69	3.3	11	5.1	--------	45	1.1
1922	90	3.8	11	4.2	--------	26	.6
1921	62	2.7	7	2.1	--------	44	.9

[1] Beginning 1947, includes acidulated scrap.
[2] Includes Hawaii, beginning in 1952; Puerto Rico in 1953; and American Samoa in 1954.
[3] Includes Hawaii and outlying areas for all years.

Series L 369–370. Sealskins Obtained From the Pribilof Islands and Land-Based Production of Whales: 1910 to 1970

Year	Sealskins obtained (369)	Whales killed [1] (370)
1970	42,179	73
1969	38,805	183
1968	58,532	202
1967	65,672	247
1966	52,866	226
1965	51,020	243
1964	64,206	274
1963	85,254	259
1962	77,915	248
1961	95,974	343
1960	40,616	271
1959	57,810	309
1958	78,919	261
1957	93,618	237
1956	122,826	145
1955	65,638	--------
1954	63,888	--------
1953	66,673	--------
1952	63,922	--------
1951	60,689	40
1950	60,090	--------
1949	70,891	49
1948	70,142	67
1947	61,447	38
1946	64,523	--------
1945	76,964	5
1944	47,652	5
1943	117,164	29
1942	150	26
1941	95,013	24
1940	65,263	29
1939	60,473	232
1938	58,364	174
1937	55,180	413
1936	52,446	483
1935	57,296	583
1934	53,470	669
1933	54,550	382
1932	49,336	319
1931	49,524	--------
1930	42,500	655
1929	40,068	722
1928	31,099	706
1927	24,942	1,102
1926	22,131	719
1925	19,860	638
1924	17,219	687
1923	15,920	908
1922	31,156	1,170
1921	23,681	129
1920	26,648	1,270
1919	27,821	1,004
1918	34,890	637
1917	8,170	673
1916	6,468	657
1915	3,947	864
1914	2,735	697
1913	2,406	397
1912	3,191	1,003
1911	12,138	
1910	12,964	--------

[1] Whales processed at Alaska and Pacific Coast States land-based stations.

Chapter M

Minerals

M 1–12. Summary of mineral operations, 1840–1967.

Source: **Series M 1–11**, U.S. Bureau of the Census, *Census of Mineral Industries, 1967*, as corrected after publication; **series M 12**, *Census of Mineral Industries, 1963*.

Figures are based on establishment reports for each operation covered in the census. These reports include all of the information shown as well as other related data. The different series are comparable, therefore, for a given year and a given industry. The comparability of figures for various census years, however, is affected somewhat by changes in the specifications for establishments covered. For 1967, excludes all single-unit establishments without paid employees. For 1963, 1958, and 1954 excludes small establishments for which each of the following three items was less than $500 for the entire year: (1) Value of products shipped and services performed for others; (2) expenses for wages, salaries, supplies, minerals received for preparation, fuel, purchased electric energy, contract work, and purchased machinery; and (3) capital expenditures for development and exploration of mineral properties, new construction and major alterations, and new and used machinery and equipment. For 1939 and 1929, in general, small establishments were excluded if each of three similar items amounted to less than $2,500, and, in general, for 1919, if value of products was less than $500 and expenditures for development work less than $5,000. For earlier years, no general size level was specified for the censuses.

M 1, number of establishments. These figures are much less comparable from one year to another than the figures for series M 2–12 since they are greatly influenced by the inclusion or exclusion of very small operations, such as the activity of prospectors, small irregular operations, and oil and gas stripper operations. Many of these were below the census level for inclusion for certain years but were included in other years (see preceding paragraph). In 1963, for mining as a whole, establishments without paid employees accounted for approximately 3 percent of value added.

M 4, value added in mining. Beginning 1954, represents gross value of shipments plus capital expenditures less cost of supplies, minerals received for preparation, fuel, purchased electric energy, contract work, and purchased machinery. For earlier years, certain data are not available from census reports, but a rough measure is included which represents value of shipments less cost of supplies, minerals received for preparation, fuel, purchased electric energy, and contract work.

M 5, production and development workers. For 1909–1954, the figures represent the average of reported employment for the mid-month pay period for the 12 months of the census year. Beginning 1958, the data represent an average of such figures for a specified month in each quarter of the year.

M 11, capital expenditures. Represents capital expenditures for development and exploration of mineral property and for new and used plant, machinery and equipment.

M 12, aggregate horsepower rating of power equipment. Represents the aggregate horsepower rating of all prime movers and electric motors driven by purchased energy in use or available for use at the end of the census year.

M 13–306. General note.

The principal sources for these series are two publications: *Mineral Resources of the United States*, published annually for 1882–1931; and *Minerals Yearbook*, published annually since 1932–1933. These volumes were prepared and issued by the U.S. Geological Survey from 1882 to 1923 and by the U.S. Bureau of Mines since 1924.

In general, production data from these sources refer to the 50 States, excluding data for U.S. outlying areas. For petroleum and petroleum products, data are included for Alaska beginning 1959 and for Hawaii beginning 1960. Except as noted in the source publications cited, however, data for other commodities have usually been compiled to include Alaska and Hawaii back as far as 1954 when they amounted to only 0.1 percent of the value of total production.

Import figures represent imports for consumption except as noted. However, as the source did not always identify the import figures, particularly for years prior to 1938, it was assumed that the figures were comparable to those identified for other years.

Unless otherwise stated, figures for imports and exports were compiled by the Bureau of Mines (or Geological Survey) from records of the Bureau of the Census. For foreign trade definitions, see the introduction in U.S. Bureau of the Census, *Foreign Commerce and Navigation of the United States, 1965*.

M 13–37. Value of mineral products, in current dollars, 1880–1970.

Source: See general note for series M 13–306, except series M 23, 1954–1969, U.S. Bureau of the Census, *Annual Survey of Manufactures* and *1967 Census of Manufactures*.

The figures for series M 13, M 14, M 20, and M 30 (the grand total and commodity subtotals) cover the period presented with two overlapping series. One on the so-called "old basis" runs from 1880 through 1924, while the other on the "new basis" is the series as currently compiled and shown for 1925 through 1970. Prior to 1925, an adjustment by Resources for the Future, Inc., Washington, D.C. has been included for iron ore and bauxite which affects series M 13 and M 30.

Minerals Yearbook, 1949, pp. 29–30, indicates the deficiencies in the earlier statistics which the "new basis" of measurement was designed to correct. These deficiencies apply mainly to fuels (series M 14–19), nonmetals (series M 20–29), and metals (series M 30–37), and are described in the text for those series. Another improvement applicable to all statistics on the "new basis" is the correction of the value grand totals and subtotals back through 1925 to exclude some mineral products made from materials of foreign origin.

In addition to the general revision described above which was made in the *Minerals Yearbook, 1949* and *1950*, other less important revisions of the grand totals and subtotals for earlier years are often carried in later editions of the *Minerals Yearbook*. Series M 13, M 14, M 20, and M 30 present the most recently revised totals and subtotals. Since these revisions are often carried in later editions of the *Minerals Yearbook*, without full supporting commodity details, the values shown here for the individual commodities are not always strictly comparable with the totals and subtotals in all years.

In general, a significant factor making for lack of long-run comparability within series, and among different series, is the failure of the basic source to use a consistent stage of production at which to measure value. Value is measured at the mining stage for some commodities and at a stage in the manufacturing process for others for which mine value figures may be difficult to collect (frequently because of the integration of mining and manufacturing production processes). Moreover, the stage at which the value of individual commodities is measured sometimes has changed. Consequently, the totals and subtotals for any year are to some extent a mixture of values at different stages in the production process and similar totals and subtotals for succeeding years may also represent different mixtures. However, double counting has generally been avoided by including a product at not more than one stage in the production process.

A less significant factor involves geographic coverage. Totals and subtotals for 1925–1953 cover only the 48 States of conterminous United States, but individual commodity figures for 1925–1946 may include production in U.S. outlying areas. For 1954–1970, the totals and subtotals include Alaska and Hawaii; for years prior to 1925, they cover Alaska, Hawaii, Philippine Islands, and Puerto Rico.

As is to be expected in long time series, the completeness of coverage has improved considerably over time. For a discussion dealing with changes in coverage for the early years, see *Mineral Resources of the United States, 1918*, part I, pp. 1a–5a, which contains an historical description of the statistical operations of the Geological Survey, then responsible for such mineral statistics.

For figures which more closely approximate a mine-value basis, see Harold Barger and Sam H. Schurr, *The Mining Industries, 1899–1939; A Study of Output, Employment and Productivity*, National Bureau of Economic Research, New York, 1944, pp. 305–309. This source shows the estimated mine values for all minerals (in million dollars of approximate value): 1899, $600; 1909, $1,200; 1919, $3,200; 1929, $4,100; and 1937, $3,800.

M 14–19, value of fuels. The individual commodities shown constitute, for practical purposes, all the mineral fuels produced (except uranium for fuels). The figures back to 1925 for total fuels (series M 14) include, in addition, asphalt and related bitumens, carbon dioxide (natural), helium, and peat. These products are closely related to the other minerals included as fuels, and work dealing with them is organized within the several fuels divisions of the Bureau of Mines. Their combined values are too small to affect seriously the total fuels figures.

M 14, total value of fuels. The most important difference between the "old" and "new" basis series is the inclusion of natural gas as valued at the well in the new series as opposed to natural gas valued at the point of consumption in the old series. In 1925, when the discontinuity occurs, natural gas was not so important, nor was the difference between well value and point of consumption value so great, as to cause a major break in the series (total value of fuels for 1925, on the "old" basis, was $3,059 million). See also text for series M 18.

M 15, bituminous coal and lignite. Represents total value of production, f.o.b. mine. Selling costs are excluded for 1880–1936 and included for 1937–1970, except for 1939 when producers were asked to exclude them but some, in fact, included them. Figures include small quantities of anthracite mined in States other than Pennsylvania.

M 16, Pennsylvania anthracite. Represents total value of production, f.o.b. mine. Data for 1951–1970 are not strictly comparable with figures for earlier years because they include output of independent operators, formerly classified as "bootleggers" but now operating under legal agreements with the owners of the coal lands. Data for 1941–1950 include some "bootleg" coal purchased by legitimate operators and prepared at their breakers.

M 17, petroleum. Represents value of crude oil at the well.

M 18, natural gas. Represents total value of "marketed production," i.e., gross withdrawals less repressuring, vented, and wasted. Beginning 1947, transmission losses and storage are included. Value is measured at the well for 1925–1970, and at the point of consumption prior to 1925. (The value at the point of consumption was $265 million in 1925.)

For 1885 to 1890, the value shown is for coal and fuel wood displaced by natural gas rather than the value of gas consumed as actually reported. For example, in 1889, the latter was $11 million.

M 19, natural-gas liquids. Represents value at the plant and includes natural gasoline, finished gasoline, naphtha, other cycle products, and beginning 1941, liquefied petroleum gases.

M 20, total nonmetals. Figures include value of nonmetals not shown separately. Figures are heavily weighted by the value of products classified as manufactures in U.S. Office of Management and Budget (formerly U.S. Bureau of the Budget), *Standard Industrial Classification Manual*. For example, cement and lime are included instead of their raw material components. Integrated operations make it difficult to obtain a value for the raw materials, which usually are not purchased on the open market, but obtained from associated operations. The value of stone includes an indeterminate amount of manufacturing because many dimension stone quarries manufacture the stone into finished products. The value of salt also includes a substantial amount of manufacturing as defined in the *Standard Industrial Classification Manual*.

Beginning 1947, the totals for nonmetals include the value of raw clay alone, but for prior years the value of clay manufactures (mainly heavy clay products, such as brick, tile, etc.) for practically the entire period. The exact definition of clay value has changed several times during the long period covered. See text for series M 22–23.

Series M 20 has a number of discontinuities. These include changes in the method of valuing clay and inadequate coverage of sand and gravel before 1905 and of clay products before 1894. Other sources of noncomparability are also present. For these reasons and because of the heavy influence of manufacturing as defined in the *Standard Industrial Classification Manual* in the total value, this series should be used with great care. By way of comparison, the mine value subtotals for nonmetals as estimated in Barger and Schurr (see text for series M 13–27) are (in million dollars of approximate value): 1899, $60; 1909, $125; 1919, $240; 1929, $500; and 1937, $390.

M 21, cement. Valuation is f.o.b. mill excluding the cost of the container. Included are portland, natural, masonry-natural, slag (formerly referred to as puzzolan), and hydraulic lime cements. (See also text for series M 188 regarding coverage of prepared masonry cement and change in 1955.) For 1912–1970, figures represent total value of shipments; for 1880–1911, figures are for value of production. For 1880–1890, figures are estimates. Early decade valuation estimates not shown in the table include: 1818–1829, $0.2 million; 1830–1839, $1 million; 1840–1849, $4 million; 1850–1859, $9 million; 1860–1869, $14 million; and 1870–1879, $19 million.

M 22–23, clay. Raw clay and clay products are both shown because total nonmetals (series M 20) includes one or the other, or parts of both, at different times. Series M 20 includes: prior to 1936, the value of all clay products (series M 23) only; for 1936–1944, the value of clay products, other than pottery and refractories (series M 23) and the value of raw clay sold (1936–1941) and sold or shipped by producers (1942–1944) as shown in series M 22; for 1945–1946, the value of clay products, other than pottery and refractories (series M 23) and the value of raw clay sold or used, except for raw clay used in the products in series M 23; for 1947–1970, the value of raw clay sold or used by producers (series M 22 except clay used in cement manufacture).

Prior to 1944, raw clay (series M 22) was mainly restricted to "merchant clay" marketed as raw clay, excluding the very great amounts of clay converted into brick and other products before sale.

Series M 23, prior to 1936, represents the total value of clay products. Beginning 1936, the figures represent the value of heavy clay products other than potteries and refractories.

M 24, lime. Represents the selling value, f.o.b. plant, excluding cost of container. Data for 1953–1970 are not strictly comparable with those for earlier years. Prior to 1953, the series has only partial coverage of captive plants; beginning 1953, coverage is essentially complete for both open-market and captive tonnage production. *Mineral Resources, 1914*, vol. II, p. 363, considers the series reliable only from 1894 on, stating that: "Although the statistics of the production of lime collected by the U.S. Geological Survey date, in one form or another, back to 1880, reliable figures showing the extent and growth of the industry have been available only since 1894 ... these early figures (prior to 1894) are much too large; but there is no adequate means of explaining the discrepancy. The statistics are sufficiently consistent to indicate a steady growth in quantity and, with a few exceptions, in value for 1880–1888, but in other respects they cannot be considered reliable."

M 25, sand and gravel. Represents the value of sand and gravel at the pit (or source). This is the total value of sand and gravel sold or used by the producer. Although the terms "sales" and "production" are used interchangeably, stocks remain small and relatively constant from year to year. Coverage includes commercial and noncommercial (government and contractor) operations. Values of industrial sand, unground and ground, are also included. Prior to 1954, ground industrial sand was included elsewhere in value of mineral products. Coverage of gravel was incomplete for 1902–1904.

M 26, stone, including slate. Stone sold or used by producers is valued f.o.b. quarries or mills. Slate is valued f.o.b. quarry or nearest point of shipment. Since manufacturing operations are often integrated with dimension stone quarries, the figures include a sizable but indeterminate value for manufacturing. Stone coverage includes granite, basalt and related rocks (traprock), marble, limestone, sandstone, and other stone. Data for 1954–1970 include ground sandstone, quartz, and quartzite used for abrasives and other purposes (formerly included elsewhere in value of nonmetals), stone for cement and lime (value excluded from nonmetals total), and shell (not formerly covered by Bureau of Mines). Value of these three categories totaled $105 million in 1954. Both dimension stone and nondimension (crushed) stone are included. Slate includes roofing slate, millstock, flagstones, granules, flour, and other. Data for 1880–1888 are incomplete, representing building stone only.

M 27, phosphate rock. Represents the value f.o.b. mine. For 1950–1970, figures refer to marketable production; for earlier years, to phosphate rock sold or used.

M 28, salt. Represents the value f.o.b. mine or refinery of common salt sold or used by producers, excluding cost of cooperage or container. Included are dry salt, both evaporated (manufactured) and rock, and also salt in brine. For 1880–1892, many manufacturers included the value of the container in the value reported.

M 29, sulfur. Represents the total value of shipments. Data for 1901–1903 included pyrites. Frasch process mine output plus other mine output is included since 1945 and recovered elemental sulfur since 1950.

M 30, total metals. Includes the value of some metals not shown separately. Adjustment in figures for years prior to 1925 have been made by Resources for the Future, Inc., Washington, D.C. and are included here. Prior to 1925, *Minerals Yearbook* figures include the value of pig iron and aluminum, both manufactured products, whereas the figures shown here include the value of iron ore and bauxite, the products of mines. Other relatively minor changes involving the substitution of mine values for manufactured values were made in the 1949 revision of the total metals figures for years after 1924, and some duplication within the totals for metals was eliminated. Because of the difficulties involved, these changes have not been applied to the pre-1925 figures shown here. However, since the iron ore and bauxite substitutions constitute the major elements in the revision, there is no major discontinuity between the pre- and post-1925 total metals figures.

The figures for gold, silver, copper, lead, and zinc for all years are based on the smelter or refinery value of the metals, not their value at the mine. The practice of valuing these products at the manufactured stage was not altered by the 1949 revision, because the complexity of their ores makes mine values difficult to derive. However, effective with the 1949 revision, the total value for each of these metals was derived by applying the average selling price of the refined metal to the recoverable mine production.

By way of comparison, the mine values for total metals as estimated in Barger and Schurr (cited in text for series M 13–37) for selected years are (in million dollars of approximate value): 1899, $189; 1909, $329; 1919, $540; 1929, $627; and 1937, $642.

M 31, iron ore. Represents total value of ore shipments. Figures for 1881, 1890, and 1891 were estimated by multiplying the arithmetic mean of the average value of the preceding year and the following year by the quantity of output for the year to be estimated. For 1906–1970, the data exclude ore containing 5 percent or more manganese, and for 1916–1941, ore for paint.

M 32, copper. For 1880–1946, figures represent the value of the smelter output from domestic ores. For 1908–1916, figures are as valued at New York City. For 1947–1970, figures represent the average price of refined copper multiplied by mine production of recoverable copper.

M 33, lead. For 1880–1946, figures represent value of refinery output from domestic ores. For 1908–1916, figures are as valued at New York City. For 1947–1970, figures represent the average price of primary refined lead multiplied by the mine production of recoverable lead.

M 34, zinc. For 1880–1946, figures represent the value of smelter output from domestic ores. For 1908–1914, figures are based on the average St. Louis quotation; for 1915–1923, on average selling price for all grades. For 1947–1970, figures represent the average price of the smelter product multiplied by the recoverable mine output.

M 35, gold. For 1880–1946, figures represent refinery or mint output multiplied by the official price. The official price of gold was $35 from January 1934 to March 15, 1968; prior to then it was $20.67, although the price of gold was unsettled in 1933 because the United States went off the gold standard in April of that year. For 1947–1970, figures represent the recoverable content of ore (mine output) multiplied by the official price per fine ounce until March 15, 1968, and Engelhard selling quotations thereafter.

M 36, silver. For 1880–1946, figures represent refinery or mint output multiplied by the price. For 1947–1970, figures represent the recoverable ore content multiplied by the New York market price of the refined metal.

M 37, molybdenum. Figures represent the value of shipments of molybdenum concentrates.

M 38–53. Value of mineral production, imports, exports, and consumption in constant (1967) dollars, 1900–1969.

Source: U.S. Bureau of the Census and U.S. Bureau of Mines, *Raw Materials in the United States Economy: 1900–1969* (Working Paper No. 35).

The figures were obtained by multiplying the physical quantity of each raw material for a given year by the average unit value of the material for 1967. For materials produced domestically, the unit value weights are average values at the mine, approximately as indicated by the 1967 Census of Mineral Industries. For materials not produced in the United States in the 1967 period, average unit value of imports was generally used. Production figures include approximately 90 mineral products which account for over 99 percent of the total value of mineral output as measured in the 1967 Census of Mineral Industries; production represents primary production only. Import and export figures include not only primary materials but also estimates of the raw material equivalents of semi-fabricated and fabricated products, in order to approximate the raw materials required for end-use products consumed in the United States. Thus, the mineral equivalents of the foreign trade in paints, other chemicals, and machinery were computed and added to the imports and exports of crude minerals. Such estimates affected most significantly the results for certain metallic minerals, particularly iron ore, copper ore, and bauxite imports and exports, which were influenced by the estimated metal content of such things as machinery and vehicles. Consumption is computed as production plus imports minus exports plus net decrease in stocks. More detailed figures are shown in the source; for example, separate series for "iron and ferroalloys," "other metals, except gold," "construction materials," and "other nonmetallic minerals (except fuels)," and for selected individual commodities. Data for Alaska and Hawaii are included for all years.

M 54–67. Indexes of physical volume of mineral production (Bureau of Mines), 1880–1970.

Source: U.S. Bureau of Mines, *Minerals Yearbook*, various issues.

These index numbers constitute an updating of the index numbers originally prepared by Y. S. Leong, "Index of the Physical Volume Production of Minerals, 1880–1948," *Journal of the American Statistical Association*, March 1950. Subsequently, Leong made revisions in his index for 1930–1948 to take account of a new natural-gas production series. Using essentially the same methods, the Bureau of Mines has brought the indexes up to date, and has converted the entire index for later years to a 1967 base. Leong included 63 series in his index, representing 98 percent of the value of all minerals produced in the United States in the base period 1935–39. The number of series is smaller in the earlier years of the index partly because new minerals came into production during the long period covered, and partly because data for minerals in production were sometimes not available in the earlier years. Estimates were used in some cases when actual production data were not available. Over the long period covered, the indexes were constructed by linking seven overlapping segments with seven different sets of value weights (value at the mine, actual or estimated). The weighting periods used were 1889–91 (for 1880–1903); 1909–13 (for 1897–1920); 1923–25 (for 1917–1939); 1935–39 (for 1929–1948); 1947–49 (for 1941–1956); 1957–59 (for 1952–1964); and 1967 (for 1962–1970). The separate segments of the indexes were spliced to form continuous series covering the entire period by selecting a particular year as the splicing origin and deriving averages of the two segments for a 3- or 5-year period centered on the splicing origin.

M 68–71. Indexes of mineral production (Federal Reserve Board), 1919–1970.

Source: Board of Governors of the Federal Reserve System, *Federal Reserve Bulletin*, various issues.

These indexes are available monthly as well as annually. The most recent revision of the index is explained in the July 1971 issue of the *Bulletin* and the previous revision is explained in the October 1962 issue. The latest revision introduced 1967 as a comparison base with 1967 value-added weights.

In this latest revision, stone and earth minerals have been divided into two component parts representing first *Standard Industrial Classification Manual* (see general note for series P 1–374) groups 141, 2, 4 and secondly groups 145, 7–9 so that the former series goes into the products group and the latter into the materials group. Also, crude oil production is now represented by three geographic areas instead of a single series for the United States. Although the revision covers only the years since 1954, the Federal Reserve Board states that with respect to the total minerals index, the "continuity of measurement back to 1919 has been preserved."

The latest revision of the index uses different value-added weights and comparison base years for each benchmark year and the years following the benchmark; 1954 through 1957, 1954 weights; 1958 through 1962, 1958 weights; 1963 through 1966, 1963 weights; and 1967 on, 1967 weights. For the period prior to 1954, 1947 through 1953, 1947 weights are used and 1939 through 1946, 1939 weights. The weight years for the period 1919 through 1938 were unchanged from the old index. Total mining indexes prior to 1967 were linked to the 1967 weighted aggregates and converted to the new 1967 comparison base.

M 72–75. Indexes of mineral production (NBER), 1899–1939.

Source: Harold Barger and Sam H. Schurr, *The Mining Industries, 1899–1939: A Study of Output, Employment and Productivity*, National Bureau of Economic Research, New York, 1944, pp. 354–355 (copyright).

These indexes were derived by combining the physical quantities of different products with unit mine values serving as weights. See the source, p. 272, for a technical description of the procedures used to construct these indexes.

The fuels index (series M 73) includes Pennsylvania anthracite, bituminous coal, petroleum, natural gas, and natural gasoline.

The nonmetals index (series M 74) includes asbestos, asphalt, barite, borates, bromine, fluorspar, tripoli, garnet, pumice, ground sand, sand, gravel, sodium salts, calcium chloride, abrasive sandstone, clay, fuller's earth, stone (dimension and nondimension), talc, gypsum, pyrites, sulfur, mica, potash, magnesite, other magnesium compounds, graphite, feldspar, and phosphate rock.

The metals index (series M 75) includes gold, silver, copper, lead, zinc, iron ore, manganese, tungsten, molybdenum, mercury, and bauxite.

M 76–92. General note.

These series are expressed in terms of British thermal units in order to have a common denominator. A British thermal unit is "the quantity of heat required to raise the temperature of one pound of water 1°F. at or near its point of maximum density."

M 76. Total production of mineral energy fuels, in B.t.u.'s, 1800–1970.

Source: This series is the sum of the figures for series M 77–80.

Totals have been derived for only the mineral fuels because of alternative possible conversion factors to apply to hydroelectricity for comparability with the other energy sources.

M 77. Production of bituminous coal, in B.t.u.'s, 1800–1970.

Source: 1800–1849, series M 93 converted to B.t.u.'s at the same rate as data for more recent years; 1850–1885, Resources for the Future, Inc., Washington, D.C., *Energy in the American Economy* (copyright); 1890–1895, converted to B.t.u.'s from physical quantities shown in successive volumes of U.S. Bureau of Mines, *Mineral Resources of the United States* and *Minerals Yearbook*; 1900–1970, *Minerals Yearbook*, annual volumes.

The B.t.u. equivalent used as a conversion factor for the data through 1954 is 13,100 B.t.u.'s per pound of coal. In recent years this heat value has not been representative of the average unit heat value of the total annual coal supply because of the large annual increases in utilization of coal of lower heat values by the electric utility industry. In 1970, the Bureau of Mines established weighted average B.t.u. values of bituminous coal and lignite produced and consumed in the United States based on known and estimated B.t.u. values of coal shipments to each major consuming sector for 1955–1970 as follows:

Year	Annual average British thermal units (B.t.u.'s) per pound [1]	
	Production	Domestic consumption
1970	12,440	12,290
1969	12,450	12,330
1968	12,530	12,430
1967	12,580	12,470
1966	12,650	12,550
1965	12,710	12,610
1964	12,750	12,640
1963	12,760	12,650
1962	12,790	12,670
1961	12,790	12,690
1960	12,830	12,740
1959	12,840	12,740
1958	12,990	12,770
1957	12,990	12,860
1956	12,990	12,870
1955	13,000	12,920

[1] The averages for U.S. consumption exclude shipments overseas and to Canada, the preponderance of which is of high B.t.u. value metallurgical coal, thus accounting for the difference in values between total production and domestic consumption.

Source: Dept. of the Interior, *Minerals Yearbook*, 1970, Bituminous and Lignite chapter.

Production statistics for bituminous coal include lignite; they cover Alaska for all years.

M 78. Production of Pennsylvania anthracite, in B.t.u.'s, 1810–1970.

Source: See source for series M 77, except 1808–1849, based on series M 123.

The B.t.u. equivalent used as a conversion factor is an average used by the Bureau of Mines, 12,700 B.t.u.'s per pound of coal.

M 79. Production of crude oil, in B.t.u.'s, 1860–1970.

Source: 1860–1895, converted to B.t.u.'s from physical quantities shown in successive volumes of U.S. Bureau of Mines, *Mineral Resources of the United States* and *Minerals Yearbook*; 1900–1970, *Minerals Yearbook*, annual volumes.

The B.t.u. equivalent used as a conversion factor through 1954 is 5,800,000 B.t.u.'s per barrel. Since 1955, B.t.u. value for crude oil is a weighted average based on average B.t.u. value of total output of petroleum products (including refinery fuel and losses) adjusted to exclude natural gas liquids inputs and their implicitly derived values. The weighted average B.t.u. values per barrel are: 1955, 5,814,200; 1956, 5,862,400; 1957, 5,864,000; 1958, 5,779,300; 1959, 5,695,000; 1960, 5,695,000; 1961, 5,792,000; 1962, 5,790,000; 1963, 5,718,300; 1964, 5,630,300; 1965, 5,592,300; 1966, 5,589,900; 1967, 5,628,540; 1968, 5,585,010; 1969, 5,601,070; and 1970, 5,620,900. Figures include commingled condensate.

See text for series M 86–87 for B.t.u. conversion factors for petroleum products.

M 80. Production of natural gas, wet, in B.t.u.'s, 1885–1970.

Source: See general note for series M 13–306.

"Natural gas, wet" refers to natural gas prior to processing at natural-gas liquid plants. Figures for 1920–1970 are termed "marketed production," and comprise gas sold or consumed by producers, including losses in transmission, amounts added to storage, and increases in gas in pipelines. Gas vented and wasted and used in repressuring is excluded. Data prior to 1920 are not strictly comparable with those for later years. Apparently, for the earlier period, neither net storage change nor transmission loss was included.

Total production, before subtraction to obtain marketed production, has been converted through 1954, at the rate of 1,075 B.t.u.'s per cubic foot. To obtain marketed production, the amounts repressured, vented, and wasted have been converted at 1,035 B.t.u.'s per cubic foot and subtracted from the B.t.u. value of total production. The new basis consists of the dry natural gas production which excludes gas used for repressuring, vented, or flared multiplied by the following B.t.u. values per cubic foot: 1,035 for 1955–1964; 1,032 for 1965–1968; and 1,031 for 1969–1970, to which is added the computed energy equivalent of the heat value of natural gas liquids production.

Comparability problems arise prior to 1900 because the figures for the very early period are based on the estimated quantity of coal and fuel wood displaced, and are not measures of gas produced.

M 81. Electricity produced from waterpower, at prevailing central station equivalent, in B.t.u.'s, 1900–1970.

Source: U.S. Bureau of Mines, *Minerals Yearbook*, annual volumes.

Figures include installations owned by manufacturing plants and mines, as well as government- and privately-owned public utilities. The fuel equivalent of waterpower is calculated from the kilowatt-hours of power produced whenever this figure is available, as it is for all public utility plants since 1919. Otherwise, the fuel equivalent is calculated from the reported horsepower of installed water wheels, assuming a capacity factor of 20 percent for factories and mines and 40 percent for public utilities. In converting waterpower to its equivalent of fuel required to generate the same power, the prevailing or average performance of all fuel-burning central electric stations

for each year in question has been used through 1946. This has dropped from 6.85 pounds of coal per kilowatt-hour in 1900 to 1.29 in 1946. Beginning with 1947, waterpower outputs are converted to theoretical energy inputs calculated from national average heat rates for fossil-fueled steam-electric plants for each year in question. The heat rates for fossil-fueled steam-electric plants are published in the Federal Power Commission's annual supplement to *Steam-Electric Plant Construction Cost and Annual Production Expenses*.

M 82. Electricity produced from waterpower, at direct calorific equivalent, in B.t.u.'s, 1890–1970.

Source: Converted at the rate of 3,412 B.t.u.'s per kilowatt-hour, direct calorific equivalent of electricity, from successive volumes of U.S. Bureau of Mines, *Mineral Resources of the United States* and *Minerals Yearbook*. This represents the same basic production series as series M 81.

M 83–92. General note.

All of the consumption figures since 1920, except series M 91 and M 92, are Bureau of Mines calculated consumption estimates. The Bureau generally defines calculated consumption as production plus imports (including shipments to noncontiguous territories) minus exports, plus or minus net change in stocks. Only in the case of bituminous coal since 1933 has the Bureau derived consumption by adding together known consumption by use. (See also text for series M 113–121.) All the consumption estimates prepared by Resources for the Future, Inc., Washington, D.C., have also been derived in accordance with the above definition except for series M 92, fuel wood consumption, which has been estimated directly.

M 83. Calculated consumption of total mineral energy fuels, in B.t.u.'s, 1850–1970.

Source: This series is the sum of series M 84–89.

See also text for series M 76.

M 84–85. Calculated consumption of bituminous coal and Pennsylvania anthracite, in B.t.u.'s, 1850–1970.

Source: 1850–1919, Resources for the Future, Inc., Washington, D.C., *Energy in the American Economy* (copyright); 1920–1970, U.S. Bureau of Mines, *Minerals Yearbook*, annual volumes.

Bituminous coal consumption for 1850–1932 represents production plus imports, minus exports, plus or minus net change in stocks. That method of derivation ignores variables such as stocks at lake and tidewater docks, stocks at other intermediate storage piles between mine and consumers, and coal in transit. For 1933–1970, consumption represents the addition of known consumption by use.

See also text for series M 77 and M 78, and general note for series M 83–92.

M 86–87. Calculated consumption of crude petroleum and petroleum products, net imports, in B.t.u.'s, 1860–1970.

Source: 1860–1919, Resources for the Future, Inc., Washington, D.C., *Energy in the American Economy* (copyright); 1920–1970, U.S. Bureau of Mines, *Minerals Yearbook*, annual volumes.

Net imports of petroleum products equals total imports minus total exports, a negative figure signifying an export surplus for that year. Series M 87 is a composite series which has been converted at the following standard Bureau of Mines factors: Gasoline and special naphtha, 5,248,000 B.t.u.'s per barrel; kerosene, 5,670,000; jet fuel, naphtha-type, 5,355,000; jet fuel, kerosene-type, 5,670,000; distillate fuel oil, 5,825,000; residual fuel oil, 6,287,000; wax, 5,537,280; lubricants, 6,064,800; asphalt, 6,636,000; petroleum coke, 6,024,000; still gas, 6,000,000; and miscellaneous petroleum products, 5,796,000.

For 1860–1919, series M 86 and 87 were combined and converted at varying rates at different times depending upon the relative importance of Pennsylvania grade, which has a lower B.t.u. content compared to other grades. From 1958–1970, series M 87 includes imports, exports, processing gains, and stock change.

See also text for series M 79.

M 88. Calculated consumption of natural gas, dry, in B.t.u.'s, 1885–1970.

Source: 1885–1919, Resources for the Future, Inc., Washington, D.C., *Energy in the American Economy* (copyright); 1920–1970, U.S. Bureau of Mines, *Minerals Yearbook*, annual volumes.

Figures were converted at the following B.t.u.'s per cubic foot: 1,035 through 1964; 1,032 for 1965–1968; and 1,031 in 1969 and 1970. Processing to recover natural gas liquids accounts for the lower B.t.u. content of the gas as compared with series M 80, "natural gas, wet." Consumption for 1920–1970 differs from "marketed production" by net change in foreign trade, net change in storage, and extraction loss, but includes losses in transmission. For 1885–1919, consumption is defined as total production (see text for series M 80) plus imports, minus exports.

M 89. Calculated consumption of natural-gas liquids, in B.t.u.'s, 1911–1970.

Source: 1911–1919, Resources for the Future, Inc., Washington, D.C., *Energy in the American Economy* (copyright); 1920–1970, U.S. Bureau of Mines, *Minerals Yearbook*, annual volumes.

For 1964 and prior years, a weighted average B.t.u. based on production is used, derived by converting natural gasoline and cycle products at 110,000 B.t.u.'s per gallon and LP-gas, including ethane, at 95,500 B.t.u.'s per gallon. After 1964, the ethane production was converted separately at 73,390 B.t.u.'s per gallon, but the same factors were used for other products.

M 90. Calculated consumption of electricity from waterpower, at prevailing central station equivalent, in B.t.u.'s, 1890–1970.

Source: 1890–1919, Resources for the Future, Inc., Washington, D.C., *Energy in the American Economy* (copyright); 1920–1970, U.S. Bureau of Mines, *Minerals Yearbook*, annual volumes.

Consumption differs from production by the quantity of imports. In the early years imports drop to zero.

See also text for series M 81.

M 91. Calculated consumption of electricity from waterpower, at direct calorific equivalent, in B.t.u.'s, 1890–1970.

Source: 1890–1919, in kilowatt-hours in Resources for the Future, Inc., Washington, D.C., *Energy in the American Economy* (copyright); 1920–1970, in kilowatt-hours in successive volumes of *Minerals Yearbook*. Entire series converted at the rate of 3,412 B.t.u.'s per kilowatt-hour, direct calorific equivalent of electricity.

This series represents the same basic consumption series as series M 90.

M 92. Calculated consumption of fuel wood, in B.t.u.'s, 1850–1970.

Source: 1800–1945, Resources for the Future, Inc., Washington, D.C., *Energy in the American Economy* (copyright); 1946–1970, based on U.S. Forest Service data as used in U.S. Bureau of the Census and U.S. Bureau of Mines Working Paper No. 35, *Raw Materials in the United States Economy: 1900–1969*.

The following conversion factors were used: 1850–1895, 20,960,000 B.t.u.'s per cord; 1900, 20,154,000 B.t.u.'s per cord; and 1901–1970, 19,407,000 B.t.u.'s per cord. These conversion factors were derived from the following fuel equivalents: prior to 1900, 1.25 cords of wood equals 1 ton of bituminous coal; in 1900, 1.30 cords of wood equals 1 ton of bituminous coal; and after 1900, because of the larger proportion of soft wood used, 1.35 cords of wood equals 1 ton of bituminous coal (J. F. Dewhurst and Associates, *America's Needs and Resources*, New York, 1955, p. 1108).

M 93–106. General note.

Coverage of bituminous coal by the Bureau of Mines includes all subbituminous coal and lignite, and anthracite and semianthracite produced outside of Pennsylvania. These series exclude Pennsylvania anthracite and, for 1955–1970, Texas lignite. In 1970, total production of lignite, except Texas, was 6.0 million of the total bituminous coal production of 602.9 million short tons. Production of small mines having an output of less than 1,000 short tons per year is not included. For all Bureau of Mines series shown here, data on Alaska are included. (In 1970, Alaskan production totaled 549,473 short tons.)

M 93. Bituminous coal, total production, 1800–1970.

Source: 1800–1885, H. N. Eavenson, *The First Century and a Quarter of American Coal Industry*, Pittsburgh, 1942; pp. 426–434; 1886–1970, see general note, series M 13–306.

Bureau of Mines production data are based on detailed annual reports furnished by producers. Output not directly reported by producers, primarily that of the small mines, is obtained with some accuracy from State mine departments or railroad carloadings.

Beginning 1951, series M 94 and M 95 do not add to series M 93 because auger production is included in series M 93.

Prior to 1886, production figures shown are those as derived by Eavenson and considered superior to the early Geological Survey figures, which appear in *Mineral Resources of the United States*. Prior to 1880, when the Geological Survey began its annual report system, Survey estimates of production came from the "decennial census, supplemented by records from State and trade sources. In the absence of other information, estimates were made for the intercensus years to round out the totals" (*Mineral Resources of the United States, 1923*, vol. II, p. 544). In reference to census data for these early years, Eavenson states: "The early census returns about coal began in 1830, and were admittedly incomplete; the next two census results are given in value and not in tons produced, and the first really good figures began in 1880" (Eavenson, cited above, p. xiii). Eavenson's estimates were made on an individual State basis and were derived from State, county, newspaper, census, and any other documented records available.

M 94–95. Bituminous coal, underground and strip production, 1914–1970.

Source: See general note for series M 13–306.

For 1914–1942, strip pit coverage includes power strip pits proper but excludes horse stripping operations and mines combining stripping and underground in the same operation. For 1943–1970, coverage includes all strip mines.

M 96–98. Bituminous coal, average value, f.o.b. mine, 1880–1970.

Source: See general note for series M 13–306.

Figures represent value received at the mines f.o.b. cars. For 1880–1936, figures exclude selling expenses; for 1937–1970, they include them. However, for 1939, *Minerals Yearbook, 1946*, states that "producers were asked to exclude ... [them] in reporting value, but a number of them included such costs" (p. 299).

Mineral Resources of the United States, 1923, vol. II, discusses at length the problem of valuation of coal not sold but used by the producer. "Coal used at the mine, coal coked by the producing company, and coal used in some other industry by that company ... is not sold, and the value placed upon it is either an estimate or the amount at which it is carried on the company's books. Either value is presumably the amount the coal would have brought if it had been sold or the amount other fuel ... would have cost if it had been purchased. In other words, the values given represent returns to the operators for coal sold plus the estimated value of coal not sold. The value thus fixed is more or less arbitrary and does not necessarily represent the current prices for coal sold commercially" (pp. 615–616).

For 1915–1942, the average value for strip mines represents power strip pits proper and excludes horse stripping operations and mines combining stripping and underground in the same operation. For 1943–1970, coverage includes all strip mines.

M 99. Bituminous coal, railroad freight charges per short ton, 1923–1970.

Source: See general note for series M 13–306.

This is an Interstate Commerce Commission series reproduced in the Bureau of Mines publications and more exactly defined as the "average revenue received by Class I steam railroads per net ton of revenue bituminous coal originated, as reported to the Interstate Commerce Commission" (*Minerals Yearbook, 1937*, p. 803).

M 100–101. Bituminous coal, foreign trade, 1867–1970.

Source: See general note for series M 13–306.

Figures for 1867–1885 and 1890–1914 are for fiscal years ending June 30; all other figures presumably represent calendar years. Figures for 1867–1889 were converted from long to short tons to form a continuously comparable series.

M 102. Bituminous coal, stocks, 1916–1970.

Source: See general note for series M 13–306.

For 1916–1932, figures were labeled "consumers' stocks"; for 1933–1970, "end-of-year stocks at industrial consumer and retail yards." Figures for 1916–1929 were estimated, mainly from data compiled from a list of 5,000 consumers whose stocks in 1918 bore a known relation to total stocks. (*Mineral Resources of the United States, 1929*, vol. II, pp. 778–779.)

M 103. Bituminous coal, number of mines, 1895–1970.

Source: See general note for series M 13–306.

Figures include only mines producing 1,000 tons per year and over. Some data for smaller mines based on incomplete information are available, however (see *Minerals Yearbook, 1945*, p. 906).

The figure for 1954 may not be strictly comparable with those for other years. In 1954, the Bureau of Mines cooperated with the Bureau of the Census in the canvass for such information, and Census standards were used. *Minerals Yearbook, 1954*, vol. II, states that "The Bureau of the Census defined a mine as 'a working or group of workings at a given locality in which operations are conducted as a unit or are unified by common management or joint handling of some part of the mining or preparation process. Individual shafts, openings, or sites should not necessarily be considered as individual mines.' The Bureau of Mines has considered individual shafts, openings, or sites as individual 'mines'" (p. 27).

M 104. Bituminous coal, mechanically cleaned, 1906–1970.

Source: See general note for series M 13–306.

For 1927–1970, figures include coal cleaned at central washeries operated by consumers in Colorado and Pennsylvania. Although pneumatic cleaning began in 1919, no data were available; therefore, such cleaning is not included until 1924. Tonnage so cleaned, however, was small during this period.

M 105. Bituminous coal, mechanically cut underground, 1891–1970.

Source: See general note for series M 13–306.

M 106. Bituminous coal, mechanically loaded underground, 1923–1970.

Source: See general note for series M 13–306.
Data for 1923–1926 exclude tonnage handled by conveyors.

M 107–111. Bituminous coal, employment, 1890–1970.

Source: See general note for series M 13–306.

Active period averages exclude periods when the mine is closed and not in operation. The Bureau of Mines publishes two sets of employment statistics—one in conjunction with the Bureau's injury statistics, the other in conjunction with the Bureau's commodity statistics. The two sets have not always agreed because of somewhat different coverage. All employment figures published here are from the bituminous coal chapter of the *Minerals Yearbook* and *Mineral Resources of the United States* (not those associated with the Bureau's injury reports). However, data on the number of men employed in 1911 are from a special inquiry made by the Bureau of Mines in connection with its accident statistics. Component figures for 1911 will not add to the total because the Bureau of Mines has revised the figure for total employment, but not the component figures.

Employment data for 1946–1970 are not strictly comparable with figures for earlier years. *Minerals Yearbook, 1953*, vol. II, p. 49, describes this change as follows: "Beginning with 1946, the figures on employment represent the average number of men working daily. Each mine is asked to report the total number of man-shifts worked during the year and the number of calendar days the mine was active during the year. The total man-shifts are divided by the total days the mine was active to determine the average number of men working daily. Before 1946 each mine was asked to report the average number of men on the rolls per pay period and number of days the mine worked. In this instance men employed were multiplied by number of days to determine total man-shifts.... Sample tests indicate that the two sets of figures, however, are reasonably comparable..."

For 1931–1953, figures for all other surface workers on active days (series M 110) include all surface employees at underground, strip, and auger mines other than those actually employed in the mining operation proper. Beginning 1954, figures for series M 110 are for auger mining only.

Although data on average hours worked per day are not shown, nominal hours of work are available for most years in the sources cited above.

M 112. Bituminous coal, man-days idle because of strikes, 1899–1970.

Source: 1899–1926, U.S. Bureau of Mines, *Mineral Resources of the United States*, annual volumes; 1927–1970, U.S. Bureau of Labor Statistics, unpublished data.

Data are believed to be substantially consistent although two different sources are used. (The Bureau of Mines figure for 1927 is 26,516,000 man-days.)

In 1943, the Bureau of Labor Statistics "established a cooperative arrangement with the Solid Fuels Administration which resulted in the receipt of additional strike leads. When this latter agency went out of existence, cooperative arrangements were made with coal associations and companies. Prior to 1943, undoubtedly many of the small, short work stoppages went unnoticed as they are seldom recorded by the press, but the number of workers and idleness in these stoppages is undoubtedly small." (*Work Stoppages, Bituminous Coal Mining Industry*, Report No. 95, August 1955, p. 7.)

"Memorial" stoppages which occurred in 1947 and 1952 are not included. For some early years (1899, 1901, 1903, 1907, and 1908), figures may include some anthracite since separation of the data was not possible.

M 113–121. Bituminous coal, domestic consumption by consumer class, 1917–1970.

Source: See general note for series M 13–306.

Data prior to 1933 may not be strictly comparable with those for later years because of revisions in series M 117–121. For a description of these revisions, see *Minerals Yearbook, 1957*, vol. II, pp. 120–121, where the revisions for 1933–1956 were first published.

M 113, total consumption. Presumably for 1917–1932, consumption was estimated through the formula of production plus imports, minus exports, plus or minus net change in stocks, rather than through the addition of known consumption by consumer class. However, for these years, components still add to the total consumption shown since the "all other uses" classification (series M 117–120) was obtained by subtracting the known consumption items from the total consumption estimate.

For 1933–1970, data are described by the Bureau of Mines as approximating total consumption. The Bureau states that any attempt to estimate total consumption of bituminous through the formula of production plus imports, minus exports, plus or minus net change in stocks, omits important items such as stocks at lake and tidewater docks, stocks at other intermediate storage piles between mines and consumers, and coal in transit, since these items are not included in the stock figures. Therefore, total consumption is estimated through the addition of known consumption by consumer class.

M 114, coal consumed by electric power utilities. For 1917–1932, the series is a Geological Survey series and includes a small amount of anthracite (the Geological Survey figure for 1933 is 30,575,000 short tons); data for 1917 and 1918 were estimated from the 1917 Census of Electrical Industries. For 1933–1970, the series is a Federal Power Commission series, and represents the latest available revised figures for bituminous coal and lignite consumed by public utility power plants in power generation, including a small quantity of coke.

M 115, coal consumed by Class I railroads. Data for 1917–1932, from the Interstate Commerce Commission, exclude consumption in shops, roundhouses, and stations, as well as all consumption by Class II and Class III railroads. (The comparable Interstate Commerce Commission figure for 1933 was 66,198,000 short tons.) For 1933–1960, figures are from the Association of American Railroads and represent consumption of bituminous coal and lignite by Class I railroads for all uses, including locomotive, powerhouse, shop, and station fuel.

M 116, coal consumed in coke plants. Separate series on coal consumption in beehive and byproduct ovens are also available in the sources for series M 113–121.

M 117–120, coal consumed in all other uses. For 1917–1932, figures are combined for bituminous coal consumed by cement mills, steel and rolling mills, other industrial, and retail dealer deliveries. The combined series was titled "all other uses" and was derived by subtracting the known consumption items from estimated total consumption (see text for series M 113).

M 119, coal consumed by other manufacturing and mining industries. For 1933–1970, figures are estimates based upon reports collected from a selected list of representative manufacturing plants.

M 120, coal consumption, retail deliveries to other consumers. For 1933–1970, figures are estimates based upon reports collected from a selected list of representative retailers. The figures include some coal shipped by truck from mine to final destination.

M 121, coal consumed in bunker foreign and lake vessels. This is a Bureau of the Census series and represents bunker coal loaded on vessels engaged in foreign trade. Such coal is not included in the export statistics and, therefore, is included under domestic consumption by use. Beginning 1933, lake vessels have been included.

M 122. Coke production, 1880–1970.

Source: See general note for series M 13–306.

Figures are collected through voluntary reports by coke-plant operators within conterminous United States. Coverage is limited to products made in high-temperature slot-type and beehive ovens. Coke made by other processes—in coal-gas retorts, by low temperature carbonization of coal, and carbonization of the residue from the refining of crude tar and petroleum—is excluded. In recent years, reports have been received from every oven-coke plant in operation and from most of the beehive plants that were in operation. Production has been estimated for the nonreporting plants (all small) and, therefore, coverage is presumed to be complete.

M 123–137. General note.

Coverage of anthracite statistics by the Bureau of Mines is limited to Pennsylvania, and includes the coal from Sullivan County, Pa., which is classified as semianthracite. Information is obtained through a mail canvass of all known anthracite operators. Producers report directly about 99 percent of total production; the remaining one percent is estimated.

The presence of anthracite near the surface of the earth resulted in the development of "bootlegging"—mining without the consent of the owner of the mineral rights. This practice grew rapidly during the depression of the 1930's and, although some information on "bootleg" operations was available during the 1940's, such production is not included in Bureau of Mines figures shown here. For 1941–1950, Bureau of Mines production data include only that part of "bootleg" production purchased by authorized operators and prepared at their breakers. For 1951–1970, however, output of these independent operators (no longer called "bootleggers" since they are now operating under legal agreements with the land owners) has been included. For 1951, output of this type was estimated at 1.5 million short tons. Estimates of "bootleg" production for earlier years may be found in the *Minerals Yearbook*.

Employment statistics for Pennsylvania anthracite have been similarly affected by this change in coverage (see *Minerals Yearbook, 1951*, for a more complete discussion). As a result of this change in coverage, production and employment figures since 1951 are not strictly comparable with similar data for earlier years.

M 123–125. Pennsylvania anthracite production, 1808–1970.

Source: 1808–1885, H. N. Eavenson, *The First Century and a Quarter of the American Coal Industry*, Pittsburgh, 1942, pp. 426–434; 1886–1970, see general note for series M 13–306.

Total production of Pennsylvania anthracite consists of production from underground mines, strip pits, culm banks, and dredging. Since figures for the latter two methods are not separately presented here, the figures for underground and strip do not add to total production. Also, see the general note for series M 123–137 for discussion of "bootleg" production and its effects on total production. Some anthracite production occurred in 1800–1807, but it amounted to less then 500 tons annually.

M 126. Pennsylvania anthracite, average value, f.o.b. mine, 1880–1970.

Source: See general note for series M 13–306.

Average value per short ton, f.o.b. mine, includes a reported value for coal not sold but used by the producer.

M 127–128. Pennsylvania anthracite, foreign trade, 1867–1970.

Source: See general note for series M 13–306.

Beginning September 1963, anthracite import data are not available because of changes in commodity classifications.

For 1867–1885, figures are for fiscal years ending June 30; 1886–1970, they are on a calendar-year basis. To obtain a comparable series throughout, data for 1867–1889 were converted from long to short tons.

M 129. Pennsylvania anthracite, net change in producers' stocks, 1913–1961.

Source: See general note for series M 13–306.

Figures represent net change in producers' stocks as of December 31, except for 1913–1918 when changes are as of March 31. Information on producers' stocks has existed in different forms since 1913. In recent years, information has been supplied by the Anthracite Institute and the Anthracite Committee. Data for 1931–1935 are from unpublished data of the Anthracite Institute and represent prepared coal on the ground at the breakers. Data for 1913–1930 are from the Cost Reports of the Federal Trade Commission (*Coal* No. 2, p. 27) and *Hearings* before the Freylinghuysen Coal Committee, S. Res. 126, 66th Congress, 1st Session (part 1, p. 308).

M 130–134.   Pennsylvania anthracite, employment, 1870–1970.

Source: 1870–1889, U. S. Bureau of Mines, *Coal Mine Fatalities in the United States, 1870–1914,* Bulletin 115, 1916, p. 290; 1890–1970, *Mineral Resources of the United States* and *Minerals Yearbook,* annual volumes.

Figures are active-period averages, excluding periods when the mine is not in operation.   Figures for 1951–1970 are not strictly comparable with earlier years because of inclusion, since 1951, of employees of independent operators (formerly known as "bootleggers"). See general note for series M 123–137.

Data for selected years since 1943 for the average number of hours worked per day are also presented in the *Minerals Yearbook,* chapters on Employment and Injuries; data for nominal hours of work in earlier years appear in Barger and Schurr, cited in text for series M 13–37.

M 135.   Pennsylvania anthracite, number of man-days idle because of strikes, 1900–1970.

Source: See source for series M 112.

M 136.   Pennsylvania anthracite, quantity cut by machines underground, 1911–1970.

Source: See general note for series M 13–306.

M 137.   Pennsylvania anthracite, quantity loaded by machines underground, 1927–1970.

Source: See general note for series M 13–306.

Figures for 1927–1928 were reported by the Pennsylvania Department of Mines.   Figures were first collected by the Bureau of Mines in 1929.

M 138–141.   Crude petroleum production, average value at well, and foreign trade, 1859–1970.

Source: See general note for series M 13–306.

M 138, production.   In recent years coverage has been virtually complete as indicated in *Minerals Yearbook, 1953,* vol. II, which states that "complete coverage of production . . . was obtained by voluntary reports from the industry, supplemented by minor estimates" (p. 358).

M 139, average value at well.   "Annual canvasses provided supplemental information on the value of crude petroleum at the well" (*Minerals Yearbook, 1953,* vol. II, p. 358).

M 140, imports.   Beginning 1934, the data have been obtained by the Bureau of Mines from the petroleum refining companies.   For recent years, imports include shipments to the States from Puerto Rico and other areas administered by the United States, which were excluded prior to 1920.   This series has been shown only since 1913 because crude and topped oil have been shown separately only since July 1912 (*Mineral Resources, 1922,* vol. II, p. 390).

M 141, exports.   Data for 1893–1896 represent fiscal years ending June 30; all other years presumably are calendar years.   For 1916 and earlier years, the figures include all crude mineral oils.   For 1928 and earlier years, reexports of foreign crude petroleum are included; prior to 1919 such reexports were negligible.   For recent years, exports include shipments from the States to Puerto Rico and other areas administered by the United States.   Prior to 1920, the figures exclude such shipments; therefore, data prior to 1920 are not strictly comparable with those for later years.   (For comparison, the 1920 export figure excluding territorial shipments is 8,757.)

M 142.   Crude petroleum, estimated proved reserves, 1899–1970.

Source: American Petroleum Institute, 1899–1948, *Petroleum Facts and Figures, 1950,* New York, 1950, p. 182; 1949–1955, same publication, 1956 issue, p. 164; 1956–1970, U.S. Bureau of Mines, *Minerals Yearbook,* annual volumes.

The *Minerals Yearbook, 1956,* vol. II (pp. 330–331) states that estimated proved reserves "include only oil recoverable under existing economic and operating conditions . . . .   Includes crude oil that may be extracted by present methods from fields completely developed or explored enough to permit reasonably accurate calculations.   The change in reserves during any year represents total new discoveries, extensions, and revisions, minus production."

For 1899–1934, figures are estimates of the American Petroleum Institute and are not based on geological surveys.   The figure for 1899 is designated in the source as representing the entire period 1859–1899. Except for 1936, figures for 1935–1970 are estimates of the Committee on Petroleum Reserves of the American Petroleum Institute.   The estimate for 1936 has been taken by the American Petroleum Institute from *The Lamp* (Standard Oil Company of New Jersey).   For 1946–1970, figures are for crude oil only.   Previously, estimates included some condensate.   (The 1945 figure on the new basis is 19,941,846 thousand barrels.)

M 143–146.   Natural gas liquids, production and value, 1911–1970.

Source: U.S. Bureau of Mines, **series M 143** and **M 145,** *Minerals Yearbook,* annual volumes, except M 145 for 1943, *Monthly Petroleum Statement No. 402;* **series M 144** and **M 146,** unpublished data.

Statistics on the production of natural-gas liquids are collected on monthly questionnaires from natural-gas processing plants, supplemented by data from State agencies on liquids recovered at pipeline compressor stations and at gas-dehydration plants.   Plant condensate delivered to a plant and fractionated into finished products was reported as output of finished products.

Natural gasoline and cycle products include all natural-gas liquids except liquefied petroleum gases and ethane.   Therefore, they include such products as natural gasoline, natural gasoline mixtures, finished gasoline, naphtha, plant condensate, kerosene, and distillate fuel produced from natural gas.   Beginning 1954, isopentane previously included in liquefied petroleum gases, is also included.

M 147–161.   General note.

Data on natural-gas consumption and value are collected by annual surveys of oil and gas producers, natural gas processing plants, gas pipeline companies and gas utility companies with separate reports obtained for each State in which they operate.   Data for production are obtained from the State agencies.

Volumes are reported at the pressure base selected by the reporting company; however, prior to 1961, if the reported pressure base deviated more than 5 percent from 14.65 pounds per square inch absolute (psia) at 60°F, it was corrected to this base.   Beginning 1961, gas volumes have been reported or converted to a pressure base of 14.73 psia at 60°F.

M 147.   Natural gas, marketed production, 1900–1970.

Source: U.S. Bureau of Mines, *Minerals Yearbook,* annual volumes.

Figures comprise gas sold or consumed by producers, including losses in transmission, amounts added to storage, and increases in gas in pipelines.   They are equal to gross production minus repressuring, vented, and wasted.   Figures for gross withdrawals may be obtained by summation of series M 147 (marketed production), series M 149 (vented and wasted), and series M 150 (repressuring).

Figures for 1900–1919 are not strictly comparable with those for later years.   Apparently, for the earlier period, neither net storage change nor transmission loss was included.

M 148.   Natural gas, average value at well, 1922–1970.

Source: U.S. Bureau of Mines, 1922–1935 and 1951–1970, *Mineral Resources of the United States* and *Minerals Yearbook,* annual volumes; 1936–1950, *Information Circular 7644,* p. 3.

In 1970, the average value at the well was 17.1 cents per thousand cubic feet as compared with 4.5 cents in 1940, when the residential use of natural gas was only slightly greater than the gas used to manufacture carbon black.

M 149–150.   Natural gas, vented and wasted, and used for repressuring, 1920–1970.

Source: See source for series M 148.

Figures for vented and wasted gas are partly estimated.   The data are compiled from information submitted by respondents, supplemented by estimates based on information from State agencies.

M 151.   Natural gas, estimated proved reserves, 1925–1970.

Source: American Gas Association, 1925–1944, *Historical Statistics of the Gas Industry*, New York, 1956, pp. 20–21; 1945–1970, *Reserves of Crude Oil, Natural Gas Liquids and Natural Gas in the United States and Canada and United States Productive Capacity as of December 31, 1970*, vol. 25, May 1971, published jointly by American Gas Association, American Petroleum Institute, and Canadian Petroleum Association. (Copyright.)

The definition of proved reserves is analogous to that for crude oil (see text for series M 142).   For 1925–1944, the source cites Lyon F. Terry, "Our Natural Gas Reserves," *Proceedings*, Natural Gas Department of the American Gas Association, 1944, p. 133; and Exhibit No. 445, Federal Power Commission Docket G-580, 1946 (witness E. De Golyer).   For 1945–1970, figures are estimates by the Committee on Natural Gas Reserves of the American Gas Association.

M 152–161.   Natural gas, consumption, 1906–1970.

Source: See source for series M 148.

Total consumption figures can be computed by summing the figures for these component series.   For 1920–1970, such totals would differ from series M 147 (marketed production) by extraction loss (in producing natural-gas liquids), net change in storage, transmission loss, and net imports or exports.   Before 1920, the definition of consumption as compared to production is unclear.   Such totals would also differ from series M 88, natural gas, dry (expressed in terms of B.t.u.'s), which includes transmission loss.

For 1906–1935, the residential figures (series M 153) appear in the source under "domestic consumption."   The figures for "other industrial" consumption (series M 161) were obtained for certain of the early years by adding component data shown in the basic source. The figures include consumption in petroleum refineries, natural-gas pipelines, electric utilities, and other industrial plants.   For 1906–1929, data for public utilities consumption came from the Geological Survey, while other components were partly estimated.

M 162–177.   Input and output of petroleum products at refineries, 1916–1970.

Source: U.S. Bureau of Mines, 1916–1930, *Petroleum Refinery Statistics, 1930*, Bulletin 367, p. 15; 1931–1970, *Minerals Yearbook*, annual volumes.

Series M 162 is the sum of petroleum refinery inputs, and excludes unfinished oils rerun (net).   Series 166 is the sum of all finished refinery products; unfinished products are excluded except that M 167 includes unfinished gasoline beginning with 1952.   For 1916–1922, this sum was not computed because of incomplete data.

For 1952–1970, jet fuel components are excluded from series M 167–169 and jet fuel included in series M 177, except as noted.

The conversion factors used by the Bureau of Mines for series M 171–175 were: Wax, 280 pounds = 1 barrel; coke, 1 short ton = 5 barrels; asphalt, 1 short ton = 5.5 barrels; and still gas, 3,600 cubic feet = 1 barrel.

M 178–187.   Petroleum products, imports and exports, 1920–1970.

Source: U.S. Bureau of Mines, 1920–1937, *Monthly Petroleum Statement No. 402*; 1938–1970, *Minerals Yearbook*, annual volumes.

Imports include shipments to the States from Puerto Rico and outlying areas of the United States; exports include shipments from the States to these areas.

Total imports (series M 178) also include motor fuel, kerosene, lubricants, wax, asphalt, and other miscellaneous petroleum products not shown separately here.   Total exports (series M 181) also include petroleum coke, petroleum asphalt, and other miscellaneous products not shown separately here.   For 1923–1937, natural gasoline exports are excluded; for other years, they are included in gasoline (series M 182).

M 188–204.   Nonmetals, 1818–1970.

Source: See general note for series M 13–306.

Of the large number of nonmetals, excluding fuels, only the more important ones and those for which more adequate data exist have been included here.   Although raw clays are among the more important nonmetals, the statistical series available are so inadequate as to result in their exclusion.   For many commodities, adequate production or shipments series exist and have been shown, but satisfactory long-run average value or price series may not exist.   Import and export series have been shown only where they are of considerable importance to the industry.

M 188, cement shipments.   For 1818–1911, represents production; for 1912–1970, represents shipments of hydraulic cement.   Coverage includes natural cement since 1818, portland cement beginning 1870, slag cement (formerly referred to as puzzolan cement) beginning 1896, and hydraulic lime cement beginning 1934.   It also includes prepared masonry cement made at natural- and slag-cement plants and, beginning 1955, prepared masonry cement made at portland-cement plants.   Portland cement shipments represented about 99 percent of the totals in series M 188 for 1954, but between 94 and 95 percent for 1955.

For 1818–1890, figures are estimated; for 1891–1970, they are based on practically complete returns from all producers.   For 1921–1970, the figures have been reported in barrels of uniform weight of 376 pounds.   However, prior to 1921, the reports were not always uniform (see *Mineral Resources of the United States, 1916*, vol. II, pp. 342–343).

Figures include Hawaiian production beginning 1960 and Puerto Rican production beginning 1939.

M 189, average value of portland cement.   Represents average value per 376-pound barrel of shipments from mills; value is that received f.o.b. mills, excluding cost of containers.   Figures include Hawaii beginning 1960 and Puerto Rico beginning 1939.   Prior to 1926, figures were identified as "average factory value per barrel in bulk."

M 190, crude gypsum mined.   Represents crude gypsum mined and ready for calcining or for uncalcined use; excludes byproduct gypsum.   Except for the first few years, coverage is believed to be complete.

M 191, lime sold by producers.   Includes quicklime, hydrated lime, and dead-burned dolomite.   For some years prior to 1921, the figures include lime produced and used by soda ash manufacturers; since 1953, they include lime used by all producers.   For 1921–1952, only small quantities of "captive" tonnage were included but, beginning 1953, coverage is assumed to be complete.   (Data for 1889–1903 are not available, and the figures for 1880–1888 are considered much too high; see text for series M 24.)

M 192, lime, average value per short ton.   Represents the selling value f.o.b. plant, excluding cost of containers.   Values for 1882–1888 were converted from average value per barrel at the kiln to an average value per short ton.   The conversion factor used was 200 pounds = 1 barrel (*Mineral Resources of the United States, 1904*, p. 840).   See also text for series M 24 and M 191.

M 193, sand and gravel sold or used.   For 1902, coverage was only partial; for 1904, most sand producers were included; since 1905, both sand and gravel are included.   Data include commercial and government-and-contractor operations.   For 1954–1970, ground sand (721 thousand short tons in 1954) is included.   See also Bureau of Mines, *Development of the Sand and Gravel Industry*, Information Circular No. 7203, 1942.

M 194, stone sold or used by producers. Includes both dimension and crushed or broken stone but, for 1916–1953, excludes stone used for abrasives, lime, and cement. For 1954–1970, includes stone used for abrasives and in making cement and lime, and shell for various uses (95 million tons in 1954). Coverage includes granite, basalt, marble, limestone, sandstone, and other stone such as mica, schist, conglomerate, argillite, and various light-colored rocks.

M 195, sulfur production from Frasch mines. Although, for most years, the major portion of sulfur production has been from Frasch process mines, these figures do not represent total sulfur output. At present, quantities of sulfur are recovered as elemental sulfur from coal and natural and refinery gases, in pyrites (see series M 198), and as byproduct sulfuric acid and other forms. In 1970 (in terms of thousands of long tons of sulfur content) Frasch production totaled 7,082; recovered elemental, 1,449; byproduct sulfuric acid, 535; and other forms, 483.

M 196–197, sulfur, crude imports and exports. Imports represent imports of crude sulfur and sulfur ore. For 1867–1883, pyrites imports are presumably included.

Although no imports of sulfur ore were reported for most of the 1940's, processors stated that during 1941–1945 at least 2,000 tons of sulfur ore were imported from Mexico. Figures for 1867–1887 are on a fiscal-year basis ending June 30; for 1888–1970, on a calendar-year basis.

Exports of crude sulfur have been separately classified since 1905. The first shipment occurred in 1904 when 3,000 tons were shipped from Louisiana to France (*Mineral Resources of the United States, 1904,* p. 1079).

M 198, pyrites production. Figures for 1922–1927 have been corrected for flotation concentrates (*Mineral Resources of the United States, 1931,* p. 145).

M 199, pyrites imports. Prior to 1884, pyrites imports were classed with sulfur ore; for 1888–1890, they were included under imports of iron ores. For early years, the restriction of not more than 3.5 percent copper content was placed on the import classification. For recent years, figures are for pyrites containing over 25 percent sulfur.

M 200, salt sold or used by producers. Coverage includes evaporated salt, rock salt, and the salt content of brine production.

M 201, potash sold by producers. Expressed in terms of K_2O equivalent, which is the standard basis for comparison of different salts of widely varying composition.

M 202, potash imports. Represents crude and refined potash materials, expressed in terms of approximate K_2O equivalent. For 1905–1912, they are based on information in a fertilizer industry report by the Federal Trade Commission; thereafter, on tabulations by the Department of Commerce (see *Mineral Resources of the United States, 1917,* vol. II, p. 401).

M 204, phosphate rock exports. Figures for 1940–1953 are also published in Bureau of Mines, *Mineral Facts and Problems,* Bulletin No. 556, p. 689. Generally, figures include high grade hard rock, land pebble, and other (colloidal matrix, soft phosphate rock, and Tennessee, Idaho, and Montana rock). Sintered matrix is included only for selected years. For 1942–1946, Florida soft rock, colloidal, and sintered matrix are excluded.

M 205–207. Iron ore, usable, production and shipments, 1860–1970.

Source: 1860–1898 and 1907–1970, U.S. Bureau of Mines, *Mineral Resources of the United States* and *Minerals Yearbook,* annual volumes; 1899–1906, see source for series M 72–75, p. 278.

The Bureau of Mines publishes several iron ore production series. Crude iron ore production as shown in series M 212–213 for 1942–1970 represents the mine product before treatment for removal of waste constituents. Figures for usable iron ore production shown here represent such output after treatment.

Ore varieties included are hematite, limonite, and magnetite. For 1942–1957, figures include byproduct material from pyrites; beginning 1958, shipments exclude byproduct ore. For 1907–1970, coverage is restricted to ore containing less than 5 percent manganese. Prior to 1907, Bureau of Mines data include ores with a higher manganese content. However, the Barger-Schurr series presented here for 1899–1906 assures comparability back to 1899. For 1860–1898, figures very probably include ores with a higher manganese content.

Data for 1882–1888 are estimated; for 1885–1888, they represent consumption of domestic ores. Corresponding consumption estimates (in thousands of long tons) for 1882–1884 are: 1882, 8,700; 1883, 8,800; and 1884, 7,718. Figures for 1875 and 1881 were estimated by I. I. Bell, *Principles of the Manufacture of Iron and Steel,* 1884, p. 451; those for 1860, 1870, and 1880 are from decennial census reports.

M 208. Iron ore, average value of shipments, 1892–1970.

Source: See general note for series M 13–306 and M 206.

Figures represent average value of shipments, f.o.b. mine.

M 209. Iron ore, price, Mesabi, non-Bessemer, 1894–1970.

Source: American Metal Market, *Metal Statistics,* New York, 1919, 1957, and 1970 editions. Reprinted with permission of American Metal Market, Fairchild Publications, Inc., N.Y., N.Y., copyright.

Prices are those at Lake Erie docks.

M 210–211. Iron ore, foreign trade, 1872–1970.

Source: See general note for series M 13–306.

For some years during the 1940's, some pyrites cinder was included in imports. For 1872–1878, figures are for fiscal years ending June 30; thereafter, for calendar years.

M 212–213. Iron ore production, by mining method, underground and open pit, 1909–1970.

Source: 1909–1929, N. Yaworski, O. E. Kiessling, C. H. Baxter, L. Eaton, and E. W. Davis, *Technology, Employment, and Output Per Man in Iron Mining,* WPA-NRP Report E-13, Philadelphia, June 1940; 1930–1970, see general note for series M 13–306.

For 1909–1941, the data are in terms of usable iron ore; beginning 1942, they represent production of crude iron ore before treatment for removal of waste constituents.

For 1909–1940, some underground production may be included in the open pit figures. For a few other years, the statistical allocation of production by method accounted for somewhat less than the total production.

M 214–216. Iron ore employment, 1880–1970.

Source: 1880–1922, see source for series M 212–213 for 1909–1929, pp. 206 and 215; 1923–1970, see general note for series M 13–306.

Figures are active period averages, excluding periods when the mines were not in operation. Slight variations occur in coverage in some years.

M 217. Pig iron shipments, 1810–1970.

Source: See general note for series M 13–306.

For 1810–1909, figures represent production; for 1910–1970, shipments. *Mineral Resources of the United States, 1910,* vol. I, p. 93, states: "The statistics for 1854 and all succeeding years (through 1909) were collected by the American Iron and Steel Association; those for 1810, 1840, and 1850 are census figures; those for the other years are largely estimates by early statisticians." Figures exclude blast furnace output of ferroalloys. Published data have been converted to long tons for comparability with related series.

M 218. Pig iron, average price, 1799–1970.

Source: American Metal Market, *Metal Statistics,* New York, 1910, 1919, 1930, 1940, 1957, and 1971 editions. Reprinted with permission of American Metal Market, Fairchild Publications, Inc., N.Y., N.Y., copyright.

Several pig iron price series have been spliced together for presentation. For 1799–1843, the series shown is titled "charcoal pig iron;" for 1844–1907, "No. 1 Foundry, Philadelphia." For 1908–1970, quotations of "basic f.o.b. Valley furnaces" are shown. Price data are available for No. 1 Foundry, Philadelphia, to 1970, but it was considered preferable to show the price of "basic" pig iron, f.o.b. Valley, for recent years (available only since 1908) because of its predominant importance today, and to splice this series with other price data for earlier years. The series spliced together exhibit similar price movements for years in which overlap occurs. For 1799–1843, the series for "charcoal" pig iron is noted in the source as representing best pig iron for 1799–1827, average of grades for 1828–1833, gray iron for 1834–1840, and No. 1 Foundry for 1841–1843. For 1844–1907, the series titled No. 1 Foundry, Philadelphia, is noted as referring to several different grades during the period; for 1844–1895, the series refers to No. 1 anthracite Foundry iron.

M 219–220. Pig iron, imports and exports, 1922–1970.

Source: See general note for series M 13–306.

Prior to 1922, pig iron imports and exports were not shown separately from ferroalloys.

M 221–234. Ferroalloying metals, 1868–1970.

Source: See general note for series M 13–306.

M 221, manganese ore, domestic output (gross weight). For 1880–1909, figures represent production; for 1910–1970, mine shipments. Coverage includes metallurgical, battery, and miscellaneous ores. For 1880–1914, figures include only ore containing 40 percent or more manganese; for 1915–1970, 35 percent or more. (See Barger and Schurr, cited for series M 72–75.)

M 222, manganese ore imports (gross weight). For recent years, figures are restricted to ores containing at least 35 percent manganese; for earlier periods, the manganese content is not specified.

For 1868–1888, figures represent only Canadian shipments to this country; figures for total imports are not available. For 1868–1872, figures are for fiscal years ending June 30. (Imports during fiscal 1873 were 939 short tons.)

M 223, chromite, domestic output (gross weight). These figures represent shipments. Data for 1880–1889 are noted as estimates; those for 1890–1910 are described as having an industry coverage of 95 percent. For later years coverage is virtually complete. Prior to 1880, cumulative output (all from Pennsylvania and Maryland) amounted to 224,000 short tons. Domestic mine production of chromite ceased in 1961 when the Federal government's last Defense Production Act contract was concluded.

M 224, chromite imports (gross weight).

M 225, tungsten concentrates, domestic output (tungsten content). For 1900–1909, data are called "production." *Mineral Resources of the United States, 1910*, vol. I, p. 740, states that "The production of tungsten ores in this country from year to year can be fairly compared . . . only since and beginning with 1906, as before that date no effort had been made to reduce the ores to a common basis of concentration." Figures for 1900–1909 were converted from tungsten concentrates to tungsten content on the basis that one short ton of 60 percent WO$_3$ contained 951.72 pounds of tungsten. For 1910–1970, figures represent shipments.

M 226, tungsten concentrates imports. For 1912–1922, figures are in terms of gross weight; for 1923–1970, tungsten content.

M 227, molybdenum ores and concentrates, domestic output (molybdenum content). Figures shown are for shipments and are believed to represent complete coverage of the industry.

M 228, molybdenum ores and concentrates exports (molybdenum content). Figures include roasted concentrates. Export figures are not separately available prior to 1940, except for 1939 gross weight (see *Foreign Commerce and Navigation, 1939*, p. 520, and *Minerals Yearbook, 1940, Review of 1939*, p. 621). However, exports were of substantial importance.

M 229, vanadium ores and concentrates, domestic output (vanadium content). Data shown are for shipments. Production occurred prior to 1911, but data for the period are not available. Data for 1927–1931 are not available because publication would disclose individual returns; data for 1934–1935 represent the vanadium content of carnotite ores only (Bureau of Mines was not at liberty to publish other data). Mine shipments of ores and concentrates for 1940–1970 were measured by receipts at mills and Government purchasing depots.

M 230, vanadium ores and concentrates imports. For 1918–1933, figures are in terms of gross weight; for 1934–1970, vanadium content. (In 1934, the vanadium content equaled 207 short tons compared to the gross weight of 1,754 short tons.) The figure for 1918 represents July through December only; imports of vanadium were not separately recorded prior to 1918.

M 231–234, nickel (content). The United States has been largely dependent on imports of ore, metal, and matte plus domestic secondary recovery from scrap for its supply of nickel. Some small quantities are also recovered as byproduct production of copper refining and other metal refineries (in 1970, 2,670 short tons).

M 231, nickel primary production (nickel content). Production from domestic ore has been of minor importance. However, because of a single mine in Riddle, Oregon, production has increased substantially—from 3,356 tons in 1955 to 13,124 tons in 1968. Production since that time has been relatively stable.

M 232, nickel secondary production (nickel content). For 1916–1918, coverage is incomplete, since the production of one large firm is only partly covered.

M 233, nickel imports (nickel content). Most nickel imports come from Canada. In 1970, 104 thousand out of 117 thousand short tons of metal (gross weight) were directly from Canada. Figures were compiled by the Bureau of Mines (or the Geological Survey) from records of the Bureau of the Census except that, for 1950–1956, they include refinery residues, data on which are reported to the Bureau of Mines by importers.

M 234, nickel, price, electrolytic (cents per pound). For 1913–1927, the source states that prices were computed from data from one large nickel company by dividing the gross amount received by the total quantity sold. For 1913–1924, prices are for March 31; for 1925–1927, December 31. (The March 31, 1925, quotation was 28.83 cents per pound.) For 1928–1941, quotations are for 2-ton minimum lots in New York City. (The New York quotation for 1942 is 35 cents per pound compared to 31.5 cents in Canada.) For 1942–1970, figures represent price quotations to United States buyers by the International Nickel Co., Inc., for electrolytic nickel in carlots f.o.b. Port Colburne, Canada. Quotations include duty paid in the United States, as follows: 2½ cents per pound, 1942–1947; 1¼ cents to September 1965; no duty to October 1967; 1¼ cents to January 1968; and no duty thereafter.

M 235–240. Copper production, imports, and exports, 1845–1970.

Source: See general note for series M 13–306.

Figures are shown for different stages of the production process. Mine output is represented by the recoverable copper content of domestic ores mined. The total domestic output of primary metal from domestic and foreign ores (i.e., excluding secondary recovery from scrap) is represented by primary refinery output. The difference between primary refinery output and the recoverable copper content of mine output in any year is accounted for to some extent by time lags and changes in stocks in the different production stages; but mainly, the difference measures the amount of new copper produced in the United States from foreign ores, concentrates, and other unrefined materials.

In addition to copper from primary sources, domestic supply includes copper recovered from scrap (called secondary production) either as unalloyed copper or in alloys and compounds. Two series are shown for secondary output: Total secondary production and recovery from old scrap only. The figures on old scrap measure what the junk pile contributes to metal supply each year, while the difference between old scrap and total secondary production is new scrap—a body of material which, in effect, is continuously being recycled in the production and fabrication of copper metal and does not constitute a true addition to supply at any time.

Primary and secondary output together measure the supply of metal in the United States produced by domestic refiners from foreign and domestic ores and scrap. To measure the supply of refined metal available for consumption in the United States it is necessary also to account for foreign trade; hence, import and export series for the refined metals are shown.

M 235, copper production, mine (recoverable content). For 1845–1905, figures represent smelter production of copper from domestic ores; for 1906–1970, they refer to the estimated recoverable copper content of domestically mined ores. The statistical differences between the two series are slight. They principally reflect time lags and changes in stocks in the two stages of production. (The comparable smelter figure for 1906 equals 458,903 short tons.)

M 236, copper production, primary refined from domestic and foreign ores. Figures represent total primary refinery production from both domestic and foreign ores.

M 237, copper, total secondary production. Figures represent secondary production from both new and old scrap.

M 239, copper refined imports. Figures represent imports of refined copper only. Imports of copper ore, concentrates, and various unrefined copper metallic materials have historically been of much greater significance than imports of copper refined in ingots, plates, or bars. An approximation of unrefined imports can be obtained by subtracting recoverable content of mine output (series M 235) from primary refinery output (series M 236). For 1916–1933, the sources used here do not always specify a precise definition of imports; for 1934–1970, figures are for "general imports."

M 241. Copper price, New York, electrolytic, f.o.b. refinery, 1850–1970.

Source: 1850–1859, U.S. Bureau of Mines, *Mineral Resources of the United States, 1929*, vol. I, p. A 123; 1860–1955 and 1969–1970, American Metal Market, *Metal Statistics*, 1919, 1957, and 1971 editions, reprinted with permission of American Metal Market, Fairchild Publications, Inc., N.Y., N.Y., copyright; 1956–1968, U.S. Bureau of Mines, *Minerals Yearbook*, annual volumes.

For 1850–1859, figures are for an unspecified grade of copper. The source cites *Weed's Copper Handbook*, vol. XI, as the basis for these data. For 1860–1899, figures refer to the New York price of Lake copper. In 1900, this price was 16.70 cents as compared with the electrolytic quotation of 16.54 cents. For 1900–1967, data are the average New York prices for electrolytic copper, f.o.b. refinery. For 1968–1970, the price is for electrolytic copper, delivered.

M 242–247. Lead production, imports, and exports, 1801–1970.

Source: See general note for series M 13–306, except for series M 243, 1801–1927, which is from U.S. Bureau of Mines, *Economic Paper No. 5*, L. A. Smith, "Summarized Data of Lead Production," 1929, pp. 12–14.

The text for series M 235–240, which discusses the interrelationships among the copper production and foreign trade series, is also generally applicable to lead.

M 242–243, lead production. Series M 242 represents the estimated recoverable lead content of domestic mine output; series M 243 represents the total primary refinery output from both domestic and foreign ores and base bullion. The two series differ by the amounts of ore and unrefined lead which are imported into this country for domestic refining (covered in series M 243) and by the amounts of lead ore and concentrates consumed outside the refineries for such products as antimonial lead and lead pigments and salts

(covered in series M 242). Other smaller differences between the two series reflect time lags and differences in stock changes at the two stages of production.

Series M 243 includes lead refined domestically from foreign ore for 1886–1970 and lead refined from foreign base bullion for 1891–1970.

M 244, lead, total secondary production. Figures represent secondary production from both new and old scrap. They include lead recovered as refined metal and in antimonial lead and other alloys.

M 246, lead imports. Although the figures purport to refer to refined lead in pigs and bars, the specific items included change frequently over the long period, and can be identified only by referring to the basic sources. For example, for 1867–1934, imports of old lead are also covered. Figures for many recent years include lead received by the Government and held in stockpile.

For 1867–1886, data are for fiscal years ending June 30.

M 247, lead exports. Figures represent exports of refined lead in pigs and bars. For 1914 and 1915, exports of lead refined domestically from foreign ores are not included. During this period, all such exports were recorded in the statistics of exports as ore and concentrates, i.e., in the form in which they were imported, and not as refined metal. Hence, the figures represent only exports of refined metal from domestic ore.

Although the figures purport to refer to refined lead in pigs and bars, the specific items included change frequently over the long period, and can be identified only by referring to the basic sources. For example, for 1920–1936, exports of old or scrap lead are also included. For 1851–1868, data are for fiscal years ending June 30.

M 248. Lead, price of pig lead at New York, 1812–1970.

Source: 1812–1883, W. R. Ingalls, *Lead and Zinc in the United States*, Hill Publishing Co., New York, 1908, p. 203; 1884–1970, American Metal Market, *Metal Statistics, 1971*, New York, 1971, p. 195, reprinted with permission of American Metal Market, Fairchild Publications, Inc., N.Y., N.Y., copyright.

Price quotations are generally available both in St. Louis and in New York. New York prices are shown because of proximity to the larger market.

M 249–254. Zinc production, imports, and exports, 1858–1970.

Source: See general note for series M 13–306, except for series M 250, 1858–1881, which is from U.S. Bureau of Mines, *Economic Paper No. 2*, E. W. Pehrson, "Summarized Data of Zinc Production," 1929, p. 19.

The text for series M 235–240, which discusses the interrelationships among the copper production and foreign trade series, is also generally applicable to zinc.

M 249–250, zinc production, mine (recoverable content) and primary smelter slab zinc. Series M 249 represents the estimated recoverable zinc content of domestic mine output; series M 250, the total primary smelter output (including electrolytic plants) from both domestic and foreign ores and base bullion. The two series differ by the amounts of ore and unsmelted zinc imported into this country for domestic smelting (covered in series M 250), and by consumption of zinc ore and concentrates outside the smelter directly in the production of zinc dust and zinc pigments and salts (covered in series M 249). Other smaller differences between the two series reflect time lags and differences in stock changes at the two stages of production.

For 1858–1903, smelter output (series M 250) is from domestic ores only. For 1904–1905, an unknown quantity of smelter output from foreign ore is included. For 1906–1970, output from both domestic and foreign ores is included.

M 251, zinc, total secondary production. Includes secondary production from both new and old scrap.

M 253, zinc imports. Figures are for zinc blocks, pigs, and slabs. For 1867–1885, figures are for fiscal years ending June 30.

M 254, zinc exports. Figures represent exports of zinc in blocks, pigs, and slabs. The specific items included, however, changed frequently over the long period and can be identified only by referring to the basic sources.

For 1864–1885, figures are for fiscal years ending June 30.

M 255. Zinc, price of slab zinc at New York, 1853–1970.

Source: 1853 and 1864, U.S. Bureau of Mines, *Mineral Resources of the United States, 1929*, vol. I, p. A 123; 1875–1879, W. R. Ingalls, *Lead and Zinc in the United States*, Hill Publishing Co., New York, 1908, p. 342; 1880–1970, American Metal Market, *Metal Statistics, 1971*, New York, 1971, pp. 331–333, reprinted with permission of American Metal Market, Fairchild Publications, Inc., N.Y., N.Y., copyright.

Quotations for slab zinc are available both at St. Louis and in New York. New York prices are shown because of proximity to the larger market.

M 256–267. Bauxite, aluminum, magnesium, and uranium, 1886–1970.

Source: See general note for series M 13–306, except for series M 262, 1895–1955, which is from American Bureau of Metal Statistics, *Yearbook, 1933*, and *Yearbook, 1956*, New York, 1934 and 1957, respectively (copyright).

M 256, bauxite domestic output. Figures represent production for 1919–1928 and 1940–1970, production or shipments for 1929–1934 (the terms are used interchangeably during this period), and shipments for all other years. For 1889–1934, the figures refer to bauxite "as shipped;" for 1935–1970, they are in terms of "dried bauxite equivalent." Because of the widely differing moisture content of the different forms (crude, dried, and calcined), dried bauxite equivalent yields a more comparable measure of the quantity of bauxite produced or shipped.

Figures for 1889–1918 are from the 1918 volume of *Mineral Resources of the United States*, vol. I, p. 516. The source states (p. 514) that the figures "are believed to represent more accurately (than other available figures) the condition of the industry."

M 257, bauxite imports. Imports of bauxite are of great importance; exports are insignificant.

For 1934–1950, the figures are in terms of "dried bauxite equivalent," an adjustment in the Department of Commerce series made by the Bureau of Mines. Figures entirely adjusted to the dried bauxite equivalent are not available for other years. However, for 1952–1970, figures for imports from Jamaica (which have a high moisture content) have been adjusted and the remaining imports presumably include only a small amount of undried bauxite.

M 258, aluminum primary production. For 1896–1906, figures represent fiscal years ending August 31. Production for September–December 1906 totaled 2,734 short tons.

M 259–260, aluminum secondary production. Total secondary production represents recoverable content from both old and new scrap processed. For 1954–1970, figures represent recoverable aluminum content and are not strictly comparable with those for previous years which are for recoverable aluminum-alloy content.

M 261, aluminum imports, crude and semicrude. Aluminum imports include metals and alloys, crude; scrap; and plates, sheets, bars, etc. Figures are for "imports for consumption" for all years except 1911–1912, for which they represent "general imports."

Although a significant quantity of crude and semicrude aluminum has been exported in recent years, export data are not shown here as the United States is normally a net importer of aluminum.

M 262, aluminum, price of primary ingot. Represents average price of primary ingot in New York City.

M 263, magnesium, primary domestic output. For 1915–1938, data are for new ingot sold or used; for 1939–1970, figures represent production. For 1943–1944, magnesium content of incendiary mixtures produced directly is excluded.

M 264–265, magnesium, secondary domestic output. Secondary production of magnesium is expressed in terms of ingot equivalent and represents the recoverable magnesium and magnesium-alloy

content of scrap processed. Total secondary output includes recoverable content of both old and new scrap processed.

M 266, primary uranium oxide (U_3O_8) production. Production data for 1911 through 1941 are estimated U_3O_8 content of ores shipped from mines in the western United States. During these years, the ores were mined essentially for radium and/or vanadium, and uranium was a byproduct. Production statistics were withheld during and immediately following World War II. For the postwar period, 1948 through 1970, production data are based on mine output statistics, provided by the U.S. Atomic Energy Commission (AEC), to which mill recovery factors were applied, giving recoverable content of ore.

M 267, imports of uranium oxide (U_3O_8). Data are not available on imports during 1910 through 1914; imports may have been very small during these years. For 1915 through 1922, available data were by value of imports only. For 1923 through 1946, data are imports for consumption; for the years 1947 through 1952, import statistics were withheld at the request of the AEC; in the post-1952 period, imports have been largely for AEC stockpiles. Pursuant to subsection 161 V of the Atomic Energy Act of 1954, as amended, foreign uranium cannot be imported for private domestic consumption.

M 268–269. Gold and silver production, 1792–1970.

Source: 1792–1834 and 1845–1903, U.S. Bureau of the Mint, *Annual Report of the Director of the Mint, 1910*, p. 99; **series M 268**, 1835–1844, U.S. Bureau of Mines, *Economic Paper No. 6*, R. H. Ridgway, "Summarized Data of Gold Production," 1929, p. 14; **series M 269**, 1835–1844, Bureau of Mines, *Economic Paper No. 8*, C. W. Merrill, "Summarized Data for Silver Production," 1930, p. 18; 1904–1938, Bureau of Mines, unpublished data; 1939–1970, see general note for series M 13–306.

For 1792–1903, figures represent production measured at the refinery stage; for 1904–1970, they represent production measured at the mining stage. For 1904, production measured at the refinery stage was 3,892,000 troy ounces for gold and 57,683,000 troy ounces for silver. The refinery figures are from the Bureau of the Mint and measure the metal from domestic ores and concentrates actually recovered in marketable form. The mine output figures are from the Bureau of Mines and measure the recoverable gold and silver content of domestically produced ores, concentrates, and bullion. Differences between the two series primarily result from time lags between the two stages of production. Other differences exist because of the difficulty at the refining stage of determining the domestic or foreign origin of the ore. The Bureau of Mines figures are defined as "calculated upon the basis of recovered or recoverable fine gold and silver shown by assays to be contained in ore, bullion, and other material produced." (*Minerals Yearbook, 1950*, p. 564.) Bureau of the Mint data are defined as "official estimates of production of gold and silver in the United States . . . based upon arrivals at U.S. mints and assay offices and at privately owned refineries" (same source, p. 580).

Data include both lode and placer production. The weight unit for both gold and silver is the fine troy ounce of 480 grains. No price series is shown for gold. In 1934, its official value was changed from $20.67 to $35 per fine ounce.

M 270. Silver, New York average price, 1850–1970.

Source: 1850–1883, U.S. Bureau of Mines, *Mineral Resources of the United States, 1929*, vol. I, p. A 123; 1884–1956, American Bureau of Metal Statistics, *Yearbook, 1933*, and *Yearbook, 1956*, New York, 1934 and 1957, respectively (copyright); 1957–1970, U.S. Bureau of Mines, *Minerals Yearbook*, annual volumes.

The U.S. Treasury no longer regularly buys domestically mined silver at a fixed price (in 1954, $0.9050505 per fine ounce). However, it remains committed to buy silver from domestic mines (since 1965) if offered at $1.25 an ounce. For more complete information, see Bureau of Mines, *Mineral Facts and Problems*, Bulletin 650.

M 271–276. Injuries and fatalities in all coal mining, 1870–1970.

Source: U.S. Bureau of Mines, **series M 271–274**, 1870–1929,

Injury Experience in Coal Mining and its predecessor, *Coal-Mine Accidents in the United States;* **series M 271–274**, 1930–1966, and **series M 275–276**, 1870–1966, *Injury Experience in Coal Mining, 1966*, Information Circular No. 8419; **series M 271–276**, 1967–1970, Bureau of Mines, *Minerals Yearbook*, annual volumes and unpublished data.

M 271–272, injuries, fatal and nonfatal. The Bureau of Mines began gathering information on nonfatal injuries in 1930. Data on number of fatalities go back to 1870 for anthracite and to 1874 for bituminous coal. Availability of information on fatalities for the 19th century and the early years of the 20th century depended on the existence of State records, which, in turn, depended mainly on whether the States had mine inspection services.

For 1870–1909, the record of fatalities is incomplete for bituminous coal. For example, coverage of Pennsylvania bituminous coal mines does not begin until 1877. Records for Maryland and Ohio extend back to 1876 and 1874, respectively, while partial records are available for Virginia as early as 1839. Incompleteness since 1870 applies only to bituminous coal. Pennsylvania anthracite records are complete since 1870, with partial data available for 1847 and 1869 (Bureau of Mines Bulletin No. 115, pp. 7, 9, 105). By 1890, the fatality records cover almost 90 percent of all production; between 1895 and 1900, about 95 percent; and between 1901 and 1909, in the neighborhood of 98–99 percent.

Additional detail is available in the source bulletins as to the causes of injury. Information is also shown classifying the nonfatal injuries into the categories of "permanent total disability," "permanent partial disability," and "temporary total disability."

M 273–276, frequency rates, fatal and nonfatal. The employment statistics used in deriving the injury and fatality frequency measures since 1890 are based on canvasses conducted by the Bureau of Mines (or the Geological Survey) with occasional figures from the Census of Mineral Industries. Although these underlying employment data are not presented here, they are available in the source bulletins. For almost all years between 1890 and the early 1930's, the underlying employment figures are those shown in series M 107–110 and M 130–133. In subsequent years, separate employment figures, collected on accident canvasses, were used for deriving the frequency rates. The latter employment figures differ somewhat from those shown in the bituminous and anthracite series (series M 107–110 and M 130–133). For 1870–1889, the frequency rates are based on employment statistics collected by the States; these statistics were less complete and presumably less accurate and comparable than those resulting from the Bureau's own canvasses in subsequent years.

M 273–274, frequency rates per million man-hours, fatal and nonfatal. The figures on man-hours of employment on which these ratios are based were derived as follows: Producers began reporting man-hours of employment to the Bureau of Mines in 1930, but during the early 1930's many mines left the man-hours question unanswered and even in the 1940's the man-hours were not always reported. For those mines not reporting man-hours, the Bureau estimated the figure by multiplying the average number of employees (active period average) by the number of days on which the mine was active, and then multiplying the product by the number of hours constituting a standard work shift in the particular mine. This method, with certain variations, was used by the Bureau to estimate man-hours in all years prior to 1930, when no direct information on man-hours was collected. Estimated man-hours, although reasonably accurate, suffered from two major shortcomings: (1) The number of active days was generally determined by the number of days on which the tipple was active, omitting days on which no coal was brought to the surface, although on such days men were often employed underground in loading coal or in repair or maintenance work; and (2) the standard work shift did not apply to all occupations and many miners were irregular in observing standard working hours (see source, Bulletin 380, pp. 8–9, and Bulletin 283, p. 64).

The 1943 bituminous coal mine wage agreement made portal-to-portal time the basis for pay rather than face or working time hours.

Since 1944, only portal-to-portal man-hours have been reported. Conversion factors were applied to man-hour data for underground bituminous coal employees back to 1930. No such adjustment was made, however, for surfacemen at underground mines or strip mine employees in the bituminous coal industry. No adjustment was deemed necessary in the anthracite industry.

M 275–276, fatalities per 1,000 300-day workers, and per 1,000 employed. The 300-day worker basis was derived by converting the average number of employees (active period average) according to the ratio between active mine days and 300 days. For the very early years, information on active days was not available; therefore the simple measure of fatalities per 1,000 was used.

For 1888 and earlier years, corresponding employment data are not available for all recorded fatalities. The rates are based on fatalities for which corresponding employment data do exist. Apparently, comparable fatality and employment data exist for all Pennsylvania anthracite back through 1870.

Source bulletins also show fatality rates per million tons mined.

M 277–280.   Injuries and fatalities in quarrying and related industries, 1911–1970.

Source: U.S. Bureau of Mines, 1911–1960, *Injury Experience in the Quarry Industry*, Information Circular No. 8171, 1960; 1961–1970, *Minerals Yearbook*, annual volumes, and unpublished data.

Separate figures are shown in the basic source according to the kind of rock produced and also for stone classified as dimension and nondimension. Nondimension stone includes all stone used in unshaped or irregular form, as for roadbuilding and cement and lime manufacture; dimension stone includes all stone that is cut or shaped for building or monumental purposes. By far, the major share of employment is in nondimension stone. The figures also cover crushing, screening, rock dressing, and the manufacture of cement and lime, insofar as these operations are conducted by the quarry companies; except for crushing and screening, these operations are classified as manufacturing in the *Standard Industrial Classification Manual*. On the other hand, quarries producing sand, gravel, and clay are excluded.

The source states that the data are comparable only since 1916 because information reported for prior years was obviously incomplete as to number of injuries, especially those causing disability for only one or two days. Additional detail is available in the source as to the causes of injuries. Also included is the classification of nonfatal injuries into the categories of "permanent total," "permanent partial," and "temporary total." The last category is further divided, for 1915–1929, into the subclasses, "temporary disabilities lasting more than 14 days" and "temporary disabilities lasting more than the remainder of the day on which the accident occurred, but not exceeding 14 days."

The employment data used in deriving the injury and fatality frequency measures are comparable with the injury data. However, they must be carefully evaluated before they are used for other purposes. For an extensive discussion of the inadequacies of the underlying employment data, see Barger and Schurr, cited in the text for series M 13–37, especially appendix C, pp. 377–393.

M 281–286.   Injuries and fatalities in metal and nonmetal mining, 1911–1970.

Source: U.S. Bureau of Mines, 1911–1954, *Injury Experience in the Metal and Nonmetal Industries*, and its predecessors: *Metal and Nonmetal Mine Accidents in the United States* and *Metal Mine Accidents in the United States;* 1955–1970, *Minerals Yearbook*, annual volumes, and unpublished data.

Employment and injury data for metal and nonmetal mines have been compiled from voluntary reports collected by the Bureau of Mines annually since 1911.

Separate figures are shown in the basic source by type of mining method. Over the entire period, there have been numerous changes in the classification systems used. In addition, data are given by kind of mine, as follows: Copper, iron ore, lead-zinc, gold-silver lode, gold placer, miscellaneous metal mines, and nonmetal mines. Included under miscellaneous metal mines are those working ores of quicksilver, manganese, tungsten, vanadium, chromium, and other metals plus pyrite mines (the cinder is used in metallurgical works for its iron and copper content) and bauxite mines (the primary source of aluminum). The nonmetallic group includes mines that produce asbestos, asphaltum, barite, borax, emery, feldspar, fluorspar, garnet, graphite, gypsum, lithium, magnesite, mica, mineral paint, phosphate rock, potash, quartz, salt, soapstone, sulfur, talc, and tripoli.

Additional detail is available in the source bulletins as to the causes of injuries, and information is shown subclassifying the nonfatal injuries. For 1911–1914, nonfatalities were simply divided into "serious"—of more than 20 days duration, and "slight"—of more than 1 but less than 20 days duration. For 1915–1919, temporary injuries were separated into "serious"—of more than 14 days duration, and "slight"—of more than 1 but less than 14 days duration. For 1930–1970, nonfatalities have been recorded as temporary or permanent with the latter subdivided into total and partial disability.

Injury data for 1931–1965, have been published in *Injury Experience in the Metallic Mineral Industries, 1965,* Information Circular, 8433 and *Injury Experience in the Nonmetallic Mineral Industries* (except stone and coal), *1964–65,* Information Circular 8481. These sources show data for men employed, average days active, and mandays and man-hours worked, as well as data for fatal and nonfatal injuries and frequency rates at mines and mills.

Frequency rate measures were originally expressed per 1,000 men employed. Shortly thereafter, in an attempt to secure a uniform time basis for comparison, the Bureau of Mines began to express all frequency rates on a 300-day worker basis (derived by converting the average number of employees on active days according to the ratio between active mine days and 300 days). These rates were extended back through 1911. Rates per million man-hours of exposure are not available prior to 1931 in the reports, although partial man-hour data by length of shift are available from 1921–1930.

The employment data used in deriving the injury frequency measures are comparable with the fatality and injury records. However, they do not necessarily reflect total employment within the industry. Despite incomplete coverage, the data are considered by the Bureau to be representative of hazard exposure.

M 287–296. Average number of men working daily in mineral industries, 1911–1970.

Source: U.S. Bureau of Mines, **series M 287,** 1911–1929, *Coal-Mine Accidents in the United States,* annual issues; 1930–1966, *Injury Experience in Coal Mining, 1966,* p. 97; and 1967–1970, *Minerals Yearbook,* annual issues. **Series M 288,** *Injury Experience and Worktime in the Coke Industry, 1970,* p. 13. **Series M 289,** *Disabling Work-Injury Experience of the Oil and Natural Gas Industry in the United States, 1970,* p. 7. **Series M 290** and **M 294,** 1931–1965, *Injury Experience in the Metallic Mineral Industries, 1965;* and 1966–1970, Mineral Industry Surveys, *Injury Experience and Worktime in the Mineral Industries,* annual issues. **Series M 291** and **M 296,** 1931–1965, *Injury Experience in the Nonmetallic Mineral Industries, 1964–65;* and 1966–1970, Mineral Industry Surveys, *Injury Experience and Worktime in the Mineral Industries,* annual issues. **Series M 292,** *Injury Experience and Worktime Data on Sand and Gravel Operations in the United States, 1958–70.* **Series M 293,** 1911–1960, *Injury Experience in Stone Quarrying, 1961;* and 1961–1970, Mineral Industry Surveys, *Injury Experience and Employment Data in the Stone Quarrying Industries,* annual issues. **Series M 295,** 1942–1965, *Injury Experience in the Metallic Mineral Industries,* annual issues; and 1966–1970, Mineral Industry Surveys, *Injury Experience and Worktime in the Mineral Industries,* annual issues.

"Men working daily" is obtained from mail canvasses of mineral mining and processing establishments started by the Bureau of Mines for health and safety information in the respective years shown in each column. The data throughout each series are in general agreement with the Standard Industrial Classification (SIC) system (see general note for series P 1–374), although separated into subclassifications so as to more closely fit accident hazards and statistics. Coverages of the industry groupings are complete subsequent to 1915 but some doubts are expressed in the early reports as to completeness of coverages during 1911–15. The sole exception to the foregoing is petroleum and natural gas (series M 289) for which the data do not follow the SIC but rather cover all activities of the reporting companies from the exploration through drilling, production, refining, all transportation, all marketing, research and engineering. Further, the data represent totals from the reports received and no attempt has been made to extrapolate for complete coverage or to estimate percent of coverage. The numbers of both on-site and central office-workers are excluded in all series except for petroleum and natural gas where such employment is included and is not separable.

The series for coke (series M 288), petroleum and natural gas (series M 289), and primary nonferrous smelters and refineries (series M 295) end with 1970; Bureau of Mines responsibilities for safety in these industries was transferred to the U.S. Department of Labor.

M 297–306. Man-hours worked in mineral industries, 1911–1970.

Source: **Series M 297,** see source for series M 287; **series M 298,** see source for series M 288; **series M 299,** see source for series M 289; **series M 300** and **M 304,** see source for series M 290 and M 294; **series M 301** and **M 306,** see source for series M 291 and M 296; **series M 302,** see source for series M 292; **series M 303,** see source for series M 293; and **series M 305,** see source for series M 295.

Producers began reporting man-hours of worktime to the Bureau of Mines in 1930, but during the early 1930's many mines left the man-hours question unanswered and even in the 1940's the man-hours were not always reported. For those mines not reporting man-hours, the Bureau estimated the figure by multiplying the average number of employees (active period average) by the number of days on which the mine was active, and then multiplying the product by the number of hours constituting a standard work shift in the particular mine. This method, with certain variations, was used by the Bureau to estimate man-hours from reported men working, days active, and length of shift of the establishment in all years prior to 1930, when no direct information on man-hours was collected. Estimated man-hours, although reasonably accurate, suffered from two major shortcomings: (1) The number of active days was generally determined by the number of days on which there was production; this omitted days on which no material was mined, although on such days men were often employed in development or in repair or maintenance work, and (2) the standard work shift did not apply to all occupations, and many miners were irregular in observing standard working hours (see U.S. Bureau of Mines, Bulletin 380, pp. 8–9; and Bulletin 283, p. 64).

The man-hours in each series, except coal mines (series M 297), whether reported or estimated, represent worktime for which pay was received and during which the employee was exposed to work hazards. Shifts started and ended at or close to the portal of a mine or plant. However, in coal mines prior to 1944, shifts started and ended at the working place. In underground workings, measurable lengths of time, for which no pay was received, were required to travel from the mine portal to the workplace and return. The November 1943 bituminous coal mine wage agreement made portal-to-portal time the basis for pay rather than face or working time hours. Since 1944, only portal-to-portal man-hours have been reported. Conversion factors, determined from a mail canvass for average travel time in 1944, were applied to man-hour data for underground bituminous employees back to 1930. No such adjustment was made, however, for surfacemen at underground mines or strip mine employees in the bituminous industry. No adjustment was deemed necessary in the anthracite industry (Bulletin 509, pp. 4–5). Hence, for coal mines (series M 297), man-hours for 1911–29 represent time at the working face whereas, beginning in 1930, they represent portal-to-portal or exposure time.

Series M 1–12.   Summary of Mineral Operations: 1840 to 1967

[In general, includes data for mining operations at manufacturing establishments. For all years prior to 1935, excludes common clay, shale, and peat (except as noted) and contract service operations; for years prior to 1929, excludes sand and gravel operations and crushed stone quarries at manufacturing plants, except as indicated]

Industry group and year	Number of establishments	Value of shipments [1] and receipts (mil. dol.)		Value added in mining (mil. dol.)	Number of persons engaged			Principal expenses (mil. dol.)			Capital expenditures (mil. dol.)	Aggregate horsepower rating of power equipment (1,000)
		Gross shipments	Net shipments		Production and development workers (1,000)	All other employees (1,000)	Man-hours of production, development, and exploration workers (millions)	Wages of production, development, and exploration workers	Salaries of all other employees	Cost of supplies, etc., and purchased machinery installed [2]		
	1	2	3	4	5	6	7	8	9	10	11	12
ALL MINERAL OPERATIONS												
1967[3]	29,688	26,208	[4]22,784	19,621	447.6	135.6	922.2	2,969	1,306	10,647	4,062	-----
1963	40,532	22,030	19,210	16,231	501.7	135.2	1,013.8	2,773	1,070	9,066	3,268	52,772
1958	37,958	18,463	16,729	13,685	585.2	169.7	1,119.5	2,702	1,133	7,585	2,807	(NA)
1954	38,858	15,160	14,465	11,752	667.8	139.6	1,291.5	2,647	819	6,148	2,728	41,045
1939[5]	24,703	(NA)	3,433	2,680	774.1	81.9	1,287.9	971	204	753	-----	14,160
1919	22,347	3,174	3,138	2,399	989.8	75.7	-----	1,310	152	774	-----	6,816
1909	25,698	1,233	1,205	928	961.1	45.4	-----	576	54	305	-----	4,720
1902[6]	52,123	-----	773	628	[7]582.0	39.9	-----	376	41	144	-----	2,753
1889	-----	-----	416	336	[8]529.6	(8)	-----	[8]217	(8)	80	-----	-----
1880	-----	-----	256	221	[8]301.2	(8)	-----	[8]95	(8)	35	-----	-----
METAL MINING												
1967[3]	1,155	2,296	[4]2,037	1,557	55.4	15.5	113.9	396	156	1,079	340	-----
1963	1,614	2,128	1,836	1,418	62.2	15.0	125.7	384	132	941	231	6,115
1958	2,351	1,826	1,562	1,180	70.8	20.8	136.2	355	131	861	215	(NA)
1954	3,668	[9]1,517	[9]1,372	[9]1,084	82.7	18.5	170.5	358	111	666	222	5,236
1939[5]	[10]2,164	(NA)	517	417	89.8	10.3	190.8	127	27	100	-----	2,264
1929[5][11]	1,799	(NA)	634	496	115.8	9.8	-----	178	27	163	-----	1,736
1919[12]	2,739	566	560	413	138.2	10.9	-----	214	25	153	-----	1,408
1909[13]	7,834	390	371	267	164.9	10.5	-----	142	15	123	-----	1,163
1902[6]	7,730	(NA)	216	168	[7]123.2	10.6	-----	96	12	48	-----	559
1889	(NA)	(NA)	159	132	104.2	6.1	-----	59	6	[14]27	-----	171
1880	4,048	(NA)	115	104	62.6	3.3	-----	[8]28	(8)	[15]9	-----	73
1870	2,969	(NA)	47	41	[8]39.9	(8)	-----	[8]20	(8)	6	-----	22
1860	7,462	55	-----	37	[8]53.6	(8)	-----	[8]27	(8)	18	-----	-----
COAL MINING												
1967[3]	4,484	3,101	2,740	2,091	115.1	16.4	224.0	812	156	1,350	341	-----
1963	7,374	2,633	2,273	1,727	129.0	16.7	237.2	701	120	1,139	233	7,005
1958	8,188	2,756	2,333	1,780	183.8	27.0	299.0	842	167	1,181	205	(NA)
1954	8,301	2,483	2,104	1,621	233.0	23.7	374.7	881	132	993	131	7,853
1939[5]	[10]6,468	(NA)	933	765	454.1	25.3	670.2	540	57	168	-----	4,465
1935[5][16]	[17]6,661	(NA)	[17]869	[17]730	527.9	23.8	-----	523	47	142	-----	(NA)
1929[5]	5,193	(NA)	1,352	1,141	601.6	32.1	-----	805	80	251	-----	4,167
1919	6,924	1,510	1,510	1,252	693.8	41.0	-----	894	82	258	-----	3,058
1909	4,765	551	551	462	657.8	22.2	-----	363	25	89	-----	1,910
1902[5][6]	6,017	-----	367	328	[7]350.8	17.5	-----	220	17	39	-----	955
1889	[18]12,552	-----	[18]160	138	291.5	8.1	-----	103	6	22	-----	(NA)
1880[5]	[19]8,419	-----	[19]96	84	[8]180.0	(8)	-----	[8]56	(8)	12	-----	132
1870[5]	1,566	-----	74	68	[8]94.8	(8)	-----	[8]44	(8)	6	-----	63
1860[5]	622	-----	20	17	[8]36.5	(8)	-----	[8]10	(8)	3	-----	-----
1850[5]	510	-----	7	7	[8]15.1	(8)	-----	[8]4	(8)	(2)	-----	-----
1840[5]	-----	-----	-----	-----	[8]6.8	(8)	-----	-----	-----	-----	-----	-----
OIL AND GAS EXTRACTION												
1967[3]	16,358	17,456	14,851	13,394	167.2	77.7	346.5	1,091	764	7,066	3,005	28,309
1963	21,242	14,513	12,423	11,020	192.0	79.5	397.3	1,093	652	6,044	2,552	(NA)
1958	18,522	11,638	10,657	9,032	214.0	98.9	440.3	1,011	690	4,799	2,194	(NA)
1954	17,591	[5][20]9,342	[5][20]9,230	[5][20]7,674	235.5	80.3	491.8	977	486	[20]3,898	2,228	20,104
1939[5]	10,909	(NA)	1,660	[20]1,242	149.0	37.2	265.0	220	98	[20]417	-----	5,101
1919[5]	9,970	932	903	614	93.7	18.0	-----	135	34	318	-----	1,827
1909	8,202	185	176	112	37.6	6.4	-----	28	7	73	-----	1,231
1902[6]	[21]31,736	(NA)	102	59	[7]22.4	5.1	-----	16	5	43	-----	1,014
1889	(NA)	(NA)	38	15	26.9	2.3	-----	9	2	23	-----	(NA)
1880[22]	(NA)	(NA)	25	18	[8]11.5	(8)	-----	[8]7	(8)	7	-----	(NA)
1870	2,314	(NA)	19	18	[8]4.5	(8)	-----	[8]4	(8)	1	-----	23
1860[23]	64	4	-----	2	[8].9	(8)	-----	(Z)	(Z)	2	-----	-----

See footnotes at end of table.

Series **M 1–12.**   Summary of Mineral Operations: 1840 to 1967—Con.

Industry group and year	Number of establishments	Value of shipments [1] and receipts (mil. dol.)		Value added in mining (mil. dol.)	Number of persons engaged			Principal expenses (mil. dol.)			Capital expenditures (mil. dol.)	Aggregate horsepower rating of power equipment (1,000)
		Gross shipments	Net shipments		Production and development workers (1,000)	All other employees (1,000)	Man-hours of production, development, and exploration workers (millions)	Wages of production, development, and exploration workers	Salaries of all other employees	Cost of supplies, etc., and purchased machinery installed [2]		
	1	2	3	4	5	6	7	8	9	10	11	12

Industry group and year	1	2	3	4	5	6	7	8	9	10	11	12
NONMETALLIC MINERALS (EXCEPT FUELS) MINING [24]												
All operations:												
1967 [3]	7,691	3,355	3,156	2,579	109.9	26.0	237.8	670	230	1,152	376	[25] 11,343
1963	10,302	2,756	2,679	2,066	118.6	24.0	253.6	596	166	[25] 942	[25] 251	(NA)
1958	8,897	2,243	2,177	1,692	116.6	23.0	243.9	494	146	[25] 744	[25] 192	[25] 7,852
1954 [26]	9,298	[5] 1,818	[5] 1,757	[5] 1,373	116.6	17.1	254.4	431	90	[25] 591	[25] 147	[25] 7,852
1939 [27]	[10] 5,162		323	256	81.3	9.1	161.8	83	22	67		2,330
1929 [28]	4,004		407	319	94.8	11.5		117	32	113		1,651
Excluding sand, gravel, common clay, and shale operations, and stone quarries operated as parts of cement and lime plants:												
1967 [3]	3,412	2,343	2,158	1,797	71.8	19.0	157.7	438	172	822	282	[25] 6,359
1963	4,082	1,768	1,704	1,306	73.2	16.7	158.1	364	122	[25] 635	[25] 173	(NA)
1958	3,882	1,412	1,348	1,032	75.1	16.3	155.3	313	106	[25] 513	[25] 133	[25] 4,657
1954 [26]	4,310	[5] 1,219	[5] 1,169	[5] 1,169	76.1	11.2	164.3	277	62	[25] 403	[25] 101	[25] 4,657
1939 [27]	[10] 2,711	(NA)	207	164	54.6	5.9	120.6	54	15	43		1,550
1929 [28]	2,694	(NA)	264	207	66.7	7.5		79	20	70		921
1919 [29]	2,714	166	166	120	64.1	5.8		66	11	45		523
1909 [30]	4,897	107	107	87	100.8	6.4		43	6	20		416
1902 [6] [31]	[10] 6,640		88	74	[7] 85.6	6.7		43	6	13		225
1889	(NA)		59	51	85.6	4.9		[8] 33	(8)	9		79
1880	1,684		21		[8] 43.9	(8)						

NA Not available.   Z Less than $500,000.

[1] Includes the estimated value of minerals produced and used in the same establishment in making manufactured products.

[2] For 1939 and years prior to 1929, excludes purchased machinery installed.

[3] First year that data for single unit establishments without paid employees were excluded from the census. For 1963, for mining as a whole, included 6,543 such establishments, accounting for approximately 3 percent of value added. The number of such establishments in 1963 for metal mining was 460; for coal mining, 1,347; for oil and gas extraction, 3,714; and for nonmetallic minerals (except fuels), 1,022.

[4] Includes gross shipments for ferroalloy ores and metallic ores, n.e.c. In 1963, the difference between gross and net shipments for these industries was $8 million.

[5] Excludes Alaska.

[6] Operators of mineral properties reported an average of 8,527 employees performing contract service operations for metal mines; 6,906 for coal mines; 12,143 for oil and gas field operations; and 592 for nonmetallic minerals (except fuels). These are not included in the employment series shown.

[7] Figures for average employment converted to a 300-day basis for establishments operating for a shorter period.

[8] "All other" employees included with production and exploration workers.

[9] Excludes the uranium-radium-vanadium ores industry.

[10] Represents number of mining operations and service establishments.

[11] Except for number of establishments, includes 27 nonproducing establishments in the nonmetallic minerals mining industries.

[12] Except for number of establishments, excludes 1 chromite mine in Alaska.

[13] Except for number of establishments, includes 2 producing and 18 nonproducing establishments in the nonmetallic minerals mining industries.

[14] Excludes the manganese ores industry.

[15] Excludes the placer gold industry.

[16] Represents producing operations only.

[17] Excludes anthracite stripping services.

[18] Includes 9,920 "Local mines and farmers' banks," producing about 2 percent of all bituminous coal and lignite, for which no data are available on labor and expenditures.

[19] Includes 5,148 bituminous coal and lignite mines, producing coal valued at $1.1 million, representing "irregular" operations for which no other data are available.

[20] For 1954 and 1939, no data obtained on value of gas received for processing at natural gas liquids plants or on value of residue gas sold or transferred. However, for 1954, estimated value (prior to processing) of natural gas liquids contained in such gas was included with value of natural gas liquids received for processing and used in computing value added. No figures for value of residue gas are included in the value of shipments and receipts shown for 1954. For 1939, cost of supplies, purchases for resale, and purchased fuels and electric energy for all oil and gas extraction industries include estimated cost of such items and subcontract work to oil and gas field services industries, for which such data were not requested in 1939. These estimates used in computing value added for such industries. For Alaska in 1958 and 1954, cost of supplies, purchased fuels and electric energy, contract work, and purchased machinery installed exceeded value of shipments and capital expenditures.

[21] Represents number of operating companies.

[22] Excludes natural gas operations.

[23] Reported as "oil, coal" and probably includes some refining as well as production of crude petroleum, or may represent primarily recovery of oil from coal.

[24] Includes operations which are parts of manufacturing establishments.

[25] For purchased machinery, capital expenditures, and horsepower, excludes data for crushed and broken stone, sand and gravel, and gypsum mining operations in manufacturing establishments. Also, for horsepower in 1963 excludes data for dimension stone establishments in manufactures.

[26] Excludes sand and gravel mining operations in manufacturing establishments. Value of sand and gravel mined and sold or used at such establishments in 1954 was $22.8 million.

[27] Except for value of shipments and value added, excludes dimension stone dressing plants operated in conjunction with quarries. Value added in dressing stone at such operations, $7.9 million, has been included in value of shipments and value added in mining.

[28] Excludes common clay and shale and peat operations. In 1939, there were 609 such mines with products valued at $6.3 million. Also excludes 27 nonproducing establishments.

[29] Except for number of establishments, excludes 1 gypsum mine and 1 marble mine in Alaska.

[30] Excludes 19 nonproducing establishments.

[31] Includes lime plants producing lime valued at $9.3 million.

MINERALS

Series M 13–37. Value of Mineral Products, in Current Dollars: 1880 to 1970

[In millions of dollars]

Year	Mineral products		Fuels						Nonmetals (except fuels)				Lime
		Total [1]	Bituminous coal and lignite	Pennsylvania anthracite	Petroleum	Natural gas	Natural-gas liquids	Total [1]	Cement	Clay Raw	Clay Products	
	13	14	15	16	17	18	19	20	21	22	23	24
1970	29,790	20,153	3,772	105	11,174	3,746	1,275	5,711	[2]1,336	[3]268	--------	286
1969	26,921	17,965	2,797	94	10,427	3,456	1,102	5,624	[2]1,354	[3]264	681	281
1968	24,971	16,820	2,546	97	9,795	3,169	1,124	5,448	1,295	[3]247	672	250
1967	23,729	16,195	2,555	96	9,376	2,899	1,180	5,206	1,211	[3]224	616	240
1966	22,968	15,088	2,421	101	8,726	2,703	1,047	5,176	1,227	[3]222	640	240
1965	21,524	14,047	2,276	122	8,158	2,495	912	4,933	1,221	[3]205	651	233
1964	20,612	13,623	2,166	149	8,017	2,388	826	4,623	1,209	[3]193	650	223
1963	19,635	13,317	2,013	154	7,966	2,328	799	4,316	1,157	[3]181	593	199
1962	18,838	12,784	1,892	134	7,774	2,145	798	4,117	1,129	[3]163	591	187
1961	18,230	12,357	1,845	140	7,566	1,996	782	3,946	1,106	[3]157	558	177
1960	18,032	12,142	1,950	147	7,420	1,790	808	3,868	1,089	[3]162	560	173
1959	17,381	11,950	1,966	172	7,473	1,557	758	3,861	1,145	[3]160	589	164
1958	16,649	11,589	1,996	188	7,380	1,317	690	3,466	1,039	[3]143	525	121
1957	18,233	12,709	2,504	228	8,079	1,202	679	3,387	961	[3]156	(NA)	135
1956	17,490	11,741	2,412	237	7,297	1,084	697	3,391	989	[3]163	(NA)	136
1955	15,911	10,780	2,092	206	6,870	978	619	3,076	884	[3]140	525	127
1954	14,170	9,919	1,770	248	6,425	883	581	2,733	763	[3]123	446	102
1953	14,418	10,257	2,248	299	6,327	775	598	2,350	698	[3]125	(NA)	112
1952	13,396	9,616	2,283	380	5,785	624	533	2,163	638	[3]131	(NA)	95
1951	13,529	9,779	2,622	406	5,690	543	508	2,079	612	[3]129	(NA)	97
1950	11,862	8,689	2,497	392	4,963	409	420	1,822	538	[3]95	(NA)	83
1949	10,580	7,920	2,134	358	4,675	344	402	1,559	475	79	(NA)	69
1948	12,273	9,502	2,990	467	5,245	333	459	1,552	446	85	268	75
1947	9,610	7,188	2,620	413	3,578	275	295	1,338	357	74	219	63
1946	7,062	5,090	1,836	413	2,443	212	182	1,243	297	[3]61	179	51
1945	6,231	4,569	1,768	324	2,094	191	188	888	175	[3]43	86	46
1944	6,310	4,574	1,811	355	2,033	190	182	836	152	37	65	49
1943	5,931	4,028	1,585	307	1,809	177	147	916	202	40	75	49
1942	5,623	3,568	1,374	272	1,643	154	122	1,056	287	27	103	44
1941	5,107	3,228	1,125	240	1,602	139	119	989	251	27	135	43
1940	4,198	2,662	879	205	1,385	120	68	784	193	20	114	34
1939	3,808	2,423	728	187	1,294	120	90	754	184	17	123	30
1938	3,518	2,436	679	181	1,373	114	87	622	157	13	89	24
1937	4,265	2,798	864	198	1,513	123	97	711	171	18	109	30
1936	3,606	2,405	771	227	1,200	119	85	685	173	16	95	27
1935	2,942	2,013	658	210	961	110	71	564	115	--------	156	22
1934	2,744	1,947	628	244	905	106	61	520	118	--------	116	17
1933	2,050	1,413	446	207	608	97	54	432	86	--------	95	14
1932	2,000	1,460	407	222	680	99	49	412	83	--------	89	12
1931	2,578	1,620	589	296	551	108	64	671	143	--------	178	19
1930	3,980	2,500	795	355	1,070	147	128	973	231	--------	275	26
1929	4,908	2,940	953	386	1,280	158	158	1,166	255	--------	373	33
1928	4,484	2,666	934	394	1,055	140	139	1,163	279	--------	374	36
1927	4,698	2,875	1,030	421	1,173	127	119	1,201	282	--------	404	39
1926	5,311	3,371	1,183	474	1,448	125	136	1,219	281	--------	430	42
1925	4,812	2,910	1,060	328	1,285	112	120	1,187	281	--------	423	43
1924	4,754	2,899	1,063	477	1,023	254	82	1,174	266	--------	416	40
1923	5,252	3,317	1,515	507	978	240	77	1,157	260	--------	425	40
1922	4,183	2,738	1,275	274	895	222	73	921	208	--------	321	33
1921	3,828	2,703	1,200	452	815	175	62	780	182	--------	271	25
1920	6,084	4,193	2,130	434	1,361	196	72	1,025	196	--------	374	38
1919	4,007	2,511	1,161	365	760	161	64	752	147	--------	275	29
1918	4,563	2,736	1,492	336	704	154	50	648	114	--------	221	27
1917	4,131	2,238	1,249	284	523	142	40	666	123	--------	233	24
1916	2,993	1,333	665	202	331	120	14	554	105	--------	207	19
1915	2,078	973	502	185	179	101	5	429	75	--------	163	14
1914	1,870	993	493	188	214	94	3	431	81	--------	165	13
1913	2,092	1,088	565	195	237	88	2	467	90	--------	181	15
1912	1,912	946	518	178	164	85	1	430	70	--------	173	14
1911	1,675	836	451	175	134	75	1	407	67	--------	162	14
1910	1,707	828	469	160	128	71	--------	410	69	--------	170	14
1909	1,571	746	405	149	128	63	--------	386	54	--------	166	14
1908	1,417	716	374	158	129	55	--------	325	44	--------	133	11
1907	1,667	789	451	164	120	54	--------	376	56	--------	159	13
1906	1,492	652	381	132	92	47	--------	362	55	--------	161	12
1905	1,313	602	335	142	84	42	--------	319	36	--------	150	11
1904	1,167	584	305	139	101	38	--------	274	26	--------	131	10
1903	1,215	634	352	152	95	36	--------	272	32	--------	131	9
1902	1,018	469	291	76	71	31	--------	254	25	--------	122	9
1901	960	442	236	113	66	27	--------	219	16	--------	110	8
1900	914	406	221	86	76	24	--------	188	13	--------	96	7
1899	798	341	168	88	65	20	--------	185	13	--------	96	7
1898	631	268	133	75	44	15	--------	151	10	--------	74	7
1897	574	254	120	79	41	14	--------	128	8	--------	62	6
1896	573	268	115	82	59	13	--------	120	6	--------	63	6
1895	555	268	116	82	58	13	--------	126	5	--------	65	7
1894	498	236	108	78	36	14	--------	127	5	--------	65	8
1893	480	252	123	86	29	14	--------	70	4	--------	(4)	(5)
1892	524	248	125	82	26	15	--------	90	5	--------	(4)	(5)
1891	504	237	117	74	31	16	--------	83	5	--------	(4)	(5)

See footnotes at end of table.

Series M 13–37. Value of Mineral Products, in Current Dollars: 1880 to 1970—Con.

[In millions of dollars]

Year	Minerals products	Fuels Total [1]	Bituminous coal and lignite	Pennsylvania anthracite	Petroleum	Natural gas liquids	Nonmetals (except fuels) Total [1]	Cement	Clay products	Lime
	13	14	15	16	17	18	20	21	23	24
1890	499	231	110	66	35	19	81	5	(4)	(5)
1889	456	208	95	66	27	21	83	5	(4)	8
1888	476	231	102	89	18	23	80	5	(4)	25
1887	448	217	98	85	19	16	77	6	(4)	23
1886	389	185	78	76	20	10	67	4	(4)	21
1885	374	183	82	77	19	5	62	3	(4)	20
1884	355	166	77	66	21	1	58	4	(4)	18
1883	383	186	82	77	26	(Z)	61	4	(4)	19
1882	378	170	76	71	24	(Z)	64	4	(4)	22
1881	340	150	60	64	25	---------	61	3	(4)	20
1880	301	120	53	42	25	---------	56	2	(4)	19

Year	Sand [6] and gravel	Stone [6] (incl. slate)	Phosphate rock	Salt	Sulfur	Metals Total [1]	Iron ore	Copper	Lead	Zinc	Gold	Silver	Molybdenum
	25	26	27	28	29	30	31	32	33	34	35	36	37
1970	1,116	1,475	203	304	152	3,926	942	1,984	179	164	63	80	190
1969	1,070	1,425	209	288	177	3,332	929	1,468	152	162	72	75	174
1968	1,020	1,318	251	272	268	2,703	836	1,008	95	143	58	70	151
1967	981	1,240	266	251	252	2,333	818	729	89	152	55	50	134
1966	985	1,261	261	230	201	2,703	854	1,034	99	166	63	56	144
1965	957	1,204	193	216	165	2,544	801	957	94	178	60	51	121
1964	893	1,135	161	201	121	2,366	802	813	75	156	51	47	97
1963	847	1,068	140	185	99	2,002	678	747	55	123	51	45	91
1962	795	1,026	134	175	109	1,937	618	757	44	116	54	40	69
1961	751	947	131	160	120	1,927	651	699	54	107	54	32	88
1960	720	953	117	161	117	2,022	724	693	58	112	58	28	87
1959	729	912	99	156	123	1,570	514	506	59	98	56	28	65
1958	653	827	94	141	111	1,594	569	515	63	84	61	31	50
1957	600	825	88	149	124	2,137	866	654	97	123	63	35	68
1956	602	7 775	98	136	166	2,358	750	939	111	149	64	35	64
1955	536	7 715	75	123	177	2,055	749	745	101	127	66	34	67
1954	503	7 622	87	105	155	1,518	526	493	89	102	64	33	64
1953	374	489	77	78	150	1,811	790	532	90	125	69	34	52
1952	345	473	72	71	117	1,617	590	448	126	223	58	36	41
1951	330	448	65	70	112	1,671	630	449	134	249	61	36	36
1950	293	402	63	60	106	1,351	483	378	116	179	74	38	38
1949	246	352	51	54	86	1,101	378	297	130	149	62	31	19
1948	252	340	51	54	90	1,219	391	362	140	168	62	34	20
1947	213	298	47	52	85	1,084	318	356	111	153	64	32	15
1946	171	243	31	45	66	729	215	173	49	82	51	19	12
1945	129	185	24	44	61	774	244	185	46	80	33	21	24
1944	125	181	21	44	56	900	257	237	50	99	36	25	28
1943	153	189	19	42	47	987	269	258	52	102	49	29	38
1942	188	211	17	38	50	999	279	257	59	110	131	40	47
1941	147	203	16	34	54	890	250	228	54	98	209	51	26
1940	111	166	12	26	41	752	189	205	43	74	210	49	17
1939	106	165	12	25	36	631	159	148	40	51	196	44	22
1938	86	145	13	23	27	460	74	110	31	42	178	41	18
1937	97	152	13	24	44	756	208	202	52	72	168	56	21
1936	90	147	11	23	35	516	132	112	36	49	153	49	12
1935	62	91	11	22	29	365	83	63	25	36	126	33	7
1934	61	102	10	23	29	277	66	39	22	31	108	21	7
1933	53	84	8	22	30	205	64	29	19	26	65	8	4
1932	58	92	6	20	20	128	13	34	15	12	51	7	1
1931	86	141	9	22	25	287	74	95	29	22	50	9	2
1930	115	187	14	25	36	507	146	181	57	47	47	20	2
1929	133	214	13	27	44	802	197	353	85	81	46	33	2
1928	119	208	12	27	38	655	156	263	73	72	46	34	2
1927	116	210	11	25	38	622	151	221	84	74	45	34	1
1926	111	201	11	25	37	721	174	244	109	92	48	39	1
1925	108	187	12	26	29	715	161	238	114	84	50	46	1
1924	97	174	10	26	25	682	151	214	91	67	52	44	(Z)
1923	91	172	12	28	26	778	241	211	76	69	52	60	(Z)
1922	65	131	10	27	22	524	158	128	52	40	49	56	(NA)
1921	56	114	12	25	17	344	90	65	36	20	50	53	(NA)
1920	66	142	25	30	30	866	285	222	76	73	51	61	(Z)
1919	46	103	12	27	10	744	197	239	45	66	60	64	(Z)
1918	38	88	8	27	28	1,179	244	471	77	90	69	66	1
1917	35	88	8	20	24	1,228	238	515	94	119	84	59	(Z)
1916	30	84	6	14	12	1,107	182	474	76	151	93	49	(Z)
1915	23	80	5	12	5	677	101	243	48	114	101	37	(Z)
1914	24	83	10	10	6	446	72	153	40	35	95	40	(Z)
1913	24	90	12	10	6	538	131	190	36	38	89	40	---------
1912	23	84	12	9	5	537	107	205	35	45	93	39	---------
1911	21	83	12	8	5	432	87	137	35	31	97	33	---------
1910	21	83	11	8	5	470	141	137	33	27	96	31	---------
1909	18	77	11	8	5	439	110	142	30	25	100	28	---------
1908	13	72	11	8	4	376	82	124	26	18	95	28	---------
1907	14	77	11	8	5	501	132	174	37	26	90	37	---------
1906	13	72	9	7	3	477	101	177	38	24	94	38	---------

See footnotes at end of table.

Series M 13–37. Value of Mineral Products, in Current Dollars: 1880 to 1970—Con.

[In millions of dollars]

Year	Nonmetals (except fuels)—Con.					Metals						
	Sand [6] and gravel	Stone [6] (incl. slate)	Phosphate rock	Salt	Sulfur	Total [1]	Iron ore	Copper	Lead	Zinc	Gold	Silver
	25	26	27	28	29	30	31	32	33	34	35	36
1905	11	69	7	6	3	392	75	139	29	24	88	34
1904	6	64	7	6	1	309	43	104	26	19	80	33
1903	1	64	5	5	1	309	66	96	24	17	74	29
1902	1	60	5	6	1	295	65	80	22	15	80	29
1901	--------	52	5	7	1	299	49	101	22	12	79	33
1900	--------	41	5	7	(Z)	319	67	101	23	11	79	36
1899	--------	39	5	7	(Z)	272	35	97	18	15	71	33
1898	--------	32	3	6	(Z)	213	22	65	15	11	64	32
1897	--------	30	3	5	(Z)	193	19	59	14	8	57	32
1896	--------	27	3	4	(Z)	185	23	50	11	6	53	40
1895	--------	29	4	4	(Z)	161	18	41	10	6	47	36
1894	--------	30	3	5	(Z)	136	14	34	10	5	40	31
1893	--------	36	4	4	(Z)	158	19	36	12	6	36	47
1892	--------	52	3	6	(Z)	186	33	40	14	8	33	56
1891	--------	50	4	5	(Z)	184	32	36	15	8	33	58
1890	--------	50	3	5	(Z)	187	35	41	13	7	33	57
1889	--------	46	3	4	(Z)	164	33	31	12	6	33	47
1888	--------	29	2	4	(Z)	164	29	38	13	5	33	43
1887	--------	28	2	4	(Z)	153	34	25	13	5	33	41
1886	--------	22	2	5	(Z)	138	28	18	12	4	35	39
1885	--------	21	4	5	(Z)	129	19	18	10	3	32	43
1884	--------	21	2	4	(Z)	130	21	19	10	3	31	42
1883	--------	22	2	4	(Z)	136	26	19	12	3	30	40
1882	--------	23	2	4	(Z)	144	31	17	13	4	32	41
1881	--------	24	2	4	(Z)	130	24	13	11	3	35	38
1880	--------	22	1	5	(Z)	125	23	13	10	3	36	35

NA Not available.   Z Less than $500,000.
[1] Includes additional mineral products not shown separately; therefore, components frequently will not add to group totals.   [2] Excludes natural and slag cement.
[3] Value of clays used in cement is included here, but excluded from total nonmetals (series M 20) to avoid duplication.
[4] Only incomplete figures available; included in total nonmetals.
[5] Not available separately; included with value of stone (series M 26).
[6] Beginning 1954, sand and sandstone (ground) included with series M 25 (sand and gravel) and M 26 (stone), respectively.   [7] Includes value of stone used for cement or lime, excluded from total nonmetals (series M 20) to avoid duplication.

Series M 38–53. Value of Mineral Production, Imports, Exports, and Consumption in Constant (1967) Dollars: 1900 to 1969

[In millions of dollars. Includes Alaska and Hawaii for all years]

Year	All minerals, total				Mineral fuels				Nonmetals (except fuels)				Metallic minerals			
	Production	Imports [1]	Exports [1]	Consumption [2]	Production	Imports	Exports	Consumption	Production	Imports	Exports	Consumption	Production	Imports [1]	Exports [1]	Consumption [2]
	38	39	40	41	42	43	44	45	46	47	48	49	50	51	52	53
1969	23,992	6,107	1,879	28,607	17,290	3,543	572	20,323	4,151	506	307	4,238	2,551	2,058	1,000	4,046
1968	23,144	6,033	1,781	27,585	16,809	3,174	538	19,313	4,031	493	307	4,167	2,304	2,366	936	4,105
1967	22,246	5,310	1,642	26,075	16,248	2,773	603	18,139	3,893	443	287	4,075	2,105	2,094	752	3,861
1966	21,615	5,334	1,523	25,658	15,361	2,793	482	17,539	3,858	458	276	4,143	2,396	2,083	765	3,976
1965	20,558	4,999	1,450	24,331	14,500	2,677	471	16,691	3,753	412	255	3,931	2,305	1,910	724	3,709
1964	19,843	4,595	1,683	23,128	14,082	2,468	486	16,018	3,501	391	238	3,665	2,260	1,736	959	3,445
1963	19,021	4,280	1,419	22,056	13,674	2,311	494	15,499	3,250	352	197	3,405	2,097	1,617	728	3,152
1962	18,300	4,251	1,172	21,445	13,060	2,267	398	14,898	3,143	338	179	3,303	2,097	1,646	595	3,244
1961	17,766	3,882	1,444	20,252	12,688	2,063	386	14,238	3,000	314	174	3,087	2,078	1,505	884	2,927
1960	17,621	3,905	1,457	20,036	12,493	1,950	423	14,057	2,920	298	181	3,040	2,208	1,657	853	2,939
1959	16,906	4,099	1,025	19,982	12,326	1,909	434	13,724	2,856	311	151	3,046	1,724	1,879	440	3,212
1958	16,189	3,911	1,220	18,887	11,738	1,824	572	13,145	2,652	250	139	2,775	1,799	1,837	509	2,967
1957	17,484	4,088	1,911	18,965	12,588	1,674	1,018	13,023	2,664	278	148	2,773	2,232	2,136	745	3,169
1956	17,320	3,731	1,627	18,856	12,553	1,529	841	12,979	2,673	271	147	2,752	2,094	1,931	639	3,125
1955	16,326	3,274	1,361	18,223	11,843	1,325	675	12,496	2,480	247	129	2,603	2,003	1,702	557	3,124
1954	14,774	2,934	1,171	16,547	10,853	1,116	566	11,474	2,273	211	119	2,360	1,648	1,607	486	2,713
1953	15,347	2,990	1,064	16,936	11,213	1,098	625	11,487	2,070	220	96	2,189	2,064	1,672	343	3,260
1952	14,933	2,764	1,209	16,157	11,042	1,016	738	11,140	2,014	215	92	2,114	1,877	1,533	379	2,903
1951	15,063	2,314	1,228	15,961	11,118	898	791	11,058	1,949	229	101	2,068	1,996	1,187	336	2,835
1950	13,534	2,559	902	15,186	10,005	905	502	10,319	1,770	215	97	1,899	1,759	1,439	303	2,968
1949	12,124	2,062	966	13,282	9,047	699	508	9,359	1,562	145	94	1,618	1,515	1,218	364	2,305
1948	13,697	1,847	1,130	13,889	10,366	553	656	9,855	1,618	175	87	1,707	1,713	1,119	387	2,327
1947	13,072	1,643	1,505	13,248	9,908	477	862	9,513	1,500	135	87	1,564	1,664	1,031	556	2,171
1946	11,642	1,420	1,111	12,027	9,007	423	691	8,602	1,360	123	77	1,410	1,275	874	343	2,015
1945	11,801	1,574	1,234	12,496	9,087	389	693	8,881	1,127	127	63	1,199	1,587	1,058	478	2,416
1944	12,184	1,443	1,567	12,474	9,184	300	755	8,751	1,104	127	51	1,192	1,896	1,016	761	2,531
1943	11,786	1,406	1,278	12,214	8,443	198	589	8,249	1,172	154	48	1,303	2,171	1,054	641	2,662
1942	11,439	1,404	1,013	11,779	7,987	121	483	7,674	1,316	136	43	1,418	2,136	1,147	487	2,687
1941	10,814	1,822	875	11,501	7,628	295	435	7,467	1,276	122	54	1,351	1,910	1,405	386	2,683
1940	9,855	1,380	1,129	9,462	7,138	249	475	6,775	1,062	93	52	1,094	1,655	1,038	602	1,593
1939	8,829	960	1,147	8,443	6,521	185	634	6,189	993	84	50	1,037	1,315	691	463	1,217
1938	7,906	933	1,080	7,181	6,080	163	633	5,637	848	66	46	837	978	704	401	707
1937	9,284	1,051	1,071	8,606	6,781	177	587	6,209	940	104	50	979	1,563	770	434	1,418
1936	8,228	1,056	767	8,104	6,191	177	454	5,957	871	79	46	902	1,166	800	267	1,245
1935	6,953	1,354	755	6,756	5,505	167	440	5,297	636	61	39	659	812	1,126	276	800
1934	6,427	743	735	6,182	5,193	154	401	5,036	609	47	40	623	625	542	294	523
1933	5,984	716	612	5,840	4,957	138	370	4,696	547	43	38	561	480	535	204	583
1932	5,463	498	559	5,347	4,506	223	356	4,510	539	30	26	535	418	245	177	302
1931	6,735	816	779	6,744	5,158	258	434	5,108	777	52	35	796	800	506	310	840
1930	8,081	886	1,061	7,677	5,843	315	545	5,538	1,022	79	44	1,052	1,216	492	472	1,078

[1] Excludes gold.   [2] Includes net consumption of gold and silver in industry and the arts only.

Series M 38–53. Value of Mineral Production, Imports, Exports, and Consumption in Constant (1967) Dollars: 1900 to 1969—Con.

[In millions of dollars]

Year	All minerals, total				Mineral fuels				Nonmetals (except fuels)				Metallic minerals			
	Production	Imports[1]	Exports[1]	Consumption[2]	Production	Imports	Exports	Consumption	Production	Imports	Exports	Consumption	Production	Imports[1]	Exports[1]	Consumption[2]
	38	39	40	41	42	43	44	45	46	47	48	49	50	51	52	53
1929	9,190	1,162	1,234	8,891	6,508	324	583	6,049	1,139	94	56	1,179	1,543	744	595	1,663
1928	8,418	1,059	1,230	8,237	5,960	265	553	5,682	1,067	83	43	1,105	1,391	711	634	1,450
1927	8,456	936	1,148	7,976	6,044	215	517	5,502	1,057	77	45	1,088	1,355	644	586	1,386
1926	8,373	1,029	1,172	8,195	5,920	249	574	5,616	1,005	87	35	1,052	1,448	693	563	1,527
1925	7,785	932	1,041	7,687	5,431	236	434	5,218	972	76	38	1,010	1,382	620	569	1,459
1924	7,444	962	1,069	7,299	5,304	280	448	5,113	884	72	32	921	1,256	610	589	1,265
1923	8,012	996	903	7,618	5,749	302	433	5,240	888	72	33	928	1,375	622	437	1,450
1922	5,890	1,023	695	6,072	4,202	422	291	4,192	701	54	31	727	987	547	373	1,153
1921	5,405	777	680	5,253	4,192	379	344	4,004	577	33	24	581	636	365	312	668
1920	6,770	942	897	6,619	4,836	322	448	4,588	664	61	38	686	1,270	559	411	1,345
1919	5,903	771	879	5,991	4,143	163	315	4,125	573	49	21	606	1,187	559	543	1,260
1918	6,796	724	1,053	6,375	4,689	120	344	4,271	557	39	16	579	1,550	565	693	1,525
1917	6,826	695	1,121	6,406	4,515	99	355	4,309	674	52	16	708	1,637	544	750	1,389
1916	6,468	625	916	6,166	4,071	69	329	3,912	730	57	12	773	1,667	499	575	1,481
1915	5,685	461	745	5,291	3,720	64	291	3,503	640	47	8	676	1,325	350	446	1,112
1914	5,317	450	724	4,827	3,589	55	270	3,303	670	57	22	704	1,058	338	432	820
1913	5,780	537	797	5,375	3,803	44	288	3,549	713	65	27	750	1,264	428	482	1,076
1912	5,406	511	716	5,117	3,534	26	249	3,353	679	63	21	722	1,193	422	446	1,042
1911	5,113	486	701	4,761	3,360	13	236	3,118	706	62	20	748	1,047	411	445	895
1910	5,178	481	592	4,870	3,333	13	196	3,106	694	61	14	740	1,151	407	382	1,024
1909	4,658	436	574	4,305	2,860	9	194	2,607	684	52	13	723	1,114	375	367	975
1908	4,301	354	537	3,903	2,818	10	187	2,581	596	39	14	621	887	305	336	701
1907	4,735	370	459	4,430	3,093	13	177	2,858	623	53	13	663	1,019	304	269	909
1906	4,270	384	459	4,104	2,617	11	156	2,486	631	54	13	671	1,022	319	290	947
1905	4,102	321	446	3,878	2,554	11	148	2,429	601	43	13	630	947	267	285	819
1904	3,598	292	446	3,340	2,289	10	129	2,154	541	41	15	566	768	241	302	620
1903	3,594	343	354	3,466	2,270	21	121	2,178	536	47	16	566	788	275	217	722
1902	3,213	339	360	3,131	1,861	16	113	1,776	553	47	14	586	799	276	233	769
1901	3,046	358	366	2,892	1,849	11	125	1,738	483	43	20	506	714	304	221	648
1900	2,863	305	395	2,654	1,683	11	120	1,561	478	38	17	499	702	256	258	594

[1] Excludes gold.
[2] Includes net consumption of gold and silver in industry and the arts only.

Series M 54–67. Indexes of Physical Volume of Mineral Production (Bureau of Mines): 1880 to 1970

[1967 = 100. Excludes Puerto Rico and outlying areas]

Year	Total minerals	Fuels			Nonmetals				Metals					
		Total	Coal	Crude oil and natural gas	Total	Construction	Chemical	Other	Total	Ferrous	Nonferrous			Other
											Total	Base	Monetary	
	54	55	56	57	58	59	60	61	62	63	64	65	66	67
1970	112.1	111.7	108.3	112.0	103.4	103.1	103.1	109.1	135.8	109.3	157.4	167.3	123.9	119.5
1969	110.1	109.1	100.9	110.5	105.5	106.6	101.4	107.3	127.9	110.9	141.7	149.6	115.5	111.0
1968	104.1	103.4	98.5	104.2	103.4	104.6	98.9	106.5	110.8	102.4	117.6	120.4	97.1	113.9
1967	100.0	100.0	100.0	100.0	100.0	100.0	100.0	100.0	100.0	100.0	100.0	100.0	100.0	100.0
1966	98.7	94.5	96.9	94.3	101.9	103.2	97.0	105.2	121.2	109.2	131.0	138.4	123.9	90.4
1965	93.5	89.2	93.7	88.5	97.6	100.6	87.8	97.2	114.5	100.9	125.6	132.7	115.0	89.8
1964	89.8	86.7	90.1	86.4	91.5	96.1	76.3	91.3	109.0	98.9	117.6	123.0	101.0	101.4
1963	86.2	84.4	85.6	84.7	86.0	90.1	69.5	85.9	100.9	87.5	113.0	118.0	98.9	100.3
1962	82.4	80.7	78.9	81.8	81.5	86.1	66.1	81.4	99.4	82.8	115.6	118.0	103.7	113.0
1961	80.1	78.6	75.8	79.9	77.8	81.7	64.0	79.7	100.3	88.2	112.6	111.5	101.4	120.4
1960	79.1	77.5	78.4	78.3	76.1	79.6	62.3	81.7	104.4	100.0	108.9	104.9	102.0	123.1
1959	77.1	76.6	78.3	77.5	77.0	81.3	60.7	81.7	82.2	73.3	91.3	84.7	99.9	106.3
1958	73.5	73.2	78.2	73.3	70.1	74.1	55.3	72.4	87.4	80.1	95.1	97.1	108.6	83.5
1957	79.1	78.9	93.9	77.2	68.6	71.2	57.8	77.2	113.1	121.8	104.1	111.0	115.2	79.5
1956	79.4	79.2	96.4	76.7	69.7	71.1	60.9	84.4	110.5	115.9	105.4	113.3	117.2	77.6
1955	75.4	74.8	89.3	72.6	65.6	67.2	56.4	79.4	109.8	124.0	95.0	103.9	117.8	64.7
1954	68.3	68.6	77.3	67.8	59.4	59.7	55.0	68.6	91.0	94.5	88.1	90.2	115.7	70.2
1953	71.2	71.7	89.4	68.7	54.7	53.7	52.1	74.3	113.6	133.3	98.5	100.0	121.5	86.0
1952	70.0	71.1	94.0	66.6	53.0	52.0	49.5	77.3	106.6	109.7	104.4	106.1	120.6	96.8
1951	71.6	73.1	106.1	65.3	50.8	48.7	47.8	83.0	113.5	127.0	100.0	107.7	124.7	77.9
1950	65.3	66.4	103.9	57.2	46.1	44.8	43.6	70.2	105.3	106.5	100.1	106.8	145.3	59.3
1949	58.6	60.2	89.8	53.1	40.1	39.1	37.9	59.7	91.1	91.5	86.9	93.8	120.2	51.5
1948	67.4	70.6	122.4	57.4	41.1	39.2	39.8	68.2	101.1	109.0	91.7	99.6	124.4	51.5
1947	64.8	68.2	127.8	52.7	38.0	35.7	38.2	63.6	98.4	100.7	92.6	100.4	126.3	53.1
1946	57.9	62.0	111.9	49.2	33.2	31.2	32.5	57.2	76.4	77.9	70.7	79.3	90.6	43.3
1945	58.5	62.9	117.6	48.6	27.9	24.3	31.7	46.0	92.3	98.1	81.4	95.4	68.8	74.0
1944	60.7	63.9	127.5	47.3	27.7	24.1	31.5	46.1	114.0	107.4	109.6	115.3	75.1	218.4
1943	58.8	59.0	121.1	42.6	30.2	28.1	29.2	52.3	132.1	119.8	129.4	127.5	96.8	310.1
1942	57.8	55.8	119.6	39.4	34.3	34.4	28.7	51.2	131.1	121.8	124.7	129.5	202.2	120.8
1941	54.8	53.4	106.6	39.5	32.3	32.9	26.2	50.4	120.9	103.1	121.4	118.6	272.4	60.6
1940	49.9	50.2	95.8	38.1	26.3	27.1	21.7	34.5	106.5	82.7	114.3	109.0	280.6	37.0
1939	45.0	46.0	84.7	35.8	24.3	26.1	18.0	30.2	87.4	59.7	101.0	92.7	266.6	24.6
1938	40.6	42.9	75.1	34.3	20.8	21.6	17.4	23.8	68.0	37.2	86.9	75.0	245.8	22.3
1937	47.0	47.9	93.5	35.9	23.1	23.0	19.6	36.6	99.6	79.5	104.8	105.0	246.3	23.9
1936	42.1	43.9	93.4	31.0	21.6	22.7	16.3	34.8	76.2	53.3	87.0	81.8	222.9	21.0

Series M 54–67.　Indexes of Physical Volume of Mineral Production (Bureau of Mines): 1880 to 1970—Con.

[1967 = 100]

Year	Total minerals	Fuels			Nonmetals				Metals		Nonferrous			
		Total	Coal	Crude oil and natural gas	Total	Construction	Chemical	Other	Total	Ferrous	Total	Base	Monetary	Other
	54	55	56	57	58	59	60	61	62	63	64	65	66	67
1935	35.5	39.0	81.2	28.1	15.3	14.7	13.7	26.5	55.5	33.8	67.8	59.4	187.7	18.5
1934	33.1	37.0	80.9	25.6	14.6	14.7	12.2	23.1	43.5	27.1	52.7	43.6	154.4	14.9
1933	30.6	35.2	69.6	25.2	12.7	12.2	11.3	22.4	34.3	19.0	43.7	37.5	124.7	9.7
1932	27.9	32.2	70.0	22.5	12.1	13.2	8.2	15.6	30.1	10.4	43.7	38.8	124.2	6.3
1931	34.5	36.9	85.8	24.5	17.5	18.9	12.7	23.1	52.9	31.8	65.0	70.9	125.5	10.1
1930	41.0	41.9	103.6	26.6	22.5	24.6	15.0	33.4	77.7	58.6	85.2	96.9	139.8	13.0
1929	46.1	46.4	116.6	29.3	25.0	28.3	14.5	36.2	99.8	73.0	111.3	128.8	153.1	13.7
1928	42.4	42.4	111.5	25.6	23.9	27.5	12.8	34.4	90.6	62.6	104.3	119.6	153.3	10.4
1927	42.5	42.9	116.1	25.2	23.7	27.6	12.2	32.7	88.3	62.0	100.8	115.2	153.7	7.7
1926	41.8	41.8	126.9	21.6	22.5	26.0	11.8	33.0	93.7	67.2	105.6	120.5	162.1	8.2
1925	38.5	38.0	109.5	20.9	21.2	24.8	10.5	32.4	90.2	62.2	103.9	116.9	169.7	7.2
1924	37.2	37.4	113.5	19.4	19.3	22.5	9.6	30.2	82.6	53.7	97.9	108.3	172.5	6.3
1923	39.5	40.3	128.8	19.5	19.3	21.6	11.4	28.6	86.9	68.4	92.9	100.2	178.0	7.1
1922	29.0	29.1	90.7	14.6	15.2	16.6	10.3	22.4	63.4	46.0	71.1	72.5	163.2	4.7
1921	27.3	29.6	103.4	12.4	12.4	13.4	8.7	15.7	41.9	28.6	48.7	43.7	148.4	3.1
1920	32.3	32.3	127.8	11.8	14.4	15.0	10.8	25.2	80.1	69.5	81.7	86.4	160.5	10.6
1919	28.0	27.3	109.6	10.2	12.4	13.2	9.0	18.7	76.2	63.8	79.9	82.2	170.5	10.1
1918	31.9	29.8	132.2	9.5	12.1	12.0	10.4	22.0	101.4	77.5	112.0	120.0	206.0	16.2
1917	31.7	27.6	127.1	9.2	14.6	16.0	10.1	22.6	108.6	86.0	118.6	123.2	237.4	18.7
1916	30.2	24.8	114.7	8.1	15.2	18.9	7.6	21.7	112.3	84.9	125.0	127.4	267.7	12.9
1915	26.6	22.5	104.7	7.3	14.5	18.8	6.3	17.7	90.9	62.0	105.2	98.8	276.6	10.1
1914	24.6	21.7	101.8	6.8	14.8	19.5	6.1	17.0	73.7	46.0	87.8	77.7	259.0	7.7
1913	26.4	22.7	111.7	6.5	15.6	20.3	6.7	18.7	83.8	68.9	90.0	81.1	256.0	8.1
1912	25.0	21.1	104.6	5.9	15.4	19.3	7.6	16.4	80.5	61.1	89.3	80.0	259.2	7.9
1911	23.2	20.1	98.9	5.7	14.2	19.0	5.4	15.3	72.4	48.7	84.2	72.0	263.1	7.1
1910	23.5	19.9	98.9	5.5	14.4	19.5	5.0	16.0	76.2	63.3	81.4	69.4	255.4	6.7
1909	22.1	18.2	91.3	4.9	14.0	19.0	5.0	14.3	75.1	57.0	83.5	70.8	264.4	6.5
1908	19.6	16.7	83.7	4.6	12.1	15.9	5.3	11.8	61.6	39.9	72.7	59.6	242.4	4.7
1907	21.1	18.2	95.3	4.3	12.7	17.1	4.7	14.2	66.1	54.9	69.1	55.8	234.8	5.9
1906	19.3	15.6	66.8	3.6	12.4	16.7	4.7	13.3	67.6	53.0	74.1	58.4	260.2	6.3
1905	18.5	15.1	78.9	3.6	11.9	16.2	4.4	11.3	62.9	47.1	70.2	56.4	239.9	6.6
1904	16.4	13.6	71.1	3.2	11.4	15.3	3.5	10.2	53.3	30.7	65.3	52.0	224.3	7.4
1903	16.3	13.5	72.3	2.8	10.4	14.6	2.8	10.3	52.1	38.7	58.4	45.4	207.2	7.5
1902	14.3	11.1	58.3	2.6	10.1	14.2	2.8	9.4	52.4	39.4	58.6	43.1	221.9	6.9
1901	13.9	11.2	59.6	2.2	9.1	13.1	2.5	9.3	48.3	32.1	56.3	39.8	218.5	5.9
1900	13.1	10.2	54.0	2.1	7.4	10.9	2.5	9.0	48.2	30.7	57.2	39.6	221.9	5.7
1899	12.5	9.8	51.3	1.9	7.3	11.4	2.3	6.2	44.3	27.5	52.9	36.3	203.0	6.4
1898	11.2	8.7	44.1	1.8	6.0	10.0	1.8	6.0	40.4	21.7	52.3	34.0	191.0	6.4
1897	10.6	8.2	40.5	1.8	6.0	10.8	1.6	4.8	37.5	19.5	47.1	31.9	177.5	5.4
1896	10.2	7.9	39.1	1.8	5.5	10.2	1.3	4.3	35.6	17.9	45.3	29.4	176.5	6.1
1895	9.9	7.9	39.7	1.6	5.5	10.7	1.4	4.2	32.3	17.9	40.4	25.2	160.7	7.2
1894	8.9	7.1	35.1	1.6	5.5	10.7	1.3	4.9	27.9	13.2	35.9	23.3	139.4	6.0
1893	9.2	7.4	37.3	1.6	5.8	11.6	1.2	4.4	28.2	12.9	36.4	22.3	147.5	5.9
1892	9.7	7.4	36.6	1.6	6.6	13.9	1.1	4.5	30.7	18.3	37.2	23.6	147.1	5.5
1891	9.2	7.2	34.6	1.8	6.3	13.4	1.0	4.7	28.1	16.3	34.2	20.7	140.3	4.5
1890	9.0	6.9	33.4	1.8	6.3	13.7	.9	3.8	27.0	18.0	31.6	18.2	134.5	4.4
1889	8.4	6.6	32.0	1.6	5.9	12.5	.8	2.5	25.3	16.3	29.8	16.8	128.7	5.1
1888	7.8	6.3	29.6	1.7	5.0	10.4	.8	2.9	23.7	13.6	29.0	16.5	122.9	6.4
1887	7.4	6.0	29.5	1.4	4.8	10.3	.7	2.8	21.8	12.8	26.6	14.1	117.1	6.6
1886	6.7	5.3	26.2	1.1	4.5	9.3	.7	2.6	20.4	11.4	25.3	12.2	117.4	5.7
1885	6.0	4.4	23.5	.7	4.3	8.9	.8	2.7	18.7	8.6	24.2	12.5	107.9	6.2
1884	5.9	4.5	24.7	.7	4.0	8.5	.6	3.1	18.3	8.6	23.6	11.7	107.6	6.1
1883	5.7	4.3	24.0	.5	3.8	8.2	.6	2.5	18.0	9.8	22.4	10.4	103.4	9.0
1882	5.5	4.1	21.5	.7	3.7	7.9	.5	2.4	17.8	9.7	22.1	8.8	105.5	10.1
1881	4.9	3.4	18.1	.7	3.6	7.7	.5	2.4	16.7	7.9	21.5	7.6	108.3	11.8
1880	4.4	3.0	15.2	.6	3.2	6.9	.5	1.9	15.9	7.9	20.5	6.2	106.3	11.6

Series M 68–71.　Indexes of Mineral Production (Federal Reserve Board): 1919 to 1970

[1967 = 100]

Year	Total mining	Coal, oil, and gas	Metal mining	Stone and earth minerals	Year	Total mining	Coal, oil, and gas	Metal mining	Stone and earth minerals	Year	Total mining	Coal, oil, and gas [1]	Metal mining	Stone and earth minerals
	68	69	70	71		68	69	70	71		68	69	70	71
1970	110	109	131	99	1961	83	82	103	77	1953	73	72	80	60
1969	107	106	125	103	1960	83	81	111	75	1952	72	69	75	58
1968	104	103	111	104	1959	81	82	86	73	1951	72	66	81	56
1967	100	100	100	100	1958	78	78	89	68	1950	66	59	75	51
1966	98	96	119	102	1957	85	85	102	69	1949	59	54	65	45
1965	94	92	114	95	1956	84	85	95	69	1948	66	57	73	46
1964	91	90	112	88	1955	80	81	91	65	1947	63	51	71	42
1963	89	89	103	83	1954	72	73	73	60	1937	46	--------	--------	--------
1962	86	85	105	80										

[1] Oil and gas only

Series M 68–71. Indexes of Mineral Production (Federal Reserve Board): 1919 to 1970—Con.

[1947–49 = 100]

Year	Total mining	Coal, oil, and gas	Metal mining	Stone and earth minerals	Year	Total mining	Coal, oil, and gas	Metal mining	Stone and earth minerals	Year	Total mining	Coal, oil, and gas	Metal mining	Stone and earth minerals
	68	69	70	71		68	69	70	71		68	69	70	71
1951	115	114	116	127	1940	76	74	115	----------	1929	68	67	115	----------
					1939	68	68	97	----------	1928	63	62	103	----------
1950	105	103	108	114	1938	62	65	74	----------	1927	64	63	99	----------
1949	94	93	94	101	1937	71	71	109	----------	1926	63	62	107	----------
1948	106	106	105	104	1936	63	65	87	----------					
1947	100	101	101	96						1925	59	57	103	----------
1946	91	93	75	----------	1935	55	58	62	----------	1924	57	56	92	----------
					1934	51	54	50	----------	1923	62	61	101	----------
1945	92	93	86	----------	1933	48	52	43	----------	1922	45	----------	----------	----------
1944	93	95	97	----------	1932	42	47	30	----------	1921	42	----------	----------	----------
1943	87	86	108	----------	1931	51	53	57	----------					
1942	84	82	127	----------						1920	53	----------	----------	----------
1941	81	80	128	----------	1930	59	59	86	----------	1919	45	----------	----------	----------

Series M 72–75. Indexes of Mineral Production (NBER): 1899 to 1939

[1929 = 100]

Year	Total mining	Fuels	Non-metals	Metals	Year	Total mining	Fuels	Non-metals	Metals	Year	Total mining	Fuels	Non-metals	Metals
	72	73	74	75		72	73	74	75		72	73	74	75
1939	94.3	99.1	75.3	89.0	1925	82.7	81.1	83.3	89.9	1911	49.4	47.0	51.5	66.0
1938	85.3	92.7	66.9	70.0	1924	79.8	79.8	76.1	82.3					
1937	99.6	103.4	78.0	99.7	1923	84.8	86.1	75.6	85.1	1910	50.2	46.8	52.0	69.4
1936	88.5	94.5	71.4	77.4	1922	61.5	61.9	59.2	61.5	1909	47.4	43.1	50.3	67.7
					1921	57.2	61.6	48.7	39.3	1908	41.6	39.5	44.0	55.3
1935	75.4	84.1	52.2	57.4						1907	44.6	43.3	45.5	57.7
1934	69.7	79.8	49.4	44.2	1920	69.8	70.3	56.8	77.5	1906	41.2	37.3	43.7	59.1
1933	64.2	75.4	43.9	35.0	1919	60.1	59.6	46.4	73.3					
1932	59.2	69.3	43.6	30.2	1918	69.4	66.0	48.3	99.1	1905	39.6	36.2	36.3	56.1
1931	73.6	79.6	67.8	54.0	1917	69.0	63.6	55.5	102.9	1904	35.4	32.8	29.4	49.7
					1916	65.4	57.2	54.9	105.0	1903	34.5	32.5	25.3	47.7
1930	88.4	90.5	90.4	78.4						1902	30.6	27.1	22.8	47.7
1929	100.0	100.0	100.0	100.0	1915	56.7	52.1	49.9	84.3	1901	29.4	26.8	20.7	44.0
1928	91.8	91.4	95.1	91.4	1914	52.1	50.3	50.8	68.5					
1927	91.9	92.3	93.6	88.7	1913	55.9	53.0	55.4	76.3	1900	27.8	24.5	21.3	43.4
1926	89.6	89.0	88.2	93.5	1912	53.0	49.6	54.8	73.2	1899	25.7	23.0	19.7	39.7

Series M 76–92. Production and Calculated Consumption of Mineral Energy Fuels, Electricity From Waterpower, and Fuel Wood, in B.t.u.'s: 1800 to 1970

[In trillions of British thermal units. A British thermal unit (B.t.u.) is the quantity of heat required to raise the temperature of one pound of water 1° F. at or near its point of maximum density]

Year	Production							Calculated consumption									
	Mineral fuels					Electricity from waterpower		Mineral fuels							Electricity from waterpower		Fuel wood
	Total	Bituminous coal	Pennsylvania anthracite	Crude petroleum	Natural gas, wet	At prevailing central station equivalent	At direct calorific equivalent	Total	Bituminous coal	Pennsylvania anthracite	Crude petroleum	Petroleum products, net imports [1]	Natural gas, dry	Natural gas, liquids	At prevailing central station equivalent	At direct calorific equivalent	
	76	77	78	79	80	81	82	83	84	85	86	87	88	89	90	91	92
1970	59,174	15,001	247	19,772	24,154	2,630	855	64,565	12,712	210	22,367	4,753	22,029	2,494	2,650	862	425
1969	55,947	13,957	266	18,886	22,838	2,648	865	62,174	12,509	224	21,796	4,166	21,020	2,459	2,659	868	441
1968	54,096	13,664	291	18,593	21,548	2,349	771	59,291	12,401	258	21,091	3,722	19,580	2,239	2,342	769	455
1967	52,402	13,904	311	18,100	20,087	2,347	768	55,841	11,982	274	20,208	3,084	18,250	2,043	2,344	767	471
1966	49,745	13,507	329	16,925	18,984	2,062	675	54,282	12,205	290	19,315	3,090	17,393	1,989	2,073	679	525
1965	46,977	13,017	378	15,930	17,652	2,059	672	51,247	11,580	328	18,506	2,882	16,098	1,853	2,058	672	577
1964	45,683	12,418	436	15,691	17,138	1,886	615	49,298	10,899	365	18,194	2,420	15,648	1,772	1,907	622	626
1963	44,188	11,712	464	15,741	16,271	1,768	576	47,507	10,353	361	18,174	2,108	14,843	1,668	1,767	575	678
1962	42,071	10,782	429	15,495	15,365	1,816	587	45,577	9,826	363	17,822	1,840	14,121	1,605	1,821	588	732
1961	40,627	10,308	443	15,185	14,691	1,656	531	43,621	9,502	404	17,348	1,641	13,228	1,498	1,680	538	790
1960	39,939	10,662	478	14,664	14,135	1,608	510	42,906	9,693	447	16,861	1,779	12,699	1,427	1,657	525	832
1959	39,128	10,581	524	14,662	13,361	1,551	482	41,547	9,332	478	16,686	1,713	11,990	1,348	1,591	495	918
1958	37,599	10,663	538	14,154	12,244	1,592	490	40,058	9,366	483	16,250	1,724	10,995	1,240	1,636	504	894
1957	40,675	12,800	644	15,346	11,885	1,422	455	40,154	10,640	528	16,960	368	10,416	1,242	1,551	467	916
1956	40,343	13,013	734	15,344	11,252	1,435	427	40,213	11,142	610	16,994	424	9,834	1,209	1,487	443	1,013
1955	37,722	12,080	665	14,445	10,532	1,360	397	38,296	10,941	599	15,956	372	9,232	1,196	1,407	410	1,037
1954	33,916	10,262	739	13,427	9,488	1,360	381	34,875	9,512	683	14,830	260	8,548	1,042	1,388	389	1,035
1953	35,554	11,981	786	13,671	9,116	1,413	374	36,147	11,182	711	14,912	180	8,156	1,006	1,439	381	1,065
1952	35,249	12,231	1,031	13,282	8,705	1,466	374	34,962	10,971	897	14,248	132	7,760	954	1,496	382	1,125
1951	36,209	13,982	1,084	13,037	8,106	1,424	356	35,321	12,285	940	13,867	107	7,248	874	1,454	364	1,155

See footnotes at end of table.

Series M 76–92. Production and Calculated Consumption of Mineral Energy Fuels, Electricity From Waterpower, and Fuel Wood, in B.t.u.'s: 1800 to 1970—Con.

[In trillions of British thermal units]

Year	Production							Calculated consumption										Fuel wood
	Mineral fuels					Electricity from waterpower		Mineral fuels							Electricity from waterpower		
	Total	Bituminous coal	Pennsylvania anthracite	Crude petroleum	Natural gas, wet	At prevailing central station equivalent	At direct calorific equivalent	Total	Bituminous coal	Pennsylvania anthracite	Crude petroleum	Petroleum products, net imports[1]	Natural gas, dry	Natural gas, liquids	At prevailing central station equivalent	At direct calorific equivalent	
	76	77	78	79	80	81	82	83	84	85	86	87	88	89	90	91	92
1950	32,937	13,527	1,120	11,449	6,841	1,415	344	32,552	11,900	1,013	12,304	402	6,150	783	1,440	350	1,171
1949	29,151	11,472	1,085	10,683	5,911	1,425	323	30,039	11,673	958	11,402	57	5,289	660	1,449	329	1,259
1948	34,490	15,707	1,451	11,717	5,615	1,369	297	32,487	13,622	1,275	12,085	−147	5,033	619	1,393	302	1,265
1947	33,758	16,522	1,453	10,771	5,012	1,296	283	31,709	14,600	1,224	11,065	−262	4,518	564	1,326	290	1,255
1946	30,133	13,989	1,537	10,057	4,550	1,406	284	29,048	13,110	1,369	10,270	−283	4,089	493	1,446	292	1,239
1945	30,891	15,134	1,395	9,939	4,423	1,442	289	30,055	14,661	1,311	10,199	−580	3,973	491	1,486	298	1,261
1944	31,759	16,233	1,618	9,732	4,176	1,344	269	30,434	15,447	1,509	9,923	−662	3,775	442	1,387	278	(NA)
1943	29,575	15,463	1,540	8,733	3,839	1,304	270	29,095	15,557	1,450	8,538	−310	3,481	379	1,347	278	(NA)
1942	28,278	15,267	1,532	8,043	3,436	1,136	228	26,720	14,149	1,435	7,987	−320	3,102	367	1,177	236	(NA)
1941	26,198	13,471	1,432	8,133	3,162	934	182	25,650	12,893	1,338	8,343	−139	2,851	364	975	189	(NA)
1940	24,208	12,072	1,308	7,849	2,979	880	171	22,991	11,290	1,245	7,662	−175	2,726	243	917	178	1,358
1939	21,753	10,345	1,308	7,337	2,763	838	158	20,717	9,854	1,262	7,327	−486	2,539	221	872	165	(NA)
1938	19,911	9,132	1,171	7,043	2,565	866	161	18,981	8,811	1,148	6,921	−456	2,348	209	899	167	(NA)
1937	23,093	11,673	1,317	7,419	2,684	871	158	21,846	11,286	1,280	7,004	−400	2,468	208	905	164	(NA)
1936	21,679	11,504	1,386	6,378	2,411	812	147	20,577	10,697	1,351	6,426	−302	2,221	184	841	152	(NA)
1935	18,997	9,756	1,325	5,780	2,136	806	146	18,276	9,336	1,298	5,799	−300	1,974	169	831	150	1,397
1934	18,104	9,415	1,452	5,267	1,970	698	125	17,216	9,008	1,410	5,136	−318	1,819	161	721	130	(NA)
1933	16,985	8,741	1,258	5,253	1,733	711	127	16,171	8,323	1,260	5,143	−299	1,600	144	729	130	(NA)
1932	15,663	8,114	1,266	4,554	1,729	713	125	15,666	8,041	1,283	4,830	−240	1,594	158	726	127	(NA)
1931	18,331	10,011	1,515	4,936	1,869	668	114	18,107	9,743	1,484	5,304	−339	1,715	200	692	119	(NA)
1930	21,367	12,249	1,762	5,208	2,148	752	122	21,503	11,921	1,718	6,148	−496	1,969	243	785	128	1,455
1929	28,852	14,017	1,875	5,842	2,118	816	128	22,909	13,612	1,815	5,894	−600	1,942	246	847	133	(NA)
1928	21,997	13,120	1,914	5,229	1,734	854	129	21,491	13,069	1,871	5,474	−711	1,588	200	890	134	(NA)
1927	22,424	13,565	2,034	5,227	1,598	776	111	21,013	13,095	1,897	5,027	−650	1,465	179	815	117	(NA)
1926	23,088	15,020	2,145	4,471	1,452	728	100	21,730	13,954	1,961	4,876	−545	1,335	149	765	105	(NA)
1925	20,939	13,625	1,570	4,430	1,314	668	87	20,198	13,079	1,627	4,641	−485	1,212	124	701	91	1,533
1924	20,309	12,672	2,233	4,141	1,263	648	77	19,768	12,681	2,050	4,228	−464	1,170	103	685	81	(NA)
1923	22,524	14,792	2,371	4,248	1,113	685	74	20,958	13,598	2,208	4,419	−389	1,032	90	727	79	(NA)
1922	16,529	11,063	1,389	3,234	843	643	67	16,540	11,185	1,443	3,390	−319	785	56	675	70	(NA)
1921	16,666	10,897	2,298	2,739	732	620	60	15,754	10,266	2,082	3,016	−342	682	50	656	63	(NA)
1920	20,627	14,899	2,276	2,569	883	738	64	19,007	13,325	2,179	3,027	−393	827	42	775	67	1,610
1919	17,441	12,206	2,238	2,195	802	718	58	16,792	11,688	2,113	2,159		793	39	766	62	(NA)
1918	20,529	15,180	2,510	2,064	775	701	55	19,686	14,588	2,385	1,911		771	31	750	58	(NA)
1917	19,787	14,457	2,530	1,945	855	700	53	18,842	13,835	2,378	1,755		850	24	755	57	(NA)
1916	17,944	13,166	2,224	1,744	810	681	49	17,052	12,631	2,106	1,497		807	11	729	52	(NA)
1915	16,163	11,597	2,260	1,630	676	659	45	15,385	11,134	2,160	1,411		673	7	691	47	1,688
1914	15,559	11,075	2,307	1,541	636	636	42	14,858	10,703	2,198	1,320		632	5	676	44	(NA)
1913	16,927	12,535	2,325	1,441	626	609	38	16,074	12,034	2,207	1,210		620	3	645	41	(NA)
1912	15,833	11,793	2,143	1,293	604	585	35	15,093	11,402	2,038	1,058		594	1	615	37	(NA)
1911	14,763	10,635	2,298	1,279	551	565	32	14,027	10,245	2,197	1,040		544	1	597	34	(NA)
1910	14,836	10,928	2,146	1,215	547	539	29	14,261	10,654	2,060	1,007		540	--------	539	29	1,765
1909	13,587	9,949	2,059	1,062	517	513	27	13,018	9,685	1,978	844		511	--------	513	27	(NA)
1908	12,295	8,713	2,115	1,035	432	476	24	11,762	8,478	2,037	820		427	--------	476	24	(NA)
1907	13,917	10,343	2,174	963	437	441	21	13,390	10,079	2,098	781		432	--------	441	21	(NA)
1906	11,946	8,983	1,811	734	418	414	19	11,507	8,793	1,748	555		411	--------	414	19	(NA)
1905	11,386	8,255	1,973	781	377	386	17	10,983	8,091	1,910	610		372	--------	386	17	1,843
1904	10,171	7,301	1,858	679	333	354	15	9,816	7,155	1,797	534		330	--------	354	15	(NA)
1903	10,205	7,408	1,895	583	319	321	13	9,924	7,315	1,843	449		317	--------	321	13	(NA)
1902	8,685	6,818	1,051	515	301	289	12	8,426	6,733	1,030	364		299	--------	289	12	(NA)
1901	8,316	5,917	1,714	402	283	264	10	7,996	5,808	1,657	250		281	--------	264	10	(NA)
1900	7,643	5,563	1,457	369	254	250	10	7,322	5,431	1,410	229		252	--------	250	10	2,015
1895	5,467	3,540	1,473	307	147	--------	3	5,265	3,511	1,439	168		147	--------	90	3	2,306
1890	4,619	2,916	1,180	266	257	--------	1	4,475	2,903	1,159	156		257	--------	22	1	2,515
1885	3,063	1,880	974	127	82	--------	--------	2,962	1,883	957	40		82	--------	--------	--------	2,683
1880	2,210	1,330	728	152	--------	--------	--------	2,150	1,337	717	96		--------	--------	--------	--------	2,851
1875	1,494	856	587	51	--------	--------	--------	1,451	862	578	11		--------	--------	--------	--------	2,872
1870	1,074	536	507	31	--------	--------	--------	1,059	545	503	11		--------	--------	--------	--------	2,893
1865	645	324	307	14	--------	--------	--------	642	328	304	10		--------	--------	--------	--------	2,767
1860	519	237	279	3	--------	--------	--------	521	243	275	3		--------	--------	--------	--------	2,641
1855	417	198	219	--------	--------	--------	--------	421	205	216	--------		--------	--------	--------	--------	2,389
1850	216	106	110	--------	--------	--------	--------	219	110	109	--------		--------	--------	--------	--------	2,138

Year	Production, mineral fuels			Year	Production, mineral fuels			Year	Production, mineral fuels	
	Total	Bituminous coal	Pennsylvania anthracite		Total	Bituminous coal	Pennsylvania anthracite		Total	Bituminous coal
	76	77	78		76	77	78		76	77
1845	122	55	67	1825	12	11	1	1805	4	4
1840	64	35	29	1820	9	9	(Z)	1800	3	3
1835	47	28	19	1815	7	7	(Z)			
1830	23	17	6	1810	5	5	(Z)			

NA Not available.   Z Less than 500 billion B.t.u.'s.   [1] Minus sign (−) denotes exports exceeded imports.

Series M 93–106. Bituminous Coal—Production, Average Value, Freight Charges, Foreign Trade, Stocks, Number of Mines, and Mechanization: 1800 to 1970

[All figures are for short tons except number of mines]

Year	Production			Average value per ton, f.o.b. mine			Railroad freight charges per short ton	Foreign trade		Stocks at end of year	Number of mines	Mechanization		
	Total [1]	Under-ground	Strip	Total	Under-ground	Strip		Imports for consump-tion	Exports			Coal mechani-cally cleaned	Coal mechani-cally cut under-ground	Coal mechani-cally loaded under-ground
	93	94	95	96	97	98	99	100	101	102	103	104	105	106
	1,000 tons	1,000 tons	1,000 tons	Dollars	Dollars	Dollars	Dollars	1,000 tons	1,000 tons	1,000 tons		1,000 tons	1,000 tons	1,000 tons
1970	602,932	338,788	244,117	6.26	7.40	4.69	3.41	36	70,908	93,743	5,601	323,452	156,063	328,640
1969	560,505	347,132	197,023	4.99	5.62	3.98	3.10	109	56,234	81,966	5,118	334,761	160,247	335,431
1968	545,245	344,142	185,836	4.67	5.22	3.75	3.01	224	50,637	87,462	5,327	340,923	166,543	329,387
1967	552,626	349,133	187,134	4.62	5.18	3.68	3.00	227	49,528	95,408	5,873	349,402	171,530	329,914
1966	533,881	338,524	180,058	4.54	5.05	3.64	3.01	178	49,302	76,808	6,749	340,626	172,503	310,281
1965	512,088	332,661	165,241	4.44	4.93	3.57	3.13	184	50,181	79,740	7,228	332,226	179,440	296,633
1964	486,998	321,808	151,859	4.45	4.92	3.55	3.11	293	47,969	77,940	7,630	310,203	184,789	281,101
1963	458,928	302,256	144,141	4.39	4.82	3.57	3.21	267	47,078	73,029	7,940	289,462	184,407	259,241
1962	422,149	281,266	130,300	4.48	4.91	3.64	3.32	232	38,413	72,578	7,740	271,633	177,963	240,920
1961	402,977	272,766	121,979	4.58	5.02	3.67	3.40	164	34,970	71,418	7,648	264,711	176,428	235,350
1960	415,512	284,888	122,630	4.69	5.14	3.74	3.40	260	36,541	73,244	7,865	273,169	193,135	245,786
1959	412,028	283,434	120,953	4.77	5.23	3.76	3.45	375	37,253	76,202	7,719	269,787	204,399	243,731
1958	410,446	286,884	116,242	4.86	5.33	3.80	3.58	307	50,293	76,285	8,264	259,035	215,898	243,573
1957	492,704	360,649	124,109	5.08	5.52	3.89	3.57	367	76,446	80,779	8,539	304,027	291,640	305,737
1956	500,874	265,774	127,055	4.82	5.20	3.74	3.45	356	68,553	78,008	8,520	292,365	309,523	307,402
1955	464,633	343,465	115,093	4.50	4.85	3.48	3.24	337	51,277	68,423	7,856	272,715	302,509	290,671
1954	391,706	289,112	98,134	4.52	4.87	3.52	3.23	199	31,041	69,201	6,453	232,764	256,822	242,970
1953	457,290	349,551	105,448	4.92	5.27	3.75	3.33	227	33,760	80,614	6,671	241,759	322,806	278,329
1952	466,841	356,425	108,910	4.90	5.24	3.81	3.35	262	47,643	76,745	7,275	227,265	340,462	268,994
1951	533,665	415,842	117,618	4.92	5.21	3.88	3.16	292	56,722	76,636	8,009	240,010	394,707	304,051
1950	516,311	392,844	123,467	4.84	5.15	3.87	3.09	347	25,468	72,516	9,429	198,699	363,809	272,725
1949	437,868	331,823	106,045	4.88	5.18	3.94	3.00	315	27,842	45,111	8,559	153,652	303,385	222,376
1948	599,518	460,012	139,506	4.99	5.26	4.11	2.74	291	45,930	69,373	9,079	180,880	417,435	295,806
1947	630,624	491,229	139,395	4.16	4.35	3.47	2.49	290	68,667	52,161	8,700	174,436	442,102	298,157
1946	533,922	420,958	112,964	3.44	3.59	2.87	2.27	435	41,197	47,157	7,333	138,670	382,134	245,341
1945	577,617	467,630	109,987	3.06	3.16	2.65	2.20	467	27,956	45,665	7,033	147,886	424,726	262,512
1944	619,576	518,678	100,898	2.92	3.01	2.48	2.21	634	26,032	57,204	6,928	158,727	469,458	274,189
1943	590,177	510,492	79,685	2.69	2.75	2.28	2.30	758	25,836	56,686	6,620	145,576	461,052	249,805
1942	582,693	515,490	67,203	2.36	2.41	1.90	2.31	498	22,943	85,889	6,972	142,187	462,345	232,903
1941	514,149	459,078	55,071	2.19	2.23	1.79	2.22	390	20,740	62,737	6,822	117,540	408,510	186,667
1940	460,772	417,604	43,167	1.91	1.94	1.56	2.22	372	16,466	50,998	6,324	102,270	369,227	147,870
1939	394,855	357,133	37,722	1.84	1.88	1.49	2.23	355	11,590	44,571	5,820	79,429	313,969	110,712
1938	348,545	318,138	30,407	1.95	(NA)	(NA)	2.27	241	10,490	40,720	5,777	63,455	278,315	85,093
1937	445,531	413,780	31,751	1.94	(NA)	(NA)	2.17	258	13,145	47,074	6,548	65,000	(NA)	83,500
1936	439,088	410,962	28,126	1.76	1.77	1.49	2.25	272	10,655	42,926	6,875	61,095	348,332	66,977
1935	372,373	348,726	23,647	1.77	1.79	1.47	2.24	202	9,742	37,017	6,315	45,361	293,664	47,177
1934	359,368	338,578	20,790	1.75	1.76	1.49	2.15	180	10,869	34,476	6,258	39,827	284,677	41,433
1933	333,631	315,360	18,270	1.34	1.34	1.33	2.20	197	9,037	32,714	5,555	34,558	267,000	37,821
1932	309,710	290,069	19,641	1.31	1.31	1.32	2.26	187	8,814	29,666	5,427	30,278	243,955	35,817
1931	382,089	363,157	18,932	1.54	1.54	1.51	2.22	206	12,126	35,500	5,642	36,172	302,263	47,562
1930	467,526	447,684	19,842	1.70	1.71	1.54	2.23	241	15,877	37,200	5,891	38,800	362,425	46,982
1929	534,989	514,721	20,268	1.78	1.79	1.57	2.25	495	17,429	40,300	6,057	36,799	403,607	37,862
1928	500,745	480,956	19,789	1.86	1.87	1.69	2.27	547	16,164	41,800	6,450	28,783	369,687	21,559
1927	517,763	499,385	18,378	1.99	1.99	1.90	(NA)	550	18,012	55,500	7,011	27,692	374,041	16,500
1926	573,367	556,444	16,923	2.06	2.07	1.89	(NA)	486	35,272	55,000	7,177	(NA)	410,913	10,545
1925	520,053	503,182	16,871	2.04	2.05	1.84	(NA)	602	17,462	49,000	7,144	(NA)	366,726	6,243
1924	483,687	470,080	13,607	2.20	2.20	2.00	(NA)	417	17,100	45,000	7,586	(NA)	336,271	3,496
1923	564,565	552,625	11,940	2.68	2.69	2.31	2.36	1,882	21,454	62,000	9,331	20,140	377,436	1,880
1922	422,268	412,059	10,209	3.02	3.02	3.07	---------	5,060	12,413	36,000	9,299	(NA)	267,033	---------
1921	415,922	410,865	5,057	2.89	2.89	2.87	---------	1,258	23,131	48,000	8,038	13,629	272,702	---------
1920	568,667	559,807	8,860	3.75	3.74	4.12	---------	1,245	38,517	45,800	8,921	17,984	339,813	---------
1919	465,860	460,225	5,635	2.49	2.49	2.33	---------	1,012	20,114	[2] 24,000	8,994	16,884	276,020	---------
1918	579,386	571,098	8,288	2.58	2.58	2.54	---------	1,457	22,351	57,900	8,319	22,017	323,931	---------
1917	551,791	546,001	5,790	2.26	2.26	2.34	---------	1,448	23,840	[3] 28,100	6,939	25,484	306,396	---------
1916	502,520	498,587	3,933	1.32	1.32	1.51	---------	1,714	21,255	[3] 27,000	5,726	22,922	283,691	---------
1915	442,624	439,792	2,832	1.13	1.13	1.18	---------	1,704	18,777	---------	5,502	20,874	243,238	---------
1914	422,704	421,423	1,281	1.17	---------	---------	---------	1,521	17,590	---------	5,592	20,264	218,399	---------
1913	478,435	---------	---------	1.18	---------	---------	---------	1,768	18,013	---------	5,776	22,070	242,422	---------
1912	450,105	---------	---------	1.15	---------	---------	---------	1,456	16,475	---------	5,747	17,539	210,539	---------
1911	405,907	---------	---------	1.11	---------	---------	---------	1,973	13,260	---------	5,887	(NA)	178,158	---------
1910	417,111	---------	---------	1.12	---------	---------	---------	1,820	11,663	---------	5,818	16,035	174,012	---------
1909	379,744	---------	---------	1.07	---------	---------	---------	1,375	10,101	---------	5,775	14,443	142,497	---------
1908	332,574	---------	---------	1.12	---------	---------	---------	2,219	11,071	---------	4,730	11,870	123,183	---------
1907	394,759	---------	---------	1.14	---------	---------	---------	1,893	9,870	---------	4,550	11,210	138,548	---------
1906	342,875	---------	---------	1.11	---------	---------	---------	2,039	8,014	---------	4,430	9,252	118,848	---------
1905	315,063	---------	---------	1.06	---------	---------	---------	1,705	7,513	---------	5,060	---------	103,396	---------
1904	278,660	---------	---------	1.10	---------	---------	---------	2,180	7,207	---------	4,650	---------	78,607	---------
1903	282,749	---------	---------	1.24	---------	---------	---------	4,044	5,836	---------	(NA)	---------	77,975	---------
1902	260,217	---------	---------	1.12	---------	---------	---------	2,174	6,049	---------	(NA)	---------	69,612	---------
1901	225,828	---------	---------	1.05	---------	---------	---------	2,215	6,455	---------	(NA)	---------	57,843	---------

NA Not available.
[1] Beginning 1951, series M 94 and M 95 do not add to total because it includes auger production.
[2] March 1, 1920.
[3] October 1.

Series M 93–106. Bituminous Coal—Production, Average Value, Freight Charges, Foreign Trade, Stocks, Number of Mines, and Mechanization: 1800 to 1970—Con.

[All figures are for short tons except number of mines]

Year	Production, total	Average value per ton, f.o.b. mine	Imports for consumption	Exports	Number of mines	Coal mechanically cut underground	Year	Production, total	Year	Production, total
	93	96	100	101	103	105		93		93
	1,000 tons	Dollars	1,000 tons	1,000 tons		1,000 tons		1,000 tons		1,000 tons
1900	212,316	1.04	1,912	6,061	(NA)	52,785	1866	13,015	1832	771
1899	193,323	.87	1,410	3,898	3,245	43,964	1865	12,349	1831	695
1898	166,594	.80	1,426	3,004	2,862	32,413	1864	11,415		
1897	147,618	.81	1,443	2,670	2,454	22,649	1863	10,480	1830	646
1896	137,640	.83	1,393	2,516	2,599	16,425	1862	9,384	1829	607
							1861	8,756	1828	569
1895	135,118	.86	1,411	2,660	2,555	(NA)			1827	532
1894	118,820	.91	1,286	2,440	-----	(NA)	1860	9,057	1826	493
1893	128,385	.96	1,234	1,986	-----	(NA)	1859	9,127		
1892	126,857	.99	1,492	1,905	-----	(NA)	1858	8,846	1825	437
1891	117,901	.99	1,182	1,652	-----	6,212	1857	8,775	1824	414
							1856	7,992	1823	370
1890	111,302	.99	1,047	1,272					1822	360
1889	95,685	.99	1,122	1,047			1855	7,543	1821	349
1888	102,040	1.00	1,216	964			1854	7,359		
1887	88,562	1.11	918	791			1853	6,100	1820	330
1886	74,645	1.05	909	610			1852	4,909	1819	320
							1851	4,590	1818	330
1885	71,773	1.13	861	765			1850	4,029	1817	303
1884	71,737	.94	839	724			1849	3,518	1816	278
1883	64,860	1.07	723	519			1848	3,080	1815	253
1882	58,917	1.12	891	352			1847	2,631	1814	235
1881	51,945	1.12	731	214			1846	2,328	1813	218
							1845	2,097	1812	203
1880	50,757	1.25	528	249			1844	1,794	1811	188
1879	40,425	-----	545	309			1843	1,615		
1878	36,418	-----	642	382			1842	1,473	1810	176
1877	34,385	-----	555	360			1841	1,355	1809	170
1876	31,822	-----	449	258					1808	165
							1840	1,345	1807	159
1875	32,657	-----	489	228			1839	1,251	1806	152
1874	30,733	-----	551	405			1838	1,141		
1873	31,601	-----	515	272			1837	1,070	1805	146
1872	27,311	-----	543	158			1836	1,067	1804	141
1871	22,857	-----	482	149					1803	127
							1835	1,059	1802	122
1870	20,471	-----	466	120			1834	912	1801	114
1869	19,903	-----	490	(NA)			1833	823	1800	108
1868	16,244	-----	441	97						
1867	13,837	-----	571	103						

NA   Not available.

Series M 107–122. Bituminous Coal—Employment, Strikes, and Domestic Consumption by Consumer Class; and Coke Production: 1880 to 1970

	Bituminous coal															Coke production (1,000 short tons)
	Employment					Man-days idle because of strikes (1,000)	Domestic consumption by consumer class (1,000 short tons)									
	Average workers on active days				Average days worked		Total	Electric power utilities	Railroads (Class I)	Coke plants	Cement mills	Steel and rolling mills	Other manufacturing and mining industries	Retail deliveries to other consumers	Bunker, foreign and lake vessels[2]	
Year	Total	Underground	Surface													
			Strip	All other[1]												
	107	108	109	110	111	112	113	114	115	116	117	118	119	120	121	122
1970	140,140	107,808	28,395	3,937	228	627	517,158	320,460	-----	96,009	7,926	5,410	74,983	12,072	298	66,525
1969	124,532	99,269	22,323	2,940	226	901	507,275	308,461	-----	92,901	8,970	5,560	76,404	14,666	313	64,709
1968	127,894	102,940	22,358	2,596	220	956	498,830	294,739	-----	90,765	9,391	5,657	82,637	15,224	417	63,653
1967	131,523	107,432	21,439	2,652	219	158	480,416	271,784	-----	92,272	6,330	8,922	83,542	17,099	467	64,580
1966	131,752	107,614	21,752	2,386	219	629	486,266	264,202	-----	95,892	9,149	7,117	89,332	19,965	609	67,402
1965	133,732	109,735	21,729	2,268	219	258	459,164	242,729	-----	94,779	8,873	7,466	85,614	19,048	655	66,854
1964	128,698	104,968	21,266	2,464	225	340	431,116	223,032	-----	88,757	8,679	7,394	82,928	19,615	711	62,145
1963	141,646	116,590	22,588	2,468	205	234	409,225	209,038	-----	77,633	8,138	7,401	82,797	23,548	670	54,524
1962	143,822	120,084	21,181	2,557	199	191	387,774	190,833	-----	74,262	7,719	7,319	78,766	28,188	687	51,910
1961	150,474	125,145	23,011	2,318	193	91	374,405	179,629	-----	73,881	7,615	7,495	77,280	27,735	770	51,711
1960	169,400	142,093	25,161	2,146	191	[3] 137	380,429	173,882	2,101	81,015	8,216	7,378	76,487	30,405	945	57,229
1959	179,636	151,895	25,759	1,982	188	[3] 1,560	366,256	165,788	2,600	79,181	8,510	6,674	73,396	29,138	969	55,864
1958	197,402	169,657	25,806	1,939	184	102	366,703	152,928	3,725	76,580	8,256	7,268	81,372	35,619	955	53,604
1957	228,635	200,519	26,168	1,948	203	136	413,668	157,398	8,401	108,020	8,633	6,938	87,202	35,712	1,364	75,951
1956	228,163	200,120	26,240	1,803	214	377	432,858	154,983	12,308	105,913	9,026	7,189	93,302	48,667	1,470	74,483
1955	225,093	197,904	25,229	1,960	210	273	423,412	140,550	15,473	107,377	8,529	7,353	89,611	53,020	1,499	75,302
1954	227,397	202,182	24,095	1,120	182	344	363,060	115,235	17,370	85,391	7,924	6,983	77,115	51,798	1,244	59,662
1953	293,106	216,435	21,395	55,276	191	418	426,798	112,283	27,735	112,874	8,167	8,764	95,160	59,976	1,839	78,837
1952	335,217	252,627	22,940	59,650	186	2,760	418,757	103,309	37,962	97,614	7,903	9,632	93,637	66,861	1,839	68,254
1951	372,897	281,868	26,102	64,927	203	887	468,904	101,898	54,005	113,448	8,507	11,260	103,188	74,378	2,220	79,331

See footnotes at end of table.

Series M 107–122. Bituminous Coal—Employment, Strikes, and Domestic Consumption by Consumer Class; and Coke Production: 1880 to 1970—Con.

Year	Total (107)	Underground (108)	Surface: Strip (109)	Surface: All other[1] (110)	Average days worked (111)	Man-days idle because of strikes (1,000) (112)	Consumption Total (113)	Electric power utilities (114)	Railroads (Class I) (115)	Coke plants (116)	Cement mills (117)	Steel and rolling mills (118)	Other manufacturing and mining industries (119)	Retail deliveries to other consumers (120)	Bunker, foreign and lake vessels[2] (121)	Coke production (1,000 short tons) (122)
1950	415,582	311,669	29,955	73,958	183	9,320	454,202	88,262	60,969	103,845	7,923	10,877	95,862	84,422	2,042	72,718
1949	433,698	326,758	29,267	77,673	157	10,700	445,538	80,610	68,123	91,236	7,966	10,529	96,629	88,389	2,056	63,637
1948	441,631	330,292	32,178	79,161	217	9,560	519,909	95,620	94,838	107,306	8,546	14,193	110,060	86,794	2,552	74,862
1947	419,182	311,369	29,783	78,030	234	2,190	545,891	86,009	109,296	104,800	7,919	14,195	123,928	96,657	3,087	73,446
1946	396,434	296,030	25,408	74,996	214	19,590	500,386	68,743	110,166	83,288	6,990	12,151	117,732	98,684	2,632	58,498
1945	383,100	290,001	23,261	69,838	261	5,010	559,567	71,603	125,120	95,349	4,203	14,241	126,562	119,297	3,192	67,308
1944	393,347	301,461	21,035	70,851	278	1,060	589,599	76,656	132,049	105,296	3,767	15,152	131,498	122,112	3,069	74,038
1943	416,007	326,763	16,643	72,601	264	7,510	593,797	74,036	130,283	102,460	5,842	15,864	142,149	120,121	3,042	71,676
1942	461,991	374,654	12,893	74,444	246	264	540,050	63,472	115,410	100,850	7,462	14,722	132,767	102,141	3,226	70,569
1941	456,981	376,765	10,861	69,355	216	6,750	492,115	59,888	97,384	93,138	6,735	15,384	121,880	94,402	3,304	65,187
1940	439,075	365,013	8,983	65,079	202	153	430,910	49,126	85,130	81,386	5,559	14,169	107,864	84,687	2,989	57,072
1939	421,788	353,476	8,791	59,521	178	7,300	376,098	42,304	79,072	63,514	5,194	13,843	100,637	68,770	2,764	44,327
1938	441,333	370,004	7,877	63,452	162	133	336,281	36,440	73,921	46,626	4,413	11,877	94,196	66,498	2,310	32,496
1937	491,864	(NA)	(NA)	(NA)	193	1,920	430,777	41,045	88,080	74,502	5,182	18,148	124,056	76,331	3,433	52,375
1936	477,204	399,367	8,043	69,794	199	533	408,293	38,104	86,391	65,942	4,711	19,019	111,030	80,044	3,052	46,275
1935	462,403	389,942	8,533	63,928	179	2,970	356,326	30,986	77,109	50,515	3,456	16,585	94,598	80,444	2,683	35,141
1934	458,011	384,947	7,652	65,412	178	1,560	343,814	29,707	76,037	45,978	3,457	15,391	87,314	83,507	2,423	31,822
1933	418,703	352,866	7,075	58,762	167	2,210	317,685	27,088	72,548	40,089	2,760	14,129	81,377	77,396	2,298	27,589
1932	406,380	345,905	6,168	54,307	146	5,910	306,917	30,290	66,498	31,917			176,862		1,350	21,789
1931	450,213	387,794	6,205	56,214	160	1,540	371,869	38,735	81,725	48,613			200,601		2,195	33,484
1930	493,202	426,742	66,460		187	883	454,990	42,898	98,400	69,805			240,390		3,497	47,972
1929	502,993	433,999	68,994		219			44,937	113,894	86,787			269,650		4,287	59,884
1928	522,150	450,960	71,190		203	5,940	498,828	41,350	112,382	77,184			263,618		4,294	52,806
1927	593,918	512,116	81,812		191	23,000	499,801	41,888	115,883	74,448			263,017		4,565	51,092
1926	593,647	510,824	82,823		215	717	532,581	41,311	122,823	82,872			277,839		7,736	56,866
1925	588,493	506,541	81,952		195	1,164	499,193	40,222	117,714	74,533			261,858		4,866	51,267
1924	619,604	531,904	87,700		171	4,219	484,004	37,556	117,247	64,975			259,766		4,460	44,270
1923	704,793	600,305	104,488		179	1,239	518,993	38,966	131,492	84,360			259,082		5,093	56,978
1922	687,958	582,409	105,549		142	53,874	426,915	34,179	113,163	54,339			220,619		4,615	37,124
1921	663,754	567,289	96,465		149	2,283	391,849	31,585	107,910	37,188			206,713		8,453	25,288
1920	639,547	529,812	109,735		220	4,099	508,595	37,124	135,414	76,191			249,380		10,486	51,345
1919	621,998	508,801	113,197		195	15,526	481,658	35,100	119,692	65,587			253,055		8,224	44,181
1918	615,305	496,252	119,053		249	439	530,593	34,500	134,214	85,028			270,662		6,189	56,478
1917	603,143	498,185	104,958		243	2,187	529,409	33,500	133,421	83,753			271,026		7,709	55,607
1916	561,102	474,244	86,858		230	2,390										54,534
1915	557,456	482,433	75,023		203	2,253										41,581
1914	583,506	506,025	77,481		195	10,834										34,556
1913	571,882	494,238	77,644		232	2,568										46,300
1912	548,632	474,513	74,119		223	5,614										43,984
1911	549,775	479,294	75,114		211	947										35,551
1910	555,533				217	19,235										41,709
1909	543,152				209	724										39,315
1908	516,264				193	5,450										26,034
1907	513,258				234	462										40,780
1906	478,425				213	13,243										36,401
1905	460,629				211	763										32,231
1904	437,832				202	3,349										23,661
1903	415,777				225	1,341										25,274
1902	370,056				230	2,462										25,402
1901	340,235				225	734										21,796
1900	304,375				234	1,378										20,533
1899	271,027				234	2,124										19,669
1898	255,717				211											16,047
1897	247,817				196											13,289
1896	244,171				192											11,789
1895	239,962				194											13,334
1894	244,603				171											9,204
1893	230,365				204											9,478
1892	212,893				219											12,011
1891	205,803				223											10,353
1890	192,204				226											11,508
1889																10,258
1888																8,540
1887																7,612
1886																6,845
1885																5,107
1884																4,874
1883																5,465
1882																4,793
1881																4,114
1880																3,338

NA Not available.
[1] Beginning 1954, covers auger mining only.
[2] Includes lake vessels beginning 1933.
[3] Includes idleness from stoppages which began in previous year.

Series M 123–137. Pennsylvania Anthracite—Production, Value, Foreign Trade, Producers' Stocks, Employment, Strikes, and Mechanization: 1808 to 1970

Year	Production Total	Production Under-ground	Production Strip	Average value per ton, f.o.b. mine	Foreign trade Exports	Foreign trade Imports for consumption	Net change in producers' stocks [1]	Employment Total	Employment Underground	Employment Strip	Employment Other surface	Average days worked	Man-days idle because of strikes	Mechanization, underground Cut by machines	Mechanization, underground Loaded by machines
	123	124	125	126	127	128	129	130	131	132	133	134	135	136	137
	1,000 short tons	*1,000 short tons*	*1,000 short tons*	*Dollars*	*1,000 short tons*	*1,000 short tons*	*1,000 short tons*						*1,000*	*1,000 short tons*	*1,000 short tons*
1970	9,729	1,742	4,541	10.83	789	---------	---------	6,000	1,414	1,809	2,777	240	11	125	1,151
1969	10,473	2,106	4,579	9.62	627	---------	---------	6,300	1,529	1,718	3,053	221	13	7	1,327
1968	11,461	2,450	4,696	8.48	518	---------	---------	6,932	1,683	1,891	3,358	217	4	61	1,475
1967	12,256	3,258	4,740	7.85	595	---------	---------	7,750	2,287	1,883	3,580	219	1	147	1,998
1966	12,941	4,088	5,253	7.78	766	---------	---------	9,292	3,332	2,085	3,875	203	8	247	2,591
1965	14,866	5,297	5,939	8.21	851	---------	---------	11,132	4,501	2,349	4,282	204	2	329	3,246
1964	17,184	5,889	7,177	8.65	1,575	---------	---------	13,144	5,193	3,075	4,876	214	1	417	3,455
1963	18,267	6,715	7,468	8.40	3,357	[2] 5	---------	13,498	5,449	3,025	5,024	216	3	240	3,666
1962	16,894	6,673	6,822	7.94	1,802	8	---------	14,010	5,779	3,008	5,223	204	15	278	3,065
1961	17,446	6,785	7,247	8.04	1,435	1	-33	15,792	6,664	3,194	5,934	196	4	236	3,378
1960	18,817	7,696	7,112	7.82	1,440	1	-230	19,051	9,041	3,470	6,540	176	9	226	4,044
1959	20,649	9,415	7,096	8.35	1,788	3	23	23,294	11,900	3,775	7,619	173	1	261	4,701
1958	21,171	10,699	6,878	8.88	2,280	4	-93	26,540	13,850	4,418	8,272	183	2	184	5,332
1957	25,338	12,616	7,543	8.99	4,332	1	158	30,825	16,822	4,546	9,457	196	2	292	6,657
1956	28,900	15,055	8,354	8.19	5,244	(Z)	-378	31,516	17,171	4,840	9,505	216	56	400	7,308
1955	26,205	14,499	7,704	7.86	3,152	(Z)	-573	[3] 33,523	[3] 19,952	[3] 4,642	[3] 8,929	[3] 197	9	394	6,661
1954	29,083	16,852	7,940	8.52	2,851	6	-377	43,996	27,294	4,837	11,865	164	76	381	6,978
1953	30,949	17,893	8,606	9.67	2,724	31	207	57,862	37,146	6,168	14,548	163	108	319	6,839
1952	40,583	24,748	10,697	9.36	4,592	29	726	65,923	43,120	7,100	15,703	201	104	386	10,034
1951	42,670	26,342	11,136	9.51	5,956	27	-286	68,995	45,483	7,647	15,865	208	81	496	10,848
1950	44,077	28,156	11,834	8.90	3,892	18	293	72,624	48,426	7,949	16,249	211	80	612	12,336
1949	42,702	27,031	10,377	8.38	4,943	(NA)	12	75,377	50,651	7,386	17,340	195	1,400	558	11,858
1948	57,140	37,175	13,353	8.17	6,676	1	252	76,215	51,629	7,005	17,581	265	274	1,017	15,742
1947	57,190	36,963	12,604	7.22	8,510	10	451	78,600	52,497	7,264	18,839	259	159	1,210	16,054
1946	60,507	38,084	12,859	6.83	6,497	10	121	78,145	51,996	6,152	19,997	271	649	1,233	15,619
1945	54,934	34,886	10,056	5.90	3,691	(Z)	-315	72,842	48,000	5,314	19,528	269	1,163	1,210	13,928
1944	63,701	41,775	10,953	5.57	4,186	12	116	77,591	51,656	5,595	20,340	292	327	1,336	14,975
1943	60,644	42,736	8,989	5.06	4,139	166	-469	79,153	54,206	5,084	19,863	270	1,836	1,625	14,746
1942	60,328	45,237	9,071	4.50	4,439	140	-476	82,121	58,926	4,526	18,669	239	226	2,286	14,741
1941	56,368	43,877	7,317	4.26	3,380	75	335	88,054	65,184	4,609	18,261	203	423	1,855	13,442
1940	51,485	41,517	6,353	3.99	2,668	135	-55	91,313	68,619	4,114	18,580	186	105	1,816	12,326
1939	51,487	42,572	5,486	3.64	2,590	298	-464	93,138	69,952	3,924	19,262	183	78	1,882	11,774
1938	46,099	38,142	5,095	3.92	1,909	363	-696	96,417	72,387	3,642	20,388	171	358	1,588	10,152
1937	51,856	42,566	5,696	3.81	1,914	396	-105	99,085	74,395	4,585	20,105	189	607	1,985	10,684
1936	54,580	44,727	6,203	4.16	1,678	615	348	102,081	76,127	4,667	21,287	192	265	2,163	10,828
1935	52,159	43,783	5,187	4.03	1,609	571	-10	103,269	78,058	4,091	21,120	189	789	1,848	9,279
1934	57,168	48,575	5,798	4.27	1,298	478	815	109,050	83,137	4,304	21,609	207	949	1,981	9,284
1933	49,541	41,032	4,932	4.17	1,035	456	-626	104,633	79,701	3,383	21,549	182	1,012	1,648	6,557
1932	49,855	43,834	3,981	4.46	1,303	607	-1,341	121,243	94,120	2,407	24,716	162	167	1,674	5,433
1931	59,646	53,460	3,813	4.97	1,778	638	98	139,431	109,280	2,232	27,919	181	655	1,587	4,385
1930	69,385	64,926	2,536	5.11	2,552	675	-119	150,804	118,750	32,054		208	117	1,410	4,468
1929	73,828	69,964	1,912	5.22	3,406	487	-548	151,501	117,856	33,645		225	239	1,160	3,470
1928	75,348	69,725	2,423	5.22	3,336	385	-1,254	160,681	123,896	36,785		217	573	1,290	2,351
1927	80,096	73,658	2,153	5.26	3,326	119	2,218	165,259	127,197	38,062		225	158	1,172	2,223
1926	84,437	78,059	2,401	5.62	4,030	814	4,000	165,386	126,231	39,155		244	5,990	932	---------
1925	61,817	57,152	1,578	5.30	3,179	383	-5,040	160,312	120,568	39,744		182	15,270	941	---------
1924	87,927	82,869	1,866	5.43	4,018	118	3,310	160,009	119,363	40,646		274	1,144	1,424	---------
1923	93,339	83,009	2,263	5.43	5,090	300	1,635	157,743	114,721	43,022		268	2,629	1,209	---------
1922	54,683	49,533	950	5.01	2,649	234	-4,530	156,849	114,279	42,570		151	19,623	503	---------
1921	90,473	85,900	2,028	5.00	4,677	9	3,855	159,499	116,817	42,682		271	823	979	---------
1920	89,598	80,454	2,054	4.85	5,404	32	-1,560	145,074	101,023	44,051		271	1,815	938	---------
1919	88,092	81,055	2,007	4.14	4,977	83	1,680	154,571	107,829	46,742		266	236	1,575	---------
1918	98,826	87,802	2,360	3.40	4,968	37	1,120	147,121	101,671	45,450		293	70	1,858	---------
1917	99,612	90,164	2,302	2.85	6,007	13	-450	154,174	109,989	44,185		285	161	1,955	---------
1916	87,578	80,931	1,988	2.31	4,666	6	-4,200	159,869	116,705	43,164		253	955	1,840	---------
1915	88,995	83,973	1,122	2.07	3,965	1	-3,100	176,552	130,963	45,589		230	215	1,308	---------
1914	90,822	---------	---------	2.07	4,290	18	2,500	179,679	133,309	46,370		245	180	917	---------
1913	91,525	---------	---------	2.13	4,653	1	1,400	175,745	127,854	47,891		257	482	556	---------
1912	84,362	---------	---------	2.11	4,131	2	---------	174,030	126,606	47,424		231	6,913	246	---------
1911	90,464	---------	---------	1.94	3,980	3	---------	172,585	---------	---------	---------	246	37	70	---------
1910	84,485			1.90	3,384	9	---------	169,497				229	16	---------	
1909	81,070			1.84	3,184	4		171,195				205	8		
1908	83,269			1.90	3,083	18		174,174				200	(NA)		
1907	85,604			1.91	3,022	11		167,234				220	(NA)		
1906	71,282			1.85	2,483	36		162,355				195	5,958		
1905	77,660			1.83	2,498	38		165,406				215	34		
1904	73,157			1.90	2,496	81		155,861				200	34		
1903	74,607			2.04	2,250	197		150,483				206	(NA)		
1902	41,374			1.84	1,017	191		148,141				116	14,210		
1901	67,472			1.67	2,233	(Z)		145,309				196	(NA)		
1900	57,368			1.49	1,853	(Z)		144,206				166	3,500		
1899	60,418			1.46	1,913	(Z)		139,608				173	---------		
1898	53,383			1.41	1,513	4		145,504				152			
1897	52,612			1.51	1,455	27		149,884				150			
1896	54,346			1.50	1,512	114		148,991				174			
1895	57,999			1.41	1,647	158		142,917				196			
1894	51,921			1.51	1,614	101		131,603				190			

See footnotes at end of table.

Series M 123–137. Pennsylvania Anthracite—Production, Value, Foreign Trade, Producers' Stocks, Employment, Strikes, and Mechanization: 1808 to 1970—Con.

Year	Production, total	Average value per ton, f.o.b. mine	Foreign trade		Employment		Year	Production, total	Year	Production, total
			Exports	Imports for consumption	Average workers on active days	Average days worked				
	123	126	127	128	130	134		123		123
	1,000 short tons	*Dollars*	*1,000 short tons*	*1,000 short tons*				*1,000 short tons*		*1,000 short tons*
1893	53,968	1.59	1,493	60	132,944	197	1865	12,077	1835	760
1892	52,473	1.57	954	73	129,050	198	1864	13,027	1834	512
1891	50,665	1.46	965	42	126,350	203	1863	12,267	1833	663
							1862	10,186	1832	502
1890	46,469	1.43	890	17	126,000	200	1861	10,245	1831	258
1889	45,547	1.44	961	23	123,676	194	1860	10,984		
1888	46,620	1.91	1,086	27	122,218	218	1859	10,092	1830	235
1887	42,088	2.01	925	16	106,517	208	1858	8,808	1829	149
1886	39,035	1.95	747	2	103,044	196	1857	8,618	1828	103
							1856	8,960	1827	80
									1826	61
1885	38,336	2.00	659	6	100,324	204	1855	8,607		
1884	37,157	1.79	727	2	101,073	192	1854	7,668	1825	43
1883	38,457	2.01	625	1	91,421	232	1853	6,653	1824	15
1882	35,121	2.01	620	(NA)	82,200	218	1852	6,412	1823	10
1881	31,920	2.01	518	1	76,031	221	1851	5,814	1822	6
1880	28,650	1.47	440	(NA)	73,373	____			1821	4
1879	30,208	____	433	1	68,847	____	1850	4,327		
1878	21,690	____	358	(NA)	63,964	____	1849	4,172	1820	4
1877	25,660	____	469	1	66,842	____	1848	4,001	1819	3
1876	22,793	____	378	2	70,474	____	1847	3,726	1818	3
							1846	3,032	1817	2
1875	23,121	____	354	(NA)	69,966	____	1845	2,626	1816	2
1874	24,267	____	450	1	53,402	____	1844	2,128		
1873	25,627	____	383	2	48,199	____	1843	1,656	1815	2
1872	24,734	____	291	(NA)	44,745	____	1842	1,441	1814	2
1871	19,465	____	151	1	37,488	____	1841	1,262	1813	2
									1812	2
1870	19,958	____	136	____	35,600	____	1840	1,129	1811	2
1869	18,341	____	318	____	____	____	1839	1,072		
1868	17,708	____	215	____	____	____	1838	978	1810	2
1867	16,067	____	216	____	____	____	1837	1,164	1809	1
1866	15,784	____	____	____	____	____	1836	925	1808	1

NA Not available.   Z Less than 500.
[1] Minus sign (−) denotes decrease.
[2] For period January-August. Beginning September 1963, data are not available separately because of change in import commodity classification.   [3] Estimated.

Series M 138–142. Crude Petroleum—Production, Value, Foreign Trade, and Proved Reserves: 1859 to 1970

[In thousands of 42-gallon barrels, except as indicated]

Year	Production	Average value at well per bbl.	Foreign trade		Estimated proved reserves, Dec. 31	Year	Production	Average value at well per bbl.	Foreign trade		Estimated proved reserves, Dec. 31
			Imports	Exports					Imports	Exports	
	138	139	140	141	142		138	139	140	141	142
1970	3,517,450	$3.18	483,293	4,991	39,001,000	1937	1,279,160	$1.18	27,484	67,234	15,507,268
1969	3,371,751	3.09	514,114	1,436	29,632,000	1936	1,099,687	1.09	32,327	50,313	13,063,400
1968	3,329,042	2.94	472,323	1,802	30,707,000						
1967	3,216,715	2.92	411,649	26,541	31,377,000	1935	996,596	.97	32,239	51,430	12,400,000
1966	3,027,763	2.88	447,120	1,477	31,452,000	1934	908,065	1.00	35,558	41,127	12,177,000
						1933	905,656	.67	31,893	36,584	12,000,000
1965	2,848,514	2.86	452,040	1,097	31,352,000	1932	785,159	.87	44,682	27,393	12,300,000
1964	2,786,822	2.88	438,643	1,363	30,991,000	1931	851,081	.65	47,250	25,535	13,000,000
1963	2,752,723	2.89	412,660	1,698	30,970,000						
1962	2,676,189	2.90	411,039	1,790	31,389,000	1930	898,011	1.19	62,129	23,705	13,600,000
1961	2,621,758	2.89	381,548	3,227	31,759,000	1929	1,007,323	1.27	78,933	26,401	13,200,000
						1928	901,474	1.17	79,767	18,966	11,000,000
1960	2,574,933	2.88	371,575	3,087	31,613,000	1927	901,129	1.30	58,383	15,844	10,500,000
1959	2,574,590	2.90	352,344	2,526	31,719,000	1926	770,874	1.88	60,382	15,407	8,800,000
1958	2,448,937	3.01	348,007	4,346	30,536,000						
1957	2,616,901	3.09	373,255	50,243	30,300,000	1925	763,743	1.68	61,824	13,337	8,500,000
1956	2,617,283	2.79	341,833	28,624	30,434,649	1924	713,940	1.43	77,775	18,239	7,500,000
						1923	732,407	1.34	82,015	17,534	7,600,000
1955	2,484,428	2.77	285,421	11,571	30,012,170	1922	557,531	1.61	127,308	10,805	7,600,000
1954	2,314,988	2.77	239,479	13,564	29,560,746	1921	472,183	1.73	125,364	9,627	7,800,000
1953	2,357,082	2.68	236,455	19,931	28,944,828						
1952	2,289,836	2.53	209,591	26,696	27,960,554	1920	442,929	3.07	106,175	9,295	7,200,000
1951	2,247,711	2.53	179,073	28,604	27,468,031	1919	378,367	2.01	52,822	6,019	6,700,000
						1918	355,928	1.98	37,736	4,901	6,200,000
1950	1,973,574	2.51	177,714	34,823	25,268,398	1917	335,316	1.56	30,127	4,098	5,900,000
1949	1,841,940	2.54	153,686	33,069	24,649,489	1916	300,767	1.10	30,570	4,096	5,900,000
1948	2,020,185	2.60	129,093	39,736	23,280,444						
1947	1,856,987	1.93	97,532	46,355	21,487,685	1915	281,104	.64	18,140	3,768	5,500,000
1946	1,733,939	1.41	86,066	42,436	20,873,560	1914	265,763	.81	17,247	2,970	5,400,000
						1913	248,446	.95	17,809	4,633	5,500,000
1945	1,713,655	1.22	74,337	32,998	20,826,813	1912	222,935	.74	____	4,493	5,400,000
1944	1,677,904	1.21	44,805	34,238	20,453,231	1911	220,449	.61	____	4,806	5,000,000
1943	1,505,613	1.20	13,833	41,342	20,064,152						
1942	1,386,645	1.19	12,297	33,834	20,082,793	1910	209,557	.61	____	4,288	4,500,000
1941	1,402,228	1.14	50,606	33,238	19,559,296	1909	183,171	.70	____	4,056	4,200,000
						1908	178,527	.72	____	3,552	4,000,000
1940	1,353,214	1.02	42,738	51,496	19,024,515	1907	166,095	.72	____	3,007	3,900,000
1939	1,264,962	1.02	33,095	72,076	18,483,012	1906	126,494	.73	____	3,525	3,800,000
1938	1,214,355	1.13	26,412	77,254	17,348,146	1905	134,717	.62	____	3,004	3,800,000

Series **M 138–142.** Crude Petroleum—Production, Value, Foreign Trade, and Proved Reserves: 1859 to 1970—Con.

[In thousands of 42-gallon barrels, except as indicated]

Year	Production	Average value at well per bbl.	Exports	Estimated proved reserves, Dec. 31	Year	Production	Average value at well per bbl.	Exports	Year	Production	Average value at well per bbl.	Exports
	138	139	141	142		138	139	141		138	139	141
1904	117,081	$0.86	2,647	3,600,000	1888	27,612	$0.65	1,846	1873	9,894	$1.83	468
1903	100,461	.94	3,012	3,400,000	1887	28,283	.67	1,920	1872	6,293	3.64	390
1902	88,767	.80	3,458	3,200,000	1886	28,065	.71	1,818	1871	5,205	4.34	269
1901	69,389	.96	3,024	3,000,000								
					1885	21,859	.88	1,939	1870	5,261	3.86	248
1900	63,621	1.19	3,290	2,900 000	1884	24,218	.85	1,897	1869	4,215	5.64	
1899	57,071	1.13	2,802	2,500,000	1883	23,450	1.10	1,405	1868	3,646	3.62	
1898	55,364	.80	2,736		1882	30,350	.78	1,072	1867	3,347	2.41	
1897	60,476	.68	2,893		1881	27,661	.92	963	1866	3,598	3.74	
1896	60,960	.96	2,641									
					1880	26,286	.94	875	1865	2,498	6.59	
1895	52,892	1.09	2,650		1879	19,914	.86	681	1864	2,116	8.06	
1894	49,344	.72	2,903		1878	15,397	1.17	573	1863	2,611	3.15	
1893	48,431	.60	2,660		1877	13,350	2.38	685	1862	3,057	1.05	
1892	50,515	.51	2,486		1876	9,133	2.52	603	1861	2,114	.49	
1891	54,293	.56	2,303									
					1875	12,163	1.35	394	1860	500	9.59	
1890	45,824	.77	2,299		1874	10,927	1.17	344	1859	2	16.00	
1889	35,164	.77	2,028									

Series **M 143–146.** Natural Gas Liquids—Production and Value: 1911 to 1970

[Quantities in millions of 42-gallon barrels, except as indicated]

Year	Natural gasoline and cycle products		Liquefied petroleum gases [1]		Year	Natural gasoline and cycle products		Liquefied petroleum gases [1]		Year	Natural gasoline and cycle products		Year	Natural gasoline and cycle products	
	Production	Average value at plant per bbl.	Production	Average value at plant per bbl.		Production	Average value at plant per bbl.	Production	Average value at plant per bbl.		Production	Average value at plant per bbl.		Production	Average value at plant per bbl.
	143	144	145	146		143	144	145	146		143	144		143	144
1970	206	$2.92	400	$1.68	1955	139	$3.05	142	$1.37	1940	56	$1.23	1925	27	$4.48
1969	202	2.99	378	1.32	1954	128	3.14	124	1.44	1939	52	1.74	1924	22	3.70
1968	199	2.87	351	1.57	1953	127	3.20	112	1.71	1938	51	1.70	1923	19	3.98
1967	188	2.91	327	1.94	1952	121	3.06	102	1.58	1937	49	1.98	1922	12	6.04
1966	179	2.89	289	1.82	1951	118	3.12	86	1.60	1936	43	1.98	1921	11	5.77
1965	174	2.85	268	1.56	1950	110	2.93	72	1.35	1935	39	1.80	1920	9	7.84
1964	167	2.78	256	1.42	1949	99	3.06	58	1.71	1934	37	1.66	1919	8	7.67
1963	156	2.82	245	1.47	1948	94	3.62	53	2.24	1933	34	1.61	1918	7	7.49
1962	149	2.99	224	1.58	1947	87	2.62	45	1.48	1932	36	1.36	1917	5	7.75
1961	145	2.83	216	1.71	1946	82	1.78	34	1.08	1931	44	1.46	1916	2	5.82
1960	139	3.00	201	1.95	1945	78	1.86	34	1.25	1930	53	2.44	1915	2	3.31
1959	133	3.07	187	1.87	1944	72	2.05	28	1.23	1929	53	2.98	1914	1	3.06
1958	133	2.95	162	1.84	1943	66	1.86	22	1.13	1928	43	3.22	1913	1	4.29
1957	137	3.05	158	1.66	1942	65	1.58	18	1.03	1927	39	3.04	1912	(Z)	4.02
1956	138	3.12	154	1.72	1941	64	1.65	17	.79	1926	32	4.20	1911	(Z)	3.01

Z Less than 500,000 barrels.   [1] Includes ethane.

Series **M 147–161.** Natural Gas—Marketed Production, Value at Well, Vented and Wasted, Repressuring, Proved Reserves, and Consumption: 1900 to 1970

[In billions of cubic feet, except as indicated]

Year	Marketed production	Average value at well (cents per 1,000 cu. ft.)	Vented and wasted	Used for repressuring	Estimated proved reserves, Dec. 31	Consumption Total	Residential	Commercial	Industrial Total	Field use [1]	Carbon black plants	Petroleum refineries	Used as pipeline fuel	Electric public utility power plants [2]	Other industrial [2]
	147	148	149	150	151	152	153	154	155	156	157	158	159	160	161
1970	21,921	17.1	489	1,376	290,746	22,046	4,837	2,056	15,152	2,305	86	1,029	722	3,894	7,116
1969	20,698	16.7	526	1,455	275,109	20,923	4,728	1,955	14,240	2,212	98	998	631	3,486	6,814
1968	19,322	16.4	517	1,486	287,350	19,460	4,450	1,801	13,209	2,065	105	974	591	3,144	6,330
1967	18,171	16.0	490	1,591	292,908	18,174	4,313	1,717	[3] 12,168	1,926	[3] 109	936	576	2,743	5,878
1966	17,207	15.7	376	1,452	289,333	17,192	4,138	1,623	[3] 11,454	1,773	[3] 115	903	535	2,609	5,519
1965	16,040	15.6	319	1,604	286,469	16,033	3,903	1,443	[3] 10,709	1,910	[3] 115	860	501	2,318	5,005
1964	15,462	15.4	340	1,638	281,251	15,452	3,767	1,367	[3] 10,327	2,082	[3] 116	821	433	2,322	4,554
1963	14,667	15.9	383	1,843	276,151	14,640	3,589	1,268	9,784	2,081	117	790	424	2,143	4,228
1962	13,801	15.5	426	1,737	272,279	13,890	3,479	1,207	9,205	1,993	133	790	382	1,966	3,941
1961	13,182	15.1	524	1,683	266,274	13,082	3,249	1,077	8,756	1,881	161	772	378	1,825	3,739
1960	12,771	14.0	563	1,753	262,326	12,510	3,103	1,020	8,386	1,780	198	775	347	1,725	3,562
1959	12,046	12.9	571	1,612	261,170	11,810	2,913	975	7,922	1,737	215	752	349	1,627	3,241
1958	11,030	11.9	633	1,483	252,762	10,761	2,714	872	7,175	1,604	211	682	312	1,373	2,992
1957	10,680	11.3	809	1,417	245,230	10,280	2,500	776	7,004	1,480	234	679	299	1,338	2,974
1956	10,082	10.8	864	1,427	236,483	9,708	2,328	717	6,662	1,421	243	679	296	1,239	2,785
1955	9,405	10.4	774	1,541	222,483	9,071	2,124	629	6,317	1,508	245	625	245	1,153	2,541
1954	8,743	10.1	724	1,519	210,561	8,403	1,894	585	5,924	1,457	251	563	231	1,165	2,256
1953	8,397	9.2	810	1,439	210,299	7,980	1,686	531	5,763	1,471	301	559	230	1,034	2,168
1952	8,013	7.8	849	1,411	198,632	7,614	1,622	516	5,476	1,484	368	536	207	910	1,970
1951	7,457	7.3	793	1,439	192,759	7,102	1,475	464	5,164	1,442	426	538	192	764	1,801
1950	6,282	6.5	801	1,399	184,585	6,026	1,198	388	4,440	1,187	411	455	126	629	1,632
1949	5,420	6.3	854	1,273	179,402	5,197	993	348	3,855	1,060	428	422	[4]	550	1,395
1948	5,148	6.5	810	1,221	172,925	4,946	896	323	3,725	1,022	481	441	--------	478	1,304
1947	4,582	6.0	1,068	1,083	165,026	4,427	802	285	3,339	934	485	364	--------	373	1,184
1946	4,153	5.3	1,102	1,038	159,704	4,013	661	242	3,110	898	478	332	--------	307	1,096
1945	4,042	4.9	896	1,062	146,987	3,900	607	230	3,063	917	432	338	--------	326	1,050
1944	3,815	5.1	1,010	883	133,500	3,697	562	221	2,914	855	356	315	--------	360	1,028
1943	3,516	5.2	684	825	110,000	3,404	529	205	2,669	781	316	244	--------	306	1,024
1942	3,146	5.1	627	753	110,000	3,046	499	184	2,363	721	336	202	--------	239	866
1941	2,894	4.9	630	644	113,800	2,805	442	145	2,218	686	365	148	--------	205	813
1940	2,734	4.5	656	363	85,000	2,656	444	135	2,076	712	369	128	--------	183	685
1939	2,538	4.9	677	171	(NA)	2,473	391	118	1,964	681	347	98	--------	191	647
1938	2,358	4.9	649	102	70,000	2,294	368	114	1,812	659	325	110	--------	170	548
1937	2,473	5.1	526	85	66,000	2,402	372	117	1,913	651	341	113	--------	171	638
1936	2,225	5.5	393	74	(NA)	2,160	343	112	1,706	618	283	93	--------	156	554
1935	1,969	5.8	481		(NA)	1,909	313	100	1,496	580	242	80	--------	125	469
1934	1,816	6.0	463		62,000	1,765	288	91	1,385	555	230	80	--------	128	393
1933	1,597	6.2	406		(NA)	1,553	283	86	1,184	491	190	66	--------	103	334
1932	1,594	6.4	408		(NA)	1,554	299	87	1,168	529	168	67	--------	107	296
1931	1,722	7.0	447		(NA)	1,679	294	81	1,304	571	196	[5]	--------	[5]	537
1930	1,979	7.6	519		46,000	1,942	296	81	1,565	723	267	--------	--------	--------	575
1929	1,952	8.2	481		(NA)	1,917	360		1,557	705	261	--------	--------	--------	591
1928	1,596	8.9	470		(NA)	1,568	321		1,247	574	175	--------	--------	--------	498
1927	1,471	8.8	434		(NA)	1,445	296		1,149	549	144	--------	--------	--------	456
1926	1,336	9.5	399		(NA)	1,313	289		1,024	478	131	--------	--------	--------	415
1925	1,210	9.4	356		23,000	1,188	272		916	424	140	--------	--------	--------	352
1924	1,162	9.3	342		--------	1,141	285		856	393	157	--------	--------	--------	306
1923	1,025	10.0	302		--------	1,007	277		730	343	109	--------	--------	--------	278
1922	776	11.1	229		--------	763	255		508	198	54	--------	--------	--------	256
1921	674		198		--------	662	248		414	182	51	--------	--------	--------	181
1920	812	--------	239		--------	798	286		512	202	41	--------	--------	--------	269
1919	746	--------	--------	--------	--------	746	256		490	170	50	--------	--------	--------	270
1918	721					721	271		450						
1917	795					795	258		537						
1916	753					753	235		518						
1915	629					629	217		412						
1914	592					592	203		389						
1913	582					582	185		397						
1912	562					562	193		368						
1911	513					513	175		338						
1910	509					509	170		339						
1909	481					481	151		330						
1908	402					402	141		261						
1907	407					407	132		275						
1906	389					389	110		279						
1905	320														
1904	257														
1903	239														
1902	206														
1901	180														
1900	128														

NA Not available.
[1] Includes pumping, drilling, extraction loss (shrinkage), and plant fuel.
[2] Consumption by electric public utility power plants includes small quantities of gas other than natural, impossible to segregate. To this extent, consumption by other industrials is understated.
[3] For 1964–1967, includes natural gas to enrich hydrocarbons.
[4] Included in "Other industrial" prior to 1950.
[5] Included in "Other industrial" prior to 1931.

Series M 162–177. Input and Output of Petroleum Products at Refineries: 1916 to 1970

Year	Input (1,000 bbl.)				Output (1,000 bbl.)												
	Total	Crude petroleum		Natural-gas liquids	Total	Gaso-line[1]	Kero-sene[2]	Distil-late	Resid-ual	Lubri-cating oil	Wax	Coke	Asphalt	Still gas	Road oil	Other finished products
		Domestic	Foreign													
	162	163	164	165	166	167	168	169	170	171	172	173	174	175	176	177
1970	4,252,075	3,485,332	482,171	284,572	4,421,218	2,130,107	94,635	895,656	257,510	66,183	6,294	107,871	146,658	163,905	9,393	543,006
1969	4,148,406	3,363,602	516,003	268,801	4,305,477	2,050,804	101,738	846,863	265,906	65,080	6,362	102,868	135,691	160,363	9,086	560,716
1968	4,037,073	3,308,044	466,316	262,713	4,179,916	1,961,470	100,545	839,373	275,814	65,684	5,887	95,190	135,460	149,796	6,826	543,871
1967	3,827,401	3,174,004	408,590	244,807	3,968,230	1,865,434	99,061	804,429	275,956	64,870	5,719	90,933	127,767	140,034	6,978	487,049
1966	3,682,803	3,000,789	446,404	235,610	3,806,970	1,813,334	100,849	784,717	263,961	65,407	5,772	88,054	129,579	135,459	7,247	412,591
1965	3,526,531	2,847,821	453,021	225,689	3,638,883	1,722,475	93,149	765,071	268,567	62,925	5,456	86,040	123,604	135,295	6,565	369,736
1964	3,436,622	2,785,895	437,434	213,293	3,543,279	1,675,278	93,474	742,046	266,825	63,668	5,352	84,325	114,879	131,257	6,371	359,804
1963	3,360,875	2,758,168	412,484	190,223	3,466,519	1,603,896	164,805	764,597	275,910	63,086	5,126	80,688	111,948	129,598	6,792	260,073
1962	3,252,478	2,659,826	409,805	182,847	3,344,112	1,570,553	156,373	719,590	295,679	61,467	5,353	78,724	109,576	130,829	7,079	208,889
1961	3,156,605	2,604,127	383,031	169,447	3,241,294	1,512,324	141,410	696,015	315,577	59,254	5,781	75,333	101,819	127,537	5,820	200,424
1960	3,119,327	2,581,568	370,966	166,793	3,194,703	1,510,134	135,772	667,050	332,147	59,389	5,896	60,010	98,671	129,480	5,970	190,184
1959	3,070,984	2,565,504	352,157	153,323	3,128,361	1,473,430	110,662	678,938	347,900	56,111	5,630	41,117	97,643	126,958	6,493	183,479
1958	2,926,673	2,444,229	345,175	137,269	2,982,358	1,411,956	110,008	631,405	363,358	51,298	5,252	37,808	89,380	125,951	5,925	150,017
1957	3,040,526	2,529,672	360,764	150,090	3,055,685	1,415,335	108,929	668,573	415,656	55,723	5,461	33,466	85,683	125,720	7,209	133,930
1956	3,040,168	2,563,655	341,451	135,062	3,059,880	1,396,787	123,480	665,687	426,699	59,211	5,367	31,095	90,636	121,993	8,027	130,898
1955	2,856,600	2,446,833	283,385	126,382	2,880,187	1,331,528	117,137	602,547	420,331	55,836	5,293	28,337	83,121	116,506	8,482	111,069
1954	2,657,113	2,300,766	238,798	117,549	2,673,555	1,232,989	123,200	542,278	416,757	53,243	5,290	24,284	74,912	102,552	7,213	91,732
1953	2,666,158	2,321,820	233,045	111,293	2,673,764	1,233,954	123,200	528,111	449,979	52,545	4,978	21,607	72,409	102,243	6,594	78,144
1952	2,545,157	2,235,198	206,061	103,898	2,551,845	1,141,467	128,767	517,920	453,897	55,600	4,331	18,123	70,312	95,275	6,998	59,155
1951	2,469,654	2,188,677	181,727	99,250	2,484,022	1,108,880	135,742	475,801	469,377	61,489	4,814	18,977	66,302	96,294	6,100	40,246
1950	2,189,506	1,918,854	176,013	94,639	2,196,866	998,093	118,512	398,912	425,217	51,735	4,462	17,224	58,240	83,743	6,928	33,800
1949	2,029,678	1,789,756	154,465	85,457	2,039,517	939,051	102,152	340,825	424,909	45,389	3,208	16,959	49,007	82,621	7,691	27,705
1948	2,124,567	1,924,335	124,014	76,218	2,118,252	895,986	121,914	379,340	479,988	51,416	3,515	14,494	51,919	81,159	7,916	30,605
1947	1,922,938	1,754,987	97,259	70,692	1,918,959	814,841	110,412	312,173	447,795	51,765	3,624	12,077	49,286	85,564	7,074	24,348
1946	1,793,058	1,645,845	84,352	62,861	1,793,086	748,411	104,385	287,896	431,364	45,645	3,003	10,621	44,911	88,136	6,175	22,539
1945	1,789,858	1,645,862	73,672	70,324	1,793,523	774,460	81,024	249,224	469,492	41,867	2,921	10,115	39,196	103,458	2,686	19,080
1944	1,732,891	1,622,514	43,170	67,207	1,715,385	722,718	78,344	239,152	461,455	41,106	2,883	9,017	38,479	102,239	1,556	18,436
1943	1,490,936	1,417,559	12,179	61,198	1,477,707	592,425	72,270	211,516	417,306	38,679	2,697	6,942	37,162	86,755	2,295	9,660
1942	1,390,698	1,319,507	14,596	56,595	1,387,591	586,971	67,474	196,714	358,901	38,626	2,502	6,692	34,631	78,924	8,039	8,117
1941	1,457,017	1,358,246	50,946	47,825	1,460,252	671,110	72,586	189,177	342,367	39,539	2,393	8,244	36,067	83,354	9,149	6,266
1940	1,333,709	1,252,364	41,798	39,547	1,333,342	597,375	73,882	183,304	316,221	36,765	1,833	7,633	29,406	75,950	7,771	3,202
1939	1,277,446	1,204,350	33,490	39,606	1,283,993	596,501	68,521	161,746	305,944	35,036	1,659	8,332	27,248	68,779	7,868	2,359
1938	1,204,976	1,138,828	26,187	39,961	1,206,880	556,012	64,580	151,774	294,890	30,826	1,555	8,011	23,878	65,890	7,543	1,921
1937	1,222,821	1,157,444	25,996	39,381	1,224,624	559,141	65,308	146,706	312,064	35,321	1,863	6,533	23,001	64,218	8,087	2,382
1936	1,102,387	1,034,637	33,933	33,817	1,102,144	504,811	56,082	125,906	287,968	30,927	1,689	6,891	21,278	57,046	7,398	2,148
1935	996,815	933,659	32,131	31,025	986,702	457,842	55,813	100,235	259,826	27,853	1,608	7,290	17,133	51,184	6,030	1,888
1934	923,798	860,776	34,860	28,162	908,883	416,932	53,855	94,972	240,381	26,373	1,674	6,500	15,623	44,391	6,310	1,872
1933	886,600	825,786	35,468	25,346	865,297	401,591	48,977	78,920	237,519	23,775	1,677	7,900	45,212	45,212	5,534	1,435
1932	846,329	777,696	42,301	26,332	827,538	392,623	43,836	69,467	225,283	22,433	1,639	9,123	13,612	40,905	6,879	1,738
1931	929,724	847,671	46,937	35,116	914,023	431,510	42,446	83,882	253,085	26,704	1,705	10,363	16,371	38,630	5,177	4,150
1930	970,617	866,615	60,832	43,170	931,372	432,241	49,208	81,551	290,947	34,201	1,956	9,895	18,194		5,425	7,754
1929	1,034,165	912,191	75,517	46,457	1,013,070	435,078	55,940		448,949	34,359	2,261	7,390	19,169		9,924	
1928	948,518	835,711	77,584	35,223	935,448	376,945	59,353		427,237	34,658	2,257	7,344	18,252		9,402	
1927	860,997	778,729	50,106	32,162	845,480	330,435	56,113		393,066	31,721	2,089	5,858	18,793		7,405	
1926	806,960	734,301	44,963	27,696	791,100	299,734	61,768		365,195	32,293	2,310	5,316	16,454		8,030	
1925	759,556	698,582	41,338	19,636	745,863	259,601	59,689		364,991	31,055	2,135	5,281	15,067		8,044	
1924	656,390	597,954	45,765	12,671	649,720	213,326	60,026		320,476	27,498	1,861	4,085	14,196		8,252	
1923	586,725	538,252	42,986	5,487	572,814	179,903	55,927		287,481	26,128	1,684	3,717	12,888		5,086	
1922	504,368	425,823	74,883	3,662		147,672	54,913		254,910	23,304						
1921	445,880	368,037	75,326	2,517		122,704	46,318		230,091	20,896						
1920	437,068	372,779	61,136	3,153		116,251	55,240		210,987	24,938						
1919	364,477	327,533	33,987	2,957		94,235	55,753		181,602	20,161						
1918	328,476	324,618	1,407	2,451		85,007	43,461		174,319	20,035						
1917		315,132				67,870	41,114		155,079	17,947						
1916		246,992				49,021	34,655		111,045	14,870						

[1] Includes special naphtha; beginning 1952, includes unfinished gasoline production.   [2] Beginning 1964, kerosene-type jet fuel is included with other finished products.

Series M 178–187. Petroluem Products—Imports and Exports: 1920 to 1970

Year	Imports (1,000 bbl.)			Exports (1,000 bbl.)						
	Total[1]	Distillate[2]	Residual	Total[1]	Gasoline	Kerosene	Distillate	Residual	Lubricants	Petroleum wax
	178	179	180	181	182	183	184	185	186	187
1970	764,769	53,826	557,845	89,467	1,370	121	898	19,785	16,090	1,808
1969	641,437	50,883	461,611	83,449	2,449	155	1,123	16,891	16,396	1,623
1968	567,046	48,148	409,928	82,742	2,083	613	1,547	20,013	18,001	1,588
1967	514,342	18,492	395,939	85,519	4,877	156	4,269	21,940	18,695	1,687
1966	492,042	13,845	376,795	70,923	5,796	254	4,377	12,895	17,112	1,888
1965	448,732	13,002	345,187	67,191	6,391	219	3,830	14,882	16,592	1,654
1964	388,093	11,785	295,771	72,516	8,039	170	5,386	18,870	18,176	1,734
1963	362,053	9,110	272,753	74,216	6,986	672	15,014	15,281	18,317	1,455
1962	348,754	11,831	264,314	59,600	6,592	337	8,224	12,850	17,693	1,429
1961	318,118	17,377	243,268	60,336	8,976	231	6,931	14,022	17,094	1,237
1960	292,536	12,771	233,208	70,819	13,456	689	9,897	18,495	15,811	1,333
1959	297,239	17,658	222,571	74,541	16,743	944	12,734	20,815	13,972	1,031
1958	272,582	14,892	182,036	96,292	27,403	1,217	18,942	25,743	13,003	911
1957	201,334	8,566	173,299	156,944	38,588	5,258	47,752	38,570	13,826	666
1956	183,758	5,159	162,869	128,762	35,572	3,297	34,535	27,877	13,859	920

See footnotes at end of table.

Series **M 178–187.** Petroleum Products—Imports and Exports: 1920 to 1970—Con.

Year	Imports (1,000 bbl.)			Exports (1,000 bbl.)						
	Total [1]	Distillate [2]	Residual	Total [1]	Gasoline	Kerosene	Distillate	Residual	Lubricants	Petroleum wax
	178	179	180	181	182	183	184	185	186	187
1955	170,143	4,413	152,035	122,617	34,521	3,335	24,605	33,799	14,298	1,248
1954	144,476	3,195	129,124	116,134	34,366	4,852	24,223	26,753	15,075	1,342
1953	141,044	3,379	131,533	126,660	37,925	7,265	32,328	25,991	12,999	1,126
1952	138,916	2,742	128,479	131,492	36,285	7,821	33,515	27,701	16,031	1,036
1951	129,121	1,767	119,166	125,448	40,136	6,843	22,555	28,999	17,429	1,349
1950	132,547	2,602	120,036	76,483	24,721	2,078	12,563	16,223	14,252	1,193
1949	81,873	1,825	75,175	86,307	39,347	2,533	12,295	12,641	12,612	1,031
1948	59,051	2,546	53,269	94,938	37,302	3,495	21,293	13,011	13,392	994
1947	61,857	4,175	54,244	118,122	47,449	7,252	29,877	10,623	14,871	1,107
1946	51,610	5,204	44,647	110,687	45,334	8,637	29,487	9,188	11,051	718
1945	39,282	4,754	31,648	149,985	88,059	6,180	33,496	11,669	6,575	566
1944	47,506	7,022	36,485	173,378	100,537	4,888	43,491	12,536	8,709	579
1943	49,579	15,269	27,210	108,615	51,577	4,752	24,957	14,894	8,863	617
1942	23,669	3,636	18,432	83,073	35,097	2,576	21,575	12,095	8,272	548
1941	46,536	5,074	37,369	75,592	27,083	3,221	16,925	14,114	9,924	761
1940	41,089	3,333	29,366	78,970	25,377	3,374	19,140	16,109	10,461	678
1939	25,965	(NA)	15,680	116,883	44,638	8,241	32,020	17,485	11,881	831
1938	27,896	(NA)	21,065	116,474	50,109	7,504	29,641	17,920	9,417	719
1937	29,673	17	22,114	102,077	34,782	8,885	30,129	15,304	10,975	829
1936	24,777	182	18,801	79,133	26,098	6,936	20,448	14,435	8,691	669
1935	20,396	15	16,115	74,343	27,399	6,651	16,249	12,699	8,499	821
1934	14,936	12,634		71,737	23,043	9,781	14,506	14,099	7,660	711
1933	13,501	13,215		67,572	26,750	8,959	11,424	9,139	8,218	885
1932	29,812	21,286		74,263	33,819	11,044	8,782	11,212	6,851	840
1931	38,837	24,998		98,859	45,716	12,712	29,231		8,128	1,038
1930	43,489	26,080		132,794	65,575	16,884	36,450		9,935	1,046
1929	29,777	20,545		136,719	62,059	20,022	39,151		10,860	1,140
1928	11,782	7,268		135,991	53,412	22,034	44,427		11,023	1,403
1927	13,353	8,124		125,805	44,951	19,537	47,391		9,776	1,216
1926	20,938	14,432		116,543	43,769	22,248	38,351		9,435	1,199
1925	16,376	12,245		100,497	31,684	21,212	36,088		9,678	1,193
1924	16,806	12,927		98,905	29,151	21,961	37,249		9,103	1,367
1923	17,638	12,286		84,447	21,094	20,347	33,372		8,372	1,178
1922	8,665	[3] 2,947		63,539	14,362	21,489	18,479		7,941	1,016
1921	3,428			62,025	13,363	18,016	22,676		6,936	807
1920	2,647			70,281	15,678	20,857	22,080		9,643	1,340

NA Not available.   [1] Includes other entries not shown separately.   [2] Beginning 1952, excludes all distillate used as jet component.   [3] Oct. through Dec. only.

Series **M 188–204.** Nonmetals: 1818 to 1970

Year	Cement		Crude gypsum mined	Lime		Sand and gravel, sold or used	Stone, sold or used by producers	Sulfur			Pyrites		Salt, sold or used by producers	Potash		Phosphate rock	
	Shipments	Average value of portland cement		Sold by producers	Average value per short ton			Production from Frasch mines	Crude imports [1]	Crude exports	Production	Imports		Sold by producers	Imports	Sold or used by producers	Exports
	188	189	190	191	192	193	194	195	196	197	198	199	200	201	202	203	204
	1,000 bbl.	Dol. per bbl.	1,000 short tons	1,000 short tons	Dol.	1,000 short tons	1,000 short tons	1,000 long tons	1,000 long tons	1,000 long tons	1,000 long tons	1,000 long tons	1,000 short tons	1,000 short tons	1,000 short tons	1,000 short tons	1,000 short tons
1970	406,304	3.32	9,436	19,788	14.53	943,941	874,512	7,082	1,537	1,429	845	130	45,896	2,669	2,612	37,923	11,738
1969	427,227	3.20	9,881	20,209	13.89	937,169	862,889	7,146	1,675	1,549	821	120	44,245	3,069	2,340	36,730	11,336
1968	414,786	3.16	10,018	18,637	13.39	917,468	819,597	7,460	1,572	1,549	872	140	41,274	2,913	2,172	37,319	12,099
1967	390,271	3.14	9,393	17,985	13.36	907,045	785,592	7,014	1,474	2,043	861	165	38,946	3,126	1,708	37,835	10,072
1966	397,459	3.12	9,647	18,057	13.27	934,481	813,374	7,002	1,514	2,326	872	160	36,463	3,133	1,491	36,443	9,248
1965	391,686	3.15	10,103	16,794	13.87	908,049	780,242	6,116	1,486	2,624	875	160	34,687	2,931	1,108	29,039	7,323
1964	383,266	3.19	10,684	16,089	13.87	868,208	725,583	5,228	1,462	1,920	847	120	31,623	3,045	737	24,731	6,374
1963	365,241	3.20	10,388	14,521	13.73	821,850	688,366	4,882	1,351	1,603	825	194	30,641	2,709	594	22,243	5,093
1962	347,117	3.29	9,969	13,753	13.58	776,701	656,954	4,985	1,040	1,537	916	302	28,807	2,722	341	21,347	4,406
1961	335,374	3.32	9,500	13,249	13.39	751,784	611,938	5,385	836	1,586	987	282	25,707	2,487	262	19,983	4,388
1960	327,087	3.37	9,825	12,935	13.35	709,792	616,784	4,943	741	1,776	1,016	306	25,479	2,602	226	19,266	4,473
1959	352,067	3.28	10,900	12,500	13.11	730,205	584,163	4,554	642	1,612	1,057	281	25,160	2,476	234	17,993	3,414
1958	322,011	3.25	9,600	9,211	13.16	684,498	535,923	4,643	591	1,578	974	343	21,912	2,336	199	16,528	3,017
1957	304,741	3.18	9,195	10,274	13.17	632,255	533,423	5,491	499	1,578	1,067	[2] 71	23,854	2,137	182	16,349	3,371
1956	325,650	3.05	10,317	10,577	12.83	626,495	507,511	6,424	212	1,651	1,070	[2] 73	24,216	2,103	181	15,804	3,007
1955	310,245	2.89	10,684	10,480	12.13	592,153	471,251	5,739	35	1,601	1,007	[2] 80	22,704	2,006	178	14,768	2,445
1954	278,385	2.76	8,996	8,629	11.79	556,537	412,060	5,515	(Z)	1,645	909	[2] 47	20,669	1,918	119	14,609	2,552
1953	261,338	2.67	8,293	9,674	11.59	440,399	306,842	5,155	1	1,242	923	190	20,789	1,732	134	14,020	2,309
1952	254,816	2.54	8,415	8,073	11.80	435,622	301,586	5,293	5	1,304	994	296	19,545	1,598	188	12,683	1,570
1951	244,629	2.54	8,666	8,256	11.74	400,634	285,542	5,278	2	1,288	1,018	221	20,207	1,408	314	12,426	1,878
1950	231,975	2.35	8,193	7,478	11.13	370,455	252,106	5,192	(NA)	1,441	931	209	16,630	1,276	201	11,484	1,971
1949	209,314	2.30	6,608	6,318	10.97	319,104	224,027	4,745	(Z)	1,431	888	121	15,572	1,121	19	10,065	1,475
1948	207,680	2.18	7,255	7,264	10.35	319,266	225,535	4,869	(NA)	1,263	929	107	16,403	1,143	27	9,709	1,139
1947	190,420	1.90	6,208	6,779	9.42	287,659	207,555	4,441	(NA)	1,299	941	127	16,054	1,053	26	10,110	1,842
1946	172,101	1.72	5,629	5,993	8.52	254,131	178,852	3,860	(NA)	1,189	813	183	15,132	928	4	7,684	783
1945	107,833	1.63	3,812	5,921	7.76	195,524	153,405	3,753	(NA)	919	723	187	15,394	870	6	6,504	550
1944	95,592	1.59	3,761	6,474	7.52	194,783	155,580	3,218	(NA)	654	789	181	15,717	818	5	6,022	492
1943	129,479	1.57	3,878	6,597	7.44	234,064	171,343	2,539	(NA)	657	802	256	15,214	732	17	5,741	401
1942	187,809	1.53	4,698	6,104	7.27	304,346	195,884	3,461	(NA)	568	720	300	13,693	681	4	5,201	592
1941	170,365	1.47	4,789	6,079	7.06	288,715	183,108	3,139	(NA)	729	645	369	12,721	531	16	5,253	1,142

See footnotes at end of table.

Series M 188–204. Nonmetals: 1818 to 1970—Con.

Year	Cement: Shipments (188)	Cement: Avg. value of portland cement (189)	Crude gypsum mined (190)	Lime: Sold by producers (191)	Lime: Avg. value per short ton (192)	Sand and gravel, sold or used (193)	Stone, sold or used by producers (194)	Sulfur: Production from Frasch mines (195)	Sulfur: Crude imports [1] (196)	Sulfur: Crude exports (197)	Pyrites: Production (198)	Pyrites: Imports (199)	Salt, sold or used by producers (200)	Potash: Sold by producers (201)	Potash: Imports (202)	Phosphate rock: Sold or used by producers (203)	Phosphate rock: Exports (204)
	1,000 bbl.	*Dol. per bbl.*	*1,000 short tons*	*1,000 short tons*	*Dol.*	*1,000 short tons*	*1,000 short tons*	*1,000 long tons*	*1,000 long tons*	*1,000 long tons*	*1,000 long tons*	*1,000 long tons*	*1,000 short tons*	*1,000 short tons*	*1,000 short tons*	*1,000 short tons*	*1,000 short tons*
1940	132,864	1.46	3,699	4,887	6.95	238,308	153,733	2,732	(NA)	746	627	407	10,360	393	119	4,483	841
1939	125,057	1.47	3,227	4,254	7.06	226,008	147,447	2,091	(Z)	628	519	482	9,278	366	100	4,208	1,063
1938	108,192	1.45	2,684	3,347	7.21	181,320	124,839	2,393	(Z)	579	556	334	8,026	286	194	4,188	1,278
1937	115,678	1.48	3,058	4,124	7.30	189,660	133,143	2,742	(Z)	675	584	524	9,242	267	351	4,431	1,179
1936	114,611	1.51	2,713	3,749	7.18	178,330	131,416	2,016	1	547	547	429	8,829	223	212	3,754	1,354
1935	76,244	1.51	1,904	2,987	7.28	123,924	83,159	1,633	2	402	514	397	7,927	225	242	3,407	1,236
1934	76,579	1.54	1,536	2,397	7.16	116,612	92,064	1,421	6	507	433	366	7,612	114	172	3,175	1,112
1933	64,761	1.33	1,335	2,269	6.28	107,755	70,222	1,406	5	523	284	373	7,605	139	172	2,789	928
1932	81,368	1.01	1,416	1,960	6.28	120,038	70,644	890	(NA)	353	190	253	6,408	56	114	1,912	687
1931	128,377	1.11	2,559	2,708	6.90	153,479	97,933	2,129	(NA)	408	331	352	7,358	64	215	2,839	1,065
1930	160,846	1.44	3,471	3,388	7.56	197,052	126,996	2,559	(Z)	593	348	355	8,054	57	342	4,397	1,373
1929	172,027	1.48	5,016	4,270	7.84	222,572	141,110	2,362	1	855	333	514	8,545	58	325	4,212	1,280
1928	178,052	1.57	5,102	4,458	8.18	209,119	133,870	1,982	5	685	313	457	8,075	60	330	3,921	1,007
1927	174,023	1.62	5,347	4,415	8.75	197,454	136,345	2,112	3	789	303	251	7,569	50	244	3,552	1,028
1926	164,219	1.71	5,635	4,560	9.11	183,101	124,496	1,890	(Z)	577	227	366	7,372	25	266	3,595	839
1925	159,047	1.77	5,678	4,581	9.30	172,001	115,851	1,409	(Z)	629	194	276	7,398	26	258	3,900	974
1924	147,466	1.81	5,043	4,072	9.72	156,230	103,184	1,221	1	482	168	247	6,803	22	200	3,212	917
1923	137,184	1.90	4,753	4,076	9.81	139,932	103,319	2,036	(Z)	473	191	264	7,131	19	210	3,368	927
1922	118,591	1.76	3,780	3,640	9.14	94,867	80,212	1,831	(Z)	486	173	279	6,793	11	201	2,708	805
1921	96,047	1.89	2,891	2,532	9.83	79,845	63,539	1,879	(Z)	286	157	216	4,981	4	79	2,312	821
1920	97,079	2.02	3,129	3,570	10.52	82,041	78,527	1,255	(Z)	477	311	333	6,840	41	225	4,596	1,198
1919	86,141	1.71	2,420	3,330	8.84	70,576	65,539	1,191	(Z)	225	421	389	6,883	46	40	2,545	424
1918	71,348	1.60	2,057	3,206	8.36	61,824	68,563	1,354	(Z)	131	464	497	7,239	39	8	2,790	160
1917	91,343	1.35	2,696	3,786	6.29	76,419	83,575	1,134	1	153	483	967	6,978	33	8	2,894	186
1916	95,394	1.10	2,758	4,073	4.54	89,092	91,831	650	21	129	439	1,245	6,363	10	8	2,220	273
1915	87,685	.86	2,448	3,623	3.98	76,603	-------	521	25	37	394	965	5,352	1	49	2,056	283
1914	87,258	.93	2,476	3,381	3.92	79,282	-------	418	24	98	337	1,027	4,873	-------	207	3,062	1,080
1913	89,541	1.00	2,600	3,595	4.07	79,556	-------	491	15	89	341	851	4,816	-------	272	3,484	1,531
1912	85,926	.81	2,501	3,529	3.96	68,355	-------	788	27	58	351	971	4,665	-------	254	3,330	1,352
1911	79,548	.84	2,324	3,393	4.03	66,847	-------	205	24	28	301	1,006	4,366	-------	274	3,419	1,397
1910	77,785	.89	2,379	3,506	4.02	69,410	-------	247	29	31	242	804	4,243	-------	280	2,974	1,213
1909	66,690	.81	2,253	3,485	3.98	59,566	-------	274	29	37	247	689	4,215	-------	173	2,619	1,144
1908	52,911	.85	1,722	2,767	4.01	37,216	-------	364	20	28	223	668	4,035	-------	136	2,672	1,331
1907	52,230	1.11	1,752	3,093	4.09	41,852	-------	189	20	36	247	628	4,159	-------	144	2,537	1,140
1906	51,000	1.13	1,541	3,198	3.90	32,932	-------	295	72	14	261	598	3,944	-------	156	2,331	-------
1905	40,102	.94	1,043	2,984	3.67	23,205	-------	220	83	12	253	512	3,635	-------	129	2,181	-------
1904	31,675	.88	941	2,708	3.68	10,680	-------	85	128	3	207	423	3,084	-------	-------	2,099	-------
1903	29,899	1.24	1,042	(NA)	(NA)	2,111	-------	7[3]	189	-------	226[3]	420	2,656	-------	-------	1,772	-------
1902	25,754	1.21	816	(NA)	(NA)	1,848	-------	7[3]	171	-------	200[3]	440	3,339	-------	-------	1,669	-------
1901	20,069	.99	634	(NA)	(NA)	-------	-------	7[4]	174	-------	235	404	2,879	-------	-------	1,662	-------
1900	17,231	1.09	594	(NA)	(NA)	-------	-------	3	167	-------	205	322	2,922	-------	-------	1,670	-------
1899	15,855	1.43	486	(NA)	(NA)	-------	-------	4	140	-------	175	270	2,759	-------	-------	1,698	-------
1898	12,344	1.62	292	(NA)	(NA)	-------	-------	1	151	-------	193	253	2,466	-------	-------	1,466	-------
1897	11,038	1.61	289	(NA)	(NA)	-------	-------	2	137	-------	143	260	2,236	-------	-------	1,164	-------
1896	9,526	1.57	224	(NA)	(NA)	-------	-------	5	138	-------	115	200	1,939	-------	-------	1,043	-------
1895	8,731	1.60	266	(NA)	(NA)	-------	-------	2	121	-------	100	190	1,914	-------	-------	1,164	-------
1894	8,362	1.73	239	(NA)	(NA)	-------	-------	(Z)	125	-------	106	164	1,816	-------	-------	1,117	-------
1893	8,002	1.96	254	(NA)	(NA)	-------	-------	1	106	-------	76	195	1,666	-------	-------	1,054	-------
1892	8,759	2.11	256	(NA)	(NA)	-------	-------	2	101	-------	110	152	1,638	-------	-------	764	-------
1891	8,223	2.13	208	(NA)	(NA)	-------	-------	1	117	-------	107	101	1,398	-------	-------	659	-------
1890	7,777	2.09	183	(NA)	(NA)	-------	-------	(NA)	163	-------	100	(NA)	1,243	-------	-------	571	-------
1889	6,832	1.67	268	(NA)	(NA)	-------	-------	(Z)	136	-------	94	(NA)	1,121	-------	-------	612	-------
1888	6,503	} 1.95	110	4,909	5.00	-------	-------	(NA)	98	-------	54	(NA)	1,128	-------	-------	506	-------
1887	6,943		95	4,675	5.00	-------	-------	3	97	-------	52	17	1,121	-------	-------	539	-------
1886	4,500		95	4,250	5.00	-------	-------	2	118	-------	55	2	1,079	-------	-------	483	-------
1885	4,150		90	4,000	5.00	-------	-------	1	97	-------	49	6	985	-------	-------	754	-------
1884	4,000	2.10	90	3,700	5.00	-------	-------	(Z)	105	-------	35	17	912	-------	-------	484	-------
1883	4,190	2.15	90	3,200	6.00	-------	-------	1	95	-------	25	-------	867	-------	-------	423	-------
1882	3,250	2.25	100	3,100	7.00	-------	-------	1	98	-------	12	-------	898	-------	-------	372	-------
1881	2,500	2.50	85	3,000	-------	-------	-------	1	105	-------	10	-------	868	-------	-------	299	-------
1880	2,073	} 3.00	90	2,800	-------	-------	-------	1	88	-------	2	-------	835	-------	-------	236	-------
1870–1879	22,082																
1860–1869	16,420																
1850–1859	11,000																
1840–1849	4,250																
1830–1839	1,000																
1818–1829	300																

Sulfur, crude imports [1] (196)

Year	Sulfur, crude imports [1] (196)	Year	Sulfur, crude imports [1] (196)	Year	Sulfur, crude imports [1] (196)	Year	Sulfur, crude imports [1] (196)
	1,000 long tons		*1,000 long tons*		*1,000 long tons*		*1,000 long tons*
1879	70	1875	40	1872	25	1869	24
1878	48	1874	41	1871	36	1868	18
1877	43	1873	46	1870	27	1867	25
1876	46						

NA Not available.   Z Less than 500 long tons.

[1] Includes elemental Frasch and recovered imports.

[2] Not strictly comparable with years prior to 1954 or after 1957. Estimated comparable totals should include an additional 232,920 long tons in 1954; 277,860 in 1955; 292,520 in 1956; and 282,000 in 1957.

[3] Tonnage calculated from combined total of domestic sulfur and sulfur content of pyrites produced.

[4] Quantity derived from figures in metric tons (*Mineral Resources of the United States, 1903*).

Series M 205–220. Iron Ore and Pig Iron: 1799 to 1970

[Quantities for iron ore in thousands of long tons; for pig iron, shipments in thousands of long tons; imports and exports in thousands of short tons]

Year	Iron ore Production	Shipments Quantity Total	Shipments Quantity Beneficiated	Average value per long ton	Price Mesabi, non-Bessemer, per long ton	Foreign trade Imports	Foreign trade Exports	Production by mining method[1] Underground	Open pit	Employment Average workers on active days	Average days worked	Average hours per shift	Pig iron Shipments	Average price per long ton[2]	Imports	Exports
	205	206	207	208	209	210	211	212	213	214	215	216	217	218	219	220
1970	89,760	87,176	79,779	$10.80	$10.80	44,876	5,492	13,209	199,252	[3]17,041	[3]319	[3]8.0	82,314	$69.69	249	310
1969	88,328	89,854	80,157	10.34	10.55	40,732	5,160	13,283	193,860	18,646	285	8.0	85,243	64.09	405	44
1968	85,865	81,934	72,781	10.21	10.55	43,941	5,884	12,703	183,229	18,000	300	8.0	79,540	63.00	786	9
1967	84,179	82,415	66,243	9.92	10.55	44,611	5,906	13,815	169,582	18,760	290	8.0	77,517	63.00	605	7
1966	90,147	90,041	70,451	9.49	10.55	46,259	7,779	18,214	164,165	20,341	284	8.0	81,146	63.00	1,187	12
1965	87,439	84,073	64,667	9.53	10.55	45,103	7,085	17,586	160,355	20,773	278	8.0	78,921	63.00	882	28
1964	84,836	84,300	64,329	9.52	10.55	42,408	6,963	10,980	162,635	20,661	267	8.0	76,512	63.00	736	176
1963	73,599	73,564	57,277	9.22	10.65	33,263	6,812	8,572	144,204	18,199	261	8.1	64,474	63.00	645	70
1962	71,829	69,969	46,942	8.84	10.65	33,409	5,898	20,626	122,676	21,010	245	8.1	58,685	65.50	500	154
1961	71,329	72,379	46,125	8.99	11.45	25,805	4,958	15,772	120,813	22,710	235	8.0	58,310	66.00	377	416
1960	88,784	82,963	46,012	8.73	11.45	34,578	5,273	19,716	135,179	27,543	246	8.0	58,582	66.00	331	112
1959	60,276	59,164	30,363	8.69	11.45	35,617	2,967	15,505	87,079	28,368	183	8.0	54,683	66.00	700	10
1958	67,709	66,288	31,968	8.59	11.45	27,544	3,573	18,244	91,558	21,333	207	8.0	50,820	66.00	210	103
1957	106,148	104,970	42,027	8.31	11.45	33,651	5,002	30,603	130,222	25,662	252	8.0	68,649	64.83	225	882
1956	97,877	97,924	38,260	7.47	10.85	30,411	5,508	26,373	119,753	26,817	234	8.0	67,063	60.69	327	269
1955	103,003	106,258	36,182	7.12	10.10	23,472	4,517	27,623	114,706	23,311	246	8.0	69,019	57.20	284	35
1954	78,129	76,954	27,756	6.99	9.90	15,792	3,146	24,222	85,065	27,840	220	8.0	51,592	56.00	291	10
1953	117,995	117,822	35,896	6.76	9.09	11,074	4,252	32,373	124,240	30,762	271	8.0	66,217	55.25	590	19
1952	97,918	97,973	27,024	6.09	8.30	9,761	5,123	28,181	100,209	31,800	248	8.0	54,674	53.08	380	14
1951	116,505	116,230	30,665	5.46	8.30	10,140	4,329	31,952	120,162	34,332	273	8.0	62,723	52.00	1,067	7
1950	98,045	97,764	26,718	4.99	7.70	8,281	2,551	28,872	96,868	31,087	264	8.0	57,702	47.04	805	7
1949	84,937	84,687	20,658	4.50	7.20	7,391	2,425	26,688	78,162	31,493	245	8.0	47,249	46.00	100	81
1948	101,003	100,822	23,629	3.91	6.20	6,092	3,081	27,229	98,996	33,075	285	8.0	53,617	41.60	219	7
1947	93,092	93,315	21,408	3.44	5.55	4,896	2,811	28,348	85,625	29,821	270	8.0	52,114	33.82	33	11
1946	70,843	70,090	15,589	3.07	4.55	2,754	1,506	20,335	63,859	28,009	222	8.1	40,246	27.13	14	96
1945	88,376	88,137	19,587	2.77	4.55	1,198	2,063	27,377	78,935	26,777	282	8.0	47,558	24.52	21	91
1944	94,118	95,136	20,303	2.70	4.45	464	2,158	28,626	72,394	29,244	280	8.0	54,461	23.50	6	162
1943	101,248	99,463	20,118	2.70	4.45	399	2,425	32,825	86,850	33,280	287	8.0	54,274	23.50	1	144
1942	105,520	105,989	23,105	2.63	4.45	731	2,515	33,633	92,894	32,774	279	8.2	52,769	23.50	(NA)	111
1941	92,410	93,054	19,376	2.68	4.45	2,344	1,908	27,217	65,192	28,587	264	8.0	49,307	23.50	4	579
1940	73,696	75,198	12,926	2.51	4.45	2,479	1,386	24,105	49,591	25,128	241	8.0	41,928	22.50	11	620
1939	51,732	54,827	9,426	2.89	4.95	2,413	1,057	18,980	32,752	21,859	222	8.0	32,091	21.10	43	198
1938	28,447	26,431	4,836	2.81	4.95	2,122	592	13,742	14,705	19,788	193	8.0	18,203	21.71	34	485
1937	72,094	72,348	12,350	2.87	4.95	2,442	1,264	23,461	48,632	25,945	247	8.0	35,224	22.99	125	876
1936	48,789	51,466	9,659	2.56	4.50	2,232	645	17,986	30,803	20,306	227	8.1	30,799	19.10	186	6
1935	30,540	33,426	6,067	2.48	4.50	1,492	661	12,613	17,927	14,987	219	8.0	21,179	18.17	147	5
1934	24,588	25,793	4,146	2.58	4.50	1,428	609	10,533	14,054	16,513	193	8.0	15,626	17.70	128	5
1933	17,553	24,624	3,556	2.59	4.50	861	155	6,217	11,336	15,125	140	8.5	14,354	15.44	178	3
1932	9,847	5,331	407	2.42	4.50	582	83	6,433	3,413	12,649	145	9.0	8,519	14.25	146	3
1931	31,132	28,516	4,676	2.60	4.50	1,466	436	17,279	13,830	22,867	201	8.9	17,813	15.88	95	8
1930	58,409	55,201	8,974	2.64	4.50	2,775	752	29,417	28,976	30,975	259	8.9	29,950	17.99	154	15
1929	73,028	75,603	9,424	2.61	4.50	3,139	1,304	32,374	40,654	30,763	281	8.9	41,549	18.20	165	52
1928	62,197	63,433	8,621	2.46	4.25	2,453	1,282	29,178	33,019	30,238	265	8.9	38,304	16.56	158	95
1927	61,741	61,232	8,115	2.47	4.25	2,621	899	30,891	30,850	34,755	264	8.9	34,867	17.71	148	57
1926	67,623	69,293	8,372	2.51	4.25	2,555	869	33,071	34,552	34,399	273	9.0	38,181	18.55	499	28
1925	61,908	63,925	8,736	2.52	4.25	2,191	631	31,937	29,971	35,757	270	8.9	36,814	19.59	494	37
1924	54,267	52,083	7,093	2.91	4.75	2,047	595	28,680	25,587	38,765	263	9.0	31,064	20.23	234	46
1923	69,351	69,811	10,687	3.45	5.55	2,768	1,117	30,228	39,123	41,294	286	9.1	38,362	25.71	412	36
1922	47,129	50,613	6,623	3.12	5.05	1,135	602	22,428	24,701	35,758	250	8.9	24,671	23.98	429	35
1921	29,491	26,653	3,728	3.37	5.55	316	440	15,645	13,846	32,348	209	9.1	16,038	21.87	--------	--------
1920	67,604	69,281	8,515	4.11	6.55	1,273	1,145	34,940	32,664	50,590	287	9.2	35,710	42.05	--------	--------
1919	60,965	56,373	7,356	3.50	5.55	476	997	32,751	28,214	51,780	280	9.1	30,230	27.49	--------	--------
1918	69,658	72,021	7,882	3.39	5.05	787	1,256	33,951	35,708	55,674	293	9.1	38,052	32.50	--------	--------
1917	75,289	75,573	8,167	3.15	5.05	972	1,132	39,839	35,450	60,594	280	9.1	38,613	39.10	--------	--------
1916	75,168	77,871	8,105	2.34	3.55	1,326	1,184	40,303	34,865	57,049	274	9.0	39,126	19.87	--------	--------
1915	55,526	55,493	5,581	1.83	2.80	1,341	708	33,365	22,161	43,385	272	8.9	30,385	13.78	--------	--------
1914	41,440	39,714	4,130	1.81	2.85	1,351	552	(NA)	(NA)	(NA)	(NA)	--------	22,263	12.89	--------	--------
1913	61,980	--------	--------	2.19	3.40	2,595	1,042	(NA)	(NA)	(NA)	(NA)	--------	30,389	14.77	--------	--------
1912	55,150	--------	--------	1.88	2.85	2,105	1,196	(NA)	(NA)	(NA)	(NA)	--------	30,181	13.90	--------	--------
1911	43,877	--------	--------	2.11	3.50	1,812	768	(NA)	(NA)	(NA)	(NA)	--------	23,257	13.10	--------	--------
1910	57,015	--------	--------	2.47	4.00	2,591	749	(NA)	(NA)	(NA)	(NA)	--------	26,674	14.73	--------	--------
1909	51,294	--------	--------	2.15	3.50	1,695	456	27,567	24,150	(NA)	(NA)	--------	25,796	15.52	--------	--------
1908	35,983	--------	--------	2.27	3.50	777	309			(NA)	(NA)	--------	15,936	15.21	--------	--------
1907	51,721	--------	--------	2.55	4.00	1,229	279			(NA)	(NA)	--------	25,781	23.89	--------	--------
1906	47,750	--------	--------	2.11	3.50	1,060	265			(NA)	(NA)	--------	25,307	20.98	--------	--------
1905	42,400	--------	--------	1.77	3.00	846	208			(NA)	(NA)	--------	22,992	17.88	--------	--------
1904	27,500	--------	--------	1.56	2.35	488	214			(NA)	(NA)	--------	16,497	15.57	--------	--------
1903	34,800	--------	--------	1.89	3.20	980	81			(NA)	(NA)	--------	18,009	19.92	--------	--------
1902	35,300	--------	--------	1.84	2.60	1,165	88			44,800	260	--------	17,821	22.19	--------	--------
1901	28,600	--------	--------	1.71	2.35	967	65			(NA)	(NA)	--------	15,879	15.87	--------	--------
1900	27,300	--------	--------	2.42	4.00	898	51			(NA)	(NA)	--------	13,789	19.98	--------	--------
1899	24,600	--------	--------	1.42	1.90	674	41			(NA)	(NA)	--------	13,621	19.36	--------	--------
1898	19,434	--------	--------	1.14	1.70	187	--------			(NA)	(NA)	--------	11,774	11.66	--------	--------
1897	17,518	--------	--------	1.08	1.80	490	--------			(NA)	(NA)	--------	9,653	12.10	--------	--------
1896	16,005	--------	--------	1.42	2.40	683	--------			(NA)	(NA)	--------	8,623	12.95	--------	--------
1895	15,958	--------	--------	1.14	1.90	524	--------			(NA)	(NA)	--------	9,446	13.10	--------	--------
1894	11,880	--------	--------	1.14	1.75	167	--------			(NA)	(NA)	--------	6,657	12.66	--------	--------

See footnotes at end of table.

Series M 205–220. Iron Ore and Pig Iron: 1799 to 1970—Con.

[Quantities for iron ore in thousands of long tons; for pig iron in thousands of short tons]

Year	Iron ore Production	Iron ore Shipments, average value per long ton	Iron ore Imports	Iron ore Employment Average workers on active days	Iron ore Employment Average days worked	Pig iron Shipments	Pig iron Average price per long ton [2]	Year	Iron ore, production	Pig iron Shipments	Pig iron Average price per long ton [2]	Year	Pig iron Shipments	Pig iron Average price per long ton [2]	Year	Pig iron Shipments	Pig iron Average price per long ton [2]
	205	208	210	214	215	217	218		205	217	218		217	218		217	218
1893	11,588	$1.66	527	(NA)	(NA)	7,124	$14.52	1870	3,832	1,665	$33.25	1845	(NA)	$29.25	1820	20	$35.00
1892	16,297	2.04	807	(NA)	(NA)	9,157	15.75	1869	(NA)	1,712	40.62	1844	(NA)	25.75	1819	(NA)	36.50
1891	14,591	(NA)	913	(NA)	(NA)	8,279	17.52	1868	(NA)	1,431	39.25	1843	(NA)	26.75	1818	(NA)	42.25
1890	16,036	(NA)	1,247	(NA)	(NA)	9,203	18.40	1867	(NA)	1,305	44.12	1842	215	28.00	1817	(NA)	47.00
1889	14,518	2.30	854	36,341	248	7,604	17.75	1866	(NA)	1,205	46.87	1841	(NA)	28.50	1816	(NA)	50.25
								1865	(NA)	832	46.12	1840	287	32.75	1815	(NA)	53.75
1888	12,063	--------	587	(NA)	(NA)	6,490	18.88	1864	(NA)	1,014	59.25	1839	(NA)	30.00	1814	(NA)	46.00
1887	11,300	--------	1,194	(NA)	(NA)	6,417	20.92	1863	(NA)	846	35.25	1838	(NA)	32.25	1813	(NA)	47.25
1886	10,000	--------	1,039	(NA)	(NA)	5,683	18.71	1862	(NA)	704	23.87	1837	(NA)	41.25	1812	(NA)	47.50
								1861	(NA)	654	20.25	1836	(NA)	41.50	1811	(NA)	44.00
1885	7,600	--------	391	(NA)	(NA)	4,045	18.00	1860	2,873	821	22.75	1835	(NA)	30.25	1810	54	38.00
1884	8,200	--------	488	(NA)	(NA)	4,098	19.87	1859	--------	751	23.37	1834	(NA)	30.25	1809	--------	40.00
1883	8,400	--------	491	(NA)	(NA)	4,596	22.37	1858	--------	629	22.25	1833	(NA)	38.25	1808	--------	40.00
1882	9,000	--------	590	(NA)	(NA)	4,623	25.75	1857	--------	712	26.37	1832	200	35.00	1807	--------	38.75
1881	7,120	--------	783	(NA)	(NA)	4,145	25.12	1856	--------	788	27.12	1831	191	35.00	1806	--------	35.75
1880	7,120	--------	493	35,000	231	3,835	28.50	1855	--------	700	27.75	1830	165	35.00	1805	--------	30.75
1879	(NA)	--------	284	--------	--------	2,742	21.50	1854	--------	657	36.87	1829	142	35.00	1804	--------	29.75
1878	(NA)	--------	28	--------	--------	2,301	17.62	1853	--------	(NA)	36.12	1828	130	35.00	1803	--------	29.25
1877	(NA)	--------	31	--------	--------	2,067	18.87	1852	--------	500	22.62	1827	(NA)	39.25	1802	--------	30.75
1876	(NA)	--------	17	--------	--------	1,869	22.25	1851	--------	(NA)	21.37	1826	(NA)	46.50	1801	--------	32.75
1875	4,018	--------	57	--------	--------	2,024	25.50	1850	--------	563	20.87	1825	(NA)	46.75	1800	--------	35.75
1874	(NA)	--------	58	--------	--------	2,401	30.25	1849	--------	650	22.75	1824	(NA)	40.00	1799	--------	36.25
1873	(NA)	--------	46	--------	--------	2,561	42.75	1848	--------	800	26.50	1823	(NA)	35.25			
1872	(NA)	--------	24	--------	--------	2,549	48.87	1847	--------	800	30.25	1822	(NA)	35.00			
1871	(NA)	--------	24	--------	--------	1,707	35.12	1846	--------	765	27.87	1821	(NA)	35.00			

NA Not available.
[1] Beginning 1942, represents mine production of crude iron ore before treatment for removal of wastes.

[2] 1908–1970, basic f.o.b. Valley furnaces; 1844–1907, No. 1 Foundry, Philadelphia; 1799–1843, charcoal pig iron. See text for minor variations within the periods.
[3] Preliminary.

Series M 221–234. Ferroalloying Metals—Manganese, Chromite, Tungsten, Molybdenum, Vanadium, and Nickel: 1868 to 1970

[Quantities in short tons, metallic content, except where specified as gross weight]

Year	Manganese ore (35% or more Mn) (gross weight) Domestic output	Manganese ore Imports	Chromite (gross weight) Domestic output [1]	Chromite Imports	Tungsten concentrates Domestic output	Tungsten concentrates Imports [2]	Molybdenum ores and concentrates Domestic output	Molybdenum ores and concentrates Exports	Vanadium ores and concentrates Domestic output	Vanadium ores and concentrates Imports [3]	Nickel Production Primary	Nickel Production Secondary	Nickel Imports	Nickel Price, electrolytic (cents per pound)
	221	222	223	224	225	226	227	228	229	230	231	232	233	234
1970	4,737	1,735,055	----------	1,405,000	3,899	642	55,191	27,868	5,793	--------	12,649	23,159	156,252	128–133
1969	5,630	1,936,175	----------	1,106,000	3,502	752	51,505	27,788	5,737	--------	13,096	18,775	129,332	103–128
1968	11,378	1,831,210	----------	1,084,000	3,933	872	46,623	14,503	7,105	31	13,124	14,061	147,950	94–103
1967	12,585	2,061,240	----------	1,240,000	3,285	850	40,798	15,000	5,088	42	13,036	20,731	143,000	85.25–94
1966	14,406	2,651,921	----------	1,864,000	3,583	2,149	45,835	12,392	5,685	72	12,231	26,777	141,000	77.75–85.25
1965	29,258	3,855,597	----------	1,518,338	3,783	1,809	38,655	14,847	5,641	(NA)	12,666	19,407	163,000	79–77.75
1964	26,058	3,024,236	----------	1,427,771	4,399	1,574	32,549	12,470	5,184	12	11,236	23,114	129,000	79
1963	10,622	2,389,520	----------	1,391,116	2,692	1,530	32,920	13,273	6,047	(NA)	10,725	18,996	119,000	79
1962	24,758	1,969,549	----------	1,445,575	4,011	2,015	25,253	7,777	7,647	(NA)	10,569	11,108	123,000	81.25–79
1961	46,088	2,147,192	82,000	1,329,131	3,924	1,062	33,377	17,831	6,359	(NA)	10,551	10,688	127,000	74–81.25
1960	80,021	2,276,970	107,000	1,386,042	3,486	1,763	34,971	15,122	8,047	3	[4] 13,680	9,431	103,000	74
1959	229,199	1,878,065	105,000	1,553,546	1,737	2,718	25,802	9,426	7,392	3	11,113	9,438	112,000	74
1958	327,309	1,798,622	143,795	1,263,437	1,803	3,271	21,164	5,983	7,266	(NA)	11,238	7,411	90,000	74
1957	366,334	2,539,173	66,157	2,282,721	2,627	7,009	28,572	12,733	7,294	(NA)	9,568	12,037	140,000	74
1956	344,735	2,222,460	207,662	2,175,056	7,014	10,430	28,563	8,991	5,636	(NA)	[5] 6,099	14,860	142,642	64.5–74
1955	287,255	2,263,847	153,253	1,833,999	7,810	10,350	32,355	7,290	4,983	93	3,356	11,540	142,000	64.5
1954	206,128	2,243,601	163,365	1,471,037	6,515	12,094	32,010	6,773	4,930	198	192	8,605	131,784	60.0–64.5
1953	157,536	3,115,023	58,817	2,226,631	4,564	14,030	26,912	3,519	4,643	359	11	8,352	118,737	56.5–60.0
1952	115,379	2,203,545	21,304	1,708,969	3,622	8,708	21,358	3,086	3,589	522	--------	7,479	108,850	56.5
1951	105,007	1,902,859	7,056	1,427,900	2,986	3,188	18,978	1,865	3,040	492	--------	8,602	93,190	50.5–56.5
1950	134,451	1,925,148	404	1,303,713	2,294	8,074	22,272	3,117	2,298	729	--------	8,795	91,347	40.0–50.5
1949	126,135	1,423,903	433	1,203,852	1,316	3,137	11,640	2,660	1,581	276	--------	5,680	91,073	40.0
1948	131,100	1,473,453	3,619	1,542,125	1,919	3,774	14,834	2,066	895	526	--------	8,850	96,880	33.75–40.0
1947	131,627	1,297,992	948	1,106,180	1,472	3,009	11,095	1,495	1,059	492	--------	9,541	80,718	35.0
1946	143,635	1,514,544	4,107	757,391	2,471	3,435	8,152	282	636	396	--------	8,248	92,500	31.5–35.0
1945	182,337	1,311,346	13,973	925,887	2,633	2,387	16,262	1,431	1,482	775	--------	6,483	107,433	31.5
1944	247,616	1,315,677	45,629	848,390	4,893	9,198	19,712	2,993	1,764	643	--------	4,321	118,293	31.5
1943	205,173	1,511,630	160,120	928,576	5,684	9,723	26,978	5,036	2,793	1,027	--------	6,917	122,492	31.5
1942	190,748	1,583,024	112,876	981,607	4,441	7,163	33,218	5,798	2,220	1,211	--------	4,142	114,275	31.5
1941	87,795	1,714,581	14,259	1,115,292	3,125	5,761	19,188	3,820	1,257	1,070	--------	5,315	106,182	35.0

See footnotes at end of table.

Series M 221–234. Ferroalloying Metals—Manganese, Chromite, Tungsten, Molybdenum, Vanadium, and Nickel: 1868 to 1970—Con.

[Quantities in short tons, metallic content, except where specified as gross weight]

Year	Manganese ore (35% or more Mn) (gross weight)		Chromite (gross weight)		Tungsten concentrates		Molybdenum ores and concentrates		Vanadium ores and concentrates		Nickel		
	Domestic output	Imports	Domestic output [1]	Imports	Domestic output	Imports [2]	Domestic output	Exports	Domestic output	Imports [3]	Production, secondary	Imports	Price, electrolytic (cents per pound)
	221	222	223	224	225	226	227	228	229	230	232	233	234
1940	44,038	1,435,928	2,982	736,612	2,531	2,805	12,664	3,292	1,082	1,288	4,152	83,760	35.0
1939	32,824	702,384	4,048	355,612	2,040	743	16,208	_____	992	1,067	2,920	58,200	35.0
1938	28,360	541,616	909	394,335	1,449	81	12,864	_____	807	692	2,300	26,200	35.0
1937	45,071	1,021,353	2,600	620,386	1,666	2,781	15,061	_____	543	630	2,400	48,500	35.0
1936	35,974	910,965	301	363,169	1,243	1,793	8,980	_____	70	172	1,965	47,600	35.0
1935	29,599	429,520	577	290,151	1,140	406	5,446	_____	26	47	1,950	34,200	35.0
1934	29,697	382,300	413	215,373	975	423	4,688	_____	7	207	1,850	21,000	35.0
1933	21,444	175,656	944	130,492	426	155	2,880	_____	2	(NA)	1,650	21,900	35.0
1932	19,910	123,910	174	99,840	188	46	1,186	_____	271	(NA)	1,450	9,400	35.0
1931	43,951	562,820	300	238,031	668	84	1,578	_____	(NA)	(NA)	2,070	15,100	35.0
1930	75,080	655,836	90	365,811	334	1,847	1,880	_____	(NA)	5,788	2,900	25,300	35.0
1929	67,625	743,981	301	355,746	395	2,987	1,952	_____	(NA)	9,760	4,350	41,500	35.0
1928	52,483	479,033	739	242,583	575	1,428	1,665	_____	(NA)	552	4,500	30,300	37.0
1927	50,110	696,715	225	249,043	554	1,085	1,141	_____	(NA)	6,943	3,380	17,900	35.43
1926	51,810	826,560	158	241,320	658	1,267	716	_____	331	8,368	3,050	19,300	35.63
1925	110,124	688,800	121	167,708	566	427	577	_____	216	2,368	2,300	21,601	32.79
1924	63,297	565,600	323	132,544	149	(NA)	149	_____	(NA)	7,059	2,240	18,542	30.33
1923	35,280	469,280	254	145,256	114	(NA)	11	_____	64	2,089	1,550	20,398	35.48
1922	15,013	476,200	398	100,891	(NA)	1,651	(NA)	_____	26	306	1,512	7,472	38.25
1921	15,155	439,719	316	91,656	3	1,614	(NA)	_____	202	5,154	945	2,198	42.04
1920	105,750	671,736	2,802	168,308	103	1,949	17	_____	527	10,337	2,200	24,246	42.32
1919	61,552	373,345	5,688	68,772	402	9,408	149	_____	284	3,013	2,447	18,330	40.41
1918	342,573	550,259	92,322	112,159	2,408	11,750	431	_____	276	886	1,393	36,613	40.82
1917	144,873	705,569	48,972	80,711	2,924	4,876	175	_____	484	_____	860	37,763	41.52
1916	35,250	645,480	52,679	129,858	2,820	3,973	103	_____	460	_____	816	36,325	41.85
1915	10,705	359,271	3,675	85,630	1,147	1,776	91	_____	627	_____	_____	28,300	41.32
1914	[6] 2,951	317,289	662	83,648	471	299	1	_____	452	_____	_____	17,549	41.37
1913	[6] 4,534	386,501	286	73,002	732	449	_____	_____	432	_____	_____	23,723	41.16
1912	[6] 1,863	336,740	225	60,400	633	824	_____	_____	300	_____	_____	23,159	_____
1911	[6] 2,752	198,074	134	42,045	542	_____	_____	_____	275	_____	_____	14,915	_____

Year	Manganese ore (40% or more Mn) (gross weight)		Chromite (gross weight)		Tungsten concentrates, domestic output	Year	Manganese ore (40% or more Mn) (gross weight)		Chromite (gross weight)	
	Domestic output	Imports	Domestic output [1]	Imports			Domestic output	Imports	Domestic output [1]	Imports
	221	222	223	224	225		221	222	223	224
1910	2,529	271,430	230	43,208	866	1888	32,702	1,324	1,680	4,973
1909	1,729	238,297	670	44,379	770	1887	38,667	1,826	3,360	1,572
1908	6,881	199,587	402	31,221	319	1886	33,816	2,036	2,240	3,759
1907	6,276	234,104	325	47,028	780	1885	26,049	1,886	3,024	13
1906	7,751	247,811	120	48,654	442	1884	11,402	675	2,240	2,998
1905	4,612	287,877	25	60,966	382	1883	6,894	1,485	3,360	_____
1904	3,523	121,541	138	27,134	352	1882	5,076	1,001	2,800	_____
1903	3,164	163,583	168	25,684	139	1881	5,482	1,908	2,240	_____
1902	8,375	263,845	353	44,318	88	1880	6,452	2,440	2,563	_____
1901	13,434	185,609	412	22,525	85	1879		2,112		_____
1900	13,184	287,002	157	19,647	22	1878		701		_____
1899	11,127	210,951	(NA)	17,688	_____	1877		998		_____
1898	17,872	128,671	(NA)	18,260	_____	1876		461		_____
1897	12,441	134,356	(NA)	12,958	_____	1875		227		_____
1896	11,299	35,268	880	9,709	_____	1874		876		_____
1895	10,693	96,444	1,949	5,858	_____	1873		1,155		_____
1894	7,065	50,014	4,122	3,886	_____	1872		1,351		_____
1893	8,644	76,287	1,624	7,116	_____	1871		1,183		_____
1892	15,246	65,601	1,680	5,522	_____	1870		1,570		_____
1891	25,146	32,284	1,537	4,994	_____	1869		547		_____
1890	21,602	38,252	4,031	4,875	_____	1868		1,139		_____
1889	27,101	4,800	2,240	6,131	_____					

NA Not available.

[1] Cumulative production prior to 1880, 224,000 short tons.
[2] Prior to 1923, gross weight; thereafter, tungsten content.
[3] Prior to 1934, gross weight; thereafter, vanadium content.
[4] Includes 1,773 tons from Cuban concentrate.
[5] Includes imported concentrate.
[6] 40 percent or more manganese; see also text for series M 221 and M 222.

Series M 235–241.   Copper: 1845 to 1970

[In short tons, except as indicated]

Year	Mine (recoverable content)	Primary refined from domestic and foreign ores	Secondary Total	Secondary From old scrap	Imports, refined	Exports, refined	Price, New York, electrolytic, f.o.b. refinery (cents per lb.)
	235	236	237	238	239	240	241
1970	1,719,657	1,765,094	1,247,602	504,071	132,143	221,211	[1]58.07
1969	1,544,579	1,742,815	1,375,493	574,890	131,171	200,269	[1]47.43
1968	1,204,621	1,437,386	1,218,340	520,772	400,278	240,745	[1]41.17
1967	954,064	1,132,982	1,159,907	482,659	330,571	159,353	37.92
1966	1,429,152	1,710,984	1,334,249	534,860	164,328	273,071	35.82
1965	1,351,734	1,711,793	1,253,250	513,436	137,443	324,965	35.19
1964	1,246,780	1,656,395	1,093,021	473,521	139,974	316,230	32.17
1963	1,213,166	1,596,351	974,426	421,843	119,219	311,479	30.82
1962	1,228,421	1,611,730	921,828	415,674	98,820	336,525	30.82
1961	1,165,155	1,550,139	848,939	411,110	66,855	428,718	30.14
1960	1,080,169	1,518,927	871,388	429,365	142,709	433,762	32.16
1959	824,846	1,098,247	930,570	471,007	214,058	158,938	30.82
1958	979,329	1,352,520	797,388	411,367	128,464	384,868	26.13
1957	1,086,859	1,454,176	841,887	444,492	162,309	346,025	29.99
1956	1,104,156	1,442,633	930,664	468,489	191,812	223,103	41.88
1955	998,570	1,342,459	989,004	514,585	202,312	199,819	37.39
1954	835,472	1,211,919	839,907	407,066	215,118	215,951	29.82
1953	926,448	1,293,117	958,464	429,388	274,111	109,580	28.92
1952	925,359	1,177,696	903,197	414,635	346,960	174,135	24.37
1951	928,330	1,206,988	932,282	458,124	238,972	133,305	24.37
1950	909,343	1,239,834	977,239	485,211	317,363	144,561	21.46
1949	752,750	927,927	713,143	383,548	275,811	137,827	19.36
1948	834,813	1,107,446	972,788	505,464	249,124	142,598	22.20
1947	847,563	1,159,970	961,741	503,376	149,478	147,642	21.15
1946	608,737	878,662	803,546	406,453	154,371	52,629	13.92
1945	772,894	1,108,599	1,006,516	497,095	531,367	48,563	11.87
1944	972,549	1,221,187	950,942	456,710	492,395	68,373	11.87
1943	1,090,818	1,379,263	1,086,047	427,521	402,762	175,859	11.87
1942	1,080,061	1,414,561	927,755	427,122	401,436	131,406	11.87
1941	958,149	1,395,309	726,396	412,699	346,994	103,602	11.87
1940	878,086	1,313,556	532,046	333,890	68,337	356,431	11.40
1939	728,320	1,009,515	499,700	286,900	16,264	372,777	11.07
1938	557,763	792,446	359,800	267,300	1,802	370,545	10.10
1937	841,998	1,066,814	532,100	408,900	7,487	295,064	13.27
1936	614,516	822,489	484,600	382,700	4,782	220,390	9.58
1935	386,491	588,805	448,900	361,700	18,071	260,735	8.76
1934	237,401	445,360	377,400	310,900	27,417	262,366	8.53
1933	190,643	370,789	338,100	260,300	5,432	124,582	7.15
1932	238,111	340,434	248,180	180,980	83,897	110,977	5.67
1931	528,875	750,721	347,000	261,300	87,225	202,698	8.24
1930	705,074	1,078,530	467,200	342,200	43,105	297,057	13.11
1929	997,555	1,370,056	626,550	464,350	67,007	411,227	18.23
1928	904,898	1,243,804	536,400	365,500	42,365	474,737	14.68
1927	824,980	1,162,882	490,200	339,400	51,640	461,233	13.05
1926	862,638	1,161,243	479,800	337,300	85,283	428,062	13.95
1925	839,059	1,102,287	420,210	291,010	49,887	484,033	14.16
1924	803,083	1,130,038	388,300	266,200	72,955	504,812	13.16
1923	738,870	989,918	410,900	270,900	[2]80,356	364,690	14.61
1922	482,292	627,758	335,900	202,800	51,572	326,333	13.56
1921	233,095	475,389	217,300	131,990	34,625	298,059	12.65
1920	612,275	763,083	312,460	168,960	54,372	275,613	17.50
1919	606,167	885,084	287,190	152,600	17,569	219,080	18.90
1918	955,011	1,197,149	352,670	176,670	19,044	345,014	29.19
1917	947,717	[3]1,210,897	383,400	194,900	3,376	515,390	29.19
1916	1,002,938	1,129,694	350,000	175,000	4,206	358,308	28.46
1915	744,036	817,102	196,187	121,187	---	---	17.47
1914	574,216	766,891	127,882	87,882	---	---	13.31
1913	617,785	807,534	136,500	91,500	---	---	15.52
1912	624,547	784,052	137,500	107,000	---	---	16.48
1911	557,382	716,938	107,000	76,000	---	---	12.55

Year	Mine (recoverable content)	Primary refined from domestic and foreign ores	Secondary Total	Secondary From old scrap	Price, New York, electrolytic, f.o.b. refinery (cents per lb.)
	235	236	237	238	241
1910	544,119	711,020	94,500	64,500	12.88
1909	563,261	695,511	---	---	13.11
1908	478,420	568,981	---	---	13.39
1907	423,576	516,258	---	---	20.86
1906	458,486	539,526	---	---	19.77
1905	444,392	---	---	---	15.98
1904	406,269	---	---	---	13.11
1903	349,022	---	---	---	13.62
1902	329,754	---	---	---	11.96
1901	301,036	---	---	---	16.40
1900	303,059	---	---	---	16.54
1899	284,333	---	---	---	17.75
1898	263,256	---	---	---	12.01
1897	247,039	---	---	---	11.30
1896	230,031	---	---	---	10.92
1895	190,307				10.70
1894	177,094				9.43
1893	164,677				10.65
1892	172,499				11.50
1891	142,061				12.88
1890	129,882				15.75
1889	113,388				13.75
1888	113,181				16.80
1887	90,739				11.25
1886	78,881				11.00
1885	82,938				11.10
1884	72,473				13.75
1883	57,763				15.88
1882	45,323				18.50
1881	35,840				18.25
1880	30,240				21.50
1879	25,760				18.62
1878	24,080				16.56
1877	23,520				19.00
1876	21,280				21.00
1875	20,160				22.69
1874	19,600				22.00
1873	17,360				28.00
1872	14,000				35.56
1871	14,560				24.12
1870	14,112				21.19
1869	14,000				24.25
1868	12,992				23.00
1867	11,200				25.38
1866	9,968				34.25
1865	9,520				39.25
1864	8,960				47.00
1863	9,520				33.88
1862	10,580				21.88
1861	8,400				22.25
1860	8,064				22.88
1859	7,056				22.00
1858	6,160				23.00
1857	5,376				25.00
1856	4,480				27.00
1855	3,360				27.00
1854	2,520				22.00
1853	2,240				22.00
1852	1,232				22.00
1851	1,008				16.60
1850	728				22.00
1849	784				---
1848	560				---
1847	336				---
1846	168				---
1845	112				---

[1] Beginning 1968, delivered price; comparable price for 1967 is 38.1 cents per pound.
[2] Imports of refined copper from Chile, as reported by the Chile Exploration Co., were included by *Mineral Resources of the United States* in place of those of the Bureau of Foreign and Domestic Commerce which were considered too low.
[3] Includes some refined copper imports.

Series **M 242–255.** Lead and Zinc: 1801 to 1970

[In short tons, except as indicated]

	Lead							Zinc						
	Production							Production						
			Secondary							Secondary				
Year	Mine (recoverable content)	Primary, refined from domestic and foreign ores	Total	From old scrap	Imports, refined	Exports, refined	Price, New York, pig lead (cents per lb.)	Mine (recoverable content)	Primary, smelter slab zinc from domestic and foreign ores	Total	From old scrap	Imports, refined	Exports, refined	Price, New York, slab zinc (cents per lb.)
	242	243	244	245	246	247	248	249	250	251	252	253	254	255
1970	571,767	666,730	597,390	506,186	244,623	7,747	15.69	534,136	877,811	339,527	72,153	260,132	288	15.82
1969	509,013	638,655	603,905	515,937	278,873	4,968	14.93	553,124	1,040,597	376,391	81,627	324,758	9,298	15.15
1968	359,156	467,310	550,879	471,267	337,620	8,281	13.21	529,446	1,020,891	354,723	79,797	304,687	33,011	14.00
1967	316,931	379,894	553,772	476,865	363,596	6,536	14.00	549,413	938,830	319,849	80,309	222,002	16,809	14.35
1966	327,368	440,735	572,834	485,329	285,788	5,435	15.12	572,558	1,025,066	360,211	86,285	280,307	1,406	15.00
1965	301,147	418,249	575,819	495,734	223,461	7,811	16.00	611,153	994,402	353,364	82,009	153,957	5,939	15.00
1964	286,010	449,429	541,582	469,661	211,140	10,175	13.62	574,858	954,084	298,394	68,064	134,118	26,515	14.07
1963	253,369	394,732	493,471	427,189	220,398	1,088	11.14	529,254	892,584	268,255	62,564	132,332	33,853	12.51
1962	236,956	376,063	444,202	393,284	257,866	2,108	9.63	505,491	[1]879,395	262,017	61,753	135,995	36,102	12.13
1961	261,921	449,565	452,792	390,538	247,427	2,133	10.87	464,390	[1]846,795	237,967	59,407	125,186	50,055	12.05
1960	246,669	382,436	469,903	408,397	213,347	1,967	11.95	435,427	[1]799,516	265,820	68,369	120,925	75,144	13.45
1959	255,586	340,931	451,387	392,762	262,632	2,756	12.21	425,303	[1]798,666	276,254	73,848	164,462	11,629	11.96
1958	267,377	470,156	401,787	343,269	351,759	1,359	12.11	412,005	[1]781,246	230,332	69,926	185,693	2,073	10.81
1957	338,216	533,533	489,229	431,883	321,708	4,339	14.66	531,735	985,796	264,104	76,789	268,824	10,785	11.90
1956	352,826	542,308	506,755	445,516	262,204	4,628	16.01	542,340	983,610	281,355	73,746	244,726	8,813	13.99
1955	338,025	479,157	502,051	449,186	263,977	403	15.14	514,671	963,504	304,775	83,549	195,059	18,069	12.80
1954	325,419	486,712	470,925	424,987	274,286	596	14.05	473,471	802,425	271,774	72,657	160,138	24,994	11.19
1953	342,644	467,891	486,737	428,750	379,119	803	13.48	547,430	916,105	294,678	64,235	227,654	17,969	11.53
1952	390,162	472,852	471,294	411,831	510,718	1,762	16.47	666,001	904,479	310,423	74,665	113,053	57,714	17.03
1951	388,164	417,693	518,110	441,658	179,021	1,281	17.49	681,189	881,633	314,377	68,174	88,043	36,510	18.75
1950	430,827	508,314	482,275	427,520	434,410	2,735	13.30	623,375	843,467	326,030	74,097	155,332	12,917	14.60
1949	409,908	477,338	412,183	364,140	272,437	969	15.36	593,203	814,782	237,813	51,651	125,564	58,709	12.86
1948	390,476	406,694	500,071	432,733	244,692	399	18.04	629,977	787,764	324,639	74,190	92,495	65,537	14.21
1947	384,221	441,010	511,970	444,578	158,705	1,523	14.67	637,608	802,495	310,793	74,979	72,063	106,669	11.01
1946	335,475	338,197	392,787	344,593	104,083	598	8.11	574,833	728,262	300,682	77,223	104,065	47,224	9.15
1945	390,831	443,585	363,039	309,849	227,311	1,408	6.50	614,358	764,561	360,444	91,266	96,760	7,782	8.65
1944	416,861	464,763	331,416	289,933	223,379	15,523	6.50	718,642	869,302	345,469	113,161	63,626	21,576	8.65
1943	453,313	469,612	342,094	310,703	244,033	2,003	6.50	744,196	942,309	368,488	84,225	56,155	97,439	8.66
1942	496,239	566,839	323,001	308,588	387,693	1,940	6.48	768,025	891,872	330,526	72,987	36,352	133,938	8.66
1941	461,426	570,967	397,416	380,280	325,999	14,359	5.79	749,125	822,020	283,967	81,154	40,288	89,309	7.87
1940	457,392	533,179	260,346	226,583	36,882	23,755	5.18	665,068	675,275	222,013	64,204	10,146	79,091	6.73
1939	413,979	484,035	241,500	210,800	4,772	74,392	5.05	583,807	507,236	189,640	45,100	30,960	4,515	5.51
1938	369,726	383,669	236,070	--------	2,001	[2]45,866	4.74	516,703	446,341	119,000	--------	7,230	(NA)	4.99
1937	464,892	467,317	290,491	--------	2,355	20,091	6.01	626,362	556,904	166,000	--------	37,208	249	6.87
1936	372,919	399,156	275,830	--------	1,979	18,313	4.71	575,574	492,132	161,000	--------	11,660	37	5.28
1935	331,103	324,560	279,879	--------	1,368	6,982	4.06	517,903	420,634	129,000	--------	4,444	1,617	4.70
1934	287,339	311,236	216,513	--------	[3]285	5,909	3.86	438,726	363,590	95,000	--------	1,725	5,105	4.51
1933	272,677	263,676	235,636	--------	45	22,835	3.87	384,280	307,182	120,000	--------	1,890	1,145	4.40
1932	292,968	281,941	211,786	--------	44	23,516	3.18	285,231	207,148	70,600	--------	310	6,471	3.25
1931	404,622	442,764	248,873	--------	[3]10	21,665	4.24	410,318	291,996	102,000	--------	274	643	3.99
1930	558,313	643,033	255,800	--------	571	48,307	5.52	595,425	498,045	127,400	--------	281	4,633	4.91
1929	[4]647,995	774,633	311,000	--------	10,089	73,251	6.83	724,478	625,447	176,200	--------	226	14,411	6.84
1928	[4]627,153	781,071	308,600	--------	10,244	116,269	6.31	695,170	602,581	181,700	--------	(NA)	25,289	6.38
1927	665,489	796,530	276,000	--------	4,967	125,267	6.75	718,541	592,516	168,300	--------	39	45,695	6.60
1926	683,917	798,941	277,300	--------	12,183	71,936	8.42	774,563	618,422	168,000	--------	(NA)	42,920	7.72
1925	684,439	766,969	226,880	--------	7,732	103,519	9.02	710,847	572,946	156,000	--------	(NA)	76,351	8.01
1924	596,068	690,493	204,500	--------	13,681	82,090	8.08	637,977	517,339	157,000	--------	11	72,583	6.70
1923	547,217	618,322	194,490	--------	21,463	50,735	7.25	610,690	510,434	164,000	--------	1	49,211	7.01
1922	477,633	532,662	159,560	--------	4,282	38,178	5.71	472,032	354,277	161,000	--------	40	30,286	6.09
1921	414,491	448,589	103,780	--------	30,955	26,624	4.55	256,640	200,500	93,000	--------	6,598	3,009	5.15
1920	496,814	529,657	124,650	--------	34,451	20,093	8.08	587,524	463,377	141,000	--------	(NA)	102,178	8.13
1919	429,589	482,220	122,100	--------	5,087	51,486	5.81	548,846	465,743	130,300	--------	32	122,002	7.39
1918	562,402	640,195	97,100	--------	570	101,247	7.46	636,091	517,927	137,000	--------	11	86,438	8.31
1917	628,464	610,769	93,500	--------	878	91,340	87.1	713,556	669,573	132,000	--------	18	201,968	9.11
1916	601,392	571,134	96,300	--------	3,194	110,380	6.83	703,169	668,343	129,200	--------	21	193,853	13.75
1915	542,098	550,055	78,900	--------	499	126,924	4.67	588,060	489,519	108,800	--------	63	131,378	14.44
1914	504,769	542,122	61,062	--------	288	58,722	3.87	415,774	353,049	84,600	--------	195	64,802	5.30
1913	483,113	462,460	72,834	--------	2,311	(NA)	4.40	413,824	346,676	89,528	--------	5,165	7,783	5.80
1912	442,126	480,894	67,168	--------	2,596	(NA)	4.48	385,621	338,806	94,111	--------	10,719	6,634	7.11
1911	426,585	486,979	54,284	--------	3,556	(NA)	4.46	331,515	286,526	74,747	--------	323	6,872	5.91
1910	382,692	470,272	55,422	--------	3,388	(NA)	4.49	324,444	269,184	68,998	--------	989	3,990	5.66
1909	385,113	446,909	41,687	--------	3,548	(NA)	4.30	302,373	255,760	48,232	--------	9,419	2,566	5.52
1908	330,237	396,564	18,533	--------	2,673	(NA)	4.23	234,064	210,424	23,226	--------	776	2,640	4.74
1907	364,715	413,389	25,487	--------	7,834	55	5.35	253,017	249,860	25,532	--------	1,709	563	6.20
1906	--------	404,746	--------	--------	12,441	74	5.66	--------	224,770	--------	--------	1,021	4,670	6.27

See footnotes at end of table.

Series M 242–255. Lead and Zinc: 1801 to 1970—Con.

[In short tons, except as indicated]

Year	Lead — Production, primary, refined from domestic and foreign ores (243)	Imports, refined (246)	Exports, refined (247)	Price, New York, pig lead (cents per lb.) (248)	Zinc — Production, primary, smelter slab zinc from domestic and foreign ores (250)	Imports, refined (253)	Exports, refined (254)	Price, New York, slab zinc (cents per lb.) (255)
1905	388,307	5,190	63	4.70	203,849	428	5,516	6.00
1904	393,452	8,667	35	4.32	186,702	341	10,147	5.17
1903	368,939	4,486	56	4.26	159,219	202	1,521	5.62
1902	367,892	6,222	3,271	4.10	156,927	448	3,237	4.90
1901	371,032	1,802	2,393	4.36	140,822	278	3,390	4.08
1900	367,773	1,837	997	4.41	123,886	884	22,410	4.40
1899	298,047	1,737	47	4.47	129,051	1,392	6,755	5.75
1898	302,148	156	59	3.78	115,399	1,303	10,499	4.57
1897	282,169	8,025	[5] 3,863	3.58	99,980	1,453	14,245	4.12
1896	257,487	5,276	[5] 8,180	2.98	81,499	520	10,130	3.94
1895	235,822	54,776	848	3.23	89,686	372	1,530	3.63
1894	213,650	19,584	(NA)	3.29	75,328	194	1,804	3.52
1893	224,320	1,980	(NA)	3.73	78,832	213	3,723	4.08
1892	208,223	775	(NA)	4.09	87,260	149	6,247	4.63
1891	198,363	1,696	(NA)	4.35	80,873	404	2,147	5.02
1890	157,844	9,668	(NA)	4.48	63,683	999	1,648	5.55
1889	[6] 178,357	1,387	(NA)	3.93	58,860	1,026	440	5.02
1888	156,015	1,291	(NA)	4.42	55,903	1,913	31	4.91
1887	156,630	3,858	(NA)	4.50	50,340	4,194	68	4.62
1886	132,189	8,791	(NA)	4.63	42,641	2,150	459	4.40
1885	126,192	2,931	(NA)	3.95	40,688	1,758	51	4.34
1884	136,297	1,536	(NA)	3.74	38,544	2,935	63	4.44
1883	140,297	2,019	(NA)	4.32	36,872	8,534	426	4.50
1882	129,780	3,040	(NA)	4.91	33,765	9,204	745	5.32
1881	114,495	2,161	(NA)	4.81	30,258	1,430	746	5.24
1880	95,725	3,362	(NA)	5.04	25,100	4,046	684	5.51
1879	90,840	608	(NA)	4.14	21,300	710	1,066	5.04
1878	89,130	3,359	(NA)	3.61	19,600	635	1,273	4.88
1877	80,380	7,292	(NA)	5.49	15,600	633	710	6.03
1876	62,940	7,165	(NA)	6.13	17,000	474	67	7.25
1875	58,590	16,385	(NA)	5.85	16,700	1,017	19	7.00
1874	51,230	23,102	(NA)	6.01	13,100	1,797	22	(NA)
1873	41,940	36,212	(NA)	6.32	9,600	3,420	37	(NA)
1872	25,720	36,543	(NA)	6.30	7,800	5,901	31	(NA)
1871	19,970	45,748	(NA)	6.08	6,900	5,580	38	(NA)
1870	17,830	42,948	(NA)	6.25	5,400	4,611	55	(NA)
1869	17,500	43,933	(NA)	6.45	4,300	6,606	(NA)	(NA)
1868	16,400	31,627	219	6.50	3,700	4,664	511	(NA)
1867	15,200	32,661	50	6.50	3,200	2,876	156	(NA)
1866	16,100	----	13	6.90	2,000	----	70	(NA)
1865	14,700	----	426	6.60	2,100	----	92	(NA)
1864	15,300	----	112	7.10	1,800	----	48	13.9
1863	14,800	----	119	6.25	1,700	----	----	(NA)
1862	14,200	----	40	6.10	1,500	----	----	(NA)
1861	14,100	----	55	5.25	1,500	----	----	(NA)
1860	15,600	----	452	5.65	800	----	----	(NA)
1859	16,400	----	157	5.50	50	----	----	(NA)
1858	15,300	----	450	5.94	20	----	----	(NA)
1857	15,800	----	435	6.18	----	----	----	(NA)
1856	16,000	----	155	6.59	----	----	----	(NA)
1855	15,800	----	83	6.87	----	----	----	(NA)
1854	16,500	----	202	6.57	----	----	----	(NA)
1853	16,800	----	50	6.45	----	----	----	5.5

Year	Lead — Production, primary, refined from domestic and foreign ores (243)	Exports, refined (247)	Price, New York, pig lead (cents per lb.) (248)
1852	15,700	374	4.80
1851	18,500	115	4.85
1850	22,000	----	4.80
1849	23,500	----	4.78
1848	25,000	----	4.26
1847	28,000	----	4.37
1846	28,000	----	4.73
1845	30,000	----	4.03
1844	26,000	----	3.90
1843	25,000	----	3.58
1842	24,000	----	3.81
1841	20,500	----	4.50
1840	17,000	----	4.89
1839	17,500	----	5.83
1838	15,000	----	5.29
1837	13,500	----	5.96
1836	15,000	----	6.37½
1835	13,000	----	6.50
1834	12,000	----	5.12½
1833	11,000	----	5.91
1832	10,000	----	5.94
1831	7,500	----	4.56–6.00
1830	8,000	----	3.75
1829	8,571	----	3.75
1828	7,452	----	5.39
1827	4,490	----	6.14
1826	2,379	----	6.75
1825	2,232	----	7.59
1824	1,987	----	6.39
1823	2,068	----	5.36
1822	1,900	----	6.35
1821	1,900	----	6.63
1820	[7] 1,500	----	6.36
1819	[7] 1,500	----	6.70
1818	[7] 1,500	----	(NA)
1817	[7] 1,500	----	(NA)
1816	[7] 1,500	----	(NA)
1815	[7] 1,500	----	17.86
1814	[7] 1,500	----	(NA)
1813	[7] 1,500	----	(NA)
1812	[7] 1,500	----	11.16
1811	[7] 1,500	----	----
1810	[7] 1,000	----	----
1809	[7] 1,000	----	----
1808	[7] 1,000	----	----
1807	[7] 1,000	----	----
1806	[7] 1,000	----	----
1805	[7] 1,000	----	----
1804	[7] 1,000	----	----
1803	[7] 1,000	----	----
1802	[7] 1,000	----	----
1801	[7] 1,000	----	----

NA Not available.
[1] Includes production of zinc in concentrates used directly in alloying operations.
[2] Includes sheets and pipes; figures not available separately.
[3] Comprises reclaimed scrap; no recorded imports of pigs and bars.
[4] Excludes output of Virginia (Bureau of Mines was not at liberty to publish).
[5] Part of this is foreign lead mistakenly designated by customs collectors as domestic lead.
[6] Derived from Bureau of the Census.
[7] Estimates based on 5-year averages.

Series M 256-267.　Bauxite, Aluminum, Magnesium, and Uranium: 1886 to 1970

Year	Bauxite Domestic output (1,000 long tons)	Bauxite Imports (1,000 long tons)	Aluminum Production Primary, from domestic and foreign ores	Aluminum Production Secondary Total	Aluminum Production Secondary From old scrap	Aluminum Imports, crude and semicrude (1,000 short tons)	Aluminum Price, primary ingot (cents per lb.)	Magnesium Primary	Magnesium Secondary Total	Magnesium Secondary From old scrap	Uranium Production[1]	Uranium Imports[2]
	256	257	258	259	260	261	262	263	264	265	266	267
1970	2,082	12,620	3,976	781	146	468	28.7	112	12	3	12,340	665
1969	1,843	12,160	3,793	901	148	558	27.2	100	13	3	11,870	1,504
1968	1,665	10,976	3,255	817	155	793	25.6	98	16	3	12,070	470
1967	1,654	11,594	3,269	698	129	539	25.0	97	13	4	10,330	1,309
1966	1,796	11,529	2,968	693	137	679	24.5	80	15	5	9,520	2,123
1965	1,654	11,199	2,754	641	160	620	24.5	81	14	4	9,860	2,986
1964	1,601	10,180	2,553	552	124	453	23.7	79	12	4	13,220	5,756
1963	1,525	9,212	2,313	506	116	466	22.6	76	9	2	13,990	8,802
1962	1,369	10,575	2,118	462	129	377	23.9	69	10	3	16,040	11,720
1961	1,228	9,206	1,904	340	102	255	25.5	41	8	5	17,390	12,915
1960	1,998	8,739	2,014	329	63	196	26.0	40	10	4	17,260	15,770
1959	1,700	8,149	1,954	360	78	302	26.9	31	10	5	15,850	18,570
1958	1,311	7,915	1,566	290	64	293	26.9	30	9	5	11,910	16,500
1957	1,416	7,098	1,648	362	72	258	27.5	81	11	5	8,530	11,826
1956	1,744	5,670	1,679	340	72	265	26.01	68	11	5	6,690	7,500
1955	1,788	4,882	1,566	336	76	239	23.67	61	10	5	3,840	[3]3,800
1954	1,995	4,988	1,461	292	60	244	21.78	70	8	3	3,010	[3]3,240
1953	1,580	4,230	1,252	369	79	359	20.93	93	12	6	1,900	[3]1,910
1952	1,667	3,462	937	305	71	151	19.41	106	11	7	1,100	(NA)
1951	1,849	2,820	837	293	77	162	19.00	41	12	6	890	(NA)
1950	1,335	2,538	719	244	76	256	17.71	16	9	5	890	(NA)
1949	1,149	2,730	603	181	45	125	17.00	12	6	3	390	(NA)
1948	1,457	2,558	623	287	96	161	15.73	10	8	4	110	(NA)
1947	1,202	1,842	572	345	164	31	15.00	12	10	5	(NA)	(⁴)
1946	1,104	851	410	278	91	57	15.00	5	5	1	(NA)	
1945	981	737	495	298	27	339	15.00	33	9	1	(NA)	1
1944	2,824	556	776	326	23	103	15.00	157	14	(Z)	(NA)	5
1943	6,233	1,542	920	314	33	136	15.00	184	11	(Z)	(NA)	106
1942	2,602	884	521	196	42	112	15.00	49	6	(Z)	(NA)	189
1941	937	1,117	309	107	43	13	16.50	16	2	(Z)	11	194
1940	439	630	206	80	46	18	18.69	6	------	------	10	120
1939	375	520	164	54	38	14	20.00	3	------	------	35	720
1938	311	456	143	39	------	9	20.00	2	------	------	31	188
1937	425	507	146	63	------	23	20.08	2	------	------	12	102
1936	380	323	112	52	------	13	20.50	2	------	------	11	171
1935	245	200	60	51	------	11	20.50	2	------	------	13	148
1934	169	167	37	46	------	9	21.58	2	------	------	4	79
1933	154	150	43	34	------	8	23.30	1	------	------	1	93
1932	96	206	52	24	------	4	23.30	(Z)	------	------	2	61
1931	196	306	89	30	------	7	23.30	(Z)	------	------	1	90

Year	Bauxite Domestic output (1,000 long tons)	Bauxite Imports (1,000 long tons)	Aluminum Production Primary, from domestic and foreign ores	Aluminum Production Secondary, total	Aluminum Imports, crude and semicrude (1,000 short tons)	Aluminum Price, primary ingot (cents per lb.)	Magnesium, domestic output, primary (1,000 short tons)	Uranium Production[1]	Uranium Imports[2]
	256	257	258	259	261	262	263	266	267
1930	331	410	115	39	13	23.79	(Z)	1	116
1929	366	381	114	48	25	23.90	(Z)	1	136
1928	375	350	105	48	19	23.90	(Z)	1	83
1927	321	357	82	46	31	25.40	(Z)	(Z)	34
1926	392	282	74	44	36	26.99	(Z)	(Z)	27
1925	317	354	70	44	21	27.19	(Z)	17	10
1924	348	202	75	27	16	27.03	(Z)	(NA)	6
1923	523	119	64	21	21	25.41	(Z)	22	3
1922	310	24	37	16	22	18.68	(Z)	27	------
1921	140	28	27	9	16	21.11	(Z)	109	------
1920	521	43	69	16	20	32.72	(Z)	169	------
1919	377	6	64	19	7	32.14	(Z)	113	------
1918	606	4	62	15	1	33.53	(Z)	106	------
1917	569	8	65	16	(Z)	51.59	(Z)	103	------
1916	425	(Z)	58	19	3	60.71	(Z)	134	------
1915	300	3	45	8	5	33.98	(Z)	20	------
1914	219	25	29	5	9	18.63		87	------
1913	211	21	24	5	13	23.64		41	------
1912	161	26	21	------	11	22.01		26	------
1911	157	43	19	------	2	20.07		25	------
1910	151	16	18	------	6	22.25			
1909	132	19	15	------	3	22.00			
1908	50	22	5	------		28.70			
1907	94	25	8	------		45.00			
1906	71	18	7	------		35.75			
1905	57	12	5	------		35.00			
1904	51	15	4	------		35.00			
1903	45	15	3	------		33.00			
1902	27	16	3	------		33.00			
1901	20	18	3	------		33.00			
1900	23	9	3	------		32.72			
1899	33	7	2	------		32.72			
1898	25	1	1	------		30.58			
1897	21		1	------		39.00			
1896	18	------	1	------		50.75			
1895	17	------	(Z)	------	------	58.66			
1894	11	------	(Z)	------	------				
1893	9	------	(Z)	------	------				
1892	11	------	(Z)	------	------				
1891	4	------	(Z)	------	------				
1890	2	------	(Z)	------	------				
1889	1	------	(Z)	------	------				
1888	------	------	(Z)	------	------				
1887	------	------	(Z)	------	------				
1886	------	------	(Z)	------	------				

NA Not available.
Z Less than 500 tons.
[1] Content of ore shipments, 1911-1941; recoverable content of ore shipments, 1948-1970.

[2] 1915-1922, data available only on value: 1915, $17,288; 1916, $5,065; 1917, $2,930; 1918, $274; 1919, $12,960; 1920, see footnote 4; 1921, $8,552; 1922, $28,685.
[3] Fiscal year data, AEC.
[4] Less than one-half ton.

Series M 268–270. Gold and Silver: 1792 to 1970

[In thousands of fine troy ounces, except price in cents per fine ounce]

Year	Gold, production	Silver Production	Silver Average price, New York	Year	Gold, production	Silver Production	Silver Average price, New York	Year	Gold, production	Silver Production	Silver Average price, New York	Year	Gold, production	Silver Production	Silver Average price, New York
	268	269	270		268	269	270		268	269	270		268	269	270
1970	1,743	45,006	177.084	1935	3,237	48,519	64.273	1900	3,830	57,647	61.330	1865	2,575	8,701	133.700
1969	1,733	41,906	179.067	1934	2,779	32,782	47.973	1899	3,437	54,764	59.580	1864	2,230	8,508	134.500
1968	1,478	32,729	214.460	1933	2,292	23,129	34.727	1898	3,118	54,438	58.260	1863	1,935	6,574	134.500
1967	1,584	32,345	154.967	1932	2,269	22,762	27.892	1897	2,775	53,860	59.790	1862	1,896	3,480	135.000
1966	1,803	43,669	129.300	1931	2,225	29,857	28.700	1896	2,568	58,835	67.060	1861	2,080	1,547	133.000
1965	1,705	39,806	129.300	1930	2,139	47,725	38.154	1895	2,255	55,727	65.280	1860	2,225	116	135.000
1964	1,456	36,334	129.300	1929	2,059	60,860	52.993	1894	1,911	49,500	63.000	1859	2,419	77	136.000
1963	1,454	35,243	127.912	1928	2,148	57,872	58.176	1893	1,739	60,000	78.200	1858	2,419	39	134.000
1962	1,543	36,798	108.375	1927	2,107	59,626	56.370	1892	1,597	63,500	87.600	1857	2,661	39	135.000
1961	1,548	34,794	92.449	1926	2,233	62,487	62.107	1891	1,605	58,330	98.800	1856	2,661	39	134.000
1960	1,667	30,766	91.375	1925	2,307	66,710	69.065	1890	1,589	54,516	104.600	1855	2,661	39	134.000
1959	1,603	31,194	91.202	1924	2,444	64,071	66.781	1889	1,595	50,094	93.600	1854	2,902	39	135.000
1958	1,739	34,111	89.044	1923	2,405	70,356	64.873	1888	1,604	45,793	94.000	1853	3,144	39	135.000
1957	1,794	38,165	90.820	1922	2,293	61,208	67.528	1887	1,603	41,722	97.800	1852	2,902	39	133.000
1956	1,827	38,722	90.830	1921	2,345	46,171	62.654	1886	1,687	39,694	99.500	1851	2,661	39	134.000
1955	1,800	37,198	89.099	1920	2,383	56,537	100.900	1885	1,538	39,909	106.500	1850	2,419	39	132.000
1954	1,837	36,941	85.250	1919	2,753	51,899	111.122	1884	1,490	37,744	111.300	1849	1,935	39	-------
1953	1,958	37,571	85.188	1918	3,213	68,059	96.772	1883	1,451	35,733	111.000	1848	484	39	-------
1952	1,893	39,452	84.941	1917	3,900	70,662	81.417	1882	1,572	36,197	114.000	1847	43	39	-------
1951	1,981	39,765	89.368	1916	4,417	78,858	65.601	1881	1,679	33,258	113.000	1846	55	39	-------
1950	2,394	42,459	74.169	1915	4,754	72,354	49.684	1880	1,742	30,319	115.000	1845	49	39	-------
1949	1,992	34,675	71.930	1914	4,418	69,623	54.811	1879	1,882	31,566	112.000	1844	55	19	-------
1948	2,014	38,096	74.361	1913	4,311	71,187	59.791	1878	2,477	35,022	115.000	1843	58	19	-------
1947	2,109	35,824	71.820	1912	4,466	66,034	60.835	1877	2,269	30,778	120.000	1842	43	19	-------
1946	1,575	22,915	80.151	1911	4,686	61,108	53.304	1876	1,932	29,996	116.000	1841	30	19	-------
1945	955	29,024	51.928	1910	4,585	57,597	53.486	1875	1,619	24,530	124.000	1840	24	19	-------
1944	998	34,474	44.750	1909	4,798	57,313	51.502	1874	1,620	28,868	127.800	1839	23	19	-------
1943	1,364	41,461	44.750	1908	4,435	50,876	52.864	1873	1,742	27,650	129.700	1838	24	19	-------
1942	3,457	54,091	38.333	1907	4,227	52,500	65.327	1872	1,742	22,236	132.200	1837	16	19	-------
1941	4,751	67,048	34.783	1906	4,703	57,362	66.791	1871	2,104	17,789	132.500	1836	26	19	-------
1940	4,870	70,436	34.773	1905	4,265	56,272	60.352	1870	2,419	12,375	132.800	1835	39	19	-------
1939	4,673	64,373	39.082	1904	3,911	56,000	57.221	1869	2,395	9,281	132.500	1834	(NA)	8	-------
1938	4,267	61,706	43.225	1903	3,560	54,300	53.570	1868	2,322	9,281	132.600	1835–1844	363	193	-------
1937	4,117	71,409	44.883	1902	3,870	55,500	52.160	1867	2,502	10,441	133.000	1792–1834	677	-------	-------
1936	3,783	61,153	45.087	1901	3,806	55,214	58.950	1866	2,588	7,734	133.900				

NA Not available.

Series M 271–286. Injuries and Fatalities in Coal Mining, Quarrying and Related Industries, and Metal and Nonmetal Mines: 1870 to 1970

Year	All coal mining — Number of injuries Fatal	Non-fatal	Frequency rate per million man-hours Fatal[1]	Non-fatal	Fatalities per 1,000 300-day workers	Fatalities per 1,000 employed	Quarrying and related industries[2] — Number of injuries Fatal	Non-fatal	Frequency rate per million man-hours[3] Fatal	Non-fatal[4]	Metal and nonmetal mining — Number of injuries Fatal	Non-fatal	Frequency rate per million man-hours[5] Fatal	Non-fatal	Frequency rate per 1,000 300-day workers Fatal	Non-fatal
	271	272	273	274	275	276	277	278	279	280	281	282	283	284	285	286
1970	260	11,552	1.0	44	2.42	1.86	43	3,666	0.2	20	93	6,637	0.4	26	0.9	62
1969	203	9,917	.9	42	2.03	1.52	53	3,389	.3	18	95	6,092	.4	24	.9	57
1968	311	9,639	1.3	41	3.15	2.31	58	3,260	.3	17	98	5,847	.4	24	1.0	57
1967	222	10,115	.9	42	2.18	1.59	46	3,267	.3	18	103	6,019	.4	24	1.0	58
1966	233	10,446	1.0	43	2.27	1.60	51	3,583	.3	19	109	6,632	.4	24	1.0	58
1965	259	11,138	1.0	45	2.47	1.74	48	3,305	.3	17	92	6,236	.3	23	.8	56
1964	242	11,070	1.0	44	2.27	1.61	61	3,367	.3	18	84	6,158	.3	24	.8	58
1963	284	11,133	1.1	44	2.65	1.81	61	3,468	.3	18	79	5,818	.3	23	.8	56
1962	289	10,944	1.1	45	2.73	1.79	67	3,299	.4	17	98	6,072	.4	23	.9	57
1961	294	11,197	1.2	44	2.71	1.75	32	4,280	.2	22	74	6,668	.3	24	.6	58
1960	325	11,902	1.2	42	2.73	1.71	39	4,668	.2	23	121	7,132	.4	24	1.0	58
1959	293	12,163	1.0	41	2.33	1.44	52	4,790	.3	24	100	6,862	.4	26	.9	62
1958	358	14,160	1.1	44	2.61	1.59	45	4,572	.2	24	97	6,411	.4	25	.9	60
1957	478	18,792	1.2	46	2.75	1.88	53	4,210	.3	23	99	7,921	.3	27	.8	66
1956	448	19,816	1.0	46	2.43	1.72	50	3,754	.3	21	[6]122	8,347	.5	32	1.1	76
1955	420	18,885	1.0	45	2.35	1.61	53	3,811	.3	22	[6]104	8,239	.5	36	1.1	87
1954	396	17,718	1.0	46	2.40	1.40	34	3,834	.2	22	105	6,780	.5	34	1.3	81
1953	461	24,258	.9	47	2.11	1.31	43	4,450	.2	23	118	8,409	.5	36	1.2	87
1952	548	30,074	.9	51	2.16	1.37	74	4,503	.4	24	135	8,707	.6	38	1.4	92
1951	785	35,553	1.1	51	2.64	1.78	57	4,945	.3	26	118	8,953	.5	39	1.2	94
1950	643	37,264	.9	52	2.11	1.33	54	4,762	.3	25	110	8,634	.5	41	1.3	98
1949	585	35,405	.9	55	1.13	1.21	66	4,826	.4	26	86	8,863	.4	43	1.0	103
1948	999	53,472	1.1	60	2.60	1.97	75	4,994	.4	28	128	9,641	.6	43	1.4	103
1947	1,158	57,660	1.2	61	2.96	2.36	75	5,504	.4	32	145	10,472	.7	47	1.6	114
1946	968	55,350	1.1	63	2.80	2.09	55	5,137	.4	32	126	9,580	.7	51	1.6	122

See footnotes at end of table.

Series **M 271–286.** Injuries and Fatalities in Coal Mining, Quarrying and Related Industries, and Metal and Nonmetal Mines: 1870 to 1970—Con.

Year	All coal mining						Quarrying and related industries [2]				Metal and nonmetal mining					
	Number of injuries		Frequency rate per million man-hours		Fatalities per 1,000 300-day workers	Fatalities per 1,000 employed	Number of injuries		Frequency rate per million man-hours [3]		Number of injuries		Frequency rate per million man-hours [5]		Frequency rate per 1,000 300-day workers	
	Fatal	Non-fatal	Fatal [1]	Non-fatal			Fatal	Non-fatal	Fatal	Non-fatal [4]	Fatal	Non-fatal	Fatal	Non-fatal	Fatal	Non-fatal
	271	272	273	274	275	276	277	278	279	280	281	282	283	284	285	286
1945	1,068	57,117	1.1	60	2.82	2.44	53	4,121	0.4	32	[7] 121	9,099	0.6	45	1.4	107
1944	1,298	63,691	1.2	59	3.05	2.86	73	4,437	.6	34	147	10,177	.8	54	1.9	130
1943	1,451	64,594	1.4	62	3.39	2.98	80	5,199	.5	33	220	13,004	.9	56	2.3	134
1942	1,471	66,774	1.4	65	3.42	2.77	112	6,349	.6	35	237	13,957	.9	56	2.3	133
1941	1,266	61,057	1.4	66	3.26	2.32	76	6,870	.4	40	230	15,772	.9	62	2.2	148
1940	1,388	57,776	1.6	69	3.92	2.60	72	5,188	.5	35	223	14,766	1.0	64	2.3	153
1939	1,078	51,773	1.4	68	3.35	2.00	48	5,204	.3	36	173	13,710	.8	66	2.0	158
1938	1,105	49,636	1.6	71	3.76	2.04	82	5,027	.6	38	156	12,722	.8	68	2.0	162
1937	1,413	66,259	1.6	73	3.69	2.40	77	6,348	.5	40	219	18,055	.9	75	2.2	181
1936	1,342	67,540	1.4	73	3.50	2.30	91	5,717	.6	39	199	14,650	1.0	72	2.4	174
1935	1,242	63,426	1.5	77	3.67	2.20	51	4,152	.5	38	164	10,206	1.0	63	2.4	150
1934	1,226	65,559	1.4	77	3.54	2.16	60	3,924	.6	41	116	7,892	1.0	68	2.4	161
1933	1,064	59,129	1.3	75	3.58	2.03	59	3,637	.7	41	95	5,925	1.0	63	2.4	153
1932	1,207	56,283	1.7	80	4.60	2.29	32	3,574	.3	38	107	5,014	1.2	54	2.9	136
1931	1,463	77,958	1.7	88	4.42	2.48	61	5,427	.5	41	158	8,709	1.0	56	2.5	140
1930	2,063	99,981	1.9	91	5.00	3.20	105	7,417	.6	40	271	15,594	--------	--------	2.9	168
1929	2,187	--------	1.9	--------	4.54	3.34	126	9,810	.6	46	350	23,092	--------	--------	3.0	200
1928	2,176	--------	1.9	--------	4.64	3.19	119	10,568	.5	47	273	22,483	--------	--------	2.5	206
1927	2,231	--------	1.8	--------	4.43	2.94	135	13,459	.6	59	352	25,133	--------	--------	3.1	222
1926	2,518	--------	1.9	--------	4.50	3.32	154	13,201	.7	57	430	30,350	--------	--------	3.5	245
1925	2,234	--------	1.9	--------	4.65	2.98	149	14,165	.6	61	371	35,132	--------	--------	3.0	284
1924	2,402	--------	2.0	--------	4.80	3.08	138	14,777	.6	62	418	33,118	--------	--------	3.5	278
1923	2,462	--------	1.8	--------	4.39	2.85	143	14,990	.6	63	367	33,563	--------	--------	3.0	275
1922	1,984	--------	2.0	--------	4.90	2.35	132	11,839	.7	61	344	26,080	--------	--------	3.5	268
1921	1,995	--------	1.7	--------	4.20	2.42	120	10,465	.7	62	230	18,604	--------	--------	3.1	250
1920	2,272	--------	1.6	--------	3.78	2.90	178	11,217	.8	52	425	32,562	--------	--------	3.2	242
1919	2,323	--------	1.8	--------	4.28	2.99	123	9,199	.7	51	468	31,506	--------	--------	3.5	234
1918	2,580	--------	1.6	--------	3.94	3.38	125	8,719	.8	52	646	42,915	--------	--------	3.6	237
1917	2,696	--------	1.7	--------	4.25	3.56	131	13,242	.6	66	852	46,286	--------	--------	4.4	241
1916	2,226	--------	1.5	--------	3.93	3.09	173	13,427	.8	63	697	[8] 48,237	--------	--------	3.6	[8] 251
1915	2,269	--------	1.7	--------	4.44	3.09	148	9,671	.6	42	553	35,295	--------	--------	3.9	249
1914	2,454	--------	1.8	--------	4.66	3.22	180	7,836	.9	41	559	30,216	--------	--------	3.9	212
1913	2,785	--------	1.8	--------	4.70	3.73	183	7,739	.8	32	683	32,971	--------	--------	3.7	180
1912	2,419	--------	1.7	--------	4.46	3.35	213	6,552	.8	25	661	30,724	--------	--------	4.1	190
1911	2,656	--------	1.9	--------	4.97	3.65	188	5,390	.8	23	695	26,577	--------	--------	4.4	170
1910	2,821	--------	[9] 2.6	--------	5.30	3.89										
1909	2,642	--------	[9] 2.3	--------	5.35	3.96										
1908	2,445	--------	[9] 2.1	--------	5.54	3.60										
1907	3,242	--------	[9] 2.6	--------	6.25	4.81										
1906	2,138	--------	[9] 1.6	--------	4.87	3.39										
1905	2,232	--------	[10] 2.0	--------	5.14	3.63										
1904	1,995	--------	[10] 2.1	--------	5.17	3.48										
1903	1,926	--------	[10] 1.9	--------	4.72	3.46										
1902	1,724	--------	--------	--------	5.15	3.38										
1901	1,574	--------	--------	--------	4.54	3.27										

Year	All coal mining			Year	All coal mining		Year	All coal mining	
	Number of injuries, fatal	Fatalities per 1,000 300-day workers	Fatalities per 1,000 employed		Number of injuries, fatal	Fatalities per 1,000 employed		Number of injuries, fatal	Fatalities per 1,000 employed
	271	275	276		271	276		271	276
1900	1,489	4.87	3.44	1889	668	2.36	1879	329	3.30
1899	1,241	4.40	3.14	1888	728	2.55	1878	260	2.62
1898	1,062	4.28	2.71	1887	535	2.20	1877	244	2.77
1897	990	4.27	2.55	1886	530	2.25	1876	256	2.83
1896	1,083	4.62	2.85	1885	574	2.58	1875	260	3.06
1895	1,142	4.68	3.04	1884	762	2.80	1874	260	3.87
1894	958	4.50	2.67	1883	593	3.34	1873	[11] 263	5.46
1893	958	4.03	2.70	1882	502	2.75	1872	[11] 223	4.98
1892	991	4.42	3.12	1881	416	2.93	1871	[11] 210	5.60
1891	956	4.30	3.08	1880	280	2.21	1870	[11] 211	5.93
1890	733	3.50	2.52						

[1] Figures for 1930–1970 are on a portal-to-portal basis; earlier years are on a working-time basis. The 1930 frequency rate for fatalities per million man-hours on a portal-to-portal basis was 1.9, the working-time rate was 2.1.
[2] Includes manufacture of cement and lime.
[3] Man-hours for 1911–1923 computed on assumption that weighted average length of workday was 9.36 hours, as shown by reports from representative operating companies for 1924.
[4] Injury rate for years before 1916 are believed not to be representative, owing to probable incompleteness of reports of slight or minor injuries.
[5] Man-hours not available prior to 1931.

[6] Nonmetal mill data were included for the first time in 1955. Clay mill data were included for the first time in 1956.
[7] Beginning with 1945, metal mill data are included.
[8] Accident reports for mines in the gold, silver, and miscellaneous metal groups are not complete as to nonfatal injuries before 1916.
[9] Data for bituminous and anthracite coal mining. Data for 1906–1909 for bituminous coal cover only the States that maintained complete records of fatal accidents. They represent 98 to 99 percent of the total production of coal in the U.S.
[10] Data for anthracite coal mining only.
[11] Data reflect only Pennsylvania anthracite fatalities; data for bituminous coal mining are not available prior to 1874.

Series M 287-296.   Average Number of Men Working Daily in Mineral Industries: 1911 to 1970

[Excludes data on iron smelting and steel industries]

Year	Coal mines	Coke	Petroleum and natural gas	Metal mines [1]	Nonmetal mines, including clay mines [1]	Sand and gravel operations	Stone quarrying and related industries	Metal mills	Primary nonferrous smelter and refineries [2]	Nonmetal mills
	287	288	289	290	291	292	293	294	295	296
1970	144,480	13,997	462,468	46,108	15,339	50,674	82,010	21,535	44,674	27,159
1969	133,302	13,617	449,606	46,500	16,400	50,161	83,149	22,300	45,200	27,900
1968	134,467	13,093	466,652	46,180	16,630	49,901	84,084	20,298	41,529	28,946
1967	139,312	13,701	445,562	48,496	18,020	52,363	84,765	20,928	43,046	31,427
1966	145,244	14,216	451,747	49,920	18,727	55,344	85,826	20,175	40,401	32,001
1965	148,734	14,521	436,935	51,420	17,214	54,159	89,580	19,484	41,627	31,215
1964	150,761	13,447	427,697	49,765	17,087	55,886	87,859	18,375	36,956	31,967
1963	157,126	13,043	461,021	47,844	15,570	52,804	91,960	18,016	34,442	33,732
1962	161,286	13,080	469,256	52,287	16,917	53,599	92,241	19,983	34,824	34,900
1961	167,568	13,534	452,721	54,251	18,281	55,726	91,371	20,518	35,547	39,031
1960	189,679	16,463	511,107	60,595	18,653	52,352	95,304	22,529	36,160	39,568
1959	203,597	16,645	559,244	58,557	18,765	59,492	91,523	19,423	36,232	40,800
1958	224,890	16,186	584,708	59,608	17,820	51,122	88,448	19,677	32,432	32,401
1957	254,725	20,264	617,596	68,457	17,921	------------	84,126	21,566	43,646	27,081
1956	260,285	20,473	585,486	68,273	15,595	------------	80,093	19,261	46,420	17,585
1955	260,089	20,681	617,274	65,143	14,504	------------	78,238	17,631	40,110	8,723
1954	283,705	19,209	580,783	66,610	12,810	------------	78,910	19,095	35,301	------------
1953	351,126	23,440	594,398	72,529	12,765	------------	83,641	19,757	35,526	------------
1952	401,329	25,241	586,138	74,626	12,447	------------	81,879	17,551	31,481	------------
1951	441,905	25,715	539,095	71,603	12,500	------------	84,802	16,339	31,680	------------
1950	483,239	24,347	517,787	68,292	11,977	------------	85,730	14,956	31,321	------------
1949	485,306	24,471	516,940	71,664	12,077	------------	82,209	16,688	30,975	------------
1948	507,333	25,157	501,253	71,436	11,950	------------	77,344	15,634	32,134	------------
1947	490,356	23,705	458,043	71,228	12,176	------------	75,245	15,937	33,145	------------
1946	463,079	21,410	432,263	65,234	11,312	------------	70,265	15,597	29,357	------------
1945	437,921	22,987	395,815	61,294	10,371	------------	58,180	15,792	30,675	------------
1944	453,937	24,766	409,165	70,413	11,261	------------	58,476	------------	39,953	------------
1943	486,516	25,765	397,345	87,880	12,713	------------	69,877	------------	45,446	------------
1942	530,861	23,909	317,810	99,769	12,677	------------	84,270	------------	31,805	------------
1941	546,692	22,641	------------	114,202	11,088	------------	86,123	------------	------------	------------
1940	533,267	19,962	------------	110,340	9,780	------------	79,509	------------	------------	------------
1939	539,375	16,609	------------	102,279	9,630	------------	79,449	------------	------------	------------
1938	541,528	13,799	------------	93,501	9,526	------------	77,497	------------	------------	------------
1937	589,856	20,042	------------	108,412	10,017	------------	84,094	------------	------------	------------
1936	584,582	17,811	------------	90,552	10,380	------------	80,022	------------	------------	------------
1935	565,202	16,125	------------	83,975	8,339	------------	73,005	------------	------------	------------
1934	566,426	15,483	------------	58,411	8,234	------------	64,331	------------	------------	------------
1933	523,182	13,598	------------	49,338	7,678	------------	61,927	------------	------------	------------
1932	527,623	12,002	------------	46,602	6,686	------------	56,866	------------	------------	------------
1931	589,705	15,564	------------	71,991	8,949	------------	69,200	------------	------------	------------
1930	644,006	19,855	------------	92,671	10,562	------------	80,633	------------	------------	------------
1929	654,494	22,459	------------	107,404	11,331	------------	85,561	------------	------------	------------
1928	682,831	19,390	------------	101,662	12,204	------------	89,667	------------	------------	------------
1927	759,177	20,667	------------	107,070	12,629	------------	91,517	------------	------------	------------
1926	759,033	23,115	------------	114,300	13,523	------------	91,146	------------	------------	------------
1925	748,805	23,254	------------	113,748	12,965	------------	91,872	------------	------------	------------
1924	779,613	20,451	------------	111,558	11,570	------------	94,242	------------	------------	------------
1923	862,536	23,729	------------	111,647	11,632	------------	92,455	------------	------------	------------
1922	844,807	19,278	------------	94,584	11,113	------------	79,081	------------	------------	------------
1921	823,253	16,204	------------	82,323	11,606	------------	77,185	------------	------------	------------
1920	784,621	28,139	------------	122,815	13,768	------------	86,488	------------	------------	------------
1919	776,569	27,741	------------	132,101	13,161	------------	75,505	------------	------------	------------
1918	762,426	32,389	------------	170,759	11,847	------------	68,332	------------	------------	------------
1917	757,317	32,417	------------	190,666	9,913	------------	82,200	------------	------------	------------
1916	720,971	31,603	------------	195,438	9,247	------------	90,797	------------	------------	------------
1915	734,008	------------	------------	144,854	7,264	------------	100,740	------------	------------	------------
1914	763,185	------------	------------	148,866	9,249	------------	87,936	------------	------------	------------
1913	747,644	------------	------------	179,470	11,806	------------	106,278	------------	------------	------------
1912	722,662	------------	------------	155,998	13,201	------------	113,105	------------	------------	------------
1911	728,348	------------	------------	152,086	13,893	------------	110,954	------------	------------	------------

[1] Beginning 1942, fluorspar mines included with nonmetal mines.

[2] Beginning 1943, includes aluminum plants.

Series M 297–306. Man-Hours Worked in Mineral Industries: 1911 to 1970

[In thousands. Excludes data on iron smelting and steel industries]

Year	Coal mines [1]	Coke	Petroleum and natural gas	Metal mines [2]	Nonmetal mines, including clay mines [2]	Sand and gravel operations	Stone quarrying and related industries	Metal mills	Primary nonferrous smelter and refineries	Nonmetal mills
	297	298	299	300	301	302	303	304	305	306
1970	260,169	39,554	972,278	107,794	32,420	95,067	184,225	57,297	124,692	62,365
1969	237,484	38,520	939,385	103,975	35,020	94,223	187,003	54,800	125,350	62,745
1968	234,417	37,546	986,952	98,693	35,633	93,156	186,620	50,182	109,012	63,781
1967	241,774	38,956	938,946	95,794	38,550	96,645	186,227	46,951	105,551	68,850
1966	243,759	40,730	954,527	111,857	41,003	104,971	190,787	51,050	109,257	72,810
1965	248,988	40,869	931,645	112,277	37,760	100,083	194,000	48,657	109,567	70,975
1964	252,405	38,418	910,525	104,204	35,977	100,891	188,000	45,243	97,807	71,461
1963	253,185	36,759	974,877	97,111	32,539	95,786	193,685	43,874	94,020	75,944
1962	248,946	37,502	984,172	103,867	32,484	97,589	193,453	49,163	90,975	74,621
1961	255,296	38,306	951,743	107,678	35,517	101,707	192,705	49,552	91,862	83,925
1960	281,528	46,066	1,063,332	119,653	36,805	95,749	202,366	53,638	91,572	86,386
1959	296,031	43,626	1,185,146	100,576	36,334	109,830	199,321	38,621	90,291	90,706
1958	322,229	45,486	1,215,722	109,523	34,648	92,456	186,821	41,799	83,974	71,161
1957	408,207	57,337	1,293,725	142,181	37,877	----------	183,394	49,795	117,694	59,765
1956	433,662	56,557	1,235,555	144,407	33,963	----------	178,281	45,440	126,138	40,675
1955	419,379	58,164	1,303,014	136,950	31,093	----------	175,775	39,837	106,004	19,843
1954	387,950	52,482	1,228,710	130,488	29,564	----------	175,817	42,121	91,554	----------
1953	513,594	64,677	1,264,020	156,605	30,488	----------	189,777	46,813	91,999	----------
1952	593,698	62,803	1,227,984	158,649	28,954	----------	186,552	41,370	83,597	----------
1951	697,247	70,190	1,147,904	159,417	30,130	----------	191,113	39,179	82,909	----------
1950	711,390	65,861	1,081,519	147,765	28,456	----------	189,535	34,815	81,615	----------
1949	642,476	62,446	1,085,827	144,368	26,948	----------	182,258	34,974	77,121	----------
1948	898,231	70,021	1,072,728	161,516	27,784	----------	179,111	36,104	84,923	----------
1947	949,539	66,119	973,155	157,024	28,809	----------	171,979	36,213	86,418	----------
1946	879,628	57,710	921,138	130,406	26,877	----------	158,528	32,082	69,591	----------
1945	958,591	64,375	926,250	141,295	24,613	----------	127,168	38,305	83,185	----------
1944	1,078,474	69,590	954,974	163,027	25,760	----------	129,302	----------	107,284	----------
1943	1,034,541	70,679	887,279	206,242	27,999	----------	155,280	----------	125,605	----------
1942	1,021,078	65,222	665,929	223,093	28,093	----------	180,836	----------	86,899	----------
1941	921,536	60,887	----------	230,453	23,225	----------	173,165	----------	----------	----------
1940	840,416	53,624	----------	211,740	18,988	----------	147,244	----------	----------	----------
1939	760,039	43,737	----------	189,554	17,281	----------	143,847	----------	----------	----------
1938	695,599	36,607	----------	170,343	17,827	----------	133,766	----------	----------	----------
1937	912,435	54,445	----------	219,008	20,536	----------	158,299	----------	----------	----------
1936	926,305	49,319	----------	180,803	21,556	----------	147,064	----------	----------	----------
1935	819,143	40,941	----------	145,134	16,168	----------	110,033	----------	----------	----------
1934	855,487	42,893	----------	100,959	15,187	----------	95,259	----------	----------	----------
1933	792,847	37,214	----------	80,006	14,134	----------	87,888	----------	----------	----------
1932	699,125	33,217	----------	80,213	11,825	----------	93,710	----------	----------	----------
1931	883,286	44,574	----------	138,237	17,941	----------	133,750	----------	----------	----------
1930	1,102,902	55,969	----------	----------	----------	----------	186,502	----------	----------	----------
1929	1,168,551	63,657	----------	----------	----------	----------	211,766	----------	----------	----------
1928	1,135,543	54,157	----------	----------	----------	----------	224,953	----------	----------	----------
1927	1,219,079	58,234	----------	----------	----------	----------	229,806	----------	----------	----------
1926	1,352,840	61,635	----------	----------	----------	----------	230,464	----------	----------	----------
1925	1,160,334	60,953	----------	----------	----------	----------	233,222	----------	----------	----------
1924	1,207,475	51,948	----------	----------	----------	----------	236,983	----------	----------	----------
1923	1,356,089	66,637	----------	----------	----------	----------	239,109	----------	----------	----------
1922	979,995	52,596	----------	----------	----------	----------	193,362	----------	----------	----------
1921	1,145,738	40,673	----------	----------	----------	----------	168,363	----------	----------	----------
1920	1,451,162	86,070	----------	----------	----------	----------	216,465	----------	----------	----------
1919	1,309,155	78,973	----------	----------	----------	----------	179,135	----------	----------	----------
1918	1,599,854	100,156	----------	----------	----------	----------	166,472	----------	----------	----------
1917	1,575,863	99,305	----------	----------	----------	----------	200,841	----------	----------	----------
1916	1,452,788	95,147	----------	----------	----------	----------	214,692	----------	----------	----------
1915	1,339,279	----------	----------	----------	----------	----------	231,512	----------	----------	----------
1914	1,378,437	----------	----------	----------	----------	----------	191,470	----------	----------	----------
1913	1,549,294	----------	----------	----------	----------	----------	244,691	----------	----------	----------
1912	1,422,694	----------	----------	----------	----------	----------	263,494	----------	----------	----------
1911	1,302,108	----------	----------	----------	----------	----------	237,043	----------	----------	----------

[1] Man-hours for 1930-70 are on a portal-to-portal basis. Prior to 1930, man-hours are on a face-to-face basis.

[2] Beginning 1942, fluorspar mines included with nonmetal mines.

★ ★ ★ ★ ★ ★ ★ ★ ★ ★   **More Recent Data for *Historical Statistics* Series**   ★ ★ ★ ★ ★ ★ ★ ★ ★ ★

Statistics for more recent years in continuation of many of the still-active series shown here appear in annual issues of the *Statistical Abstract of the United States*, beginning with the 1975 edition. For direct linkage of the historical series to the tables in the *Abstract*, see Appendix I in the *Abstract*.

★ ★

Appendix:

Contributors to This Edition of Historical Statistics

[Listed below, by chapter and subject, are the names of persons other than those listed on pp. viii–x, who contributed new or revised data or text additions and revisions to this edition, to the extent they could be identified. In some cases, manuscript was provided for the book without specific identification of the persons engaged in its compilation, preparation, or review]

Subject	Contributor	Subject	Contributor
Chapter A		**Chapter D—Con.**	
State areas	Robert C. Klove, Bureau of the Census	Employee earnings and wage supplements	F. Beatrice Coleman, Bureau of Economic Analysis
Households and families	Arthur J. Norton and Robert O. Grymes, Bureau of the Census	Hours and earnings, selected industries	Gerald Storch, Bureau of Labor Statistics
Chapter B		Wage rates and hours, printing and building trades	John Fitsock and Thomas Mobley, Bureau of Labor Statistics
Health expenditures	Barbara Cooper, Dorothy P. Rice, and Alfred M. Skolnik, Social Security Administration	Engineering salaries	John Alden, Engineering Manpower Commission
Medical care price indexes	Marie Schlegel, Bureau of Labor Statistics	Work stoppages	Albert A. Balman and Norman J. Samuels, Bureau of Labor Statistics
Physicians, dentists, nurses, hospitals	Genevieve Strahan, Public Health Service	Injury rates, selected industries	Joseph Musselwhite, Bureau of Railroad Safety
Reportable disease rates	W. Jere Housworth, Gladys Reynolds, and William Stewart, Center for Disease Control	**Chapter E**	
Hospitals	Bernard Ferber, American Hospital Association	Implicit price deflators	Allan H. Young, Bureau of Economic Analysis
Mental health care	Richard Walker, Social and Rehabilitation Service, and Shirley G. Willner, National Institute of Mental Health	Wholesale price indexes	Craig Howell and William Thomas, Bureau of Labor Statistics
Nutrition	Kathryn R. Coleman and Berta Friend, Department of Agriculture	Wholesale prices	Joseph A. Clorety, Jr., and Lloyd Wigren, Bureau of Labor Statistics
Fluoridation	John Small, Public Health Service	Retail prices, selected foods	Kenneth V. Dalton, Bureau of Labor Statistics
Chapter C		Retail price indexes, fuels	Richard Bahr and Rod Meany, Bureau of Labor Statistics
Native population, by residence and place of birth	Larry Long, Bureau of the Census	**Chapter F**	
Intercensal migration	James B. Tarver, University of Georgia	Gross national product and national income	Edward O. Bassett, Jacqueline Bauman, Leo M. Bernstein, John A. Gorman, and Jack J. Gottsegen, Bureau of Economic Analysis
Farm population movement	Vera Banks, Department of Agriculture	National wealth and saving	Helen S. Tice, Board of Governors of the Federal Reserve System
Population mobility	Kristin A. Hansen, Bureau of the Census	Nonresidential and residential capital	Bruce Levine, John C. Musgrave, and Robert C. Wasson, Bureau of Economic Analysis
Immigration and naturalization	Marvin Gibson, Robert G. Prosek, and Nellie W. Schneider, Immigration and Naturalization Service	Individuals' saving	Jeannette M. Honsa, Securities and Exchange Commission
Citizenship and ethnicity	Karen A. Crook and Nampeo R. McKenney, Bureau of the Census	**Chapter G**	
Chapter D		Money income distribution	Robert W. Cleveland and Mary F. Henson, Bureau of the Census
Labor force characteristics	Paula J. Schneider, Bureau of the Census	Personal income distribution	Daniel B. Radner, Bureau of Economic Analysis
Women in the labor force	Carl Rosenfeld, Bureau of Labor Statistics	Consumption expenditures of farm families	Frances M. Magrabi, Department of Agriculture
Persons with a job but not at work and civilians employed	John Stinson, Bureau of Labor Statistics	Per capita food consumption	Kathryn R. Coleman, Department of Agriculture

Appendix: Contributors to This Edition—Con.

Subject	Contributor	Subject	Contributor
Chapter H		**Chapter H—Con.**	
Workers covered under social insurance programs	John E. Bregger, Bureau of Labor Statistics	Boxing	Nat Fleischer, The Ring
Old-age, survivors, disability, and health insurance	Harry Shulman, Social Security Administration	Personal expenditures for recreation	Edward O. Bassett, Bureau of Economic Analysis
Civil Service retirement	Stewart C. Reiman and Edwin Hustead, Civil Service Commission	Passports	Emil W. Kontak and Eleanor L. Schwartz, Passport Office
Railroad retirement	Samuel A. Block and Robert B. McNab, Railroad Retirement Board	Foreign visitors	Etienne H. Miller, Bureau of Economic Analysis
Unemployment insurance	John Hunter and T. James Walker, Manpower Administration	Homicides and suicides	Robert J. Armstrong, Public Health Service
Public and old-age assistance	Harold Coleman, Anne L. Henneman, and Sigmund Schor, Social and Rehabilitation Service	Arrests	Walter Crone, Federal Bureau of Investigation
Child health and welfare programs	Donald A. Trauger, Public Health Service	Juvenile Court	Louise T. Jackson, Public Health Service
Vocational rehabilitation	Althea H. Peters, Social and Rehabilitation Service	Juvenile delinquents	Arthur J. Norton, Bureau of the Census
Private philanthropy	Ralph L. Nelson, Queens College	Prisoners	Donald Miller, Bureau of Prisons
School enrollment and years of school completed	Charles E. Johnson, Jr., and Larry E. Suter, Bureau of the Census	**Chapter J**	
		Territorial acquisition	G. C. Gardner, Jr., and Kenneth W. Knox, General Services Administration
Catholic schools	Frank H. Bredeweg, National Catholic Education Association	Public lands	Julia Angel and Fred Heine, Bureau of Land Management
Doctorates	David W. Breneman and Clarebeth M. Cunningham, National Research Council	Indian lands	Betty Jo Counselman, Bureau of Indian Affairs
Roman Catholic membership	Arthur R. Kenedy, P. J. Kenedy & Sons	Livestock grazing on national forest land	Elizabeth Truhan, Forest Service
Protestant Episcopal membership	E. Allen Kelley, Morehouse-Gorham Co.	Oil and gas leases	John Duletsky and Walter Harris, Geological Survey
Methodist membership	John L. Schreiber, The United Methodist Church	Land area, use, and ownership	H. Thomas Frey and Howard L. Hill, Department of Agriculture
Southern Baptist membership	Wilmer C. Fields, Southern Baptist Convention Press	Land drainage and irrigation	Earl R. Franklin, Bureau of the Census
National parks	Jacob Bassan, National Park Service	Water wells	Ruth C. Knape, Bureau of Domestic Commerce
Recreational use of national forests	William Everard and Gordon R. Sanford, Forest Service	Climate	Dick M. Whiting, National Climatic Center
State parks	Diana Dunn, National Recreation and Park Association; Merle Van Horne, National Park Service	Tornadoes, floods, cyclones	Richard M. DeAngelis, National Oceanic and Atmospheric Administration
Bowling	Bruce Pluckhahn, American Bowling Congress	**Chapter K**	
Horseracing	A. E. Clark and Warren D. Schweder, The National Association of State Racing Commissioners	General note on agricultural statistics	John E. Cochrane and Joseph Reis, Department of Agriculture
		Agriculture census data	Thomas D. Monroe, Bureau of the Census
Baseball	David J. Grote, The National League of Professional Baseball Clubs; John J. Sheehan, The American League of Professional Baseball Clubs	Farm property and real estate	Ivery D. Clifton, Department of Agriculture
		Farm employment, wages, and man-hours	Jennie Frederick, James R. Garrett, and Donald D. Durost, Department of Agriculture
		Fertilizer and lime	David N. Harrington, Department of Agriculture

Appendix: Contributors to This Edition—Con.

Subject	Contributor	Subject	Contributor
Chapter K—Con.		**Chapter L**—Con.	
Balance sheet and country bank deposits	Carson D. Evans, Department of Agriculture	Newsprint	Leo V. Barry, Jr., Bureau of Economic Analysis
Farm income and expenses	Earl E. Miller, Department of Agriculture	Wholesale price indexes	Craig Howell, Bureau of Labor Statistics
Farm-to-retail price spreads	Henry T. Badger, Department of Agriculture	Fish and fishery products	Hoyt A. Wheeland, National Marine Fisheries Service
Farm mortgage debt, loans, interest	Nan Mitchem, Department of Agriculture	Landed catch, Pacific Coast States	Bernard E. Skud, International Pacific Halibut Commission
Farm property taxes	Jerome M. Stam, Department of Agriculture	**Chapter M**	
Supply and utilization of farm food commodities	Rachel Modina, Department of Agriculture	General review	Arthur W. Berger, Bureau of Mines
Farm productivity	Polly Dunn, Earle Gavett, and Donald D. Durost, Department of Agriculture	Operations summary, production, trade	John P. McNamee, Bureau of the Census
Crop areas, production, prices, stocks	Dorothy Majors, Department of Agriculture	Mineral production indexes	Mary H. Hillard, Board of Governors of the Federal Reserve System
Livestock	Madge Cobb, Department of Agriculture	Mineral energy fuels and waterpower	Charles R. Readling, Bureau of Mines
Poultry and eggs	Irene Wilkinson, Department of Agriculture	Petroleum and natural gas	William B. Harper, Bureau of Mines
Chapter L		Petroleum products	William G. Carrico and Charles Hennig, Bureau of Mines
Forest land and timber industries	William Everard and Robert B. Phelps, Forest Service	Nickel	Horace T. Reno, Bureau of Mines
Lumber and lumber products	Rosemary Keesling, Forest Service	Uranium	Walter C. Woodmansee, Bureau of Mines
Paper and board	Benjamin Slatin, American Paper Institute	Silver	John R. Welch, Bureau of Mines
		Employment, man-hours, accidents	Forrest T. Moyer, Bureau of Mines

[Entries are series numbers. Each statistical series has been allocated to the time period for which the earliest figure in the series appears. For most series, an entry for a given time period means that the figures are presented for that and all later time periods]

Chapter	Before 1800	1800–1819	1820–1839	1840–1859	1860–1879	1880–1889	1890–1899
A. Population	A 1–2, 5, 7, 43, 49–52, 57, 63–66, 69, 92, 99, 119–134, 172–179, 184–189, 195–200, 202–210, 217–218, 221, 228, 230–232, 240–241, 243–244, 249–251, 253, 256–257, 263, 288, 291, 335–349	A 3–4, 48, 62, 146–148, 219, 224–225, 229, 233, 235, 244, 246	A 47, 61, 91, 93, 98, 100, 143–145, 149–151, 211, 214, 220, 236, 262	A 45–46, 59–60, 106–107, 113–114, 135, 139, 190–194, 215, 226, 234, 242, 248, 254–255, 260	A 94–97, 101–105, 108–112, 115–118, 152–157, 201, 213, 216, 223, 227, 237–239, 258–259, 261	A 9–10, 12–13, 44, 58, 73–81	A 54–56, 70–72, 136–138, 140–142, 158–171, 245, 247, 252, 320–334
B. Vital Statistics and Health and Medical Care		B 6, 9, 67, 69–81, 83–92, 278, 281–282	B 5, 82	B 68, 93, 96, 126–135, 148, 275–276, 283, 285	B 193–213	B 279–280, 288–290	
C. Migration			C 89–96, 98–102, 104–105, 109–115, 119–120, 130–136, 138–142	C 1–7, 10–24, 228–240, 242–245, 248, 251–255, 258–260, 262–264, 268, 273, 278–289, 293–294	C 8–9, 25–60, 62–73, 97, 103, 106, 116–118, 137, 241, 246, 249, 265, 267, 274–275, 290–292, 295	C 61	C 121–129, 159, 161, 181, 188–194
D. Labor	D 715–717	D 167–172, 174–176, 178, 180–181, 705–711	D 75–77, 152–153, 156–157, 166, 718–721	D 154–155, 158–165, 173, 177, 179, 712, 714	D 11–13, 16–17, 19, 26–28, 78–84, 683–686, 688, 728–738, 921–926	D 713, 845, 977–980, 982–985	D 14, 24–25, 29–41, 49–51, 53–55, 57–60, 62, 85–86, 687, 765–783, 786–801, 814, 846–876, 940–945, 952–969
E. Prices and Price Indexes	E 52–60, 62–63, 90–111, 115–117	E 112–114, 118–129, 131–133, 135	E 183	E 61, 130, 134, 174–182, 184	E 214		E 23, 40, 42–51, 87–89, 185–187, 189, 191–195, 197, 202
F. National Income and Wealth			F 238–249	F 287–294, 423, 425–429, 431–436, 438, 445, 447, 449–453, 455–460, 462, 469	F 1–5, 10–16, 71–83, 85, 88–91, 93, 96–110, 112, 115–118, 120, 123–129, 210–225, 250–260	F 295–296, 424, 430, 448, 454, 535–539	F 6–9, 540–551, 638–652, 656–659, 661–667
G. Consumer Income and Expenditures				G 889, 907	G 573–581, 911	G 564–572, 582–587	G 881–884, 887–888, 906
H. Social Statistics	H 803		H 801	H 433–441, 789, 792, 805–807, 809–810	H 420, 422, 424, 492–493, 496, 502–503, 520–522, 524, 526–528, 598–601, 664–665, 668, 689, 694–698, 706–707, 751–754, 757, 760–762, 764, 791, 894–898	H 418–419, 426, 494, 498–499, 504, 666–667, 756, 763, 1168–1170	H 1–3, 16–17, 21, 28, 32, 40, 427, 429–430, 432, 487, 489–490, 545, 548–549, 552, 554, 557–558, 560–561, 708–709, 717, 747–748, 758–759, 788, 790, 793, 800, 815–816, 862–863

[Entries are series numbers. Each statistical series has been allocated to the time period for which the earliest figure in the series appears. For most series, an entry for a given time period means that the figures are presented for that and all later time periods]

Chapter	1900–1909	1910–1919	1920–1929	1930–1939	1940–1949	1950–1970
A. Population	A 11, 14–18, 23–42, 180–183, 350	A 19, 22, 309–312, 351–352	A 20	A 6, 8	A 289–290, 292–308, 313–319, 359–371	A 21, 53, 67–68, 82–90, 212, 222, 264–287, 353–358
B. Vital Statistics and Health and Medical Care	B 1, 8, 36–41, 107–125, 149–152, 154–163, 165–192, 277, 319–320, 329, 345–350, 423–424, 444, 446–452	B 7, 42–66, 94–95, 97–98, 139–147, 164, 286–287, 292–293, 295–296, 299, 301–304	B 3–4, 10, 136–138, 214–217, 221–228, 230–233, 235–250, 252–254, 256–259, 261, 284, 294, 300, 321–328, 330, 351–358, 371, 373, 375, 377, 379, 425–427, 445	B 2, 99–105, 262–274, 291, 298, 372, 374, 376, 378, 380–388, 401–402, 407–408, 429–437	B 11–35, 106, 153, 220, 229, 234, 251, 255, 260, 305–318, 331–334, 337–338, 341–344, 359–370, 389–400, 403–406, 409–422, 428, 438–443, 453–456	B 218–219, 297, 335–336, 339–340, 457–459
C. Migration	C 162, 168–169, 180, 182–183, 195–202, 205–208, 210–211, 213–215, 218, 223–224, 227, 256, 296–301	C 158, 166–167, 203–204, 216–217, 219–221, 225–226, 257, 269–272	C 76–80, 143–154, 157, 160, 170–179, 184–187, 247, 250, 261, 266	C 108, 209, 212, 222, 302–311, 313–326, 328–331	C 81–88, 107, 163–165	C 74–75, 155–156, 276–277, 312, 327
D. Labor	D 1–10, 127–130, 133–134, 137–139, 145, 182–240, 242–264, 266–271, 273–278, 280–281, 285–295, 297–308, 310, 312–331, 334–340, 342–344, 346–377, 379–391, 393–406, 408–412, 414–430, 432–446, 448–449, 451–460, 463–466, 468–472, 474–481, 483, 485–486, 488–491, 495, 497–545, 547–563, 565–577, 579–607, 609–661, 663–679, 681–682, 723–727, 739–764, 784–785, 802–804, 811–813, 818–823, 826–829	D 265, 272, 279, 296, 309, 311, 332–333, 341, 345, 378, 392, 407, 413, 431, 450, 461, 467, 473, 482, 484, 487, 492–494, 496, 564, 578, 608, 680, 824–825, 830–844, 1022, 1024–1028	D 140–141, 241, 282–284, 462, 722, 807, 810, 893–907, 909–916, 918–920, 970–973, 975–976, 981, 1029, 1034, 1036	D 15, 18, 131–132, 135–136, 146–147, 546, 662, 805–806, 808–809, 815–817, 877–888, 892, 908, 917, 927–931, 934–937, 939, 946–951, 974, 986–989, 994–996, 998–1000, 1002–1008, 1010–1012, 1014–1016, 1030–1033, 1035	D 20–23, 42, 52, 56, 61, 63–74, 87–115, 142–144, 148–151, 447, 689–704, 889–891, 990–993, 997, 1001, 1009, 1013, 1017–1021	D 43–48, 116–126, 932–933, 938, 1023
E. Prices and Price Indexes		E 24–25, 41, 73–74, 78, 84, 137, 150, 155–156, 188, 190, 196, 198–201, 203, 212–213	E 1–22, 28–29, 31–32, 34, 36–38, 204	E 30, 35, 138–146, 149, 152–153, 157–173, 205–211	E 26–27, 33, 39, 64–72, 75–77, 79–83, 85–86, 147	E 136, 148, 151, 154
F. National Income and Wealth	F 31, 186–191, 377–380, 383–384, 386–396, 400–410, 412–422, 437, 439–444, 446, 461, 463–468	F 84, 86–87, 92, 94–95, 111, 113–114, 119, 121–122, 653–654, 660	F 17–30, 32–67, 70, 144–185, 192–209, 226–237, 261–275, 278–286, 297–298, 300–308, 310–348, 385, 411, 470–534, 552–560, 562–565, 595–619, 621–637, 655	F 68–69, 276–277, 620	F 130–143, 309, 381–382, 397–399, 566–594, 668–723	F 299, 349–376, 561
G. Consumer Income and Expenditure	G 470–494, 554–563, 850–856, 885, 890–893, 895, 897–898, 900, 903–905, 908–910, 912–914	G 337–352, 534–553, 588–601, 849, 894, 899, 902, 915	G 269–313, 319–331, 333–336, 416–421, 423–469, 772–797, 843–848, 896	G 314–318, 332, 353–415, 422, 515–533, 679–696, 754–771, 828–842, 857–865, 886, 901	G 1–138, 179–181, 184–206, 208–268, 643–678, 735–753, 813–827, 866–880	G 139–178, 182–183, 207, 495–514, 602–642, 697–734, 798–812
H. Social Statistics	H 431, 550–551, 555, 559, 562, 755, 804, 808, 811–813, 868–870, 878–882, 884–885, 887–892, 899, 971–974, 979–986, 1013, 1017, 1021, 1023, 1025	H 5, 417, 423, 425, 486, 488, 495, 497, 500, 505–507, 547, 556, 563–564, 567–568, 570–573, 575–576, 578–582, 584–585, 690–693, 716, 814, 851–852, 856–857, 860–861, 877, 921, 924–931, 939–945, 948–951, 975–976, 978	H 4, 8, 13–15, 18–20, 22–23, 25–26, 29–30, 33, 35–37, 39, 41–43, 45, 47, 260–266, 393–404, 421, 478–479, 483, 491, 501, 523, 525, 529–530, 535–537, 540–542, 546, 553, 565–566, 569, 587–597, 699, 718–721, 723, 725–726, 739, 741, 743, 765–787, 802, 833–835, 850, 853–855, 858–859, 864, 873–875, 883, 886, 893, 932–938, 1135–1146, 1148–1151, 1153–1154	H 6–7, 9–10, 27, 31, 34, 38, 44, 48–55, 57–64, 66–68, 174–181, 183–185, 238–240, 242–244, 267–274, 276–278, 280–283, 285–287, 290, 293, 296, 299, 302, 333–343, 346–351, 353–377, 380, 382–389, 392, 405–416, 428, 477, 480–482, 485, 513–519, 531–534, 538–539, 543–544, 574, 583, 656–661, 722, 724, 727–738, 745–746, 749–750, 817–819, 821–823, 832, 839–842, 849, 876, 962–970, 999–1011, 1147, 1152, 1155–1167	H 11–12, 24, 56, 69, 115–132, 134–156, 158–173, 186–189, 191–195, 197–202, 204–211, 213–219, 221–225, 227–237, 241, 245–246, 249–250, 252–257, 305–332, 344–345, 378–379, 381, 390–391, 442–448, 463–476, 508–512, 602–617, 641–653, 684–688, 700–705, 710–715, 740, 742, 820, 836–837, 843–848, 865, 867, 871–872, 900–914, 917–920, 946–947, 977, 987, 990–998, 1020, 1022, 1029–1037, 1040–1046, 1049–1050, 1054–1058, 1062–1068, 1070–1110, 1112–1124	H 46, 65, 70–114, 133, 157, 182, 190, 196, 203, 212, 220, 226, 247–248, 251, 258–259, 275, 279, 284, 288–289, 291–292, 294–295, 297–298, 300–301, 303–304, 352, 449–462, 484, 577, 586, 618–640, 654–655, 662–663, 669–683, 744, 794–799, 824–831, 838, 866, 915–916, 922–923, 952–961, 988–989, 1012, 1014–1016, 1018–1019, 1024, 1026–1028, 1038–1039, 1047–1048, 1051–1053, 1059–1061, 1069, 1111, 1125–1134

[Entries are series numbers. Each statistical series has been allocated to the time period for which the earliest figure in the series appears. For most series, an entry for a given time period means that the figures are presented for that and all later time periods]

Chapter	Before 1800	1800–1819	1820–1839	1840–1859	1860–1879	1880–1889	1890–1899
J. Land, Water, and Climate	J 1–2, 4–7, 26, 32, 248, 254	J 3, 9, 20, 250–251, 253, 255	J 21, 23–25, 249, 252, 256–259, 264–267	J 22, 50–52, 56, 61, 260–263	J 10, 13, 15	J 14, 16, 18, 27–28, 55, 59–60, 62–65, 164–166, 201, 206–208, 239–241, 276–277	J 86–87, 89, 91, 179–184, 191–193, 197–200, 202, 215–220, 233–235, 242–244
K. Agriculture	K 554	K 240–250, 445–459	K 407–409, 503, 507, 512, 515, 527, 530, 551, 608	K 4–7, 10–12, 14–15, 17–40, 45–63, 65–67, 72, 74, 76, 78–79, 193, 518, 533, 536, 595, 598–599, 601–602	K 13, 41–44, 68–71, 73, 75, 77, 178–181, 414, 502, 504, 506, 508, 511, 513–514, 516, 526, 528–529, 531–532, 534–535, 537, 550, 552–553, 555, 557, 559–573, 596, 600, 607	K 1–2, 8, 82, 85–86, 89, 109–113, 124–128, 162–173, 517, 597	K 64, 93–98, 373–374, 519, 538–540, 558, 584–585, 587, 590–591, 593
L. Forestry and Fisheries	L 98–99, 211	L 100, 172			L 113–127, 129–135, 137, 166, 169, 268	L 224, 229, 236–241, 243, 245–250, 252, 263–267, 270–273, 275–278, 280–282, 286, 290–291	L 101, 104, 107, 110, 128, 136, 167–168, 170–171, 174, 178–187, 242, 251, 274, 283–285
M. Minerals	M 218, 268	M 76–78, 93, 123, 188, 217, 243, 248	M 269	M 1, 3–5, 8, 83–85, 92, 138–139, 235, 241, 247, 250, 255, 270	M 2, 9–10, 12, 79, 86–87, 100–101, 127–128, 130, 141, 189, 196, 205, 210, 222, 246, 253–254, 271, 276	M 6, 13–18, 20–21, 24, 26–36, 54–67, 80, 88, 96, 122, 126, 134, 190–192, 195, 198–200, 203, 208, 214–215, 221, 223–224, 256, 258	M 23, 72–75, 82, 90–91, 103, 105, 107, 111–112, 142, 209, 211, 257, 262, 275
N. Construction and Housing			N 114		N 70–71, 111–113, 115–117, 138	N 62–65, 72–77, 139, 156, 162–164, 167, 196–199	N 192–195, 232–245, 259–260, 262–269, 272, 302–307
P. Manufactures				P 1, 5, 9–10	P 17, 69, 73, 107–112, 123, 126–146, 149–172, 174, 176, 227–228, 231–232, 235–236, 239–241, 253, 262–268, 270, 294–295, 318–332, 334–336, 339–344, 347, 349–353, 355–360, 362, 364–374	P 4, 7–8, 70, 124–125, 173, 230, 233–234, 293, 302, 307, 348	P 16, 40–41, 45, 47, 49, 51–58, 60–62, 64–65, 67–68, 71–72, 214–215, 224, 247–249, 251–252, 260–261, 286, 290, 296–301, 333, 337, 345
Q. Transportation	Q 418, 425, 429–434, 436, 506–508, 518–523	Q 419, 435, 464–466, 481–483, 485–486, 559–563	Q 321, 329, 512–514, 556–558, 564	Q 347–349, 351–352, 459–463, 484, 509–511, 515–517, 548–551	Q 274, 278, 283, 322–328, 346, 350, 353–355, 417, 426, 437, 552	Q 47–49, 275–277, 279–282, 427–428	Q 96, 264–273, 284, 287–291, 295, 301, 304, 306–307, 311–312, 314, 317–318, 330, 339–341, 343–345, 356, 358–363, 367–371, 373–377, 398–407, 473–480
R. Communications	R 163–165, 190			R 71–72, 166–167, 246–247	R 1–2, 6, 46–55, 73–74, 89, 168, 188–189	R 9–10, 17, 19–20, 23, 25–29, 92, 169, 192	R 7–8, 11–12, 91, 193–194

Time Period Index

1900-1970

[Entries are series numbers. Each statistical series has been allocated to the time period for which the earliest figure in the series appears. For most series, an entry for a given time period means that the figures are presented for that and all later time periods]

Chapter	1900–1909	1910–1919	1920–1929	1930–1939	1940–1949	1950–1970
J. Land, Water, and Climate	J 8, 17, 33–34, 57–58, 92–109, 173–178, 188–190, 194–196, 209–214, 221–223, 225, 227–232, 278	J 53–54, 167–172, 185–187, 203–205, 224, 226, 245–247, 268–273	J 11–12, 30, 45–49, 66–84, 274–275	J 19, 35–38, 88, 236–237	J 29, 39–44, 85, 90, 110–163, 238	J 31
K. Agriculture	K 80–81, 83–84, 87–88, 100, 114–123, 130–134, 136–140, 142–146, 148–152, 192, 251–252, 254–255, 392–403, 520–522, 541–549, 556, 575, 578–580, 583, 586, 588–589, 592, 594, 603–604, 606, 609–611, 617–618	K 16, 101–104, 174–177, 182–187, 189, 194–203, 259–260, 264–267, 269–302, 344–365, 367–372, 376, 410–413, 415–429, 460–463, 466–468, 471–477, 481–482, 485–501, 523–524, 576–577, 581–582, 605, 619	K 3, 9, 129, 135, 141, 147, 153, 188, 220–229, 231–239, 375, 377, 379, 381–388, 390–391, 404–406, 478–480, 505, 509–510, 525, 574, 612–613, 620–623	K 105–108, 154–161, 230, 256–258, 261–263, 268, 303–334, 339–341, 366, 378, 380, 430–444, 483–484, 614–616	K 90–92, 99, 190–191, 204–219, 253, 335–338, 342–343, 389, 464–465, 469–470	
L. Forestry and Fisheries	L 10–11, 15–18, 22–29, 56–78, 80–84, 87–97, 173, 175–177, 206, 262, 292, 294–295, 298, 304	L 12–14, 19, 30, 44–46, 102, 105–106, 108–109, 199–203, 205, 279, 287, 289, 319–320, 369–370	L 20–21, 47–49, 52–55, 79, 103, 111–112, 188–190, 208–210, 225–228, 230–235, 244, 253, 288, 296–297, 299–303, 305–310, 313, 315–318, 338–351, 354–360, 362–365, 367–368	L 37–43, 50–51, 191–198, 204, 254–261, 269, 311–312, 314, 321–327, 333, 361, 366	L 31–36, 85–86, 207, 293, 328–332, 352–353	L 1–9, 138–165, 212–223, 334–337
M. Minerals	M 25, 38–53, 81, 104, 135, 147, 152–155, 193, 197, 202, 204, 212–213, 225, 236, 242, 244, 249, 251, 261, 273	M 19, 37, 68, 89, 94–95, 97–98, 102, 108–110, 113–121, 124–125, 129, 131–133, 136, 140, 143–144, 156–157, 161–165, 167–171, 194, 201, 206–207, 216, 226–227, 229–230, 232–234, 237–240, 259, 263, 266, 277–282, 285–288, 290–291, 293, 297–298, 303	M 69–70, 99, 106, 137, 148–151, 166, 172–174, 176–187, 219–220, 267	M 7, 22, 158, 160, 175, 245, 252, 260, 272, 274, 283–284, 300–301	M 71, 145–146, 228, 264–265, 289, 294–295, 299, 304–305	M 11, 159, 231, 292, 296, 302, 306
N. Construction and Housing	N 78, 159–161	N 1–8, 11–21, 25–29, 32–35, 37, 40–47, 49, 55–61, 66–69, 79–81, 83–93, 96–101, 108, 118–132, 135–137, 261	N 9–10, 23–24, 30–31, 36, 38–39, 48, 50, 52–54, 82, 94–95, 140, 143, 148–149, 151–152, 155, 200–202, 205–206, 208–210, 213–214, 216–218, 221–222, 224–226, 229–230, 273, 276, 278–282, 284, 301	N 22, 51, 102–107, 109–110, 133–134, 157–158, 165–166, 168–169, 180, 182–184, 203–204, 211–212, 219–220, 227–228, 270–271, 274, 277, 283, 285–296, 300	N 141–142, 144–147, 150, 153–154, 170–172, 174–176, 178–179, 181, 185–191, 207, 215, 223, 231, 246–248, 275, 297	N 173, 177, 249–258, 298–299
P. Manufactures	P 3, 15, 197, 212–213, 216–220, 250, 269, 279, 303, 310–311, 314, 317, 346, 361	P 13, 50, 147–148, 175, 229, 244, 254–259, 281–282, 308–309, 316, 338, 354, 363	P 14, 46, 113–121, 221, 237–238, 242–243, 271, 277, 283–285, 288–289, 304–306, 312, 315	P 12, 42–44, 48, 205, 208, 210, 222–223, 225–226, 236a, 246, 291–292	P 6, 11, 18–21, 23–39, 63, 66, 74–106, 122, 177–196, 198–199, 201, 203, 206–207, 209, 211, 245, 272–276, 278, 280, 287, 313	P 2, 22, 59, 200, 202, 204
Q. Transportation	Q 56, 148–153, 155, 300, 305, 313, 316, 372, 542–545	Q 65–68, 82–95, 156–158, 208–219, 222–223, 225, 242, 293–294, 296–297, 331–338, 357, 391–392, 411, 438–448, 546, 553–555, 565–567, 573–576	Q 50–52, 54–55, 57–58, 60–64, 97–128, 154, 199–201, 226–232, 241, 243–244, 251, 257–263, 285–286, 298–299, 308, 319–320, 342, 364–366, 378–379, 384–389, 393–397, 408–410, 412, 414, 420–424, 524–540, 577–578, 580–584, 586, 588, 604, 606–607, 609–610, 614, 619, 624–627, 634–636	Q 12–35, 53, 59, 69–81, 159–162, 202–207, 224, 233–240, 245–250, 252–253, 256, 292, 309–310, 315, 380–383, 390, 413, 487–505, 579, 585, 587, 589, 591–603, 605, 608, 615–618, 628–633, 637	Q 36–46, 129–147, 163–196, 220–221, 254–255, 302–303, 449–458, 467–472, 547, 568–569, 590, 611–613, 620–623	Q 1–11, 197–198, 415–416, 541, 570–572
R. Communications	R 13–14, 18, 21–22, 30, 75–77, 79, 81, 83–84, 86–88, 90, 244–245, 248–251, 256–257	R 15–16, 24, 31–38, 40–45, 56–63, 65–68, 80, 82, 140, 145–146, 191, 252, 254	R 3–5, 39, 64, 78, 85, 93, 102, 104, 141, 170, 172–187, 224–226, 228, 230–231, 253, 255	R 69–70, 106–122, 143, 147, 171, 232–243	R 94–96, 103, 105, 123–138, 144, 148–150, 153–161, 218–223, 227, 229	R 97–101, 139, 142, 151–152, 162, 195–217

[Entries are series numbers.   Each statistical series has been allocated to the time period for which the earliest figure in the series appears.   For most series, an entry for a given time period means that the figures are presented for that and all later time periods]

Chapter	Before 1800	1800–1819	1820–1839	1840–1859	1860–1879	1880–1889	1890–1899
S. Energy				S 1, 3–10, 12	S 11	S 13	S 2
T. Distribution and Services					T 1–2, 15–16, 220–221, 225, 228, 231, 233–234, 236, 239–241, 243–244, 384–385, 388–390, 444	T 222, 227, 229–230	T 223–224, 232
U. International Transactions and Foreign Commerce	U 1–3, 8–10, 13–15, 17–23, 40, 190–193, 196, 275, 277–280, 296, 298, 300, 317, 324–328, 335	U 274, 276, 281, 287, 294	U 4, 11, 16, 187–189, 194–195, 197–200, 207–224, 282, 286, 289, 295, 297, 299, 301, 307–308, 310, 318–323, 329–330, 333–334, 336–348, 351–352	U 26, 33, 285, 303, 306, 331–332, 349–350	U 7, 24, 27, 34, 37, 201–202, 206, 225–248, 264–273, 305	U 283–284, 288, 290–293, 309, 311–315	U 28–30, 302, 304
V. Business Enterprise				V 20, 23–24, 27, 30	V 271–274, 279–280, 283–284	V 275–278	V 39–40
W. Productivity and Technological Development	W 99		W 96, 106	W 104	W 58, 60–61, 82, 85, 87–88, 92, 107	W 1–8, 13, 55–56, 97	W 12, 89
X. Financial Markets and Institutions	X 879	X 420–421, 423, 437, 561–563, 565–567, 569–579, 882–883	X 564, 568, 580–587, 697	X 476, 792, 890–891, 894–895, 897–900, 903–904, 906–908, 915, 917	X 410–411, 415–418, 424–427, 429, 433–436, 479–482, 495–498, 634–636, 639, 643, 648, 653–654, 656–658, 661, 665, 670, 675–676, 678–684, 687–690, 741–745, 768, 773–775, 885, 893, 896, 901–902, 909–914, 916	X 685–686, 769–772, 794–795	X 419, 428, 444–445, 448, 588–609, 616–619, 637–638, 640–642, 644–647, 649–652, 655, 659–660, 662–664, 666–669, 671–674, 677, 691, 694, 821–833, 880, 887, 889
Y. Government	Y 1–16, 79–82, 189–190, 192–200, 202, 204–205, 207–208, 210, 215–221, 228–229, 231, 238, 241–242, 250–251, 253–254, 259–261, 263, 266–267, 335–338, 352–356, 457–459, 461–463, 493, 849–855, 904–907, 911–916, 971, 984–985, 996	Y 17–19, 90–91, 94, 98, 101–102, 104–105, 113–114, 116–117, 119, 122–124, 126, 129–130, 201, 222, 234–235, 239–240, 245, 256, 308–310, 312–317	Y 20–28, 31, 34–35, 38, 41–42, 45–50, 52–53, 57–58, 60–61, 63, 66–67, 70, 73–74, 83–84, 87, 97, 103, 106, 108–109, 135–136, 139, 142–143, 146, 149–150, 153–158, 160–161, 165–166, 168–169, 171, 174–175, 178, 181–182, 191, 206, 209, 225, 243, 246	Y 32, 37, 43, 71, 77, 88, 93, 99, 127, 133, 140, 145, 151, 179, 185, 203, 226, 230, 236, 244, 258, 264, 270, 494–495, 497–498	Y 44, 51, 55–56, 65, 68, 76, 89, 100, 107, 111–112, 121, 132, 152, 159, 163–164, 173, 176, 184, 187–188, 227, 237, 248–249, 269, 358, 362, 364–366, 373, 496, 856–857, 859–860, 862–866, 871–887, 890–891, 898–903, 943–955, 957–960, 972, 993, 995, 998–999, 1004–1005	Y 33, 141, 233, 247, 255, 262, 268, 271, 311, 501–502, 973	Y 40, 54, 62, 69, 72, 75, 78, 96, 110, 118, 125, 128, 131, 134, 148, 162, 170, 177, 180, 183, 186, 211–214, 265, 867–870, 888–889, 892–897, 956, 961, 974–976
Z. Colonial and Pre-Federal Statistics	Z 1–615						

[Entries are series numbers. Each statistical series has been allocated to the time period for which the earliest figure in the series appears. For most series, an entry for a given time period means that the figures are presented for that and all later time periods]

Chapter	1900–1909	1910–1919	1920–1929	1930–1939	1940–1949	1950–1970
S. Energy	S 15–24, 32–36, 40, 44–46, 48–49, 52–53, 57, 74–88, 90–91, 94, 109, 112–114, 116, 119–120	S 37–39, 41–43, 108, 118, 121–124, 126–132	S 14, 50–51, 54–56, 58–59, 66, 71, 92–93, 95, 100–107, 110–111, 160–167, 176–189	S 115, 117, 133–151, 190–218	S 25–31, 47, 60–63, 67–70, 72–73, 89, 125, 152–157, 168–175	S 64–65, 96–99, 158–159
T. Distribution and Services	T 226, 235, 237–238, 242, 386–387	T 272–273	T 3–5, 7–14, 17–19, 21–33, 35–42, 70–71, 75, 79–81, 84, 87–112, 116–172, 176–219, 245–270, 274–286, 288–290, 292–293, 300–302, 304–306, 308–310, 312–314, 316–318, 320–322, 324–326, 328–330, 332–334, 336–338, 340–342, 344–346, 348–350, 352–353, 360–362, 364–366, 368–369, 438–439, 485–491	T 43–45, 47–50, 52–55, 57–69, 72–74, 76–78, 82–83, 85, 113–115, 173–175, 271, 287, 291, 294–299, 303, 307, 311, 315, 319, 323, 327, 331, 335, 339, 343, 347, 351, 354–359, 363, 367, 370–374, 391, 393, 398, 400–415, 418–437, 440–443, 445–454, 459–479, 482–484	T 6, 20, 34, 46, 51, 56, 57–69, 72–74, 397, 399, 416–417, 455–458, 480–481	T 86, 392
U. International Transactions and Foreign Commerce	U 5, 25, 316	U 6, 12, 31–32, 35–36, 38, 203–205	U 41–44, 46, 249–263	U 47–51, 55, 59, 63, 67, 74	U 39, 75–96, 102–186	U 45, 52–54, 56–58, 60–62, 64–66, 68–73, 97–101
V. Business Enterprise	V 216, 225–231, 234–246, 249–270	V 38, 41–65, 213–215, 219–224, 232–233, 247–248, 281–282, 285–305	V 13–19, 25–26, 28–29, 66–77, 108–119, 123–128, 167–177, 217–218	V 1–12, 120–122, 129–140, 178–212	V 21–22, 31–37, 78–107, 141–166, 306–332	
W. Productivity and Technological Development	W 30, 83, 100–102	W 31, 36–38, 40, 43, 47, 50–54, 57, 64, 67–81, 84, 90–91, 93–95, 108	W 59, 86	W 14–21, 32, 34–35, 39, 41, 44–45, 48, 65, 98, 103, 105	W 9–11, 22–29, 32a–33, 42, 46, 49, 62–63, 66, 126–132, 134, 136–138, 140–141	W 109–125, 133, 135, 139, 142–180
X. Financial Markets and Institutions	X 430, 475, 487–491, 493–494, 531, 717–721, 732–736, 834–835	X 393–395, 397–399, 402–409, 412–414, 422, 431–432, 438–443, 447, 449, 454–456, 470–474, 477–478, 492, 510–516, 532–535, 547–560, 610–615, 693, 695–696, 706–715, 796–810, 812–820, 845–853, 884, 886, 888, 892, 947–956	X 400–401, 459–469, 483–486, 746–755, 793, 836, 842, 855, 864, 866–867, 869, 905, 933–946	X 450–451, 499–509, 517–530, 540–546, 620–633, 692, 714, 722–731, 737–739, 756–767, 776–787, 789–791, 811, 840–841, 843–844, 854, 856, 858–863, 865, 868, 870–878, 881, 918–932	X 1–121, 124–277, 279–298, 300–301, 303–342, 344–357, 359–392, 396, 446, 452–453, 457–458, 536–539, 698–705, 740, 788, 837–839, 857, 957–961	X 122–123, 278, 299, 302, 343, 358, 962
Y. Government	Y 64, 120, 172, 257, 381–382, 386, 388–389, 466–467, 469–471, 505–507, 510–514, 522, 524–528, 530–531, 533–552, 554, 556–561, 567–569, 572–573, 575–581, 583, 590–592, 594–598, 600–601, 603–608, 610, 612–618, 620–622, 624, 627–631, 652–657, 660–664, 671–677, 679–680, 682–699, 701–705, 710–716, 719, 724–725, 727–729, 736–741, 743–744, 746–753, 756–760, 762–765, 767–769, 771, 773–774, 776–778, 783, 785–791, 793–794, 796–802, 805–810, 812, 817, 819–833, 835, 837–842, 844, 962, 982, 1000–1003, 1006–1009	Y 30, 59, 86, 115, 138, 167, 224, 252, 357, 359–360, 370–372, 383–384, 387, 390, 402–407, 414–425, 429–443, 445–449, 468, 499, 503, 509, 515–516, 529, 562–563, 571, 602, 623, 665–666, 678, 706–707, 722, 726, 742, 770, 792, 804, 814–815, 843, 846–847, 861, 970, 977, 983, 986, 988, 992	Y 332–334, 339–341, 363, 385, 391–392, 408–410, 444, 450–456, 504, 508, 521, 532, 555, 566, 570, 584–585, 588, 599, 609, 619, 626, 632–633, 636, 658–659, 670, 681, 709, 717–718, 721, 730–731, 735, 745, 754–755, 779–780, 782, 795, 811, 963, 994, 997, 1010–1022, 1026–1031	Y 342, 361, 367–369, 374–380, 411, 488–492, 500, 517–520, 553, 564–565, 574, 587, 589, 611, 625, 635, 637–651, 667–669, 700, 708, 720, 723, 732–734, 761, 766, 775, 781, 813, 816, 834, 836, 845, 1023–1025	Y 272–307, 318–331, 343–351, 393–397, 399–401, 412–413, 426–428, 460, 472–487, 582, 586, 634, 772, 803, 848, 908–910, 917–942, 964, 978, 987, 989–990	Y 29, 36, 39, 85, 92, 95, 137, 144, 147, 223, 232, 398, 464–465, 523, 593, 784, 818, 858, 965–969, 979–981, 991
Z. Colonial and Pre-Federal Statistics						

Subject Index

[Numbers in *italics* refer to text pages]

[Numbers in *italics* refer to text pages]

[Numbers in *italics* refer to text pages]

[Numbers in *italics* refer to text pages]

[Numbers in *italics* refer to text pages]

[Numbers in *italics* refer to text pages]

[Numbers in *italics* refer to text pages]

[Numbers in *italics* refer to text pages]

Library of Congress Cataloging in Publication Data

United States. Bureau of the Census.
   **Historical statistics of the United States,
colonial times to 1970.**

Includes bibliographical references and indexes.

   1. United States—Statistics.   I. Title.
HA202.B87 1976   317.3   75-38832

☆ U.S. GOVERNMENT PRINTING OFFICE : 1976 O—499—508